World Tables 1991

Published for The World Bank
The Johns Hopkins University Press
Baltimore and London

40707

This publication has been prepared by the Socio-Economic Data Division of the World Bank's International Economics Department. The World Bank does not accept responsibility for the accuracy or completeness of this publication. Any judgments expressed are those of the World Bank staff or consultants and do not necessarily reflect the views of the Board of Directors or the governments they represent.

The complete backlist of publications from the World Bank is shown in the annual *Index of Publications*, which contains an alphabetical title list and indexes of subjects, authors, and countries and regions. The latest edition is available free of charge from the Publications Sales Unit, The World Bank, 1818 H Street, N.W., Washington, D.C. 20433, U.S.A., or from Publications, The World Bank, 66, avenue d'Iéna, 75116 Paris, France.

ISBN   0-8018-4252-2
ISSN   1043-5573

Library of Congress Catalog No.: 89-647121

Contents

Symbols and Conventions

. .	data not available, or nonexistent
Scientific notation e.g. .63E-2	data with insignificant digits, using units appropriate for the latest year
0,0.0, .0E-0	zero, or less than half the unit shown and not known more precisely
A, B, C, etc.	general issue of methodology; see Codes for General and Country Notes
f	country specific issue of methodology; see Country Notes
Billion	1,000,000,000

1987 is the base year for constant price series data.

The cutoff date for all data is February 22, 1991.

The data in this book are also available on diskette, using the World Bank's ☆STARS☆ compression and retrieval system. For information about ordering copies of ☆STARS☆ data, see the Introduction.

Introduction

This 1991 edition of the *World Tables* (WT) updates core socio-economic indicators given on country and topical pages in the 1989-90 edition. The data cover the period 1969 to 1989 and projections for 1990 for some of the series in the topical pages. The base year for constant prices has been moved from 1980 to 1987; see Sources and Methods for details of the rebasing and "chain-linking" of the constant price series.

After an extensive review of comments from users, changes have been made in the country pages of this edition. To streamline presentation of national accounts, use of resources is presented before origin, and several new indicators have been added. They are: GDP at constant market prices, consumer price index, urban population as percent of total, and female primary school enrollment ratio. Several indicators shown in the previous edition have been dropped. They are: export price indices of non-fuel primary product, fuel and manufactures, constant price data on total exports and imports, and crude birth rate.

Four new countries (Bulgaria, Equatorial Guinea, Islamic Republic of Iran and São Tomé and Principe) have been added to the country list. The Republic of Yemen, which was formed by the union of Yemen Arab Republic and People's Democratic Republic of Yemen, has not been included as the compilation of data for the new country is still continuing. For the Federal Republic of Germany, the data do not reflect its union with the German Democratic Republic as the data for the unified country are still being compiled. WT contains data for 139 economies.

The *World Tables* disseminates, with little delay, country estimates used by the Bank in analysis of economic and social trends in developing countries, which emphasizes Bank borrowers. To make the volume a more useful resource, other economies are covered to the extent that they provide internationally comparable measures in readily usable form; these are not subject to detailed scrutiny by Bank staff. Data for high-income OECD economies are based on reports of the Organisation for Economic Co-operation and Development (OECD) and the International Monetary

Fund (IMF). National publications are used for the remaining economies. Such sources, generally specified in the Country Notes, should be consulted by readers wishing to be assured of the most timely and complete reports.

Country time series are also used by the Bank to measure trends in groups of countries, notably for the Bank's *World Development Report* (WDR) and *World Development Indicators* (WDI). The *World Tables* topical pages fill a gap between the country pages and measures for analytical groupings of countries given in the WDR and WDI; how group indicators are derived from country time series is more evident in the topical pages and is explained more fully below.

The *World Tables* is issued annually in diskettes and tapes as well as in book form, with a midyear update in electronic form. The tables report annual time series. The book and the diskettes have the same time coverage (1969-89 for country pages and 1969-90 for topical pages); the tape contains data from 1950 for some countries and series. The diskettes contain the country pages and topical pages in ☆STARS☆ software. ☆STARS☆ software compresses WT data into diskettes and allows easy retrieval of data into Lotus, Javelin or ASCII format. Information on prices and payment terms for the book, diskette, and tape versions of *World Tables* may be obtained by contacting World Bank Publications, 300 Raritan Center Parkway, Edison N.J. 08816-7816, U.S.A., or by calling 201-225-2165.

TOPICAL PAGES

Topical pages cover two double-page spreads and report annual data for 1969-89 and projections for 1990. Topical pages recast some indicators from country pages as a global backdrop for analyzing how low- and middle-income economies have fared in recent decades. Economies are grouped first by geographic region and, in a sub-table, by income groups and other analytical groupings used in the WDI. The last few lines of each sub-table indicate trends for high-income economies.

The Bank's classification of economies is directly

related to analytic and geographic objectives. The Bank's *analytic* classification is based primarily on *income*, with GNP per capita providing the major dividing line between low, middle and high-income economies. Economies are also grouped according to *geographic* regions of special Bank development focus (Sub-Sahara Africa), level of *external indebtedness* (severely indebted), composition of *major export* (fuel, manufactures, primary nonfuel), and by *Bank status* (IDA borrowers, blend, current Bank borrowers, other Bank member countries). The analytic groups of economies shown here represent only a few of these classifications of economies used in the Bank.

Since only sparse data are available on the selected topics for some economies such as some of the historically planned economies of Eastern Europe and the USSR, no attempt is made to report global indicators. With this exception, all economies of the world are included in group aggregates in the sub-tables, including those not selected for separate presentation on the topical pages.

Simple addition is used when a variable is expressed in reasonably comparable units of account, say *imports in current dollars*.

Indicators that do not seem naturally additive, say *quantities of diverse imports*, are usually combined by a price-weighting scheme, say *dollar values of the diverse imports in 1987*, which in the case of export and import price index numbers are those re-based to 1987 in the Country Tables. Fixed (Laspeyres) weights are normally used for quantities, with moving (Paasche) weights for prices to fulfill the expectation that [value = price x quantity]. The identity also means that one part of the identity can be derived from the other two; the one derived being described as implicit, for example, *implicit deflators in national accounts*.

The weighting scheme has been incorporated into the indicator by scaling the volume indicator to match the 1987 weights. The ratio of the sums of imports in current and constant dollars can then provide the implicit deflator for imports. It should be emphasized, however, that use of single base year joined in a chain linked series raises problems over a period encompassing profound structural changes and significant movements in relative prices, as certainly occurred during 1969-90. The problems exist in indicators for a single country and are simply more apparent when country indicators are agglomerated.

It is debatable whether an analytical ratio, say *imports to GDP*, should be a weighted average of country ratios or a ratio of separately aggregated numerator and denominator. The results will be different, sometimes significantly so. WT first estimates the numerator and

denominator for the group and then calculates the group ratio.

The World Tables strives for group time series that retain the same country composition over time and across topics. It does so by permitting group measures to be compiled only if the country data available for a given year account for *at least two-thirds of the full group*, as defined by 1987 benchmarks. So long as that criterion is met, uncurrent reporters (and those not providing ample history) are assumed to behave like the portion of the group that does provide estimates.

The same technique applies to regional groupings in the main part of the topical pages; for these, however, South Africa is omitted from Sub-Saharan Africa.

The benchmarking procedure underlying group measures requires that some weight be assigned to each economy within the group. For an economy reporting inadequate data in every year, Bank staff must choose some arbitrary 1987 base value within a broad range of plausible estimates. Readers should keep in mind that the purpose is to maintain an appropriate relationship across topics, despite myriad country problems, and that nothing meaningful can be deduced about behavior at the country level by working back from group indicators. In addition, the weighting process may result in discrepancies between summed subgroup figures and overall totals.

Contributions to Growth of GDP

Several topical pages express sources and uses of gross domestic production (or expenditure) as "contributions" to growth of GDP. The term "contribution" combines information about growth rates and percentage shares of GDP components. This form of presentation, sometimes referred to as "percentage points of GDP," shows by how much GDP would have changed if other GDP components were unchanged.

For example, if agriculture has a 9% growth rate and accounts for a third of GDP, it contributes 3 percentage points to GDP growth. If industry and services remained unchanged, GDP's growth rate would have been 3%. In practice, contributions are obtained by expressing the year-to-year change in a component, for instance, agriculture, as a percentage of GDP in the earlier year.

National accounts in constant 1987 prices are used. Regional aggregation requires that country estimates be expressed in 1987 US dollars and then summed. Even so, regional aggregation raises an index number problem closely related to the partial rebasing issue arising at the country level (see Sources and Methods), which is resolved in a similar manner. Moreover, regional measures of the contribution to GDP of resource balance are actually the difference between separately compiled measures for exports and imports (of goods and nonfactor services); regional measures for private consumption are then derived as a residual (GDP less government consumption, investment, and the net export of goods and nonfactor services).

COVERAGE OF COUNTRY PAGES

Most time series selected for the country pages are concerned with national accounts and international transactions (foreign trade, balance of payments, and external debt). The Bank uses methodologies and historical data files developed by other international organizations, but adds information obtained by Bank staff directly from national sources, when it can be fitted to internationally agreed classification schemes.

For other data sets (manufacturing, monetary and fiscal, and social indicators), WT recasts a few of the time series made available to the Bank by other international agencies, but readers should refer to publications of the agencies concerned for fuller information. A more diverse selection of indicators, not in time series form, is given in the WDI.

WT provides limited time series on external debt, since the Bank's *World Debt Tables* is the authoritative source. Similarly, a wider range of social indicators is available in the Bank's *Social Indicators of Development*. These may also be obtained from World Bank Publications (see above).

The country pages are in alphabetical order. A list of countries covered on page 655 also notes the original base years for constant price national accounts prior to partial rebasing (see Sources and Methods).

BASIC CONCEPTS

As far as is practicable, the WT economic indicators conform to the UN System of National Accounts (SNA), and its social indicators conform to methodologies of UN specialized agencies. In some areas of economic statistics, additional guidelines have been developed that are broadly in line with the SNA but differ in some respects. For example, the IMF has played a leading role in helping national compilers elaborate balance of payments, monetary, and government finance statistics. While further revision of the SNA, already under study, may reduce definitional and classification differences, few are resolved in the WT amalgam of statistical sources.

Where possible, however, the Bank harmonizes related data sets drawn from diverse sources. This conceptual process, perhaps as much as national estimates obtained by Bank staff, imparts a unique quality to the national accounts and international transactions data reported in WT. The Bank has devised for its analytical purposes certain methods and concepts such as partial rebasing, gross domestic income (GDY), and gross national income (GNY).

The concepts and methods are described in Sources and Methods and in the Glossary of Terms. It should be emphasized, however, that the notes are selective rather than encyclopedic. Readers interested in more comprehensive and technically precise descriptions should consult the basic references noted in Sources and Methods.

STATISTICAL ISSUES

A concerted effort has been made to standardize data and to note exceptions to standards. However, full comparability cannot be ensured, and care must be taken in interpreting the indicators. The data are drawn from sources thought to be most authoritative, but many of them are subject to considerable margins of error. This is particularly true for the most recent year or two, since conventional statistical reports take time to digest.

Moreover, intercountry and intertemporal comparisons always involve complex technical problems, which have no full and unequivocal solution.

The statistical systems in many developing economies are weak, and this affects the availability and reliability of the data. Readers are urged to take these limitations into account in interpreting the indicators, particularly when making comparisons across economies. WT addresses issues of data reliability partly by omitting questionable estimates but also by flagging methodological issues that can influence analysis.

Country pages for about a dozen Bank members have been omitted for lack of adequate data; some time series on other country pages are blank or uncertain.

Unless otherwise stated, data are reported for calendar years.

Sources and Methods

The **GNP per capita** figures are calculated according to the *World Bank Atlas* method of converting data in national currency to US dollars. In this method, the conversion factor for any year is the average exchange rate for that year and the two preceding years, adjusted for differences in rates of inflation between the country and the United States. This averaging smooths fluctuations in prices and exchange rates. The resulting estimate of GNP in US dollars is divided by the midyear population to obtain the per capita GNP in current US dollars.

The following formulas describe the procedures for computing the conversion factor for year t:

$$(e^*_{t-2,t}) = \frac{1}{3} \left[e_{t-2} \left(\frac{P_t}{P_{t-2}} \Big/ \frac{P_t^\$}{P_{t-2}^\$} \right) + e_{t-1} \left(\frac{P_t}{P_{t-1}} \Big/ \frac{P_t^\$}{P_{t-1}^\$} \right) + e_t \right]$$

and for calculating per capita GNP in US dollars for year t:

$$(Y_t^\$) = (Y_t / N_t \div e^*_{t-2,t})$$

where

$Y_t^\$$ = per capita GNP in US\$ for year t

Y_t = current GNP (local currency) for year t

P_t = GNP deflator for year t

e_t = annual average exchange rate (local currency/US dollars) for year t

N_t = midyear population for year t

$P_t^\$$ = US GNP deflator for year t

The **conversion factor** line on each country page reports the underlying annual observations used for this *Atlas* method. As a rule, it is the official exchange rate reported in the IMF's *International Financial Statistics* (IFS), line *rf*.

Exceptions arise where *World Tables* recasts IFS-style measures to report on a fiscal year basis or to average multiple exchange rates; in highly exceptional cases, further refinements are made by Bank staff (see Country Conversion Factors for a list of all three exceptions).

Where multiple exchange rate practices are officially maintained and the spread between rates is analytically significant a transactions-weighted average is given, if possible. However, no account of unofficial parallel market rates is taken in the calculations. When the official exchange rate, including any multiple rate, is judged to diverge by an exceptionally large margin from the rate effectively applied to international transactions, a different conversion factor is used by the Bank. Where national compilers used an official exchange rate to assign a national currency value to international transactions, however, that rate must be used to convert the same items to dollars, regardless of whether it was the rate actually applied to international transactions. In these cases, country pages report both the *conversion factor*, underlying the *Atlas* method of converting values of international transactions, and an *additional conversion factor* underlying the *Atlas* method of converting the remaining components of GNP.

Current **population** estimates and estimates of fertility and mortality are made by the World Bank from data provided by the UN Population Division, the UN Statistical Office, country statistical offices, and other sources. In many cases, the data take into account the results of recent population censuses. Refugees not permanently settled in the country of asylum are generally considered to be part of the population of their country of origin.

Statistical background for the estimates is available in the UN annual *Population and Vital Statistics Report* and the Bank's annual *World Population Projections*.

USE AND ORIGIN OF RESOURCES

The time series are based mainly on national sources as collected by World Bank regional country economists. They generally accord with the System of National Accounts (SNA). Most definitions of indicators given below are those in UN SNA, series F, no. 2, revision 3.

For most countries, GDP by industrial origin is the sum of value added measured at producer prices.

Data are expressed in national currency units and shown in current prices, and in "chain-linked" 1987 constant prices. Chain linking describes the process when, to facilitate international comparisons, constant price data for most economies are partially rebased to three base years and linked together. 1970 is the base year for data from 1960 to 1975, 1980 for 1976 to 1982, and 1987 for 1983 and beyond. These three constant price time series are chain-linked to provide long-term trend analysis.

This is accomplished for each of the three sub-periods by rescaling; this moves the year in which current and constant price versions of the same time series have the same value, without altering the trend of either. Components of GDP are individually rescaled and summed up to provide GDP and its subaggregates. In this process, a rescaling deviation may occur between constant price GDP by industrial origin and constant price GDP by expenditure. Such rescaling deviations are absorbed in private consumption, etc. on the assumption that GDP by industrial origin is a more reliable estimate than GDP by expenditure.

This approach takes into account the effects of changes in intersectoral relative prices between the original and new base period (original base periods are noted in the country list on page 654). Because private consumption is calculated as a residual, the national accounting identities are maintained. This method of accounting does, however, involve "burying" in private consumption whatever statistical discrepancies arise on the expenditures side in the rebasing and chain linking process. Large discrepancies are flagged in the General Notes.

Partial rebasing requires constant price estimates by industrial origin at the rather aggregated level shown in these tables. If sufficient data are not available for partially rebasing to 1987, then 1980 is used, or the original base year if 1980 data are not available. If only GDP or GNP is available, the original constant price estimates of GDP are directly rescaled to 1987 prices.

DOMESTIC PRICES/DEFLATORS

These data are based on national accounts data, discussed above. **Overall (GDP)** and **domestic absorption** prices are implicit deflators, that is, they are ratios of current and constant price estimates of relevant aggregates. Domestic prices for **agriculture, industry,** and **manufacturing** are, in principle, price indexes of value added; the **consumer price index** reflects prices of goods and services used for private consumption of households. For most countries, price indexes are implicit deflators derived from volume and value estimates.

MANUFACTURING ACTIVITY

The primary source is the United Nations Industrial Development Organization (UNIDO) database. To improve cross-country comparability, UNIDO has standardized the coverage of establishments to those with five or more employees.

The concepts and definitions are in accordance with the *International Recommendations for Industrial Statistics*, published by the United Nations. The term *employees* refers to two categories defined by the UN: *employees* and *persons engaged*. The term *employees* excludes working proprietors, active business partners, and unpaid family workers, whereas the term *persons engaged* includes them. Most countries report data on *employees*, but some, as indicated in the *Notes* column, report data on *persons engaged*. Both terms exclude homeworkers. The number of employees or persons engaged usually refers to the average number employed throughout the year.

Real earnings per employee (wages and salaries) covers all payments in cash or kind made by the employer during the year, in connection with work done. The payments include (a) all regular and overtime cash payments, bonuses, and cost of living allowances; (b) wages and salaries paid during vacation and sick leave; (c) taxes and social insurance contributions and the like, payable by the employees and deducted by the employer; and (d) payments in kind.

The value of gross **real output per employee** is estimated on the basis of either production or shipments. On the production basis, it consists of (a) the value of all products of the establishment, (b) the value of industrial services rendered to others, (c) the value of goods shipped in the same condition as received, (d) the value of electricity sold, and (e) the net change between the value of work-in-progress at the beginning and the end of the reference period. In the case of estimates compiled on a shipment basis, the net change between the beginning and the end of the reference period in the value of stocks of finished goods is also included. **Value added** is defined as the current value of gross output less the current cost of (a) materials, fuels, and other supplies consumed; (b) contract and commission work done by others; (c) repair and maintenance work done by others; and (d) goods shipped in the same condition as received.

MONETARY HOLDINGS

The primary source is the IMF's *International Financial Statistics* (IFS) database. The concepts and definitions are from the Fund's *A Guide to Money and Banking Statistics in IFS*.

For most countries, the **money supply broadly defined** comprises money (IFS line 34) and quasi-money (IFS line 35), the normal forms of financial liquidity that economic transactors hold in the monetary system. By definition, holdings of nonresidents and the central government are excluded.

In some countries, other (nonmonetary) financial institutions may also incur quasi-monetary liabilities, that is, they may issue financial instruments on terms similar to those for quasi-money. Where these are significant, **money supply broadly defined** is a measure of liquid liabilities comprising the monetary and quasi-monetary liabilities of both monetary and nonmonetary financial institutions.

GOVERNMENT DEFICIT OR SURPLUS

The primary source is the IMF's *Government Finance Statistics Yearbook* (GFSY). GFSY data are reported by countries using the system of common definitions and classifications found in the IMF *Manual on Government Finance Statistics (1986)*.

The inadequate statistical coverage of state, provincial, and local governments has dictated the use of central government data only. This may seriously understate or distort the role of government, especially in large countries where lower levels of government are important. A *general note* (E) indicates instances where this is thought to be likely.

Grants, reported separately in GFSY, are here included in **current revenue**; government lending operations (GFSY lending minus repayments) are classified as **capital payments**.

FOREIGN TRADE (CUSTOMS BASIS)

Exports and imports cover international movements of goods across customs borders; generally, exports are valued f.o.b. (free on board) and imports c.i.f. (cost, insurance, and freight).

The primary source is the UN trade data system made available through the UN International Computing Center (Geneva). Apart from greater currentness, the UN trade data system accords with the UN *Yearbook of International Trade Statistics*; that is, the data are based on countries' customs returns.

For the most recent years, secondary sources are often used, notably estimates obtained directly from national sources by World Bank staff. Secondary sources are based on aggregated reports from national authorities that become available before the detailed reports submitted to the UN are released.

Export and import price indexes for developing countries are World Bank estimates. For industrial economies, the indexes are from the UN *Yearbook of International Trade Statistics* and *Monthly Bulletin of Statistics*, and the IFS.

BALANCE OF PAYMENTS

The primary sources are the files from the IMF's *Balance of Payments Statistics Yearbook*. The methodology is described in the Fund's *Balance of Payments Manual* (fourth edition). Supplementary data, usually most recent estimates, are obtained from national sources or estimated by World Bank staff.

For **long-term loans** (net disbursements, gross disbursements, and repayments), data are reported to the World Bank's Debtor Reporting System (DRS). Any difference between the IMF balance of payments long-term capital and those in the DRS is shown as **other long-term capital**.

It is not yet possible to reconcile related measures in the sections on balance of payments, foreign trade, and national accounts. This reflects differences in definitions used, timing, recording, and valuation of transactions as well as the nature of basic data sources. Both general and country notes indicate classification and coverage issues that produce discrepancies. The Country Pages report related time series on international transactions in each section in order to help readers make their own judgments about how such discrepancies may affect the analytical purpose at hand.

EXTERNAL DEBT (TOTAL)

External debt statistics are presented by type of borrower instead of by type of creditor.

The source of debt data is the DRS, supplemented by World Bank estimates. The DRS is concerned solely with low- and middle-income economies and does not collect data on external debt for other groups of borrowers, nor from economies that are not members of the World Bank. The figures on debt refer to amounts disbursed and outstanding, expressed in US dollars converted at official exchange rates. Total disbursements and total repayments are also reported as separate items of the balance of payments. Valuation adjustments explain differences between the change in debt outstanding and the net movements shown in the balance of payment items.

Data on **international reserves** and **gold holdings** are from the IFS data files.

SOCIAL INDICATORS

The primary sources of social indicators data are the data files and publications of specialized international agencies, such as Food and Agriculture Organization,

International Labour Organisation, United Nations Educational, Scientific, and Cultural Organization, the UN Statistical Office, and World Health Organization. Supplementary sources are the Population Council, UN Research Institute for Social Development (UNRISD), and World Bank data files. Some demographic and labor force indicators are estimated by interpolating census observations.

The index of **food production per capita** shows the average annual quantity of food produced per capita. For this index, food is defined as comprising nuts, fruits, pulses, cereals, vegetables, starchy roots, sugar beet, sugar cane, edible oils, livestock, and livestock products. Quantities of food are measured net of animal feed, seeds for use in agriculture, and food lost in processing and distribution.

The data on **primary school enrollment** are estimates of children of all ages enrolled in primary school. Figures are expressed as the ratio of pupils to the population of children in the country's school age group. While many countries consider primary school age to be 6 to 11 years, others do not. For some countries with universal primary education, the gross enrollment ratios may exceed 100 percent because some pupils are younger or older than the country's standard primary-school age.

The data on **secondary school enrollment** are calculated in the same manner, and the definition of secondary school age also differs among countries. It is most commonly considered to be 12 to 17 years.

Many indicators are based on census or household surveys, which occur infrequently. Thus some reported figures are interpolated or extrapolated estimates.

Glossary of Terms

in order of appearance on country pages

Current GNP per capita
GNP per capita estimates at current purchaser values (market prices), in US dollars, are calculated according to *World Bank Atlas* methodology.

Population
Total population – midyear estimates.

USE AND ORIGIN OF RESOURCES
(current and constant prices)

Gross national product (GNP)
Comprises gross domestic product (GDP) at purchaser values (market prices) plus net factor income from abroad.

Net factor income from abroad (current prices)
Includes the net compensation of employees (with less than one year of residence in the host country) and the net property and entrepreneurial income components of the System of National Accounts (SNA). The major components of the latter are investment income and interest on short- and long-term capital.

Gross domestic product (GDP)
Gross domestic product at purchaser values (market prices) is the sum of GDP at factor cost and indirect taxes, less subsidies.

Resource balance
Equals exports of goods and nonfactor services less imports of goods and nonfactor services.

Exports/imports of goods and nonfactor services
Consists of transactions of residents of a given country with the rest of the world, and covers insurance, merchandise, transportation, travel, and other nonfactor services such as government transactions and various fees but excludes dividends, interest, and other investment income receipts or payments, as well as labor income.

Domestic absorption
Equals private consumption, and general government consumption, plus gross domestic investment.

Private consumption
Equals the market value of all goods and services purchased or received as income in kind by individuals and nonprofit institutions. It excludes purchases of dwellings, but includes the imputed rent of owner-occupied dwellings. The line is called **Private consumption, etc.** because it includes any statistical discrepancy in the use of resources. At constant prices, it also includes the rescaling deviation from partial rebasing (see Sources and Methods).

General government consumption
Equals the sum of (i) purchases, less sales, of consumer goods and services, reduced by the value of the own-account production of fixed assets, (ii) compensation of employees, (iii) consumption of fixed assets, and (iv) any payments of indirect taxes.

Gross domestic investment
The sum of gross domestic fixed investment and the change in stocks.

Fixed investment
Made up of all outlays (purchases and own-account production) of industries, producers of government services, and producers of private nonprofit services on additions of new and imported durable goods to their stocks of fixed assets, reduced by the proceeds of net sales (sales less purchases) of similar second-hand and scrapped goods. Excluded is the outlay of producers of government services on durable goods primarily for military purposes, which is classified by the SNA as current consumption.

Indirect taxes, net
Equals total indirect taxes less subsidies.

GDP at factor cost (producer prices)
Derived as the sum of the value added in the agriculture, industry, and services sectors. If the value added of these sectors is calculated at purchaser values (mar-

ket prices), GDP at factor cost is derived by subtracting the net indirect taxes from the GDP at purchaser values (market prices).

Agriculture (value added)
Comprises agricultural and livestock production and services, fishing, hunting, logging, and forestry.

Industry (value added)
Comprises mining and quarrying; manufacturing; construction; and electricity, gas, and water.

Services (value added)
Includes all service activities, that is, transport, storage, and communications; wholesale and retail trade; banking, insurance, and real estate; ownership of dwellings; public administration and defense; and other services. The line is called **Services, etc.**, because it includes any statistical discrepancy in the origin of resources.

Gross domestic saving (at current prices)
Equals gross domestic product minus total consumption, etc. (or gross domestic investment plus the resource balance). *Gross Domestic Saving* (at constant prices) equals gross domestic income minus total consumption, etc. (or gross domestic investment plus the resource balance plus the terms of trade adjustment).

Gross national saving (at current prices)
Equals gross domestic saving plus net factor income and net current transfers from abroad.

Capacity to import
Value of exports of goods and nonfactor services deflated by the import price index.

Terms of trade adjustment
Equals capacity to import less exports of goods and nonfactor services in constant prices.

Gross domestic income (constant prices)
Derived as the sum of GDP and the terms of trade adjustment.

Gross national income
Derived as the sum of GNP and the terms of trade adjustment.

DOMESTIC PRICES/DEFLATORS

Overall (GDP)
The deflator is derived by dividing current price estimates of GDP at purchaser values (market prices) by constant price estimates; also called the implicit GDP deflator.

Domestic absorption
The deflator is derived by dividing current price domestic absorption estimates by constant price estimates.

Agriculture, industry, manufacturing
Price indexes are mostly implicit deflators derived from volume and value estimates.

Consumer price index
Comprises the price index of goods and services used for private final consumption of households.

MANUFACTURING ACTIVITY

Employment
The average number of employees or persons engaged during the year. For further information about these classifications, see Sources and Methods.

Real earnings per employee
Derived by deflating nominal earnings per employee data from UNIDO by the consumer price index.

Real output per employee
Obtained as UNIDO data on gross output per employee in current prices deflated by price indexes of value added in manufacturing, where available, or in industry, where not.

Earnings as % of value added
Derived by dividing total nominal earnings of employees by nominal value added, to show labor's share in income generated in the manufacturing sector.

MONETARY HOLDINGS

Money supply, broadly defined
Comprises the monetary and quasi-monetary liabilities of a country's financial institutions to residents other than the central government.

Money
The sum of currency outside banks plus demand deposits held in the financial system by the rest of the domestic economy, other than central government.

Currency outside banks
Comprises bank notes and coin accepted as legal tender in the domestic economy, excluding amounts held by the monetary system, central government, and nonresidents.

Demand deposits
Deposits payable on demand. Typically comprises accounts transferable by checks and any alternative

instruments, forms, and mechanisms for transferring money.

Quasi-money
Comprises time and savings deposits, and similar bank accounts that the issuer will readily exchange for money. Where nonmonetary financial institutions are important issuers of quasi-monetary liabilities, these are also included in the measure of monetary holdings.

GOVERNMENT DEFICIT OR SURPLUS

Government deficit or surplus
Defined as the sum of current and capital revenue and all grants received, less the sum of current and capital expenditure and government lending minus repayments.

Current revenue
Comprises tax revenue and nontax revenue. Capital receipts are excluded. Tax revenue covers tax on income, profits, social security contributions, taxes on property, domestic taxes on goods and services, etc. Nontax revenue consists of grants, property income and operating surpluses of departmental enterprises, receipts from public enterprises, administrative fees and charges, fines, etc.

Current expenditure
Expenditure for goods and services, interest payments, and subsidies and other current transfers. Excludes capital payments.

Current budget balance
The excess of current revenue over current expenditure.

Capital receipts
Proceeds from the sale of nonfinancial capital assets, including land, intangible assets, stocks, and fixed capital assets of buildings, construction, and equipment of more than a minimum value and usable for more than one year in the process of production, and receipts of unrequited transfers for capital purposes from nongovernmental sources.

Capital payments
Expenditure for acquisition of land, intangible assets, government stocks, and nonmilitary and nonfinancial assets; also for capital grants and lending minus repayments.

FOREIGN TRADE (CUSTOMS BASIS)

Value of exports, fob/imports, cif
With some exceptions, covers international movements of goods only across customs borders. Exports are valued fob (free on board), imports cif (cost, insurance, and freight), unless otherwise specified.

Nonfuel primary products
Comprises commodities in SITC revision 1, Sections 0, 1, 2, 4, and Division 68 (food and live animals, beverages and tobacco, inedible crude materials, oils, fats, waxes, and nonferrous metals).

Fuels
Comprises commodities in SITC revision 1, Section 3 (mineral fuels and lubricants and related materials).

Manufactures
Comprises commodities in SITC revision 1, Sections 5 through 9 (chemicals and related products, basic manufactures, machinery and transport equipment, other manufactured articles and goods not elsewhere classified) excluding Division 68 (nonferrous metals).

Terms of trade
The relative level of export prices compared with import prices, calculated as the ratio of a country's index of average export price to the average import price index.

Export price, fob/import price, cif
Price index measuring changes in the aggregate price level of a country's merchandise exports and imports over time.

BALANCE OF PAYMENTS

Exports/imports of goods and services
Comprises all transactions involving a change of ownership of goods and services between residents of a country and the rest of the world. It includes merchandise, nonfactor services, and factor services.

Merchandise, fob
Comprises the market value of movable goods, including nonmonetary gold. It also includes the market value of related distributive services up to the customs frontier of the exporting economy, that is, fob (free on board) value. The few types of goods that are not covered by the merchandise account include travellers' purchases abroad, which are included in travel, and purchases of goods by diplomatic and military personnel, which are classified under other official goods, services, and income.

Nonfactor services
Comprises shipment, passenger and other transport services, and travel, as well as current account transactions not separately reported (e.g., not classified as merchandise, nonfactor services, or transfers). These include transactions with nonresidents by government agencies and their personnel abroad, and also transactions by private residents with foreign governments and government personnel stationed in the reporting country.

Factor services
Comprises services of labor and capital, thus covering income from direct investment abroad, interest, dividends, and property and labor income.

Long-term interest
Comprises interest on the disbursed portion of outstanding public and private loans repayable in foreign currencies, goods, or services. It may include commitment charges on undisbursed loans.

Private current transfers, net
Comprises net transfer payments—between private persons and nonofficial organizations of the reporting country and the rest of the world—that carry no provisions for repayments. Included are workers' remittances; transfers by migrants; gifts, dowries, and inheritances; and alimony and other support remittances.

Workers' remittances
Comprises remittances of income by migrants who have come to an economy to stay for a year or more and who are employed by their new economy, where they are considered to be residents.

Current account balance before official transfers
Comprises the sum of the net exports of goods and nonfactor services, net factor service income, and net private transfers.

Net official transfers
Comprises net transfer payment between governments of the reporting country and the rest of the world.

Current account balance after official transfers
Comprises the sum of the net exports of goods and nonfactor services, net factor service income, and net transfers; official capital grants are always included.

Long-term capital, net
Comprises changes, apart from valuation adjustments in residents' long-term foreign liabilities less their long-term assets, excluding any long-term items classified as reserves.

Direct investment
Comprises all capital transactions that are made to acquire a lasting interest in an enterprise operating in an economy other than that of the investor, where the investor's purpose is to have an effective voice in the management of the enterprise. Direct investment includes items such as equity capital, reinvestment of earnings, and other long- and short-term capital.

Long-term loans
Comprises all public, publicly guaranteed, and private nonguaranteed loans that have an original or extended maturity of more than a year and that are repayable in foreign currencies, goods, or services. These data are as reported in the Bank's Debtor Reporting System and accord with the stock data on external debt, discussed below.

Disbursements
Comprises the total amounts drawn on public, publicly guaranteed, and private nonguaranteed loans, net of commitment cancellations.

Repayments
Comprises repayments (amortization) of the principal of public, publicly guaranteed, and private nonguaranteed loans.

Other long-term capital
Comprises the difference between long-term capital, as defined above, and the similar item reported in IMF balance of payments statistics.

Other capital, net
Comprises the sum of short-term capital, net errors and omissions, and capital transactions not included elsewhere.

Change in reserves
Comprises the net change in a country's holdings of international reserves resulting from transactions on the current and capital accounts. These include changes in holdings of monetary gold, SDRs, reserve position in the Fund, foreign exchange assets, and other claims on nonresidents that are available to the central authority. The measure is net of liabilities constituting foreign authorities' reserves, and counterpart items for valuation of monetary gold and SDRs, which are reported separately in IMF sources.

Conversion factor (annual average)
Is the annual average of market exchange rates for countries quoting rates in units of national currency

per US dollar. (See Sources and Methods for details of additional conversion factors.)

EXTERNAL DEBT

Long-term debt (by debtor)
Is all external obligation of both public and private debtors with maturity of more than one year. It comprises both publicly guaranteed and nonguaranteed debt.

Central government
Is the borrower when the name of the republic, kingdom, etc., or any agencies and departments of central government, appears as the obligor in the contract.

Rest of general government
Is the borrower when the name of the state, province, city, etc., or any agencies and departments of local government, appears as the obligor in the contract.

Nonfinancial public enterprises
Are those described in the SNA definition of "nonfinancial public enterprises."

Private sector, including non-guaranteed
Private sector borrowers are other than those listed above.

Short-term debt
Is the sum of public and private external obligations with original or extended maturity of a year or less.

International reserves excluding gold
Comprises a country's monetary authorities' (central banks, currency boards, exchange stabilization funds, and treasuries) holdings of SDRs, reserve position in the Fund, and foreign exchange.

Gold holdings (at market price)
Are official holdings of gold (fine troy ounces) valued at year-end London market prices.

SOCIAL INDICATORS

Total fertility rate
Is the average number of children that would be born alive to a woman during her lifetime if she were to bear children at each age in accordance with prevailing age-specific fertility rates.

Infant mortality rate
Is the number of infants per thousand live births, in a given year, who die before reaching one year of age.

Life expectancy at birth
Is the number of years a newborn infant would live if prevailing patterns of mortality for all people at the time of his or her birth were to stay the same throughout his or her life.

Urban population, % of total
Is the urban population as a percentage of the total population

Food production per capita
Is the index of annual production of all food commodities adjusted for population growth. Production excludes animal feed and seed for agriculture.

Labor force, agriculture (%)
Is the labor force in farming, forestry, hunting, and fishing as a percentage of total labor force, which comprises so-called "economically active" persons, including armed forces and unemployed but excluding housewives and students.

Labor force, female (%)
Female labor force as a percentage of total labor force.

Primary school enrollment ratio
Gross enrollment of all ages at primary level as a percentage of children in the country's primary school age group.

Primary school enrollment ratio, female
Gross enrollment of females of all ages at primary level as a percentage of children in the country's primary school age group.

Secondary school enrollment ratio
Computed in a similar manner to primary enrollment, but includes pupils enrolled in vocational or teacher-training secondary schools.

Topical Pages

Table 1. Gross national product per capita

US dollars, Atlas methodology	1970	1971	1972	1973	1974	1975	1976	1977	1978	1979	1980
SUB-SAHARAN AFRICA	*150*	*170*	*190*	*210*	*260*	*300*	*360*	*400*	*420*	*490*	*560*
Excluding Nigeria	*160*	*170*	*180*	*190*	*230*	*260*	*280*	*300*	*330*	*370*	*420*
Benin	110	100	110	130	150	160	180	200	220	260	320
Botswana	130	150	190	240	340	350	420	430	490	600	780
Burkina Faso	80	80	80	100	120	130	150	160	170	210	240
Burundi	70	90	80	80	90	100	120	140	150	170	200
Cameroon	180	180	180	210	270	310	360	410	500	600	760
Cape Verde	..	..	200	230	290	310	350	320	320	360	520
Central African Rep.	110	100	110	120	150	170	200	230	260	280	320
Chad	100	90	100	100	120	150	150	160	170	150	160
Comoros	100	110	110	140	150	170	190	200	220	260	340
Congo, People's Rep of the	240	260	290	340	430	530	520	490	530	650	850
Cote D'Ivoire	270	280	290	310	390	510	560	640	840	1,010	1,180
Ethiopia	60	70	70	70	80	90	90	90	100	110	120
Gabon	660	690	740	890	1,660	2,730	4,170	3,800	2,870	3,190	3,900
Gambia, The	100	120	130	140	200	210	230	250	260	350	350
Ghana	250	270	250	260	290	280	280	300	350	380	410
Guinea-Bissau	..	..	160	160	170	190	170	160	170	170	130
Kenya	130	160	180	180	210	230	240	270	310	370	420
Lesotho	100	110	110	150	200	230	250	290	330	360	410
Liberia	300	310	320	320	370	410	460	500	530	580	580
Madagascar	170	170	180	190	230	280	280	300	310	370	430
Malawi	60	80	80	90	110	120	120	130	160	170	180
Mali	70	70	80	80	90	120	140	170	170	210	240
Mauritania	180	170	180	200	260	300	340	360	360	400	440
Mauritius	280	300	340	430	590	710	860	930	1,020	1,200	1,180
Mozambique	..	..	..	..	..	..	..	..	..	..	..
Niger	160	170	160	160	200	230	230	250	300	360	440
Nigeria	150	190	230	270	360	440	600	700	720	870	1,030
Rwanda	60	60	60	70	70	90	120	160	180	210	240
Senegal	220	210	230	240	280	350	400	400	380	460	510
Seychelles	350	410	470	580	700	800	870	960	1,120	1,610	2,000
Sierra Leone	160	160	160	170	190	210	210	220	220	270	320
Somalia	90	90	100	110	110	160	180	170	150	130	140
Sudan	140	150	160	150	200	260	330	390	410	400	430
Swaziland	270	320	330	370	460	590	580	590	600	720	820
Tanzania	100	100	110	120	140	160	180	190	220	250	280
Togo	140	140	150	170	210	260	270	310	350	360	420
Uganda	190	200	210	210	220	220	270	280	280	290	280
Zaire	260	270	280	340	390	430	430	470	510	600	630
Zambia	440	430	430	430	530	550	540	500	500	510	600
Zimbabwe	310	330	360	400	530	570	560	540	530	590	710
SOUTH ASIA	*110*	*110*	*110*	*120*	*140*	*160*	*160*	*170*	*180*	*190*	*230*
Bangladesh	100	100	80	80	100	130	140	110	110	120	140
India	110	110	110	130	140	170	160	170	190	200	240
Nepal	80	80	80	80	100	110	120	120	120	130	140
Pakistan	170	170	160	130	130	130	170	190	220	240	290
Sri Lanka	170	170	160	170	200	220	230	220	220	230	260
EAST ASIA AND PACIFIC	*140*	*140*	*140*	*160*	*190*	*220*	*230*	*250*	*300*	*350*	*400*
China	130	130	130	150	160	180	170	190	220	260	300
Fiji	400	450	520	660	840	1,030	1,190	1,290	1,350	1,580	1,750
Indonesia	80	90	90	110	150	210	270	320	380	400	470
Korea, Republic of	270	310	330	390	480	580	750	910	1,190	1,520	1,620
Malaysia	390	410	450	550	700	820	920	1,010	1,150	1,400	1,690
Papua New Guinea	260	280	300	370	450	530	520	540	650	710	760
Philippines	230	220	220	250	300	360	420	450	510	590	680
Solomon islands	..	..	..	..	..	290	270	300	320	440	400
Thailand	210	210	220	250	300	360	410	460	530	590	670
Vanuatu	..	..	..	..	..	..	..	..	..	..	..

1981	1982	1983	1984	1985	1986	1987	1988	1989	1990	
590	*590*	*520*	*480*	*470*	*420*	*340*	*330*	*330*	*..*	*SUB-SAHARAN AFRICA*
430	*420*	*380*	*340*	*320*	*330*	*330*	*350*	*360*	*..*	*Excluding Nigeria*
340	330	280	260	260	280	310	370	380	..	Benin
1,040	1,020	1,070	1,050	920	980	1,010	1,230	1,600	..	Botswana
250	250	220	190	190	210	250	310	320	..	Burkina Faso
250	240	250	240	250	240	250	240	220	..	Burundi
900	900	870	820	810	890	920	980	1,000	990	Cameroon
520	500	480	450	440	460	550	680	760	..	Cape Verde
330	340	280	280	270	290	320	370	390	..	Central African Rep.
160	150	140	130	150	150	140	180	190	..	Chad
380	350	330	310	300	320	370	440	450	..	Comoros
1,100	1,320	1,240	1,150	1,040	910	910	890	940	940	Congo, People's Rep of the
1,150	990	790	690	650	710	790	880	790	..	Cote D'Ivoire
120	120	120	120	110	120	120	120	120	..	Ethiopia
4,260	4,370	3,830	3,580	3,560	3,630	2,890	2,780	2,960	..	Gabon
370	350	290	250	210	170	190	210	240	..	Gambia, The
410	380	350	370	370	390	390	400	390	..	Ghana
170	190	200	190	190	160	170	170	180	..	Guinea-Bissau
430	400	350	330	310	330	340	370	370	..	Kenya
480	550	510	480	390	340	340	410	470	..	Lesotho
590	550	500	470	470	450	450	..	..	..	Liberia
410	400	380	340	310	290	270	250	230	..	Madagascar
180	190	180	180	170	160	150	160	180	200	Malawi
240	220	170	160	150	180	200	240	270	..	Mali
480	450	460	410	400	420	410	460	490	..	Mauritania
1,260	1,210	1,120	1,080	1,100	1,230	1,470	1,730	1,990	2,240	Mauritius
..	190	160	180	180	220	150	100	80	..	Mozambique
440	380	310	240	230	240	250	300	290	..	Niger
1,090	1,110	980	900	930	710	370	280	250	270	Nigeria
260	260	270	260	270	300	310	330	320	..	Rwanda
490	500	440	380	380	430	520	650	650	..	Senegal
2,270	2,350	2,350	2,330	2,520	2,650	3,040	3,640	4,170	..	Seychelles
370	380	380	360	360	390	280	250	220	..	Sierra Leone
160	170	150	150	160	150	170	170	170	..	Somalia
460	450	400	350	320	370	380	380	..	..	Sudan
1,010	1,010	930	890	740	660	640	820	900	..	Swaziland
300	310	320	310	310	270	200	150	120	..	Tanzania
410	350	290	260	250	270	310	370	390	..	Togo
220	240	220	220	230	230	220	240	250	..	Uganda
590	540	460	340	270	240	240	260	260	..	Zaire
720	660	560	460	370	260	240	290	390	..	Zambia
860	900	850	730	620	560	540	570	650	650	Zimbabwe
260	*270*	*270*	*270*	*270*	*280*	*290*	*320*	*320*	*330*	*SOUTH ASIA*
160	160	150	140	150	160	160	170	180	..	Bangladesh
270	280	280	280	290	290	310	340	340	350	India
160	160	160	170	170	160	160	180	180	..	Nepal
330	360	350	350	340	340	330	350	360	..	Pakistan
290	330	340	350	390	410	410	420	430	..	Sri Lanka
440	*450*	*460*	*460*	*460*	*440*	*450*	*500*	*560*	*..*	*EAST ASIA AND PACIFIC*
320	320	320	320	330	310	310	330	360	..	China
2,000	1,870	1,700	1,770	1,640	1,760	1,590	1,500	1,640	..	Fiji
550	610	610	580	540	520	490	480	500	550	Indonesia
1,830	1,930	2,110	2,240	2,320	2,570	2,950	3,600	4,400	5,440	Korea, Republic of
1,880	1,900	1,900	2,040	1,970	1,850	1,830	1,930	2,160	..	Malaysia
820	780	760	750	740	740	760	850	890	..	Papua New Guinea
770	790	740	630	570	560	590	630	700	760	Philippines
500	570	550	620	520	580	550	550	570	..	Solomon islands
750	780	810	840	800	790	850	1,030	1,230	..	Thailand
..	..	..	..	930	900	780	830	860	..	Vanuatu

Table 1. Gross national product per capita (cont'd.)

US dollars, Atlas methodology	1970	1971	1972	1973	1974	1975	1976	1977	1978	1979	1980
LATIN AMERICA AND CARIBBEAN	*590*	*630*	*670*	*780*	*960*	*1,120*	*1,260*	*1,350*	*1,460*	*1,670*	*1,920*
Argentina	920	1,000	1,040	1,240	1,630	1,810	1,680	1,610	1,570	1,800	1,970
Bahamas	2,700	2,900	2,900	3,260	2,950	2,730	3,000	3,330	3,670	5,100	5,830
Barbados	750	830	910	1,040	1,220	1,520	1,740	1,960	2,250	2,670	3,130
Belize	430	470	520	570	660	790	840	860	910	1,080	1,170
Bolivia	230	250	270	290	320	360	400	410	440	470	490
Brazil	450	500	570	710	880	1,070	1,300	1,470	1,640	1,870	2,070
Chile	840	990	1,080	1,080	1,140	860	880	1,030	1,330	1,680	2,100
Colombia	340	360	390	430	500	550	600	680	840	1,010	1,180
Costa Rica	560	610	660	750	860	950	1,070	1,320	1,560	1,790	1,960
Dominican Republic	330	370	430	490	570	660	760	840	900	1,010	1,080
Ecuador	290	290	300	370	430	540	680	790	930	1,080	1,260
El Salvador	290	300	310	330	380	430	500	590	700	760	750
Grenada	..	..	..	..	..	..	..	..	..	..	..
Guatemala	360	380	390	430	500	570	660	790	900	1,030	1,120
Guyana	380	410	400	410	510	640	660	620	620	650	720
Haiti	90	100	100	110	130	150	170	180	200	220	250
Honduras	270	280	290	310	340	360	400	460	530	600	640
Jamaica	720	770	910	960	1,090	1,260	1,330	1,440	1,420	1,290	1,160
Mexico	820	800	820	940	1,120	1,360	1,500	1,490	1,580	1,820	2,320
Nicaragua	380	390	390	430	560	630	700	780	740	560	690
Panama	680	740	770	840	920	1,030	1,080	1,120	1,290	1,420	1,630
Paraguay	260	270	300	350	440	550	620	720	830	1,030	1,340
Peru	520	580	620	700	850	1,000	1,040	970	840	850	990
St. Vincent and The Grenadines	220	230	300	290	310	340	360	380	430	470	540
Trinidad and Tobago	810	840	960	1,100	1,340	1,920	2,440	2,770	3,310	3,740	4,690
Uruguay	780	910	910	990	1,140	1,370	1,440	1,450	1,650	2,110	2,800
Venezuela	1,240	1,260	1,340	1,540	1,920	2,380	2,890	3,160	3,390	3,730	4,070
MIDDLE EAST AND NORTH AFRICA	*340*	*350*	*390*	*470*	*610*	*810*	*1,050*	*1,160*	*1,190*	*1,330*	*1,430*
Algeria	360	340	430	500	670	870	1,060	1,180	1,380	1,650	1,940
Egypt, Arab Republic of	230	250	260	280	280	320	360	410	410	440	500
Iran, Islamic Rep. of	380	420	500	690	940	1,310	1,890	2,180	1,980	2,110	2,030
Jordan	..	..	..	..	..	..	..	..	..	..	..
Morocco	260	280	300	340	410	500	560	600	650	770	930
Oman	360	370	400	390	560	1,280	2,840	2,860	2,790	3,080	3,660
Syrian Arab Republic	350	390	460	460	650	890	1,020	1,010	1,120	1,200	1,410
Tunisia	280	320	400	430	560	710	800	850	930	1,080	1,280
Turkey	400	400	410	470	630	830	1,000	1,110	1,210	1,360	1,390
Yemen, Republic of	..	..	..	..	..	..	..	..	..	..	..
EUROPE	..	..	..	..	..	..	..	..	..	..	..
Bulgaria	..	..	..	..	..	..	..	..	..	..	..
Greece	1,170	1,300	1,460	1,720	1,940	2,370	2,650	2,850	3,270	3,860	4,370
Hungary	..	..	..	..	..	..	..	1,310	1,500	1,680	1,930
Malta	760	820	900	1,030	1,220	1,540	1,700	1,860	2,090	2,500	3,150
Poland	..	..	..	..	..	..	..	..	..	..	..
Portugal	700	820	940	1,200	1,420	1,540	1,700	1,830	1,890	2,090	2,380
Romania	..	..	..	..	..	..	..	..	..	..	..
Yugoslavia	660	740	780	870	1,150	1,380	1,620	1,970	2,400	2,880	3,250
Low- & middle-income economies	220	230	240	280	340	400	450	480	530	610	700
Severely indebted	530	570	610	710	870	1,030	1,160	1,230	1,340	1,530	1,770
Low-income economies	120	120	130	140	160	180	190	210	230	260	310
Low-income Africa	140	160	180	190	240	280	330	370	390	450	520
China and India	120	120	120	140	150	180	170	180	210	230	270
Other low-income	100	100	100	100	120	150	180	200	230	250	280
Middle-income economies	490	520	560	660	820	980	1,150	1,240	1,360	1,560	1,770
High-income OECD members	3,190	3,460	3,870	4,520	5,160	5,800	6,470	7,150	8,090	9,400	10,650
European Community members	2,360	2,580	2,940	3,570	4,250	4,900	5,440	6,000	6,780	8,220	9,760
Japan	1,950	2,140	2,540	3,240	3,820	4,490	4,970	5,690	7,020	8,620	9,870
United States	4,950	5,320	5,780	6,410	6,890	7,400	8,180	9,040	10,100	11,150	12,000
Other high-income economies /a	800	930	1,100	1,310	1,780	2,370	3,330	3,940	4,380	5,160	6,080

a. Economies classified by the United Nations or otherwise regarded by their authorities as developing.

1981	1982	1983	1984	1985	1986	1987	1988	1989	1990	
2,140	2,120	1,900	1,800	1,730	1,720	1,730	1,800	1,950	..	*LATIN AMERICA AND CARIBBEAN*
1,960	1,880	1,970	2,150	2,140	2,380	2,400	2,570	2,160	2,260	Argentina
5,650	6,600	7,110	8,190	8,950	9,530	10,360	10,680	11,370	..	Bahamas
3,520	3,760	4,010	4,420	4,640	5,180	5,350	5,910	6,370	..	Barbados
1,220	1,140	1,090	1,100	1,140	1,240	1,390	1,560	1,720	..	Belize
560	530	480	450	420	440	510	590	620	..	Bolivia
2,030	2,070	1,840	1,730	1,670	1,810	1,960	2,120	2,540	..	Brazil
2,600	2,220	1,930	1,680	1,450	1,350	1,370	1,510	1,770	1,890	Chile
1,320	1,390	1,380	1,370	1,280	1,220	1,180	1,180	1,190	1,200	Colombia
1,540	1,150	1,060	1,250	1,400	1,550	1,650	1,680	1,780	1,940	Costa Rica
1,180	1,280	1,230	1,010	790	750	750	720	790	..	Dominican Republic
1,490	1,490	1,320	1,160	1,170	1,140	1,060	1,090	1,020	1,010	Ecuador
750	740	760	820	840	830	860	960	1,070	1,090	El Salvador
..	..	..	..	..	1,360	1,500	1,710	1,900	..	Grenada
1,200	1,190	1,170	1,180	1,200	1,050	950	900	910	910	Guatemala
730	610	520	500	510	500	400	400	340	..	Guyana
270	270	280	290	310	340	350	360	360	..	Haiti
690	690	700	720	740	760	820	860	900	610	Honduras
1,240	1,310	1,360	1,150	910	870	960	1,080	1,260	..	Jamaica
3,000	2,820	2,290	2,130	2,180	1,890	1,770	1,750	1,990	2,360	Mexico
810	850	860	860	840	850	870	..	..	..	Nicaragua
1,820	1,950	1,950	1,980	2,060	2,170	2,210	1,810	1,760	1,830	Panama
1,680	1,740	1,640	1,490	1,170	950	890	970	1,030	1,150	Paraguay
1,240	1,380	1,150	1,120	980	1,080	1,170	1,040	1,010	1,090	Peru
650	750	840	900	1,000	1,060	1,140	1,360	..	..	St. Vincent and The Grenadines
5,890	6,630	6,400	6,400	5,940	4,970	4,060	3,410	3,230	..	Trinidad and Tobago
3,590	3,410	2,450	1,940	1,680	1,910	2,210	2,440	2,620	..	Uruguay
4,730	4,920	4,790	4,250	3,830	3,570	3,180	3,130	2,450	2,420	Venezuela
1,610	1,750	1,790	1,800	1,860	1,840	1,800	1,740	1,650	..	*MIDDLE EAST AND NORTH AFRICA*
2,240	2,420	2,420	2,440	2,570	2,660	2,740	2,450	2,250	2,110	Algeria
550	600	620	640	660	670	690	660	630	..	Egypt, Arab Republic of
2,600	3,240	3,660	3,920	4,210	4,180	3,870	3,590	3,190	..	Iran, Islamic Rep. of
..	..	..	..	1,880	1,940	2,040	2,000	1,730	..	Jordan
870	860	730	660	610	650	680	830	880	960	Morocco
5,830	7,110	7,220	7,280	7,550	6,660	5,810	4,980	5,220	..	Oman
1,660	1,770	1,800	1,720	1,720	1,520	1,220	1,100	..	..	Syrian Arab Republic
1,380	1,310	1,240	1,210	1,170	1,110	1,180	1,230	1,260	1,390	Tunisia
1,440	1,290	1,180	1,100	1,080	1,110	1,220	1,280	1,370	1,610	Turkey
..	..	..	..	..	..	..	..	..	..	Yemen, Republic of
..	..	..	..	..	..	..	..	..	..	*EUROPE*
..	2,450	2,260	2,150	2,040	2,170	2,560	2,750	2,320	..	Bulgaria
4,470	4,320	3,950	3,800	3,610	3,650	3,990	4,770	5,340	..	Greece
2,150	2,260	2,150	2,050	1,940	2,020	2,250	2,450	2,580	2,680	Hungary
3,590	3,790	3,510	3,440	3,390	3,580	4,170	5,180	5,820	..	Malta
..	1,540	1,800	2,060	2,080	2,030	1,850	1,850	1,780	..	Poland
2,500	2,500	2,250	1,990	1,970	2,270	2,830	3,650	4,250	..	Portugal
..	..	..	..	..	..	..	..	..	..	Romania
3,450	3,230	2,640	2,270	2,040	2,290	2,510	2,720	2,920	..	Yugoslavia
780	790	750	740	730	720	720	760	800	..	**Low- & middle-income economies**
1,960	1,940	1,750	1,670	1,620	1,620	1,630	1,710	1,830	..	Severely indebted
340	340	330	330	330	310	310	320	330	..	Low-income economies
540	540	480	440	430	380	280	260	260	..	Low-income Africa
300	300	300	300	310	300	310	330	350	..	China and India
320	350	350	340	320	320	310	310	330	..	Other low-income
1,970	2,000	1,900	1,850	1,800	1,810	1,840	1,940	2,050	..	Middle-income economies
11,430	11,380	11,350	11,720	12,080	12,980	14,720	17,440	19,240	..	**High-income OECD members**
10,220	9,850	9,090	8,730	8,590	9,410	11,270	14,220	15,980	..	European Community members
10,390	10,280	10,320	10,560	11,240	12,840	15,800	20,960	23,810	..	Japan
13,270	13,610	14,510	15,890	16,760	17,530	18,570	19,820	21,000	..	United States
7,310	7,790	7,520	7,010	6,530	6,510	6,750	7,400	8,280	..	**Other high-income economies** /a

Table 2. Gross national income per capita

1987 US dollars	1970	1971	1972	1973	1974	1975	1976	1977	1978	1979	1980
SUB-SAHARAN AFRICA	*290*	*290*	*290*	*300*	*360*	*330*	*350*	*360*	*350*	*340*	*380*
Excluding Nigeria	*350*	*340*	*340*	*350*	*370*	*350*	*360*	*380*	*360*	*360*	*370*
Benin	440	420	420	450	430	390	380	400	400	410	410
Botswana	290	300	340	430	530	470	510	500	490	630	760
Burkina Faso	240	240	240	240	260	250	270	270	260	260	260
Burundi	150	200	180	200	190	180	210	250	210	220	210
Cameroon	670	650	610	630	700	660	650	740	780	820	910
Cape Verde	..	..	..	220	250	240	270	300	310	360	510
Central African Rep.	480	480	480	470	450	410	470	500	500	460	430
Chad	210	200	200	180	190	190	190	180	180	130	130
Comoros	..	..	..	..	..	..	..	..	..	..	..
Congo, People's Rep of the	670	700	680	800	950	820	800	690	670	730	900
Cote D'Ivoire	830	840	830	870	920	920	1,010	1,140	1,160	1,080	1,050
Ethiopia	..	..	..	..	..	..	..	..	..	..	..
Gabon	3,130	3,200	3,230	3,260	6,250	6,440	7,830	6,730	4,970	5,250	6,570
Gambia, The	200	220	230	220	260	250	240	270	240	250	220
Ghana	490	460	430	490	510	440	390	430	450	440	440
Guinea-Bissau	200	200	200	200	200	200	180	160	170	170	120
Kenya	320	350	390	380	370	350	350	400	380	390	380
Lesotho	200	210	230	290	320	350	380	430	460	440	420
Liberia	..	..	..	..	..	..	..	..	..	..	..
Madagascar	410	400	390	370	360	340	330	330	300	320	300
Malawi	160	180	180	180	190	190	180	190	200	180	170
Mali	180	180	190	180	170	190	210	220	210	230	220
Mauritania	550	540	510	480	570	540	580	520	480	480	490
Mauritius	740	760	860	910	1,300	1,360	1,280	1,300	1,320	1,350	1,150
Mozambique	..	..	..	..	..	..	..	..	..	..	130
Niger	430	450	410	310	370	290	290	320	340	400	400
Nigeria	160	190	180	210	390	310	350	370	360	320	470
Rwanda	300	300	290	290	280	280	290	300	310	340	350
Senegal	720	700	720	660	670	690	730	700	640	670	630
Seychelles	..	..	..	..	..	..	..	..	..	..	..
Sierra Leone	210	210	200	210	210	200	180	190	190	200	200
Somalia	150	160	160	150	120	160	160	200	210	190	170
Sudan	420	440	410	360	400	430	490	560	530	460	450
Swaziland	..	..	..	..	..	..	..	..	..	..	..
Tanzania	220	220	220	220	200	200	210	200	190	180	170
Togo	450	370	370	380	520	380	440	470	490	440	460
Uganda	..	..	..	..	..	..	..	..	..	..	..
Zaire	380	350	340	380	380	310	290	290	260	260	320
Zambia	800	600	630	700	680	420	450	390	350	380	350
Zimbabwe	..	..	..	..	..	..	740	670	640	630	690
SOUTH ASIA	*240*	*240*	*230*	*230*	*230*	*230*	*240*	*250*	*260*	*240*	*250*
Bangladesh	170	150	130	130	140	140	150	150	150	150	150
India	250	250	240	240	240	250	250	270	280	250	260
Nepal	..	..	..	..	..	..	..	..	..	..	..
Pakistan	250	230	220	230	240	220	230	230	250	250	270
Sri Lanka	250	250	240	260	260	250	280	320	330	330	330
EAST ASIA AND PACIFIC	*180*	*190*	*190*	*210*	*220*	*220*	*220*	*240*	*270*	*280*	*290*
China	110	120	120	130	130	130	130	130	150	160	170
Fiji	1,230	1,270	1,340	1,470	1,670	1,750	1,730	1,800	1,780	1,920	1,870
Indonesia	160	170	170	180	210	220	220	240	260	290	340
Korea, Republic of	970	1,040	1,080	1,220	1,280	1,310	1,500	1,640	1,810	1,900	1,710
Malaysia	950	940	960	1,140	1,210	1,130	1,300	1,400	1,450	1,620	1,740
Papua New Guinea	910	920	970	1,120	1,070	950	980	990	1,010	1,060	950
Philippines	510	520	520	570	580	590	590	620	640	680	680
Solomon islands	..	..	..	..	..	..	..	..	..	..	490
Thailand	510	500	510	580	560	560	590	630	670	690	700
Vanuatu	..	..	..	..	..	..	..	..	..	..	..

1981	1982	1983	1984	1985	1986	1987	1988	1989	1990	
370	*350*	*340*	*330*	*320*	*300*	*290*	*290*	*290*	..	*SUB-SAHARAN AFRICA*
370	*360*	*350*	*350*	*340*	*340*	*330*	*330*	*320*	..	*Excluding Nigeria*
420	430	410	400	430	410	380	370	390	..	Benin
720	660	690	690	820	1,000	1,080	1,270	1,600	..	Botswana
270	290	280	270	290	310	310	320	310	..	Burkina Faso
220	210	220	210	230	230	220	230	..	..	Burundi
990	1,020	1,060	1,090	1,140	1,200	1,110	990	930	870	Cameroon
520	530	560	570	590	610	660	670	670	..	Cape Verde
400	420	380	410	410	410	380	370	370	..	Central African Rep.
130	130	150	140	170	160	150	170	170	170	Chad
..	..	510	490	490	490	460	..	..	..	Comoros
1,030	1,460	1,480	1,580	1,300	870	990	750	780	790	Congo, People's Rep of the
980	940	900	910	880	920	900	850	710	570	Cote D'Ivoire
..	..	..	..	..	..	..	..	..	..	Ethiopia
6,400	6,070	5,630	5,220	4,930	3,660	3,000	2,680	..	..	Gabon
230	230	210	200	200	180	200	220	210	..	Gambia, The
410	350	330	350	360	360	360	380	..	..	Ghana
160	170	160	170	180	170	170	180	190	..	Guinea-Bissau
370	350	340	340	330	350	350	360	360	..	Kenya
430	470	460	460	430	410	400	420	420	420	Lesotho
..	..	..	..	..	..	..	..	..	..	Liberia
260	250	250	250	240	250	230	230	230	..	Madagascar
170	170	160	170	170	160	150	150	150	150	Malawi
220	230	210	220	210	240	240	240	250	..	Mali
510	480	480	440	460	480	450	440	470	..	Mauritania
1,140	1,130	1,160	1,190	1,260	1,480	1,680	1,670	1,740	1,860	Mauritius
130	120	100	110	90	90	90	80	90	90	Mozambique
400	390	380	300	300	310	300	300	270	..	Niger
440	370	320	310	300	220	220	200	220	230	Nigeria
360	360	370	360	350	360	330	330	290	..	Rwanda
610	650	650	610	620	630	640	660	630	640	Senegal
..	..	..	..	..	..	..	..	..	..	Seychelles
210	200	190	190	170	190	180	170	170	..	Sierra Leone
190	200	170	160	170	170	170	160	160	..	Somalia
440	480	470	430	390	420	420	380	410	..	Sudan
..	..	..	..	..	..	..	..	..	..	Swaziland
150	150	140	140	140	140	130	140	130	120	Tanzania
440	410	370	380	380	390	370	380	390	..	Togo
..	..	..	..	..	..	..	..	..	..	Uganda
310	300	280	270	260	240	230	240	230	..	Zaire
330	260	270	260	270	250	240	280	250	240	Zambia
740	720	700	660	670	620	570	650	700	670	Zimbabwe
260	*260*	*270*	*280*	*290*	*300*	*300*	*320*	*320*	*330*	*SOUTH ASIA*
160	150	160	160	160	160	170	170	160	170	Bangladesh
270	270	290	290	300	310	320	340	350	360	India
..	..	..	..	..	..	..	..	..	..	Nepal
270	280	280	290	300	310	320	330	330	340	Pakistan
330	350	380	400	400	410	410	410	410	..	Sri Lanka
300	*310*	*340*	*360*	*380*	*400*	*430*	*470*	*490*	*520*	*EAST ASIA AND PACIFIC*
180	190	200	220	250	260	280	310	310	320	China
1,840	1,680	1,570	1,670	1,580	1,700	1,520	..	..	..	Fiji
370	360	380	400	410	410	420	430	450	480	Indonesia
1,770	1,900	2,110	2,280	2,400	2,740	3,090	3,450	3,730	4,040	Korea, Republic of
1,730	1,750	1,790	1,950	1,830	1,660	1,790	1,950	2,090	2,260	Malaysia
840	790	810	820	820	810	820	850	760	690	Papua New Guinea
680	660	660	600	560	560	580	630	670	670	Philippines
450	460	460	680	480	430	490	550	..	..	Solomon islands
710	710	760	790	790	830	880	1,030	1,150	1,240	Thailand
..	..	910	1,070	1,040	900	780	..	..	..	Vanuatu

Table 2. Gross national income per capita (cont'd.)

1987 US dollars	1970	1971	1972	1973	1974	1975	1976	1977	1978	1979	1980
LATIN AMERICA AND CARIBBEAN	*1,350*	*1,410*	*1,480*	*1,580*	*1,630*	*1,630*	*1,700*	*1,750*	*1,750*	*1,810*	*1,900*
Argentina	2,630	2,720	2,730	2,810	2,870	2,800	2,760	2,880	2,740	2,910	2,950
Bahamas	..	..	..	..	..	..	..	5,880	5,990	8,170	8,650
Barbados	..	..	..	..	..	..	..	..	..	..	..
Belize	..	..	..	..	..	..	..	..	..	..	..
Bolivia	790	800	820	850	920	890	930	930	900	890	870
Brazil	1,200	1,300	1,430	1,610	1,690	1,720	1,860	1,920	1,900	1,960	2,060
Chile	1,580	1,670	1,590	1,520	1,510	1,090	1,150	1,230	1,300	1,430	1,510
Colombia	760	790	830	880	900	890	940	990	1,040	1,050	1,070
Costa Rica	1,380	1,390	1,440	1,510	1,500	1,500	1,600	1,800	1,790	1,780	1,740
Dominican Republic	500	540	630	680	700	710	700	730	720	730	730
Ecuador	720	730	760	860	1,030	1,030	1,110	1,200	1,200	1,290	1,330
El Salvador	1,080	1,080	1,120	1,160	1,150	1,170	1,320	1,500	1,390	1,350	1,170
Grenada	..	..	..	..	..	..	..	..	..	..	..
Guatemala	890	880	900	950	950	940	990	1,110	1,090	1,070	1,060
Guyana	690	720	650	590	800	990	770	720	680	610	650
Haiti	330	350	350	340	350	340	370	370	380	390	410
Honduras	770	760	790	830	800	780	860	950	980	980	950
Jamaica	1,470	1,440	1,610	1,590	1,600	1,630	1,420	1,400	1,370	1,230	1,130
Mexico	1,310	1,320	1,380	1,440	1,490	1,520	1,550	1,550	1,640	1,770	1,920
Nicaragua	1,430	1,410	1,360	1,360	1,580	1,500	1,570	1,700	1,460	950	1,150
Panama	1,750	1,890	1,940	1,960	1,940	1,940	1,870	1,810	1,990	1,990	2,030
Paraguay	570	590	620	670	700	690	760	870	900	850	1,070
Peru	1,270	1,270	1,260	1,320	1,390	1,340	1,320	1,290	1,230	1,320	1,350
St. Vincent and The Grenadines	..	..	..	..	..	..	..	830	890	850	870
Trinidad and Tobago	3,600	3,750	3,890	3,910	4,050	4,560	4,890	5,090	5,690	5,790	6,290
Uruguay	2,150	2,160	2,150	2,220	2,130	2,210	2,290	2,280	2,400	2,550	2,670
Venezuela	..	..	..	..	3,140	3,110	3,300	3,410	3,250	3,270	3,360
MIDDLE EAST AND NORTH AFRICA	*1,250*	*1,310*	*1,430*	*1,590*	*1,730*	*1,750*	*1,950*	*2,020*	*1,810*	*1,760*	*1,610*
Algeria	1,720	1,630	1,870	1,900	2,250	2,200	2,320	2,370	2,450	2,630	2,740
Egypt, Arab Republic of	370	370	370	400	410	420	480	520	520	580	640
Iran, Islamic Rep. of	2,770	2,960	3,260	3,890	4,170	4,120	4,770	4,940	3,950	3,630	2,830
Jordan	..	..	..	..	..	..	..	..	..	..	..
Morocco	560	580	570	580	620	660	680	690	690	710	750
Oman	..	..	..	..	..	..	..	..	..	..	..
Syrian Arab Republic	630	700	780	740	1,040	1,220	1,270	1,200	1,260	1,320	1,400
Tunisia	690	750	880	860	970	990	990	1,000	1,050	1,130	1,210
Turkey	820	870	920	930	970	1,010	1,080	1,100	1,100	1,060	1,010
Yemen, Republic of	..	..	..	..	..	..	..	..	..	..	..
EUROPE	*..*	*..*	*..*	*..*	*..*	*..*	*..*	*..*	*..*	*..*	*2,390*
Bulgaria	..	..	..	..	..	..	..	..	..	..	2,480
Greece	3,200	3,420	3,700	3,980	3,790	3,940	4,130	4,230	4,430	4,510	4,560
Hungary	..	..	..	1,470	1,490	1,880	1,970	2,070	2,140	2,150	2,160
Malta	2,110	2,160	2,250	2,320	2,430	2,850	3,200	3,360	3,530	3,670	3,990
Poland	..	..	..	..	..	..	..	..	..	..	1,610
Portugal	2,250	2,520	2,760	3,080	3,070	2,700	2,750	2,920	2,980	3,120	3,150
Romania	..	..	..	..	..	..	..	..	..	..	..
Yugoslavia	1,780	1,920	1,980	2,020	2,250	2,250	2,350	2,520	2,750	2,840	2,880
Low- & middle-income economies	460	480	490	530	550	560	580	610	610	620	640
Severely indebted	1,230	1,280	1,340	1,440	1,490	1,500	1,570	1,610	1,610	1,680	1,760
Low-income economies	180	180	180	180	190	190	190	210	220	210	230
Low-income Africa	240	240	240	250	300	260	280	300	280	270	310
China and India	170	170	170	170	170	180	180	190	200	200	210
Other low-income	170	170	160	170	180	180	190	200	210	220	250
Middle-income economies	1,240	1,300	1,370	1,490	1,560	1,560	1,660	1,720	1,700	1,740	1,750
High-income OECD members	11,550	11,810	12,330	12,950	12,700	12,560	13,140	13,520	14,040	14,360	14,290
European Community members	9,950	10,160	10,540	11,010	10,940	10,810	11,270	11,530	11,940	12,300	12,290
Japan	11,460	11,910	12,790	13,600	12,940	13,000	13,490	14,080	14,830	15,230	15,410
United States	14,140	14,360	14,900	15,580	15,140	14,840	15,440	15,960	16,590	16,760	16,340
Other high-income economies /a	..	..	..	..	..	..	..	..	..	..	..

a. Economies classified by the United Nations or otherwise regarded by their authorities as developing.

1981	1982	1983	1984	1985	1986	1987	1988	1989	1990	
1,840	*1,740*	*1,620*	*1,670*	*1,680*	*1,700*	*1,720*	*1,690*	*1,700*	*1,680*	*LATIN AMERICA AND CARIBBEAN*
2,710	2,420	2,460	2,510	2,360	2,470	2,450	2,360	2,210	2,180	Argentina
7,860	8,340	8,540	9,480	10,190	10,410	10,630	..	..	..	Bahamas
..	..	..	..	..	..	..	..	..	..	Barbados
..	..	..	..	..	..	..	..	..	..	Belize
850	770	700	690	630	600	590	570	580	..	Bolivia
1,890	1,830	1,720	1,780	1,890	2,040	2,070	2,030	2,080	1,960	Brazil
1,500	1,200	1,190	1,170	1,200	1,260	1,390	1,520	1,630	1,570	Chile
1,050	1,030	1,030	1,040	1,040	1,110	1,100	1,080	1,130	1,110	Colombia
1,550	1,370	1,430	1,530	1,530	1,680	1,620	1,630	1,650	1,670	Costa Rica
730	720	740	770	690	710	710	710	740	650	Dominican Republic
1,310	1,240	1,180	1,170	1,180	1,070	1,000	1,060	1,050	1,080	Ecuador
1,000	920	900	910	930	970	920	950	940	930	El Salvador
..	..	..	..	..	..	..	..	..	..	Grenada
1,010	930	890	870	830	820	810	830	830	830	Guatemala
590	480	390	370	370	410	340	400	..	..	Guyana
390	370	370	360	360	360	350	340	330	310	Haiti
900	820	800	800	810	800	820	830	820	660	Honduras
1,100	1,120	1,130	1,070	960	1,030	1,070	1,040	1,020	980	Jamaica
2,050	1,960	1,740	1,780	1,790	1,590	1,620	1,630	1,670	1,730	Mexico
1,130	1,090	1,110	1,080	1,040	980	980	660	580	540	Nicaragua
2,100	2,070	2,070	2,120	2,150	2,230	2,170	1,720	1,680	1,660	Panama
1,110	1,050	960	950	950	890	910	960	990	1,040	Paraguay
1,360	1,330	1,120	1,140	1,120	1,200	1,300	1,130	1,000	940	Peru
940	1,030	1,090	1,140	1,270	1,320	1,250	..	..	..	St. Vincent and The Grenadines
6,430	6,150	5,380	4,820	4,420	3,720	3,690	3,480	3,330	3,270	Trinidad and Tobago
2,720	2,410	2,150	2,040	2,020	2,290	2,450	2,460	2,520	2,460	Uruguay
3,330	3,010	2,770	2,970	2,790	2,480	2,550	2,520	2,360	2,920	Venezuela
1,650	*1,750*	*1,820*	*1,850*	*1,890*	*1,760*	*1,740*	*1,710*	*1,700*	*..*	*MIDDLE EAST AND NORTH AFRICA*
2,820	2,810	2,890	2,910	2,980	2,670	2,720	2,450	2,500	2,580	Algeria
640	660	700	710	710	680	650	660	660	640	Egypt, Arab Republic of
2,970	3,360	3,580	3,650	3,710	3,230	3,120	3,020	3,030	..	Iran, Islamic Rep. of
..	..	2,100	2,020	1,960	2,190	2,130	2,040	1,860	..	Jordan
690	740	720	720	740	810	780	840	820	820	Morocco
..	..	..	..	..	..	..	..	..	..	Oman
1,500	1,470	1,440	1,350	1,340	1,250	1,100	1,190	..	..	Syrian Arab Republic
1,250	1,210	1,230	1,250	1,250	1,160	1,200	1,170	1,190	1,260	Tunisia
1,010	1,020	1,030	1,080	1,110	1,200	1,260	1,280	1,240	1,330	Turkey
..	..	..	..	..	..	..	..	..	..	Yemen, Republic of
2,330	*2,310*	*2,320*	*2,340*	*2,370*	*2,460*	*2,490*	*2,550*	*2,570*	*..*	*EUROPE*
2,580	2,580	2,690	2,780	2,830	2,940	3,130	3,250	3,030	..	Bulgaria
4,540	4,490	4,420	4,440	4,520	4,520	4,580	4,780	4,860	..	Greece
2,200	2,240	2,250	2,280	2,260	2,260	2,370	2,390	2,400	2,250	Hungary
4,170	4,380	4,200	4,370	4,550	4,630	4,860	5,350	5,580	..	Malta
1,400	1,340	1,410	1,470	1,540	1,600	1,620	1,680	1,630	1,360	Poland
3,070	3,080	3,040	2,890	3,010	3,300	3,490	3,680	3,900	..	Portugal
..	..	..	..	..	..	..	..	..	..	Romania
2,870	2,860	2,790	2,770	2,720	2,890	2,780	2,700	2,770	2,640	Yugoslavia
640	630	630	650	660	670	680	700	710	710	**Low- & middle-income economies**
1,690	1,600	1,520	1,550	1,560	1,580	1,600	1,590	1,590	1,550	Severely indebted
240	240	250	260	270	280	290	300	310	320	Low-income economies
300	280	260	250	240	220	220	210	220	..	Low-income Africa
220	220	240	250	270	280	300	320	330	340	China and India
260	260	270	280	280	280	290	290	300	310	Other low-income
1,730	1,700	1,680	1,720	1,730	1,730	1,760	1,770	1,790	1,790	Middle-income economies
14,360	14,260	14,590	15,170	15,600	16,110	16,570	17,220	17,710	..	**High-income OECD members**
12,120	12,190	12,390	12,630	12,940	13,490	13,880	14,410	14,840	..	European Community members
15,820	16,190	16,580	17,220	17,970	18,860	19,550	20,590	21,350	..	Japan
16,520	16,000	16,470	17,420	17,820	18,160	18,560	19,180	19,620	..	United States
..	..	..	..	..	..	..	..	..	..	**Other high-income economies** /a

Table 3. Private consumption per capita

1987 US dollars	1970	1971	1972	1973	1974	1975	1976	1977	1978	1979	1980
SUB-SAHARAN AFRICA	*200*	*210*	*200*	*190*	*210*	*220*	*230*	*230*	*260*	*220*	*240*
Excluding Nigeria	*240*	*250*	*250*	*240*	*250*	*250*	*250*	*260*	*260*	*260*	*260*
Benin	350	340	340	350	330	310	310	340	340	340	330
Botswana	340	310	320	410	430	420	420	410	440	530	570
Burkina Faso	210	210	200	190	200	200	210	230	230	240	250
Burundi	120	180	170	170	160	180	190	200	180	190	190
Cameroon	530	560	540	520	560	550	560	610	600	690	750
Cape Verde	..	..	..	310	250	270	290	310	370	370	460
Central African Rep.	300	300	310	290	310	320	350	400	400	360	370
Chad	..	..	..	..	..	..	..	..	..	..	..
Comoros	..	..	..	..	..	..	..	..	..	..	..
Congo, People's Rep of the	530	500	480	440	420	420	520	420	460	390	460
Cote D'Ivoire	440	470	480	510	500	560	550	540	610	600	410
Ethiopia	..	..	..	..	..	..	..	..	..	..	..
Gabon	1,530	1,580	1,630	1,820	1,640	1,660	1,820	1,900	2,360	2,040	1,990
Gambia, The	..	..	..	..	..	..	..	..	..	..	..
Ghana	380	370	310	360	410	330	310	320	360	340	360
Guinea-Bissau	130	170	200	220	230	190	170	140	120	100	80
Kenya	140	200	230	200	230	220	200	200	220	230	220
Lesotho	170	180	220	260	300	330	360	360	390	380	320
Liberia	..	..	..	..	..	..	..	..	..	..	..
Madagascar	370	380	360	340	320	320	290	290	280	310	310
Malawi	110	140	140	130	130	130	130	140	130	130	140
Mali	140	140	150	150	160	170	190	180	190	200	200
Mauritania	430	420	400	360	400	360	400	360	330	340	340
Mauritius	530	560	550	550	770	880	900	960	1,000	1,020	900
Mozambique	..	..	..	..	..	..	..	..	..	..	100
Niger	370	390	350	240	330	240	230	250	250	310	330
Nigeria	110	130	100	100	150	180	190	200	270	140	220
Rwanda	270	260	260	240	250	230	230	230	260	290	310
Senegal	550	540	530	500	490	520	550	520	500	530	510
Seychelles	..	..	..	..	..	..	..	..	..	..	..
Sierra Leone	..	..	..	..	..	..	..	..	160	180	180
Somalia	130	140	110	110	90	130	130	210	170	160	160
Sudan	270	300	310	260	270	310	340	410	410	360	330
Swaziland	..	..	..	..	..	..	..	..	..	..	..
Tanzania	..	..	..	..	..	..	160	150	170	140	140
Togo	290	190	200	210	230	170	230	220	210	200	240
Uganda	..	..	..	..	..	..	..	..	..	..	..
Zaire	260	270	280	290	290	270	250	240	210	210	200
Zambia	260	240	230	180	180	180	210	200	180	230	200
Zimbabwe	..	..	..	..	..	..	530	490	470	480	510
SOUTH ASIA	*180*	*170*	*170*	*160*	*160*	*170*	*160*	*180*	*180*	*170*	*170*
Bangladesh	..	..	..	..	..	..	..	..	..	..	..
India	180	180	170	170	160	170	170	180	190	170	180
Nepal	..	..	..	..	..	..	..	..	..	..	..
Pakistan	220	210	180	180	190	190	190	200	210	220	230
Sri Lanka	200	200	180	200	200	210	210	230	240	240	260
EAST ASIA AND PACIFIC	*130*	*130*	*130*	*140*	*140*	*150*	*150*	*160*	*170*	*180*	*190*
China	80	80	80	80	80	90	80	90	90	100	110
Fiji	890	950	1,000	1,160	1,250	1,240	1,260	1,290	1,270	1,290	1,210
Indonesia	150	150	140	140	160	170	170	170	190	200	210
Korea, Republic of	670	740	740	820	850	880	960	990	1,060	1,160	1,110
Malaysia	570	590	610	650	690	670	700	750	810	880	960
Papua New Guinea	460	470	500	520	520	520	520	560	590	570	590
Philippines	360	370	380	380	390	390	380	400	420	440	440
Solomon islands	..	..	..	..	..	..	..	..	..	..	400
Thailand	350	330	350	380	380	380	400	420	430	470	480
Vanuatu	..	..	..	..	..	..	..	..	..	..	..

1981	1982	1983	1984	1985	1986	1987	1988	1989	1990	
280	*270*	*260*	*240*	*240*	*230*	*220*	*220*	*210*	*..*	*SUB-SAHARAN AFRICA*
260	*260*	*260*	*250*	*250*	*250*	*250*	*250*	*240*	*..*	*Excluding Nigeria*
350	370	330	350	350	360	330	330	330	..	Benin
550	560	490	460	570	460	540	640	940	..	Botswana
250	250	240	220	230	250	250	260	270	..	Burkina Faso
190	190	190	200	210	200	170	180	..	..	Burundi
760	740	720	680	720	760	800	780	660	650	Cameroon
450	430	460	480	500	510	480	490	490	..	Cape Verde
320	350	300	330	330	350	330	330	320	..	Central African Rep.
..	..	150	130	180	170	150	170	160	160	Chad
..	..	330	380	380	360	390	..	..	..	Comoros
490	760	600	620	640	580	660	530	490	410	Congo, People's Rep of the
520	510	510	560	540	590	660	590	540	450	Cote D'Ivoire
..	..	..	..	..	..	..	..	..	..	Ethiopia
1,940	1,950	2,060	1,590	1,520	2,050	1,550	1,370	..	..	Gabon
..	..	..	..	..	..	..	..	..	..	Gambia, The
320	260	270	290	300	300	300	290	..	..	Ghana
130	140	130	140	150	140	150	150	150	..	Guinea-Bissau
200	210	200	210	190	220	230	230	230	..	Kenya
350	350	380	370	330	310	320	320	270	260	Lesotho
..	..	..	..	..	..	..	..	..	..	Liberia
250	250	240	230	240	230	210	210	210	..	Madagascar
130	120	120	130	120	120	110	120	130	120	Malawi
200	210	200	200	210	210	200	200	200	..	Mali
360	380	470	390	370	370	370	390	410	..	Mauritania
890	840	840	880	920	950	1,070	1,150	1,200	1,240	Mauritius
100	100	100	100	90	90	90	90	90	80	Mozambique
330	350	320	290	270	280	260	250	230	..	Niger
360	350	290	240	230	190	160	160	160	160	Nigeria
310	310	320	300	280	290	270	260	230	..	Rwanda
500	510	520	480	510	500	510	520	490	500	Senegal
..	..	..	..	..	..	..	..	..	..	Seychelles
180	170	150	150	140	130	130	120	120	..	Sierra Leone
170	200	180	180	170	160	150	140	150	..	Somalia
340	360	390	360	370	340	340	320	340	..	Sudan
..	..	..	..	..	..	..	..	..	..	Swaziland
120	110	120	120	120	120	120	120	110	110	Tanzania
250	260	240	260	250	270	260	280	280	..	Togo
..	..	..	..	..	..	..	..	..	..	Uganda
200	200	200	190	190	190	190	190	180	..	Zaire
210	170	180	170	190	170	200	220	..	..	Zambia
570	590	530	420	450	380	290	330	440	440	Zimbabwe
170	*180*	*190*	*200*	*200*	*210*	*210*	*220*	*220*	*230*	*SOUTH ASIA*
..	..	140	150	150	140	150	150	150	150	Bangladesh
180	180	200	200	200	210	220	230	240	240	India
..	..	..	..	..	..	..	..	..	..	Nepal
220	220	230	230	240	240	240	250	250	260	Pakistan
270	300	320	300	320	330	320	330	320	..	Sri Lanka
190	*200*	*210*	*220*	*230*	*240*	*250*	*270*	*290*	*300*	*EAST ASIA AND PACIFIC*
110	110	120	140	150	150	160	170	180	180	China
1,330	1,180	1,090	1,150	1,090	1,100	1,030	..	..	..	Fiji
220	230	250	250	250	250	260	260	270	270	Indonesia
1,150	1,220	1,310	1,390	1,460	1,560	1,670	1,810	1,970	2,130	Korea, Republic of
980	990	1,000	1,040	1,020	910	910	1,020	1,140	1,210	Malaysia
580	550	550	530	570	540	540	530	510	420	Papua New Guinea
440	460	480	470	430	420	440	470	510	520	Philippines
400	300	330	370	350	340	370	490	..	..	Solomon islands
460	460	510	510	500	520	550	690	780	860	Thailand
..	..	500	560	560	530	510	..	..	..	Vanuatu

Table 3. Private consumption per capita (cont'd.)

1987 US dollars	1970	1971	1972	1973	1974	1975	1976	1977	1978	1979	1980
LATIN AMERICA AND CARIBBEAN	*900*	*950*	*990*	*1,030*	*1,070*	*1,060*	*1,110*	*1,140*	*1,150*	*1,220*	*1,270*
Argentina	1,760	1,780	1,800	1,860	1,960	1,920	1,730	1,720	1,690	1,900	2,010
Bahamas	..	..	..	..	..	..	..	3,890	4,410	6,170	5,970
Barbados	..	..	..	..	..	..	..	..	..	..	..
Belize	..	..	..	..	..	..	..	..	..	..	..
Bolivia	430	430	390	440	440	380	440	450	480	490	510
Brazil	780	850	930	1,010	1,090	1,060	1,180	1,230	1,230	1,320	1,380
Chile	1,160	1,290	1,360	1,250	1,010	840	820	960	1,020	1,090	1,160
Colombia	550	580	610	630	630	650	670	680	720	730	740
Costa Rica	970	950	990	1,010	1,030	1,020	1,020	1,120	1,190	1,190	1,130
Dominican Republic	430	460	510	530	560	520	570	580	570	550	640
Ecuador	500	510	530	560	590	630	680	710	720	750	780
El Salvador	860	860	880	920	920	930	1,000	1,090	1,100	1,010	900
Grenada	..	..	..	..	..	..	..	..	..	..	..
Guatemala	720	730	750	770	780	780	830	880	890	890	880
Guyana	270	250	300	330	330	280	350	350	270	210	250
Haiti	280	300	300	290	310	290	310	320	320	320	340
Honduras	590	570	580	630	590	590	650	710	700	700	710
Jamaica	720	780	980	730	890	900	900	950	860	790	750
Mexico	940	960	990	1,020	1,040	1,070	1,090	1,060	1,130	1,210	1,290
Nicaragua	1,230	1,220	1,190	1,200	1,320	1,310	1,330	1,390	1,280	890	940
Panama	1,070	1,100	1,060	1,060	1,160	1,090	1,060	1,120	1,220	1,260	1,310
Paraguay	450	480	480	500	540	540	570	630	640	570	830
Peru	910	910	920	880	900	910	920	910	860	880	850
St. Vincent and The Grenadines	..	..	..	..	..	..	..	..	..	..	..
Trinidad and Tobago	2,980	2,930	3,050	3,060	3,040	2,960	3,200	3,540	3,790	3,860	3,910
Uruguay	1,780	1,780	1,800	1,800	1,780	1,840	1,790	1,780	1,830	1,910	2,060
Venezuela	..	..	..	..	1,310	1,550	1,730	1,840	1,890	1,830	1,920
MIDDLE EAST AND NORTH AFRICA	*950*	*960*	*1,020*	*1,090*	*1,060*	*1,000*	*1,120*	*1,240*	*1,130*	*1,090*	*920*
Algeria	1,120	1,020	1,150	1,100	1,120	1,120	1,180	1,180	1,140	1,260	1,220
Egypt, Arab Republic of	..	..	..	..	370	360	370	410	430	500	540
Iran, Islamic Rep. of	2,240	2,210	2,290	2,600	2,350	2,040	2,430	2,850	2,350	2,060	1,310
Jordan	..	..	..	..	..	..	..	..	..	..	..
Morocco	430	440	440	450	460	480	510	520	540	550	580
Oman	..	..	..	..	..	..	..	..	..	..	..
Syrian Arab Republic	460	510	540	540	740	880	900	860	920	930	990
Tunisia	390	420	490	510	530	580	600	640	660	680	740
Turkey	580	640	690	670	700	720	770	790	800	770	710
Yemen, Republic of	..	..	..	..	..	..	..	..	..	..	..
EUROPE	*..*	*..*	*..*	*..*	*..*	*..*	*..*	*..*	*..*	*..*	*1,340*
Bulgaria	..	..	..	..	..	..	..	..	..	..	1,600
Greece	1,880	2,010	2,160	2,180	2,190	2,330	2,430	2,510	2,600	2,570	2,570
Hungary	900	930	1,000	1,050	1,090	1,140	1,160	1,210	1,240	1,290	1,320
Malta	1,770	1,760	1,780	1,790	1,900	1,900	2,060	2,300	2,240	2,240	2,370
Poland	..	..	..	..	..	..	..	..	..	..	1,010
Portugal	1,290	1,520	1,550	1,760	1,990	1,900	1,940	1,950	1,900	1,880	1,860
Romania	..	..	..	..	..	..	..	..	..	..	..
Yugoslavia	870	1,010	940	960	1,290	1,200	1,100	1,300	1,490	1,550	1,480
Low- & middle-income economies	320	320	330	340	350	350	360	380	390	390	400
Severely indebted	820	860	890	930	970	970	1,000	1,030	1,050	1,110	1,160
Low-income economies	130	130	120	120	130	130	130	140	150	140	150
Low-income Africa	160	170	160	160	180	180	180	190	220	180	200
China and India	120	120	120	120	120	120	120	130	130	130	140
Other low-income	130	120	110	110	130	130	130	130	140	150	160
Middle-income economies	830	870	900	950	980	970	1,020	1,060	1,060	1,090	1,080
High-income OECD members	6,750	6,920	7,260	7,560	7,520	7,650	7,980	8,230	8,500	8,710	8,750
European Community members	5,650	5,780	6,040	6,270	6,330	6,410	6,620	6,830	7,040	7,290	7,370
Japan	6,490	6,780	7,280	7,810	7,650	7,910	8,160	8,460	8,800	9,210	9,450
United States	8,650	8,810	9,190	9,470	9,280	9,380	9,790	10,120	10,440	10,500	10,360
Other high-income economies /a	..	..	..	..	..	..	..	..	..	..	..

a. Economies classified by the United Nations or otherwise regarded by their authorities as developing.

1981	1982	1983	1984	1985	1986	1987	1988	1989	1990	
1,250	*1,200*	*1,160*	*1,190*	*1,170*	*1,200*	*1,180*	*1,160*	*1,180*	*1,180*	*LATIN AMERICA AND CARIBBEAN*
1,920	1,710	1,770	1,870	1,750	1,850	1,800	1,740	1,730	1,750	Argentina
5,520	5,410	5,380	6,810	7,020	7,120	7,200	..	..	..	Bahamas
..	..	..	..	..	..	..	..	..	..	Barbados
..	..	..	..	..	..	..	..	..	..	Belize
590	500	520	530	560	540	520	480	480	..	Bolivia
1,290	1,310	1,280	1,320	1,320	1,380	1,340	1,320	1,350	1,310	Brazil
1,290	1,050	980	990	950	980	1,020	1,110	1,190	1,180	Chile
740	730	730	740	750	760	780	770	800	800	Colombia
1,070	960	970	1,020	1,030	1,050	1,080	1,090	1,140	1,220	Costa Rica
590	620	630	580	570	590	590	550	540	410	Dominican Republic
810	790	770	770	770	750	760	750	740	730	Ecuador
810	750	740	760	780	770	760	760	750	790	El Salvador
..	..	..	..	..	..	..	..	..	..	Grenada
860	790	740	740	700	680	710	720	720	720	Guatemala
330	290	290	240	290	310	300	330	..	..	Guyana
330	300	300	290	290	300	300	290	280	280	Haiti
680	660	630	610	610	600	620	640	630	600	Honduras
700	750	750	770	720	740	760	..	..	..	Jamaica
1,370	1,260	1,150	1,170	1,190	1,150	1,120	1,140	1,210	1,250	Mexico
830	760	710	660	590	540	510	410	420	370	Nicaragua
1,260	1,280	1,340	1,450	1,450	1,370	1,340	1,090	1,240	1,300	Panama
820	810	710	740	750	720	750	710	760	770	Paraguay
850	840	770	800	810	870	910	820	720	760	Peru
..	..	..	..	..	..	..	..	..	..	St. Vincent and The Grenadines
4,140	4,120	3,850	3,180	2,380	2,270	2,220	2,150	2,060	1,880	Trinidad and Tobago
2,090	1,880	1,700	1,590	1,600	1,760	1,930	1,900	1,930	1,860	Uruguay
1,960	1,970	1,810	1,800	1,710	1,720	1,700	1,740	1,600	1,690	Venezuela
930	*1,130*	*1,100*	*1,210*	*1,230*	*1,150*	*1,150*	*1,140*	*1,120*	*..*	*MIDDLE EAST AND NORTH AFRICA*
1,270	1,320	1,340	1,350	1,410	1,390	1,380	1,270	1,330	1,390	Algeria
540	540	550	580	600	590	580	580	570	580	Egypt, Arab Republic of
1,350	2,190	1,990	2,420	2,450	2,030	2,010	2,010	1,900	..	Iran, Islamic Rep. of
..	..	1,600	1,500	1,550	1,720	1,620	1,640	1,530	..	Jordan
540	560	540	550	540	550	550	570	570	560	Morocco
..	..	..	..	..	..	..	..	..	..	Oman
1,160	1,060	1,060	930	950	890	800	850	..	..	Syrian Arab Republic
770	770	790	810	810	810	810	820	820	840	Tunisia
680	700	720	780	770	830	870	870	890	910	Turkey
..	..	..	..	..	..	..	..	..	..	Yemen, Republic of
1,350	*1,310*	*1,340*	*1,340*	*1,370*	*1,430*	*1,460*	*1,480*	*1,490*	*..*	*EUROPE*
1,690	1,650	1,760	1,770	1,850	1,860	2,050	1,990	1,890	..	Bulgaria
2,750	2,920	2,910	2,900	3,060	3,110	3,230	3,260	3,240	..	Greece
1,360	1,390	1,410	1,440	1,470	1,490	1,560	1,510	1,520	1,420	Hungary
2,370	2,410	2,460	2,640	2,880	2,930	3,000	3,310	3,500	..	Malta
950	830	860	890	950	990	1,010	1,030	1,020	870	Poland
1,890	1,910	1,950	1,920	1,930	2,030	2,350	2,640	2,780	..	Portugal
..	..	..	..	..	..	..	..	..	..	Romania
1,450	1,400	1,370	1,330	1,260	1,380	1,220	1,160	1,200	1,170	Yugoslavia
400	410	410	430	430	430	430	450	460	460	**Low- & middle-income economies**
1,140	1,090	1,060	1,090	1,080	1,100	1,090	1,080	1,100	1,080	Severely indebted
160	160	170	170	180	180	180	190	200	200	Low-income economies
230	230	210	200	190	180	170	170	170	..	Low-income Africa
140	140	160	160	170	180	180	200	210	210	China and India
160	170	180	180	180	180	180	190	190	190	Other low-income
1,090	1,100	1,080	1,120	1,120	1,120	1,130	1,140	1,160	1,160	Middle-income economies
8,800	8,860	9,080	9,320	9,610	9,900	10,180	10,490	10,710	..	**High-income OECD members**
7,390	7,440	7,530	7,610	7,790	8,060	8,330	8,620	8,830	..	European Community members
9,590	9,880	10,190	10,400	10,660	10,880	11,190	11,550	11,800	..	Japan
10,390	10,360	10,750	11,190	11,590	11,950	12,230	12,550	12,760	..	United States
..	..	..	..	..	..	..	..	..	..	**Other high-income economies** /a

Table 4. Gross domestic investment per capita

1987 US dollars	1970	1971	1972	1973	1974	1975	1976	1977	1978	1979	1980
SUB-SAHARAN AFRICA	*60*	*70*	*60*	*70*	*80*	*90*	*100*	*110*	*90*	*80*	*90*
Excluding Nigeria	*70*	*70*	*70*	*70*	*90*	*80*	*80*	*90*	*80*	*80*	*80*
Benin	50	40	60	60	90	80	80	70	70	100	130
Botswana	90	130	160	200	190	160	150	110	140	170	210
Burkina Faso	30	40	50	60	70	70	60	60	60	50	50
Burundi	10	20	0	10	20	10	20	20	30	30	20
Cameroon	80	100	100	110	100	110	100	130	190	170	190
Cape Verde	..	..	..	80	80	70	110	150	130	170	210
Central African Rep.	80	90	80	90	50	40	40	40	40	30	20
Chad	..	..	..	..	..	..	..	..	..	..	..
Comoros	..	..	..	..	..	..	..	..	..	..	..
Congo, People's Rep of the	270	310	350	400	460	520	390	300	230	240	350
Cote D'Ivoire	240	230	210	260	240	240	290	400	450	400	460
Ethiopia	..	..	..	..	..	..	..	..	..	..	..
Gabon	890	970	1,110	1,220	3,260	3,840	5,240	3,910	1,430	1,690	1,650
Gambia, The	10	10	10	10	10	20	20	30	60	40	50
Ghana	90	90	50	60	80	70	50	80	50	50	50
Guinea-Bissau	190	150	130	100	80	70	70	80	100	110	80
Kenya	140	140	120	140	130	90	90	120	150	110	140
Lesotho	20	30	30	40	40	50	80	110	90	110	130
Liberia	..	..	..	..	..	..	..	..	..	..	..
Madagascar	40	50	40	40	40	40	30	30	30	50	40
Malawi	70	50	70	60	70	80	60	60	90	70	60
Mali	30	30	30	30	20	30	30	40	40	40	40
Mauritania	40	40	60	40	130	190	240	200	140	110	160
Mauritius	90	140	160	260	310	320	300	290	310	320	180
Mozambique	..	..	..	..	..	..	..	..	..	..	30
Niger	60	40	60	80	70	60	60	60	80	90	80
Nigeria	50	70	70	80	80	120	150	160	120	100	110
Rwanda	20	20	20	20	20	30	30	30	30	20	40
Senegal	120	120	120	120	130	110	130	120	110	90	90
Seychelles	..	..	..	..	..	..	..	..	..	..	..
Sierra Leone	40	30	20	20	30	30	20	20	20	20	30
Somalia	20	20	20	20	20	20	30	50	50	40	70
Sudan	50	50	40	40	70	70	110	90	70	60	60
Swaziland	..	..	..	..	..	..	..	..	..	..	..
Tanzania	50	60	40	50	50	40	50	50	50	50	50
Togo	90	100	110	110	110	150	120	210	250	230	140
Uganda	..	..	..	..	..	..	..	..	..	..	..
Zaire	20	30	20	30	30	20	20	30	20	30	30
Zambia	300	320	320	300	360	300	160	140	130	70	110
Zimbabwe	130	150	160	170	220	200	140	110	70	70	110
SOUTH ASIA	*50*	*50*	*40*	*50*	*50*	*50*	*50*	*50*	*60*	*60*	*60*
Bangladesh	30	20	10	20	10	10	10	10	20	20	30
India	50	50	50	60	60	60	60	60	70	60	60
Nepal	..	..	..	..	..	..	..	..	..	..	..
Pakistan	50	50	40	40	40	40	40	40	50	50	50
Sri Lanka	40	40	40	30	50	40	50	50	70	100	110
EAST ASIA AND PACIFIC	*50*	*50*	*50*	*50*	*60*	*60*	*60*	*70*	*80*	*90*	*90*
China	30	30	30	30	30	40	30	40	50	50	50
Fiji	280	310	340	360	320	340	340	340	360	470	500
Indonesia	20	30	30	40	50	50	50	60	70	70	70
Korea, Republic of	220	240	220	270	340	330	370	460	590	670	520
Malaysia	230	230	240	300	380	290	320	380	400	440	510
Papua New Guinea	520	550	360	220	230	220	200	210	210	250	250
Philippines	110	110	110	120	140	170	190	180	190	210	210
Solomon islands	..	..	..	..	..	..	..	..	..	..	160
Thailand	140	140	120	160	150	150	150	180	210	190	190
Vanuatu	..	..	..	..	..	..	..	..	..	..	..

1981	1982	1983	1984	1985	1986	1987	1988	1989	1990	
90	*80*	*70*	*50*	*60*	*60*	*50*	*50*	*50*	*50*	*SUB-SAHARAN AFRICA*
80	*80*	*70*	*60*	*70*	*70*	*60*	*60*	*60*	*60*	*Excluding Nigeria*
140	150	70	50	60	50	50	50	50	70	Benin
210	190	130	120	190	140	80	130	260	..	Botswana
50	60	50	50	70	70	70	70	60	60	Burkina Faso
30	20	40	30	30	40	50	40	50	50	Burundi
260	250	260	240	250	390	280	160	170	150	Cameroon
220	260	250	240	240	280	290	300	300	300	Cape Verde
30	40	60	60	60	50	50	30	30	50	Central African Rep.
..	..	0	10	10	10	20	10	20	20	Chad
..	..	160	210	140	130	110	70	60	60	Comoros
600	800	650	560	510	330	220	180	150	250	Congo, People's Rep of the
350	290	250	120	170	130	110	140	90	50	Cote D'Ivoire
..	..	..	..	..	..	..	..	..	..	Ethiopia
2,230	1,940	1,740	1,780	1,910	1,580	910	930	..	..	Gabon
40	40	40	50	40	40	40	40	40	50	Gambia, The
40	30	30	30	40	40	50	60	..	..	Ghana
60	80	80	80	90	80	60	70	100	60	Guinea-Bissau
130	100	80	80	100	80	90	90	100	80	Kenya
130	140	80	100	120	100	100	120	210	220	Lesotho
..	..	..	..	..	..	..	..	..	..	Liberia
30	20	20	20	20	20	20	30	30	30	Madagascar
40	50	50	30	40	20	20	30	30	30	Malawi
40	40	30	30	40	50	60	60	70	60	Mali
190	230	90	120	120	120	100	90	80	100	Mauritania
220	180	180	210	220	290	450	540	500	580	Mauritius
30	30	20	20	10	20	20	30	30	30	Mozambique
80	60	60	0	40	30	30	40	30	30	Niger
110	80	60	30	40	40	30	30	30	40	Nigeria
30	50	40	50	60	50	50	60	50	50	Rwanda
90	90	90	90	80	90	100	100	100	90	Senegal
..	..	..	..	..	..	..	..	..	..	Seychelles
30	20	20	20	20	20	20	20	20	20	Sierra Leone
50	60	50	50	60	50	50	30	40	30	Somalia
60	100	70	60	20	50	40	40	40	30	Sudan
..	..	..	..	..	..	..	..	..	..	Swaziland
40	40	30	30	40	30	30	40	40	50	Tanzania
140	110	80	80	110	90	80	80	80	80	Togo
..	..	..	..	..	..	..	..	..	..	Uganda
30	40	30	30	30	30	30	40	30	20	Zaire
100	70	50	50	60	80	40	60	..	..	Zambia
140	100	120	130	110	100	110	130	100	100	Zimbabwe
70	*60*	*60*	*60*	*70*	*70*	*70*	*70*	*70*	*70*	*SOUTH ASIA*
30	20	20	20	20	20	20	20	20	20	Bangladesh
70	70	70	70	80	70	70	80	80	80	India
..	..	..	..	..	..	..	..	..	..	Nepal
50	60	60	60	60	60	60	60	60	60	Pakistan
100	100	100	100	90	90	100	90	90	90	Sri Lanka
90	*90*	*100*	*110*	*130*	*130*	*150*	*160*	*170*	*180*	*EAST ASIA AND PACIFIC*
50	50	60	70	90	100	110	120	120	120	China
520	360	310	270	260	290	220	..	..	..	Fiji
130	120	120	120	140	140	140	130	140	160	Indonesia
530	560	630	710	730	810	920	1,030	1,310	1,540	Korea, Republic of
590	650	690	710	550	470	450	530	630	760	Malaysia
240	260	270	240	170	170	180	240	180	200	Papua New Guinea
210	200	190	100	80	70	90	110	120	120	Philippines
150	130	140	140	150	140	140	160	..	..	Solomon islands
210	180	220	230	210	200	230	260	280	300	Thailand
..	..	250	260	290	270	290	..	..	..	Vanuatu

Table 4. Gross domestic investment per capita (cont'd.)

1987 US dollars	1970	1971	1972	1973	1974	1975	1976	1977	1978	1979	1980
LATIN AMERICA AND CARIBBEAN	*340*	*350*	*370*	*410*	*470*	*480*	*480*	*500*	*500*	*500*	*540*
Argentina	720	780	780	730	720	730	760	910	750	810	870
Bahamas	..	..	..	..	..	..	..	810	770	1,060	1,580
Barbados	..	..	..	..	..	..	..	..	..	..	..
Belize	..	..	..	..	..	..	..	..	..	..	..
Bolivia	300	320	380	330	320	450	390	400	390	330	240
Brazil	310	340	390	470	540	580	570	550	560	550	600
Chile	310	300	210	190	330	150	150	180	210	270	350
Colombia	190	190	180	190	230	180	190	220	230	220	240
Costa Rica	290	350	320	370	390	350	430	510	500	530	550
Dominican Republic	90	110	120	150	170	180	160	170	170	180	190
Ecuador	210	250	210	230	310	350	320	380	410	390	410
El Salvador	120	150	130	170	210	180	200	280	280	210	140
Grenada	..	..	..	..	..	..	..	..	..	..	..
Guatemala	130	140	120	140	180	150	200	210	230	190	160
Guyana	300	250	210	310	270	460	390	270	190	260	250
Haiti	20	20	30	30	40	40	50	50	60	70	60
Honduras	160	120	120	140	190	140	150	190	230	230	210
Jamaica	750	740	640	850	630	680	480	310	340	320	270
Mexico	360	330	350	390	450	460	430	420	460	530	630
Nicaragua	190	190	130	250	340	190	190	310	130	-50	150
Panama	480	570	640	640	590	560	540	370	450	470	540
Paraguay	90	90	100	140	150	160	190	200	250	280	330
Peru	220	250	210	320	430	400	340	280	260	290	390
St. Vincent and The Grenadines	..	..	..	..	..	..	..	210	240	280	300
Trinidad and Tobago	410	640	560	500	720	870	980	1,000	1,260	1,280	1,550
Uruguay	220	240	200	190	200	250	300	350	400	490	510
Venezuela	..	..	..	..	880	1,050	1,220	1,500	1,430	1,100	890
MIDDLE EAST AND NORTH AFRICA	*250*	*250*	*280*	*310*	*390*	*520*	*550*	*560*	*460*	*440*	*510*
Algeria	490	470	530	640	850	900	900	1,020	1,190	1,070	1,060
Egypt, Arab Republic of	50	40	40	50	80	120	120	130	140	150	150
Iran, Islamic Rep. of	470	480	580	620	740	1,140	1,210	1,150	730	720	970
Jordan	..	..	..	..	..	..	..	..	..	..	..
Morocco	110	120	90	100	110	180	210	240	170	170	170
Oman	..	..	..	..	..	..	..	..	1,130	1,280	1,270
Syrian Arab Republic	100	120	150	90	210	230	290	320	270	270	310
Tunisia	260	260	310	280	320	340	350	350	380	390	380
Turkey	200	190	200	220	270	320	330	350	260	260	270
Yemen, Republic of	..	..	..	..	..	..	..	..	..	..	..
EUROPE	..	..	..	..	..	..	..	..	..	..	*750*
Bulgaria	..	..	..	..	..	..	..	..	..	..	790
Greece	1,040	1,100	1,220	1,540	1,180	1,150	1,160	1,160	1,230	1,340	1,270
Hungary	480	580	510	510	620	680	690	750	880	730	710
Malta	770	690	630	550	610	610	750	780	790	850	930
Poland	..	..	..	..	..	..	..	..	..	..	570
Portugal	880	960	1,090	1,260	1,140	790	860	1,030	1,090	1,170	1,290
Romania	..	..	..	..	..	..	..	..	..	..	..
Yugoslavia	370	400	360	400	430	470	480	560	540	660	630
Low- & middle-income economies	110	120	120	130	150	160	160	170	170	170	180
Severely indebted	320	340	350	390	440	460	470	490	490	490	530
Low-income economies	40	40	40	40	40	50	50	50	60	60	60
Low-income Africa	50	50	50	60	60	70	80	90	70	60	70
China and India	40	40	40	40	40	50	40	50	60	60	60
Other low-income	30	30	30	30	30	30	40	40	40	50	50
Middle-income economies	320	330	340	380	430	470	470	500	480	490	530
High-income OECD members	2,510	2,550	2,680	2,960	2,830	2,440	2,680	2,780	2,880	3,020	2,910
European Community members	2,460	2,430	2,480	2,720	2,650	2,270	2,540	2,520	2,530	2,690	2,670
Japan	3,770	3,720	4,010	4,510	4,120	3,770	3,880	4,020	4,270	4,530	4,460
United States	1,900	2,060	2,270	2,510	2,300	1,810	2,130	2,420	2,650	2,610	2,290
Other high-income economies /a	..	..	..	..	..	..	..	..	..	..	..

a. Economies classified by the United Nations or otherwise regarded by their authorities as developing.

1981	1982	1983	1984	1985	1986	1987	1988	1989	1990	
510	*430*	*320*	*320*	*340*	*360*	*370*	*360*	*340*	*340*	*LATIN AMERICA AND CARIBBEAN*
660	520	460	400	320	370	430	390	290	280	Argentina
1,570	1,860	1,830	1,640	2,070	2,010	2,130	..	..	..	Bahamas
..	..	..	..	..	..	..	..	..	..	Barbados
..	..	..	..	..	..	..	..	..	..	Belize
230	170	100	70	80	50	70	70	80	80	Bolivia
510	460	350	350	410	490	470	430	450	430	Brazil
420	140	120	200	180	210	260	270	350	340	Chile
270	280	260	240	220	220	230	240	220	210	Colombia
340	250	320	350	370	470	470	430	440	420	Costa Rica
170	130	140	150	140	140	190	200	240	260	Dominican Republic
350	380	250	240	260	260	240	240	240	230	Ecuador
130	120	110	110	100	120	120	130	180	130	El Salvador
..	..	..	..	..	..	..	..	..	..	Grenada
180	140	110	120	90	90	120	110	110	120	Guatemala
230	150	130	150	160	180	140	130	..	..	Guyana
70	60	60	60	50	40	50	40	40	40	Haiti
170	100	110	160	150	120	130	120	120	90	Honduras
340	320	330	290	290	230	270	300	240	200	Jamaica
710	520	370	390	420	320	330	370	370	400	Mexico
220	170	180	180	170	160	150	150	130	110	Nicaragua
600	560	420	370	380	410	410	150	60	270	Panama
370	300	240	230	230	230	240	240	210	210	Paraguay
460	410	250	220	190	250	310	270	200	140	Peru
280	270	250	290	330	360	390	..	..	..	St. Vincent and The Grenadines
1,270	1,320	1,160	1,130	1,150	990	780	640	620	690	Trinidad and Tobago
460	380	240	240	190	200	250	250	220	310	Uruguay
860	900	430	560	570	580	650	730	330	490	Venezuela
540	*410*	*530*	*470*	*470*	*480*	*430*	*390*	*430*	*..*	*MIDDLE EAST AND NORTH AFRICA*
1,070	1,040	1,070	1,060	1,020	930	840	770	760	720	Algeria
150	170	170	180	190	160	130	140	130	130	Egypt, Arab Republic of
1,090	510	1,040	740	720	840	740	630	800	..	Iran, Islamic Rep. of
..	..	640	550	470	510	490	380	310	..	Jordan
170	190	150	160	180	200	170	200	210	220	Morocco
1,510	1,960	2,030	2,930	3,010	2,200	1,080	..	..	..	Oman
310	310	310	300	310	280	210	210	..	..	Syrian Arab Republic
430	420	400	420	360	280	260	210	280	320	Tunisia
290	270	260	260	290	320	330	300	280	320	Turkey
..	..	..	..	..	..	..	..	..	..	Yemen, Republic of
700	*680*	*640*	*630*	*640*	*660*	*650*	*670*	*700*	*..*	*EUROPE*
870	860	860	920	920	1,070	1,040	1,150	1,090	..	Bulgaria
1,080	1,000	990	950	1,010	910	810	920	1,100	..	Greece
720	670	620	600	580	640	660	640	640	600	Hungary
1,120	1,510	1,300	1,270	1,270	1,170	1,270	1,550	1,580	..	Malta
440	420	440	460	470	490	490	530	540	320	Poland
1,310	1,380	1,080	870	870	990	990	990	1,080	..	Portugal
..	..	..	..	..	..	..	..	..	..	Romania
630	610	600	610	590	580	600	570	570	520	Yugoslavia
180	160	160	160	170	170	170	180	180	180	**Low- & middle-income economies**
490	420	320	320	330	350	350	350	340	320	Severely indebted
60	60	60	60	80	80	80	90	90	90	Low-income economies
70	60	40	30	40	40	30	40	40	40	Low-income Africa
60	60	60	70	90	90	100	100	100	100	China and India
70	70	70	70	70	70	70	70	70	80	Other low-income
520	450	420	410	410	420	410	410	430	430	Middle-income economies
2,850	2,670	2,730	3,050	3,080	3,170	3,360	3,660	3,890	..	**High-income OECD members**
2,380	2,380	2,380	2,470	2,500	2,610	2,750	3,010	3,190	..	European Community members
4,550	4,550	4,460	4,710	5,010	5,240	5,670	6,420	7,090	..	Japan
2,420	1,970	2,200	2,840	2,720	2,710	2,830	2,970	3,000	..	United States
..	..	..	..	..	..	..	..	..	..	**Other high-income economies** /a

Table 5. Gross national income

Average annual growth (percent)	1970	1971	1972	1973	1974	1975	1976	1977	1978	1979	1980
SUB-SAHARAN AFRICA	*5.7*	*4.2*	*0.8*	*6.8*	*24.6*	*-7.1*	*8.7*	*7.7*	*-1.0*	*-0.7*	*16.6*
Excluding Nigeria	*3.4*	*0.9*	*2.1*	*4.1*	*9.2*	*-3.2*	*7.2*	*6.7*	*-1.0*	*1.9*	*6.1*
Benin	4.3	-0.7	2.7	8.5	-2.2	-5.7	0.2	7.5	1.8	5.1	4.9
Botswana	3.6	7.2	20.4	30.1	28.6	-8.6	12.7	2.8	1.9	32.2	24.2
Burkina Faso	-0.6	1.2	1.8	1.5	9.4	-0.5	10.8	1.3	-1.6	3.7	2.6
Burundi	37.5	32.3	-5.3	9.6	-3.3	-1.9	18.8	21.2	-12.3	4.6	-4.2
Cameroon	5.1	-0.8	-2.4	5.2	14.4	-2.8	2.1	16.4	9.7	7.4	14.6
Cape Verde	..	..	..	..	12.5	-4.3	15.0	13.9	4.4	15.5	47.2
Central African Rep.	4.4	-0.1	1.1	0.8	-2.4	-8.0	17.6	9.6	2.1	-4.4	-5.6
Chad	2.4	-2.4	3.4	-7.0	7.9	0.2	1.5	0.0	0.2	-25.1	-1.8
Comoros	..	..	..	..	..	..	..	..	..	..	..
Congo, People's Rep of the	3.1	7.4	0.3	19.3	22.6	-11.2	1.1	-11.2	0.5	12.7	27.9
Cote D'Ivoire	8.9	4.9	2.5	9.9	9.8	4.4	14.4	17.2	5.5	-2.9	0.8
Ethiopia	..	..	..	..	..	..	..	..	..	..	..
Gabon	19.4	6.5	5.6	6.0	101.6	8.0	27.5	-10.2	-22.9	10.3	31.0
Gambia, The	-1.2	8.7	8.0	-2.6	22.9	-1.4	0.6	15.7	-8.3	11.3	-10.2
Ghana	1.6	-2.8	-3.7	16.0	7.0	-11.6	-8.5	10.5	7.4	-1.6	3.3
Guinea-Bissau	..	0.8	4.4	1.9	4.0	3.8	-3.8	-5.9	14.2	4.3	-25.7
Kenya	0.4	13.5	16.2	1.4	1.4	-3.8	6.2	18.9	-1.1	4.2	3.1
Lesotho	14.3	10.0	9.5	29.9	14.2	11.0	12.0	15.5	10.0	-1.1	-1.3
Liberia	..	..	..	..	..	..	..	..	..	..	..
Madagascar	7.9	0.8	-0.8	-3.2	-0.9	-0.8	-2.2	1.9	-3.8	6.4	-1.1
Malawi	5.5	17.5	2.9	5.7	7.1	3.2	0.1	8.8	6.7	-5.6	-3.4
Mali	4.9	1.3	5.0	-3.5	-4.5	13.6	16.7	7.2	-2.8	9.0	-2.2
Mauritania	14.6	-1.3	-2.0	-3.5	20.6	-2.2	9.0	-7.4	-4.9	0.8	5.0
Mauritius	3.7	4.8	14.0	6.4	45.0	6.1	-4.0	3.0	3.9	3.8	-13.4
Mozambique	..	..	..	..	..	..	..	..	..	..	..
Niger	1.8	6.3	-6.1	-22.0	22.5	-18.9	2.9	12.9	10.7	19.3	3.3
Nigeria	19.6	21.9	-4.7	19.7	87.7	-16.5	12.6	10.4	-0.8	-7.9	48.5
Rwanda	6.1	1.6	-0.2	3.8	-0.2	3.1	7.5	9.1	5.1	13.3	6.4
Senegal	11.9	0.3	5.1	-5.3	4.8	6.3	8.4	-2.0	-5.8	8.5	-3.9
Seychelles	..	..	..	..	..	..	..	..	..	..	..
Sierra Leone	10.0	-0.9	-3.4	7.2	1.8	-3.8	-5.8	6.2	1.8	6.7	3.1
Somalia	6.2	4.2	5.1	-1.0	-19.7	38.3	1.5	30.2	6.3	-6.8	-8.0
Sudan	4.5	7.0	-2.3	-9.4	11.7	13.0	17.6	16.6	-1.4	-10.3	-0.4
Swaziland	..	..	..	..	..	..	..	..	..	..	..
Tanzania	8.0	3.8	4.8	1.5	-4.1	1.1	9.9	-0.8	-5.8	-1.5	-2.9
Togo	2.4	-17.0	2.8	4.7	42.3	-25.1	18.5	8.7	6.9	-7.2	6.6
Uganda	..	..	..	..	..	..	..	..	..	..	..
Zaire	2.1	-4.8	0.4	15.5	0.4	-13.9	-4.7	2.8	-7.7	4.3	24.4
Zambia	-20.6	-23.0	8.5	14.1	0.6	-36.7	11.8	-10.8	-9.4	12.9	-4.8
Zimbabwe	..	..	..	..	..	..	..	-6.0	-1.8	1.0	12.3
SOUTH ASIA	*5.7*	*1.0*	*-0.9*	*2.5*	*0.9*	*6.8*	*4.1*	*7.7*	*5.9*	*-4.4*	*5.8*
Bangladesh	5.8	-6.6	-14.1	1.8	9.4	2.5	11.9	1.6	6.4	4.5	2.3
India	5.4	1.9	0.1	1.9	-0.2	8.3	3.2	8.2	5.7	-6.7	5.5
Nepal	..	..	..	..	..	..	..	..	..	..	..
Pakistan	9.5	-2.0	-1.3	8.1	4.4	-2.1	5.4	6.0	7.9	4.9	10.1
Sri Lanka	5.9	1.3	-4.1	9.4	2.4	0.3	11.9	14.9	5.1	2.3	2.9
EAST ASIA AND PACIFIC	*15.3*	*6.4*	*4.6*	*11.2*	*5.0*	*4.7*	*3.5*	*9.4*	*11.3*	*8.3*	*4.7*
China	25.9	7.4	3.9	8.0	1.1	7.4	-4.6	8.8	14.1	7.4	6.5
Fiji	13.7	5.3	7.9	11.8	15.4	7.1	0.7	6.3	0.9	9.5	-0.5
Indonesia	7.2	6.9	3.7	9.4	22.5	2.8	5.7	11.2	8.7	14.6	20.0
Korea, Republic of	8.7	9.5	6.0	15.0	7.2	4.8	15.9	11.4	11.8	6.4	-8.5
Malaysia	3.9	1.6	5.0	20.8	8.8	-4.5	18.5	9.9	6.3	13.9	10.1
Papua New Guinea	8.4	3.6	7.9	17.6	-1.5	-9.6	6.3	3.4	3.7	7.7	-7.9
Philippines	5.6	4.5	4.4	12.0	4.6	3.4	3.9	7.2	6.5	8.9	3.3
Solomon islands	..	..	..	..	..	..	..	..	..	..	..
Thailand	6.6	0.4	6.5	15.7	1.0	1.9	8.8	8.3	9.7	5.2	4.5
Vanuatu	..	..	..	..	..	..	..	..	..	..	..

1981	1982	1983	1984	1985	1986	1987	1988	1989	1990	
0.4	*-2.4*	*-1.9*	*0.3*	*1.7*	*-3.2*	*-0.4*	*1.0*	*3.2*	..	*SUB-SAHARAN AFRICA*
2.1	*2.4*	*0.8*	*1.3*	*1.3*	*3.3*	*-0.4*	*2.1*	*1.5*	..	*Excluding Nigeria*
3.9	6.6	-2.2	1.3	9.6	-1.5	-4.2	2.4	7.7	..	Benin
-1.5	-4.7	7.3	3.9	22.7	26.5	11.2	21.8	29.5	..	Botswana
4.0	9.8	1.8	-1.1	8.2	8.7	2.9	8.8	-0.3	..	Burkina Faso
8.4	-2.8	8.2	1.2	12.4	2.8	-1.5	6.9	..	..	Burundi
12.9	5.7	7.9	5.6	7.7	9.4	-5.1	-7.4	-3.1	-2.8	Cameroon
3.9	4.6	7.3	4.8	6.8	5.7	11.0	3.8	2.6	..	Cape Verde
-3.0	7.4	-7.9	10.5	3.0	2.0	-4.3	1.9	2.1	..	Central African Rep.
1.1	7.8	13.0	1.1	22.6	-4.5	-3.5	17.6	0.9	3.0	Chad
..	..	..	-1.0	5.2	3.1	-2.0	..	..	..	Comoros
18.0	47.6	5.0	10.3	-14.5	-30.6	16.5	-21.7	7.3	5.1	Congo, People's Rep of the
-3.1	0.0	-0.6	5.1	0.0	9.1	1.6	-1.3	-13.1	-15.6	Cote D'Ivoire
..	..	..	..	..	..	..	..	..	..	Ethiopia
2.0	-0.6	-2.9	-3.2	-1.6	-23.7	-15.9	-8.5	..	..	Gabon
9.9	2.7	-8.3	-0.6	5.9	-8.3	14.0	11.8	1.3	..	Gambia, The
-4.7	-13.2	-2.1	11.8	4.5	4.6	4.6	6.4	..	..	Ghana
36.5	3.8	-1.0	7.2	5.7	-2.0	3.9	3.6	10.0	..	Guinea-Bissau
0.0	-0.7	0.9	4.3	1.1	10.0	3.0	6.5	3.3	..	Kenya
5.0	12.2	-1.4	3.9	-3.5	-2.3	0.8	7.7	3.0	1.8	Lesotho
..	..	..	..	..	..	..	..	..	..	Liberia
-10.8	-0.5	1.6	1.0	0.8	4.5	-4.7	3.1	1.8	..	Madagascar
0.5	2.6	2.2	9.6	0.3	-3.9	0.8	1.7	4.6	2.7	Malawi
3.4	7.6	-4.3	4.3	-2.0	16.0	4.4	1.5	9.1	..	Mali
7.5	-4.5	2.5	-5.7	8.7	7.6	-5.7	1.4	9.2	..	Mauritania
1.3	0.0	3.8	3.8	6.5	18.4	14.6	0.5	5.6	7.9	Mauritius
2.7	-9.1	-11.3	6.6	-9.0	2.7	-5.8	0.3	9.9	6.4	Mozambique
4.0	1.9	-0.1	-17.1	2.8	8.3	-2.6	2.9	-6.3	..	Niger
-3.2	-13.3	-9.4	-2.5	2.9	-23.6	-0.3	-3.8	10.3	10.2	Nigeria
7.5	2.9	6.1	-1.8	1.7	6.0	-4.0	1.3	-6.8	..	Rwanda
-0.9	11.3	2.5	-3.0	4.0	4.0	6.0	4.9	-1.2	5.0	Senegal
..	..	..	..	..	..	..	..	..	..	Seychelles
7.0	-2.6	-3.2	2.2	-4.4	14.3	-6.4	0.4	-1.1	..	Sierra Leone
11.9	7.1	-11.4	-5.0	10.6	2.5	5.7	-2.4	1.8	..	Somalia
0.9	12.3	1.3	-5.2	-6.9	9.9	3.3	-5.9	10.2	..	Sudan
..	..	..	..	..	..	..	..	..	..	Swaziland
-4.8	-1.2	0.5	5.4	-2.4	8.9	-3.0	4.5	3.4	-6.9	Tanzania
-2.5	-3.9	-5.7	5.3	3.9	6.1	-1.4	7.1	5.9	..	Togo
..	..	..	..	..	..	..	..	..	..	Uganda
1.3	-1.9	-2.7	-1.5	-2.2	-1.8	-4.1	8.6	0.9	..	Zaire
-2.1	-17.0	6.3	-1.2	7.5	-3.6	1.1	21.1	-6.2	-3.3	Zambia
10.7	1.5	1.3	-2.0	4.9	-4.4	-4.4	18.0	9.8	-1.9	Zimbabwe
6.3	*3.2*	*7.3*	*3.9*	*6.0*	*4.5*	*4.0*	*8.2*	*4.1*	*4.2*	*SOUTH ASIA*
6.0	-0.7	4.2	5.5	5.0	3.0	4.1	2.5	1.3	5.3	Bangladesh
6.7	3.1	7.7	3.4	6.3	4.9	4.1	9.6	4.2	4.1	India
..	..	..	..	..	..	..	..	..	..	Nepal
4.2	5.1	6.2	6.0	7.0	4.5	7.2	7.8	4.0	5.0	Pakistan
1.9	7.7	10.0	5.4	2.5	3.1	1.4	2.2	0.4	..	Sri Lanka
5.5	*5.3*	*8.6*	*9.2*	*6.7*	*6.6*	*10.3*	*10.3*	*6.9*	*6.1*	*EAST ASIA AND PACIFIC*
5.5	7.9	8.8	12.7	11.3	6.7	11.0	9.5	4.2	4.0	China
0.4	-7.2	-4.3	8.4	-3.7	9.4	-8.8	..	..	..	Fiji
12.9	-0.7	6.8	7.0	4.8	1.3	6.0	2.8	7.7	7.9	Indonesia
5.2	8.8	12.6	9.5	6.4	15.3	13.7	12.8	9.3	9.2	Korea, Republic of
2.1	3.7	5.3	11.7	-3.7	-6.9	10.9	11.3	10.0	10.9	Malaysia
-10.1	-3.3	5.6	3.8	1.5	2.0	3.1	6.2	-8.7	-6.7	Papua New Guinea
2.2	0.1	2.6	-7.1	-4.9	3.1	6.2	10.4	8.8	1.9	Philippines
-4.7	6.8	2.5	53.1	-26.3	-7.5	17.3	15.3	..	..	Solomon islands
2.5	2.2	10.1	6.1	1.4	6.6	8.1	19.2	13.4	8.7	Thailand
..	..	..	19.8	0.1	-11.6	-10.5	..	..	..	Vanuatu

Table 5. Gross national income (cont'd.)

Average annual growth (percent)	1970	1971	1972	1973	1974	1975	1976	1977	1978	1979	1980
LATIN AMERICA AND CARIBBEAN	*12.7*	*6.8*	*7.5*	*9.6*	*6.2*	*2.2*	*6.8*	*5.4*	*2.3*	*6.3*	*7.0*
Argentina	3.1	5.3	1.9	4.7	4.1	-0.8	0.1	6.0	-3.2	7.9	2.9
Bahamas	..	..	..	..	..	..	..	..	4.0	39.7	8.0
Barbados	..	..	..	..	..	..	..	..	..	..	..
Belize	..	..	..	..	..	..	..	..	..	..	..
Bolivia	5.4	3.2	5.5	6.2	10.7	-1.4	7.2	2.6	0.1	1.7	-0.5
Brazil	10.6	11.0	12.6	15.5	7.3	4.5	10.4	5.4	1.5	5.6	7.6
Chile	-0.9	7.4	-2.9	-2.8	0.8	-26.9	7.2	8.6	7.9	11.5	7.3
Colombia	10.1	5.4	8.7	8.4	4.4	1.0	8.3	7.2	7.4	3.3	5.0
Costa Rica	9.3	3.6	5.9	8.1	1.6	2.8	9.4	14.7	2.4	1.8	-0.2
Dominican Republic	11.7	11.0	19.7	10.9	6.6	4.2	1.2	6.0	0.9	4.4	2.4
Ecuador	9.5	3.6	7.2	17.3	22.9	3.5	10.8	11.1	2.8	10.8	6.1
El Salvador	9.5	3.0	6.9	6.3	1.8	3.5	15.9	15.6	-5.4	-0.6	-11.8
Grenada	..	..	..	..	..	..	..	..	..	..	..
Guatemala	9.3	2.0	4.9	8.1	3.5	1.0	8.5	15.7	0.5	1.4	1.5
Guyana	-2.3	6.2	-7.5	-7.2	36.7	25.7	-21.5	-5.6	-4.9	-9.6	7.2
Haiti	1.0	8.1	0.5	0.1	4.9	-1.2	10.9	2.5	4.1	4.8	8.0
Honduras	1.6	1.7	6.6	8.7	0.2	-0.2	14.4	14.8	6.3	3.7	0.9
Jamaica	13.6	-0.6	13.0	0.5	2.0	3.4	-11.7	-0.5	-0.8	-9.3	-7.0
Mexico	41.9	4.1	8.1	8.1	6.7	5.2	4.5	2.7	8.6	10.3	11.6
Nicaragua	0.9	2.6	-0.8	3.8	19.1	-1.7	7.4	11.5	-12.1	-33.1	24.8
Panama	6.7	11.1	5.5	4.0	1.5	2.4	-1.0	-1.0	12.2	2.2	4.0
Paraguay	5.6	6.6	7.0	11.5	7.2	1.7	13.0	17.6	7.4	-2.9	30.5
Peru	5.0	2.7	1.7	7.5	8.3	-0.3	1.0	0.2	-1.7	10.0	5.1
St. Vincent and The Grenadines	..	..	..	..	..	..	..	..	9.6	-3.0	3.3
Trinidad and Tobago	5.2	5.0	4.6	1.3	4.4	13.6	8.4	5.4	13.4	3.4	10.3
Uruguay	6.5	1.0	-0.3	3.3	-4.0	3.9	4.0	0.0	6.0	7.2	5.1
Venezuela	..	..	..	..	..	2.6	9.9	6.9	-1.4	4.2	6.2
MIDDLE EAST AND NORTH AFRICA	*8.1*	*7.6*	*12.1*	*14.1*	*11.7*	*3.7*	*14.5*	*6.0*	*-8.2*	*0.3*	*-6.6*
Algeria	9.4	-2.5	18.6	5.0	22.0	0.8	8.6	5.2	6.6	10.6	7.8
Egypt, Arab Republic of	5.4	3.2	1.3	8.8	3.7	5.8	15.9	12.2	2.1	13.2	13.4
Iran, Islamic Rep. of	10.9	10.2	14.1	23.1	10.4	1.9	19.1	6.7	-17.9	-5.6	-20.0
Jordan	..	..	..	..	..	..	..	..	..	..	..
Morocco	3.8	6.4	1.2	3.7	9.5	8.4	6.1	3.5	1.9	5.8	8.2
Oman	..	..	..	..	..	..	..	..	..	..	..
Syrian Arab Republic	-8.5	15.0	14.5	-0.9	44.7	21.2	7.5	-1.6	7.9	8.5	9.8
Tunisia	8.9	10.2	19.2	-0.8	14.6	4.3	2.0	4.1	7.7	10.8	9.5
Turkey	4.7	9.5	7.9	4.2	6.3	7.3	8.9	4.1	2.8	-1.7	-2.8
Yemen, Republic of	..	..	..	..	..	..	..	..	..	..	..
EUROPE	*..*	*..*	*..*	*..*	*..*	*..*	*..*	*..*	*..*	*..*	*..*
Bulgaria	..	..	..	..	..	..	..	..	..	..	..
Greece	7.8	7.6	8.7	8.1	-4.4	4.8	6.1	4.1	6.1	3.0	2.1
Hungary	..	..	..	..	1.2	27.4	5.2	5.5	3.9	0.9	0.5
Malta	5.6	1.9	3.6	3.0	5.4	19.1	14.2	7.9	8.2	6.0	10.0
Poland	..	..	..	..	..	..	..	..	..	..	..
Portugal	7.1	7.2	9.3	11.7	0.9	-8.5	4.8	7.1	3.3	5.7	2.0
Romania	..	..	..	..	..	..	..	..	..	..	..
Yugoslavia	3.8	9.2	4.0	2.8	12.5	1.1	5.6	8.2	9.9	4.2	2.0
Low- & middle-income economies	9.9	5.9	5.7	9.2	7.1	2.8	6.9	6.4	2.6	3.6	4.7
Severely indebted	12.4	6.7	7.0	9.8	6.3	3.1	6.7	5.3	2.3	6.6	6.8
Low-income economies	10.4	3.7	0.9	5.2	6.3	3.5	2.3	8.5	7.0	0.6	9.4
Low-income Africa	4.8	4.6	0.3	7.1	25.0	-9.7	7.8	9.1	-1.0	-2.6	19.3
China and India	12.8	4.1	1.7	4.5	0.4	7.9	-0.3	8.4	9.3	-0.4	6.0
Other low-income	6.9	1.0	-1.7	6.4	12.3	1.7	6.8	7.8	7.5	9.0	12.9
Middle-income economies	9.6	6.9	8.0	10.9	7.4	2.5	8.7	5.6	1.0	4.8	3.0
High-income OECD members	3.9	3.4	5.3	5.8	-1.0	-0.3	5.2	3.6	4.5	3.0	0.2
European Community members	5.1	2.9	4.5	5.1	-0.2	-0.9	4.5	2.6	3.9	3.3	0.3
Japan	11.1	5.3	8.9	7.3	-3.0	2.1	4.5	5.4	6.2	3.6	2.0
United States	-0.1	2.9	4.8	5.6	-1.9	-1.0	5.0	4.4	5.1	2.1	-1.3
Other high-income economies /a	..	..	..	..	..	..	..	..	..	..	..

a. Economies classified by the United Nations or otherwise regarded by their authorities as developing.

1981	1982	1983	1984	1985	1986	1987	1988	1989	1990	
-1.2	-3.3	-4.3	4.8	2.9	3.2	3.4	0.3	2.4	1.0	*LATIN AMERICA AND CARIBBEAN*
-6.6	-9.3	2.9	3.4	-4.5	5.8	0.6	-2.7	-5.2	-0.1	Argentina
-7.4	8.5	4.8	13.5	8.9	3.9	3.8	..	..	..	Bahamas
..	..	..	..	..	..	..	..	..	..	Barbados
..	..	..	..	..	..	..	..	..	..	Belize
0.9	-7.5	-5.6	0.3	-5.3	-2.8	0.7	-0.4	5.6	..	Bolivia
-6.3	-0.7	-4.0	6.0	8.1	10.7	3.2	0.4	4.5	-4.0	Brazil
1.0	-19.0	0.8	-0.1	4.6	6.8	11.9	11.6	9.1	-2.6	Chile
-0.2	0.8	1.5	3.0	2.1	8.8	1.0	0.3	6.6	0.4	Colombia
-9.1	-9.4	7.1	9.6	2.4	12.4	-1.4	2.7	4.0	3.5	Costa Rica
2.2	1.7	5.1	6.8	-9.1	5.7	1.8	2.6	7.0	-10.3	Dominican Republic
1.0	-2.6	-2.2	1.9	3.7	-6.6	-4.3	9.1	1.5	5.1	Ecuador
-13.6	-6.8	-1.4	2.1	2.9	6.9	-3.5	5.0	1.0	1.3	El Salvador
..	..	..	..	..	..	..	..	..	..	Grenada
-2.1	-4.8	-2.2	0.6	-1.4	2.2	1.7	4.8	3.6	3.0	Guatemala
-8.5	-17.4	-17.8	-4.7	0.5	9.7	-16.5	19.8	..	..	Guyana
-3.1	-4.7	1.8	-0.2	-0.2	2.2	-1.0	-1.9	-0.2	-2.8	Haiti
-1.8	-5.9	1.6	3.5	4.3	2.5	5.6	4.4	1.9	-16.8	Honduras
-0.8	3.6	2.0	-3.0	-9.8	9.3	4.7	-2.5	-0.6	-3.5	Jamaica
8.8	-2.2	-8.9	4.5	2.6	-9.5	4.4	2.4	4.8	5.8	Mexico
1.9	-0.8	5.7	0.5	-0.8	-1.9	3.1	-29.8	-10.7	-3.8	Nicaragua
5.8	1.1	2.0	4.6	3.7	6.2	-0.7	-19.4	0.1	0.9	Panama
7.2	-2.5	-5.4	2.3	2.5	-3.2	5.6	9.2	5.8	7.7	Paraguay
2.9	0.0	-13.7	4.1	-0.2	10.3	9.9	-10.6	-9.6	-3.8	Peru
9.4	10.7	7.4	5.5	12.8	5.6	-4.4	..	..	..	St. Vincent and The Grenadines
3.8	-2.7	-11.1	-8.7	-6.7	-14.2	0.9	-4.2	-2.8	0.3	Trinidad and Tobago
2.5	-10.8	-10.3	-4.1	-0.7	14.1	7.7	1.1	2.9	-1.6	Uruguay
2.1	-6.7	-5.6	10.4	-3.5	-8.9	5.9	1.3	-3.8	26.7	Venezuela
5.6	9.1	6.8	4.6	4.7	-4.0	1.6	0.8	2.5	..	*MIDDLE EAST AND NORTH AFRICA*
5.9	2.9	6.2	3.8	5.7	-7.6	4.6	-7.7	5.4	6.2	Algeria
3.5	5.5	7.9	5.0	2.8	-2.3	-0.9	4.1	1.5	-0.3	Egypt, Arab Republic of
8.0	16.5	9.6	4.9	4.7	-10.2	-0.6	0.1	3.6	..	Iran, Islamic Rep. of
..	..	..	0.0	1.1	15.5	0.4	-0.3	-5.4	-15.1	Jordan
-5.3	9.7	-0.8	4.0	5.1	12.1	-1.0	10.6	0.1	2.6	Morocco
..	..	..	..	..	..	..	..	..	..	Oman
11.3	1.2	1.3	-3.2	3.4	-3.4	-9.3	12.8	..	..	Syrian Arab Republic
6.0	-0.5	4.8	3.9	2.7	-5.3	5.9	0.3	4.2	7.8	Tunisia
2.4	3.3	3.2	7.4	5.7	10.0	7.5	3.8	-0.8	9.9	Turkey
..	..	..	..	..	..	..	..	..	..	Yemen, Republic of
-2.1	-0.2	1.0	1.3	2.1	4.0	1.7	2.9	1.0	..	*EUROPE*
4.3	0.1	4.6	3.5	1.8	4.1	6.9	3.8	-6.5	..	Bulgaria
0.5	-0.6	-1.0	1.0	2.2	0.3	1.5	4.8	1.8	..	Greece
1.7	1.9	0.4	0.9	-0.9	-0.1	4.5	0.9	0.0	-6.9	Hungary
4.5	4.4	-5.4	2.2	2.2	2.1	5.1	10.9	5.0	..	Malta
-11.8	-3.5	5.8	5.5	5.7	4.4	1.7	4.5	-2.8	-15.8	Poland
-1.6	1.2	-0.6	-4.2	5.0	10.0	6.3	5.8	6.5	..	Portugal
..	..	..	..	..	..	..	..	..	..	Romania
0.4	0.6	-1.7	0.0	-1.3	7.0	-3.3	-2.0	3.3	-4.2	Yugoslavia
2.0	1.1	2.3	4.9	4.1	2.7	4.4	4.4	3.5	2.9	**Low- & middle-income economies**
-1.9	-2.7	-3.3	4.4	2.9	3.2	3.6	1.4	1.8	-0.6	Severely indebted
5.3	2.8	6.0	6.5	7.1	3.8	6.3	7.4	4.5	4.6	Low-income economies
-1.2	-5.1	-3.8	-0.6	1.3	-5.1	-0.1	1.8	5.2	..	Low-income Africa
6.2	5.4	8.2	8.0	8.9	5.8	7.7	9.6	4.2	4.0	China and India
8.5	1.2	6.2	6.2	4.9	2.1	4.7	2.9	5.6	6.6	Other low-income
0.8	0.5	0.8	4.2	2.9	2.2	3.6	3.0	3.1	1.9	Middle-income economies
1.2	-0.1	2.9	4.5	3.4	3.9	3.4	4.6	3.4	..	**High-income OECD members**
-1.1	0.8	1.8	2.1	2.7	4.5	3.2	4.1	3.3	..	European Community members
3.4	3.0	3.1	4.5	5.0	5.6	4.2	5.8	4.0	..	Japan
2.2	-2.1	3.9	6.8	3.3	2.9	3.1	4.4	3.1	..	United States
..	..	..	..	..	..	..	..	..	..	**Other high-income economies** /a

Table 6. Gross domestic product

Average annual growth (percent)	1970	1971	1972	1973	1974	1975	1976	1977	1978	1979	1980
SUB-SAHARAN AFRICA	*8.2*	*7.5*	*3.0*	*2.9*	*7.3*	*0.7*	*6.3*	*3.4*	*0.1*	*3.1*	*3.2*
Excluding Nigeria	*5.5*	*6.5*	*3.4*	*1.6*	*6.2*	*1.9*	*5.4*	*2.6*	*1.8*	*1.9*	*3.1*
Benin	2.1	-1.4	6.3	3.8	3.0	-5.0	1.4	4.7	1.7	6.4	6.5
Botswana	4.2	18.7	32.3	21.9	19.9	-1.3	15.0	2.2	18.6	12.0	15.3
Burkina Faso	0.1	1.2	3.2	-0.1	9.1	2.2	8.2	1.4	4.7	5.1	0.1
Burundi	26.6	44.6	-7.0	7.9	-0.7	0.7	7.9	11.5	-0.9	1.7	1.0
Cameroon	2.9	3.8	2.3	5.5	10.7	-0.8	4.3	8.5	14.7	13.3	15.6
Cape Verde	..	-7.0	-4.6	-0.7	-2.8	3.2	0.0	0.7	10.6	11.0	37.7
Central African Rep.	3.1	0.9	2.4	2.2	5.9	0.3	4.7	3.6	2.5	-2.7	-4.6
Chad	2.0	-2.2	1.1	-8.1	5.0	9.0	3.0	2.2	-0.5	-21.4	-6.0
Comoros	..	..	..	..	..	..	..	..	..	..	..
Congo, People's Rep of the	6.3	7.9	8.7	8.3	9.9	10.3	2.3	-10.8	6.1	12.0	18.8
Cote D'Ivoire	9.6	11.6	6.4	4.3	6.2	10.2	5.8	-0.2	13.9	2.9	-0.8
Ethiopia	6.5	4.2	5.1	3.3	1.3	0.2	2.7	2.7	-1.1	6.4	4.4
Gabon	8.7	10.3	11.3	10.2	39.5	19.2	35.6	-12.6	-24.1	0.5	2.5
Gambia, The	-9.9	11.5	7.2	4.6	19.8	-2.1	9.9	3.0	-5.6	17.3	-9.8
Ghana	9.7	5.4	-3.0	2.9	7.3	-13.4	-3.5	1.8	9.8	-1.7	0.6
Guinea-Bissau	..	1.1	4.3	4.0	4.3	6.9	4.8	-7.7	13.6	0.5	-18.9
Kenya	-4.7	22.5	18.3	5.8	3.6	1.3	2.2	9.4	6.8	7.5	5.4
Lesotho	2.2	6.1	9.6	29.9	11.0	-13.5	11.0	21.8	18.3	2.9	-3.0
Liberia	6.6	4.9	4.2	-2.3	4.5	-2.3	5.9	2.6	5.1	3.2	-4.5
Madagascar	5.3	4.7	-1.5	-3.0	2.0	1.3	-3.1	2.4	-2.6	9.9	0.8
Malawi	0.4	16.4	6.1	2.4	7.1	6.2	4.8	5.0	10.0	4.6	0.5
Mali	6.2	3.4	5.2	-2.5	-2.4	13.9	13.6	6.8	-2.7	10.9	-1.3
Mauritania	10.2	1.0	1.3	-6.2	10.3	-6.4	8.0	-1.3	-0.4	4.6	4.0
Mauritius	-0.4	3.8	8.0	13.3	8.8	0.4	12.3	7.8	5.7	5.6	-10.4
Mozambique	..	..	..	..	..	..	..	..	..	..	..
Niger	3.1	5.7	-5.2	-17.0	8.8	-2.8	0.7	7.8	13.5	7.1	4.8
Nigeria	19.8	11.6	1.3	7.7	11.4	-3.3	9.5	6.1	-5.5	7.2	3.4
Rwanda	6.0	1.2	0.3	3.4	0.8	2.7	7.0	5.0	9.2	10.0	10.2
Senegal	8.6	0.2	6.1	-5.4	3.8	7.6	8.8	-2.6	-5.9	9.4	-2.7
Seychelles	8.9	15.8	6.3	9.1	1.3	3.1	11.3	7.9	7.1	16.3	-2.6
Sierra Leone	10.5	3.0	-0.9	2.8	5.3	2.6	-4.3	0.6	-3.1	8.0	3.1
Somalia	4.6	2.6	10.1	-1.9	-20.4	34.6	-0.4	25.2	5.1	-3.6	-4.2
Sudan	4.9	6.9	-2.1	-8.1	10.1	12.7	18.4	15.2	-1.6	-10.4	1.0
Swaziland	2.5	13.6	4.4	11.3	3.3	2.9	-2.3	1.3	13.2	-0.3	-4.8
Tanzania	7.1	3.9	7.1	6.2	2.1	4.0	3.3	0.0	2.1	2.5	2.7
Togo	0.8	0.1	8.1	4.2	4.7	2.5	-2.0	6.5	11.1	-5.1	14.7
Uganda	1.3	6.4	-1.1	-3.0	1.6	-5.3	2.6	1.5	-6.6	-14.8	-4.8
Zaire	3.3	6.4	0.1	8.6	3.5	-4.9	-5.5	0.4	-5.5	-0.2	2.4
Zambia	2.7	0.5	10.3	-0.4	6.6	-2.3	6.0	-4.7	0.8	-3.1	3.0
Zimbabwe	22.6	8.9	8.3	2.6	6.4	-2.1	0.3	-7.1	-2.8	3.6	10.6
SOUTH ASIA	*5.7*	*1.1*	*-1.1*	*3.6*	*2.2*	*8.1*	*2.8*	*6.4*	*6.0*	*-3.3*	*6.4*
Bangladesh	6.0	-4.8	-12.9	1.9	12.1	3.4	12.2	1.3	6.5	4.5	1.3
India	5.2	1.6	-0.6	3.4	1.2	9.2	1.8	7.2	5.8	-5.2	6.5
Nepal	2.6	-1.2	3.1	-0.5	6.3	1.5	4.4	3.0	4.4	2.4	-2.3
Pakistan	11.3	0.5	0.8	7.1	3.4	4.1	5.3	4.0	8.1	3.7	10.4
Sri Lanka	3.1	2.3	-2.3	9.5	3.8	6.5	3.5	5.1	5.4	6.4	5.8
EAST ASIA AND PACIFIC	*15.5*	*7.3*	*4.9*	*9.8*	*4.3*	*6.7*	*2.9*	*8.5*	*10.3*	*6.9*	*4.4*
China	26.1	7.7	3.7	8.3	1.1	8.3	-5.4	7.9	12.5	7.0	6.4
Fiji	12.8	7.2	7.4	11.3	2.6	0.5	2.7	5.9	1.9	12.2	-1.6
Indonesia	7.4	7.0	6.3	8.7	7.7	5.0	6.9	9.0	7.7	6.2	7.9
Korea, Republic of	8.9	10.0	5.8	15.2	8.9	7.7	13.5	11.0	10.9	7.4	-3.3
Malaysia	6.0	5.5	9.7	11.9	8.2	0.8	11.7	7.8	6.8	9.5	7.4
Papua New Guinea	10.9	6.3	5.6	6.5	2.6	-0.9	-3.4	0.8	8.5	1.8	-2.3
Philippines	4.6	4.9	5.6	8.5	5.0	6.6	7.8	6.2	5.5	6.3	5.3
Solomon islands	5.1	2.4	-28.3	11.6	26.3	-11.9	13.8	14.4	8.9	24.8	-6.0
Thailand	9.6	4.9	4.2	9.8	4.3	4.8	9.3	9.6	10.6	5.0	4.7
Vanuatu	..	..	..	..	..	..	..	..	..	..	-11.4

22

1981	1982	1983	1984	1985	1986	1987	1988	1989	1990	
1.6	*2.7*	*0.1*	*-0.6*	*3.7*	*4.8*	*0.2*	*2.9*	*3.0*	*1.6*	*SUB-SAHARAN AFRICA*
3.8	*3.5*	*1.8*	*1.0*	*2.6*	*5.4*	*1.2*	*2.5*	*2.4*	*0.7*	*Excluding Nigeria*
9.0	6.8	-2.0	2.0	6.4	-1.7	-3.9	1.2	2.4	1.1	Benin
7.4	-1.1	24.0	19.2	8.3	8.2	10.3	9.2	13.4	..	Botswana
4.5	10.0	0.8	-1.8	9.8	10.0	1.8	7.4	-0.2	1.7	Burkina Faso
13.5	-3.1	7.0	0.0	11.6	3.8	4.1	3.6	6.5	2.5	Burundi
12.9	2.6	7.8	5.8	7.6	8.0	-6.5	-7.7	-3.4	-1.2	Cameroon
8.5	2.8	9.5	3.8	8.7	2.9	7.0	3.2	5.5	4.0	Cape Verde
-2.2	7.5	-6.7	9.4	3.9	1.0	-3.4	1.6	2.3	3.6	Central African Rep.
1.0	5.3	15.7	2.0	21.8	-4.1	-3.4	17.6	0.9	3.0	Chad
..	..	..	4.3	2.8	2.1	1.9	0.7	0.2	2.0	Comoros
13.9	26.1	7.7	7.0	-1.2	-6.8	0.7	0.5	0.3	-0.1	Congo, People's Rep of the
4.3	1.6	-1.2	-1.0	3.7	3.7	-0.2	-1.8	-1.3	-6.1	Cote D'Ivoire
2.1	1.6	5.1	-2.1	-6.8	6.7	9.1	3.8	2.3	-2.5	Ethiopia
-4.0	2.7	0.9	6.4	6.3	11.4	-18.4	0.1	4.0	5.5	Gabon
10.2	12.7	-5.3	3.0	0.6	2.8	6.0	8.0	4.7	4.5	Gambia, The
-2.9	-6.5	-4.5	8.8	5.1	5.1	4.6	6.2	6.1	4.1	Ghana
18.9	4.4	-3.2	5.5	4.3	-1.0	6.0	6.8	5.0	3.0	Guinea-Bissau
4.1	1.9	1.5	1.7	4.3	7.1	5.9	6.0	4.6	4.2	Kenya
1.1	3.7	-5.7	7.6	3.2	-0.9	7.3	12.3	4.1	7.8	Lesotho
-1.2	-2.0	-1.6	-2.1	-0.8	-1.7	-1.0	..	..	..	Liberia
-9.8	-1.9	0.9	1.7	1.2	1.9	1.1	3.8	4.9	4.6	Madagascar
-5.3	2.5	3.7	5.7	4.5	-0.5	1.6	2.9	5.4	3.7	Malawi
4.6	6.7	-4.5	1.3	-0.4	17.9	1.4	2.4	9.2	0.3	Mali
3.8	-2.1	4.9	-7.2	2.9	5.6	3.1	3.7	3.4	0.3	Mauritania
5.4	5.8	0.3	4.7	7.4	10.3	10.5	6.5	3.5	6.4	Mauritius
0.5	-3.4	-12.8	1.5	-8.0	1.9	5.2	5.6	3.1	3.0	Mozambique
1.2	-1.2	-1.8	-16.9	3.1	6.4	-2.4	5.0	-3.5	3.1	Niger
-5.7	-0.2	-6.2	-7.3	8.7	2.0	-4.6	4.8	5.8	5.3	Nigeria
8.8	1.7	6.3	-4.6	3.0	5.2	-0.4	0.1	-6.9	-2.7	Rwanda
-0.5	14.8	2.5	-4.7	3.8	4.6	4.1	5.1	-1.5	4.5	Senegal
-7.0	-1.5	2.1	3.6	9.6	2.4	4.1	6.2	5.6	5.3	Seychelles
8.7	0.0	-3.1	2.3	-3.4	-1.9	5.4	0.0	-0.7	2.6	Sierra Leone
8.0	3.6	-9.2	3.4	8.1	3.7	6.1	-1.3	2.7	3.5	Somalia
2.1	12.7	2.1	-5.0	-6.3	9.7	1.1	-1.9	7.4	-5.8	Sudan
6.7	1.2	-0.8	3.8	2.4	8.8	1.2	9.2	4.7	4.6	Swaziland
-1.0	-0.3	-0.5	4.6	1.5	5.4	4.1	5.2	4.3	4.5	Tanzania
-3.4	-3.7	-5.2	5.9	3.2	3.4	1.5	5.0	3.7	1.9	Togo
7.5	11.7	9.6	-8.5	-1.9	-1.5	5.7	6.1	6.4	6.3	Uganda
3.5	-0.4	1.5	2.4	2.2	4.3	0.6	3.2	-2.0	-1.9	Zaire
6.1	-2.7	-2.1	-1.1	1.7	0.2	3.0	5.5	0.1	0.9	Zambia
12.5	2.6	1.6	-2.5	6.7	2.7	-1.4	-1.5	13.4	3.0	Zimbabwe
6.6	*3.9*	*6.8*	*3.9*	*6.1*	*4.6*	*4.3*	*8.2*	*4.5*	*4.5*	*SOUTH ASIA*
6.8	0.8	3.6	4.1	3.6	5.1	3.6	1.9	2.2	5.6	Bangladesh
6.5	3.7	7.4	3.8	6.2	4.7	4.5	9.7	4.5	4.4	India
8.3	3.8	-3.0	9.7	6.1	4.3	3.9	7.8	2.3	2.0	Nepal
7.9	6.5	6.8	5.1	7.3	5.6	6.3	7.9	5.0	4.9	Pakistan
5.6	7.5	3.9	-0.3	9.8	4.4	0.7	2.7	2.1	4.8	Sri Lanka
5.7	*5.8*	*8.8*	*9.1*	*7.3*	*7.4*	*8.9*	*9.7*	*5.4*	*6.0*	*EAST ASIA AND PACIFIC*
4.9	8.3	9.8	13.3	12.5	7.9	10.1	9.9	3.2	3.7	China
6.3	-6.0	-4.2	8.5	-3.4	7.9	-6.5	0.1	12.7	5.2	Fiji
7.4	-0.4	8.8	6.8	2.6	5.8	4.9	5.8	7.3	6.6	Indonesia
6.9	7.4	12.1	9.2	6.9	12.3	11.6	11.3	6.4	9.3	Korea, Republic of
6.9	6.0	6.4	7.8	-1.0	1.2	5.3	8.8	8.8	9.0	Malaysia
0.2	0.3	3.0	-0.5	4.3	3.3	3.5	3.0	-1.8	-1.2	Papua New Guinea
3.8	2.9	1.1	-6.5	-4.6	1.4	5.0	6.4	5.7	3.6	Philippines
13.4	2.9	13.9	1.2	0.8	19.8	1.7	4.3	5.7	..	Solomon islands
6.3	4.0	7.2	7.2	3.4	4.6	8.6	15.0	12.5	10.0	Thailand
4.2	10.7	5.6	6.8	1.1	-2.0	0.5	3.0	2.5	..	Vanuatu

Table 6. Gross domestic product (cont'd.)

Average annual growth (percent)	1970	1971	1972	1973	1974	1975	1976	1977	1978	1979	1980
LATIN AMERICA AND CARIBBEAN	*6.9*	*6.3*	*7.0*	*8.6*	*6.5*	*3.3*	*5.9*	*4.8*	*3.6*	*6.1*	*6.0*
Argentina	5.2	3.8	2.1	3.6	5.5	-0.5	-0.2	6.5	-3.4	7.2	1.9
Bahamas	-5.6	1.6	-3.5	7.6	-16.8	-14.8	5.2	9.2	14.2	26.1	6.5
Barbados	9.7	4.5	1.9	1.3	-4.7	4.0	0.0	4.3	6.1	7.7	4.7
Belize	4.8	4.0	10.2	5.4	13.6	3.6	0.0	6.5	7.9	6.3	3.6
Bolivia	-0.3	4.9	5.4	5.3	5.1	6.6	6.1	4.2	3.4	0.0	-0.9
Brazil	8.7	11.3	12.3	14.4	9.0	5.2	9.8	4.6	3.2	6.8	9.3
Chile	2.0	9.1	-1.1	-5.5	0.8	-13.2	3.6	9.8	8.4	8.3	7.8
Colombia	7.1	6.0	7.6	6.7	5.7	2.1	4.8	4.1	8.4	5.4	4.1
Costa Rica	7.6	6.8	8.2	7.7	5.4	2.0	5.4	8.9	6.2	5.0	0.7
Dominican Republic	18.1	10.9	10.4	12.9	5.8	4.8	6.7	4.9	2.3	4.3	6.1
Ecuador	6.5	6.6	16.6	28.4	5.8	5.3	9.7	6.4	7.0	5.4	4.6
El Salvador	3.1	4.8	5.4	4.9	6.5	5.3	3.7	5.8	6.7	-1.6	-8.5
Grenada	..	..	..	..	..	..	..	..	..	..	..
Guatemala	5.7	5.6	7.3	6.8	6.4	2.0	7.4	7.8	5.0	4.7	3.7
Guyana	4.6	3.0	-2.8	1.5	7.9	7.9	1.4	-2.7	-1.5	-2.1	1.8
Haiti	-0.3	8.4	1.4	1.2	6.3	-2.3	8.6	0.5	4.8	7.3	7.6
Honduras	3.8	3.9	5.9	7.9	-0.9	2.5	10.5	10.5	8.3	6.3	1.3
Jamaica	11.9	3.1	9.1	0.4	-3.3	-0.8	-7.0	-2.8	0.4	-2.0	-6.2
Mexico	7.3	4.2	8.5	8.2	6.1	5.7	4.2	3.2	8.2	9.3	8.4
Nicaragua	-0.2	3.3	2.0	6.5	14.2	-0.2	4.8	8.8	-7.9	-26.5	4.6
Panama	7.0	9.6	4.6	5.4	2.6	1.7	1.6	1.1	9.8	4.6	15.4
Paraguay	4.8	5.4	6.4	7.2	8.3	6.4	6.8	10.7	10.9	11.1	14.5
Peru	5.5	4.2	2.6	5.2	9.3	3.5	1.9	0.4	0.2	5.8	4.5
St. Vincent and The Grenadines	10.7	3.0	25.8	-11.1	-8.8	-7.6	5.5	5.1	10.8	2.0	2.1
Trinidad and Tobago	3.5	1.0	5.8	1.7	3.6	0.7	8.3	6.7	10.9	2.4	7.6
Uruguay	6.0	0.2	-1.4	0.3	3.1	6.0	4.0	1.3	5.4	6.2	5.9
Venezuela	7.7	1.5	1.3	7.1	2.1	2.9	7.7	6.3	2.4	0.8	-4.5
MIDDLE EAST AND NORTH AFRICA	*8.4*	*1.1*	*8.5*	*8.2*	*3.5*	*5.5*	*14.9*	*6.3*	*-5.9*	*-0.7*	*-6.1*
Algeria	8.8	-7.6	19.8	3.0	7.4	5.1	8.4	5.3	9.2	7.4	0.9
Egypt, Arab Republic of	6.0	4.2	2.6	5.1	3.9	10.1	15.4	13.1	7.7	7.9	10.8
Iran, Islamic Rep. of	12.2	2.2	12.9	15.0	3.8	2.4	17.5	6.7	-17.1	-9.2	-19.3
Jordan	..	..	..	..	..	..	..	..	..	..	..
Morocco	4.9	5.6	2.4	3.4	5.4	6.7	11.0	4.9	2.9	4.6	9.1
Oman	13.9	0.9	9.8	-14.3	11.5	24.4	20.5	1.0	-3.7	1.1	3.8
Syrian Arab Republic	-6.0	9.4	16.7	-5.5	26.6	22.6	8.9	-1.4	7.9	4.2	8.4
Tunisia	6.8	11.0	18.7	-0.4	8.1	7.1	7.9	3.4	6.4	6.6	7.4
Turkey	4.8	9.2	6.6	4.2	8.6	8.9	8.8	4.7	3.3	-0.9	-0.7
Yemen, Republic of	..	..	..	..	..	..	..	..	..	..	..
EUROPE	..	..	..	..	..	..	..	..	..	..	..
Bulgaria	..	..	..	..	..	..	..	..	..	..	..
Greece	8.0	7.1	8.9	7.3	-3.2	6.0	6.0	3.0	6.8	3.4	2.1
Hungary	4.9	6.3	6.2	7.0	5.9	6.2	3.5	6.7	4.6	1.6	0.0
Malta	12.6	2.5	5.8	9.8	9.9	19.6	17.0	12.2	11.2	10.5	7.0
Poland	..	..	..	..	..	..	..	..	..	..	..
Portugal	9.1	6.6	8.0	11.2	1.2	-4.3	6.9	5.6	3.4	5.7	4.6
Romania	..	..	..	..	..	..	..	..	..	..	..
Yugoslavia	4.8	8.8	3.5	2.6	14.8	0.7	5.3	8.3	9.2	5.3	2.6
Low- & middle-income economies	8.3	5.0	5.3	7.3	5.0	4.5	6.5	5.8	3.2	3.4	3.1
Severely indebted	6.7	6.4	6.8	8.6	6.6	3.9	6.2	4.8	3.4	6.2	5.9
Low-income economies	10.8	4.5	1.3	5.1	3.2	6.0	1.3	6.8	6.5	1.2	5.9
Low-income Africa	8.0	7.7	1.9	2.5	6.4	-1.1	5.3	5.4	-0.9	1.9	2.4
China and India	12.9	4.1	1.2	5.5	1.1	8.8	-1.4	7.5	8.7	0.2	6.4
Other low-income	7.2	2.8	1.1	6.3	6.9	4.4	7.0	6.1	7.2	5.3	7.1
Middle-income economies	7.3	5.2	7.0	8.2	5.7	3.9	8.5	5.4	1.9	4.3	2.1
High-income OECD members	3.6	3.2	5.1	5.8	0.7	-0.3	5.3	3.8	4.1	3.3	1.5
European Community members	4.5	2.7	4.1	5.7	2.2	-1.1	4.8	2.9	3.1	3.5	1.4
Japan	10.8	4.4	8.4	8.2	-1.2	2.6	4.8	5.3	5.1	5.2	4.4
United States	-0.2	2.8	4.9	4.8	-0.7	-1.0	4.8	4.6	5.2	2.1	-0.1
Other high-income economies /a	8.1	11.3	12.0	9.9	5.3	0.5	9.6	9.7	6.7	9.8	6.3

a. Economies classified by the United Nations or otherwise regarded by their authorities as developing.

1981	1982	1983	1984	1985	1986	1987	1988	1989	1990	
-0.3	*-1.3*	*-2.8*	*3.7*	*3.6*	*4.4*	*3.0*	*0.6*	*1.3*	*-0.7*	*LATIN AMERICA AND CARIBBEAN*
-6.9	-5.5	2.9	2.5	-4.4	5.4	2.3	-2.7	-3.8	-1.1	Argentina
-9.2	6.7	3.6	14.2	4.8	1.8	3.0	-1.2	2.1	..	Bahamas
-3.2	-5.0	0.2	3.3	0.3	10.4	0.6	6.9	3.6	-2.9	Barbados
1.4	-1.7	-0.6	5.6	2.0	3.8	14.6	9.9	8.9	..	Belize
0.9	-4.4	-6.5	1.0	0.0	-3.7	1.7	3.4	3.5	2.9	Bolivia
-4.4	0.6	-3.5	5.2	8.2	8.1	3.3	0.0	3.6	-3.3	Brazil
5.6	-14.2	-0.7	6.3	2.4	5.7	5.7	7.4	9.9	1.6	Chile
2.1	1.0	1.6	3.6	3.3	6.1	5.4	3.6	3.3	3.5	Colombia
-2.3	-7.0	2.8	7.9	0.8	5.5	4.8	3.5	5.7	4.0	Costa Rica
0.0	6.0	4.4	0.3	-2.2	3.0	6.5	1.3	3.8	-7.4	Dominican Republic
4.1	1.1	-2.1	4.1	4.2	3.0	-6.3	11.4	0.1	1.3	Ecuador
-8.2	-5.5	0.6	2.2	2.4	1.1	2.7	3.1	1.0	2.5	El Salvador
..	..	..	..	7.2	3.5	7.8	6.8	5.1	..	Grenada
0.7	-3.5	-2.6	0.5	-0.6	0.1	3.1	4.3	4.0	3.9	Guatemala
1.8	-13.6	-6.6	0.1	1.0	1.6	-0.1	-1.4	-3.5	16.1	Guyana
-2.7	-3.5	0.8	0.3	0.2	0.7	-0.4	-1.2	-0.9	-1.2	Haiti
1.5	-2.0	-0.3	2.7	3.6	2.9	5.3	5.0	2.1	-4.5	Honduras
2.5	0.8	2.4	-1.4	-5.0	2.3	5.5	0.8	3.0	2.6	Jamaica
8.8	-0.6	-4.2	3.7	2.7	-3.9	1.7	1.3	3.1	3.4	Mexico
5.4	-0.8	4.6	-2.1	-4.3	-2.0	-0.8	-9.3	-2.5	-2.0	Nicaragua
4.2	5.6	0.4	-0.5	4.7	3.4	2.3	-15.7	-0.9	3.0	Panama
8.6	-1.5	-5.0	3.1	4.0	-0.1	4.4	6.5	6.1	5.1	Paraguay
4.5	0.2	-12.5	4.6	2.2	9.3	8.5	-8.0	-11.4	-4.3	Peru
8.1	9.4	5.6	6.2	7.2	1.6	-0.5	9.1	26.5	..	St. Vincent and The Grenadines
3.8	-4.7	-7.1	-6.8	-7.5	-3.1	-6.1	-3.9	-1.8	-1.4	Trinidad and Tobago
1.8	-9.5	-6.0	-1.4	0.1	7.6	6.2	0.4	1.3	1.1	Uruguay
-0.3	-2.1	-3.8	1.4	0.2	6.5	3.6	5.8	-8.3	-1.2	Venezuela
2.2	*8.5*	*6.3*	*4.1*	*4.2*	*-1.5*	*0.8*	*2.4*	*3.2*	*..*	*MIDDLE EAST AND NORTH AFRICA*
3.0	6.4	5.4	4.1	5.3	2.0	2.2	-2.6	5.6	2.5	Algeria
4.0	10.7	7.7	6.1	6.6	2.6	2.5	3.9	2.4	0.5	Egypt, Arab Republic of
8.1	15.0	10.1	5.0	5.2	-7.8	-1.6	1.7	3.9	..	Iran, Islamic Rep. of
..	..	..	2.1	1.5	9.5	4.3	-0.7	-4.1	-7.4	Jordan
-2.8	9.6	-0.6	4.2	6.2	7.9	-2.1	10.1	1.2	4.4	Morocco
16.7	10.6	18.1	15.7	15.6	6.3	1.4	..	..	..	Oman
9.5	2.9	1.8	-4.1	3.3	-0.7	-9.5	13.6	..	..	Syrian Arab Republic
5.5	-0.5	4.7	5.8	5.8	-1.5	5.7	1.3	3.5	6.4	Tunisia
4.2	4.9	3.8	5.9	5.1	8.3	7.5	3.7	1.3	7.9	Turkey
..	..	..	..	..	..	..	..	..	..	Yemen, Republic of
-1.0	*0.1*	*1.5*	*2.5*	*2.2*	*2.9*	*1.4*	*2.2*	*1.3*	*..*	*EUROPE*
4.9	1.9	4.0	3.3	2.5	4.2	6.0	2.6	-1.5	..	Bulgaria
0.0	0.5	0.1	2.8	3.0	0.7	-0.1	3.9	2.4	..	Greece
3.9	1.8	0.7	2.6	-0.1	1.5	4.3	-0.3	-0.1	-6.4	Hungary
3.3	2.3	-0.6	0.9	2.6	4.0	4.2	8.7	5.0	..	Malta
-10.0	-4.8	5.6	5.6	5.1	4.2	2.0	4.1	0.5	-14.0	Poland
1.0	3.1	-0.1	-1.6	3.3	4.3	4.3	4.5	5.0	..	Portugal
..	..	..	..	..	..	..	..	..	..	Romania
1.2	0.6	-1.1	1.7	-0.6	3.6	-2.0	-1.6	0.8	-3.5	Yugoslavia
2.3	2.6	2.8	4.5	4.5	3.8	3.8	4.4	3.2	2.2	**Low- & middle-income economies**
-0.9	-0.9	-2.0	3.5	3.5	4.3	2.9	1.2	1.2	-1.9	Severely indebted
5.0	4.4	6.7	6.2	7.4	5.8	5.9	8.0	4.1	4.1	Low-income economies
-0.3	1.9	-1.2	-2.5	2.9	4.1	0.8	4.0	3.9	2.2	Low-income Africa
5.7	5.9	8.5	8.4	9.4	6.4	7.5	9.8	3.8	4.0	China and India
7.1	2.0	6.7	5.5	4.1	4.8	3.9	4.4	5.6	5.8	Other low-income
1.3	1.9	1.4	3.9	3.3	3.0	2.9	2.8	2.7	1.1	Middle-income economies
1.7	-0.1	2.7	4.6	3.4	2.8	3.5	4.4	3.4	..	**High-income OECD members**
0.2	0.8	1.6	2.4	2.4	2.6	2.8	3.9	3.3	..	European Community members
3.9	2.8	3.2	4.8	4.7	2.6	4.0	5.5	4.9	..	Japan
2.0	-2.5	3.7	6.8	3.5	3.1	3.8	4.4	2.8	..	United States
3.8	-1.8	1.3	2.9	-0.1	4.6	6.7	6.2	5.0	..	**Other high-income economies /a**

Table 7. Agriculture: contribution to growth of gross domestic product

Percentage points	1970	1971	1972	1973	1974	1975	1976	1977	1978	1979	1980
SUB-SAHARAN AFRICA	*3.1*	*1.7*	*0.4*	*0.2*	*2.0*	*-1.1*	*0.8*	*1.2*	*0.0*	*-0.2*	*0.6*
Excluding Nigeria	*1.7*	*1.5*	*1.5*	*-0.7*	*1.3*	*-0.1*	*1.2*	*0.9*	*1.0*	*0.0*	*0.3*
Benin	..	-1.6	1.5	0.7	-1.7	-2.0	4.1	-0.2	4.1	2.0	1.3
Botswana	-5.6	4.5	7.9	5.3	9.5	-3.1	0.3	1.0	-1.5	0.0	-0.6
Burkina Faso	..	0.5	-0.1	-2.2	5.6	-0.3	1.5	-2.1	1.9	-2.2	0.7
Burundi	24.0	32.4	-6.6	7.8	-2.7	3.0	2.5	2.7	-1.7	0.9	1.1
Cameroon	1.8	0.5	2.1	1.5	1.8	0.4	0.5	0.5	1.2	4.4	2.5
Cape Verde	..	..	..	..	..	..	..	..	..	..	..
Central African Rep.	0.7	1.3	0.2	0.3	1.6	0.9	1.3	0.7	1.2	-0.6	-0.6
Chad	-0.3	-1.1	1.5	-6.2	1.4	3.8	-0.5	0.5	0.6	-4.3	2.0
Comoros	..	..	..	..	..	..	..	..	..	..	..
Congo, People's Rep of the	1.8	0.8	0.8	0.7	0.7	0.6	-0.8	0.6	-0.1	1.1	1.2
Cote D'Ivoire	2.4	4.1	0.3	2.9	-5.1	3.8	2.3	-1.9	4.2	0.2	4.8
Ethiopia	1.4	1.1	2.0	0.4	-0.3	-1.0	1.4	-0.2	-0.7	1.2	2.4
Gabon	..	..	..	..	..	..	..	..	..	..	..
Gambia, The	-3.5	4.1	2.5	1.7	7.0	-2.2	0.5	-0.1	-4.6	1.6	-1.8
Ghana	6.0	2.6	2.1	-1.1	4.8	-11.1	-0.8	-2.8	9.3	2.0	1.2
Guinea-Bissau	..	-5.2	5.0	-0.5	2.1	0.8	4.4	-7.5	7.9	-4.4	-18.9
Kenya	-3.3	6.6	4.4	1.0	-0.9	2.6	0.7	3.6	1.4	1.0	0.4
Lesotho	..	2.2	-14.4	8.7	10.9	-12.9	-2.5	10.1	4.7	1.4	-15.2
Liberia	..	..	..	..	..	..	..	..	..	..	..
Madagascar	..	-0.6	0.6	0.3	2.7	-0.2	-2.7	1.0	-1.9	2.0	0.7
Malawi	-0.6	7.3	4.2	-2.8	0.8	0.4	4.4	4.4	1.2	1.2	-2.6
Mali	5.1	1.5	1.0	-6.9	-3.7	13.6	8.7	4.9	-4.7	9.4	-2.0
Mauritania	-1.8	-5.0	13.7	-8.6	-0.1	-6.0	0.9	1.8	-0.9	0.6	3.6
Mauritius	..	2.8	4.7	1.7	-0.5	-9.3	2.4	0.0	0.0	0.8	-6.6
Mozambique	..	..	..	..	..	..	..	..	..	..	..
Niger	2.6	2.4	-4.4	-14.5	7.7	-7.9	-2.9	4.6	4.4	-1.9	1.5
Nigeria	8.0	2.3	-3.0	3.4	3.9	-3.8	-0.5	2.1	-2.7	-0.9	1.3
Rwanda	3.6	1.1	-2.2	1.9	7.3	-2.8	12.6	0.4	1.4	10.3	-0.8
Senegal	1.7	-4.6	5.6	-4.4	5.6	1.1	4.2	-2.0	-6.6	6.2	-4.8
Seychelles	..	..	..	..	..	..	..	-0.6	-0.6	1.1	0.0
Sierra Leone	0.0	0.6	-0.3	0.5	-0.2	1.1	1.4	1.5	9.6	3.7	-1.2
Somalia	..	-0.9	3.3	-2.3	-18.2	32.3	1.9	19.4	2.2	-3.6	2.5
Sudan	10.0	4.3	-0.7	-4.4	8.0	2.5	1.7	7.4	0.8	-6.9	-2.4
Swaziland	..	..	..	..	..	..	..	..	..	..	..
Tanzania	2.7	-0.8	5.3	0.6	-2.7	5.1	-3.2	0.7	-1.0	0.4	2.1
Togo	-2.3	-0.2	1.7	0.9	0.4	0.8	-1.4	-1.6	4.1	-1.2	4.2
Uganda	0.8	-1.6	2.3	3.3	-0.7	-0.2	0.5	1.9	-0.3	-10.5	-4.5
Zaire	-4.1	0.7	0.4	0.9	0.5	-0.3	1.3	-0.9	0.0	0.8	0.8
Zambia	0.4	0.2	0.4	-0.1	0.4	0.4	0.7	0.1	0.1	-0.6	-0.2
Zimbabwe	-1.4	3.8	2.2	-3.3	2.5	-0.9	1.6	-3.4	1.4	0.0	0.2
SOUTH ASIA	*3.1*	*-0.8*	*-2.0*	*2.2*	*0.2*	*4.1*	*-1.3*	*3.2*	*1.3*	*-3.8*	*3.9*
Bangladesh	3.3	-2.7	-6.5	0.2	6.4	-0.6	6.7	-1.7	4.7	-0.8	0.1
India	3.1	-0.8	-2.2	3.0	-0.6	5.3	-2.5	4.0	0.9	-5.0	4.5
Nepal	..	..	..	..	..	..	..	..	..	..	..
Pakistan	3.5	-1.1	1.2	0.6	1.4	-0.7	1.4	0.8	0.9	0.9	1.9
Sri Lanka	1.4	-0.9	1.1	-0.3	1.9	-0.8	0.4	3.3	1.8	0.6	1.0
EAST ASIA AND PACIFIC	*3.1*	*1.2*	*-0.1*	*3.1*	*1.5*	*0.8*	*1.1*	*-0.1*	*1.1*	*1.8*	*-0.7*
China	6.2	1.2	-0.7	4.2	2.0	1.0	0.5	-1.1	2.5	2.7	-0.8
Fiji	2.5	-1.5	-0.2	1.5	-0.8	0.1	0.8	3.3	-0.3	3.8	-1.5
Indonesia	1.8	2.1	0.5	3.1	1.2	0.0	1.4	0.4	1.4	1.8	1.9
Korea, Republic of	-0.5	1.0	0.6	2.0	1.9	1.1	2.5	0.7	-2.2	1.3	-3.6
Malaysia	..	..	..	..	..	..	..	..	..	..	..
Papua New Guinea	1.1	0.8	0.9	0.5	1.2	1.1	0.4	0.2	1.2	0.5	1.3
Philippines	0.6	1.2	1.0	1.5	0.7	0.9	1.9	1.2	0.9	1.0	1.1
Solomon islands	..	..	..	..	..	..	..	..	..	..	..
Thailand	1.0	1.1	-0.5	2.2	0.7	1.0	1.4	0.5	2.6	-0.4	0.4
Vanuatu	..	..	..	..	..	..	..	..	..	..	-4.0

1981	1982	1983	1984	1985	1986	1987	1988	1989	1990	
-0.5	*1.6*	*-0.6*	*-0.6*	*1.0*	*2.5*	*0.0*	*1.0*	*1.6*	*..*	*SUB-SAHARAN AFRICA*
0.8	*1.9*	*-0.8*	*-0.3*	*0.3*	*2.4*	*0.6*	*0.8*	*1.7*	*..*	*Excluding Nigeria*
-2.8	0.6	0.3	0.5	4.5	3.9	-2.0	6.0	..	..	Benin
-1.3	-0.5	-1.8	-1.1	-0.4	0.6	-0.2	0.7	0.0	..	Botswana
2.5	0.9	0.1	-0.3	6.5	3.8	-1.6	4.5	-1.1	..	Burkina Faso
10.5	-6.0	2.0	-2.1	7.3	2.3	2.5	1.3	..	..	Burundi
3.7	1.1	-2.1	2.1	-2.8	3.0	1.2	-0.8	0.1	-0.6	Cameroon
-1.1	-3.6	-0.1	0.2	3.2	1.0	1.7	0.6	0.6	..	Cape Verde
-0.7	0.6	-1.5	3.6	1.4	3.0	-0.6	1.6	1.3	..	Central African Rep.
-5.9	2.4	5.6	-6.6	14.5	-7.6	-1.3	11.4	-4.9	1.1	Chad
..	..	..	1.2	1.7	1.1	3.1	1.1	0.9	..	Comoros
0.6	0.7	0.5	-0.2	0.1	0.6	0.6	0.3	0.7	0.5	Congo, People's Rep of the
0.9	-0.6	-4.4	1.0	3.6	4.4	-1.2	2.3	2.0	0.7	Cote D'Ivoire
1.2	-0.6	2.3	-4.7	-7.3	3.7	5.9	-0.3	2.4	-0.5	Ethiopia
..	..	..	..	..	..	..	..	..	..	Gabon
11.3	7.2	-7.9	2.2	1.4	3.9	1.2	0.1	2.2	..	Gambia, The
-1.5	-3.1	-4.0	5.4	0.4	1.8	0.0	1.8	2.4	1.3	Ghana
11.0	2.4	-0.8	1.4	2.8	1.9	4.9	1.5	3.6	..	Guinea-Bissau
2.0	2.4	0.6	-1.2	1.3	1.6	1.3	1.5	1.3	..	Kenya
1.7	-5.6	7.4	-5.9	-1.0	-1.0	1.1	5.2	-4.2	1.6	Lesotho
..	..	..	..	..	..	..	..	..	..	Liberia
-1.3	1.2	0.8	1.0	0.4	1.0	0.8	0.8	1.8	..	Madagascar
-3.0	2.3	1.7	2.2	0.2	0.2	0.3	0.7	1.2	1.2	Malawi
-1.0	4.4	-7.1	-4.2	-2.8	14.3	-0.9	0.5	7.3	..	Mali
3.0	0.6	5.7	-7.6	0.9	3.3	1.1	-0.3	0.6	-1.4	Mauritania
3.1	3.2	-2.4	0.1	1.7	1.7	-0.4	-0.8	-1.1	1.2	Mauritius
0.0	0.0	-9.2	5.0	0.5	0.4	3.6	4.6	1.2	1.8	Mozambique
-0.2	-0.7	3.1	-3.1	5.0	2.9	-5.0	..	..	..	Niger
-4.6	0.8	0.0	-1.8	3.9	2.6	-2.4	1.6	1.2	1.1	Nigeria
-2.9	5.8	2.2	-4.0	-2.4	1.1	-0.7	-0.9	-4.4	..	Rwanda
-1.2	5.2	1.1	-4.1	1.6	2.1	0.6	1.7	-1.5	1.6	Senegal
1.9	-2.0	0.6	-0.8	-0.3	0.2	0.4	..	..	..	Seychelles
0.3	1.2	-0.3	0.1	3.8	-1.2	2.8	0.2	0.1	0.7	Sierra Leone
8.4	1.8	-7.6	8.0	6.1	-0.8	5.2	2.4	1.1	..	Somalia
-1.5	13.3	-3.5	-1.6	-4.2	6.6	0.2	-4.8	8.3	..	Sudan
..	..	..	..	..	..	..	..	..	..	Swaziland
0.5	0.8	1.6	2.4	3.6	3.5	2.7	2.8	3.5	2.6	Tanzania
0.1	-2.3	0.2	8.0	1.3	1.6	0.5	2.1	2.5	..	Togo
4.7	4.1	5.6	-7.5	1.7	0.4	3.8	4.0	3.9	3.5	Uganda
0.6	0.9	0.6	0.8	0.8	0.7	0.9	0.6	0.8	..	Zaire
0.8	-1.1	0.7	0.6	0.4	0.9	-0.3	2.3	..	..	Zambia
1.9	-1.0	-2.0	2.6	3.3	-1.0	-2.6	3.1	0.2	0.4	Zimbabwe
2.4	*-0.1*	*3.4*	*0.1*	*0.5*	*-0.1*	*0.1*	*4.0*	*0.5*	*0.5*	*SOUTH ASIA*
2.8	0.5	2.4	0.8	0.5	3.0	-0.1	-0.4	0.1	3.7	Bangladesh
2.2	-0.6	3.9	0.0	0.1	-0.6	0.2	5.4	0.2	0.2	India
..	..	..	..	..	..	..	..	..	..	Nepal
3.1	1.4	1.3	-1.4	2.9	1.6	0.9	0.7	1.8	1.1	Pakistan
2.1	0.8	1.5	-0.1	2.5	0.8	-1.7	0.6	-0.3	..	Sri Lanka
2.0	*2.4*	*1.9*	*2.6*	*0.7*	*0.9*	*0.7*	*1.1*	*0.7*	*0.7*	*EAST ASIA AND PACIFIC*
2.8	4.7	3.5	5.3	0.7	1.4	1.7	1.1	1.0	1.3	China
2.8	0.4	-4.4	5.3	-3.3	4.1	-1.7	-0.5	3.2	0.6	Fiji
1.3	0.3	0.6	1.0	1.0	0.6	0.5	1.1	1.0	0.4	Indonesia
2.1	1.2	1.2	-0.2	0.5	0.6	-0.9	0.9	-0.2	-0.1	Korea, Republic of
..	..	..	..	..	..	..	..	..	..	Malaysia
2.4	-0.5	0.3	0.9	-0.9	0.5	1.6	1.1	0.5	-0.2	Papua New Guinea
0.8	0.7	-0.4	0.4	0.8	0.8	-0.3	0.9	1.0	0.3	Philippines
..	..	..	..	..	..	..	..	..	..	Solomon islands
1.0	0.6	0.8	1.0	1.1	0.1	-0.4	2.0	1.0	0.1	Thailand
4.5	-2.8	7.3	1.7	-0.5	-1.4	-0.1	..	..	..	Vanuatu

Table 7. Agriculture: contribution to growth of gross domestic product (cont'd.)

Percentage points	1970	1971	1972	1973	1974	1975	1976	1977	1978	1979	1980
LATIN AMERICA AND CARIBBEAN	*0.2*	*0.6*	*0.3*	*0.4*	*0.3*	*0.3*	*0.3*	*0.7*	*0.2*	*0.2*	*0.3*
Argentina	-1.4	0.2	0.2	1.4	0.4	-0.4	0.6	0.3	0.4	0.4	-0.7
Bahamas	..	..	..	..	..	..	..	..	..	..	..
Barbados	0.9	-1.5	-2.1	0.5	-0.6	-0.4	0.8	0.2	0.0	0.8	0.6
Belize	..	..	..	..	2.0	0.8	-2.3	7.2	1.4	-0.4	0.2
Bolivia	0.9	1.6	1.5	1.2	1.0	2.0	1.3	-0.2	0.5	0.8	0.4
Brazil	0.1	1.2	0.5	0.0	0.1	0.6	0.2	1.0	-0.2	0.4	0.8
Chile	..	..	..	..	..	..	..	..	..	..	..
Colombia	0.8	0.2	1.6	0.5	1.1	1.1	0.7	0.6	1.6	1.0	0.4
Costa Rica	1.0	1.1	1.2	1.2	-0.4	0.6	0.1	0.4	1.2	0.1	-0.1
Dominican Republic	7.4	1.2	0.8	1.8	0.0	-0.5	1.3	0.3	0.8	0.2	0.8
Ecuador	1.6	1.2	0.9	0.2	1.4	0.4	0.5	0.4	-0.6	0.4	0.7
El Salvador	1.0	0.6	0.2	0.3	1.5	0.9	-1.2	0.5	1.8	0.5	-0.8
Grenada	..	..	..	..	..	..	..	..	..	..	..
Guatemala	..	..	..	..	..	..	..	..	..	..	..
Guyana	-0.2	1.6	-2.5	0.0	4.0	-1.0	0.9	-0.8	2.1	-1.9	0.1
Haiti	..	..	..	..	..	..	..	..	..	..	..
Honduras	-1.3	2.4	0.5	1.5	-2.3	-1.6	2.5	1.3	1.5	1.7	-0.2
Jamaica	0.3	0.7	0.1	-0.8	0.2	0.1	0.0	0.2	0.6	-0.7	-0.3
Mexico	0.6	0.6	0.1	0.4	0.3	0.2	0.1	0.7	0.6	-0.2	0.6
Nicaragua	2.9	1.2	0.0	2.8	3.2	0.5	0.5	1.7	2.0	-5.2	-7.5
Panama	-0.1	1.1	-0.4	0.1	-0.7	0.8	0.6	0.6	1.0	-0.5	-0.5
Paraguay	2.0	0.5	1.2	2.0	3.1	2.6	1.2	2.1	1.5	1.9	2.3
Peru	1.4	-0.3	-0.8	-0.1	0.6	-0.1	0.2	-0.1	0.0	0.5	-0.7
St. Vincent and The Grenadines	..	..	..	..	..	..	..	..	3.5	-3.2	-2.4
Trinidad and Tobago	0.9	-0.3	0.7	-0.6	-0.1	0.2	-0.2	0.0	-0.2	-0.2	-0.3
Uruguay	1.4	-0.9	-1.4	0.3	0.4	0.7	0.2	0.4	-0.8	0.0	1.7
Venezuela	0.3	0.1	-0.1	0.3	0.3	0.3	-0.2	0.4	0.2	0.1	0.1
MIDDLE EAST AND NORTH AFRICA	*0.4*	*1.0*	*1.0*	*-0.5*	*1.5*	*1.2*	*0.9*	*-0.7*	*0.7*	*0.6*	*0.9*
Algeria	..	0.4	0.0	-0.7	2.3	3.0	-0.3	-0.9	1.2	1.0	1.3
Egypt, Arab Republic of	1.1	0.6	3.5	1.4	0.1	2.5	0.5	-1.0	1.7	1.2	1.0
Iran, Islamic Rep. of	0.7	0.6	0.8	0.8	0.8	0.9	0.8	-0.5	0.2	1.0	0.2
Jordan	..	..	..	..	..	..	..	..	..	..	..
Morocco	1.0	2.3	-0.5	-2.2	0.4	-1.2	2.6	-2.2	2.7	-0.3	2.3
Oman	..	..	..	..	..	..	..	..	..	0.8	0.7
Syrian Arab Republic	-8.6	2.0	14.4	-15.0	16.7	0.2	5.1	-3.8	6.0	-4.3	9.6
Tunisia	1.3	4.2	5.1	-2.3	3.0	1.0	1.4	-2.2	1.1	-0.9	1.7
Turkey	0.6	3.3	-0.4	-2.5	2.2	2.3	1.6	-0.2	0.5	0.5	0.4
Yemen, Republic of	..	..	..	..	..	..	..	..	..	..	..
EUROPE	*..*	*..*	*..*	*..*	*..*	*..*	*..*	*..*	*..*	*..*	*..*
Bulgaria	..	..	..	..	..	..	..	..	..	..	..
Greece	2.1	0.8	1.3	-0.1	0.9	1.2	-0.3	-1.4	1.8	-1.1	2.1
Hungary	-2.4	1.2	0.5	1.0	0.5	0.4	-0.6	1.8	0.1	-0.2	0.5
Malta	..	..	..	..	..	..	..	..	..	..	..
Poland	..	..	..	..	..	..	..	..	..	..	..
Portugal	..	..	..	..	..	..	..	..	..	..	..
Romania	..	..	..	..	..	..	..	..	..	..	..
Yugoslavia	-1.1	1.1	0.7	1.5	1.0	-0.4	1.1	1.0	-0.9	0.5	0.0
Low- & middle-income economies	1.3	0.7	0.1	0.9	0.9	0.9	0.4	0.6	0.6	0.0	0.6
Severely indebted	0.1	0.7	0.3	0.4	0.3	0.3	0.4	0.6	0.2	0.2	0.4
Low-income economies	3.8	0.5	-1.0	2.6	1.2	1.8	-0.2	1.5	1.4	-0.8	1.6
Low-income Africa	3.6	1.8	-0.1	0.3	2.4	-1.6	0.5	2.0	-0.1	-1.0	0.4
China and India	4.3	0.1	-1.5	3.6	0.6	3.3	-1.1	1.7	1.6	-1.4	1.9
Other low-income	2.5	0.6	-0.4	1.2	2.4	0.0	2.3	0.4	2.1	1.3	1.9
Middle-income economies	0.2	0.9	0.6	0.2	0.8	0.6	0.6	0.2	0.3	0.4	0.3
High-income OECD members	..	0.1	0.2	0.3	0.0	0.0	-0.1	-0.4	0.1	0.1	-0.1
European Community members	..	0.3	0.0	0.5	0.1	-0.2	-0.1	-1.2	0.2	0.1	0.0
Japan	-0.8	-0.3	0.7	0.3	-0.1	0.0	-0.2	-0.1	0.0	0.1	-0.3
United States	0.1	0.0	0.0	0.0	0.0	0.1	-0.1	0.0	0.0	0.1	0.0
Other high-income economies /a	0.2	0.1	0.2	0.1	0.1	-0.1	0.3	0.2	0.1	0.2	0.0

a. Economies classified by the United Nations or otherwise regarded by their authorities as developing.

1981	1982	1983	1984	1985	1986	1987	1988	1989	1990	
0.5	*0.1*	*0.0*	*0.4*	*0.5*	*-0.3*	*0.7*	*0.2*	*-0.2*	*0.0*	*LATIN AMERICA AND CARIBBEAN*
0.2	1.0	0.3	0.5	-0.2	-0.4	0.3	0.2	-2.4	-0.1	Argentina
..	..	..	..	..	..	..	..	..	..	Bahamas
-1.8	-0.2	0.3	0.9	-0.1	0.4	-1.1	-0.5	-0.7	0.3	Barbados
-0.1	1.1	-1.4	0.6	-0.3	-1.0	4.8	0.3	0.6	..	Belize
-0.2	1.8	-4.7	5.8	2.8	-1.6	-0.1	0.3	-0.5	..	Bolivia
0.6	0.0	0.0	0.2	0.9	-0.8	1.2	0.1	0.2	-0.3	Brazil
..	..	..	..	..	..	..	..	..	..	Chile
0.6	-0.4	0.5	0.3	0.3	0.6	1.1	0.5	0.9	0.5	Colombia
0.9	-0.9	0.8	1.9	-1.1	0.9	0.8	0.8	1.0	1.0	Costa Rica
-2.5	4.2	0.5	0.0	-0.6	-0.1	0.5	-0.2	0.3	0.1	Dominican Republic
0.9	0.3	-1.8	1.2	1.2	1.3	0.4	1.3	0.5	1.2	Ecuador
-1.0	-0.7	-0.5	0.5	-0.2	-0.4	0.3	-0.1	0.1	0.3	El Salvador
1.3	-2.3	0.5	2.6	-1.4	-0.1	6.2	-3.8	0.4	..	Grenada
..	..	..	..	..	..	..	..	..	..	Guatemala
0.6	-0.4	-1.0	1.0	0.0	1.1	-1.8	-2.4	..	..	Guyana
..	..	..	..	..	..	..	..	..	..	Haiti
0.8	-0.1	-0.1	0.3	0.6	0.5	0.9	0.4	0.3	0.4	Honduras
0.1	-0.5	0.4	0.6	-0.2	-0.1	0.2	-0.3	0.1	0.1	Jamaica
0.5	-0.2	0.2	0.2	0.3	-0.1	0.1	-0.1	-0.4	0.3	Mexico
2.9	0.9	1.9	-1.8	-1.5	-2.8	-1.0	-3.0	0.8	-0.6	Nicaragua
0.8	-0.2	0.3	0.2	0.5	-0.2	0.7	-0.5	0.3	0.2	Panama
2.6	0.1	-0.7	1.6	1.3	-1.7	1.9	3.3	3.0	..	Paraguay
0.8	0.3	-1.1	1.2	0.4	0.7	0.5	0.8	-0.4	-0.1	Peru
5.8	1.0	1.5	1.2	1.6	0.8	-0.9	4.1	0.5	..	St. Vincent and The Grenadines
0.0	0.1	0.6	0.0	-2.0	-0.7	0.3	-0.3	1.5	0.2	Trinidad and Tobago
0.6	-0.9	0.3	-0.9	0.6	0.6	0.3	0.1	0.2	0.1	Uruguay
-0.1	0.2	0.0	0.0	0.5	0.5	0.2	0.3	-0.3	0.1	Venezuela
0.7	*1.1*	*0.2*	*0.8*	*1.4*	*1.0*	*0.1*	*1.0*	*0.1*	*..*	*MIDDLE EAST AND NORTH AFRICA*
0.0	-0.9	-0.2	0.7	2.6	0.6	0.8	-0.6	1.5	..	Algeria
0.4	1.0	0.7	0.5	0.7	0.4	0.4	0.5	0.4	0.3	Egypt, Arab Republic of
2.2	2.0	0.7	1.4	1.6	0.9	0.6	0.9	0.6	..	Iran, Islamic Rep. of
..	..	..	-1.4	0.7	0.2	1.7	1.0	-0.8	0.5	Jordan
-4.8	4.3	-1.6	0.5	2.5	5.6	-4.5	4.6	-0.3	0.9	Morocco
0.1	0.3	0.6	0.3	0.6	-0.4	-0.4	0.3	..	..	Oman
1.2	-0.7	-0.1	-2.3	1.6	1.5	-3.7	8.4	..	..	Syrian Arab Republic
1.1	-1.8	0.4	1.9	2.8	-2.2	2.8	-4.2	0.8	3.7	Tunisia
0.0	1.3	0.0	0.7	0.5	1.5	0.4	1.5	-2.1	1.9	Turkey
..	..	..	..	..	..	..	..	..	..	Yemen, Republic of
0.0	*0.8*	*-0.6*	*0.7*	*-0.7*	*0.6*	*-0.3*	*0.2*	*..*	*..*	*EUROPE*
0.8	1.0	-3.0	1.7	-3.3	2.8	-2.1	-0.2	-0.2	..	Bulgaria
-0.3	0.4	-1.6	1.2	0.3	-0.5	-0.1	1.0	0.0	..	Greece
0.6	1.7	0.0	0.8	-0.7	0.6	-0.5	1.2	-0.3	-1.3	Hungary
..	..	..	..	..	..	..	..	..	..	Malta
..	..	..	..	..	..	..	..	..	..	Poland
..	..	..	..	..	..	..	..	..	..	Portugal
..	..	..	..	..	..	..	..	..	..	Romania
0.4	1.0	-0.1	0.3	-1.0	0.9	0.2	-0.5	0.4	..	Yugoslavia
0.9	0.8	0.7	0.9	0.6	0.5	0.4	1.0	0.4	0.4	**Low- & middle-income economies**
0.4	0.3	-0.1	0.3	0.6	0.0	0.4	0.4	-0.2	0.0	Severely indebted
1.8	1.8	2.6	1.8	0.7	0.9	0.7	2.2	1.0	0.9	Low-income economies
-1.2	2.0	-0.1	-1.1	1.2	2.6	0.0	1.1	2.2	..	Low-income Africa
2.5	2.0	3.7	2.7	0.4	0.5	1.0	2.9	0.7	0.8	China and India
2.2	0.9	1.2	0.7	1.4	1.2	0.2	0.3	1.4	1.2	Other low-income
0.6	0.5	-0.1	0.5	0.6	0.4	0.2	0.5	0.0	..	Middle-income economies
0.1	0.1	-0.1	0.2	0.1	0.0	0.0	..	..	..	**High-income OECD members**
0.0	0.2	0.0	0.1	0.0	0.1	0.0	0.0	..	..	European Community members
-0.1	0.2	0.0	0.1	0.0	-0.1	0.0	0.0	..	..	Japan
0.3	0.0	-0.4	0.2	0.3	0.1	0.0	..	..	..	United States
0.1	0.2	0.2	0.3	0.3	0.3	0.4	0.2	0.1	..	**Other high-income economies /a**

Table 8. Industry: contribution to growth of gross domestic product

Percentage points	1970	1971	1972	1973	1974	1975	1976	1977	1978	1979	1980
SUB-SAHARAN AFRICA	*4.7*	*3.8*	*2.7*	*0.6*	*2.7*	*-1.4*	*2.9*	*1.1*	*-0.3*	*3.0*	*1.1*
Excluding Nigeria	*1.8*	*1.4*	*0.9*	*1.1*	*1.1*	*0.5*	*0.6*	*0.7*	*0.3*	*1.0*	*2.0*
Benin	..	-0.9	1.5	-0.2	2.8	-1.7	-1.1	1.2	-0.6	1.1	0.0
Botswana	26.2	4.6	10.3	7.0	5.8	0.6	7.9	-1.3	16.4	2.4	5.8
Burkina Faso	..	1.2	0.6	3.9	-4.0	5.8	3.5	-5.7	2.1	-0.8	1.1
Burundi	0.6	8.8	-0.2	0.2	0.3	0.1	1.0	2.4	1.3	0.1	1.3
Cameroon	-0.2	2.0	-0.6	0.7	0.9	0.6	1.3	3.1	1.9	7.7	7.5
Cape Verde	..	..	..	..	..	..	..	..	..	..	..
Central African Rep.	1.0	-0.1	1.6	0.4	1.2	-0.1	-0.7	1.2	1.8	-0.8	0.2
Chad	0.4	0.2	0.2	0.1	0.9	1.4	1.5	0.2	-0.7	-6.5	-2.8
Comoros	..	..	..	..	..	..	..	..	..	..	..
Congo, People's Rep of the	3.6	0.2	1.6	3.4	6.1	7.4	3.2	-6.9	1.4	7.5	8.4
Cote D'Ivoire	5.9	4.7	1.6	-0.9	-0.4	2.9	3.1	2.4	5.5	2.2	2.5
Ethiopia	1.6	1.4	0.7	0.4	-0.1	-0.2	-0.6	0.2	-0.5	2.0	1.4
Gabon	..	..	..	..	..	..	..	..	..	..	..
Gambia, The	-1.1	1.3	0.8	0.5	2.2	-0.7	0.1	0.3	3.2	-0.9	1.9
Ghana	1.5	0.3	-2.2	3.9	-0.1	-0.2	-0.7	1.0	-1.9	-3.0	0.1
Guinea-Bissau	..	-1.6	1.5	-0.6	0.2	3.2	-7.3	3.6	5.9	0.0	-2.5
Kenya	-0.8	3.9	7.2	1.5	0.2	0.1	-0.1	2.4	2.0	0.7	1.0
Lesotho	..	-2.4	5.4	4.7	2.4	-0.8	5.2	10.0	3.7	4.2	5.6
Liberia	..	..	..	..	..	..	..	..	..	..	..
Madagascar	..	-1.5	0.2	-0.3	1.0	0.0	-1.5	0.5	0.6	2.1	-0.5
Malawi	0.7	1.0	3.0	-0.2	1.4	3.2	-0.7	1.1	2.2	0.2	0.2
Mali	1.2	-2.7	1.3	0.2	0.0	1.0	0.6	1.2	-0.2	-1.7	-0.1
Mauritania	2.0	1.2	-2.1	-0.6	3.1	-2.1	2.4	-2.3	0.8	2.0	-1.3
Mauritius	..	1.2	2.5	3.7	5.7	-0.1	5.5	2.5	1.9	0.3	-2.6
Mozambique	..	..	..	..	..	..	..	..	..	..	..
Niger	-1.9	1.8	0.1	1.9	-2.1	2.3	2.3	1.9	3.6	7.0	1.0
Nigeria	16.1	12.1	8.6	-0.6	8.1	-6.7	10.3	2.5	-1.8	9.4	-1.2
Rwanda	..	..	..	..	..	..	..	2.1	1.3	0.4	5.1
Senegal	1.9	0.6	0.5	-0.8	2.4	1.5	1.7	4.1	-2.4	0.1	1.7
Seychelles	..	..	..	..	..	..	..	0.1	1.6	4.4	-0.3
Sierra Leone	7.3	-1.1	-1.9	0.1	0.0	1.4	-3.7	-2.8	-4.4	1.5	3.8
Somalia	..	0.7	0.3	-3.4	0.3	-0.8	1.8	1.5	-5.5	1.9	0.5
Sudan	-0.6	-0.1	-0.7	-1.1	2.0	1.7	2.8	1.0	-1.3	-0.4	1.2
Swaziland	..	..	..	..	..	..	..	..	..	..	..
Tanzania	0.5	1.7	0.6	0.3	0.1	-0.2	1.2	-0.3	-0.1	0.7	0.0
Togo	-1.3	0.4	3.0	2.0	1.7	0.5	1.8	3.5	0.1	-0.1	3.8
Uganda	-0.2	0.2	-0.6	-1.0	0.1	-1.6	-0.6	-0.2	-1.6	-2.0	-1.3
Zaire	4.9	2.1	0.1	2.7	2.0	-1.4	-2.8	-0.6	-2.3	-2.0	1.3
Zambia	-1.0	0.9	6.0	0.4	4.3	-1.4	1.3	-3.2	2.0	-2.4	1.1
Zimbabwe	5.2	2.5	4.2	4.3	1.0	-0.3	-1.9	-3.1	-1.7	2.2	3.8
SOUTH ASIA	*0.6*	*0.4*	*0.3*	*0.8*	*0.6*	*1.4*	*1.8*	*1.5*	*2.0*	*-0.2*	*0.9*
Bangladesh	0.0	-2.1	-3.9	3.6	1.2	3.6	0.6	0.8	0.2	2.6	-0.6
India	0.3	0.7	0.9	0.5	0.5	1.3	2.1	1.7	2.2	-0.8	0.8
Nepal	..	..	..	..	..	..	..	..	..	..	..
Pakistan	2.8	0.7	-1.0	2.3	1.9	0.5	1.0	1.5	2.1	1.7	2.5
Sri Lanka	2.5	0.1	-0.3	1.7	-1.0	0.5	2.0	-1.1	3.8	2.7	1.4
EAST ASIA AND PACIFIC	*6.5*	*3.2*	*2.6*	*4.1*	*1.5*	*3.2*	*1.8*	*4.7*	*4.9*	*2.7*	*2.5*
China	10.9	4.4	1.8	3.0	0.3	4.8	-1.5	5.1	6.3	3.3	4.4
Fiji	2.8	0.0	2.0	2.5	-1.1	-1.2	0.7	2.6	0.0	3.8	0.3
Indonesia	4.5	1.3	6.4	7.3	2.7	0.3	4.7	5.1	1.3	1.5	2.9
Korea, Republic of	3.3	2.7	2.1	6.2	3.8	3.3	5.8	5.2	7.0	2.9	-0.3
Malaysia	..	..	..	..	..	..	..	..	..	..	..
Papua New Guinea	..	..	..	..	..	..	..	..	..	..	..
Philippines	2.0	2.4	3.4	4.2	1.8	3.0	3.7	2.9	2.2	2.8	1.7
Solomon islands	..	..	..	..	..	..	..	..	..	..	..
Thailand	2.7	2.5	2.5	3.1	1.3	1.4	4.9	5.0	3.8	2.2	1.2
Vanuatu	..	..	..	..	..	..	..	..	..	..	..

1981	1982	1983	1984	1985	1986	1987	1988	1989	1990	
-0.2	*0.1*	*-0.7*	*-0.1*	*0.7*	*0.5*	*-0.3*	*0.9*	*0.8*	*1.0*	*SUB-SAHARAN AFRICA*
1.5	*0.5*	*1.3*	*0.7*	*-0.1*	*1.0*	*0.0*	*0.3*	*0.1*	*..*	*Excluding Nigeria*
2.0	3.2	0.1	1.2	0.7	-1.2	0.2	-0.1	..	..	Benin
7.2	-3.0	19.8	16.2	1.6	2.0	2.3	2.1	7.1	..	Botswana
-0.4	2.0	0.2	0.4	-0.7	3.3	1.4	1.8	-0.8	..	Burkina Faso
1.1	0.1	1.8	0.2	1.4	0.2	1.2	0.5	..	..	Burundi
7.9	4.9	7.0	1.6	-2.7	3.3	-6.2	-2.3	-2.4	0.4	Cameroon
1.8	0.0	2.7	-0.1	2.4	0.3	1.0	0.9	1.4	..	Cape Verde
-1.1	-0.1	1.1	0.4	0.5	-0.5	0.6	0.3	1.9	..	Central African Rep.
4.0	1.7	3.6	3.0	0.4	1.6	-1.2	1.8	2.9	0.6	Chad
..	..	..	1.2	-0.6	0.1	-1.8	-1.6	-0.8	..	Comoros
-1.3	12.2	5.9	3.1	-1.8	-3.1	1.1	-0.7	0.5	-0.2	Congo, People's Rep of the
3.1	-4.8	0.8	0.8	-1.1	-1.4	1.7	-1.5	-1.5	-2.3	Cote D'Ivoire
0.5	0.5	0.8	0.8	0.1	0.7	0.8	0.2	0.3	-0.6	Ethiopia
..	..	..	..	..	..	..	..	..	..	Gabon
-2.9	-1.3	1.6	-0.3	0.0	1.4	0.8	-0.4	1.9	..	Gambia, The
-2.9	-2.7	-1.7	1.2	2.3	1.1	1.7	1.6	1.4	1.7	Ghana
-0.8	1.5	-0.3	5.4	1.1	-2.5	-3.3	1.5	0.6	..	Guinea-Bissau
0.8	0.3	0.1	0.4	1.1	0.7	1.0	1.0	1.1	..	Kenya
-4.7	8.7	-16.6	7.8	5.1	-1.7	3.7	5.1	6.8	3.4	Lesotho
..	..	..	..	..	..	..	..	..	..	Liberia
-3.7	-2.0	0.2	1.5	0.1	0.5	0.7	0.2	0.2	..	Madagascar
-0.6	0.0	0.6	-0.1	1.4	-0.3	0.3	1.3	1.5	0.7	Malawi
2.3	0.5	0.6	2.1	0.8	1.3	-0.7	0.6	0.6	..	Mali
0.0	-0.7	-1.0	5.3	0.9	0.8	-0.2	1.0	2.6	0.0	Mauritania
1.0	1.2	0.1	2.5	3.8	4.9	3.8	3.1	1.8	2.5	Mauritius
0.1	-3.0	-2.5	-3.7	-3.7	1.9	0.2	1.1	1.2	0.9	Mozambique
1.1	-0.9	-2.6	-1.4	-0.7	0.2	1.0	..	..	..	Niger
-5.4	-1.1	-7.4	-2.8	4.3	-1.3	-1.6	3.3	4.0	2.7	Nigeria
0.6	-0.5	3.5	-0.7	-0.7	1.0	0.2	0.0	-0.8	..	Rwanda
1.5	4.1	0.6	-0.5	0.6	1.4	2.2	1.2	-0.9	0.8	Senegal
-1.6	-2.3	0.0	1.5	2.6	0.5	0.3	..	..	..	Seychelles
-2.3	-2.2	-2.9	2.1	-3.5	1.5	0.1	-0.7	-0.1	2.1	Sierra Leone
-1.8	1.3	-1.6	0.3	0.2	2.4	0.5	-0.9	0.4	..	Somalia
1.2	1.6	1.8	-0.9	0.1	0.5	0.5	0.2	-0.1	..	Sudan
..	..	..	..	..	..	..	..	..	..	Swaziland
-0.9	-0.1	-1.7	0.6	-0.4	0.1	0.3	0.4	0.6	0.5	Tanzania
-3.8	0.6	-1.5	-2.1	1.3	0.4	0.9	2.1	0.7	..	Togo
-0.2	0.8	0.7	-0.2	-0.6	-0.5	1.1	1.4	1.0	0.8	Uganda
1.8	-1.0	0.1	1.5	-0.4	1.9	-0.2	0.5	-1.5	..	Zaire
2.3	-0.3	-1.5	-1.3	0.5	0.1	1.2	2.9	..	..	Zambia
2.8	-0.3	-0.9	-1.1	2.3	1.5	1.3	1.3	2.5	1.8	Zimbabwe
1.7	*1.2*	*2.0*	*1.5*	*1.7*	*1.8*	*1.5*	*2.0*	*1.5*	*1.7*	*SOUTH ASIA*
0.9	0.4	0.1	1.0	0.8	0.3	0.9	0.9	0.7	0.8	Bangladesh
2.0	1.2	2.4	1.6	1.9	2.1	1.6	2.2	1.7	1.8	India
..	..	..	..	..	..	..	..	..	..	Nepal
0.0	2.4	1.1	1.6	1.8	1.9	2.0	2.4	1.1	1.9	Pakistan
0.7	0.7	0.5	1.8	0.9	1.6	1.6	1.2	1.0	..	Sri Lanka
1.4	*1.4*	*4.0*	*4.3*	*4.1*	*3.8*	*5.2*	*6.7*	*3.7*	*3.2*	*EAST ASIA AND PACIFIC*
0.7	2.5	3.9	6.0	8.0	4.2	6.3	9.5	4.2	2.4	China
1.6	-1.5	-1.8	0.5	-1.5	2.5	-2.8	-1.6	3.9	0.9	Fiji
1.9	-2.9	5.4	3.5	-0.1	2.4	1.9	1.9	2.9	3.1	Indonesia
2.5	3.0	6.2	5.7	2.8	6.5	6.9	5.1	2.9	5.2	Korea, Republic of
..	..	..	..	..	..	..	..	..	..	Malaysia
-3.6	0.2	2.6	-1.8	4.0	3.6	-0.4	2.0	-3.6	0.5	Papua New Guinea
1.8	0.7	0.3	-3.8	-3.6	-0.7	2.5	2.8	2.3	1.7	Philippines
..	..	..	..	..	..	..	..	..	..	Solomon islands
1.9	1.0	2.7	2.9	-0.1	2.4	4.0	6.6	6.2	4.9	Thailand
..	..	..	1.2	0.3	0.7	2.3	..	..	..	Vanuatu

Table 8. Industry: contribution to growth of gross domestic product (cont'd.)

Percentage points	1970	1971	1972	1973	1974	1975	1976	1977	1978	1979	1980
LATIN AMERICA AND CARIBBEAN	2.8	2.3	3.3	4.3	2.3	0.8	2.8	1.5	2.6	2.8	2.3
Argentina	-0.5	2.5	1.3	0.5	2.3	-0.3	0.2	3.3	-3.1	3.0	-0.5
Bahamas	..	..	..	..	..	..	..	..	..	..	..
Barbados	1.1	0.2	1.0	1.4	-1.1	-0.2	3.5	-1.2	1.3	3.0	1.0
Belize	..	..	..	..	2.8	1.2	0.5	2.5	1.9	0.9	2.4
Bolivia	-1.1	2.2	3.8	7.4	-0.2	0.4	1.8	1.1	-1.1	-2.6	0.1
Brazil	3.7	4.9	5.9	7.2	3.6	2.0	5.0	1.3	4.8	3.1	4.3
Chile	..	..	..	..	..	..	..	..	..	..	..
Colombia	1.7	2.3	3.3	3.2	1.8	0.0	1.5	0.5	2.5	1.7	1.2
Costa Rica	2.0	2.3	2.9	2.1	2.8	0.9	2.3	2.9	2.1	1.7	0.3
Dominican Republic	4.0	3.9	3.9	5.1	1.4	2.1	2.0	1.3	-0.4	2.1	0.7
Ecuador	1.4	3.0	12.6	21.0	-0.9	-0.3	5.3	0.8	3.5	2.5	-0.2
El Salvador	0.8	1.6	1.7	1.0	1.3	2.3	1.3	2.4	0.8	-0.7	-2.7
Grenada	..	..	..	..	..	..	..	..	..	..	..
Guatemala	..	..	..	..	..	..	..	..	..	..	..
Guyana	2.0	1.5	-2.9	-1.1	3.7	4.0	-1.8	-1.4	-3.1	-0.7	1.3
Haiti	..	..	..	..	..	..	..	..	..	..	..
Honduras	0.9	0.6	1.6	3.0	1.2	0.1	1.2	3.0	3.1	3.9	-1.8
Jamaica	7.4	1.4	3.1	-0.2	-0.6	-2.1	-5.7	-2.8	-0.5	-1.4	-4.2
Mexico	3.2	0.6	3.4	3.8	2.5	1.9	1.9	0.8	3.8	4.2	3.5
Nicaragua	2.6	0.7	1.2	0.9	3.8	-0.2	1.1	3.0	-2.5	-7.4	3.3
Panama	2.0	2.8	0.9	2.5	-0.7	0.7	0.8	-1.8	2.7	1.6	2.3
Paraguay	1.7	1.6	1.5	2.1	1.8	0.6	1.9	4.1	3.7	3.6	7.7
Peru	2.9	1.2	1.4	2.2	3.3	0.3	1.2	0.4	1.1	2.9	2.0
St. Vincent and The Grenadines	..	..	..	..	..	..	..	..	2.3	4.4	1.4
Trinidad and Tobago	1.5	1.5	3.2	1.0	3.2	-0.3	6.1	1.1	6.6	1.4	2.3
Uruguay	0.4	-0.2	0.5	-0.8	0.8	3.0	1.3	1.6	3.1	2.7	1.0
Venezuela	6.5	-0.7	-1.1	3.5	-2.0	-3.2	2.2	1.6	1.4	1.0	-2.1
MIDDLE EAST AND NORTH AFRICA	4.9	-3.0	6.8	3.5	-0.4	0.0	4.2	0.9	-3.3	-2.5	-4.6
Algeria	..	-8.5	17.9	2.7	-9.7	-2.3	5.1	3.4	4.5	1.7	0.6
Egypt, Arab Republic of	2.0	1.2	0.4	-0.5	-1.1	4.2	3.9	5.7	4.6	2.7	4.3
Iran, Islamic Rep. of	6.1	-3.5	5.4	3.9	0.8	-1.5	3.7	-0.7	-6.9	-5.1	-8.9
Jordan	..	..	..	..	..	..	..	..	..	..	..
Morocco	1.1	2.6	2.1	2.1	2.4	3.8	3.5	3.0	-0.4	2.8	-0.5
Oman	..	..	..	..	..	..	..	..	..	-3.4	-0.2
Syrian Arab Republic	1.8	4.5	2.3	-0.1	5.0	6.4	2.1	-1.5	0.7	0.5	-0.2
Tunisia	2.5	2.0	4.1	0.3	1.2	4.5	-0.3	2.3	2.9	3.6	3.1
Turkey	1.3	1.6	1.9	3.3	2.5	2.9	3.2	2.9	2.1	-1.2	-1.5
Yemen, Republic of	..	..	..	..	..	..	..	..	..	..	..
EUROPE	..	..	..	..	..	..	..	..	..	..	..
Bulgaria	..	..	..	..	..	..	..	..	..	..	..
Greece	2.5	3.7	3.9	4.0	-3.7	1.8	2.9	1.5	2.0	1.9	-0.8
Hungary	2.6	2.6	2.5	3.0	3.2	2.8	2.3	2.6	2.2	2.1	-0.7
Malta	..	..	..	..	..	..	..	..	..	..	..
Poland	..	..	..	..	..	..	..	..	..	..	..
Portugal	..	..	..	..	..	..	..	..	..	..	..
Romania	..	..	..	..	..	..	..	..	..	..	..
Yugoslavia	2.9	3.0	8.5	1.7	4.6	3.4	1.9	4.6	4.5	3.3	1.6
Low- & middle-income economies	3.8	1.5	3.3	3.3	1.4	1.2	2.6	2.1	1.8	1.6	0.9
Severely indebted	2.8	2.4	3.2	4.3	2.4	1.2	3.0	1.7	2.5	2.9	2.3
Low-income economies	4.2	2.2	1.7	1.9	1.2	1.6	1.3	2.8	2.6	1.4	2.1
Low-income Africa	5.1	4.1	2.9	0.5	3.1	-2.2	3.3	1.0	-0.8	2.8	0.1
China and India	4.5	2.3	1.3	1.6	0.4	3.0	0.4	3.2	4.1	1.1	2.6
Other low-income	2.6	0.4	2.0	4.4	1.8	0.9	2.7	2.9	1.3	1.6	1.9
Middle-income economies	3.5	1.2	4.1	3.9	1.5	1.0	3.2	1.8	1.5	1.7	0.3
High-income OECD members	0.7	1.0	2.0	3.0	-0.9	-2.3	2.4	0.5	1.6	1.2	0.2
European Community members	..	1.4	1.3	2.8	-0.6	-3.7	2.9	-1.7	0.8	1.6	0.5
Japan	4.9	2.3	3.2	4.0	-1.0	-0.5	2.4	1.4	2.7	2.1	2.1
United States	-1.5	0.0	2.0	2.6	-1.2	-2.0	2.0	1.8	1.7	0.5	-1.0
Other high-income economies /a	6.6	6.7	6.6	5.3	1.7	-1.2	4.6	4.7	3.5	3.7	0.1

a. Economies classified by the United Nations or otherwise regarded by their authorities as developing.

1981	1982	1983	1984	1985	1986	1987	1988	1989	1990	
-1.5	*-0.7*	*-2.0*	*1.8*	*1.6*	*2.6*	*0.8*	*-0.4*	*0.5*	*-0.9*	*LATIN AMERICA AND CARIBBEAN*
-4.7	-2.4	2.0	0.3	-2.7	3.5	0.6	-1.7	-2.9	-1.0	Argentina
..	..	..	..	..	..	..	..	..	..	Bahamas
-0.2	-1.6	0.7	0.6	-1.2	1.4	-0.3	1.5	1.2	-0.9	Barbados
0.8	-0.8	-0.7	-0.2	0.0	0.9	3.2	2.3	3.0	..	Belize
-0.9	-2.7	-1.6	-4.4	-3.6	-2.2	0.5	3.5	4.9	..	Bolivia
-4.1	0.1	-2.6	2.7	3.8	5.2	0.5	-1.2	1.7	-2.5	Brazil
..	..	..	..	..	..	..	..	..	..	Chile
-0.3	-0.1	1.0	2.2	1.9	3.7	2.2	0.8	1.1	1.4	Colombia
-1.2	-3.8	1.1	3.0	0.4	1.8	1.4	0.5	1.5	1.1	Costa Rica
0.8	-1.2	2.3	0.1	-1.9	1.4	4.5	-0.2	1.3	1.0	Dominican Republic
2.5	0.1	2.4	1.2	1.5	0.4	-7.6	9.4	-1.7	1.0	Ecuador
-2.3	-1.6	0.5	0.1	0.9	0.6	0.7	-2.7	0.5	0.5	El Salvador
3.4	1.5	-2.4	-0.8	1.7	1.6	2.4	2.1	2.7	..	Grenada
..	..	..	..	..	..	..	..	..	..	Guatemala
-0.8	-7.5	-7.5	0.7	1.3	-0.8	0.3	-1.0	..	..	Guyana
..	..	..	..	..	..	..	..	..	..	Haiti
-2.1	1.1	0.5	1.4	-0.2	1.3	0.3	1.7	1.0	0.2	Honduras
0.5	-0.8	1.2	-1.5	-2.7	1.8	2.8	0.5	2.1	1.2	Jamaica
3.4	-0.8	-3.3	1.7	1.7	-2.1	0.9	0.4	2.2	0.8	Mexico
0.6	-0.6	1.2	0.2	-0.6	0.8	-0.4	-5.9	-0.7	-0.4	Nicaragua
0.1	1.9	-2.5	-1.1	0.4	0.8	0.5	-5.0	-0.3	1.7	Panama
2.0	-1.3	-1.9	0.9	0.1	0.5	0.4	0.7	-1.7	..	Paraguay
0.4	0.1	-5.7	1.6	0.9	3.4	3.1	-3.8	-4.2	-1.8	Peru
0.6	1.2	0.9	0.8	0.7	2.3	2.6	1.3	0.1	..	St. Vincent and The Grenadines
0.9	-5.2	-4.1	-2.9	-1.2	-3.2	-3.4	-1.6	-0.7	0.0	Trinidad and Tobago
-1.0	-4.5	-3.8	0.1	-1.6	3.1	3.7	-0.7	-0.5	-0.4	Uruguay
-0.8	-1.5	-2.1	2.9	-0.4	3.0	1.5	2.6	-3.6	0.6	Venezuela
2.8	*3.9*	*2.9*	*1.1*	*1.4*	*0.0*	*0.0*	*1.2*	*0.7*	*..*	*MIDDLE EAST AND NORTH AFRICA*
5.2	3.4	6.1	4.0	2.7	-0.1	-4.7	1.6	-1.4	..	Algeria
1.1	0.7	2.0	2.6	2.3	0.5	0.7	1.1	0.5	-0.7	Egypt, Arab Republic of
2.4	5.8	1.9	-1.0	-0.1	-1.8	0.4	0.4	1.2	..	Iran, Islamic Rep. of
..	..	..	2.4	-3.3	1.8	0.2	0.0	0.7	-2.8	Jordan
0.9	1.0	0.5	0.5	1.9	0.3	0.5	2.9	-0.3	1.4	Morocco
12.0	6.5	15.5	11.1	12.9	8.3	0.7	..	..	..	Oman
-0.1	1.1	1.0	-1.6	1.5	2.3	-3.8	2.0	..	..	Syrian Arab Republic
2.4	0.0	2.3	1.4	0.6	-0.3	0.0	0.7	1.5	1.3	Tunisia
1.8	1.3	2.1	2.8	1.9	3.0	3.2	0.8	1.1	2.8	Turkey
..	..	..	..	..	..	..	..	..	..	Yemen, Republic of
..	*..*	*..*	*..*	*..*	*..*	*..*	*..*	*..*	*..*	*EUROPE*
2.8	4.9	4.3	3.6	3.0	3.2	3.3	1.5	0.1	..	Bulgaria
-0.5	-0.7	0.1	0.4	1.1	0.0	-0.5	1.6	0.9	..	Greece
2.9	0.5	0.8	0.6	-1.0	-0.2	1.6	-0.9	-1.0	-4.1	Hungary
..	..	..	..	..	..	..	..	..	..	Malta
..	..	..	..	..	..	..	..	..	..	Poland
..	..	..	..	..	..	..	..	..	..	Portugal
..	..	..	..	..	..	..	..	..	..	Romania
1.1	-0.9	-0.7	1.7	1.0	2.0	1.1	-0.3	0.4	..	Yugoslavia
0.6	0.7	0.9	2.1	2.0	2.1	1.9	2.3	1.6	..	**Low- & middle-income economies**
-1.2	-0.5	-1.8	1.5	1.3	2.2	0.8	-0.2	0.5	-1.0	Severely indebted
0.8	0.9	2.3	2.9	3.7	2.5	3.1	4.8	2.7	2.1	Low-income economies
-1.6	-0.3	-2.2	-0.6	1.3	0.2	0.0	1.5	1.4	1.4	Low-income Africa
1.4	1.8	3.2	3.8	5.1	3.2	4.2	6.4	3.1	2.1	China and India
1.2	-0.9	2.9	2.3	0.4	1.6	1.5	1.5	2.0	2.3	Other low-income
0.5	0.6	0.2	1.8	1.2	1.9	1.2	1.0	1.0	..	Middle-income economies
0.2	-0.6	1.0	2.3	1.2	0.3	1.2	..	..	..	**High-income OECD members**
-0.6	-0.6	0.3	0.5	0.6	0.3	0.2	..	..	..	European Community members
1.4	1.4	1.5	3.2	2.3	0.5	2.6	3.4	..	..	Japan
0.2	-1.6	1.2	3.1	0.9	0.2	1.1	..	..	..	United States
0.5	-3.7	-0.3	-0.6	-1.7	5.3	1.3	2.8	3.0	..	**Other high-income economies** /a

Table 9. Services: contribution to growth of gross domestic product

Percentage points	1970	1971	1972	1973	1974	1975	1976	1977	1978	1979	1980
SUB-SAHARAN AFRICA	*0.5*	*2.1*	*-0.1*	*2.1*	*2.6*	*3.1*	*2.6*	*1.2*	*0.4*	*0.3*	*1.5*
Excluding Nigeria	*2.0*	*3.6*	*1.0*	*1.3*	*3.8*	*1.5*	*3.6*	*1.1*	*0.6*	*0.9*	*0.7*
Benin	..	1.1	3.3	3.3	1.9	-1.4	-1.6	3.7	-1.8	3.4	5.3
Botswana	-16.4	9.6	14.1	9.5	4.7	1.2	6.8	2.5	3.6	9.6	10.2
Burkina Faso	..	-0.4	2.7	-1.8	7.5	-3.2	3.2	9.3	0.7	8.2	-1.7
Burundi	2.0	3.4	-0.1	-0.1	1.6	-2.4	4.5	6.3	-0.6	0.6	-1.4
Cameroon	1.3	1.3	0.8	3.3	8.1	-1.8	2.6	4.9	11.5	1.2	5.6
Cape Verde	..	..	..	..	..	..	..	..	..	..	..
Central African Rep.	1.4	-0.2	0.6	1.5	3.1	-0.5	4.1	1.7	-0.5	-1.3	-4.2
Chad	1.8	-1.3	-0.7	-2.0	2.7	3.8	2.0	1.6	-0.3	-10.7	-5.2
Comoros	..	..	..	..	..	..	..	..	..	..	..
Congo, People's Rep of the	0.9	6.9	6.3	4.2	3.1	2.3	-0.1	-4.5	4.8	3.4	9.2
Cote D'Ivoire	1.3	2.8	4.5	2.2	11.7	3.5	0.3	-0.7	4.1	0.5	-8.2
Ethiopia	3.5	1.7	2.5	2.4	1.7	1.4	1.9	2.7	0.0	3.2	0.6
Gabon	..	..	..	..	..	..	..	..	..	..	..
Gambia, The	-5.2	6.2	3.9	2.5	10.6	0.8	9.3	2.8	-4.1	16.6	-9.8
Ghana	2.2	2.6	-2.9	0.2	2.6	-2.1	-2.0	3.7	2.5	-0.6	-0.7
Guinea-Bissau	..	7.9	-2.1	5.2	2.0	2.9	7.7	-3.8	-0.2	4.9	2.5
Kenya	-0.5	12.0	6.7	3.3	4.4	-1.3	1.6	3.4	3.4	5.8	4.0
Lesotho	..	6.3	18.5	16.5	-2.2	0.2	8.4	1.7	9.9	-2.7	6.6
Liberia	..	..	..	..	..	..	..	..	..	..	..
Madagascar	..	6.8	-2.3	-3.0	-1.7	1.4	1.1	1.0	-1.3	5.7	0.5
Malawi	0.3	8.1	-1.1	5.5	4.9	2.6	1.0	-0.4	6.5	3.2	2.9
Mali	-0.1	4.6	2.9	4.2	1.3	-0.7	4.3	0.7	2.1	3.2	0.8
Mauritania	10.0	4.8	-10.4	2.9	7.4	1.7	4.8	-0.9	-0.3	2.0	1.7
Mauritius	..	-0.2	0.7	7.9	3.6	9.8	4.4	5.3	3.8	4.5	-1.1
Mozambique	..	..	..	..	..	..	..	..	..	..	..
Niger	2.3	1.5	-0.8	-4.4	3.2	2.8	1.3	1.2	5.5	2.1	2.4
Nigeria	-4.2	-2.8	-4.2	4.9	-0.6	7.2	-0.2	1.5	-1.0	-1.4	3.3
Rwanda	..	..	..	..	..	..	..	2.5	6.5	-0.7	5.9
Senegal	5.0	4.2	0.1	-0.2	-4.2	5.1	2.9	-4.7	3.1	3.1	0.4
Seychelles	..	..	..	..	..	..	..	8.4	6.1	10.8	-2.3
Sierra Leone	3.2	3.6	1.2	2.2	5.5	0.1	-1.9	2.0	-8.3	2.9	0.6
Somalia	..	2.8	6.5	3.8	-2.6	3.2	-4.1	4.3	8.4	-1.8	-7.2
Sudan	-4.4	2.7	-0.8	-2.6	0.1	8.5	13.9	6.7	-1.1	-3.1	2.2
Swaziland	..	..	..	..	..	..	..	..	..	..	..
Tanzania	3.9	3.1	1.2	5.3	4.7	-0.9	5.4	-0.3	3.1	1.4	0.6
Togo	4.4	-0.1	3.4	1.3	2.6	1.1	-2.4	4.6	6.9	-3.7	6.7
Uganda	0.7	7.8	-2.8	-5.3	2.1	-3.4	2.7	-0.1	-4.7	-2.4	1.0
Zaire	2.5	3.6	-0.4	4.9	1.0	-3.1	-4.0	1.9	-3.2	0.9	0.4
Zambia	3.3	-0.6	3.9	-0.7	1.8	-1.3	4.0	-1.6	-1.3	-0.2	2.1
Zimbabwe	18.8	2.6	1.9	1.6	2.9	-0.8	0.6	-0.6	-2.5	1.4	6.5
SOUTH ASIA	*2.0*	*1.5*	*0.5*	*0.6*	*1.4*	*2.6*	*2.3*	*1.7*	*2.7*	*0.8*	*1.7*
Bangladesh	2.7	0.0	-2.6	-1.8	4.5	0.4	4.9	2.1	1.6	2.7	1.8
India	1.8	1.8	0.7	0.0	1.4	2.6	2.2	1.5	2.6	0.6	1.1
Nepal	..	..	..	..	..	..	..	..	..	..	..
Pakistan	4.9	0.9	0.6	4.2	0.0	4.4	2.8	1.7	5.1	1.0	6.0
Sri Lanka	-0.7	3.1	-3.1	8.1	2.9	6.9	1.1	2.9	-0.2	3.1	3.4
EAST ASIA AND PACIFIC	*5.9*	*2.9*	*2.4*	*2.6*	*1.3*	*2.6*	*0.0*	*4.0*	*4.3*	*2.4*	*2.5*
China	9.0	2.2	2.6	1.1	-1.2	2.4	-4.4	3.9	3.7	1.0	2.7
Fiji	7.5	8.8	5.6	7.3	4.5	1.6	1.2	0.0	2.2	4.6	-0.4
Indonesia	1.0	3.6	-0.6	-1.7	3.8	4.7	0.8	3.5	5.0	2.9	3.2
Korea, Republic of	6.1	6.3	3.1	7.0	3.3	3.3	5.2	5.1	6.2	3.2	0.6
Malaysia	..	..	..	..	..	..	..	..	..	..	..
Papua New Guinea	..	..	..	..	..	..	..	..	..	..	..
Philippines	2.1	1.3	1.1	2.8	2.4	2.6	2.2	2.2	2.4	2.5	2.5
Solomon islands	..	..	..	..	..	..	..	..	..	..	..
Thailand	5.8	1.4	2.2	4.5	2.3	2.4	3.1	4.2	4.2	3.3	3.1
Vanuatu	..	..	..	..	..	..	..	..	..	..	..

1981	1982	1983	1984	1985	1986	1987	1988	1989	1990	
2.4	*0.9*	*1.4*	*0.1*	*1.9*	*1.8*	*0.5*	*1.0*	*0.6*	..	*SUB-SAHARAN AFRICA*
1.5	*1.1*	*1.3*	*0.5*	*2.4*	*2.0*	*0.7*	*1.3*	*0.7*	..	*Excluding Nigeria*
9.9	2.9	-2.4	0.2	1.1	-4.4	-2.2	-4.6	..	..	Benin
1.5	2.4	5.9	4.1	7.1	5.6	8.2	6.4	6.3	..	Botswana
2.4	7.1	0.5	-1.9	3.9	2.9	2.0	1.1	1.7	..	Burkina Faso
1.9	2.9	3.2	1.9	2.9	1.3	0.4	1.8	..	..	Burundi
1.3	-3.3	2.8	2.1	13.1	1.8	-1.5	-4.7	-1.1	-1.1	Cameroon
7.8	6.4	6.9	3.7	3.0	1.6	4.4	1.7	3.5	..	Cape Verde
-0.5	6.9	-6.3	5.4	2.0	-1.5	-3.4	-0.3	-1.0	..	Central African Rep.
2.8	1.3	6.4	5.6	6.9	2.0	-0.9	4.4	3.0	1.3	Chad
..	..	..	1.8	1.7	0.9	0.6	1.2	0.1	..	Comoros
14.7	13.2	1.4	4.0	0.5	-4.3	-0.9	0.9	-0.9	-0.4	Congo, People's Rep of the
0.3	7.0	2.3	-2.7	1.3	0.7	-0.7	-2.6	-1.8	-4.4	Cote D'Ivoire
0.3	1.8	2.0	1.8	0.3	2.3	2.3	3.9	-0.3	-1.5	Ethiopia
..	..	..	..	..	..	..	..	..	..	Gabon
1.8	6.7	1.0	1.1	-0.8	-2.6	4.1	8.3	0.6	..	Gambia, The
1.5	-0.7	1.2	2.2	2.4	2.2	2.9	2.8	2.2	1.1	Ghana
8.7	0.5	-2.1	-1.2	0.4	-0.5	4.4	3.8	0.8	..	Guinea-Bissau
1.3	-0.9	0.7	2.5	1.9	4.8	3.6	3.5	2.2	..	Kenya
4.1	0.5	3.5	5.7	-1.0	1.8	2.5	1.9	1.5	2.7	Lesotho
..	..	..	..	..	..	..	..	..	..	Liberia
-4.8	-1.1	-0.1	-0.8	0.7	0.3	-0.3	2.8	2.9	..	Madagascar
-1.7	0.2	1.4	3.5	3.0	-0.4	1.0	0.9	2.7	1.9	Malawi
3.3	1.8	2.0	3.4	1.6	2.2	2.9	1.4	1.2	..	Mali
0.8	-1.9	0.2	-5.0	1.0	1.5	2.2	3.1	0.2	1.7	Mauritania
1.2	1.4	2.6	2.1	1.8	3.7	7.1	4.2	2.8	2.7	Mauritius
0.4	-0.4	-1.1	0.3	-4.8	-0.4	1.4	-0.1	0.8	0.4	Mozambique
0.4	0.4	-2.3	-12.5	-1.2	3.3	1.6	..	..	..	Niger
4.3	0.1	1.2	-2.6	0.5	0.6	-0.6	-0.1	0.7	1.5	Nigeria
11.1	-3.6	0.6	0.0	6.0	3.1	0.1	0.9	-1.7	..	Rwanda
-0.7	5.5	0.8	-0.1	1.6	1.1	1.4	2.2	0.9	2.1	Senegal
-7.2	2.8	1.5	2.9	7.3	1.7	3.4	..	..	..	Seychelles
10.6	1.0	0.1	0.0	-3.7	-2.2	2.5	0.5	-0.7	-0.2	Sierra Leone
1.3	0.5	0.1	-4.8	1.8	2.2	0.4	-2.8	1.2	..	Somalia
2.4	-2.2	3.7	-2.5	-2.1	2.6	0.4	2.7	-0.8	..	Sudan
..	..	..	..	..	..	..	..	..	..	Swaziland
-0.6	-0.9	-0.4	1.6	-1.7	1.8	1.0	2.0	0.2	1.4	Tanzania
0.3	-2.0	-3.9	-0.1	0.5	1.4	0.0	0.8	0.5	..	Togo
3.0	6.9	3.3	-0.8	-2.9	-1.4	0.7	0.6	1.5	2.0	Uganda
1.2	-0.3	0.8	0.2	1.8	1.7	-0.1	2.2	-1.3	..	Zaire
3.0	-1.3	-1.4	-0.3	0.8	-0.8	2.0	0.3	..	..	Zambia
7.8	3.9	4.6	-4.0	1.2	2.1	-0.1	-5.9	10.6	0.8	Zimbabwe
2.6	*2.8*	*1.5*	*2.3*	*3.9*	*2.9*	*2.7*	*2.2*	*2.4*	*2.3*	*SOUTH ASIA*
3.0	0.0	1.2	2.2	2.3	1.8	2.7	1.5	1.4	1.1	Bangladesh
2.3	3.1	1.1	2.2	4.2	3.2	2.8	2.1	2.7	2.5	India
..	..	..	..	..	..	..	..	..	..	Nepal
4.9	2.7	4.3	4.9	2.6	2.1	3.5	4.8	2.0	1.9	Pakistan
2.8	6.0	1.9	-2.0	6.4	2.1	0.8	1.0	1.5	..	Sri Lanka
2.4	*2.0*	*2.9*	*2.2*	*2.5*	*2.6*	*3.0*	*1.9*	*1.0*	*2.1*	*EAST ASIA AND PACIFIC*
1.4	1.1	2.3	2.0	3.8	2.3	2.0	-0.7	-2.1	0.0	China
1.9	-4.9	1.9	2.7	1.4	1.3	-2.1	2.3	5.6	3.6	Fiji
4.2	2.2	2.8	2.2	1.8	2.8	2.5	2.8	3.5	3.1	Indonesia
2.3	3.2	4.6	3.7	3.6	5.2	5.6	5.2	3.7	4.2	Korea, Republic of
..	..	..	..	..	..	..	..	..	..	Malaysia
1.4	0.6	0.1	0.4	1.3	-0.8	2.3	0.0	1.3	-1.5	Papua New Guinea
1.2	1.5	1.2	-3.1	-1.8	1.2	2.8	2.7	2.3	1.6	Philippines
..	..	..	..	..	..	..	..	..	..	Solomon islands
3.3	2.4	3.6	3.3	2.3	2.2	4.9	6.4	5.3	4.9	Thailand
..	..	..	3.9	1.3	-1.2	-1.6	..	..	..	Vanuatu

Table 9. Services: contribution to growth of gross domestic product (cont'd.)

Percentage points	1970	1971	1972	1973	1974	1975	1976	1977	1978	1979	1980
LATIN AMERICA AND CARIBBEAN	*3.9*	*3.4*	*3.5*	*3.9*	*3.9*	*2.1*	*2.9*	*2.6*	*0.7*	*3.1*	*3.3*
Argentina	7.1	1.2	0.5	1.7	2.8	0.2	-1.1	2.9	-0.7	3.8	3.1
Bahamas	..	..	..	..	..	..	..	..	..	..	..
Barbados	7.7	5.9	2.9	-0.7	-3.0	4.6	-4.2	5.2	4.8	3.9	3.1
Belize	..	..	..	8.8	1.6	1.7	-3.2	4.6	5.9	1.0
Bolivia	-0.2	1.1	0.0	-3.3	4.4	4.2	2.9	3.3	3.9	1.8	-1.4
Brazil	4.9	5.3	5.9	7.2	5.4	2.5	4.6	2.3	-1.3	3.2	4.2
Chile	..	..	..	..	..	..	..	..	..	..	..
Colombia	4.7	3.5	2.8	3.0	2.8	1.0	2.6	2.9	4.4	2.7	2.5
Costa Rica	4.6	3.4	4.0	4.4	2.9	0.5	3.0	5.6	2.9	3.2	0.5
Dominican Republic	6.7	5.8	5.6	6.0	4.4	3.2	3.4	3.2	1.9	2.1	4.6
Ecuador	3.4	2.5	3.1	7.2	5.3	5.2	3.9	5.2	4.0	2.6	4.1
El Salvador	1.4	2.6	3.5	3.7	3.8	2.1	3.5	3.0	4.1	-1.4	-5.0
Grenada	..	..	..	..	..	..	..	..	..	..	..
Guatemala	..	..	..	..	..	..	..	..	..	..	..
Guyana	2.7	-0.2	2.6	2.6	0.2	4.8	2.3	-0.4	-0.5	0.5	0.3
Haiti	..	..	..	..	..	..	..	..	..	..	..
Honduras	4.2	0.8	3.8	3.4	0.3	4.0	6.9	6.1	3.7	0.7	3.3
Jamaica	4.2	0.9	5.9	1.4	-2.9	1.2	-1.3	-0.1	0.4	0.1	-1.8
Mexico	3.5	2.9	5.0	4.0	3.3	3.6	2.3	1.8	3.9	5.3	4.3
Nicaragua	-5.7	1.4	0.9	2.8	7.2	-0.5	3.2	4.1	-7.4	-13.9	8.7
Panama	5.1	5.8	4.2	2.7	4.0	0.2	0.1	2.3	6.2	3.5	13.6
Paraguay	1.1	3.4	3.7	3.0	3.5	3.3	3.7	4.4	5.8	5.6	4.5
Peru	1.2	3.3	2.0	3.1	5.4	3.3	0.5	0.0	-0.8	2.4	3.2
St. Vincent and The Grenadines	..	..	..	..	..	..	..	..	5.0	0.8	3.1
Trinidad and Tobago	1.2	-0.1	1.8	1.3	0.5	0.8	2.4	5.5	4.5	1.1	5.6
Uruguay	4.2	1.3	-0.5	0.8	1.9	2.3	2.4	-0.7	3.1	3.5	3.2
Venezuela	1.0	2.1	2.5	3.3	3.9	5.7	5.7	4.3	0.9	-0.4	-2.5
MIDDLE EAST AND NORTH AFRICA	*3.1*	*3.0*	*0.7*	*5.2*	*2.4*	*4.3*	*9.8*	*6.1*	*-3.2*	*1.2*	*-2.4*
Algeria	..	0.5	1.9	1.1	14.8	4.4	3.6	2.8	3.5	4.8	-1.1
Egypt, Arab Republic of	2.9	2.4	-1.3	4.3	4.8	3.4	11.0	8.3	1.4	4.0	5.5
Iran, Islamic Rep. of	5.4	5.1	6.7	10.3	2.3	3.0	13.0	7.9	-10.3	-5.1	-10.6
Jordan	..	..	..	..	..	..	..	..	..	..	..
Morocco	2.9	0.7	0.8	3.5	2.6	4.1	4.9	4.2	0.6	2.0	7.3
Oman	..	..	..	..	..	..	..	..	..	3.7	3.3
Syrian Arab Republic	0.8	2.9	0.0	9.7	4.9	16.0	1.8	3.9	1.2	8.0	-1.0
Tunisia	2.9	4.7	9.6	1.5	3.9	1.5	6.8	3.3	2.5	3.9	2.6
Turkey	3.0	4.3	5.1	3.4	3.9	3.7	3.9	2.0	0.7	-0.3	0.4
Yemen, Republic of	..	..	..	..	..	..	..	..	..	..	..
EUROPE	..	..	..	..	..	..	..	..	..	..	..
Bulgaria	..	..	..	..	..	..	..	..	..	..	..
Greece	3.4	2.6	3.7	3.5	-0.4	3.1	3.5	2.9	2.9	2.5	0.8
Hungary	4.7	2.6	3.2	3.0	2.2	3.1	1.9	2.3	2.3	-0.3	0.2
Malta	..	..	..	..	..	..	..	..	..	..	..
Poland	..	..	..	..	..	..	..	..	..	..	..
Portugal	..	..	..	..	..	..	..	..	..	..	..
Romania	..	..	..	..	..	..	..	..	..	..	..
Yugoslavia	3.0	4.7	-5.6	-0.6	9.2	-2.3	2.3	2.8	5.5	1.4	1.0
Low- & middle-income economies	3.3	2.7	2.0	3.2	2.7	2.4	3.5	3.2	0.8	1.8	1.6
Severely indebted	3.8	3.3	3.3	3.9	3.9	2.3	2.8	2.5	0.7	3.0	3.2
Low-income economies	2.8	1.8	0.7	0.7	0.8	2.7	0.2	2.6	2.5	0.6	2.2
Low-income Africa	-0.7	1.8	-1.0	1.7	1.0	2.7	1.5	2.4	0.0	0.1	1.8
China and India	4.1	1.8	1.4	0.4	0.1	2.5	-0.7	2.6	3.0	0.5	1.9
Other low-income	2.0	1.9	-0.5	0.7	2.8	3.5	2.0	2.8	3.9	2.4	3.3
Middle-income economies	3.6	3.1	2.3	4.0	3.3	2.3	4.7	3.4	0.2	2.2	1.5
High-income OECD members	..	2.1	2.9	2.5	1.6	2.0	3.0	3.7	2.5	2.0	1.4
European Community members	..	1.0	2.8	2.3	2.6	2.8	2.0	5.7	2.2	1.9	0.8
Japan	6.7	2.4	4.6	3.8	-0.1	3.1	2.6	4.0	2.4	3.1	2.6
United States	1.2	2.8	2.9	2.2	0.6	0.9	2.8	2.8	3.4	1.5	1.0
Other high-income economies /a	1.2	4.5	5.3	4.5	2.8	1.3	4.1	4.1	4.0	4.5	3.9

a. Economies classified by the United Nations or otherwise regarded by their authorities as developing.

1981	1982	1983	1984	1985	1986	1987	1988	1989	1990	
0.7	*-0.7*	*-0.8*	*1.5*	*1.5*	*2.1*	*1.6*	*0.8*	*1.0*	*0.1*	*LATIN AMERICA AND CARIBBEAN*
-2.4	-4.1	0.7	1.6	-1.5	2.3	1.5	-1.2	1.4	0.0	Argentina
..	..	..	..	..	..	..	..	..	..	Bahamas
-1.2	-3.2	-0.9	1.8	1.5	8.6	1.9	5.9	3.0	-2.3	Barbados
0.7	-2.0	1.5	5.2	2.3	3.9	6.6	7.2	5.2	..	Belize
2.1	-3.4	-0.3	-0.4	0.8	0.2	1.3	-0.4	-0.9	..	Bolivia
-1.0	0.6	-0.8	2.3	3.5	3.6	1.6	1.0	1.7	-0.6	Brazil
..	..	..	..	..	..	..	..	..	..	Chile
1.8	1.5	0.0	1.1	1.0	1.8	2.0	2.3	1.3	1.6	Colombia
-1.9	-2.3	1.0	3.0	1.5	2.8	2.6	2.1	3.2	1.9	Costa Rica
1.7	3.1	1.6	0.2	0.3	1.7	1.5	1.7	2.1	-8.5	Dominican Republic
0.7	0.8	-2.6	1.7	1.6	1.2	0.9	0.7	1.3	-1.0	Ecuador
-4.9	-3.2	0.6	1.6	1.6	0.9	1.7	5.9	0.4	1.7	El Salvador
..	..	..	..	6.9	2.0	-0.9	8.5	2.0	..	Grenada
..	..	..	..	..	..	..	..	..	..	Guatemala
2.0	-5.7	1.9	-1.6	-0.2	1.3	1.4	2.0	..	..	Guyana
..	..	..	..	..	..	..	..	..	..	Haiti
2.8	-3.0	-0.6	1.0	3.2	1.1	4.1	3.0	0.8	-5.2	Honduras
1.9	2.1	0.8	-0.5	-2.1	0.7	2.6	0.5	0.8	1.2	Jamaica
4.9	0.3	-1.0	1.8	0.8	-1.6	0.7	1.0	1.3	2.4	Mexico
1.8	-1.1	1.5	-0.5	-2.1	0.0	0.6	-0.4	-2.6	-1.0	Nicaragua
3.3	3.8	2.6	0.5	3.8	2.9	1.1	-10.2	-1.0	1.1	Panama
4.0	-0.3	-2.5	0.6	2.6	1.1	2.1	2.5	4.8	..	Paraguay
3.3	-0.2	-5.8	1.9	0.9	5.2	4.9	-5.0	-6.8	-2.4	Peru
1.7	7.2	3.2	4.2	4.9	-1.4	-2.2	3.7	25.9	..	St. Vincent and The Grenadines
3.0	0.4	-3.6	-3.9	-4.2	0.8	-3.0	-2.0	-2.6	-1.7	Trinidad and Tobago
2.1	-4.2	-2.5	-0.6	1.1	4.0	2.2	1.0	1.6	1.4	Uruguay
0.6	-0.7	-1.7	-1.5	0.2	3.0	1.8	2.9	-4.4	-1.9	Venezuela
-1.4	*3.4*	*3.1*	*2.2*	*1.5*	*-2.5*	*0.7*	*0.1*	*2.4*	*..*	*MIDDLE EAST AND NORTH AFRICA*
-2.2	4.0	-0.5	-0.5	0.0	1.4	6.1	-3.5	5.6	..	Algeria
2.4	9.0	5.0	3.0	3.6	1.7	1.4	2.3	1.5	0.9	Egypt, Arab Republic of
3.5	7.2	7.6	4.6	3.8	-6.9	-2.6	0.4	2.1	..	Iran, Islamic Rep. of
..	..	..	1.0	4.0	7.5	2.5	-1.7	-4.0	-5.2	Jordan
1.2	4.3	0.6	3.2	1.8	2.0	1.8	2.6	1.9	2.1	Morocco
4.7	3.8	2.0	4.2	2.2	-1.6	1.1	..	..	..	Oman
8.5	2.6	1.0	-0.2	0.1	-4.5	-1.9	3.2	..	..	Syrian Arab Republic
2.0	1.2	2.0	2.5	2.4	1.0	2.8	4.8	1.2	1.5	Tunisia
2.4	2.3	1.8	2.4	2.7	3.7	3.9	1.4	2.3	3.1	Turkey
..	..	..	..	..	..	..	..	..	..	Yemen, Republic of
..	*..*	*..*	*..*	*..*	*..*	*..*	*..*	*..*	*..*	*EUROPE*
1.2	-4.0	2.7	-2.0	2.7	-1.7	4.8	1.3	-1.4	..	Bulgaria
0.8	0.8	1.6	1.3	1.6	1.1	0.5	1.3	1.5	..	Greece
0.4	-0.4	-0.1	1.3	1.6	1.1	3.2	-0.6	1.2	-1.0	Hungary
..	..	..	..	..	..	..	..	..	..	Malta
..	..	..	..	..	..	..	..	..	..	Poland
..	..	..	..	..	..	..	..	..	..	Portugal
..	..	..	..	..	..	..	..	..	..	Romania
-0.2	0.5	-0.3	-0.3	-0.6	0.7	-3.3	-0.8	-0.1	..	Yugoslavia
0.7	1.0	1.2	1.5	1.9	1.2	1.6	1.1	1.2	..	**Low- & middle-income economies**
-0.1	-0.7	-0.1	1.6	1.6	2.1	1.6	1.0	1.0	-1.0	Severely indebted
2.3	1.7	1.8	1.6	3.0	2.4	2.0	1.0	0.5	1.2	Low-income economies
2.6	0.3	1.1	-0.9	0.4	1.3	0.8	1.5	0.4	..	Low-income Africa
1.9	2.0	1.7	1.8	3.8	2.6	2.2	0.5	0.0	1.1	China and India
3.7	2.0	2.6	2.5	2.2	2.0	2.3	2.6	2.2	2.4	Other low-income
0.2	0.8	1.2	1.6	1.5	0.8	1.4	1.3	1.7	..	Middle-income economies
1.4	0.3	1.9	2.2	2.2	2.4	2.3	..	..	..	**High-income OECD members**
0.8	1.2	1.2	1.8	1.9	2.3	2.6	..	..	..	European Community members
2.6	1.2	1.6	1.6	2.4	2.2	1.4	2.1	..	..	Japan
1.5	-0.9	3.0	3.4	2.4	2.7	2.7	..	..	..	United States
3.4	2.5	2.2	2.9	1.4	2.2	5.2	3.9	1.4	..	**Other high-income economies /a**

Table 10. Total consumption: contribution to growth of gross domestic product

Percentage points	1970	1971	1972	1973	1974	1975	1976	1977	1978	1979	1980
SUB-SAHARAN AFRICA	*2.6*	*7.2*	*-0.9*	*0.5*	*7.6*	*4.8*	*3.1*	*6.2*	*8.7*	*-8.1*	*6.2*
Excluding Nigeria	*2.6*	*6.5*	*1.4*	*0.4*	*4.6*	*1.6*	*2.6*	*5.4*	*3.5*	*2.0*	*1.0*
Benin	3.2	0.3	3.3	4.7	-3.1	-3.0	-0.9	8.6	3.1	2.2	3.3
Botswana	2.7	-4.5	9.1	24.6	19.2	2.9	6.4	4.9	10.2	14.2	13.4
Burkina Faso	-4.0	-0.4	-2.6	-2.4	6.3	7.2	6.0	9.7	1.0	6.9	3.6
Burundi	37.2	45.9	-4.3	4.4	-2.1	8.7	4.1	14.8	-3.1	6.4	-1.0
Cameroon	0.4	7.7	-0.2	0.7	9.2	0.7	5.2	9.0	2.9	13.6	10.8
Cape Verde	..	..	..	..	-12.3	8.0	9.8	11.4	16.2	3.4	28.2
Central African Rep.	3.2	-1.5	1.9	-0.5	-0.6	2.4	7.1	12.0	4.4	-3.8	2.1
Chad	..	..	..	..	..	..	..	..	..	..	..
Comoros	..	..	..	..	..	..	..	..	..	..	..
Congo, People's Rep of the	7.8	-0.9	-0.6	-1.6	-0.6	3.7	12.4	-10.4	9.4	-6.2	13.9
Cote D'Ivoire	6.8	9.6	2.6	6.8	2.4	10.5	3.6	2.7	12.8	3.0	-9.1
Ethiopia	..	..	..	..	..	..	..	..	..	..	..
Gabon	3.4	5.2	8.8	5.1	0.3	8.6	6.2	3.9	4.6	-5.6	6.1
Gambia, The	-11.6	30.5	-2.0	4.9	5.5	-13.2	30.0	6.0	25.3	-20.6	-3.4
Ghana	-2.0	0.6	-8.3	8.9	15.0	-15.0	-3.1	6.1	14.7	-5.6	6.5
Guinea-Bissau	..	16.7	21.7	12.1	11.7	-16.9	-1.5	-16.8	1.2	-10.4	-6.6
Kenya	-9.2	33.0	13.9	-5.5	11.6	3.3	-2.8	6.1	10.6	8.3	-1.9
Lesotho	11.0	16.9	33.0	36.2	27.3	21.7	26.1	6.7	21.7	3.5	-6.9
Liberia	..	..	..	..	..	..	..	..	..	..	..
Madagascar	6.1	7.2	-3.5	-3.5	-4.0	0.6	-5.5	4.4	-1.0	13.4	1.4
Malawi	-10.6	24.3	-1.6	0.9	0.5	5.6	3.5	5.3	1.9	6.2	4.8
Mali	4.5	0.5	9.4	-1.3	9.4	7.4	9.2	-0.5	8.2	10.1	-1.3
Mauritania	9.7	0.4	-1.2	-2.1	10.2	-2.3	24.4	-5.0	-5.2	0.7	-5.6
Mauritius	8.7	5.9	1.4	-0.1	23.8	11.8	7.5	7.2	4.8	2.8	-6.9
Mozambique	..	..	..	..	..	..	..	..	..	..	..
Niger	-4.2	4.5	-5.7	-22.9	28.7	-20.0	0.5	7.1	3.0	15.0	7.0
Nigeria	2.8	9.8	-9.0	1.3	17.2	13.6	4.3	8.6	24.3	-41.0	22.0
Rwanda	3.7	1.7	0.8	-1.0	5.7	-0.6	4.2	6.3	10.6	10.0	10.1
Senegal	6.3	1.1	1.2	-2.3	1.5	7.9	6.2	0.3	0.1	8.6	-0.8
Seychelles	..	..	..	..	..	..	..	..	..	..	..
Sierra Leone	5.3	4.2	-1.5	7.9	4.0	-3.4	-2.6	5.1	4.4	13.0	2.6
Somalia	3.5	7.2	-1.2	4.9	-15.4	34.4	-0.9	53.9	-8.3	13.7	-23.3
Sudan	2.4	9.1	0.1	-10.6	4.3	13.8	8.4	18.9	1.7	-8.2	-0.1
Swaziland	..	..	..	..	..	..	..	..	..	..	..
Tanzania	5.3	5.3	11.5	6.1	3.1	1.9	-7.2	-3.4	18.8	-10.1	-0.4
Togo	1.4	-20.3	5.5	3.4	5.2	-7.3	17.3	-0.1	-0.7	2.7	10.7
Uganda	..	..	..	..	..	..	..	..	..	..	..
Zaire	3.6	5.5	1.3	9.6	2.3	-4.7	-6.0	1.5	-9.2	-0.2	0.1
Zambia	-15.4	2.1	2.6	-10.3	-0.7	4.5	7.6	-0.1	-6.1	12.8	-1.9
Zimbabwe	..	..	..	..	..	..	..	-1.8	2.8	5.4	9.3
SOUTH ASIA	*6.1*	*-0.1*	*-0.6*	*-1.2*	*1.9*	*5.1*	*2.0*	*6.6*	*5.4*	*-3.6*	*5.4*
Bangladesh	8.4	-2.9	-5.1	-14.7	22.4	3.0	14.0	-5.3	9.9	3.6	1.1
India	4.7	0.5	0.5	-1.0	-0.4	6.1	0.6	7.5	4.9	-5.9	5.5
Nepal	..	..	..	..	..	..	..	..	..	..	..
Pakistan	22.0	-4.3	-8.6	2.6	10.0	-0.6	5.1	6.2	7.9	9.0	8.2
Sri Lanka	-3.6	0.2	-5.9	11.3	1.6	1.5	2.5	8.4	5.6	2.2	6.5
EAST ASIA AND PACIFIC	*8.5*	*3.7*	*3.8*	*5.7*	*4.3*	*3.8*	*1.5*	*4.9*	*6.5*	*5.5*	*4.9*
China	13.5	2.6	4.4	4.7	2.6	3.4	-2.6	5.3	6.8	3.9	6.9
Fiji	11.7	7.1	6.6	12.5	7.8	1.6	5.9	4.1	0.6	5.7	-3.5
Indonesia	1.0	3.0	-1.0	3.9	7.2	5.7	3.1	3.4	7.1	5.7	7.9
Korea, Republic of	9.0	9.8	3.0	8.6	6.4	5.3	7.0	4.0	7.0	6.6	-0.8
Malaysia	3.7	4.4	5.8	5.8	7.0	0.8	4.8	6.6	6.4	6.3	10.4
Papua New Guinea	2.2	3.3	5.6	2.2	2.1	1.7	-1.1	3.3	5.6	0.7	1.7
Philippines	2.1	3.7	5.2	4.6	4.9	2.0	0.9	4.8	4.9	5.2	2.5
Solomon islands	..	..	..	..	..	..	..	..	..	..	..
Thailand	6.4	-1.5	6.4	8.4	2.2	4.4	7.3	6.2	4.6	10.3	2.5
Vanuatu	..	..	..	..	..	..	..	..	..	..	..

1981	1982	1983	1984	1985	1986	1987	1988	1989	1990	
13.7	*2.2*	*-2.2*	*-3.3*	*0.8*	*1.2*	*1.3*	*2.3*	*1.4*	*1.1*	*SUB-SAHARAN AFRICA*
2.8	*2.4*	*2.0*	*-0.3*	*2.0*	*4.3*	*3.5*	*3.0*	*1.3*	*0.7*	*Excluding Nigeria*
7.2	8.4	-5.7	7.1	5.2	2.7	-4.9	1.7	0.8	-0.1	Benin
2.5	8.4	-3.9	0.5	16.2	-6.8	10.2	13.1	27.6	..	Botswana
5.4	5.5	0.6	-4.7	5.7	10.1	1.4	5.0	7.7	-0.5	Burkina Faso
2.9	6.7	1.8	5.0	8.7	0.2	-5.0	3.3	4.4	6.4	Burundi
4.6	0.1	1.2	-1.0	5.9	5.8	6.6	0.0	-9.0	1.0	Cameroon
0.4	3.9	10.0	8.3	7.9	7.7	-2.9	3.9	0.4	5.3	Cape Verde
-10.8	8.3	-12.5	9.2	3.8	6.6	-3.4	1.9	0.4	3.9	Central African Rep.
..	..	..	-3.0	41.9	-2.2	-8.3	15.6	1.1	2.4	Chad
..	..	..	14.5	5.0	-2.5	9.1	..	..	..	Comoros
6.6	34.0	-7.7	6.3	4.0	-4.8	5.8	-9.9	-3.7	-5.8	Congo, People's Rep of the
7.2	0.0	1.0	3.5	-3.8	8.3	9.5	-4.6	-3.4	-8.7	Cote D'Ivoire
..	..	..	..	..	..	..	..	..	..	Ethiopia
2.7	5.8	6.0	-7.6	2.3	14.4	-15.7	-3.1	..	..	Gabon
22.2	-1.4	-12.7	5.7	-2.1	0.1	3.5	6.5	3.5	2.2	Gambia, The
-3.6	-14.9	3.9	7.0	5.0	4.9	1.1	2.3	..	..	Ghana
31.4	10.5	-3.0	6.6	5.8	-3.2	8.9	4.3	2.0	5.0	Guinea-Bissau
-3.0	3.8	0.4	4.4	-4.9	13.0	5.3	5.1	2.2	3.8	Kenya
14.5	4.2	20.5	2.0	-13.5	-5.9	9.3	7.1	-30.8	-0.1	Lesotho
..	..	..	..	..	..	..	..	..	..	Liberia
-14.1	0.1	-1.2	-1.0	4.8	0.8	-5.4	3.2	1.2	4.0	Madagascar
-2.4	-2.5	0.8	9.5	2.7	1.3	-2.8	4.0	9.8	1.8	Malawi
2.9	5.4	1.0	2.1	7.5	3.2	-1.7	0.8	4.8	7.1	Mali
0.3	3.2	18.2	-14.2	-2.4	2.2	4.1	6.4	5.3	-0.8	Mauritania
-0.1	-2.4	1.3	3.8	3.2	2.7	9.5	5.6	3.9	3.2	Mauritius
3.0	1.0	-1.6	-0.4	-10.3	5.9	2.3	3.0	5.2	-3.3	Mozambique
1.7	7.8	-3.2	-5.4	-2.8	5.8	-3.3	-0.2	-3.6	4.3	Niger
47.8	1.1	-17.5	-16.3	-4.0	-11.6	-8.1	-0.7	2.0	3.2	Nigeria
8.8	0.8	6.7	-6.0	0.6	6.0	-2.1	-0.2	-6.0	-4.4	Rwanda
1.9	5.2	3.3	-3.2	7.0	1.4	3.5	3.7	-2.3	4.9	Senegal
..	..	..	..	..	..	..	..	..	..	Seychelles
0.9	0.2	-8.3	-2.8	-2.8	-5.1	5.3	-2.7	3.6	1.6	Sierra Leone
19.1	7.7	-1.4	-1.6	-0.5	7.8	-1.2	-7.0	11.8	4.3	Somalia
3.7	3.4	8.0	-3.2	2.0	0.9	3.4	-1.7	7.6	-6.0	Sudan
..	..	..	..	..	..	..	..	..	..	Swaziland
-10.2	-3.6	5.2	8.6	1.1	10.8	2.2	0.0	-0.4	1.3	Tanzania
0.3	3.1	-5.6	9.3	-0.5	14.2	-1.1	7.1	2.4	0.9	Togo
..	..	..	..	..	..	..	..	..	..	Uganda
4.3	2.5	1.4	-2.2	3.1	0.6	5.2	6.3	-5.3	1.8	Zaire
6.3	-12.0	1.6	-0.2	7.6	-4.5	11.2	8.8	..	..	Zambia
15.9	7.6	-5.3	-12.3	8.6	-6.6	-7.5	9.9	21.9	2.9	Zimbabwe
2.4	*4.8*	*7.1*	*3.6*	*3.8*	*4.7*	*3.5*	*6.4*	*3.4*	*4.0*	*SOUTH ASIA*
4.5	0.6	6.0	4.6	5.6	2.2	3.2	4.5	1.9	4.9	Bangladesh
2.5	4.9	7.7	3.2	3.1	5.6	3.8	7.2	3.4	3.9	India
..	..	..	..	..	..	..	..	..	..	Nepal
-1.2	4.6	5.2	6.2	7.4	0.7	4.4	7.9	4.8	3.9	Pakistan
3.0	10.9	6.6	-3.1	10.5	2.6	0.0	3.1	-0.5	4.1	Sri Lanka
4.3	*3.5*	*6.2*	*5.0*	*3.6*	*2.2*	*4.1*	*6.8*	*6.2*	*3.2*	*EAST ASIA AND PACIFIC*
5.5	3.1	6.6	7.6	6.1	1.8	4.1	6.3	5.4	0.8	China
7.7	-5.0	-2.6	5.8	-3.6	2.6	-3.6	..	..	..	Fiji
4.9	4.2	6.7	2.7	1.1	1.8	2.3	2.9	3.3	4.2	Indonesia
3.6	4.7	5.9	4.7	4.0	5.3	5.2	6.1	5.9	5.6	Korea, Republic of
5.0	3.6	2.9	2.7	0.2	-4.6	1.6	8.1	8.3	5.2	Malaysia
-0.5	-3.4	0.6	-0.1	6.6	-2.1	2.8	-0.4	0.3	-12.3	Papua New Guinea
2.4	4.8	3.5	0.0	-4.2	0.3	6.1	7.4	8.6	3.4	Philippines
5.2	-21.2	12.7	14.6	0.2	1.5	10.6	28.0	..	..	Solomon islands
0.8	1.2	9.3	2.1	1.7	3.5	5.3	16.7	12.4	8.6	Thailand
..	..	..	10.8	5.5	-3.8	-5.4	..	..	..	Vanuatu

Table 10. Total consumption: contribution to growth of gross domestic product (cont'd.)

Percentage points	1970	1971	1972	1973	1974	1975	1976	1977	1978	1979	1980
LATIN AMERICA AND CARIBBEAN	*6.6*	*5.5*	*4.8*	*5.2*	*4.7*	*2.1*	*5.1*	*3.4*	*3.1*	*5.9*	*5.3*
Argentina	2.6	2.5	1.3	4.0	5.6	-0.2	-5.3	1.3	0.3	9.0	5.1
Bahamas	..	..	..	..	..	..	..	..	10.1	24.3	-0.4
Barbados	..	..	..	..	..	..	..	..	..	..	..
Belize	..	..	..	..	..	..	..	..	..	..	..
Bolivia	2.7	2.2	-2.9	9.3	2.6	-4.3	9.1	3.0	4.5	5.5	3.0
Brazil	10.2	9.4	8.6	8.9	7.0	0.8	9.4	3.9	2.1	6.9	4.7
Chile	0.3	12.3	7.2	-6.0	-14.5	-13.4	-0.3	13.0	7.4	7.3	4.8
Colombia	6.1	6.7	5.5	4.7	2.0	3.1	4.9	2.6	6.5	4.4	3.7
Costa Rica	8.4	1.9	5.8	3.7	4.3	2.3	3.0	9.0	6.5	2.6	-1.4
Dominican Republic	17.1	9.3	11.0	6.4	10.0	-6.2	8.7	3.1	1.5	0.5	16.4
Ecuador	5.4	3.7	5.2	7.1	9.8	8.5	7.9	7.4	3.4	5.2	5.8
El Salvador	5.5	3.0	5.1	7.3	2.1	3.1	9.4	10.7	3.8	-5.5	-7.8
Grenada	..	..	..	..	..	..	..	..	..	..	..
Guatemala	6.1	4.4	4.9	5.1	4.0	2.5	9.1	7.6	4.5	2.5	2.3
Guyana	3.6	-1.2	11.1	9.8	1.3	1.5	22.2	-6.9	-17.5	-9.4	10.9
Haiti	-0.3	8.1	0.9	-1.4	5.8	-3.6	9.5	3.0	2.6	2.7	7.8
Honduras	4.8	0.2	4.9	6.9	-0.8	4.0	12.0	10.2	2.5	3.2	5.1
Jamaica	9.8	4.1	14.7	-11.3	10.5	1.5	2.5	3.9	-5.3	-4.5	-1.9
Mexico	4.3	4.4	5.7	5.3	4.5	5.2	3.5	0.1	6.8	7.7	7.1
Nicaragua	0.3	2.2	1.1	2.6	10.2	2.6	4.0	5.8	-3.0	-20.5	9.9
Panama	4.8	6.3	2.7	2.1	7.4	0.1	0.4	5.4	8.2	4.3	5.2
Paraguay	1.5	6.4	2.5	3.7	8.3	2.6	6.6	12.1	4.0	-5.5	31.5
Peru	13.8	2.5	3.8	0.0	3.7	4.4	3.1	2.8	-3.7	1.9	1.9
St. Vincent and The Grenadines	..	..	..	..	..	..	..	..	-8.2	4.0	3.2
Trinidad and Tobago	0.2	0.2	4.7	1.0	-0.1	1.6	6.9	7.1	7.1	5.0	2.6
Uruguay	8.5	0.6	-0.8	2.4	-0.4	2.7	-0.7	-0.7	3.8	5.2	5.9
Venezuela	..	..	..	..	..	9.6	8.8	6.0	3.0	0.6	4.9
MIDDLE EAST AND NORTH AFRICA	..	..	..	..	..	..	..	..	..	..	..
Algeria	4.2	-2.1	10.4	-0.8	3.0	5.0	5.5	2.8	1.5	7.7	2.7
Egypt, Arab Republic of	9.5	5.7	3.3	4.9	13.7	6.2	5.2	10.3	6.5	13.8	12.0
Iran, Islamic Rep. of	9.2	2.0	8.1	12.8	2.3	-3.1	14.7	9.1	-8.8	-10.5	-21.8
Jordan	..	..	..	..	..	..	..	..	..	..	..
Morocco	4.2	2.9	2.3	3.9	4.6	8.5	12.3	3.2	4.7	5.3	4.5
Oman	..	..	..	..	..	..	..	..	..	..	..
Syrian Arab Republic	-5.0	10.9	7.7	4.2	30.6	23.7	3.9	-0.5	9.3	7.9	7.0
Tunisia	11.1	5.7	11.5	4.5	4.7	8.4	4.9	6.5	4.1	3.9	9.3
Turkey	1.4	11.4	6.6	0.0	6.8	4.9	7.5	3.6	3.7	-1.2	-2.8
Yemen, Republic of	..	..	..	..	..	..	..	..	..	..	..
EUROPE	..	..	..	..	..	..	..	..	..	..	..
Bulgaria	..	..	..	..	..	..	..	..	..	..	..
Greece	4.3	5.3	5.7	1.9	2.1	6.3	4.4	4.1	3.7	1.1	0.4
Hungary	..	3.7	4.6	4.1	3.8	3.3	1.8	3.6	2.4	3.2	0.6
Malta	17.0	-1.0	0.8	0.6	7.2	4.2	11.1	11.4	2.0	3.1	4.8
Poland	..	..	..	..	..	..	..	..	..	..	..
Portugal	1.9	7.8	2.0	8.6	10.5	0.1	4.6	2.2	-0.5	1.0	0.9
Romania	..	..	..	..	..	..	..	..	..	..	..
Yugoslavia	9.0	9.5	-1.0	2.7	19.8	-2.2	-2.1	11.1	9.5	4.4	-1.8
Low- & middle-income economies	6.1	3.9	2.9	4.1	4.8	2.8	4.7	4.7	3.3	1.9	2.6
Severely indebted	6.1	5.1	4.4	5.1	4.5	2.5	4.7	3.2	3.0	6.0	4.6
Low-income economies	6.5	2.3	0.5	1.1	3.9	4.4	0.9	6.1	6.5	-2.2	6.6
Low-income Africa	1.3	7.4	-1.7	-0.2	8.7	4.1	2.1	7.3	9.5	-12.6	7.6
China and India	7.9	1.4	2.1	1.5	0.9	4.9	-0.8	6.6	5.7	-1.5	6.1
Other low-income	7.1	0.3	-3.1	1.1	9.4	3.3	5.6	3.2	7.1	5.6	6.8
Middle-income economies	6.1	4.6	3.8	5.4	5.2	2.2	6.1	4.2	2.0	3.7	1.2
High-income OECD members	2.6	2.5	4.1	3.4	0.7	2.1	3.5	2.7	3.0	2.4	1.1
European Community members	3.7	2.6	3.8	3.3	1.3	1.7	2.6	2.3	2.8	2.9	1.3
Japan	5.2	3.9	5.8	5.4	0.2	3.7	2.9	3.3	3.6	3.8	2.4
United States	0.7	1.8	3.6	2.4	-0.4	1.6	3.4	3.2	3.3	1.3	0.3
Other high-income economies /a	..	..	..	..	..	..	..	..	..	..	..

a. Economies classified by the United Nations or otherwise regarded by their authorities as developing.

1981	1982	1983	1984	1985	1986	1987	1988	1989	1990	
0.6	*-1.2*	*-1.5*	*2.8*	*1.7*	*3.7*	*1.6*	*0.4*	*2.4*	*1.1*	*LATIN AMERICA AND CARIBBEAN*
-2.0	-7.7	3.9	5.1	-3.9	5.5	0.6	-4.7	-0.9	-1.7	Argentina
-2.7	0.2	2.2	17.2	3.4	2.0	2.0	..	..	..	Bahamas
..	..	..	..	..	..	..	..	..	..	Barbados
..	..	..	..	..	..	..	..	..	..	Belize
8.4	-6.7	4.0	2.0	3.2	0.1	-1.1	-2.3	3.7	0.7	Bolivia
-3.1	3.1	-0.4	2.7	3.8	6.1	1.8	0.1	3.2	-1.0	Brazil
9.2	-13.7	-3.8	2.1	-1.9	3.2	3.7	7.4	6.8	0.6	Chile
1.7	1.2	0.7	3.1	2.6	2.8	3.2	1.1	4.4	2.2	Colombia
-2.9	-5.3	1.7	5.3	2.0	2.7	3.7	2.8	4.7	6.5	Costa Rica
-4.2	7.2	2.6	-4.7	1.5	4.5	1.1	-3.7	0.4	-15.5	Dominican Republic
4.2	0.8	-1.0	1.0	1.5	0.0	2.5	0.4	1.1	0.4	Ecuador
-7.5	-5.8	0.2	3.5	4.0	0.4	1.3	2.4	0.6	4.5	El Salvador
..	..	..	..	..	..	..	..	..	..	Grenada
0.6	-4.6	-2.7	1.7	-1.3	0.0	6.2	4.5	2.9	1.4	Guatemala
10.2	-15.5	-0.6	-22.7	10.9	5.7	-0.7	8.0	..	..	Guyana
-0.8	-5.7	1.6	-1.6	2.5	2.7	0.4	-1.5	0.1	-0.4	Haiti
0.2	-0.1	-0.8	1.2	3.2	4.0	4.9	5.3	1.0	-3.2	Honduras
-3.4	5.6	0.5	1.8	-3.3	2.0	2.4	7.5	7.8	-2.5	Jamaica
6.5	-4.1	-4.2	3.3	2.7	-1.2	-0.3	2.9	5.3	4.3	Mexico
-4.4	-0.9	4.2	1.5	-2.3	-1.5	0.1	-8.6	-7.2	-0.8	Nicaragua
2.2	4.0	2.9	6.3	1.8	-0.2	1.1	-14.1	8.2	3.5	Panama
2.5	1.0	-6.9	5.4	3.6	-0.1	5.5	-0.8	8.6	3.2	Paraguay
1.6	2.3	-5.0	2.9	2.6	7.5	5.6	-6.6	-10.0	4.5	Peru
4.8	19.1	2.2	-3.1	3.2	8.1	1.7	..	..	..	St. Vincent and The Grenadines
6.8	0.0	-5.4	-11.4	-10.6	-2.1	-0.5	-2.5	-2.0	-3.6	Trinidad and Tobago
2.7	-7.6	-7.0	-4.3	1.2	8.1	7.7	-1.0	2.0	-2.8	Uruguay
3.8	2.5	-4.2	1.4	-1.8	2.9	1.3	4.4	-3.9	7.9	Venezuela
..	..	..	..	..	..	..	..	..	..	*MIDDLE EAST AND NORTH AFRICA*
4.6	4.5	3.4	3.0	4.9	0.9	1.3	-2.3	4.5	3.1	Algeria
5.1	2.6	5.3	8.3	5.2	0.6	-0.1	2.3	1.3	-0.2	Egypt, Arab Republic of
3.7	30.6	-4.4	13.2	3.9	-12.9	0.6	2.7	-1.5	..	Iran, Islamic Rep. of
..	..	..	1.2	3.6	12.4	-0.7	4.6	-4.0	-10.4	Jordan
-2.3	5.9	-1.4	3.3	2.7	6.0	0.8	3.6	3.4	0.2	Morocco
..	..	..	..	..	..	..	..	..	..	Oman
16.5	-3.5	3.6	-5.0	2.2	-4.1	-7.9	8.7	..	..	Syrian Arab Republic
5.6	2.7	4.0	4.8	2.7	1.4	1.5	2.2	2.4	3.6	Tunisia
-1.1	2.9	4.4	6.8	1.3	7.5	5.2	1.5	2.7	9.6	Turkey
..	..	..	..	..	..	..	..	..	..	Yemen, Republic of
0.4	*-0.8*	*1.5*	*0.8*	*2.2*	*3.0*	*2.2*	*1.2*	*0.8*	*..*	*EUROPE*
3.9	-1.1	4.9	0.9	3.4	1.2	7.0	-1.7	-2.7	..	Bulgaria
5.9	4.8	0.6	0.6	4.6	1.1	3.2	1.8	0.8	..	Greece
2.0	1.7	1.0	1.3	1.6	1.2	2.7	-1.7	-0.4	-4.7	Hungary
1.2	1.6	0.3	2.8	5.5	2.2	3.3	8.2	6.1	..	Malta
-3.1	-7.4	3.1	3.0	5.2	3.0	1.7	1.3	-1.1	-8.8	Poland
1.8	1.2	2.0	-0.1	1.0	3.6	9.7	9.0	4.4	..	Portugal
..	..	..	..	..	..	..	..	..	..	Romania
-2.3	-1.2	-1.6	-0.8	-1.6	6.1	-4.2	-2.5	2.0	0.7	Yugoslavia
2.7	2.8	1.4	3.5	2.4	1.8	2.4	3.1	3.0	2.1	**Low- & middle-income economies**
0.4	-0.9	-0.7	2.7	1.7	3.6	1.8	0.7	2.0	0.0	Severely indebted
5.8	3.6	5.3	3.5	3.7	2.7	3.0	5.4	4.0	2.5	Low-income economies
16.3	1.5	-3.1	-4.8	-0.4	-0.5	-0.3	2.2	2.0	1.7	Low-income Africa
3.9	4.1	7.2	5.3	4.6	3.6	4.0	6.7	4.5	2.2	China and India
3.5	4.0	5.7	3.6	3.6	1.5	2.3	3.1	3.2	4.2	Other low-income
1.5	2.5	-0.1	3.5	1.8	1.5	2.1	2.0	2.5	..	Middle-income economies
1.1	1.1	2.2	2.5	3.0	2.9	2.5	2.5	1.9	..	**High-income OECD members**
0.7	0.8	1.1	1.0	1.9	2.7	2.7	2.6	1.7	..	European Community members
1.8	2.4	2.6	1.9	2.0	2.1	1.9	2.3	1.6	..	Japan
1.2	0.8	3.4	4.3	4.6	3.6	2.7	2.6	2.1	..	United States
..	..	..	..	..	..	..	..	..	..	Other high-income economies /a

Table 11. Gross domestic investment: contribution to growth of gross domestic product

Percentage points	1970	1971	1972	1973	1974	1975	1976	1977	1978	1979	1980
SUB-SAHARAN AFRICA	*5.1*	*2.4*	*-0.1*	*2.7*	*3.5*	*2.8*	*3.8*	*2.6*	*-4.3*	*-2.1*	*3.1*
Excluding Nigeria	*3.7*	*1.5*	*-0.4*	*2.2*	*4.5*	*-0.2*	*1.2*	*1.8*	*-1.6*	*-0.9*	*2.8*
Benin	-0.8	-0.3	4.9	0.2	6.8	0.0	0.4	-1.7	-1.1	7.7	8.8
Botswana	10.1	12.5	13.6	9.8	0.8	-4.2	-1.1	-6.7	6.9	4.8	6.8
Burkina Faso	0.6	5.5	5.2	4.0	2.9	-0.2	0.2	-2.2	0.8	-3.7	0.4
Burundi	-3.8	5.3	-5.7	2.8	3.5	-2.4	3.1	4.1	1.9	0.3	-0.6
Cameroon	3.3	2.9	1.1	1.1	-1.4	2.3	-1.2	5.3	8.6	-1.0	2.2
Cape Verde	..	..	..	..	1.4	-3.3	11.6	14.4	-6.0	11.8	10.5
Central African Rep.	1.7	0.7	0.0	0.8	-7.0	-1.9	0.6	0.1	-0.3	-1.3	-2.3
Chad	..	..	..	..	..	..	..	..	..	..	..
Comoros	..	..	..	..	..	..	..	..	..	..	..
Congo, People's Rep of the	-3.0	7.4	8.0	8.6	9.2	10.4	-14.4	-9.0	-8.6	2.3	14.7
Cote D'Ivoire	4.9	-0.1	-0.9	5.3	-0.5	0.6	5.6	11.1	6.0	-2.6	6.3
Ethiopia	..	..	..	..	..	..	..	..	..	..	..
Gabon	3.1	4.0	5.7	4.8	59.2	15.6	29.4	-15.8	-39.9	7.6	0.9
Gambia, The	-2.2	0.9	1.2	-0.4	0.3	6.0	0.4	3.3	12.7	-6.2	2.0
Ghana	4.4	0.8	-8.1	2.8	5.3	-2.3	-3.3	5.8	-6.0	0.4	-1.0
Guinea-Bissau	..	-14.3	-10.5	-11.4	-10.7	-1.8	3.2	5.3	13.8	11.8	-18.1
Kenya	15.2	0.8	-3.9	7.8	-2.3	-12.3	3.2	10.4	8.6	-10.2	10.1
Lesotho	0.7	4.6	3.3	10.1	-1.1	6.9	15.8	20.7	-6.0	7.4	9.8
Liberia	..	..	..	..	..	..	..	..	..	..	..
Madagascar	-1.1	2.2	-3.1	0.5	0.7	-0.5	-1.8	-0.6	0.1	6.8	-0.7
Malawi	17.2	-6.7	10.5	-4.8	5.8	6.9	-9.7	0.2	23.0	-13.3	-4.9
Mali	-2.7	0.9	0.2	-0.9	-3.8	4.6	-0.4	3.6	-0.4	1.3	-0.6
Mauritania	0.9	0.4	2.9	-2.5	16.7	11.0	9.7	-4.6	-11.5	-3.9	8.3
Mauritius	-5.1	5.7	2.3	11.2	4.9	1.1	-1.0	-0.3	2.0	1.1	-9.6
Mozambique	..	..	..	..	..	..	..	..	..	..	..
Niger	4.8	-2.8	2.9	5.5	-0.9	-3.3	0.4	2.0	4.3	3.5	-2.2
Nigeria	10.9	6.0	1.0	4.5	0.7	12.1	12.6	5.4	-12.7	-6.3	4.4
Rwanda	0.6	1.7	0.3	0.1	0.9	2.8	0.8	1.6	-0.3	-1.9	3.6
Senegal	3.0	0.4	1.6	0.4	1.5	-2.2	2.5	-0.7	-0.8	-2.1	0.1
Seychelles	..	..	..	..	..	..	..	..	..	..	..
Sierra Leone	5.3	-7.0	-4.0	0.7	4.3	0.4	-4.5	0.0	0.7	1.7	3.6
Somalia	-0.1	-0.1	3.5	-0.2	0.3	1.5	4.3	11.0	5.7	-5.5	17.8
Sudan	1.3	-1.0	-2.5	1.5	7.7	1.2	8.9	-3.2	-2.6	-2.3	1.2
Swaziland	..	..	..	..	..	..	..	..	..	..	..
Tanzania	11.2	6.1	-7.1	1.3	3.4	-2.4	3.0	4.8	-0.6	0.8	-2.1
Togo	2.3	2.4	2.5	1.3	0.6	11.7	-6.6	23.3	8.8	-2.9	-18.0
Uganda	..	..	..	..	..	..	..	..	..	..	..
Zaire	0.2	2.0	-0.1	0.6	0.6	-0.6	-1.7	5.7	-6.3	4.1	3.2
Zambia	24.3	8.4	2.6	-4.0	19.0	-11.8	-35.2	-3.8	-1.1	-15.2	13.0
Zimbabwe	4.3	3.7	2.1	2.1	8.9	-3.1	-7.9	-3.8	-6.8	1.2	7.8
SOUTH ASIA	*1.5*	*1.3*	*-1.6*	*2.5*	*0.4*	*1.2*	*1.2*	*1.1*	*3.1*	*-0.3*	*1.7*
Bangladesh	-1.3	-3.7	-6.9	6.1	-0.6	-1.2	0.5	1.6	2.7	0.5	4.7
India	1.5	2.0	-1.4	2.9	0.4	1.3	1.2	0.9	3.2	-0.8	1.4
Nepal	..	..	..	..	..	..	..	..	..	..	..
Pakistan	3.5	0.0	-1.1	0.7	-0.9	2.0	0.3	2.2	0.8	0.9	1.5
Sri Lanka	1.9	-1.2	1.2	-3.2	6.3	-1.4	4.3	-0.6	8.1	7.5	6.5
EAST ASIA AND PACIFIC	*7.3*	*1.9*	*-0.6*	*4.3*	*2.6*	*1.9*	*0.2*	*3.9*	*6.5*	*3.4*	*-1.2*
China	14.5	2.7	-0.9	4.2	0.5	3.4	-2.5	3.3	8.8	3.9	-0.6
Fiji	0.1	2.7	2.8	1.8	-2.3	1.7	0.2	0.3	1.6	7.1	2.2
Indonesia	2.9	2.4	2.4	2.4	2.9	2.4	1.1	2.9	2.9	2.1	0.3
Korea, Republic of	-0.5	1.8	-1.4	5.4	6.9	-0.8	3.6	6.4	8.3	5.2	-7.2
Malaysia	6.5	0.3	1.8	5.9	7.9	-6.6	2.7	5.2	2.1	3.6	5.2
Papua New Guinea	24.7	4.5	-19.3	-14.1	1.3	-0.2	-2.3	1.7	0.7	5.1	1.1
Philippines	-0.9	0.8	-0.7	2.3	5.0	5.8	4.5	0.1	2.4	3.4	1.4
Solomon islands	..	..	..	..	..	..	..	..	..	..	..
Thailand	2.0	-0.9	-1.9	9.2	-1.2	0.7	-0.1	6.6	5.5	-1.5	0.5
Vanuatu	..	..	..	..	..	..	..	..	..	..	..

1981	1982	1983	1984	1985	1986	1987	1988	1989	1990	
1.4	*-2.0*	*-3.5*	*-3.2*	*1.7*	*1.0*	*-1.8*	*0.5*	*0.3*	*0.3*	*SUB-SAHARAN AFRICA*
1.0	*0.2*	*-2.7*	*-1.4*	*1.3*	*1.4*	*-1.4*	*0.3*	*0.1*	*-0.6*	*Excluding Nigeria*
4.3	2.3	-17.3	-3.2	1.7	-0.4	-0.8	1.0	1.3	4.3	Benin
0.5	-0.8	-7.5	-0.3	6.6	-3.8	-4.7	4.0	10.7	..	Botswana
0.0	5.3	-1.6	0.3	7.3	0.4	-0.6	3.5	-5.0	1.7	Burkina Faso
4.8	-4.2	10.3	-3.9	-2.5	3.8	6.2	-3.2	4.5	0.5	Burundi
7.8	0.5	1.6	-1.4	1.8	12.5	-8.3	-9.6	1.7	-2.3	Cameroon
3.5	8.3	-0.5	-0.8	0.9	7.9	3.1	1.4	1.0	1.7	Cape Verde
1.2	2.9	4.3	1.5	0.6	-1.6	-1.4	-3.1	0.3	4.8	Central African Rep.
..	..	..	2.5	4.5	0.6	2.7	-3.1	1.2	0.3	Chad
..	..	..	12.0	-12.9	-1.2	-3.9	-7.2	-2.0	0.8	Comoros
30.5	22.0	-10.0	-5.6	-2.1	-13.6	-9.2	-2.8	-2.2	10.2	Congo, People's Rep of the
-8.6	-4.2	-2.3	-12.4	5.5	-3.3	-1.0	3.2	-5.0	-4.3	Cote D'Ivoire
..	..	..	..	..	..	..	..	..	..	Ethiopia
16.7	-5.1	-3.4	3.4	5.7	-7.6	-15.8	1.3	..	..	Gabon
-0.5	-3.3	1.0	4.2	-0.2	0.6	0.6	0.6	0.6	3.0	Gambia, The
-0.9	-2.3	0.0	1.3	2.2	-0.3	4.0	2.0	..	..	Ghana
-8.7	10.5	-1.4	2.5	4.6	0.0	-13.5	6.8	14.3	-15.2	Guinea-Bissau
-1.2	-8.1	-3.5	1.0	6.0	-4.2	3.7	2.3	1.6	-2.6	Kenya
0.5	8.3	-25.0	9.0	12.5	-9.6	1.1	10.4	38.9	8.1	Lesotho
..	..	..	..	..	..	..	..	..	..	Liberia
-4.2	-1.9	-0.1	0.4	0.1	0.4	0.9	1.2	0.7	1.5	Madagascar
-9.1	5.5	2.9	-12.8	7.5	-10.6	3.2	4.0	1.2	-1.1	Malawi
1.5	0.7	-3.6	1.4	3.8	7.3	1.9	2.8	2.2	-2.9	Mali
6.7	8.9	-26.5	6.5	1.0	-0.6	-1.9	-1.2	-1.7	2.6	Mauritania
3.3	-2.9	-0.2	2.7	1.0	4.9	9.7	5.7	-1.8	4.5	Mauritius
1.0	-1.1	-12.2	2.5	-2.6	7.5	3.4	4.9	0.7	5.2	Mozambique
0.6	-2.7	-0.9	-13.6	12.2	-4.5	1.0	2.5	-1.9	0.2	Niger
2.7	-9.5	-6.7	-10.3	3.4	-0.4	-3.5	1.3	1.1	3.7	Nigeria
-0.4	4.0	-2.0	3.4	3.9	-0.9	-0.2	1.7	-1.8	-0.2	Rwanda
0.2	1.0	0.6	-0.4	-1.1	1.9	2.6	-0.6	0.2	-0.4	Senegal
..	..	..	..	..	..	..	..	..	..	Seychelles
3.3	-4.3	-0.6	0.3	-1.5	3.1	-4.4	1.7	-0.1	0.4	Sierra Leone
-11.5	4.2	-5.5	3.6	3.4	-4.3	3.4	-9.1	4.3	-4.0	Somalia
0.2	10.3	-5.8	-1.7	-9.5	9.0	-1.7	-1.3	-0.1	-0.6	Sudan
..	..	..	..	..	..	..	..	..	..	Swaziland
-0.8	2.4	-9.6	3.6	2.0	0.5	-0.7	4.7	5.3	2.8	Tanzania
-0.9	-5.2	-5.3	0.4	8.5	-3.9	-3.5	0.9	0.9	2.1	Togo
..	..	..	..	..	..	..	..	..	..	Uganda
-0.6	2.5	-1.5	0.1	0.5	1.8	-0.8	1.9	-0.5	-3.2	Zaire
-3.6	-6.3	-5.1	1.1	1.4	8.9	-12.2	5.4	..	..	Zambia
5.8	-5.2	2.5	3.0	-2.8	-1.1	3.1	3.4	-4.2	0.0	Zimbabwe
3.7	*-1.1*	*-0.1*	*0.4*	*3.6*	*-0.4*	*0.2*	*2.7*	*0.4*	*0.3*	*SOUTH ASIA*
0.5	-0.3	-3.0	0.6	1.5	-0.2	0.9	-0.8	0.3	0.5	Bangladesh
4.5	-1.7	0.0	0.5	4.3	-0.5	0.1	3.5	0.3	0.2	India
..	..	..	..	..	..	..	..	..	..	Nepal
1.1	2.6	1.2	0.9	1.9	0.9	0.7	0.0	0.0	0.5	Pakistan
-3.9	1.5	0.6	-0.6	-2.8	1.8	0.5	-0.5	-0.3	0.8	Sri Lanka
2.4	*1.3*	*2.9*	*3.0*	*5.1*	*2.3*	*3.3*	*3.3*	*2.2*	*2.6*	*EAST ASIA AND PACIFIC*
-1.5	2.9	3.7	6.2	11.3	3.7	4.0	4.1	-1.1	0.5	China
1.7	-7.8	-2.8	-2.0	-0.6	2.3	-3.9	..	..	..	Fiji
16.6	-1.8	1.0	0.7	4.5	1.9	-0.1	-1.6	3.8	3.3	Indonesia
0.5	2.1	3.7	4.2	1.1	3.4	4.3	3.8	8.2	6.7	Korea, Republic of
5.3	4.8	2.8	2.0	-7.1	-3.8	-0.4	5.1	5.7	6.7	Malaysia
-1.2	3.6	1.4	-2.7	-8.1	0.8	1.4	8.3	-7.2	3.8	Papua New Guinea
0.7	-1.0	-1.4	-11.8	-3.6	-1.2	4.2	2.7	2.5	0.7	Philippines
-0.6	-3.8	4.3	-0.5	3.3	0.3	-0.4	6.6	..	..	Solomon islands
2.8	-3.1	5.6	1.9	-1.3	-1.6	4.6	4.3	2.0	2.1	Thailand
..	..	..	2.2	4.6	-1.5	2.5	..	..	..	Vanuatu

Table 11. Gross domestic investment: contribution to growth of gross domestic product (cont'd.)

Percentage points	1970	1971	1972	1973	1974	1975	1976	1977	1978	1979	1980
LATIN AMERICA AND CARIBBEAN	*1.1*	*2.0*	*1.6*	*3.8*	*4.2*	*1.6*	*0.7*	*1.9*	*0.5*	*0.8*	*3.2*
Argentina	0.6	2.9	0.3	-1.3	0.3	0.4	1.7	5.6	-4.9	2.7	2.5
Bahamas	..	..	..	..	..	..	..	..	-0.3	4.0	5.6
Barbados	..	..	..	..	..	..	..	..	..	..	..
Belize	..	..	..	..	..	..	..	..	..	..	..
Bolivia	-1.1	4.4	9.5	-5.6	-0.3	16.9	-5.0	1.3	0.4	-5.9	-9.0
Brazil	-0.1	3.7	4.4	6.8	4.9	3.2	0.2	0.0	0.9	0.1	3.4
Chile	1.7	-0.7	-5.4	-1.6	11.0	-12.8	0.0	2.2	3.2	4.5	5.8
Colombia	3.6	1.0	-0.6	1.9	4.2	-4.4	1.8	3.3	1.6	-0.1	2.3
Costa Rica	2.8	5.2	-1.8	4.0	2.0	-2.2	5.8	5.9	-0.1	2.6	2.0
Dominican Republic	3.9	3.3	2.5	5.5	4.4	2.1	-1.7	1.9	0.7	2.0	2.2
Ecuador	1.8	8.2	-4.8	3.0	9.2	5.4	-1.8	6.4	4.1	-1.0	2.9
El Salvador	1.3	2.7	-0.9	3.8	4.2	-1.9	1.7	7.5	0.7	-5.2	-5.7
Grenada	..	..	..	..	..	..	..	..	..	..	..
Guatemala	2.9	2.5	-2.8	2.6	5.4	-3.1	6.3	2.4	2.2	-3.0	-2.8
Guyana	5.1	-8.1	-7.5	19.4	-5.8	34.6	-10.9	-19.2	-14.4	12.2	-0.6
Haiti	2.5	0.2	1.3	1.4	1.0	2.2	2.8	0.5	1.6	2.5	0.1
Honduras	1.0	-3.7	-0.3	3.9	5.7	-4.9	1.2	5.8	5.1	0.9	-1.1
Jamaica	0.7	0.2	-5.5	12.8	-12.5	4.1	-12.7	-11.4	2.5	-0.8	-3.9
Mexico	5.3	-1.3	2.6	3.9	4.7	1.5	-0.7	-0.1	3.2	4.9	6.7
Nicaragua	-0.1	0.4	-3.9	8.2	6.1	-7.6	0.3	7.1	-9.4	-10.8	16.8
Panama	4.7	6.5	4.7	1.3	-1.8	-1.1	-0.3	-9.1	5.1	1.8	4.1
Paraguay	-0.1	1.5	2.0	6.1	2.4	1.5	4.7	3.0	6.9	4.6	6.2
Peru	-11.1	2.9	-2.3	9.5	9.5	-1.7	-3.7	-3.6	-1.3	3.5	7.9
St. Vincent and The Grenadines	..	..	..	..	..	..	..	..	4.2	5.0	2.5
Trinidad and Tobago	3.4	5.5	-1.8	-1.2	4.9	3.3	2.7	0.6	5.4	0.7	5.0
Uruguay	1.3	0.7	-1.8	-0.5	0.4	2.5	2.3	2.2	2.1	3.9	1.0
Venezuela	..	..	..	..	..	6.6	6.7	9.9	-0.6	-8.7	-5.4
MIDDLE EAST AND NORTH AFRICA	*2.0*	*0.5*	*2.7*	*2.2*	*5.5*	*8.4*	*2.3*	*1.6*	*-4.8*	*0.0*	*4.2*
Algeria	5.3	-0.4	4.3	6.0	11.3	3.3	1.2	6.6	8.5	-3.3	0.9
Egypt, Arab Republic of	0.7	-1.7	0.4	3.7	7.0	11.9	-0.1	3.3	2.9	3.1	-0.4
Iran, Islamic Rep. of	0.9	0.8	3.3	1.7	3.5	10.1	2.6	-0.5	-8.1	0.3	7.7
Jordan	..	..	..	..	..	..	..	..	..	..	..
Morocco	3.3	2.1	-3.8	0.6	3.1	11.9	4.9	4.6	-8.5	0.3	1.1
Oman	..	..	..	..	..	..	..	..	..	5.5	1.4
Syrian Arab Republic	-3.2	2.5	5.0	-6.4	15.0	1.9	5.8	3.7	-3.4	0.3	4.1
Tunisia	-1.2	0.6	7.5	-2.5	5.6	2.1	2.3	0.7	3.6	2.2	0.3
Turkey	4.8	0.2	1.9	3.0	6.2	6.2	1.4	3.2	-7.9	0.1	2.1
Yemen, Republic of	..	..	..	..	..	..	..	..	..	..	..
EUROPE	*..*	*..*	*..*	*..*	*..*	*..*	*..*	*..*	*..*	*..*	*..*
Bulgaria	..	..	..	..	..	..	..	..	..	..	..
Greece	3.7	2.1	3.8	9.3	-9.4	-0.4	0.6	0.3	2.3	2.8	-1.4
Hungary	5.2	7.7	-5.0	0.1	7.1	3.7	0.7	3.1	6.7	-7.1	-1.2
Malta	0.6	-6.0	-4.2	-4.3	3.6	0.2	6.3	2.0	0.9	2.4	2.7
Poland	..	..	..	..	..	..	..	..	..	..	..
Portugal	8.0	1.3	5.5	6.1	-3.3	-10.8	3.4	6.5	2.3	3.1	4.1
Romania	..	..	..	..	..	..	..	..	..	..	..
Yugoslavia	3.0	2.0	-1.6	2.1	1.7	1.9	0.8	3.6	-0.7	4.5	-1.0
Low- & middle-income economies	3.1	1.8	0.5	3.5	3.1	2.6	1.0	2.1	0.7	1.0	2.3
Severely indebted	1.1	2.1	1.4	3.6	4.4	2.4	1.0	2.1	0.5	0.6	3.1
Low-income economies	5.3	1.9	-0.9	3.0	1.0	2.2	0.5	2.3	3.2	0.6	1.1
Low-income Africa	5.6	2.5	-0.6	2.4	2.1	3.0	3.9	3.5	-4.5	-2.9	2.8
China and India	6.3	2.3	-1.2	3.4	0.4	2.2	-0.4	1.9	5.6	1.3	0.4
Other low-income	2.1	0.2	-0.2	1.8	1.6	1.7	0.9	2.2	2.7	2.0	1.5
Middle-income economies	2.1	1.7	1.1	3.6	4.0	2.7	1.2	2.0	-0.3	1.2	2.7
High-income OECD members	1.3	0.5	1.3	2.6	-0.8	-3.0	2.1	0.9	0.9	1.1	-0.6
European Community members	1.5	-0.1	0.7	2.5	-0.6	-3.4	2.5	-0.1	0.2	1.4	0.0
Japan	6.3	-0.1	3.1	4.4	-2.4	-2.2	1.1	1.3	2.1	2.1	-0.2
United States	-1.0	1.4	1.6	1.9	-1.3	-3.2	2.3	2.1	1.7	0.0	-1.8
Other high-income economies /a	..	..	..	..	..	..	..	..	..	..	..

a. Economies classified by the United Nations or otherwise regarded by their authorities as developing.

1981	1982	1983	1984	1985	1986	1987	1988	1989	1990	
-1.0	*-3.9*	*-5.9*	*0.6*	*1.4*	*1.4*	*1.0*	*0.0*	*-0.8*	*0.4*	*LATIN AMERICA AND CARIBBEAN*
-6.9	-4.8	-2.2	-2.0	-3.1	2.3	2.3	-1.4	-3.7	-0.3	Argentina
0.1	3.6	0.1	-1.6	4.3	-0.2	1.4	..	..	..	Bahamas
..	..	..	..	..	..	..	..	..	..	Barbados
..	..	..	..	..	..	..	..	..	..	Belize
-0.4	-6.9	-9.3	-3.1	0.7	-3.8	3.7	1.0	0.9	1.2	Bolivia
-3.7	-2.2	-5.3	0.5	3.7	4.5	-0.3	-1.4	1.3	-0.7	Brazil
5.0	-17.0	-1.9	6.6	-1.0	1.9	3.7	1.4	5.5	-0.8	Chile
3.0	1.3	-0.6	-1.5	-2.2	0.9	1.3	1.5	-1.4	-0.4	Colombia
-11.5	-4.9	5.2	2.2	1.6	6.8	0.9	-1.7	1.2	-0.5	Costa Rica
-2.7	-4.2	1.5	0.9	-0.9	0.8	7.9	2.1	6.0	3.3	Dominican Republic
-4.6	3.6	-9.9	-0.3	1.7	0.7	-0.7	0.1	0.5	-0.3	Ecuador
-0.5	-1.3	-1.2	0.4	-0.7	2.4	-0.6	2.3	4.9	-4.9	El Salvador
..	..	..	..	..	..	..	..	..	..	Grenada
2.4	-3.4	-2.5	0.8	-2.6	0.0	3.4	0.0	0.3	1.4	Guatemala
-3.6	-12.8	-4.5	5.2	2.2	3.8	-7.5	-2.3	..	..	Guyana
1.8	-2.8	0.8	0.7	-2.3	-2.1	0.6	-0.1	-0.1	-1.3	Haiti
-3.5	-7.2	2.3	5.5	-0.1	-2.7	1.1	-0.7	0.1	-2.3	Honduras
6.6	-1.1	0.9	-2.7	0.0	-4.7	4.2	2.1	-4.4	-3.4	Jamaica
5.0	-8.7	-7.4	1.3	2.2	-4.8	0.8	2.7	0.7	1.9	Mexico
6.2	-3.0	1.2	0.1	-0.1	-0.2	-0.2	0.0	-1.5	-2.0	Nicaragua
3.1	-1.0	-5.6	-2.0	1.1	1.4	0.4	-11.1	-4.4	11.8	Panama
5.4	-5.8	-5.2	0.4	0.3	0.9	1.6	1.0	-2.4	0.7	Paraguay
5.8	-2.4	-11.8	-2.1	-2.0	5.2	5.4	-2.6	-5.2	-5.4	Peru
-1.7	-0.7	-1.6	4.0	2.8	3.0	2.8	..	..	..	St. Vincent and The Grenadines
-4.2	1.1	-2.4	-0.2	0.8	-3.1	-4.5	-3.4	-0.3	2.2	Trinidad and Tobago
-1.7	-3.1	-5.6	0.2	-2.0	0.4	2.0	0.2	-1.0	3.3	Uruguay
0.0	2.0	-16.3	5.7	0.9	1.0	3.1	3.7	-14.2	7.0	Venezuela
3.2	*-7.5*	*7.9*	*-2.7*	*0.8*	*1.4*	*-2.5*	*-1.6*	*2.8*	*..*	*MIDDLE EAST AND NORTH AFRICA*
1.5	0.1	2.4	0.8	-0.2	-2.2	-2.4	-1.6	0.3	-0.7	Algeria
2.0	3.2	1.0	2.6	2.0	-3.3	-4.0	1.1	-0.2	-0.2	Egypt, Arab Republic of
5.7	-19.5	17.3	-8.2	0.3	4.0	-2.6	-2.8	6.5	..	Iran, Islamic Rep. of
..	..	..	-3.2	-3.3	2.9	0.1	-4.7	-2.5	-1.4	Jordan
0.1	3.7	-4.1	1.5	2.6	3.3	-3.0	4.0	1.9	1.5	Morocco
8.5	12.8	4.0	20.6	3.9	-11.5	-17.4	..	..	..	Oman
0.5	0.7	0.8	0.4	1.5	-1.3	-5.6	0.6	..	..	Syrian Arab Republic
4.9	-0.2	-0.8	2.9	-4.3	-5.2	-1.8	-3.5	6.0	4.1	Tunisia
2.0	-1.3	-0.1	0.4	3.1	3.2	1.4	-1.6	-1.1	3.2	Turkey
..	..	..	..	..	..	..	..	..	..	Yemen, Republic of
-2.1	*-0.6*	*-1.2*	*-0.3*	*0.3*	*1.1*	*-0.3*	*0.8*	*1.3*	*..*	*EUROPE*
3.5	-0.5	0.0	2.3	0.2	5.3	-0.9	3.3	-1.6	..	Bulgaria
-4.0	-1.6	-0.2	-0.6	1.3	-2.0	-2.2	2.3	4.0	..	Greece
0.7	-2.5	-2.2	-0.7	-0.9	2.2	0.9	-0.9	0.2	-1.7	Hungary
5.1	9.8	-5.6	-1.5	-0.6	-2.1	2.2	6.4	0.8	..	Malta
-7.5	-1.0	1.6	1.9	1.1	1.3	0.0	2.5	1.0	-12.8	Poland
1.1	2.4	-8.7	-5.9	0.2	3.8	0.0	0.0	2.5	..	Portugal
..	..	..	..	..	..	..	..	..	..	Romania
0.3	-0.7	-0.1	0.6	-0.4	-0.4	0.7	-0.9	0.2	-1.5	Yugoslavia
0.9	-2.6	-0.4	0.3	2.0	1.2	0.6	1.1	0.9	0.7	**Low- & middle-income economies**
-1.6	-3.6	-5.3	0.0	1.4	1.3	0.8	0.4	-0.5	-0.7	Severely indebted
2.9	-0.2	0.5	1.8	6.1	1.5	1.4	2.6	0.2	0.7	Low-income economies
0.5	-2.3	-4.6	-3.2	1.5	0.8	-0.8	1.3	0.9	0.9	Low-income Africa
1.6	0.5	1.8	3.3	7.8	1.7	2.1	3.8	-0.5	0.4	China and India
8.8	-0.4	0.2	0.5	2.8	1.0	0.2	-1.0	2.3	2.1	Other low-income
0.2	-3.6	-0.8	-0.4	0.4	1.1	0.3	0.5	1.3	0.7	Middle-income economies
-0.3	-1.1	0.5	2.3	0.4	0.7	1.3	2.0	1.4	..	**High-income OECD members**
-2.3	0.0	0.0	0.8	0.2	0.9	1.1	1.9	1.3	..	European Community members
0.8	0.2	-0.4	1.7	1.9	1.4	2.4	4.0	3.4	..	Japan
1.0	-2.7	1.6	4.2	-0.5	0.1	0.8	1.0	0.3	..	United States
..	..	..	..	..	..	..	..	..	..	Other high-income economies /a

Table 12. Resource balance: contribution to growth of gross domestic product

Percentage points	1970	1971	1972	1973	1974	1975	1976	1977	1978	1979	1980
SUB-SAHARAN AFRICA	*0.6*	*-2.1*	*3.9*	*-0.3*	*-3.7*	*-7.0*	*-0.7*	*-5.4*	*-4.3*	*13.3*	*-6.1*
Excluding Nigeria	*-0.7*	*-1.5*	*2.4*	*-0.9*	*-2.8*	*0.5*	*1.6*	*-4.6*	*-0.1*	*0.8*	*-0.7*
Benin	-0.3	-1.3	-1.9	-1.0	-0.6	-2.0	1.9	-2.1	-0.3	-3.5	-5.7
Botswana	-8.6	10.8	9.6	-12.6	-0.1	0.0	9.8	4.0	1.4	-7.0	-4.9
Burkina Faso	3.6	-4.0	0.6	-1.7	-0.1	-4.7	2.0	-6.0	3.0	2.0	-3.9
Burundi	-6.8	-6.6	3.0	0.7	-2.2	-5.6	0.7	-7.4	0.2	-5.0	2.6
Cameroon	-0.8	-6.8	1.4	3.7	2.9	-3.8	0.2	-5.9	3.2	0.6	2.6
Cape Verde	..	..	..	..	8.1	-1.6	-21.5	-25.1	0.4	-4.2	-0.9
Central African Rep.	-1.9	1.8	0.5	2.0	13.5	-0.2	-3.0	-8.5	-1.7	2.4	-4.4
Chad	-2.7	0.8	-2.4	-5.9	-1.2	2.7	2.4	-1.8	2.3	3.2	0.7
Comoros	..	..	..	..	..	..	..	..	..	..	..
Congo, People's Rep of the	1.5	1.4	1.4	1.3	1.3	-3.8	4.4	8.6	5.4	15.9	-9.8
Cote D'Ivoire	-2.1	2.1	4.8	-7.9	4.3	-1.0	-3.4	-14.0	-4.9	2.5	2.1
Ethiopia	..	..	..	..	..	..	..	..	..	..	..
Gabon	2.2	1.0	-3.2	0.3	-20.0	-5.0	0.0	-0.7	11.2	-1.5	-4.5
Gambia, The	3.9	-19.9	8.0	0.1	14.0	5.1	-20.5	-6.3	-43.6	44.1	-8.3
Ghana	7.3	4.0	13.5	-8.8	-12.9	4.0	2.9	-10.1	1.1	3.6	-4.9
Guinea-Bissau	..	-1.3	-6.9	3.3	3.3	25.6	3.1	3.8	-1.4	-0.9	5.8
Kenya	-10.7	-11.3	8.3	3.5	-5.6	10.3	1.8	-7.1	-12.4	9.4	-2.9
Lesotho	-9.5	-15.3	-26.7	-16.4	-15.2	-42.1	-30.9	-5.5	2.6	-8.1	-5.9
Liberia	..	..	..	..	..	..	..	..	..	..	..
Madagascar	0.3	-4.8	5.1	0.1	5.3	1.2	4.2	-1.4	-1.7	-10.4	0.1
Malawi	-6.2	-1.2	-2.9	6.3	0.8	-6.3	11.0	-0.5	-15.0	11.7	0.6
Mali	4.4	2.1	-4.4	-0.3	-8.0	1.9	4.9	3.6	-10.4	-0.5	0.7
Mauritania	-0.4	0.1	-0.3	-1.6	-16.6	-15.2	-26.1	8.3	16.3	7.9	1.2
Mauritius	-4.0	-7.9	4.3	2.2	-19.9	-12.4	5.8	0.9	-1.1	1.7	6.2
Mozambique	..	..	..	..	..	..	..	..	..	..	..
Niger	2.4	3.9	-2.4	0.4	-19.1	20.5	-0.2	-1.4	6.2	-11.3	0.0
Nigeria	6.1	-4.2	9.2	1.8	-6.5	-29.0	-7.4	-7.9	-17.0	54.4	-22.9
Rwanda	1.7	-2.2	-0.8	4.3	-5.8	0.6	2.0	-2.9	-1.2	1.9	-3.5
Senegal	-0.8	-1.3	3.2	-3.5	0.8	2.0	0.1	-2.2	-5.1	2.9	-2.0
Seychelles	..	..	..	..	..	..	..	..	..	..	..
Sierra Leone	-0.1	5.8	4.5	-5.8	-3.0	5.5	2.9	-4.5	-8.2	-6.6	-3.1
Somalia	1.2	-4.5	7.9	-6.6	-5.3	-1.3	-3.8	-39.7	7.7	-11.8	1.4
Sudan	1.2	-1.2	0.3	1.0	-2.0	-2.3	1.1	-0.5	-0.6	0.1	-0.2
Swaziland	..	..	..	..	..	..	..	..	..	..	..
Tanzania	-9.4	-7.5	2.8	-1.1	-4.4	4.5	7.6	-1.3	-16.1	11.8	5.3
Togo	-3.0	18.0	0.0	-0.4	-1.1	-2.0	-12.7	-16.6	3.0	-4.8	22.0
Uganda	..	..	..	..	..	..	..	..	..	..	..
Zaire	-0.5	-1.1	-1.2	-1.7	0.6	0.4	2.1	-6.9	10.0	-4.1	-0.8
Zambia	-6.2	-10.0	5.1	13.9	-11.7	5.0	33.6	-0.7	7.9	-0.7	-8.1
Zimbabwe	..	..	..	..	..	..	..	-1.5	1.1	-3.0	-6.5
SOUTH ASIA	*-1.9*	*-0.1*	*1.1*	*2.2*	*-0.1*	*1.9*	*-0.3*	*-1.2*	*-2.5*	*0.6*	*-0.7*
Bangladesh	-1.2	1.8	-0.9	10.5	-9.7	1.6	-2.4	5.0	-6.0	0.4	-4.5
India	-1.0	-0.9	0.3	1.5	1.2	1.8	-0.1	-1.2	-2.3	1.4	-0.4
Nepal	..	..	..	..	..	..	..	..	..	..	..
Pakistan	-14.3	4.7	10.5	3.8	-5.6	2.7	-0.2	-4.4	-0.6	-6.2	0.7
Sri Lanka	4.8	3.3	2.4	1.5	-4.1	6.4	-3.4	-2.7	-8.4	-3.3	-7.2
EAST ASIA AND PACIFIC	*-0.3*	*1.7*	*1.7*	*-0.1*	*-2.6*	*1.0*	*1.3*	*-0.3*	*-2.7*	*-2.0*	*0.7*
China	-2.0	2.4	0.2	-0.6	-2.0	1.6	-0.3	-0.8	-3.1	-0.8	0.1
Fiji	1.1	-2.6	-1.9	-3.0	-2.9	-2.9	-3.3	1.5	-0.3	-0.5	-0.3
Indonesia	3.4	1.6	5.0	2.4	-2.4	-3.1	2.7	2.7	-2.3	-1.6	-0.3
Korea, Republic of	0.4	-1.6	4.2	1.2	-4.4	3.2	2.9	0.6	-4.3	-4.3	4.7
Malaysia	-4.2	0.9	2.2	0.2	-6.7	6.7	4.2	-4.0	-1.7	-0.4	-8.2
Papua New Guinea	-16.0	-1.5	19.3	18.5	-0.8	-2.4	-0.1	-4.2	2.3	-3.9	-5.2
Philippines	3.4	0.4	1.0	1.6	-5.0	-1.2	2.5	1.3	-1.7	-2.3	1.4
Solomon islands	..	..	..	..	..	..	..	..	..	..	..
Thailand	1.1	7.3	-0.3	-7.8	3.3	-0.4	2.1	-3.1	0.5	-3.8	1.7
Vanuatu	..	..	..	..	..	..	..	..	..	..	..

1981	1982	1983	1984	1985	1986	1987	1988	1989	1990	
-13.4	*2.5*	*5.8*	*6.0*	*1.1*	*2.6*	*0.7*	*0.1*	*1.3*	*0.1*	*SUB-SAHARAN AFRICA*
0.0	*0.8*	*2.5*	*2.6*	*-0.7*	*-0.2*	*-0.9*	*-0.8*	*1.1*	*0.7*	*Excluding Nigeria*
-2.4	-3.8	20.9	-1.9	-0.5	-4.0	1.7	-1.5	0.3	-3.2	Benin
4.4	-8.7	35.3	18.9	-14.6	18.7	4.8	-7.9	-24.9	..	Botswana
-0.9	-0.8	1.8	2.6	-3.2	-0.6	0.9	-1.1	-2.9	0.5	Burkina Faso
5.8	-5.6	-5.0	-1.1	5.4	-0.2	2.9	3.5	-2.3	-4.4	Burundi
0.5	2.0	5.0	8.2	-0.1	-10.3	-4.9	1.9	4.0	0.1	Cameroon
4.5	-9.4	0.0	-3.7	-0.1	-12.6	6.8	-2.2	4.1	-3.0	Cape Verde
7.4	-3.7	1.5	-1.3	-0.5	-4.1	1.4	2.8	1.5	-5.1	Central African Rep.
6.6	-6.4	2.3	2.6	-24.6	-2.5	2.2	5.1	-1.4	0.3	Chad
..	..	..	-22.1	10.7	5.8	-3.3	..	..	..	Comoros
-23.1	-29.9	25.5	6.3	-3.1	11.5	4.1	13.2	6.2	-4.6	Congo, People's Rep of the
5.7	5.8	0.1	8.0	2.0	-1.3	-8.7	-0.4	7.1	6.9	Cote D'Ivoire
..	..	..	..	..	..	..	..	..	..	Ethiopia
-23.4	2.1	-1.8	10.7	-1.6	4.7	13.1	1.9	..	..	Gabon
-11.6	17.5	6.4	-6.9	3.0	2.1	1.9	0.9	0.6	-0.7	Gambia, The
1.6	10.7	-8.3	0.5	-2.2	0.5	-0.5	2.0	..	..	Ghana
-3.8	-16.6	1.1	-3.7	-6.1	2.2	10.6	-4.3	-11.3	13.3	Guinea-Bissau
8.2	6.1	4.5	-3.8	3.3	-1.7	-3.1	-1.4	0.7	3.0	Kenya
-13.9	-8.8	-1.3	-3.4	4.2	14.6	-3.0	-5.3	-4.1	-0.2	Lesotho
..	..	..	..	..	..	..	..	..	..	Liberia
8.5	-0.1	2.2	2.3	-3.7	0.7	5.6	-0.6	3.0	-0.9	Madagascar
6.2	-0.5	0.0	9.0	-5.7	8.8	1.2	-5.0	-5.5	3.0	Malawi
0.2	0.6	-1.8	-2.2	-11.7	7.4	1.3	-1.1	2.1	-3.9	Mali
-3.2	-14.1	13.2	0.4	4.3	4.0	0.9	-1.5	-0.2	-1.5	Mauritania
2.2	11.1	-0.8	-1.7	3.1	2.7	-8.7	-4.8	1.3	-1.3	Mauritius
-3.5	-3.3	1.1	-0.5	5.0	-11.5	-0.5	-2.4	-2.8	1.1	Mozambique
-1.2	-6.3	2.3	2.1	-6.3	5.1	-0.1	2.7	1.9	-1.3	Niger
-56.2	8.2	18.0	19.4	9.3	14.0	7.1	4.2	2.7	-1.6	Nigeria
0.4	-3.1	1.5	-2.1	-1.5	0.1	2.0	-1.4	1.0	1.9	Rwanda
-2.7	8.6	-1.4	-1.1	-2.2	1.3	-2.0	2.0	0.6	0.0	Senegal
..	..	..	..	..	..	..	..	..	..	Seychelles
4.4	4.1	5.8	4.8	0.9	0.0	4.5	1.0	-4.2	0.5	Sierra Leone
0.4	-8.4	-2.3	1.4	5.2	0.2	3.9	14.8	-13.3	3.2	Somalia
-1.8	-1.0	-0.1	-0.2	1.2	-0.2	-0.6	1.1	-0.1	0.8	Sudan
..	..	..	..	..	..	..	..	..	..	Swaziland
10.1	0.9	4.0	-7.6	-1.6	-5.9	2.5	0.6	-0.6	0.5	Tanzania
-2.8	-1.6	5.7	-3.9	-4.8	-6.9	6.1	-3.0	0.4	-1.2	Togo
..	..	..	..	..	..	..	..	..	..	Uganda
-0.2	-5.4	1.7	4.5	-1.4	1.9	-3.9	-5.0	3.8	-0.5	Zaire
3.4	15.7	1.4	-2.0	-7.2	-4.2	3.9	-8.8	2.8	-6.0	Zambia
-9.1	0.2	4.4	6.8	0.9	10.5	3.1	-14.8	-4.3	0.1	Zimbabwe
0.5	*0.2*	*-0.2*	*-0.1*	*-1.3*	*0.3*	*0.6*	*-0.8*	*0.6*	*0.3*	*SOUTH ASIA*
1.7	0.5	0.7	-1.0	-3.5	3.1	-0.5	-1.8	0.0	0.3	Bangladesh
-0.5	0.5	-0.4	0.1	-1.2	-0.4	0.6	-1.0	0.8	0.3	India
..	..	..	..	..	..	..	..	..	..	Nepal
8.1	-0.6	0.4	-2.0	-1.9	3.9	1.2	0.0	0.1	0.5	Pakistan
6.5	-4.9	-3.3	3.4	2.0	0.1	0.2	0.1	3.0	-0.1	Sri Lanka
-1.0	*0.9*	*-0.3*	*1.1*	*-1.5*	*2.9*	*1.5*	*-0.4*	*-2.9*	*0.1*	*EAST ASIA AND PACIFIC*
1.0	2.2	-0.5	-0.6	-4.9	2.3	2.0	-0.5	-1.2	2.4	China
-3.1	6.9	1.1	4.6	0.8	3.0	0.9	..	..	..	Fiji
-14.1	-2.8	1.2	3.4	-3.0	2.1	2.7	4.4	0.3	-0.9	Indonesia
2.8	0.5	2.4	0.4	1.8	3.6	2.2	1.3	-7.7	-3.0	Korea, Republic of
-3.4	-2.4	0.7	3.1	5.9	9.6	4.2	-4.3	-5.2	-2.9	Malaysia
1.9	0.1	1.0	2.2	5.8	4.6	-0.7	-4.9	5.1	7.3	Papua New Guinea
0.8	-0.9	-0.9	5.3	3.2	2.3	-5.2	-3.8	-5.5	-0.4	Philippines
8.8	28.0	-3.2	-12.8	-2.7	18.0	-8.5	-30.3	..	..	Solomon islands
2.7	5.9	-7.7	3.2	3.0	2.7	-1.3	-5.9	-2.0	-0.7	Thailand
..	..	..	-6.1	-9.0	3.3	3.4	..	..	..	Vanuatu

Table 12. Resource balance: contribution to growth of gross domestic product (cont'd.)

Percentage points	1970	1971	1972	1973	1974	1975	1976	1977	1978	1979	1980
LATIN AMERICA AND CARIBBEAN	*-0.8*	*-1.1*	*0.6*	*-0.4*	*-2.3*	*-0.4*	*0.1*	*-0.5*	*0.1*	*-0.5*	*-2.4*
Argentina	2.0	-1.6	0.5	0.9	-0.4	-0.7	3.3	-0.4	1.1	-4.5	-5.6
Bahamas	..	..	..	..	..	..	..	..	4.4	-2.2	1.3
Barbados	..	..	..	..	..	..	..	..	..	..	..
Belize	..	..	..	..	..	..	..	..	..	..	..
Bolivia	-1.9	-1.8	-1.3	1.6	2.9	-6.0	2.1	-0.1	-1.6	0.4	5.1
Brazil	-1.4	-1.8	-0.7	-1.3	-2.9	1.2	0.1	0.8	0.2	-0.3	1.2
Chile	0.0	-2.5	-2.9	2.0	4.3	13.0	3.9	-5.4	-2.3	-3.5	-2.8
Colombia	-2.6	-1.7	2.7	0.1	-0.5	3.4	-1.9	-1.8	0.4	1.1	-1.9
Costa Rica	-3.7	-0.3	4.2	0.0	-1.0	1.8	-3.3	-6.0	-0.2	-0.2	0.1
Dominican Republic	-2.9	-1.6	-3.1	1.0	-8.6	8.9	-0.2	-0.1	0.2	1.8	-12.5
Ecuador	-0.8	-5.3	16.1	18.3	-13.2	-8.6	3.6	-7.5	-0.5	1.2	-4.1
El Salvador	-3.7	-0.9	1.2	-6.2	0.3	4.1	-7.4	-12.4	2.2	9.0	5.0
Grenada	..	..	..	..	..	..	..	..	..	..	..
Guatemala	-3.3	-1.3	5.2	-0.9	-3.0	2.6	-8.0	-2.1	-1.8	5.2	4.3
Guyana	-4.2	12.2	-6.5	-27.7	12.4	-28.2	-9.9	23.5	30.4	-4.9	-8.5
Haiti	-2.5	0.2	-0.8	1.2	-0.5	-0.9	-3.7	-3.0	0.6	2.1	-0.3
Honduras	-2.0	7.4	1.3	-2.8	-5.8	3.4	-2.8	-5.6	0.6	2.2	-2.6
Jamaica	1.4	-1.2	-0.1	-1.1	-1.2	-6.3	3.2	4.7	3.2	3.3	-0.4
Mexico	-2.3	1.1	0.2	-1.0	-3.2	-1.0	1.4	3.2	-1.8	-3.4	-5.4
Nicaragua	-0.3	0.7	4.8	-4.3	-2.1	4.8	0.6	-4.1	4.6	4.9	-22.0
Panama	-2.5	-3.3	-2.8	2.0	-3.0	2.7	1.5	4.7	-3.5	-1.5	6.2
Paraguay	3.5	-2.5	1.9	-2.7	-2.3	2.3	-4.6	-4.4	0.0	12.0	-23.3
Peru	2.8	-1.1	1.2	-4.3	-3.9	0.8	2.6	1.2	5.2	0.4	-5.2
St. Vincent and The Grenadines	..	..	..	..	..	..	..	..	14.8	-7.0	-3.6
Trinidad and Tobago	0.0	-4.7	2.9	1.9	-1.3	-4.2	-1.3	-1.0	-1.5	-3.3	-0.1
Uruguay	-3.8	-1.1	1.2	-1.6	3.1	0.7	2.4	-0.3	-0.6	-2.9	-1.0
Venezuela	..	..	..	..	..	-13.3	-7.7	-9.7	0.0	8.9	-4.0
MIDDLE EAST AND NORTH AFRICA	..	..	..	..	..	..	..	..	..	..	..
Algeria	-0.7	-5.1	5.1	-2.2	-6.9	-3.2	1.7	-4.2	-0.7	3.0	-2.8
Egypt, Arab Republic of	-4.2	0.3	-1.1	-3.6	-16.9	-8.1	10.3	-0.5	-1.7	-9.1	-0.8
Iran, Islamic Rep. of	2.2	-0.7	1.5	0.4	-1.9	-4.5	0.2	-1.9	-0.2	1.0	-5.2
Jordan	..	..	..	..	..	..	..	..	..	..	..
Morocco	-2.5	0.6	3.8	-1.0	-2.4	-13.6	-6.2	-2.9	6.7	-1.1	3.5
Oman	..	..	..	..	..	..	..	..	..	..	..
Syrian Arab Republic	2.2	-4.0	4.0	-3.3	-19.0	-3.0	-0.7	-4.6	1.9	-4.1	-2.7
Tunisia	-3.1	4.7	-0.3	-2.3	-2.2	-3.5	0.7	-3.8	-1.2	0.5	-2.2
Turkey	-1.4	-2.4	-1.9	1.3	-4.5	-2.2	-0.2	-2.1	7.5	0.3	-0.1
Yemen, Republic of	..	..	..	..	..	..	..	..	..	..	..
EUROPE	..	..	..	..	..	..	..	..	..	..	..
Bulgaria	..	..	..	..	..	..	..	..	..	..	..
Greece	0.0	-0.3	-0.6	-3.8	4.0	0.1	1.0	-1.4	0.9	-0.5	3.0
Hungary	..	-5.0	6.6	2.8	-5.0	-0.8	0.9	0.0	-4.5	5.4	0.6
Malta	-5.0	9.4	9.2	13.5	-0.9	15.1	-0.3	-1.2	8.3	4.9	-0.4
Poland	..	..	..	..	..	..	..	..	..	..	..
Portugal	-0.8	-2.4	0.5	-3.5	-6.0	6.4	-1.0	-3.2	1.5	1.7	-0.4
Romania	..	..	..	..	..	..	..	..	..	..	..
Yugoslavia	-7.2	-2.6	6.2	-2.2	-6.8	0.9	6.7	-6.4	0.4	-3.6	5.3
Low- & middle-income economies	-0.9	-0.7	1.9	-0.3	-2.9	-0.8	0.8	-1.0	-0.8	0.4	-1.8
Severely indebted	-0.4	-0.9	1.0	-0.1	-2.4	-1.0	0.4	-0.4	-0.1	-0.5	-1.9
Low-income economies	-1.0	0.3	1.8	1.0	-1.7	-0.5	-0.1	-1.5	-3.2	2.8	-1.8
Low-income Africa	1.1	-2.2	4.2	0.3	-4.4	-8.2	-0.7	-5.4	-5.9	17.4	-8.1
China and India	-1.3	0.5	0.3	0.6	-0.3	1.7	-0.2	-1.0	-2.6	0.4	-0.1
Other low-income	-2.0	2.4	4.4	3.4	-4.0	-0.6	0.4	0.7	-2.6	-2.3	-1.2
Middle-income economies	-0.9	-1.2	2.0	-0.8	-3.5	-0.9	1.2	-0.8	0.2	-0.6	-1.8
High-income OECD members	-0.3	0.1	-0.3	-0.2	0.9	0.6	-0.3	0.2	0.2	-0.1	0.9
European Community members	-0.7	0.3	-0.3	-0.1	1.4	0.5	-0.3	0.7	0.1	-0.8	0.1
Japan	-0.6	0.6	-0.5	-1.6	1.0	1.1	0.8	0.7	-0.6	-0.7	2.3
United States	0.2	-0.3	-0.3	0.6	1.0	0.6	-0.9	-0.7	0.3	0.8	1.4
Other high-income economies /a	..	..	..	..	..	..	..	..	..	..	..

a. Economies classified by the United Nations or otherwise regarded by their authorities as developing.

1981	1982	1983	1984	1985	1986	1987	1988	1989	1990	
0.0	*3.7*	*4.7*	*0.3*	*0.5*	*-0.7*	*0.4*	*0.2*	*-0.3*	*-2.2*	*LATIN AMERICA AND CARIBBEAN*
2.0	6.9	1.2	-0.6	2.6	-2.4	-0.5	3.3	0.8	0.9	Argentina
-6.7	2.9	1.3	-1.5	-2.9	0.1	-0.4	..	..	..	Bahamas
..	..	..	..	..	..	..	..	..	..	Barbados
..	..	..	..	..	..	..	..	..	..	Belize
-7.1	9.2	-1.2	2.1	-3.9	0.0	-0.9	4.7	-1.1	1.0	Bolivia
2.4	-0.2	2.3	2.0	0.7	-2.6	1.7	1.3	-1.0	-1.6	Brazil
-8.6	16.6	4.9	-2.4	5.3	0.6	-1.7	-1.5	-2.3	1.7	Chile
-2.6	-1.5	1.5	1.9	2.9	2.5	0.9	1.0	0.2	1.8	Colombia
12.2	3.3	-4.1	0.4	-2.8	-4.0	0.2	2.4	-0.2	-2.0	Costa Rica
7.0	3.0	0.3	4.1	-2.8	-2.3	-2.5	2.9	-2.6	4.7	Dominican Republic
4.5	-3.3	8.9	3.4	1.0	2.2	-8.1	10.9	-1.5	1.2	Ecuador
-0.2	1.6	1.6	-1.6	-1.0	-1.8	2.1	-1.6	-4.5	2.9	El Salvador
..	..	..	..	..	..	..	..	..	..	Grenada
-2.3	4.4	2.6	-2.0	3.3	0.1	-6.4	-0.1	0.8	1.0	Guatemala
-4.8	14.7	-1.5	17.6	-12.1	-7.9	8.1	-7.1	..	..	Guyana
-3.7	5.1	-1.7	1.1	-0.1	0.0	-1.4	0.4	-0.8	0.5	Haiti
4.8	5.3	-1.8	-4.0	0.5	1.6	-0.7	0.5	1.0	1.0	Honduras
-0.7	-3.7	1.0	-0.5	-1.7	5.0	-1.1	-8.8	-0.4	8.5	Jamaica
-2.8	12.2	7.4	-0.9	-2.2	2.2	1.2	-4.2	-3.0	-2.9	Mexico
3.6	3.1	-0.8	-3.7	-1.9	-0.3	-0.6	-0.8	6.2	0.8	Nicaragua
-1.1	2.6	3.2	-4.8	1.8	2.2	0.8	9.6	-4.6	-12.3	Panama
0.7	3.3	7.1	-2.6	0.1	-0.9	-2.7	6.2	-0.2	1.3	Paraguay
-2.9	0.3	4.2	3.8	1.6	-3.4	-2.5	1.2	3.8	-3.4	Peru
5.0	-8.9	5.0	5.3	1.2	-9.5	-5.0	..	..	..	St. Vincent and The Grenadines
1.2	-5.8	0.8	4.8	2.3	2.1	-1.1	2.0	0.4	-0.1	Trinidad and Tobago
0.8	1.1	6.6	2.7	0.8	-0.9	-3.5	1.2	0.4	0.6	Uruguay
-4.1	-6.5	16.7	-5.6	1.0	2.5	-0.9	-2.3	9.8	-16.2	Venezuela
..	..	..	..	..	..	..	..	..	..	*MIDDLE EAST AND NORTH AFRICA*
-3.1	1.8	-0.4	0.3	0.6	3.3	3.3	1.3	0.8	0.1	Algeria
-3.2	4.9	1.4	-4.8	-0.6	5.3	6.6	0.5	1.2	0.9	Egypt, Arab Republic of
-1.3	3.9	-2.7	0.0	1.1	1.0	0.4	1.9	-1.1	..	Iran, Islamic Rep. of
..	..	..	4.0	1.2	-5.8	4.9	-0.5	2.3	4.4	Jordan
-0.5	0.1	4.9	-0.5	0.9	-1.4	0.1	2.4	-4.2	2.7	Morocco
..	..	..	..	..	..	..	..	..	..	Oman
-7.5	5.8	-2.6	0.6	-0.4	4.6	4.0	4.2	..	..	Syrian Arab Republic
-4.9	-2.9	1.5	-1.9	7.3	2.4	6.0	2.6	-4.8	-1.2	Tunisia
3.3	3.2	-0.5	-1.3	0.6	-2.5	0.9	3.8	-0.3	-5.0	Turkey
..	..	..	..	..	..	..	..	..	..	Yemen, Republic of
0.8	*1.5*	*1.3*	*2.0*	*-0.3*	*-1.2*	*-0.5*	*0.3*	*-0.9*	*..*	*EUROPE*
-2.4	3.5	-1.0	0.2	-1.1	-2.3	-0.1	1.0	2.8	..	Bulgaria
-1.8	-2.7	-0.3	2.8	-2.9	1.6	-1.1	-0.2	-2.4	..	Greece
1.1	2.6	1.9	2.0	-0.9	-1.9	0.7	2.3	0.0	0.0	Hungary
-3.0	-9.1	4.8	-0.4	-2.3	3.9	-1.3	-5.9	-2.0	..	Malta
0.6	3.7	0.8	0.8	-1.2	-0.1	0.2	0.3	0.6	7.6	Poland
-1.8	-0.5	6.5	4.4	2.1	-3.1	-5.4	-4.5	-1.9	..	Portugal
..	..	..	..	..	..	..	..	..	..	Romania
3.2	2.5	0.6	1.9	1.4	-2.2	1.6	1.8	-1.5	-2.7	Yugoslavia
-1.2	2.4	1.8	0.8	0.1	0.8	0.8	0.2	-0.8	-0.6	**Low- & middle-income economies**
0.3	3.5	4.0	0.7	0.3	-0.7	0.2	0.2	-0.3	-1.2	Severely indebted
-3.7	1.0	0.9	0.9	-2.3	1.6	1.5	-0.1	-0.1	0.9	Low-income economies
-17.1	2.7	6.5	5.4	1.8	3.9	1.9	0.5	1.0	-0.4	Low-income Africa
0.2	1.3	-0.4	-0.2	-3.1	1.0	1.3	-0.7	-0.3	1.4	China and India
-5.2	-1.6	0.9	1.4	-2.3	2.3	1.4	2.2	0.1	-0.5	Other low-income
-0.3	3.0	2.2	0.8	1.1	0.4	0.5	0.3	-1.1	..	Middle-income economies
0.8	-0.1	-0.1	-0.2	0.1	-0.8	-0.3	-0.1	0.1	..	**High-income OECD members**
1.8	0.0	0.4	0.6	0.3	-0.9	-0.9	-0.6	0.2	..	European Community members
1.2	0.3	1.0	1.2	0.8	-1.0	-0.3	-0.9	-0.1	..	Japan
-0.2	-0.6	-1.3	-1.7	-0.5	-0.6	0.3	0.9	0.4	..	United States
..	..	..	..	..	..	..	..	..	..	**Other high-income economies** /a

Table 13. Gross domestic investment: percentage of gross domestic product

Percentage points	1970	1971	1972	1973	1974	1975	1976	1977	1978	1979	1980
SUB-SAHARAN AFRICA	*15.1*	*16.9*	*17.5*	*17.7*	*17.5*	*20.8*	*23.1*	*23.0*	*21.1*	*18.9*	*19.9*
Excluding Nigeria	*16.1*	*17.3*	*17.0*	*16.8*	*19.4*	*20.1*	*19.9*	*20.0*	*18.4*	*18.0*	*19.3*
Benin	14.2	12.6	16.4	16.0	22.3	23.7	20.4	21.8	19.7	23.3	18.6
Botswana	42.2	47.7	52.5	49.9	51.7	47.7	42.0	31.3	39.6	38.3	41.0
Burkina Faso	12.3	17.9	20.8	24.8	30.7	27.8	27.5	23.5	22.0	19.7	18.2
Burundi	4.5	7.6	3.2	5.3	4.1	7.6	9.1	11.1	14.0	14.9	13.9
Cameroon	16.0	16.6	18.2	19.9	17.1	20.0	17.6	21.8	22.7	21.7	18.9
Cape Verde	..	..	..	19.7	16.7	16.0	27.2	38.7	34.6	46.6	41.9
Central African Rep.	18.9	19.7	19.2	22.1	14.6	13.9	12.1	11.7	11.0	9.7	7.0
Chad	18.1	17.8	16.5	-3.8	20.7	23.0	19.1	20.8	18.2	..	..
Comoros	..	..	..	..	..	..	..	..	..	..	..
Congo, People's Rep of the	24.2	26.6	29.1	32.0	35.1	39.1	31.0	26.6	27.3	26.0	35.8
Cote D'Ivoire	22.5	21.8	20.9	23.2	22.0	22.4	23.0	27.3	29.8	28.0	28.2
Ethiopia	11.5	11.8	12.7	11.4	9.9	10.4	9.6	8.8	7.5	8.7	10.0
Gabon	32.0	32.0	48.1	37.6	51.8	62.7	73.5	58.1	35.0	32.9	28.1
Gambia, The	4.6	6.1	7.6	7.9	4.2	11.6	10.9	14.1	30.1	25.9	25.0
Ghana	14.2	14.1	7.1	9.0	13.0	12.7	8.9	11.1	5.4	6.5	5.6
Guinea-Bissau	29.6	28.0	22.8	20.9	16.8	15.4	16.3	19.8	21.7	21.8	29.6
Kenya	24.4	23.9	22.3	25.8	25.8	18.1	20.2	23.7	29.8	22.3	29.2
Lesotho	11.4	15.8	15.2	18.6	17.7	18.7	36.1	25.0	25.9	34.6	42.4
Liberia	22.2	20.1	21.2	14.5	19.7	34.0	31.5	32.8	29.7	30.1	27.3
Madagascar	9.9	11.2	8.8	9.1	8.7	8.1	8.1	8.1	9.6	16.1	15.0
Malawi	25.7	19.2	24.4	22.4	27.3	33.7	26.3	24.7	38.4	30.2	24.8
Mali	16.2	17.0	18.1	17.9	14.3	16.5	14.2	16.5	16.9	16.4	17.0
Mauritania	22.0	22.8	30.4	8.6	16.1	34.5	42.4	39.1	31.0	25.5	36.2
Mauritius	9.9	14.5	15.3	24.9	25.2	26.3	31.8	30.0	30.7	31.2	20.7
Mozambique	..	..	..	..	..	..	..	..	..	..	18.9
Niger	9.8	7.8	11.1	14.9	15.1	14.3	14.2	19.7	23.0	25.8	36.6
Nigeria	13.0	16.3	18.3	19.4	14.6	21.8	27.1	26.7	24.8	20.1	20.5
Rwanda	7.0	9.1	9.6	9.4	10.5	13.7	13.8	15.1	16.6	12.0	16.1
Senegal	15.7	16.2	17.0	18.9	22.2	17.8	16.5	17.5	17.4	14.4	15.3
Seychelles	..	..	..	..	..	..	38.9	40.0	43.3	32.9	38.3
Sierra Leone	16.6	15.3	11.7	11.7	15.8	15.7	11.3	13.1	11.3	13.4	16.2
Somalia	11.7	11.9	13.6	14.3	26.9	22.5	29.9	21.4	28.7	23.0	42.4
Sudan	13.6	11.8	9.2	11.7	18.4	17.5	23.2	17.1	14.4	13.2	15.1
Swaziland	19.2	19.9	22.3	23.4	26.9	17.8	29.6	27.0	43.9	39.7	40.7
Tanzania	22.5	26.4	21.8	21.1	22.0	21.1	22.9	26.1	25.2	26.1	23.0
Togo	15.1	18.9	20.7	21.7	16.4	27.7	24.9	34.3	52.7	48.8	30.1
Uganda	13.3	15.2	11.0	8.2	10.7	7.6	5.8	5.5	7.8	6.4	6.1
Zaire	9.6	11.8	11.9	10.7	10.9	11.4	9.3	13.7	7.6	8.2	6.4
Zambia	28.2	37.1	35.3	29.2	36.7	40.6	23.7	24.7	23.9	14.1	23.3
Zimbabwe	20.4	22.4	26.4	25.4	27.5	26.3	17.9	19.1	11.9	12.7	18.8
SOUTH ASIA	*16.3*	*17.0*	*15.9*	*17.0*	*17.9*	*18.2*	*19.4*	*19.0*	*21.0*	*21.6*	*22.0*
Bangladesh	11.3	8.2	4.7	8.9	7.6	6.2	10.2	12.0	11.6	11.3	15.1
India	17.1	18.5	17.1	18.3	19.8	20.8	20.9	19.8	22.3	22.9	22.8
Nepal	6.0	7.8	7.3	9.2	8.8	14.5	15.1	16.0	18.3	15.8	18.3
Pakistan	15.8	15.6	14.2	12.9	13.4	16.2	17.2	19.3	17.9	17.9	18.5
Sri Lanka	18.9	17.1	17.3	13.7	15.7	15.6	16.2	14.4	20.0	25.8	33.8
EAST ASIA AND PACIFIC	*26.5*	*27.0*	*25.5*	*27.2*	*27.6*	*28.7*	*27.1*	*27.6*	*30.8*	*32.9*	*30.4*
China	28.5	29.0	27.1	29.0	28.9	30.3	28.5	29.0	33.4	34.9	32.2
Fiji	22.2	24.8	24.0	22.2	18.9	20.6	21.5	23.2	22.8	30.1	31.8
Indonesia	15.8	18.4	21.8	20.8	19.5	23.7	24.1	23.4	23.9	26.6	24.3
Korea, Republic of	24.7	25.1	20.8	24.5	31.6	27.1	25.3	27.3	31.4	35.5	31.7
Malaysia	22.4	22.4	23.3	25.5	30.8	25.3	23.6	25.8	26.7	28.9	30.4
Papua New Guinea	41.6	42.8	27.8	15.5	17.4	20.0	18.6	21.6	22.6	23.5	25.2
Philippines	21.2	20.9	19.3	20.2	25.2	29.5	31.0	28.8	28.9	31.1	30.7
Solomon islands	..	..	..	..	..	..	..	..	..	..	36.4
Thailand	25.6	24.2	21.7	27.0	26.6	26.7	24.0	26.9	28.2	27.2	26.4
Vanuatu	..	..	..	..	..	..	..	..	..	..	..

1981	1982	1983	1984	1985	1986	1987	1988	1989	1990	
20.4	*17.3*	*14.0*	*10.8*	*12.1*	*15.1*	*15.9*	*15.6*	*15.0*	*15.5*	*SUB-SAHARAN AFRICA*
19.4	*19.1*	*16.4*	*15.5*	*16.4*	*17.7*	*17.2*	*16.8*	*16.0*	*..*	*Excluding Nigeria*
19.2	34.1	11.6	7.4	13.3	12.5	12.3	13.0	9.2	11.9	Benin
43.6	44.2	29.4	24.4	30.1	17.9	6.3	10.3	23.9	..	Botswana
17.0	21.6	20.6	20.1	26.0	22.5	21.5	23.4	19.2	20.6	Burkina Faso
17.0	14.5	17.8	18.4	14.1	15.9	21.2	18.5	..	..	Burundi
24.7	23.4	24.4	20.8	24.9	30.8	24.1	15.7	18.0	15.9	Cameroon
45.3	52.9	48.8	44.0	45.1	45.8	44.3	41.7	42.3	37.0	Cape Verde
8.7	6.7	11.8	12.3	14.5	12.2	11.8	8.9	9.3	11.8	Central African Rep.
..	..	3.1	5.4	8.2	9.1	12.3	7.8	9.0	9.5	Chad
..	..	29.0	45.8	29.6	23.6	23.3	16.0	13.9	14.4	Comoros
48.2	59.7	38.4	30.4	30.3	29.5	19.7	17.4	12.8	20.9	Congo, People's Rep of the
25.9	23.2	20.6	10.9	12.6	11.1	11.7	15.2	10.3	..	Cote D'Ivoire
10.4	11.8	11.2	12.3	14.0	12.7	14.6	15.3	13.3	11.3	Ethiopia
36.3	35.0	35.3	33.5	37.3	45.0	28.2	31.9	25.9	..	Gabon
23.0	16.8	17.3	19.3	15.8	20.4	18.5	17.9	22.0	22.4	Gambia, The
4.6	3.4	3.7	7.0	9.6	9.6	13.3	14.0	..	..	Ghana
25.7	28.3	22.7	30.0	32.0	24.3	33.3	34.2	40.2	25.3	Guinea-Bissau
27.7	21.8	20.8	20.7	25.5	21.8	24.4	25.3	25.5	22.3	Kenya
42.9	49.7	33.6	41.6	50.0	45.4	44.9	46.2	65.5	67.6	Lesotho
16.3	14.3	11.8	10.2	8.7	9.7	..	..	..	..	Liberia
11.5	8.5	8.4	8.6	8.4	8.9	10.0	13.0	13.2	14.3	Madagascar
17.6	21.4	22.8	12.9	18.6	12.3	14.7	18.0	18.7	16.9	Malawi
17.5	17.6	14.6	15.2	19.5	22.9	23.1	24.7	26.6	21.1	Mali
41.9	47.1	17.8	25.1	24.3	23.0	20.5	17.7	14.7	16.2	Mauritania
25.3	18.2	17.5	22.0	23.5	21.9	25.3	30.6	29.3	29.3	Mauritius
20.3	19.3	10.0	10.6	6.9	9.7	23.8	32.5	33.4	39.1	Mozambique
20.3	18.2	12.8	3.2	12.7	10.1	9.2	11.0	9.5	9.2	Niger
21.4	15.4	11.4	6.0	7.5	9.7	11.4	12.3	12.5	14.8	Nigeria
13.3	17.8	13.5	15.8	17.3	15.9	15.6	15.7	15.1	16.4	Rwanda
16.4	15.8	16.2	15.8	13.7	14.6	15.3	14.5	15.3	14.3	Senegal
32.6	32.3	21.2	21.7	22.7	22.8	21.0	..	..	..	Seychelles
19.1	13.4	14.3	12.7	10.0	11.2	10.4	11.6	11.3	11.4	Sierra Leone
27.6	29.3	22.4	24.2	24.8	23.7	28.5	18.7	21.4	18.9	Somalia
14.3	22.8	16.0	13.8	4.5	12.8	10.3	10.0	9.1	9.0	Sudan
31.0	32.2	35.0	31.6	32.0	24.5	15.1	15.9	..	..	Swaziland
20.6	21.0	13.6	15.3	15.7	19.5	22.8	21.2	..	..	Tanzania
30.2	26.3	22.1	21.2	28.8	24.0	20.2	20.2	20.6	22.3	Togo
6.0	7.9	9.1	8.9	9.9	12.5	13.2	12.9	13.0	14.9	Uganda
7.1	5.9	7.9	7.9	9.3	12.5	13.0	12.7	12.8	10.1	Zaire
19.3	16.8	13.8	14.7	14.1	22.1	15.0	12.7	9.1	..	Zambia
23.1	21.2	15.9	19.0	21.1	19.4	19.1	19.7	20.7	21.4	Zimbabwe
24.2	*22.5*	*21.5*	*21.2*	*23.6*	*22.7*	*21.6*	*22.5*	*21.6*	*21.2*	*SOUTH ASIA*
16.0	15.0	13.6	12.3	12.5	12.3	12.6	11.9	11.7	..	Bangladesh
25.7	23.5	22.3	22.4	25.4	24.3	22.9	24.4	23.6	22.9	India
17.6	17.1	19.6	18.7	22.9	21.0	21.6	20.5	19.5	18.3	Nepal
18.8	19.3	18.8	18.3	18.3	18.8	19.1	18.0	17.6	..	Pakistan
27.8	29.9	28.3	26.0	23.4	23.3	22.9	22.3	21.4	21.2	Sri Lanka
29.5	*29.0*	*29.8*	*29.7*	*32.5*	*32.3*	*33.0*	*33.6*	*34.2*	*..*	*EAST ASIA AND PACIFIC*
29.2	29.7	30.4	32.4	38.7	39.3	39.2	38.9	36.4	..	China
34.3	25.6	21.1	18.9	19.1	18.1	13.9	13.1	15.9	..	Fiji
29.6	27.5	28.7	26.2	28.0	28.3	31.4	31.5	34.7	35.9	Indonesia
29.5	28.6	28.8	29.8	29.3	28.8	29.2	29.8	34.5	37.3	Korea, Republic of
35.0	37.3	37.8	33.6	27.6	26.0	23.4	26.0	29.6	..	Malaysia
27.2	32.2	29.4	27.0	19.8	19.9	20.7	27.5	23.5	..	Papua New Guinea
30.6	28.3	26.7	17.0	13.9	12.9	15.6	17.3	18.6	18.8	Philippines
33.9	30.0	36.8	23.0	26.3	26.9	27.3	38.6	..	..	Solomon islands
26.3	23.1	25.9	24.9	24.0	22.0	25.8	28.8	31.1	..	Thailand
..	..	25.7	23.9	28.3	29.0	34.4	31.7	..	..	Vanuatu

Table 13. Gross domestic investment: percentage of gross domestic product (cont'd.)

Percentage points	1970	1971	1972	1973	1974	1975	1976	1977	1978	1979	1980
LATIN AMERICA AND CARIBBEAN	*21.3*	*20.8*	*20.5*	*21.2*	*23.1*	*25.0*	*23.6*	*24.1*	*24.5*	*23.8*	*24.3*
Argentina	21.6	20.8	20.8	18.0	19.3	25.9	26.8	27.2	24.4	22.7	22.2
Bahamas	..	..	..	..	..	..	..	12.5	11.3	12.8	18.3
Barbados	26.1	23.1	22.3	22.2	22.8	19.2	27.0	19.5	22.9	23.5	25.3
Belize	..	..	..	..	..	..	..	..	..	..	..
Bolivia	23.8	24.1	29.6	29.1	21.4	36.9	28.3	27.3	24.0	20.0	14.8
Brazil	20.5	21.1	21.2	23.2	25.4	26.8	23.1	22.1	23.0	22.8	23.3
Chile	16.5	14.5	12.2	7.9	21.2	13.1	12.8	14.4	17.8	17.8	21.0
Colombia	20.2	19.4	18.1	18.3	21.5	17.0	17.6	18.8	18.3	18.2	19.1
Costa Rica	20.5	24.3	22.0	24.0	26.7	21.6	23.7	24.3	23.5	25.3	26.6
Dominican Republic	19.1	17.9	19.7	22.1	23.3	24.5	22.5	21.8	23.7	25.4	25.1
Ecuador	18.2	23.2	20.0	19.5	22.5	26.7	23.8	26.5	28.4	25.3	26.1
El Salvador	12.9	15.6	14.2	18.3	22.6	22.1	19.6	23.4	23.8	18.1	13.3
Grenada	..	..	..	..	..	..	..	..	..	..	32.9
Guatemala	12.8	14.4	12.1	13.7	18.6	16.1	21.4	20.0	21.6	18.7	15.9
Guyana	22.8	18.6	19.8	27.2	26.4	33.1	37.4	29.1	20.5	31.0	29.8
Haiti	11.4	11.4	13.9	15.9	16.5	14.7	15.8	15.5	16.8	18.7	16.9
Honduras	20.9	17.1	15.9	19.1	26.2	19.0	19.2	23.1	27.2	26.5	24.5
Jamaica	31.5	32.1	27.3	31.5	24.3	25.8	18.2	12.2	15.0	19.2	15.7
Mexico	21.3	18.9	19.0	20.0	21.8	22.3	21.0	21.6	22.3	24.7	27.2
Nicaragua	18.4	17.7	13.1	24.2	31.5	21.3	18.7	26.8	13.3	-5.7	16.8
Panama	27.8	30.4	31.8	33.6	33.6	30.8	31.6	23.7	26.6	28.1	27.7
Paraguay	14.7	14.6	15.1	19.0	21.0	24.1	24.6	24.7	27.2	28.6	27.9
Peru	15.5	17.9	15.2	20.3	25.9	24.7	21.9	19.2	19.4	21.7	27.5
St. Vincent and The Grenadines	..	..	..	..	..	..	..	28.1	28.8	35.0	40.3
Trinidad and Tobago	25.9	34.0	31.3	26.0	21.8	27.3	24.6	26.7	30.2	29.1	30.6
Uruguay	11.5	12.6	11.8	12.6	11.5	13.5	14.8	15.2	16.0	17.3	17.3
Venezuela	32.9	32.2	33.2	31.0	26.1	32.8	36.2	43.1	43.9	33.2	26.4
MIDDLE EAST AND NORTH AFRICA	*19.3*	*19.6*	*21.3*	*21.0*	*23.0*	*29.3*	*29.3*	*29.5*	*26.9*	*24.9*	*29.0*
Algeria	36.4	35.5	34.3	40.3	39.7	45.2	43.1	46.8	52.1	42.5	39.1
Egypt, Arab Republic of	13.9	13.2	12.3	13.1	22.5	33.4	28.4	29.2	31.7	32.8	27.5
Iran, Islamic Rep. of	18.9	21.4	22.7	19.5	18.3	28.8	28.5	27.3	22.0	20.4	32.5
Jordan	..	..	..	..	..	..	..	..	..	..	..
Morocco	18.5	17.9	15.3	16.9	20.6	25.2	28.1	34.2	25.4	24.5	24.2
Oman	13.8	28.5	29.8	26.2	30.6	35.6	35.9	30.6	28.9	26.0	22.3
Syrian Arab Republic	13.7	14.8	20.1	12.4	24.8	25.0	31.4	35.5	27.4	26.2	27.5
Tunisia	21.1	21.5	22.7	21.3	25.8	28.0	30.7	30.5	30.8	29.4	29.4
Turkey	19.8	17.8	20.9	19.0	21.6	23.2	25.1	25.2	18.7	18.6	21.9
Yemen, Republic of	..	..	..	..	..	..	..	..	..	..	..
EUROPE	*..*	*..*	*..*	*..*	*..*	*..*	*..*	*..*	*..*	*..*	*32.8*
Bulgaria	..	..	..	..	..	..	..	..	..	..	34.0
Greece	28.1	27.9	29.6	35.8	29.3	27.0	26.3	26.4	27.7	30.1	25.0
Hungary	33.6	37.7	31.7	29.7	35.8	37.8	35.9	37.2	41.3	34.0	30.7
Malta	32.7	29.0	25.0	22.1	27.1	23.5	27.5	26.0	23.4	25.5	24.6
Poland	..	..	..	..	..	..	..	..	..	..	26.3
Portugal	26.2	26.3	28.9	29.7	28.5	24.3	25.9	29.0	30.5	29.5	34.1
Romania	..	..	..	..	..	..	..	..	..	..	..
Yugoslavia	32.3	32.8	28.1	28.4	30.2	33.5	31.9	35.8	34.3	38.3	39.9
Low- & middle-income economies	22.4	22.7	22.1	23.2	24.2	26.3	25.8	26.2	26.8	26.8	27.0
Severely indebted	21.8	21.4	20.9	21.4	23.6	26.0	24.7	25.5	25.8	24.8	25.3
Low-income economies	21.0	21.9	21.1	22.5	21.9	23.7	23.7	23.7	25.8	26.4	25.5
Low-income Africa	14.3	16.3	16.4	16.3	15.7	19.2	21.8	21.9	20.3	17.9	19.0
China and India	24.1	25.0	23.4	25.1	25.4	26.9	25.5	25.3	29.2	30.6	28.8
Other low-income	14.4	14.2	15.3	15.7	15.4	17.3	20.0	20.5	20.7	22.5	22.5
Middle-income economies	23.2	23.2	22.6	23.5	25.3	27.8	26.8	27.4	27.2	26.9	27.8
High-income OECD members	18.9	19.7	20.7	22.7	22.7	19.9	21.5	21.9	22.3	22.8	22.0
European Community members	22.3	22.1	21.9	23.6	24.0	20.8	23.4	22.7	22.1	23.0	23.0
Japan	37.6	34.8	34.9	37.9	37.6	33.3	32.1	31.0	31.0	32.5	32.3
United States	12.0	13.9	15.5	16.6	15.7	13.3	15.5	17.3	18.4	18.1	16.0
Other high-income economies /a	23.3	23.4	23.2	24.0	20.8	21.8	25.1	27.7	30.9	28.9	25.5

a. Economies classified by the United Nations or otherwise regarded by their authorities as developing.

1981	1982	1983	1984	1985	1986	1987	1988	1989	1990	
24.2	*21.7*	*17.4*	*16.8*	*17.7*	*17.7*	*20.4*	*20.9*	*19.5*	..	*LATIN AMERICA AND CARIBBEAN*
18.8	15.9	17.3	11.3	8.5	8.8	16.4	16.4	12.0	11.9	Argentina
18.8	21.5	20.3	16.3	19.2	18.4	18.8	..	..	..	Bahamas
27.6	22.6	19.9	16.2	15.4	16.0	16.0	17.5	18.4	18.3	Barbados
27.2	24.6	18.9	23.5	20.3	19.9	24.9	28.5	31.4	..	Belize
13.8	13.8	8.7	7.2	10.2	7.9	11.1	11.9	12.8	13.5	Bolivia
23.0	21.0	16.5	15.3	17.0	19.2	22.1	21.8	22.4	..	Brazil
22.7	11.3	9.8	13.6	13.7	14.6	16.9	17.0	20.4	19.4	Chile
20.6	20.5	19.9	19.0	19.0	18.0	19.8	21.9	19.6	21.9	Colombia
29.0	24.7	24.2	22.7	25.4	25.2	27.1	23.8	24.4	23.3	Costa Rica
23.6	20.0	21.1	21.3	20.0	19.7	25.3	22.8	25.8	..	Dominican Republic
23.2	25.2	17.6	17.2	18.2	20.9	22.7	22.0	21.6	20.5	Ecuador
14.2	13.2	12.1	12.0	10.8	13.3	12.4	12.8	16.3	12.1	El Salvador
47.9	50.9	41.6	32.0	33.4	39.0	34.0	32.9	..	..	Grenada
17.0	14.1	11.1	11.6	11.5	10.3	13.8	13.8	13.5	13.5	Guatemala
29.5	24.2	21.0	27.4	29.8	33.8	31.9	21.1	..	..	Guyana
16.9	16.6	16.3	15.9	14.2	10.9	12.9	12.5	12.3	..	Haiti
20.7	13.5	14.9	19.0	18.0	14.2	14.7	13.1	12.9	14.3	Honduras
20.4	20.9	22.3	23.0	25.0	18.5	22.6	27.1	..	..	Jamaica
27.4	22.9	20.8	19.9	21.9	18.3	19.2	20.6	17.3	14.4	Mexico
23.6	18.8	22.5	22.2	23.1	16.9	15.8	..	..	..	Nicaragua
30.1	27.7	21.4	16.7	15.4	16.7	17.5	6.9	2.6	12.4	Panama
28.0	25.1	21.1	22.5	22.0	25.0	25.1	24.4	21.0	22.4	Paraguay
31.4	31.3	23.5	22.2	21.6	22.4	22.8	25.7	19.9	20.6	Peru
33.2	28.8	25.5	27.9	28.2	28.2	30.6	24.0	..	..	St. Vincent and The Grenadines
27.6	28.3	26.0	21.6	19.2	22.2	20.0	17.2	18.6	..	Trinidad and Tobago
15.4	14.4	10.0	9.9	8.2	8.2	9.7	9.8	9.2	..	Uruguay
24.4	27.7	12.2	17.5	18.5	20.9	24.6	28.0	12.8	15.9	Venezuela
30.7	*22.5*	*26.7*	*23.5*	*23.2*	*26.5*	*24.3*	*24.5*	*26.8*	..	*MIDDLE EAST AND NORTH AFRICA*
37.0	37.3	37.6	35.1	33.2	33.5	30.0	31.3	30.9	31.8	Algeria
29.5	30.1	28.7	27.5	26.7	23.7	18.0	24.2	23.6	..	Egypt, Arab Republic of
34.4	13.3	25.9	18.6	18.2	24.3	23.6	23.7	29.9	..	Iran, Islamic Rep. of
..	..	34.8	30.9	26.3	22.4	22.7	18.9	18.4	18.2	Jordan
26.1	28.2	24.0	25.3	27.1	22.7	20.7	21.4	24.1	23.5	Morocco
23.0	26.6	26.5	30.0	27.6	32.1	18.0	16.6	..	..	Oman
23.2	23.7	23.6	23.7	23.8	23.3	18.6	16.6	..	..	Syrian Arab Republic
32.3	31.7	29.6	32.0	26.6	23.2	20.4	19.3	22.8	24.7	Tunisia
22.0	20.6	19.6	19.5	21.0	24.4	25.4	23.9	22.4	23.1	Turkey
..	..	..	..	..	..	..	..	..	..	Yemen, Republic of
30.7	*30.4*	*29.0*	*28.5*	*29.1*	*30.1*	*26.0*	*30.1*	*32.8*	..	*EUROPE*
35.5	33.5	32.9	33.2	32.2	35.9	32.9	34.4	32.2	..	Bulgaria
25.4	21.1	21.9	20.4	21.3	19.4	17.5	18.4	18.5	..	Greece
29.7	28.5	26.5	25.7	25.0	26.9	26.7	25.5	26.4	24.9	Hungary
27.1	31.5	30.0	28.9	28.1	25.5	27.5	28.8	29.1	..	Malta
18.5	28.0	25.0	26.3	27.7	28.9	28.8	32.6	32.9	..	Poland
36.1	37.0	29.1	23.2	21.7	23.3	27.7	29.8	30.4	..	Portugal
..	..	..	..	..	..	..	..	..	..	Romania
38.9	35.6	35.7	37.2	38.8	38.4	21.0	37.7	47.9	..	Yugoslavia
26.9	24.4	23.6	22.6	23.7	24.6	24.7	25.8	26.1	..	**Low- & middle-income economies**
24.5	23.0	18.9	18.0	18.9	18.9	21.1	21.8	20.6	..	Severely indebted
25.5	24.2	23.7	23.6	26.9	27.8	28.4	29.2	28.4	..	Low-income economies
18.9	15.4	12.1	8.9	10.1	12.8	14.9	15.1	14.5	15.1	Low-income Africa
27.9	27.2	27.1	28.4	33.1	32.6	31.7	32.8	31.4	..	China and India
26.0	24.7	24.9	22.7	23.6	23.2	24.4	24.2	25.9	..	Other low-income
27.6	24.5	23.6	22.1	22.1	23.2	23.1	24.3	25.1	..	Middle-income economies
21.2	19.4	19.1	20.4	19.7	19.8	20.3	21.4	21.8	..	**High-income OECD members**
20.5	20.0	19.5	19.7	19.4	19.4	19.8	20.9	21.6	..	European Community members
31.2	30.1	28.3	28.3	28.5	28.0	29.2	31.1	32.9	..	Japan
17.0	14.4	15.0	17.9	16.3	15.7	15.3	15.3	15.1	..	United States
25.2	26.5	27.0	28.4	22.2	21.8	21.9	23.8	23.0	..	**Other high-income economies** /a

Table 14. Gross domestic savings: percentage of gross domestic product

Percentage points	1970	1971	1972	1973	1974	1975	1976	1977	1978	1979	1980
SUB-SAHARAN AFRICA	*16.1*	*15.4*	*17.3*	*19.1*	*23.2*	*17.4*	*21.1*	*20.4*	*16.2*	*18.1*	*21.2*
Excluding Nigeria	*17.5*	*14.7*	*15.7*	*16.8*	*18.4*	*13.8*	*16.5*	*16.1*	*12.5*	*12.3*	*13.2*
Benin	6.5	4.7	3.9	7.1	5.9	2.1	-0.5	1.2	0.0	1.9	-6.3
Botswana	1.7	14.7	27.5	28.0	27.6	22.5	22.9	14.3	12.3	22.6	28.5
Burkina Faso	2.4	4.1	6.7	8.9	15.5	5.7	9.7	1.9	2.5	-0.4	-3.1
Burundi	3.6	1.9	-0.2	3.0	-1.7	-3.1	6.2	11.4	5.5	4.4	0.3
Cameroon	17.6	12.5	12.6	16.6	19.7	17.1	12.9	19.1	18.2	14.5	15.7
Cape Verde	..	..	..	-23.4	-12.7	-12.5	-22.4	-27.1	-32.4	-23.3	-8.0
Central African Rep.	3.6	6.5	5.6	7.9	5.8	-5.7	4.1	1.5	-0.7	-1.7	-9.6
Chad	9.8	10.5	9.7	-14.8	8.8	6.8	4.5	2.3	1.8	-23.9	-16.9
Comoros	..										
Congo, People's Rep of the	1.2	6.5	5.6	20.2	28.8	11.3	4.8	6.9	10.0	24.7	35.7
Cote D'Ivoire	29.2	25.6	25.4	25.7	29.3	22.6	28.5	33.6	28.8	24.9	22.2
Ethiopia	11.2	9.9	10.8	13.4	13.3	7.5	8.7	5.7	1.9	3.4	4.9
Gabon	43.7	46.0	48.9	38.7	66.0	64.3	73.0	58.4	49.9	54.0	61.2
Gambia, The	9.4	-0.8	7.8	1.2	8.8	21.5	-1.6	8.0	-13.3	12.8	2.7
Ghana	12.8	9.6	12.6	14.1	9.6	13.7	8.5	10.0	4.0	6.6	4.9
Guinea-Bissau	3.4	-2.2	-8.5	-13.8	-17.4	-5.4	-6.4	-3.5	-5.8	-10.7	-6.0
Kenya	23.6	17.4	20.2	24.5	18.5	13.5	20.9	27.0	20.0	16.4	18.1
Lesotho	-32.2	-42.6	-49.9	-45.9	-66.0	-70.4	-83.3	-74.5	-47.4	-66.2	-59.7
Liberia	42.0	38.1	40.6	32.6	31.9	38.4	34.2	25.6	24.6	26.9	27.3
Madagascar	7.5	4.6	4.8	4.5	4.0	3.1	5.8	4.5	2.7	0.3	-1.4
Malawi	10.8	7.1	9.7	12.4	16.4	17.0	17.8	20.1	20.5	12.6	10.8
Mali	10.2	9.7	8.0	4.5	-15.5	-4.4	3.5	9.3	-2.5	-2.0	-1.9
Mauritania	29.7	30.4	27.5	9.8	5.8	13.0	2.9	-1.3	0.0	-0.6	6.9
Mauritius	11.2	10.1	17.5	22.8	31.1	27.3	24.9	19.3	18.4	19.5	10.5
Mozambique	..	..	..	..	..	..	..	..	..	..	0.5
Niger	2.5	4.5	4.8	6.7	-1.6	2.6	2.1	10.0	17.7	17.5	22.6
Nigeria	12.8	16.7	20.5	24.1	30.4	22.7	26.9	26.0	21.1	25.3	29.5
Rwanda	3.3	2.5	1.6	7.6	1.3	5.2	9.0	11.7	7.6	10.3	4.2
Senegal	11.1	8.9	13.3	8.8	15.6	12.5	8.4	11.3	4.7	4.2	-0.4
Seychelles	..	..	..	..	..	..	22.9	36.0	42.0	26.9	27.1
Sierra Leone	14.6	14.2	11.7	10.9	8.7	6.4	2.8	6.6	3.9	0.7	-0.8
Somalia	6.5	5.3	8.8	1.4	4.3	8.1	16.1	-17.5	-1.6	-28.2	-12.9
Sudan	15.2	10.2	7.6	11.9	14.5	6.1	13.2	10.7	6.3	6.6	3.4
Swaziland	25.1	31.4	30.2	38.1	49.5	33.9	37.7	23.7	22.1	6.6	7.4
Tanzania	20.5	21.7	18.3	14.9	7.4	8.6	20.7	22.8	10.0	13.3	9.8
Togo	25.9	25.8	21.5	21.9	53.5	17.4	25.6	23.4	39.8	22.6	24.8
Uganda	16.4	11.3	13.4	11.4	10.4	5.5	7.4	6.8	2.9	8.2	-0.4
Zaire	17.4	15.5	14.3	15.6	16.8	11.2	10.1	11.1	9.9	10.9	16.2
Zambia	45.1	35.0	36.9	45.0	46.1	21.0	28.8	22.1	20.5	23.1	19.3
Zimbabwe	21.4	20.7	29.2	27.4	27.0	25.1	21.8	21.5	15.4	12.5	15.8
SOUTH ASIA	*14.3*	*15.0*	*14.5*	*16.4*	*15.6*	*16.1*	*18.1*	*18.1*	*18.1*	*17.5*	*16.6*
Bangladesh	7.2	3.8	-3.4	9.9	0.6	1.0	-2.8	6.9	2.2	1.5	2.1
India	16.4	17.6	16.7	17.7	18.7	20.5	21.7	20.3	21.1	20.7	19.2
Nepal	2.6	4.0	5.1	5.4	3.7	10.0	11.7	13.5	13.4	11.6	11.1
Pakistan	9.0	8.7	9.2	10.1	6.4	4.9	7.9	9.5	8.6	5.8	6.9
Sri Lanka	15.8	15.1	15.7	12.5	8.2	8.1	13.9	18.1	15.3	13.8	11.2
EAST ASIA AND PACIFIC	*25.6*	*26.5*	*25.7*	*28.0*	*27.3*	*27.7*	*27.4*	*28.3*	*30.3*	*32.2*	*30.7*
China	28.7	29.9	28.1	29.8	28.8	30.6	29.0	29.5	33.2	34.6	32.2
Fiji	18.9	17.0	14.7	8.7	13.7	20.0	16.8	20.4	18.4	24.7	26.9
Indonesia	13.9	16.8	22.6	22.5	27.9	25.9	26.3	28.2	26.3	33.6	37.1
Korea, Republic of	15.0	14.8	16.1	21.6	20.6	18.5	24.1	27.5	28.5	28.2	24.3
Malaysia	26.6	23.9	22.0	31.0	31.1	25.8	33.7	33.1	32.2	37.8	32.9
Papua New Guinea	6.1	5.9	10.8	25.5	24.5	13.9	19.6	20.3	19.1	23.4	15.1
Philippines	20.9	20.1	18.6	23.7	22.1	22.7	24.7	25.0	23.9	25.6	25.0
Solomon islands	4.2	6.2	6.8	1.5	5.2	-15.0	3.7	21.6	16.9	35.4	6.8
Thailand	21.2	21.3	20.7	25.6	24.3	22.1	21.5	21.5	23.9	20.5	20.1
Vanuatu	..	..	..	..	..	..	..	..	..	..	..

1981	1982	1983	1984	1985	1986	1987	1988	1989	1990	
14.9	*10.8*	*9.8*	*10.9*	*12.3*	*11.4*	*12.4*	*11.1*	*12.4*	*15.3*	*SUB-SAHARAN AFRICA*
12.1	*12.2*	*11.5*	*13.9*	*13.7*	*13.3*	*11.7*	*10.4*	*10.6*	*..*	*Excluding Nigeria*
-14.9	-2.6	0.1	-6.4	5.1	0.1	1.2	0.9	5.0	..	Benin
22.4	7.8	16.8	23.8	28.4	38.6	34.0	35.8	37.1	..	Botswana
-4.1	-1.0	-0.2	2.5	3.9	2.4	6.8	10.6	2.2	..	Burkina Faso
5.6	-0.9	1.5	4.3	5.1	7.5	4.5	5.1	..	..	Burundi
22.3	23.1	28.8	32.7	35.9	31.5	19.6	12.9	19.3	17.2	Cameroon
-3.9	-3.4	-4.3	-10.9	-11.4	-12.0	4.5	1.3	4.0	..	Cape Verde
-1.9	-6.8	-1.2	-0.3	-0.3	-1.7	-2.7	-2.8	-1.3	..	Central African Rep.
-10.7	-9.8	-8.6	-3.4	-19.3	-22.1	-17.7	-13.4	-13.4	..	Chad
..	..	2.8	-10.8	-9.1	-3.5	-9.2	-10.7	-9.3	-18.1	Comoros
30.1	46.5	44.6	46.4	31.1	7.4	19.6	8.2	18.7	29.9	Congo, People's Rep of the
18.8	20.3	18.9	22.4	25.8	23.0	16.3	16.0	13.1	..	Cote D'Ivoire
3.6	2.0	2.7	1.9	2.8	2.2	3.5	4.4	5.4	..	Ethiopia
59.0	56.9	53.2	54.2	51.0	27.9	28.5	24.5	33.0	..	Gabon
-5.8	-0.1	-3.8	-4.6	7.3	4.4	7.0	7.1	8.3	..	Gambia, The
4.0	3.7	0.6	6.6	7.6	7.9	11.1	13.8	..	..	Ghana
1.2	-5.2	-3.6	-8.3	-11.0	-1.3	3.6	-5.9	-1.9	..	Guinea-Bissau
19.6	18.1	20.4	19.4	24.5	21.9	19.3	20.1	19.7	..	Kenya
-68.3	-73.5	-99.0	-94.1	-78.4	-75.7	-75.8	-56.9	-54.9	..	Lesotho
18.8	12.5	10.0	14.4	14.3	18.4	..	..	..	..	Liberia
0.2	-1.0	1.4	3.7	0.3	4.3	5.4	6.5	8.0	..	Madagascar
11.7	15.1	15.2	14.8	12.9	10.1	12.5	8.9	4.0	4.4	Malawi
-0.3	0.5	-4.8	-3.4	-14.2	-1.2	6.2	7.0	11.4	..	Mali
12.6	3.0	-12.1	-1.9	8.8	15.4	13.7	6.1	7.9	..	Mauritania
14.8	15.4	17.1	18.7	21.6	28.6	27.4	25.5	21.5	21.4	Mauritius
0.0	-3.3	-10.8	-6.2	-3.1	-1.1	-11.2	-17.2	-19.4	-16.6	Mozambique
8.7	7.8	7.5	-1.6	2.4	5.6	4.5	6.7	3.2	..	Niger
18.0	9.3	8.0	7.7	10.8	7.4	16.9	14.8	21.0	27.3	Nigeria
1.4	5.2	4.4	8.8	8.2	8.3	6.3	6.4	6.1	..	Rwanda
-4.7	4.7	2.0	5.6	1.7	7.1	8.3	9.2	10.7	..	Senegal
17.0	8.8	-1.0	8.2	7.2	5.6	9.9	..	..	..	Seychelles
4.4	1.9	7.5	11.1	8.8	9.6	11.1	15.2	4.8	..	Sierra Leone
-16.0	-12.8	-26.6	-22.3	-11.5	-16.5	-9.9	-6.3	-14.0	..	Somalia
1.0	8.3	1.5	6.2	-3.8	5.6	7.0	1.8	2.2	..	Sudan
1.4	2.0	-1.1	-4.6	-3.5	12.6	15.5	14.2	..	..	Swaziland
12.1	13.6	8.4	7.2	7.4	5.5	0.0	-4.8	-10.0	..	Tanzania
23.5	17.7	20.9	19.1	20.0	12.3	11.6	10.6	13.2	..	Togo
-0.6	1.2	3.9	6.3	7.8	8.4	6.4	3.6	2.1	1.5	Uganda
15.8	11.3	13.2	18.8	16.9	16.4	10.0	9.8	15.7	..	Zaire
6.8	8.0	15.2	16.5	14.1	22.1	15.0	10.6	5.0	..	Zambia
15.8	15.3	12.8	19.5	22.3	23.7	23.2	24.6	21.4	19.4	Zimbabwe
19.2	*17.6*	*17.4*	*17.2*	*18.7*	*18.8*	*18.1*	*18.5*	*17.8*	*17.2*	*SOUTH ASIA*
3.5	1.0	1.2	1.6	1.8	2.4	3.6	2.5	1.1	..	Bangladesh
22.5	20.7	20.0	20.0	22.3	21.6	20.3	21.1	20.7	20.0	India
10.9	9.9	8.6	9.9	14.0	11.7	12.3	10.8	7.2	3.6	Nepal
9.3	8.3	8.5	7.7	6.3	10.9	13.9	12.4	11.3	..	Pakistan
11.7	11.5	13.5	20.0	11.7	11.8	12.6	11.8	11.9	..	Sri Lanka
28.7	*28.5*	*29.0*	*30.2*	*31.0*	*32.5*	*35.5*	*35.7*	*34.7*	*..*	*EAST ASIA AND PACIFIC*
30.0	31.6	31.5	32.8	34.5	36.1	39.1	38.0	35.7	..	China
19.9	19.2	15.7	17.8	18.7	20.3	16.7	15.5	15.3	..	Fiji
33.7	27.9	29.0	29.7	29.8	27.3	32.9	34.0	37.2	38.3	Indonesia
24.5	26.0	28.3	29.9	30.5	34.8	37.3	38.3	37.3	36.7	Korea, Republic of
28.8	28.6	32.1	35.5	32.7	32.1	37.3	36.3	33.9	..	Malaysia
6.7	8.5	12.2	13.3	9.5	12.0	14.1	18.7	11.3	..	Papua New Guinea
25.1	21.6	19.9	16.9	16.9	19.1	16.4	17.9	17.5	15.8	Philippines
1.7	15.5	15.3	19.2	7.5	-0.6	-5.0	-3.0	..	..	Solomon islands
20.0	21.4	18.7	20.6	21.2	24.1	26.1	27.3	28.7	..	Thailand
..	..	12.3	18.5	6.9	-2.9	4.9	9.8	..	..	Vanuatu

Table 14. Gross domestic savings: percentage of gross domestic product (cont'd.)

Percentage points	1970	1971	1972	1973	1974	1975	1976	1977	1978	1979	1980
LATIN AMERICA AND CARIBBEAN	*20.6*	*19.7*	*19.5*	*21.1*	*22.1*	*22.5*	*22.3*	*22.9*	*22.6*	*22.5*	*22.9*
Argentina	21.6	21.6	21.7	20.8	20.4	25.5	31.2	30.3	28.3	23.0	20.0
Bahamas	..	..	..	..	..	..	..	29.0	26.5	21.5	25.8
Barbados	7.0	10.4	9.0	10.6	15.8	9.2	8.3	4.8	15.0	13.9	19.3
Belize	..	..	..	..	..	..	..	..	..	14.2	11.6
Bolivia	24.2	21.3	26.9	28.7	30.1	30.8	26.3	24.6	16.6	16.8	18.7
Brazil	20.1	19.4	19.6	22.0	19.5	22.9	20.7	21.4	21.8	20.7	21.0
Chile	17.1	13.5	8.7	6.1	21.8	11.1	17.1	12.6	14.5	15.0	16.8
Colombia	18.4	15.4	17.7	19.3	20.4	18.8	20.7	22.4	21.1	19.9	19.7
Costa Rica	13.8	13.9	15.6	17.9	11.9	13.2	17.7	18.8	15.6	15.0	16.2
Dominican Republic	11.8	9.7	14.9	18.3	12.1	22.2	15.2	17.6	16.8	19.0	15.4
Ecuador	13.6	13.7	16.4	22.7	27.6	20.3	22.4	23.5	22.8	25.9	25.9
El Salvador	13.2	13.7	15.3	15.5	14.2	17.0	20.0	24.3	14.6	17.9	14.2
Grenada	..	..	..	..	..	..	..	..	..	..	0.0
Guatemala	13.6	13.0	12.5	14.4	15.3	14.3	15.4	18.2	15.8	14.2	13.1
Guyana	22.2	22.4	18.5	10.5	28.3	33.0	12.5	13.5	20.5	21.6	19.3
Haiti	7.5	8.0	9.0	11.2	9.3	6.5	6.9	6.6	7.9	8.8	8.1
Honduras	14.7	16.3	17.0	18.2	14.3	10.0	14.8	18.6	22.6	22.4	17.3
Jamaica	27.4	25.0	19.0	21.9	14.1	15.4	9.4	10.8	16.4	17.7	13.6
Mexico	18.7	17.1	17.4	18.1	18.9	19.0	18.8	20.6	20.7	22.3	24.9
Nicaragua	16.0	15.5	18.9	14.5	18.0	12.2	19.9	21.1	16.6	8.2	-2.3
Panama	24.5	26.6	26.9	29.6	24.2	23.5	24.6	20.1	21.9	19.3	24.4
Paraguay	13.5	12.0	15.0	19.7	18.7	18.6	21.2	21.7	23.5	23.1	14.5
Peru	17.4	17.0	14.6	18.3	18.4	13.6	13.7	12.4	20.0	30.3	27.5
St. Vincent and The Grenadines	..	..	..	..	..	..	..	-15.4	7.8	-1.7	-2.5
Trinidad and Tobago	27.0	28.8	24.7	31.7	46.3	45.1	40.3	39.3	34.6	34.8	42.1
Uruguay	10.1	11.4	12.2	13.8	8.9	9.9	14.1	12.3	13.5	12.8	11.7
Venezuela	37.0	37.7	36.1	39.3	48.1	39.7	36.9	36.2	32.7	34.5	33.3
MIDDLE EAST AND NORTH AFRICA	*21.1*	*20.6*	*22.1*	*25.3*	*32.4*	*27.4*	*30.8*	*27.7*	*23.0*	*27.7*	*28.7*
Algeria	29.3	26.1	29.1	34.0	43.0	36.0	39.0	35.6	37.5	40.8	43.1
Egypt, Arab Republic of	9.4	8.1	6.6	8.0	5.7	12.3	16.7	18.5	16.4	14.2	15.2
Iran, Islamic Rep. of	24.9	25.4	26.5	35.0	44.2	37.7	39.0	31.6	23.6	33.6	29.3
Jordan	..	..	..	..	..	..	..	..	..	..	..
Morocco	14.5	15.2	14.6	15.6	20.0	14.3	8.7	13.8	11.7	11.6	13.7
Oman	67.8	62.1	45.5	38.8	56.6	52.5	52.2	44.9	38.5	46.4	47.3
Syrian Arab Republic	10.1	9.9	14.6	8.7	15.2	12.5	16.6	13.0	11.1	9.3	10.3
Tunisia	16.6	19.5	21.6	18.8	26.2	23.2	22.7	20.3	21.1	24.4	24.0
Turkey	17.5	14.3	18.1	16.8	15.2	15.0	18.3	17.1	15.1	15.4	14.1
Yemen, Republic of	..	..	..	..	..	..	..	..	..	..	..
EUROPE	..	..	..	..	..	..	..	..	..	..	*29.0*
Bulgaria	..	..	..	..	..	..	..	..	..	..	33.2
Greece	19.7	19.8	21.2	24.8	19.8	17.0	18.0	18.0	20.6	22.4	19.7
Hungary	31.3	31.4	33.0	34.2	31.3	30.3	31.8	32.7	32.1	30.7	28.5
Malta	2.7	3.3	2.0	2.5	-1.7	10.0	15.8	11.6	16.3	20.3	19.2
Poland	..	..	..	..	..	..	..	..	..	..	23.4
Portugal	19.6	19.2	24.2	22.7	13.2	11.9	12.5	14.0	18.1	18.7	19.0
Romania	..	..	..	..	..	..	..	..	..	..	..
Yugoslavia	27.1	26.5	25.6	24.8	20.5	25.7	29.3	29.6	29.5	31.4	35.6
Low- & middle-income economies	21.4	21.3	21.5	23.7	24.5	23.8	24.9	24.9	24.4	25.8	26.0
Severely indebted	21.1	20.3	20.0	21.7	22.6	22.7	22.6	23.4	22.9	22.8	23.2
Low-income economies	20.5	21.2	21.2	23.0	23.0	22.5	23.2	23.4	23.9	25.7	25.6
Low-income Africa	15.4	14.8	16.5	18.4	21.9	15.8	19.7	19.0	14.9	17.5	20.9
China and India	24.0	25.2	23.9	25.4	24.8	26.9	26.2	25.9	28.7	29.6	27.4
Other low-income	10.3	10.2	12.5	15.8	16.6	14.8	17.6	20.7	18.7	21.9	25.7
Middle-income economies	21.9	21.3	21.7	24.0	25.4	24.4	25.7	25.7	24.6	25.9	26.2
High-income OECD members	19.3	20.6	21.5	23.5	22.7	20.8	21.9	22.2	23.2	23.0	21.9
European Community members	22.9	23.2	22.9	24.0	23.3	21.3	23.2	23.2	23.4	23.1	22.0
Japan	38.9	37.4	37.2	38.0	36.7	33.2	32.8	32.6	32.7	31.8	31.4
United States	12.1	14.5	15.7	17.9	16.8	15.2	16.5	17.4	18.6	18.9	17.2
Other high-income economies /a	28.2	34.2	38.4	39.3	53.3	51.3	50.6	48.1	43.8	42.1	46.2

a. Economies classified by the United Nations or otherwise regarded by their authorities as developing.

1981	1982	1983	1984	1985	1986	1987	1988	1989	1990	
22.6	*21.6*	*21.4*	*21.9*	*22.5*	*19.9*	*22.9*	*23.4*	*22.5*	*..*	*LATIN AMERICA AND CARIBBEAN*
18.3	19.1	22.1	15.5	15.2	11.1	16.7	20.1	19.0	17.5	Argentina
23.9	27.7	28.9	21.6	24.7	24.3	24.3	..	..	..	Bahamas
12.6	16.4	14.6	16.9	19.3	18.3	16.5	19.5	16.4	..	Barbados
14.7	7.9	6.8	16.1	12.9	20.8	22.4	21.3	19.3	..	Belize
11.8	17.8	11.5	10.5	8.5	5.0	4.7	6.4	9.0	..	Bolivia
22.6	20.4	18.9	20.8	22.0	21.7	25.2	26.7	25.6	..	Brazil
12.4	9.4	12.5	12.6	16.5	18.4	21.0	24.2	23.7	21.4	Chile
17.1	16.2	17.1	18.4	20.3	24.8	23.8	24.1	23.8	26.7	Colombia
24.1	27.6	23.4	23.1	23.6	26.1	23.0	21.8	20.5	15.0	Costa Rica
19.4	15.0	17.2	24.0	14.5	15.2	15.3	17.4	18.0	..	Dominican Republic
24.2	22.9	21.6	23.7	24.1	21.0	16.4	20.2	19.5	21.4	Ecuador
8.1	8.2	6.6	5.2	3.3	10.1	5.3	6.3	6.0	1.4	El Salvador
6.7	1.7	-1.4	2.8	4.3	4.8	6.1	10.1	..	..	Grenada
10.5	10.2	9.5	9.4	10.5	11.8	7.3	8.0	8.3	8.3	Guatemala
7.6	9.1	2.5	18.2	12.9	19.6	18.3	16.7	..	..	Guyana
1.7	6.4	5.9	6.8	6.1	5.1	5.0	4.5	4.6	..	Haiti
14.4	11.6	11.2	12.3	13.5	12.8	11.8	10.8	11.2	9.0	Honduras
10.0	9.3	10.2	16.4	14.7	20.7	22.9	18.7	..	..	Jamaica
24.8	27.9	30.3	27.7	27.0	22.9	26.2	22.9	18.3	14.3	Mexico
4.2	8.7	11.9	9.2	16.1	8.8	13.8	..	..	..	Nicaragua
25.8	23.5	21.8	15.0	15.9	20.3	19.4	18.8	11.3	7.6	Panama
16.4	15.3	17.7	16.2	13.1	15.3	14.9	22.6	14.6	21.0	Paraguay
25.4	25.6	22.4	25.9	26.3	20.2	20.0	23.7	22.3	18.9	Peru
6.1	-2.1	3.9	14.4	22.1	17.2	10.1	5.5	..	..	St. Vincent and The Grenadines
37.3	20.9	16.0	19.9	25.6	13.8	21.2	22.1	25.5	..	Trinidad and Tobago
11.4	11.3	11.6	14.0	12.1	13.0	11.4	13.8	15.1	..	Uruguay
29.3	25.1	20.5	28.7	27.7	19.9	25.1	21.0	26.6	34.0	Venezuela
27.1	*23.1*	*25.3*	*21.4*	*22.0*	*23.6*	*23.6*	*24.4*	*25.5*	*..*	*MIDDLE EAST AND NORTH AFRICA*
40.7	39.2	39.7	37.4	36.4	29.4	31.9	30.9	31.0	36.6	Algeria
14.1	15.2	17.8	14.0	14.5	13.8	6.6	8.2	6.9	..	Egypt, Arab Republic of
29.3	18.8	26.2	18.3	18.1	22.2	22.9	23.4	28.4	..	Iran, Islamic Rep. of
..	..	-10.5	-9.7	-10.4	-3.9	-1.2	-3.6	-1.5	-7.4	Jordan
11.5	13.8	15.2	14.7	18.1	16.4	16.3	20.9	18.5	18.3	Morocco
49.6	42.0	42.1	42.7	40.2	18.0	41.2	27.9	..	..	Oman
5.9	12.6	10.2	12.1	11.2	13.3	9.9	12.5	..	..	Syrian Arab Republic
23.9	21.2	20.9	20.3	20.4	15.9	19.4	19.7	18.7	20.3	Tunisia
16.7	17.3	15.3	15.3	17.8	21.5	23.4	25.9	21.3	18.9	Turkey
..	..	..	..	..	..	..	..	..	..	Yemen, Republic of
27.3	*28.8*	*28.2*	*29.6*	*29.9*	*30.8*	*26.5*	*32.0*	*33.8*	*..*	*EUROPE*
31.3	30.9	29.5	29.9	27.3	29.2	27.9	32.8	29.8	..	Bulgaria
18.9	10.8	11.6	12.1	9.7	10.8	10.2	12.2	9.4	..	Greece
28.6	29.3	28.4	28.9	27.1	25.5	26.2	28.2	29.8	28.2	Hungary
18.7	15.3	15.0	13.7	12.3	14.6	16.9	16.6	15.7	..	Malta
16.3	30.0	26.8	28.3	29.1	30.3	31.2	35.3	33.0	..	Poland
15.9	16.8	16.8	15.0	18.3	20.8	21.1	20.2	20.7	..	Portugal
..	..	..	..	..	..	..	..	..	..	Romania
36.4	35.5	35.9	38.0	40.6	40.1	23.9	43.8	53.4	..	Yugoslavia
24.4	23.2	23.6	23.7	24.3	24.3	25.7	26.9	26.8	..	**Low- & middle-income economies**
22.6	23.0	22.7	23.1	23.4	20.9	23.5	24.3	23.3	..	Severely indebted
23.5	21.8	21.8	22.4	23.7	24.2	26.4	26.7	26.4	..	**Low-income economies**
13.3	8.3	7.0	7.6	9.1	7.6	9.6	8.9	10.2	14.4	Low-income Africa
27.1	27.3	26.8	27.7	29.3	29.6	30.5	30.9	29.9	..	China and India
24.4	20.2	20.7	20.9	20.1	19.0	22.0	22.3	23.8	25.1	Other low-income
24.9	23.8	24.5	24.2	24.6	24.4	25.3	26.9	27.0	..	**Middle-income economies**
21.8	20.0	19.8	20.7	19.9	20.5	20.7	21.9	22.2	..	**High-income OECD members**
20.5	20.2	20.4	20.9	21.0	21.7	21.4	22.0	22.7	..	European Community members
31.8	30.9	30.2	31.2	32.3	32.4	33.0	34.0	34.9	..	Japan
18.1	15.2	14.8	16.3	14.3	13.4	12.8	13.8	14.1	..	United States
48.6	35.2	29.2	29.2	26.0	24.6	27.8	27.7	28.7	..	**Other high-income economies** /a

Table 15. Private consumption: percentage of gross domestic product

Percentage points	1970	1971	1972	1973	1974	1975	1976	1977	1978	1979	1980
SUB-SAHARAN AFRICA	*69.9*	*70.0*	*68.5*	*66.7*	*64.4*	*69.0*	*66.1*	*65.8*	*69.6*	*68.8*	*66.8*
Excluding Nigeria	*65.0*	*66.7*	*66.8*	*66.4*	*65.0*	*69.3*	*66.9*	*67.4*	*71.6*	*72.3*	*71.7*
Benin	81.6	82.9	83.6	80.7	83.5	86.6	90.0	88.7	89.8	88.3	95.7
Botswana	78.0	66.9	57.0	59.7	55.5	58.0	57.1	61.6	62.3	57.2	51.6
Burkina Faso	90.4	88.5	85.8	82.7	75.9	80.9	79.8	87.6	87.0	89.1	93.5
Burundi	86.6	87.5	87.2	85.4	89.1	91.6	85.1	77.5	80.7	82.8	86.5
Cameroon	70.5	75.3	75.3	71.8	69.2	72.0	76.4	71.1	72.0	76.3	75.5
Cape Verde	..	..	..	114.7	100.4	96.6	102.7	101.5	110.0	100.3	93.3
Central African Rep.	75.3	73.6	74.6	71.5	75.4	88.5	82.2	86.0	86.4	86.2	94.5
Chad	63.6	62.1	62.6	84.0	63.7	67.9	71.8	73.7	72.8	..	..
Comoros	..	..	..	..	..	..	..	..	..	..	..
Congo, People's Rep of the	81.8	76.3	77.0	62.3	53.4	70.7	77.5	73.7	67.1	54.9	46.8
Cote D'Ivoire	57.3	58.5	59.0	58.5	54.5	60.4	55.3	52.7	54.9	56.9	60.0
Ethiopia	78.9	80.3	78.5	75.9	76.1	79.4	76.9	80.2	81.1	82.0	79.9
Gabon	36.6	35.3	33.4	45.7	24.7	23.5	16.5	23.5	36.5	33.9	25.6
Gambia, The	78.6	86.6	78.1	84.0	77.5	63.3	86.0	75.8	91.3	70.9	75.1
Ghana	74.4	77.4	74.8	75.0	78.2	73.3	79.2	77.4	84.7	83.1	83.9
Guinea-Bissau	76.7	80.5	85.7	89.3	92.2	82.5	81.5	85.0	84.7	88.5	77.0
Kenya	60.2	64.7	62.2	59.0	64.4	68.2	61.6	55.8	60.5	64.4	62.1
Lesotho	120.4	126.1	133.1	132.1	149.9	151.2	163.9	157.2	129.7	144.8	123.9
Liberia	46.9	49.5	47.5	56.0	57.7	51.5	54.1	60.7	60.7	58.4	56.4
Madagascar	79.4	80.5	81.6	83.3	84.8	86.1	83.0	84.5	85.4	87.4	89.3
Malawi	72.8	78.0	76.4	74.2	69.4	68.9	68.1	66.4	62.7	68.4	69.9
Mali	79.9	80.2	80.4	87.1	103.8	94.1	88.7	81.5	92.2	92.1	91.5
Mauritania	56.2	55.1	53.2	71.5	76.9	67.3	65.2	65.3	65.3	70.9	67.8
Mauritius	75.3	76.6	69.4	66.4	59.4	61.6	62.8	67.2	67.9	67.3	75.5
Mozambique	..	..	..	..	..	..	..	..	..	..	76.2
Niger	88.8	87.2	85.9	84.7	93.5	86.6	84.9	75.7	70.7	71.1	67.1
Nigeria	81.4	77.5	72.6	68.6	63.5	68.5	64.9	63.7	66.8	64.5	61.5
Rwanda	88.0	87.6	87.8	81.0	86.7	78.2	74.3	71.0	76.6	76.6	83.3
Senegal	74.0	75.4	71.7	75.5	69.7	72.2	75.9	72.6	76.9	76.7	78.4
Seychelles	..	..	..	..	..	..	54.8	40.3	32.8	46.8	44.2
Sierra Leone	73.6	76.9	79.3	78.4	81.0	82.5	86.8	83.9	87.1	90.0	92.4
Somalia	83.2	85.0	70.8	79.1	71.1	71.6	67.0	103.4	82.8	88.5	97.3
Sudan	63.8	68.8	74.8	69.6	71.0	80.1	74.3	77.4	82.2	80.9	80.6
Swaziland	54.2	52.2	49.7	43.3	30.2	49.4	44.5	55.7	56.1	73.3	67.9
Tanzania	68.8	66.7	69.2	70.5	75.4	74.1	63.0	62.3	72.6	70.3	77.1
Togo	58.3	55.2	58.2	59.8	32.4	60.9	51.9	58.8	41.4	52.0	52.8
Uganda	..	..	..	..	..	..	..	..	..	..	..
Zaire	67.6	70.4	73.7	73.3	70.7	76.4	79.7	78.6	80.3	79.0	74.9
Zambia	39.4	41.4	39.7	33.3	34.9	51.4	44.8	51.5	55.6	53.1	55.2
Zimbabwe	66.9	67.8	59.8	61.0	61.1	62.1	63.5	61.1	65.6	68.5	64.5
SOUTH ASIA	*74.9*	*74.0*	*76.6*	*76.1*	*75.9*	*75.1*	*72.4*	*72.7*	*72.6*	*72.8*	*73.8*
Bangladesh	79.5	..	..	86.0	94.6	95.8	98.6	87.8	92.9	92.1	91.5
India	74.8	72.8	74.0	73.9	72.8	70.2	68.6	70.6	69.6	69.6	71.1
Nepal	..	..	..	..	..	82.4	80.8	79.2	79.2	79.9	82.2
Pakistan	80.9	80.9	78.8	78.3	83.8	84.4	81.3	79.3	80.6	83.8	83.1
Sri Lanka	72.3	72.4	71.8	76.5	80.2	82.6	76.1	73.3	75.2	77.1	80.3
EAST ASIA AND PACIFIC	*61.1*	*59.6*	*60.6*	*59.1*	*60.4*	*59.4*	*59.8*	*58.9*	*56.9*	*56.7*	*57.8*
China	57.1	55.5	57.2	56.2	57.3	55.4	56.7	56.2	52.6	53.9	56.3
Fiji	67.1	68.5	70.8	78.7	74.3	68.0	69.6	64.1	65.3	58.4	57.2
Indonesia	78.1	74.7	69.1	67.8	65.0	65.1	64.3	61.9	63.0	56.8	52.3
Korea, Republic of	75.5	75.5	73.7	70.0	69.7	70.5	65.1	61.9	61.2	62.0	64.2
Malaysia	57.7	59.2	58.5	53.2	53.4	56.5	50.9	50.2	51.7	48.3	50.5
Papua New Guinea	63.8	63.3	58.9	47.2	46.3	52.6	50.1	53.7	55.3	53.9	60.9
Philippines	70.9	71.4	72.0	67.8	68.9	67.7	65.6	65.8	67.1	66.0	67.0
Solomon islands	..	..	..	..	..	..	..	..	..	..	70.2
Thailand	67.5	67.1	68.4	64.7	66.4	67.6	67.5	67.9	64.9	67.5	67.5
Vanuatu	..	..	..	..	..	..	..	..	..	..	..

1981	1982	1983	1984	1985	1986	1987	1988	1989	1990	
72.8	76.2	76.4	74.7	74.9	73.7	70.7	72.5	71.8	..	*SUB-SAHARAN AFRICA*
73.0	73.2	73.8	70.1	70.6	71.3	71.8	73.1	73.2	..	*Excluding Nigeria*
103.6	92.2	89.0	96.2	81.8	85.8	84.2	89.6	86.6	..	Benin
51.9	61.6	54.4	48.3	44.9	37.6	42.1	41.6	43.3	..	Botswana
94.4	86.6	85.2	82.5	84.0	84.5	80.2	77.2	84.6	..	Burkina Faso
78.4	85.9	78.7	78.2	78.7	75.3	76.7	77.5	..	..	Burundi
68.9	68.2	62.3	57.9	55.1	59.7	69.5	75.8	69.0	71.1	Cameroon
88.8	84.3	83.6	88.0	87.7	84.6	72.1	74.5	76.4	..	Cape Verde
86.9	90.9	84.3	86.0	86.5	86.7	85.1	86.9	86.7	..	Central African Rep.
..	..	100.0	89.2	102.7	102.3	95.1	95.5	92.2	..	Chad
..	..	68.7	82.5	79.5	75.9	82.7	81.4	80.4	..	Comoros
56.5	40.0	39.8	38.8	52.5	67.7	59.4	69.9	60.3	49.0	Congo, People's Rep of the
63.8	62.5	64.2	62.3	60.3	61.8	68.2	65.3	68.5	..	Cote D'Ivoire
80.7	81.8	80.0	79.7	77.7	78.9	77.2	72.0	68.8	..	Ethiopia
26.7	27.3	29.5	27.2	30.4	46.8	47.8	52.1	47.2	..	Gabon
80.1	79.9	83.2	86.4	76.3	72.9	73.0	76.0	75.1	..	Gambia, The
87.2	89.8	90.8	86.0	83.1	81.0	78.9	76.3	..	..	Ghana
70.3	75.7	78.1	83.6	86.8	87.6	84.8	89.1	86.6	..	Guinea-Bissau
61.9	63.5	61.2	63.3	58.1	59.7	62.1	62.6	61.1	..	Kenya
134.8	141.6	167.3	164.5	145.3	141.8	144.9	128.0	135.9	..	Lesotho
61.9	65.9	70.9	68.6	64.7	64.5	..	..	..	..	Liberia
88.2	90.3	89.0	86.7	90.1	86.9	85.6	85.6	84.0	..	Madagascar
70.4	67.4	68.3	69.5	69.4	70.1	69.6	75.2	81.1	..	Malawi
90.4	89.7	93.9	92.6	102.4	90.3	82.8	82.3	78.5	..	Mali
65.7	79.1	93.7	84.7	76.4	71.0	73.1	79.9	78.9	..	Mauritania
71.3	70.8	69.5	68.5	66.9	60.9	61.1	61.9	66.1	66.5	Mauritius
74.3	79.7	82.2	80.2	80.6	75.7	90.1	95.1	94.5	..	Mozambique
80.4	80.5	81.1	91.4	86.8	82.9	83.8	82.9	84.7	..	Niger
72.3	79.3	79.0	79.1	79.1	80.8	69.8	74.0	70.2	63.7	Nigeria
78.6	81.9	83.9	81.0	80.5	79.7	80.7	80.7	80.1	..	Rwanda
82.2	75.3	78.2	74.1	79.8	75.9	74.6	74.5	73.0	..	Senegal
51.2	56.2	68.2	61.2	58.2	56.4	..	..	..	..	Seychelles
88.6	89.5	83.6	82.0	84.0	83.8	82.8	74.5	85.4	..	Sierra Leone
93.9	99.5	106.8	105.3	93.0	93.0	85.2	85.9	91.1	..	Somalia
83.0	81.0	89.3	84.1	94.2	80.8	80.1	84.3	83.3	..	Sudan
71.9	72.3	77.7	77.1	79.6	62.3	63.6	65.1	..	..	Swaziland
75.4	72.6	78.2	77.2	77.2	79.7	86.7	92.6	..	..	Tanzania
57.4	63.1	61.9	64.3	63.4	67.7	67.4	71.4	69.3	..	Togo
..	..	93.0	84.0	83.2	83.0	85.9	89.0	90.8	90.7	Uganda
74.3	78.6	79.0	72.5	76.1	76.1	78.4	76.6	74.8	..	Zaire
64.9	64.3	60.7	58.3	67.6	61.8	69.6	76.7	84.8	..	Zambia
67.0	65.0	68.9	59.2	55.5	54.5	49.1	52.0	54.5	56.4	Zimbabwe
71.2	72.3	72.4	72.3	70.2	69.5	69.7	69.4	68.7	69.8	*SOUTH ASIA*
89.8	92.0	93.0	91.8	91.1	88.9	87.7	88.2	90.7	..	Bangladesh
67.9	69.0	69.8	69.4	66.6	66.6	67.3	67.1	67.0	67.7	India
82.1	81.6	81.3	80.9	76.1	78.1	76.7	79.0	81.6	..	Nepal
80.6	81.3	80.1	80.2	81.6	76.3	72.6	72.0	72.0	..	Pakistan
80.9	80.4	78.5	72.2	78.3	78.0	77.6	78.6	78.5	..	Sri Lanka
59.6	60.5	59.9	58.4	58.6	57.9	56.1	56.5	..	..	*EAST ASIA AND PACIFIC*
58.5	58.6	57.6	55.3	56.0	56.0	54.8	56.4	..	..	China
63.7	62.5	64.0	62.9	62.2	61.2	65.0	69.2	70.4	..	Fiji
55.3	60.5	60.6	60.2	59.0	61.7	57.7	57.1	53.4	51.9	Indonesia
63.9	62.5	61.0	60.1	59.4	55.1	52.8	51.5	52.5	..	Korea, Republic of
53.1	53.1	52.1	49.8	52.0	51.0	47.4	49.4	52.1	..	Malaysia
66.2	64.7	64.5	63.5	67.0	64.8	63.3	60.2	64.0	..	Papua New Guinea
66.8	69.9	72.4	76.5	75.9	73.1	75.3	73.2	73.2	74.7	Philippines
74.7	61.2	60.8	57.3	64.4	67.3	74.1	69.2	..	..	Solomon islands
67.2	65.2	68.3	66.1	64.7	62.6	62.0	62.3	61.3	..	Thailand
..	..	51.6	48.5	57.2	65.0	60.5	51.4	..	..	Vanuatu

Table 15. Private consumption: percentage of gross domestic product (cont'd.)

Percentage points	1970	1971	1972	1973	1974	1975	1976	1977	1978	1979	1980
LATIN AMERICA AND CARIBBEAN	*69.3*	*70.1*	*70.1*	*68.4*	*67.5*	*66.5*	*67.0*	*66.8*	*66.9*	*67.0*	*66.5*
Argentina	68.2	69.6	69.1	67.6	66.3	61.2	59.0	60.3	60.1	65.6	66.8
Bahamas	..	..	..	..	..	..	..	55.7	58.1	65.9	61.7
Barbados	79.9	76.1	77.9	74.9	72.3	74.2	74.4	77.9	68.0	70.5	63.3
Belize	..	..	..	..	..	..	..	..	..	..	..
Bolivia	66.2	68.5	63.1	61.5	60.6	58.7	63.0	63.6	70.6	68.0	67.1
Brazil	68.6	69.6	69.7	67.5	70.7	66.5	68.8	69.2	68.6	69.5	69.8
Chile	70.1	71.3	75.2	80.8	62.4	73.2	68.9	72.8	71.1	70.7	70.7
Colombia	72.4	73.7	72.8	71.3	70.9	72.3	71.1	69.9	70.3	70.8	70.2
Costa Rica	73.7	72.2	70.0	68.2	73.8	71.6	66.3	65.2	67.6	66.9	65.5
Dominican Republic	76.6	80.1	76.2	73.4	78.0	71.6	80.9	78.3	77.5	73.4	77.0
Ecuador	75.3	76.0	73.5	67.0	59.8	65.2	63.6	61.7	63.4	61.2	59.6
El Salvador	76.1	76.1	74.1	74.1	74.9	71.8	68.0	64.5	72.5	68.9	71.8
Grenada	..	..	..	..	..	..	..	..	..	..	72.4
Guatemala	78.4	80.0	80.0	79.2	78.1	78.9	77.8	75.3	77.0	78.7	78.9
Guyana	60.8	59.6	62.0	64.7	54.7	47.4	59.3	60.7	56.2	52.2	51.8
Haiti	83.0	81.8	81.8	80.3	83.3	84.5	84.7	85.1	82.7	81.7	81.9
Honduras	73.8	71.8	71.0	71.6	74.0	77.7	72.3	68.9	65.7	65.9	69.4
Jamaica	60.9	62.6	67.3	61.8	68.0	66.2	69.8	68.5	63.6	63.1	66.0
Mexico	74.8	76.0	74.8	73.6	72.9	71.6	71.3	69.6	69.4	67.7	65.1
Nicaragua	74.6	74.8	71.6	77.3	74.3	78.6	70.5	69.4	71.0	74.0	82.5
Panama	60.6	57.7	55.2	53.1	57.7	57.3	55.7	60.0	58.4	60.5	56.5
Paraguay	77.5	79.5	77.0	73.8	75.8	75.1	72.5	72.1	69.8	71.2	79.4
Peru	70.4	70.6	72.3	68.8	70.1	74.1	74.1	73.5	68.8	61.0	61.3
St. Vincent and The Grenadines	..	..	..	..	..	..	..	91.0	67.6	77.7	78.3
Trinidad and Tobago	60.0	55.3	59.3	54.0	42.3	42.6	47.5	47.9	52.0	51.3	45.9
Uruguay	74.5	72.3	75.5	72.0	76.2	76.5	72.1	75.4	74.1	75.4	75.8
Venezuela	51.9	50.6	52.2	49.6	42.0	48.9	50.8	51.5	55.6	54.3	54.9
MIDDLE EAST AND NORTH AFRICA	*61.5*	*60.7*	*59.4*	*56.6*	*50.1*	*53.2*	*51.3*	*55.1*	*58.0*	*55.2*	*54.1*
Algeria	55.8	57.0	55.3	51.4	46.3	51.1	48.5	51.1	48.5	45.6	43.2
Egypt, Arab Republic of	65.9	66.0	66.6	63.8	73.5	62.9	58.5	62.0	63.1	68.7	69.2
Iran, Islamic Rep. of	59.1	55.9	53.5	47.5	35.1	39.0	39.7	49.3	53.7	47.1	49.8
Jordan	..	..	..	..	..	..	..	..	..	..	..
Morocco	73.4	72.5	73.0	72.7	68.0	69.4	68.9	65.6	67.5	67.0	67.9
Oman	19.4	17.1	24.9	24.0	8.7	15.9	20.5	26.8	32.8	26.1	27.7
Syrian Arab Republic	72.5	72.4	67.8	70.0	67.1	66.4	63.3	67.4	69.0	69.1	66.5
Tunisia	66.5	64.8	63.9	66.0	60.6	62.2	62.1	63.5	62.5	60.4	61.5
Turkey	69.7	72.3	69.9	70.7	73.3	72.7	69.0	69.4	71.4	71.0	73.4
Yemen, Republic of	..	..	..	..	..	..	..	..	..	..	..
EUROPE	*..*	*..*	*..*	*..*	*..*	*..*	*..*	*..*	*..*	*..*	*57.3*
Bulgaria	..	..	..	..	..	..	..	..	..	..	61.1
Greece	67.6	67.7	66.6	63.8	66.4	67.8	66.9	66.0	63.4	61.3	63.9
Hungary	58.4	58.1	57.2	56.3	58.2	59.2	58.1	57.4	57.4	58.8	61.2
Malta	77.8	76.8	78.7	77.8	81.3	71.6	66.6	71.9	67.1	63.2	64.7
Poland	..	..	..	..	..	..	..	..	..	..	67.4
Portugal	66.5	67.3	62.5	64.5	72.6	73.1	73.7	72.0	68.0	67.5	66.6
Romania	..	..	..	..	..	..	..	..	..	..	..
Yugoslavia	55.2	56.9	57.5	59.2	62.1	56.1	53.2	52.9	53.0	51.5	48.8
Low- & middle-income economies	66.1	65.8	66.0	64.4	63.6	63.4	62.5	62.5	62.7	62.0	62.1
Severely indebted	68.9	69.6	69.7	68.0	67.1	66.3	66.5	66.1	66.3	66.5	66.1
Low-income economies	66.6	65.4	66.5	65.4	65.8	65.6	64.8	64.4	63.6	63.2	63.6
Low-income Africa	70.8	70.9	69.6	68.0	66.0	70.8	67.8	67.5	71.2	70.0	67.9
China and India	63.9	62.1	63.4	62.7	63.4	60.7	61.4	62.0	59.0	59.5	61.7
Other low-income	76.4	75.5	77.4	73.5	75.4	77.4	73.1	69.0	70.6	68.1	64.8
Middle-income economies	66.0	66.3	65.8	63.8	62.3	62.1	61.3	61.6	62.3	61.5	61.3
High-income OECD members	59.9	59.6	59.5	58.6	58.9	60.3	60.0	60.0	59.5	59.6	60.1
European Community members	58.7	58.4	58.7	58.0	58.4	59.6	58.8	59.0	58.6	58.9	59.4
Japan	52.5	53.6	54.0	53.6	54.5	57.3	57.6	57.8	57.6	58.6	58.8
United States	62.8	62.3	62.1	61.3	61.6	63.0	62.9	62.6	61.9	61.8	62.8
Other high-income economies /a	52.0	47.9	45.4	43.5	32.9	33.7	33.0	34.5	38.3	38.3	36.6

a. Economies classified by the United Nations or otherwise regarded by their authorities as developing.

1981	1982	1983	1984	1985	1986	1987	1988	1989	1990	
66.4	67.2	67.7	67.9	67.0	69.1	65.3	65.5	67.5	..	*LATIN AMERICA AND CARIBBEAN*
68.0	69.8	64.8	73.5	73.8	77.1	69.4	69.4	71.0	75.4	Argentina
62.3	59.1	57.4	65.4	62.9	63.5	63.7	..	..	..	Bahamas
70.6	67.1	69.0	66.2	61.9	64.0	66.4	63.1	67.2	..	Barbados
64.6	68.5	69.0	62.1	64.9	57.8	58.1	60.6	62.7	..	Belize
77.4	65.8	69.9	65.6	78.0	83.3	83.0	80.1	79.9	..	Bolivia
68.1	69.7	71.6	71.0	68.3	67.8	62.5	61.2	65.4	..	Brazil
74.5	75.3	73.3	73.0	69.3	68.9	67.6	65.3	66.4	69.0	Chile
72.5	72.9	71.9	70.6	69.0	65.3	66.4	66.0	66.0	63.5	Colombia
60.1	57.8	61.5	61.3	60.6	58.5	62.0	62.6	63.3	69.8	Costa Rica
71.1	75.2	73.7	67.6	77.5	76.5	78.5	76.3	75.7	..	Dominican Republic
61.6	63.1	65.9	64.1	64.5	66.9	70.7	68.9	71.3	69.5	Ecuador
76.0	76.1	77.5	78.8	81.2	77.9	81.0	80.9	81.8	87.1	El Salvador
68.0	74.5	76.6	74.1	72.7	73.7	72.7	71.3	..	..	Grenada
81.6	82.0	82.9	82.9	82.6	81.1	84.9	84.1	83.9	85.0	Guatemala
63.4	63.8	66.3	63.7	69.0	61.9	65.9	55.1	..	..	Guyana
87.1	82.2	83.4	82.4	82.0	84.5	84.8	85.8	85.5	..	Haiti
72.0	74.5	74.3	73.0	71.6	70.2	71.3	72.7	72.8	77.5	Honduras
69.3	68.8	69.7	67.1	69.6	63.9	62.5	65.9	..	..	Jamaica
64.4	61.6	60.9	63.1	63.8	68.0	65.3	68.8	70.7	75.0	Mexico
73.9	67.9	56.7	55.4	48.2	55.8	52.0	..	..	..	Nicaragua
53.3	54.0	56.7	63.0	62.8	57.7	57.5	59.0	67.0	71.8	Panama
76.9	77.7	75.3	77.4	80.4	78.0	78.5	71.8	79.3	72.1	Paraguay
63.2	61.8	65.0	62.9	62.4	68.2	67.3	66.3	67.8	65.1	Peru
70.5	78.6	73.0	63.7	58.0	67.3	..	..	..	..	St. Vincent and The Grenadines
49.9	62.8	66.7	61.2	51.0	62.3	56.7	57.5	56.4	..	Trinidad and Tobago
74.4	73.1	74.5	73.5	74.8	74.0	76.0	73.3	71.9	..	Uruguay
57.9	62.4	67.6	61.0	61.8	68.9	64.7	68.4	64.1	56.2	Venezuela
55.3	59.4	58.1	62.6	63.0	63.7	62.1	62.1	61.5	..	*MIDDLE EAST AND NORTH AFRICA*
45.5	46.0	45.4	47.7	47.9	52.7	49.5	53.0	53.5	49.1	Algeria
66.9	67.0	65.0	67.9	68.2	69.6	79.4	78.3	80.5	..	Egypt, Arab Republic of
50.6	64.0	58.5	67.2	67.1	64.8	64.3	64.7	60.7	..	Iran, Islamic Rep. of
..	..	83.8	81.0	83.0	77.0	74.1	77.0	77.7	81.6	Jordan
69.4	67.9	68.1	69.8	66.0	68.2	68.1	63.6	65.4	67.0	Morocco
25.8	31.9	31.4	30.8	33.9	51.5	..	..	..	..	Oman
73.4	65.4	67.8	65.2	65.1	65.4	71.9	71.6	..	..	Syrian Arab Republic
61.3	62.3	62.2	63.2	63.0	66.7	64.2	64.2	64.5	63.5	Tunisia
72.4	71.8	74.5	75.6	73.6	69.6	67.5	65.3	67.8	68.0	Turkey
..	..	..	..	..	..	..	..	..	..	Yemen, Republic of
57.1	55.1	56.4	56.5	56.0	55.2	54.9	54.8	53.3	..	*EUROPE*
62.5	61.9	62.6	62.6	64.2	62.3	64.7	60.1	62.9	..	Bulgaria
63.2	70.9	69.6	68.4	69.9	69.7	69.9	67.2	69.0	..	Greece
61.3	60.8	61.5	61.4	62.8	63.9	63.5	60.6	59.3	61.0	Hungary
64.0	66.2	67.0	68.9	70.0	68.0	65.2	66.1	66.3	..	Malta
74.2	61.8	64.4	62.4	61.5	60.6	59.8	56.5	..	..	Poland
69.3	68.8	68.6	70.5	67.5	65.6	65.5	66.5	66.2	..	Portugal
..	..	..	..	..	..	..	..	..	..	Romania
48.6	49.4	49.8	48.3	46.1	46.3	43.0	47.9	40.3	..	Yugoslavia
63.3	64.4	64.1	64.5	64.1	64.1	62.2	62.3	62.4	..	**Low- & middle-income economies**
66.4	66.1	66.8	67.2	66.4	68.3	65.0	64.7	67.2	..	Severely indebted
65.6	67.6	67.1	65.9	65.6	65.3	63.7	64.0	..	..	Low-income economies
75.0	79.5	79.7	78.9	79.2	79.0	76.0	77.3	77.4	..	Low-income Africa
62.2	62.8	62.5	60.9	60.5	60.8	60.5	60.9	..	..	China and India
66.2	69.8	69.8	69.6	69.5	70.3	68.1	67.8	64.6	..	Other low-income
62.2	62.9	62.5	63.7	63.2	63.6	61.5	61.5	62.3	..	Middle-income economies
60.1	61.3	61.8	61.2	61.7	61.5	61.5	61.0	60.7	..	**High-income OECD members**
60.2	60.4	60.2	59.9	59.9	59.6	59.9	59.6	59.3	..	European Community members
58.2	59.1	59.7	58.9	58.0	57.6	57.5	56.8	56.2	..	Japan
62.0	64.2	65.0	64.0	65.1	65.9	66.3	66.0	65.5	..	United States
34.8	42.0	46.7	47.3	49.9	52.0	50.5	52.3	51.8	..	**Other high-income economies** /a

Table 16. Current account balance before official transfers

Percentage of GDP	1970	1971	1972	1973	1974	1975	1976	1977	1978	1979	1980
SUB-SAHARAN AFRICA	..	..	..	..	..	..	..	..	..	..	..
Excluding Nigeria	..	..	..	..	..	..	..	..	..	..	..
Benin	-8.5	-8.6	-13.2	-8.9	-14.8	-19.1	-22.1	-20.8	-19.9	-14.0	-17.2
Botswana	-41.8	-37.6	-34.7	-24.6	-7.1	-12.2	-8.9	-14.6	-28.9	-14.3	-23.2
Burkina Faso	-5.2	-8.0	-8.8	-10.1	-14.5	-18.4	-13.5	-18.3	-16.4	-15.6	-15.2
Burundi	-1.0	-5.8	-3.6	-2.1	-5.6	-10.6	-2.5	-1.7	-9.9	-9.9	-13.9
Cameroon	-4.1	-5.0	-7.6	-2.0	-1.7	-7.2	-4.8	-3.7	-4.5	-2.7	-6.4
Cape Verde	..	..	..	..	..	..	..	..	-33.0	-37.2	-17.6
Central African Rep.	-13.4	-12.1	-12.2	-11.6	-18.0	-22.7	-9.7	-11.3	-12.6	-14.5	-17.6
Chad	-10.0	-9.6	-9.0	-13.4	-13.7	-22.0	-14.9	-19.9	-20.8	-6.2	-2.2
Comoros	..	..	..	..	..	..	..	..	..	..	..
Congo, People's Rep of the	-19.4	-24.5	-28.1	-16.6	-19.8	-37.2	-35.6	-28.8	-26.4	-11.9	-13.5
Cote D'Ivoire	-5.1	-9.2	-8.5	-10.9	-3.5	-10.8	-6.0	-3.5	-11.1	-15.2	-17.5
Ethiopia	-2.4	-3.0	-0.3	2.6	0.8	-3.0	-0.3	-2.7	-5.1	-4.8	-4.5
Gabon	-4.7	2.4	-7.1	-9.1	12.7	1.4	0.3	2.5	1.6	7.0	8.2
Gambia, The	0.1	-4.8	-2.2	-7.0	-0.9	6.1	-15.1	-7.2	-31.2	-25.2	-47.8
Ghana	-3.4	-6.4	4.3	4.4	-6.9	-0.1	-3.8	-4.5	-3.0	1.0	-1.2
Guinea-Bissau	..	..	..	..	..	..	..	..	..	..	..
Kenya	-5.4	-10.3	-5.1	-6.6	-11.9	-8.6	-4.6	-0.8	-13.9	-9.3	-13.8
Lesotho	-1.4	-7.1	-15.5	-12.6	-22.9	-14.1	-27.4	-20.3	-16.4	-27.1	-31.8
Liberia	-6.6	-4.7	-3.8	-2.2	-8.5	6.3	4.3	-5.4	-3.9	-1.7	0.9
Madagascar	-3.8	-6.6	-3.8	-4.0	-4.8	-6.1	-4.5	-3.7	-5.8	-14.0	-15.4
Malawi	-15.8	-11.2	-14.1	-8.4	-7.7	-14.1	-10.3	-10.9	-22.5	-29.5	-25.0
Mali	-6.4	-7.6	-8.3	-15.5	-27.9	-19.6	-9.5	-5.8	-17.3	-14.6	-14.4
Mauritania	-6.4	-4.8	-8.7	-9.2	-5.3	-30.5	-45.5	-46.3	-43.7	-37.3	-35.4
Mauritius	2.4	-3.3	3.3	-0.5	6.8	1.8	-5.5	-10.5	-12.4	-12.8	-11.5
Mozambique	..	..	..	..	..	..	..	..	..	..	-17.5
Niger	-5.0	-2.0	-4.4	-6.3	-12.0	-6.7	-12.3	-13.2	-18.0	-13.2	-16.9
Nigeria	-3.0	-2.7	-2.0	0.0	14.2	0.1	-0.7	-1.7	-6.0	2.2	5.1
Rwanda	-5.6	-9.0	-11.4	-2.6	-11.8	-11.7	-5.7	-6.0	-16.0	-7.5	-13.4
Senegal	-7.7	-10.5	-6.9	-14.4	-10.8	-9.4	-9.6	-8.1	-15.9	-14.0	-17.5
Seychelles	1.1	-18.2	-24.1	-23.9	-14.8	-18.6	-19.3	-17.4	-16.1	-16.7	-20.4
Sierra Leone	-4.7	-5.7	-2.9	-7.4	-14.5	-11.4	-10.6	-10.0	-16.0	-20.7	-19.0
Somalia	-5.7	-4.9	-5.4	-12.7	-21.4	-14.1	-13.5	-27.8	-16.4	-44.7	-46.2
Sudan	-2.2	-1.9	-2.3	1.2	-8.1	-10.9	-8.1	-4.5	-6.5	-5.9	-8.2
Swaziland	..	..	..	..	10.4	11.4	7.9	-0.7	-25.8	-37.9	-38.9
Tanzania	-2.9	-7.4	-4.9	-6.8	-15.4	-12.4	-2.7	-4.8	-14.7	-11.1	-9.1
Togo	-5.4	-8.6	-13.1	-10.1	16.6	-19.1	-9.8	-16.7	-32.7	-33.4	-15.9
Uganda	1.0	-4.2	0.6	1.8	-1.1	-2.9	1.3	2.1	-5.5	0.5	-7.0
Zaire	-2.8	-5.2	-6.5	-4.4	-4.9	-6.8	-9.4	-12.7	2.0	1.0	-3.8
Zambia	6.0	-14.9	-11.2	4.6	0.3	-29.5	-5.0	-9.2	-11.4	0.1	-14.0
Zimbabwe	-1.7	-4.1	-0.7	-1.3	-3.4	-6.7	-0.7	..	..	..	-5.6
SOUTH ASIA	..	..	..	..	..	..	..	..	..	..	..
Bangladesh	-3.5	-4.8	-9.5	-6.4	-6.1	-7.1	-12.2	-6.4	-8.0	-7.3	-11.2
India	-1.0	-1.2	-0.7	-0.7	-1.0	-0.1	1.3	1.4	-0.3	-0.7	-1.7
Nepal	-2.9	-3.2	-1.2	-2.7	-4.7	-2.8	-0.6	-2.4	-3.5	-3.0	-5.1
Pakistan	-7.0	-5.6	-3.1	-2.0	-6.2	-10.4	-7.1	-7.0	-3.4	-5.7	-4.8
Sri Lanka	-3.6	-2.7	-2.5	-1.7	-6.4	-6.3	-2.3	3.0	-4.5	-11.0	-19.7
EAST ASIA AND PACIFIC	..	..	..	..	..	..	..	..	..	..	..
China	-0.1	-0.1	-0.1	0.4	-0.5	-0.2	0.2	0.3	0.1	0.0	0.3
Fiji	-8.2	-12.7	-12.5	-15.2	-5.9	-4.1	-7.5	-4.0	-4.6	-7.8	-5.0
Indonesia	-3.9	-4.2	-3.3	-3.1	2.0	-3.5	-2.3	-0.2	-2.6	1.7	3.6
Korea, Republic of	-7.9	-9.3	-3.9	-2.5	-11.0	-9.3	-1.6	-0.1	-2.2	-6.5	-8.6
Malaysia	0.0	-2.8	-4.8	1.1	-5.6	-5.3	5.0	3.1	0.5	4.2	-1.3
Papua New Guinea	-37.0	-41.3	-18.0	2.4	-0.1	-10.2	-6.9	-7.9	-15.8	-7.6	-22.7
Philippines	-1.9	-1.3	-1.2	3.2	-2.5	-6.8	-6.7	-4.2	-5.0	-5.5	-5.8
Solomon islands	..	..	..	..	..	-39.9	-17.0	-8.7	-18.1	-7.0	-27.0
Thailand	-4.2	-2.9	-1.0	-0.7	-0.8	-4.4	-2.7	-5.6	-4.9	-7.8	-6.9
Vanuatu	..	..	..	..	..	..	..	..	..	..	..

1981	1982	1983	1984	1985	1986	1987	1988	1989	1990	
..	..	..	..	..	..	..	..	..	..	**SUB-SAHARAN AFRICA**
..	..	..	..	..	..	..	..	..	..	*Excluding Nigeria*
-26.4	-37.9	-10.5	-12.9	-11.2	-9.9	-9.4	-10.0	-3.4	..	Benin
-34.1	-19.5	-13.4	-9.9	3.8	4.9	36.2	12.7	6.9	..	Botswana
-14.1	-18.0	-15.9	-12.6	-13.1	-11.4	-9.5	-9.0	-12.7	-11.1	Burkina Faso
-13.0	-17.7	-16.5	-16.5	-10.3	-11.4	-17.8	-14.5	-15.1	..	Burundi
-6.1	-5.3	-1.7	1.8	4.0	-5.7	-9.8	-7.2	-2.7	..	Cameroon
-30.6	-35.3	-37.2	-34.1	-37.6	-23.5	-15.2	-15.2	..	..	Cape Verde
-11.2	-15.3	-16.3	-15.4	-16.6	-19.1	-18.6	-16.0	-14.4	-15.9	Central African Rep.
-3.3	-7.4	-13.0	-12.1	-30.3	-33.1	-32.5	-24.1	-23.8	..	Chad
..	-26.3	-27.9	-59.7	-40.3	-29.1	-30.3	-22.9	-17.9	..	Comoros
-25.3	-16.7	-20.9	7.7	-9.3	-35.7	-12.6	-23.0	-5.6	-12.7	Congo, People's Rep of the
-16.9	-13.8	-14.1	-1.5	0.6	-3.9	-7.8	-13.0	-11.2	..	Cote D'Ivoire
-6.4	-9.0	-7.0	-8.6	-8.8	-7.0	-8.8	-8.2	-6.3	-8.4	Ethiopia
9.7	7.9	2.0	2.5	-4.8	-31.1	-13.9	-19.4	-5.6	..	Gabon
-49.2	-26.0	-25.8	-1.2	-0.4	-1.8	0.6	-33.5	-7.7	..	Gambia, The
-12.0	-4.8	-6.1	-4.1	-5.4	-2.9	-4.3	-5.0	-5.9	-9.0	Ghana
..	-48.0	-44.0	-47.3	-48.1	-50.8	-35.4	-47.2	-56.7	..	Guinea-Bissau
-9.9	-5.5	-2.7	-3.9	-3.6	-2.6	-8.0	-8.4	-10.5	..	Kenya
-34.6	-23.7	-25.2	-29.2	-26.0	-30.2	-14.5	-34.6	-38.3	-10.0	Lesotho
0.6	-8.0	-20.3	-9.6	-3.2	-7.5	-14.3	..	..	..	Liberia
-12.4	-11.0	-9.2	-9.2	-8.9	-8.3	-10.0	-12.3	-11.1	..	Madagascar
-15.6	-13.0	-13.8	-6.1	-13.2	-10.1	-6.9	-9.6	-10.9	-8.6	Malawi
-17.4	-16.6	-18.8	-19.3	-31.1	-23.5	-16.4	-16.8	-15.3	-14.3	Mali
-35.3	-49.4	-37.9	-29.9	-35.0	-36.7	-26.3	-20.6	-15.7	-18.3	Mauritania
-14.1	-5.8	-2.9	-6.2	-4.0	5.1	2.1	-4.1	-3.8	..	Mauritius
-20.3	-23.4	-22.2	-18.8	-13.0	-14.0	-47.0	-52.2	-61.9	..	Mozambique
-15.8	-19.5	-11.1	-9.9	-19.2	-6.6	-9.7	-8.3	-11.9	-10.6	Niger
-6.4	-7.8	-4.8	0.2	2.8	0.8	-0.3	-0.7	-0.9	5.7	Nigeria
-13.1	-13.6	-10.7	-8.9	-10.3	-9.6	-11.7	-11.1	-10.7	..	Rwanda
-25.9	-17.4	-18.1	-17.7	-17.7	-11.9	-10.2	-9.5	-8.5	..	Senegal
-20.5	-34.1	-27.5	-18.7	-19.9	-23.4	-17.4	-20.2	-21.8	..	Seychelles
-14.0	-16.1	-3.4	-4.4	-0.9	9.5	-6.0	-1.0	..	-14.2	Sierra Leone
-30.1	-44.0	-39.5	-41.4	-34.3	-37.3	-45.1	-30.2	-42.6	-43.8	Somalia
-10.8	-17.4	-12.0	-8.5	-9.6	-9.1	-7.1	-11.2	-7.4	..	Sudan
-28.2	-34.4	-33.9	-31.1	-29.6	-13.1	3.1	-3.5	-10.9	..	Swaziland
-6.0	-7.6	-4.4	-5.1	-5.9	-8.1	-21.8	-24.8	-21.9	..	Tanzania
-11.8	-18.9	-14.5	-6.8	-12.9	-15.7	-15.0	-9.8	-8.9	-7.9	Togo
-7.4	-7.1	-4.3	-3.0	-1.3	-1.9	-5.0	-7.0	-8.9	..	Uganda
-6.2	-5.2	-4.6	-7.0	-6.9	-7.0	-11.2	-10.2	-9.4	-13.2	Zaire
-19.1	-15.3	-9.3	-6.0	-17.9	-19.3	-8.2	-7.0	-1.4	-8.0	Zambia
-11.3	-11.0	-8.1	-3.7	-3.2	-1.0	-0.6	0.8	-3.1	-7.0	Zimbabwe
..	..	..	..	..	..	..	..	..	..	**SOUTH ASIA**
-10.0	-12.0	-9.1	-6.8	-8.2	-7.0	-5.5	-5.9	-6.9	..	Bangladesh
-2.0	-1.7	-1.5	-1.8	-2.7	-2.6	-2.5	-3.3	-3.0	-3.3	India
-4.6	-6.0	-9.8	-8.1	-7.4	-8.0	-7.6	-7.4	-10.1	..	Nepal
-3.6	-5.0	-1.8	-3.2	-5.4	-3.9	-2.2	-4.4	-4.8	-4.1	Pakistan
-13.7	-14.5	-12.1	-3.4	-9.8	-9.1	-7.4	-8.6	-7.7	..	Sri Lanka
..	..	..	..	..	..	..	..	..	..	**EAST ASIA AND PACIFIC**
1.0	2.2	1.5	0.8	-4.1	-3.1	-0.3	-1.2	-1.1	1.5	China
-16.3	-9.5	-8.1	-3.9	-4.0	-1.8	-2.9	1.5	-4.5	-4.4	Fiji
-0.9	-5.8	-7.5	-2.2	-2.2	-5.1	-3.0	-1.8	-1.6	..	Indonesia
-6.8	-3.6	-2.0	-1.5	-1.0	4.3	7.5	8.2	2.4	..	Korea, Republic of
-10.0	-13.5	-11.7	-5.0	-2.1	-0.6	8.1	5.2	-0.6	-1.8	Malaysia
-32.1	-31.4	-24.6	-22.8	-15.4	-12.1	-13.4	-11.9	-18.8	-17.8	Papua New Guinea
-5.8	-8.4	-8.7	-4.8	-0.7	2.4	-1.9	-1.7	-4.1	..	Philippines
-34.1	-19.7	-19.4	-5.5	-20.3	-26.6	-26.7	-34.5	-38.1	..	Solomon islands
-7.7	-3.1	-7.6	-5.4	-4.4	0.2	-1.0	-3.1	-3.8	-4.7	Thailand
..	-23.3	-17.4	-7.1	-19.1	-21.3	-31.5	-20.1	..	..	Vanuatu

Table 16. Current account balance before official transfers (cont'd.)

Percentage of GDP	1970	1971	1972	1973	1974	1975	1976	1977	1978	1979	1980
LATIN AMERICA AND CARIBBEAN	..	..	..	..	..	..	..	..	..	..	..
Argentina	-0.7	-1.5	-0.9	1.8	..	-3.3	1.7	2.7	4.3	-1.0	-8.4
Bahamas	..	..	..	-22.1	-19.8	6.4	12.4	8.5	4.1	0.4	-2.6
Barbados	-23.7	-18.0	-19.4	-18.9	-14.2	-10.4	-15.1	-11.0	-6.1	-5.8	-3.1
Belize	..	..	..	..	..	..	..	..	..	..	..
Bolivia	0.2	-0.7	-1.0	0.2	7.7	-8.1	-3.3	-5.9	-15.1	-16.1	-1.7
Brazil	-2.0	-3.4	-2.9	-2.7	-7.2	-5.7	-4.3	-2.9	-3.5	-4.7	-5.5
Chile	-1.2	-2.0	-3.9	-2.8	-2.7	-6.9	1.3	-4.2	-7.2	-5.8	-7.3
Colombia	-4.6	-6.2	-2.5	-0.8	-3.1	-1.4	1.0	1.9	1.0	1.6	-0.6
Costa Rica	-7.8	-11.0	-8.3	-7.3	-16.0	-11.1	-8.4	-7.4	-10.3	-13.7	-13.6
Dominican Republic	-6.9	-7.8	-2.4	-4.2	-8.3	-2.2	-3.3	-2.9	-6.6	-6.5	-10.9
Ecuador	-7.3	-10.2	-4.5	-0.5	0.6	-5.5	-0.6	-5.7	-9.6	-7.0	-5.7
El Salvador	0.7	-1.4	0.8	-3.4	-8.6	-5.3	0.8	0.8	-9.5	0.4	0.0
Grenada	..	..	..	..	..	..	..	..	..	..	-19.8
Guatemala	-0.4	-2.4	-0.5	0.3	-3.2	-1.8	-1.8	-0.7	-4.5	-3.0	-2.1
Guyana	..	-2.7	-5.3	-21.1	-2.2	-4.6	-31.7	-22.0	-4.6	-16.0	-21.4
Haiti	1.0	-6.0	-6.3	-7.8	-10.8	-17.0	-15.3	-7.1	-8.4	-8.6	-9.4
Honduras	-9.3	-3.6	-2.0	-4.2	-11.9	-11.1	-8.5	-8.3	-9.0	-9.3	-13.0
Jamaica	-10.6	-10.7	-10.6	-12.7	-3.5	-10.1	-10.3	-1.4	-2.3	-6.1	-6.6
Mexico	-2.9	-2.0	-2.0	-2.4	-3.8	-4.4	-3.7	-2.2	-3.0	-3.9	-5.5
Nicaragua	-5.5	-5.7	2.0	-8.9	-17.7	-12.7	-2.7	-9.2	-1.7	5.7	-25.8
Panama	-7.7	-7.8	-9.2	-9.0	-14.9	-10.3	-10.2	-8.8	-9.7	-12.9	-10.9
Paraguay	-3.2	-3.9	-1.2	-2.0	-4.1	-5.6	-4.2	-2.8	-4.6	-6.2	-13.5
Peru	2.0	-0.9	-0.7	-2.8	-5.6	-9.6	-8.0	-6.9	-2.0	3.9	-1.2
St. Vincent and The Grenadines	..	..	..	..	..	..	..	..	0.0	-14.9	-23.2
Trinidad and Tobago	-12.7	-18.1	-10.9	-1.8	13.9	14.0	11.0	6.0	1.7	-0.3	5.7
Uruguay	-2.3	-2.6	2.0	0.6	-3.6	-5.5	-2.2	-4.0	-2.6	-4.9	-7.1
Venezuela	-0.7	0.0	-0.6	4.4	19.4	6.8	0.8	-7.1	-11.9	0.6	6.8
MIDDLE EAST AND NORTH AFRICA	..	..	..	..	..	..	..	..	..	..	..
Algeria	-3.3	-3.5	-2.5	-5.1	4.3	-10.8	-5.1	-11.1	-13.5	-4.9	0.5
Egypt, Arab Republic of	-5.9	-5.7	-5.3	-5.8	-17.7	-21.2	-10.2	-9.9	-9.2	-10.6	-6.6
Iran, Islamic Rep. of	-4.4	-0.9	-2.3	0.6	26.9	9.2	11.5	3.5	0.2	13.3	-2.6
Jordan	..	..	..	..	..	..	..	..	..	..	..
Morocco	-4.1	-2.2	0.3	1.0	2.5	-6.3	-15.1	-16.9	-10.5	-9.8	-8.1
Oman	..	..	..	..	9.4	-7.2	-0.6	0.3	-2.5	9.9	14.0
Syrian Arab Republic	-3.3	-3.0	-0.5	-0.8	-4.8	-8.2	-15.4	-17.0	-8.6	-6.9	-9.7
Tunisia	-6.1	-1.2	-1.6	-3.7	0.6	-4.9	-10.3	-12.3	-8.5	-5.1	-5.3
Turkey	-0.5	-0.2	1.2	3.1	-2.0	-4.7	-4.9	-6.6	-2.4	-2.1	-6.0
Yemen, Republic of	..	..	..	..	..	..	..	..	..	..	..
EUROPE	..	..	..	..	..	..	..	..	..	..	..
Bulgaria	..	..	..	..	..	..	..	..	..	..	..
Greece	-4.3	-3.1	-3.2	-7.3	-6.1	-4.2	-4.2	..	-3.0	-4.9	..
Hungary	..	..	..	..	..	..	..	..	..	..	..
Malta	-12.9	-4.9	3.7	7.9	-3.4	11.3	9.9	5.9	7.6	2.7	1.8
Poland	..	..	..	..	..	..	..	..	..	..	-6.3
Portugal	-2.6	2.1	..	..	..	-4.9	..	..	..	-0.3	-4.3
Romania	..	..	..	..	..	..	..	..	..	..	..
Yugoslavia	-2.8	-2.7	2.7	2.4	-3.6	-2.1	0.5	-2.9	-2.3	-5.3	-3.2
Low- & middle-income economies	..	..	..	..	..	..	..	..	..	..	..
Severely indebted	..	..	..	..	..	..	..	..	..	..	..
Low-income economies	..	..	..	..	..	..	..	..	..	..	..
Low-income Africa	..	..	..	..	..	..	..	..	..	..	..
China and India	..	..	..	..	..	..	..	..	..	..	..
Other low-income	..	..	..	..	..	..	..	..	..	..	..
Middle-income economies	..	..	..	..	..	..	..	..	..	..	..
High-income OECD members	..	..	..	..	..	..	..	..	..	..	..
European Community members	..	..	..	..	..	..	..	..	..	..	..
Japan	1.1	2.6	2.3	0.0	-1.0	-0.1	0.7	1.6	1.7	-0.8	-0.9
United States	0.5	0.1	-0.2	0.7	0.6	1.4	0.5	-0.5	-0.5	0.2	0.3
Other high-income economies /a	..	..	..	..	..	..	..	..	..	..	..

a. Economies classified by the United Nations or otherwise regarded by their authorities as developing.

1981	1982	1983	1984	1985	1986	1987	1988	1989	1990	
..	..	..	..	..	..	..	..	..	..	*LATIN AMERICA AND CARIBBEAN*
-8.2	-4.1	-3.8	-3.2	-1.4	-3.6	-5.3	-1.7	-2.2	-0.2	Argentina
-6.5	-5.4	-3.0	-3.0	-7.2	-1.6	-6.6	-5.1	-6.5	..	Bahamas
-11.9	-4.2	-4.4	1.8	4.1	-0.7	-2.8	1.3	-8.2	..	Barbados
..	..	..	-7.5	-1.9	0.0	-2.5	-4.6	-9.2	..	Belize
-13.5	-6.4	-7.2	-8.8	-11.7	-12.2	-12.5	-9.8	-8.8	..	Bolivia
-4.4	-5.7	-3.3	0.0	-0.1	-2.0	-0.5	1.3	0.2	-0.9	Brazil
-14.7	-9.7	-5.9	-11.3	-8.4	-7.0	-4.6	-1.3	-4.3	-5.2	Chile
-5.4	-7.8	-7.8	-3.7	-5.2	1.1	0.9	-0.5	0.1	..	Colombia
-15.6	-10.5	-10.4	-7.1	-7.7	-4.4	-9.8	-8.5	-9.6	-12.7	Costa Rica
-5.5	-6.3	-6.4	-4.4	-4.9	-4.3	-8.7	-4.7	-4.3	-3.9	Dominican Republic
-7.3	-9.8	-6.9	-2.8	0.3	-5.2	-11.6	-6.2	-6.1	..	Ecuador
-7.9	-6.8	-5.4	-5.9	-6.2	-3.0	-4.8	-5.0	-7.9	-6.9	El Salvador
-35.5	-42.0	-31.4	-20.1	-21.9	-27.5	-21.7	-15.3	..	..	Grenada
-6.7	-4.6	-2.5	-4.0	-2.5	-0.6	-7.6	-6.2	-5.1	-6.2	Guatemala
-31.6	-28.9	-32.9	-22.6	-20.4	-28.8	-35.5	-24.3	-51.0	..	Guyana
-15.1	-10.8	-10.7	-10.0	-9.5	-6.5	-6.8	-8.8	..	-8.5	Haiti
-11.6	-8.7	-8.4	-12.0	-9.6	-7.7	-8.4	-7.8	-6.8	-15.1	Honduras
-12.3	-14.2	-11.1	-15.7	-18.4	-3.1	-6.6	0.2	-9.9	-6.2	Jamaica
-6.4	-3.7	3.6	2.3	0.2	-1.4	2.6	-1.5	-2.8	-2.4	Mexico
-26.6	-23.0	-23.4	-22.8	-29.1	-29.3	-23.8	..	..	..	Nicaragua
-11.3	-11.8	-7.0	-6.1	-5.3	-1.6	-2.5	4.0	-1.5	..	Panama
-11.3	-9.1	-2.7	-5.9	-7.0	-12.8	-13.8	-9.5	-2.1	..	Paraguay
-7.5	-6.9	-5.5	-1.8	0.0	-5.1	-6.1	-6.6	1.2	..	Peru
-8.0	-17.3	-6.1	-3.5	0.3	-2.3	-16.8	-13.5	..	..	St. Vincent and The Grenadines
5.8	-7.3	-12.5	-6.4	-1.2	-8.9	-4.7	-3.5	-3.4	-1.7	Trinidad and Tobago
-4.1	-2.7	-1.3	-2.7	-2.5	0.6	-1.8	0.2	1.7	-0.5	Uruguay
5.2	-5.3	5.5	7.8	5.4	-3.7	-2.9	-9.6	5.7	13.7	Venezuela
..	..	..	..	..	..	..	..	..	..	*MIDDLE EAST AND NORTH AFRICA*
0.2	-0.4	-0.2	0.2	1.7	-3.5	0.2	-3.9	-2.6	2.0	Algeria
-10.1	-13.7	-8.4	-9.9	-13.6	-14.8	-10.6	-9.2	-8.5	-7.5	Egypt, Arab Republic of
										Iran, Islamic Rep. of
..	..	-24.9	-20.1	-20.9	-11.7	-15.3	-14.2	-15.9	-26.1	Jordan
-12.7	-13.2	-7.1	-8.5	-7.8	-2.2	-0.1	0.7	-4.7	-1.7	Morocco
15.0	5.9	4.3	1.0	0.9	-14.0	10.4	..	..	..	Oman
-13.8	-10.1	-12.1	-11.5	-11.5	-9.1	-7.6	-6.9	..	..	Syrian Arab Republic
-5.2	-8.7	-7.6	-10.1	-7.7	-7.5	-1.0	1.0	-3.7	-3.4	Tunisia
-3.4	-2.0	-4.2	-3.3	-2.3	-2.9	-1.7	1.8	0.7	-2.6	Turkey
..	..	..	..	..	..	..	..	..	..	Yemen, Republic of
..	..	..	..	..	..	..	..	..	..	*EUROPE*
..	..	..	..	..	..	..	..	..	..	Bulgaria
-6.9	-6.4	-7.8	-8.4	-12.4	-7.8	-6.3	-5.5	-9.7	..	Greece
..	-2.3	-0.9	0.2	-2.2	-5.7	-2.6	-2.0	-2.0	-0.6	Hungary
3.0	-1.9	-3.3	-2.2	-4.1	-1.8	-1.1	-2.2	0.2	..	Malta
-8.0	-3.0	-2.1	-1.4	-1.4	-1.5	-0.6	..	-2.7	..	Poland
..	..	..	-2.9	1.5	3.2	0.8	-3.2	-3.1	..	Portugal
..	..	..	..	..	..	..	..	..	..	Romania
..	..	0.6	1.1	1.8	1.7	1.9	4.0	3.2	0.4	Yugoslavia
..	..	..	..	..	..	..	..	..	..	**Low- & middle-income economies**
..	..	..	..	..	..	..	..	..	..	Severely indebted
..	..	..	..	..	..	..	..	..	..	Low-income economies
..	..	..	..	..	..	..	..	..	..	Low-income Africa
..	..	..	..	..	..	..	..	..	..	China and India
..	..	..	..	..	..	..	..	..	..	Other low-income
..	..	..	..	..	..	..	..	..	..	Middle-income economies
..	..	..	..	..	..	..	..	..	..	**High-income OECD members**
..	..	..	..	..	..	..	..	..	..	European Community members
0.5	0.8	1.9	2.9	3.8	4.5	3.8	2.9	2.1	..	Japan
0.3	0.0	-1.0	-2.5	-2.9	-3.3	-3.4	-2.4	-1.9	..	United States
..	..	..	..	..	..	..	..	..	..	**Other high-income economies** /a

Table 17. Value of merchandise exports

Millions of US dollars	1970	1971	1972	1973	1974	1975	1976	1977	1978	1979	1980
SUB-SAHARAN AFRICA	*7,832*	*8,062*	*9,509*	*13,450*	*22,846*	*20,468*	*24,549*	*28,600*	*26,776*	*39,183*	*51,729*
Excluding Nigeria	*6,605*	*6,270*	*7,349*	*10,004*	*13,652*	*12,478*	*13,981*	*16,753*	*16,218*	*21,472*	*25,761*
Benin	58	70	67	93	93	116	86	129	126	133	223
Botswana	22	28	58	85	121	142	176	180	222	436	503
Burkina Faso	25	25	36	44	66	74	83	95	108	133	161
Burundi	24	19	26	30	30	32	54	89	69	105	65
Cameroon	231	213	225	362	491	470	535	704	805	1,170	1,447
Cape Verde	2	2	2	2	2	2	2	2	3	5	9
Central African Rep.	43	44	41	55	57	54	70	105	110	122	147
Chad	25	26	34	36	35	40	63	107	99	72	72
Comoros	5	6	6	5	9	10	12	9	9	10	11
Congo, People's Rep of the	28	35	46	79	208	179	190	174	161	524	980
Cote D'Ivoire	469	456	553	861	1,214	1,182	1,631	2,155	2,323	2,507	3,142
Ethiopia	122	126	168	237	267	229	278	334	310	422	425
Gabon	140	178	228	330	768	943	1,135	1,343	1,107	1,848	2,173
Gambia, The	16	15	19	21	40	49	36	48	39	58	31
Ghana	433	341	393	565	647	737	765	951	992	1,041	1,257
Guinea-Bissau	7	5	6	8	9	7	6	13	12	13	11
Kenya	305	314	372	516	661	647	824	1,195	1,023	1,107	1,389
Lesotho	6	4	8	13	14	13	17	14	32	45	58
Liberia	217	222	244	324	400	394	463	454	496	547	597
Madagascar	145	147	164	203	244	301	283	347	399	408	402
Malawi	59	72	81	99	121	139	166	200	185	223	285
Mali	36	36	37	58	64	37	85	125	112	148	205
Mauritania	89	94	119	155	182	174	178	157	123	147	196
Mauritius	69	65	107	138	313	2	215	310	326	376	431
Mozambique	157	160	175	227	296	20	150	149	163	254	281
Niger	32	38	54	63	53	91	134	160	283	448	580
Nigeria	1,228	1,793	2,161	3,448	9,195	7,992	10,569	11,848	10,560	17,713	25,968
Rwanda	25	22	20	51	54	58	114	127	112	203	134
Senegal	161	125	216	195	391	462	485	623	421	533	477
Seychelles	2	2	3	4	7	6	9	11	15	22	21
Sierra Leone	102	99	118	131	146	146	107	131	178	194	207
Somalia	31	38	57	57	64	89	81	71	110	106	133
Sudan	295	332	361	417	441	429	578	661	483	583	594
Swaziland	71	78	82	107	179	199	183	168	196	231	368
Tanzania	238	251	300	344	388	349	490	559	472	511	537
Togo	68	73	70	72	215	141	159	199	262	291	476
Uganda	246	235	261	300	316	264	352	588	350	436	345
Zaire	735	687	738	1,001	1,382	865	809	1,110	899	2,004	2,507
Zambia	1,001	679	758	1,142	1,407	812	1,041	897	869	1,376	1,360
Zimbabwe	370	404	515	693	864	936	974	877	891	1,217	1,423
SOUTH ASIA	*3,535*	*3,500*	*3,952*	*4,858*	*6,170*	*6,520*	*7,922*	*9,045*	*9,861*	*12,055*	*13,368*
Bangladesh	..	..	321	326	368	265	362	435	553	662	759
India	2,026	2,043	2,422	2,968	3,906	4,365	5,526	6,355	6,650	7,850	8,332
Nepal	48	48	58	63	66	100	98	81	91	108	109
Pakistan	723	666	698	947	1,102	1,049	1,167	1,174	1,475	2,056	2,618
Sri Lanka	338	327	326	405	523	559	567	763	846	981	1,049
EAST ASIA AND PACIFIC	*8,038*	*8,862*	*11,239*	*19,685*	*29,958*	*29,602*	*35,993*	*43,837*	*51,475*	*67,899*	*87,416*
China	2,260	2,640	3,440	5,820	6,950	7,260	6,860	7,590	9,115	12,525	18,265
Fiji	68	68	73	78	144	159	127	173	216	249	361
Indonesia	1,055	1,200	1,778	3,211	7,426	7,130	8,556	10,853	11,643	15,590	21,909
Korea, Republic of	835	1,068	1,624	3,225	4,460	5,081	7,715	10,016	12,695	15,052	17,483
Malaysia	1,687	1,639	1,722	3,040	4,234	3,847	5,295	6,079	7,387	11,075	12,939
Papua New Guinea	79	113	149	294	710	580	456	613	756	877	1,033
Philippines	1,060	1,116	1,029	1,797	2,651	2,218	2,508	3,080	3,349	4,601	5,788
Solomon islands	..	..	..	..	..	..	..	..	..	..	73
Thailand	710	827	1,067	1,566	2,449	2,195	2,978	3,490	4,085	5,297	6,505
Vanuatu	12	13	15	21	30	11	17	37	42	47	36

1981	1982	1983	1984	1985	1986	1987	1988	1989	1990	
41,461	*33,859*	*31,455*	*34,895*	*35,421*	*29,132*	*31,124*	*31,552*	*35,948*	..	*SUB-SAHARAN AFRICA*
23,615	*21,705*	*21,085*	*23,004*	*22,855*	*22,363*	*23,747*	*24,600*	..	..	*Excluding Nigeria*
184	144	122	147	152	94	168	189	..	..	Benin
413	456	637	674	745	858	1,521	1,418	..	..	Botswana
159	126	130	138	131	148	198	208	521	..	Burkina Faso
71	88	77	98	112	167	90	128	..	..	Burundi
1,764	1,616	1,830	2,080	2,322	1,995	1,714	1,642	1,828	..	Cameroon
6	3	2	3	3	3	5	..	..	..	Cape Verde
118	112	115	115	132	130	130	132	..	..	Central African Rep.
83	58	74	111	88	99	111	..	..	..	Chad
16	20	20	7	15	19	12	19	..	..	Comoros
1,115	1,213	1,097	1,265	1,145	673	914	835	..	..	Congo, People's Rep of the
2,535	2,288	2,092	2,707	2,972	3,179	2,982	2,429	3,110	..	Cote D'Ivoire
378	404	403	417	333	455	355	429	..	..	Ethiopia
2,201	2,161	1,975	2,011	1,974	1,074	1,286	1,200	..	..	Gabon
27	44	48	49	43	44	45	50	..	..	Gambia, The
1,063	873	536	575	663	914	1,056	1,044	..	..	Ghana
14	12	9	17	12	10	15	..	..	..	Guinea-Bissau
1,183	1,045	979	1,083	988	1,217	961	1,071	1,115	..	Kenya
51	35	35	28	22	25	47	54	..	..	Lesotho
529	477	438	452	436	404	382	392	..	..	Liberia
324	330	310	340	287	320	310	282	..	..	Madagascar
274	246	244	314	250	243	277	292	..	..	Malawi
154	146	167	192	181	192	217	252	..	..	Mali
270	240	315	294	374	349	428	455	..	..	Mauritania
324	367	368	372	435	676	918	1,131	..	..	Mauritius
281	229	132	96	77	79	97	105	..	..	Mozambique
455	380	335	303	251	330	361	256	..	..	Niger
17,846	12,154	10,370	11,891	12,566	6,769	7,365	7,006	7,707	..	Nigeria
113	109	124	143	126	184	121	125	..	..	Rwanda
500	548	581	613	498	584	645	740	..	..	Senegal
17	15	20	26	28	18	22	31	..	..	Seychelles
136	111	120	133	130	143	129	110	..	..	Sierra Leone
175	171	98	55	91	89	94	59	..	..	Somalia
538	432	581	722	595	497	482	501	661	..	Sudan
388	325	304	237	176	267	311	..	..	..	Swaziland
564	413	379	340	255	348	347	402	460	..	Tanzania
378	345	274	240	243	275	297	337	..	..	Togo
243	349	372	399	348	395	320	369	..	..	Uganda
2,030	1,530	1,388	1,558	1,526	1,521	1,594	2,032	..	..	Zaire
998	932	997	884	815	689	869	1,179	1,048	..	Zambia
1,406	1,273	1,128	1,154	1,113	1,254	1,358	1,592	..	..	Zimbabwe
13,820	*13,829*	*15,128*	*15,598*	*15,008*	*16,376*	*19,988*	*22,581*	..	..	*SOUTH ASIA*
662	671	705	811	934	819	1,074	1,231	1,324	..	Bangladesh
8,698	9,225	9,770	10,192	9,465	10,460	12,888	14,824	..	..	India
134	115	94	128	160	142	151	193	..	..	Nepal
2,779	2,377	3,075	2,592	2,739	3,384	4,178	4,522	5,321	..	Pakistan
1,036	1,014	1,066	1,454	1,333	1,215	1,393	1,476	..	..	Sri Lanka
93,574	*91,453*	*97,091*	*109,390*	*108,326*	*113,174*	*145,444*	*179,474*	*178,621*	..	*EAST ASIA AND PACIFIC*
21,554	21,820	22,175	25,922	27,326	31,148	39,542	47,540	46,022	..	China
298	284	240	256	237	274	334	366	..	..	Fiji
22,260	19,747	20,961	20,345	18,711	14,787	17,206	19,504	20,855	..	Indonesia
21,250	21,850	24,437	29,248	30,283	34,702	47,172	60,697	61,000	..	Korea, Republic of
11,734	12,027	14,100	16,484	15,632	13,830	17,911	21,110	21,548	..	Malaysia
864	791	820	892	912	1,033	1,172	1,448	..	..	Papua New Guinea
5,722	5,021	5,001	5,391	4,629	4,842	5,649	7,074	7,273	..	Philippines
66	58	62	93	70	66	..	..	..	..	Solomon islands
7,035	6,957	6,368	7,413	7,121	8,835	11,659	15,869	14,280	..	Thailand
32	23	30	44	30	14	17	19	..	..	Vanuatu

Table 17. Value of merchandise exports (cont'd.)

Millions of US dollars	1970	1971	1972	1973	1974	1975	1976	1977	1978	1979	1980
LATIN AMERICA AND CARIBBEAN	15,921	15,758	18,439	26,894	43,479	39,578	45,316	53,144	57,318	75,706	99,102
Argentina	1,773	1,740	1,941	3,266	3,931	2,961	3,912	5,642	6,394	7,808	8,021
Bahamas	88	267	343	530	1,795	2,216	2,616	2,409	2,118	3,784	4,906
Barbados	39	42	45	54	86	107	86	96	130	152	196
Belize	19	19	26	32	45	67	42	62	80	87	111
Bolivia	190	181	201	261	557	444	568	632	629	760	942
Brazil	2,739	2,904	3,991	6,199	7,951	8,670	10,128	12,120	12,659	15,244	20,100
Chile	1,234	961	856	1,249	2,481	1,649	2,209	2,138	2,462	3,894	4,705
Colombia	728	689	863	1,176	1,417	1,465	1,745	2,443	3,038	3,300	3,950
Costa Rica	231	225	281	345	440	494	600	840	919	934	1,032
Dominican Republic	214	241	354	443	649	894	716	780	676	869	962
Ecuador	190	199	326	532	1,124	974	1,258	1,436	1,558	2,104	2,480
El Salvador	236	243	302	358	463	531	743	973	801	1,131	1,074
Grenada	..	..	..	..	..	..	..	..	..	..	17
Guatemala	290	283	328	436	572	623	760	1,160	1,112	1,161	1,486
Guyana	133	149	147	137	270	364	268	261	291	290	389
Haiti	48	53	63	95	130	143	176	216	241	240	341
Honduras	170	183	193	247	253	293	392	511	602	721	813
Jamaica	335	330	366	390	731	784	633	778	747	817	965
Mexico	1,205	1,321	1,845	2,632	2,957	2,993	3,468	4,284	6,301	8,817	15,308
Nicaragua	175	183	246	275	377	372	539	633	646	633	414
Panama	110	117	123	138	211	287	237	250	244	292	353
Paraguay	65	67	86	128	173	188	202	327	356	385	400
Peru	1,044	893	944	1,050	1,517	1,291	1,360	1,726	1,941	3,491	3,898
St. Vincent and The Grenadines	4	3	3	5	7	8	9	10	16	15	16
Trinidad and Tobago	482	521	558	696	2,038	1,773	2,219	2,180	2,043	2,610	4,080
Uruguay	233	206	214	322	381	381	536	599	682	787	1,060
Venezuela	3,197	3,110	3,126	4,773	11,258	9,010	9,466	9,627	9,270	14,318	19,293
MIDDLE EAST AND NORTH AFRICA	6,399	6,856	8,655	12,736	32,060	29,668	34,034	38,816	39,287	58,463	70,263
Algeria	1,009	857	1,306	1,906	4,260	4,291	4,972	5,809	6,126	9,863	13,871
Egypt, Arab Republic of	870	927	887	1,117	1,588	1,596	1,785	2,015	2,458	3,320	4,759
Iran, Islamic Rep. of	2,445	2,677	3,812	6,076	21,575	20,114	22,580	25,943	..	17,800	14,082
Jordan	34	32	48	58	155	153	209	249	297	402	561
Morocco	488	499	634	877	1,706	1,543	1,262	1,300	1,511	1,959	2,403
Oman	206	221	242	344	1,211	1,436	1,566	1,573	1,598	2,280	3,748
Syrian Arab Republic	203	195	287	351	784	930	1,055	1,063	1,060	1,645	2,108
Tunisia	183	216	311	386	914	856	789	929	1,126	1,791	2,234
Turkey	589	677	885	1,317	1,538	1,401	1,960	1,753	2,288	2,261	2,910
Yemen, Republic of	..	..	..	..	..	..	..	..	..	..	..
EUROPE	16,239	17,794	21,953	29,262	36,315	41,675	46,038	51,770	59,563	70,594	78,290
Bulgaria	2,004	2,182	2,627	3,301	3,836	4,691	5,382	6,351	7,478	8,869	10,372
Greece	643	663	871	1,454	2,030	2,278	2,558	2,757	3,375	3,877	5,142
Hungary	1,726	1,847	2,403	3,354	3,942	4,519	4,932	5,840	6,434	7,938	8,677
Malta	39	45	67	98	134	167	228	289	342	424	483
Poland	3,548	3,872	4,927	6,432	8,321	10,289	11,024	12,273	14,114	16,249	13,870
Portugal	949	1,053	1,294	1,862	2,302	1,940	1,820	2,013	2,411	3,480	4,629
Romania	..	..	..	..	..	..	..	..	..	..	..
Yugoslavia	1,679	1,836	2,237	3,020	3,805	4,072	4,896	4,896	5,546	6,800	8,978
Low- & middle-income economies	59,503	62,494	75,903	109,760	177,743	174,563	199,823	232,600	255,546	337,911	419,675
Severely indebted	19,859	20,056	23,972	34,742	51,660	49,924	56,466	65,631	72,375	93,822	113,403
Low-income economies	13,133	13,875	16,727	24,423	38,646	36,929	43,359	50,742	52,140	71,676	95,083
Low-income Africa	5,820	6,035	6,945	9,781	17,016	14,634	18,272	21,166	19,303	29,190	39,047
China and India	4,286	4,683	5,862	8,788	10,856	11,625	12,386	13,945	15,765	20,375	26,597
Other low-income	2,984	3,058	3,763	5,670	10,615	10,463	12,330	15,171	16,612	21,933	29,790
Middle-income economies	46,357	48,612	59,156	85,325	139,018	137,486	156,368	181,764	203,577	266,253	324,593
High-income OECD members	218,607	245,224	289,742	395,189	528,174	564,723	627,145	710,521	850,460	1,043,171	1,226,368
European Community members	113,685	131,068	156,811	213,409	279,711	303,276	333,066	388,632	471,215	591,274	678,076
Japan	19,319	24,019	28,591	36,931	55,538	55,754	67,203	80,470	97,502	102,965	129,542
United States	43,224	44,130	49,778	71,339	98,507	107,592	114,992	120,133	142,536	176,788	216,916
Other high-income economies /a	11,258	15,053	19,566	29,781	72,746	64,358	82,665	93,396	98,867	145,690	214,502

a. Economies classified by the United Nations or otherwise regarded by their authorities as developing.

1981	1982	1983	1984	1985	1986	1987	1988	1989	1990	
105,366	95,273	94,928	103,123	96,403	79,404	90,240	102,957	..	..	*LATIN AMERICA AND CARIBBEAN*
9,143	7,625	7,836	8,107	8,396	6,852	6,360	8,941	9,162	..	Argentina
3,515	2,451	2,561	2,346	1,431	825	733	733	..	..	Bahamas
244	263	321	391	352	275	156	173	..	..	Barbados
119	91	78	90	87	75	87	95	95	..	Belize
912	828	755	725	623	564	566	601	..	..	Bolivia
23,300	20,200	21,900	27,000	25,600	22,396	26,225	33,780	30,954	..	Brazil
3,836	3,710	3,836	3,650	3,823	4,222	5,091	7,046	5,591	..	Chile
3,160	3,110	3,080	3,480	3,550	5,110	5,024	5,100	6,368	..	Colombia
1,011	877	867	967	976	1,125	1,155	1,320	..	..	Costa Rica
1,188	768	782	868	735	718	711	890	..	..	Dominican Republic
2,168	2,291	2,348	2,621	2,905	2,172	2,021	2,192	..	..	Ecuador
797	699	736	725	679	757	634	648	..	..	El Salvador
19	19	19	18	22	28	..	..	..	..	Grenada
1,115	1,120	1,159	1,127	1,060	1,103	1,084	1,105	..	..	Guatemala
346	241	189	210	206	229	243	266	..	..	Guyana
273	296	272	313	333	285	261	286	..	..	Haiti
713	656	672	725	765	854	827	919	..	..	Honduras
985	739	713	714	549	596	649	755	..	..	Jamaica
20,041	21,230	22,312	24,196	22,108	16,237	20,887	20,761	22,266	..	Mexico
476	391	435	387	302	247	300	236	..	..	Nicaragua
319	310	303	307	335	341	350	280	..	..	Panama
399	396	326	361	324	573	952	1,097	..	..	Paraguay
3,249	3,293	3,015	3,147	2,966	2,531	2,661	2,695	..	..	Peru
24	32	41	54	63	68	52	68	..	..	St. Vincent and The Grenadines
3,760	3,090	2,353	2,173	2,161	1,386	1,462	1,412	..	..	Trinidad and Tobago
1,220	1,020	1,050	925	855	1,090	1,190	1,405	1,488	..	Uruguay
20,125	16,499	14,571	15,841	14,660	9,122	10,567	10,112	..	..	Venezuela
66,245	70,495	66,452	62,069	64,173	44,810	50,370	52,995	..	..	*MIDDLE EAST AND NORTH AFRICA*
14,396	13,144	12,583	12,795	13,034	8,066	9,029	7,830	8,690	..	Algeria
5,048	5,033	5,368	5,936	6,076	5,193	4,040	4,576	4,878	5,111	Egypt, Arab Republic of
12,522	19,526	19,508	12,527	13,384	8,322	..	..	..	..	Iran, Islamic Rep. of
732	739	579	752	789	714	930	1,019	..	..	Jordan
2,320	2,059	2,062	2,172	2,165	2,428	2,807	3,625	3,336	..	Morocco
4,696	4,423	4,256	4,421	4,971	2,888	3,805	3,123	..	..	Oman
2,103	2,026	1,923	1,854	1,637	1,037	1,357	1,345	..	..	Syrian Arab Republic
2,504	1,984	1,872	1,796	1,738	1,759	2,152	2,395	2,449	..	Tunisia
4,702	5,890	5,905	7,389	8,255	7,583	10,190	11,695	13,190	..	Turkey
..	..	..	..	..	..	..	..	..	..	Yemen, Republic of
77,401	78,270	79,740	83,659	84,415	92,079	102,361	110,416	..	..	*EUROPE*
10,689	11,428	12,130	12,850	13,348	14,192	15,921	17,223	..	..	Bulgaria
4,250	4,297	4,412	4,864	4,536	5,660	6,489	5,400	..	..	Greece
8,712	8,799	8,722	8,560	8,555	9,157	9,571	9,949	..	..	Hungary
448	411	363	395	400	497	605	711	..	..	Malta
10,656	11,214	11,572	11,647	11,489	12,074	12,204	13,959	..	..	Poland
4,180	4,171	4,602	5,208	5,685	7,160	9,167	10,556	11,027	..	Portugal
..	..	..	..	..	..	..	..	..	..	Romania
10,929	10,752	9,914	10,255	10,642	10,298	11,397	12,580	14,461	..	Yugoslavia
413,101	396,019	398,920	422,294	418,555	393,228	461,974	524,079	..	..	**Low- & middle-income economies**
117,754	109,760	110,723	120,645	115,432	100,349	112,622	128,619	..	..	Severely indebted
89,170	79,825	80,361	86,039	85,267	81,551	97,108	111,099	113,597	..	Low-income economies
29,106	22,008	19,620	21,663	21,762	16,712	17,469	18,226	20,240	..	Low-income Africa
30,252	31,045	31,945	36,114	36,791	41,608	52,430	62,364	60,373	..	China and India
29,932	27,164	29,022	28,510	27,073	23,351	27,248	30,504	33,212	..	Other low-income
323,932	316,203	318,569	336,264	333,298	311,682	364,795	412,845	..	..	Middle-income economies
1,212,054	1,150,347	1,135,998	1,212,314	1,254,721	1,448,387	1,707,980	1,953,302	..	..	**High-income OECD members**
625,496	604,548	589,542	602,996	640,817	780,517	940,994	1,046,838	..	..	European Community members
151,910	138,584	146,804	170,038	175,858	209,081	229,055	264,772	..	..	Japan
230,506	210,929	199,144	216,008	211,419	211,897	252,567	315,313	..	..	United States
227,778	177,089	146,993	154,384	143,189	143,035	183,124	217,381	..	..	**Other high-income economies** /a

Table 18. Value of merchandise imports

Millions of US dollars	1970	1971	1972	1973	1974	1975	1976	1977	1978	1979	1980
SUB-SAHARAN AFRICA	*7,345*	*8,752*	*9,141*	*11,423*	*15,960*	*20,750*	*22,314*	*28,337*	*33,206*	*33,302*	*46,140*
Excluding Nigeria	*6,289*	*7,245*	*7,640*	*9,566*	*13,185*	*14,711*	*14,119*	*17,315*	*20,442*	*23,031*	*29,498*
Benin	64	76	93	112	164	197	219	246	312	320	331
Botswana	57	83	109	166	185	218	209	276	353	521	691
Burkina Faso	57	73	94	130	180	216	195	260	296	370	446
Burundi	22	30	31	32	40	63	58	91	98	153	167
Cameroon	242	250	299	335	437	598	595	747	1,009	1,271	1,538
Cape Verde	16	20	24	34	34	40	30	38	54	56	91
Central African Rep.	57	51	56	69	84	110	100	136	156	159	221
Chad	62	62	61	82	87	133	116	189	217	85	74
Comoros	9	10	12	15	26	23	13	16	19	28	29
Congo, People's Rep of the	57	79	90	125	123	165	168	183	242	266	500
Cote D'Ivoire	387	398	453	714	967	1,127	1,295	1,752	2,310	2,389	3,015
Ethiopia	173	188	189	213	273	294	353	391	505	567	721
Gabon	80	91	133	190	332	469	503	716	682	673	686
Gambia, The	17	21	23	32	38	49	65	73	100	141	132
Ghana	410	434	292	448	818	788	862	1,144	1,003	853	1,129
Guinea-Bissau	27	31	32	44	43	38	37	37	49	61	53
Kenya	442	560	554	655	1,026	987	923	1,286	1,706	1,656	2,590
Lesotho	32	39	56	87	120	160	207	229	273	373	490
Liberia	150	162	179	194	288	331	399	464	481	507	534
Madagascar	170	213	202	203	281	367	290	353	460	698	677
Malawi	86	109	130	142	188	251	206	232	338	398	440
Mali	45	59	74	126	179	190	150	159	286	361	439
Mauritania	72	72	85	135	188	235	304	334	302	323	363
Mauritius	76	83	120	170	309	331	358	445	498	566	619
Mozambique	323	335	327	465	464	417	300	328	521	571	800
Niger	58	53	66	87	96	99	127	196	306	462	608
Nigeria	1,059	1,511	1,505	1,862	2,781	6,041	8,195	11,020	12,763	10,274	16,642
Rwanda	29	33	35	41	72	102	128	125	202	224	277
Senegal	192	218	279	359	498	582	644	762	756	931	1,038
Seychelles	10	15	21	25	28	32	44	46	53	90	99
Sierra Leone	117	113	121	158	222	159	166	181	278	316	425
Somalia	46	56	72	112	154	162	176	206	275	394	461
Sudan	311	355	354	480	656	957	952	983	878	916	1,499
Swaziland	60	67	69	96	138	180	200	224	311	434	538
Tanzania	272	338	363	447	760	718	645	730	1,141	1,077	1,227
Togo	76	85	94	95	116	269	218	305	497	558	638
Uganda	172	250	162	162	213	206	172	241	255	197	293
Zaire	533	619	766	782	940	933	840	852	797	826	1,117
Zambia	477	559	563	532	787	929	655	671	628	750	1,111
Zimbabwe	329	397	416	549	753	814	612	618	592	937	1,448
SOUTH ASIA	*4,597*	*4,620*	*4,137*	*5,706*	*9,007*	*10,956*	*10,055*	*11,426*	*14,215*	*18,595*	*25,039*
Bangladesh	..	..	611	834	1,032	1,200	1,137	1,058	1,338	1,711	2,254
India	2,094	2,406	2,230	3,146	5,167	6,385	5,710	6,601	7,854	10,142	14,090
Nepal	85	70	88	96	110	171	214	244	339	379	342
Pakistan	1,171	926	682	966	1,729	2,153	2,183	2,455	3,161	4,061	5,351
Sri Lanka	387	328	336	422	688	745	552	701	942	1,449	2,035
EAST ASIA AND PACIFIC	*10,873*	*11,801*	*13,453*	*20,873*	*33,061*	*35,158*	*38,148*	*44,441*	*57,021*	*74,710*	*91,971*
China	2,330	2,210	2,860	5,160	7,620	7,486	6,578	7,214	10,893	15,675	19,550
Fiji	104	128	158	204	273	267	263	306	366	470	561
Indonesia	1,258	1,379	1,611	2,969	5,231	6,196	7,700	8,495	9,493	10,364	14,139
Korea, Republic of	1,983	2,394	2,522	4,240	6,844	7,271	8,765	10,803	14,966	20,296	22,228
Malaysia	1,390	1,485	1,674	2,517	4,297	3,851	4,177	5,004	6,364	8,708	11,602
Papua New Guinea	300	356	336	356	503	556	502	642	770	903	1,176
Philippines	1,210	1,319	1,388	1,790	3,468	3,776	3,953	4,270	5,143	6,613	8,295
Solomon islands	13	15	17	18	27	33	30	33	42	70	89
Thailand	1,293	1,287	1,484	2,073	3,156	3,279	3,572	4,613	5,314	7,132	9,450
Vanuatu	13	18	29	35	50	40	39	52	63	73	73

1981	1982	1983	1984	1985	1986	1987	1988	1989	1990	
49,640	*42,354*	*35,419*	*32,120*	*31,993*	*32,619*	*34,960*	*35,557*	..	..	*SUB-SAHARAN AFRICA*
28,763	*26,294*	*23,165*	*22,756*	*23,103*	*25,154*	*27,158*	*28,196*	..	..	*Excluding Nigeria*
543	464	283	285	312	370	418	439	..	..	Benin
799	686	735	707	583	684	849	1,027	..	..	Botswana
422	436	377	319	405	525	540	566	214	..	Burkina Faso
161	214	194	187	189	203	206	204	..	..	Burundi
1,421	1,243	1,250	1,213	1,163	1,717	2,168	1,767	1,722	..	Cameroon
95	97	105	82	81	92	112	..	..	..	Cape Verde
171	166	160	182	222	253	259	236	..	..	Central African Rep.
108	109	157	171	240	288	366	..	..	..	Chad
32	33	34	43	36	37	52	51	..	..	Comoros
828	807	746	737	752	629	570	609	..	..	Congo, People's Rep of the
2,393	2,184	1,814	1,497	1,749	2,055	2,370	1,917	2,520	..	Cote D'Ivoire
737	785	875	928	993	1,102	1,066	1,129	..	..	Ethiopia
843	799	852	888	976	1,118	836	853	..	..	Gabon
145	151	118	100	93	99	109	126	..	..	Gambia, The
1,106	705	600	640	731	783	836	881	..	..	Ghana
55	52	58	57	63	72	..	..	..	..	Guinea-Bissau
2,081	1,603	1,390	1,529	1,455	1,649	1,755	1,975	1,945	..	Kenya
564	514	561	504	364	415	523	591	..	..	Lesotho
477	422	412	369	284	235	208	216	..	..	Liberia
473	439	411	412	465	374	386	386	..	..	Madagascar
350	311	311	270	287	260	295	402	..	..	Malawi
365	332	353	368	432	438	447	479	..	..	Mali
436	482	427	341	358	430	474	519	..	..	Mauritania
554	464	440	471	529	676	1,010	1,112	..	..	Mauritius
801	836	636	540	424	543	625	706	..	..	Mozambique
604	573	367	341	354	379	417	490	..	..	Niger
20,877	16,060	12,254	9,364	8,890	7,466	7,816	7,435	6,862	..	Nigeria
279	297	277	282	313	348	352	372	..	..	Rwanda
1,076	992	1,025	1,035	898	1,014	1,174	1,165	..	..	Senegal
93	98	88	88	99	106	114	153	..	..	Seychelles
311	298	160	157	149	141	132	149	..	..	Sierra Leone
426	542	416	535	380	440	452	307	..	..	Somalia
1,519	1,754	1,534	1,370	1,114	990	694	975	1,402	..	Sudan
506	440	464	381	281	352	365	..	..	..	Swaziland
1,176	1,134	795	847	1,028	1,048	1,150	1,237	1,364	..	Tanzania
504	487	350	310	358	408	409	413	..	..	Togo
345	377	377	344	327	344	477	573	..	..	Uganda
1,019	913	842	877	919	1,008	1,149	1,190	..	..	Zaire
1,062	831	690	730	654	663	745	848	808	..	Zambia
1,696	1,639	1,205	955	1,031	1,099	1,055	1,189	..	..	Zimbabwe
26,943	*25,483*	*25,534*	*26,673*	*28,972*	*27,737*	*30,890*	*35,914*	..	..	*SOUTH ASIA*
2,649	2,581	2,246	2,353	2,647	2,364	2,620	2,987	3,204	..	Bangladesh
15,654	14,387	14,782	15,424	17,295	16,801	18,985	22,500	..	..	India
369	395	447	416	453	459	569	688	..	..	Nepal
5,413	5,233	5,341	5,873	5,890	5,377	5,827	6,590	6,515	..	Pakistan
1,804	1,770	1,789	1,847	1,988	1,948	2,085	2,262	..	..	Sri Lanka
102,559	*100,302*	*107,248*	*113,724*	*122,548*	*121,451*	*140,176*	*179,351*	*185,385*	..	*EAST ASIA AND PACIFIC*
19,482	18,546	21,346	27,350	42,526	43,172	43,392	55,278	56,891	..	China
631	514	483	450	442	437	380	454	..	..	Fiji
18,527	19,996	19,853	16,853	14,230	13,103	14,453	15,833	16,733	..	Indonesia
26,028	24,236	26,174	30,609	31,119	31,518	40,925	51,811	58,000	..	Korea, Republic of
13,052	14,042	14,669	14,849	12,746	11,447	12,506	16,551	17,128	..	Malaysia
1,261	1,170	1,120	1,110	1,008	1,130	1,222	1,380	..	..	Papua New Guinea
8,478	8,262	7,977	6,424	5,445	5,393	7,144	8,729	9,305	..	Philippines
91	71	74	79	83	72	..	..	..	..	Solomon islands
10,055	8,527	10,279	10,518	9,239	9,124	12,955	20,285	16,100	..	Thailand
58	52	63	67	70	58	68	69	..	..	Vanuatu

Table 18. Value of merchandise imports (cont'd.)

Millions of US dollars	1970	1971	1972	1973	1974	1975	1976	1977	1978	1979	1980
LATIN AMERICA AND CARIBBEAN	**16,381**	**18,207**	**20,757**	**27,362**	**46,849**	**49,365**	**50,682**	**56,864**	**64,893**	**81,624**	**108,898**
Argentina	1,689	1,846	1,904	2,235	3,635	3,945	3,029	4,158	3,832	6,692	10,539
Bahamas	332	511	485	764	2,112	2,482	2,893	2,871	2,482	3,985	5,507
Barbados	117	122	142	168	204	216	237	272	312	421	522
Belize	33	36	43	44	64	88	73	90	106	132	150
Bolivia	159	170	179	230	366	574	594	586	770	842	665
Brazil	2,845	3,696	4,776	6,992	14,163	13,578	13,714	13,254	15,016	19,731	24,900
Chile	980	1,049	1,168	1,562	2,137	1,733	1,672	2,418	3,276	4,777	6,185
Colombia	843	929	859	1,062	1,597	1,495	1,708	2,028	2,836	3,233	4,660
Costa Rica	317	350	373	455	720	694	800	1,059	1,212	1,446	1,597
Dominican Republic	304	358	388	489	808	889	878	975	987	1,213	1,640
Ecuador	273	339	325	396	781	985	952	1,165	1,499	1,986	2,215
El Salvador	214	247	278	374	563	598	718	943	1,024	1,012	976
Grenada	..	..	..	..	..	..	..	29	33	43	49
Guatemala	284	303	328	427	701	733	838	1,053	1,261	1,362	1,559
Guyana	134	135	143	177	255	344	364	315	279	318	365
Haiti	59	66	85	113	166	196	246	287	311	368	492
Honduras	221	193	193	262	380	404	453	579	699	826	1,009
Jamaica	525	551	620	664	936	1,123	911	859	880	992	1,178
Mexico	2,461	2,407	2,935	4,146	6,057	6,572	6,033	5,589	8,053	12,587	19,517
Nicaragua	198	210	218	326	559	517	532	762	780	415	882
Panama	357	396	441	502	822	892	848	859	942	1,184	1,448
Paraguay	91	98	93	149	229	262	289	435	521	687	803
Peru	622	750	796	1,024	1,595	2,380	1,798	1,598	1,601	1,951	3,062
St. Vincent and The Grenadines	15	18	18	19	26	25	24	30	36	46	57
Trinidad and Tobago	543	663	762	792	1,847	1,489	1,976	1,809	1,980	2,105	3,180
Uruguay	233	222	187	285	461	517	599	669	716	1,173	1,650
Venezuela	1,869	2,079	2,430	2,806	4,186	6,004	7,663	10,938	11,766	10,670	11,827
MIDDLE EAST AND NORTH AFRICA	**7,537**	**8,681**	**10,756**	**15,129**	**27,818**	**39,524**	**41,046**	**50,520**	**53,408**	**58,039**	**73,131**
Algeria	1,257	1,227	1,492	2,259	4,036	5,974	5,307	7,102	8,667	8,407	10,525
Egypt, Arab Republic of	787	920	898	914	2,351	3,934	3,862	4,815	6,727	7,073	8,047
Iran, Islamic Rep. of	1,693	2,081	2,593	3,659	6,544	11,586	12,506	14,448	13,549	9,738	12,246
Jordan	185	215	267	328	487	731	1,022	1,381	1,499	1,949	2,394
Morocco	684	697	764	1,098	1,901	2,547	2,593	3,169	2,950	3,674	4,182
Oman	18	33	49	117	393	671	667	875	947	1,246	1,732
Syrian Arab Republic	350	438	539	613	1,229	1,669	1,959	2,656	2,444	3,324	4,118
Tunisia	305	342	459	606	1,120	1,418	1,526	1,821	2,158	2,842	3,509
Turkey	886	1,088	1,508	2,049	3,720	4,640	4,993	5,694	4,479	4,946	7,573
Yemen, Republic of	..	..	..	..	..	..	..	..	..	..	..
EUROPE	**19,325**	**21,637**	**25,153**	**34,701**	**48,126**	**54,101**	**58,521**	**66,432**	**75,835**	**90,316**	**100,658**
Bulgaria	1,831	2,120	2,567	3,266	4,326	5,408	5,626	6,393	7,651	8,514	9,650
Greece	1,958	2,098	2,346	3,473	4,385	5,321	6,051	6,853	7,655	9,594	10,531
Hungary	1,877	2,248	2,356	3,018	4,453	5,400	5,517	6,509	7,967	8,659	9,212
Malta	161	156	174	240	357	375	421	513	569	753	938
Poland	3,210	3,593	4,745	6,953	9,327	11,155	12,898	13,420	14,744	16,142	16,915
Portugal	1,590	1,824	2,227	3,073	4,641	3,863	4,316	4,964	5,229	6,509	9,293
Romania	..	..	..	..	..	..	..	..	..	..	..
Yugoslavia	2,874	3,297	3,233	4,783	7,520	7,699	7,367	8,973	9,770	14,037	15,064
Low- & middle-income economies	68,902	77,235	86,516	118,979	185,711	216,148	225,413	261,489	303,075	361,019	458,815
Severely indebted	19,483	21,860	25,557	34,777	55,776	62,653	64,905	72,841	83,332	101,770	127,204
Low-income economies	14,424	15,911	16,556	23,282	34,904	42,835	44,277	52,130	63,368	71,776	97,213
Low-income Africa	5,430	6,573	6,672	8,020	11,378	15,594	17,201	21,651	25,365	23,824	34,252
China and India	4,424	4,616	5,090	8,306	12,787	13,871	12,288	13,815	18,747	25,817	33,640
Other low-income	4,623	4,677	4,716	6,788	10,583	13,159	14,664	16,431	19,020	22,625	29,929
Middle-income economies	54,517	61,362	69,969	95,711	150,829	173,334	181,164	209,380	239,712	289,272	361,599
High-income OECD members	224,118	248,626	295,404	405,484	575,852	577,179	665,382	753,470	882,850	1,134,660	1,357,197
European Community members	120,961	134,428	159,937	223,207	306,603	313,311	357,913	401,188	474,687	623,130	748,700
Japan	18,883	19,712	23,471	38,313	62,094	57,865	64,505	70,561	78,731	110,108	139,892
United States	39,952	45,563	55,563	69,476	100,997	96,904	121,795	147,863	182,196	217,387	250,280
Other high-income economies /a	10,802	12,465	14,999	23,050	33,744	36,448	46,873	60,160	75,651	95,595	121,931

a. Economies classified by the United Nations or otherwise regarded by their authorities as developing.

1981	1982	1983	1984	1985	1986	1987	1988	1989	1990	
115,002	*92,937*	*71,588*	*70,895*	*68,528*	*69,046*	*77,768*	*86,485*	..	..	*LATIN AMERICA AND CARIBBEAN*
9,430	5,337	4,504	4,585	3,814	4,724	5,818	5,322	6,696	..	Argentina
4,214	3,067	3,252	3,037	2,209	1,618	1,701	1,547	..	..	Bahamas
572	551	621	659	602	593	515	582	..	..	Barbados
162	128	112	130	102	104	127	158	181	..	Belize
917	578	589	492	552	716	776	604	..	..	Bolivia
24,100	21,100	16,800	15,200	14,300	15,555	16,581	16,047	19,647	..	Brazil
6,331	4,117	3,186	3,770	3,300	3,157	4,023	4,843	5,172	..	Chile
5,200	5,460	4,970	4,490	4,130	3,850	4,322	5,002	..	..	Colombia
1,274	945	993	1,091	1,098	1,148	1,377	1,409	..	..	Costa Rica
1,668	1,444	1,471	1,446	1,487	1,433	1,783	1,849	..	..	Dominican Republic
1,907	1,737	1,487	1,616	1,767	1,810	2,250	1,714	..	..	Ecuador
1,045	945	892	977	961	935	975	1,052	..	..	El Salvador
56	59	58	51	62	75	78	..	..	..	Grenada
2,009	1,388	1,135	1,277	1,175	960	1,479	1,557	..	..	Guatemala
438	282	246	214	248	217	226	236	..	..	Guyana
527	448	412	435	449	367	378	453	..	..	Haiti
945	690	823	893	888	875	895	868	..	..	Honduras
1,487	1,373	1,531	1,130	1,124	964	1,207	1,449	..	..	Jamaica
24,161	15,041	8,023	11,788	13,994	12,032	12,731	19,592	17,098	..	Mexico
994	775	799	848	964	857	923	892	..	..	Nicaragua
1,562	1,568	1,411	1,412	1,383	1,229	1,306	751	..	..	Panama
915	822	629	741	530	830	1,180	1,271	..	..	Paraguay
3,803	3,721	2,722	2,212	2,023	2,909	3,562	3,080	..	..	Peru
58	65	70	77	79	92	99	108	..	..	St. Vincent and The Grenadines
3,120	3,700	2,582	1,919	1,533	1,370	1,219	1,127	..	..	Trinidad and Tobago
1,630	1,110	788	776	708	870	1,140	1,157	1,348	..	Uruguay
13,106	12,944	8,710	7,594	8,234	9,565	10,567	12,662	..	..	Venezuela
83,350	*77,530*	*82,202*	*79,223*	*71,896*	*64,681*	*64,167*	*68,870*	..	..	*MIDDLE EAST AND NORTH AFRICA*
11,302	10,679	10,332	10,263	9,814	9,234	7,028	7,432	9,719	..	Algeria
8,840	9,078	10,275	10,766	11,594	10,581	8,453	10,771	11,662	12,184	Egypt, Arab Republic of
12,499	11,955	18,320	15,370	11,635	10,521	9,570	9,454	..	..	Iran, Islamic Rep. of
3,146	3,218	3,016	2,784	2,733	2,413	2,710	2,732	..	..	Jordan
4,353	4,315	3,597	3,907	3,850	3,790	4,229	4,773	..	..	Morocco
2,171	2,683	2,492	2,640	3,028	2,402	1,822	2,202	..	..	Oman
5,040	4,014	4,542	4,116	3,967	2,703	2,546	2,223	..	..	Syrian Arab Republic
3,771	3,396	3,100	3,115	2,757	2,890	3,022	3,640	3,702	..	Tunisia
8,864	8,794	9,235	10,757	11,515	11,104	14,163	14,340	17,307	..	Turkey
..	..	..	..	..	..	..	..	..	..	Yemen, Republic of
96,245	*91,118*	*88,815*	*89,956*	*92,347*	*101,902*	*112,902*	*118,216*	..	..	*EUROPE*
10,801	11,527	12,283	12,714	13,656	15,249	16,095	16,582	..	..	Bulgaria
8,781	10,012	9,500	9,611	10,138	11,241	12,908	11,978	..	..	Greece
9,123	8,836	8,481	8,084	8,143	9,583	9,855	9,346	..	..	Hungary
855	789	733	717	759	880	1,139	1,343	..	..	Malta
12,795	10,244	10,590	10,547	10,836	11,208	10,844	12,064	..	..	Poland
9,946	9,605	8,257	7,975	7,650	9,393	13,438	16,108	16,353	..	Portugal
..	..	..	..	..	..	..	..	..	..	Romania
15,757	14,100	12,155	11,996	12,163	11,749	12,549	13,152	..	..	Yugoslavia
490,393	443,220	421,795	425,195	425,926	430,313	475,831	543,668	..	..	**Low- & middle-income economies**
127,644	103,734	83,654	83,097	83,315	87,889	96,828	106,793	..	..	Severely indebted
107,023	99,869	96,792	98,621	113,049	110,888	117,079	137,080	140,317	..	Low-income economies
37,499	31,630	25,681	22,775	22,273	21,754	22,905	23,845	23,039	..	Low-income Africa
35,136	32,933	36,128	42,774	59,821	59,973	62,377	77,778	..	..	China and India
34,791	36,114	35,671	33,754	31,268	29,369	32,445	35,876	37,347	..	Other low-income
383,370	343,348	324,997	326,567	312,822	319,380	358,780	406,553	..	..	Middle-income economies
1,292,886	1,216,333	1,200,217	1,315,091	1,365,473	1,523,370	1,800,658	2,038,890	..	..	**High-income OECD members**
662,411	633,026	608,797	620,038	648,135	760,471	929,093	1,053,048	..	..	European Community members
140,830	130,319	125,017	134,257	127,512	119,424	146,048	183,252	..	..	Japan
271,213	253,033	267,971	338,190	358,705	381,363	422,407	458,682	..	..	United States
136,346	140,229	138,287	138,120	122,520	127,673	163,271	205,897	..	..	**Other high-income economies** /a

Table 19. Growth of merchandise exports

Average annual growth (percent)	1970	1971	1972	1973	1974	1975	1976	1977	1978	1979	1980
SUB-SAHARAN AFRICA	*25.6*	*17.5*	*12.0*	*3.6*	*-16.2*	*-0.6*	*6.0*	*0.6*	*-7.2*	*16.0*	*-0.3*
Excluding Nigeria	*5.8*	*2.9*	*8.8*	*-4.7*	*-2.1*	*7.0*	*-5.3*	*0.8*	*-2.5*	*13.1*	*6.2*
Benin	32.1	24.2	-14.0	-21.3	6.4	41.4	-46.5	5.0	7.2	1.9	46.8
Botswana	19.4	27.1	88.4	10.3	19.0	12.4	20.3	3.5	13.0	64.9	6.9
Burkina Faso	-11.3	-7.7	35.2	-23.6	48.5	30.6	-9.6	14.7	5.9	5.5	12.0
Burundi	63.6	-14.6	20.6	-6.4	-8.7	9.1	-17.1	10.1	2.0	39.0	-29.9
Cameroon	-0.3	1.5	-2.9	9.7	8.8	8.6	-22.7	-5.1	19.9	32.1	9.8
Cape Verde	..	..	..	..	..	..	..	..	..	..	..
Central African Rep.	1.5	2.5	-14.1	-0.9	-12.1	2.2	-8.8	26.2	18.2	-7.9	5.0
Chad	..	..	..	..	..	..	..	..	..	..	..
Comoros	..	..	..	..	..	..	..	..	..	..	..
Congo, People's Rep of the	-23.0	20.2	29.4	80.7	14.4	-10.8	-2.6	-19.1	-5.2	118.0	22.8
Cote D'Ivoire	-4.7	5.4	17.3	6.2	5.1	9.0	-4.5	-4.2	10.8	-5.4	26.1
Ethiopia	-15.1	11.6	10.6	5.6	16.9	-15.2	-31.0	-21.3	18.3	20.5	14.7
Gabon	-1.7	12.5	1.4	16.5	-11.1	24.5	7.5	11.1	-21.2	19.7	-22.2
Gambia, The	-15.7	-7.7	11.7	-34.3	86.3	48.5	-31.5	12.8	-22.4	51.1	-50.4
Ghana	62.6	-5.2	1.9	-6.6	-18.8	31.9	-25.4	-17.1	4.6	-7.4	34.1
Guinea-Bissau	..	..	..	..	..	..	..	..	..	..	..
Kenya	8.5	-3.0	-2.5	0.5	-18.0	6.2	-0.5	7.5	-2.8	-8.2	10.2
Lesotho	-8.9	-30.0	82.6	14.5	-8.2	-2.0	26.6	-19.0	103.7	15.1	21.8
Liberia	2.1	10.2	9.6	-6.5	11.1	-8.3	12.6	-7.1	15.2	-11.6	-4.4
Madagascar	13.9	0.3	1.2	-5.2	-5.5	32.3	-33.4	-8.4	31.3	-10.8	-0.6
Malawi	6.4	13.2	6.4	2.1	-17.2	14.8	23.5	2.1	-3.3	0.7	8.0
Mali	104.4	-5.4	-0.3	3.9	0.5	-33.9	80.0	49.5	-16.0	34.6	18.6
Mauritania	-11.6	18.4	33.5	18.2	-20.4	-15.3	4.7	-12.8	-13.9	0.4	20.3
Mauritius	-3.0	1.1	18.6	8.2	0.4	-22.5	22.3	7.6	7.6	4.2	2.0
Mozambique	..	..	..	..	..	..	..	..	..	..	..
Niger	20.1	28.2	26.6	1.8	-38.1	55.4	38.2	13.9	53.0	47.6	31.4
Nigeria	70.8	38.2	15.5	11.9	-28.1	-9.3	21.5	0.4	-12.2	19.5	-7.6
Rwanda	48.2	0.5	-18.5	97.0	-7.1	8.1	25.3	-14.8	8.7	44.0	-27.4
Senegal	24.4	-17.5	42.3	-25.1	3.4	28.0	9.2	18.2	-29.0	3.8	-22.0
Seychelles	6.5	-30.4	63.3	-7.2	-22.1	14.2	28.8	13.1	34.7	1.9	-30.6
Sierra Leone	-9.4	-0.2	14.1	-18.4	-20.0	3.7	-31.2	-10.6	51.5	-9.3	3.0
Somalia	-10.8	18.9	22.3	-21.5	34.2	51.3	-21.9	-11.7	14.2	-26.5	30.6
Sudan	17.1	-2.1	-2.0	-30.9	-4.5	17.0	4.4	16.8	-29.6	11.2	-12.2
Swaziland	..	..	..	..	..	..	..	..	..	..	..
Tanzania	-3.0	1.4	11.1	-22.5	-24.0	-0.8	10.8	-7.9	-8.1	-5.6	1.1
Togo	-7.7	17.1	-10.5	-22.9	7.9	-26.3	27.8	19.2	46.1	1.1	28.9
Uganda	5.2	2.4	0.7	-12.5	0.2	-11.4	-32.8	15.3	-22.1	14.5	-15.9
Zaire	4.0	18.6	9.0	-23.2	9.9	-7.2	-22.2	31.2	-20.2	70.7	19.2
Zambia	-1.0	-11.7	11.6	-10.2	5.2	-5.3	14.4	-7.9	-7.2	10.1	-10.1
Zimbabwe	4.2	9.6	22.0	0.7	4.5	12.7	-6.8	-14.6	0.0	20.0	2.7
SOUTH ASIA	*-11.2*	*-0.7*	*6.4*	*-4.4*	*-2.4*	*4.7*	*27.7*	*3.9*	*1.0*	*6.4*	*-4.2*
Bangladesh	..	..	..	-16.2	-15.2	-24.4	36.8	9.3	20.2	4.9	12.0
India	-18.1	3.6	12.2	0.2	0.2	2.3	36.6	7.2	-2.4	4.3	-11.5
Nepal	-9.7	-8.1	3.7	-12.9	-14.8	50.3	1.5	-19.7	-2.6	-0.7	10.2
Pakistan	7.4	-14.2	-7.6	-19.8	-6.2	20.0	5.9	-16.3	16.2	17.7	15.1
Sri Lanka	10.4	-4.5	-1.9	5.1	-6.7	16.8	-7.4	0.9	14.6	4.0	..
EAST ASIA AND PACIFIC	*7.6*	*9.1*	*20.2*	*22.0*	*-3.7*	*7.6*	*13.4*	*11.3*	*10.3*	*5.6*	*9.2*
China	2.8	11.2	11.5	20.1	-3.2	12.2	-7.3	0.7	16.1	17.2	24.6
Fiji	14.7	-13.1	-12.0	-20.1	-30.5	21.5	8.8	44.1	24.2	-9.2	-20.7
Indonesia	6.3	6.3	53.7	22.1	-14.5	3.2	8.0	13.2	5.8	-4.5	-2.0
Korea, Republic of	21.7	23.3	50.0	61.0	12.0	11.3	36.5	28.0	15.1	-0.1	10.0
Malaysia	4.9	1.7	-6.4	9.5	-2.7	7.3	22.7	-2.0	6.8	14.8	-0.8
Papua New Guinea	5.8	66.9	20.7	18.9	90.4	-13.5	-31.2	4.2	30.5	0.5	20.5
Philippines	21.3	6.7	-13.7	18.2	-9.0	10.9	14.8	18.8	8.6	10.6	15.5
Solomon islands	..	..	..	..	..	..	..	..	..	..	..
Thailand	8.3	20.0	23.5	2.6	0.6	3.5	41.2	7.2	-0.1	10.9	10.6
Vanuatu	..	..	..	..	..	..	..	..	..	..	..

1981	1982	1983	1984	1985	1986	1987	1988	1989	1990	
-17.7	*-9.2*	*-4.6*	*8.9*	*8.4*	*1.2*	*0.7*	*-0.2*	*..*	*..*	*SUB-SAHARAN AFRICA*
-3.1	*-1.4*	*-3.6*	*6.8*	*5.6*	*3.4*	*4.6*	*-4.6*	*..*	*..*	*Excluding Nigeria*
-19.1	-10.1	-7.6	16.8	16.0	-18.3	49.6	13.8	..	..	Benin
-17.6	18.2	42.6	7.2	12.8	2.7	61.8	-21.6	..	..	Botswana
9.6	-10.9	-7.6	9.5	13.6	19.0	7.8	5.6	..	..	Burkina Faso
29.4	16.0	-8.2	17.8	17.8	20.4	-21.6	22.3	..	..	Burundi
16.1	-4.6	16.6	12.0	16.9	9.6	-13.6	-11.9	..	..	Cameroon
..	..	..	..	..	..	..	..	..	..	Cape Verde
-9.4	-3.9	5.5	-4.5	24.7	-10.5	1.4	-10.5	..	..	Central African Rep.
..	..	..	..	..	..	..	..	..	..	Chad
..	..	..	..	..	..	..	..	..	..	Comoros
12.9	20.6	-3.6	15.7	-5.1	-7.9	11.7	6.9	..	..	Congo, People's Rep of the
-6.8	-7.0	-9.2	15.5	18.0	3.2	3.9	-21.2	..	..	Cote D'Ivoire
2.6	5.3	-0.8	-5.0	-17.6	11.4	6.8	6.6	..	..	Ethiopia
0.2	5.4	1.5	5.4	5.7	-21.1	-0.1	2.2	..	..	Gabon
-17.1	119.3	0.4	-4.2	6.9	9.4	5.3	-9.2	..	..	Gambia, The
0.2	-3.6	-46.4	-2.6	23.5	53.3	7.8	4.5	..	..	Ghana
..	..	..	..	..	..	..	..	..	..	Guinea-Bissau
-10.4	-3.1	-7.0	0.3	4.6	11.8	-5.5	5.7	..	..	Kenya
-10.0	-26.1	-0.1	-10.2	-21.5	-2.3	74.3	7.4	..	..	Lesotho
0.6	-10.7	-3.7	6.3	1.8	-6.9	-12.1	-4.1	..	..	Liberia
-8.6	0.0	-4.1	6.9	-17.6	-2.9	14.9	-19.2	..	..	Madagascar
2.9	-1.0	-2.8	30.3	-4.5	-5.5	15.1	-6.8	..	..	Malawi
-21.2	10.8	4.6	16.0	12.2	16.7	-8.5	16.5	..	..	Mali
40.8	-4.4	42.1	-10.1	24.7	-6.2	25.8	-9.6	..	..	Mauritania
-19.8	22.7	2.6	7.5	15.7	29.3	18.5	12.4	..	..	Mauritius
..	..	..	..	..	..	..	..	..	..	Mozambique
-22.2	-14.2	-11.9	-11.1	-16.0	43.8	21.0	-31.7	..	..	Niger
-36.5	-24.6	-7.1	14.7	15.3	-3.9	-8.7	12.2	..	..	Nigeria
-4.6	-8.0	17.1	5.1	-11.4	12.5	0.8	-13.3	..	..	Rwanda
3.4	22.8	7.6	3.8	-9.6	21.9	2.7	11.0	..	..	Senegal
-21.3	0.2	34.2	-7.0	54.3	13.6	-3.4	41.8	..	..	Seychelles
-31.9	-17.2	8.7	7.7	4.1	7.2	-11.4	-19.4	..	..	Sierra Leone
40.1	2.4	-44.9	-40.5	73.8	-0.9	-4.3	-41.6	..	..	Somalia
-10.0	-9.4	25.9	30.1	2.4	-10.3	-15.1	1.0	..	..	Sudan
..	..	..	..	..	..	..	..	..	..	Swaziland
19.3	-24.6	-8.7	-12.8	-18.7	17.6	7.5	7.3	..	..	Tanzania
-19.1	4.4	-12.3	-14.5	14.3	11.8	11.6	4.4	..	..	Togo
-15.3	36.1	9.8	-1.6	-8.7	-13.1	26.3	-1.9	..	..	Uganda
-4.5	-16.9	-12.6	13.4	1.8	-7.2	3.9	-3.1	..	..	Zaire
-9.6	9.6	0.0	0.7	-9.3	-13.2	-1.0	-5.3	..	..	Zambia
2.8	1.5	-12.9	4.1	6.4	15.2	-7.1	9.0	..	..	Zimbabwe
-3.8	*3.5*	*6.1*	*2.1*	*2.6*	*8.8*	*13.3*	*7.2*	*..*	*..*	*SOUTH ASIA*
-9.7	0.5	5.5	8.2	6.4	3.0	21.7	6.1	..	..	Bangladesh
-5.0	6.2	1.8	3.7	-1.7	6.8	15.8	9.8	..	..	India
19.9	-13.4	-11.6	34.7	24.2	-16.7	1.0	18.2	..	..	Nepal
8.0	-5.7	30.6	-12.0	12.7	27.2	11.5	2.8	..	..	Pakistan
..	4.1	-1.5	20.8	14.5	-3.4	6.3	-1.3	..	..	Sri Lanka
10.9	*5.9*	*10.6*	*13.2*	*4.4*	*13.6*	*15.1*	*12.5*	*..*	*..*	*EAST ASIA AND PACIFIC*
20.6	6.1	9.4	15.3	7.1	16.4	13.9	14.4	..	..	China
5.4	40.3	-16.2	22.4	9.8	15.6	7.0	-10.4	..	..	Fiji
-6.1	-4.7	19.2	0.0	-0.4	13.0	-0.3	5.6	..	..	Indonesia
19.2	7.1	14.6	18.2	6.3	16.4	25.8	13.3	..	..	Korea, Republic of
1.4	15.2	15.4	13.7	3.2	7.2	9.7	9.0	..	..	Malaysia
-3.5	-7.0	3.3	3.4	12.6	14.0	12.4	15.1	..	..	Papua New Guinea
8.0	-2.5	-3.1	5.8	-6.3	3.4	3.4	9.2	..	..	Philippines
..	..	..	..	..	..	..	..	..	..	Solomon islands
20.8	19.4	-8.8	23.1	5.5	11.8	22.6	21.0	..	..	Thailand
..	..	..	..	..	..	..	..	..	..	Vanuatu

Table 19. Growth of merchandise exports (cont'd.)

Average annual growth (percent)	1970	1971	1972	1973	1974	1975	1976	1977	1978	1979	1980
LATIN AMERICA AND CARIBBEAN	*2.2*	*-14.0*	*0.6*	*7.4*	*-17.6*	*-3.7*	*3.3*	*4.0*	*10.8*	*6.5*	*5.7*
Argentina	1.7	-4.0	2.7	26.5	0.5	-24.4	31.1	39.9	7.7	-1.7	-8.4
Bahamas	..	..	..	..	..	..	..	..	..	..	..
Barbados	-7.0	13.2	-13.3	-17.9	-15.3	19.6	1.3	10.8	36.5	-1.9	-6.7
Belize	..	..	..	..	..	..	..	..	..	..	..
Bolivia	-15.9	14.3	14.4	-8.8	5.6	-5.4	13.7	-6.7	-10.3	-5.2	3.7
Brazil	9.4	7.0	25.2	9.1	7.5	13.9	1.7	0.5	14.4	11.7	23.2
Chile	15.4	-2.1	-13.0	-14.8	70.9	0.8	23.6	1.7	10.4	14.9	8.6
Colombia	-1.9	-1.8	9.9	12.8	-10.4	3.6	-12.1	1.1	36.5	-0.5	16.1
Costa Rica	10.9	7.5	9.6	-1.0	7.4	11.2	-1.5	10.6	20.3	-12.8	7.8
Dominican Republic	8.1	10.1	28.0	0.7	-20.3	49.9	-7.6	-10.6	-3.9	17.6	-9.7
Ecuador	23.8	16.1	105.7	90.5	-23.3	-10.8	9.1	-7.6	10.7	9.6	-10.7
El Salvador	-6.8	9.2	13.3	-8.0	6.7	19.5	-9.3	-1.4	2.6	18.9	-5.3
Grenada	..	..	..	..	..	..	..	..	..	..	..
Guatemala	-1.0	0.9	4.3	0.3	5.1	16.0	-7.8	20.5	8.8	-5.0	17.0
Guyana	19.2	9.7	-14.7	-19.4	4.9	19.2	-1.5	-3.2	2.9	-10.7	5.4
Haiti	12.6	11.8	15.3	20.8	4.1	13.5	2.8	3.9	13.5	-8.5	30.0
Honduras	-2.8	3.1	-5.9	2.2	-14.5	13.9	8.7	9.5	24.1	0.7	7.3
Jamaica	40.5	-1.8	3.0	-14.0	23.6	5.5	-19.2	10.5	-5.9	-5.8	8.6
Mexico	-12.7	4.6	27.5	11.5	-12.2	0.5	3.0	14.6	48.3	8.4	25.5
Nicaragua	2.1	4.4	22.8	-21.1	18.6	10.6	6.8	2.6	8.7	-17.2	-39.7
Panama	-6.8	-2.7	-16.4	-13.7	-17.4	39.6	-23.4	-1.7	-2.7	-5.4	-4.3
Paraguay	3.9	-5.5	17.4	-12.6	30.0	24.4	1.9	45.7	8.9	-8.2	0.7
Peru	14.1	-5.2	-7.0	-32.5	22.3	20.2	-13.0	18.9	16.8	41.0	0.3
St. Vincent and The Grenadines	..	..	..	..	..	..	..	..	..	..	..
Trinidad and Tobago	0.9	-15.5	-4.0	-8.4	-20.7	-11.1	18.6	-10.3	-6.8	-9.6	-1.3
Uruguay	11.3	-13.1	-20.5	-0.3	22.9	15.0	30.4	10.2	2.6	-4.1	18.9
Venezuela	1.3	-24.7	-10.2	9.2	-40.3	-17.9	-1.9	-7.1	-4.4	7.9	-15.5
MIDDLE EAST AND NORTH AFRICA	..	..	..	..	..	..	..	..	..	..	..
Algeria	10.8	-30.2	46.3	3.7	-38.9	2.9	8.7	7.5	4.2	12.3	-13.2
Egypt, Arab Republic of	16.9	-1.0	-8.5	-26.1	-13.0	10.5	-4.3	13.3	18.3	2.2	-6.2
Iran, Islamic Rep. of	..	..	..	..	..	..	..	..	..	..	..
Jordan	2.2	-4.5	41.9	-2.2	55.3	-9.6	65.4	18.9	12.7	11.3	24.3
Morocco	-0.1	-0.8	19.8	13.9	1.8	-18.4	9.5	-1.0	8.8	8.8	8.0
Oman	..	..	..	..	..	..	..	..	..	..	..
Syrian Arab Republic	13.1	-6.5	19.3	-9.1	23.1	29.1	2.0	-5.8	-2.1	16.1	-14.0
Tunisia	3.4	6.6	31.0	-1.5	21.7	0.9	-8.8	5.9	24.5	13.5	-6.6
Turkey	6.5	13.1	32.0	10.7	-8.0	-5.8	28.7	-11.2	18.7	-16.7	18.4
Yemen, Republic of	..	..	..	..	..	..	..	..	..	..	..
EUROPE	..	..	..	..	..	..	..	..	..	..	..
Bulgaria	..	..	..	..	..	..	..	..	..	..	..
Greece	13.5	3.8	23.2	37.2	6.1	11.0	7.5	0.4	15.0	-7.1	15.5
Hungary	..	..	..	..	..	..	..	..	..	..	..
Malta	-4.4	5.0	33.1	10.8	-4.5	24.7	36.0	17.8	11.5	3.8	1.7
Poland	..	..	..	..	..	..	..	..	..	..	..
Portugal	8.1	2.9	6.9	9.6	1.7	-22.3	-0.8	9.9	3.4	21.0	9.2
Romania	..	..	..	..	..	..	..	..	..	..	..
Yugoslavia	5.3	9.6	14.6	8.0	-0.3	3.7	18.2	-3.4	1.6	3.0	16.3
Low- & middle-income economies	6.3	-3.4	10.1	7.7	-11.3	1.3	8.0	6.0	7.8	8.2	5.9
Severely indebted	2.5	-13.8	0.9	9.9	-17.1	-4.6	5.1	5.3	10.6	8.3	6.9
Low-income economies	11.4	12.0	16.5	7.3	-12.9	2.4	8.9	4.1	1.2	8.5	2.3
Low-income Africa	33.9	20.5	11.4	2.8	-20.4	-4.0	8.6	0.9	-8.5	15.9	-1.7
China and India	-8.5	7.5	11.9	10.8	-1.8	7.9	10.7	4.0	6.5	11.0	8.4
Other low-income	5.8	-3.9	30.9	10.9	-13.6	4.5	7.2	8.5	7.1	-0.5	0.2
Middle-income economies	4.5	-8.9	7.3	7.9	-10.6	0.8	7.6	6.9	10.9	8.0	7.4
High-income OECD members	9.6	7.4	7.1	6.7	11.1	-2.0	9.5	6.6	4.4	4.0	5.8
European Community members	9.6	8.4	7.0	6.6	8.8	-1.9	10.1	7.8	4.0	4.7	2.5
Japan	13.9	20.3	7.0	5.0	17.0	3.6	21.4	10.0	0.1	-2.5	17.9
United States	6.9	0.1	7.3	16.5	15.6	-0.7	1.7	1.0	9.9	5.8	12.4
Other high-income economies /a	20.8	13.8	17.3	9.7	-11.9	-8.8	20.7	5.2	4.4	10.8	4.5

a. Economies classified by the United Nations or otherwise regarded by their authorities as developing.

1981	1982	1983	1984	1985	1986	1987	1988	1989	1990	
6.9	-2.9	7.0	12.7	1.6	-4.6	5.2	9.0	..	..	*LATIN AMERICA AND CARIBBEAN*
12.2	-4.8	-4.0	5.5	12.0	-14.7	-10.0	19.6	..	..	Argentina
..	..	..	..	..	..	..	..	..	..	Bahamas
36.8	28.2	24.5	31.1	-11.3	-20.4	-49.0	1.5	..	..	Barbados
..	..	..	..	..	..	..	..	..	..	Belize
2.7	-2.0	-8.1	-2.6	-9.9	12.9	16.5	-12.2	..	..	Bolivia
17.9	-4.9	15.6	22.3	3.4	-19.1	12.4	19.3	..	..	Brazil
-6.1	10.6	-2.0	3.1	8.0	11.0	2.8	4.5	..	..	Chile
-11.5	-5.4	-2.1	9.1	5.5	26.7	22.6	-2.0	..	..	Colombia
3.0	-10.7	-1.3	15.2	2.7	1.0	12.2	1.1	..	..	Costa Rica
33.6	-23.7	5.5	19.3	-11.4	-15.1	6.8	10.8	..	..	Dominican Republic
-13.3	10.5	0.6	16.5	15.9	4.3	-12.6	18.2	..	..	Ecuador
-16.2	-13.6	8.3	-5.2	-3.2	-12.4	12.4	-11.1	..	..	El Salvador
..	..	..	..	..	..	..	..	..	..	Grenada
-14.8	4.7	3.8	-1.8	-1.7	-10.4	9.7	-9.5	..	..	Guatemala
-7.7	-19.6	-17.8	22.8	4.6	5.7	10.3	-5.7	..	..	Guyana
-12.4	10.0	-5.3	17.1	7.1	-28.6	-7.1	0.4	..	..	Haiti
-6.1	-6.3	0.0	13.4	7.8	0.8	6.6	-5.3	..	..	Honduras
4.0	-22.8	1.0	3.3	-23.1	-1.8	5.3	7.2	..	..	Jamaica
23.9	3.1	21.7	12.0	-4.2	3.4	8.5	2.7	..	..	Mexico
30.0	-15.7	9.2	-8.9	-15.2	-27.4	34.7	-27.6	..	..	Nicaragua
-1.2	0.6	-2.2	11.2	15.0	0.0	2.0	-29.5	..	..	Panama
4.0	8.7	-25.5	12.7	10.3	83.9	46.6	-2.0	..	..	Paraguay
-8.5	15.7	-6.1	6.8	-1.4	-9.1	-8.5	-14.8	..	..	Peru
..	..	..	..	..	..	..	..	..	..	St. Vincent and The Grenadines
-13.0	-7.5	-14.7	-3.4	3.3	0.2	-12.6	8.7	..	..	Trinidad and Tobago
12.2	-6.2	4.5	-7.8	-3.9	20.8	-2.2	13.2	..	..	Uruguay
-4.7	-10.2	-2.3	12.1	-1.5	7.9	-4.9	10.3	..	..	Venezuela
..	..	..	..	..	..	..	..	..	..	*MIDDLE EAST AND NORTH AFRICA*
-6.8	0.7	5.1	4.5	4.4	8.8	-1.0	6.1	..	..	Algeria
1.3	10.5	6.2	16.4	21.0	7.8	-26.7	5.1	..	..	Egypt, Arab Republic of
..	..	..	..	..	..	..	..	..	..	Iran, Islamic Rep. of
39.1	8.2	-19.3	29.4	10.4	-21.8	28.5	-1.5	..	..	Jordan
2.9	0.0	8.6	3.8	4.5	5.6	7.5	16.0	..	..	Morocco
..	..	..	..	..	..	..	..	..	..	Oman
-5.6	9.9	4.0	0.5	-11.2	-3.1	7.1	10.4	..	..	Syrian Arab Republic
11.4	-6.0	2.4	1.5	1.5	8.6	14.2	7.3	..	..	Tunisia
69.2	38.0	2.3	29.9	17.4	-15.8	21.7	5.7	..	..	Turkey
..	..	..	..	..	..	..	..	..	..	Yemen, Republic of
..	..	..	..	..	..	..	..	..	..	*EUROPE*
..	..	..	..	..	..	..	..	..	..	Bulgaria
-9.8	3.1	9.9	15.2	-2.9	20.5	5.3	-24.5	..	..	Greece
..	..	..	..	..	..	..	..	..	..	Hungary
2.7	-17.2	7.0	12.5	3.1	5.0	11.3	9.0	..	..	Malta
..	..	..	..	..	..	..	..	..	..	Poland
0.7	16.7	18.0	13.3	7.8	17.6	5.2	6.8	..	..	Portugal
..	..	..	..	..	..	..	..	..	..	Romania
19.3	-5.7	-8.0	6.8	8.1	-6.2	0.2	0.4	..	..	Yugoslavia
2.6	0.9	6.6	10.6	4.4	4.4	8.7	7.6	..	..	**Low- & middle-income economies**
8.6	-1.9	7.0	12.8	1.6	-4.7	4.3	9.5	..	..	Severely indebted
-4.5	-2.5	6.3	7.6	4.6	10.2	7.8	9.3	..	..	Low-income economies
-23.5	-14.8	-7.6	8.5	7.5	-0.2	-2.2	4.3	..	..	Low-income Africa
11.3	6.1	7.0	11.9	4.7	13.9	14.3	13.3	..	..	China and India
-3.6	-3.3	16.8	0.1	2.8	11.9	1.8	4.7	..	..	Other low-income
5.5	2.1	6.7	11.6	4.3	2.4	9.0	7.1	..	..	Middle-income economies
3.8	-2.0	1.4	10.2	4.5	2.3	5.6	6.3	..	..	**High-income OECD members**
3.8	-0.3	1.9	8.6	5.3	3.8	4.2	4.6	..	..	European Community members
11.4	-2.0	7.9	16.1	5.8	-1.2	-0.1	4.5	..	..	Japan
-1.3	-9.3	-8.0	8.5	-0.1	-1.5	17.2	14.8	..	..	United States
-1.5	-10.9	-4.4	10.5	-2.8	14.3	12.4	14.6	..	..	**Other high-income economies** /a

Table 20. Growth of merchandise imports

Average annual growth (percent)	1970	1971	1972	1973	1974	1975	1976	1977	1978	1979	1980
SUB-SAHARAN AFRICA	*8.6*	*8.2*	*-3.4*	*-0.7*	*2.4*	*28.1*	*9.5*	*15.6*	*2.5*	*-15.2*	*21.2*
Excluding Nigeria	*4.8*	*4.8*	*-2.1*	*-1.6*	*-1.1*	*9.1*	*-2.7*	*10.7*	*3.7*	*-4.5*	*8.8*
Benin	11.4	11.1	12.1	1.8	9.4	10.1	6.7	-1.4	15.6	-11.6	-5.4
Botswana	31.2	28.7	17.5	21.2	-22.6	11.5	-7.3	21.4	15.4	23.7	18.1
Burkina Faso	-9.0	17.6	15.6	6.5	-8.4	22.2	-7.8	22.1	-1.9	9.5	5.7
Burundi	4.5	9.9	-6.6	-19.9	-8.6	51.6	-9.9	47.8	-3.1	35.3	-7.4
Cameroon	10.7	-4.6	9.1	-8.2	-6.7	28.4	-0.8	13.6	20.9	7.8	7.6
Cape Verde	..	..	..	..	..	..	..	..	..	..	..
Central African Rep.	-14.8	-15.5	2.4	0.4	-2.7	19.9	-11.3	25.8	1.9	-11.2	23.2
Chad	..	..	..	..	..	..	..	..	..	..	..
Comoros	..	..	..	..	..	..	..	..	..	..	..
Congo, People's Rep of the	-34.0	32.0	3.4	18.4	-25.8	24.4	0.1	0.1	14.3	-6.3	65.2
Cote D'Ivoire	9.2	-5.3	6.5	22.7	0.0	11.4	14.5	23.5	17.1	-11.9	6.5
Ethiopia	8.0	1.1	-10.0	-7.1	-11.7	-0.6	19.0	1.7	14.9	-6.5	6.7
Gabon	-3.7	7.0	34.3	20.3	41.6	29.4	5.3	28.5	-18.5	-13.7	-6.3
Gambia, The	-29.0	18.1	1.4	16.6	-18.4	24.9	34.4	1.7	21.6	23.5	-11.1
Ghana	9.2	-1.4	-33.2	13.7	27.8	-6.5	7.5	23.9	-22.3	-28.1	9.2
Guinea-Bissau	..	..	..	..	..	..	..	..	..	..	..
Kenya	15.2	9.7	-6.0	-5.8	3.4	-9.9	-9.4	29.1	19.6	-18.9	25.1
Lesotho	-8.7	12.7	25.7	24.4	3.4	26.0	23.3	1.4	6.4	15.6	19.4
Liberia	32.7	0.4	-0.5	-12.1	2.9	10.7	20.4	5.1	-9.3	-11.6	-15.0
Madagascar	-8.5	10.8	-9.7	-21.3	-12.0	31.8	-21.7	12.7	14.4	29.8	-11.6
Malawi	7.6	27.6	8.1	-12.0	-7.5	24.6	-20.0	4.8	31.2	-0.4	-3.7
Mali	5.9	19.7	18.5	14.9	-15.9	27.9	-17.0	-1.9	56.0	11.4	3.8
Mauritania	0.1	-13.0	7.1	22.7	-0.8	14.8	31.5	2.1	-19.4	-8.7	-4.3
Mauritius	-3.6	-0.6	36.2	10.8	21.7	7.0	10.6	14.8	-2.9	-3.1	-5.2
Mozambique	..	..	..	..	..	..	..	..	..	..	..
Niger	13.0	-7.4	12.5	5.3	-28.0	-3.1	39.5	40.7	34.1	31.3	5.5
Nigeria	34.7	26.1	-9.2	3.8	18.3	100.7	34.7	22.9	0.8	-30.1	44.7
Rwanda	14.9	9.2	-2.9	-0.7	12.7	36.7	28.5	-9.9	44.9	-5.0	10.4
Senegal	-11.8	6.2	15.6	-3.7	-5.4	21.1	12.1	8.6	-11.7	5.4	-9.3
Seychelles	26.8	36.9	24.3	-1.1	-27.3	10.3	38.7	-3.9	3.6	44.3	-7.5
Sierra Leone	-5.0	-6.4	-2.9	-0.4	-0.4	-31.1	3.8	0.9	37.5	-3.9	16.8
Somalia	-21.0	4.9	26.4	26.2	1.4	-4.8	9.7	10.7	19.3	23.9	1.8
Sudan	6.3	0.5	-11.6	7.0	-4.3	43.5	3.8	-4.8	-22.9	-8.7	26.7
Swaziland	..	..	..	..	..	..	..	..	..	..	..
Tanzania	27.8	13.2	-2.7	2.2	0.7	-8.1	-7.8	5.9	41.2	-18.3	-8.5
Togo	6.7	7.0	2.3	-14.8	-9.8	104.1	-17.2	25.5	49.1	-6.0	-5.0
Uganda	-6.0	33.2	-41.2	-16.0	5.2	-9.5	-22.9	32.8	-5.8	-35.3	27.9
Zaire	-1.4	4.2	12.1	-18.2	-13.5	-5.7	-13.5	-4.0	-18.0	-10.9	20.5
Zambia	2.6	-0.7	-9.3	-19.0	0.6	10.8	-31.1	-6.0	-17.4	1.0	29.5
Zimbabwe	10.5	6.7	-4.8	6.3	-2.6	2.8	-25.8	-7.7	-15.0	35.2	31.8
SOUTH ASIA	*0.7*	*-1.6*	*-16.9*	*9.6*	*-3.3*	*17.3*	*-6.6*	*7.1*	*14.7*	*9.8*	*8.9*
Bangladesh	..	..	..	19.4	-28.1	16.9	4.3	-12.0	16.6	10.1	12.9
India	3.2	14.4	-11.1	8.2	-2.6	18.2	-11.2	9.1	11.2	6.4	8.5
Nepal	25.8	-22.6	21.0	-13.3	-27.4	48.8	19.1	7.1	29.4	-8.4	-29.7
Pakistan	3.9	-23.9	-36.9	13.7	22.2	18.3	3.2	4.3	14.1	9.4	12.4
Sri Lanka	-22.6	-22.9	-11.2	8.2	-3.2	6.5	-15.6	23.7	26.3	32.6	14.2
EAST ASIA AND PACIFIC	*9.1*	*0.5*	*1.1*	*22.2*	*20.0*	*1.5*	*6.5*	*6.5*	*16.5*	*11.2*	*4.4*
China	28.0	-7.3	14.1	31.8	25.1	4.0	-14.2	-1.7	38.4	25.2	10.1
Fiji	12.5	8.5	11.2	0.7	-8.7	-6.8	-3.3	4.8	6.9	10.1	2.1
Indonesia	6.4	7.1	5.8	49.8	32.1	12.3	21.7	0.1	-1.9	-5.6	16.8
Korea, Republic of	7.1	12.7	-1.9	25.1	15.1	2.9	18.5	14.5	26.7	10.7	-13.4
Malaysia	13.4	-2.7	-7.3	16.6	23.2	-16.4	8.0	10.3	14.0	17.8	15.9
Papua New Guinea	29.9	9.8	-11.9	-14.9	-1.4	8.2	-11.4	16.2	6.8	0.0	10.9
Philippines	-3.3	-1.8	-6.0	1.5	26.7	3.0	2.0	-1.1	10.1	7.6	3.9
Solomon islands	..	..	..	..	..	..	..	..	..	..	..
Thailand	0.1	-8.2	4.5	13.5	1.6	-2.8	4.7	18.8	4.4	11.1	8.9
Vanuatu	..	..	..	..	..	..	..	..	..	..	..

1981	1982	1983	1984	1985	1986	1987	1988	1989	1990	
7.3	-10.1	-16.0	-9.5	-0.3	-4.1	-1.5	-4.6	..	..	*SUB-SAHARAN AFRICA*
-5.5	-3.0	-9.3	-1.4	2.2	6.3	-0.6	-1.6	..	..	*Excluding Nigeria*
64.5	-12.0	-37.4	-28.1	11.1	44.9	11.9	6.7	..	..	Benin
16.5	-11.5	9.7	-1.1	-17.8	13.7	12.6	11.7	..	..	Botswana
-10.6	6.9	-11.8	-11.5	30.3	23.2	-4.0	-3.9	..	..	Burkina Faso
-3.3	38.1	-7.4	-0.8	1.1	0.6	-5.5	-8.2	..	..	Burundi
-6.3	-8.2	2.0	-2.6	-4.9	32.4	17.5	-26.3	..	..	Cameroon
..	..	..	..	..	..	..	..	..	..	Cape Verde
-23.6	-1.1	-1.4	17.3	21.0	5.3	-6.1	-14.1	..	..	Central African Rep.
..	..	..	..	..	..	..	..	..	..	Chad
..	..	..	..	..	..	..	..	..	..	Comoros
65.6	1.1	-5.0	1.7	3.4	-22.6	-15.9	-2.9	..	..	Congo, People's Rep of the
-25.4	-3.0	-13.3	-13.8	15.2	16.7	4.5	-22.1	..	..	Cote D'Ivoire
0.6	8.5	15.3	10.3	6.3	4.4	-6.7	5.6	..	..	Ethiopia
23.5	-2.3	8.4	6.4	9.9	-1.7	-29.1	-6.5	..	..	Gabon
-3.5	7.1	-14.0	-25.4	3.1	3.4	5.0	3.5	..	..	Gambia, The
-6.3	-35.3	-7.1	10.5	13.8	10.3	-4.6	2.9	..	..	Ghana
..	..	..	..	..	..	..	..	..	..	Guinea-Bissau
-23.0	-20.2	-12.3	13.9	-1.9	23.4	-5.2	10.9	..	..	Kenya
16.7	-3.0	4.3	-11.3	-23.4	6.6	19.3	4.8	..	..	Lesotho
-13.5	-4.6	0.8	-5.0	-23.5	-14.5	-20.2	2.0	..	..	Liberia
-31.1	-12.1	-2.5	-0.6	20.2	-18.2	-8.1	3.1	..	..	Madagascar
-23.6	-8.0	2.0	-10.8	8.4	-14.6	3.1	28.2	..	..	Malawi
-18.0	-5.1	8.7	4.2	22.8	-1.8	-7.1	4.1	..	..	Mali
23.5	17.9	-11.8	-15.8	6.3	11.5	5.3	0.5	..	..	Mauritania
-15.0	-10.3	-2.4	11.8	14.4	24.3	37.0	4.1	..	..	Mauritius
..	..	..	..	..	..	..	..	..	..	Mozambique
4.3	0.9	-37.6	-2.2	5.3	1.3	2.6	8.1	..	..	Niger
25.5	-17.6	-24.5	-21.7	-5.1	-25.4	-4.1	-13.9	..	..	Nigeria
0.2	9.4	-5.9	2.9	10.8	6.1	-7.2	3.8	..	..	Rwanda
-3.1	3.0	7.3	1.0	-9.7	6.2	11.4	-3.4	..	..	Senegal
-4.6	11.5	-10.4	-33.7	74.9	10.4	-2.8	31.1	..	..	Seychelles
-26.8	-0.4	-44.8	-0.3	-4.3	-9.6	-13.3	4.9	..	..	Sierra Leone
-4.3	30.8	-21.7	30.2	-28.3	7.1	-4.1	-38.3	..	..	Somalia
2.4	20.8	-10.4	-9.9	-17.4	-18.5	-28.8	37.5	..	..	Sudan
..	..	..	..	..	..	..	..	..	..	Swaziland
-8.6	3.1	-28.1	10.3	23.2	2.6	-1.5	3.7	..	..	Tanzania
-16.5	0.4	-26.5	-10.8	14.4	8.2	-4.3	-6.8	..	..	Togo
15.6	12.4	3.3	-6.5	-7.8	5.5	25.7	14.1	..	..	Uganda
-9.5	-7.4	-6.1	6.8	5.7	1.8	4.8	-4.9	..	..	Zaire
-5.5	-19.2	-14.9	3.7	-7.7	-0.1	1.3	7.8	..	..	Zambia
11.2	1.7	-23.9	-17.9	9.8	3.0	-12.9	5.5	..	..	Zimbabwe
7.5	2.2	4.0	5.3	13.7	-1.4	0.1	10.6	..	..	*SOUTH ASIA*
20.2	1.7	-12.1	7.7	13.5	-8.0	-1.0	6.6	..	..	Bangladesh
12.0	2.5	6.9	5.8	19.3	-0.4	1.4	12.3	..	..	India
7.6	15.0	36.6	-5.9	14.1	-3.0	10.2	13.5	..	..	Nepal
-1.5	-0.4	5.9	8.8	3.6	-1.7	-2.0	9.6	..	..	Pakistan
-12.1	2.5	8.1	6.2	7.5	0.0	-3.1	4.3	..	..	Sri Lanka
12.0	2.3	11.2	11.1	10.8	-5.3	2.7	16.7	..	..	*EAST ASIA AND PACIFIC*
1.4	-1.1	20.7	33.5	60.3	-10.4	-9.4	17.8	..	..	China
8.7	-17.0	0.1	-3.9	-1.3	-0.1	-21.1	16.1	..	..	Fiji
34.3	9.4	-0.5	-9.9	-17.4	-5.3	-3.1	0.6	..	..	Indonesia
16.7	-0.2	13.9	21.7	4.6	3.9	13.6	13.7	..	..	Korea, Republic of
10.3	13.9	7.9	6.1	-14.6	-15.9	-0.7	21.4	..	..	Malaysia
4.0	-1.1	-1.4	3.1	-7.5	9.0	-1.5	6.4	..	..	Papua New Guinea
-1.0	2.8	-0.6	-16.6	-16.1	3.1	18.5	17.5	..	..	Philippines
..	..	..	..	..	..	..	..	..	..	Solomon islands
5.3	-12.9	29.8	4.6	-10.9	-1.0	26.5	36.0	..	..	Thailand
..	..	..	..	..	..	..	..	..	..	Vanuatu

Table 20. Growth of merchandise imports (cont'd.)

Average annual growth (percent)	1970	1971	1972	1973	1974	1975	1976	1977	1978	1979	1980
LATIN AMERICA AND CARIBBEAN	10.0	5.1	3.7	5.0	13.0	2.7	-0.9	3.1	2.8	5.3	15.0
Argentina	-1.7	6.0	-11.0	0.7	16.4	2.8	-26.2	26.7	-16.9	45.5	45.9
Bahamas	..	..	..	..	..	..	..	..	..	..	..
Barbados	9.8	-2.8	3.9	-4.2	-12.5	1.4	7.5	5.5	2.7	15.2	9.4
Belize	..	..	..	..	..	..	..	..	..	..	..
Bolivia	-9.9	0.2	-3.6	5.3	26.0	49.1	4.9	-8.6	15.0	-4.2	-28.0
Brazil	22.3	20.5	17.1	15.5	27.1	-7.8	-4.5	-11.3	2.1	3.8	0.3
Chile	3.6	1.7	-1.8	0.9	-13.2	-13.1	-7.8	41.3	20.6	24.2	11.5
Colombia	16.6	4.0	-15.7	-0.2	20.7	-10.4	10.4	7.5	24.9	-2.5	26.6
Costa Rica	21.2	3.6	-0.2	1.8	13.3	-9.9	14.0	21.5	1.3	1.4	-4.4
Dominican Republic	15.0	11.1	2.1	-0.8	8.2	5.5	-1.5	-1.2	-9.1	0.7	15.9
Ecuador	8.5	17.5	-15.7	-5.8	46.8	22.1	-4.2	12.7	12.2	15.7	1.4
El Salvador	-7.0	14.9	0.9	11.4	11.1	-1.8	19.3	20.4	-4.1	-15.9	-18.7
Grenada	..	..	..	..	..	..	..	..	..	..	..
Guatemala	7.2	6.2	3.9	5.6	15.8	-3.3	14.7	14.8	6.2	-7.0	-6.9
Guyana	8.5	-8.8	-2.4	3.2	-7.0	28.2	4.1	-21.7	-20.9	-4.5	-0.7
Haiti	16.8	3.2	15.6	8.2	10.2	6.7	22.9	9.6	-3.1	2.2	19.4
Honduras	13.7	-16.3	-8.4	10.2	-2.4	-2.5	13.4	17.5	6.9	1.3	5.5
Jamaica	13.8	1.4	0.0	-14.0	-10.2	18.0	-22.1	-13.3	-7.3	-6.7	-6.5
Mexico	9.7	-6.0	11.4	16.4	1.5	4.3	-6.3	-16.5	27.4	37.0	40.0
Nicaragua	8.1	-0.7	-5.9	20.6	25.2	-15.2	1.4	31.6	-10.2	-56.3	84.2
Panama	10.8	-5.8	-0.3	-6.0	-7.9	2.6	-6.2	-7.7	0.9	3.1	2.2
Paraguay	1.5	-6.4	-11.6	21.4	-1.1	8.3	4.9	33.3	12.3	10.7	-4.7
Peru	-3.3	18.9	0.3	5.6	10.1	39.4	-25.1	-18.9	-8.9	6.3	40.0
St. Vincent and The Grenadines	..	..	..	..	..	..	..	..	..	..	..
Trinidad and Tobago	12.2	-5.4	1.0	-21.8	-13.1	-16.8	27.0	-14.8	1.8	-11.6	20.7
Uruguay	21.3	-15.9	-21.5	8.6	4.3	10.0	12.0	3.7	-3.7	34.9	19.4
Venezuela	5.1	4.4	6.8	-5.9	20.8	33.2	26.7	31.0	-5.5	-21.5	-0.6
MIDDLE EAST AND NORTH AFRICA	7.0	3.7	11.3	8.4	34.0	28.0	4.0	17.6	-2.8	2.1	6.7
Algeria	20.7	-6.4	6.6	24.2	37.4	36.3	-9.4	23.5	8.4	-16.5	11.2
Egypt, Arab Republic of	21.2	-1.1	-12.4	-27.2	77.8	70.7	4.7	20.7	21.5	-8.8	-0.3
Iran, Islamic Rep. of	..	..	..	..	..	..	..	..	..	..	..
Jordan	-7.5	9.2	8.3	-3.3	14.0	43.8	36.8	29.9	-5.3	9.9	6.1
Morocco	14.8	-5.8	2.0	7.3	18.1	29.9	8.3	14.7	-18.1	2.8	-6.5
Oman	..	..	..	..	..	..	..	..	..	..	..
Syrian Arab Republic	-16.6	6.2	12.5	-9.3	49.2	33.2	17.2	23.5	-19.7	12.9	4.4
Tunisia	16.0	5.2	31.2	4.5	27.0	24.3	8.8	10.4	5.7	8.6	4.6
Turkey	9.7	22.4	24.5	10.5	11.3	21.6	8.2	4.4	-29.5	-10.7	13.4
Yemen, Republic of	..	..	..	..	..	..	..	..	..	..	..
EUROPE	..	..	..	..	..	..	..	..	..	..	..
Bulgaria	..	..	..	..	..	..	..	..	..	..	..
Greece	17.3	-2.0	6.2	20.6	-17.1	17.7	10.2	5.0	-0.9	3.6	-5.7
Hungary	..	..	..	..	..	..	..	..	..	..	..
Malta	4.9	-9.4	5.2	6.9	10.0	0.1	11.2	12.5	-1.2	14.1	9.7
Poland	..	..	..	..	..	..	..	..	..	..	..
Portugal	20.8	1.3	6.7	6.7	6.3	-21.6	9.2	7.8	-3.5	2.8	21.7
Romania	..	..	..	..	..	..	..	..	..	..	..
Yugoslavia	28.3	8.3	-11.9	21.9	11.3	0.7	-9.5	12.1	-1.5	20.9	-10.8
Low- & middle-income economies	10.8	4.0	-0.6	9.1	13.6	8.5	1.8	7.4	5.0	4.1	12.4
Severely indebted	7.8	5.2	4.6	8.2	15.9	5.1	-1.0	4.6	2.3	6.5	13.5
Low-income economies	8.9	3.0	-5.4	11.8	9.9	18.3	3.9	8.2	8.9	-3.0	16.6
Low-income Africa	10.2	9.6	-6.7	-3.6	3.5	32.6	11.8	15.9	2.2	-19.4	25.4
China and India	13.7	4.0	-0.3	19.7	12.3	9.7	-12.9	3.1	25.7	17.5	9.5
Other low-income	0.2	-12.0	-10.6	25.3	14.4	12.3	13.5	1.7	4.4	2.7	13.7
Middle-income economies	11.4	4.3	0.9	8.3	14.7	5.7	1.0	7.2	3.7	6.6	11.0
High-income OECD members	12.0	3.1	6.7	8.3	-7.4	-3.1	10.9	3.7	6.9	5.7	0.9
European Community members	12.3	4.3	5.6	8.8	-9.6	-1.2	10.3	2.6	7.4	8.8	2.8
Japan	23.8	-4.5	8.4	11.6	-12.0	-4.5	4.3	2.1	6.3	6.1	-3.3
United States	6.2	6.0	12.2	5.1	-5.8	-7.8	19.9	10.2	13.3	-3.1	-4.8
Other high-income economies /a	10.8	7.6	11.2	20.9	7.5	2.5	26.1	19.0	12.0	7.3	11.6

a. Economies classified by the United Nations or otherwise regarded by their authorities as developing.

1981	1982	1983	1984	1985	1986	1987	1988	1989	1990	
5.1	-17.5	-24.0	3.7	2.5	-0.4	1.6	4.4	..	..	*LATIN AMERICA AND CARIBBEAN*
-10.4	-43.1	-12.5	3.4	-17.2	15.6	11.9	-13.7	..	..	Argentina
..	..	..	..	..	..	..	..	..	..	Bahamas
9.2	-0.4	15.1	10.8	-10.2	-4.3	-20.7	8.6	..	..	Barbados
..	..	..	..	..	..	..	..	..	..	Belize
37.6	-35.2	3.7	-15.8	12.2	15.0	0.7	-28.9	..	..	Bolivia
-10.6	-9.2	-18.7	-6.0	-0.5	26.8	-5.5	-1.9	..	..	Brazil
6.6	-33.3	-21.0	18.8	-11.2	-6.9	16.6	13.3	..	..	Chile
10.6	9.7	-7.9	-6.8	-7.8	-12.2	2.4	5.8	..	..	Colombia
-21.0	-25.2	8.0	14.3	1.4	-0.6	8.6	-1.9	..	..	Costa Rica
-5.6	-9.1	3.7	3.5	6.4	1.6	12.2	-0.1	..	..	Dominican Republic
-19.8	0.7	-14.4	10.7	9.6	-9.2	12.4	-30.0	..	..	Ecuador
3.9	-8.9	-2.0	18.6	-0.6	-8.6	-5.0	2.1	..	..	El Salvador
..	..	..	..	..	..	..	..	..	..	Grenada
15.5	-25.3	-15.9	20.4	-7.1	-18.0	38.8	-0.1	..	..	Guatemala
17.5	-33.4	-10.5	-11.6	17.8	-14.9	-3.2	0.3	..	..	Guyana
5.3	-13.8	-10.0	7.4	4.8	-18.9	-5.0	12.5	..	..	Haiti
-7.7	-27.6	22.1	14.8	0.9	-6.2	-7.8	-5.9	..	..	Honduras
28.2	0.3	13.1	-23.3	1.9	-9.3	13.8	13.5	..	..	Jamaica
24.8	-35.2	-47.7	47.4	21.1	-22.2	-6.3	39.0	..	..	Mexico
10.2	-19.0	5.9	9.6	16.2	-14.0	-1.9	-9.1	..	..	Nicaragua
8.3	4.9	-8.5	3.0	0.7	-11.8	-3.9	-43.0	..	..	Panama
11.3	-2.5	-20.8	16.0	-26.5	68.8	31.9	5.5	..	..	Paraguay
25.2	3.1	-27.5	-15.9	-8.1	27.8	13.6	-22.2	..	..	Peru
..	..	..	..	..	..	..	..	..	..	St. Vincent and The Grenadines
-4.1	34.4	-20.0	-24.3	-20.0	-19.5	-18.0	-14.3	..	..	Trinidad and Tobago
-3.2	-32.6	-25.9	-1.1	-5.4	32.4	17.7	-2.9	..	..	Uruguay
10.9	2.0	-32.1	-11.0	11.0	1.6	2.0	9.4	..	..	Venezuela
17.1	-5.4	-1.1	2.4	-4.8	-11.5	-6.1	..	..	..	*MIDDLE EAST AND NORTH AFRICA*
8.6	-2.1	-2.1	1.6	-5.6	-15.1	-28.3	-5.0	..	..	Algeria
7.9	8.9	15.7	5.9	9.9	-15.3	-24.4	14.7	..	..	Egypt, Arab Republic of
..	..	..	..	..	..	..	..	..	..	Iran, Islamic Rep. of
31.4	3.4	-3.2	-6.9	0.2	-12.1	2.1	-3.1	..	..	Jordan
0.1	9.1	-15.9	9.2	0.8	7.5	0.8	5.4	..	..	Morocco
..	..	..	..	..	..	..	..	..	..	Oman
13.6	-17.5	20.7	-10.5	1.1	-26.7	-16.6	-24.4	..	..	Syrian Arab Republic
7.5	0.1	-8.2	2.5	-10.2	0.4	-4.8	9.2	..	..	Tunisia
17.9	4.7	11.7	19.8	10.8	4.6	12.9	-0.1	..	..	Turkey
..	..	..	..	..	..	..	..	..	..	Yemen, Republic of
..	..	..	..	..	..	..	..	..	..	*EUROPE*
..	..	..	..	..	..	..	..	..	..	Bulgaria
-16.8	12.5	-2.0	3.2	5.7	16.9	3.3	-13.2	..	..	Greece
..	..	..	..	..	..	..	..	..	..	Hungary
-9.7	-5.1	-3.5	-0.6	7.1	9.8	18.7	9.8	..	..	Malta
..	..	..	..	..	..	..	..	..	..	Poland
5.9	1.3	-13.4	-4.5	1.7	30.9	27.8	14.5	..	..	Portugal
..	..	..	..	..	..	..	..	..	..	Romania
4.8	-7.7	-12.9	-1.0	4.9	-0.6	-3.9	2.1	..	..	Yugoslavia
9.0	-7.2	-6.3	4.2	2.9	-3.2	1.4	8.3	..	..	**Low- & middle-income economies**
3.5	-17.8	-23.7	3.0	2.6	2.3	2.3	5.8	..	..	Severely indebted
11.2	-2.8	-1.4	4.6	19.2	-7.4	-4.9	9.4	..	..	Low-income economies
10.0	-11.9	-19.0	-11.1	-1.7	-9.3	-3.5	-2.3	..	..	Low-income Africa
5.4	0.3	15.1	23.2	47.1	-7.8	-6.4	16.1	..	..	China and India
19.1	6.0	-0.5	-4.4	-8.3	-3.5	-1.9	4.2	..	..	Other low-income
8.3	-8.7	-8.1	4.1	-3.5	-1.2	4.3	7.8	..	..	Middle-income economies
-4.2	-0.2	2.6	12.3	7.7	9.9	6.0	6.3	..	..	**High-income OECD members**
-10.1	2.0	0.0	5.0	7.6	9.9	7.6	7.0	..	..	European Community members
0.3	0.0	0.7	11.0	0.3	7.7	16.1	16.0	..	..	Japan
7.1	-4.0	11.3	30.4	11.8	11.0	1.1	0.7	..	..	United States
10.9	7.8	0.9	1.9	-10.3	-2.0	15.3	16.9	..	..	Other high-income economies /a

Country Pages

ALGERIA	1969	1970	1971	1972	1973	1974	1975	1976	1977	1978	1979
CURRENT GNP PER CAPITA (US $)	330	360	330	450	520	670	870	1,060	1,180	1,380	1,650
POPULATION (thousands)	13,340	13,746	14,169	14,609	15,064	15,534	16,018	16,516	17,030	17,559	18,105
USE AND ORIGIN OF RESOURCES					*(Billions of current Algerian Dinars)*						
Gross National Product (GNP)	21.04	23.51	24.77	30.27	34.33	55.26	60.93	72.83	85.72	102.48	124.02
Net Factor Income from Abroad	0.00	-0.56	-0.28	-0.15	-0.26	-0.30	-0.64	-1.24	-1.52	-2.35	-4.21
GDP at Market Prices	21.04	24.07	25.04	30.41	34.59	55.56	61.57	74.07	87.24	104.83	128.22
Resource Balance	-0.92	-1.70	-2.34	-1.59	-2.17	1.83	-5.69	-3.03	-9.78	-15.26	-2.17
Exports of Goods & NFServices	4.95	5.31	4.57	6.16	8.75	21.40	20.71	24.36	26.55	26.69	39.91
Imports of Goods & NFServices	5.87	7.01	6.91	7.76	10.92	19.57	26.40	27.39	36.33	41.95	42.08
Domestic Absorption	21.97	25.77	27.39	32.01	36.76	53.73	67.26	77.11	97.02	120.10	130.40
Private Consumption, etc.	12.04	13.44	14.28	16.81	17.79	25.72	31.45	35.93	44.62	50.88	58.48
General Gov't Consumption	3.17	3.58	4.22	4.76	5.03	5.93	7.97	9.25	11.59	14.60	17.48
Gross Domestic Investment	6.76	8.75	8.89	10.44	13.94	22.08	27.84	31.93	40.81	54.62	54.43
Fixed Investment	6.17	8.16	8.34	9.81	12.42	16.96	23.97	31.36	38.43	50.79	50.37
Indirect Taxes, net	..	1.65	1.45	1.89	2.05	10.31	11.43	14.04	17.13	20.57	23.59
GDP at factor cost	..	22.42	23.60	28.53	32.55	45.25	50.15	60.04	70.11	84.26	104.63
Agriculture	2.22	2.43	2.62	2.83	2.73	4.05	6.08	6.97	6.98	8.72	11.14
Industry	8.12	9.27	8.95	12.61	15.94	24.09	23.07	30.01	35.85	41.97	52.81
Manufacturing	2.78	3.37	3.47	4.09	4.78	3.72	4.32	5.72	6.53	8.84	10.67
Services, etc.	..	10.72	12.03	13.09	13.87	17.12	21.00	23.06	27.28	33.56	40.68
Gross Domestic Saving	5.84	7.05	6.54	8.85	11.77	23.91	22.15	28.90	31.03	39.36	52.26
Gross National Saving	..	7.46	7.37	9.71	12.85	24.94	22.91	29.26	30.66	38.18	49.26
					(Billions of 1987 Algerian Dinars)						
Gross National Product	121.43	132.30	118.81	152.32	157.69	169.71	177.46	191.13	201.13	218.51	232.20
GDP at Market Prices	124.49	135.44	120.14	153.06	158.87	170.63	179.33	194.39	204.70	223.53	240.07
Resource Balance	14.82	13.98	7.00	13.44	10.13	-0.62	-5.94	-3.04	-10.96	-12.41	-5.83
Exports of Goods & NFServices	31.11	32.32	23.94	33.19	34.95	32.85	33.05	34.17	34.00	36.09	38.64
Imports of Goods & NFServices	16.29	18.34	16.94	19.75	24.82	33.47	38.99	37.21	44.97	48.51	44.46
Domestic Absorption	85.83	98.30	102.38	119.23	129.09	163.34	183.36	194.62	220.55	240.89	247.22
Private Consumption, etc.	45.84	50.82	53.72	63.11	63.94	80.10	89.04	96.22	106.74	106.61	116.99
General Gov't Consumption	14.14	14.99	16.68	18.73	18.64	19.18	24.73	26.64	29.46	33.01	36.21
Gross Domestic Investment	25.85	32.49	31.98	37.39	46.51	64.06	69.58	71.75	84.34	101.27	94.01
Fixed Investment	24.19	31.28	31.05	36.20	42.78	51.53	62.67	73.76	83.13	99.29	91.41
GDP at factor cost	..	128.38	114.70	146.13	152.17	140.53	147.83	159.60	166.41	180.97	197.12
Agriculture	10.68	11.54	12.04	12.08	11.11	14.47	18.64	18.20	16.79	18.75	20.43
Industry	52.01	56.62	45.74	67.19	71.00	56.63	53.48	60.86	66.13	73.43	76.36
Manufacturing	5.01	5.93	5.83	6.71	7.70	5.69	6.07	7.66	8.32	10.15	11.53
Services, etc.	..	60.44	61.61	64.60	67.06	74.63	86.46	89.51	90.69	94.94	110.73
Memo Items:											
Capacity to Import	13.73	13.89	11.20	15.69	19.89	36.60	30.59	33.10	32.86	30.86	42.17
Terms of Trade Adjustment	-17.38	-18.44	-12.75	-17.50	-15.06	3.75	-2.46	-1.08	-1.14	-5.23	3.53
Gross Domestic Income	107.11	117.01	107.39	135.56	143.81	174.38	176.87	193.32	203.56	218.30	243.60
Gross National Income	104.06	113.87	106.06	134.82	142.62	173.46	175.00	190.05	199.99	213.28	235.73
DOMESTIC PRICES/DEFLATORS					*(Index 1987 = 100)*						
Overall (GDP)	16.9	17.8	20.8	19.9	21.8	32.6	34.3	38.1	42.6	46.9	53.4
Domestic Absorption	25.6	26.2	26.8	26.8	28.5	32.9	36.7	39.6	44.0	49.9	52.7
Agriculture	20.8	21.0	21.7	23.4	24.6	28.0	32.6	38.3	41.6	46.5	54.5
Industry	15.6	16.4	19.6	18.8	22.5	42.5	43.1	49.3	54.2	57.2	69.2
Manufacturing	55.5	56.8	59.5	60.9	62.0	65.4	71.2	74.7	78.5	87.0	92.6
Consumer Price Index	22.3	23.8	24.4	25.3	26.9	28.1	30.7	33.4	37.4	43.8	48.9
MANUFACTURING ACTIVITY											
Employment (1987=100)	..	..	..	..	..	..	..	..	..	..	..
Real Earnings per Empl. (1987=100)	..	..	..	..	..	..	..	..	..	..	..
Real Output per Empl. (1987=100)	..	..	..	..	..	..	..	..	..	..	..
Earnings as % of Value Added	44.7	45.2	46.4	45.1	44.9	53.9	55.6	54.5	54.8	52.7	54.5
MONETARY HOLDINGS					*(Billions of current Algerian Dinars)*						
Money Supply, Broadly Defined	12.37	13.45	14.59	19.00	21.42	27.12	35.44	45.88	55.25	71.99	86.29
Money	11.01	11.63	12.95	16.75	18.92	24.25	31.97	41.07	48.55	62.13	72.21
Currency Outside Banks	4.16	4.74	5.70	7.05	8.82	10.45	12.74	17.24	20.58	27.29	35.40
Demand Deposits	6.85	6.89	7.25	9.70	10.11	13.80	19.23	23.83	27.98	34.84	36.81
Quasi-Money	1.36	1.83	1.64	2.25	2.50	2.87	3.47	4.81	6.69	9.86	14.08
GOVERNMENT DEFICIT (-) OR SURPLUS					*(Millions of current Algerian Dinars)*						
Current Revenue	..	..	..	..	..	..	..	..	..	..	..
Current Expenditure	..	..	..	..	..	..	..	..	..	..	..
Current Budget Balance	..	..	..	..	..	..	..	..	..	..	..
Capital Receipts	..	..	..	..	..	..	..	..	..	..	..
Capital Payments	..	..	..	..	..	..	..	..	..	..	..

1980	1981	1982	1983	1984	1985	1986	1987	1988	1989 estimate	NOTES	ALGERIA
1,940	2,240	2,420	2,420	2,460	2,580	2,650	2,680	2,430	2,220	..	CURRENT GNP PER CAPITA (US $)
18,669	19,254	19,862	20,495	21,173	21,848	22,497	23,124	23,753	24,453	..	POPULATION (thousands)
				(Billions of current Algerian Dinars)							USE AND ORIGIN OF RESOURCES
157.91	186.06	201.52	227.89	257.19	284.83	289.83	305.27	295.07	349.44	..	Gross National Product (GNP)
-4.60	-5.41	-6.03	-5.87	-6.66	-6.77	-6.72	-7.44	-11.90	-14.46	..	Net Factor Income from Abroad
162.51	191.47	207.55	233.75	263.86	291.60	296.55	312.71	306.97	363.90	..	GDP at Market Prices
6.46	7.10	3.99	5.06	6.02	9.28	-12.09	5.95	-1.32	0.20	..	Resource Balance
55.80	66.18	64.22	65.34	67.69	68.63	38.71	45.83	49.81	76.50	..	Exports of Goods & NFServices
49.34	59.08	60.23	60.29	61.67	59.35	50.80	39.89	51.13	76.30	..	Imports of Goods & NFServices
156.04	184.37	203.56	228.69	257.84	282.32	308.64	306.76	308.29	363.70	..	Domestic Absorption
70.18	87.18	95.56	106.18	125.83	139.72	156.41	154.88	162.56	194.60	..	Private Consumption, etc.
22.35	26.35	30.66	34.69	39.48	45.83	52.89	58.00	49.53	56.50	..	General Gov't Consumption
63.51	70.84	77.34	87.82	92.53	96.77	99.33	93.88	96.20	112.60	..	Gross Domestic Investment
54.88	63.04	71.49	80.32	87.48	92.77	101.33	92.88	96.10	111.50	..	Fixed Investment
30.36	37.65	39.35	43.32	51.77	53.19	52.96	59.13	50.16	61.23	..	Indirect Taxes, net
132.15	153.82	168.20	190.43	212.09	238.41	243.59	253.58	256.81	302.67	..	GDP at factor cost
13.25	16.58	16.47	16.97	18.28	23.95	26.07	31.50	38.37	47.08	..	Agriculture
70.94	81.93	88.40	100.80	112.71	120.81	111.63	109.93	112.61	134.56	..	Industry
12.47	14.63	16.58	19.91	26.13	29.08	34.77	34.31	32.21	34.30	..	Manufacturing
47.96	55.31	63.33	72.67	81.09	93.64	105.88	112.14	105.83	121.04	..	Services, etc.
69.98	77.94	81.33	92.88	98.55	106.05	87.25	99.83	94.88	112.80	..	Gross Domestic Saving
66.44	73.84	76.90	88.14	92.82	101.12	84.12	94.92	85.26	102.29	..	Gross National Saving
				(Billions of 1987 Algerian Dinars)							
235.38	242.47	257.86	272.86	288.09	304.17	307.84	305.27	294.32	304.11	..	Gross National Product
242.23	249.52	265.58	279.88	295.55	311.40	314.98	312.71	306.19	316.69	H	GDP at Market Prices
-12.32	-19.72	-15.36	-16.32	-15.46	-13.88	-4.11	5.95	10.13	12.58	..	Resource Balance
33.66	33.76	37.20	39.51	41.76	43.06	43.49	45.83	47.35	50.61	..	Exports of Goods & NFServices
45.98	53.47	52.56	55.82	57.22	56.93	47.60	39.89	37.21	38.03	..	Imports of Goods & NFServices
267.80	285.14	291.76	309.42	322.77	328.55	325.01	306.76	302.65	313.00	..	Domestic Absorption
129.09	139.93	143.71	152.62	160.86	164.40	166.54	154.88	154.57	161.84	..	Private Consumption, etc.
42.51	45.44	47.99	50.53	53.51	56.29	57.31	58.00	59.27	61.29	..	General Gov't Consumption
96.20	99.76	100.06	106.27	108.39	107.85	101.16	93.88	88.81	89.88	..	Gross Domestic Investment
91.52	94.41	97.09	102.08	105.75	107.91	103.51	92.88	88.30	89.36	..	Fixed Investment
197.73	200.69	213.90	228.25	238.81	253.82	259.03	253.58	257.76	266.11	..	GDP at factor cost
22.99	23.03	21.19	20.72	22.19	28.03	29.53	31.50	29.90	33.63	..	Agriculture
77.56	87.60	94.29	107.02	115.81	122.00	121.79	109.93	113.94	110.28	..	Industry
12.20	22.71	23.18	30.19	36.72	40.18	41.67	34.31	30.90	25.85	..	Manufacturing
105.96	89.98	98.31	94.36	90.32	92.53	98.74	112.14	112.26	127.23	..	Services, etc.
											Memo Items:
52.00	59.90	56.05	60.51	62.80	65.84	36.27	45.83	36.26	38.13	..	Capacity to Import
18.35	26.14	18.85	21.00	21.04	22.78	-7.21	0.00	-11.09	-12.48	..	Terms of Trade Adjustment
260.58	275.66	284.42	300.88	316.59	334.18	307.77	312.71	295.10	304.21	..	Gross Domestic Income
253.73	268.62	276.71	293.86	309.13	326.95	300.63	305.27	283.23	291.63	..	Gross National Income
				(Index 1987 = 100)							DOMESTIC PRICES/DEFLATORS
67.1	76.7	78.2	83.5	89.3	93.6	94.1	100.0	100.3	114.9	..	Overall (GDP)
58.3	64.7	69.8	73.9	79.9	85.9	95.0	100.0	101.9	116.2	..	Domestic Absorption
57.7	72.0	77.7	81.9	82.4	85.4	88.3	100.0	128.4	140.0	..	Agriculture
91.5	93.5	93.8	94.2	97.3	99.0	91.7	100.0	98.8	122.0	..	Industry
102.2	64.4	71.5	66.0	71.2	72.4	83.4	100.0	104.3	132.7	..	Manufacturing
53.5	61.3	65.4	70.5	75.0	82.8	93.1	100.0	105.9	..	..	Consumer Price Index
											MANUFACTURING ACTIVITY
..	..	..	..	..	..	..	..	..	..	..	Employment (1987=100)
..	..	..	..	..	..	..	..	..	..	..	Real Earnings per Empl. (1987=100)
..	..	..	..	..	..	..	..	..	..	..	Real Output per Empl. (1987=100)
55.8	..	..	..	..	..	..	..	..	..	..	Earnings as % of Value Added
				(Billions of current Algerian Dinars)							MONETARY HOLDINGS
103.83	121.23	154.12	185.02	216.63	249.46	257.62	295.83	339.14	366.26	D	Money Supply, Broadly Defined
84.43	97.92	125.30	152.76	180.43	202.23	204.75	223.87	252.21	250.01	..	Money
42.34	48.06	49.16	60.02	67.46	76.64	89.36	96.89	109.75	119.87	..	Currency Outside Banks
42.09	49.87	76.14	92.74	112.97	125.59	115.39	126.98	142.45	130.14	..	Demand Deposits
19.40	23.31	28.82	32.26	36.20	47.23	52.87	71.96	86.94	116.25	..	Quasi-Money
				(Millions of current Algerian Dinars)							GOVERNMENT DEFICIT (-) OR SURPLUS
..	..	..	..	..	..	..	..	..	..	..	Current Revenue
..	..	..	..	..	..	..	..	..	..	..	Current Expenditure
..	..	..	..	..	..	..	..	..	..	..	Current Budget Balance
..	..	..	..	..	..	..	..	..	..	..	Capital Receipts
..	..	..	..	..	..	..	..	..	..	..	Capital Payments

ALGERIA	1969	1970	1971	1972	1973	1974	1975	1976	1977	1978	1979
FOREIGN TRADE (CUSTOMS BASIS)					*(Millions of current US dollars)*						
Value of Exports, fob	934	1,009	857	1,306	1,906	4,260	4,291	4,972	5,809	6,126	9,863
Nonfuel Primary Products	230	232	142	159	262	234	233	274	195	206	184
Fuels	632	709	641	1,080	1,582	3,941	3,964	4,654	5,577	5,885	9,640
Manufactures	72	68	73	67	62	86	94	44	38	35	40
Value of Imports, cif	1,009	1,257	1,227	1,492	2,259	4,036	5,974	5,307	7,102	8,667	8,407
Nonfuel Primary Products	208	233	263	347	473	1,040	1,520	1,109	1,520	1,726	1,878
Fuels	16	27	43	34	36	60	102	84	97	130	165
Manufactures	785	998	922	1,112	1,749	2,936	4,353	4,113	5,485	6,812	6,364
					(Index 1987 = 100)						
Terms of Trade	38.2	36.1	42.1	38.4	44.4	124.7	112.4	122.3	122.6	110.2	136.1
Export Prices, fob	10.5	10.2	12.4	13.0	18.2	66.7	65.3	69.6	75.7	76.6	109.9
Import Prices, cif	27.5	28.4	29.6	33.8	41.1	53.5	58.1	56.9	61.7	69.5	80.8
BALANCE OF PAYMENTS					*(Millions of current US dollars)*						
Exports of Goods & Services	..	1,129	935	1,348	2,133	5,268	4,854	5,536	6,384	6,735	10,109
Merchandise, fob	..	1,010	816	1,224	1,950	4,944	4,501	5,221	6,009	6,340	9,484
Nonfactor Services	..	98	107	106	160	176	281	235	288	326	468
Factor Services	..	21	11	18	23	148	73	80	87	69	156
Imports of Goods & Services	..	1,487	1,339	1,740	2,914	5,015	6,888	6,822	8,988	10,588	12,061
Merchandise, fob	..	1,078	996	1,303	2,141	3,667	5,452	4,693	6,198	7,293	7,805
Nonfactor Services	..	245	246	326	513	715	1,009	1,299	1,532	1,959	2,391
Factor Services	..	164	97	111	259	633	427	830	1,259	1,336	1,865
Long-Term Interest	..	10	17	52	69	220	217	348	417	614	1,253
Private Current Transfers, net	..	195	225	224	337	319	355	386	278	295	313
Workers' Remittances	..	211	238	272	332	351	412	433	349	393	417
Curr. A/C Bal before Off. Transf.	..	-163	-180	-167	-444	572	-1,678	-900	-2,327	-3,558	-1,639
Net Official Transfers	..	37	222	41	-2	-396	20	18	4	20	8
Curr. A/C Bal after Off. Transf.	..	-125	42	-126	-445	176	-1,658	-882	-2,323	-3,538	-1,631
Long-Term Capital, net	..	59	4	199	1,015	529	1,373	1,740	1,897	3,647	2,432
Direct Investment	..	45	-151	17	50	358	85	184	173	135	10
Long-Term Loans	..	279	257	281	1,366	350	1,308	1,644	2,496	4,208	2,834
Disbursements	..	313	310	420	1,599	842	1,560	2,084	3,142	5,112	4,397
Repayments	..	35	53	138	233	492	252	440	646	904	1,563
Other Long-Term Capital	..	-265	-102	-100	-402	-179	-19	-87	-772	-696	-412
Other Capital, net	..	-16	-46	2	14	-141	-49	-235	79	-16	-317
Change in Reserves	..	83	0	-75	-583	-564	334	-622	347	-93	-484
Memo Item:					*(Algerian Dinars per US dollar)*						
Conversion Factor (Annual Avg)	4.940	4.940	4.910	4.480	3.960	4.180	3.950	4.160	4.150	3.970	3.850
				(Millions of US dollars), outstanding at end of year							
EXTERNAL DEBT (Total)	..	945	1,261	1,550	2,991	3,416	4,633	6,149	10,618	15,750	18,519
Long-Term Debt (by debtor)	..	945	1,261	1,550	2,991	3,416	4,633	6,149	8,932	13,765	16,586
Central Bank, incl. IMF credit	..	20	51	236	948	887	1,222	1,448	1,831	2,844	3,173
Central Government	..	438	484	487	623	703	695	687	752	837	1,027
Rest of General Government	..	0	0	0	0	0	0	0	0	0	0
Non-financial Public Enterprises	..	487	725	828	1,420	1,826	2,715	4,015	6,349	10,084	12,386
Priv. Sector, incl non-guaranteed	..	0	0	0	0	0	0	0	0	0	0
Short-Term Debt	..	0	0	0	0	0	0	0	1,686	1,985	1,933
Memo Items:					*(Millions of US dollars)*						
Int'l Reserves Excluding Gold	204.3	147.9	298.6	285.1	912.2	1,454.3	1,128.3	1,764.9	1,683.6	1,980.5	2,658.8
Gold Holdings (at market price)	206.4	204.4	238.7	355.1	614.1	1,020.4	767.4	737.3	907.1	1,249.1	2,858.5
SOCIAL INDICATORS											
Total Fertility Rate	7.4	7.4	7.4	7.4	7.3	7.3	7.3	7.2	7.2	7.0	6.9
Infant Mortality Rate	142.8	139.2	135.6	132.0	128.0	124.0	120.0	116.0	112.0	107.2	102.4
Life Expectancy at Birth	52.6	53.3	53.9	54.5	55.1	55.7	56.3	56.9	57.5	58.1	58.7
Urban Population, % of total	39.1	39.5	39.7	39.8	40.0	40.1	40.3	40.5	40.7	40.8	41.0
Food Prod. per capita (1987=100)	108.8	109.1	108.2	107.7	99.8	101.9	116.7	104.0	87.8	89.3	90.5
Labor Force, Agriculture (%)	49.2	47.3	45.5	43.8	42.1	40.6	39.2	37.4	35.7	34.1	32.6
Labor Force, Female (%)	5.8	6.0	6.3	6.5	6.7	6.9	7.1	7.3	7.6	7.8	8.0
Primary Schl. Enroll. Ratio	..	76.0	..	..	..	..	93.0	..	95.0	95.0	95.0
Primary Schl. Enroll. Ratio, Female	..	58.0	..	..	..	..	75.0	..	79.0	80.0	81.0
Secondary Schl. Enroll. Ratio	..	11.0	..	..	..	..	20.0	23.0	27.0	29.0	31.0

1980	1981	1982	1983	1984	1985	1986	1987	1988	1989 estimate	NOTES	ALGERIA
				(Millions of current US dollars)							**FOREIGN TRADE (CUSTOMS BASIS)**
13,871	14,396	13,144	12,583	12,795	13,034	8,066	9,029	7,830	8,690	f	Value of Exports, fob
194	204	148	104	118	105	89	71	159	..	..	Nonfuel Primary Products
13,628	14,124	12,908	12,365	12,548	12,826	7,870	8,816	7,433	8,107	..	Fuels
49	68	89	114	129	103	107	142	238	239	..	Manufactures
10,525	11,302	10,679	10,332	10,263	9,814	9,234	7,028	7,432	9,719	f	Value of Imports, cif
2,718	2,865	2,658	2,728	2,536	3,050	2,540	2,384	2,610	..	..	Nonfuel Primary Products
259	230	165	214	211	184	274	160	183	312	..	Fuels
7,548	8,207	7,856	7,390	7,516	6,579	6,420	4,484	4,639	6,749	..	Manufactures
				(Index 1987 = 100)							
195.8	220.5	207.1	190.7	189.7	182.8	93.8	100.0	73.4	..	..	Terms of Trade
178.1	198.3	179.8	163.7	159.2	155.4	88.4	100.0	81.8	..	..	Export Prices, fob
90.9	89.9	86.8	85.8	83.9	85.0	94.2	100.0	111.3	..	..	Import Prices, cif
				(Millions of current US dollars)							**BALANCE OF PAYMENTS**
14,500	15,072	14,366	13,608	13,570	13,756	8,785	9,704	8,162	10,121	..	Exports of Goods & Services
13,652	14,117	13,509	12,742	12,792	13,034	8,065	9,029	7,620	9,476	..	Merchandise, fob
476	474	528	679	599	531	549	565	470	592	..	Nonfactor Services
372	481	328	186	179	191	172	110	71	53	..	Factor Services
14,552	15,291	14,878	13,931	13,676	13,120	11,779	10,080	10,592	11,894	..	Imports of Goods & Services
9,596	10,088	9,889	9,516	9,235	8,811	7,879	6,616	6,675	8,188	..	Merchandise, fob
2,715	2,720	2,670	2,436	2,583	2,573	2,035	1,455	1,347	1,748	..	Nonfactor Services
2,241	2,483	2,319	1,979	1,859	1,736	1,865	2,009	2,571	1,958	..	Factor Services
1,436	1,361	1,427	1,274	1,376	1,409	1,564	1,576	1,811	1,851	..	Long-Term Interest
277	304	347	237	186	367	765	522	385	519	..	Private Current Transfers, net
406	447	507	392	329	313	358	487	379	355	..	Workers' Remittances
225	85	-165	-86	80	1,004	-2,229	146	-2,045	-1,254	..	Curr. A/C Bal before Off. Transf.
24	5	-18	1	-5	11	-1	-5	5	..	..	Net Official Transfers
249	90	-183	-85	74	1,015	-2,230	141	-2,040	-1,254	..	Curr. A/C Bal after Off. Transf.
897	6	-956	-852	-404	-36	353	21	764	357	..	Long-Term Capital, net
315	-1	-65	-14	-14	-2	11	-11	8	-59	..	Direct Investment
916	246	-338	206	567	484	960	735	1,432	-197	..	Long-Term Loans
3,398	2,798	2,617	3,523	4,175	3,988	4,545	4,575	5,912	5,024	..	Disbursements
2,481	2,552	2,955	3,317	3,608	3,504	3,585	3,840	4,480	5,221	..	Repayments
-334	-239	-553	-1,044	-958	-518	-617	-703	-676	613	..	Other Long-Term Capital
195	24	69	517	-3	42	379	-514	316	250	..	Other Capital, net
-1,341	-120	1,070	421	333	-1,020	1,498	352	960	647	..	Change in Reserves
				(Algerian Dinars per US dollar)							**Memo Item:**
3.840	4.320	4.590	4.790	4.980	5.030	4.700	4.850	5.910	7.610	..	Conversion Factor (Annual Avg)
				(Millions of US dollars), outstanding at end of year							
19,377	18,397	17,728	16,285	15,944	18,374	22,796	24,748	25,074	26,067	..	**EXTERNAL DEBT (Total)**
17,052	16,090	14,977	14,328	14,185	16,512	19,644	23,432	23,454	24,228	..	Long-Term Debt (by debtor)
3,076	2,981	2,854	2,661	4,119	6,652	9,821	12,255	13,691	14,415	..	Central Bank, incl. IMF credit
1,017	1,062	1,037	1,061	830	1,035	1,231	1,976	2,470	2,595	..	Central Government
1	3	42	125	277	324	295	243	20	11	..	Rest of General Government
12,958	12,044	11,044	10,481	8,958	8,501	8,297	8,958	7,266	7,193	..	Non-financial Public Enterprises
0	0	0	0	0	0	0	1	7	14	..	Priv. Sector, incl non-guaranteed
2,325	2,307	2,751	1,957	1,759	1,862	3,152	1,315	1,620	1,840	..	Short-Term Debt
				(Millions of US dollars)							**Memo Items:**
3,772.6	3,695.4	2,422.0	1,880.4	1,464.2	2,819.0	1,660.2	1,640.5	900.2	847.0	..	Int'l Reserves Excluding Gold
3,291.2	2,219.3	2,550.8	2,129.8	1,721.2	1,825.6	2,182.3	2,702.6	2,290.4	2,238.7	..	Gold Holdings (at market price)
											SOCIAL INDICATORS
6.7	6.5	6.4	6.2	6.0	5.8	5.7	5.5	5.4	5.3	..	Total Fertility Rate
97.6	92.8	88.0	85.2	82.4	79.6	76.8	74.0	71.9	69.8	..	Infant Mortality Rate
59.3	59.9	60.5	61.2	61.9	62.6	63.3	64.0	64.4	64.8	..	Life Expectancy at Birth
41.2	41.5	41.8	42.0	42.3	42.6	43.0	43.4	43.9	44.3	..	Urban Population, % of total
101.4	91.2	85.7	88.7	90.6	103.8	99.2	100.0	88.4	87.4	..	Food Prod. per capita (1987=100)
31.1	..	..	..	..	..	..	..	..	..	..	Labor Force, Agriculture (%)
8.2	8.4	8.5	8.7	8.8	8.9	9.1	9.2	9.3	9.5	..	Labor Force, Female (%)
95.0	..	94.0	94.0	94.0	93.0	95.0	96.0	96.0	..	..	Primary Schl. Enroll. Ratio
81.0	81.0	81.0	82.0	83.0	82.0	85.0	81.0	87.0	..	..	Primary Schl. Enroll. Ratio, Female
33.0	..	..	43.0	47.0	51.0	53.0	55.0	54.0	..	..	Secondary Schl. Enroll. Ratio

ANTIGUA AND BARBUDA	1969	1970	1971	1972	1973	1974	1975	1976	1977	1978	1979
CURRENT GNP PER CAPITA (US $)	..	..	..	..	..	..	..	..	..	..	..
POPULATION (thousands)	64	66	67	68	69	70	71	71	72	73	74
USE AND ORIGIN OF RESOURCES				*(Millions of current Eastern Caribbean Dollars)*							
Gross National Product (GNP)	85.50	91.70	95.90	109.30	118.20	131.50	142.10	135.10	162.20	182.70	229.30
Net Factor Income from Abroad	0.00	0.00	0.00	0.00	0.00	0.00	0.00	0.00	-0.30	-2.20	-4.90
GDP at Market Prices	85.50	91.70	95.90	109.30	118.20	131.50	142.10	135.10	162.50	184.90	234.20
Resource Balance	..	..	..	..	..	..	..	..	..	..	-75.10
Exports of Goods & NFServices	..	..	..	..	..	..	..	..	..	..	135.50
Imports of Goods & NFServices	..	..	..	..	..	..	..	..	..	..	210.60
Domestic Absorption	..	..	..	..	..	..	..	..	..	..	..
Private Consumption, etc.	..	..	..	..	..	..	..	..	..	..	..
General Gov't Consumption	..	..	..	..	..	..	..	..	..	..	..
Gross Domestic Investment	..	..	..	..	..	..	..	..	..	..	..
Fixed Investment	..	..	..	..	..	..	..	..	..	..	..
Indirect Taxes, net	..	..	..	..	..	..	..	..	20.50	25.60	16.80
GDP at factor cost	..	..	..	..	..	..	..	..	142.00	159.30	217.40
Agriculture	..	..	..	..	..	..	..	..	..	..	..
Industry	..	..	..	..	..	..	..	..	..	..	..
Manufacturing	..	..	..	..	..	..	..	..	..	..	..
Services, etc.	..	..	..	..	..	..	..	..	..	..	..
Gross Domestic Saving	..	..	..	..	..	..	..	..	..	..	..
Gross National Saving	..	..	..	..	..	..	..	..	..	..	..
				(Millions of 1987 Eastern Caribbean Dollars)							
Gross National Product	..	..	..	..	..	..	..	..	..	..	..
GDP at Market Prices	..	..	..	..	..	..	..	..	..	..	..
Resource Balance	..	..	..	..	..	..	..	..	..	..	..
Exports of Goods & NFServices	..	..	..	..	..	..	..	..	..	..	..
Imports of Goods & NFServices	..	..	..	..	..	..	..	..	..	..	..
Domestic Absorption	..	..	..	..	..	..	..	..	..	..	..
Private Consumption, etc.	..	..	..	..	..	..	..	..	..	..	..
General Gov't Consumption	..	..	..	..	..	..	..	..	..	..	..
Gross Domestic Investment	..	..	..	..	..	..	..	..	..	..	..
Fixed Investment	..	..	..	..	..	..	..	..	..	..	..
GDP at factor cost	..	..	..	..	..	..	..	..	293.67	333.83	356.05
Agriculture	..	..	..	..	..	..	..	..	33.97	45.38	36.04
Industry	..	..	..	..	..	..	..	..	42.48	52.19	56.23
Manufacturing	..	..	..	..	..	..	..	..	10.32	11.57	13.38
Services, etc.	..	..	..	..	..	..	..	..	220.38	241.42	266.54
Memo Items:											
Capacity to Import	..	..	..	..	..	..	..	..	..	..	..
Terms of Trade Adjustment	..	..	..	..	..	..	..	..	..	..	..
Gross Domestic Income	..	..	..	..	..	..	..	..	..	..	..
Gross National Income	..	..	..	..	..	..	..	..	..	..	..
DOMESTIC PRICES/DEFLATORS				*(Index 1987 = 100)*							
Overall (GDP)	..	..	..	..	..	..	..	..	..	..	..
Domestic Absorption	..	..	..	..	..	..	..	..	..	..	..
Agriculture	..	..	..	..	..	..	..	..	..	..	..
Industry	..	..	..	..	..	..	..	..	..	..	..
Manufacturing	..	..	..	..	..	..	..	..	..	..	..
Consumer Price Index	..	..	..	..	..	..	..	..	..	..	..
MANUFACTURING ACTIVITY											
Employment (1987=100)	..	..	..	..	..	..	..	..	..	..	..
Real Earnings per Empl. (1987=100)	..	..	..	..	..	..	..	..	..	..	..
Real Output per Empl. (1987=100)	..	..	..	..	..	..	..	..	..	..	..
Earnings as % of Value Added	..	..	..	..	..	..	..	..	..	..	..
MONETARY HOLDINGS				*(Millions of current Eastern Caribbean Dollars)*							
Money Supply, Broadly Defined	..	..	..	..	..	..	98.02	106.49	102.53	113.21	130.74
Money	..	..	..	..	..	..	18.97	24.26	30.91	29.37	34.81
Currency Outside Banks	..	..	..	..	..	..	10.77	11.92	13.15	15.13	17.09
Demand Deposits	..	..	..	..	..	..	8.20	12.35	17.76	14.24	17.72
Quasi-Money	..	..	..	..	..	..	79.05	82.23	71.61	83.84	95.93
GOVERNMENT DEFICIT (-) OR SURPLUS				*(Millions of current Eastern Caribbean Dollars)*							
Current Revenue	..	..	..	..	..	..	..	..	..	..	..
Current Expenditure	..	..	..	..	..	..	..	..	..	..	..
Current Budget Balance	..	..	..	..	..	..	..	..	..	..	..
Capital Receipts	..	..	..	..	..	..	..	..	..	..	..
Capital Payments	..	..	..	..	..	..	..	..	..	..	..

1980	1981	1982	1983	1984	1985	1986	1987	1988	1989 estimate	NOTES	ANTIGUA AND BARBUDA
..	..	1,780	2,030	2,250	2,550	2,980	3,310	3,810	..	..	**CURRENT GNP PER CAPITA** (US $)
75	75	75	75	76	76	76	77	78	78	..	**POPULATION** (thousands)
			(Millions of current Eastern Caribbean Dollars)								**USE AND ORIGIN OF RESOURCES**
299.80	334.90	364.20	419.90	469.20	536.90	628.60	711.50	820.60	..	..	Gross National Product (GNP)
-3.20	-5.40	-10.00	-2.70	-1.10	-7.30	-12.70	-32.40	-50.50	..	..	Net Factor Income from Abroad
303.00	340.30	374.20	422.60	470.30	544.20	641.30	743.90	871.10	929.50	..	GDP at Market Prices
-74.80	-110.90	-127.70	-50.50	-36.50	-93.40	-374.50	-239.50	..	..	..	Resource Balance
281.10	280.60	272.70	268.10	451.70	482.30	540.20	594.50	..	..	..	Exports of Goods & NFServices
355.90	391.50	400.40	318.60	488.20	575.70	914.70	834.00	..	..	..	Imports of Goods & NFServices
..	..	..	..	..	..	..	..	..	..	..	Domestic Absorption
..	..	..	..	..	..	..	..	..	..	..	Private Consumption, etc.
..	..	..	..	..	..	..	..	..	..	..	General Gov't Consumption
..	..	..	..	..	..	..	..	..	..	..	Gross Domestic Investment
..	..	..	..	..	..	..	..	..	..	..	Fixed Investment
45.80	50.90	57.10	66.50	65.90	79.40	115.80	129.70	140.30	..	..	Indirect Taxes, net
257.20	289.40	317.10	356.10	404.40	464.80	525.50	614.20	730.80	806.60	..	GDP at factor cost
18.30	18.60	19.70	21.80	19.30	23.20	24.60	29.30	32.10	32.00	..	Agriculture
46.60	53.40	46.30	50.70	63.10	77.80	101.90	132.90	168.10	203.30	..	Industry
13.70	14.60	16.80	17.60	19.30	20.30	21.50	23.00	24.10	24.70	..	Manufacturing
192.30	217.40	251.10	283.60	322.00	363.80	399.00	452.00	530.60	571.30	..	Services, etc.
..	..	..	..	..	..	..	..	..	..	..	Gross Domestic Saving
..	..	..	..	..	..	..	..	..	..	..	Gross National Saving
			(Millions of 1987 Eastern Caribbean Dollars)								
467.95	487.13	486.89	533.64	561.94	602.01	676.49	711.50	779.95	..	..	Gross National Product
472.14	494.54	499.28	536.20	563.22	610.47	689.10	743.90	779.95	807.29	..	GDP at Market Prices
..	..	..	..	..	..	..	..	..	..	..	Resource Balance
..	..	..	..	..	..	..	..	..	..	..	Exports of Goods & NFServices
..	..	..	..	..	..	..	..	..	..	..	Imports of Goods & NFServices
..	..	..	..	..	..	..	..	..	..	..	Domestic Absorption
..	..	..	..	..	..	..	..	..	..	..	Private Consumption, etc.
..	..	..	..	..	..	..	..	..	..	..	General Gov't Consumption
..	..	..	..	..	..	..	..	..	..	..	Gross Domestic Investment
..	..	..	..	..	..	..	..	..	..	..	Fixed Investment
401.13	420.85	423.11	452.20	484.37	521.33	564.75	614.20	660.55	701.20	..	GDP at factor cost
36.04	32.15	30.34	30.08	24.11	24.63	26.19	29.30	30.86	31.92	..	Agriculture
72.62	82.53	68.57	69.18	75.45	87.99	109.23	132.90	147.87	172.14	..	Industry
15.89	19.38	19.38	19.79	20.63	21.19	22.02	23.00	23.42	24.12	..	Manufacturing
294.73	307.39	324.75	352.94	384.80	408.70	429.33	452.00	481.82	497.14	..	Services, etc.
											Memo Items:
..	..	..	..	..	..	..	..	..	..	..	Capacity to Import
..	..	..	..	..	..	..	..	..	..	..	Terms of Trade Adjustment
..	..	..	..	..	..	..	..	..	..	..	Gross Domestic Income
..	..	..	..	..	..	..	..	..	..	..	Gross National Income
			(Index 1987 = 100)								**DOMESTIC PRICES/DEFLATORS**
64.2	68.8	74.9	78.8	83.5	89.1	93.1	100.0	111.7	115.1	..	Overall (GDP)
..	..	..	..	..	..	..	..	..	..	..	Domestic Absorption
50.8	57.8	64.9	72.5	80.0	94.2	93.9	100.0	104.0	100.3	..	Agriculture
64.2	64.7	67.5	73.3	83.6	88.4	93.3	100.0	113.7	118.1	..	Industry
86.2	75.4	86.7	88.9	93.6	95.8	97.6	100.0	102.9	102.4	..	Manufacturing
..	..	..	..	..	..	..	..	..	..	..	Consumer Price Index
											MANUFACTURING ACTIVITY
..	..	..	..	..	..	..	..	..	..	..	Employment (1987=100)
..	..	..	..	..	..	..	..	..	..	..	Real Earnings per Empl. (1987=100)
..	..	..	..	..	..	..	..	..	..	..	Real Output per Empl. (1987=100)
..	..	..	..	..	..	..	..	..	..	..	Earnings as % of Value Added
			(Millions of current Eastern Caribbean Dollars)								**MONETARY HOLDINGS**
145.37	168.54	191.25	236.80	286.08	319.92	378.13	449.44	503.58	568.92	..	Money Supply, Broadly Defined
38.57	43.16	41.70	51.10	58.40	68.45	87.37	110.62	127.99	141.06	..	Money
15.26	16.27	16.32	17.47	23.97	26.50	32.46	42.24	51.31	61.47	..	Currency Outside Banks
23.31	26.89	25.38	33.62	34.44	41.95	54.91	68.39	76.68	79.59	..	Demand Deposits
106.79	125.38	149.55	185.71	227.68	251.47	290.76	338.82	375.59	427.86	..	Quasi-Money
			(Millions of current Eastern Caribbean Dollars)								
..	..	..	..	..	..	..	..	..	..	..	**GOVERNMENT DEFICIT (-) OR SURPLUS**
..	..	..	..	..	..	..	..	..	..	..	Current Revenue
..	..	..	..	..	..	..	..	..	..	..	Current Expenditure
..	..	..	..	..	..	..	..	..	..	..	Current Budget Balance
..	..	..	..	..	..	..	..	..	..	..	Capital Receipts
..	..	..	..	..	..	..	..	..	..	..	Capital Payments

ANTIGUA AND BARBUDA	1969	1970	1971	1972	1973	1974	1975	1976	1977	1978	1979
FOREIGN TRADE (CUSTOMS BASIS)				*(Millions of current US dollars)*							
Value of Exports, fob	..	..	..	..	..	..	..	..	..	..	..
Nonfuel Primary Products	..	..	..	..	..	..	..	..	..	..	..
Fuels	..	..	..	..	..	..	..	..	..	..	..
Manufactures	..	..	..	..	..	..	..	..	..	..	..
Value of Imports, cif	..	..	..	..	..	..	..	..	..	..	..
Nonfuel Primary Products	..	..	..	..	..	..	..	..	..	..	..
Fuels	..	..	..	..	..	..	..	..	..	..	..
Manufactures	..	..	..	..	..	..	..	..	..	..	..
					(Index 1987 = 100)						
Terms of Trade	..	..	..	..	..	..	..	..	..	..	..
Export Prices, fob	..	..	..	..	..	..	..	..	..	..	..
Import Prices, cif	..	..	..	..	..	..	..	..	..	..	..
BALANCE OF PAYMENTS				*(Millions of current US dollars)*							
Exports of Goods & Services	..	..	..	..	..	..	..	..	31.60	42.20	51.00
Merchandise, fob	..	..	..	..	..	..	..	..	6.60	12.60	12.00
Nonfactor Services	..	..	..	..	..	..	..	..	24.70	29.50	38.20
Factor Services	..	..	..	..	..	..	..	..	0.30	0.10	0.80
Imports of Goods & Services	..	..	..	..	..	..	..	..	44.00	49.60	80.60
Merchandise, fob	..	..	..	..	..	..	..	..	37.00	42.09	67.72
Nonfactor Services	..	..	..	..	..	..	..	..	6.50	7.01	10.28
Factor Services	..	..	..	..	..	..	..	..	0.50	0.50	2.60
Long-Term Interest	..	..	..	..	..	..	..	..	..	..	..
Private Current Transfers, net	..	..	..	..	..	..	..	..	1.20	3.70	8.20
Workers' Remittances	..	..	..	..	..	..	..	..	..	..	..
Curr. A/C Bal before Off. Transf.	..	..	..	..	..	..	..	..	-11.20	-3.70	-21.40
Net Official Transfers	..	..	..	..	..	..	..	..	1.60	1.50	1.90
Curr. A/C Bal after Off. Transf.	..	..	..	..	..	..	..	..	-9.60	-2.20	-19.50
Long-Term Capital, net	..	..	..	..	..	..	..	..	8.84	3.50	17.43
Direct Investment	..	..	..	..	..	..	..	..	2.20	-6.90	8.50
Long-Term Loans	..	..	..	..	..	..	..	..	..	..	..
Disbursements	..	..	..	..	..	..	..	..	..	..	..
Repayments	..	..	..	..	..	..	..	..	..	..	..
Other Long-Term Capital	..	..	..	..	..	..	..	..	6.64	10.40	8.93
Other Capital, net	..	..	..	..	..	..	..	..	-3.71	-0.53	7.43
Change in Reserves	..	..	..	..	..	..	..	-2.35	4.46	-0.77	-5.36
Memo Item:				*(Eastern Caribbean Dollars per US dollar)*							
Conversion Factor (Annual Avg)	2.000	2.000	1.970	1.920	1.960	2.050	2.170	2.610	2.700	2.700	2.700
				(Millions of US dollars), outstanding at end of year							
EXTERNAL DEBT (Total)	..	..	..	..	..	..	..	..	..	..	..
Long-Term Debt (by debtor)	..	..	..	..	..	..	..	..	..	..	..
Central Bank, incl. IMF credit	..	..	..	..	..	..	..	..	..	..	..
Central Government	..	..	..	..	..	..	..	..	..	..	..
Rest of General Government	..	..	..	..	..	..	..	..	..	..	..
Non-financial Public Enterprises	..	..	..	..	..	..	..	..	..	..	..
Priv. Sector, incl non-guaranteed	..	..	..	..	..	..	..	..	..	..	..
Short-Term Debt	..	..	..	..	..	..	..	..	..	..	..
Memo Items:				*(Thousands of US dollars)*							
Int'l Reserves Excluding Gold	..	..	..	..	..	..	7,316	9,666	5,104	5,973	11,233
Gold Holdings (at market price)	..	..	..	..	..	..	..	..	..	..	..
SOCIAL INDICATORS											
Total Fertility Rate	..	..	..	..	2.6	2.5	2.5	2.4	2.3	2.3	2.2
Infant Mortality Rate	..	..	..	..	..	..	..	..	..	..	..
Life Expectancy at Birth	66.4	66.9	67.3	67.8	68.2	68.7	69.1	69.5	70.0	70.4	70.9
Urban Population, % of total	34.3	33.7	33.1	32.5	32.0	31.4	30.8	30.8	30.8	30.8	30.8
Food Prod. per capita (1987=100)	90.4	91.4	114.8	93.6	93.0	91.5	91.2	93.1	93.6	106.8	86.3
Labor Force, Agriculture (%)	..	..	..	..	..	..	..	..	..	..	..
Labor Force, Female (%)	..	..	..	..	..	..	..	..	..	..	..
Primary Schl. Enroll. Ratio	..	..	..	..	..	..	..	..	..	..	..
Primary Schl. Enroll. Ratio, Female	..	..	..	..	..	..	..	..	..	..	..
Secondary Schl. Enroll. Ratio	..	..	..	..	..	..	..	..	..	..	..

1980	1981	1982	1983	1984	1985	1986	1987	1988	1989 estimate	NOTES	ANTIGUA AND BARBUDA
				(Millions of current US dollars)							**FOREIGN TRADE (CUSTOMS BASIS)**
59.50	51.40	49.30	36.50	35.00	28.00	28.00	..	..	..	..	Value of Exports, fob
..	..	..	..	..	..	..	..	..	..	..	Nonfuel Primary Products
..	..	..	..	..	..	..	..	..	..	..	Fuels
..	..	..	..	..	..	..	..	..	..	..	Manufactures
126.20	136.50	136.60	148.70	165.20	192.20	262.00	..	..	..	..	Value of Imports, cif
..	..	..	..	..	..	..	..	..	..	..	Nonfuel Primary Products
..	..	..	..	..	..	..	..	..	..	..	Fuels
..	..	..	..	..	..	..	..	..	..	..	Manufactures
				(Index 1987 = 100)							
..	..	..	..	..	..	..	..	..	..	..	Terms of Trade
..	..	..	..	..	..	..	..	..	..	..	Export Prices, fob
..	..	..	..	..	..	..	..	..	..	..	Import Prices, cif
				(Millions of current US dollars)							**BALANCE OF PAYMENTS**
106.90	107.10	107.60	104.30	172.40	181.00	203.10	222.80	..	..	..	Exports of Goods & Services
59.50	51.40	49.30	36.50	35.20	28.30	30.90	28.50	..	..	..	Merchandise, fob
44.60	52.50	51.70	62.80	132.10	150.30	169.70	191.70	..	..	..	Nonfactor Services
2.80	3.20	6.60	5.00	5.10	2.40	2.50	2.60	..	..	..	Factor Services
135.80	150.20	158.60	124.00	186.30	218.30	346.90	324.80	..	..	..	Imports of Goods & Services
114.72	125.26	126.72	99.72	150.17	174.80	284.15	258.25	..	..	..	Merchandise, fob
17.09	19.74	21.59	18.28	30.63	38.40	55.55	50.65	..	..	..	Nonfactor Services
4.00	5.20	10.30	6.00	5.50	5.10	7.20	15.90	..	..	..	Factor Services
..	..	..	..	..	..	..	..	..	..	..	Long-Term Interest
7.00	7.80	8.70	10.60	12.50	13.50	14.50	17.00	..	..	..	Private Current Transfers, net
..	..	..	..	..	..	..	..	..	..	..	Workers' Remittances
-21.90	-35.30	-42.30	-9.10	-1.40	-23.80	-129.30	-85.00	..	..	..	Curr. A/C Bal before Off. Transf.
3.10	2.60	0.70	..	2.00	0.70	2.70	1.70	..	..	..	Net Official Transfers
-18.80	-32.70	-41.60	-9.10	0.60	-23.10	-126.60	-83.30	..	..	..	Curr. A/C Bal after Off. Transf.
23.57	36.71	30.40	-1.10	-0.40	10.80	121.90	76.60	..	..	..	Long-Term Capital, net
19.60	22.40	23.00	5.00	4.40	15.60	17.70	29.20	..	..	..	Direct Investment
..	..	..	..	..	..	..	..	..	..	..	Long-Term Loans
..	..	..	..	..	..	..	..	..	..	..	Disbursements
..	..	..	..	..	..	..	..	..	..	..	Repayments
3.97	14.31	7.40	-6.10	-4.80	-4.80	104.20	47.40	..	..	..	Other Long-Term Capital
-7.98	-4.39	12.40	11.60	6.90	15.60	13.90	11.19	..	..	..	Other Capital, net
3.21	0.38	-1.20	-1.40	-7.10	-3.30	-9.20	-4.49	-2.43	-0.04	..	Change in Reserves
				(Eastern Caribbean Dollars per US dollar)							**Memo Item:**
2.700	2.700	2.700	2.700	2.700	2.700	2.700	2.700	2.700	2.700	..	Conversion Factor (Annual Avg)
				(Millions of US dollars), outstanding at end of year							
..	..	..	..	..	..	..	..	..	..	..	**EXTERNAL DEBT (Total)**
..	..	..	..	..	..	..	..	..	..	..	Long-Term Debt (by debtor)
..	..	..	..	..	..	..	..	..	..	..	Central Bank, incl. IMF credit
..	..	..	..	..	..	..	..	..	..	..	Central Government
..	..	..	..	..	..	..	..	..	..	..	Rest of General Government
..	..	..	..	..	..	..	..	..	..	..	Non-financial Public Enterprises
..	..	..	..	..	..	..	..	..	..	..	Priv. Sector, incl non-guaranteed
..	..	..	..	..	..	..	..	..	..	..	Short-Term Debt
				(Thousands of US dollars)							**Memo Items:**
7,817	7,336	8,520	9,930	15,440	16,580	28,260	25,600	28,030	28,070	..	Int'l Reserves Excluding Gold
..	..	..	..	..	..	..	..	..	..	..	Gold Holdings (at market price)
											SOCIAL INDICATORS
2.1	2.1	2.0	2.0	2.0	1.9	1.9	1.9	1.9	1.9	..	Total Fertility Rate
31.5	30.1	28.7	27.3	25.8	24.4	23.0	21.6	20.9	20.3	..	Infant Mortality Rate
71.3	71.8	72.2	72.4	72.6	72.7	72.9	73.0	73.2	73.4	..	Life Expectancy at Birth
30.8	30.8	30.8	30.8	30.8	30.8	31.0	31.3	31.5	31.8	..	Urban Population, % of total
95.0	94.6	93.3	94.3	87.8	104.2	101.2	100.0	98.9	95.8	..	Food Prod. per capita (1987=100)
..	..	..	..	..	..	..	..	..	..	..	Labor Force, Agriculture (%)
..	..	..	..	..	..	..	..	..	..	..	Labor Force, Female (%)
..	..	..	..	..	..	..	..	..	..	..	Primary Schl. Enroll. Ratio
..	..	..	..	..	..	..	..	..	..	..	Primary Schl. Enroll. Ratio, Female
..	..	..	..	..	..	..	..	..	..	..	Secondary Schl. Enroll. Ratio

ARGENTINA	1969	1970	1971	1972	1973	1974	1975	1976	1977	1978	1979
CURRENT GNP PER CAPITA (US $)	900	920	1,000	1,040	1,240	1,630	1,810	1,680	1,610	1,570	1,800
POPULATION (thousands)	23,597	23,963	24,360	24,770	25,190	25,618	26,052	26,489	26,928	27,366	27,803

USE AND ORIGIN OF RESOURCES *(Billions of current Argentine Australes)*

	1969	1970	1971	1972	1973	1974	1975	1976	1977	1978	1979
Gross National Product (GNP)	8.00E-6	8.70E-6	1.24E-5	2.04E-5	3.51E-5	4.82E-5	1.42E-4	7.49E-4	2.07E-3	5.17E-3	1.41E-2
Net Factor Income from Abroad	-1.00E-7	-1.00E-7	-1.00E-7	-3.00E-7	-4.00E-7	-4.00E-7	-1.30E-6	-9.50E-6	-2.70E-5	-5.91E-5	-1.43E-4
GDP at Market Prices	8.10E-6	8.80E-6	1.25E-5	2.07E-5	3.55E-5	4.86E-5	1.43E-4	7.59E-4	2.09E-3	5.23E-3	1.43E-2
Resource Balance	0.00E+0	0.00E+0	-1.00E-7	1.00E-7	9.00E-7	4.00E-7	-3.00E-7	3.33E-5	6.50E-5	2.05E-4	3.50E-5
Exports of Goods & NFServices	7.00E-7	8.00E-7	1.00E-6	2.00E-6	3.60E-6	4.50E-6	1.13E-5	9.39E-5	2.73E-4	6.10E-4	1.26E-3
Imports of Goods & NFServices	7.00E-7	8.00E-7	1.10E-6	1.90E-6	2.70E-6	4.10E-6	1.16E-5	6.06E-5	2.08E-4	4.05E-4	1.22E-3
Domestic Absorption	8.10E-6	8.80E-6	1.24E-5	2.05E-5	3.45E-5	4.81E-5	1.44E-4	7.26E-4	2.03E-3	5.03E-3	1.42E-2
Private Consumption, etc.	5.60E-6	6.00E-6	8.50E-6	1.42E-5	2.39E-5	3.21E-5	8.78E-5	4.48E-4	1.26E-3	3.14E-3	9.34E-3
General Gov't Consumption	8.00E-7	9.00E-7	1.30E-6	2.00E-6	4.20E-6	6.60E-6	1.88E-5	7.42E-5	1.97E-4	6.09E-4	1.64E-3
Gross Domestic Investment	1.70E-6	1.90E-6	2.60E-6	4.30E-6	6.40E-6	9.40E-6	3.70E-5	2.04E-4	5.69E-4	1.28E-3	3.24E-3
Fixed Investment	1.70E-6	1.90E-6	2.60E-6	4.30E-6	6.40E-6	9.40E-6	3.70E-5	2.04E-4	5.69E-4	1.28E-3	2.99E-3
Indirect Taxes, net	9.00E-7	1.00E-6	1.40E-6	2.40E-6	4.00E-6	5.50E-6	1.63E-5	8.65E-5	2.39E-4	5.97E-4	1.26E-3
GDP at factor cost	7.20E-6	7.80E-6	1.11E-5	1.83E-5	3.15E-5	4.31E-5	1.27E-4	6.72E-4	1.85E-3	4.64E-3	1.30E-2
Agriculture	8.89E-7	9.00E-7	1.60E-6	2.70E-6	5.00E-6	5.90E-6	1.13E-5	7.38E-5	2.03E-4	4.70E-4	1.33E-3
Industry	3.02E-6	3.10E-6	4.40E-6	7.30E-6	1.19E-5	1.65E-5	5.58E-5	3.00E-4	7.79E-4	1.90E-3	4.95E-3
Manufacturing	2.22E-6	2.30E-6	3.30E-6	5.60E-6	9.00E-6	1.23E-5	4.11E-5	2.22E-4	5.76E-4	1.34E-3	3.50E-3
Services, etc.	3.29E-6	3.80E-6	5.10E-6	8.30E-6	1.46E-5	2.07E-5	5.96E-5	2.98E-4	8.73E-4	2.27E-3	6.70E-3
Gross Domestic Saving	1.70E-6	1.90E-6	2.70E-6	4.50E-6	7.40E-6	9.90E-6	3.64E-5	2.37E-4	6.34E-4	1.48E-3	3.27E-3
Gross National Saving	..	1.80E-6	2.60E-6	4.20E-6	7.00E-6	..	3.51E-5	2.28E-4	6.08E-4	1.43E-3	3.13E-3

(Millions of 1987 Argentine Australes)

	1969	1970	1971	1972	1973	1974	1975	1976	1977	1978	1979
Gross National Product	126,076	132,780	138,835	140,496	145,321	153,550	152,768	152,401	162,293	156,608	167,704
GDP at Market Prices	132,853	139,791	145,156	148,203	153,551	162,022	161,244	160,851	171,334	165,554	177,477
Resource Balance	-5,001	-2,310	-4,513	-3,745	-2,456	-3,070	-4,157	1,131	466,940	2,426	-5,107
Exports of Goods & NFServices	8,720	8,824	7,948	8,109	9,243	9,265	8,404	11,052	14,071	15,325	14,834
Imports of Goods & NFServices	13,720	11,135	12,461	11,854	11,699	12,334	12,560	9,921	13,604	12,899	19,941
Domestic Absorption	137,853	142,102	149,669	151,948	156,007	165,092	165,400	159,720	170,867	163,128	182,583
Private Consumption, etc.	86,874	90,363	93,235	95,359	100,371	107,760	107,335	98,068	99,357	99,341	113,202
General Gov't Consumption	14,934	14,901	15,575	15,295	16,283	17,543	17,563	18,357	19,145	19,760	20,858
Gross Domestic Investment	36,046	36,838	40,859	41,295	39,354	39,789	40,502	43,295	52,366	44,028	48,524
Fixed Investment	36,219	36,836	39,821	40,276	37,347	38,851	38,930	42,987	51,973	45,323	48,390
GDP at factor cost	116,863	123,350	128,083	130,753	135,459	142,959	142,295	141,904	151,185	146,048	156,604
Agriculture	17,976	16,306	16,563	16,882	18,690	19,200	18,673	19,554	20,032	20,590	21,180
Industry	47,476	46,926	49,960	51,688	52,336	55,456	54,980	55,259	59,883	55,261	59,592
Manufacturing	34,152	33,273	35,325	36,736	38,193	40,436	39,404	38,209	41,194	36,860	40,525
Services, etc.	51,243	59,707	61,038	61,620	64,055	67,727	67,886	66,723	70,664	69,855	75,159

Memo Items:

	1969	1970	1971	1972	1973	1974	1975	1976	1977	1978	1979
Capacity to Import	13,720	11,135	11,328	12,478	15,599	13,538	12,235	15,373	17,856	19,428	20,511
Terms of Trade Adjustment	5,000	2,310	3,380	4,369	6,356	4,273	3,832	4,321	3,784	4,103	5,677
Gross Domestic Income	137,853	142,102	148,537	152,572	159,907	166,295	165,075	165,172	175,119	169,657	183,154
Gross National Income	131,077	135,090	142,215	144,865	151,677	157,823	156,600	156,722	166,077	160,710	173,381

DOMESTIC PRICES/DEFLATORS *(Index 1987 = 100)*

	1969	1970	1971	1972	1973	1974	1975	1976	1977	1978	1979
Overall (GDP)	6.10E-6	6.30E-6	8.61E-6	1.40E-5	2.31E-5	3.00E-5	8.87E-5	4.72E-4	1.22E-3	3.16E-3	8.03E-3
Domestic Absorption	5.88E-6	6.19E-6	8.28E-6	1.35E-5	2.21E-5	2.91E-5	8.68E-5	4.54E-4	1.19E-3	3.08E-3	7.79E-3
Agriculture	4.94E-6	5.52E-6	9.66E-6	1.60E-5	2.68E-5	3.07E-5	6.05E-5	3.77E-4	1.01E-3	2.28E-3	6.29E-3
Industry	6.37E-6	6.61E-6	8.81E-6	1.41E-5	2.27E-5	2.98E-5	1.01E-4	5.44E-4	1.30E-3	3.43E-3	8.31E-3
Manufacturing	6.51E-6	6.91E-6	9.34E-6	1.52E-5	2.36E-5	3.04E-5	1.04E-4	5.81E-4	1.40E-3	3.64E-3	8.64E-3
Consumer Price Index	5.00E-6	6.00E-6	8.00E-6	1.30E-5	2.20E-5	2.70E-5	7.80E-5	4.25E-4	1.17E-3	3.24E-3	8.40E-3

MANUFACTURING ACTIVITY

	1969	1970	1971	1972	1973	1974	1975	1976	1977	1978	1979
Employment (1987=100)	..	144.7	148.8	151.9	158.0	166.6	172.1	165.6	154.9	140.1	137.0
Real Earnings per Empl. (1987=100)	..	91.3	98.6	94.1	102.1	118.6	122.7	80.2	78.4	77.4	86.8
Real Output per Empl. (1987=100)	..	52.4	55.4	56.6	58.7	57.0	53.1	54.7	63.0	62.3	70.9
Earnings as % of Value Added	..	29.9	30.6	28.1	32.4	35.6	32.2	20.4	19.8	21.0	22.9

MONETARY HOLDINGS *(Billions of current Argentine Australes)*

	1969	1970	1971	1972	1973	1974	1975	1976	1977	1978	1979
Money Supply, Broadly Defined	2.40E-6	2.80E-6	3.00E-6	5.30E-6	9.70E-6	1.50E-5	3.60E-5	1.59E-4	5.17E-4	1.46E-3	4.35E-3
Money	1.70E-6	1.80E-6	2.00E-6	3.30E-6	5.70E-6	9.00E-6	2.80E-5	1.05E-4	2.26E-4	5.87E-4	1.40E-3
Currency Outside Banks	7.00E-7	8.00E-7	1.00E-6	1.30E-6	2.70E-6	4.00E-6	1.20E-5	4.10E-5	1.07E-4	3.33E-4	7.87E-4
Demand Deposits	1.00E-6	1.00E-6	1.00E-6	2.00E-6	3.00E-6	5.00E-6	1.60E-5	6.40E-5	1.19E-4	2.54E-4	6.09E-4
Quasi-Money	7.00E-7	1.00E-6	1.00E-6	2.00E-6	4.00E-6	6.00E-6	8.00E-6	5.40E-5	2.91E-4	8.78E-4	2.96E-3

GOVERNMENT DEFICIT (-) OR SURPLUS *(Millions of current Argentine Australes)*

	1969	1970	1971	1972	1973	1974	1975	1976	1977	1978	1979
	..	..	..	..	..	..	..	..	..	..	..
Current Revenue	..	..	..	..	..	..	..	..	..	1.00E+0	3
Current Expenditure	..	..	..	..	..	..	..	..	..	1.00E+0	3
Current Budget Balance	..	..	..	..	..	..	..	..	..	0.00E+0	0
Capital Receipts	..	..	..	..	..	..	..	..	..	..	..
Capital Payments	..	..	..	..	..	..	..	..	..	0.00E+0	0

1980	1981	1982	1983	1984	1985	1986	1987	1988	1989 estimate	NOTES	ARGENTINA
1,970	1,960	1,880	1,970	2,150	2,140	2,380	2,400	2,570	2,160	A	**CURRENT GNP PER CAPITA (US $)**
28,237	28,667	29,092	29,512	29,925	30,331	30,730	31,121	31,506	31,883	..	**POPULATION (thousands)**
				(Billions of current Argentine Australes)							**USE AND ORIGIN OF RESOURCES**
2.80E-2	5.31E-2	1.35E-1	6.26E-1	4.89	36.40	70.14	163.48	776.59	22,892.56	..	Gross National Product (GNP)
-3.33E-4	-1.64E-3	-1.26E-2	-5.71E-2	-0.39	-3.19	-4.17	-9.62	-44.88	-2,188.75	..	Net Factor Income from Abroad
2.83E-2	5.48E-2	1.48E-1	6.83E-1	5.28	39.59	74.31	173.10	821.47	25,081.32	..	GDP at Market Prices
-6.16E-4	-2.37E-4	4.76E-3	3.33E-2	0.23	2.63	1.67	0.55	30.74	1,751.95	..	Resource Balance
1.94E-3	5.17E-3	1.99E-2	1.00E-1	0.68	6.19	8.30	17.44	98.92	4,056.30	..	Exports of Goods & NFServices
2.56E-3	5.41E-3	1.51E-2	6.69E-2	0.45	3.56	6.62	16.89	68.18	2,304.34	..	Imports of Goods & NFServices
2.90E-2	5.50E-2	1.43E-1	6.49E-1	5.06	36.96	72.64	172.55	790.73	23,329.36	..	Domestic Absorption
1.89E-2	3.72E-2	1.03E-1	4.42E-1	3.88	29.22	57.32	120.11	569.99	17,802.97	..	Private Consumption, etc.
3.74E-3	7.47E-3	1.65E-2	8.91E-2	0.58	4.38	8.76	24.04	86.06	2,508.13	..	General Gov't Consumption
6.28E-3	1.03E-2	2.34E-2	1.18E-1	0.60	3.37	6.56	28.40	134.68	3,018.26	..	Gross Domestic Investment
5.78E-3	1.04E-2	2.15E-2	1.17E-1	0.61	3.78	6.71	28.68	130.17	2,940.01	..	Fixed Investment
3.23E-3	6.24E-3	1.68E-2	7.78E-2	0.60	4.52	8.47	19.74	93.66	2,616.73	..	Indirect Taxes, net
2.51E-2	4.85E-2	1.31E-1	6.05E-1	4.68	35.08	65.84	153.36	727.81	22,464.57	..	GDP at factor cost
2.16E-3	4.38E-3	1.54E-2	7.65E-2	0.59	4.44	8.33	22.41	108.55	3,106.82	..	Agriculture
9.28E-3	1.74E-2	4.98E-2	2.63E-1	2.03	15.24	28.61	52.80	244.91	7,345.57	..	Industry
6.27E-3	1.16E-2	3.71E-2	1.86E-1	1.44	10.80	20.27	35.94	163.20	4,924.21	..	Manufacturing
1.37E-2	2.67E-2	6.56E-2	2.65E-1	2.05	15.39	28.89	78.16	374.35	12,012.19	..	Services, etc.
5.67E-3	1.00E-2	2.82E-2	1.51E-1	0.82	6.00	8.23	28.95	165.42	4,770.22	..	Gross Domestic Saving
5.34E-3	8.38E-3	1.56E-2	9.42E-2	0.43	2.81	4.07	19.31	120.54	2,584.85	..	Gross National Saving
				(Millions of 1987 Argentine Australes)							
170,305	156,255	146,529	150,337	154,290	149,222	160,068	163,484	158,888	147,782	..	Gross National Product
180,920	168,409	159,155	163,790	167,822	160,464	169,131	173,100	168,362	161,993	I f	GDP at Market Prices
-15,113	-11,531	169,271	2,077	1,068	5,355	1,466	546,697	6,258	7,687	..	Resource Balance
14,071	14,845	15,368	16,556	16,436	18,507	17,003	17,439	20,709	21,799	..	Exports of Goods & NFServices
29,184	26,376	15,199	14,479	15,368	13,153	15,538	16,893	14,451	14,112	..	Imports of Goods & NFServices
196,033	179,940	158,986	161,713	166,754	155,110	167,666	172,553	162,104	154,306	..	Domestic Absorption
121,917	117,893	106,467	112,118	119,980	113,847	121,577	120,111	117,463	118,090	..	Private Consumption, etc.
21,137	21,465	19,939	20,481	20,907	20,546	21,629	24,042	18,577	16,411	..	General Gov't Consumption
52,980	40,582	32,580	29,114	25,866	20,717	24,460	28,401	26,064	19,806	..	Gross Domestic Investment
50,983	41,998	30,439	28,856	26,244	23,176	24,997	28,678	24,898	..	..	Fixed Investment
159,732	148,653	140,373	144,465	148,020	141,518	149,165	153,364	148,626	142,257	I f	GDP at factor cost
20,016	20,399	21,817	22,216	22,933	22,630	22,008	22,407	22,646	19,124	..	Agriculture
58,874	51,328	47,777	50,520	50,995	46,985	51,962	52,802	50,219	45,970	..	Industry
39,082	32,915	31,234	34,405	35,721	32,027	36,149	35,943	33,438	31,710	..	Manufacturing
79,399	75,951	70,754	71,730	74,092	71,903	75,195	78,155	75,762	77,163	..	Services, etc.
											Memo Items:
22,162	25,221	19,986	21,682	22,971	22,867	19,457	17,439	20,967	24,842	..	Capacity to Import
8,091	10,375	4,618	5,125	6,535	4,360	2,454	0	257,884	3,043	..	Terms of Trade Adjustment
189,011	178,784	163,773	168,915	174,357	164,824	171,585	173,100	168,619	165,036	..	Gross Domestic Income
178,395	166,631	151,146	155,462	160,825	153,582	162,522	163,484	159,146	150,825	..	Gross National Income
				(Index 1987 = 100)							**DOMESTIC PRICES/DEFLATORS**
1.57E-2	3.25E-2	9.27E-2	4.17E-1	3.1	24.7	43.9	100.0	487.9	15483.0	..	Overall (GDP)
1.48E-2	3.06E-2	8.99E-2	4.02E-1	3.0	23.8	43.3	100.0	487.8	15118.9	..	Domestic Absorption
1.08E-2	2.15E-2	7.06E-2	3.45E-1	2.6	19.6	37.9	100.0	479.3	16245.9	..	Agriculture
1.58E-2	3.40E-2	1.04E-1	5.20E-1	4.0	32.4	55.1	100.0	487.7	15979.0	..	Industry
1.61E-2	3.54E-2	1.19E-1	5.41E-1	4.0	33.7	56.1	100.0	488.1	15529.0	..	Manufacturing
1.69E-2	3.45E-2	9.13E-2	4.05E-1	2.9	22.7	43.2	100.0	443.0	14085.1	..	Consumer Price Index
											MANUFACTURING ACTIVITY
125.7	109.4	103.1	106.7	109.7	105.2	101.1	100.0	100.7	..	J	Employment (1987=100)
97.5	89.6	80.0	103.4	124.5	102.5	108.5	100.0	95.0	..	J	Real Earnings per Empl. (1987=100)
73.7	71.9	73.7	77.1	68.9	64.5	75.8	100.0	92.2	..	J	Real Output per Empl. (1987=100)
26.4	23.2	16.2	19.2	25.3	20.5	21.1	19.1	17.9	..	J	Earnings as % of Value Added
				(Billions of current Argentine Australes)							**MONETARY HOLDINGS**
8.23E-3	1.75E-2	4.59E-2	2.30E-1	1.64	8.43	17.76	48.42	259.89	5,958.37	..	Money Supply, Broadly Defined
2.75E-3	4.67E-3	1.62E-2	7.50E-2	0.45	3.03	5.60	12.58	55.08	2,311.38	..	Money
1.64E-3	3.02E-3	8.74E-3	4.63E-2	0.31	2.02	3.99	9.26	43.19	1,822.35	..	Currency Outside Banks
1.10E-3	1.65E-3	7.50E-3	2.87E-2	0.14	1.01	1.61	3.32	11.90	489.03	..	Demand Deposits
5.48E-3	1.28E-2	2.97E-2	1.55E-1	1.19	5.40	12.16	35.84	204.81	3,646.99	..	Quasi-Money
				(Millions of current Argentine Australes)							
-1	-5	-11	-87	-267	-29,240	-19,640	-66,750	-208,710	..	..	**GOVERNMENT DEFICIT (-) OR SURPLUS**
6	9	23	106	783	8,286	151,760	324,310	103,000	..	..	Current Revenue
7	10	26	134	805	8,583	147,040	326,650	107,000	..	..	Current Expenditure
-1	-1	-3	-28	-22	-297	472	-234	-48,784	..	..	Current Budget Balance
..	..	..	..	..	..		3	196	309	..	Capital Receipts
1	4	8	59	245	2,627	2,439	6,637	163,021	..	..	Capital Payments

ARGENTINA	1969	1970	1971	1972	1973	1974	1975	1976	1977	1978	1979
FOREIGN TRADE (CUSTOMS BASIS)					*(Millions of current US dollars)*						
Value of Exports, fob	1,612	1,773	1,740	1,941	3,266	3,931	2,961	3,912	5,642	6,394	7,808
Nonfuel Primary Products	1,386	1,519	1,468	1,540	2,527	2,958	2,224	2,919	4,265	4,669	5,871
Fuels	6	8	9	6	6	12	15	20	28	52	49
Manufactures	220	247	264	395	733	961	723	973	1,349	1,674	1,888
Value of Imports, cif	1,571	1,689	1,846	1,904	2,235	3,635	3,945	3,029	4,158	3,832	6,692
Nonfuel Primary Products	367	374	390	411	552	780	763	511	615	566	1,096
Fuels	106	80	123	72	170	528	522	536	682	477	1,109
Manufactures	1,098	1,234	1,332	1,422	1,514	2,327	2,660	1,982	2,861	2,790	4,488
					(Index 1987 = 100)						
Terms of Trade	164.4	162.7	161.4	151.2	172.4	147.8	139.5	135.1	128.4	121.8	126.0
Export Prices, fob	40.4	43.7	44.7	48.5	64.5	77.3	77.0	77.6	80.0	84.2	104.6
Import Prices, cif	24.6	26.9	27.7	32.1	37.4	52.3	55.2	57.4	62.3	69.1	83.0
BALANCE OF PAYMENTS					*(Millions of current US dollars)*						
Exports of Goods & Services	..	2,148	2,131	2,318	3,747	4,714	3,587	4,691	6,738	7,836	9,916
Merchandise, fob	..	1,773	1,740	1,941	3,266	3,930	2,961	3,918	5,651	6,401	7,810
Nonfactor Services	..	331	360	359	433	623	537	691	937	1,083	1,366
Factor Services	..	44	31	17	48	161	89	82	150	352	740
Imports of Goods & Services	..	2,308	2,518	2,541	3,047	4,596	4,878	4,058	5,643	6,048	10,486
Merchandise, fob	..	1,499	1,653	1,685	1,978	3,216	3,510	2,765	3,799	3,488	6,028
Nonfactor Services	..	487	512	460	564	808	813	703	913	1,473	2,745
Factor Services	..	322	354	395	505	572	555	590	931	1,087	1,713
Long-Term Interest	..	338	343	367	461	511	495	470	551	754	957
Private Current Transfers, net	..	0	0	0	0	..	6	24	32	48	35
Workers' Remittances	..	..	..	..	..	..	..	..	..	..	..
Curr. A/C Bal before Off. Transf.	..	-160	-387	-223	700	118	-1,286	657	1,127	1,836	-535
Net Official Transfers	..	-3	-3	-4	11	..	-1	-6	-1	20	22
Curr. A/C Bal after Off. Transf.	..	-163	-390	-227	711	118	-1,287	651	1,126	1,856	-513
Long-Term Capital, net	..	120	338	187	42	-2	-285	805	473	1,390	2,994
Direct Investment	..	11	11	10	10	10	..	..	143	227	147
Long-Term Loans	..	135	343	265	320	464	-52	1,119	426	1,278	4,566
Disbursements	..	907	1,068	1,027	1,234	1,460	920	2,173	1,577	3,316	5,865
Repayments	..	772	726	761	915	996	972	1,053	1,151	2,038	1,299
Other Long-Term Capital	..	-26	-16	-88	-288	-476	-233	-314	-96	-115	-1,719
Other Capital, net	..	119	-393	-25	90	-41	494	-538	246	-1,111	1,679
Change in Reserves	..	-76	445	65	-842	-75	1,078	-918	-1,845	-2,135	-4,160
Memo Item:					*(Argentine Australes per US dollar)*						
Conversion Factor (Annual Avg)	3.50E-7	3.79E-7	4.52E-7	5.00E-7	5.00E-7	5.00E-7	3.66E-6	1.40E-5	4.08E-5	7.96E-5	1.32E-4
Additional Conversion Factor	4.00E-7	4.00E-7	5.00E-7	8.00E-7	9.00E-7	9.00E-7	3.70E-6	2.00E-5	5.00E-5	1.22E-4	2.79E-4
EXTERNAL DEBT (Total)				*(Millions of US dollars), outstanding at end of year*							
	..	5,171	5,564	6,028	6,429	6,789	8,171	9,880	11,445	13,276	20,950
Long-Term Debt (by debtor)	..	5,171	5,564	6,028	6,429	6,789	6,873	8,258	8,721	9,848	14,039
Central Bank, incl. IMF credit	..	105	86	416	625	411	526	1,227	1,007	118	174
Central Government	..	702	894	943	905	1,117	1,087	1,447	1,391	1,988	2,819
Rest of General Government	..	65	47	41	43	36	30	42	42	71	277
Non-financial Public Enterprises	..	875	956	955	1,137	1,391	1,385	1,536	1,876	2,793	2,718
Priv. Sector, incl non-guaranteed	..	3,424	3,581	3,673	3,719	3,835	3,846	4,007	4,405	4,878	8,051
Short-Term Debt	..	0	0	0	0	0	1,297	1,622	2,724	3,428	6,911
Memo Items:					*(Millions of US dollars)*						
Int'l Reserves Excluding Gold	402.8	532.6	192.4	313.3	1,148.7	1,144.3	287.8	1,444.9	3,153.8	4,966.5	9,388.0
Gold Holdings (at market price)	135.5	149.2	111.9	259.1	448.6	745.3	560.4	538.5	690.2	966.8	2,238.5
SOCIAL INDICATORS											
Total Fertility Rate	3.1	3.1	3.1	3.1	3.2	3.2	3.3	3.3	3.4	3.3	3.3
Infant Mortality Rate	53.2	51.8	50.4	49.0	47.4	45.8	44.2	42.6	41.0	40.0	39.0
Life Expectancy at Birth	66.5	66.8	67.0	67.3	67.6	67.9	68.1	68.4	68.7	68.9	69.1
Urban Population, % of total	77.9	78.4	78.8	79.3	79.7	80.2	80.6	81.0	81.4	81.9	82.3
Food Prod. per capita (1987=100)	95.7	99.9	87.3	78.8	77.7	91.1	97.7	101.6	103.6	101.5	111.9
Labor Force, Agriculture (%)	16.4	16.0	15.7	15.4	15.1	14.8	14.5	14.2	13.9	13.6	13.3
Labor Force, Female (%)	24.5	24.9	25.1	25.3	25.6	25.8	26.0	26.2	26.3	26.5	26.7
Primary Schl. Enroll. Ratio	..	105.0	..	..	..	..	106.0	109.0	111.0	..	112.0
Primary Schl. Enroll. Ratio, Female	..	106.0	..	..	..	..	106.0	109.0	111.0	..	..
Secondary Schl. Enroll. Ratio	..	44.0	..	..	..	..	54.0	57.0	56.0	56.0	56.0

1980	1981	1982	1983	1984	1985	1986	1987	1988	1989 estimate	NOTES	ARGENTINA
											FOREIGN TRADE (CUSTOMS BASIS)
8,021	9,143	7,625	7,836	8,107	8,396	6,852	6,360	8,941	9,162	f	Value of Exports, fob
5,883	6,724	5,228	6,219	6,353	5,988	4,894	4,262	6,481	..	..	Nonfuel Primary Products
278	620	548	334	332	614	154	85	160	..	..	Fuels
1,861	1,800	1,849	1,283	1,423	1,795	1,804	2,013	2,300	2,528	..	Manufactures
10,539	9,430	5,337	4,504	4,585	3,814	4,724	5,818	5,322	6,696	f	Value of Imports, cif
1,299	1,039	722	626	694	492	798	813	608	..	..	Nonfuel Primary Products
1,086	1,022	682	463	478	462	439	664	401	..	..	Fuels
8,155	7,370	3,933	3,414	3,413	2,860	3,488	4,341	4,313	5,293	..	Manufactures

(Index 1987 = 100)

1980	1981	1982	1983	1984	1985	1986	1987	1988	1989 estimate	NOTES	
131.0	133.3	117.3	130.3	129.8	119.5	106.7	100.0	110.8	..	..	Terms of Trade
117.3	119.2	104.4	111.7	109.6	101.3	96.9	100.0	117.5	..	..	Export Prices, fob
89.5	89.4	89.0	85.8	84.4	84.8	90.8	100.0	106.1	..	..	Import Prices, cif

(Millions of current US dollars)

											BALANCE OF PAYMENTS
11,202	11,805	9,755	9,764	9,909	10,329	8,841	8,400	11,284	12,056	f	Exports of Goods & Services
8,021	9,143	7,623	7,835	8,100	8,396	6,852	6,360	9,134	9,573	..	Merchandise, fob
1,872	1,710	1,562	1,453	1,507	1,643	1,581	1,774	1,933	2,200	..	Nonfactor Services
1,309	952	570	476	302	290	408	266	217	283	..	Factor Services
15,999	16,495	12,142	12,216	12,406	11,281	11,702	12,631	12,899	13,356	f	Imports of Goods & Services
9,394	8,431	4,859	4,119	4,118	3,518	4,406	5,392	4,900	3,864	..	Merchandise, fob
3,687	3,180	1,655	1,700	1,843	1,767	2,080	2,235	2,373	2,391	..	Nonfactor Services
2,918	4,884	5,628	6,397	6,445	5,996	5,216	5,004	5,626	7,101	..	Factor Services
1,337	2,044	2,435	2,419	3,280	4,396	3,707	3,660	2,781	1,519	..	Long-Term Interest
23	-22	34	16	2	0	2	-8	0	8	..	Private Current Transfers, net
..	..	..	..	..	..	..	..	..	..	..	Workers' Remittances
-4,774	-4,712	-2,353	-2,436	-2,495	-952	-2,859	-4,239	-1,615	-1,292	..	Curr. A/C Bal before Off. Transf.
0	0	0	0	0	0	0	0	0	..	..	Net Official Transfers
-4,774	-4,712	-2,353	-2,436	-2,495	-952	-2,859	-4,239	-1,615	-1,292	..	Curr. A/C Bal after Off. Transf.
4,255	9,754	3,784	1,717	-322	4,790	2,275	2,471	1,464	2,189	f	Long-Term Capital, net
568	730	197	183	268	919	574	-19	1,147	1,028	..	Direct Investment
2,855	6,396	5,759	1,465	-3	2,567	644	1,612	491	-433	..	Long-Term Loans
4,708	8,346	7,054	2,832	821	3,584	2,687	3,152	1,888	1,079	..	Disbursements
1,853	1,950	1,294	1,367	824	1,017	2,043	1,540	1,398	1,512	..	Repayments
832	2,628	-2,172	69	-587	1,304	1,057	878	-174	1,594	..	Other Long-Term Capital
-2,186	-8,313	-2,062	-1,587	2,789	-2,590	-299	-275	2,071	-2,170	f	Other Capital, net
2,705	3,271	631	2,306	28	-1,248	883	2,043	-1,920	1,273	..	Change in Reserves

(Argentine Australes per US dollar)

											Memo Item:
1.84E-4	4.40E-4	2.59E-3	1.05E-2	0.068	0.602	0.943	2.140	8.750	423.340	..	Conversion Factor (Annual Avg)
4.99E-4	9.50E-4	2.59E-3	1.05E-2	0.068	0.602	0.943	2.140	8.750	423.340	..	Additional Conversion Factor

(Millions of US dollars), outstanding at end of year

											EXTERNAL DEBT (Total)
27,157	35,657	43,634	45,920	48,857	50,945	52,450	58,425	58,706	64,745	..	Long-Term Debt (by debtor)
16,774	22,736	27,113	37,006	38,138	44,215	48,040	54,894	52,992	56,329	..	Central Bank, incl. IMF credit
170	251	5,068	12,995	13,852	26,952	30,504	41,335	39,685	42,200	..	Central Government
3,480	4,238	4,485	2,625	2,422	4,889	5,313	6,814	6,695	7,998	..	Rest of General Government
475	479	433	504	509	379	345	163	144	117	..	Non-financial Public Enterprises
3,399	2,978	2,922	3,266	4,672	4,195	4,345	2,839	2,908	2,632	..	Priv. Sector, incl non-guaranteed
9,250	14,790	14,205	17,616	16,683	7,799	7,533	3,743	3,560	3,382	..	Short-Term Debt
10,383	12,921	16,521	8,913	10,718	6,730	4,410	3,531	5,714	8,416	..	

(Millions of US dollars)

											Memo Items:
6,719.5	3,268.4	2,506.4	1,172.4	1,242.6	3,273.0	2,718.0	1,617.0	3,363.5	1,463.3	..	Int'l Reserves Excluding Gold
2,577.3	1,737.9	1,997.6	1,667.9	1,347.9	1,429.6	1,709.4	2,117.0	1,794.0	1,753.6	..	Gold Holdings (at market price)

											SOCIAL INDICATORS
3.2	3.2	3.1	3.1	3.1	3.0	3.0	3.0	2.9	2.9	..	Total Fertility Rate
38.0	37.0	36.0	35.2	34.4	33.6	32.8	32.0	31.2	30.4	..	Infant Mortality Rate
69.3	69.5	69.7	69.9	70.0	70.2	70.4	70.6	70.8	70.9	..	Life Expectancy at Birth
82.7	83.1	83.5	83.8	84.2	84.6	84.9	85.2	85.6	85.9	..	Urban Population, % of total
105.7	113.0	116.5	112.1	103.3	99.8	96.7	100.0	106.6	93.1	..	Food Prod. per capita (1987=100)
13.0	..	..	..	..	..	..	..	..	..	..	Labor Force, Agriculture (%)
26.9	27.0	27.1	27.2	27.4	27.5	27.6	27.7	27.8	28.0	..	Labor Force, Female (%)
106.0	..	108.0	107.0	107.0	107.0	109.0	110.0	..	..	..	Primary Schl. Enroll. Ratio
106.0	107.0	107.0	107.0	107.0	108.0	109.0	110.0	..	..	..	Primary Schl. Enroll. Ratio, Female
..	..	..	60.0	65.0	71.0	74.0	74.0	..	..	..	Secondary Schl. Enroll. Ratio

AUSTRALIA	1969	1970	1971	1972	1973	1974	1975	1976	1977	1978	1979
CURRENT GNP PER CAPITA (US $)	2,760	2,970	3,180	3,440	4,140	5,140	6,360	7,430	7,650	8,090	8,820
POPULATION (thousands)	12,263	12,507	12,937	13,177	13,380	13,723	13,893	14,033	14,192	14,358	14,514
USE AND ORIGIN OF RESOURCES					*(Billions of current Australian Dollars)*						
Gross National Product (GNP)	29.79	32.78	36.76	40.97	48.99	58.21	69.15	81.53	89.75	99.62	113.24
Net Factor Income from Abroad	-0.49	-0.48	-0.51	-0.55	-0.41	-0.50	-0.84	-1.05	-1.21	-1.52	-1.94
GDP at Market Prices	30.28	33.26	37.27	41.52	49.40	58.72	69.99	82.58	90.96	101.14	115.18
Resource Balance	-0.10	0.02	0.03	1.19	1.26	-1.11	0.56	0.21	-0.84	-1.70	0.52
Exports of Goods & NFServices	4.33	4.94	5.34	6.24	7.56	8.81	10.56	12.48	13.95	14.80	19.74
Imports of Goods & NFServices	4.44	4.92	5.31	5.05	6.30	9.92	10.00	12.27	14.79	16.50	19.22
Domestic Absorption	30.39	33.24	37.24	40.33	48.13	59.82	69.44	82.37	91.80	102.84	114.65
Private Consumption, etc.	17.86	19.46	21.85	24.33	28.37	34.86	41.12	47.34	53.24	59.79	66.41
General Gov't Consumption	4.99	5.40	5.98	6.56	7.64	9.44	12.01	14.40	16.14	18.15	19.83
Gross Domestic Investment	7.54	8.38	9.41	9.44	12.13	15.52	16.31	20.63	22.42	24.90	28.41
Fixed Investment	0.00	8.81	10.18	10.81	12.27	14.05	16.51	19.63	21.48	23.96	27.06
Indirect Taxes, net	2.87	3.08	3.41	3.87	4.53	5.68	6.93	8.67	9.33	10.22	11.96
GDP at factor cost	27.41	30.18	33.86	37.65	44.86	53.04	63.06	73.91	81.63	90.92	103.22
Agriculture	2.16	1.93	2.19	2.91	3.95	3.40	3.53	4.06	4.02	6.22	7.19
Industry	11.83	12.98	14.35	15.56	18.07	21.52	25.52	29.79	32.74	35.50	41.00
Manufacturing	7.42	8.08	8.76	9.41	10.89	12.55	14.49	16.80	18.24	19.42	22.08
Services, etc.	16.29	18.36	20.73	23.05	27.38	33.80	40.95	48.73	54.20	59.41	66.98
Gross Domestic Saving	7.43	8.40	9.44	10.63	13.39	14.42	16.86	20.84	21.58	23.20	28.94
Gross National Saving	..	7.99	8.98	10.13	12.98	13.89	15.96	19.73	20.35	21.71	27.09
					(Billions of 1987 Australian Dollars)						
Gross National Product	152.17	160.87	169.08	173.89	185.61	188.99	191.44	199.20	201.11	207.76	215.19
GDP at Market Prices	154.82	163.38	171.54	176.35	187.33	190.80	193.95	201.94	203.95	211.04	219.03
Resource Balance	-5.43	-4.53	-2.58	0.78	-4.84	-12.78	-5.14	-5.91	-5.86	-6.32	-3.90
Exports of Goods & NFServices	18.46	20.73	22.50	23.84	23.38	22.72	24.74	27.49	27.66	28.61	31.87
Imports of Goods & NFServices	23.89	25.26	25.07	23.06	28.22	35.50	29.88	33.40	33.51	34.93	35.76
Domestic Absorption	160.25	167.90	174.12	175.56	192.17	203.58	199.09	207.84	209.81	217.35	222.93
Private Consumption, etc.	90.18	94.30	98.64	104.11	111.25	117.32	118.47	119.78	122.18	126.34	127.94
General Gov't Consumption	24.35	25.18	25.98	26.90	28.85	30.65	33.14	35.09	35.91	37.79	38.12
Gross Domestic Investment	45.72	48.42	49.49	44.56	52.07	55.61	47.48	52.97	51.71	53.22	56.87
Fixed Investment	0.00	44.84	48.00	47.28	49.58	48.09	47.65	49.76	49.31	50.86	52.82
GDP at factor cost	139.47	147.62	155.37	159.28	169.00	171.26	173.87	179.89	182.46	189.24	195.61
Agriculture	..	..	..	..	..	9.09	9.83	10.24	9.89	11.92	10.53
Industry	..	..	..	..	..	66.04	65.81	69.38	69.16	70.54	73.48
Manufacturing	..	..	..	..	..	38.06	37.41	38.80	38.63	39.63	41.92
Services, etc.	..	..	..	..	..	114.85	117.47	121.30	124.20	127.38	134.42
Memo Items:											
Capacity to Import	23.33	25.37	25.22	28.49	33.88	31.54	31.54	33.97	31.61	31.33	36.73
Terms of Trade Adjustment	4.87	4.64	2.72	4.65	10.50	8.82	6.80	6.48	3.96	2.72	4.87
Gross Domestic Income	159.68	168.02	174.26	181.00	197.83	199.62	200.75	208.41	207.91	213.76	223.90
Gross National Income	157.03	165.52	171.80	178.54	196.11	197.81	198.24	205.68	205.06	210.48	220.06
DOMESTIC PRICES/DEFLATORS					*(Index 1987 = 100)*						
Overall (GDP)	19.6	20.4	21.7	23.5	26.4	30.8	36.1	40.9	44.6	47.9	52.6
Domestic Absorption	19.0	19.8	21.4	23.0	25.0	29.4	34.9	39.6	43.8	47.3	51.4
Agriculture	..	..	..	..	..	37.4	35.9	39.6	40.7	52.2	68.2
Industry	..	..	..	..	..	32.6	38.8	42.9	47.3	50.3	55.8
Manufacturing	..	..	..	..	..	33.0	38.7	43.3	47.2	49.0	52.7
Consumer Price Index	20.3	21.1	22.4	23.7	25.9	29.8	34.3	39.0	43.8	47.2	51.5
MANUFACTURING ACTIVITY											
Employment (1987=100)	122.3	125.8	126.2	126.1	125.5	129.4	121.2	116.8	114.3	111.4	111.4
Real Earnings per Empl. (1987=100)	73.2	75.8	77.9	81.7	83.1	86.2	95.2	96.6	97.7	98.4	96.9
Real Output per Empl. (1987=100)	..	..	..	..	..	62.9	64.8	66.8	71.3	75.8	80.6
Earnings as % of Value Added	52.3	52.5	53.9	54.1	54.3	54.5	56.0	55.9	54.8	54.9	54.0
MONETARY HOLDINGS					*(Billions of current Australian Dollars)*						
Money Supply, Broadly Defined	14.93	15.70	17.07	20.42	24.71	26.96	32.55	52.67	58.13	65.90	74.83
Money	5.21	5.45	5.75	6.90	8.05	7.99	9.81	10.68	11.39	12.71	14.66
Currency Outside Banks	1.19	1.33	1.48	1.66	1.96	2.36	2.76	3.13	3.55	3.96	4.37
Demand Deposits	4.01	4.12	4.27	5.23	6.09	5.64	7.05	7.55	7.84	8.75	10.29
Quasi-Money	9.73	10.25	11.32	13.53	16.66	18.97	22.75	41.99	46.74	53.19	60.17
GOVERNMENT DEFICIT (-) OR SURPLUS					*(Millions of current Australian Dollars)*						
GOVERNMENT DEFICIT (-) OR SURPLUS	..	-260	-78	130	-409	-241	-2,482	-3,609	-2,743	-3,297	-3,419
Current Revenue	..	7,308	8,219	9,087	9,691	12,253	15,725	18,818	22,046	24,179	26,316
Current Expenditure	..	5,844	6,597	7,374	8,431	9,982	13,623	17,980	26,825	24,077	26,751
Current Budget Balance	..	1,464	1,622	1,713	1,260	2,271	2,102	838	-4,779	102	-435
Capital Receipts	..	15	22	44	49	43	21	35	32	39	26
Capital Payments	..	1,739	1,722	1,627	1,718	2,555	4,605	4,482	-2,005	3,439	3,010

1980	1981	1982	1983	1984	1985	1986	1987	1988	1989 estimate	NOTES	AUSTRALIA
9,730	11,010	11,600	11,530	12,050	11,770	11,400	11,250	12,330	14,440	..	**CURRENT GNP PER CAPITA** (US $)
14,692	14,927	15,178	15,369	15,544	15,758	15,974	16,249	16,532	16,765	..	**POPULATION** (thousands)
				(Billions of current Australian Dollars)							**USE AND ORIGIN OF RESOURCES**
129.14	145.56	160.82	174.13	197.86	220.57	241.29	269.22	302.44	342.46	C f	Gross National Product (GNP)
-2.13	-2.96	-3.58	-4.64	-6.49	-7.78	-8.48	-9.85	-12.77	-13.84	..	Net Factor Income from Abroad
131.28	148.52	164.40	178.77	204.34	228.35	249.77	279.07	315.21	356.30	..	GDP at Market Prices
-0.89	-4.22	-5.32	-2.57	-4.36	-5.99	-6.74	-3.52	-3.28	-8.80	..	Resource Balance
22.46	22.49	24.78	26.27	31.09	37.91	40.15	46.07	52.28	57.17	..	Exports of Goods & NFServices
23.35	26.71	30.09	28.84	35.45	43.90	46.89	49.59	55.56	65.96	..	Imports of Goods & NFServices
132.17	152.74	169.72	181.34	208.71	234.34	256.52	282.59	318.49	365.09	..	Domestic Absorption
76.17	86.30	97.24	107.74	121.47	134.03	148.75	164.97	183.18	210.59	..	Private Consumption, etc.
23.06	26.54	30.20	33.92	38.13	42.38	46.99	50.10	54.26	59.77	..	General Gov't Consumption
32.94	39.90	42.28	39.68	49.10	57.93	60.77	67.52	81.05	94.74	..	Gross Domestic Investment
31.65	38.06	41.38	40.88	47.30	56.02	59.76	66.27	77.37	89.85	..	Fixed Investment
14.22	15.82	18.23	20.42	23.95	28.16	29.12	34.41	38.76	41.98	..	Indirect Taxes, net
117.05	132.69	146.18	158.34	180.39	200.19	220.66	244.66	276.45	314.32	..	GDP at factor cost
6.85	7.19	5.67	8.58	8.87	8.80	9.58	11.34	13.31	..	B	Agriculture
47.83	52.79	57.98	62.33	71.34	78.77	82.29	89.73	99.38	..	B	Industry
25.40	28.46	29.82	32.18	36.29	39.25	41.65	46.69	53.36	..	B	Manufacturing
76.60	88.54	100.75	107.86	124.13	140.78	157.90	178.00	202.53	..	B	Services, etc.
32.05	35.68	36.97	37.11	44.74	51.94	54.03	64.00	77.77	85.94	..	Gross Domestic Saving
30.15	32.98	33.68	32.92	38.77	45.14	46.76	55.85	67.19	74.72	..	Gross National Saving
				(Billions of 1987 Australian Dollars)							
220.47	226.69	225.68	225.78	241.19	253.66	259.24	269.22	276.94	290.94	C f	Gross National Product
224.26	231.45	230.84	231.93	249.29	262.72	268.33	279.07	288.93	303.00	..	GDP at Market Prices
-6.10	-10.95	-11.27	-7.47	-10.43	-9.41	-6.13	-3.52	-9.76	-19.75	..	Resource Balance
31.39	30.21	32.11	31.32	36.28	39.86	41.90	46.07	47.43	49.19	..	Exports of Goods & NFServices
37.48	41.15	43.38	38.79	46.71	49.28	48.03	49.59	57.19	68.94	..	Imports of Goods & NFServices
230.36	242.39	242.10	239.40	259.72	272.14	274.46	282.59	298.69	322.75	..	Domestic Absorption
132.84	137.50	140.80	142.68	151.31	156.37	160.14	164.97	170.85	183.98	..	Private Consumption, etc.
39.56	40.95	40.80	43.02	45.07	47.61	49.40	50.10	51.45	53.84	..	General Gov't Consumption
57.95	63.94	60.51	53.70	63.34	68.16	64.92	67.52	76.39	84.94	..	Gross Domestic Investment
55.44	60.70	59.29	54.27	59.10	65.22	64.04	66.27	72.64	79.49	..	Fixed Investment
199.31	206.14	204.69	204.84	219.37	229.93	237.13	244.66	252.53	265.82	..	GDP at factor cost
9.10	10.83	8.49	11.70	11.99	11.65	12.05	11.34	11.61	..	..	Agriculture
75.08	77.99	74.39	72.75	79.67	84.90	84.48	89.73	95.26	..	..	Industry
42.36	44.11	40.94	39.56	42.41	43.77	44.34	46.69	49.31	..	..	Manufacturing
140.14	142.05	148.82	147.48	157.64	166.17	171.80	178.00	182.06	..	..	Services, etc.
											Memo Items:
36.05	34.65	35.71	35.34	40.96	42.56	41.12	46.07	53.81	59.74	..	Capacity to Import
4.67	4.45	3.61	4.01	4.68	2.69	-0.77	0.00	6.39	10.55	..	Terms of Trade Adjustment
228.93	235.89	234.44	235.94	253.97	265.42	267.55	279.07	295.32	313.56	..	Gross Domestic Income
225.13	231.14	229.29	229.79	245.87	256.36	258.46	269.22	283.32	301.49	..	Gross National Income
				(Index 1987 = 100)							**DOMESTIC PRICES/DEFLATORS**
58.5	64.2	71.2	77.1	82.0	86.9	93.1	100.0	109.1	117.6	..	Overall (GDP)
57.4	63.0	70.1	75.7	80.4	86.1	93.5	100.0	106.6	113.1	..	Domestic Absorption
75.3	66.3	66.7	73.3	74.0	75.5	79.5	100.0	114.7	..	..	Agriculture
63.7	67.7	77.9	85.7	89.6	92.8	97.4	100.0	104.3	..	..	Industry
60.0	64.5	72.8	81.3	85.6	89.7	93.9	100.0	108.2	..	..	Manufacturing
56.7	62.2	69.2	76.2	79.2	84.5	92.2	100.0	107.2	115.3	..	Consumer Price Index
											MANUFACTURING ACTIVITY
112.2	112.4	112.2	102.5	98.5	99.7	99.8	100.0	103.6	..	..	Employment (1987=100)
97.5	99.1	101.8	103.5	104.1	103.6	101.5	100.0	100.2	..	..	Real Earnings per Empl. (1987=100)
83.9	87.6	86.0	84.3	89.7	94.3	97.9	100.0	101.7	..	..	Real Output per Empl. (1987=100)
52.1	52.3	54.1	55.9	51.0	48.9	48.0	47.1	46.5	..	..	Earnings as % of Value Added
				(Billions of current Australian Dollars)							**MONETARY HOLDINGS**
87.42	99.14	111.32	124.46	138.24	159.81	175.22	195.49	230.25	270.56	D	Money Supply, Broadly Defined
17.22	18.06	18.03	20.80	22.49	23.30	25.95	31.22	40.47	43.50	..	Money
4.98	5.53	6.02	6.88	7.86	8.63	9.54	10.84	12.27	13.02	..	Currency Outside Banks
12.25	12.53	12.01	13.91	14.64	14.67	16.41	20.38	28.20	30.48	..	Demand Deposits
70.20	81.08	93.28	103.67	115.75	136.51	149.27	164.27	189.78	227.06	..	Quasi-Money
				(Millions of current Australian Dollars)							
-2,017	-1,051	-580	-4,608	-8,035	-6,760	-5,872	-3,394	1,454	..	C	**GOVERNMENT DEFICIT (-) OR SURPLUS**
30,561	35,964	41,782	45,639	49,975	58,771	66,007	73,830	81,862	..	..	Current Revenue
29,677	34,022	38,891	45,712	53,064	60,198	66,471	72,011	76,655	..	..	Current Expenditure
884	1,942	2,891	-73	-3,089	-1,427	-464	1,819	5,207	..	..	Current Budget Balance
28	285	40	64	79	137	233	268	738	..	..	Capital Receipts
2,929	3,278	3,511	4,599	5,025	5,470	5,641	5,481	4,491	..	..	Capital Payments

AUSTRALIA	1969	1970	1971	1972	1973	1974	1975	1976	1977	1978	1979
FOREIGN TRADE (CUSTOMS BASIS)					*(Millions of current US dollars)*						
Value of Exports, fob	4,045	4,621	5,073	6,306	9,596	11,000	11,877	13,126	13,306	14,522	18,888
Nonfuel Primary Products	3,018	3,393	3,651	4,567	6,764	7,513	8,088	8,630	8,561	8,310	11,393
Fuels	191	251	317	389	589	954	1,384	1,648	1,783	2,013	2,269
Manufactures	836	978	1,105	1,350	2,243	2,534	2,405	2,847	2,963	4,198	5,226
Value of Imports, cif	4,538	5,056	5,228	5,028	7,393	11,982	10,697	12,232	13,511	15,567	18,190
Nonfuel Primary Products	569	614	611	625	977	1,452	1,065	1,286	1,525	1,630	1,878
Fuels	335	276	249	236	303	1,008	1,045	1,170	1,364	1,415	1,937
Manufactures	3,633	4,167	4,368	4,167	6,113	9,522	8,588	9,776	10,623	12,522	14,375
					(Index 1987 = 100)						
Terms of Trade	137.5	138.0	127.6	145.1	178.1	167.9	137.9	144.4	131.7	122.1	127.9
Export Prices, fob	35.3	38.8	39.6	49.5	74.2	92.4	82.5	88.6	89.5	93.3	114.2
Import Prices, cif	25.7	28.1	31.1	34.1	41.7	55.1	59.8	61.3	68.0	76.4	89.3
BALANCE OF PAYMENTS					*(Millions of current US dollars)*						
Exports of Goods & Services	..	5,705	6,267	7,751	11,329	13,533	14,468	15,574	15,851	17,358	22,480
Merchandise, fob	..	4,623	5,064	6,276	9,271	10,765	11,691	12,976	13,197	14,115	18,578
Nonfactor Services	..	902	967	1,107	1,399	2,001	2,178	2,087	2,126	2,621	3,142
Factor Services	..	180	236	369	658	767	599	511	528	622	760
Imports of Goods & Services	..	6,467	7,075	7,205	10,770	16,089	15,120	17,327	18,732	21,648	24,891
Merchandise, fob	..	4,108	4,476	4,294	6,464	10,631	9,481	10,943	12,174	14,025	16,060
Nonfactor Services	..	1,357	1,517	1,697	2,449	3,492	3,501	3,921	4,109	4,724	5,224
Factor Services	..	1,001	1,082	1,214	1,857	1,966	2,138	2,462	2,450	2,899	3,607
Long-Term Interest	..	..	..	..	..	..	..	..	..	..	..
Private Current Transfers, net	..	80	56	66	-11	-32	-82	-72	-21	24	104
Workers' Remittances	..	..	..	..	..	..	..	..	..		
Curr. A/C Bal before Off. Transf.	..	-682	-752	612	548	-2,588	-734	-1,825	-2,902	-4,266	-2,306
Net Official Transfers	..	-95	-82	-150	-141	-248	-331	-185	-231	-294	-354
Curr. A/C Bal after Off. Transf.	..	-777	-833	462	407	-2,836	-1,065	-2,010	-3,133	-4,560	-2,660
Long-Term Capital, net	..	1,045	1,881	1,721	-963	866	812	1,502	2,191	3,300	2,476
Direct Investment	..	778	1,045	926	-112	1,088	295	777	873	1,442	1,111
Long-Term Loans	..	..	..	..	..	..	..	..	..	..	..
Disbursements	..	..	..	..	..	..	..	..	..	..	..
Repayments	..	..	..	..	..	..	..	..	..	..	..
Other Long-Term Capital	..	267	836	795	-852	-222	517	725	1,318	1,859	1,365
Other Capital, net	..	77	322	534	237	337	-621	124	-213	1,173	-517
Change in Reserves	..	-345	-1,369	-2,717	319	1,633	874	384	1,155	87	701
Memo Item:					*(Australian Dollars per US dollar)*						
Conversion Factor (Annual Avg)	0.890	0.890	0.890	0.860	0.780	0.680	0.730	0.790	0.870	0.890	0.880
					(Millions US dollars), outstanding at end of year						
EXTERNAL DEBT (Total)	..	..	..	..	..	..	..	..	..	..	..
Long-Term Debt (by debtor)	..	..	..	..	..	..	..	..	..	..	..
Central Bank, incl. IMF credit	..	..	..	..	..	..	..	..	..	..	..
Central Government	..	..	..	..	..	..	..	..	..	..	..
Rest of General Government	..	..	..	..	..	..	..	..	..	..	..
Non-financial Public Enterprises	..	..	..	..	..	..	..	..	..	..	..
Priv. Sector, incl non-guaranteed	..	..	..	..	..	..	..	..	..	..	..
Short-Term Debt	..	..	..	..	..	..	..	..	..	..	..
Memo Items:					*(Millions of US dollars)*						
Int'l Reserves Excluding Gold	998.0	1,454.0	3,034.0	5,860.0	5,386.0	3,953.0	2,954.0	2,870.0	2,058.0	2,062.0	1,424.0
Gold Holdings (at market price)	264.0	255.0	324.0	480.0	827.0	1,376.0	1,035.0	992.0	1,262.0	1,761.0	4,062.0
SOCIAL INDICATORS											
Total Fertility Rate	2.9	2.9	3.0	2.7	2.5	2.4	2.2	2.1	2.0	2.0	1.9
Infant Mortality Rate	17.9	17.9	17.3	16.7	16.5	16.1	14.2	13.8	12.4	12.1	11.3
Life Expectancy at Birth	71.2	71.4	71.5	71.7	72.1	72.4	72.8	73.1	73.5	73.8	74.2
Urban Population, % of total	84.8	85.2	85.3	85.5	85.6	85.8	85.9	85.9	85.9	85.8	85.8
Food Prod. per capita (1987=100)	92.7	92.0	96.3	91.8	105.3	97.7	104.4	108.6	103.3	124.4	116.7
Labor Force, Agriculture (%)	8.3	8.1	7.9	7.8	7.7	7.6	7.4	7.3	7.2	7.1	7.0
Labor Force, Female (%)	30.8	31.2	31.9	32.6	33.2	33.8	34.4	35.1	35.7	36.4	37.0
Primary Schl. Enroll. Ratio	..	115.0	..	..	..	..	107.0	108.0	109.0	111.0	111.0
Primary Schl. Enroll. Ratio, Female	..	115.0	..	..	..	..	107.0	108.0	109.0	111.0	111.0
Secondary Schl. Enroll. Ratio	..	82.0	..	..	..	..	87.0	88.0	88.0	87.0	86.0

1980	1981	1982	1983	1984	1985	1986	1987	1988	1989 estimate	NOTES	AUSTRALIA
				(Millions of current US dollars)							**FOREIGN TRADE (CUSTOMS BASIS)**
21,985	22,160	21,415	19,841	22,720	22,292	21,838	25,283	..	..	..	Value of Exports, fob
13,346	12,913	12,835	10,782	12,709	11,876	12,244	13,920	..	..	..	Nonfuel Primary Products
2,419	3,376	3,845	4,454	5,392	5,869	4,810	5,064	..	..	..	Fuels
6,220	5,871	4,736	4,605	4,618	4,548	4,784	6,300	..	..	..	Manufactures
22,399	26,215	26,667	21,458	25,919	25,889	26,104	29,318	..	..	..	Value of Imports, cif
2,282	2,303	2,144	2,014	2,389	2,250	2,253	2,676	..	..	..	Nonfuel Primary Products
3,098	3,563	3,849	2,324	2,336	1,749	1,207	1,427	..	..	..	Fuels
17,018	20,348	20,674	17,120	21,194	21,889	22,644	25,214	..	..	..	Manufactures
				(Index 1987 = 100)							
129.7	126.2	118.9	122.3	127.6	122.1	108.4	100.0	..	..	..	Terms of Trade
132.5	124.0	112.3	109.7	110.7	102.9	98.9	100.0	..	..	..	Export Prices, fob
102.2	98.2	94.4	89.7	86.8	84.3	91.3	100.0	..	..	..	Import Prices, cif
				(Millions of current US dollars)							**BALANCE OF PAYMENTS**
26,323	26,552	26,411	25,167	29,093	27,999	28,612	34,916	44,007	49,261	..	Exports of Goods & Services
21,560	21,214	20,793	19,501	22,769	22,275	22,189	26,270	32,778	36,452	..	Merchandise, fob
3,736	4,304	4,518	4,311	4,596	4,206	4,775	6,013	8,064	8,552	..	Nonfactor Services
1,028	1,034	1,099	1,355	1,729	1,519	1,648	2,633	3,165	4,256	..	Factor Services
30,510	34,921	34,674	31,010	37,664	37,337	38,935	44,335	55,613	67,339	..	Imports of Goods & Services
20,191	23,538	23,406	19,470	23,653	23,592	24,264	26,749	33,892	40,381	..	Merchandise, fob
6,201	6,985	7,138	6,490	7,391	7,072	7,073	8,011	9,805	11,670	..	Nonfactor Services
4,117	4,397	4,130	5,050	6,620	6,674	7,597	9,574	11,917	15,289	..	Factor Services
..	..	..	..	..	..	..	..	..	..	..	Long-Term Interest
275	298	300	412	451	686	817	1,196	1,706	2,073	..	Private Current Transfers, net
..	..	..	..	..	..	..	..	..	..	..	Workers' Remittances
-3,912	-8,071	-7,963	-5,431	-8,120	-8,651	-9,506	-8,224	-9,900	-16,005	..	Curr. A/C Bal before Off. Transf.
-336	-399	-496	-437	-458	-262	-225	-178	-229	-176	..	Net Official Transfers
-4,248	-8,470	-8,459	-5,868	-8,577	-8,913	-9,731	-8,401	-10,129	-16,181	..	Curr. A/C Bal after Off. Transf.
4,152	6,448	11,994	7,497	6,397	7,463	9,523	7,434	12,064	16,521	..	Long-Term Capital, net
1,365	1,551	1,610	2,464	-1,033	397	107	-2,099	1,569	8,953	..	Direct Investment
..	..	..	..	..	..	..	..	..	..	..	Long-Term Loans
..	..	..	..	..	..	..	..	..	..	..	Disbursements
..	..	..	..	..	..	..	..	..	..	..	Repayments
2,787	4,897	10,384	5,033	7,429	7,066	9,416	9,533	10,496	7,569	..	Other Long-Term Capital
694	1,879	1,367	1,403	874	-832	913	1,338	3,316	288	..	Other Capital, net
-598	143	-4,902	-3,031	1,307	2,282	-705	-371	-5,251	-628	..	Change in Reserves
				(Australian Dollars per US dollar)							Memo Item:
0.900	0.860	0.910	1.070	1.100	1.300	1.430	1.510	1.280	1.260	..	Conversion Factor (Annual Avg)
				(Millions US dollars), outstanding at end of year							
..	..	..	..	..	..	..	..	..	..	..	**EXTERNAL DEBT (Total)**
..	..	..	..	..	..	..	..	..	..	..	Long-Term Debt (by debtor)
..	..	..	..	..	..	..	..	..	..	..	Central Bank, incl. IMF credit
..	..	..	..	..	..	..	..	..	..	..	Central Government
..	..	..	..	..	..	..	..	..	..	..	Rest of General Government
..	..	..	..	..	..	..	..	..	..	..	Non-financial Public Enterprises
..	..	..	..	..	..	..	..	..	..	..	Priv. Sector, incl non-guaranteed
..	..	..	..	..	..	..	..	..	..	..	Short-Term Debt
				(Millions of US dollars)							Memo Items:
1,690.0	1,671.0	6,371.0	8,962.0	7,441.0	5,768.0	7,246.0	8,744.0	13,598.0	13,780.0	..	Int'l Reserves Excluding Gold
4,677.0	3,153.0	3,624.0	3,026.0	2,445.0	2,593.0	3,100.0	3,840.0	3,255.0	3,181.0	..	Gold Holdings (at market price)
											SOCIAL INDICATORS
1.9	2.0	2.0	2.0	2.0	1.9	1.9	1.9	1.9	1.9	..	Total Fertility Rate
10.7	9.9	10.3	9.6	9.2	9.9	9.9	9.8	9.2	9.2	..	Infant Mortality Rate
74.5	74.9	75.2	75.4	75.6	75.8	75.9	76.1	76.3	76.5	..	Life Expectancy at Birth
85.8	85.7	85.7	85.6	85.6	85.5	85.5	85.5	85.5	85.5	..	Urban Population, % of total
96.7	105.8	89.3	117.4	110.6	105.5	105.9	100.0	104.1	100.7	..	Food Prod. per capita (1987=100)
6.9	..	..	..	..	..	..	..	..	..	..	Labor Force, Agriculture (%)
37.5	37.6	37.6	37.7	37.7	37.8	37.9	37.9	38.0	38.1	..	Labor Force, Female (%)
111.0	..	..	108.0	108.0	106.0	106.0	106.0	..	..	..	Primary Schl. Enroll. Ratio
110.0	107.0	106.0	108.0	107.0	105.0	106.0	105.0	..	..	..	Primary Schl. Enroll. Ratio, Female
84.0	..	..	90.0	94.0	96.0	97.0	98.0	..	..	..	Secondary Schl. Enroll. Ratio

AUSTRIA	1969	1970	1971	1972	1973	1974	1975	1976	1977	1978	1979
CURRENT GNP PER CAPITA (US $)	1,770	1,950	2,180	2,520	3,120	3,960	4,760	5,380	6,130	6,870	8,450
POPULATION (thousands)	7,384	7,426	7,456	7,495	7,525	7,533	7,537	7,540	7,544	7,547	7,551
USE AND ORIGIN OF RESOURCES					*(Billions of current Austrian Schillings)*						
Gross National Product (GNP)	333.3	373.9	417.7	476.8	540.1	615.6	652.5	719.7	789.3	833.9	910.6
Net Factor Income from Abroad	-1.7	-2.0	-1.9	-2.7	-3.4	-3.0	-3.6	-5.0	-6.9	-8.4	-7.8
GDP at Market Prices	335.0	375.9	419.6	479.5	543.5	618.6	656.1	724.7	796.1	842.3	918.4
Resource Balance	3.9	3.5	3.0	2.8	2.1	-2.0	4.3	-11.1	-21.3	0.3	-3.6
Exports of Goods & NFServices	95.0	116.7	128.6	146.5	166.0	204.2	209.0	236.2	257.1	280.7	327.7
Imports of Goods & NFServices	91.0	113.1	125.6	143.7	163.9	206.2	204.8	247.2	278.3	280.4	331.3
Domestic Absorption	331.1	372.3	416.6	476.7	541.4	620.6	651.8	735.8	817.4	842.0	922.1
Private Consumption, etc.	189.9	205.3	230.5	259.4	291.8	330.6	368.1	410.5	456.5	468.7	511.5
General Gov't Consumption	63.2	68.2	74.0	82.0	90.0	104.7	117.4	127.8	138.7	154.1	166.0
Gross Domestic Investment	78.0	98.8	112.1	135.3	159.6	185.2	166.3	197.6	222.2	219.1	244.6
Fixed Investment	82.2	95.4	115.6	139.1	149.3	172.7	174.4	191.9	213.1	214.8	232.2
Indirect Taxes, net	48.7	55.2	62.4	74.6	88.0	94.0	92.5	98.7	112.6	112.8	124.3
GDP at factor cost	286.3	320.7	357.2	405.0	455.4	524.6	563.6	626.0	683.6	729.5	794.2
Agriculture	23.3	25.8	25.1	28.2	31.4	33.1	33.1	36.4	36.0	39.3	40.3
Industry	150.8	170.5	190.8	219.2	231.4	265.1	268.4	294.0	318.8	334.7	368.1
Manufacturing	111.5	126.7	140.9	158.3	166.7	190.6	187.7	208.7	223.0	234.6	260.1
Services, etc.	160.8	179.6	203.7	232.1	280.7	320.3	354.7	394.3	441.3	468.2	510.1
Gross Domestic Saving	82.0	102.3	115.1	138.1	161.7	183.2	170.6	186.5	200.9	219.4	241.0
Gross National Saving	..	100.6	113.4	134.7	156.7	177.3	164.6	179.6	192.0	211.1	233.9
					(Billions of 1987 Austrian Schillings)						
Gross National Product	878.0	933.8	981.0	1,040.6	1,091.8	1,136.6	1,131.7	1,181.8	1,233.4	1,232.4	1,292.7
GDP at Market Prices	882.4	938.7	985.4	1,046.6	1,098.8	1,142.1	1,137.9	1,190.0	1,244.1	1,244.8	1,303.8
Resource Balance	-2.3	-0.3	-0.1	-4.7	-15.5	-6.5	0.5	-17.7	-25.0	-0.9	-1.1
Exports of Goods & NFServices	183.9	215.5	229.3	252.6	266.3	294.8	287.8	319.6	333.1	357.5	399.2
Imports of Goods & NFServices	186.2	215.8	229.4	257.3	281.8	301.3	287.3	337.3	358.1	358.5	400.3
Domestic Absorption	884.7	939.0	985.5	1,051.3	1,114.3	1,148.6	1,137.5	1,207.8	1,269.1	1,245.7	1,304.9
Private Consumption, etc.	489.6	506.8	539.5	571.5	602.2	620.3	640.4	666.6	702.3	693.1	722.8
General Gov't Consumption	170.2	175.8	181.6	189.1	194.7	205.8	214.0	223.1	230.4	238.0	245.1
Gross Domestic Investment	224.9	256.4	264.4	290.6	317.4	322.4	283.1	318.1	336.4	314.6	337.1
Fixed Investment	218.4	239.4	272.4	305.5	306.5	318.7	302.9	314.5	330.5	317.0	328.2
GDP at factor cost	752.4	799.6	837.6	881.8	917.3	968.1	976.9	1,028.0	1,069.1	1,078.3	1,128.1
Agriculture	36.3	37.4	34.6	34.8	37.0	38.5	40.4	41.8	40.3	42.9	43.7
Industry	337.9	360.5	384.4	412.1	434.9	450.9	431.6	451.8	473.6	474.2	500.5
Manufacturing	231.0	247.6	262.1	282.0	296.6	306.8	288.5	306.7	322.2	325.2	346.1
Services, etc.	503.9	537.0	565.1	598.6	624.3	650.0	664.2	694.7	729.5	726.0	757.9
Memo Items:											
Capacity to Import	194.2	222.6	234.9	262.3	285.4	298.4	293.3	322.2	330.7	358.9	395.9
Terms of Trade Adjustment	10.3	7.1	5.6	9.7	19.1	3.5	5.5	2.6	-2.4	1.3	-3.3
Gross Domestic Income	892.7	945.8	991.0	1,056.3	1,117.8	1,145.6	1,143.5	1,192.7	1,241.7	1,246.1	1,300.5
Gross National Income	888.3	940.8	986.5	1,050.4	1,110.9	1,140.2	1,137.2	1,184.4	1,231.0	1,233.7	1,289.5
DOMESTIC PRICES/DEFLATORS					*(Index 1987 = 100)*						
Overall (GDP)	38.0	40.0	42.6	45.8	49.5	54.2	57.7	60.9	64.0	67.7	70.4
Domestic Absorption	37.4	39.7	42.3	45.3	48.6	54.0	57.3	60.9	64.4	67.6	70.7
Agriculture	64.3	68.9	72.7	81.1	84.7	85.8	81.9	87.2	89.5	91.7	92.0
Industry	44.6	47.3	49.6	53.2	53.2	58.8	62.2	65.1	67.3	70.6	73.6
Manufacturing	48.3	51.2	53.8	56.1	56.2	62.1	65.1	68.1	69.2	72.1	75.2
Consumer Price Index	39.8	41.6	43.5	46.3	49.8	54.5	59.1	63.4	66.9	69.3	71.9
MANUFACTURING ACTIVITY											
Employment (1987=100)	94.4	102.3	107.2	109.7	111.9	110.8	105.0	109.4	109.4	108.3	109.0
Real Earnings per Empl. (1987=100)	60.7	63.4	65.9	69.1	72.9	76.8	80.0	79.3	82.2	85.7	86.9
Real Output per Empl. (1987=100)	53.5	57.0	58.2	61.0	64.7	72.4	73.2	74.8	78.4	79.6	83.1
Earnings as % of Value Added	47.1	47.1	47.7	48.5	52.0	51.5	56.2	55.9	58.4	58.4	57.3
MONETARY HOLDINGS					*(Billions of current Austrian Schillings)*						
Money Supply, Broadly Defined	190.6	215.1	247.0	285.8	323.2	363.6	430.5	503.2	548.9	627.4	678.3
Money	60.8	64.8	73.7	89.2	95.9	101.4	115.9	125.5	127.3	137.9	125.4
Currency Outside Banks	32.7	34.0	37.3	42.9	46.1	48.7	52.3	55.2	58.7	63.2	67.0
Demand Deposits	28.1	30.8	36.4	46.4	49.8	52.7	63.5	70.4	68.6	74.7	58.4
Quasi-Money	129.8	150.4	173.3	196.6	227.3	262.3	314.6	377.6	421.6	489.5	552.8
GOVERNMENT DEFICIT (-) OR SURPLUS					*(Billions of current Austrian Schillings)*						
GOVERNMENT DEFICIT (-) OR SURPLUS	..	-1.80	0.24	-0.85	-8.96	-9.76	-26.34	-34.06	-30.21	-34.92	-35.31
Current Revenue	..	110.06	124.63	142.93	163.80	189.51	205.49	226.70	254.14	290.01	317.76
Current Expenditure	..	99.94	111.72	126.44	144.72	171.27	203.15	230.63	255.66	291.79	314.92
Current Budget Balance	..	10.12	12.91	16.49	19.08	18.24	2.34	-3.93	-1.52	-1.78	2.84
Capital Receipts	..	0.27	0.14	0.17	0.17	0.21	0.27	0.37	0.42	0.40	0.40
Capital Payments	..	12.19	12.81	17.51	28.21	28.21	28.95	30.50	29.11	33.54	38.55

1980	1981	1982	1983	1984	1985	1986	1987	1988	1989 estimate	NOTES	AUSTRIA
9,980	10,140	9,800	9,300	9,080	9,040	9,860	11,950	15,450	17,360	..	**CURRENT GNP PER CAPITA (US $)**
7,554	7,558	7,571	7,549	7,552	7,555	7,565	7,573	7,595	7,598	..	**POPULATION (thousands)**
(Billions of current Austrian Schillings)											**USE AND ORIGIN OF RESOURCES**
986.4	1,047.2	1,125.1	1,192.3	1,268.2	1,341.3	1,403.5	1,464.8	1,556.7	1,657.0	..	Gross National Product (GNP)
-8.3	-8.8	-8.4	-8.8	-8.6	-7.1	-12.0	-12.9	-13.8	-14.7	..	Net Factor Income from Abroad
994.7	1,056.0	1,133.5	1,201.1	1,276.7	1,348.4	1,415.5	1,477.7	1,570.6	1,671.7	..	GDP at Market Prices
-19.6	-14.1	19.0	15.8	2.1	2.3	13.0	7.7	4.6	8.5	..	Resource Balance
366.2	404.4	431.4	449.7	497.6	549.2	522.9	527.3	586.6	669.0	..	Exports of Goods & NFServices
385.7	418.5	412.4	433.9	495.5	546.9	510.0	519.6	582.0	660.5	..	Imports of Goods & NFServices
1,014.3	1,070.1	1,114.5	1,185.4	1,274.7	1,346.0	1,402.5	1,470.0	1,566.0	1,663.2	..	Domestic Absorption
552.7	596.7	640.7	694.7	732.7	775.3	802.9	834.8	874.9	927.0	..	Private Consumption, etc.
178.7	195.2	214.3	226.9	237.8	255.0	270.7	280.4	289.1	303.0	..	General Gov't Consumption
282.9	278.2	259.4	263.8	304.2	315.7	328.9	354.8	401.9	433.2	..	Gross Domestic Investment
254.4	270.7	262.2	269.6	288.2	312.7	331.2	347.1	373.7	401.9	..	Fixed Investment
132.8	142.3	150.7	161.7	180.2	186.7	188.0	197.8	208.8	226.0	..	Indirect Taxes, net
861.9	913.7	982.8	1,039.4	1,096.6	1,161.6	1,227.5	1,280.0	1,361.8	1,445.7	..	GDP at factor cost
44.3	43.4	43.7	44.1	48.7	45.0	47.4	49.2	50.1	..	B	Agriculture
393.4	410.4	436.6	454.6	471.3	497.6	519.1	537.6	580.7	..	B	Industry
276.7	288.9	308.1	322.8	340.1	362.8	376.2	383.6	418.0	..	B	Manufacturing
557.0	602.1	653.2	702.4	756.8	805.8	848.9	890.9	939.7	..	B	Services, etc.
263.3	264.0	278.5	279.6	306.3	318.1	341.9	362.5	406.5	441.8	..	Gross Domestic Saving
254.2	254.4	269.4	270.1	297.3	309.9	330.0	349.5	393.2	428.3	..	Gross National Saving
(Billions of 1987 Austrian Schillings)											
1,330.7	1,327.2	1,342.5	1,369.3	1,387.9	1,425.2	1,436.7	1,464.8	1,525.3	1,583.4	..	Gross National Product
1,341.9	1,338.0	1,352.3	1,379.2	1,397.1	1,432.5	1,448.9	1,477.7	1,538.9	1,597.3	..	GDP at Market Prices
-5.2	18.5	44.5	36.3	22.1	27.0	18.5	7.7	2.3	10.7	..	Resource Balance
420.0	440.5	452.4	466.8	495.2	529.3	515.0	527.3	573.9	637.7	..	Exports of Goods & NFServices
425.2	421.9	407.9	430.5	473.1	502.3	496.4	519.6	571.6	627.0	..	Imports of Goods & NFServices
1,347.0	1,319.5	1,307.8	1,342.9	1,375.0	1,405.5	1,430.4	1,470.0	1,536.6	1,586.5	..	Domestic Absorption
733.0	736.4	747.6	783.0	779.2	798.3	810.8	834.8	858.0	885.9	..	Private Consumption, etc.
251.6	257.2	263.1	268.9	269.5	274.8	279.3	280.4	282.3	285.1	..	General Gov't Consumption
362.4	325.9	297.1	291.0	326.3	332.4	340.3	354.8	396.3	415.5	..	Gross Domestic Investment
337.9	333.3	306.1	304.3	310.7	326.3	337.5	347.1	367.2	384.2	..	Fixed Investment
1,165.5	1,162.9	1,176.4	1,196.8	1,202.9	1,237.7	1,257.3	1,280.0	1,333.7	1,381.1	..	GDP at factor cost
45.5	43.9	50.0	47.9	50.4	48.0	48.7	49.2	51.1	..	..	Agriculture
510.7	501.3	496.4	501.6	511.3	527.4	531.8	537.6	564.8	..	..	Industry
354.4	349.8	351.2	356.9	367.1	381.2	383.4	383.6	406.1	..	..	Manufacturing
784.1	792.4	804.4	829.8	835.5	857.1	868.4	890.9	923.0	..	..	Services, etc.
											Memo Items:
403.6	407.7	426.7	446.1	475.1	504.5	509.1	527.3	576.1	635.1	..	Capacity to Import
-16.4	-32.8	-25.6	-20.7	-20.1	-24.9	-5.9	0.0	2.3	-2.6	..	Terms of Trade Adjustment
1,325.5	1,305.2	1,326.6	1,358.6	1,377.0	1,407.7	1,443.0	1,477.7	1,541.2	1,594.7	..	Gross Domestic Income
1,314.4	1,294.4	1,316.8	1,348.6	1,367.8	1,400.3	1,430.8	1,464.8	1,527.6	1,580.8	..	Gross National Income
(Index 1987 = 100)											**DOMESTIC PRICES/DEFLATORS**
74.1	78.9	83.8	87.1	91.4	94.1	97.7	100.0	102.1	104.7	..	Overall (GDP)
75.3	81.1	85.2	88.3	92.7	95.8	98.0	100.0	101.9	104.8	..	Domestic Absorption
97.3	98.8	87.5	92.2	96.7	93.8	97.3	100.0	98.0	..	..	Agriculture
77.0	81.9	87.9	90.6	92.2	94.3	97.6	100.0	102.8	..	..	Industry
78.1	82.6	87.7	90.5	92.6	95.2	98.1	100.0	102.9	..	..	Manufacturing
76.4	81.6	86.0	88.9	94.0	97.0	98.6	100.0	101.9	104.5	..	Consumer Price Index
											MANUFACTURING ACTIVITY
109.0	106.6	103.5	104.2	103.2	103.5	102.1	100.0	100.3	101.4	..	Employment (1987=100)
88.2	90.0	91.8	91.9	91.2	93.3	96.9	100.0	105.2	..	..	Real Earnings per Empl. (1987=100)
88.5	92.2	93.9	95.8	100.7	102.7	99.6	100.0	104.5	..	..	Real Output per Empl. (1987=100)
58.6	58.5	58.2	56.7	55.5	55.6	56.0	55.8	56.5	..	..	Earnings as % of Value Added
(Billions of current Austrian Schillings)											**MONETARY HOLDINGS**
765.0	843.6	936.1	984.7	1,047.3	1,110.2	1,205.9	1,296.5	1,371.9	1,469.3	..	Money Supply, Broadly Defined
145.1	141.6	153.3	170.4	176.4	181.9	193.5	213.5	232.2	235.0	..	Money
71.6	73.2	75.7	84.1	83.9	84.5	87.9	93.0	98.7	102.6	..	Currency Outside Banks
73.4	68.5	77.5	86.3	92.5	97.4	105.7	120.5	133.5	132.4	..	Demand Deposits
620.0	702.0	782.8	814.3	870.9	928.3	1,012.4	1,083.0	1,139.7	1,234.3	..	Quasi-Money
(Billions of current Austrian Schillings)											
-33.57	-32.52	-54.53	-71.84	-58.22	-63.33	-84.22	-81.55	-78.40	..	E	**GOVERNMENT DEFICIT (-) OR SURPLUS**
346.98	382.46	397.57	417.64	456.97	476.12	497.45	516.35	557.07	..	..	Current Revenue
338.12	370.13	405.34	433.57	461.64	484.60	520.81	550.50	568.13	..	..	Current Expenditure
8.86	12.33	-7.77	-15.93	-4.67	-8.48	-23.36	-34.15	-11.06	..	..	Current Budget Balance
0.43	0.47	0.51	0.53	0.46	0.58	0.84	0.72	0.97	..	..	Capital Receipts
42.86	45.32	47.27	56.44	54.01	55.43	61.70	48.12	68.31	..	..	Capital Payments

AUSTRIA	1969	1970	1971	1972	1973	1974	1975	1976	1977	1978	1979
FOREIGN TRADE (CUSTOMS BASIS)					*(Millions of current US dollars)*						
Value of Exports, fob	2,412	2,857	3,169	3,883	5,285	7,161	7,518	8,507	9,808	12,174	15,478
Nonfuel Primary Products	442	493	519	619	868	1,068	943	1,232	1,378	1,745	2,327
Fuels	60	72	64	77	113	144	155	159	189	191	223
Manufactures	1,911	2,291	2,586	3,187	4,303	5,950	6,420	7,116	8,241	10,238	12,928
Value of Imports, cif	2,825	3,549	4,189	5,216	7,121	9,023	9,392	11,523	14,248	15,975	20,231
Nonfuel Primary Products	642	777	819	950	1,392	1,743	1,622	1,898	2,339	2,567	3,266
Fuels	204	294	340	370	533	1,096	1,187	1,409	1,465	1,715	2,499
Manufactures	1,980	2,479	3,029	3,896	5,196	6,184	6,584	8,216	10,444	11,694	14,465
					(Index 1987 = 100)						
Terms of Trade	113.0	117.3	111.3	110.2	113.0	98.8	105.2	97.6	97.4	102.7	102.2
Export Prices, fob	25.5	26.8	27.9	30.9	39.3	48.1	54.3	52.0	56.8	67.0	78.8
Import Prices, cif	22.6	22.8	25.1	28.0	34.7	48.6	51.6	53.2	58.2	65.3	77.1
BALANCE OF PAYMENTS					*(Millions of current US dollars)*						
Exports of Goods & Services	..	4,331	5,037	6,173	8,543	11,270	12,454	13,748	16,273	20,598	26,005
Merchandise, fob	..	2,837	3,143	3,842	5,238	7,504	7,553	8,468	9,728	12,189	15,454
Nonfactor Services	..	1,358	1,723	2,155	3,040	3,222	4,289	4,646	5,795	7,406	8,966
Factor Services	..	136	170	177	265	544	611	634	750	1,002	1,584
Imports of Goods & Services	..	4,415	5,132	6,296	8,710	11,306	12,545	14,753	18,333	21,294	27,175
Merchandise, fob	..	3,516	4,076	4,969	6,804	8,812	9,508	11,048	13,553	15,472	19,726
Nonfactor Services	..	687	811	1,033	1,465	1,787	2,217	2,789	3,614	4,243	5,277
Factor Services	..	212	246	294	440	707	820	916	1,166	1,579	2,172
Long-Term Interest	..	..	..	..	..	..	..	..	..	..	..
Private Current Transfers, net	..	11	9	-30	-82	-157	-137	-103	-122	2	53
Workers' Remittances	..	13	19	27	40	66	73	89	103	136	177
Curr. A/C Bal before Off. Transf.	..	-73	-87	-152	-249	-193	-228	-1,108	-2,183	-695	-1,118
Net Official Transfers	..	-2	-4	-5	-5	-10	-3	-11	-17	-11	-23
Curr. A/C Bal after Off. Transf.	..	-75	-91	-157	-254	-203	-231	-1,119	-2,200	-706	-1,141
Long-Term Capital, net	..	14	-18	78	-227	403	1,062	-72	604	1,404	-521
Direct Investment	..	104	107	107	122	157	53	35	11	53	103
Long-Term Loans	..	..	..	..	..	..	..	..	..	..	..
Disbursements	..	..	..	..	..	..	..	..	..	..	..
Repayments	..	..	..	..	..	..	..	..	..	..	..
Other Long-Term Capital	..	-90	-125	-29	-349	245	1,009	-107	593	1,351	-624
Other Capital, net	..	242	482	445	310	188	341	1,076	1,251	652	640
Change in Reserves	..	-181	-373	-366	171	-388	-1,172	116	344	-1,350	1,022
Memo Item:					*(Austrian Schillings per US dollar)*						
Conversion Factor (Annual Avg)	26.000	26.000	24.960	23.120	19.580	18.690	17.420	17.940	16.530	14.520	13.370
				(Millions US dollars), outstanding at end of year							
EXTERNAL DEBT (Total)	..	..	..	..	..	..	..	..	..	..	..
Long-Term Debt (by debtor)	..	..	..	..	..	..	..	..	..	..	..
Central Bank, incl. IMF credit	..	..	..	..	..	..	..	..	..	..	..
Central Government	..	..	..	..	..	..	..	..	..	..	..
Rest of General Government	..	..	..	..	..	..	..	..	..	..	..
Non-financial Public Enterprises	..	..	..	..	..	..	..	..	..	..	..
Priv. Sector, incl non-guaranteed	..	..	..	..	..	..	..	..	..	..	..
Short-Term Debt	..	..	..	..	..	..	..	..	..	..	..
Memo Items:					*(Millions of US dollars)*						
Int'l Reserves Excluding Gold	822	1,044	1,547	1,927	1,992	2,535	3,583	3,561	3,351	5,047	4,075
Gold Holdings (at market price)	719	762	909	1,353	2,344	3,894	2,928	2,814	3,463	4,758	10,808
SOCIAL INDICATORS											
Total Fertility Rate	2.5	2.3	2.2	2.1	2.0	1.9	1.8	1.7	1.6	1.6	1.7
Infant Mortality Rate	25.4	25.9	26.1	25.2	23.8	23.5	20.5	18.2	16.9	14.9	14.8
Life Expectancy at Birth	70.1	70.3	70.4	70.6	70.8	71.1	71.4	71.7	72.0	72.2	72.4
Urban Population, % of total	51.5	51.7	52.0	52.3	52.5	52.8	53.1	53.4	53.7	54.0	54.3
Food Prod. per capita (1987=100)	84.4	81.1	81.2	77.8	82.8	86.9	88.3	88.3	87.6	90.8	92.0
Labor Force, Agriculture (%)	15.7	14.8	14.2	13.6	13.0	12.5	11.9	11.3	10.7	10.1	9.6
Labor Force, Female (%)	38.9	38.7	38.9	39.1	39.3	39.5	39.6	39.8	39.9	40.1	40.2
Primary Schl. Enroll. Ratio	..	104.0	..	..	..	..	102.0	102.0	100.0	100.0	99.0
Primary Schl. Enroll. Ratio, Female	..	103.0	..	..	..	..	101.0	102.0	100.0	99.0	98.0
Secondary Schl. Enroll. Ratio	..	72.0	..	..	..	..	74.0	75.0	72.0	72.0	72.0

1980	1981	1982	1983	1984	1985	1986	1987	1988	1989 estimate	NOTES	AUSTRIA
				(Millions of current US dollars)							**FOREIGN TRADE (CUSTOMS BASIS)**
17,478	15,840	15,690	15,423	15,712	17,102	22,517	27,163	28,111	..	..	Value of Exports, fob
2,723	2,310	2,116	2,137	2,175	2,128	2,621	3,100	3,302	..	..	Nonfuel Primary Products
274	276	241	217	234	346	273	479	392	..	..	Fuels
14,480	13,255	13,333	13,070	13,304	14,628	19,622	23,583	24,417	..	..	Manufactures
24,415	21,013	19,514	19,322	19,573	20,803	26,793	32,638	36,579	..	..	Value of Imports, cif
3,781	3,229	3,002	2,866	3,072	3,139	3,796	4,340	4,957	..	..	Nonfuel Primary Products
3,781	3,920	3,150	2,667	2,955	3,090	2,320	2,358	2,078	..	..	Fuels
16,852	13,863	13,362	13,788	13,546	14,574	20,678	25,940	29,544	..	..	Manufactures
				(Index 1987 = 100)							
95.0	83.7	87.8	86.5	82.3	85.1	99.3	100.0	95.0	..	..	Terms of Trade
83.9	72.8	71.8	67.7	63.6	64.5	79.6	100.0	102.0	..	..	Export Prices, fob
88.4	87.1	81.7	78.2	77.2	75.8	80.1	100.0	107.4	..	..	Import Prices, cif
				(Millions of current US dollars)							**BALANCE OF PAYMENTS**
31,315	28,720	28,628	27,826	27,919	30,106	38,473	46,617	53,404	56,402	..	Exports of Goods & Services
17,027	15,603	15,363	15,155	15,471	16,683	21,565	26,558	30,056	31,607	..	Merchandise, fob
11,749	9,920	10,078	10,039	9,540	10,194	13,081	15,508	17,943	17,881	..	Nonfactor Services
2,538	3,197	3,187	2,632	2,908	3,229	3,827	4,551	5,405	6,914	..	Factor Services
32,951	30,096	27,913	27,498	28,122	30,286	38,344	46,966	53,827	56,517	..	Imports of Goods & Services
23,644	20,646	18,814	18,794	19,485	21,089	26,176	31,702	36,358	38,970	..	Merchandise, fob
6,124	5,708	5,418	5,586	5,302	5,631	7,538	9,688	10,946	9,641	..	Nonfactor Services
3,182	3,742	3,682	3,118	3,335	3,567	4,630	5,576	6,523	7,906	..	Factor Services
..	..	..	..	..	..	..	..	..	..	..	Long-Term Interest
-58	-57	-37	-38	-22	-55	2	-10	38	93	..	Private Current Transfers, net
215	198	201	188	176	184	269	365	410	420	..	Workers' Remittances
-1,694	-1,433	677	290	-226	-235	130	-358	-385	-22	..	Curr. A/C Bal before Off. Transf.
-31	-30	-36	-44	-39	-39	-44	-71	-74	-72	..	Net Official Transfers
-1,725	-1,464	641	246	-264	-273	86	-429	-458	-94	..	Curr. A/C Bal after Off. Transf.
550	814	-557	-1,343	-308	-313	-1,656	893	599	92	..	Long-Term Capital, net
139	117	129	104	92	195	-39	145	190	-75	..	Direct Investment
..	..	..	..	..	..	..	..	..	..	..	Long-Term Loans
..	..	..	..	..	..	..	..	..	..	..	Disbursements
..	..	..	..	..	..	..	..	..	..	..	Repayments
411	698	-687	-1,447	-400	-508	-1,617	748	408	168	..	Other Long-Term Capital
2,516	1,028	124	606	642	674	2,299	-60	255	998	..	Other Capital, net
-1,341	-379	-208	491	-70	-88	-728	-404	-395	-996	..	Change in Reserves
				(Austrian Schillings per US dollar)							**Memo Item:**
12.940	15.930	17.060	17.960	20.010	20.690	15.270	12.640	12.350	13.230	..	Conversion Factor (Annual Avg)
				(Millions US dollars), outstanding at end of year							
..	..	..	..	..	..	..	..	..	..	..	**EXTERNAL DEBT (Total)**
..	..	..	..	..	..	..	..	..	..	..	Long-Term Debt (by debtor)
..	..	..	..	..	..	..	..	..	..	..	Central Bank, incl. IMF credit
..	..	..	..	..	..	..	..	..	..	..	Central Government
..	..	..	..	..	..	..	..	..	..	..	Rest of General Government
..	..	..	..	..	..	..	..	..	..	..	Non-financial Public Enterprises
..	..	..	..	..	..	..	..	..	..	..	Priv. Sector, incl non-guaranteed
..	..	..	..	..	..	..	..	..	..	..	Short-Term Debt
				(Millions of US dollars)							**Memo Items:**
5,281	5,285	5,300	4,515	4,244	4,767	6,162	7,532	7,368	8,598	..	Int'l Reserves Excluding Gold
12,445	8,392	9,649	8,060	6,516	6,912	8,265	10,237	8,675	8,284	..	Gold Holdings (at market price)
											SOCIAL INDICATORS
1.7	1.6	1.6	1.6	1.5	1.5	1.5	1.5	1.5	1.5	..	Total Fertility Rate
13.9	12.6	12.8	12.0	11.5	11.2	10.3	9.9	8.1	8.6	..	Infant Mortality Rate
72.7	72.9	73.1	73.5	73.9	74.3	74.7	75.1	75.4	75.6	..	Life Expectancy at Birth
54.6	54.9	55.2	55.5	55.8	56.1	56.4	56.7	57.1	57.4	..	Urban Population, % of total
97.4	92.2	104.1	99.0	103.0	100.7	101.1	100.0	106.2	99.4	..	Food Prod. per capita (1987=100)
9.0	..	..	..	..	..	..	..	..	..	..	Labor Force, Agriculture (%)
40.4	40.3	40.3	40.3	40.2	40.2	40.2	40.1	40.1	40.1	..	Labor Force, Female (%)
98.0	..	98.0	98.0	97.0	99.0	100.0	101.0	..	..	..	Primary Schl. Enroll. Ratio
98.0	98.0	98.0	97.0	97.0	98.0	100.0	101.0	..	..	..	Primary Schl. Enroll. Ratio, Female
73.0	..	74.0	74.0	76.0	79.0	79.0	80.0	..	..	..	Secondary Schl. Enroll. Ratio

BAHAMAS	1969	1970	1971	1972	1973	1974	1975	1976	1977	1978	1979
CURRENT GNP PER CAPITA (US $)	2,780	2,700	2,900	2,900	3,260	2,950	2,730	3,000	3,330	3,670	5,100
POPULATION (thousands)	164	171	174	178	181	185	189	193	197	201	206
USE AND ORIGIN OF RESOURCES					*(Millions of current Bahamian Dollars)*						
Gross National Product (GNP)	474.7	475.3	505.2	520.6	591.1	557.2	525.3	565.7	628.2	702.7	1,016.4
Net Factor Income from Abroad	-64.0	-64.2	-68.2	-70.3	-79.8	-75.2	-70.9	-76.4	-84.8	-129.7	-123.4
GDP at Market Prices	538.7	539.5	573.4	590.9	670.9	632.4	596.2	642.1	713.0	832.4	1,139.8
Resource Balance	..	..	..	..	..	..	..	..	117.7	126.1	98.8
Exports of Goods & NFServices	..	..	..	..	..	..	..	..	589.3	688.1	785.0
Imports of Goods & NFServices	..	..	..	..	..	..	..	..	471.6	562.0	686.2
Domestic Absorption	..	..	..	..	..	..	..	..	595.3	706.3	1,041.0
Private Consumption, etc.	..	..	..	..	..	..	..	..	396.8	483.5	751.0
General Gov't Consumption	..	..	..	..	..	..	..	..	109.3	128.4	143.8
Gross Domestic Investment	..	..	..	..	..	..	..	..	89.2	94.4	146.2
Fixed Investment	..	..	..	..	..	..	..	..	81.3	85.9	135.3
Indirect Taxes, net	..	..	..	..	..	..	..	..	..	..	125.9
GDP at factor cost	..	..	..	..	..	..	..	..	..	..	1,013.9
Agriculture	..	..	..	..	..	..	..	..	..	..	..
Industry	..	..	..	..	..	..	..	..	..	..	..
Manufacturing	..	..	..	..	..	..	..	..	..	..	..
Services, etc.	..	..	..	..	..	..	..	..	..	..	..
Gross Domestic Saving	..	..	..	..	..	..	..	..	206.9	220.5	245.0
Gross National Saving	..	..	..	..	..	..	..	..	103.5	68.6	105.8
					(Millions of 1987 Bahamian Dollars)						
Gross National Product	1,533.0	1,446.3	1,469.9	1,418.5	1,525.9	1,270.3	1,082.0	1,138.2	1,242.4	1,359.7	1,854.2
GDP at Market Prices	1,734.0	1,636.0	1,662.6	1,604.5	1,725.9	1,436.7	1,224.0	1,287.5	1,405.4	1,604.7	2,023.9
Resource Balance	..	..	..	..	..	..	..	..	269.9	331.1	295.4
Exports of Goods & NFServices	..	..	..	..	..	..	..	..	1,011.6	1,115.5	1,156.7
Imports of Goods & NFServices	..	..	..	..	..	..	..	..	741.8	784.4	861.3
Domestic Absorption	..	..	..	..	..	..	..	..	1,135.5	1,273.6	1,728.5
Private Consumption, etc.	..	..	..	..	..	..	..	..	766.7	886.7	1,271.0
General Gov't Consumption	..	..	..	..	..	..	..	..	209.9	232.1	238.5
Gross Domestic Investment	..	..	..	..	..	..	..	..	159.0	154.7	219.0
Fixed Investment	..	..	..	..	..	..	..	..	144.9	140.8	202.6
GDP at factor cost	..	..	..	..	..	..	..	..	..	..	1,824.2
Agriculture	..	..	..	..	..	..	..	..	..	..	..
Industry	..	..	..	..	..	..	..	..	..	..	..
Manufacturing	..	..	..	..	..	..	..	..	..	..	..
Services, etc.	..	..	..	..	..	..	..	..	..	..	..
Memo Items:											
Capacity to Import	..	..	..	..	..	..	..	..	926.9	960.4	985.3
Terms of Trade Adjustment	..	..	..	..	..	..	..	..	-84.7	-155.1	-171.4
Gross Domestic Income	..	..	..	..	..	..	..	..	1,320.6	1,449.6	1,852.5
Gross National Income	..	..	..	..	..	..	..	..	1,157.7	1,204.6	1,682.8
DOMESTIC PRICES/DEFLATORS					*(Index 1987 = 100)*						
Overall (GDP)	31.1	33.0	34.5	36.8	38.9	44.0	48.7	49.9	50.7	51.9	56.3
Domestic Absorption	..	..	..	..	..	..	..	..	52.4	55.5	60.2
Agriculture	..	..	..	..	..	..	..	..	..	..	..
Industry	..	..	..	..	..	..	..	..	..	..	..
Manufacturing	..	..	..	..	..	..	..	..	..	..	..
Consumer Price Index	30.8	32.7	34.2	36.5	38.5	43.6	48.1	50.2	51.8	54.9	59.9
MANUFACTURING ACTIVITY											
Employment (1987=100)	..	..	..	..	..	..	..	..	..	..	..
Real Earnings per Empl. (1987=100)	..	..	..	..	..	..	..	..	..	..	..
Real Output per Empl. (1987=100)	..	..	..	..	..	..	..	..	..	..	..
Earnings as % of Value Added	..	..	..	..	..	..	..	..	39.8	93.8	45.3
MONETARY HOLDINGS					*(Millions of current Bahamian Dollars)*						
Money Supply, Broadly Defined	200.8	183.6	189.2	204.5	252.9	254.2	276.9	356.8	338.3	388.2	456.9
Money	88.0	80.5	68.8	84.9	80.4	77.8	73.7	77.5	89.5	107.1	138.3
Currency Outside Banks	17.4	17.8	15.3	21.3	20.2	19.3	20.1	20.5	23.3	26.5	29.8
Demand Deposits	70.6	62.7	53.5	63.6	60.2	58.5	53.6	57.0	66.2	80.6	108.5
Quasi-Money	112.8	103.1	120.4	119.6	172.5	176.4	203.2	279.3	248.8	281.1	318.6
					(Millions of current Bahamian Dollars)						
GOVERNMENT DEFICIT (-) OR SURPLUS	..	..	..	..	1.90	-40.10	-0.40	-6.90	-9.80	-13.60	6.70
Current Revenue	..	..	..	..	107.60	118.00	137.20	152.10	156.00	185.20	226.50
Current Expenditure	..	..	..	..	97.30	103.00	113.40	127.70	140.70	149.80	180.40
Current Budget Balance	..	..	..	..	10.30	15.00	23.80	24.40	15.30	35.40	46.10
Capital Receipts	..	..	..	..	..	..	..	..	..	..	..
Capital Payments	..	..	..	..	8.40	55.10	24.20	31.30	25.10	49.00	39.40

1980	1981	1982	1983	1984	1985	1986	1987	1988	1989 estimate	NOTES	BAHAMAS
5,830	5,650	6,600	7,110	8,190	8,950	9,530	10,360	10,680	11,370	..	**CURRENT GNP PER CAPITA (US $)**
210	214	219	224	229	232	236	240	244	248	..	**POPULATION (thousands)**
			(Millions of current Bahamian Dollars)								**USE AND ORIGIN OF RESOURCES**
1,221.7	1,287.7	1,463.4	1,609.5	1,892.6	2,158.1	2,309.2	2,551.9	2,649.6	2,851.2	..	Gross National Product (GNP)
-113.6	-138.8	-114.9	-123.3	-148.5	-162.6	-163.3	-162.1	-168.3	-181.2	..	Net Factor Income from Abroad
1,335.3	1,426.5	1,578.3	1,732.8	2,041.1	2,320.7	2,472.5	2,714.0	2,817.9	3,032.4	..	GDP at Market Prices
100.2	71.5	98.4	148.2	107.8	128.1	146.2	149.8	..	..	..	Resource Balance
939.8	961.2	1,038.3	1,153.5	1,297.9	1,503.6	1,577.9	1,664.3	..	..	..	Exports of Goods & NFServices
839.6	889.7	939.9	1,005.3	1,190.1	1,375.5	1,431.7	1,514.5	..	..	..	Imports of Goods & NFServices
1,235.1	1,355.0	1,479.9	1,584.5	1,933.3	2,192.6	2,326.3	2,564.2	..	..	..	Domestic Absorption
823.9	888.9	932.2	994.3	1,335.6	1,458.6	1,570.7	1,727.7	..	..	..	Private Consumption, etc.
167.0	197.3	208.9	238.0	264.0	289.1	300.1	326.4	..	..	..	General Gov't Consumption
244.2	268.8	338.8	352.2	333.7	444.9	455.5	510.1	..	..	..	Gross Domestic Investment
212.9	238.9	298.7	310.7	326.5	407.8	425.2	508.1	..	..	..	Fixed Investment
146.6	152.6	157.0	179.0	254.0	303.1	322.8	335.4	..	..	..	Indirect Taxes, net
1,188.7	1,273.9	1,421.3	1,553.8	1,787.1	2,017.6	2,149.7	2,378.6	..	..	..	GDP at factor cost
..	..	..	..	41.7	44.2	44.8	49.6	..	..	..	Agriculture
..	..	..	..	246.6	279.6	301.0	344.6	..	..	..	Industry
..	..	..	..	..	..	..	..	..	..	..	Manufacturing
..	..	..	..	1,498.8	1,693.8	1,803.9	1,984.4	..	..	..	Services, etc.
344.4	340.3	437.2	500.5	441.5	573.0	601.7	659.9	..	..	..	Gross Domestic Saving
211.1	187.6	304.6	366.9	278.4	395.8	424.4	480.0	..	..	..	Gross National Saving
			(Millions of 1987 Bahamian Dollars)								
2,025.4	1,780.4	1,952.0	2,009.9	2,281.8	2,385.0	2,462.2	2,551.9	2,541.8	2,595.1	..	Gross National Product
2,155.6	1,956.7	2,088.0	2,163.1	2,469.8	2,588.6	2,635.2	2,714.0	2,681.2	2,737.5	..	GDP at Market Prices
322.0	177.9	234.2	260.9	229.5	158.4	160.5	149.8	..	..	..	Resource Balance
1,273.4	1,166.1	1,265.9	1,376.1	1,551.5	1,643.5	1,686.4	1,664.3	..	..	..	Exports of Goods & NFServices
951.4	988.2	1,031.6	1,115.2	1,322.0	1,485.1	1,526.0	1,514.5	..	..	..	Imports of Goods & NFServices
1,833.6	1,778.8	1,853.8	1,902.2	2,240.2	2,430.2	2,474.7	2,564.2	..	..	..	Domestic Absorption
1,253.9	1,180.4	1,184.6	1,205.7	1,559.0	1,628.3	1,680.7	1,727.7	..	..	..	Private Consumption, etc.
247.1	262.7	262.3	287.0	306.4	321.4	319.9	326.4	..	..	..	General Gov't Consumption
332.6	335.8	406.9	409.4	374.8	480.5	474.1	510.1	..	..	..	Gross Domestic Investment
289.8	298.3	358.8	360.9	366.6	440.4	442.5	508.1	..	..	..	Fixed Investment
1,948.6	1,762.0	1,900.7	1,957.0	2,184.5	2,263.8	2,299.3	2,378.6	..	..	..	GDP at factor cost
..	..	..	..	..	..	..	..	..	..	..	Agriculture
..	..	..	..	..	..	..	..	..	..	..	Industry
..	..	..	..	..	..	..	..	..	..	..	Manufacturing
..	..	..	..	..	..	..	..	..	..	..	Services, etc.
											Memo Items:
1,065.0	1,067.6	1,139.6	1,279.5	1,441.7	1,623.4	1,681.8	1,664.3	..	..	..	Capacity to Import
-208.5	-98.5	-126.2	-96.5	-109.8	-20.1	-4.6	0.0	..	..	..	Terms of Trade Adjustment
1,947.1	1,858.2	1,961.8	2,066.6	2,360.0	2,568.5	2,630.5	2,714.0	..	..	..	Gross Domestic Income
1,817.0	1,681.9	1,825.7	1,913.4	2,172.0	2,364.9	2,457.6	2,551.9	..	..	..	Gross National Income
			(Index 1987 = 100)								**DOMESTIC PRICES/DEFLATORS**
61.9	72.9	75.6	80.1	82.6	89.6	93.8	100.0	105.1	110.8	..	Overall (GDP)
67.4	76.2	79.8	83.3	86.3	90.2	94.0	100.0	..	..	..	Domestic Absorption
..	..	..	..	..	..	..	..	..	..	..	Agriculture
..	..	..	..	..	..	..	..	..	..	..	Industry
..	..	..	..	..	..	..	..	..	..	..	Manufacturing
67.2	74.6	79.1	82.3	85.5	89.5	94.3	100.0	104.1	109.8	..	Consumer Price Index
											MANUFACTURING ACTIVITY
..	..	..	..	..	..	..	..	..	..	..	Employment (1987=100)
..	..	..	..	..	..	..	..	..	..	..	Real Earnings per Empl. (1987=100)
..	..	..	..	..	..	..	..	..	..	..	Real Output per Empl. (1987=100)
42.6	100.1	81.0	41.0	..	..	39.1	..	..	..	..	Earnings as % of Value Added
			(Millions of current Bahamian Dollars)								**MONETARY HOLDINGS**
520.3	583.4	684.7	792.6	857.9	937.9	1,065.6	1,241.3	1,323.6	1,417.2	D	Money Supply, Broadly Defined
136.3	143.5	159.7	176.9	187.7	208.1	249.2	277.7	297.1	298.3	..	Money
33.4	37.4	41.1	45.5	51.0	57.8	65.0	74.8	78.8	79.5	..	Currency Outside Banks
102.9	106.1	118.6	131.4	136.7	150.3	184.2	202.9	218.3	218.8	..	Demand Deposits
384.0	439.9	525.0	615.7	670.2	729.8	816.4	963.6	1,026.5	1,118.9	..	Quasi-Money
			(Millions of current Bahamian Dollars)								**GOVERNMENT DEFICIT (-) OR SURPLUS**
18.90	-33.90	-45.10	-52.20	14.40	4.50	-17.40	..	..	..	..	
270.40	314.20	311.30	337.90	376.70	430.60	451.20	..	..	..	..	Current Revenue
228.10	261.40	289.00	318.10	343.80	385.00	436.00	..	..	..	..	Current Expenditure
42.30	52.80	22.30	19.80	32.90	45.60	15.20	..	..	..	..	Current Budget Balance
..	..	..	..	..	..	..	..	..	..	..	Capital Receipts
23.40	86.70	67.40	72.00	18.50	41.10	32.60	..	..	..	..	Capital Payments

BAHAMAS	1969	1970	1971	1972	1973	1974	1975	1976	1977	1978	1979
FOREIGN TRADE (CUSTOMS BASIS)					*(Millions of current US dollars)*						
Value of Exports, fob	53.2	87.5	266.5	343.4	529.8	1,795.4	2,216.1	2,616.0	2,408.7	2,118.1	3,783.5
Nonfuel Primary Products	..	..	..	..	..	..	..	..	..	..	..
Fuels	..	..	..	..	..	..	..	..	..	..	..
Manufactures	..	..	..	..	..	..	..	..	..	..	..
Value of Imports, cif	296.3	331.9	511.3	484.9	764.2	2,111.5	2,482.1	2,892.6	2,871.3	2,482.2	3,985.0
Nonfuel Primary Products	..	..	..	..	..	..	..	..	..	..	..
Fuels	..	..	..	..	..	..	..	..	..	..	..
Manufactures	..	..	..	..	..	..	..	..	..	..	..
					(Index 1987 = 100)						
Terms of Trade	..	..	..	..	..	..	..	..	..	..	..
Export Prices, fob	..	..	..	..	..	..	..	..	..	..	..
Import Prices, cif	..	..	..	..	..	..	..	..	..	..	..
BALANCE OF PAYMENTS					*(Millions of current US dollars)*						
Exports of Goods & Services	..	..	..	..	593.7	696.0	712.8	694.0	712.4	836.4	952.7
Merchandise, fob	..	..	..	..	95.0	122.8	117.3	149.3	135.9	146.4	170.5
Nonfactor Services	..	..	..	..	374.8	444.0	470.7	540.2	572.5	683.1	771.3
Factor Services	..	..	..	..	123.9	129.2	124.8	4.5	4.0	6.9	10.9
Imports of Goods & Services	..	..	..	..	721.5	800.8	659.9	597.6	633.1	780.4	932.9
Merchandise, fob	..	..	..	..	388.8	411.1	340.6	389.5	390.4	467.9	597.5
Nonfactor Services	..	..	..	..	120.6	140.2	130.4	127.0	152.7	175.3	188.0
Factor Services	..	..	..	..	212.1	249.5	188.8	81.1	90.0	137.2	147.4
Long-Term Interest	..	2.7	2.4	2.2	2.7	3.8	4.8	5.5	4.6	4.9	6.8
Private Current Transfers, net	..	..	..	..	-20.3	-20.1	-14.9	-16.5	-18.6	-22.2	-15.8
Workers' Remittances	..	..	..	..	..	..	..	..	..	..	..
Curr. A/C Bal before Off. Transf.	..	..	..	..	-148.1	-125.0	38.0	79.9	60.7	33.8	4.0
Net Official Transfers	..	..	..	..	3.0	2.4	4.7	4.9	5.4	7.5	11.8
Curr. A/C Bal after Off. Transf.	..	..	..	..	-145.1	-122.5	42.7	84.8	66.1	41.3	15.8
Long-Term Capital, net	..	..	..	..	90.6	113.0	37.7	9.6	40.7	-25.3	8.8
Direct Investment	..	..	..	..	79.4	111.1	48.8	14.6	31.4	-1.1	9.6
Long-Term Loans	..	-4.6	-4.6	1.5	18.6	18.9	16.0	-7.2	0.5	12.1	-4.4
Disbursements	..	0.0	0.0	6.2	23.3	23.6	23.3	0.6	30.8	23.5	15.6
Repayments	..	4.6	4.6	4.7	4.7	4.7	7.3	7.8	30.3	11.4	20.0
Other Long-Term Capital	..	..	..	..	-7.4	-17.0	-27.1	2.2	8.8	-36.3	3.6
Other Capital, net	..	..	..	..	61.6	16.0	-76.7	-100.3	-87.7	-25.0	-9.8
Change in Reserves	..	4.4	-7.8	-7.6	-7.2	-6.5	-3.7	5.9	-19.1	9.0	-14.8
Memo Item:					*(Bahamian Dollars per US dollar)*						
Conversion Factor (Annual Avg)	1.020	1.000	1.000	1.000	1.000	1.000	1.000	1.000	1.000	1.000	1.000
					(Millions of US dollars), outstanding at end of year						
EXTERNAL DEBT (Total)	..	..	..	..	..	..	..	..	..	..	..
Long-Term Debt (by debtor)	..	..	..	..	..	..	..	..	..	..	..
Central Bank, incl. IMF credit	..	..	..	..	..	..	..	..	..	..	..
Central Government	..	..	..	..	..	..	..	..	..	..	..
Rest of General Government	..	..	..	..	..	..	..	..	..	..	..
Non-financial Public Enterprises	..	..	..	..	..	..	..	..	..	..	..
Priv. Sector, incl non-guaranteed	..	..	..	..	..	..	..	..	..	..	..
Short-Term Debt	..	..	..	..	..	..	..	..	..	..	..
Memo Items:					*(Millions of US dollars)*						
Int'l Reserves Excluding Gold	26.1	21.7	29.5	37.1	43.2	49.8	53.3	47.4	67.1	58.1	77.5
Gold Holdings (at market price)	..	..	..	..	..	..	..	..	1.4	2.9	8.8
SOCIAL INDICATORS											
Total Fertility Rate	..	3.4	3.4	3.4	3.1	2.8	2.5	3.0	3.4	3.3	3.3
Infant Mortality Rate	36.7	35.0	32.0	29.0	27.3	25.5	34.2	24.7	27.7	32.5	25.9
Life Expectancy at Birth	65.6	64.9	65.2	65.5	65.6	65.8	65.9	66.0	66.2	66.3	66.4
Urban Population, % of total	58.0	57.8	57.6	57.4	57.1	56.9	56.7	56.7	56.7	56.7	56.7
Food Prod. per capita (1987=100)	110.0	132.8	77.6	87.7	72.3	81.9	85.7	96.0	90.4	91.9	90.7
Labor Force, Agriculture (%)	..	..	..	..	..	..	..	..	..	..	..
Labor Force, Female (%)	..	..	..	..	..	..	..	..	..	..	..
Primary Schl. Enroll. Ratio	..	..	..	..	..	..	..	..	..	..	..
Primary Schl. Enroll. Ratio, Female	..	..	..	..	..	..	..	..	..	..	..
Secondary Schl. Enroll. Ratio	..	..	..	..	..	..	..	..	..	..	..

1980	1981	1982	1983	1984	1985	1986	1987	1988	1989 estimate	NOTES	BAHAMAS
				(Millions of current US dollars)							**FOREIGN TRADE (CUSTOMS BASIS)**
4,906.0	3,515.0	2,451.0	2,561.0	2,346.0	1,431.0	825.0	733.0	733.0	..	..	Value of Exports, fob
44.0	46.4	53.8	44.2	55.6	54.6	..	..	..	..	..	Nonfuel Primary Products
4,706.0	3,339.0	2,239.0	2,336.0	2,084.0	1,135.0	..	..	..	..	..	Fuels
156.0	129.6	158.2	180.8	206.4	241.4	..	..	..	..	..	Manufactures
5,507.0	4,214.0	3,067.0	3,252.0	3,037.0	2,209.0	1,618.0	1,701.0	1,547.0	..	..	Value of Imports, cif
170.4	118.0	195.3	171.6	195.2	202.4	..	..	..	..	..	Nonfuel Primary Products
4,830.5	3,781.1	2,402.5	3,080.4	2,319.9	1,400.2	..	..	..	..	..	Fuels
506.1	314.9	469.2	419.6	521.9	606.4	..	..	..	..	..	Manufactures
				(Index 1987 = 100)							
..	..	..	..	..	..	..	..	..	..	..	Terms of Trade
..	..	..	..	..	..	..	..	..	..	..	Export Prices, fob
..	..	..	..	..	..	..	..	..	..	..	Import Prices, cif
				(Millions of current US dollars)							**BALANCE OF PAYMENTS**
1,160.1	1,160.6	1,158.8	1,263.3	1,327.8	1,536.3	1,607.2	1,662.5	1,628.4	1,702.2	..	Exports of Goods & Services
200.5	176.2	212.7	225.1	261.9	295.8	293.4	273.1	273.6	259.2	..	Merchandise, fob
946.6	967.4	922.3	1,022.9	1,047.1	1,220.1	1,294.3	1,371.3	1,339.5	1,426.9	..	Nonfactor Services
13.0	17.0	23.8	15.3	18.8	20.4	19.5	18.1	15.3	16.1	..	Factor Services
1,174.5	1,239.9	1,225.8	1,304.9	1,374.1	1,688.3	1,633.6	1,824.9	1,742.2	1,882.6	..	Imports of Goods & Services
800.8	796.7	754.5	822.1	866.2	1,096.2	1,012.8	1,154.7	1,058.9	1,151.9	..	Merchandise, fob
223.1	267.0	312.5	325.5	320.3	385.0	413.8	464.8	497.4	525.7	..	Nonfactor Services
150.6	176.2	158.8	157.3	187.6	207.1	207.0	205.4	185.9	205.0	..	Factor Services
7.6	9.0	25.2	27.0	25.9	20.0	22.0	14.4	15.9	14.3	..	Long-Term Interest
-19.7	-13.9	-17.7	-10.3	-14.6	-14.6	-14.0	-17.8	-28.9	-17.9	..	Private Current Transfers, net
..	..	..	..	..	..	..	..	..	..	..	Workers' Remittances
-34.1	-93.2	-84.7	-51.9	-60.9	-166.6	-40.4	-180.2	-142.7	-198.3	..	Curr. A/C Bal before Off. Transf.
17.8	11.1	21.5	17.4	15.4	17.9	13.7	14.2	14.4	18.9	..	Net Official Transfers
-16.3	-82.1	-63.2	-34.5	-45.5	-148.7	-26.7	-166.0	-128.3	-179.4	..	Curr. A/C Bal after Off. Transf.
9.5	145.6	74.8	19.3	-6.8	-35.8	-0.8	-27.0	24.0	26.1	..	Long-Term Capital, net
4.1	34.4	2.8	-6.0	-4.9	-30.2	-13.2	10.8	36.7	25.0	..	Direct Investment
-6.5	71.4	66.4	6.1	-27.5	-24.6	11.9	-29.9	-18.1	-23.0	..	Long-Term Loans
11.2	102.3	84.5	23.4	1.7	6.2	33.1	6.3	18.6	10.1	..	Disbursements
17.7	30.9	18.1	17.3	29.2	30.8	21.2	36.2	36.7	33.1	..	Repayments
11.9	39.8	5.6	19.2	25.6	19.0	0.5	-7.9	5.4	24.1	..	Other Long-Term Capital
17.5	-58.2	2.4	25.8	91.4	203.9	75.1	133.4	105.1	199.5	..	Other Capital, net
-10.7	-5.3	-14.0	-10.6	-39.1	-19.4	-47.6	59.6	-0.8	-46.2	..	Change in Reserves
				(Bahamian Dollars per US dollar)							Memo Item:
1.000	1.000	1.000	1.000	1.000	1.000	1.000	1.000	1.000	1.000	..	Conversion Factor (Annual Avg)
				(Millions of US dollars), outstanding at end of year							
..	..	..	..	..	..	..	..	..	..	..	**EXTERNAL DEBT (Total)**
..	..	..	..	..	..	..	..	..	..	..	Long-Term Debt (by debtor)
..	..	..	..	..	..	..	..	..	..	..	Central Bank, incl. IMF credit
..	..	..	..	..	..	..	..	..	..	..	Central Government
..	..	..	..	..	..	..	..	..	..	..	Rest of General Government
..	..	..	..	..	..	..	..	..	..	..	Non-financial Public Enterprises
..	..	..	..	..	..	..	..	..	..	..	Priv. Sector, incl non-guaranteed
..	..	..	..	..	..	..	..	..	..	..	Short-Term Debt
				(Millions of US dollars)							Memo Items:
92.3	100.2	113.5	122.0	161.1	182.5	231.5	170.1	172.0	146.8	..	Int'l Reserves Excluding Gold
..	..	..	..	..	..	..	..	..	..	..	Gold Holdings (at market price)
											SOCIAL INDICATORS
3.3	3.3	3.2	3.0	2.8	2.7	2.5	2.3	2.3	2.2	..	Total Fertility Rate
30.0	22.3	33.2	21.6	22.9	26.7	27.3	27.9	27.1	26.3	..	Infant Mortality Rate
66.6	66.7	66.8	66.9	67.1	67.2	67.3	67.5	67.7	68.0	..	Life Expectancy at Birth
56.7	56.9	57.0	57.2	57.3	57.5	57.8	58.1	58.5	58.8	..	Urban Population, % of total
102.3	102.0	99.1	99.4	104.4	98.0	99.4	100.0	98.4	97.2	..	Food Prod. per capita (1987=100)
..	..	..	..	..	..	..	..	..	..	..	Labor Force, Agriculture (%)
..	..	..	..	..	..	..	..	..	..	..	Labor Force, Female (%)
..	..	..	..	..	..	..	..	..	..	..	Primary Schl. Enroll. Ratio
..	..	..	..	..	..	..	..	..	..	..	Primary Schl. Enroll. Ratio, Female
..	..	..	..	..	..	..	..	..	..	..	Secondary Schl. Enroll. Ratio

BAHRAIN	1969	1970	1971	1972	1973	1974	1975	1976	1977	1978	1979
CURRENT GNP PER CAPITA (US $)	..	..	..	..	..	..	..	..	..	..	..
POPULATION (thousands)	204	210	216	227	238	250	262	275	289	303	319

USE AND ORIGIN OF RESOURCES *(Millions of current Bahrain Dinars)*

	1969	1970	1971	1972	1973	1974	1975	1976	1977	1978	1979
Gross National Product (GNP)	..	..	..	..	..	..	..	..	..	..	..
Net Factor Income from Abroad	..	..	..	..	..	..	..	..	..	..	..
GDP at Market Prices	..	..	..	..	..	..	..	..	..	..	..
Resource Balance	..	..	..	..	..	..	..	..	..	..	..
Exports of Goods & NFServices	..	..	..	..	..	..	..	..	..	..	..
Imports of Goods & NFServices	..	..	..	..	..	..	..	..	..	..	..
Domestic Absorption	..	..	..	..	..	..	..	..	..	..	..
Private Consumption, etc.	..	..	..	..	..	..	..	..	..	..	..
General Gov't Consumption	..	..	..	..	..	..	..	..	..	..	..
Gross Domestic Investment	..	..	..	..	..	..	..	..	..	..	..
Fixed Investment	..	..	..	..	..	..	..	..	..	..	..
Indirect Taxes, net	..	..	..	..	..	..	..	..	..	..	..
GDP at factor cost	..	..	..	..	..	..	..	..	..	..	..
Agriculture	..	..	..	..	..	..	..	..	..	..	..
Industry	..	..	..	..	..	..	..	..	..	..	..
Manufacturing	..	..	..	..	..	..	..	..	..	..	..
Services, etc.	..	..	..	..	..	..	..	..	..	..	..
Gross Domestic Saving	..	..	..	..	..	..	..	..	..	..	..
Gross National Saving	..	..	..	..	..	..	..	..	..	..	..

(Millions of 1987 Bahrain Dinars)

	1969	1970	1971	1972	1973	1974	1975	1976	1977	1978	1979
Gross National Product	..	..	..	..	..	..	..	..	..	..	..
GDP at Market Prices	..	..	..	..	..	..	..	..	..	..	..
Resource Balance	..	..	..	..	..	..	..	..	..	..	..
Exports of Goods & NFServices	..	..	..	..	..	..	..	..	..	..	..
Imports of Goods & NFServices	..	..	..	..	..	..	..	..	..	..	..
Domestic Absorption	..	..	..	..	..	..	..	..	..	..	..
Private Consumption, etc.	..	..	..	..	..	..	..	..	..	..	..
General Gov't Consumption	..	..	..	..	..	..	..	..	..	..	..
Gross Domestic Investment	..	..	..	..	..	..	..	..	..	..	..
Fixed Investment	..	..	..	..	..	..	..	..	..	..	..
GDP at factor cost	..	..	..	..	..	..	..	..	..	..	..
Agriculture	..	..	..	..	..	..	..	..	..	..	..
Industry	..	..	..	..	..	..	..	..	..	..	..
Manufacturing	..	..	..	..	..	..	..	..	..	..	..
Services, etc.	..	..	..	..	..	..	..	..	..	..	..
Memo Items:											
Capacity to Import	..	..	..	..	..	..	..	..	..	..	..
Terms of Trade Adjustment	..	..	..	..	..	..	..	..	..	..	..
Gross Domestic Income	..	..	..	..	..	..	..	..	..	..	..
Gross National Income	..	..	..	..	..	..	..	..	..	..	..

DOMESTIC PRICES/DEFLATORS *(Index 1987 = 100)*

	1969	1970	1971	1972	1973	1974	1975	1976	1977	1978	1979
Overall (GDP)	..	..	..	..	..	..	..	..	..	..	..
Domestic Absorption	..	..	..	..	..	..	..	..	..	..	..
Agriculture	..	..	..	..	..	..	..	..	..	..	..
Industry	..	..	..	..	..	..	..	..	..	..	..
Manufacturing	..	..	..	..	..	..	..	..	..	..	..
Consumer Price Index	25.8	26.2	27.8	29.2	33.3	41.5	48.2	59.0	69.5	80.5	82.2

MANUFACTURING ACTIVITY

	1969	1970	1971	1972	1973	1974	1975	1976	1977	1978	1979
Employment (1987=100)	..	..	..	..	..	..	..	..	..	..	..
Real Earnings per Empl. (1987=100)	..	..	..	..	..	..	..	..	..	..	..
Real Output per Empl. (1987=100)	..	..	..	..	..	..	..	..	..	..	..
Earnings as % of Value Added	..	..	..	..	..	..	..	..	..	..	..

MONETARY HOLDINGS *(Millions of current Bahrain Dinars)*

	1969	1970	1971	1972	1973	1974	1975	1976	1977	1978	1979
Money Supply, Broadly Defined	48.4	56.4	73.1	87.9	99.6	145.8	184.2	303.8	355.5	402.3	411.9
Money	34.4	37.9	48.6	55.2	59.4	61.3	77.8	127.9	152.5	171.3	186.1
Currency Outside Banks	17.2	18.9	21.2	23.8	14.9	16.9	24.0	34.2	43.8	44.1	49.9
Demand Deposits	17.2	19.1	27.3	31.4	44.5	44.4	53.8	93.7	108.7	127.2	136.2
Quasi-Money	14.0	18.5	24.6	32.7	40.3	84.5	106.5	175.9	203.0	231.0	225.8

GOVERNMENT DEFICIT (-) OR SURPLUS *(Millions of current Bahrain Dinars)*

	1969	1970	1971	1972	1973	1974	1975	1976	1977	1978	1979
GOVERNMENT DEFICIT (-) OR SURPLUS	..	..	..	..	..	39.60	5.50	-36.20	-12.90	-30.60	22.10
Current Revenue	..	..	..	..	..	117.50	129.00	186.70	255.10	273.90	304.30
Current Expenditure	..	..	..	..	..	38.20	61.60	78.40	100.20	137.00	156.80
Current Budget Balance	..	..	..	..	..	79.30	67.40	108.30	154.90	136.90	147.50
Capital Receipts	..	..	..	..	..	..	..	..	..	..	..
Capital Payments	..	..	..	..	..	39.70	61.90	144.50	167.80	167.50	125.40

1980	1981	1982	1983	1984	1985	1986	1987	1988	1989 estimate	NOTES	BAHRAIN
..	..	8,830	9,440	9,680	8,380	7,710	6,840	6,360	..	..	**CURRENT GNP PER CAPITA (US $)**
334	353	374	390	407	425	442	458	473	489	..	POPULATION (thousands)
				(Millions of current Bahrain Dinars)							**USE AND ORIGIN OF RESOURCES**
1,111.5	1,288.9	1,332.8	1,343.6	1,411.0	1,283.2	1,085.1	1,084.1	1,094.9	..	..	Gross National Product (GNP)
-46.6	-15.0	-38.0	-60.8	-57.5	-109.7	-113.1	-107.7	-168.0	..	..	Net Factor Income from Abroad
1,158.1	1,303.9	1,370.8	1,404.4	1,468.5	1,392.9	1,198.2	1,191.8	1,262.9	..	..	GDP at Market Prices
102.7	145.0	167.3	52.4	38.8	159.3	205.7	138.3	143.5	..	..	Resource Balance
1,437.3	1,709.8	1,631.0	1,357.8	1,416.9	1,392.3	1,143.1	1,232.6	1,139.0	..	..	Exports of Goods & NFServices
1,334.6	1,564.8	1,463.7	1,305.4	1,378.1	1,233.0	937.4	1,094.3	995.5	..	..	Imports of Goods & NFServices
1,055.4	1,158.9	1,203.5	1,352.0	1,429.7	1,233.6	992.5	1,053.5	1,119.4	..	..	Domestic Absorption
370.3	427.7	472.9	481.6	502.2	450.5	408.3	453.5	514.2	..	..	Private Consumption, etc.
150.9	188.6	233.3	254.5	302.2	312.8	312.4	310.9	339.9	..	..	General Gov't Consumption
534.2	542.6	497.3	615.9	625.3	470.3	271.8	289.1	265.3	..	..	Gross Domestic Investment
356.9	380.5	451.9	576.1	647.0	487.8	390.8	359.2	344.8	..	..	Fixed Investment
40.3	50.2	60.4	62.7	58.5	44.9	26.6	28.3	33.2	..	..	Indirect Taxes, net
1,117.8	1,253.7	1,310.4	1,341.7	1,410.0	1,348.0	1,171.7	1,163.5	1,229.7	..	..	GDP at factor cost
11.4	13.2	14.5	16.2	16.4	16.4	16.4	16.0	15.4	..	..	Agriculture
684.3	753.7	724.9	676.8	719.7	696.6	521.5	524.7	544.6	..	..	Industry
187.9	202.3	170.1	167.2	182.8	138.8	166.1	191.0	235.3	..	..	Manufacturing
462.4	537.0	631.4	711.4	732.4	679.9	660.3	651.1	702.9	..	..	Services, etc.
636.9	687.6	664.6	668.3	664.1	629.6	477.5	427.4	408.8	..	..	Gross Domestic Saving
555.1	632.5	582.4	569.1	559.4	436.6	264.9	231.2	..	..	..	Gross National Saving
				(Millions of 1987 Bahrain Dinars)							
1,161.8	1,134.4	1,036.1	1,084.9	1,140.4	1,054.5	1,103.3	1,084.1	1,105.2	..	..	Gross National Product
1,210.7	1,147.8	1,065.7	1,133.9	1,186.9	1,144.9	1,219.0	1,191.8	1,274.3	..	H	GDP at Market Prices
5.8	-11.8	15.9	-14.2	29.8	111.3	201.4	138.3	133.3	..	..	Resource Balance
1,020.6	1,109.3	1,055.9	972.3	1,087.0	1,073.0	1,258.8	1,232.6	1,267.8	..	..	Exports of Goods & NFServices
1,014.7	1,121.1	1,040.0	986.4	1,057.3	961.7	1,057.4	1,094.3	1,134.5	..	..	Imports of Goods & NFServices
1,154.7	1,119.6	1,039.3	1,123.6	1,139.8	1,029.3	1,009.0	1,053.5	1,146.8	..	..	Domestic Absorption
437.5	437.6	463.9	462.1	472.0	437.0	402.1	453.5	514.8	..	..	Private Consumption, etc.
177.4	192.8	221.5	231.6	258.1	274.0	301.4	310.9	335.9	..	..	General Gov't Consumption
539.8	489.2	353.8	429.9	409.7	318.3	305.6	289.1	296.1	..	..	Gross Domestic Investment
280.3	282.9	329.8	420.3	488.5	422.9	381.2	359.2	342.5	..	..	Fixed Investment
1,188.1	1,107.7	1,006.3	1,071.3	1,130.7	1,099.6	1,192.5	1,163.5	1,232.9	..	..	GDP at factor cost
12.4	12.7	15.1	15.1	15.4	15.1	15.0	16.0	16.6	..	..	Agriculture
664.0	599.7	463.6	486.7	529.7	521.1	576.7	524.7	543.2	..	..	Industry
136.4	144.7	148.2	137.9	149.0	124.9	202.6	191.0	199.6	..	..	Manufacturing
513.5	520.0	586.1	632.1	641.8	608.8	627.3	651.1	714.5	..	..	Services, etc.
											Memo Items:
1,092.8	1,224.9	1,158.9	1,026.0	1,087.0	1,086.0	1,289.4	1,232.6	1,298.1	..	..	Capacity to Import
72.2	115.6	103.0	53.8	0.0	13.0	30.6	0.0	30.3	..	..	Terms of Trade Adjustment
1,282.9	1,263.4	1,168.7	1,187.7	1,186.9	1,157.9	1,249.6	1,191.8	1,304.6	..	..	Gross Domestic Income
1,234.0	1,250.0	1,139.1	1,138.7	1,140.4	1,067.5	1,133.9	1,084.1	1,135.5	..	..	Gross National Income
				(Index 1987 = 100)							**DOMESTIC PRICES/DEFLATORS**
95.7	113.6	128.6	123.9	123.7	121.7	98.3	100.0	99.1	..	..	Overall (GDP)
91.4	103.5	115.8	120.3	125.4	119.8	98.4	100.0	97.6	..	..	Domestic Absorption
91.8	104.0	96.2	107.4	106.2	108.8	109.4	100.0	92.5	..	..	Agriculture
103.1	125.7	156.4	139.1	135.9	133.7	90.4	100.0	100.3	..	..	Industry
137.8	139.8	114.8	121.3	122.7	111.1	82.0	100.0	117.9	..	..	Manufacturing
85.4	95.1	103.6	106.6	107.0	104.2	101.8	100.0	100.3	101.8	..	Consumer Price Index
											MANUFACTURING ACTIVITY
..	..	..	..	..	..	..	..	..	..	..	Employment (1987=100)
..	..	..	..	..	..	..	..	..	..	..	Real Earnings per Empl. (1987=100)
..	..	..	..	..	..	..	..	..	..	..	Real Output per Empl. (1987=100)
..	..	..	..	..	..	..	..	..	..	..	Earnings as % of Value Added
				(Millions of current Bahrain Dinars)							**MONETARY HOLDINGS**
524.1	730.5	780.2	843.1	827.8	903.3	885.2	968.5	1,007.6	1,052.4	..	Money Supply, Broadly Defined
192.2	248.8	266.9	250.0	239.3	243.1	235.7	246.7	238.9	234.7	..	Money
58.3	63.3	70.5	73.5	78.2	79.0	80.0	84.1	84.4	84.8	..	Currency Outside Banks
133.9	185.4	196.5	176.5	161.1	164.2	155.7	162.6	154.5	149.9	..	Demand Deposits
331.8	481.8	513.3	593.1	588.5	660.2	649.5	721.8	768.7	817.8	..	Quasi-Money
				(Millions of current Bahrain Dinars)							
68.00	110.80	32.10	-96.20	-23.00	13.70	-51.90	-122.20	49.10	..	..	**GOVERNMENT DEFICIT (-) OR SURPLUS**
445.70	536.60	554.20	490.50	523.00	541.40	459.80	414.00	395.50	..	..	Current Revenue
191.60	230.90	298.70	313.20	328.60	344.20	354.50	300.00	331.90	..	..	Current Expenditure
254.10	305.70	255.50	177.30	194.40	197.20	105.30	114.00	63.60	..	..	Current Budget Balance
..	..	..	..	..	..	..	..	2.70	..	..	Capital Receipts
186.10	194.90	223.40	273.50	217.40	183.50	157.20	236.20	17.20	..	..	Capital Payments

BAHRAIN	1969	1970	1971	1972	1973	1974	1975	1976	1977	1978	1979
FOREIGN TRADE (CUSTOMS BASIS)					*(Millions of current US dollars)*						
Value of Exports, fob	226.0	235.9	318.1	323.0	406.8	1,162.7	1,147.3	1,633.5	1,859.4	1,867.2	2,470.5
Nonfuel Primary Products	21.6	12.8	11.7	15.7	22.4	105.0	100.8	143.5	138.5	202.8	148.1
Fuels	178.9	183.7	259.0	252.9	328.0	982.2	934.5	1,289.8	1,462.1	1,487.4	2,159.7
Manufactures	25.5	39.4	47.4	54.4	56.4	75.5	112.0	200.2	258.8	177.0	162.8
Value of Imports, cif	208.0	247.0	302.4	377.5	532.5	1,199.0	1,158.2	1,669.6	2,030.9	2,032.9	2,477.5
Nonfuel Primary Products	22.6	37.9	42.4	50.5	65.3	84.7	86.1	153.9	162.9	194.4	231.7
Fuels	92.1	79.5	84.3	152.3	218.4	764.1	588.6	708.3	925.4	879.8	1,276.7
Manufactures	93.3	129.6	175.8	174.7	248.8	350.3	483.5	807.4	942.6	958.7	969.0
					(Index 1987 = 100)						
Terms of Trade	71.0	59.7	58.8	71.0	73.8	112.8	108.7	118.7	119.0	108.6	119.5
Export Prices, fob	9.0	9.2	11.4	13.1	18.1	65.6	62.5	69.5	76.7	76.4	108.5
Import Prices, cif	12.7	15.3	19.5	18.5	24.5	58.2	57.5	58.6	64.5	70.3	90.8
BALANCE OF PAYMENTS					*(Millions of current US dollars)*						
Exports of Goods & Services	..	246.0	300.0	392.0	541.0	1,436.0	1,404.8	1,786.2	2,181.0	2,362.9	2,924.9
Merchandise, fob	..	218.0	265.0	348.0	479.0	1,272.0	1,203.0	1,517.9	1,848.9	1,891.8	2,499.1
Nonfactor Services	..	15.0	19.0	24.0	34.0	89.0	156.3	201.5	255.8	364.2	313.7
Factor Services	..	13.0	16.0	20.0	28.0	75.0	45.5	66.7	76.3	106.9	112.2
Imports of Goods & Services	..	291.0	356.0	425.0	607.0	1,324.0	1,531.5	2,062.7	2,502.7	2,710.0	3,152.1
Merchandise, fob	..	247.0	303.0	361.0	516.0	1,126.0	1,090.0	1,510.1	1,837.0	1,873.3	2,094.8
Nonfactor Services	..	40.0	48.0	58.0	83.0	180.0	179.3	243.2	296.2	342.8	369.7
Factor Services	..	4.0	5.0	6.0	8.0	18.0	262.2	309.4	369.5	494.0	687.6
Long-Term Interest	..	..	..	..	..	..	..	..	..	..	..
Private Current Transfers, net	..	-44.0	-54.0	-63.0	-92.0	-198.0	-76.4	-84.9	-101.1	-131.1	-93.5
Workers' Remittances	..	..	..	..	..	..	..	..	..	..	..
Curr. A/C Bal before Off. Transf.	..	-89.0	-110.0	-96.0	-158.0	-86.0	-203.0	-361.5	-422.8	-478.3	-320.7
Net Official Transfers	..	0.0	0.0	0.0	0.0	0.0	..	1.3	98.8	90.6	98.0
Curr. A/C Bal after Off. Transf.	..	-89.0	-110.0	-96.0	-158.0	-86.0	-203.0	-360.2	-324.0	-387.7	-222.7
Long-Term Capital, net	..	73.2	57.2	44.5	-13.8	56.2	88.0	279.8	402.1	146.3	170.6
Direct Investment	..	..	..	..	..	..	..	..	..	23.0	145.2
Long-Term Loans	..	..	..	..	..	..	..	..	..	..	..
Disbursements	..	..	..	..	..	..	..	..	..	..	..
Repayments	..	..	..	..	..	..	..	..	..	..	..
Other Long-Term Capital	..	73.2	57.2	44.5	-13.8	56.2	88.0	279.8	402.1	123.4	25.4
Other Capital, net	..	19.0	76.0	49.0	152.0	97.0	284.0	227.0	-10.8	223.1	173.7
Change in Reserves	..	-3.2	-23.2	2.5	19.8	-67.2	-168.9	-146.6	-67.3	18.2	-121.6
Memo Item:					*(Bahrain Dinars per US dollar)*						
Conversion Factor (Annual Avg)	0.480	0.480	0.470	0.440	0.400	0.390	0.400	0.400	0.400	0.390	0.380
				(Millions of US dollars), outstanding at end of year							
EXTERNAL DEBT (Total)	..	..	..	..	..	..	..	..	..	..	..
Long-Term Debt (by debtor)	..	..	..	..	..	..	..	..	..	..	..
Central Bank, incl. IMF credit	..	..	..	..	..	..	..	..	..	..	..
Central Government	..	..	..	..	..	..	..	..	..	..	..
Rest of General Government	..	..	..	..	..	..	..	..	..	..	..
Non-financial Public Enterprises	..	..	..	..	..	..	..	..	..	..	..
Priv. Sector, incl non-guaranteed	..	..	..	..	..	..	..	..	..	..	..
Short-Term Debt	..	..	..	..	..	..	..	..	..	..	..
Memo Items:					*(Millions of US dollars)*						
Int'l Reserves Excluding Gold	59.6	62.8	86.0	83.5	64.0	131.3	289.5	436.4	503.9	493.4	613.9
Gold Holdings (at market price)	8.3	8.9	10.3	15.4	26.6	44.4	21.0	20.2	24.7	33.9	76.8
SOCIAL INDICATORS											
Total Fertility Rate	6.6	6.4	6.2	5.9	5.9	5.8	5.7	5.6	5.5	5.4	5.4
Infant Mortality Rate	68.8	64.2	59.6	55.0	51.6	48.2	44.8	41.4	38.0	36.8	35.6
Life Expectancy at Birth	61.4	62.1	62.8	63.5	63.9	64.2	64.6	65.0	65.3	65.7	66.0
Urban Population, % of total	78.3	78.2	78.4	78.6	78.9	79.1	79.3	79.5	79.8	80.0	80.3
Food Prod. per capita (1987=100)	..	..	..	..	..	..	..	..	..	..	..
Labor Force, Agriculture (%)	7.7	7.2	6.7	6.2	5.7	5.3	5.0	4.4	3.9	3.6	3.3
Labor Force, Female (%)	5.0	4.9	6.0	6.9	7.8	8.5	9.2	9.8	10.2	10.5	10.8
Primary Schl. Enroll. Ratio	..	99.0	..	..	..	..	96.0	..	97.0	99.0	102.0
Primary Schl. Enroll. Ratio, Female	..	84.0	..	..	..	..	85.0	..	87.0	90.0	93.0
Secondary Schl. Enroll. Ratio	..	51.0	..	..	..	..	52.0	..	50.0	52.0	54.0

1980	1981	1982	1983	1984	1985	1986	1987	1988	1989 estimate	NOTES	BAHRAIN
				(Millions of current US dollars)							**FOREIGN TRADE (CUSTOMS BASIS)**
3,794.8	4,347.0	3,791.0	3,200.0	3,139.3	2,820.0	2,344.0	2,344.0	2,269.0	..	..	Value of Exports, fob
128.8	176.8	245.4	269.6	223.9	148.0	209.0	162.0	..	..	..	Nonfuel Primary Products
3,552.8	3,882.0	2,984.6	2,586.0	2,712.1	2,442.0	1,970.0	1,967.0	1,773.0	..	..	Fuels
113.2	288.2	561.0	344.4	203.3	230.0	165.0	215.0	303.0	..	..	Manufactures
3,479.2	4,124.0	3,615.4	3,342.0	3,523.6	3,158.5	2,426.6	2,613.0	2,635.0	..	..	Value of Imports, cif
311.4	253.8	265.4	242.8	251.9	213.5	229.0	249.0	..	..	..	Nonfuel Primary Products
2,029.3	2,517.0	1,900.4	1,832.1	1,941.1	1,815.8	987.0	1,025.0	1,035.0	..	..	Fuels
1,138.5	1,353.3	1,449.6	1,267.1	1,330.6	1,129.2	1,210.6	1,339.0	1,350.0	..	..	Manufactures
				(Index 1987 = 100)							
140.4	137.6	134.8	124.5	129.2	123.2	93.1	100.0	..	..	..	Terms of Trade
172.0	178.2	154.2	138.5	140.7	134.7	79.7	100.0	..	..	..	Export Prices, fob
122.5	129.5	114.4	111.2	108.9	109.4	85.6	100.0	..	..	..	Import Prices, cif
				(Millions of current US dollars)							**BALANCE OF PAYMENTS**
4,080.1	5,055.9	4,752.4	3,901.9	4,375.0	4,124.2	3,244.4	3,513.0	..	..	..	Exports of Goods & Services
3,433.1	4,177.1	3,695.0	3,119.4	3,204.0	2,896.8	2,202.1	2,429.5	..	..	..	Merchandise, fob
332.9	360.9	567.6	366.8	802.1	914.9	764.4	834.3	..	..	..	Nonfactor Services
314.1	517.8	489.9	415.7	368.9	312.5	277.9	249.2	..	..	..	Factor Services
3,983.5	4,714.1	4,398.9	3,839.6	4,168.9	3,971.3	3,166.8	3,544.0	..	..	..	Imports of Goods & Services
2,987.5	3,559.3	3,167.8	2,935.6	3,131.7	2,796.0	2,164.6	2,442.3	..	..	..	Merchandise, fob
473.7	610.1	729.8	499.5	542.0	484.8	327.1	462.8	..	..	..	Nonfactor Services
522.3	544.7	501.3	404.5	495.2	690.4	675.0	638.8	..	..	..	Factor Services
..	..	..	..	..	..	..	..	..	..	..	Long-Term Interest
-93.4	-106.6	-117.6	-102.1	-125.5	-221.5	-264.6	-235.4	..	..	..	Private Current Transfers, net
..	..	..	..	..	..	..	..	..	..	..	Workers' Remittances
3.2	235.1	235.9	-39.9	80.6	-68.6	-187.0	-266.3	-176.6	..	..	Curr. A/C Bal before Off. Transf.
181.2	194.4	189.6	142.6	124.5	120.2	120.7	113.3	366.5	..	..	Net Official Transfers
184.3	429.5	425.6	102.7	205.1	51.6	-66.2	-153.0	189.9	..	..	Curr. A/C Bal after Off. Transf.
10.3	-2.9	-94.9	41.2	151.3	36.4	-86.4	-68.1	..	..	..	Long-Term Capital, net
-418.0	..	28.5	64.1	140.7	104.8	-31.9	-40.7	..	..	..	Direct Investment
..	..	..	..	..	..	..	..	..	..	..	Long-Term Loans
..	..	..	..	..	..	..	..	..	..	..	Disbursements
..	..	..	..	..	..	..	..	..	..	..	Repayments
428.4	-2.9	-123.4	-22.9	10.6	-68.4	-54.5	-27.4	..	..	..	Other Long-Term Capital
148.3	162.7	-335.0	-252.4	-366.5	182.2	24.3	-101.1	-83.7	..	..	Other Capital, net
-343.0	-589.3	4.4	108.5	10.1	-270.2	128.4	322.2	-106.2	200.4	..	Change in Reserves
				(Bahrain Dinars per US dollar)							Memo Item:
0.380	0.380	0.380	0.380	0.380	0.380	0.380	0.380	0.380	..	..	Conversion Factor (Annual Avg)
				(Millions of US dollars), outstanding at end of year							
..	..	..	..	..	..	..	..	..	..	..	**EXTERNAL DEBT** (Total)
..	..	..	..	..	..	..	..	..	..	..	Long-Term Debt (by debtor)
..	..	..	..	..	..	..	..	..	..	..	Central Bank, incl. IMF credit
..	..	..	..	..	..	..	..	..	..	..	Central Government
..	..	..	..	..	..	..	..	..	..	..	Rest of General Government
..	..	..	..	..	..	..	..	..	..	..	Non-financial Public Enterprises
..	..	..	..	..	..	..	..	..	..	..	Priv. Sector, incl non-guaranteed
..	..	..	..	..	..	..	..	..	..	..	Short-Term Debt
				(Millions of US dollars)							Memo Items:
953.4	1,544.1	1,534.8	1,426.4	1,302.4	1,659.7	1,489.4	1,148.5	1,251.7	1,050.0	..	Int'l Reserves Excluding Gold
88.4	59.6	68.5	57.2	46.2	49.0	58.6	72.6	61.5	60.1	..	Gold Holdings (at market price)
											SOCIAL INDICATORS
5.3	5.2	5.1	5.0	4.9	4.8	4.7	4.6	4.5	4.4	..	Total Fertility Rate
34.4	33.2	32.0	30.8	29.6	28.4	27.2	26.0	25.2	24.3	..	Infant Mortality Rate
66.4	66.7	67.1	67.3	67.5	67.7	67.9	68.1	68.3	68.5	..	Life Expectancy at Birth
80.5	80.7	81.0	81.2	81.5	81.7	81.9	82.2	82.4	82.7	..	Urban Population, % of total
..	..	..	..	..	..	..	..	..	..	..	Food Prod. per capita (1987=100)
3.0	..	..	..	..	..	..	..	..	..	..	Labor Force, Agriculture (%)
11.1	11.0	10.9	10.9	10.8	10.8	10.7	10.6	10.6	10.5	..	Labor Force, Female (%)
104.0	..	104.0	108.0	110.0	111.0	111.0	110.0	..	..	..	Primary Schl. Enroll. Ratio
97.0	95.0	99.0	104.0	108.0	110.0	110.0	108.0	..	..	..	Primary Schl. Enroll. Ratio, Female
65.0	..	78.0	77.0	82.0	86.0	86.0	85.0	..	..	..	Secondary Schl. Enroll. Ratio

BANGLADESH	1969	1970	1971	1972	1973	1974	1975	1976	1977	1978	1979
CURRENT GNP PER CAPITA (US $)	100	100	100	80	80	100	130	140	110	110	120
POPULATION (millions)	65	67	69	71	73	75	77	79	81	83	85
USE AND ORIGIN OF RESOURCES					*(Billions of current Bangladesh Taka)*						
Gross National Product (GNP)	30.14	32.01	30.99	27.70	45.23	71.15	125.69	107.33	104.88	145.88	172.48
Net Factor Income from Abroad	0.25	0.27	0.11	-0.04	0.12	0.06	-0.05	-0.13	-0.48	-0.48	-0.33
GDP at Market Prices	29.89	31.73	30.88	27.74	45.11	71.09	125.74	107.46	105.36	146.37	172.82
Resource Balance	-1.05	-1.33	-1.37	-2.24	0.45	-4.98	-6.57	-13.96	-5.35	-13.87	-16.87
Exports of Goods & NFServices	2.44	2.64	1.94	1.57	2.71	2.41	3.66	4.98	7.14	7.55	8.99
Imports of Goods & NFServices	3.49	3.97	3.31	3.81	2.26	7.39	10.22	18.94	12.49	21.42	25.86
Domestic Absorption	30.94	33.06	32.25	29.97	44.66	76.06	132.31	121.42	110.71	160.23	189.69
Private Consumption, etc.	23.24	25.22	29.71	28.67	38.81	67.26	120.49	105.98	92.48	135.99	159.24
General Gov't Consumption	3.96	4.24	..	..	1.82	3.40	4.02	4.49	5.59	7.20	10.94
Gross Domestic Investment	3.74	3.60	2.54	1.30	4.03	5.40	7.80	10.95	12.65	17.05	19.51
Fixed Investment	..	..	..	..	..	..	..	..	..	..	..
Indirect Taxes, net	1.00	1.10	1.07	0.96	1.07	2.11	1.79	6.07	5.49	7.17	8.91
GDP at factor cost	28.89	30.63	29.81	26.78	44.04	68.98	123.95	101.39	99.87	139.20	163.91
Agriculture	16.56	17.31	15.76	16.53	26.10	41.50	78.62	57.34	53.67	80.09	91.35
Industry	2.75	2.77	2.37	1.68	4.56	7.28	14.17	13.88	14.70	19.87	25.98
Manufacturing	1.75	1.84	1.69	1.10	2.90	4.27	8.38	8.17	8.66	13.36	15.83
Services, etc.	10.58	11.65	12.75	9.52	14.46	22.30	32.94	36.24	36.99	46.41	55.49
Gross Domestic Saving	2.69	2.27	1.17	-0.93	4.48	0.43	1.23	-3.01	7.30	3.18	2.64
Gross National Saving	..	..	1.35	-0.89	4.87	0.65	1.60	-2.70	7.75	4.39	4.53
					(Billions of 1987 Bangladesh Taka)						
Gross National Product	313.86	332.63	315.00	273.01	279.46	312.57	322.78	361.91	365.24	389.57	407.63
GDP at Market Prices	311.30	329.89	314.06	273.40	278.69	312.30	322.92	362.33	366.88	390.86	408.43
Resource Balance	-29.32	-33.02	-26.97	-29.91	-1.15	-28.15	-23.30	-30.90	-12.87	-34.91	-33.41
Exports of Goods & NFServices	16.30	18.01	13.03	10.05	18.67	15.53	18.55	17.39	22.84	24.41	24.24
Imports of Goods & NFServices	45.62	51.03	40.00	39.96	19.82	43.68	41.85	48.30	35.71	59.32	57.65
Domestic Absorption	340.61	362.91	341.03	303.31	279.84	340.45	346.22	393.24	379.75	425.76	441.84
Private Consumption, etc.	..	..	..	..	..	..	..	..	..	..	..
General Gov't Consumption	..	..	..	..	..	..	..	..	..	..	..
Gross Domestic Investment	55.19	51.28	38.93	17.27	33.93	32.20	28.60	30.26	36.11	45.90	47.91
Fixed Investment	..	..	..	..	..	..	..	..	..	..	..
GDP at factor cost	300.95	318.55	303.35	264.18	272.18	303.12	318.45	342.05	347.85	371.87	387.62
Agriculture	188.05	198.24	189.31	169.04	169.50	187.21	185.32	206.94	200.69	218.02	214.84
Industry	33.14	33.03	26.11	13.80	23.65	27.06	38.42	40.26	43.29	44.15	54.25
Manufacturing	16.42	17.15	14.54	7.97	13.21	15.53	25.01	26.82	27.91	28.33	32.24
Services, etc.	94.70	102.69	101.27	91.50	88.34	101.01	99.87	116.51	123.61	129.93	138.68
Memo Items:											
Capacity to Import	31.85	33.91	23.46	16.51	23.77	14.25	14.97	12.70	20.42	20.91	20.03
Terms of Trade Adjustment	15.55	15.91	10.43	6.46	5.10	-1.27	-3.59	-4.69	-2.42	-3.49	-4.21
Gross Domestic Income	326.85	345.79	324.49	279.86	283.79	311.03	319.34	357.64	364.45	387.36	404.22
Gross National Income	329.42	348.54	325.43	279.47	284.56	311.30	319.19	357.22	362.82	386.07	403.42
DOMESTIC PRICES/DEFLATORS					*(Index 1987 = 100)*						
Overall (GDP)	9.6	9.6	9.8	10.1	16.2	22.8	38.9	29.7	28.7	37.4	42.3
Domestic Absorption	9.1	9.1	9.5	9.9	16.0	22.3	38.2	30.9	29.2	37.6	42.9
Agriculture	8.8	8.7	8.3	9.8	15.4	22.2	42.4	27.7	26.7	36.7	42.5
Industry	8.3	8.4	9.1	12.2	19.3	26.9	36.9	34.5	34.0	45.0	47.9
Manufacturing	10.7	10.7	11.6	13.9	21.9	27.5	33.5	30.5	31.0	47.2	49.1
Consumer Price Index	7.9	8.1	8.1	11.4	17.0	26.3	32.0	32.8	34.3	36.1	41.4
MANUFACTURING ACTIVITY											
Employment (1987=100)	59.3	46.4	52.9	44.4	41.2	75.9	80.2	82.6	81.3	88.5	90.1
Real Earnings per Empl. (1987=100)	107.3	132.9	140.5	106.4	83.0	75.1	68.6	73.4	73.7	85.9	100.5
Real Output per Empl. (1987=100)	83.7	95.0	73.2	53.8	49.4	47.4	57.1	83.3	99.3	70.7	79.4
Earnings as % of Value Added	24.4	26.4	33.8	35.0	30.0	35.6	32.7	32.4	27.0	29.6	34.5
MONETARY HOLDINGS					*(Billions of current Bangladesh Taka)*						
Money Supply, Broadly Defined	..	..	..	..	..	13.99	14.74	17.47	21.61	27.30	33.40
Money	..	..	..	..	..	8.39	8.28	9.22	11.67	14.64	18.36
Currency Outside Banks	..	..	..	..	3.21	4.10	3.62	3.82	4.90	6.33	7.11
Demand Deposits	..	..	..	..	..	4.29	4.66	5.40	6.76	8.31	11.24
Quasi-Money	..	..	..	..	..	5.60	6.46	8.25	9.94	12.67	15.05
					(Millions of current Bangladesh Taka)						
GOVERNMENT DEFICIT (-) OR SURPLUS	..	..	..	..	-864.00	-330.00	1,444.00	-3,728.00	209.00	4,274.00	874.00
Current Revenue	..	..	..	..	4,022.00	5,970.00	11,863.00	10,763.00	15,912.00	21,672.00	24,098.00
Current Expenditure	..	..	..	..	..	..	..	..	..	..	..
Current Budget Balance	..	..	..	..	..	..	..	..	..	..	..
Capital Receipts	..	..	..	..	..	..	..	..	..	..	..
Capital Payments	..	..	..	..	..	..	..	..	..	..	..

1980	1981	1982	1983	1984	1985	1986	1987	1988	1989 estimate	NOTES	BANGLADESH
140	160	160	150	140	150	160	160	170	180	..	**CURRENT GNP PER CAPITA (US $)**
88	90	92	95	98	101	103	106	109	112	..	**POPULATION (millions)**
				(Billions of current Bangladesh Taka)							**USE AND ORIGIN OF RESOURCES**
198.21	232.90	263.19	285.83	348.31	414.64	461.41	537.40	585.98	646.14	C f	Gross National Product (GNP)
0.22	-0.37	-1.95	-2.59	-1.61	-2.38	-3.78	-3.77	-4.22	-4.30	f	Net Factor Income from Abroad
197.98	233.26	265.14	288.42	349.92	417.02	465.19	541.16	590.20	650.44	C	GDP at Market Prices
-25.57	-29.17	-37.08	-35.71	-37.31	-44.34	-46.14	-48.29	-55.16	-68.59	..	Resource Balance
11.34	15.25	16.85	21.36	26.01	30.28	31.17	39.81	46.43	50.07	..	Exports of Goods & NFServices
36.91	44.42	53.93	57.07	63.32	74.62	77.31	88.10	101.59	118.66	..	Imports of Goods & NFServices
223.56	262.44	302.22	324.14	387.24	461.36	511.34	589.46	645.36	719.03	..	Domestic Absorption
181.08	209.56	243.82	268.19	321.06	379.75	413.60	474.39	520.44	589.71	..	Private Consumption, etc.
12.68	15.64	18.56	16.73	23.09	29.61	40.47	47.08	54.89	53.34	..	General Gov't Consumption
29.80	37.23	39.84	39.21	43.08	52.01	57.27	67.99	70.03	75.98	..	Gross Domestic Investment
29.80	37.23	39.84	39.21	43.08	52.01	57.27	67.99	70.03	75.98	..	Fixed Investment
10.35	13.46	13.82	15.47	18.85	21.79	25.52	30.08	32.70	37.35	..	Indirect Taxes, net
187.63	219.80	251.32	272.95	331.07	395.23	439.68	511.08	557.50	613.09	B C	GDP at factor cost
99.50	108.95	121.84	135.87	169.33	212.49	222.41	259.93	268.39	288.06	..	Agriculture
29.49	36.70	42.53	44.71	50.98	59.50	66.11	72.59	82.62	93.57	..	Industry
19.56	22.86	25.70	28.07	30.95	34.63	37.33	40.21	43.42	47.97	f	Manufacturing
69.00	87.61	100.77	107.84	129.61	145.03	176.67	208.65	239.19	268.81	..	Services, etc.
4.23	8.06	2.76	3.50	5.77	7.67	11.13	19.70	14.87	7.39	..	Gross Domestic Saving
7.70	14.51	10.19	16.37	20.05	18.64	25.16	38.56	35.66	30.07	..	Gross National Saving
				(Billions of 1987 Bangladesh Taka)							
414.02	440.80	441.94	457.24	477.80	494.29	518.17	537.40	547.63	560.12	C f	Gross National Product
413.56	441.48	445.13	461.23	479.97	497.15	522.37	541.16	551.60	563.84	C	GDP at Market Prices
-51.93	-44.77	-42.44	-39.45	-44.28	-61.05	-45.70	-48.29	-58.02	-57.79	..	Resource Balance
25.00	28.73	30.54	31.27	31.74	30.02	34.17	39.81	42.59	45.53	..	Exports of Goods & NFServices
76.93	73.49	72.98	70.72	76.02	91.07	79.87	88.10	100.61	103.33	..	Imports of Goods & NFServices
465.48	486.25	487.57	500.68	524.26	558.20	568.08	589.46	609.62	621.63	..	Domestic Absorption
..	..	..	420.98	436.95	458.58	458.96	474.39	492.19	501.68	..	Private Consumption, etc.
..	..	..	25.43	30.49	35.53	45.99	47.08	53.65	54.77	..	General Gov't Consumption
67.05	69.12	67.66	54.27	56.82	64.09	63.13	67.99	63.77	65.18	..	Gross Domestic Investment
..	..	..	..	..	..	..	..	..	..	..	Fixed Investment
392.06	416.20	422.08	436.65	454.28	471.30	493.72	511.08	521.09	531.46	B C	GDP at factor cost
215.19	226.70	228.76	239.32	243.16	245.45	260.27	259.93	257.59	258.27	..	Agriculture
51.65	55.54	57.23	57.57	62.35	66.21	67.72	72.59	77.28	81.26	..	Industry
32.90	34.69	35.24	34.67	35.94	37.11	37.79	40.21	41.30	42.45	f	Manufacturing
146.72	159.11	158.75	164.34	174.47	185.49	194.38	208.65	216.74	224.30	..	Services, etc.
											Memo Items:
23.64	25.23	22.81	26.47	31.22	36.96	32.20	39.81	45.98	43.60	..	Capacity to Import
-1.37	-3.50	-7.73	-4.80	-0.52	6.93	-1.97	0.00	3.39	-1.93	..	Terms of Trade Adjustment
412.19	437.98	437.40	456.43	479.46	504.08	520.41	541.16	554.99	561.91	..	Gross Domestic Income
412.65	437.30	434.21	452.44	477.28	501.22	516.20	537.40	551.02	558.20	..	Gross National Income
				(Index 1987 = 100)							**DOMESTIC PRICES/DEFLATORS**
47.9	52.8	59.6	62.5	72.9	83.9	89.1	100.0	107.0	115.4	..	Overall (GDP)
48.0	54.0	62.0	64.7	73.9	82.7	90.0	100.0	105.9	115.7	..	Domestic Absorption
46.2	48.1	53.3	56.8	69.6	86.6	85.5	100.0	104.2	111.5	..	Agriculture
57.1	66.1	74.3	77.7	81.8	89.9	97.6	100.0	106.9	115.1	..	Industry
59.4	65.9	72.9	81.0	86.1	93.3	98.8	100.0	105.1	113.0	..	Manufacturing
47.0	54.6	61.4	67.2	74.3	82.2	91.3	100.0	109.3	120.3	..	Consumer Price Index
											MANUFACTURING ACTIVITY
92.6	98.5	102.1	100.8	101.4	105.2	104.9	100.0	96.8	..	J	Employment (1987=100)
106.2	102.2	93.0	91.4	94.0	95.3	105.2	100.0	100.3	..	J	Real Earnings per Empl. (1987=100)
81.8	81.1	82.7	80.2	91.9	92.0	94.3	100.0	106.9	..	J	Real Output per Empl. (1987=100)
31.3	34.0	32.2	28.7	26.9	29.8	29.7	28.8	27.9	..	J	Earnings as % of Value Added
				(Billions of current Bangladesh Taka)							**MONETARY HOLDINGS**
33.56	43.93	45.97	58.98	83.86	105.34	123.38	138.71	164.08	190.78	..	Money Supply, Broadly Defined
20.17	22.72	23.34	31.64	42.27	45.95	50.00	51.00	53.16	60.00	..	Money
8.27	9.14	9.74	13.44	17.25	17.67	19.03	22.49	25.28	27.29	..	Currency Outside Banks
11.90	13.57	13.59	18.19	25.02	28.28	30.97	28.51	27.88	32.72	..	Demand Deposits
13.39	21.21	22.64	27.35	41.59	59.39	73.39	87.71	110.92	130.78	..	Quasi-Money
				(Millions of current Bangladesh Taka)							**GOVERNMENT DEFICIT (-) OR SURPLUS**
4,976.00	-7,396.00	3,135.00	9,003.00	2,873.00	-5,924.00	..	..	..	..	C	GOVERNMENT DEFICIT (-) OR SURPLUS
28,068.00	30,078.00	41,232.00	44,257.00	44,355.00	48,124.00	..	..	..	..		Current Revenue
..	..	..	..	..	..	..	..	..	..		Current Expenditure
..	..	..	..	..	..	..	..	..	..		Current Budget Balance
..	..	..	..	..	..	..	..	..	..		Capital Receipts
..	..	..	..	..	..	..	..	..	..		Capital Payments

BANGLADESH	1969	1970	1971	1972	1973	1974	1975	1976	1977	1978	1979
FOREIGN TRADE (CUSTOMS BASIS)				*(Millions of current US dollars)*							
Value of Exports, fob	..	..	..	321.0	326.0	367.6	264.8	361.7	435.0	552.8	661.6
Nonfuel Primary Products	..	..	..	123.8	126.7	151.1	84.3	137.9	177.1	199.8	223.6
Fuels	..	..	..	0.2	0.3	0.2	0.2	1.4	6.7	6.7	4.0
Manufactures	..	..	..	197.0	199.0	216.4	180.2	222.5	251.3	346.4	434.1
Value of Imports, cif	..	..	..	611.0	834.0	1,032.0	1,199.5	1,136.5	1,057.5	1,338.0	1,710.5
Nonfuel Primary Products	..	..	..	363.0	384.2	544.3	631.0	469.9	403.8	463.6	509.7
Fuels	..	..	..	32.0	93.8	92.0	97.0	120.0	172.0	193.9	247.0
Manufactures	..	..	..	216.0	356.0	395.7	471.5	546.6	481.7	680.4	953.8
				(Index 1987 = 100)							
Terms of Trade	..	..	..	125.7	133.3	103.1	98.8	108.7	113.1	110.1	108.2
Export Prices, fob	..	..	..	46.8	56.8	75.5	72.0	71.9	79.1	83.6	95.4
Import Prices, cif	..	..	..	37.3	42.6	73.3	72.8	66.1	70.0	75.9	88.2
BALANCE OF PAYMENTS				*(Millions of current US dollars)*							
Exports of Goods & Services	..	526.0	344.0	355.0	411.7	417.5	439.5	450.9	488.6	598.6	765.1
Merchandise, fob	..	420.0	295.0	260.0	354.2	369.7	344.0	371.9	404.6	489.8	609.7
Nonfactor Services	..	61.0	40.0	76.0	43.1	34.4	82.5	62.9	59.4	82.2	113.8
Factor Services	..	45.0	9.0	19.0	14.4	13.4	13.0	16.1	24.6	26.6	41.6
Imports of Goods & Services	..	769.8	664.9	800.8	816.7	984.1	1,477.8	1,361.4	988.0	1,489.7	1,738.8
Merchandise, fob	..	660.0	570.0	683.0	780.0	925.0	1,403.0	1,275.0	875.0	1,349.0	1,556.0
Nonfactor Services	..	105.0	94.0	113.0	35.0	48.7	56.3	51.1	57.5	82.0	118.9
Factor Services	..	4.8	0.9	4.8	1.7	10.4	18.5	35.3	55.5	58.7	63.9
Long-Term Interest	..	0.0	0.0	0.0	4.1	9.2	16.6	28.2	29.7	37.0	40.4
Private Current Transfers, net	..	9.8	9.9	9.8	34.3	19.4	35.0	28.8	60.2	113.1	142.9
Workers' Remittances	..	0.0	0.0	0.0	0.0	0.0	8.5	15.5	44.8	102.1	127.0
Curr. A/C Bal before Off. Transf.	..	-234.0	-311.0	-436.0	-370.7	-547.2	-1,003.3	-881.7	-439.2	-778.0	-830.8
Net Official Transfers	..	120.0	160.0	210.0	431.0	173.8	382.3	244.7	264.8	392.6	553.2
Curr. A/C Bal after Off. Transf.	..	-114.0	-151.0	-226.0	60.3	-373.4	-621.0	-637.0	-174.4	-385.4	-277.6
Long-Term Capital, net	..	160.0	140.0	95.0	95.5	190.9	506.0	504.9	256.8	456.4	474.1
Direct Investment	..	..	..	..	0.0	0.0	0.0	0.0	0.0	0.0	0.0
Long-Term Loans	..	0.0	0.0	59.8	308.9	502.0	550.0	256.9	273.8	432.8	516.9
Disbursements	..	0.0	0.0	59.8	315.1	517.9	605.4	297.2	316.1	486.9	592.6
Repayments	..	0.0	0.0	0.0	6.2	15.9	55.4	40.3	42.3	54.1	75.7
Other Long-Term Capital	..	160.0	140.0	35.2	-213.4	-311.1	-44.0	248.0	-17.0	23.6	-42.8
Other Capital, net	..	0.0	0.0	65.3	-252.4	89.9	160.0	-1.6	47.9	-118.9	-49.3
Change in Reserves	..	-46.0	11.0	65.7	96.6	92.6	-45.0	133.7	-130.3	47.9	-147.2
Memo Item:				*(Bangladesh Taka per US dollar)*							
Conversion Factor (Annual Avg)	4.760	4.760	4.760	6.030	7.780	7.970	8.880	14.850	15.470	15.120	15.220
				(Millions of US dollars), outstanding at end of year							
EXTERNAL DEBT (Total)	..	15	15	161	496	1,253	1,812	2,117	2,456	3,026	3,196
Long-Term Debt (by debtor)	..	15	15	161	495	1,253	1,810	2,111	2,425	2,949	3,080
Central Bank, incl. IMF credit	..	0	0	68	75	169	212	298	282	328	373
Central Government	..	15	15	93	401	1,059	1,561	1,798	2,126	2,604	2,688
Rest of General Government	..	..	..	..	..	..	..	..	..	..	..
Non-financial Public Enterprises	..	0	0	0	18	25	36	15	17	18	19
Priv. Sector, incl non-guaranteed	..	0	0	0	0	0	0	0	0	0	0
Short-Term Debt	..	0	0	0	1	0	2	6	31	77	116
Memo Items:				*(Millions of US dollars)*							
Int'l Reserves Excluding Gold	..	..	..	270.5	143.2	138.2	148.3	288.9	232.7	315.2	386.3
Gold Holdings (at market price)	..	..	..	..	..	..	..	..	8.8	6.0	27.4
SOCIAL INDICATORS											
Total Fertility Rate	7.0	7.0	7.0	7.0	6.9	6.7	6.6	6.4	6.3	6.2	6.2
Infant Mortality Rate	140.0	140.0	140.0	140.0	139.4	138.8	138.2	137.6	137.0	135.2	133.4
Life Expectancy at Birth	44.9	44.9	44.9	44.9	45.2	45.6	46.0	46.4	46.8	47.1	47.5
Urban Population, % of total	7.3	7.6	7.9	8.2	8.5	8.8	9.1	9.4	9.6	9.9	10.1
Food Prod. per capita (1987=100)	134.1	123.3	110.9	105.8	113.9	107.2	115.5	107.4	113.0	113.1	108.7
Labor Force, Agriculture (%)	81.9	81.4	80.7	80.0	79.4	78.7	78.1	77.4	76.7	76.1	75.4
Labor Force, Female (%)	5.3	5.4	5.5	5.6	5.7	5.7	5.8	5.9	6.0	6.1	6.2
Primary Schl. Enroll. Ratio	..	54.0	..	..	..	..	73.0	79.0	72.0	67.0	65.0
Primary Schl. Enroll. Ratio, Female	..	35.0	..	..	..	..	51.0	57.0	40.0	46.0	50.0
Secondary Schl. Enroll. Ratio	..	..	..	..	..	..	26.0	21.0	21.0	18.0	15.0

1980	1981	1982	1983	1984	1985	1986	1987	1988	1989 estimate	NOTES	BANGLADESH
											FOREIGN TRADE (CUSTOMS BASIS)
758.9	662.0	671.1	704.9	811.2	934.0	819.0	1,074.0	1,231.0	1,324.0	C	Value of Exports, fob
249.2	214.8	239.0	245.3	269.8	291.6	266.8	270.0	361.0	..	..	Nonfuel Primary Products
0.0	0.0	15.0	26.2	15.2	23.4	7.2	13.0	19.0	..	..	Fuels
509.7	447.2	417.0	433.4	526.2	619.0	545.0	791.0	851.0	845.9	..	Manufactures
2,253.5	2,649.0	2,581.0	2,246.0	2,353.0	2,647.0	2,364.0	2,620.0	2,987.0	3,204.0	C	Value of Imports, cif
642.5	571.0	584.3	637.9	700.7	872.3	521.1	919.0	969.1	..	..	Nonfuel Primary Products
416.0	509.0	485.7	370.1	300.0	404.7	375.9	352.0	293.9	..	f	Fuels
1,195.0	1,569.0	1,511.0	1,238.0	1,352.3	1,370.0	1,467.0	1,349.0	1,724.0	..	f	Manufactures
				(Index 1987 = 100)							
94.9	93.8	98.7	99.2	108.5	118.4	103.8	100.0	101.0	..	..	Terms of Trade
97.7	94.4	95.2	94.7	100.8	109.0	92.8	100.0	108.1	..	..	Export Prices, fob
102.9	100.6	96.4	95.5	92.9	92.1	89.4	100.0	106.9	..	..	Import Prices, cif
				(Millions of current US dollars)							**BALANCE OF PAYMENTS**
976.4	984.9	874.0	916.0	1,090.0	1,220.0	1,079.0	1,335.8	1,541.1	1,677.0	C f	Exports of Goods & Services
722.3	710.7	626.0	686.0	811.0	934.0	819.0	1,074.0	1,231.0	1,286.0	..	Merchandise, fob
162.6	222.3	214.0	213.0	222.4	228.0	223.9	226.6	255.2	272.0	..	Nonfactor Services
91.5	51.9	34.0	17.0	56.6	58.0	36.1	35.2	54.9	119.0	..	Factor Services
2,622.1	2,792.4	2,890.0	2,651.0	2,664.0	3,011.2	2,749.1	3,033.1	3,440.6	3,915.0	C f	Imports of Goods & Services
2,372.0	2,533.0	2,572.0	2,309.0	2,353.0	2,647.0	2,364.0	2,620.0	2,987.0	3,375.0	..	Merchandise, fob
172.8	184.8	187.0	156.0	190.0	216.6	222.9	256.3	265.7	317.0	..	Nonfactor Services
77.3	74.6	131.0	186.0	121.0	147.6	162.2	156.8	187.9	223.0	..	Factor Services
46.9	54.8	59.1	65.4	72.0	90.9	108.4	138.3	140.6	138.8	..	Long-Term Interest
210.1	379.0	424.0	628.0	626.8	476.8	586.0	731.0	788.0	836.0	f	Private Current Transfers, net
197.4	362.3	368.3	575.7	526.6	363.7	497.4	617.4	737.0	771.0	..	Workers' Remittances
-1,435.6	-1,428.5	-1,592.0	-1,107.0	-947.2	-1,314.4	-1,084.1	-966.3	-1,111.5	-1,402.0	..	Curr. A/C Bal before Off. Transf.
592.1	584.4	697.3	720.0	708.0	700.8	962.6	656.9	823.0	672.9	f	Net Official Transfers
-843.5	-844.1	-894.7	-387.0	-239.2	-613.6	-121.5	-309.4	-288.5	-729.1	..	Curr. A/C Bal after Off. Transf.
682.8	553.0	499.8	551.5	470.2	546.2	152.4	681.1	652.0	644.3	C f	Long-Term Capital, net
0.0	0.0	0.0	0.0	0.2	-0.4	2.1	2.4	0.0	..	..	Direct Investment
595.7	467.4	578.5	476.0	511.3	559.0	917.3	787.8	710.5	840.6	..	Long-Term Loans
658.3	547.2	671.9	538.5	596.0	668.9	1,067.5	951.7	908.2	1,014.9	..	Disbursements
62.6	79.8	93.4	62.5	84.7	109.9	150.2	163.9	197.7	174.3	..	Repayments
87.1	85.6	-78.7	75.5	-41.3	-12.4	-767.0	-109.1	-58.5	-196.3	..	Other Long-Term Capital
-42.9	-107.8	-112.6	35.8	124.0	-9.6	97.1	-168.7	-219.0	179.6	C f	Other Capital, net
203.6	398.9	507.5	-200.3	-355.0	77.0	-128.0	-203.0	-144.5	-94.8	..	Change in Reserves
				(Bangladesh Taka per US dollar)							**Memo Item:**
15.480	16.340	20.040	23.760	24.950	26.000	29.890	30.630	31.250	32.140	..	Conversion Factor (Annual Avg)
				(Millions of US dollars), outstanding at end of year							
4,056	4,455	5,019	5,435	5,632	6,629	8,032	9,891	10,389	10,712	..	**EXTERNAL DEBT** (Total)
3,844	4,227	4,810	5,265	5,499	6,494	7,907	9,817	10,339	10,644	..	Long-Term Debt (by debtor)
451	486	571	584	477	540	568	875	868	738	..	Central Bank, incl. IMF credit
3,371	3,720	4,217	4,661	5,005	5,937	7,295	8,919	9,452	9,892	..	Central Government
..	..	..	..	..	..	..	..	..	..	..	Rest of General Government
22	21	23	20	17	17	44	23	19	14	..	Non-financial Public Enterprises
0	0	0	0	0	0	0	0	0	..	..	Priv. Sector, incl non-guaranteed
212	228	209	170	133	135	125	74	50	68	..	Short-Term Debt
				(Millions of US dollars)							**Memo Items:**
299.6	138.4	182.6	524.1	389.9	336.5	409.1	843.1	1,046.1	501.5	..	Int'l Reserves Excluding Gold
31.5	21.3	24.4	21.4	16.5	17.5	20.9	25.9	30.4	30.6	..	Gold Holdings (at market price)
											SOCIAL INDICATORS
6.1	6.1	6.0	5.9	5.8	5.7	5.6	5.5	5.5	5.4	..	Total Fertility Rate
131.6	129.8	128.0	126.2	124.4	122.6	120.8	119.0	117.6	116.2	..	Infant Mortality Rate
47.9	48.3	48.6	49.1	49.5	49.9	50.3	50.8	51.0	51.2	..	Life Expectancy at Birth
10.4	10.7	11.0	11.3	11.6	11.9	12.2	12.6	12.9	13.3	..	Urban Population, % of total
110.7	107.1	107.9	107.6	104.7	105.5	103.7	100.0	98.4	105.2	..	Food Prod. per capita (1987=100)
74.8	..	..	..	..	..	..	..	..	..	..	Labor Force, Agriculture (%)
6.3	6.4	6.5	6.6	6.7	6.8	6.9	7.0	7.1	7.2	..	Labor Force, Female (%)
62.0	..	61.0	62.0	62.0	60.0	60.0	59.0	70.0	..	..	Primary Schl. Enroll. Ratio
46.0	52.0	51.0	47.0	55.0	50.0	50.0	49.0	64.0	..	..	Primary Schl. Enroll. Ratio, Female
18.0	..	..	18.0	19.0	18.0	18.0	18.0	18.0	..	..	Secondary Schl. Enroll. Ratio

BARBADOS	1969	1970	1971	1972	1973	1974	1975	1976	1977	1978	1979
CURRENT GNP PER CAPITA (US $)	680	750	830	910	1,040	1,220	1,520	1,740	1,960	2,250	2,670
POPULATION (thousands)	238	239	240	242	243	245	246	246	247	248	247

USE AND ORIGIN OF RESOURCES *(Millions of current Barbados Dollars)*

	1969	1970	1971	1972	1973	1974	1975	1976	1977	1978	1979
Gross National Product (GNP)	308.7	361.6	402.1	444.6	554.6	704.2	809.8	877.8	989.9	1,115.4	1,345.3
Net Factor Income from Abroad	-0.1	-1.4	-0.8	-3.8	-3.3	5.1	-2.6	4.4	-3.7	3.3	-3.1
GDP at Market Prices	308.8	363.0	402.9	448.4	557.9	699.1	812.4	873.4	993.6	1,112.1	1,348.4
Resource Balance	-50.5	-69.4	-51.0	-59.5	-64.7	-49.0	-81.5	-163.8	-146.4	-87.8	-130.0
Exports of Goods & NFServices	190.2	216.0	246.7	290.8	336.5	435.6	409.3	395.1	503.0	645.6	867.8
Imports of Goods & NFServices	240.7	285.4	297.7	350.3	401.2	484.6	490.8	558.9	649.4	733.4	997.8
Domestic Absorption	359.3	432.4	453.9	507.9	622.6	748.1	893.9	1,037.2	1,140.0	1,199.9	1,478.4
Private Consumption, etc.	243.4	289.9	306.7	349.3	417.9	505.2	602.9	649.9	773.8	755.7	950.9
General Gov't Consumption	41.7	47.7	54.2	58.8	80.8	83.4	134.8	151.4	172.1	189.7	210.3
Gross Domestic Investment	74.2	94.8	93.0	99.8	123.9	159.5	156.2	235.9	194.1	254.5	317.2
Fixed Investment	74.2	94.8	93.0	99.8	123.9	159.5	156.2	235.9	194.1	254.5	317.2
Indirect Taxes, net	35.5	43.1	47.7	53.3	59.0	58.7	111.8	85.4	103.5	127.6	152.2
GDP at factor cost	273.3	319.9	355.2	395.1	498.9	640.4	700.6	788.0	890.1	984.5	1,196.2
Agriculture	32.7	35.1	33.4	39.0	51.7	68.5	93.4	76.8	91.8	91.7	109.8
Industry	55.1	62.5	69.7	76.5	92.2	125.8	130.1	153.9	181.2	210.1	252.1
Manufacturing	..	25.4	29.6	34.2	43.8	62.6	71.9	84.8	102.6	112.4	136.4
Services, etc.	185.5	222.3	252.1	279.6	355.0	446.1	477.1	557.3	617.1	682.7	834.3
Gross Domestic Saving	23.7	25.4	42.0	40.3	59.2	110.5	74.7	72.1	47.7	166.7	187.2
Gross National Saving	..	31.8	48.8	45.1	67.2	128.7	85.8	98.2	69.6	199.1	218.1

(Millions of 1987 Barbados Dollars)

	1969	1970	1971	1972	1973	1974	1975	1976	1977	1978	1979
Gross National Product	1,853.7	2,026.1	2,122.1	2,148.5	2,181.1	2,107.0	2,168.5	2,187.0	2,260.7	2,415.9	2,588.4
GDP at Market Prices	1,876.8	2,058.6	2,152.0	2,192.5	2,220.2	2,116.3	2,201.4	2,201.9	2,296.2	2,437.1	2,625.3
Resource Balance	..	..	..	..	..	..	..	..	..	..	..
Exports of Goods & NFServices	..	..	..	..	..	..	..	..	..	..	..
Imports of Goods & NFServices	..	..	..	..	..	..	..	..	..	..	..
Domestic Absorption	..	..	..	..	..	..	..	..	..	..	..
Private Consumption, etc.	..	..	..	..	..	..	..	..	..	..	..
General Gov't Consumption	..	..	..	..	..	..	..	..	..	..	..
Gross Domestic Investment	..	..	..	..	..	..	..	..	..	..	..
Fixed Investment	..	..	..	..	..	..	..	..	..	..	..
GDP at factor cost	1,616.6	1,766.2	1,848.4	1,883.7	1,935.5	1,889.7	1,850.3	1,936.5	2,005.1	2,102.9	2,270.4
Agriculture	254.5	269.6	243.0	204.4	214.5	203.0	196.1	210.1	214.5	214.5	232.0
Industry	356.7	374.3	377.2	396.1	423.3	402.5	398.0	462.3	439.3	465.2	527.6
Manufacturing	..	175.5	191.3	211.3	226.5	215.8	238.9	279.2	274.0	280.6	319.9
Services, etc.	1,029.8	1,143.9	1,235.9	1,278.5	1,296.6	1,282.5	1,254.6	1,265.0	1,350.1	1,421.9	1,510.8

Memo Items:

	1969	1970	1971	1972	1973	1974	1975	1976	1977	1978	1979
Capacity to Import	..	..	..	..	..	..	..	..	..	..	..
Terms of Trade Adjustment	..	..	..	..	..	..	..	..	..	..	..
Gross Domestic Income	..	..	..	..	..	..	..	..	..	..	..
Gross National Income	..	..	..	..	..	..	..	..	..	..	..

DOMESTIC PRICES/DEFLATORS *(Index 1987 = 100)*

	1969	1970	1971	1972	1973	1974	1975	1976	1977	1978	1979
Overall (GDP)	16.5	17.6	18.7	20.5	25.1	33.0	36.9	39.7	43.3	45.6	51.4
Domestic Absorption	..	..	..	..	..	..	..	..	..	..	..
Agriculture	12.8	13.0	13.7	19.1	24.1	33.8	47.6	36.6	42.8	42.7	47.3
Industry	15.4	16.7	18.5	19.3	21.8	31.3	32.7	33.3	41.2	45.2	47.8
Manufacturing	..	14.5	15.5	16.2	19.3	29.0	30.1	30.4	37.4	40.1	42.6
Consumer Price Index	16.2	17.4	18.7	21.0	24.5	34.0	40.9	43.0	46.6	51.0	57.7

MANUFACTURING ACTIVITY

	1969	1970	1971	1972	1973	1974	1975	1976	1977	1978	1979
Employment (1987=100)	..	77.2	87.8	92.0	97.9	86.9	90.3	95.9	108.6	87.0	96.3
Real Earnings per Empl. (1987=100)	..	79.4	77.0	79.3	75.9	68.9	60.7	63.4	63.1	70.6	64.0
Real Output per Empl. (1987=100)	..	108.6	101.3	108.9	106.9	105.9	107.1	113.0	91.8	112.1	114.1
Earnings as % of Value Added	..	56.7	54.9	51.9	51.1	46.9	53.1	56.2	61.7	51.6	53.7

MONETARY HOLDINGS *(Millions of current Barbados Dollars)*

	1969	1970	1971	1972	1973	1974	1975	1976	1977	1978	1979
Money Supply, Broadly Defined	169.4	193.9	228.5	240.1	253.8	311.2	362.4	413.0	455.5	512.6	645.9
Money	56.8	55.7	62.5	67.8	74.0	88.3	105.5	113.5	135.2	160.7	222.2
Currency Outside Banks	15.7	21.2	21.4	23.7	26.8	33.9	40.8	46.7	55.2	65.8	80.2
Demand Deposits	41.1	34.5	41.1	44.1	47.2	54.4	64.7	66.8	80.0	94.9	142.0
Quasi-Money	112.6	138.2	166.0	172.3	179.7	222.9	257.0	299.5	320.3	351.9	423.6

GOVERNMENT DEFICIT (-) OR SURPLUS *(Millions of current Barbados Dollars)*

	1969	1970	1971	1972	1973	1974	1975	1976	1977	1978	1979
	..	..	..	-8.00	-33.80	-22.00	-20.00	-58.50	-62.80	-4.30	-20.90
Current Revenue	..	..	..	119.50	138.60	177.50	214.20	230.30	267.00	330.00	377.50
Current Expenditure	..	..	..	102.00	139.10	161.00	185.30	227.20	244.60	261.00	..
Current Budget Balance	..	..	..	17.50	-0.50	16.50	28.90	3.10	22.40	69.00	..
Capital Receipts	..	..	..	..	..	..	..	..	..	..	..
Capital Payments	..	..	..	25.50	33.30	38.50	48.90	61.60	85.20	73.30	..

1980	1981	1982	1983	1984	1985	1986	1987	1988	1989 estimate	NOTES	BARBADOS
3,130	3,520	3,760	4,010	4,420	4,640	5,180	5,350	5,910	6,370	..	CURRENT GNP PER CAPITA (US $)
249	250	251	252	253	253	254	254	254	255	..	POPULATION (thousands)
											USE AND ORIGIN OF RESOURCES
				(Millions of current Barbados Dollars)							
1,683.2	1,904.6	1,984.8	2,082.6	2,280.5	2,392.3	2,568.8	2,824.5	3,077.2	3,356.4	..	Gross National Product (GNP)
4.7	0.0	-5.2	-30.1	-22.3	-28.8	-77.2	-89.2	-19.8	-93.0	..	Net Factor Income from Abroad
1,678.5	1,904.6	1,990.0	2,112.7	2,302.8	2,421.1	2,646.0	2,913.7	3,097.0	3,449.4	..	GDP at Market Prices
-100.2	-285.5	-124.7	-112.6	15.9	95.2	61.2	15.5	61.3	-68.2	..	Resource Balance
1,129.4	1,072.5	1,215.5	1,353.7	1,573.8	1,558.7	1,495.9	1,340.1	1,536.8	1,732.7	..	Exports of Goods & NFServices
1,229.6	1,358.0	1,340.2	1,466.3	1,557.9	1,463.5	1,434.7	1,324.6	1,475.5	1,800.9	..	Imports of Goods & NFServices
1,778.7	2,190.1	2,114.7	2,225.2	2,286.9	2,325.9	2,584.9	2,898.2	3,035.6	3,517.6	..	Domestic Absorption
1,062.0	1,343.9	1,335.2	1,457.9	1,525.4	1,497.8	1,692.3	1,934.0	1,955.0	2,318.0	f	Private Consumption, etc.
292.4	321.2	329.0	346.1	387.6	456.3	468.8	497.5	537.3	564.2	..	General Gov't Consumption
424.3	525.0	450.5	421.2	373.9	371.8	423.8	466.7	543.3	635.4	f	Gross Domestic Investment
424.3	525.0	450.5	421.2	373.9	371.8	423.8	466.7	449.6	..	..	Fixed Investment
194.7	198.4	205.8	213.7	228.2	229.3	348.7	414.8	431.6	522.6	..	Indirect Taxes, net
1,483.8	1,706.2	1,784.2	1,899.0	2,074.6	2,191.8	2,297.3	2,498.9	2,665.4	2,926.8	B	GDP at factor cost
152.2	128.9	122.0	135.6	139.2	150.1	213.2	207.4	199.9	193.0	..	Agriculture
331.8	379.7	388.4	440.4	493.2	449.2	473.3	537.5	549.0	611.3	..	Industry
169.0	189.7	205.5	238.7	264.1	231.7	238.9	276.8	261.2	289.6	f	Manufacturing
999.8	1,197.6	1,273.8	1,323.0	1,442.2	1,592.5	1,610.8	1,754.0	1,916.5	2,122.5	..	Services, etc.
324.1	239.5	325.8	308.7	389.8	467.0	484.9	482.2	604.7	567.2	..	Gross Domestic Saving
372.0	287.9	355.0	312.2	400.7	467.7	445.1	431.2	665.7	530.5	..	Gross National Saving
				(Millions of 1987 Barbados Dollars)							
2,724.9	2,630.1	2,491.2	2,467.0	2,569.9	2,593.0	2,850.2	2,824.5	3,012.6	3,006.3	..	Gross National Product
2,749.6	2,661.3	2,527.6	2,532.9	2,616.4	2,623.5	2,896.7	2,913.7	3,115.1	3,226.8	..	GDP at Market Prices
											Resource Balance
..	..	..	..	..	..	..	..	..	..	..	Exports of Goods & NFServices
..	..	..	..	..	..	..	..	..	..	..	Imports of Goods & NFServices
											Domestic Absorption
..	..	..	..	..	..	..	..	..	..	..	Private Consumption, etc.
..	..	..	..	..	..	..	..	..	..	..	General Gov't Consumption
..	..	..	..	..	..	..	..	..	..	..	Gross Domestic Investment
..	..	..	..	..	..	..	..	..	..	..	Fixed Investment
2,369.4	2,324.1	2,209.4	2,219.3	2,299.1	2,318.8	2,439.7	2,498.9	2,586.8	2,680.1	B	GDP at factor cost
244.7	202.7	197.9	205.3	224.9	223.7	233.5	207.4	195.3	177.8	..	Agriculture
551.3	545.5	508.7	525.0	538.5	511.3	543.9	537.5	574.6	606.3	..	Industry
326.8	315.1	298.2	305.1	311.6	282.0	296.4	276.8	295.4	310.9	f	Manufacturing
1,573.5	1,575.5	1,501.9	1,488.9	1,535.8	1,583.8	1,662.3	1,754.0	1,817.0	1,896.0	..	Services, etc.
											Memo Items:
..	..	..	..	..	..	..	..	..	..	..	Capacity to Import
..	..	..	..	..	..	..	..	..	..	..	Terms of Trade Adjustment
..	..	..	..	..	..	..	..	..	..	..	Gross Domestic Income
..	..	..	..	..	..	..	..	..	..	..	Gross National Income
				(Index 1987 = 100)							DOMESTIC PRICES/DEFLATORS
61.0	71.6	78.7	83.4	88.0	92.3	91.3	100.0	99.4	106.9	..	Overall (GDP)
										..	Domestic Absorption
62.2	63.6	61.6	66.0	61.9	67.1	91.3	100.0	102.4	108.6	..	Agriculture
60.2	69.6	76.4	83.9	91.6	87.9	87.0	100.0	95.5	100.8	..	Industry
51.7	60.2	68.9	78.2	84.8	82.2	80.6	100.0	88.4	93.1	..	Manufacturing
66.0	75.6	83.4	87.8	91.9	95.5	96.8	100.0	104.9	111.3	..	Consumer Price Index
											MANUFACTURING ACTIVITY
83.9	89.6	117.6	125.9	122.2	98.7	107.8	100.0	..	..	G	Employment (1987=100)
83.0	79.6	81.8	86.3	96.0	102.2	100.5	100.0	..	..	G	Real Earnings per Empl. (1987=100)
138.7	127.7	106.8	99.6	107.3	117.7	118.8	100.0	..	..	G	Real Output per Empl. (1987=100)
63.0	60.2	69.8	64.0	67.5	77.9	71.8	69.0	..	..	..	Earnings as % of Value Added
				(Millions of current Barbados Dollars)							MONETARY HOLDINGS
741.3	856.3	926.5	1,029.9	1,110.9	1,208.3	1,315.5	1,567.6	1,733.1	1,775.3	D	Money Supply, Broadly Defined
244.8	249.6	251.5	312.9	305.7	353.5	395.4	466.9	524.8	459.0	..	Money
101.5	111.2	110.6	114.1	118.1	123.5	137.4	156.6	171.3	182.7	..	Currency Outside Banks
143.3	138.3	140.9	198.7	187.6	230.0	258.0	310.3	353.4	276.3	..	Demand Deposits
496.5	606.7	675.0	717.0	805.2	854.8	920.2	1,100.7	1,208.3	1,316.2	..	Quasi-Money
				(Millions of current Barbados Dollars)							GOVERNMENT DEFICIT (-) OR SURPLUS
-60.90	-128.80	-76.10	-25.70	-91.00	-71.40	-79.70	-213.80	-88.70	..	C F	GOVERNMENT DEFICIT (-) OR SURPLUS
476.00	512.20	572.50	636.90	666.10	748.50	775.10	844.20	1,036.70	..	..	Current Revenue
393.10	484.90	513.90	532.30	613.60	674.90	698.30	860.20	900.40	..	..	Current Expenditure
82.90	27.30	58.60	104.60	52.50	73.60	76.80	-16.00	136.30	..	..	Current Budget Balance
..	0.70	..	..	..	..	..	0.20	..	..	..	Capital Receipts
143.80	156.80	134.70	130.30	143.50	145.00	156.50	198.00	225.00	..	..	Capital Payments

BARBADOS	1969	1970	1971	1972	1973	1974	1975	1976	1977	1978	1979
FOREIGN TRADE (CUSTOMS BASIS)					*(Millions of current US dollars)*						
Value of Exports, fob	37.13	39.04	41.88	44.73	53.49	86.05	107.27	86.09	96.18	129.81	151.74
Nonfuel Primary Products	22.58	23.23	21.98	22.74	26.47	40.53	62.11	36.90	38.24	38.65	45.29
Fuels	4.56	4.07	7.26	6.01	4.97	18.02	14.44	11.36	12.62	25.24	13.52
Manufactures	9.99	11.74	12.64	15.98	22.04	27.49	30.72	37.84	45.33	65.92	92.93
Value of Imports, cif	97.28	117.27	121.84	141.66	167.62	203.96	216.39	236.58	271.61	312.35	420.75
Nonfuel Primary Products	27.82	32.65	35.13	42.41	51.84	60.90	59.73	65.93	71.06	82.90	93.94
Fuels	7.40	6.50	7.97	8.29	11.13	32.35	36.54	30.79	36.01	36.23	59.17
Manufactures	62.06	78.12	78.74	90.96	104.65	110.71	120.12	139.86	164.54	193.22	267.64
					(Index 1987 = 100)						
Terms of Trade	105.9	109.1	96.8	106.5	125.5	171.4	170.7	133.1	123.4	109.0	111.0
Export Prices, fob	26.1	29.5	28.0	34.5	50.2	95.4	99.5	78.8	79.5	78.6	93.7
Import Prices, cif	24.7	27.1	28.9	32.4	40.0	55.7	58.3	59.3	64.5	72.2	84.4
BALANCE OF PAYMENTS					*(Millions of current US dollars)*						
Exports of Goods & Services	..	101.65	110.74	125.23	149.35	189.80	220.78	210.21	260.01	329.54	441.55
Merchandise, fob	..	35.75	33.27	37.68	47.93	67.31	94.45	76.11	85.36	110.97	131.51
Nonfactor Services	..	59.15	71.65	81.04	92.38	112.46	114.05	123.82	166.73	206.78	294.39
Factor Services	..	6.75	5.82	6.51	9.03	10.03	12.28	10.28	7.92	11.78	15.66
Imports of Goods & Services	..	148.65	151.25	174.99	208.96	244.64	269.39	287.01	327.34	377.47	497.64
Merchandise, fob	..	106.90	112.16	128.04	152.56	185.51	197.02	219.09	250.20	288.02	379.11
Nonfactor Services	..	34.65	31.04	37.11	44.25	46.80	56.09	59.19	64.88	75.97	95.71
Factor Services	..	7.10	8.05	9.84	12.15	12.32	16.29	8.73	12.26	13.47	22.82
Long-Term Interest	..	0.80	0.70	0.70	0.30	2.60	2.40	2.00	1.70	3.40	5.30
Private Current Transfers, net	..	3.90	3.85	4.48	5.77	6.38	6.78	10.83	12.76	14.47	16.90
Workers' Remittances	..	..	..	..	..	..	..	..	..	..	..
Curr. A/C Bal before Off. Transf.	..	-43.10	-36.66	-45.28	-53.85	-48.46	-41.83	-65.98	-54.56	-33.46	-39.18
Net Official Transfers	..	1.30	1.52	2.03	1.53	0.63	0.50	1.80	3.19	2.19	4.97
Curr. A/C Bal after Off. Transf.	..	-41.80	-35.14	-43.25	-52.32	-47.83	-41.33	-64.18	-51.38	-31.27	-34.21
Long-Term Capital, net	..	11.10	16.36	19.62	24.81	1.85	20.89	22.96	35.03	11.88	-7.51
Direct Investment	..	8.45	14.79	17.23	4.80	2.24	22.13	5.94	4.48	8.90	5.07
Long-Term Loans	..	0.00	0.30	-5.60	17.90	1.30	-0.30	4.80	19.10	15.00	4.00
Disbursements	..	0.00	0.30	0.90	21.10	2.50	1.40	6.80	26.10	19.40	10.90
Repayments	..	0.00	0.00	6.50	3.20	1.20	1.70	2.00	7.00	4.40	6.90
Other Long-Term Capital	..	2.65	1.27	7.99	2.11	-1.69	-0.94	12.22	11.45	-12.02	-16.58
Other Capital, net	..	24.85	30.48	26.70	27.10	39.32	29.15	29.21	17.99	40.47	46.50
Change in Reserves	..	5.85	-11.70	-3.07	0.41	6.66	-8.70	12.02	-1.64	-21.08	-4.79
Memo Item:					*(Barbados Dollars per US dollar)*						
Conversion Factor (Annual Avg)	2.000	2.000	1.970	1.920	1.960	2.050	2.020	2.000	2.010	2.010	2.010
				(Millions of US dollars), outstanding at end of year							
EXTERNAL DEBT (Total)	..	..	..	..	..	..	..	..	..	..	..
Long-Term Debt (by debtor)	..	..	..	..	..	..	..	..	..	..	..
Central Bank, incl. IMF credit	..	..	..	..	..	..	..	..	..	..	..
Central Government	..	..	..	..	..	..	..	..	..	..	..
Rest of General Government	..	..	..	..	..	..	..	..	..	..	..
Non-financial Public Enterprises	..	..	..	..	..	..	..	..	..	..	..
Priv. Sector, incl non-guaranteed	..	..	..	..	..	..	..	..	..	..	..
Short-Term Debt	..	..	..	..	..	..	..	..	..	..	..
Memo Items:					*(Millions of US dollars)*						
Int'l Reserves Excluding Gold	12.47	16.58	18.86	27.99	32.37	39.15	39.58	27.98	37.01	59.84	66.12
Gold Holdings (at market price)	..	..	..	..	..	..	..	..	..	..	..
SOCIAL INDICATORS											
Total Fertility Rate	3.2	3.0	2.9	2.7	2.6	2.5	2.4	2.3	2.2	2.2	2.1
Infant Mortality Rate	40.8	38.2	35.6	33.0	31.8	30.6	29.4	28.2	27.0	24.6	22.2
Life Expectancy at Birth	68.3	68.7	69.0	69.4	69.8	70.1	70.5	70.9	71.2	71.5	71.8
Urban Population, % of total	37.1	37.4	37.6	37.9	38.1	38.4	38.6	38.9	39.2	39.5	39.8
Food Prod. per capita (1987=100)	135.2	152.2	135.9	121.9	119.8	116.9	106.0	112.4	123.6	119.0	128.1
Labor Force, Agriculture (%)	19.0	18.2	17.2	16.3	15.5	14.7	14.0	13.1	12.2	11.4	10.6
Labor Force, Female (%)	40.1	39.9	40.7	41.4	42.1	42.7	43.3	44.2	45.0	45.8	46.5
Primary Schl. Enroll. Ratio	..	102.0	..	..	..	..	103.0	109.0	116.0	122.0	115.0
Primary Schl. Enroll. Ratio, Female	..	101.0	..	..	..	..	103.0	111.0	116.0	122.0	114.0
Secondary Schl. Enroll. Ratio	..	69.0	..	..	..	..	77.0	77.0	81.0	81.0	85.0

1980	1981	1982	1983	1984	1985	1986	1987	1988	1989 estimate	NOTES	BARBADOS
				(Millions of current US dollars)							**FOREIGN TRADE (CUSTOMS BASIS)**
196.00	244.00	263.00	321.00	391.00	352.00	274.70	155.89	173.00	..	f	Value of Exports, fob
72.59	45.85	55.35	71.25	78.07	63.72	41.58	46.97	45.03	..	..	Nonfuel Primary Products
27.02	70.30	47.33	63.35	60.93	89.28	45.12	32.92	32.97	..	..	Fuels
96.39	127.85	160.32	186.40	252.00	199.00	188.00	76.00	95.00	..	..	Manufactures
522.00	572.00	551.00	621.00	658.60	601.90	593.00	515.00	582.00	..	f	Value of Imports, cif
112.06	115.64	109.29	124.67	107.36	105.73	112.30	88.02	91.98	..	..	Nonfuel Primary Products
80.17	91.50	89.23	99.80	90.24	106.17	60.70	77.98	77.02	..	..	Fuels
329.77	364.86	352.48	396.53	461.00	390.00	420.00	349.00	413.00	..	..	Manufactures
				(Index 1987 = 100)							
135.5	122.9	106.9	107.0	103.8	103.5	98.5	100.0	105.1	..	..	Terms of Trade
129.7	118.1	99.3	97.4	90.4	91.8	89.9	100.0	109.3	..	..	Export Prices, fob
95.8	96.1	92.9	91.0	87.1	88.7	91.3	100.0	104.0	..	..	Import Prices, cif
				(Millions of current US dollars)							**BALANCE OF PAYMENTS**
572.66	555.46	626.31	698.35	827.28	794.71	760.35	688.41	803.26	728.80	f	Exports of Goods & Services
180.78	162.78	208.22	272.16	339.73	300.45	244.27	131.41	144.83	153.50	..	Merchandise, fob
371.35	370.16	396.11	405.01	458.66	464.82	476.91	523.44	627.65	554.30	..	Nonfactor Services
20.53	22.52	21.98	21.18	28.89	29.43	39.18	33.56	30.78	21.00	..	Factor Services
619.75	692.04	685.13	761.00	822.80	759.96	787.80	748.22	823.05	897.70	f	Imports of Goods & Services
480.78	527.17	507.03	571.47	606.22	559.19	522.60	458.36	517.87	690.70	..	Merchandise, fob
118.33	133.50	144.68	148.66	165.47	149.06	194.70	208.22	234.28	139.50	..	Nonfactor Services
20.63	31.37	33.41	40.87	51.11	51.71	70.50	81.64	70.90	67.50	..	Factor Services
5.80	8.80	15.70	17.10	14.90	20.10	31.10	32.90	37.60	39.20	..	Long-Term Interest
21.48	24.06	17.10	16.71	16.51	14.67	18.59	18.99	40.17	28.00	..	Private Current Transfers, net
..	..	..	..	..	..	..	..	..	..	..	Workers' Remittances
-25.61	-112.51	-41.71	-45.94	20.98	49.42	-8.85	-40.82	20.38	-140.90	..	Curr. A/C Bal before Off. Transf.
-0.05	-6.12	6.07	3.98	-1.84	-9.15	-6.96	-12.48	-12.03	46.50	..	Net Official Transfers
-25.66	-118.63	-35.65	-41.96	19.14	40.27	-15.81	-53.30	8.35	-94.40	..	Curr. A/C Bal after Off. Transf.
22.77	70.60	8.05	21.68	-19.39	11.49	12.33	69.41	26.35	-25.40	f	Long-Term Capital, net
2.19	7.16	4.13	2.24	-1.49	2.59	4.97	4.57	10.54	7.00	..	Direct Investment
29.70	79.70	53.20	68.90	26.20	48.20	88.10	-11.50	75.50	-29.50	..	Long-Term Loans
38.40	87.10	60.40	80.20	39.20	72.00	114.10	28.50	109.70	15.50	..	Disbursements
8.70	7.40	7.20	11.30	13.00	23.80	26.00	40.00	34.20	45.00	..	Repayments
-9.12	-16.26	-49.27	-49.46	-44.10	-39.30	-80.74	76.33	-59.69	-2.90	..	Other Long-Term Capital
20.52	69.27	29.38	9.56	-13.34	-29.50	23.58	-9.89	3.28	99.66	f	Other Capital, net
-17.64	-21.24	-1.79	10.73	13.59	-22.25	-20.10	-6.22	-37.99	20.14	..	Change in Reserves
				(Barbados Dollars per US dollar)							**Memo Item:**
2.010	2.010	2.010	2.010	2.010	2.010	2.010	2.010	2.010	2.010	..	Conversion Factor (Annual Avg)
				(Millions of US dollars), outstanding at end of year							
..	..	..	..	..	..	..	..	..	..	..	**EXTERNAL DEBT** (Total)
..	..	..	..	..	..	..	..	..	..	..	Long-Term Debt (by debtor)
..	..	..	..	..	..	..	..	..	..	..	Central Bank, incl. IMF credit
..	..	..	..	..	..	..	..	..	..	..	Central Government
..	..	..	..	..	..	..	..	..	..	..	Rest of General Government
..	..	..	..	..	..	..	..	..	..	..	Non-financial Public Enterprises
..	..	..	..	..	..	..	..	..	..	..	Priv. Sector, incl non-guaranteed
..	..	..	..	..	..	..	..	..	..	..	Short-Term Debt
				(Millions of US dollars)							**Memo Items:**
78.92	100.56	121.60	123.28	132.52	139.77	151.71	145.21	135.46	109.47	..	Int'l Reserves Excluding Gold
1.65	2.41	2.77	2.31	1.87	1.98	2.37	2.93	2.49	2.43	..	Gold Holdings (at market price)
											SOCIAL INDICATORS
2.0	2.0	1.9	1.9	1.9	1.8	1.8	1.8	1.8	1.8	..	Total Fertility Rate
19.8	17.4	15.0	14.1	13.1	12.9	12.6	16.2	16.0	15.8	..	Infant Mortality Rate
72.1	72.4	72.7	73.0	73.3	73.7	74.0	74.3	74.6	74.8	..	Life Expectancy at Birth
40.1	40.5	40.9	41.4	41.8	42.2	42.7	43.2	43.7	44.2	..	Urban Population, % of total
143.6	123.4	113.9	103.6	106.0	102.8	113.4	100.0	103.4	96.0	..	Food Prod. per capita (1987=100)
9.9	..	..	..	..	..	..	..	..	..	..	Labor Force, Agriculture (%)
47.2	47.2	47.2	47.2	47.2	47.2	47.2	47.3	47.3	47.3	..	Labor Force, Female (%)
100.0	101.0	103.0	108.0	110.0	..	..	..	..	..	..	Primary Schl. Enroll. Ratio
100.0	99.0	99.0	107.0	108.0	..	..	..	..	..	..	Primary Schl. Enroll. Ratio, Female
90.0	89.0	89.0	91.0	93.0	..	..	..	..	..	..	Secondary Schl. Enroll. Ratio

BELGIUM	1969	1970	1971	1972	1973	1974	1975	1976	1977	1978	1979
CURRENT GNP PER CAPITA (US $)	2,450	2,700	2,950	3,390	4,150	5,170	6,050	6,980	7,780	8,980	10,690
POPULATION (thousands)	9,613	9,638	9,673	9,709	9,738	9,768	9,795	9,811	9,822	9,830	9,837
USE AND ORIGIN OF RESOURCES					*(Billions of current Belgian Francs)*						
Gross National Product (GNP)	1,159.7	1,291.8	1,411.9	1,580.7	1,791.6	2,102.7	2,325.8	2,650.1	2,858.9	3,067.7	3,260.2
Net Factor Income from Abroad	8.4	10.9	9.5	12.2	9.3	11.8	12.7	17.3	12.1	10.1	-3.5
GDP at Market Prices	1,151.3	1,280.9	1,402.4	1,568.5	1,782.3	2,090.9	2,313.1	2,632.8	2,846.8	3,057.6	3,263.7
Resource Balance	9.4	28.7	28.5	51.6	33.9	8.9	3.0	5.0	-23.8	-30.8	-66.3
Exports of Goods & NFServices	483.3	562.0	609.5	683.4	845.6	1,117.2	1,065.0	1,265.9	1,473.7	1,539.8	1,796.5
Imports of Goods & NFServices	473.9	533.3	581.0	631.8	811.8	1,108.2	1,062.1	1,260.9	1,497.5	1,570.5	1,862.8
Domestic Absorption	1,141.9	1,252.2	1,373.9	1,516.9	1,748.5	2,082.0	2,310.2	2,627.8	2,870.6	3,088.4	3,330.1
Private Consumption, etc.	716.8	769.5	849.1	948.0	1,082.5	1,257.0	1,420.3	1,612.9	1,768.3	1,891.2	2,059.5
General Gov't Consumption	186.8	197.9	220.7	246.2	275.0	322.1	379.2	441.0	489.1	544.0	588.1
Gross Domestic Investment	238.3	284.8	304.1	322.8	390.9	502.8	510.8	573.9	613.2	653.2	682.4
Fixed Investment	245.0	267.3	278.8	302.6	342.9	419.9	467.1	522.5	557.4	597.2	604.8
Indirect Taxes, net	134.4	148.2	159.7	165.1	181.2	215.6	233.6	271.1	294.0	317.1	331.9
GDP at factor cost	1,016.9	1,132.7	1,242.7	1,403.4	1,601.2	1,875.3	2,079.6	2,361.7	2,552.8	2,740.5	2,931.8
Agriculture	51.2	46.0	49.3	63.5	69.3	62.2	68.2	78.6	71.4	78.6	75.6
Industry	479.0	541.5	570.2	631.8	719.8	859.4	889.8	1,010.0	1,081.2	1,146.1	1,207.4
Manufacturing	368.0	411.3	424.8	475.7	544.2	644.0	634.2	717.1	758.4	798.6	841.2
Services, etc.	621.1	693.4	782.9	873.3	993.3	1,169.3	1,355.1	1,544.1	1,694.2	1,832.9	1,980.7
Gross Domestic Saving	247.7	313.5	332.6	374.3	424.8	511.7	513.7	578.9	589.4	622.4	616.1
Gross National Saving	..	..	..	..	..	..	..	..	..	..	..
					(Billions of 1987 Belgian Francs)						
Gross National Product	3,380.3	3,580.1	3,708.3	3,913.6	4,143.5	4,317.8	4,256.4	4,503.2	4,518.8	4,643.2	4,722.3
GDP at Market Prices	3,356.3	3,549.2	3,682.8	3,882.8	4,121.1	4,292.8	4,232.7	4,473.2	4,499.1	4,627.4	4,727.4
Resource Balance	84.1	-10.8	3.6	27.5	-49.7	-67.3	-43.1	-35.6	-95.6	-106.1	-164.4
Exports of Goods & NFServices	1,349.4	1,412.9	1,502.5	1,652.4	1,889.8	2,017.8	1,837.4	2,051.8	2,312.5	2,390.7	2,560.2
Imports of Goods & NFServices	1,265.3	1,423.7	1,499.0	1,624.9	1,939.5	2,085.1	1,880.5	2,087.4	2,408.1	2,496.8	2,724.6
Domestic Absorption	3,272.3	3,560.0	3,679.3	3,855.3	4,170.7	4,360.1	4,275.8	4,508.8	4,594.7	4,733.6	4,891.7
Private Consumption, etc.	2,130.3	2,211.7	2,318.7	2,464.8	2,637.4	2,702.9	2,732.6	2,863.8	2,905.2	2,974.7	3,098.8
General Gov't Consumption	550.4	568.3	601.8	637.4	671.4	696.8	729.4	758.7	779.1	824.9	847.1
Gross Domestic Investment	591.6	780.0	758.7	753.0	861.9	960.5	813.7	886.4	910.4	934.0	945.9
Fixed Investment	696.0	757.5	742.6	763.9	817.3	877.8	861.6	894.3	895.3	918.8	895.3
GDP at factor cost	2,974.6	3,128.8	3,256.8	3,464.7	3,687.9	3,838.9	3,800.8	4,007.7	4,025.4	4,137.9	4,234.6
Agriculture	88.1	85.9	90.4	89.9	93.4	97.5	81.1	77.9	81.0	90.4	90.8
Industry	1,019.7	1,109.2	1,154.2	1,229.6	1,323.2	1,377.8	1,325.9	1,422.3	1,450.5	1,481.8	1,513.9
Manufacturing	685.0	745.4	775.3	836.2	910.5	944.5	883.3	949.3	955.5	970.8	996.7
Services, etc.	2,268.0	2,360.3	2,441.5	2,562.7	2,693.6	2,806.2	2,825.4	2,970.3	2,959.9	3,047.5	3,115.2
Memo Items:											
Capacity to Import	1,290.4	1,500.3	1,572.4	1,757.5	2,020.4	2,101.9	1,885.7	2,095.7	2,369.8	2,447.9	2,627.6
Terms of Trade Adjustment	-58.9	87.5	69.8	105.1	130.5	84.1	48.3	43.8	57.3	57.2	67.3
Gross Domestic Income	3,297.4	3,636.6	3,752.7	3,987.9	4,251.6	4,376.9	4,281.0	4,517.1	4,556.4	4,684.7	4,794.7
Gross National Income	3,321.3	3,667.5	3,778.1	4,018.8	4,274.0	4,402.0	4,304.7	4,547.0	4,576.1	4,700.5	4,789.7
DOMESTIC PRICES/DEFLATORS					*(Index 1987 = 100)*						
Overall (GDP)	34.3	36.1	38.1	40.4	43.2	48.7	54.6	58.9	63.3	66.1	69.0
Domestic Absorption	34.9	35.2	37.3	39.3	41.9	47.7	54.0	58.3	62.5	65.2	68.1
Agriculture	58.1	53.6	54.5	70.6	74.2	63.8	84.1	100.9	88.1	86.9	83.3
Industry	47.0	48.8	49.4	51.4	54.4	62.4	67.1	71.0	74.5	77.3	79.8
Manufacturing	53.7	55.2	54.8	56.9	59.8	68.2	71.8	75.5	79.4	82.3	84.4
Consumer Price Index	32.7	34.0	35.5	37.4	40.0	45.1	50.8	55.5	59.4	62.1	64.9
MANUFACTURING ACTIVITY											
Employment (1987=100)	146.2	152.8	153.3	151.5	146.2	147.8	138.7	133.1	128.0	122.5	119.2
Real Earnings per Empl. (1987=100)	59.7	61.6	66.2	70.7	76.1	80.8	83.3	87.6	90.0	92.2	95.7
Real Output per Empl. (1987=100)	35.5	40.2	43.8	46.0	54.8	60.7	57.2	65.3	66.7	67.6	72.6
Earnings as % of Value Added	46.7	46.4	48.4	47.5	46.1	46.9	49.7	49.1	48.8	48.8	49.1
MONETARY HOLDINGS					*(Millions of current Belgian Francs)*						
Money Supply, Broadly Defined	689.2	741.2	838.6	971.0	1,101.0	1,200.2	1,384.4	1,554.1	1,686.8	1,818.7	1,935.6
Money	353.5	378.1	420.3	484.2	520.3	552.6	639.4	684.1	741.0	784.4	804.1
Currency Outside Banks	178.1	183.2	196.4	216.8	231.5	248.9	281.2	299.5	327.4	349.7	359.0
Demand Deposits	175.4	194.9	223.9	267.4	288.8	303.7	358.2	384.6	413.6	434.7	445.1
Quasi-Money	335.7	363.1	418.3	486.8	580.7	647.6	745.0	870.0	945.8	1,034.3	1,131.5
					(Millions of current Belgian Francs)						
GOVERNMENT DEFICIT (-) OR SURPLUS	..	-21,200	-39,600	-67,900	-61,800	-46,600	-109,000	-147,500	-168,300	-209,200	-247,700
Current Revenue	..	448,900	495,100	555,700	649,600	780,500	927,300	1.0596M	1.183M	1.3001M	1.3976M
Current Expenditure	..	416,700	463,000	545,300	634,500	742,400	939,800	1.0914M	1.2255M	1.3601M	1.4944M
Current Budget Balance	..	32,200	32,100	10,400	15,100	38,100	-12,500	-31,800	-42,500	-60,000	-96,800
Capital Receipts	..	500	600	300	500	1,100	600	400	500	600	500
Capital Payments	..	53,900	72,300	78,600	77,400	85,800	97,100	116,100	126,300	149,801	151,400

1980	1981	1982	1983	1984	1985	1986	1987	1988	1989 estimate	NOTES	BELGIUM
12,440	12,090	10,770	9,360	8,710	8,460	9,360	11,400	14,520	16,390	..	**CURRENT GNP PER CAPITA (US $)**
9,847	9,852	9,856	9,856	9,853	9,858	9,862	9,870	9,878	9,886	..	**POPULATION (thousands)**
				(Billions of current Belgian Francs)							**USE AND ORIGIN OF RESOURCES**
3,507.9	3,640.8	3,934.0	4,168.0	4,492.0	4,791.7	5,063.7	5,277.8	5,603.5	6,092.2	..	Gross National Product (GNP)
-18.3	-21.2	-48.0	-53.0	-48.5	-63.0	-53.3	-44.0	-52.5	-24.7	..	Net Factor Income from Abroad
3,526.2	3,662.0	3,982.0	4,221.0	4,540.5	4,854.7	5,117.0	5,321.8	5,656.0	6,116.8	..	GDP at Market Prices
-98.8	-71.6	-58.3	60.9	61.2	100.1	180.3	138.5	156.0	144.3	..	Resource Balance
2,026.4	2,283.6	2,637.9	2,923.5	3,336.9	3,479.1	3,369.3	3,474.5	3,866.5	4,460.3	..	Exports of Goods & NFServices
2,125.2	2,355.2	2,696.2	2,862.6	3,275.6	3,379.0	3,189.0	3,336.0	3,710.5	4,316.0	..	Imports of Goods & NFServices
3,624.9	3,733.6	4,040.2	4,160.1	4,479.2	4,754.6	4,936.7	5,183.3	5,500.1	5,972.5	..	Domestic Absorption
2,223.4	2,396.6	2,620.4	2,762.6	2,963.1	3,198.8	3,302.4	3,446.2	3,588.5	3,831.5	..	Private Consumption, etc.
643.6	696.6	734.2	756.9	792.4	849.1	877.9	893.8	898.0	936.9	..	General Gov't Consumption
757.9	640.3	685.6	640.7	723.8	706.6	756.5	843.2	1,013.5	1,204.2	..	Gross Domestic Investment
674.5	611.7	644.0	649.6	696.6	739.6	776.5	828.5	977.0	1,155.4	..	Fixed Investment
361.8	382.3	425.2	454.7	469.0	491.4	506.4	555.6	579.8	640.2	..	Indirect Taxes, net
3,164.4	3,279.7	3,556.8	3,766.3	4,071.5	4,363.3	4,610.6	4,766.2	5,076.2	5,476.7	..	GDP at factor cost
79.4	88.2	97.8	109.7	112.3	112.2	114.2	109.6	115.8	..	B	Agriculture
1,266.6	1,211.0	1,325.4	1,384.1	1,455.0	1,573.9	1,597.3	1,605.3	1,739.3	..	B	Industry
861.3	829.9	933.0	974.8	1,029.7	1,120.9	1,148.9	1,148.0	1,236.9	..	B	Manufacturing
2,180.1	2,362.8	2,558.8	2,727.3	2,973.1	3,168.6	3,405.5	3,606.8	3,800.9	..	B	Services, etc.
659.2	568.8	627.4	701.6	785.0	806.7	936.8	981.8	1,169.5	1,348.5	..	Gross Domestic Saving
..	..	..	..	..	..	..	..	..	..	..	Gross National Saving
				(Billions of 1987 Belgian Francs)							
4,898.2	4,850.7	4,892.9	4,909.9	5,022.1	5,054.8	5,163.7	5,277.8	5,491.7	5,753.1	..	Gross National Product
4,923.5	4,877.9	4,950.3	4,969.9	5,074.3	5,119.0	5,217.6	5,321.8	5,543.4	5,776.2	..	GDP at Market Prices
-87.7	68.7	102.4	220.5	224.3	237.3	193.5	138.5	148.5	124.3	..	Resource Balance
2,645.1	2,727.4	2,785.9	2,874.7	3,038.2	3,079.0	3,244.7	3,474.5	3,760.3	4,061.1	..	Exports of Goods & NFServices
2,732.8	2,658.7	2,683.5	2,654.3	2,813.9	2,841.7	3,051.1	3,336.0	3,611.8	3,936.8	..	Imports of Goods & NFServices
5,011.3	4,809.1	4,847.9	4,749.4	4,850.0	4,881.8	5,024.1	5,183.3	5,394.9	5,651.9	..	Domestic Absorption
3,174.4	3,171.1	3,222.6	3,192.7	3,225.7	3,292.0	3,370.9	3,446.2	3,515.5	3,627.3	..	Private Consumption, etc.
860.5	862.9	849.1	847.6	848.5	870.7	882.5	893.8	887.6	891.0	..	General Gov't Consumption
976.4	775.1	776.1	709.1	775.8	719.1	770.8	843.2	991.8	1,133.6	..	Gross Domestic Investment
936.1	786.8	770.9	736.2	749.5	754.3	787.3	828.5	961.0	1,098.3	..	Fixed Investment
4,419.9	4,386.1	4,441.5	4,454.9	4,569.6	4,618.4	4,704.9	4,766.2	4,972.2	5,165.1	..	GDP at factor cost
94.6	99.0	104.9	102.2	111.8	110.3	115.4	109.6	118.4	..	..	Agriculture
1,558.1	1,488.7	1,507.8	1,547.8	1,559.2	1,573.1	1,566.3	1,605.3	1,696.6	..	..	Industry
1,021.2	1,016.7	1,057.6	1,106.0	1,128.2	1,139.0	1,131.4	1,148.0	1,206.1	..	..	Manufacturing
3,267.1	3,297.2	3,344.2	3,319.9	3,403.2	3,435.6	3,535.9	3,606.8	3,728.4	..	..	Services, etc.
											Memo Items:
2,605.8	2,577.9	2,625.5	2,710.7	2,866.5	2,925.9	3,223.7	3,474.5	3,763.6	4,068.5	..	Capacity to Import
-39.3	-149.5	-160.4	-164.0	-171.7	-153.1	-21.0	0.0	3.3	7.4	..	Terms of Trade Adjustment
4,884.3	4,728.3	4,789.9	4,805.9	4,902.6	4,965.9	5,196.6	5,321.8	5,546.7	5,783.5	..	Gross Domestic Income
4,858.9	4,701.2	4,732.4	4,745.9	4,850.4	4,901.8	5,142.7	5,277.8	5,495.0	5,760.5	..	Gross National Income
				(Index 1987 = 100)							**DOMESTIC PRICES/DEFLATORS**
71.6	75.1	80.4	84.9	89.5	94.8	98.1	100.0	102.0	105.9	..	Overall (GDP)
72.3	77.6	83.3	87.6	92.4	97.4	98.3	100.0	102.0	105.7	..	Domestic Absorption
83.9	89.1	93.3	107.3	100.4	101.7	98.9	100.0	97.8	..	..	Agriculture
81.3	81.3	87.9	89.4	93.3	100.0	102.0	100.0	102.5	..	..	Industry
84.3	81.6	88.2	88.1	91.3	98.4	101.5	100.0	102.5	..	..	Manufacturing
69.2	74.5	81.0	87.2	92.7	97.2	98.5	100.0	101.2	104.3	..	Consumer Price Index
											MANUFACTURING ACTIVITY
116.5	110.8	106.7	103.8	103.0	101.1	101.3	100.0	..	..	..	Employment (1987=100)
97.7	98.3	97.5	95.1	93.8	93.1	97.3	100.0	..	..	..	Real Earnings per Empl. (1987=100)
79.5	82.7	84.6	90.0	91.8	91.6	94.1	100.0	..	..	..	Real Output per Empl. (1987=100)
49.9	53.2	49.4	47.7	46.5	46.2	46.3	46.2	..	..	..	Earnings as % of Value Added
				(Millions of current Belgian Francs)							**MONETARY HOLDINGS**
1,996.6	2,110.3	2,237.2	2,411.7	2,527.4	2,699.6	2,931.4	3,174.9	3,381.2	3,752.2	D	Money Supply, Broadly Defined
806.1	823.5	855.8	929.8	932.5	962.4	1,037.3	1,086.0	1,145.9	1,208.0	..	Money
364.2	370.1	369.5	383.3	381.9	379.9	400.5	410.7	415.0	422.6	..	Currency Outside Banks
441.9	453.4	486.3	546.5	550.6	582.5	636.8	675.3	730.9	785.4	..	Demand Deposits
1,190.5	1,286.8	1,381.4	1,481.9	1,594.9	1,737.2	1,894.1	2,088.9	2,235.3	2,544.2	..	Quasi-Money
				(Millions of current Belgian Francs)							**GOVERNMENT DEFICIT (-) OR SURPLUS**
-282,000	-446,900	-431,600	-515,900	-596,100	-537,600	-497,300	-404,000	-419,500	..	..	Current Revenue
1.5104M	1.5978M	1.7829M	1.8584M	2.0424M	2.203M	2.2733M	2.3719M	2.4597M	..	..	Current Revenue
1.6098M	1.8406M	2.0106M	2.1668M	2.3254M	2.4571M	2.5628M	2.5946M	2.6951M	..	..	Current Expenditure
-99,400	-242,801	-227,700	-308,400	-283,000	-254,099	-289,501	-222,700	-235,400	..	..	Current Budget Balance
600	700	1,900	1,700	700	1,100	700	700	1,200	..	..	Capital Receipts
183,200	204,799	205,800	209,199	313,800	284,600	208,500	182,000	185,300	..	..	Capital Payments

BELGIUM	1969	1970	1971	1972	1973	1974	1975	1976	1977	1978	1979
FOREIGN TRADE (CUSTOMS BASIS)					*(Millions of current US dollars)*						
Value of Exports, fob	10,065	11,609	12,391	16,044	22,393	28,126	28,760	32,783	37,450	44,793	56,083
Nonfuel Primary Products	2,160	2,451	2,330	2,914	4,366	5,286	4,873	5,559	6,447	7,382	9,201
Fuels	332	310	332	466	639	938	1,393	1,572	2,012	1,912	3,526
Manufactures	7,572	8,849	9,729	12,663	17,388	21,902	22,495	25,652	28,991	35,498	43,357
Value of Imports, cif	9,989	11,362	12,856	15,589	21,916	29,446	30,191	35,161	40,140	48,268	60,186
Nonfuel Primary Products	3,180	3,577	3,530	4,125	6,086	7,720	7,215	8,514	9,346	10,733	13,536
Fuels	893	1,035	1,223	1,567	1,900	4,219	4,323	4,982	5,637	5,986	8,555
Manufactures	5,915	6,751	8,103	9,897	13,931	17,507	18,652	21,666	25,157	31,549	38,095
					(Index 1987 = 100)						
Terms of Trade	122.9	137.6	124.3	134.1	130.2	112.0	111.7	109.5	107.6	110.4	111.4
Export Prices, fob	29.1	33.6	32.8	38.4	48.7	60.6	62.7	63.2	67.3	76.8	92.5
Import Prices, cif	23.7	24.4	26.4	28.6	37.4	54.1	56.1	57.7	62.5	69.6	83.1
BALANCE OF PAYMENTS					*(Millions of current US dollars)*						
Exports of Goods & Services	..	12,358	13,600	17,173	24,741	33,732	33,832	37,334	46,240	56,441	73,952
Merchandise, fob	..	9,062	9,804	12,789	18,425	24,215	23,077	26,065	31,224	38,204	49,186
Nonfactor Services	..	2,176	2,501	2,920	3,940	5,266	6,178	6,734	9,622	10,712	13,063
Factor Services	..	1,120	1,295	1,463	2,377	4,251	4,576	4,534	5,393	7,525	11,703
Imports of Goods & Services	..	11,487	12,790	15,665	23,038	32,522	33,037	36,379	46,172	56,511	76,136
Merchandise, fob	..	8,598	9,589	11,998	17,545	24,193	23,905	27,307	34,203	40,848	53,813
Nonfactor Services	..	1,857	2,040	2,431	3,368	4,438	5,064	5,207	7,159	8,795	10,966
Factor Services	..	1,032	1,162	1,236	2,125	3,890	4,068	3,865	4,809	6,869	11,357
Long-Term Interest	..	..	..	..	..	..	..	..	..	..	..
Private Current Transfers, net	..	33	44	34	62	10	-108	-196	-163	-284	-345
Workers' Remittances	..	154	186	199	280	294	286	263	322	461	471
Curr. A/C Bal before Off. Transf.	..	904	853	1,542	1,765	1,220	687	759	-95	-355	-2,528
Net Official Transfers	..	-187	-206	-234	-370	-389	-506	-324	-459	-468	-552
Curr. A/C Bal after Off. Transf.	..	717	647	1,308	1,395	831	181	435	-554	-823	-3,080
Long-Term Capital, net	..	-363	-546	-898	-731	-211	-280	149	-313	-270	511
Direct Investment	..	140	221	209	450	658	717	520	810	876	-211
Long-Term Loans	..	..	..	..	..	..	..	..	..	..	..
Disbursements	..	..	..	..	..	..	..	..	..	..	..
Repayments	..	..	..	..	..	..	..	..	..	..	..
Other Long-Term Capital	..	-503	-767	-1,107	-1,180	-869	-997	-371	-1,123	-1,146	722
Other Capital, net	..	-123	281	178	329	-1,182	78	-1,860	422	1,078	-531
Change in Reserves	..	-230	-382	-588	-994	562	21	1,276	445	15	3,100
Memo Item:					*(Belgian Francs per US dollar)*						
Conversion Factor (Annual Avg)	50.000	50.000	48.870	44.010	38.980	38.950	36.780	38.610	35.840	31.490	29.320
				(Millions of US dollars), outstanding at end of year							
EXTERNAL DEBT (Total)	..	..	..	..	..	..	..	..	..	..	..
Long-Term Debt (by debtor)	..	..	..	..	..	..	..	..	..	..	..
Central Bank, incl. IMF credit	..	..	..	..	..	..	..	..	..	..	..
Central Government	..	..	..	..	..	..	..	..	..	..	..
Rest of General Government	..	..	..	..	..	..	..	..	..	..	..
Non-financial Public Enterprises	..	..	..	..	..	..	..	..	..	..	..
Priv. Sector, incl non-guaranteed	..	..	..	..	..	..	..	..	..	..	..
Short-Term Debt	..	..	..	..	..	..	..	..	..	..	..
Memo Items:					*(Millions of US dollars)*						
Int'l Reserves Excluding Gold	868	1,377	1,797	2,232	3,319	3,538	4,069	3,491	3,956	3,966	5,443
Gold Holdings (at market price)	1,528	1,570	1,925	2,796	4,734	7,865	5,915	5,683	7,002	9,625	17,516
SOCIAL INDICATORS											
Total Fertility Rate	2.2	2.2	2.2	2.1	1.9	1.8	1.7	1.7	1.7	1.7	1.7
Infant Mortality Rate	21.2	21.1	20.4	18.8	17.7	17.4	16.1	15.3	13.6	13.3	12.3
Life Expectancy at Birth	71.1	71.2	71.2	71.3	71.4	71.8	71.9	72.1	72.3	72.6	72.9
Urban Population, % of total	94.1	94.3	94.4	94.4	94.5	94.5	94.6	94.8	94.9	95.1	95.2
Food Prod. per capita (1987=100)	..	..	..	..	..	..	..	..	..	..	..
Labor Force, Agriculture (%)	5.1	4.8	4.6	4.4	4.2	4.0	3.8	3.6	3.4	3.2	3.0
Labor Force, Female (%)	30.1	30.5	30.8	31.2	31.5	31.9	32.2	32.6	32.9	33.2	33.6
Primary Schl. Enroll. Ratio	..	103.0	..	..	..	..	102.0	101.0	102.0	101.0	101.0
Primary Schl. Enroll. Ratio, Female	..	104.0	..	..	..	..	102.0	102.0	102.0	101.0	101.0
Secondary Schl. Enroll. Ratio	..	81.0	..	..	..	..	84.0	85.0	85.0	87.0	87.0

1980	1981	1982	1983	1984	1985	1986	1987	1988	1989 estimate	NOTES	BELGIUM
				(Millions of current US dollars)							**FOREIGN TRADE (CUSTOMS BASIS)**
63,967	55,228	51,695	51,676	51,416	53,316	68,649	82,951	88,953	..	..	Value of Exports, fob
11,217	9,693	8,994	8,707	9,108	9,017	11,013	13,175	14,854	..	..	Nonfuel Primary Products
5,310	4,961	4,440	4,292	4,016	3,439	3,295	3,058	3,135	..	..	Fuels
47,440	40,574	38,261	38,676	38,293	40,860	54,342	66,718	70,964	..	..	Manufactures
71,192	61,417	57,213	53,653	54,746	55,561	68,025	82,598	91,098	..	..	Value of Imports, cif
15,764	13,361	12,253	11,828	12,148	11,933	13,667	15,997	18,522	..	..	Nonfuel Primary Products
12,361	12,523	11,886	9,450	10,242	9,257	7,233	7,688	6,646	..	..	Fuels
43,067	35,533	33,074	32,376	32,357	34,371	47,126	58,913	65,930	..	..	Manufactures
				(Index 1987 = 100)							
107.8	95.0	92.2	93.1	89.0	92.1	105.6	100.0	97.0	..	..	Terms of Trade
103.4	89.8	82.6	79.8	74.8	75.0	88.9	100.0	105.5	..	..	Export Prices, fob
95.9	94.5	89.6	85.7	84.1	81.4	84.2	100.0	108.8	..	..	Import Prices, cif
				(Millions of current US dollars)							**BALANCE OF PAYMENTS**
88,925	87,258	82,097	76,701	77,366	80,803	101,196	124,352	141,609	161,837	..	Exports of Goods & Services
55,155	48,597	46,061	45,662	46,213	47,336	59,955	76,088	85,496	89,987	..	Merchandise, fob
15,158	14,276	12,964	12,493	11,995	12,443	17,288	20,409	22,565	24,598	..	Nonfactor Services
18,612	24,384	23,072	18,546	19,159	21,024	23,953	27,856	33,547	47,252	..	Factor Services
92,625	90,186	83,515	76,097	76,590	79,479	97,195	120,132	136,259	156,922	..	Imports of Goods & Services
60,310	53,204	49,508	47,478	47,431	47,808	59,399	76,268	84,273	89,020	..	Merchandise, fob
13,493	12,367	10,525	9,775	9,816	10,400	13,742	16,036	18,407	21,030	..	Nonfactor Services
18,823	24,615	23,482	18,843	19,344	21,270	24,055	27,828	33,579	46,872	..	Factor Services
..	..	..	..	..	..	..	..	..	..		Long-Term Interest
-374	-409	-250	-181	-176	-129	-212	-114	41	47	..	Private Current Transfers, net
534	455	388	394	358	385	482	554	628	585	..	Workers' Remittances
-4,074	-3,338	-1,667	422	601	1,196	3,789	4,107	5,391	4,962	..	Curr. A/C Bal before Off. Transf.
-857	-831	-927	-918	-656	-527	-734	-1,313	-1,796	-1,765	..	Net Official Transfers
-4,931	-4,168	-2,594	-495	-55	669	3,055	2,794	3,594	3,197	..	Curr. A/C Bal after Off. Transf.
3,986	3,747	1,473	-2,339	-2,228	-4,558	-6,777	-1,960	-3,750	-2,437	..	Long-Term Capital, net
1,349	1,283	1,403	935	96	755	-993	-427	1,428	245	..	Direct Investment
..	..	..	..	..	..	..	..	..	..	..	Long-Term Loans
..	..	..	..	..	..	..	..	..	..	..	Disbursements
..	..	..	..	..	..	..	..	..	..	..	Repayments
2,637	2,464	70	-3,274	-2,324	-5,313	-5,784	-1,532	-5,178	-2,683	..	Other Long-Term Capital
1,368	-1,888	347	2,468	2,893	4,117	4,113	1,439	51	-3,078	..	Other Capital, net
-423	2,309	774	366	-611	-228	-392	-2,273	104	2,319	..	Change in Reserves
				(Belgian Francs per US dollar)							Memo Item:
29.240	37.130	45.690	51.130	57.780	59.380	44.670	37.330	36.770	39.400	..	Conversion Factor (Annual Avg)
			(Millions of US dollars), outstanding at end of year								
..	..	..	..	..	..	..	..	..	..	..	**EXTERNAL DEBT (Total)**
..	..	..	..	..	..	..	..	..	..	..	Long-Term Debt (by debtor)
..	..	..	..	..	..	..	..	..	..	..	Central Bank, incl. IMF credit
..	..	..	..	..	..	..	..	..	..	..	Central Government
..	..	..	..	..	..	..	..	..	..	..	Rest of General Government
..	..	..	..	..	..	..	..	..	..	..	Non-financial Public Enterprises
..	..	..	..	..	..	..	..	..	..	..	Priv. Sector, incl non-guaranteed
..	..	..	..	..	..	..	..	..	..	..	Short-Term Debt
				(Millions of US dollars)							Memo Items:
7,823	4,952	3,927	4,714	4,564	4,849	5,538	9,620	9,333	10,766	..	Int'l Reserves Excluding Gold
20,151	13,588	15,618	13,041	10,539	11,178	13,362	16,279	13,813	12,121	..	Gold Holdings (at market price)
											SOCIAL INDICATORS
1.7	1.7	1.6	1.6	1.6	1.5	1.5	1.6	1.6	1.6	..	Total Fertility Rate
12.1	11.5	11.1	10.5	10.7	9.4	9.7	9.7	9.4	9.2	..	Infant Mortality Rate
73.2	73.4	73.7	73.9	74.1	74.3	74.5	74.7	74.9	75.1	..	Life Expectancy at Birth
95.4	95.6	95.8	95.9	96.1	96.3	96.4	96.5	96.7	96.8	..	Urban Population, % of total
..	..	..	..	..	..	..	..	..	..	..	Food Prod. per capita (1987=100)
2.8	..	..	..	..	..	..	..	..	..	..	Labor Force, Agriculture (%)
33.9	33.9	33.9	33.9	33.8	33.8	33.8	33.8	33.8	33.7	..	Labor Force, Female (%)
104.0	..	98.0	97.0	97.0	98.0	96.0	100.0	..	..	..	Primary Schl. Enroll. Ratio
113.0	100.0	98.0	97.0	98.0	98.0	97.0	100.0	..	..	..	Primary Schl. Enroll. Ratio, Female
91.0	..	89.0	92.0	97.0	98.0	99.0	99.0	..	..	..	Secondary Schl. Enroll. Ratio

BELIZE	1969	1970	1971	1972	1973	1974	1975	1976	1977	1978	1979
CURRENT GNP PER CAPITA (US $)	430	430	470	520	570	660	790	840	860	910	1,080
POPULATION (thousands)	117	120	122	123	125	127	129	132	135	138	141
USE AND ORIGIN OF RESOURCES					*(Millions of current Belize Dollars)*						
Gross National Product (GNP)	76.20	86.00	93.40	101.00	121.00	158.00	191.50	197.40	224.10	259.00	293.00
Net Factor Income from Abroad	-2.80	-2.90	-3.70	-4.70	-6.70	-18.50	-22.20	-18.70	-11.20	-13.60	-10.60
GDP at Market Prices	79.00	88.90	97.10	105.70	127.70	176.50	213.70	216.10	235.30	272.60	303.60
Resource Balance	..	..	..	..	..	..	..	..	..	..	..
Exports of Goods & NFServices	..	..	..	..	..	..	..	..	..	..	..
Imports of Goods & NFServices	..	..	..	..	..	..	..	..	..	..	..
Domestic Absorption	..	..	..	..	..	..	..	..	..	..	..
Private Consumption, etc.	..	..	..	..	..	..	..	..	..	..	..
General Gov't Consumption	..	..	..	..	..	..	..	..	..	..	..
Gross Domestic Investment	..	..	..	..	..	..	..	..	..	..	..
Fixed Investment	..	..	..	..	..	..	..	..	..	..	..
Indirect Taxes, net	..	..	..	..	..	..	..	..	..	20.70	26.70
GDP at factor cost	..	..	..	..	..	..	..	..	..	251.90	276.90
Agriculture	..	..	..	..	..	..	..	..	..	79.00	85.20
Industry	..	..	..	..	..	..	..	..	..	62.10	60.70
Manufacturing	..	..	..	..	..	..	..	..	..	45.10	41.90
Services, etc.	..	..	..	..	..	..	..	..	..	110.80	131.00
Gross Domestic Saving	..	..	..	..	..	..	..	..	..	..	43.00
Gross National Saving	..	..	..	..	..	..	..	..	..	..	..
					(Millions of 1987 Belize Dollars)						
Gross National Product	213.49	223.65	237.24	254.92	263.56	269.30	282.54	312.36	332.64	358.24	395.58
GDP at Market Prices	210.53	220.65	229.39	252.83	266.36	302.48	313.35	313.24	333.59	360.01	382.68
Resource Balance	..	..	..	..	..	..	..	..	..	..	..
Exports of Goods & NFServices	..	..	..	..	..	..	..	..	..	..	..
Imports of Goods & NFServices	..	..	..	..	..	..	..	..	..	..	..
Domestic Absorption	..	..	..	..	..	..	..	..	..	..	..
Private Consumption, etc.	..	..	..	..	..	..	..	..	..	..	..
General Gov't Consumption	..	..	..	..	..	..	..	..	..	..	..
Gross Domestic Investment	..	..	..	..	..	..	..	..	..	..	..
Fixed Investment	..	..	..	..	..	..	..	..	..	..	..
GDP at factor cost	..	..	..	..	249.87	267.97	278.80	270.16	310.89	315.93	326.48
Agriculture	..	..	..	..	57.59	62.53	64.66	58.38	77.80	82.07	80.72
Industry	..	..	..	..	47.57	54.59	57.84	59.24	65.94	72.00	74.70
Manufacturing	..	..	..	..	32.39	37.86	38.60	37.44	45.22	47.33	44.91
Services, etc.	..	..	..	..	145.91	151.55	157.09	154.61	165.79	158.96	169.55
Memo Items:											
Capacity to Import	..	..	..	..	..	..	..	..	..	..	..
Terms of Trade Adjustment	..	..	..	..	..	..	..	..	..	..	..
Gross Domestic Income	..	..	..	..	..	..	..	..	..	..	..
Gross National Income	..	..	..	..	..	..	..	..	..	..	..
DOMESTIC PRICES/DEFLATORS					*(Index 1987 = 100)*						
Overall (GDP)	37.5	40.3	42.3	41.8	47.9	58.4	68.2	69.0	70.5	75.7	79.3
Domestic Absorption	..	..	..	..	..	..	..	..	..	..	..
Agriculture	..	..	..	..	..	..	..	..	..	96.3	105.6
Industry	..	..	..	..	..	..	..	..	..	86.3	81.3
Manufacturing	..	..	..	..	..	..	..	..	..	95.3	93.3
Consumer Price Index	..	..	..	..	..	..	..	..	..	..	..
MANUFACTURING ACTIVITY											
Employment (1987=100)	..	..	..	..	..	..	..	..	..	..	..
Real Earnings per Empl. (1987=100)	..	..	..	..	..	..	..	..	..	..	..
Real Output per Empl. (1987=100)	..	..	..	..	..	..	..	..	..	..	..
Earnings as % of Value Added	..	..	..	..	..	..	..	..	..	..	..
MONETARY HOLDINGS					*(Millions of current Belize Dollars)*						
Money Supply, Broadly Defined	..	..	..	..	..	..	..	71.58	73.43	92.93	95.94
Money	..	..	..	..	..	..	..	21.30	24.69	36.01	36.89
Currency Outside Banks	..	..	..	..	..	..	..	11.27	12.55	16.72	16.67
Demand Deposits	..	..	..	..	..	..	..	10.03	12.14	19.29	20.22
Quasi-Money	..	..	..	..	..	..	..	50.28	48.74	56.92	59.04
					(Thousands of current Belize Dollars)						
GOVERNMENT DEFICIT (-) OR SURPLUS	..	..	..	..	..	..	..	..	-12,112	-2,613	-5,018
Current Revenue	..	..	..	..	..	..	..	..	49,880	62,000	71,001
Current Expenditure	..	..	..	..	..	..	..	..	38,574	43,735	51,599
Current Budget Balance	..	..	..	..	..	..	..	..	11,306	18,265	19,402
Capital Receipts	..	..	..	..	..	..	..	..	200	491	684
Capital Payments	..	..	..	..	..	..	..	..	23,618	21,369	25,104

1980	1981	1982	1983	1984	1985	1986	1987	1988	1989 estimate	NOTES	BELIZE
1,170	1,220	1,140	1,090	1,100	1,140	1,240	1,390	1,560	1,720	..	**CURRENT GNP PER CAPITA (US $)**
144	148	152	157	162	166	171	175	180	184	..	**POPULATION (thousands)**
				(Millions of current Belize Dollars)							**USE AND ORIGIN OF RESOURCES**
333.80	350.60	327.00	336.80	366.50	371.40	411.90	489.30	567.90	626.50	..	Gross National Product (GNP)
-14.20	-3.80	-10.40	-11.00	-27.20	-20.90	-10.50	-14.30	-10.00	-13.40	..	Net Factor Income from Abroad
348.00	354.40	337.40	347.80	393.70	392.30	422.40	503.60	577.90	639.90	..	GDP at Market Prices
..	-44.50	-56.20	-42.00	-29.20	-28.90	3.90	-12.60	-41.70	-77.40	..	Resource Balance
..	206.00	172.00	185.50	224.30	208.70	245.40	286.10	339.70	361.70	..	Exports of Goods & NFServices
..	250.50	228.20	227.50	253.50	237.60	241.50	298.70	381.40	439.10	..	Imports of Goods & NFServices
..	398.90	393.60	389.80	422.90	421.20	418.50	516.20	619.60	717.30	..	Domestic Absorption
..	229.00	231.20	239.90	244.60	254.50	244.30	292.60	350.20	401.10	..	Private Consumption, etc.
..	73.40	79.50	84.20	85.60	87.10	90.20	98.40	104.80	115.50	..	General Gov't Consumption
..	96.50	82.90	65.70	92.70	79.60	84.00	125.20	164.60	200.70	..	Gross Domestic Investment
..	..	..	..	..	71.60	80.00	119.20	158.60	193.70	..	Fixed Investment
39.90	45.00	45.80	45.40	54.70	57.10	68.20	84.70	..	..	..	Indirect Taxes, net
308.10	309.40	291.60	302.40	339.00	335.20	354.20	418.90	..	..	B	GDP at factor cost
91.70	86.20	67.50	67.90	72.90	69.40	73.40	95.20	..	..	..	Agriculture
73.60	66.40	56.90	55.50	73.60	68.00	73.30	94.70	..	..	..	Industry
50.10	42.60	31.90	37.50	45.00	37.70	37.70	52.90	..	..	..	Manufacturing
142.80	156.80	167.20	179.00	192.50	197.80	207.50	229.00	..	..	..	Services, etc.
40.40	52.00	26.70	23.70	63.50	50.70	87.90	112.60	122.90	123.30	..	Gross Domestic Saving
..	..	..	..	68.10	69.00	108.10	128.70	143.40	151.30	..	Gross National Saving
				(Millions of 1987 Belize Dollars)							
406.26	411.97	384.07	376.88	381.15	396.48	432.41	489.30	542.82	589.30	..	Gross National Product
396.56	402.23	395.53	393.00	414.95	423.39	439.43	503.60	553.40	602.67	..	GDP at Market Prices
..	..	..	..	..	..	..	..	..	..	..	Resource Balance
..	..	..	..	..	..	..	..	..	..	..	Exports of Goods & NFServices
..	..	..	..	..	..	..	..	..	..	..	Imports of Goods & NFServices
..	..	..	..	..	..	..	..	..	..	..	Domestic Absorption
..	..	..	..	..	..	..	..	..	..	..	Private Consumption, etc.
..	..	..	..	..	..	..	..	..	..	..	General Gov't Consumption
..	..	..	..	..	..	..	..	..	..	..	Gross Domestic Investment
..	..	..	..	..	..	..	..	..	..	..	Fixed Investment
339.04	347.73	349.04	342.46	351.83	359.93	369.38	418.90	451.65	489.75	..	GDP at factor cost
81.50	81.17	84.87	79.93	81.84	80.83	77.35	95.20	96.55	99.35	..	Agriculture
82.59	85.40	82.70	80.21	79.57	79.67	82.92	94.70	104.54	118.27	..	Industry
50.90	52.90	52.27	51.74	47.33	47.75	48.90	52.90	53.43	57.74	..	Manufacturing
173.80	180.83	180.13	182.31	190.42	199.42	209.12	229.00	250.56	272.13	..	Services, etc.
											Memo Items:
..	..	..	..	..	..	..	..	..	..	..	Capacity to Import
..	..	..	..	..	..	..	..	..	..	..	Terms of Trade Adjustment
..	..	..	..	..	..	..	..	..	..	..	Gross Domestic Income
..	..	..	..	..	..	..	..	..	..	..	Gross National Income
				(Index 1987 = 100)							**DOMESTIC PRICES/DEFLATORS**
87.8	88.1	85.3	88.5	94.9	92.7	96.1	100.0	104.4	106.2	..	Overall (GDP)
..	..	..	..	..	..	..	..	..	..	..	Domestic Absorption
112.5	106.2	79.5	84.9	89.1	85.9	94.9	100.0	..	..	..	Agriculture
89.1	77.7	68.8	69.2	92.5	85.3	88.4	100.0	..	..	..	Industry
98.4	80.5	61.0	72.5	95.1	79.0	77.1	100.0	..	..	..	Manufacturing
72.2	80.3	85.8	90.0	93.4	96.8	97.7	100.0	..	..	..	Consumer Price Index
											MANUFACTURING ACTIVITY
..	..	..	..	..	..	..	..	..	..	..	Employment (1987=100)
..	..	..	..	..	..	..	..	..	..	..	Real Earnings per Empl. (1987=100)
..	..	..	..	..	..	..	..	..	..	..	Real Output per Empl. (1987=100)
..	..	..	..	..	..	..	..	..	..	..	Earnings as % of Value Added
				(Millions of current Belize Dollars)							**MONETARY HOLDINGS**
108.20	117.81	125.07	148.16	154.63	167.73	199.10	241.65	252.11	287.27	..	Money Supply, Broadly Defined
41.65	39.56	39.40	42.41	50.01	58.61	71.03	84.30	81.78	99.87	..	Money
17.51	19.01	20.61	21.53	22.77	22.64	25.90	29.56	34.11	40.44	..	Currency Outside Banks
24.14	20.55	18.79	20.88	27.24	35.97	45.13	54.74	47.67	59.43	..	Demand Deposits
66.55	78.25	85.67	105.75	104.62	109.12	128.06	157.35	170.33	187.40	..	Quasi-Money
				(Thousands of current Belize Dollars)							
-5,916	..	..	..	..	..	..	..	..	..	C F	**GOVERNMENT DEFICIT (-) OR SURPLUS**
84,972	88,794	97,638	95,521	97,884	..	..	..	..	..	..	Current Revenue
65,414	77,910	83,958	84,038	93,569	99,891	..	..	..	..	..	Current Expenditure
19,558	10,884	13,680	11,483	4,315	..	..	..	..	..	..	Current Budget Balance
281	288	302	341	511	157	..	..	..	..	..	Capital Receipts
25,755	..	..	..	..	..	..	..	..	..	..	Capital Payments

BELIZE	1969	1970	1971	1972	1973	1974	1975	1976	1977	1978	1979
FOREIGN TRADE (CUSTOMS BASIS)					*(Millions of current US dollars)*						
Value of Exports, fob	17.00	19.00	19.00	26.00	32.00	45.00	67.00	42.00	62.00	80.00	87.00
Nonfuel Primary Products	..	..	..	..	..	..	..	..	..	..	..
Fuels	..	..	..	..	..	..	..	..	..	..	..
Manufactures	..	..	..	..	..	..	..	..	..	..	..
Value of Imports, cif	30.00	33.00	36.00	43.00	44.00	64.00	88.00	73.00	90.00	106.00	132.00
Nonfuel Primary Products	..	..	..	..	..	..	..	..	..	..	..
Fuels	..	..	..	..	..	..	..	..	..	..	..
Manufactures	..	..	..	..	..	..	..	..	..	..	..
					(Index 1987 = 100)						
Terms of Trade	..	..	..	..	..	..	..	..	..	..	..
Export Prices, fob	..	..	..	..	..	..	..	..	..	..	..
Import Prices, cif	..	..	..	..	..	..	..	..	..	..	..
BALANCE OF PAYMENTS					*(Millions of current US dollars)*						
Exports of Goods & Services	..	..	..	..	..	..	..	..	..	..	..
Merchandise, fob	..	..	..	..	..	..	..	..	..	..	..
Nonfactor Services	..	..	..	..	..	..	..	..	..	..	..
Factor Services	..	..	..	..	..	..	..	..	..	..	..
Imports of Goods & Services	..	..	..	..	..	..	..	..	..	..	..
Merchandise, fob	..	..	..	..	..	..	..	..	..	..	..
Nonfactor Services	..	..	..	..	..	..	..	..	..	..	..
Factor Services	..	..	..	..	..	..	..	..	..	..	..
Long-Term Interest	..	0.00	0.00	0.00	0.30	0.20	0.30	0.20	0.30	0.30	0.60
Private Current Transfers, net	..	..	..	..	..	..	..	..	..	..	..
Workers' Remittances	..	..	..	..	..	..	..	..	..	..	..
Curr. A/C Bal before Off. Transf.	..	..	..	..	..	..	..	..	..	..	..
Net Official Transfers	..	..	..	..	..	..	..	..	..	..	..
Curr. A/C Bal after Off. Transf.	..	..	..	..	..	..	..	..	..	..	..
Long-Term Capital, net	..	..	..	..	..	..	..	..	..	..	..
Direct Investment	..	..	..	..	..	..	..	..	..	..	..
Long-Term Loans	..	4.30	0.00	0.00	-0.20	0.40	0.20	4.90	4.30	8.70	11.10
Disbursements	..	4.30	0.00	0.00	0.60	0.40	5.10	4.50	8.80	11.30	
Repayments	..	0.00	0.00	0.00	0.20	0.20	0.20	0.20	0.20	0.10	0.20
Other Long-Term Capital	..	..	..	..	..	..	..	..	..	..	..
Other Capital, net	..	..	..	..	..	..	..	..	..	..	..
Change in Reserves	..	..	..	..	..	..	..	..	-2.53	-5.96	3.51
Memo Item:					*(Belize Dollars per US dollar)*						
Conversion Factor (Annual Avg)	1.670	1.670	1.640	1.600	1.630	1.710	1.810	2.230	2.000	2.000	2.000
				(Millions of US dollars), outstanding at end of year							
EXTERNAL DEBT (Total)	..	4.10	4.30	5.10	4.80	5.30	4.80	9.10	20.70	33.30	71.70
Long-Term Debt (by debtor)	..	4.10	4.30	5.10	4.80	5.30	4.80	9.10	13.70	22.30	33.70
Central Bank, incl. IMF credit	..	0.00	0.00	0.00	0.00	0.00	0.20	4.10	4.90	6.40	8.20
Central Government	..	4.10	4.30	5.10	4.80	5.30	4.60	5.00	8.80	13.60	16.80
Rest of General Government	..	..	..	..	..	..	..	..	..	..	..
Non-financial Public Enterprises	..	0.00	0.00	0.00	0.00	0.00	0.00	0.00	0.00	2.30	8.70
Priv. Sector, incl non-guaranteed	..	..	..	..	..	..	..	..	..	..	..
Short-Term Debt	..	..	..	..	..	..	..	..	7.00	11.00	38.00
Memo Items:					*(Thousands of US dollars)*						
Int'l Reserves Excluding Gold	..	..	..	..	..	..	..	5,491	8,021	13,978	10,463
Gold Holdings (at market price)	..	..	..	..	..	..	..	..	..	..	..
SOCIAL INDICATORS											
Total Fertility Rate	5.6	6.9	6.4	6.3	6.3	6.2	6.1	6.0	5.9	5.8	5.8
Infant Mortality Rate	..	..	..	..	..	..	..	..	..	..	..
Life Expectancy at Birth	..	..	..	..	..	..	..	..	..	..	..
Urban Population, % of total	51.2	50.9	50.6	50.3	50.0	49.7	49.4	49.4	49.4	49.4	49.4
Food Prod. per capita (1987=100)	76.8	86.3	86.5	87.6	92.0	98.8	90.2	80.0	103.3	113.4	100.7
Labor Force, Agriculture (%)	..	..	..	..	..	..	..	..	..	..	..
Labor Force, Female (%)	..	..	..	..	..	..	..	..	..	..	..
Primary Schl. Enroll. Ratio	..	..	..	..	..	..	..	..	..	..	..
Primary Schl. Enroll. Ratio, Female	..	..	..	..	..	..	..	..	..	..	..
Secondary Schl. Enroll. Ratio	..	..	..	..	..	..	..	..	..	..	..

1980	1981	1982	1983	1984	1985	1986	1987	1988	1989 estimate	NOTES	BELIZE
											FOREIGN TRADE (CUSTOMS BASIS)
				(Millions of current US dollars)							
111.00	119.00	91.00	78.00	90.30	86.60	74.50	86.90	95.40	95.00	..	Value of Exports, fob
..	..	..	..	..	..	..	..	..	..	..	Nonfuel Primary Products
..	..	..	..	..	..	..	..	..	..	..	Fuels
..	..	..	..	..	..	..	..	..	..	..	Manufactures
150.00	162.00	128.00	112.00	130.00	102.40	103.80	127.00	157.60	180.80	..	Value of Imports, cif
..	..	..	..	..	..	..	..	..	..	..	Nonfuel Primary Products
..	..	..	..	..	..	..	..	..	..	..	Fuels
..	..	..	..	..	..	..	..	..	..	..	Manufactures
				(Index 1987 = 100)							
..	..	..	..	..	..	..	..	..	..	..	Terms of Trade
..	..	..	..	..	..	..	..	..	..	..	Export Prices, fob
..	..	..	..	..	..	..	..	..	..	..	Import Prices, cif
				(Millions of current US dollars)							**BALANCE OF PAYMENTS**
..	..	..	..	129.90	131.15	144.60	164.70	201.85	219.95	..	Exports of Goods & Services
..	..	..	..	93.20	90.15	92.60	102.85	119.40	124.40	..	Merchandise, fob
..	..	..	..	35.40	38.10	42.35	55.40	71.55	82.95	..	Nonfactor Services
..	..	..	..	1.30	2.90	9.65	6.45	10.90	12.60	..	Factor Services
..	..	..	..	160.50	154.50	160.05	186.25	230.35	270.10	..	Imports of Goods & Services
..	..	..	..	116.30	113.80	108.30	126.95	161.30	188.50	..	Merchandise, fob
..	..	..	..	29.30	27.35	38.90	45.70	53.15	62.30	..	Nonfactor Services
..	..	..	..	14.90	13.35	12.85	13.60	15.90	19.30	..	Factor Services
0.90	1.80	2.50	2.60	3.30	5.90	4.70	4.00	4.00	6.00	..	Long-Term Interest
..	..	..	..	15.90	19.60	15.35	15.20	15.25	20.70	..	Private Current Transfers, net
..	..	..	..	17.65	20.65	16.85	15.85	12.90	17.90	..	Workers' Remittances
..	..	..	..	-14.70	-3.75	-0.10	-6.35	-13.25	-29.45	..	Curr. A/C Bal before Off. Transf.
..	..	..	..	9.40	12.80	12.05	15.75	10.60	10.40	..	Net Official Transfers
..	..	..	..	-5.30	9.05	11.95	9.40	-2.65	-19.05	..	Curr. A/C Bal after Off. Transf.
..	..	..	..	-0.10	10.40	8.25	7.40	23.30	29.90	..	Long-Term Capital, net
..	..	..	..	-3.70	3.70	4.60	6.85	14.00	18.65	..	Direct Investment
13.20	11.10	9.20	15.20	6.00	14.40	-0.10	4.20	8.70	11.10	..	Long-Term Loans
13.70	12.50	11.70	18.60	8.70	24.50	8.70	12.20	17.40	17.70	..	Disbursements
0.50	1.40	2.50	3.40	2.70	10.10	8.80	8.00	8.70	6.60	..	Repayments
..	..	..	..	-2.40	-7.70	3.75	-3.65	0.60	0.15	..	Other Long-Term Capital
..	..	..	..	1.31	-17.13	-8.40	-4.93	1.12	4.66	..	Other Capital, net
-2.21	2.34	0.53	4.31	4.09	-2.32	-11.80	-11.87	-21.77	-15.51	..	Change in Reserves
				(Belize Dollars per US dollar)							**Memo Item:**
2.000	2.000	2.000	2.000	2.000	2.000	2.000	2.000	2.000	2.000	..	Conversion Factor (Annual Avg)
				(Millions of US dollars), outstanding at end of year							
62.90	60.20	69.60	100.00	97.10	118.20	120.60	136.70	131.40	134.40	..	**EXTERNAL DEBT (Total)**
46.90	56.00	62.20	78.20	79.20	105.10	108.90	122.30	126.30	129.60	..	Long-Term Debt (by debtor)
9.20	10.10	11.20	18.00	21.40	31.10	33.30	35.30	32.30	25.70	..	Central Bank, incl. IMF credit
21.00	28.90	33.30	40.90	41.30	62.00	65.80	76.20	76.30	85.80	..	Central Government
..	..	..	..	..	..	..	..	..	..	..	Rest of General Government
16.70	17.00	17.70	19.30	16.50	12.00	9.80	10.80	17.70	18.10	..	Non-financial Public Enterprises
..	..	..	..	..	..	..	..	..	..	..	Priv. Sector, incl non-guaranteed
16.00	4.20	7.40	21.80	17.90	13.10	11.70	14.40	5.10	4.80	..	Short-Term Debt
				(Thousands of US dollars)							**Memo Items:**
12,676	10,335	9,838	9,306	6,072	14,813	26,897	36,415	51,657	59,880	..	Int'l Reserves Excluding Gold
..	..	..	..	..	..	..	..	..	..	..	Gold Holdings (at market price)
											SOCIAL INDICATORS
5.7	5.6	5.5	5.4	5.3	5.2	5.1	5.0	4.9	4.8	..	Total Fertility Rate
..	..	60.0	58.0	56.0	54.0	52.0	50.0	48.5	47.0	..	Infant Mortality Rate
..	..	65.1	65.5	65.8	66.1	66.4	66.7	67.1	67.4	..	Life Expectancy at Birth
49.4	49.5	49.6	49.8	49.9	50.0	50.3	50.6	51.0	51.3	..	Urban Population, % of total
109.2	107.1	112.8	109.9	103.5	97.8	94.9	100.0	95.3	97.3	..	Food Prod. per capita (1987=100)
..	..	..	..	..	..	..	..	..	..	..	Labor Force, Agriculture (%)
..	..	..	..	..	..	..	..	..	..	..	Labor Force, Female (%)
..	..	..	..	..	..	..	..	..	..	..	Primary Schl. Enroll. Ratio
..	..	..	..	..	..	..	..	..	..	..	Primary Schl. Enroll. Ratio, Female
..	..	..	..	..	..	..	..	..	..	..	Secondary Schl. Enroll. Ratio

BENIN	1969	1970	1971	1972	1973	1974	1975	1976	1977	1978	1979
CURRENT GNP PER CAPITA (US $)	110	110	100	110	130	150	160	180	200	220	260
POPULATION (thousands)	2,589	2,657	2,728	2,801	2,875	2,951	3,029	3,109	3,191	3,276	3,367

USE AND ORIGIN OF RESOURCES

(Billions of current CFA Francs)

	1969	1970	1971	1972	1973	1974	1975	1976	1977	1978	1979
Gross National Product (GNP)	69.52	74.57	74.44	83.85	91.75	108.41	118.13	136.22	150.34	171.13	206.02
Net Factor Income from Abroad	-0.65	-0.69	-0.86	-0.55	0.00	-0.55	-0.26	0.02	-0.05	0.07	0.08
GDP at Market Prices	70.17	75.26	75.30	84.40	91.75	108.96	118.39	136.20	150.39	171.06	205.94
Resource Balance	-6.65	-5.81	-5.92	-10.51	-8.23	-17.87	-25.56	-28.52	-30.97	-33.60	-44.06
Exports of Goods & NFServices	14.71	20.34	23.85	21.62	25.59	27.78	30.63	31.51	43.33	50.34	64.24
Imports of Goods & NFServices	21.36	26.15	29.77	32.13	33.82	45.65	56.19	60.03	74.30	83.94	108.30
Domestic Absorption	76.82	81.07	81.22	94.91	99.98	126.83	143.95	164.72	181.36	204.66	250.00
Private Consumption, etc.	58.26	61.40	62.46	70.60	74.08	90.99	102.53	122.59	133.34	153.56	181.75
General Gov't Consumption	7.67	8.98	9.27	10.49	11.20	11.50	13.42	14.34	15.31	17.43	20.25
Gross Domestic Investment	10.89	10.69	9.49	13.82	14.70	24.34	28.00	27.79	32.71	33.67	48.00
Fixed Investment	..	..	..	..	..	..	..	..	..	..	..
Indirect Taxes, net	7.53	7.53	8.33	8.74	9.24	9.07	10.18	13.34	15.89	15.89	18.20
GDP at factor cost	62.64	67.73	66.97	75.66	82.51	99.89	108.21	122.86	134.50	155.17	187.74
Agriculture	33.12	33.47	31.73	35.41	37.85	42.15	44.26	55.42	58.72	72.45	88.29
Industry	5.88	7.73	7.42	9.09	10.15	14.79	15.01	14.44	15.49	19.42	24.17
Manufacturing	..	5.27	5.66	6.25	6.82	9.21	9.58	8.26	8.96	12.20	12.08
Services, etc.	23.64	26.53	27.82	31.16	34.51	42.95	48.94	53.00	60.29	63.30	75.28
Gross Domestic Saving	4.24	4.88	3.57	3.31	6.47	6.47	2.44	-0.73	1.74	0.07	3.94
Gross National Saving	..	4.19	3.21	3.55	7.21	7.01	5.38	5.68	11.02	12.49	19.14

(Billions of 1987 CFA Francs)

	1969	1970	1971	1972	1973	1974	1975	1976	1977	1978	1979
Gross National Product	319.29	325.95	320.76	342.56	358.02	366.91	349.64	355.39	372.00	378.63	403.02
GDP at Market Prices	322.24	329.00	324.49	344.79	358.03	368.80	350.41	355.34	372.14	378.50	402.88
Resource Balance	-44.50	-45.61	-49.95	-56.20	-59.76	-61.98	-69.45	-62.81	-70.41	-71.63	-84.77
Exports of Goods & NFServices	48.74	55.28	70.77	74.07	68.88	68.25	68.70	66.24	70.92	77.78	105.70
Imports of Goods & NFServices	93.24	100.89	120.72	130.28	128.64	130.22	138.14	129.05	141.33	149.41	190.48
Domestic Absorption	366.75	374.61	374.45	400.99	417.79	430.78	419.86	418.15	442.55	450.13	487.66
Private Consumption, etc.	275.59	280.20	280.96	286.41	299.18	292.15	283.59	285.91	323.87	335.47	340.07
General Gov't Consumption	51.90	57.75	57.93	63.08	66.45	62.22	59.79	54.33	46.97	46.95	50.66
Gross Domestic Investment	39.26	36.66	35.55	51.50	52.16	76.42	76.48	77.92	71.71	67.71	96.93
Fixed Investment	..	..	..	..	..	..	..	..	..	..	..
GDP at factor cost	301.51	310.73	304.51	324.70	340.04	359.07	337.51	337.89	351.79	361.40	386.91
Agriculture	..	133.97	129.09	133.56	135.93	130.15	123.10	136.97	136.41	150.67	157.85
Industry	..	31.00	28.08	32.71	32.01	41.68	35.69	31.93	35.90	33.82	37.73
Manufacturing	..	16.59	16.73	17.55	16.47	19.82	17.40	14.46	18.06	16.59	14.80
Services, etc.	..	139.87	143.00	154.23	169.65	186.26	179.74	165.51	177.25	171.25	186.05
Memo Items:											
Capacity to Import	64.23	78.47	96.71	87.66	97.34	79.25	75.30	67.74	82.42	89.60	112.98
Terms of Trade Adjustment	15.49	23.19	25.95	13.59	28.45	11.00	6.61	1.50	11.50	11.82	7.28
Gross Domestic Income	337.73	352.19	350.44	358.38	386.49	379.80	357.02	356.84	383.64	390.32	410.17
Gross National Income	334.78	349.14	346.70	356.15	386.47	377.91	356.25	356.89	383.50	390.45	410.31

DOMESTIC PRICES/DEFLATORS

(Index 1987 = 100)

	1969	1970	1971	1972	1973	1974	1975	1976	1977	1978	1979
Overall (GDP)	21.8	22.9	23.2	24.5	25.6	29.5	33.8	38.3	40.4	45.2	51.1
Domestic Absorption	20.9	21.6	21.7	23.7	23.9	29.4	34.3	39.4	41.0	45.5	51.3
Agriculture	..	25.0	24.6	26.5	27.8	32.4	36.0	40.5	43.0	48.1	55.9
Industry	..	24.9	26.4	27.8	31.7	35.5	42.1	45.2	43.2	57.4	64.1
Manufacturing	..	31.8	33.8	35.6	41.4	46.5	55.1	57.1	49.6	73.5	81.6
Consumer Price Index	..	..	..	..	..	..	..	..	..	..	..

MANUFACTURING ACTIVITY

	1969	1970	1971	1972	1973	1974	1975	1976	1977	1978	1979
Employment (1987=100)	..	..	..	..	..	..	..	..	..	..	..
Real Earnings per Empl. (1987=100)	..	..	..	..	..	..	..	..	..	..	..
Real Output per Empl. (1987=100)	..	..	..	..	..	..	..	..	..	..	..
Earnings as % of Value Added	..	..	..	..	..	19.2	20.9	24.3	23.9	25.1	25.4

MONETARY HOLDINGS

(Millions of current CFA Francs)

	1969	1970	1971	1972	1973	1974	1975	1976	1977	1978	1979
Money Supply, Broadly Defined	8,553	10,028	12,263	13,897	14,786	18,449	31,859	30,631	34,918	39,017	40,741
Money	8,189	9,631	11,521	12,709	12,325	15,730	26,869	25,631	29,318	31,017	33,741
Currency Outside Banks	3,969	4,510	4,966	5,801	6,017	6,067	8,446	9,364	9,924	7,955	13,255
Demand Deposits	4,220	5,121	6,555	6,908	6,308	9,663	18,423	16,267	19,394	23,062	20,486
Quasi-Money	364	397	742	1,188	2,461	2,719	4,990	5,000	5,600	8,000	7,000

(Millions of current CFA Francs)

	1969	1970	1971	1972	1973	1974	1975	1976	1977	1978	1979
GOVERNMENT DEFICIT (-) OR SURPLUS	..	..	..	..	..	..	..	..	1,434	5,052	-1,010
Current Revenue	..	..	..	..	..	..	..	..	41,982	40,695	45,898
Current Expenditure	..	..	..	..	..	..	..	..	22,416	18,853	26,315
Current Budget Balance	..	..	..	..	..	..	..	..	19,566	21,842	19,583
Capital Receipts	..	..	..	..	..	..	..	15	13	12	7
Capital Payments	..	..	..	..	..	..	..	..	18,145	16,802	20,600

1980	1981	1982	1983	1984	1985	1986	1987	1988	1989 estimate	NOTES	BENIN
320	340	330	280	260	260	280	310	370	380	..	**CURRENT GNP PER CAPITA (US $)**
3,464	3,568	3,677	3,793	3,915	4,043	4,174	4,310	4,449	4,593	..	**POPULATION (thousands)**
				(Billions of current CFA Francs)							**USE AND ORIGIN OF RESOURCES**
241.70	283.16	338.05	368.36	409.85	486.91	491.70	488.40	516.10	522.23	f	Gross National Product (GNP)
-0.61	-3.17	-1.97	-5.07	-7.34	-12.94	-11.32	-12.80	-9.50	-14.07	..	Net Factor Income from Abroad
242.31	286.33	340.02	373.43	417.19	499.85	503.20	501.20	525.60	536.30	f	GDP at Market Prices
-60.21	-97.56	-125.00	-43.00	-57.78	-41.10	-62.40	-55.80	-63.80	-22.30		Resource Balance
68.25	81.23	105.00	92.00	102.60	115.10	89.70	105.60	99.10	105.60	..	Exports of Goods & NFServices
128.46	178.79	230.00	135.00	160.38	156.20	152.10	161.40	162.90	127.90	..	Imports of Goods & NFServices
302.52	383.89	465.02	416.43	474.97	540.95	565.42	557.00	589.40	558.60	..	Domestic Absorption
231.86	296.76	313.34	332.22	401.53	408.75	431.72	421.90	471.20	464.30	..	Private Consumption, etc.
25.66	32.13	35.57	40.98	42.50	65.60	70.60	73.50	49.70	45.00	..	General Gov't Consumption
45.00	55.00	116.11	43.23	30.94	66.60	63.10	61.60	68.50	49.30	..	Gross Domestic Investment
..	..	..	..	..	65.60	60.00	63.50	61.00	54.30	..	Fixed Investment
22.26	32.70	41.10	31.60	27.60	26.95	27.12	27.23	24.90	25.50	..	Indirect Taxes, net
220.05	253.63	298.92	341.83	389.59	472.90	475.90	473.97	500.70	510.80	..	GDP at factor cost
105.23	114.56	135.26	160.20	176.70	180.50	201.00	188.70	214.60	232.50	..	Agriculture
26.86	36.60	47.57	51.03	59.70	73.40	57.20	64.44	61.50	61.70	..	Industry
12.84	12.57	20.49	18.50	16.30	21.10	18.40	25.00	23.70	24.40	..	Manufacturing
87.96	102.47	116.09	130.60	153.19	219.00	217.70	220.83	224.60	216.60	..	Services, etc.
-15.21	-42.56	-8.89	0.23	-26.84	25.50	0.70	5.80	4.70	27.00	..	Gross Domestic Saving
6.87	-11.22	21.83	4.16	-17.49	36.15	13.17	18.39	21.05	30.96	..	Gross National Saving
				(Billions of 1987 CFA Francs)							
428.06	463.10	497.01	483.47	491.04	517.46	509.96	488.40	498.04	504.84	..	Gross National Product
429.16	467.98	499.74	489.64	499.22	530.94	521.77	501.20	507.35	519.53	I	GDP at Market Prices
-107.54	-117.99	-135.94	-31.54	-40.94	-43.45	-64.80	-55.80	-63.09	-61.56	..	Resource Balance
117.17	127.93	151.76	122.00	124.83	121.57	93.12	105.60	92.82	97.00	..	Exports of Goods & NFServices
224.70	245.92	287.70	153.54	165.77	165.02	157.93	161.40	155.91	158.56	..	Imports of Goods & NFServices
536.70	585.97	635.68	521.18	540.16	574.39	586.57	557.00	570.44	581.09	..	Domestic Absorption
344.70	370.28	404.56	376.94	407.68	429.43	447.24	421.90	441.14	451.13	..	Private Consumption, etc.
59.52	64.94	69.76	69.08	73.02	77.19	73.80	73.50	62.77	56.83	..	General Gov't Consumption
132.48	150.76	161.36	75.15	59.46	67.77	65.53	61.60	66.53	73.13	..	Gross Domestic Investment
..	..	..	..	..	..	..	..	..	..	..	Fixed Investment
408.42	438.92	469.96	460.48	469.76	502.78	494.15	473.97	482.73	..	I	GDP at factor cost
162.76	151.13	153.94	155.48	157.83	179.13	198.72	188.70	217.02	..	..	Agriculture
37.67	45.83	60.06	60.33	66.01	69.22	63.25	64.44	63.97	..	..	Industry
14.62	13.72	22.37	20.20	17.75	20.86	24.27	25.00	25.75	..	..	Manufacturing
205.82	248.27	259.41	244.67	245.92	254.44	232.18	220.83	201.74	..	..	Services, etc.
											Memo Items:
119.38	111.73	131.34	104.64	106.05	121.60	93.14	105.60	94.85	130.92	..	Capacity to Import
2.22	-16.20	-20.42	-17.37	-18.78	0.03	0.01	0.00	2.03	33.92	..	Terms of Trade Adjustment
431.38	451.78	479.32	472.27	480.44	530.97	521.78	501.20	509.38	553.44	..	Gross Domestic Income
430.28	446.90	476.59	466.11	472.26	517.49	509.98	488.40	500.07	538.75	..	Gross National Income
				(Index 1987 = 100)							**DOMESTIC PRICES/DEFLATORS**
56.5	61.2	68.0	76.3	83.6	94.1	96.4	100.0	103.6	103.2	..	Overall (GDP)
56.4	65.5	73.2	79.9	87.9	94.2	96.4	100.0	103.3	96.1	..	Domestic Absorption
64.7	75.8	87.9	103.0	112.0	100.8	101.1	100.0	98.9	..	..	Agriculture
71.3	79.9	79.2	84.6	90.4	106.0	90.4	100.0	96.1	..	..	Industry
87.8	91.6	91.6	91.6	91.8	101.1	75.8	100.0	92.0	..	..	Manufacturing
..	..	..	..	..	..	..	..	..	..	..	Consumer Price Index
											MANUFACTURING ACTIVITY
..	..	..	..	..	..	..	..	..	..	..	Employment (1987=100)
..	..	..	..	..	..	..	..	..	..	..	Real Earnings per Empl. (1987=100)
..	..	..	..	..	..	..	..	..	..	..	Real Output per Empl. (1987=100)
24.8	25.0	..	..	..	..	..	..	..	..	..	Earnings as % of Value Added
				(Millions of current CFA Francs)							**MONETARY HOLDINGS**
61,407	75,436	98,438	97,000	110,610	111,620	109,142	96,814	97,862	104,192	..	Money Supply, Broadly Defined
45,407	60,436	83,438	82,000	89,489	87,090	78,926	61,844	71,954	84,372	..	Money
17,047	28,103	28,844	22,511	26,954	20,262	26,166	19,606	23,685	36,391	..	Currency Outside Banks
28,360	32,333	54,594	59,489	62,535	66,828	52,760	42,238	48,269	47,981	..	Demand Deposits
16,000	15,000	15,000	15,000	21,121	24,530	30,216	34,970	25,908	19,820	..	Quasi-Money
				(Millions of current CFA Francs)							**GOVERNMENT DEFICIT (-) OR SURPLUS**
..	..	..	..	..	..	..	..	..	..	..	Current Revenue
..	..	..	..	..	..	..	..	..	..	..	Current Expenditure
..	..	..	..	..	..	..	..	..	..	..	Current Budget Balance
..	..	..	..	..	..	..	..	..	..	..	Capital Receipts
..	..	..	..	..	..	..	..	..	..	..	Capital Payments

BENIN	1969	1970	1971	1972	1973	1974	1975	1976	1977	1978	1979
FOREIGN TRADE (CUSTOMS BASIS)					*(Millions of current US dollars)*						
Value of Exports, fob	42.80	58.00	69.70	67.30	93.00	93.00	116.10	85.90	129.10	125.60	132.90
Nonfuel Primary Products	39.47	51.78	65.38	61.54	85.79	72.02	98.59	74.20	119.41	114.28	120.77
Fuels	0.03	0.09	0.02	0.02	0.02	4.53	0.30	0.33	0.50	0.37	0.43
Manufactures	3.30	6.13	4.30	5.74	7.19	16.45	17.21	11.36	9.19	10.95	11.70
Value of Imports, cif	54.72	63.56	76.32	93.17	111.73	164.30	197.00	218.80	246.24	312.00	320.00
Nonfuel Primary Products	12.19	13.03	16.65	23.70	28.03	32.59	43.21	52.59	67.83	82.02	82.90
Fuels	1.91	2.42	2.77	4.02	6.37	16.07	15.22	12.41	12.29	16.85	21.83
Manufactures	40.62	48.11	56.90	65.45	77.33	115.64	138.57	153.80	166.12	213.13	215.28
					(Index 1987 = 100)						
Terms of Trade	160.8	158.3	141.7	146.1	217.7	152.2	123.4	164.0	205.6	170.2	152.4
Export Prices, fob	42.7	43.8	42.4	47.6	83.6	78.6	69.4	96.0	137.3	124.6	129.4
Import Prices, cif	26.6	27.7	29.9	32.6	38.4	51.6	56.2	58.5	66.8	73.2	84.9
BALANCE OF PAYMENTS					*(Millions of current US dollars)*						
Exports of Goods & Services	..	71.50	83.75	84.79	115.40	119.07	147.73	119.88	165.03	168.16	182.31
Merchandise, fob	..	58.00	69.71	67.31	92.99	92.99	116.10	85.86	129.06	125.56	132.91
Nonfactor Services	..	11.90	12.24	15.31	18.95	22.01	28.13	30.83	32.55	38.67	43.36
Factor Services	..	1.60	1.81	2.17	3.46	4.07	3.50	3.19	3.42	3.93	6.05
Imports of Goods & Services	..	94.60	108.92	132.13	155.45	190.69	268.28	272.70	330.40	373.93	388.65
Merchandise, fob	..	66.00	78.43	94.35	115.52	148.27	205.64	208.57	255.51	284.77	288.96
Nonfactor Services	..	24.50	25.58	33.44	36.48	40.64	57.88	60.98	71.27	85.49	94.91
Factor Services	..	4.10	4.91	4.34	3.46	1.79	4.76	3.16	3.61	3.67	4.78
Long-Term Interest	..	0.40	0.90	0.50	0.40	0.70	0.80	0.90	0.90	2.00	3.10
Private Current Transfers, net	..	0.00	1.81	3.15	3.34	4.55	14.93	26.71	37.97	54.73	71.08
Workers' Remittances	..	2.20	4.01	5.65	6.56	7.31	17.59	28.04	39.18	56.24	72.92
Curr. A/C Bal before Off. Transf.	..	-23.10	-23.37	-44.19	-36.72	-67.07	-105.63	-126.11	-127.39	-151.04	-135.26
Net Official Transfers	..	20.10	21.46	35.61	22.41	37.79	52.25	61.30	70.73	60.71	83.41
Curr. A/C Bal after Off. Transf.	..	-3.00	-1.91	-8.58	-14.31	-29.27	-53.38	-64.82	-56.66	-90.33	-51.85
Long-Term Capital, net	..	7.60	8.83	8.69	11.68	19.04	17.71	17.89	17.24	26.57	31.93
Direct Investment	..	6.70	2.81	4.78	3.46	-2.34	1.89	2.45	3.13	0.75	3.37
Long-Term Loans	..	1.00	5.00	4.30	9.20	11.50	11.40	23.80	30.20	34.20	147.50
Disbursements	..	2.40	7.70	6.70	11.10	16.90	16.70	27.20	33.20	37.40	150.90
Repayments	..	1.40	2.70	2.40	1.90	5.40	5.30	3.40	3.00	3.20	3.40
Other Long-Term Capital	..	-0.10	1.02	-0.39	-0.97	9.89	4.42	-8.36	-16.09	-8.39	-118.94
Other Capital, net	..	1.66	-1.11	2.28	4.17	10.69	15.81	52.09	39.55	57.30	16.29
Change in Reserves	..	-6.26	-5.81	-2.39	-1.55	-0.46	19.85	-5.17	-0.12	6.47	3.63
Memo Item:					*(CFA Francs per US dollar)*						
Conversion Factor (Annual Avg)	259.710	277.710	277.130	252.210	222.700	240.500	214.320	238.980	245.670	225.640	212.720
					(Millions of US dollars), outstanding at end of year						
EXTERNAL DEBT (Total)	..	40.5	48.0	43.5	56.1	70.3	80.4	101.9	161.8	233.2	396.4
Long-Term Debt (by debtor)	..	40.5	48.0	43.5	56.1	70.3	80.4	101.9	134.8	171.8	299.0
Central Bank, incl. IMF credit	..	1.5	2.7	2.8	3.1	3.9	4.2	3.8	6.3	15.6	15.9
Central Government	..	26.8	33.8	29.5	41.3	49.9	60.8	82.2	109.9	117.4	132.9
Rest of General Government	..	0.0	0.0	0.0	0.0	0.0	0.0	0.0	0.0	0.0	0.0
Non-financial Public Enterprises	..	12.2	11.5	11.2	11.7	16.5	15.4	15.9	18.6	38.8	150.2
Priv. Sector, incl non-guaranteed	..	..	..	..	..	..	..	..	..	..	..
Short-Term Debt	..	..	..	..	..	..	..	..	27.0	61.4	97.4
Memo Items:					*(Thousands of US dollars)*						
Int'l Reserves Excluding Gold	7,470.0	15,510.0	24,596.0	28,416.5	33,081.0	34,602.6	15,034.9	19,231.4	20,359.6	15,515.2	14,241.3
Gold Holdings (at market price)	..	..	..	..	..	..	..	..	923.7	1,898.4	5,683.2
SOCIAL INDICATORS											
Total Fertility Rate	6.9	6.9	6.9	6.9	6.8	6.7	6.6	6.6	6.5	6.5	6.5
Infant Mortality Rate	156.4	154.6	152.8	151.0	146.8	142.6	138.4	134.2	130.0	128.0	126.0
Life Expectancy at Birth	43.7	44.0	44.2	44.5	44.8	45.0	45.3	45.6	45.8	46.2	46.7
Urban Population, % of total	15.1	16.0	17.1	18.2	19.3	20.4	21.5	22.8	24.2	25.5	26.9
Food Prod. per capita (1987=100)	96.7	98.3	96.8	96.3	98.1	92.6	89.8	97.2	94.7	103.3	104.4
Labor Force, Agriculture (%)	81.3	80.9	79.8	78.6	77.6	76.5	75.6	74.4	73.3	72.2	71.2
Labor Force, Female (%)	47.8	47.9	48.0	48.1	48.2	48.3	48.4	48.6	48.7	48.8	48.8
Primary Schl. Enroll. Ratio	..	36.0	..	..	..	..	50.0	..	52.0	58.0	60.0
Primary Schl. Enroll. Ratio, Female	..	22.0	..	..	..	..	31.0	..	33.0	37.0	40.0
Secondary Schl. Enroll. Ratio	..	5.0	..	..	..	..	9.0	..	11.0	11.0	12.0

1980	1981	1982	1983	1984	1985	1986	1987	1988	1989 estimate	NOTES	BENIN
											FOREIGN TRADE (CUSTOMS BASIS)
				(Millions of current US dollars)							
222.50	184.00	143.60	121.94	146.70	152.00	93.90	168.00	189.00	..	f	Value of Exports, fob
101.30	71.36	63.42	80.21	64.49	68.69	38.51	83.41	85.22	..	..	Nonfuel Primary Products
111.59	105.85	74.13	34.10	68.08	67.02	35.00	45.34	55.21	..	..	Fuels
9.61	6.79	6.05	7.64	14.13	16.29	20.39	39.25	48.57	..	..	Manufactures
331.00	543.00	464.00	283.00	285.00	312.00	370.00	418.00	439.00	..	f	Value of Imports, cif
89.03	144.84	126.01	76.16	29.84	32.57	68.01	59.81	72.04	..	..	Nonfuel Primary Products
12.11	23.54	12.10	9.87	187.18	203.81	89.46	117.61	136.92	..	..	Fuels
229.86	374.62	325.90	196.96	67.98	75.62	212.53	240.58	230.03	..	..	Manufactures
				(Index 1987 = 100)							
158.9	162.8	145.6	137.1	100.9	91.4	84.5	100.0	100.4	..	..	Terms of Trade
147.6	150.8	130.9	120.2	123.9	110.6	83.6	100.0	98.8	..	..	Export Prices, fob
92.9	92.6	89.9	87.7	122.8	121.0	99.0	100.0	98.5	..	..	Import Prices, cif
				(Millions of current US dollars)							**BALANCE OF PAYMENTS**
306.30	256.00	214.50	241.70	234.80	242.40	258.10	351.60	332.70	331.30	f	Exports of Goods & Services
222.40	184.00	143.60	175.80	170.30	176.50	186.30	260.10	231.80	234.40	..	Merchandise, fob
83.80	71.80	70.60	65.60	64.50	65.90	71.80	91.50	100.90	96.90	..	Nonfactor Services
0.10	0.20	0.30	0.30	0.00	0.00	0.00	0.00	0.00	..	..	Factor Services
611.00	661.30	706.20	367.90	396.60	419.70	471.20	592.90	583.70	445.60	f	Imports of Goods & Services
499.20	522.40	575.70	250.80	266.20	276.20	332.40	407.70	415.00	293.50	..	Merchandise, fob
108.80	135.50	124.20	103.50	100.80	114.70	106.10	142.60	131.80	108.00	..	Nonfactor Services
3.00	3.40	6.30	13.60	29.60	28.80	32.70	42.60	36.90	44.10	..	Factor Services
2.90	3.10	6.00	13.20	16.80	13.60	21.70	14.90	7.60	12.20	..	Long-Term Interest
107.40	127.00	99.50	23.60	38.20	52.50	68.70	84.50	86.80	56.50	f	Private Current Transfers, net
107.40	127.00	99.50	23.60	38.20	52.50	68.70	84.50	81.60	56.50	..	Workers' Remittances
-197.30	-278.30	-392.20	-102.60	-123.60	-124.80	-144.40	-156.80	-176.70	-57.80	..	Curr. A/C Bal before Off. Transf.
63.40	81.70	64.50	55.10	38.00	29.10	34.60	58.50	71.30	54.90	..	Net Official Transfers
-133.90	-196.60	-327.70	-47.50	-85.60	-95.70	-109.80	-98.30	-105.40	-2.90	..	Curr. A/C Bal after Off. Transf.
65.80	100.60	213.00	159.70	71.90	92.90	21.60	13.10	-11.20	65.90	f	Long-Term Capital, net
4.30	2.10	-0.50	-0.50	-0.50	0.70	1.20	1.30	1.30	1.30	..	Direct Investment
56.10	100.30	219.90	91.80	16.80	11.90	38.70	54.30	46.30	144.40	..	Long-Term Loans
61.90	107.20	228.50	102.60	37.80	38.00	71.40	69.50	56.50	151.30	..	Disbursements
5.80	6.90	8.60	10.80	21.00	26.10	32.70	15.20	10.20	6.90	..	Repayments
5.40	-1.80	-6.40	68.40	55.60	80.30	-18.30	-42.50	-58.80	-79.80	..	Other Long-Term Capital
49.00	180.30	-35.30	-113.20	21.90	-11.00	92.20	9.00	115.60	32.90	f	Other Capital, net
19.10	-84.30	150.00	1.00	-8.20	13.80	-4.00	76.20	1.00	-95.90	..	Change in Reserves
				(CFA Francs per US dollar)							Memo Item:
211.300	271.730	328.620	381.070	436.960	449.260	346.300	300.540	297.850	319.010	..	Conversion Factor (Annual Avg)
				(Millions of US dollars), outstanding at end of year							
417.3	485.8	665.3	706.5	674.3	812.3	943.6	1,140.5	1,059.9	1,177.0	..	**EXTERNAL DEBT (Total)**
343.9	401.4	587.1	624.1	587.2	668.8	775.3	934.5	912.9	1,056.5	..	Long-Term Debt (by debtor)
28.7	28.1	29.6	28.0	25.8	27.9	26.5	26.5	20.6	18.4	..	Central Bank, incl. IMF credit
176.2	198.4	343.5	381.9	369.4	413.4	482.0	579.4	596.7	731.4	..	Central Government
0.0	0.0	0.0	0.0	0.0	0.0	0.0	0.0	0.0	0.0	..	Rest of General Government
139.0	174.9	214.0	214.2	192.0	227.5	266.8	328.6	295.6	306.7	..	Non-financial Public Enterprises
..	..	..	..	..	..	..	..	..	..	..	Priv. Sector, incl non-guaranteed
73.4	84.4	78.2	82.4	87.1	143.5	168.3	206.0	147.0	120.5	..	Short-Term Debt
				(Thousands of US dollars)							Memo Items:
8,145.8	57,641.5	4,943.4	3,674.7	2,452.3	4,102.6	3,899.0	3,595.0	4,225.8	3,399.6	..	Int'l Reserves Excluding Gold
6,543.4	4,412.3	5,071.6	4,234.6	3,422.1	3,629.7	4,339.0	5,373.5	4,553.8	4,451.1	..	Gold Holdings (at market price)
											SOCIAL INDICATORS
6.5	6.5	6.5	6.5	6.5	6.5	6.5	6.5	6.4	6.3	..	Total Fertility Rate
124.0	122.0	120.0	119.2	118.4	117.6	116.8	116.0	114.5	113.0	..	Infant Mortality Rate
47.1	47.6	48.0	48.5	48.9	49.4	49.9	50.3	50.6	50.8	..	Life Expectancy at Birth
28.2	29.6	31.0	32.4	33.8	35.2	36.9	38.6	39.7	40.9	..	Urban Population, % of total
95.1	91.7	90.8	91.5	108.8	110.9	113.4	100.0	112.1	118.9	..	Food Prod. per capita (1987=100)
70.2	..	..	..	..	..	..	..	..	..	..	Labor Force, Agriculture (%)
48.9	48.8	48.7	48.5	48.4	48.3	48.1	47.9	47.7	47.6	..	Labor Force, Female (%)
64.0	..	70.0	67.0	67.0	65.0	63.0	..	..	..	..	Primary Schl. Enroll. Ratio
40.0	42.0	45.0	44.0	44.0	43.0	43.0	..	..	..	..	Primary Schl. Enroll. Ratio, Female
16.0	..	22.0	21.0	20.0	17.0	16.0	..	..	..	..	Secondary Schl. Enroll. Ratio

BHUTAN	1969	1970	1971	1972	1973	1974	1975	1976	1977	1978	1979
CURRENT GNP PER CAPITA (US $)	..	..	..	..	..	..	..	..	..	..	..
POPULATION (thousands)	963	976	983	995	1,011	1,028	1,047	1,068	1,091	1,115	1,140

USE AND ORIGIN OF RESOURCES *(Millions of current Bhutanese Ngultrum)*

	1969	1970	1971	1972	1973	1974	1975	1976	1977	1978	1979
Gross National Product (GNP)	..	..	..	..	..	..	..	..	..	..	..
Net Factor Income from Abroad	..	..	..	..	..	..	..	..	..	..	..
GDP at Market Prices	..	..	..	..	..	..	..	..	..	..	..
Resource Balance	..	..	..	..	..	..	..	..	..	..	..
Exports of Goods & NFServices	..	..	..	..	..	..	..	..	..	..	..
Imports of Goods & NFServices	..	..	..	..	..	..	..	..	..	..	..
Domestic Absorption	..	..	..	..	..	..	..	..	..	..	..
Private Consumption, etc.	..	..	..	..	..	..	..	..	..	..	..
General Gov't Consumption	..	..	..	..	..	..	..	..	..	..	..
Gross Domestic Investment	..	..	..	..	..	..	..	..	..	..	..
Fixed Investment	..	..	..	..	..	..	..	..	..	..	..
Indirect Taxes, net	..	..	..	..	..	..	..	..	..	..	..
GDP at factor cost	..	..	..	..	..	..	..	..	..	..	..
Agriculture	..	..	..	..	..	..	..	..	..	..	..
Industry	..	..	..	..	..	..	..	..	..	..	..
Manufacturing	..	..	..	..	..	..	..	..	..	..	..
Services, etc.	..	..	..	..	..	..	..	..	..	..	..
Gross Domestic Saving	..	..	..	..	..	..	..	..	..	..	..
Gross National Saving	..	..	..	..	..	..	..	..	..	..	..

(Millions of 1987 Bhutanese Ngultrum)

	1969	1970	1971	1972	1973	1974	1975	1976	1977	1978	1979
Gross National Product	..	..	..	..	..	..	..	..	..	..	..
GDP at Market Prices	..	..	..	..	..	..	..	..	..	..	..
Resource Balance	..	..	..	..	..	..	..	..	..	..	..
Exports of Goods & NFServices	..	..	..	..	..	..	..	..	..	..	..
Imports of Goods & NFServices	..	..	..	..	..	..	..	..	..	..	..
Domestic Absorption	..	..	..	..	..	..	..	..	..	..	..
Private Consumption, etc.	..	..	..	..	..	..	..	..	..	..	..
General Gov't Consumption	..	..	..	..	..	..	..	..	..	..	..
Gross Domestic Investment	..	..	..	..	..	..	..	..	..	..	..
Fixed Investment	..	..	..	..	..	..	..	..	..	..	..
GDP at factor cost	..	..	..	..	..	..	..	..	..	..	..
Agriculture	..	..	..	..	..	..	..	..	..	..	..
Industry	..	..	..	..	..	..	..	..	..	..	..
Manufacturing	..	..	..	..	..	..	..	..	..	..	..
Services, etc.	..	..	..	..	..	..	..	..	..	..	..
Memo Items:											
Capacity to Import	..	..	..	..	..	..	..	..	..	..	..
Terms of Trade Adjustment	..	..	..	..	..	..	..	..	..	..	..
Gross Domestic Income	..	..	..	..	..	..	..	..	..	..	..
Gross National Income	..	..	..	..	..	..	..	..	..	..	..

DOMESTIC PRICES/DEFLATORS *(Index 1987 = 100)*

	1969	1970	1971	1972	1973	1974	1975	1976	1977	1978	1979
Overall (GDP)	..	..	..	..	..	..	..	..	..	..	..
Domestic Absorption	..	..	..	..	..	..	..	..	..	..	..
Agriculture	..	..	..	..	..	..	..	..	..	..	..
Industry	..	..	..	..	..	..	..	..	..	..	..
Manufacturing	..	..	..	..	..	..	..	..	..	..	..
Consumer Price Index	..	..	..	..	..	..	..	..	..	..	..

MANUFACTURING ACTIVITY

	1969	1970	1971	1972	1973	1974	1975	1976	1977	1978	1979
Employment (1987=100)	..	..	..	..	..	..	..	..	..	..	..
Real Earnings per Empl. (1987=100)	..	..	..	..	..	..	..	..	..	..	..
Real Output per Empl. (1987=100)	..	..	..	..	..	..	..	..	..	..	..
Earnings as % of Value Added	..	..	..	..	..	..	..	..	..	..	..

MONETARY HOLDINGS *(Millions of current Bhutanese Ngultrum)*

	1969	1970	1971	1972	1973	1974	1975	1976	1977	1978	1979
Money Supply, Broadly Defined	..	..	..	..	..	..	..	..	..	..	..
Money	..	..	..	..	..	..	..	..	..	..	..
Currency Outside Banks	..	..	..	..	..	..	..	..	..	..	..
Demand Deposits	..	..	..	..	..	..	..	..	..	..	..
Quasi-Money	..	..	..	..	..	..	..	..	..	..	..

(Millions of current Bhutanese Ngultrum)

GOVERNMENT DEFICIT (-) OR SURPLUS	1969	1970	1971	1972	1973	1974	1975	1976	1977	1978	1979
Current Revenue	..	..	..	..	..	..	..	..	..	..	..
Current Expenditure	..	..	..	..	..	..	..	..	..	..	..
Current Budget Balance	..	..	..	..	..	..	..	..	..	..	..
Capital Receipts	..	..	..	..	..	..	..	..	..	..	..
Capital Payments	..	..	..	..	..	..	..	..	..	..	..

1980	1981	1982	1983	1984	1985	1986	1987	1988	1989 estimate	NOTES	BHUTAN
..	..	110	110	130	130	140	180	190	..	..	**CURRENT GNP PER CAPITA (US $)**
1,165	1,188	1,212	1,237	1,261	1,286	1,313	1,343	1,373	1,403	..	**POPULATION (thousands)**
				(Millions of current Bhutanese Ngultrum)							**USE AND ORIGIN OF RESOURCES**
912.9	1,031.6	1,200.1	1,332.2	1,717.7	1,941.7	2,334.6	3,258.0	3,596.6	..	..	Gross National Product (GNP)
-200.0	-269.7	-321.6	-456.1	-387.8	-449.7	-467.0	-349.5	-344.3	..	..	Net Factor Income from Abroad
1,112.9	1,301.3	1,521.7	1,788.3	2,105.5	2,391.4	2,801.6	3,607.5	3,940.9	4,374.0	..	GDP at Market Prices
-256.7	-408.8	-474.4	-561.2	-608.7	-760.3	-747.3	-435.1	-782.9	..	..	Resource Balance
145.4	207.4	213.2	227.8	290.2	367.5	550.5	767.5	1,200.8	..	..	Exports of Goods & NFServices
402.1	616.2	687.6	789.0	898.9	1,127.8	1,297.8	1,202.6	1,983.7	..	..	Imports of Goods & NFServices
1,369.6	1,710.0	1,996.0	2,350.0	2,714.3	3,151.7	3,548.9	4,042.6	4,723.8	..	..	Domestic Absorption
748.6	922.2	1,053.8	1,195.1	1,435.8	1,506.3	1,837.5	2,320.8	2,636.7	..	..	Private Consumption, etc.
275.9	287.3	326.7	442.9	513.2	560.9	576.3	633.6	568.7	..	..	General Gov't Consumption
345.1	500.5	615.5	712.0	765.3	1,084.5	1,135.1	1,088.2	1,518.4	..	..	Gross Domestic Investment
330.4	425.8	555.7	690.7	754.9	1,002.9	1,103.1	1,249.7	1,508.0	..	..	Fixed Investment
17.9	21.2	23.6	34.8	45.6	41.8	43.0	76.7	82.8	..	..	Indirect Taxes, net
1,095.0	1,280.1	1,498.1	1,753.5	2,059.9	2,349.6	2,758.6	3,530.8	3,858.1	4,399.0	..	GDP at factor cost
621.4	676.7	804.3	934.2	1,117.6	1,236.2	1,399.2	1,623.5	1,746.3	..	..	Agriculture
133.6	217.9	274.5	352.0	415.2	445.8	538.6	968.6	963.5	..	..	Industry
35.8	63.5	70.1	96.5	109.5	128.3	137.1	204.7	226.5	..	..	Manufacturing
340.0	385.5	419.3	467.3	527.1	667.6	820.8	938.7	1,148.3	..	..	Services, etc.
88.4	91.8	141.2	150.3	156.5	324.2	387.8	653.1	735.5	..	..	Gross Domestic Saving
..	..	..	-305.8	-231.3	-125.5	-79.2	303.6	391.2	..	..	Gross National Saving
				(Millions of 1987 Bhutanese Ngultrum)							
1,621.6	1,724.6	1,806.0	1,849.1	2,169.3	2,227.7	2,514.4	3,258.0	3,396.8	..	..	Gross National Product
1,980.6	2,179.8	2,294.4	2,486.9	2,663.1	2,748.1	3,021.8	3,607.5	3,722.4	3,882.7	..	GDP at Market Prices
..	..	..	..	..	..	..	..	..	..	..	Resource Balance
..	..	..	..	..	..	..	..	..	..	..	Exports of Goods & NFServices
..	..	..	..	..	..	..	..	..	..	..	Imports of Goods & NFServices
..	..	..	..	..	..	..	..	..	..	..	Domestic Absorption
..	..	..	..	..	..	..	..	..	..	..	Private Consumption, etc.
..	..	..	..	..	..	..	..	..	..	..	General Gov't Consumption
667.5	875.6	998.3	1,062.3	974.1	1,311.0	1,109.3	1,088.2	1,525.9	..	..	Gross Domestic Investment
632.7	737.6	894.3	1,023.2	947.5	1,195.7	1,055.9	1,249.7	1,501.5	..	..	Fixed Investment
1,948.6	2,144.0	2,258.6	2,438.3	2,605.1	2,699.9	2,975.1	3,530.8	3,644.2	3,801.2	..	GDP at factor cost
1,089.7	1,115.5	1,213.9	1,301.5	1,414.3	1,462.3	1,544.9	1,623.5	1,647.9	1,707.1	..	Agriculture
254.8	384.7	443.4	501.6	499.1	501.6	563.3	968.6	966.1	1,031.2	..	Industry
69.8	115.2	116.2	122.6	131.0	147.0	138.4	204.7	215.0	290.9	..	Manufacturing
591.7	638.7	599.5	635.2	691.8	736.0	866.8	938.7	1,030.2	1,062.9	..	Services, etc.
											Memo Items:
..	..	..	..	..	..	..	..	..	..	..	Capacity to Import
..	..	..	..	..	..	..	..	..	..	..	Terms of Trade Adjustment
..	..	..	..	..	..	..	..	..	..	..	Gross Domestic Income
..	..	..	..	..	..	..	..	..	..	..	Gross National Income
				(Index 1987 = 100)							**DOMESTIC PRICES/DEFLATORS**
56.2	59.7	66.3	71.9	79.1	87.0	92.7	100.0	105.9	112.7	..	Overall (GDP)
..	..	..	..	..	..	..	..	..	..	..	Domestic Absorption
57.0	60.7	66.3	71.8	79.0	84.5	90.6	100.0	106.0	..	..	Agriculture
52.4	56.6	61.9	70.2	83.2	88.9	95.6	100.0	99.7	..	..	Industry
51.3	55.1	60.3	78.7	83.6	87.3	99.0	100.0	105.3	..	..	Manufacturing
55.0	60.5	66.4	78.4	83.9	85.5	94.0	100.0	110.1	119.7	..	Consumer Price Index
											MANUFACTURING ACTIVITY
..	..	..	..	..	..	..	..	..	..	..	Employment (1987=100)
..	..	..	..	..	..	..	..	..	..	..	Real Earnings per Empl. (1987=100)
..	..	..	..	..	..	..	..	..	..	..	Real Output per Empl. (1987=100)
..	..	..	..	..	..	..	..	..	..	..	Earnings as % of Value Added
				(Millions of current Bhutanese Ngultrum)							**MONETARY HOLDINGS**
65.3	74.3	85.7	103.8	157.4	202.9	231.6	316.8	..	..	..	Money Supply, Broadly Defined
..	..	..	177.2	209.8	261.7	277.0	316.8	412.1	546.3	..	Money
..	..	..	22.1	46.2	70.4	90.7	103.5	149.1	188.1	..	Currency Outside Banks
..	..	..	155.1	163.6	191.3	186.3	213.3	263.0	358.2	..	Demand Deposits
..	..	..	-73.4	-52.4	-58.8	-45.4	0.0	..	..	..	Quasi-Money
				(Millions of current Bhutanese Ngultrum)							**GOVERNMENT DEFICIT (-) OR SURPLUS**
..	..	10.0	-23.0	32.0	-207.0	-98.0	..	32.0	..	..	Current Revenue
..	..	498.0	673.0	787.0	966.0	1,116.0	..	1,762.0	..	..	Current Revenue
..	..	213.0	223.0	304.0	441.0	423.0	..	775.0	..	..	Current Expenditure
..	..	285.0	450.0	482.0	525.0	693.0	..	987.0	..	..	Current Budget Balance
..	..	1.0	2.0	4.0	4.0	7.0	..	10.0	..	..	Capital Receipts
..	..	275.0	476.0	454.0	736.0	798.0	..	965.0	..	..	Capital Payments

BHUTAN	1969	1970	1971	1972	1973	1974	1975	1976	1977	1978	1979
FOREIGN TRADE (CUSTOMS BASIS)					*(Thousands of current US dollars)*						
Value of Exports, fob	..	..	..	..	..	..	..	..	..	..	2,971
Nonfuel Primary Products	..	..	..	..	..	..	..	..	..	..	..
Fuels	..	..	..	..	..	..	..	..	..	..	..
Manufactures	..	..	..	..	..	..	..	..	..	..	..
Value of Imports, cif	..	..	..	..	..	..	..	..	..	..	15,375
Nonfuel Primary Products	..	..	..	..	..	..	..	..	..	..	..
Fuels	..	..	..	..	..	..	..	..	..	..	..
Manufactures	..	..	..	..	..	..	..	..	..	..	..
					(Index 1987 = 100)						
Terms of Trade	..	..	..	..	..	..	..	..	..	..	..
Export Prices, fob	..	..	..	..	..	..	..	..	..	..	..
Import Prices, cif	..	..	..	..	..	..	..	..	..	..	..
BALANCE OF PAYMENTS					*(Millions of current US dollars)*						
Exports of Goods & Services	..	..	..	..	..	..	..	..	..	..	..
Merchandise, fob	..	..	..	..	..	..	..	..	..	..	..
Nonfactor Services	..	..	..	..	..	..	..	..	..	..	..
Factor Services	..	..	..	..	..	..	..	..	..	..	..
Imports of Goods & Services	..	..	..	..	..	..	..	..	..	..	..
Merchandise, fob	..	..	..	..	..	..	..	..	..	..	..
Nonfactor Services	..	..	..	..	..	..	..	..	..	..	..
Factor Services	..	..	..	..	..	..	..	..	..	..	..
Long-Term Interest	..	0.00	0.00	0.00	0.00	0.00	0.00	0.00	0.00	0.00	0.00
Private Current Transfers, net	..	..	..	..	..	..	..	..	..	..	..
Workers' Remittances	..	..	..	..	..	..	..	..	..	..	..
Curr. A/C Bal before Off. Transf.	..	..	..	..	..	..	..	..	..	..	..
Net Official Transfers	..	..	..	..	..	..	..	..	..	..	..
Curr. A/C Bal after Off. Transf.	..	..	..	..	..	..	..	..	..	..	..
Long-Term Capital, net	..	..	..	..	..	..	..	..	..	..	..
Direct Investment	..	..	..	..	..	..	..	..	..	..	..
Long-Term Loans	..	0.00	0.00	0.00	0.00	0.00	0.00	0.00	0.00	0.00	0.00
Disbursements	..	0.00	0.00	0.00	0.00	0.00	0.00	0.00	0.00	0.00	0.00
Repayments	..	0.00	0.00	0.00	0.00	0.00	0.00	0.00	0.00	0.00	0.00
Other Long-Term Capital	..	..	..	..	..	..	..	..	..	..	..
Other Capital, net	..	..	..	..	..	..	..	..	..	..	..
Change in Reserves	..	..	..	..	..	..	..	..	..	..	..
Memo Item:					*(Bhutanese Ngultrum per US dollar)*						
Conversion Factor (Annual Avg)	7.500	7.500	7.500	7.590	7.740	8.100	8.380	8.960	8.740	8.190	8.130
				(Thousands of US dollars), outstanding at end of year							
EXTERNAL DEBT (Total)	..	0	0	0	0	0	0	0	0	0	0
Long-Term Debt (by debtor)	..	0	0	0	0	0	0	0	0	0	0
Central Bank, incl. IMF credit	..	..	..	..	..	..	..	..	..	..	..
Central Government	..	0	0	0	0	0	0	0	0	0	0
Rest of General Government	..	..	..	..	..	..	..	..	..	..	..
Non-financial Public Enterprises	..	..	..	..	..	..	..	..	..	..	..
Priv. Sector, incl non-guaranteed	..	..	..	..	..	..	..	..	..	..	..
Short-Term Debt	..	0	0	0	0	0	0	0	0	0	0
Memo Items:					*(Thousands of US dollars)*						
Int'l Reserves Excluding Gold	..	..	..	..	..	..	..	..	..	..	..
Gold Holdings (at market price)	..	..	..	..	..	..	..	..	..	..	..
SOCIAL INDICATORS											
Total Fertility Rate	6.0	6.0	6.0	6.0	6.0	6.0	6.0	6.0	6.0	6.0	6.1
Infant Mortality Rate	159.6	157.4	155.2	153.0	151.8	150.6	149.4	148.2	147.0	145.4	143.8
Life Expectancy at Birth	41.3	41.6	41.9	42.3	42.8	43.3	43.8	44.3	44.8	45.0	45.3
Urban Population, % of total	3.0	3.1	3.2	3.3	3.3	3.4	3.5	3.6	3.7	3.7	3.8
Food Prod. per capita (1987=100)	75.3	75.6	76.0	76.5	76.8	77.3	77.9	78.3	78.8	79.5	79.8
Labor Force, Agriculture (%)	94.2	94.1	93.9	93.8	93.6	93.4	93.3	93.1	92.9	92.7	92.6
Labor Force, Female (%)	35.0	34.8	34.7	34.6	34.5	34.4	34.3	34.1	34.0	33.9	33.8
Primary Schl. Enroll. Ratio	..	6.0	..	..	..	..	..	9.0	10.0	10.0	11.0
Primary Schl. Enroll. Ratio, Female	..	1.0	..	..	..	..	..	5.0	6.0	6.0	7.0
Secondary Schl. Enroll. Ratio	..	1.0	..	..	..	..	1.0	1.0	..	1.0	1.0

1980	1981	1982	1983	1984	1985	1986	1987	1988	1989 estimate	NOTES	BHUTAN
				(Thousands of current US dollars)							**FOREIGN TRADE (CUSTOMS BASIS)**
17,000	19,200	16,500	15,900	18,200	21,900	30,300	54,900	..	..	..	Value of Exports, fob
..	..	..	..	..	..	..	..	..	..	..	Nonfuel Primary Products
..	..	..	..	..	..	..	..	..	..	..	Fuels
..	..	..	..	..	..	..	..	..	..	..	Manufactures
57,000	65,600	67,100	71,200	76,900	76,200	99,900	88,500	..	..	..	Value of Imports, cif
..	..	..	..	..	..	..	..	..	..	..	Nonfuel Primary Products
..	..	..	..	..	..	..	..	..	..	..	Fuels
..	..	..	..	..	..	..	..	..	..	..	Manufactures
				(Index 1987 = 100)							
..	..	..	..	..	..	..	..	..	..	..	Terms of Trade
..	..	..	..	..	..	..	..	..	..	..	Export Prices, fob
..	..	..	..	..	..	..	..	..	..	..	Import Prices, cif
				(Millions of current US dollars)							**BALANCE OF PAYMENTS**
..	..	..	..	..	..	..	..	..	..	..	Exports of Goods & Services
..	..	17.20	15.80	18.90	21.00	28.30	48.90	62.00	69.70	..	Merchandise, fob
..	..	..	9.00	10.60	10.70	12.50	13.70	14.30	12.80	..	Nonfactor Services
..	..	..	..	..	..	..	..	..	..	..	Factor Services
..	..	..	..	..	..	..	..	..	..	..	Imports of Goods & Services
..	..	66.70	69.90	69.80	84.60	93.90	89.00	103.90	114.90	..	Merchandise, fob
..	..	..	51.10	46.20	42.80	45.60	44.70	43.50	33.80	..	Nonfactor Services
..	..	..	..	..	..	..	..	..	..	..	Factor Services
0.00	0.00	0.00	0.00	0.00	0.00	0.20	0.50	0.70	2.30	..	Long-Term Interest
..	..	..	0.00	0.00	0.00	0.00	0.00	0.00	..	..	Private Current Transfers, net
..	..	..	..	..	..	..	..	..	..	..	Workers' Remittances
..	..	..	-96.20	-86.50	-95.70	-98.70	-71.10	-71.10	-66.20	..	Curr. A/C Bal before Off. Transf.
0.00	..	..	67.50	58.20	69.70	75.80	72.30	69.50	62.80	..	Net Official Transfers
..	..	..	-28.70	-28.30	-26.00	-22.90	1.20	-1.60	-3.40	..	Curr. A/C Bal after Off. Transf.
..	..	..	..	..	..	..	..	..	..	..	Long-Term Capital, net
..	..	..	..	..	..	..	..	..	..	..	Direct Investment
0.00	0.30	0.80	0.70	1.10	5.50	11.40	16.30	29.60	9.90	..	Long-Term Loans
0.00	0.30	0.80	0.70	1.10	5.50	11.40	16.30	30.20	11.70	..	Disbursements
0.00	0.00	0.00	0.00	0.00	0.00	0.00	0.00	0.60	1.80	..	Repayments
..	..	..	..	..	..	..	..	..	..	..	Other Long-Term Capital
..	..	..	..	..	..	..	..	..	..	..	Other Capital, net
..	..	..	..	..	..	..	..	..	..	..	Change in Reserves
				(Bhutanese Ngultrum per US dollar)							**Memo Item:**
7.860	8.660	9.460	10.100	11.360	12.370	12.610	12.960	13.920	16.230	..	Conversion Factor (Annual Avg)
				(Thousands of US dollars), outstanding at end of year							
0	300	1,100	1,800	2,700	8,800	21,000	40,700	68,300	79,200	..	**EXTERNAL DEBT (Total)**
0	300	1,100	1,800	2,700	8,800	21,000	40,700	68,300	77,200	..	Long-Term Debt (by debtor)
..	..	..	..	..	..	..	..	..	..	..	Central Bank, incl. IMF credit
0	300	1,100	1,800	2,700	8,800	21,000	40,700	68,300	77,200	..	Central Government
..	..	..	..	..	..	..	..	..	..	..	Rest of General Government
..	..	..	..	..	..	..	..	..	..	..	Non-financial Public Enterprises
..	..	..	..	..	..	..	..	..	..	..	Priv. Sector, incl non-guaranteed
0	0	0	0	0	0	0	0	0	2,000	..	Short-Term Debt
				(Thousands of US dollars)							**Memo Items:**
..	31,114.0	35,510.0	40,221.0	44,813.0	50,303.0	61,002.0	84,549.0	92,669.0	66,318.0	..	Int'l Reserves Excluding Gold
..	..	..	..	..	..	..	..	..	..	..	Gold Holdings (at market price)
											SOCIAL INDICATORS
6.1	6.2	6.2	6.1	5.9	5.8	5.7	5.5	5.5	5.5	..	Total Fertility Rate
142.2	140.6	139.0	136.8	134.6	132.4	130.2	128.0	126.6	125.3	..	Infant Mortality Rate
45.5	45.7	45.9	46.3	46.7	47.1	47.5	47.9	48.1	48.3	..	Life Expectancy at Birth
3.9	4.0	4.1	4.1	4.2	4.3	4.5	4.7	4.9	5.1	..	Urban Population, % of total
80.6	80.8	80.7	81.8	87.3	87.0	88.9	100.0	96.0	97.1	..	Food Prod. per capita (1987=100)
92.4	..	..	..	..	..	..	..	..	..	..	Labor Force, Agriculture (%)
33.7	33.5	33.3	33.2	33.0	32.9	32.7	32.6	32.4	32.3	..	Labor Force, Female (%)
16.0	..	22.0	24.0	26.0	27.0	24.0	..	26.0	..	..	Primary Schl. Enroll. Ratio
..	..	15.0	16.0	18.0	19.0	17.0	..	20.0	..	..	Primary Schl. Enroll. Ratio, Female
..	..	3.0	4.0	4.0	4.0	4.0	..	5.0	..	..	Secondary Schl. Enroll. Ratio

BOLIVIA	1969	1970	1971	1972	1973	1974	1975	1976	1977	1978	1979
CURRENT GNP PER CAPITA (US $)	230	230	250	270	290	320	360	400	410	440	470
POPULATION (thousands)	4,222	4,325	4,431	4,541	4,655	4,772	4,894	5,020	5,150	5,285	5,425

USE AND ORIGIN OF RESOURCES *(Millions of current Bolivianos)*

	1969	1970	1971	1972	1973	1974	1975	1976	1977	1978	1979
Gross National Product (GNP)	1.11E-2	1.19E-2	1.31E-2	1.66E-2	2.51E-2	4.17E-2	4.75E-2	5.45E-2	6.23E-2	7.27E-2	8.55E-2
Net Factor Income from Abroad	-3.62E-4	-2.84E-4	-1.79E-4	-3.09E-4	-4.88E-4	-8.22E-4	-7.92E-4	-8.96E-4	-1.68E-3	-2.33E-3	-3.93E-3
GDP at Market Prices	1.15E-2	1.21E-2	1.33E-2	1.69E-2	2.56E-2	4.25E-2	4.83E-2	5.54E-2	6.40E-2	7.50E-2	8.95E-2
Resource Balance	-2.71E-4	5.13E-5	-3.71E-4	-4.58E-4	-1.00E-4	3.68E-3	-2.93E-3	-1.09E-3	-1.72E-3	-5.55E-3	-2.84E-3
Exports of Goods & NFServices	2.72E-3	2.99E-3	2.80E-3	3.56E-3	7.06E-3	1.49E-2	1.26E-2	1.52E-2	1.74E-2	1.71E-2	2.20E-2
Imports of Goods & NFServices	2.99E-3	2.94E-3	3.18E-3	4.02E-3	7.16E-3	1.13E-2	1.55E-2	1.63E-2	1.91E-2	2.26E-2	2.48E-2
Domestic Absorption	1.18E-2	1.21E-2	1.37E-2	1.74E-2	2.57E-2	3.88E-2	5.12E-2	5.65E-2	6.57E-2	8.06E-2	9.23E-2
Private Consumption, etc.	7.97E-3	8.03E-3	9.11E-3	1.07E-2	1.57E-2	2.58E-2	2.84E-2	3.49E-2	4.07E-2	5.30E-2	6.08E-2
General Gov't Consumption	1.06E-3	1.17E-3	1.35E-3	1.70E-3	2.49E-3	3.95E-3	5.04E-3	5.93E-3	7.57E-3	9.54E-3	1.36E-2
Gross Domestic Investment	2.75E-3	2.88E-3	3.20E-3	5.00E-3	7.45E-3	9.10E-3	1.78E-2	1.57E-2	1.75E-2	1.80E-2	1.79E-2
Fixed Investment	2.13E-3	2.20E-3	2.43E-3	3.57E-3	5.63E-3	7.41E-3	1.25E-2	1.25E-2	1.41E-2	1.60E-2	1.66E-2
Indirect Taxes, net	7.54E-4	1.04E-3	1.10E-3	1.41E-3	2.64E-3	5.60E-3	5.85E-3	6.54E-3	7.72E-3	8.48E-3	1.02E-2
GDP at factor cost	1.08E-2	1.11E-2	1.22E-2	1.55E-2	2.29E-2	3.69E-2	4.24E-2	4.88E-2	5.63E-2	6.65E-2	7.93E-2
Agriculture	2.26E-3	2.41E-3	2.70E-3	3.33E-3	5.09E-3	8.88E-3	9.82E-3	1.10E-2	1.24E-2	1.39E-2	1.63E-2
Industry	3.52E-3	3.91E-3	3.98E-3	5.84E-3	9.81E-3	1.69E-2	1.55E-2	1.82E-2	2.11E-2	2.44E-2	2.83E-2
Manufacturing	1.50E-3	1.61E-3	1.77E-3	2.16E-3	3.26E-3	5.18E-3	5.94E-3	7.04E-3	8.16E-3	9.36E-3	1.18E-2
Services, etc.	5.73E-3	5.82E-3	6.61E-3	7.75E-3	1.07E-2	1.67E-2	2.29E-2	2.62E-2	3.04E-2	3.67E-2	4.49E-2
Gross Domestic Saving	2.47E-3	2.93E-3	2.83E-3	4.55E-3	7.35E-3	1.28E-2	1.49E-2	1.46E-2	1.57E-2	1.25E-2	1.50E-2
Gross National Saving	..	2.67E-3	2.68E-3	4.30E-3	6.95E-3	1.20E-2	1.41E-2	1.38E-2	1.41E-2	1.03E-2	1.13E-2

(Millions of 1987 Bolivianos)

	1969	1970	1971	1972	1973	1974	1975	1976	1977	1978	1979
Gross National Product	6,380	6,400	6,790	7,120	7,490	7,860	8,420	8,930	9,210	9,480	9,350
GDP at Market Prices	6,590	6,570	6,890	7,260	7,640	8,030	8,560	9,090	9,470	9,790	9,780
Resource Balance	-500	-630	-740	-830	-710	-490	-970	-800	-810	-960	-920
Exports of Goods & NFServices	1,470	1,190	1,330	1,470	1,630	1,620	1,550	1,710	1,680	1,630	1,650
Imports of Goods & NFServices	1,970	1,820	2,070	2,300	2,340	2,110	2,520	2,510	2,490	2,590	2,570
Domestic Absorption	7,090	7,190	7,630	8,090	8,350	8,530	9,540	9,880	10,300	10,700	10,700
Private Consumption, etc.	3,710	3,830	3,910	3,630	4,200	4,310	3,840	4,550	4,780	5,170	5,480
General Gov't Consumption	670	730	790	880	980	1,070	1,190	1,260	1,300	1,340	1,560
Gross Domestic Investment	2,710	2,630	2,920	3,580	3,170	3,140	4,500	4,070	4,190	4,230	3,650
Fixed Investment	2,020	1,920	2,110	2,360	2,300	2,510	3,010	3,150	3,330	3,650	3,360
GDP at factor cost	..	..	..	..	..	..	..	..	..	9,500	9,520
Agriculture	1,650	1,720	1,820	1,920	2,010	2,090	2,250	2,360	2,350	2,400	2,470
Industry	3,020	2,950	3,100	3,360	3,900	3,880	3,910	4,070	4,170	4,070	3,810
Manufacturing	988	1,040	1,080	1,160	1,220	1,360	1,440	1,560	1,670	1,750	1,710
Services, etc.	2,000	1,990	2,080	2,140	2,100	2,370	2,660	2,890	3,120	3,400	3,530

Memo Items:

	1969	1970	1971	1972	1973	1974	1975	1976	1977	1978	1979
Capacity to Import	1,790	1,850	1,830	2,040	2,310	2,800	2,040	2,340	2,260	1,950	2,270
Terms of Trade Adjustment	322	657	500	567	678	1,180	498	628	585	324	623
Gross Domestic Income	6,910	7,220	7,390	7,830	8,320	9,220	9,060	9,710	10,100	10,100	10,400
Gross National Income	6,700	7,060	7,290	7,690	8,170	9,040	8,920	9,560	9,800	9,800	9,970

DOMESTIC PRICES/DEFLATORS *(Index 1987 = 100)*

	1969	1970	1971	1972	1973	1974	1975	1976	1977	1978	1979
Overall (GDP)	1.75E-4	1.85E-4	1.93E-4	2.33E-4	3.35E-4	5.29E-4	5.64E-4	6.09E-4	6.76E-4	7.67E-4	9.14E-4
Domestic Absorption	1.66E-4	1.68E-4	1.79E-4	2.15E-4	3.07E-4	4.55E-4	5.37E-4	5.71E-4	6.39E-4	7.50E-4	8.63E-4
Agriculture	1.36E-4	1.40E-4	1.48E-4	1.73E-4	2.53E-4	4.26E-4	4.36E-4	4.67E-4	5.30E-4	5.80E-4	6.57E-4
Industry	1.17E-4	1.32E-4	1.28E-4	1.74E-4	2.52E-4	4.35E-4	3.97E-4	4.46E-4	5.06E-4	6.00E-4	7.44E-4
Manufacturing	1.52E-4	1.55E-4	1.65E-4	1.86E-4	2.67E-4	3.82E-4	4.12E-4	4.51E-4	4.89E-4	5.36E-4	6.89E-4
Consumer Price Index	2.19E-4	2.28E-4	2.36E-4	2.51E-4	3.31E-4	5.39E-4	5.82E-4	6.08E-4	6.57E-4	7.25E-4	8.69E-4

MANUFACTURING ACTIVITY

	1969	1970	1971	1972	1973	1974	1975	1976	1977	1978	1979
Employment (1987=100)	..	48.5	46.0	48.5	56.7	69.4	72.3	69.3	68.5	61.9	65.3
Real Earnings per Empl. (1987=100)	..	209.5	232.3	246.4	231.1	193.3	196.4	216.9	230.9	237.6	240.6
Real Output per Empl. (1987=100)	..	185.4	210.0	214.9	200.5	188.2	187.2	211.9	243.0	322.5	281.0
Earnings as % of Value Added	..	43.4	43.3	42.1	40.2	42.2	41.8	39.4	38.6	32.6	34.2

MONETARY HOLDINGS *(Thousands of current Bolivianos)*

	1969	1970	1971	1972	1973	1974	1975	1976	1977	1978	1979
Money Supply, Broadly Defined	1.70E+0	1.90E+0	2.30E+0	2.80E+0	3.80E+0	5.40E+0	6.70E+0	9.90E+0	1.28E+1	1.45E+1	1.66E+1
Money	1.40E+0	1.50E+0	1.80E+0	2.20E+0	3.00E+0	4.30E+0	4.80E+0	6.50E+0	7.90E+0	8.80E+0	1.03E+1
Currency Outside Banks	1.00E+0	1.20E+0	1.30E+0	1.60E+0	2.10E+0	2.70E+0	3.10E+0	4.00E+0	4.90E+0	5.80E+0	7.20E+0
Demand Deposits	3.20E-1	3.80E-1	4.84E-1	6.12E-1	8.96E-1	1.50E+0	1.70E+0	2.50E+0	3.00E+0	3.00E+0	3.10E+0
Quasi-Money	3.06E-1	3.81E-1	4.93E-1	6.34E-1	8.07E-1	1.20E+0	2.00E+0	3.40E+0	5.00E+0	5.70E+0	6.30E+0

GOVERNMENT DEFICIT (-) OR SURPLUS *(Thousands of current Bolivianos)*

	1969	1970	1971	1972	1973	1974	1975	1976	1977	1978	1979
Current Revenue	..	..	..	..	..	..	..	..	..	..	..
Current Expenditure	..	..	..	..	..	..	..	..	..	..	..
Current Budget Balance	..	..	..	..	..	..	..	..	..	..	..
Capital Receipts	..	..	..	..	..	..	..	..	..	..	..
Capital Payments	..	..	..	..	..	..	..	..	..	..	..

1980	1981	1982	1983	1984	1985	1986	1987	1988	1989 estimate	NOTES	BOLIVIA
490	560	530	480	450	420	440	510	590	620	A	**CURRENT GNP PER CAPITA (US $)**
5,570	5,720	5,875	6,035	6,200	6,371	6,547	6,729	6,917	7,110	..	**POPULATION (thousands)**
				(Millions of current Bolivianos)							**USE AND ORIGIN OF RESOURCES**
1.16E-1	1.60E-1	3.45E-1	1.20E+0	18.3	2,033.5	6,719.5	8,125.1	9,630.3	11,478.1	..	Gross National Product (GNP)
-7.20E-3	-9.90E-3	-2.98E-2	-9.84E-2	-1.3	-191.2	-591.9	-533.2	-620.9	-681.7	..	Net Factor Income from Abroad
1.23E-1	1.70E-1	3.75E-1	1.30E+0	19.6	2,224.8	7,311.4	8,658.4	10,251.3	12,159.8	..	GDP at Market Prices
4.90E-3	-3.60E-3	1.50E-2	3.83E-2	0.6	-38.2	-213.6	-552.0	-567.8	-453.3	..	Resource Balance
2.56E-2	2.50E-2	6.06E-2	1.96E-1	2.4	321.9	1,349.9	1,344.8	1,582.2	2,344.2	..	Exports of Goods & NFServices
2.07E-2	2.86E-2	4.56E-2	1.58E-1	1.8	360.1	1,563.5	1,896.7	2,150.0	2,797.5	..	Imports of Goods & NFServices
1.18E-1	1.74E-1	3.60E-1	1.30E+0	19.0	2,263.0	7,525.0	9,210.3	10,819.1	12,613.1	..	Domestic Absorption
8.26E-2	1.32E-1	2.47E-1	9.30E-1	12.9	1,735.5	6,092.9	7,187.8	8,206.8	9,711.1	..	Private Consumption, etc.
1.73E-2	1.85E-2	6.15E-2	2.46E-1	4.7	300.4	855.5	1,060.4	1,390.4	1,348.6	..	General Gov't Consumption
1.82E-2	2.36E-2	5.18E-2	1.15E-1	1.4	227.0	576.6	962.1	1,222.0	1,553.4	..	Gross Domestic Investment
1.76E-2	1.87E-2	5.17E-2	1.14E-1	1.7	161.1	695.0	893.2	1,324.0	1,540.3	..	Fixed Investment
3.30E-3	4.30E-3	4.90E-3	6.20E-3	0.0	17.7	88.7	111.1	96.5	82.5	..	Indirect Taxes, net
1.20E-1	1.66E-1	3.70E-1	1.30E+0	19.6	2,207.0	7,222.6	8,547.3	10,154.8	12,077.3	B	GDP at factor cost
2.26E-2	2.86E-2	7.84E-2	3.74E-1	7.3	878.9	2,556.0	2,836.0	3,357.5	3,875.6	..	Agriculture
4.27E-2	5.21E-2	1.44E-1	4.10E-1	5.7	744.0	2,173.8	2,459.5	3,085.2	3,642.8	..	Industry
1.80E-2	2.45E-2	3.34E-2	1.35E-1	1.7	275.2	951.4	1,094.6	1,335.5	..	..	Manufacturing
5.76E-2	8.96E-2	1.53E-1	5.46E-1	6.6	601.9	2,581.6	3,362.8	3,808.6	4,641.4	..	Services, etc.
2.30E-2	2.01E-2	6.68E-2	1.53E-1	2.1	188.8	363.0	410.1	654.2	1,100.1	..	Gross Domestic Saving
1.61E-2	1.05E-2	3.81E-2	6.44E-2	0.8	6.3	-193.3	-86.1	63.1	473.9	..	Gross National Saving
				(Millions of 1987 Bolivianos)							
9,100	9,190	8,570	8,050	8,180	8,010	7,830	8,130	8,420	8,610	..	Gross National Product
9,690	9,780	9,360	8,750	8,830	8,830	8,510	8,660	8,950	9,270	..	GDP at Market Prices
-420	-1,110	-200	-320	-140	-480	-470	-560	-140	-240	..	Resource Balance
1,270	1,220	1,250	1,200	1,130	1,310	1,280	1,340	1,640	1,700	..	Exports of Goods & NFServices
1,690	2,330	1,450	1,520	1,270	1,790	1,750	1,900	1,780	1,940	..	Imports of Goods & NFServices
10,100	10,900	9,560	9,060	8,970	9,310	8,990	9,210	9,100	9,510	..	Domestic Absorption
5,810	6,950	5,990	6,490	6,760	7,380	7,300	7,190	6,750	6,980	..	Private Consumption, etc.
1,530	1,210	1,510	1,380	1,290	950	1,040	1,060	1,300	1,400	..	General Gov't Consumption
2,780	2,740	2,070	1,190	921	988	649	962	1,050	1,130	..	Gross Domestic Investment
2,720	2,200	2,080	1,200	1,020	765	809	893	1,140	1,130	..	Fixed Investment
9,430	9,490	9,270	8,710	8,810	8,760	8,410	8,550	8,870	9,170	B	GDP at factor cost
2,510	2,490	2,660	2,220	2,730	2,980	2,840	2,840	2,860	2,820	..	Agriculture
3,820	3,730	3,460	3,310	2,930	2,610	2,420	2,460	2,760	3,200	..	Industry
1,720	1,590	1,390	1,330	1,140	1,040	1,060	1,090	1,140	1,510	..	Manufacturing
3,430	3,570	3,340	3,210	3,170	3,240	3,250	3,360	3,330	3,250	..	Services, etc.
											Memo Items:
2,090	2,040	1,930	1,890	1,720	1,600	1,510	1,340	1,310	1,630	..	Capacity to Import
819	815	684	685	588	289	237	0	-325	-7,204	..	Terms of Trade Adjustment
10,500	10,600	10,000	9,430	9,420	9,120	8,750	8,660	8,630	9,200	..	Gross Domestic Income
9,920	10,000	9,250	8,740	8,760	8,300	8,070	8,130	8,090	8,540	..	Gross National Income
				(Index 1987 = 100)							**DOMESTIC PRICES/DEFLATORS**
1.27E-3	1.74E-3	4.01E-3	1.52E-2	0.2	25.2	85.9	100.0	114.5	131.2	..	Overall (GDP)
1.17E-3	1.60E-3	3.76E-3	1.42E-2	0.2	24.3	83.7	100.0	118.9	132.6	..	Domestic Absorption
8.99E-4	1.15E-3	2.95E-3	1.68E-2	0.3	29.5	89.9	100.0	117.4	137.5	..	Agriculture
1.12E-3	1.40E-3	4.16E-3	1.24E-2	0.2	28.5	90.0	100.0	111.7	113.9	..	Industry
1.05E-3	1.54E-3	2.40E-3	1.02E-2	0.1	26.6	89.9	100.0	117.4	..	..	Manufacturing
1.28E-3	1.65E-3	3.84E-3	1.42E-2	0.2	23.2	87.3	100.0	116.0	133.4	..	Consumer Price Index
											MANUFACTURING ACTIVITY
70.0	70.2	79.1	82.0	89.2	94.0	99.5	100.0	106.1	..	G	Employment (1987=100)
201.7	196.7	134.2	184.2	231.8	127.9	82.9	100.0	92.2	..	G	Real Earnings per Empl. (1987=100)
284.4	224.1	258.0	217.1	226.6	118.6	92.1	100.0	97.1	..	G	Real Output per Empl. (1987=100)
29.7	27.3	25.9	32.3	37.8	26.1	23.8	27.5	25.8	..	..	Earnings as % of Value Added
				(Thousands of current Bolivianos)							**MONETARY HOLDINGS**
2.31E+1	2.94E+1	9.72E+1	2.65E+2	4,053.40	..	..	..	..	..	..	Money Supply, Broadly Defined
1.47E+1	1.76E+1	5.78E+1	1.78E+2	3,369.80	..	..	..	..	..	..	Money
9.50E+0	1.09E+1	3.91E+1	1.25E+2	2,887.60	..	..	..	..	..	..	Currency Outside Banks
5.20E+0	6.70E+0	1.87E+1	5.28E+1	482.20	..	..	..	..	..	..	Demand Deposits
8.40E+0	1.18E+1	3.94E+1	8.76E+1	683.60	..	..	..	..	..	..	Quasi-Money
				(Thousands of current Bolivianos)							
..	..	-100	-200	-6,200	..	-5,500	66,700	-793,000	..	C F	**GOVERNMENT DEFICIT (-) OR SURPLUS**
..	..	..	..	700	233,000	1,010,000	1,180,000	1,440,000	..	..	Current Revenue
..	..	100	200	6,800	..	911,000	1,080,000	1,250,000	..	..	Current Expenditure
..	..	-100	-200	-6,100	..	103,000	92,500	185,000	..	..	Current Budget Balance
..	..	..	..	..	..	..	..	3,100	..	..	Capital Receipts
..	..	0	0	100	..	108,000	25,800	268,000	..	..	Capital Payments

BOLIVIA	1969	1970	1971	1972	1973	1974	1975	1976	1977	1978	1979
FOREIGN TRADE (CUSTOMS BASIS)					*(Millions of current US dollars)*						
Value of Exports, fob	172.30	190.20	181.10	201.20	260.50	556.50	444.10	568.20	631.70	628.80	759.80
Nonfuel Primary Products	151.22	175.72	156.34	164.41	204.69	377.96	298.95	404.34	480.55	511.33	619.29
Fuels	20.16	8.61	20.03	34.38	48.48	165.92	129.00	149.40	117.29	106.57	105.93
Manufactures	0.92	5.86	4.73	2.41	7.34	12.63	16.15	14.46	33.86	10.90	34.58
Value of Imports, cif	164.95	159.15	169.63	178.61	230.00	366.20	573.99	593.45	586.28	769.48	841.54
Nonfuel Primary Products	31.04	35.40	39.92	41.66	54.55	88.31	109.28	98.12	92.71	119.45	131.45
Fuels	1.78	1.97	2.12	1.59	2.22	3.81	12.56	10.70	8.46	10.89	7.08
Manufactures	132.13	121.78	127.59	135.36	173.23	274.08	452.15	484.63	485.11	639.14	703.01
					(Index 1987 = 100)						
Terms of Trade	108.3	132.8	104.0	92.5	107.3	171.8	137.8	157.3	173.4	168.5	188.1
Export Prices, fob	30.5	40.0	33.3	32.4	46.0	92.9	78.4	88.2	105.1	116.6	148.6
Import Prices, cif	28.1	30.1	32.1	35.0	42.8	54.1	56.9	56.1	60.6	69.2	79.0
BALANCE OF PAYMENTS					*(Millions of current US dollars)*						
Exports of Goods & Services	..	207.1	202.3	223.0	294.1	597.7	494.6	636.2	700.7	706.0	873.4
Merchandise, fob	..	190.4	181.6	201.3	260.8	556.5	444.7	563.0	634.3	627.3	759.8
Nonfactor Services	..	14.2	16.1	21.2	26.1	36.9	40.9	60.4	60.8	76.2	105.2
Factor Services	..	2.5	4.5	0.5	7.2	4.3	9.0	12.8	5.6	2.5	8.4
Imports of Goods & Services	..	206.8	211.8	240.1	297.0	474.3	667.5	706.9	833.6	1,064.5	1,321.6
Merchandise, fob	..	135.2	144.3	153.2	193.2	324.1	469.9	512.3	579.0	723.9	738.4
Nonfactor Services	..	43.7	45.5	64.1	71.3	118.2	147.8	145.7	180.0	221.8	390.7
Factor Services	..	27.9	22.0	22.8	32.4	32.0	49.9	48.9	74.6	118.8	192.5
Long-Term Interest	..	7.2	8.2	12.5	17.0	18.5	25.5	39.4	60.6	89.5	129.2
Private Current Transfers, net	..	1.5	2.1	4.9	4.9	3.0	3.4	3.2	2.3	5.5	10.5
Workers' Remittances	..	..	..	..	..	..	..	..	..	..	..
Curr. A/C Bal before Off. Transf.	..	1.8	-7.4	-12.2	2.0	126.4	-139.9	-64.3	-130.6	-353.0	-437.7
Net Official Transfers	..	2.4	5.0	8.6	10.5	10.6	9.7	10.8	12.7	21.5	40.7
Curr. A/C Bal after Off. Transf.	..	4.2	-2.4	-3.6	12.5	137.0	-130.2	-53.5	-117.9	-331.5	-397.0
Long-Term Capital, net	..	33.2	55.9	92.8	37.0	100.1	158.9	215.2	325.1	273.4	249.0
Direct Investment	..	-75.9	1.9	-10.5	4.6	25.9	53.4	-8.1	-1.2	11.5	35.0
Long-Term Loans	..	38.8	47.6	95.9	7.8	73.4	116.1	247.5	345.3	284.1	222.6
Disbursements	..	57.7	66.9	126.9	41.1	127.1	170.3	321.5	451.1	562.8	384.3
Repayments	..	18.9	19.3	31.0	33.3	53.7	54.2	74.0	105.8	278.7	161.7
Other Long-Term Capital	..	70.3	6.4	7.5	24.5	0.8	-10.6	-24.2	-19.0	-22.2	-8.6
Other Capital, net	..	-38.4	-54.7	-88.0	-52.7	-113.2	-68.8	-105.9	-145.3	-13.2	106.5
Change in Reserves	..	1.0	1.3	-1.3	3.2	-123.8	40.0	-55.8	-61.9	71.3	41.5
Memo Item:					*(Bolivianos per US dollar)*						
Conversion Factor (Annual Avg)	1.19E-5	1.19E-5	1.19E-5	1.33E-5	2.00E-5	2.00E-5	2.00E-5	2.00E-5	2.00E-5	2.00E-5	2.04E-5
Additional Conversion Factor	1.19E-5	1.19E-5	1.19E-5	1.33E-5	2.00E-5	2.60E-5	2.80E-5	2.80E-5	2.90E-5	3.20E-5	3.30E-5
				(Millions of US dollars), outstanding at end of year							
EXTERNAL DEBT (Total)	..	497.3	547.2	644.9	674.2	748.0	856.5	1,090.3	1,733.4	2,161.9	2,550.7
Long-Term Debt (by debtor)	..	497.3	547.2	644.9	674.2	748.0	856.5	1,090.3	1,448.4	1,797.9	2,022.7
Central Bank, incl. IMF credit	..	25.1	28.2	40.8	60.9	69.3	87.3	83.4	101.7	183.6	205.8
Central Government	..	302.9	312.0	356.3	371.4	418.4	459.5	587.9	735.0	809.3	874.8
Rest of General Government	..	0.1	0.7	2.5	4.1	3.3	2.1	2.5	23.2	47.4	53.1
Non-financial Public Enterprises	..	133.2	180.6	218.7	214.2	233.5	271.8	368.9	532.2	639.9	738.4
Priv. Sector, incl non-guaranteed	..	36.0	25.7	26.6	23.6	23.5	35.8	47.6	56.3	117.7	150.6
Short-Term Debt	..	0.0	0.0	0.0	0.0	0.0	0.0	0.0	285.0	364.0	528.0
Memo Items:					*(Millions of US dollars)*						
Int'l Reserves Excluding Gold	30.00	33.00	40.00	44.00	55.00	176.00	140.00	151.00	211.00	170.00	178.00
Gold Holdings (at market price)	12.00	14.00	17.00	26.00	46.00	76.00	57.00	56.00	99.00	146.00	350.00
SOCIAL INDICATORS											
Total Fertility Rate	6.5	6.5	6.5	6.5	6.5	6.5	6.4	6.4	6.4	6.4	6.3
Infant Mortality Rate	154.6	153.4	152.2	151.0	148.4	145.8	143.2	140.6	138.0	135.2	132.4
Life Expectancy at Birth	45.7	46.1	46.4	46.7	47.1	47.5	47.9	48.3	48.6	49.1	49.5
Urban Population, % of total	40.6	40.8	40.9	41.1	41.2	41.4	41.5	42.1	42.6	43.2	43.7
Food Prod. per capita (1987=100)	89.9	92.2	93.0	97.7	99.3	101.2	106.7	107.8	99.4	97.3	95.3
Labor Force, Agriculture (%)	52.5	52.1	51.5	50.9	50.3	49.8	49.2	48.6	48.0	47.5	46.9
Labor Force, Female (%)	21.4	21.5	21.6	21.7	21.8	21.9	22.0	22.1	22.2	22.3	22.4
Primary Schl. Enroll. Ratio	..	76.0	..	..	..	..	85.0	89.0	89.0	..	..
Primary Schl. Enroll. Ratio, Female	..	62.0	..	..	..	..	76.0	76.0	..	..	..
Secondary Schl. Enroll. Ratio	..	24.0	..	..	..	..	31.0	30.0	32.0	..	..

1980	1981	1982	1983	1984	1985	1986	1987	1988	1989 estimate	NOTES	BOLIVIA
				(Millions of current US dollars)							**FOREIGN TRADE (CUSTOMS BASIS)**
942.20	912.40	827.70	755.20	724.50	623.40	563.80	565.80	601.00	..	f	Value of Exports, fob
691.60	572.97	435.72	360.10	329.47	248.79	225.74	166.17	253.48	..	..	Nonfuel Primary Products
222.24	314.39	372.40	388.29	390.54	370.37	327.51	387.96	330.09	..	..	Fuels
28.36	25.04	19.59	6.82	4.49	4.24	10.55	11.67	17.43	..	..	Manufactures
665.00	917.10	577.50	589.10	491.60	551.90	716.20	776.00	604.00	..	f	Value of Imports, cif
103.87	143.17	90.16	91.97	74.54	80.38	104.01	135.75	106.02	..	..	Nonfuel Primary Products
6.76	9.37	5.79	5.94	9.89	10.25	9.77	11.70	18.98	..	..	Fuels
554.37	764.56	481.55	491.19	407.17	461.27	602.42	628.55	479.00	..	..	Manufactures
				(Index 1987 = 100)							
205.0	192.9	183.7	185.4	184.4	175.9	124.9	100.0	110.4	..	..	Terms of Trade
177.7	167.6	155.1	154.0	151.7	144.9	116.1	100.0	121.0	..	..	Export Prices, fob
86.7	86.9	84.4	83.1	82.3	82.4	93.0	100.0	109.5	..	..	Import Prices, cif
				(Millions of current US dollars)							**BALANCE OF PAYMENTS**
1,045.7	1,021.6	918.4	899.0	848.0	737.4	684.2	666.4	689.0	890.7	f	Exports of Goods & Services
942.2	912.4	827.7	755.1	724.5	623.4	545.5	518.7	542.5	723.5	..	Merchandise, fob
87.9	93.0	82.3	103.0	93.5	96.5	121.1	131.5	128.3	143.3	..	Nonfactor Services
15.6	16.2	8.4	40.9	30.0	17.5	17.6	16.2	18.2	23.9	..	Factor Services
1,111.6	1,525.9	1,136.8	1,143.3	1,110.7	1,099.3	1,168.4	1,210.4	1,128.7	1,310.7	f	Imports of Goods & Services
574.4	827.7	496.0	496.0	412.3	462.8	596.5	646.3	590.9	729.5	..	Merchandise, fob
256.5	316.8	218.7	241.6	250.5	243.6	243.7	266.4	251.2	295.0	..	Nonfactor Services
280.7	381.4	422.1	405.7	447.9	392.9	328.2	297.7	286.6	286.2	..	Factor Services
173.2	179.7	190.8	205.3	213.4	157.2	98.5	76.7	94.5	95.0	..	Long-Term Interest
12.7	13.3	16.7	40.2	21.8	19.7	18.5	18.0	12.7	20.6	..	Private Current Transfers, net
0.0	0.5	0.5	0.5	0.5	0.3	0.5	0.6	0.8	0.8	..	Workers' Remittances
-53.2	-491.0	-201.7	-204.1	-240.9	-342.2	-465.7	-526.0	-427.0	-399.4	..	Curr. A/C Bal before Off. Transf.
46.8	26.2	28.8	66.0	66.7	60.3	81.7	103.3	171.6	135.7	..	Net Official Transfers
-6.4	-464.8	-172.9	-138.1	-174.2	-281.9	-384.0	-422.7	-255.4	-263.7	..	Curr. A/C Bal after Off. Transf.
276.8	459.0	25.9	288.2	-144.2	-229.8	-54.0	23.2	266.2	228.0	f	Long-Term Capital, net
46.5	75.6	31.0	6.9	7.0	10.0	10.0	36.4	-12.0	-25.4	..	Direct Investment
311.5	251.4	185.0	45.4	60.3	-37.3	225.0	168.9	175.3	186.9	..	Long-Term Loans
456.8	379.6	309.0	152.2	210.6	137.1	328.6	256.7	330.8	326.9	..	Disbursements
145.3	128.2	124.0	106.8	150.3	174.4	103.6	87.8	155.5	140.0	..	Repayments
-81.2	132.0	-190.1	235.9	-211.5	-202.5	-289.0	-182.1	102.9	66.5	..	Other Long-Term Capital
-422.6	-191.4	32.6	121.3	471.9	534.9	603.4	385.5	-39.7	-140.6	f	Other Capital, net
152.2	197.2	114.5	-271.4	-153.5	-23.2	-165.5	14.0	28.9	176.3	..	Change in Reserves
				(Bolivianos per US dollar)							Memo Item:
2.45E-5	2.45E-5	6.41E-5	2.32E-4	0.003	0.440	1.920	2.050	2.350	2.690	..	Conversion Factor (Annual Avg)
4.00E-5	4.70E-5	1.19E-4	4.68E-4	0.007	0.758	1.920	2.050	2.350	2.690	..	Additional Conversion Factor
				(Millions of US dollars), outstanding at end of year							
2,699.8	3,218.8	3,328.6	4,069.4	4,317.0	4,804.7	5,574.5	5,840.3	5,430.9	4,358.6	..	**EXTERNAL DEBT (Total)**
2,399.8	2,916.0	3,092.2	3,758.1	3,808.0	4,148.6	4,817.2	5,009.6	4,822.6	4,056.6	..	Long-Term Debt (by debtor)
313.9	311.3	315.7	319.8	319.7	295.4	481.3	421.1	392.0	403.9	..	Central Bank, incl. IMF credit
1,114.4	1,649.7	1,795.1	2,334.2	2,474.7	2,581.0	3,062.7	3,626.2	3,550.6	2,792.1	..	Central Government
55.6	58.9	59.5	61.0	61.3	61.5	48.5	48.3	41.8	38.5	..	Rest of General Government
776.0	775.9	759.5	640.8	589.9	634.8	660.6	706.9	635.6	619.5	..	Non-financial Public Enterprises
139.9	120.2	162.4	402.3	362.4	575.9	564.1	207.1	202.6	202.6	..	Priv. Sector, incl non-guaranteed
300.0	302.8	236.4	311.3	509.0	656.1	757.3	830.7	608.3	302.0	..	Short-Term Debt
				(Millions of US dollars)							Memo Items:
106.00	100.00	156.00	160.00	252.00	200.00	164.00	97.00	106.00	205.00	..	Int'l Reserves Excluding Gold
447.00	329.00	407.00	349.00	281.00	292.00	350.00	433.00	367.00	358.00	..	Gold Holdings (at market price)
											SOCIAL INDICATORS
6.3	6.3	6.3	6.2	6.2	6.1	6.1	6.1	6.0	5.9	..	Total Fertility Rate
129.6	126.8	124.0	121.2	118.4	115.6	112.8	110.0	108.2	106.4	..	Infant Mortality Rate
49.9	50.3	50.7	51.2	51.7	52.2	52.6	53.1	53.4	53.7	..	Life Expectancy at Birth
44.3	45.0	45.7	46.4	47.1	47.8	48.5	49.2	50.0	50.7	..	Urban Population, % of total
97.6	101.4	103.5	76.4	95.3	100.7	96.8	100.0	102.9	97.7	..	Food Prod. per capita (1987=100)
46.4	..	..	..	..	..	..	..	..	..	..	Labor Force, Agriculture (%)
22.5	22.9	23.2	23.5	23.9	24.2	24.5	24.9	25.2	25.5	..	Labor Force, Female (%)
84.0	86.0	85.0	87.0	91.0	..	87.0	91.0	..	..	..	Primary Schl. Enroll. Ratio
78.0	78.0	..	81.0	85.0	..	82.0	85.0	..	..	..	Primary Schl. Enroll. Ratio, Female
36.0	34.0	35.0	35.0	37.0	..	37.0	37.0	..	..	..	Secondary Schl. Enroll. Ratio

BOTSWANA	1969	1970	1971	1972	1973	1974	1975	1976	1977	1978	1979
CURRENT GNP PER CAPITA (US $)	120	130	150	190	240	340	350	420	430	490	600
POPULATION (thousands)	604	624	647	673	699	727	755	784	812	841	871

USE AND ORIGIN OF RESOURCES					*(Millions of current Botswana Pula)*						
Gross National Product (GNP)	49.9	58.6	71.9	88.3	129.5	180.3	188.1	248.0	290.7	328.4	470.3
Net Factor Income from Abroad	-1.3	-1.3	-6.1	-15.3	-21.1	-8.0	-24.9	-25.9	-24.4	-31.9	-45.8
GDP at Market Prices	51.2	59.9	78.0	103.6	150.6	188.3	213.0	273.9	315.1	360.3	516.1
Resource Balance	-20.3	-24.3	-25.7	-25.9	-33.0	-45.4	-53.8	-52.3	-53.5	-98.1	-81.0
Exports of Goods & NFServices	11.7	13.6	20.4	39.8	55.2	76.4	93.8	135.2	155.5	161.1	275.9
Imports of Goods & NFServices	32.0	37.9	46.1	65.7	88.2	121.8	147.6	187.5	209.0	259.2	356.9
Domestic Absorption	71.5	84.2	103.7	129.5	183.6	233.7	266.8	326.2	368.6	458.4	597.1
Private Consumption, etc.	43.0	46.7	52.2	59.1	89.9	104.6	123.6	156.5	194.2	224.6	295.2
General Gov't Consumption	11.3	12.2	14.3	16.0	18.6	31.7	41.5	54.7	75.7	91.3	104.3
Gross Domestic Investment	17.2	25.3	37.2	54.4	75.1	97.4	101.7	115.0	98.7	142.5	197.6
Fixed Investment	9.9	17.3	30.3	54.5	64.3	79.6	57.3	79.1	77.8	110.1	162.9
Indirect Taxes, net	2.1	4.0	5.6	11.2	12.0	14.2	18.1	22.9	29.2	40.9	61.6
GDP at factor cost	49.1	55.9	72.4	92.4	138.6	174.1	194.9	251.0	285.9	319.4	454.5
Agriculture	23.2	19.8	25.7	34.2	49.7	62.4	61.2	65.7	74.4	71.7	81.7
Industry	5.2	16.5	21.5	28.6	41.6	49.5	60.5	84.4	91.8	107.3	193.1
Manufacturing	2.8	3.5	4.6	6.1	8.9	10.1	15.5	20.9	25.3	24.4	42.8
Services, etc.	22.8	23.6	30.8	40.8	59.3	76.4	91.3	123.8	148.9	181.3	241.3
Gross Domestic Saving	-3.1	1.0	11.5	28.5	42.1	52.0	47.9	62.7	45.2	44.4	116.6
Gross National Saving	..	0.4	8.3	20.9	34.2	72.5	17.5	41.6	26.0	17.8	72.5

					(Millions of 1987 Botswana Pula)						
Gross National Product	287.4	300.2	337.5	420.0	511.8	690.9	629.4	745.7	776.8	919.4	1,017.7
GDP at Market Prices	307.2	320.2	380.1	502.7	612.7	734.9	725.3	834.3	852.9	1,011.1	1,132.1
Resource Balance	-221.2	-247.7	-213.2	-176.7	-239.8	-240.4	-240.6	-169.7	-136.5	-124.4	-195.1
Exports of Goods & NFServices	86.7	100.7	150.9	275.3	313.3	378.2	388.8	522.5	530.1	633.6	740.1
Imports of Goods & NFServices	307.9	348.4	364.2	451.9	553.1	618.5	629.4	692.2	666.6	758.0	935.3
Domestic Absorption	528.4	567.9	593.3	679.4	852.5	975.2	965.9	1,003.9	989.4	1,135.6	1,327.2
Private Consumption, etc.	380.2	385.9	367.0	392.0	518.2	562.7	583.3	606.4	610.3	678.1	832.8
General Gov't Consumption	71.7	74.3	78.8	88.1	85.8	159.2	160.2	183.4	220.5	240.1	228.6
Gross Domestic Investment	76.5	107.6	147.6	199.2	248.5	253.3	222.4	214.2	158.5	217.3	265.8
Fixed Investment	..	..	..	..	..	395.0	243.0	277.1	233.5	313.2	404.5
GDP at factor cost	..	..	..	..	..	..	..	..	..	..	..
Agriculture	95.5	78.3	92.5	122.5	149.2	207.1	184.0	186.5	194.7	182.1	181.7
Industry	26.4	106.9	121.6	160.8	196.2	231.5	236.0	293.0	282.3	422.4	446.8
Manufacturing	21.5	25.7	30.9	40.7	50.2	56.7	79.8	102.3	112.7	105.5	142.0
Services, etc.	179.3	144.7	177.2	234.2	285.6	321.1	327.2	375.9	399.3	422.7	521.5

Memo Items:											
Capacity to Import	112.6	125.0	161.2	273.8	346.2	388.0	400.0	499.1	496.0	471.1	723.0
Terms of Trade Adjustment	25.9	24.3	10.2	-1.5	32.8	9.8	11.2	-23.4	-34.1	-162.5	-17.1
Gross Domestic Income	333.1	344.5	390.3	501.2	645.5	744.7	736.5	810.9	818.7	848.7	1,114.9
Gross National Income	313.3	324.5	347.8	418.5	544.7	700.7	640.6	722.2	742.7	756.9	1,000.6

DOMESTIC PRICES/DEFLATORS					*(Index 1987 = 100)*						
Overall (GDP)	16.7	18.7	20.5	20.6	24.6	25.6	29.4	32.8	36.9	35.6	45.6
Domestic Absorption	13.5	14.8	17.5	19.1	21.5	24.0	27.6	32.5	37.3	40.4	45.0
Agriculture	24.3	25.3	27.8	27.9	33.3	30.1	33.3	35.2	38.2	39.4	45.0
Industry	19.7	15.4	17.7	17.8	21.2	21.4	25.6	28.8	32.5	25.4	43.2
Manufacturing	13.0	13.6	14.9	15.0	17.7	17.8	19.4	20.4	22.4	23.1	30.1
Consumer Price Index	..	..	..	..	..	25.2	28.2	31.5	35.6	38.9	43.4

MANUFACTURING ACTIVITY											
Employment (1987=100)	..	..	15.7	18.0	19.4	22.4	26.2	29.1	28.2	30.3	37.3
Real Earnings per Empl. (1987=100)	..	..	..	..	..	..	..	..	..	..	..
Real Output per Empl. (1987=100)	..	..	..	..	..	..	..	..	..	..	..
Earnings as % of Value Added	..	..	..	27.6	..	39.6	51.6	20.6	37.1	50.4	29.7

MONETARY HOLDINGS					*(Millions of current Botswana Pula)*						
Money Supply, Broadly Defined	..	..	..	..	..	..	..	86.2	108.6	120.9	199.0
Money	..	..	..	..	..	..	..	43.5	58.2	60.9	82.1
Currency Outside Banks	..	..	..	..	..	..	..	10.4	12.4	15.8	17.9
Demand Deposits	..	..	..	..	..	..	..	33.1	45.8	45.2	64.2
Quasi-Money	..	..	..	..	..	..	..	42.7	50.4	60.0	116.9

GOVERNMENT DEFICIT (-) OR SURPLUS					*(Millions of current Botswana Pula)*						
GOVERNMENT DEFICIT (-) OR SURPLUS	..	..	-11.2	-21.0	-14.1	-5.7	1.2	-20.8	-4.6	-6.9	21.4
Current Revenue	..	..	19.2	28.9	45.6	65.9	89.3	84.0	115.1	160.1	242.3
Current Expenditure	..	..	18.1	20.2	26.0	36.0	46.8	63.5	75.8	100.0	137.0
Current Budget Balance	..	..	1.1	8.7	19.6	29.9	42.5	20.6	39.4	60.1	105.2
Capital Receipts	..	..	0.0	..	..	..	..	0.8	0.3	0.7	0.9
Capital Payments	..	..	12.3	29.7	33.7	35.6	41.2	42.1	44.3	67.7	84.8

1980	1981	1982	1983	1984	1985	1986	1987	1988	1989 estimate	NOTES	BOTSWANA
780	1,040	1,020	1,070	1,050	920	980	1,010	1,230	1,600	..	CURRENT GNP PER CAPITA (US $)
902	933	966	1,000	1,035	1,070	1,106	1,143	1,180	1,217	..	POPULATION (thousands)
				(Millions of current Botswana Pula)							USE AND ORIGIN OF RESOURCES
655.0	771.1	781.8	996.3	1,127.4	1,377.8	1,961.6	2,244.8	2,919.7	4,408.6	C	Gross National Product (GNP)
-54.5	-19.1	-11.1	-53.4	-174.7	-282.9	-273.7	-402.7	-478.2	-579.3	..	Net Factor Income from Abroad
709.5	790.2	792.9	1,049.7	1,302.1	1,660.7	2,235.3	2,647.5	3,397.9	4,987.9	C f	GDP at Market Prices
-88.4	-167.7	-288.5	-131.5	-7.8	-27.9	463.5	733.8	865.1	654.5	..	Resource Balance
357.8	398.0	349.9	618.3	772.3	970.3	1,591.6	2,132.9	2,674.9	3,173.5	..	Exports of Goods & NFServices
446.2	565.7	638.4	749.8	780.1	998.2	1,128.1	1,399.1	1,809.8	2,519.0	..	Imports of Goods & NFServices
797.9	957.9	1,081.4	1,181.2	1,309.9	1,688.6	1,771.6	1,913.7	2,532.8	4,333.4	..	Domestic Absorption
366.3	409.8	488.4	571.2	629.3	746.3	840.1	1,115.7	1,412.3	2,159.7	..	Private Consumption, etc.
140.7	203.2	242.6	301.9	362.8	443.1	531.8	630.4	770.7	979.8	..	General Gov't Consumption
290.9	344.9	350.4	308.1	317.8	499.2	399.7	167.6	349.8	1,193.9	..	Gross Domestic Investment
248.8	306.6	304.6	320.3	337.6	484.0	411.9	550.5	743.0	1,114.5	..	Fixed Investment
102.0	120.6	118.8	131.9	165.4	155.0	..	..	..	..	..	Indirect Taxes, net
607.5	669.6	674.1	917.8	1,136.7	1,505.7	2,037.4	..	..	..	B C f	GDP at factor cost
83.3	90.5	87.8	77.2	76.1	82.9	94.0	107.0	136.2	149.1	..	Agriculture
291.3	310.6	270.7	440.4	590.7	814.2	1,183.3	1,251.6	1,645.3	2,851.5	..	Industry
29.2	49.3	71.2	78.7	82.0	88.0	125.9	161.9	166.8	309.4	..	Manufacturing
334.9	389.1	434.4	532.1	635.3	763.6	958.0	1,288.9	1,616.4	1,987.3	..	Services, etc.
202.5	177.2	61.9	176.6	310.0	471.3	863.4	901.4	1,214.9	1,848.4	..	Gross Domestic Saving
146.9	156.7	50.6	122.8	125.8	182.4	584.8	510.1	761.7	1,237.6	..	Gross National Saving
				(Millions of 1987 Botswana Pula)							
1,183.6	1,347.1	1,345.5	1,622.0	1,812.9	1,835.6	2,131.6	2,244.8	2,478.9	2,826.5	C	Gross National Product
1,305.8	1,402.1	1,386.8	1,719.0	2,049.0	2,218.5	2,400.0	2,647.5	2,890.6	3,277.9	C	GDP at Market Prices
-250.4	-192.5	-313.8	176.2	501.4	202.8	617.7	733.8	525.0	-193.5	..	Resource Balance
716.3	871.3	776.8	1,280.3	1,581.6	1,534.3	1,844.6	2,132.9	2,158.7	1,811.6	..	Exports of Goods & NFServices
966.7	1,063.7	1,090.6	1,104.0	1,080.2	1,331.5	1,226.9	1,399.1	1,633.7	2,005.1	..	Imports of Goods & NFServices
1,556.2	1,594.5	1,700.6	1,542.7	1,547.7	2,015.7	1,782.3	1,913.7	2,365.6	3,471.4	..	Domestic Absorption
943.7	931.9	991.7	894.5	858.6	1,113.0	916.8	1,115.7	1,380.9	2,078.8	..	Private Consumption, etc.
269.6	313.5	371.7	414.6	459.9	537.5	583.8	630.4	710.9	809.7	..	General Gov't Consumption
342.9	349.1	337.2	233.6	229.2	365.3	281.6	167.6	273.8	582.8	..	Gross Domestic Investment
537.3	571.7	534.3	457.2	453.7	647.0	489.4	550.5	650.7	848.1	..	Fixed Investment
..	..	..	..	..	..	..	..	..	..	B C	GDP at factor cost
174.8	157.4	150.6	126.1	106.8	98.2	111.6	107.0	125.3	125.3	..	Agriculture
512.0	606.4	564.7	840.0	1,118.0	1,151.4	1,195.7	1,251.6	1,308.2	1,514.7	..	Industry
95.1	120.5	149.2	138.1	143.3	116.6	147.9	161.9	170.0	179.5	..	Manufacturing
636.7	649.9	685.2	752.9	824.2	968.9	1,092.7	1,288.9	1,457.2	1,638.0	..	Services, etc.
											Memo Items:
775.2	748.4	597.7	910.4	1,069.4	1,294.3	1,730.9	2,132.9	2,414.7	2,526.0	..	Capacity to Import
58.9	-122.9	-179.0	-369.9	-512.2	-240.0	-113.7	0.0	255.9	714.4	..	Terms of Trade Adjustment
1,364.7	1,279.2	1,207.8	1,349.1	1,536.9	1,978.5	2,286.3	2,647.5	3,146.6	3,992.4	..	Gross Domestic Income
1,242.5	1,224.3	1,166.5	1,252.2	1,300.7	1,595.5	2,018.0	2,244.8	2,734.8	3,540.9	..	Gross National Income
				(Index 1987 = 100)							DOMESTIC PRICES/DEFLATORS
54.3	56.4	57.2	61.1	63.5	74.9	93.1	100.0	117.5	152.2	..	Overall (GDP)
51.3	60.1	63.6	76.6	84.6	83.8	99.4	100.0	107.1	124.8	..	Domestic Absorption
47.7	57.5	58.3	61.2	71.3	84.4	84.2	100.0	108.7	119.0	..	Agriculture
56.9	51.2	47.9	52.4	52.8	70.7	99.0	100.0	125.8	188.3	..	Industry
30.7	40.9	47.7	57.0	57.2	75.5	85.1	100.0	98.1	172.4	..	Manufacturing
49.3	57.5	63.9	70.5	76.6	82.8	91.1	100.0	108.4	120.9	..	Consumer Price Index
											MANUFACTURING ACTIVITY
37.3	44.9	56.1	66.0	66.0	68.0	83.0	100.0	111.6	..	G	Employment (1987=100)
..	..	..	..	..	..	..	..	..	..	G	Real Earnings per Empl. (1987=100)
..	..	..	..	..	..	..	..	..	..	G	Real Output per Empl. (1987=100)
49.2	46.5	35.6	37.2	41.1	39.3	35.9	..	..	..	..	Earnings as % of Value Added
				(Millions of current Botswana Pula)							MONETARY HOLDINGS
236.9	226.5	245.6	316.3	368.9	557.4	606.2	1,013.3	1,228.3	1,797.3	..	Money Supply, Broadly Defined
90.6	114.8	127.4	137.3	150.6	188.2	243.4	312.1	406.5	506.5	..	Money
24.4	29.6	29.0	30.2	35.2	43.4	58.5	68.6	95.8	117.6	..	Currency Outside Banks
66.2	85.1	98.4	107.2	115.4	144.8	184.9	243.6	310.7	388.9	..	Demand Deposits
146.3	111.7	118.2	178.9	218.3	369.2	362.7	701.2	821.9	1,290.8	..	Quasi-Money
				(Millions of current Botswana Pula)							
-1.3	-18.3	-20.1	103.2	188.3	413.8	539.8	502.4	790.2	..	C	GOVERNMENT DEFICIT (-) OR SURPLUS
299.9	311.4	385.7	554.5	787.9	1,116.3	1,508.4	1,798.5	2,513.8	..	..	Current Revenue
178.6	211.9	270.1	316.1	416.3	497.6	727.5	962.5	1,215.7	..	..	Current Expenditure
121.3	99.5	115.6	238.4	371.6	618.8	780.9	836.0	1,298.1	..	..	Current Budget Balance
1.8	3.7	1.9	1.7	3.2	4.4	3.6	4.4	7.1	..	..	Capital Receipts
124.4	121.5	137.6	136.9	186.5	209.3	244.7	338.0	514.9	..	..	Capital Payments

BOTSWANA	1969	1970	1971	1972	1973	1974	1975	1976	1977	1978	1979
FOREIGN TRADE (CUSTOMS BASIS)					*(Millions of current US dollars)*						
Value of Exports, fob	18.0	22.0	28.0	58.0	85.0	121.0	142.0	176.0	180.0	222.0	436.0
Nonfuel Primary Products	17.1	16.5	18.7	31.9	55.2	70.1	92.2	126.2	114.9	114.9	176.9
Fuels	0.0	0.0	0.0	0.1	0.1	0.1	0.2	0.2	0.2	0.2	0.4
Manufactures	0.9	5.5	9.3	26.0	29.7	50.8	49.6	49.6	64.9	106.9	258.6
Value of Imports, cif	43.0	57.0	83.0	109.0	166.0	185.0	218.0	209.0	276.0	353.0	521.0
Nonfuel Primary Products	11.6	15.0	22.0	29.5	45.0	50.1	58.8	56.4	74.3	96.6	134.9
Fuels	4.1	6.0	8.0	10.4	15.8	17.6	21.6	20.7	27.9	30.4	72.4
Manufactures	27.3	36.0	53.0	69.1	105.2	117.3	137.6	131.9	173.8	226.0	313.6
					(Index 1987 = 100)						
Terms of Trade	147.4	149.3	132.1	130.0	137.5	114.2	112.9	112.5	102.2	100.6	100.4
Export Prices, fob	34.6	35.4	35.5	39.0	51.8	62.0	64.7	66.6	65.9	71.9	85.6
Import Prices, cif	23.5	23.7	26.8	30.0	37.7	54.2	57.3	59.2	64.4	71.4	85.2
BALANCE OF PAYMENTS					*(Millions of current US dollars)*						
Exports of Goods & Services	..	58.0	85.0	102.0	157.0	159.0	219.9	275.9	311.3	332.8	575.6
Merchandise, fob	..	26.0	38.0	57.0	92.0	120.0	142.0	169.7	191.6	223.4	442.2
Nonfactor Services	..	31.0	46.0	43.0	63.0	36.0	30.8	46.8	51.4	50.5	61.1
Factor Services	..	1.0	1.0	2.0	2.0	3.0	47.1	59.3	68.3	58.9	72.3
Imports of Goods & Services	..	94.0	130.0	161.0	225.0	221.0	273.6	310.5	370.7	465.4	666.6
Merchandise, fob	..	57.0	78.0	98.0	137.0	165.0	181.2	180.2	226.4	295.0	442.1
Nonfactor Services	..	34.0	46.0	50.0	70.0	41.0	46.7	78.4	89.9	101.8	128.3
Factor Services	..	3.0	6.0	13.0	18.0	15.0	45.7	51.9	54.4	68.6	96.2
Long-Term Interest	..	0.4	0.6	1.2	2.2	3.0	3.4	3.2	3.5	4.6	5.8
Private Current Transfers, net	..	1.0	4.0	10.0	19.0	42.0	-7.4	5.5	6.2	6.4	2.1
Workers' Remittances	..	..	..	..	..	..	..	..	..	..	..
Curr. A/C Bal before Off. Transf.	..	-35.0	-41.0	-49.0	-49.0	-20.0	-37.9	-29.1	-53.2	-126.2	-89.0
Net Official Transfers	..	5.0	4.0	10.0	1.0	2.0	2.3	14.4	32.3	14.7	35.0
Curr. A/C Bal after Off. Transf.	..	-30.0	-37.0	-39.0	-48.0	-18.0	-35.6	-14.7	-20.9	-111.5	-54.0
Long-Term Capital, net	..	15.0	92.0	156.0	142.0	124.0	50.2	19.8	-10.5	67.7	99.9
Direct Investment	..	6.0	38.0	60.0	53.0	46.0	-38.3	11.2	12.0	40.8	127.9
Long-Term Loans	..	5.5	15.4	44.9	41.4	18.2	21.0	24.8	13.4	7.7	12.1
Disbursements	..	5.7	15.7	45.3	41.7	18.5	24.7	25.9	15.8	11.3	15.6
Repayments	..	0.2	0.3	0.4	0.3	0.3	3.7	1.1	2.4	3.6	3.5
Other Long-Term Capital	..	3.5	38.6	51.1	47.6	59.8	67.4	-16.2	-35.8	19.2	-40.1
Other Capital, net	..	15.5	-42.0	-64.0	-52.0	-55.0	..	66.8	49.1	83.0	70.1
Change in Reserves	..	-0.5	-13.0	-53.0	-42.0	-51.0	..	-71.9	-17.7	-39.3	-116.0
Memo Item:					*(Botswana Pula per US dollar)*						
Conversion Factor (Annual Avg)	0.720	0.720	0.710	0.730	0.760	0.670	0.680	0.830	0.860	0.820	0.830
				(Millions of US dollars), outstanding at end of year							
EXTERNAL DEBT (Total)	..	17.40	33.20	74.80	114.90	134.10	147.30	165.20	183.80	123.50	127.70
Long-Term Debt (by debtor)	..	17.40	33.20	74.80	114.90	134.10	147.30	165.20	180.80	120.50	110.70
Central Bank, incl. IMF credit	..	0.00	0.00	0.00	0.00	0.00	0.00	0.00	0.00	0.00	0.00
Central Government	..	17.40	33.20	74.80	114.90	134.10	147.30	165.20	178.70	117.90	107.80
Rest of General Government	..	..	..	..	..	..	..	..	..	..	..
Non-financial Public Enterprises	..	0.00	0.00	0.00	0.00	0.00	0.00	0.00	2.10	2.60	2.90
Priv. Sector, incl non-guaranteed	..	0.00	0.00	0.00	0.00	0.00	0.00	0.00	0.00	0.00	0.00
Short-Term Debt	..	..	..	..	..	..	..	..	3.00	3.00	17.00
Memo Items:					*(Millions of US dollars)*						
Int'l Reserves Excluding Gold	..	..	..	..	..	..	.. ..	..	74.9	100.1	150.6	267.3
Gold Holdings (at market price)	..	..	..	..	..	..	..	..	..	..	..
SOCIAL INDICATORS											
Total Fertility Rate	6.9	6.9	6.9	6.9	6.9	6.8	6.8	6.7	6.7	6.7	6.7
Infant Mortality Rate	104.0	101.0	98.0	95.0	92.4	89.8	87.2	84.6	82.0	75.6	69.2
Life Expectancy at Birth	49.3	49.7	50.1	50.5	50.9	51.3	51.7	52.1	52.5	55.0	57.4
Urban Population, % of total	7.5	8.4	9.1	9.8	10.6	11.3	12.0	12.7	13.3	14.0	14.6
Food Prod. per capita (1987=100)	262.9	256.4	286.2	269.2	238.0	248.1	211.1	237.1	209.3	167.1	183.0
Labor Force, Agriculture (%)	86.1	85.5	83.8	82.3	80.8	79.4	78.1	76.3	74.7	73.2	71.7
Labor Force, Female (%)	44.0	43.8	43.1	42.5	41.8	41.3	40.7	40.1	39.5	38.9	38.4
Primary Schl. Enroll. Ratio	..	65.0	..	..	..	..	72.0	82.0	89.0	91.0	95.0
Primary Schl. Enroll. Ratio, Female	..	67.0	..	..	..	..	79.0	90.0	98.0	101.0	105.0
Secondary Schl. Enroll. Ratio	..	7.0	..	..	..	..	16.0	18.0	20.0	21.0	21.0

1980	1981	1982	1983	1984	1985	1986	1987	1988	1989 estimate	NOTES	BOTSWANA
											(Millions of current US dollars)
											FOREIGN TRADE (CUSTOMS BASIS)
503.0	413.0	456.0	637.0	673.6	744.5	857.7	1,520.9	1,418.0	..	f	Value of Exports, fob
150.1	191.9	166.4	240.9	266.3	281.6	297.9	920.6	877.6	..	..	Nonfuel Primary Products
0.1	0.4	0.4	0.5	0.5	0.5	0.2	0.3	0.4	..	..	Fuels
352.8	220.7	289.2	395.6	406.8	462.4	559.6	600.0	540.0	..	..	Manufactures
691.0	799.0	686.0	735.0	706.8	583.1	684.1	849.0	1,027.0	..	f	Value of Imports, cif
171.1	199.4	174.7	185.9	168.6	127.4	155.7	211.4	258.6	..	..	Nonfuel Primary Products
90.4	104.8	103.5	106.5	92.2	93.1	41.5	60.1	78.4	..	..	Fuels
429.5	494.9	407.8	442.6	446.0	362.5	486.9	577.5	690.0	..	..	Manufactures
											(Index 1987 = 100)
96.5	96.8	93.1	93.3	94.7	92.4	100.6	100.0	109.8	..	..	Terms of Trade
92.4	92.0	86.0	84.2	83.0	81.3	91.2	100.0	118.9	..	..	Export Prices, fob
95.8	95.1	92.3	90.2	87.7	88.0	90.7	100.0	108.3	..	..	Import Prices, cif
											(Millions of current US dollars)
											BALANCE OF PAYMENTS
747.5	604.4	645.5	836.0	877.6	888.8	1,069.0	1,912.9	1,823.9	1,939.0	..	Exports of Goods & Services
544.5	401.3	460.6	640.3	677.7	727.6	852.5	1,591.5	1,478.3	1,818.7	..	Merchandise, fob
100.9	97.0	102.5	113.0	107.2	76.3	100.0	149.6	153.1	120.3	..	Nonfactor Services
102.2	106.0	82.4	82.7	92.7	84.9	116.5	171.8	192.5	..	..	Factor Services
953.5	948.6	813.3	965.2	982.8	846.5	1,009.3	1,393.5	1,582.6	1,750.4	..	Imports of Goods & Services
602.5	687.1	579.8	615.3	583.4	493.8	608.4	803.9	883.2	1,227.0	..	Merchandise, fob
177.0	176.5	155.8	186.9	173.1	119.1	138.7	186.8	217.7	235.5	..	Nonfactor Services
174.0	85.0	77.7	163.1	226.2	233.6	262.2	402.8	481.8	287.9	..	Factor Services
6.7	6.8	9.8	12.9	15.3	20.5	27.8	33.5	34.0	33.0	..	Long-Term Interest
-1.4	-1.7	-0.2	-0.4	-7.3	-3.2	-2.6	6.8	13.7	-15.6	..	Private Current Transfers, net
..	..	..	..	..	..	..	..	..	..	..	Workers' Remittances
-207.4	-345.9	-168.0	-129.6	-112.5	39.2	57.1	526.2	255.0	173.0	..	Curr. A/C Bal before Off. Transf.
64.6	50.9	23.3	47.3	42.6	42.1	53.8	166.7	184.6	193.0	..	Net Official Transfers
-142.8	-295.0	-144.7	-82.3	-69.9	81.3	110.9	692.8	439.5	366.0	..	Curr. A/C Bal after Off. Transf.
135.6	121.7	105.8	64.0	114.8	105.0	99.6	-84.3	39.9	183.1	..	Long-Term Capital, net
109.2	88.3	21.1	22.5	61.9	52.1	70.4	113.6	39.9	128.5	..	Direct Investment
21.2	25.8	55.1	25.4	59.8	41.4	17.0	63.5	14.3	28.8	..	Long-Term Loans
27.2	27.8	59.1	37.3	76.6	68.1	34.4	99.4	52.5	64.4	..	Disbursements
6.0	2.0	4.0	11.9	16.8	26.7	17.4	35.9	38.2	35.6	..	Repayments
5.2	7.5	29.6	16.1	-6.9	11.5	12.2	-261.4	-14.3	25.8	..	Other Long-Term Capital
97.7	99.5	93.8	142.0	79.4	68.0	91.1	-47.0	-97.1	29.1	..	Other Capital, net
-90.4	73.8	-54.9	-123.6	-124.3	-254.3	-301.6	-561.5	-382.3	-578.2	..	Change in Reserves
											(Botswana Pula per US dollar)
											Memo Item:
0.790	0.780	0.920	1.090	1.140	1.610	1.910	1.820	1.690	1.990	..	Conversion Factor (Annual Avg)
											(Millions of US dollars), outstanding at end of year
133.20	157.60	203.10	225.60	260.70	333.60	387.00	513.30	501.60	520.20	..	**EXTERNAL DEBT (Total)**
129.20	149.60	200.10	221.60	255.70	331.60	383.90	509.00	497.80	516.60	..	Long-Term Debt (by debtor)
0.00	0.00	0.00	0.00	0.50	1.10	1.40	1.40	1.20	1.10	..	Central Bank, incl. IMF credit
117.10	130.00	181.40	198.90	200.10	232.50	264.00	364.70	367.10	393.70	..	Central Government
..	..	..	..	..	..	..	..	..	..	..	Rest of General Government
12.10	16.90	16.30	20.90	53.80	96.60	117.10	141.50	128.60	121.30	..	Non-financial Public Enterprises
0.00	2.70	2.40	1.80	1.30	1.40	1.40	1.40	0.90	0.50	..	Priv. Sector, incl non-guaranteed
4.00	8.00	3.00	4.00	5.00	2.00	3.10	4.30	3.80	3.60	..	Short-Term Debt
											(Millions of US dollars)
											Memo Items:
343.7	253.4	293.0	395.7	474.3	783.2	1,197.7	2,057.1	2,258.1	2,841.1	..	Int'l Reserves Excluding Gold
..	..	..	..	..	..	..	..	..	..	..	Gold Holdings (at market price)
											SOCIAL INDICATORS
6.7	6.7	6.8	6.5	6.2	5.9	5.6	5.3	5.1	5.0	..	Total Fertility Rate
62.8	56.4	50.0	48.3	46.7	45.0	43.4	41.7	40.5	39.3	..	Infant Mortality Rate
59.8	62.3	64.7	65.1	65.5	65.9	66.3	66.7	66.9	67.2	..	Life Expectancy at Birth
15.3	16.1	16.9	17.6	18.4	19.2	20.3	21.4	22.1	22.9	..	Urban Population, % of total
146.6	167.5	160.4	145.1	132.4	126.2	115.8	100.0	125.1	113.6	..	Food Prod. per capita (1987=100)
70.3	..	..	..	..	..	..	..	..	..	..	Labor Force, Agriculture (%)
37.8	37.5	37.2	36.9	36.6	36.3	36.0	35.7	35.4	35.2	..	Labor Force, Female (%)
92.0	..	96.0	99.0	103.0	108.0	112.0	114.0	..	..	..	Primary Schl. Enroll. Ratio
100.0	110.0	104.0	106.0	109.0	112.0	115.0	117.0	..	..	..	Primary Schl. Enroll. Ratio, Female
21.0	..	21.0	21.0	27.0	30.0	32.0	..	..	..	..	Secondary Schl. Enroll. Ratio

BRAZIL	1969	1970	1971	1972	1973	1974	1975	1976	1977	1978	1979
CURRENT GNP PER CAPITA (US $)	410	450	500	570	710	880	1,070	1,300	1,470	1,640	1,870
POPULATION (millions)	94	96	98	101	103	106	108	111	113	116	119

USE AND ORIGIN OF RESOURCES *(Billions of current Brazilian Cruzados)*

	1969	1970	1971	1972	1973	1974	1975	1976	1977	1978	1979
Gross National Product (GNP)	1.49E-1	1.92E-1	2.58E-1	3.44E-1	4.81E-1	7.07E-1	9.91E-1	2.00E+0	2.00E+0	4.00E+0	6.00E+0
Net Factor Income from Abroad	-3.24E-3	-1.84E-3	-2.46E-3	-3.31E-3	-4.47E-3	-6.18E-3	-1.43E-2	-2.48E-2	-4.02E-2	-8.38E-2	-1.63E-1
GDP at Market Prices	1.52E-1	1.94E-1	2.60E-1	3.47E-1	4.85E-1	7.14E-1	1.00E+0	2.00E+0	2.00E+0	4.00E+0	6.00E+0
Resource Balance	1.00E-4	-8.16E-4	-4.48E-3	-5.50E-3	-5.97E-3	-4.19E-2	-3.99E-2	-3.90E-2	-1.66E-2	-4.31E-2	-1.24E-1
Exports of Goods & NFServices	1.01E-2	1.37E-2	1.67E-2	2.52E-2	4.02E-2	5.72E-2	7.58E-2	1.15E-1	1.81E-1	2.42E-1	4.32E-1
Imports of Goods & NFServices	1.00E-2	1.45E-2	2.12E-2	3.07E-2	4.61E-2	9.91E-2	1.16E-1	1.54E-1	1.97E-1	2.85E-1	5.56E-1
Domestic Absorption	1.52E-1	1.95E-1	2.65E-1	3.53E-1	4.91E-1	7.55E-1	1.00E+0	2.00E+0	3.00E+0	4.00E+0	6.00E+0
Private Consumption, etc.	1.02E-1	1.33E-1	1.81E-1	2.42E-1	3.28E-1	5.05E-1	6.68E-1	1.00E+0	2.00E+0	2.00E+0	4.00E+0
General Gov't Consumption	1.65E-2	2.20E-2	2.87E-2	3.73E-2	5.07E-2	6.95E-2	1.07E-1	1.71E-1	2.35E-1	3.50E-1	5.90E-1
Gross Domestic Investment	3.41E-2	3.99E-2	5.49E-2	7.35E-2	1.13E-1	1.81E-1	2.70E-1	3.77E-1	5.50E-1	8.33E-1	1.00E+0
Fixed Investment	..	3.66E-2	5.14E-2	7.05E-2	1.04E-1	1.63E-1	2.45E-1	3.66E-1	5.32E-1	8.05E-1	1.00E+0
Indirect Taxes, net	2.47E-2	3.10E-2	3.83E-2	5.15E-2	6.95E-2	9.34E-2	1.18E-1	1.95E-1	2.96E-1	4.17E-1	6.14E-1
GDP at factor cost	1.28E-1	1.63E-1	2.22E-1	2.96E-1	4.16E-1	6.20E-1	8.87E-1	1.00E+0	2.00E+0	3.00E+0	5.00E+0
Agriculture	1.69E-2	2.02E-2	2.86E-2	3.84E-2	5.56E-2	8.01E-2	1.07E-1	1.87E-1	3.22E-1	3.73E-1	6.00E-1
Industry	4.78E-2	6.25E-2	8.51E-2	1.14E-1	1.62E-1	2.48E-1	3.56E-1	5.70E-1	8.48E-1	1.00E+0	2.00E+0
Manufacturing	3.69E-2	4.79E-2	6.50E-2	8.69E-2	1.24E-1	1.89E-1	2.69E-1	4.36E-1	6.44E-1	9.86E-1	2.00E+0
Services, etc.	6.31E-2	8.06E-2	1.08E-1	1.44E-1	1.98E-1	2.92E-1	4.23E-1	6.77E-1	1.00E+0	2.00E+0	3.00E+0
Gross Domestic Saving	3.41E-2	3.91E-2	5.04E-2	6.80E-2	1.07E-1	1.39E-1	2.30E-1	3.37E-1	5.33E-1	7.90E-1	1.00E+0
Gross National Saving	..	3.72E-2	4.79E-2	6.46E-2	1.02E-1	1.33E-1	2.16E-1	3.13E-1	..	7.07E-1	1.00E+0

(Billions of 1987 Brazilian Cruzados)

	1969	1970	1971	1972	1973	1974	1975	1976	1977	1978	1979
Gross National Product	4,000.0	4,390.0	4,890.0	5,490.0	6,280.0	6,860.0	7,170.0	7,870.0	8,220.0	8,430.0	8,960.0
GDP at Market Prices	4,090.0	4,440.0	4,950.0	5,550.0	6,350.0	6,930.0	7,290.0	8,000.0	8,370.0	8,640.0	9,230.0
Resource Balance	-70.0	-140.0	-220.0	-240.0	-320.0	-500.0	-420.0	-410.0	-350.0	-340.0	-350.0
Exports of Goods & NFServices	230.0	240.0	250.0	320.0	360.0	370.0	410.0	410.0	410.0	460.0	510.0
Imports of Goods & NFServices	300.0	380.0	470.0	560.0	680.0	870.0	830.0	820.0	760.0	800.0	860.0
Domestic Absorption	4,170.0	4,580.0	5,160.0	5,800.0	6,670.0	7,430.0	7,710.0	8,410.0	8,720.0	8,970.0	9,580.0
Private Consumption, etc.	2,530.0	2,920.0	3,290.0	3,670.0	4,090.0	4,530.0	4,480.0	5,110.0	5,460.0	5,590.0	6,130.0
General Gov't Consumption	480.0	510.0	560.0	600.0	680.0	680.0	780.0	840.0	800.0	840.0	910.0
Gross Domestic Investment	1,150.0	1,150.0	1,310.0	1,530.0	1,910.0	2,220.0	2,450.0	2,460.0	2,460.0	2,540.0	2,550.0
Fixed Investment	..	1,100.0	1,270.0	1,490.0	1,800.0	2,040.0	2,230.0	2,390.0	2,360.0	2,480.0	2,570.0
GDP at factor cost	3,660.0	4,020.0	4,480.0	5,030.0	5,760.0	6,280.0	6,600.0	7,250.0	7,580.0	7,810.0	8,340.0
Agriculture	460.0	470.0	520.0	540.0	540.0	540.0	580.0	590.0	670.0	650.0	680.0
Industry	1,520.0	1,650.0	1,850.0	2,110.0	2,470.0	2,680.0	2,810.0	3,140.0	3,240.0	3,600.0	3,840.0
Manufacturing	1,110.0	1,210.0	1,350.0	1,540.0	1,800.0	1,940.0	2,010.0	2,250.0	2,310.0	2,560.0	2,730.0
Services, etc.	1,670.0	1,900.0	2,110.0	2,380.0	2,750.0	3,080.0	3,230.0	3,550.0	3,700.0	3,610.0	3,860.0

Memo Items:

	1969	1970	1971	1972	1973	1974	1975	1976	1977	1978	1979
Capacity to Import	310.0	360.0	370.0	460.0	590.0	500.0	550.0	610.0	700.0	670.0	670.0
Terms of Trade Adjustment	80.0	110.0	120.0	150.0	230.0	130.0	130.0	200.0	290.0	210.0	160.0
Gross Domestic Income	420.0	4,560.0	5,060.0	5,700.0	6,580.0	7,060.0	7,420.0	8,200.0	8,660.0	8,850.0	9,390.0
Gross National Income	4,080.0	4,510.0	5,010.0	5,640.0	6,510.0	6,990.0	7,310.0	8,070.0	8,510.0	8,640.0	9,120.0

DOMESTIC PRICES/DEFLATORS *(Index 1987 = 100)*

	1969	1970	1971	1972	1973	1974	1975	1976	1977	1978	1979
Overall (GDP)	3.73E-3	4.37E-3	5.26E-3	6.25E-3	7.64E-3	1.03E-2	1.38E-2	2.04E-2	2.98E-2	4.20E-2	6.57E-2
Domestic Absorption	3.66E-3	4.26E-3	5.13E-3	6.08E-3	7.37E-3	1.02E-2	1.36E-2	1.98E-2	2.87E-2	4.09E-2	6.46E-2
Agriculture	3.64E-3	4.30E-3	5.55E-3	7.16E-3	1.04E-2	1.48E-2	1.85E-2	3.13E-2	4.82E-2	5.74E-2	8.82E-2
Industry	3.15E-3	3.79E-3	4.61E-3	5.38E-3	6.56E-3	9.27E-3	1.27E-2	1.82E-2	2.62E-2	3.58E-2	5.76E-2
Manufacturing	3.33E-3	3.96E-3	4.81E-3	5.64E-3	6.90E-3	9.78E-3	1.34E-2	1.93E-2	2.79E-2	3.85E-2	6.18E-2
Consumer Price Index	5.16E-3	6.31E-3	7.58E-3	8.83E-3	9.96E-3	1.27E-2	1.64E-2	2.33E-2	3.34E-2	4.64E-2	7.08E-2

MANUFACTURING ACTIVITY

	1969	1970	1971	1972	1973	1974	1975	1976	1977	1978	1979
Employment (1987=100)	47.6	49.7	52.8	57.4	74.7	79.1	82.5	87.8	92.7	98.3	102.0
Real Earnings per Empl. (1987=100)	45.3	61.0	68.2	77.4	79.1	84.3	80.8	88.3	89.8	94.0	98.1
Real Output per Empl. (1987=100)	51.4	57.1	58.1	64.4	69.2	75.7	81.7	79.6	77.8	79.4	78.7
Earnings as % of Value Added	16.7	22.3	23.6	25.4	23.3	21.9	18.9	20.1	20.9	21.2	20.7

MONETARY HOLDINGS *(Millions of current Brazilian Cruzados)*

	1969	1970	1971	1972	1973	1974	1975	1976	1977	1978	1979
Money Supply, Broadly Defined	39.110	50.110	0.055	0.083	0.127	0.175	0.276	0.416	0.636	0.959	1.680
Money	0.027	0.035	0.042	0.059	0.087	0.117	0.169	0.231	0.319	0.434	0.759
Currency Outside Banks	0.005	0.007	0.009	0.012	0.016	0.022	0.031	0.046	0.065	0.093	0.167
Demand Deposits	0.022	0.028	0.033	0.047	0.071	0.095	0.138	0.185	0.254	0.341	0.592
Quasi-Money	39.080	50.080	0.013	0.024	0.040	0.058	0.107	0.185	0.317	0.525	0.917

(Billions of current Brazilian Cruzados)

	1969	1970	1971	1972	1973	1974	1975	1976	1977	1978	1979
GOVERNMENT DEFICIT (-) OR SURPLUS	..	..	..	..	..	..	..	..	..	0.000	..
Current Revenue	..	..	..	0.000	0.000	0.000	0.000	0.000	0.001	0.001	0.001
Current Expenditure	..	..	..	..	..	0.000	0.000	0.000	0.000	0.001	0.001
Current Budget Balance	..	..	..	..	..	0.000	0.000	0.000	0.000	0.000	0.000
Capital Receipts	..	..	..	..	..	..	..	..	..	..	...
Capital Payments	..	..	..	..	..	0.000	0.000	0.000	0.000	0.000	0.000

1980	1981	1982	1983	1984	1985	1986	1987	1988	1989 estimate	NOTES	BRAZIL
2,070	2,030	2,070	1,840	1,730	1,670	1,810	1,960	2,120	2,540	..	CURRENT GNP PER CAPITA (US $)
121	124	127	130	133	136	138	141	144	147	..	POPULATION (millions)
(Billions of current Brazilian Cruzados)											USE AND ORIGIN OF RESOURCES
1.20E+1	2.40E+1	4.80E+1	1.12E+2	372	1,340	3,546	11,464	88,533	1,310,000	f	Gross National Product (GNP)
-3.96E-1	-9.97E-1	-3.00E+0	-7.00E+0	-22	-74	-163	-436	-3,419	-56,217	..	Net Factor Income from Abroad
1.20E+1	2.50E+1	5.10E+1	1.19E+2	394	1,413	3,709	11,900	91,952	1,370,000	f	GDP at Market Prices
-2.78E-1	-9.30E-2	-3.35E-1	3.00E+0	22	71	90	377	4,502	44,494	..	Resource Balance
1.00E+0	2.00E+0	4.00E+0	1.30E+1	52	169	323	1,091	9,423	102,000	..	Exports of Goods & NFServices
1.00E+0	2.00E+0	4.00E+0	1.10E+1	31	98	233	714	4,922	57,530	..	Imports of Goods & NFServices
1.30E+1	2.50E+1	5.10E+1	1.16E+2	372	1,342	3,619	11,523	87,451	1,320,000	..	Domestic Absorption
9.00E+0	1.70E+1	3.60E+1	8.50E+1	280	965	2,515	7,437	56,264	894,000	..	Private Consumption, etc.
1.00E+0	2.00E+0	5.00E+0	1.10E+1	32	137	391	1,462	11,150	122,000	..	General Gov't Consumption
3.00E+0	6.00E+0	1.10E+1	2.00E+1	60	240	713	2,624	20,036	306,000	..	Gross Domestic Investment
3.00E+0	5.00E+0	1.00E+1	1.90E+1	65	240	713	2,624	20,036	306,000	..	Fixed Investment
1.00E+0	3.00E+0	5.00E+0	1.20E+1	34	124	413	1,202	8,213	..	..	Indirect Taxes, net
1.10E+1	2.20E+1	4.60E+1	1.07E+2	360	1,289	3,296	10,698	83,739	..	f	GDP at factor cost
1.00E+0	2.00E+0	4.00E+0	1.10E+1	37	131	328	950	7,297	..	..	Agriculture
5.00E+0	1.00E+1	2.10E+1	4.60E+1	159	562	1,416	4,733	36,406	..	..	Industry
4.00E+0	7.00E+0	1.50E+1	3.40E+1	114	403	992	3,248	25,944	..	..	Manufacturing
5.00E+0	1.00E+1	2.10E+1	5.00E+1	163	596	1,551	5,015	40,036	..	..	Services, etc.
3.00E+0	6.00E+0	1.00E+1	2.20E+1	82	311	803	3,001	24,538	350,000	..	Gross Domestic Saving
2.00E+0	5.00E+0	8.00E+0	1.60E+1	60	238	641	2,569	21,145	294,000	..	Gross National Saving
(Billions of 1987 Brazilian Cruzados)											
9,740.0	9,220.0	9,160.0	8,800.0	9,270.0	10,100.0	11,000.0	11,500.0	11,400.0	11,800.0	..	Gross National Product
10,100.0	9,640.0	9,700.0	9,360.0	9,850.0	10,700.0	11,500.0	11,900.0	11,900.0	12,300.0	f	GDP at Market Prices
-250.0	0.0	-20.0	190.0	380.0	450.0	170.0	380.0	530.0	420.0	..	Resource Balance
620.0	760.0	690.0	780.0	960.0	1,020.0	910.0	1,090.0	1,230.0	1,300.0	..	Exports of Goods & NFServices
870.0	760.0	710.0	590.0	570.0	570.0	740.0	710.0	700.0	880.0	..	Imports of Goods & NFServices
10,300.0	9,640.0	9,720.0	9,170.0	9,470.0	10,200.0	11,300.0	11,500.0	11,400.0	11,900.0	..	Domestic Absorption
6,550.0	6,270.0	6,500.0	6,540.0	6,890.0	7,050.0	7,510.0	7,440.0	7,460.0	7,790.0	..	Private Consumption, etc.
910.0	880.0	950.0	870.0	780.0	900.0	1,180.0	1,460.0	1,450.0	1,500.0	..	General Gov't Consumption
2,860.0	2,490.0	2,270.0	1,760.0	1,800.0	2,170.0	2,650.0	2,620.0	2,450.0	2,610.0	..	Gross Domestic Investment
2,810.0	2,440.0	2,300.0	1,900.0	1,940.0	2,170.0	2,650.0	2,620.0	2,500.0	..	..	Fixed Investment
9,140.0	8,710.0	8,770.0	8,460.0	8,880.0	9,580.0	10,400.0	10,700.0	10,700.0	11,100.0	..	GDP at factor cost
740.0	800.0	800.0	800.0	820.0	900.0	820.0	950.0	960.0	980.0	..	Agriculture
4,200.0	3,830.0	3,830.0	3,610.0	3,840.0	4,180.0	4,680.0	4,730.0	4,600.0	4,780.0	..	Industry
2,980.0	2,670.0	2,670.0	2,510.0	2,670.0	2,890.0	3,220.0	3,250.0	3,140.0	3,190.0	..	Manufacturing
4,250.0	4,090.0	4,140.0	4,060.0	4,220.0	4,500.0	4,860.0	5,010.0	5,140.0	5,330.0	..	Services, etc.
Memo Items:											
690.0	730.0	660.0	750.0	980.0	990.0	1,020.0	1,090.0	1,350.0	1,570.0	..	Capacity to Import
70.0	20.0	-30.0	-40.0	20.0	-40.0	110.0	0.0	120.0	270.0	..	Terms of Trade Adjustment
10,200.0	9,610.0	9,670.0	9,320.0	9,870.0	10,600.0	11,600.0	11,900.0	12,000.0	12,600.0	..	Gross Domestic Income
9,810.0	9,190.0	9,130.0	8,760.0	9,290.0	10,000.0	11,100.0	11,500.0	11,500.0	12,000.0	..	Gross National Income
(Index 1987 = 100)											DOMESTIC PRICES/DEFLATORS
1.23E-1	2.56E-1	5.26E-1	1.30E+0	4.0	13.3	32.2	100.0	773.0	11,088.1	..	Overall (GDP)
1.23E-1	2.57E-1	5.28E-1	1.30E+0	3.9	13.1	31.9	100.0	769.4	11,100.5	..	Domestic Absorption
1.65E-1	2.88E-1	4.90E-1	1.40E+0	4.6	14.6	39.8	100.0	756.8	..	..	Agriculture
1.17E-1	2.50E-1	5.35E-1	1.30E+0	4.1	13.5	30.3	100.0	790.7	..	..	Industry
1.26E-1	2.68E-1	5.76E-1	1.30E+0	4.3	13.9	30.8	100.0	827.2	..	..	Manufacturing
1.29E-1	2.66E-1	5.26E-1	1.27E+0	3.8	12.4	30.3	100.0	782.3	10,850.3	..	Consumer Price Index
											MANUFACTURING ACTIVITY
106.9	92.1	90.9	82.8	87.6	95.5	106.2	100.0	98.1	..	G	Employment (1987=100)
90.7	103.2	111.6	102.8	95.3	98.7	102.5	100.0	98.6	..	G	Real Earnings per Empl. (1987=100)
80.8	83.8	78.7	91.2	93.3	91.8	91.9	100.0	94.0	..	G	Real Output per Empl. (1987=100)
17.2	18.3	19.4	16.1	13.7	14.5	16.5	15.1	15.0	..	..	Earnings as % of Value Added
(Millions of current Brazilian Cruzados)											MONETARY HOLDINGS
2.880	6.260	13.110	36.350	127.020	467.880	..	..	..	..	D	Money Supply, Broadly Defined
1.290	2.350	3.960	8.040	24.440	106.150	..	..	..	..	..	Money
0.290	0.523	1.010	1.880	6.250	23.850	..	..	..	..	..	Currency Outside Banks
0.998	1.830	2.950	6.160	18.190	82.300	..	..	..	..	..	Demand Deposits
1.590	3.910	9.150	28.310	102.580	361.730	..	..	..	..	..	Quasi-Money
(Billions of current Brazilian Cruzados)											
0.000	-0.001	-0.001	-0.005	-0.019	-0.154	-0.488	-1.390	-13.210	..	E	GOVERNMENT DEFICIT (-) OR SURPLUS
0.003	0.006	0.013	0.030	0.091	0.363	0.829	3.970	37.090	..	..	Current Revenue
0.002	0.005	0.010	0.024	0.078	0.349	1.000	2.970	28.050	..	..	Current Expenditure
0.001	0.001	0.003	0.006	0.012	0.014	-0.171	1.000	9.040	..	..	Current Budget Balance
..	0.000	0.000	0.001	0.001	0.005	0.000	0.027	0.221	..	..	Capital Receipts
0.001	0.002	0.004	0.012	0.032	0.173	0.317	2.420	22.470	..	..	Capital Payments

BRAZIL	1969	1970	1971	1972	1973	1974	1975	1976	1977	1978	1979
FOREIGN TRADE (CUSTOMS BASIS)					*(Millions of current US dollars)*						
Value of Exports, fob	2,311	2,739	2,904	3,991	6,199	7,951	8,669	10,128	12,120	12,659	15,244
Nonfuel Primary Products	2,062	2,335	2,350	3,167	4,779	5,769	6,098	7,377	8,763	8,128	9,140
Fuels	3	16	24	40	84	111	201	251	217	196	228
Manufactures	245	388	530	784	1,337	2,071	2,371	2,500	3,141	4,335	5,876
Value of Imports, cif	2,263	2,845	3,696	4,776	6,992	14,163	13,578	13,713	13,254	15,016	19,731
Nonfuel Primary Products	512	531	591	690	1,287	2,199	1,607	1,922	1,832	2,435	3,642
Fuels	292	351	523	643	1,054	3,372	3,551	4,332	4,502	4,937	7,314
Manufactures	1,459	1,962	2,581	3,443	4,652	8,591	8,421	7,459	6,920	7,645	8,776
					(Index 1987 = 100)						
Terms of Trade	194.8	205.4	188.7	187.7	210.8	157.8	145.3	158.0	172.6	142.0	121.0
Export Prices, fob	41.3	44.8	44.4	48.7	69.3	82.7	79.2	91.0	108.4	99.0	106.7
Import Prices, cif	21.2	21.8	23.5	25.9	32.9	52.4	54.5	57.6	62.8	69.7	88.2
BALANCE OF PAYMENTS					*(Millions of current US dollars)*						
Exports of Goods & Services	..	3,117	3,334	4,508	7,037	9,371	9,939	11,283	13,510	14,489	17,998
Merchandise, fob	..	2,739	2,891	3,941	6,093	7,814	8,492	9,961	11,923	12,473	15,244
Nonfactor Services	..	320	388	421	603	824	926	887	1,080	1,191	1,464
Factor Services	..	58	55	145	341	734	521	435	507	825	1,290
Imports of Goods & Services	..	3,975	4,985	6,204	9,222	16,934	16,950	17,841	18,622	21,597	28,493
Merchandise, fob	..	2,507	3,256	4,193	6,154	12,562	12,042	12,347	12,023	13,631	17,961
Nonfactor Services	..	788	939	1,151	1,626	2,354	2,281	2,340	2,623	2,863	3,763
Factor Services	..	680	790	860	1,442	2,019	2,627	3,154	3,976	5,103	6,769
Long-Term Interest	..	224	297	425	748	1,472	2,055	1,719	2,026	3,131	4,760
Private Current Transfers, net	..	-3	-7	-17	11	4	13	7	..	69	12
Workers' Remittances	..	..	..	..	..	..	..	..	..	..	5
Curr. A/C Bal before Off. Transf.	..	-861	-1,658	-1,713	-2,174	-7,560	-6,998	-6,551	-5,116	-7,039	-10,483
Net Official Transfers	..	24	20	23	17	-2	-10	-3	4	3	5
Curr. A/C Bal after Off. Transf.	..	-837	-1,638	-1,690	-2,158	-7,562	-7,008	-6,554	-5,112	-7,036	-10,478
Long-Term Capital, net	..	1,217	1,668	3,543	4,100	6,231	4,936	6,108	6,040	10,088	6,460
Direct Investment	..	407	536	570	1,341	1,268	1,190	1,372	1,687	1,882	2,223
Long-Term Loans	..	1,336	1,430	3,552	2,662	6,290	4,825	5,639	5,827	9,527	5,827
Disbursements	..	1,792	1,995	4,311	3,812	8,210	7,067	8,162	9,494	14,727	12,341
Repayments	..	456	564	758	1,150	1,920	2,242	2,523	3,668	5,200	6,513
Other Long-Term Capital	..	-526	-298	-580	96	-1,327	-1,079	-903	-1,474	-1,321	-1,590
Other Capital, net	..	114	453	579	354	347	1,007	3,118	-407	1,576	1,231
Change in Reserves	..	-494	-483	-2,431	-2,296	984	1,065	-2,672	-521	-4,628	2,787
Memo Item:					*(Brazilian Cruzados per US dollar)*						
Conversion Factor (Annual Avg)	0.0041	0.0046	0.0053	0.0059	0.0061	0.0068	0.0081	0.0107	0.0141	0.0181	0.0270
				(Billions of US dollars), outstanding at end of year							
EXTERNAL DEBT (Total)	..	5.13	6.63	10.17	12.94	19.42	23.75	29.05	41.41	53.85	60.72
Long-Term Debt (by debtor)	..	5.13	6.63	10.17	12.94	19.42	23.75	29.05	35.42	46.78	52.08
Central Bank, incl. IMF credit	..	0.39	0.51	0.70	1.16	2.06	2.68	3.06	3.58	5.07	5.33
Central Government	..	1.41	1.55	2.07	2.50	3.25	3.51	3.82	4.43	5.64	7.30
Rest of General Government	..	0.12	0.17	0.25	0.40	0.58	0.95	1.45	1.42	1.74	2.30
Non-financial Public Enterprises	..	1.39	1.82	2.64	3.36	4.81	6.28	8.58	11.77	16.43	19.36
Priv. Sector, incl non-guaranteed	..	1.81	2.58	4.51	5.52	8.71	10.34	12.13	14.22	17.90	17.79
Short-Term Debt	..	0.00	0.00	0.00	0.00	0.00	0.00	0.00	5.99	7.07	8.63
Memo Items:					*(Millions of US dollars)*						
Int'l Reserves Excluding Gold	611.3	1,141.7	1,696.2	4,132.8	6,359.9	5,215.7	3,980.4	6,488.0	7,192.0	11,826.4	8,966.3
Gold Holdings (at market price)	45.4	48.2	57.7	86.1	149.0	247.5	186.1	178.8	249.9	363.6	872.4
SOCIAL INDICATORS											
Total Fertility Rate	5.1	4.9	4.8	4.7	4.6	4.5	4.4	4.3	4.2	4.1	4.1
Infant Mortality Rate	96.4	94.6	92.8	91.0	88.6	86.2	83.8	81.4	79.0	77.4	75.8
Life Expectancy at Birth	58.7	59.0	59.4	59.8	60.2	60.6	61.0	61.4	61.8	62.1	62.5
Urban Population, % of total	54.7	55.8	57.0	58.2	59.4	60.6	61.8	62.9	64.1	65.2	66.4
Food Prod. per capita (1987=100)	77.9	81.0	81.0	82.7	80.4	84.4	86.1	89.5	91.6	84.8	86.2
Labor Force, Agriculture (%)	45.5	44.9	43.3	41.8	40.4	39.1	37.9	36.4	34.9	33.6	32.3
Labor Force, Female (%)	21.4	21.7	22.3	22.9	23.4	23.9	24.4	25.0	25.5	26.0	26.5
Primary Schl. Enroll. Ratio	..	..	82.0	..	..	..	88.0	..	89.0	92.0	97.0
Primary Schl. Enroll. Ratio, Female	..	..	82.0	..	..	..	87.0	..	88.0	91.0	96.0
Secondary Schl. Enroll. Ratio	..	26.0	17.0	..	..	..	26.0	30.0	32.0	32.0	32.0

1980	1981	1982	1983	1984	1985	1986	1987	1988	1989 estimate	NOTES	BRAZIL
				(Millions of current US dollars)							**FOREIGN TRADE (CUSTOMS BASIS)**
20,100	23,300	20,200	21,900	27,000	25,600	22,396	26,225	33,780	30,954	..	Value of Exports, fob
11,973	12,658	10,785	11,831	13,729	12,511	11,253	13,229	16,234	..	..	Nonfuel Primary Products
358	1,178	1,444	1,158	1,824	1,625	981	1,246	1,395	..	..	Fuels
7,770	9,465	7,971	8,911	11,447	11,464	10,162	11,750	16,151	14,214	..	Manufactures
24,900	24,100	21,100	16,800	15,200	14,300	15,555	16,581	16,047	19,647	..	Value of Imports, cif
3,974	3,212	2,668	2,049	2,164	2,095	3,505	2,800	3,307	..	..	Nonfuel Primary Products
10,737	12,171	11,293	9,391	8,030	6,758	4,160	4,466	4,504	..	..	Fuels
10,190	8,716	7,140	5,360	5,005	5,447	7,890	9,315	8,235	9,349	..	Manufactures
				(Index 1987 = 100)							
102.9	93.4	88.3	84.6	88.6	86.0	108.3	100.0	109.5	..	..	Terms of Trade
114.2	112.3	102.4	96.0	96.8	88.8	96.0	100.0	107.9	..	..	Export Prices, fob
111.0	120.2	115.9	113.5	109.3	103.3	88.6	100.0	98.6	..	..	Import Prices, cif
				(Millions of current US dollars)							**BALANCE OF PAYMENTS**
23,275	26,923	23,469	24,341	30,205	29,309	25,131	28,730	36,424	36,900	f	Exports of Goods & Services
20,132	23,276	20,173	21,898	27,002	25,634	22,348	26,210	33,700	34,000	..	Merchandise, fob
1,725	2,246	1,794	1,713	1,936	2,079	1,812	1,947	1,950	1,990	..	Nonfactor Services
1,418	1,401	1,502	730	1,267	1,596	971	573	824	900	..	Factor Services
36,250	38,873	39,773	31,286	30,334	29,737	30,522	30,250	32,100	36,000	f	Imports of Goods & Services
22,955	22,091	19,395	15,429	13,916	13,168	14,044	15,052	14,600	17,100	..	Merchandise, fob
4,833	5,109	5,366	4,105	3,679	3,760	4,355	4,275	2,900	3,220	..	Nonfactor Services
8,462	11,673	15,012	11,752	12,739	12,809	12,123	10,923	14,600	15,700	..	Factor Services
6,333	7,991	9,389	8,030	7,636	7,457	6,422	6,420	11,743	4,366	..	Long-Term Interest
127	189	-10	106	161	139	89	113	100	100	..	Private Current Transfers, net
4	14	6	2	4	2	0	0	0	..	..	Workers' Remittances
-12,848	-11,761	-16,314	-6,839	32	-289	-5,302	-1,407	4,450	1,040	..	Curr. A/C Bal before Off. Transf.
42	10	2	2	10	16	-2	-43	0	..	..	Net Official Transfers
-12,806	-11,751	-16,312	-6,837	42	-273	-5,304	-1,450	4,450	1,040	..	Curr. A/C Bal after Off. Transf.
6,207	11,647	8,011	7,744	8,080	1,105	-265	-995	3,160	1,010	f	Long-Term Capital, net
1,544	2,313	2,534	1,373	1,556	1,267	177	1,087	2,680	782	..	Direct Investment
4,619	8,712	8,001	4,614	5,373	490	128	-845	2,259	-1,983	..	Long-Term Loans
11,449	16,124	15,535	8,330	9,896	2,493	3,427	2,465	5,784	3,034	..	Disbursements
6,829	7,412	7,534	3,715	4,523	2,003	3,299	3,310	3,525	5,018	..	Repayments
44	622	-2,524	1,757	1,151	-652	-570	-1,237	-1,779	2,211	..	Other Long-Term Capital
2,893	657	1,466	-1,493	-3,244	-958	1,941	4,085	-5,832	-678	f	Other Capital, net
3,706	-553	6,835	586	-4,878	126	3,628	-1,640	-1,778	-1,372	..	Change in Reserves
				(Brazilian Cruzados per US dollar)							**Memo Item:**
0.0527	0.0931	0.1800	0.5770	1.8500	6.2000	13.6500	39.2300	262.3800	2,833.9200	..	Conversion Factor (Annual Avg)
				(Billions of US dollars), outstanding at end of year							
70.96	80.88	92.81	98.10	105.01	105.52	113.04	123.56	115.65	111.30	..	**EXTERNAL DEBT (Total)**
57.43	65.55	75.36	83.89	94.07	96.25	103.76	109.90	104.74	92.73	..	Long-Term Debt (by debtor)
6.41	7.54	8.48	17.05	24.39	20.26	25.84	31.45	60.65	53.56	..	Central Bank, incl. IMF credit
7.76	7.59	8.09	9.47	11.64	14.50	19.83	23.31	18.23	19.42	..	Central Government
2.60	3.12	3.27	3.46	3.96	5.40	5.49	5.25	0.98	0.98	..	Rest of General Government
21.99	25.51	30.36	30.52	32.98	37.18	36.37	33.89	12.77	12.15	..	Non-financial Public Enterprises
18.67	21.79	25.17	23.39	21.10	18.92	16.23	15.99	12.11	6.61	..	Priv. Sector, incl non-guaranteed
13.53	15.32	17.45	14.20	10.95	9.27	9.29	13.66	10.91	18.58	..	Short-Term Debt
				(Millions of US dollars)							**Memo Items:**
5,769.3	6,603.5	3,927.9	4,355.1	11,507.9	10,604.6	5,803.0	6,299.2	6,971.8	7,535.4	..	Int'l Reserves Excluding Gold
1,105.9	876.1	69.4	206.4	452.9	1,013.4	950.7	1,177.8	1,118.3	1,193.4	..	Gold Holdings (at market price)
											SOCIAL INDICATORS
4.0	3.9	3.8	3.7	3.7	3.6	3.5	3.5	3.4	3.3	..	Total Fertility Rate
74.2	72.6	71.0	69.4	67.8	66.2	64.6	63.0	61.5	59.9	..	Infant Mortality Rate
62.8	63.1	63.4	63.7	64.0	64.3	64.6	64.9	65.2	65.6	..	Life Expectancy at Birth
67.5	68.5	69.6	70.6	71.7	72.7	73.5	74.4	75.2	76.1	..	Urban Population, % of total
93.2	92.3	97.5	91.3	94.1	100.7	94.1	100.0	105.4	106.0	..	Food Prod. per capita (1987 = 100)
31.2	..	..	..	..	..	..	..	..	..	..	Labor Force, Agriculture (%)
26.9	27.0	27.0	27.1	27.1	27.2	27.2	27.3	27.3	27.4	..	Labor Force, Female (%)
99.0	..	..	103.0	103.0	101.0	103.0	103.0			..	Primary Schl. Enroll. Ratio
97.0	..	..	99.0	..	..	..	..			..	Primary Schl. Enroll. Ratio, Female
34.0	..	..	35.0	35.2	36.4	39.1	38.9	..	..	..	Secondary Schl. Enroll. Ratio

BULGARIA	1969	1970	1971	1972	1973	1974	1975	1976	1977	1978	1979
CURRENT GNP PER CAPITA (US $)	..	..	..	..	..	..	..	..	..	..	..
POPULATION (thousands)	8,434	8,490	8,536	8,576	8,621	8,679	8,721	8,759	8,804	8,814	8,826

USE AND ORIGIN OF RESOURCES *(Billions of current Bulgarian Leva)*

	1969	1970	1971	1972	1973	1974	1975	1976	1977	1978	1979
Gross National Product (GNP)	..	..	..	..	..	..	..	..	..	..	..
Net Factor Income from Abroad	..	..	..	..	..	..	..	..	..	..	..
GDP at Market Prices	..	..	..	..	..	..	..	..	..	..	..
Resource Balance	..	..	..	..	..	..	..	..	..	..	..
Exports of Goods & NFServices	..	..	..	..	..	..	..	..	..	..	..
Imports of Goods & NFServices	..	..	..	..	..	..	..	..	..	..	..
Domestic Absorption	..	..	..	..	..	..	..	..	..	..	..
Private Consumption, etc.	..	..	..	..	..	..	..	..	..	..	..
General Gov't Consumption	..	..	..	..	..	..	..	..	..	..	..
Gross Domestic Investment	..	..	..	..	..	..	..	..	..	..	..
Fixed Investment	..	..	..	..	..	..	..	..	..	..	..
Indirect Taxes, net	..	..	..	..	..	..	..	..	..	..	..
GDP at factor cost	..	..	..	..	..	..	..	..	..	..	..
Agriculture	..	..	..	..	..	..	..	..	..	..	..
Industry	..	..	..	..	..	..	..	..	..	..	..
Manufacturing	..	..	..	..	..	..	..	..	..	..	..
Services, etc.	..	..	..	..	..	..	..	..	..	..	..
Gross Domestic Saving	..	..	..	..	..	..	..	..	..	..	..
Gross National Saving	..	..	..	..	..	..	..	..	..	..	..

(Billions of 1987 Bulgarian Leva)

	1969	1970	1971	1972	1973	1974	1975	1976	1977	1978	1979
Gross National Product	..	..	..	..	..	..	..	..	..	..	..
GDP at Market Prices	..	..	..	..	..	..	..	..	..	..	..
Resource Balance	..	..	..	..	..	..	..	..	..	..	..
Exports of Goods & NFServices	..	..	..	..	..	..	..	..	..	..	..
Imports of Goods & NFServices	..	..	..	..	..	..	..	..	..	..	..
Domestic Absorption	..	..	..	..	..	..	..	..	..	..	..
Private Consumption, etc.	..	..	..	..	..	..	..	..	..	..	..
General Gov't Consumption	..	..	..	..	..	..	..	..	..	..	..
Gross Domestic Investment	..	..	..	..	..	..	..	..	..	..	..
Fixed Investment	..	..	..	..	..	..	..	..	..	..	..
GDP at factor cost	..	..	..	..	..	..	..	..	..	..	..
Agriculture	..	..	..	..	..	..	..	..	..	..	..
Industry	..	..	..	..	..	..	..	..	..	..	..
Manufacturing	..	..	..	..	..	..	..	..	..	..	..
Services, etc.	..	..	..	..	..	..	..	..	..	..	..

Memo Items:

	1969	1970	1971	1972	1973	1974	1975	1976	1977	1978	1979
Capacity to Import	..	..	..	..	..	..	..	..	..	..	..
Terms of Trade Adjustment	..	..	..	..	..	..	..	..	..	..	..
Gross Domestic Income	..	..	..	..	..	..	..	..	..	..	..
Gross National Income	..	..	..	..	..	..	..	..	..	..	..

DOMESTIC PRICES/DEFLATORS *(Index 1987 = 100)*

	1969	1970	1971	1972	1973	1974	1975	1976	1977	1978	1979
Overall (GDP)	..	..	..	..	..	..	..	..	..	..	..
Domestic Absorption	..	..	..	..	..	..	..	..	..	..	..
Agriculture	..	..	..	..	..	..	..	..	..	..	..
Industry	..	..	..	..	..	..	..	..	..	..	..
Manufacturing	..	..	..	..	..	..	..	..	..	..	..
Consumer Price Index	..	..	..	..	..	..	..	..	..	..	..

MANUFACTURING ACTIVITY

	1969	1970	1971	1972	1973	1974	1975	1976	1977	1978	1979
Employment (1987=100)	78.2	80.2	82.3	84.3	86.1	89.5	91.0	91.9	92.7	93.5	94.6
Real Earnings per Empl. (1987=100)	..	..	..	..	..	..	..	..	..	..	..
Real Output per Empl. (1987=100)	..	..	..	..	..	..	..	..	..	..	..
Earnings as % of Value Added	..	..	..	..	..	..	..	..	..	..	..

MONETARY HOLDINGS *(Millions of current Bulgarian Leva)*

	1969	1970	1971	1972	1973	1974	1975	1976	1977	1978	1979
Money Supply, Broadly Defined	..	..	..	..	..	..	..	..	..	..	..
Money	..	..	..	..	..	..	..	..	..	..	..
Currency Outside Banks	..	..	..	..	..	..	..	..	..	..	..
Demand Deposits	..	..	..	..	..	..	..	..	..	..	..
Quasi-Money	..	..	..	..	..	..	..	..	..	..	..

GOVERNMENT DEFICIT (-) OR SURPLUS *(Millions of current Bulgarian Leva)*

	1969	1970	1971	1972	1973	1974	1975	1976	1977	1978	1979
Current Revenue	..	..	..	..	..	..	..	..	..	..	..
Current Expenditure	..	..	..	..	..	..	..	..	..	..	..
Current Budget Balance	..	..	..	..	..	..	..	..	..	..	..
Capital Receipts	..	..	..	..	..	..	..	..	..	..	..
Capital Payments	..	..	..	..	..	..	..	..	..	..	..

1980	1981	1982	1983	1984	1985	1986	1987	1988	1989 estimate	NOTES	BULGARIA
..	..	2,450	2,260	2,150	2,040	2,170	2,560	2,750	2,320	..	**CURRENT GNP PER CAPITA (US $)**
8,862	8,878	8,894	8,909	8,925	8,941	8,956	8,971	8,986	9,001	..	**POPULATION (thousands)**
											USE AND ORIGIN OF RESOURCES
				(Billions of current Bulgarian Leva)							
25,383,000	27,546,000	28,781,000	29,669,000	31,611,000	32,480,000	34,194,000	36,124,000	37,629,000	38,397,000	..	Gross National Product (GNP)
-408,100	-271,900	-232,300	-145,500	-60,300	-115,500	-230,200	-407,800	-716,600	-1,079,000	..	Net Factor Income from Abroad
25,791,000	27,818,000	29,013,000	29,815,000	31,671,000	32,595,000	34,424,000	36,531,000	38,345,000	39,475,000	..	GDP at Market Prices
-197,400	-1,166,000	-779,100	-1,024,000	-1,058,000	-1,596,000	-2,311,000	-1,825,000	-637,200	-943,900	..	Resource Balance
6,673,000	7,027,700	7,945,500	8,227,100	8,956,900	9,119,400	10,025,000	10,255,000	12,482,000	12,116,000	..	Exports of Goods & NFServices
6,870,400	8,193,600	8,724,600	9,251,100	10,015,000	10,716,000	12,335,000	12,081,000	13,119,000	13,060,000	..	Imports of Goods & NFServices
25,988,000	28,984,000	29,792,000	30,839,000	32,729,000	34,191,000	36,734,000	38,357,000	38,982,000	40,419,000	..	Domestic Absorption
15,763,000	17,383,000	17,966,000	18,676,000	19,829,000	20,940,000	21,430,000	23,624,000	23,040,000	24,848,000	..	Private Consumption, etc.
1,457,000	1,729,000	2,096,000	2,356,000	2,383,500	2,756,500	2,954,100	2,712,800	2,744,500	2,870,000	..	General Gov't Consumption
8,768,000	9,872,000	9,730,500	9,806,900	10,516,000	10,495,000	12,350,000	12,020,000	13,197,000	12,701,000	..	Gross Domestic Investment
7,289,000	7,690,000	7,973,000	7,974,900	8,111,700	8,612,800	9,290,900	9,817,300	10,260,000	10,285,000	..	Fixed Investment
..	..	..	..	..	..	..	..	..	..	..	Indirect Taxes, net
..	..	..	..	..	..	..	..	..	..	..	GDP at factor cost
3,718,700	4,624,900	4,983,800	4,317,000	5,008,000	3,868,600	4,447,400	4,309,300	4,394,100	4,457,000	..	Agriculture
13,869,000	14,448,000	16,802,000	17,984,000	18,988,000	20,382,000	22,035,000	22,454,000	23,379,000	23,432,000	..	Industry
..	..	..	..	..	..	..	..	..	..	..	Manufacturing
8,203,600	8,744,900	7,227,600	7,513,500	7,675,100	8,344,400	7,941,800	9,768,400	10,572,000	11,586,000	..	Services, etc.
8,570,600	8,706,100	8,951,400	8,782,900	9,458,100	8,898,700	10,040,000	10,195,000	12,560,000	11,757,000	..	Gross Domestic Saving
..	..	..	..	..	..	..	..	..	..	..	Gross National Saving
				(Billions of 1987 Bulgarian Leva)							
27,664,000	29,213,000	29,819,000	31,097,000	32,218,000	32,957,000	34,241,000	36,124,000	36,720,000	35,567,000	..	Gross National Product
28,118,000	29,493,000	30,050,000	31,242,000	32,275,000	33,067,000	34,464,000	36,531,000	37,484,000	36,929,000	..	GDP at Market Prices
-796,910	-1,477,000	-446,380	-736,160	-682,920	-1,044,000	-1,800,000	-1,825,000	-1,457,000	-414,860	..	Resource Balance
7,232,900	7,272,500	8,511,300	8,520,100	8,828,000	9,168,900	10,138,000	10,255,000	12,534,000	12,521,000	..	Exports of Goods & NFServices
8,029,800	8,749,300	8,957,600	9,256,200	9,510,900	10,213,000	11,938,000	12,081,000	13,991,000	12,935,000	..	Imports of Goods & NFServices
28,915,000	30,970,000	30,497,000	31,978,000	32,958,000	34,111,000	36,264,000	38,357,000	38,941,000	37,343,000	..	Domestic Absorption
18,265,000	19,228,000	18,812,000	20,198,000	20,338,000	21,208,000	21,415,000	23,624,000	22,977,000	21,905,000	..	Private Consumption, etc.
1,662,100	1,782,800	1,864,900	1,964,400	2,090,900	2,320,200	2,523,200	2,712,800	2,739,800	2,807,900	..	General Gov't Consumption
8,987,600	9,958,900	9,819,800	9,816,300	10,529,000	10,583,000	12,326,000	12,020,000	13,224,000	12,630,000	..	Gross Domestic Investment
7,289,000	7,690,000	7,973,000	7,974,900	8,111,700	8,612,800	9,290,900	9,817,300	10,260,000	10,285,000	..	Fixed Investment
..	..	..	..	..	..	..	..	..	..	..	GDP at factor cost
5,045,800	5,271,300	5,576,600	4,665,600	5,210,600	4,136,300	5,048,100	4,309,300	4,235,400	4,153,200	..	Agriculture
14,630,000	15,430,000	16,872,000	18,161,000	19,275,000	20,257,000	21,309,000	22,454,000	23,000,000	23,035,000	..	Industry
..	..	..	..	..	..	..	..	..	..	..	Manufacturing
8,627,100	8,981,100	7,844,600	8,415,500	7,789,600	8,673,900	8,107,500	9,768,400	10,249,000	9,740,700	..	Services, etc.
											Memo Items:
..	..	..	..	..	..	..	..	..	..	..	Capacity to Import
..	..	..	..	..	..	..	..	..	..	..	Terms of Trade Adjustment
28,684,000	29,725,000	29,697,000	30,954,000	31,953,000	32,590,000	34,028,000	36,531,000	38,262,000	36,409,000	..	Gross Domestic Income
28,231,000	29,445,000	29,465,000	30,808,000	31,896,000	32,480,000	33,805,000	36,124,000	37,497,000	35,047,000	..	Gross National Income
				(Index 1987 = 100)							**DOMESTIC PRICES/DEFLATORS**
91.7	94.3	96.5	95.4	98.1	98.6	99.9	100.0	102.3	106.9	..	Overall (GDP)
89.9	93.6	97.7	96.4	99.3	100.2	101.3	100.0	100.1	108.2	..	Domestic Absorption
73.7	87.7	89.4	92.5	96.1	93.5	88.1	100.0	103.7	107.3	..	Agriculture
94.8	93.6	99.6	99.0	98.5	100.6	103.4	100.0	101.6	101.7	..	Industry
..	..	..	..	..	..	..	..	..	..	..	Manufacturing
..	..	..	..	..	..	..	..	..	..	..	Consumer Price Index
											MANUFACTURING ACTIVITY
95.8	97.2	98.3	98.1	98.7	100.0	100.9	100.0	101.8	..	..	Employment (1987=100)
..	..	..	..	..	..	..	..	..	..	..	Real Earnings per Empl. (1987=100)
..	..	..	..	..	..	..	..	..	..	..	Real Output per Empl. (1987=100)
..	..	..	..	..	..	..	..	..	..	..	Earnings as % of Value Added
				(Millions of current Bulgarian Leva)							**MONETARY HOLDINGS**
..	..	..	..	..	..	..	..	..	..	..	Money Supply, Broadly Defined
..	..	..	..	..	..	..	..	..	..	..	Money
..	..	..	..	..	..	..	..	..	..	..	Currency Outside Banks
..	..	..	..	..	..	..	..	..	..	..	Demand Deposits
..	..	..	..	..	..	..	..	..	..	..	Quasi-Money
				(Millions of current Bulgarian Leva)							**GOVERNMENT DEFICIT (-) OR SURPLUS**
..	..	..	..	..	..	..	..	..	..	..	Current Revenue
..	..	..	..	..	..	..	..	..	..	..	Current Expenditure
..	..	..	..	..	..	..	..	..	..	..	Current Budget Balance
..	..	..	..	..	..	..	..	..	..	..	Capital Receipts
..	..	..	..	..	..	..	..	..	..	..	Capital Payments

BULGARIA	1969	1970	1971	1972	1973	1974	1975	1976	1977	1978	1979
FOREIGN TRADE (CUSTOMS BASIS)					*(Millions of current US dollars)*						
Value of Exports, fob	1,796	2,004	2,182	2,627	3,301	3,836	4,691	5,382	6,351	7,478	8,869
Nonfuel Primary Products	..	..	..	..	..	..	..	..	..	..	..
Fuels	..	..	..	..	..	..	..	..	..	..	..
Manufactures	..	..	..	..	..	..	..	..	..	..	..
Value of Imports, cif	1,749	1,831	2,120	2,567	3,266	4,326	5,408	5,626	6,393	7,651	8,514
Nonfuel Primary Products	..	..	..	..	..	..	..	..	..	..	..
Fuels	..	..	..	..	..	..	..	..	..	..	..
Manufactures	..	..	..	..	..	..	..	..	..	..	..
					(Index 1987 = 100)						
Terms of Trade	..	..	..	..	..	..	..	..	..	..	..
Export Prices, fob	..	..	..	..	..	..	..	..	..	..	..
Import Prices, cif	..	..	..	..	..	..	..	..	..	..	..
BALANCE OF PAYMENTS					*(Current US dollars)*						
Exports of Goods & Services	..	..	..	..	..	..	..	..	..	..	..
Merchandise, fob	..	..	..	..	..	..	..	..	..	..	..
Nonfactor Services	..	..	..	..	..	..	..	..	..	..	..
Factor Services	..	..	..	..	..	..	..	..	..	..	..
Imports of Goods & Services	..	..	..	..	..	..	..	..	..	..	..
Merchandise, fob	..	..	..	..	..	..	..	..	..	..	..
Nonfactor Services	..	..	..	..	..	..	..	..	..	..	..
Factor Services	..	..	..	..	..	..	..	..	..	..	..
Long-Term Interest	..	..	..	..	..	..	..	..	..	..	..
Private Current Transfers, net	..	..	..	..	..	..	..	..	..	..	..
Workers' Remittances	..	..	..	..	..	..	..	..	..	..	..
Curr. A/C Bal before Off. Transf.	..	..	..	..	..	..	..	..	..	..	..
Net Official Transfers	..	..	..	..	..	..	..	..	..	..	..
Curr. A/C Bal after Off. Transf.	..	..	..	..	..	..	..	..	..	..	..
Long-Term Capital, net	..	..	..	..	..	..	..	..	..	..	..
Direct Investment	..	..	..	..	..	..	..	..	..	..	..
Long-Term Loans	..	..	..	..	..	..	..	..	..	..	..
Disbursements	..	..	..	..	..	..	..	..	..	..	..
Repayments	..	..	..	..	..	..	..	..	..	..	..
Other Long-Term Capital	..	..	..	..	..	..	..	..	..	..	..
Other Capital, net	..	..	..	..	..	..	..	..	..	..	..
Change in Reserves	..	..	..	..	..	..	..	..	..	..	..
Memo Item:					*(Bulgarian Leva per US dollar)*						
Conversion Factor (Annual Avg)	..	..	..	..	..	..	..	..	..	..	..
				(Millions US dollars), outstanding at end of year							
EXTERNAL DEBT (Total)	..	..	..	..	..	..	..	..	..	..	..
Long-Term Debt (by debtor)	..	..	..	..	..	..	..	..	..	..	..
Central Bank, incl. IMF credit	..	..	..	..	..	..	..	..	..	..	..
Central Government	..	..	..	..	..	..	..	..	..	..	..
Rest of General Government	..	..	..	..	..	..	..	..	..	..	..
Non-financial Public Enterprises	..	..	..	..	..	..	..	..	..	..	..
Priv. Sector, incl non-guaranteed	..	..	..	..	..	..	..	..	..	..	..
Short-Term Debt	..	..	..	..	..	..	..	..	..	..	..
Memo Items:					*Millions US dollars)*						
Int'l Reserves Excluding Gold	..	..	..	..	..	..	..	..	..	..	..
Gold Holdings (at market price)	..	..	..	..	..	..	..	..	..	..	..
SOCIAL INDICATORS											
Total Fertility Rate	2.3	2.2	2.1	2.0	2.2	2.3	2.2	2.3	2.2	2.1	2.1
Infant Mortality Rate	30.5	27.3	24.9	26.2	26.2	25.5	23.1	23.5	23.7	22.2	21.2
Life Expectancy at Birth	69.8	69.9	70.0	70.0	70.1	70.1	70.1	70.2	70.2	70.5	70.7
Urban Population, % of total	51.0	52.3	53.3	54.4	55.4	56.5	57.5	58.5	59.5	60.5	61.5
Food Prod. per capita (1987=100)	85.3	82.2	84.6	89.0	88.4	81.7	87.3	95.0	90.3	94.2	101.2
Labor Force, Agriculture (%)	36.9	34.8	33.1	31.4	29.8	28.1	26.5	24.8	23.2	21.5	19.8
Labor Force, Female (%)	44.1	44.2	44.5	44.8	45.1	45.4	45.6	45.8	45.9	46.0	46.1
Primary Schl. Enroll. Ratio	..	101.0	..	..	..	..	99.0	99.0	99.0	97.0	96.0
Primary Schl. Enroll. Ratio, Female	..	100.0	..	..	..	..	99.0	99.0	98.0	96.0	95.0
Secondary Schl. Enroll. Ratio	..	79.0	..	..	..	..	89.0	90.0	90.0	89.0	87.0

BULGARIA

1980	1981	1982	1983	1984	1985	1986	1987	1988	1989 estimate	NOTES	BULGARIA
				(Millions of current US dollars)							**FOREIGN TRADE (CUSTOMS BASIS)**
10,372	10,689	11,428	12,130	12,850	13,348	14,192	15,921	17,223	..	..	Value of Exports, fob
..	..	..	..	..	..	..	..	..	..	..	Nonfuel Primary Products
..	..	..	..	..	..	..	..	..	..	..	Fuels
..	..	..	..	..	..	..	..	..	..	..	Manufactures
9,650	10,801	11,527	12,283	12,714	13,656	15,249	16,095	16,582	..	..	Value of Imports, cif
..	..	..	..	..	..	..	..	..	..	..	Nonfuel Primary Products
..	..	..	..	..	..	..	..	..	..	..	Fuels
..	..	..	..	..	..	..	..	..	..	..	Manufactures
				(Index 1987 = 100)							
..	..	..	..	..	..	..	..	..	..	..	Terms of Trade
..	..	..	..	..	..	..	..	..	..	..	Export Prices, fob
..	..	..	..	..	..	..	..	..	..	..	Import Prices, cif
				(Current US dollars)							**BALANCE OF PAYMENTS**
..	..	..	..	..	..	..	..	..	..	..	Exports of Goods & Services
..	..	..	..	..	..	..	..	..	..	..	Merchandise, fob
..	..	..	..	..	..	..	..	..	..	..	Nonfactor Services
..	..	..	..	..	..	..	..	..	..	..	Factor Services
..	..	..	..	..	..	..	..	..	..	..	Imports of Goods & Services
..	..	..	..	..	..	..	..	..	..	..	Merchandise, fob
..	..	..	..	..	..	..	..	..	..	..	Nonfactor Services
..	..	..	..	..	..	..	..	..	..	..	Factor Services
..	..	..	..	..	..	..	..	..	..	..	Long-Term Interest
..	..	..	..	..	..	..	..	..	..	..	Private Current Transfers, net
..	..	..	..	..	..	..	..	..	..	..	Workers' Remittances
..	..	..	..	..	..	..	..	..	..	..	Curr. A/C Bal before Off. Transf.
..	..	..	..	..	..	..	..	..	..	..	Net Official Transfers
..	..	..	..	..	..	..	..	..	..	..	Curr. A/C Bal after Off. Transf.
..	..	..	..	..	..	..	..	..	..	..	Long-Term Capital, net
..	..	..	..	..	..	..	..	..	..	..	Direct Investment
..	..	..	..	..	..	..	..	..	..	..	Long-Term Loans
..	..	..	..	..	..	..	..	..	..	..	Disbursements
..	..	..	..	..	..	..	..	..	..	..	Repayments
..	..	..	..	..	..	..	..	..	..	..	Other Long-Term Capital
..	..	..	..	..	..	..	..	..	..	..	Other Capital, net
..	..	..	..	..	..	..	..	..	..	..	Change in Reserves
				(Bulgarian Leva per US dollar)							Memo Item:
..	..	..	..	..	..	..	..	..	..	..	Conversion Factor (Annual Avg)
				(Millions US dollars), outstanding at end of year							**EXTERNAL DEBT (Total)**
..	..	..	..	..	..	..	..	..	..	..	Long-Term Debt (by debtor)
..	..	..	..	..	..	..	..	..	..	..	Central Bank, incl. IMF credit
..	..	..	..	..	..	..	..	..	..	..	Central Government
..	..	..	..	..	..	..	..	..	..	..	Rest of General Government
..	..	..	..	..	..	..	..	..	..	..	Non-financial Public Enterprises
..	..	..	..	..	..	..	..	..	..	..	Priv. Sector, incl non-guaranteed
..	..	..	..	..	..	..	..	..	..	..	Short-Term Debt
				Millions US dollars)							Memo Items:
..	..	..	..	..	..	..	..	..	..	..	Int'l Reserves Excluding Gold
..	..	..	..	..	..	..	..	..	..	..	Gold Holdings (at market price)
											SOCIAL INDICATORS
2.1	2.0	2.0	2.0	2.0	2.0	1.9	1.9	1.9	1.9	..	Total Fertility Rate
20.2	19.5	18.2	16.8	16.2	15.4	14.5	14.7	14.3	13.8	..	Infant Mortality Rate
70.9	71.1	71.4	71.5	71.6	71.8	71.9	72.1	72.2	72.4	..	Life Expectancy at Birth
62.5	63.3	64.1	65.0	65.8	66.6	67.3	68.1	68.8	69.6	..	Urban Population, % of total
97.0	103.0	109.5	100.8	107.8	94.5	106.5	100.0	98.8	102.9	..	Food Prod. per capita (1987=100)
18.1	..	..	..	..	..	..	..	..	..	..	Labor Force, Agriculture (%)
46.3	46.2	46.2	46.2	46.2	46.2	46.3	46.3	46.3	46.3	..	Labor Force, Female (%)
98.0	..	102.0	102.0	102.0	102.0	104.0	104.0			..	Primary Schl. Enroll. Ratio
98.0	99.0	102.0	101.0	102.0	102.0	103.0	103.0			..	Primary Schl. Enroll. Ratio, Female
84.0	..	82.0	86.0	92.0	102.0	75.0	76.0	..	..	..	Secondary Schl. Enroll. Ratio

BURKINA FASO	1969	1970	1971	1972	1973	1974	1975	1976	1977	1978	1979
CURRENT GNP PER CAPITA (US $)	80	80	80	80	100	120	130	150	160	170	210
POPULATION (thousands)	5,526	5,633	5,736	5,843	5,956	6,075	6,202	6,337	6,482	6,636	6,797

USE AND ORIGIN OF RESOURCES *(Billions of current CFA Francs)*

	1969	1970	1971	1972	1973	1974	1975	1976	1977	1978	1979
Gross National Product (GNP)	112.90	116.70	122.64	134.16	140.22	166.69	182.89	213.91	253.45	292.39	327.96
Net Factor Income from Abroad	2.60	4.30	4.80	4.80	6.80	6.30	4.30	6.90	6.90	-3.00	-2.00
GDP at Market Prices	110.30	112.40	117.84	129.36	133.42	160.39	178.59	207.01	246.55	295.39	329.96
Resource Balance	-10.96	-11.20	-16.25	-18.27	-21.20	-24.37	-39.40	-36.87	-53.30	-57.55	-66.28
Exports of Goods & NFServices	7.66	7.32	7.74	9.87	10.04	15.91	15.66	20.25	23.40	26.30	32.44
Imports of Goods & NFServices	18.62	18.52	24.00	28.14	31.24	40.28	55.05	57.12	76.70	83.85	98.72
Domestic Absorption	121.25	123.60	134.10	147.63	154.63	184.76	217.99	243.88	299.85	352.94	396.24
Private Consumption, etc.	101.72	101.59	104.26	110.96	110.29	121.72	144.43	165.16	216.08	256.95	294.06
General Gov't Consumption	6.80	8.14	8.76	9.79	11.24	13.81	23.91	21.85	25.77	30.92	37.11
Gross Domestic Investment	12.73	13.86	21.08	26.88	33.10	49.23	49.65	56.86	58.00	65.07	65.07
Fixed Investment	..	..	..	..	..	..	..	..	..	..	59.57
Indirect Taxes, net	3.88	4.30	6.49	6.48	7.66	9.03	10.47	14.26	18.44	20.01	13.50
GDP at factor cost	106.41	108.09	111.35	122.88	125.76	151.37	168.12	192.75	228.11	275.38	316.46
Agriculture	34.64	33.64	35.34	40.45	38.44	48.46	50.56	58.87	68.68	87.20	95.01
Industry	29.49	29.79	34.09	35.98	41.71	43.97	55.31	65.37	62.66	75.60	81.33
Manufacturing	16.98	18.02	19.71	22.82	24.38	28.53	31.12	35.27	38.90	43.57	50.31
Services, etc.	42.29	44.67	41.93	46.45	45.61	58.94	62.25	68.51	96.76	112.58	140.12
Gross Domestic Saving	1.77	2.66	4.82	8.61	11.90	24.86	10.25	19.99	4.70	7.52	-1.21
Gross National Saving	..	11.40	15.60	19.08	26.67	38.17	21.51	35.62	21.45	16.85	14.46

(Billions of 1987 CFA Francs)

	1969	1970	1971	1972	1973	1974	1975	1976	1977	1978	1979
Gross National Product	399.20	405.40	411.30	422.67	427.97	461.76	465.33	508.02	512.84	518.45	546.88
GDP at Market Prices	389.87	390.32	395.05	407.64	407.33	444.54	454.54	491.92	498.94	522.56	549.44
Resource Balance	-69.32	-55.44	-70.97	-68.49	-75.40	-75.88	-96.90	-87.98	-117.70	-102.69	-92.30
Exports of Goods & NFServices	23.17	26.21	26.52	35.66	32.92	35.36	34.75	32.00	33.53	48.95	60.72
Imports of Goods & NFServices	92.49	81.66	97.49	104.15	108.32	111.24	131.65	119.99	151.23	151.65	153.01
Domestic Absorption	459.19	445.77	466.02	476.13	482.73	520.42	551.44	579.90	616.65	625.25	641.73
Private Consumption, etc.	383.03	362.91	360.77	345.42	333.53	357.05	374.42	402.17	453.51	457.58	488.79
General Gov't Consumption	25.32	29.86	30.61	35.53	37.79	40.06	54.80	54.42	50.64	51.40	56.22
Gross Domestic Investment	50.84	53.00	74.63	95.18	111.41	123.30	122.22	123.30	112.49	116.27	96.73
Fixed Investment	..	..	..	..	..	..	..	..	..	..	88.90
GDP at factor cost	..	373.13	377.58	392.46	388.57	424.72	432.80	463.19	466.77	492.89	527.19
Agriculture	..	151.70	153.52	153.07	144.49	166.16	164.81	171.13	161.20	170.23	159.26
Industry	..	110.18	114.54	116.85	132.13	116.69	141.18	156.39	129.93	139.89	135.80
Manufacturing	..	59.06	60.76	66.44	69.85	70.98	74.39	77.23	78.36	81.20	84.11
Services, etc.	..	121.89	121.09	131.42	122.26	149.75	137.87	147.61	181.45	189.35	233.53

Memo Items:

	1969	1970	1971	1972	1973	1974	1975	1976	1977	1978	1979
Capacity to Import	38.05	32.26	31.45	36.53	34.81	43.94	37.44	42.54	46.14	47.57	50.28
Terms of Trade Adjustment	14.88	6.05	4.94	0.87	1.89	8.58	2.69	10.53	12.61	-1.39	-10.44
Gross Domestic Income	404.75	396.37	399.99	408.51	409.22	453.12	457.23	502.45	511.55	521.17	539.00
Gross National Income	414.08	411.45	416.24	423.54	429.86	470.35	468.02	518.55	525.45	517.07	536.44

DOMESTIC PRICES/DEFLATORS *(Index 1987 = 100)*

	1969	1970	1971	1972	1973	1974	1975	1976	1977	1978	1979
Overall (GDP)	28.3	28.8	29.8	31.7	32.8	36.1	39.3	42.1	49.4	56.5	60.1
Domestic Absorption	26.4	27.7	28.8	31.0	32.0	35.5	39.5	42.1	48.6	56.4	61.7
Agriculture	..	22.2	23.0	26.4	26.6	29.2	30.7	34.4	42.6	51.2	59.7
Industry	..	27.0	29.8	30.8	31.6	37.7	39.2	41.8	48.2	54.0	59.9
Manufacturing	..	30.5	32.4	34.3	34.9	40.2	41.8	45.7	49.6	53.7	59.8
Consumer Price Index	31.0	31.5	32.2	31.2	33.6	36.6	43.4	39.8	51.7	56.0	64.3

MANUFACTURING ACTIVITY

	1969	1970	1971	1972	1973	1974	1975	1976	1977	1978	1979
Employment (1987=100)	..	..	..	..	..	..	..	..	..	..	..
Real Earnings per Empl. (1987=100)	..	..	..	..	..	..	..	..	..	..	..
Real Output per Empl. (1987=100)	..	..	..	..	..	..	..	..	..	..	..
Earnings as % of Value Added	..	..	..	..	..	11.1	13.3	15.4	17.5	20.7	22.8

MONETARY HOLDINGS *(Billions of current CFA Francs)*

	1969	1970	1971	1972	1973	1974	1975	1976	1977	1978	1979
Money Supply, Broadly Defined	8.71	9.36	9.93	10.59	14.49	17.53	24.32	31.55	35.57	42.52	46.24
Money	8.51	9.14	9.47	9.89	13.50	16.38	22.50	27.55	30.78	34.40	34.76
Currency Outside Banks	5.54	5.74	5.65	5.77	7.13	8.51	10.65	12.85	14.75	13.50	17.36
Demand Deposits	2.97	3.40	3.82	4.11	6.36	7.86	11.85	14.71	16.03	20.90	17.41
Quasi-Money	0.20	0.23	0.46	0.71	0.99	1.16	1.82	4.00	4.79	8.12	11.48

GOVERNMENT DEFICIT (-) OR SURPLUS *(Millions of current CFA Francs)*

	1969	1970	1971	1972	1973	1974	1975	1976	1977	1978	1979
GOVERNMENT DEFICIT (-) OR SURPLUS	..	..	..	..	354	2,212	-1,664	-1,272	4,313	1,495	-5,622
Current Revenue	..	..	..	..	12,850	15,971	16,644	21,728	31,384	32,542	35,550
Current Expenditure	..	..	..	..	10,255	11,457	14,487	17,503	22,343	27,203	34,661
Current Budget Balance	..	..	..	..	2,595	4,514	2,157	4,225	9,041	5,339	889
Capital Receipts	..	..	..	..	12	2	18	37	30	..	1
Capital Payments	..	..	..	..	2,253	2,304	3,839	5,534	4,758	3,844	6,512

1980	1981	1982	1983	1984	1985	1986	1987	1988	1989 estimate	NOTES	BURKINA FASO
240	250	250	220	190	190	210	250	310	320	..	**CURRENT GNP PER CAPITA (US $)**
6,962	7,134	7,312	7,496	7,688	7,888	8,096	8,312	8,539	8,776	..	**POPULATION (thousands)**
				(Billions of current CFA Francs)							**USE AND ORIGIN OF RESOURCES**
360.50	425.08	508.45	536.98	558.11	643.00	695.00	765.00	852.00	814.00	f	Gross National Product (GNP)
-1.00	-3.00	-3.00	-4.00	-3.00	0.00	-4.00	-4.00	-4.00	-5.00	..	Net Factor Income from Abroad
361.50	428.08	511.45	540.98	561.11	643.00	699.00	769.00	856.00	819.00	..	GDP at Market Prices
-76.89	-90.15	-115.28	-112.61	-98.62	-142.00	-140.00	-113.00	-109.00	-139.00	..	Resource Balance
38.58	47.34	49.97	50.85	64.00	63.00	56.00	73.00	78.00	70.00	..	Exports of Goods & NFServices
115.47	137.49	165.25	163.46	162.62	205.00	196.00	186.00	187.00	209.00	..	Imports of Goods & NFServices
438.40	518.23	626.73	653.59	659.73	785.00	839.00	882.00	965.00	958.00	..	Domestic Absorption
337.97	404.22	443.02	461.12	463.03	540.00	591.00	617.00	661.00	693.00	..	Private Consumption, etc.
34.76	41.27	73.46	81.03	84.06	78.00	91.00	100.00	104.00	108.00	..	General Gov't Consumption
65.67	72.74	110.25	111.45	112.64	167.00	157.00	165.00	200.00	157.00	..	Gross Domestic Investment
59.27	68.64	102.25	108.45	109.64	135.00	158.00	194.00	184.00	163.00	..	Fixed Investment
16.00	17.70	22.00	18.00	17.00	25.00	26.00	29.00	31.00	35.00	..	Indirect Taxes, net
345.50	410.38	489.45	522.98	544.11	618.00	673.00	740.00	825.00	784.00	..	GDP at factor cost
100.79	125.04	137.94	146.41	158.06	206.00	225.00	233.00	275.00	278.00	..	Agriculture
85.44	95.84	114.99	131.39	134.80	140.00	159.00	182.00	203.00	204.00	..	Industry
51.17	59.30	70.71	83.16	82.12	88.00	94.00	107.00	112.00	115.00	..	Manufacturing
159.27	189.50	236.52	245.17	251.25	272.00	289.00	325.00	347.00	302.00	..	Services, etc.
-11.22	-17.41	-5.03	-1.17	14.03	25.00	17.00	52.00	91.00	18.00	..	Gross Domestic Saving
11.40	12.26	21.13	28.76	42.26	87.50	79.30	98.10	136.20	59.00	..	Gross National Saving
				(Billions of 1987 CFA Francs)							
549.02	572.21	628.26	633.27	623.23	687.16	751.72	765.00	821.92	819.99	I	Gross National Product
550.05	574.74	632.27	637.27	625.89	687.16	755.72	769.00	825.92	824.23	..	GDP at Market Prices
-113.71	-118.74	-123.30	-112.18	-95.86	-115.90	-119.90	-113.00	-121.39	-145.02	..	Resource Balance
54.71	61.91	53.27	41.76	47.51	56.15	59.90	73.00	69.26	58.03	..	Exports of Goods & NFServices
168.43	180.65	176.58	153.94	143.38	172.05	179.80	186.00	190.65	203.05	..	Imports of Goods & NFServices
663.77	693.48	755.57	749.46	721.75	803.06	875.62	882.00	947.32	969.26	..	Domestic Absorption
514.83	539.73	542.27	549.49	517.52	553.24	613.73	617.00	658.59	716.09	..	Private Consumption, etc.
50.23	55.25	84.47	81.05	83.33	83.33	92.42	100.00	96.97	103.03	..	General Gov't Consumption
98.70	98.50	128.83	118.92	120.90	166.49	169.46	165.00	191.76	150.14	..	Gross Domestic Investment
90.43	93.82	121.87	116.40	118.39	134.31	171.62	194.00	176.09	156.69	..	Fixed Investment
521.28	546.55	602.34	614.41	607.61	659.87	726.72	740.00	795.22	791.82	..	GDP at factor cost
163.20	176.37	181.29	181.82	179.89	219.59	244.73	233.00	266.53	258.14	..	Agriculture
141.44	139.37	150.57	151.75	154.40	150.28	171.98	182.00	195.36	188.68	..	Industry
91.88	84.32	93.62	94.21	93.33	93.62	101.98	107.00	107.00	107.00	..	Manufacturing
220.06	233.68	271.23	280.84	273.32	290.00	310.00	325.00	333.33	345.00	..	Services, etc.
											Memo Items:
56.27	62.20	53.40	47.89	56.43	52.87	51.37	73.00	79.52	68.01	..	Capacity to Import
1.55	0.29	0.12	6.13	8.91	-3.28	-8.53	0.00	10.27	9.98	..	Terms of Trade Adjustment
551.61	575.03	632.39	643.40	634.81	683.88	747.19	769.00	836.19	834.22	..	Gross Domestic Income
550.57	572.50	628.38	639.40	632.14	683.88	743.19	765.00	832.19	829.97	..	Gross National Income
				(Index 1987 = 100)							**DOMESTIC PRICES/DEFLATORS**
65.7	74.5	80.9	84.9	89.7	93.6	92.5	100.0	103.6	99.4	..	Overall (GDP)
66.0	74.7	82.9	87.2	91.4	97.8	95.8	100.0	101.9	98.8	..	Domestic Absorption
61.8	70.9	76.1	80.5	87.9	93.8	91.9	100.0	103.2	107.7	..	Agriculture
60.4	68.8	76.4	86.6	87.3	93.2	92.5	100.0	103.9	108.1	..	Industry
55.7	70.3	75.5	88.3	88.0	94.0	92.2	100.0	104.7	107.5	..	Manufacturing
72.2	77.7	87.0	94.3	98.9	105.7	102.9	100.0	104.4	103.9	..	Consumer Price Index
											MANUFACTURING ACTIVITY
..	..	..	..	..	..	..	..	..	..	..	Employment (1987 = 100)
..	..	..	..	..	..	..	..	..	..	..	Real Earnings per Empl. (1987 = 100)
..	..	..	..	..	..	..	..	..	..	..	Real Output per Empl. (1987 = 100)
23.0	21.2	19.8	18.3	..	..	..	..	..	..	..	Earnings as % of Value Added
				(Billions of current CFA Francs)							**MONETARY HOLDINGS**
53.22	63.72	71.38	80.06	92.77	93.32	114.19	127.51	148.69	154.17	..	Money Supply, Broadly Defined
41.67	48.83	54.36	60.33	66.50	69.54	85.43	91.18	100.87	105.27	..	Money
19.90	24.83	27.03	31.74	31.24	30.97	43.43	43.71	49.31	53.28	..	Currency Outside Banks
21.77	24.00	27.34	28.60	35.26	38.57	42.00	47.47	51.56	52.00	..	Demand Deposits
11.55	14.89	17.01	19.72	26.26	23.78	28.77	36.33	47.83	48.89	..	Quasi-Money
				(Millions of current CFA Francs)							**GOVERNMENT DEFICIT (-) OR SURPLUS**
879	-4,674	-6,185	562	-3,350	6,339	-747	1,976	..	..	F	Current Revenue
43,109	48,674	54,527	54,540	63,071	71,488	79,162	89,924	..	..	..	Current Expenditure
35,305	41,140	55,354	47,987	60,854	56,639	71,690	..	..	..	..	Current Budget Balance
7,804	7,534	-827	6,553	2,217	14,849	7,472	..	..	..	..	Capital Receipts
30	46	33	..	17	100	78	40	..	..	..	Capital Payments
6,955	12,254	5,391	5,991	5,584	8,610	8,632	..	..	..	..	

BURKINA FASO	1969	1970	1971	1972	1973	1974	1975	1976	1977	1978	1979
FOREIGN TRADE (CUSTOMS BASIS)					*(Millions of current US dollars)*						
Value of Exports, fob	26.50	24.60	24.60	36.00	44.20	66.00	73.50	83.10	94.80	107.80	132.70
Nonfuel Primary Products	25.50	23.41	23.04	32.80	41.64	60.60	68.67	78.11	89.44	99.57	115.50
Fuels	0.06	0.09	0.09	0.14	0.23	0.02	0.05	0.11	0.05	0.15	0.76
Manufactures	0.94	1.09	1.47	3.06	2.33	5.38	4.78	4.88	5.30	8.08	16.44
Value of Imports, cif	62.00	56.50	73.00	94.00	130.00	180.00	216.00	195.00	260.00	296.00	370.00
Nonfuel Primary Products	16.60	15.33	20.67	27.96	39.02	66.31	52.50	43.68	60.88	92.17	92.91
Fuels	4.11	4.63	6.45	8.05	9.19	11.67	19.10	15.30	22.06	25.19	41.91
Manufactures	41.30	36.54	45.88	57.99	81.79	102.02	144.40	136.01	177.06	178.64	235.17
					(Index 1987 = 100)						
Terms of Trade	165.5	172.9	170.6	165.7	205.1	136.4	118.4	151.2	137.7	127.4	130.2
Export Prices, fob	41.1	43.0	46.6	50.4	81.0	81.5	69.4	86.9	86.4	92.8	108.3
Import Prices, cif	24.8	24.9	27.3	30.4	39.5	59.7	58.7	57.5	62.8	72.8	83.1
BALANCE OF PAYMENTS					*(Millions of current US dollars)*						
Exports of Goods & Services	..	30.80	33.20	45.06	58.41	84.37	95.19	106.49	118.53	136.46	181.37
Merchandise, fob	..	24.60	24.57	36.05	44.23	65.98	73.49	83.06	94.83	107.81	132.70
Nonfactor Services	..	4.10	6.12	6.30	8.46	9.36	14.31	17.02	17.49	23.72	41.57
Factor Services	..	2.10	2.51	2.71	5.72	9.04	7.39	6.41	6.21	4.93	7.10
Imports of Goods & Services	..	67.70	88.96	112.48	154.86	210.50	281.31	260.37	341.98	406.14	506.83
Merchandise, fob	..	44.90	58.07	74.37	104.31	147.76	187.79	167.45	220.69	255.40	312.13
Nonfactor Services	..	20.70	27.88	34.09	44.59	51.44	74.06	77.00	94.88	134.71	178.38
Factor Services	..	2.10	3.01	4.02	5.96	11.29	19.46	15.93	26.40	16.03	16.31
Long-Term Interest	..	0.40	0.50	0.50	0.80	1.10	1.50	1.60	1.70	2.60	4.50
Private Current Transfers, net	..	16.00	21.56	22.47	35.76	29.15	32.47	36.51	40.12	54.64	83.07
Workers' Remittances	..	18.00	20.96	26.17	35.53	33.65	46.25	49.93	59.66	77.95	109.53
Curr. A/C Bal before Off. Transf.	..	-20.90	-34.20	-44.95	-60.68	-96.97	-153.65	-117.37	-183.32	-215.05	-242.39
Net Official Transfers	..	29.40	35.00	48.42	63.18	91.72	99.35	84.85	100.33	155.51	185.87
Curr. A/C Bal after Off. Transf.	..	8.50	0.80	3.47	2.50	-5.26	-54.30	-32.51	-82.99	-59.54	-56.52
Long-Term Capital, net	..	1.34	2.14	-5.48	17.69	13.03	19.04	18.69	40.18	27.76	64.04
Direct Investment	..	0.40	0.80	-1.00	4.19	2.41	-0.38	2.05	4.60	0.39	1.13
Long-Term Loans	..	-0.10	1.40	4.10	9.20	13.30	17.50	24.20	41.60	34.30	62.40
Disbursements	..	1.70	2.90	5.60	11.50	15.80	21.20	27.30	45.40	38.80	67.10
Repayments	..	1.80	1.50	1.50	2.30	2.50	3.70	3.10	3.80	4.50	4.70
Other Long-Term Capital	..	1.04	-0.06	-8.58	4.31	-2.68	1.92	-7.56	-6.03	-6.93	0.51
Other Capital, net	..	2.26	-1.14	4.31	-8.81	8.54	29.00	15.30	24.37	7.21	13.11
Change in Reserves	..	-12.10	-1.80	-2.31	-11.39	-16.31	6.26	-1.47	18.44	24.57	-20.63
Memo Item:					*(CFA Francs per US dollar)*						
Conversion Factor (Annual Avg)	259.710	277.710	277.130	252.210	222.700	240.500	214.320	238.980	245.670	225.640	212.720
				(Millions of US dollars), outstanding at end of year							
EXTERNAL DEBT (Total)	..	20.70	23.60	20.00	31.20	47.20	62.50	85.20	164.40	262.60	295.00
Long-Term Debt (by debtor)	..	20.70	23.60	20.00	31.20	47.20	62.50	85.20	134.40	184.60	257.00
Central Bank, incl. IMF credit	..	0.00	0.00	0.00	0.00	0.00	0.00	0.00	0.00	6.10	11.40
Central Government	..	16.60	16.90	10.30	16.40	24.90	39.60	59.00	99.60	136.50	189.70
Rest of General Government	..	0.10	0.10	0.10	0.10	0.00	0.00	0.00	0.00	0.00	0.00
Non-financial Public Enterprises	..	1.00	1.10	1.10	2.60	4.20	5.10	5.80	11.80	13.20	26.40
Priv. Sector, incl non-guaranteed	..	3.00	5.50	8.50	12.10	18.10	17.80	20.40	23.00	28.80	29.50
Short-Term Debt	..	..	..	..	..	..	..	..	30.00	78.00	38.00
Memo Items:					*(Millions of US dollars)*						
Int'l Reserves Excluding Gold	25.8	36.4	43.0	47.5	62.6	83.6	76.5	71.4	56.2	36.3	61.6
Gold Holdings (at market price)	..	..	..	..	..	..	..	..	0.9	1.9	5.7
SOCIAL INDICATORS											
Total Fertility Rate	6.4	6.4	6.4	6.4	6.4	6.4	6.5	6.5	6.5	6.5	6.5
Infant Mortality Rate	174.6	170.4	166.2	162.0	161.0	160.0	159.0	158.0	157.0	155.4	153.8
Life Expectancy at Birth	40.0	40.4	40.8	41.2	41.6	42.0	42.4	42.8	43.2	43.6	44.0
Urban Population, % of total	5.6	5.7	5.8	5.9	6.1	6.2	6.3	6.4	6.6	6.7	6.9
Food Prod. per capita (1987=100)	109.7	110.3	105.1	96.4	82.1	88.2	98.0	86.4	88.1	92.3	95.2
Labor Force, Agriculture (%)	88.4	88.3	88.1	87.9	87.8	87.6	87.5	87.3	87.1	87.0	86.8
Labor Force, Female (%)	48.4	48.3	48.3	48.2	48.2	48.2	48.1	48.1	48.0	47.9	47.9
Primary Schl. Enroll. Ratio	..	13.0	..	..	..	..	16.0	15.0	16.0	17.0	18.0
Primary Schl. Enroll. Ratio, Female	..	10.0	..	..	..	..	12.0	11.0	12.0	12.0	13.0
Secondary Schl. Enroll. Ratio	..	1.0	..	..	..	..	2.0	2.0	2.0	2.0	3.0

	1980	1981	1982	1983	1984	1985	1986	1987	1988	1989 estimate	NOTES	BURKINA FASO
												FOREIGN TRADE (CUSTOMS BASIS)
(Millions of current US dollars)												
	160.60	159.40	126.40	130.00	138.00	130.90	148.00	198.00	208.00	520.80	f	Value of Exports, fob
	143.12	135.95	108.92	116.36	118.26	108.27	129.33	193.98	203.79	..	..	Nonfuel Primary Products
	0.18	0.28	0.00	0.00	0.00	0.00	0.00	0.00	0.00	..	..	Fuels
	17.30	23.17	17.48	13.64	19.74	22.63	18.67	4.02	4.21	..	..	Manufactures
	446.00	422.00	436.00	377.00	319.00	405.00	525.00	540.00	566.00	214.40	f	Value of Imports, cif
	103.53	117.10	123.30	108.60	74.48	90.23	128.83	114.02	131.27	..	..	Nonfuel Primary Products
	58.93	65.63	71.80	64.53	54.50	61.95	9.34	13.63	15.23	..	..	Fuels
	283.54	239.27	240.90	203.86	190.02	252.82	386.83	412.35	419.50	..	..	Manufactures
(Index 1987 = 100)												
	123.3	105.4	97.1	110.3	111.7	95.7	86.4	100.0	91.2	..	..	Terms of Trade
	117.0	105.9	94.3	104.9	101.6	84.8	80.6	100.0	99.5	..	..	Export Prices, fob
	94.9	100.4	97.1	95.1	91.0	88.6	93.3	100.0	109.1	..	..	Import Prices, cif
												BALANCE OF PAYMENTS
(Millions of current US dollars)												
	225.24	209.10	183.69	156.54	174.99	172.44	200.98	278.83	298.14	267.71	..	Exports of Goods & Services
	160.59	159.36	126.43	112.93	140.87	135.49	149.00	229.92	249.12	215.04	..	Merchandise, fob
	49.10	40.86	48.25	37.72	27.12	27.16	39.85	34.94	34.92	39.50	..	Nonfactor Services
	15.55	8.88	9.02	5.89	7.01	9.79	12.13	13.97	14.10	13.17	..	Factor Services
	596.37	552.21	553.11	471.78	408.80	498.59	622.59	688.42	722.19	738.85	..	Imports of Goods & Services
	368.33	348.44	359.85	308.90	270.11	352.80	441.24	475.14	486.83	501.55	..	Merchandise, fob
	208.40	185.08	173.97	146.90	124.27	135.11	157.09	185.00	208.16	208.77	..	Nonfactor Services
	19.63	18.69	19.28	15.97	14.43	10.68	24.26	28.28	27.20	28.53	..	Factor Services
	6.30	6.10	7.50	7.60	6.00	9.90	11.90	14.40	13.60	16.00	..	Long-Term Interest
	111.82	120.22	88.73	89.04	71.48	139.12	191.46	166.70	165.18	144.19	..	Private Current Transfers, net
	150.27	153.32	110.27	113.16	90.19	125.90	191.74	173.35	165.19	147.33	..	Workers' Remittances
	-259.31	-222.89	-280.68	-226.20	-162.33	-187.03	-230.15	-242.89	-258.87	-326.95	..	Curr. A/C Bal before Off. Transf.
	210.58	180.80	188.61	166.10	158.87	127.10	211.09	201.97	204.47	235.73	..	Net Official Transfers
	-48.73	-42.09	-92.07	-60.10	-3.46	-59.93	-19.06	-40.92	-54.40	-91.22	..	Curr. A/C Bal after Off. Transf.
	53.46	37.22	56.23	78.93	45.08	54.36	79.99	104.54	71.49	-3.56	..	Long-Term Capital, net
	0.02	2.43	1.95	1.98	1.67	12.46	2.89	5.99	1.68	1.57	..	Direct Investment
	58.00	75.70	70.30	81.90	41.60	41.90	76.90	98.50	68.60	83.80	..	Long-Term Loans
	68.60	83.30	78.00	89.40	53.80	57.10	96.00	112.80	90.30	99.60	..	Disbursements
	10.60	7.60	7.70	7.50	12.20	15.20	19.10	14.30	21.70	15.80	..	Repayments
	-4.56	-40.91	-16.02	-4.95	1.81	0.00	0.20	0.05	1.21	-88.93	..	Other Long-Term Capital
	6.19	19.15	35.64	17.51	-6.87	-0.37	-6.32	-29.41	18.50	46.19	..	Other Capital, net
	-10.92	-14.29	0.20	-36.35	-34.76	5.94	-54.61	-34.21	-35.59	48.59	..	Change in Reserves
												Memo Item:
(CFA Francs per US dollar)												
	211.300	271.730	328.620	381.070	436.960	449.260	346.300	300.540	297.850	319.010	..	Conversion Factor (Annual Avg)
(Millions of US dollars), outstanding at end of year												**EXTERNAL DEBT (Total)**
	333.60	345.50	372.90	417.60	429.40	534.60	669.60	866.00	877.80	756.30	..	
	298.60	310.50	340.90	390.50	399.30	489.60	613.60	786.70	800.60	685.80	..	Long-Term Debt (by debtor)
	15.40	14.00	13.70	14.40	12.90	13.20	12.10	10.80	8.00	5.30	..	Central Bank, incl. IMF credit
	231.70	249.50	291.80	334.80	345.80	426.30	545.10	711.10	736.20	637.60	..	Central Government
	0.00	0.00	0.00	0.00	0.00	0.00	0.00	0.00	0.00	..	..	Rest of General Government
	25.70	27.00	28.70	36.20	36.80	46.40	53.30	61.70	54.10	41.20	..	Non-financial Public Enterprises
	25.80	20.00	6.70	5.10	3.80	3.70	3.10	3.10	2.30	1.70	..	Priv. Sector, incl non-guaranteed
	35.00	35.00	32.00	27.10	30.10	45.00	56.00	79.30	77.20	70.50	..	Short-Term Debt
												Memo Items:
(Millions of US dollars)												
	68.2	70.8	61.8	85.0	106.3	139.5	233.5	322.6	320.9	265.5	..	Int'l Reserves Excluding Gold
	6.6	4.5	5.1	4.2	3.4	3.6	4.3	5.4	4.6	4.5	..	Gold Holdings (at market price)
												SOCIAL INDICATORS
	6.5	6.5	6.5	6.5	6.5	6.5	6.5	6.5	6.5	6.5	..	Total Fertility Rate
	152.2	150.6	149.0	146.8	144.6	142.4	140.2	138.0	136.7	135.3	..	Infant Mortality Rate
	44.4	44.8	45.3	45.7	46.0	46.4	46.8	47.2	47.4	47.6	..	Life Expectancy at Birth
	7.0	7.2	7.4	7.5	7.7	7.9	8.2	8.5	8.7	8.8	..	Urban Population, % of total
	86.8	91.6	89.8	90.2	88.1	102.9	112.3	100.0	110.1	103.6	..	Food Prod. per capita (1987=100)
	86.7	..	..	..	..	..	..	..	..	..	..	Labor Force, Agriculture (%)
	47.8	47.7	47.5	47.3	47.2	47.0	46.9	46.7	46.5	46.4	..	Labor Force, Female (%)
	18.0	..	24.0	26.0	26.0	29.0	31.0	32.0	..	31.0	..	Primary Schl. Enroll. Ratio
	14.0	17.0	18.0	19.0	19.0	21.0	23.0	24.0	..	24.0	..	Primary Schl. Enroll. Ratio, Female
	3.0	..	3.0	4.0	4.0	5.0	5.0	6.0	..	6.0	..	Secondary Schl. Enroll. Ratio

BURUNDI	1969	1970	1971	1972	1973	1974	1975	1976	1977	1978	1979
CURRENT GNP PER CAPITA (US $)	50	70	90	80	80	90	100	120	140	150	170
POPULATION (thousands)	3,295	3,350	3,420	3,494	3,569	3,644	3,720	3,795	3,868	3,943	4,024
USE AND ORIGIN OF RESOURCES					*(Billions of current Burundi Francs)*						
Gross National Product (GNP)	15.59	20.59	21.33	20.60	23.69	26.48	32.47	37.70	48.35	53.62	69.51
Net Factor Income from Abroad	-1.05	-0.65	-0.79	-1.00	-0.67	-0.71	-0.68	-0.97	-1.23	-1.30	-0.91
GDP at Market Prices	16.64	21.24	22.12	21.60	24.36	27.19	33.15	38.68	49.58	54.92	70.42
Resource Balance	-0.41	-0.20	-1.27	-0.72	-0.56	-1.57	-3.56	-1.13	0.15	-4.68	-7.44
Exports of Goods & NFServices	1.61	2.27	1.87	2.53	2.68	2.65	2.74	5.31	8.67	6.43	9.98
Imports of Goods & NFServices	2.01	2.47	3.14	3.26	3.25	4.22	6.30	6.44	8.52	11.11	17.43
Domestic Absorption	17.05	21.44	23.39	22.32	24.92	28.76	36.71	39.81	49.43	59.60	77.87
Private Consumption, etc.	14.29	18.40	19.37	18.84	20.80	24.24	30.37	32.92	38.42	44.31	58.31
General Gov't Consumption	1.38	2.08	2.34	2.79	2.82	3.42	3.83	3.37	5.50	7.58	9.05
Gross Domestic Investment	1.38	0.96	1.68	0.69	1.29	1.10	2.51	3.52	5.52	7.71	10.50
Fixed Investment	1.38	0.85	1.12	1.14	1.39	1.77	3.07	3.52	5.52	7.71	10.50
Indirect Taxes, net	1.16	1.59	1.44	1.50	1.66	2.00	2.20	3.17	6.38	6.11	7.89
GDP at factor cost	15.48	19.65	20.69	20.09	22.69	25.19	30.95	35.50	43.20	48.81	62.54
Agriculture	..	13.88	14.33	13.12	15.42	16.59	20.32	23.00	27.39	29.64	37.91
Industry	..	2.00	2.16	2.33	2.83	3.30	4.17	4.54	6.00	7.86	10.36
Manufacturing	..	1.43	1.62	1.77	2.27	2.58	2.84	3.16	3.88	4.53	6.55
Services, etc.	..	3.77	4.20	4.64	4.44	5.30	6.45	7.96	9.81	11.32	14.26
Gross Domestic Saving	0.97	0.76	0.41	-0.03	0.73	-0.47	-1.04	2.38	5.67	3.03	3.06
Gross National Saving	..	0.17	-0.32	-0.98	0.12	-1.09	-1.61	1.61	4.72	2.05	2.35
					(Billions of 1987 Burundi Francs)						
Gross National Product	40.96	53.63	77.52	71.44	78.38	77.95	78.97	84.70	94.25	93.74	96.36
GDP at Market Prices	44.01	55.70	80.54	74.91	80.83	80.24	80.80	87.22	97.22	96.31	97.91
Resource Balance	-8.12	-11.11	-14.79	-12.36	-11.86	-13.62	-18.09	-17.52	-23.98	-23.76	-28.58
Exports of Goods & NFServices	7.00	6.53	6.36	7.88	7.14	6.62	7.83	6.70	5.72	8.08	9.01
Imports of Goods & NFServices	15.12	17.63	21.15	20.24	19.00	20.24	25.91	24.22	29.70	31.84	37.60
Domestic Absorption	52.13	66.81	95.33	87.27	92.69	93.86	98.89	104.73	121.20	120.06	126.49
Private Consumption, etc.	39.14	51.32	76.13	71.88	75.60	73.71	80.56	86.80	94.20	89.40	96.57
General Gov't Consumption	7.64	11.83	12.60	13.36	12.95	13.16	13.27	10.38	15.92	17.70	16.66
Gross Domestic Investment	5.35	3.66	6.60	2.03	4.14	6.99	5.05	7.55	11.08	12.96	13.26
Fixed Investment	..	..	..	..	..	..	..	..	..	..	..
GDP at factor cost	40.05	50.45	75.22	69.70	75.30	74.40	75.40	80.17	85.20	85.94	87.59
Agriculture	24.19	33.80	50.15	45.16	50.58	48.56	50.80	52.65	54.81	53.34	54.13
Industry	2.30	2.54	6.98	6.82	6.94	7.20	7.24	7.99	9.94	11.08	11.17
Manufacturing	4.85	5.06	5.53	5.40	5.57	5.77	5.75	6.11	6.39	6.83	7.11
Services, etc.	21.34	20.86	17.83	17.98	17.17	18.15	16.76	18.99	20.00	21.23	22.01
Memo Items:											
Capacity to Import	12.08	16.22	12.59	15.76	15.70	12.71	11.29	19.96	30.22	18.43	21.54
Terms of Trade Adjustment	5.07	9.69	6.23	7.87	8.56	6.09	3.46	13.26	24.50	10.35	12.53
Gross Domestic Income	49.08	65.40	86.77	82.79	89.39	86.32	84.26	100.48	121.72	106.66	110.44
Gross National Income	46.04	63.32	83.75	79.32	86.94	84.04	82.43	97.96	118.75	104.09	108.89
DOMESTIC PRICES/DEFLATORS					*(Index 1987 = 100)*						
Overall (GDP)	37.8	38.1	27.5	28.8	30.1	33.9	41.0	44.3	51.0	57.0	71.9
Domestic Absorption	32.7	32.1	24.5	25.6	26.9	30.6	37.1	38.0	40.8	49.6	61.6
Agriculture	..	41.0	28.6	29.1	30.5	34.2	40.0	43.7	50.0	55.6	70.0
Industry	..	78.5	30.9	34.2	40.8	45.8	57.6	56.8	60.4	70.9	92.8
Manufacturing	..	28.3	29.3	32.7	40.7	44.8	49.5	51.8	60.8	66.3	92.2
Consumer Price Index	19.9	19.9	20.7	21.4	22.7	26.3	30.4	32.5	34.7	43.1	58.8
MANUFACTURING ACTIVITY											
Employment (1987=100)	..	..	..	..	..	..	..	..	..	..	..
Real Earnings per Empl. (1987=100)	..	..	..	..	..	..	..	..	..	..	..
Real Output per Empl. (1987=100)	..	..	..	..	..	..	..	..	..	..	..
Earnings as % of Value Added	..	..	29.5	28.8	26.7	26.5	28.7	25.6	25.5	19.3	13.2
MONETARY HOLDINGS					*(Millions of current Burundi Francs)*						
Money Supply, Broadly Defined	1,731	2,138	2,444	2,440	2,988	3,451	3,350	4,713	6,550	8,902	9,477
Money	1,653	2,001	2,321	2,310	2,825	3,307	3,208	4,548	6,154	8,406	9,058
Currency Outside Banks	1,032	1,192	1,333	1,370	1,548	1,873	1,709	2,411	3,225	4,542	4,876
Demand Deposits	622	809	988	940	1,277	1,434	1,499	2,137	2,930	3,864	4,182
Quasi-Money	77	138	124	131	163	144	141	165	396	496	419
GOVERNMENT DEFICIT (-) OR SURPLUS					*(Millions of current Burundi Francs)*						
Current Revenue	..	..	..	..	..	-86	-1,081	-237	-791	-1,610	-3,758
Current Expenditure	..	..	..	..	4,719	5,658	5,729	8,435	9,821	10,970	12,471
Current Budget Balance	..	..	..	..	..	..	..	..	..	..	..
Capital Receipts	..	..	..	..	1	2	17	2	21	5	9
Capital Payments	..	..	..	..	..	..	..	..	..	..	..

1980	1981	1982	1983	1984	1985	1986	1987	1988	1989 estimate	NOTES	BURUNDI
200	250	240	250	240	250	240	250	240	220	..	**CURRENT GNP PER CAPITA** (US $)
4,114	4,213	4,321	4,437	4,562	4,696	4,837	4,986	5,140	5,299	..	**POPULATION** (thousands)
			(Billions of current Burundi Francs)								**USE AND ORIGIN OF RESOURCES**
82.17	85.39	88.84	100.44	117.23	137.58	134.91	136.92	150.54	167.84	..	Gross National Product (GNP)
-0.63	-1.81	-2.36	-2.45	-3.22	-3.77	-5.93	-3.56	-3.04	-0.71	..	Net Factor Income from Abroad
82.80	87.20	91.20	102.89	120.45	141.35	140.84	140.48	153.58	168.55	..	GDP at Market Prices
-11.21	-9.98	-14.00	-16.84	-17.05	-12.65	-11.87	-23.42	-20.46	..	..	Resource Balance
7.29	7.89	9.24	9.27	12.12	15.08	15.64	13.60	18.92	..	..	Exports of Goods & NFServices
18.50	17.87	23.23	26.11	29.18	27.73	27.51	37.02	39.39	..	..	Imports of Goods & NFServices
94.01	97.18	105.20	119.73	137.51	154.00	152.71	163.90	174.05	..	..	Domestic Absorption
71.64	68.35	78.32	80.96	94.18	111.28	106.03	107.79	119.10	..	..	Private Consumption, etc.
10.88	14.00	13.69	20.41	21.13	22.79	24.25	26.31	26.57	..	..	General Gov't Consumption
11.49	14.83	13.18	18.36	22.19	19.93	22.43	29.80	28.37	..	..	Gross Domestic Investment
11.49	11.83	13.80	19.44	20.78	19.85	19.18	29.16	25.69	..	..	Fixed Investment
6.20	4.50	6.80	8.88	13.03	15.15	17.72	14.03	19.34	..	..	Indirect Taxes, net
76.60	82.70	84.40	94.01	107.42	126.19	123.12	126.45	134.24		..	GDP at factor cost
47.87	50.39	48.08	53.83	64.59	77.66	72.06	71.49	75.09	..	..	Agriculture
9.70	11.07	12.96	14.58	14.87	16.41	16.64	18.59	20.07	..	..	Industry
5.70	6.40	7.50	8.41	9.26	10.17	10.79	11.91	12.90	..	..	Manufacturing
19.03	21.24	23.36	25.60	27.96	32.13	34.42	36.37	39.08	..	..	Services, etc.
0.28	4.85	-0.81	1.52	5.14	7.28	10.56	6.38	7.91	..	..	Gross Domestic Saving
0.01	3.45	-3.00	-0.62	2.32	4.71	5.50	3.70	6.27	..	..	Gross National Saving
			(Billions of 1987 Burundi Francs)								
97.91	109.77	105.86	113.46	113.08	126.22	128.73	136.92	144.42	146.54	..	Gross National Product
98.91	112.26	108.80	116.44	116.48	130.00	134.96	140.48	145.54	155.04	..	GDP at Market Prices
-26.04	-20.28	-26.57	-32.05	-33.29	-27.04	-27.30	-23.42	-18.49	-21.84	..	Resource Balance
6.36	10.11	10.91	9.19	11.24	12.49	12.13	13.60	13.43	15.38	..	Exports of Goods & NFServices
32.40	30.39	37.48	41.24	44.53	39.53	39.43	37.02	31.92	37.22	..	Imports of Goods & NFServices
124.95	132.54	135.38	148.50	149.77	157.04	162.26	163.90	164.02	176.88	..	Domestic Absorption
95.88	96.61	103.43	105.84	111.92	121.71	119.43	107.79	112.57	..	..	Private Consumption, etc.
16.39	18.48	19.20	18.71	18.45	18.82	21.39	26.31	26.12	..	..	General Gov't Consumption
12.68	17.45	12.74	23.95	19.40	16.51	21.44	29.80	25.33	31.83	..	Gross Domestic Investment
..	..	..	..	..	..	..	..	..	..	..	Fixed Investment
90.87	104.14	98.69	104.48	104.28	116.97	120.88	126.45	130.04	..	..	GDP at factor cost
55.07	64.66	58.36	60.35	58.16	65.80	68.52	71.49	73.14	..	f	Agriculture
12.34	13.32	13.38	15.20	15.44	16.85	17.10	18.59	19.22	..	f	Industry
7.61	8.67	8.43	8.55	9.39	10.32	10.80	11.91	12.26	..	..	Manufacturing
23.26	25.81	26.82	28.93	30.68	34.32	35.27	36.37	37.68	..	..	Services, etc.
											Memo Items:
12.77	13.42	14.90	14.65	18.50	21.50	22.42	13.60	15.34	..	..	Capacity to Import
6.41	3.31	3.99	5.46	7.26	9.01	10.29	0.00	1.90	..	..	Terms of Trade Adjustment
105.32	115.58	112.79	121.90	123.74	139.01	145.24	140.48	147.44	..	..	Gross Domestic Income
104.32	113.08	109.86	118.92	120.34	135.23	139.01	136.92	146.32	..	..	Gross National Income
			(Index 1987 = 100)								**DOMESTIC PRICES/DEFLATORS**
83.7	77.7	83.8	88.4	103.4	108.7	104.4	100.0	105.5	108.7	..	Overall (GDP)
75.2	73.3	77.7	80.6	91.8	98.1	94.1	100.0	106.1	..	..	Domestic Absorption
86.9	77.9	82.4	89.2	111.1	118.0	105.2	100.0	102.7	..	..	Agriculture
78.5	83.1	96.9	95.9	96.3	97.4	97.3	100.0	104.4	..	..	Industry
74.9	73.8	89.0	98.3	98.6	98.6	99.9	100.0	105.3	..	..	Manufacturing
60.3	67.5	71.4	77.3	88.5	91.7	93.4	100.0	104.5	116.7	..	Consumer Price Index
											MANUFACTURING ACTIVITY
..	..	..	..	..	..	..	..	..	..	..	Employment (1987=100)
..	..	..	..	..	..	..	..	..	..	..	Real Earnings per Empl. (1987=100)
..	..	..	..	..	..	..	..	..	..	..	Real Output per Empl. (1987=100)
14.4	..	..	18.1	..	..	..	..	..	..	..	Earnings as % of Value Added
			(Millions of current Burundi Francs)								**MONETARY HOLDINGS**
12,495	15,649	15,305	19,241	19,979	23,912	24,096	24,520	27,696	31,304	..	Money Supply, Broadly Defined
9,651	12,238	10,827	13,647	14,536	18,182	19,658	19,453	19,962	20,547	..	Money
4,971	7,059	6,419	7,262	7,498	7,253	8,008	8,734	9,605	9,868	..	Currency Outside Banks
4,679	5,179	4,408	6,385	7,038	10,929	11,650	10,719	10,357	10,679	..	Demand Deposits
2,844	3,411	4,478	5,593	5,444	5,730	4,438	5,067	7,735	10,756	..	Quasi-Money
			(Millions of current Burundi Francs)								
-3,234	-4,933	..	..	..	..	..	..	..	..	..	**GOVERNMENT DEFICIT (-) OR SURPLUS**
14,708	16,096	..	..	..	..	..	..	..	..	..	Current Revenue
..	10,060	..	..	..	..	..	..	..	..	..	Current Expenditure
..	6,036	..	..	..	..	..	..	..	..	..	Current Budget Balance
12	22	..	..	..	..	..	..	..	..	..	Capital Receipts
..	10,991	..	..	..	..	..	..	..	..	..	Capital Payments

BURUNDI	1969	1970	1971	1972	1973	1974	1975	1976	1977	1978	1979
FOREIGN TRADE (CUSTOMS BASIS)					*(Millions of current US dollars)*						
Value of Exports, fob	11.88	24.36	18.54	26.00	30.07	29.57	31.62	53.56	89.00	69.00	104.88
Nonfuel Primary Products	11.39	24.03	17.92	25.36	29.26	28.90	30.55	52.62	87.11	67.80	103.47
Fuels	0.01	0.02	0.06	0.01	0.21	0.16	0.16	0.28	0.47	0.36	0.55
Manufactures	0.48	0.31	0.56	0.63	0.60	0.51	0.91	0.66	1.42	0.84	0.86
Value of Imports, cif	21.74	22.36	29.93	31.27	31.47	40.32	62.71	57.96	90.89	98.00	152.72
Nonfuel Primary Products	4.56	7.12	8.51	9.49	9.95	12.02	14.58	14.57	20.95	19.34	25.09
Fuels	1.62	2.54	1.99	1.91	1.97	3.03	3.69	5.07	6.21	7.92	14.24
Manufactures	15.57	12.70	19.43	19.87	19.55	25.27	44.44	38.32	63.73	70.74	113.39
					(Index 1987 = 100)						
Terms of Trade	141.6	180.3	131.9	137.2	135.0	103.7	99.1	197.4	280.8	191.8	182.2
Export Prices, fob	33.9	42.5	37.9	44.0	54.4	58.6	57.5	117.5	177.3	134.7	147.4
Import Prices, cif	24.0	23.6	28.7	32.1	40.3	56.5	58.0	59.5	63.1	70.3	80.9
BALANCE OF PAYMENTS					*(Millions of current US dollars)*						
Exports of Goods & Services	..	26.50	22.00	29.70	34.80	34.90	35.90	62.80	98.90	78.70	115.50
Merchandise, fob	..	24.50	19.60	26.60	31.10	31.30	32.30	56.90	93.20	69.50	102.00
Nonfactor Services	..	1.40	1.70	2.40	2.70	2.40	2.50	4.60	3.10	4.40	6.60
Factor Services	..	0.60	0.70	0.70	1.00	1.20	1.10	1.30	2.60	4.80	6.90
Imports of Goods & Services	..	29.50	37.40	39.20	42.00	55.40	81.90	76.40	111.60	142.60	194.90
Merchandise, fob	..	22.40	29.90	31.30	31.40	43.10	61.70	58.20	76.30	96.50	145.00
Nonfactor Services	..	5.80	5.90	5.90	9.50	10.50	18.30	16.60	18.40	26.90	32.80
Factor Services	..	1.30	1.60	2.00	1.10	1.80	1.90	1.60	16.90	19.20	17.10
Long-Term Interest	..	0.20	0.20	0.30	0.20	0.20	0.40	0.50	0.60	0.90	1.30
Private Current Transfers, net	..	0.60	0.70	0.60	0.70	1.10	1.50	2.30	3.20	3.60	2.20
Workers' Remittances	..	..	..	..	..	..	..	..	..	..	..
Curr. A/C Bal before Off. Transf.	..	-2.40	-14.70	-8.90	-6.50	-19.40	-44.50	-11.30	-9.50	-60.30	-77.20
Net Official Transfers	..	4.70	5.50	4.70	5.90	8.70	11.80	18.20	25.70	29.00	17.80
Curr. A/C Bal after Off. Transf.	..	2.30	-9.20	-4.20	-0.60	-10.70	-32.70	6.90	16.20	-31.30	-59.40
Long-Term Capital, net	..	7.60	7.00	6.20	11.50	16.30	31.50	15.30	31.80	45.40	64.00
Direct Investment	..	0.20	..	..	..	0.20	..	..	..	..	..
Long-Term Loans	..	1.00	0.10	-1.00	0.30	1.50	9.30	2.80	15.50	17.10	31.70
Disbursements	..	1.40	0.50	0.60	1.00	2.20	10.90	5.10	17.90	19.00	34.60
Repayments	..	0.40	0.40	1.60	0.70	0.70	1.60	2.30	2.40	1.90	2.90
Other Long-Term Capital	..	6.40	6.90	7.20	11.20	14.60	22.20	12.50	16.30	28.30	32.30
Other Capital, net	..	-6.37	4.67	2.41	-8.38	-12.97	16.39	-3.86	-2.79	-26.35	-11.49
Change in Reserves	..	-3.53	-2.47	-4.41	-2.52	7.37	-15.19	-18.34	-45.21	12.25	6.89
Memo Item:					*(Burundi Francs per US dollar)*						
Conversion Factor (Annual Avg)	87.500	87.500	87.500	87.500	80.030	78.750	78.750	86.250	90.000	90.000	90.000
					(Millions of US dollars), outstanding at end of year						
EXTERNAL DEBT (Total)	..	15.00	13.60	6.90	7.70	9.40	19.30	22.40	47.20	74.70	136.10
Long-Term Debt (by debtor)	..	15.00	13.60	6.90	7.70	9.40	19.30	22.40	42.20	69.70	123.10
Central Bank, incl. IMF credit	..	7.70	5.80	0.00	0.00	0.00	2.40	3.40	8.10	14.90	35.20
Central Government	..	5.80	6.20	5.30	5.80	7.10	13.00	15.90	32.10	50.80	82.70
Rest of General Government	..	..	..	..	..	..	..	..	..	..	..
Non-financial Public Enterprises	..	0.00	0.00	0.00	0.00	0.00	2.00	1.10	0.00	1.80	1.60
Priv. Sector, incl non-guaranteed	..	1.50	1.60	1.60	1.90	2.30	1.90	2.00	2.00	2.20	3.60
Short-Term Debt	..	0.00	0.00	0.00	0.00	0.00	0.00	0.00	5.00	5.00	13.00
Memo Items:					*(Thousands of US dollars)*						
Int'l Reserves Excluding Gold	7,420.0	15,360.0	17,685.0	18,487.0	21,483.0	14,189.0	30,713.0	49,030.0	94,406.0	81,304.0	89,987.0
Gold Holdings (at market price)	34.0	36.0	42.0	62.0	108.0	179.0	135.0	129.0	1,500.0	2,055.0	6,738.0
SOCIAL INDICATORS											
Total Fertility Rate	6.4	6.4	6.4	6.4	6.4	6.4	6.5	6.5	6.5	6.5	6.5
Infant Mortality Rate	138.0	137.0	136.0	135.0	134.0	133.0	132.0	131.0	130.0	124.6	119.2
Life Expectancy at Birth	44.6	44.7	44.8	44.9	45.0	45.2	45.4	45.5	45.7	45.9	46.1
Urban Population, % of total	2.2	2.2	2.4	2.5	2.7	2.8	3.0	3.2	3.4	3.7	3.9
Food Prod. per capita (1987=100)	107.6	107.4	107.0	99.5	108.3	96.6	108.7	109.2	108.4	112.2	95.9
Labor Force, Agriculture (%)	93.6	93.5	93.4	93.3	93.3	93.2	93.1	93.0	93.0	92.9	92.8
Labor Force, Female (%)	49.8	49.7	49.7	49.6	49.6	49.5	49.5	49.4	49.3	49.3	49.2
Primary Schl. Enroll. Ratio	..	30.0	..	..	..	..	22.0	..	23.0	23.0	25.0
Primary Schl. Enroll. Ratio, Female	..	20.0	..	..	..	..	17.0	..	18.0	18.0	20.0
Secondary Schl. Enroll. Ratio	..	2.0	..	..	..	..	3.0	2.0	2.0	3.0	3.0

1980	1981	1982	1983	1984	1985	1986	1987	1988	1989 estimate	NOTES	BURUNDI
											(Millions of current US dollars) **FOREIGN TRADE (CUSTOMS BASIS)**
65.26	71.00	88.00	77.10	98.00	111.60	167.00	90.00	128.00	..	..	Value of Exports, fob
60.64	66.81	82.86	72.50	93.36	103.16	147.44	77.57	107.00	..	..	Nonfuel Primary Products
0.31	0.37	0.46	0.40	0.40	0.37	0.20	0.25	0.00	..	..	Fuels
4.31	3.82	4.68	4.20	4.25	8.07	19.36	12.18	21.00	..	..	Manufactures
167.22	161.00	214.00	194.00	186.90	188.80	202.50	206.10	204.00	..	..	Value of Imports, cif
29.37	28.25	37.33	33.90	31.17	30.63	32.59	33.57	30.17	..	..	Nonfuel Primary Products
26.46	22.14	29.36	27.04	23.71	23.18	9.66	11.68	9.83	..	..	Fuels
111.39	110.61	147.31	133.06	132.02	134.99	160.25	160.85	164.00	..	..	Manufactures
											(Index 1987 = 100)
136.7	115.5	128.1	125.0	139.0	134.4	156.7	100.0	107.8	..	..	Terms of Trade
130.8	110.0	117.5	112.2	121.1	117.0	145.4	100.0	116.3	..	..	Export Prices, fob
95.7	95.3	91.7	89.8	87.1	87.1	92.8	100.0	107.9	..	..	Import Prices, cif
											(Millions of current US dollars) **BALANCE OF PAYMENTS**
92.00	97.00	108.20	98.60	102.70	128.36	142.94	113.17	139.16	114.90	f	Exports of Goods & Services
66.30	74.90	87.80	80.60	87.80	113.65	129.14	98.34	124.36	93.25	..	Merchandise, fob
14.70	12.80	14.90	16.10	13.40	13.16	11.74	11.91	11.92	12.77	..	Nonfactor Services
11.00	9.30	5.50	1.90	1.50	1.56	2.07	2.92	2.88	8.89	..	Factor Services
223.70	227.80	289.60	284.40	272.40	258.98	290.88	322.55	307.38	284.24	f	Imports of Goods & Services
168.00	161.00	214.00	184.00	184.00	149.70	165.31	159.17	166.06	152.16	..	Merchandise, fob
37.70	37.40	43.90	72.10	60.00	89.34	102.86	132.04	116.02	106.64	..	Nonfactor Services
18.00	29.40	31.70	28.30	28.40	19.94	22.71	31.34	25.30	25.44	..	Factor Services
1.90	1.60	2.30	3.30	8.00	8.50	12.00	15.10	16.60	14.40	..	Long-Term Interest
4.00	4.60	1.90	3.30	3.40	9.98	7.67	7.16	10.02	8.60	..	Private Current Transfers, net
..	..	..	..	..	..	..	..	..	..	..	Workers' Remittances
-127.70	-126.20	-179.50	-182.50	-166.30	-120.63	-140.26	-202.21	-158.20	-160.74	..	Curr. A/C Bal before Off. Transf.
32.00	37.40	15.10	26.70	40.60	78.47	102.69	105.73	87.16	131.61	..	Net Official Transfers
-95.70	-88.80	-164.40	-155.80	-125.70	-42.16	-37.58	-96.48	-71.04	-29.13	..	Curr. A/C Bal after Off. Transf.
77.00	65.00	93.00	143.00	111.00	55.40	61.65	115.89	79.31	63.51	f	Long-Term Capital, net
1.10	0.60	1.50	0.40	0.90	0.54	1.52	1.37	1.20	0.57	..	Direct Investment
34.70	26.10	51.80	102.80	72.10	58.00	79.40	121.20	79.80	68.40	..	Long-Term Loans
39.00	29.70	55.10	106.40	79.40	69.20	94.30	141.30	98.70	87.60	..	Disbursements
4.30	3.60	3.30	3.60	7.30	11.20	14.90	20.10	18.90	19.20	..	Repayments
41.20	38.30	39.70	39.80	38.00	-3.14	-19.27	-6.68	-1.68	-5.46	..	Other Long-Term Capital
20.57	-10.88	40.37	15.89	13.01	-2.52	-5.14	-30.69	-16.19	-12.52	..	Other Capital, net
-1.87	34.68	31.03	-3.09	1.69	-10.72	-18.93	11.28	7.92	-21.86	..	Change in Reserves
											Memo Item: *(Burundi Francs per US dollar)*
90.000	90.000	90.000	92.950	119.710	120.690	114.170	123.560	140.400	158.670	..	Conversion Factor (Annual Avg)
											(Millions of US dollars), outstanding at end of year
165.80	178.60	227.50	306.00	344.00	446.50	555.50	763.30	793.80	866.80	..	**EXTERNAL DEBT (Total)**
153.80	168.60	211.50	296.00	332.00	414.90	531.40	725.90	780.80	849.80	..	Long-Term Debt (by debtor)
40.40	36.70	35.50	30.40	21.40	21.40	30.40	30.30	42.60	53.00	..	Central Bank, incl. IMF credit
111.20	130.20	173.40	255.80	301.80	383.70	490.30	685.50	729.70	789.70	..	Central Government
..	..	..	..	..	..	..	..	..	..	..	Rest of General Government
1.00	1.10	1.10	1.30	1.10	1.60	1.90	2.00	2.90	2.90	..	Non-financial Public Enterprises
1.20	0.60	1.50	8.50	7.70	8.20	8.80	8.10	5.60	4.20	..	Priv. Sector, incl non-guaranteed
12.00	10.00	16.00	10.00	12.00	31.60	24.10	37.40	13.00	17.00	..	Short-Term Debt
											Memo Items: *(Thousands of US dollars)*
94,502.0	61,300.0	29,489.0	26,939.0	19,731.0	29,472.0	69,073.0	60,732.0	69,384.0	99,621.0	..	Int'l Reserves Excluding Gold
10,152.0	6,846.0	7,869.0	6,570.0	5,310.0	5,632.0	6,732.0	8,337.0	7,065.0	6,906.0	..	Gold Holdings (at market price)
											SOCIAL INDICATORS
6.5	6.5	6.5	6.6	6.6	6.7	6.7	6.8	6.8	6.8	..	Total Fertility Rate
113.7	108.3	102.9	97.3	91.7	86.2	80.6	75.0	73.0	71.1	..	Infant Mortality Rate
46.3	46.4	46.6	47.0	47.5	47.9	48.4	48.8	49.0	49.3	..	Life Expectancy at Birth
4.1	4.4	4.7	5.0	5.3	5.6	6.1	6.5	6.8	7.0	..	Urban Population, % of total
95.8	101.2	99.3	95.5	91.5	98.6	99.6	100.0	100.5	86.1	..	Food Prod. per capita (1987=100)
92.7	..	..	..	..	..	..	..	..	..	..	Labor Force, Agriculture (%)
49.1	49.0	48.8	48.6	48.4	48.3	48.1	47.9	47.7	47.5	..	Labor Force, Female (%)
29.0	..	..	44.0	49.0	53.0	59.0	67.0	70.0	..	..	Primary Schl. Enroll. Ratio
22.0	25.0	..	35.0	40.0	44.0	50.0	..	..	..	..	Primary Schl. Enroll. Ratio, Female
3.0	..	..	3.0	4.0	4.0	4.0	..	..	..	..	Secondary Schl. Enroll. Ratio

CAMEROON	1969	1970	1971	1972	1973	1974	1975	1976	1977	1978	1979
CURRENT GNP PER CAPITA (US $)	170	180	180	180	210	270	310	360	410	500	600
POPULATION (thousands)	6,352	6,506	6,667	6,840	7,026	7,226	7,439	7,667	7,910	8,167	8,431
USE AND ORIGIN OF RESOURCES					*(Billions of current CFA Francs)*						
Gross National Product (GNP)	272.8	304.8	316.5	347.2	390.9	477.2	563.7	639.7	773.9	987.5	1,167.1
Net Factor Income from Abroad	-13.3	-13.4	-24.1	-30.4	-32.9	-42.1	-48.6	-52.8	-60.1	-64.7	-92.0
GDP at Market Prices	286.1	318.2	340.6	377.6	423.8	519.3	612.3	692.5	834.0	1,052.2	1,259.1
Resource Balance	1.5	4.9	-14.1	-21.5	-14.0	13.7	-17.5	-32.7	-22.9	-47.0	-90.2
Exports of Goods & NFServices	66.9	83.4	78.4	77.0	87.7	132.1	138.9	156.8	209.0	248.9	265.4
Imports of Goods & NFServices	65.4	78.5	92.5	98.5	101.7	118.4	156.4	189.5	231.9	295.9	355.6
Domestic Absorption	284.6	313.3	354.7	399.1	437.8	505.6	629.8	725.2	856.9	1,099.2	1,349.3
Private Consumption, etc.	215.2	224.2	256.5	284.2	304.5	359.6	440.8	528.9	593.2	757.6	960.4
General Gov't Consumption	38.8	38.1	41.5	46.0	49.0	57.3	66.7	74.5	81.9	102.8	116.3
Gross Domestic Investment	30.6	51.0	56.7	68.9	84.3	88.7	122.3	121.8	181.8	238.8	272.6
Fixed Investment	..	..	..	..	..	..	100.3	118.8	163.5	204.7	251.7
Indirect Taxes, net	22.6	20.4	18.4	29.6	46.9	70.7	96.5	116.0	80.4	108.2	83.5
GDP at factor cost	263.5	297.8	322.2	348.0	376.9	448.6	515.8	576.5	753.6	944.0	1,175.6
Agriculture	87.9	99.8	105.6	120.7	130.5	153.4	178.3	191.2	280.6	329.9	388.1
Industry	55.6	59.3	65.5	71.2	78.9	92.8	111.7	131.3	153.4	167.9	259.9
Manufacturing	28.1	32.6	35.2	39.2	43.4	51.0	63.0	73.0	74.7	86.7	101.9
Services, etc.	142.6	159.1	169.5	185.7	214.4	273.1	322.3	370.0	400.0	554.4	611.1
Gross Domestic Saving	32.1	55.9	42.6	47.4	70.3	102.4	104.8	89.1	158.9	191.8	182.4
Gross National Saving	..	40.5	16.4	14.4	31.7	55.6	51.5	32.3	98.4	124.3	83.4
					(Billions of 1987 CFA Francs)						
Gross National Product	1,227.7	1,268.1	1,265.0	1,282.6	1,359.2	1,495.4	1,489.7	1,562.8	1,694.1	1,975.0	2,215.7
GDP at Market Prices	1,283.1	1,320.1	1,369.9	1,401.9	1,478.5	1,637.2	1,624.9	1,695.2	1,838.6	2,108.6	2,388.8
Resource Balance	-79.0	-89.7	-180.0	-160.7	-108.7	-65.6	-127.1	-123.0	-222.2	-163.2	-149.6
Exports of Goods & NFServices	282.0	307.2	301.8	316.9	325.2	369.7	331.6	384.9	339.1	446.8	529.7
Imports of Goods & NFServices	360.9	396.9	481.9	477.6	433.9	435.3	458.7	508.0	561.3	610.0	679.4
Domestic Absorption	1,362.0	1,409.8	1,549.9	1,562.6	1,587.2	1,702.8	1,752.0	1,818.2	2,060.8	2,271.9	2,538.4
Private Consumption, etc.	1,081.5	1,092.7	1,197.5	1,174.4	1,169.2	1,278.4	1,299.9	1,362.0	1,542.6	1,566.6	1,841.2
General Gov't Consumption	149.3	143.5	140.2	160.8	175.4	201.8	191.9	214.9	186.9	215.5	228.1
Gross Domestic Investment	131.3	173.6	212.2	227.3	242.7	222.6	260.2	241.3	331.3	489.8	469.1
Fixed Investment	..	..	..	..	..	..	..	..	..	..	..
GDP at factor cost	..	..	..	..	..	..	..	..	..	..	..
Agriculture	467.8	490.6	497.0	525.8	546.4	572.9	579.9	587.6	595.4	617.9	710.2
Industry	217.8	214.9	240.9	232.6	242.3	255.5	264.8	285.1	337.4	372.7	535.3
Manufacturing	105.6	108.8	123.6	125.2	125.4	127.7	138.2	147.1	167.0	192.5	199.5
Services, etc.	595.7	615.2	628.9	644.9	689.7	808.9	780.2	822.4	905.8	1,118.1	1,143.3
Memo Items:											
Capacity to Import	369.2	421.7	408.4	373.4	374.2	485.6	407.4	420.3	505.8	513.1	507.1
Terms of Trade Adjustment	87.2	114.5	106.6	56.4	49.0	116.0	75.8	35.4	166.8	66.3	-22.7
Gross Domestic Income	1,370.3	1,434.6	1,476.5	1,458.3	1,527.5	1,753.2	1,700.7	1,730.6	2,005.4	2,175.0	2,366.1
Gross National Income	1,315.0	1,382.6	1,371.6	1,339.0	1,408.2	1,611.4	1,565.5	1,598.2	1,860.9	2,041.3	2,193.0
DOMESTIC PRICES/DEFLATORS					*(Index 1987 = 100)*						
Overall (GDP)	22.3	24.1	24.9	26.9	28.7	31.7	37.7	40.9	45.4	49.9	52.7
Domestic Absorption	20.9	22.2	22.9	25.5	27.6	29.7	35.9	39.9	41.6	48.4	53.2
Agriculture	18.8	20.3	21.2	23.0	23.9	26.8	30.7	32.5	47.1	53.4	54.6
Industry	25.5	27.6	27.2	30.6	32.6	36.3	42.2	46.0	45.5	45.1	48.5
Manufacturing	26.6	30.0	28.5	31.3	34.6	39.9	45.6	49.6	44.7	45.0	51.1
Consumer Price Index	18.3	19.4	20.2	21.8	24.1	28.2	32.1	35.2	40.4	45.5	48.5
MANUFACTURING ACTIVITY											
Employment (1987=100)	..	..	..	..	..	..	..	..	..	..	..
Real Earnings per Empl. (1987=100)	..	..	..	..	..	..	..	..	..	..	..
Real Output per Empl. (1987=100)	..	..	..	..	..	..	..	..	..	..	..
Earnings as % of Value Added	..	29.5	31.0	25.3	..	32.6	39.0	39.8	40.6	39.6	37.0
MONETARY HOLDINGS					*(Billions of current CFA Francs)*						
Money Supply, Broadly Defined	40.43	45.47	50.87	56.44	69.68	93.38	104.74	132.07	182.64	211.30	259.23
Money	35.17	38.40	42.87	46.26	54.73	71.82	75.10	94.16	125.77	145.93	183.39
Currency Outside Banks	17.88	19.55	20.90	21.88	25.91	30.99	32.23	36.90	48.92	58.47	68.24
Demand Deposits	17.29	18.85	21.96	24.39	28.83	40.83	42.87	57.26	76.85	87.46	115.15
Quasi-Money	5.26	7.07	8.00	10.18	14.95	21.56	29.64	37.91	56.87	65.36	75.84
GOVERNMENT DEFICIT (-) OR SURPLUS					*(Billions of current CFA Francs)*						
	..	..	..	..	..	..	-12.98	-15.85	-3.02	4.07	31.72
Current Revenue	..	..	..	..	..	..	90.96	109.61	132.75	178.78	222.43
Current Expenditure	..	..	..	..	..	..	73.36	77.73	95.92	124.42	133.90
Current Budget Balance	..	..	..	..	..	..	17.60	31.88	36.83	54.36	88.53
Capital Receipts	..	..	..	..	..	..	..	..	..	..	..
Capital Payments	..	..	..	..	..	..	30.58	47.73	39.85	50.29	56.81

1980	1981	1982	1983	1984	1985	1986	1987	1988	1989 estimate	NOTES	CAMEROON
760	900	900	870	820	810	890	920	980	1,000	..	**CURRENT GNP PER CAPITA (US $)**
8,701	8,978	9,262	9,554	9,855	10,166	10,491	10,830	11,184	11,554	..	**POPULATION (thousands)**
				(Billions of current CFA Francs)							**USE AND ORIGIN OF RESOURCES**
1,427.3	1,800.4	2,158.1	2,609.5	3,059.6	3,595.9	3,949.0	3,818.0	3,568.0	3,383.0	C	Gross National Product (GNP)
-141.6	-179.6	-145.3	-175.0	-213.0	-243.0	-217.0	-151.0	-127.0	-112.0	..	Net Factor Income from Abroad
1,568.9	1,980.0	2,303.4	2,784.5	3,272.6	3,838.9	4,166.0	3,969.0	3,695.0	3,495.0	C	GDP at Market Prices
-49.1	-45.9	-6.0	121.8	390.3	422.1	28.6	-177.3	-102.0	45.0	..	Resource Balance
378.0	516.0	599.0	797.0	1,085.0	1,318.0	985.0	666.0	611.0	670.0	..	Exports of Goods & NFServices
427.1	561.9	605.0	675.2	694.7	895.9	956.4	843.3	713.0	625.0	..	Imports of Goods & NFServices
1,618.0	2,025.9	2,309.4	2,662.7	2,882.3	3,416.8	4,137.4	4,146.3	3,797.0	3,450.0	..	Domestic Absorption
1,185.3	1,365.2	1,571.4	1,734.3	1,894.7	2,116.2	2,488.8	2,756.6	2,800.0	2,410.0	..	Private Consumption, etc.
136.8	172.3	199.3	248.3	306.4	345.3	364.0	433.0	417.0	412.0	..	General Gov't Consumption
295.9	488.4	538.7	680.1	681.2	955.3	1,284.6	956.7	580.0	628.0	..	Gross Domestic Investment
282.4	441.4	507.2	654.5	661.8	939.0	1,255.2	950.3	..	..	..	Fixed Investment
118.2	..	..	..	..	121.0	144.3	186.6	165.6	154.3	..	Indirect Taxes, net
1,450.7	..	..	..	..	3,717.9	4,021.7	3,782.4	3,529.4	3,340.7	B C	GDP at factor cost
437.0	527.4	633.9	656.0	758.7	790.4	907.9	976.0	954.0	939.0	..	Agriculture
406.0	617.9	810.4	1,085.9	1,333.4	1,317.4	1,373.1	1,137.0	1,055.0	945.0	..	Industry
124.1	173.7	247.0	290.9	358.5	422.5	536.6	522.8	498.2	456.2	..	Manufacturing
725.9	834.7	859.1	1,042.6	1,180.5	1,731.1	1,885.0	1,856.0	1,686.0	1,611.0	..	Services, etc.
246.8	442.5	532.7	801.9	1,071.5	1,377.4	1,313.2	779.4	478.0	673.0	..	Gross Domestic Saving
88.4	248.8	363.5	597.0	830.7	1,119.6	1,073.2	588.4	308.0	534.0	..	Gross National Saving
				(Billions of 1987 CFA Francs)							
2,513.0	2,838.2	2,999.5	3,235.1	3,416.1	3,678.2	4,025.1	3,818.0	3,536.3	3,425.0	C	Gross National Product
2,762.2	3,118.9	3,201.4	3,449.7	3,651.2	3,930.5	4,246.1	3,969.0	3,662.1	3,538.3	C	GDP at Market Prices
-86.5	-72.2	-8.3	150.9	435.4	432.0	29.0	-177.3	-101.1	45.6	..	Resource Balance
665.5	812.8	832.5	987.3	1,210.3	1,349.3	1,003.8	666.0	605.6	678.3	..	Exports of Goods & NFServices
751.9	885.0	840.8	836.4	775.0	917.2	974.8	843.3	706.7	632.7	..	Imports of Goods & NFServices
2,848.7	3,191.1	3,209.7	3,298.8	3,215.8	3,498.4	4,217.1	4,146.3	3,763.2	3,492.8	..	Domestic Absorption
2,086.9	2,177.3	2,171.6	2,183.3	2,122.8	2,328.5	2,536.7	2,756.6	2,775.1	2,439.9	..	Private Consumption, etc.
240.9	278.3	288.5	314.5	342.0	352.0	371.0	433.0	413.3	417.2	..	General Gov't Consumption
521.0	735.4	749.7	801.1	751.1	818.0	1,309.3	956.7	574.8	635.7	..	Gross Domestic Investment
..	..	..	..	..	..	..	..	..	..	..	Fixed Investment
..	..	..	..	..	3,806.6	4,099.1	3,782.4	3,498.0	3,382.1	B C	GDP at factor cost
769.3	870.5	903.8	835.3	909.1	807.5	925.3	976.0	945.4	950.5	..	Agriculture
714.8	934.1	1,086.7	1,312.4	1,368.5	1,270.5	1,399.5	1,137.0	1,045.6	956.7	..	Industry
218.4	289.6	389.8	415.7	410.0	473.9	547.1	522.8	493.6	461.7	..	Manufacturing
1,278.1	1,314.3	1,210.9	1,301.9	1,373.6	1,852.5	1,921.3	1,856.0	1,671.1	1,631.2	..	Services, etc.
											Memo Items:
665.5	812.7	832.5	987.3	1,210.4	1,349.4	1,004.0	666.0	605.6	678.3	..	Capacity to Import
0.0	-0.1	0.0	0.0	0.1	0.1	0.1	0.0	0.0	0.0	..	Terms of Trade Adjustment
2,762.3	3,118.8	3,201.4	3,449.7	3,651.2	3,930.6	4,246.3	3,969.0	3,662.1	3,538.3	..	Gross Domestic Income
2,513.0	2,838.1	2,999.5	3,235.2	3,416.1	3,678.4	4,025.2	3,818.0	3,536.3	3,425.0	..	Gross National Income
				(Index 1987 = 100)							**DOMESTIC PRICES/DEFLATORS**
56.8	63.5	71.9	80.7	89.6	97.7	98.1	100.0	100.9	98.8	..	Overall (GDP)
56.8	63.5	71.9	80.7	89.6	97.7	98.1	100.0	100.9	98.8	..	Domestic Absorption
56.8	60.6	70.1	78.5	83.5	97.9	98.1	100.0	100.9	98.8	..	Agriculture
56.8	66.1	74.6	82.7	97.4	103.7	98.1	100.0	100.9	98.8	..	Industry
56.8	60.0	63.4	70.0	87.4	89.2	98.1	100.0	100.9	98.8	..	Manufacturing
53.1	58.8	66.6	77.7	86.5	87.6	94.4	100.0	108.6	108.6	..	Consumer Price Index
											MANUFACTURING ACTIVITY
..	..	..	..	..	..	..	..	..	..	..	Employment (1987=100)
..	..	..	..	..	..	..	..	..	..	..	Real Earnings per Empl. (1987=100)
..	..	..	..	..	..	..	..	..	..	..	Real Output per Empl. (1987=100)
34.6	35.5	34.0	32.1	30.2	..	..	..	..	..	..	Earnings as % of Value Added
				(Billions of current CFA Francs)							**MONETARY HOLDINGS**
314.51	404.41	481.91	610.92	734.73	863.42	829.93	676.62	693.15	761.03	..	Money Supply, Broadly Defined
207.32	257.72	296.98	375.57	409.26	425.58	446.87	385.91	384.62	444.05	..	Money
78.08	101.81	107.59	127.63	134.41	148.30	167.65	171.11	161.66	162.85	..	Currency Outside Banks
129.24	155.91	189.39	247.94	274.85	277.28	279.21	214.80	222.96	281.20	..	Demand Deposits
107.18	146.69	184.92	235.35	325.47	437.84	383.07	290.71	308.52	316.98	..	Quasi-Money
				(Billions of current CFA Francs)							
7.24	-58.50	-55.22	33.87	..	..	..	..	..	..	C	**GOVERNMENT DEFICIT (-) OR SURPLUS**
230.74	314.54	389.21	668.14	795.32	..	912.22	731.18	613.00	..	..	Current Revenue
148.68	248.42	256.44	344.57	428.84	466.19	556.20	493.98	458.78	..	..	Current Expenditure
82.06	66.12	132.77	323.57	366.48	..	356.02	237.20	154.22	..	..	Current Budget Balance
..	..	1.23	3.69	0.09	..	11.64	11.60	20.20	..	..	Capital Receipts
74.82	124.62	189.22	293.39	..	388.98	..	..	..	..	..	Capital Payments

CAMEROON	1969	1970	1971	1972	1973	1974	1975	1976	1977	1978	1979
FOREIGN TRADE (CUSTOMS BASIS)					*(Millions of current US dollars)*						
Value of Exports, fob	232.1	230.8	212.5	225.3	361.6	490.9	469.9	534.8	704.0	805.0	1,170.0
Nonfuel Primary Products	214.1	211.5	192.3	203.2	328.3	447.2	421.3	483.3	660.9	749.2	836.2
Fuels	0.1	0.0	0.1	0.4	0.6	1.0	1.4	2.0	13.2	25.3	266.4
Manufactures	17.9	19.3	20.0	21.7	32.8	42.6	47.2	49.6	29.9	30.6	67.4
Value of Imports, cif	207.2	242.1	249.5	298.8	334.7	437.3	598.3	594.7	746.9	1,008.5	1,270.6
Nonfuel Primary Products	26.9	32.9	37.2	39.7	47.6	67.3	76.4	67.2	102.3	113.2	152.7
Fuels	11.9	13.1	15.3	17.8	21.4	42.4	60.2	53.2	67.2	72.4	137.1
Manufactures	168.3	196.0	197.0	241.3	265.7	327.6	461.7	474.3	577.4	822.9	980.9
					(Index 1987 = 100)						
Terms of Trade	145.6	137.7	115.6	115.0	137.9	122.8	101.6	149.3	187.2	159.8	150.5
Export Prices, fob	35.2	35.2	31.9	34.8	50.9	63.5	56.0	82.5	114.4	109.1	120.0
Import Prices, cif	24.2	25.5	27.6	30.3	36.9	51.7	55.1	55.2	61.1	68.2	79.7
BALANCE OF PAYMENTS					*(Millions of current US dollars)*						
Exports of Goods & Services	..	279.3	294.3	320.0	521.2	583.8	672.3	721.2	979.0	1,318.6	1,718.0
Merchandise, fob	..	218.7	235.7	239.3	409.5	493.2	512.0	584.2	809.1	1,095.8	1,354.1
Nonfactor Services	..	56.7	51.7	75.0	108.1	86.8	147.9	133.7	161.8	206.5	351.5
Factor Services	..	3.9	6.9	5.6	3.6	3.7	12.4	3.3	8.1	16.3	12.4
Imports of Goods & Services	..	319.4	347.6	417.8	531.5	601.9	848.4	851.2	1,103.6	1,506.0	1,843.8
Merchandise, fob	..	190.8	223.1	257.6	310.6	389.9	540.3	554.9	719.2	951.5	1,270.8
Nonfactor Services	..	122.4	114.2	146.4	194.1	175.7	249.4	251.9	335.1	464.1	464.7
Factor Services	..	6.2	10.3	13.8	26.8	36.3	58.8	44.4	49.3	90.4	108.3
Long-Term Interest	..	4.9	6.1	7.1	11.1	13.1	17.2	20.9	31.1	48.3	71.3
Private Current Transfers, net	..	-7.2	-7.4	-10.2	-25.6	-19.4	-22.1	-16.7	-1.5	-12.2	-32.7
Workers' Remittances	..	..	..	..	..	..	..	..	..	..	3.5
Curr. A/C Bal before Off. Transf.	..	-47.3	-60.8	-108.0	-35.9	-37.5	-198.3	-146.7	-126.1	-199.7	-158.4
Net Official Transfers	..	17.5	16.3	16.4	19.2	20.6	45.8	54.7	33.7	13.3	32.7
Curr. A/C Bal after Off. Transf.	..	-29.8	-44.4	-91.6	-16.7	-17.0	-152.5	-92.1	-92.4	-186.4	-125.7
Long-Term Capital, net	..	42.4	36.8	17.0	51.5	32.1	59.4	112.9	111.2	121.6	279.7
Direct Investment	..	16.0	1.7	3.3	-0.7	13.5	25.3	8.2	4.3	33.7	59.9
Long-Term Loans	..	33.1	26.0	69.8	31.1	41.8	104.6	162.6	320.8	281.3	507.5
Disbursements	..	39.5	35.3	81.2	50.0	60.3	132.3	189.9	357.4	353.3	599.4
Repayments	..	6.4	9.3	11.4	18.9	18.5	27.7	27.3	36.6	72.0	91.9
Other Long-Term Capital	..	-6.7	9.1	-56.0	21.1	-23.2	-70.5	-57.9	-213.9	-193.3	-287.7
Other Capital, net	..	16.8	-9.0	40.2	-32.1	2.8	33.6	-28.3	-20.9	70.3	-80.0
Change in Reserves	..	-29.4	16.6	34.4	-2.7	-18.0	59.5	7.5	2.1	-5.6	-74.0
Memo Item:					*(CFA Francs per US dollar)*						
Conversion Factor (Annual Avg)	246.850	274.330	277.710	265.390	240.960	230.050	222.420	225.090	247.780	238.590	216.650
					(Millions of US dollars), outstanding at end of year						
EXTERNAL DEBT (Total)	..	140.4	174.1	215.5	259.0	316.3	420.1	590.7	1,056.9	1,478.2	2,116.8
Long-Term Debt (by debtor)	..	140.4	174.1	215.5	259.0	315.1	419.4	590.7	945.5	1,314.1	1,877.9
Central Bank, incl. IMF credit	..	0.0	0.0	0.0	0.0	5.7	14.2	39.4	41.2	61.6	65.8
Central Government	..	69.8	83.4	66.7	92.1	117.2	183.0	283.7	415.4	559.2	748.7
Rest of General Government	..	0.2	0.1	0.1	0.0	0.0	0.0	0.0	0.0	0.0	0.0
Non-financial Public Enterprises	..	47.7	65.8	117.2	133.4	144.5	172.7	198.6	400.4	532.1	798.0
Priv. Sector, incl non-guaranteed	..	22.7	24.8	31.5	33.5	47.7	49.5	69.0	88.5	161.2	265.0
Short-Term Debt	..	..	..	..	..	1.2	0.7	0.0	111.4	164.1	238.9
Memo Items:					*(Millions of US dollars)*						
Int'l Reserves Excluding Gold	48.1	80.8	73.6	43.6	51.2	78.5	28.8	43.8	42.4	52.3	125.7
Gold Holdings (at market price)	..	..	..	..	..	..	..	..	2.5	3.4	15.2
SOCIAL INDICATORS											
Total Fertility Rate	5.6	5.8	5.9	6.0	6.1	6.2	6.3	6.4	6.5	6.5	6.5
Infant Mortality Rate	129.2	125.8	122.4	119.0	117.4	115.8	114.2	112.6	111.0	109.4	107.8
Life Expectancy at Birth	48.1	48.9	49.8	50.6	50.9	51.2	51.5	51.8	52.1	52.4	52.7
Urban Population, % of total	19.5	20.3	21.6	22.9	24.3	25.6	26.9	28.5	30.0	31.6	33.1
Food Prod. per capita (1987=100)	105.4	111.9	113.9	117.0	118.2	123.4	123.3	115.5	114.9	105.1	105.1
Labor Force, Agriculture (%)	84.0	83.4	82.0	80.6	79.2	77.9	76.7	75.2	73.8	72.5	71.1
Labor Force, Female (%)	37.6	37.5	37.3	37.1	36.9	36.7	36.5	36.3	36.1	35.9	35.7
Primary Schl. Enroll. Ratio	..	89.0	..	..	..	..	97.0	99.0	101.0	103.0	104.0
Primary Schl. Enroll. Ratio, Female	..	75.0	..	..	..	..	87.0	88.0	91.0	93.0	94.0
Secondary Schl. Enroll. Ratio	..	7.0	..	..	..	..	13.0	15.0	16.0	17.0	18.0

1980	1981	1982	1983	1984	1985	1986	1987	1988	1989 estimate	NOTES	CAMEROON
											FOREIGN TRADE (CUSTOMS BASIS)
				(Millions of current US dollars)							
1,447.0	1,764.0	1,616.2	1,830.0	2,080.0	2,322.0	1,995.0	1,714.0	1,642.0	1,828.1	f	Value of Exports, fob
893.1	619.2	480.9	561.1	647.0	723.9	754.0	759.0	676.5	..	..	Nonfuel Primary Products
503.9	1,058.6	1,051.1	1,183.3	1,342.8	1,489.2	1,083.0	803.0	773.5	807.0	..	Fuels
50.1	86.2	84.2	85.6	90.2	108.9	158.0	152.0	192.0	164.0	..	Manufactures
1,538.4	1,421.0	1,243.2	1,249.7	1,213.0	1,163.0	1,717.0	2,168.0	1,767.4	1,721.5	f	Value of Imports, cif
157.0	155.8	145.8	142.8	126.4	116.1	302.2	706.5	449.4	..	..	Nonfuel Primary Products
179.3	108.7	45.3	65.6	103.8	109.1	29.1	24.0	18.0		..	Fuels
1,202.1	1,156.5	1,052.1	1,041.4	982.8	937.8	1,385.7	1,437.5	1,300.0	1,512.6	..	Manufactures
				(Index 1987 = 100)							
150.7	160.4	161.6	159.3	162.2	153.7	108.0	100.0	98.3	..	..	Terms of Trade
135.2	141.9	136.3	132.3	134.3	128.3	100.6	100.0	108.8	..	..	Export Prices, fob
89.7	88.5	84.3	83.1	82.8	83.5	93.1	100.0	110.6	..	..	Import Prices, cif
				(Millions of current US dollars)							**BALANCE OF PAYMENTS**
1,827.7	2,218.3	2,032.6	2,259.6	2,588.3	2,819.0	2,897.1	2,255.4	2,097.0	2,111.6	C f	Exports of Goods & Services
1,418.1	1,763.1	1,617.1	1,829.6	2,080.2	2,337.0	2,292.8	1,826.7	1,645.1	1,733.5	..	Merchandise, fob
388.6	430.5	402.4	417.3	461.3	461.0	551.5	389.3	406.2	366.8	..	Nonfactor Services
21.0	24.7	13.1	12.7	46.9	21.0	52.8	39.4	45.7	11.3	..	Factor Services
2,226.2	2,676.5	2,368.6	2,311.2	2,380.0	2,458.0	3,441.1	3,347.8	2,865.8	2,321.9	C f	Imports of Goods & Services
1,452.3	1,611.4	1,285.4	1,166.2	1,194.7	1,088.0	1,477.0	1,734.0	1,484.0	1,156.3	..	Merchandise, fob
589.4	776.5	753.6	737.5	718.9	810.0	1,284.7	1,072.0	909.8	803.2	..	Nonfactor Services
184.5	288.6	329.6	407.4	466.4	560.0	679.4	541.8	472.0	362.4	..	Factor Services
119.2	137.3	150.6	139.1	166.1	136.2	188.7	178.4	192.3	111.3	..	Long-Term Interest
-79.5	-52.0	-72.8	-78.5	-63.7	-33.0	-66.4	-133.1	-144.4	-84.6	..	Private Current Transfers, net
11.0	21.1	17.3	25.6	14.2	1.0	2.0	3.0	3.4	3.0	..	Workers' Remittances
-478.0	-510.2	-408.8	-130.1	144.6	328.0	-610.4	-1,225.5	-913.2	-294.9	..	Curr. A/C Bal before Off. Transf.
82.9	62.6	57.0	75.1	56.5	0.0	0.0	0.0	0.0	..	..	Net Official Transfers
-395.1	-447.6	-351.8	-55.0	201.1	328.0	-610.4	-1,225.5	-913.2	-294.9	..	Curr. A/C Bal after Off. Transf.
615.2	441.0	262.9	297.7	73.9	26.0	-126.2	561.1	227.0	349.9	C f	Long-Term Capital, net
105.2	30.5	27.6	57.8	92.1	21.0	0.0	31.0	34.0	31.3	..	Direct Investment
497.8	328.0	166.9	341.9	210.0	-157.8	84.5	91.6	287.0	521.8	..	Long-Term Loans
611.8	452.6	362.8	508.9	407.0	306.5	509.2	488.4	662.8	714.2	..	Disbursements
114.0	124.6	195.9	167.0	197.0	464.3	424.7	396.8	375.8	192.4	..	Repayments
12.2	82.5	68.4	-102.0	-228.2	162.8	-210.7	438.5	-94.0	-203.2	..	Other Long-Term Capital
-74.9	-94.7	37.7	-35.4	-491.5	-315.4	536.5	116.5	639.2	-205.5	C f	Other Capital, net
-145.2	101.3	51.2	-207.3	216.5	-38.6	200.1	547.9	47.0	150.5	..	Change in Reserves
				(CFA Francs per US dollar)							Memo Item:
209.210	235.270	296.680	354.660	409.520	471.130	386.600	318.660	291.710	315.360	..	Conversion Factor (Annual Avg)
				(Millions of US dollars), outstanding at end of year							
2,512.7	2,548.3	2,716.7	2,738.9	2,721.6	2,939.9	3,709.8	4,039.1	4,224.5	4,743.4	..	**EXTERNAL DEBT (Total)**
2,242.2	2,303.0	2,320.3	2,411.0	2,339.5	2,411.2	2,926.2	3,316.8	3,460.8	4,198.6	..	Long-Term Debt (by debtor)
58.8	43.9	38.3	35.2	30.1	27.4	22.2	16.1	100.4	113.2	..	Central Bank, incl. IMF credit
885.1	911.9	955.1	991.9	995.8	1,232.7	1,534.9	1,848.9	2,092.5	3,098.5	..	Central Government
0.0	0.0	0.0	0.0	0.0	0.0	0.0	0.0	0.0		..	Rest of General Government
983.8	970.6	863.4	776.1	645.7	704.1	800.5	866.0	743.9	529.3	..	Non-financial Public Enterprises
314.5	376.6	463.5	607.8	667.9	447.0	568.6	585.8	524.0	457.6	..	Priv. Sector, incl non-guaranteed
270.5	245.3	396.4	327.9	382.1	528.7	783.6	722.3	763.7	544.8	..	Short-Term Debt
				(Millions of US dollars)							Memo Items:
188.9	85.2	67.2	159.1	53.9	132.5	59.0	63.8	150.5	79.9	..	Int'l Reserves Excluding Gold
17.5	11.8	13.6	11.3	9.3	9.8	11.7	14.5	12.3	12.0	..	Gold Holdings (at market price)
											SOCIAL INDICATORS
6.5	6.5	6.5	6.5	6.5	6.5	6.5	6.5	6.5	6.4	..	Total Fertility Rate
106.2	104.6	103.0	101.2	99.4	97.6	95.8	94.0	92.3	90.5	..	Infant Mortality Rate
53.0	53.3	53.6	54.1	54.6	55.1	55.6	56.2	56.4	56.7	..	Life Expectancy at Birth
34.7	36.2	37.8	39.3	40.9	42.4	44.1	45.9	47.1	48.2	..	Urban Population, % of total
101.8	104.3	103.5	102.2	100.9	101.6	102.6	100.0	99.8	98.8	..	Food Prod. per capita (1987=100)
69.9	..	..	..	..	..	..	..	..	..	..	Labor Force, Agriculture (%)
35.5	35.2	35.0	34.8	34.6	34.4	34.2	33.9	33.7	33.5	..	Labor Force, Female (%)
104.0	105.0	107.0	106.0	107.0	108.0	109.0	..	..	..	..	Primary Schl. Enroll. Ratio
94.0	96.0	98.0	96.0	97.0	98.0	100.0	..	..	..	..	Primary Schl. Enroll. Ratio, Female
19.0	19.0	21.0	22.0	23.0	24.0	26.0	..	..	..	..	Secondary Schl. Enroll. Ratio

CANADA	1969	1970	1971	1972	1973	1974	1975	1976	1977	1978	1979
CURRENT GNP PER CAPITA (US $)	3,640	3,880	4,320	4,850	5,590	6,510	7,330	8,390	8,920	9,510	10,040
POPULATION (thousands)	21,028	21,324	21,592	21,822	22,072	22,364	22,697	22,993	23,273	23,517	23,747
USE AND ORIGIN OF RESOURCES					*(Billions of current Canadian Dollars)*						
Gross National Product (GNP)	81.82	87.76	95.78	107.17	125.64	149.87	169.00	194.39	213.31	235.65	268.94
Net Factor Income from Abroad	-1.21	-1.35	-1.51	-1.46	-1.73	-2.24	-2.54	-3.54	-4.57	-5.95	-7.15
GDP at Market Prices	83.03	89.12	97.29	108.63	127.37	152.11	171.54	197.92	217.88	241.60	276.10
Resource Balance	0.18	2.24	1.62	1.01	1.74	0.48	-2.40	-0.99	-0.09	1.12	1.82
Exports of Goods & NFServices	17.86	20.07	21.18	23.77	29.79	37.82	38.97	44.28	51.17	61.16	75.07
Imports of Goods & NFServices	17.69	17.83	19.55	22.75	28.05	37.35	41.37	45.28	51.26	60.04	73.25
Domestic Absorption	82.85	86.88	95.67	107.61	125.63	151.63	173.94	198.92	217.97	240.48	274.27
Private Consumption, etc.	49.06	51.13	55.52	62.83	71.94	84.90	97.42	111.74	122.56	137.34	153.55
General Gov't Consumption	18.14	20.55	21.99	23.54	26.44	30.91	36.38	38.27	43.41	47.39	52.29
Gross Domestic Investment	15.64	15.20	18.16	21.25	27.25	35.82	40.13	48.90	52.00	55.75	68.44
Fixed Investment	16.89	17.58	19.69	21.57	25.58	30.60	36.13	40.86	44.84	49.52	58.22
Indirect Taxes, net	10.54	11.09	12.05	13.63	15.31	17.87	17.09	20.99	23.19	24.82	26.64
GDP at factor cost	72.48	78.02	85.24	95.00	112.06	134.24	154.45	176.93	194.69	216.78	249.46
Agriculture	..	..	..	..	..	..	..	..	..	..	..
Industry	..	..	..	..	..	..	..	..	..	..	..
Manufacturing	..	..	..	..	..	..	..	..	..	..	..
Services, etc.	..	..	..	..	..	..	..	..	..	..	..
Gross Domestic Saving	15.82	17.44	19.78	22.26	28.99	36.30	37.73	47.91	51.91	56.87	70.26
Gross National Saving	..	16.17	18.45	20.98	27.50	34.48	35.58	44.80	47.69	51.20	63.54
					(Billions of 1987 Canadian Dollars)						
Gross National Product	272.15	278.76	294.73	312.51	336.57	351.08	360.01	381.07	393.25	410.28	425.49
GDP at Market Prices	276.12	283.29	299.60	316.77	341.20	356.22	365.49	388.01	402.03	420.42	436.70
Resource Balance	6.72	12.04	11.79	9.84	8.63	0.27	-2.18	-1.09	4.03	9.22	4.59
Exports of Goods & NFServices	52.33	56.88	59.84	64.52	71.33	69.92	65.19	72.09	78.49	89.20	93.68
Imports of Goods & NFServices	45.62	44.83	48.04	54.68	62.70	69.65	67.37	73.18	74.46	79.97	89.09
Domestic Absorption	269.41	271.25	287.81	306.93	332.57	355.95	367.67	389.10	398.01	411.20	432.11
Private Consumption, etc.	156.73	157.89	167.23	181.57	195.82	207.10	213.84	228.93	234.55	245.99	253.90
General Gov't Consumption	59.16	64.70	67.53	69.36	73.39	77.51	82.53	84.15	88.01	89.48	89.99
Gross Domestic Investment	53.52	48.65	53.04	56.00	63.36	71.33	71.30	76.03	75.45	75.73	88.21
Fixed Investment	54.95	55.13	59.46	62.03	68.19	72.72	76.94	80.50	82.17	84.72	91.95
GDP at factor cost	241.89	246.37	260.82	277.70	300.89	315.75	329.06	347.14	357.70	378.22	395.01
Agriculture	..	..	..	..	..	..	..	..	..	..	..
Industry	..	..	..	..	..	..	..	..	..	..	..
Manufacturing	..	..	..	..	..	..	..	..	..	..	..
Services, etc.	..	..	..	..	..	..	..	..	..	..	..
Memo Items:											
Capacity to Import	46.08	50.46	52.04	57.12	66.59	70.54	63.46	71.58	74.33	81.47	91.31
Terms of Trade Adjustment	-6.26	-6.41	-7.80	-7.41	-4.74	0.62	-1.72	-0.52	-4.16	-7.73	-2.37
Gross Domestic Income	269.87	276.87	291.80	309.37	336.46	356.84	363.76	387.49	397.87	412.69	434.32
Gross National Income	265.90	272.35	286.92	305.11	331.83	351.70	358.29	380.55	389.09	402.55	423.12
DOMESTIC PRICES/DEFLATORS					*(Index 1987 = 100)*						
Overall (GDP)	30.1	31.5	32.5	34.3	37.3	42.7	46.9	51.0	54.2	57.5	63.2
Domestic Absorption	30.8	32.0	33.2	35.1	37.8	42.6	47.3	51.1	54.8	58.5	63.5
Agriculture	..	..	..	..	..	..	..	..	..	..	..
Industry	..	..	..	..	..	..	..	..	..	..	..
Manufacturing	..	..	..	..	..	..	..	..	..	..	..
Consumer Price Index	28.7	29.7	30.5	32.0	34.4	38.2	42.3	45.5	49.1	53.5	58.4
MANUFACTURING ACTIVITY											
Employment (1987=100)	90.0	88.0	87.6	90.1	94.1	96.0	93.7	93.7	91.6	96.2	99.7
Real Earnings per Empl. (1987=100)	80.9	83.9	87.5	89.8	90.6	92.5	93.3	98.7	101.2	99.6	99.8
Real Output per Empl. (1987=100)	..	..	..	..	..	..	..	..	..	..	..
Earnings as % of Value Added	50.6	53.0	52.3	51.6	49.5	46.6	49.5	51.2	50.4	48.8	46.8
MONETARY HOLDINGS					*(Billions of current Canadian Dollars)*						
Money Supply, Broadly Defined	43.23	46.31	49.92	55.83	70.32	83.72	97.62	116.83	135.48	159.57	188.43
Money	15.30	15.57	17.61	19.77	21.50	21.83	25.97	26.36	29.10	31.12	31.56
Currency Outside Banks	3.33	3.56	3.99	4.56	5.20	5.86	6.78	7.32	8.08	8.95	9.45
Demand Deposits	11.97	12.01	13.63	15.21	16.30	15.97	19.19	19.04	21.01	22.17	22.11
Quasi-Money	27.93	30.74	32.30	36.05	48.82	61.90	71.65	90.47	106.38	128.44	156.86
					(Billions of current Canadian Dollars)						
GOVERNMENT DEFICIT (-) OR SURPLUS	..	..	-1.72	..	..	-1.97	-5.70	-6.30	-9.41	-11.95	-10.56
Current Revenue	..	..	18.14	..	..	31.62	34.89	37.72	38.24	41.64	48.22
Current Expenditure	..	..		..	..	28.87	34.85	38.41	43.71	49.15	54.62
Current Budget Balance	..	..		..	..	2.75	0.04	-0.69	-5.47	-7.52	-6.40
Capital Receipts	..	..	..	..	..						
Capital Payments	..	..	..	..	..	4.72	5.74	5.61	3.94	4.44	4.16

1980	1981	1982	1983	1984	1985	1986	1987	1988	1989 estimate	NOTES	CANADA
10,680	11,860	12,020	12,770	13,690	14,160	14,150	15,190	16,940	19,020	..	**CURRENT GNP PER CAPITA (US $)**
24,043	24,343	24,632	24,890	25,128	25,359	25,612	25,652	25,950	26,302	..	**POPULATION (thousands)**
				(Billions of current Canadian Dollars)							**USE AND ORIGIN OF RESOURCES**
302.06	344.66	361.77	394.11	431.25	463.66	488.08	533.81	583.10	628.69	..	Gross National Product (GNP)
-7.83	-11.34	-12.67	-11.60	-13.49	-14.33	-16.55	-16.52	-18.41	-19.84	..	Net Factor Income from Abroad
309.89	355.99	374.44	405.72	444.74	477.99	504.63	550.33	601.51	648.54	..	GDP at Market Prices
5.68	3.88	14.06	13.67	15.46	11.60	4.47	5.01	3.92	-2.33	..	Resource Balance
87.60	96.88	96.67	103.46	126.05	134.94	137.47	144.37	157.31	159.48	..	Exports of Goods & NFServices
81.92	93.00	82.61	89.79	110.60	123.35	132.99	139.36	153.39	161.81	..	Imports of Goods & NFServices
304.21	352.12	360.38	392.05	429.28	466.39	500.16	545.32	597.59	650.87	..	Domestic Absorption
172.56	196.02	210.15	229.37	250.78	274.63	295.85	323.36	352.50	384.31	..	Private Consumption, etc.
59.25	68.79	78.65	84.57	89.09	95.52	100.34	105.32	112.44	119.76	..	General Gov't Consumption
72.40	87.31	71.58	78.10	89.41	96.24	103.97	116.64	132.64	146.80	..	Gross Domestic Investment
69.72	86.12	84.09	87.60	92.73	104.56	113.91	131.94	154.09	170.12	..	Fixed Investment
27.27	36.46	38.91	40.14	42.71	47.21	53.53	57.81	65.10	72.30	..	Indirect Taxes, net
282.62	319.54	335.53	365.58	402.02	430.78	451.10	492.53	536.41	576.23	..	GDP at factor cost
..	..	..	..	..	..	..	..	..	..	..	Agriculture
..	..	..	..	..	..	..	..	..	..	..	Industry
..	..	..	..	..	..	..	..	..	..	..	Manufacturing
..	..	..	..	..	..	..	..	..	..	..	Services, etc.
78.08	91.18	85.64	91.77	104.87	107.83	108.44	121.65	136.57	144.47	..	Gross Domestic Saving
70.98	80.79	74.09	81.17	92.42	94.62	93.19	107.84	122.87	130.19	..	Gross National Saving
				(Billions of 1987 Canadian Dollars)							
431.83	444.56	429.49	444.87	472.62	495.67	509.31	533.81	560.71	576.06	..	Gross National Product
443.18	459.45	444.67	458.74	487.68	510.93	526.76	550.33	577.91	594.45	..	GDP at Market Prices
2.74	-1.00	12.20	10.74	13.19	11.01	7.67	5.01	-0.70	-13.63	..	Resource Balance
96.23	100.46	98.28	104.57	123.08	130.42	135.51	144.37	158.08	156.61	..	Exports of Goods & NFServices
93.49	101.46	86.08	93.84	109.89	119.41	127.84	139.36	158.78	170.24	..	Imports of Goods & NFServices
440.43	460.45	432.47	448.01	474.49	499.92	519.09	545.32	578.61	608.08	..	Domestic Absorption
258.69	264.98	257.55	264.69	280.68	296.11	307.12	323.36	340.07	352.81	..	Private Consumption, etc.
92.54	94.88	97.13	98.54	99.74	102.88	104.64	105.32	108.58	110.99	..	General Gov't Consumption
89.20	100.59	77.78	84.77	94.07	100.92	107.33	116.64	129.96	144.28	..	Gross Domestic Investment
101.23	113.16	100.72	100.00	102.14	111.80	118.14	131.94	149.32	159.90	..	Fixed Investment
403.65	411.52	397.98	410.76	439.94	460.61	470.35	492.53	517.10	529.70	..	GDP at factor cost
..	..	..	..	..	..	..	..	..	..	..	Agriculture
..	..	..	..	..	..	..	..	..	..	..	Industry
..	..	..	..	..	..	..	..	..	..	..	Manufacturing
..	..	..	..	..	..	..	..	..	..	..	Services, etc.
											Memo Items:
99.97	105.70	100.73	108.12	125.25	130.63	132.14	144.37	162.84	167.78	..	Capacity to Import
3.74	5.23	2.45	3.55	2.16	0.22	-3.37	0.00	4.76	11.17	..	Terms of Trade Adjustment
446.92	464.68	447.12	462.29	489.84	511.14	523.39	550.33	582.67	605.63	..	Gross Domestic Income
435.57	449.79	431.94	448.42	474.79	495.88	505.95	533.81	565.47	587.23	..	Gross National Income
				(Index 1987 = 100)							**DOMESTIC PRICES/DEFLATORS**
69.9	77.5	84.2	88.4	91.2	93.6	95.8	100.0	104.1	109.1	..	Overall (GDP)
69.1	76.5	83.3	87.5	90.5	93.3	96.4	100.0	103.3	107.0	..	Domestic Absorption
..	..	..	..	..	..	..	..	..	..	..	Agriculture
..	..	..	..	..	..	..	..	..	..	..	Industry
..	..	..	..	..	..	..	..	..	..	..	Manufacturing
64.3	72.3	80.1	84.8	88.5	92.0	95.8	100.0	104.0	109.2	..	Consumer Price Index
											MANUFACTURING ACTIVITY
99.6	99.3	91.4	89.8	92.3	94.9	97.0	100.0	101.6	102.2	..	Employment (1987=100)
99.8	99.5	99.1	100.3	101.8	102.2	101.2	100.0	103.3	104.3	..	Real Earnings per Empl. (1987=100)
..	..	..	..	..	..	..	..	..	..	..	Real Output per Empl. (1987=100)
47.4	47.3	51.3	48.5	45.8	45.6	45.3	43.7	43.6	43.5	..	Earnings as % of Value Added
				(Billions of current Canadian Dollars)							**MONETARY HOLDINGS**
211.37	242.73	256.16	263.89	281.94	302.08	331.02	362.82	406.77	461.89	D	Money Supply, Broadly Defined
34.75	36.75	39.82	44.09	52.44	68.91	80.22	85.20	90.12	95.45	..	Money
10.40	10.71	11.62	12.80	13.50	14.61	15.59	16.92	18.24	19.64	..	Currency Outside Banks
24.35	26.04	28.20	31.30	38.94	54.31	64.63	68.27	71.88	75.80	..	Demand Deposits
176.62	205.98	216.34	219.80	229.50	233.17	250.80	277.63	316.65	366.45	..	Quasi-Money
				(Billions of current Canadian Dollars)							**GOVERNMENT DEFICIT (-) OR SURPLUS**
-10.73	-8.43	-20.81	-25.16	-28.87	-28.68	-20.11	-14.00	-17.50	..	C E	GOVERNMENT DEFICIT (-) OR SURPLUS
57.49	72.28	73.24	77.33	85.30	91.10	99.23	111.66	119.44	..	..	Current Revenue
64.75	74.84	88.02	97.02	108.78	115.06	117.13	124.94	134.03	..	..	Current Expenditure
-7.25	-2.56	-14.78	-19.69	-23.48	-23.96	-17.90	-13.28	-14.59	..	..	Current Budget Balance
..	..	..	..	..	..	..	..	..	..	..	Capital Receipts
3.48	5.87	6.03	5.47	5.39	4.72	2.21	0.72	2.91	..	..	Capital Payments

CANADA	1969	1970	1971	1972	1973	1974	1975	1976	1977	1978	1979
FOREIGN TRADE (CUSTOMS BASIS)					*(Millions of current US dollars)*						
Value of Exports, fob	13,754	16,185	17,675	20,178	25,207	32,783	32,300	38,370	41,293	44,080	55,117
Nonfuel Primary Products	5,551	6,918	7,214	7,981	10,627	13,045	11,904	14,250	15,076	15,342	19,717
Fuels	744	978	1,262	1,734	2,466	5,179	5,334	5,300	5,171	4,816	7,281
Manufactures	7,460	8,288	9,199	10,463	12,115	14,560	15,063	18,821	21,046	23,923	28,119
Value of Imports, cif	14,004	14,253	16,541	20,042	24,746	34,414	36,212	40,356	42,257	46,548	56,953
Nonfuel Primary Products	1,990	2,113	2,293	2,697	3,675	4,950	4,827	5,332	5,552	6,044	7,497
Fuels	707	800	971	1,149	1,405	3,613	4,362	4,365	4,195	4,209	5,286
Manufactures	11,307	11,340	13,278	16,196	19,666	25,851	27,023	30,659	32,510	36,295	44,169
					(Index 1987 = 100)						
Terms of Trade	106.8	109.4	100.7	96.0	116.4	90.9	98.5	103.1	93.1	88.0	87.5
Export Prices, fob	32.0	33.5	33.6	35.3	52.9	57.2	66.2	71.4	70.7	75.2	87.9
Import Prices, cif	29.9	30.6	33.3	36.8	45.5	63.0	67.2	69.3	76.0	85.4	100.5
BALANCE OF PAYMENTS					*(Billions of current US dollars)*						
Exports of Goods & Services	..	20.19	21.95	25.03	31.00	40.13	39.99	46.46	49.80	55.62	66.37
Merchandise, fob	..	16.71	18.30	21.20	26.55	34.48	34.02	40.01	43.19	48.16	57.65
Nonfactor Services	..	2.48	2.66	2.80	3.21	4.18	4.27	4.80	4.91	5.40	6.46
Factor Services	..	1.00	0.98	1.04	1.23	1.48	1.70	1.64	1.70	2.06	2.26
Imports of Goods & Services	..	19.31	21.82	25.53	30.99	41.97	44.87	51.15	54.19	59.85	70.93
Merchandise, fob	..	13.66	15.63	19.03	23.37	32.39	34.29	38.13	40.05	43.98	53.47
Nonfactor Services	..	3.36	3.71	3.99	4.65	5.82	6.38	7.64	8.16	8.63	9.09
Factor Services	..	2.29	2.48	2.51	2.97	3.76	4.20	5.37	5.98	7.24	8.37
Long-Term Interest	..	..	..	..	..	..	..	..	..	..	..
Private Current Transfers, net	..	0.08	0.17	0.18	0.24	0.43	0.38	0.43	0.33	0.24	0.37
Workers' Remittances	..	..	..	..	..	..	..	..	..	..	..
Curr. A/C Bal before Off. Transf.	..	0.96	0.30	-0.32	0.25	-1.41	-4.51	-4.26	-4.07	-3.99	-4.19
Net Official Transfers	..	0.05	0.06	0.05	0.06	0.08	-0.07	0.11	-0.03	-0.29	0.05
Curr. A/C Bal after Off. Transf.	..	1.01	0.36	-0.28	0.31	-1.32	-4.57	-4.15	-4.10	-4.29	-4.14
Long-Term Capital, net	..	0.52	0.27	1.33	0.22	0.89	3.76	7.75	3.36	3.12	2.44
Direct Investment	..	0.51	0.73	0.34	-0.14	0.08	-0.15	-1.06	-0.47	-1.43	-0.73
Long-Term Loans	..	..	..	..	..	..	..	..	..	..	..
Disbursements	..	..	..	..	..	..	..	..	..	..	..
Repayments	..	..	..	..	..	..	..	..	..	..	..
Other Long-Term Capital	..	0.01	-0.45	0.99	0.36	0.82	3.91	8.81	3.83	4.55	3.17
Other Capital, net	..	-1.27	-0.90	-1.09	-0.56	0.62	0.97	-3.07	-0.60	0.97	0.76
Change in Reserves	..	-0.25	0.26	0.04	0.04	-0.18	-0.16	-0.53	1.35	0.19	0.94
Memo Item:					*(Canadian Dollars per US dollar)*						
Conversion Factor (Annual Avg)	1.080	1.050	1.010	0.990	1.000	0.980	1.020	0.990	1.060	1.140	1.170
					(Millions US dollars), outstanding at end of year						
EXTERNAL DEBT (Total)	..	..	..	..	..	..	..	..	..	..	..
Long-Term Debt (by debtor)	..	..	..	..	..	..	..	..	..	..	..
Central Bank, incl. IMF credit	..	..	..	..	..	..	..	..	..	..	..
Central Government	..	..	..	..	..	..	..	..	..	..	..
Rest of General Government	..	..	..	..	..	..	..	..	..	..	..
Non-financial Public Enterprises	..	..	..	..	..	..	..	..	..	..	..
Priv. Sector, incl non-guaranteed	..	..	..	..	..	..	..	..	..	..	..
Short-Term Debt	..	..	..	..	..	..	..	..	..	..	..
Memo Items:					*(Millions of US dollars)*						
Int'l Reserves Excluding Gold	2,234	3,888	4,839	5,216	4,841	4,885	4,385	4,924	3,653	3,544	2,856
Gold Holdings (at market price)	877	844	990	1,424	2,464	4,094	3,079	2,913	3,630	5,001	11,356
SOCIAL INDICATORS											
Total Fertility Rate	2.3	2.3	2.1	2.0	1.9	1.8	1.8	1.8	1.8	1.8	1.8
Infant Mortality Rate	19.3	18.8	17.5	17.1	15.5	15.0	14.2	13.4	12.3	11.9	10.9
Life Expectancy at Birth	72.3	72.5	72.6	72.8	73.0	73.2	73.4	73.6	73.8	74.1	74.4
Urban Population, % of total	75.1	75.7	75.7	75.7	75.6	75.6	75.6	75.6	75.6	75.7	75.7
Food Prod. per capita (1987=100)	86.5	77.8	88.4	85.8	84.8	77.9	85.5	95.7	93.4	95.1	85.4
Labor Force, Agriculture (%)	8.2	7.8	7.5	7.2	7.0	6.7	6.5	6.2	6.0	5.7	5.5
Labor Force, Female (%)	31.9	32.5	33.4	34.2	35.0	35.7	36.4	37.2	37.9	38.6	39.2
Primary Schl. Enroll. Ratio	..	101.0	..	..	..	..	99.0	100.0	100.0	101.0	101.0
Primary Schl. Enroll. Ratio, Female	..	100.0	..	..	..	..	99.0	100.0	100.0	100.0	100.0
Secondary Schl. Enroll. Ratio	..	65.0	..	..	..	..	91.0	91.0	89.0	88.0	88.0

1980	1981	1982	1983	1984	1985	1986	1987	1988	1989 estimate	NOTES	CANADA
											FOREIGN TRADE (CUSTOMS BASIS)
(Millions of current US dollars)											
63,105	68,281	66,977	72,420	84,844	85,737	84,381	92,886	111,364	..	..	Value of Exports, fob
23,500	23,258	21,311	22,486	24,281	22,191	22,676	26,851	31,636	..	..	Nonfuel Primary Products
9,010	9,451	9,601	10,017	11,117	12,047	8,146	9,382	10,158	..	..	Fuels
30,595	35,573	36,065	39,917	49,446	51,499	53,559	56,653	69,570	..	..	Manufactures
62,838	70,342	58,360	65,077	77,789	80,640	85,068	92,594	112,180	..	..	Value of Imports, cif
9,063	9,069	7,652	8,211	9,078	8,460	9,163	14,925	11,573	..	..	Nonfuel Primary Products
7,778	8,620	5,887	4,488	5,016	4,886	4,020	4,249	4,460	..	..	Fuels
45,996	52,653	44,821	52,378	63,694	67,294	71,884	73,420	96,147	..	..	Manufactures
(Index 1987 = 100)											
88.9	96.0	100.7	105.7	109.6	109.3	100.7	100.0	107.1	..	..	Terms of Trade
102.0	105.8	104.8	106.1	106.9	105.1	98.8	100.0	109.9	..	..	Export Prices, fob
114.7	110.2	104.1	100.4	97.5	96.2	98.0	100.0	102.6	..	..	Import Prices, cif
(Billions of current US dollars)											**BALANCE OF PAYMENTS**
77.99	84.14	82.74	88.46	102.16	104.33	104.98	115.28	138.27	144.72	..	Exports of Goods & Services
67.48	72.52	70.49	75.68	88.62	89.65	89.03	97.97	115.77	123.22	..	Merchandise, fob
7.41	8.29	7.81	8.24	8.64	9.14	10.39	11.24	13.29	14.33	..	Nonfactor Services
3.11	3.33	4.44	4.54	4.90	5.54	5.55	6.08	9.21	7.18	..	Factor Services
79.86	90.36	81.67	86.83	100.76	106.39	113.35	123.79	149.98	163.15	..	Imports of Goods & Services
59.48	65.94	55.50	60.71	72.66	77.07	81.35	89.09	106.64	116.36	..	Merchandise, fob
10.58	11.63	11.46	12.17	12.79	13.27	14.64	16.42	18.74	20.89	..	Nonfactor Services
9.80	12.78	14.71	13.95	15.32	16.04	17.35	18.28	24.60	25.89	..	Factor Services
..	..	..	..	..	..	..	..	..	..	..	Long-Term Interest
0.62	0.78	0.91	0.81	0.80	0.82	0.93	2.04	3.83	4.70	..	Private Current Transfers, net
..	..	..	..	..	..	..	..	..	..	..	Workers' Remittances
-1.24	-5.43	1.98	2.44	2.20	-1.24	-7.44	-6.47	-7.87	-13.72	..	Curr. A/C Bal before Off. Transf.
0.28	0.32	0.25	0.05	-0.20	-0.22	0.14	-0.45	-0.33	-0.37	..	Net Official Transfers
-0.97	-5.11	2.23	2.49	2.00	-1.47	-7.30	-6.92	-8.20	-14.09	..	Curr. A/C Bal after Off. Transf.
-0.32	0.87	5.77	0.17	2.99	3.31	13.76	8.17	8.07	19.68	..	Long-Term Capital, net
-3.17	-8.68	-2.28	-3.77	-0.84	-4.85	-1.65	-2.05	-3.09	-0.81	..	Direct Investment
..	..	..	..	..	..	..	..	..	..	..	Long-Term Loans
..	..	..	..	..	..	..	..	..	..	..	Disbursements
..	..	..	..	..	..	..	..	..	..	..	Repayments
2.85	9.55	8.04	3.95	3.82	8.16	15.41	10.22	11.16	20.49	..	Other Long-Term Capital
0.63	4.39	-8.58	-2.21	-5.85	-1.92	-5.98	2.09	7.69	-5.30	..	Other Capital, net
0.66	-0.15	0.58	-0.45	0.87	0.07	-0.48	-3.34	-7.56	-0.29	..	Change in Reserves
(Canadian Dollars per US dollar)											**Memo Item:**
1.170	1.200	1.230	1.230	1.300	1.370	1.390	1.330	1.230	1.180	..	Conversion Factor (Annual Avg)
(Millions US dollars), outstanding at end of year											
..	..	..	..	..	..	..	..	..	..	..	**EXTERNAL DEBT (Total)**
..	..	..	..	..	..	..	..	..	..	..	Long-Term Debt (by debtor)
..	..	..	..	..	..	..	..	..	..	..	Central Bank, incl. IMF credit
..	..	..	..	..	..	..	..	..	..	..	Central Government
..	..	..	..	..	..	..	..	..	..	..	Rest of General Government
..	..	..	..	..	..	..	..	..	..	..	Non-financial Public Enterprises
..	..	..	..	..	..	..	..	..	..	..	Priv. Sector, incl non-guaranteed
..	..	..	..	..	..	..	..	..	..	..	Short-Term Debt
(Millions of US dollars)											**Memo Items:**
3,041	3,492	3,000	3,465	2,491	2,503	3,251	7,277	15,391	16,055	..	Int'l Reserves Excluding Gold
12,369	8,134	9,258	7,695	6,208	6,575	7,710	8,965	7,031	6,457	..	Gold Holdings (at market price)
											SOCIAL INDICATORS
1.8	1.7	1.7	1.7	1.6	1.7	1.7	1.7	1.7	1.7	..	Total Fertility Rate
10.4	9.6	9.1	8.5	8.1	7.9	7.9	7.3	7.1	6.9	..	Infant Mortality Rate
74.7	75.0	75.4	75.6	75.9	76.1	76.4	76.7	76.9	77.1	..	Life Expectancy at Birth
75.7	75.7	75.8	75.8	75.9	75.9	76.0	76.1	76.2	76.3	..	Urban Population, % of total
90.8	98.1	103.9	96.8	95.2	98.0	106.8	100.0	88.4	94.5	..	Food Prod. per capita (1987=100)
5.3	..	..	..	..	..	..	..	..	..	..	Labor Force, Agriculture (%)
39.8	39.8	39.8	39.8	39.8	39.8	39.8	39.8	39.8	39.8	..	Labor Force, Female (%)
103.0	..	107.0	106.0	106.0	105.0	105.0	105.0	..	..	..	Primary Schl. Enroll. Ratio
103.0	106.0	106.0	105.0	105.0	104.0	104.0	104.0	..	..	..	Primary Schl. Enroll. Ratio, Female
93.0	..	99.0	102.0	103.0	103.0	103.0	104.0	..	..	..	Secondary Schl. Enroll. Ratio

CAPE VERDE	1969	1970	1971	1972	1973	1974	1975	1976	1977	1978	1979
CURRENT GNP PER CAPITA (US $)	..	..	..	200	230	290	310	350	320	320	360
POPULATION (thousands)	264	269	271	272	273	274	276	278	281	285	290
USE AND ORIGIN OF RESOURCES					*(Millions of current Cape Verde Escudos)*						
Gross National Product (GNP)	..	1,434	1,497	1,743	1,701	2,133	2,367	2,367	2,567	3,081	3,651
Net Factor Income from Abroad	..	-51	-53	-62	-60	-75	-84	-84	-91	-109	-129
GDP at Market Prices	..	1,484	1,549	1,805	1,761	2,209	2,450	2,450	2,658	3,190	3,779
Resource Balance	..	..	..	..	-758	-649	-697	-1,216	-1,748	-2,134	-2,642
Exports of Goods & NFServices	..	..	..	..	364	317	266	197	88	316	529
Imports of Goods & NFServices	..	..	..	..	1,121	967	964	1,412	1,836	2,450	3,171
Domestic Absorption	..	..	..	..	2,519	2,858	3,148	3,666	4,406	5,324	6,422
Private Consumption, etc.	..	..	..	..	2,019	2,218	2,367	2,515	2,698	3,508	3,791
General Gov't Consumption	..	..	..	..	154	272	390	484	680	713	868
Gross Domestic Investment	..	..	..	..	346	369	391	667	1,028	1,102	1,763
Fixed Investment	..	..	..	..	..	..	..	..	..	..	..
Indirect Taxes, net	..	90	100	104	110	117	122	120	137	204	228
GDP at factor cost	..	1,394	1,449	1,701	1,652	2,092	2,328	2,330	2,521	2,986	3,551
Agriculture	..	..	..	..	214	223	304	405	429	592	821
Industry	..	..	..	..	421	392	433	490	454	650	757
Manufacturing	..	..	..	..	..	..	..	..	..	..	..
Services, etc.	..	..	..	..	1,126	1,593	1,713	1,555	1,775	1,948	2,202
Gross Domestic Saving	..	..	..	..	-412	-281	-306	-549	-720	-1,032	-880
Gross National Saving	..	..	..	..	..	..	..	..	..	-274	-54
					(Millions of 1987 Cape Verde Escudos)						
Gross National Product	..	6,491	6,038	5,760	5,719	5,857	5,396	6,348	6,390	7,070	7,847
GDP at Market Prices	..	7,438	6,920	6,601	6,553	6,373	6,573	6,570	6,613	7,317	8,122
Resource Balance	..	..	..	..	-1,751	-1,221	-1,320	-2,732	-4,384	-4,355	-4,659
Exports of Goods & NFServices	..	..	..	..	2,807	1,964	1,429	1,500	428	1,344	1,395
Imports of Goods & NFServices	..	..	..	..	4,558	3,184	2,749	4,232	4,812	5,699	6,054
Domestic Absorption	..	..	..	..	8,304	7,593	7,894	9,302	10,997	11,673	12,781
Private Consumption, etc.	..	..	..	..	6,228	5,016	5,353	5,866	6,240	7,546	7,793
General Gov't Consumption	..	..	..	..	535	943	1,113	1,245	1,623	1,387	1,388
Gross Domestic Investment	..	..	..	..	1,541	1,634	1,427	2,190	3,135	2,740	3,600
Fixed Investment	..	..	..	..	..	..	..	..	..	..	..
GDP at factor cost	..	..	..	..	..	..	..	..	..	..	..
Agriculture	..	..	..	..	..	..	..	..	..	..	..
Industry	..	..	..	..	..	..	..	..	..	..	..
Manufacturing	..	..	..	..	..	..	..	..	..	..	..
Services, etc.	..	..	..	..	..	..	..	..	..	..	..
Memo Items:											
Capacity to Import	..	..	..	..	1,478	1,045	760	589	229	735	1,009
Terms of Trade Adjustment	..	..	..	..	-1,329	-919	-669	-911	-199	-609	-386
Gross Domestic Income	..	..	..	..	5,224	5,454	5,904	5,660	6,415	6,708	7,736
Gross National Income	..	..	..	..	4,390	4,939	4,726	5,437	6,191	6,461	7,461
DOMESTIC PRICES/DEFLATORS					*(Index 1987 = 100)*						
Overall (GDP)	..	20.0	22.4	27.3	26.9	34.7	37.3	37.3	40.2	43.6	46.5
Domestic Absorption	..	..	..	..	30.3	37.6	39.9	39.4	40.1	45.6	50.2
Agriculture	..	..	..	..	..	..	..	..	..	..	..
Industry	..	..	..	..	..	..	..	..	..	..	..
Manufacturing	..	..	..	..	..	..	..	..	..	..	..
Consumer Price Index	..	..	..	..	..	..	..	..	..	..	..
MANUFACTURING ACTIVITY											
Employment (1987=100)	..	..	..	..	..	..	..	..	..	..	..
Real Earnings per Empl. (1987=100)	..	..	..	..	..	..	..	..	..	..	..
Real Output per Empl. (1987=100)	..	..	..	..	..	..	..	..	..	..	..
Earnings as % of Value Added	..	..	..	..	..	..	..	..	..	..	..
MONETARY HOLDINGS					*(Millions of current Cape Verde Escudos)*						
Money Supply, Broadly Defined	..	..	..	..	..	..	..	1,022	1,441	1,674	1,966
Money	..	..	..	..	..	..	..	1,000	1,411	1,615	1,823
Currency Outside Banks	..	..	..	..	..	..	..	465	537	638	736
Demand Deposits	..	..	..	..	..	..	..	536	874	977	1,086
Quasi-Money	..	..	..	..	..	..	..	21	30	59	143
					(Millions of current Cape Verde Escudos)						
GOVERNMENT DEFICIT (-) OR SURPLUS	..	..	..	..	..	..	..	..	..	..	..
Current Revenue	..	..	..	..	..	..	..	..	..	..	..
Current Expenditure	..	..	..	..	..	..	..	..	..	..	..
Current Budget Balance	..	..	..	..	..	..	..	..	..	..	..
Capital Receipts	..	..	..	..	..	..	..	..	..	..	..
Capital Payments	..	..	..	..	..	..	..	..	..	..	..

1980	1981	1982	1983	1984	1985	1986	1987	1988	1989 estimate	NOTES	CAPE VERDE
520	520	500	480	450	440	460	550	680	760	..	**CURRENT GNP PER CAPITA (US $)**
296	302	309	317	325	334	343	352	360	369	..	**POPULATION (thousands)**
				(Millions of current Cape Verde Escudos)							**USE AND ORIGIN OF RESOURCES**
5,748	6,601	8,036	9,620	10,875	12,315	15,082	16,798	18,920	21,993	..	Gross National Product (GNP)
33	-191	-163	-309	-334	-310	-204	-180	-34	-70	..	Net Factor Income from Abroad
5,715	6,792	8,199	9,929	11,209	12,625	15,286	16,978	18,954	22,062	..	GDP at Market Prices
-2,851	-3,343	-4,612	-5,279	-6,155	-7,137	-8,837	-6,757	-7,656	-8,447	..	Resource Balance
976	1,458	1,879	2,445	2,552	2,856	2,691	3,745	3,183	3,188	..	Exports of Goods & NFServices
3,827	4,801	6,491	7,724	8,707	9,993	11,527	10,503	10,839	11,636	..	Imports of Goods & NFServices
8,566	10,135	12,811	15,209	17,364	19,761	24,122	23,736	26,610	30,509	..	Domestic Absorption
5,332	6,029	6,910	8,304	9,859	11,066	12,926	12,244	14,130	16,855	..	Private Consumption, etc.
842	1,028	1,566	2,055	2,570	2,999	4,194	3,973	4,585	4,326	..	General Gov't Consumption
2,392	3,078	4,335	4,850	4,935	5,696	7,002	7,519	7,895	9,328	..	Gross Domestic Investment
2,214	3,271	4,222	4,840	4,966	5,958	6,440	..	..	..	..	Fixed Investment
468	552	616	715	834	876	1,088	1,215	1,305	1,436	..	Indirect Taxes, net
5,247	6,240	7,583	9,214	10,375	11,749	14,197	15,763	17,649	20,626	B	GDP at factor cost
1,068	1,093	1,035	1,255	1,376	1,720	2,182	2,548	2,759	3,180	..	Agriculture
962	1,156	1,292	1,656	1,925	2,189	2,624	2,898	3,170	3,773	..	Industry
291	289	389	524	604	807	1,005	1,270	1,520	1,931	..	Manufacturing
3,685	4,542	5,872	7,017	7,908	8,716	10,480	11,533	13,026	15,109	..	Services, etc.
-459	-265	-277	-429	-1,220	-1,441	-1,835	762	239	881	..	Gross Domestic Saving
1,169	1,301	1,425	1,750	282	284	102	3,053	3,052	..	..	Gross National Saving
				(Millions of 1987 Cape Verde Escudos)							
11,250	11,834	12,249	13,280	13,800	15,093	15,648	16,799	17,484	18,420	..	Gross National Product
11,183	12,128	12,470	13,658	14,176	15,412	15,861	16,978	17,517	18,483	..	GDP at Market Prices
-4,736	-4,231	-5,372	-5,372	-5,879	-5,894	-7,842	-6,758	-7,124	-6,400	..	Resource Balance
1,984	2,449	2,628	3,184	2,983	3,439	3,060	3,745	3,028	3,143	..	Exports of Goods & NFServices
6,720	6,679	8,000	8,556	8,862	9,332	10,902	10,503	10,152	9,543	..	Imports of Goods & NFServices
15,919	16,358	17,842	19,030	20,055	21,306	23,702	23,736	24,641	24,882	..	Domestic Absorption
9,892	9,772	9,671	10,517	11,336	12,075	12,584	12,244	12,774	13,090	..	Private Consumption, etc.
1,578	1,741	2,316	2,715	3,030	3,415	4,092	3,973	4,109	3,862	..	General Gov't Consumption
4,449	4,845	5,855	5,798	5,690	5,816	7,027	7,519	7,758	7,930	..	Gross Domestic Investment
..	..	..	..	..	..	..	..	..	..	..	Fixed Investment
10,266	11,140	11,532	12,672	13,120	14,343	14,731	15,763	16,311	17,279	B	GDP at factor cost
2,200	2,078	1,647	1,638	1,670	2,129	2,282	2,548	2,650	2,752	..	Agriculture
1,821	2,017	2,020	2,361	2,348	2,694	2,743	2,898	3,044	3,288	..	Industry
717	607	740	869	835	1,096	1,050	1,270	1,461	1,607	..	Manufacturing
7,209	8,067	8,816	9,660	10,159	10,589	10,836	11,533	11,823	12,443	..	Services, etc.
											Memo Items:
1,713	2,028	2,316	2,708	2,597	2,668	2,545	3,745	2,981	2,615	..	Capacity to Import
-270	-421	-312	-476	-386	-771	-516	0	-47	-528	..	Terms of Trade Adjustment
10,913	11,707	12,158	13,181	13,790	14,642	15,345	16,978	17,470	17,954	..	Gross Domestic Income
10,980	11,413	11,937	12,803	13,415	14,322	15,132	16,799	17,437	17,891	..	Gross National Income
				(Index 1987 = 100)							**DOMESTIC PRICES/DEFLATORS**
51.1	56.0	65.8	72.7	79.1	81.9	96.4	100.0	108.2	119.4	..	Overall (GDP)
53.8	62.0	71.8	79.9	86.6	92.7	101.8	100.0	108.0	122.6	..	Domestic Absorption
48.5	52.6	62.8	76.7	82.4	80.8	95.6	100.0	104.1	115.6	..	Agriculture
52.9	57.3	64.0	70.2	82.0	81.3	95.7	100.0	104.1	114.7	..	Industry
40.5	47.6	52.6	60.3	72.4	73.6	95.7	100.0	104.1	120.2	..	Manufacturing
..	..	..	74.1	82.4	86.9	96.3	100.0	..	..	..	Consumer Price Index
											MANUFACTURING ACTIVITY
..	..	..	..	..	..	..	..	..	..	..	Employment (1987=100)
..	..	..	..	..	..	..	..	..	..	..	Real Earnings per Empl. (1987=100)
..	..	..	..	..	..	..	..	..	..	..	Real Output per Empl. (1987=100)
..	..	..	..	..	..	..	..	..	..	..	Earnings as % of Value Added
				(Millions of current Cape Verde Escudos)							**MONETARY HOLDINGS**
2,563	3,047	..	..	..	..	..	..	..	..	..	Money Supply, Broadly Defined
2,302	2,553	3,228	3,956	4,202	4,843	5,621	5,710	6,038	6,411	..	Money
872	1,041	1,282	1,333	1,434	1,628	1,826	1,956	2,219	2,490	..	Currency Outside Banks
1,430	1,512	1,946	2,623	2,768	3,215	3,794	3,755	3,819	3,920	..	Demand Deposits
261	494	..	..	..	..	..	..	..	..	..	Quasi-Money
				(Millions of current Cape Verde Escudos)							
..	..	..	..	..	..	..	..	..	..	..	**GOVERNMENT DEFICIT (-) OR SURPLUS**
..	..	..	..	..	..	..	..	..	..	..	Current Revenue
..	..	..	..	..	..	..	..	..	..	..	Current Expenditure
..	..	..	..	..	..	..	..	..	..	..	Current Budget Balance
..	..	..	..	..	..	..	..	..	..	..	Capital Receipts
..	..	..	..	..	..	..	..	..	..	..	Capital Payments

CAPE VERDE	1969	1970	1971	1972	1973	1974	1975	1976	1977	1978	1979
FOREIGN TRADE (CUSTOMS BASIS)					*(Millions of current US dollars)*						
Value of Exports, fob	..	2.00	2.00	2.00	2.00	2.00	2.00	2.00	2.00	3.00	5.00
Nonfuel Primary Products	..	..	..	..	..	..	..	..	..	..	..
Fuels	..	..	..	..	..	..	..	..	..	..	..
Manufactures	..	..	..	..	..	..	..	..	..	..	..
Value of Imports, cif	..	16.00	20.00	24.00	34.00	34.00	40.00	30.00	38.00	54.00	56.00
Nonfuel Primary Products	..	..	..	..	..	..	..	..	..	..	..
Fuels	..	..	..	..	..	..	..	..	..	..	..
Manufactures	..	..	..	..	..	..	..	..	..	..	..
					(Index 1987 = 100)						
Terms of Trade	..	..	..	..	..	..	..	..	..	..	..
Export Prices, fob	..	..	..	..	..	..	..	..	..	..	..
Import Prices, cif	..	..	..	..	..	..	..	..	..	..	..
BALANCE OF PAYMENTS					*(Thousands of current US dollars)*						
Exports of Goods & Services	..	..	..	..	..	..	..	..	..	..	..
Merchandise, fob	..	..	..	..	..	..	..	..	..	..	..
Nonfactor Services	..	..	..	..	..	..	..	..	..	..	..
Factor Services	..	..	..	..	..	..	..	..	..	..	..
Imports of Goods & Services	..	..	..	..	..	..	..	..	..	..	..
Merchandise, fob	..	..	..	..	..	..	..	..	..	..	..
Nonfactor Services	..	..	..	..	..	..	..	..	..	..	..
Factor Services	..	..	..	..	..	..	..	..	..	..	..
Long-Term Interest	..	0.00	0.00	0.00	0.00	0.00	0.00	0.10	0.10	0.10	0.10
Private Current Transfers, net	..	..	..	..	..	..	..	..	..	24.40	25.51
Workers' Remittances	..	..	..	..	..	..	..	..	..	..	..
Curr. A/C Bal before Off. Transf.	..	..	..	..	..	..	..	..	..	-29.66	-37.53
Net Official Transfers	..	..	..	..	..	..	..	..	..	0.00	0.00
Curr. A/C Bal after Off. Transf.	..	..	..	..	..	..	..	..	..	-29.66	-37.53
Long-Term Capital, net	..	..	..	..	..	..	..	..	..	22.54	37.22
Direct Investment	..	..	..	..	..	..	..	..	..	..	..
Long-Term Loans	..	0.00	0.00	0.00	0.00	0.00	0.50	11.30	2.30	1.40	2.90
Disbursements	..	0.00	0.00	0.00	0.00	0.00	0.50	11.30	2.30	1.50	3.00
Repayments	..	0.00	0.00	0.00	0.00	0.00	0.00	0.00	0.00	0.10	0.10
Other Long-Term Capital	..	..	..	..	..	..	..	..	..	21.14	34.32
Other Capital, net	..	..	..	..	..	..	..	..	..	4.66	6.19
Change in Reserves	..	..	..	..	..	..	..	..	..	2.46	-5.88
Memo Item:					*(Cape Verde Escudos per US dollar)*						
Conversion Factor (Annual Avg)	28.750	28.750	28.320	27.010	24.670	25.410	25.550	30.140	34.050	35.500	37.430
				(Millions of US dollars), outstanding at end of year							
EXTERNAL DEBT (Total)	..	..	..	..	..	..	0.5	11.7	13.7	19.9	18.6
Long-Term Debt (by debtor)	..	..	..	..	..	..	0.5	11.7	13.7	14.9	17.6
Central Bank, incl. IMF credit	..	..	..	..	..	..	..	..	..	..	..
Central Government	..	..	..	..	..	..	0.5	11.7	13.7	14.9	17.6
Rest of General Government	..	..	..	..	..	..	..	..	..	..	..
Non-financial Public Enterprises	..	..	..	..	..	..	0.0	0.0	0.0	0.0	0.0
Priv. Sector, incl non-guaranteed	..	..	..	..	..	..	..	..	..	..	..
Short-Term Debt	..	..	..	..	..	..	..	..	..	5.0	1.0
Memo Items:					*(Thousands of US dollars)*						
Int'l Reserves Excluding Gold	..	..	..	..	..	..	..	32,695	42,024	39,368	42,322
Gold Holdings (at market price)	..	..	..	..	..	..	..	..	..	..	..
SOCIAL INDICATORS											
Total Fertility Rate	7.4	7.5	7.4	7.2	7.1	7.0	6.9	6.7	6.6	6.5	6.3
Infant Mortality Rate	..	..	..	82.0	79.6	77.2	74.8	72.4	70.0	66.4	62.8
Life Expectancy at Birth	55.6	56.1	56.5	57.0	57.4	57.8	58.3	58.7	59.2	59.7	60.2
Urban Population, % of total	19.3	19.5	19.9	20.3	20.7	21.1	21.4	21.8	22.2	22.6	23.0
Food Prod. per capita (1987=100)	79.9	70.8	59.7	57.7	56.2	55.3	57.4	63.6	58.8	66.1	60.9
Labor Force, Agriculture (%)	64.6	64.1	62.8	61.6	60.3	59.1	58.0	56.7	55.4	54.1	52.9
Labor Force, Female (%)	23.7	23.6	24.0	24.4	24.8	25.2	25.6	26.0	26.5	26.9	27.3
Primary Schl. Enroll. Ratio	..	66.0	..	..	..	..	145.0	..	..	..	..
Primary Schl. Enroll. Ratio, Female	..	..	..	..	..	..	138.0	..	..	..	..
Secondary Schl. Enroll. Ratio	..	..	..	..	..	..	8.0	..	..	..	..

1980	1981	1982	1983	1984	1985	1986	1987	1988	1989 estimate	NOTES	CAPE VERDE
				(Millions of current US dollars)							**FOREIGN TRADE (CUSTOMS BASIS)**
9.00	6.00	3.00	2.00	3.00	3.00	3.00	5.00	..	..	..	Value of Exports, fob
..	..	..	..	..	..	..	..	..	..	..	Nonfuel Primary Products
..	..	..	..	..	..	..	..	..	..	..	Fuels
..	..	..	..	..	..	..	..	..	..	..	Manufactures
91.00	95.00	97.00	105.00	82.00	81.00	92.00	112.00	..	..	..	Value of Imports, cif
..	..	..	..	..	..	..	..	..	..	..	Nonfuel Primary Products
..	..	..	..	..	..	..	..	..	..	..	Fuels
..	..	..	..	..	..	..	..	..	..	..	Manufactures
				(Index 1987 = 100)							
..	..	..	..	..	..	..	..	..	..	..	Terms of Trade
..	..	..	..	..	..	..	..	..	..	..	Export Prices, fob
..	..	..	..	..	..	..	..	..	..	..	Import Prices, cif
				(Thousands of current US dollars)							**BALANCE OF PAYMENTS**
..	..	..	..	..	..	..	..	..	..	..	Exports of Goods & Services
9.11	6.25	3.75	1.90	6.90	6.10	5.10	12.20	4.40	..	..	Merchandise, fob
..	..	..	..	..	..	..	..	..	..	..	Nonfactor Services
..	..	..	..	..	..	..	..	..	..	..	Factor Services
..	..	..	..	..	..	..	..	..	..	..	Imports of Goods & Services
..	..	96.70	104.50	82.40	92.30	91.50	100.60	104.70	..	f	Merchandise, fob
..	..	..	..	..	..	..	..	..	..	..	Nonfactor Services
..	..	..	..	..	..	..	..	..	..	..	Factor Services
0.10	0.20	0.90	2.00	3.00	2.60	2.00	3.40	3.50	2.10	f	Long-Term Interest
39.70	36.10	32.00	34.71	21.63	22.20	26.70	34.10	39.50	..	..	Private Current Transfers, net
..	..	..	..	..	..	..	..	..	..	..	Workers' Remittances
-25.06	-42.73	-49.68	-51.46	-45.10	-51.75	-44.90	-35.60	-40.10	..	f	Curr. A/C Bal before Off. Transf.
0.00	0.00	35.30	38.80	38.70	37.30	42.20	47.00	41.80	..	f	Net Official Transfers
-25.06	-42.73	-14.38	-12.66	-6.40	-14.45	-2.70	11.40	1.70	..	..	Curr. A/C Bal after Off. Transf.
31.79	39.82	20.11	15.04	10.30	13.36	8.30	3.60	7.10	..	f	Long-Term Capital, net
..	..	..	..	..	..	..	..	..	..	..	Direct Investment
2.80	20.40	21.90	16.10	13.80	19.20	8.40	3.70	7.50	5.40	..	Long-Term Loans
2.90	20.50	22.50	17.10	16.10	21.30	10.80	7.30	11.00	8.50	..	Disbursements
0.10	0.10	0.60	1.00	2.30	2.10	2.40	3.60	3.50	3.10	..	Repayments
28.99	19.42	-1.79	-1.06	-3.50	-5.84	-0.10	-0.10	-0.40	..	..	Other Long-Term Capital
-1.00	3.48	5.78	5.83	1.60	6.49	-1.80	-1.90	-0.70	..	f	Other Capital, net
-5.73	-0.57	-11.51	-8.21	-5.50	-5.40	-3.80	-13.10	-8.10	..	..	Change in Reserves
				(Cape Verde Escudos per US dollar)							**Memo Item:**
40.170	48.690	58.290	71.690	84.760	91.630	80.140	72.470	72.070	77.980	..	Conversion Factor (Annual Avg)
				(Millions of US dollars), outstanding at end of year							
20.2	38.6	57.8	70.2	74.7	96.8	115.4	132.6	129.4	129.6	..	**EXTERNAL DEBT (Total)**
20.2	38.6	57.8	70.2	74.7	95.8	108.5	122.0	124.6	126.4	..	Long-Term Debt (by debtor)
..	..	..	..	..	..	..	..	..	..	..	Central Bank, incl. IMF credit
20.2	21.2	28.2	32.7	42.9	61.3	71.3	89.6	95.8	99.7	..	Central Government
..	..	..	..	..	..	..	..	..	..	..	Rest of General Government
0.0	17.4	29.6	37.5	31.8	34.5	37.2	32.4	28.8	26.7	..	Non-financial Public Enterprises
..	..	..	..	..	..	..	..	..	..	..	Priv. Sector, incl non-guaranteed
0.0	0.0	0.0	0.0	0.0	1.0	6.9	10.6	4.8	3.2	..	Short-Term Debt
				(Thousands of US dollars)							**Memo Items:**
42,401	37,829	42,739	45,902	40,990	55,358	56,360	80,730	81,333	74,738	..	Int'l Reserves Excluding Gold
..	..	..	..	..	..	..	..	..	..	..	Gold Holdings (at market price)
											SOCIAL INDICATORS
6.2	6.0	5.8	5.6	5.5	5.4	5.3	5.2	5.1	5.0	..	Total Fertility Rate
59.2	55.6	52.0	50.4	48.8	47.2	45.6	44.0	43.0	42.0	..	Infant Mortality Rate
60.7	62.0	63.4	63.7	64.1	64.5	64.9	65.3	65.4	65.6	..	Life Expectancy at Birth
23.4	23.9	24.3	24.8	25.2	25.7	26.3	26.9	27.3	27.6	..	Urban Population, % of total
85.3	63.8	61.6	54.7	64.7	60.2	74.1	100.0	90.6	73.8	..	Food Prod. per capita (1987=100)
51.7	..	..	..	..	..	..	..	..	..	..	Labor Force, Agriculture (%)
27.7	28.0	28.2	28.4	28.6	28.8	28.9	29.0	29.0	29.1	..	Labor Force, Female (%)
112.0	..	106.0	110.0	109.0	109.0	108.0	..	..	..	..	Primary Schl. Enroll. Ratio
108.0	..	102.0	107.0	107.0	106.0	105.0	..	..	..	..	Primary Schl. Enroll. Ratio, Female
8.0	..	..	10.0	11.0	13.0	14.0	..	..	..	..	Secondary Schl. Enroll. Ratio

CENTRAL AFRICAN REPUBLIC	1969	1970	1971	1972	1973	1974	1975	1976	1977	1978	1979
CURRENT GNP PER CAPITA (US $)	110	110	100	110	120	150	170	200	230	260	280
POPULATION (thousands)	1,851	1,879	1,902	1,928	1,958	1,993	2,034	2,081	2,136	2,196	2,258
USE AND ORIGIN OF RESOURCES					*(Billions of current CFA Francs)*						
Gross National Product (GNP)	46.80	49.60	52.60	55.50	57.00	71.90	80.50	107.10	123.60	136.40	151.10
Net Factor Income from Abroad	-0.10	-0.10	-0.10	-0.10	-0.10	-0.10	-0.10	0.10	0.10	0.10	0.20
GDP at Market Prices	46.90	49.70	52.70	55.60	57.10	72.00	80.60	107.00	123.50	136.30	150.90
Resource Balance	-7.00	-7.60	-7.00	-7.60	-8.10	-6.30	-15.80	-8.50	-12.50	-15.90	-17.10
Exports of Goods & NFServices	11.20	13.90	13.90	12.10	14.40	19.00	18.40	25.40	32.70	33.70	35.20
Imports of Goods & NFServices	18.20	21.50	20.90	19.70	22.50	25.30	34.20	33.90	45.20	49.60	52.30
Domestic Absorption	53.90	57.30	59.70	63.20	65.20	78.30	96.40	115.50	136.00	152.20	168.00
Private Consumption, etc.	36.10	37.40	38.80	41.50	40.80	54.30	71.30	88.00	106.20	117.80	130.10
General Gov't Consumption	9.80	10.50	10.50	11.00	11.80	13.50	13.90	14.60	15.40	19.40	23.30
Gross Domestic Investment	8.00	9.40	10.40	10.70	12.60	10.50	11.20	12.90	14.40	15.00	14.60
Fixed Investment	..	..	..	..	..	..	..	..	14.50	12.50	16.70
Indirect Taxes, net	3.30	2.90	3.30	3.90	4.50	4.90	5.10	5.80	7.20	7.20	8.10
GDP at factor cost	43.60	46.80	49.40	51.70	52.60	67.10	75.50	101.20	116.30	129.10	142.80
Agriculture	16.50	16.60	18.40	19.90	20.60	26.50	28.50	40.60	46.80	51.30	55.80
Industry	12.10	12.20	13.30	14.10	14.10	15.10	17.30	20.50	22.90	28.80	32.20
Manufacturing	2.30	3.20	3.30	3.80	4.10	5.20	5.70	6.20	7.60	10.80	11.80
Services, etc.	15.00	18.00	17.70	17.70	17.90	25.50	29.70	40.10	46.60	49.00	54.80
Gross Domestic Saving	1.00	1.80	3.40	3.10	4.50	4.20	-4.60	4.40	1.90	-0.90	-2.50
Gross National Saving	..	0.62	1.85	1.88	3.23	2.25	-7.33	2.02	-0.48	-3.80	-4.06
					(Billions of 1987 CFA Francs)						
Gross National Product	250.21	257.94	259.27	265.99	271.97	288.04	288.83	303.45	314.32	321.80	313.84
GDP at Market Prices	248.41	256.07	258.41	264.56	270.49	286.43	287.21	300.84	311.63	319.35	310.85
Resource Balance	-45.73	-50.36	-45.82	-44.52	-39.33	-2.78	-3.41	-11.89	-37.45	-42.64	-34.90
Exports of Goods & NFServices	41.62	47.06	48.31	43.29	50.82	72.16	87.21	71.95	68.39	66.72	68.60
Imports of Goods & NFServices	87.35	97.42	94.14	87.81	90.16	74.94	90.62	83.83	105.85	109.36	103.50
Domestic Absorption	294.13	306.43	304.24	309.08	309.82	289.21	290.62	312.73	349.08	361.99	345.76
Private Consumption, etc.	166.83	171.64	172.04	178.47	173.48	186.95	198.21	220.54	259.86	263.26	246.80
General Gov't Consumption	84.70	87.87	83.51	81.93	85.49	70.45	66.10	64.12	60.95	71.24	75.60
Gross Domestic Investment	42.60	46.92	48.69	48.69	50.85	31.80	26.31	28.07	28.27	27.48	23.36
Fixed Investment	..	..	..	..	..	..	..	..	28.32	22.85	26.56
GDP at factor cost	229.82	239.92	241.02	245.15	248.32	266.98	269.46	279.70	294.42	297.94	290.61
Agriculture	92.27	93.91	96.96	97.43	98.14	102.13	104.47	108.00	109.87	113.40	111.75
Industry	24.98	27.18	26.86	30.63	31.73	34.72	34.56	32.68	35.98	41.16	38.80
Manufacturing	..	..	..	..	..	22.56	21.02	21.64	23.49	28.44	25.96
Services, etc.	123.92	128.87	127.55	120.61	120.61	132.84	133.17	144.41	153.99	144.74	142.09
Memo Items:											
Capacity to Import	53.75	62.98	62.61	53.94	57.70	56.28	48.76	62.81	76.57	74.30	69.66
Terms of Trade Adjustment	12.13	15.92	14.29	10.64	6.88	-15.88	-38.46	-9.13	8.18	7.58	1.06
Gross Domestic Income	260.54	271.99	272.71	275.20	277.36	270.55	248.75	291.71	319.81	326.93	311.91
Gross National Income	262.34	273.86	273.57	276.64	278.85	272.16	250.37	294.32	322.50	329.39	314.90
DOMESTIC PRICES/DEFLATORS					*(Index 1987 = 100)*						
Overall (GDP)	18.9	19.4	20.4	21.0	21.1	25.1	28.1	35.6	39.6	42.7	48.5
Domestic Absorption	18.3	18.7	19.6	20.4	21.0	27.1	33.2	36.9	39.0	42.0	48.6
Agriculture	17.9	17.7	19.0	20.4	21.0	25.9	27.3	37.6	42.6	45.2	49.9
Industry	48.4	44.9	49.5	46.0	44.4	43.5	50.1	62.7	63.7	70.0	83.0
Manufacturing	..	..	..	..	..	23.0	27.1	28.7	32.4	38.0	45.4
Consumer Price Index	..	..	..	..	..	..	..	..	..	..	..
MANUFACTURING ACTIVITY											
Employment (1987=100)	..	..	..	..	..	..	..	..	..	..	..
Real Earnings per Empl. (1987=100)	..	..	..	..	..	..	..	..	..	..	..
Real Output per Empl. (1987=100)	..	..	..	..	..	..	..	..	..	..	..
Earnings as % of Value Added	..	..	..	..	30.1	27.3	31.4	31.6	30.8	49.6	..
MONETARY HOLDINGS					*(Millions of current CFA Francs)*						
Money Supply, Broadly Defined	7,559	8,381	8,365	9,768	10,427	13,629	13,682	19,346	20,487	22,508	27,104
Money	6,700	7,547	7,547	8,917	9,213	12,477	12,274	17,075	18,200	20,517	26,131
Currency Outside Banks	4,665	4,958	4,901	5,528	5,752	7,380	7,482	8,957	11,160	13,358	17,938
Demand Deposits	2,035	2,589	2,646	3,389	3,461	5,097	4,792	8,118	7,040	7,159	8,193
Quasi-Money	859	834	818	851	1,214	1,152	1,408	2,271	2,287	1,991	973
					(Millions of current CFA Francs)						
GOVERNMENT DEFICIT (-) OR SURPLUS	..	..	..	..	..	..	..	..	..	..	..
Current Revenue	..	..	..	..	..	..	..	..	..	..	..
Current Expenditure	..	..	..	..	..	..	..	..	..	..	..
Current Budget Balance	..	..	..	..	..	..	..	..	..	..	..
Capital Receipts	..	..	..	..	..	..	..	..	..	..	..
Capital Payments	..	..	..	..	..	..	..	..	..	..	..

1980	1981	1982	1983	1984	1985	1986	1987	1988	1989 estimate	NOTES	CENTRAL AFRICAN REPUBLIC
320	330	340	280	280	270	290	320	370	390	..	**CURRENT GNP PER CAPITA (US $)**
2,320	2,383	2,447	2,512	2,578	2,646	2,717	2,791	2,869	2,951	..	**POPULATION (thousands)**
				(Billions of current CFA Francs)							**USE AND ORIGIN OF RESOURCES**
168.90	190.10	244.60	247.50	274.50	311.20	338.60	316.70	326.80	347.10	..	Gross National Product (GNP)
0.50	1.30	-1.30	-3.50	-4.20	-5.00	-4.30	-5.80	-6.30	-5.40	..	Net Factor Income from Abroad
168.40	188.80	245.90	251.00	278.70	316.20	342.90	322.50	333.10	352.50	..	GDP at Market Prices
-28.00	-20.00	-33.20	-32.80	-35.00	-46.50	-47.60	-46.70	-38.90	-37.30	..	Resource Balance
44.00	48.50	54.60	60.50	65.40	79.80	64.30	59.10	58.60	67.70	..	Exports of Goods & NFServices
72.00	68.50	87.80	93.30	100.40	126.30	111.90	105.80	97.50	105.00	..	Imports of Goods & NFServices
196.40	208.80	279.10	283.80	313.70	362.70	390.50	369.20	372.00	389.80	..	Domestic Absorption
159.10	164.00	223.60	211.70	239.70	273.40	297.30	274.40	289.60	305.70	f	Private Consumption, etc.
25.50	28.30	39.10	42.40	39.70	43.60	51.30	56.80	52.70	51.40	..	General Gov't Consumption
11.80	16.50	16.40	29.70	34.30	45.70	41.90	38.00	29.70	32.70	f	Gross Domestic Investment
11.70	15.20	15.70	26.30	33.80	49.10	41.70	37.80	29.40	31.90	..	Fixed Investment
9.90	11.10	14.10	13.70	18.70	22.40	25.80	18.90	17.70	18.30	..	Indirect Taxes, net
158.50	177.70	231.80	237.30	260.00	293.80	317.10	303.60	315.40	334.20	..	GDP at factor cost
63.40	70.50	96.60	95.80	109.27	117.30	132.10	127.00	134.00	141.00	..	Agriculture
31.80	33.60	30.35	34.83	39.00	40.30	38.90	42.10	43.80	51.10	..	Industry
11.40	13.20	17.90	20.60	21.70	21.52	20.51	23.80	26.00	33.00	..	Manufacturing
63.30	73.60	104.85	106.67	111.73	136.20	146.10	134.50	137.60	142.10	..	Services, etc.
-16.20	-3.50	-16.80	-3.10	-0.70	-0.80	-5.70	-8.70	-9.20	-4.60	..	Gross Domestic Saving
-19.22	-5.97	-23.68	-12.25	-9.79	-11.11	-16.74	-21.63	-23.56	-17.93	..	Gross National Saving
				(Billions of 1987 CFA Francs)							
299.79	294.55	312.25	288.68	316.04	327.61	328.83	316.70	321.50	329.31	..	Gross National Product
296.62	289.96	311.63	290.88	318.24	330.55	333.71	322.50	327.75	335.14	..	GDP at Market Prices
-48.50	-26.63	-37.45	-32.74	-36.53	-38.03	-51.47	-46.70	-37.73	-32.73	..	Resource Balance
82.40	85.54	68.39	70.06	70.48	73.20	64.21	59.10	54.09	59.10	..	Exports of Goods & NFServices
130.90	112.17	105.85	102.80	107.02	111.23	115.68	105.80	91.83	91.83	..	Imports of Goods & NFServices
345.11	316.58	349.08	323.62	354.77	368.58	385.18	369.20	365.49	367.86	..	Domestic Absorption
257.58	227.89	259.86	229.95	254.42	264.08	286.38	274.40	282.68	285.05	f	Private Consumption, etc.
71.24	68.87	60.95	51.85	54.22	56.60	56.20	56.80	54.81	53.81	..	General Gov't Consumption
16.29	19.83	28.27	41.81	46.13	47.90	42.60	38.00	28.00	29.00	f	Gross Domestic Investment
16.01	17.77	26.95	36.91	45.45	50.39	42.22	37.80	27.85	28.85	..	Fixed Investment
285.47	281.69	294.42	274.56	300.72	312.30	311.63	303.60	311.07	317.39	..	GDP at factor cost
110.11	108.23	109.87	105.41	115.27	119.50	129.00	127.00	132.00	136.00	..	Agriculture
39.28	36.13	35.98	39.28	40.38	41.79	40.10	42.10	43.10	49.12	..	Industry
25.35	22.87	23.49	23.80	24.11	25.04	25.35	23.80	25.78	31.73	..	Manufacturing
137.14	140.44	153.99	129.87	145.07	151.01	142.53	134.50	135.96	132.27	..	Services, etc.
											Memo Items:
80.00	79.42	65.82	66.66	69.71	70.28	66.47	59.10	55.19	59.21	..	Capacity to Import
-2.41	-6.12	-2.57	-3.40	-0.77	-2.92	2.26	0.00	1.10	0.11	..	Terms of Trade Adjustment
294.21	283.83	309.06	287.48	317.47	327.63	335.97	322.50	328.85	335.24	..	Gross Domestic Income
297.38	288.43	309.68	285.28	315.27	324.69	331.09	316.70	322.60	329.42	..	Gross National Income
				(Index 1987 = 100)							**DOMESTIC PRICES/DEFLATORS**
56.8	65.1	78.9	86.3	87.6	95.7	102.8	100.0	101.6	105.2	..	Overall (GDP)
56.9	66.0	80.0	87.7	88.4	98.4	101.4	100.0	101.8	106.0	..	Domestic Absorption
57.6	65.1	87.9	90.9	94.8	98.2	102.4	100.0	101.5	103.7	..	Agriculture
81.0	93.0	84.4	88.7	96.6	96.4	97.0	100.0	101.6	104.0	..	Industry
45.0	57.7	76.2	86.6	90.0	86.0	80.9	100.0	100.8	104.0	..	Manufacturing
..	71.5	81.0	92.9	95.2	105.2	107.5	100.0	96.0	96.7	..	Consumer Price Index
											MANUFACTURING ACTIVITY
..	..	..	..	..	..	..	..	..	..	J	Employment (1987 = 100)
..	..	..	..	..	..	..	..	..	..	J	Real Earnings per Empl. (1987 = 100)
..	..	..	..	..	..	..	..	..	..	J	Real Output per Empl. (1987 = 100)
47.9	45.4	62.6	56.2	..	48.8	85.3	..	..	..	J	Earnings as % of Value Added
				(Millions of current CFA Francs)							**MONETARY HOLDINGS**
36,617	45,329	43,286	47,928	52,114	56,545	58,356	60,025	60,907	64,410	..	Money Supply, Broadly Defined
34,612	42,322	40,557	44,779	48,244	51,536	52,186	53,548	52,741	56,660	..	Money
24,367	31,956	31,218	34,313	37,236	37,147	40,606	41,462	41,581	42,240	..	Currency Outside Banks
10,245	10,366	9,339	10,466	11,008	14,389	11,580	12,086	11,160	14,420	..	Demand Deposits
2,005	3,007	2,729	3,149	3,870	5,009	6,170	6,477	8,166	7,750	..	Quasi-Money
				(Millions of current CFA Francs)							
..	-6,671	..	..	..	..	..	..	..	..	..	**GOVERNMENT DEFICIT (-) OR SURPLUS**
..	35,036	..	..	42,129	44,944	43,228	73,162	73,534	..	..	Current Revenue
..	34,977	..	..	39,661	43,198	46,130	50,935	49,710	..	..	Current Expenditure
..	59	..	..	2,468	1,746	-2,902	22,227	23,824	..	..	Current Budget Balance
..	15	..	..						..	..	Capital Receipts
..	7,179	..	..	27,767	44,065	42,367	36,180	34,140	..	..	Capital Payments

CENTRAL AFRICAN REPUBLIC	1969	1970	1971	1972	1973	1974	1975	1976	1977	1978	1979
FOREIGN TRADE (CUSTOMS BASIS)					*(Millions of current US dollars)*						
Value of Exports, fob	36.90	43.40	43.90	40.50	55.00	57.40	54.00	69.50	104.50	110.30	122.20
Nonfuel Primary Products	19.09	24.09	27.24	27.34	36.58	44.97	41.20	57.24	79.55	68.85	67.93
Fuels	0.11	0.09	0.05	0.03	0.25	0.00	0.00	0.00	0.00	0.00	0.00
Manufactures	17.70	19.22	16.60	13.13	18.17	12.43	12.80	12.26	24.95	41.45	54.27
Value of Imports, cif	52.70	56.60	50.70	56.40	69.00	83.50	109.80	99.60	136.30	156.10	158.70
Nonfuel Primary Products	8.85	10.59	10.34	10.67	12.55	15.01	19.68	19.76	24.29	29.61	28.13
Fuels	4.42	0.79	0.84	1.12	0.66	1.07	0.90	1.42	1.31	2.48	3.86
Manufactures	39.43	45.22	39.52	44.62	55.80	67.42	89.22	78.41	110.70	124.01	126.71
					(Index 1987 = 100)						
Terms of Trade	128.9	118.4	110.1	108.9	122.5	117.1	98.2	135.5	148.5	117.9	123.9
Export Prices, fob	29.5	34.1	33.7	36.2	49.6	58.9	54.2	76.5	91.2	81.5	98.0
Import Prices, cif	22.9	28.8	30.6	33.2	40.5	50.3	55.2	56.5	61.4	69.1	79.1
BALANCE OF PAYMENTS					*(Millions of current US dollars)*						
Exports of Goods & Services	..	60.80	60.38	57.98	78.08	78.89	80.98	101.60	130.62	146.67	159.83
Merchandise, fob	..	43.40	43.93	40.50	54.96	57.37	54.03	69.50	104.50	110.29	122.24
Nonfactor Services	..	17.00	16.05	16.83	22.65	20.69	25.98	30.59	23.36	32.69	35.00
Factor Services	..	0.40	0.40	0.65	0.48	0.84	0.97	1.50	2.76	3.69	2.59
Imports of Goods & Services	..	80.80	78.23	80.45	102.52	125.19	154.08	134.50	177.49	209.48	254.24
Merchandise, fob	..	39.60	44.83	46.25	50.67	62.90	82.93	75.85	103.89	119.03	132.90
Nonfactor Services	..	39.00	30.49	31.49	48.28	59.05	68.24	56.46	70.24	87.92	113.34
Factor Services	..	2.20	2.91	2.71	3.58	3.25	2.91	2.19	3.36	2.53	8.01
Long-Term Interest	..	0.70	0.60	0.60	1.20	1.20	2.10	0.90	1.20	1.40	0.40
Private Current Transfers, net	..	-3.90	-5.22	-4.45	-5.25	-7.70	-12.26	-10.39	-10.11	-13.29	-8.28
Workers' Remittances	..	..	..	..	..	..	..	..	..	..	..
Curr. A/C Bal before Off. Transf.	..	-23.90	-23.07	-26.93	-29.68	-54.00	-85.35	-43.29	-56.98	-76.10	-102.69
Net Official Transfers	..	12.40	14.14	28.01	26.70	39.45	48.08	48.78	38.09	51.78	86.86
Curr. A/C Bal after Off. Transf.	..	-11.50	-8.93	1.09	-2.98	-14.55	-37.27	5.48	-18.89	-24.32	-15.82
Long-Term Capital, net	..	-0.10	6.82	-3.04	-0.36	18.04	20.03	16.63	9.79	11.19	37.98
Direct Investment	..	0.90	0.30	1.19	-0.48	5.65	4.25	3.46	-2.93	4.75	22.43
Long-Term Loans	..	-0.60	2.50	14.90	15.80	6.10	9.80	9.30	21.20	19.10	12.80
Disbursements	..	1.80	4.10	16.00	19.30	9.60	13.40	11.20	24.30	21.70	13.10
Repayments	..	2.40	1.60	1.10	3.50	3.50	3.60	1.90	3.10	2.60	0.30
Other Long-Term Capital	..	-0.40	4.02	-19.13	-15.68	6.29	5.98	3.86	-8.48	-12.66	2.75
Other Capital, net	..	10.18	-0.93	2.05	3.29	-5.90	16.79	-10.76	14.10	7.61	-3.81
Change in Reserves	..	1.41	3.03	-0.10	0.05	2.41	0.45	-11.35	-4.99	5.52	-18.35
Memo Item:					*(CFA Francs per US dollar)*						
Conversion Factor (Annual Avg)	259.710	277.710	277.130	252.210	222.700	240.500	214.320	238.980	245.670	225.640	212.720
				(Millions of US dollars), outstanding at end of year							
EXTERNAL DEBT (Total)	..	24.10	28.10	36.30	55.20	67.10	77.00	90.30	125.80	135.20	149.80
Long-Term Debt (by debtor)	..	24.10	28.10	36.30	55.20	67.10	77.00	90.30	115.80	126.20	133.80
Central Bank, incl. IMF credit	..	0.00	0.00	0.00	0.00	3.30	5.70	11.10	11.60	20.40	17.90
Central Government	..	12.60	15.10	18.10	26.00	29.30	37.30	35.70	44.00	62.90	72.70
Rest of General Government	..	0.10	0.10	0.00	0.00	0.00	0.00	0.00	0.00	0.00	0.00
Non-financial Public Enterprises	..	8.90	10.40	15.60	26.70	32.20	32.20	41.70	58.40	41.30	41.60
Priv. Sector, incl non-guaranteed	..	2.50	2.50	2.60	2.50	2.30	1.80	1.80	1.80	1.60	1.60
Short-Term Debt	..	..	..	..	..	..	..	..	10.00	9.00	16.00
Memo Items:					*(Millions of US dollars)*						
Int'l Reserves Excluding Gold	1.2	1.4	0.2	1.7	1.8	1.7	3.8	18.8	25.4	24.1	44.1
Gold Holdings (at market price)	..	..	..	..	..	..	..	..	0.9	1.9	5.8
SOCIAL INDICATORS											
Total Fertility Rate	4.8	4.9	4.9	5.0	5.1	5.2	5.3	5.4	5.5	5.5	5.5
Infant Mortality Rate	142.8	139.2	135.6	132.0	130.0	128.0	126.0	124.0	122.0	120.4	118.8
Life Expectancy at Birth	41.9	42.4	42.9	43.4	43.8	44.3	44.7	45.1	45.5	45.9	46.4
Urban Population, % of total	29.7	30.4	31.2	31.9	32.7	33.4	34.2	35.0	35.8	36.6	37.4
Food Prod. per capita (1987=100)	104.2	105.5	108.9	111.1	114.4	115.1	114.4	111.4	114.1	113.9	111.6
Labor Force, Agriculture (%)	84.0	82.9	81.8	80.8	79.7	78.7	77.7	76.6	75.5	74.4	73.4
Labor Force, Female (%)	49.2	49.1	49.0	48.9	48.8	48.7	48.6	48.5	48.4	48.2	48.1
Primary Schl. Enroll. Ratio	..	64.0	..	..	..	..	73.0	..	70.0	69.0	70.0
Primary Schl. Enroll. Ratio, Female	..	41.0	..	..	..	..	51.0	..	47.0	48.0	49.0
Secondary Schl. Enroll. Ratio	..	4.0	..	..	..	..	8.0	9.0	10.0	10.0	11.0

1980	1981	1982	1983	1984	1985	1986	1987	1988	1989 estimate	NOTES	CENTRAL AFRICAN REPUBLIC
				(Millions of current US dollars)							**FOREIGN TRADE (CUSTOMS BASIS)**
147.20	117.70	111.50	114.60	114.70	131.65	130.00	130.00	132.00	..	f	Value of Exports, fob
108.68	81.25	76.55	79.35	83.23	93.28	92.00	81.00	79.00	..	..	Nonfuel Primary Products
0.00	0.00	0.00	0.00	0.00	0.00	0.00	0.00	0.00	..	..	Fuels
38.52	36.45	34.95	35.25	31.47	38.37	38.00	49.00	53.00	..	..	Manufactures
221.00	170.80	165.70	160.00	182.00	222.00	253.00	259.00	236.00	..	f	Value of Imports, cif
52.02	37.75	36.60	21.43	25.16	27.99	31.17	35.00	32.02	..	..	Nonfuel Primary Products
6.98	9.05	10.10	18.57	16.84	23.01	29.83	13.00	17.98	..	..	Fuels
162.00	124.00	119.00	120.00	140.00	171.00	192.00	211.00	186.00	..	..	Manufactures
				(Index 1987 = 100)							
125.8	109.7	110.3	109.8	118.7	108.4	110.5	100.0	106.9	..	..	Terms of Trade
112.4	99.2	97.8	95.3	99.9	92.0	101.4	100.0	113.5	..	..	Export Prices, fob
89.3	90.4	88.6	86.8	84.1	84.8	91.8	100.0	106.1	..	..	Import Prices, cif
				(Millions of current US dollars)							**BALANCE OF PAYMENTS**
205.38	177.39	170.93	162.17	151.94	184.49	188.33	197.70	202.00	213.00	f	Exports of Goods & Services
147.20	117.69	124.41	123.40	114.43	131.05	129.49	127.09	135.00	155.00	..	Merchandise, fob
53.83	51.72	41.55	35.67	34.78	46.79	56.00	67.84	62.00	56.00	..	Nonfactor Services
4.35	7.97	4.97	3.10	2.73	6.66	2.84	2.77	5.00	2.00	..	Factor Services
329.22	241.32	268.34	254.98	238.83	289.82	357.81	374.02	353.60	347.10	f	Imports of Goods & Services
185.11	144.56	149.71	137.52	140.06	167.75	201.00	197.67	178.10	179.10	f	Merchandise, fob
142.33	92.09	106.40	103.67	86.38	108.05	141.65	154.42	149.00	149.90	..	Nonfactor Services
1.79	4.67	12.24	13.79	12.39	14.03	15.16	21.93	26.50	18.10	..	Factor Services
0.40	0.90	2.30	6.60	5.60	6.60	9.20	8.50	7.30	7.10	..	Long-Term Interest
-16.67	-13.89	-16.98	-14.83	-11.20	-11.81	-19.46	-23.71	-27.06	-24.86	..	Private Current Transfers, net
..	..	..	..	..	..	..	..	..	..	..	Workers' Remittances
-140.51	-77.82	-114.39	-107.64	-98.09	-117.15	-188.94	-200.03	-178.66	-158.96	..	Curr. A/C Bal before Off. Transf.
97.46	73.64	71.75	78.33	64.64	68.53	102.42	124.80	162.00	150.80	..	Net Official Transfers
-43.05	-4.18	-42.64	-29.31	-33.45	-48.62	-86.52	-75.23	-16.66	-8.16	..	Curr. A/C Bal after Off. Transf.
46.57	15.00	2.19	35.77	49.79	55.38	94.01	85.08	39.10	36.30	f	Long-Term Capital, net
5.34	5.78	8.81	4.03	4.90	2.39	6.90	9.33	..	..	..	Direct Investment
30.30	27.80	16.60	18.50	27.60	42.50	71.70	84.50	78.30	60.40	..	Long-Term Loans
31.30	30.50	19.00	29.50	36.10	47.50	78.00	93.70	82.50	66.20	..	Disbursements
1.00	2.70	2.40	11.00	8.50	5.00	6.30	9.20	4.20	5.80	..	Repayments
10.93	-18.58	-23.22	13.24	17.29	10.50	15.41	-8.75	-39.20	-24.10	..	Other Long-Term Capital
6.96	-6.89	24.88	-8.43	-9.02	-26.92	-3.72	-2.03	-38.24	-12.54	..	Other Capital, net
-10.47	-3.93	15.57	1.97	-7.32	20.15	-3.76	-7.82	15.80	-15.60	..	Change in Reserves
				(CFA Francs per US dollar)							**Memo Item:**
211.300	271.730	328.620	381.070	436.960	449.260	346.300	300.540	297.850	319.010	..	Conversion Factor (Annual Avg)
				(Millions of US dollars), outstanding at end of year							
194.60	233.40	253.20	258.30	264.90	348.00	467.90	626.10	671.40	715.60	..	**EXTERNAL DEBT (Total)**
170.00	213.90	233.80	243.40	251.30	329.80	439.40	596.60	633.90	677.50	..	Long-Term Debt (by debtor)
23.50	37.70	37.70	40.00	35.10	39.00	41.80	51.90	50.30	35.30	..	Central Bank, incl. IMF credit
98.10	146.90	148.80	159.70	184.20	245.70	334.30	458.70	504.20	557.40	..	Central Government
0.00	0.00	0.00	0.00	0.00	0.00	0.00	0.00	0.00	..	..	Rest of General Government
47.00	29.30	47.30	43.70	30.80	43.30	61.40	84.00	77.50	83.00	..	Non-financial Public Enterprises
1.40	0.00	0.00	0.00	1.20	1.80	1.90	2.00	1.90	1.80	..	Priv. Sector, incl non-guaranteed
24.60	19.50	19.40	14.90	13.60	18.20	28.50	29.50	37.50	38.10	..	Short-Term Debt
				(Millions of US dollars)							**Memo Items:**
55.0	69.3	46.4	46.8	52.7	49.6	65.4	96.7	108.5	113.2	..	Int'l Reserves Excluding Gold
6.7	4.5	5.2	4.4	3.4	3.6	4.3	5.4	4.6	4.5	..	Gold Holdings (at market price)
											SOCIAL INDICATORS
5.5	5.5	5.5	5.6	5.6	5.6	5.7	5.8	5.7	5.7	..	Total Fertility Rate
117.2	115.6	114.0	112.0	110.0	108.0	106.0	104.0	102.2	100.4	..	Infant Mortality Rate
46.8	47.3	47.7	48.2	48.6	49.1	49.5	50.0	50.2	50.5	..	Life Expectancy at Birth
38.2	39.0	39.9	40.7	41.6	42.4	43.4	44.5	45.2	45.9	..	Urban Population, % of total
112.7	113.1	111.8	107.3	102.4	98.3	103.7	100.0	101.2	100.9	..	Food Prod. per capita (1987=100)
72.4	..	..	..	..	..	..	..	..	..	..	Labor Force, Agriculture (%)
48.0	47.8	47.6	47.4	47.1	46.9	46.7	46.4	46.2	46.0	..	Labor Force, Female (%)
71.0	..	74.0	77.0	79.0	77.0	66.0	66.0	..	..	..	Primary Schl. Enroll. Ratio
51.0	52.0	51.0	55.0	57.0	59.0	50.0	51.0	..	..	..	Primary Schl. Enroll. Ratio, Female
14.0	..	..	16.0	16.0	16.0	13.0	12.0	..	..	..	Secondary Schl. Enroll. Ratio

CHAD	1969	1970	1971	1972	1973	1974	1975	1976	1977	1978	1979
CURRENT GNP PER CAPITA (US $)	100	100	90	100	100	120	150	150	160	170	150
POPULATION (thousands)	3,584	3,652	3,723	3,796	3,871	3,949	4,030	4,113	4,199	4,288	4,381

USE AND ORIGIN OF RESOURCES					*(Billions of current CFA Francs)*						
Gross National Product (GNP)	85.81	91.30	97.28	104.86	101.84	110.86	129.73	145.07	160.36	175.04	148.56
Net Factor Income from Abroad	-0.50	0.00	0.00	1.00	0.30	0.30	-0.70	-0.60	-1.40	-1.90	-1.82
GDP at Market Prices	86.31	91.30	97.28	103.86	101.54	110.56	130.43	145.67	161.76	176.94	150.39
Resource Balance	-5.50	-7.50	-7.10	-7.10	-11.20	-13.20	-21.20	-21.30	-29.90	-29.00	-36.00
Exports of Goods & NFServices	16.20	21.10	22.00	21.50	22.70	28.90	26.70	33.30	35.30	41.30	38.00
Imports of Goods & NFServices	21.70	28.60	29.10	28.60	33.90	42.10	47.90	54.60	65.20	70.30	74.00
Domestic Absorption	91.81	98.80	104.38	110.96	112.74	123.76	151.63	166.97	191.66	205.94	186.38
Private Consumption, etc.	53.73	58.05	60.42	64.98	85.32	70.39	88.62	104.62	119.23	128.83	..
General Gov't Consumption	21.76	24.27	26.61	28.79	31.30	30.46	32.97	34.48	38.83	44.89	..
Gross Domestic Investment	16.32	16.48	17.34	17.19	-3.87	22.92	30.04	27.87	33.60	32.22	..
Fixed Investment	..	..	..	..	..	..	..	..	..	..	..
Indirect Taxes, net	6.60	7.40	7.60	6.20	5.80	7.10	6.70	7.30	1.28	1.46	0.95
GDP at factor cost	79.71	83.90	89.68	97.66	95.74	103.46	123.73	138.37	160.48	175.48	149.43
Agriculture	38.65	39.52	42.23	45.82	43.21	47.34	56.24	60.80	66.99	74.50	72.40
Industry	14.62	15.17	16.20	17.73	19.82	21.87	25.77	26.71	29.24	30.81	20.89
Manufacturing	13.66	14.17	15.20	16.49	18.29	20.10	23.70	24.22	26.28	27.41	..
Services, etc.	33.04	36.61	38.84	40.31	38.51	41.36	48.42	58.16	65.53	71.63	57.10
Gross Domestic Saving	10.82	8.98	10.24	10.09	-15.07	9.72	8.84	6.57	3.70	3.22	-36.00
Gross National Saving	..	7.26	8.32	8.92	-16.82	7.85	6.40	4.98	-1.15	-1.25	-39.80

					(Billions of 1987 CFA Francs)						
Gross National Product	210.80	214.95	210.20	212.42	195.22	204.85	221.40	228.30	232.36	230.79	181.18
GDP at Market Prices	210.10	214.25	209.51	211.72	194.58	204.23	222.63	229.27	234.39	233.29	183.27
Resource Balance	-26.12	-31.83	-30.02	-35.11	-47.66	-50.02	-44.55	-39.26	-43.32	-37.99	-30.58
Exports of Goods & NFServices	40.23	50.08	53.28	45.82	47.15	34.63	39.43	51.15	51.15	49.17	46.22
Imports of Goods & NFServices	66.34	81.91	83.30	80.93	94.81	84.65	83.98	90.41	94.47	87.17	76.80
Domestic Absorption	236.22	246.08	239.53	246.83	242.23	254.25	267.18	268.53	277.71	271.28	213.85
Private Consumption, etc.	..	..	..	..	..	..	..	..	..	..	..
General Gov't Consumption	..	..	..	..	..	..	..	..	..	..	..
Gross Domestic Investment	..	..	..	..	..	..	..	..	..	..	..
Fixed Investment	..	..	..	..	..	..	..	..	..	..	..
GDP at factor cost	..	..	..	..	..	..	..	..	232.54	231.36	182.11
Agriculture	99.22	98.68	96.26	99.49	86.31	89.00	96.80	95.73	96.94	98.23	88.23
Industry	32.10	32.96	33.47	33.95	34.19	35.95	38.72	42.02	42.37	40.62	25.46
Manufacturing	..	..	..	..	..	..	..	..	..	..	..
Services, etc.	79.55	83.14	80.23	78.94	74.07	79.27	87.11	91.52	95.08	94.45	69.58

Memo Items:											
Capacity to Import	49.53	60.43	62.98	60.84	63.49	58.11	46.81	55.14	51.15	51.21	39.44
Terms of Trade Adjustment	9.30	10.35	9.70	15.02	16.33	23.48	7.38	3.99	0.00	2.03	-6.78
Gross Domestic Income	219.40	224.59	219.20	226.74	210.91	227.71	230.01	233.26	234.39	235.32	176.49
Gross National Income	220.10	225.30	219.90	227.44	211.55	228.32	228.78	232.29	232.36	232.82	174.40

DOMESTIC PRICES/DEFLATORS					*(Index 1987 = 100)*						
Overall (GDP)	41.1	42.6	46.4	49.1	52.2	54.1	58.6	63.5	69.0	75.8	82.1
Domestic Absorption	38.9	40.2	43.6	45.0	46.5	48.7	56.8	62.2	69.0	75.9	87.2
Agriculture	39.0	40.0	43.9	46.1	50.1	53.2	58.1	63.5	69.1	75.8	82.1
Industry	45.5	46.0	48.4	52.2	58.0	60.8	66.6	63.6	69.0	75.8	82.1
Manufacturing	..	..	..	..	..	..	..	..	..	..	..
Consumer Price Index	..	..	..	..	..	..	..	..	..	..	..

MANUFACTURING ACTIVITY											
Employment (1987=100)	..	..	..	..	..	..	..	..	..	..	..
Real Earnings per Empl. (1987=100)	..	..	..	..	..	..	..	..	..	..	..
Real Output per Empl. (1987=100)	..	..	..	..	..	..	..	..	..	..	..
Earnings as % of Value Added	..	..	..	..	..	..	13.5	..	..	..	..

MONETARY HOLDINGS					*(Millions of current CFA Francs)*						
Money Supply, Broadly Defined	8,042	9,195	9,782	10,125	10,660	15,122	16,687	20,830	23,709	29,419	33,236
Money	7,677	8,603	9,269	9,635	9,796	14,133	15,513	19,494	22,508	27,565	31,572
Currency Outside Banks	4,908	5,311	6,196	6,903	6,487	8,527	10,883	12,999	14,365	16,492	22,539
Demand Deposits	2,769	3,292	3,073	2,732	3,309	5,606	4,630	6,495	8,143	11,073	9,033
Quasi-Money	365	592	513	490	864	989	1,174	1,336	1,201	1,854	1,664

GOVERNMENT DEFICIT (-) OR SURPLUS					*(Millions of current CFA Francs)*						
GOVERNMENT DEFICIT (-) OR SURPLUS	..	..	..	-2,783	-3,910	-2,543	-2,130	-2,848	..	..	..
Current Revenue	..	..	..	12,852	13,450	16,707	18,191	20,292	..	..	..
Current Expenditure	..	..	..	12,554	14,164	15,571	15,371	19,085	..	..	..
Current Budget Balance	..	..	..	298	-714	1,136	2,820	1,207	..	..	..
Capital Receipts	..	..	..	..	..	..	..	..	..	..	..
Capital Payments	..	..	..	3,081	3,196	3,679	4,950	4,055	..	..	..

1980	1981	1982	1983	1984	1985	1986	1987	1988	1989 estimate	NOTES	CHAD
160	160	150	140	130	150	150	140	180	190	..	**CURRENT GNP PER CAPITA (US $)**
4,477	4,577	4,681	4,789	4,901	5,018	5,140	5,267	5,398	5,537	..	**POPULATION (thousands)**
				(Billions of current CFA Francs)							**USE AND ORIGIN OF RESOURCES**
152.76	167.58	192.78	222.18	278.66	325.45	257.21	241.15	309.61	319.72	..	Gross National Product (GNP)
-0.87	-0.16	-0.22	-1.10	-4.00	-2.45	-3.06	-3.06	-3.97	-4.11	..	Net Factor Income from Abroad
153.63	167.74	193.00	223.29	282.66	327.90	260.26	244.21	313.58	323.83	..	GDP at Market Prices
-26.00	-18.00	-19.00	-26.00	-25.00	-90.11	-81.26	-73.34	-66.58	-72.56	..	Resource Balance
37.00	36.00	18.00	52.00	72.00	55.29	49.55	54.04	66.35	71.50	..	Exports of Goods & NFServices
63.00	54.00	37.00	78.00	97.00	145.40	130.82	127.39	132.94	144.06	..	Imports of Goods & NFServices
179.63	185.74	212.00	249.29	307.66	418.00	341.53	317.56	380.16	396.39	..	Domestic Absorption
..	..	197.00	223.25	252.12	336.72	266.35	232.22	299.51	298.56	..	Private Consumption, etc.
..	..	15.00	19.19	40.23	54.51	51.43	55.33	56.11	68.82	..	General Gov't Consumption
..	..	..	6.85	15.32	26.77	23.75	30.00	24.53	29.01	..	Gross Domestic Investment
..	..	..	6.85	15.32	26.77	23.75	30.00	24.53	29.01	..	Fixed Investment
0.49	0.73	0.85	5.37	12.81	13.23	10.68	12.37	17.02	17.65	..	Indirect Taxes, net
153.14	167.01	192.15	217.92	269.85	314.67	249.58	231.84	296.56	306.18	B	GDP at factor cost
81.96	78.80	90.00	101.29	107.42	141.30	96.17	90.02	128.76	116.01	f	Agriculture
18.15	26.35	32.00	38.90	58.03	54.88	49.77	45.33	54.19	64.61	..	Industry
..	..	..	36.77	54.34	49.52	44.77	40.19	48.47	56.76	..	Manufacturing
53.51	62.59	71.00	83.10	117.21	131.72	114.32	108.87	130.62	143.22	..	Services, etc.
-26.00	-18.00	-19.00	-19.15	-9.68	-63.34	-57.51	-43.34	-42.05	-43.55	..	Gross Domestic Saving
-27.74	-18.32	-19.43	-21.34	-14.42	-62.72	-62.44	-49.36	-51.12	-48.36	..	Gross National Saving
				(Billions of 1987 CFA Francs)							
171.33	173.82	183.07	210.97	213.30	261.55	249.79	241.15	283.58	286.15	..	Gross National Product
172.30	173.98	183.28	212.02	216.37	263.52	252.76	244.21	287.21	289.83	..	GDP at Market Prices
-29.21	-17.87	-28.98	-24.69	-19.13	-72.42	-78.92	-73.34	-60.98	-64.94	..	Resource Balance
41.68	37.58	20.29	49.38	55.11	44.43	48.13	54.04	60.78	63.99	..	Exports of Goods & NFServices
70.89	55.45	49.27	74.06	74.25	116.85	127.05	127.39	121.76	128.93	..	Imports of Goods & NFServices
201.51	191.85	212.26	236.71	235.50	335.93	331.68	317.55	348.20	354.77	..	Domestic Absorption
..	..	..	211.98	192.98	270.61	258.67	232.22	274.33	267.21	..	Private Consumption, etc.
..	..	18.22	30.79	43.81	49.94	55.33	51.40	61.59		..	General Gov't Consumption
..	..	..	6.50	11.73	21.51	23.07	30.00	22.47	25.97	..	Gross Domestic Investment
..	..	..	..	..	..	..	..	..	..	..	Fixed Investment
171.75	173.23	182.46	206.92	206.56	252.89	242.38	231.84	271.63	274.03	B	GDP at factor cost
91.92	81.74	85.91	96.18	82.23	113.56	93.40	90.02	117.94	103.83	f	Agriculture
20.36	27.33	30.26	36.93	43.31	44.10	48.34	45.33	49.64	57.82	..	Industry
..	..	..	34.91	41.60	39.80	43.48	40.19	44.39	50.80	..	Manufacturing
60.02	64.91	67.12	78.91	90.83	105.86	111.02	108.87	119.64	128.18	..	Services, etc.
											Memo Items:
41.64	36.97	23.97	49.38	55.11	44.43	48.13	54.04	60.78	63.99	..	Capacity to Import
-0.05	-0.62	3.68	0.00	0.00	0.00	0.00	0.00	0.00	0.00	..	Terms of Trade Adjustment
172.25	173.37	186.97	212.02	216.36	263.52	252.76	244.21	287.21	289.83	..	Gross Domestic Income
171.28	173.20	186.75	210.97	213.30	261.55	249.79	241.15	283.58	286.15	..	Gross National Income
				(Index 1987 = 100)							**DOMESTIC PRICES/DEFLATORS**
89.2	96.4	105.3	105.3	130.6	124.4	103.0	100.0	109.2	111.7	..	Overall (GDP)
89.1	96.8	99.9	105.3	130.6	124.4	103.0	100.0	109.2	111.7	..	Domestic Absorption
89.2	96.4	104.8	105.3	130.6	124.4	103.0	100.0	109.2	111.7	..	Agriculture
89.2	96.4	105.8	105.3	134.0	124.4	103.0	100.0	109.2	111.7	..	Industry
..	..	..	105.3	130.6	124.4	103.0	100.0	109.2	111.7	..	Manufacturing
..	..	..	96.7	116.3	122.3	106.4	100.0	115.5	109.8	..	Consumer Price Index
											MANUFACTURING ACTIVITY
..	..	..	..	..	..	..	..	..	..	..	Employment (1987 = 100)
..	..	..	..	..	..	..	..	..	..	..	Real Earnings per Empl. (1987 = 100)
..	..	..	..	..	..	..	..	..	..	..	Real Output per Empl. (1987 = 100)
..	..	..	..	..	..	..	..	..	..	..	Earnings as % of Value Added
				(Millions of current CFA Francs)							**MONETARY HOLDINGS**
28,142	33,162	34,649	42,389	67,759	71,898	72,714	75,381	69,030	70,750	..	Money Supply, Broadly Defined
26,478	31,680	33,163	40,753	65,125	68,344	69,138	70,596	64,683	66,440	..	Money
17,445	22,143	23,609	29,196	44,925	47,354	46,665	46,702	42,007	43,090	..	Currency Outside Banks
9,033	9,537	9,554	11,557	20,200	20,990	22,473	23,894	22,676	23,350	..	Demand Deposits
1,664	1,482	1,486	1,636	2,634	3,554	3,576	4,785	4,347	4,310	..	Quasi-Money
				(Millions of current CFA Francs)							
..	..	..	..	..	..		..	..	..	..	**GOVERNMENT DEFICIT (-) OR SURPLUS**
..	..	..	..	..	..	21,535	..	..	..	..	Current Revenue
..	..	..	..	..	..		..	..	..	..	Current Expenditure
..	..	..	..	..	..	..	..	..	..	..	Current Budget Balance
..	..	..	..	..	..	..	..	..	..	..	Capital Receipts
..	..	..	..	..	..	..	..	..	..	..	Capital Payments

CHAD	1969	1970	1971	1972	1973	1974	1975	1976	1977	1978	1979
FOREIGN TRADE (CUSTOMS BASIS)					*(Millions of current US dollars)*						
Value of Exports, fob	31.07	24.71	26.37	34.15	35.95	35.06	40.03	63.00	107.00	99.00	72.17
Nonfuel Primary Products	..	..	..	..	..	..	..	..	..	..	..
Fuels	..	..	..	..	..	..	..	..	..	..	..
Manufactures	..	..	..	..	..	..	..	..	..	..	..
Value of Imports, cif	54.00	62.00	61.98	61.36	82.37	87.14	133.00	116.00	189.00	217.00	85.00
Nonfuel Primary Products	..	..	..	..	..	..	..	..	..	..	..
Fuels	..	..	..	..	..	..	..	..	..	..	..
Manufactures	..	..	..	..	..	..	..	..	..	..	..
					(Index 1987 = 100)						
Terms of Trade	..	..	..	..	..	..	..	..	..	..	..
Export Prices, fob	..	..	..	..	..	..	..	..	..	..	..
Import Prices, cif	..	..	..	..	..	..	..	..	..	..	..
BALANCE OF PAYMENTS					*(Millions of current US dollars)*						
Exports of Goods & Services	..	69.80	73.22	78.39	93.82	109.44	104.42	128.61	132.38	..	..
Merchandise, fob	..	39.80	42.33	39.85	48.76	70.47	57.91	100.79	106.55	98.95	88.27
Nonfactor Services	..	28.80	29.99	37.24	43.27	37.16	44.32	25.86	24.19	20.59	4.60
Factor Services	..	1.20	0.90	1.30	1.79	1.80	2.19	1.96	1.64	..	..
Imports of Goods & Services	..	96.50	100.10	107.05	145.80	163.32	229.96	215.20	249.56	271.17	127.06
Merchandise, fob	..	52.50	53.06	58.52	73.55	82.74	126.15	115.34	142.20	163.38	64.09
Nonfactor Services	..	41.70	44.53	45.82	68.55	76.97	100.90	97.56	103.42	104.13	54.41
Factor Services	..	2.30	2.51	2.71	3.70	3.61	2.91	2.31	3.94	3.66	8.56
Long-Term Interest	..	0.40	0.90	0.70	0.50	0.70	1.40	0.80	0.60	0.70	0.20
Private Current Transfers, net	..	-6.20	-6.92	-8.58	-9.18	-9.02	-8.13	-4.16	-14.03	-11.37	-9.29
Workers' Remittances	..	..	..	..	..	..	..	..	..	..	..
Curr. A/C Bal before Off. Transf.	..	-32.90	-33.80	-37.24	-61.16	-62.90	-133.68	-90.75	-131.21	-163.00	-43.49
Net Official Transfers	..	34.50	37.11	37.35	54.36	58.69	73.33	85.55	102.69	116.56	41.94
Curr. A/C Bal after Off. Transf.	..	1.60	3.31	0.11	-6.80	-4.21	-60.34	-5.20	-28.52	-46.44	-1.55
Long-Term Capital, net	..	3.60	7.32	-13.14	4.65	14.67	37.76	58.65	33.05	34.57	-3.97
Direct Investment	..	0.60	0.30	-0.11	6.08	13.83	20.28	26.78	21.15	33.09	-1.29
Long-Term Loans	..	3.30	9.00	-1.20	10.60	23.50	18.00	6.50	37.00	38.40	22.60
Disbursements	..	5.80	14.80	2.40	13.40	26.10	23.10	10.20	39.80	40.90	24.40
Repayments	..	2.50	5.80	3.60	2.80	2.60	5.10	3.70	2.80	2.50	1.80
Other Long-Term Capital	..	-0.30	-1.98	-11.83	-12.03	-22.66	-0.52	25.36	-25.10	-36.92	-25.28
Other Capital, net	..	-8.48	-3.89	10.51	-6.53	-0.07	10.21	-39.74	-8.55	5.76	3.16
Change in Reserves	..	3.28	-6.75	2.52	8.67	-10.39	12.38	-13.71	4.02	6.10	2.36
Memo Item:					*(CFA Francs per US dollar)*						
Conversion Factor (Annual Avg)	259.710	277.710	277.130	252.210	222.700	240.500	214.320	238.980	245.670	225.640	212.720
				(Millions of US dollars), outstanding at end of year							
EXTERNAL DEBT (Total)	..	34.90	46.60	35.80	46.80	74.80	90.80	100.20	145.70	210.80	236.70
Long-Term Debt (by debtor)	..	34.90	46.60	35.80	46.80	74.80	90.80	100.20	141.70	196.80	223.70
Central Bank, incl. IMF credit	..	6.00	6.90	6.50	5.40	8.40	8.00	13.50	14.10	20.40	20.00
Central Government	..	23.10	35.00	24.80	37.00	58.30	74.60	76.30	90.30	108.50	124.40
Rest of General Government	..	0.30	0.20	0.20	0.10	0.10	0.10	0.00	0.00	0.00	0.00
Non-financial Public Enterprises	..	5.50	4.50	4.30	4.30	8.00	8.10	10.40	37.30	67.90	79.30
Priv. Sector, incl non-guaranteed	..	0.00	0.00	0.00	0.00	0.00	0.00	0.00	0.00	0.00	0.00
Short-Term Debt	..	..	..	..	..	..	..	..	4.00	14.00	13.00
Memo Items:					*(Thousands of US dollars)*						
Int'l Reserves Excluding Gold	1,275.0	2,309.0	11,224.0	10,075.0	1,471.0	15,267.0	3,059.0	23,274.0	18,783.0	11,790.0	11,267.0
Gold Holdings (at market price)	..	..	..	..	..	..	..	..	924.0	1,921.0	5,837.0
SOCIAL INDICATORS											
Total Fertility Rate	6.0	6.0	6.0	6.0	6.0	5.9	5.9	5.9	5.9	5.9	5.9
Infant Mortality Rate	173.8	171.2	168.6	166.0	163.6	161.2	158.8	156.4	154.0	151.8	149.6
Life Expectancy at Birth	37.8	38.2	38.6	39.0	39.4	39.8	40.2	40.6	41.0	41.4	41.8
Urban Population, % of total	11.0	11.4	12.2	12.9	13.7	14.4	15.2	16.3	17.4	18.6	19.7
Food Prod. per capita (1987=100)	112.5	106.9	105.0	97.9	90.8	91.5	95.0	96.8	96.8	99.9	101.1
Labor Force, Agriculture (%)	90.5	90.2	89.4	88.7	88.0	87.4	86.7	86.0	85.3	84.6	83.9
Labor Force, Female (%)	23.0	23.0	22.9	22.9	22.8	22.7	22.7	22.6	22.6	22.5	22.4
Primary Schl. Enroll. Ratio	..	35.0	..	..	..	..	35.0	35.0	..	..	..
Primary Schl. Enroll. Ratio, Female	..	17.0	..	..	..	..	18.0	19.0	..	..	..
Secondary Schl. Enroll. Ratio	..	2.0	..	..	..	..	3.0	3.0	..	..	..

1980	1981	1982	1983	1984	1985	1986	1987	1988	1989 estimate	NOTES	CHAD
											FOREIGN TRADE (CUSTOMS BASIS)
					(Millions of current US dollars)						
72.38	83.40	57.70	73.90	111.00	88.00	99.00	111.00	..	..	..	Value of Exports, fob
..	..	..	..	..	..	..	..	..	..	..	Nonfuel Primary Products
..	..	..	..	..	..	..	..	..	..	..	Fuels
..	..	..	..	..	..	..	..	..	..	..	Manufactures
74.00	108.00	109.00	157.00	171.00	240.00	288.00	366.00	..	..	..	Value of Imports, cif
..	..	..	..	..	..	..	..	..	..	..	Nonfuel Primary Products
..	..	..	..	..	..	..	..	..	..	..	Fuels
..	..	..	..	..	..	..	..	..	..	..	Manufactures
					(Index 1987 = 100)						
..	..	..	..	..	..	..	..	..	..	..	Terms of Trade
..	..	..	..	..	..	..	..	..	..	..	Export Prices, fob
..	..	..	..	..	..	..	..	..	..	..	Import Prices, cif
					(Millions of current US dollars)						**BALANCE OF PAYMENTS**
..	..	61.99	106.84	147.85	99.49	146.64	182.71	224.92	225.33	f	Exports of Goods & Services
70.99	83.41	57.72	78.22	109.68	61.84	98.60	109.45	144.04	146.00	..	Merchandise, fob
0.38	4.11	2.36	24.24	36.84	32.60	44.50	70.38	78.74	78.70	..	Nonfactor Services
..	..	1.91	4.38	1.33	5.04	3.54	2.88	2.14	0.63	..	Factor Services
83.17	107.60	104.73	180.09	224.69	327.44	390.12	436.92	461.79	465.06	f	Imports of Goods & Services
55.28	81.21	81.69	99.15	128.33	166.29	212.06	225.91	228.40	235.40	..	Merchandise, fob
24.21	25.32	22.09	77.61	90.07	153.86	165.70	197.96	217.92	216.15	..	Nonfactor Services
3.68	1.07	0.95	3.34	6.29	7.29	12.37	13.06	15.46	13.51	..	Factor Services
0.00	0.10	0.20	0.20	0.30	2.10	1.70	3.10	3.50	1.70	..	Long-Term Interest
-4.11	-0.59	-0.66	-2.83	-1.68	6.85	-5.39	-9.84	-17.13	-2.21	..	Private Current Transfers, net
..	..	..	..	..	0.03	1.23	1.35	0.35	0.04	..	Workers' Remittances
-15.91	-20.67	-43.40	-76.08	-78.52	-221.11	-248.88	-264.05	-254.00	-241.94	..	Curr. A/C Bal before Off. Transf.
28.21	44.11	61.92	114.06	87.57	133.87	189.51	238.52	277.65	237.25	..	Net Official Transfers
12.31	23.44	18.53	37.98	9.05	-87.24	-59.37	-25.53	23.65	-4.69	f	Curr. A/C Bal after Off. Transf.
-4.17	-1.93	-1.11	-18.13	4.36	67.51	49.28	55.76	-50.99	80.41	f	Long-Term Capital, net
-0.43	-0.11	-0.12	-0.09	9.19	53.39	27.77	0.17	-12.55	-11.62	..	Direct Investment
2.60	9.10	3.60	13.70	7.50	-0.30	28.50	40.50	58.10	76.60	..	Long-Term Loans
5.20	9.70	4.60	13.90	10.50	9.80	31.50	42.80	60.50	80.00	..	Disbursements
2.60	0.60	1.00	0.20	3.00	10.10	3.00	2.30	2.40	3.40	..	Repayments
-6.34	-10.92	-4.58	-31.74	-12.33	14.42	-6.99	15.10	-96.54	15.43	..	Other Long-Term Capital
-13.17	-22.97	-14.84	-2.48	10.54	-2.09	-4.99	-13.68	13.69	-41.04	f	Other Capital, net
5.03	1.46	-2.58	-17.37	-23.95	21.82	15.08	-16.56	13.64	-34.68	..	Change in Reserves
					(CFA Francs per US dollar)						Memo Item:
211.300	271.730	328.620	381.070	436.960	449.260	346.300	300.540	297.850	319.010	..	Conversion Factor (Annual Avg)
				(Millions of US dollars), outstanding at end of year							
218.30	201.40	168.00	168.60	157.80	186.00	237.30	320.00	357.40	368.20	..	**EXTERNAL DEBT (Total)**
207.70	190.60	160.50	163.20	155.00	165.80	206.40	282.00	320.00	340.50	..	Long-Term Debt (by debtor)
16.40	16.90	14.70	13.80	9.30	13.00	11.90	21.10	18.00	24.80	..	Central Bank, incl. IMF credit
120.50	118.00	118.00	125.60	122.50	124.10	145.40	181.20	222.70	288.00	..	Central Government
0.00	0.00	0.00	0.00	0.00	0.00	0.00	0.00	0.30	0.40	..	Rest of General Government
70.80	55.70	27.80	23.80	23.20	28.70	49.10	75.90	73.50	27.10	..	Non-financial Public Enterprises
0.00	0.00	0.00	0.00	0.00	0.00	0.00	3.80	5.50	0.20	..	Priv. Sector, incl non-guaranteed
10.60	10.80	7.50	5.40	2.80	20.20	30.90	38.00	37.40	27.70	..	Short-Term Debt
					(Thousands of US dollars)						Memo Items:
5,053.0	7,315.0	12,405.0	27,999.0	44,162.0	33,460.0	15,910.0	52,108.0	61,109.0	128,943.0	..	Int'l Reserves Excluding Gold
6,720.0	4,532.0	5,209.0	4,349.0	3,422.0	3,630.0	4,339.0	5,374.0	4,554.0	4,451.0	..	Gold Holdings (at market price)
											SOCIAL INDICATORS
5.9	5.9	5.9	5.9	5.9	5.9	5.9	5.9	5.9	5.9	..	Total Fertility Rate
147.4	145.2	143.0	140.8	138.6	136.4	134.2	132.0	129.9	127.8	..	Infant Mortality Rate
42.2	42.6	43.0	43.5	44.0	44.5	45.0	45.5	45.9	46.3	..	Life Expectancy at Birth
18.7	22.0	23.3	24.5	25.8	22.9	24.0	25.2	26.4	32.2	..	Urban Population, % of total
104.0	101.3	100.9	102.7	89.5	105.5	105.2	100.0	107.7	100.3	..	Food Prod. per capita (1987=100)
83.3	..	..	..	..	..	..	..	..	..	..	Labor Force, Agriculture (%)
22.4	22.2	22.1	22.0	21.8	21.7	21.6	21.5	21.3	21.2	..	Labor Force, Female (%)
..	..	..	..	38.0	43.0	43.0	51.0	..	..	..	Primary Schl. Enroll. Ratio
..	..	..	..	21.0	24.0	24.0	29.0	..	..	..	Primary Schl. Enroll. Ratio, Female
..	..	..	..	6.0	..	6.0	6.0	..	..	..	Secondary Schl. Enroll. Ratio

CHILE	1969	1970	1971	1972	1973	1974	1975	1976	1977	1978	1979
CURRENT GNP PER CAPITA (US $)	810	840	990	1,080	1,080	1,140	860	880	1,030	1,330	1,680
POPULATION (thousands)	9,325	9,504	9,682	9,855	10,024	10,189	10,350	10,508	10,662	10,815	10,975

USE AND ORIGIN OF RESOURCES *(Billions of current Chilean Pesos)*

	1969	1970	1971	1972	1973	1974	1975	1976	1977	1978	1979
Gross National Product (GNP)	6.65E-2	9.60E-2	1.25E-1	2.32E-1	1.10E+0	9.10E+0	34.1	124.5	281.9	476.5	752.7
Net Factor Income from Abroad	-2.10E-3	-2.40E-3	-1.50E-3	-2.90E-3	-1.22E-2	-1.44E-1	-1.4	-4.2	-5.9	-11.0	-19.5
GDP at Market Prices	6.86E-2	9.84E-2	1.27E-1	2.34E-1	1.10E+0	9.20E+0	35.4	128.7	287.8	487.5	772.2
Resource Balance	1.60E-3	6.00E-4	-1.30E-3	-8.20E-3	-2.13E-2	6.23E-2	-0.7	5.6	-5.2	-16.3	-21.9
Exports of Goods & NFServices	1.16E-2	1.48E-2	1.44E-2	2.36E-2	1.60E-1	1.90E+0	9.0	32.3	59.3	100.4	179.7
Imports of Goods & NFServices	1.00E-2	1.42E-2	1.57E-2	3.18E-2	1.82E-1	1.80E+0	9.7	26.8	64.5	116.7	201.6
Domestic Absorption	6.70E-2	9.78E-2	1.28E-1	2.43E-1	1.20E+0	9.10E+0	36.1	123.1	293.0	503.8	794.1
Private Consumption, etc.	4.90E-2	6.90E-2	9.05E-2	1.76E-1	9.27E-1	5.70E+0	25.9	88.7	209.5	346.6	546.3
General Gov't Consumption	7.60E-3	1.26E-2	1.94E-2	3.77E-2	1.51E-1	1.40E+0	5.6	18.0	41.9	70.3	110.4
Gross Domestic Investment	1.04E-2	1.62E-2	1.84E-2	2.86E-2	9.07E-2	1.90E+0	4.6	16.4	41.5	86.8	137.4
Fixed Investment	9.80E-3	1.48E-2	1.85E-2	3.07E-2	1.47E-1	1.60E+0	6.3	17.1	38.3	71.6	115.0
Indirect Taxes, net	6.70E-3	1.04E-2	1.24E-2	2.00E-2	1.20E-1	1.40E+0	5.0	17.7	41.3	67.4	95.8
GDP at factor cost	6.19E-2	8.80E-2	1.15E-1	2.14E-1	1.00E+0	7.80E+0	30.5	111.0	246.4	420.1	676.4
Agriculture	4.70E-3	6.70E-3	1.03E-2	1.95E-2	7.64E-2	5.23E-1	2.3	10.9	28.3	37.1	56.1
Industry	2.94E-2	4.07E-2	4.90E-2	8.86E-2	4.70E-1	4.50E+0	13.5	51.4	103.9	175.5	288.0
Manufacturing	1.72E-2	2.51E-2	3.10E-2	5.48E-2	3.11E-1	2.70E+0	7.2	29.9	62.6	109.2	164.0
Services, etc.	3.45E-2	5.10E-2	6.77E-2	1.26E-1	6.00E-1	4.20E+0	19.6	66.4	155.6	274.9	428.1
Gross Domestic Saving	1.20E-2	1.68E-2	1.71E-2	2.04E-2	6.94E-2	2.00E+0	3.9	22.0	36.3	70.5	115.5
Gross National Saving	..	1.44E-2	1.56E-2	1.76E-2	5.77E-2	1.90E+0	2.6	18.2	32.2	61.9	99.3

(Billions of 1980 Chilean Pesos)

	1969	1970	1971	1972	1973	1974	1975	1976	1977	1978	1979
Gross National Product	797.6	819.5	904.4	898.9	844.9	847.9	718.9	749.6	833.1	900.8	970.5
GDP at Market Prices	821.6	838.4	914.5	903.9	853.8	860.7	747.0	773.8	849.7	920.7	997.2
Resource Balance	-86.3	-86.1	-100.5	-120.8	-107.7	-76.7	1.7	26.2	-0.3	-11.1	-29.7
Exports of Goods & NFServices	90.6	92.5	93.3	79.2	81.4	118.8	121.6	151.2	169.2	188.1	214.7
Imports of Goods & NFServices	176.9	178.6	193.8	199.9	189.1	195.5	119.9	125.0	169.5	199.2	244.3
Domestic Absorption	907.9	924.5	1,015.0	1,024.7	961.5	937.4	745.3	747.7	850.0	931.8	1,026.9
Private Consumption, etc.	653.5	651.3	734.6	783.9	731.7	608.5	532.6	534.9	617.1	665.2	709.2
General Gov't Consumption	95.7	101.4	114.0	120.5	122.6	134.3	120.5	120.4	125.0	133.5	145.7
Gross Domestic Investment	158.7	171.9	166.4	120.3	107.2	194.6	92.2	92.4	107.9	133.2	172.0
Fixed Investment	151.5	161.3	157.6	125.9	118.3	140.9	108.8	92.7	107.0	125.6	146.8
GDP at factor cost	741.5	749.9	825.4	827.0	764.4	726.7	642.3	667.4	727.4	793.3	873.5
Agriculture	60.4	62.3	61.6	56.5	50.8	64.4	67.3	66.2	73.2	70.5	74.8
Industry	342.4	348.9	383.5	375.2	348.5	368.2	287.9	299.2	316.8	339.8	370.8
Manufacturing	201.7	205.7	233.7	238.9	220.4	214.8	160.1	169.7	184.1	201.2	217.1
Services, etc.	418.9	427.3	469.4	472.3	454.5	428.1	391.9	408.4	459.7	510.4	551.6
Memo Items:											
Capacity to Import	205.2	186.1	177.8	148.4	166.9	202.2	111.3	151.1	155.8	171.4	217.8
Terms of Trade Adjustment	114.6	93.6	84.5	69.2	85.5	83.4	-10.3	-0.1	-13.3	-16.7	3.2
Gross Domestic Income	936.2	932.0	999.0	973.1	939.3	944.1	736.7	773.7	836.4	903.9	1,000.4
Gross National Income	912.2	913.1	988.9	968.1	930.5	931.3	708.6	749.5	819.7	884.1	973.7

DOMESTIC PRICES/DEFLATORS *(Index 1980 = 100)*

	1969	1970	1971	1972	1973	1974	1975	1976	1977	1978	1979
Overall (GDP)	8.35E-3	1.17E-2	1.39E-2	2.59E-2	1.34E-1	1.10E+0	4.7	16.6	33.9	53.0	77.4
Domestic Absorption	7.38E-3	1.06E-2	1.26E-2	2.37E-2	1.21E-1	9.75E-1	4.8	16.5	34.5	54.1	77.3
Agriculture	7.79E-3	1.08E-2	1.67E-2	3.45E-2	1.50E-1	8.12E-1	3.5	16.4	38.6	52.6	75.0
Industry	8.59E-3	1.17E-2	1.28E-2	2.36E-2	1.35E-1	1.20E+0	4.7	17.2	32.8	51.6	77.7
Manufacturing	8.53E-3	1.22E-2	1.33E-2	2.29E-2	1.41E-1	1.30E+0	4.5	17.6	34.0	54.3	75.5
Consumer Price Index	4.78E-3	6.33E-3	7.60E-3	1.33E-2	6.13E-2	3.71E-1	1.8	5.5	10.5	14.8	19.7

MANUFACTURING ACTIVITY

	1969	1970	1971	1972	1973	1974	1975	1976	1977	1978	1979
Employment (1987=100)	109.0	111.9	113.5	119.1	121.5	116.5	108.4	100.8	103.9	101.9	100.4
Real Earnings per Empl. (1987=100)	37.4	40.9	53.3	59.3	42.1	52.8	51.9	61.4	66.1	78.3	91.1
Real Output per Empl. (1987=100)	..	..	..	..	..	..	..	..	..	..	..
Earnings as % of Value Added	18.3	18.6	22.8	29.6	16.3	12.1	12.3	14.6	17.5	17.9	18.2

MONETARY HOLDINGS *(Billions of current Chilean Pesos)*

	1969	1970	1971	1972	1973	1974	1975	1976	1977	1978	1979
Money Supply, Broadly Defined	1.06E-2	1.60E-2	3.17E-2	8.00E-2	4.41E-1	2.02E+0	7.500	25.890	45.940	103.700	179.710
Money	6.06E-3	1.00E-2	2.13E-2	..	..	..	..	9.720	..	33.940	55.090
Currency Outside Banks	2.36E-3	4.38E-3	8.97E-3	..	..	..	..	4.480	..	16.390	24.870
Demand Deposits	3.70E-3	5.65E-3	1.23E-2	..	..	..	..	5.240	..	17.550	30.210
Quasi-Money	4.55E-3	5.96E-3	1.04E-2	..	..	..	..	16.170	..	69.760	124.620

(Billions of current Chilean Pesos)

	1969	1970	1971	1972	1973	1974	1975	1976	1977	1978	1979
GOVERNMENT DEFICIT (-) OR SURPLUS	..	..	..	-0.03	-0.08	-0.49	0.05	1.80	-3.20	-0.52	37.20
Current Revenue	..	..	..	0.07	0.32	2.60	12.30	39.70	89.10	154.20	252.40
Current Expenditure	..	..	..	0.08	0.31	2.10	9.70	33.10	81.40	135.60	195.10
Current Budget Balance	..	..	..	-0.01	0.01	0.47	2.60	6.50	7.70	18.60	57.30
Capital Receipts	..	..	..	..	0.01	0.04	0.12	1.40	2.40	3.20	11.10
Capital Payments	..	..	..	0.02	0.10	1.00	2.70	6.20	13.30	22.30	31.20

1980	1981	1982	1983	1984	1985	1986	1987	1988	1989 estimate	NOTES	CHILE
2,100	2,600	2,220	1,930	1,680	1,450	1,350	1,370	1,510	1,770	..	**CURRENT GNP PER CAPITA (US $)**
11,145	11,333	11,526	11,721	11,919	12,121	12,330	12,543	12,760	12,980	..	POPULATION (thousands)
				(Billions of current Chilean Pesos)							**USE AND ORIGIN OF RESOURCES**
1,043.4	1,220.3	1,149.0	1,430.7	1,710.6	2,291.2	2,882.1	3,814.4	4,984.0	6,224.0	..	Gross National Product (GNP)
-31.9	-52.8	-90.1	-127.0	-182.8	-285.4	-364.0	-345.4	-427.0	-521.0	..	Net Factor Income from Abroad
1,075.3	1,273.1	1,239.1	1,557.7	1,893.4	2,576.6	3,246.1	4,159.8	5,411.0	6,745.0	f	GDP at Market Prices
-44.7	-131.6	-23.5	42.4	-20.1	71.1	124.0	170.6	389.0	221.0	..	Resource Balance
245.4	209.0	239.9	374.5	459.5	749.2	994.2	1,394.3	2,022.0	2,541.0	..	Exports of Goods & NFServices
290.1	340.6	263.4	332.1	479.6	678.1	870.2	1,223.7	1,633.0	2,320.0	..	Imports of Goods & NFServices
1,120.0	1,404.7	1,262.6	1,515.3	1,913.5	2,505.6	3,122.1	3,989.2	5,022.0	6,524.0	..	Domestic Absorption
760.5	948.2	932.7	1,141.9	1,381.7	1,785.2	2,237.3	2,811.0	3,534.8	4,479.0	..	Private Consumption, etc.
133.9	167.4	190.1	220.7	273.8	367.1	410.7	475.1	568.5	667.0	..	General Gov't Consumption
225.6	289.0	139.9	152.8	258.0	353.2	474.1	703.1	918.7	1,378.0	..	Gross Domestic Investment
178.9	236.8	181.5	186.5	233.8	366.4	472.7	666.8	882.7	1,250.0	..	Fixed Investment
129.8	181.5	168.2	..	..	..	..	..	..	..		Indirect Taxes, net
945.5	1,091.7	1,070.9	..	..	..	..	..	..	..	B f	GDP at factor cost
77.7	80.7	69.4	88.8	..	..	..	..	..	..	..	Agriculture
401.1	466.4	438.5	604.2	..	..	..	..	..	..	..	Industry
230.5	284.2	233.5	320.8	..	..	..	..	..	..	..	Manufacturing
596.4	726.0	731.3	864.7	..	..	..	..	..	..	..	Services, etc.
180.9	157.4	116.4	195.2	237.9	424.3	598.1	873.7	1,307.7	1,599.0	..	Gross Domestic Saving
151.5	106.0	28.3	72.4	59.7	146.4	241.8	542.6	896.1	1,093.5	..	Gross National Saving
				(Billions of 1980 Chilean Pesos)							
1,043.4	1,085.3	905.2	899.1	935.3	978.0	1,033.6	1,114.4	1,186.3	1,313.1	..	Gross National Product
1,075.3	1,135.0	973.6	967.0	1,028.3	1,053.3	1,112.5	1,176.4	1,263.4	1,389.6	f	GDP at Market Prices
-44.7	-112.2	20.2	54.0	40.1	80.6	88.8	79.6	70.2	57.5	..	Resource Balance
245.4	223.4	234.0	235.4	251.4	268.7	295.1	321.0	340.7	396.3	..	Exports of Goods & NFServices
290.1	335.7	213.7	181.4	211.3	188.1	206.3	241.4	270.5	338.8	..	Imports of Goods & NFServices
1,120.0	1,247.3	953.3	913.0	988.2	972.7	1,023.7	1,096.8	1,193.2	1,332.1	..	Domestic Absorption
760.5	842.3	729.9	707.1	721.0	714.9	750.4	788.3	863.0	935.8	..	Private Consumption, etc.
133.9	129.7	127.9	127.2	129.1	128.8	126.1	123.4	129.4	131.2	..	General Gov't Consumption
225.6	275.3	95.5	78.7	138.1	129.0	147.2	185.0	200.9	265.1	..	Gross Domestic Investment
178.9	208.9	138.0	117.5	128.0	147.0	157.4	182.8	202.4	245.6	..	Fixed Investment
945.5	973.3	841.3	..	..	..	..	..	..	..	B f	GDP at factor cost
77.7	80.6	79.7	77.7	83.5	88.2	96.0	99.1	103.5	109.5	..	Agriculture
401.1	426.4	362.8	365.4	392.8	407.0	428.7	449.7	482.8	529.7	..	Industry
230.5	236.4	186.9	192.6	211.5	213.9	231.0	243.7	264.3	291.3	..	Manufacturing
596.4	628.0	531.0	523.9	552.0	558.0	587.7	627.6	677.1	750.4	..	Services, etc.
											Memo Items:
245.4	206.0	194.7	204.5	202.5	207.8	235.7	275.0	334.9	371.1	..	Capacity to Import
0.0	-17.4	-39.3	-30.9	-48.9	-60.9	-59.4	-46.0	-5.7	-25.2	..	Terms of Trade Adjustment
1,075.3	1,117.6	934.3	936.1	979.4	992.4	1,053.1	1,130.4	1,257.7	1,364.4	..	Gross Domestic Income
1,043.4	1,067.9	865.9	868.2	886.4	917.2	974.2	1,068.4	1,180.6	1,287.9	..	Gross National Income
				(Index 1980 = 100)							**DOMESTIC PRICES/DEFLATORS**
100.0	112.2	127.3	161.1	184.1	244.6	291.8	353.6	428.3	485.4	..	Overall (GDP)
100.0	112.6	132.4	166.0	193.6	257.6	305.0	363.7	420.9	489.8	..	Domestic Absorption
100.0	100.1	87.0	114.3	..	..	..	..	..	..	..	Agriculture
100.0	109.4	120.8	165.3	..	..	..	..	..	..	..	Industry
100.0	120.2	124.9	166.5	..	..	..	..	..	..	..	Manufacturing
26.6	31.9	35.0	44.6	53.4	69.8	83.4	100.0	114.7	134.2	f	Consumer Price Index
											MANUFACTURING ACTIVITY
94.9	88.3	69.8	69.5	77.4	85.1	97.3	100.0	101.2	..	..	Employment (1987 = 100)
101.4	122.3	126.2	114.1	106.8	98.0	99.6	100.0	106.0	..	..	Real Earnings per Empl. (1987 = 100)
..	..	..	..	..	..	..	..	..	..	..	Real Output per Empl. (1987 = 100)
18.4	23.0	20.3	17.1	15.4	13.7	16.6	16.8	16.6	..	..	Earnings as % of Value Added
				(Billions of current Chilean Pesos)							**MONETARY HOLDINGS**
307.160	411.790	577.100	701.710	891.170	717.680	..	..	..	..	..	Money Supply, Broadly Defined
85.300	81.860	92.150	112.190	130.280	..	..	..	..	..	..	Money
35.560	44.490	42.960	51.880	64.180	..	..	..	..	..	..	Currency Outside Banks
49.740	37.370	49.200	60.310	66.090	..	..	..	..	..	..	Demand Deposits
221.860	329.930	484.950	589.520	760.890	..	..	..	..	..	..	Quasi-Money
				(Billions of current Chilean Pesos)							**GOVERNMENT DEFICIT (-) OR SURPLUS**
58.20	33.00	-12.20	-40.90	-56.20	-60.70	-31.40	20.00	-12.20	..	..	Current Revenue
358.70	406.40	368.30	429.00	544.10	745.90	914.30	1,194.00	1,534.30	..	..	Current Revenue
272.30	341.40	395.00	463.00	563.00	725.80	861.50	1,064.40	1,413.80	..	..	Current Expenditure
86.50	64.90	-26.70	-34.00	-18.90	20.10	52.80	129.60	120.50	..	..	Current Budget Balance
8.40	13.00	6.10	3.10	3.30	6.20	6.60	11.60	16.00	..	..	Capital Receipts
36.60	44.90	-8.40	10.10	40.50	87.00	90.90	121.20	148.70	..	..	Capital Payments

CHILE	1969	1970	1971	1972	1973	1974	1975	1976	1977	1978	1979
FOREIGN TRADE (CUSTOMS BASIS)					*(Millions of current US dollars)*						
Value of Exports, fob	1,067.9	1,233.6	961.2	855.4	1,249.4	2,480.6	1,648.7	2,208.5	2,138.4	2,462.1	3,894.0
Nonfuel Primary Products	1,026.0	1,178.4	909.8	806.9	1,200.9	2,351.3	1,469.1	1,943.3	1,842.8	2,154.4	3,510.4
Fuels	0.7	0.4	0.9	2.8	2.6	19.9	14.3	34.6	58.6	41.8	54.9
Manufactures	41.2	54.8	50.5	45.7	46.0	109.3	165.4	230.5	237.0	265.9	328.7
Value of Imports, cif	891.0	980.0	1,049.0	1,168.0	1,562.0	2,137.0	1,733.0	1,672.0	2,418.0	3,276.0	4,777.0
Nonfuel Primary Products	213.2	210.0	271.1	384.3	518.4	847.8	405.7	544.7	431.0	714.7	802.7
Fuels	64.8	60.8	95.5	106.2	114.2	305.3	342.9	196.7	485.0	550.1	1,014.1
Manufactures	613.0	709.2	682.4	677.5	929.4	983.9	984.4	930.6	1,502.0	2,011.2	2,960.1
					(Index 1987 = 100)						
Terms of Trade	277.0	261.2	197.7	178.4	230.9	170.1	120.3	124.6	115.9	107.6	126.2
Export Prices, fob	67.6	67.7	53.9	55.2	94.6	109.9	72.5	78.5	74.8	78.0	107.3
Import Prices, cif	24.4	25.9	27.3	30.9	41.0	64.6	60.3	63.0	64.5	72.4	85.1
BALANCE OF PAYMENTS					*(Millions of current US dollars)*						
Exports of Goods & Services	..	1,274.0	1,142.4	984.7	1,467.5	2,351.2	1,842.0	2,425.0	2,621.0	2,984.0	4,746.0
Merchandise, fob	..	1,113.0	1,000.0	851.2	1,316.1	2,151.5	1,590.0	2,116.0	2,186.0	2,460.0	3,835.0
Nonfactor Services	..	134.0	130.4	132.5	146.6	175.6	248.0	297.0	417.0	481.0	785.0
Factor Services	..	27.0	12.0	1.1	4.8	24.1	4.0	12.0	18.0	43.0	126.0
Imports of Goods & Services	..	1,371.0	1,347.0	1,463.5	1,760.8	2,657.8	2,344.0	2,325.0	3,268.0	4,169.0	6,040.0
Merchandise, fob	..	867.0	926.8	1,011.9	1,329.2	1,901.4	1,520.0	1,473.0	2,151.0	2,886.0	4,190.0
Nonfactor Services	..	281.0	289.9	302.9	317.1	461.8	529.0	507.0	720.0	735.0	1,027.0
Factor Services	..	223.0	130.4	148.7	114.4	294.6	295.0	345.0	397.0	548.0	823.0
Long-Term Interest	..	104.4	108.5	50.0	64.9	114.2	195.4	253.6	264.8	384.3	582.6
Private Current Transfers, net	..	2.0	3.0	5.4	4.8	6.0	4.0	32.0	80.0	75.0	88.0
Workers' Remittances	..	..	..	..	..	..	..	..	..	..	..
Curr. A/C Bal before Off. Transf.	..	-95.0	-201.6	-473.4	-288.5	-300.7	-498.0	132.0	-567.0	-1,110.0	-1,206.0
Net Official Transfers	..	4.0	4.0	2.2	9.5	8.4	8.0	16.0	16.0	22.0	17.0
Curr. A/C Bal after Off. Transf.	..	-91.0	-197.6	-471.2	-279.0	-292.2	-490.0	148.0	-551.0	-1,088.0	-1,189.0
Long-Term Capital, net	..	140.0	-114.3	107.5	-63.2	16.8	172.0	46.0	49.0	1,510.0	1,685.1
Direct Investment	..	-79.0	-66.2	-1.1	-4.8	-556.8	50.0	-1.0	16.0	177.0	233.0
Long-Term Loans	..	448.2	-57.0	165.1	186.4	509.7	44.7	13.6	195.9	1,136.6	1,466.4
Disbursements	..	655.3	222.7	291.6	358.1	760.6	464.6	653.9	995.4	2,232.6	2,784.5
Repayments	..	207.1	279.7	126.5	171.7	250.9	419.9	640.3	799.5	1,096.0	1,318.1
Other Long-Term Capital	..	-229.2	8.9	-56.5	-244.8	64.0	77.3	33.4	-162.9	196.4	-14.3
Other Capital, net	..	37.3	53.0	226.7	388.5	154.6	92.6	84.4	633.3	307.6	551.3
Change in Reserves	..	-86.3	258.9	137.0	-46.3	120.8	225.4	-278.4	-131.3	-729.6	-1,047.4
Memo Item:					*(Chilean Pesos per US dollar)*						
Conversion Factor (Annual Avg)	0.0090	0.0120	0.0124	0.0195	0.1110	0.8320	4.9100	13.0500	21.5300	31.6600	37.2500
					(Millions of US dollars), outstanding at end of year						
EXTERNAL DEBT (Total)	..	2,570	2,618	3,050	3,275	4,522	4,762	4,849	5,884	7,374	9,361
Long-Term Debt (by debtor)	..	2,570	2,618	3,050	3,275	4,522	4,762	4,849	5,020	6,273	7,726
Central Bank, incl. IMF credit	..	75	122	366	443	774	950	1,123	1,093	1,337	1,577
Central Government	..	719	715	945	939	1,573	1,681	1,541	1,440	1,293	1,193
Rest of General Government	..	1	1	1	1	0	0	0	0	0	0
Non-financial Public Enterprises	..	1,171	1,255	1,244	1,384	1,528	1,384	1,301	1,392	1,945	2,068
Priv. Sector, incl non-guaranteed	..	604	525	495	508	647	745	882	1,095	1,697	2,888
Short-Term Debt	..	0	0	0	0	0	0	0	864	1,101	1,635
Memo Items:					*(Millions of US dollars)*						
Int'l Reserves Excluding Gold	296.0	341.8	170.1	96.8	121.6	41.1	55.9	405.1	426.5	1,090.1	1,938.3
Gold Holdings (at market price)	47.7	49.9	58.7	87.9	154.5	268.2	181.9	180.0	225.0	314.1	780.3
SOCIAL INDICATORS											
Total Fertility Rate	4.1	4.0	3.8	3.6	3.5	3.3	3.2	3.0	2.9	2.9	2.9
Infant Mortality Rate	85.0	80.0	75.0	70.0	65.2	60.4	55.6	50.8	46.0	41.4	36.8
Life Expectancy at Birth	61.8	62.4	63.0	63.6	64.3	65.0	65.7	66.4	67.2	67.9	68.7
Urban Population, % of total	74.5	75.2	75.8	76.4	77.1	77.7	78.3	78.9	79.5	80.0	80.6
Food Prod. per capita (1987=100)	92.5	96.7	95.1	88.2	78.0	88.8	92.0	88.4	95.7	89.7	95.8
Labor Force, Agriculture (%)	23.8	23.2	22.5	21.7	21.0	20.4	19.7	19.0	18.3	17.7	17.0
Labor Force, Female (%)	22.3	22.4	22.9	23.4	23.9	24.4	24.8	25.3	25.9	26.3	26.8
Primary Schl. Enroll. Ratio	..	107.0	..	..	..	..	118.0	116.0	117.0	118.0	119.0
Primary Schl. Enroll. Ratio, Female	..	107.0	..	..	..	..	118.0	116.0	117.0	117.0	118.0
Secondary Schl. Enroll. Ratio	..	39.0	..	..	..	..	48.0	49.0	50.0	52.0	55.0

1980	1981	1982	1983	1984	1985	1986	1987	1988	1989 estimate	NOTES	CHILE
				(Millions of current US dollars)							**FOREIGN TRADE (CUSTOMS BASIS)**
4,705.0	3,836.0	3,710.0	3,836.0	3,650.0	3,822.9	4,222.4	5,091.0	7,046.0	5,591.3	..	Value of Exports, fob
4,197.1	3,474.6	3,339.6	3,450.4	3,240.5	3,437.7	3,831.2	4,598.3	5,928.0	..	..	Nonfuel Primary Products
59.8	66.3	61.2	63.0	59.5	61.2	34.2	44.7	60.0	..	..	Fuels
448.1	295.1	309.2	322.6	350.0	324.0	357.0	448.0	1,058.0	511.1	..	Manufactures
6,185.0	6,331.0	4,117.0	3,186.0	3,770.0	3,300.0	3,157.0	4,023.0	4,843.0	5,171.7	..	Value of Imports, cif
1,144.4	962.4	659.6	513.1	616.2	494.1	318.9	265.3	223.2	..	..	Nonfuel Primary Products
1,140.5	925.0	660.3	509.6	679.7	582.3	191.1	330.9	269.8	..	..	Fuels
3,900.1	4,443.6	2,797.1	2,163.3	2,474.1	2,223.6	2,647.1	3,426.8	4,350.0	3,524.3	..	Manufactures
				(Index 1987 = 100)							
120.9	109.3	98.0	105.5	97.8	96.2	93.2	100.0	124.5	..	..	Terms of Trade
119.4	103.7	90.7	95.7	88.3	85.7	85.3	100.0	132.4	..	..	Export Prices, fob
98.8	94.9	92.6	90.7	90.4	89.1	91.5	100.0	106.3	..	..	Import Prices, cif
				(Millions of current US dollars)							**BALANCE OF PAYMENTS**
6,276.0	5,614.0	5,154.0	4,831.0	4,636.0	4,669.0	5,349.0	6,492.0	8,451.0	9,718.0	..	Exports of Goods & Services
4,705.0	3,836.0	3,706.0	3,831.0	3,650.0	3,804.0	4,199.0	5,224.0	7,052.0	8,080.0	..	Merchandise, fob
1,263.0	1,172.0	936.0	797.0	664.0	664.0	922.0	1,085.0	1,214.0	1,398.0	..	Nonfactor Services
308.0	606.0	512.0	203.0	322.0	201.0	228.0	183.0	185.0	240.0	..	Factor Services
8,360.0	10,455.0	7,567.0	6,045.0	6,854.0	6,058.0	6,570.0	7,426.0	8,795.0	10,863.0	..	Imports of Goods & Services
5,469.0	6,513.0	3,643.0	2,845.0	3,288.0	2,954.0	3,099.0	3,994.0	4,833.0	6,502.0	..	Merchandise, fob
1,554.0	1,741.0	1,377.0	1,204.0	1,181.0	967.0	1,318.0	1,506.0	1,808.0	2,114.0	..	Nonfactor Services
1,337.0	2,201.0	2,547.0	1,996.0	2,385.0	2,137.0	2,153.0	1,926.0	2,154.0	2,247.0	..	Factor Services
918.3	1,419.8	1,942.8	1,361.1	1,983.0	1,637.4	1,404.8	1,389.4	1,007.4	1,286.6	..	Long-Term Interest
64.0	36.0	41.0	54.0	47.0	47.0	40.0	65.0	63.0	58.0	..	Private Current Transfers, net
..	..	..	..	..	..	..	..	..	..	..	Workers' Remittances
-2,020.0	-4,805.0	-2,372.0	-1,160.0	-2,171.0	-1,342.0	-1,181.0	-869.0	-281.0	-1,087.0	..	Curr. A/C Bal before Off. Transf.
49.0	72.0	68.0	43.0	60.0	14.0	44.0	61.0	114.0	182.0	..	Net Official Transfers
-1,971.0	-4,733.0	-2,304.0	-1,117.0	-2,111.0	-1,328.0	-1,137.0	-808.0	-167.0	-905.0	..	Curr. A/C Bal after Off. Transf.
2,242.0	3,579.0	1,659.0	-3.0	3,516.0	900.0	804.0	833.0	1,310.0	645.0	..	Long-Term Capital, net
170.0	362.0	384.0	132.0	67.0	62.0	57.0	97.0	109.0	259.0	..	Direct Investment
2,089.4	3,400.0	1,428.1	1,048.8	1,207.2	1,120.6	810.2	597.5	1,086.8	676.5	..	Long-Term Loans
3,551.2	5,198.6	2,678.3	1,961.7	1,651.3	1,450.0	1,170.4	937.7	1,684.4	1,514.5	..	Disbursements
1,461.8	1,798.6	1,250.2	912.9	444.1	329.4	360.2	340.2	597.6	838.0	..	Repayments
-17.4	-183.0	-153.1	-1,183.8	2,241.8	-282.6	-63.2	138.5	114.2	-290.5	..	Other Long-Term Capital
974.2	1,221.0	-513.2	579.0	-1,386.3	329.7	106.1	33.3	-409.5	699.7	..	Other Capital, net
-1,245.2	-67.0	1,158.2	541.0	-18.7	98.3	226.9	-58.3	-733.5	-439.7	..	Change in Reserves
				(Chilean Pesos per US dollar)							**Memo Item:**
39.0000	39.0000	50.9100	78.8400	98.6600	161.0800	193.0200	219.5400	245.0500	267.1600	..	Conversion Factor (Annual Avg)
				(Millions of US dollars), outstanding at end of year							
12,081	15,664	17,315	17,928	19,737	20,384	21,144	21,502	19,578	18,241	..	**EXTERNAL DEBT (Total)**
9,521	12,675	13,977	15,329	17,823	18,716	19,455	19,485	17,376	15,268	..	Long-Term Debt (by debtor)
1,404	1,000	1,177	3,139	4,572	5,314	5,479	4,924	4,059	3,164	..	Central Bank, incl. IMF credit
1,105	982	965	998	3,905	5,887	7,995	9,961	9,365	7,461	..	Central Government
0	0	0	0	0	0	0	0	0	..	..	Rest of General Government
2,191	2,429	3,001	2,964	2,808	2,721	2,495	2,109	1,577	1,485	..	Non-financial Public Enterprises
4,821	8,263	8,834	8,228	6,537	4,793	3,486	2,491	2,374	3,158	..	Priv. Sector, incl non-guaranteed
2,560	2,989	3,338	2,599	1,914	1,668	1,689	2,017	2,202	2,973	..	Short-Term Debt
				(Millions of US dollars)							**Memo Items:**
3,123.2	3,213.3	1,815.0	2,036.3	2,302.9	2,449.9	2,351.3	2,503.8	3,160.5	..	..	Int'l Reserves Excluding Gold
1,004.5	676.5	782.2	583.3	471.4	500.0	597.7	740.2	627.3	..	..	Gold Holdings (at market price)
											SOCIAL INDICATORS
2.8	2.8	2.8	2.8	2.8	2.8	2.7	2.7	2.7	2.6	..	Total Fertility Rate
32.2	27.6	23.0	22.4	21.8	21.2	20.6	20.0	19.6	19.1	..	Infant Mortality Rate
69.5	70.2	71.0	71.1	71.2	71.3	71.4	71.5	71.7	71.8	..	Life Expectancy at Birth
81.2	81.7	82.2	82.6	83.1	83.6	84.0	84.4	84.8	85.2	..	Urban Population, % of total
95.1	101.4	97.9	91.4	95.5	95.2	98.6	100.0	103.5	107.9	..	Food Prod. per capita (1987=100)
16.5	..	..	..	..	..	..	..	..	..	..	Labor Force, Agriculture (%)
27.2	27.4	27.6	27.7	27.8	28.0	28.1	28.2	28.3	28.4	..	Labor Force, Female (%)
109.0	..	108.0	108.0	107.0	106.0	105.0	103.0	102.0	..	..	Primary Schl. Enroll. Ratio
108.0	..	106.0	107.0	106.0	104.0	104.0	..	101.0	..	..	Primary Schl. Enroll. Ratio, Female
53.0	..	58.0	63.0	66.0	67.0	68.0	70.0	74.0	..	..	Secondary Schl. Enroll. Ratio

CHINA	1969	1970	1971	1972	1973	1974	1975	1976	1977	1978	1979
CURRENT GNP PER CAPITA (US $)	110	130	130	130	150	160	180	170	190	220	260
POPULATION (millions)	796	818	841	862	882	900	916	931	944	956	969
USE AND ORIGIN OF RESOURCES					*(Billions of current Chinese Yuan)*						
Gross National Product (GNP)	192.7	229.5	247.5	254.5	267.1	279.6	298.1	289.0	314.8	358.8	400.2
Net Factor Income from Abroad	0.0	0.0	0.0	0.0	-9.0	0.0	0.0	0.0	0.0	0.0	0.4
GDP at Market Prices	192.7	229.5	247.5	254.5	276.1	279.6	298.1	289.0	314.8	358.8	399.9
Resource Balance	1.8	0.5	2.2	2.6	2.2	-0.4	0.7	1.6	1.8	-0.6	-1.3
Exports of Goods & NFServices	6.5	6.2	7.5	9.1	12.8	15.2	15.6	14.7	15.3	17.7	23.1
Imports of Goods & NFServices	4.8	5.7	5.3	6.5	10.6	15.6	14.9	13.1	13.5	18.3	24.4
Domestic Absorption	191.0	229.0	245.2	251.9	273.9	280.0	297.4	287.3	313.0	359.5	401.2
Private Consumption, etc.	123.4	131.1	137.3	145.6	155.3	160.3	165.1	164.0	177.0	188.8	215.4
General Gov't Consumption	29.1	32.5	36.2	37.3	38.5	38.8	41.9	41.2	44.7	50.8	46.2
Gross Domestic Investment	38.5	65.4	71.7	69.0	80.1	80.9	90.4	82.2	91.2	119.8	139.5
Fixed Investment	..	..	..	..	..	..	..	..	..	..	100.7
Indirect Taxes, net	..										
GDP at factor cost	..	..	..	..	..	..	..	..	..	..	..
Agriculture	82.0	90.4	93.7	93.9	102.9	107.0	109.9	110.6	108.6	117.6	146.4
Industry	74.6	97.2	109.8	114.9	124.2	124.6	141.0	135.0	152.2	177.2	194.3
Manufacturing	55.9	75.0	84.7	88.3	94.8	92.1	104.0	96.0	110.0	131.3	145.2
Services, etc.	36.2	42.0	44.0	45.7	49.0	48.1	47.2	43.4	54.0	64.0	59.2
Gross Domestic Saving	40.2	65.9	74.0	71.6	82.3	80.6	91.1	83.8	93.0	119.2	138.3
Gross National Saving	..	65.9	73.9	71.6	73.3	80.6	91.1	83.8	93.0	120.2	139.7
					(Billions of 1987 Chinese Yuan)						
Gross National Product	275.68	347.66	374.61	388.49	420.74	425.19	460.35	435.49	469.72	528.58	566.12
GDP at Market Prices	275.68	347.67	374.62	388.50	420.75	425.20	460.36	435.50	469.73	528.59	565.58
Resource Balance	8.34	2.95	11.46	12.12	9.77	1.30	7.90	6.39	3.12	-11.37	-15.56
Exports of Goods & NFServices	31.08	28.43	33.93	39.96	44.86	42.67	49.93	41.64	40.81	42.16	52.75
Imports of Goods & NFServices	22.73	25.49	22.47	27.84	35.09	41.37	42.03	35.25	37.69	53.53	68.30
Domestic Absorption	267.34	344.72	363.15	376.38	410.98	423.89	452.46	429.11	466.61	539.96	581.14
Private Consumption, etc.	197.42	232.61	239.24	255.04	272.59	283.49	295.89	284.61	306.38	334.91	353.96
General Gov't Consumption	18.50	20.64	23.03	23.67	24.43	24.44	26.30	25.75	27.25	30.76	32.24
Gross Domestic Investment	51.42	91.47	100.88	97.67	113.96	115.96	130.27	118.74	132.98	174.29	194.94
Fixed Investment	..	..	..	..	..	..	..	..	..	..	140.65
GDP at factor cost	..	..	..	..	..	..	..	..	..	..	..
Agriculture	169.99	187.17	191.35	188.73	205.19	213.40	217.85	219.94	215.23	226.90	241.43
Industry	82.24	112.16	127.38	134.16	145.74	147.21	167.51	160.79	182.89	212.60	229.83
Manufacturing	..	..	..	..	..	..	..	..	..	..	..
Services, etc.	41.48	60.71	64.45	71.04	75.83	70.31	79.22	57.12	72.25	88.41	92.88
Memo Items:											
Capacity to Import	31.18	27.87	32.02	38.80	42.40	40.36	43.92	39.62	42.63	51.66	64.66
Terms of Trade Adjustment	0.10	-0.57	-1.91	-1.16	-2.46	-2.32	-6.01	-2.02	1.82	9.51	11.91
Gross Domestic Income	275.78	347.10	372.71	387.33	418.29	422.88	454.36	433.49	471.55	538.09	577.50
Gross National Income	275.77	347.10	372.70	387.32	418.28	422.87	454.35	433.48	471.54	538.08	578.04
DOMESTIC PRICES/DEFLATORS					*(Index 1987 = 100)*						
Overall (GDP)	69.9	66.0	66.1	65.5	65.6	65.8	64.7	66.4	67.0	67.9	70.7
Domestic Absorption	71.4	66.4	67.5	66.9	66.6	66.1	65.7	67.0	67.1	66.6	69.0
Agriculture	48.2	48.3	49.0	49.7	50.1	50.1	50.4	50.3	50.4	51.8	60.6
Industry	90.7	86.7	86.2	85.7	85.2	84.7	84.1	84.0	83.2	83.4	84.6
Manufacturing	..	..	..	..	..	..	..	..	..	..	..
Consumer Price Index	..	..	..	..	..	..	61.7	61.9	63.5	64.0	65.3
MANUFACTURING ACTIVITY											
Employment (1987=100)	..	..	..	..	..	..	..	..	..	..	..
Real Earnings per Empl. (1987=100)	..	..	..	..	..	..	..	..	..	..	..
Real Output per Empl. (1987=100)	..	..	..	..	..	..	..	..	..	..	..
Earnings as % of Value Added	..	..	..	..	..	..	..	..	..	..	..
MONETARY HOLDINGS					*(Billions of current Chinese Yuan)*						
Money Supply, Broadly Defined	..	..	..	..	..	..	..	..	85.84	88.97	132.78
Money	..	..	..	..	..	..	..	..	58.01	58.04	92.15
Currency Outside Banks	..	..	..	..	..	..	..	..	19.54	21.20	26.77
Demand Deposits	..	..	..	..	..	..	..	..	38.47	36.84	65.38
Quasi-Money	..	..	..	..	..	..	..	..	27.83	30.93	40.63
GOVERNMENT DEFICIT (-) OR SURPLUS					*(Millions of current Chinese Yuan)*						
Current Revenue	..	..	..	..	..	..	..	..	..	..	..
Current Expenditure	..	..	..	..	..	..	..	..	..	..	..
Current Budget Balance	..	..	..	..	..	..	..	..	..	..	..
Capital Receipts	..	..	..	..	..	..	..	..	..	..	..
Capital Payments	..	..	..	..	..	..	..	..	..	..	..

1980	1981	1982	1983	1984	1985	1986	1987	1988	1989 estimate	NOTES	CHINA
300	320	320	320	320	330	310	310	330	360	..	**CURRENT GNP PER CAPITA (US $)**
981	994	1,008	1,022	1,033	1,045	1,058	1,073	1,088	1,105	..	**POPULATION (millions)**
											USE AND ORIGIN OF RESOURCES
			(Billions of current Chinese Yuan)								
447.4	477.8	518.9	579.9	694.8	854.9	972.1	1,132.8	1,383.2	1,567.3	..	Gross National Product (GNP)
0.3	0.3	0.4	1.4	2.4	0.8	0.1	-2.9	-2.6	-5.8	..	Net Factor Income from Abroad
447.2	477.5	518.6	578.5	692.4	854.1	972.0	1,135.7	1,385.8	1,573.1	f	GDP at Market Prices
-0.5	3.9	10.0	6.3	2.7	-36.1	-31.0	-1.1	-12.4	-11.3	..	Resource Balance
28.8	41.4	46.5	48.5	66.2	88.0	117.1	159.8	193.2	213.8	..	Exports of Goods & NFServices
29.3	37.5	36.5	42.3	63.6	124.1	148.2	160.8	205.6	225.1	..	Imports of Goods & NFServices
447.3	473.6	508.5	572.2	689.8	890.2	1,003.0	1,136.8	1,398.2	1,584.4	..	Domestic Absorption
251.2	279.3	304.1	332.9	383.1	478.5	544.0	621.8	781.7	..	..	Private Consumption, etc.
52.1	54.9	50.4	63.3	82.5	81.0	76.7	70.0	77.7	..	..	General Gov't Consumption
144.0	139.4	154.0	176.0	224.2	330.7	382.2	445.0	538.9	572.2	..	Gross Domestic Investment
107.4	96.1	123.0	143.0	183.3	254.3	302.0	364.1	449.7	400.0	..	Fixed Investment
..	..	..	..	..	..	..	..	..	..	..	Indirect Taxes, net
..	..	..	..	..	..	..	..	..	..	B f	GDP at factor cost
160.7	182.9	209.7	234.9	275.9	302.7	335.2	384.3	449.5	..	..	Agriculture
218.7	223.0	237.1	261.2	308.3	384.2	440.5	519.4	639.5	..	..	Industry
160.7	161.7	172.4	188.3	226.3	284.3	320.5	..	..	..	..	Manufacturing
67.7	71.6	71.8	82.3	108.2	167.2	196.4	232.0	296.7	..	..	Services, etc.
143.9	143.3	164.0	182.2	226.8	294.6	351.2	443.9	526.4	560.9	..	Gross Domestic Saving
145.1	144.4	165.4	184.5	229.9	295.9	352.2	441.9	522.6	554.4	..	Gross National Saving
			(Billions of 1987 Chinese Yuan)								
602.18	631.63	684.15	752.48	853.54	957.70	1,032.07	1,132.77	1,245.57	1,282.48	..	Gross National Product
601.79	631.27	683.67	750.68	850.67	956.80	1,031.99	1,135.71	1,247.92	1,287.29	f	GDP at Market Prices
-14.87	-8.96	5.21	2.13	-2.00	-43.69	-21.50	-1.06	-6.98	-21.79	..	Resource Balance
64.76	79.63	84.55	85.01	99.49	109.11	134.69	159.79	187.33	195.88	..	Exports of Goods & NFServices
79.63	88.59	79.34	82.87	101.49	152.80	156.19	160.85	194.31	217.66	..	Imports of Goods & NFServices
616.66	640.23	678.45	748.54	852.67	1,000.49	1,053.50	1,136.77	1,254.90	1,309.07	..	Domestic Absorption
391.34	412.78	429.87	470.48	522.20	570.42	584.99	621.85	685.43	746.18	..	Private Consumption, etc.
33.95	45.40	48.06	52.49	58.06	61.58	64.34	69.96	78.36	85.58	..	General Gov't Consumption
191.37	182.05	200.52	225.58	272.40	368.48	404.17	444.96	491.11	477.31	..	Gross Domestic Investment
142.74	125.47	160.20	183.27	222.72	283.39	319.30	364.09	409.80	333.65	..	Fixed Investment
..	..	..	..	..	..	..	..	..	..	B f	GDP at factor cost
237.08	253.90	283.62	307.72	347.73	353.64	366.73	384.32	396.62	409.72	..	Agriculture
254.88	259.21	274.77	301.70	346.64	414.59	454.39	519.36	626.87	678.90	..	Industry
..	..	..	..	..	..	..	..	..	..	..	Manufacturing
105.96	116.58	125.07	141.26	156.29	188.56	210.88	232.03	224.43	198.67	..	Services, etc.
											Memo Items:
78.21	97.75	101.16	95.13	105.74	108.33	123.51	159.79	182.56	206.77	..	Capacity to Import
13.46	18.12	16.61	10.12	6.25	-0.77	-11.18	0.00	-4.77	10.90	..	Terms of Trade Adjustment
615.24	649.39	700.28	760.79	856.91	956.02	1,020.81	1,135.71	1,243.15	1,298.18	..	Gross Domestic Income
615.64	649.74	700.77	762.60	859.78	956.93	1,020.89	1,132.77	1,240.80	1,293.38	..	Gross National Income
			(Index 1987 = 100)								**DOMESTIC PRICES/DEFLATORS**
74.3	75.6	75.9	77.1	81.4	89.3	94.2	100.0	111.0	122.2	..	Overall (GDP)
72.5	74.0	75.0	76.4	80.9	89.0	95.2	100.0	111.4	121.0	..	Domestic Absorption
67.8	72.0	73.9	76.3	79.4	85.6	91.4	100.0	113.3	..	..	Agriculture
85.8	86.0	86.3	86.6	89.0	92.7	96.9	100.0	102.0	..	..	Industry
..	..	..	..	..	..	..	..	..	..	..	Manufacturing
70.1	71.9	73.4	74.8	76.8	85.9	91.9	100.0	120.7	140.4	..	Consumer Price Index
											MANUFACTURING ACTIVITY
..	..	..	..	..	..	..	..	..	..	..	Employment (1987=100)
..	..	..	..	..	..	..	..	..	..	..	Real Earnings per Empl. (1987=100)
..	..	..	..	..	..	..	..	..	..	..	Real Output per Empl. (1987=100)
..	..	..	..	..	13.3	14.5	..	..	..	..	Earnings as % of Value Added
			(Billions of current Chinese Yuan)								**MONETARY HOLDINGS**
167.11	197.77	226.57	271.28	359.85	487.53	634.86	795.74	960.21	1,139.31	..	Money Supply, Broadly Defined
114.88	134.52	148.84	174.89	251.47	301.73	385.90	457.40	548.74	583.42	..	Money
34.62	39.63	43.91	52.98	79.21	98.78	121.84	145.45	213.26	234.21	..	Currency Outside Banks
80.26	94.89	104.93	121.91	172.26	202.95	264.06	311.95	335.48	349.21	..	Demand Deposits
52.23	63.25	77.73	96.39	108.38	185.80	248.96	338.34	411.47	555.89	..	Quasi-Money
			(Millions of current Chinese Yuan)								**GOVERNMENT DEFICIT (-) OR SURPLUS**
..	..	..	..	..	..	..	..	..	..	..	Current Revenue
..	..	..	..	..	..	..	..	..	..	..	Current Expenditure
..	..	..	..	..	..	..	..	..	..	..	Current Budget Balance
..	..	..	..	..	..	..	..	..	..	..	Capital Receipts
..	..	..	..	..	..	..	..	..	..	f	Capital Payments

CHINA	1969	1970	1971	1972	1973	1974	1975	1976	1977	1978	1979
FOREIGN TRADE (CUSTOMS BASIS)					*(Millions of current US dollars)*						
Value of Exports, fob	2,200	2,260	2,640	3,440	5,820	6,950	7,260	6,860	7,590	9,115	12,525
Nonfuel Primary Products	1,177	1,220	1,380	1,768	2,878	3,181	3,170	2,724	2,843	2,999	3,391
Fuels	18	21	26	26	78	617	1,033	826	1,068	1,409	2,654
Manufactures	1,004	1,019	1,233	1,647	2,864	3,152	3,056	3,310	3,680	4,708	6,480
Value of Imports, cif	1,830	2,330	2,210	2,860	5,160	7,620	7,486	6,578	7,214	10,893	15,675
Nonfuel Primary Products	912	939	814	1,288	2,497	3,331	2,337	1,965	2,931	3,673	4,991
Fuels	4	11	6	12	5	48	50	14	59	66	21
Manufactures	915	1,381	1,390	1,560	2,658	4,241	5,099	4,599	4,224	7,155	10,662
					(Index 1987 = 100)						
Terms of Trade	101.2	101.6	104.3	107.5	110.7	115.7	114.1	113.5	111.7	106.0	108.1
Export Prices, fob	33.6	33.5	35.2	41.1	58.0	71.5	66.6	67.9	74.5	77.1	90.4
Import Prices, cif	33.2	33.0	33.8	38.3	52.4	61.8	58.4	59.8	66.7	72.8	83.6
BALANCE OF PAYMENTS					*(Millions of current US dollars)*						
Exports of Goods & Services	..	..	..	..	..	..	..	..	8,770	10,749	15,143
Merchandise, fob	..	2,309	2,803	3,652	5,677	7,108	7,689	6,943	8,050	9,750	13,660
Nonfactor Services	..	128	81	132	103	128	139	440	500	763	1,178
Factor Services	..	..	..	..	..	..	..	..	220	236	305
Imports of Goods & Services	..	..	..	..	..	..	..	..	8,286	11,134	15,731
Merchandise, fob	..	2,280	2,144	2,819	5,031	7,791	7,926	6,660	7,627	9,986	14,369
Nonfactor Services	..	238	862	1,099	220	168	171	465	521	904	1,301
Factor Services	..	..	..	..	..	..	..	..	138	244	61
Long-Term Interest	..	0	0	0	0	0	0	0	0	0	61
Private Current Transfers, net	..	0	0	0	0	0	0	0	0	597	656
Workers' Remittances	..	..	..	..	..	..	..	..	..	0	0
Curr. A/C Bal before Off. Transf.	..	-81	-122	-134	529	-723	-269	258	484	212	68
Net Official Transfers	..	0	0	0	0	0	0	0	-70	-69	-30
Curr. A/C Bal after Off. Transf.	..	-81	-122	-134	529	-723	-269	258	414	143	38
Long-Term Capital, net	..	..	..	..	..	..	..	..	-990	-761	852
Direct Investment	..	..	..	..	..	..	..	..	..	..	..
Long-Term Loans	..	0	0	0	0	0	0	0	0	583	1,779
Disbursements	..	0	0	0	0	0	0	0	0	583	1,779
Repayments	..	0	0	0	0	0	0	0	0	0	0
Other Long-Term Capital	..	..	..	..	..	..	..	..	-990	-1,344	-927
Other Capital, net	..	..	..	..	..	..	..	..	670	-130	2
Change in Reserves	..	..	..	..	..	..	..	..	-94	748	-892
Memo Item:					*(Chinese Yuan per US dollar)*						
Conversion Factor (Annual Avg)	2.460	2.460	2.460	2.250	1.990	1.960	1.860	1.940	1.860	1.680	1.550
				(Millions of US dollars), outstanding at end of year							
EXTERNAL DEBT (Total)	..	0	0	0	0	0	0	0	0	623	2,183
Long-Term Debt (by debtor)	..	0	0	0	0	0	0	0	0	623	2,183
Central Bank, incl. IMF credit	..	0	0	0	0	0	0	0	0	0	76
Central Government	..	0	0	0	0	0	0	0	0	27	226
Rest of General Government	..	0	0	0	0	0	0	0	0	0	0
Non-financial Public Enterprises	..	0	0	0	0	0	0	0	0	596	1,880
Priv. Sector, incl non-guaranteed	..	0	0	0	0	0	0	0	0	0	0
Short-Term Debt	..	0	0	0	0	0	0	0	0	0	0
Memo Items:					*(Millions of US dollars)*						
Int'l Reserves Excluding Gold	..	..	..	..	..	..	..	..	2,345.0	1,557.0	2,154.0
Gold Holdings (at market price)	..	..	..	..	..	..	..	..	2,111.0	2,893.0	6,554.0
SOCIAL INDICATORS											
Total Fertility Rate	5.8	5.8	5.1	4.9	4.4	3.8	3.4	2.9	2.7	2.6	2.3
Infant Mortality Rate	73.0	69.0	66.0	61.0	56.0	51.0	46.0	41.0	39.0	38.0	43.0
Life Expectancy at Birth	61.0	61.7	62.5	63.2	63.8	64.3	64.8	65.2	65.6	66.1	66.5
Urban Population, % of total	17.6	17.5	17.4	17.3	17.2	17.2	17.3	17.4	17.5	17.8	18.5
Food Prod. per capita (1987=100)	62.5	67.1	68.7	66.5	70.2	69.3	70.2	69.0	67.3	73.4	77.9
Labor Force, Agriculture (%)	78.8	78.3	77.9	77.5	77.0	76.7	76.3	75.8	75.4	75.0	74.6
Labor Force, Female (%)	41.6	41.7	41.8	42.0	42.1	42.3	42.4	42.6	42.7	42.9	43.0
Primary Schl. Enroll. Ratio	..	89.0	..	..	..	..	126.0	..	106.0	124.0	122.0
Primary Schl. Enroll. Ratio, Female	..	..	..	..	..	..	115.0	..	..	114.0	112.0
Secondary Schl. Enroll. Ratio	..	24.0	..	..	..	..	47.0	..	83.0	63.0	56.0

1980	1981	1982	1983	1984	1985	1986	1987	1988	1989 estimate	NOTES	CHINA
				(Millions of current US dollars)							**FOREIGN TRADE (CUSTOMS BASIS)**
18,265	21,554	21,820	22,175	25,922	27,326	31,148	39,542	47,540	46,022	..	Value of Exports, fob
5,088	5,127	4,864	4,950	5,749	6,762	7,746	7,769	9,208	..	..	Nonfuel Primary Products
4,388	4,677	5,314	4,656	6,027	7,144	3,677	5,043	3,792	..	..	Fuels
8,789	11,750	11,642	12,569	14,146	13,420	19,725	26,730	34,540	29,246	..	Manufactures
19,550	19,482	18,546	21,346	27,350	42,526	43,172	43,392	55,278	56,890	..	Value of Imports, cif
6,910	6,863	7,275	5,689	6,123	7,040	4,905	5,957	4,571	..	..	Nonfuel Primary Products
177	108	180	111	139	172	515	700	841	..	..	Fuels
12,463	12,512	11,091	15,546	21,088	35,314	37,752	36,735	49,866		..	Manufactures
				(Index 1987 = 100)							
111.7	111.2	110.3	107.4	113.5	115.2	99.5	100.0	97.1	..	..	Terms of Trade
105.8	103.5	98.8	91.8	93.0	91.6	89.7	100.0	105.1	..	..	Export Prices, fob
94.7	93.0	89.6	85.4	82.0	79.5	90.1	100.0	108.2	..	..	Import Prices, cif
				(Millions of current US dollars)							**BALANCE OF PAYMENTS**
20,382	24,987	25,601	26,082	30,564	31,435	35,028	43,958	53,410	57,859	f	Exports of Goods & Services
18,188	22,010	22,330	22,230	26,129	27,350	30,942	39,437	47,541	52,486	..	Merchandise, fob
1,682	2,280	2,254	2,324	2,427	2,607	2,986	3,494	4,365	3,697	..	Nonfactor Services
512	697	1,017	1,528	2,008	1,478	1,100	1,027	1,504	1,676	..	Factor Services
20,267	22,551	20,103	22,212	28,407	43,448	43,982	45,033	57,454	62,349	f	Imports of Goods & Services
18,294	20,185	17,680	19,616	25,135	38,745	39,343	39,629	50,665	54,233	..	Merchandise, fob
1,656	1,827	1,600	1,775	2,275	3,507	3,561	3,587	4,586	4,909	..	Nonfactor Services
317	539	823	821	997	1,196	1,078	1,817	2,203	3,207	..	Factor Services
317	518	541	523	610	586	644	1,126	1,610	2,508	..	Long-Term Interest
640	464	530	436	305	171	255	249	-331	-211	..	Private Current Transfers, net
0	0	541	446	317	180	208	166	129	138	..	Workers' Remittances
755	2,900	6,028	4,306	2,462	-11,842	-8,699	-826	-4,375	-4,701	..	Curr. A/C Bal before Off. Transf.
-70	108	-44	75	137	73	124	-25	3	171	..	Net Official Transfers
685	3,008	5,984	4,381	2,599	-11,769	-8,575	-851	-4,372	-4,530	..	Curr. A/C Bal after Off. Transf.
1,830	523	453	1,097	1,471	4,264	6,934	5,815	7,053	3,212	f	Long-Term Capital, net
57	265	430	636	1,124	1,030	1,425	1,669	2,344	1,400	..	Direct Investment
1,927	596	535	986	1,070	4,006	4,851	6,130	6,781	4,500	..	Long-Term Loans
2,540	1,800	1,837	2,375	2,357	5,302	6,725	8,047	9,130	6,902	..	Disbursements
613	1,204	1,302	1,389	1,287	1,297	1,874	1,916	2,349	2,401	..	Repayments
-154	-338	-512	-525	-723	-772	658	-1,984	-2,072	-2,688	..	Other Long-Term Capital
-1,848	-1,324	-346	-1,911	-2,863	2,217	-504	-738	-1,018	-412	f	Other Capital, net
-667	-2,207	-6,091	-3,567	-1,207	5,288	2,145	-4,226	-1,663	1,730	..	Change in Reserves
				(Chinese Yuan per US dollar)							**Memo Item:**
1.500	1.700	1.890	1.980	2.320	2.940	3.450	3.720	3.720	3.770	..	Conversion Factor (Annual Avg)
			(Millions of US dollars), outstanding at end of year								
4,503	5,797	8,359	9,609	12,082	16,722	23,746	35,304	42,406	44,857	..	**EXTERNAL DEBT (Total)**
4,503	5,797	6,059	5,625	6,482	10,303	17,670	27,083	33,600	37,950	..	Long-Term Debt (by debtor)
363	1,461	1,517	1,123	1,240	3,809	6,561	10,587	14,198	15,649	..	Central Bank, incl. IMF credit
575	976	1,508	1,990	2,464	4,195	6,004	8,011	8,556	8,794	..	Central Government
0	0	0	0	0	1	3	3	3	2	..	Rest of General Government
3,566	3,360	3,033	2,512	2,779	2,299	5,103	8,482	10,844	13,459	..	Non-financial Public Enterprises
0	0	0	0	0	0	0	0	0	47	..	Priv. Sector, incl non-guaranteed
0	0	2,300	3,984	5,600	6,419	6,076	8,221	8,806	6,907	..	Short-Term Debt
				(Millions of US dollars)							**Memo Items:**
2,545.0	5,058.0	11,349.0	14,987.0	17,366.0	12,728.0	11,453.0	16,305.0	18,541.0	17,960.0	..	Int'l Reserves Excluding Gold
7,546.0	5,048.0	5,803.0	4,845.0	3,915.0	4,153.0	4,964.0	6,148.0	5,210.0	5,093.0	..	Gold Holdings (at market price)
											SOCIAL INDICATORS
2.5	3.0	2.3	2.3	2.2	2.3	2.3	2.4	2.4	2.4	..	Total Fertility Rate
41.0	41.0	39.0	37.6	36.2	34.8	33.4	32.0	31.1	30.3	..	Infant Mortality Rate
66.9	67.4	67.8	68.1	68.5	68.8	69.1	69.5	69.7	69.9	..	Life Expectancy at Birth
19.2	19.4	20.2	23.5	31.9	36.6	41.4	46.6	49.6	52.8	..	Urban Population, % of total
76.9	78.4	84.1	89.5	95.0	94.6	97.6	100.0	98.6	100.1	..	Food Prod. per capita (1987=100)
74.2	..	..	..	..	..	..	..	..	..	..	Labor Force, Agriculture (%)
43.2	43.2	43.2	43.2	43.2	43.2	43.2	43.2	43.2	43.2	..	Labor Force, Female (%)
112.0	..	112.0	113.0	118.0	124.0	129.0	132.0	..	..	..	Primary Schl. Enroll. Ratio
103.0	106.0	101.0	102.0	107.0	114.0	120.0	124.0			..	Primary Schl. Enroll. Ratio, Female
46.0	..	36.0	35.0	37.0	39.0	42.0	43.0	..	..	..	Secondary Schl. Enroll. Ratio

COLOMBIA	1969	1970	1971	1972	1973	1974	1975	1976	1977	1978	1979
CURRENT GNP PER CAPITA (US $)	320	340	360	390	430	500	550	600	680	840	1,010
POPULATION (thousands)	20,805	21,360	21,877	22,394	22,916	23,448	23,991	24,550	25,127	25,719	26,314
USE AND ORIGIN OF RESOURCES					*(Billions of current Colombian Pesos)*						
Gross National Product (GNP)	110	129	152	185	238	317	397	521	708	902	1,182
Net Factor Income from Abroad	-3	-3	-4	-4	-5	-5	-8	-11	-8	-8	-7
GDP at Market Prices	113	133	156	190	243	322	405	532	716	909	1,189
Resource Balance	-1	-2	-6	-1	2	-4	7	17	26	26	21
Exports of Goods & NFServices	15	19	20	27	37	47	64	91	121	151	181
Imports of Goods & NFServices	16	21	26	28	35	50	57	74	95	125	160
Domestic Absorption	114	135	162	190	241	326	398	515	690	884	1,168
Private Consumption, etc.	83	96	115	138	173	229	293	378	500	640	841
General Gov't Consumption	10	12	17	18	23	28	36	44	55	78	111
Gross Domestic Investment	21	27	30	34	44	69	69	93	134	166	216
Fixed Investment	19	24	27	30	38	53	62	85	104	140	183
Indirect Taxes, net	9	10	11	13	17	22	32	50	75	99	123
GDP at factor cost	104	123	145	177	227	300	373	483	641	810	1,066
Agriculture	29	33	37	46	59	79	97	126	179	210	255
Industry	31	37	43	55	74	98	118	164	217	273	351
Manufacturing	22	27	32	41	55	75	94	129	171	211	267
Services, etc.	53	63	76	89	110	146	190	242	320	427	583
Gross Domestic Saving	20	24	24	33	47	66	76	110	161	192	237
Gross National Saving	..	21	20	29	42	61	69	101	154	186	234
					(Billions of 1987 Colombian Pesos)						
Gross National Product	3,685.6	3,980.9	4,229.7	4,552.0	4,865.0	5,158.9	5,257.5	5,504.5	5,749.9	6,240.1	6,591.5
GDP at Market Prices	3,852.8	4,126.4	4,373.3	4,707.5	5,023.7	5,311.8	5,425.1	5,683.5	5,915.6	6,415.4	6,761.4
Resource Balance	46.9	-53.5	-122.6	-3.6	3.3	-20.9	159.1	54.6	-50.4	-28.0	41.9
Exports of Goods & NFServices	598.4	604.6	634.9	717.9	738.7	698.8	799.7	774.2	739.4	925.5	1,002.8
Imports of Goods & NFServices	551.6	658.1	757.6	721.5	735.4	719.8	640.6	719.6	789.8	953.4	960.9
Domestic Absorption	3,805.9	4,179.8	4,495.9	4,711.0	5,020.4	5,332.8	5,266.0	5,628.9	5,966.0	6,443.4	6,719.5
Private Consumption, etc.	2,678.5	2,869.3	3,053.6	3,313.8	3,491.7	3,602.2	3,756.4	4,004.0	4,131.8	4,471.1	4,684.5
General Gov't Consumption	301.9	345.5	436.1	415.5	457.8	447.3	457.6	475.0	497.5	543.1	610.4
Gross Domestic Investment	825.5	965.1	1,006.3	981.7	1,070.9	1,283.3	1,052.0	1,150.0	1,336.8	1,429.2	1,424.7
Fixed Investment	693.0	802.0	840.9	824.4	896.0	973.8	936.5	1,025.6	1,032.8	1,129.4	1,172.4
GDP at factor cost	3,526.7	3,762.7	3,994.3	4,328.9	4,659.4	4,883.3	4,981.5	5,195.1	5,390.1	5,725.4	5,971.2
Agriculture	852.9	882.2	889.4	958.9	981.6	1,036.0	1,092.6	1,129.4	1,166.3	1,260.9	1,322.0
Industry	1,271.8	1,335.4	1,430.1	1,573.7	1,725.5	1,817.0	1,819.5	1,900.1	1,928.1	2,074.8	2,184.6
Manufacturing	800.0	850.6	923.2	1,022.1	1,109.3	1,201.7	1,216.6	1,269.9	1,288.2	1,416.6	1,503.3
Services, etc.	1,708.4	1,887.3	2,039.8	2,165.5	2,320.4	2,462.5	2,515.9	2,656.9	2,823.0	3,081.2	3,256.4
Memo Items:											
Capacity to Import	507.6	580.1	574.2	698.5	787.6	669.6	723.2	882.8	1,009.2	1,148.8	1,087.5
Terms of Trade Adjustment	-90.9	-24.6	-60.8	-19.4	48.8	-29.3	-76.5	108.6	269.8	223.3	84.7
Gross Domestic Income	3,761.9	4,101.8	4,312.5	4,688.1	5,072.5	5,282.5	5,348.6	5,792.1	6,185.4	6,638.7	6,846.1
Gross National Income	3,594.8	3,956.3	4,168.9	4,532.6	4,913.8	5,129.7	5,181.0	5,613.1	6,019.8	6,463.4	6,676.2
DOMESTIC PRICES/DEFLATORS					*(Index 1987 = 100)*						
Overall (GDP)	2.9	3.2	3.6	4.0	4.8	6.1	7.5	9.4	12.1	14.2	17.6
Domestic Absorption	3.0	3.2	3.6	4.0	4.8	6.1	7.6	9.2	11.6	13.7	17.4
Agriculture	3.4	3.8	4.1	4.8	6.0	7.6	8.9	11.1	15.4	16.6	19.3
Industry	2.4	2.7	3.0	3.5	4.3	5.4	6.5	8.6	11.3	13.1	16.1
Manufacturing	2.8	3.2	3.4	4.0	5.0	6.2	7.7	10.1	13.3	14.9	17.8
Consumer Price Index	3.4	3.7	4.0	4.5	5.5	6.8	8.4	10.1	13.4	15.8	19.7
MANUFACTURING ACTIVITY											
Employment (1987=100)	70.5	74.8	77.0	83.5	92.1	97.5	99.5	102.3	106.0	108.8	112.4
Real Earnings per Empl. (1987=100)	75.6	82.6	86.6	84.5	77.3	75.0	73.5	75.6	74.0	88.0	84.7
Real Output per Empl. (1987=100)	58.8	57.2	62.5	61.6	59.0	64.9	61.3	60.9	57.8	63.3	69.9
Earnings as % of Value Added	23.2	24.9	24.0	23.3	23.0	19.9	20.6	19.8	19.6	22.4	19.7
MONETARY HOLDINGS					*(Billions of current Colombian Pesos)*						
Money Supply, Broadly Defined	25.6	28.9	32.0	40.2	53.1	65.6	97.4	135.1	181.8	240.0	301.5
Money	19.4	22.4	25.1	31.9	41.6	49.1	58.9	79.4	103.5	132.9	165.9
Currency Outside Banks	6.5	7.8	8.5	10.7	12.4	15.9	20.8	28.8	40.5	53.7	67.3
Demand Deposits	12.9	14.6	16.5	21.1	29.2	33.2	38.1	50.6	63.0	79.2	98.6
Quasi-Money	6.2	6.5	7.0	8.4	11.4	16.5	38.5	55.8	78.3	107.1	135.6
GOVERNMENT DEFICIT (-) OR SURPLUS	..	..	-2.5	-4.7	-5.6	-4.1	-0.9	5.3	4.5	6.2	-9.2
Current Revenue	..	..	17.3	20.1	25.2	34.2	51.3	63.6	84.0	110.8	139.0
Current Expenditure	..	..	11.5	13.3	14.7	22.3	34.5	38.3	51.7	74.2	124.3
Current Budget Balance	..	..	5.8	6.8	10.5	11.9	16.8	25.3	32.3	36.6	14.7
Capital Receipts	..	..	..	..	..	..	..	..	0.1	0.1	..
Capital Payments	..	..	8.3	11.5	16.1	16.0	17.7	20.0	27.9	30.5	23.9

Note: The "GOVERNMENT DEFICIT" section header is above *(Billions of current Colombian Pesos)*.

1980	1981	1982	1983	1984	1985	1986	1987	1988	1989 estimate	NOTES	COLOMBIA
1,180	1,320	1,390	1,380	1,370	1,280	1,220	1,180	1,180	1,190	..	**CURRENT GNP PER CAPITA (US $)**
26,906	27,498	28,091	28,685	29,281	29,879	30,481	31,090	31,707	32,335	..	**POPULATION (thousands)**
											USE AND ORIGIN OF RESOURCES
			(Billions of current Colombian Pesos)								
1,573	1,972	2,460	2,991	3,757	4,824	6,549	8,262	10,877	14,111	..	Gross National Product (GNP)
-6	-10	-37	-63	-99	-142	-239	-562	-754	-978	..	Net Factor Income from Abroad
1,579	1,983	2,497	3,054	3,857	4,966	6,788	8,824	11,631	15,089	..	GDP at Market Prices
10	-71	-107	-85	-22	64	465	356	247	634	..	Resource Balance
256	235	273	319	458	686	1,279	1,496	1,875	2,721	..	Exports of Goods & NFServices
246	306	379	404	481	622	814	1,140	1,627	2,087	..	Imports of Goods & NFServices
1,569	2,054	2,604	3,139	3,879	4,902	6,323	8,469	11,384	14,455	..	Domestic Absorption
1,109	1,438	1,820	2,197	2,722	3,425	4,436	5,855	7,675	9,960	..	Private Consumption, etc.
159	207	273	335	426	531	666	868	1,158	1,535	..	General Gov't Consumption
301	409	512	608	731	946	1,222	1,745	2,550	2,959	..	Gross Domestic Investment
265	350	436	525	654	870	1,204	1,517	2,201	2,819	..	Fixed Investment
158	167	215	254	361	517	797	1,031	..	..	..	Indirect Taxes, net
1,421	1,815	2,283	2,800	3,496	4,449	5,991	7,794	..	..	..	GDP at factor cost
306	382	469	572	671	844	1,186	1,594	1,961	2,535	..	Agriculture
499	607	771	962	1,283	1,718	2,455	3,093	4,104	5,489	..	Industry
367	423	530	641	853	1,080	1,526	1,793	2,438	3,058	..	Manufacturing
775	994	1,257	1,521	1,902	2,404	3,146	4,137	5,566	7,064	..	Services, etc.
311	338	405	523	709	1,009	1,687	2,101	2,797	3,593	..	Gross Domestic Saving
313	341	378	471	639	932	1,603	1,783	2,335	3,009	..	Gross National Saving
			(Billions of 1987 Colombian Pesos)								
6,875.1	7,000.2	7,034.4	7,132.5	7,291.3	7,505.8	7,840.4	8,262.4	8,565.8	8,933.7	..	Gross National Product
7,040.6	7,190.4	7,261.7	7,377.9	7,640.3	7,891.0	8,376.0	8,824.4	9,146.0	9,443.6	..	GDP at Market Prices
-87.1	-267.7	-377.5	-268.4	-128.5	89.7	283.7	355.9	442.7	458.2	..	Resource Balance
1,054.0	929.3	914.8	906.6	1,000.1	1,143.6	1,380.4	1,495.7	1,547.6	1,652.3	..	Exports of Goods & NFServices
1,141.1	1,197.0	1,292.3	1,175.1	1,128.5	1,053.9	1,096.7	1,139.8	1,104.9	1,194.1	..	Imports of Goods & NFServices
7,127.7	7,458.1	7,639.2	7,646.3	7,768.7	7,801.3	8,092.3	8,468.5	8,703.3	8,985.4	..	Domestic Absorption
4,860.4	4,956.1	5,008.7	5,060.9	5,261.3	5,426.4	5,637.9	5,855.4	5,940.9	6,246.9	..	Private Consumption, etc.
687.7	713.3	746.4	741.9	772.5	807.3	818.6	868.4	884.2	983.8	..	General Gov't Consumption
1,579.6	1,788.7	1,884.1	1,843.6	1,734.9	1,567.6	1,635.9	1,744.7	1,878.3	1,754.7	..	Gross Domestic Investment
1,326.8	1,410.0	1,451.7	1,468.9	1,487.1	1,409.5	1,517.2	1,517.2	1,790.8	..	..	Fixed Investment
6,300.7	6,469.6	6,508.3	6,630.1	6,833.7	7,045.0	7,413.0	7,793.5	..	..	..	GDP at factor cost
1,351.3	1,394.6	1,368.1	1,406.6	1,431.3	1,454.8	1,503.9	1,594.0	1,641.4	1,721.8	..	Agriculture
2,262.4	2,241.8	2,232.8	2,308.6	2,467.5	2,614.6	2,906.1	3,093.5	3,166.7	3,265.3	..	Industry
1,521.5	1,481.3	1,459.9	1,476.6	1,565.0	1,611.3	1,707.1	1,792.9	1,833.6	1,895.6	..	Manufacturing
3,428.4	3,553.8	3,659.8	3,662.7	3,741.5	3,821.6	3,966.0	4,136.9	4,338.0	4,456.5	..	Services, etc.
											Memo Items:
1,186.5	920.1	928.4	928.3	1,076.1	1,161.8	1,722.6	1,495.7	1,272.8	1,556.9	..	Capacity to Import
132.5	-9.2	13.6	21.6	76.0	18.2	342.2	0.0	-274.8	-95.3	..	Terms of Trade Adjustment
7,173.1	7,181.2	7,275.3	7,399.5	7,716.3	7,909.2	8,718.2	8,824.4	8,871.2	9,348.3	..	Gross Domestic Income
7,007.7	6,990.9	7,048.0	7,154.1	7,367.4	7,524.0	8,182.6	8,262.4	8,290.9	8,838.4	..	Gross National Income
			(Index 1987 = 100)								**DOMESTIC PRICES/DEFLATORS**
22.4	27.6	34.4	41.4	50.5	62.9	81.0	100.0	127.2	159.8	..	Overall (GDP)
22.0	27.5	34.1	41.1	49.9	62.8	78.1	100.0	130.8	160.9	..	Domestic Absorption
22.6	27.4	34.3	40.6	46.9	58.0	78.9	100.0	119.5	147.3	..	Agriculture
22.0	27.1	34.5	41.7	52.0	65.7	84.5	100.0	129.6	168.1	..	Industry
24.2	28.5	36.3	43.4	54.5	67.0	89.4	100.0	133.0	161.3	..	Manufacturing
24.9	31.7	39.5	47.4	55.0	68.2	81.1	100.0	128.1	161.2	..	Consumer Price Index
											MANUFACTURING ACTIVITY
112.3	109.1	106.3	102.7	100.5	97.2	99.4	100.0	100.5	..	..	Employment (1987=100)
80.5	81.5	83.3	87.3	94.3	93.2	93.3	100.0	103.3	..	..	Real Earnings per Empl. (1987=100)
66.7	70.6	67.9	71.6	76.4	85.4	84.4	100.0	98.8	..	..	Real Output per Empl. (1987=100)
18.4	19.0	20.5	21.0	19.9	17.9	15.9	15.9	16.1	..	..	Earnings as % of Value Added
			(Billions of current Colombian Pesos)								**MONETARY HOLDINGS**
447.2	615.3	773.9	1,010.3	1,243.7	1,495.3	..	..	..	..	D	Money Supply, Broadly Defined
212.4	256.4	321.4	396.7	492.4	545.3	..	1,019.6	1,282.0	..	..	Money
84.1	101.6	130.3	167.7	211.7	186.7	..	418.8	530.7	..	..	Currency Outside Banks
128.3	154.7	191.1	229.1	280.7	358.5	..	600.7	751.4	..	..	Demand Deposits
234.8	359.0	452.5	613.6	751.3	950.1	..	..	..	..	..	Quasi-Money
			(Billions of current Colombian Pesos)								
-27.8	-60.4	-118.1	-127.9	-166.5	-158.2	-107.4	-61.0	..	..	F	**GOVERNMENT DEFICIT (-) OR SURPLUS**
189.4	229.2	283.4	347.9	428.6	587.1	828.7	1,138.7	..	..	..	Current Revenue
164.9	218.0	302.7	381.0	506.5	567.9	730.9	975.0	..	..	..	Current Expenditure
24.5	11.2	-19.3	-33.1	-77.9	19.2	97.8	163.7	..	..	..	Current Budget Balance
0.1	0.2	..	0.1	0.1	0.8	0.9	12.2	..	..	..	Capital Receipts
52.4	71.8	98.8	94.9	88.7	178.2	206.1	236.9	..	..	..	Capital Payments

COLOMBIA	1969	1970	1971	1972	1973	1974	1975	1976	1977	1978	1979
FOREIGN TRADE (CUSTOMS BASIS)					*(Millions of current US dollars)*						
Value of Exports, fob	602.9	727.7	689.1	863.4	1,175.5	1,416.7	1,464.9	1,744.6	2,443.0	3,038.3	3,300.4
Nonfuel Primary Products	465.6	595.8	527.4	625.5	804.6	901.3	1,053.8	1,289.8	1,881.6	2,377.5	2,453.7
Fuels	77.0	73.2	70.2	65.3	61.9	117.2	105.6	71.0	95.8	130.9	131.8
Manufactures	60.3	58.7	91.5	172.6	309.0	398.2	305.5	383.8	465.6	529.8	714.9
Value of Imports, cif	685.3	842.9	929.4	858.9	1,061.5	1,597.2	1,494.8	1,708.1	2,028.3	2,836.3	3,233.2
Nonfuel Primary Products	112.8	131.8	166.7	147.0	224.4	367.4	257.8	342.1	398.1	488.5	561.1
Fuels	8.1	8.8	11.0	5.5	4.5	4.4	15.3	42.7	137.7	206.3	325.8
Manufactures	564.3	702.4	751.7	706.5	832.7	1,225.4	1,221.7	1,323.4	1,492.5	2,141.5	2,346.3
					(Index 1987 = 100)						
Terms of Trade	99.0	115.5	105.0	109.2	106.4	114.9	109.8	143.8	180.4	146.8	136.9
Export Prices, fob	27.4	33.7	32.5	37.0	44.6	60.1	60.0	81.2	112.5	102.5	111.9
Import Prices, cif	27.6	29.1	30.9	33.9	42.0	52.3	54.6	56.5	62.4	69.8	81.7
BALANCE OF PAYMENTS					*(Millions of current US dollars)*						
Exports of Goods & Services	..	1,019.0	996.9	1,228.3	1,588.0	1,947.9	2,180.4	2,849.8	3,502.0	4,099.5	4,851.0
Merchandise, fob	..	788.0	754.2	978.6	1,262.6	1,494.5	1,683.2	2,201.9	2,660.0	3,155.4	3,441.0
Nonfactor Services	..	189.0	214.6	223.7	279.0	363.2	422.2	558.8	717.9	770.6	1,091.0
Factor Services	..	42.0	28.1	26.1	46.5	90.2	75.0	89.2	124.1	173.4	319.0
Imports of Goods & Services	..	1,348.0	1,485.0	1,454.3	1,677.3	2,350.7	2,400.3	2,738.0	3,172.6	3,914.1	4,514.9
Merchandise, fob	..	802.0	902.5	849.6	982.7	1,511.4	1,414.9	1,654.0	1,969.7	2,552.2	2,977.8
Nonfactor Services	..	324.0	381.0	376.7	431.4	557.6	592.4	639.2	766.2	851.9	940.9
Factor Services	..	222.0	201.4	228.0	263.2	281.8	392.9	444.7	436.7	510.1	596.2
Long-Term Interest	..	59.2	67.1	81.1	103.4	133.0	135.6	156.9	153.8	195.3	251.7
Private Current Transfers, net	..	-4.0	0.0	8.7	11.9	18.4	30.0	39.0	39.5	44.1	99.0
Workers' Remittances	..	6.0	8.0	8.7	11.9	15.6	18.0	42.0	42.0	43.8	63.0
Curr. A/C Bal before Off. Transf.	..	-333.0	-488.1	-217.3	-77.4	-384.4	-189.9	150.9	368.9	229.4	435.0
Net Official Transfers	..	40.0	34.1	26.1	22.7	32.5	18.2	12.0	6.5	28.8	3.0
Curr. A/C Bal after Off. Transf.	..	-293.0	-454.0	-191.2	-54.7	-351.9	-171.7	162.9	375.4	258.1	438.0
Long-Term Capital, net	..	227.0	194.3	263.6	285.4	228.4	302.1	79.1	225.0	108.0	755.4
Direct Investment	..	39.0	40.1	17.4	22.7	34.9	33.1	14.0	43.0	66.0	103.0
Long-Term Loans	..	115.2	185.2	282.6	243.4	117.6	326.8	149.4	186.3	50.7	679.2
Disbursements	..	252.6	356.7	469.8	449.7	400.8	505.3	366.0	411.5	335.2	1,130.2
Repayments	..	137.4	171.5	187.2	206.3	283.2	178.5	216.6	225.2	284.5	451.0
Other Long-Term Capital	..	72.8	-31.1	-36.4	19.4	75.9	-57.7	-84.3	-4.3	-8.7	-26.8
Other Capital, net	..	82.5	241.8	88.1	-69.5	29.1	-68.2	372.2	47.7	202.9	302.8
Change in Reserves	..	-16.5	18.0	-160.5	-161.3	94.4	-62.3	-614.2	-648.1	-569.0	-1,496.2
Memo Item:					*(Colombian Pesos per US dollar)*						
Conversion Factor (Annual Avg)	17.320	18.440	19.930	21.870	23.640	26.060	30.930	34.690	36.770	39.100	42.550
					(Millions of US dollars), outstanding at end of year						
EXTERNAL DEBT (Total)	..	1,635	1,837	2,067	2,320	2,446	2,746	2,882	5,053	5,102	5,869
Long-Term Debt (by debtor)	..	1,635	1,837	2,067	2,320	2,446	2,746	2,882	3,089	3,175	3,857
Central Bank, incl. IMF credit	..	210	227	198	207	221	217	219	232	268	320
Central Government	..	637	709	859	1,035	1,107	1,257	1,249	1,244	1,270	1,635
Rest of General Government	..	172	182	209	258	294	318	349	376	374	363
Non-financial Public Enterprises	..	260	299	339	392	464	540	623	803	864	1,036
Priv. Sector, incl non-guaranteed	..	356	420	462	428	359	414	441	434	399	503
Short-Term Debt	..	..	..	..	..	..	..	..	1,964	1,927	2,012
Memo Items:					*(Millions of US dollars)*						
Int'l Reserves Excluding Gold	195.0	189.1	188.0	309.0	516.2	431.1	474.7	1,100.8	1,747.2	2,366.4	3,843.8
Gold Holdings (at market price)	26.2	18.2	17.5	27.8	48.2	80.0	157.9	190.4	285.5	443.2	1,186.3
SOCIAL INDICATORS											
Total Fertility Rate	5.6	5.3	5.0	4.7	4.6	4.5	4.4	4.2	4.1	4.0	3.9
Infant Mortality Rate	78.4	76.6	74.8	73.0	70.2	67.4	64.6	61.8	59.0	55.4	51.8
Life Expectancy at Birth	60.6	61.0	61.3	61.6	62.1	62.6	63.0	63.5	64.0	64.6	65.3
Urban Population, % of total	56.5	57.2	57.9	58.6	59.4	60.1	60.8	61.5	62.2	62.8	63.5
Food Prod. per capita (1987=100)	84.3	85.8	88.6	88.1	85.5	89.1	94.1	98.2	96.4	100.5	102.8
Labor Force, Agriculture (%)	40.3	39.3	38.7	38.2	37.7	37.2	36.7	36.2	35.7	35.2	34.7
Labor Force, Female (%)	21.1	21.3	21.4	21.5	21.6	21.8	21.9	22.0	22.1	22.2	22.3
Primary Schl. Enroll. Ratio	..	108.0	..	..	..	..	118.0	..	125.0	129.0	133.0
Primary Schl. Enroll. Ratio, Female	..	110.0	..	..	..	..	120.0	..	127.0	131.0	135.0
Secondary Schl. Enroll. Ratio	..	25.0	..	..	..	..	39.0	..	43.0	45.0	48.0

1980	1981	1982	1983	1984	1985	1986	1987	1988	1989 estimate	NOTES	COLOMBIA
											FOREIGN TRADE (CUSTOMS BASIS)
				(Millions of current US dollars)							
3,950.0	3,160.0	3,110.0	3,080.0	3,480.0	3,550.0	5,110.0	5,024.4	5,100.0	6,367.9	..	Value of Exports, fob
3,033.9	2,074.4	2,090.8	2,034.0	2,350.1	2,315.0	3,652.0	2,306.9	2,511.6	..	..	Nonfuel Primary Products
112.4	248.0	268.0	451.0	518.0	578.0	665.0	1,634.4	1,311.4	..	..	Fuels
803.7	837.6	751.2	595.0	611.9	657.0	793.0	1,083.0	1,277.0	1,286.2	..	Manufactures
4,660.0	5,200.0	5,460.0	4,970.0	4,490.0	4,130.0	3,850.0	4,322.0	5,002.0	..	..	Value of Imports, cif
822.9	820.1	872.8	802.0	759.3	686.0	627.0	700.9	802.7	..	..	Nonfuel Primary Products
567.6	730.8	663.0	648.5	474.7	484.0	153.0	121.1	180.3	..	..	Fuels
3,269.5	3,649.1	3,924.2	3,519.5	3,256.0	2,960.0	3,070.0	3,500.0	4,019.0	..	..	Manufactures
				(Index 1987 = 100)							
124.1	111.1	120.7	123.5	132.0	127.8	136.8	100.0	94.7	..	..	Terms of Trade
115.4	104.3	108.4	109.6	113.6	109.8	124.7	100.0	103.6	..	..	Export Prices, fob
93.0	93.8	89.8	88.8	86.1	85.9	91.2	100.0	109.4	..	..	Import Prices, cif
				(Millions of current US dollars)							**BALANCE OF PAYMENTS**
5,860.4	5,014.1	4,974.2	4,103.0	5,328.0	4,616.0	6,614.0	7,029.0	6,996.0	7,648.0	f	Exports of Goods & Services
3,986.3	3,157.7	3,113.8	2,970.0	4,273.0	3,650.0	5,331.0	5,661.0	5,343.0	6,029.0	..	Merchandise, fob
1,331.0	1,131.4	1,309.1	814.0	894.0	826.0	1,097.0	1,155.0	1,383.0	1,315.0	..	Nonfactor Services
543.2	725.0	551.3	319.0	161.0	140.0	186.0	213.0	270.0	304.0	..	Factor Services
6,231.3	7,217.4	8,197.3	7,270.0	7,028.0	6,886.0	7,016.0	7,694.0	8,160.0	8,634.0	f	Imports of Goods & Services
4,283.4	4,730.1	5,357.6	4,464.0	4,027.0	3,673.0	3,409.0	3,793.0	4,516.0	4,548.0	..	Merchandise, fob
1,159.5	1,284.1	1,335.1	1,290.0	1,288.0	1,420.0	1,677.0	1,699.0	1,591.0	1,674.0	..	Nonfactor Services
788.4	1,203.2	1,504.7	1,516.0	1,713.0	1,793.0	1,930.0	2,202.0	2,053.0	2,412.0	..	Factor Services
309.9	460.8	704.5	625.0	620.3	867.4	978.1	1,184.0	1,213.4	1,383.7	..	Long-Term Interest
164.0	241.3	167.2	145.0	289.0	455.0	801.0	1,009.0	975.0	1,028.0	..	Private Current Transfers, net
68.0	99.0	71.0	63.0	71.0	105.0	393.0	616.0	448.0	459.0	..	Workers' Remittances
-206.8	-1,962.0	-3,056.0	-3,022.0	-1,411.0	-1,815.0	399.0	344.0	-189.0	42.0	..	Curr. A/C Bal before Off. Transf.
1.0	0.7	2.2	19.0	10.0	6.0	-16.0	-8.0	-11.0	..	..	Net Official Transfers
-205.8	-1,961.3	-3,053.8	-3,003.0	-1,401.0	-1,809.0	383.0	336.0	-200.0	42.0	..	Curr. A/C Bal after Off. Transf.
815.4	1,579.8	1,615.1	1,527.7	1,822.0	2,350.0	2,469.0	191.0	840.0	662.0	f	Long-Term Capital, net
51.1	228.0	337.0	513.7	561.0	1,016.0	642.0	293.0	165.0	546.0	..	Direct Investment
808.3	1,401.1	1,255.1	1,048.6	1,357.6	1,329.9	1,634.8	-100.8	619.0	105.0	..	Long-Term Loans
1,071.2	1,774.6	1,653.0	1,662.2	2,039.6	2,083.7	2,755.7	1,311.4	2,343.8	2,256.4	..	Disbursements
262.9	373.5	397.9	613.6	682.0	753.8	1,120.9	1,412.2	1,724.8	2,151.4	..	Repayments
-44.0	-49.3	23.0	-34.6	-96.6	4.1	192.2	-1.2	56.0	11.0	..	Other Long-Term Capital
309.0	321.3	588.9	-369.3	-805.7	-386.1	-1,556.0	-136.0	-446.0	-310.0	f	Other Capital, net
-918.6	60.1	849.8	1,844.6	384.7	-154.9	-1,296.0	-391.0	-194.0	-394.0	..	Change in Reserves
											Memo Item:
				(Colombian Pesos per US dollar)							
47.280	54.490	64.080	78.850	100.820	142.310	194.260	242.610	299.200	382.900	..	Conversion Factor (Annual Avg)
			(Millions of US dollars), outstanding at end of year								
6,941	8,716	10,306	11,412	12,039	14,241	15,363	17,249	17,202	17,037	..	**EXTERNAL DEBT (Total)**
4,604	5,942	7,182	8,152	9,171	11,142	13,767	15,595	15,593	15,423	..	Long-Term Debt (by debtor)
384	405	423	516	448	526	695	1,295	1,151	1,047	..	Central Bank, incl. IMF credit
2,030	2,513	2,784	2,872	3,167	3,692	4,347	4,501	4,733	4,984	..	Central Government
419	578	689	820	866	1,191	1,399	1,714	1,751	1,797	..	Rest of General Government
1,212	1,489	2,003	2,584	3,192	4,100	5,666	6,478	6,352	6,272	..	Non-financial Public Enterprises
559	956	1,284	1,361	1,497	1,635	1,659	1,607	1,606	1,323	..	Priv. Sector, incl non-guaranteed
2,337	2,774	3,124	3,260	2,868	3,099	1,597	1,654	1,609	1,614	..	Short-Term Debt
				(Millions of US dollars)							**Memo Items:**
4,830.8	4,740.5	3,861.4	1,900.9	1,364.1	1,595.0	2,695.8	3,086.1	3,247.8	3,616.1	..	Int'l Reserves Excluding Gold
1,642.9	1,338.0	1,744.0	1,611.1	421.4	602.3	785.3	330.2	452.1	246.2	..	Gold Holdings (at market price)
											SOCIAL INDICATORS
3.8	3.6	3.5	3.4	3.4	3.3	3.2	3.1	3.1	3.0	..	Total Fertility Rate
48.2	44.6	41.0	40.8	40.6	40.4	40.2	40.0	39.3	38.5	..	Infant Mortality Rate
65.9	66.5	67.2	67.4	67.6	67.8	68.0	68.2	68.4	68.5	..	Life Expectancy at Birth
64.2	64.8	65.5	66.1	66.8	67.4	68.0	68.6	69.1	69.7	..	Urban Population, % of total
100.6	102.1	99.3	96.2	98.4	97.4	99.8	100.0	104.6	106.6	..	Food Prod. per capita (1987=100)
34.2	..	..	..	..	..	..	..	..	..	..	Labor Force, Agriculture (%)
22.5	22.4	22.4	22.3	22.3	22.2	22.2	22.1	22.0	22.0	..	Labor Force, Female (%)
128.0	..	..	121.0	119.0	117.0	114.0	..	..	..	..	Primary Schl. Enroll. Ratio
130.0	132.0	115.0	122.0	119.0	119.0	115.0	..	..	..	..	Primary Schl. Enroll. Ratio, Female
44.0	..	..	46.0	49.0	50.0	56.0	..	..	..	..	Secondary Schl. Enroll. Ratio

COMOROS	1969	1970	1971	1972	1973	1974	1975	1976	1977	1978	1979
CURRENT GNP PER CAPITA (US $)	90	100	110	110	140	150	170	190	200	220	260
POPULATION (thousands)	260	266	272	279	285	292	298	302	308	315	324

USE AND ORIGIN OF RESOURCES
(Millions of current Comorian Francs)

	1969	1970	1971	1972	1973	1974	1975	1976	1977	1978	1979
Gross National Product (GNP)	6,123	6,856	8,041	8,539	9,447	14,305	12,797	12,361	13,771	16,494	19,656
Net Factor Income from Abroad	..	..	..	..	..	..	..	..	..	..	..
GDP at Market Prices	..	..	..	..	..	..	..	..	..	..	..
Resource Balance	..	..	..	..	..	..	..	..	..	..	..
Exports of Goods & NFServices	..	..	..	..	..	..	..	..	..	..	..
Imports of Goods & NFServices	..	..	..	..	..	..	..	..	..	..	..
Domestic Absorption	..	..	..	..	..	..	..	..	..	..	..
Private Consumption, etc.	..	..	..	..	..	..	..	..	..	..	..
General Gov't Consumption	..	..	..	..	..	..	..	..	..	..	..
Gross Domestic Investment	..	..	..	..	..	..	..	..	..	..	..
Fixed Investment	..	..	..	..	..	..	..	..	..	..	..
Indirect Taxes, net	..	..	..	..	..	..	..	..	..	..	..
GDP at factor cost	..	..	..	..	..	..	..	..	..	..	..
Agriculture	..	..	..	..	..	..	..	..	..	..	..
Industry	..	..	..	..	..	..	..	..	..	..	..
Manufacturing	..	..	..	..	..	..	..	..	..	..	..
Services, etc.	..	..	..	..	..	..	..	..	..	..	..
Gross Domestic Saving	..	..	..	..	..	..	..	..	..	..	..
Gross National Saving	..	..	..	..	..	..	..	..	..	..	..

(Millions of 1987 Comorian Francs)

	1969	1970	1971	1972	1973	1974	1975	1976	1977	1978	1979
Gross National Product	31,366	34,968	38,477	39,721	43,699	38,129	34,291	34,291	35,814	37,121	38,442
GDP at Market Prices	..	..	..	..	..	..	..	..	..	..	..
Resource Balance	..	..	..	..	..	..	..	..	..	..	..
Exports of Goods & NFServices	..	..	..	..	..	..	..	..	..	..	..
Imports of Goods & NFServices	..	..	..	..	..	..	..	..	..	..	..
Domestic Absorption	..	..	..	..	..	..	..	..	..	..	..
Private Consumption, etc.	..	..	..	..	..	..	..	..	..	..	..
General Gov't Consumption	..	..	..	..	..	..	..	..	..	..	..
Gross Domestic Investment	..	..	..	..	..	..	..	..	..	..	..
Fixed Investment	..	..	..	..	..	..	..	..	..	..	..
GDP at factor cost	..	..	..	..	..	..	..	..	..	..	..
Agriculture	..	..	..	..	..	..	..	..	..	..	..
Industry	..	..	..	..	..	..	..	..	..	..	..
Manufacturing	..	..	..	..	..	..	..	..	..	..	..
Services, etc.	..	..	..	..	..	..	..	..	..	..	..
Memo Items:											
Capacity to Import	..	..	..	..	..	..	..	..	..	..	..
Terms of Trade Adjustment	..	..	..	..	..	..	..	..	..	..	..
Gross Domestic Income	..	..	..	..	..	..	..	..	..	..	..
Gross National Income	..	..	..	..	..	..	..	..	..	..	..

DOMESTIC PRICES/DEFLATORS
(Index 1987 = 100)

	1969	1970	1971	1972	1973	1974	1975	1976	1977	1978	1979
Overall (GDP)	..	..	..	..	..	..	..	..	..	..	..
Domestic Absorption	..	..	..	..	..	..	..	..	..	..	..
Agriculture	..	..	..	..	..	..	..	..	..	..	..
Industry	..	..	..	..	..	..	..	..	..	..	..
Manufacturing	..	..	..	..	..	..	..	..	..	..	..
Consumer Price Index	..	..	..	..	..	..	..	..	..	..	..

MANUFACTURING ACTIVITY

	1969	1970	1971	1972	1973	1974	1975	1976	1977	1978	1979
Employment (1987=100)	..	..	..	..	..	..	..	..	..	..	..
Real Earnings per Empl. (1987=100)	..	..	..	..	..	..	..	..	..	..	..
Real Output per Empl. (1987=100)	..	..	..	..	..	..	..	..	..	..	..
Earnings as % of Value Added	..	..	..	..	..	..	..	..	..	..	..

MONETARY HOLDINGS
(Millions of current Comorian Francs)

	1969	1970	1971	1972	1973	1974	1975	1976	1977	1978	1979
Money Supply, Broadly Defined	..	..	..	..	..	..	..	..	..	..	..
Money	..	..	..	..	..	..	..	..	..	..	..
Currency Outside Banks	..	..	..	..	..	..	..	..	..	..	..
Demand Deposits	..	..	..	..	..	..	..	..	..	..	..
Quasi-Money	..	..	..	..	..	..	..	..	..	..	..

(Millions of current Comorian Francs)

	1969	1970	1971	1972	1973	1974	1975	1976	1977	1978	1979
GOVERNMENT DEFICIT (-) OR SURPLUS	..	..	..	..	..	..	..	..	..	..	..
Current Revenue	..	..	..	..	..	..	..	..	..	..	..
Current Expenditure	..	..	..	..	..	..	..	..	..	..	..
Current Budget Balance	..	..	..	..	..	..	..	..	..	..	..
Capital Receipts	..	..	..	..	..	..	..	..	..	..	..
Capital Payments	..	..	..	..	..	..	..	..	..	..	..

1980	1981	1982	1983	1984	1985	1986	1987	1988	1989 estimate	NOTES	COMOROS
340	380	350	330	310	300	320	370	440	450	..	**CURRENT GNP PER CAPITA (US $)**
333	343	355	367	381	395	410	426	442	459	..	**POPULATION (thousands)**
			(Millions of current Comorian Francs)								**USE AND ORIGIN OF RESOURCES**
25,551	30,115	36,150	42,321	46,832	51,262	56,117	59,335	61,251	63,252	..	Gross National Product (GNP)
..	..	-1,609	-175	-136	-350	-153	-337	-417	-432	..	Net Factor Income from Abroad
..	..	37,759	42,496	46,968	51,612	56,270	59,672	61,668	63,684	..	GDP at Market Prices
..	..	..	-11,135	-26,587	-19,966	-15,255	-19,382	-16,424	-14,782	..	Resource Balance
..	..	..	8,426	4,236	8,943	9,251	6,431	7,700	6,300	..	Exports of Goods & NFServices
..	..	..	19,561	30,823	28,909	24,506	25,813	24,124	21,082	..	Imports of Goods & NFServices
..	..	..	53,631	73,555	71,578	71,525	79,054	78,092	78,466	..	Domestic Absorption
..	..	..	29,207	38,727	41,016	42,700	49,335	50,170	51,173	..	Private Consumption, etc.
..	..	..	12,084	13,305	15,310	15,552	15,819	18,085	18,447	..	General Gov't Consumption
..	..	..	12,340	21,523	15,252	13,273	13,900	9,837	8,846	..	Gross Domestic Investment
..	..	..	11,366	15,740	13,410	11,773	9,838	7,704	7,246	..	Fixed Investment
..	..	..	..	..	..	..	..	..	..		Indirect Taxes, net
..	..	..	..	..	..	..	..	..	..	B	GDP at factor cost
..	..	13,724	14,861	16,266	18,640	21,049	21,363	24,606	26,174	..	Agriculture
..	..	5,236	6,038	7,195	7,261	7,286	8,413	6,351	6,495	..	Industry
..	..	1,431	1,516	1,716	1,893	2,062	2,148	2,424	2,420	..	Manufacturing
..	..	18,799	21,597	23,507	25,711	27,935	29,896	30,711	31,015	..	Services, etc.
..	..	..	1,205	-5,064	-4,714	-1,982	-5,482	-6,587	-5,936	..	Gross Domestic Saving
..	..	..	208	-6,502	-5,369	-2,835	-5,540	-6,075	-5,521	..	Gross National Saving
			(Millions of 1987 Comorian Francs)								
45,141	49,969	49,640	53,284	55,637	56,965	58,380	59,335	59,680	59,775		Gross National Product
..	..	..	53,505	55,792	57,346	58,541	59,672	60,084	60,190	..	GDP at Market Prices
..	..	..	-14,883	-26,727	-20,755	-17,435	-19,382	..	..	..	Resource Balance
..	..	..	5,789	4,051	6,765	7,112	6,431	..	..	..	Exports of Goods & NFServices
..	..	..	20,672	30,779	27,521	24,547	25,813	..	..	..	Imports of Goods & NFServices
..	..	..	68,387	82,519	78,102	75,976	79,054	..	..	..	Domestic Absorption
..	..	..	36,552	43,595	45,054	44,463	49,335	..	..	..	Private Consumption, etc.
..	..	..	14,185	14,875	16,193	15,358	15,819	16,882	18,035	..	General Gov't Consumption
..	..	..	17,650	24,049	16,855	16,154	13,900	9,620	8,405	..	Gross Domestic Investment
..	..	..	16,439	17,533	14,818	14,203	9,838	7,534	6,884	..	Fixed Investment
..	..	..	..	..	..	..	..	..	..	B	GDP at factor cost
..	..	..	17,331	17,992	18,922	19,547	21,363	22,030	22,581	..	Agriculture
..	..	..	9,132	9,770	9,420	9,461	8,413	7,463	6,977	..	Industry
..	..	..	1,721	1,846	1,935	2,072	2,148	2,222	2,110	..	Manufacturing
..	..	..	27,042	28,030	29,005	29,533	29,896	30,591	30,632	..	Services, etc.
											Memo Items:
..	..	..	8,905	4,230	8,514	9,266	6,431	..	..	..	Capacity to Import
..	..	..	3,115	179	1,748	2,155	0	..	..	..	Terms of Trade Adjustment
..	..	..	56,620	55,971	59,094	60,696	59,672	..	..	..	Gross Domestic Income
..	..	..	56,399	55,816	58,713	60,535	59,335	..	..	..	Gross National Income
			(Index 1987 = 100)								**DOMESTIC PRICES/DEFLATORS**
..	..	..	79.4	84.2	90.0	96.1	100.0	102.6	105.8	..	Overall (GDP)
..	..	..	78.4	89.1	91.6	94.1	100.0	..	..	..	Domestic Absorption
..	..	..	85.7	90.4	98.5	107.7	100.0	111.7	115.9	..	Agriculture
..	..	..	66.1	73.6	77.1	77.0	100.0	85.1	93.1	..	Industry
..	..	..	88.1	92.9	97.8	99.5	100.0	109.1	114.7	..	Manufacturing
..	..	..	..	..	..	..	..	..	..		Consumer Price Index
											MANUFACTURING ACTIVITY
..	..	..	..	..	..	..	..	..	..	..	Employment (1987 = 100)
..	..	..	..	..	..	..	..	..	..	..	Real Earnings per Empl. (1987 = 100)
..	..	..	..	..	..	..	..	..	..	..	Real Output per Empl. (1987 = 100)
..	..	..	..	..	..	..	..	..	..	..	Earnings as % of Value Added
			(Millions of current Comorian Francs)								**MONETARY HOLDINGS**
..	..	6,370	8,521	7,213	8,192	8,664	10,847	12,438	14,864	..	Money Supply, Broadly Defined
..	..	5,202	7,292	6,254	7,177	7,232	7,812	8,879	10,256	..	Money
..	..	2,434	3,427	3,142	3,448	3,118	3,151	3,688	3,618	..	Currency Outside Banks
..	..	2,768	3,865	3,112	3,729	4,114	4,661	5,191	6,638	..	Demand Deposits
..	..	1,168	1,229	959	1,015	1,432	3,035	3,559	4,608	..	Quasi-Money
			(Millions of current Comorian Francs)								**GOVERNMENT DEFICIT (-) OR SURPLUS**
..	..	-4,084	-6,353	-8,586	-8,126	-4,816	..	..	..	..	Current Revenue
..	..	9,551	13,501	16,111	16,017	18,509	..	..	..	..	Current Expenditure
..	..	9,362	12,208	14,585	15,324	17,921	..	..	..	..	Current Budget Balance
..	..	189	1,293	1,526	693	588	..	..	..	..	Capital Receipts
..	..	..	..	..	..	..	..	..	..	..	Capital Payments
..	..	4,273	7,645	10,113	8,819	5,404	..	..	..	..	

COMOROS	1969	1970	1971	1972	1973	1974	1975	1976	1977	1978	1979
FOREIGN TRADE (CUSTOMS BASIS)					*(Thousands of current US dollars)*						
Value of Exports, fob	..	5,000	6,000	6,000	5,000	9,000	10,000	12,000	9,000	9,000	10,000
Nonfuel Primary Products	..	..	..	..	..	..	..	..	..	..	..
Fuels	..	..	..	..	..	..	..	..	..	..	..
Manufactures	..	..	..	..	..	..	..	..	..	..	..
Value of Imports, cif	..	9,000	10,000	12,000	15,000	26,000	23,000	13,000	16,000	19,000	28,000
Nonfuel Primary Products	..	..	..	..	..	..	..	..	..	..	..
Fuels	..	..	..	..	..	..	..	..	..	..	..
Manufactures	..	..	..	..	..	..	..	..	..	..	..
					(Index 1987 = 100)						
Terms of Trade	..	..	..	..	..	..	..	..	..	..	..
Export Prices, fob	..	..	..	..	..	..	..	..	..	..	..
Import Prices, cif	..	..	..	..	..	..	..	..	..	..	..
BALANCE OF PAYMENTS					*(Thousands of current US dollars)*						
Exports of Goods & Services	..	..	..	..	..	..	..	..	..	..	..
Merchandise, fob	..	..	..	..	..	..	..	..	..	..	..
Nonfactor Services	..	..	..	..	..	..	..	..	..	..	..
Factor Services	..	..	..	..	..	..	..	..	..	..	..
Imports of Goods & Services	..	..	..	..	..	..	..	..	..	..	..
Merchandise, fob	..	..	..	..	..	..	..	..	..	..	..
Nonfactor Services	..	..	..	..	..	..	..	..	..	..	..
Factor Services	..	..	..	..	..	..	..	..	..	..	..
Long-Term Interest	..	0.00	0.00	0.00	0.00	0.00	0.10	0.10	0.10	0.10	0.20
Private Current Transfers, net	..	..	..	..	..	..	..	..	..	..	..
Workers' Remittances	..	..	..	..	..	..	..	..	..	..	..
Curr. A/C Bal before Off. Transf.	..	..	..	..	..	..	..	..	..	..	..
Net Official Transfers	..	..	..	..	..	..	..	..	..	..	..
Curr. A/C Bal after Off. Transf.	..	..	..	..	..	..	..	..	..	..	..
Long-Term Capital, net	..	..	..	..	..	..	..	..	..	..	..
Direct Investment	..	..	..	..	..	..	..	..	..	..	..
Long-Term Loans	..	0.00	0.00	0.20	0.00	2.30	0.50	14.20	4.30	3.50	10.10
Disbursements	..	0.00	0.00	0.30	0.10	2.40	0.90	14.60	4.60	3.60	10.10
Repayments	..	0.00	0.00	0.10	0.10	0.10	0.40	0.40	0.30	0.10	0.00
Other Long-Term Capital	..	..	..	..	..	..	..	..	..	..	..
Other Capital, net	..	..	..	..	..	..	..	..	..	..	..
Change in Reserves	..	..	..	..	..	..	..	..	0.00	..	0.00
Memo Item:					*(Comorian Francs per US dollar)*						
Conversion Factor (Annual Avg)	259.710	277.710	277.130	252.210	222.700	240.500	214.320	238.980	225.670	225.640	212.720
				(Millions of US dollars), outstanding at end of year							
EXTERNAL DEBT (Total)	..	1.20	1.20	1.50	1.70	4.30	4.70	18.50	24.40	28.90	39.50
Long-Term Debt (by debtor)	..	1.20	1.20	1.50	1.70	4.30	4.70	18.50	23.40	27.90	38.50
Central Bank, incl. IMF credit	..	0.00	0.00	0.00	0.00	0.00	0.00	0.00	0.00	0.00	0.00
Central Government	..	1.20	1.20	1.40	1.50	4.10	4.60	18.40	23.30	27.80	38.30
Rest of General Government	..	0.00	0.00	0.00	0.00	0.00	0.00	0.00	0.00	0.00	0.00
Non-financial Public Enterprises	..	0.00	0.00	0.10	0.20	0.20	0.10	0.10	0.10	0.10	0.20
Priv. Sector, incl non-guaranteed	..	..	..	..	..	..	..	..	..	..	..
Short-Term Debt	..	..	..	..	..	..	..	..	1.00	1.00	1.00
Memo Items:					*(Thousands of US dollars)*						
Int'l Reserves Excluding Gold	..	..	..	..	..	..	..	..	..	..	..
Gold Holdings (at market price)	..	..	..	..	..	..	..	..	..	..	..
SOCIAL INDICATORS											
Total Fertility Rate	7.0	7.0	7.0	7.0	7.0	7.0	7.0	7.0	7.0	7.0	7.0
Infant Mortality Rate	144.0	141.0	138.0	135.0	132.0	129.0	126.0	123.0	120.0	117.8	115.6
Life Expectancy at Birth	47.8	48.3	48.7	49.2	49.6	50.1	50.6	51.0	51.5	52.0	52.4
Urban Population, % of total	10.0	11.3	13.3	15.3	17.3	19.3	21.3	21.7	22.1	22.4	22.8
Food Prod. per capita (1987=100)	115.9	116.0	116.5	114.2	113.3	110.5	106.6	100.9	89.0	86.4	84.2
Labor Force, Agriculture (%)	86.9	86.7	86.2	85.8	85.5	85.1	84.8	84.4	84.0	83.6	83.3
Labor Force, Female (%)	42.8	42.8	42.8	42.7	42.7	42.6	42.6	42.5	42.5	42.5	42.4
Primary Schl. Enroll. Ratio	..	34.0	..	..	46.0	..	..	..	..	..	..
Primary Schl. Enroll. Ratio, Female	..	21.0	..	..	29.0	..	..	..	..	..	..
Secondary Schl. Enroll. Ratio	..	3.0	..	..	7.0	..	..	..	..	..	..

1980	1981	1982	1983	1984	1985	1986	1987	1988	1989 estimate	NOTES	COMOROS
					(Thousands of current US dollars)						**FOREIGN TRADE (CUSTOMS BASIS)**
11,190	16,420	19,580	19,470	7,050	15,230	18,460	12,000	19,000	..	..	Value of Exports, fob
..	..	..	..	..	..	..	..	..	..	..	Nonfuel Primary Products
..	..	..	..	..	..	..	..	..	..	..	Fuels
..	..	..	..	..	..	..	..	..	..	..	Manufactures
29,000	32,000	33,000	34,000	43,000	36,000	37,000	52,000	51,000	..	..	Value of Imports, cif
..	..	..	..	..	..	..	..	..	..	..	Nonfuel Primary Products
..	..	..	..	..	..	..	..	..	..	..	Fuels
..	..	..	..	..	..	..	..	..	..	..	Manufactures
					(Index 1987 = 100)						
..	..	..	..	..	..	..	..	..	..	..	Terms of Trade
..	..	..	..	..	..	..	..	..	..	..	Export Prices, fob
..	..	..	..	..	..	..	..	..	..	..	Import Prices, cif
					(Thousands of current US dollars)						**BALANCE OF PAYMENTS**
14.06	18.33	23.41	23.38	10.73	20.48	28.63	27.84	40.06	39.64	..	Exports of Goods & Services
11.19	16.42	19.58	19.47	7.05	15.69	20.37	11.60	21.48	18.05	..	Merchandise, fob
2.24	1.10	2.56	2.64	2.65	4.22	6.76	14.44	16.85	17.55	..	Nonfactor Services
0.63	0.81	1.27	1.27	1.04	0.57	1.50	1.80	1.74	4.04	..	Factor Services
34.33	50.76	51.23	52.38	71.91	66.08	73.94	88.87	90.54	77.94	..	Imports of Goods & Services
22.37	24.88	25.10	28.80	32.65	28.22	28.54	44.15	44.29	35.65	..	Merchandise, fob
11.92	25.31	25.41	21.85	37.66	35.89	42.27	41.80	42.29	39.61	..	Nonfactor Services
0.04	0.56	0.71	1.73	1.61	1.97	3.13	2.92	3.96	2.69	..	Factor Services
0.30	0.40	0.80	1.20	1.60	1.50	0.80	0.90	0.30	0.70	..	Long-Term Interest
0.10	0.48	-2.40	-2.16	-2.98	-0.68	-2.02	0.93	3.12	2.66	..	Private Current Transfers, net
1.62	1.22	2.37	1.84	2.14	4.23	4.76	6.80	7.38	7.89	..	Workers' Remittances
-20.17	-31.95	-30.23	-31.16	-64.16	-46.28	-47.34	-60.11	-47.33	-35.65	..	Curr. A/C Bal before Off. Transf.
11.26	23.79	19.27	20.11	31.44	32.02	31.65	38.74	40.80	38.51	..	Net Official Transfers
-8.91	-8.16	-10.96	-11.05	-32.72	-14.26	-15.69	-21.37	-6.53	2.86	..	Curr. A/C Bal after Off. Transf.
-17.04	-11.22	-15.42	-21.53	-27.65	-20.54	-20.51	-3.40	0.26	1.03	..	Long-Term Capital, net
..	..	..	..	..	..	..	7.55	3.77	3.27	..	Direct Investment
13.00	11.00	16.20	17.80	23.10	21.80	23.70	12.60	8.30	5.20	..	Long-Term Loans
13.00	11.10	16.30	18.10	24.10	22.20	24.80	13.00	8.30	5.20	..	Disbursements
0.00	0.10	0.10	0.30	1.00	0.40	1.10	0.40	0.00	..	..	Repayments
-30.04	-22.22	-31.62	-39.33	-50.75	-42.34	-44.21	-23.54	-11.81	-7.43	..	Other Long-Term Capital
22.44	22.89	30.09	34.66	54.52	40.91	39.67	33.55	9.83	1.45	..	Other Capital, net
3.51	-3.51	-3.71	-2.08	5.85	-6.12	-3.48	-8.79	-3.56	-5.35	..	Change in Reserves
					(Comorian Francs per US dollar)						Memo Item:
211.280	271.730	328.600	381.060	436.960	449.260	346.300	300.530	297.850	319.010	..	Conversion Factor (Annual Avg)
					(Millions of US dollars), outstanding at end of year						
44.00	54.50	68.70	85.60	104.30	133.30	166.20	202.90	198.70	175.50	..	**EXTERNAL DEBT** (Total)
43.00	52.50	67.70	83.60	101.30	129.30	158.60	187.70	187.40	162.30	..	Long-Term Debt (by debtor)
0.00	0.00	0.00	0.00	0.00	0.00	0.00	0.20	0.40	0.20	..	Central Bank, incl. IMF credit
43.00	52.50	66.50	81.40	96.40	119.60	144.40	164.40	161.90	158.10	..	Central Government
0.00	0.00	0.00	0.00	0.00	0.00	0.00	0.00	0.00	..	..	Rest of General Government
0.00	0.00	1.20	2.20	4.90	9.70	14.20	23.10	25.10	4.00	..	Non-financial Public Enterprises
..	..	..	..	..	..	..	..	..	..	..	Priv. Sector, incl non-guaranteed
1.00	2.00	1.00	2.00	3.00	4.00	7.60	15.20	11.30	13.20	..	Short-Term Debt
					(Thousands of US dollars)						Memo Items:
6,373	8,392	10,831	10,794	3,509	11,748	17,546	30,674	23,541	30,773	..	Int'l Reserves Excluding Gold
..	..	..	221	176	186	223	..	..	..	..	Gold Holdings (at market price)
											SOCIAL INDICATORS
7.0	7.0	7.0	7.0	7.0	7.0	7.0	7.0	6.9	6.8	..	Total Fertility Rate
113.4	111.2	109.0	107.0	105.0	103.0	101.0	99.0	97.0	95.0	..	Infant Mortality Rate
52.9	53.3	53.8	54.2	54.7	55.1	55.6	56.0	56.4	56.7	..	Life Expectancy at Birth
23.2	23.6	24.0	24.4	24.8	25.2	25.8	26.4	26.8	27.2	..	Urban Population, % of total
91.3	79.8	81.4	86.0	83.0	85.5	88.4	100.0	89.0	92.4	..	Food Prod. per capita (1987=100)
83.0	..	..	..	..	..	..	..	..	..	..	Labor Force, Agriculture (%)
42.4	42.2	42.0	41.8	41.6	41.4	41.2	41.0	40.8	40.6	..	Labor Force, Female (%)
95.0	..	90.0	..	..	87.0	76.0	..	92.0	..	..	Primary Schl. Enroll. Ratio
79.0	..	..	..	..	75.0	70.0	..	..	..	..	Primary Schl. Enroll. Ratio, Female
23.0	..	..	..	..	31.0	36.0	..	..	..	..	Secondary Schl. Enroll. Ratio

CONGO, PEOPLE'S REPUBLIC OF THE	1969	1970	1971	1972	1973	1974	1975	1976	1977	1978	1979
CURRENT GNP PER CAPITA (US $)	240	240	260	290	340	430	530	520	490	530	650
POPULATION (thousands)	1,178	1,208	1,238	1,269	1,302	1,338	1,380	1,424	1,471	1,521	1,574

USE AND ORIGIN OF RESOURCES *(Billions of current CFA Francs)*

	1969	1970	1971	1972	1973	1974	1975	1976	1977	1978	1979
Gross National Product (GNP)	67.60	74.20	86.70	101.90	114.00	135.70	157.90	170.60	178.70	185.60	234.60
Net Factor Income from Abroad	-1.30	-1.80	-2.00	-1.60	-6.80	-5.20	-6.50	-9.70	-9.30	-12.70	-20.40
GDP at Market Prices	68.90	76.00	88.70	103.50	120.80	140.90	164.40	180.30	188.00	198.30	255.00
Resource Balance	-17.10	-17.50	-17.80	-24.30	-14.20	-8.80	-45.80	-47.20	-37.00	-34.40	-3.10
Exports of Goods & NFServices	22.10	26.40	28.90	29.30	38.20	75.00	59.00	72.80	85.70	86.70	120.90
Imports of Goods & NFServices	39.20	43.90	46.70	53.60	52.40	83.80	104.80	120.00	122.70	121.10	124.00
Domestic Absorption	86.00	93.50	106.50	127.80	135.00	149.70	210.20	227.50	225.00	232.70	258.10
Private Consumption, etc.	55.40	62.20	67.70	79.70	75.20	75.20	116.30	139.70	138.60	133.00	139.90
General Gov't Consumption	12.20	12.90	15.20	18.00	21.20	25.10	29.60	31.90	36.40	45.50	52.00
Gross Domestic Investment	18.40	18.40	23.60	30.10	38.60	49.40	64.30	55.90	50.00	54.20	66.20
Fixed Investment	..	..	..	..	..	47.30	61.50	53.60	48.90	46.40	56.40
Indirect Taxes, net	10.90	9.70	11.80	11.90	12.90	14.50	21.60	21.00	26.70	21.80	35.40
GDP at factor cost	58.00	66.30	76.90	91.60	107.90	126.40	142.80	159.30	161.30	176.50	219.60
Agriculture	12.20	13.60	15.20	17.00	19.00	21.30	23.80	24.30	29.00	31.80	36.50
Industry	13.40	18.20	19.40	22.00	26.70	35.80	53.30	67.80	59.50	58.50	92.80
Manufacturing	..	..	..	..	..	..	..	..	..	18.60	21.50
Services, etc.	43.30	44.20	54.10	64.50	75.10	83.80	87.30	88.20	99.50	108.00	125.70
Gross Domestic Saving	1.30	0.90	5.80	5.80	24.40	40.60	18.50	8.70	13.00	19.80	63.10
Gross National Saving	..	-2.07	1.55	0.99	15.90	21.62	4.95	-8.72	-4.53	4.10	35.97

(Billions of 1987 CFA Francs)

	1969	1970	1971	1972	1973	1974	1975	1976	1977	1978	1979
Gross National Product	203.63	215.40	232.66	255.00	264.42	297.65	330.07	333.46	298.26	312.29	344.25
GDP at Market Prices	213.37	226.77	244.61	265.94	288.01	316.58	349.09	357.15	318.55	337.94	378.43
Resource Balance	-126.53	-123.31	-120.12	-116.70	-113.27	-109.62	-121.73	-106.44	-75.81	-58.75	-4.92
Exports of Goods & NFServices	91.94	119.11	123.29	127.70	132.11	136.75	136.99	141.16	156.49	171.58	179.24
Imports of Goods & NFServices	218.48	242.42	243.41	244.40	245.38	246.37	258.72	247.61	232.30	230.33	184.16
Domestic Absorption	348.18	359.60	377.46	399.05	421.94	446.03	485.99	468.24	406.74	408.27	395.37
Private Consumption, etc.	192.12	202.14	199.72	198.08	194.38	187.65	190.69	225.18	196.18	220.95	195.22
General Gov't Consumption	52.32	60.10	63.59	67.34	71.10	75.39	79.42	77.54	77.27	81.56	86.66
Gross Domestic Investment	103.75	97.37	114.15	133.63	156.46	182.98	215.88	165.52	133.29	105.76	113.48
Fixed Investment	..	..	..	..	..	..	..	..	..	..	..
GDP at factor cost	..	..	..	..	..	..	..	..	..	..	359.70
Agriculture	44.55	48.45	50.15	52.10	54.05	55.99	57.94	55.26	57.46	57.21	60.86
Industry	49.86	57.47	58.04	61.97	70.97	88.63	112.01	123.03	98.45	102.85	128.04
Manufacturing	..	..	..	..	..	..	..	..	..	26.61	26.61
Services, etc.	134.91	137.99	154.61	171.33	183.82	188.48	188.80	183.65	173.81	190.56	196.03

Memo Items:	1969	1970	1971	1972	1973	1974	1975	1976	1977	1978	1979
Capacity to Import	123.17	145.79	150.63	133.60	178.89	220.50	145.65	150.22	162.25	164.90	179.56
Terms of Trade Adjustment	31.23	26.68	27.35	5.90	46.78	83.75	8.67	9.05	5.76	-6.68	0.32
Gross Domestic Income	244.60	253.44	271.96	271.84	334.79	400.33	357.75	366.20	324.32	331.26	378.75
Gross National Income	234.86	242.07	260.00	260.90	311.19	381.40	338.73	342.51	304.03	305.60	344.57

DOMESTIC PRICES/DEFLATORS *(Index 1987 = 100)*

	1969	1970	1971	1972	1973	1974	1975	1976	1977	1978	1979
Overall (GDP)	32.3	33.5	36.3	38.9	41.9	44.5	47.1	50.5	59.0	58.7	67.4
Domestic Absorption	24.7	26.0	28.2	32.0	32.0	33.6	43.3	48.6	55.3	57.0	65.3
Agriculture	27.4	28.1	30.3	32.6	35.2	38.0	41.1	44.0	50.5	55.6	60.0
Industry	26.9	31.7	33.4	35.5	37.6	40.4	47.6	55.1	60.4	56.9	72.5
Manufacturing	..	..	..	..	..	..	..	..	..	69.9	80.8
Consumer Price Index	24.1	24.5	25.5	28.0	28.9	30.5	35.8	38.4	43.8	48.4	52.3

MANUFACTURING ACTIVITY	1969	1970	1971	1972	1973	1974	1975	1976	1977	1978	1979
Employment (1987=100)	..	..	..	..	..	..	..	..	..	..	..
Real Earnings per Empl. (1987=100)	..	..	..	..	..	..	..	..	..	..	..
Real Output per Empl. (1987=100)	..	..	..	..	..	..	..	..	..	..	..
Earnings as % of Value Added	34.3	33.8	35.1	40.6	44.3	49.8	46.7	43.8	..	..	..

MONETARY HOLDINGS *(Billions of current CFA Francs)*

	1969	1970	1971	1972	1973	1974	1975	1976	1977	1978	1979
Money Supply, Broadly Defined	11.63	13.40	14.90	15.90	18.48	25.60	29.07	33.89	34.50	36.89	44.91
Money	10.85	12.47	13.74	14.65	17.07	23.73	26.91	31.27	30.63	32.96	39.61
Currency Outside Banks	5.06	5.42	6.38	7.77	8.88	11.61	14.03	15.05	15.86	16.31	18.96
Demand Deposits	5.79	7.05	7.36	6.88	8.18	12.12	12.88	16.21	14.76	16.65	20.65
Quasi-Money	0.78	0.92	1.16	1.26	1.42	1.87	2.16	2.62	3.87	3.92	5.30

(Billions of current CFA Francs)

	1969	1970	1971	1972	1973	1974	1975	1976	1977	1978	1979
GOVERNMENT DEFICIT (-) OR SURPLUS	..	-1.09	-2.40	..	..	..	..	..	..	..	..
Current Revenue	..	16.70	17.61	18.80	19.60	43.77	47.83	46.92	..	..	..
Current Expenditure	..	16.11	17.66	..	..	..	..	..	..	..	..
Current Budget Balance	..	0.59	-0.05	..	..	..	..	..	..	..	..
Capital Receipts	..	0.01	..	..	0.50	0.35	..	1.38	..	..	..
Capital Payments	..	1.69	2.35	..	..	..	..	..	..	..	..

1980	1981	1982	1983	1984	1985	1986	1987	1988	1989 estimate	NOTES	CONGO, PEOPLE'S REPUBLIC OF THE
850	1,100	1,320	1,240	1,150	1,040	910	910	890	940	..	**CURRENT GNP PER CAPITA (US $)**
1,630	1,688	1,748	1,809	1,873	1,938	2,004	2,071	2,139	2,208	..	**POPULATION (thousands)**
			(Billions of current CFA Francs)								**USE AND ORIGIN OF RESOURCES**
325.70	501.20	654.10	732.90	871.00	867.60	563.60	613.80	569.90	640.50	..	Gross National Product (GNP)
-34.70	-40.50	-55.90	-66.30	-87.50	-103.20	-76.80	-76.80	-91.20	-83.30	..	Net Factor Income from Abroad
360.40	541.70	710.00	799.20	958.50	970.80	640.40	690.60	661.10	723.80	..	GDP at Market Prices
-0.40	-97.90	-94.00	49.40	153.40	7.60	-141.40	-0.80	-60.70	42.60	..	Resource Balance
216.30	314.30	392.40	463.10	590.70	551.30	271.40	301.80	280.60	369.60	..	Exports of Goods & NFServices
216.70	412.20	486.40	413.70	437.30	543.70	412.80	302.60	341.30	327.00	..	Imports of Goods & NFServices
360.80	639.60	804.00	749.80	805.10	963.20	781.80	691.40	721.80	681.20	..	Domestic Absorption
168.50	305.90	284.10	318.40	372.10	509.50	433.40	410.00	461.80	436.50	..	Private Consumption, etc.
63.40	72.80	95.80	124.20	141.70	159.70	159.80	145.20	144.80	152.10	..	General Gov't Consumption
128.90	260.90	424.10	307.20	291.30	294.00	188.60	136.20	115.20	92.60	..	Gross Domestic Investment
118.70	239.70	404.70	302.90	277.30	276.90	182.90	144.00	113.10	103.90	..	Fixed Investment
17.50	21.80	30.30	29.00	37.10	34.20	28.00	25.50	29.20	29.40	..	Indirect Taxes, net
342.90	519.90	679.70	770.20	921.40	936.60	612.40	665.10	631.90	694.40	B	GDP at factor cost
42.10	42.70	55.80	60.60	66.30	72.30	77.40	82.40	90.90	99.10	..	Agriculture
168.00	275.70	373.20	434.20	542.40	523.40	208.50	247.20	206.20	256.70	..	Industry
27.00	34.30	33.90	44.10	46.50	54.60	61.30	59.80	58.90	61.80	f	Manufacturing
150.30	223.30	281.00	304.40	349.80	375.10	354.50	361.00	364.00	368.00	..	Services, etc.
128.50	163.00	330.10	356.60	444.70	301.60	47.20	135.40	54.50	135.20	..	Gross Domestic Saving
80.20	113.73	258.67	274.64	337.55	181.58	-43.80	41.52	-53.57	37.54	..	Gross National Saving
			(Billions of 1987 CFA Francs)								
399.39	465.62	576.82	618.99	648.72	639.69	611.22	613.80	612.01	621.59	..	Gross National Product
449.63	512.32	646.06	696.08	744.50	735.74	685.61	690.60	694.36	696.56	H	GDP at Market Prices
-41.95	-145.92	-298.93	-134.38	-90.61	-113.71	-29.12	-0.80	90.34	133.16	..	Resource Balance
218.25	238.45	260.24	305.16	335.05	313.28	302.39	301.80	322.38	342.37	..	Exports of Goods & NFServices
260.20	384.37	559.17	439.54	425.66	426.99	331.51	302.60	232.04	209.21	..	Imports of Goods & NFServices
501.96	689.15	960.33	846.25	850.26	859.88	722.59	691.40	613.19	575.48	..	Domestic Absorption
234.55	280.19	412.43	342.05	366.64	380.60	354.85	410.00	350.03	337.40	..	Private Consumption, etc.
98.20	102.76	128.89	150.04	168.68	180.16	168.32	145.20	146.28	136.42	..	General Gov't Consumption
169.22	306.20	419.01	354.16	314.94	299.13	199.42	136.20	116.88	101.66	..	Gross Domestic Investment
..	..	..	..	..	..	..	..	..	..	..	Fixed Investment
422.78	485.02	609.92	661.22	701.10	696.67	656.59	665.10	664.12	666.05	B H	GDP at factor cost
65.49	68.37	71.79	75.02	73.76	74.30	78.62	82.40	84.56	89.60	..	Agriculture
159.73	153.66	216.26	254.06	275.86	262.50	239.82	247.20	242.63	246.32	..	Industry
30.92	37.05	39.49	51.93	55.08	60.37	56.65	59.80	56.80	56.65	f	Manufacturing
227.46	310.36	369.65	367.00	394.88	398.93	367.18	361.00	367.18	360.65	..	Services, etc.
											Memo Items:
259.72	293.08	451.11	492.03	574.97	432.96	217.95	301.80	190.77	236.47	..	Capacity to Import
41.47	54.63	190.87	186.86	239.92	119.68	-84.44	0.00	-131.61	-105.90	..	Terms of Trade Adjustment
491.10	566.95	836.93	882.94	984.42	855.41	601.17	690.60	562.75	590.66	..	Gross Domestic Income
440.86	520.25	767.69	805.85	888.65	759.37	526.78	613.80	480.40	515.69	..	Gross National Income
			(Index 1987 = 100)								**DOMESTIC PRICES/DEFLATORS**
80.2	105.7	109.9	114.8	128.7	131.9	93.4	100.0	95.2	103.9	..	Overall (GDP)
71.9	92.8	83.7	88.6	94.7	112.0	108.2	100.0	117.7	118.4	..	Domestic Absorption
64.3	62.5	77.7	80.8	89.9	97.3	98.4	100.0	107.5	110.6	..	Agriculture
105.2	179.4	172.6	170.9	196.6	199.4	86.9	100.0	85.0	104.2	..	Industry
87.3	92.6	85.9	84.9	84.4	90.4	108.2	100.0	103.7	109.1	..	Manufacturing
56.1	65.6	74.1	79.8	90.0	95.5	97.8	100.0	103.7	108.0	..	Consumer Price Index
											MANUFACTURING ACTIVITY
..	..	..	..	..	..	..	..	..	..	..	Employment (1987=100)
..	..	..	..	..	..	..	..	..	..	..	Real Earnings per Empl. (1987=100)
..	..	..	..	..	..	..	..	..	..	..	Real Output per Empl. (1987=100)
..	34.3	45.1	42.0	53.7	48.5	..	..	..	..	..	Earnings as % of Value Added
			(Billions of current CFA Francs)								**MONETARY HOLDINGS**
61.41	92.12	115.95	113.83	122.26	147.49	130.49	138.46	137.51	141.39	..	Money Supply, Broadly Defined
54.34	75.11	97.60	90.49	101.34	111.86	97.51	102.33	94.90	96.26	..	Money
22.85	30.64	43.19	42.92	43.68	48.14	49.39	55.26	50.60	49.91	..	Currency Outside Banks
31.50	44.47	54.41	47.58	57.66	63.73	48.11	47.08	44.30	46.35	..	Demand Deposits
7.06	17.01	18.35	23.33	20.92	35.62	32.99	36.13	42.61	45.13	..	Quasi-Money
			(Billions of current CFA Francs)								
-18.76	13.62	-93.38	-26.65	..	..	..	..	..	..	E F	**GOVERNMENT DEFICIT (-) OR SURPLUS**
159.93	215.05	262.89	284.01	..	..	..	..	..	..		Current Revenue
..	118.35	176.36	181.34	..	..	..	..	..	..		Current Expenditure
..	96.70	86.53	102.67	..	..	..	..	..	..		Current Budget Balance
0.07	..	..	..	..	..	..	..	..	..		Capital Receipts
..	96.30	179.91	129.32	..	..	..	..	..	..		Capital Payments

CONGO, PEOPLE'S REPUBLIC OF THE	1969	1970	1971	1972	1973	1974	1975	1976	1977	1978	1979
FOREIGN TRADE (CUSTOMS BASIS)					*(Millions of current US dollars)*						
Value of Exports, fob	34.5	28.2	35.0	46.0	78.5	207.8	178.9	189.5	173.6	160.9	523.9
Nonfuel Primary Products	20.2	18.9	21.0	23.1	23.1	31.6	27.0	29.2	45.8	35.6	51.4
Fuels	0.5	0.3	0.5	2.6	28.2	158.0	131.2	136.9	99.1	93.5	433.7
Manufactures	13.7	9.0	13.5	20.2	27.2	18.2	20.7	23.5	28.8	31.8	38.8
Value of Imports, cif	78.6	57.2	78.9	89.7	125.1	123.3	164.8	167.6	183.1	242.0	266.4
Nonfuel Primary Products	14.0	12.1	13.6	17.4	19.2	22.0	28.7	29.2	40.7	58.1	75.5
Fuels	2.5	1.2	2.0	2.4	3.5	10.6	13.0	15.1	2.7	19.4	17.2
Manufactures	62.1	44.0	63.3	70.0	102.4	90.7	123.1	123.3	139.7	164.6	173.7
					(Index 1987 = 100)						
Terms of Trade	94.4	90.9	89.9	82.9	66.6	115.9	104.1	111.5	115.7	97.8	124.4
Export Prices, fob	24.7	26.2	27.1	27.5	26.0	60.1	58.0	63.1	71.5	69.9	104.4
Import Prices, cif	26.2	28.9	30.1	33.1	39.0	51.9	55.7	56.6	61.8	71.5	84.0
BALANCE OF PAYMENTS					*(Millions of current US dollars)*						
Exports of Goods & Services	..	80.2	105.1	115.2	173.0	304.9	276.9	293.1	348.6	380.4	568.7
Merchandise, fob	..	58.0	75.3	78.1	122.2	261.2	230.8	221.6	266.7	308.2	495.7
Nonfactor Services	..	22.0	28.2	34.7	47.7	41.3	43.0	68.5	77.2	68.8	69.7
Factor Services	..	0.2	1.6	2.4	3.1	2.4	3.2	3.1	4.8	3.4	3.3
Imports of Goods & Services	..	129.0	175.5	217.8	255.5	363.8	529.2	529.5	535.2	599.3	679.1
Merchandise, fob	..	72.0	98.6	119.2	126.8	193.4	272.0	235.1	234.1	282.1	363.0
Nonfactor Services	..	50.0	68.3	89.9	105.3	152.1	224.9	254.1	258.6	259.2	219.8
Factor Services	..	7.0	8.6	8.7	23.4	18.3	32.4	40.3	42.5	58.0	96.3
Long-Term Interest	..	3.0	3.0	2.9	4.6	5.6	9.2	11.8	11.9	8.2	32.4
Private Current Transfers, net	..	-4.2	-8.1	-12.7	-7.6	-57.2	-32.9	-32.3	-33.5	-13.3	-31.7
Workers' Remittances	..	0.8	..	..	..	..	..	..	..	..	..
Curr. A/C Bal before Off. Transf.	..	-53.0	-78.5	-115.3	-90.1	-116.2	-285.2	-268.7	-220.1	-232.2	-142.1
Net Official Transfers	..	8.0	11.8	17.5	11.8	23.1	36.3	41.3	26.7	51.6	42.7
Curr. A/C Bal after Off. Transf.	..	-45.0	-66.7	-97.8	-78.3	-93.1	-248.9	-227.3	-193.3	-180.6	-99.4
Long-Term Capital, net	..	59.0	58.1	85.7	74.4	72.6	159.3	138.5	135.7	172.5	72.6
Direct Investment	..	30.0	48.7	66.3	68.3	46.1	15.4	1.4	2.0	4.1	16.5
Long-Term Loans	..	12.6	16.8	22.4	29.1	57.9	112.7	34.4	47.6	144.6	149.9
Disbursements	..	18.4	22.3	27.1	36.5	70.6	132.6	45.9	69.5	156.9	187.9
Repayments	..	5.8	5.5	4.7	7.4	12.7	19.9	11.5	21.9	12.3	38.0
Other Long-Term Capital	..	16.4	-7.5	-3.1	-23.0	-31.3	31.2	102.8	86.1	23.8	-93.7
Other Capital, net	..	-12.2	8.3	10.2	0.2	39.2	79.2	84.3	49.3	-2.0	54.8
Change in Reserves	..	-1.8	0.3	2.0	3.7	-18.7	10.4	4.5	8.4	10.1	-28.1
Memo Item:					*(CFA Francs per US dollar)*						
Conversion Factor (Annual Avg)	259.710	277.710	277.130	252.210	222.700	240.500	214.320	238.980	245.670	225.640	212.720
					(Millions of US dollars), outstanding at end of year						
EXTERNAL DEBT (Total)	..	118.8	141.5	164.0	196.0	268.1	364.6	388.9	594.8	798.7	1,044.7
Long-Term Debt (by debtor)	..	118.5	140.8	162.5	192.6	263.5	359.3	381.1	465.2	674.1	852.1
Central Bank, incl. IMF credit	..	0.6	0.5	0.3	2.3	3.8	10.3	14.5	31.9	46.6	53.8
Central Government	..	73.8	93.2	111.5	138.5	202.7	290.0	302.4	365.0	545.4	688.8
Rest of General Government	..	0.3	0.3	0.2	0.5	0.5	0.3	0.3	0.2	0.3	0.2
Non-financial Public Enterprises	..	14.5	19.0	24.2	26.7	33.6	30.4	39.1	43.3	58.8	74.4
Priv. Sector, incl non-guaranteed	..	29.3	27.8	26.3	24.6	22.9	28.3	24.8	24.8	23.0	34.9
Short-Term Debt	..	0.3	0.7	1.5	3.4	4.6	5.3	7.8	129.6	124.6	192.6
Memo Items:					*(Thousands of US dollars)*						
Int'l Reserves Excluding Gold	5,741.7	8,884.8	10,820.1	10,338.0	7,858.0	24,101.2	13,814.5	12,168.2	13,530.0	9,429.1	42,232.5
Gold Holdings (at market price)	..	..	..	..	..	..	..	..	923.7	1,921.0	5,836.8
SOCIAL INDICATORS											
Total Fertility Rate	5.9	5.9	6.0	6.0	6.0	6.0	6.0	6.0	6.0	6.0	6.0
Infant Mortality Rate	126.6	126.1	125.5	125.0	125.0	125.0	124.9	124.9	124.9	124.7	124.5
Life Expectancy at Birth	45.4	45.8	46.2	46.6	47.0	47.4	47.8	48.2	48.6	49.0	49.4
Urban Population, % of total	34.6	34.8	35.0	35.2	35.4	35.6	35.8	47.6	45.0	42.5	39.9
Food Prod. per capita (1987=100)	104.6	103.4	104.1	101.2	100.9	100.4	102.6	101.6	99.4	98.1	99.0
Labor Force, Agriculture (%)	65.2	65.0	64.7	64.5	64.2	64.0	63.7	63.4	63.2	62.9	62.7
Labor Force, Female (%)	40.2	40.2	40.2	40.1	40.1	40.0	40.0	40.0	39.9	39.9	39.8
Primary Schl. Enroll. Ratio	..	..	..	..	..	133.0	..	..	..	..	..
Primary Schl. Enroll. Ratio, Female	..	..	..	..	..	..	..	..	..	..	..
Secondary Schl. Enroll. Ratio	..	..	..	..	..	33.0	..	..	..	..	..

1980	1981	1982	1983	1984	1985	1986	1987	1988	1989 estimate	NOTES	CONGO, PEOPLE'S REPUBLIC OF THE
											FOREIGN TRADE (CUSTOMS BASIS)
				(Millions of current US dollars)							
979.6	1,114.8	1,212.5	1,096.6	1,265.0	1,145.0	673.0	914.0	835.0	..	..	Value of Exports, fob
60.2	106.8	134.6	112.1	131.2	119.2	114.3	168.2	148.5	..	..	Nonfuel Primary Products
855.7	907.0	952.0	878.0	1,016.0	909.1	438.4	597.2	599.5	..	..	Fuels
63.7	101.0	125.9	106.5	117.8	116.8	120.3	148.7	87.0	..	..	Manufactures
500.0	828.0	807.0	746.0	737.0	752.0	629.0	570.0	609.0	..	..	Value of Imports, cif
107.5	193.1	190.0	173.8	160.8	162.4	140.7	109.2	165.0	..	..	Nonfuel Primary Products
69.3	95.4	92.0	86.9	83.9	68.4	32.7	42.2	41.0	..	..	Fuels
323.3	539.5	525.1	485.3	492.3	521.2	455.6	418.6	403.0	..	..	Manufactures
				(Index 1987 = 100)							
166.7	168.0	157.1	151.5	155.5	150.2	88.6	100.0	77.7	..	..	Terms of Trade
159.1	160.3	144.6	135.6	135.2	128.9	82.2	100.0	85.4	..	..	Export Prices, fob
95.4	95.4	92.0	89.5	86.9	85.8	92.8	100.0	110.0	..	..	Import Prices, cif
				(Millions of current US dollars)							**BALANCE OF PAYMENTS**
1,029.3	1,173.3	1,205.7	1,159.4	1,355.2	1,228.6	783.8	1,004.4	942.9	1,186.0	f	Exports of Goods & Services
910.6	1,072.7	1,108.5	1,066.2	1,268.4	1,144.8	672.6	876.7	843.2	1,092.0	..	Merchandise, fob
110.6	84.0	77.6	87.8	80.3	74.7	103.1	97.2	92.3	85.0	..	Nonfactor Services
8.0	16.6	19.6	5.4	6.5	9.1	8.1	30.5	7.5	9.0	..	Factor Services
1,194.9	1,645.7	1,519.2	1,556.2	1,142.4	1,392.8	1,403.4	1,238.2	1,396.2	1,268.0	f	Imports of Goods & Services
545.2	803.6	663.8	649.5	617.6	630.1	512.4	419.9	522.7	447.0	..	Merchandise, fob
480.1	713.3	697.3	727.4	391.3	525.6	656.8	532.1	560.1	554.0	..	Nonfactor Services
169.6	128.8	158.0	179.3	133.5	237.2	234.2	286.2	313.3	267.0	..	Factor Services
36.7	93.8	93.8	97.0	98.5	132.3	92.1	83.2	83.5	94.2	..	Long-Term Interest
-64.4	-32.3	-47.2	-41.1	-45.0	-37.5	-41.0	-56.8	-56.6	-45.0	..	Private Current Transfers, net
0.8	..	..	..	..	..	..	..	..	..	..	Workers' Remittances
-230.0	-504.6	-360.7	-437.9	167.9	-201.7	-660.6	-290.6	-509.9	-127.0	..	Curr. A/C Bal before Off. Transf.
63.3	43.9	29.2	37.0	42.3	40.4	59.9	67.9	64.4	62.0	..	Net Official Transfers
-166.7	-460.7	-331.5	-400.9	210.2	-161.3	-600.7	-222.7	-445.5	-65.0	f	Curr. A/C Bal after Off. Transf.
242.4	135.5	451.2	175.0	-55.4	27.8	-56.3	173.2	7.7	222.9	f	Long-Term Capital, net
40.0	30.8	35.3	56.1	34.9	12.7	22.4	43.4	9.1	..	..	Direct Investment
457.5	239.2	504.8	280.2	212.2	204.5	125.0	155.7	329.6	-41.1	..	Long-Term Loans
491.1	342.8	627.1	494.8	454.1	453.5	366.1	460.4	607.9	134.3	..	Disbursements
33.6	103.6	122.3	214.6	241.9	249.0	241.1	304.7	278.3	175.4	..	Repayments
-255.1	-134.6	-88.9	-161.3	-302.6	-189.3	-203.8	-26.0	-331.0	264.0	..	Other Long-Term Capital
-16.6	387.8	-201.3	193.6	-163.2	132.0	647.6	44.5	439.8	-247.5	f	Other Capital, net
-59.1	-62.6	81.6	32.3	8.4	1.5	9.5	5.0	-2.1	89.6	..	Change in Reserves
				(CFA Francs per US dollar)							Memo Item:
211.300	271.730	328.620	381.070	436.960	449.260	346.300	300.540	297.850	319.010	..	Conversion Factor (Annual Avg)
				(Millions of US dollars), outstanding at end of year							
1,495.8	1,474.5	1,942.4	2,006.5	2,055.3	3,040.4	3,483.1	4,351.8	4,158.1	4,316.1	..	**EXTERNAL DEBT (Total)**
1,249.7	1,358.7	1,756.7	1,834.9	1,861.8	2,361.2	2,781.8	3,450.3	3,560.9	3,546.4	..	Long-Term Debt (by debtor)
47.3	34.6	31.3	115.2	93.0	110.9	121.7	146.4	131.5	109.8	..	Central Bank, incl. IMF credit
829.7	876.2	1,130.6	1,132.7	1,200.9	1,517.0	1,925.1	2,616.0	2,732.0	2,780.0	..	Central Government
0.2	0.1	0.1	0.1	6.1	7.6	2.8	2.4	1.7	1.7	..	Rest of General Government
88.4	99.4	122.1	163.0	171.9	225.8	238.7	252.3	211.7	193.7	..	Non-financial Public Enterprises
284.1	348.4	472.6	423.9	389.9	499.9	493.5	433.2	484.0	461.2	..	Priv. Sector, incl non-guaranteed
246.1	115.8	185.7	171.6	193.5	679.2	701.3	901.5	597.2	769.7	..	Short-Term Debt
				(Thousands of US dollars)							Memo Items:
85,899.0	123,369.0	37,014.5	7,360.1	4,113.8	3,963.4	6,818.5	3,398.1	3,836.1	16,180.9	..	Int'l Reserves Excluding Gold
6,720.3	4,531.5	5,208.7	4,349.1	3,422.1	3,629.7	4,339.0	5,373.5	4,553.8	4,451.1	..	Gold Holdings (at market price)
											SOCIAL INDICATORS
6.0	6.0	6.0	6.1	6.2	6.3	6.4	6.5	6.5	6.5	..	Total Fertility Rate
124.4	124.2	124.0	123.0	122.0	121.0	120.0	119.0	117.4	115.9	..	Infant Mortality Rate
49.8	50.2	50.6	51.0	51.4	51.8	52.2	52.6	53.1	53.5	..	Life Expectancy at Birth
37.3	37.7	38.2	38.6	39.1	39.5	40.2	40.9	41.3	41.8	..	Urban Population, % of total
100.5	103.3	100.9	99.9	100.7	100.0	97.2	100.0	99.4	97.2	..	Food Prod. per capita (1987=100)
62.4	..	..	..	..	..	..	..	..	..	..	Labor Force, Agriculture (%)
39.8	39.7	39.6	39.5	39.4	39.3	39.2	39.1	39.0	38.9	..	Labor Force, Female (%)
..	..	..	..	..	..	..	..	..	..	..	Primary Schl. Enroll. Ratio
..	..	..	..	..	..	..	..	..	..	..	Primary Schl. Enroll. Ratio, Female
..	..	..	..	..	..	..	..	..	..	..	Secondary Schl. Enroll. Ratio

COSTA RICA	1969	1970	1971	1972	1973	1974	1975	1976	1977	1978	1979
CURRENT GNP PER CAPITA (US $)	510	560	610	660	750	860	950	1,070	1,320	1,560	1,790
POPULATION (thousands)	1,679	1,727	1,775	1,823	1,871	1,919	1,968	2,017	2,066	2,116	2,167
USE AND ORIGIN OF RESOURCES					*(Billions of current Costa Rican Colones)*						
Gross National Product (GNP)	5.54	6.43	7.04	7.96	9.88	12.89	16.28	20.08	25.70	29.31	33.31
Net Factor Income from Abroad	-0.11	-0.09	-0.10	-0.25	-0.28	-0.33	-0.52	-0.60	-0.63	-0.88	-1.28
GDP at Market Prices	5.66	6.52	7.14	8.22	10.16	13.22	16.80	20.68	26.33	30.19	34.58
Resource Balance	-0.29	-0.44	-0.74	-0.53	-0.62	-1.96	-1.43	-1.24	-1.44	-2.37	-3.55
Exports of Goods & NFServices	1.54	1.84	1.94	2.52	3.16	4.43	5.05	5.98	8.13	8.51	9.31
Imports of Goods & NFServices	1.83	2.28	2.69	3.05	3.78	6.39	6.48	7.22	9.57	10.88	12.86
Domestic Absorption	5.95	6.97	7.88	8.74	10.78	15.17	18.23	21.92	27.77	32.56	38.14
Private Consumption, etc.	4.11	4.81	5.15	5.75	6.93	9.75	12.04	13.72	17.17	20.41	23.14
General Gov't Consumption	0.71	0.82	0.99	1.18	1.42	1.89	2.56	3.31	4.21	5.07	6.24
Gross Domestic Investment	1.13	1.34	1.74	1.81	2.44	3.53	3.64	4.89	6.39	7.08	8.75
Fixed Investment	1.02	1.27	1.58	1.80	2.25	3.17	3.69	4.85	5.89	6.95	9.05
Indirect Taxes, net	0.58	0.73	0.77	0.74	1.00	1.45	2.12	2.57	3.41	4.00	4.22
GDP at factor cost	5.08	5.80	6.37	7.47	9.17	11.77	14.69	18.11	22.92	26.19	30.37
Agriculture	1.30	1.47	1.44	1.60	1.96	2.52	3.42	4.21	5.76	6.16	6.40
Industry	1.34	1.58	1.80	2.08	2.57	3.58	4.60	5.67	6.89	7.87	9.15
Manufacturing	..	..	..	..	..	..	..	..	..	..	..
Services, etc.	3.01	3.48	3.90	4.54	5.63	7.12	8.79	10.79	13.68	16.16	19.04
Gross Domestic Saving	0.84	0.90	1.00	1.28	1.82	1.58	2.21	3.65	4.95	4.71	5.20
Gross National Saving	..	0.83	0.92	1.05	1.58	1.32	1.77	3.15	4.46	3.97	4.07
					(Millions of 1987 Costa Rican Colones)						
Gross National Product	134,960	145,878	155,923	166,250	179,660	190,593	192,777	202,523	221,158	233,335	243,244
GDP at Market Prices	136,345	146,670	156,627	169,449	182,575	192,395	196,255	206,917	225,389	239,340	251,195
Resource Balance	-8,458	-13,473	-13,896	-7,318	-7,267	-9,019	-5,497	-12,022	-24,380	-24,754	-25,251
Exports of Goods & NFServices	31,671	36,548	39,666	46,435	49,819	53,437	52,383	55,222	59,726	65,662	67,802
Imports of Goods & NFServices	40,129	50,021	53,562	53,753	57,087	62,455	57,880	67,245	84,105	90,416	93,053
Domestic Absorption	144,803	160,143	170,523	176,767	189,843	201,414	201,752	218,939	249,768	264,093	276,446
Private Consumption, etc.	95,375	104,791	106,052	113,399	118,049	123,499	126,259	129,559	144,992	158,184	161,350
General Gov't Consumption	21,611	23,688	25,195	26,968	28,602	31,016	32,773	35,330	38,424	39,832	42,905
Gross Domestic Investment	27,818	31,664	39,276	36,400	43,192	46,899	42,721	54,050	66,353	66,078	72,191
Fixed Investment	21,689	25,996	30,253	31,671	34,353	37,701	37,235	46,057	51,783	55,994	64,553
GDP at factor cost	..	..	..	..	..	..	..	..	..	..	235,959
Agriculture	32,306	33,633	35,185	37,092	39,187	38,524	39,693	39,890	40,769	43,460	43,675
Industry	30,764	33,501	36,857	41,455	44,987	50,186	51,966	56,504	62,455	67,168	71,149
Manufacturing	..	..	..	..	..	..	..	..	..	..	..
Services, etc.	73,283	79,512	84,475	90,656	98,112	103,623	104,572	110,653	122,430	129,042	136,807
Memo Items:											
Capacity to Import	33,686	40,343	38,780	44,429	47,730	43,321	45,139	55,684	71,453	70,717	67,358
Terms of Trade Adjustment	2,015	3,795	-887	-2,006	-2,090	-10,116	-7,245	462	11,728	5,055	-445
Gross Domestic Income	138,360	150,465	155,741	167,443	180,486	182,279	189,011	207,379	237,116	244,394	250,750
Gross National Income	136,976	149,673	155,036	164,244	177,570	180,477	185,533	202,985	232,886	238,390	242,799
DOMESTIC PRICES/DEFLATORS					*(Index 1987 = 100)*						
Overall (GDP)	4.1	4.4	4.6	4.8	5.6	6.9	8.6	10.0	11.7	12.6	13.8
Domestic Absorption	4.1	4.3	4.6	4.9	5.7	7.5	9.0	10.0	11.1	12.3	13.8
Agriculture	4.0	4.4	4.1	4.3	5.0	6.5	8.6	10.6	14.1	14.2	14.7
Industry	4.4	4.7	4.9	5.0	5.7	7.1	8.9	10.0	11.0	11.7	12.9
Manufacturing	..	..	..	..	..	..	..	..	..	..	..
Consumer Price Index	5.9	6.1	6.3	6.6	7.6	9.9	11.7	12.1	12.6	13.3	14.6
MANUFACTURING ACTIVITY											
Employment (1987=100)	..	..	..	..	..	..	..	..	..	..	..
Real Earnings per Empl. (1987=100)	..	..	..	..	..	..	..	..	..	..	..
Real Output per Empl. (1987=100)	..	..	..	..	..	..	..	..	..	..	..
Earnings as % of Value Added	41.9	41.4	41.9	41.8	40.0	38.4	39.5	40.1	38.6	40.0	40.5
MONETARY HOLDINGS					*(Billions of current Costa Rican Colones)*						
Money Supply, Broadly Defined	1.19	1.28	1.81	2.17	2.64	3.45	4.90	6.59	8.66	11.07	14.87
Money	0.96	1.01	1.32	1.50	1.87	2.15	2.77	3.41	4.50	5.62	6.23
Currency Outside Banks	0.35	0.38	0.43	0.52	0.64	0.73	0.85	1.12	1.41	1.70	1.95
Demand Deposits	0.61	0.63	0.88	0.98	1.23	1.41	1.92	2.29	3.09	3.92	4.27
Quasi-Money	0.24	0.27	0.49	0.66	0.77	1.30	2.13	3.18	4.16	5.44	8.64
					(Millions of current Costa Rican Colones)						
GOVERNMENT DEFICIT (-) OR SURPLUS	..	..	..	-360	-380	-90	-370	-700	-820	-1,510	-2,340
Current Revenue	..	..	..	1,260	1,620	2,450	3,030	3,650	4,390	5,750	6,320
Current Expenditure	..	..	..	1,260	1,570	2,000	2,750	3,500	4,170	5,870	7,040
Current Budget Balance	..	..	..	0	50	450	280	150	220	-120	-720
Capital Receipts	..	..	..	..	..	..	..	..	..	..	..
Capital Payments	..	..	..	360	430	540	650	850	1,040	1,390	1,620

1980	1981	1982	1983	1984	1985	1986	1987	1988	1989 estimate	NOTES	COSTA RICA
1,960	1,540	1,150	1,060	1,250	1,400	1,550	1,650	1,680	1,780	..	**CURRENT GNP PER CAPITA (US $)**
2,218	2,270	2,323	2,377	2,432	2,489	2,547	2,608	2,670	2,735	..	**POPULATION (thousands)**
(Billions of current Costa Rican Colones)											**USE AND ORIGIN OF RESOURCES**
39.42	50.67	81.42	115.64	149.21	183.79	231.50	265.70	324.20	399.30	..	Gross National Product (GNP)
-1.99	-6.43	-16.09	-13.67	-13.80	-14.12	-15.10	-18.60	-25.40	-26.20	..	Net Factor Income from Abroad
41.41	57.10	97.51	129.31	163.01	197.90	246.60	284.30	349.60	425.50	..	GDP at Market Prices
-4.28	-2.80	2.85	-0.96	0.60	-3.50	2.10	-11.70	-7.00	-16.60	..	Resource Balance
10.96	24.71	43.96	46.60	56.00	60.80	77.30	90.10	120.70	147.50	..	Exports of Goods & NFServices
15.25	27.51	41.11	47.57	55.40	64.30	75.20	101.80	127.70	164.10	..	Imports of Goods & NFServices
45.69	59.91	94.66	130.28	162.41	201.40	244.50	296.00	356.60	442.10	..	Domestic Absorption
27.14	34.34	56.40	79.48	99.91	119.90	144.30	176.30	218.70	269.30	..	Private Consumption, etc.
7.54	8.99	14.19	19.53	25.50	31.20	38.00	42.70	54.60	68.90	..	General Gov't Consumption
11.00	16.58	24.07	31.27	37.00	50.30	62.20	77.00	83.30	103.90	..	Gross Domestic Investment
9.89	13.74	19.81	23.27	32.68	38.20	46.00	56.30	66.20	84.00	..	Fixed Investment
4.86	6.78	11.31	18.62	23.91	26.69	32.10	22.60	..	..	..	Indirect Taxes, net
36.54	50.32	86.19	110.69	139.10	171.21	214.50	261.70	..	..	B	GDP at factor cost
7.37	13.14	23.88	28.45	34.57	37.30	51.50	51.40	62.80	73.10	..	Agriculture
11.17	15.20	25.10	37.00	48.01	57.10	68.06	78.50	95.00	114.40	..	Industry
..	..	..	..	..	..	..	..	..	..	f	Manufacturing
22.87	28.76	48.52	63.87	80.43	103.50	127.04	154.40	191.80	238.00	..	Services, etc.
6.72	13.77	26.92	30.31	37.60	46.80	64.30	65.30	76.30	87.30	..	Gross Domestic Saving
4.90	7.93	11.94	17.57	25.22	34.83	51.29	49.13	53.93	64.37	..	Gross National Saving
(Millions of 1987 Costa Rican Colones)											
242,521	232,827	209,581	219,301	238,581	241,811	254,810	265,700	273,587	290,133	..	Gross National Product
253,072	247,354	230,104	236,499	255,079	257,215	271,384	284,300	294,170	310,970	..	GDP at Market Prices
-25,002	5,877	13,934	4,471	5,361	-1,796	-12,136	-11,700	-4,839	-5,364	..	Resource Balance
64,857	72,069	68,136	67,242	74,823	71,836	74,442	90,100	98,007	111,514	..	Exports of Goods & NFServices
89,859	66,192	54,202	62,771	69,462	73,632	86,578	101,800	102,846	116,878	..	Imports of Goods & NFServices
278,075	241,477	216,170	232,028	249,719	259,011	283,520	296,000	299,009	316,334	..	Domestic Absorption
157,299	152,288	140,271	145,450	156,399	161,186	167,114	176,300	182,936	195,298	..	Private Consumption, etc.
43,529	41,087	40,040	38,863	40,378	40,787	41,779	42,700	43,982	45,520	..	General Gov't Consumption
77,247	48,102	35,859	47,715	52,942	57,038	74,626	77,000	72,090	75,516	..	Gross Domestic Investment
58,473	43,908	31,698	34,319	43,293	45,621	51,025	56,300	54,243	60,209	..	Fixed Investment
239,075	234,735	220,671	222,044	241,315	241,057	248,583	261,700	..	..	B	GDP at factor cost
43,457	45,673	43,525	45,265	49,813	47,060	49,327	51,400	53,763	56,719	..	Agriculture
71,975	68,949	59,652	62,086	69,086	70,138	74,715	78,500	80,012	84,408	..	Industry
..	..	..	..	..	..	..	..	..	..	f	Manufacturing
138,112	133,026	126,892	129,148	136,181	140,017	147,342	154,400	160,395	169,843	..	Services, etc.
											Memo Items:
64,621	59,449	57,954	61,498	70,215	69,624	88,996	90,100	97,208	105,055	..	Capacity to Import
-236	-12,620	-10,181	-5,743	-4,609	-2,212	14,554	0	-799	-6,459	..	Terms of Trade Adjustment
252,836	234,734	219,922	230,756	250,471	255,003	285,938	284,300	293,371	304,511	..	Gross Domestic Income
242,285	220,208	199,400	213,557	233,972	239,599	269,364	265,700	272,789	283,675	..	Gross National Income
(Index 1987 = 100)											**DOMESTIC PRICES/DEFLATORS**
16.4	23.1	42.4	54.7	63.9	76.9	90.9	100.0	118.8	136.8	..	Overall (GDP)
16.4	24.8	43.8	56.1	65.0	77.8	86.2	100.0	119.3	139.8	..	Domestic Absorption
17.0	28.8	54.9	62.8	69.4	79.3	104.4	100.0	116.8	128.9	..	Agriculture
15.5	22.0	42.1	59.6	69.5	81.4	91.1	100.0	118.7	135.5	..	Industry
..	..	..	..	..	..	..	..	..	..		Manufacturing
17.2	23.6	44.8	59.4	66.5	76.5	85.6	100.0	120.8	140.8	..	Consumer Price Index
											MANUFACTURING ACTIVITY
..	..	..	..	..	..	92.3	100.0	102.5	..	..	Employment (1987=100)
..	..	..	..	..	..	100.2	100.0	92.8	..	..	Real Earnings per Empl. (1987=100)
..	..	..	..	..	..	105.9	100.0	101.7	..	G	Real Output per Empl. (1987=100)
42.9	..	..	..	..	..	29.6	32.8	30.6	..	..	Earnings as % of Value Added
(Billions of current Costa Rican Colones)											**MONETARY HOLDINGS**
17.24	32.27	40.99	56.14	65.76	76.00	92.16	107.15	150.23	174.83	..	Money Supply, Broadly Defined
7.27	10.83	18.45	25.62	30.13	32.44	42.49	42.61	65.27	63.97	..	Money
2.26	3.50	5.44	6.94	8.59	9.94	13.24	14.78	24.73	21.92	..	Currency Outside Banks
5.02	7.33	13.01	18.68	21.54	22.50	29.25	27.83	40.53	42.05	..	Demand Deposits
9.96	21.44	22.55	30.52	35.63	43.56	49.67	64.53	84.96	110.86	..	Quasi-Money
(Millions of current Costa Rican Colones)											
-3,060	-1,640	-860	-2,600	-1,200	-2,470	-11,040	-8,290	10	..	..	**GOVERNMENT DEFICIT (-) OR SURPLUS**
7,380	10,190	17,030	28,110	36,380	41,010	54,560	70,080	87,720	..	..	Current Revenue
8,810	10,620	17,490	27,000	33,080	36,970	53,700	67,330	74,230	..	..	Current Expenditure
-1,430	-430	-460	1,110	3,300	4,040	860	2,750	13,490	..	..	Current Budget Balance
..	..	..	..	..	..	..	..	10	30	..	Capital Receipts
1,630	1,210	400	3,710	4,500	6,510	11,900	11,050	13,510	..	..	Capital Payments

COSTA RICA	1969	1970	1971	1972	1973	1974	1975	1976	1977	1978	1979
FOREIGN TRADE (CUSTOMS BASIS)					*(Millions of current US dollars)*						
Value of Exports, fob	189.7	231.2	225.4	280.9	344.5	440.3	494.1	600.4	839.5	919.4	934.3
Nonfuel Primary Products	153.7	184.7	172.4	221.1	264.1	321.5	364.2	428.5	635.5	655.3	705.2
Fuels	0.2	1.0	1.8	0.6	0.4	0.6	0.3	0.8	0.8	0.9	0.8
Manufactures	35.9	45.5	51.1	59.2	79.9	118.2	129.6	171.2	203.3	263.1	228.3
Value of Imports, cif	245.1	316.7	349.7	372.8	455.3	719.7	694.0	800.3	1,059.3	1,211.7	1,446.1
Nonfuel Primary Products	31.6	44.6	51.6	48.8	61.0	108.7	89.2	95.0	115.1	122.8	152.5
Fuels	10.6	12.3	15.8	20.1	31.5	65.1	73.8	73.8	102.2	117.7	189.5
Manufactures	202.9	259.8	282.4	303.8	362.9	545.8	531.0	631.4	842.0	971.2	1,104.1
					(Index 1987 = 100)						
Terms of Trade	151.0	155.8	132.5	141.0	145.7	124.3	117.3	143.1	166.0	133.8	132.5
Export Prices, fob	38.0	41.8	37.9	43.1	53.4	63.6	64.2	79.2	100.1	91.1	106.2
Import Prices, cif	25.2	26.8	28.6	30.6	36.7	51.2	54.7	55.3	60.3	68.1	80.2
BALANCE OF PAYMENTS					*(Millions of current US dollars)*						
Exports of Goods & Services	..	277.9	281.4	344.2	418.8	539.6	600.5	710.6	969.1	1,025.0	1,111.3
Merchandise, fob	..	231.0	225.3	278.8	344.8	440.2	493.1	592.4	827.8	863.9	942.1
Nonfactor Services	..	45.9	55.5	64.1	71.4	95.2	103.2	112.6	130.9	143.8	156.1
Factor Services	..	1.0	0.7	1.3	2.6	4.2	4.2	5.7	10.4	17.3	13.1
Imports of Goods & Services	..	357.9	403.3	450.8	537.9	815.4	827.8	925.2	1,210.5	1,404.8	1,681.7
Merchandise, fob	..	286.8	317.2	337.1	412.1	648.9	627.2	695.4	925.1	1,049.4	1,257.2
Nonfactor Services	..	54.3	68.3	74.8	82.4	120.5	130.4	148.6	195.3	224.8	261.7
Factor Services	..	16.8	17.8	38.9	43.4	45.9	70.2	81.3	90.1	130.6	162.8
Long-Term Interest	..	14.2	15.3	17.7	23.6	31.2	36.9	41.0	51.5	84.6	116.2
Private Current Transfers, net	..	3.4	3.5	4.0	7.0	8.7	9.5	11.2	15.4	15.9	16.5
Workers' Remittances	..	..	..	..	..	..	..	..	..	..	..
Curr. A/C Bal before Off. Transf.	..	-76.6	-118.4	-102.6	-112.1	-267.1	-217.8	-203.4	-226.0	-363.9	-553.9
Net Official Transfers	..	2.5	3.9	2.6	-0.1	1.0	0.1	2.0	0.4	0.7	-4.3
Curr. A/C Bal after Off. Transf.	..	-74.1	-114.4	-100.0	-112.2	-266.1	-217.7	-201.5	-225.6	-363.2	-558.2
Long-Term Capital, net	..	43.8	57.1	80.1	92.4	135.9	238.0	217.4	298.8	352.7	354.7
Direct Investment	..	26.4	22.1	25.8	37.7	46.3	69.0	60.7	62.5	47.0	42.4
Long-Term Loans	..	18.9	35.1	53.1	61.4	83.6	157.8	156.3	247.6	211.6	198.8
Disbursements	..	59.9	78.1	103.3	118.2	157.8	260.1	275.9	399.0	515.3	464.9
Repayments	..	41.0	43.0	50.2	56.8	74.2	102.3	119.6	151.4	303.7	266.1
Other Long-Term Capital	..	-1.5	-0.1	1.2	-6.7	6.0	11.2	0.4	-11.3	94.1	113.5
Other Capital, net	..	15.0	63.5	23.6	46.2	79.4	-18.3	35.8	33.3	-16.6	120.5
Change in Reserves	..	15.3	-6.1	-3.7	-26.4	50.8	-2.0	-51.8	-106.4	27.1	83.0
Memo Item:					*(Costa Rican Colones per US dollar)*						
Conversion Factor (Annual Avg)	6.630	6.630	6.630	6.630	6.650	7.930	8.570	8.570	8.570	8.570	8.570
					(Millions of US dollars), outstanding at end of year						
EXTERNAL DEBT (Total)	..	246.0	282.6	339.2	401.6	508.5	684.4	842.8	1,317.2	1,679.0	2,109.8
Long-Term Debt (by debtor)	..	246.0	282.6	339.2	401.6	508.5	684.4	842.8	1,094.2	1,395.0	1,756.8
Central Bank, incl. IMF credit	..	27.0	28.6	33.3	39.8	79.5	131.6	175.8	261.8	281.0	478.2
Central Government	..	50.0	65.3	87.9	110.2	120.6	147.3	174.1	213.1	317.7	410.6
Rest of General Government	..	0.9	4.4	5.1	5.4	4.5	7.3	6.5	5.8	5.2	4.3
Non-financial Public Enterprises	..	54.4	62.8	72.6	85.3	110.6	153.6	194.9	247.7	334.6	418.9
Priv. Sector, incl non-guaranteed	..	113.7	121.5	140.3	160.9	193.3	244.6	291.5	365.8	456.5	444.8
Short-Term Debt	..	..	..	..	..	..	..	..	223.0	284.0	353.0
Memo Items:					*(Millions of US dollars)*						
Int'l Reserves Excluding Gold	27.1	14.2	27.2	40.6	48.5	42.1	48.8	95.4	190.5	193.9	118.6
Gold Holdings (at market price)	2.1	2.2	2.6	3.9	6.7	11.1	8.4	8.0	12.1	18.1	44.5
SOCIAL INDICATORS											
Total Fertility Rate	5.2	4.9	4.6	4.3	4.3	4.2	4.1	4.0	3.9	3.8	3.7
Infant Mortality Rate	67.1	61.5	56.5	54.4	44.8	37.5	37.8	33.1	27.9	23.8	23.3
Life Expectancy at Birth	66.6	67.1	67.6	68.1	68.6	69.2	69.7	70.3	70.8	71.3	71.9
Urban Population, % of total	39.4	39.7	40.0	40.3	40.6	41.4	42.2	43.0	43.7	44.5	45.2
Food Prod. per capita (1987=100)	100.6	106.9	111.3	113.3	115.0	108.9	118.9	118.7	118.2	116.0	117.0
Labor Force, Agriculture (%)	43.3	42.6	41.2	39.9	38.7	37.6	36.6	35.2	34.0	32.8	31.8
Labor Force, Female (%)	17.8	18.0	18.4	18.8	19.1	19.4	19.7	20.0	20.4	20.7	21.0
Primary Schl. Enroll. Ratio	..	110.0	..	..	..	..	107.0	108.0	109.0	107.0	107.0
Primary Schl. Enroll. Ratio, Female	..	109.0	..	..	..	..	106.0	108.0	108.0	107.0	106.0
Secondary Schl. Enroll. Ratio	..	28.0	..	..	..	..	42.0	43.0	44.0	..	48.0

1980	1981	1982	1983	1984	1985	1986	1987	1988	1989 estimate	NOTES	COSTA RICA
											FOREIGN TRADE (CUSTOMS BASIS)
				(Millions of current US dollars)							
1,031.5	1,010.5	876.8	867.0	966.8	976.0	1,125.2	1,154.7	1,320.0	..	..	Value of Exports, fob
671.4	676.4	620.9	602.3	664.1	636.8	716.3	681.0	778.4	..	..	Nonfuel Primary Products
6.2	12.5	8.0	8.2	8.4	8.5	4.5	6.3	5.9	..	..	Fuels
353.9	321.6	247.9	256.5	294.4	330.7	404.5	467.4	535.7	..	..	Manufactures
1,596.5	1,274.2	945.2	993.0	1,091.0	1,098.2	1,147.5	1,376.7	1,409.0	..	..	Value of Imports, cif
198.0	157.9	114.0	120.8	121.6	111.5	102.3	79.6	110.0	..	..	Nonfuel Primary Products
245.7	205.3	188.9	186.2	171.6	171.4	94.3	144.1	164.0	..	..	Fuels
1,152.7	911.0	642.3	686.1	797.8	815.3	950.9	1,153.0	1,135.0	..	..	Manufactures
				(Index 1987 = 100)							
117.4	110.6	108.3	111.5	112.4	111.3	120.7	100.0	108.3	..	..	Terms of Trade
108.7	103.4	100.5	100.6	97.4	95.8	109.3	100.0	113.0	..	..	Export Prices, fob
92.6	93.5	92.7	90.2	86.7	86.1	90.5	100.0	104.4	..	..	Import Prices, cif
				(Millions of current US dollars)							**BALANCE OF PAYMENTS**
1,218.6	1,199.3	1,143.4	1,172.6	1,313.7	1,270.2	1,440.2	1,492.3	1,658.8	1,891.6	f	Exports of Goods & Services
1,000.9	1,002.6	869.0	852.5	997.5	939.1	1,084.8	1,106.7	1,180.7	1,322.7	..	Merchandise, fob
196.9	172.9	247.7	280.2	278.5	281.3	310.0	344.5	439.4	509.2	..	Nonfactor Services
20.8	23.8	26.7	39.9	37.7	49.8	45.4	41.1	38.7	59.7	..	Factor Services
1,897.0	1,639.1	1,451.0	1,524.1	1,605.7	1,614.9	1,672.1	1,974.7	2,092.7	2,434.3	f	Imports of Goods & Services
1,375.2	1,090.6	804.9	894.3	992.9	1,001.0	1,045.2	1,245.2	1,278.6	1,577.2	..	Merchandise, fob
282.5	213.4	237.5	249.9	255.0	274.0	296.0	382.9	416.6	446.2	..	Nonfactor Services
239.3	335.1	408.6	379.9	357.8	339.9	330.9	346.6	397.5	410.9	..	Factor Services
170.6	135.1	109.0	528.9	243.3	341.7	216.2	145.3	185.5	161.5	..	Long-Term Interest
19.8	27.2	29.6	22.9	31.9	42.6	37.4	38.7	40.0	40.1	..	Private Current Transfers, net
..	..	..	..	..	..	0.0	0.0	0.0	..	..	Workers' Remittances
-658.6	-409.0	-273.0	-326.0	-260.1	-302.1	-194.5	-443.7	-393.9	-502.6	..	Curr. A/C Bal before Off. Transf.
-5.3	-0.1	6.3	46.1	109.0	176.1	114.5	187.3	215.4	120.7	..	Net Official Transfers
-663.9	-409.1	-266.7	-279.9	-151.1	-126.0	-80.0	-256.4	-178.5	-381.9	..	Curr. A/C Bal after Off. Transf.
402.2	217.6	22.1	1,175.3	67.4	343.4	-55.9	-363.1	-98.0	71.9	f	Long-Term Capital, net
48.1	66.2	26.5	55.3	52.0	65.2	57.4	75.8	121.4	114.9	..	Direct Investment
369.4	187.9	122.3	292.6	101.1	171.3	-12.4	10.8	-20.8	-3.3	..	Long-Term Loans
532.5	366.0	243.1	429.8	238.5	312.1	189.5	86.6	126.3	127.7	..	Disbursements
163.1	178.1	120.8	137.2	137.4	140.8	201.9	75.8	147.1	131.0	..	Repayments
-15.3	-36.5	-126.7	827.4	-85.7	106.9	-100.9	-449.7	-198.6	-39.7	..	Other Long-Term Capital
223.7	146.8	358.0	-823.0	79.8	-103.1	228.8	662.3	510.7	459.6	f	Other Capital, net
38.0	44.8	-113.4	-72.4	3.9	-114.3	-92.9	-42.8	-234.2	-149.6	..	Change in Reserves
				(Costa Rican Colones per US dollar)							Memo Item:
8.570	21.760	37.410	41.090	44.530	50.450	55.990	62.780	75.800	81.500	..	Conversion Factor (Annual Avg)
				(Millions of US dollars), outstanding at end of year							
2,735.3	3,286.0	3,627.2	4,163.7	3,972.8	4,370.1	4,528.8	4,691.1	4,531.7	4,468.3	..	**EXTERNAL DEBT (Total)**
2,160.3	2,666.2	2,851.6	3,668.5	3,637.5	3,994.0	4,057.0	4,112.2	3,920.7	3,818.6	..	Long-Term Debt (by debtor)
663.5	1,072.2	1,134.5	1,239.8	1,230.8	1,233.6	1,100.9	1,073.5	900.5	862.4	..	Central Bank, incl. IMF credit
505.2	546.0	657.3	1,522.6	1,563.0	1,938.8	2,105.4	2,111.8	2,127.9	2,110.1	..	Central Government
3.2	2.2	2.2	1.5	1.1	18.0	13.6	13.6	13.4	9.0	..	Rest of General Government
535.6	641.9	634.4	534.7	508.4	492.4	525.5	608.8	560.5	531.6	..	Non-financial Public Enterprises
452.8	403.9	423.2	369.9	334.2	311.2	311.6	304.5	318.4	305.5	..	Priv. Sector, incl non-guaranteed
575.0	619.8	775.6	495.2	335.3	376.1	471.8	578.9	611.0	649.7	..	Short-Term Debt
				(Millions of US dollars)							Memo Items:
145.6	131.4	226.1	311.3	405.0	506.4	523.4	488.9	668.0	742.6	..	Int'l Reserves Excluding Gold
51.3	11.5	23.7	33.4	7.1	19.0	27.1	30.3	8.7	3.3	..	Gold Holdings (at market price)
											SOCIAL INDICATORS
3.7	3.6	3.5	3.5	3.4	3.4	3.3	3.3	3.2	3.1	..	Total Fertility Rate
20.1	17.9	19.3	18.6	18.9	18.6	18.3	18.0	17.6	17.2	..	Infant Mortality Rate
72.4	73.0	73.5	73.8	74.0	74.2	74.4	74.6	74.8	74.9	..	Life Expectancy at Birth
46.0	45.7	45.4	45.1	44.8	44.5	44.5	44.5	44.5	44.5	..	Urban Population, % of total
109.9	107.1	99.1	100.2	103.0	100.9	100.6	100.0	98.1	99.0	..	Food Prod. per capita (1987=100)
30.8	..	..	..	..	..	..	..	..	..	..	Labor Force, Agriculture (%)
21.3	21.4	21.4	21.5	21.6	21.6	21.7	21.7	21.7	21.7	..	Labor Force, Female (%)
105.0	..	103.0	102.0	98.0	97.0	98.0	98.0	..	..	..	Primary Schl. Enroll. Ratio
104.0	105.0	102.0	100.0	97.0	96.0	97.0	97.0	..	..	..	Primary Schl. Enroll. Ratio, Female
48.0	..	46.0	44.0	41.0	40.0	41.0	41.0	..	..	..	Secondary Schl. Enroll. Ratio

COTE D'IVOIRE	1969	1970	1971	1972	1973	1974	1975	1976	1977	1978	1979
CURRENT GNP PER CAPITA (US $)	260	270	280	290	310	390	510	560	640	840	1,010
POPULATION (thousands)	5,285	5,510	5,744	5,985	6,235	6,491	6,755	7,026	7,305	7,592	7,888

USE AND ORIGIN OF RESOURCES *(Billions of current CFA Francs)*

	1969	1970	1971	1972	1973	1974	1975	1976	1977	1978	1979
Gross National Product (GNP)	334.6	380.3	407.2	433.8	509.5	679.6	767.2	1,006.9	1,406.9	1,610.5	1,742.4
Net Factor Income from Abroad	-19.3	-22.0	-29.0	-32.3	-49.6	-59.4	-67.3	-107.1	-132.3	-172.3	-202.5
GDP at Market Prices	353.9	402.3	436.2	466.1	559.1	739.0	834.5	1,114.0	1,539.2	1,782.8	1,944.9
Resource Balance	34.3	26.8	16.5	21.0	14.1	54.1	1.2	61.2	96.9	-16.3	-59.5
Exports of Goods & NFServices	130.1	143.9	140.5	156.2	199.9	337.7	306.5	465.0	656.1	651.1	673.0
Imports of Goods & NFServices	95.8	117.1	124.0	135.2	185.8	283.6	305.3	403.8	559.2	667.4	732.5
Domestic Absorption	319.6	375.5	419.7	445.1	545.0	684.9	833.3	1,052.8	1,442.3	1,799.1	2,004.4
Private Consumption, etc.	207.3	230.4	255.1	275.1	327.3	402.5	504.2	616.4	811.9	978.1	1,106.7
General Gov't Consumption	43.2	54.6	69.5	72.7	88.1	119.7	141.8	180.3	209.7	290.4	353.8
Gross Domestic Investment	69.1	90.5	95.1	97.3	129.6	162.7	187.3	256.1	420.7	530.6	543.9
Fixed Investment	61.3	83.1	91.5	94.2	121.9	143.6	183.9	247.2	397.6	528.8	527.1
Indirect Taxes, net	69.5	83.9	79.1	83.8	110.2	164.5	149.8	299.8	501.5	448.6	448.4
GDP at factor cost	284.4	318.4	357.1	382.3	448.9	574.5	684.7	814.2	1,037.7	1,334.2	1,496.5
Agriculture	118.8	128.2	134.7	138.9	173.6	188.2	235.7	272.7	373.5	461.4	513.5
Industry	54.6	74.4	85.9	92.0	99.2	118.9	142.2	182.3	233.3	293.8	331.8
Manufacturing	32.7	41.4	45.1	51.7	56.8	75.6	78.4	104.8	117.6	137.0	158.1
Services, etc.	111.0	115.8	136.5	151.4	176.1	267.4	306.8	359.2	430.9	579.0	651.2
Gross Domestic Saving	103.4	117.3	111.6	118.3	143.7	216.8	188.5	317.3	517.6	514.3	484.4
Gross National Saving	..	79.9	64.3	63.4	66.7	123.9	81.8	141.0	300.6	238.6	159.3

(Billions of 1987 CFA Francs)

	1969	1970	1971	1972	1973	1974	1975	1976	1977	1978	1979
Gross National Product	1,324.7	1,451.8	1,607.0	1,712.1	1,750.4	1,900.5	2,106.5	2,154.5	2,120.3	2,383.9	2,451.0
GDP at Market Prices	1,437.7	1,575.5	1,758.0	1,871.0	1,950.7	2,071.1	2,282.2	2,413.6	2,409.7	2,744.2	2,824.5
Resource Balance	233.2	203.5	237.1	321.3	174.3	258.5	238.3	159.8	-178.6	-296.6	-227.9
Exports of Goods & NFServices	728.3	783.9	829.6	928.8	909.5	1,043.7	1,002.2	1,119.8	1,031.0	1,090.3	1,115.1
Imports of Goods & NFServices	495.0	580.5	592.5	607.5	735.2	785.3	763.8	960.0	1,209.6	1,386.8	1,343.0
Domestic Absorption	1,204.5	1,372.0	1,520.9	1,549.7	1,776.4	1,812.7	2,043.8	2,253.9	2,588.3	3,040.8	3,052.4
Private Consumption, etc.	670.9	723.9	817.8	864.6	952.6	968.0	1,144.4	1,158.1	1,186.4	1,393.7	1,427.0
General Gov't Consumption	201.2	245.6	302.5	300.7	340.8	371.5	412.9	481.3	518.6	619.0	669.5
Gross Domestic Investment	332.4	402.5	400.6	384.4	483.0	473.2	486.6	614.4	883.3	1,028.0	956.0
Fixed Investment	267.2	335.2	351.1	339.0	412.9	377.6	438.0	541.2	774.1	943.4	851.9
GDP at factor cost	1,079.2	1,173.0	1,362.0	1,446.8	1,490.7	1,604.7	1,829.0	1,756.1	1,608.4	1,992.2	2,092.6
Agriculture	600.5	626.1	674.3	678.0	719.8	643.5	704.0	746.4	713.9	781.8	784.9
Industry	197.0	260.6	316.0	338.1	325.8	319.5	365.7	422.6	464.8	553.6	597.9
Manufacturing	..	..	..	..	..	..	..	..	..	..	..
Services, etc.	336.8	342.8	418.8	466.0	486.3	607.2	707.3	610.3	509.0	694.8	742.0

Memo Items:

	1969	1970	1971	1972	1973	1974	1975	1976	1977	1978	1979
Capacity to Import	672.3	713.3	671.4	701.8	791.0	935.1	766.8	1,105.5	1,419.2	1,353.0	1,233.9
Terms of Trade Adjustment	-56.0	-70.6	-158.3	-227.0	-118.5	-108.7	-235.3	-14.3	388.2	262.7	118.8
Gross Domestic Income	1,381.7	1,504.9	1,599.7	1,644.0	1,832.2	1,962.5	2,046.8	2,399.4	2,797.9	3,006.9	2,943.3
Gross National Income	1,268.7	1,381.2	1,448.7	1,485.1	1,631.9	1,791.9	1,871.2	2,140.3	2,508.6	2,646.6	2,569.8

DOMESTIC PRICES/DEFLATORS *(Index 1987 = 100)*

	1969	1970	1971	1972	1973	1974	1975	1976	1977	1978	1979
Overall (GDP)	24.6	25.5	24.8	24.9	28.7	35.7	36.6	46.2	63.9	65.0	68.9
Domestic Absorption	26.5	27.4	27.6	28.7	30.7	37.8	40.8	46.7	55.7	59.2	65.7
Agriculture	19.8	20.5	20.0	20.5	24.1	29.2	33.5	36.5	52.3	59.0	65.4
Industry	27.7	28.5	27.2	27.2	30.5	37.2	38.9	43.1	50.2	53.1	55.5
Manufacturing	..	..	..	..	..	..	..	..	..	..	..
Consumer Price Index	20.9	22.8	22.5	22.5	25.0	29.4	32.7	36.7	46.8	52.8	61.6

MANUFACTURING ACTIVITY

	1969	1970	1971	1972	1973	1974	1975	1976	1977	1978	1979
Employment (1987=100)	..	..	..	..	..	..	..	..	..	..	..
Real Earnings per Empl. (1987=100)	..	..	..	..	..	..	..	..	..	..	..
Real Output per Empl. (1987=100)	..	..	..	..	..	..	..	..	..	..	..
Earnings as % of Value Added	26.1	27.1	26.2	25.6	27.6	25.0	29.8	29.7	26.1	29.3	30.5

MONETARY HOLDINGS *(Billions of current CFA Francs)*

	1969	1970	1971	1972	1973	1974	1975	1976	1977	1978	1979
Money Supply, Broadly Defined	91.92	106.78	117.60	122.83	147.91	223.21	244.56	349.75	524.49	581.61	566.16
Money	69.77	83.54	92.08	103.16	117.94	162.81	179.84	260.10	383.08	415.55	433.78
Currency Outside Banks	33.99	39.83	46.95	51.48	57.02	77.47	89.63	106.74	137.27	164.47	193.71
Demand Deposits	35.78	43.71	45.13	51.68	60.92	85.34	90.21	153.36	245.81	251.08	240.07
Quasi-Money	22.15	23.24	25.52	19.67	29.97	60.40	64.72	89.65	141.41	166.06	132.38

(Billions of current CFA Francs)

	1969	1970	1971	1972	1973	1974	1975	1976	1977	1978	1979
GOVERNMENT DEFICIT (-) OR SURPLUS	..	..	..	..	..	..	..	..	..	..	-168.30
Current Revenue	..	..	..	..	..	..	..	..	..	..	467.11
Current Expenditure	..	..	..	..	..	..	..	..	..	..	..
Current Budget Balance	..	..	..	..	..	..	..	..	..	..	..
Capital Receipts	..	..	..	..	..	..	..	..	..	..	..
Capital Payments	..	..	..	..	..	..	..	..	..	..	..

1980	1981	1982	1983	1984	1985	1986	1987	1988	1989 estimate	NOTES	COTE D'IVOIRE
1,180	1,150	990	790	690	650	710	790	880	790	..	**CURRENT GNP PER CAPITA (US $)**
8,194	8,512	8,842	9,188	9,551	9,933	10,337	10,767	11,225	11,713	..	**POPULATION (thousands)**
				(Billions of current CFA Francs)							**USE AND ORIGIN OF RESOURCES**
2,102.7	2,150.8	2,319.8	2,388.1	2,661.9	2,832.0	2,998.0	2,907.7	2,981.5	2,698.8	..	Gross National Product (GNP)
-118.9	-140.7	-166.7	-193.8	-207.4	-305.8	-246.3	-210.1	-89.4	-270.6	f	Net Factor Income from Abroad
2,221.6	2,291.5	2,486.5	2,581.9	2,869.3	3,137.8	3,244.3	3,117.8	3,070.9	2,969.4	..	GDP at Market Prices
-134.6	-162.8	-72.2	-43.2	330.2	414.3	389.2	142.0	24.6	84.4	f	Resource Balance
756.0	806.0	905.7	942.8	1,314.1	1,437.9	1,269.2	1,102.7	973.5	1,047.0	..	Exports of Goods & NFServices
890.6	968.8	977.9	986.0	983.9	1,023.6	880.0	960.7	948.9	962.6	..	Imports of Goods & NFServices
2,356.2	2,454.3	2,558.7	2,625.1	2,539.1	2,723.5	2,855.1	2,975.8	3,046.3	2,885.0	..	Domestic Absorption
1,333.6	1,462.0	1,553.9	1,658.5	1,787.8	1,891.7	2,004.8	2,125.4	2,005.9	2,034.3	..	Private Consumption, etc.
395.9	398.0	427.8	435.0	438.0	437.1	491.7	485.4	573.6	544.9	..	General Gov't Consumption
626.7	594.3	577.0	531.6	313.3	394.7	358.6	365.0	466.8	305.8	..	Gross Domestic Investment
581.8	558.4	538.7	469.5	352.6	359.3	386.2	361.9	466.8	305.8	..	Fixed Investment
429.4	373.5	450.1	502.8	728.4	792.9	696.3	772.4	736.8	682.9	..	Indirect Taxes, net
1,792.2	1,918.0	2,036.4	2,079.1	2,140.9	2,344.9	2,548.0	2,345.4	2,334.1	2,286.5	..	GDP at factor cost
597.9	655.8	650.2	633.8	788.4	833.5	916.1	969.3	1,025.6	1,051.0	..	Agriculture
357.4	375.8	462.9	487.8	506.8	618.0	613.9	628.3	595.8	548.5	..	Industry
195.6	201.0	263.5	301.6	334.2	399.2	412.3	..	..	..	..	Manufacturing
836.9	886.4	923.3	957.5	845.7	893.4	1,018.0	747.8	712.7	687.0	..	Services, etc.
492.1	431.5	504.8	488.4	643.5	809.0	747.8	507.0	491.4	390.2	..	Gross Domestic Saving
222.0	156.4	209.5	172.8	308.9	377.9	353.5	154.0	259.0	-1.3	..	Gross National Saving
				(Billions of 1987 CFA Francs)							
2,635.7	2,727.6	2,756.8	2,703.8	2,688.6	2,706.4	2,875.3	2,907.7	2,977.1	2,767.0	..	Gross National Product
2,802.4	2,922.7	2,968.9	2,933.3	2,905.2	3,013.8	3,124.2	3,117.8	3,060.3	3,020.0	..	GDP at Market Prices
-169.6	-10.5	157.7	160.8	396.6	454.5	414.9	142.0	130.0	347.7	f	Resource Balance
1,257.2	1,344.6	1,364.0	1,254.7	1,383.3	1,371.0	1,323.8	1,102.7	1,056.1	1,213.8	..	Exports of Goods & NFServices
1,426.9	1,355.2	1,206.3	1,093.9	986.8	916.6	908.8	960.7	926.1	866.0	..	Imports of Goods & NFServices
2,972.0	2,933.3	2,811.3	2,772.5	2,508.7	2,559.4	2,709.3	2,975.8	2,930.4	2,672.3	..	Domestic Absorption
998.4	1,324.8	1,357.7	1,410.5	1,613.8	1,624.8	1,831.4	2,125.4	1,977.1	1,890.3	..	Private Consumption, etc.
840.7	717.4	684.3	661.0	559.0	438.6	482.0	485.4	489.7	471.5	..	General Gov't Consumption
1,132.8	891.0	769.3	700.9	335.8	496.0	395.9	365.0	463.5	310.5	..	Gross Domestic Investment
968.3	770.8	661.3	569.9	348.0	415.7	392.5	361.9	..	..	..	Fixed Investment
2,089.7	2,220.8	2,258.0	2,257.7	2,169.3	2,417.8	2,508.6	2,345.4	2,325.9	2,324.6	..	GDP at factor cost
886.3	904.9	892.5	793.9	816.1	893.1	1,000.3	969.3	1,022.6	1,069.7	..	Agriculture
650.6	715.4	608.4	627.1	644.7	620.0	585.0	628.3	593.1	557.5	..	Industry
..	..	..	..	..	..	..	..	..	..	..	Manufacturing
662.9	713.9	792.4	836.7	708.5	904.7	923.3	747.8	710.1	697.4	..	Services, etc.
											Memo Items:
1,211.2	1,127.4	1,117.3	1,046.0	1,317.9	1,287.6	1,310.8	1,102.7	950.1	942.0	..	Capacity to Import
-46.0	-217.2	-246.7	-208.7	-65.4	-83.5	-13.0	0.0	-106.0	-271.8	..	Terms of Trade Adjustment
2,756.3	2,705.6	2,722.2	2,724.5	2,839.8	2,930.4	3,111.2	3,117.8	2,954.4	2,748.2	..	Gross Domestic Income
2,589.7	2,510.4	2,510.1	2,495.0	2,623.1	2,622.9	2,862.4	2,907.7	2,871.1	2,495.2	..	Gross National Income
				(Index 1987 = 100)							**DOMESTIC PRICES/DEFLATORS**
79.3	78.4	83.8	88.0	98.8	104.1	103.8	100.0	100.3	98.3	..	Overall (GDP)
79.3	83.7	91.0	94.7	101.2	106.4	105.4	100.0	104.0	108.0	..	Domestic Absorption
67.5	72.5	72.9	79.8	96.6	93.3	91.6	100.0	100.3	98.3	..	Agriculture
54.9	52.5	76.1	77.8	78.6	99.7	104.9	100.0	100.5	98.4	..	Industry
..	..	..	..	..	..	..	..	..	..	..	Manufacturing
70.6	76.9	82.5	87.4	91.1	92.8	99.6	100.0	107.0	108.1	..	Consumer Price Index
											MANUFACTURING ACTIVITY
..	..	..	..	..	..	..	..	..	..	..	Employment (1987=100)
..	..	..	..	..	..	..	..	..	..	..	Real Earnings per Empl. (1987=100)
..	..	..	..	..	..	..	..	..	..	..	Real Output per Empl. (1987=100)
30.3	33.0	31.0	..	..	..	..	..	..	..	..	Earnings as % of Value Added
				(Billions of current CFA Francs)							**MONETARY HOLDINGS**
581.82	639.65	660.34	691.95	826.05	939.44	963.90	929.95	944.00	867.72	..	Money Supply, Broadly Defined
438.73	464.39	460.31	488.01	574.57	620.18	636.43	598.58	577.96	511.21	..	Money
210.94	229.83	219.13	231.99	278.71	307.07	317.66	304.71	298.45	254.14	..	Currency Outside Banks
227.79	234.56	241.18	256.02	295.86	313.11	318.77	293.87	279.51	257.07	..	Demand Deposits
143.09	175.26	200.03	203.94	251.48	319.26	327.47	331.37	366.04	356.51	..	Quasi-Money
				(Billions of current CFA Francs)							
-233.19	..	..	..	-90.03	..	..	..	..	..	..	**GOVERNMENT DEFICIT (-) OR SURPLUS**
517.40	..	..	..	816.10	..	..	..	..	..	..	Current Revenue
409.57	..	..	..	748.50	..	..	..	..	..	..	Current Expenditure
107.83	..	..	..	67.60	..	..	..	..	..	..	Current Budget Balance
0.16	..	..	..	..	..	..	..	..	..	..	Capital Receipts
341.18	..	..	..	157.63	..	..	..	..	..	..	Capital Payments

COTE D'IVOIRE	1969	1970	1971	1972	1973	1974	1975	1976	1977	1978	1979
FOREIGN TRADE (CUSTOMS BASIS)					*(Millions of current US dollars)*						
Value of Exports, fob	458.1	468.8	455.6	552.9	860.6	1,214.3	1,181.6	1,630.8	2,154.8	2,322.9	2,506.8
Nonfuel Primary Products	428.8	437.9	424.7	488.7	769.4	1,069.7	974.3	1,446.1	1,912.3	2,081.6	2,182.4
Fuels	4.1	2.9	2.5	11.4	19.6	45.3	66.9	63.0	81.9	86.0	112.4
Manufactures	25.1	28.0	28.4	52.8	71.6	99.3	140.4	121.7	160.5	155.3	212.0
Value of Imports, cif	334.1	387.2	398.1	452.8	713.5	966.7	1,126.5	1,295.4	1,751.4	2,309.6	2,388.9
Nonfuel Primary Products	55.4	70.8	74.0	90.5	160.6	189.7	191.2	206.8	286.8	358.1	417.4
Fuels	17.4	18.5	19.1	29.0	33.1	137.6	156.6	166.4	199.9	221.3	272.7
Manufactures	261.3	298.0	305.0	333.3	519.8	639.3	778.7	922.2	1,264.7	1,730.2	1,698.8
					(Index 1987 = 100)						
Terms of Trade	122.0	123.5	104.8	101.6	115.9	114.8	98.0	141.1	177.9	153.7	149.5
Export Prices, fob	30.5	32.8	30.2	31.3	45.9	61.6	55.0	79.5	109.7	106.8	121.9
Import Prices, cif	25.0	26.6	28.9	30.8	39.6	53.6	56.1	56.3	61.7	69.5	81.5
BALANCE OF PAYMENTS					*(Millions of current US dollars)*						
Exports of Goods & Services	..	565.7	576.3	696.9	995.3	1,445.7	1,503.4	1,998.3	2,779.2	3,086.6	3,292.6
Merchandise, fob	..	497.1	496.0	595.7	861.8	1,253.0	1,238.9	1,735.1	2,412.1	2,615.9	2,722.8
Nonfactor Services	..	53.5	65.4	84.4	116.9	167.3	225.8	235.2	324.8	410.4	510.5
Factor Services	..	15.1	14.9	16.8	16.6	25.4	38.7	28.0	42.3	60.3	59.2
Imports of Goods & Services	..	583.6	654.8	765.2	1,145.5	1,414.1	1,740.6	1,988.4	2,656.4	3,507.3	4,104.0
Merchandise, fob	..	375.1	400.4	460.2	701.1	894.4	1,012.1	1,161.3	1,597.2	2,042.9	2,233.4
Nonfactor Services	..	145.6	173.0	228.3	324.5	397.6	548.8	640.9	822.7	1,095.2	1,351.1
Factor Services	..	62.9	81.4	76.7	119.9	122.1	179.6	186.2	236.5	369.1	519.5
Long-Term Interest	..	12.1	16.0	19.0	28.9	42.5	59.1	71.0	110.9	189.5	257.3
Private Current Transfers, net	..	-55.5	-66.0	-89.4	-123.1	-139.3	-183.8	-289.6	-344.8	-458.2	-576.3
Workers' Remittances	..	..	..	..	..	..	..	..	..	..	..
Curr. A/C Bal before Off. Transf.	..	-73.4	-144.5	-157.6	-273.4	-107.7	-421.0	-279.7	-221.9	-879.0	-1,387.7
Net Official Transfers	..	35.5	39.0	61.0	54.0	46.7	42.0	30.5	45.2	40.3	4.7
Curr. A/C Bal after Off. Transf.	..	-37.9	-105.5	-96.6	-219.3	-61.0	-379.0	-249.2	-176.7	-838.6	-1,383.0
Long-Term Capital, net	..	69.4	96.8	25.2	219.9	173.7	270.2	276.2	570.7	839.3	715.0
Direct Investment	..	30.7	15.7	18.7	51.0	32.6	69.1	44.8	14.7	83.3	74.7
Long-Term Loans	..	51.2	82.5	42.5	205.9	109.5	308.5	270.3	724.6	832.6	706.4
Disbursements	..	81.7	114.2	84.5	252.6	190.9	391.7	396.5	905.8	1,085.6	1,108.2
Repayments	..	30.5	31.7	42.0	46.7	81.4	83.2	126.2	181.2	253.0	401.8
Other Long-Term Capital	..	-12.5	-1.5	-36.0	-37.0	31.6	-107.4	-38.9	-168.6	-76.6	-66.1
Other Capital, net	..	3.6	-11.7	-0.3	-6.9	-51.1	16.4	3.0	-275.3	165.4	339.1
Change in Reserves	..	-35.1	20.5	71.8	6.3	-61.6	92.4	-30.0	-118.7	-166.1	328.9
Memo Item:					*(CFA Francs per US dollar)*						
Conversion Factor (Annual Avg)	259.710	277.710	277.130	252.210	222.700	240.500	214.320	238.980	245.670	225.640	212.720
				(Millions of US dollars), outstanding at end of year							
EXTERNAL DEBT (Total)	..	267	366	413	615	756	1,040	1,298	2,559	3,816	4,755
Long-Term Debt (by debtor)	..	267	366	413	615	756	1,040	1,298	2,081	3,087	3,898
Central Bank, incl. IMF credit	..	17	17	20	28	52	64	102	101	151	157
Central Government	..	177	265	281	342	362	539	626	1,136	1,679	2,237
Rest of General Government	..	1	1	1	0	0	0	0	0	0	0
Non-financial Public Enterprises	..	61	70	100	213	293	356	480	670	939	1,237
Priv. Sector, incl non-guaranteed	..	11	14	13	32	49	81	90	174	318	267
Short-Term Debt	..	..	..	..	..	..	..	..	478	729	857
Memo Items:					*(Thousands of US dollars)*						
Int'l Reserves Excluding Gold	73,900	118,840	89,433	87,178	88,373	65,667	102,760	76,403	184,808	447,966	147,031
Gold Holdings (at market price)	..	..	..	..	..	..	..	..	3,695	7,571	22,784
SOCIAL INDICATORS											
Total Fertility Rate	7.4	7.4	7.4	7.4	7.4	7.4	7.4	7.4	7.4	7.4	7.4
Infant Mortality Rate	137.4	134.6	131.8	129.0	126.4	123.8	121.2	118.6	116.0	113.8	111.6
Life Expectancy at Birth	44.0	44.5	45.0	45.5	46.0	46.5	47.0	47.5	48.0	48.5	49.0
Urban Population, % of total	26.5	27.4	28.4	29.3	30.3	31.2	32.2	33.2	34.2	35.1	36.1
Food Prod. per capita (1987=100)	92.0	89.6	94.7	87.0	88.3	93.3	106.3	99.9	99.5	101.9	105.7
Labor Force, Agriculture (%)	77.2	76.5	75.2	74.0	72.9	71.9	70.9	69.6	68.4	67.3	66.3
Labor Force, Female (%)	38.3	38.1	37.8	37.4	37.1	36.9	36.6	36.2	35.9	35.5	35.2
Primary Schl. Enroll. Ratio	..	58.0	..	..	..	..	62.0	64.0	66.0	70.0	72.0
Primary Schl. Enroll. Ratio, Female	..	45.0	..	..	..	..	47.0	64.0	..	..	..
Secondary Schl. Enroll. Ratio	..	9.0	..	..	..	..	13.0	13.0	14.0	17.0	20.0

1980	1981	1982	1983	1984	1985	1986	1987	1988	1989 estimate	NOTES	COTE D'IVOIRE
											FOREIGN TRADE (CUSTOMS BASIS)
3,142.0	2,535.2	2,287.9	2,092.0	2,707.0	2,972.1	3,179.2	2,982.0	2,429.0	3,109.7	..	Value of Exports, fob
2,657.7	2,081.8	1,743.3	1,615.0	2,187.5	2,446.1	2,782.7	2,577.4	2,066.0	..	..	Nonfuel Primary Products
188.9	191.2	298.0	239.2	319.5	259.0	107.5	122.1	63.0	..	..	Fuels
295.4	262.2	246.7	237.7	200.0	267.0	289.0	282.5	300.0	317.1	..	Manufactures
3,015.0	2,393.1	2,183.7	1,813.5	1,496.9	1,749.2	2,055.0	2,370.0	1,917.0	2,520.4	..	Value of Imports, cif
606.8	545.1	469.1	413.6	271.5	301.9	500.4	631.0	392.0	..	..	Nonfuel Primary Products
504.4	527.5	469.1	336.3	253.6	378.6	264.4	325.4	296.0	..	..	Fuels
1,903.8	1,320.5	1,245.6	1,063.6	971.8	1,068.7	1,290.2	1,413.5	1,229.0	1,558.3	..	Manufactures
				(Index 1987 = 100)							
125.4	102.1	105.2	110.7	129.5	118.8	122.3	100.0	99.5	..	..	Terms of Trade
121.1	104.9	101.7	102.5	114.8	106.9	110.7	100.0	103.3	..	..	Export Prices, fob
96.6	102.7	96.7	92.6	88.7	90.0	90.6	100.0	103.8	..	..	Import Prices, cif
				(Millions of current US dollars)							**BALANCE OF PAYMENTS**
3,639.7	2,915.4	2,843.8	2,538.2	3,032.8	3,199.5	3,726.2	3,770.3	2,995.8	3,322.2	f	Exports of Goods & Services
3,012.6	2,435.1	2,347.2	2,066.3	2,624.8	2,761.0	3,187.4	3,091.5	2,354.2	2,708.7	..	Merchandise, fob
564.2	434.3	450.7	425.1	370.3	398.9	471.3	589.6	562.4	578.4	..	Nonfactor Services
63.0	46.0	46.0	46.7	37.8	39.6	67.6	89.2	79.2	35.1	..	Factor Services
4,760.5	3,847.6	3,498.4	3,173.7	2,842.6	2,878.7	3,667.6	4,103.3	3,851.0	3,987.0	f	Imports of Goods & Services
2,613.6	2,067.9	1,789.7	1,635.2	1,487.3	1,409.9	1,639.9	1,838.7	1,538.7	1,680.8	..	Merchandise, fob
1,521.2	1,215.9	1,155.5	983.3	823.9	763.0	1,311.9	1,479.7	1,458.8	1,340.1	..	Nonfactor Services
625.7	563.8	553.2	555.3	531.4	705.8	715.8	784.9	853.5	966.1	..	Factor Services
383.1	444.0	551.1	519.0	573.7	634.1	771.9	518.0	444.3	426.5	..	Long-Term Interest
-715.6	-494.6	-391.4	-319.6	-291.1	-278.9	-427.4	-475.5	-480.1	-379.0	..	Private Current Transfers, net
..	..	..	..	..	..	..	..	..	..	..	Workers' Remittances
-1,836.4	-1,426.8	-1,045.9	-955.2	-100.9	41.8	-368.8	-808.6	-1,335.3	-1,043.8	..	Curr. A/C Bal before Off. Transf.
9.9	15.5	29.8	26.5	28.1	26.0	71.0	60.2	57.4	60.8	..	Net Official Transfers
-1,826.5	-1,411.3	-1,016.1	-928.7	-72.8	67.9	-297.7	-748.3	-1,277.8	-983.0	..	Curr. A/C Bal after Off. Transf.
1,032.8	921.1	898.6	533.5	300.5	203.2	163.2	288.8	386.4	-466.4	f	Long-Term Capital, net
94.7	32.8	47.5	37.5	21.7	29.2	70.7	51.6	56.7	..	..	Direct Investment
1,119.9	809.9	1,504.5	506.3	941.6	728.5	460.7	691.3	586.4	451.4	..	Long-Term Loans
1,675.3	1,421.0	2,105.9	1,116.1	1,430.4	1,286.1	1,225.6	1,491.0	1,202.6	1,130.5	..	Disbursements
555.4	611.1	601.4	609.8	488.8	557.6	764.9	799.7	616.2	679.1	..	Repayments
-181.8	78.5	-653.3	-10.3	-662.9	-554.4	-368.3	-454.1	-256.7	-917.8	..	Other Long-Term Capital
681.9	113.1	-32.4	250.5	-253.9	-244.6	224.5	600.6	567.7	1,570.6	f	Other Capital, net
111.8	377.1	149.9	144.7	26.2	-26.6	-90.0	-141.1	323.7	-121.2	..	Change in Reserves
				(CFA Francs per US dollar)							**Memo Item:**
211.300	271.730	328.620	381.070	436.960	449.260	346.300	300.540	297.850	319.010	..	Conversion Factor (Annual Avg)
			(Millions of US dollars), outstanding at end of year								
5,847	6,651	7,862	7,819	8,106	9,746	11,088	13,555	13,977	15,412	..	**EXTERNAL DEBT (Total)**
4,788	5,486	6,756	6,933	7,467	9,014	10,284	12,178	12,145	12,596	..	Long-Term Debt (by debtor)
195	560	677	802	748	783	784	724	609	453	..	Central Bank, incl. IMF credit
2,721	2,971	3,619	3,507	3,633	4,536	5,434	7,101	7,023	7,295	..	Central Government
0	0	0	0	0	0	0	0	0	..	..	Rest of General Government
1,409	1,319	1,263	1,228	1,068	1,103	1,087	1,072	803	768	..	Non-financial Public Enterprises
464	636	1,196	1,395	2,018	2,593	2,978	3,282	3,710	4,080	..	Priv. Sector, incl non-guaranteed
1,059	1,165	1,106	886	639	732	804	1,377	1,832	2,816	..	Short-Term Debt
				(Thousands of US dollars)							**Memo Items:**
19,704	17,847	2,195	19,721	5,367	4,732	19,556	8,902	10,418	14,986	..	Int'l Reserves Excluding Gold
26,233	17,689	20,332	16,977	13,719	14,552	17,395	21,542	18,256	17,844	..	Gold Holdings (at market price)
											SOCIAL INDICATORS
7.4	7.4	7.4	7.4	7.4	7.4	7.4	7.4	7.3	7.3	..	Total Fertility Rate
109.4	107.2	105.0	103.2	101.4	99.6	97.8	96.0	94.5	93.0	..	Infant Mortality Rate
49.5	50.0	50.5	50.9	51.3	51.7	52.1	52.5	52.7	52.9	..	Life Expectancy at Birth
37.1	38.1	39.1	40.0	41.0	42.0	43.2	44.3	45.1	45.8	..	Urban Population, % of total
103.6	104.1	96.4	92.1	105.2	101.7	99.0	100.0	104.0	96.1	..	Food Prod. per capita (1987=100)
65.2	..	..	..	..	..	..	..	..	..	..	Labor Force, Agriculture (%)
34.9	34.9	34.8	34.8	34.7	34.7	34.6	34.5	34.4	34.3	..	Labor Force, Female (%)
74.0	..	..	..	71.0	70.0	..	..	..	..	..	Primary Schl. Enroll. Ratio
59.0	..	..	..	59.0	58.0	..	..	..	..	..	Primary Schl. Enroll. Ratio, Female
18.0	..	19.0	19.0	18.0	19.0	18.0	19.0	..	..	..	Secondary Schl. Enroll. Ratio

CYPRUS	1969	1970	1971	1972	1973	1974	1975	1976	1977	1978	1979
CURRENT GNP PER CAPITA (US $)	..	..	..	..	..	..	..	..	..	..	..
POPULATION (thousands)	608	615	614	613	611	610	609	611	614	618	623

USE AND ORIGIN OF RESOURCES *(Millions of current Cyprus Pounds)*

	1969	1970	1971	1972	1973	1974	1975	1976	1977	1978	1979
Gross National Product (GNP)	..	..	..	..	..	..	259.0	336.2	431.6	516.0	638.2
Net Factor Income from Abroad	..	..	..	..	..	..	2.0	2.3	8.5	9.5	8.4
GDP at Market Prices	..	..	..	..	..	..	257.0	333.9	423.1	506.5	629.8
Resource Balance	..	..	..	..	..	..	-54.5	-43.0	-84.4	-104.3	-120.2
Exports of Goods & NFServices	..	..	..	..	..	..	91.2	166.1	202.3	214.4	281.4
Imports of Goods & NFServices	..	..	..	..	..	..	145.7	209.1	286.7	318.7	401.6
Domestic Absorption	..	..	..	..	..	..	311.5	376.9	507.5	610.8	750.0
Private Consumption, etc.	..	..	..	..	..	..	208.7	233.7	300.7	356.0	425.6
General Gov't Consumption	..	..	..	..	..	..	44.9	54.5	59.2	66.3	80.5
Gross Domestic Investment	..	..	..	..	..	..	57.9	88.7	147.6	188.5	243.9
Fixed Investment	..	..	..	..	..	..	50.5	70.3	124.6	170.4	219.5
Indirect Taxes, net	..	..	..	..	..	..	..	..	..	..	..
GDP at factor cost	..	..	..	..	..	..	..	..	..	..	..
Agriculture	..	..	..	..	..	..	40.4	53.1	55.9	55.3	64.5
Industry	..	..	..	..	..	..	64.7	96.3	131.1	167.8	209.2
Manufacturing	..	..	..	..	..	..	36.8	57.6	75.2	92.6	110.8
Services, etc.	..	..	..	..	..	..	151.9	184.5	236.1	283.4	356.1
Gross Domestic Saving	..	..	..	..	..	..	3.4	45.7	63.2	84.2	123.7
Gross National Saving	..	..	..	..	..	..	10.5	53.4	77.6	102.1	141.1

(Millions of 1987 Cyprus Pounds)

	1969	1970	1971	1972	1973	1974	1975	1976	1977	1978	1979
Gross National Product	..	..	..	..	..	..	706.4	847.8	997.6	1,072.7	1,172.5
GDP at Market Prices	..	..	..	..	..	..	701.0	841.8	977.8	1,053.0	1,157.0
Resource Balance	..	..	..	..	..	..	-113.1	-113.2	-159.4	-166.5	-179.7
Exports of Goods & NFServices	..	..	..	..	..	..	173.0	285.9	349.7	371.2	448.2
Imports of Goods & NFServices	..	..	..	..	..	..	286.1	399.1	509.1	537.7	627.9
Domestic Absorption	..	..	..	..	..	..	814.1	954.9	1,137.2	1,219.5	1,336.7
Private Consumption, etc.	..	..	..	..	..	..	532.8	596.3	666.0	704.5	754.8
General Gov't Consumption	..	..	..	..	..	..	134.5	156.0	157.7	156.2	163.1
Gross Domestic Investment	..	..	..	..	..	..	146.8	202.6	313.5	358.8	418.8
Fixed Investment	..	..	..	..	..	..	125.2	164.0	269.5	327.1	380.5
GDP at factor cost	..	..	..	..	..	..	..	..	..	..	..
Agriculture	..	..	..	..	..	..	104.0	112.8	113.0	109.2	113.2
Industry	..	..	..	..	..	..	198.4	261.8	327.2	363.0	400.8
Manufacturing	..	..	..	..	..	..	105.0	136.8	158.0	171.7	187.3
Services, etc.	..	..	..	..	..	..	399.5	468.7	539.7	582.9	645.2

Memo Items:

	1969	1970	1971	1972	1973	1974	1975	1976	1977	1978	1979
Capacity to Import	..	..	..	..	..	..	179.1	317.0	359.2	361.7	440.0
Terms of Trade Adjustment	..	..	..	..	..	..	6.1	31.1	9.5	-9.4	-8.2
Gross Domestic Income	..	..	..	..	..	..	707.1	872.8	987.4	1,043.5	1,148.7
Gross National Income	..	..	..	..	..	..	712.5	878.9	1,007.1	1,063.2	1,164.3

DOMESTIC PRICES/DEFLATORS *(Index 1987 = 100)*

	1969	1970	1971	1972	1973	1974	1975	1976	1977	1978	1979
Overall (GDP)	..	..	..	..	..	..	36.7	39.7	43.3	48.1	54.4
Domestic Absorption	..	..	..	..	..	..	38.3	39.5	44.6	50.1	56.1
Agriculture	..	..	..	..	..	..	38.8	47.1	49.5	50.6	57.0
Industry	..	..	..	..	..	..	32.6	36.8	40.1	46.2	52.2
Manufacturing	..	..	..	..	..	..	35.1	42.1	47.6	53.9	59.2
Consumer Price Index	32.0	32.7	34.1	35.8	38.5	41.0	46.9	48.7	52.2	56.1	61.4

MANUFACTURING ACTIVITY

	1969	1970	1971	1972	1973	1974	1975	1976	1977	1978	1979
Employment (1987=100)	54.7	57.6	60.1	66.2	67.6	54.7	46.5	54.4	67.5	76.5	82.1
Real Earnings per Empl. (1987=100)	39.9	41.6	42.2	45.9	50.2	56.3	49.4	50.3	54.8	59.6	67.3
Real Output per Empl. (1987=100)	..	..	..	..	..	..	85.5	92.6	85.9	78.9	84.4
Earnings as % of Value Added	38.6	37.8	35.7	35.1	37.0	40.6	36.2	30.0	32.6	34.8	38.3

MONETARY HOLDINGS *(Millions of current Cyprus Pounds)*

	1969	1970	1971	1972	1973	1974	1975	1976	1977	1978	1979
Money Supply, Broadly Defined	109.3	120.4	145.0	175.2	197.0	228.5	229.7	275.1	316.0	363.3	433.5
Money	38.0	42.6	46.7	57.4	60.8	67.0	62.1	80.0	85.9	100.8	129.5
Currency Outside Banks	17.2	18.4	21.8	26.3	29.7	35.8	33.7	39.3	43.2	51.2	64.0
Demand Deposits	20.8	24.2	25.0	31.2	31.1	31.3	28.3	40.7	42.8	49.6	65.5
Quasi-Money	71.3	77.8	98.3	117.7	136.1	161.4	167.6	195.1	230.1	262.5	304.0

GOVERNMENT DEFICIT (-) OR SURPLUS *(Millions of current Cyprus Pounds)*

	1969	1970	1971	1972	1973	1974	1975	1976	1977	1978	1979
GOVERNMENT DEFICIT (-) OR SURPLUS	..	1.42	0.45	-4.39	-12.15	-20.90	-20.38	-24.90	-12.71	-28.84	-41.64
Current Revenue	..	41.25	46.97	52.35	60.31	61.12	66.82	78.70	106.72	113.31	136.58
Current Expenditure	..	31.94	37.29	45.34	60.95	72.23	76.18	83.93	91.84	100.95	129.25
Current Budget Balance	..	9.31	9.68	7.01	-0.64	-11.11	-9.36	-5.23	14.88	12.36	7.33
Capital Receipts	..	0.12	0.06	0.03	0.11	0.03	0.07	0.07	0.09	0.19	0.19
Capital Payments	..	8.01	9.29	11.53	11.62	9.82	11.09	19.74	27.68	41.39	49.16

1980	1981	1982	1983	1984	1985	1986	1987	1988	1989 estimate	NOTES	CYPRUS
..	..	..	..	..	..	4,480	5,300	6,580	7,050	..	**CURRENT GNP PER CAPITA (US $)**
629	637	645	653	660	666	673	680	687	694	..	**POPULATION (thousands)**
				(Millions of current Cyprus Pounds)							**USE AND ORIGIN OF RESOURCES**
772.3	887.4	1,036.6	1,136.2	1,339.3	1,485.1	1,600.8	1,780.7	1,995.6	2,205.2	..	Gross National Product (GNP)
12.0	11.5	12.1	-0.4	2.6	4.9	2.8	2.0	3.5	5.4	..	Net Factor Income from Abroad
760.3	875.9	1,024.5	1,136.6	1,336.7	1,480.2	1,598.0	1,778.7	1,992.1	2,199.8	..	GDP at Market Prices
-135.4	-114.5	-136.5	-154.2	-166.4	-149.6	-54.2	-3.2	-50.5	-135.6	..	Resource Balance
344.1	440.2	521.9	573.0	731.0	722.4	721.0	842.5	959.8	1,151.6	..	Exports of Goods & NFServices
479.5	554.7	658.4	727.2	897.4	872.0	775.2	845.7	1,010.3	1,287.2	..	Imports of Goods & NFServices
895.7	990.4	1,161.0	1,290.8	1,503.1	1,629.8	1,652.2	1,781.9	2,042.6	2,335.4	..	Domestic Absorption
504.3	566.2	683.8	775.9	864.3	971.6	1,011.3	1,084.2	1,235.2	1,390.3	..	Private Consumption, etc.
103.9	128.0	152.1	172.6	189.5	208.5	225.9	246.8	275.0	293.9	..	General Gov't Consumption
287.5	296.2	325.1	342.3	449.3	449.7	415.0	450.9	532.4	651.2	..	Gross Domestic Investment
260.0	275.9	304.7	316.0	412.5	403.0	384.0	414.3	475.2	596.4	..	Fixed Investment
..	..	..	..	..	..	..	..	..	..	..	Indirect Taxes, net
..	..	..	..	..	..	..	..	..	..	B	GDP at factor cost
72.9	81.1	95.0	89.8	119.6	111.0	117.3	132.3	143.2	155.6	..	Agriculture
255.8	283.9	316.3	342.0	388.2	420.9	439.7	487.6	547.0	592.0	..	Industry
133.4	154.2	174.5	187.9	215.2	231.9	240.5	273.9	309.1	334.0	..	Manufacturing
431.6	510.9	613.2	704.8	828.9	948.3	1,041.0	1,158.8	1,301.9	1,452.2	..	Services, etc.
152.1	181.7	188.6	188.1	282.9	300.1	360.8	447.7	481.9	515.6	..	Gross Domestic Saving
175.6	204.7	212.5	200.0	298.2	318.6	375.9	462.4	496.9	532.3	..	Gross National Saving
				(Millions of 1987 Cyprus Pounds)							
1,243.0	1,271.8	1,347.3	1,405.4	1,532.2	1,606.6	1,665.0	1,780.7	1,933.0	2,042.0	..	Gross National Product
1,223.7	1,255.3	1,331.3	1,405.9	1,529.2	1,601.4	1,662.1	1,778.7	1,929.7	2,037.1	..	GDP at Market Prices
-167.6	-114.3	-156.6	-148.9	-181.7	-147.1	-61.2	-3.2	-27.5	-99.1	..	Resource Balance
496.7	566.6	611.4	661.3	761.2	753.0	740.4	842.5	954.9	1,110.3	..	Exports of Goods & NFServices
664.2	680.9	768.0	810.3	942.9	900.1	801.5	845.7	982.4	1,209.4	..	Imports of Goods & NFServices
1,391.2	1,369.6	1,487.8	1,554.8	1,710.9	1,748.5	1,723.2	1,781.9	1,957.2	2,136.2	..	Domestic Absorption
776.6	781.4	879.5	936.3	993.1	1,049.5	1,063.7	1,084.2	1,189.8	1,287.2	..	Private Consumption, etc.
176.9	190.1	197.5	209.8	217.8	226.2	234.3	246.8	265.5	274.4	..	General Gov't Consumption
437.7	398.1	410.7	408.7	500.0	472.8	425.2	450.9	501.9	574.6	..	Gross Domestic Investment
400.4	374.6	388.7	380.2	462.2	426.5	396.3	414.3	447.2	527.0	..	Fixed Investment
..	..	..	..	..	..	..	..	..	..	B	GDP at factor cost
119.6	118.7	119.2	117.9	128.9	128.6	127.9	132.3	146.8	149.1	..	Agriculture
420.1	406.3	415.2	423.4	444.1	450.2	456.6	487.6	518.8	536.4	..	Industry
202.2	215.0	227.9	232.3	247.2	252.8	253.5	273.9	292.6	301.5	..	Manufacturing
686.2	731.6	797.6	864.5	956.2	1,022.6	1,077.6	1,158.8	1,264.0	1,351.6	..	Services, etc.
											Memo Items:
476.7	540.3	608.8	638.5	768.1	745.7	745.5	842.5	933.3	1,082.0	..	Capacity to Import
-20.0	-26.3	-2.7	-22.9	6.9	-7.3	5.1	0.0	-21.6	-28.3	..	Terms of Trade Adjustment
1,203.7	1,229.0	1,328.6	1,383.0	1,536.1	1,594.1	1,667.2	1,778.7	1,908.1	2,008.8	..	Gross Domestic Income
1,223.0	1,245.5	1,344.7	1,382.5	1,539.0	1,599.3	1,670.1	1,780.7	1,911.4	2,013.7	..	Gross National Income
				(Index 1987 = 100)							**DOMESTIC PRICES/DEFLATORS**
62.1	69.8	77.0	80.8	87.4	92.4	96.1	100.0	103.2	108.0	..	Overall (GDP)
64.4	72.3	78.0	83.0	87.9	93.2	95.9	100.0	104.4	109.3	..	Domestic Absorption
61.0	68.3	79.7	76.1	92.8	86.3	91.7	100.0	97.6	104.4	..	Agriculture
60.9	69.9	76.2	80.8	87.4	93.5	96.3	100.0	105.4	110.4	..	Industry
66.0	71.7	76.6	80.9	87.1	91.7	94.9	100.0	105.6	110.8	..	Manufacturing
69.7	77.2	82.2	86.3	91.5	96.1	97.3	100.0	103.4	107.3	..	Consumer Price Index
											MANUFACTURING ACTIVITY
86.6	90.6	92.0	92.6	95.9	98.5	95.9	100.0	105.5	..	J	Employment (1987=100)
73.0	78.6	85.3	89.2	91.2	93.5	97.3	100.0	103.7	..	J	Real Earnings per Empl. (1987=100)
93.4	99.4	99.8	101.7	103.8	100.8	97.9	100.0	100.1	..	J	Real Output per Empl. (1987=100)
37.6	44.0	46.1	47.6	46.7	46.9	46.4	44.8	45.0	..	J	Earnings as % of Value Added
				(Millions of current Cyprus Pounds)							**MONETARY HOLDINGS**
501.2	601.4	709.5	791.1	899.4	992.3	1,095.5	1,238.4	1,456.1	1,686.2	..	Money Supply, Broadly Defined
153.3	188.3	218.5	248.4	259.4	285.3	282.5	314.0	358.9	385.0	..	Money
75.9	89.5	101.6	115.9	122.2	127.9	130.7	142.6	157.6	169.1	..	Currency Outside Banks
77.4	98.8	116.8	132.6	137.1	157.4	151.9	171.5	201.3	215.9	..	Demand Deposits
347.9	413.1	491.0	542.7	640.1	707.0	813.0	924.4	1,097.1	1,301.1	..	Quasi-Money
				(Millions of current Cyprus Pounds)							**GOVERNMENT DEFICIT (-) OR SURPLUS**
-70.01	-46.75	-48.48	-81.34	-73.11	-65.40	-58.07	-75.06	-62.65	..	..	Current Revenue
173.63	203.22	252.19	288.66	344.07	389.86	426.40	460.59	535.76	..	..	Current Revenue
165.09	212.44	249.35	301.24	337.18	362.92	381.09	425.54	481.26	..	..	Current Expenditure
8.54	-9.22	2.84	-12.58	6.89	26.94	45.31	35.05	54.50	..	..	Current Budget Balance
0.14	0.12	0.16	0.75	0.28	0.24	0.69	1.12	0.30	..	..	Capital Receipts
78.69	37.65	51.48	69.51	80.28	92.58	104.07	111.23	117.45	..	..	Capital Payments

CYPRUS	1969	1970	1971	1972	1973	1974	1975	1976	1977	1978	1979
FOREIGN TRADE (CUSTOMS BASIS)					*(Millions of current US dollars)*						
Value of Exports, fob	88.2	108.4	114.8	133.8	173.1	152.2	151.2	256.9	317.5	343.7	456.3
Nonfuel Primary Products	84.5	91.1	95.5	110.2	138.0	114.3	91.5	151.4	175.2	172.9	205.6
Fuels	0.0	0.0	0.0	0.5	0.1	0.6	0.6	9.9	5.9	8.3	23.1
Manufactures	3.7	17.3	19.3	23.1	34.9	37.3	59.1	95.5	136.5	162.5	227.6
Value of Imports, cif	202.4	235.1	259.0	315.4	449.0	406.1	305.5	429.8	619.1	748.2	999.8
Nonfuel Primary Products	36.2	45.2	50.0	63.9	119.9	93.3	85.6	114.1	129.9	153.4	190.6
Fuels	15.6	16.9	20.8	22.0	25.1	52.2	48.8	65.1	86.3	83.1	125.5
Manufactures	150.6	173.0	188.2	229.5	304.0	260.6	171.1	250.5	402.8	511.8	683.7
					(Index 1987 = 100)						
Terms of Trade	178.7	166.5	144.6	135.2	123.0	106.1	102.5	104.1	106.7	104.9	106.9
Export Prices, fob	42.6	42.3	39.8	41.6	49.8	58.0	62.1	63.5	68.4	74.7	89.5
Import Prices, cif	23.8	25.4	27.5	30.8	40.5	54.6	60.6	61.0	64.1	71.2	83.7
BALANCE OF PAYMENTS					*(Millions of current US dollars)*						
Exports of Goods & Services	..	229.2	264.6	329.9	423.2	365.5	301.0	459.4	565.4	658.6	896.6
Merchandise, fob	..	102.4	109.0	121.9	163.6	142.4	142.3	250.2	304.3	326.6	421.5
Nonfactor Services	..	111.3	140.9	191.2	236.4	192.5	133.3	179.8	214.6	271.2	400.9
Factor Services	..	15.5	14.6	16.8	23.2	30.5	25.4	29.5	46.5	60.8	74.2
Imports of Goods & Services	..	268.0	298.7	373.8	516.3	498.9	410.5	533.5	728.1	888.3	1,183.3
Merchandise, fob	..	206.3	227.4	281.4	402.1	379.1	301.2	397.8	558.8	683.8	906.2
Nonfactor Services	..	47.9	58.0	78.4	92.7	99.7	89.2	111.6	143.6	169.5	226.6
Factor Services	..	13.8	13.3	14.0	21.5	20.1	20.0	24.1	25.7	35.1	50.5
Long-Term Interest	..	2.4	2.8	2.4	3.0	3.8	4.9	5.3	8.6	13.4	24.8
Private Current Transfers, net	..	13.7	16.3	16.1	12.0	17.3	13.8	13.2	14.5	22.5	25.4
Workers' Remittances	..	..	..	..	..	..	10.9	16.3	17.3	25.7	29.3
Curr. A/C Bal before Off. Transf.	..	-25.1	-17.8	-27.8	-81.1	-116.1	-95.7	-60.9	-148.2	-207.2	-261.3
Net Official Transfers	..	3.4	2.7	2.6	2.9	43.7	58.4	47.5	58.3	45.0	46.3
Curr. A/C Bal after Off. Transf.	..	-21.7	-15.0	-25.2	-78.2	-72.4	-37.3	-13.4	-89.9	-162.2	-215.0
Long-Term Capital, net	..	24.8	27.2	34.9	47.6	45.7	13.5	62.6	77.7	143.5	127.5
Direct Investment	..	20.2	29.6	36.4	37.2	32.4	18.1	32.4	41.4	57.0	70.5
Long-Term Loans	..	4.3	-17.3	-0.8	16.7	17.1	4.7	18.0	58.4	65.7	52.2
Disbursements	..	7.4	6.8	4.3	22.0	21.9	9.8	27.3	67.7	78.1	67.7
Repayments	..	3.1	24.1	5.1	5.3	4.8	5.1	9.3	9.3	12.4	15.5
Other Long-Term Capital	..	0.3	14.9	-0.7	-6.3	-3.8	-9.3	12.2	-22.1	20.8	4.8
Other Capital, net	..	25.3	38.8	19.0	15.5	-14.5	-8.7	-4.4	35.4	37.5	75.4
Change in Reserves	..	-28.4	-51.0	-28.7	15.1	41.2	32.5	-44.8	-23.2	-18.7	12.0
Memo Item:					*(Cyprus Pounds per US dollar)*						
Conversion Factor (Annual Avg)	..	..	..	..	..	..	0.370	0.410	0.410	0.370	0.350
					(Millions of US dollars), outstanding at end of year						
EXTERNAL DEBT (Total)	..	56.0	41.2	39.9	57.2	84.0	85.8	144.4	275.3	370.2	462.5
Long-Term Debt (by debtor)	..	56.0	41.2	39.9	57.2	84.0	85.8	144.4	214.3	284.2	349.5
Central Bank, incl. IMF credit	..	0.0	0.0	0.0	0.0	7.8	9.5	50.0	52.3	42.9	50.0
Central Government	..	26.0	10.1	10.5	17.6	21.3	26.1	52.1	96.9	144.2	179.2
Rest of General Government	..	0.0	0.0	0.6	2.0	3.0	3.1	3.3	3.3	3.3	3.2
Non-financial Public Enterprises	..	29.3	30.3	27.5	36.2	48.4	43.4	35.3	55.8	81.9	96.8
Priv. Sector, incl non-guaranteed	..	0.7	0.8	1.3	1.4	3.5	3.7	3.7	6.0	11.9	20.3
Short-Term Debt	..	0.0	0.0	0.0	0.0	0.0	0.0	0.0	61.0	86.0	113.0
Memo Items:					*(Millions of US dollars)*						
Int'l Reserves Excluding Gold	161.9	194.0	268.7	303.3	288.7	250.1	197.7	274.5	313.5	345.7	353.1
Gold Holdings (at market price)	15.1	16.0	18.7	27.8	48.0	79.8	60.0	57.7	72.6	100.1	235.0
SOCIAL INDICATORS											
Total Fertility Rate	2.6	2.4	2.3	2.2	2.2	2.2	2.2	2.2	2.2	2.2	2.2
Infant Mortality Rate	29.0	29.0	29.0	29.0	27.2	25.4	23.6	21.8	20.0	19.2	18.4
Life Expectancy at Birth	70.8	71.0	71.2	71.4	71.9	72.3	72.8	73.2	73.7	74.0	74.2
Urban Population, % of total	40.3	40.8	41.3	41.8	42.4	42.9	43.4	44.0	44.6	45.1	45.7
Food Prod. per capita (1987=100)	180.4	163.7	200.1	195.4	137.8	157.2	110.8	114.7	117.3	115.3	115.7
Labor Force, Agriculture (%)	38.8	38.5	37.2	35.9	34.7	33.4	32.3	31.0	29.7	28.4	27.2
Labor Force, Female (%)	33.6	33.6	33.7	33.8	33.9	34.0	34.1	34.2	34.4	34.5	34.6
Primary Schl. Enroll. Ratio	..	..	..	..	..	..	..	..	..	..	..
Primary Schl. Enroll. Ratio, Female	..	..	..	..	..	..	..	..	..	..	..
Secondary Schl. Enroll. Ratio	..	..	..	..	..	..	..	..	..	..	..

1980	1981	1982	1983	1984	1985	1986	1987	1988	1989 estimate	NOTES	CYPRUS
				(Millions of current US dollars)							**FOREIGN TRADE (CUSTOMS BASIS)**
532.8	559.0	554.0	494.2	575.0	476.3	506.0	622.0	767.0	..	..	Value of Exports, fob
209.6	215.6	228.5	178.8	217.8	169.1	201.0	220.0	276.0	..	..	Nonfuel Primary Products
27.9	31.7	38.5	41.4	36.2	38.6	30.0	32.0	30.0	..	..	Fuels
295.4	311.7	286.9	274.0	321.0	268.6	275.0	370.0	461.0	..	..	Manufactures
1,195.1	1,101.4	1,206.8	1,207.8	1,350.8	1,233.5	1,263.4	1,463.3	1,859.0	..	..	Value of Imports, cif
214.4	212.5	217.3	242.8	242.3	211.5	239.3	250.3	300.2	..	..	Nonfuel Primary Products
222.5	238.7	246.7	227.7	247.9	224.9	161.1	183.0	226.3	..	..	Fuels
758.2	650.2	742.8	737.3	860.6	797.0	863.0	1,030.0	1,332.6	..	..	Manufactures
				(Index 1987 = 100)							
97.7	92.6	94.0	93.8	92.5	95.0	101.0	100.0	101.7	..	..	Terms of Trade
95.7	93.8	90.3	88.3	84.4	85.5	92.3	100.0	106.9	..	..	Export Prices, fob
97.9	101.3	96.1	94.2	91.2	90.0	91.4	100.0	105.2	..	..	Import Prices, cif
				(Millions of current US dollars)							**BALANCE OF PAYMENTS**
1,107.2	1,180.3	1,246.6	1,225.7	1,384.6	1,328.9	1,564.2	1,942.2	2,273.7	2,581.7	..	Exports of Goods & Services
489.2	507.6	499.2	438.1	522.6	416.9	451.6	566.4	645.5	717.3	..	Merchandise, fob
520.3	570.4	632.1	684.7	752.1	796.3	983.1	1,234.5	1,468.4	1,673.7	..	Nonfactor Services
97.7	102.3	115.3	102.9	110.0	115.6	129.5	141.3	159.9	190.7	..	Factor Services
1,421.9	1,390.7	1,474.2	1,484.5	1,630.9	1,530.8	1,620.2	1,894.2	2,317.5	2,776.2	..	Imports of Goods & Services
1,079.2	1,042.6	1,090.3	1,093.5	1,224.9	1,121.9	1,141.6	1,326.8	1,666.9	2,072.1	..	Merchandise, fob
279.0	273.4	294.3	287.5	300.3	301.5	354.5	428.2	494.6	540.4	..	Nonfactor Services
63.7	74.7	89.6	103.5	105.7	107.4	124.1	139.3	156.0	163.7	..	Factor Services
29.3	41.5	49.5	62.6	66.1	67.5	78.6	95.1	93.7	100.7	..	Long-Term Interest
32.6	27.3	24.8	23.4	21.6	22.2	23.7	26.4	24.6	22.9	..	Private Current Transfers, net
..	..	..	..	..	..	..	..	0.0	..	..	Workers' Remittances
-282.1	-183.2	-202.8	-235.5	-224.7	-179.7	-32.2	74.4	-19.1	-171.6	..	Curr. A/C Bal before Off. Transf.
40.8	35.4	46.7	50.9	21.9	18.6	21.6	17.5	27.4	15.6	..	Net Official Transfers
-241.3	-147.8	-156.1	-184.6	-202.8	-161.1	-10.6	91.9	8.4	-156.0	..	Curr. A/C Bal after Off. Transf.
217.2	188.6	220.0	136.3	204.5	113.6	171.2	45.9	51.2	363.7	..	Long-Term Capital, net
85.0	78.3	71.5	68.4	52.7	58.0	46.3	52.0	62.1	69.9	..	Direct Investment
108.3	104.7	134.4	66.8	151.1	73.3	131.8	22.3	-31.6	104.0	..	Long-Term Loans
138.5	139.4	184.1	134.3	212.0	166.8	245.8	199.3	150.8	316.8	..	Disbursements
30.2	34.7	49.7	67.5	60.9	93.5	114.0	177.0	182.4	212.8	..	Repayments
24.0	5.6	14.1	1.2	0.7	-17.6	-6.9	-28.3	20.7	189.8	..	Other Long-Term Capital
61.1	47.1	76.3	89.9	94.2	17.9	-1.1	-74.1	11.1	20.8	..	Other Capital, net
-37.1	-88.0	-140.2	-41.7	-95.9	29.6	-159.5	-63.7	-70.7	-228.5	..	Change in Reserves
				(Cyprus Pounds per US dollar)							**Memo Item:**
0.350	0.420	0.480	0.530	0.590	0.610	0.520	0.480	0.470	0.490	..	Conversion Factor (Annual Avg)
				(Millions of US dollars), outstanding at end of year							
545.4	622.5	729.7	860.1	1,022.6	1,349.3	1,618.5	2,015.8	2,042.3	2,105.2	..	**EXTERNAL DEBT** (Total)
437.4	511.5	622.7	660.1	764.6	940.3	1,197.5	1,418.6	1,323.8	1,433.2	..	Long-Term Debt (by debtor)
39.0	25.2	13.6	5.7	3.1	0.0	0.0	0.0	0.0	..	..	Central Bank, incl. IMF credit
256.2	304.0	405.7	446.2	503.8	605.4	876.0	1,072.2	1,022.3	1,013.2	..	Central Government
3.4	3.2	3.1	2.9	2.5	2.8	3.0	3.4	3.0	2.5	..	Rest of General Government
110.1	135.3	154.4	159.0	215.6	278.1	269.8	300.3	264.8	379.3	..	Non-financial Public Enterprises
28.7	43.8	45.9	46.3	39.6	54.0	48.7	42.7	33.7	38.2	..	Priv. Sector, incl non-guaranteed
108.0	111.0	107.0	200.0	258.0	409.0	421.0	597.2	718.5	672.0	..	Short-Term Debt
				(Millions of US dollars)							**Memo Items:**
368.3	426.4	523.2	519.1	540.6	595.3	752.8	873.5	927.9	1,124.0	..	Int'l Reserves Excluding Gold
270.6	182.5	209.7	175.1	141.5	150.1	179.4	222.2	188.3	184.1	..	Gold Holdings (at market price)
											SOCIAL INDICATORS
2.3	2.3	2.4	2.3	2.3	2.3	2.3	2.3	2.3	2.3	..	Total Fertility Rate
17.6	16.8	16.0	15.1	14.2	13.3	12.4	11.5	11.1	10.7	..	Infant Mortality Rate
74.4	74.7	74.9	75.1	75.2	75.4	75.5	75.7	75.9	76.1	..	Life Expectancy at Birth
46.3	46.9	47.6	48.2	48.9	49.5	50.2	50.8	51.5	52.1	..	Urban Population, % of total
118.9	108.3	113.4	90.9	108.4	104.0	96.2	100.0	116.1	124.3	..	Food Prod. per capita (1987=100)
26.0	..	..	..	..	..	..	..	..	..	..	Labor Force, Agriculture (%)
34.8	34.9	34.9	35.0	35.1	35.2	35.3	35.3	35.4	35.5	..	Labor Force, Female (%)
104.0	..	..	96.0	98.0	103.0	106.0	106.0	..	..	..	Primary Schl. Enroll. Ratio
104.0	..	..	95.0	97.0	102.0	106.0	106.0	..	..	..	Primary Schl. Enroll. Ratio, Female
95.0	..	..	98.0	97.0	94.0	91.0	87.0	..	..	..	Secondary Schl. Enroll. Ratio

DENMARK	1969	1970	1971	1972	1973	1974	1975	1976	1977	1978	1979
CURRENT GNP PER CAPITA (US $)	2,950	3,130	3,450	3,980	4,820	5,760	6,910	8,040	8,930	10,010	11,880
POPULATION (thousands)	4,891	4,929	4,963	4,992	5,022	5,045	5,060	5,073	5,088	5,104	5,117
USE AND ORIGIN OF RESOURCES					*(Billions of current Danish Kroner)*						
Gross National Product (GNP)	107.18	118.41	130.71	149.98	172.03	192.35	214.59	249.26	276.24	306.74	340.27
Net Factor Income from Abroad	-0.14	-0.21	-0.41	-0.75	-0.83	-1.28	-1.66	-1.96	-3.07	-4.60	-6.58
GDP at Market Prices	107.32	118.63	131.12	150.73	172.86	193.63	216.26	251.21	279.30	311.34	346.85
Resource Balance	-2.31	-3.54	-2.40	0.79	-3.28	-5.81	-2.00	-11.68	-10.20	-6.76	-9.77
Exports of Goods & NFServices	29.43	33.08	36.19	40.71	49.28	61.37	65.07	72.42	80.48	86.48	101.50
Imports of Goods & NFServices	31.74	36.62	38.59	39.92	52.56	67.18	67.07	84.09	90.68	93.24	111.27
Domestic Absorption	109.63	122.17	133.52	149.94	176.14	199.44	218.26	262.89	289.50	318.09	356.63
Private Consumption, etc.	61.76	68.16	73.19	80.55	94.19	105.31	119.87	142.30	158.78	174.76	195.76
General Gov't Consumption	21.20	24.22	27.60	31.58	36.68	43.66	48.99	60.52	66.77	76.25	86.83
Gross Domestic Investment	26.66	29.79	32.73	37.81	45.27	50.48	49.39	60.07	63.95	67.09	74.04
Fixed Investment	25.81	28.43	31.38	37.08	42.74	45.51	44.42	56.94	60.90	66.91	72.73
Indirect Taxes, net	15.53	17.29	19.25	21.89	23.76	23.98	27.54	33.09	39.11	46.32	54.57
GDP at factor cost	91.79	101.33	111.87	128.84	149.10	169.65	188.71	218.12	240.19	265.02	292.28
Agriculture	..	..	..	..	..	..	..	..	..	..	..
Industry	..	..	..	..	..	..	..	..	..	..	..
Manufacturing	..	..	..	..	..	..	..	..	..	..	..
Services, etc.	..	..	..	..	..	..	..	..	..	..	..
Gross Domestic Saving	24.35	26.25	30.33	38.61	42.00	44.66	47.39	48.40	53.76	60.33	64.27
Gross National Saving	..	25.97	29.88	37.74	41.10	43.21	45.53	46.16	50.62	55.55	57.33
					(Billions of 1987 Danish Kroner)						
Gross National Product	464.93	474.10	486.11	510.79	529.43	523.63	519.54	553.13	560.26	566.20	583.84
GDP at Market Prices	465.57	475.00	487.66	513.39	532.04	527.08	523.59	557.49	566.53	574.90	595.28
Resource Balance	-27.02	-33.38	-26.30	-21.97	-30.79	-20.05	-14.99	-32.63	-26.97	-25.47	-21.78
Exports of Goods & NFServices	103.16	108.94	115.00	121.42	130.91	135.49	133.08	138.52	144.22	145.92	158.12
Imports of Goods & NFServices	130.19	142.32	141.30	143.39	161.70	155.55	148.07	171.14	171.19	171.39	179.90
Domestic Absorption	492.59	508.38	513.96	535.36	562.83	547.13	538.58	590.12	593.51	600.36	617.06
Private Consumption, etc.	273.53	281.96	280.98	286.51	298.87	291.84	303.48	324.58	329.06	331.73	336.81
General Gov't Consumption	96.57	103.22	108.86	115.11	119.71	123.91	126.41	132.05	135.22	143.60	152.02
Gross Domestic Investment	122.49	123.20	124.12	133.73	144.25	131.38	108.69	133.49	129.23	125.03	128.23
Fixed Investment	117.30	119.86	122.19	133.50	138.13	125.90	110.31	129.20	126.04	127.43	126.87
GDP at factor cost	395.04	402.10	412.81	434.57	455.30	460.86	455.26	482.42	485.61	486.67	500.05
Agriculture	..	..	..	..	..	..	..	..	..	..	..
Industry	..	..	..	..	..	..	..	..	..	..	..
Manufacturing	..	..	..	..	..	..	..	..	..	..	..
Services, etc.	..	..	..	..	..	..	..	..	..	..	..
Memo Items:											
Capacity to Import	120.72	128.56	132.50	146.23	151.61	142.09	143.65	147.38	151.94	158.97	164.10
Terms of Trade Adjustment	17.56	19.62	17.50	24.81	20.71	6.60	10.58	8.87	7.72	13.04	5.98
Gross Domestic Income	483.13	494.62	505.16	538.20	552.74	533.68	534.17	566.35	574.26	587.94	601.26
Gross National Income	482.49	493.72	503.62	535.60	550.14	530.23	530.11	562.00	567.98	579.24	589.82
DOMESTIC PRICES/DEFLATORS					*(Index 1987 = 100)*						
Overall (GDP)	23.1	25.0	26.9	29.4	32.5	36.7	41.3	45.1	49.3	54.2	58.3
Domestic Absorption	22.3	24.0	26.0	28.0	31.3	36.5	40.5	44.5	48.8	53.0	57.8
Agriculture	..	..	..	..	..	..	..	..	..	..	..
Industry	..	..	..	..	..	..	..	..	..	..	..
Manufacturing	..	..	..	..	..	..	..	..	..	..	..
Consumer Price Index	23.3	24.8	26.2	28.0	30.6	35.2	38.6	42.1	46.8	51.5	56.4
MANUFACTURING ACTIVITY											
Employment (1987=100)	98.0	103.9	100.6	102.0	105.8	102.3	92.9	93.5	95.6	95.2	96.4
Real Earnings per Empl. (1987=100)	74.9	76.3	81.8	84.0	85.9	91.3	96.6	99.2	97.5	96.6	97.7
Real Output per Empl. (1987=100)	..	..	..	..	..	..	..	..	..	..	..
Earnings as % of Value Added	54.5	56.4	58.1	56.6	57.0	59.1	59.1	57.4	57.5	57.6	57.7
MONETARY HOLDINGS					*(Billions of current Danish Kroner)*						
Money Supply, Broadly Defined	51.88	54.39	59.21	67.12	76.27	82.70	104.99	117.30	128.19	136.44	150.38
Money	27.13	27.47	29.61	33.64	37.59	39.36	51.27	54.51	58.85	68.30	75.05
Currency Outside Banks	5.23	4.87	4.92	5.56	5.99	6.04	7.63	8.44	9.91	10.75	11.57
Demand Deposits	21.90	22.60	24.69	28.08	31.60	33.32	43.64	46.07	48.94	57.55	63.47
Quasi-Money	24.75	26.92	29.60	33.48	38.68	43.34	53.72	62.79	69.34	68.14	75.33
GOVERNMENT DEFICIT (-) OR SURPLUS					*(Billions of current Danish Kroner)*						
	..	2.95	3.57	4.09	6.14	1.34	-4.35	-0.52	-2.73	-1.07	-2.58
Current Revenue	..	41.83	47.63	53.57	58.64	67.27	71.24	83.17	91.70	106.80	122.09
Current Expenditure	..	35.39	40.34	45.67	48.38	61.01	69.79	77.44	88.35	101.61	118.61
Current Budget Balance	..	6.44	7.29	7.90	10.26	6.25	1.45	5.73	3.35	5.19	3.48
Capital Receipts	..	0.11	0.09	0.19	0.15	0.21	0.16	1.00	0.21	0.62	0.61
Capital Payments	..	3.60	3.81	4.00	4.28	5.13	5.96	7.25	6.29	6.87	6.67

1980	1981	1982	1983	1984	1985	1986	1987	1988	1989 estimate	NOTES	DENMARK
13,120	12,850	12,110	11,390	11,160	11,310	12,650	14,990	18,540	20,510	..	**CURRENT GNP PER CAPITA (US $)**
5,123	5,122	5,118	5,114	5,112	5,114	5,121	5,127	5,130	5,132	..	**POPULATION (thousands)**
			(Billions of current Danish Kroner)								**USE AND ORIGIN OF RESOURCES**
364.54	395.07	446.58	494.05	541.37	588.80	638.98	667.90	695.39	734.20	..	Gross National Product (GNP)
-9.28	-12.69	-17.82	-18.43	-23.86	-26.17	-27.49	-27.95	-28.65	-26.84	..	Net Factor Income from Abroad
373.82	407.76	464.40	512.48	565.23	614.98	666.47	695.86	724.04	761.04	..	GDP at Market Prices
-3.95	3.03	2.06	10.13	7.20	2.13	-2.93	12.81	21.76	26.58	..	Resource Balance
122.26	149.08	168.95	186.25	207.57	225.59	213.61	220.07	237.01	267.05	..	Exports of Goods & NFServices
126.21	146.05	166.89	176.12	200.37	223.46	216.54	207.26	215.25	240.47	..	Imports of Goods & NFServices
377.77	404.73	462.34	502.34	558.03	612.85	669.40	683.05	702.29	734.45	..	Domestic Absorption
208.85	228.45	255.57	279.89	307.85	337.12	366.60	377.47	386.36	403.84	..	Private Consumption, etc.
99.73	113.22	131.10	140.54	146.18	155.48	159.36	176.21	186.98	194.10	..	General Gov't Consumption
69.19	63.06	75.67	81.91	104.00	120.25	143.44	129.36	128.95	136.51	..	Gross Domestic Investment
70.31	63.44	75.05	81.83	97.69	114.61	138.17	134.55	134.81	138.92	..	Fixed Investment
57.80	62.67	67.05	74.67	83.61	94.56	110.82	113.97	115.63	116.00	..	Indirect Taxes, net
316.02	345.09	397.34	437.80	481.62	520.42	555.65	581.89	608.42	645.04	..	GDP at factor cost
..	..	..	..	..	..	..	..	..	..	..	Agriculture
..	..	..	..	..	..	..	..	..	..	..	Industry
..	..	..	..	..	..	..	..	..	..	..	Manufacturing
..	..	..	..	..	..	..	..	..	..	..	Services, etc.
65.24	66.10	77.73	92.04	111.21	122.38	140.51	142.17	150.71	163.10	..	Gross Domestic Saving
55.45	52.53	59.58	72.75	87.28	95.62	112.11	113.83	121.47	136.84	..	Gross National Saving
			(Billions of 1987 Danish Kroner)								
578.04	569.48	582.32	598.35	620.63	647.00	671.03	667.90	667.47	677.53	..	Gross National Product
592.64	587.37	605.11	620.35	647.58	675.35	699.96	695.86	694.72	702.17	..	GDP at Market Prices
-1.46	14.99	13.26	19.21	16.42	11.48	-1.86	12.81	25.04	31.04	..	Resource Balance
166.27	179.90	184.41	193.36	200.07	209.99	210.06	220.07	234.76	249.79	..	Exports of Goods & NFServices
167.73	164.91	171.14	174.15	183.65	198.52	211.92	207.26	209.72	218.74	..	Imports of Goods & NFServices
594.10	572.38	591.84	601.14	631.16	663.88	701.82	683.04	669.68	671.12	..	Domestic Absorption
327.52	322.36	326.73	336.10	347.06	363.29	381.95	377.47	372.79	371.92	..	Private Consumption, etc.
158.52	162.69	167.69	167.62	166.93	171.15	171.98	176.21	174.65	173.69	..	General Gov't Consumption
108.07	87.33	97.42	97.41	117.16	129.44	147.89	129.36	122.23	125.52	..	Gross Domestic Investment
110.88	89.57	95.92	97.69	110.28	124.13	145.36	134.55	128.14	126.41	..	Fixed Investment
501.52	498.93	519.44	531.29	553.23	572.96	583.35	581.89	584.79	596.64	..	GDP at factor cost
..	..	..	..	..	..	..	..	..	..	..	Agriculture
..	..	..	..	..	..	..	..	..	..	..	Industry
..	..	..	..	..	..	..	..	..	..	..	Manufacturing
..	..	..	..	..	..	..	..	..	..	..	Services, etc.
											Memo Items:
162.48	168.33	173.25	184.17	190.25	200.40	209.05	220.07	230.92	242.92	..	Capacity to Import
-3.79	-11.57	-11.16	-9.19	-9.82	-9.59	-1.01	0.00	-3.84	-6.86	..	Terms of Trade Adjustment
588.85	575.80	593.95	611.16	637.76	665.76	698.95	695.86	690.88	695.30	..	Gross Domestic Income
574.25	557.91	571.16	589.16	610.81	637.41	670.02	667.90	663.64	670.67	..	Gross National Income
			(Index 1987 = 100)								**DOMESTIC PRICES/DEFLATORS**
63.1	69.4	76.7	82.6	87.3	91.1	95.2	100.0	104.2	108.4	..	Overall (GDP)
63.6	70.7	78.1	83.6	88.4	92.3	95.4	100.0	104.9	109.4	..	Domestic Absorption
..	..	..	..	..	..	..	..	..	..	..	Agriculture
..	..	..	..	..	..	..	..	..	..	..	Industry
..	..	..	..	..	..	..	..	..	..	..	Manufacturing
63.4	70.8	78.0	83.4	88.6	92.7	96.2	100.0	104.6	109.6	..	Consumer Price Index
											MANUFACTURING ACTIVITY
94.5	89.9	89.5	89.3	93.7	100.4	102.4	100.0	100.7	101.6	..	Employment (1987=100)
97.1	94.9	96.1	96.9	95.4	93.7	96.9	100.0	101.0	..	..	Real Earnings per Empl. (1987=100)
..	..	..	..	..	..	..	..	..	..	..	Real Output per Empl. (1987=100)
56.8	55.1	54.4	52.5	51.7	51.8	52.7	53.3	53.2	..	..	Earnings as % of Value Added
			(Billions of current Danish Kroner)								**MONETARY HOLDINGS**
167.99	186.21	206.82	247.57	309.79	366.67	401.19	417.79	..	..	..	Money Supply, Broadly Defined
83.21	93.03	105.24	114.18	153.84	195.77	214.95	243.28	278.14	279.76	..	Money
12.36	13.57	14.18	15.42	16.37	17.57	18.82	31.43	27.87	32.83	..	Currency Outside Banks
70.85	79.46	91.05	98.76	137.47	178.19	196.14	211.85	250.27	246.93	..	Demand Deposits
84.78	93.18	101.59	133.40	155.95	170.90	186.24	174.51	..	..	..	Quasi-Money
			(Billions of current Danish Kroner)								**GOVERNMENT DEFICIT (-) OR SURPLUS**
-10.00	-24.69	-37.52	-35.15	-22.24	-3.73	30.08	27.82	..	..	E	
135.23	148.10	166.21	192.19	223.32	251.18	283.31	294.34	305.10	..	..	Current Revenue
137.09	162.04	191.50	213.75	233.94	242.58	243.69	257.15	277.76	..	..	Current Expenditure
-1.86	-13.94	-25.30	-21.56	-10.62	8.60	39.62	37.18	27.33	..	..	Current Budget Balance
3.67	0.23	0.27	0.39	0.38	0.33	2.34	1.31	1.13	..	..	Capital Receipts
11.81	10.99	12.50	13.99	11.99	12.66	11.88	10.68	..	..	..	Capital Payments

DENMARK	1969	1970	1971	1972	1973	1974	1975	1976	1977	1978	1979
FOREIGN TRADE (CUSTOMS BASIS)					*(Millions of current US dollars)*						
Value of Exports, fob	2,958	3,285	3,601	4,312	6,116	7,683	8,663	8,980	9,911	11,676	14,342
Nonfuel Primary Products	1,328	1,429	1,556	1,831	2,654	3,085	3,479	3,577	4,014	4,961	5,906
Fuels	56	82	81	89	132	288	292	335	317	298	562
Manufactures	1,574	1,774	1,963	2,392	3,330	4,310	4,892	5,068	5,580	6,417	7,874
Value of Imports, cif	3,800	4,385	4,582	5,027	7,714	9,857	10,326	12,404	13,227	14,777	18,412
Nonfuel Primary Products	725	869	849	967	1,486	1,761	1,640	2,133	2,539	2,847	3,464
Fuels	384	459	557	549	821	1,889	1,920	2,038	2,227	2,303	3,603
Manufactures	2,691	3,057	3,177	3,511	5,407	6,206	6,766	8,232	8,461	9,627	11,345
					(Index 1987 = 100)						
Terms of Trade	124.8	124.9	124.1	123.5	126.6	96.4	97.8	98.6	94.9	99.3	99.3
Export Prices, fob	28.8	29.7	32.0	36.4	47.3	52.9	56.7	59.6	63.6	73.9	89.0
Import Prices, cif	23.1	23.8	25.8	29.5	37.3	54.8	57.9	60.4	67.0	74.4	89.7
BALANCE OF PAYMENTS					*(Millions of current US dollars)*						
Exports of Goods & Services	..	4,549	5,152	6,230	8,711	10,895	12,124	12,894	14,487	17,134	16,486
Merchandise, fob	..	3,317	3,610	4,363	6,191	7,703	8,652	9,053	10,011	11,807	14,574
Nonfactor Services	..	1,148	1,462	1,769	2,353	2,968	3,223	3,586	4,113	4,785	4,710
Factor Services	..	84	80	98	167	224	249	255	363	543	1,912
Imports of Goods & Services	..	5,050	5,525	6,203	9,409	12,033	12,690	15,026	16,594	19,187	21,295
Merchandise, fob	..	4,077	4,322	4,793	7,380	9,490	9,956	11,931	12,726	14,163	17,966
Nonfactor Services	..	844	1,052	1,191	1,703	2,061	2,159	2,480	2,958	3,596	3,180
Factor Services	..	129	151	218	326	482	574	616	911	1,429	3,329
Long-Term Interest	..	..	..	..	..	..	..	..	..	..	..
Private Current Transfers, net	..	-9	-6	-17	-11	-29	-34	-47	-11	-32	-67
Workers' Remittances	..	..	..	..	..	..	..	..	..	..	..
Curr. A/C Bal before Off. Transf.	..	-510	-379	10	-709	-1,167	-600	-2,179	-2,118	-2,085	-3,338
Net Official Transfers	..	-34	-45	-73	241	186	110	265	396	583	366
Curr. A/C Bal after Off. Transf.	..	-544	-424	-63	-468	-981	-490	-1,914	-1,722	-1,502	-2,972
Long-Term Capital, net	..	111	376	266	511	344	134	1,863	2,478	2,435	933
Direct Investment	..	75	73	16	114	..	188	-254	-85	56	103
Long-Term Loans	..	..	..	..	..	..	..	..	..	..	..
Disbursements	..	..	..	..	..	..	..	..	..	..	..
Repayments	..	..	..	..	..	..	..	..	..	..	..
Other Long-Term Capital	..	36	303	250	397	344	-54	2,117	2,564	2,379	829
Other Capital, net	..	444	226	-112	399	199	313	70	-39	564	1,967
Change in Reserves	..	-11	-178	-91	-443	438	42	-19	-717	-1,496	72
Memo Item:					*(Danish Kroner per US dollar)*						
Conversion Factor (Annual Avg)	7.500	7.500	7.420	6.950	6.050	6.090	5.750	6.050	6.000	5.510	5.260
				(Millions US dollars), outstanding at end of year							
EXTERNAL DEBT (Total)	..	..	..	..	..	..	..	..	..	..	..
Long-Term Debt (by debtor)	..	..	..	..	..	..	..	..	..	..	..
Central Bank, incl. IMF credit	..	..	..	..	..	..	..	..	..	..	..
Central Government	..	..	..	..	..	..	..	..	..	..	..
Rest of General Government	..	..	..	..	..	..	..	..	..	..	..
Non-financial Public Enterprises	..	..	..	..	..	..	..	..	..	..	..
Priv. Sector, incl non-guaranteed	..	..	..	..	..	..	..	..	..	..	..
Short-Term Debt	..	..	..	..	..	..	..	..	..	..	..
Memo Items:					*(Millions of US dollars)*						
Int'l Reserves Excluding Gold	357	419	653	786	1,247	858	803	841	1,589	3,129	3,236
Gold Holdings (at market price)	89	69	79	118	204	338	254	244	318	447	840
SOCIAL INDICATORS											
Total Fertility Rate	2.0	1.9	2.0	2.0	1.9	1.9	1.9	1.7	1.7	1.7	1.6
Infant Mortality Rate	14.8	14.2	13.5	12.2	11.5	10.7	10.4	10.2	8.7	8.8	8.8
Life Expectancy at Birth	73.1	73.2	73.4	73.5	73.6	73.7	73.8	74.0	74.1	74.1	74.1
Urban Population, % of total	79.2	79.7	80.2	80.7	81.1	81.6	82.1	82.4	82.8	83.1	83.5
Food Prod. per capita (1987=100)	79.9	72.9	77.5	74.3	73.7	84.1	77.5	74.0	83.2	82.3	84.8
Labor Force, Agriculture (%)	11.8	11.2	10.8	10.4	10.0	9.6	9.2	8.8	8.4	8.0	7.7
Labor Force, Female (%)	35.7	36.0	36.9	37.7	38.5	39.3	40.0	40.8	41.6	42.4	43.2
Primary Schl. Enroll. Ratio	..	96.0	..	..	..	..	104.0	101.0	99.0	98.0	98.0
Primary Schl. Enroll. Ratio, Female	..	97.0	..	..	..	..	..	102.0	100.0	99.0	98.0
Secondary Schl. Enroll. Ratio	..	78.0	..	..	..	..	80.0	80.0	83.0	99.0	102.0

1980	1981	1982	1983	1984	1985	1986	1987	1988	1989	NOTES	DENMARK
				(Millions of current US dollars)							**FOREIGN TRADE (CUSTOMS BASIS)**
16,407	15,697	14,953	15,601	15,486	16,469	20,558	24,697	27,816	..	..	Value of Exports, fob
6,589	6,304	6,110	5,899	5,748	5,967	7,581	8,924	9,370	..	..	Nonfuel Primary Products
566	505	385	780	801	903	643	734	613	..	..	Fuels
9,252	8,888	8,458	8,922	8,936	9,599	12,334	15,039	17,833	..	..	Manufactures
19,315	17,521	16,834	16,179	16,536	17,985	22,726	25,334	26,458	..	..	Value of Imports, cif
3,664	3,323	3,017	3,066	3,052	3,036	3,997	4,642	4,977	..	..	Nonfuel Primary Products
4,328	4,216	3,790	3,163	2,999	3,097	2,009	1,996	1,673	..	..	Fuels
11,323	9,982	10,027	9,950	10,485	11,852	16,719	18,696	19,808	..	..	Manufactures
				(Index 1987 = 100)							
89.8	83.7	83.9	86.6	85.6	89.4	98.3	100.0	102.7	..	..	Terms of Trade
93.7	86.0	80.6	80.0	76.3	77.2	88.7	100.0	105.7	..	..	Export Prices, fob
104.4	102.7	96.0	92.3	89.1	86.3	90.2	100.0	103.0	..	..	Import Prices, cif
				(Millions of current US dollars)							**BALANCE OF PAYMENTS**
19,245	23,176	22,241	22,511	22,444	24,091	29,674	36,170	40,420	42,768	..	Exports of Goods & Services
16,786	16,136	15,685	16,210	16,079	17,116	21,307	25,695	27,537	28,718	..	Merchandise, fob
4,904	5,853	5,410	5,310	5,208	5,567	6,372	7,848	9,291	9,649	..	Nonfactor Services
2,459	1,187	1,146	991	1,157	1,409	1,995	2,627	3,592	4,401	..	Factor Services
23,057	24,891	24,315	23,499	24,149	26,685	33,886	38,951	41,980	44,039	..	Imports of Goods & Services
18,809	17,064	16,479	15,974	16,285	17,887	22,357	24,900	25,664	26,285	..	Merchandise, fob
3,583	4,663	4,538	4,511	4,465	4,925	6,066	7,302	8,427	8,824	..	Nonfactor Services
4,248	3,164	3,298	3,013	3,399	3,873	5,464	6,750	7,890	8,930	..	Factor Services
..	..	..	..	..	..	..	..	..	..	..	Long-Term Interest
-89	-124	-39	-94	-7	-55	-112	-56	-88	80	..	Private Current Transfers, net
..	..	..	..	..	..	..	..	..	..	..	Workers' Remittances
-2,578	-1,839	-2,113	-1,082	-1,712	-2,648	-4,325	-2,838	-1,648	-1,192	..	Curr. A/C Bal before Off. Transf.
112	-37	-146	-94	76	-80	-166	-164	-131	-223	..	Net Official Transfers
-2,466	-1,875	-2,259	-1,176	-1,637	-2,728	-4,490	-3,001	-1,779	-1,414	..	Curr. A/C Bal after Off. Transf.
2,546	1,349	2,398	2,466	1,900	4,451	3,563	8,153	2,909	-3,268	..	Long-Term Capital, net
-92	-39	52	-97	-88	..	..	..	..	..	..	Direct Investment
..	..	..	..	..	..	..	..	..	..	..	Long-Term Loans
..	..	..	..	..	..	..	..	..	..	..	Disbursements
..	..	..	..	..	..	..	..	..	..	..	Repayments
2,638	1,388	2,346	2,562	1,988	4,451	3,563	8,153	2,909	-3,268	..	Other Long-Term Capital
-4	-187	-436	85	-631	-201	-1,052	-708	186	860	..	Other Capital, net
-77	713	297	-1,375	367	-1,522	1,979	-4,443	-1,316	3,821	..	Change in Reserves
				(Danish Kroner per US dollar)							Memo Item:
5.640	7.120	8.330	9.150	10.360	10.600	8.090	6.840	6.730	7.310	..	Conversion Factor (Annual Avg)
			(Millions US dollars), outstanding at end of year								
..	..	..	..	..	..	..	..	..	..	..	**EXTERNAL DEBT (Total)**
..	..	..	..	..	..	..	..	..	..	..	Long-Term Debt (by debtor)
..	..	..	..	..	..	..	..	..	..	..	Central Bank, incl. IMF credit
..	..	..	..	..	..	..	..	..	..	..	Central Government
..	..	..	..	..	..	..	..	..	..	..	Rest of General Government
..	..	..	..	..	..	..	..	..	..	..	Non-financial Public Enterprises
..	..	..	..	..	..	..	..	..	..	..	Priv. Sector, incl non-guaranteed
..	..	..	..	..	..	..	..	..	..	..	Short-Term Debt
				(Millions of US dollars)							Memo Items:
3,387	2,548	2,266	3,621	3,009	5,429	4,964	10,066	10,765	6,397	..	Int'l Reserves Excluding Gold
960	648	744	621	502	533	637	788	668	657	..	Gold Holdings (at market price)
											SOCIAL INDICATORS
1.5	1.4	1.4	1.4	1.4	1.4	1.5	1.5	1.5	1.5	..	Total Fertility Rate
8.4	7.9	8.2	7.7	7.7	7.9	8.2	8.3	8.2	8.1	..	Infant Mortality Rate
74.1	74.3	74.3	74.5	74.5	74.5	74.6	74.8	74.9	75.1	..	Life Expectancy at Birth
83.8	84.1	84.3	84.6	84.8	85.1	85.4	85.6	85.9	86.1	..	Urban Population, % of total
84.3	85.6	94.1	87.8	107.4	104.5	102.0	100.0	100.8	104.2	..	Food Prod. per capita (1987=100)
7.3	..	..	..	..	..	..	..	..	..	..	Labor Force, Agriculture (%)
43.9	44.0	44.0	44.1	44.2	44.2	44.3	44.4	44.5	44.5	..	Labor Force, Female (%)
96.0	..	98.0	99.0	98.0	98.0	99.0	..	..	..	..	Primary Schl. Enroll. Ratio
95.0	98.0	98.0	99.0	99.0	98.0	99.0	..	..	..	..	Primary Schl. Enroll. Ratio, Female
105.0	..	105.0	103.0	103.0	105.0	107.0	..	..	..	..	Secondary Schl. Enroll. Ratio

DOMINICA	1969	1970	1971	1972	1973	1974	1975	1976	1977	1978	1979
CURRENT GNP PER CAPITA (US $)	250	290	320	340	350	350	380	420	470	560	500
POPULATION (thousands)	68	68	69	70	70	71	71	71	72	72	73

USE AND ORIGIN OF RESOURCES *(Millions of current East Caribbean Dollars)*

	1969	1970	1971	1972	1973	1974	1975	1976	1977	1978	1979
Gross National Product (GNP)	32.30	40.30	43.00	45.60	49.60	56.90	60.20	74.30	98.24	109.80	112.50
Net Factor Income from Abroad	0.00	0.00	0.00	0.00	0.00	0.00	0.00	0.00	0.00	0.00	-0.30
GDP at Market Prices	32.30	40.30	43.00	45.60	49.60	56.90	60.20	74.30	98.24	109.80	112.80
Resource Balance	..	..	..	..	..	..	..	..	..	..	-62.40
Exports of Goods & NFServices	..	..	..	..	..	..	..	..	..	..	51.00
Imports of Goods & NFServices	..	..	..	..	..	..	..	..	..	..	113.40
Domestic Absorption	..	..	..	..	..	..	..	..	..	..	..
Private Consumption, etc.	..	..	..	..	..	..	..	..	..	..	..
General Gov't Consumption	..	..	..	..	..	..	..	..	..	..	..
Gross Domestic Investment	..	..	..	..	..	..	..	..	..	..	..
Fixed Investment	..	..	..	..	..	..	..	..	..	..	..
Indirect Taxes, net	..	..	..	..	..	..	..	..	13.40	14.40	7.00
GDP at factor cost	..	..	..	..	..	..	..	..	84.84	95.40	105.80
Agriculture	..	..	..	..	..	..	..	..	31.93	35.50	34.78
Industry	..	..	..	..	..	..	..	..	12.51	14.23	15.57
Manufacturing	..	..	..	..	..	..	..	..	4.24	5.85	5.02
Services, etc.	..	..	..	..	..	..	..	..	40.40	45.67	55.45
Gross Domestic Saving	..	..	..	..	..	..	..	..	..	..	..
Gross National Saving	..	..	..	..	..	..	..	..	..	..	..

(Millions of 1987 East Caribbean Dollars)

	1969	1970	1971	1972	1973	1974	1975	1976	1977	1978	1979
Gross National Product	219.72	247.47	262.38	266.73	254.81	222.24	208.48	215.82	225.31	251.66	190.34
GDP at Market Prices	219.25	246.94	261.82	266.16	254.26	221.77	208.03	215.36	224.83	251.12	190.32
Resource Balance	..	..	..	..	..	..	..	..	..	..	..
Exports of Goods & NFServices	..	..	..	..	..	..	..	..	..	..	..
Imports of Goods & NFServices	..	..	..	..	..	..	..	..	..	..	..
Domestic Absorption	..	..	..	..	..	..	..	..	..	..	..
Private Consumption, etc.	..	..	..	..	..	..	..	..	..	..	..
General Gov't Consumption	..	..	..	..	..	..	..	..	..	..	..
Gross Domestic Investment	..	..	..	..	..	..	..	..	..	..	..
Fixed Investment	..	..	..	..	..	..	..	..	..	..	..
GDP at factor cost	..	..	..	..	..	..	..	..	194.69	218.69	178.45
Agriculture	..	..	..	..	..	..	..	..	68.78	76.49	52.04
Industry	..	..	..	..	..	..	..	..	22.38	25.47	24.79
Manufacturing	..	..	..	..	..	..	..	..	7.87	10.86	9.00
Services, etc.	..	..	..	..	..	..	..	..	99.69	112.64	101.59

Memo Items:

	1969	1970	1971	1972	1973	1974	1975	1976	1977	1978	1979
Capacity to Import	..	..	..	..	..	..	..	..	..	..	..
Terms of Trade Adjustment	..	..	..	..	..	..	..	..	..	..	..
Gross Domestic Income	..	..	..	..	..	..	..	..	..	..	..
Gross National Income	..	..	..	..	..	..	..	..	..	..	..

DOMESTIC PRICES/DEFLATORS *(Index 1987 = 100)*

	1969	1970	1971	1972	1973	1974	1975	1976	1977	1978	1979
Overall (GDP)	14.7	16.3	16.4	17.1	19.5	25.7	28.9	34.5	43.7	43.7	59.3
Domestic Absorption	..	..	..	..	..	..	..	..	..	..	..
Agriculture	..	..	..	..	..	..	..	..	46.4	46.4	66.8
Industry	..	..	..	..	..	..	..	..	55.9	55.9	62.8
Manufacturing	..	..	..	..	..	..	..	..	53.9	53.9	55.8
Consumer Price Index	16.1	18.0	18.7	19.4	21.7	29.2	35.0	38.8	72.4	45.8	..

MANUFACTURING ACTIVITY

	1969	1970	1971	1972	1973	1974	1975	1976	1977	1978	1979
Employment (1987=100)	..	..	..	..	..	..	..	..	..	..	..
Real Earnings per Empl. (1987=100)	..	..	..	..	..	..	..	..	..	..	..
Real Output per Empl. (1987=100)	..	..	..	..	..	..	..	..	..	..	..
Earnings as % of Value Added	..	..	..	..	..	..	..	..	..	..	..

MONETARY HOLDINGS *(Millions of current East Caribbean Dollars)*

	1969	1970	1971	1972	1973	1974	1975	1976	1977	1978	1979
Money Supply, Broadly Defined	..	..	..	..	..	..	36.65	41.25	45.15	53.94	77.60
Money	..	..	..	..	..	..	8.54	9.36	11.53	17.49	30.09
Currency Outside Banks	..	..	..	..	..	..	2.77	3.65	4.81	5.15	7.33
Demand Deposits	..	..	..	..	..	..	5.77	5.70	6.72	12.34	22.75
Quasi-Money	..	..	..	..	..	..	28.11	31.89	33.63	36.45	47.52

(Thousands of current East Caribbean Dollars)

	1969	1970	1971	1972	1973	1974	1975	1976	1977	1978	1979
GOVERNMENT DEFICIT (-) OR SURPLUS	..	..	..	..	..	..	..	-4,490	200	-2,720	-8,110
Current Revenue	..	..	..	..	..	..	..	21,660	30,970	43,280	52,080
Current Expenditure	..	..	..	..	..	..	..	19,460	23,740	35,190	37,810
Current Budget Balance	..	..	..	..	..	..	..	2,200	7,230	8,090	14,270
Capital Receipts	..	..	..	..	..	..	..	20	30	20	50
Capital Payments	..	..	..	..	..	..	..	6,710	7,060	10,830	22,430

1980	1981	1982	1983	1984	1985	1986	1987	1988	1989 estimate	NOTES	DOMINICA
700	950	1,020	990	1,070	1,120	1,280	1,480	1,690	..	..	**CURRENT GNP PER CAPITA (US $)**
73	74	75	77	78	80	81	81	82	82	..	**POPULATION (thousands)**
			(Millions of current East Caribbean Dollars)								**USE AND ORIGIN OF RESOURCES**
158.50	182.50	196.90	208.00	233.80	252.30	289.90	328.40	385.30	..	..	Gross National Product (GNP)
0.80	1.30	0.50	-5.70	-8.70	-14.30	-16.50	-13.80	-9.20	..	..	Net Factor Income from Abroad
157.70	181.20	196.40	213.70	242.50	266.60	306.40	342.20	394.50	412.10	..	GDP at Market Prices
-109.40	-79.60	-51.30	-37.00	-58.10	-58.90	-14.10	-27.80	-62.70	..	..	Resource Balance
41.30	61.60	84.00	97.20	99.60	103.40	145.20	160.70	183.30	..	..	Exports of Goods & NFServices
150.70	141.20	135.30	134.20	157.70	162.30	159.30	188.50	246.00	..	..	Imports of Goods & NFServices
..	..	..	..	..	..	..	..	..	..	..	Domestic Absorption
..	..	..	..	..	..	..	..	..	..	..	Private Consumption, etc.
..	..	..	..	..	..	..	..	..	..	..	General Gov't Consumption
..	..	..	..	..	..	..	..	..	..	..	Gross Domestic Investment
..	..	..	..	..	..	..	..	..	..	..	Fixed Investment
14.00	28.30	32.80	33.30	39.80	43.30	53.13	60.44	70.19	..	..	Indirect Taxes, net
143.70	152.90	163.60	180.40	202.70	223.30	253.27	281.76	324.31	340.00	..	GDP at factor cost
44.05	48.48	49.78	52.50	56.80	62.39	76.64	82.59	95.41	91.80	..	Agriculture
30.05	30.97	33.48	33.26	36.95	37.07	36.76	41.82	53.60	55.90	..	Industry
6.93	10.23	13.39	14.12	12.36	14.37	16.88	18.25	21.00	24.30	..	Manufacturing
69.60	73.45	80.34	94.64	108.95	123.84	139.87	157.35	175.30	192.30	..	Services, etc.
..	..	..	..	..	..	..	..	..	..	..	Gross Domestic Saving
..	..	..	..	..	..	..	..	..	..	..	Gross National Saving
			(Millions of 1987 East Caribbean Dollars)								
227.22	263.69	272.14	265.58	277.82	275.96	301.20	328.40	355.08	..	..	Gross National Product
225.59	261.41	270.80	272.84	289.14	294.36	319.25	342.20	363.57	361.78	..	GDP at Market Prices
..	..	..	..	..	..	..	..	..	..	..	Resource Balance
..	..	..	..	..	..	..	..	..	..	..	Exports of Goods & NFServices
..	..	..	..	..	..	..	..	..	..	..	Imports of Goods & NFServices
..	..	..	..	..	..	..	..	..	..	..	Domestic Absorption
..	..	..	..	..	..	..	..	..	..	..	Private Consumption, etc.
..	..	..	..	..	..	..	..	..	..	..	General Gov't Consumption
..	..	..	..	..	..	..	..	..	..	..	Gross Domestic Investment
..	..	..	..	..	..	..	..	..	..	..	Fixed Investment
205.26	220.57	225.79	230.32	241.64	246.48	264.00	281.76	302.48	299.07	..	GDP at factor cost
50.97	62.30	63.74	64.28	67.79	66.09	78.63	82.59	87.65	76.47	..	Agriculture
36.65	35.65	35.68	35.36	40.48	40.26	38.19	41.82	49.73	50.62	..	Industry
11.51	13.55	15.91	16.23	14.61	16.52	17.23	18.25	20.05	22.46	..	Manufacturing
118.59	121.57	125.62	130.68	133.37	140.13	147.18	157.35	165.10	171.98	..	Services, etc.
											Memo Items:
..	..	..	..	..	..	..	..	..	..	..	Capacity to Import
..	..	..	..	..	..	..	..	..	..	..	Terms of Trade Adjustment
..	..	..	..	..	..	..	..	..	..	..	Gross Domestic Income
..	..	..	..	..	..	..	..	..	..	..	Gross National Income
			(Index 1987 = 100)								**DOMESTIC PRICES/DEFLATORS**
69.9	69.3	72.5	78.3	83.9	90.6	96.0	100.0	108.5	113.9	..	Overall (GDP)
..	..	..	..	..	..	..	..	..	..	..	Domestic Absorption
86.4	77.8	78.1	81.7	83.8	94.4	97.5	100.0	108.9	120.0	..	Agriculture
82.0	86.9	93.8	94.1	91.3	92.1	96.3	100.0	107.8	110.4	..	Industry
60.2	75.5	84.2	87.0	84.6	87.0	98.0	100.0	104.7	108.2	..	Manufacturing
71.8	81.3	84.9	88.4	90.3	92.2	95.0	100.0	101.8	108.2	..	Consumer Price Index
											MANUFACTURING ACTIVITY
..	..	..	..	..	..	..	..	..	..	..	Employment (1987=100)
..	..	..	..	..	..	..	..	..	..	..	Real Earnings per Empl. (1987=100)
..	..	..	..	..	..	..	..	..	..	..	Real Output per Empl. (1987=100)
..	..	..	..	..	..	..	..	..	..	..	Earnings as % of Value Added
			(Millions of current East Caribbean Dollars)								**MONETARY HOLDINGS**
79.47	81.29	96.26	105.71	122.59	128.20	147.27	190.85	209.35	232.42	..	Money Supply, Broadly Defined
27.11	26.44	25.41	25.40	32.40	31.22	37.03	58.67	61.24	57.04	..	Money
7.48	7.73	6.58	6.39	12.22	9.64	6.64	20.77	22.83	20.69	..	Currency Outside Banks
19.63	18.71	18.83	19.01	20.18	21.58	30.39	37.89	38.41	36.35	..	Demand Deposits
52.36	54.84	70.85	80.31	90.19	96.98	110.24	132.18	148.11	175.38	..	Quasi-Money
			(Thousands of current East Caribbean Dollars)							C	**GOVERNMENT DEFICIT (-) OR SURPLUS**
..	..	..	..	..	..	..	..	..	..		Current Revenue
..	..	..	..	..	..	..	..	..	..		Current Expenditure
..	..	..	..	..	..	..	..	..	..		Current Budget Balance
..	..	..	..	..	..	..	..	..	..		Capital Receipts
..	..	..	..	..	..	..	..	..	..		Capital Payments
1980	1981	1982	1983	1984	1985	1986	1987	1988	1989	NOTES	

DOMINICA	1969	1970	1971	1972	1973	1974	1975	1976	1977	1978	1979
FOREIGN TRADE (CUSTOMS BASIS)					*(Thousands of current US dollars)*						
Value of Exports, fob	..	..	..	..	..	..	..	11,100	12,000	15,900	9,800
Nonfuel Primary Products	..	..	..	..	..	..	..	..	..	..	..
Fuels	..	..	..	..	..	..	..	..	..	..	..
Manufactures	..	..	..	..	..	..	..	..	..	..	..
Value of Imports, cif	..	..	..	..	..	..	..	17,300	19,900	25,900	35,800
Nonfuel Primary Products	..	..	..	..	..	..	..	..	..	..	..
Fuels	..	..	..	..	..	..	..	..	..	..	..
Manufactures	..	..	..	..	..	..	..	..	..	..	..
					(Index 1987 = 100)						
Terms of Trade	..	..	..	..	..	..	..	..	..	..	..
Export Prices, fob	..	..	..	..	..	..	..	..	..	..	..
Import Prices, cif	..	..	..	..	..	..	..	..	..	..	..
BALANCE OF PAYMENTS					*(Thousands of current US dollars)*						
Exports of Goods & Services	..	..	..	..	..	..	..	14,002	15,300	19,200	19,600
Merchandise, fob	..	..	..	..	..	..	..	11,099	12,000	15,900	9,800
Nonfactor Services	..	..	..	..	..	..	..	2,501	3,000	3,100	9,500
Factor Services	..	..	..	..	..	..	..	402	300	200	300
Imports of Goods & Services	..	..	..	..	..	..	..	19,299	22,500	29,700	40,700
Merchandise, fob	..	..	..	..	..	..	..	17,272	19,907	25,907	35,818
Nonfactor Services	..	..	..	..	..	..	..	1,828	2,293	3,393	4,481
Factor Services	..	..	..	..	..	..	..	199	300	400	400
Long-Term Interest	..	..	..	..	..	..	..	..	..	..	..
Private Current Transfers, net	..	..	..	..	..	..	..	1,300	1,700	3,600	6,800
Workers' Remittances	..	..	..	..	..	..	..	1,300	3,200	5,800	8,700
Curr. A/C Bal before Off. Transf.	..	..	..	..	..	..	..	-3,997	-5,500	-6,900	-14,300
Net Official Transfers	..	..	..	..	..	..	..	2,899	4,000	5,600	20,600
Curr. A/C Bal after Off. Transf.	..	..	..	..	..	..	..	-1,098	-1,500	-1,300	6,300
Long-Term Capital, net	..	..	..	..	..	..	..	1,499	2,000	1,100	600
Direct Investment	..	..	..	..	..	..	..	..	..	..	..
Long-Term Loans	..	..	..	..	..	..	..	..	..	..	..
Disbursements	..	..	..	..	..	..	..	..	..	..	..
Repayments	..	..	..	..	..	..	..	..	..	..	..
Other Long-Term Capital	..	..	..	..	..	..	..	1,499	2,000	1,100	600
Other Capital, net	..	..	..	..	..	..	..	-4	459	296	-1,341
Change in Reserves	..	..	..	..	..	..	..	-398	-959	-96	-5,559
Memo Item:					*(East Caribbean Dollars per US dollar)*						
Conversion Factor (Annual Avg)	2.000	2.000	1.970	1.920	1.960	2.050	2.170	2.610	2.700	2.700	2.700
					(Millions of US dollars), outstanding at end of year						
EXTERNAL DEBT (Total)	..	..	..	..	..	..	..	..	..	..	..
Long-Term Debt (by debtor)	..	..	..	..	..	..	..	..	..	..	..
Central Bank, incl. IMF credit	..	..	..	..	..	..	..	..	..	..	..
Central Government	..	..	..	..	..	..	..	..	..	..	..
Rest of General Government	..	..	..	..	..	..	..	..	..	..	..
Non-financial Public Enterprises	..	..	..	..	..	..	..	..	..	..	..
Priv. Sector, incl non-guaranteed	..	..	..	..	..	..	..	..	..	..	..
Short-Term Debt	..	..	..	..	..	..	..	..	..	..	..
Memo Items:					*(Thousands of US dollars)*						
Int'l Reserves Excluding Gold	..	..	..	..	..	..	345	1,173	2,230	1,925	9,836
Gold Holdings (at market price)	..	..	..	..	..	..	..	..	..	..	..
SOCIAL INDICATORS											
Total Fertility Rate	..	..	..	5.5	5.3	5.1	4.9	4.7	4.5	4.3	4.1
Infant Mortality Rate	..	..	..	..	38.7	28.1	26.9	24.0	27.0	21.9	12.3
Life Expectancy at Birth	..	..	..	..	..	..	..	..	..	..	..
Urban Population, % of total	..	..	..	..	..	..	..	..	..	..	..
Food Prod. per capita (1987=100)	88.2	77.4	74.3	74.8	71.5	77.3	81.0	88.8	90.8	100.0	70.0
Labor Force, Agriculture (%)	..	..	..	..	..	..	..	..	..	..	..
Labor Force, Female (%)	..	..	..	..	..	..	..	..	..	..	..
Primary Schl. Enroll. Ratio	..	..	..	..	..	..	..	..	..	..	..
Primary Schl. Enroll. Ratio, Female	..	..	..	..	..	..	..	..	..	..	..
Secondary Schl. Enroll. Ratio	..	..	..	..	..	..	..	..	..	..	..

1980	1981	1982	1983	1984	1985	1986	1987	1988	1989 est.	NOTES	DOMINICA
				(Thousands of current US dollars)							**FOREIGN TRADE (CUSTOMS BASIS)**
10,100	19,700	25,100	27,800	26,100	28,800	44,600	46,500	55,600	..	..	Value of Exports, fob
..	..	..	..	..	..	..	..	..	..	..	Nonfuel Primary Products
..	..	..	..	..	..	..	..	..	..	..	Fuels
..	..	..	..	..	..	..	..	..	..	..	Manufactures
48,400	45,200	43,200	42,800	50,700	52,000	50,500	60,300	79,500	..	..	Value of Imports, cif
..	..	..	..	..	..	..	..	..	..	..	Nonfuel Primary Products
..	..	..	..	..	..	..	..	..	..	..	Fuels
..	..	..	..	..	..	..	..	..	..	..	Manufactures
				(Index 1987 = 100)							
..	..	..	..	..	..	..	..	..	..	..	Terms of Trade
..	..	..	..	..	..	..	..	..	..	..	Export Prices, fob
..	..	..	..	..	..	..	..	..	..	..	Import Prices, cif
				(Thousands of current US dollars)							**BALANCE OF PAYMENTS**
16,300	24,400	32,700	37,259	..	..	..	..	..	..	..	Exports of Goods & Services
10,100	19,700	25,100	27,800	25,600	28,400	43,400	48,000	55,600	..	..	Merchandise, fob
5,600	3,700	6,600	8,200	11,800	10,200	10,800	11,800	13,500	..	..	Nonfactor Services
600	1,000	1,000	1,259	..	..	..	..	..	..	..	Factor Services
55,000	52,600	50,900	51,404	62,100	65,700	65,400	74,989	95,700	..	..	Imports of Goods & Services
48,359	45,178	43,178	42,815	50,722	52,000	50,637	60,274	79,548	..	..	Merchandise, fob
6,341	6,922	6,922	6,885	9,478	11,800	12,863	13,026	14,452	..	..	Nonfactor Services
300	500	800	1,704	1,900	1,900	1,900	1,689	1,700	..	..	Factor Services
..	..	..	..	..	..	..	..	..	..	..	Long-Term Interest
6,300	5,800	4,600	5,000	6,300	6,500	6,700	7,600	8,400	..	..	Private Current Transfers, net
8,600	8,500	7,500	9,400	10,800	11,100	9,300	10,700	11,700	..	..	Workers' Remittances
-32,400	-22,400	-13,600	-9,144	-18,400	-20,600	-4,500	-7,589	-18,200	..	..	Curr. A/C Bal before Off. Transf.
18,100	9,598	5,795	7,394	11,298	14,299	10,781	9,388	8,880	..	..	Net Official Transfers
-14,300	-12,802	-7,805	-1,750	-7,102	-6,301	6,281	1,799	-9,320	..	..	Curr. A/C Bal after Off. Transf.
1,467	2,678	8,356	6,000	7,100	7,500	6,900	14,000	10,400	..	..	Long-Term Capital, net
..	..	200	200	2,300	3,000	2,700	8,600	6,900	..	..	Direct Investment
..	..	..	..	..	..	..	..	..	..	..	Long-Term Loans
..	..	..	..	..	..	..	..	..	..	..	Disbursements
..	..	..	..	..	..	..	..	..	..	..	Repayments
1,467	2,678	8,156	5,800	4,800	4,500	4,200	5,400	3,500	..	..	Other Long-Term Capital
8,889	1,611	-2,086	-8,626	5,765	-1,675	-7,103	-7,129	-747	..	..	Other Capital, net
3,944	8,514	1,536	4,376	-5,763	476	-6,078	-8,671	-333	335	..	Change in Reserves
				(East Caribbean Dollars per US dollar)							Memo Item:
2.700	2.700	2.700	2.700	2.700	2.700	2.700	2.700	2.700	2.700	..	Conversion Factor (Annual Avg)
				(Millions of US dollars), outstanding at end of year							
..	..	..	..	..	..	..	..	..	..	..	**EXTERNAL DEBT (Total)**
..	..	..	..	..	..	..	..	..	..	..	Long-Term Debt (by debtor)
..	..	..	..	..	..	..	..	..	..	..	Central Bank, incl. IMF credit
..	..	..	..	..	..	..	..	..	..	..	Central Government
..	..	..	..	..	..	..	..	..	..	..	Rest of General Government
..	..	..	..	..	..	..	..	..	..	..	Non-financial Public Enterprises
..	..	..	..	..	..	..	..	..	..	..	Priv. Sector, incl non-guaranteed
..	..	..	..	..	..	..	..	..	..	..	Short-Term Debt
				(Thousands of US dollars)							Memo Items:
5,078	3,057	4,329	1,479	5,250	3,271	9,593	18,427	14,064	11,684	..	Int'l Reserves Excluding Gold
..	..	..	..	..	..	..	..	..	..	..	Gold Holdings (at market price)
											SOCIAL INDICATORS
3.9	3.7	3.5	3.4	3.4	3.3	3.2	3.1	3.0	3.0	..	Total Fertility Rate
12.6	10.2	20.0	13.9	14.9	15.9	17.0	18.0	17.6	17.1	..	Infant Mortality Rate
..	..	73.5	73.6	73.7	73.8	73.9	74.1	74.3	74.5	..	Life Expectancy at Birth
..	..	..	..	..	..	..	..	..	..	..	Urban Population, % of total
56.7	70.2	76.8	82.0	77.8	85.1	97.5	100.0	105.6	84.7	..	Food Prod. per capita (1987=100)
..	..	..	..	..	..	..	..	..	..	..	Labor Force, Agriculture (%)
..	..	..	..	..	..	..	..	..	..	..	Labor Force, Female (%)
..	..	..	..	..	..	..	..	..	..	..	Primary Schl. Enroll. Ratio
..	..	..	..	..	..	..	..	..	..	..	Primary Schl. Enroll. Ratio, Female
..	..	..	..	..	..	..	..	..	..	..	Secondary Schl. Enroll. Ratio

DOMINICAN REPUBLIC	1969	1970	1971	1972	1973	1974	1975	1976	1977	1978	1979
CURRENT GNP PER CAPITA (US $)	290	330	370	430	490	570	660	760	840	900	1,010
POPULATION (thousands)	4,299	4,423	4,547	4,672	4,797	4,922	5,048	5,175	5,302	5,430	5,562

USE AND ORIGIN OF RESOURCES
(Millions of current Dominican Pesos)

	1969	1970	1971	1972	1973	1974	1975	1976	1977	1978	1979
Gross National Product (GNP)	1,207	1,476	1,664	2,027	2,351	2,920	3,598	3,945	4,508	4,771	5,551
Net Factor Income from Abroad	-23	-9	-2	40	6	-5	-2	-6	-80	-3	52
GDP at Market Prices	1,231	1,485	1,667	1,987	2,345	2,926	3,599	3,952	4,587	4,774	5,499
Resource Balance	-94	-109	-135	-96	-89	-331	-83	-289	-191	-326	-349
Exports of Goods & NFServices	227	256	275	411	513	730	998	825	918	828	1,135
Imports of Goods & NFServices	321	365	410	506	602	1,060	1,080	1,114	1,109	1,154	1,484
Domestic Absorption	1,324	1,595	1,802	2,083	2,434	3,256	3,682	4,240	4,778	5,100	5,848
Private Consumption, etc.	945	1,139	1,335	1,514	1,722	2,282	2,578	3,197	3,590	3,699	4,034
General Gov't Consumption	156	172	169	178	194	292	222	152	189	271	420
Gross Domestic Investment	223	284	298	392	518	683	882	891	1,000	1,130	1,394
Fixed Investment	192	246	294	427	498	644	803	789	939	1,032	1,335
Indirect Taxes, net	151	160	181	205	229	398	432	386	450	403	456
GDP at factor cost	1,080	1,325	1,486	1,782	2,116	2,528	3,167	3,565	4,138	4,371	5,043
Agriculture	262	345	371	409	521	648	773	753	921	886	1,027
Industry	327	388	450	549	658	833	1,139	1,238	1,353	1,383	1,651
Manufacturing	230	275	306	347	399	545	752	815	871	874	929
Services, etc.	642	752	846	1,029	1,166	1,445	1,688	1,960	2,313	2,505	2,821
Gross Domestic Saving	130	175	162	296	429	353	799	602	808	804	1,045
Gross National Saving	..	196	176	365	464	381	832	719	865	947	1,274

(Millions of 1987 Dominican Pesos)

	1969	1970	1971	1972	1973	1974	1975	1976	1977	1978	1979
Gross National Product	7,481.4	8,328.9	9,291.4	10,485.1	11,623.8	12,246.1	12,850.8	13,699.0	14,164.3	14,713.5	15,519.5
GDP at Market Prices	7,109.9	8,398.2	9,316.2	10,284.6	11,611.5	12,280.0	12,869.6	13,736.0	14,402.9	14,737.9	15,374.1
Resource Balance	-893.8	-1,098.4	-1,233.3	-1,520.4	-1,421.1	-2,424.6	-1,330.6	-1,358.2	-1,378.6	-1,347.3	-1,081.5
Exports of Goods & NFServices	1,874.9	2,150.5	2,222.0	2,553.9	2,514.4	2,031.2	3,096.8	2,716.9	2,654.8	2,484.2	3,034.6
Imports of Goods & NFServices	2,768.7	3,248.9	3,455.3	4,074.3	3,935.5	4,455.8	4,427.4	4,075.2	4,033.4	3,831.5	4,116.1
Domestic Absorption	8,003.7	9,496.6	10,549.5	11,805.0	13,032.6	14,704.6	14,200.1	15,094.2	15,781.5	16,085.2	16,455.5
Private Consumption, etc.	6,052.3	7,244.1	8,068.2	9,092.9	9,739.0	10,670.5	10,073.7	11,358.6	11,722.1	11,841.9	11,777.3
General Gov't Consumption	625.5	651.3	604.7	601.7	616.0	845.1	678.9	510.0	573.6	663.4	806.1
Gross Domestic Investment	1,325.8	1,601.3	1,876.7	2,110.4	2,677.6	3,189.0	3,447.5	3,225.6	3,485.8	3,579.9	3,872.2
Fixed Investment	1,124.0	1,416.6	1,897.6	2,254.2	2,673.6	2,934.6	3,293.5	3,032.0	3,329.2	3,311.4	3,764.7
GDP at factor cost	6,243.4	7,499.5	8,315.0	9,231.9	10,489.2	10,620.9	11,328.2	12,397.6	12,993.8	13,498.3	14,102.4
Agriculture	1,401.0	1,926.0	2,029.2	2,106.2	2,288.1	2,288.6	2,231.2	2,395.2	2,437.0	2,548.1	2,575.9
Industry	1,559.0	1,843.3	2,172.3	2,539.7	3,062.9	3,220.5	3,478.7	3,741.7	3,922.1	3,865.6	4,170.8
Manufacturing	1,241.1	1,477.1	1,668.0	1,804.7	2,045.0	2,142.1	2,298.2	2,453.2	2,591.5	2,588.3	2,707.4
Services, etc.	4,163.5	4,617.1	5,075.0	5,566.7	6,130.9	6,683.4	7,106.3	7,531.6	7,999.4	8,288.9	8,591.9

Memo Items:

	1969	1970	1971	1972	1973	1974	1975	1976	1977	1978	1979
Capacity to Import	1,959.5	2,275.9	2,313.9	3,305.1	3,353.1	3,066.5	4,088.1	3,019.7	3,338.0	2,749.1	3,147.2
Terms of Trade Adjustment	84.6	125.4	92.0	751.2	838.7	1,035.3	991.3	302.8	683.3	264.9	112.6
Gross Domestic Income	7,194.5	8,523.6	9,408.2	11,035.8	12,450.2	13,315.3	13,860.8	14,038.8	15,086.2	15,002.8	15,486.6
Gross National Income	7,566.0	8,454.3	9,383.3	11,236.3	12,462.6	13,281.4	13,842.0	14,001.8	14,847.6	14,978.5	15,632.1

DOMESTIC PRICES/DEFLATORS
(Index 1987 = 100)

	1969	1970	1971	1972	1973	1974	1975	1976	1977	1978	1979
Overall (GDP)	17.3	17.7	17.9	19.3	20.2	23.8	28.0	28.8	31.8	32.4	35.8
Domestic Absorption	16.5	16.8	17.1	17.6	18.7	22.1	25.9	28.1	30.3	31.7	35.5
Agriculture	18.7	17.9	18.3	19.4	22.8	28.3	34.6	31.4	37.8	34.8	39.9
Industry	21.0	21.1	20.7	21.6	21.5	25.9	32.7	33.1	34.5	35.8	39.6
Manufacturing	18.5	18.6	18.4	19.2	19.5	25.4	32.7	33.2	33.6	33.8	34.3
Consumer Price Index	13.3	13.8	14.3	15.5	17.9	20.2	23.1	24.9	28.1	29.1	31.8

MANUFACTURING ACTIVITY

	1969	1970	1971	1972	1973	1974	1975	1976	1977	1978	1979
Employment (1987=100)	..	..	..	..	..	..	..	..	..	..	..
Real Earnings per Empl. (1987=100)	..	..	..	..	..	..	..	..	..	..	..
Real Output per Empl. (1987=100)	..	..	..	..	..	..	..	..	..	..	..
Earnings as % of Value Added	37.5	35.3	33.2	34.4	30.5	26.5	24.2	22.7	22.1	23.4	25.8

MONETARY HOLDINGS
(Millions of current Dominican Pesos)

	1969	1970	1971	1972	1973	1974	1975	1976	1977	1978	1979
Money Supply, Broadly Defined	243.0	289.8	356.1	442.4	559.8	798.8	947.0	997.6	1,158.3	1,183.7	1,392.1
Money	149.3	171.7	188.1	222.5	260.1	364.2	379.7	390.4	460.0	458.0	598.4
Currency Outside Banks	72.5	81.2	83.5	98.9	116.2	140.6	157.7	172.3	203.2	223.9	273.5
Demand Deposits	76.8	90.5	104.6	123.6	143.9	223.6	222.1	218.2	256.8	234.0	324.9
Quasi-Money	93.7	118.1	168.0	220.0	299.7	434.6	567.3	607.2	698.4	725.7	793.7

(Millions of current Dominican Pesos)

	1969	1970	1971	1972	1973	1974	1975	1976	1977	1978	1979
GOVERNMENT DEFICIT (-) OR SURPLUS	..	..	..	-3.2	-20.6	-41.8	56.3	-10.6	-0.1	-70.4	-315.0
Current Revenue	..	..	..	348.2	386.0	499.1	684.2	616.8	671.3	679.2	731.9
Current Expenditure	..	..	..	215.4	234.1	275.8	302.2	344.3	390.1	460.0	630.9
Current Budget Balance	..	..	..	132.8	151.9	223.3	382.0	272.5	281.2	219.2	101.0
Capital Receipts	..	..	..	13.3	11.5	14.2	10.4	5.4	6.6	15.5	7.8
Capital Payments	..	..	..	149.3	184.0	279.3	336.1	288.5	287.9	305.1	423.8

1980	1981	1982	1983	1984	1985	1986	1987	1988	1989 estimate	NOTES	DOMINICAN REPUBLIC
1,080	1,180	1,280	1,230	1,010	790	750	750	720	790	A	**CURRENT GNP PER CAPITA (US $)**
5,697	5,836	5,977	6,122	6,268	6,416	6,564	6,712	6,859	7,002	..	**POPULATION (thousands)**
			(Millions of current Dominican Pesos)								**USE AND ORIGIN OF RESOURCES**
6,354	6,990	7,710	8,326	10,114	13,268	15,055	18,249	26,330	40,717	..	Gross National Product (GNP)
-277	-277	-255	-297	-241	-704	-725	-1,177	-1,941	-1,468	..	Net Factor Income from Abroad
6,631	7,267	7,964	8,623	10,355	13,972	15,780	19,426	28,270	42,185	..	GDP at Market Prices
-647	-306	-392	-336	280	-771	-704	-1,950	-1,526	-3,277	..	Resource Balance
1,271	1,513	1,141	1,242	3,780	4,088	4,041	5,432	10,067	13,620	..	Exports of Goods & NFServices
1,919	1,818	1,533	1,578	3,500	4,859	4,745	7,382	11,593	16,897	..	Imports of Goods & NFServices
7,278	7,573	8,357	8,959	10,075	14,744	16,484	21,375	29,796	45,462	..	Domestic Absorption
5,109	5,163	5,987	6,356	7,002	10,833	12,078	15,251	21,558	31,949	..	Private Consumption, etc.
504	693	779	786	871	1,112	1,297	1,205	1,783	2,643	..	General Gov't Consumption
1,665	1,716	1,591	1,817	2,203	2,799	3,109	4,919	6,455	10,871	..	Gross Domestic Investment
1,584	1,655	1,491	1,754	2,169	2,747	3,023	4,802	6,368	..	..	Fixed Investment
507	541	473	574	824	..	..	..	..	..	..	Indirect Taxes, net
6,124	6,726	7,492	8,049	9,532	..	..	..	..	..	B	GDP at factor cost
1,336	1,350	1,412	1,485	1,916	2,271	2,648	3,034	5,028	6,416	..	Agriculture
1,877	2,008	2,279	2,503	2,928	3,372	3,738	5,352	7,275	10,765	..	Industry
1,015	1,133	1,455	1,528	1,708	2,198	2,363	3,272	4,541	6,644	..	Manufacturing
3,418	3,910	4,274	4,635	5,512	8,330	9,394	11,039	15,968	25,004	..	Services, etc.
1,018	1,411	1,198	1,481	2,483	2,028	2,405	2,970	4,929	7,593	..	Gross Domestic Saving
941	1,317	1,133	1,379	2,447	2,077	2,382	2,791	4,994	8,066	..	Gross National Saving
			(Millions of 1987 Dominican Pesos)								
15,600.8	15,654.2	16,721.1	17,410.6	17,649.4	16,804.5	17,373.0	18,248.8	18,294.4	19,699.9	..	Gross National Product
16,309.7	16,313.0	17,294.0	18,056.8	18,105.7	17,707.1	18,241.2	19,425.7	19,676.1	20,421.0	..	GDP at Market Prices
-3,001.3	-1,859.4	-1,374.6	-1,322.5	-589.8	-1,096.6	-1,495.2	-1,949.7	-1,388.5	-1,891.9	..	Resource Balance
4,706.1	5,028.0	4,355.7	4,575.0	4,807.0	4,742.3	4,806.1	5,432.2	5,904.5	6,103.7	..	Exports of Goods & NFServices
7,707.4	6,887.4	5,730.3	5,897.5	5,396.8	5,838.8	6,301.3	7,381.9	7,293.0	7,995.6	..	Imports of Goods & NFServices
19,311.0	18,172.5	18,668.6	19,379.3	18,695.5	18,803.7	19,736.4	21,375.4	21,064.6	22,312.9	..	Domestic Absorption
14,111.0	13,149.9	14,304.6	14,714.4	13,878.1	14,094.1	14,795.6	15,251.0	14,421.6	14,505.3	..	Private Consumption, etc.
987.1	1,257.5	1,277.5	1,315.4	1,309.7	1,366.9	1,464.6	1,205.2	1,319.9	1,310.8	..	General Gov't Consumption
4,212.9	3,765.2	3,086.5	3,349.5	3,507.8	3,342.7	3,476.2	4,919.2	5,323.0	6,496.8	..	Gross Domestic Investment
4,007.9	3,674.3	2,861.4	3,223.2	3,504.4	3,291.8	3,405.8	4,801.7	5,301.7	..	..	Fixed Investment
15,064.9	15,093.6	16,273.5	16,859.5	16,671.6	..	..	..	..	..	B	GDP at factor cost
2,701.5	2,298.1	2,981.0	3,073.1	3,073.6	2,964.3	2,948.6	3,034.0	2,993.3	3,058.0	..	Agriculture
4,278.6	4,414.8	4,213.6	4,603.3	4,618.5	4,277.7	4,533.5	5,352.4	5,319.6	5,583.1	..	Industry
2,843.6	2,920.3	3,015.8	3,046.9	2,973.4	2,762.1	2,954.1	3,271.6	3,154.7	3,210.5	..	Manufacturing
9,331.9	9,717.2	10,124.7	10,380.4	10,413.6	10,465.2	10,759.0	11,039.3	11,363.2	11,779.9	..	Services, etc.
											Memo Items:
5,106.8	5,729.1	4,265.5	4,642.2	5,829.2	4,911.8	5,366.6	5,432.2	6,333.0	6,444.8	..	Capacity to Import
400.7	701.2	-90.2	67.2	1,022.2	169.6	560.4	0.0	428.5	341.1	..	Terms of Trade Adjustment
16,710.4	17,014.2	17,203.8	18,124.0	19,127.9	17,876.7	18,801.6	19,425.7	20,104.7	20,762.2	..	Gross Domestic Income
16,001.5	16,355.4	16,630.9	17,477.8	18,671.6	16,974.1	17,933.4	18,248.8	18,723.0	20,041.1	..	Gross National Income
			(Index 1987 = 100)								**DOMESTIC PRICES/DEFLATORS**
40.7	44.5	46.1	47.8	57.2	78.9	86.5	100.0	143.7	206.6	..	Overall (GDP)
37.7	41.7	44.8	46.2	53.9	78.4	83.5	100.0	141.5	203.7	..	Domestic Absorption
49.5	58.7	47.4	48.3	62.3	76.6	89.8	100.0	168.0	209.8	..	Agriculture
43.9	45.5	54.1	54.4	63.4	78.8	82.5	100.0	136.8	192.8	..	Industry
35.7	38.8	48.2	50.1	57.4	79.6	80.0	100.0	144.0	207.0	..	Manufacturing
37.1	39.9	43.0	45.0	57.2	78.6	86.3	100.0	144.4	210.0	..	Consumer Price Index
											MANUFACTURING ACTIVITY
..	..	..	..	..	..	..	..	..	..	..	Employment (1987=100)
..	..	..	..	..	..	..	..	..	..	..	Real Earnings per Empl. (1987=100)
..	..	..	..	..	..	..	..	..	..	..	Real Output per Empl. (1987=100)
26.9	25.9	23.0	22.8	..	..	..	..	..	..	..	Earnings as % of Value Added
			(Millions of current Dominican Pesos)								**MONETARY HOLDINGS**
1,494.1	1,723.6	1,994.2	2,211.8	2,768.5	3,394.7	5,107.2	6,020.5	8,761.9	11,370.5	D	Money Supply, Broadly Defined
579.6	660.5	731.5	781.4	1,159.5	1,355.2	1,988.6	2,609.4	4,168.3	5,284.5	..	Money
274.9	323.8	357.8	414.7	592.8	677.2	937.4	1,312.8	1,876.3	2,682.9	..	Currency Outside Banks
304.7	336.7	373.6	366.7	566.7	678.0	1,051.2	1,296.6	2,292.1	2,601.7	..	Demand Deposits
914.5	1,063.1	1,262.7	1,430.4	1,609.0	2,039.5	3,118.5	3,411.1	4,593.5	6,086.0	..	Quasi-Money
			(Millions of current Dominican Pesos)								**GOVERNMENT DEFICIT (-) OR SURPLUS**
-172.9	-181.4	-246.6	-216.4	..	..	..	..	..	..	..	Current Revenue
945.9	984.1	818.6	986.3	..	..	..	..	..	..	..	Current Expenditure
752.8	809.1	824.4	908.0	..	..	..	..	2,317.0	..	..	Current Budget Balance
193.1	175.0	-5.8	78.3	..	..	..	..	..	..	..	Capital Receipts
9.6	10.2	7.7	14.0	19.3	11.4	9.4	17.5	19.7	..	..	Capital Payments
375.6	366.6	248.5	308.7	..	..	..	..	3,061.1	..	..	

DOMINICAN REPUBLIC	1969	1970	1971	1972	1973	1974	1975	1976	1977	1978	1979
FOREIGN TRADE (CUSTOMS BASIS)					*(Millions of current US dollars)*						
Value of Exports, fob	183.4	214.0	240.8	353.4	443.2	648.7	893.8	716.4	780.4	675.5	868.6
Nonfuel Primary Products	175.5	203.8	228.7	284.9	341.8	535.0	761.4	567.0	653.2	548.2	675.0
Fuels	0.0	0.0	0.0	0.0	0.0	0.0	0.0	0.5	0.0	0.0	0.0
Manufactures	7.9	10.2	12.0	68.6	101.4	113.8	132.4	149.0	127.1	127.3	193.6
Value of Imports, cif	246.0	304.0	358.0	388.0	489.0	808.0	889.0	878.0	975.0	987.0	1,213.0
Nonfuel Primary Products	48.9	60.2	65.5	65.2	116.6	181.9	154.6	233.2	205.9	202.5	255.9
Fuels	20.1	21.0	30.9	40.2	58.7	134.0	200.8	14.0	202.7	222.9	321.5
Manufactures	177.0	222.8	261.5	282.6	313.7	492.1	533.6	630.8	566.4	561.6	635.6
					(Index 1987 = 100)						
Terms of Trade	174.7	175.5	169.2	182.9	179.3	215.6	189.9	164.4	178.3	144.2	129.2
Export Prices, fob	41.1	44.4	45.3	52.0	64.8	119.0	109.4	94.9	115.7	104.2	113.8
Import Prices, cif	23.5	25.3	26.8	28.4	36.1	55.2	57.6	57.7	64.9	72.2	88.1
BALANCE OF PAYMENTS					*(Millions of current US dollars)*						
Exports of Goods & Services	..	258.5	291.7	412.6	516.4	735.2	1,015.2	853.1	939.5	848.8	1,166.8
Merchandise, fob	..	214.0	240.7	347.6	442.1	636.8	893.8	716.4	780.5	675.5	868.6
Nonfactor Services	..	43.0	49.5	63.5	71.5	93.4	116.2	127.8	146.7	152.5	266.3
Factor Services	..	1.5	1.5	1.5	2.8	5.0	5.2	8.9	12.3	20.8	31.9
Imports of Goods & Services	..	391.6	438.5	490.2	643.6	1,011.2	1,127.0	1,108.1	1,207.7	1,310.5	1,703.9
Merchandise, fob	..	278.0	309.7	337.7	421.9	673.0	772.7	763.6	849.3	862.4	1,137.5
Nonfactor Services	..	86.2	98.5	104.1	142.0	243.4	236.3	226.4	247.7	291.6	346.8
Factor Services	..	27.4	30.3	48.4	79.7	94.8	118.0	118.1	110.7	156.5	219.6
Long-Term Interest	..	12.6	13.5	16.3	20.0	23.5	32.8	34.3	48.4	61.1	77.9
Private Current Transfers, net	..	30.4	16.3	29.0	28.8	33.2	34.2	122.9	136.1	146.3	177.0
Workers' Remittances	..	25.1	14.5	24.0	24.0	26.8	28.0	112.0	123.6	131.6	161.3
Curr. A/C Bal before Off. Transf.	..	-102.7	-130.5	-48.6	-98.4	-242.8	-77.6	-132.1	-132.1	-315.4	-360.1
Net Official Transfers	..	0.8	1.1	1.6	1.8	1.8	4.8	2.9	3.5	3.5	28.8
Curr. A/C Bal after Off. Transf.	..	-101.9	-129.4	-47.0	-96.6	-241.0	-72.8	-129.2	-128.6	-311.9	-331.3
Long-Term Capital, net	..	109.5	81.5	82.2	69.6	161.3	159.2	167.5	218.9	160.4	160.3
Direct Investment	..	71.6	65.0	43.5	34.5	53.6	63.9	60.0	71.5	63.6	17.1
Long-Term Loans	..	33.0	37.9	44.1	35.1	107.8	95.3	115.3	137.0	119.7	124.0
Disbursements	..	59.9	70.6	75.6	76.8	151.6	157.7	188.7	226.9	223.0	351.4
Repayments	..	26.9	32.7	31.5	41.7	43.8	62.4	73.4	89.9	103.3	227.4
Other Long-Term Capital	..	4.9	-21.4	-5.4	0.0	-0.1	0.0	-7.8	10.4	-22.9	19.2
Other Capital, net	..	-12.6	63.2	-30.0	59.9	79.6	-93.1	-60.9	-47.7	115.1	126.5
Change in Reserves	..	5.0	-15.3	-5.2	-32.9	0.1	6.7	22.6	-42.6	36.4	44.5
Memo Item:					*(Dominican Pesos per US dollar)*						
Conversion Factor (Annual Avg)	1.000	1.000	1.000	1.000	1.000	1.000	1.000	1.000	1.000	1.000	1.000
				(Millions of US dollars), outstanding at end of year							
EXTERNAL DEBT (Total)	..	359.7	402.8	439.4	470.2	577.5	672.8	811.5	1,121.1	1,334.3	1,603.8
Long-Term Debt (by debtor)	..	359.7	402.8	439.4	470.2	577.5	672.8	811.5	957.1	1,079.3	1,286.8
Central Bank, incl. IMF credit	..	32.9	40.8	38.1	49.4	52.4	61.2	97.0	167.2	212.8	294.0
Central Government	..	146.4	151.7	172.0	178.6	179.2	183.6	183.8	202.8	290.6	437.5
Rest of General Government	..	0.0	0.0	0.0	1.3	2.9	2.3	2.7	2.0	1.3	0.6
Non-financial Public Enterprises	..	24.2	19.8	34.1	45.2	81.3	112.9	188.5	226.4	224.9	216.4
Priv. Sector, incl non-guaranteed	..	156.2	190.5	195.2	195.7	261.7	312.8	339.5	358.7	349.7	338.3
Short-Term Debt	..	0.0	0.0	0.0	0.0	0.0	0.0	0.0	164.0	255.0	317.0
Memo Items:					*(Millions of US dollars)*						
Int'l Reserves Excluding Gold	36.8	29.1	52.8	55.3	84.3	87.1	112.6	123.5	180.1	154.1	238.6
Gold Holdings (at market price)	3.0	3.2	3.8	5.6	9.7	16.0	12.1	11.6	17.2	23.5	57.9
SOCIAL INDICATORS											
Total Fertility Rate	6.3	6.0	5.8	5.6	5.4	5.3	5.1	4.9	4.7	4.6	4.5
Infant Mortality Rate	100.6	98.4	96.2	94.0	92.0	90.0	88.0	86.0	84.0	82.2	80.4
Life Expectancy at Birth	58.2	58.7	59.3	59.9	60.3	60.8	61.2	61.6	62.1	62.5	62.9
Urban Population, % of total	39.3	40.3	41.3	42.3	43.3	44.3	45.3	46.3	47.4	48.4	49.5
Food Prod. per capita (1987=100)	111.6	116.7	120.0	119.6	117.7	119.5	111.2	115.4	115.3	116.4	113.2
Labor Force, Agriculture (%)	55.6	54.8	53.7	52.8	51.9	51.0	50.2	49.2	48.2	47.3	46.5
Labor Force, Female (%)	10.8	10.9	11.1	11.2	11.4	11.5	11.7	11.8	12.0	12.1	12.2
Primary Schl. Enroll. Ratio	..	100.0	..	..	..	..	104.0	..	95.0	102.0	104.0
Primary Schl. Enroll. Ratio, Female	..	100.0	..	..	..	..	..	..	96.0	..	..
Secondary Schl. Enroll. Ratio	..	21.0	..	..	..	..	36.0	..	..	38.0	39.0

				(Millions of current US dollars)							**FOREIGN TRADE (CUSTOMS BASIS)**
961.9	1,188.0	767.7	781.7	868.1	735.2	717.6	711.2	890.0	..	..	Value of Exports, fob
795.8	1,002.1	665.2	626.9	668.7	535.2	509.8	557.1	661.0	..	..	Nonfuel Primary Products
0.0	0.0	0.0	0.0	0.0	0.0	0.0	0.0	0.0	..	..	Fuels
166.1	185.9	102.5	154.8	199.4	200.0	207.8	154.1	229.0	..	..	Manufactures
1,640.0	1,668.0	1,444.0	1,471.0	1,446.0	1,487.0	1,433.0	1,782.5	1,849.0	..	..	Value of Imports, cif
337.1	340.3	268.5	259.8	285.4	279.7	272.1	318.0	364.3	..	..	Nonfuel Primary Products
416.5	548.4	492.9	533.5	427.4	407.5	200.9	260.7	316.3	..	..	Fuels
886.5	779.4	682.6	677.7	733.3	799.8	960.0	1,203.8	1,168.4	..	..	Manufactures
				(Index 1987 = 100)							
135.7	116.4	103.4	101.6	99.6	98.5	119.4	100.0	108.8	..	..	Terms of Trade
139.6	129.0	109.2	105.3	98.0	93.7	107.7	100.0	113.0	..	..	Export Prices, fob
102.8	110.8	105.6	103.7	98.4	95.1	90.2	100.0	103.9	..	..	Import Prices, cif
				(Millions of current US dollars)							**BALANCE OF PAYMENTS**
1,313.1	1,524.4	1,146.2	1,248.7	1,375.4	1,344.4	1,425.1	1,571.6	1,758.5	2,150.0	..	Exports of Goods & Services
961.9	1,188.0	767.7	785.2	868.1	738.5	722.1	711.0	894.0	926.0	..	Merchandise, fob
309.4	324.6	374.1	456.6	501.5	584.3	686.0	845.0	852.0	1,210.0	..	Nonfactor Services
41.8	11.8	4.4	6.9	5.8	21.6	17.0	11.6	8.5	10.0	..	Factor Services
2,237.5	2,106.8	1,793.8	1,881.6	1,803.8	1,808.3	1,902.7	2,268.0	2,296.0	2,662.0	..	Imports of Goods & Services
1,519.7	1,451.7	1,257.3	1,279.0	1,257.1	1,285.9	1,351.7	1,590.0	1,610.0	1,950.0	..	Merchandise, fob
399.0	366.7	277.3	298.6	299.5	274.5	284.3	360.0	367.0	467.0	..	Nonfactor Services
318.8	288.4	259.2	304.0	247.2	247.9	266.7	318.0	326.0	242.0	..	Factor Services
120.7	143.7	126.0	130.3	111.3	139.2	187.0	106.6	151.7	85.3	..	Long-Term Interest
199.8	182.9	190.0	195.0	205.0	242.0	242.0	259.6	328.1	306.1	..	Private Current Transfers, net
183.1	182.9	190.0	195.0	205.0	242.0	242.0	260.0	328.0	306.0	..	Workers' Remittances
-724.6	-399.5	-457.6	-437.9	-223.4	-221.9	-235.6	-441.4	-218.9	-288.9	..	Curr. A/C Bal before Off. Transf.
4.7	10.1	15.0	20.0	60.0	114.3	29.0	95.4	90.9	83.9	..	Net Official Transfers
-719.9	-389.4	-442.6	-417.9	-163.4	-107.6	-206.6	-346.0	-128.0	-205.0	..	Curr. A/C Bal after Off. Transf.
349.0	236.1	283.3	557.9	294.1	185.5	141.8	59.5	249.0	192.0	..	Long-Term Capital, net
92.7	79.7	-1.4	48.2	68.5	36.2	50.0	89.0	106.0	110.0	..	Direct Investment
346.5	162.4	274.8	69.5	218.0	166.4	94.1	56.2	55.3	82.0	..	Long-Term Loans
481.5	298.8	454.9	256.6	309.6	251.0	195.3	159.4	163.5	198.7	..	Disbursements
135.0	136.4	180.1	187.1	91.6	84.6	101.2	103.2	108.2	116.7	..	Repayments
-90.2	-6.0	9.9	440.2	7.6	-17.1	-2.3	-85.7	87.7	0.0	..	Other Long-Term Capital
325.8	184.4	-89.0	-258.0	-41.4	-3.3	118.1	152.5	1.0	11.0	..	Other Capital, net
45.1	-31.1	248.3	118.0	-89.3	-74.6	-53.3	134.0	-122.0	2.0	..	Change in Reserves
				(Dominican Pesos per US dollar)							**Memo Item:**
1.000	1.000	1.090	1.260	2.060	3.110	2.900	3.840	6.110	6.340	..	Conversion Factor (Annual Avg)
			(Millions of US dollars), outstanding at end of year								
2,002.3	2,293.9	2,518.8	2,927.0	3,112.5	3,503.3	3,645.2	3,863.9	3,947.0	4,065.6	..	**EXTERNAL DEBT (Total)**
1,521.9	1,656.0	1,989.6	2,629.0	2,741.5	3,139.9	3,337.9	3,590.4	3,572.4	3,507.6	..	Long-Term Debt (by debtor)
305.5	338.6	363.6	1,048.4	1,006.1	1,097.1	1,324.0	1,436.6	1,418.8	1,325.9	..	Central Bank, incl. IMF credit
580.8	684.5	909.1	960.6	1,083.3	1,488.0	1,547.2	1,692.6	1,713.2	1,744.6	..	Central Government
0.1	0.0	0.0	0.0	0.0	0.0	0.0	0.0	0.0		..	Rest of General Government
346.6	368.7	434.5	406.6	459.5	371.4	292.2	300.2	294.0	303.5	..	Non-financial Public Enterprises
288.9	264.2	282.4	213.4	192.6	183.4	174.5	161.0	146.4	133.6	..	Priv. Sector, incl non-guaranteed
480.4	637.9	529.2	298.0	371.0	363.4	307.3	273.5	374.6	558.0	..	Short-Term Debt
				(Millions of US dollars)							**Memo Items:**
201.8	225.2	129.0	171.3	253.5	340.1	376.3	182.2	254.0	164.0	..	Int'l Reserves Excluding Gold
77.2	56.5	41.6	29.4	5.6	5.9	7.0	8.7	7.4	7.2	..	Gold Holdings (at market price)
											SOCIAL INDICATORS
4.4	4.3	4.2	4.1	4.0	3.9	3.8	3.8	3.7	3.6	..	Total Fertility Rate
78.6	76.8	75.0	73.0	71.0	69.0	67.0	65.0	63.4	61.9	..	Infant Mortality Rate
63.3	63.7	64.1	64.5	64.8	65.2	65.6	66.0	66.3	66.5	..	Life Expectancy at Birth
50.5	51.5	52.6	53.6	54.7	55.7	56.6	57.6	58.5	59.5	..	Urban Population, % of total
107.6	107.1	109.1	112.7	112.6	104.0	101.5	100.0	98.6	108.7	..	Food Prod. per capita (1987=100)
45.7	..	..	..	..	..	..	..	..	..	..	Labor Force, Agriculture (%)
12.4	12.7	13.0	13.2	13.5	13.7	14.0	14.3	14.5	14.7	..	Labor Force, Female (%)
114.0	..	109.0	112.0	121.0	124.0	133.0	..	..	..	..	Primary Schl. Enroll. Ratio
..	..	115.0	117.0	123.0	126.0	135.0	..	..	..	..	Primary Schl. Enroll. Ratio, Female
43.0	..	50.0	50.0	50.0	50.0	47.0	..	..	..	..	Secondary Schl. Enroll. Ratio

ECUADOR	1969	1970	1971	1972	1973	1974	1975	1976	1977	1978	1979
CURRENT GNP PER CAPITA (US $)	280	290	290	300	370	430	540	680	790	930	1,080
POPULATION (thousands)	5,865	6,051	6,240	6,433	6,629	6,830	7,035	7,244	7,457	7,675	7,897
USE AND ORIGIN OF RESOURCES					*(Billions of current Ecuadoran Sucres)*						
Gross National Product (GNP)	29.6	34.3	39.1	45.2	58.7	87.1	105.3	128.9	158.9	185.8	224.0
Net Factor Income from Abroad	-0.5	-0.7	-0.9	-1.7	-3.5	-5.7	-2.5	-4.1	-7.5	-5.5	-9.9
GDP at Market Prices	30.1	35.0	40.0	46.9	62.2	92.8	107.7	132.9	166.4	191.3	234.0
Resource Balance	-1.8	-1.6	-3.8	-1.7	2.0	4.8	-7.0	-1.8	-5.0	-10.8	1.3
Exports of Goods & NFServices	3.9	4.9	6.0	8.8	15.5	33.6	28.2	34.2	41.3	40.8	60.6
Imports of Goods & NFServices	5.7	6.5	9.8	10.5	13.5	28.8	35.2	36.0	46.3	51.6	59.3
Domestic Absorption	32.0	36.6	43.8	48.5	60.2	88.0	114.7	134.7	171.4	202.1	232.7
Private Consumption, etc.	23.6	26.4	30.4	34.4	41.7	55.5	70.3	84.5	102.6	121.2	143.3
General Gov't Consumption	3.1	3.9	4.1	4.7	6.4	11.6	15.6	18.6	24.7	26.5	30.1
Gross Domestic Investment	5.3	6.4	9.3	9.4	12.1	20.8	28.8	31.6	44.1	54.4	59.3
Fixed Investment	4.8	5.8	8.7	8.4	10.9	16.9	24.9	29.5	39.3	50.1	55.4
Indirect Taxes, net	3.1	3.8	4.6	5.5	7.7	10.4	10.7	10.6	13.4	16.5	19.1
GDP at factor cost	27.0	31.3	35.4	41.4	54.5	82.4	97.0	122.4	152.9	174.9	214.9
Agriculture	7.3	8.4	9.2	10.5	12.2	17.4	19.3	22.6	27.7	28.5	31.7
Industry	7.1	8.6	10.7	13.1	20.1	35.4	36.5	47.0	57.3	66.1	90.3
Manufacturing	5.7	6.4	7.5	8.8	10.8	14.3	17.2	22.9	29.9	36.3	44.9
Services, etc.	15.7	18.0	20.1	23.2	29.9	40.0	51.9	63.3	81.4	96.8	112.0
Gross Domestic Saving	3.5	4.8	5.5	7.7	14.1	25.6	21.8	29.8	39.1	43.7	60.6
Gross National Saving	..	4.3	4.8	6.2	10.8	20.3	19.7	25.9	31.7	38.4	50.7
					(Billions of 1987 Ecuadoran Sucres)						
Gross National Product	626.94	673.07	715.02	823.14	1,035.32	1,090.60	1,194.64	1,300.12	1,387.87	1,481.79	1,540.40
GDP at Market Prices	638.82	680.10	725.28	845.40	1,085.13	1,148.50	1,208.96	1,325.97	1,410.23	1,508.52	1,590.42
Resource Balance	-125.32	-130.12	-166.08	-49.58	104.73	-38.05	-137.03	-94.06	-193.67	-200.57	-182.14
Exports of Goods & NFServices	94.14	99.81	111.30	219.11	387.70	369.34	338.26	366.85	348.48	359.70	377.69
Imports of Goods & NFServices	219.46	229.92	277.38	268.69	282.97	407.39	475.30	460.91	542.15	560.27	559.83
Domestic Absorption	764.14	810.22	891.36	894.98	980.39	1,186.55	1,346.00	1,420.03	1,603.90	1,709.09	1,772.56
Private Consumption, etc.	490.40	515.81	542.71	576.19	628.62	685.80	756.97	836.88	897.75	945.03	1,012.42
General Gov't Consumption	73.29	82.41	80.55	85.15	93.14	142.68	169.42	185.40	223.07	223.51	234.84
Gross Domestic Investment	200.46	212.00	268.10	233.64	258.63	358.07	419.61	397.75	483.08	540.55	525.29
Fixed Investment	197.73	205.97	260.80	213.95	242.02	306.38	377.88	383.36	442.72	501.54	499.98
GDP at factor cost	568.75	603.43	638.41	744.00	950.87	1,019.53	1,087.80	1,220.54	1,296.05	1,378.64	1,460.94
Agriculture	147.35	157.88	165.79	172.45	174.26	189.88	194.29	199.90	204.61	196.72	202.33
Industry	141.93	151.16	171.66	262.98	440.40	431.13	427.35	491.12	501.35	550.47	587.70
Manufacturing	88.71	131.71	138.25	151.01	164.92	182.10	209.81	237.45	265.74	287.45	315.33
Services, etc.	369.65	392.30	408.34	421.85	468.13	530.08	593.88	638.90	711.52	767.04	805.35
Memo Items:											
Capacity to Import	149.04	173.64	169.97	225.42	325.09	474.67	381.12	437.70	483.67	443.24	572.04
Terms of Trade Adjustment	54.90	73.84	58.66	6.30	-62.61	105.33	42.86	70.85	135.19	83.54	194.35
Gross Domestic Income	693.72	753.94	783.95	851.70	1,022.51	1,253.83	1,251.82	1,396.82	1,545.42	1,592.06	1,784.77
Gross National Income	681.84	746.91	773.69	829.44	972.71	1,195.93	1,237.50	1,370.97	1,523.07	1,565.33	1,734.75
DOMESTIC PRICES/DEFLATORS					*(Index 1987 = 100)*						
Overall (GDP)	4.7	5.1	5.5	5.5	5.7	8.1	8.9	10.0	11.8	12.7	14.7
Domestic Absorption	4.2	4.5	4.9	5.4	6.1	7.4	8.5	9.5	10.7	11.8	13.1
Agriculture	4.9	5.3	5.5	6.1	7.0	9.2	10.0	11.3	13.5	14.5	15.6
Industry	5.0	5.7	6.3	5.0	4.6	8.2	8.5	9.6	11.4	12.0	15.4
Manufacturing	6.4	4.8	5.5	5.8	6.6	7.8	8.2	9.7	11.3	12.6	14.2
Consumer Price Index	5.4	5.7	6.2	6.6	7.5	9.3	10.7	11.8	13.4	14.9	16.5
MANUFACTURING ACTIVITY											
Employment (1987=100)	40.8	43.7	45.9	48.9	53.8	60.8	68.4	74.1	80.0	90.7	97.8
Real Earnings per Empl. (1987=100)	60.0	62.5	65.6	68.4	67.1	64.1	66.3	70.8	70.8	71.1	76.4
Real Output per Empl. (1987=100)	50.5	73.2	72.4	73.4	75.7	81.1	80.0	83.3	88.7	89.4	87.1
Earnings as % of Value Added	27.1	26.7	25.7	28.0	27.4	24.8	29.1	26.3	25.4	21.4	24.8
MONETARY HOLDINGS					*(Billions of current Ecuadoran Sucres)*						
Money Supply, Broadly Defined	6.30	7.73	8.89	10.97	14.43	21.03	23.08	28.81	35.96	39.74	52.18
Money	4.75	5.99	6.72	8.38	11.30	16.87	18.34	22.81	29.88	32.92	41.95
Currency Outside Banks	1.75	2.33	2.41	2.89	3.62	4.78	5.39	7.57	9.13	10.27	12.34
Demand Deposits	3.00	3.66	4.30	5.49	7.68	12.09	12.96	15.24	20.75	22.65	29.61
Quasi-Money	1.55	1.75	2.18	2.59	3.13	4.17	4.74	6.01	6.09	6.82	10.23
					(Millions of current Ecuadoran Sucres)						
GOVERNMENT DEFICIT (-) OR SURPLUS	..	..	..	..	124	-3	-666	-2,160	-5,388	-2,296	-1,520
Current Revenue	..	..	..	..	7,973	11,390	12,391	14,653	16,452	19,057	23,078
Current Expenditure	..	..	..	..	..	..	..	..	..	..	..
Current Budget Balance	..	..	..	..	..	..	..	..	..	..	..
Capital Receipts	..	..	..	..	..	..	..	..	..	..	..
Capital Payments	..	..	..	..	..	..	..	..	..	..	..

1980	1981	1982	1983	1984	1985	1986	1987	1988	1989 estimate	NOTES	ECUADOR
1,260	1,490	1,490	1,320	1,160	1,170	1,140	1,060	1,090	1,020	A	CURRENT GNP PER CAPITA (US $)
8,123	8,354	8,589	8,828	9,071	9,317	9,566	9,819	10,073	10,329	..	POPULATION (thousands)
					(Billions of current Ecuadoran Sucres)						USE AND ORIGIN OF RESOURCES
278.8	330.4	384.8	518.5	740.1	1,028.2	1,272.7	1,672.2	2,909.4	5,088.8	..	Gross National Product (GNP)
-14.5	-18.3	-30.9	-41.8	-72.6	-81.8	-110.5	-122.3	-195.0	-375.8	..	Net Factor Income from Abroad
293.3	348.7	415.7	560.3	812.6	1,109.9	1,383.2	1,794.5	3,104.3	5,464.6	..	GDP at Market Prices
-0.7	3.5	-9.5	22.4	52.4	65.3	2.2	-112.2	-55.4	-109.9	..	Resource Balance
73.8	75.9	87.6	133.1	209.9	296.9	314.7	431.5	865.3	1,482.6	..	Exports of Goods & NFServices
74.5	72.4	97.0	110.6	157.4	231.7	312.5	543.7	920.8	1,592.5	..	Imports of Goods & NFServices
294.1	345.2	425.2	537.8	760.2	1,044.7	1,381.0	1,906.7	3,159.8	5,574.5	..	Domestic Absorption
174.9	214.7	262.2	369.3	520.6	715.7	925.8	1,269.4	2,140.1	3,896.9	..	Private Consumption, etc.
42.6	49.7	58.1	70.1	99.6	127.3	166.7	230.4	337.0	499.6	..	General Gov't Consumption
76.6	80.8	104.8	98.4	140.0	201.7	288.5	406.8	682.7	1,177.9	..	Gross Domestic Investment
69.3	77.6	94.2	93.0	125.2	178.3	260.0	406.6	666.9	1,125.7	..	Fixed Investment
24.4	32.6	35.7	46.7	67.7	128.4	156.5	204.5	350.6	652.5	..	Indirect Taxes, net
268.9	316.0	380.0	513.6	744.9	981.6	1,226.8	1,590.0	2,753.7	4,812.1	B	GDP at factor cost
35.6	41.6	50.4	73.0	110.0	148.0	208.7	274.6	468.1	803.0	..	Agriculture
111.7	137.0	167.6	227.5	335.6	451.8	485.9	579.3	1,111.7	2,113.7	..	Industry
51.8	60.0	73.9	103.6	168.0	210.3	274.2	350.3	650.4	1,203.5	..	Manufacturing
146.1	170.0	197.8	259.8	367.0	510.2	688.6	940.6	1,524.5	2,547.8	..	Services, etc.
75.9	84.3	95.4	120.9	192.4	267.0	290.7	294.7	627.2	1,068.1	..	Gross Domestic Saving
61.4	65.9	64.5	79.1	119.8	185.2	180.2	172.4	432.3	692.2	..	Gross National Saving
					(Billions of 1987 Ecuadoran Sucres)							
1,598.86	1,659.02	1,638.97	1,604.52	1,640.77	1,739.04	1,787.30	1,672.21	1,937.54	1,940.15	..	Gross National Product
1,663.24	1,731.08	1,750.45	1,713.94	1,784.00	1,859.70	1,914.78	1,794.50	1,999.34	2,000.47	f	GDP at Market Prices
-247.67	-173.16	-230.75	-74.93	-16.93	1.53	43.34	-112.16	83.08	52.23	..	Resource Balance
368.80	386.23	367.07	376.04	423.17	473.84	514.58	431.54	570.24	562.33	..	Exports of Goods & NFServices
616.48	559.39	597.81	450.96	440.10	472.31	471.23	543.70	487.16	510.10	..	Imports of Goods & NFServices
1,910.91	1,904.24	1,981.20	1,788.87	1,800.93	1,858.16	1,871.44	1,906.66	1,916.26	1,948.24	..	Domestic Absorption
1,083.46	1,147.26	1,160.57	1,158.20	1,184.82	1,222.00	1,224.79	1,269.41	1,289.95	1,309.38	..	Private Consumption, etc.
256.02	262.25	263.48	247.53	238.52	228.53	226.64	230.42	217.73	220.23	..	General Gov't Consumption
571.43	494.74	557.15	383.14	377.60	407.63	420.02	406.83	408.58	418.63	..	Gross Domestic Investment
530.63	492.20	495.61	366.05	349.48	373.50	389.61	406.60	396.89	394.92	..	Fixed Investment
1,524.74	1,569.05	1,599.86	1,572.12	1,636.21	1,645.56	1,698.88	1,589.97	1,773.91	1,761.75	B	GDP at factor cost
213.03	227.59	232.15	199.89	221.16	242.98	267.88	274.58	298.25	307.32	..	Agriculture
584.41	626.68	628.20	670.28	690.32	716.31	724.12	579.28	747.82	713.62	..	Industry
326.82	355.50	360.68	355.79	349.21	350.03	344.31	350.26	358.21	344.69	..	Manufacturing
875.36	884.08	898.25	843.76	872.52	900.41	922.78	940.64	953.28	979.53	..	Services, etc.
											Memo Items:
610.44	586.15	539.51	542.46	586.73	605.35	474.60	431.54	457.82	474.91	..	Capacity to Import
241.64	199.92	172.45	166.43	163.57	131.51	-39.98	0.00	-112.42	-87.42	..	Terms of Trade Adjustment
1,904.87	1,931.00	1,922.90	1,880.37	1,947.57	1,991.20	1,874.81	1,794.50	1,886.93	1,913.05	..	Gross Domestic Income
1,840.50	1,858.94	1,811.42	1,770.94	1,804.34	1,870.55	1,747.33	1,672.21	1,825.12	1,852.73	..	Gross National Income
					(Index 1987 = 100)						DOMESTIC PRICES/DEFLATORS
17.6	20.1	23.7	32.7	45.6	59.7	72.2	100.0	155.3	273.2	..	Overall (GDP)
15.4	18.1	21.5	30.1	42.2	56.2	73.8	100.0	164.9	286.1	..	Domestic Absorption
16.7	18.3	21.7	36.5	49.7	60.9	77.9	100.0	156.9	261.3	..	Agriculture
19.1	21.9	26.7	33.9	48.6	63.1	67.1	100.0	148.7	296.2	..	Industry
15.8	16.9	20.5	29.1	48.1	60.1	79.6	100.0	181.6	349.2	..	Manufacturing
18.6	21.7	25.2	37.4	49.0	62.8	77.2	100.0	158.2	277.9	..	Consumer Price Index
											MANUFACTURING ACTIVITY
103.4	95.3	92.8	87.2	87.7	89.6	94.1	100.0	101.6	..	J	Employment (1987=100)
105.9	113.5	115.0	98.7	99.7	99.3	104.6	100.0	99.6	..	J	Real Earnings per Empl. (1987=100)
88.0	96.5	99.5	100.7	93.5	91.4	96.2	100.0	88.9	..	J	Real Output per Empl. (1987=100)
39.4	43.3	52.8	34.8	34.6	39.8	36.0	34.7	34.1	..	J	Earnings as % of Value Added
					(Billions of current Ecuadoran Sucres)						MONETARY HOLDINGS
66.17	75.70	93.63	118.01	169.28	216.96	268.20	383.90	621.58	..	..	Money Supply, Broadly Defined
53.58	61.81	73.13	95.15	129.06	153.18	183.40	246.19	372.61	..	..	Money
15.29	17.41	20.52	25.42	35.31	42.70	54.60	74.78	123.96	..	..	Currency Outside Banks
38.30	44.39	52.61	69.72	93.74	110.47	128.80	171.41	248.65	..	..	Demand Deposits
12.59	13.90	20.50	22.87	40.22	63.79	84.80	137.71	248.97	..	..	Quasi-Money
					(Millions of current Ecuadoran Sucres)						GOVERNMENT DEFICIT (-) OR SURPLUS
-4,119	-16,837	-18,480	-14,047	-6,785	21,971	-31,031	-40,997	-1,372	..	..	Current Revenue
37,549	39,297	45,996	60,187	99,872	189,472	186,907	236,762	411,242	..	..	Current Revenue
34,872	43,135	49,336	..	..	..	..	..	..	..	..	Current Expenditure
2,677	-3,838	-3,340	..	..	..	..	..	..	..	..	Current Budget Balance
..	..	..	..	..	..	17	..	..	..	..	Capital Receipts
6,796	12,999	15,140	..	..	..	..	..	..	..	..	Capital Payments

ECUADOR	1969	1970	1971	1972	1973	1974	1975	1976	1977	1978	1979
FOREIGN TRADE (CUSTOMS BASIS)					*(Millions of current US dollars)*						
Value of Exports, fob	152.5	189.9	199.1	326.3	532.1	1,123.5	973.9	1,257.6	1,436.3	1,557.5	2,104.2
Nonfuel Primary Products	148.1	185.7	193.0	259.0	236.1	405.3	364.3	492.0	692.9	800.3	868.6
Fuels	0.6	0.9	2.0	59.9	282.8	696.7	588.0	740.5	713.3	718.4	1,178.2
Manufactures	3.8	3.3	4.0	7.4	13.2	21.5	21.6	25.1	30.0	38.8	57.4
Value of Imports, cif	239.4	272.9	338.5	325.0	396.4	781.3	984.6	951.5	1,165.4	1,498.6	1,986.0
Nonfuel Primary Products	30.9	27.2	39.1	44.3	57.0	99.1	115.2	112.0	125.5	164.2	228.9
Fuels	16.5	17.1	28.4	21.4	12.1	137.6	20.5	11.3	10.4	13.6	21.7
Manufactures	192.0	228.7	271.0	259.2	327.3	544.7	848.9	828.2	1,029.5	1,320.8	1,735.4
					(Index 1987 = 100)						
Terms of Trade	160.3	153.5	131.3	91.9	60.7	124.5	117.2	137.5	156.4	133.8	144.0
Export Prices, fob	37.7	37.9	34.2	27.3	23.4	64.3	62.4	73.9	91.4	89.5	110.3
Import Prices, cif	23.5	24.7	26.1	29.7	38.4	51.6	53.3	53.7	58.4	66.9	76.6
BALANCE OF PAYMENTS					*(Millions of current US dollars)*						
Exports of Goods & Services	..	258.9	265.7	367.0	633.0	1,333.2	1,126.7	1,431.8	1,626.2	1,738.4	2,472.9
Merchandise, fob	..	234.9	238.0	323.2	584.7	1,225.4	1,012.8	1,307.2	1,400.8	1,529.2	2,150.5
Nonfactor Services	..	23.7	27.0	41.7	42.3	82.5	96.9	111.4	201.9	174.3	260.2
Factor Services	..	0.3	0.7	2.1	6.0	25.4	17.0	13.2	23.5	34.9	62.2
Imports of Goods & Services	..	388.8	437.7	459.7	653.3	1,326.6	1,379.0	1,469.1	2,005.8	2,482.6	3,133.0
Merchandise, fob	..	249.6	306.8	284.1	397.5	875.2	1,006.3	1,047.9	1,360.5	1,704.0	2,096.8
Nonfactor Services	..	109.7	94.4	107.8	111.6	225.1	288.6	263.9	413.7	462.7	556.4
Factor Services	..	29.5	36.5	67.7	144.2	226.3	84.1	157.3	231.6	315.9	479.8
Long-Term Interest	..	10.1	10.8	13.8	20.1	25.2	31.5	41.8	68.9	135.7	268.7
Private Current Transfers, net	..	7.7	7.9	7.8	8.3	15.8	13.5	7.9	0.4	12.0	0.4
Workers' Remittances	..	..	..	..	..	..	..	..	..	..	..
Curr. A/C Bal before Off. Transf.	..	-122.2	-164.1	-84.9	-11.9	22.4	-238.8	-29.4	-379.2	-732.2	-659.7
Net Official Transfers	..	9.2	7.8	7.5	18.5	15.3	18.8	22.8	35.8	28.9	29.4
Curr. A/C Bal after Off. Transf.	..	-113.0	-156.3	-77.4	6.6	37.6	-220.0	-6.6	-343.4	-703.3	-630.3
Long-Term Capital, net	..	110.4	180.6	159.4	77.1	105.2	199.7	157.0	591.0	782.0	566.7
Direct Investment	..	88.6	162.1	80.8	52.3	76.8	95.3	-19.9	34.5	48.6	63.4
Long-Term Loans	..	21.4	19.9	84.1	29.0	86.1	241.1	159.8	633.2	577.3	559.3
Disbursements	..	47.6	53.9	121.3	71.5	176.3	305.2	270.1	760.8	768.1	1,411.2
Repayments	..	26.2	34.0	37.2	42.5	90.2	64.1	110.3	127.6	190.8	851.9
Other Long-Term Capital	..	0.4	-1.3	-5.5	-4.2	-57.7	-136.7	17.1	-76.7	156.1	-56.0
Other Capital, net	..	8.6	-35.7	-13.0	8.5	-33.2	-43.7	23.0	-126.3	-88.4	89.0
Change in Reserves	..	-6.0	11.3	-68.9	-92.2	-109.7	64.0	-173.4	-121.3	9.7	-25.4
Memo Item:					*(Ecuadoran Sucres per US dollar)*						
Conversion Factor (Annual Avg)	18.000	20.920	25.000	25.000	25.000	25.000	25.000	25.000	25.000	25.000	25.000
				(Millions of US dollars), outstanding at end of year							
EXTERNAL DEBT (Total)	..	256	270	358	382	471	709	870	2,374	3,976	4,525
Long-Term Debt (by debtor)	..	256	270	358	382	471	709	870	1,518	2,778	3,376
Central Bank, incl. IMF credit	..	22	14	18	10	12	23	39	64	122	96
Central Government	..	89	99	161	173	136	213	256	608	1,330	1,673
Rest of General Government	..	35	38	41	47	58	60	65	97	100	115
Non-financial Public Enterprises	..	47	48	53	60	74	107	175	260	566	600
Priv. Sector, incl non-guaranteed	..	63	70	85	92	190	306	335	489	661	892
Short-Term Debt	..	0	0	0	0	0	0	0	856	1,198	1,149
Memo Items:					*(Millions of US dollars)*						
Int'l Reserves Excluding Gold	42.9	55.2	37.1	121.1	210.4	318.6	253.4	477.4	623.1	635.8	722.0
Gold Holdings (at market price)	22.2	20.4	23.3	23.1	43.3	72.0	54.1	52.0	66.0	92.0	212.1
SOCIAL INDICATORS											
Total Fertility Rate	6.4	6.3	6.2	6.1	5.9	5.8	5.7	5.5	5.4	5.3	5.2
Infant Mortality Rate	102.2	99.8	97.4	95.0	92.4	89.8	87.2	84.6	82.0	79.6	77.2
Life Expectancy at Birth	57.6	58.1	58.5	58.9	59.4	59.9	60.4	60.9	61.4	62.0	62.6
Urban Population, % of total	39.0	39.5	40.1	40.7	41.2	41.8	42.4	43.4	44.4	45.3	46.3
Food Prod. per capita (1987=100)	105.3	106.2	107.0	99.8	98.6	105.8	104.2	103.2	102.7	98.1	97.0
Labor Force, Agriculture (%)	51.3	50.6	49.3	48.0	46.8	45.6	44.5	43.2	41.9	40.8	39.6
Labor Force, Female (%)	16.3	16.3	16.6	16.9	17.2	17.4	17.7	18.1	18.4	18.7	19.0
Primary Schl. Enroll. Ratio	..	97.0	..	..	..	..	104.0	104.0	106.0	108.0	112.0
Primary Schl. Enroll. Ratio, Female	..	95.0	..	..	..	..	102.0	102.0	104.0	106.0	109.0
Secondary Schl. Enroll. Ratio	..	22.0	..	..	..	..	40.0	..	..	..	49.0

1980	1981	1982	1983	1984	1985	1986	1987	1988	1989 estimate	NOTES	ECUADOR
				(Millions of current US dollars)							**FOREIGN TRADE (CUSTOMS BASIS)**
2,480.2	2,167.9	2,290.8	2,348.0	2,621.0	2,904.7	2,171.5	2,021.3	2,192.0	..	..	Value of Exports, fob
843.0	754.0	750.3	562.7	726.0	882.8	1,093.9	1,118.7	1,065.8	..	..	Nonfuel Primary Products
1,562.9	1,341.1	1,471.3	1,733.3	1,833.8	1,929.9	982.6	818.0	987.2	..	..	Fuels
74.3	72.8	69.2	52.0	61.2	92.0	95.0	84.6	139.0	..	..	Manufactures
2,215.3	1,906.8	1,736.7	1,487.0	1,616.0	1,767.0	1,810.0	2,250.0	1,714.0	..	..	Value of Imports, cif
267.1	177.1	179.0	217.1	216.0	229.0	140.1	178.5	158.0	..	..	Nonfuel Primary Products
28.2	249.7	27.6	24.9	27.0	27.0	39.9	61.5	59.0	..	..	Fuels
1,920.0	1,480.0	1,530.0	1,245.0	1,373.0	1,511.0	1,630.0	2,010.0	1,497.0	..	..	Manufactures
				(Index 1987 = 100)							
172.7	162.1	171.4	174.6	170.4	163.3	103.8	100.0	84.4	..	..	Terms of Trade
145.6	146.7	140.3	143.0	137.0	131.0	93.9	100.0	91.8	..	..	Export Prices, fob
84.3	90.5	81.8	81.9	80.4	80.2	90.4	100.0	108.8	..	..	Import Prices, cif
				(Millions of current US dollars)							**BALANCE OF PAYMENTS**
2,975.0	2,995.0	2,739.0	2,688.0	2,971.0	3,327.0	2,654.0	2,465.0	2,657.0	2,883.0	..	Exports of Goods & Services
2,520.0	2,527.0	2,327.0	2,348.0	2,621.0	2,905.0	2,186.0	2,021.0	2,202.0	2,354.0	..	Merchandise, fob
367.0	398.6	386.0	315.0	291.0	393.0	444.0	434.0	446.0	507.0	..	Nonfactor Services
88.0	69.4	26.0	25.0	59.0	29.0	24.0	10.0	9.0	22.0	..	Factor Services
3,646.8	4,018.0	3,955.0	3,422.0	3,255.0	3,293.0	3,240.0	3,687.0	3,295.0	3,512.0	..	Imports of Goods & Services
2,241.8	2,353.0	2,187.0	1,421.0	1,567.0	1,611.0	1,631.0	2,054.0	1,614.0	1,693.0	..	Merchandise, fob
681.9	806.3	722.0	1,033.0	507.0	594.0	579.0	620.0	586.0	651.0	..	Nonfactor Services
723.1	858.7	1,046.0	968.0	1,181.0	1,088.0	1,030.0	1,013.0	1,095.0	1,168.0	..	Factor Services
365.3	539.4	764.7	540.7	842.2	745.1	681.1	258.9	291.9	410.4	..	Long-Term Interest
0.0	0.0	0.0	0.0	0.0	0.0	0.0	0.0	0.0	..	..	Private Current Transfers, net
..	..	..	..	..	..	..	..	..	..	..	Workers' Remittances
-671.8	-1,023.0	-1,216.0	-734.0	-284.0	34.0	-586.0	-1,222.0	-638.0	-629.0	..	Curr. A/C Bal before Off. Transf.
30.2	25.0	20.0	24.0	20.0	80.0	45.0	132.0	1,042.0	97.0	..	Net Official Transfers
-641.6	-998.0	-1,196.0	-710.0	-264.0	114.0	-541.0	-1,090.0	404.0	-532.0	..	Curr. A/C Bal after Off. Transf.
763.0	1,076.8	164.0	1,372.0	360.0	474.0	740.0	1,088.0	180.0	466.0	..	Long-Term Capital, net
70.0	60.0	40.0	50.0	50.0	62.0	70.0	75.0	80.0	80.0	..	Direct Investment
753.9	1,291.4	-91.5	88.5	614.6	369.8	788.1	352.1	367.1	460.3	..	Long-Term Loans
1,288.8	2,096.8	1,083.1	283.9	835.8	640.4	1,161.9	694.5	924.7	922.0	..	Disbursements
534.9	805.4	1,174.6	195.4	221.2	270.6	373.8	342.4	557.6	461.7	..	Repayments
-60.9	-274.6	215.5	1,233.5	-304.6	42.2	-118.1	660.9	-267.1	-74.3	..	Other Long-Term Capital
124.9	-446.4	586.2	-622.9	-104.1	-458.1	-334.5	-95.6	-636.2	272.6	..	Other Capital, net
-246.3	367.6	445.8	-39.1	8.1	-129.9	135.5	97.6	52.2	-206.6	..	Change in Reserves
				(Ecuadoran Sucres per US dollar)							Memo Item:
25.000	25.000	33.400	52.900	79.500	91.500	122.790	170.460	301.610	526.350	..	Conversion Factor (Annual Avg)
				(Millions of US dollars), outstanding at end of year							
5,997	7,666	7,705	7,595	8,305	8,705	9,337	10,482	10,750	11,311	..	**EXTERNAL DEBT (Total)**
4,422	5,645	5,514	6,429	7,022	7,716	8,833	9,586	9,556	9,904	..	Long-Term Debt (by debtor)
93	108	123	392	473	806	1,105	1,172	1,050	1,072	..	Central Bank, incl. IMF credit
2,125	2,759	2,487	4,213	5,317	5,754	6,380	7,022	7,412	7,697	..	Central Government
135	211	196	185	158	149	147	152	140	185	..	Rest of General Government
832	1,026	992	894	787	805	1,069	1,095	799	762	..	Non-financial Public Enterprises
1,237	1,542	1,717	745	287	203	132	144	155	188	..	Priv. Sector, incl non-guaranteed
1,575	2,021	2,191	1,166	1,283	989	504	896	1,194	1,407	..	Short-Term Debt
				(Millions of US dollars)							Memo Items:
1,013.0	632.4	304.2	644.5	611.2	718.2	644.2	491.1	397.6	540.4	..	Int'l Reserves Excluding Gold
244.2	164.7	189.3	158.0	127.7	135.5	161.9	200.5	170.0	166.1	..	Gold Holdings (at market price)
											SOCIAL INDICATORS
5.0	4.9	4.8	4.7	4.6	4.5	4.4	4.3	4.2	4.1	..	Total Fertility Rate
74.8	72.4	70.0	68.6	67.2	65.8	64.4	63.0	62.1	61.3	..	Infant Mortality Rate
63.1	63.7	64.3	64.5	64.8	65.0	65.2	65.5	65.6	65.8	..	Life Expectancy at Birth
47.3	48.3	49.3	50.3	51.3	52.3	53.2	54.1	55.1	56.0	..	Urban Population, % of total
99.8	99.3	100.1	84.2	90.4	99.8	99.9	100.0	105.4	108.0	..	Food Prod. per capita (1987=100)
38.6	..	..	..	..	..	..	..	..	..	..	Labor Force, Agriculture (%)
19.3	19.3	19.3	19.3	19.3	19.3	19.3	19.3	19.3	19.3	..	Labor Force, Female (%)
113.0	115.0	116.0	117.0	114.0	117.0	118.0	117.0	..	..	..	Primary Schl. Enroll. Ratio
111.0	113.0	112.0	117.0	..	116.0	117.0	116.0	..	..	..	Primary Schl. Enroll. Ratio, Female
51.0	53.0	55.0	52.0	55.0	55.0	56.0	56.0	..	..	..	Secondary Schl. Enroll. Ratio

EGYPT, ARAB REPUBLIC OF	1969	1970	1971	1972	1973	1974	1975	1976	1977	1978	1979
CURRENT GNP PER CAPITA (US $)	210	230	250	260	280	280	320	360	410	410	440
POPULATION (thousands)	32,368	33,053	33,655	34,264	34,898	35,569	36,289	37,067	37,911	38,819	39,781
USE AND ORIGIN OF RESOURCES					*(Millions of current Egyptian Pounds)*						
Gross National Product (GNP)	2,809	3,033	3,212	3,363	3,757	4,282	5,107	6,555	8,102	9,358	11,957
Net Factor Income from Abroad	-24	-26	-29	-27	-49	-57	-111	-172	-242	-437	-748
GDP at Market Prices	2,834	3,058	3,241	3,390	3,806	4,339	5,218	6,727	8,344	9,795	12,705
Resource Balance	-94	-140	-165	-196	-197	-726	-1,101	-789	-894	-1,496	-2,364
Exports of Goods & NFServices	403	434	447	452	532	890	1,053	1,498	1,876	2,130	3,777
Imports of Goods & NFServices	496	573	612	649	729	1,616	2,154	2,287	2,770	3,626	6,141
Domestic Absorption	2,928	3,198	3,406	3,586	4,003	5,065	6,319	7,516	9,238	11,291	15,069
Private Consumption, etc.	1,882	2,016	2,139	2,259	2,429	3,191	3,280	3,936	5,176	6,178	8,724
General Gov't Consumption	679	756	839	909	1,074	899	1,298	1,670	1,628	2,012	2,172
Gross Domestic Investment	367	427	429	418	500	975	1,741	1,910	2,434	3,101	4,173
Fixed Investment	342	353	363	378	462	685	1,282	1,471	1,873	2,685	3,763
Indirect Taxes, net	388	432	449	388	342	142	162	562	810	774	604
GDP at factor cost	2,446	2,627	2,792	3,002	3,464	4,197	5,056	6,165	7,534	9,021	12,101
Agriculture	730	773	814	933	1,062	1,280	1,468	1,744	2,038	2,286	2,530
Industry	679	740	787	804	852	1,052	1,360	1,615	2,051	2,583	4,337
Manufacturing	..	..	..	..	..	746	880	993	1,120	1,319	1,650
Services, etc.	1,037	1,114	1,191	1,265	1,550	1,865	2,228	2,806	3,445	4,152	5,234
Gross Domestic Saving	274	287	263	222	303	249	640	1,121	1,540	1,605	1,809
Gross National Saving	..	276	251	243	308	282	707	1,278	1,673	1,878	2,834
					(Millions of 1987 Egyptian Pounds)						
Gross National Product	12,959	13,737	14,430	14,804	15,556	16,153	17,635	20,280	22,855	24,269	25,799
GDP at Market Prices	13,408	14,212	14,807	15,191	15,965	16,582	18,258	21,077	23,829	25,659	27,685
Resource Balance	-2,960	-3,525	-3,489	-3,655	-4,200	-6,896	-8,234	-6,347	-6,457	-6,872	-9,203
Exports of Goods & NFServices	3,164	3,477	3,429	3,603	3,422	3,558	4,387	5,595	6,134	6,149	5,931
Imports of Goods & NFServices	6,124	7,002	6,918	7,258	7,622	10,454	12,621	11,942	12,591	13,021	15,134
Domestic Absorption	16,368	17,737	18,296	18,846	20,165	23,478	26,492	27,424	30,286	32,531	36,888
Private Consumption, etc.	..	..	..	..	..	16,605	16,627	17,288	20,004	21,222	25,107
General Gov't Consumption	..	..	..	..	..	3,367	4,381	4,668	4,116	4,445	4,110
Gross Domestic Investment	1,908	2,004	1,757	1,812	2,381	3,506	5,484	5,468	6,166	6,864	7,671
Fixed Investment	..	..	..	..	..	2,306	3,780	3,942	4,441	5,564	6,475
GDP at factor cost	11,227	11,871	12,407	12,956	14,214	14,994	16,617	19,061	21,202	23,220	25,487
Agriculture	5,242	5,368	5,438	5,877	6,052	6,070	6,443	6,532	6,350	6,704	6,978
Industry	3,580	3,806	3,952	3,999	3,930	3,780	4,408	5,064	6,157	7,135	7,772
Manufacturing	..	..	..	..	..	..	..	..	..	..	..
Services, etc.	3,511	3,784	4,056	4,223	5,129	6,045	6,648	8,213	9,175	9,776	11,062
Memo Items:											
Capacity to Import	4,969	5,296	5,050	5,064	5,562	5,757	6,170	7,822	8,527	7,649	9,308
Terms of Trade Adjustment	1,805	1,819	1,621	1,461	2,140	2,199	1,783	2,227	2,393	1,500	3,377
Gross Domestic Income	15,213	16,031	16,429	16,652	18,105	18,781	20,041	23,304	26,223	27,159	31,062
Gross National Income	14,764	15,556	16,051	16,265	17,697	18,353	19,418	22,507	25,248	25,769	29,176
DOMESTIC PRICES/DEFLATORS					*(Index 1987 = 100)*						
Overall (GDP)	21.1	21.5	21.9	22.3	23.8	26.2	28.6	31.9	35.0	38.2	45.9
Domestic Absorption	17.9	18.0	18.6	19.0	19.9	21.6	23.9	27.4	30.5	34.7	40.9
Agriculture	13.9	14.4	15.0	15.9	17.6	21.1	22.8	26.7	32.1	34.1	36.3
Industry	19.0	19.4	19.9	20.1	21.7	27.8	30.9	31.9	33.3	36.2	55.8
Manufacturing	..	..	..	..	..	..	..	..	..	..	..
Consumer Price Index	13.8	14.3	14.7	15.0	15.8	17.4	19.1	21.1	23.7	26.4	29.0
MANUFACTURING ACTIVITY											
Employment (1987=100)	..	..	..	..	..	..	..	..	..	..	..
Real Earnings per Empl. (1987=100)	..	..	..	..	..	..	..	..	..	..	..
Real Output per Empl. (1987=100)	..	..	..	..	..	..	..	..	..	..	..
Earnings as % of Value Added	55.5	53.7	50.3	50.5	49.5	42.9	52.8	53.4	48.6	54.8	54.1
MONETARY HOLDINGS					*(Millions of current Egyptian Pounds)*						
Money Supply, Broadly Defined	999	1,053	1,084	1,255	1,536	2,000	2,430	3,061	4,103	5,212	6,844
Money	746	783	846	989	1,205	1,503	1,863	2,239	2,943	3,553	4,354
Currency Outside Banks	496	525	559	631	777	948	1,156	1,388	1,749	2,184	2,657
Demand Deposits	250	258	288	358	428	555	707	851	1,194	1,369	1,697
Quasi-Money	253	270	238	266	331	498	567	822	1,160	1,659	2,490
GOVERNMENT DEFICIT (-) OR SURPLUS					*(Millions of current Egyptian Pounds)*						
GOVERNMENT DEFICIT (-) OR SURPLUS	..	..	..	..	..	..	-938	-1,557	-1,114	-1,246	-1,964
Current Revenue	..	..	..	..	..	..	2,235	2,424	3,301	3,778	4,363
Current Expenditure	..	..	..	..	..	..	2,418	2,662	3,209	3,488	4,516
Current Budget Balance	..	..	..	..	..	..	-183	-238	92	290	-153
Capital Receipts	..	..	..	..	..	..	54	105	147	42	323
Capital Payments	..	..	..	..	..	..	809	1,424	1,353	1,578	2,134

1980	1981	1982	1983	1984	1985	1986	1987	1988	1989 estimate	NOTES	EGYPT, ARAB REPUBLIC OF
500	550	600	620	640	660	670	690	660	630	A	CURRENT GNP PER CAPITA (US $)
40,792	41,852	42,958	44,105	45,287	46,497	47,713	48,935	50,161	51,390	..	POPULATION (thousands)
				(Millions of current Egyptian Pounds)							USE AND ORIGIN OF RESOURCES
15,446	16,088	19,332	22,557	26,585	29,995	34,280	40,782	49,753	59,429	C	Gross National Product (GNP)
-1,051	-1,232	-1,449	-1,613	-1,919	-3,136	-4,076	-4,466	-4,800	-5,259	..	Net Factor Income from Abroad
16,497	17,320	20,781	24,170	28,504	33,132	38,356	45,249	54,553	64,688	C	GDP at Market Prices
-2,038	-2,673	-3,096	-2,646	-3,837	-4,018	-3,783	-5,178	-8,736	-10,837	..	Resource Balance
5,034	5,780	5,618	6,159	6,371	6,598	6,034	8,006	12,944	14,010	..	Exports of Goods & NFServices
7,072	8,453	8,714	8,805	10,208	10,616	9,817	13,184	21,680	24,847	..	Imports of Goods & NFServices
18,535	19,993	23,877	26,816	32,341	37,150	42,139	50,427	63,289	75,525	..	Domestic Absorption
11,411	11,588	13,923	15,712	19,367	22,600	26,706	35,947	42,729	52,067	..	Private Consumption, etc.
2,585	3,294	3,704	4,160	5,140	5,712	6,340	6,330	7,373	8,189	..	General Gov't Consumption
4,539	5,111	6,250	6,944	7,834	8,838	9,093	8,150	13,187	15,269	..	Gross Domestic Investment
4,062	4,702	6,150	7,144	7,634	8,338	8,593	8,050	13,037	15,029	..	Fixed Investment
757	768	684	929	1,103	1,180	2,125	3,218	2,499	3,530	..	Indirect Taxes, net
15,740	16,552	20,097	23,241	27,401	31,952	36,231	42,031	52,054	61,158	C	GDP at factor cost
2,875	3,326	3,932	4,564	5,494	6,386	7,531	8,640	10,052	11,345	..	Agriculture
5,789	6,245	6,521	6,970	8,024	9,125	9,715	12,329	15,614	18,053	..	Industry
1,928	2,144	2,670	3,068	3,624	4,316	4,805	..	..	..	..	Manufacturing
7,076	6,981	9,644	11,707	13,883	16,441	18,985	21,062	26,388	31,760	..	Services, etc.
2,501	2,438	3,154	4,298	3,997	4,820	5,310	2,972	4,451	4,432	..	Gross Domestic Saving
3,338	3,248	3,096	4,918	4,848	4,149	3,331	512	2,037	2,795	..	Gross National Saving
				(Millions of 1987 Egyptian Pounds)							
28,390	29,313	32,633	35,231	37,340	38,492	39,086	40,783	43,082	44,487	C	Gross National Product
30,678	31,894	35,302	38,020	40,336	42,999	44,137	45,249	47,023	48,144	C	GDP at Market Prices
-9,424	-10,402	-8,843	-8,341	-10,163	-10,385	-8,085	-5,178	-4,939	-4,370	..	Resource Balance
6,940	6,838	6,126	6,784	7,199	7,494	7,528	8,006	8,870	8,873	..	Exports of Goods & NFServices
16,364	17,240	14,969	15,125	17,362	17,879	15,613	13,184	13,809	13,243	..	Imports of Goods & NFServices
40,102	42,296	44,145	46,361	50,499	53,384	52,222	50,427	51,962	52,514	..	Domestic Absorption
28,157	28,806	29,744	31,086	33,604	35,609	35,823	35,947	36,976	37,538	..	Private Consumption, etc.
4,383	5,309	5,187	5,711	6,354	6,435	6,481	6,330	6,356	6,418	..	General Gov't Consumption
7,562	8,181	9,214	9,564	10,541	11,340	9,918	8,150	8,630	8,558	..	Gross Domestic Investment
6,335	7,046	8,487	9,223	9,612	10,006	8,721	8,050	8,530	8,410	..	Fixed Investment
28,279	29,421	32,787	35,316	37,468	39,940	40,997	42,031	43,723	45,095	C	GDP at factor cost
7,222	7,349	7,645	7,866	8,031	8,288	8,463	8,640	8,856	9,033	..	Agriculture
8,871	9,196	9,408	10,057	10,990	11,857	12,057	12,329	12,794	13,013	..	Industry
..	..	..	..	..	..	..	..	..	..	..	Manufacturing
12,354	13,005	15,829	17,393	18,447	19,795	20,477	21,062	22,073	23,049	..	Services, etc.
											Memo Items:
11,649	11,788	9,651	10,580	10,836	11,112	9,597	8,006	8,245	7,467	..	Capacity to Import
4,709	4,950	3,525	3,796	3,637	3,618	2,069	0	-625	-1,406	..	Terms of Trade Adjustment
35,387	36,844	38,827	41,816	43,973	46,617	46,206	45,249	46,398	46,738	..	Gross Domestic Income
33,099	34,264	36,157	39,026	40,977	42,110	41,154	40,783	42,457	43,081	..	Gross National Income
				(Index 1987 = 100)							DOMESTIC PRICES/DEFLATORS
53.8	54.3	58.9	63.6	70.7	77.1	86.9	100.0	116.0	134.4	..	Overall (GDP)
46.2	47.3	54.1	57.8	64.0	69.6	80.7	100.0	121.8	143.8	..	Domestic Absorption
39.8	45.3	51.4	58.0	68.4	77.1	89.0	100.0	113.5	125.6	..	Agriculture
65.3	67.9	69.3	69.3	73.0	77.0	80.6	100.0	122.0	138.7	..	Industry
..	..	..	..	..	..	..	..	..	..	..	Manufacturing
35.0	38.6	44.3	51.4	60.2	67.4	83.5	100.0	117.7	142.7	..	Consumer Price Index
											MANUFACTURING ACTIVITY
..	..	..	..	..	..	..	..	..	..	..	Employment (1987=100)
..	..	..	..	..	..	..	..	..	..	..	Real Earnings per Empl. (1987=100)
..	..	..	..	..	..	..	..	..	..	..	Real Output per Empl. (1987=100)
57.0	63.8	59.4	61.6	59.5	56.0	56.4	..	..	..	..	Earnings as % of Value Added
				(Millions of current Egyptian Pounds)							MONETARY HOLDINGS
10,364	13,566	17,792	21,817	25,929	30,676	37,102	44,878	54,549	64,093	..	Money Supply, Broadly Defined
6,775	7,646	9,552	10,933	12,443	14,696	15,973	18,241	20,579	22,471	..	Money
3,398	4,291	5,503	6,475	7,097	8,284	8,803	9,537	10,406	10,934	..	Currency Outside Banks
3,377	3,355	4,049	4,457	5,346	6,411	7,170	8,704	10,173	11,537	..	Demand Deposits
3,589	5,920	8,240	10,885	13,486	15,980	21,129	26,637	33,970	41,622	..	Quasi-Money
				(Millions of current Egyptian Pounds)							
..	-1,096	-3,554	-2,364	-3,258	-3,439	-4,655	-2,613	-4,715	..	F	GOVERNMENT DEFICIT (-) OR SURPLUS
..	7,893	9,116	10,714	11,951	13,245	15,214	16,590	19,137	..	..	Current Revenue
..	6,333	9,347	9,637	12,519	12,891	15,054	15,008	18,634	..	..	Current Expenditure
..	1,560	-231	1,077	-568	354	160	1,582	503	..	..	Current Budget Balance
..	188	601	363	395	655	668	1,261	1,006	..	..	Capital Receipts
..	2,844	3,924	3,804	3,085	4,448	5,483	5,456	6,224	..	..	Capital Payments

EGYPT, ARAB REPUBLIC OF	1969	1970	1971	1972	1973	1974	1975	1976	1977	1978	1979
FOREIGN TRADE (CUSTOMS BASIS)					*(Millions of current US dollars)*						
Value of Exports, fob	824	870	927	887	1,117	1,588	1,596	1,785	2,015	2,458	3,320
Nonfuel Primary Products	572	585	634	564	721	988	792	761	866	752	702
Fuels	48	79	73	68	113	201	327	644	720	1,203	2,245
Manufactures	204	207	220	256	283	399	478	380	429	504	373
Value of Imports, cif	638	787	920	898	914	2,351	3,934	3,862	4,815	6,727	7,073
Nonfuel Primary Products	232	274	370	361	380	1,225	1,703	1,344	1,586	2,224	2,039
Fuels	56	74	71	60	23	66	272	221	109	101	164
Manufactures	349	439	479	478	511	1,060	1,958	2,296	3,120	4,401	4,870
					(Index 1987 = 100)						
Terms of Trade	100.9	89.5	81.5	76.5	93.1	105.3	97.7	121.7	117.3	105.3	120.7
Export Prices, fob	25.0	22.6	24.3	25.4	43.2	70.7	64.3	75.1	74.8	77.1	101.9
Import Prices, cif	24.7	25.2	29.8	33.2	46.4	67.1	65.8	61.7	63.8	73.3	84.4
BALANCE OF PAYMENTS					*(Millions of current US dollars)*						
Exports of Goods & Services	..	962	1,005	1,017	1,304	2,338	2,589	3,391	4,001	4,243	5,707
Merchandise, fob	..	817	851	813	1,000	1,818	1,875	2,169	2,346	2,558	3,987
Nonfactor Services	..	143	153	203	300	433	628	1,150	1,542	1,541	1,414
Factor Services	..	2	1	1	4	87	86	72	113	144	306
Imports of Goods & Services	..	1,447	1,518	1,592	1,986	4,165	5,471	5,596	6,417	7,419	10,156
Merchandise, fob	..	1,084	1,131	1,170	1,429	3,618	4,608	4,659	5,110	5,998	7,817
Nonfactor Services	..	297	312	352	429	341	533	523	769	614	964
Factor Services	..	66	74	69	128	206	330	414	538	807	1,375
Long-Term Interest	..	56	54	76	102	99	147	141	336	402	288
Private Current Transfers, net	..	33	38	110	123	231	456	842	960	1,815	2,534
Workers' Remittances	..	29	27	104	117	189	366	755	897	1,761	2,445
Curr. A/C Bal before Off. Transf.	..	-452	-474	-465	-559	-1,596	-2,426	-1,363	-1,456	-1,361	-1,915
Net Official Transfers	..	304	268	290	579	1,261	986	705	382	291	72
Curr. A/C Bal after Off. Transf.	..	-148	-207	-174	20	-335	-1,440	-658	-1,074	-1,070	-1,843
Long-Term Capital, net	..	2	20	304	204	66	955	1,009	2,499	1,933	2,195
Direct Investment	..	..	..	..	..	87	225	444	477	387	1,375
Long-Term Loans	..	87	278	225	-29	153	2,257	942	2,288	1,702	1,894
Disbursements	..	397	570	612	562	640	2,765	1,456	3,001	2,491	2,655
Repayments	..	310	292	388	591	487	508	515	713	789	761
Other Long-Term Capital	..	-85	-258	79	233	-174	-1,527	-377	-266	-156	-1,074
Other Capital, net	..	134	128	-115	-54	90	59	157	-73	113	262
Change in Reserves	..	12	58	-14	-171	179	426	-508	-1,352	-976	-614
Memo Item:					*(Egyptian Pounds per US dollar)*						
Conversion Factor (Annual Avg)	0.410	0.400	0.390	0.390	0.400	0.480	0.460	0.500	0.570	0.660	0.700
					(Millions of US dollars), outstanding at end of year						
EXTERNAL DEBT (Total)	..	1,831	2,157	2,326	2,448	2,679	4,792	5,890	12,761	13,807	16,041
Long-Term Debt (by debtor)	..	1,831	2,157	2,326	2,448	2,679	4,792	5,890	8,474	10,499	12,565
Central Bank, incl. IMF credit	..	302	262	246	420	526	1,947	2,430	2,838	3,027	3,051
Central Government	..	623	872	875	982	959	1,656	2,145	4,157	5,732	6,958
Rest of General Government	..	0	0	0	0	0	0	0	0	3	11
Non-financial Public Enterprises	..	906	1,024	1,205	1,044	1,189	1,184	1,284	1,416	1,659	2,358
Priv. Sector, incl non-guaranteed	..	0	0	0	1	5	5	32	64	79	187
Short-Term Debt	..	0	0	0	0	0	0	0	4,287	3,308	3,476
Memo Items:					*(Millions of US dollars)*						
Int'l Reserves Excluding Gold	51.0	74.1	57.1	51.5	259.6	251.8	193.9	239.6	430.7	491.7	529.5
Gold Holdings (at market price)	94.1	91.0	106.1	157.8	273.0	453.6	341.1	327.7	401.2	558.9	1,265.7
SOCIAL INDICATORS											
Total Fertility Rate	6.2	5.9	5.7	5.5	5.5	5.4	5.4	5.3	5.3	5.2	5.1
Infant Mortality Rate	162.0	158.0	154.0	150.0	144.0	138.0	132.0	126.0	120.0	116.0	112.0
Life Expectancy at Birth	50.7	51.1	51.6	52.1	52.5	52.9	53.3	53.7	54.1	54.8	55.5
Urban Population, % of total	41.9	42.2	42.5	42.7	43.0	43.2	43.5	43.7	44.0	44.2	44.5
Food Prod. per capita (1987=100)	97.5	95.7	98.0	98.2	97.6	97.1	98.0	98.1	92.5	92.7	92.8
Labor Force, Agriculture (%)	52.5	52.0	51.3	50.6	50.0	49.4	48.8	48.1	47.5	46.8	46.2
Labor Force, Female (%)	7.1	7.1	7.3	7.4	7.5	7.7	7.8	8.0	8.1	8.3	8.5
Primary Schl. Enroll. Ratio	..	72.0	..	..	..	..	71.0	73.0	73.0	74.0	75.0
Primary Schl. Enroll. Ratio, Female	..	57.0	..	..	..	..	57.0	57.0	57.0	58.0	61.0
Secondary Schl. Enroll. Ratio	..	35.0	..	..	..	..	43.0	45.0	47.0	49.0	50.0

1980	1981	1982	1983	1984	1985	1986	1987	1988	1989 estimate	NOTES	EGYPT, ARAB REPUBLIC OF
				(Millions of current US dollars)							**FOREIGN TRADE (CUSTOMS BASIS)**
4,759	5,048	5,033	5,368	5,936	6,076	5,193	4,040	4,576	4,878	C f	Value of Exports, fob
781	889	806	653	795	808	696	592	621	..	..	Nonfuel Primary Products
3,590	3,755	3,737	4,165	4,485	4,608	3,858	2,658	2,792	2,887	..	Fuels
388	404	490	550	656	660	639	790	1,163	1,244	..	Manufactures
8,047	8,839	9,078	10,275	10,766	11,594	10,581	8,453	10,771	11,662	C f	Value of Imports, cif
2,800	3,566	3,292	3,220	3,610	3,730	3,432	2,612	2,975	..	..	Nonfuel Primary Products
214	265	371	584	484	469	303	189	188	199	..	Fuels
5,033	5,008	5,415	6,471	6,672	7,395	6,846	5,652	7,608	8,220	..	Manufactures
				(Index 1987 = 100)							
161.6	166.2	159.0	163.3	156.7	135.3	99.6	100.0	97.0	..	..	Terms of Trade
155.8	163.1	147.2	147.8	140.4	118.8	94.2	100.0	107.8	..	..	Export Prices, fob
96.4	98.1	92.5	90.5	89.6	87.8	94.7	100.0	111.1	..	..	Import Prices, cif
				(Millions of current US dollars)							**BALANCE OF PAYMENTS**
7,087	8,207	8,430	8,870	9,561	9,754	8,754	8,061	9,081	10,373	..	Exports of Goods & Services
4,686	5,617	5,779	5,248	5,924	6,075	5,193	4,040	4,499	3,755	..	Merchandise, fob
2,116	2,186	2,183	2,604	2,558	2,636	2,647	3,231	3,779	5,698	..	Nonfactor Services
284	404	468	1,018	1,079	1,043	914	790	803	919	..	Factor Services
11,300	13,481	13,917	14,411	16,556	18,011	17,074	14,684	15,337	17,454	..	Imports of Goods & Services
8,577	10,334	10,380	9,619	11,328	11,593	10,581	8,453	10,771	11,419	..	Merchandise, fob
980	1,078	1,285	1,896	2,086	2,091	2,300	2,176	1,851	4,241	..	Nonfactor Services
1,744	2,069	2,252	2,896	3,142	4,327	4,193	4,055	2,715	1,794	..	Factor Services
441	680	703	953	963	1,022	1,210	643	1,029	1,193	..	Long-Term Interest
2,696	2,918	1,986	3,191	3,957	3,522	2,995	2,866	3,408	4,253	..	Private Current Transfers, net
2,696	2,855	1,935	3,165	3,931	3,496	2,973	2,845	3,386	4,254	..	Workers' Remittances
-1,517	-2,356	-3,501	-2,350	-3,038	-4,735	-5,325	-3,757	-2,848	-2,828	..	Curr. A/C Bal before Off. Transf.
97	279	395	675	760	1,171	1,287	1,052	980	1,137	..	Net Official Transfers
-1,420	-2,077	-3,106	-1,675	-2,278	-3,564	-4,038	-2,705	-1,868	-1,691	..	Curr. A/C Bal after Off. Transf.
2,076	2,001	1,920	2,112	1,932	1,156	1,173	-697	2,759	2,415	..	Long-Term Capital, net
541	836	885	966	1,275	1,289	1,275	869	973	1,586	..	Direct Investment
2,206	2,323	3,261	2,228	2,379	2,144	982	1,293	1,443	684	..	Long-Term Loans
3,260	3,641	4,708	3,741	3,825	3,740	2,432	2,054	2,511	2,146	..	Disbursements
1,054	1,318	1,446	1,513	1,446	1,596	1,450	761	1,068	1,462	..	Repayments
-672	-1,158	-2,226	-1,082	-1,722	-2,277	-1,084	-2,859	343	146	..	Other Long-Term Capital
43	-57	1,203	452	485	2,821	3,277	4,105	-491	-1,287	..	Other Capital, net
-698	133	-17	-889	-139	-413	-412	-703	-400	562	..	Change in Reserves
				(Egyptian Pounds per US dollar)							Memo Item:
0.720	0.740	0.810	0.860	0.930	0.960	1.070	1.270	1.760	1.940	..	Conversion Factor (Annual Avg)
				(Millions of US dollars), outstanding at end of year							
20,384	23,576	28,795	31,598	34,864	40,218	42,997	49,121	49,485	48,799	..	**EXTERNAL DEBT (Total)**
16,450	20,061	23,891	26,554	29,211	34,115	36,143	42,854	42,963	40,993	..	Long-Term Debt (by debtor)
2,885	2,595	2,814	2,856	2,675	2,554	2,634	2,963	2,863	3,500	..	Central Bank, incl. IMF credit
10,482	13,491	16,326	18,433	21,024	24,947	26,312	32,623	33,229	30,659	..	Central Government
17	19	21	27	23	33	42	50	42	40	..	Rest of General Government
2,800	3,635	4,267	4,616	4,895	5,684	6,078	6,008	5,601	5,633	..	Non-financial Public Enterprises
266	321	463	622	593	897	1,077	1,210	1,227	1,161	..	Priv. Sector, incl non-guaranteed
3,933	3,515	4,904	5,044	5,653	6,103	6,855	6,267	6,522	7,806	..	Short-Term Debt
				(Millions of US dollars)							Memo Items:
1,046.0	716.2	698.1	771.1	736.2	792.1	829.0	1,378.3	1,263.4	1,520.1	..	Int'l Reserves Excluding Gold
1,433.7	966.7	1,111.2	927.8	749.8	795.3	950.7	1,177.3	997.7	975.2	..	Gold Holdings (at market price)
											SOCIAL INDICATORS
5.1	5.0	5.0	4.9	4.8	4.7	4.7	4.6	4.5	4.5	..	Total Fertility Rate
108.0	104.0	100.0	97.0	94.0	91.0	88.0	85.0	82.8	80.5	..	Infant Mortality Rate
56.3	57.0	57.7	58.6	59.4	60.3	61.2	62.1	62.5	63.0	..	Life Expectancy at Birth
44.7	45.1	45.4	45.8	46.1	46.5	47.0	47.4	47.9	48.3	..	Urban Population, % of total
90.0	89.1	95.3	95.2	93.4	95.0	97.2	100.0	98.8	97.1	..	Food Prod. per capita (1987=100)
45.7	..	..	..	..	..	..	..	..	..	..	Labor Force, Agriculture (%)
8.6	8.8	8.9	9.1	9.2	9.3	9.5	9.7	9.8	9.9	..	Labor Force, Female (%)
78.0	..	82.0	84.0	86.0	87.0	88.0	90.0	..	..	..	Primary Schl. Enroll. Ratio
65.0	..	70.0	73.0	76.0	78.0	79.0	79.0	..	..	..	Primary Schl. Enroll. Ratio, Female
54.0	..	57.0	59.0	60.0	66.0	68.0	69.0	..	..	..	Secondary Schl. Enroll. Ratio

EL SALVADOR	1969	1970	1971	1972	1973	1974	1975	1976	1977	1978	1979
CURRENT GNP PER CAPITA (US $)	290	290	300	310	330	380	430	500	590	700	760
POPULATION (thousands)	3,475	3,588	3,696	3,798	3,894	3,989	4,085	4,180	4,272	4,361	4,446
USE AND ORIGIN OF RESOURCES					*(Millions of current Salvadoran Colones)*						
Gross National Product (GNP)	2,362	2,549	2,679	2,855	3,294	3,891	4,412	5,689	7,095	7,562	8,547
Net Factor Income from Abroad	-20	-22	-25	-27	-38	-53	-66	-17	-72	-130	-60
GDP at Market Prices	2,382	2,571	2,704	2,882	3,332	3,944	4,478	5,706	7,167	7,692	8,607
Resource Balance	-62	8	-50	32	-94	-332	-228	21	62	-713	-15
Exports of Goods & NFServices	556	643	669	842	1,003	1,284	1,485	2,178	2,767	2,328	3,182
Imports of Goods & NFServices	617	635	719	810	1,096	1,615	1,713	2,157	2,705	3,041	3,197
Domestic Absorption	2,444	2,563	2,754	2,850	3,425	4,275	4,706	5,685	7,105	8,405	8,622
Private Consumption, etc.	1,892	1,957	2,057	2,135	2,467	2,954	3,214	3,880	4,622	5,575	5,933
General Gov't Consumption	249	276	275	308	349	429	501	686	805	996	1,133
Gross Domestic Investment	303	331	422	408	609	892	991	1,120	1,679	1,834	1,556
Fixed Investment	274	298	359	474	521	719	1,031	1,145	1,520	1,652	1,512
Indirect Taxes, net	162	196	199	223	268	329	353	562	848	645	855
GDP at factor cost	2,220	2,375	2,505	2,659	3,064	3,615	4,125	5,144	6,319	7,047	7,752
Agriculture	607	731	729	728	922	999	1,028	1,614	2,374	2,049	2,508
Industry	573	600	644	712	769	915	1,115	1,246	1,488	1,664	1,851
Manufacturing	466	485	519	563	611	707	831	933	1,047	1,205	1,338
Services, etc.	1,201	1,240	1,331	1,442	1,641	2,030	2,335	2,845	3,304	3,979	4,248
Gross Domestic Saving	241	339	372	440	515	561	762	1,140	1,741	1,122	1,541
Gross National Saving	..	348	387	435	507	551	760	1,184	1,744	1,104	1,593
					(Millions of 1987 Salvadoran Colones)						
Gross National Product	17,409.0	17,940.0	18,795.8	19,798.0	20,732.0	22,050.5	23,205.4	24,325.5	25,524.3	27,073.1	26,914.5
GDP at Market Prices	17,251.0	17,787.6	18,644.1	19,643.9	20,613.7	21,954.9	23,128.6	23,989.8	25,388.7	27,083.2	26,650.2
Resource Balance	-700.7	-1,330.7	-1,487.2	-1,263.0	-2,476.5	-2,421.7	-1,513.9	-3,218.7	-6,181.8	-5,616.2	-3,170.6
Exports of Goods & NFServices	3,843.7	3,520.7	3,827.2	4,485.7	4,314.5	4,601.7	5,157.4	4,670.0	4,122.6	4,968.3	6,764.5
Imports of Goods & NFServices	4,544.4	4,851.3	5,314.4	5,748.8	6,791.0	7,023.4	6,671.3	7,888.7	10,304.4	10,584.5	9,935.0
Domestic Absorption	17,951.7	19,118.3	20,131.3	20,906.9	23,090.2	24,376.6	24,642.5	27,208.5	31,570.5	32,699.4	29,820.8
Private Consumption, etc.	14,509.2	15,361.1	15,981.7	16,683.9	17,918.9	18,419.9	18,951.9	20,811.6	23,261.5	23,956.6	22,408.8
General Gov't Consumption	1,427.6	1,520.2	1,431.3	1,679.3	1,872.8	1,800.3	1,958.1	2,266.0	2,379.2	2,640.5	2,705.8
Gross Domestic Investment	2,014.9	2,237.0	2,718.4	2,543.7	3,298.4	4,156.4	3,732.5	4,130.8	5,929.9	6,102.2	4,706.2
Fixed Investment	1,758.8	1,968.6	2,231.6	2,932.3	2,667.8	3,051.7	3,945.5	4,066.4	5,148.7	5,285.5	4,459.3
GDP at factor cost	..	..	..	..	..	..	..	..	..	..	..
Agriculture	2,562.4	2,730.4	2,832.7	2,874.5	2,925.4	3,225.0	3,427.4	3,157.0	3,270.7	3,729.1	3,862.7
Industry	3,642.8	3,775.8	4,069.3	4,381.2	4,579.4	4,847.5	5,354.8	5,666.1	6,240.0	6,436.8	6,254.4
Manufacturing	3,141.4	3,258.9	3,486.4	3,620.2	3,879.7	4,105.8	4,297.6	4,673.8	4,918.4	5,141.5	4,883.5
Services, etc.	11,109.0	11,212.3	11,662.3	12,419.5	13,279.1	13,932.1	14,337.0	15,636.5	16,437.9	17,240.3	16,620.6
Memo Items:											
Capacity to Import	4,088.8	4,912.5	4,943.3	5,974.5	6,210.7	5,581.7	5,783.2	7,964.8	10,539.8	8,104.0	9,889.4
Terms of Trade Adjustment	245.1	1,391.8	1,116.2	1,488.7	1,896.2	980.0	625.7	3,294.8	6,417.2	3,135.8	3,124.9
Gross Domestic Income	17,496.2	19,179.5	19,760.3	21,132.6	22,509.9	22,934.9	23,754.4	27,284.5	31,805.9	30,218.9	29,775.1
Gross National Income	17,654.1	19,331.9	19,912.0	21,286.7	22,628.1	23,030.6	23,831.1	27,620.3	31,941.5	30,208.9	30,039.4
DOMESTIC PRICES/DEFLATORS					*(Index 1987 = 100)*						
Overall (GDP)	13.8	14.5	14.5	14.7	16.2	18.0	19.4	23.8	28.2	28.4	32.3
Domestic Absorption	13.6	13.4	13.7	13.6	14.8	17.5	19.1	20.9	22.5	25.7	28.9
Agriculture	23.7	26.8	25.7	25.3	31.5	31.0	30.0	51.1	72.6	54.9	64.9
Industry	15.7	15.9	15.8	16.3	16.8	18.9	20.8	22.0	23.9	25.9	29.6
Manufacturing	14.8	14.9	14.9	15.5	15.7	17.2	19.3	20.0	21.3	23.4	27.4
Consumer Price Index	10.8	11.1	11.2	11.3	12.1	14.1	16.8	18.0	20.1	22.8	26.1
MANUFACTURING ACTIVITY											
Employment (1987=100)	..	..	..	..	..	..	..	..	..	..	..
Real Earnings per Empl. (1987=100)	..	..	..	..	..	..	..	..	..	..	..
Real Output per Empl. (1987=100)	..	..	..	..	..	..	..	..	..	..	..
Earnings as % of Value Added	26.8	28.0	25.3	23.3	24.6	23.3	22.6	22.5	19.2	25.2	29.0
MONETARY HOLDINGS					*(Millions of current Salvadoran Colones)*						
Money Supply, Broadly Defined	561.9	595.5	658.2	807.1	957.6	1,116.3	1,352.7	1,770.4	2,003.6	2,241.4	2,445.7
Money	288.1	295.3	315.4	389.6	466.0	556.6	648.1	916.7	988.3	1,086.9	1,320.9
Currency Outside Banks	133.5	136.1	145.2	174.9	201.1	240.6	252.9	379.6	432.0	500.5	743.0
Demand Deposits	154.6	159.2	170.2	214.7	264.9	316.0	395.3	537.1	556.3	586.4	578.0
Quasi-Money	273.8	300.2	342.8	417.5	491.5	559.7	704.6	853.7	1,015.3	1,154.4	1,124.8
GOVERNMENT DEFICIT (-) OR SURPLUS					*(Millions of current Salvadoran Colones)*						
	..	-15.2	-27.9	-29.7	-12.2	-27.1	-71.5	-28.4	91.0	-107.3	-85.9
Current Revenue	..	278.0	294.9	332.1	395.5	483.9	561.7	806.8	1,173.8	1,009.9	1,187.5
Current Expenditure	..	230.0	241.2	272.7	310.4	372.8	441.6	543.5	652.0	754.8	833.7
Current Budget Balance	..	48.0	53.7	59.4	85.1	111.1	120.1	263.3	521.8	255.1	353.8
Capital Receipts	..	8.7	..	9.0	3.8	0.1	..	0.1	0.2	..	1.2
Capital Payments	..	71.9	81.6	98.1	101.1	138.3	191.6	291.8	431.0	362.4	440.9

1980	1981	1982	1983	1984	1985	1986	1987	1988	1989 estimate	NOTES	EL SALVADOR
750	750	740	760	820	840	830	860	960	1,070	A	**CURRENT GNP PER CAPITA (US $)**
4,525	4,572	4,625	4,663	4,707	4,767	4,846	4,934	5,032	5,143	..	**POPULATION (thousands)**
			(Millions of current Salvadoran Colones)								**USE AND ORIGIN OF RESOURCES**
8,789	8,427	8,660	9,795	11,251	13,834	19,128	22,778	26,856	31,673	..	Gross National Product (GNP)
-128	-219	-306	-357	-406	-497	-635	-363	-510	-559	..	Net Factor Income from Abroad
8,917	8,647	8,966	10,152	11,657	14,331	19,763	23,141	27,366	32,232	..	GDP at Market Prices
82	-527	-454	-550	-791	-1,084	-630	-1,645	-1,772	-3,313	..	Resource Balance
3,046	2,383	2,188	2,486	2,536	3,199	5,130	4,395	4,327	4,186	..	Exports of Goods & NFServices
2,964	2,909	2,642	3,036	3,327	4,283	5,760	6,040	6,099	7,499	..	Imports of Goods & NFServices
8,835	9,173	9,420	10,702	12,448	15,415	20,393	24,786	29,138	35,545	..	Domestic Absorption
6,405	6,574	6,821	7,871	9,184	11,640	15,392	18,744	22,151	26,364	..	Private Consumption, etc.
1,247	1,369	1,414	1,607	1,869	2,220	2,382	3,181	3,484	3,930	..	General Gov't Consumption
1,183	1,231	1,185	1,224	1,394	1,554	2,619	2,860	3,503	5,251	..	Gross Domestic Investment
1,210	1,173	1,131	1,180	1,336	1,723	2,619	3,152	3,417	4,224	..	Fixed Investment
642	661	..	..	..	..	..	..	..	..	..	Indirect Taxes, net
8,275	7,986	..	..	..	..	..	..	..	..	B	GDP at factor cost
2,480	2,106	2,075	2,160	2,320	2,611	3,996	3,198	3,801	3,767	..	Agriculture
1,846	1,847	1,896	2,175	2,492	3,139	4,051	5,252	5,670	6,864	..	Industry
1,339	1,359	1,382	1,572	1,837	2,346	3,059	4,045	4,808	5,836	..	Manufacturing
4,591	4,693	4,995	5,817	6,846	8,581	11,716	14,690	17,895	21,601	..	Services, etc.
1,265	704	731	673	604	471	1,989	1,215	1,731	1,938	..	Gross Domestic Saving
1,181	583	646	560	493	297	2,080	1,754	2,231	2,589	..	Gross National Saving
			(Millions of 1987 Salvadoran Colones)								
24,453.5	22,236.6	20,829.6	20,952.8	21,423.7	21,931.0	22,159.1	22,777.6	23,645.4	23,897.6	..	Gross National Product
24,388.3	22,395.2	21,159.2	21,294.8	21,772.5	22,284.7	22,522.4	23,140.6	23,854.0	24,099.3	..	GDP at Market Prices
-1,835.2	-1,876.1	-1,512.4	-1,166.4	-1,503.5	-1,716.8	-2,107.6	-1,645.5	-2,026.2	-3,088.2	..	Resource Balance
5,782.2	4,922.7	4,349.0	4,866.8	4,652.8	4,473.3	3,910.0	4,394.6	3,981.8	3,286.6	..	Exports of Goods & NFServices
7,617.3	6,798.8	5,861.5	6,033.2	6,156.3	6,190.1	6,017.6	6,040.1	6,008.0	6,374.8	..	Imports of Goods & NFServices
26,223.4	24,271.3	22,671.7	22,461.2	23,276.0	24,001.5	24,630.0	24,786.1	25,880.2	27,187.5	..	Domestic Absorption
20,469.2	18,549.6	17,254.4	17,272.5	17,883.8	18,566.6	18,551.9	18,744.3	19,229.6	19,404.1	..	Private Consumption, etc.
2,555.2	2,645.3	2,637.5	2,660.5	2,788.7	2,977.4	3,088.7	3,181.3	3,260.5	3,222.4	..	General Gov't Consumption
3,199.0	3,076.4	2,779.7	2,528.2	2,603.5	2,457.5	2,989.4	2,860.5	3,390.0	4,561.0	..	Gross Domestic Investment
3,209.8	2,863.2	2,591.8	2,382.8	2,438.3	2,686.8	2,889.0	3,152.0	3,226.5	3,481.9	..	Fixed Investment
..	..	..	..	..	..	..	..	..	..	B	GDP at factor cost
3,661.6	3,428.3	3,267.6	3,164.0	3,269.4	3,230.2	3,133.5	3,198.4	3,167.9	3,182.7	..	Agriculture
5,534.5	4,974.3	4,626.7	4,739.1	4,766.6	4,959.2	5,088.8	5,252.0	4,628.1	4,756.3	..	Industry
4,358.6	3,903.5	3,575.6	3,647.0	3,694.6	3,832.9	3,928.1	4,044.8	..	..	..	Manufacturing
15,134.7	13,869.4	13,120.5	13,391.6	13,736.6	14,095.3	14,300.1	14,690.2	16,058.0	16,160.3	..	Services, etc.
											Memo Items:
7,827.3	5,567.7	4,854.2	4,939.7	4,693.0	4,623.7	5,359.4	4,394.6	4,262.5	3,558.5	..	Capacity to Import
2,045.1	645.0	505.2	72.9	40.2	150.4	1,449.4	0.0	280.7	271.8	..	Terms of Trade Adjustment
26,433.4	23,040.2	21,664.4	21,367.7	21,812.7	22,435.2	23,971.8	23,140.6	24,134.7	24,371.2	..	Gross Domestic Income
26,498.6	22,881.6	21,334.8	21,025.7	21,463.9	22,081.4	23,608.5	22,777.6	23,926.1	24,169.4	..	Gross National Income
			(Index 1987 = 100)								**DOMESTIC PRICES/DEFLATORS**
36.6	38.6	42.4	47.7	53.5	64.3	87.7	100.0	114.7	133.7	..	Overall (GDP)
33.7	37.8	41.5	47.6	53.5	64.2	82.8	100.0	112.6	130.7	..	Domestic Absorption
67.7	61.4	63.5	68.3	71.0	80.8	127.5	100.0	120.0	118.4	..	Agriculture
33.3	37.1	41.0	45.9	52.3	63.3	79.6	100.0	122.5	144.3	..	Industry
30.7	34.8	38.6	43.1	49.7	61.2	77.9	100.0	..	..	..	Manufacturing
30.6	35.1	39.3	44.5	49.6	60.7	80.1	100.0	119.8	140.9	..	Consumer Price Index
											MANUFACTURING ACTIVITY
..	..	..	..	..	..	..	..	..	..	G J	Employment (1987=100)
..	..	..	..	..	..	..	..	..	..	G J	Real Earnings per Empl. (1987=100)
..	..	..	..	..	..	..	..	..	..	G J	Real Output per Empl. (1987=100)
31.4	30.1	25.3	21.9	21.3	19.5	..	..	..	..	J	Earnings as % of Value Added
			(Millions of current Salvadoran Colones)								**MONETARY HOLDINGS**
2,563.2	2,834.1	3,232.5	3,575.3	4,235.5	5,374.4	6,904.5	7,371.0	8,218.7	9,130.2	..	Money Supply, Broadly Defined
1,428.5	1,437.2	1,633.0	1,595.9	1,830.4	2,306.3	2,757.7	2,762.4	2,996.2	3,370.3	..	Money
718.7	703.0	731.9	724.4	836.3	1,079.8	1,156.5	1,298.0	1,326.2	1,727.1	..	Currency Outside Banks
709.9	734.1	901.1	871.5	994.1	1,226.5	1,601.2	1,464.4	1,670.0	1,643.2	..	Demand Deposits
1,134.7	1,397.0	1,599.5	1,979.4	2,405.1	3,068.1	4,146.8	4,608.6	5,222.5	5,759.9	..	Quasi-Money
			(Millions of current Salvadoran Colones)								**GOVERNMENT DEFICIT (-) OR SURPLUS**
-512.3	-648.3	-680.2	-543.3	-521.4	-106.7	185.0	142.0	-77.6	..	..	Current Revenue
1,015.1	1,085.0	1,085.6	1,210.1	1,697.5	2,439.4	2,917.0	3,077.7	2,960.7	..	..	Current Revenue
1,046.0	1,183.3	1,293.6	1,298.3	1,707.6	1,833.5	2,465.3	2,535.9	2,679.5	..	..	Current Expenditure
-30.9	-98.3	-208.0	-88.2	-10.1	605.9	451.7	541.8	281.2	..	..	Current Budget Balance
1.2	0.1	..	3.1	3.5	0.3	2.4	0.1	..	..	..	Capital Receipts
482.6	550.1	472.2	458.2	514.8	712.9	269.1	399.9	358.8	..	..	Capital Payments

EL SALVADOR	1969	1970	1971	1972	1973	1974	1975	1976	1977	1978	1979
FOREIGN TRADE (CUSTOMS BASIS)					*(Millions of current US dollars)*						
Value of Exports, fob	202.1	236.2	243.2	301.7	358.3	462.5	531.4	743.3	972.8	801.0	1,131.0
Nonfuel Primary Products	135.1	169.6	168.7	217.1	247.0	318.1	386.5	563.4	770.5	578.0	871.0
Fuels	2.8	1.1	1.1	1.6	1.9	3.9	6.3	6.0	6.6	5.8	8.7
Manufactures	64.2	65.4	73.4	83.0	109.3	140.5	138.5	173.9	195.6	217.2	251.3
Value of Imports, cif	209.3	213.6	247.4	278.1	373.8	563.4	598.0	717.9	942.4	1,023.9	1,012.0
Nonfuel Primary Products	41.2	38.9	41.0	42.2	63.1	88.6	94.5	110.1	135.5	158.9	173.6
Fuels	8.8	5.2	13.1	12.8	21.5	52.4	50.3	52.6	92.3	80.1	95.4
Manufactures	159.2	169.4	193.4	223.1	289.2	422.4	453.2	555.1	714.7	785.0	743.0
					(Index 1987 = 100)						
Terms of Trade	126.1	144.0	134.7	132.4	141.7	126.3	112.4	172.3	209.9	148.6	150.1
Export Prices, fob	31.7	39.7	37.4	40.9	52.9	64.0	61.5	94.9	125.9	101.0	120.0
Import Prices, cif	25.1	27.6	27.8	30.9	37.3	50.6	54.7	55.0	60.0	68.0	80.0
BALANCE OF PAYMENTS					*(Millions of current US dollars)*						
Exports of Goods & Services	..	260.5	271.4	339.3	402.3	518.7	600.0	899.6	1,126.4	959.6	1,355.7
Merchandise, fob	..	236.1	243.9	301.7	358.4	464.5	533.0	744.6	973.5	801.6	1,132.3
Nonfactor Services	..	19.8	23.7	34.1	39.6	49.2	60.3	117.4	115.1	121.4	133.5
Factor Services	..	4.6	3.8	3.5	4.4	5.1	6.7	37.6	37.8	36.6	89.9
Imports of Goods & Services	..	266.1	302.9	339.0	459.8	671.2	720.4	905.2	1,135.1	1,296.8	1,385.7
Merchandise, fob	..	194.7	226.0	249.7	339.8	522.2	550.7	681.0	861.0	951.1	954.7
Nonfactor Services	..	57.2	62.5	73.1	99.5	109.2	122.6	171.4	208.6	256.8	300.6
Factor Services	..	14.2	14.4	16.2	20.5	39.8	47.0	52.8	65.5	88.8	130.3
Long-Term Interest	..	9.1	9.6	10.9	14.6	16.9	18.8	26.3	31.3	37.0	41.2
Private Current Transfers, net	..	12.4	16.1	8.9	11.8	17.2	25.1	24.4	30.4	44.9	44.9
Workers' Remittances	..	..	..	..	..	..	..	..	33.6	45.3	49.2
Curr. A/C Bal before Off. Transf.	..	6.8	-15.3	9.2	-45.7	-135.3	-95.2	18.8	21.6	-292.3	14.9
Net Official Transfers	..	1.9	1.1	3.1	1.8	1.1	2.3	4.8	9.2	6.5	6.5
Curr. A/C Bal after Off. Transf.	..	8.7	-14.2	12.4	-43.9	-134.2	-92.9	23.6	30.8	-285.8	21.4
Long-Term Capital, net	..	6.0	21.1	62.2	37.0	193.1	138.7	72.7	38.3	175.7	78.4
Direct Investment	..	3.7	7.0	6.6	6.0	20.1	13.1	12.9	18.6	23.4	-10.0
Long-Term Loans	..	9.2	18.9	46.7	3.3	94.1	52.3	73.5	41.9	74.0	27.1
Disbursements	..	31.3	48.5	73.9	46.5	140.5	132.1	134.7	136.5	134.6	90.0
Repayments	..	22.1	29.6	27.2	43.2	46.4	79.8	61.2	94.6	60.6	62.9
Other Long-Term Capital	..	-6.9	-4.9	8.9	27.7	79.0	73.2	-13.7	-22.3	78.3	61.2
Other Capital, net	..	-12.5	-13.9	-59.6	-3.5	-44.2	-16.1	-12.0	-28.2	165.6	-233.6
Change in Reserves	..	-2.2	7.1	-15.0	10.4	-14.7	-29.7	-84.3	-40.9	-55.4	133.8
Memo Item:					*(Salvadoran Colones per US dollar)*						
Conversion Factor (Annual Avg)	2.500	2.500	2.500	2.500	2.500	2.500	2.500	2.500	2.500	2.500	2.500
				(Millions of US dollars), outstanding at end of year							
EXTERNAL DEBT (Total)	..	182.6	206.1	252.0	244.3	360.3	412.3	480.4	723.3	910.0	886.5
Long-Term Debt (by debtor)	..	182.6	206.1	252.0	244.3	360.3	412.3	480.4	507.3	581.0	608.5
Central Bank, incl. IMF credit	..	24.9	29.9	31.5	12.2	94.2	73.4	53.0	52.5	66.0	83.0
Central Government	..	34.4	38.9	53.6	60.7	62.4	68.8	83.8	104.2	147.9	200.1
Rest of General Government	..	..	..	..	..	..	..	..	..	..	..
Non-financial Public Enterprises	..	32.0	31.9	30.5	30.8	38.0	71.6	136.2	99.8	103.2	108.0
Priv. Sector, incl non-guaranteed	..	91.3	105.4	136.4	140.6	165.7	198.5	207.4	250.8	263.9	217.4
Short-Term Debt	..	0.0	0.0	0.0	0.0	0.0	0.0	0.0	216.0	329.0	278.0
Memo Items:					*(Millions of US dollars)*						
Int'l Reserves Excluding Gold	46.5	45.4	46.2	63.9	41.3	77.6	107.0	185.4	211.3	268.1	142.6
Gold Holdings (at market price)	17.4	18.5	21.5	31.5	54.5	90.6	68.1	65.5	82.6	113.2	260.2
SOCIAL INDICATORS											
Total Fertility Rate	6.4	6.3	6.2	6.1	6.0	5.9	5.9	5.8	5.7	5.6	5.5
Infant Mortality Rate	106.0	103.0	100.0	97.0	94.0	91.0	88.0	85.0	82.0	79.6	77.2
Life Expectancy at Birth	57.1	57.6	58.2	58.7	58.5	58.2	57.9	57.7	57.4	57.4	57.3
Urban Population, % of total	39.3	39.4	39.6	39.8	40.0	40.2	40.4	40.6	40.8	41.1	41.3
Food Prod. per capita (1987=100)	93.1	101.5	102.8	93.6	106.1	103.6	114.7	114.3	110.1	120.4	121.2
Labor Force, Agriculture (%)	56.5	56.0	54.5	53.1	51.8	50.6	49.4	48.0	46.7	45.5	44.3
Labor Force, Female (%)	20.1	20.4	20.9	21.4	21.8	22.2	22.6	23.1	23.6	24.1	24.5
Primary Schl. Enroll. Ratio	..	85.0	..	..	..	..	75.0	..	76.0	78.0	79.0
Primary Schl. Enroll. Ratio, Female	..	83.0	..	..	..	..	74.0	..	76.0	77.0	79.0
Secondary Schl. Enroll. Ratio	..	22.0	..	..	..	..	19.0	21.0	23.0	25.0	26.0

1980	1981	1982	1983	1984	1985	1986	1987	1988	1989 estimate	NOTES	EL SALVADOR
				(Millions of current US dollars)							**FOREIGN TRADE (CUSTOMS BASIS)**
1,074.0	797.0	699.0	736.0	725.4	679.0	756.6	634.0	648.0	..	..	Value of Exports, fob
799.1	594.5	524.2	553.8	544.8	490.7	577.7	433.6	454.5	..	..	Nonfuel Primary Products
20.1	21.3	12.4	14.2	13.4	13.9	4.4	5.7	5.0	..	..	Fuels
254.7	181.2	162.3	168.0	167.2	174.4	174.4	194.7	188.5	..	..	Manufactures
975.9	1,044.5	944.8	892.0	977.4	961.4	935.0	975.0	1,051.6	..	..	Value of Imports, cif
210.2	214.2	200.1	188.0	177.6	167.8	172.9	158.9	202.5	..	..	Nonfuel Primary Products
173.2	218.0	232.5	206.7	156.7	146.4	56.5	79.2	87.9	..	..	Fuels
592.5	612.3	512.3	497.3	643.1	647.2	705.6	736.9	761.3	..	..	Manufactures
				(Index 1987 = 100)							
126.8	108.9	111.3	112.3	126.3	123.3	147.3	100.0	108.9	..	..	Terms of Trade
120.3	106.5	108.0	105.0	109.1	105.5	134.1	100.0	115.0	..	..	Export Prices, fob
94.9	97.7	97.1	93.5	86.4	85.6	91.1	100.0	105.6	..	..	Import Prices, cif
				(Millions of current US dollars)							**BALANCE OF PAYMENTS**
1,270.8	970.2	867.8	930.8	954.2	951.4	1,055.9	950.7	962.8	802.1	f	Exports of Goods & Services
1,075.3	798.0	699.6	758.0	725.9	679.0	777.9	589.6	610.6	496.0	f	Merchandise, fob
140.1	126.4	118.5	137.8	167.7	226.7	245.2	320.2	331.5	264.0	f	Nonfactor Services
55.4	45.8	49.8	35.0	60.6	45.7	32.7	40.9	20.6	41.1	f	Factor Services
1,289.1	1,281.0	1,195.0	1,230.3	1,315.3	1,323.6	1,322.3	1,353.7	1,437.6	1,503.0	f	Imports of Goods & Services
897.0	898.4	799.8	832.2	914.5	895.0	902.3	938.7	966.5	1,160.0	f	Merchandise, fob
273.5	262.6	250.3	242.0	238.9	289.4	278.7	278.5	338.0	202.0	f	Nonfactor Services
118.6	120.0	144.9	156.0	161.9	139.3	141.3	136.5	133.0	143.0	f	Factor Services
35.5	38.9	43.7	67.4	74.3	75.5	74.1	76.2	66.3	57.8	..	Long-Term Interest
17.4	39.2	88.4	97.4	118.0	129.4	149.6	180.5	202.1	242.0	..	Private Current Transfers, net
10.9	42.2	77.7	92.5	114.2	126.2	138.6	167.4	194.4	242.0	..	Workers' Remittances
-1.0	-271.6	-238.8	-202.1	-243.1	-242.9	-116.9	-222.6	-272.7	-463.0	..	Curr. A/C Bal before Off. Transf.
31.6	21.2	119.0	174.1	189.6	214.2	233.7	358.4	298.5	277.0	f	Net Official Transfers
30.6	-250.4	-119.8	-28.0	-53.5	-28.7	116.9	135.8	25.8	-186.0	..	Curr. A/C Bal after Off. Transf.
148.4	185.5	189.3	316.7	83.8	99.4	66.1	-36.7	29.2	66.8	..	Long-Term Capital, net
5.9	-5.7	-1.0	28.1	12.4	12.4	24.1	18.3	17.0	..	f	Direct Investment
74.4	198.4	228.8	227.4	127.4	57.9	-2.4	7.8	29.8	83.5	f	Long-Term Loans
109.5	236.0	283.4	334.9	256.8	194.3	131.1	125.0	143.8	185.6	..	Disbursements
35.1	37.6	54.6	107.5	129.4	136.4	133.5	117.2	114.0	102.1	..	Repayments
68.2	-7.2	-38.5	61.2	-55.9	29.1	44.4	-62.8	-17.6	-16.7	..	Other Long-Term Capital
-259.9	-19.2	-62.1	-259.5	-37.2	-49.7	-124.5	-20.9	-79.8	239.8	..	Other Capital, net
80.9	84.2	-7.4	-29.3	6.9	-21.0	-58.4	-78.2	24.8	-120.6	..	Change in Reserves
				(Salvadoran Colones per US dollar)							**Memo Item:**
2.500	2.500	2.570	2.730	2.820	3.670	5.000	5.000	5.000	5.500	..	Conversion Factor (Annual Avg)
				(Millions of US dollars), outstanding at end of year							
911.0	1,127.0	1,418.9	1,673.0	1,730.0	1,757.1	1,712.9	1,751.9	1,760.4	1,850.5	..	**EXTERNAL DEBT (Total)**
691.0	915.0	1,212.9	1,579.0	1,628.0	1,672.9	1,619.3	1,658.3	1,641.1	1,701.7	..	Long-Term Debt (by debtor)
133.0	237.4	359.2	570.3	567.8	496.5	394.7	333.8	262.7	211.3	..	Central Bank, incl. IMF credit
254.7	383.2	541.4	704.3	802.0	910.7	972.4	1,061.2	1,140.8	1,283.4	..	Central Government
..	..	..	..	..	..	..	..	..	..	..	Rest of General Government
125.0	127.6	158.1	160.4	120.6	129.4	124.1	138.1	128.7	115.6	..	Non-financial Public Enterprises
178.3	166.8	154.2	144.0	137.4	136.3	128.1	125.2	108.9	91.4	..	Priv. Sector, incl non-guaranteed
220.0	212.0	206.0	94.0	102.0	84.2	93.6	93.6	119.3	148.8	..	Short-Term Debt
				(Millions of US dollars)							**Memo Items:**
77.7	71.9	108.5	160.2	165.8	179.6	169.7	186.1	161.6	265.9	..	Int'l Reserves Excluding Gold
304.0	205.0	235.6	178.8	144.7	153.4	183.4	227.1	192.5	188.2	..	Gold Holdings (at market price)
											SOCIAL INDICATORS
5.4	5.3	5.2	5.1	5.1	5.0	4.9	4.9	4.8	4.7	..	Total Fertility Rate
74.8	72.4	70.0	67.8	65.6	63.4	61.2	59.0	57.3	55.6	..	Infant Mortality Rate
57.3	57.2	57.2	58.2	59.2	60.2	61.2	62.2	62.6	62.9	..	Life Expectancy at Birth
41.5	41.7	42.0	42.2	42.5	42.7	43.0	43.4	43.7	44.1	..	Urban Population, % of total
115.3	104.4	94.6	95.7	108.2	106.4	108.1	100.0	108.5	98.5	..	Food Prod. per capita (1987=100)
43.2	..	..	..	..	..	..	..	..	..	..	Labor Force, Agriculture (%)
24.9	24.9	25.0	25.0	25.0	25.1	25.1	25.1	25.1	25.1	..	Labor Force, Female (%)
75.0	..	..	73.0	74.0	..	..	79.0	..	..	..	Primary Schl. Enroll. Ratio
75.0	..	..	73.0	75.0	..	..	81.0	..	..	..	Primary Schl. Enroll. Ratio, Female
24.0	..	23.0	26.0	27.0	..	..	29.0	..	..	..	Secondary Schl. Enroll. Ratio

EQUATORIAL GUINEA	1969	1970	1971	1972	1973	1974	1975	1976	1977	1978	1979
CURRENT GNP PER CAPITA (US $)	..	..	..	..	..	..	..	..	..	..	..
POPULATION (thousands)	285	291	276	261	247	235	226	216	211	209	212
USE AND ORIGIN OF RESOURCES					*(Millions of current CFA Francs)*						
Gross National Product (GNP)	4,706	4,680	4,541	4,194	4,743	5,453	6,010	6,961	7,929	..	..
Net Factor Income from Abroad	0	37	29	-11	12	21	23	27	30	..	..
GDP at Market Prices	4,706	4,643	4,512	4,205	4,731	5,432	5,987	6,935	7,899	..	..
Resource Balance	747	-436	-137	-403	-720	-896	-469	-380	-447	..	..
Exports of Goods & NFServices	1,699	1,658	2,096	1,463	1,814	2,300	2,573	3,259	3,713	..	..
Imports of Goods & NFServices	952	2,094	2,233	1,866	2,533	3,196	3,042	3,640	4,161	..	..
Domestic Absorption	3,959	5,079	4,648	4,608	5,450	6,328	6,456	7,315	8,346	..	..
Private Consumption, etc.	2,663	3,125	2,693	2,679	3,397	4,108	3,927	4,414	5,000	..	..
General Gov't Consumption	980	1,031	1,035	1,053	1,201	1,316	1,632	1,988	2,281	..	..
Gross Domestic Investment	316	923	920	876	853	904	897	913	1,065	..	..
Fixed Investment	..	..	..	..	..	..	..	..	..	..	..
Indirect Taxes, net	365	350	338	315	355	490	..	..	..	..	..
GDP at factor cost	4,341	4,293	4,174	3,890	4,376	4,942	..	..	..	..	..
Agriculture	..	..	..	..	..	..	..	..	..	..	..
Industry	..	..	..	..	..	..	..	..	..	..	..
Manufacturing	..	..	..	..	..	..	..	..	..	..	..
Services, etc.	..	..	..	..	..	..	..	..	..	..	..
Gross Domestic Saving	1,063	487	783	473	134	7	428	533	618	..	..
Gross National Saving	..	386	712	373	137	..	..	..	..	..	..
					..						
Gross National Product	..	..	..	..	..	..	..	..	..	..	..
GDP at Market Prices	..	..	..	..	..	..	..	..	..	..	..
Resource Balance	..	..	..	..	..	..	..	..	..	..	..
Exports of Goods & NFServices	..	..	..	..	..	..	..	..	..	..	..
Imports of Goods & NFServices	..	..	..	..	..	..	..	..	..	..	..
Domestic Absorption	..	..	..	..	..	..	..	..	..	..	..
Private Consumption, etc.	..	..	..	..	..	..	..	..	..	..	..
General Gov't Consumption	..	..	..	..	..	..	..	..	..	..	..
Gross Domestic Investment	..	..	..	..	..	..	..	..	..	..	..
Fixed Investment	..	..	..	..	..	..	..	..	..	..	..
GDP at factor cost	..	..	..	..	..	..	..	..	..	..	..
Agriculture	..	..	..	..	..	..	..	..	..	..	..
Industry	..	..	..	..	..	..	..	..	..	..	..
Manufacturing	..	..	..	..	..	..	..	..	..	..	..
Services, etc.	..	..	..	..	..	..	..	..	..	..	..
Memo Items:											
Capacity to Import	..	..	..	..	..	..	..	..	..	..	..
Terms of Trade Adjustment	..	..	..	..	..	..	..	..	..	..	..
Gross Domestic Income	..	..	..	..	..	..	..	..	..	..	..
Gross National Income	..	..	..	..	..	..	..	..	..	..	..
DOMESTIC PRICES/DEFLATORS					*(Index 1987 = 100)*						
Overall (GDP)	..	..	..	..	..	..	..	..	..	..	..
Domestic Absorption	..	..	..	..	..	..	..	..	..	..	..
Agriculture	..	..	..	..	..	..	..	..	..	..	..
Industry	..	..	..	..	..	..	..	..	..	..	..
Manufacturing	..	..	..	..	..	..	..	..	..	..	..
Consumer Price Index	..	..	..	..	..	..	..	..	..	..	..
MANUFACTURING ACTIVITY											
Employment (1987=100)	..	..	..	..	..	..	..	..	..	..	..
Real Earnings per Empl. (1987=100)	..	..	..	..	..	..	..	..	..	..	..
Real Output per Empl. (1987=100)	..	..	..	..	..	..	..	..	..	..	..
Earnings as % of Value Added	..	..	..	..	..	..	..	..	..	..	..
MONETARY HOLDINGS					*(Millions of current CFA Francs)*						
Money Supply, Broadly Defined	..	..	..	..	..	..	..	..	..	..	..
Money	..	..	..	..	..	..	..	..	..	..	..
Currency Outside Banks	..	..	..	..	..	..	..	..	..	..	..
Demand Deposits	..	..	..	..	..	..	..	..	..	..	..
Quasi-Money	..	..	..	..	..	..	..	..	..	..	..
					(Millions of current CFA Francs)						
GOVERNMENT DEFICIT (-) OR SURPLUS	..	..	..	..	..	..	..	..	..	..	..
Current Revenue	..	..	..	..	..	..	..	..	..	..	..
Current Expenditure	..	..	..	..	..	..	..	..	..	..	..
Current Budget Balance	..	..	..	..	..	..	..	..	..	..	..
Capital Receipts	..	..	..	..	..	..	..	..	..	..	..
Capital Payments	..	..	..	..	..	..	..	..	..	..	..

1980	1981	1982	1983	1984	1985	1986	1987	1988	1989 estimate	NOTES	EQUATORIAL GUINEA
..	..	..	..	..	..	..	310	390	390	..	**CURRENT GNP PER CAPITA (US $)**
219	238	257	276	296	315	322	329	336	344	..	**POPULATION (thousands)**
				(Millions of current CFA Francs)							**USE AND ORIGIN OF RESOURCES**
..	..	..	..	..	34,531	35,272	36,879	39,741	39,793	..	Gross National Product (GNP)
..	..	..	..	..	-1,887	-1,316	-1,623	-2,323	-2,201	..	Net Factor Income from Abroad
..	..	..	..	..	36,418	36,588	38,502	42,064	41,994	..	GDP at Market Prices
..	..	-7,910	-2,869	-7,166	-1,093	-5,122	-12,834	-15,522	-14,550	..	Resource Balance
..	..	3,296	5,163	9,438	10,561	8,781	10,662	10,287	9,250	..	Exports of Goods & NFServices
..	..	11,206	8,032	16,604	11,654	13,903	23,496	25,809	23,800	..	Imports of Goods & NFServices
..	..	..	..	..	37,511	41,710	51,336	57,586	56,544	..	Domestic Absorption
..	..	..	..	..	22,944	23,416	29,776	31,927	33,447	..	Private Consumption, etc.
..	..	..	..	..	9,833	10,976	9,240	13,881	13,858	..	General Gov't Consumption
..	..	..	..	..	4,734	7,318	12,320	11,778	9,239	..	Gross Domestic Investment
..	..	..	..	..	4,734	7,318	12,320	11,778	9,239	..	Fixed Investment
..	..	..	..	..	2,328	2,064	1,877	1,929	2,174	..	Indirect Taxes, net
..	..	..	..	..	34,090	34,524	36,625	40,135	39,820	..	GDP at factor cost
..	..	..	..	..	20,675	20,735	21,332	20,997	21,562	..	Agriculture
..	..	..	..	..	3,505	2,256	2,934	3,605	2,949	..	Industry
..	..	..	..	..	..	..	..	..	..	..	Manufacturing
..	..	..	..	..	12,238	13,597	14,236	17,462	17,483	..	Services, etc.
..	..	..	..	..	3,641	2,196	-514	-3,744	-5,311	..	Gross Domestic Saving
..	..	..	..	..	1,754	1,261	-2,888	-7,199	-8,022	..	Gross National Saving
..	..	..	..	..	35,302.3	35,468.8	36,879.0	39,594.0	40,018.5	..	Gross National Product
..	..	..	..	..	36,915.3	36,939.8	38,502.0	41,781.5	41,966.8	..	GDP at Market Prices
..	..	..	..	..	-7,099.0	-12,256.0	-12,834.0	-15,505.0	-11,060.0	..	Resource Balance
..	..	..	..	..	12,567.4	10,556.2	10,662.0	10,342.2	8,583.5	..	Exports of Goods & NFServices
..	..	..	..	..	19,666.4	22,811.8	23,496.0	25,847.2	19,643.4	..	Imports of Goods & NFServices
..	..	..	..	..	44,014.3	49,195.4	51,336.0	57,286.5	53,026.8	..	Domestic Absorption
..	..	..	..	..	28,784.1	31,155.3	29,776.0	31,322.5	29,309.1	..	Private Consumption, etc.
..	..	..	..	..	10,091.8	10,999.8	9,240.0	14,137.6	14,137.6	..	General Gov't Consumption
..	..	..	..	..	5,138.3	7,040.3	12,320.0	11,826.5	9,580.1	..	Gross Domestic Investment
..	..	..	..	..	5,138.3	7,040.3	12,320.0	11,826.5	9,580.1	..	Fixed Investment
..	..	..	..	..	34,597.5	34,876.9	36,625.0	40,260.3	40,658.5	..	GDP at factor cost
..	..	..	..	..	20,710.7	20,710.7	21,332.0	20,905.5	21,532.8	..	Agriculture
..	..	..	..	..	1,910.3	1,830.0	2,934.0	4,270.0	3,539.9	..	Industry
..	..	..	..	..	..	..	..	..	..	..	Manufacturing
..	..	..	..	..	14,294.2	14,399.1	14,236.0	16,606.0	16,894.1	..	Services, etc.
											Memo Items:
..	..	..	..	..	17,821.9	14,407.7	10,662.0	10,302.2	7,634.5	..	Capacity to Import
..	..	..	..	..	5,254.5	3,851.5	0.0	-40.0	-948.9	..	Terms of Trade Adjustment
..	..	..	..	..	42,169.8	40,791.3	38,502.0	41,741.5	41,017.9	..	Gross Domestic Income
..	..	..	..	..	40,556.9	39,320.3	36,879.0	39,554.1	39,069.6	..	Gross National Income
				(Index 1987 = 100)							**DOMESTIC PRICES/DEFLATORS**
..	..	..	..	..	98.7	99.0	100.0	100.7	100.1	..	Overall (GDP)
..	..	..	..	..	85.2	84.8	100.0	100.5	106.6	..	Domestic Absorption
..	..	..	..	..	99.8	100.1	100.0	100.4	100.1	..	Agriculture
..	..	..	..	..	183.5	123.3	100.0	84.4	83.3	..	Industry
..	..	..	..	..	..	..	..	..	..	..	Manufacturing
..	..	..	..	..	139.6	114.8	100.0	102.3	108.4	..	Consumer Price Index
											MANUFACTURING ACTIVITY
..	..	..	..	..	..	..	..	..	..	..	Employment (1987=100)
..	..	..	..	..	..	..	..	..	..	..	Real Earnings per Empl. (1987=100)
..	..	..	..	..	..	..	..	..	..	..	Real Output per Empl. (1987=100)
..	..	..	..	..	..	..	..	..	..	..	Earnings as % of Value Added
				(Millions of current CFA Francs)							**MONETARY HOLDINGS**
..	..	..	..	..	8,972.0	10,539.0	9,434.0	6,175.0	..	..	Money Supply, Broadly Defined
..	..	..	..	..	8,047.0	9,919.0	9,004.0	5,629.0	..	..	Money
..	..	..	..	..	5,239.0	7,475.0	6,687.0	2,478.0	..	..	Currency Outside Banks
..	..	..	..	..	2,808.0	2,444.0	2,317.0	3,151.0	..	..	Demand Deposits
..	..	..	..	..	925.0	620.0	430.0	546.0	..	..	Quasi-Money
				(Millions of current CFA Francs)							**GOVERNMENT DEFICIT (-) OR SURPLUS**
..	..	..	..	..	..	..	..	..	..	..	Current Revenue
..	..	..	..	..	..	..	..	..	..	..	Current Expenditure
..	..	..	..	..	..	..	..	..	..	..	Current Budget Balance
..	..	..	..	..	..	..	..	..	..	..	Capital Receipts
..	..	..	..	..	..	..	..	..	..	..	Capital Payments

EQUATORIAL GUINEA	1969	1970	1971	1972	1973	1974	1975	1976	1977	1978	1979
FOREIGN TRADE (CUSTOMS BASIS)					*(Thousands of current US dollars)*						
Value of Exports, fob	..	..	..	..	..	..	..	..	..	..	..
Nonfuel Primary Products	..	..	..	..	..	..	..	..	..	..	..
Fuels	..	..	..	..	..	..	..	..	..	..	..
Manufactures	..	..	..	..	..	..	..	..	..	..	..
Value of Imports, cif	..	..	..	..	..	..	..	..	..	..	..
Nonfuel Primary Products	..	..	..	..	..	..	..	..	..	..	..
Fuels	..	..	..	..	..	..	..	..	..	..	..
Manufactures	..	..	..	..	..	..	..	..	..	..	..
					(Index 1987 = 100)						
Terms of Trade	..	..	..	..	..	..	..	..	..	..	..
Export Prices, fob	..	..	..	..	..	..	..	..	..	..	..
Import Prices, cif	..	..	..	..	..	..	..	..	..	..	..
BALANCE OF PAYMENTS					*(Thousands of current US dollars)*						
Exports of Goods & Services	..	27.0	31.0	23.0	22.0	37.0	..	..	..	..	..
Merchandise, fob	..	25.0	28.0	19.0	19.0	34.0	..	..	..	..	..
Nonfactor Services	..	1.0	2.0	3.0	3.0	2.0	..	..	..	..	..
Factor Services	..	1.0	1.0	0.0	0.0	1.0	..	..	..	..	..
Imports of Goods & Services	..	31.0	32.0	29.0	..	21.0	..	..	..	..	..
Merchandise, fob	..	21.0	25.0	24.0	18.0	14.0	..	..	..	..	..
Nonfactor Services	..	9.0	7.0	5.0	5.0	6.0	..	..	..	..	..
Factor Services	..	1.0	0.0	1.0	..	1.0	..	..	..	..	..
Long-Term Interest	..	0.0	0.0	0.0	0.0	0.0	0.0	0.0	0.0	0.0	0.0
Private Current Transfers, net	..	-2.0	-1.0	-1.0	0.0	..	..	..	..	..	..
Workers' Remittances	..	..	..	..	..	..	..	..	..	..	..
Curr. A/C Bal before Off. Transf.	..	-6.0	-3.0	-8.0	-1.0	16.0	..	..	..	..	..
Net Official Transfers	..	..	1.0	0.0	0.0	..	..	..	..	..	..
Curr. A/C Bal after Off. Transf.	..	-6.0	-2.0	-8.0	-1.0	16.0	..	..	..	..	..
Long-Term Capital, net	..	2.0	2.0	4.0	1.0	1.0	..	..	..	..	..
Direct Investment	..	..	..	..	..	..	..	..	..	..	..
Long-Term Loans	..	0.0	4.0	5.0	5.0	4.0	1.0	2.0	2.0	-1.0	1.0
Disbursements	..	0.0	4.0	5.0	5.0	4.0	1.0	2.0	3.0	0.0	2.0
Repayments	..	0.0	0.0	0.0	0.0	0.0	0.0	0.0	1.0	1.0	1.0
Other Long-Term Capital	..	2.0	-2.0	0.0	-4.0	-3.0	..	..	..	..	..
Other Capital, net	..	6.0	-3.0	-3.0	7.0	-6.0	..	..	..	..	..
Change in Reserves	..	-2.0	3.0	7.0	-6.0	-11.0	0.0	-2.0	2.0	0.0	2.0
Memo Item:					*(CFA Francs per US dollar)*						
Conversion Factor (Annual Avg)	70.000	70.000	69.550	64.290	58.270	57.700	57.510	66.890	75.890	76.660	67.130
				(Millions of US dollars), outstanding at end of year							
EXTERNAL DEBT (Total)	..	5.0	9.1	13.9	19.8	25.8	25.2	28.4	49.4	39.2	40.6
Long-Term Debt (by debtor)	..	5.0	9.1	13.9	19.8	25.8	25.2	28.4	34.4	37.2	38.6
Central Bank, incl. IMF credit	..	5.0	5.0	5.0	5.0	5.0	5.0	5.0	7.1	7.2	7.0
Central Government	..	0.0	4.1	8.9	14.8	20.8	20.2	23.4	27.3	30.0	31.6
Rest of General Government	..	..	..	..	..	..	..	..	..	..	..
Non-financial Public Enterprises	..	..	..	..	..	..	..	..	..	..	..
Priv. Sector, incl non-guaranteed	..	0.0	0.0	0.0	0.0	0.0	0.0	0.0	0.0	0.0	0.0
Short-Term Debt	..	0.0	0.0	0.0	0.0	0.0	0.0	0.0	15.0	2.0	2.0
Memo Items:					*(Thousands of US dollars)*						
Int'l Reserves Excluding Gold	..	..	..	..	..	..	..	..	..	..	..
Gold Holdings (at market price)	..	..	..	..	..	..	..	..	..	..	..
SOCIAL INDICATORS											
Total Fertility Rate	5.0	5.0	5.0	5.0	5.0	5.0	5.0	5.0	5.0	5.0	5.0
Infant Mortality Rate	167.8	165.2	162.6	160.0	157.8	155.6	153.4	151.2	149.0	146.6	144.2
Life Expectancy at Birth	39.2	39.5	39.8	40.2	40.5	40.9	41.2	41.5	41.9	42.2	42.5
Urban Population, % of total	37.6	39.0	40.5	42.0	43.6	45.1	46.6	48.0	49.4	50.9	52.3
Food Prod. per capita (1987=100)	..	..	..	..	..	..	..	..	..	..	..
Labor Force, Agriculture (%)	75.7	75.0	74.1	73.1	72.2	71.3	70.5	69.5	68.5	67.6	66.7
Labor Force, Female (%)	41.8	41.8	41.8	41.7	41.7	41.6	41.6	41.5	41.5	41.4	41.3
Primary Schl. Enroll. Ratio	..	76.0	..	..	78.0	..	..	..	..	..	..
Primary Schl. Enroll. Ratio, Female	..	67.0	..	..	69.0	..	..	..	..	..	..
Secondary Schl. Enroll. Ratio	..	16.0	..	..	..	..	11.0	..	..	..	..

1980	1981	1982	1983	1984	1985	1986	1987	1988	1989 estimate	NOTES	EQUATORIAL GUINEA
				(Thousands of current US dollars)							**FOREIGN TRADE (CUSTOMS BASIS)**
14,700.0	15,700.0	15,000.0	18,000.0	21,000.0	24,000.0	26,000.0	29,000.0	32,000.0	..	..	Value of Exports, fob
..	..	..	..	..	..	..	..	..	..	..	Nonfuel Primary Products
..	..	..	..	..	..	..	..	..	..	..	Fuels
..	..	..	..	..	..	..	..	..	..	..	Manufactures
58,000.0	48,700.0	50,000.0	27,000.0	36,000.0	32,000.0	34,000.0	41,000.0	41,000.0	..	..	Value of Imports, cif
..	..	..	..	..	..	..	..	..	..	..	Nonfuel Primary Products
..	..	..	..	..	..	..	..	..	..	..	Fuels
..	..	..	..	..	..	..	..	..	..	..	Manufactures
				(Index 1987 = 100)							
..	..	..	..	..	..	..	..	..	..	..	Terms of Trade
..	..	..	..	..	..	..	..	..	..	..	Export Prices, fob
..	..	..	..	..	..	..	..	..	..	..	Import Prices, cif
				(Thousands of current US dollars)							**BALANCE OF PAYMENTS**
..	..	..	18.0	22.0	25.0	29.0	37.0	37.0	32.0	..	Exports of Goods & Services
15.0	16.0	15.0	18.0	21.0	24.0	26.0	29.0	29.0	23.0	..	Merchandise, fob
0.0	0.0	0.0	0.0	0.0	0.0	1.0	6.0	6.0	6.0	..	Nonfactor Services
..	..	..	0.0	0.0	0.0	2.0	2.0	2.0	2.0	..	Factor Services
..	..	..	33.0	37.0	35.0	55.0	77.0	87.0	76.0	..	Imports of Goods & Services
58.0	49.0	50.0	27.0	36.0	25.0	27.0	36.0	39.0	32.0	..	Merchandise, fob
0.0	0.0	0.0	0.0	0.0	6.0	22.0	33.0	38.0	35.0	..	Nonfactor Services
..	..	..	6.0	1.0	4.0	6.0	8.0	10.0	9.0	..	Factor Services
0.0	0.0	0.0	0.0	0.0	1.0	1.0	3.0	2.0	0.0	..	Long-Term Interest
..	..	0.0	0.0	0.0	0.0	1.0	-3.0	-4.0	-2.0	..	Private Current Transfers, net
..	..	..	..	..	..	..	..	..	..	..	Workers' Remittances
-43.0	-33.0	-35.0	-15.0	-16.0	-11.0	-26.0	-42.0	-54.0	-46.0	..	Curr. A/C Bal before Off. Transf.
..	..	5.0	6.0	7.0	9.0	22.0	27.0	48.0	38.0	..	Net Official Transfers
-43.0	-33.0	-30.0	-9.0	-8.0	-2.0	-4.0	-15.0	-6.0	-8.0	..	Curr. A/C Bal after Off. Transf.
24.0	16.0	30.0	8.0	0.0	1.0	3.0	14.0	15.0	16.0	..	Long-Term Capital, net
..	..	..	..	..	0.0	0.0	0.0	0.0	..	..	Direct Investment
18.0	16.0	30.0	8.0	0.0	8.0	18.0	18.0	20.0	19.0	..	Long-Term Loans
20.0	20.0	33.0	9.0	1.0	9.0	20.0	24.0	22.0	19.0	..	Disbursements
2.0	4.0	3.0	2.0	1.0	1.0	1.0	7.0	1.0	..	..	Repayments
6.0	0.0	0.0	0.0	0.0	-7.0	-16.0	-3.0	-5.0	-3.0	..	Other Long-Term Capital
6.0	9.0	1.0	0.0	15.0	5.0	2.0	-1.0	-9.0	-8.0	..	Other Capital, net
13.0	9.0	0.0	2.0	-6.0	-3.0	-1.0	2.0	0.0	0.0	..	Change in Reserves
				(CFA Francs per US dollar)							**Memo Item:**
108.880	184.600	219.720	286.860	321.520	449.260	346.300	300.540	297.850	319.010	..	Conversion Factor (Annual Avg)
				(Millions of US dollars), outstanding at end of year							
75.6	92.4	116.9	122.4	116.4	132.2	158.5	195.7	210.6	227.8	..	**EXTERNAL DEBT (Total)**
68.6	85.0	106.3	110.1	93.2	125.7	150.4	184.7	198.7	212.9	..	Long-Term Debt (by debtor)
21.1	27.4	32.5	36.4	28.1	21.7	19.9	21.6	24.1	18.8	..	Central Bank, incl. IMF credit
35.6	37.7	54.1	56.7	49.3	98.9	124.6	156.0	167.8	191.9	..	Central Government
..	..	..	..	..	..	..	..	..	..	..	Rest of General Government
..	..	..	..	..	..	..	..	..	..	..	Non-financial Public Enterprises
11.9	19.9	19.7	17.0	15.8	5.1	5.9	7.1	6.8	2.2	..	Priv. Sector, incl non-guaranteed
7.0	7.4	10.6	12.3	23.2	6.5	8.1	11.0	11.9	14.9	..	Short-Term Debt
				(Thousands of US dollars)							**Memo Items:**
..	..	2,773.6	1,300.0	1,381.0	3,465.5	2,676.4	568.6	5,031.3	828.3	..	Int'l Reserves Excluding Gold
..	..	..	..	..	..	..	..	..	..	..	Gold Holdings (at market price)
											SOCIAL INDICATORS
5.0	5.0	5.0	5.1	5.2	5.3	5.4	5.5	5.5	5.5	..	Total Fertility Rate
141.8	139.4	137.0	135.0	133.0	131.0	129.0	127.0	125.0	123.0	..	Infant Mortality Rate
42.9	43.2	43.5	43.9	44.3	44.7	45.1	45.5	45.9	46.3	..	Life Expectancy at Birth
53.7	54.9	56.1	57.3	58.5	59.7	60.9	62.1	62.9	63.7	..	Urban Population, % of total
..	..	..	..	..	..	..	..	..	..	..	Food Prod. per capita (1987=100)
65.8	..	..	..	..	..	..	..	..	..	..	Labor Force, Agriculture (%)
41.3	41.2	41.0	40.9	40.8	40.6	40.5	40.4	40.2	40.1	..	Labor Force, Female (%)
84.0	84.0	94.0	108.0							..	Primary Schl. Enroll. Ratio
..	..	..	..	..	..	..	..	..	..	..	Primary Schl. Enroll. Ratio, Female
..	..	9.0	..	..	..	..	..	..	..	..	Secondary Schl. Enroll. Ratio

ETHIOPIA	1969	1970	1971	1972	1973	1974	1975	1976	1977	1978	1979
CURRENT GNP PER CAPITA (US $)	60	60	70	70	70	80	90	90	90	100	110
POPULATION (thousands)	28,190	28,937	29,704	30,493	31,300	32,122	32,954	33,824	34,733	35,683	36,677

USE AND ORIGIN OF RESOURCES *(Millions of current Ethiopian Birr)*

	1969	1970	1971	1972	1973	1974	1975	1976	1977	1978	1979
Gross National Product (GNP)	4,030	4,441	4,691	4,712	4,955	5,513	5,516	5,993	6,851	7,295	7,982
Net Factor Income from Abroad	-26	-20	-19	-32	-50	-39	-35	-3	-4	0	-5
GDP at Market Prices	4,056	4,461	4,710	4,744	5,005	5,551	5,551	5,996	6,855	7,295	7,987
Resource Balance	-87	-14	-88	-93	101	189	-164	-58	-216	-405	-425
Exports of Goods & NFServices	400	489	468	487	653	827	683	760	840	866	943
Imports of Goods & NFServices	487	504	556	580	552	638	847	818	1,056	1,271	1,368
Domestic Absorption	4,143	4,475	4,798	4,837	4,905	5,362	5,715	6,054	7,071	7,700	8,413
Private Consumption, etc.	3,188	3,519	3,783	3,726	3,798	4,227	4,405	4,610	5,497	5,915	6,546
General Gov't Consumption	411	443	461	508	538	586	730	866	968	1,240	1,168
Gross Domestic Investment	544	512	554	603	569	549	580	578	606	545	699
Fixed Investment	533	512	554	603	569	549	580	578	606	545	699
Indirect Taxes, net	237	288	301	327	376	410	421	474	690	749	901
GDP at factor cost	3,819	4,173	4,409	4,417	4,629	5,141	5,130	5,522	6,164	6,546	7,086
Agriculture	2,120	2,327	2,405	2,286	2,331	2,605	2,450	2,768	3,227	3,497	3,656
Industry	588	602	672	707	748	796	855	824	892	894	1,046
Manufacturing	337	372	420	440	464	508	569	586	636	636	758
Services, etc.	1,112	1,244	1,333	1,424	1,550	1,739	1,825	1,930	2,046	2,154	2,383
Gross Domestic Saving	457	498	467	510	670	739	416	520	390	140	274
Gross National Saving	..	472	443	485	644	738	411	561	420	171	317

(Millions of 1980 Ethiopian Birr)

	1969	1970	1971	1972	1973	1974	1975	1976	1977	1978	1979
Gross National Product	5,971.5	6,365.9	6,633.9	6,952.6	7,150.9	7,264.4	7,282.2	7,525.1	7,729.7	7,648.7	8,136.2
GDP at Market Prices	6,009.6	6,395.2	6,661.6	6,999.6	7,223.9	7,315.9	7,328.3	7,528.5	7,734.0	7,649.0	8,141.5
Resource Balance	-154.7	-190.6	-182.3	-202.9	25.1	158.6	-184.7	-25.1	-225.1	-400.5	-376.5
Exports of Goods & NFServices	781.1	766.3	823.4	815.8	945.4	1,126.7	1,038.6	1,133.6	1,159.1	1,016.7	995.6
Imports of Goods & NFServices	935.8	956.9	1,005.7	1,018.7	920.2	968.1	1,223.3	1,158.7	1,384.2	1,417.2	1,372.1
Domestic Absorption	6,164.3	6,585.8	6,843.9	7,202.5	7,198.7	7,157.3	7,513.0	7,553.5	7,959.1	8,049.5	8,517.9
Private Consumption, etc.	4,677.7	5,163.5	5,350.3	5,493.7	5,534.2	5,601.7	5,709.7	5,447.5	5,828.1	6,116.8	6,582.3
General Gov't Consumption	603.0	630.3	648.1	746.5	774.4	770.8	968.6	1,092.7	1,096.4	1,304.8	1,190.4
Gross Domestic Investment	883.5	792.0	845.5	962.3	890.1	784.7	834.7	1,013.3	1,034.6	627.9	745.2
Fixed Investment	..	..	..	..	..	..	834.7	1,013.3	1,034.6	627.9	745.2
GDP at factor cost	5,649.8	5,971.7	6,223.1	6,502.0	6,663.5	6,757.0	6,749.9	6,909.8	6,925.1	6,832.9	7,219.2
Agriculture	3,361.0	3,439.6	3,509.0	3,633.8	3,660.0	3,639.9	3,569.6	3,667.7	3,654.9	3,607.9	3,694.9
Industry	778.6	871.7	955.0	997.7	1,027.0	1,019.7	1,005.0	966.5	978.7	947.2	1,085.9
Manufacturing	442.8	567.5	619.7	645.1	677.2	670.4	662.7	652.3	657.4	657.8	772.2
Services, etc.	1,510.2	1,660.5	1,759.2	1,870.6	1,976.5	2,097.4	2,175.3	2,275.6	2,291.4	2,277.8	2,438.4

Memo Items:

	1969	1970	1971	1972	1973	1974	1975	1976	1977	1978	1979
Capacity to Import	768.3	929.6	847.1	855.3	1,088.1	1,255.6	986.3	1,076.6	1,100.7	965.5	945.5
Terms of Trade Adjustment	-12.8	163.2	23.6	39.5	142.7	128.9	-52.4	-57.1	-58.4	-51.2	-50.1
Gross Domestic Income	5,996.8	6,558.5	6,685.2	7,039.2	7,366.6	7,444.8	7,276.0	7,471.4	7,675.6	7,597.8	8,091.3
Gross National Income	5,958.7	6,529.2	6,657.6	6,992.2	7,293.6	7,393.3	7,229.8	7,468.0	7,671.3	7,597.5	8,086.1

DOMESTIC PRICES/DEFLATORS *(Index 1980 = 100)*

	1969	1970	1971	1972	1973	1974	1975	1976	1977	1978	1979
Overall (GDP)	67.5	69.7	70.7	67.8	69.3	75.9	75.7	79.6	88.6	95.4	98.1
Domestic Absorption	67.2	67.9	70.1	67.2	68.1	74.9	76.1	80.1	88.8	95.7	98.8
Agriculture	63.1	67.7	68.5	62.9	63.7	71.6	68.6	75.5	88.3	96.9	99.0
Industry	75.5	69.0	70.3	70.8	72.9	78.1	85.1	85.3	91.1	94.4	96.4
Manufacturing	76.1	65.6	67.7	68.2	68.5	75.7	85.9	89.8	96.7	96.7	98.2
Consumer Price Index	29.0	31.9	32.1	30.1	32.8	35.6	38.0	48.8	56.9	65.0	75.5

MANUFACTURING ACTIVITY

	1969	1970	1971	1972	1973	1974	1975	1976	1977	1978	1979
Employment (1987=100)	51.6	52.4	54.2	56.3	57.8	60.5	63.3	62.3	65.7	69.3	78.6
Real Earnings per Empl. (1987=100)	140.3	132.3	139.5	152.4	148.2	143.8	139.1	122.0	114.0	102.4	92.3
Real Output per Empl. (1987=100)	39.7	53.4	56.9	60.7	65.0	65.1	55.7	60.4	57.8	55.4	70.6
Earnings as % of Value Added	26.8	23.8	24.0	23.5	23.6	23.3	21.7	23.0	25.3	25.3	20.6

MONETARY HOLDINGS *(Millions of current Ethiopian Birr)*

	1969	1970	1971	1972	1973	1974	1975	1976	1977	1978	1979
Money Supply, Broadly Defined	604.8	639.7	651.3	755.9	981.8	1,134.6	1,243.9	1,402.9	1,651.9	1,861.4	2,107.9
Money	454.8	453.2	436.7	490.7	618.5	753.9	942.1	953.0	1,178.7	1,378.2	1,571.9
Currency Outside Banks	319.1	323.2	303.8	339.5	403.8	532.9	689.0	574.6	769.4	894.7	1,012.4
Demand Deposits	135.7	130.0	132.9	151.2	214.7	221.0	253.1	378.4	409.3	483.5	559.5
Quasi-Money	150.1	186.5	214.6	265.2	363.3	380.7	301.8	449.9	473.2	483.2	536.0

(Millions of current Ethiopian Birr)

	1969	1970	1971	1972	1973	1974	1975	1976	1977	1978	1979
GOVERNMENT DEFICIT (-) OR SURPLUS	..	..	..	-64.2	-49.2	-43.8	-226.2	-325.1	-232.5	-421.9	-254.5
Current Revenue	..	..	..	586.2	651.1	716.2	804.8	853.2	1,093.6	1,252.8	1,601.3
Current Expenditure	..	..	..	545.2	581.2	646.9	848.1	966.7	1,090.9	1,405.6	1,595.7
Current Budget Balance	..	..	..	41.0	69.9	69.3	-43.3	-113.5	2.7	-152.8	5.6
Capital Receipts	..	..	..	0.8	1.6	1.4	1.7	1.9	2.7	3.3	3.3
Capital Payments	..	..	..	106.0	120.7	114.5	184.6	213.5	237.9	272.4	263.4

1980	1981	1982	1983	1984	1985	1986	1987	1988	1989 estimate	NOTES	ETHIOPIA
120	120	120	120	120	110	120	120	120	120	..	**CURRENT GNP PER CAPITA (US $)**
37,717	38,785	39,883	41,010	42,169	43,350	44,605	45,939	47,356	48,861	..	**POPULATION (thousands)**
											USE AND ORIGIN OF RESOURCES
				(Millions of current Ethiopian Birr)							
8,512	8,888	9,149	10,003	9,961	9,821	10,773	11,119	11,646	12,335	C	Gross National Product (GNP)
13	-15	-18	-28	-40	-68	-60	-77	-121	-156	..	Net Factor Income from Abroad
8,499	8,903	9,167	10,031	10,001	9,890	10,832	11,196	11,767	12,491	C	GDP at Market Prices
-440	-603	-900	-848	-1,043	-1,103	-1,137	-1,244	-1,289	-982	..	Resource Balance
1,178	1,147	1,059	1,142	1,267	1,136	1,371	1,276	1,303	1,484	..	Exports of Goods & NFServices
1,619	1,750	1,959	1,991	2,310	2,240	2,508	2,520	2,592	2,466	..	Imports of Goods & NFServices
8,939	9,506	10,067	10,879	11,044	10,993	11,969	12,440	13,056	13,473	..	Domestic Absorption
6,792	7,185	7,499	8,027	7,969	7,687	8,546	8,643	8,474	8,589	f	Private Consumption, etc.
1,293	1,400	1,487	1,733	1,841	1,924	2,045	2,164	2,777	3,223	..	General Gov't Consumption
854	922	1,082	1,119	1,234	1,382	1,378	1,633	1,805	1,661	f	Gross Domestic Investment
854	922	1,082	1,119	1,234	1,382	1,378	1,633	1,805	1,661	..	Fixed Investment
874	806	871	948	1,057	979	1,115	1,196	1,279	1,282	..	Indirect Taxes, net
7,625	8,097	8,297	9,083	8,944	8,910	9,718	9,999	10,488	11,209	C	GDP at factor cost
3,872	4,072	4,062	4,389	4,070	3,916	4,354	4,318	4,327	4,666	..	Agriculture
1,189	1,258	1,297	1,402	1,476	1,495	1,596	1,737	1,775	1,843	..	Industry
830	871	902	984	1,009	1,023	1,073	1,167	1,200	1,230	..	Manufacturing
2,563	2,767	2,938	3,292	3,397	3,500	3,767	3,944	4,386	4,701	..	Services, etc.
414	319	182	271	190	279	241	389	516	680	..	Gross Domestic Saving
469	355	257	419	373	511	615	649	844	910	..	Gross National Saving
				(Millions of 1980 Ethiopian Birr)							
8,512.4	8,660.9	8,796.7	9,237.4	9,024.0	8,367.9	8,939.0	9,751.5	10,068.8	10,298.2	C	Gross National Product
8,498.9	8,675.1	8,814.2	9,263.2	9,059.5	8,427.0	8,990.9	9,814.7	10,178.7	10,420.9	C	GDP at Market Prices
-440.3	-373.9	-812.2	-798.6	-805.0	-1,074.2	-1,426.7	..	..	..	..	Resource Balance
1,178.2	1,166.9	1,114.9	1,219.1	1,415.8	1,129.1	1,054.9	..	..	..	..	Exports of Goods & NFServices
1,618.5	1,540.8	1,927.1	2,017.7	2,220.8	2,203.3	2,481.6	..	..	..	..	Imports of Goods & NFServices
8,939.2	9,049.0	9,626.4	10,061.9	9,864.5	9,501.2	10,417.7	..	..	..	..	Domestic Absorption
6,792.0	6,733.4	7,068.5	7,272.4	6,952.9	6,864.2	7,647.2	..	..	..	f	Private Consumption, etc.
1,293.2	1,369.8	1,435.5	1,609.6	1,687.7	1,706.3	1,764.3	..	..	..	..	General Gov't Consumption
854.0	945.7	1,122.4	1,179.8	1,224.0	930.7	1,006.1	..	..	..	f	Gross Domestic Investment
854.0	945.7	1,122.4	1,179.8	1,224.0	930.7	1,006.1	..	..	..	..	Fixed Investment
7,624.7	7,858.7	7,951.2	8,375.0	8,068.2	7,504.7	8,006.9	8,725.0	9,037.5	9,303.1	C	GDP at factor cost
3,871.9	3,966.9	3,916.0	4,100.8	3,695.1	3,094.4	3,380.0	3,866.9	3,837.1	4,058.2	..	Agriculture
1,189.4	1,230.2	1,268.2	1,334.3	1,404.6	1,414.3	1,467.1	1,532.7	1,552.3	1,578.8	..	Industry
830.0	866.9	900.6	951.3	983.0	993.2	1,036.8	1,087.4	1,112.1	1,133.7	..	Manufacturing
2,563.4	2,661.6	2,767.0	2,939.9	2,968.6	2,996.0	3,159.7	3,325.3	3,648.0	3,666.1	..	Services, etc.
											Memo Items:
1,178.2	1,009.9	1,041.8	1,157.7	1,217.8	1,118.0	1,356.6	..	..	..	..	Capacity to Import
0.0	-157.1	-73.2	-61.4	-198.0	-11.1	301.7	..	..	..	..	Terms of Trade Adjustment
8,498.9	8,518.0	8,741.1	9,201.9	8,861.5	8,415.9	9,292.7	..	..	..	..	Gross Domestic Income
8,512.4	8,503.9	8,723.5	9,176.0	8,826.0	8,356.8	9,240.8	..	..	..	..	Gross National Income
				(Index 1980 = 100)							**DOMESTIC PRICES/DEFLATORS**
100.0	102.6	104.0	108.3	110.4	117.4	120.5	114.1	115.6	119.9	..	Overall (GDP)
100.0	105.1	104.6	108.1	112.0	115.7	114.9	..	..	..	..	Domestic Absorption
100.0	102.6	103.7	107.0	110.2	126.5	128.8	111.7	112.8	115.0	..	Agriculture
100.0	102.3	102.2	105.1	105.1	105.7	108.8	113.3	114.4	116.7	..	Industry
100.0	100.5	100.1	103.5	102.7	103.0	103.5	107.4	107.9	108.5	..	Manufacturing
78.9	83.7	88.6	88.0	95.4	113.6	102.5	100.0	107.1	115.5	f	Consumer Price Index
											MANUFACTURING ACTIVITY
80.6	83.2	86.1	87.6	94.4	92.6	95.6	100.0	103.0	..	G J	Employment (1987=100)
94.5	91.6	89.1	96.1	89.2	80.9	91.6	100.0	94.1	..	G J	Real Earnings per Empl. (1987=100)
87.0	91.4	97.6	96.8	95.3	99.5	99.4	100.0	102.2	..	G J	Real Output per Empl. (1987=100)
18.0	18.7	19.0	19.7	19.7	20.3	19.2	19.5	19.7	..	J	Earnings as % of Value Added
				(Millions of current Ethiopian Birr)							**MONETARY HOLDINGS**
2,196.5	2,438.3	2,689.4	3,198.4	3,449.0	3,994.0	4,467.8	4,754.4	5,291.4	6,048.3	..	Money Supply, Broadly Defined
1,568.3	1,719.9	1,892.3	2,142.2	2,309.3	2,702.2	3,272.8	3,341.4	3,721.6	4,321.9	..	Money
1,029.2	1,039.2	1,149.9	1,250.5	1,272.1	1,417.6	1,640.2	1,744.1	1,962.4	2,340.5	..	Currency Outside Banks
539.1	680.7	742.4	891.7	1,037.1	1,284.6	1,632.6	1,597.3	1,759.2	1,981.3	..	Demand Deposits
628.2	718.4	797.1	1,056.1	1,139.7	1,291.8	1,195.0	1,413.0	1,569.8	1,726.5	..	Quasi-Money
				(Millions of current Ethiopian Birr)							**GOVERNMENT DEFICIT (-) OR SURPLUS**
-380.5	-334.2	-491.5	-1,352.3	-621.5	-868.8	-813.1	-754.9	..	..	C	
1,764.4	1,974.5	2,117.8	2,402.7	2,522.4	2,885.8	3,160.9	3,154.6	..	..	..	Current Revenue
1,858.8	1,969.9	2,180.7	2,766.8	2,492.0	3,078.6	3,109.0	3,063.3	..	..	..	Current Expenditure
-94.4	4.6	-62.9	-364.1	30.4	-192.8	51.9	91.3	..	..	..	Current Budget Balance
6.8	7.6	9.1	15.0	14.5	11.5	12.6	15.2	..	..	..	Capital Receipts
292.9	346.4	437.7	1,003.2	666.4	687.5	877.6	861.4	..	..	..	Capital Payments

ETHIOPIA	1969	1970	1971	1972	1973	1974	1975	1976	1977	1978	1979
FOREIGN TRADE (CUSTOMS BASIS)					*(Millions of current US dollars)*						
Value of Exports, fob	119.4	122.3	125.6	168.4	236.7	266.7	229.4	278.3	333.6	309.8	422.2
Nonfuel Primary Products	114.8	114.6	119.6	161.0	225.8	251.5	202.3	265.6	324.8	294.6	399.4
Fuels	1.4	1.4	2.0	1.1	1.6	4.7	9.9	7.0	6.2	12.1	20.3
Manufactures	3.2	6.3	4.0	6.3	9.3	10.5	17.1	5.8	2.5	3.1	2.4
Value of Imports, cif	155.3	173.1	187.7	189.4	213.1	272.9	294.0	353.2	391.4	505.3	567.4
Nonfuel Primary Products	18.0	21.4	21.9	20.4	24.8	28.7	28.3	32.1	33.2	46.8	60.0
Fuels	11.3	13.4	17.7	15.7	20.0	38.7	51.3	53.3	62.0	60.3	110.2
Manufactures	126.0	138.2	148.1	153.3	168.3	205.5	214.3	267.9	296.2	398.1	397.2
					(Index 1987 = 100)						
Terms of Trade	140.5	164.3	141.0	152.5	167.6	111.5	104.3	181.8	253.9	177.5	167.1
Export Prices, fob	32.7	39.4	36.3	44.0	58.6	56.5	57.3	100.7	153.3	120.4	136.2
Import Prices, cif	23.3	24.0	25.7	28.9	34.9	50.7	54.9	55.4	60.4	67.9	81.5
BALANCE OF PAYMENTS					*(Millions of current US dollars)*						
Exports of Goods & Services	..	185.3	194.4	247.2	347.7	390.4	346.4	384.6	422.3	430.8	465.4
Merchandise, fob	..	122.3	126.4	165.6	239.0	266.7	230.0	260.4	312.2	324.0	359.9
Nonfactor Services	..	56.5	63.3	78.1	100.0	103.2	100.0	106.8	93.4	94.2	95.5
Factor Services	..	6.5	4.7	3.6	8.7	20.4	16.4	17.4	16.7	12.6	10.0
Imports of Goods & Services	..	225.5	248.7	256.7	297.9	386.8	442.7	413.9	528.7	626.5	672.5
Merchandise, fob	..	144.3	158.9	157.8	178.8	249.7	275.9	278.2	368.0	470.9	589.0
Nonfactor Services	..	67.0	73.4	76.3	90.6	105.6	133.4	117.0	142.3	142.9	71.0
Factor Services	..	14.2	16.4	22.6	28.5	31.5	33.4	18.7	18.5	12.7	12.5
Long-Term Interest	..	6.3	7.0	8.1	8.9	9.7	11.0	10.4	11.3	12.4	13.0
Private Current Transfers, net	..	-2.6	-1.8	2.8	11.3	18.2	15.0	21.2	16.6	14.8	23.3
Workers' Remittances	..	..	..	..	..	..	..	..	..	..	..
Curr. A/C Bal before Off. Transf.	..	-42.8	-56.2	-6.6	61.2	21.8	-81.3	-8.1	-89.9	-180.9	-183.8
Net Official Transfers	..	10.6	10.9	14.8	14.2	33.7	29.7	29.4	42.6	53.2	59.7
Curr. A/C Bal after Off. Transf.	..	-32.2	-45.2	8.1	75.3	55.4	-51.6	21.3	-47.3	-127.7	-124.1
Long-Term Capital, net	..	16.5	36.3	32.1	53.4	50.9	68.6	59.9	50.6	36.7	70.6
Direct Investment	..	3.9	5.7	9.7	30.9	28.9	19.3	4.3	5.8	..	..
Long-Term Loans	..	12.7	31.2	19.6	24.2	24.8	61.3	60.2	38.3	48.3	94.6
Disbursements	..	27.6	44.4	32.9	37.3	36.2	75.7	73.9	52.1	63.0	110.2
Repayments	..	14.9	13.2	13.3	13.1	11.4	14.4	13.7	13.8	14.7	15.6
Other Long-Term Capital	..	-0.1	-0.6	2.9	-1.7	-2.8	-12.0	-4.6	6.5	-11.6	-24.0
Other Capital, net	..	12.6	3.0	-9.1	-23.1	-16.6	-23.6	-37.4	-76.8	58.8	8.1
Change in Reserves	..	3.1	5.9	-31.2	-105.6	-89.7	6.6	-43.7	73.5	32.2	45.4
Memo Item:					*(Ethiopian Birr per US dollar)*						
Conversion Factor (Annual Avg)	2.500	2.500	2.490	2.300	2.100	2.070	2.070	2.070	2.070	2.070	2.070
				(Millions of US dollars), outstanding at end of year							
EXTERNAL DEBT (Total)	..	169.0	203.9	226.2	256.4	283.1	343.5	402.1	500.3	563.0	728.8
Long-Term Debt (by debtor)	..	169.0	203.9	226.2	256.4	283.1	343.5	402.1	447.3	511.0	664.8
Central Bank, incl. IMF credit	..	0.0	0.0	0.0	0.0	0.0	0.0	0.0	0.0	14.6	73.5
Central Government	..	98.3	137.1	163.6	194.4	218.0	273.5	337.1	383.0	422.9	503.7
Rest of General Government	..	10.9	11.6	11.6	10.8	9.8	9.0	6.9	6.2	5.1	4.8
Non-financial Public Enterprises	..	47.6	43.2	37.8	37.1	38.3	39.0	35.4	33.8	39.7	57.3
Priv. Sector, incl non-guaranteed	..	12.2	12.0	13.2	14.1	17.0	22.0	22.7	24.3	28.7	25.5
Short-Term Debt	..	0.0	0.0	0.0	0.0	0.0	0.0	0.0	53.0	52.0	64.0
Memo Items:					*(Thousands of US dollars)*						
Int'l Reserves Excluding Gold	62,390	63,300	59,294	83,204	166,027	263,550	276,684	294,735	213,316	152,926	172,727
Gold Holdings (at market price)	9,469	8,446	10,340	16,160	28,848	51,288	38,569	37,056	47,176	64,636	146,432
SOCIAL INDICATORS											
Total Fertility Rate	5.8	5.8	5.8	5.8	5.8	5.9	5.9	6.0	6.0	6.3	6.6
Infant Mortality Rate	159.2	157.8	156.4	155.0	153.8	152.6	151.4	150.2	149.0	151.0	153.0
Life Expectancy at Birth	43.2	43.3	43.4	43.5	43.7	43.9	44.1	44.3	44.5	44.1	43.8
Urban Population, % of total	8.4	8.6	8.8	9.0	9.1	9.3	9.5	9.7	9.9	10.1	10.3
Food Prod. per capita (1987=100)	123.0	124.1	117.8	116.6	115.2	107.2	110.3	107.2	102.2	110.3	119.3
Labor Force, Agriculture (%)	85.2	85.0	84.4	83.9	83.4	82.9	82.4	81.8	81.3	80.8	80.3
Labor Force, Female (%)	40.0	40.0	39.9	39.8	39.8	39.7	39.7	39.6	39.5	39.5	39.4
Primary Schl. Enroll. Ratio	..	16.0	..	..	..	..	24.0	25.0	24.0	29.0	37.0
Primary Schl. Enroll. Ratio, Female	..	10.0	..	..	..	..	15.0	..	..	18.0	25.0
Secondary Schl. Enroll. Ratio	..	4.0	..	..	..	..	6.0	8.0	7.0	9.0	10.0

1980	1981	1982	1983	1984	1985	1986	1987	1988	1989	NOTES	ETHIOPIA
				(Millions of current US dollars)							**FOREIGN TRADE (CUSTOMS BASIS)**
424.8	378.1	404.4	403.0	416.8	333.1	455.0	355.0	429.0	..	..	Value of Exports, fob
392.0	343.0	370.0	368.4	388.9	306.8	441.2	339.9	412.6	..	..	Nonfuel Primary Products
31.5	29.9	30.9	30.9	25.0	23.7	10.8	11.8	12.4	..	..	Fuels
1.2	5.3	3.5	3.7	2.9	2.6	3.0	3.3	4.0	..	..	Manufactures
721.4	737.3	785.0	875.0	928.2	993.4	1,102.0	1,066.0	1,129.0	..	..	Value of Imports, cif
80.3	95.3	103.9	113.4	112.3	111.5	92.0	73.3	82.9	..	..	Nonfuel Primary Products
178.5	171.0	193.3	213.0	195.1	227.2	162.8	200.1	254.5	..	..	Fuels
462.6	470.9	487.8	548.5	620.8	654.7	847.2	792.6	791.6	..	..	Manufactures
				(Index 1987 = 100)							
123.0	105.1	108.8	113.0	127.9	123.1	141.9	100.0	113.0	..	..	Terms of Trade
119.5	103.7	105.3	105.8	115.2	111.6	136.8	100.0	113.4	..	..	Export Prices, fob
97.1	98.7	96.8	93.6	90.1	90.7	96.4	100.0	100.3	..	..	Import Prices, cif
				(Millions of current US dollars)							**BALANCE OF PAYMENTS**
590.5	564.6	537.6	577.5	626.5	558.5	679.3	632.8	636.4	722.8	C f	Exports of Goods & Services
459.2	411.3	375.8	391.5	449.2	359.0	446.2	383.9	373.6	436.3	..	Merchandise, fob
109.9	142.8	135.7	160.2	162.5	189.9	216.0	232.2	255.5	280.6	..	Nonfactor Services
21.4	10.5	26.1	25.8	14.8	9.6	17.1	16.7	7.3	5.9	..	Factor Services
796.6	863.0	981.2	1,000.9	1,149.7	1,124.4	1,257.2	1,270.8	1,317.7	1,287.8	C f	Imports of Goods & Services
691.9	743.6	848.4	856.3	1,026.4	974.7	1,087.2	1,080.5	1,098.6	1,033.6	..	Merchandise, fob
89.8	101.8	97.9	105.2	89.3	107.1	124.1	136.6	153.1	172.5	..	Nonfactor Services
14.9	17.6	34.9	39.4	34.0	42.6	45.9	53.7	66.0	81.7	..	Factor Services
16.9	16.8	21.4	23.7	30.9	34.9	45.7	52.3	77.7	71.7	..	Long-Term Interest
20.0	24.7	45.2	84.9	107.2	145.0	209.5	162.6	217.4	186.9	..	Private Current Transfers, net
..	..	..	..	..	..	..	..	..	..	..	Workers' Remittances
-186.1	-273.7	-398.4	-338.5	-416.0	-420.9	-368.4	-475.4	-463.9	-378.1	..	Curr. A/C Bal before Off. Transf.
59.9	59.9	67.5	92.5	161.9	298.3	293.2	211.8	187.8	209.2	..	Net Official Transfers
-126.2	-213.8	-330.9	-246.0	-254.1	-122.6	-75.2	-263.6	-276.1	-168.9	..	Curr. A/C Bal after Off. Transf.
150.0	161.6	309.2	203.6	180.3	162.3	277.3	181.3	280.9	204.0	C f	Long-Term Capital, net
..	..	..	..	..	..	..	..	..	..	..	Direct Investment
84.4	287.9	80.3	201.5	201.0	282.4	236.0	308.8	305.8	123.1	..	Long-Term Loans
101.7	313.3	113.1	245.1	251.7	348.5	343.9	436.9	465.9	296.7	..	Disbursements
17.3	25.4	32.8	43.6	50.7	66.1	107.9	128.1	160.1	173.6	..	Repayments
65.6	-126.3	228.9	2.1	-20.7	-120.1	41.3	-127.5	-24.9	80.9	C	Other Long-Term Capital
-64.1	-7.0	81.7	-29.1	31.5	7.9	-36.9	62.4	-83.7	-17.1	C f	Other Capital, net
40.3	59.2	-60.0	71.5	42.3	-47.6	-165.2	19.9	78.9	-18.0	..	Change in Reserves
				(Ethiopian Birr per US dollar)							Memo Item:
2.070	2.070	2.070	2.070	2.070	2.070	2.070	2.070	2.070	2.070	..	Conversion Factor (Annual Avg)
				(Millions of US dollars), outstanding at end of year							**EXTERNAL DEBT (Total)**
804.4	1,138.6	1,239.1	1,386.5	1,524.2	1,869.2	2,215.2	2,709.5	2,980.7	3,012.8	..	
747.9	1,079.7	1,170.7	1,323.9	1,456.9	1,791.9	2,131.9	2,611.9	2,847.9	2,905.9	..	Long-Term Debt (by debtor)
79.4	144.8	160.6	133.6	98.3	71.1	84.1	75.7	55.0	30.2	..	Central Bank, incl. IMF credit
550.6	764.2	843.8	1,020.2	1,095.0	1,374.2	1,678.5	2,080.1	2,303.0	2,464.8	..	Central Government
3.9	2.0	0.0	0.0	0.0	0.0	0.0	0.0	0.0	..	..	Rest of General Government
87.1	145.9	146.9	152.6	245.5	327.5	348.6	431.2	451.3	379.1	..	Non-financial Public Enterprises
26.9	22.8	19.4	17.5	18.1	19.1	20.7	24.9	38.6	31.8	..	Priv. Sector, incl non-guaranteed
56.5	58.9	68.4	62.6	67.3	77.3	83.3	97.6	132.8	106.9	..	Short-Term Debt
				(Thousands of US dollars)							Memo Items:
80,129	266,705	181,841	125,874	44,341	147,998	250,500	122,688	64,227	46,053	..	Int'l Reserves Excluding Gold
182,156	103,350	95,492	79,734	64,435	68,343	81,698	101,177	85,742	76,992	..	Gold Holdings (at market price)
											SOCIAL INDICATORS
6.9	7.2	7.5	7.5	7.5	7.5	7.5	7.5	7.5	7.5	..	Total Fertility Rate
139.0	157.0	159.0	154.6	150.2	145.8	141.4	137.0	131.0	133.2	..	Infant Mortality Rate
43.5	43.1	42.8	43.6	44.5	45.3	46.2	47.1	47.3	47.6	..	Life Expectancy at Birth
10.5	10.7	10.9	11.2	11.4	11.6	12.0	12.3	12.5	12.7	..	Urban Population, % of total
112.0	108.0	116.1	106.3	94.8	100.5	107.9	100.0	100.1	100.4	..	Food Prod. per capita (1987=100)
79.8	..	..	..	..	..	..	..	..	..	..	Labor Force, Agriculture (%)
39.3	39.1	39.0	38.8	38.6	38.4	38.2	38.0	37.8	37.6	..	Labor Force, Female (%)
35.0	..	40.0	39.0	34.0	36.0	32.0	34.0	35.0	..	..	Primary Schl. Enroll. Ratio
25.0	32.0	29.0	29.0	28.0	27.0	28.0	28.0	..	..	..	Primary Schl. Enroll. Ratio, Female
9.0	..	10.0	11.0	12.0	13.0	14.0	15.0	..	..	..	Secondary Schl. Enroll. Ratio

FIJI	1969	1970	1971	1972	1973	1974	1975	1976	1977	1978	1979
CURRENT GNP PER CAPITA (US $)	350	400	450	520	660	840	1,030	1,190	1,290	1,350	1,580
POPULATION (thousands)	508	520	531	543	554	565	576	587	599	610	622

USE AND ORIGIN OF RESOURCES *(Millions of current Fiji Dollars)*

	1969	1970	1971	1972	1973	1974	1975	1976	1977	1978	1979
Gross National Product (GNP)	151.4	183.6	201.8	252.1	333.7	448.2	556.4	622.5	651.5	697.7	839.7
Net Factor Income from Abroad	-7.9	-8.2	-10.1	-9.2	-4.6	-1.8	-6.0	-1.0	-8.6	-4.5	-12.5
GDP at Market Prices	159.3	191.8	211.9	261.3	338.3	450.0	562.4	623.5	660.1	702.2	852.2
Resource Balance	-6.9	-6.2	-16.5	-24.3	-45.6	-23.5	-3.6	-29.5	-18.2	-31.0	-46.3
Exports of Goods & NFServices	78.9	92.8	105.5	119.9	153.2	221.1	241.8	235.1	289.9	299.5	385.8
Imports of Goods & NFServices	85.8	99.0	122.0	144.2	198.8	244.6	245.4	264.6	308.1	330.5	432.1
Domestic Absorption	166.2	198.0	228.4	285.6	383.9	473.5	566.0	653.0	678.3	733.2	898.5
Private Consumption, etc.	104.4	128.7	145.1	185.1	266.3	334.4	382.5	433.7	423.0	458.2	497.7
General Gov't Consumption	22.1	26.8	30.7	37.9	42.4	54.0	67.5	85.3	102.3	115.1	143.9
Gross Domestic Investment	39.7	42.5	52.6	62.6	75.2	85.1	116.0	134.0	153.0	159.9	256.9
Fixed Investment	36.0	34.8	45.9	53.1	65.7	74.2	103.4	119.5	128.9	149.8	197.3
Indirect Taxes, net	18.8	22.9	27.3	30.8	37.7	39.5	47.0	52.9	54.4	59.2	72.8
GDP at factor cost	140.5	168.9	184.6	230.5	300.6	410.5	515.4	570.6	605.7	643.0	779.4
Agriculture	38.8	48.2	45.7	57.6	75.7	105.0	132.0	147.0	141.3	141.1	168.0
Industry	33.7	39.8	39.8	52.4	66.6	91.0	115.0	128.0	125.4	126.1	167.9
Manufacturing	20.1	23.7	21.1	27.0	31.6	48.0	60.0	67.0	69.4	70.8	98.5
Services, etc.	68.0	80.9	99.1	120.5	158.3	214.5	268.4	295.6	339.0	375.8	443.5
Gross Domestic Saving	32.8	36.3	36.1	38.3	29.6	61.6	112.4	104.5	134.8	128.9	210.6
Gross National Saving	..	27.1	25.7	29.8	24.3	58.0	104.4	99.1	122.6	121.0	191.0

(Millions of 1987 Fiji Dollars)

	1969	1970	1971	1972	1973	1974	1975	1976	1977	1978	1979
Gross National Product	730.82	830.22	890.31	964.68	1,095.28	1,135.18	1,133.80	1,166.18	1,233.13	1,265.06	1,407.93
GDP at Market Prices	769.12	867.89	930.64	999.83	1,112.93	1,141.88	1,147.70	1,179.07	1,248.48	1,271.80	1,427.17
Resource Balance	-3.22	5.00	-17.26	-35.08	-64.97	-97.25	-130.04	-168.32	-151.07	-155.22	-162.05
Exports of Goods & NFServices	386.20	426.36	474.13	512.20	569.68	540.37	495.26	472.04	551.79	548.56	656.48
Imports of Goods & NFServices	389.42	421.35	491.39	547.28	634.65	637.62	625.30	640.36	702.86	703.78	818.52
Domestic Absorption	772.34	862.88	947.89	1,034.91	1,177.90	1,239.12	1,277.74	1,347.39	1,399.55	1,427.02	1,589.22
Private Consumption, etc.	499.17	574.40	627.52	674.58	798.97	879.75	885.04	921.28	959.61	964.34	998.38
General Gov't Consumption	90.06	104.89	113.04	127.31	128.24	134.54	148.07	179.02	189.58	192.36	230.35
Gross Domestic Investment	183.11	183.60	207.33	233.02	250.69	224.84	244.64	247.09	250.36	270.33	360.49
Fixed Investment	182.10	161.97	197.62	217.19	238.43	209.99	231.78	234.56	238.06	256.72	310.46
GDP at factor cost	668.81	753.23	803.92	867.80	979.01	1,004.50	1,005.42	1,032.50	1,094.27	1,114.03	1,248.19
Agriculture	196.40	213.31	201.68	200.10	212.78	205.38	206.44	214.36	248.89	245.72	287.81
Industry	196.63	215.68	215.68	231.98	254.00	243.20	231.56	238.76	265.42	265.21	307.55
Manufacturing	77.77	88.66	81.04	84.62	87.41	90.53	90.99	98.77	107.95	115.57	136.41
Services, etc.	287.69	335.81	393.90	442.37	517.13	557.34	566.79	579.00	582.60	604.60	656.85

Memo Items:

	1969	1970	1971	1972	1973	1974	1975	1976	1977	1978	1979
Capacity to Import	358.10	394.97	424.93	455.05	489.08	576.36	616.13	568.96	661.34	637.76	730.82
Terms of Trade Adjustment	-28.10	-31.39	-49.20	-57.15	-80.60	35.99	120.87	96.92	109.55	89.21	74.34
Gross Domestic Income	741.03	836.50	881.44	942.68	1,032.32	1,177.86	1,268.57	1,275.99	1,358.03	1,361.01	1,501.51
Gross National Income	702.72	798.82	841.11	907.53	1,014.68	1,171.17	1,254.66	1,263.10	1,342.69	1,354.27	1,482.27

DOMESTIC PRICES/DEFLATORS *(Index 1987 = 100)*

	1969	1970	1971	1972	1973	1974	1975	1976	1977	1978	1979
Overall (GDP)	20.7	22.1	22.8	26.1	30.4	39.4	49.0	52.9	52.9	55.2	59.7
Domestic Absorption	21.5	22.9	24.1	27.6	32.6	38.2	44.3	48.5	48.5	51.4	56.5
Agriculture	19.8	22.6	22.7	28.8	35.6	51.1	63.9	68.6	56.8	57.4	58.4
Industry	17.1	18.5	18.5	22.6	26.2	37.4	49.7	53.6	47.2	47.5	54.6
Manufacturing	25.8	26.7	26.0	31.9	36.1	53.0	65.9	67.8	64.3	61.3	72.2
Consumer Price Index	21.4	22.3	24.3	29.7	32.9	37.7	42.6	47.5	50.8	54.0	58.2

MANUFACTURING ACTIVITY

	1969	1970	1971	1972	1973	1974	1975	1976	1977	1978	1979
Employment (1987=100)	..	63.4	64.0	63.9	69.6	75.9	71.2	86.0	85.5	85.6	90.2
Real Earnings per Empl. (1987=100)	..	..	..	..	..	..	..	..	..	..	..
Real Output per Empl. (1987=100)	..	..	..	..	..	..	..	..	..	..	..
Earnings as % of Value Added	..	43.6	59.4	50.1	42.6	37.1	37.5	48.4	46.0	54.6	41.4

MONETARY HOLDINGS *(Millions of current Fiji Dollars)*

	1969	1970	1971	1972	1973	1974	1975	1976	1977	1978	1979
Money Supply, Broadly Defined	55.40	65.47	77.96	95.44	108.11	150.46	191.27	193.88	230.05	247.45	298.30
Money	31.77	37.34	42.74	52.32	56.55	69.06	84.02	85.38	84.05	98.45	112.32
Currency Outside Banks	9.56	11.16	13.07	14.95	17.19	21.52	27.34	30.70	34.02	38.79	45.24
Demand Deposits	22.21	26.18	29.67	37.37	39.36	47.54	56.68	54.68	50.03	59.66	67.08
Quasi-Money	23.63	28.14	35.22	43.12	51.57	81.39	107.25	108.49	146.00	149.00	185.98

GOVERNMENT DEFICIT (-) OR SURPLUS *(Millions of current Fiji Dollars)*

	1969	1970	1971	1972	1973	1974	1975	1976	1977	1978	1979
GOVERNMENT DEFICIT (-) OR SURPLUS	..	-5.25	-3.23	-4.02	-11.16	-16.04	-7.65	-23.62	-35.18	-30.57	-24.78
Current Revenue	..	43.36	50.17	55.08	68.20	80.02	109.32	124.07	134.11	157.04	194.00
Current Expenditure	..	39.12	46.08	44.17	55.60	70.03	87.17	108.47	119.38	140.00	165.32
Current Budget Balance	..	4.24	4.09	10.91	12.60	9.99	22.15	15.60	14.73	17.04	28.68
Capital Receipts	..	..	..	..	..	..	..	..	..	..	..
Capital Payments	..	9.49	7.32	14.93	23.76	26.03	29.80	39.22	49.91	47.61	53.46

1980	1981	1982	1983	1984	1985	1986	1987	1988	1989 estimate	NOTES	FIJI
1,750	2,000	1,870	1,700	1,770	1,640	1,760	1,590	1,500	1,640	..	**CURRENT GNP PER CAPITA (US $)**
634	646	659	672	686	700	711	722	732	743	..	**POPULATION (thousands)**
			(Millions of current Fiji Dollars)								**USE AND ORIGIN OF RESOURCES**
969.1	1,046.9	1,079.5	1,106.3	1,234.2	1,265.2	1,411.4	1,369.4	1,457.2	1,726.8	..	Gross National Product (GNP)
-14.6	-9.2	-33.8	-35.9	-40.8	-50.9	-59.6	-51.6	-80.8	-115.2	..	Net Factor Income from Abroad
983.7	1,056.1	1,113.3	1,142.2	1,275.0	1,316.1	1,471.0	1,421.0	1,538.0	1,842.0	f	GDP at Market Prices
-48.6	-152.2	-71.3	-62.0	-13.6	-5.0	32.0	40.0	37.0	-11.0	..	Resource Balance
470.0	454.4	481.3	498.1	546.2	584.0	609.0	658.0	849.0	1,063.0	..	Exports of Goods & NFServices
518.6	606.6	552.6	560.1	559.8	589.0	577.0	618.0	812.0	1,074.0	..	Imports of Goods & NFServices
1,032.3	1,208.4	1,184.4	1,204.2	1,289.1	1,321.1	1,439.0	1,381.0	1,501.0	1,853.0	..	Domestic Absorption
562.4	673.1	696.1	731.1	802.8	818.0	900.0	923.0	1,064.0	1,296.0	..	Private Consumption, etc.
156.7	173.1	203.8	231.6	245.0	252.0	273.0	260.0	235.0	264.0	..	General Gov't Consumption
313.2	362.2	284.5	241.5	241.3	251.1	266.0	198.0	202.0	293.0	..	Gross Domestic Investment
249.8	280.5	262.6	239.2	218.0	239.1	215.0	193.0	190.0	263.0	..	Fixed Investment
82.7	102.5	92.8	110.4	123.6	139.0	136.0	136.0	153.0	182.0	..	Indirect Taxes, net
901.0	953.6	1,020.5	1,031.8	1,151.4	1,177.1	1,335.0	1,285.0	1,385.0	1,660.0	f	GDP at factor cost
199.5	189.7	206.8	189.9	220.2	215.7	277.1	304.9	328.6	393.9	..	Agriculture
198.3	202.6	217.6	203.4	216.4	229.5	266.3	268.6	289.4	346.8	..	Industry
107.6	100.1	108.9	94.4	112.5	111.3	136.6	130.5	140.7	168.6	..	Manufacturing
503.2	561.3	596.1	638.5	714.8	731.9	791.6	711.5	767.0	919.3	..	Services, etc.
264.6	209.9	213.4	179.5	227.2	246.1	298.0	238.0	239.0	282.0	..	Gross Domestic Saving
248.1	193.2	176.8	141.6	182.3	184.5	232.4	160.6	153.0	145.1	..	Gross National Saving
			(Millions of 1987 Fiji Dollars)								
1,385.37	1,482.97	1,365.27	1,305.92	1,415.51	1,363.34	1,491.59	1,369.40	1,335.43	1,504.77	..	Gross National Product
1,404.63	1,493.36	1,404.43	1,344.76	1,458.48	1,408.38	1,520.08	1,421.00	1,422.87	1,603.66	f	GDP at Market Prices
-165.71	-208.58	-105.26	-89.27	-27.39	-16.18	25.93	40.00	..	..	..	Resource Balance
642.77	631.16	642.77	631.16	673.42	672.08	686.36	658.00			..	Exports of Goods & NFServices
808.49	839.74	748.03	720.43	700.81	688.26	660.43	618.00			..	Imports of Goods & NFServices
1,570.35	1,701.94	1,509.69	1,434.03	1,485.87	1,424.55	1,494.15	1,381.00			..	Domestic Absorption
950.91	1,066.01	966.30	910.14	981.63	945.58	974.48	923.00			..	Private Consumption, etc.
227.20	219.97	244.43	263.71	270.56	254.63	262.59	260.00			..	General Gov't Consumption
392.24	415.96	298.96	260.18	233.67	224.35	257.07	198.00			..	Gross Domestic Investment
353.13	352.39	304.92	264.11	233.45	223.47	259.12	193.00			..	Fixed Investment
1,227.58	1,300.65	1,286.22	1,235.88	1,337.27	1,273.61	1,375.04	1,285.00	1,286.05	1,449.99	f	GDP at factor cost
269.14	304.02	309.30	253.29	318.64	274.96	327.62	304.90	298.03	339.07	..	Agriculture
311.78	331.46	311.99	289.13	295.27	274.95	306.70	268.60	247.65	298.02	..	Industry
125.68	138.28	134.39	120.86	141.54	123.35	147.14	130.50	123.50	146.52	..	Manufacturing
651.69	671.46	668.71	693.45	723.36	723.70	740.72	711.50	740.37	812.90	..	Services, etc.
											Memo Items:
732.72	629.04	651.52	640.68	683.78	682.42	697.06	658.00	..	..	..	Capacity to Import
89.95	-2.12	8.74	9.52	10.37	10.34	10.70	0.00	..	..	..	Terms of Trade Adjustment
1,494.58	1,491.24	1,413.18	1,354.28	1,468.84	1,418.71	1,530.77	1,421.00	..	..	..	Gross Domestic Income
1,475.32	1,480.86	1,374.01	1,315.44	1,425.87	1,373.68	1,502.29	1,369.40	..	..	..	Gross National Income
			(Index 1987 = 100)								**DOMESTIC PRICES/DEFLATORS**
70.0	70.7	79.3	84.9	87.4	93.4	96.8	100.0	108.1	114.9	..	Overall (GDP)
65.7	71.0	78.5	84.0	86.8	92.7	96.3	100.0	..	..	..	Domestic Absorption
74.1	62.4	66.9	75.0	69.1	78.4	84.6	100.0	110.3	116.2	..	Agriculture
63.6	61.1	69.7	70.3	73.3	83.5	86.8	100.0	116.9	116.4	..	Industry
85.6	72.4	81.0	78.1	79.5	90.2	92.8	100.0	113.9	115.1	..	Manufacturing
66.6	74.0	79.2	84.6	89.0	93.0	94.6	100.0	111.8	118.7	..	Consumer Price Index
											MANUFACTURING ACTIVITY
96.2	88.9	92.3	96.4	105.1	100.6	103.4	100.0	..	..	..	Employment (1987=100)
..	..	..	..	..	..	..	..	..	..	..	Real Earnings per Empl. (1987=100)
..	..	..	..	..	..	..	..	..	..	..	Real Output per Empl. (1987=100)
43.0	48.4	47.0	55.1	55.9	58.6	..	..	..	..	..	Earnings as % of Value Added
			(Millions of current Fiji Dollars)								**MONETARY HOLDINGS**
335.13	352.58	381.20	432.22	480.07	489.37	574.98	598.18	721.32	789.20	..	Money Supply, Broadly Defined
100.68	118.43	123.55	134.76	135.97	137.79	172.10	168.31	272.92	263.58	..	Money
44.06	48.73	52.77	58.73	61.03	61.76	63.13	64.91	67.73	77.98	..	Currency Outside Banks
56.63	69.71	70.79	76.04	74.93	76.03	108.97	103.40	205.19	185.59	..	Demand Deposits
234.45	234.15	257.64	297.46	344.11	351.59	402.88	429.87	448.40	525.62	..	Quasi-Money
			(Millions of current Fiji Dollars)								**GOVERNMENT DEFICIT (-) OR SURPLUS**
-29.54	-45.26	-70.33	-43.29	-38.73	-35.44	-70.57	-73.92	-11.89	..	..	Current Revenue
224.35	262.85	264.80	293.65	329.16	339.69	340.06	336.18	389.84	..	..	Current Revenue
193.63	213.38	244.57	281.47	316.74	318.49	327.30	349.41	333.66	..	..	Current Expenditure
30.72	49.47	20.23	12.18	12.42	21.20	12.76	-13.23	56.18	..	..	Current Budget Balance
..	..	..	..	..	..	..	..	..	..	..	Capital Receipts
60.26	94.73	90.56	55.47	51.15	56.64	83.33	60.69	68.07	..	..	Capital Payments

FIJI	1969	1970	1971	1972	1973	1974	1975	1976	1977	1978	1979
FOREIGN TRADE (CUSTOMS BASIS)					*(Millions of current US dollars)*						
Value of Exports, fob	57.26	67.70	67.79	73.01	78.44	143.67	159.32	126.84	173.20	215.54	249.19
Nonfuel Primary Products	45.84	52.11	51.87	55.48	56.90	109.21	127.07	91.60	131.71	154.29	190.29
Fuels	5.76	7.47	8.19	8.48	8.56	18.63	19.32	22.42	24.68	38.76	30.29
Manufactures	5.66	8.12	7.73	9.05	12.98	15.83	12.93	12.82	16.81	22.49	28.61
Value of Imports, cif	89.43	103.91	128.09	158.15	203.45	273.06	267.34	262.68	306.22	366.26	469.64
Nonfuel Primary Products	21.60	24.94	30.29	37.53	49.66	64.86	57.85	58.24	72.17	89.56	94.78
Fuels	9.62	11.45	13.42	15.71	18.20	42.90	46.58	42.17	59.03	63.90	86.58
Manufactures	58.21	67.52	84.38	104.91	135.59	165.30	162.91	162.27	175.02	212.80	288.28
					(Index 1987 = 100)						
Terms of Trade	130.4	130.1	132.1	145.6	153.3	274.6	238.7	171.8	146.4	131.1	143.4
Export Prices, fob	29.3	30.2	34.9	42.7	57.4	151.1	138.0	100.9	95.7	95.9	122.1
Import Prices, cif	22.5	23.2	26.4	29.3	37.4	55.0	57.8	58.7	65.4	73.1	85.1
BALANCE OF PAYMENTS					*(Millions of current US dollars)*						
Exports of Goods & Services	..	109.00	126.58	151.13	198.37	286.23	295.16	264.89	325.51	369.52	475.46
Merchandise, fob	..	62.10	63.39	71.01	82.73	142.75	157.60	120.86	164.47	184.47	242.40
Nonfactor Services	..	44.40	59.38	74.37	108.60	130.13	126.03	137.73	153.09	176.20	219.00
Factor Services	..	2.50	3.81	5.75	7.03	13.35	11.53	6.30	7.96	8.86	14.05
Imports of Goods & Services	..	125.90	157.57	191.63	262.39	316.78	320.78	311.96	350.55	403.27	546.39
Merchandise, fob	..	92.50	113.34	139.19	194.68	234.52	230.93	226.80	258.50	298.17	412.38
Nonfactor Services	..	21.20	28.69	35.61	54.96	66.63	62.41	67.45	75.30	90.93	106.62
Factor Services	..	12.20	15.55	16.83	12.76	15.63	27.44	17.71	16.75	14.17	27.39
Long-Term Interest	..	1.10	0.80	1.20	1.80	3.80	4.00	4.20	4.80	6.40	6.30
Private Current Transfers, net	..	-1.20	-0.40	0.87	-0.83	-2.29	-2.43	-4.89	-3.97	-4.02	-8.51
Workers' Remittances	..	..	..	..	..	..	..	..	..	..	..
Curr. A/C Bal before Off. Transf.	..	-18.10	-31.39	-39.63	-64.85	-32.83	-28.05	-51.95	-29.00	-37.77	-79.45
Net Official Transfers	..	3.80	3.81	7.71	6.68	3.97	1.70	1.34	2.92	2.01	13.19
Curr. A/C Bal after Off. Transf.	..	-14.30	-27.58	-31.92	-58.18	-28.86	-26.35	-50.62	-26.08	-35.76	-66.26
Long-Term Capital, net	..	15.50	14.14	27.90	43.16	49.07	45.41	15.33	36.26	1.18	55.52
Direct Investment	..	6.40	6.52	8.47	13.23	12.03	10.93	..	..	..	10.17
Long-Term Loans	..	0.70	3.40	6.10	24.80	9.30	9.00	10.30	19.10	-3.90	23.00
Disbursements	..	2.30	4.10	7.30	26.50	12.40	12.40	14.60	24.00	8.00	30.50
Repayments	..	1.60	0.70	1.20	1.70	3.10	3.40	4.30	4.90	11.90	7.50
Other Long-Term Capital	..	8.40	4.22	13.33	5.12	27.74	25.48	5.03	17.16	5.08	22.35
Other Capital, net	..	-0.70	22.66	28.23	23.25	13.68	30.75	12.90	6.32	13.03	16.20
Change in Reserves	..	-0.50	-9.22	-24.21	-8.23	-33.88	-49.81	22.39	-16.50	21.54	-5.46
Memo Item:					*(Fiji Dollars per US dollar)*						
Conversion Factor (Annual Avg)	0.870	0.870	0.860	0.820	0.790	0.800	0.820	0.900	0.920	0.850	0.840
				(Millions of US dollars), outstanding at end of year							
EXTERNAL DEBT (Total)	..	11.70	14.80	20.80	47.20	54.50	59.30	63.90	120.40	103.20	141.40
Long-Term Debt (by debtor)	..	11.70	14.80	20.80	47.20	54.50	59.30	63.90	94.40	93.20	118.40
Central Bank, incl. IMF credit	..	0.00	0.00	0.00	0.00	0.40	0.00	0.00	7.90	8.50	8.60
Central Government	..	11.70	13.70	14.60	37.00	41.40	46.20	51.30	73.10	72.00	81.20
Rest of General Government	..	..	..	..	..	..	..	..	..	..	..
Non-financial Public Enterprises	..	0.00	1.10	6.20	10.20	11.90	11.70	10.70	11.60	11.00	27.00
Priv. Sector, incl non-guaranteed	..	0.00	0.00	0.00	0.00	0.80	1.40	1.90	1.80	1.70	1.60
Short-Term Debt	..	0.00	0.00	0.00	0.00	0.00	0.00	0.00	26.00	10.00	23.00
Memo Items:					*(Millions of US dollars)*						
Int'l Reserves Excluding Gold	26.8	27.4	39.6	69.4	74.0	109.2	148.6	116.3	147.1	134.7	136.5
Gold Holdings (at market price)	..	..	..	..	..	..	..	..	0.9	1.9	5.7
SOCIAL INDICATORS											
Total Fertility Rate	4.2	4.1	3.9	3.7	3.7	3.7	3.6	3.6	3.6	3.6	3.6
Infant Mortality Rate	51.0	49.0	47.0	45.0	43.4	41.8	40.2	38.6	37.0	35.8	34.6
Life Expectancy at Birth	63.7	64.2	64.6	65.1	65.5	66.0	66.4	66.8	67.2	67.6	67.9
Urban Population, % of total	34.4	34.8	35.2	35.6	35.9	36.3	36.7	37.1	37.5	37.9	38.3
Food Prod. per capita (1987=100)	132.1	140.8	125.4	110.0	110.5	98.9	95.3	96.1	106.5	108.5	134.2
Labor Force, Agriculture (%)	52.2	51.5	50.9	50.3	49.7	49.1	48.6	48.1	47.6	47.1	46.6
Labor Force, Female (%)	11.4	11.9	12.5	13.1	13.7	14.2	14.7	15.3	15.9	16.4	16.9
Primary Schl. Enroll. Ratio	..	105.0	..	..	..	..	115.0	112.0	110.0	110.0	109.0
Primary Schl. Enroll. Ratio, Female	..	103.0	..	..	..	..	115.0	111.0	110.0	110.0	108.0
Secondary Schl. Enroll. Ratio	..	52.0	..	..	..	..	66.0	55.0	58.0	60.0	62.0

1980	1981	1982	1983	1984	1985	1986	1987	1988	1989 estimate	NOTES	FIJI
				(Millions of current US dollars)							**FOREIGN TRADE (CUSTOMS BASIS)**
361.43	297.66	284.00	240.00	256.00	236.60	273.50	334.00	366.00	..	..	Value of Exports, fob
272.18	206.42	178.90	161.74	169.81	151.10	203.29	248.93	232.04	..	..	Nonfuel Primary Products
57.53	60.19	59.77	49.10	56.61	57.85	34.15	43.07	36.96	..	..	Fuels
31.72	31.05	45.34	29.17	29.58	27.64	36.05	42.00	97.00	..	..	Manufactures
561.26	631.08	513.70	483.16	449.80	441.50	437.40	380.00	454.00	..	..	Value of Imports, cif
98.36	112.03	94.34	96.37	74.43	70.25	68.44	57.00	61.01	..	..	Nonfuel Primary Products
129.46	162.03	146.70	112.21	105.19	103.10	56.73	62.00	73.99	..	..	Fuels
333.44	357.02	272.66	274.58	270.18	268.15	312.23	261.00	319.00	..	..	Manufactures
				(Index 1987 = 100)							
223.9	169.1	117.3	125.8	113.1	95.7	96.5	100.0	118.9	..	..	Terms of Trade
223.2	174.4	118.5	119.5	104.1	87.6	87.6	100.0	122.3	..	..	Export Prices, fob
99.7	103.1	101.1	95.0	92.0	91.5	90.8	100.0	102.9	..	..	Import Prices, cif
				(Millions of current US dollars)							**BALANCE OF PAYMENTS**
600.11	561.42	543.50	511.28	526.26	523.34	555.27	550.67	637.60	767.44	..	Exports of Goods & Services
343.31	278.39	251.39	217.05	227.87	207.68	245.70	303.56	351.37	383.06	..	Merchandise, fob
233.74	252.24	269.58	273.56	277.47	301.29	290.45	226.07	257.81	369.16	..	Nonfactor Services
23.06	30.78	22.53	20.67	20.92	14.37	19.12	21.04	28.42	15.23	..	Factor Services
657.83	753.97	653.74	600.60	568.15	559.34	573.70	563.31	617.88	809.04	..	Imports of Goods & Services
492.96	544.86	440.23	421.19	390.70	382.57	368.31	329.05	399.88	544.00	..	Merchandise, fob
124.64	167.51	154.76	130.39	128.33	131.13	155.81	173.94	170.75	214.22	..	Nonfactor Services
40.23	41.60	58.76	49.01	49.12	45.64	49.58	60.32	47.25	50.83	..	Factor Services
9.50	16.50	22.30	23.00	24.30	24.60	25.20	26.00	24.80	31.70	..	Long-Term Interest
-2.33	-8.80	-2.99	-1.99	-3.78	-9.29	-5.27	-20.78	-3.62	-14.65	..	Private Current Transfers, net
..	..	..	..	0.00	..	..	0.00	19.10	..	..	Workers' Remittances
-60.04	-201.35	-113.23	-91.31	-45.66	-45.28	-23.71	-33.42	16.09	-56.24	..	Curr. A/C Bal before Off. Transf.
35.19	25.86	20.47	26.68	18.77	32.96	14.75	10.32	33.69	34.50	..	Net Official Transfers
-24.86	-175.49	-92.76	-64.63	-26.89	-12.32	-8.96	-23.10	49.78	-21.74	..	Curr. A/C Bal after Off. Transf.
74.10	104.01	75.96	58.73	28.52	1.71	-23.59	-51.90	1.10	-54.96	..	Long-Term Capital, net
34.22	34.62	35.91	32.02	23.04	0.86	-13.98	-27.79	-5.50	-23.81	..	Direct Investment
67.00	70.60	44.90	41.00	17.00	2.70	-12.90	-18.60	6.80	-37.40	..	Long-Term Loans
78.20	80.10	56.80	55.50	43.70	33.90	18.40	18.10	43.50	20.10	..	Disbursements
11.20	9.50	11.90	14.50	26.70	31.20	31.30	36.70	36.70	57.50	..	Repayments
-27.12	-1.21	-4.86	-14.29	-11.52	-1.85	3.29	-5.51	-0.20	6.25	..	Other Long-Term Capital
-9.00	47.89	-5.35	-0.35	5.86	5.77	63.14	11.90	61.21	62.84	..	Other Capital, net
-40.24	23.59	22.16	6.26	-7.49	4.84	-30.59	63.10	-112.09	13.86	..	Change in Reserves
				(Fiji Dollars per US dollar)							**Memo Item:**
0.820	0.850	0.930	1.020	1.080	1.150	1.130	1.240	1.430	1.480	..	Conversion Factor (Annual Avg)
				(Millions of US dollars), outstanding at end of year							
280.90	372.20	401.90	437.40	413.30	443.70	440.80	466.20	466.60	398.20	..	**EXTERNAL DEBT (Total)**
244.90	333.20	379.90	411.40	391.30	424.70	420.80	444.70	435.20	384.20	..	Long-Term Debt (by debtor)
0.00	0.00	14.90	14.10	13.20	14.50	7.90	6.70	4.00	0.80	..	Central Bank, incl. IMF credit
112.80	140.90	149.40	148.40	142.00	145.30	155.90	171.70	177.40	158.50	..	Central Government
..	..	..	..	..	..	..	..	..	..	..	Rest of General Government
65.40	94.80	114.20	142.30	136.00	155.60	153.50	156.50	146.20	120.80	..	Non-financial Public Enterprises
66.70	97.50	101.40	106.60	100.10	109.30	103.50	109.80	107.60	104.10	..	Priv. Sector, incl non-guaranteed
36.00	39.00	22.00	26.00	22.00	19.00	20.00	21.50	31.40	14.00	..	Short-Term Debt
				(Millions of US dollars)							**Memo Items:**
167.5	135.1	126.9	115.8	117.4	130.8	171.1	132.2	233.4	211.6	..	Int'l Reserves Excluding Gold
6.5	4.4	5.1	4.2	3.4	3.6	4.3	0.4	0.3	0.3	..	Gold Holdings (at market price)
											SOCIAL INDICATORS
3.5	3.5	3.5	3.4	3.4	3.4	3.3	3.3	3.2	3.1	..	Total Fertility Rate
33.4	32.2	31.0	29.0	27.0	25.0	23.0	21.0	20.4	19.7	..	Infant Mortality Rate
68.3	68.6	69.0	69.2	69.5	69.8	70.1	70.4	70.6	70.8	..	Life Expectancy at Birth
38.7	39.2	39.7	40.2	40.7	41.2	41.8	42.3	42.9	43.4	..	Urban Population, % of total
118.4	128.8	131.2	92.5	138.2	110.1	128.6	100.0	101.9	102.2	..	Food Prod. per capita (1987=100)
46.2	..	..	..	..	..	..	..	..	..	..	Labor Force, Agriculture (%)
17.4	17.7	18.0	18.3	18.6	18.9	19.2	19.4	19.7	19.9	..	Labor Force, Female (%)
131.0	..	..	130.0	129.0	129.0	129.0	..	..	..	..	Primary Schl. Enroll. Ratio
129.0	..	..	129.0	129.0	128.0	129.0	..	..	..	..	Primary Schl. Enroll. Ratio, Female
57.0	..	..	56.0	56.0	54.0	56.0	..	..	..	..	Secondary Schl. Enroll. Ratio

FINLAND	1969	1970	1971	1972	1973	1974	1975	1976	1977	1978	1979
CURRENT GNP PER CAPITA (US $)	2,200	2,380	2,550	2,900	3,510	4,360	5,410	6,170	6,690	7,200	8,630
POPULATION (thousands)	4,624	4,606	4,616	4,640	4,666	4,691	4,711	4,726	4,739	4,753	4,765
USE AND ORIGIN OF RESOURCES					*(Billions of current Finnish Markkaa)*						
Gross National Product (GNP)	40.62	45.32	49.76	57.98	70.55	89.01	102.77	115.79	127.30	140.67	164.10
Net Factor Income from Abroad	-0.37	-0.43	-0.50	-0.65	-0.82	-1.04	-1.52	-1.86	-2.48	-2.69	-2.77
GDP at Market Prices	40.99	45.74	50.26	58.62	71.36	90.05	104.29	117.64	129.78	143.37	166.88
Resource Balance	0.37	-0.58	-0.88	0.21	-0.43	-3.31	-6.12	-2.29	2.19	5.61	2.68
Exports of Goods & NFServices	9.89	11.75	12.24	14.97	18.18	24.78	24.78	29.51	36.91	43.00	52.51
Imports of Goods & NFServices	9.52	12.33	13.13	14.77	18.60	28.10	30.90	31.80	34.72	37.39	49.82
Domestic Absorption	40.61	46.32	51.14	58.42	71.79	93.37	110.41	119.93	127.59	137.76	164.19
Private Consumption, etc.	23.37	25.13	27.53	32.78	39.58	45.91	57.53	68.52	71.70	75.65	89.84
General Gov't Consumption	6.98	7.46	8.43	9.85	11.67	14.61	18.12	21.31	24.00	26.34	29.87
Gross Domestic Investment	10.26	13.72	15.18	15.78	20.55	32.85	34.77	30.10	31.89	35.77	44.48
Fixed Investment	10.60	12.38	13.94	16.27	19.97	25.31	31.19	32.08	33.80	34.98	38.50
Indirect Taxes, net	4.40	4.74	5.42	6.37	7.72	8.37	8.87	10.22	12.57	14.88	16.59
GDP at factor cost	36.59	41.00	44.83	52.26	63.64	81.69	95.42	107.42	117.21	128.49	150.29
Agriculture	..	..	..	..	..	..	..	..	..	..	..
Industry	..	..	..	..	..	..	..	..	..	..	..
Manufacturing	..	..	..	..	..	..	..	..	..	..	..
Services, etc.	..	..	..	..	..	..	..	..	..	..	..
Gross Domestic Saving	10.64	13.15	14.30	15.99	20.12	29.54	28.65	27.81	34.08	41.37	47.16
Gross National Saving	..	12.73	13.83	15.34	19.31	28.51	27.12	25.92	31.55	38.62	44.33
					(Billions of 1987 Finnish Markkaa)						
Gross National Product	208.42	223.90	228.41	245.49	261.58	269.60	271.58	272.14	271.53	273.07	298.45
GDP at Market Prices	210.30	226.01	230.68	248.21	264.59	272.72	275.64	276.56	276.88	278.29	303.49
Resource Balance	0.30	-4.82	-5.11	-0.39	-3.60	-8.17	-16.75	-8.99	0.96	9.27	4.07
Exports of Goods & NFServices	44.84	48.75	48.14	55.11	59.12	58.74	50.54	56.98	65.94	71.83	78.12
Imports of Goods & NFServices	44.54	53.58	53.26	55.50	62.72	66.92	67.29	65.97	64.98	62.56	74.05
Domestic Absorption	210.00	230.84	235.79	248.60	268.19	280.90	292.39	285.54	275.91	269.02	299.42
Private Consumption, etc.	115.78	121.63	124.81	137.53	147.53	142.65	152.89	160.13	151.21	148.80	162.33
General Gov't Consumption	35.47	37.40	39.56	42.62	45.01	47.03	50.28	53.14	55.38	57.67	59.85
Gross Domestic Investment	58.76	71.80	71.43	68.45	75.66	91.21	89.23	72.27	69.32	62.54	77.23
Fixed Investment	56.15	63.14	65.52	69.80	75.74	78.38	83.04	75.71	73.07	68.01	70.06
GDP at factor cost	187.56	202.25	205.52	221.08	235.64	247.42	252.04	252.28	249.80	249.46	273.33
Agriculture	..	..	..	..	..	..	..	..	..	..	..
Industry	..	..	..	..	..	..	..	..	..	..	..
Manufacturing	..	..	..	..	..	..	..	..	..	..	..
Services, etc.	..	..	..	..	..	..	..	..	..	..	..
Memo Items:											
Capacity to Import	46.28	51.08	49.68	56.27	61.28	59.03	53.97	61.23	69.08	71.95	78.04
Terms of Trade Adjustment	1.45	2.32	1.54	1.16	2.16	0.28	3.43	4.24	3.13	0.12	-0.09
Gross Domestic Income	211.75	228.34	232.22	249.37	266.75	273.01	279.07	280.80	280.01	278.40	303.41
Gross National Income	209.87	226.23	229.95	246.65	263.74	269.89	275.02	276.38	274.66	273.18	298.37
DOMESTIC PRICES/DEFLATORS					*(Index 1987 = 100)*						
Overall (GDP)	19.5	20.2	21.8	23.6	27.0	33.0	37.8	42.5	46.9	51.5	55.0
Domestic Absorption	19.3	20.1	21.7	23.5	26.8	33.2	37.8	42.0	46.2	51.2	54.8
Agriculture	..	..	..	..	..	..	..	..	..	..	..
Industry	..	..	..	..	..	..	..	..	..	..	..
Manufacturing	..	..	..	..	..	..	..	..	..	..	..
Consumer Price Index	20.8	21.4	22.8	24.4	27.1	31.6	37.2	42.5	47.9	51.6	55.5
MANUFACTURING ACTIVITY											
Employment (1987=100)	90.1	99.1	101.9	104.8	109.1	112.4	111.4	110.9	107.8	104.7	108.4
Real Earnings per Empl. (1987=100)	59.7	63.6	66.6	71.8	74.9	78.5	81.7	82.7	78.9	80.3	83.6
Real Output per Empl. (1987=100)	..	..	..	..	..	..	..	..	..	..	..
Earnings as % of Value Added	45.5	47.1	50.3	50.2	48.9	44.1	49.5	50.1	49.2	45.3	43.4
MONETARY HOLDINGS					*(Billions of current Finnish Markkaa)*						
Money Supply, Broadly Defined	16.91	19.48	21.98	25.71	29.67	34.90	42.70	46.67	51.99	59.92	70.75
Money	3.13	3.45	4.03	4.96	6.11	7.27	9.77	9.60	9.87	11.50	14.09
Currency Outside Banks	1.20	1.29	1.48	1.55	1.78	2.15	2.51	2.54	2.84	3.48	3.91
Demand Deposits	1.92	2.16	2.55	3.41	4.33	5.12	7.26	7.06	7.03	8.01	10.18
Quasi-Money	13.78	16.04	17.96	20.75	23.56	27.63	32.93	37.07	42.12	48.43	56.66
					(Billions of current Finnish Markkaa)						
GOVERNMENT DEFICIT (-) OR SURPLUS	..	..	..	0.72	2.04	0.76	-2.32	-0.03	-1.94	-2.64	-4.10
Current Revenue	..	..	..	15.64	19.51	23.69	29.08	36.53	39.60	40.95	45.79
Current Expenditure	..	..	..	11.82	13.84	18.38	24.73	29.18	33.02	36.61	42.61
Current Budget Balance	..	..	..	3.82	5.67	5.30	4.35	7.35	6.58	4.34	3.18
Capital Receipts	..	..	..	0.00	0.01	0.01	0.02	0.03	0.03	0.11	0.03
Capital Payments	..	..	..	3.11	3.64	4.56	6.69	7.41	8.55	7.10	7.32

1980	1981	1982	1983	1984	1985	1986	1987	1988	1989 estimate	NOTES	FINLAND
10,160	11,060	11,410	10,900	10,780	10,950	12,180	14,570	18,570	22,060	..	**CURRENT GNP PER CAPITA (US $)**
4,780	4,800	4,824	4,863	4,882	4,908	4,918	4,932	4,951	4,974	..	**POPULATION (thousands)**
											USE AND ORIGIN OF RESOURCES
				(Billions of current Finnish Markkaa)							
189.27	214.04	240.31	268.80	300.39	328.26	352.65	383.56	431.72	484.18	..	Gross National Product (GNP)
-3.24	-4.40	-5.35	-5.79	-7.10	-6.71	-7.58	-8.01	-8.61	-9.67	..	Net Factor Income from Abroad
192.51	218.45	245.66	274.60	307.50	334.97	360.23	391.57	440.33	493.84	..	GDP at Market Prices
-1.57	3.15	2.07	1.35	8.08	3.28	5.65	2.26	-1.23	-8.19	..	Resource Balance
63.50	72.35	75.78	82.71	94.18	98.17	95.62	99.98	108.99	117.20	..	Exports of Goods & NFServices
65.06	69.20	73.71	81.36	86.10	94.89	89.97	97.72	110.22	125.39	..	Imports of Goods & NFServices
194.07	215.29	243.58	273.25	299.42	331.69	354.59	389.31	441.56	502.03	..	Domestic Absorption
101.80	113.32	130.84	148.14	162.07	183.86	200.59	217.56	243.01	270.27	..	Private Consumption, etc.
34.89	40.83	46.66	53.33	59.74	68.22	74.00	81.34	88.83	98.53	..	General Gov't Consumption
57.38	61.14	66.08	71.79	77.61	79.61	79.99	90.42	109.72	133.23	..	Gross Domestic Investment
47.66	54.77	61.78	69.93	73.66	80.05	82.79	91.25	105.80	126.01	..	Fixed Investment
19.49	22.46	25.44	28.10	33.74	37.46	41.19	45.91	55.62	62.44	..	Indirect Taxes, net
173.02	195.99	220.21	246.50	273.75	297.51	319.04	345.67	384.71	431.40	..	GDP at factor cost
..	..	..	..	..	..	..	..	..	..	..	Agriculture
..	..	..	..	..	..	..	..	..	..	..	Industry
..	..	..	..	..	..	..	..	..	..	..	Manufacturing
..	..	..	..	..	..	..	..	..	..	..	Services, etc.
55.82	64.29	68.15	73.13	85.69	82.89	85.64	92.68	108.49	125.05	..	Gross Domestic Saving
52.50	59.84	62.68	67.21	78.45	76.14	77.26	83.95	99.52	114.55	..	Gross National Saving
				(Billions of 1987 Finnish Markkaa)							
314.38	318.31	329.14	339.17	348.80	361.55	371.32	383.56	403.87	424.38	..	Gross National Product
319.63	324.68	336.31	346.30	356.92	368.81	379.25	391.57	412.03	432.69	..	GDP at Market Prices
4.50	12.42	9.58	9.41	13.47	9.09	7.73	2.26	-5.02	-13.59	..	Resource Balance
84.69	88.87	87.91	90.07	94.96	96.11	97.41	99.98	103.90	105.56	..	Exports of Goods & NFServices
80.19	76.45	78.33	80.66	81.48	87.02	89.68	97.72	108.91	119.15	..	Imports of Goods & NFServices
315.13	312.26	326.73	336.89	343.45	359.72	371.52	389.31	417.05	446.28	..	Domestic Absorption
164.78	165.29	173.92	180.99	185.64	197.88	209.02	217.56	230.92	241.78	..	Private Consumption, etc.
62.39	65.07	67.38	69.88	71.83	75.54	77.87	81.34	83.35	86.19	..	General Gov't Consumption
87.96	81.89	85.43	86.01	85.97	86.30	84.63	90.42	102.77	118.31	..	Gross Domestic Investment
77.37	79.04	82.55	85.90	84.09	86.54	86.55	91.25	100.24	112.67	..	Fixed Investment
288.02	292.30	302.34	311.85	318.43	328.34	336.24	345.67	359.19	376.60	..	GDP at factor cost
..	..	..	..	..	..	..	..	..	..	..	Agriculture
..	..	..	..	..	..	..	..	..	..	..	Industry
..	..	..	..	..	..	..	..	..	..	..	Manufacturing
..	..	..	..	..	..	..	..	..	..	..	Services, etc.
											Memo Items:
78.26	79.94	80.53	81.99	89.13	90.02	95.31	99.98	107.70	111.37	..	Capacity to Import
-6.43	-8.94	-7.38	-8.08	-5.83	-6.09	-2.10	0.00	3.80	5.82	..	Terms of Trade Adjustment
313.20	315.74	328.93	338.22	351.09	362.73	377.14	391.57	415.84	438.50	..	Gross Domestic Income
307.95	309.37	321.76	331.09	342.97	355.47	369.22	383.56	407.67	430.19	..	Gross National Income
				(Index 1987 = 100)							**DOMESTIC PRICES/DEFLATORS**
60.2	67.3	73.0	79.3	86.2	90.8	95.0	100.0	106.9	114.1	..	Overall (GDP)
61.6	68.9	74.6	81.1	87.2	92.2	95.4	100.0	105.9	112.5	..	Domestic Absorption
..	..	..	..	..	..	..	..	..	..	..	Agriculture
..	..	..	..	..	..	..	..	..	..	..	Industry
..	..	..	..	..	..	..	..	..	..	..	Manufacturing
61.9	69.4	76.0	82.4	88.2	93.4	96.1	100.0	105.1	112.1	..	Consumer Price Index
											MANUFACTURING ACTIVITY
113.9	113.7	111.5	109.2	107.8	106.3	101.9	100.0	97.4	99.5	..	Employment (1987=100)
84.4	86.1	87.0	88.1	90.3	93.0	96.7	100.0	103.2	..	..	Real Earnings per Empl. (1987=100)
..	..	..	..	..	..	..	..	..	..	..	Real Output per Empl. (1987=100)
44.1	45.4	45.6	44.4	42.6	43.3	49.1	45.7	44.0	..	..	Earnings as % of Value Added
				(Billions of current Finnish Markkaa)							**MONETARY HOLDINGS**
81.41	94.38	107.06	121.34	140.25	165.59	178.73	200.25	246.38	269.76	..	Money Supply, Broadly Defined
14.98	17.19	19.92	21.43	24.95	27.69	27.84	30.34	35.92	41.44	..	Money
4.30	4.82	5.17	5.63	5.88	6.14	6.36	7.26	8.42	8.77	..	Currency Outside Banks
10.67	12.36	14.75	15.80	19.07	21.55	21.48	23.08	27.50	32.67	..	Demand Deposits
66.43	77.19	87.14	99.91	115.30	137.90	150.90	169.91	210.46	228.31	..	Quasi-Money
				(Billions of current Finnish Markkaa)							
-4.15	-1.97	-5.07	-7.96	-3.11	-2.70	0.39	-6.69	1.75	..	E	**GOVERNMENT DEFICIT (-) OR SURPLUS**
52.89	62.50	70.01	78.34	88.88	100.40	113.27	116.53	137.17	..	..	Current Revenue
48.19	55.47	65.39	76.53	82.35	92.59	101.09	110.74	119.08	..	..	Current Expenditure
4.71	7.02	4.62	1.81	6.53	7.82	12.18	5.79	18.09	..	..	Current Budget Balance
0.07	0.04	0.07	0.21	0.15	0.08	0.13	0.56	0.11	..	..	Capital Receipts
8.93	9.04	9.75	9.98	9.79	10.60	11.91	13.04	16.44	..	..	Capital Payments

FINLAND	1969	1970	1971	1972	1973	1974	1975	1976	1977	1978	1979
FOREIGN TRADE (CUSTOMS BASIS)					*(Millions of current US dollars)*						
Value of Exports, fob	1,985	2,306	2,356	2,947	3,719	5,522	5,489	6,339	7,668	8,572	11,175
Nonfuel Primary Products	661	750	727	814	1,057	1,435	1,230	1,497	1,818	1,936	2,838
Fuels	12	19	5	6	10	47	23	100	165	223	303
Manufactures	1,312	1,538	1,624	2,127	2,652	4,040	4,236	4,741	5,686	6,413	8,034
Value of Imports, cif	2,023	2,637	2,796	3,198	4,210	6,850	7,600	7,391	7,608	7,865	11,390
Nonfuel Primary Products	393	488	443	524	720	1,113	1,196	1,098	1,218	1,276	1,735
Fuels	229	302	383	420	527	1,504	1,447	1,586	1,794	1,746	3,018
Manufactures	1,401	1,847	1,970	2,254	2,963	4,233	4,957	4,708	4,596	4,842	6,637
					(Index 1987 = 100)						
Terms of Trade	109.4	105.8	110.6	110.1	100.8	85.9	95.4	91.4	87.8	86.6	90.4
Export Prices, fob	24.7	24.7	27.6	30.7	36.0	48.0	55.7	55.7	59.4	64.1	81.4
Import Prices, cif	22.6	23.3	24.9	27.9	35.7	55.8	58.4	60.9	67.7	73.9	90.0
BALANCE OF PAYMENTS					*(Millions of current US dollars)*						
Exports of Goods & Services	..	2,773	2,908	3,613	4,725	6,576	6,742	7,680	9,211	10,589	13,717
Merchandise, fob	..	2,294	2,352	2,929	3,820	5,487	5,508	6,295	7,609	8,504	11,100
Nonfactor Services	..	411	464	571	768	845	1,095	1,246	1,452	1,859	2,246
Factor Services	..	68	91	113	137	244	139	139	150	227	372
Imports of Goods & Services	..	3,008	3,247	3,740	5,096	7,768	8,850	8,752	9,267	9,864	13,776
Merchandise, fob	..	2,471	2,628	2,985	4,070	6,367	7,224	6,960	7,167	7,408	10,734
Nonfactor Services	..	371	421	506	685	920	1,072	1,172	1,337	1,575	1,961
Factor Services	..	166	198	250	341	481	553	620	762	881	1,080
Long-Term Interest	..	..	..	..	..	..	..	..	..	..	..
Private Current Transfers, net	..	2	6	1	1	5	-2	-8	-12	-15	-16
Workers' Remittances	..										..
Curr. A/C Bal before Off. Transf.	..	-233	-333	-126	-370	-1,187	-2,110	-1,081	-67	711	-75
Net Official Transfers	..	-7	-8	9	-15	-23	-34	-37	-38	-36	-94
Curr. A/C Bal after Off. Transf.	..	-240	-341	-117	-386	-1,210	-2,143	-1,117	-105	674	-169
Long-Term Capital, net	..	79	378	333	69	236	1,307	955	449	880	203
Direct Investment	..	-34	-21	-24	-2	6	43	27	-24	-29	-97
Long-Term Loans	..	..	..	..	..	..	..	..	..	..	..
Disbursements	..	..	..	..	..	..	..	..	..	..	..
Repayments	..	..	..	..	..	..	..	..	..	..	..
Other Long-Term Capital	..	113	399	357	71	230	1,265	928	473	909	301
Other Capital, net	..	255	155	-195	131	948	611	54	-301	-844	356
Change in Reserves	..	-94	-193	-21	186	27	225	108	-43	-710	-391
Memo Item:					*(Finnish Markkaa per US dollar)*						
Conversion Factor (Annual Avg)	4.200	4.200	4.180	4.150	3.820	3.770	3.680	3.860	4.030	4.120	3.900
					(Millions US dollars), outstanding at end of year						
EXTERNAL DEBT (Total)	..	..	..	..	..	..	..	..	..	..	..
Long-Term Debt (by debtor)	..	..	..	..	..	..	..	..	..	..	..
Central Bank, incl. IMF credit	..	..	..	..	..	..	..	..	..	..	..
Central Government	..	..	..	..	..	..	..	..	..	..	..
Rest of General Government	..	..	..	..	..	..	..	..	..	..	..
Non-financial Public Enterprises	..	..	..	..	..	..	..	..	..	..	..
Priv. Sector, incl non-guaranteed	..	..	..	..	..	..	..	..	..	..	..
Short-Term Debt	..	..	..	..	..	..	..	..	..	..	..
Memo Items:					*(Millions of US dollars)*						
Int'l Reserves Excluding Gold	281.9	424.6	623.1	667.6	574.3	595.9	433.2	462.1	531.1	1,222.9	1,540.0
Gold Holdings (at market price)	45.3	30.8	60.9	90.6	92.4	153.6	115.5	111.0	149.2	213.6	504.9
SOCIAL INDICATORS											
Total Fertility Rate	1.9	1.8	1.7	1.6	1.5	1.6	1.7	1.7	1.7	1.7	1.6
Infant Mortality Rate	13.8	13.2	12.6	12.0	11.5	11.0	9.5	9.8	9.0	7.5	7.6
Life Expectancy at Birth	70.0	70.3	70.5	70.7	71.0	71.3	71.6	71.9	72.2	72.5	72.9
Urban Population, % of total	49.0	50.3	51.3	52.2	53.2	54.1	55.1	57.4	59.7	59.7	59.7
Food Prod. per capita (1987=100)	98.6	99.3	105.6	103.7	96.8	100.8	104.8	114.3	101.6	103.5	108.1
Labor Force, Agriculture (%)	20.4	19.6	18.8	18.1	17.3	16.5	15.8	15.0	14.3	13.5	12.8
Labor Force, Female (%)	43.4	43.7	43.9	44.2	44.5	44.7	45.0	45.3	45.6	45.9	46.1
Primary Schl. Enroll. Ratio	..	82.0	..	..	..	..	102.0	101.0	100.0	98.0	97.0
Primary Schl. Enroll. Ratio, Female	..	79.0	..	..	..	..	101.0	100.0	100.0	98.0	96.0
Secondary Schl. Enroll. Ratio	..	102.0	..	..	..	..	89.0	91.0	93.0	96.0	97.0

1980	1981	1982	1983	1984	1985	1986	1987	1988	1989 estimate	NOTES	FINLAND
											FOREIGN TRADE (CUSTOMS BASIS)
				(Millions of current US dollars)							
14,140	14,007	13,127	12,510	13,498	13,609	16,325	20,039	21,639	..	..	Value of Exports, fob
3,658	3,363	2,529	2,530	2,804	2,530	2,742	3,500	3,788	..	..	Nonfuel Primary Products
618	591	532	646	743	580	395	444	369	..	..	Fuels
9,864	10,052	10,066	9,334	9,950	10,499	13,188	16,095	17,482	..	..	Manufactures
15,632	14,190	13,380	12,846	12,435	13,226	15,324	19,860	20,911	..	..	Value of Imports, cif
2,272	1,925	1,946	1,725	1,762	1,761	2,044	2,539	2,873	..	..	Nonfuel Primary Products
4,546	4,357	3,654	3,454	3,101	3,218	2,345	2,672	2,013	..	..	Fuels
8,814	7,909	7,781	7,667	7,572	8,247	10,936	14,649	16,025	..	..	Manufactures
				(Index 1987 = 100)							
87.0	83.2	85.3	83.0	84.6	84.3	95.8	100.0	103.5	..	..	Terms of Trade
93.9	88.4	84.1	78.7	77.7	75.7	86.9	100.0	112.1	..	..	Export Prices, fob
107.9	106.2	98.5	94.9	91.9	89.7	90.8	100.0	108.3	..	..	Import Prices, cif
				(Millions of current US dollars)							**BALANCE OF PAYMENTS**
17,332	17,276	16,291	15,351	16,327	16,778	19,730	23,884	27,820	29,730	..	Exports of Goods & Services
14,070	13,662	12,842	12,172	13,087	13,351	16,005	19,079	21,826	22,882	..	Merchandise, fob
2,729	2,908	2,719	2,525	2,433	2,423	2,752	3,538	3,975	4,296	..	Nonfactor Services
533	706	731	654	808	1,004	973	1,267	2,019	2,552	..	Factor Services
18,621	17,545	16,919	16,142	16,163	17,368	20,069	25,206	30,069	34,198	..	Imports of Goods & Services
14,727	13,285	12,627	12,010	11,596	12,473	14,363	17,700	20,686	23,100	..	Merchandise, fob
2,492	2,533	2,447	2,438	2,582	2,812	3,235	4,410	5,350	6,042	..	Nonfactor Services
1,401	1,728	1,845	1,694	1,985	2,082	2,470	3,096	4,033	5,056	..	Factor Services
..	..	..	..	..	..	..	..	..	..	..	Long-Term Interest
-20	-10	-27	-23	-22	-7	-157	-162	-87	-195	..	Private Current Transfers, net
..	..	..	..	..	..	..	..	..	..	..	Workers' Remittances
-1,308	-279	-655	-814	143	-597	-495	-1,484	-2,337	-4,663	..	Curr. A/C Bal before Off. Transf.
-102	-106	-108	-121	-153	-169	-236	-328	-425	-465	..	Net Official Transfers
-1,410	-385	-763	-935	-10	-766	-731	-1,812	-2,762	-5,128	..	Curr. A/C Bal after Off. Transf.
-150	490	236	352	356	624	103	68	1,470	2,242	..	Long-Term Capital, net
-109	-127	-243	-249	-370	-280	-430	-807	-1,700	-2,598	..	Direct Investment
..	..	..	..	..	..	..	..	..	..	..	Long-Term Loans
..	..	..	..	..	..	..	..	..	..	..	Disbursements
..	..	..	..	..	..	..	..	..	..	..	Repayments
-41	618	478	601	727	904	534	875	3,169	4,840	..	Other Long-Term Capital
1,839	-330	727	355	1,471	728	-1,652	5,766	1,547	1,828	..	Other Capital, net
-280	224	-200	228	-1,817	-586	2,280	-4,022	-255	1,058	..	Change in Reserves
				(Finnish Markkaa per US dollar)							Memo Item:
3.730	4.320	4.820	5.570	6.010	6.200	5.070	4.400	4.180	4.290	..	Conversion Factor (Annual Avg)
				(Millions US dollars), outstanding at end of year							
..	..	..	..	..	..	..	..	..	..	..	**EXTERNAL DEBT (Total)**
..	..	..	..	..	..	..	..	..	..	..	Long-Term Debt (by debtor)
..	..	..	..	..	..	..	..	..	..	..	Central Bank, incl. IMF credit
..	..	..	..	..	..	..	..	..	..	..	Central Government
..	..	..	..	..	..	..	..	..	..	..	Rest of General Government
..	..	..	..	..	..	..	..	..	..	..	Non-financial Public Enterprises
..	..	..	..	..	..	..	..	..	..	..	Priv. Sector, incl non-guaranteed
..	..	..	..	..	..	..	..	..	..	..	Short-Term Debt
				(Millions of US dollars)							Memo Items:
1,870.2	1,483.7	1,517.5	1,237.7	2,754.3	3,749.9	1,787.1	6,417.5	6,369.2	5,111.1	..	Int'l Reserves Excluding Gold
581.3	504.5	580.2	484.5	391.6	625.2	747.4	946.4	802.1	802.8	..	Gold Holdings (at market price)
											SOCIAL INDICATORS
1.7	1.7	1.8	1.8	1.8	1.7	1.7	1.7	1.7	1.7	..	Total Fertility Rate
7.6	6.5	6.0	6.2	6.3	6.3	6.5	6.5	6.4	6.4	..	Infant Mortality Rate
73.2	73.5	73.9	74.1	74.3	74.5	74.7	74.9	75.1	75.3	..	Life Expectancy at Birth
59.8	59.9	59.9	59.9	59.8	59.8	59.8	59.8	59.8	59.8	..	Urban Population, % of total
107.8	96.1	109.6	120.4	119.3	115.5	114.5	100.0	102.7	113.9	..	Food Prod. per capita (1987=100)
12.0	..	..	..	..	..	..	..	..	..	..	Labor Force, Agriculture (%)
46.4	46.5	46.5	46.6	46.6	46.6	46.7	46.8	46.9	46.9	..	Labor Force, Female (%)
96.0	..	100.0	102.0	103.0	103.0	103.0	101.0	..	..	..	Primary Schl. Enroll. Ratio
96.0	98.0	99.0	102.0	102.0	102.0	103.0	101.0	..	..	..	Primary Schl. Enroll. Ratio, Female
98.0	..	98.0	101.0	103.0	104.0	104.0	106.0	..	..	..	Secondary Schl. Enroll. Ratio

FRANCE	1969	1970	1971	1972	1973	1974	1975	1976	1977	1978	1979
CURRENT GNP PER CAPITA (US $)	2,810	2,990	3,140	3,490	4,210	5,080	6,010	6,700	7,540	8,430	10,010
POPULATION (thousands)	50,318	50,772	51,251	51,701	52,118	52,460	52,699	52,909	53,145	53,376	53,606

USE AND ORIGIN OF RESOURCES

(Billions of current French Francs)

	1969	1970	1971	1972	1973	1974	1975	1976	1977	1978	1979
Gross National Product (GNP)	713.5	796.8	887.1	990.1	1,132.2	1,307.1	1,470.3	1,703.5	1,921.7	2,187.3	2,489.7
Net Factor Income from Abroad	2.9	3.3	2.9	2.1	2.3	4.1	2.4	2.9	3.9	4.8	8.6
GDP at Market Prices	710.5	793.5	884.2	987.9	1,129.8	1,303.0	1,467.9	1,700.6	1,917.8	2,182.6	2,481.1
Resource Balance	-3.0	4.4	9.8	10.6	9.5	-13.2	17.3	-12.5	2.2	28.7	14.4
Exports of Goods & NFServices	99.8	125.5	145.2	165.3	198.5	269.5	279.6	332.8	393.0	445.3	526.7
Imports of Goods & NFServices	102.8	121.1	135.4	154.7	188.9	282.7	262.3	345.3	390.8	416.6	512.3
Domestic Absorption	713.6	789.1	874.4	977.4	1,120.3	1,316.2	1,450.5	1,713.1	1,915.6	2,153.9	2,466.7
Private Consumption, etc.	416.2	457.5	507.8	567.8	640.6	745.0	856.7	987.8	1,112.6	1,258.7	1,434.4
General Gov't Consumption	133.0	145.5	160.3	176.8	196.0	227.7	265.4	292.9	335.2	390.0	443.8
Gross Domestic Investment	164.4	186.1	206.4	232.8	283.6	343.5	328.3	432.4	467.7	505.2	588.6
Fixed Investment	172.1	190.1	216.9	244.9	286.1	334.6	351.9	404.8	436.2	487.5	554.4
Indirect Taxes, net	96.5	103.0	115.5	130.7	146.2	160.5	176.4	211.5	223.7	260.2	309.4
GDP at factor cost	614.0	690.5	768.6	857.2	983.7	1,142.5	1,291.5	1,489.0	1,694.1	1,922.4	2,171.7
Agriculture	..	6.8	8.8	9.8	12.1	14.5	14.5	16.1	91.2	104.5	118.5
Industry	..	418.5	458.0	482.6	539.5	592.5	562.1	670.0	679.8	766.5	859.8
Manufacturing	..	378.8	417.8	446.1	509.1	556.1	505.7	591.5	496.4	564.3	635.6
Services, etc.	..	368.2	417.4	495.5	578.2	696.0	891.3	1,014.5	1,146.8	1,311.6	1,502.9
Gross Domestic Saving	161.4	190.5	216.1	243.4	293.2	330.3	345.7	419.9	470.0	533.9	603.0
Gross National Saving	..	190.1	214.3	240.9	290.6	328.9	341.5	416.1	466.9	530.4	601.8

(Billions of 1987 French Francs)

	1969	1970	1971	1972	1973	1974	1975	1976	1977	1978	1979
Gross National Product	3,311.8	3,501.7	3,607.3	3,779.7	3,930.9	4,057.4	4,039.8	4,211.6	4,348.5	4,494.9	4,646.7
GDP at Market Prices	3,297.9	3,486.9	3,595.0	3,771.2	3,922.2	4,044.1	4,032.9	4,204.0	4,339.3	4,484.7	4,630.0
Resource Balance	-75.3	-44.2	-33.1	-43.8	-70.5	-26.9	32.2	-26.5	27.9	52.3	35.0
Exports of Goods & NFServices	411.2	478.2	522.5	585.3	648.2	705.6	693.7	750.4	805.7	853.3	916.9
Imports of Goods & NFServices	486.5	522.5	555.5	629.1	718.7	732.5	661.6	776.9	777.7	800.9	881.9
Domestic Absorption	3,373.2	3,531.2	3,628.1	3,815.0	3,992.6	4,071.0	4,000.7	4,230.5	4,311.3	4,432.3	4,595.1
Private Consumption, etc.	1,969.8	2,063.8	2,105.8	2,221.1	2,281.2	2,314.1	2,378.3	2,485.0	2,556.4	2,649.3	2,724.7
General Gov't Consumption	594.3	618.9	643.6	666.4	689.1	697.1	727.1	757.2	775.3	815.0	839.4
Gross Domestic Investment	809.2	848.5	878.7	927.5	1,022.3	1,059.8	895.3	988.3	979.7	968.1	1,030.9
Fixed Investment	791.1	827.6	887.6	941.1	1,020.8	1,033.9	967.2	998.8	980.6	1,001.2	1,032.6
GDP at factor cost	2,852.6	3,038.3	3,120.8	3,267.8	3,400.3	3,548.3	3,548.4	3,681.8	3,837.6	3,950.8	4,054.0
Agriculture	..	235.7	276.0	296.7	341.6	344.0	313.2	313.3	133.0	147.0	159.2
Industry	..	1,912.8	2,026.4	2,049.5	2,174.4	2,028.5	1,715.4	1,843.6	1,493.9	1,523.8	1,553.6
Manufacturing	..	1,622.1	1,724.6	1,756.6	1,869.8	1,719.0	1,410.4	1,497.0	1,118.5	1,142.7	1,170.3
Services, etc.	..	1,180.4	1,175.9	1,286.4	1,304.7	1,578.5	1,933.6	1,975.1	2,713.8	2,813.3	2,915.1

Memo Items:

	1969	1970	1971	1972	1973	1974	1975	1976	1977	1978	1979
Capacity to Import	472.1	541.6	595.5	672.1	754.9	698.4	705.3	748.7	782.2	856.0	906.7
Terms of Trade Adjustment	60.9	63.4	73.1	86.8	106.7	-7.3	11.6	-1.7	-23.5	2.8	-10.2
Gross Domestic Income	3,358.8	3,550.3	3,668.1	3,858.0	4,028.8	4,036.9	4,044.5	4,202.3	4,315.8	4,487.4	4,619.8
Gross National Income	3,372.7	3,565.1	3,680.4	3,866.5	4,037.5	4,050.2	4,051.4	4,209.9	4,325.0	4,497.7	4,636.5

DOMESTIC PRICES/DEFLATORS

(Index 1987 = 100)

	1969	1970	1971	1972	1973	1974	1975	1976	1977	1978	1979
Overall (GDP)	21.5	22.8	24.6	26.2	28.8	32.2	36.4	40.5	44.2	48.7	53.6
Domestic Absorption	21.2	22.3	24.1	25.6	28.1	32.3	36.3	40.5	44.4	48.6	53.7
Agriculture	..	2.9	3.2	3.3	3.5	4.2	4.6	5.1	68.6	71.1	74.4
Industry	..	21.9	22.6	23.5	24.8	29.2	32.8	36.3	45.5	50.3	55.3
Manufacturing	..	23.4	24.2	25.4	27.2	32.4	35.9	39.5	44.4	49.4	54.3
Consumer Price Index	22.5	23.8	25.2	26.7	28.7	32.6	36.4	39.9	43.7	47.6	52.8

MANUFACTURING ACTIVITY

	1969	1970	1971	1972	1973	1974	1975	1976	1977	1978	1979
Employment (1987=100)	118.7	121.8	123.6	125.5	128.7	130.4	126.7	125.5	125.1	123.4	121.3
Real Earnings per Empl. (1987=100)	..	..	..	..	..	..	..	..	..	..	..
Real Output per Empl. (1987=100)	..	66.4	69.5	72.4	76.3	79.4	75.8	81.1	80.5	79.9	85.4
Earnings as % of Value Added	..	..	..	..	..	..	..	..	66.7	64.8	64.1

MONETARY HOLDINGS

(Billions of current French Francs)

	1969	1970	1971	1972	1973	1974	1975	1976	1977	1978	1979
Money Supply, Broadly Defined	427.4	489.7	577.6	681.4	783.9	916.3	1,075.2	1,228.5	1,443.5	1,634.4	1,868.3
Money	209.7	232.5	259.9	299.0	327.9	377.7	425.2	457.0	507.8	665.9	751.4
Currency Outside Banks	72.6	75.9	78.0	84.0	89.5	97.8	106.6	116.1	121.5	131.9	139.2
Demand Deposits	137.0	156.6	181.9	215.0	238.4	279.9	318.6	340.9	386.3	534.0	612.2
Quasi-Money	217.7	257.2	317.7	382.4	456.0	538.6	650.0	771.5	935.7	968.5	1,116.9

GOVERNMENT DEFICIT (-) OR SURPLUS

(Billions of current French Francs)

	1969	1970	1971	1972	1973	1974	1975	1976	1977	1978	1979
GOVERNMENT DEFICIT (-) OR SURPLUS	..	..	..	6.8	4.7	5.8	-37.8	-17.1	-22.3	-29.6	-37.0
Current Revenue	..	..	..	333.8	372.9	457.5	516.4	627.8	699.0	793.2	942.1
Current Expenditure	..	..	..	299.0	335.3	414.0	502.7	578.0	669.2	784.2	905.1
Current Budget Balance	..	..	..	34.8	37.6	43.5	13.7	49.8	29.8	9.0	37.0
Capital Receipts	..	..	..	0.8	2.6	2.2	1.6	3.8	2.9	0.9	1.0
Capital Payments	..	..	..	30.1	30.7	39.3	52.8	64.4	50.6	51.2	64.9

1980	1981	1982	1983	1984	1985	1986	1987	1988	1989 estimate	NOTES	FRANCE
11,870	12,430	11,900	10,640	9,940	9,750	10,770	12,960	16,200	17,830	..	CURRENT GNP PER CAPITA (US $)
53,880	54,182	54,480	54,728	54,947	55,170	55,394	55,630	55,874	56,119	..	POPULATION (thousands)
(Billions of current French Francs)											USE AND ORIGIN OF RESOURCES
2,820.9	3,175.1	3,628.0	3,994.8	4,338.4	4,674.5	5,035.8	5,305.2	5,679.2	6,087.5	..	Gross National Product (GNP)
12.6	10.3	2.0	-11.7	-23.5	-25.7	-16.7	-15.7	-13.3	-17.7	..	Net Factor Income from Abroad
2,808.3	3,164.8	3,626.0	4,006.5	4,361.9	4,700.1	5,052.5	5,320.9	5,692.4	6,105.2	..	GDP at Market Prices
-34.4	-30.6	-68.8	-6.8	28.5	31.3	52.1	8.0	3.8	22.5	..	Resource Balance
604.4	714.4	790.4	900.7	1,053.2	1,124.2	1,074.2	1,102.9	1,222.0	1,428.5	..	Exports of Goods & NFServices
638.8	745.0	859.2	907.5	1,024.8	1,092.8	1,022.1	1,094.9	1,218.2	1,406.0	..	Imports of Goods & NFServices
2,842.7	3,195.4	3,694.8	4,013.3	4,333.4	4,668.8	5,000.4	5,312.9	5,688.6	6,082.7	..	Domestic Absorption
1,645.1	1,897.5	2,191.8	2,422.9	2,640.5	2,858.5	3,042.3	3,231.3	3,421.6	3,649.5	..	Private Consumption, etc.
517.4	604.1	711.7	793.5	866.4	923.0	972.7	1,015.9	1,071.0	1,132.2	..	General Gov't Consumption
680.2	693.9	791.4	796.8	826.5	887.3	985.4	1,065.7	1,196.1	1,301.0	..	Gross Domestic Investment
645.8	712.8	785.5	828.6	868.1	942.2	1,001.3	1,081.5	1,208.4	1,321.6	..	Fixed Investment
356.2	386.8	451.6	499.5	546.6	595.2	618.5	656.4	720.1	762.2	..	Indirect Taxes, net
2,452.1	2,778.0	3,174.5	3,507.0	3,815.3	4,104.9	4,434.0	4,664.5	4,972.3	5,342.9	..	GDP at factor cost
119.0	130.9	166.2	169.6	175.2	182.3	189.2	188.0	189.7	..	B	Agriculture
947.3	1,029.8	1,148.4	1,256.6	1,338.7	1,434.0	1,526.6	1,565.2	1,670.5	..	B	Industry
679.5	733.5	821.5	901.0	956.3	1,033.1	1,111.1	1,127.6	1,207.7	..	B	Manufacturing
1,742.0	2,004.0	2,311.4	2,580.3	2,848.0	3,083.8	3,336.7	3,567.7	3,832.2	..	B	Services, etc.
645.8	663.2	722.6	790.1	855.0	918.7	1,037.5	1,073.7	1,199.9	1,323.6	..	Gross Domestic Saving
648.0	661.2	711.6	765.1	822.7	881.2	1,008.7	1,044.2	1,172.1	1,288.6	..	Gross National Saving
(Billions of 1987 French Francs)											
4,726.6	4,776.2	4,884.7	4,901.7	4,954.1	5,048.6	5,177.4	5,305.2	5,514.5	5,716.0	..	Gross National Product
4,705.2	4,760.6	4,881.8	4,915.7	4,980.2	5,075.7	5,194.5	5,320.9	5,527.4	5,732.3	..	GDP at Market Prices
37.8	91.2	51.8	111.5	157.5	136.5	58.5	8.0	4.8	37.0	..	Resource Balance
941.7	976.3	959.8	995.2	1,064.9	1,085.2	1,073.5	1,102.9	1,194.4	1,325.5	..	Exports of Goods & NFServices
903.9	885.1	908.0	883.7	907.4	948.7	1,014.9	1,094.9	1,189.6	1,288.5	..	Imports of Goods & NFServices
4,667.4	4,669.4	4,829.9	4,804.2	4,822.7	4,939.2	5,136.0	5,312.9	5,522.6	5,695.3	..	Domestic Absorption
2,756.9	2,813.1	2,908.3	2,936.3	2,966.9	3,036.6	3,143.7	3,231.3	3,332.7	3,438.2	..	Private Consumption, etc.
860.5	887.1	920.1	939.0	949.8	971.2	987.8	1,015.9	1,045.0	1,061.5	..	General Gov't Consumption
1,050.0	969.2	1,001.6	928.9	906.0	931.5	1,004.5	1,065.7	1,144.9	1,195.7	..	Gross Domestic Investment
1,059.7	1,039.7	1,025.4	988.9	963.1	994.3	1,027.6	1,081.5	1,174.1	1,239.3	..	Fixed Investment
4,120.5	4,196.8	4,292.5	4,319.6	4,373.9	4,447.7	4,560.2	4,664.5	4,827.8	5,017.9	..	GDP at factor cost
156.1	155.1	181.0	172.1	180.1	181.6	182.9	188.0	188.3	..	..	Agriculture
1,560.2	1,560.2	1,565.8	1,574.7	1,555.9	1,555.8	1,565.3	1,565.2	1,634.8	..	..	Industry
1,162.5	1,154.6	1,164.7	1,169.4	1,148.0	1,143.6	1,138.9	1,127.6	1,183.1	..	..	Manufacturing
2,989.4	3,047.4	3,131.8	3,168.9	3,244.2	3,338.3	3,446.3	3,567.7	3,704.3	..	..	Services, etc.
											Memo Items:
855.3	848.7	835.3	877.1	932.6	975.9	1,066.6	1,102.9	1,193.3	1,309.1	..	Capacity to Import
-86.4	-127.6	-124.6	-118.1	-132.2	-109.3	-6.8	0.0	-1.1	-16.4	..	Terms of Trade Adjustment
4,618.8	4,633.0	4,757.2	4,797.6	4,847.9	4,966.4	5,187.7	5,320.9	5,526.3	5,715.9	..	Gross Domestic Income
4,640.2	4,648.6	4,760.2	4,783.6	4,821.9	4,939.3	5,170.5	5,305.2	5,513.4	5,699.6	..	Gross National Income
(Index 1987 = 100)											DOMESTIC PRICES/DEFLATORS
59.7	66.5	74.3	81.5	87.6	92.6	97.3	100.0	103.0	106.5	..	Overall (GDP)
60.9	68.4	76.5	83.5	89.9	94.5	97.4	100.0	103.0	106.8	..	Domestic Absorption
76.2	84.4	91.8	98.5	97.3	100.4	103.4	100.0	100.7	..	..	Agriculture
60.7	66.0	73.3	79.8	86.0	92.2	97.5	100.0	102.2	..	..	Industry
58.5	63.5	70.5	77.0	83.3	90.3	97.6	100.0	102.1	..	..	Manufacturing
59.8	67.8	75.8	83.1	89.3	94.4	96.8	100.0	102.7	106.3	..	Consumer Price Index
											MANUFACTURING ACTIVITY
119.6	115.5	113.9	111.5	108.0	104.8	102.8	100.0	98.1	98.3	..	Employment (1987=100)
..	..	..	..	..	..	..	..	..	..	..	Real Earnings per Empl. (1987=100)
92.2	96.9	98.6	99.3	103.6	104.2	97.8	100.0	107.1	..	..	Real Output per Empl. (1987=100)
68.4	70.2	70.1	68.7	68.2	66.3	..	..	..	..	..	Earnings as % of Value Added
(Billions of current French Francs)											MONETARY HOLDINGS
2,044.9	2,271.0	2,536.7	2,817.8	3,443.4	3,338.3	3,573.7	4,095.4	4,452.0	4,836.8	D	Money Supply, Broadly Defined
801.2	899.8	985.0	1,108.4	1,219.2	1,312.4	1,406.8	1,471.1	1,531.6	1,652.6	..	Money
143.8	160.9	177.1	191.7	198.8	207.3	214.1	221.8	235.7	246.4	..	Currency Outside Banks
657.4	738.9	807.9	916.7	1,020.4	1,105.1	1,192.7	1,249.3	1,295.9	1,406.2	..	Demand Deposits
1,243.7	1,371.2	1,551.7	1,709.4	2,224.2	2,025.9	2,166.9	2,624.3	2,920.4	3,184.2	..	Quasi-Money
(Billions of current French Francs)											GOVERNMENT DEFICIT (-) OR SURPLUS
-2.0	-73.2	-121.9	-140.7	-116.3	-127.7	-170.2	-63.2	-127.0	..	..	
1,124.3	1,287.7	1,496.0	1,672.6	1,835.2	1,979.4	2,100.8	2,229.9	2,363.4	..	..	Current Revenue
1,050.9	1,264.7	1,499.1	1,698.9	1,862.7	2,013.7	2,131.1	2,223.7	2,339.8	..	..	Current Expenditure
73.4	23.0	-3.1	-26.3	-27.5	-34.3	-30.3	6.2	23.6	..	..	Current Budget Balance
0.8	1.3	3.0	1.2	2.3	1.9	2.1	4.9	2.3	..	..	Capital Receipts
71.0	88.4	139.7	106.4	108.9	109.1	137.6	92.9	136.3	..	..	Capital Payments

FRANCE	1969	1970	1971	1972	1973	1974	1975	1976	1977	1978	1979
FOREIGN TRADE (CUSTOMS BASIS)					*(Billions of current US dollars)*						
Value of Exports, fob	14.88	17.74	20.42	25.84	35.66	45.14	51.60	55.46	63.36	76.49	97.96
Nonfuel Primary Products	3.79	4.11	4.83	6.38	9.20	11.09	10.82	11.65	12.89	16.21	20.25
Fuels	0.35	0.38	0.45	0.58	0.76	1.21	1.41	1.61	1.89	2.05	3.49
Manufactures	10.74	13.25	15.13	18.88	25.70	32.84	39.38	42.20	48.58	58.24	74.22
Value of Imports, cif	17.22	18.92	21.14	26.72	37.05	52.17	53.61	64.02	70.28	81.86	106.71
Nonfuel Primary Products	5.26	5.60	5.60	6.88	9.97	12.16	12.17	13.95	16.47	18.69	22.52
Fuels	1.96	2.29	2.93	3.53	4.58	11.94	12.26	14.37	15.09	15.94	22.95
Manufactures	9.99	11.04	12.60	16.30	22.50	28.07	29.17	35.70	38.71	47.24	61.24
					(Index 1987 = 100)						
Terms of Trade	130.2	131.9	128.9	129.9	132.8	100.2	108.8	103.5	98.0	102.9	102.9
Export Prices, fob	28.7	29.5	31.0	34.8	46.1	52.8	59.8	58.9	61.5	71.2	85.5
Import Prices, cif	22.0	22.4	24.1	26.8	34.7	52.6	55.0	57.0	62.8	69.2	83.1
BALANCE OF PAYMENTS					*(Billions of current US dollars)*						
Exports of Goods & Services	..	25.29	28.92	35.78	49.97	63.51	73.31	78.68	90.51	114.20	144.87
Merchandise, fob	..	17.95	20.43	25.89	34.87	44.00	49.91	53.92	61.18	74.56	94.28
Nonfactor Services	..	5.61	6.72	7.81	11.34	14.17	18.07	19.21	22.70	30.01	35.81
Factor Services	..	1.73	1.78	2.08	3.76	5.34	5.34	5.56	6.63	9.63	14.78
Imports of Goods & Services	..	24.61	27.49	34.24	46.79	65.09	67.94	79.60	88.10	103.86	135.71
Merchandise, fob	..	17.69	19.57	24.83	34.44	48.80	48.78	58.91	64.47	74.45	97.50
Nonfactor Services	..	5.38	6.24	7.23	9.01	11.47	13.65	14.98	17.37	20.70	25.27
Factor Services	..	1.54	1.69	2.18	3.35	4.82	5.52	5.71	6.26	8.71	12.93
Long-Term Interest	..	..	..	..	..	..	..	..	..	..	..
Private Current Transfers, net	..	-0.66	-0.85	-0.90	-1.11	-1.15	-1.53	-1.41	-1.41	-1.82	-2.30
Workers' Remittances	..	0.13	0.15	0.18	0.20	0.21	0.24	0.24	0.27	0.34	0.40
Curr. A/C Bal before Off. Transf.	..	0.02	0.58	0.64	2.07	-2.73	3.85	-2.33	1.01	8.52	6.86
Net Official Transfers	..	-0.22	-0.42	-0.74	-0.64	-1.12	-1.10	-1.04	-1.42	-1.45	-1.72
Curr. A/C Bal after Off. Transf.	..	-0.20	0.16	-0.10	1.44	-3.86	2.74	-3.37	-0.41	7.06	5.14
Long-Term Capital, net	..	0.10	0.01	-0.65	-2.48	-0.26	-1.50	-2.19	0.89	-3.43	-5.20
Direct Investment	..	0.25	0.13	0.09	0.19	1.34	0.23	-0.66	0.89	0.57	0.60
Long-Term Loans	..	..	..	..	..	..	..	..	..	..	..
Disbursements	..	..	..	..	..	..	..	..	..	..	..
Repayments	..	..	..	..	..	..	..	..	..	..	..
Other Long-Term Capital	..	-0.15	-0.12	-0.74	-2.67	-1.60	-1.73	-1.53	0.00	-4.00	-5.80
Other Capital, net	..	1.91	3.11	2.36	-0.85	3.77	2.27	2.52	0.20	-0.63	1.81
Change in Reserves	..	-1.81	-3.28	-1.61	1.89	0.35	-3.51	3.04	-0.68	-3.00	-1.75
Memo Item:					*(French Francs per US dollar)*						
Conversion Factor (Annual Avg)	5.190	5.550	5.540	5.040	4.450	4.810	4.290	4.780	4.910	4.510	4.250
					(Millions US dollars), outstanding at end of year						
EXTERNAL DEBT (Total)	..	..	..	..	..	..	..	..	..	..	..
Long-Term Debt (by debtor)	..	..	..	..	..	..	..	..	..	..	..
Central Bank, incl. IMF credit	..	..	..	..	..	..	..	..	..	..	..
Central Government	..	..	..	..	..	..	..	..	..	..	..
Rest of General Government	..	..	..	..	..	..	..	..	..	..	..
Non-financial Public Enterprises	..	..	..	..	..	..	..	..	..	..	..
Priv. Sector, incl non-guaranteed	..	..	..	..	..	..	..	..	..	..	..
Short-Term Debt	..	..	..	..	..	..	..	..	..	..	..
Memo Items:					*(Millions of US dollars)*						
Int'l Reserves Excluding Gold	286	1,428	4,428	6,189	4,268	4,526	8,457	5,620	5,872	9,278	17,579
Gold Holdings (at market price)	3,567	3,771	4,392	6,535	11,327	18,824	14,156	13,613	16,770	23,050	41,941
SOCIAL INDICATORS											
Total Fertility Rate	2.5	2.5	2.5	2.4	2.3	2.1	1.9	1.8	1.9	1.8	1.9
Infant Mortality Rate	19.6	18.2	17.2	16.0	15.4	14.6	13.8	12.5	11.4	10.7	10.0
Life Expectancy at Birth	71.9	72.0	72.2	72.3	72.6	72.9	73.2	73.5	73.8	74.0	74.1
Urban Population, % of total	70.2	71.0	71.4	71.8	72.2	72.6	73.0	73.0	73.1	73.1	73.2
Food Prod. per capita (1987=100)	81.6	87.1	86.9	83.3	90.3	92.7	86.6	87.5	81.5	87.3	95.3
Labor Force, Agriculture (%)	14.4	13.6	13.1	12.6	12.1	11.6	11.1	10.6	10.1	9.6	9.1
Labor Force, Female (%)	35.9	36.2	36.5	36.8	37.1	37.4	37.7	38.0	38.4	38.7	39.0
Primary Schl. Enroll. Ratio	..	117.0	..	..	..	..	109.0	109.0	111.0	112.0	112.0
Primary Schl. Enroll. Ratio, Female	..	117.0	..	..	..	..	..	109.0	110.0	111.0	111.0
Secondary Schl. Enroll. Ratio	..	74.0	..	..	..	..	82.0	83.0	83.0	83.0	84.0

1980	1981	1982	1983	1984	1985	1986	1987	1988	1989 estimate	NOTES	FRANCE
				(Billions of current US dollars)							**FOREIGN TRADE (CUSTOMS BASIS)**
110.87	101.25	92.36	91.14	93.16	97.46	119.07	143.08	161.70	..	..	Value of Exports, fob
24.73	22.85	20.08	20.49	20.89	21.46	25.39	30.21	35.25	..	..	Nonfuel Primary Products
4.49	4.72	3.66	3.46	3.40	3.75	3.19	3.17	3.34	..	..	Fuels
81.65	73.68	68.62	67.19	68.87	72.24	90.49	109.70	123.11	..	..	Manufactures
134.33	120.28	115.45	105.27	103.61	107.59	127.85	157.52	176.75	..	..	Value of Imports, cif
25.61	21.68	20.28	19.53	19.56	19.57	23.65	27.72	31.90	..	..	Nonfuel Primary Products
35.73	34.67	30.83	25.75	24.91	23.95	16.14	16.93	14.60	..	..	Fuels
73.00	63.93	64.35	59.99	59.15	64.08	88.06	112.87	130.25	..	..	Manufactures
				(Index 1987 = 100)							
97.0	87.2	87.6	88.3	89.0	93.9	98.9	100.0	104.8	..	..	Terms of Trade
95.3	84.4	78.9	76.3	74.7	76.3	86.0	100.0	111.1	..	..	Export Prices, fob
98.2	96.7	90.1	86.3	84.0	81.3	87.0	100.0	106.0	..	..	Import Prices, cif
				(Billions of current US dollars)							**BALANCE OF PAYMENTS**
171.82	168.78	153.77	145.28	147.70	154.28	187.80	221.00	248.02	273.37	..	Exports of Goods & Services
107.52	100.87	91.50	89.71	92.21	95.93	119.36	141.66	160.64	171.32	..	Merchandise, fob
42.89	41.25	36.45	34.77	34.65	36.04	43.51	50.89	55.40	64.53	..	Nonfactor Services
21.42	26.66	25.81	20.80	20.85	22.31	24.92	28.46	31.99	37.53	..	Factor Services
171.86	169.36	161.23	146.63	145.68	151.69	180.78	220.04	244.84	269.25	..	Imports of Goods & Services
120.93	110.84	107.29	98.46	96.87	101.20	121.44	150.32	168.73	181.67	..	Merchandise, fob
31.65	33.01	27.78	25.52	25.13	25.45	32.18	38.92	42.12	48.03	..	Nonfactor Services
19.27	25.50	26.16	22.65	23.69	25.03	27.16	30.80	33.99	39.55	..	Factor Services
..	..	..	..	..	..	..	..	..	..	..	Long-Term Interest
-2.45	-2.27	-1.96	-1.74	-1.01	-1.31	-1.74	-2.30	-2.44	-2.71	..	Private Current Transfers, net
0.45	0.35	0.32	0.34	0.34	0.23	0.32	0.40	0.44	0.57	..	Workers' Remittances
-2.49	-2.84	-9.42	-3.09	1.01	1.28	5.28	-1.33	0.75	1.42	..	Curr. A/C Bal before Off. Transf.
-1.71	-1.97	-2.66	-2.08	-1.88	-1.32	-2.85	-3.11	-4.29	-5.72	..	Net Official Transfers
-4.21	-4.81	-12.08	-5.17	-0.88	-0.03	2.43	-4.45	-3.55	-4.30	..	Curr. A/C Bal after Off. Transf.
-8.48	-8.89	0.85	9.31	4.37	3.23	-7.47	2.21	-1.01	6.25	..	Long-Term Capital, net
0.19	-2.08	-1.26	0.01	0.28	0.35	-2.15	-4.07	-6.01	-8.76	..	Direct Investment
..	..	..	..	..	..	..	..	..	..	..	Long-Term Loans
..	..	..	..	..	..	..	..	..	..	..	Disbursements
..	..	..	..	..	..	..	..	..	..	..	Repayments
-8.67	-6.81	2.11	9.30	4.10	2.87	-5.32	6.28	5.00	15.01	..	Other Long-Term Capital
18.75	8.93	7.63	0.02	-0.71	-0.81	6.46	-6.09	4.46	-4.42	..	Other Capital, net
-6.06	4.77	3.61	-4.17	-2.79	-2.38	-1.42	8.33	0.10	2.47	..	Change in Reserves
				(French Francs per US dollar)							Memo Item:
4.230	5.430	6.570	7.620	8.740	8.990	6.930	6.010	5.960	6.380	..	Conversion Factor (Annual Avg)
				(Millions US dollars), outstanding at end of year							
..	..	..	..	..	..	..	..	..	..	..	**EXTERNAL DEBT (Total)**
..	..	..	..	..	..	..	..	..	..	..	Long-Term Debt (by debtor)
..	..	..	..	..	..	..	..	..	..	..	Central Bank, incl. IMF credit
..	..	..	..	..	..	..	..	..	..	..	Central Government
..	..	..	..	..	..	..	..	..	..	..	Rest of General Government
..	..	..	..	..	..	..	..	..	..	..	Non-financial Public Enterprises
..	..	..	..	..	..	..	..	..	..	..	Priv. Sector, incl non-guaranteed
..	..	..	..	..	..	..	..	..	..	..	Short-Term Debt
				(Millions of US dollars)							Memo Items:
27,340	22,262	16,531	19,851	20,940	26,589	31,454	33,050	25,365	24,611	..	Int'l Reserves Excluding Gold
48,252	32,536	37,398	31,227	25,235	26,766	31,996	39,625	33,580	32,823	..	Gold Holdings (at market price)
											SOCIAL INDICATORS
1.9	1.9	1.9	1.8	1.8	1.8	1.8	1.8	1.8	1.8	..	Total Fertility Rate
10.0	9.7	9.5	9.1	8.3	8.3	8.0	7.8	7.7	7.4	..	Infant Mortality Rate
74.3	74.4	74.6	74.9	75.2	75.4	75.7	76.0	76.3	76.5	..	Life Expectancy at Birth
73.2	73.2	73.3	73.3	73.4	73.4	73.5	73.7	73.8	74.0	..	Urban Population, % of total
95.3	91.9	97.6	93.0	101.0	98.5	97.7	100.0	99.9	96.4	..	Food Prod. per capita (1987=100)
8.6	..	..	..	..	..	..	..	..	..	..	Labor Force, Agriculture (%)
39.3	39.4	39.4	39.5	39.6	39.6	39.7	39.7	39.8	39.8	..	Labor Force, Female (%)
111.0	..	109.0	108.0	106.0	109.0	111.0	113.0	..	..	..	Primary Schl. Enroll. Ratio
110.0	109.0	108.0	107.0	105.0	107.0	110.0	113.0	..	..	..	Primary Schl. Enroll. Ratio, Female
85.0	..	88.0	90.0	89.0	90.0	91.0	92.0	..	..	..	Secondary Schl. Enroll. Ratio

GABON	1969	1970	1971	1972	1973	1974	1975	1976	1977	1978	1979
CURRENT GNP PER CAPITA (US $)	620	660	690	740	890	1,660	2,730	4,170	3,800	2,870	3,190
POPULATION (thousands)	493	504	525	550	578	607	637	668	698	728	761

USE AND ORIGIN OF RESOURCES *(Billions of current CFA Francs)*

	1969	1970	1971	1972	1973	1974	1975	1976	1977	1978	1979
Gross National Product (GNP)	76.8	84.9	98.5	101.3	148.3	341.3	429.6	676.4	653.0	488.0	567.7
Net Factor Income from Abroad	-5.9	-4.6	-6.6	-7.2	-12.8	-30.4	-32.8	-42.7	-37.2	-51.2	-76.9
GDP at Market Prices	82.7	89.5	105.1	108.5	161.1	371.7	462.4	719.1	690.2	539.2	644.6
Resource Balance	0.5	10.5	14.7	0.9	1.9	53.1	7.5	-3.7	2.3	80.0	135.9
Exports of Goods & NFServices	45.2	44.5	69.7	79.3	94.8	213.9	229.0	327.8	356.1	333.0	377.0
Imports of Goods & NFServices	44.7	34.0	55.0	78.4	92.9	160.8	221.5	331.5	353.8	253.0	241.1
Domestic Absorption	82.2	79.0	90.4	107.6	159.2	318.6	454.9	722.8	687.9	459.2	508.7
Private Consumption, etc.	42.1	32.8	37.1	36.2	73.6	91.8	108.6	118.3	162.2	196.6	218.6
General Gov't Consumption	11.6	17.6	19.7	19.2	25.1	34.4	56.5	76.0	124.9	73.8	77.9
Gross Domestic Investment	28.5	28.6	33.6	52.2	60.5	192.4	289.8	528.5	400.8	188.8	212.2
Fixed Investment	..	27.2	32.2	51.5	52.3	156.3	258.2	435.5	338.0	224.0	203.1
Indirect Taxes, net	11.0	13.5	9.7	5.3	13.5	20.3	31.9	38.5	50.8	38.7	37.8
GDP at factor cost	71.7	76.0	95.4	103.2	147.6	351.4	430.5	680.6	639.4	500.5	606.8
Agriculture	15.4	16.6	14.5	14.2	18.7	30.5	29.6	36.0	37.7	35.1	48.0
Industry	37.7	42.6	47.9	55.6	77.1	235.5	288.0	448.4	402.1	311.8	398.1
Manufacturing	5.9	6.1	7.5	8.4	10.7	13.6	19.7	27.8	32.6	32.2	32.3
Services, etc.	29.6	30.3	42.7	38.7	65.3	105.7	144.8	234.7	250.4	192.3	198.5
Gross Domestic Saving	29.0	39.1	48.3	53.1	62.4	245.5	297.3	524.8	403.1	268.8	348.1
Gross National Saving	..	32.5	39.2	42.8	45.3	209.1	255.7	470.0	349.7	199.8	238.5

(Billions of 1987 CFA Francs)

	1969	1970	1971	1972	1973	1974	1975	1976	1977	1978	1979
Gross National Product	424.77	459.53	500.66	558.39	590.11	887.37	1,066.49	1,432.93	1,251.56	905.62	915.31
GDP at Market Prices	440.08	478.27	527.34	587.12	646.91	902.35	1,075.51	1,458.68	1,275.25	968.48	973.16
Resource Balance	29.11	38.61	43.62	26.86	28.46	-100.96	-146.28	-146.62	-156.49	-13.46	-28.03
Exports of Goods & NFServices	191.25	212.31	224.72	239.06	240.66	361.56	446.71	520.71	503.06	522.07	429.18
Imports of Goods & NFServices	162.14	173.71	181.10	212.20	212.20	462.52	592.99	667.32	659.55	535.53	457.21
Domestic Absorption	410.97	439.67	483.72	560.26	618.45	1,003.31	1,221.79	1,605.30	1,431.74	981.93	1,001.19
Private Consumption, etc.	221.07	231.72	249.20	269.04	315.96	299.91	318.70	365.16	399.06	517.25	465.75
General Gov't Consumption	69.37	73.79	81.09	107.80	91.08	109.34	168.33	188.90	211.57	152.38	149.69
Gross Domestic Investment	120.52	134.15	153.42	183.42	211.41	594.06	734.76	1,051.24	821.11	312.30	385.74
Fixed Investment	..	..	..	..	..	..	..	..	..	..	..
GDP at factor cost	..	..	..	..	..	..	..	..	..	..	..
Agriculture	..	..	..	..	..	..	..	..	..	..	..
Industry	..	..	..	..	..	..	..	..	..	..	..
Manufacturing	..	..	..	..	..	..	..	..	..	..	..
Services, etc.	..	..	..	..	..	..	..	..	..	..	..
Memo Items:											
Capacity to Import	163.95	227.35	229.50	214.64	216.54	615.25	613.07	659.88	663.84	704.87	714.92
Terms of Trade Adjustment	-27.30	15.04	4.78	-24.43	-24.12	253.70	166.36	139.17	160.78	182.79	285.75
Gross Domestic Income	412.78	493.31	532.12	562.70	622.79	1,156.05	1,241.87	1,597.85	1,436.03	1,151.27	1,258.90
Gross National Income	397.47	474.56	505.44	533.96	565.99	1,141.07	1,232.85	1,572.10	1,412.34	1,088.41	1,201.06

DOMESTIC PRICES/DEFLATORS *(Index 1987 = 100)*

	1969	1970	1971	1972	1973	1974	1975	1976	1977	1978	1979
Overall (GDP)	18.8	18.7	19.9	18.5	24.9	41.2	43.0	49.3	54.1	55.7	66.2
Domestic Absorption	20.0	18.0	18.7	19.2	25.7	31.8	37.2	45.0	48.0	46.8	50.8
Agriculture	..	..	..	..	..	..	..	..	..	..	..
Industry	..	..	..	..	..	..	..	..	..	..	..
Manufacturing	..	..	..	..	..	..	..	..	..	..	..
Consumer Price Index	19.1	19.8	20.5	21.3	22.6	25.3	32.5	39.0	44.4	49.2	53.1

MANUFACTURING ACTIVITY

	1969	1970	1971	1972	1973	1974	1975	1976	1977	1978	1979
Employment (1987=100)	..	..	..	..	..	..	..	..	..	..	..
Real Earnings per Empl. (1987=100)	..	..	..	..	..	..	..	..	..	..	..
Real Output per Empl. (1987=100)	..	..	..	..	..	..	..	..	..	..	..
Earnings as % of Value Added	..	..	..	40.1	39.8	45.1	48.6	44.5	42.3	44.5	..

MONETARY HOLDINGS *(Billions of current CFA Francs)*

	1969	1970	1971	1972	1973	1974	1975	1976	1977	1978	1979
Money Supply, Broadly Defined	12.42	13.49	15.33	19.71	26.11	44.00	70.95	132.49	129.58	112.78	122.35
Money	11.43	12.53	14.50	18.41	22.84	38.11	58.97	104.06	95.76	89.84	85.42
Currency Outside Banks	4.25	4.98	5.81	7.00	9.14	15.29	21.71	32.73	30.51	30.48	29.86
Demand Deposits	7.18	7.55	8.69	11.41	13.70	22.82	37.26	71.33	65.26	59.37	55.56
Quasi-Money	0.99	0.95	0.83	1.30	3.27	5.89	11.98	28.43	33.82	22.94	36.93

GOVERNMENT DEFICIT (-) OR SURPLUS *(Billions of current CFA Francs)*

	1969	1970	1971	1972	1973	1974	1975	1976	1977	1978	1979
GOVERNMENT DEFICIT (-) OR SURPLUS	..	..	..	..	-17.63	-15.46	-36.97	-158.13	..	..	-3.50
Current Revenue	..	..	..	..	38.82	89.16	167.31	188.43	..	..	275.00
Current Expenditure	..	..	..	..	..	..	..	..	..	..	..
Current Budget Balance	..	..	..	..	..	..	..	..	..	..	..
Capital Receipts	..	..	..	..	0.05	0.03	0.08	0.63	..	..	..
Capital Payments	..	..	..	..	..	..	..	..	..	..	..

1980	1981	1982	1983	1984	1985	1986	1987	1988	1989 estimate	NOTES	GABON
3,900	4,260	4,370	3,830	3,580	3,560	3,630	2,890	2,780	2,960	..	CURRENT GNP PER CAPITA (US $)
797	835	875	916	957	997	1,023	1,050	1,077	1,105	..	POPULATION (thousands)

(Billions of current CFA Francs) — USE AND ORIGIN OF RESOURCES

1980	1981	1982	1983	1984	1985	1986	1987	1988	1989	NOTES	
814.7	960.4	1,086.0	1,179.9	1,438.1	1,536.6	1,115.5	947.6	880.6	995.1	..	Gross National Product (GNP)
-89.8	-89.2	-102.9	-107.1	-97.9	-109.4	-85.4	-73.0	-82.7	-102.0	..	Net Factor Income from Abroad
904.5	1,049.6	1,188.9	1,287.0	1,536.0	1,646.0	1,200.9	1,020.6	963.3	1,097.1	..	GDP at Market Prices
299.2	237.9	260.7	229.9	317.9	226.3	-205.0	3.0	-71.4	78.2	..	Resource Balance
585.2	665.0	732.3	792.5	946.8	897.3	401.0	405.9	362.2	526.8	..	Exports of Goods & NFServices
286.0	427.1	471.6	562.6	628.9	671.0	606.0	402.9	433.6	448.6	..	Imports of Goods & NFServices
605.3	811.7	928.2	1,057.1	1,218.1	1,419.7	1,405.9	1,017.6	1,034.7	1,018.9	..	Domestic Absorption
231.6	280.7	325.1	380.1	418.5	499.8	561.8	488.3	501.9	517.7	..	Private Consumption, etc.
119.7	149.5	186.8	222.3	284.4	306.3	304.0	241.5	225.4	217.0	..	General Gov't Consumption
254.0	381.5	416.3	454.7	515.2	613.6	540.1	287.8	307.4	284.2	..	Gross Domestic Investment
246.2	347.1	384.5	469.4	478.5	596.8	537.0	294.6	319.3	294.1	..	Fixed Investment
55.7	64.0	74.3	78.2	86.7	104.9	91.5	63.2	66.0	62.0	B	Indirect Taxes, net
848.8	985.6	1,114.6	1,208.8	1,449.3	1,541.1	1,109.4	957.4	897.3	1,035.1	B	GDP at factor cost
65.3	66.9	72.9	83.0	96.6	102.2	109.3	107.4	108.0	112.5	..	Agriculture
556.3	642.1	738.6	769.0	974.1	1,004.9	538.2	469.8	377.0	510.2	..	Industry
49.8	53.7	63.5	77.0	97.3	117.5	110.0	96.8	98.7	89.0	..	Manufacturing
282.9	340.6	377.4	435.0	465.3	538.9	553.4	443.4	478.3	474.4	..	Services, etc.
553.2	619.4	677.0	684.6	833.1	839.9	335.1	290.8	236.0	362.4	..	Gross Domestic Saving
430.1	504.9	546.6	541.3	694.8	681.4	191.1	173.4	107.2	217.5	..	Gross National Saving

(Billions of 1987 CFA Francs)

1980	1981	1982	1983	1984	1985	1986	1987	1988	1989	NOTES	
945.38	909.24	937.13	950.16	979.89	1,042.72	1,161.84	947.60	948.67	986.42	..	Gross National Product
997.46	957.61	983.72	992.48	1,056.49	1,123.05	1,251.34	1,020.60	1,021.75	1,062.41	..	GDP at Market Prices
-71.71	-304.72	-284.63	-302.25	-196.23	-213.29	-160.83	3.00	22.89	..	..	Resource Balance
460.03	397.87	391.61	423.49	444.43	439.54	418.88	405.90	380.53	..	..	Exports of Goods & NFServices
531.74	702.60	676.24	725.73	640.66	652.83	579.71	402.90	357.64	..	..	Imports of Goods & NFServices
1,069.17	1,262.33	1,268.35	1,294.73	1,252.72	1,336.34	1,412.17	1,017.60	998.86	..	..	Domestic Absorption
477.72	485.90	513.12	566.05	456.00	456.11	630.89	488.30	441.84	..	..	Private Consumption, etc.
197.35	216.18	244.24	250.77	285.55	309.25	295.96	241.50	256.25	..	..	General Gov't Consumption
394.10	560.25	510.99	477.90	511.17	570.98	485.33	287.80	300.77	..	..	Gross Domestic Investment
..	..	..	..	..	..	..	..	..	..	..	Fixed Investment
..	..	..	..	..	..	..	..	..	..	..	GDP at factor cost
..	..	..	..	..	..	..	..	..	..	..	Agriculture
..	..	..	..	..	..	..	..	..	..	..	Industry
..	..	..	..	..	..	..	..	..	..	..	Manufacturing
..	..	..	..	..	..	..	..	..	..	..	Services, etc.

Memo Items:

1980	1981	1982	1983	1984	1985	1986	1987	1988	1989	NOTES	
1,088.01	1,093.95	1,050.06	1,022.29	964.50	873.00	383.61	405.90	298.75	..	..	Capacity to Import
627.98	696.08	658.45	598.81	520.07	433.46	-35.28	0.00	-81.78	..	..	Terms of Trade Adjustment
1,625.45	1,653.69	1,642.17	1,591.29	1,576.56	1,556.51	1,216.07	1,020.60	939.97	..	..	Gross Domestic Income
1,573.36	1,605.32	1,595.58	1,548.97	1,499.96	1,476.18	1,126.56	947.60	866.89	..	..	Gross National Income

(Index 1987 = 100) — DOMESTIC PRICES/DEFLATORS

1980	1981	1982	1983	1984	1985	1986	1987	1988	1989	NOTES	
90.7	109.6	120.9	129.7	145.4	146.6	96.0	100.0	94.3	103.3	..	Overall (GDP)
56.6	64.3	73.2	81.6	97.2	106.2	99.6	100.0	103.6	..	..	Domestic Absorption
..	..	..	..	..	..	..	..	..	..	..	Agriculture
..	..	..	..	..	..	..	..	..	..	..	Industry
..	..	..	..	..	..	..	..	..	..	..	Manufacturing
59.7	64.9	75.7	83.6	88.5	95.0	101.0	100.0	90.2	96.5	..	Consumer Price Index

MANUFACTURING ACTIVITY

1980	1981	1982	1983	1984	1985	1986	1987	1988	1989	NOTES	
..	..	..	..	..	..	..	..	..	..	..	Employment (1987=100)
..	..	..	..	..	..	..	..	..	..	..	Real Earnings per Empl. (1987=100)
..	..	..	..	..	..	..	..	..	..	..	Real Output per Empl. (1987=100)
50.4	56.4	57.7	..	..	..	..	..	..	..	..	Earnings as % of Value Added

(Billions of current CFA Francs) — MONETARY HOLDINGS

1980	1981	1982	1983	1984	1985	1986	1987	1988	1989	NOTES	
152.07	176.16	199.64	235.32	272.80	305.97	274.90	238.73	248.58	278.62	..	Money Supply, Broadly Defined
93.96	114.50	125.56	142.59	167.75	176.55	152.39	133.26	146.47	170.90	..	Money
34.93	36.74	43.98	48.39	52.64	55.78	47.39	49.46	50.15	57.50	..	Currency Outside Banks
59.03	77.76	81.58	94.20	115.11	120.77	105.00	83.80	96.32	113.40	..	Demand Deposits
58.11	61.67	74.08	92.73	105.05	129.41	122.51	105.46	102.11	107.72	..	Quasi-Money

(Billions of current CFA Francs)

1980	1981	1982	1983	1984	1985	1986	1987	1988	1989	NOTES	
55.10	8.20	35.10	-16.30	3.10	1.10	..	..	..	..	F	GOVERNMENT DEFICIT (-) OR SURPLUS
353.50	422.80	488.10	509.29	606.70	648.40	..	..	..	..		Current Revenue
..	..	..	253.10	290.20	298.50	..	..	..	..		Current Expenditure
..	..	..	256.19	316.50	349.90	..	..	..	..		Current Budget Balance
0.30	0.40	0.30	0.11	0.10	..	..	..	..	..		Capital Receipts
..	..	..	272.60	313.50	348.80	..	..	..	..		Capital Payments

GABON	1969	1970	1971	1972	1973	1974	1975	1976	1977	1978	1979
FOREIGN TRADE (CUSTOMS BASIS)					*(Millions of current US dollars)*						
Value of Exports, fob	142.0	140.4	178.4	227.6	330.3	767.9	942.6	1,135.0	1,343.0	1,107.2	1,848.4
Nonfuel Primary Products	82.8	77.9	87.2	140.1	169.0	180.3	183.3	226.2	248.6	310.4	389.4
Fuels	50.2	51.6	78.2	68.9	141.9	562.9	749.1	895.8	1,065.3	782.2	1,415.6
Manufactures	9.1	10.9	13.0	18.6	19.4	24.8	10.2	13.0	29.1	14.6	43.4
Value of Imports, cif	77.9	79.8	90.9	133.3	189.7	331.9	469.2	503.2	716.0	682.0	673.0
Nonfuel Primary Products	12.2	12.3	13.9	20.7	27.8	47.9	66.6	66.5	101.1	145.7	140.5
Fuels	1.2	1.1	1.1	1.6	2.2	4.0	6.0	3.9	7.8	8.4	10.2
Manufactures	64.6	66.5	75.9	111.0	159.8	280.1	396.6	432.8	607.1	527.9	522.3
					(Index 1987 = 100)						
Terms of Trade	48.8	46.1	48.9	56.4	59.4	125.7	113.4	124.7	119.9	107.3	130.9
Export Prices, fob	13.2	13.2	14.9	18.8	23.4	61.3	60.5	67.7	72.1	75.4	105.2
Import Prices, cif	27.0	28.7	30.6	33.4	39.5	48.8	53.3	54.3	60.1	70.2	80.4
BALANCE OF PAYMENTS					*(Millions of current US dollars)*						
Exports of Goods & Services	..	207.9	251.6	310.9	442.6	1,005.4	1,247.3	1,357.7	1,487.0	1,482.9	2,031.2
Merchandise, fob	..	173.7	225.1	268.0	396.5	956.9	1,149.2	1,217.3	1,300.4	1,308.6	1,815.0
Nonfactor Services	..	31.4	24.9	40.0	42.3	39.3	85.8	127.0	172.7	169.9	208.8
Factor Services	..	2.8	1.7	3.0	3.8	9.1	12.3	13.4	13.9	4.4	7.3
Imports of Goods & Services	..	215.8	233.5	329.3	488.9	784.7	1,175.1	1,299.4	1,349.8	1,366.7	1,665.6
Merchandise, fob	..	99.3	106.9	155.6	231.0	349.7	516.9	527.3	589.2	557.9	554.8
Nonfactor Services	..	97.2	101.1	142.0	196.7	299.7	492.7	580.1	595.3	577.7	741.9
Factor Services	..	19.3	25.5	31.7	61.2	135.3	165.5	192.0	165.2	231.1	368.8
Long-Term Interest	..	2.6	3.4	4.2	10.9	10.7	15.0	25.3	31.0	71.5	101.3
Private Current Transfers, net	..	-7.2	-9.0	-12.2	-19.4	-25.0	-41.2	-50.6	-65.8	-79.1	-153.7
Workers' Remittances	..	..	..	..	..	..	..	..	..	..	0.1
Curr. A/C Bal before Off. Transf.	..	-15.1	9.1	-30.5	-65.7	195.7	31.1	7.7	71.3	37.1	211.9
Net Official Transfers	..	12.5	8.8	26.8	22.7	23.5	42.4	44.6	27.6	36.7	35.8
Curr. A/C Bal after Off. Transf.	..	-2.6	18.0	-3.7	-43.0	219.1	73.5	52.3	98.9	73.9	247.6
Long-Term Capital, net	..	6.3	18.1	0.9	41.4	116.5	276.5	197.7	-17.5	100.0	31.5
Direct Investment	..	-0.7	15.7	17.4	15.9	76.4	159.9	1.0	14.6	56.5	48.3
Long-Term Loans	..	16.6	32.0	79.8	138.2	105.8	328.0	333.4	132.0	-55.7	149.4
Disbursements	..	25.9	47.0	98.0	189.9	135.8	377.4	396.1	228.5	146.3	374.5
Repayments	..	9.3	15.0	18.2	51.7	30.0	49.4	62.7	96.5	202.0	225.1
Other Long-Term Capital	..	-9.6	-29.7	-96.3	-112.7	-65.6	-211.4	-136.8	-164.1	99.1	-166.2
Other Capital, net	..	1.1	-29.0	-1.1	24.4	-284.9	-303.9	-267.1	-192.5	-165.6	-295.5
Change in Reserves	..	-4.8	-7.0	3.9	-22.8	-50.7	-46.0	17.1	111.2	-8.2	16.3
Memo Item:					*(CFA Francs per US dollar)*						
Conversion Factor (Annual Avg)	259.710	277.710	277.130	252.210	222.700	240.500	214.320	238.980	245.670	225.640	212.720
				(Millions of US dollars), outstanding at end of year							
EXTERNAL DEBT (Total)	..	90.9	127.5	200.7	346.2	462.0	771.7	1,079.2	1,476.3	1,511.8	1,721.6
Long-Term Debt (by debtor)	..	90.9	127.5	200.7	346.2	462.0	771.7	1,079.2	1,255.3	1,297.8	1,480.6
Central Bank, incl. IMF credit	..	16.1	18.9	22.6	21.6	25.7	25.3	20.1	18.5	27.7	36.2
Central Government	..	35.7	71.1	134.5	265.7	341.0	567.8	850.6	1,010.5	1,021.4	1,139.4
Rest of General Government	..	0.1	1.3	4.2	3.2	2.3	1.1	0.1	0.0	10.6	8.8
Non-financial Public Enterprises	..	13.3	16.3	24.9	29.9	52.2	104.6	136.2	156.9	174.0	247.3
Priv. Sector, incl non-guaranteed	..	25.7	19.9	14.5	25.8	40.8	72.9	72.2	69.4	64.1	48.9
Short-Term Debt	..	0.0	0.0	0.0	0.0	0.0	0.0	0.0	221.0	214.0	241.0
Memo Items:					*(Thousands of US dollars)*						
Int'l Reserves Excluding Gold	8,286	14,740	25,387	23,227	47,858	103,293	146,069	116,155	9,905	22,574	20,135
Gold Holdings (at market price)	..	..	..	..	..	..	..	..	1,056	2,147	6,451
SOCIAL INDICATORS											
Total Fertility Rate	4.2	4.2	4.2	4.3	4.3	4.3	4.3	4.4	4.4	4.4	4.4
Infant Mortality Rate	141.0	138.0	135.0	132.0	130.0	128.0	126.0	124.0	122.0	120.0	118.0
Life Expectancy at Birth	43.8	44.2	44.6	45.0	45.4	45.8	46.3	46.7	47.1	47.6	48.0
Urban Population, % of total	24.7	25.6	26.6	27.6	28.6	29.6	30.6	31.6	32.7	33.7	34.8
Food Prod. per capita (1987=100)	135.2	137.9	136.1	130.1	126.1	125.5	125.1	124.9	124.0	125.8	124.7
Labor Force, Agriculture (%)	80.2	79.6	79.2	78.8	78.4	78.0	77.5	77.1	76.7	76.3	75.9
Labor Force, Female (%)	40.1	40.0	40.0	39.9	39.8	39.8	39.7	39.6	39.6	39.5	39.4
Primary Schl. Enroll. Ratio	..	85.0	..	..	..	..	102.0	..	..	..	..
Primary Schl. Enroll. Ratio, Female	..	81.0	..	..	..	..	100.0	..	..	..	..
Secondary Schl. Enroll. Ratio	..	8.0	..	..	..	..	17.0	..	..	..	..

1980	1981	1982	1983	1984	1985	1986	1987	1988	1989 estimate	NOTES	GABON
				(Millions of current US dollars)							**FOREIGN TRADE (CUSTOMS BASIS)**
2,172.8	2,200.7	2,160.6	1,975.3	2,011.4	1,974.4	1,074.2	1,286.4	1,200.0	..	f	Value of Exports, fob
340.5	418.1	412.6	404.3	469.7	486.1	438.2	535.8	481.5	..	..	Nonfuel Primary Products
1,806.3	1,712.1	1,697.3	1,485.3	1,416.6	1,345.9	501.2	612.8	553.9	..	..	Fuels
26.0	70.5	50.7	85.7	125.1	142.4	134.9	137.9	164.5	..	..	Manufactures
686.0	842.7	798.5	852.2	888.0	976.0	1,118.0	835.6	853.0	..	f	Value of Imports, cif
141.4	148.4	146.5	167.4	155.9	165.6	270.0	179.0	213.7	..	..	Nonfuel Primary Products
9.4	22.5	8.2	15.1	19.1	18.4	7.9	10.8	16.4	..	..	Fuels
535.2	671.8	643.8	669.7	713.0	792.0	840.1	645.9	623.0	..	..	Manufactures
				(Index 1987 = 100)							
181.9	184.8	177.4	162.3	160.1	148.7	88.0	100.0	83.6	..	..	Terms of Trade
159.0	160.7	149.6	134.8	130.2	121.0	83.4	100.0	91.3	..	..	Export Prices, fob
87.4	87.0	84.4	83.0	81.3	81.4	94.8	100.0	109.2	..	..	Import Prices, cif
				(Millions of current US dollars)							**BALANCE OF PAYMENTS**
2,433.9	2,533.0	2,350.7	2,218.3	2,203.4	2,119.1	1,215.9	1,417.2	1,423.7	1,877.3	..	Exports of Goods & Services
2,084.4	2,200.2	2,160.4	2,000.1	2,017.8	1,951.4	1,074.2	1,286.4	1,195.6	1,620.6	..	Merchandise, fob
324.6	307.6	170.3	200.8	137.8	138.5	123.6	114.8	212.9	244.2	..	Nonfactor Services
24.9	25.2	20.0	17.3	47.7	29.2	18.1	16.0	15.1	12.5	..	Factor Services
1,926.0	2,064.6	1,982.1	2,056.8	2,023.6	2,185.9	2,126.6	1,742.9	1,895.8	1,936.9	..	Imports of Goods & Services
686.1	841.2	722.6	725.5	733.2	854.7	979.1	731.8	791.2	755.5	..	Merchandise, fob
789.4	868.2	926.1	1,031.5	1,018.5	1,058.3	882.7	752.4	811.9	849.5	..	Nonfactor Services
450.5	355.2	333.3	299.8	271.8	272.8	264.8	258.7	292.7	331.9	..	Factor Services
118.7	87.5	94.9	52.6	60.8	56.8	51.2	42.8	74.7	107.1	..	Long-Term Interest
-157.5	-93.1	-83.6	-95.1	-92.5	-109.2	-169.1	-147.8	-154.6	-134.6	..	Private Current Transfers, net
0.0	0.2	0.1	0.3	0.1	0.1	0.2	0.3	0.1	..	..	Workers' Remittances
350.4	375.3	285.0	66.4	87.4	-176.0	-1,079.9	-473.6	-626.8	-194.2	..	Curr. A/C Bal before Off. Transf.
33.4	28.0	24.3	5.6	25.3	13.5	22.3	24.4	11.2	18.8	..	Net Official Transfers
383.9	403.3	309.4	72.0	112.7	-162.5	-1,057.6	-449.1	-615.6	-175.4	..	Curr. A/C Bal after Off. Transf.
-35.8	-95.9	92.9	71.8	172.6	212.6	570.1	533.5	637.7	304.7	..	Long-Term Capital, net
23.5	47.5	127.0	106.1	4.8	11.1	103.7	82.2	121.4	80.0	..	Direct Investment
-108.5	-161.1	-91.5	-58.5	56.6	133.2	328.5	187.7	223.4	65.8	..	Long-Term Loans
170.5	60.8	95.5	103.5	250.1	301.1	451.7	210.7	251.4	128.4	..	Disbursements
279.0	221.9	187.0	162.0	193.5	167.9	123.2	23.0	28.0	62.6	..	Repayments
49.1	17.8	57.5	24.2	111.2	68.3	137.9	263.7	292.8	158.9	..	Other Long-Term Capital
-252.1	-189.6	-255.8	-233.3	-246.0	-99.0	355.9	-284.0	-23.5	-165.1	..	Other Capital, net
-95.9	-117.8	-146.5	89.5	-39.2	48.9	131.6	199.7	1.4	35.8	..	Change in Reserves
				(CFA Francs per US dollar)							**Memo Item:**
211.300	271.730	328.620	381.070	436.960	449.260	346.300	300.540	297.850	319.010	..	Conversion Factor (Annual Avg)
				(Millions of US dollars), outstanding at end of year							
1,513.1	1,134.9	1,000.0	914.0	920.5	1,207.3	1,940.8	2,543.8	2,800.5	3,175.5	..	**EXTERNAL DEBT (Total)**
1,285.1	987.8	827.0	680.9	669.5	945.3	1,461.7	2,138.3	2,398.3	2,613.3	..	Long-Term Debt (by debtor)
32.4	26.7	23.6	16.5	9.0	10.1	44.1	67.9	137.1	137.8	..	Central Bank, incl. IMF credit
997.3	775.1	671.7	570.1	591.2	834.4	1,240.4	1,844.7	2,067.9	2,286.3	..	Central Government
6.9	3.3	0.7	0.5	0.3	0.0	0.0	0.0	0.0		..	Rest of General Government
215.2	164.4	122.6	88.1	66.1	98.0	174.5	223.3	191.6	185.4	..	Non-financial Public Enterprises
33.3	18.3	8.4	5.7	2.9	2.8	2.7	2.4	1.7	3.8	..	Priv. Sector, incl non-guaranteed
228.0	147.1	173.0	233.1	251.0	262.0	479.1	405.5	402.2	562.2	..	Short-Term Debt
				(Thousands of US dollars)							**Memo Items:**
107,503	198,854	311,885	186,898	199,450	192,546	126,350	11,999	65,692	34,566	..	Int'l Reserves Excluding Gold
7,428	5,009	5,757	4,807	3,885	4,120	4,925	6,100	5,169	5,053	..	Gold Holdings (at market price)
											SOCIAL INDICATORS
4.5	4.5	4.5	4.7	4.9	5.1	5.3	5.5	5.5	5.6	..	Total Fertility Rate
116.0	114.0	112.0	110.2	108.4	106.6	114.0	103.0	101.1	99.2	..	Infant Mortality Rate
48.4	48.9	49.3	49.9	50.5	51.1	51.7	52.3	52.6	52.9	..	Life Expectancy at Birth
35.8	36.8	37.8	38.9	39.9	40.9	50.0	43.3	50.0	44.9	..	Urban Population, % of total
124.3	116.6	114.4	112.6	108.0	102.4	102.2	100.0	98.5	95.8	..	Food Prod. per capita (1987=100)
75.4	..	..	..	..	..	..	..	..	..	..	Labor Force, Agriculture (%)
39.4	39.2	39.0	38.7	38.5	38.3	38.1	37.9	37.7	37.5	..	Labor Force, Female (%)
..	..	..	..	..	..	..	..	..	..	..	Primary Schl. Enroll. Ratio
..	..	..	..	..	..	..	..	..	..	..	Primary Schl. Enroll. Ratio, Female
..	..	..	..	..	..	..	..	..	..	..	Secondary Schl. Enroll. Ratio

GAMBIA, THE	1969	1970	1971	1972	1973	1974	1975	1976	1977	1978	1979
CURRENT GNP PER CAPITA (US $)	110	100	120	130	140	200	210	230	250	260	350
POPULATION (thousands)	451	463	475	488	502	517	533	551	570	591	612
USE AND ORIGIN OF RESOURCES					*(Millions of current Gambian Dalasis)*						
Gross National Product (GNP)	96.7	111.8	108.5	117.7	128.8	196.0	220.5	274.0	347.3	355.3	401.5
Net Factor Income from Abroad	-5.4	-4.0	-4.7	-5.9	-3.6	0.6	-0.6	-4.3	-7.7	-6.5	-18.9
GDP at Market Prices	102.1	115.8	113.2	123.6	132.4	195.4	221.1	278.3	355.0	361.8	420.4
Resource Balance	-1.9	5.6	-7.8	0.2	-8.8	8.9	21.9	-34.7	-21.4	-156.9	-54.7
Exports of Goods & NFServices	55.7	48.4	45.3	55.8	57.8	103.7	131.7	127.5	166.6	138.6	207.1
Imports of Goods & NFServices	57.6	42.8	53.1	55.6	66.6	94.8	109.8	162.2	188.0	295.5	261.8
Domestic Absorption	104.0	110.2	121.0	123.4	141.2	186.5	199.2	313.0	376.4	518.7	475.2
Private Consumption, etc.	81.4	91.0	98.0	96.5	111.2	151.4	140.0	239.3	269.0	330.2	298.1
General Gov't Consumption	13.6	13.9	16.1	17.5	19.6	26.9	33.5	43.5	57.5	79.6	68.4
Gross Domestic Investment	9.0	5.3	6.9	9.4	10.4	8.2	25.7	30.2	49.9	108.9	108.7
Fixed Investment	..	..	..	..	..	..	..	..	..	..	..
Indirect Taxes, net	10.4	14.4	10.6	11.7	12.7	14.7	17.6	33.1	46.5	46.9	60.9
GDP at factor cost	91.7	101.4	102.6	111.9	119.7	180.7	203.5	245.2	308.5	314.9	359.5
Agriculture	32.9	33.0	36.5	39.9	42.6	63.0	70.5	92.5	103.8	96.5	112.3
Industry	8.5	9.4	9.4	10.2	10.9	16.3	20.8	27.2	33.3	43.0	48.1
Manufacturing	3.0	3.4	3.4	3.6	3.9	5.8	6.6	11.8	14.3	13.6	13.8
Services, etc.	50.3	59.0	56.7	61.8	66.2	101.4	112.2	125.5	171.4	175.4	199.1
Gross Domestic Saving	7.1	10.9	-0.9	9.6	1.6	17.1	47.6	-4.5	28.5	-48.0	54.0
Gross National Saving	..	7.4	-5.0	4.8	-1.4	18.0	46.6	-6.0	23.0	-54.3	33.4
					(Millions of 1987 Gambian Dalasis)						
Gross National Product	595.07	545.01	602.81	642.25	687.91	851.38	828.10	899.04	918.48	871.28	993.10
GDP at Market Prices	629.61	567.29	632.69	678.33	709.84	850.60	832.40	915.21	942.69	889.95	1,043.68
Resource Balance	-67.70	-43.16	-155.85	-105.23	-104.55	-5.22	38.11	-132.18	-189.79	-600.77	-208.40
Exports of Goods & NFServices	443.34	339.57	287.68	366.28	371.80	418.17	508.12	533.30	511.50	394.83	518.26
Imports of Goods & NFServices	511.05	382.72	443.53	471.50	476.35	423.38	470.01	665.48	701.29	995.61	726.65
Domestic Absorption	697.31	610.44	788.53	783.56	814.39	855.82	794.29	1,047.39	1,132.48	1,490.73	1,252.08
Private Consumption, etc.	..	..	..	..	..	..	..	..	..	..	..
General Gov't Consumption	..	..	..	..	..	..	..	..	..	..	..
Gross Domestic Investment	32.12	18.26	23.34	31.20	28.66	30.97	81.81	85.04	115.32	235.03	180.03
Fixed Investment	..	..	..	..	..	..	..	..	..	..	..
GDP at factor cost	541.62	488.14	544.05	583.52	610.30	731.31	685.57	724.33	733.34	705.97	819.14
Agriculture	191.71	172.59	192.42	206.11	215.79	258.53	242.47	246.01	245.07	211.31	222.83
Industry	59.36	53.28	59.59	64.03	66.83	80.15	74.78	75.71	77.82	100.95	94.46
Manufacturing	24.32	21.98	24.32	26.19	27.36	32.73	30.16	34.37	33.44	34.37	4.44
Services, etc.	283.90	256.19	285.32	306.15	320.12	383.58	359.90	397.31	405.83	388.55	508.08
Memo Items:											
Capacity to Import	494.19	432.80	378.38	473.20	413.41	463.13	563.76	523.11	621.46	466.97	574.83
Terms of Trade Adjustment	50.85	93.23	90.70	106.92	41.61	44.97	55.63	-10.19	109.96	72.14	56.57
Gross Domestic Income	680.46	660.52	723.38	785.25	751.45	895.57	888.04	905.02	1,052.65	962.09	1,100.25
Gross National Income	645.92	638.24	693.51	749.18	729.51	896.35	883.74	888.85	1,028.45	943.42	1,049.68
DOMESTIC PRICES/DEFLATORS					*(Index 1987 = 100)*						
Overall (GDP)	16.2	20.4	17.9	18.2	18.7	23.0	26.6	30.4	37.7	40.7	40.3
Domestic Absorption	14.9	18.1	15.3	15.7	17.3	21.8	25.1	29.9	33.2	34.8	38.0
Agriculture	17.2	19.1	19.0	19.4	19.7	24.4	29.1	37.6	42.4	45.7	50.4
Industry	14.3	17.6	15.8	15.9	16.3	20.3	27.8	35.9	42.8	42.6	50.9
Manufacturing	12.3	15.5	14.0	13.7	14.3	17.7	21.9	34.3	42.8	39.6	310.6
Consumer Price Index	10.5	10.3	10.6	11.5	12.3	13.5	17.0	19.9	22.3	24.3	25.8
MANUFACTURING ACTIVITY											
Employment (1987=100)	..	..	..	..	..	..	..	..	..	..	..
Real Earnings per Empl. (1987=100)	..	..	..	..	..	..	..	..	..	..	..
Real Output per Empl. (1987=100)	..	..	..	..	..	..	..	..	..	..	..
Earnings as % of Value Added	..	..	..	..	..	..	43.2	43.7	40.8	60.8	40.5
MONETARY HOLDINGS					*(Millions of current Gambian Dalasis)*						
Money Supply, Broadly Defined	16.75	19.36	19.44	27.07	38.42	42.24	47.90	69.91	61.45	89.68	82.19
Money	14.08	16.45	16.36	22.78	31.80	33.03	37.34	49.42	39.80	57.78	57.78
Currency Outside Banks	10.19	12.12	12.73	14.94	25.21	24.06	27.15	32.08	19.79	34.53	36.53
Demand Deposits	3.89	4.33	3.63	7.84	6.59	8.97	10.19	17.34	20.01	23.25	21.25
Quasi-Money	2.67	2.91	3.08	4.29	6.62	9.21	10.56	20.49	21.65	31.90	24.41
					(Millions of current Gambian Dalasis)						
GOVERNMENT DEFICIT (-) OR SURPLUS	..	..	..	..	0.30	-2.79	-6.61	-6.65	-26.49	-35.85	-38.42
Current Revenue	..	..	..	19.37	22.87	26.94	35.02	47.46	64.56	102.57	88.71
Current Expenditure	..	..	..	..	18.04	20.70	30.93	39.91	54.45	61.61	62.66
Current Budget Balance	..	..	..	..	4.83	6.24	4.09	7.55	10.11	40.96	26.05
Capital Receipts	..	..	..	0.01	0.02	0.01	0.02	0.04	0.03	0.20	0.15
Capital Payments	..	..	..	..	4.55	9.04	10.72	14.24	36.63	77.01	64.62

1980	1981	1982	1983	1984	1985	1986	1987	1988	1989 estimate	NOTES	GAMBIA, THE
350	370	350	290	250	210	170	190	210	240	..	**CURRENT GNP PER CAPITA (US $)**
634	656	678	701	724	748	772	797	822	848	..	**POPULATION (thousands)**
			(Millions of current Gambian Dalasis)								**USE AND ORIGIN OF RESOURCES**
390.2	436.9	495.6	550.3	607.6	734.5	861.6	1,073.1	1,322.4	1,591.1	C	Gross National Product (GNP)
-19.2	-24.5	-32.3	-48.1	-65.1	-124.8	-216.5	-177.8	-167.1	-201.9	..	Net Factor Income from Abroad
409.4	461.4	527.9	598.4	672.7	859.3	1,078.1	1,250.9	1,489.5	1,793.0	C	GDP at Market Prices
-91.4	-132.9	-89.3	-126.3	-160.3	-73.6	-172.5	-143.8	-160.4	-246.2	..	Resource Balance
241.2	190.6	213.7	323.2	327.2	393.5	753.3	786.9	1,011.9	1,218.2	..	Exports of Goods & NFServices
332.6	323.5	303.0	449.5	487.5	467.1	925.8	930.7	1,172.3	1,464.4	..	Imports of Goods & NFServices
500.8	594.3	617.2	724.8	833.4	932.9	1,250.6	1,394.7	1,649.9	2,039.2	..	Domestic Absorption
307.3	369.7	421.9	497.8	581.5	655.7	785.7	913.1	1,132.3	1,346.0	..	Private Consumption, etc.
91.1	118.2	106.5	123.3	122.3	141.1	245.4	250.5	251.0	298.7	..	General Gov't Consumption
102.3	106.3	88.8	103.7	129.6	136.1	219.5	231.1	266.6	394.5	..	Gross Domestic Investment
..	..	..	..	..	..	..	..	..	..	..	Fixed Investment
42.1	53.6	66.3	77.6	96.4	141.8	166.5	210.4	328.0	354.0	..	Indirect Taxes, net
367.3	407.8	461.6	520.8	576.2	717.5	911.5	1,040.5	1,161.5	1,439.1	C	GDP at factor cost
111.9	154.8	195.9	167.8	188.2	246.9	322.0	361.7	396.2	493.6	..	Agriculture
59.9	48.8	45.7	77.3	89.3	71.1	95.5	110.3	119.4	167.3	..	Industry
26.7	22.7	23.3	51.6	58.7	44.1	57.0	65.0	66.4	99.9	..	Manufacturing
195.5	204.2	220.0	275.7	298.7	399.5	494.0	568.5	645.9	778.2	..	Services, etc.
10.9	-26.6	-0.5	-22.7	-31.1	62.5	47.0	87.3	106.2	148.3	..	Gross Domestic Saving
-2.0	-44.0	-26.2	-63.7	-78.6	-37.9	-95.2	4.9	24.8	-2.9	..	Gross National Saving
			(Millions of 1987 Gambian Dalasis)								
895.57	979.33	1,053.82	1,024.01	1,035.89	973.24	946.65	1,073.10	1,204.61	1,264.68	..	Gross National Product
941.86	1,037.69	1,169.76	1,107.98	1,141.24	1,148.30	1,180.08	1,250.90	1,350.80	1,414.87	C I	GDP at Market Prices
-294.86	-403.82	-222.67	-148.19	-224.15	-190.35	-166.63	-143.80	-132.52	-124.45	..	Resource Balance
606.37	439.96	496.15	550.49	659.18	678.95	757.73	786.90	869.80	908.94	..	Exports of Goods & NFServices
901.23	843.78	718.82	698.68	883.33	869.30	924.36	930.70	1,002.32	1,033.39	..	Imports of Goods & NFServices
1,236.72	1,441.51	1,392.43	1,256.17	1,365.39	1,338.65	1,346.71	1,394.70	1,483.32	1,539.32	..	Domestic Absorption
..	..	..	..	..	..	..	..	..	..	..	Private Consumption, etc.
..	..	..	..	..	..	..	..	..	..	..	General Gov't Consumption
200.59	195.97	161.54	173.79	220.24	217.93	224.44	231.10	238.96	247.30	..	Gross Domestic Investment
..	..	..	..	..	..	..	..	..	..	..	Fixed Investment
776.04	848.07	955.50	897.08	926.35	914.47	991.62	1,040.50	1,052.15	1,125.70	C I	GDP at factor cost
207.81	295.76	357.14	281.71	301.35	314.46	350.13	361.70	362.69	386.02	..	Agriculture
110.11	87.49	76.88	92.07	89.27	89.67	102.82	110.30	106.42	126.19	..	Industry
-4.44	41.85	45.13	59.62	55.65	55.65	61.49	65.00	59.90	72.01	..	Manufacturing
459.16	456.91	512.24	523.30	535.73	510.35	538.67	568.50	583.04	613.49	..	Services, etc.
											Memo Items:
653.57	497.14	506.97	502.36	592.87	732.33	752.13	786.90	865.18	859.66	..	Capacity to Import
47.20	57.18	10.82	-48.13	-66.31	53.37	-5.61	0.00	-4.62	-49.29	..	Terms of Trade Adjustment
989.06	1,094.87	1,180.58	1,059.85	1,074.93	1,201.68	1,174.48	1,250.90	1,346.18	1,365.59	..	Gross Domestic Income
942.77	1,036.51	1,064.64	975.88	969.58	1,026.61	941.05	1,073.10	1,199.99	1,215.39	..	Gross National Income
			(Index 1987 = 100)								**DOMESTIC PRICES/DEFLATORS**
43.5	44.5	45.1	54.0	58.9	74.8	91.4	100.0	110.3	126.7	..	Overall (GDP)
40.5	41.2	44.3	57.7	61.0	69.7	92.9	100.0	111.2	132.5	..	Domestic Absorption
53.8	52.3	54.9	59.6	62.5	78.5	92.0	100.0	109.2	127.9	..	Agriculture
54.4	55.8	59.4	84.0	100.0	79.3	92.9	100.0	112.2	132.6	..	Industry
-601.0	54.2	51.6	86.5	105.5	79.3	92.7	100.0	110.8	138.7	..	Manufacturing
27.5	29.2	32.4	35.8	43.7	51.7	81.0	100.0	111.7	120.9	..	Consumer Price Index
											MANUFACTURING ACTIVITY
..	..	..	..	..	..	..	..	..	..	J	Employment (1987=100)
..	..	..	..	..	..	..	..	..	..	J	Real Earnings per Empl. (1987=100)
..	..	..	..	..	..	..	..	..	..	J	Real Output per Empl. (1987=100)
25.3	25.8	31.7	..	..	..	..	..	..	..	J	Earnings as % of Value Added
			(Millions of current Gambian Dalasis)								**MONETARY HOLDINGS**
90.70	109.66	127.02	160.96	169.78	256.95	275.64	343.53	394.19	476.18	..	Money Supply, Broadly Defined
61.28	76.97	87.22	100.32	99.58	162.10	166.49	197.83	213.52	260.25	..	Money
36.76	42.62	55.92	57.18	58.38	85.67	91.18	95.02	111.99	134.78	..	Currency Outside Banks
24.52	34.35	31.30	43.14	41.20	76.43	75.31	102.81	101.53	125.47	..	Demand Deposits
29.42	32.69	39.80	60.64	70.20	94.85	109.15	145.70	180.67	215.93	..	Quasi-Money
			(Millions of current Gambian Dalasis)								
-18.32	-50.10	-33.86	..	..	..	..	..	..	..	C	**GOVERNMENT DEFICIT (-) OR SURPLUS**
109.00	97.39	135.03	..	..	..	..	..	..	..		Current Revenue
68.17	84.86	119.74	114.63	133.46	134.40	173.93	..	..	..		Current Expenditure
40.83	12.53	15.29	..	..	..	..	..	..	..		Current Budget Balance
0.05	0.03	0.04	1.24	0.11	0.65	3.15	0.68	..	..		Capital Receipts
59.20	62.66	49.19	..	..	..	..	..	..	..		Capital Payments

GAMBIA, THE	1969	1970	1971	1972	1973	1974	1975	1976	1977	1978	1979
FOREIGN TRADE (CUSTOMS BASIS)					*(Millions of current US dollars)*						
Value of Exports, fob	17.21	15.64	14.72	18.52	20.70	40.17	48.98	35.95	47.56	39.00	58.00
Nonfuel Primary Products	17.20	15.40	14.41	18.05	19.77	39.16	48.07	34.59	45.24	37.29	55.45
Fuels	0.01	0.00	0.02	0.04	0.20	0.35	0.33	0.29	0.29	0.26	0.38
Manufactures	0.00	0.24	0.29	0.43	0.73	0.66	0.58	1.07	2.03	1.45	2.17
Value of Imports, cif	22.39	16.89	21.14	22.83	31.66	37.56	48.74	65.13	73.07	100.00	141.00
Nonfuel Primary Products	5.88	5.75	6.22	5.85	8.03	12.05	13.29	19.61	21.19	29.05	41.11
Fuels	0.68	0.61	0.66	0.80	1.45	1.98	4.35	4.13	4.87	6.83	9.51
Manufactures	15.83	10.53	14.26	16.18	22.18	23.53	31.10	41.39	47.01	64.12	90.38
					(Index 1987 = 100)						
Terms of Trade	207.2	210.3	202.5	214.2	306.2	219.5	173.4	186.7	198.5	186.4	160.6
Export Prices, fob	58.3	62.9	64.1	72.3	122.9	128.0	105.1	112.5	132.0	139.4	137.3
Import Prices, cif	28.1	29.9	31.7	33.7	40.1	58.3	60.6	60.3	66.5	74.8	85.5
BALANCE OF PAYMENTS					*(Millions of current US dollars)*						
Exports of Goods & Services	..	20.00	21.26	26.82	29.14	54.23	68.88	56.42	67.83	55.28	78.18
Merchandise, fob	..	17.76	18.31	21.57	20.64	43.73	56.69	43.72	53.47	40.08	53.75
Nonfactor Services	..	1.50	2.06	4.17	6.66	9.20	9.42	10.09	12.29	13.27	22.51
Factor Services	..	0.74	0.89	1.07	1.84	1.30	2.77	2.61	2.07	1.93	1.92
Imports of Goods & Services	..	20.22	24.29	28.79	35.06	55.43	61.95	75.73	80.47	111.83	136.43
Merchandise, fob	..	15.92	19.13	21.80	26.57	41.37	47.35	59.54	62.64	81.00	94.74
Nonfactor Services	..	2.43	2.86	4.09	5.88	11.44	12.24	15.31	17.40	26.15	37.27
Factor Services	..	1.87	2.31	2.90	2.61	2.62	2.36	0.88	0.43	4.68	4.42
Long-Term Interest	..	0.00	0.00	0.00	0.00	0.10	0.00	0.00	0.10	0.20	0.30
Private Current Transfers, net	..	0.26	0.29	0.53	0.38	0.20	-0.23	1.27	0.98	0.09	-0.88
Workers' Remittances	..	..	..	..	..	..	..	..	..	..	..
Curr. A/C Bal before Off. Transf.	..	0.04	-2.74	-1.44	-5.54	-1.00	6.70	-18.03	-11.65	-56.46	-59.13
Net Official Transfers	..	0.41	1.77	1.24	1.44	6.69	4.59	1.37	3.88	12.88	25.99
Curr. A/C Bal after Off. Transf.	..	0.45	-0.97	-0.21	-4.10	5.69	11.29	-16.66	-7.78	-43.59	-33.14
Long-Term Capital, net	..	1.28	1.69	3.76	4.64	4.32	1.87	2.47	4.34	10.14	16.56
Direct Investment	..	0.11	1.71	1.66	1.41	1.21	0.11	0.94	..	2.00	11.68
Long-Term Loans	..	0.70	0.10	2.30	1.50	3.30	2.40	3.40	9.00	14.80	22.70
Disbursements	..	0.80	0.30	2.60	1.80	3.70	2.80	3.70	9.50	15.00	22.90
Repayments	..	0.10	0.20	0.30	0.30	0.40	0.40	0.30	0.50	0.20	0.20
Other Long-Term Capital	..	0.47	-0.12	-0.20	1.73	-0.20	-0.64	-1.86	-4.66	-6.66	-17.83
Other Capital, net	..	-0.12	0.95	-1.84	10.14	-5.48	0.85	7.09	4.69	20.24	0.75
Change in Reserves	..	-1.61	-1.66	-1.72	-10.68	-4.52	-14.01	7.10	-1.26	13.21	15.83
Memo Item:					*(Gambian Dalasis per US dollar)*						
Conversion Factor (Annual Avg)	2.080	2.080	1.970	1.920	1.680	1.700	2.010	2.340	2.190	2.000	1.790
					(Millions of US dollars), outstanding at end of year						
EXTERNAL DEBT (Total)	..	5.10	5.50	7.40	8.90	12.20	13.40	15.50	38.00	49.70	81.20
Long-Term Debt (by debtor)	..	5.10	5.50	7.40	8.90	12.20	13.40	15.50	31.00	39.70	61.20
Central Bank, incl. IMF credit	..	0.00	0.00	0.00	0.00	0.00	0.00	0.00	5.20	15.20	13.70
Central Government	..	5.10	5.50	7.40	8.90	12.20	13.40	14.30	22.90	23.90	42.50
Rest of General Government	..	..	..	..	..	..	..	..	..	..	..
Non-financial Public Enterprises	..	0.00	0.00	0.00	0.00	0.00	0.00	1.20	2.90	0.60	2.40
Priv. Sector, incl non-guaranteed	..	0.00	0.00	0.00	0.00	0.00	0.00	0.00	0.00	0.00	2.60
Short-Term Debt	..	0.00	0.00	0.00	0.00	0.00	0.00	0.00	7.00	10.00	20.00
Memo Items:					*(Thousands of US dollars)*						
Int'l Reserves Excluding Gold	5,990	8,110	10,939	11,385	16,241	28,046	28,552	20,635	24,395	26,072	1,929
Gold Holdings (at market price)	..	..	..	..	..	..	..	..	..	..	..
SOCIAL INDICATORS											
Total Fertility Rate	6.5	6.5	6.5	6.5	6.5	6.5	6.5	6.5	6.5	6.5	6.5
Infant Mortality Rate	187.4	184.6	181.8	179.0	176.4	173.8	171.2	168.6	166.0	163.6	161.2
Life Expectancy at Birth	35.7	36.1	36.5	36.9	37.3	37.7	38.1	38.5	38.9	39.3	39.8
Urban Population, % of total	14.7	15.0	15.3	15.6	16.0	16.3	16.6	16.9	17.2	17.5	17.8
Food Prod. per capita (1987=100)	180.3	182.0	186.4	160.9	177.1	171.8	173.2	154.3	115.7	144.4	97.7
Labor Force, Agriculture (%)	86.8	86.6	86.3	86.1	85.8	85.6	85.3	85.1	84.8	84.5	84.3
Labor Force, Female (%)	42.7	42.7	42.7	42.6	42.6	42.6	42.6	42.5	42.5	42.4	42.3
Primary Schl. Enroll. Ratio	..	24.0	..	..	..	..	33.0	31.0	33.0	37.0	42.0
Primary Schl. Enroll. Ratio, Female	..	15.0	..	..	..	..	21.0	20.0	21.0	24.0	28.0
Secondary Schl. Enroll. Ratio	..	7.0	..	..	..	..	10.0	11.0	11.0	11.0	12.0

1980	1981	1982	1983	1984	1985	1986	1987	1988	1989 estimate	NOTES	GAMBIA, THE
											FOREIGN TRADE (CUSTOMS BASIS)
				(Millions of current US dollars)							
31.00	27.00	44.00	48.00	48.90	43.30	44.10	45.10	50.00	..	..	Value of Exports, fob
29.62	25.81	42.05	45.87	46.86	41.09	40.76	41.34	46.64	..	..	Nonfuel Primary Products
0.20	0.18	0.29	0.32	0.32	0.30	0.33	0.44	0.31	..	..	Fuels
1.18	1.01	1.66	1.81	1.72	1.91	3.01	3.33	3.06	..	..	Manufactures
131.80	145.00	150.60	117.60	100.20	93.30	99.40	109.00	126.00	..	..	Value of Imports, cif
18.37	56.98	78.23	35.27	55.34	50.65	55.51	62.06	74.50	..	..	Nonfuel Primary Products
8.90	9.79	10.17	7.95	10.94	9.45	3.54	4.29	4.83	..	..	Fuels
104.53	78.23	62.20	74.38	33.92	33.20	40.35	42.65	46.67	..	..	Manufactures
				(Index 1987 = 100)							
164.7	151.7	116.2	139.1	129.6	119.0	107.5	100.0	109.3	..	..	Terms of Trade
147.9	155.4	115.4	125.5	133.5	110.6	103.0	100.0	122.1	..	..	Export Prices, fob
89.8	102.4	99.4	90.2	103.0	93.0	95.8	100.0	111.7	..	..	Import Prices, cif
				(Millions of current US dollars)							**BALANCE OF PAYMENTS**
..	..	83.84	81.96	118.45	87.22	93.56	125.66	137.01	167.93	..	Exports of Goods & Services
48.29	45.13	58.56	54.55	90.73	62.80	64.87	74.51	74.40	100.20	..	Merchandise, fob
17.96	20.16	24.32	27.19	27.73	24.42	28.69	50.33	61.17	65.73	..	Nonfactor Services
..	..	0.96	0.22	0.00	0.00	0.00	0.81	1.44	2.01	..	Factor Services
181.45	173.00	141.99	137.29	125.32	94.18	107.00	139.72	147.53	191.76	..	Imports of Goods & Services
137.69	128.69	94.41	89.70	99.43	74.84	84.57	94.95	105.92	125.35	..	Merchandise, fob
41.56	41.59	36.17	29.92	25.88	19.30	21.48	25.56	27.24	50.60	..	Nonfactor Services
2.20	2.72	11.41	17.66	0.01	0.05	0.95	19.21	14.37	15.81	..	Factor Services
0.40	2.10	2.10	1.70	1.40	0.50	4.70	5.00	4.80	4.10	..	Long-Term Interest
3.62	3.55	2.89	2.69	4.91	6.29	10.71	13.49	12.78	6.68	..	Private Current Transfers, net
..	..	..	0.00	0.00	0.00	0.00	0.00	..	..	..	Workers' Remittances
-111.58	-104.17	-55.27	-52.63	-1.95	-0.68	-2.73	1.04	-71.01	-17.15	..	Curr. A/C Bal before Off. Transf.
37.66	54.66	32.80	19.65	10.02	7.97	6.94	36.21	41.91	33.87	..	Net Official Transfers
-73.92	-49.51	-22.46	-32.98	8.07	7.29	4.21	37.25	-29.10	16.72	..	Curr. A/C Bal after Off. Transf.
3.73	14.18	17.76	-5.43	-10.13	1.98	-9.78	33.83	11.49	12.88	..	Long-Term Capital, net
..	2.28	..	..	0.50	2.20	6.10	1.48	1.17	14.79	..	Direct Investment
50.80	39.30	21.00	8.80	10.40	13.30	31.80	28.60	8.80	22.20	..	Long-Term Loans
51.20	39.90	29.40	13.70	13.80	13.80	35.30	37.10	15.00	29.10	..	Disbursements
0.40	0.60	8.40	4.90	3.40	0.50	3.50	8.50	6.20	6.90	..	Repayments
-47.07	-27.41	-3.24	-14.23	-21.03	-13.52	-47.68	3.76	1.52	-24.10	..	Other Long-Term Capital
63.89	45.47	-19.76	29.59	3.97	-8.67	8.49	-56.50	35.86	-36.27	..	Other Capital, net
6.30	-10.14	24.46	8.82	-1.91	-0.60	-2.92	-14.58	-18.25	6.67	..	Change in Reserves
				(Gambian Dalasis per US dollar)							Memo Item:
1.750	2.180	2.480	2.940	4.110	4.990	7.310	6.750	7.030	8.050	..	Conversion Factor (Annual Avg)
				(Millions of US dollars), outstanding at end of year							
136.80	176.10	207.00	211.70	230.00	245.30	270.10	326.80	321.50	341.80	..	**EXTERNAL DEBT (Total)**
113.50	157.60	187.40	186.80	184.60	209.60	241.60	303.40	307.50	329.50	..	Long-Term Debt (by debtor)
16.20	25.30	40.00	35.10	32.90	33.00	29.50	37.80	34.60	37.70	..	Central Bank, incl. IMF credit
82.70	117.40	122.00	125.60	126.70	150.20	192.80	248.80	265.80	285.20	..	Central Government
..	..	..	..	..	..	..	..	..	..	..	Rest of General Government
4.20	3.50	3.10	2.70	2.30	3.00	1.20	1.30	1.00	0.90	..	Non-financial Public Enterprises
10.40	11.40	22.30	23.40	22.70	23.40	18.10	15.50	6.10	5.70	..	Priv. Sector, incl non-guaranteed
23.30	18.50	19.60	24.90	45.40	35.70	28.50	23.40	14.00	12.30	..	Short-Term Debt
				(Thousands of US dollars)							Memo Items:
5,670	3,948	8,387	2,918	2,259	1,734	13,563	25,757	19,049	20,589	..	Int'l Reserves Excluding Gold
..	..	..	..	..	..	..	..	..	..	..	Gold Holdings (at market price)
											SOCIAL INDICATORS
6.5	6.5	6.5	6.5	6.5	6.5	6.5	6.5	6.5	6.5	..	Total Fertility Rate
158.8	156.4	154.0	151.8	149.6	147.4	145.2	143.0	140.9	138.9	..	Infant Mortality Rate
40.2	40.6	41.0	41.5	41.9	42.4	42.9	43.4	43.7	44.0	..	Life Expectancy at Birth
18.1	18.5	18.9	19.3	19.7	20.1	20.7	21.3	21.7	22.1	..	Urban Population, % of total
100.2	126.6	143.9	106.8	108.9	99.3	108.1	100.0	96.9	102.7	..	Food Prod. per capita (1987=100)
84.0	..	..	..	..	..	..	..	..	..	..	Labor Force, Agriculture (%)
42.3	42.1	41.9	41.7	41.5	41.3	41.1	40.9	40.7	40.5	..	Labor Force, Female (%)
51.0	..	62.0	68.0	..	68.0	67.0	65.0	57.0	..	..	Primary Schl. Enroll. Ratio
35.0	41.0	45.0	51.0	..	52.0	52.0	51.0	46.0	..	..	Primary Schl. Enroll. Ratio, Female
11.0	..	17.0	..	..	17.0	17.0	16.0	..	..	..	Secondary Schl. Enroll. Ratio

GERMANY, FEDERAL REPUBLIC OF *	1969	1970	1971	1972	1973	1974	1975	1976	1977	1978	1979
CURRENT GNP PER CAPITA (US $)	2,550	2,860	3,240	3,830	4,750	5,720	6,670	7,480	8,250	9,510	11,560
POPULATION (thousands)	60,067	60,651	61,302	61,672	61,976	62,054	61,829	61,531	61,401	61,327	61,359

USE AND ORIGIN OF RESOURCES — *(Billions of current Deutsche Mark)*

	1969	1970	1971	1972	1973	1974	1975	1976	1977	1978	1979
Gross National Product (GNP)	597.7	675.7	751.8	825.1	918.9	985.7	1,029.4	1,126.2	1,199.3	1,291.6	1,396.5
Net Factor Income from Abroad	0.9	0.4	1.2	1.4	1.6	1.0	2.5	4.5	1.4	6.3	4.3
GDP at Market Prices	596.8	675.3	750.6	823.7	917.3	984.7	1,026.9	1,121.7	1,197.9	1,285.3	1,392.2
Resource Balance	17.8	13.9	15.1	17.7	28.7	44.1	30.4	29.2	29.1	37.7	11.2
Exports of Goods & NFServices	137.5	152.8	169.9	185.0	217.1	279.0	271.4	309.2	325.8	344.9	377.3
Imports of Goods & NFServices	119.7	139.0	154.8	167.3	188.4	234.9	241.1	280.0	296.7	307.2	366.1
Domestic Absorption	579.9	661.8	736.7	807.4	890.2	941.6	999.0	1,097.0	1,170.2	1,253.9	1,385.3
Private Consumption, etc.	330.8	368.7	408.8	451.9	495.6	534.2	585.7	632.2	682.6	729.8	785.0
General Gov't Consumption	119.2	128.8	142.8	157.4	175.6	195.6	215.5	227.8	239.4	255.5	274.3
Gross Domestic Investment	129.9	164.3	185.1	198.0	218.9	211.8	197.9	237.1	248.3	268.6	326.0
Fixed Investment	145.7	170.2	193.8	209.5	222.7	218.0	218.6	235.3	253.0	274.0	307.4
Indirect Taxes, net	76.7	77.3	86.1	94.4	102.4	106.2	109.9	119.8	127.9	137.9	152.0
GDP at factor cost	520.2	598.0	664.5	729.3	814.9	878.5	917.0	1,001.9	1,070.0	1,147.4	1,240.2
Agriculture	23.5	21.8	22.8	24.7	26.6	25.9	28.5	31.1	31.8	32.2	31.0
Industry	290.3	333.7	361.3	387.8	430.9	456.0	454.9	500.6	529.9	561.6	607.7
Manufacturing	229.6	259.4	278.0	296.6	333.3	355.7	354.1	389.7	414.5	437.9	470.4
Services, etc.	283.1	319.8	366.5	411.2	459.8	502.8	543.5	590.0	636.2	691.5	753.5
Gross Domestic Saving	146.8	177.8	198.9	214.4	246.0	254.9	225.7	261.8	276.0	300.0	332.9
Gross National Saving	..	172.3	192.8	208.0	238.9	246.5	219.0	256.6	268.2	296.6	327.5

(Billions of 1987 Deutsche Mark)

	1969	1970	1971	1972	1973	1974	1975	1976	1977	1978	1979
Gross National Product	1,329.7	1,396.9	1,436.8	1,495.9	1,567.1	1,569.9	1,547.3	1,633.6	1,676.9	1,731.7	1,800.2
GDP at Market Prices	1,327.9	1,396.2	1,434.5	1,493.5	1,564.4	1,568.4	1,543.6	1,627.2	1,675.1	1,723.2	1,794.7
Resource Balance	44.0	26.0	18.5	22.4	42.5	78.7	53.9	56.9	58.0	55.1	34.3
Exports of Goods & NFServices	270.7	288.3	306.9	327.1	360.3	403.6	376.7	413.7	427.5	445.0	465.2
Imports of Goods & NFServices	226.7	262.2	288.4	304.7	317.8	324.9	322.8	356.7	369.4	389.9	430.9
Domestic Absorption	1,283.8	1,370.1	1,415.9	1,471.0	1,521.9	1,489.7	1,489.7	1,570.3	1,617.1	1,668.2	1,760.5
Private Consumption, etc.	693.5	743.6	776.1	808.7	835.1	841.1	863.8	892.5	934.5	962.6	997.9
General Gov't Consumption	244.3	254.9	268.0	279.3	293.1	304.8	316.1	320.8	325.4	337.8	349.2
Gross Domestic Investment	346.0	371.6	371.8	383.0	393.8	343.8	309.8	356.9	357.2	367.7	413.3
Fixed Investment	319.4	349.5	370.6	380.5	379.2	342.9	324.6	336.5	348.4	364.8	391.1
GDP at factor cost	1,159.5	1,237.3	1,269.5	1,321.7	1,389.8	1,401.3	1,380.3	1,455.9	1,499.0	1,539.5	1,601.1
Agriculture	24.9	25.7	25.2	24.5	26.4	27.6	26.2	25.8	27.3	28.1	26.9
Industry	633.1	667.2	678.3	703.6	741.4	729.9	693.2	743.0	757.9	771.0	807.4
Manufacturing	483.8	509.0	514.0	530.7	564.4	560.4	534.3	575.3	587.1	597.9	625.6
Services, etc.	670.4	704.2	733.5	769.9	800.3	813.5	825.8	861.3	892.4	926.1	963.6

Memo Items:

	1969	1970	1971	1972	1973	1974	1975	1976	1977	1978	1979
Capacity to Import	260.3	288.4	316.6	337.0	366.3	385.8	363.4	393.9	405.6	437.7	444.1
Terms of Trade Adjustment	-10.4	0.1	9.6	9.8	6.0	-17.7	-13.2	-19.8	-21.8	-7.2	-21.1
Gross Domestic Income	1,317.5	1,396.3	1,444.1	1,503.3	1,570.4	1,550.7	1,530.4	1,607.4	1,653.3	1,716.0	1,773.7
Gross National Income	1,319.3	1,397.0	1,446.4	1,505.7	1,573.1	1,552.2	1,534.1	1,613.9	1,655.1	1,724.4	1,779.1

DOMESTIC PRICES/DEFLATORS — *(Index 1987 = 100)*

	1969	1970	1971	1972	1973	1974	1975	1976	1977	1978	1979
Overall (GDP)	44.9	48.4	52.3	55.2	58.6	62.8	66.5	68.9	71.5	74.6	77.6
Domestic Absorption	45.2	48.3	52.0	54.9	58.5	63.2	67.1	69.9	72.4	75.2	78.7
Agriculture	94.3	84.8	90.2	100.9	100.9	94.0	108.8	120.7	116.7	114.6	115.4
Industry	45.9	50.0	53.3	55.1	58.1	62.5	65.6	67.4	69.9	72.8	75.3
Manufacturing	47.5	51.0	54.1	55.9	59.0	63.5	66.3	67.7	70.6	73.2	75.2
Consumer Price Index	48.7	50.3	53.0	55.9	59.8	63.9	67.7	70.7	73.3	75.2	78.3

MANUFACTURING ACTIVITY

	1969	1970	1971	1972	1973	1974	1975	1976	1977	1978	1979
Employment (1987=100)	117.2	121.7	120.7	118.2	119.0	115.9	108.1	105.5	106.2	105.5	105.9
Real Earnings per Empl. (1987=100)	58.1	64.9	68.3	70.8	74.3	77.9	79.0	82.5	85.3	87.9	89.8
Real Output per Empl. (1987=100)	57.8	58.2	58.9	61.7	64.9	69.6	70.1	78.5	86.5	87.3	93.5
Earnings as % of Value Added	43.6	46.3	47.4	47.7	47.9	49.1	49.4	47.7	48.5	48.2	47.9

MONETARY HOLDINGS — *(Billions of current Deutsche Mark)*

	1969	1970	1971	1972	1973	1974	1975	1976	1977	1978	1979
Money Supply, Broadly Defined	340.5	373.0	423.4	483.4	529.5	569.1	634.0	683.5	752.2	827.4	873.0
Money	95.4	103.7	116.9	133.4	135.7	150.2	171.7	177.3	198.6	227.5	234.1
Currency Outside Banks	34.7	36.9	40.3	45.7	47.4	51.5	56.5	60.6	67.5	76.2	79.9
Demand Deposits	60.7	66.8	76.6	87.7	88.2	98.7	115.2	116.7	131.1	151.3	154.3
Quasi-Money	245.1	269.4	306.6	350.0	393.8	418.8	462.3	506.2	553.6	599.9	638.9

(Billions of current Deutsche Mark)

	1969	1970	1971	1972	1973	1974	1975	1976	1977	1978	1979
GOVERNMENT DEFICIT (-) OR SURPLUS	..	6.94	6.37	5.83	12.43	-6.43	-37.16	-31.21	-25.57	-26.49	-27.63
Current Revenue	..	166.10	186.69	208.22	242.26	260.36	272.99	302.23	329.27	352.40	377.62
Current Expenditure	..	143.54	161.62	184.78	208.38	241.54	283.61	303.65	325.23	348.84	371.51
Current Budget Balance	..	22.56	25.07	23.44	33.88	18.82	-10.62	-1.42	4.04	3.56	6.11
Capital Receipts	..	0.12	0.10	0.12	0.13	0.12	0.10	0.32	0.10	0.12	0.12
Capital Payments	..	15.74	18.80	17.73	21.58	25.37	26.64	30.11	29.71	30.17	33.86

* Data for the former German Democratic Republic are excluded.

1980	1981	1982	1983	1984	1985	1986	1987	1988	1989 estimate	NOTES	GERMANY, FEDERAL REPUBLIC OF
13,340	13,290	12,270	11,450	11,220	10,970	11,990	14,400	18,460	20,750	..	**CURRENT GNP PER CAPITA (US $)**
61,566	61,682	61,638	61,423	61,175	61,024	61,066	61,199	61,268	61,337	..	**POPULATION (thousands)**
				(Billions of current Deutsche Mark)							**USE AND ORIGIN OF RESOURCES**
1,485.2	1,545.1	1,597.1	1,680.5	1,769.9	1,844.4	1,945.2	2,017.8	2,121.8	2,269.4	..	Gross National Product (GNP)
6.3	4.2	-0.8	5.6	14.1	13.8	13.8	11.3	11.1	..	..	Net Factor Income from Abroad
1,478.9	1,540.9	1,597.9	1,674.9	1,755.8	1,830.6	1,931.4	2,006.4	2,110.7	..	..	GDP at Market Prices
-3.0	15.0	37.5	38.1	55.1	80.5	115.0	112.9	120.8	141.4	..	Resource Balance
422.3	481.8	517.6	524.8	590.8	647.7	638.2	638.6	687.8	785.8	..	Exports of Goods & NFServices
425.3	466.8	480.1	486.7	535.7	567.3	523.2	525.7	567.1	644.4	..	Imports of Goods & NFServices
1,488.2	1,530.1	1,559.6	1,642.4	1,714.8	1,763.9	1,830.2	1,904.9	2,001.0	2,128.1	..	Domestic Absorption
840.8	888.5	918.0	964.0	1,004.5	1,038.1	1,068.0	1,112.5	1,156.7	1,216.2	..	Private Consumption, etc.
297.9	322.1	334.8	346.1	363.9	379.0	386.8	394.7	408.5	422.0	..	General Gov't Consumption
349.5	319.5	306.8	332.3	346.4	346.8	375.4	397.7	435.9	489.8	..	Gross Domestic Investment
335.9	337.6	332.9	353.4	364.7	372.1	385.3	397.9	426.8	479.1	..	Fixed Investment
162.9	169.2	172.5	182.7	190.0	192.5	195.0	201.0	209.2	231.2	..	Indirect Taxes, net
1,316.1	1,371.7	1,425.4	1,492.2	1,565.8	1,638.1	1,736.4	1,805.5	1,901.4	..	..	GDP at factor cost
30.4	31.7	36.3	32.2	34.6	32.2	33.7	29.9	32.2	..	B	Agriculture
632.2	641.6	657.0	685.1	710.5	745.6	788.0	805.0	..	..	B	Industry
482.8	489.7	502.9	525.0	547.2	583.6	621.0	632.7	662.4	..	B	Manufacturing
816.3	867.7	904.6	957.6	1,010.6	1,052.8	1,109.8	1,171.5	..	..	B	Services, etc.
340.2	330.3	345.1	364.8	387.4	413.5	476.7	499.2	545.5	..	..	Gross Domestic Saving
335.9	323.5	333.4	359.4	390.1	416.7	480.2	500.6	545.5	..	..	Gross National Saving
				(Billions of 1987 Deutsche Mark)							
1,826.7	1,826.9	1,809.3	1,843.7	1,902.8	1,940.7	1,984.2	2,017.8	2,091.4	2,181.0	..	Gross National Product
1,819.2	1,822.2	1,810.4	1,837.8	1,888.3	1,926.7	1,970.3	2,006.4	2,080.4	..	..	GDP at Market Prices
42.9	88.1	105.7	100.4	125.6	148.3	131.6	112.9	117.0	151.3	..	Resource Balance
489.9	529.8	546.8	544.0	592.9	633.0	633.3	638.6	675.6	749.6	..	Exports of Goods & NFServices
447.0	441.6	441.1	443.6	467.3	484.7	501.7	525.7	558.6	598.3	..	Imports of Goods & NFServices
1,776.3	1,734.0	1,704.6	1,737.4	1,762.7	1,778.4	1,838.7	1,893.5	1,963.4	..	..	Domestic Absorption
1,007.5	1,006.0	998.3	1,009.5	1,014.9	1,029.9	1,062.9	1,101.1	1,130.6	..	..	Private Consumption, etc.
358.4	364.9	361.9	362.7	371.6	379.3	389.1	394.7	403.4	403.6	..	General Gov't Consumption
410.5	363.1	344.5	365.3	376.2	369.1	386.8	397.7	429.3	464.1	..	Gross Domestic Investment
402.1	382.7	362.6	374.1	376.9	377.2	389.5	397.9	421.5	457.7	..	Fixed Investment
1,624.2	1,630.4	1,622.6	1,644.5	1,691.8	1,731.6	1,773.1	1,805.5	1,873.9	..	..	GDP at factor cost
27.2	27.4	32.3	29.5	32.0	30.3	32.9	29.9	32.0	..	..	Agriculture
807.0	790.3	768.3	778.0	793.3	809.4	812.7	805.0	..	..	..	Industry
625.6	616.1	601.4	608.2	624.7	645.8	645.9	632.7	658.7	..	..	Manufacturing
987.6	1,006.1	1,008.7	1,030.4	1,062.9	1,086.9	1,124.7	1,171.5	..	..	..	Services, etc.
											Memo Items:
443.8	455.8	475.5	478.4	515.3	553.5	612.0	638.6	677.5	729.6	..	Capacity to Import
-46.0	-74.0	-71.3	-65.7	-77.6	-79.5	-21.3	0.0	1.9	..	..	Terms of Trade Adjustment
1,773.2	1,748.2	1,739.1	1,772.2	1,810.7	1,847.1	1,949.0	2,006.4	2,082.3	..	..	Gross Domestic Income
1,780.7	1,752.9	1,738.0	1,778.1	1,825.3	1,861.1	1,962.9	2,017.8	2,093.3	2,161.0	..	Gross National Income
				(Index 1987 = 100)							**DOMESTIC PRICES/DEFLATORS**
81.3	84.6	88.3	91.1	93.0	95.0	98.0	100.0	101.5	..	..	Overall (GDP)
83.8	88.2	91.5	94.5	97.3	99.2	99.5	100.6	101.9	..	..	Domestic Absorption
111.5	115.6	112.5	109.4	108.3	106.4	102.3	100.0	100.6	..	..	Agriculture
78.3	81.2	85.5	88.1	89.6	92.1	97.0	100.0	..	..	..	Industry
77.2	79.5	83.6	86.3	87.6	90.4	96.1	100.0	100.6	..	..	Manufacturing
82.6	87.8	92.4	95.5	97.7	99.9	99.8	100.0	101.3	104.1	..	Consumer Price Index
											MANUFACTURING ACTIVITY
107.3	104.7	100.9	97.6	96.7	98.1	100.0	100.0	99.9	100.5	G	Employment (1987=100)
90.7	90.0	89.3	90.1	91.1	92.9	96.8	100.0	102.6	..	G	Real Earnings per Empl. (1987=100)
97.5	101.2	102.0	105.2	111.5	114.2	103.4	100.0	105.4	..	G	Real Output per Empl. (1987=100)
50.3	44.5	43.9	43.0	41.9	41.7	42.6	42.7	41.8	..	..	Earnings as % of Value Added
				(Billions of current Deutsche Mark)							**MONETARY HOLDINGS**
914.4	950.0	1,012.4	1,067.7	1,120.8	1,199.7	1,268.0	1,333.1	1,404.5	1,472.5	D	Money Supply, Broadly Defined
243.4	239.6	256.7	278.2	294.7	314.5	340.2	365.7	408.3	431.6	..	Money
84.0	84.2	88.6	96.4	99.8	103.9	112.1	124.1	142.6	147.9	..	Currency Outside Banks
159.4	155.4	168.1	181.8	195.0	210.6	228.1	241.6	265.7	283.7	..	Demand Deposits
671.1	710.4	755.6	789.6	826.1	885.3	927.7	967.4	996.2	1,040.9	..	Quasi-Money
				(Billions of current Deutsche Mark)							
-26.91	-36.31	-32.02	-32.95	-32.31	-20.00	-17.56	-21.57	-37.28	..	E	**GOVERNMENT DEFICIT (-) OR SURPLUS**
425.69	451.53	480.43	493.75	527.00	554.19	575.41	591.35	609.64	..	..	Current Revenue
415.25	450.59	475.39	489.50	518.86	533.64	553.70	578.35	609.40	..	..	Current Expenditure
10.44	0.94	5.04	4.25	8.14	20.55	21.71	13.00	0.24	..	..	Current Budget Balance
0.14	0.17	0.30	0.24	0.21	0.24	0.25	0.19	0.35	..	..	Capital Receipts
37.49	36.97	36.20	37.59	38.27	38.35	35.54	34.74	34.68	..	..	Capital Payments

GERMANY, FEDERAL REPUBLIC OF	1969	1970	1971	1972	1973	1974	1975	1976	1977	1978	1979
FOREIGN TRADE (CUSTOMS BASIS)					*(Billions of current US dollars)*						
Value of Exports, fob	29.05	34.19	39.04	46.21	67.44	89.17	90.02	102.03	117.93	142.09	171.44
Nonfuel Primary Products	2.34	2.73	3.00	3.62	5.96	8.20	7.57	8.70	10.45	12.33	15.91
Fuels	0.81	1.01	1.16	1.21	1.72	3.08	2.81	2.93	3.12	4.51	5.69
Manufactures	25.90	30.45	34.88	41.38	59.76	77.88	79.64	90.40	104.36	125.25	149.84
Value of Imports, cif	24.93	29.81	34.34	39.76	54.50	68.98	74.21	87.78	100.70	120.67	157.68
Nonfuel Primary Products	9.71	10.84	11.10	12.71	17.72	20.52	20.38	23.64	26.89	30.02	36.54
Fuels	2.21	2.63	3.50	3.67	6.21	13.31	13.10	15.83	17.23	19.50	30.87
Manufactures	13.01	16.34	19.74	23.38	30.57	35.15	40.73	48.31	56.58	71.14	90.27
					(Index 1987 = 100)						
Terms of Trade	104.7	110.1	111.9	110.3	116.8	92.4	99.2	97.8	96.1	103.5	98.9
Export Prices, fob	24.9	26.9	28.8	31.9	41.7	49.2	54.4	55.7	59.8	70.9	81.6
Import Prices, cif	23.8	24.4	25.7	28.9	35.7	53.2	54.9	57.0	62.2	68.6	82.5
BALANCE OF PAYMENTS					*(Billions of current US dollars)*						
Exports of Goods & Services	..	42.97	48.01	56.96	81.04	106.74	110.37	123.40	141.13	172.68	206.99
Merchandise, fob	..	34.32	37.31	44.79	65.09	86.99	87.65	98.46	113.29	136.04	163.91
Nonfactor Services	..	6.21	7.67	8.64	11.13	13.84	16.48	17.99	20.36	25.95	29.44
Factor Services	..	2.45	3.03	3.53	4.82	5.91	6.24	6.95	7.49	10.69	13.63
Imports of Goods & Services	..	39.48	44.05	51.98	70.63	90.23	98.96	112.47	129.48	154.49	201.33
Merchandise, fob	..	28.62	30.64	36.39	49.25	65.09	70.74	82.43	93.82	111.90	147.47
Nonfactor Services	..	7.90	9.62	11.25	15.65	18.04	21.42	22.85	26.36	32.51	39.58
Factor Services	..	2.96	3.80	4.34	5.72	7.10	6.79	7.18	9.31	10.08	14.28
Long-Term Interest	..	..	..	..	..	..	..	..	..	..	..
Private Current Transfers, net	..	-1.59	-2.10	-2.43	-3.27	-3.65	-3.75	-3.84	-3.94	-4.79	-5.30
Workers' Remittances	..	..	..	..	..	..	..	..	..	..	..
Curr. A/C Bal before Off. Transf.	..	1.90	1.85	2.55	7.15	12.86	7.66	7.10	7.71	13.40	0.36
Net Official Transfers	..	-1.05	-0.87	-1.36	-1.93	-2.23	-3.24	-3.38	-3.70	-4.25	-5.95
Curr. A/C Bal after Off. Transf.	..	0.85	0.98	1.18	5.22	10.63	4.42	3.72	4.00	9.15	-5.60
Long-Term Capital, net	..	0.25	0.92	0.70	2.17	-2.27	-7.18	-0.73	-5.36	-1.38	6.64
Direct Investment	..	-0.30	0.11	0.04	0.39	0.21	-1.31	-1.23	-1.25	-2.01	-2.81
Long-Term Loans	..	..	..	..	..	..	..	..	..	..	..
Disbursements	..	..	..	..	..	..	..	..	..	..	..
Repayments	..	..	..	..	..	..	..	..	..	..	..
Other Long-Term Capital	..	0.55	0.82	0.67	1.78	-2.49	-5.87	0.49	-4.11	0.63	9.45
Other Capital, net	..	4.95	2.91	2.73	2.08	-9.05	1.67	0.58	4.22	1.93	-4.14
Change in Reserves	..	-6.05	-4.81	-4.62	-9.48	0.69	1.09	-3.56	-2.86	-9.69	3.09
Memo Item:					*(Deutsche Mark per US dollar)*						
Conversion Factor (Annual Avg)	3.940	3.660	3.490	3.190	2.670	2.590	2.460	2.520	2.320	2.010	1.830
					(Millions US dollars), outstanding at end of year						
EXTERNAL DEBT (Total)	..	..	..	..	..	..	..	..	..	..	..
Long-Term Debt (by debtor)	..	..	..	..	..	..	..	..	..	..	..
Central Bank, incl. IMF credit	..	..	..	..	..	..	..	..	..	..	..
Central Government	..	..	..	..	..	..	..	..	..	..	..
Rest of General Government	..	..	..	..	..	..	..	..	..	..	..
Non-financial Public Enterprises	..	..	..	..	..	..	..	..	..	..	..
Priv. Sector, incl non-guaranteed	..	..	..	..	..	..	..	..	..	..	..
Short-Term Debt	..	..	..	..	..	..	..	..	..	..	..
Memo Items:					*(Millions of US dollars)*						
Int'l Reserves Excluding Gold	3,050	9,630	14,231	19,326	28,206	27,359	26,216	30,019	34,708	48,474	52,549
Gold Holdings (at market price)	4,103	4,249	5,081	7,616	13,202	21,935	16,495	15,848	19,513	26,812	48,769
SOCIAL INDICATORS											
Total Fertility Rate	2.2	2.0	1.9	1.7	1.5	1.5	1.5	1.5	1.4	1.4	1.4
Infant Mortality Rate	23.2	23.4	23.1	22.4	22.7	21.1	19.7	17.4	15.4	14.7	13.6
Life Expectancy at Birth	70.4	70.5	70.5	70.6	70.9	71.2	71.6	71.9	72.3	72.6	72.9
Urban Population, % of total	80.9	81.3	81.7	82.0	82.4	82.7	83.1	83.4	83.6	83.9	84.1
Food Prod. per capita (1987=100)	80.7	82.1	83.8	80.1	81.2	84.4	82.4	81.5	85.6	89.3	89.0
Labor Force, Agriculture (%)	8.1	7.5	7.3	7.1	7.0	6.8	6.6	6.5	6.3	6.1	5.9
Labor Force, Female (%)	36.1	36.2	36.4	36.6	36.8	37.0	37.2	37.4	37.6	37.8	38.0
Primary Schl. Enroll. Ratio	..	..	..	..	..	..	..	..	..	..	..
Primary Schl. Enroll. Ratio, Female	..	..	..	..	..	..	..	..	..	..	..
Secondary Schl. Enroll. Ratio	..	36.0	..	..	..	..	42.0	..	..	..	47.0

1980	1981	1982	1983	1984	1985	1986	1987	1988	1989 estimate	NOTES	GERMANY, FEDERAL REPUBLIC OF
				(Billions of current US dollars)							**FOREIGN TRADE (CUSTOMS BASIS)**
191.64	175.28	175.46	168.75	171.01	183.33	242.40	293.79	322.56	..	..	Value of Exports, fob
19.05	17.27	16.21	16.12	16.71	16.97	21.05	24.68	28.63	..	..	Nonfuel Primary Products
7.14	6.97	6.47	5.63	5.55	5.06	3.88	3.89	4.15	..	..	Fuels
165.45	151.04	152.77	147.00	148.75	161.30	217.47	265.22	289.78	..	..	Manufactures
185.92	162.69	154.05	152.01	152.87	157.60	189.65	227.33	249.00	..	..	Value of Imports, cif
41.79	34.59	32.73	32.23	32.82	32.97	39.73	45.16	50.67	..	..	Nonfuel Primary Products
41.90	39.80	36.43	32.40	31.17	31.35	21.88	21.96	19.13	..	..	Fuels
102.22	88.30	84.90	87.37	88.88	93.28	128.04	160.21	179.20	..	..	Manufactures
				(Index 1987 = 100)							
90.8	80.6	83.6	84.3	77.7	81.0	95.7	100.0	99.6	..	..	Terms of Trade
87.1	75.5	73.8	71.4	63.9	64.9	83.9	100.0	102.9	..	..	Export Prices, fob
95.9	93.6	88.3	84.7	82.2	80.2	87.6	100.0	103.4	..	..	Import Prices, cif
				(Billions of current US dollars)							**BALANCE OF PAYMENTS**
233.94	215.50	215.62	207.89	209.52	223.78	298.17	360.13	395.09	422.79	..	Exports of Goods & Services
183.22	166.82	165.81	159.90	161.38	173.66	231.02	278.09	308.19	324.48	..	Merchandise, fob
34.93	33.20	33.76	31.75	31.01	32.41	41.74	48.53	48.62	50.95	..	Nonfactor Services
15.79	15.49	16.04	16.24	17.12	17.70	25.40	33.51	38.28	47.36	..	Factor Services
234.87	207.78	199.91	192.63	189.37	196.82	245.59	297.80	326.59	348.90	..	Imports of Goods & Services
174.36	150.63	141.08	138.48	139.09	145.15	175.29	208.22	228.78	247.77	..	Merchandise, fob
44.35	40.39	40.10	37.96	35.10	35.78	47.17	57.66	61.92	62.76	..	Nonfactor Services
16.16	16.76	18.73	16.19	15.17	15.89	23.13	31.93	35.89	38.37	..	Factor Services
..	..	..	..	..	..	..	..	..	..	..	Long-Term Interest
-5.85	-4.85	-4.47	-4.32	-4.00	-3.58	-4.73	-5.54	-6.35	-6.17	..	Private Current Transfers, net
..	..	..	..	..	..	..	..	..	..	..	Workers' Remittances
-6.79	2.87	11.23	10.94	16.15	23.38	47.85	56.79	62.14	67.72	..	Curr. A/C Bal before Off. Transf.
-7.13	-6.15	-6.24	-5.54	-6.40	-6.39	-7.76	-10.68	-11.69	-12.24	..	Net Official Transfers
-13.92	-3.28	5.00	5.40	9.75	16.99	40.09	46.11	50.46	55.48	..	Curr. A/C Bal after Off. Transf.
3.02	3.56	-5.96	-3.22	-6.80	-4.60	14.66	-13.36	-51.93	-11.65	..	Long-Term Capital, net
-3.60	-3.54	-1.65	-1.59	-3.76	-4.45	-9.01	-7.26	-9.92	-6.99	..	Direct Investment
..	..	..	..	..	..	..	..	..	..	..	Long-Term Loans
..	..	..	..	..	..	..	..	..	..	..	Disbursements
..	..	..	..	..	..	..	..	..	..	..	Repayments
6.62	7.10	-4.31	-1.63	-3.04	-0.15	23.67	-6.09	-42.01	-4.66	..	Other Long-Term Capital
-4.75	1.29	3.88	-3.41	-4.08	-11.50	-53.20	-12.40	-16.96	-54.43	..	Other Capital, net
15.65	-1.56	-2.92	1.23	1.13	-0.89	-1.54	-20.35	18.43	10.61	..	Change in Reserves
				(Deutsche Mark per US dollar)							Memo Item:
1.820	2.260	2.430	2.550	2.850	2.940	2.170	1.800	1.760	1.880	..	Conversion Factor (Annual Avg)
			(Millions US dollars), outstanding at end of year								
..	..	..	..	..	..	..	..	..	..	..	**EXTERNAL DEBT (Total)**
..	..	..	..	..	..	..	..	..	..	..	Long-Term Debt (by debtor)
..	..	..	..	..	..	..	..	..	..	..	Central Bank, incl. IMF credit
..	..	..	..	..	..	..	..	..	..	..	Central Government
..	..	..	..	..	..	..	..	..	..	..	Rest of General Government
..	..	..	..	..	..	..	..	..	..	..	Non-financial Public Enterprises
..	..	..	..	..	..	..	..	..	..	..	Priv. Sector, incl non-guaranteed
..	..	..	..	..	..	..	..	..	..	..	Short-Term Debt
				(Millions of US dollars)							Memo Items:
48,592	43,719	44,762	42,674	40,141	44,380	51,734	78,756	58,528	60,709	..	Int'l Reserves Excluding Gold
56,110	37,835	43,489	36,312	29,345	31,125	37,207	46,078	39,048	38,168	..	Gold Holdings (at market price)
											SOCIAL INDICATORS
1.4	1.4	1.4	1.3	1.3	1.3	1.3	1.4	1.5	1.5	..	Total Fertility Rate
12.7	11.6	10.9	10.2	9.6	8.9	8.7	8.3	8.1	7.8	..	Infant Mortality Rate
73.2	73.2	73.3	73.9	74.1	74.3	74.6	74.8	75.0	75.3	..	Life Expectancy at Birth
84.4	84.6	84.8	85.1	85.3	85.5	85.7	85.9	86.0	86.2	..	Urban Population, % of total
90.8	90.1	97.3	95.3	101.6	98.0	105.0	100.0	103.0	98.2	..	Food Prod. per capita (1987=100)
5.8	..	..	..	..	..	..	..	..	..	..	Labor Force, Agriculture (%)
38.1	38.0	38.0	37.9	37.8	37.7	37.6	37.5	37.4	37.3	..	Labor Force, Female (%)
99.0	..	100.0	99.0	97.0	98.0	101.0	103.0	..	..	..	Primary Schl. Enroll. Ratio
99.0	..	99.0	99.0	96.0	98.0	101.0		..	..	..	Primary Schl. Enroll. Ratio, Female
94.0	..	..	..	93.0	93.0	94.0	..	..	..	..	Secondary Schl. Enroll. Ratio

GHANA	1969	1970	1971	1972	1973	1974	1975	1976	1977	1978	1979
CURRENT GNP PER CAPITA (US $)	230	250	270	250	260	290	280	280	300	350	380
POPULATION (thousands)	8,424	8,614	8,877	9,138	9,388	9,621	9,835	10,023	10,177	10,322	10,501
USE AND ORIGIN OF RESOURCES					*(Millions of current Ghanaian Cedis)*						
Gross National Product (GNP)	1,952	2,214	2,454	2,779	3,475	4,629	5,241	6,478	11,123	20,938	28,123
Net Factor Income from Abroad	-49	-45	-47	-37	-26	-31	-42	-48	-40	-48	-99
GDP at Market Prices	2,001	2,259	2,500	2,815	3,501	4,660	5,283	6,526	11,163	20,986	28,222
Resource Balance	-12	-31	-112	154	177	-162	49	-22	-118	-279	20
Exports of Goods & NFServices	395	482	394	583	751	854	1,023	1,025	1,172	1,754	3,170
Imports of Goods & NFServices	407	513	506	428	574	1,016	973	1,047	1,289	2,033	3,150
Domestic Absorption	2,013	2,290	2,612	2,661	3,324	4,822	5,234	6,548	11,281	21,265	28,202
Private Consumption, etc.	1,492	1,680	1,935	2,106	2,626	3,645	3,873	5,170	8,637	17,766	23,454
General Gov't Consumption	285	290	324	355	382	569	688	799	1,409	2,371	2,903
Gross Domestic Investment	236	320	353	200	316	608	672	580	1,235	1,128	1,845
Fixed Investment	200	271	311	244	268	555	614	642	1,049	1,062	1,899
Indirect Taxes, net	242	309	301	303	281	418	541	672	867	1,398	1,524
GDP at factor cost	1,758	1,950	2,199	2,512	3,220	4,242	4,742	5,854	10,296	19,588	26,698
Agriculture	919	1,051	1,104	1,313	1,715	2,383	2,518	3,300	6,274	12,742	16,924
Industry	383	412	457	499	651	845	1,110	1,254	1,768	2,524	3,466
Manufacturing	248	258	275	306	409	502	737	857	1,204	1,813	2,447
Services, etc.	699	797	940	1,003	1,135	1,432	1,655	1,972	3,121	5,721	7,832
Gross Domestic Saving	224	289	241	354	493	446	721	558	1,117	849	1,865
Gross National Saving	..	233	185	314	459	410	708	505	1,070	792	1,759
					(Millions of 1987 Ghanaian Cedis)						
Gross National Product	580,177	639,927	676,512	659,748	682,243	732,529	634,329	612,384	624,503	685,856	674,358
GDP at Market Prices	597,100	654,834	690,518	669,927	689,341	739,887	641,087	618,695	629,974	691,914	680,388
Resource Balance	-34,559	8,994	35,188	128,095	69,247	-19,856	9,452	28,364	-34,082	-26,933	-2,295
Exports of Goods & NFServices	197,221	236,047	220,901	256,401	255,190	200,316	196,548	206,332	154,936	148,209	145,691
Imports of Goods & NFServices	231,780	227,052	185,712	128,305	185,943	220,172	187,096	177,967	189,018	175,142	147,986
Domestic Absorption	631,659	645,840	655,330	541,832	620,094	759,744	631,634	590,331	664,056	718,847	682,683
Private Consumption, etc.	496,605	474,950	484,155	420,966	492,196	584,374	473,217	451,702	472,242	551,455	528,500
General Gov't Consumption	48,525	58,276	53,189	58,726	46,965	57,979	58,378	59,735	76,879	90,386	74,276
Gross Domestic Investment	86,529	112,614	117,985	62,140	80,934	117,390	100,040	78,895	114,935	77,005	79,907
Fixed Investment	..	..	..	..	..	..	..	..	..	..	..
GDP at factor cost	..	..	..	..	..	..	..	..	..	..	..
Agriculture	318,215	354,043	370,848	385,080	377,403	410,659	328,804	323,385	305,876	364,150	377,873
Industry	136,402	145,411	147,410	132,545	158,460	157,559	156,193	152,013	158,178	146,354	125,563
Manufacturing	85,225	89,016	83,533	75,900	93,803	88,465	96,649	92,281	95,298	91,954	76,464
Services, etc.	163,472	178,564	193,713	177,752	181,425	196,852	184,230	171,397	194,346	203,196	192,110
Memo Items:											
Capacity to Import	224,829	213,368	144,643	174,548	243,281	185,066	196,533	174,212	171,735	151,124	148,925
Terms of Trade Adjustment	27,608	-22,678	-76,258	-81,853	-11,909	-15,250	-16	-32,120	16,799	2,915	3,234
Gross Domestic Income	624,708	632,156	614,260	588,074	677,432	724,638	641,071	586,576	646,772	694,828	683,623
Gross National Income	607,785	617,248	600,254	577,895	670,334	717,279	634,313	580,265	641,301	688,770	677,592
DOMESTIC PRICES/DEFLATORS					*(Index 1987 = 100)*						
Overall (GDP)	0.3	0.3	0.4	0.4	0.5	0.6	0.8	1.1	1.8	3.0	4.1
Domestic Absorption	0.3	0.4	0.4	0.5	0.5	0.6	0.8	1.1	1.7	3.0	4.1
Agriculture	0.3	0.3	0.3	0.3	0.5	0.6	0.8	1.0	2.1	3.5	4.5
Industry	0.3	0.3	0.3	0.4	0.4	0.5	0.7	0.8	1.1	1.7	2.8
Manufacturing	0.3	0.3	0.3	0.4	0.4	0.6	0.8	0.9	1.3	2.0	3.2
Consumer Price Index	0.2	0.2	0.2	0.3	0.3	0.4	0.5	0.7	1.6	2.7	4.2
MANUFACTURING ACTIVITY											
Employment (1987=100)	..	..	..	..	..	..	..	..	..	..	..
Real Earnings per Empl. (1987=100)	..	..	..	..	..	..	..	..	..	..	..
Real Output per Empl. (1987=100)	..	..	..	..	..	..	..	..	..	..	..
Earnings as % of Value Added	24.1	23.0	22.0	22.1	19.5	21.2	20.5	17.1	17.1	21.8	18.3
MONETARY HOLDINGS					*(Millions of current Ghanaian Cedis)*						
Money Supply, Broadly Defined	388	427	475	668	794	1,005	1,386	1,903	3,044	5,131	5,942
Money	290	306	321	463	564	697	1,009	1,429	2,393	4,126	4,680
Currency Outside Banks	151	151	159	239	245	336	486	707	1,157	2,122	2,459
Demand Deposits	139	155	162	223	319	361	523	722	1,236	2,004	2,221
Quasi-Money	99	121	154	205	230	308	377	474	651	1,005	1,262
					(Millions of current Ghanaian Cedis)						
GOVERNMENT DEFICIT (-) OR SURPLUS	..	..	..	-161	-187	-196	-401	-736	-1,057	-1,897	-1,800
Current Revenue	..	..	..	422	392	584	810	870	1,171	1,393	2,600
Current Expenditure	..	..	..	440	453	624	910	1,102	1,361	2,541	3,500
Current Budget Balance	..	..	..	-18	-61	-40	-100	-232	-190	-1,148	-900
Capital Receipts	..	..	..	..	..	..	..	..	..	..	..
Capital Payments	..	..	..	143	126	156	301	504	867	749	900

1980	1981	1982	1983	1984	1985	1986	1987	1988	1989 estimate	NOTES	GHANA
410	410	380	350	370	370	390	390	400	390	A	**CURRENT GNP PER CAPITA (US $)**
10,740	11,030	11,366	11,747	12,168	12,620	13,073	13,526	13,977	14,425	..	**POPULATION (thousands)**
				(Millions of current Ghanaian Cedis)							**USE AND ORIGIN OF RESOURCES**
42,670	72,404	86,226	182,398	266,918	337,280	498,796	724,844	1,031,340	1,386,300	..	Gross National Product (GNP)
-182	-222	-225	-1,640	-4,082	-5,720	-12,204	-20,459	-26,875	-33,400	..	Net Factor Income from Abroad
42,852	72,626	86,451	184,038	271,000	343,000	511,000	745,303	1,058,220	1,419,700	..	GDP at Market Prices
-295	-412	308	-5,790	-1,000	-7,000	-8,600	-16,900	-2,900	..	..	Resource Balance
3,628	3,454	2,886	11,238	20,000	33,000	81,800	157,800	217,700	..	..	Exports of Goods & NFServices
3,923	3,866	2,578	17,028	21,000	40,000	90,400	174,700	220,600	..	..	Imports of Goods & NFServices
43,147	73,038	86,143	189,828	272,000	350,000	519,600	762,203	1,061,120	..	..	Domestic Absorption
35,953	63,333	77,620	167,147	233,000	285,000	413,900	588,103	807,716	..	..	Private Consumption, etc.
4,784	6,384	5,603	15,780	20,000	32,000	56,600	74,700	104,800	..	..	General Gov't Consumption
2,410	3,321	2,920	6,901	19,000	33,000	49,100	99,400	148,600	..	..	Gross Domestic Investment
2,613	3,430	3,053	6,922	18,542	32,600	48,600	..	..	..	..	Fixed Investment
1,524	2,867	2,937	..	..	..	..	..	..	..	..	Indirect Taxes, net
41,328	69,759	83,514	..	..	..	..	..	..	..	B	GDP at factor cost
24,821	38,553	49,572	109,927	133,232	154,003	244,317	377,481	521,529	694,000	..	Agriculture
5,086	6,654	5,401	12,199	28,631	57,209	87,723	118,947	171,375	247,400	..	Industry
3,346	4,338	3,117	7,101	17,306	39,562	57,021	73,710	106,845	149,200	..	Manufacturing
12,945	27,419	31,478	61,912	109,137	131,788	178,960	248,875	365,312	478,300	..	Services, etc.
2,115	2,909	3,228	1,111	18,000	26,000	40,500	82,500	145,700	..	..	Gross Domestic Saving
1,924	2,675	3,000	-545	14,677	22,052	34,728	93,034	153,709	..	..	Gross National Saving
				(Millions of 1987 Ghanaian Cedis)							
676,487	657,174	614,509	587,596	634,796	663,278	693,204	724,844	771,314	818,426	..	Gross National Product
684,201	664,105	621,029	593,386	645,315	677,947	712,698	745,303	791,580	839,850	I	GDP at Market Prices
-35,929	-24,975	45,944	-5,587	-2,742	-16,695	-13,251	-16,900	-2,293	..	..	Resource Balance
125,894	114,746	132,237	71,750	78,554	83,628	125,894	157,800	166,065	..	..	Exports of Goods & NFServices
161,823	139,722	86,293	77,337	81,296	100,323	139,145	174,700	168,358	..	..	Imports of Goods & NFServices
720,130	689,080	575,085	598,973	648,057	694,641	725,949	762,203	793,872	..	..	Domestic Absorption
563,953	526,244	438,259	463,992	516,489	550,928	583,196	588,103	598,427	..	..	Private Consumption, etc.
83,264	96,322	85,638	83,942	73,089	70,800	72,072	74,700	81,314	..	..	General Gov't Consumption
72,913	66,515	51,188	51,039	58,479	72,913	70,681	99,400	114,131	..	..	Gross Domestic Investment
..	..	..	..	..	..	..	..	..	..	..	Fixed Investment
..	..	..	..	..	..	..	..	..	..	B I	GDP at factor cost
386,099	376,175	355,676	330,867	362,988	365,338	377,350	377,481	391,060	410,202	..	Agriculture
125,985	105,856	87,838	77,421	84,318	99,240	106,841	118,947	131,053	142,384	..	Industry
75,415	60,856	48,397	43,019	48,528	60,332	67,021	73,710	80,530	86,904	..	Manufacturing
187,658	190,441	180,980	185,098	198,009	213,369	228,507	248,875	269,466	287,264	..	Services, etc.
											Memo Items:
149,655	124,831	96,603	51,040	77,425	82,766	125,908	157,800	166,144	..	..	Capacity to Import
23,761	10,085	-35,634	-20,710	-1,129	-862	14	0	80	..	..	Terms of Trade Adjustment
707,961	674,190	585,395	572,677	644,186	677,085	712,712	745,303	791,659	..	..	Gross Domestic Income
700,248	667,260	578,875	566,886	633,667	662,416	693,218	724,844	771,393	..	..	Gross National Income
				(Index 1987 = 100)							**DOMESTIC PRICES/DEFLATORS**
6.3	10.9	13.9	31.0	42.0	50.6	71.7	100.0	133.7	169.0	..	Overall (GDP)
6.0	10.6	15.0	31.7	42.0	50.4	71.6	100.0	133.7	..	..	Domestic Absorption
6.4	10.2	13.9	33.2	36.7	42.2	64.7	100.0	133.4	169.2	..	Agriculture
4.0	6.3	6.1	15.8	34.0	57.6	82.1	100.0	130.8	173.8	..	Industry
4.4	7.1	6.4	16.5	35.7	65.6	85.1	100.0	132.7	171.7	..	Manufacturing
6.3	13.7	16.7	37.3	52.1	57.4	71.5	100.0	131.4	164.5	..	Consumer Price Index
											MANUFACTURING ACTIVITY
..	..	..	..	..	..	..	..	..	..	G	Employment (1987=100)
..	..	..	..	..	..	..	..	..	..	G	Real Earnings per Empl. (1987=100)
..	..	..	..	..	..	..	..	..	..	G	Real Output per Empl. (1987=100)
20.0	20.6	20.5	17.6	11.0	12.9	14.3	..	..	..	..	Earnings as % of Value Added
				(Millions of current Ghanaian Cedis)							**MONETARY HOLDINGS**
7,949	12,029	14,837	20,804	31,962	46,718	69,112	105,970	155,010	239,750	..	Money Supply, Broadly Defined
6,085	9,413	11,203	16,717	26,849	38,308	55,156	84,170	122,030	186,390	..	Money
3,521	6,049	6,957	10,389	17,631	22,557	32,348	48,980	67,880	82,920	..	Currency Outside Banks
2,564	3,364	4,246	6,328	9,218	15,750	22,808	35,190	54,150	103,470	..	Demand Deposits
1,864	2,616	3,634	4,086	5,113	8,410	13,957	21,800	32,980	53,360	..	Quasi-Money
				(Millions of current Ghanaian Cedis)							**GOVERNMENT DEFICIT (-) OR SURPLUS**
-1,808	-4,707	-4,848	-4,933	-4,843	-7,579	299	4,059	3,911	..	F	**GOVERNMENT DEFICIT (-) OR SURPLUS**
2,951	3,279	4,856	10,242	22,642	40,311	73,626	111,046	153,791	..	..	Current Revenue
4,179	6,330	8,603	13,401	23,326	38,461	60,834	80,703	111,002	..	..	Current Expenditure
-1,228	-3,051	-3,747	-3,159	-684	1,850	12,792	30,343	42,789	..	..	Current Budget Balance
..	..	..	..	..	..	..	..	..	..	..	Capital Receipts
580	1,656	1,101	1,774	4,159	9,429	12,493	26,284	38,878	..	..	Capital Payments

GHANA	1969	1970	1971	1972	1973	1974	1975	1976	1977	1978	1979
FOREIGN TRADE (CUSTOMS BASIS)					*(Millions of current US dollars)*						
Value of Exports, fob	301.5	432.9	341.4	393.1	565.1	646.6	737.0	765.2	951.1	992.4	1,041.0
Nonfuel Primary Products	290.9	422.8	326.4	373.6	519.9	614.9	696.7	722.3	906.1	943.8	989.0
Fuels	2.0	0.7	2.7	3.1	3.7	12.4	20.4	16.4	15.3	23.0	32.0
Manufactures	8.6	9.3	12.3	16.4	41.6	19.4	19.9	26.5	29.6	25.6	20.0
Value of Imports, cif	347.3	410.0	433.6	292.2	447.6	817.7	787.9	862.0	1,143.5	1,002.6	852.7
Nonfuel Primary Products	70.8	100.3	89.8	73.3	132.3	179.0	139.1	162.2	160.0	155.7	109.5
Fuels	22.4	23.9	26.5	33.7	40.1	135.7	131.2	128.7	179.5	138.6	175.9
Manufactures	254.1	285.8	317.3	185.2	275.3	503.1	517.6	571.2	803.9	708.2	567.3
					(Index 1987 = 100)						
Terms of Trade	150.7	123.2	95.6	107.0	122.2	120.6	101.1	138.2	193.5	171.2	164.0
Export Prices, fob	37.0	32.7	27.2	30.7	47.3	66.7	57.7	80.2	120.3	120.0	136.1
Import Prices, cif	24.6	26.5	28.5	28.7	38.7	55.3	57.1	58.1	62.2	70.1	83.0
BALANCE OF PAYMENTS					*(Millions of current US dollars)*						
Exports of Goods & Services	..	476.5	389.3	442.9	653.8	746.5	895.4	894.0	1,020.4	997.4	1,164.6
Merchandise, fob	..	427.0	334.6	384.3	585.0	679.0	801.0	779.0	889.6	892.8	1,065.7
Nonfactor Services	..	45.4	51.9	54.9	62.0	63.3	90.0	112.4	128.3	103.3	97.0
Factor Services	..	4.1	2.8	3.6	6.8	4.2	4.4	2.5	2.5	1.3	1.9
Imports of Goods & Services	..	542.5	535.4	347.9	539.6	942.1	922.3	994.8	1,158.6	1,101.6	1,121.4
Merchandise, fob	..	375.1	368.2	222.9	372.1	708.2	650.5	690.3	860.2	780.3	803.1
Nonfactor Services	..	127.5	127.9	100.0	144.8	207.1	231.0	260.3	261.0	292.6	258.1
Factor Services	..	39.9	39.3	25.0	22.7	26.8	40.8	44.3	37.4	28.7	60.2
Long-Term Interest	..	12.2	15.3	7.0	12.1	13.0	19.4	18.7	15.6	23.9	29.9
Private Current Transfers, net	..	-10.0	-8.7	-2.9	-6.3	-3.6	24.3	-4.3	-6.1	-5.1	-2.6
Workers' Remittances	..	..	..	..	..	..	..	..	..	..	1.3
Curr. A/C Bal before Off. Transf.	..	-76.0	-154.9	92.1	107.9	-199.3	-2.7	-105.1	-144.4	-109.3	40.6
Net Official Transfers	..	8.3	9.0	16.2	18.8	27.8	20.3	31.0	64.6	63.4	81.4
Curr. A/C Bal after Off. Transf.	..	-67.7	-145.8	108.2	126.7	-171.5	17.6	-74.0	-79.7	-45.9	122.0
Long-Term Capital, net	..	102.1	65.0	41.3	31.5	8.4	92.4	-13.4	89.0	93.6	85.6
Direct Investment	..	67.8	30.6	11.5	14.4	10.5	70.9	-18.3	19.2	9.7	-2.8
Long-Term Loans	..	27.7	24.7	34.1	21.0	17.0	-3.9	11.3	80.7	71.6	79.3
Disbursements	..	41.8	37.9	41.5	32.1	31.1	31.1	44.8	100.4	113.0	119.9
Repayments	..	14.1	13.2	7.4	11.1	14.1	35.0	33.5	19.7	41.4	40.6
Other Long-Term Capital	..	6.6	9.7	-4.4	-4.0	-19.0	25.5	-6.4	-11.0	12.3	9.1
Other Capital, net	..	-41.0	87.6	-84.3	-82.9	103.1	-112.6	28.1	100.2	37.9	-238.6
Change in Reserves	..	6.6	-6.7	-65.2	-75.3	59.9	2.5	59.3	-109.4	-85.5	31.0
Memo Item:					*(Ghanaian Cedis per US dollar)*						
Conversion Factor (Annual Avg)	1.020	1.020	1.030	1.330	1.160	1.150	1.150	1.150	1.150	1.760	2.750
Additional Conversion Factor	1.020	1.020	1.030	1.320	1.420	1.610	1.880	2.360	3.500	5.730	7.020
					(Millions of US dollars), outstanding at end of year						
EXTERNAL DEBT (Total)	..	548.7	531.2	583.4	735.6	717.2	729.3	716.9	1,058.4	1,269.0	1,272.5
Long-Term Debt (by debtor)	..	543.6	524.2	566.8	709.9	708.1	723.4	713.9	837.7	910.6	1,072.1
Central Bank, incl. IMF credit	..	46.1	19.9	1.9	0.0	0.0	45.2	44.8	46.9	66.4	130.2
Central Government	..	317.5	329.3	387.9	460.8	530.2	514.3	505.5	607.1	652.5	742.4
Rest of General Government	..	..	..	..	..	..	..	..	..	..	..
Non-financial Public Enterprises	..	169.8	164.8	167.8	167.0	102.0	86.4	77.2	85.2	109.4	136.8
Priv. Sector, incl non-guaranteed	..	10.2	10.2	9.2	82.1	75.9	77.5	86.4	98.5	82.3	62.7
Short-Term Debt	..	5.1	7.0	16.6	25.7	9.1	5.9	3.0	220.7	358.4	200.4
Memo Items:					*(Millions of US dollars)*						
Int'l Reserves Excluding Gold	66.2	36.6	36.1	93.7	176.1	71.5	124.7	91.7	148.6	277.2	289.1
Gold Holdings (at market price)	5.6	6.0	7.0	10.4	18.0	29.8	22.4	21.6	33.0	49.5	112.1
SOCIAL INDICATORS											
Total Fertility Rate	6.7	6.7	6.7	6.6	6.6	6.6	6.6	6.5	6.5	6.5	6.5
Infant Mortality Rate	112.4	110.6	108.8	107.0	106.0	105.0	104.0	103.0	102.0	101.2	100.4
Life Expectancy at Birth	48.8	49.2	49.6	50.0	50.2	50.4	50.6	50.8	51.0	51.2	51.4
Urban Population, % of total	28.4	29.0	29.2	29.3	29.5	29.6	29.8	30.0	30.2	30.3	30.5
Food Prod. per capita (1987=100)	113.5	121.1	119.2	109.6	113.5	122.9	112.2	100.4	92.4	90.2	94.0
Labor Force, Agriculture (%)	58.9	58.4	58.1	57.8	57.6	57.3	57.1	56.8	56.6	56.3	56.1
Labor Force, Female (%)	42.4	42.2	42.2	42.1	42.0	41.9	41.9	41.8	41.7	41.6	41.5
Primary Schl. Enroll. Ratio	..	64.0	..	..	..	..	71.0	71.0	71.0	71.0	69.0
Primary Schl. Enroll. Ratio, Female	..	54.0	..	..	..	..	62.0	62.0	61.0	62.0	60.0
Secondary Schl. Enroll. Ratio	..	14.0	..	..	..	..	37.0	36.0	36.0	36.0	36.0

1980	1981	1982	1983	1984	1985	1986	1987	1988	1989 estimate	NOTES	GHANA
				(Millions of current US dollars)							**FOREIGN TRADE (CUSTOMS BASIS)**
1,257.0	1,063.0	873.0	536.0	575.0	663.0	914.0	1,056.0	1,044.0	..	f	Value of Exports, fob
1,212.0	931.0	789.0	506.0	529.0	572.0	868.0	987.0	964.4	..	..	Nonfuel Primary Products
20.0	99.0	69.0	12.0	38.0	81.0	24.0	41.0	41.4	..	..	Fuels
25.0	33.0	15.0	18.0	8.0	10.0	22.0	28.0	38.3	..	..	Manufactures
1,128.6	1,106.0	705.0	600.0	640.0	731.0	783.0	836.0	881.0	..	..	Value of Imports, cif
145.9	123.0	93.0	78.0	75.0	78.0	72.1	82.0	91.7	..	..	Nonfuel Primary Products
300.9	350.0	242.0	161.0	161.0	199.0	122.9	144.0	151.7	..	..	Fuels
681.8	633.0	370.0	361.0	404.0	454.0	588.0	610.0	637.6	..	..	Manufactures
				(Index 1987 = 100)							
121.8	98.3	85.0	106.3	121.3	112.8	104.5	100.0	92.4	..	..	Terms of Trade
122.5	103.4	88.1	100.9	111.2	103.8	93.3	100.0	94.6	..	..	Export Prices, fob
100.5	105.1	103.6	94.9	91.6	92.0	89.3	100.0	102.4	..	..	Import Prices, cif
				(Millions of current US dollars)							**BALANCE OF PAYMENTS**
1,213.1	831.8	713.9	477.6	611.7	676.0	818.5	906.1	958.7	889.1	f	Exports of Goods & Services
1,103.6	710.7	607.0	439.1	565.9	632.4	773.4	826.8	881.0	807.2	..	Merchandise, fob
106.7	119.1	103.9	38.2	43.8	38.0	39.7	72.4	71.4	75.5	..	Nonfactor Services
2.8	2.0	3.0	0.3	2.0	5.6	5.4	6.9	6.3	6.4	..	Factor Services
1,263.5	1,335.6	905.0	724.1	812.8	952.3	1,056.1	1,327.8	1,393.0	1,401.8	f	Imports of Goods & Services
908.3	954.3	588.7	499.7	533.0	668.7	712.5	951.5	993.4	999.0	..	Merchandise, fob
266.4	291.6	224.7	134.4	162.9	167.5	227.6	237.5	255.0	272.6	..	Nonfactor Services
88.8	89.7	91.6	90.0	116.9	116.1	116.0	138.8	144.6	130.2	..	Factor Services
30.0	26.1	28.7	44.6	29.4	30.9	45.1	57.6	63.7	63.0	..	Long-Term Interest
-3.3	-4.2	-1.2	-1.8	21.1	32.6	72.1	201.6	172.4	202.1	..	Private Current Transfers, net
0.5	0.8	0.9	0.4	4.5	0.4	0.6	0.7	6.0	6.0	..	Workers' Remittances
-53.7	-508.0	-192.3	-248.3	-180.0	-243.7	-165.5	-220.1	-261.9	-310.6	..	Curr. A/C Bal before Off. Transf.
82.9	87.2	83.7	74.2	141.2	109.5	122.5	123.2	196.1	213.1	..	Net Official Transfers
29.2	-420.8	-108.6	-174.1	-38.8	-134.2	-43.0	-96.9	-65.8	-97.5	..	Curr. A/C Bal after Off. Transf.
64.1	93.7	128.1	33.8	204.2	45.1	146.3	232.4	183.9	202.6	f	Long-Term Capital, net
15.6	16.3	16.3	2.4	2.0	5.6	4.3	4.7	5.0	15.0	..	Direct Investment
98.1	81.3	58.7	106.3	51.5	122.4	274.9	221.7	219.9	298.2	..	Long-Term Loans
168.9	114.8	98.3	172.9	121.6	189.3	364.6	338.0	360.5	442.6	..	Disbursements
70.8	33.5	39.6	66.6	70.1	66.9	89.7	116.3	140.6	144.4	..	Repayments
-49.6	-3.8	53.1	-74.9	150.7	-82.9	-132.9	6.0	-41.0	-110.6	..	Other Long-Term Capital
-189.0	291.1	-20.7	-115.4	-232.7	149.5	-133.5	-69.7	52.2	54.9	f	Other Capital, net
95.7	35.9	1.3	255.7	67.3	-60.4	30.2	-65.8	-170.3	-160.0	..	Change in Reserves
				(Ghanaian Cedis per US dollar)							**Memo Item:**
2.750	2.750	2.750	8.830	35.990	54.370	89.200	153.730	202.350	270.000	..	Conversion Factor (Annual Avg)
9.640	17.200	21.420	45.360	61.320	76.160	89.290	147.000	202.350	270.000	..	Additional Conversion Factor
			(Millions of US dollars), outstanding at end of year								
1,314.4	1,461.8	1,397.0	1,598.4	1,897.7	2,174.3	2,652.1	3,133.8	3,112.6	3,077.7	..	**EXTERNAL DEBT (Total)**
1,183.5	1,175.9	1,191.0	1,508.6	1,659.4	1,991.2	2,472.1	3,025.5	3,045.9	3,049.1	..	Long-Term Debt (by debtor)
105.2	85.2	75.4	331.4	516.3	706.0	882.2	1,004.6	867.2	798.6	..	Central Bank, incl. IMF credit
855.8	844.1	849.1	914.8	908.6	1,005.6	1,286.5	1,676.6	1,855.5	1,959.8	..	Central Government
..	..	..	..	..	..	..	..	..	..	..	Rest of General Government
168.7	195.4	209.3	214.4	181.5	218.9	235.4	269.8	249.0	227.5	..	Non-financial Public Enterprises
53.8	51.2	57.2	48.0	53.0	60.7	68.0	74.5	74.2	63.2	..	Priv. Sector, incl non-guaranteed
130.9	285.9	206.0	89.8	238.3	183.1	180.0	108.3	66.7	28.6	..	Short-Term Debt
				(Millions of US dollars)							**Memo Items:**
180.4	145.6	138.9	144.8	301.6	478.5	513.0	195.1	221.3	347.3	..	Int'l Reserves Excluding Gold
149.1	122.8	175.5	146.5	135.7	73.6	111.0	136.5	89.0	88.6	..	Gold Holdings (at market price)
											SOCIAL INDICATORS
6.5	6.5	6.5	6.5	6.5	6.4	6.4	6.4	6.3	6.2	..	Total Fertility Rate
99.6	98.8	98.0	96.4	94.8	93.2	91.6	90.0	88.4	86.9	..	Infant Mortality Rate
51.6	51.8	52.0	52.4	52.8	53.2	53.6	54.0	54.2	54.4	..	Life Expectancy at Birth
30.7	30.9	31.0	31.2	31.3	31.5	31.9	32.3	32.5	32.8	..	Urban Population, % of total
92.3	91.6	85.8	71.0	121.2	102.5	99.5	100.0	99.2	102.8	..	Food Prod. per capita (1987=100)
55.8	..	..	..	..	..	..	..	..	..	..	Labor Force, Agriculture (%)
41.4	41.2	41.0	40.9	40.7	40.6	40.4	40.2	40.0	39.9	..	Labor Force, Female (%)
80.0	..	77.0	78.0	76.0	76.0	72.0	71.0		..	..	Primary Schl. Enroll. Ratio
71.0	68.0	67.0	68.0	66.0	..	63.0	63.0		..	..	Primary Schl. Enroll. Ratio, Female
41.0	..	38.0	38.0	41.0	40.0	39.0	40.0		..	..	Secondary Schl. Enroll. Ratio

GREECE	1969	1970	1971	1972	1973	1974	1975	1976	1977	1978	1979
CURRENT GNP PER CAPITA (US $)	1,060	1,170	1,300	1,460	1,720	1,940	2,370	2,650	2,850	3,270	3,860
POPULATION (thousands)	8,773	8,793	8,831	8,889	8,929	8,962	9,047	9,167	9,309	9,430	9,548

USE AND ORIGIN OF RESOURCES *(Billions of current Greek Drachmas)*

	1969	1970	1971	1972	1973	1974	1975	1976	1977	1978	1979
Gross National Product (GNP)	271.5	304.4	338.2	387.3	497.2	582.1	691.4	849.9	994.0	1,193.8	1,472.2
Net Factor Income from Abroad	5.0	5.5	7.9	9.6	13.1	17.9	19.2	24.9	30.3	32.4	43.5
GDP at Market Prices	266.5	298.9	330.3	377.7	484.2	564.2	672.2	824.9	963.7	1,161.4	1,428.8
Resource Balance	-23.9	-25.0	-26.8	-31.4	-53.2	-53.9	-67.2	-67.9	-81.0	-81.7	-111.3
Exports of Goods & NFServices	25.9	30.0	34.1	44.3	68.9	90.8	113.3	145.1	162.3	204.4	249.6
Imports of Goods & NFServices	49.8	55.0	60.9	75.7	122.1	144.7	180.6	213.1	243.3	286.1	360.8
Domestic Absorption	290.4	323.9	357.1	409.1	537.3	618.1	739.4	892.9	1,044.7	1,243.1	1,540.0
Private Consumption, etc.	187.4	202.2	223.5	251.5	308.7	374.7	456.0	551.8	636.1	736.6	875.8
General Gov't Consumption	33.9	37.7	41.4	45.9	55.4	78.1	102.0	124.3	153.8	185.2	233.5
Gross Domestic Investment	69.0	84.0	92.2	111.7	173.2	165.4	181.3	216.7	254.7	321.4	430.7
Fixed Investment	65.6	70.7	83.3	104.8	135.7	125.5	140.0	175.0	221.4	278.0	369.2
Indirect Taxes, net	37.5	40.9	42.9	47.7	55.9	56.9	79.0	96.2	119.1	144.7	183.6
GDP at factor cost	229.0	258.0	287.4	330.0	428.2	507.3	593.2	728.7	844.6	1,016.7	1,245.2
Agriculture	43.1	47.1	52.3	61.5	87.3	100.4	111.0	136.2	141.5	177.1	198.2
Industry	70.2	81.0	91.7	106.7	142.0	155.2	178.9	222.8	263.8	312.9	401.3
Manufacturing	40.8	49.3	55.6	61.9	86.2	102.6	118.1	146.5	165.3	191.3	238.5
Services, etc.	115.7	130.0	143.4	161.8	198.9	251.8	303.3	369.8	439.3	526.7	645.8
Gross Domestic Saving	45.1	59.0	65.4	80.3	120.0	111.4	114.1	148.8	173.8	239.7	319.4
Gross National Saving	..	74.8	87.4	107.0	154.8	148.6	156.8	202.9	238.0	308.1	406.0

(Billions of 1987 Greek Drachmas)

	1969	1970	1971	1972	1973	1974	1975	1976	1977	1978	1979
Gross National Product	3,504.9	3,781.3	4,070.8	4,433.0	4,768.7	4,602.9	4,851.3	5,156.4	5,336.3	5,676.5	5,874.7
GDP at Market Prices	3,422.5	3,694.8	3,957.8	4,309.3	4,624.8	4,474.6	4,743.0	5,029.7	5,181.4	5,534.0	5,719.5
Resource Balance	-342.2	-343.9	-355.3	-380.6	-546.4	-359.2	-355.9	-310.0	-382.5	-337.4	-366.3
Exports of Goods & NFServices	313.8	352.6	394.4	484.7	597.9	598.6	662.3	770.8	784.4	913.0	973.8
Imports of Goods & NFServices	656.1	696.5	749.7	865.3	1,144.3	957.9	1,018.2	1,080.8	1,167.0	1,250.4	1,340.0
Domestic Absorption	3,764.8	4,038.7	4,313.1	4,689.9	5,171.2	4,833.9	5,098.9	5,339.7	5,564.0	5,871.4	6,085.7
Private Consumption, etc.	2,120.5	2,235.9	2,404.9	2,597.8	2,636.2	2,654.4	2,849.2	3,017.3	3,167.9	3,325.1	3,328.1
General Gov't Consumption	531.8	563.2	591.0	624.5	667.0	747.5	836.7	879.7	937.1	969.9	1,026.6
Gross Domestic Investment	1,112.4	1,239.5	1,317.2	1,467.6	1,868.0	1,431.9	1,412.9	1,442.7	1,458.9	1,576.4	1,731.0
Fixed Investment	1,062.7	1,048.0	1,194.8	1,379.0	1,484.5	1,104.9	1,107.3	1,182.8	1,274.8	1,351.1	1,470.1
GDP at factor cost	2,864.4	3,102.5	3,349.6	3,655.3	3,959.5	3,899.0	4,099.2	4,334.1	4,443.7	4,734.9	4,888.3
Agriculture	645.5	705.1	729.1	772.3	767.2	804.2	850.0	838.6	776.6	857.2	803.3
Industry	877.9	948.7	1,063.8	1,194.4	1,339.8	1,191.5	1,260.2	1,377.7	1,443.6	1,534.4	1,626.6
Manufacturing	474.2	548.0	607.1	655.0	770.0	748.2	789.1	867.9	880.3	938.1	989.9
Services, etc.	1,366.6	1,477.9	1,581.6	1,711.1	1,861.5	1,909.6	1,996.0	2,124.5	2,228.5	2,349.6	2,463.3
Memo Items:											
Capacity to Import	341.2	379.8	419.9	506.2	645.8	600.8	639.2	736.2	778.6	893.3	926.7
Terms of Trade Adjustment	27.4	27.2	25.4	21.5	47.9	2.2	-23.1	-34.6	-5.8	-19.8	-47.0
Gross Domestic Income	3,449.9	3,721.9	3,983.2	4,330.8	4,672.7	4,476.9	4,719.9	4,995.1	5,175.6	5,514.3	5,672.5
Gross National Income	3,532.3	3,808.5	4,096.2	4,454.5	4,816.6	4,605.1	4,828.2	5,121.8	5,330.5	5,656.8	5,827.7

DOMESTIC PRICES/DEFLATORS *(Index 1987 = 100)*

	1969	1970	1971	1972	1973	1974	1975	1976	1977	1978	1979
Overall (GDP)	7.8	8.1	8.3	8.8	10.5	12.6	14.2	16.4	18.6	21.0	25.0
Domestic Absorption	7.7	8.0	8.3	8.7	10.4	12.8	14.5	16.7	18.8	21.2	25.3
Agriculture	6.7	6.7	7.2	8.0	11.4	12.5	13.1	16.2	18.2	20.7	24.7
Industry	8.0	8.5	8.6	8.9	10.6	13.0	14.2	16.2	18.3	20.4	24.7
Manufacturing	8.6	9.0	9.2	9.5	11.2	13.7	15.0	16.9	18.8	20.4	24.1
Consumer Price Index	7.0	7.2	7.4	7.7	8.9	11.3	12.8	14.6	16.3	18.4	21.9

MANUFACTURING ACTIVITY

	1969	1970	1971	1972	1973	1974	1975	1976	1977	1978	1979
Employment (1987=100)	72.8	78.4	81.9	84.6	89.6	94.8	97.7	104.2	106.0	106.9	107.8
Real Earnings per Empl. (1987=100)	60.7	63.3	66.2	70.3	72.5	70.9	77.2	84.6	90.6	94.0	99.1
Real Output per Empl. (1987=100)	49.1	50.4	52.1	55.9	60.9	64.6	68.5	69.2	71.6	79.1	86.7
Earnings as % of Value Added	32.4	31.5	31.7	32.9	29.8	31.6	35.9	37.6	38.9	39.0	39.0

MONETARY HOLDINGS *(Billions of current Greek Drachmas)*

	1969	1970	1971	1972	1973	1974	1975	1976	1977	1978	1979
Money Supply, Broadly Defined	117.4	139.0	170.5	212.1	250.0	301.4	375.4	472.2	586.2	797.3	947.4
Money	48.9	54.6	63.6	75.9	93.7	112.2	130.6	159.6	186.6	228.2	265.4
Currency Outside Banks	35.7	39.1	43.3	50.8	65.3	80.6	92.2	112.3	133.4	161.8	184.7
Demand Deposits	13.2	15.5	20.4	25.1	28.4	31.6	38.5	47.3	53.2	66.4	80.8
Quasi-Money	68.5	84.4	106.8	136.2	156.3	189.2	244.8	312.6	399.6	569.1	682.0

(Billions of current Greek Drachmas)

	1969	1970	1971	1972	1973	1974	1975	1976	1977	1978	1979
GOVERNMENT DEFICIT (-) OR SURPLUS	..	..	..	-6.5	-13.0	-23.4	-26.1	-32.4	-47.4	-49.8	-55.3
Current Revenue	..	..	..	98.5	123.0	143.7	179.5	239.5	283.9	348.9	427.3
Current Expenditure	..	..	..	77.7	100.4	132.4	163.0	215.9	256.5	321.7	407.1
Current Budget Balance	..	..	..	20.8	22.6	11.3	16.6	23.7	27.4	27.2	20.2
Capital Receipts	..	..	..	1.6	0.5	1.2	0.5	0.6	0.5	0.9	1.4
Capital Payments	..	..	..	28.9	36.1	36.0	43.2	56.7	75.4	77.9	76.9

1980	1981	1982	1983	1984	1985	1986	1987	1988	1989 estimate	NOTES	GREECE
4,370	4,470	4,320	3,950	3,800	3,610	3,650	3,990	4,770	5,340	..	**CURRENT GNP PER CAPITA (US $)**
9,643	9,729	9,790	9,847	9,896	9,934	9,964	9,990	10,013	10,039	..	**POPULATION (thousands)**
			(Billions of current Greek Drachmas)								**USE AND ORIGIN OF RESOURCES**
1,767.5	2,109.1	2,632.4	3,108.2	3,806.6	4,582.1	5,412.1	6,192.6	7,389.3	8,596.4	..	Gross National Product (GNP)
56.6	59.0	57.8	30.4	1.9	-34.0	-68.0	-63.0	-57.0	-78.4	..	Net Factor Income from Abroad
1,710.9	2,050.1	2,574.7	3,077.8	3,804.7	4,616.1	5,480.1	6,255.6	7,446.3	8,674.8	..	GDP at Market Prices
-91.2	-133.7	-265.3	-315.9	-314.5	-535.9	-470.2	-456.6	-463.0	-789.8	..	Resource Balance
357.7	422.4	473.0	609.5	824.6	977.6	1,233.1	1,536.8	1,800.9	2,110.7	..	Exports of Goods & NFServices
448.9	556.1	738.3	925.4	1,139.1	1,513.5	1,703.3	1,993.4	2,263.9	2,900.5	f	Imports of Goods & NFServices
1,802.2	2,183.8	2,839.9	3,393.7	4,119.2	5,152.0	5,950.3	6,712.2	7,909.2	9,464.6	f	Domestic Absorption
1,093.9	1,294.6	1,825.4	2,141.1	2,601.5	3,227.5	3,820.7	4,374.4	5,006.6	5,984.0	..	Private Consumption, etc.
280.0	368.5	471.2	579.4	742.8	942.1	1,067.2	1,243.0	1,533.1	1,878.0	..	General Gov't Consumption
428.2	520.6	543.3	673.2	774.8	982.4	1,062.4	1,094.8	1,369.5	1,602.6	f	Gross Domestic Investment
413.7	456.3	513.5	624.0	702.9	880.4	1,017.9	1,056.0	1,292.6	1,587.3	f	Fixed Investment
187.2	190.1	264.0	345.9	443.1	481.0	648.4	850.4	..	..	..	Indirect Taxes, net
1,523.7	1,860.0	2,310.7	2,731.9	3,361.6	4,135.1	4,831.7	5,405.2	..	..	..	GDP at factor cost
270.1	329.3	424.4	462.8	591.4	713.8	791.9	875.0	..	..	..	Agriculture
474.3	570.4	672.7	811.5	981.9	1,209.3	1,450.5	1,580.4	..	..	..	Industry
297.0	361.3	422.6	503.1	614.8	752.5	907.4	971.0	..	..	..	Manufacturing
779.4	960.2	1,213.5	1,457.7	1,788.3	2,212.0	2,589.2	2,949.8	..	..	..	Services, etc.
337.0	386.9	278.0	357.3	460.4	446.5	592.2	638.2	906.6	812.8	..	Gross Domestic Saving
439.9	505.5	405.2	469.7	565.6	522.6	660.7	760.7	1,092.6	958.7	..	Gross National Saving
			(Billions of 1987 Greek Drachmas)								
6,009.8	5,991.7	5,981.8	5,912.6	6,041.4	6,180.4	6,188.1	6,192.6	6,453.3	6,609.5	..	Gross National Product
5,840.0	5,840.4	5,867.9	5,873.2	6,037.1	6,220.3	6,261.6	6,255.6	6,502.3	6,658.2	I	GDP at Market Prices
-191.8	-298.5	-458.9	-476.1	-312.9	-485.8	-384.7	-456.6	-469.5	-627.5	..	Resource Balance
1,041.3	979.6	908.9	981.7	1,148.0	1,163.1	1,326.3	1,536.8	1,654.4	1,700.2	..	Exports of Goods & NFServices
1,233.1	1,278.1	1,367.8	1,457.8	1,460.9	1,648.9	1,711.0	1,993.4	2,123.8	2,327.7	f	Imports of Goods & NFServices
6,031.8	6,138.9	6,326.7	6,349.3	6,350.0	6,706.1	6,646.3	6,712.2	6,971.8	7,285.7	f	Domestic Absorption
3,350.8	3,622.8	3,876.3	3,879.0	3,881.1	4,122.1	4,195.1	4,374.4	4,419.3	4,407.9	..	Private Consumption, etc.
1,028.7	1,098.9	1,124.1	1,155.0	1,190.2	1,228.1	1,220.6	1,243.0	1,311.6	1,377.3	..	General Gov't Consumption
1,652.3	1,417.3	1,326.3	1,315.4	1,278.7	1,356.0	1,230.5	1,094.8	1,240.9	1,500.6	f	Gross Domestic Investment
1,375.0	1,271.8	1,247.3	1,231.0	1,161.3	1,220.6	1,145.0	1,056.0	1,150.9	1,247.3	f	Fixed Investment
5,007.4	5,013.3	5,045.3	5,048.2	5,203.5	5,376.4	5,409.7	5,405.2	5,638.8	5,773.7	I	GDP at factor cost
906.4	891.7	913.1	831.8	889.9	906.4	881.0	875.0	927.4	928.9	..	Agriculture
1,587.3	1,563.3	1,527.5	1,530.2	1,549.3	1,606.2	1,608.1	1,580.4	1,668.3	1,719.8	..	Industry
991.3	988.4	967.1	950.3	961.8	995.8	994.9	971.0	1,014.4	..	..	Manufacturing
2,519.1	2,562.2	2,607.7	2,686.2	2,764.3	2,863.7	2,920.6	2,949.8	3,043.0	3,124.9	..	Services, etc.
											Memo Items:
982.5	970.7	876.3	960.2	1,057.6	1,065.1	1,238.7	1,536.8	1,689.5	1,693.9	..	Capacity to Import
-58.8	-8.9	-32.6	-21.5	-90.4	-98.0	-87.6	0.0	35.1	-6.3	..	Terms of Trade Adjustment
5,781.2	5,831.5	5,835.3	5,851.7	5,946.7	6,122.3	6,174.0	6,255.6	6,537.4	6,651.9	..	Gross Domestic Income
5,951.0	5,982.9	5,949.2	5,891.1	5,951.0	6,082.4	6,100.5	6,192.6	6,488.4	6,603.1	..	Gross National Income
			(Index 1987 = 100)								**DOMESTIC PRICES/DEFLATORS**
29.3	35.1	43.9	52.4	63.0	74.2	87.5	100.0	114.5	130.3	..	Overall (GDP)
29.9	35.6	44.9	53.4	64.9	76.8	89.5	100.0	113.4	129.9	..	Domestic Absorption
29.8	36.9	46.5	55.6	66.5	78.8	89.9	100.0	..	..	..	Agriculture
29.9	36.5	44.0	53.0	63.4	75.3	90.2	100.0	..	..	..	Industry
30.0	36.6	43.7	52.9	63.9	75.6	91.2	100.0	..	..	..	Manufacturing
27.3	34.0	41.1	49.4	58.5	69.8	85.9	100.0	113.5	129.1	..	Consumer Price Index
											MANUFACTURING ACTIVITY
108.8	109.3	105.3	102.2	102.2	101.3	101.3	100.0	..	..	..	Employment (1987=100)
97.6	96.4	105.6	104.0	109.4	109.6	108.3	100.0	..	..	..	Real Earnings per Empl. (1987=100)
89.3	92.3	89.8	92.7	95.0	99.7	101.5	100.0	..	..	..	Real Output per Empl. (1987=100)
39.0	39.8	44.9	42.8	43.2	42.4	42.8	43.0	..	..	..	Earnings as % of Value Added
			(Billions of current Greek Drachmas)								**MONETARY HOLDINGS**
1,159.8	1,536.7	1,973.3	2,374.3	3,070.3	3,851.6	4,579.7	5,642.4	..	..	D	Money Supply, Broadly Defined
308.8	377.4	459.1	525.6	630.9	743.3	896.0	1,000.0	..	..	..	Money
211.8	263.7	305.2	348.2	408.2	513.5	550.1	641.4	..	..	..	Currency Outside Banks
97.0	113.7	153.9	177.4	222.7	229.8	345.9	358.6	..	..	..	Demand Deposits
851.0	1,159.3	1,514.2	1,848.7	2,439.4	3,108.3	3,683.8	4,642.4	..	..	..	Quasi-Money
			(Billions of current Greek Drachmas)								**GOVERNMENT DEFICIT (-) OR SURPLUS**
-85.5	-223.7	-477.5	-160.9	-534.0	-661.3	..	..	..	..	..	Current Revenue
524.7	600.8	871.6	1,192.7	1,368.0	1,671.3	..	..	..	..	..	Current Revenue
532.2	728.4	1,206.4	1,162.2	1,661.0	2,033.7	..	..	..	..	..	Current Expenditure
-7.5	-127.6	-334.8	30.6	-293.0	-362.4	..	..	..	..	..	Current Budget Balance
1.6	2.3	3.6	0.2	4.2	3.6	..	..	..	..	..	Capital Receipts
79.6	98.4	146.3	191.7	245.2	302.5	..	..	..	..	..	Capital Payments

GREECE	1969	1970	1971	1972	1973	1974	1975	1976	1977	1978	1979
FOREIGN TRADE (CUSTOMS BASIS)					*(Millions of current US dollars)*						
Value of Exports, fob	554	643	662	871	1,454	2,030	2,278	2,558	2,757	3,375	3,877
Nonfuel Primary Products	388	414	454	549	713	942	1,024	1,156	1,251	1,512	1,646
Fuels	6	6	6	11	203	183	252	150	133	321	459
Manufactures	160	222	202	311	537	905	1,003	1,253	1,373	1,543	1,773
Value of Imports, cif	1,594	1,958	2,098	2,346	3,473	4,385	5,321	6,051	6,852	7,655	9,594
Nonfuel Primary Products	369	399	448	486	813	981	991	982	1,134	1,231	1,620
Fuels	119	135	153	231	427	974	1,178	1,234	1,041	1,429	2,036
Manufactures	1,106	1,425	1,496	1,629	2,233	2,429	3,152	3,835	4,678	4,995	5,938
					(Index 1987 = 100)						
Terms of Trade	161.0	157.2	142.8	144.7	143.5	123.9	121.6	123.1	122.4	115.7	118.3
Export Prices, fob	38.6	39.5	39.3	41.9	51.0	67.1	67.8	70.9	76.0	81.0	100.2
Import Prices, cif	24.0	25.1	27.5	28.9	35.5	54.1	55.8	57.6	62.1	70.0	84.7
BALANCE OF PAYMENTS					*(Millions of current US dollars)*						
Exports of Goods & Services	..	1,100	1,314	1,692	2,401	3,254	3,647	4,202	4,833	5,905	7,680
Merchandise, fob	..	612	627	835	1,230	1,774	1,960	2,228	2,522	2,999	3,932
Nonfactor Services	..	471	668	818	1,105	1,370	1,559	1,838	2,193	2,742	3,495
Factor Services	..	17	19	39	66	111	129	136	118	164	253
Imports of Goods & Services	..	1,868	2,129	2,664	4,323	5,041	5,272	5,940	6,833	7,842	10,732
Merchandise, fob	..	1,509	1,727	2,161	3,582	4,125	4,320	4,922	5,686	6,498	8,948
Nonfactor Services	..	267	307	392	591	690	720	738	859	1,001	1,340
Factor Services	..	92	95	112	149	226	232	280	288	343	444
Long-Term Interest	..	..	..	..	..	..	..	..	..	..	..
Private Current Transfers, net	..	344	469	572	732	642	733	800	922	981	1,164
Workers' Remittances	..	333	457	560	715	625	716	777	899	951	1,137
Curr. A/C Bal before Off. Transf.	..	-424	-346	-401	-1,190	-1,145	-891	-938	-1,078	-956	-1,888
Net Official Transfers	..	2	2	1	1	2	15	10	..	1	1
Curr. A/C Bal after Off. Transf.	..	-422	-344	-400	-1,189	-1,143	-877	-928	-1,078	-955	-1,887
Long-Term Capital, net	..	280	236	496	795	759	789	544	862	1,040	1,331
Direct Investment	..	50	42	55	62	67	24	305	387	428	613
Long-Term Loans	..	..	..	..	..	..	..	..	..	..	..
Disbursements	..	..	..	..	..	..	..	..	..	..	..
Repayments	..	..	..	..	..	..	..	..	..	..	..
Other Long-Term Capital	..	230	193	441	733	692	765	239	475	612	718
Other Capital, net	..	119	292	375	382	227	-96	312	387	49	513
Change in Reserves	..	23	-184	-472	11	156	183	72	-171	-134	43
Memo Item:					*(Greek Drachmas per US dollar)*						
Conversion Factor (Annual Avg)	30.000	30.000	30.000	30.000	29.630	30.000	32.050	36.520	36.840	36.740	37.040
					(Millions of US dollars), outstanding at end of year						
EXTERNAL DEBT (Total)	..	..	..	..	..	..	..	..	..	..	..
Long-Term Debt (by debtor)	..	..	..	..	..	..	..	..	..	..	..
Central Bank, incl. IMF credit	..	..	..	..	..	..	..	..	..	..	..
Central Government	..	..	..	..	..	..	..	..	..	..	..
Rest of General Government	..	..	..	..	..	..	..	..	..	..	..
Non-financial Public Enterprises	..	..	..	..	..	..	..	..	..	..	..
Priv. Sector, incl non-guaranteed	..	..	..	..	..	..	..	..	..	..	..
Short-Term Debt	..	..	..	..	..	..	..	..	..	..	..
Memo Items:					*(Millions of US dollars)*						
Int'l Reserves Excluding Gold	187.2	193.6	412.4	898.8	898.9	781.7	963.6	880.6	1,048.3	1,305.0	1,342.8
Gold Holdings (at market price)	130.6	124.4	122.4	226.8	393.1	673.3	509.0	492.0	615.3	852.0	1,949.7
SOCIAL INDICATORS											
Total Fertility Rate	2.5	2.3	2.3	2.3	2.3	2.4	2.4	2.4	2.3	2.3	2.3
Infant Mortality Rate	31.8	29.6	26.9	27.3	24.1	23.9	24.0	22.5	20.4	19.3	18.7
Life Expectancy at Birth	71.6	71.8	72.2	72.7	72.7	72.8	72.9	73.0	73.1	73.5	73.9
Urban Population, % of total	51.5	52.5	53.1	53.6	54.2	54.7	55.3	55.8	56.3	56.7	57.2
Food Prod. per capita (1987=100)	78.4	86.7	84.1	89.7	89.8	98.5	103.1	98.3	95.3	99.9	95.6
Labor Force, Agriculture (%)	43.2	42.2	41.1	40.0	38.8	37.7	36.6	35.4	34.2	33.1	32.0
Labor Force, Female (%)	25.6	25.7	25.7	25.8	25.8	25.9	25.9	25.9	26.0	26.0	26.0
Primary Schl. Enroll. Ratio	..	107.0	..	..	..	..	104.0	104.0	103.0	103.0	100.0
Primary Schl. Enroll. Ratio, Female	..	106.0	..	..	..	..	104.0	103.0	103.0	103.0	99.0
Secondary Schl. Enroll. Ratio	..	63.0	..	..	..	..	78.0	80.0	81.0	81.0	81.0

1980	1981	1982	1983	1984	1985	1986	1987	1988	1989 estimate	NOTES	GREECE
											FOREIGN TRADE (CUSTOMS BASIS)
				(Millions of current US dollars)							
5,142	4,249	4,297	4,412	4,864	4,536	5,660	6,489	5,400	..	..	Value of Exports, fob
1,901	1,580	1,680	1,912	1,998	1,749	2,241	2,579	2,098	..	..	Nonfuel Primary Products
800	404	462	305	492	546	371	436	306	..	..	Fuels
2,441	2,266	2,154	2,194	2,374	2,241	3,048	3,474	2,996	..	..	Manufactures
10,531	8,781	10,012	9,500	9,611	10,138	11,241	12,908	11,978	..	..	Value of Imports, cif
1,725	1,613	1,916	1,880	1,982	1,950	1,994	3,307	3,024	..	..	Nonfuel Primary Products
2,464	1,933	2,871	2,606	2,583	2,993	1,587	1,786	609	..	..	Fuels
6,343	5,234	5,225	5,013	5,045	5,195	7,659	7,815	8,345	..	..	Manufactures
				(Index 1987 = 100)							
116.6	106.6	103.1	99.5	97.2	93.5	102.1	100.0	103.0	..	..	Terms of Trade
115.0	105.3	103.3	96.5	92.3	88.7	91.8	100.0	110.2	..	..	Export Prices, fob
98.6	98.8	100.2	96.9	95.0	94.8	89.9	100.0	106.9	..	..	Import Prices, cif
				(Millions of current US dollars)							**BALANCE OF PAYMENTS**
8,374	9,183	7,891	7,166	7,333	7,111	7,905	10,216	11,378	11,173	..	Exports of Goods & Services
4,093	4,772	4,141	4,106	4,394	4,293	4,513	5,612	5,933	5,994	..	Merchandise, fob
4,029	4,065	3,492	2,930	2,756	2,664	3,286	4,419	5,176	4,896	..	Nonfactor Services
252	346	258	130	183	154	106	185	269	283	..	Factor Services
11,670	12,828	11,382	10,811	11,097	12,053	11,948	14,474	15,985	17,729	..	Imports of Goods & Services
9,650	10,149	8,910	8,400	8,624	9,346	8,936	11,112	12,005	13,377	..	Merchandise, fob
1,475	1,773	1,612	1,446	1,320	1,417	1,589	1,736	2,188	2,424	..	Nonfactor Services
545	906	860	965	1,153	1,290	1,423	1,626	1,792	1,928	..	Factor Services
..	..	..	..	..	..	..	..	..	..	..	Long-Term Interest
1,087	1,076	1,039	931	917	797	975	1,370	1,713	1,381	..	Private Current Transfers, net
1,066	1,057	1,016	912	898	775	942	1,334	1,675	1,350	..	Workers' Remittances
-2,209	-2,569	-2,452	-2,714	-2,847	-4,145	-3,068	-2,888	-2,894	-5,175	..	Curr. A/C Bal before Off. Transf.
..	161	560	836	715	869	1,392	1,665	1,936	2,602	..	Net Official Transfers
-2,209	-2,408	-1,892	-1,878	-2,132	-3,276	-1,676	-1,223	-958	-2,573	..	Curr. A/C Bal after Off. Transf.
1,994	1,589	1,239	2,110	1,773	2,766	2,151	1,387	1,438	1,941	..	Long-Term Capital, net
672	520	436	439	485	447	471	683	907	752	..	Direct Investment
..	..	..	..	..	..	..	..	..	..	..	Long-Term Loans
..	..	..	..	..	..	..	..	..	..	..	Disbursements
..	..	..	..	..	..	..	..	..	..	..	Repayments
1,322	1,069	803	1,671	1,288	2,319	1,680	704	531	1,189	..	Other Long-Term Capital
78	661	541	-132	490	369	-205	642	668	291	..	Other Capital, net
137	158	112	-100	-131	141	-270	-806	-1,148	341	..	Change in Reserves
				(Greek Drachmas per US dollar)							Memo Item:
42.620	55.410	66.800	88.060	112.720	138.120	139.980	135.430	141.860	162.420	..	Conversion Factor (Annual Avg)
				(Millions of US dollars), outstanding at end of year							**EXTERNAL DEBT (Total)**
..	..	..	..	..	..	..	..	..	..	..	Long-Term Debt (by debtor)
..	..	..	..	..	..	..	..	..	..	..	Central Bank, incl. IMF credit
..	..	..	..	..	..	..	..	..	..	..	Central Government
..	..	..	..	..	..	..	..	..	..	..	Rest of General Government
..	..	..	..	..	..	..	..	..	..	..	Non-financial Public Enterprises
..	..	..	..	..	..	..	..	..	..	..	Priv. Sector, incl non-guaranteed
..	..	..	..	..	..	..	..	..	..	..	Short-Term Debt
				(Millions of US dollars)							Memo Items:
1,345.9	1,022.0	861.1	900.5	954.2	868.0	1,518.7	2,681.4	3,619.4	3,223.5	..	Int'l Reserves Excluding Gold
2,260.7	1,531.6	1,769.1	1,480.2	1,265.9	1,348.2	1,293.1	1,617.9	1,392.8	1,361.4	..	Gold Holdings (at market price)
											SOCIAL INDICATORS
2.2	2.1	2.0	1.9	1.8	1.7	1.6	1.6	1.6	1.6	..	Total Fertility Rate
17.9	16.3	15.1	14.6	14.3	14.1	12.2	12.6	12.3	11.9	..	Infant Mortality Rate
74.3	74.7	75.2	75.4	75.6	75.9	76.1	76.4	76.6	76.7	..	Life Expectancy at Birth
57.7	58.2	58.7	59.1	59.6	60.1	60.6	61.1	61.6	62.1	..	Urban Population, % of total
108.6	108.1	111.0	104.2	104.8	112.7	107.8	100.0	104.8	106.0	..	Food Prod. per capita (1987=100)
30.9	..	..	..	..	..	..	..	..	..	..	Labor Force, Agriculture (%)
26.1	26.1	26.2	26.3	26.3	26.4	26.4	26.5	26.5	26.6	..	Labor Force, Female (%)
103.0	104.0	105.0	105.0	105.0	104.0	..	..	..	..	..	Primary Schl. Enroll. Ratio
103.0	104.0	105.0	105.0	105.0	104.0	..	..	..	..	..	Primary Schl. Enroll. Ratio, Female
81.0	84.0	84.0	85.0	88.0	90.0	..	..	..	..	..	Secondary Schl. Enroll. Ratio

GRENADA	1969	1970	1971	1972	1973	1974	1975	1976	1977	1978	1979
CURRENT GNP PER CAPITA (US $)	..	..	..	..	..	..	..	..	..	..	..
POPULATION (thousands)	..	..	..	..	..	..	..	..	..	..	..
USE AND ORIGIN OF RESOURCES				*(Millions of current Eastern Caribbean Dollars)*							
Gross National Product (GNP)	..	..	..	..	..	..	..	..	..	..	..
Net Factor Income from Abroad	..	..	..	..	..	..	..	..	..	..	..
GDP at Market Prices	..	..	..	..	..	..	..	..	..	..	..
Resource Balance	..	..	..	..	..	..	..	..	..	..	..
Exports of Goods & NFServices	..	..	..	..	..	..	..	..	..	..	..
Imports of Goods & NFServices	..	..	..	..	..	..	..	..	..	..	..
Domestic Absorption	..	..	..	..	..	..	..	..	..	..	..
Private Consumption, etc.	..	..	..	..	..	..	..	..	..	..	..
General Gov't Consumption	..	..	..	..	..	..	..	..	..	..	..
Gross Domestic Investment	..	..	..	..	..	..	..	..	..	..	..
Fixed Investment	..	..	..	..	..	..	..	..	..	..	..
Indirect Taxes, net	..	..	..	..	..	..	..	..	..	..	..
GDP at factor cost	..	..	..	..	..	..	..	..	..	..	..
Agriculture	..	..	..	..	..	..	..	..	..	..	..
Industry	..	..	..	..	..	..	..	..	..	..	..
Manufacturing	..	..	..	..	..	..	..	..	..	..	..
Services, etc.	..	..	..	..	..	..	..	..	..	..	..
Gross Domestic Saving	..	..	..	..	..	..	..	..	..	..	..
Gross National Saving	..	..	..	..	..	..	..	..	..	..	..
				(Millions of 1984 Eastern Caribbean Dollars)							
Gross National Product	..	..	..	..	..	..	..	..	..	..	..
GDP at Market Prices	..	..	..	..	..	..	..	..	..	..	..
Resource Balance	..	..	..	..	..	..	..	..	..	..	..
Exports of Goods & NFServices	..	..	..	..	..	..	..	..	..	..	..
Imports of Goods & NFServices	..	..	..	..	..	..	..	..	..	..	..
Domestic Absorption	..	..	..	..	..	..	..	..	..	..	..
Private Consumption, etc.	..	..	..	..	..	..	..	..	..	..	..
General Gov't Consumption	..	..	..	..	..	..	..	..	..	..	..
Gross Domestic Investment	..	..	..	..	..	..	..	..	..	..	..
Fixed Investment	..	..	..	..	..	..	..	..	..	..	..
GDP at factor cost	..	..	..	..	..	..	..	..	..	..	..
Agriculture	..	..	..	..	..	..	..	..	..	..	..
Industry	..	..	..	..	..	..	..	..	..	..	..
Manufacturing	..	..	..	..	..	..	..	..	..	..	..
Services, etc.	..	..	..	..	..	..	..	..	..	..	..
Memo Items:											
Capacity to Import	..	..	..	..	..	..	..	..	..	..	..
Terms of Trade Adjustment	..	..	..	..	..	..	..	..	..	..	..
Gross Domestic Income	..	..	..	..	..	..	..	..	..	..	..
Gross National Income	..	..	..	..	..	..	..	..	..	..	..
DOMESTIC PRICES/DEFLATORS				*(Index 1984 = 100)*							
Overall (GDP)	..	..	..	..	..	..	..	..	..	..	..
Domestic Absorption	..	..	..	..	..	..	..	..	..	..	..
Agriculture	..	..	..	..	..	..	..	..	..	..	..
Industry	..	..	..	..	..	..	..	..	..	..	..
Manufacturing	..	..	..	..	..	..	..	..	..	..	..
Consumer Price Index	..	..	..	..	..	..	..	33.1	39.2	46.3	56.3
MANUFACTURING ACTIVITY											
Employment (1987=100)	..	..	..	..	..	..	..	..	..	..	..
Real Earnings per Empl. (1987=100)	..	..	..	..	..	..	..	..	..	..	..
Real Output per Empl. (1987=100)	..	..	..	..	..	..	..	..	..	..	..
Earnings as % of Value Added	..	..	..	..	..	..	..	..	..	..	..
MONETARY HOLDINGS				*(Millions of current Eastern Caribbean Dollars)*							
Money Supply, Broadly Defined	..	42.68	45.41	53.91	55.48	54.48	66.67	79.28	88.07	104.13	123.40
Money	..	10.81	11.87	14.31	15.62	15.78	19.38	26.70	29.51	38.04	45.65
Currency Outside Banks	..	6.09	6.90	8.28	8.39	9.71	12.65	15.32	18.33	23.67	28.50
Demand Deposits	..	4.72	4.97	6.03	7.23	6.07	6.73	11.38	11.18	14.37	17.15
Quasi-Money	..	31.87	33.54	39.60	39.86	38.69	47.29	52.58	58.55	66.09	77.75
				(Thousands of current Eastern Caribbean Dollars)							
GOVERNMENT DEFICIT (-) OR SURPLUS	..	..	..	..	..	-5,250	-5,080	-6,370	-1,660	..	..
Current Revenue	..	..	..	..	..	18,620	21,120	29,750	35,110	..	..
Current Expenditure	..	..	..	..	..	19,380	22,760	33,250	31,120	..	..
Current Budget Balance	..	..	..	..	..	-760	-1,640	-3,500	3,990	..	..
Capital Receipts	..	..	..	..	..	80	130	60	130	..	..
Capital Payments	..	..	..	..	..	4,570	3,570	2,930	5,780	..	..

1980	1981	1982	1983	1984	1985	1986	1987	1988	1989 estimate	NOTES	GRENADA
..	..	..	..	..	..	1,360	1,500	1,710	1,900	..	**CURRENT GNP PER CAPITA (US $)**
87	88	91	92	93	94	90	94	94	94	..	**POPULATION (thousands)**
				(Millions of current Eastern Caribbean Dollars)							**USE AND ORIGIN OF RESOURCES**
163.80	187.10	202.60	210.30	273.20	307.10	345.90	398.10	440.90	492.00	..	Gross National Product (GNP)
-5.90	-13.50	-13.50	-11.90	-4.10	-5.10	-4.90	-7.30	-8.60	-12.50	..	Net Factor Income from Abroad
169.70	200.60	216.10	222.20	277.30	312.20	350.80	405.40	449.50	504.50	..	GDP at Market Prices
-55.90	-82.60	-106.40	-95.50	-80.70	-91.00	-119.90	-113.10	-102.60	..	..	Resource Balance
106.90	106.90	103.10	104.80	107.50	142.80	182.80	212.00	225.70	..	..	Exports of Goods & NFServices
162.80	189.50	209.50	200.30	188.20	233.80	302.70	325.10	328.30	..	..	Imports of Goods & NFServices
225.60	283.20	322.50	317.70	358.00	403.20	470.50	518.50	552.10	..	..	Domestic Absorption
122.90	136.40	161.10	170.20	205.40	227.00	258.60	294.90	320.30	..	..	Private Consumption, etc.
46.80	50.80	51.40	55.00	64.00	71.90	75.40	85.80	84.00	..	..	General Gov't Consumption
55.90	96.00	110.00	92.50	88.60	104.30	136.70	137.80	147.80	..	..	Gross Domestic Investment
..	..	..	..	..	..	..	..	..	..	..	Fixed Investment
..	..	..	..	..	..	..	..	..	..	..	Indirect Taxes, net
167.60	180.90	196.60	204.50	223.40	246.20	282.00	320.50	350.20	374.00	..	GDP at factor cost
41.40	44.80	40.70	41.30	44.90	44.20	52.90	69.50	72.00	73.70	..	Agriculture
21.80	29.70	35.50	32.80	32.70	39.10	45.20	54.20	63.40	71.80	..	Industry
6.60	8.70	10.20	10.50	9.80	12.50	13.20	16.00	18.40	18.40	..	Manufacturing
104.40	106.40	120.40	130.40	145.80	162.90	183.90	196.80	214.80	228.50	..	Services, etc.
0.00	13.40	3.60	-3.00	7.90	13.30	16.80	24.70	45.20	..	..	Gross Domestic Saving
25.15	27.98	19.80	23.98	32.42	36.06	39.98	49.26	77.90	..	..	Gross National Saving
				(Millions of 1984 Eastern Caribbean Dollars)							
..	..	..	..	273.20	292.10	302.90	325.60	347.40	362.90	..	Gross National Product
..	..	..	..	277.30	297.20	307.60	331.50	354.10	372.10	..	GDP at Market Prices
..	..	..	..	..	..	..	..	..	..	..	Resource Balance
..	..	..	..	..	..	..	..	..	..	..	Exports of Goods & NFServices
..	..	..	..	..	..	..	..	..	..	..	Imports of Goods & NFServices
..	..	..	..	..	..	..	..	..	..	..	Domestic Absorption
..	..	..	..	..	..	..	..	..	..	..	Private Consumption, etc.
..	..	..	..	..	..	..	..	..	..	..	General Gov't Consumption
..	..	..	..	..	..	..	..	..	..	..	Gross Domestic Investment
..	..	..	..	..	..	..	..	..	..	..	Fixed Investment
194.50	198.50	209.10	212.00	223.40	234.40	247.30	273.30	275.80	291.60	..	GDP at factor cost
40.60	43.10	38.80	39.70	44.90	42.00	41.80	56.40	46.40	47.50	..	Agriculture
29.50	36.20	39.20	34.30	32.70	36.40	40.20	46.20	52.00	59.30	..	Industry
8.90	10.70	11.90	11.60	9.80	11.70	11.80	13.80	15.20	1.70	..	Manufacturing
124.40	119.20	131.10	138.00	145.80	156.00	165.30	170.70	177.40	184.80	..	Services, etc.
											Memo Items:
..	..	..	..	..	..	..	..	..	..	..	Capacity to Import
..	..	..	..	..	..	..	..	..	..	..	Terms of Trade Adjustment
..	..	..	..	..	..	..	..	..	..	..	Gross Domestic Income
..	..	..	..	..	..	..	..	..	..	..	Gross National Income
				(Index 1984 = 100)							**DOMESTIC PRICES/DEFLATORS**
..	..	..	..	100.0	105.0	114.0	122.3	126.9	135.6	..	Overall (GDP)
..	..	..	..	..	..	..	..	..	..	..	Domestic Absorption
102.0	103.9	104.9	104.0	100.0	105.2	126.6	123.2	155.2	155.2	..	Agriculture
73.9	82.0	90.6	95.6	100.0	107.4	112.4	117.3	121.9	121.1	..	Industry
74.2	81.3	85.7	90.5	100.0	106.8	111.9	115.9	121.1	1082.4	..	Manufacturing
68.2	81.0	87.3	92.6	97.8	100.4	100.9	100.0	104.0	109.8	f	Consumer Price Index
											MANUFACTURING ACTIVITY
..	..	..	..	..	..	..	..	..	..	..	Employment (1987=100)
..	..	..	..	..	..	..	..	..	..	..	Real Earnings per Empl. (1987=100)
..	..	..	..	..	..	..	..	..	..	..	Real Output per Empl. (1987=100)
..	..	..	..	..	..	..	..	..	..	..	Earnings as % of Value Added
				(Millions of current Eastern Caribbean Dollars)							**MONETARY HOLDINGS**
130.95	141.16	146.61	146.96	148.42	177.21	226.95	254.05	302.56	326.59	..	Money Supply, Broadly Defined
48.45	53.32	59.57	58.10	50.71	54.12	69.34	74.43	83.21	88.64	..	Money
32.58	37.41	39.95	41.36	20.58	25.07	30.69	33.07	35.13	31.40	..	Currency Outside Banks
15.86	15.91	19.62	16.74	30.13	29.05	38.65	41.37	48.08	57.24	..	Demand Deposits
82.51	87.83	87.03	88.86	97.71	123.09	157.61	179.62	219.34	237.95	..	Quasi-Money
				(Thousands of current Eastern Caribbean Dollars)							**GOVERNMENT DEFICIT (-) OR SURPLUS**
..	..	..	..	..	..	..	..	..	..	..	Current Revenue
..	..	..	..	..	..	..	..	..	..	..	Current Expenditure
..	..	..	..	..	..	..	..	..	..	..	Current Budget Balance
..	..	..	..	..	..	..	..	..	..	..	Capital Receipts
..	..	..	..	..	..	..	..	..	..	..	Capital Payments

GRENADA	1969	1970	1971	1972	1973	1974	1975	1976	1977	1978	1979
FOREIGN TRADE (CUSTOMS BASIS)					*(Thousands of current US dollars)*						
Value of Exports, fob	..	..	..	..	..	..	..	..	..	..	..
Nonfuel Primary Products	..	..	..	..	..	..	..	..	..	..	..
Fuels	..	..	..	..	..	..	..	..	..	..	..
Manufactures	..	..	..	..	..	..	..	..	..	..	..
Value of Imports, cif	..	..	..	..	..	..	..	..	28,500	33,400	42,600
Nonfuel Primary Products	..	..	..	..	..	..	..	..	..	..	..
Fuels	..	..	..	..	..	..	..	..	..	..	..
Manufactures	..	..	..	..	..	..	..	..	..	..	..
					(Index 1987 = 100)						
Terms of Trade	..	..	..	..	..	..	..	..	..	..	..
Export Prices, fob	..	..	..	..	..	..	..	..	..	..	..
Import Prices, cif	..	..	..	..	..	..	..	..	..	..	..
BALANCE OF PAYMENTS					*(Millions of current US dollars)*						
Exports of Goods & Services	..	..	..	..	..	..	..	..	29.16	33.60	41.35
Merchandise, fob	..	..	..	..	..	..	..	..	14.26	16.90	21.40
Nonfactor Services	..	..	..	..	..	..	..	..	14.60	16.40	19.15
Factor Services	..	..	..	..	..	..	..	..	0.30	0.30	0.80
Imports of Goods & Services	..	..	..	..	..	..	..	..	33.09	40.35	55.66
Merchandise, fob	..	..	..	..	..	..	..	..	28.54	33.35	42.64
Nonfactor Services	..	..	..	..	..	..	..	..	4.35	6.60	12.42
Factor Services	..	..	..	..	..	..	..	..	0.20	0.40	0.60
Long-Term Interest	..	0.10	0.20	0.50	0.50	0.40	0.40	0.40	0.40	0.30	0.40
Private Current Transfers, net	..	..	..	..	..	..	..	..	4.50	7.00	6.30
Workers' Remittances	..	..	..	..	..	..	..	..	..	..	..
Curr. A/C Bal before Off. Transf.	..	..	..	..	..	..	..	..	0.57	0.25	-8.01
Net Official Transfers	..	..	..	..	..	..	..	..	0.74	0.80	6.90
Curr. A/C Bal after Off. Transf.	..	..	..	..	..	..	..	..	1.31	1.05	-1.11
Long-Term Capital, net	..	..	..	..	..	..	..	..	1.49	2.29	2.21
Direct Investment	..	..	..	..	..	..	..	..	-0.10	1.40	..
Long-Term Loans	..	3.00	0.20	-0.20	0.20	0.60	0.80	-0.20	1.60	2.40	1.10
Disbursements		3.00	0.40	0.00	0.40	0.90	1.20	0.90	1.80	3.20	1.40
Repayments	..	0.00	0.20	0.20	0.20	0.30	0.40	1.10	0.20	0.80	0.30
Other Long-Term Capital	..	..	..	..	..	..	..	..	-0.01	-1.51	1.11
Other Capital, net	..	..	..	..	..	..	..	..	-2.93	-1.54	1.43
Change in Reserves	..	-5.32	-0.51	0.22	0.60	-0.36	0.51	-3.34	0.13	-1.79	-2.53
Memo Item:					*(Eastern Caribbean Dollars per US dollar)*						
Conversion Factor (Annual Avg)	2.000	2.000	1.970	1.920	1.960	2.050	2.170	2.610	2.700	2.700	2.700
					(Thousands of US dollars), outstanding at end of year						
EXTERNAL DEBT (Total)	..	7,600	8,000	7,800	7,800	8,200	8,900	8,800	11,700	14,600	17,700
Long-Term Debt (by debtor)	..	7,600	8,000	7,800	7,800	8,200	8,900	8,800	10,700	13,600	15,700
Central Bank, incl. IMF credit	..	0	0	0	0	0	900	1,400	1,700	2,700	3,200
Central Government	..	7,600	8,000	7,800	7,800	8,200	7,500	6,600	8,100	9,900	10,800
Rest of General Government	..	..	..	..	..	..	..	..	..	..	..
Non-financial Public Enterprises	..	0	0	0	0	0	500	800	900	1,000	1,700
Priv. Sector, incl non-guaranteed	..	..	..	..	..	..	..	..	..	..	..
Short-Term Debt	..	0	0	0	0	0	0	0	1,000	1,000	2,000
Memo Items:					*(Thousands of US dollars)*						
Int'l Reserves Excluding Gold	..	5,316	5,821	5,604	5,004	5,363	5,036	8,113	7,650	9,703	12,220
Gold Holdings (at market price)	..	..	..	..	..	..	..	..	..	..	..
SOCIAL INDICATORS											
Total Fertility Rate	4.6	4.6	4.5	4.5	4.4	4.3	4.3	4.2	4.1	4.0	3.9
Infant Mortality Rate	..	32.8	36.9	41.0	40.8	40.6	40.4	40.2	40.0	39.8	39.6
Life Expectancy at Birth	64.7	64.9	65.1	65.3	65.5	65.7	65.9	66.1	66.3	66.5	66.7
Urban Population, % of total	..	..	..	..	..	..	..	..	..	..	..
Food Prod. per capita (1987=100)	114.6	112.5	106.3	100.8	101.8	98.0	99.0	108.9	105.3	109.1	113.3
Labor Force, Agriculture (%)	..	..	..	..	..	..	..	..	..	..	..
Labor Force, Female (%)	..	..	..	..	..	..	..	..	..	..	..
Primary Schl. Enroll. Ratio	..	..	..	..	..	..	..	..	..	..	..
Primary Schl. Enroll. Ratio, Female	..	..	..	..	..	..	..	..	..	..	..
Secondary Schl. Enroll. Ratio	..	..	..	..	..	..	..	..	..	..	..

1980	1981	1982	1983	1984	1985	1986	1987	1988	1989 estimate	NOTES	GRENADA
				(Thousands of current US dollars)							**FOREIGN TRADE (CUSTOMS BASIS)**
17,400	19,000	18,600	18,800	18,100	22,100	27,800	..	..	..	..	Value of Exports, fob
..	..	..	..	..	..	..	..	..	..	..	Nonfuel Primary Products
..	..	..	..	..	..	..	..	..	..	..	Fuels
..	..	..	..	..	..	..	..	..	..	..	Manufactures
48,800	56,100	59,000	57,900	51,100	62,100	74,600	77,700	..	..	..	Value of Imports, cif
..	..	..	..	..	..	..	..	..	..	..	Nonfuel Primary Products
..	..	..	..	..	..	..	..	..	..	..	Fuels
..	..	..	..	..	..	..	..	..	..	..	Manufactures
				(Index 1987 = 100)							
..	..	..	..	..	..	..	..	..	..	..	Terms of Trade
..	..	..	..	..	..	..	..	..	..	..	Export Prices, fob
..	..	..	..	..	..	..	..	..	..	..	Import Prices, cif
				(Millions of current US dollars)							**BALANCE OF PAYMENTS**
39.10	39.00	38.30	39.60	41.20	54.09	69.29	80.04	85.16	..	..	Exports of Goods & Services
17.40	19.00	18.50	19.30	18.20	22.30	28.80	31.60	32.81	..	..	Merchandise, fob
20.60	18.70	18.30	18.60	21.60	30.59	38.89	46.94	50.83	..	..	Nonfactor Services
1.10	1.30	1.50	1.70	1.40	1.20	1.60	1.50	1.52	..	..	Factor Services
63.06	75.76	82.90	79.80	72.40	89.73	115.43	124.43	126.00	..	..	Imports of Goods & Services
48.79	56.07	59.03	57.88	51.12	65.56	85.97	92.80	94.50	..	..	Merchandise, fob
11.07	13.39	17.37	15.82	18.38	21.07	26.07	27.73	27.20	..	..	Nonfactor Services
3.20	6.30	6.50	6.10	2.90	3.10	3.40	3.90	4.30	..	..	Factor Services
0.50	0.40	0.60	0.80	1.10	1.10	1.00	1.90	2.40	1.10	..	Long-Term Interest
11.50	10.40	11.00	14.40	10.60	10.32	10.40	11.80	15.30	..	..	Private Current Transfers, net
..	..	..	..	..	..	..	..	..	..	..	Workers' Remittances
-12.46	-26.36	-33.60	-25.80	-20.60	-25.32	-35.74	-32.59	-25.54	..	..	Curr. A/C Bal before Off. Transf.
12.73	12.49	15.90	10.90	24.40	27.90	25.50	8.19	6.30	..	..	Net Official Transfers
0.27	-13.87	-17.70	-14.90	3.80	2.58	-10.24	-24.40	-19.25	..	..	Curr. A/C Bal after Off. Transf.
1.21	7.61	10.74	15.91	8.04	4.91	10.95	23.90	23.16	..	..	Long-Term Capital, net
..	..	1.90	2.50	2.80	4.11	5.00	12.70	17.00	..	..	Direct Investment
0.10	7.00	12.40	13.20	2.80	1.10	3.90	8.20	5.20	5.60	..	Long-Term Loans
1.00	7.50	13.00	16.20	4.70	2.90	6.50	10.70	8.20	6.30	..	Disbursements
0.90	0.50	0.60	3.00	1.90	1.80	2.60	2.50	3.00	0.70	..	Repayments
1.11	0.61	-3.56	0.21	2.44	-0.30	2.05	3.00	0.96	..	..	Other Long-Term Capital
0.11	2.50	4.97	-0.92	-11.30	1.46	1.23	3.82	-9.42	..	..	Other Capital, net
-1.60	3.76	1.99	-0.09	-0.54	-8.95	-1.94	-3.32	5.51	1.20	..	Change in Reserves
				(Eastern Caribbean Dollars per US dollar)							**Memo Item:**
2.700	2.700	2.700	2.700	2.700	2.700	2.700	2.700	2.700	2.700	..	Conversion Factor (Annual Avg)
				(Thousands of US dollars), outstanding at end of year							
16,600	29,900	40,000	53,200	50,100	52,500	56,600	71,400	75,500	78,300	..	**EXTERNAL DEBT (Total)**
15,600	27,900	38,000	50,700	48,300	50,900	54,400	67,700	66,500	68,200	..	Long-Term Debt (by debtor)
2,800	8,300	7,000	7,700	6,200	4,200	2,600	2,100	1,100	500	..	Central Bank, incl. IMF credit
11,100	17,600	28,600	39,100	37,700	41,900	46,300	59,400	59,600	62,100	..	Central Government
..	..	..	..	..	..	..	..	..	..	..	Rest of General Government
1,700	2,000	2,400	3,900	4,400	4,800	5,500	6,200	5,800	5,600	..	Non-financial Public Enterprises
..	..	..	..	..	..	..	..	..	..	..	Priv. Sector, incl non-guaranteed
1,000	2,000	2,000	2,500	1,800	1,600	2,200	3,700	9,000	10,100	..	Short-Term Debt
				(Thousands of US dollars)							**Memo Items:**
12,909	16,097	9,233	14,142	14,234	20,812	20,565	23,331	17,447	15,894	..	Int'l Reserves Excluding Gold
..	..	..	..	..	..	..	..	..	..	..	Gold Holdings (at market price)
											SOCIAL INDICATORS
3.8	3.7	3.6	3.6	3.5	3.4	3.4	3.3	3.2	3.1	..	Total Fertility Rate
39.4	39.2	39.0	38.0	37.0	36.0	35.0	34.0	33.1	32.2	..	Infant Mortality Rate
66.9	67.2	67.4	67.6	67.8	68.1	68.3	68.6	68.9	69.2	..	Life Expectancy at Birth
..	..	..	..	..	..	..	..	..	..	..	Urban Population, % of total
107.3	114.7	105.1	101.2	105.3	95.2	96.3	100.0	101.4	98.3	..	Food Prod. per capita (1987=100)
..	..	..	..	..	..	..	..	..	..	..	Labor Force, Agriculture (%)
..	..	..	..	..	..	..	..	..	..	..	Labor Force, Female (%)
..	..	..	..	..	..	..	..	..	..	..	Primary Schl. Enroll. Ratio
..	..	..	..	..	..	..	..	..	..	..	Primary Schl. Enroll. Ratio, Female
..	..	..	..	..	..	..	..	..	..	..	Secondary Schl. Enroll. Ratio

GUATEMALA	1969	1970	1971	1972	1973	1974	1975	1976	1977	1978	1979
CURRENT GNP PER CAPITA (US $)	340	360	380	390	430	500	570	660	790	900	1,030
POPULATION (thousands)	5,103	5,246	5,393	5,544	5,699	5,858	6,022	6,190	6,364	6,542	6,726
USE AND ORIGIN OF RESOURCES				*(Millions of current Guatemalan Quetzales)*							
Gross National Product (GNP)	1,678	1,862	1,941	2,054	2,521	3,112	3,577	4,292	5,448	6,044	6,890
Net Factor Income from Abroad	-38	-42	-44	-48	-48	-50	-69	-74	-33	-26	-12
GDP at Market Prices	1,715	1,904	1,985	2,101	2,569	3,161	3,646	4,365	5,481	6,071	6,903
Resource Balance	6	15	-28	8	17	-103	-66	-262	-99	-351	-311
Exports of Goods & NFServices	305	354	343	397	536	708	792	942	1,340	1,304	1,474
Imports of Goods & NFServices	299	339	371	389	519	811	858	1,204	1,439	1,655	1,784
Domestic Absorption	1,709	1,889	2,013	2,093	2,552	3,264	3,712	4,628	5,579	6,422	7,214
Private Consumption, etc.	1,379	1,493	1,588	1,682	2,034	2,470	2,875	3,396	4,127	4,675	5,432
General Gov't Consumption	135	151	139	157	167	207	250	297	355	435	488
Gross Domestic Investment	196	244	285	255	352	588	587	934	1,098	1,312	1,294
Fixed Investment	231	239	264	272	357	468	571	900	1,039	1,218	1,286
Indirect Taxes, net	121	132	138	144	170	227	252	316	492	536	543
GDP at factor cost	1,595	1,772	1,847	1,958	2,399	2,935	3,394	4,049	4,988	5,535	6,360
Agriculture	..	..	..	..	..	..	..	..	..	..	..
Industry	..	..	..	..	..	..	..	..	..	..	..
Manufacturing	..	..	..	..	..	..	..	..	..	..	..
Services, etc.	..	..	..	..	..	..	..	..	..	..	..
Gross Domestic Saving	202	259	258	263	369	485	521	672	1,000	961	983
Gross National Saving	..	234	240	246	364	492	530	796	1,061	1,050	1,094
				(Millions of 1958 Guatemalan Quetzales)							
Gross National Product	1,651.7	1,750.9	1,845.9	1,981.2	2,126.9	2,269.4	2,306.2	2,481.0	2,707.7	2,842.5	2,977.8
GDP at Market Prices	1,695.9	1,792.7	1,892.8	2,031.6	2,169.4	2,307.7	2,352.7	2,526.5	2,723.8	2,859.9	2,994.7
Resource Balance	82.1	52.7	48.3	117.4	127.4	110.9	145.4	73.2	63.5	41.1	136.4
Exports of Goods & NFServices	353.9	346.0	360.4	412.1	451.6	481.6	497.5	530.3	563.3	562.7	619.2
Imports of Goods & NFServices	271.8	293.3	312.1	294.7	324.2	370.7	352.1	457.1	499.8	521.6	482.8
Domestic Absorption	1,613.8	1,740.0	1,844.5	1,914.2	2,042.0	2,196.8	2,207.3	2,453.3	2,660.3	2,818.8	2,858.3
Private Consumption, etc.	1,323.3	1,399.5	1,479.9	1,576.6	1,665.5	1,727.2	1,777.9	1,897.1	2,048.8	2,151.3	2,242.6
General Gov't Consumption	112.7	125.6	116.3	128.6	128.7	134.8	148.5	165.0	176.1	187.2	198.9
Gross Domestic Investment	177.8	214.9	248.3	209.0	247.8	334.8	280.9	391.2	435.4	480.3	416.8
Fixed Investment	212.7	209.6	227.4	226.1	251.9	247.2	270.6	371.4	405.8	435.7	413.4
GDP at factor cost	..	..	..	..	..	..	..	..	..	..	..
Agriculture	462.9	489.7	524.3	574.7	605.1	643.8	659.9	689.6	716.5	739.1	760.1
Industry	323.3	334.6	356.1	381.2	416.5	432.1	435.1	507.9	568.8	606.2	644.6
Manufacturing	273.3	283.0	303.2	319.8	345.8	361.6	356.3	393.5	435.6	463.7	489.6
Services, etc.	909.7	968.4	1,012.4	1,075.7	1,147.8	1,231.8	1,257.7	1,329.0	1,438.5	1,514.6	1,590.0
Memo Items:											
Capacity to Import	277.6	306.4	288.6	300.6	335.1	323.6	325.0	357.5	465.5	410.9	398.7
Terms of Trade Adjustment	-76.3	-39.6	-71.8	-111.5	-116.5	-158.0	-172.5	-172.8	-97.8	-151.8	-220.5
Gross Domestic Income	1,619.6	1,753.1	1,821.0	1,920.1	2,052.9	2,149.7	2,180.2	2,353.7	2,626.0	2,708.1	2,774.2
Gross National Income	1,575.4	1,711.3	1,774.1	1,869.7	2,010.4	2,111.4	2,133.7	2,308.2	2,609.9	2,690.7	2,757.3
DOMESTIC PRICES/DEFLATORS				*(Index 1958 = 100)*							
Overall (GDP)	101.1	106.2	104.9	103.4	118.4	137.0	155.0	172.8	201.2	212.3	230.5
Domestic Absorption	105.9	108.6	109.1	109.4	125.0	148.6	168.2	188.6	209.7	227.8	252.4
Agriculture	..	..	..	..	..	..	..	..	..	..	..
Industry	..	..	..	..	..	..	..	..	..	..	..
Manufacturing	..	..	..	..	..	..	..	..	..	..	..
Consumer Price Index	17.8	18.2	18.1	18.2	20.7	24.1	27.3	30.2	33.9	36.7	40.9
MANUFACTURING ACTIVITY											
Employment (1987=100)	..	..	90.0	96.3	91.7	99.4	101.8	108.1	114.7	122.4	124.2
Real Earnings per Empl. (1987=100)	..	..	134.5	138.2	141.6	128.1	127.9	114.7	101.3	102.5	114.1
Real Output per Empl. (1987=100)	..	..	..	..	..	..	..	..	..	..	..
Earnings as % of Value Added	..	..	26.7	29.9	27.0	24.4	24.0	21.0	18.3	18.3	21.5
MONETARY HOLDINGS				*(Millions of current Guatemalan Quetzales)*							
Money Supply, Broadly Defined	309.2	343.7	383.3	476.9	579.8	668.3	808.5	1,051.8	1,249.1	1,423.6	1,537.2
Money	160.9	172.8	178.9	214.4	264.3	305.4	353.6	493.8	594.1	664.0	734.9
Currency Outside Banks	91.3	96.5	99.0	114.1	137.3	158.3	175.4	236.6	284.4	324.6	365.4
Demand Deposits	69.6	76.3	79.9	100.3	127.0	147.1	178.2	257.2	309.7	339.4	369.5
Quasi-Money	148.3	170.9	204.4	262.5	315.5	362.9	454.9	558.0	655.0	759.6	802.3
GOVERNMENT DEFICIT (-) OR SURPLUS				*(Millions of current Guatemalan Quetzales)*							
	..	..	..	-45.15	-37.94	-45.57	-30.59	-111.25	-51.19	-71.15	-149.12
Current Revenue	..	..	..	183.17	212.22	279.64	327.38	409.08	589.26	661.24	666.14
Current Expenditure	..	..	..	153.74	170.80	213.04	262.49	310.86	392.54	465.50	525.37
Current Budget Balance	..	..	..	29.43	41.42	66.60	64.89	98.22	196.72	195.74	140.77
Capital Receipts	..	..	..	..	..	..	..	0.56	0.23	0.25	0.29
Capital Payments	..	..	..	74.58	79.36	112.17	95.48	210.03	248.14	267.14	290.18

1980	1981	1982	1983	1984	1985	1986	1987	1988	1989 estimate	NOTES	GUATEMALA
1,120	1,200	1,190	1,170	1,180	1,200	1,050	950	900	910	A	CURRENT GNP PER CAPITA (US $)
6,916	7,112	7,314	7,523	7,739	7,963	8,195	8,436	8,686	8,946	..	POPULATION (thousands)
											USE AND ORIGIN OF RESOURCES
(Millions of current Guatemalan Quetzales)											
7,808	8,505	8,596	8,937	9,267	10,966	15,402	17,170	20,072	23,115	..	Gross National Product (GNP)
-71	-103	-121	-113	-203	-214	-436	-425	-471	-521	..	Net Factor Income from Abroad
7,879	8,607	8,717	9,050	9,470	11,180	15,838	17,595	20,543	23,636	..	GDP at Market Prices
-215	-560	-340	-141	-204	-116	231	-1,141	-1,197	-1,242	..	Resource Balance
1,748	1,471	1,289	1,176	1,231	1,336	2,542	2,807	3,309	4,121	..	Exports of Goods & NFServices
1,963	2,032	1,629	1,317	1,435	1,452	2,311	3,948	4,506	5,363	..	Imports of Goods & NFServices
8,094	9,168	9,057	9,191	9,674	11,296	15,607	18,736	21,740	24,878	..	Domestic Absorption
6,217	7,022	7,149	7,501	7,852	9,233	12,846	14,932	17,271	19,836	..	Private Consumption, etc.
627	680	675	688	726	777	1,124	1,374	1,637	1,843	..	General Gov't Consumption
1,250	1,466	1,233	1,002	1,096	1,285	1,636	2,431	2,832	3,199	..	Gross Domestic Investment
1,294	1,443	1,309	950	912	1,225	1,593	2,150	2,742	3,200	..	Fixed Investment
597	561	539	461	437	586	..	..	..	..	..	Indirect Taxes, net
7,282	8,047	8,178	8,589	9,033	10,594	..	..	..	..	B	GDP at factor cost
..	..	..	..	..	..	..	..	5,305	4,269	..	Agriculture
..	..	..	..	..	..	..	..	3,659	6,045	..	Industry
..	..	..	..	..	..	..	..	..	..	..	Manufacturing
..	..	..	..	..	..	..	..	11,579	13,323	..	Services, etc.
1,035	905	893	861	892	1,170	1,868	1,289	1,635	1,957	..	Gross Domestic Saving
1,073	892	834	778	718	975	1,527	1,117	1,535	1,900	..	Gross National Saving
(Millions of 1958 Guatemalan Quetzales)											
3,069.3	3,079.0	2,964.1	2,890.4	2,877.0	2,884.0	2,863.0	2,966.0	3,096.0	3,221.0	..	Gross National Product
3,106.9	3,127.4	3,016.6	2,939.6	2,954.0	2,936.0	2,940.0	3,032.0	3,163.0	3,288.0	..	GDP at Market Prices
209.9	134.2	175.9	186.8	153.0	204.0	176.0	100.0	109.0	149.0	..	Resource Balance
651.1	557.3	510.2	454.7	440.0	454.0	390.0	414.0	437.0	497.0	..	Exports of Goods & NFServices
441.2	423.1	334.3	267.9	287.0	250.0	214.0	314.0	328.0	348.0	..	Imports of Goods & NFServices
2,897.0	2,993.2	2,840.7	2,752.8	2,801.0	2,732.0	2,764.0	2,932.0	3,054.0	3,139.0	..	Domestic Absorption
2,318.9	2,350.8	2,279.7	2,247.1	2,273.0	2,265.0	2,284.0	2,363.0	2,471.0	2,544.0	..	Private Consumption, etc.
222.7	232.6	229.7	229.9	236.0	231.0	243.0	258.0	273.0	279.0	..	General Gov't Consumption
355.4	409.8	331.3	275.2	292.0	236.0	237.0	311.0	310.0	316.0	..	Gross Domestic Investment
372.6	401.5	357.6	258.2	235.0	220.0	229.0	262.0	300.0	317.0	..	Fixed Investment
..	..	..	..	..	..	..	..	..	..	..	GDP at factor cost
772.0	781.4	758.0	744.9	757.0	759.0	753.0	780.0	818.0	847.0	..	Agriculture
683.2	680.1	640.7	602.7	583.6	577.0	591.0	609.0	639.0	663.0	..	Industry
517.3	501.2	475.1	466.0	468.4	465.0	468.0	476.0	..	..	..	Manufacturing
1,651.7	1,665.9	1,617.9	1,592.0	1,613.4	1,600.0	1,596.0	1,643.0	1,706.0	1,778.0	..	Services, etc.
											Memo Items:
392.8	306.4	264.5	239.2	246.3	230.1	235.4	223.2	240.9	267.4	..	Capacity to Import
-258.3	-250.9	-245.7	-215.5	-193.7	-223.9	-154.6	-190.8	-196.1	-229.6	..	Terms of Trade Adjustment
2,848.6	2,876.5	2,770.9	2,724.1	2,760.3	2,712.1	2,785.4	2,841.2	2,966.9	3,058.4	..	Gross Domestic Income
2,811.0	2,828.1	2,718.4	2,674.9	2,683.3	2,660.1	2,708.4	2,775.2	2,899.9	2,991.4	..	Gross National Income
(Index 1958 = 100)											
											DOMESTIC PRICES/DEFLATORS
253.6	275.2	289.0	307.9	320.6	380.8	538.7	580.3	649.5	718.9	..	Overall (GDP)
279.4	306.3	318.8	333.9	345.4	413.5	564.6	639.0	711.9	792.5	..	Domestic Absorption
..	..	..	..	..	..	..	..	648.5	504.0	..	Agriculture
..	..	..	..	..	..	..	..	572.6	911.7	..	Industry
..	..	..	..	..	..	..	..	..	..	..	Manufacturing
45.3	50.5	50.7	53.0	54.8	65.0	89.0	100.0	110.8	123.5	f	Consumer Price Index
											MANUFACTURING ACTIVITY
128.5	119.4	118.6	114.2	114.5	113.8	106.8	100.0	144.6	..	G	Employment (1987 = 100)
113.0	121.1	124.0	122.1	124.5	116.1	95.7	100.0	100.0	..	G	Real Earnings per Empl. (1987 = 100)
..	..	..	..	..	..	..	..	..	..	..	Real Output per Empl. (1987 = 100)
22.5	21.9	25.9	23.0	23.7	22.3	22.0	19.4	18.9	..	..	Earnings as % of Value Added
(Millions of current Guatemalan Quetzales)											
											MONETARY HOLDINGS
1,692.4	1,906.7	2,190.7	2,155.1	2,399.1	3,192.9	3,875.1	4,167.8	4,995.0	5,800.6	..	Money Supply, Broadly Defined
752.8	775.9	786.6	833.8	869.4	1,346.5	1,608.4	1,765.6	2,019.0	2,437.8	..	Money
381.0	405.2	404.6	437.9	460.9	697.8	804.6	931.2	1,069.0	1,329.2	..	Currency Outside Banks
371.8	370.7	382.0	395.9	408.5	648.7	803.8	834.4	950.0	1,108.6	..	Demand Deposits
939.6	1,130.8	1,404.1	1,321.3	1,529.7	1,846.4	2,266.7	2,402.2	2,976.0	3,362.8	..	Quasi-Money
(Millions of current Guatemalan Quetzales)											
-307.28	-535.40	-416.91	-317.99	-360.72	-201.61	-91.55	-133.72	-218.13	..	F	GOVERNMENT DEFICIT (-) OR SURPLUS
883.29	895.89	880.88	874.00	664.38	862.25	1,461.88	1,851.91	2,291.24	..	..	Current Revenue
728.98	818.27	804.67	888.20	761.03	819.93	1,230.61	1,723.94	2,088.86	..	..	Current Expenditure
154.31	77.62	76.21	-14.20	-96.65	42.32	231.27	127.97	202.38	..	..	Current Budget Balance
1.35	2.65	0.59	..	0.16	0.24	..	0.02	0.09	..	..	Capital Receipts
462.94	615.67	493.71	303.79	264.23	244.17	322.82	261.71	420.60	..	..	Capital Payments

GUATEMALA	1969	1970	1971	1972	1973	1974	1975	1976	1977	1978	1979
FOREIGN TRADE (CUSTOMS BASIS)					*(Millions of current US dollars)*						
Value of Exports, fob	255.3	290.2	283.1	328.1	436.2	572.1	623.4	760.3	1,160.2	1,111.6	1,160.9
Nonfuel Primary Products	191.0	208.9	204.9	241.7	318.8	418.7	468.1	580.8	957.2	881.8	892.6
Fuels	0.1	0.1	0.2	0.1	0.1	0.4	0.4	0.3	0.2	0.3	0.4
Manufactures	64.2	81.2	78.1	86.3	117.2	153.0	154.9	179.2	202.8	229.5	268.0
Value of Imports, cif	250.2	284.3	303.3	327.7	427.4	700.5	732.6	838.4	1,052.5	1,260.7	1,361.8
Nonfuel Primary Products	32.7	40.7	41.1	40.0	52.3	86.1	86.8	77.3	89.9	119.8	134.9
Fuels	5.3	6.2	15.3	25.0	31.5	94.0	103.3	106.0	148.4	160.7	145.9
Manufactures	212.2	237.3	246.9	262.7	343.7	520.4	542.5	655.1	814.1	980.2	1,080.9
					(Index 1987 = 100)						
Terms of Trade	133.9	145.0	139.6	149.1	160.0	141.2	122.6	162.6	188.2	146.9	139.1
Export Prices, fob	35.4	40.6	39.3	43.7	57.8	72.2	67.8	89.8	113.7	100.1	110.1
Import Prices, cif	26.5	28.0	28.1	29.3	36.1	51.1	55.3	55.2	60.4	68.1	79.1
BALANCE OF PAYMENTS					*(Millions of current US dollars)*						
Exports of Goods & Services	..	353.7	342.2	397.7	541.7	720.1	797.5	1,007.7	1,369.6	1,349.1	1,552.0
Merchandise, fob	..	297.1	286.9	335.9	442.0	582.3	641.0	760.4	1,160.2	1,092.4	1,221.4
Nonfactor Services	..	52.4	51.8	58.1	89.9	119.7	141.9	208.3	161.0	183.6	228.0
Factor Services	..	4.2	3.6	3.7	9.8	18.2	14.6	39.0	48.4	73.1	102.6
Imports of Goods & Services	..	379.1	416.7	439.2	576.4	878.6	941.0	1,284.1	1,500.7	1,735.2	1,884.2
Merchandise, fob	..	266.6	290.0	294.8	391.4	631.5	672.4	950.7	1,087.0	1,283.8	1,401.7
Nonfactor Services	..	70.1	81.2	95.1	129.3	181.0	188.0	250.4	338.3	360.7	382.5
Factor Services	..	42.4	45.5	49.3	55.7	66.1	80.6	83.0	75.4	90.7	100.0
Long-Term Interest	..	7.0	8.6	8.6	10.2	11.1	12.5	14.6	20.0	32.7	48.2
Private Current Transfers, net	..	17.4	26.3	31.2	43.2	56.6	78.3	197.7	93.9	115.0	123.2
Workers' Remittances	..	..	..	..	..	..	..	..	..	..	..
Curr. A/C Bal before Off. Transf.	..	-8.0	-48.2	-10.3	8.5	-101.9	-65.2	-78.7	-37.2	-271.1	-209.0
Net Official Transfers	..	0.1	-1.0	-1.2	-0.7	-1.2	-0.5	1.2	1.9	0.6	3.4
Curr. A/C Bal after Off. Transf.	..	-7.9	-49.2	-11.5	7.7	-103.1	-65.7	-77.5	-35.3	-270.5	-205.6
Long-Term Capital, net	..	53.6	39.2	25.5	49.4	58.1	146.3	83.2	198.2	263.2	241.5
Direct Investment	..	29.4	28.6	15.9	34.8	47.4	80.0	12.5	97.5	127.2	117.0
Long-Term Loans	..	21.2	13.9	5.6	28.4	29.2	49.8	45.2	108.9	156.3	184.1
Disbursements	..	43.2	36.4	44.4	47.2	60.7	72.3	74.4	141.8	202.7	248.9
Repayments	..	22.0	22.5	38.8	18.8	31.5	22.5	29.2	32.9	46.4	64.8
Other Long-Term Capital	..	3.0	-3.3	4.1	-13.9	-18.5	16.5	25.5	-8.2	-20.3	-59.6
Other Capital, net	..	-30.3	20.1	25.0	23.8	33.8	23.6	213.8	18.8	75.6	-61.6
Change in Reserves	..	-15.4	-10.1	-39.0	-81.0	11.2	-104.2	-219.5	-181.7	-68.3	25.7
Memo Item:					*(Guatemalan Quetzales per US dollar)*						
Conversion Factor (Annual Avg)	1.000	1.000	1.000	1.000	1.000	1.000	1.000	1.000	1.000	1.000	1.000
					(Millions of US dollars), outstanding at end of year						
EXTERNAL DEBT (Total)	..	120.3	134.2	139.8	165.9	195.1	243.3	288.5	652.2	813.0	1,039.7
Long-Term Debt (by debtor)	..	120.3	134.2	139.8	165.9	195.1	243.3	288.5	397.2	554.0	738.7
Central Bank, incl. IMF credit	..	16.6	15.3	12.0	6.3	7.0	9.7	7.1	6.1	8.2	16.4
Central Government	..	66.9	64.4	63.8	71.9	66.6	80.1	92.8	139.3	207.4	271.1
Rest of General Government	..	4.4	3.2	0.3	1.5	5.4	6.1	7.1	8.7	8.2	8.5
Non-financial Public Enterprises	..	17.6	30.4	33.0	36.1	41.1	47.4	56.5	63.1	80.2	130.7
Priv. Sector, incl non-guaranteed	..	14.8	20.9	30.7	50.1	75.0	100.0	125.0	180.0	250.0	312.0
Short-Term Debt	..	0.0	0.0	0.0	0.0	0.0	0.0	0.0	255.0	259.0	301.0
Memo Items:					*(Millions of US dollars)*						
Int'l Reserves Excluding Gold	54.1	60.8	74.7	116.3	191.3	181.3	283.8	491.0	668.9	741.5	696.3
Gold Holdings (at market price)	20.1	18.7	21.6	31.9	55.2	91.7	68.9	66.2	83.6	116.3	267.4
SOCIAL INDICATORS											
Total Fertility Rate	6.5	6.5	6.5	6.5	6.4	6.4	6.4	6.4	6.4	6.3	6.3
Infant Mortality Rate	102.8	100.2	97.6	95.0	92.4	89.8	87.2	84.6	82.0	79.6	77.2
Life Expectancy at Birth	51.7	52.5	53.2	54.0	54.5	55.0	55.4	55.9	56.4	56.9	57.4
Urban Population, % of total	35.4	35.7	36.0	36.3	36.5	36.8	37.1	36.2	35.3	34.5	33.6
Food Prod. per capita (1987=100)	91.2	93.1	92.3	95.0	97.7	96.6	99.9	101.9	102.0	100.3	98.0
Labor Force, Agriculture (%)	61.8	61.3	60.8	60.4	59.9	59.5	59.1	58.6	58.1	57.7	57.3
Labor Force, Female (%)	13.1	13.1	13.2	13.3	13.3	13.4	13.5	13.5	13.6	13.7	13.7
Primary Schl. Enroll. Ratio	..	57.0	..	..	..	..	61.0	61.0	63.0	65.0	67.0
Primary Schl. Enroll. Ratio, Female	..	51.0	..	..	..	..	56.0	56.0	58.0	60.0	61.0
Secondary Schl. Enroll. Ratio	..	8.0	..	..	..	..	12.0	13.0	13.0	14.0	16.0

1980	1981	1982	1983	1984	1985	1986	1987	1988	1989 estimate	NOTES	GUATEMALA
				(Millions of current US dollars)							**FOREIGN TRADE (CUSTOMS BASIS)**
1,486.1	1,114.8	1,120.0	1,159.0	1,127.0	1,060.1	1,103.4	1,084.1	1,105.0	..	..	Value of Exports, fob
1,111.4	768.4	794.0	821.6	777.7	744.7	741.9	689.5	680.0	..	..	Nonfuel Primary Products
15.6	21.8	17.7	18.6	19.5	10.4	5.1	6.2	6.0	..	..	Fuels
359.1	324.6	308.2	318.8	329.8	305.0	356.3	388.4	419.0	..	..	Manufactures
1,559.1	2,009.3	1,388.0	1,135.0	1,277.4	1,174.9	960.0	1,479.4	1,557.0	..	..	Value of Imports, cif
174.4	178.6	131.2	108.0	124.1	107.3	92.1	138.6	150.7	..	..	Nonfuel Primary Products
377.4	760.1	449.6	370.7	319.8	283.7	118.6	172.5	150.3	..	..	Fuels
1,007.3	1,070.6	807.2	656.3	833.5	783.9	749.3	1,168.3	1,256.0	..	..	Manufactures
				(Index 1987 = 100)							
123.7	97.6	101.2	103.8	110.0	106.3	123.9	100.0	106.9	..	..	Terms of Trade
120.4	106.0	101.7	101.4	100.4	96.1	111.6	100.0	112.6	..	..	Export Prices, fob
97.3	108.6	100.5	97.7	91.3	90.4	90.1	100.0	105.3	..	..	Import Prices, cif
				(Millions of current US dollars)							**BALANCE OF PAYMENTS**
1,834.0	1,525.9	1,312.2	1,205.0	1,261.2	1,191.3	1,203.2	1,167.3	1,300.7	1,520.4	f	Exports of Goods & Services
1,519.8	1,291.3	1,170.4	1,091.7	1,132.2	1,059.7	1,043.8	977.9	1,073.3	1,190.0	..	Merchandise, fob
210.8	154.8	107.5	80.2	96.0	101.1	123.3	158.3	195.8	310.0	..	Nonfactor Services
103.4	79.8	34.3	33.1	33.0	30.5	36.1	31.1	31.6	20.4	..	Factor Services
2,107.1	2,189.5	1,774.0	1,459.5	1,667.3	1,457.3	1,295.9	1,803.1	1,939.0	2,105.0	f	Imports of Goods & Services
1,472.6	1,540.0	1,284.3	1,056.0	1,182.2	1,076.7	875.7	1,333.2	1,413.2	1,510.0	..	Merchandise, fob
486.1	483.7	341.5	257.5	245.3	180.0	170.0	259.5	317.9	386.0	..	Nonfactor Services
148.4	165.8	148.2	146.0	239.8	200.6	250.2	210.4	207.9	205.0	..	Factor Services
59.5	63.5	76.8	88.9	94.9	116.0	154.1	154.1	118.3	95.9	..	Long-Term Interest
108.6	89.5	61.9	29.8	28.0	18.9	50.6	101.0	141.7	165.0	..	Private Current Transfers, net
..	..	..	..	..	..	..	..	42.7	..	..	Workers' Remittances
-164.5	-574.1	-399.9	-224.7	-378.1	-247.1	-42.1	-534.8	-496.6	-418.0	..	Curr. A/C Bal before Off. Transf.
1.2	1.4	0.8	0.8	0.7	0.8	24.5	92.3	82.6	105.0	..	Net Official Transfers
-163.3	-572.7	-399.1	-223.9	-377.4	-246.3	-17.6	-442.5	-414.0	-313.0	..	Curr. A/C Bal after Off. Transf.
238.1	397.7	339.4	283.5	194.0	241.7	44.6	136.8	108.0	235.0	f	Long-Term Capital, net
110.7	127.1	77.1	45.0	38.0	61.8	68.8	150.2	329.7	80.2	..	Direct Investment
92.5	279.7	278.7	225.0	92.6	111.9	35.9	-52.5	-36.9	22.1	..	Long-Term Loans
170.1	344.3	337.3	313.5	254.3	264.4	175.4	99.1	180.6	181.7	..	Disbursements
77.6	64.6	58.6	88.5	161.7	152.5	139.5	151.6	217.5	159.6	..	Repayments
34.9	-9.1	-16.4	13.5	63.4	68.0	-60.1	39.1	-184.8	132.7	..	Other Long-Term Capital
-332.7	-126.3	21.3	-50.0	200.0	111.8	81.9	251.7	167.2	196.4	f	Other Capital, net
257.9	301.3	38.4	-9.6	-16.6	-107.2	-108.9	54.0	138.8	-118.4	..	Change in Reserves
				(Guatemalan Quetzales per US dollar)							Memo Item:
1.000	1.000	1.000	1.000	1.000	1.150	2.190	2.500	2.550	2.900	..	Conversion Factor (Annual Avg)
				(Millions of US dollars), outstanding at end of year							**EXTERNAL DEBT (Total)**
1,165.9	1,264.3	1,537.2	1,799.5	2,352.5	2,622.6	2,752.5	2,770.4	2,576.5	2,601.2	..	Long-Term Debt (by debtor)
830.9	1,127.9	1,417.5	1,680.3	2,202.2	2,357.7	2,441.7	2,487.9	2,281.1	2,271.5	..	Central Bank, incl. IMF credit
40.7	260.1	370.8	547.4	1,126.6	1,133.9	1,080.2	1,027.9	809.9	770.6	..	Central Government
336.8	424.8	517.4	603.0	624.2	696.4	782.7	850.2	895.7	911.2	..	Rest of General Government
7.3	6.7	6.6	5.8	4.8	3.8	3.3	2.2	1.6	1.3	..	Non-financial Public Enterprises
164.0	225.9	354.1	369.2	340.6	416.6	454.0	488.8	458.1	475.6	..	Priv. Sector, incl non-guaranteed
282.1	210.4	168.6	154.9	106.0	107.0	121.5	118.8	115.8	112.8	..	Short-Term Debt
335.0	136.4	119.7	119.2	150.3	264.9	310.8	282.5	295.4	329.7	..	
				(Millions of US dollars)							Memo Items:
444.7	149.7	112.2	210.0	274.4	300.9	362.1	287.8	201.2	306.0	..	Int'l Reserves Excluding Gold
307.9	207.6	238.6	199.3	161.0	170.8	204.2	253.1	214.6	217.5	..	Gold Holdings (at market price)
											SOCIAL INDICATORS
6.2	6.2	6.1	6.1	6.0	5.9	5.8	5.8	5.7	5.6	..	Total Fertility Rate
74.8	72.4	70.0	67.8	65.6	63.4	61.2	59.0	57.3	55.6	..	Infant Mortality Rate
58.0	58.5	59.0	59.6	60.2	60.8	61.4	62.0	62.3	62.6	..	Life Expectancy at Birth
32.7	32.7	32.7	32.7	32.7	32.7	32.7	32.7	32.7	32.7	..	Urban Population, % of total
96.9	101.2	104.1	101.8	98.1	101.3	101.9	100.0	101.4	102.9	..	Food Prod. per capita (1987=100)
56.8	..	..	..	..	..	..	..	..	..	..	Labor Force, Agriculture (%)
13.8	14.1	14.4	14.6	14.9	15.1	15.4	15.6	15.9	16.1	..	Labor Force, Female (%)
71.0	..	70.0	75.0	76.0	76.0	76.0	77.0	..	..	..	Primary Schl. Enroll. Ratio
65.0	..	65.0	69.0	..	70.0	70.0	..	..	..	..	Primary Schl. Enroll. Ratio, Female
18.0	..	17.0	17.0	19.0	19.0	20.0	21.0	..	..	..	Secondary Schl. Enroll. Ratio

GUINEA-BISSAU	1969	1970	1971	1972	1973	1974	1975	1976	1977	1978	1979
CURRENT GNP PER CAPITA (US $)	..	..	..	160	160	170	190	170	160	170	170
POPULATION (thousands)	519	526	537	552	573	598	628	662	701	742	779

USE AND ORIGIN OF RESOURCES *(Millions of current Guinea-Bissau Pesos)*

	1969	1970	1971	1972	1973	1974	1975	1976	1977	1978	1979
Gross National Product (GNP)	..	2,810	2,749	3,070	3,428	3,904	4,615	4,492	4,368	5,234	5,801
Net Factor Income from Abroad	..	0	0	0	0	0	102	-316	-232	-299	-84
GDP at Market Prices	..	2,810	2,749	3,070	3,428	3,904	4,513	4,808	4,600	5,533	5,885
Resource Balance	..	-736	-829	-960	-1,188	-1,336	-937	-1,090	-1,072	-1,523	-1,917
Exports of Goods & NFServices	..	112	114	134	208	196	234	254	428	472	527
Imports of Goods & NFServices	..	848	943	1,094	1,396	1,532	1,171	1,343	1,500	1,995	2,444
Domestic Absorption	..	3,546	3,578	4,030	4,616	5,240	5,450	5,897	5,672	7,056	7,802
Private Consumption, etc.	..	2,155	2,213	2,632	3,061	3,598	3,722	3,918	3,909	4,686	5,208
General Gov't Consumption	..	560	595	699	839	985	1,033	1,197	853	1,169	1,309
Gross Domestic Investment	..	831	770	698	716	656	695	782	910	1,200	1,285
Fixed Investment	..	..	..	..	..	..	..	..	..	..	..
Indirect Taxes, net	..	125	128	134	168	178	107	169	159	202	336
GDP at factor cost	..	2,685	2,621	2,936	3,259	3,726	4,406	4,639	4,441	5,332	5,549
Agriculture	..	1,333	1,233	1,405	1,470	1,615	2,156	2,312	2,123	2,856	3,036
Industry	..	597	607	689	836	995	1,145	747	1,041	1,106	1,169
Manufacturing	..	597	..	..	..	..	..	..	..	..	..
Services, etc.	..	880	909	975	1,122	1,293	1,212	1,749	1,436	1,571	1,680
Gross Domestic Saving	..	95	-59	-262	-472	-680	-242	-308	-162	-322	-632
Gross National Saving	..	..	..	..	..	..	..	..	..	..	..

(Millions of 1987 Guinea-Bissau Pesos)

	1969	1970	1971	1972	1973	1974	1975	1976	1977	1978	1979
Gross National Product	..	60,708.4	61,371.2	64,015.4	66,591.2	69,480.3	76,186.9	72,421.3	67,961.6	77,202.8	80,831.6
GDP at Market Prices	..	60,738.6	61,401.8	64,047.3	66,624.3	69,514.9	74,342.7	77,879.3	71,846.6	81,641.3	82,018.8
Resource Balance	..	-41,194.0	-42,003.0	-46,245.0	-44,106.0	-41,906.0	-24,091.0	-21,814.0	-18,855.0	-19,849.0	-20,581.0
Exports of Goods & NFServices	..	7,393.1	7,115.4	7,756.6	10,664.0	9,415.4	14,765.5	12,320.2	15,038.1	13,680.4	13,680.4
Imports of Goods & NFServices	..	48,587.3	49,118.6	54,001.3	54,769.5	51,321.0	38,856.9	34,134.1	33,892.9	33,529.9	34,261.6
Domestic Absorption	..	101,933.0	103,405.0	110,292.0	110,730.0	111,421.0	98,434.2	99,693.2	90,701.4	101,491.0	102,600.0
Private Consumption, etc.	..	39,662.0	49,618.8	62,051.8	69,421.6	76,728.0	65,351.4	63,084.8	53,015.9	51,727.6	43,683.8
General Gov't Consumption	..	7,468.7	7,643.2	8,536.0	8,884.3	9,377.4	8,994.6	10,171.5	7,150.8	9,326.7	8,854.6
Gross Domestic Investment	..	54,802.1	46,143.0	39,704.2	32,424.0	25,315.1	24,088.1	26,437.0	30,534.8	40,436.5	50,061.6
Fixed Investment	..	..	..	..	..	..	..	..	..	..	..
GDP at factor cost	..	..	..	..	..	..	..	..	..	..	..
Agriculture	..	40,210.2	37,030.6	40,089.1	39,750.5	41,139.0	41,725.2	44,994.5	39,172.5	44,883.0	41,291.3
Industry	..	12,435.7	11,472.8	12,369.1	11,957.0	12,095.7	14,298.9	8,876.6	11,651.0	15,911.8	15,906.4
Manufacturing	..	..	..	..	..	..	..	..	..	..	..
Services, etc.	..	8,440.6	10,190.6	9,978.9	11,420.7	12,770.2	15,157.0	20,821.2	18,514.5	17,649.7	22,803.4

Memo Items:

	1969	1970	1971	1972	1973	1974	1975	1976	1977	1978	1979
Capacity to Import	..	6,437.8	5,952.4	6,601.4	8,149.3	6,562.1	7,764.8	6,442.5	9,672.7	7,941.3	7,387.8
Terms of Trade Adjustment	..	-955.3	-1,163.0	-1,155.1	-2,514.7	-2,853.3	-7,000.8	-5,877.7	-5,365.4	-5,739.2	-6,292.6
Gross Domestic Income	..	59,783.3	60,238.7	62,892.1	64,109.6	66,661.6	67,342.0	72,001.7	66,481.2	75,902.2	75,726.2
Gross National Income	..	59,753.1	60,208.2	62,860.3	64,076.5	66,627.0	69,186.2	66,543.6	62,596.2	71,463.6	74,539.1

DOMESTIC PRICES/DEFLATORS *(Index 1987 = 100)*

	1969	1970	1971	1972	1973	1974	1975	1976	1977	1978	1979
Overall (GDP)	..	4.6	4.5	4.8	5.1	5.6	6.1	6.2	6.4	6.8	7.2
Domestic Absorption	..	3.5	3.5	3.7	4.2	4.7	5.5	5.9	6.3	7.0	7.6
Agriculture	..	3.3	3.3	3.5	3.7	3.9	5.2	5.1	5.4	6.4	7.4
Industry	..	4.8	5.3	5.6	7.0	8.2	8.0	8.4	8.9	7.0	7.3
Manufacturing	..	..	..	..	..	..	..	..	..	..	..
Consumer Price Index	..	..	..	..	..	..	..	..	..	..	..

MANUFACTURING ACTIVITY

	1969	1970	1971	1972	1973	1974	1975	1976	1977	1978	1979
Employment (1987=100)	..	..	..	..	..	..	..	..	..	..	..
Real Earnings per Empl. (1987=100)	..	..	..	..	..	..	..	..	..	..	..
Real Output per Empl. (1987=100)	..	..	..	..	..	..	..	..	..	..	..
Earnings as % of Value Added	..	..	..	..	..	..	..	..	..	..	..

MONETARY HOLDINGS *(Millions of current Guinea-Bissau Pesos)*

	1969	1970	1971	1972	1973	1974	1975	1976	1977	1978	1979
Money Supply, Broadly Defined	..	..	..	..	..	..	..	..	..	..	..
Money	..	..	..	..	..	..	..	..	..	..	..
Currency Outside Banks	..	..	..	..	..	..	..	..	..	..	..
Demand Deposits	..	..	..	..	..	..	..	..	..	..	..
Quasi-Money	..	..	..	..	..	..	..	..	..	..	..

(Millions of current Guinea-Bissau Pesos)

	1969	1970	1971	1972	1973	1974	1975	1976	1977	1978	1979
GOVERNMENT DEFICIT (-) OR SURPLUS	..	..	..	..	..	..	..	..	..	..	..
Current Revenue	..	..	..	..	..	..	..	..	..	..	..
Current Expenditure	..	..	..	..	..	..	..	..	..	..	..
Current Budget Balance	..	..	..	..	..	..	..	..	..	..	..
Capital Receipts	..	..	..	..	..	..	..	..	..	..	..
Capital Payments	..	..	..	..	..	..	..	..	..	..	..

1980	1981	1982	1983	1984	1985	1986	1987	1988	1989 estimate	NOTES	GUINEA-BISSAU
130	170	190	200	190	190	160	170	170	180	A	**CURRENT GNP PER CAPITA (US $)**
809	824	839	854	870	886	903	921	940	960	..	**POPULATION (thousands)**
											USE AND ORIGIN OF RESOURCES
				(Millions of current Guinea-Bissau Pesos)							
5,223	6,567	7,944	9,578	16,644	24,942	46,544	89,563	167,800	302,500	..	Gross National Product (GNP)
-33	-71	-117	-24	-56	-296	-423	-2,777	-3,900	-4,000	..	Net Factor Income from Abroad
5,257	6,638	8,061	9,602	16,700	25,238	46,967	92,340	171,700	306,500	f	GDP at Market Prices
-1,869	-1,628	-2,696	-2,520	-6,398	-10,866	-11,992	-27,461	-69,000	-129,000	..	Resource Balance
439	743	632	577	2,270	2,488	3,588	13,387	28,800	64,400	..	Exports of Goods & NFServices
2,308	2,371	3,328	3,097	8,668	13,354	15,580	40,848	97,800	193,400	..	Imports of Goods & NFServices
7,126	8,266	10,757	12,122	23,098	36,104	58,960	119,800	240,700	435,500	..	Domestic Absorption
4,046	4,666	6,106	7,502	13,965	21,909	41,135	78,275	152,904	265,530	f	Private Consumption, etc.
1,525	1,891	2,373	2,444	4,124	6,116	6,423	10,776	29,000	46,897	..	General Gov't Consumption
1,555	1,709	2,278	2,176	5,009	8,079	11,402	30,749	58,796	123,073	f	Gross Domestic Investment
..	..	..	..	..	..	..	..	..	..	..	Fixed Investment
321	499	506	..	..	..	1,544	3,037	5,359	9,500	..	Indirect Taxes, net
4,935	6,139	7,555	..	..	..	45,423	89,303	166,341	297,000	B f	GDP at factor cost
2,328	3,271	3,769	4,075	6,933	10,719	21,271	43,756	78,400	144,000	..	Agriculture
1,033	1,057	1,161	1,100	2,359	3,592	9,309	14,417	27,400	48,500	..	Industry
..	..	..	..	..	..	5,400	10,530	18,540	31,900	..	Manufacturing
1,895	2,311	3,130	4,427	7,408	10,927	16,387	34,167	65,900	114,000	..	Services, etc.
-314	81	-418	-344	-1,389	-2,787	-591	3,289	-10,204	-5,927	..	Gross Domestic Saving
..	..	-1,093	-827	-1,961	-3,626	-1,320	-607	-12,437	-7,753	..	Gross National Saving
				(Millions of 1987 Guinea-Bissau Pesos)							
66,085.6	78,193.1	81,296.2	80,154.5	84,615.4	88,875.7	86,197.4	89,563.2	93,787.8	97,963.7	..	Gross National Product
66,539.9	79,112.6	82,620.9	79,964.7	84,367.2	87,996.5	87,115.9	92,339.9	98,617.1	103,550.0	f	GDP at Market Prices
-15,859.0	-18,360.0	-31,469.0	-30,538.0	-33,462.0	-38,630.0	-36,698.0	-27,461.0	-31,418.0	-42,553.0	..	Resource Balance
16,943.5	12,143.7	10,869.1	10,064.3	13,758.3	9,960.5	11,017.0	13,387.1	14,529.3	15,144.5	..	Exports of Goods & NFServices
32,802.3	30,503.2	42,337.8	40,602.3	47,220.5	48,590.1	47,715.3	40,847.6	45,947.6	57,698.0	..	Imports of Goods & NFServices
82,398.7	97,472.2	114,090.0	110,503.0	117,829.0	126,626.0	123,814.0	119,800.0	130,035.0	146,103.0	..	Domestic Absorption
38,130.7	58,612.6	65,044.5	62,386.7	68,091.8	72,309.7	69,387.4	78,275.2	81,448.1	80,370.5	f	Private Consumption, etc.
9,012.2	9,419.4	11,331.5	11,535.8	11,143.5	11,823.2	11,953.1	10,776.2	11,566.9	14,635.0	..	General Gov't Consumption
35,255.8	29,440.2	37,713.7	36,580.2	38,594.0	42,493.1	42,473.7	30,749.0	37,020.3	51,097.7	f	Gross Domestic Investment
..	..	..	..	..	..	..	..	..	..		Fixed Investment
..	..	..	..	..	..	84,242.5	89,302.9	95,537.8	100,339.0	B f	GDP at factor cost
25,808.1	33,127.5	35,015.1	34,316.1	35,413.6	37,786.7	39,475.8	43,755.6	45,178.1	48,715.4	..	Agriculture
13,839.2	13,278.9	14,474.3	14,226.8	18,506.7	19,447.8	17,275.9	14,417.2	15,789.4	16,408.2	..	Industry
..	..	..	..	..	..	10,048.6	10,530.0	10,651.4	10,779.5	..	Manufacturing
27,578.3	33,032.1	33,288.7	31,421.8	30,446.9	30,762.0	30,364.2	34,167.1	37,649.5	38,426.1	..	Services, etc.
											Memo Items:
6,243.6	9,558.8	8,040.1	7,564.6	12,366.2	9,052.9	10,987.1	13,387.1	13,530.6	19,212.8	..	Capacity to Import
-10,700.0	-2,584.9	-2,829.0	-2,499.7	-1,392.1	-907.6	-29.9	0.0	-998.7	4,068.3	..	Terms of Trade Adjustment
55,840.0	76,527.7	79,791.9	77,465.0	82,975.1	87,088.9	87,085.9	92,339.9	97,618.4	107,618.0	..	Gross Domestic Income
55,385.7	75,608.2	78,467.2	77,654.7	83,223.3	87,968.1	86,167.5	89,563.2	92,789.1	102,032.0	..	Gross National Income
				(Index 1987 = 100)							**DOMESTIC PRICES/DEFLATORS**
7.9	8.4	9.8	12.0	19.8	28.7	53.9	100.0	174.1	296.0	..	Overall (GDP)
8.6	8.5	9.4	11.0	19.6	28.5	47.6	100.0	185.1	298.1	..	Domestic Absorption
9.0	9.9	10.8	11.9	19.6	28.4	53.9	100.0	173.5	295.6	..	Agriculture
7.5	8.0	8.0	7.7	12.7	18.5	53.9	100.0	173.5	295.6	..	Industry
..	..	..	..	..	..	53.7	100.0	174.1	295.9	..	Manufacturing
..	..	..	..	..	..	..	..	..	..	..	Consumer Price Index
											MANUFACTURING ACTIVITY
..	..	..	..	..	..	..	..	..	..	..	Employment (1987=100)
..	..	..	..	..	..	..	..	..	..	..	Real Earnings per Empl. (1987=100)
..	..	..	..	..	..	..	..	..	..	..	Real Output per Empl. (1987=100)
..	..	..	..	..	..	..	..	..	..	..	Earnings as % of Value Added
				(Millions of current Guinea-Bissau Pesos)							**MONETARY HOLDINGS**
..	..	2,779	3,402	4,541	6,433	8,753	22,395	38,650	..	..	Money Supply, Broadly Defined
..	..	..	..	..	..	8,650	16,724	30,859	..	..	Money
..	..	..	..	..	..	5,468	9,309	15,976	..	..	Currency Outside Banks
..	..	..	..	..	..	3,183	7,416	14,883	..	..	Demand Deposits
..	..	..	..	..	..	102	5,671	7,792	..	..	Quasi-Money
				(Millions of current Guinea-Bissau Pesos)							**GOVERNMENT DEFICIT (-) OR SURPLUS**
..	..	..	-2,215	-4,615	-7,163	-7,530	-17,893	-31,557	..	..	Current Revenue
..	..	..	2,510	5,141	8,406	11,494	34,583	59,035	..	..	Current Expenditure
..	..	..	2,311	3,602	5,581	8,363	15,694	29,180	..	..	Current Budget Balance
..	..	..	199	1,539	2,825	3,131	18,889	29,855	..	..	Capital Receipts
..	..	..	5	7	7	9	13	14	..	..	Capital Payments
..	..	..	2,419	6,161	9,995	10,670	36,795	61,426	..	..	

GUINEA-BISSAU	1969	1970	1971	1972	1973	1974	1975	1976	1977	1978	1979
FOREIGN TRADE (CUSTOMS BASIS)				*(Thousands of current US dollars)*							
Value of Exports, fob	..	7,000	5,000	6,000	8,000	9,000	7,000	6,000	13,000	12,000	13,000
Nonfuel Primary Products	..	..	..	..	..	..	..	..	..	..	..
Fuels	..	..	..	..	..	..	..	..	..	..	..
Manufactures	..	..	..	..	..	..	..	..	..	..	..
Value of Imports, cif	..	27,000	31,000	32,000	44,000	43,000	38,000	37,000	37,000	49,000	61,000
Nonfuel Primary Products	..	..	..	..	..	..	..	..	..	..	..
Fuels	..	..	..	..	..	..	..	..	..	..	..
Manufactures	..	..	..	..	..	..	..	..	..	..	..
					(Index 1987 = 100)						
Terms of Trade	..	..	..	..	..	..	..	..	..	..	..
Export Prices, fob	..	..	..	..	..	..	..	..	..	..	..
Import Prices, cif	..	..	..	..	..	..	..	..	..	..	..
BALANCE OF PAYMENTS				*(Millions of current US dollars)*							
Exports of Goods & Services	..	..	..	..	..	..	..	..	..	..	..
Merchandise, fob	..	..	..	..	..	..	..	..	..	..	..
Nonfactor Services	..	..	..	..	..	..	..	..	..	..	..
Factor Services	..	..	..	..	..	..	..	..	..	..	..
Imports of Goods & Services	..	..	..	..	..	..	..	..	..	..	..
Merchandise, fob	..	..	..	..	..	..	..	..	..	..	..
Nonfactor Services	..	..	..	..	..	..	..	..	..	..	..
Factor Services	..	..	..	..	..	..	..	..	..	..	..
Long-Term Interest	..	0.00	0.00	0.00	0.00	0.00	0.00	0.00	0.00	0.20	1.00
Private Current Transfers, net	..	..	..	..	..	..	..	..	..	..	..
Workers' Remittances	..	..	..	..	..	..	..	..	..	..	..
Curr. A/C Bal before Off. Transf.	..	..	..	..	..	..	..	..	..	..	..
Net Official Transfers	..	..	..	..	..	..	..	..	..	..	..
Curr. A/C Bal after Off. Transf.	..	..	..	..	..	..	..	..	..	..	..
Long-Term Capital, net	..	..	..	..	..	..	..	..	..	..	..
Direct Investment	..	..	..	..	..	..	..	..	..	..	..
Long-Term Loans	..	0.00	0.00	0.00	0.00	0.00	7.50	12.70	8.50	20.60	17.80
Disbursements	..	0.00	0.00	0.00	0.00	0.00	7.50	12.70	8.80	21.40	19.20
Repayments	..	0.00	0.00	0.00	0.00	0.00	0.00	0.00	0.30	0.80	1.40
Other Long-Term Capital	..	..	..	..	..	..	..	..	..	..	..
Other Capital, net	..	..	..	..	..	..	..	..	..	..	..
Change in Reserves	..	..	..	..	..	..	..	..	-0.93	0.98	1.82
Memo Item:				*(Guinea-Bissau Pesos per US dollar)*							
Conversion Factor (Annual Avg)	28.80	28.80	28.30	27.10	24.50	25.40	25.50	30.20	33.60	35.00	34.10
Additional Conversion Factor	28.75	35.69	35.00	35.00	38.35	39.52	41.41	42.78	40.01	45.11	49.65
				(Millions of US dollars), outstanding at end of year							
EXTERNAL DEBT (Total)	..	0.0	0.0	0.0	0.0	0.0	7.0	18.8	27.1	52.1	70.0
Long-Term Debt (by debtor)	..	0.0	0.0	0.0	0.0	0.0	7.0	18.7	25.8	46.6	66.2
Central Bank, incl. IMF credit	..	0.0	0.0	0.0	0.0	0.0	0.0	0.0	0.0	0.0	6.4
Central Government	..	0.0	0.0	0.0	0.0	0.0	7.0	18.7	25.5	46.2	56.8
Rest of General Government	..	..	..	..	..	..	..	..	..	..	..
Non-financial Public Enterprises	..	0.0	0.0	0.0	0.0	0.0	0.0	0.0	0.3	0.4	3.0
Priv. Sector, incl non-guaranteed	..	..	..	..	..	..	..	..	..	..	..
Short-Term Debt	..	0.0	0.0	0.0	0.0	0.0	0.0	0.1	1.3	5.5	3.8
Memo Items:				*(Thousands of US dollars)*							
Int'l Reserves Excluding Gold	..	..	..	..	..	..	..	..	..	..	..
Gold Holdings (at market price)	..	..	..	..	..	..	..	..	..	..	..
SOCIAL INDICATORS											
Total Fertility Rate	5.9	5.9	5.9	5.9	5.9	5.9	6.0	6.0	6.0	6.0	6.0
Infant Mortality Rate	187.6	185.4	183.2	181.0	179.0	177.0	175.0	173.0	171.0	168.6	166.2
Life Expectancy at Birth	35.4	35.5	35.5	35.6	35.7	35.8	35.8	35.9	36.0	36.3	36.7
Urban Population, % of total	17.6	18.1	18.6	19.2	19.7	20.3	20.8	21.4	22.0	22.6	23.2
Food Prod. per capita (1987=100)	88.6	89.5	80.5	82.2	78.9	78.7	91.3	99.6	69.1	74.5	70.3
Labor Force, Agriculture (%)	84.5	84.1	83.9	83.7	83.6	83.4	83.2	83.0	82.8	82.6	82.5
Labor Force, Female (%)	42.6	42.6	42.6	42.6	42.6	42.6	42.6	42.6	42.6	42.6	42.6
Primary Schl. Enroll. Ratio	..	39.0	..	..	..	..	64.0	..	..	106.0	98.0
Primary Schl. Enroll. Ratio, Female	..	23.0	..	..	..	..	39.0	41.0	..	..	..
Secondary Schl. Enroll. Ratio	..	8.0	..	..	..	..	3.0	..	..	..	..

1980	1981	1982	1983	1984	1985	1986	1987	1988	1989 estimate	NOTES	GUINEA-BISSAU
											FOREIGN TRADE (CUSTOMS BASIS)
				(Thousands of current US dollars)							
11,000	14,000	12,000	9,000	17,400	11,600	10,000	15,000	..	..	..	Value of Exports, fob
..	..	..	..	..	..	..	..	..	..	..	Nonfuel Primary Products
..	..	..	..	..	..	..	..	..	..	..	Fuels
..	..	..	..	..	..	..	..	..	..	..	Manufactures
53,200	54,600	52,400	58,100	57,400	63,000	71,600	..	..	..	..	Value of Imports, cif
..	..	..	..	..	..	..	..	..	..	..	Nonfuel Primary Products
..	..	..	..	..	..	..	..	..	..	..	Fuels
..	..	..	..	..	..	..	..	..	..	..	Manufactures
				(Index 1987 = 100)							
..	..	..	..	..	..	..	..	..	..		Terms of Trade
..	..	..	..	..	..	..	..	..	..		Export Prices, fob
..	..	..	..	..	..	..	..	..	..		Import Prices, cif
				(Millions of current US dollars)							**BALANCE OF PAYMENTS**
..	..	..	..	..	..	17.70	23.90	25.80	25.80	f	Exports of Goods & Services
..	..	11.80	8.60	17.40	11.60	9.70	15.40	15.90	14.20	..	Merchandise, fob
..	..	5.60	6.70	8.00	6.50	8.00	8.50	9.90	11.60	..	Nonfactor Services
..	..	..	..	..	..	0.00	0.00	0.00	..	..	Factor Services
..	..	82.90	76.40	86.00	90.50	80.10	80.40	100.30	123.00	f	Imports of Goods & Services
..	..	61.50	58.40	60.10	59.50	51.20	44.70	58.90	69.10	..	Merchandise, fob
..	..	18.20	14.90	21.80	25.70	22.40	28.10	30.80	41.60	..	Nonfactor Services
..	..	3.20	3.10	4.10	5.30	6.50	7.60	10.60	12.30	..	Factor Services
1.10	1.30	1.00	0.70	0.50	1.80	0.70	4.50	2.70	3.20	..	Long-Term Interest
..	..	-14.00	-10.90	-4.90	-3.40	-1.50	-2.00	1.50	1.20	..	Private Current Transfers, net
..	..	..	..	..	..	..	..	1.50	1.20	..	Workers' Remittances
..	..	-79.50	-72.00	-65.50	-75.80	-63.90	-58.50	-73.00	-96.00	..	Curr. A/C Bal before Off. Transf.
..	..	44.50	43.00	29.30	30.50	43.50	45.60	44.00	58.30	..	Net Official Transfers
..	..	-35.00	-29.00	-36.20	-45.30	-20.40	-12.90	-29.00	-37.70	..	Curr. A/C Bal after Off. Transf.
..	..	18.90	16.70	36.50	63.00	22.90	52.70	38.00	33.70	f	Long-Term Capital, net
..	..	..	..	..	..	..	..	..	..	..	Direct Investment
66.20	16.50	16.00	15.80	27.80	57.00	19.90	40.80	23.10	33.60	..	Long-Term Loans
69.20	19.10	17.60	17.40	30.90	59.30	22.00	44.50	25.10	37.60	..	Disbursements
3.00	2.60	1.60	1.60	3.10	2.30	2.10	3.70	2.00	4.00	..	Repayments
..	..	2.90	0.90	8.70	6.00	3.00	11.90	14.90	0.10	..	Other Long-Term Capital
..	..	0.20	-0.70	0.00	-1.10	-6.70	-28.80	3.30	-3.70	f	Other Capital, net
-0.01	3.12	15.90	13.00	-0.30	-16.60	4.20	-11.00	-12.30	7.70	..	Change in Reserves
											Memo Item:
				(Guinea-Bissau Pesos per US dollar)							
33.80	37.30	39.90	42.10	105.30	159.60	204.00	559.30	1,111.10	1,811.40	..	Conversion Factor (Annual Avg)
49.86	42.90	48.70	58.70	120.60	160.00	373.30	559.33	1,111.06	1,811.42	..	Additional Conversion Factor
				(Millions of US dollars), outstanding at end of year							
132.4	138.9	156.7	184.7	239.7	303.8	329.3	427.3	431.0	458.1	..	**EXTERNAL DEBT (Total)**
127.3	134.3	141.6	147.2	189.9	263.0	306.3	396.9	395.2	431.8	..	Long-Term Debt (by debtor)
17.4	17.0	18.5	16.5	43.5	42.9	42.1	43.1	41.0	43.0	..	Central Bank, incl. IMF credit
106.3	112.7	117.6	125.5	143.6	216.8	260.5	352.1	352.9	387.7	..	Central Government
..	..	..	..	..	..	..	..	..	..	..	Rest of General Government
3.6	4.6	5.5	5.2	2.8	3.3	3.7	1.7	1.3	1.1	..	Non-financial Public Enterprises
..	..	..	..	..	..	..	..	..	..	..	Priv. Sector, incl non-guaranteed
5.1	4.6	15.1	37.5	49.8	40.8	23.0	30.4	35.8	26.3	..	Short-Term Debt
				(Thousands of US dollars)							Memo Items:
..	..	..	..	..	..	30,015	9,822	14,711	..	..	Int'l Reserves Excluding Gold
..	..	..	..	..	..	..	..	..	..	..	Gold Holdings (at market price)
											SOCIAL INDICATORS
6.0	6.0	6.0	6.0	6.0	6.0	6.0	6.0	6.0	6.0	..	Total Fertility Rate
163.8	161.4	159.0	156.2	153.4	150.6	147.8	180.0	143.2	141.4	..	Infant Mortality Rate
37.0	37.3	37.7	38.0	38.4	38.7	39.0	39.4	39.6	39.8	..	Life Expectancy at Birth
23.8	24.5	25.1	25.8	26.4	27.1	28.1	29.0	29.6	30.2	..	Urban Population, % of total
68.4	80.6	90.7	78.3	88.9	89.1	95.4	100.0	98.3	101.7	..	Food Prod. per capita (1987=100)
82.3	..	..	..	..	..	..	..	..	..	..	Labor Force, Agriculture (%)
42.6	42.4	42.3	42.1	42.0	41.8	41.6	41.4	41.2	41.0	..	Labor Force, Female (%)
67.0	66.0	63.0	62.0	60.0	..	58.0	..	..	..	..	Primary Schl. Enroll. Ratio
41.0	40.0	40.0	40.0	40.0	..	39.0	..	..	..	..	Primary Schl. Enroll. Ratio, Female
6.0	8.0	10.0	11.0	11.0	..	7.0	..	..	..	..	Secondary Schl. Enroll. Ratio

GUYANA	1969	1970	1971	1972	1973	1974	1975	1976	1977	1978	1979
CURRENT GNP PER CAPITA (US $)	..	380	410	400	410	510	640	660	620	620	650
POPULATION (thousands)	..	670	683	696	710	724	730	735	742	747	754

USE AND ORIGIN OF RESOURCES
(Millions of current Guyana Dollars)

	1969	1970	1971	1972	1973	1974	1975	1976	1977	1978	1979
Gross National Product (GNP)	457.6	493.1	528.1	577.1	613.1	905.4	1,154.5	1,075.3	1,057.5	1,203.1	1,249.0
Net Factor Income from Abroad	-41.0	-42.5	-36.0	-22.2	-31.7	-49.3	-33.0	-60.9	-67.1	-64.5	-77.0
GDP at Market Prices	498.6	535.6	564.1	599.3	644.8	954.7	1,187.5	1,136.2	1,124.6	1,267.6	1,326.0
Resource Balance	19.0	-2.9	21.0	-7.8	-107.7	18.4	-0.3	-283.2	-175.0	-0.2	-124.9
Exports of Goods & NFServices	295.4	302.4	329.5	344.4	336.5	652.5	889.2	750.7	710.9	799.7	793.1
Imports of Goods & NFServices	276.4	305.3	308.5	352.2	444.2	634.1	889.5	1,033.9	885.9	799.9	918.0
Domestic Absorption	479.6	538.5	543.1	607.1	752.5	936.3	1,187.8	1,419.0	1,299.7	1,267.9	1,451.0
Private Consumption, etc.	296.7	325.7	336.3	371.3	417.3	522.0	562.3	673.7	682.7	711.9	692.0
General Gov't Consumption	79.1	90.9	101.7	116.9	159.7	162.2	232.9	320.1	290.0	296.0	348.0
Gross Domestic Investment	103.8	121.9	105.1	118.9	175.5	252.1	392.6	425.2	327.0	260.0	411.0
Fixed Investment	98.0	112.6	102.8	108.3	154.8	198.1	350.3	381.0	290.0	242.0	325.0
Indirect Taxes, net	60.7	65.6	65.7	68.6	68.4	84.9	90.0	97.8	105.3	132.0	147.0
GDP at factor cost	437.9	470.0	498.4	530.7	576.4	869.8	1,097.5	1,038.4	1,019.3	1,135.6	1,179.0
Agriculture	89.4	90.1	101.7	104.2	106.3	264.1	341.4	236.0	210.8	256.6	263.5
Industry	173.9	189.3	190.6	196.3	191.8	287.8	376.9	364.9	364.0	391.0	400.5
Manufacturing	52.5	57.0	61.3	63.9	64.3	120.3	161.6	134.9	122.9	137.5	146.0
Services, etc.	174.6	190.6	206.1	230.2	278.3	317.9	379.2	437.5	444.5	488.0	515.0
Gross Domestic Saving	122.8	119.0	126.1	111.1	67.8	270.5	392.3	142.4	151.9	259.7	286.0
Gross National Saving	..	75.5	89.7	89.4	34.3	216.1	349.0	70.3	75.8	195.8	209.5

(Millions of 1987 Guyana Dollars)

	1969	1970	1971	1972	1973	1974	1975	1976	1977	1978	1979
Gross National Product	3,469.3	3,659.9	3,957.8	3,843.2	3,866.7	4,209.0	4,693.3	4,643.4	4,511.0	4,488.3	4,376.2
GDP at Market Prices	3,471.4	3,629.4	3,736.5	3,630.4	3,686.5	3,978.6	4,293.1	4,353.4	4,237.2	4,173.5	4,086.8
Resource Balance	-762.0	-907.1	-465.4	-707.6	-1,711.8	-1,256.1	-2,378.1	-2,804.6	-1,782.3	-492.8	-696.0
Exports of Goods & NFServices	4,879.7	4,820.9	4,984.1	4,612.0	4,332.8	4,177.1	4,290.6	4,126.9	3,570.0	3,884.3	3,489.6
Imports of Goods & NFServices	5,641.6	5,728.0	5,449.5	5,319.6	6,044.6	5,433.2	6,668.7	6,931.5	5,352.2	4,377.1	4,185.6
Domestic Absorption	4,233.4	4,536.5	4,201.9	4,338.0	5,398.3	5,234.7	6,671.2	7,158.0	6,019.5	4,666.3	4,782.7
Private Consumption, etc.	1,773.3	1,732.3	1,664.1	2,037.5	2,267.6	2,335.5	1,996.7	2,522.2	2,519.3	1,948.8	1,557.7
General Gov't Consumption	647.9	814.6	840.8	882.8	1,009.6	990.8	1,390.8	1,818.0	1,520.2	1,348.3	1,345.1
Gross Domestic Investment	1,812.1	1,989.6	1,697.0	1,417.7	2,121.1	1,908.4	3,283.7	2,817.8	1,979.9	1,369.2	1,879.9
Fixed Investment	..	..	..	..	..	..	..	2,601.7	1,808.4	1,312.1	1,540.3
GDP at factor cost	2,986.4	3,126.1	3,231.3	3,131.0	3,217.5	3,481.3	3,800.9	3,860.6	3,746.5	3,645.8	3,586.6
Agriculture	834.8	830.1	881.2	800.3	800.3	928.1	894.0	928.1	897.4	974.9	906.8
Industry	1,435.9	1,496.5	1,543.4	1,449.6	1,415.5	1,534.8	1,675.5	1,607.3	1,551.9	1,436.8	1,411.2
Manufacturing	411.9	409.3	480.9	465.6	440.0	552.6	608.8	624.2	628.8	644.7	670.2
Services, etc.	861.1	928.6	949.7	976.8	1,061.2	1,094.4	1,293.4	1,371.8	1,340.1	1,278.3	1,302.4

Memo Items:

	1969	1970	1971	1972	1973	1974	1975	1976	1977	1978	1979
Capacity to Import	6,029.4	5,673.6	5,820.5	5,201.8	4,579.0	5,590.9	6,666.5	5,032.9	4,295.0	4,376.0	3,616.1
Terms of Trade Adjustment	1,149.8	852.7	836.4	589.8	246.3	1,413.7	2,375.9	906.0	725.0	491.7	126.5
Gross Domestic Income	4,621.2	4,482.1	4,572.9	4,220.2	3,932.8	5,392.4	6,668.9	5,259.4	4,962.2	4,665.2	4,213.3
Gross National Income	4,619.1	4,512.6	4,794.2	4,433.0	4,113.0	5,622.8	7,069.2	5,549.4	5,235.9	4,980.0	4,502.7

DOMESTIC PRICES/DEFLATORS
(Index 1987 = 100)

	1969	1970	1971	1972	1973	1974	1975	1976	1977	1978	1979
Overall (GDP)	14.4	14.8	15.1	16.5	17.5	24.0	27.7	26.1	26.5	30.4	32.4
Domestic Absorption	11.3	11.9	12.9	14.0	13.9	17.9	17.8	19.8	21.6	27.2	30.3
Agriculture	10.7	10.9	11.5	13.0	13.3	28.5	38.2	25.4	23.5	26.3	29.1
Industry	12.1	12.6	12.3	13.5	13.6	18.8	22.5	22.7	23.5	27.2	28.4
Manufacturing	12.7	13.9	12.7	13.7	14.6	21.8	26.5	21.6	19.5	21.3	21.8
Consumer Price Index	10.8	11.2	11.3	11.8	12.7	14.9	16.1	17.6	19.0	21.9	25.8

MANUFACTURING ACTIVITY

	1969	1970	1971	1972	1973	1974	1975	1976	1977	1978	1979
Employment (1987=100)	..	..	..	..	..	..	..	..	..	..	..
Real Earnings per Empl. (1987=100)	..	..	..	..	..	..	..	..	..	..	..
Real Output per Empl. (1987=100)	..	..	..	..	..	..	..	..	..	..	..
Earnings as % of Value Added	..	..	..	..	..	..	..	..	..	..	..

MONETARY HOLDINGS
(Millions of current Guyana Dollars)

	1969	1970	1971	1972	1973	1974	1975	1976	1977	1978	1979
Money Supply, Broadly Defined	160.5	173.9	202.0	246.3	291.8	339.1	475.8	523.8	646.1	716.3	770.8
Money	60.6	61.4	69.4	87.5	100.6	133.1	207.4	221.5	284.9	300.4	288.2
Currency Outside Banks	35.7	37.3	40.7	48.1	55.6	63.6	91.6	105.2	142.8	156.4	148.3
Demand Deposits	24.9	24.1	28.7	39.4	44.9	69.5	115.8	116.3	142.1	143.9	139.9
Quasi-Money	99.9	112.5	132.5	158.8	191.2	205.9	268.4	302.3	361.2	415.9	482.6

(Millions of current Guyana Dollars)

	1969	1970	1971	1972	1973	1974	1975	1976	1977	1978	1979
GOVERNMENT DEFICIT (-) OR SURPLUS	..	-24.30	-33.00	-39.20	-104.70	-22.20	-77.50	-313.10	-133.40	-128.70	-232.40
Current Revenue	..	143.30	140.10	162.50	177.40	322.80	503.10	399.10	380.50	404.20	480.50
Current Expenditure	..	..	..	..	199.50	258.80	302.80	388.60	391.20	402.50	450.20
Current Budget Balance	..	..	..	..	-22.10	64.00	200.30	10.50	-10.70	1.70	30.30
Capital Receipts	..	0.80	0.60	0.90	2.40	..	..	..	..	0.20	0.30
Capital Payments	..	..	..	..	85.00	86.20	277.80	323.60	122.70	130.60	263.00

1980	1981	1982	1983	1984	1985	1986	1987	1988	1989 estimate	NOTES	GUYANA
720	730	610	520	500	510	500	400	400	340	..	**CURRENT GNP PER CAPITA (US $)**
760	766	772	779	785	790	794	797	799	800	..	**POPULATION (thousands)**
(Millions of current Guyana Dollars)											**USE AND ORIGIN OF RESOURCES**
1,403.0	1,433.0	1,284.0	1,255.7	1,401.3	1,651.5	1,806.9	2,633.8	3,192.0	6,252.0	..	Gross National Product (GNP)
-105.0	-164.0	-162.0	-212.3	-261.7	-298.5	-363.1	-871.2	-946.0	-1,011.3	..	Net Factor Income from Abroad
1,508.0	1,597.0	1,446.0	1,468.0	1,663.0	1,950.0	2,170.0	3,505.0	4,138.0	7,263.3	..	GDP at Market Prices
-158.4	-350.2	-219.0	-272.7	-152.9	-330.3	-306.3	-477.0	-184.0	-494.0	..	Resource Balance
1,041.9	1,031.9	794.4	675.3	938.0	1,047.7	1,056.0	2,676.1	2,602.0	2,446.0	..	Exports of Goods & NFServices
1,200.3	1,382.1	1,013.4	948.0	1,090.9	1,378.0	1,362.3	3,153.1	2,786.0	2,940.0	..	Imports of Goods & NFServices
1,666.4	1,947.2	1,665.0	1,740.7	1,815.9	2,280.4	2,476.6	3,982.0	4,322.0	..	..	Domestic Absorption
781.4	1,012.2	923.0	973.7	1,058.9	1,346.4	1,342.6	2,311.0	2,282.0	..	..	Private Consumption, etc.
436.0	464.0	392.0	458.0	301.0	352.0	401.0	552.0	1,165.0	..	..	General Gov't Consumption
449.0	471.0	350.0	309.0	456.0	582.0	733.0	1,119.0	875.0	..	..	Gross Domestic Investment
404.0	441.0	350.0	309.0	456.0	466.0	595.0	946.0	..	..	..	Fixed Investment
172.0	247.0	196.0	268.0	259.0	314.0	333.0	441.0	560.0	..	..	Indirect Taxes, net
1,336.0	1,350.0	1,250.0	1,200.0	1,404.0	1,636.0	1,837.0	3,064.0	3,578.0	..	..	GDP at factor cost
312.0	300.0	292.0	291.0	347.0	439.0	490.0	894.0	878.0	..	..	Agriculture
478.0	412.0	362.0	273.0	348.0	397.0	501.0	955.0	1,115.0	..	f	Industry
162.0	201.0	179.0	158.0	183.0	227.0	271.0	440.0	543.0	..	..	Manufacturing
546.0	638.0	596.0	636.0	709.0	800.0	846.0	1,215.0	1,585.0	..	f	Services, etc.
290.6	120.8	131.0	36.3	303.1	251.6	426.4	642.0	691.0	..	..	Gross Domestic Saving
188.1	-31.2	-48.6	-188.8	45.4	-55.5	81.7	-183.3	-231.0	..	..	Gross National Saving
(Millions of 1987 Guyana Dollars)											
4,396.3	4,344.8	3,721.8	3,213.3	3,165.7	3,158.2	3,142.1	2,633.8	2,651.7	2,514.6	..	Gross National Product
4,158.9	4,231.8	3,658.0	3,415.7	3,418.8	3,454.6	3,509.1	3,505.0	3,457.5	3,336.6	I	GDP at Market Prices
-1,043.6	-1,244.6	-622.7	-677.2	-75.0	-487.1	-761.3	-477.0	-725.3	..	..	Resource Balance
3,589.1	3,376.6	2,590.2	2,418.5	2,648.0	2,731.8	2,576.7	2,676.1	2,622.4	..	..	Exports of Goods & NFServices
4,632.7	4,621.2	3,212.9	3,095.7	2,722.9	3,219.0	3,338.0	3,153.1	3,347.6	..	..	Imports of Goods & NFServices
5,202.6	5,476.4	4,280.7	4,092.9	3,493.8	3,941.7	4,270.4	3,982.0	4,182.8	..	..	Domestic Absorption
1,870.2	2,483.3	2,213.9	2,179.5	1,838.2	2,203.7	2,372.4	2,311.0	2,600.6	..	..	Private Consumption, etc.
1,477.2	1,287.0	901.1	913.7	479.7	487.5	514.8	552.0	542.6	..	..	General Gov't Consumption
1,855.1	1,706.1	1,165.7	999.7	1,176.0	1,250.5	1,383.2	1,119.0	1,039.6	..	..	Gross Domestic Investment
1,728.0	1,656.9	1,199.8	1,028.9	1,210.4	1,095.7	1,212.9	946.0	..	..	..	Fixed Investment
3,646.2	3,636.0	3,256.9	2,949.5	3,015.7	3,051.1	3,062.6	3,064.0	2,955.8	..	I	GDP at factor cost
911.0	932.3	919.5	885.5	915.3	915.3	949.3	894.0	821.6	..	..	Agriculture
1,458.1	1,428.2	1,155.4	912.4	933.7	972.1	946.5	955.0	925.2	..	f	Industry
675.4	716.3	624.2	521.9	491.2	475.8	475.8	440.0	434.9	..	..	Manufacturing
1,314.5	1,311.5	1,202.9	1,151.7	1,166.8	1,163.8	1,166.8	1,215.0	1,209.0	..	f	Services, etc.
											Memo Items:
4,021.3	3,450.3	2,518.6	2,205.2	2,341.3	2,447.4	2,587.5	2,676.1	3,126.6	..	..	Capacity to Import
432.3	73.6	-71.6	-213.3	-306.7	-284.5	10.8	0.0	504.2	..	..	Terms of Trade Adjustment
4,591.2	4,305.4	3,586.4	3,202.4	3,112.1	3,170.2	3,519.9	3,505.0	3,961.7	..	..	Gross Domestic Income
4,828.5	4,418.5	3,650.2	3,000.0	2,859.0	2,873.8	3,152.9	2,633.8	3,155.9	..	..	Gross National Income
(Index 1987 = 100)											**DOMESTIC PRICES/DEFLATORS**
36.3	37.7	39.5	43.0	48.6	56.4	61.8	100.0	119.7	217.7	..	Overall (GDP)
32.0	35.6	38.9	42.5	52.0	57.9	58.0	100.0	103.3	..	..	Domestic Absorption
34.2	32.2	31.8	32.9	37.9	48.0	51.6	100.0	106.9	..	..	Agriculture
32.8	28.8	31.3	29.9	37.3	40.8	52.9	100.0	120.5	..	..	Industry
24.0	28.1	28.7	30.3	37.3	47.7	57.0	100.0	124.9	..	..	Manufacturing
29.4	35.9	43.5	50.0	62.6	72.0	77.7	100.0	139.9	..	..	Consumer Price Index
											MANUFACTURING ACTIVITY
..	..	..	..	..	..	..	..	..	..	..	Employment (1987 = 100)
..	..	..	..	..	..	..	..	..	..	..	Real Earnings per Empl. (1987 = 100)
..	..	..	..	..	..	..	..	..	..	..	Real Output per Empl. (1987 = 100)
..	..	..	..	..	..	..	..	..	..	..	Earnings as % of Value Added
(Millions of current Guyana Dollars)											**MONETARY HOLDINGS**
929.4	1,085.5	1,384.2	1,671.7	1,991.0	2,431.0	2,906.5	4,331.8	..	8,867.7	D	Money Supply, Broadly Defined
328.1	350.8	436.0	508.9	618.6	739.6	880.8	1,332.5	2,095.2	2,922.6	..	Money
167.0	186.0	231.0	268.9	335.8	421.6	508.8	726.2	1,057.8	1,506.0	..	Currency Outside Banks
161.1	164.7	205.0	240.0	282.8	318.0	372.0	606.4	1,037.4	1,416.7	..	Demand Deposits
601.4	734.7	948.2	1,162.8	1,372.4	1,691.4	2,025.7	2,999.3	..	5,945.0	..	Quasi-Money
(Millions of current Guyana Dollars)											**GOVERNMENT DEFICIT (-) OR SURPLUS**
-440.20	-453.00	..	..	..	..	..	..	..	..	..	Current Revenue
539.70	666.40	651.00	673.00	..	959.40	..	..	..	..	..	Current Expenditure
..	..	..	887.10	1,260.40	..	..	..	..	..	..	Current Budget Balance
..	..	..	-214.10	..	..	..	..	..	..	..	Capital Receipts
..	..	..	..	..	3.20	..	..	..	..	..	Capital Payments

GUYANA	1969	1970	1971	1972	1973	1974	1975	1976	1977	1978	1979
FOREIGN TRADE (CUSTOMS BASIS)					*(Millions of current US dollars)*						
Value of Exports, fob	116.84	133.43	149.18	147.02	137.08	270.20	364.18	268.21	261.25	291.00	289.88
Nonfuel Primary Products	112.53	126.40	140.39	137.92	126.91	258.51	348.77	227.03	211.88	243.22	272.75
Fuels	0.01	0.01	0.04	0.01	0.01	0.10	0.21	0.18	0.05	0.46	0.07
Manufactures	4.30	7.02	8.75	9.09	10.16	11.59	15.20	41.00	49.32	47.32	17.06
Value of Imports, cif	118.00	134.06	135.00	143.34	177.00	254.88	343.90	364.00	315.00	279.00	318.00
Nonfuel Primary Products	23.05	22.55	25.54	24.17	31.67	44.28	50.31	57.33	51.57	50.90	61.29
Fuels	10.69	11.52	11.89	13.52	23.02	46.52	57.30	54.19	63.08	68.75	69.19
Manufactures	84.26	99.99	97.57	105.65	122.31	164.08	236.29	252.48	200.35	159.36	187.51
					(Index 1987 = 100)						
Terms of Trade	199.5	182.4	168.4	178.9	173.0	209.9	225.5	165.8	151.0	146.0	136.5
Export Prices, fob	45.7	43.7	44.6	51.5	59.6	111.9	126.5	94.6	95.2	103.0	114.9
Import Prices, cif	22.9	24.0	26.5	28.8	34.4	53.3	56.1	57.0	63.0	70.5	84.2
BALANCE OF PAYMENTS					*(Millions of current US dollars)*						
Exports of Goods & Services	..	146.60	163.19	163.83	157.60	293.08	371.77	294.75	..	..	314.94
Merchandise, fob	..	129.00	145.93	143.64	135.66	270.11	351.38	279.51	259.33	295.61	292.71
Nonfactor Services	..	16.60	16.45	18.78	20.50	21.65	18.94	13.62	16.16	18.16	18.55
Factor Services	..	1.00	0.80	1.41	1.43	1.32	1.46	1.62	..	..	3.69
Imports of Goods & Services	..	167.90	170.61	179.14	221.38	300.30	390.35	431.44	369.10	336.86	398.24
Merchandise, fob	..	119.90	120.36	128.87	159.39	230.31	305.84	330.89	286.71	253.49	288.78
Nonfactor Services	..	31.10	31.29	38.22	48.52	49.79	64.11	75.04	60.75	60.08	71.37
Factor Services	..	16.90	18.96	12.05	13.47	20.20	20.40	25.51	21.65	23.29	38.08
Long-Term Interest	..	3.40	3.60	6.40	8.10	8.70	10.30	19.80	15.20	17.30	25.20
Private Current Transfers, net	..	-0.50	-0.20	0.22	-0.83	-2.29	-4.37	-4.39	-3.53	0.24	0.20
Workers' Remittances	..	..	..	..	..	..	..	..	..	..	..
Curr. A/C Bal before Off. Transf.	..	-21.80	-7.62	-15.09	-64.61	-9.50	-22.95	-141.08	-97.14	-22.86	-83.10
Net Official Transfers	..	..	1.00	-1.19	0.12	-1.20	-1.70	-1.73	-0.39	-6.71	0.20
Curr. A/C Bal after Off. Transf.	..	-21.80	-6.62	-16.29	-64.49	-10.70	-24.65	-142.81	-97.53	-29.57	-82.90
Long-Term Capital, net	..	17.10	6.94	8.82	18.22	43.10	89.85	44.79	41.33	32.82	14.31
Direct Investment	..	9.00	-55.77	2.50	8.23	1.32	0.85	-26.09	-1.76	..	0.59
Long-Term Loans	..	11.60	14.10	8.80	16.10	29.70	98.50	56.90	42.50	27.40	32.80
Disbursements	..	13.80	15.50	11.20	21.10	35.00	105.00	70.00	59.20	59.70	98.90
Repayments	..	2.20	1.40	2.40	5.00	5.30	6.50	13.10	16.70	32.30	66.10
Other Long-Term Capital	..	-3.50	48.61	-2.47	-6.11	12.08	-9.50	13.98	0.60	5.42	-19.07
Other Capital, net	..	2.45	1.39	15.65	20.22	13.64	-15.45	10.07	44.78	13.27	11.62
Change in Reserves	..	2.25	-1.71	-8.19	26.05	-46.03	-49.75	87.95	11.42	-16.52	56.97
Memo Item:					*(Guyana Dollars per US dollar)*						
Conversion Factor (Annual Avg)	2.000	2.000	1.980	2.090	2.110	2.230	2.360	2.550	2.550	2.550	2.550
					(Millions of US dollars), outstanding at end of year						
EXTERNAL DEBT (Total)	..	82.7	156.4	157.7	178.1	219.8	305.7	394.3	492.1	574.1	640.1
Long-Term Debt (by debtor)	..	82.7	156.4	157.7	178.1	219.8	305.7	394.3	448.1	501.1	574.1
Central Bank, incl. IMF credit	..	0.0	2.2	0.0	4.7	6.1	0.0	25.9	35.0	58.8	73.4
Central Government	..	62.3	130.0	133.8	149.4	184.4	246.3	290.1	311.5	328.4	376.6
Rest of General Government	..	..	..	..	..	..	..	..	..	..	..
Non-financial Public Enterprises	..	20.4	24.2	23.9	24.0	29.3	59.4	78.3	101.6	113.9	124.1
Priv. Sector, incl non-guaranteed	..	..	..	..	..	..	..	..	..	..	..
Short-Term Debt	..	0.0	0.0	0.0	0.0	0.0	0.0	0.0	44.0	73.0	66.0
Memo Items:					*(Thousands of US dollars)*						
Int'l Reserves Excluding Gold	20,550.0	20,400.0	26,156.0	36,750.3	13,973.7	62,572.1	100,497.0	27,282.9	22,976.2	58,265.7	17,528.0
Gold Holdings (at market price)	..	..	..	..	..	..	..	..	..	..	..
SOCIAL INDICATORS											
Total Fertility Rate	5.6	5.4	5.1	4.9	4.7	4.5	4.3	4.1	3.9	3.8	3.7
Infant Mortality Rate	80.8	80.2	79.6	79.0	76.6	74.2	71.8	69.4	67.0	66.2	65.4
Life Expectancy at Birth	59.5	59.7	59.8	60.0	60.1	60.3	60.4	60.6	60.7	60.8	60.9
Urban Population, % of total	29.4	29.4	29.4	29.5	29.5	29.6	29.6	29.8	30.0	30.1	30.3
Food Prod. per capita (1987=100)	177.4	158.5	174.2	148.5	136.7	160.3	141.1	148.9	128.8	158.5	141.4
Labor Force, Agriculture (%)	32.5	31.9	31.3	30.8	30.2	29.8	29.3	28.7	28.2	27.7	27.2
Labor Force, Female (%)	20.5	20.7	21.2	21.6	22.0	22.4	22.8	23.1	23.5	23.8	24.1
Primary Schl. Enroll. Ratio	..	98.0	..	..	..	..	95.0	99.0	98.0	98.0	102.0
Primary Schl. Enroll. Ratio, Female	..	96.0	..	..	..	..	95.0	98.0	98.0	97.0	101.0
Secondary Schl. Enroll. Ratio	..	55.0	..	..	..	..	54.0	61.0	61.0	60.0	59.0

1980	1981	1982	1983	1984	1985	1986	1987	1988	1989 estimate	NOTES	GUYANA
											FOREIGN TRADE (CUSTOMS BASIS)
				(Millions of current US dollars)							
389.00	346.00	241.00	189.00	210.00	206.40	228.48	243.12	266.00	..	..	Value of Exports, fob
352.78	313.68	219.33	171.82	191.06	185.64	191.55	204.96	244.14	..	..	Nonfuel Primary Products
0.20	0.20	0.13	0.10	0.07	0.08	0.06	0.07	0.07	..	..	Fuels
36.02	32.13	21.55	17.09	18.87	20.69	36.87	38.09	21.79	..	..	Manufactures
365.00	438.00	282.00	246.00	214.00	248.00	217.00	225.56	236.40	..	..	Value of Imports, cif
68.54	82.46	53.20	46.36	41.14	44.66	73.55	73.00	118.08	..	..	Nonfuel Primary Products
80.88	97.79	62.70	54.72	47.08	52.33	25.23	34.61	42.52	..	..	Fuels
215.58	257.75	166.10	144.91	125.78	151.00	118.22	117.94	75.80	..	..	Manufactures
				(Index 1987 = 100)							
150.5	141.9	127.1	124.4	114.4	109.3	111.3	100.0	111.0	..	..	Terms of Trade
146.4	141.0	122.1	116.5	105.4	99.0	103.7	100.0	116.0	..	..	Export Prices, fob
97.3	99.4	96.1	93.6	92.2	90.6	93.2	100.0	104.5	..	..	Import Prices, cif
				(Millions of current US dollars)							**BALANCE OF PAYMENTS**
410.51	372.44	264.37	225.20	246.37	..	247.40	274.60	260.50	244.90	..	Exports of Goods & Services
388.86	346.42	241.43	193.33	216.88	214.02	217.40	232.20	208.90	197.50	..	Merchandise, fob
19.76	22.97	22.60	31.53	29.23	48.00	29.80	42.10	51.30	47.10	..	Nonfactor Services
1.88	3.06	0.33	0.33	0.26	..	0.20	0.30	0.30	0.30	..	Factor Services
538.23	556.12	397.91	381.69	345.63	353.43	404.10	412.80	373.50	395.40	..	Imports of Goods & Services
386.43	399.64	254.17	225.73	201.64	209.09	259.50	261.90	215.60	224.70	..	Merchandise, fob
107.33	98.88	94.47	98.13	99.05	104.03	59.40	61.30	63.00	69.30	..	Nonfactor Services
44.47	57.60	49.28	57.82	44.95	40.32	85.20	89.60	94.90	101.40	..	Factor Services
26.60	35.90	21.60	24.40	19.40	11.50	16.30	14.40	12.10	10.20	..	Long-Term Interest
0.98	4.27	-5.87	-4.27	1.04	-2.02	4.30	4.70	2.40	7.10	..	Private Current Transfers, net
..	..	2.30	1.17	..	..	..	..	..	..	..	Workers' Remittances
-126.75	-179.41	-139.41	-160.75	-98.22	-93.42	-146.40	-127.60	-100.50	-136.50	..	Curr. A/C Bal before Off. Transf.
-1.76	-4.08	-1.90	3.27	3.60	-3.20	6.00	5.90	10.10	6.90	..	Net Official Transfers
-128.51	-183.50	-141.31	-157.49	-94.62	-96.62	-140.40	-121.70	-90.40	-129.60	..	Curr. A/C Bal after Off. Transf.
74.47	114.88	10.17	-32.93	-27.73	-36.02	-2.80	-11.40	-18.00	-44.80	..	Long-Term Capital, net
0.59	-1.78	4.43	4.73	4.49	1.81	-12.00	5.40	4.70	5.00	..	Direct Investment
64.70	96.50	52.70	32.60	12.70	48.60	52.30	30.30	21.60	31.10	..	Long-Term Loans
107.30	139.80	75.70	54.60	27.00	60.30	65.40	41.80	30.50	44.80	..	Disbursements
42.60	43.30	23.00	22.00	14.30	11.70	13.10	11.50	8.90	13.70	..	Repayments
9.18	20.16	-46.97	-70.27	-44.92	-86.43	-43.10	-47.10	-44.30	-80.90	..	Other Long-Term Capital
10.75	50.83	130.75	190.74	146.25	137.15	145.73	132.52	104.01	175.46	..	Other Capital, net
43.29	17.79	0.40	-0.32	-23.90	-4.50	-2.53	0.58	4.39	-1.06	..	Change in Reserves
				(Guyana Dollars per US dollar)							**Memo Item:**
2.550	2.810	3.000	3.000	3.830	4.250	4.270	9.760	10.000	27.160	..	Conversion Factor (Annual Avg)
				(Millions of US dollars), outstanding at end of year							
788.5	868.0	951.4	1,200.9	1,264.8	1,482.1	1,615.3	1,712.7	1,678.0	1,713.0	..	**EXTERNAL DEBT (Total)**
678.5	758.9	793.3	802.2	776.5	867.9	955.9	1,064.8	1,044.8	1,093.1	..	Long-Term Debt (by debtor)
114.1	126.7	137.1	136.7	132.1	152.1	165.5	190.8	189.5	177.3	..	Central Bank, incl. IMF credit
436.4	524.7	563.3	585.4	578.8	652.0	697.5	763.3	758.7	850.1	..	Central Government
..	..	..	..	..	..	..	..	..	..	..	Rest of General Government
128.0	107.5	92.9	80.1	65.6	63.8	92.9	110.7	96.6	65.7	..	Non-financial Public Enterprises
..	..	..	..	..	..	..	..	..	..	..	Priv. Sector, incl non-guaranteed
110.0	109.1	158.1	398.7	488.3	614.2	659.4	647.9	633.2	619.9	..	Short-Term Debt
				(Thousands of US dollars)							**Memo Items:**
12,700.0	6,910.5	10,557.1	6,490.0	5,850.0	6,470.0	9,000.0	8,430.0	4,040.0	13,350.0	..	Int'l Reserves Excluding Gold
..	..	..	..	..	..	..	..	..	..	..	Gold Holdings (at market price)
											SOCIAL INDICATORS
3.5	3.4	3.3	3.2	3.2	3.1	3.1	3.1	3.0	2.9	..	Total Fertility Rate
64.6	63.8	63.0	61.6	60.2	58.8	57.4	56.0	54.6	53.2	..	Infant Mortality Rate
61.0	61.1	61.2	61.6	62.0	62.4	62.8	63.2	63.5	63.7	..	Life Expectancy at Birth
30.5	30.8	31.2	31.5	31.9	32.2	32.7	33.2	33.6	34.1	..	Urban Population, % of total
132.5	143.4	134.5	117.3	111.1	106.1	108.8	100.0	94.2	96.8	..	Food Prod. per capita (1987=100)
26.8	..	..	..	..	..	..	..	..	..	..	Labor Force, Agriculture (%)
24.4	24.5	24.6	24.7	24.7	24.8	24.9	24.9	24.9	25.0	..	Labor Force, Female (%)
100.0	99.0	95.0	90.0	..	..	..	..	..	..	..	Primary Schl. Enroll. Ratio
99.0	99.0	..	..	..	..	..	..	..	..	..	Primary Schl. Enroll. Ratio, Female
60.0	60.0	57.0	55.0	..	..	..	..	..	..	..	Secondary Schl. Enroll. Ratio

HAITI	1969	1970	1971	1972	1973	1974	1975	1976	1977	1978	1979
CURRENT GNP PER CAPITA (US $)	90	90	100	100	110	130	150	170	180	200	220
POPULATION (thousands)	4,408	4,500	4,592	4,684	4,775	4,866	4,957	5,047	5,137	5,227	5,319

USE AND ORIGIN OF RESOURCES — *(Millions of current Haitian Gourdes)*

	1969	1970	1971	1972	1973	1974	1975	1976	1977	1978	1979
Gross National Product (GNP)	1,872	1,954	2,207	2,354	2,821	3,460	3,573	4,359	4,878	4,928	5,531
Net Factor Income from Abroad	-18	-18	-20	-23	-22	-30	-35	-36	-61	-74	-67
GDP at Market Prices	1,890	1,972	2,227	2,377	2,843	3,489	3,608	4,395	4,939	5,001	5,597
Resource Balance	-56	-77	-76	-118	-133	-250	-297	-391	-440	-443	-557
Exports of Goods & NFServices	242	272	304	296	350	422	528	736	905	1,018	1,094
Imports of Goods & NFServices	298	349	380	413	483	672	825	1,128	1,345	1,461	1,651
Domestic Absorption	1,946	2,049	2,303	2,494	2,976	3,739	3,905	4,786	5,379	5,444	6,154
Private Consumption, etc.	1,605	1,636	1,821	1,944	2,283	2,908	3,048	3,721	4,201	4,135	4,573
General Gov't Consumption	175	188	227	219	241	257	326	372	411	469	532
Gross Domestic Investment	166	225	254	331	451	574	532	694	767	840	1,049
Fixed Investment	..	..	..	..	..	..	..	..	..	..	..
Indirect Taxes, net	..	..	..	..	..	..	..	..	..	..	..
GDP at factor cost	..	..	..	..	..	..	..	..	..	..	..
Agriculture	..	..	..	..	..	..	..	..	..	..	..
Industry	..	..	..	..	..	..	..	..	..	..	..
Manufacturing	..	..	..	..	..	..	..	..	..	..	..
Services, etc.	..	..	..	..	..	..	..	..	..	..	..
Gross Domestic Saving	110	148	178	213	319	325	235	303	327	397	492
Gross National Saving	..	204	145	198	273	266	27	77	421	467	596

(Millions of 1976 Haitian Gourdes)

	1969	1970	1971	1972	1973	1974	1975	1976	1977	1978	1979
Gross National Product	3,470.0	3,453.0	3,748.0	3,794.5	3,849.4	4,094.8	4,013.1	4,359.0	4,362.0	4,560.0	4,907.6
GDP at Market Prices	3,516.0	3,504.0	3,800.0	3,852.5	3,898.4	4,144.8	4,048.7	4,395.0	4,416.0	4,628.0	4,966.0
Resource Balance	-71.0	-177.0	-165.0	-203.0	-142.0	-164.0	-209.2	-391.0	-551.6	-517.2	-397.0
Exports of Goods & NFServices	383.0	412.0	491.0	520.0	610.0	649.0	654.3	736.5	726.9	797.8	893.8
Imports of Goods & NFServices	454.0	589.0	656.0	723.0	752.0	813.0	863.5	1,127.5	1,278.5	1,315.0	1,290.8
Domestic Absorption	3,587.0	3,681.0	3,965.0	4,055.5	4,040.4	4,308.8	4,257.9	4,786.0	4,967.6	5,145.2	5,363.0
Private Consumption, etc.	3,007.0	2,981.0	3,202.0	3,274.5	3,232.4	3,486.8	3,334.4	3,720.8	3,865.9	3,898.8	3,969.3
General Gov't Consumption	382.0	403.0	460.0	423.0	391.0	359.0	356.2	371.5	382.9	448.8	464.6
Gross Domestic Investment	198.0	297.0	303.0	358.0	417.0	463.0	567.3	693.7	718.8	797.6	929.1
Fixed Investment	183.0	282.0	286.0	341.0	400.0	446.0	577.1	..	..	..	..
GDP at factor cost	..	..	..	..	..	..	..	..	..	..	..
Agriculture	1,439.0	1,409.0	1,499.1	1,491.4	1,476.9	1,614.2	1,596.2	1,675.0	1,575.0	1,604.0	1,708.0
Industry	582.2	592.7	646.6	690.8	761.7	856.7	823.9	996.0	1,061.0	1,128.0	1,234.0
Manufacturing	415.0	422.0	447.0	486.0	507.0	556.0	546.0	664.0	721.0	772.0	851.0
Services, etc.	1,494.8	1,502.3	1,654.3	1,670.3	1,659.8	1,673.9	1,628.6	1,724.0	1,780.0	1,896.0	2,024.0

Memo Items:

	1969	1970	1971	1972	1973	1974	1975	1976	1977	1978	1979
Capacity to Import	368.6	459.0	524.6	517.6	545.5	510.9	552.8	736.5	860.3	916.3	855.3
Terms of Trade Adjustment	-14.4	47.0	33.6	-2.4	-64.5	-138.1	-101.5	0.0	133.4	118.5	-38.5
Gross Domestic Income	3,501.6	3,551.0	3,833.6	3,850.1	3,833.9	4,006.7	3,947.2	4,395.0	4,549.4	4,746.5	4,927.5
Gross National Income	3,455.6	3,500.0	3,781.6	3,792.1	3,784.9	3,956.7	3,911.6	4,359.0	4,495.4	4,678.5	4,869.1

DOMESTIC PRICES/DEFLATORS — *(Index 1976 = 100)*

	1969	1970	1971	1972	1973	1974	1975	1976	1977	1978	1979
Overall (GDP)	53.8	56.3	58.6	61.7	72.9	84.2	89.1	100.0	111.8	108.1	112.7
Domestic Absorption	54.3	55.7	58.1	61.5	73.6	86.8	91.7	100.0	108.3	105.8	114.7
Agriculture	..	..	..	..	..	..	..	..	..	..	..
Industry	..	..	..	..	..	..	..	..	..	..	..
Manufacturing	..	..	..	..	..	..	..	..	..	..	..
Consumer Price Index	25.4	25.7	28.2	29.1	35.7	41.0	47.9	51.3	54.6	53.1	60.1

MANUFACTURING ACTIVITY

	1969	1970	1971	1972	1973	1974	1975	1976	1977	1978	1979
Employment (1987=100)	34.0	32.0	34.0	40.7	46.1	51.6	60.0	63.8	73.2	72.5	80.9
Real Earnings per Empl. (1987=100)	90.8	92.0	96.1	84.5	69.7	62.2	52.9	60.9	59.4	71.7	72.9
Real Output per Empl. (1987=100)	..	..	..	..	..	..	..	..	..	..	..
Earnings as % of Value Added	..	..	..	..	..	..	..	..	..	..	..

MONETARY HOLDINGS — *(Millions of current Haitian Gourdes)*

	1969	1970	1971	1972	1973	1974	1975	1976	1977	1978	1979
Money Supply, Broadly Defined	224.4	248.6	290.0	381.6	487.3	583.7	734.8	1,015.2	1,216.8	1,431.5	1,872.7
Money	175.6	190.6	214.6	271.2	332.8	342.4	402.6	549.6	629.1	717.8	1,107.8
Currency Outside Banks	105.0	114.6	126.1	147.7	172.9	182.7	189.5	243.2	265.5	311.4	418.5
Demand Deposits	70.6	76.0	88.5	123.5	159.9	159.7	213.0	306.4	363.6	406.4	689.3
Quasi-Money	48.8	58.0	75.4	110.3	154.5	241.3	332.2	465.6	587.8	713.7	764.9

GOVERNMENT DEFICIT (-) OR SURPLUS — *(Millions of current Haitian Gourdes)*

	1969	1970	1971	1972	1973	1974	1975	1976	1977	1978	1979
GOVERNMENT DEFICIT (-) OR SURPLUS	..	..	..	..	..	..	..	..	..	..	-225.7
Current Revenue	..	..	..	..	..	..	..	..	..	..	823.8
Current Expenditure	..	..	..	309.9	313.8	422.1	527.5	641.8	757.7	666.5	878.2
Current Budget Balance	..	..	..	..	..	..	..	..	..	..	-54.4
Capital Receipts	..	..	..	..	..	..	..	..	..	..	..
Capital Payments	..	..	..	31.6	29.4	27.9	107.8	174.3	229.4	255.0	171.3

1980	1981	1982	1983	1984	1985	1986	1987	1988	1989 estimate	NOTES	HAITI
250	270	270	280	290	310	340	350	360	360	..	CURRENT GNP PER CAPITA (US $)
5,413	5,510	5,609	5,711	5,815	5,922	6,031	6,142	6,254	6,368	..	POPULATION (thousands)
				(Millions of current Haitian Gourdes)							USE AND ORIGIN OF RESOURCES
7,230	7,323	7,341	8,026	8,991	9,948	11,141	10,707	10,919	11,721	C	Gross National Product (GNP)
-80	-74	-84	-123	-91	-99	-77	-105	-135	-128	..	Net Factor Income from Abroad
7,309	7,397	7,425	8,148	9,082	10,047	11,218	10,812	11,054	11,849	C	GDP at Market Prices
-649	-1,124	-755	-848	-821	-821	-658	-856	-882	-913	..	Resource Balance
1,580	1,243	1,465	1,427	1,587	1,520	1,458	1,412	1,382	1,442	..	Exports of Goods & NFServices
2,229	2,367	2,220	2,276	2,408	2,341	2,116	2,268	2,264	2,355	f	Imports of Goods & NFServices
7,958	8,521	8,180	8,996	9,903	10,868	11,876	11,668	11,936	12,762	..	Domestic Absorption
5,984	6,443	6,102	6,794	7,488	8,241	9,484	9,172	9,486	10,127	..	Private Consumption, etc.
736	826	848	871	974	1,197	1,168	1,096	1,067	1,177	..	General Gov't Consumption
1,238	1,252	1,230	1,331	1,441	1,431	1,225	1,400	1,384	1,458	f	Gross Domestic Investment
..	..	..	1,331	1,441	1,431	1,225	1,400	1,209	..	f	Fixed Investment
..	..	..	645	716	912	1,025	524	910	..	..	Indirect Taxes, net
..	..	..	7,503	8,366	9,135	10,193	10,288	10,144	..	B C	GDP at factor cost
..	..	..	..	..	..	..	..	3,461	..	..	Agriculture
..	..	..	..	..	..	..	..	4,200	..	..	Industry
..	..	..	..	..	..	..	..	1,811	..	..	Manufacturing
..	..	..	..	..	..	..	..	3,393	..	..	Services, etc.
589	128	475	483	620	609	567	544	501	545	..	Gross Domestic Saving
770	378	639	592	755	753	750	720	683	714	..	Gross National Saving
				(Millions of 1976 Haitian Gourdes)							
5,290.3	5,152.4	4,971.9	5,012.6	5,021.4	5,030.1	5,077.5	5,041.2	4,967.5	4,928.7	C	Gross National Product
5,342.0	5,197.3	5,017.9	5,055.8	5,071.1	5,079.7	5,113.0	5,091.0	5,029.5	4,983.4	C	GDP at Market Prices
-410.3	-659.6	-330.8	-438.1	-366.8	-373.4	-375.1	-465.0	-439.5	-491.4	..	Resource Balance
1,133.0	862.6	1,058.4	957.9	1,017.1	954.7	868.4	836.0	829.0	824.0	..	Exports of Goods & NFServices
1,543.3	1,522.2	1,389.2	1,396.0	1,383.9	1,328.1	1,243.5	1,301.0	1,268.5	1,315.4	f	Imports of Goods & NFServices
5,752.3	5,856.9	5,348.7	5,493.9	5,437.9	5,453.1	5,488.1	5,556.0	5,469.0	5,474.8	..	Domestic Absorption
4,265.9	4,249.5	3,938.4	4,061.4	3,944.7	4,021.3	4,236.3	4,309.5	4,257.1	4,249.9	..	Private Consumption, etc.
552.4	563.4	533.6	508.2	526.1	596.5	537.8	500.0	473.0	493.3	..	General Gov't Consumption
934.0	1,044.0	876.7	924.3	967.1	835.3	714.0	746.5	738.9	731.6	f	Gross Domestic Investment
..	..	..	924.3	967.1	835.3	714.0	746.5	572.0	..	f	Fixed Investment
5,108.0	4,961.0	4,652.0	4,656.0	4,673.0	4,620.0	4,645.0	4,657.8	4,615.3	4,589.4	..	GDP at factor cost
1,723.0	1,699.0	1,627.0	1,566.0	1,621.0	1,629.0	1,671.0	1,666.0	1,635.2	1,602.4	..	Agriculture
1,361.0	1,249.0	1,223.0	1,221.0	1,177.0	1,190.0	1,149.0	1,141.0	1,141.4	1,159.0	..	Industry
970.0	856.0	843.0	888.0	836.0	812.0	789.0	773.0	773.3	773.7	..	Manufacturing
2,258.0	2,249.3	2,167.9	2,268.8	2,273.1	2,260.7	2,293.0	2,284.0	2,252.9	2,222.0	..	Services, etc.
											Memo Items:
1,094.1	799.4	916.5	875.6	912.1	862.1	856.7	809.9	774.3	805.4	..	Capacity to Import
-38.9	-63.2	-141.9	-82.3	-105.0	-92.6	-11.7	-26.1	-54.7	-18.6	..	Terms of Trade Adjustment
5,303.1	5,134.1	4,876.0	4,973.5	4,966.1	4,987.1	5,101.3	5,064.9	4,974.8	4,964.8	..	Gross Domestic Income
5,251.4	5,089.2	4,830.0	4,930.3	4,916.4	4,937.5	5,065.8	5,015.1	4,912.8	4,910.1	..	Gross National Income
				(Index 1976 = 100)							DOMESTIC PRICES/DEFLATORS
136.8	142.3	148.0	161.2	179.1	197.8	219.4	212.4	219.8	237.8	..	Overall (GDP)
138.3	145.5	152.9	163.8	182.1	199.3	216.4	210.0	218.3	233.1	..	Domestic Absorption
..	..	..	..	..	..	..	..	211.6	..	..	Agriculture
..	..	..	..	..	..	..	..	368.0	..	..	Industry
..	..	..	..	..	..	..	..	234.1	..	..	Manufacturing
70.8	78.5	84.2	92.9	98.8	109.3	112.9	100.0	104.1	..	f	Consumer Price Index
											MANUFACTURING ACTIVITY
86.2	88.3	95.7	105.4	97.1	99.5	109.3	100.0	94.7	..	..	Employment (1987=100)
65.2	73.5	75.5	70.2	70.0	67.7	75.7	100.0	102.6	..	..	Real Earnings per Empl. (1987=100)
..	..	..	..	..	..	..	..	..	..	..	Real Output per Empl. (1987=100)
..	..	..	..	..	..	..	..	..	..	..	Earnings as % of Value Added
				(Millions of current Haitian Gourdes)							MONETARY HOLDINGS
1,938.2	2,175.0	2,247.0	2,347.7	8,806.1	1,442.4	3,276.5	3,693.6	3,312.9	4,558.8	..	Money Supply, Broadly Defined
945.4	1,166.5	1,164.3	1,174.7	3,588.0	1,076.1	1,789.9	2,097.9	1,635.2	2,633.6	..	Money
418.1	487.4	565.6	599.5	691.0	763.2	829.1	979.5	205.0	1,458.8	..	Currency Outside Banks
527.3	679.1	598.7	575.2	2,897.0	312.9	960.8	1,118.3	1,430.2	1,174.8	..	Demand Deposits
992.8	1,008.5	1,082.7	1,173.0	5,218.1	366.4	1,486.7	1,595.7	1,677.7	1,925.2	..	Quasi-Money
				(Millions of current Haitian Gourdes)							
-341.7	..	-236.3	..	..	..	..	..	..	..	C	GOVERNMENT DEFICIT (-) OR SURPLUS
926.5	..	1,113.3	1,345.9	1,590.8	1,929.7	1,596.8	..	..	..	..	Current Revenue
1,012.5	1,299.7	1,205.4	1,406.8	..	1,798.5	1,709.8	1,959.3	..	..	..	Current Expenditure
-86.0	..	-92.1	-60.9	..	131.2	-113.0	..	..	..	..	Current Budget Balance
..	..	..	..	..	..	..	..	..	..	..	Capital Receipts
255.7	160.4	144.2	..	..	..	..	..	..	..	..	Capital Payments

HAITI	1969	1970	1971	1972	1973	1974	1975	1976	1977	1978	1979
FOREIGN TRADE (CUSTOMS BASIS)					*(Millions of current US dollars)*						
Value of Exports, fob	38.80	48.10	52.50	63.20	95.00	130.20	142.90	176.30	216.30	240.60	239.70
Nonfuel Primary Products	29.28	29.92	35.02	29.98	35.63	44.82	48.86	73.36	92.55	97.16	72.70
Fuels	0.00	0.00	0.00	0.00	0.00	0.00	0.00	0.00	0.00	0.00	0.00
Manufactures	9.52	18.18	17.48	33.22	59.37	85.38	94.04	102.94	123.75	143.44	167.00
Value of Imports, cif	45.30	59.00	66.20	84.80	112.70	165.60	196.30	246.10	286.90	311.40	367.80
Nonfuel Primary Products	12.57	12.08	16.16	18.74	22.39	32.10	47.05	70.63	65.88	67.37	71.34
Fuels	3.68	2.91	3.79	3.92	4.35	12.38	12.91	17.12	23.57	24.52	34.53
Manufactures	29.05	44.01	46.25	62.14	85.96	121.12	136.34	158.35	197.45	219.51	261.93
					(Index 1987 = 100)						
Terms of Trade	140.5	138.7	124.5	117.4	118.9	117.4	102.3	120.4	133.6	116.9	110.1
Export Prices, fob	33.7	37.1	36.2	37.8	47.1	62.0	59.9	72.0	84.9	83.2	90.6
Import Prices, cif	24.0	26.7	29.1	32.2	39.6	52.8	58.6	59.8	63.6	71.2	82.3
BALANCE OF PAYMENTS					*(Millions of current US dollars)*						
Exports of Goods & Services	..	53.00	..	..	52.92	59.24	67.70	129.44	175.40	213.26	215.54
Merchandise, fob	..	39.10	29.72	26.42	31.06	37.22	41.82	99.68	137.64	149.92	137.98
Nonfactor Services	..	13.80	18.80	21.02	21.62	21.78	25.58	28.76	36.44	61.30	74.94
Factor Services	..	0.10	..	..	0.24	0.24	0.30	1.00	1.32	2.04	2.62
Imports of Goods & Services	..	63.80	72.62	78.98	92.44	128.94	155.90	225.64	276.40	325.80	346.18
Merchandise, fob	..	41.90	47.22	51.76	58.52	87.32	111.70	164.20	199.92	207.46	220.06
Nonfactor Services	..	18.30	20.24	21.82	27.36	33.56	36.76	53.26	63.12	101.62	110.10
Factor Services	..	3.60	5.16	5.40	6.56	8.06	7.44	8.18	13.36	16.72	16.02
Long-Term Interest	..	0.40	0.30	0.30	0.50	0.50	1.20	1.50	3.80	4.50	3.50
Private Current Transfers, net	..	14.80	-2.80	1.40	-4.72	-5.72	-34.48	-37.88	30.92	28.72	34.10
Workers' Remittances	..	16.50	1.32	2.44	1.70	2.44	2.60	3.66	75.02	76.00	84.78
Curr. A/C Bal before Off. Transf.	..	4.00	-26.90	-30.14	-44.24	-75.42	-122.68	-134.08	-70.08	-83.82	-96.54
Net Official Transfers	..	7.10	5.74	7.48	8.76	11.20	13.44	31.92	32.58	39.18	41.76
Curr. A/C Bal after Off. Transf.	..	11.10	-21.16	-22.66	-35.48	-64.22	-109.24	-102.16	-37.50	-44.64	-54.78
Long-Term Capital, net	..	2.60	2.70	15.26	1.30	10.34	36.12	33.92	67.98	40.08	42.22
Direct Investment	..	2.80	3.40	4.06	6.98	7.94	2.64	7.78	8.00	10.00	12.00
Long-Term Loans	..	0.90	-1.20	1.10	-2.20	4.80	10.80	35.40	48.10	38.50	35.90
Disbursements	..	4.30	3.00	4.60	3.00	10.40	17.10	44.10	63.10	52.60	44.40
Repayments	..	3.40	4.20	3.50	5.20	5.60	6.30	8.70	15.00	14.10	8.50
Other Long-Term Capital	..	-1.10	0.50	10.10	-3.48	-2.40	22.68	-9.26	11.88	-8.42	-5.68
Other Capital, net	..	-12.47	26.52	15.57	34.29	43.00	60.17	79.35	-18.18	18.66	20.71
Change in Reserves	..	-1.23	-8.06	-8.17	-0.11	10.88	12.95	-11.11	-12.30	-14.10	-8.15
Memo Item:					*(Haitian Gourdes per US dollar)*						
Conversion Factor (Annual Avg)	5.000	5.000	5.000	5.000	5.000	5.000	5.000	5.000	5.000	5.000	5.000
				(Millions of US dollars), outstanding at end of year							
EXTERNAL DEBT (Total)	..	42.90	39.90	43.40	41.00	49.50	69.60	102.60	156.40	201.00	254.10
Long-Term Debt (by debtor)	..	42.90	39.90	43.40	41.00	49.50	69.60	102.60	148.40	195.00	235.10
Central Bank, incl. IMF credit	..	2.90	1.20	0.00	0.00	4.00	17.50	25.40	33.70	56.60	70.20
Central Government	..	35.90	35.10	36.80	34.00	32.10	38.70	53.30	88.50	111.00	132.00
Rest of General Government	..	..	..	..	..	..	..	..	..	..	..
Non-financial Public Enterprises	..	4.10	3.60	6.60	7.00	13.40	13.40	23.90	26.20	27.40	32.90
Priv. Sector, incl non-guaranteed	..	0.00	0.00	0.00	0.00	0.00	0.00	0.00	0.00	0.00	0.00
Short-Term Debt	..	0.00	0.00	0.00	0.00	0.00	0.00	0.00	8.00	6.00	19.00
Memo Items:					*(Thousands of US dollars)*						
Int'l Reserves Excluding Gold	3,500	4,300	10,387	17,882	17,032	19,700	12,430	27,941	33,844	38,638	55,015
Gold Holdings (at market price)	..	..	..	..	..	289	217	208	926	2,195	9,118
SOCIAL INDICATORS											
Total Fertility Rate	6.0	5.9	5.8	5.8	5.7	5.6	5.5	5.4	5.4	5.3	5.2
Infant Mortality Rate	165.2	161.8	158.4	155.0	151.8	148.6	145.4	142.2	139.0	136.8	134.6
Life Expectancy at Birth	47.1	47.6	48.0	48.5	48.9	49.4	49.8	50.2	50.7	51.1	51.5
Urban Population, % of total	19.4	19.8	20.3	20.7	21.2	21.6	22.1	22.6	23.1	23.6	24.1
Food Prod. per capita (1987=100)	103.7	104.0	105.0	106.1	105.0	105.7	104.1	105.1	98.7	103.6	105.1
Labor Force, Agriculture (%)	74.9	74.4	73.9	73.5	73.0	72.6	72.2	71.7	71.3	70.8	70.4
Labor Force, Female (%)	46.7	46.6	46.3	46.1	45.8	45.6	45.4	45.1	44.8	44.5	44.2
Primary Schl. Enroll. Ratio	..	..	53.0	..	..	..	60.0	61.0	60.0	60.0	64.0
Primary Schl. Enroll. Ratio, Female	..	..	..	..	..	..	..	..	55.0	55.0	59.0
Secondary Schl. Enroll. Ratio	..	..	6.0	..	..	..	8.0	10.0	11.0	12.0	12.0

1980	1981	1982	1983	1984	1985	1986	1987	1988	1989 estimate	NOTES	HAITI
				(Millions of current US dollars)							**FOREIGN TRADE (CUSTOMS BASIS)**
341.00	273.20	296.20	272.40	312.90	332.60	285.00	260.70	286.00	..	C f	Value of Exports, fob
141.30	74.70	74.80	72.90	69.40	67.10	72.70	48.80	75.75	..	..	Nonfuel Primary Products
0.00	0.00	0.10	2.70	0.00	0.00	0.00	0.00	0.00	..	..	Fuels
199.70	198.50	221.30	196.80	243.50	265.50	212.30	211.90	210.25	..	..	Manufactures
492.10	527.20	448.20	412.00	435.00	449.20	367.20	378.20	453.00	..	C f	Value of Imports, cif
74.60	93.90	100.60	123.40	128.09	127.03	114.44	120.50	72.50	..	..	Nonfuel Primary Products
61.40	64.70	55.60	61.30	61.41	63.87	50.76	42.00	37.10	..	..	Fuels
356.10	368.60	292.00	227.30	245.50	258.30	202.00	215.70	343.40	..	..	Manufactures
				(Index 1987 = 100)							
107.6	96.7	96.6	91.8	91.7	92.4	110.1	100.0	102.6	..	..	Terms of Trade
99.2	90.8	89.4	86.9	85.2	84.6	101.5	100.0	109.2	..	..	Export Prices, fob
92.2	93.9	92.6	94.6	93.0	91.6	92.3	100.0	106.4	..	..	Import Prices, cif
				(Millions of current US dollars)							**BALANCE OF PAYMENTS**
308.78	245.66	278.48	294.54	323.54	342.28	296.62	325.60	256.78	272.44	C	Exports of Goods & Services
215.80	151.12	177.14	186.56	214.58	223.00	190.78	210.12	156.06	181.32	..	Merchandise, fob
89.88	90.40	97.72	103.28	104.46	114.18	101.28	110.28	94.48	86.48	..	Nonfactor Services
3.10	4.14	3.62	4.70	4.50	5.10	4.56	5.20	6.24	4.64	..	Factor Services
498.36	533.80	488.75	516.07	549.56	581.97	493.42	527.82	514.30	..	C	Imports of Goods & Services
319.00	360.14	301.92	325.90	337.86	344.70	303.24	311.18	283.86	..	..	Merchandise, fob
161.96	156.46	169.14	171.32	189.10	212.38	170.24	190.52	197.12	188.84	..	Nonfactor Services
17.40	17.20	17.69	18.85	22.60	24.89	19.94	26.12	33.32	30.14	..	Factor Services
5.10	5.60	6.30	6.10	6.20	7.00	7.30	8.60	8.10	9.20	..	Long-Term Interest
52.10	64.78	49.70	46.40	45.00	48.54	52.02	56.24	63.42	59.34	..	Private Current Transfers, net
106.44	126.62	97.04	89.88	90.00	95.78	105.42	113.16	124.10	122.80	..	Workers' Remittances
-137.48	-223.36	-160.57	-175.13	-181.02	-191.15	-144.78	-145.98	-194.10	..	..	Curr. A/C Bal before Off. Transf.
36.64	74.56	62.00	64.00	78.00	96.50	99.84	114.82	129.46	..	..	Net Official Transfers
-100.84	-148.80	-98.57	-111.13	-103.02	-94.65	-44.94	-31.16	-64.64	..	..	Curr. A/C Bal after Off. Transf.
41.42	75.38	34.16	39.25	58.35	18.71	4.83	27.30	-5.17	14.52	C	Long-Term Capital, net
13.00	8.34	7.08	8.42	4.46	4.92	4.82	4.68	10.10	9.36	..	Direct Investment
31.80	101.60	57.50	34.50	48.60	55.50	32.40	75.80	35.00	14.30	..	Long-Term Loans
47.10	116.70	65.90	41.80	58.30	66.10	39.30	90.00	50.10	28.90	..	Disbursements
15.30	15.10	8.40	7.30	9.70	10.60	6.90	14.20	15.10	14.60	..	Repayments
-3.38	-34.56	-30.42	-3.67	5.29	-41.71	-32.39	-53.18	-50.27	-9.14	..	Other Long-Term Capital
30.23	35.25	44.69	42.94	23.51	78.52	60.42	5.19	90.95	..	C	Other Capital, net
29.19	38.17	19.73	28.94	21.17	-2.58	-20.31	-1.33	-21.13	-10.35	..	Change in Reserves
				(Haitian Gourdes per US dollar)							Memo Item:
5.000	5.000	5.000	5.000	5.000	5.000	5.000	5.000	5.000	5.000	..	Conversion Factor (Annual Avg)
			(Millions of US dollars), outstanding at end of year								
302.40	423.00	536.10	569.40	664.10	717.00	710.00	843.90	817.80	802.30	..	**EXTERNAL DEBT (Total)**
288.40	399.00	463.10	523.40	575.40	617.60	654.00	753.50	730.30	725.50	..	Long-Term Debt (by debtor)
99.70	122.90	148.00	186.10	204.80	211.80	196.50	201.30	172.60	170.80	..	Central Bank, incl. IMF credit
152.90	228.00	261.10	286.60	324.00	359.90	411.60	510.00	518.40	528.10	..	Central Government
..	..	..	..	..	..	..	..	..	..	..	Rest of General Government
28.40	41.10	48.50	45.80	42.40	41.10	40.00	38.60	36.30	26.60	..	Non-financial Public Enterprises
7.40	7.00	5.50	4.90	4.20	4.80	5.90	3.60	3.00	..	..	Priv. Sector, incl non-guaranteed
14.00	24.00	73.00	46.00	88.70	99.40	56.00	90.40	87.50	76.80	..	Short-Term Debt
				(Thousands of US dollars)							Memo Items:
16,226	24,047	4,225	8,968	12,978	6,388	15,879	16,999	12,994	12,597	..	Int'l Reserves Excluding Gold
10,498	7,079	8,136	6,794	5,490	5,823	6,961	8,621	7,364	7,232	..	Gold Holdings (at market price)
											SOCIAL INDICATORS
5.2	5.1	5.1	5.0	4.9	4.9	4.8	4.7	4.7	4.6	..	Total Fertility Rate
132.4	130.2	128.0	125.8	123.6	121.4	119.2	117.0	115.9	114.7	..	Infant Mortality Rate
51.9	52.3	52.7	53.1	53.5	53.9	54.3	54.7	55.0	55.2	..	Life Expectancy at Birth
24.6	25.1	25.6	26.2	26.7	27.2	27.8	28.4	29.1	29.7	..	Urban Population, % of total
100.9	99.8	98.5	100.8	101.3	102.5	101.9	100.0	94.3	91.0	..	Food Prod. per capita (1987=100)
70.0	..	..	..	..	..	..	..	..	..	..	Labor Force, Agriculture (%)
44.0	43.7	43.5	43.3	43.1	42.8	42.6	42.3	42.1	41.9	..	Labor Force, Female (%)
74.0	67.0	81.0	87.0	90.0	95.0	..	..	..	..	..	Primary Schl. Enroll. Ratio
68.0	63.0	76.0	82.0	84.0	89.0	..	..	..	..	..	Primary Schl. Enroll. Ratio, Female
13.0	12.0	15.0	17.0	19.0	17.0	..	..	..	..	..	Secondary Schl. Enroll. Ratio

HONDURAS	1969	1970	1971	1972	1973	1974	1975	1976	1977	1978	1979
CURRENT GNP PER CAPITA (US $)	260	270	280	290	310	340	360	400	460	530	600
POPULATION (thousands)	2,553	2,627	2,708	2,794	2,885	2,980	3,081	3,186	3,296	3,412	3,533
USE AND ORIGIN OF RESOURCES					*(Millions of current Honduran Lempiras)*						
Gross National Product (GNP)	1,298.8	1,400.8	1,413.0	1,551.0	1,759.0	2,042.0	2,190.0	2,580.0	3,201.0	3,627.0	4,184.0
Net Factor Income from Abroad	-37.2	-45.2	-49.0	-55.0	-66.0	-27.0	-58.0	-116.0	-138.0	-171.0	-241.0
GDP at Market Prices	1,336.0	1,446.0	1,462.0	1,606.0	1,825.0	2,069.0	2,248.0	2,696.0	3,339.0	3,798.0	4,425.0
Resource Balance	-38.6	-89.6	-12.0	17.0	-16.0	-247.0	-202.0	-120.0	-148.0	-175.0	-184.0
Exports of Goods & NFServices	373.8	403.6	434.0	470.0	588.0	665.0	690.0	909.0	1,163.0	1,380.0	1,679.0
Imports of Goods & NFServices	412.4	493.2	446.0	453.0	604.0	912.0	892.0	1,029.0	1,311.0	1,555.0	1,863.0
Domestic Absorption	1,374.6	1,535.6	1,474.0	1,589.0	1,841.0	2,316.0	2,450.0	2,816.0	3,487.0	3,973.0	4,609.0
Private Consumption, etc.	967.3	1,067.6	1,049.0	1,140.0	1,307.0	1,532.0	1,746.0	1,950.0	2,300.0	2,497.0	2,915.0
General Gov't Consumption	148.5	166.0	175.0	193.0	186.0	242.0	278.0	348.0	417.0	442.0	520.0
Gross Domestic Investment	258.8	302.0	250.0	256.0	348.0	542.0	426.0	518.0	770.0	1,034.0	1,174.0
Fixed Investment	244.5	268.0	253.0	245.0	325.0	433.0	476.0	550.0	711.0	941.0	1,004.0
Indirect Taxes, net	117.2	139.0	143.0	151.0	170.0	199.0	221.0	286.0	407.0	426.0	496.0
GDP at factor cost	1,218.8	1,307.0	1,319.0	1,455.0	1,655.0	1,870.0	2,027.0	2,410.0	2,932.0	3,372.0	3,929.0
Agriculture	437.2	424.0	413.0	450.0	511.0	550.0	554.0	688.0	898.0	945.0	1,038.0
Industry	268.1	290.0	299.0	329.0	397.0	474.0	505.0	560.0	679.0	836.0	978.0
Manufacturing	164.7	181.0	196.0	221.0	261.0	294.0	319.0	363.0	443.0	520.0	606.0
Services, etc.	513.5	593.0	607.0	676.0	747.0	846.0	968.0	1,162.0	1,355.0	1,591.0	1,913.0
Gross Domestic Saving	220.2	212.4	238.0	273.0	332.0	295.0	224.0	398.0	622.0	859.0	990.0
Gross National Saving	..	173.0	195.2	224.5	272.9	295.1	175.8	288.6	491.7	696.9	762.8
					(Millions of 1987 Honduran Lempiras)						
Gross National Product	3,868.1	3,994.7	4,140.4	4,387.9	4,726.0	4,855.9	4,915.7	5,311.9	5,842.9	6,305.3	6,677.3
GDP at Market Prices	3,982.9	4,134.7	4,294.0	4,548.7	4,907.7	4,863.5	4,986.3	5,508.4	6,084.2	6,591.8	7,007.6
Resource Balance	-246.4	-326.2	-21.3	35.8	-93.2	-378.6	-211.1	-351.2	-658.8	-619.3	-475.3
Exports of Goods & NFServices	1,037.8	1,129.4	1,278.6	1,281.0	1,411.4	1,271.6	1,321.0	1,335.1	1,331.5	1,621.8	1,902.7
Imports of Goods & NFServices	1,284.3	1,455.6	1,300.0	1,245.2	1,504.6	1,650.2	1,532.0	1,686.2	1,990.3	2,241.1	2,378.0
Domestic Absorption	4,229.3	4,460.9	4,315.3	4,512.9	5,000.8	5,242.1	5,197.3	5,859.6	6,743.0	7,211.1	7,482.9
Private Consumption, etc.	2,983.9	3,100.6	3,091.3	3,268.8	3,627.0	3,508.5	3,660.4	4,137.2	4,650.8	4,768.1	4,935.7
General Gov't Consumption	465.8	539.2	557.2	591.0	545.2	626.8	670.6	793.9	841.7	879.5	923.3
Gross Domestic Investment	779.6	821.0	666.8	653.2	828.6	1,106.8	866.4	928.4	1,250.4	1,563.4	1,623.9
Fixed Investment	737.2	722.3	662.7	621.0	768.4	871.2	948.6	971.0	1,139.2	1,401.3	1,370.1
GDP at factor cost	3,624.3	3,712.1	3,867.1	4,113.6	4,424.5	4,389.0	4,492.6	4,918.8	5,336.2	5,846.8	6,389.0
Agriculture	1,033.1	987.5	1,076.8	1,097.8	1,160.8	1,057.1	986.2	1,096.5	1,162.1	1,240.9	1,342.0
Industry	775.1	807.9	832.0	894.0	1,016.3	1,068.0	1,073.1	1,124.8	1,272.9	1,440.0	1,669.1
Manufacturing	398.6	470.2	501.3	553.7	624.2	627.4	652.0	697.9	792.9	851.9	907.6
Services, etc.	1,750.1	1,872.4	1,896.3	2,071.6	2,193.1	2,231.0	2,430.2	2,695.1	2,900.3	3,169.2	3,374.4
Memo Items:											
Capacity to Import	1,164.1	1,191.2	1,265.0	1,291.9	1,464.8	1,203.3	1,185.1	1,489.6	1,765.6	1,988.9	2,143.1
Terms of Trade Adjustment	126.2	61.8	-13.6	10.9	53.3	-68.3	-135.9	154.5	434.1	367.1	240.4
Gross Domestic Income	4,109.1	4,196.4	4,280.5	4,559.7	4,961.0	4,795.2	4,850.4	5,662.9	6,518.3	6,958.8	7,248.1
Gross National Income	3,994.3	4,056.5	4,126.8	4,398.8	4,779.3	4,787.5	4,779.9	5,466.5	6,277.0	6,672.4	6,917.8
DOMESTIC PRICES/DEFLATORS					*(Index 1987 = 100)*						
Overall (GDP)	33.5	35.0	34.0	35.3	37.2	42.5	45.1	48.9	54.9	57.6	63.1
Domestic Absorption	32.5	34.4	34.2	35.2	36.8	44.2	47.1	48.1	51.7	55.1	61.6
Agriculture	42.3	42.9	38.4	41.0	44.0	52.0	56.2	62.7	77.3	76.2	77.3
Industry	34.6	35.9	35.9	36.8	39.1	44.4	47.1	49.8	53.3	58.1	58.6
Manufacturing	41.3	38.5	39.1	39.9	41.8	46.9	48.9	52.0	55.9	61.0	66.8
Consumer Price Index	30.0	30.8	31.5	32.7	34.4	38.8	42.0	44.1	47.8	50.5	56.7
MANUFACTURING ACTIVITY											
Employment (1987=100)	..	..	..	..	..	..	..	..	..	..	..
Real Earnings per Empl. (1987=100)	..	..	..	..	..	..	..	..	..	..	..
Real Output per Empl. (1987=100)	..	..	..	..	..	..	..	..	..	..	..
Earnings as % of Value Added	35.3	..	37.5	36.9	37.3	38.0	37.5	..	..	..	..
MONETARY HOLDINGS					*(Millions of current Honduran Lempiras)*						
Money Supply, Broadly Defined	263.2	300.3	333.1	378.5	460.6	474.4	532.0	692.6	839.4	1,008.6	1,107.2
Money	148.1	158.9	169.4	192.9	238.4	242.4	262.7	361.0	411.3	480.4	545.6
Currency Outside Banks	73.4	76.8	80.2	90.1	112.2	108.8	114.8	173.3	193.2	215.4	270.1
Demand Deposits	74.7	82.1	89.2	102.8	126.2	133.6	147.9	187.7	218.1	265.0	275.5
Quasi-Money	115.1	141.4	163.7	185.6	222.2	232.0	269.3	331.6	428.1	528.2	561.6
GOVERNMENT DEFICIT (-) OR SURPLUS					*(Millions of current Honduran Lempiras)*						
	..	..	..	-44.70	-8.20	-18.40	-63.40	-64.00	..	..	..
Current Revenue	..	172.80	179.40	205.60	241.80	278.00	308.30	390.40	476.90	519.10	631.60
Current Expenditure	..	..	..	186.20	198.10	201.60	235.50	288.40	..	..	..
Current Budget Balance	..	..	..	19.40	43.70	76.40	72.80	102.00	..	..	..
Capital Receipts	..	..	..	1.00	0.10	0.10	1.30	..	..	..	..
Capital Payments	..	..	..	65.10	52.00	94.90	137.50	166.00	..	..	..

1980	1981	1982	1983	1984	1985	1986	1987	1988	1989 estimate	NOTES	HONDURAS
640	690	690	700	720	740	760	820	860	900	..	**CURRENT GNP PER CAPITA** (US $)
3,662	3,797	3,938	4,083	4,232	4,383	4,535	4,687	4,837	4,981	..	**POPULATION** (thousands)
				(Millions of current Honduran Lempiras)							**USE AND ORIGIN OF RESOURCES**
4,781.0	5,247.0	5,359.0	5,731.0	6,106.0	6,628.0	7,090.0	7,653.0	8,389.0	9,244.0	..	Gross National Product (GNP)
-307.0	-306.0	-403.0	-304.0	-356.0	-380.0	-506.0	-475.0	-524.0	-526.0	..	Net Factor Income from Abroad
5,088.0	5,553.0	5,762.0	6,035.0	6,462.0	7,008.0	7,596.0	8,128.0	8,913.0	9,770.0	..	GDP at Market Prices
-370.0	-354.0	-105.0	-223.0	-437.0	-319.0	-105.0	-237.0	-205.0	-162.0	..	Resource Balance
1,886.0	1,771.0	1,537.0	1,606.0	1,699.0	1,811.0	2,022.0	1,945.0	2,037.0	2,189.0	..	Exports of Goods & NFServices
2,256.0	2,125.0	1,642.0	1,829.0	2,136.0	2,130.0	2,127.0	2,182.0	2,242.0	2,351.0	..	Imports of Goods & NFServices
5,458.0	5,907.0	5,867.0	6,258.0	6,899.0	7,327.0	7,701.0	8,365.0	9,118.0	9,932.0	..	Domestic Absorption
3,532.0	3,998.0	4,291.0	4,484.0	4,716.0	5,017.0	5,329.0	5,798.0	6,484.0	7,112.0	..	Private Consumption, etc.
678.0	758.0	800.0	877.0	952.0	1,046.0	1,297.0	1,371.0	1,468.0	1,562.0	..	General Gov't Consumption
1,248.0	1,151.0	776.0	897.0	1,231.0	1,264.0	1,075.0	1,196.0	1,166.0	1,258.0	..	Gross Domestic Investment
1,235.0	1,051.0	966.0	1,073.0	1,246.0	1,252.0	1,088.0	1,035.0	1,141.0	1,278.0	..	Fixed Investment
539.0	597.0	577.0	616.0	705.0	842.0	829.0	945.0	1,016.0	1,129.0	..	Indirect Taxes, net
4,549.0	4,956.0	5,185.0	5,419.0	5,757.0	6,166.0	6,767.0	7,183.0	7,897.0	8,641.0	..	GDP at factor cost
1,132.0	1,166.0	1,186.0	1,226.0	1,253.0	1,328.0	1,495.0	1,518.0	1,630.0	1,779.0	..	Agriculture
1,143.0	1,180.0	1,335.0	1,392.0	1,502.0	1,540.0	1,658.0	1,707.0	1,930.0	2,172.0	..	Industry
687.0	726.0	766.0	832.0	913.0	926.0	962.0	1,055.0	1,230.0	1,390.0	..	Manufacturing
2,274.0	2,610.0	2,664.0	2,801.0	3,002.0	3,298.0	3,614.0	3,958.0	4,337.0	4,690.0	..	Services, etc.
878.0	797.0	671.0	674.0	794.0	945.0	970.0	959.0	961.0	1,096.0	..	Gross Domestic Saving
586.0	508.8	286.0	389.4	458.6	589.8	490.0	516.0	472.0	602.0	..	Gross National Saving
				(Millions of 1987 Honduran Lempiras)							
6,721.0	6,889.2	6,604.7	6,709.8	6,874.4	7,088.9	7,165.9	7,653.0	7,993.8	8,180.6	..	Gross National Product
7,101.6	7,209.6	7,064.2	7,046.2	7,238.5	7,499.2	7,716.7	8,128.0	8,533.5	8,712.9	..	GDP at Market Prices
-660.2	-319.3	62.8	-61.7	-342.2	-302.6	-185.5	-237.0	-199.6	-116.9	..	Resource Balance
1,802.8	1,843.9	1,626.5	1,781.6	1,811.0	1,859.2	1,940.3	1,945.0	2,015.5	2,108.4	..	Exports of Goods & NFServices
2,463.0	2,163.3	1,563.7	1,843.3	2,153.2	2,161.8	2,125.8	2,182.0	2,215.1	2,225.2	..	Imports of Goods & NFServices
7,761.8	7,528.9	7,001.4	7,107.9	7,580.7	7,801.8	7,902.2	8,365.0	8,733.1	8,829.8	..	Domestic Absorption
5,199.3	5,191.9	5,219.9	5,149.6	5,199.1	5,373.6	5,460.1	5,798.0	6,169.4	6,229.6	..	Private Consumption, etc.
1,018.8	1,042.7	1,008.8	1,020.8	1,058.6	1,114.3	1,329.2	1,371.0	1,426.7	1,452.6	..	General Gov't Consumption
1,543.8	1,294.3	772.6	937.4	1,323.0	1,313.9	1,112.8	1,196.0	1,137.0	1,147.6	..	Gross Domestic Investment
1,505.6	1,163.1	960.5	1,100.5	1,317.9	1,282.2	1,108.0	1,035.0	1,099.0	1,146.7	..	Fixed Investment
6,344.0	6,427.6	6,350.1	6,320.0	6,442.3	6,591.0	6,859.2	7,183.0	7,560.5	7,720.6	..	GDP at factor cost
1,331.5	1,382.7	1,374.9	1,365.7	1,382.7	1,423.5	1,457.6	1,518.0	1,545.6	1,567.9	..	Agriculture
1,557.1	1,424.5	1,496.9	1,526.1	1,617.4	1,601.9	1,684.6	1,707.0	1,825.9	1,899.9	..	Industry
881.4	860.1	828.9	873.2	946.9	930.5	958.3	1,055.0	1,143.5	1,176.2	..	Manufacturing
3,464.0	3,637.3	3,481.9	3,428.1	3,442.1	3,565.6	3,717.0	3,958.0	4,189.1	4,252.8	..	Services, etc.
											Memo Items:
2,059.1	1,802.9	1,463.7	1,618.6	1,712.7	1,838.1	2,020.9	1,945.0	2,012.6	2,071.9	..	Capacity to Import
256.3	-41.0	-162.8	-163.1	-98.4	-21.2	80.6	0.0	-2.9	-36.5	..	Terms of Trade Adjustment
7,357.9	7,168.5	6,901.4	6,883.1	7,140.2	7,478.1	7,797.2	8,128.0	8,530.6	8,676.4	..	Gross Domestic Income
6,977.2	6,848.2	6,441.9	6,546.7	6,776.0	7,067.8	7,246.5	7,653.0	7,990.9	8,144.1	..	Gross National Income
				(Index 1987 = 100)							**DOMESTIC PRICES/DEFLATORS**
71.6	77.0	81.6	85.6	89.3	93.4	98.4	100.0	104.4	112.1	..	Overall (GDP)
70.3	78.5	83.8	88.0	91.0	93.9	97.5	100.0	104.4	112.5	..	Domestic Absorption
85.0	84.3	86.3	89.8	90.6	93.3	102.6	100.0	105.5	113.5	..	Agriculture
73.4	82.8	89.2	91.2	92.9	96.1	98.4	100.0	105.7	114.3	..	Industry
77.9	84.4	92.4	95.3	96.4	99.5	100.4	100.0	107.6	118.2	..	Manufacturing
66.9	73.2	79.8	86.4	90.5	93.5	97.6	100.0	104.5	114.8	..	Consumer Price Index
											MANUFACTURING ACTIVITY
..	..	..	..	..	..	..	..	..	..	G	Employment (1987 = 100)
..	..	..	..	..	..	..	..	..	..	G	Real Earnings per Empl. (1987 = 100)
..	..	..	..	..	..	..	..	..	..	G	Real Output per Empl. (1987 = 100)
..	..	..	..	..	..	..	..	..	..	..	Earnings as % of Value Added
				(Millions of current Honduran Lempiras)							**MONETARY HOLDINGS**
1,212.3	1,320.9	1,579.2	1,851.7	2,056.4	2,009.5	2,203.0	2,707.7	3,085.3	3,513.8	D	Money Supply, Broadly Defined
610.3	637.4	716.9	814.9	846.0	855.6	955.3	1,119.1	1,252.6	1,523.7	..	Money
274.6	302.2	313.6	361.9	383.5	410.2	425.8	491.5	570.3	676.0	..	Currency Outside Banks
335.7	335.2	403.3	453.0	462.5	445.4	529.5	627.6	682.3	847.7	..	Demand Deposits
602.0	683.5	862.3	1,036.8	1,210.4	1,153.9	1,247.7	1,588.6	1,832.7	1,990.1	..	Quasi-Money
				(Millions of current Honduran Lempiras)							
..		..	..	..	..	..	..	..	..	F	**GOVERNMENT DEFICIT (-) OR SURPLUS**
748.20	741.20								..	..	Current Revenue
..	..	..	..	..	..	..	..	..	..	..	Current Expenditure
..	..	..	..	..	..	..	..	..	..	..	Current Budget Balance
..	..	..	..	..	..	..	..	..	..	..	Capital Receipts
..	..	..	..	..	..	..	..	..	..	..	Capital Payments

HONDURAS	1969	1970	1971	1972	1973	1974	1975	1976	1977	1978	1979
FOREIGN TRADE (CUSTOMS BASIS)					*(Millions of current US dollars)*						
Value of Exports, fob	165.8	169.7	182.8	193.1	246.8	253.3	293.3	391.8	510.7	601.8	720.9
Nonfuel Primary Products	147.3	149.8	174.8	183.5	228.6	211.0	249.5	351.9	461.0	541.2	640.0
Fuels	4.8	6.3	3.0	3.4	4.1	14.5	12.3	1.1	0.6	0.5	0.3
Manufactures	13.8	13.7	5.1	6.2	14.0	27.8	31.5	38.8	49.0	60.1	80.6
Value of Imports, cif	184.3	220.7	193.4	192.8	262.2	380.1	404.3	453.1	579.4	699.2	825.8
Nonfuel Primary Products	23.3	28.4	21.3	24.2	30.1	46.2	60.4	56.6	64.9	79.2	84.7
Fuels	12.8	14.7	17.4	19.2	26.1	63.4	68.5	48.2	69.3	76.0	106.8
Manufactures	148.2	177.5	154.6	149.4	206.1	270.5	275.3	348.3	445.2	544.0	634.3
					(Index 1987 = 100)						
Terms of Trade	148.4	148.4	148.2	152.7	154.6	125.0	116.3	144.7	158.3	133.2	135.8
Export Prices, fob	34.8	36.6	38.3	42.9	53.7	64.4	65.5	80.5	95.8	91.0	108.2
Import Prices, cif	23.4	24.7	25.8	28.1	34.7	51.6	56.3	55.6	60.5	68.3	79.6
BALANCE OF PAYMENTS					*(Millions of current US dollars)*						
Exports of Goods & Services	..	198.8	217.7	237.4	297.6	336.8	350.9	463.4	593.9	706.5	859.2
Merchandise, fob	..	178.2	194.6	212.1	266.6	300.3	309.6	411.7	529.9	626.1	756.5
Nonfactor Services	..	18.3	20.9	22.8	27.1	31.5	34.7	42.0	50.8	61.3	81.5
Factor Services	..	2.3	2.3	2.5	3.9	4.9	6.5	9.6	13.2	19.1	21.2
Imports of Goods & Services	..	269.2	247.2	256.7	339.0	474.6	480.6	581.3	736.6	881.0	1,071.8
Merchandise, fob	..	203.4	178.0	176.5	243.4	387.5	372.3	432.5	550.1	654.5	783.5
Nonfactor Services	..	40.9	42.1	50.3	58.5	67.8	73.2	81.5	104.6	122.1	147.0
Factor Services	..	24.9	27.1	29.9	37.1	19.3	35.1	67.4	81.9	104.3	141.3
Long-Term Interest	..	3.5	5.0	6.4	9.7	12.1	16.2	21.8	30.6	43.3	60.0
Private Current Transfers, net	..	2.9	3.1	3.3	3.5	13.5	4.9	3.3	3.8	4.4	6.9
Workers' Remittances	..	..	..	..	..	..	..	..	..	..	..
Curr. A/C Bal before Off. Transf.	..	-67.5	-26.4	-16.0	-38.0	-122.9	-124.9	-114.7	-138.9	-170.0	-205.6
Net Official Transfers	..	3.7	3.7	3.3	3.5	19.0	12.8	9.9	10.3	12.8	13.5
Curr. A/C Bal after Off. Transf.	..	-63.8	-22.7	-12.7	-34.6	-103.9	-112.1	-104.8	-128.7	-157.2	-192.1
Long-Term Capital, net	..	40.1	35.3	23.5	32.3	63.3	131.5	103.7	148.8	175.5	170.1
Direct Investment	..	8.4	7.3	3.0	6.6	-1.1	7.0	5.3	8.9	13.1	28.2
Long-Term Loans	..	32.2	29.2	24.5	4.2	67.7	98.7	98.4	139.7	161.7	149.7
Disbursements	..	38.5	37.7	37.6	21.0	89.2	127.5	135.8	199.7	236.2	268.8
Repayments	..	6.3	8.5	13.1	16.8	21.5	28.8	37.4	60.0	74.5	119.1
Other Long-Term Capital	..	-0.5	-1.2	-4.1	21.5	-3.3	25.8	0.0	0.1	0.7	-7.8
Other Capital, net	..	11.3	-13.6	1.0	10.8	23.7	34.5	38.9	46.4	-8.7	42.1
Change in Reserves	..	12.3	0.9	-11.8	-8.6	17.0	-53.9	-37.9	-66.5	-9.6	-20.1
Memo Item:					*(Honduran Lempiras per US dollar)*						
Conversion Factor (Annual Avg)	2.000	2.000	2.000	2.000	2.000	2.000	2.000	2.000	2.000	2.000	2.000
				(Millions of US dollars), outstanding at end of year							
EXTERNAL DEBT (Total)	..	109.4	138.5	163.9	196.0	281.0	379.5	478.1	752.4	932.7	1,182.1
Long-Term Debt (by debtor)	..	109.4	138.5	163.9	196.0	281.0	379.5	478.1	603.4	759.7	918.1
Central Bank, incl. IMF credit	..	7.2	6.5	5.9	6.7	27.1	52.9	69.6	55.9	56.5	76.2
Central Government	..	67.0	79.0	94.7	105.0	126.6	177.7	209.0	262.4	346.7	422.9
Rest of General Government	..	0.0	0.0	0.0	0.0	0.0	0.3	3.7	4.6	6.8	6.8
Non-financial Public Enterprises	..	16.0	16.7	18.7	21.9	38.1	51.3	72.2	115.6	146.7	191.6
Priv. Sector, incl non-guaranteed	..	19.2	36.3	44.6	62.4	89.2	97.3	123.6	164.9	203.0	220.6
Short-Term Debt	..	0.0	0.0	0.0	0.0	0.0	0.0	0.0	149.0	173.0	264.0
Memo Items:					*(Thousands of US dollars)*						
Int'l Reserves Excluding Gold	30,810	20,130	21,774	35,087	41,656	44,302	96,969	130,830	179,772	184,436	209,170
Gold Holdings (at market price)	120	116	135	201	348	578	435	418	2,276	3,119	7,066
SOCIAL INDICATORS											
Total Fertility Rate	7.4	7.4	7.4	7.4	7.2	7.1	6.9	6.7	6.6	6.5	6.4
Infant Mortality Rate	117.8	115.2	112.6	110.0	107.0	104.0	101.0	98.0	95.0	92.4	89.8
Life Expectancy at Birth	52.1	52.7	53.3	54.0	54.7	55.4	56.2	56.9	57.7	58.5	59.4
Urban Population, % of total	28.3	28.9	29.6	30.3	30.9	31.6	32.3	33.0	33.7	34.5	35.2
Food Prod. per capita (1987=100)	123.5	121.0	126.1	128.4	120.9	110.5	99.1	105.4	110.6	115.4	106.1
Labor Force, Agriculture (%)	65.4	64.9	64.4	64.0	63.5	63.1	62.7	62.2	61.7	61.3	60.9
Labor Force, Female (%)	14.0	14.2	14.4	14.5	14.7	14.8	14.9	15.1	15.3	15.4	15.6
Primary Schl. Enroll. Ratio	..	87.0	..	..	..	..	88.0	88.0	..	89.0	89.0
Primary Schl. Enroll. Ratio, Female	..	87.0	..	..	..	..	86.0	88.0	..	89.0	85.0
Secondary Schl. Enroll. Ratio	..	14.0	..	..	..	..	16.0	17.0	19.0	23.0	..

1980	1981	1982	1983	1984	1985	1986	1987	1988	1989 estimate	NOTES	HONDURAS
				(Millions of current US dollars)							**FOREIGN TRADE (CUSTOMS BASIS)**
813.4	712.5	655.7	671.8	725.4	764.6	854.2	826.7	919.0	..	..	Value of Exports, fob
707.9	626.9	597.5	606.4	646.9	675.8	757.5	721.0	808.4	..	..	Nonfuel Primary Products
3.8	2.4	0.6	4.2	4.8	5.4	4.5	5.6	5.5	..	..	Fuels
101.7	83.2	57.6	61.2	73.7	83.4	92.3	100.1	105.1	..	..	Manufactures
1,008.7	944.9	689.9	823.0	893.4	888.1	875.0	895.0	868.0	..	..	Value of Imports, cif
119.6	114.5	79.6	96.4	94.5	90.2	63.9	58.1	86.5	..	..	Nonfuel Primary Products
160.7	149.4	150.3	184.1	154.9	134.0	91.0	126.2	132.7	..	..	Fuels
728.4	681.0	460.0	542.4	644.0	663.9	720.0	710.7	648.8	..	..	Manufactures
				(Index 1987 = 100)							
123.3	113.4	110.5	115.9	116.8	115.9	122.3	100.0	114.0	..	..	Terms of Trade
113.7	106.1	104.2	106.7	101.6	99.4	110.2	100.0	117.4	..	..	Export Prices, fob
92.2	93.5	94.3	92.1	87.0	85.8	90.1	100.0	103.0	..	..	Import Prices, cif
				(Millions of current US dollars)							**BALANCE OF PAYMENTS**
967.5	903.2	783.5	815.0	863.2	918.2	1,022.1	981.9	1,028.8	1,105.4	f	Exports of Goods & Services
850.2	783.8	676.5	698.7	737.0	789.6	891.2	844.3	893.0	966.7	..	Merchandise, fob
91.3	99.8	90.4	102.3	110.3	113.8	117.8	125.5	123.6	125.8	..	Nonfactor Services
25.8	19.6	16.5	13.9	15.8	14.8	13.1	12.0	12.1	12.9	..	Factor Services
1,305.8	1,233.4	1,041.8	1,078.7	1,259.6	1,267.9	1,327.7	1,338.0	1,392.7	1,452.0	f	Imports of Goods & Services
954.1	898.6	680.7	756.3	884.8	879.2	874.1	893.9	916.6	964.0	..	Merchandise, fob
172.5	162.0	142.3	156.1	181.2	183.5	187.4	193.8	201.8	208.7	..	Nonfactor Services
179.1	172.8	218.8	166.3	193.6	205.2	266.2	250.3	274.2	279.3	..	Factor Services
83.0	95.9	111.6	96.6	88.1	100.8	114.0	93.6	128.7	45.7	..	Long-Term Interest
7.5	8.9	9.0	9.7	10.3	12.4	13.0	16.0	17.5	16.0	..	Private Current Transfers, net
..	..	..	..	..	..	..	..	..	..	..	Workers' Remittances
-330.8	-321.3	-249.3	-254.0	-386.2	-337.3	-292.5	-340.1	-346.5	-330.7	..	Curr. A/C Bal before Off. Transf.
14.0	18.6	21.0	34.8	69.7	133.2	145.3	115.3	117.5	56.0	..	Net Official Transfers
-316.8	-302.7	-228.3	-219.2	-316.5	-204.1	-147.2	-224.8	-229.0	-274.6	..	Curr. A/C Bal after Off. Transf.
257.7	222.0	134.0	147.7	261.5	219.8	31.0	78.6	66.8	7.2	f	Long-Term Capital, net
5.8	-3.6	13.8	21.0	20.4	27.5	30.0	38.8	46.8	37.3	..	Direct Investment
258.0	233.0	163.8	170.5	186.1	265.3	111.5	81.0	131.2	77.3	..	Long-Term Loans
345.2	330.3	256.2	253.7	269.6	347.5	216.7	250.3	307.2	152.9	..	Disbursements
87.2	97.3	92.4	83.2	83.5	82.2	105.2	169.3	176.0	75.6	..	Repayments
-6.1	-7.4	-43.5	-43.8	54.9	-73.0	-110.5	-41.2	-111.2	-107.5	..	Other Long-Term Capital
-18.7	6.9	10.0	28.1	39.9	-33.0	146.0	223.7	183.2	222.3	f	Other Capital, net
77.8	73.8	84.2	43.4	15.0	17.4	-29.8	-77.4	-21.1	45.1	..	Change in Reserves
				(Honduran Lempiras per US dollar)							Memo Item:
2.000	2.000	2.000	2.000	2.000	2.000	2.000	2.000	2.000	2.000	..	Conversion Factor (Annual Avg)
				(Millions of US dollars), outstanding at end of year							
1,470.2	1,702.7	1,841.9	2,125.5	2,284.3	2,731.5	2,973.8	3,302.1	3,303.7	3,349.6	..	**EXTERNAL DEBT (Total)**
1,198.0	1,461.2	1,690.2	1,983.7	2,085.5	2,428.6	2,612.8	2,892.8	2,891.4	2,942.6	..	Long-Term Debt (by debtor)
83.6	134.9	208.0	254.2	227.9	271.8	241.5	205.3	193.3	267.2	..	Central Bank, incl. IMF credit
564.9	670.0	821.5	986.3	1,141.0	1,370.9	1,556.2	1,833.8	1,945.6	1,989.5	..	Central Government
6.8	6.8	6.1	5.3	5.0	4.2	3.8	3.2	3.1	1.9	..	Rest of General Government
205.7	294.9	317.9	375.6	385.6	471.0	524.1	582.1	504.7	468.1	..	Non-financial Public Enterprises
337.0	354.6	336.7	362.3	326.0	310.7	287.2	268.4	244.7	215.9	..	Priv. Sector, incl non-guaranteed
272.2	241.5	151.7	141.8	198.8	302.9	361.0	409.3	412.3	407.0	..	Short-Term Debt
				(Thousands of US dollars)							Memo Items:
149,826	101,018	112,228	113,617	128,157	105,800	111,300	106,000	50,000	21,100	..	Int'l Reserves Excluding Gold
9,432	6,360	7,310	6,104	4,933	5,232	6,254	7,746	6,564	6,416	..	Gold Holdings (at market price)
											SOCIAL INDICATORS
6.3	6.2	6.2	6.0	5.9	5.8	5.7	5.6	5.5	5.4	..	Total Fertility Rate
87.2	84.6	82.0	79.4	76.8	74.2	71.6	69.0	67.7	66.4	..	Infant Mortality Rate
60.2	61.1	61.9	62.3	62.8	63.2	63.6	64.0	64.2	64.5	..	Life Expectancy at Birth
35.9	36.7	37.4	38.2	38.9	39.7	40.5	41.3	42.0	42.8	..	Urban Population, % of total
114.3	119.3	110.5	100.7	100.2	97.4	95.1	100.0	99.0	100.2	..	Food Prod. per capita (1987=100)
60.5	..	..	..	..	..	..	..	..	..	..	Labor Force, Agriculture (%)
15.7	16.1	16.4	16.7	17.0	17.3	17.6	18.0	18.3	18.6	..	Labor Force, Female (%)
93.0	..	99.0	101.0	100.0	102.0	106.0	..	..	..	..	Primary Schl. Enroll. Ratio
94.0	..	98.0	100.0	101.0	103.0	108.0	..	..	..	..	Primary Schl. Enroll. Ratio, Female
30.0	..	32.0	33.0	32.0	35.0	32.0	..	..	..	..	Secondary Schl. Enroll. Ratio

HONG KONG	1969	1970	1971	1972	1973	1974	1975	1976	1977	1978	1979
CURRENT GNP PER CAPITA (US $)	790	900	1,020	1,220	1,570	1,900	2,180	2,700	3,200	3,750	4,260
POPULATION (thousands)	3,922	3,942	4,012	4,089	4,173	4,263	4,360	4,443	4,510	4,597	4,979
USE AND ORIGIN OF RESOURCES					*(Billions of current Hong Kong Dollars)*						
Gross National Product (GNP)	..	..	..	..	..	..	..	..	..	..	..
Net Factor Income from Abroad	..	..	..	..	..	..	..	..	..	..	..
GDP at Market Prices	18.38	21.88	25.18	30.38	39.10	44.58	46.46	59.34	68.90	81.16	107.05
Resource Balance	0.86	0.78	-0.06	1.17	0.96	0.32	0.48	4.05	1.60	-2.90	-3.12
Exports of Goods & NFServices	17.45	20.33	22.42	25.48	33.29	38.52	38.51	53.16	57.11	68.64	95.19
Imports of Goods & NFServices	16.58	19.55	22.48	24.31	32.33	38.21	38.02	49.11	55.51	71.54	98.31
Domestic Absorption	17.52	21.10	25.24	29.21	38.14	44.26	45.98	55.29	67.31	84.06	110.16
Private Consumption, etc.	12.95	14.78	17.04	19.62	26.18	29.74	31.20	35.36	43.33	54.16	66.89
General Gov't Consumption	1.41	1.64	1.74	2.11	2.59	3.20	3.53	4.03	4.72	5.55	6.83
Gross Domestic Investment	3.16	4.68	6.45	7.48	9.38	11.33	11.26	15.91	19.26	24.35	36.44
Fixed Investment	3.02	4.51	6.26	7.25	9.08	10.65	10.53	12.93	17.56	22.29	33.19
Indirect Taxes, net	0.95	1.06	1.18	1.50	1.69	1.59	1.92	2.42	2.86	3.52	4.06
GDP at factor cost	17.43	20.82	23.99	28.88	37.41	42.99	44.54	56.91	66.04	77.64	102.99
Agriculture	0.36	0.38	0.41	0.44	0.53	0.54	0.53	0.64	0.72	0.86	0.99
Industry	6.55	7.56	8.55	9.98	12.07	12.51	13.39	17.36	20.11	24.31	32.33
Manufacturing	5.25	6.14	6.70	7.73	9.37	9.44	10.34	13.70	15.65	18.33	24.72
Services, etc.	10.52	12.89	15.04	18.46	24.81	29.94	30.62	38.91	45.21	52.47	69.67
Gross Domestic Saving	4.02	5.46	6.39	8.65	10.34	11.64	11.74	19.95	20.86	21.46	33.33
Gross National Saving	..	..	..	..	..	..	..	..	..	..	..
					(Billions of 1987 Hong Kong Dollars)						
Gross National Product	..	..	..	..	..	..	..	..	..	..	..
GDP at Market Prices	82.16	89.89	96.45	107.06	120.65	123.31	123.55	144.68	162.77	178.22	199.01
Resource Balance	7.09	6.70	1.07	4.31	4.94	7.88	5.19	10.09	6.41	-2.11	-2.31
Exports of Goods & NFServices	68.29	75.52	78.72	85.59	94.71	90.78	91.22	116.87	121.35	136.99	161.63
Imports of Goods & NFServices	61.20	68.82	77.65	81.29	89.77	82.90	86.03	106.79	114.93	139.10	163.94
Domestic Absorption	75.07	83.18	95.38	102.75	115.71	115.43	118.36	134.60	156.36	180.33	201.33
Private Consumption, etc.	48.18	53.08	59.91	64.23	72.91	71.55	73.56	79.22	93.23	110.62	120.99
General Gov't Consumption	7.20	7.66	7.79	8.42	9.23	10.06	10.69	11.39	12.54	13.91	15.22
Gross Domestic Investment	19.69	22.45	27.68	30.10	33.57	33.82	34.10	43.99	50.59	55.80	65.12
Fixed Investment	19.02	21.71	26.89	29.22	32.58	32.11	32.74	37.31	46.95	51.62	59.39
GDP at factor cost	77.94	85.53	91.98	101.73	115.38	118.92	118.53	138.84	156.14	170.53	191.46
Agriculture	..	..	..	..	..	..	..	..	..	..	..
Industry	..	..	..	..	..	..	..	..	..	..	..
Manufacturing	..	..	..	..	..	..	..	..	..	..	..
Services, etc.	..	..	..	..	..	..	..	..	..	..	..
Memo Items:											
Capacity to Import	64.37	71.56	77.45	85.19	92.44	83.59	87.12	115.59	118.25	133.47	158.75
Terms of Trade Adjustment	-3.92	-3.96	-1.27	-0.40	-2.28	-7.20	-4.10	-1.29	-3.10	-3.52	-2.88
Gross Domestic Income	78.25	85.92	95.17	106.66	118.38	116.11	119.46	143.39	159.67	174.70	196.13
Gross National Income	78.25	85.92	95.17	106.66	118.38	116.11	119.46	143.39	159.67	174.70	196.13
DOMESTIC PRICES/DEFLATORS					*(Index 1987 = 100)*						
Overall (GDP)	22.4	24.3	26.1	28.4	32.4	36.2	37.6	41.0	42.3	45.5	53.8
Domestic Absorption	23.3	25.4	26.5	28.4	33.0	38.3	38.8	41.1	43.0	46.6	54.7
Agriculture	..	..	..	..	..	..	..	..	..	..	..
Industry	..	..	..	..	..	..	..	..	..	..	..
Manufacturing	..	..	..	..	..	..	..	..	..	..	..
Consumer Price Index	24.4	26.1	27.0	28.7	33.9	38.8	39.9	41.4	43.7	46.2	51.6
MANUFACTURING ACTIVITY											
Employment (1987=100)	55.5	58.2	59.8	61.3	69.2	64.3	73.3	85.6	83.9	84.2	94.4
Real Earnings per Empl. (1987=100)	..	..	..	..	56.6	51.4	53.0	57.8	62.0	77.4	77.8
Real Output per Empl. (1987=100)	..	..	..	..	..	..	..	..	..	..	..
Earnings as % of Value Added	..	..	..	..	53.2	53.5	52.5	51.3	53.2	55.6	51.3
MONETARY HOLDINGS					*(Billions of current Hong Kong Dollars)*						
Money Supply, Broadly Defined	..	..	..	..	..	..	..	..	..	70.15	79.73
Money	..	..	..	..	..	..	..	..	..	20.11	20.85
Currency Outside Banks	..	..	..	..	..	..	..	..	..	..	..
Demand Deposits	..	..	..	..	..	..	..	..	..	..	..
Quasi-Money	..	..	..	..	..	..	..	..	..	50.04	58.88
					(Millions of current Hong Kong Dollars)						
GOVERNMENT DEFICIT (-) OR SURPLUS	..	..	..	..	..	..	..	..	..	..	..
Current Revenue	..	..	..	..	..	..	..	..	..	..	..
Current Expenditure	..	..	..	..	..	..	..	..	..	..	..
Current Budget Balance	..	..	..	..	..	..	..	..	..	..	..
Capital Receipts	..	..	..	..	..	..	..	..	..	..	..
Capital Payments	..	..	..	..	..	..	..	..	..	..	..

1980	1981	1982	1983	1984	1985	1986	1987	1988	1989 estimate	NOTES	HONG KONG
5,210	6,080	6,330	6,140	6,330	6,080	6,900	8,190	9,250	10,320	f	**CURRENT GNP PER CAPITA (US $)**
5,039	5,120	5,202	5,285	5,370	5,456	5,533	5,613	5,681	5,735	..	**POPULATION (thousands)**
				(Billions of current Hong Kong Dollars)							**USE AND ORIGIN OF RESOURCES**
..	..	..	..	..	..	..	..	..	..	..	Gross National Product (GNP)
..	..	..	..	..	..	..	..	..	..	..	Net Factor Income from Abroad
137.08	164.97	186.33	207.56	248.73	261.19	300.82	369.27	431.61	491.59	f	GDP at Market Prices
-6.30	-9.24	-6.77	-4.18	10.45	14.84	14.05	22.72	22.11	38.83	..	Resource Balance
120.40	149.32	157.99	197.62	265.29	281.00	330.82	448.87	578.48	665.65	..	Exports of Goods & NFServices
126.71	158.56	164.76	201.81	254.84	266.16	316.77	426.14	556.37	626.81	..	Imports of Goods & NFServices
143.38	174.22	193.10	211.75	238.28	246.36	286.77	346.55	409.50	452.76	..	Domestic Absorption
85.26	102.45	118.93	138.83	158.60	169.86	191.68	221.76	257.01	285.00	..	Private Consumption, etc.
8.83	12.40	14.91	16.72	18.29	19.92	22.97	25.78	30.01	36.27	..	General Gov't Consumption
49.29	59.36	59.26	56.20	61.38	56.58	72.12	99.02	122.48	131.49	..	Gross Domestic Investment
45.55	55.41	57.86	51.87	55.58	55.12	65.94	89.27	112.94	129.83	..	Fixed Investment
5.20	6.12	6.23	8.10	9.89	12.33	14.75	18.65	21.45	..	..	Indirect Taxes, net
131.88	158.86	180.10	199.46	238.83	248.86	286.07	350.63	410.15	..	f	GDP at factor cost
1.11	1.12	1.23	1.24	1.27	1.24	1.33	1.36	1.44	..	..	Agriculture
41.04	50.45	52.84	61.47	73.74	72.16	85.07	102.11	114.95	..	..	Industry
30.55	36.05	36.39	44.14	55.54	53.07	62.78	75.76	84.15	..	..	Manufacturing
89.74	107.28	126.02	136.75	163.82	175.47	199.67	247.16	293.76	..	..	Services, etc.
42.99	50.12	52.49	52.01	71.83	71.42	86.17	121.74	144.59	170.32	..	Gross Domestic Saving
..	..	..	..	..	..	..	..	..	..	..	Gross National Saving
				(Billions of 1987 Hong Kong Dollars)							
..	..	..	..	..	..	..	..	..	..	..	Gross National Product
220.64	241.42	248.70	264.86	289.97	289.64	324.09	369.27	395.83	405.78	f	GDP at Market Prices
-8.85	-8.15	-7.48	-1.29	10.86	8.60	14.45	22.72	24.19	30.86	..	Resource Balance
185.39	211.05	207.85	236.59	283.26	298.43	344.03	448.87	558.25	610.15	..	Exports of Goods & NFServices
194.24	219.20	215.33	237.89	272.40	289.83	329.57	426.14	534.06	579.29	..	Imports of Goods & NFServices
229.50	249.56	256.18	266.15	279.11	281.04	309.64	346.55	371.64	374.92	..	Domestic Absorption
136.24	146.28	154.58	166.83	176.82	183.58	200.22	221.76	241.35	248.40	..	Private Consumption, etc.
16.39	20.03	21.14	22.26	22.87	23.29	24.74	25.78	27.10	28.67	..	General Gov't Consumption
76.87	83.25	80.47	77.06	79.42	74.17	84.68	99.02	103.20	97.84	..	Gross Domestic Investment
71.12	77.43	78.72	72.13	73.28	72.66	77.93	89.27	94.66	95.63	..	Fixed Investment
212.33	232.51	240.43	254.66	278.44	275.94	308.28	350.63	376.27	..	f	GDP at factor cost
..	..	..	..	..	..	..	..	..	..	..	Agriculture
..	..	..	..	..	..	..	..	..	..	..	Industry
..	..	..	..	..	..	..	..	..	..	..	Manufacturing
..	..	..	..	..	..	..	..	..	..	..	Services, etc.
											Memo Items:
184.58	206.42	206.48	232.95	283.57	305.99	344.19	448.87	555.28	615.18	..	Capacity to Import
-0.81	-4.63	-1.37	-3.64	0.31	7.56	0.16	0.00	-2.96	5.03	..	Terms of Trade Adjustment
219.84	236.79	247.33	261.22	290.28	297.20	324.26	369.27	392.87	410.81	..	Gross Domestic Income
219.84	236.79	247.33	261.22	290.28	297.20	324.26	369.27	392.87	410.81	..	Gross National Income
				(Index 1987 = 100)							**DOMESTIC PRICES/DEFLATORS**
62.1	68.3	74.9	78.4	85.8	90.2	92.8	100.0	109.0	121.1	..	Overall (GDP)
62.5	69.8	75.4	79.6	85.4	87.7	92.6	100.0	110.2	120.8	..	Domestic Absorption
..	..	..	..	..	..	..	..	..	..	..	Agriculture
..	..	..	..	..	..	..	..	..	..	..	Industry
..	..	..	..	..	..	..	..	..	..	..	Manufacturing
59.3	67.5	74.6	82.0	88.9	92.0	95.0	100.0	107.4	117.8	..	Consumer Price Index
											MANUFACTURING ACTIVITY
99.2	105.5	94.8	99.2	101.2	96.2	99.9	100.0	102.9	..	G	Employment (1987=100)
74.3	74.0	75.7	75.9	80.5	84.3	91.8	100.0	102.0	..	G	Real Earnings per Empl. (1987=100)
..	..	..	..	..	..	..	..	..	..	G	Real Output per Empl. (1987=100)
52.0	51.5	51.6	48.4	59.0	63.4	59.5	56.8	56.3	..	..	Earnings as % of Value Added
				(Billions of current Hong Kong Dollars)							**MONETARY HOLDINGS**
110.36	135.74	..	..	..	..	..	..	..	..	D	Money Supply, Broadly Defined
24.12	25.06	..	..	..	..	..	..	..	..	..	Money
..	..	..	..	..	..	..	..	..	..	..	Currency Outside Banks
..	..	..	..	..	..	..	..	..	..	..	Demand Deposits
86.23	110.68	..	..	..	..	..	..	..	..	..	Quasi-Money
				(Millions of current Hong Kong Dollars)							**GOVERNMENT DEFICIT (-) OR SURPLUS**
..	..	..	..	..	..	..	..	..	..	..	Current Revenue
..	..	..	..	..	..	..	..	..	..	..	Current Expenditure
..	..	..	..	..	..	..	..	..	..	..	Current Budget Balance
..	..	..	..	..	..	..	..	..	..	..	Capital Receipts
..	..	..	..	..	..	..	..	..	..	..	Capital Payments

HONG KONG	1969	1970	1971	1972	1973	1974	1975	1976	1977	1978	1979
FOREIGN TRADE (CUSTOMS BASIS)					*(Millions of current US dollars)*						
Value of Exports, fob	2,178	2,514	2,871	3,477	5,051	5,907	6,019	8,522	9,624	11,499	15,156
Nonfuel Primary Products	159	171	180	225	344	424	389	615	656	764	1,013
Fuels	7	7	8	8	11	20	19	25	35	42	58
Manufactures	2,012	2,336	2,683	3,244	4,696	5,463	5,611	7,882	8,933	10,693	14,085
Value of Imports, cif	2,457	2,905	3,387	3,895	5,631	6,710	6,757	8,909	10,457	13,451	17,137
Nonfuel Primary Products	747	835	964	1,076	1,581	1,926	2,005	2,398	2,629	3,015	3,398
Fuels	79	85	109	120	153	419	429	552	643	666	979
Manufactures	1,631	1,985	2,314	2,700	3,897	4,364	4,323	5,960	7,186	9,770	12,760
					(Index 1987 = 100)						
Terms of Trade	94.2	96.1	104.3	115.1	132.6	130.4	110.9	116.1	107.6	91.3	94.0
Export Prices, fob	25.7	27.5	31.6	38.4	54.5	68.4	61.9	66.4	66.7	63.4	75.0
Import Prices, cif	27.3	28.6	30.3	33.4	41.1	52.5	55.8	57.2	62.0	69.4	79.8
BALANCE OF PAYMENTS					*(Millions of current US dollars)*						
Exports of Goods & Services	..	3,474	3,888	4,708	6,783	8,201	8,509	11,651	13,241	15,986	20,935
Merchandise, fob	..	2,514	2,872	3,442	5,041	5,969	6,027	8,512	9,624	11,517	15,181
Nonfactor Services	..	840	879	1,078	1,413	1,687	1,753	2,377	2,637	3,149	3,850
Factor Services	..	120	137	188	329	545	729	762	980	1,320	1,904
Imports of Goods & Services	..	3,249	3,785	4,354	6,394	7,870	7,940	10,412	12,396	16,049	20,736
Merchandise, fob	..	2,910	3,394	3,866	5,633	6,785	6,774	8,915	10,476	13,516	17,262
Nonfactor Services	..	316	366	447	635	807	907	1,145	1,443	1,769	2,393
Factor Services	..	23	25	41	126	278	259	352	477	764	1,081
Long-Term Interest	..	..	..	..	..	..	..	..	..	..	..
Private Current Transfers, net	..	..	..	..	..	..	..	..	..	..	..
Workers' Remittances	..	..	..	..	..	..	..	..	..	..	..
Curr. A/C Bal before Off. Transf.	..	225	103	354	389	331	569	1,239	845	-63	199
Net Official Transfers	..	0	0	0	0	0	0	0	0	0	0
Curr. A/C Bal after Off. Transf.	..	225	103	354	389	331	569	1,239	845	-63	199
Long-Term Capital, net	..	-1	-1	-1	0	16	4	41	88	29	103
Direct Investment	..	..	..	..	..	..	..	..	..	..	..
Long-Term Loans	..	..	..	..	..	..	..	..	..	..	..
Disbursements	..	..	..	..	..	..	..	..	..	..	..
Repayments	..	..	..	..	..	..	..	..	..	..	..
Other Long-Term Capital	..	-1	-1	-1	0	16	4	41	88	29	103
Other Capital, net	..	..	..	..	..	..	..	..	..	..	..
Change in Reserves	..	..	..	..	..	..	..	..	..	..	..
Memo Item:					*(Hong Kong Dollars per US dollar)*						
Conversion Factor (Annual Avg)	6.060	6.060	5.980	5.640	5.150	5.030	4.940	4.900	4.660	4.680	5.000
					(Millions of US dollars), outstanding at end of year						
EXTERNAL DEBT (Total)	..	..	..	..	..	..	..	..	..	..	..
Long-Term Debt (by debtor)	..	..	..	..	..	..	..	..	..	..	..
Central Bank, incl. IMF credit	..	..	..	..	..	..	..	..	..	..	..
Central Government	..	..	..	..	..	..	..	..	..	..	..
Rest of General Government	..	..	..	..	..	..	..	..	..	..	..
Non-financial Public Enterprises	..	..	..	..	..	..	..	..	..	..	..
Priv. Sector, incl non-guaranteed	..	..	..	..	..	..	..	..	..	..	..
Short-Term Debt	..	..	..	..	..	..	..	..	..	..	..
Memo Items:					*Millions US dollars)*						
Int'l Reserves Excluding Gold	..	..	..	..	..	..	..	..	..	..	..
Gold Holdings (at market price)	..	..	..	..	..	..	..	..	..	..	..
SOCIAL INDICATORS											
Total Fertility Rate	3.6	3.3	3.1	2.9	2.8	2.7	2.5	2.4	2.3	2.2	2.1
Infant Mortality Rate	20.6	19.4	18.2	17.0	16.9	16.8	14.9	13.7	13.5	11.8	12.3
Life Expectancy at Birth	69.9	70.0	70.0	70.0	71.0	71.3	71.5	71.8	72.1	72.7	73.4
Urban Population, % of total	89.6	89.7	89.9	90.1	90.2	90.4	90.6	90.8	91.0	91.2	91.4
Food Prod. per capita (1987 = 100)	319.0	330.1	316.5	328.6	268.2	265.9	220.2	201.1	225.0	197.2	224.2
Labor Force, Agriculture (%)	0.0	0.0	0.0	0.0	0.0	0.0	0.0	0.0	0.0	0.0	0.0
Labor Force, Female (%)	..	..	..	..	..	..	..	..	..	..	..
Primary Schl. Enroll. Ratio	..	117.0	..	..	..	..	119.0	114.0	115.0	113.0	111.0
Primary Schl. Enroll. Ratio, Female	..	115.0	..	..	..	..	117.0	112.0	113.0	111.0	109.0
Secondary Schl. Enroll. Ratio	..	36.0	..	..	..	..	49.0	52.0	54.0	57.0	60.0

1980	1981	1982	1983	1984	1985	1986	1987	1988	1989 estimate	NOTES	HONG KONG
											FOREIGN TRADE (CUSTOMS BASIS)
(Millions of current US dollars)											
19,703	21,737	20,964	21,951	28,317	30,185	35,440	48,473	63,161	..	..	Value of Exports, fob
1,410	1,575	1,587	1,755	2,017	2,281	2,587	3,472	5,043	..	..	Nonfuel Primary Products
84	96	101	107	131	145	207	221	282	..	..	Fuels
18,208	20,066	19,277	20,089	26,169	27,758	32,645	44,780	57,836	..	..	Manufactures
22,027	24,671	23,461	24,009	28,567	29,580	35,365	48,462	63,894	..	..	Value of Imports, cif
4,145	4,303	4,383	4,415	4,731	4,841	5,306	6,757	8,532	..	..	Nonfuel Primary Products
1,217	1,955	1,884	1,595	1,568	1,384	1,135	1,215	1,219	..	..	Fuels
16,665	18,414	17,194	17,999	22,268	23,355	28,925	40,491	54,143	..	..	Manufactures
(Index 1987 = 100)											
93.3	101.8	99.5	92.6	93.4	96.7	100.8	100.0	100.2	..	..	Terms of Trade
81.9	90.2	86.0	77.9	76.4	77.9	91.1	100.0	108.6	..	..	Export Prices, fob
87.8	88.6	86.4	84.1	81.7	80.5	90.4	100.0	108.4	..	..	Import Prices, cif
(Millions of current US dollars)											**BALANCE OF PAYMENTS**
24,190	26,646	26,039	27,199	33,968	36,187	42,116	53,168	..	..	..	Exports of Goods & Services
19,731	21,791	20,986	22,119	28,325	30,186	35,449	45,835	..	..	..	Merchandise, fob
3,686	4,001	4,184	4,265	4,594	4,800	5,372	5,923	..	..	..	Nonfactor Services
773	854	869	815	1,049	1,201	1,295	1,410	..	..	..	Factor Services
25,448	28,269	27,126	27,756	32,555	34,318	40,564	51,969	..	..	..	Imports of Goods & Services
22,453	24,838	23,685	24,304	28,754	29,861	35,564	46,559	..	..	..	Merchandise, fob
2,643	3,027	3,036	3,046	3,354	3,928	4,423	4,769	..	..	..	Nonfactor Services
352	404	405	406	447	529	577	641	..	..	..	Factor Services
..	..	..	..	..	..	..	..	..	..	..	Long-Term Interest
..	..	..	..	..	..	..	..	..	..	..	Private Current Transfers, net
..	..	..	..	..	..	..	..	..	..	..	Workers' Remittances
-1,258	-1,623	-1,087	-557	1,413	1,869	1,552	1,199	..	..	..	Curr. A/C Bal before Off. Transf.
0	0	0	0	0	0	0	0	..	..	..	Net Official Transfers
-1,258	-1,623	-1,087	-557	1,413	1,869	1,552	1,199	..	..	..	Curr. A/C Bal after Off. Transf.
329	125	208	206	224	270	295	321	..	..	..	Long-Term Capital, net
250	300	200	200	243	257	282	282	..	..	..	Direct Investment
..	..	..	..	..	..	..	..	..	..	..	Long-Term Loans
..	..	..	..	..	..	..	..	..	..	..	Disbursements
..	..	..	..	..	..	..	..	..	..	..	Repayments
79	-175	8	6	-19	13	13	39	..	..	..	Other Long-Term Capital
250	300	200	200	243	257	282	0	..	..	..	Other Capital, net
679	1,198	679	151	-1,880	-2,396	-2,129	-1,520	..	..	..	Change in Reserves
(Hong Kong Dollars per US dollar)											Memo Item:
4.980	5.590	6.070	7.270	7.820	7.790	7.800	7.800	7.810	7.800	..	Conversion Factor (Annual Avg)
(Millions of US dollars), outstanding at end of year											
..	..	..	..	..	..	..	..	..	..	..	**EXTERNAL DEBT** (Total)
..	..	..	..	..	..	..	..	..	..	..	Long-Term Debt (by debtor)
..	..	..	..	..	..	..	..	..	..	..	Central Bank, incl. IMF credit
..	..	..	..	..	..	..	..	..	..	..	Central Government
..	..	..	..	..	..	..	..	..	..	..	Rest of General Government
..	..	..	..	..	..	..	..	..	..	..	Non-financial Public Enterprises
..	..	..	..	..	..	..	..	..	..	..	Priv. Sector, incl non-guaranteed
..	..	..	..	..	..	..	..	..	..	..	Short-Term Debt
Millions US dollars)											
..	..	..	..	..	..	..	..	..	..	..	Memo Items:
..	..	..	..	..	..	..	..	..	..	..	Int'l Reserves Excluding Gold
..	..	..	..	..	..	..	..	..	..	..	Gold Holdings (at market price)
											SOCIAL INDICATORS
2.0	1.9	1.8	1.8	1.7	1.7	1.6	1.6	1.6	1.6	..	Total Fertility Rate
11.2	9.7	9.9	9.4	8.8	8.3	7.9	7.4	7.2	7.0	..	Infant Mortality Rate
74.1	74.7	75.4	75.5	75.5	76.0	76.5	77.0	77.2	77.4	..	Life Expectancy at Birth
91.6	91.8	91.9	92.1	92.2	92.4	92.6	92.7	92.9	93.0	..	Urban Population, % of total
189.1	219.0	158.7	149.0	155.5	183.9	91.8	100.0	143.5	140.3	..	Food Prod. per capita (1987 = 100)
0.0	..	..	..	..	..	..	..	..	..	..	Labor Force, Agriculture (%)
..	..	..	..	..	..	..	..	..	..	..	Labor Force, Female (%)
106.0	106.0	106.0	106.0	104.0	104.0	104.0	106.0	..	..	..	Primary Schl. Enroll. Ratio
105.0	105.0	105.0	105.0	103.0	103.0	103.0	105.0	..	..	..	Primary Schl. Enroll. Ratio, Female
64.0	66.0	67.0	68.0	72.0	72.0	73.0	74.0	..	..	..	Secondary Schl. Enroll. Ratio

HUNGARY	1969	1970	1971	1972	1973	1974	1975	1976	1977	1978	1979
CURRENT GNP PER CAPITA (US $)	..	..	..	..	..	..	..	..	1,310	1,500	1,680
POPULATION (thousands)	10,303	10,337	10,365	10,394	10,436	10,471	10,532	10,589	10,637	10,673	10,698
USE AND ORIGIN OF RESOURCES					*(Billions of current Hungarian Forint)*						
Gross National Product (GNP)	..	..	..	..	..	..	475.2	524.4	574.9	619.7	668.7
Net Factor Income from Abroad	..	..	..	..	..	..	-7.5	-4.5	-7.1	-10.0	-13.6
GDP at Market Prices	312.4	332.5	360.8	391.0	429.0	448.9	482.7	528.9	582.0	629.7	682.3
Resource Balance	6.9	-7.7	-22.5	4.8	19.6	-19.9	-36.0	-21.3	-26.3	-57.7	-22.3
Exports of Goods & NFServices	..	100.2	108.4	133.4	163.9	186.8	200.2	205.2	240.6	243.9	283.3
Imports of Goods & NFServices	..	107.9	130.9	128.6	144.2	206.7	236.2	226.5	266.9	301.6	305.6
Domestic Absorption	305.5	340.2	383.3	386.2	409.4	468.8	518.7	550.2	608.3	687.4	704.6
Private Consumption, etc.	..	194.1	209.6	223.5	241.7	261.4	286.0	307.3	334.0	361.7	401.2
General Gov't Consumption	..	34.4	37.8	38.6	40.5	46.9	50.3	53.2	57.8	65.8	71.3
Gross Domestic Investment	95.4	111.7	135.9	124.1	127.2	160.5	182.4	189.7	216.5	259.9	232.1
Fixed Investment	83.1	100.3	113.1	116.8	123.1	139.2	161.0	168.2	197.7	214.4	220.8
Indirect Taxes, net	..	..	..	..	..	..	..	..	..	..	..
GDP at factor cost	..	..	..	..	..	..	..	..	..	..	..
Agriculture	64.7	60.6	69.1	70.7	82.3	84.7	86.4	94.7	105.4	107.8	108.8
Industry	139.4	150.5	163.8	178.6	200.5	224.9	247.8	259.1	285.6	308.5	332.4
Manufacturing	..	..	..	..	..	..	..	..	..	..	..
Services, etc.	108.3	121.5	128.0	141.7	146.2	139.3	148.5	175.1	191.0	213.4	241.1
Gross Domestic Saving	102.3	104.0	113.4	128.9	146.8	140.7	146.4	168.4	190.2	202.2	209.8
Gross National Saving	..	..	..	..	..	..	142.2	166.8	184.9	195.9	197.8
					(Billions of 1987 Hungarian Forint)						
Gross National Product	..	..	..	..	637.31	674.69	889.48	927.17	985.97	1,027.55	1,039.56
GDP at Market Prices	634.12	665.12	707.17	750.80	803.30	850.72	903.65	935.39	998.25	1,044.33	1,060.70
Resource Balance	..	-80.51	-114.05	-67.42	-46.63	-87.06	-93.54	-85.01	-84.69	-129.54	-73.36
Exports of Goods & NFServices	..	157.18	168.56	200.81	230.21	238.23	248.58	267.22	303.31	309.24	345.21
Imports of Goods & NFServices	..	237.69	282.62	268.23	276.84	325.29	342.12	352.23	387.99	438.79	418.58
Domestic Absorption	..	745.63	821.23	818.23	849.93	937.78	997.19	1,020.40	1,082.94	1,173.88	1,134.06
Private Consumption, etc.	..	434.82	454.30	486.07	515.90	537.70	562.27	575.36	605.62	619.57	647.73
General Gov't Consumption	..	77.88	82.68	83.14	84.43	93.10	96.45	99.84	103.43	113.51	119.19
Gross Domestic Investment	200.12	232.93	284.25	249.02	249.60	306.98	338.47	345.21	373.88	440.79	367.14
Fixed Investment	167.54	195.90	216.62	214.29	221.24	245.45	273.66	273.66	306.89	321.74	324.15
GDP at factor cost	..	..	..	..	..	..	..	..	..	..	..
Agriculture	135.88	120.55	128.31	131.61	138.77	142.62	145.82	140.14	157.32	158.80	156.70
Industry	234.32	250.64	267.87	285.42	307.87	333.56	357.09	377.79	401.82	423.67	445.53
Manufacturing	..	..	..	..	..	..	..	..	..	..	..
Services, etc.	262.61	295.17	311.66	335.01	357.30	375.63	402.74	421.03	441.66	465.36	462.14
Memo Items:											
Capacity to Import	..	220.74	234.07	278.15	314.46	294.03	289.98	319.10	349.76	354.84	388.03
Terms of Trade Adjustment	..	63.57	65.51	77.34	84.25	55.80	41.39	51.88	46.45	45.60	42.82
Gross Domestic Income	..	728.68	772.68	828.14	887.56	906.52	945.05	987.28	1,044.71	1,089.93	1,103.52
Gross National Income	..	..	..	..	721.56	730.49	930.88	979.05	1,032.42	1,073.15	1,082.38
DOMESTIC PRICES/DEFLATORS					*(Index 1987 = 100)*						
Overall (GDP)	49.3	50.0	51.0	52.1	53.4	52.8	53.4	56.5	58.3	60.3	64.3
Domestic Absorption	..	45.6	46.7	47.2	48.2	50.0	52.0	53.9	56.2	58.6	62.1
Agriculture	47.6	50.2	53.9	53.7	59.3	59.4	59.2	67.6	67.0	67.9	69.4
Industry	59.5	60.0	61.1	62.6	65.1	67.4	69.4	68.6	71.1	72.8	74.6
Manufacturing	..	..	..	..	..	..	..	..	..	..	..
Consumer Price Index	..	..	..	42.6	44.0	44.8	46.5	49.0	50.9	53.3	58.0
MANUFACTURING ACTIVITY											
Employment (1987=100)	123.8	124.7	122.6	122.0	123.9	125.4	124.9	116.3	116.2	116.3	114.4
Real Earnings per Empl. (1987=100)	..	..	..	70.9	74.9	78.9	80.9	91.5	93.8	96.5	93.2
Real Output per Empl. (1987=100)	33.9	36.7	39.8	42.5	44.3	47.2	52.7	61.9	65.0	68.5	71.9
Earnings as % of Value Added	28.6	27.9	26.0	25.0	24.9	24.0	23.2	24.6	28.5	28.9	27.2
MONETARY HOLDINGS					*(Billions of current Hungarian Forint)*						
Money Supply, Broadly Defined	..	..	..	..	..	..	..	..	..	..	..
Money	..	..	..	..	..	..	..	..	..	..	..
Currency Outside Banks	..	..	..	..	..	..	..	..	..	..	..
Demand Deposits	..	..	..	..	..	..	..	..	..	..	..
Quasi-Money	..	..	..	..	..	..	..	..	..	..	..
					(Billions of current Hungarian Forint)						
GOVERNMENT DEFICIT (-) OR SURPLUS	..	..	..	..	..	..	..	..	..	..	..
Current Revenue	..	..	..	..	..	..	..	..	..	..	..
Current Expenditure	..	..	..	..	..	..	..	..	..	..	..
Current Budget Balance	..	..	..	..	..	..	..	..	..	..	..
Capital Receipts	..	..	..	..	..	..	..	..	..	..	..
Capital Payments	..	..	..	..	..	..	..	..	..	..	..

1980	1981	1982	1983	1984	1985	1986	1987	1988	1989 estimate	NOTES	HUNGARY
1,930	2,150	2,260	2,150	2,050	1,940	2,020	2,250	2,450	2,580	..	**CURRENT GNP PER CAPITA (US $)**
10,710	10,713	10,711	10,700	10,679	10,657	10,640	10,621	10,604	10,587	..	**POPULATION (thousands)**
			(Billions of current Hungarian Forint)								**USE AND ORIGIN OF RESOURCES**
708.4	751.5	824.7	877.1	949.3	995.9	1,047.8	1,181.2	1,355.8	1,633.5	..	Gross National Product (GNP)
-12.6	-28.4	-23.2	-19.3	-29.1	-37.8	-41.0	-45.2	-53.7	-83.2	..	Net Factor Income from Abroad
721.0	779.9	847.9	896.4	978.4	1,033.7	1,088.8	1,226.4	1,409.5	1,716.7	..	GDP at Market Prices
-15.6	-8.2	6.8	17.1	30.9	21.4	-15.4	-5.9	38.7	58.3	..	Resource Balance
281.8	308.2	321.8	360.7	402.0	436.2	431.6	464.4	530.4	617.2	..	Exports of Goods & NFServices
297.4	316.4	315.0	343.6	371.1	414.8	447.0	470.3	491.7	558.9	..	Imports of Goods & NFServices
736.6	788.1	841.1	879.3	947.5	1,012.3	1,104.2	1,232.3	1,370.8	1,658.4	..	Domestic Absorption
441.2	477.7	515.1	551.2	600.5	649.3	695.5	778.5	854.5	1,018.4	..	Private Consumption, etc.
74.1	79.1	84.2	90.9	95.2	104.6	116.0	126.3	157.4	186.5	..	General Gov't Consumption
221.3	231.3	241.8	237.2	251.8	258.4	292.7	327.5	358.9	453.5	..	Gross Domestic Investment
207.7	206.7	213.9	220.1	225.4	232.1	261.2	303.5	295.5	345.0	..	Fixed Investment
..	..	..	..	..	..	..	..	..	..	..	Indirect Taxes, net
..	..	..	..	..	..	..	..	..	..	B	GDP at factor cost
123.5	136.8	148.5	152.9	166.1	166.6	182.6	189.2	209.5	239.1	..	Agriculture
296.8	323.8	350.1	369.3	400.8	425.9	440.0	494.6	527.0	618.3	..	Industry
..	..	..	..	..	..	..	..	..	..	..	Manufacturing
300.7	319.3	349.3	374.2	411.5	441.2	466.2	542.6	673.0	859.3	..	Services, etc.
205.7	223.1	248.6	254.3	282.7	279.8	277.3	321.6	397.6	511.8	..	Gross Domestic Saving
194.6	196.4	227.7	237.3	256.7	245.2	239.9	281.3	349.9	436.3	..	Gross National Saving
			(Billions of 1987 Hungarian Forint)								
1,042.34	1,062.21	1,091.99	1,106.58	1,125.57	1,116.45	1,131.83	1,181.17	1,176.25	1,164.36	..	Gross National Product
1,061.09	1,102.36	1,122.72	1,131.11	1,160.45	1,158.98	1,176.21	1,226.40	1,223.03	1,221.39	..	GDP at Market Prices
-66.82	-54.83	-26.07	-4.24	18.20	8.32	-13.73	-5.90	21.89	22.26	..	Resource Balance
347.23	365.87	378.81	404.09	430.92	453.36	443.27	464.40	494.32	498.94	..	Exports of Goods & NFServices
414.06	420.70	404.88	408.34	412.73	445.04	457.00	470.30	472.43	476.68	..	Imports of Goods & NFServices
1,127.92	1,157.19	1,148.79	1,135.36	1,142.25	1,150.66	1,189.94	1,232.30	1,201.15	1,199.13	..	Domestic Absorption
665.40	682.75	700.08	710.81	723.97	738.22	746.60	778.50	751.06	755.28	..	Private Consumption, etc.
107.75	112.00	113.84	114.12	115.54	120.35	125.88	126.30	133.24	124.18	..	General Gov't Consumption
354.77	362.44	334.86	310.42	302.74	292.09	317.47	327.50	316.84	319.67	..	Gross Domestic Investment
305.48	292.33	287.66	277.90	267.58	259.38	276.35	303.50	275.78	287.52	..	Fixed Investment
..	..	..	..	..	..	..	..	..	..	B	GDP at factor cost
162.51	169.06	187.59	187.72	196.49	188.46	195.13	189.20	204.15	200.32	..	Agriculture
438.15	468.69	474.48	483.74	489.97	477.81	475.93	494.60	483.89	471.15	..	Industry
..	..	..	..	..	..	..	..	..	..	..	Manufacturing
463.46	467.11	460.68	459.65	473.99	492.71	505.15	542.60	534.99	549.91	..	Services, etc.
											Memo Items:
392.34	409.80	413.62	428.66	447.09	468.00	441.26	464.40	509.61	526.41	..	Capacity to Import
45.10	43.93	34.81	24.56	16.17	14.64	-2.01	0.00	15.30	27.46	..	Terms of Trade Adjustment
1,106.20	1,146.29	1,157.53	1,155.68	1,176.62	1,173.62	1,174.20	1,226.40	1,238.33	1,248.85	..	Gross Domestic Income
1,087.44	1,106.14	1,126.81	1,131.15	1,141.74	1,131.08	1,129.82	1,181.17	1,191.54	1,191.82	..	Gross National Income
			(Index 1987 = 100)								**DOMESTIC PRICES/DEFLATORS**
67.9	70.7	75.5	79.2	84.3	89.2	92.6	100.0	115.2	140.6	..	Overall (GDP)
65.3	68.1	73.2	77.4	83.0	88.0	92.8	100.0	114.1	138.3	..	Domestic Absorption
76.0	80.9	79.2	81.5	84.5	88.4	93.6	100.0	102.6	119.4	..	Agriculture
67.7	69.1	73.8	76.3	81.8	89.1	92.5	100.0	108.9	131.2	..	Industry
..	..	..	..	..	..	..	..	..	..	..	Manufacturing
63.4	66.3	70.9	75.5	82.0	87.8	92.4	100.0	116.3	136.0	..	Consumer Price Index
											MANUFACTURING ACTIVITY
111.3	108.8	106.1	102.1	101.4	102.8	102.1	100.0	97.2	92.6	..	Employment (1987=100)
89.1	92.5	91.7	90.6	94.9	96.9	98.9	100.0	111.0	..	..	Real Earnings per Empl. (1987=100)
89.1	96.0	96.5	101.8	103.0	98.5	98.9	100.0	98.8	..	..	Real Output per Empl. (1987=100)
33.7	32.9	32.5	32.1	32.6	33.5	34.2	32.8	39.3	..	..	Earnings as % of Value Added
			(Billions of current Hungarian Forint)								**MONETARY HOLDINGS**
..	..	..	..	..	..	554.37	595.10	..	..	..	Money Supply, Broadly Defined
..	..	187.61	192.22	200.86	239.70	266.45	306.62	301.99	355.09	..	Money
..	..	84.87	94.79	105.42	116.75	130.88	153.77	164.45	180.62	..	Currency Outside Banks
..	..	102.74	97.43	95.44	122.95	135.57	152.85	137.54	174.47	..	Demand Deposits
..	..	..	..	..	..	287.92	288.48	..	..	..	Quasi-Money
			(Billions of current Hungarian Forint)								
..	-22.10	-16.10	-6.40	15.70	-10.10	-30.90	-40.30	-3.20	..	..	**GOVERNMENT DEFICIT (-) OR SURPLUS**
..	416.80	438.70	484.50	535.20	538.70	606.80	660.40	789.90	..	..	Current Revenue
..	380.00	399.00	438.60	463.40	491.70	592.20	651.50	738.70	..	..	Current Expenditure
..	36.80	39.70	45.90	71.80	47.00	14.60	8.90	51.20	..	..	Current Budget Balance
..	1.30	..	1.00	..	0.30	..	..	..	..	..	Capital Receipts
..	60.20	55.80	53.30	56.10	57.40	45.50	49.20	54.40	..	..	Capital Payments

HUNGARY	1969	1970	1971	1972	1973	1974	1975	1976	1977	1978	1979
FOREIGN TRADE (CUSTOMS BASIS)				*(Millions of current US dollars)*							
Value of Exports, fob	1,553	1,726	1,847	2,403	3,354	3,942	4,519	4,932	5,840	6,434	7,938
Nonfuel Primary Products	..	..	..	..	..	..	..	1,457	1,722	1,822	2,164
Fuels	..	..	..	..	..	..	..	146	179	222	333
Manufactures	..	..	..	..	..	..	..	3,328	3,939	4,390	5,441
Value of Imports, cif	1,444	1,877	2,248	2,356	3,018	4,453	5,400	5,517	6,509	7,967	8,659
Nonfuel Primary Products	..	..	..	..	..	..	..	1,275	1,513	1,640	1,732
Fuels	..	..	..	..	..	..	..	683	803	1,083	1,384
Manufactures	..	..	..	..	..	..	..	3,558	4,192	5,244	5,543
					(Index 1987 = 100)						
Terms of Trade	..	..	..	..	..	..	..	..	..	..	..
Export Prices, fob	..	..	..	..	..	..	..	..	..	..	..
Import Prices, cif	..	..	..	..	..	..	..	..	..	..	..
BALANCE OF PAYMENTS				*(Millions of current US dollars)*							
Exports of Goods & Services	..	2,144	2,108	2,707	3,683	4,628	5,333	5,518	6,473	7,275	8,678
Merchandise, fob	..	1,819	1,864	2,421	3,327	4,021	4,765	5,042	5,877	6,565	7,949
Nonfactor Services	..	307	229	262	313	538	492	386	504	603	625
Factor Services	..	18	15	24	43	69	77	90	92	107	103
Imports of Goods & Services	..	2,204	2,498	2,672	3,501	5,046	6,059	6,208	7,330	8,812	9,662
Merchandise, fob	..	1,921	2,206	2,325	2,957	4,421	5,277	5,528	6,496	7,752	8,509
Nonfactor Services	..	204	212	253	415	444	534	482	569	688	669
Factor Services	..	79	80	93	129	181	248	198	264	372	484
Long-Term Interest	..	0	0	0	0	0	0	0	0	8	15
Private Current Transfers, net	..	36	42	60	73	80	75	69	44	99	42
Workers' Remittances	..	..	..	..	..	..	..	..	..	..	..
Curr. A/C Bal before Off. Transf.	..	-25	-347	95	256	-339	-651	-620	-813	-1,437	-942
Net Official Transfers	..	..	..	..	..	..	..	..	..	..	..
Curr. A/C Bal after Off. Transf.	..	-25	-347	95	256	-339	-651	-620	-813	-1,437	-942
Long-Term Capital, net	..	..	217	137	5	143	413	419	637	1,143	943
Direct Investment	..	..	..	..	..	..	..	..	-6	-4	6
Long-Term Loans	..	0	0	0	0	0	0	0	43	151	96
Disbursements	..	0	0	0	0	0	0	0	43	151	191
Repayments	..	0	0	0	0	0	0	0	0	0	95
Other Long-Term Capital	..	..	217	137	5	143	413	419	600	996	841
Other Capital, net	..	..	..	-59	30	416	124	136	242	426	-167
Change in Reserves	..	..	..	-172	-290	-220	114	66	-67	-132	166
Memo Item:				*(Hungarian Forint per US dollar)*							
Conversion Factor (Annual Avg)	60.000	60.000	59.820	55.260	48.970	46.750	43.970	41.570	40.960	37.910	35.580
				(Millions of US dollars), outstanding at end of year							
EXTERNAL DEBT (Total)	..	0	0	0	0	0	0	0	43	8,118	8,861
Long-Term Debt (by debtor)	..	0	0	0	0	0	0	0	43	4,695	5,689
Central Bank, incl. IMF credit	..	0	0	0	0	0	0	0	0	4,652	5,646
Central Government	..	0	0	0	0	0	0	0	0	0	0
Rest of General Government	..	..	..	..	..	..	..	..	..	..	..
Non-financial Public Enterprises	..	0	0	0	0	0	0	0	43	43	43
Priv. Sector, incl non-guaranteed	..	0	0	0	0	0	0	0	0	0	0
Short-Term Debt	..	0	0	0	0	0	0	0	0	3,423	3,172
Memo Items:				*(Millions of US dollars)*							
Int'l Reserves Excluding Gold	..	..	..	..	..	..	..	..	..	..	..
Gold Holdings (at market price)	..	..	63.1	108.4	204.3	248.0	133.4	178.1	211.5	447.0	909.8
SOCIAL INDICATORS											
Total Fertility Rate	2.0	2.0	1.9	1.9	2.0	2.3	2.4	2.3	2.2	2.1	2.0
Infant Mortality Rate	35.7	35.9	35.1	33.2	33.8	34.3	32.8	29.8	26.2	24.4	23.7
Life Expectancy at Birth	69.6	69.6	69.7	69.7	69.7	69.8	69.8	69.8	69.7	69.6	69.6
Urban Population, % of total	45.0	45.6	46.5	47.4	48.3	49.2	50.1	50.8	51.5	52.1	52.8
Food Prod. per capita (1987=100)	77.2	66.9	74.8	78.9	82.7	83.0	87.0	80.8	87.8	89.0	87.4
Labor Force, Agriculture (%)	26.3	25.1	24.4	23.7	23.0	22.3	21.7	21.0	20.3	19.6	18.9
Labor Force, Female (%)	39.4	39.8	40.3	40.7	41.1	41.6	42.0	42.4	42.7	43.1	43.5
Primary Schl. Enroll. Ratio	..	97.0	..	..	..	..	99.0	99.0	98.0	97.0	96.0
Primary Schl. Enroll. Ratio, Female	..	97.0	..	..	..	..	99.0	99.0	98.0	97.0	96.0
Secondary Schl. Enroll. Ratio	..	63.0	..	..	..	..	63.0	..	..	..	70.0

1980	1981	1982	1983	1984	1985	1986	1987	1988	1989 estimate	NOTES	HUNGARY
				(Millions of current US dollars)							**FOREIGN TRADE (CUSTOMS BASIS)**
8,677	8,712	8,799	8,722	8,560	8,555	9,157	9,571	9,949	..	..	Value of Exports, fob
2,547	2,708	2,615	2,477	2,404	2,252	2,340	2,386	2,566	..	..	Nonfuel Primary Products
420	413	581	806	739	437	368	402	460	..	..	Fuels
5,709	5,591	5,603	5,440	5,418	5,866	6,450	6,783	6,923	..	..	Manufactures
9,212	9,123	8,836	8,481	8,084	8,143	9,583	9,855	9,346	..	..	Value of Imports, cif
1,958	1,851	1,462	1,473	1,430	1,343	1,630	1,635	1,591	..	..	Nonfuel Primary Products
1,512	1,518	1,843	1,939	1,821	1,796	1,952	1,675	1,536	..	..	Fuels
5,741	5,755	5,531	5,069	4,833	5,004	6,000	6,545	6,219	..	..	Manufactures
				(Index 1987 = 100)							
..	..	..	..	..	..	..	..	..	..	..	Terms of Trade
..	..	..	..	..	..	..	..	..	..	..	Export Prices, fob
..	..	..	..	..	..	..	..	..	..	..	Import Prices, cif
				(Millions of current US dollars)							**BALANCE OF PAYMENTS**
10,176	10,335	10,421	10,378	10,688	10,012	11,024	12,030	12,159	12,798	f	Exports of Goods & Services
8,877	8,901	9,038	8,978	9,090	8,578	9,198	9,965	9,989	10,493	..	Merchandise, fob
806	1,191	1,264	1,268	1,439	1,229	1,565	1,822	1,932	2,074	..	Nonfactor Services
493	244	119	132	159	205	261	243	238	231	..	Factor Services
10,801	11,276	11,018	10,614	10,715	10,532	12,465	12,812	12,849	13,500	f	Imports of Goods & Services
9,020	8,855	8,628	8,544	8,310	8,130	9,663	9,887	9,406	9,450	..	Merchandise, fob
900	1,057	1,158	1,163	1,396	1,330	1,550	1,655	2,112	2,425	..	Nonfactor Services
881	1,365	1,232	907	1,009	1,072	1,252	1,270	1,331	1,625	..	Factor Services
606	672	808	795	893	907	936	1,138	1,100	1,185	..	Long-Term Interest
48	48	63	56	66	65	78	105	118	130	..	Private Current Transfers, net
..	..	0	0	0	0	0	0	0	..	..	Workers' Remittances
-577	-893	-534	-180	39	-455	-1,363	-677	-572	-572	..	Curr. A/C Bal before Off. Transf.
..	..	0	0	0	0	0	0	0	..	..	Net Official Transfers
-577	-893	-534	-180	39	-455	-1,363	-677	-572	-572	..	Curr. A/C Bal after Off. Transf.
778	990	290	297	1,749	1,600	844	226	289	1,134	f	Long-Term Capital, net
0	2	..	..	..	..	..	..	..	125	..	Direct Investment
741	941	225	148	1,010	2,025	1,028	1,108	318	594	..	Long-Term Loans
1,552	1,880	1,203	1,404	2,852	4,214	3,861	3,217	2,151	2,245	..	Disbursements
811	939	978	1,255	1,842	2,189	2,832	2,109	1,833	1,651	..	Repayments
38	48	65	149	739	-425	-184	-882	-29	415	..	Other Long-Term Capital
283	-540	-529	702	-1,046	-629	495	-698	246	-153	f	Other Capital, net
-484	443	773	-819	-742	-516	24	1,149	37	-409	..	Change in Reserves
				(Hungarian Forint per US dollar)							**Memo Item:**
32.530	34.310	36.630	42.670	48.040	50.120	45.830	46.970	50.410	59.070	..	Conversion Factor (Annual Avg)
				(Millions of US dollars), outstanding at end of year							**EXTERNAL DEBT (Total)**
9,757	9,781	10,216	10,745	10,984	13,955	16,914	19,592	19,626	20,605	..	
6,409	6,933	6,955	6,842	8,006	10,936	13,420	16,489	16,263	17,299	..	Long-Term Debt (by debtor)
6,338	6,674	6,699	6,599	7,460	9,942	12,089	15,077	14,848	15,985	..	Central Bank, incl. IMF credit
0	0	0	0	12	186	252	323	451	567	..	Central Government
..	..	..	..	..	..	..	..	..	..	..	Rest of General Government
71	186	183	171	399	400	427	373	283	130	..	Non-financial Public Enterprises
0	73	73	71	136	408	653	716	680	617	..	Priv. Sector, incl non-guaranteed
3,347	2,848	3,261	3,904	2,977	3,019	3,494	3,103	3,363	3,307	..	Short-Term Debt
				(Millions of US dollars)							**Memo Items:**
..	..	..	1,231.2	1,560.0	2,153.1	2,302.0	1,634.3	1,467.2	1,246.0	..	Int'l Reserves Excluding Gold
1,219.7	669.8	295.2	584.5	636.0	760.9	917.1	794.4	653.5	600.3	..	Gold Holdings (at market price)
											SOCIAL INDICATORS
1.9	1.9	1.8	1.8	1.7	1.8	1.8	1.8	1.8	1.8	..	Total Fertility Rate
23.1	20.6	19.7	19.0	20.2	20.4	19.0	17.0	15.8	15.8	..	Infant Mortality Rate
69.5	69.6	69.6	69.7	69.8	69.9	70.1	70.2	70.3	70.5	..	Life Expectancy at Birth
53.5	54.5	55.4	56.4	57.3	58.3	58.7	59.1	59.5	59.9	..	Urban Population, % of total
94.1	92.8	103.3	97.9	103.6	98.1	100.0	100.0	106.5	103.5	..	Food Prod. per capita (1987=100)
18.2	..	..	..	..	..	..	..	..	..	..	Labor Force, Agriculture (%)
43.9	44.0	44.1	44.2	44.3	44.4	44.5	44.6	44.7	44.8	..	Labor Force, Female (%)
96.0	..	99.0	99.0	99.0	98.0	98.0	97.0	..	..	..	Primary Schl. Enroll. Ratio
97.0	..	99.0	99.0	99.0	99.0	98.0	97.0	..	..	..	Primary Schl. Enroll. Ratio, Female
69.0	..	73.0	73.0	73.0	72.0	70.0	70.0	..	..	..	Secondary Schl. Enroll. Ratio

ICELAND	1969	1970	1971	1972	1973	1974	1975	1976	1977	1978	1979
CURRENT GNP PER CAPITA (US $)	2,370	2,420	2,820	3,380	4,190	5,520	6,370	7,080	8,200	9,930	11,800
POPULATION (thousands)	203	204	206	209	212	215	218	220	222	224	226

USE AND ORIGIN OF RESOURCES *(Billions of current Icelandic Kronur)*

	1969	1970	1971	1972	1973	1974	1975	1976	1977	1978	1979
Gross National Product (GNP)	0.34	0.43	0.55	0.69	0.96	1.40	1.98	2.79	4.05	6.31	9.36
Net Factor Income from Abroad	-0.01	0.00	-0.01	-0.01	-0.01	-0.02	-0.05	-0.07	-0.09	-0.16	-0.24
GDP at Market Prices	0.35	0.44	0.56	0.70	0.97	1.42	2.03	2.87	4.14	6.47	9.60
Resource Balance	0.01	0.01	-0.03	-0.01	-0.01	-0.14	-0.16	0.03	-0.01	0.23	0.18
Exports of Goods & NFServices	0.16	0.21	0.22	0.26	0.37	0.47	0.72	1.05	1.44	2.47	3.81
Imports of Goods & NFServices	0.15	0.20	0.25	0.27	0.38	0.61	0.88	1.02	1.45	2.24	3.63
Domestic Absorption	0.34	0.43	0.59	0.71	0.99	1.55	2.19	2.83	4.15	6.24	9.42
Private Consumption, etc.	0.21	0.27	0.34	0.42	0.56	0.85	1.18	1.59	2.33	3.72	5.55
General Gov't Consumption	0.06	0.07	0.08	0.11	0.15	0.22	0.37	0.51	0.67	1.05	1.62
Gross Domestic Investment	0.07	0.09	0.17	0.18	0.28	0.48	0.64	0.74	1.14	1.47	2.26
Fixed Investment	0.08	0.10	0.16	0.18	0.28	0.44	0.59	0.74	1.08	1.53	2.23
Indirect Taxes, net	0.00	0.00	0.00	0.00	0.00	0.00	0.00	0.60	0.84	1.24	1.80
GDP at factor cost	0.35	0.44	0.56	0.70	0.97	1.42	2.03	2.27	3.30	5.23	7.81
Agriculture	..	..	..	..	..	..	..	..	..	..	..
Industry	..	..	..	..	..	..	..	..	..	..	..
Manufacturing	..	..	..	..	..	..	..	..	..	..	..
Services, etc.	..	..	..	..	..	..	..	..	..	..	..
Gross Domestic Saving	0.08	0.10	0.14	0.17	0.27	0.35	0.47	0.77	1.13	1.70	2.44
Gross National Saving	..	0.09	0.13	0.17	0.26	0.33	0.42	0.70	..	1.54	2.19

(Millions of 1987 Icelandic Kronur)

	1969	1970	1971	1972	1973	1974	1975	1976	1977	1978	1979
Gross National Product	80,570	87,409	98,679	104,747	109,664	115,879	116,653	122,403	133,817	142,581	150,408
GDP at Market Prices	81,806	88,204	99,391	105,908	110,857	117,259	119,212	125,397	136,553	146,062	154,036
Resource Balance	5,477	4,229	-3,326	-119	-3,568	-9,022	-2,481	3,222	-250	5,020	7,151
Exports of Goods & NFServices	26,994	31,720	30,476	33,739	36,603	36,302	37,253	41,574	45,839	52,787	56,095
Imports of Goods & NFServices	21,517	27,492	33,803	33,859	40,171	45,324	39,733	38,352	46,089	47,767	48,945
Domestic Absorption	76,330	83,975	102,717	106,027	114,426	126,281	121,693	122,175	136,803	141,041	146,885
Private Consumption, etc.	43,852	50,270	57,943	62,723	65,636	71,090	66,198	68,728	77,038	84,128	86,698
General Gov't Consumption	11,971	13,026	14,018	16,053	17,417	18,893	20,656	21,693	22,163	23,739	25,035
Gross Domestic Investment	20,506	20,679	30,756	27,251	31,373	36,298	34,839	31,753	37,603	33,174	35,152
Fixed Investment	17,548	18,900	27,355	27,090	32,819	35,891	32,762	31,780	35,609	34,474	34,544
GDP at factor cost	82,768	89,241	100,559	107,153	112,161	118,638	120,614	99,757	108,886	118,300	126,313
Agriculture	..	..	..	..	..	..	..	..	..	..	..
Industry	..	..	..	..	..	..	..	..	..	..	..
Manufacturing	..	..	..	..	..	..	..	..	..	..	..
Services, etc.	..	..	..	..	..	..	..	..	..	..	..

Memo Items:

	1969	1970	1971	1972	1973	1974	1975	1976	1977	1978	1979
Capacity to Import	22,867	29,119	29,154	32,573	38,717	35,278	32,324	39,507	45,742	52,710	51,369
Terms of Trade Adjustment	-4,127	-2,601	-1,322	-1,167	2,114	-1,024	-4,928	-2,067	-97	-77	-4,727
Gross Domestic Income	77,679	85,603	98,069	104,741	112,971	116,235	114,284	123,330	136,457	145,984	149,309
Gross National Income	76,443	84,808	97,357	103,580	111,778	114,855	111,725	120,336	133,720	142,503	145,681

DOMESTIC PRICES/DEFLATORS *(Index 1987 = 100)*

	1969	1970	1971	1972	1973	1974	1975	1976	1977	1978	1979
Overall (GDP)	0.4	0.5	0.6	0.7	0.9	1.2	1.7	2.3	3.0	4.4	6.2
Domestic Absorption	0.4	0.5	0.6	0.7	0.9	1.2	1.8	2.3	3.0	4.4	6.4
Agriculture	..	..	..	..	..	..	..	..	..	..	..
Industry	..	..	..	..	..	..	..	..	..	..	..
Manufacturing	..	..	..	..	..	..	..	..	..	..	..
Consumer Price Index	0.5	0.6	0.6	0.7	0.8	1.1	1.7	2.2	2.9	4.2	6.2

MANUFACTURING ACTIVITY

	1969	1970	1971	1972	1973	1974	1975	1976	1977	1978	1979
Employment (1987=100)	62.2	67.6	71.0	73.0	72.3	73.4	75.8	78.4	82.1	83.8	87.4
Real Earnings per Empl. (1987=100)	52.6	60.2	63.4	78.1	88.0	92.2	78.6	76.8	84.5	91.2	97.4
Real Output per Empl. (1987=100)	..	..	..	..	..	..	..	..	..	..	..
Earnings as % of Value Added	57.9	58.0	59.8	61.6	59.4	61.3	60.0	56.6	58.7	58.9	54.6

MONETARY HOLDINGS *(Millions of current Icelandic Kronur)*

	1969	1970	1971	1972	1973	1974	1975	1976	1977	1978	1979
Money Supply, Broadly Defined	139	173	209	247	327	420	542	720	1,038	1,540	2,421
Money	38	46	57	69	96	125	167	208	305	430	629
Currency Outside Banks	11	14	17	21	27	35	44	57	88	124	160
Demand Deposits	27	32	39	48	69	90	123	151	217	306	469
Quasi-Money	101	126	152	178	231	296	375	513	732	1,110	1,792

GOVERNMENT DEFICIT (-) OR SURPLUS *(Millions of current Icelandic Kronur)*

	1969	1970	1971	1972	1973	1974	1975	1976	1977	1978	1979
	..	..	..	-18	-30	-66	-122	-69	-173	-156	-193
Current Revenue	..	..	..	194	285	415	579	763	1,068	1,717	2,626
Current Expenditure	..	..	..	154	212	344	496	595	862	1,435	2,243
Current Budget Balance	..	..	..	39	74	71	83	168	205	282	383
Capital Receipts	..	..	..	..	0	2	9	10	4	3	4
Capital Payments	..	..	..	57	104	140	213	247	382	441	580

1980	1981	1982	1983	1984	1985	1986	1987	1988	1989 estimate	NOTES	ICELAND
13,560	14,810	14,530	12,360	11,730	11,650	13,400	16,910	20,230	21,240	..	CURRENT GNP PER CAPITA (US $)
228	231	234	237	239	241	243	246	249	252	..	POPULATION (thousands)
(Billions of current Icelandic Kronur)											USE AND ORIGIN OF RESOURCES
15.07	23.50	36.67	62.78	82.90	113.42	152.19	201.91	247.02	285.21	..	Gross National Product (GNP)
-0.41	-0.81	-1.50	-3.07	-4.55	-5.58	-6.23	-6.20	-8.33	-9.61	..	Net Factor Income from Abroad
15.48	24.32	38.16	65.85	87.45	119.00	158.42	208.11	255.36	294.82	..	GDP at Market Prices
0.10	-0.19	-1.64	1.77	0.46	0.72	6.75	-1.01	-1.14	11.03	..	Resource Balance
5.74	8.73	12.72	27.04	34.27	49.75	63.10	73.47	84.16	111.26	..	Exports of Goods & NFServices
5.64	8.93	14.36	25.27	33.81	49.03	56.35	74.48	85.30	100.23	..	Imports of Goods & NFServices
15.38	24.51	39.81	64.08	87.00	118.28	151.67	209.12	256.49	283.80	..	Domestic Absorption
8.83	14.21	23.11	38.33	50.61	69.84	92.06	127.43	151.05	167.05	..	Private Consumption, etc.
2.54	4.10	6.72	12.44	15.95	22.37	29.17	36.80	47.34	57.47	..	General Gov't Consumption
4.00	6.20	9.98	13.31	20.43	26.08	30.44	44.88	58.10	59.28	..	Gross Domestic Investment
3.92	5.95	9.14	14.17	19.79	26.65	32.15	45.50	55.44	59.72	..	Fixed Investment
3.03	5.02	7.81	12.28	17.67	22.85	29.74	41.53	51.07	..	..	Indirect Taxes, net
12.45	19.30	30.35	53.57	69.78	96.15	128.69	166.58	204.29	..	..	GDP at factor cost
..	..	..	..	..	..	..	..	..	..	..	Agriculture
..	..	..	..	..	..	..	..	..	..	..	Industry
..	..	..	..	..	..	..	..	..	..	..	Manufacturing
..	..	..	..	..	..	..	..	..	..	..	Services, etc.
4.10	6.01	8.33	15.08	20.89	26.80	37.20	43.88	56.96	70.31	..	Gross Domestic Saving
3.68	5.19	6.80	12.00	16.40	21.27	31.20	37.71	48.66	60.75	..	Gross National Saving
(Millions of 1987 Icelandic Kronur)											
158,844	164,182	166,409	158,585	163,652	170,062	183,988	201,910	199,410	192,174	..	Gross National Product
162,819	169,502	172,822	166,108	172,380	178,169	191,397	208,113	206,159	198,352	..	GDP at Market Prices
7,201	4,577	-696	7,754	4,812	6,015	9,994	-1,009	-1,777	6,374	..	Resource Balance
57,609	58,341	52,747	58,171	59,915	66,482	70,613	73,471	70,372	71,287	..	Exports of Goods & NFServices
50,408	53,764	53,443	50,417	55,103	60,467	60,619	74,479	72,150	64,913	..	Imports of Goods & NFServices
155,618	164,925	173,518	158,355	167,568	172,154	181,403	209,122	207,936	191,978	..	Domestic Absorption
89,807	95,950	101,169	95,155	97,821	101,824	110,481	127,434	122,532	113,311	..	Private Consumption, etc.
25,567	27,445	29,142	30,518	30,578	32,476	34,695	36,804	38,340	38,724	..	General Gov't Consumption
40,244	41,530	43,207	32,681	39,170	37,854	36,227	44,884	47,064	39,943	..	Gross Domestic Investment
39,435	39,817	39,616	34,755	37,939	38,702	38,240	45,500	44,898	40,239	..	Fixed Investment
132,472	135,939	139,019	136,150	138,537	145,134	156,193	166,581	164,787	..	..	GDP at factor cost
..	..	..	..	..	..	..	..	..	..	..	Agriculture
..	..	..	..	..	..	..	..	..	..	..	Industry
..	..	..	..	..	..	..	..	..	..	..	Manufacturing
..	..	..	..	..	..	..	..	..	..	..	Services, etc.
											Memo Items:
51,283	52,600	47,326	53,948	55,849	61,357	67,882	73,471	71,187	72,056	..	Capacity to Import
-6,326	-5,741	-5,420	-4,223	-4,067	-5,125	-2,731	0	815	769	..	Terms of Trade Adjustment
156,493	163,761	167,401	161,885	168,314	173,044	188,666	208,113	206,974	199,121	..	Gross Domestic Income
152,518	158,441	160,989	154,362	159,585	164,937	181,257	201,910	200,225	192,943	..	Gross National Income
(Index 1987 = 100)											DOMESTIC PRICES/DEFLATORS
9.5	14.3	22.1	39.6	50.7	66.8	82.8	100.0	123.9	148.6	..	Overall (GDP)
9.9	14.9	22.9	40.5	51.9	68.7	83.6	100.0	123.4	147.8	..	Domestic Absorption
..	..	..	..	..	..	..	..	..	..	..	Agriculture
..	..	..	..	..	..	..	..	..	..	..	Industry
..	..	..	..	..	..	..	..	..	..	..	Manufacturing
9.8	14.7	22.2	41.0	52.9	69.7	84.9	100.0	125.8	151.9	..	Consumer Price Index
											MANUFACTURING ACTIVITY
90.8	92.3	92.7	93.6	95.7	95.9	97.0	100.0	101.3	..	G	Employment (1987=100)
88.1	90.7	93.5	78.2	75.0	81.2	85.3	100.0	..	..	G	Real Earnings per Empl. (1987=100)
..	..	..	..	..	..	..	..	..	..	G	Real Output per Empl. (1987=100)
50.5	54.3	51.9	57.4	52.7	56.1	58.0	65.1	..	..	..	Earnings as % of Value Added
(Millions of current Icelandic Kronur)											MONETARY HOLDINGS
4,003	6,868	10,856	19,448	26,031	38,453	52,003	70,423	87,304	110,815	..	Money Supply, Broadly Defined
1,010	1,628	2,076	3,698	7,669	15,201	22,592	34,454	44,231	61,121	..	Money
224	406	527	770	966	1,251	1,734	2,244	2,639	3,046	..	Currency Outside Banks
786	1,222	1,549	2,928	6,703	13,950	20,857	32,210	41,592	58,075	..	Demand Deposits
2,993	5,240	8,780	15,750	18,362	23,252	29,411	35,969	43,073	49,694	..	Quasi-Money
(Millions of current Icelandic Kronur)											
-193	-172	-958	-1,998	-1,610	-4,719	-7,639	-2,677	..	..	E	GOVERNMENT DEFICIT (-) OR SURPLUS
4,089	6,623	10,762	17,492	23,630	31,231	41,671	55,012	..	..	..	Current Revenue
3,388	5,342	9,017	16,505	19,665	28,644	42,939	49,882	..	..	..	Current Expenditure
700	1,281	1,745	987	3,964	2,587	-1,268	5,129	..	..	..	Current Budget Balance
2	1	10	21	4	25	267	242	..	..	..	Capital Receipts
895	1,454	2,713	3,006	5,578	7,331	6,639	8,048	..	..	..	Capital Payments

ICELAND	1969	1970	1971	1972	1973	1974	1975	1976	1977	1978	1979
FOREIGN TRADE (CUSTOMS BASIS)					*(Millions of current US dollars)*						
Value of Exports, fob	107.7	146.9	150.1	191.4	290.7	329.3	307.5	404.0	512.6	640.9	790.8
Nonfuel Primary Products	102.1	141.7	143.2	181.6	277.2	310.4	290.8	379.8	479.7	608.5	738.9
Fuels	0.0	0.0	0.0	0.0	0.0	0.0	0.0	0.0	0.0	0.0	0.0
Manufactures	5.6	5.2	6.9	9.8	13.5	19.0	16.7	24.3	32.9	32.4	51.9
Value of Imports, cif	123.2	157.1	220.7	233.4	327.2	524.5	488.3	470.0	606.9	673.5	825.0
Nonfuel Primary Products	29.1	34.0	39.5	42.6	48.4	76.4	73.6	77.5	88.0	97.5	114.4
Fuels	12.2	14.5	17.9	17.9	25.9	63.6	62.0	57.7	77.9	79.2	161.8
Manufactures	81.9	108.7	163.3	172.9	252.9	384.6	352.7	334.8	441.1	496.9	548.8
					(Index 1987 = 100)						
Terms of Trade	152.7	165.0	156.5	146.2	163.1	134.0	101.2	117.7	132.1	128.0	116.9
Export Prices, fob	32.1	36.5	39.1	40.3	54.5	64.0	52.6	63.1	77.1	83.3	91.2
Import Prices, cif	21.0	22.1	25.0	27.6	33.4	47.7	52.0	53.6	58.4	65.1	78.0
BALANCE OF PAYMENTS					*(Millions of current US dollars)*						
Exports of Goods & Services	..	234.8	251.7	294.9	414.9	476.0	491.1	577.7	729.5	908.2	1,084.3
Merchandise, fob	..	146.2	150.8	191.7	291.0	329.4	306.5	402.0	512.6	640.3	779.6
Nonfactor Services	..	85.1	97.2	99.8	118.9	140.7	182.5	172.5	212.1	262.0	292.8
Factor Services	..	3.5	3.7	3.4	5.0	5.9	2.1	3.2	4.8	5.9	11.9
Imports of Goods & Services	..	232.3	300.7	320.9	447.3	637.0	593.1	600.8	777.8	888.2	1,102.6
Merchandise, fob	..	143.5	200.6	215.5	326.0	476.7	441.9	427.9	564.7	618.4	754.1
Nonfactor Services	..	71.3	85.0	84.0	93.2	125.3	118.3	117.2	149.8	192.1	253.5
Factor Services	..	17.5	15.1	21.4	28.0	35.0	32.9	55.7	63.3	77.7	95.0
Long-Term Interest	..	..	..	..	..	..	..	..	..	..	..
Private Current Transfers, net	..	0.0	-0.1	0.8	1.7	1.4	0.5	1.1	..	-0.3	-1.4
Workers' Remittances	..	..	..	..	..	..	..	..	..	..	..
Curr. A/C Bal before Off. Transf.	..	2.5	-49.0	-25.3	-30.8	-159.6	-101.5	-22.0	-47.6	19.7	-19.7
Net Official Transfers	..	-0.4	..	-0.5	14.5	-0.8	-1.2	-0.8	-0.7	-0.8	-1.5
Curr. A/C Bal after Off. Transf.	..	2.1	-49.0	-25.8	-16.2	-160.4	-102.7	-22.8	-48.3	18.9	-21.2
Long-Term Capital, net	..	-2.9	53.2	24.1	22.9	109.0	134.3	64.7	111.7	78.1	94.9
Direct Investment	..	4.5	19.8	2.8	-1.5	13.2	42.4	4.5	4.2	8.1	3.1
Long-Term Loans	..	..	..	..	..	..	..	..	..	..	..
Disbursements	..	..	..	..	..	..	..	..	..	..	..
Repayments	..	..	..	..	..	..	..	..	..	..	..
Other Long-Term Capital	..	-7.4	33.4	21.3	24.4	95.7	92.0	60.2	107.5	70.0	91.8
Other Capital, net	..	21.6	10.1	13.2	9.3	-16.8	-50.2	-38.4	-47.2	-45.7	-37.0
Change in Reserves	..	-20.8	-14.2	-11.5	-16.0	68.3	18.6	-3.5	-16.2	-51.3	-36.7
Memo Item:					*(Icelandic Kronur per US dollar)*						
Conversion Factor (Annual Avg)	0.880	0.880	0.880	0.880	0.900	1.000	1.540	1.820	1.990	2.710	3.530
					(Millions US dollars), outstanding at end of year						
EXTERNAL DEBT (Total)	..	..	..	..	..	..	..	..	..	..	..
Long-Term Debt (by debtor)	..	..	..	..	..	..	..	..	..	..	..
Central Bank, incl. IMF credit	..	..	..	..	..	..	..	..	..	..	..
Central Government	..	..	..	..	..	..	..	..	..	..	..
Rest of General Government	..	..	..	..	..	..	..	..	..	..	..
Non-financial Public Enterprises	..	..	..	..	..	..	..	..	..	..	..
Priv. Sector, incl non-guaranteed	..	..	..	..	..	..	..	..	..	..	..
Short-Term Debt	..	..	..	..	..	..	..	..	..	..	..
Memo Items:					*(Millions of US dollars)*						
Int'l Reserves Excluding Gold	37.50	52.72	68.85	83.05	98.40	47.25	45.60	79.38	98.34	135.83	161.94
Gold Holdings (at market price)	1.02	1.08	1.27	1.88	3.26	5.59	4.21	4.04	6.43	9.94	25.09
SOCIAL INDICATORS											
Total Fertility Rate	3.0	2.8	2.9	3.1	2.9	2.7	2.6	2.5	2.3	2.4	2.4
Infant Mortality Rate	11.6	13.2	12.9	11.3	9.6	11.7	12.5	7.7	9.5	11.3	9.5
Life Expectancy at Birth	73.8	74.0	74.1	74.3	74.7	75.1	75.5	75.9	76.3	76.4	76.5
Urban Population, % of total	84.5	84.9	85.3	85.7	86.0	86.4	86.8	87.1	87.4	87.6	87.9
Food Prod. per capita (1987=100)	101.3	101.2	103.7	112.4	108.9	116.7	115.6	106.5	104.0	114.9	108.4
Labor Force, Agriculture (%)	17.9	17.2	16.4	15.7	15.0	14.3	13.6	12.9	12.2	11.5	10.8
Labor Force, Female (%)	33.4	34.0	34.9	35.8	36.6	37.4	38.1	38.9	39.7	40.4	41.1
Primary Schl. Enroll. Ratio	..	97.0	..	..	..	..	100.0	99.0	..	96.0	96.0
Primary Schl. Enroll. Ratio, Female	..	100.0	..	..	..	..	102.0	100.0	..	..	..
Secondary Schl. Enroll. Ratio	..	80.0	..	..	..	..	80.0	83.0	..	83.0	80.0

1980	1981	1982	1983	1984	1985	1986	1987	1988	1989 estimate	NOTES	ICELAND
				(Millions of current US dollars)							**FOREIGN TRADE (CUSTOMS BASIS)**
931.2	894.6	684.9	748.4	744.2	813.8	1,095.8	1,375.1	1,431.0	..	..	Value of Exports, fob
853.1	825.0	619.1	677.1	651.1	733.0	995.2	1,247.3	1,248.0	..	..	Nonfuel Primary Products
0.0	0.0	0.0	0.0	0.0	0.0	..	0.0	0.0	..	..	Fuels
78.1	69.6	65.8	71.3	93.1	80.8	100.6	127.8	183.0	..	..	Manufactures
1,000.1	1,021.0	941.6	815.3	843.6	904.0	1,115.3	1,581.4	1,588.0	..	..	Value of Imports, cif
148.2	144.2	134.2	130.5	128.5	128.0	147.8	179.8	189.0	..	..	Nonfuel Primary Products
167.3	168.1	146.3	132.5	132.9	142.1	107.1	117.3	101.0	..	..	Fuels
684.6	708.7	661.1	552.3	582.2	633.9	860.4	1,284.3	1,298.0	..	..	Manufactures
				(Index 1987 = 100)							
129.2	128.7	116.6	116.3	109.4	102.7	..	100.0	101.6	..	..	Terms of Trade
115.3	110.5	95.1	93.2	84.9	78.5	..	100.0	104.7	..	..	Export Prices, fob
89.3	85.8	81.6	80.1	77.6	76.4	85.6	100.0	103.1	..	..	Import Prices, cif
				(Millions of current US dollars)							**BALANCE OF PAYMENTS**
1,213.5	1,221.6	1,054.3	1,100.0	1,106.0	1,224.4	1,569.7	1,945.8	1,983.2	1,941.5	..	Exports of Goods & Services
919.8	896.4	685.5	742.0	743.2	814.0	1,096.8	1,376.1	1,425.4	1,401.5	..	Merchandise, fob
279.8	302.8	340.6	342.5	347.1	394.3	453.2	541.9	531.6	516.9	..	Nonfactor Services
13.9	22.4	28.2	15.5	15.7	16.1	19.7	27.8	26.2	23.1	..	Factor Services
1,288.4	1,366.2	1,312.4	1,154.9	1,238.1	1,339.7	1,556.5	2,136.0	2,203.5	2,031.8	..	Imports of Goods & Services
899.9	925.5	837.6	721.6	756.6	814.3	1,000.0	1,428.2	1,439.4	1,267.3	..	Merchandise, fob
262.8	282.0	308.5	280.7	310.9	362.9	373.6	509.9	535.6	494.8	..	Nonfactor Services
125.7	158.7	166.3	152.6	170.6	162.5	182.9	197.9	228.5	269.7	..	Factor Services
..	..	..	..	..	..	..	..	..	..		Long-Term Interest
-3.0	-1.6	-3.4	-0.6	2.1	1.3	5.7	0.9	0.7	0.9	..	Private Current Transfers, net
..	..	..	..	..	..	..	..	..	..	..	Workers' Remittances
-77.9	-146.2	-261.5	-55.5	-130.0	-114.0	18.9	-189.3	-219.6	-89.4	..	Curr. A/C Bal before Off. Transf.
-1.2	-1.7	-1.7	-1.4	-1.3	-1.1	-1.7	-1.7	-1.9	-3.9	..	Net Official Transfers
-79.1	-147.9	-263.2	-56.9	-131.3	-115.1	17.2	-191.0	-221.5	-93.3	..	Curr. A/C Bal after Off. Transf.
153.0	191.3	214.1	93.5	113.0	155.3	156.7	178.1	207.8	259.7	..	Long-Term Capital, net
22.3	53.0	35.8	-23.4	13.7	23.6	6.4	1.7	-15.9	-35.6	..	Direct Investment
..	..	..	..	..	..	..	..	..	..	..	Long-Term Loans
..	..	..	..	..	..	..	..	..	..	..	Disbursements
..	..	..	..	..	..	..	..	..	..	..	Repayments
130.7	138.3	178.3	116.9	99.3	131.7	150.3	176.4	223.7	295.3	..	Other Long-Term Capital
-39.7	28.5	-46.5	-25.7	3.1	23.9	-75.0	-5.2	14.9	-111.8	..	Other Capital, net
-34.2	-71.9	95.6	-10.9	15.2	-64.1	-98.9	18.1	-1.2	-54.6	..	Change in Reserves
				(Icelandic Kronur per US dollar)							**Memo Item:**
4.800	7.220	12.350	24.840	31.690	41.510	41.100	38.680	43.010	57.040	..	Conversion Factor (Annual Avg)
				(Millions US dollars), outstanding at end of year							**EXTERNAL DEBT (Total)**
..	..	..	..	..	..	..	..	..	..	..	Long-Term Debt (by debtor)
..	..	..	..	..	..	..	..	..	..	..	Central Bank, incl. IMF credit
..	..	..	..	..	..	..	..	..	..	..	Central Government
..	..	..	..	..	..	..	..	..	..	..	Rest of General Government
..	..	..	..	..	..	..	..	..	..	..	Non-financial Public Enterprises
..	..	..	..	..	..	..	..	..	..	..	Priv. Sector, incl non-guaranteed
..	..	..	..	..	..	..	..	..	..	..	Short-Term Debt
				(Millions of US dollars)							**Memo Items:**
173.81	229.53	145.17	149.29	127.60	205.54	309.84	311.31	290.74	337.32	..	Int'l Reserves Excluding Gold
28.89	19.48	22.39	18.69	15.11	16.02	19.15	23.72	20.10	19.65	..	Gold Holdings (at market price)
											SOCIAL INDICATORS
2.5	2.4	2.3	2.2	2.1	1.9	1.9	2.1	2.1	2.1	..	Total Fertility Rate
7.7	7.2	6.7	6.2	6.1	5.7	5.4	7.2	7.1	7.1	..	Infant Mortality Rate
76.6	76.7	76.8	76.9	77.1	77.2	77.4	77.5	77.7	77.8	..	Life Expectancy at Birth
88.2	88.4	88.7	88.9	89.2	89.4	89.6	89.8	90.1	90.3	..	Urban Population, % of total
111.1	110.3	111.6	109.6	108.7	112.0	104.4	100.0	90.8	88.3	..	Food Prod. per capita (1987=100)
10.2	..	..	..	..	..	..	..	..	..	..	Labor Force, Agriculture (%)
41.8	41.9	42.0	42.1	42.2	42.3	42.3	42.4	42.5	42.6	..	Labor Force, Female (%)
99.0	..	99.0	101.0	100.0	99.0	99.0	..	..	..	..	Primary Schl. Enroll. Ratio
..	..	101.0	102.0	..	99.0	100.0	..	..	..	..	Primary Schl. Enroll. Ratio, Female
85.0	..	88.0	88.0	89.0	92.0	..	..	..	..	..	Secondary Schl. Enroll. Ratio

INDIA	1969	1970	1971	1972	1973	1974	1975	1976	1977	1978	1979
CURRENT GNP PER CAPITA (US $)	100	110	110	110	130	140	170	160	170	190	200
POPULATION (millions)	535	548	560	573	586	600	613	628	642	657	672

USE AND ORIGIN OF RESOURCES					*(Billions of current Indian Rupees)*						
Gross National Product (GNP)	401.7	429.8	460.5	507.8	618.1	730.7	785.9	847.7	959.8	1,042.0	1,146.2
Net Factor Income from Abroad	-2.2	-1.8	-2.1	-2.3	-2.0	-1.6	-1.7	-1.2	-0.9	0.1	2.6
GDP at Market Prices	403.9	431.6	462.6	510.0	620.1	732.3	787.6	848.9	960.7	1,041.9	1,143.6
Resource Balance	-1.3	-3.2	-4.3	-2.1	-3.3	-8.1	-3.0	6.5	4.9	-12.6	-25.3
Exports of Goods & NFServices	16.3	16.1	17.7	21.5	26.5	36.4	48.9	60.8	66.2	68.7	80.6
Imports of Goods & NFServices	17.6	19.3	22.0	23.6	29.8	44.5	51.9	54.3	61.3	81.3	105.9
Domestic Absorption	405.1	434.8	466.7	512.1	623.3	740.4	790.6	842.5	955.9	1,054.4	1,168.8
Private Consumption, etc.	305.9	322.6	336.7	377.6	458.5	533.2	552.7	582.5	678.1	725.0	795.7
General Gov't Consumption	34.4	38.4	44.6	47.3	51.6	62.4	73.8	82.3	87.6	97.2	111.7
Gross Domestic Investment	64.8	73.8	85.5	87.2	113.3	144.8	164.1	177.8	190.2	232.2	261.4
Fixed Investment	59.0	63.0	70.8	81.3	90.7	110.0	133.3	153.0	172.2	188.8	213.1
Indirect Taxes, net	30.6	34.6	40.1	45.3	50.5	62.0	75.6	83.6	87.2	103.1	119.1
GDP at factor cost	373.3	397.1	422.5	464.7	569.5	670.4	712.0	765.4	873.5	938.8	1,024.4
Agriculture	174.0	179.4	183.2	201.5	265.6	291.0	288.4	294.6	348.8	358.5	370.9
Industry	80.3	87.0	96.1	106.0	123.1	154.4	169.0	191.7	216.5	243.4	273.8
Manufacturing	54.5	59.5	66.0	73.3	88.7	114.0	118.6	131.2	147.0	169.2	193.8
Services, etc.	119.0	130.7	143.2	157.2	180.8	225.1	254.6	279.0	308.2	336.9	379.7
Gross Domestic Saving	63.6	70.6	81.3	85.2	110.0	136.7	161.1	184.2	194.9	219.7	236.2
Gross National Saving	..	69.4	80.0	83.7	109.3	137.1	163.3	189.1	203.5	229.2	253.9

					(Billions of 1987 Indian Rupees)						
Gross National Product	1,636.2	1,725.7	1,751.9	1,741.1	1,802.4	1,828.5	1,996.7	2,034.0	2,181.8	2,306.0	2,196.3
GDP at Market Prices	1,646.7	1,732.6	1,760.0	1,749.4	1,809.1	1,830.7	1,998.9	2,034.4	2,180.8	2,306.6	2,185.6
Resource Balance	-58.2	-74.3	-89.6	-84.0	-57.3	-36.1	-3.9	-5.2	-29.5	-79.3	-46.3
Exports of Goods & NFServices	76.5	74.0	78.4	86.6	86.6	95.6	113.9	140.2	134.8	135.6	151.1
Imports of Goods & NFServices	134.7	148.4	168.0	170.6	143.9	131.6	117.8	145.4	164.3	214.9	197.5
Domestic Absorption	1,704.9	1,806.9	1,849.6	1,833.4	1,866.4	1,866.8	2,002.8	2,039.6	2,210.3	2,385.9	2,231.9
Private Consumption, etc.	1,228.7	1,292.6	1,285.4	1,293.0	1,277.6	1,278.4	1,373.5	1,372.0	1,518.9	1,610.7	1,462.7
General Gov't Consumption	139.8	152.9	168.7	169.3	167.7	159.8	176.5	190.5	196.3	210.8	223.8
Gross Domestic Investment	336.4	361.4	395.4	371.0	421.0	428.6	452.8	477.2	495.1	564.4	545.4
Fixed Investment	313.4	314.9	334.4	351.7	348.1	337.4	370.0	416.6	456.6	460.9	447.5
GDP at factor cost	1,484.7	1,560.3	1,575.7	1,569.5	1,641.8	1,660.8	1,810.4	1,833.0	1,969.9	2,078.3	1,970.2
Agriculture	648.7	694.7	681.7	647.5	694.1	683.5	771.7	727.1	800.0	818.5	713.9
Industry	354.8	360.0	370.3	384.2	391.5	399.3	421.3	458.4	489.2	532.4	516.0
Manufacturing	215.4	220.5	227.7	236.6	247.2	254.4	259.7	282.5	300.1	337.1	326.3
Services, etc.	481.7	505.3	523.8	538.9	556.6	578.7	618.3	647.9	680.9	727.4	740.8

Memo Items:											
Capacity to Import	124.8	123.8	135.2	155.4	128.0	107.7	111.0	162.9	177.4	181.6	150.3
Terms of Trade Adjustment	48.3	49.7	56.7	68.8	41.3	12.1	-2.9	22.7	42.7	46.0	-0.8
Gross Domestic Income	1,695.0	1,782.3	1,816.8	1,818.2	1,850.4	1,842.8	1,996.0	2,057.1	2,223.5	2,352.6	2,184.7
Gross National Income	1,684.5	1,775.4	1,808.6	1,809.8	1,843.7	1,840.6	1,993.8	2,056.7	2,224.4	2,352.0	2,195.4

DOMESTIC PRICES/DEFLATORS					*(Index 1987 = 100)*						
Overall (GDP)	24.5	24.9	26.3	29.2	34.3	40.0	39.4	41.7	44.1	45.2	52.3
Domestic Absorption	23.8	24.1	25.2	27.9	33.4	39.7	39.5	41.3	43.2	44.2	52.4
Agriculture	26.8	25.8	26.9	31.1	38.3	42.6	37.4	40.5	43.6	43.8	52.0
Industry	22.6	24.2	25.9	27.6	31.4	38.7	40.1	41.8	44.2	45.7	53.1
Manufacturing	25.3	27.0	29.0	31.0	35.9	44.8	45.7	46.4	49.0	50.2	59.4
Consumer Price Index	24.3	25.6	26.4	28.1	32.8	42.2	44.6	41.2	44.6	45.8	48.6

MANUFACTURING ACTIVITY											
Employment (1987=100)	64.9	68.1	72.1	72.7	75.2	77.6	81.4	83.8	89.3	91.4	97.3
Real Earnings per Empl. (1987=100)	71.8	74.1	82.1	83.4	75.6	69.6	70.3	76.6	75.6	79.4	82.8
Real Output per Empl. (1987=100)	49.0	49.9	49.9	51.9	48.8	49.9	52.9	57.3	58.2	62.9	59.3
Earnings as % of Value Added	45.7	46.5	60.8	54.2	47.8	43.6	47.2	43.3	49.9	48.6	49.5

MONETARY HOLDINGS					*(Billions of current Indian Rupees)*						
Money Supply, Broadly Defined	97.5	109.0	126.9	145.3	172.6	192.8	218.2	271.5	322.1	388.3	455.9
Money	60.4	67.6	76.5	86.2	101.0	111.3	122.3	152.8	178.5	157.6	176.9
Currency Outside Banks	37.6	41.6	45.6	49.1	57.8	61.4	64.4	73.2	84.2	94.6	108.0
Demand Deposits	22.7	26.1	30.8	37.1	43.3	49.9	57.9	79.6	94.3	63.1	68.9
Quasi-Money	37.2	41.4	50.4	59.2	71.5	81.5	95.8	118.8	143.6	230.7	279.0

GOVERNMENT DEFICIT (-) OR SURPLUS					*(Billions of current Indian Rupees)*						
GOVERNMENT DEFICIT (-) OR SURPLUS	..	..	..	..	..	-23.6	-32.0	-36.9	-37.9	-50.8	-63.0
Current Revenue	..	..	..	..	..	75.8	93.6	104.2	115.6	130.9	146.2
Current Expenditure	..	..	..	..	..	65.6	80.8	92.6	101.7	116.4	140.0
Current Budget Balance	..	..	..	..	..	10.3	12.8	11.6	13.8	14.5	6.3
Capital Receipts	..	..	..	..	..	0.5	0.9	1.1	1.2	1.4	1.6
Capital Payments	..	..	..	..	..	34.3	45.7	49.6	52.9	66.7	70.8

1980	1981	1982	1983	1984	1985	1986	1987	1988	1989 estimate	NOTES	INDIA
240	270	280	280	280	290	290	310	340	340	..	**CURRENT GNP PER CAPITA (US $)**
687	703	718	734	750	765	782	799	816	833	..	**POPULATION (millions)**
											USE AND ORIGIN OF RESOURCES
				(Billions of current Indian Rupees)							
1,361.8	1,594.7	1,769.4	2,057.3	2,289.6	2,607.0	2,907.5	3,293.5	3,868.4	4,339.1	C f	Gross National Product (GNP)
3.7	0.5	-6.5	-11.3	-17.2	-19.0	-26.1	-32.0	-43.2	-55.1	..	Net Factor Income from Abroad
1,358.1	1,594.2	1,775.9	2,068.6	2,306.8	2,626.0	2,933.6	3,325.5	3,911.6	4,394.2	C f	GDP at Market Prices
-48.9	-52.3	-48.8	-47.5	-54.2	-81.3	-80.2	-85.9	-129.0	-124.7	..	Resource Balance
88.5	101.7	107.9	127.6	157.1	156.3	174.9	210.3	263.2	350.7	..	Exports of Goods & NFServices
137.4	154.0	156.7	175.0	211.3	237.6	255.1	296.2	392.2	475.4	..	Imports of Goods & NFServices
1,407.0	1,646.5	1,824.6	2,116.1	2,361.0	2,707.4	3,013.8	3,411.4	4,040.3	4,518.9	..	Domestic Absorption
966.0	1,082.6	1,224.9	1,443.9	1,600.9	1,748.4	1,954.5	2,239.7	2,623.1	2,944.4	..	Private Consumption, etc.
130.8	153.5	182.7	211.4	243.5	291.7	346.3	410.3	463.3	538.3	..	General Gov't Consumption
310.2	410.4	417.0	460.7	516.5	667.3	713.1	761.4	953.8	1,036.2	..	Gross Domestic Investment
262.8	314.5	357.7	399.9	454.2	535.7	620.2	674.5	802.0	873.8	..	Fixed Investment
135.9	165.4	187.4	208.7	228.1	284.4	329.3	381.4	422.6	474.9	..	Indirect Taxes, net
1,222.3	1,428.8	1,588.5	1,859.9	2,078.7	2,341.6	2,604.4	2,944.1	3,489.0	3,919.4	C f	GDP at factor cost
464.8	523.7	556.2	667.7	712.3	764.8	815.7	916.5	1,137.4	1,188.8	..	Agriculture
316.3	380.9	432.6	507.4	578.5	664.8	749.5	845.7	980.0	1,122.0	..	Industry
216.4	252.6	280.7	330.5	372.4	429.8	476.9	541.6	629.9	721.1	..	Manufacturing
441.1	524.1	599.7	684.9	787.8	911.9	1,039.1	1,181.8	1,371.5	1,608.6	..	Services, etc.
261.3	358.1	368.3	413.3	462.3	585.9	632.9	675.5	825.1	911.5	..	Gross Domestic Saving
287.4	378.6	386.6	429.2	474.8	595.5	636.1	678.4	823.4	901.1	..	Gross National Saving
				(Billions of 1987 Indian Rupees)							
2,336.9	2,482.6	2,560.7	2,743.1	2,840.4	3,015.9	3,153.1	3,293.5	3,607.2	3,764.1	C	Gross National Product
2,326.7	2,477.5	2,568.7	2,758.1	2,861.7	3,037.8	3,181.7	3,325.5	3,647.5	3,811.7	C I	GDP at Market Prices
-55.0	-66.3	-54.6	-64.0	-61.5	-95.4	-106.1	-85.9	-118.1	-90.2	..	Resource Balance
155.8	157.4	159.0	169.0	185.4	180.6	194.6	210.3	233.1	263.5	..	Exports of Goods & NFServices
210.8	223.7	213.6	233.1	246.8	276.0	300.7	296.2	351.2	353.8	..	Imports of Goods & NFServices
2,381.7	2,543.8	2,623.3	2,822.2	2,923.2	3,133.3	3,287.8	3,411.4	3,765.6	3,901.9	..	Domestic Absorption
1,570.1	1,616.8	1,713.4	1,899.3	1,964.3	2,017.8	2,153.6	2,239.7	2,457.7	2,552.5	..	Private Consumption, etc.
235.7	246.1	271.5	283.7	305.9	340.8	375.5	410.3	430.4	460.4	..	General Gov't Consumption
575.9	680.9	638.3	639.2	653.0	774.6	758.7	761.4	877.5	888.9	..	Gross Domestic Investment
496.2	530.3	553.3	559.6	579.3	614.6	656.7	674.5	728.8	740.3	..	Fixed Investment
2,108.0	2,235.2	2,301.9	2,488.9	2,586.4	2,713.8	2,826.9	2,944.1	3,250.5	3,396.8	C I	GDP at factor cost
803.0	848.9	835.4	924.7	925.0	927.7	911.9	916.5	1,075.9	1,081.3	..	Agriculture
532.6	574.8	602.0	656.5	695.8	744.9	801.5	845.7	910.8	965.4	..	Industry
326.9	353.2	376.2	413.5	440.3	474.6	510.8	541.6	586.2	609.3	..	Manufacturing
773.1	811.8	865.0	907.7	965.6	1,041.2	1,113.6	1,181.8	1,263.8	1,350.1	..	Services, etc.
											Memo Items:
135.8	147.8	147.1	169.8	183.5	181.5	206.1	210.3	235.7	261.0	..	Capacity to Import
-20.1	-9.6	-11.9	0.8	-1.8	0.9	11.6	0.0	2.7	-2.5	..	Terms of Trade Adjustment
2,306.7	2,467.9	2,556.8	2,758.9	2,859.9	3,038.8	3,193.2	3,325.5	3,650.1	3,809.1	..	Gross Domestic Income
2,316.8	2,473.0	2,548.9	2,743.9	2,838.6	3,016.8	3,164.7	3,293.5	3,609.8	3,761.6	..	Gross National Income
				(Index 1987 = 100)							**DOMESTIC PRICES/DEFLATORS**
58.4	64.3	69.1	75.0	80.6	86.4	92.2	100.0	107.2	115.3	..	Overall (GDP)
59.1	64.7	69.6	75.0	80.8	86.4	91.7	100.0	107.3	115.8	..	Domestic Absorption
57.9	61.7	66.6	72.2	77.0	82.4	89.5	100.0	105.7	109.9	..	Agriculture
59.4	66.3	71.9	77.3	83.1	89.3	93.5	100.0	107.6	116.2	..	Industry
66.2	71.5	74.6	79.9	84.6	90.6	93.4	100.0	107.5	118.3	..	Manufacturing
54.2	61.3	66.1	73.9	80.1	84.5	91.9	100.0	109.4	116.1	..	Consumer Price Index
											MANUFACTURING ACTIVITY
100.3	99.9	102.6	99.6	98.5	94.9	97.0	100.0	..	..	G	Employment (1987=100)
80.9	79.4	85.0	89.4	95.8	96.8	94.8	100.0	..	..	G	Real Earnings per Empl. (1987=100)
60.0	66.7	72.7	74.8	81.8	89.5	93.0	100.0	..	..	G	Real Output per Empl. (1987=100)
50.7	47.9	49.0	48.1	50.3	46.3	46.2	46.5	..	..	..	Earnings as % of Value Added
				(Billions of current Indian Rupees)							**MONETARY HOLDINGS**
527.7	618.0	720.9	840.4	988.4	1,152.5	1,356.0	1,575.4	1,858.8	2,149.0	D	Money Supply, Broadly Defined
204.6	232.5	273.7	308.6	365.6	412.4	478.7	543.2	632.8	746.9	..	Money
126.3	137.4	157.4	181.3	218.1	239.4	268.0	315.6	356.4	434.5	..	Currency Outside Banks
78.3	95.0	116.3	127.2	147.5	173.0	210.7	227.6	276.3	312.4	..	Demand Deposits
323.1	385.5	447.2	531.9	622.8	740.1	877.3	1,032.2	1,226.1	1,402.1	..	Quasi-Money
				(Billions of current Indian Rupees)							
-88.6	-87.3	-107.3	-133.3	-175.8	-222.5	-272.0	-278.8	-330.9	..	C E	**GOVERNMENT DEFICIT (-) OR SURPLUS**
163.6	196.3	225.9	254.9	297.0	361.3	420.1	477.8	554.7	..	..	Current Revenue
159.1	181.3	213.3	248.5	301.9	370.9	444.3	515.8	608.5	..	..	Current Expenditure
4.5	15.0	12.7	6.4	-4.9	-9.6	-24.2	-38.0	-53.8	..	..	Current Budget Balance
1.9	3.4	3.1	3.6	3.9	4.8	5.0	7.9	7.0	..	..	Capital Receipts
95.0	105.7	123.1	143.3	174.8	217.7	252.8	248.7	284.1	..	..	Capital Payments

INDIA	1969	1970	1971	1972	1973	1974	1975	1976	1977	1978	1979
FOREIGN TRADE (CUSTOMS BASIS)					*(Millions of current US dollars)*						
Value of Exports, fob	1,834	2,026	2,043	2,422	2,968	3,906	4,365	5,526	6,355	6,650	7,850
Nonfuel Primary Products	812	949	932	1,073	1,353	1,839	2,354	2,486	2,590	2,429	2,974
Fuels	14	17	11	16	40	26	39	35	34	24	20
Manufactures	1,008	1,061	1,100	1,333	1,576	2,041	1,972	3,004	3,731	4,197	4,857
Value of Imports, cif	2,118	2,094	2,406	2,230	3,146	5,167	6,385	5,710	6,601	7,854	10,142
Nonfuel Primary Products	825	838	773	593	1,009	1,475	2,120	1,933	1,998	1,910	1,813
Fuels	86	162	245	266	436	1,446	1,419	1,390	1,640	1,973	3,546
Manufactures	1,206	1,095	1,387	1,371	1,701	2,247	2,846	2,387	2,962	3,970	4,783
Terms of Trade	83.9	118.2	114.5	116.0	*(Index 1987 = 100)* 108.8	84.7	88.6	81.5	82.5	82.7	77.2
Export Prices, fob	23.8	32.1	31.2	33.0	40.3	53.0	57.9	53.6	57.5	61.7	69.8
Import Prices, cif	28.4	27.2	27.3	28.4	37.1	62.5	65.4	65.8	69.7	74.6	90.5
BALANCE OF PAYMENTS					*(Millions of current US dollars)*						
Exports of Goods & Services	..	2,140	2,380	2,830	3,450	4,690	5,780	7,010	8,030	8,860	10,776
Merchandise, fob	..	1,870	2,090	2,460	3,020	3,990	4,830	5,740	6,340	6,770	7,680
Nonfactor Services	..	270	290	330	380	580	820	1,060	1,380	1,610	2,300
Factor Services	..	0	0	40	50	120	130	210	310	480	796
Imports of Goods & Services	..	2,810	3,240	3,370	4,130	5,890	6,310	6,430	7,580	10,360	13,590
Merchandise, fob	..	2,290	2,680	2,780	3,500	5,210	5,480	5,390	6,470	9,010	11,860
Nonfactor Services	..	280	280	270	320	360	510	690	690	890	1,260
Factor Services	..	240	280	320	310	320	320	350	420	460	470
Long-Term Interest	..	193	219	241	255	268	263	279	303	379	395
Private Current Transfers, net	..	80	110	100	160	260	470	690	1,080	1,150	1,852
Workers' Remittances	..	80	110	140	190	280	490	710	1,090	1,130	1,872
Curr. A/C Bal before Off. Transf.	..	-590	-750	-440	-520	-940	-60	1,270	1,530	-350	-962
Net Official Transfers	..	210	400	110	90	120	340	380	430	450	577
Curr. A/C Bal after Off. Transf.	..	-380	-350	-330	-430	-820	280	1,650	1,960	100	-385
Long-Term Capital, net	..	580	610	470	560	960	1,350	1,040	760	590	656
Direct Investment	..	0	0	0	0	0	0	0	0	0	0
Long-Term Loans	..	594	622	494	542	868	1,342	1,043	820	592	658
Disbursements	..	908	959	865	953	1,395	1,881	1,577	1,387	1,259	1,369
Repayments	..	314	336	371	412	526	539	534	567	667	712
Other Long-Term Capital	..	-14	-12	-24	18	92	8	-3	-60	-2	-1
Other Capital, net	..	-180	-230	-80	-250	-700	-1,050	-790	-350	920	55
Change in Reserves	..	-20	-30	-60	120	560	-580	-1,900	-2,370	-1,610	-326
Memo Item:					*(Indian Rupees per US dollar)*						
Conversion Factor (Annual Avg)	7.500	7.500	7.440	7.710	7.790	7.980	8.650	8.940	8.560	8.210	8.080
EXTERNAL DEBT (Total)				*(Millions of US dollars), outstanding at end of year*							
Long-Term Debt (by debtor)	..	7,937	8,892	9,805	10,575	12,235	13,234	13,971	15,504	16,461	17,892
Central Bank, incl. IMF credit	..	7,937	8,892	9,805	10,575	12,235	13,234	13,971	15,072	15,810	17,194
Central Government	..	95	112	137	234	800	991	639	306	168	1,204
Rest of General Government	..	5,927	6,702	7,530	8,100	9,049	9,834	10,938	12,178	12,906	13,292
Non-financial Public Enterprises	..	72	72	69	63	58	47	43	41	37	32
Priv. Sector, incl non-guaranteed	..	1,393	1,550	1,608	1,684	1,712	1,726	1,680	1,855	1,917	1,892
Short-Term Debt	..	451	456	461	494	616	636	672	692	782	773
	..	..	..	..	..	..	..	..	432	651	698
Memo Items:					*(Millions of US dollars)*						
Int'l Reserves Excluding Gold	683.0	763.3	942.4	916.3	848.8	1,027.7	1,089.1	2,791.7	4,872.0	6,426.3	7,432.5
Gold Holdings (at market price)	244.8	259.9	303.4	451.3	780.5	1,296.9	975.3	937.0	1,213.4	1,889.8	4,382.9
SOCIAL INDICATORS											
Total Fertility Rate	5.9	5.8	5.7	5.6	5.5	5.4	5.3	5.3	5.2	5.1	5.0
Infant Mortality Rate	141.0	139.0	137.0	135.0	133.2	131.4	129.6	127.8	126.0	122.8	119.6
Life Expectancy at Birth	47.0	47.5	48.0	48.4	49.1	49.7	50.4	51.1	51.7	52.4	53.0
Urban Population, % of total	19.6	19.8	20.1	20.5	20.8	21.2	21.5	21.9	22.3	22.6	23.0
Food Prod. per capita (1987=100)	91.1	94.7	94.0	87.4	92.2	86.1	95.6	93.5	98.5	99.2	92.5
Labor Force, Agriculture (%)	72.0	71.7	71.5	71.3	71.1	70.9	70.7	70.5	70.3	70.1	69.9
Labor Force, Female (%)	29.8	29.7	29.4	29.2	28.9	28.7	28.5	28.2	27.9	27.7	27.4
Primary Schl. Enroll. Ratio	..	73.0	..	..	..	..	79.0	79.0	78.0	76.0	81.0
Primary Schl. Enroll. Ratio, Female	..	56.0	..	..	..	..	62.0	63.0	64.0	61.0	65.0
Secondary Schl. Enroll. Ratio	..	26.0	..	..	..	..	26.0	26.0	27.0	28.0	30.0

1980	1981	1982	1983	1984	1985	1986	1987	1988	1989 estimate	NOTES	INDIA
				(Millions of current US dollars)							**FOREIGN TRADE (CUSTOMS BASIS)**
8,332	8,698	9,225	9,770	10,192	9,465	10,460	12,888	14,824	..	..	Value of Exports, fob
3,125	2,586	3,220	2,909	3,079	2,751	3,248	3,387	3,513	..	..	Nonfuel Primary Products
32	197	657	914	714	648	397	503	549	..	f	Fuels
5,175	5,916	5,348	5,947	6,399	6,066	6,815	8,998	10,762	..	f	Manufactures
14,090	15,654	14,387	14,782	15,424	17,295	16,801	18,985	22,500	..	..	Value of Imports, cif
2,302	2,563	2,465	2,257	2,507	2,443	2,549	2,863	3,196	..	..	Nonfuel Primary Products
6,168	6,308	4,735	4,684	4,550	4,078	1,679	2,829	2,938	..	..	Fuels
5,621	6,783	7,187	7,841	8,367	10,774	12,573	13,293	16,366	..	f	Manufactures
				(Index 1987 = 100)							
72.3	80.1	89.1	96.4	98.3	98.8	104.7	100.0	99.3	..	..	Terms of Trade
83.8	92.1	91.9	95.6	96.1	90.8	93.9	100.0	104.8	..	..	Export Prices, fob
115.9	115.0	103.2	99.1	97.8	91.9	89.7	100.0	105.5	..	..	Import Prices, cif
				(Millions of current US dollars)							**BALANCE OF PAYMENTS**
12,364	12,306	11,801	12,819	13,709	13,318	14,178	16,661	18,581	21,441	C f	Exports of Goods & Services
8,332	8,697	8,389	9,090	9,769	9,461	10,460	12,644	14,208	16,850	..	Merchandise, fob
2,949	2,697	2,887	3,280	3,447	3,310	3,217	3,571	3,976	4,196	..	Nonfactor Services
1,083	912	525	449	493	547	501	446	397	395	..	Factor Services
18,135	18,107	17,473	18,517	19,716	21,518	22,496	25,756	30,475	32,229	C f	Imports of Goods & Services
15,892	15,552	14,386	14,782	15,424	17,295	17,728	19,812	23,849	25,052	..	Merchandise, fob
1,516	1,696	1,884	2,192	2,350	2,124	2,222	3,027	3,244	3,477	..	Nonfactor Services
727	859	1,202	1,543	1,942	2,099	2,546	2,917	3,382	3,700	..	Factor Services
503	549	721	933	1,025	1,311	1,725	2,069	2,510	2,954	..	Long-Term Interest
2,860	2,314	2,625	2,691	2,609	2,305	2,327	2,698	2,979	2,750	..	Private Current Transfers, net
2,786	2,339	2,526	2,587	2,542	2,220	2,287	2,621	2,850	2,650	..	Workers' Remittances
-2,911	-3,487	-3,047	-3,007	-3,398	-5,895	-5,991	-6,397	-8,915	-8,038	..	Curr. A/C Bal before Off. Transf.
643	497	399	367	453	359	403	410	406	500	..	Net Official Transfers
-2,268	-2,990	-2,648	-2,640	-2,945	-5,536	-5,588	-5,987	-8,509	-7,538	..	Curr. A/C Bal after Off. Transf.
1,760	1,992	2,671	2,880	3,531	4,206	5,190	5,698	6,942	6,419	C f	Long-Term Capital, net
8	10	65	63	62	160	208	181	287	425	..	Direct Investment
1,424	1,629	1,966	1,908	2,697	2,545	2,912	3,791	4,370	4,221	..	Long-Term Loans
2,180	2,376	2,898	2,991	3,788	3,854	5,201	5,683	6,319	6,142	..	Disbursements
756	747	932	1,083	1,091	1,309	2,289	1,893	1,949	1,921	..	Repayments
328	353	640	909	771	1,501	2,070	1,726	2,285	1,773	..	Other Long-Term Capital
-853	-2,051	-1,486	-663	-390	2,141	1,118	1,032	1,345	1,276	C f	Other Capital, net
1,360	3,049	1,463	424	-196	-812	-720	-743	222	-157	..	Change in Reserves
				(Indian Rupees per US dollar)							**Memo Item:**
7.890	8.930	9.630	10.310	11.890	12.240	12.790	12.970	14.480	16.660	..	Conversion Factor (Annual Avg)
				(Millions of US dollars), outstanding at end of year							
20,561	22,567	27,376	31,891	33,857	40,886	48,026	55,034	57,254	62,509	..	**EXTERNAL DEBT (Total)**
19,635	21,363	25,485	29,255	31,001	37,757	44,729	51,515	53,482	57,820	..	Long-Term Debt (by debtor)
2,489	3,227	5,562	7,641	7,789	9,750	11,338	12,496	12,472	12,844	..	Central Bank, incl. IMF credit
14,224	14,696	15,907	17,012	17,293	20,702	24,374	28,289	29,041	31,108	..	Central Government
27	22	18	15	18	21	19	74	63	125	..	Rest of General Government
2,135	2,143	2,564	2,993	4,063	5,080	6,514	7,537	8,520	10,036	..	Non-financial Public Enterprises
760	1,276	1,433	1,595	1,838	2,203	2,483	3,119	3,387	3,707	..	Priv. Sector, incl non-guaranteed
926	1,204	1,891	2,636	2,856	3,129	3,297	3,519	3,772	4,689	..	Short-Term Debt
				(Millions of US dollars)							**Memo Items:**
6,943.9	4,692.9	4,315.1	4,937.3	5,842.3	6,420.3	6,395.7	6,453.6	4,899.3	3,858.6	..	Int'l Reserves Excluding Gold
5,065.9	3,416.0	3,926.4	3,278.5	2,693.6	3,072.8	4,084.4	5,058.2	4,286.5	4,189.9	..	Gold Holdings (at market price)
											SOCIAL INDICATORS
5.0	4.9	4.8	4.7	4.6	4.5	4.4	4.3	4.2	4.1	..	Total Fertility Rate
116.4	113.2	110.0	107.8	105.6	103.4	101.2	99.0	97.2	95.4	..	Infant Mortality Rate
53.7	54.3	55.0	55.5	56.1	56.7	57.3	57.8	58.2	58.5	..	Life Expectancy at Birth
23.4	23.8	24.2	24.7	25.1	25.5	26.0	26.5	27.0	27.5	..	Urban Population, % of total
93.0	98.4	94.7	105.8	105.7	105.4	103.3	100.0	110.1	112.0	..	Food Prod. per capita (1987=100)
69.7	..	..	..	..	..	..	..	..	..	..	Labor Force, Agriculture (%)
27.2	27.0	26.8	26.6	26.4	26.2	26.0	25.8	25.6	25.4	..	Labor Force, Female (%)
83.0	82.0	85.0	92.0	93.0	95.0	98.0	..	..	..	..	Primary Schl. Enroll. Ratio
67.0	66.0	69.0	75.0	76.0	79.0	81.0	..	..	..	..	Primary Schl. Enroll. Ratio, Female
32.0	34.0	35.0	35.0	37.0	39.0	39.0	..	..	..	..	Secondary Schl. Enroll. Ratio

INDONESIA	1969	1970	1971	1972	1973	1974	1975	1976	1977	1978	1979
CURRENT GNP PER CAPITA (US $)	70	80	90	90	110	150	210	270	320	380	400
POPULATION (millions)	115	118	120	123	126	130	133	136	139	142	145

USE AND ORIGIN OF RESOURCES *(Billions of current Indonesian Rupiahs)*

	1969	1970	1971	1972	1973	1974	1975	1976	1977	1978	1979
Gross National Product (GNP)	2,887	3,540	3,878	4,756	7,002	10,984	13,004	16,122	19,749	23,540	32,860
Net Factor Income from Abroad	19	15	3	-60	-124	-315	-338	-200	-336	-462	-1,484
GDP at Market Prices	2,868	3,525	3,875	4,816	7,126	11,300	13,341	16,321	20,084	24,002	34,345
Resource Balance	-139	-69	-59	38	122	943	292	357	969	587	2,402
Exports of Goods & NFServices	262	458	563	815	1,449	3,255	3,097	3,870	4,824	5,317	10,147
Imports of Goods & NFServices	402	528	622	776	1,328	2,312	2,805	3,513	3,855	4,730	7,746
Domestic Absorption	3,008	3,594	3,934	4,778	7,004	10,357	13,050	15,964	19,116	23,416	31,943
Private Consumption, etc.	2,428	2,754	2,894	3,328	4,833	7,342	8,687	10,500	12,422	15,126	19,516
General Gov't Consumption	191	282	328	398	688	809	1,206	1,530	1,997	2,556	3,277
Gross Domestic Investment	389	558	712	1,052	1,483	2,206	3,157	3,934	4,696	5,734	9,150
Fixed Investment	..	..	..	..	..	..	..	..	..	..	7,668
Indirect Taxes, net	135	188	229	236	328	447	520	635	846	1,029	1,305
GDP at factor cost	2,734	3,337	3,646	4,580	6,798	10,853	12,821	15,686	19,238	22,973	33,040
Agriculture	1,347	1,584	1,656	1,848	2,726	3,517	4,026	4,840	5,940	6,745	9,374
Industry	514	659	806	1,215	1,891	3,862	4,466	5,560	6,880	8,578	12,944
Manufacturing	292	363	357	521	756	1,036	1,308	1,691	2,115	2,816	4,003
Services, etc.	1,007	1,282	1,414	1,753	2,509	3,920	4,850	5,921	7,265	8,680	12,027
Gross Domestic Saving	250	489	653	1,090	1,605	3,149	3,449	4,292	5,665	6,321	11,551
Gross National Saving	..	504	656	1,030	1,481	2,833	3,111	4,092	5,330	5,858	10,067

(Billions of 1987 Indonesian Rupiahs)

	1969	1970	1971	1972	1973	1974	1975	1976	1977	1978	1979
Gross National Product	36,937	39,658	42,428	45,151	49,093	52,463	55,126	59,290	64,339	69,165	73,016
GDP at Market Prices	40,839	43,842	46,901	49,853	54,171	58,331	61,259	65,491	71,368	76,882	81,616
Resource Balance	7,049	8,443	9,130	11,457	12,640	11,349	9,533	11,189	12,961	11,353	10,134
Exports of Goods & NFServices	10,740	12,576	14,551	17,637	20,924	22,298	21,757	25,461	27,868	28,146	28,790
Imports of Goods & NFServices	3,691	4,133	5,421	6,181	8,285	10,949	12,225	14,272	14,907	16,793	18,657
Domestic Absorption	30,918	32,786	34,575	36,057	39,975	45,413	50,321	52,365	56,215	63,493	69,517
Private Consumption, etc.	25,089	25,411	25,943	26,084	27,986	32,252	34,701	35,750	36,929	41,163	44,808
General Gov't Consumption	2,194	2,556	2,763	2,987	3,812	3,413	4,451	4,776	5,559	6,539	7,323
Gross Domestic Investment	3,635	4,819	5,869	6,985	8,177	9,747	11,169	11,839	13,727	15,792	17,386
Fixed Investment	..	..	..	..	..	..	..	..	..	..	16,975
GDP at factor cost	..	..	..	..	..	..	..	..	..	..	..
Agriculture	14,444	15,197	16,121	16,372	17,898	18,565	18,565	19,443	19,688	20,705	22,082
Industry	11,544	13,367	13,929	16,925	20,556	22,011	22,208	25,079	28,442	29,396	30,538
Manufacturing	2,336	2,557	2,638	3,036	3,499	4,064	4,565	5,006	5,696	6,654	7,754
Services, etc.	12,967	13,752	15,058	15,740	15,839	17,857	20,681	20,929	22,911	26,599	28,919
Memo Items:											
Capacity to Import	2,409	3,590	4,907	6,487	9,045	15,413	13,496	15,725	18,653	18,877	24,441
Terms of Trade Adjustment	-8,331	-8,986	-9,645	-11,150	-11,879	-6,885	-8,261	-9,736	-9,215	-9,269	-4,350
Gross Domestic Income	32,508	34,856	37,256	38,702	42,292	51,446	52,998	55,754	62,153	67,612	77,266
Gross National Income	28,606	30,672	32,783	34,001	37,214	45,578	46,864	49,554	55,124	59,895	68,666

DOMESTIC PRICES/DEFLATORS *(Index 1987 = 100)*

	1969	1970	1971	1972	1973	1974	1975	1976	1977	1978	1979
Overall (GDP)	7.0	8.0	8.3	9.7	13.2	19.4	21.8	24.9	28.1	31.2	42.1
Domestic Absorption	9.7	11.0	11.4	13.3	17.5	22.8	25.9	30.5	34.0	36.9	45.9
Agriculture	9.3	10.4	10.3	11.3	15.2	18.9	21.7	24.9	30.2	32.6	42.5
Industry	4.5	4.9	5.8	7.2	9.2	17.5	20.1	22.2	24.2	29.2	42.4
Manufacturing	12.5	14.2	13.5	17.2	21.6	25.5	28.7	33.8	37.1	42.3	51.6
Consumer Price Index	9.9	11.1	11.6	12.3	16.2	22.8	27.1	32.5	36.0	39.0	46.1

MANUFACTURING ACTIVITY

	1969	1970	1971	1972	1973	1974	1975	1976	1977	1978	1979
Employment (1987=100)	..	..	..	..	..	..	..	..	..	..	..
Real Earnings per Empl. (1987=100)	..	..	..	..	..	..	..	..	..	..	..
Real Output per Empl. (1987=100)	..	..	..	..	..	..	..	..	..	..	..
Earnings as % of Value Added	..	26.4	23.0	23.5	20.9	23.9	20.5	21.6	20.6	20.3	19.6

MONETARY HOLDINGS *(Billions of current Indonesian Rupiahs)*

	1969	1970	1971	1972	1973	1974	1975	1976	1977	1978	1979
Money Supply, Broadly Defined	233	330	468	696	994	1,454	2,022	2,651	3,133	3,822	5,159
Money	183	250	319	474	671	942	1,274	1,601	2,006	2,488	3,316
Currency Outside Banks	116	155	198	269	375	497	650	779	979	1,240	1,545
Demand Deposits	68	96	121	205	296	445	625	822	1,027	1,248	1,771
Quasi-Money	50	80	148	222	323	512	747	1,050	1,127	1,334	1,842

GOVERNMENT DEFICIT (-) OR SURPLUS *(Billions of current Indonesian Rupiahs)*

	1969	1970	1971	1972	1973	1974	1975	1976	1977	1978	1979
	..	..	..	-117	-163	-167	-468	-693	-393	-754	-764
Current Revenue	..	..	..	644	1,020	1,832	2,300	2,968	3,634	4,378	7,050
Current Expenditure	..	..	..	413	695	1,282	1,519	1,809	2,113	2,570	3,959
Current Budget Balance	..	..	..	231	325	550	781	1,159	1,521	1,808	3,091
Capital Receipts	..	..	..	..	..	..	..	..	..	..	..
Capital Payments	..	..	..	348	488	718	1,249	1,852	1,914	2,562	3,855

1980	1981	1982	1983	1984	1985	1986	1987	1988	1989 estimate	NOTES	INDONESIA
470	550	610	610	580	540	520	490	480	500	..	**CURRENT GNP PER CAPITA (US $)**
148	152	155	158	161	165	168	171	175	178	..	**POPULATION (millions)**
				(Billions of current Indonesian Rupiahs)							**USE AND ORIGIN OF RESOURCES**
46,903	56,496	59,611	74,304	85,719	93,063	98,558	118,810	135,123	158,196	..	Gross National Product (GNP)
-2,011	-1,925	-3,036	-3,319	-4,166	-3,934	-4,125	-6,007	-6,897	-8,133	..	Net Factor Income from Abroad
48,914	58,421	62,646	77,623	89,885	96,997	102,683	124,817	142,020	166,329	..	GDP at Market Prices
6,277	2,367	253	221	3,154	1,699	-1,026	1,919	3,494	4,108	..	Resource Balance
16,162	16,401	15,324	19,847	22,999	21,534	20,010	29,875	34,666	42,503	..	Exports of Goods & NFServices
9,886	14,034	15,071	19,626	19,845	19,835	21,036	27,956	31,172	38,395	..	Imports of Goods & NFServices
42,637	56,054	62,393	77,402	86,731	95,298	103,709	122,898	138,526	162,221	..	Domestic Absorption
25,595	32,293	37,924	47,064	54,066	57,201	63,355	71,988	81,045	88,751	..	Private Consumption, etc.
5,148	6,452	7,229	8,077	9,122	10,893	11,329	11,764	12,756	15,698	..	General Gov't Consumption
11,894	17,309	17,241	22,261	23,543	27,204	29,025	39,146	44,725	57,772	..	Gross Domestic Investment
10,550	14,135	15,822	19,468	20,136	22,367	24,782	30,980	36,803	45,650	..	Fixed Investment
1,635	1,752	2,133	2,547	..	..	..	..	..	..	..	Indirect Taxes, net
47,278	56,669	60,514	75,076	..	..	..	..	..	..	B	GDP at factor cost
11,725	13,649	15,001	17,765	20,420	22,513	24,871	29,116	34,193	38,998	..	Agriculture
20,405	24,076	23,745	30,915	35,162	34,772	34,648	45,252	51,452	62,195	..	Industry
6,353	7,067	7,482	9,896	13,113	15,503	17,185	21,150	26,252	30,573	..	Manufacturing
16,783	20,696	23,901	28,943	34,304	39,712	43,164	50,450	56,374	65,135	..	Services, etc.
18,171	19,676	17,494	22,482	26,697	28,903	27,999	41,065	48,219	61,880	..	Gross Domestic Saving
16,160	17,751	14,458	19,172	22,585	25,037	23,965	35,199	41,489	53,968	..	Gross National Saving
				(Billions of 1987 Indonesian Rupiahs)							
79,303	85,887	86,740	94,346	101,169	104,754	112,113	118,810	127,092	136,860	..	Gross National Product
88,093	94,632	94,301	102,608	109,576	112,479	119,004	124,817	131,996	141,672	H	GDP at Market Prices
9,909	-2,494	-5,123	-3,998	-461	-3,695	-1,351	1,919	7,459	7,847	..	Resource Balance
30,382	24,899	22,656	23,030	24,537	22,622	26,064	29,875	30,188	32,318	..	Exports of Goods & NFServices
20,473	27,393	27,779	27,028	24,998	26,317	27,415	27,956	22,729	24,470	..	Imports of Goods & NFServices
76,088	96,656	99,268	106,725	110,358	116,836	120,768	122,898	124,641	134,060	..	Domestic Absorption
49,698	54,748	58,158	64,905	67,496	68,193	69,685	71,988	74,782	77,885	..	Private Consumption, etc.
8,765	9,628	10,494	10,299	10,651	11,464	11,783	11,764	12,654	13,981	..	General Gov't Consumption
17,625	32,280	30,616	31,521	32,211	37,179	39,300	39,146	37,205	42,193	..	Gross Domestic Investment
21,450	24,210	25,693	26,690	25,085	26,893	29,369	30,980	34,550	39,166	..	Fixed Investment
..	..	..	..	..	..	..	..	..	..	B H	GDP at factor cost
23,610	24,744	25,009	25,576	26,653	27,786	28,505	29,116	30,476	31,797	..	Agriculture
32,888	34,564	31,856	36,913	40,497	40,334	43,017	45,252	47,622	51,411	..	Industry
9,516	10,264	10,387	12,892	15,736	17,496	19,122	21,150	23,687	25,841	..	Manufacturing
31,509	35,317	37,878	40,120	42,426	44,359	47,482	50,450	53,899	58,465	..	Services, etc.
											Memo Items:
33,472	32,013	28,246	27,332	28,971	28,571	26,078	29,875	25,277	27,088	..	Capacity to Import
3,090	7,114	5,589	4,302	4,434	5,949	13	0	-4,911	-5,229	..	Terms of Trade Adjustment
91,182	101,747	99,890	106,911	114,010	118,428	119,017	124,817	127,085	136,443	..	Gross Domestic Income
82,393	93,002	92,329	98,648	105,603	110,703	112,126	118,810	122,181	131,631	..	Gross National Income
				(Index 1987 = 100)							**DOMESTIC PRICES/DEFLATORS**
55.5	61.7	66.4	75.6	82.0	86.2	86.3	100.0	107.6	117.4	..	Overall (GDP)
56.0	58.0	62.9	72.5	78.6	81.6	85.9	100.0	111.1	121.0	..	Domestic Absorption
49.7	55.2	60.0	69.5	76.6	81.0	87.3	100.0	112.2	122.6	..	Agriculture
62.0	69.7	74.5	83.8	86.8	86.2	80.5	100.0	108.0	121.0	..	Industry
66.8	68.9	72.0	76.8	83.3	88.6	89.9	100.0	110.8	118.3	..	Manufacturing
54.4	61.1	66.9	74.8	82.6	86.5	91.5	100.0	108.0	115.0	..	Consumer Price Index
											MANUFACTURING ACTIVITY
..	..	..	..	..	..	..	..	..	..	J	Employment (1987=100)
..	..	..	..	..	..	..	..	..	..	J	Real Earnings per Empl. (1987=100)
..	..	..	..	..	..	..	..	..	..	J	Real Output per Empl. (1987=100)
16.4	17.7	19.8	20.0	17.6	19.0	19.0	..	..	..	J	Earnings as % of Value Added
				(Billions of current Indonesian Rupiahs)							**MONETARY HOLDINGS**
7,707	9,705	11,074	14,670	17,937	23,177	27,615	33,904	42,072	58,526	..	Money Supply, Broadly Defined
5,011	6,474	7,120	7,576	8,581	10,124	11,631	12,705	14,392	20,558	..	Money
2,169	2,546	2,934	3,340	3,712	4,460	5,338	5,802	6,245	7,908	..	Currency Outside Banks
2,842	3,929	4,185	4,236	4,869	5,663	6,293	6,903	8,146	12,651	..	Demand Deposits
2,696	3,231	3,954	7,093	9,356	13,054	15,984	21,200	27,681	37,967	..	Quasi-Money
				(Billions of current Indonesian Rupiahs)							
-1,102	-1,172	-1,191	-1,862	1,219	-948	-3,621	-1,028	-4,179	..	C	**GOVERNMENT DEFICIT (-) OR SURPLUS**
10,406	13,763	12,815	15,511	18,724	20,347	21,324	24,747	24,088	..	..	Current Revenue
5,731	6,882	6,996	8,412	9,429	11,426	13,560	17,481	20,738	..	..	Current Expenditure
4,675	6,881	5,819	7,099	9,295	8,921	7,764	7,266	3,350	..	..	Current Budget Balance
..	..	..	..	..	..	..	..	..	..	..	Capital Receipts
5,777	8,053	7,010	8,961	8,076	9,869	11,385	8,294	7,529	..	..	Capital Payments

INDONESIA	1969	1970	1971	1972	1973	1974	1975	1976	1977	1978	1979
FOREIGN TRADE (CUSTOMS BASIS)					*(Millions of current US dollars)*						
Value of Exports, fob	800	1,055	1,199	1,778	3,211	7,426	7,130	8,556	10,853	11,643	15,590
Nonfuel Primary Products	405	694	700	827	1,533	2,145	1,704	2,419	3,283	3,431	4,936
Fuels	379	346	478	913	1,609	5,211	5,339	6,014	7,379	7,986	10,166
Manufactures	16	15	22	37	69	70	88	124	191	225	488
Value of Imports, cif	1,122	1,258	1,379	1,611	2,969	5,231	6,196	7,700	8,495	9,493	10,364
Nonfuel Primary Products	214	208	180	223	441	1,037	1,069	1,490	1,805	2,210	2,311
Fuels	26	19	36	41	54	251	334	598	1,009	831	1,150
Manufactures	882	1,031	1,163	1,346	2,474	3,943	4,793	5,612	5,681	6,452	6,903
					(Index 1987 = 100)						
Terms of Trade	46.1	54.2	56.6	49.5	59.5	120.6	106.3	115.6	117.6	104.7	127.0
Export Prices, fob	12.6	15.6	16.7	16.1	23.8	64.5	60.0	66.6	74.7	75.7	106.2
Import Prices, cif	27.4	28.8	29.5	32.6	40.1	53.5	56.4	57.6	63.5	72.3	83.6
BALANCE OF PAYMENTS					*(Millions of current US dollars)*						
Exports of Goods & Services	..	..	..	..	3,306	7,464	7,025	8,774	10,929	11,327	15,552
Merchandise, fob	..	1,173	1,311	1,793	3,215	7,265	6,888	8,613	10,763	11,035	15,154
Nonfactor Services	..	16	28	45	52	71	93	111	114	234	315
Factor Services	..	..	..	..	38	127	44	50	51	58	83
Imports of Goods & Services	..	1,565	1,757	2,222	3,836	6,915	8,160	9,696	11,004	12,754	14,602
Merchandise, fob	..	1,116	1,230	1,445	2,663	4,634	5,469	6,815	7,478	8,386	9,245
Nonfactor Services	..	316	355	430	544	952	1,306	1,669	1,840	2,349	2,889
Factor Services	..	133	173	347	629	1,329	1,385	1,212	1,686	2,018	2,468
Long-Term Interest	..	46	57	86	118	186	322	489	610	720	1,049
Private Current Transfers, net	..	0	0	0	0	0	0	0	0	0	0
Workers' Remittances	..	..	..	..	..	..	..	..	..	..	..
Curr. A/C Bal before Off. Transf.	..	-376	-418	-385	-530	548	-1,135	-922	-75	-1,427	950
Net Official Transfers	..	66	46	51	55	49	27	15	24	14	30
Curr. A/C Bal after Off. Transf.	..	-310	-372	-334	-476	598	-1,109	-907	-51	-1,413	980
Long-Term Capital, net	..	290	377	501	521	492	2,244	2,262	1,491	1,596	1,320
Direct Investment	..	83	139	207	15	-49	476	344	235	279	226
Long-Term Loans	..	516	529	976	1,288	1,507	2,264	2,153	1,356	862	655
Disbursements	..	636	691	1,190	1,615	2,017	2,945	3,004	2,727	2,975	2,670
Repayments	..	120	162	215	327	510	682	851	1,372	2,113	2,016
Other Long-Term Capital	..	-309	-291	-683	-783	-966	-496	-235	-100	455	440
Other Capital, net	..	-3	-35	211	295	-401	-1,986	-453	-444	-11	-856
Change in Reserves	..	23	30	-377	-341	-688	851	-902	-996	-171	-1,444
Memo Item:					*(Indonesian Rupiahs per US dollar)*						
Conversion Factor (Annual Avg)	326.000	365.000	393.400	415.000	415.000	415.000	415.000	415.000	415.000	442.000	623.100
				(Millions of US dollars), outstanding at end of year							
EXTERNAL DEBT (Total)	..	3,096	4,248	5,243	6,563	8,211	10,372	12,634	16,477	18,053	18,631
Long-Term Debt (by debtor)	..	3,096	4,248	5,243	6,563	8,211	10,372	12,634	14,552	16,267	16,523
Central Bank, incl. IMF credit	..	139	136	116	23	0	575	626	486	108	92
Central Government	..	2,408	3,272	3,658	4,237	4,845	5,763	7,524	9,345	11,359	11,704
Rest of General Government	..	1	1	1	1	2	0	0	0	0	0
Non-financial Public Enterprises	..	86	188	554	1,017	1,521	1,664	1,860	1,879	1,760	1,588
Priv. Sector, incl non-guaranteed	..	463	651	914	1,286	1,844	2,369	2,624	2,842	3,040	3,140
Short-Term Debt	..	0	0	0	0	0	0	0	1,925	1,786	2,108
Memo Items:					*(Millions of US dollars)*						
Int'l Reserves Excluding Gold	117.7	156.0	185.3	572.2	804.7	1,489.5	584.3	1,496.5	2,508.7	2,626.1	4,061.8
Gold Holdings (at market price)	4.0	4.3	2.5	7.9	6.4	10.6	8.0	7.7	27.9	50.6	143.4
SOCIAL INDICATORS											
Total Fertility Rate	5.5	5.5	5.4	5.4	5.3	5.1	5.0	4.9	4.8	4.6	4.5
Infant Mortality Rate	120.0	118.0	116.0	114.0	112.2	110.4	108.6	106.8	105.0	103.0	101.0
Life Expectancy at Birth	46.7	47.4	48.2	49.0	49.7	50.5	51.2	51.9	52.7	53.3	54.0
Urban Population, % of total	16.8	17.1	17.6	18.0	18.5	18.9	19.4	20.0	20.5	21.1	21.6
Food Prod. per capita (1987=100)	65.2	69.2	68.5	69.4	72.3	73.3	72.6	71.5	72.2	75.2	76.8
Labor Force, Agriculture (%)	67.1	66.3	65.3	64.4	63.5	62.6	61.8	60.8	59.8	58.9	58.0
Labor Force, Female (%)	29.9	30.2	30.4	30.5	30.6	30.7	30.8	31.0	31.1	31.2	31.2
Primary Schl. Enroll. Ratio	..	80.0	..	..	..	..	86.0	84.0	90.0	99.0	107.0
Primary Schl. Enroll. Ratio, Female	..	73.0	..	..	..	..	78.0	79.0	83.0	92.0	99.0
Secondary Schl. Enroll. Ratio	..	16.0	..	..	..	..	20.0	20.0	21.0	22.0	24.0

1980	1981	1982	1983	1984	1985	1986	1987	1988	1989 estimate	NOTES	INDONESIA
				(Millions of current US dollars)							**FOREIGN TRADE** (CUSTOMS BASIS)
21,909	22,260	19,747	20,961	20,345	18,711	14,787	17,206	19,504	20,855	..	Value of Exports, fob
5,633	3,763	2,690	3,350	3,585	3,753	3,826	4,025	5,439	..	..	Nonfuel Primary Products
15,743	17,764	16,189	15,993	14,598	12,503	8,097	8,843	8,530	..	..	Fuels
533	733	868	1,618	2,162	2,455	2,864	4,338	5,535	7,222	..	Manufactures
14,139	18,527	19,996	19,853	16,853	14,230	13,103	14,453	15,833	16,732	..	Value of Imports, cif
2,637	3,195	2,382	2,455	2,182	1,579	1,633	1,210	1,222	..	..	Nonfuel Primary Products
2,289	2,459	4,296	5,033	3,288	3,696	2,443	2,510	2,788	..	..	Fuels
9,213	12,874	13,318	12,365	11,383	8,954	9,027	10,732	11,823	13,240	..	Manufactures
				(Index 1987 = 100)							
156.0	172.9	163.1	145.6	150.0	135.4	97.5	100.0	98.6	..	..	Terms of Trade
152.3	164.8	153.4	136.6	132.6	122.5	85.7	100.0	107.3	..	..	Export Prices, fob
97.7	95.3	94.0	93.8	88.4	90.4	87.9	100.0	108.9	..	..	Import Prices, cif
				(Millions of current US dollars)							**BALANCE OF PAYMENTS**
22,241	24,878	21,274	19,866	22,152	20,139	15,972	18,832	21,370	25,085	f	Exports of Goods & Services
21,795	23,348	19,747	18,689	20,754	18,527	14,396	17,206	19,509	22,688	..	Merchandise, fob
327	449	504	546	570	844	844	1,065	1,369	1,875	..	Nonfactor Services
119	1,081	1,023	631	828	768	732	561	492	522	..	Factor Services
19,432	25,694	26,732	26,318	24,175	22,150	20,142	21,187	23,021	26,750	f	Imports of Goods & Services
12,624	16,542	17,854	17,726	15,047	12,705	11,938	12,532	13,831	16,275	..	Merchandise, fob
3,477	4,998	4,862	4,311	4,239	5,135	4,256	4,440	4,606	5,358	..	Nonfactor Services
3,330	4,154	4,016	4,281	4,889	4,310	3,948	4,215	4,584	5,117	..	Factor Services
1,182	1,428	1,554	1,613	1,909	1,919	2,344	2,617	2,919	2,981	..	Long-Term Interest
0	0	0	10	53	61	71	86	99	125	..	Private Current Transfers, net
..	..	..	10	53	61	71	86	99	125	..	Workers' Remittances
2,810	-816	-5,458	-6,442	-1,970	-1,950	-4,099	-2,269	-1,552	-1,540	..	Curr. A/C Bal before Off. Transf.
201	250	134	104	114	27	188	171	155	172	..	Net Official Transfers
3,011	-566	-5,324	-6,338	-1,856	-1,923	-3,911	-2,098	-1,397	-1,368	..	Curr. A/C Bal after Off. Transf.
2,153	2,151	5,096	5,323	2,981	1,880	2,882	2,510	1,796	2,786	f	Long-Term Capital, net
180	133	225	292	222	310	258	446	542	735	..	Direct Investment
1,613	2,055	2,468	3,889	2,664	1,247	1,901	2,370	1,722	2,191	..	Long-Term Loans
3,245	3,845	4,410	5,915	4,943	4,336	4,816	6,424	7,261	7,292	..	Disbursements
1,632	1,790	1,942	2,026	2,280	3,089	2,915	4,054	5,539	5,101	..	Repayments
360	-37	2,403	1,142	95	323	723	-306	-468	-140	..	Other Long-Term Capital
-2,558	-1,959	-1,625	1,198	-144	553	26	218	-500	-968	f	Other Capital, net
-2,606	374	1,853	-183	-981	-510	1,003	-630	101	-450	..	Change in Reserves
				(Indonesian Rupiahs per US dollar)							**Memo Item:**
627.000	631.800	661.400	909.300	1,025.900	1,110.600	1,282.600	1,643.800	1,685.700	1,770.100	..	Conversion Factor (Annual Avg)
				(Millions of US dollars), outstanding at end of year							**EXTERNAL DEBT** (Total)
20,944	22,762	26,304	29,978	31,861	36,670	43,090	52,468	52,798	53,110	..	
18,169	19,487	21,518	25,339	26,453	30,621	36,780	46,108	46,071	46,084	..	Long-Term Debt (by debtor)
89	73	57	486	441	69	68	727	623	608	..	Central Bank, incl. IMF credit
13,135	14,037	16,565	19,914	20,986	25,821	32,277	40,890	41,048	40,769	..	Central Government
0	0	0	0	0	0	0	0	0	..	..	Rest of General Government
1,804	1,799	1,696	1,539	1,226	921	607	386	234	81	..	Non-financial Public Enterprises
3,142	3,579	3,200	3,400	3,800	3,810	3,828	4,105	4,166	4,626	..	Priv. Sector, incl non-guaranteed
2,775	3,274	4,787	4,639	5,408	6,049	6,310	6,360	6,727	7,026	..	Short-Term Debt
				(Millions of US dollars)							**Memo Items:**
5,391.7	5,014.2	3,144.5	3,718.4	4,773.0	4,974.2	4,051.3	5,592.3	5,048.3	5,453.5	..	Int'l Reserves Excluding Gold
1,411.3	1,233.8	1,418.2	1,184.2	957.0	1,015.0	1,213.4	1,502.6	1,273.4	1,245.9	..	Gold Holdings (at market price)
											SOCIAL INDICATORS
4.3	4.2	4.1	3.9	3.8	3.7	3.6	3.5	3.4	3.3	..	Total Fertility Rate
99.0	97.0	95.0	90.2	85.4	80.6	75.8	71.0	68.3	65.6	..	Infant Mortality Rate
54.7	55.3	56.0	56.8	57.7	58.5	59.3	60.2	60.6	61.1	..	Life Expectancy at Birth
22.2	22.8	23.4	24.1	24.7	25.3	26.0	26.7	27.4	28.1	..	Urban Population, % of total
82.6	85.7	85.2	89.4	96.1	95.9	101.5	100.0	101.6	101.7	..	Food Prod. per capita (1987 = 100)
57.2	..	..	..	..	..	..	..	..	..	..	Labor Force, Agriculture (%)
31.3	31.3	31.3	31.3	31.3	31.3	31.3	31.2	31.2	31.2	..	Labor Force, Female (%)
107.0	111.0	113.0	115.0	118.0	118.0	118.0	..	..	..	..	Primary Schl. Enroll. Ratio
100.0	105.0	109.0	112.0	115.0	114.0	115.0	..	..	..	..	Primary Schl. Enroll. Ratio, Female
29.0	31.0	35.0	37.0	39.0	41.0	46.0	..	..	..	..	Secondary Schl. Enroll. Ratio

IRAN, ISLAMIC REPUBLIC OF	1969	1970	1971	1972	1973	1974	1975	1976	1977	1978	1979
CURRENT GNP PER CAPITA (US $)	350	380	420	500	690	940	1,310	1,890	2,180	1,980	2,110
POPULATION (thousands)	27,577	28,429	29,381	30,358	31,350	32,347	33,344	34,336	35,319	36,302	37,306
USE AND ORIGIN OF RESOURCES					*(Billions of current Iranian Rials)*						
Gross National Product (GNP)	704	798	968	1,235	1,836	3,079	3,497	4,692	5,850	5,344	6,391
Net Factor Income from Abroad	-70	-86	-46	-29	-24	-11	-15	-5	-98	-186	56
GDP at Market Prices	774	884	1,014	1,264	1,861	3,090	3,512	4,697	5,948	5,530	6,335
Resource Balance	33	53	41	48	289	802	313	492	259	86	840
Exports of Goods & NFServices	172	211	255	328	643	1,478	1,440	1,787	1,751	1,189	1,762
Imports of Goods & NFServices	140	158	214	280	355	676	1,127	1,295	1,491	1,103	923
Domestic Absorption	741	831	973	1,217	1,572	2,288	3,199	4,205	5,688	5,444	5,496
Private Consumption, etc.	464	523	567	677	883	1,084	1,369	1,863	2,933	2,972	2,982
General Gov't Consumption	121	142	189	253	325	639	817	1,004	1,134	1,255	1,223
Gross Domestic Investment	156	167	217	287	363	564	1,013	1,338	1,622	1,217	1,290
Fixed Investment	156	167	217	287	363	530	999	1,589	1,790	1,696	1,191
Indirect Taxes, net	51	57	65	74	77	19	80	126	185	175	-3
GDP at factor cost	723	827	949	1,190	1,784	3,071	3,432	4,571	5,762	5,354	6,338
Agriculture	148	161	173	202	234	303	334	426	459	543	768
Industry	302	351	412	511	920	1,878	1,997	2,538	2,761	2,166	2,634
Manufacturing	100	114	138	171	232	313	383	490	493	437	454
Services, etc.	273	315	364	477	629	889	1,101	1,606	2,542	2,645	2,937
Gross Domestic Saving	189	220	258	335	652	1,367	1,326	1,830	1,881	1,303	2,130
Gross National Saving	..	134	212	305	627	1,356	1,311	1,825	1,783	1,117	2,185
					(Billions of 1987 Iranian Rials)						
Gross National Product	11,619	12,960	14,072	16,057	18,822	19,570	20,023	23,587	25,108	20,802	18,944
GDP at Market Prices	12,856	14,426	14,739	16,642	19,135	19,869	20,347	23,909	25,502	21,148	19,202
Resource Balance	1,427	1,712	1,613	1,832	1,904	1,539	635	674	213	150	362
Exports of Goods & NFServices	1,892	2,233	2,291	2,640	2,848	2,802	2,516	2,803	2,551	1,736	1,502
Imports of Goods & NFServices	465	521	678	808	943	1,263	1,881	2,129	2,339	1,586	1,140
Domestic Absorption	11,429	12,715	13,126	14,810	17,230	18,330	19,711	23,235	25,290	20,999	18,839
Private Consumption, etc.	8,274	9,238	9,407	10,076	11,831	10,996	9,840	12,083	14,590	12,369	11,116
General Gov't Consumption	1,329	1,542	1,668	2,193	2,576	3,847	4,385	5,143	4,811	4,800	3,833
Gross Domestic Investment	1,825	1,935	2,051	2,542	2,823	3,487	5,486	6,009	5,888	3,830	3,890
Fixed Investment	1,765	1,871	1,983	2,457	2,730	3,164	5,227	7,059	6,422	5,548	3,441
GDP at factor cost	12,506	14,073	14,305	16,368	18,542	19,728	19,875	23,254	24,693	20,464	19,188
Agriculture	2,021	2,115	2,197	2,317	2,450	2,593	2,770	2,922	2,799	2,842	3,047
Industry	5,143	5,907	5,410	6,181	6,818	6,966	6,677	7,417	7,248	5,532	4,486
Manufacturing	640	710	802	946	1,113	1,317	1,533	1,760	1,513	1,315	1,167
Services, etc.	3,107	3,554	3,971	4,718	5,620	6,665	7,345	9,861	12,264	10,715	11,278
Memo Items:											
Capacity to Import	575	694	809	945	1,711	2,762	2,403	2,938	2,745	1,710	2,177
Terms of Trade Adjustment	-1,318	-1,539	-1,482	-1,695	-1,137	-39	-113	135	194	-26	675
Gross Domestic Income	11,538	12,888	13,256	14,947	17,998	19,830	20,234	24,044	25,696	21,122	19,877
Gross National Income	10,301	11,421	12,590	14,362	17,685	19,531	19,910	23,722	25,302	20,776	19,618
DOMESTIC PRICES/DEFLATORS					*(Index 1987 = 100)*						
Overall (GDP)	6.0	6.1	6.9	7.6	9.7	15.6	17.3	19.6	23.3	26.1	33.0
Domestic Absorption	6.5	6.5	7.4	8.2	9.1	12.5	16.2	18.1	22.5	25.9	29.2
Agriculture	7.3	7.6	7.9	8.7	9.6	11.7	12.1	14.6	16.4	19.1	25.2
Industry	5.9	5.9	7.6	8.3	13.5	27.0	29.9	34.2	38.1	39.2	58.7
Manufacturing	15.7	16.0	17.2	18.1	20.8	23.8	25.0	27.8	32.6	33.3	38.9
Consumer Price Index	9.4	9.6	10.0	10.6	11.6	13.3	15.0	16.7	21.3	23.8	26.3
MANUFACTURING ACTIVITY											
Employment (1987=100)	..	..	..	..	..	..	..	..	..	..	..
Real Earnings per Empl. (1987=100)	..	..	..	..	..	..	..	..	..	..	..
Real Output per Empl. (1987=100)	..	..	..	..	..	..	..	..	..	..	..
Earnings as % of Value Added	21.3	24.7	24.7	25.0	25.8	23.1	27.4	29.8	30.9	..	70.4
MONETARY HOLDINGS					*(Billions of current Iranian Rials)*						
Money Supply, Broadly Defined	212	250	310	419	546	779	1,050	1,511	1,905	2,351	3,186
Money	112	128	155	214	278	381	458	668	822	1,078	1,689
Currency Outside Banks	32	37	42	56	70	102	148	206	252	511	769
Demand Deposits	80	92	113	158	208	280	310	462	570	567	920
Quasi-Money	100	121	155	204	268	398	592	843	1,083	1,273	1,497
GOVERNMENT DEFICIT (-) OR SURPLUS					*(Billions of current Iranian Rials)*						
	..	-54	-31	-57	-13	140	12	-38	-262	-450	-231
Current Revenue	..	189	275	323	491	1,427	1,627	1,896	2,193	1,736	1,781
Current Expenditure	..	152	203	253	338	982	1,152	1,284	1,472	1,563	1,602
Current Budget Balance	..	37	72	70	154	445	475	611	721	173	178
Capital Receipts	..	..	..	..	..	..	..	..	..	..	..
Capital Payments	..	91	103	127	167	305	463	649	983	623	410

1980	1981	1982	1983	1984	1985	1986	1987	1988	1989 estimate	NOTES	IRAN, ISLAMIC REPUBLIC OF
2,030	2,600	3,240	3,660	3,920	4,210	4,180	3,870	3,590	3,190	..	**CURRENT GNP PER CAPITA (US $)**
38,345	39,420	40,537	41,702	42,925	44,212	45,578	47,029	48,569	50,204	..	**POPULATION (thousands)**
				(Billions of current Iranian Rials)							**USE AND ORIGIN OF RESOURCES**
6,628	8,380	11,152	14,021	15,151	16,522	18,107	21,231	26,342	33,344	C	Gross National Product (GNP)
6	31	0	-7	-11	-34	-19	-19	-39	-50	..	Net Factor Income from Abroad
6,622	8,349	11,152	14,027	15,162	16,556	18,126	21,270	26,387	33,394	C	GDP at Market Prices
-209	-424	613	35	-35	-15	-382	-140	-78	-480	..	Resource Balance
880	876	1,864	1,885	1,570	1,251	553	748	744	1,059	..	Exports of Goods & NFServices
1,089	1,300	1,251	1,851	1,605	1,266	935	888	822	1,539	..	Imports of Goods & NFServices
6,830	8,773	10,539	13,993	15,197	16,571	18,507	21,410	26,465	33,873	..	Domestic Absorption
3,301	4,224	7,142	8,207	10,195	11,111	11,737	13,687	17,074	20,271	..	Private Consumption, etc.
1,380	1,676	1,910	2,151	2,190	2,443	2,371	2,707	3,140	3,625	..	General Gov't Consumption
2,150	2,873	1,486	3,634	2,813	3,018	4,400	5,016	6,251	9,978	..	Gross Domestic Investment
1,407	1,575	1,821	2,879	3,098	2,841	2,606	2,658	2,997	4,048	..	Fixed Investment
161	125	204	447	561	608	613	665	685	985	..	Indirect Taxes, net
6,460	8,224	10,948	13,581	14,601	15,948	17,513	20,605	25,702	32,409	C	GDP at factor cost
1,080	1,502	2,000	2,223	2,606	2,848	3,734	4,813	6,101	7,455	..	Agriculture
2,138	2,612	3,900	4,588	4,522	4,274	3,455	3,918	4,209	4,951	..	Industry
700	972	1,130	1,299	1,473	1,470	1,496	1,651	1,903	1,892	..	Manufacturing
3,243	4,109	5,047	6,770	7,473	8,826	10,323	11,875	15,391	20,003	..	Services, etc.
1,941	2,449	2,099	3,669	2,778	3,002	4,018	4,876	6,172	9,498	..	Gross Domestic Saving
1,948	..	..	..	..	..	..	..	..	..	..	Gross National Saving
				(Billions of 1987 Iranian Rials)							
15,280	16,530	19,002	20,932	22,054	23,332	21,492	21,231	21,589	22,430	C	Gross National Product
15,495	16,755	19,273	21,224	22,289	23,450	21,611	21,270	21,637	22,481	C	GDP at Market Prices
-634	-830	-174	-697	-708	-473	-229	-140	257	18	..	Resource Balance
476	428	1,008	1,036	840	761	665	748	1,014	1,272	..	Exports of Goods & NFServices
1,110	1,258	1,182	1,733	1,548	1,234	894	888	757	1,253	..	Imports of Goods & NFServices
16,129	17,585	19,447	21,922	22,997	23,922	21,840	21,410	21,380	22,463	..	Domestic Absorption
7,257	7,686	12,844	12,019	15,029	15,707	13,412	13,687	14,176	13,829	..	Private Consumption, etc.
3,501	3,653	3,624	3,596	3,392	3,575	2,856	2,707	2,793	2,808	..	General Gov't Consumption
5,371	6,247	2,979	6,307	4,576	4,641	5,571	5,016	4,411	5,825	..	Gross Domestic Investment
3,361	3,423	3,509	4,837	4,866	4,227	3,249	2,658	2,552	2,903	..	Fixed Investment
15,101	16,487	18,901	20,530	21,455	22,588	20,883	20,605	21,064	21,740	C	GDP at factor cost
3,081	3,420	3,751	3,881	4,163	4,497	4,690	4,813	5,001	5,135	..	Agriculture
2,786	3,152	4,112	4,467	4,264	4,242	3,833	3,918	4,004	4,256	..	Industry
1,483	1,853	1,595	1,795	2,024	1,969	1,822	1,651	1,584	1,342	..	Manufacturing
9,888	10,477	11,028	12,182	13,028	13,849	12,361	11,875	12,059	12,349	..	Services, etc.
											Memo Items:
898	848	1,761	1,765	1,514	1,219	529	748	685	863	..	Capacity to Import
421	420	753	730	674	458	-136	0	-329	-409	..	Terms of Trade Adjustment
15,916	17,175	20,026	21,954	22,963	23,908	21,474	21,270	21,308	22,072	..	Gross Domestic Income
15,701	16,950	19,755	21,661	22,728	23,790	21,356	21,231	21,260	22,021	..	Gross National Income
				(Index 1987 = 100)							**DOMESTIC PRICES/DEFLATORS**
42.7	49.8	57.9	66.1	68.0	70.6	83.9	100.0	121.9	148.5	..	Overall (GDP)
42.3	49.9	54.2	63.8	66.1	69.3	84.7	100.0	123.8	150.8	..	Domestic Absorption
35.1	43.9	53.3	57.3	62.6	63.3	79.6	100.0	122.0	145.2	..	Agriculture
76.7	82.9	94.9	102.7	106.0	100.8	90.2	100.0	105.1	116.3	..	Industry
47.2	52.5	70.9	72.3	72.8	74.6	82.1	100.0	120.2	141.1	..	Manufacturing
31.7	39.3	46.7	55.9	62.9	65.7	77.8	100.0	128.7	157.4	..	Consumer Price Index
											MANUFACTURING ACTIVITY
..	..	..	..	..	..	..	..	..	..	..	Employment (1987=100)
..	..	..	..	..	..	..	..	..	..	..	Real Earnings per Empl. (1987=100)
..	..	..	..	..	..	..	..	..	..	..	Real Output per Empl. (1987=100)
55.5	45.2	54.0	54.3	55.0	..	..	..	..	..	..	Earnings as % of Value Added
				(Billions of current Iranian Rials)							**MONETARY HOLDINGS**
4,025	4,683	5,884	6,983	8,045	10,965	..	..	..	..	..	Money Supply, Broadly Defined
2,258	2,637	3,293	3,922	..	..	..	..	..	..	..	Money
1,108	1,248	1,465	1,757	..	..	..	..	..	..	..	Currency Outside Banks
1,150	1,389	1,828	2,165	..	..	..	..	..	..	..	Demand Deposits
1,767	2,046	2,591	3,061	..	..	..	..	..	..	..	Quasi-Money
				(Billions of current Iranian Rials)							
-915	-841	-603	-842	-597	-594	-1,353	-1,419	-2,104	..	C	**GOVERNMENT DEFICIT (-) OR SURPLUS**
1,430	1,923	2,698	2,994	2,989	2,964	2,017	2,511	2,501	..	..	Current Revenue
1,838	2,169	2,422	2,739	2,754	2,846	2,755	3,255	3,794	..	..	Current Expenditure
-408	-246	276	255	235	117	-738	-744	-1,293	..	..	Current Budget Balance
..	..	..	..	..	..	..	..	..	..	..	Capital Receipts
507	594	879	1,097	832	712	615	675	811	..	..	Capital Payments

IRAN, ISLAMIC REPUBLIC OF	1969	1970	1971	1972	1973	1974	1975	1976	1977	1978	1979
FOREIGN TRADE (CUSTOMS BASIS)					*(Millions of current US dollars)*						
Value of Exports, fob	2,213	2,445	2,677	3,812	6,076	21,575	20,114	22,580	25,943	..	17,800
Nonfuel Primary Products	..	..	..	..	..	..	..	..	..	..	..
Fuels	..	..	..	..	..	..	..	..	..	..	..
Manufactures	..	..	..	..	..	..	..	..	..	..	..
Value of Imports, cif	1,525	1,693	2,081	2,593	3,659	6,544	11,586	12,506	14,448	13,549	9,738
Nonfuel Primary Products	..	..	..	..	..	..	..	..	..	..	..
Fuels	..	..	..	..	..	..	..	..	..	..	..
Manufactures	..	..	..	..	..	..	..	..	..	..	..
Terms of Trade					*(Index 1987 = 100)*						
Export Prices, fob	..	..	..	..	..	..	..	..	..	..	..
Import Prices, cif	..	..	..	..	..	..	..	..	..	..	..
BALANCE OF PAYMENTS					*(Millions of current US dollars)*						
Exports of Goods & Services	..	2,613	3,957	4,284	6,770	22,711	22,904	27,980	28,544	21,879	26,991
Merchandise, fob	..	2,417	3,724	3,966	6,122	21,356	20,432	24,719	24,076	17,675	24,171
Nonfactor Services	..	186	223	303	598	959	1,770	2,651	3,699	3,104	1,580
Factor Services	..	10	10	15	50	396	702	610	769	1,100	1,240
Imports of Goods & Services	..	3,124	4,079	4,676	6,614	10,410	18,178	20,303	25,603	21,760	15,008
Merchandise, fob	..	1,658	2,069	2,591	3,985	7,257	12,898	13,860	16,718	11,803	8,521
Nonfactor Services	..	561	686	815	1,317	2,409	4,572	5,773	8,201	9,177	5,690
Factor Services	..	905	1,324	1,270	1,311	744	708	670	684	780	797
Long-Term Interest	..	..	..	..	..	..	..	..	..	..	..
Private Current Transfers, net	..	0	0	0	-1	-1	-1	0	0	0	0
Workers' Remittances	..	..	..	..	..	..	..	..	..	..	..
Curr. A/C Bal before Off. Transf.	..	-511	-122	-392	155	12,299	4,724	7,677	2,941	119	11,983
Net Official Transfers	..	4	4	4	-1	-32	-17	-17	-125	-15	-15
Curr. A/C Bal after Off. Transf.	..	-507	-118	-388	154	12,267	4,707	7,660	2,816	104	11,968
Long-Term Capital, net	..	462	740	622	1,189	-1,939	-2,869	-925	1,706	-73	-2,000
Direct Investment	..	25	65	91	561	324	141	..	..	..	..
Long-Term Loans	..	..	..	..	..	..	..	..	..	..	..
Disbursements	..	..	..	..	..	..	..	..	..	..	..
Repayments	..	..	..	..	..	..	..	..	..	..	..
Other Long-Term Capital	..	437	675	531	627	-2,262	-3,010	-925	1,706	-73	-2,000
Other Capital, net	..	-192	-235	250	-1,312	-3,172	-1,771	-4,322	-2,432	-746	-6,899
Change in Reserves	..	237	-387	-485	-30	-7,156	-67	-2,413	-2,090	715	-3,069
Memo Item:					*(Iranian Rials per US dollar)*						
Conversion Factor (Annual Avg)	75.750	75.750	75.750	75.750	68.880	67.630	68.170	70.530	70.580	70.480	70.480
EXTERNAL DEBT (Total)				*(Millions of US dollars), outstanding at end of year*							
Long-Term Debt (by debtor)	..	..	..	..	..	..	..	..	..	..	..
Central Bank, incl. IMF credit	..	..	..	..	..	..	..	..	..	..	..
Central Government	..	..	..	..	..	..	..	..	..	..	..
Rest of General Government	..	..	..	..	..	..	..	..	..	..	..
Non-financial Public Enterprises	..	..	..	..	..	..	..	..	..	..	..
Priv. Sector, incl non-guaranteed	..	..	..	..	..	..	..	..	..	..	..
Short-Term Debt	..	..	..	..	..	..	..	..	..	..	..
Memo Items:					*(Millions of US dollars)*						
Int'l Reserves Excluding Gold	152.0	77.0	479.3	818.3	1,078.5	8,223.2	8,743.6	8,681.3	12,105.8	11,977.2	15,209.6
Gold Holdings (at market price)	158.9	139.9	163.3	242.9	420.2	697.2	524.3	503.7	623.4	863.4	1,998.1
SOCIAL INDICATORS											
Total Fertility Rate	6.8	6.7	6.6	6.5	6.4	6.3	6.2	6.1	6.1	6.0	5.9
Infant Mortality Rate	135.8	131.2	126.6	122.0	117.6	113.2	108.8	104.4	100.0	95.6	91.2
Life Expectancy at Birth	54.3	54.8	55.3	55.9	56.4	57.0	57.5	58.0	58.6	59.0	59.4
Urban Population, % of total	40.2	41.0	41.9	42.9	43.8	44.8	45.7	46.4	47.1	47.7	48.4
Food Prod. per capita (1987=100)	89.6	89.7	88.4	93.6	93.7	96.3	99.9	106.1	100.9	106.0	100.4
Labor Force, Agriculture (%)	44.6	43.8	42.9	42.1	41.3	40.6	39.9	39.1	38.4	37.6	37.0
Labor Force, Female (%)	13.1	13.3	13.5	13.7	13.9	14.1	14.3	14.5	14.8	15.0	15.2
Primary Schl. Enroll. Ratio	..	72.0	..	..	..	..	93.0	98.0	101.0	..	..
Primary Schl. Enroll. Ratio, Female	..	52.0	..	..	..	..	71.0	77.0	80.0	..	..
Secondary Schl. Enroll. Ratio	..	27.0	..	..	..	..	45.0	48.0	42.0	..	..

1980	1981	1982	1983	1984	1985	1986	1987	1988	1989 estimate	NOTES	IRAN, ISLAMIC REPUBLIC OF
				(Millions of current US dollars)							**FOREIGN TRADE (CUSTOMS BASIS)**
14,082	12,522	19,526	19,508	12,527	13,384	8,322	..	..	..	..	Value of Exports, fob
..	..	..	..	..	..	..	..	..	..	..	Nonfuel Primary Products
..	..	..	..	..	..	..	..	..	..	..	Fuels
..	..	..	..	..	..	..	..	..	..	..	Manufactures
12,246	12,499	11,955	18,320	15,370	11,635	10,521	9,570	9,454	..	..	Value of Imports, cif
..	..	..	..	..	..	..	..	..	..	..	Nonfuel Primary Products
..	..	..	..	..	..	..	..	..	..	..	Fuels
..	..	..	..	..	..	..	..	..	..	..	Manufactures
				(Index 1987 = 100)							
..	..	..	..	..	..	..	..	..	..	..	Terms of Trade
..	..	..	..	..	..	..	..	..	..	..	Export Prices, fob
..	..	..	..	..	..	..	..	..	..	..	Import Prices, cif
				(Millions of current US dollars)							**BALANCE OF PAYMENTS**
14,073	13,282	21,573	22,842	18,156	14,938	7,778	11,076	..	..	..	Exports of Goods & Services
12,338	11,831	20,452	21,507	17,087	14,175	7,171	10,639	..	..	..	Merchandise, fob
731	556	509	540	475	370	242	231	..	..	..	Nonfactor Services
1,004	895	612	795	594	393	365	206	..	..	..	Factor Services
16,509	16,728	15,840	22,484	18,570	15,414	12,933	13,552	..	..	..	Imports of Goods & Services
10,888	13,138	12,552	18,027	14,729	12,006	10,585	11,197	..	..	..	Merchandise, fob
5,223	3,315	3,061	4,273	3,698	3,308	2,282	2,289	..	..	..	Nonfactor Services
398	275	227	184	143	100	66	66	..	..	..	Factor Services
..	..	..	..	..	..	..	..	..	..	..	Long-Term Interest
0	..	..	..	..	..	..	..	..	..	..	Private Current Transfers, net
..	..	..	..	..	..	..	..	..	..	..	Workers' Remittances
-2,436	-3,446	5,733	358	-414	-476	-5,155	-2,476	..	..	..	Curr. A/C Bal before Off. Transf.
-2	..	..	..	..	..	..	..	..	..	..	Net Official Transfers
-2,438	-3,446	5,733	358	-414	-476	-5,155	-2,476	..	..	..	Curr. A/C Bal after Off. Transf.
-6,533	-947	-2,186	-835	-663	-570	-1,258	-1,079	..	..	..	Long-Term Capital, net
..	..	..	..	..	..	..	..	..	..	..	Direct Investment
..	..	..	..	..	..	..	..	..	..	..	Long-Term Loans
..	..	..	..	..	..	..	..	..	..	..	Disbursements
..	..	..	..	..	..	..	..	..	..	..	Repayments
-6,533	-947	-2,186	-835	-663	-570	-1,258	-1,079	..	..	..	Other Long-Term Capital
-876	4,023	1,340	-772	-3,059	1,601	5,199	3,331	..	..	..	Other Capital, net
9,847	370	-4,887	1,249	4,136	-555	1,214	224	271	-111	..	Change in Reserves
				(Iranian Rials per US dollar)							Memo Item:
71.570	80.030	84.450	87.230	91.900	87.730	76.550	144.910	177.970	215.700	..	Conversion Factor (Annual Avg)
			(Millions of US dollars), outstanding at end of year								
..	..	..	..	..	..	..	..	..	..	..	**EXTERNAL DEBT (Total)**
..	..	..	..	..	..	..	..	..	..	..	Long-Term Debt (by debtor)
..	..	..	..	..	..	..	..	..	..	..	Central Bank, incl. IMF credit
..	..	..	..	..	..	..	..	..	..	..	Central Government
..	..	..	..	..	..	..	..	..	..	..	Rest of General Government
..	..	..	..	..	..	..	..	..	..	..	Non-financial Public Enterprises
..	..	..	..	..	..	..	..	..	..	..	Priv. Sector, incl non-guaranteed
..	..	..	..	..	..	..	..	..	..	..	Short-Term Debt
				(Millions of US dollars)							Memo Items:
10,222.9	1,605.4	5,701.2	..	..	..	..	..	..	..	..	Int'l Reserves Excluding Gold
2,907.4	2,407.7	2,706.2	..	..	..	..	..	..	..	..	Gold Holdings (at market price)
											SOCIAL INDICATORS
5.8	5.7	5.6	5.6	5.6	5.6	5.6	5.6	5.6	5.5	..	Total Fertility Rate
86.8	82.4	78.0	75.4	72.8	70.2	67.6	65.0	63.7	62.4	..	Infant Mortality Rate
59.8	60.2	60.6	61.0	61.4	61.8	62.2	62.6	62.8	63.0	..	Life Expectancy at Birth
49.1	49.7	50.2	50.8	51.3	51.9	52.5	53.1	53.7	54.3	..	Urban Population, % of total
100.9	110.1	109.8	102.8	102.2	102.3	102.3	100.0	88.6	82.9	..	Food Prod. per capita (1987=100)
36.4	..	..	..	..	..	..	..	..	..	..	Labor Force, Agriculture (%)
15.3	15.7	15.9	16.2	16.5	16.7	17.0	17.3	17.5	17.8	..	Labor Force, Female (%)
87.0	..	97.0	102.0	103.0	107.0	110.0	114.0	..	..	..	Primary Schl. Enroll. Ratio
..	..	82.0	89.0	92.0	97.0	100.0	105.0	..	..	..	Primary Schl. Enroll. Ratio, Female
..	..	39.0	40.0	42.0	45.0	46.0	48.0	..	..	..	Secondary Schl. Enroll. Ratio

IRELAND	1969	1970	1971	1972	1973	1974	1975	1976	1977	1978	1979
CURRENT GNP PER CAPITA (US $)	1,230	1,300	1,460	1,720	2,020	2,340	2,610	2,660	3,000	3,430	4,120
POPULATION (thousands)	2,926	2,950	2,978	3,024	3,073	3,124	3,177	3,228	3,272	3,314	3,368
USE AND ORIGIN OF RESOURCES					*(Millions of current Irish Pounds)*						
Gross National Product (GNP)	1,467	1,648	1,882	2,284	2,741	3,041	3,796	4,617	5,593	6,527	7,631
Net Factor Income from Abroad	28	28	27	30	13	19	4	-36	-108	-228	-283
GDP at Market Prices	1,438	1,620	1,856	2,255	2,729	3,021	3,792	4,653	5,701	6,755	7,914
Resource Balance	-130	-130	-134	-121	-182	-436	-231	-369	-521	-666	-1,299
Exports of Goods & NFServices	537	600	669	775	1,027	1,272	1,618	2,151	2,813	3,371	3,931
Imports of Goods & NFServices	666	729	803	896	1,209	1,708	1,849	2,520	3,334	4,038	5,230
Domestic Absorption	1,596	1,778	2,016	2,405	2,923	3,477	4,027	4,986	6,114	7,193	8,930
Private Consumption, etc.	1,019	1,131	1,276	1,468	1,734	2,050	2,478	2,972	3,601	4,111	4,923
General Gov't Consumption	233	271	321	377	448	559	730	837	970	1,156	1,431
Gross Domestic Investment	345	375	418	560	741	868	819	1,176	1,542	1,926	2,576
Fixed Investment	314	343	406	477	632	674	798	1,042	1,247	1,612	2,144
Indirect Taxes, net	205	236	272	320	407	435	481	670	754	811	878
GDP at factor cost	1,233	1,385	1,584	1,935	2,322	2,587	3,311	3,983	4,947	5,944	7,036
Agriculture	..	..	..	..	..	..	..	..	..	..	..
Industry	..	..	..	..	..	..	..	..	..	..	..
Manufacturing	..	..	..	..	..	..	..	..	..	..	..
Services, etc.	..	..	..	..	..	..	..	..	..	..	..
Gross Domestic Saving	187	218	258	410	547	413	584	844	1,129	1,488	1,561
Gross National Saving	..	277	318	475	599	475	634	857	1,074	1,317	1,323
					(Millions of 1987 Irish Pounds)						
Gross National Product	10,990	11,348	11,740	12,582	13,097	13,655	13,938	14,009	14,994	15,817	16,251
GDP at Market Prices	10,741	11,115	11,532	12,370	12,988	13,523	13,877	14,078	15,246	16,345	16,819
Resource Balance	-969	-924	-986	-1,087	-1,590	-1,432	-579	-950	-1,040	-1,385	-2,023
Exports of Goods & NFServices	3,233	3,376	3,515	3,641	4,039	4,067	4,359	4,713	5,374	6,036	6,427
Imports of Goods & NFServices	4,202	4,300	4,501	4,728	5,628	5,499	4,938	5,663	6,414	7,421	8,450
Domestic Absorption	11,710	12,039	12,518	13,457	14,578	14,956	14,456	15,027	16,285	17,730	18,842
Private Consumption, etc.	7,154	7,363	7,607	8,023	8,489	8,688	8,792	8,809	9,515	10,271	10,545
General Gov't Consumption	1,790	1,924	2,092	2,240	2,393	2,573	2,741	2,814	2,872	3,107	3,249
Gross Domestic Investment	2,766	2,751	2,819	3,194	3,696	3,695	2,923	3,404	3,898	4,352	5,048
Fixed Investment	2,398	2,407	2,607	2,753	3,251	2,988	2,878	3,169	3,319	3,926	4,494
GDP at factor cost	9,172	9,455	9,780	10,513	10,877	11,590	12,139	12,031	13,233	14,368	14,979
Agriculture	..	..	..	..	..	..	..	..	..	..	..
Industry	..	..	..	..	..	..	..	..	..	..	..
Manufacturing	..	..	..	..	..	..	..	..	..	..	..
Services, etc.	..	..	..	..	..	..	..	..	..	..	..
Memo Items:											
Capacity to Import	3,383	3,537	3,751	4,090	4,781	4,096	4,322	4,834	5,411	6,197	6,352
Terms of Trade Adjustment	150	160	237	449	743	29	-37	121	37	160	-75
Gross Domestic Income	10,891	11,275	11,769	12,819	13,731	13,552	13,840	14,199	15,283	16,505	16,744
Gross National Income	11,141	11,509	11,977	13,030	13,840	13,684	13,901	14,130	15,031	15,977	16,176
DOMESTIC PRICES/DEFLATORS					*(Index 1987 = 100)*						
Overall (GDP)	13.4	14.6	16.1	18.2	21.0	22.3	27.3	33.1	37.4	41.3	47.1
Domestic Absorption	13.6	14.8	16.1	17.9	20.1	23.2	27.9	33.2	37.5	40.6	47.4
Agriculture	..	..	..	..	..	..	..	..	..	..	..
Industry	..	..	..	..	..	..	..	..	..	..	..
Manufacturing	..	..	..	..	..	..	..	..	..	..	..
Consumer Price Index	13.4	14.5	15.8	17.2	19.2	22.4	27.1	32.0	36.3	39.1	44.3
MANUFACTURING ACTIVITY											
Employment (1987=100)	103.8	105.6	104.8	105.5	111.4	112.2	103.9	105.3	109.1	110.5	121.4
Real Earnings per Empl. (1987=100)	56.8	60.3	63.8	67.7	71.7	74.6	79.3	78.8	80.3	87.3	88.8
Real Output per Empl. (1987=100)	..	..	..	..	..	..	..	..	..	..	..
Earnings as % of Value Added	47.1	48.7	48.5	48.5	46.4	45.3	46.0	42.0	42.4	41.1	42.3
MONETARY HOLDINGS					*(Millions of current Irish Pounds)*						
Money Supply, Broadly Defined	990	1,084	1,177	1,352	1,682	2,033	2,456	2,770	3,261	4,142	4,914
Money	389	415	440	518	572	624	748	875	1,072	1,367	1,479
Currency Outside Banks	137	155	173	191	219	245	292	342	390	476	582
Demand Deposits	252	260	267	327	354	380	456	533	682	892	896
Quasi-Money	601	669	738	834	1,109	1,409	1,708	1,895	2,189	2,775	3,435
					(Millions of current Irish Pounds)						
GOVERNMENT DEFICIT (-) OR SURPLUS	..	-89	-98	-125	-183	-357	-472	-470	-534	-768	-944
Current Revenue	..	506	598	695	842	956	1,209	1,629	1,933	2,256	2,728
Current Expenditure	..	481	560	663	810	987	1,406	1,750	2,065	2,531	3,081
Current Budget Balance	..	25	38	32	32	-31	-197	-121	-132	-275	-353
Capital Receipts	..	..	..	..	..	..	..	..	..	..	..
Capital Payments	..	114	136	157	215	326	275	349	402	493	591

1980	1981	1982	1983	1984	1985	1986	1987	1988	1989 estimate	NOTES	IRELAND
5,040	5,580	5,520	5,120	5,010	4,880	5,200	6,380	7,740	8,500	..	CURRENT GNP PER CAPITA (US $)
3,401	3,443	3,480	3,504	3,529	3,540	3,541	3,543	3,538	3,537	..	POPULATION (thousands)
				(Millions of current Irish Pounds)							USE AND ORIGIN OF RESOURCES
9,002	10,852	12,457	13,595	14,790	15,701	16,727	18,031	18,784	20,388	..	Gross National Product (GNP)
-358	-505	-928	-1,184	-1,639	-1,966	-1,957	-1,957	-2,542		..	Net Factor Income from Abroad
9,360	11,357	13,384	14,779	16,428	17,667	18,684	19,988	21,326	..	..	GDP at Market Prices
-1,262	-1,613	-987	-415	-35	342	491	1,306	1,971	2,300	..	Resource Balance
4,639	5,501	6,431	7,743	9,773	10,738	10,352	11,775	13,520	16,264	..	Exports of Goods & NFServices
5,902	7,114	7,418	8,158	9,808	10,397	9,862	10,469	11,549	13,964	..	Imports of Goods & NFServices
10,264	12,466	13,443	14,011	14,824	15,359	16,237	16,725	16,813	18,088	..	Domestic Absorption
5,791	6,994	7,145	7,640	7,982	8,450	8,847	9,403	9,444	10,028	..	Private Consumption, etc.
1,860	2,260	2,646	2,857	3,067	3,295	3,527	3,571	3,551	3,597	..	General Gov't Consumption
2,613	3,211	3,652	3,513	3,776	3,614	3,863	3,751	3,818	4,463	..	Gross Domestic Investment
2,434	3,100	3,389	3,347	3,533	3,401	3,503	3,551	3,617	4,161	..	Fixed Investment
1,116	1,412	1,762	2,023	2,312	2,444	2,622	2,624	3,076	3,328	..	Indirect Taxes, net
8,244	9,945	11,622	12,756	14,116	15,223	16,062	17,364	18,250	..	..	GDP at factor cost
..	..	..	..	..	..	..	..	..	..	..	Agriculture
..	..	..	..	..	..	..	..	..	..	..	Industry
..	..	..	..	..	..	..	..	..	..	..	Manufacturing
..	..	..	..	..	..	..	..	..	..	..	Services, etc.
1,709	2,102	3,593	4,282	5,380	5,921	6,310	7,014	8,331	..	..	Gross Domestic Saving
1,411	1,658	2,730	3,144	3,711	3,936	4,312	4,950	5,709	..	..	Gross National Saving
				(Millions of 1987 Irish Pounds)							
16,686	17,124	17,002	16,731	17,134	17,283	17,083	18,031	18,268	18,993	..	Gross National Product
17,295	17,857	18,232	18,183	19,015	19,426	19,111	19,988	20,722	..	..	GDP at Market Prices
-1,235	-1,239	-598	-200	328	654	414	1,306	1,920	2,130	..	Resource Balance
6,835	6,969	7,355	8,123	9,471	10,094	10,385	11,775	12,798	14,275	..	Exports of Goods & NFServices
8,070	8,208	7,952	8,323	9,144	9,440	9,971	10,469	10,878	12,145	..	Imports of Goods & NFServices
18,530	19,096	18,830	18,383	18,688	18,772	18,697	18,682	18,802	..	..	Domestic Absorption
10,661	10,864	10,270	10,367	10,572	11,011	10,988	11,360	11,825	..	..	Private Consumption, etc.
3,480	3,491	3,605	3,592	3,567	3,625	3,711	3,571	3,417	3,330	..	General Gov't Consumption
4,389	4,741	4,956	4,425	4,549	4,136	3,999	3,751	3,560	3,980	..	Gross Domestic Investment
4,327	4,643	4,488	4,084	4,026	3,693	3,620	3,551	3,492	3,856	..	Fixed Investment
15,318	15,740	15,881	15,697	16,354	16,757	16,385	17,364	17,741	..	..	GDP at factor cost
..	..	..	..	..	..	..	..	..	..	..	Agriculture
..	..	..	..	..	..	..	..	..	..	..	Industry
..	..	..	..	..	..	..	..	..	..	..	Manufacturing
..	..	..	..	..	..	..	..	..	..	..	Services, etc.
											Memo Items:
6,344	6,347	6,895	7,900	9,111	9,751	10,468	11,775	12,734	14,146	..	Capacity to Import
-491	-622	-460	-224	-360	-344	82	0	-64	..	..	Terms of Trade Adjustment
16,803	17,235	17,772	17,960	18,655	19,083	19,193	19,988	20,659	..	..	Gross Domestic Income
16,195	16,501	16,542	16,507	16,774	16,940	17,165	18,031	18,204	18,864	..	Gross National Income
				(Index 1987 = 100)							DOMESTIC PRICES/DEFLATORS
54.1	63.6	73.4	81.3	86.4	90.9	97.8	100.0	102.9	..	..	Overall (GDP)
55.4	65.3	71.4	76.2	79.3	81.8	86.8	89.5	89.4	..	..	Domestic Absorption
..	..	..	..	..	..	..	..	..	..	..	Agriculture
..	..	..	..	..	..	..	..	..	..	..	Industry
..	..	..	..	..	..	..	..	..	..	..	Manufacturing
52.4	63.1	73.9	81.6	88.6	93.4	97.0	100.0	102.2	106.3	..	Consumer Price Index
											MANUFACTURING ACTIVITY
120.5	118.8	114.2	107.8	104.6	100.0	98.8	100.0	102.6	..	G	Employment (1987=100)
90.0	86.6	84.4	86.6	88.7	92.0	94.2	100.0	106.8	..	G	Real Earnings per Empl. (1987=100)
..	..	..	..	..	..	..	..	..	..	G	Real Output per Empl. (1987=100)
43.6	41.2	39.6	35.8	33.2	32.5	33.1	32.1	31.3	..	..	Earnings as % of Value Added
				(Millions of current Irish Pounds)							MONETARY HOLDINGS
5,954	6,832	7,043	7,486	8,257	8,750	8,620	9,559	9,654	10,749	D	Money Supply, Broadly Defined
1,686	1,743	1,838	2,048	2,245	2,289	2,382	2,640	2,826	3,112	..	Money
663	739	811	907	923	970	1,025	1,107	1,212	1,310	..	Currency Outside Banks
1,023	1,004	1,027	1,142	1,322	1,318	1,357	1,532	1,614	1,802	..	Demand Deposits
4,268	5,088	5,205	5,438	6,012	6,461	6,238	6,919	6,828	7,637	..	Quasi-Money
				(Millions of current Irish Pounds)							GOVERNMENT DEFICIT (-) OR SURPLUS
-1,224	-1,662	-1,984	-1,849	-1,756	-2,080	-2,123	-1,934	..	..	..	
3,550	4,427	5,607	6,516	7,188	7,669	8,117	8,732	..	..	..	Current Revenue
3,950	5,046	6,484	7,357	7,960	8,776	9,273	9,793	..	..	..	Current Expenditure
-400	-619	-877	-841	-772	-1,107	-1,156	-1,061	..	..	..	Current Budget Balance
..	..	..	..	..	..	..	..	..	..	..	Capital Receipts
824	1,043	1,107	1,008	984	973	967	873	..	..	..	Capital Payments

IRELAND	1969	1970	1971	1972	1973	1974	1975	1976	1977	1978	1979
FOREIGN TRADE (CUSTOMS BASIS)					*(Millions of current US dollars)*						
Value of Exports, fob	891	1,035	1,308	1,611	2,131	2,629	3,179	3,313	4,400	5,681	7,173
Nonfuel Primary Products	523	583	688	819	1,079	1,243	1,661	1,546	1,951	2,565	3,059
Fuels	22	25	16	16	16	35	42	22	29	23	34
Manufactures	346	427	604	776	1,036	1,352	1,475	1,745	2,420	3,093	4,080
Value of Imports, cif	1,413	1,568	1,835	2,102	2,793	3,813	3,769	4,192	5,381	7,102	9,850
Nonfuel Primary Products	323	344	355	426	599	802	726	793	1,023	1,218	1,662
Fuels	107	127	166	158	190	531	531	562	678	718	1,187
Manufactures	983	1,097	1,314	1,517	2,004	2,481	2,512	2,837	3,680	5,166	7,001
					(Index 1987 = 100)						
Terms of Trade	115.8	132.1	139.5	137.2	126.0	99.7	100.1	98.7	94.5	99.7	100.4
Export Prices, fob	28.0	32.7	37.1	41.7	48.7	53.8	57.2	57.8	60.3	71.2	84.6
Import Prices, cif	24.2	24.7	26.6	30.4	38.6	54.0	57.2	58.6	63.9	71.4	84.2
BALANCE OF PAYMENTS					*(Millions of current US dollars)*						
Exports of Goods & Services	..	1,539	1,754	2,101	2,730	3,319	3,947	4,248	5,286	6,942	8,683
Merchandise, fob	..	1,092	1,271	1,580	2,090	2,479	3,032	3,326	4,229	5,604	6,949
Nonfactor Services	..	306	331	331	397	508	568	561	715	896	1,169
Factor Services	..	141	152	190	243	331	347	360	343	442	565
Imports of Goods & Services	..	1,842	2,065	2,376	3,196	4,311	4,462	4,992	6,396	8,677	11,929
Merchandise, fob	..	1,524	1,711	1,958	2,617	3,561	3,518	3,935	5,049	6,669	9,269
Nonfactor Services	..	220	239	269	350	407	550	572	739	1,024	1,372
Factor Services	..	98	115	149	229	342	395	485	608	984	1,288
Long-Term Interest	..	..	..	..	..	..	..	..	..	..	..
Private Current Transfers, net	..	75	82	89	97	101	102	88	92	109	93
Workers' Remittances	..	..	..	..	..	..	..	..	..	..	..
Curr. A/C Bal before Off. Transf.	..	-228	-229	-186	-370	-892	-413	-656	-1,018	-1,626	-3,153
Net Official Transfers	..	30	29	36	116	203	290	228	495	777	1,053
Curr. A/C Bal after Off. Transf.	..	-198	-200	-150	-254	-688	-124	-428	-522	-849	-2,100
Long-Term Capital, net	..	102	-15	33	277	218	388	655	195	965	854
Direct Investment	..	32	25	31	52	51	158	173	136	375	337
Long-Term Loans	..	..	..	..	..	..	..	..	..	..	..
Disbursements	..	..	..	..	..	..	..	..	..	..	..
Repayments	..	..	..	..	..	..	..	..	..	..	..
Other Long-Term Capital	..	70	-40	1	224	167	230	483	59	590	518
Other Capital, net	..	88	423	204	-21	603	86	102	735	27	659
Change in Reserves	..	8	-209	-87	-1	-132	-350	-329	-408	-142	586
Memo Item:					*(Irish Pounds per US dollar)*						
Conversion Factor (Annual Avg)	0.420	0.420	0.410	0.400	0.410	0.430	0.450	0.560	0.570	0.520	0.490
					(Millions US dollars), outstanding at end of year						
EXTERNAL DEBT (Total)	..	..	..	..	..	..	..	..	..	..	..
Long-Term Debt (by debtor)	..	..	..	..	..	..	..	..	..	..	..
Central Bank, incl. IMF credit	..	..	..	..	..	..	..	..	..	..	..
Central Government	..	..	..	..	..	..	..	..	..	..	..
Rest of General Government	..	..	..	..	..	..	..	..	..	..	..
Non-financial Public Enterprises	..	..	..	..	..	..	..	..	..	..	..
Priv. Sector, incl non-guaranteed	..	..	..	..	..	..	..	..	..	..	..
Short-Term Debt	..	..	..	..	..	..	..	..	..	..	..
Memo Items:					*(Millions of US dollars)*						
Int'l Reserves Excluding Gold	652.1	680.7	978.0	1,109.4	1,007.2	1,247.2	1,512.6	1,818.5	2,351.1	2,668.4	2,212.0
Gold Holdings (at market price)	39.2	17.1	19.9	29.7	48.1	83.4	62.7	60.2	78.0	101.0	196.2
SOCIAL INDICATORS											
Total Fertility Rate	3.8	3.9	4.0	3.9	3.7	3.6	3.4	3.3	3.3	3.2	3.2
Infant Mortality Rate	20.6	19.5	18.0	18.0	18.0	17.8	17.5	15.5	15.5	14.9	12.8
Life Expectancy at Birth	71.1	71.1	71.1	71.3	71.4	71.6	71.7	71.9	72.0	72.2	72.4
Urban Population, % of total	51.1	51.7	52.1	52.5	52.8	53.2	53.6	53.9	54.3	54.6	55.0
Food Prod. per capita (1987=100)	78.1	76.4	86.1	81.5	76.6	88.1	99.8	86.3	97.0	101.6	92.1
Labor Force, Agriculture (%)	27.3	26.3	25.5	24.7	23.9	23.1	22.4	21.6	20.8	20.0	19.3
Labor Force, Female (%)	26.2	26.3	26.5	26.8	27.0	27.2	27.5	27.6	27.7	27.8	28.0
Primary Schl. Enroll. Ratio	..	106.0	..	..	..	..	103.0	106.0	105.0	104.0	100.0
Primary Schl. Enroll. Ratio, Female	..	106.0	..	..	..	..	103.0	105.0	105.0	104.0	100.0
Secondary Schl. Enroll. Ratio	..	74.0	..	..	..	..	86.0	91.0	92.0	92.0	90.0

1980	1981	1982	1983	1984	1985	1986	1987	1988	1989 estimate	NOTES	IRELAND
				(Millions of current US dollars)							**FOREIGN TRADE (CUSTOMS BASIS)**
8,473	7,784	8,060	8,609	9,627	10,399	12,604	15,970	18,736	..	..	Value of Exports, fob
3,509	2,913	2,782	2,772	2,907	3,016	3,732	4,900	5,461	..	..	Nonfuel Primary Products
55	51	51	99	116	132	98	115	103	..	..	Fuels
4,909	4,820	5,227	5,737	6,604	7,251	8,773	10,955	13,173	..	..	Manufactures
11,133	10,595	9,696	9,169	9,658	10,049	11,564	13,613	15,558	..	..	Value of Imports, cif
1,862	1,846	1,611	1,591	1,634	1,700	2,020	2,272	2,582	..	..	Nonfuel Primary Products
1,647	1,556	1,435	1,237	1,198	1,195	981	1,005	868	..	..	Fuels
7,624	7,193	6,651	6,342	6,825	7,154	8,563	10,336	12,108	..	..	Manufactures
				(Index 1987 = 100)							
91.5	97.4	75.9	78.5	81.0	96.1	98.7	100.0	101.8	..	..	Terms of Trade
88.6	91.1	67.3	67.6	67.4	78.2	90.8	100.0	110.9	..	..	Export Prices, fob
96.8	93.6	88.6	86.1	83.2	81.4	91.9	100.0	109.0	..	..	Import Prices, cif
				(Millions of current US dollars)							**BALANCE OF PAYMENTS**
10,418	9,681	9,864	10,197	11,249	12,189	14,864	18,619	21,932	24,366	..	Exports of Goods & Services
8,229	7,696	7,933	8,438	9,421	10,131	12,365	15,569	18,392	20,355	..	Merchandise, fob
1,381	1,209	1,219	1,174	1,166	1,302	1,621	2,029	2,266	2,344	..	Nonfactor Services
808	776	712	584	663	756	878	1,021	1,274	1,667	..	Factor Services
13,754	13,120	12,633	12,242	13,086	13,925	16,835	19,552	22,817	25,425	..	Imports of Goods & Services
10,452	9,950	9,096	8,690	9,183	9,500	11,223	12,948	14,563	16,348	..	Merchandise, fob
1,593	1,435	1,375	1,372	1,372	1,471	1,966	2,522	2,952	2,957	..	Nonfactor Services
1,710	1,734	2,162	2,179	2,531	2,954	3,647	4,083	5,302	6,120	..	Factor Services
..	..	..	..	..	..	..	..	..	..	..	Long-Term Interest
123	97	91	57	-33	-21	-55	-160	-121	-94	..	Private Current Transfers, net
..	..	..	..	..	..	..	..	..	..	..	Workers' Remittances
-3,213	-3,342	-2,677	-1,988	-1,870	-1,757	-2,027	-1,093	-1,006	-1,153	..	Curr. A/C Bal before Off. Transf.
1,081	741	743	769	833	1,068	1,348	1,468	1,659	1,670	..	Net Official Transfers
-2,132	-2,601	-1,935	-1,219	-1,038	-690	-680	375	653	517	..	Curr. A/C Bal after Off. Transf.
1,326	1,690	1,661	995	800	835	1,050	827	-261	-1,215	..	Long-Term Capital, net
286	203	242	170	121	164	-43	89	92	85	..	Direct Investment
..	..	..	..	..	..	..	..	..	..	..	Long-Term Loans
..	..	..	..	..	..	..	..	..	..	..	Disbursements
..	..	..	..	..	..	..	..	..	..	..	Repayments
1,039	1,486	1,419	825	679	672	1,093	738	-352	-1,300	..	Other Long-Term Capital
1,519	904	395	412	195	-97	-467	-317	201	-239	..	Other Capital, net
-712	8	-121	-188	43	-48	96	-885	-593	937	..	Change in Reserves
				(Irish Pounds per US dollar)							**Memo Item:**
0.490	0.620	0.700	0.800	0.920	0.950	0.740	0.670	0.660	0.710	..	Conversion Factor (Annual Avg)
				(Millions US dollars), outstanding at end of year							
..	..	..	..	..	..	..	..	..	..	..	**EXTERNAL DEBT (Total)**
..	..	..	..	..	..	..	..	..	..	..	Long-Term Debt (by debtor)
..	..	..	..	..	..	..	..	..	..	..	Central Bank, incl. IMF credit
..	..	..	..	..	..	..	..	..	..	..	Central Government
..	..	..	..	..	..	..	..	..	..	..	Rest of General Government
..	..	..	..	..	..	..	..	..	..	..	Non-financial Public Enterprises
..	..	..	..	..	..	..	..	..	..	..	Priv. Sector, incl non-guaranteed
..	..	..	..	..	..	..	..	..	..	..	Short-Term Debt
				(Millions of US dollars)							**Memo Items:**
2,860.3	2,651.3	2,622.1	2,639.6	2,352.4	2,939.6	3,236.3	4,796.2	5,086.8	4,057.4	..	Int'l Reserves Excluding Gold
210.7	142.6	164.3	137.1	110.8	117.5	140.5	173.9	147.4	144.0	..	Gold Holdings (at market price)
											SOCIAL INDICATORS
3.2	3.1	3.0	2.8	2.6	2.5	2.4	2.3	2.3	2.3	..	Total Fertility Rate
11.1	10.3	10.5	10.1	9.6	8.8	8.7	7.4	7.2	7.0	..	Infant Mortality Rate
72.6	72.8	73.0	73.2	73.3	73.5	73.7	73.9	74.1	74.3	..	Life Expectancy at Birth
55.3	55.6	56.0	56.3	56.7	57.0	57.4	57.8	58.3	58.7	..	Urban Population, % of total
100.3	82.7	88.7	91.8	99.4	99.1	99.9	100.0	95.8	94.1	..	Food Prod. per capita (1987=100)
18.6	..	..	..	..	..	..	..	..	..	..	Labor Force, Agriculture (%)
28.1	28.3	28.4	28.6	28.8	28.9	29.0	29.1	29.2	29.3	..	Labor Force, Female (%)
100.0	99.0	100.0	99.0	100.0	100.0	..	..	..	..	..	Primary Schl. Enroll. Ratio
100.0	100.0	100.0	99.0	100.0	100.0	..	..	..	..	..	Primary Schl. Enroll. Ratio, Female
90.0	92.0	94.0	96.0	97.0	98.0	..	..	..	..	..	Secondary Schl. Enroll. Ratio

ISRAEL	1969	1970	1971	1972	1973	1974	1975	1976	1977	1978	1979
CURRENT GNP PER CAPITA (US $)	1,760	1,830	2,100	2,450	2,680	3,310	3,890	4,080	4,090	4,250	4,730
POPULATION (thousands)	2,877	2,974	3,069	3,148	3,278	3,377	3,455	3,533	3,613	3,690	3,786

USE AND ORIGIN OF RESOURCES *(Millions of current Israel New Sheqalims)*

	1969	1970	1971	1972	1973	1974	1975	1976	1977	1978	1979
Gross National Product (GNP)	2.00E+0	2.00E+0	2.00E+0	3.00E+0	4.00E+0	6.00E+0	8.00E+0	1.10E+1	1.50E+1	2.50E+1	47
Net Factor Income from Abroad	-2.80E-2	-3.52E-2	-4.28E-2	-5.70E-2	-1.11E-1	-1.57E-1	-2.80E-1	-3.52E-1	-3.60E-1	-7.12E-1	-2
GDP at Market Prices	2.00E+0	2.00E+0	2.00E+0	3.00E+0	4.00E+0	6.00E+0	8.00E+0	1.10E+1	1.60E+1	2.60E+1	49
Resource Balance	-2.70E-1	-3.83E-1	-3.95E-1	-3.64E-1	-9.63E-1	-1.00E+0	-2.00E+0	-2.00E+0	-2.00E+0	-4.00E+0	-7
Exports of Goods & NFServices	4.43E-1	4.88E-1	6.80E-1	8.68E-1	1.00E+0	2.00E+0	2.00E+0	3.00E+0	6.00E+0	1.10E+1	19
Imports of Goods & NFServices	7.13E-1	8.71E-1	1.00E+0	1.00E+0	2.00E+0	3.00E+0	4.00E+0	5.00E+0	7.00E+0	1.50E+1	26
Domestic Absorption	2.00E+0	2.00E+0	3.00E+0	4.00E+0	5.00E+0	7.00E+0	1.10E+1	1.30E+1	1.80E+1	3.00E+1	56
Private Consumption, etc.	1.00E+0	1.00E+0	1.00E+0	2.00E+0	3.00E+0	3.00E+0	5.00E+0	6.00E+0	9.00E+0	1.50E+1	28
General Gov't Consumption	4.92E-1	6.73E-1	7.94E-1	9.29E-1	2.00E+0	2.00E+0	3.00E+0	4.00E+0	5.00E+0	9.00E+0	15
Gross Domestic Investment	4.31E-1	5.37E-1	7.43E-1	9.73E-1	1.00E+0	2.00E+0	2.00E+0	3.00E+0	4.00E+0	6.00E+0	12
Fixed Investment	3.96E-1	5.02E-1	6.94E-1	9.19E-1	1.00E+0	2.00E+0	2.00E+0	3.00E+0	3.00E+0	6.00E+0	12
Indirect Taxes, net	..	..	..	..	..	..	..	..	..	..	..
GDP at factor cost	..	..	..	..	..	..	..	..	..	..	..
Agriculture	9.52E-2	1.03E-1	1.26E-1	1.51E-1	1.86E-1	2.85E-1	3.98E-1	5.68E-1	7.76E-1	1.00E+0	2
Industry	4.74E-1	5.89E-1	7.45E-1	9.71E-1	1.00E+0	2.00E+0	2.00E+0	3.00E+0	4.00E+0	8.00E+0	14
Manufacturing	..	..	..	..	..	..	..	..	..	..	..
Services, etc.	..	..	..	..	..	..	..	..	..	..	..
Gross Domestic Saving	1.61E-1	1.54E-1	3.47E-1	6.09E-1	3.27E-1	5.02E-1	4.15E-1	7.80E-1	2.00E+0	2.00E+0	5
Gross National Saving		2.75E-1	5.13E-1	8.48E-1	6.94E-1	6.74E-1	6.16E-1	1.00E+0	2.00E+0	3.00E+0	6

(Millions of 1980 Israel New Sheqalims)

	1969	1970	1971	1972	1973	1974	1975	1976	1977	1978	1979
Gross National Product	60.64	64.93	72.23	82.41	84.09	89.91	92.45	93.62	94.49	98.78	104.31
GDP at Market Prices	62.16	66.70	74.19	84.32	87.14	93.10	96.19	97.45	97.45	102.15	108.57
Resource Balance	-13.71	-18.32	-17.88	-14.75	-29.24	-26.58	-29.22	-22.98	-17.63	-20.93	-19.15
Exports of Goods & NFServices	18.01	19.63	24.36	27.52	29.03	30.70	31.25	36.10	40.06	42.20	43.68
Imports of Goods & NFServices	31.72	37.94	42.24	42.28	58.27	57.28	60.47	59.08	57.69	63.14	62.83
Domestic Absorption	75.87	85.02	92.07	99.07	116.38	119.68	125.41	120.43	115.08	123.08	127.72
Private Consumption, etc.	36.21	37.30	39.46	43.30	46.88	50.48	50.61	53.05	55.62	60.09	64.86
General Gov't Consumption	21.29	26.89	27.24	26.72	38.83	39.90	43.96	39.68	34.36	37.24	34.02
Gross Domestic Investment	18.37	20.83	25.37	29.06	30.68	29.29	30.83	27.70	25.09	25.75	28.84
Fixed Investment	..	19.02	23.12	26.30	29.11	28.20	28.32	25.28	22.40	23.68	26.55
GDP at factor cost	..	..	..	..	..	..	..	..	..	..	..
Agriculture	..	..	..	..	..	..	..	..	..	..	..
Industry	..	..	..	..	..	..	..	..	..	..	..
Manufacturing	..	..	..	..	..	..	..	..	..	..	..
Services, etc.	..	..	..	..	..	..	..	..	..	..	..
Memo Items:											
Capacity to Import	19.71	21.26	26.71	29.78	30.87	31.40	31.56	37.49	43.24	45.65	45.72
Terms of Trade Adjustment	1.70	1.64	2.36	2.26	1.84	0.69	0.31	1.38	3.18	3.45	2.04
Gross Domestic Income	63.86	68.34	76.54	86.58	88.98	93.79	96.50	98.84	100.63	105.60	110.61
Gross National Income	62.34	66.57	74.58	84.67	85.93	90.60	92.76	95.01	97.67	102.23	106.35

DOMESTIC PRICES/DEFLATORS *(Index 1980 = 100)*

	1969	1970	1971	1972	1973	1974	1975	1976	1977	1978	1979
Overall (GDP)	2.70	2.90	3.30	3.90	4.80	6.50	8.80	11.40	16.20	25.30	44.70
Domestic Absorption	2.60	2.80	3.10	3.60	4.40	6.10	8.40	10.80	15.30	24.50	43.60
Agriculture	..	..	..	..	..	..	..	..	..	..	..
Industry	..	..	..	..	..	..	..	..	..	..	..
Manufacturing	..	..	..	..	..	..	..	..	..	..	..
Consumer Price Index	7.30E-3	7.70E-3	8.70E-3	9.80E-3	1.17E-2	1.64E-2	2.28E-2	3.00E-2	4.04E-2	6.08E-2	0.11

MANUFACTURING ACTIVITY

	1969	1970	1971	1972	1973	1974	1975	1976	1977	1978	1979
Employment (1987=100)	64.3	67.5	71.8	75.8	80.3	82.2	80.9	81.5	82.9	85.6	89.5
Real Earnings per Empl. (1987=100)	39.7	41.8	42.4	45.0	42.3	41.7	47.9	53.0	55.7	53.6	95.6
Real Output per Empl. (1987=100)	..	..	..	..	..	..	..	..	..	..	..
Earnings as % of Value Added	36.3	36.2	36.7	36.9	36.5	33.4	35.4	37.5	36.4	24.0	51.1

MONETARY HOLDINGS *(Millions of current Israel New Sheqalims)*

	1969	1970	1971	1972	1973	1974	1975	1976	1977	1978	1979
Money Supply, Broadly Defined	0.32	0.27	0.16	2.00	3.00	3.00	4.00	7.00	11.00	19.00	38.00
Money	0.12	0.13	0.16	0.20	1.00	1.00	1.00	2.00	2.00	3.00	3.00
Currency Outside Banks	0.12	0.13	0.16	0.20	0.28	0.33	0.42	0.51	0.69	0.98	1.00
Demand Deposits	0.00	0.00	0.00	0.00	1.00	1.00	1.00	1.00	1.00	2.00	2.00
Quasi-Money	0.20	0.14	0.00	2.00	2.00	2.00	3.00	5.00	9.00	16.00	35.00

GOVERNMENT DEFICIT (-) OR SURPLUS *(Millions of current Israel New Sheqalims)*

	1969	1970	1971	1972	1973	1974	1975	1976	1977	1978	1979
	..	..	..	-0.50	-0.80	-1.00	-2.00	-2.00	-3.00	-3.00	-7.00
Current Revenue	..	..	..	1.00	2.00	3.00	4.00	6.00	9.00	14.00	31.00
Current Expenditure	..	..	..	1.00	2.00	3.00	5.00	7.00	10.00	15.00	32.00
Current Budget Balance	..	..	..	-0.30	-0.50	-0.70	-0.70	-0.80	-1.00	-0.70	-2.00
Capital Receipts	..	..	..	..	..	..	..	..	..	..	..
Capital Payments	..	..	..	0.20	0.30	0.60	0.90	1.00	1.00	2.00	5.00

1980	1981	1982	1983	1984	1985	1986	1987	1988	1989 estimate	NOTES	ISRAEL
5,390	6,250	6,510	6,780	6,680	6,570	6,780	7,600	8,940	9,750	..	**CURRENT GNP PER CAPITA (US $)**
3,878	3,956	4,031	4,105	4,170	4,233	4,305	4,375	4,444	4,525	..	**POPULATION (thousands)**
			(Millions of current Israel New Sheqalims)								**USE AND ORIGIN OF RESOURCES**
112	270	621	1,604	7,710	29,133	46,244	59,295	71,748	86,022	f	Gross National Product (GNP)
-4	-6	-14	-35	-333	-1,129	-1,522	-1,817	-1,801	-2,191	..	Net Factor Income from Abroad
116	276	635	1,639	8,043	30,262	47,766	61,112	73,549	88,213	f	GDP at Market Prices
-13	-35	-76	-177	-696	-2,022	-2,541	-5,609	-4,696	-3,293	..	Resource Balance
46	106	213	508	2,886	12,123	16,759	21,383	23,488	30,238	..	Exports of Goods & NFServices
59	141	289	686	3,582	14,145	19,300	26,992	28,184	33,531	f	Imports of Goods & NFServices
129	311	712	1,816	8,739	32,284	50,307	66,721	78,245	91,506	..	Domestic Absorption
59	145	343	909	4,158	16,544	27,732	36,071	43,284	51,679	..	Private Consumption, etc.
45	110	229	547	2,925	10,475	13,946	19,755	22,820	25,953	..	General Gov't Consumption
25	56	140	360	1,656	5,265	8,629	10,895	12,141	13,874	..	Gross Domestic Investment
24	58	135	355	1,556	5,275	7,871	10,967	12,467	13,856	..	Fixed Investment
..	..	..	..	..	..	..	..	..	..	..	Indirect Taxes, net
..	..	..	..	..	..	..	..	..	..	..	GDP at factor cost
5	12	22	45	242	1,041	1,581	..	..	..	..	Agriculture
27	61	140	355	1,817	5,976	8,530	..	..	..	..	Industry
..	..	..	..	..	..	..	..	..	..	..	Manufacturing
..	..	..	..	..	..	..	..	..	..	..	Services, etc.
12	21	64	183	960	3,243	6,088	5,286	7,445	10,581	..	Gross Domestic Saving
14	29	71	193	852	3,088	6,326	5,652	7,475	11,391	..	Gross National Saving
			(Millions of 1980 Israel New Sheqalims)								
112.22	119.23	121.44	125.73	124.10	129.09	135.36	144.48	147.56	148.16	f	Gross National Product
116.03	122.00	124.20	128.57	129.73	134.20	140.02	149.09	151.50	152.12	f	GDP at Market Prices
-12.71	-15.98	-19.70	-22.56	-16.26	-11.08	-14.04	-21.95	-21.25	-12.78	..	Resource Balance
46.18	48.43	46.98	48.03	54.61	59.26	62.38	69.12	67.58	70.58	..	Exports of Goods & NFServices
58.88	64.41	66.68	70.60	70.88	70.35	76.42	91.06	88.83	83.36	..	Imports of Goods & NFServices
128.73	137.98	143.91	151.13	145.99	145.28	154.06	171.04	172.75	164.89	..	Domestic Absorption
58.84	66.51	71.85	78.11	72.60	73.04	83.81	92.70	95.86	93.12	..	Private Consumption, etc.
44.71	47.61	44.68	42.88	45.41	47.23	42.75	50.04	49.13	44.75	..	General Gov't Consumption
25.18	23.86	27.38	30.13	27.98	25.01	27.51	28.30	27.76	27.02	..	Gross Domestic Investment
24.34	25.31	26.60	29.95	26.57	24.51	24.36	27.66	27.54	26.03	..	Fixed Investment
..	..	..	..	..	..	..	..	..	..	..	GDP at factor cost
..	..	..	..	..	..	..	..	..	..	..	Agriculture
..	..	..	..	..	..	..	..	..	..	..	Industry
..	..	..	..	..	..	..	..	..	..	..	Manufacturing
..	..	..	..	..	..	..	..	..	..	..	Services, etc.
											Memo Items:
46.18	48.44	49.05	52.33	57.11	60.29	66.36	72.14	74.03	75.17	..	Capacity to Import
0.00	0.00	2.08	4.30	2.49	1.03	3.98	3.02	6.45	4.59	..	Terms of Trade Adjustment
116.03	122.00	126.28	132.86	132.22	135.23	144.00	152.12	157.95	156.71	..	Gross Domestic Income
112.22	119.24	123.51	130.03	126.59	130.12	139.34	147.50	154.00	152.75	..	Gross National Income
			(Index 1980 = 100)								**DOMESTIC PRICES/DEFLATORS**
100.00	226.20	511.30	1,274.70	6,199.90	22,549.80	34,113.60	40,989.20	48,546.40	57,989.80	..	Overall (GDP)
100.00	225.30	494.40	1,201.80	5,986.00	22,221.20	32,653.80	39,009.00	45,293.80	55,493.90	..	Domestic Absorption
..	..	..	..	..	..	..	..	..	..	..	Agriculture
..	..	..	..	..	..	..	..	..	..	..	Industry
..	..	..	..	..	..	..	..	..	..	..	Manufacturing
0.25	0.54	1.20	2.94	13.92	56.33	83.46	100.00	116.30	139.80	f	Consumer Price Index
											MANUFACTURING ACTIVITY
85.5	87.8	91.2	93.4	93.4	96.7	96.9	100.0	95.0	89.2	J	Employment (1987=100)
108.1	111.0	113.1	136.6	70.6	110.0	69.8	100.0	78.3	..	J	Real Earnings per Empl. (1987=100)
..	..	..	..	..	..	..	..	..	..	..	Real Output per Empl. (1987=100)
53.5	52.0	64.3	65.6	51.3	58.7	39.8	63.3	42.7	..	J	Earnings as % of Value Added
			(Millions of current Israel New Sheqalims)								**MONETARY HOLDINGS**
93	224	543	1,671	10,190	27,361	33,039	42,037	51,390	62,214	..	Money Supply, Broadly Defined
8	13	28	68	305	1,051	2,238	3,346	3,723	5,374	..	Money
3	4	9	25	123	481	974	1,365	1,643	2,224	..	Currency Outside Banks
5	9	20	43	182	570	1,264	1,981	2,080	3,150	..	Demand Deposits
85	211	515	1,603	9,885	26,310	30,801	38,691	47,667	56,840	..	Quasi-Money
			(Millions of current Israel New Sheqalims)								
-18	-58	-101	-412	-1,440	-951	333	-2,000	-6,143	..	C	**GOVERNMENT DEFICIT (-) OR SURPLUS**
70	158	381	1,108	5,791	20,949	29,104	33,055	34,355	..	..	Current Revenue
78	190	424	1,319	6,587	19,267	25,792	31,548	33,868	..	..	Current Expenditure
-8	-32	-42	-211	-796	1,682	3,312	1,507	488	..	..	Current Budget Balance
..	..	..	..	..	..	..	..	..	..	..	Capital Receipts
10	26	58	202	644	2,634	2,979	3,507	6,631	..	..	Capital Payments

ISRAEL	1969	1970	1971	1972	1973	1974	1975	1976	1977	1978	1979
FOREIGN TRADE (CUSTOMS BASIS)					*(Millions of current US dollars)*						
Value of Exports, fob	724	776	960	1,149	1,509	1,825	1,941	2,416	3,083	3,924	4,553
Nonfuel Primary Products	207	229	263	286	320	394	455	535	630	730	898
Fuels	0	0	0	0	0	0	0	0	0	0	1
Manufactures	516	547	697	863	1,189	1,431	1,486	1,880	2,453	3,195	3,654
Value of Imports, cif	1,646	2,084	2,375	2,447	4,235	5,380	5,975	5,645	5,745	7,162	8,428
Nonfuel Primary Products	354	468	489	484	840	1,094	1,327	1,158	1,124	1,256	1,522
Fuels	88	102	119	122	297	800	914	931	876	947	1,515
Manufactures	1,204	1,513	1,767	1,841	3,098	3,486	3,734	3,556	3,745	4,959	5,391
					(Index 1987 = 100)						
Terms of Trade	132.0	145.4	143.7	127.6	124.9	123.9	121.8	118.1	114.0	111.6	109.8
Export Prices, fob	33.5	39.2	41.6	40.4	47.5	67.1	70.5	69.6	72.5	78.1	92.7
Import Prices, cif	25.4	27.0	29.0	31.7	38.0	54.1	57.9	59.0	63.5	70.0	84.4
BALANCE OF PAYMENTS					*(Millions of current US dollars)*						
Exports of Goods & Services	..	1,402	1,874	2,120	2,697	3,563	3,688	4,397	5,459	6,619	8,031
Merchandise, fob	..	808	1,002	1,219	1,563	2,004	2,178	2,669	3,403	4,074	4,759
Nonfactor Services	..	498	703	709	821	1,109	1,083	1,299	1,557	1,921	2,277
Factor Services	..	96	169	192	313	450	427	429	499	624	995
Imports of Goods & Services	..	2,614	3,096	3,219	5,263	6,756	7,537	7,466	7,818	9,712	11,586
Merchandise, fob	..	1,931	2,205	2,287	3,965	4,995	5,520	5,248	5,364	6,693	7,883
Nonfactor Services	..	438	593	549	759	967	1,079	1,269	1,462	1,780	2,064
Factor Services	..	245	298	383	539	794	938	949	992	1,239	1,639
Long-Term Interest	..	..	..	..	..	..	..	..	..	..	..
Private Current Transfers, net	..	446	550	708	1,139	740	759	776	803	825	1,001
Workers' Remittances	..	..	..	..	..	..	..	..	..	..	..
Curr. A/C Bal before Off. Transf.	..	-766	-672	-391	-1,427	-2,453	-3,090	-2,293	-1,556	-2,268	-2,554
Net Official Transfers	..	204	240	341	1,050	990	1,332	1,657	1,269	1,400	1,836
Curr. A/C Bal after Off. Transf.	..	-562	-432	-50	-377	-1,463	-1,758	-636	-287	-868	-718
Long-Term Capital, net	..	677	626	731	999	601	1,027	1,234	1,005	1,016	1,254
Direct Investment	..	40	53	114	149	84	43	41	75	32	10
Long-Term Loans	..	..	..	..	..	..	..	..	..	..	..
Disbursements	..	..	..	..	..	..	..	..	..	..	..
Repayments	..	..	..	..	..	..	..	..	..	..	..
Other Long-Term Capital	..	637	573	617	850	517	984	1,193	930	984	1,244
Other Capital, net	..	-108	17	-133	-74	20	575	-414	-504	797	-324
Change in Reserves	..	-7	-211	-548	-548	842	156	-184	-214	-945	-211
Memo Item:					*(Israel New Sheqalims per US dollar)*						
Conversion Factor (Annual Avg)	0.00035	0.00035	0.00037	0.00042	0.00042	0.00045	0.00063	0.00079	0.00105	0.00175	0.00254
					(Millions of US dollars), outstanding at end of year						
EXTERNAL DEBT (Total)	..	..	..	..	..	..	..	..	..	..	..
Long-Term Debt (by debtor)	..	..	..	..	..	..	..	..	..	..	..
Central Bank, incl. IMF credit	..	..	..	..	..	..	..	..	..	..	..
Central Government	..	..	..	..	..	..	..	..	..	..	..
Rest of General Government	..	..	..	..	..	..	..	..	..	..	..
Non-financial Public Enterprises	..	..	..	..	..	..	..	..	..	..	..
Priv. Sector, incl non-guaranteed	..	..	..	..	..	..	..	..	..	..	..
Short-Term Debt	..	..	..	..	..	..	..	..	..	..	..
Memo Items:					*(Millions of US dollars)*						
Int'l Reserves Excluding Gold	366.7	405.2	689.8	1,178.9	1,768.3	1,153.4	1,137.1	1,328.3	1,521.6	2,625.1	3,063.5
Gold Holdings (at market price)	46.0	46.3	54.1	74.2	123.1	205.0	154.4	148.6	192.0	264.6	630.3
SOCIAL INDICATORS											
Total Fertility Rate	3.8	3.8	3.8	3.8	3.7	3.6	3.6	3.5	3.4	3.4	3.3
Infant Mortality Rate	23.5	25.3	23.0	24.2	22.8	23.4	22.9	20.1	18.1	16.3	15.9
Life Expectancy at Birth	71.0	71.2	71.7	71.1	71.7	71.7	72.0	73.0	73.2	73.1	73.0
Urban Population, % of total	83.5	84.2	84.7	85.2	85.6	86.1	86.6	87.0	87.4	87.8	88.2
Food Prod. per capita (1987=100)	88.3	86.3	93.4	105.9	94.8	103.6	106.2	100.0	100.8	97.0	93.7
Labor Force, Agriculture (%)	10.1	9.7	9.3	8.9	8.6	8.2	7.9	7.6	7.2	6.9	6.5
Labor Force, Female (%)	29.6	30.0	30.4	30.8	31.1	31.5	31.8	32.2	32.5	32.8	33.2
Primary Schl. Enroll. Ratio	..	96.0	..	..	..	..	97.0	96.0	97.0	96.0	96.0
Primary Schl. Enroll. Ratio, Female	..	95.0	..	..	..	..	97.0	97.0	97.0	97.0	97.0
Secondary Schl. Enroll. Ratio	..	57.0	..	..	..	..	66.0	66.0	67.0	68.0	71.0

1980	1981	1982	1983	1984	1985	1986	1987	1988	1989 estimate	NOTES	ISRAEL
											FOREIGN TRADE (CUSTOMS BASIS)
				(Millions of current US dollars)							
5,540	5,664	5,280	5,112	5,804	6,257	7,135	8,475	9,605	..	..	Value of Exports, fob
988	1,074	1,034	989	1,065	1,044	1,083	1,237	1,402	..	..	Nonfuel Primary Products
1	0	0	1	1	1	1	1	1	..	..	Fuels
4,551	4,590	4,246	4,122	4,738	5,212	6,052	7,236	8,201	..	..	Manufactures
9,682	10,125	10,236	9,614	9,849	10,112	10,814	14,354	15,030	..	..	Value of Imports, cif
1,626	1,913	1,667	1,413	1,570	1,510	1,521	1,815	1,900	..	..	Nonfuel Primary Products
2,563	2,628	2,373	1,691	1,723	1,659	871	1,218	1,275	..	..	Fuels
5,492	5,584	6,196	6,510	6,557	6,943	8,422	11,321	11,855	..	..	Manufactures
				(Index 1987 = 100)							
103.6	98.4	101.3	105.1	103.7	103.7	102.5	100.0	100.9	..	..	Terms of Trade
106.0	101.9	97.5	95.4	92.6	90.8	93.0	100.0	107.5	..	..	Export Prices, fob
102.3	103.6	96.3	90.8	89.3	87.5	90.8	100.0	106.5	..	..	Import Prices, cif
				(Millions of current US dollars)							**BALANCE OF PAYMENTS**
9,828	10,499	10,324	10,232	10,582	10,887	11,820	13,914	15,312	16,667	..	Exports of Goods & Services
5,840	5,970	5,621	5,611	6,257	6,678	7,742	9,140	10,111	10,917	..	Merchandise, fob
2,709	2,700	2,565	2,732	2,846	3,064	2,966	3,603	3,839	4,159	..	Nonfactor Services
1,279	1,829	2,138	1,889	1,479	1,145	1,112	1,171	1,362	1,591	..	Factor Services
13,430	14,559	14,683	14,884	15,163	14,776	15,580	19,622	20,498	20,395	..	Imports of Goods & Services
8,946	9,411	8,798	8,760	8,758	9,040	9,614	12,898	13,158	12,736	..	Merchandise, fob
2,242	2,540	2,821	3,032	3,058	2,662	2,942	3,542	3,961	4,314	..	Nonfactor Services
2,242	2,608	3,064	3,092	3,347	3,074	3,024	3,182	3,379	3,345	..	Factor Services
..	..	..	..	..	..	..	..	..	..	..	Long-Term Interest
1,060	1,313	880	809	767	826	1,183	1,369	1,145	1,566	..	Private Current Transfers, net
..	..	..	..	..	..	..	..	..	..	..	Workers' Remittances
-2,542	-2,747	-3,479	-3,843	-3,814	-3,063	-2,577	-4,339	-4,041	-2,162	..	Curr. A/C Bal before Off. Transf.
1,965	1,787	1,583	1,899	2,514	4,172	4,197	3,471	3,418	3,310	..	Net Official Transfers
-577	-960	-1,896	-1,944	-1,300	1,109	1,620	-868	-623	1,148	..	Curr. A/C Bal after Off. Transf.
1,237	1,144	1,121	2,342	1,065	-69	348	421	-573	-115	..	Long-Term Capital, net
48	4	-122	-31	19	48	48	165	164	102	..	Direct Investment
..	..	..	..	..	..	..	..	..	..	..	Long-Term Loans
..	..	..	..	..	..	..	..	..	..	..	Disbursements
..	..	..	..	..	..	..	..	..	..	..	Repayments
1,189	1,140	1,243	2,373	1,046	-117	300	256	-737	-217	..	Other Long-Term Capital
-119	366	1,694	-965	-272	-643	-977	1,091	34	356	..	Other Capital, net
-541	-550	-919	567	507	-397	-991	-644	1,162	-1,389	..	Change in Reserves
				(Israel New Sheqalims per US dollar)							Memo Item:
0.00512	0.01140	0.02430	0.05620	0.293	1.18	1.49	1.59	1.60	1.92	..	Conversion Factor (Annual Avg)
				(Millions of US dollars), outstanding at end of year							
..	..	..	..	..	..	..	..	..	..	..	**EXTERNAL DEBT (Total)**
..	..	..	..	..	..	..	..	..	..	..	Long-Term Debt (by debtor)
..	..	..	..	..	..	..	..	..	..	..	Central Bank, incl. IMF credit
..	..	..	..	..	..	..	..	..	..	..	Central Government
..	..	..	..	..	..	..	..	..	..	..	Rest of General Government
..	..	..	..	..	..	..	..	..	..	..	Non-financial Public Enterprises
..	..	..	..	..	..	..	..	..	..	..	Priv. Sector, incl non-guaranteed
..	..	..	..	..	..	..	..	..	..	..	Short-Term Debt
				(Millions of US dollars)							Memo Items:
3,351.4	3,496.7	3,839.3	3,651.2	3,060.3	3,680.2	4,659.6	5,876.1	4,015.6	5,276.2	..	Int'l Reserves Excluding Gold
703.9	474.2	495.3	387.2	313.5	332.6	397.5	492.3	417.6	407.8	..	Gold Holdings (at market price)
											SOCIAL INDICATORS
3.2	3.2	3.1	3.1	3.1	3.1	3.0	3.0	3.0	2.9	..	Total Fertility Rate
15.1	15.5	13.9	14.4	13.1	11.9	11.6	11.4	11.1	10.8	..	Infant Mortality Rate
72.9	73.7	74.5	74.6	74.8	75.0	75.2	75.4	75.5	75.7	..	Life Expectancy at Birth
88.6	88.9	89.3	89.6	90.0	90.3	90.6	90.8	91.1	91.3	..	Urban Population, % of total
85.5	81.6	88.7	96.7	90.8	99.9	90.1	100.0	86.8	88.5	..	Food Prod. per capita (1987=100)
6.2	..	..	..	..	..	..	..	..	..	..	Labor Force, Agriculture (%)
33.5	33.5	33.5	33.5	33.5	33.5	33.5	33.6	33.6	33.6	..	Labor Force, Female (%)
95.0	..	97.0	98.0	97.0	97.0	95.0	95.0	..	..	..	Primary Schl. Enroll. Ratio
..	..	97.0	99.0	99.0	98.0	97.0	97.0	..	..	..	Primary Schl. Enroll. Ratio, Female
73.0	..	73.0	74.0	81.0	80.0	83.0	83.0	..	..	..	Secondary Schl. Enroll. Ratio

ITALY	1969	1970	1971	1972	1973	1974	1975	1976	1977	1978	1979
CURRENT GNP PER CAPITA (US $)	1,830	1,990	2,150	2,380	2,840	3,370	3,700	4,040	4,390	4,890	6,080
POPULATION (thousands)	53,538	53,822	54,074	54,381	54,751	55,111	55,441	55,718	55,955	56,155	56,318
USE AND ORIGIN OF RESOURCES					*(Billions of current Italian Lire)*						
Gross National Product (GNP)	59,865	67,311	73,333	80,146	97,009	122,094	138,214	174,355	214,207	253,386	310,435
Net Factor Income from Abroad	331	311	338	336	271	-96	-419	-514	-223	-21	845
GDP at Market Prices	59,534	67,000	72,995	79,810	96,738	122,190	138,633	174,869	214,430	253,407	309,590
Resource Balance	145	-505	-173	-341	-2,933	-6,221	-1,515	-4,001	-957	1,546	-1,803
Exports of Goods & NFServices	8,888	9,995	11,140	12,694	15,218	22,896	26,332	35,859	45,627	54,032	68,359
Imports of Goods & NFServices	8,743	10,500	11,312	13,035	18,151	29,117	27,847	39,859	46,584	52,486	70,162
Domestic Absorption	59,389	67,505	73,168	80,151	99,671	128,411	140,148	178,870	215,387	251,861	311,393
Private Consumption, etc.	36,102	40,652	44,116	48,421	59,197	74,531	87,208	105,899	128,514	150,263	184,439
General Gov't Consumption	10,008	10,846	12,097	13,509	15,785	19,652	23,484	23,963	30,073	36,480	45,720
Gross Domestic Investment	13,279	16,007	16,954	18,222	24,689	34,228	29,457	49,008	56,801	65,118	81,234
Fixed Investment	17,213	18,765	19,540	21,038	26,256	33,081	35,526	42,172	50,839	58,200	71,214
Indirect Taxes, net	4,928	5,596	5,790	5,543	6,622	8,202	6,887	10,063	12,990	14,145	15,317
GDP at factor cost	54,606	61,403	67,205	74,267	90,116	113,988	131,746	164,806	201,440	239,261	294,273
Agriculture	..	5,228	5,415	5,507	7,216	8,395	10,007	11,642	13,921	16,318	19,250
Industry	..	27,645	29,795	31,788	38,736	50,160	57,455	72,449	87,138	101,035	122,218
Manufacturing	..	18,135	19,536	21,054	26,056	34,919	38,425	51,467	61,825	71,281	87,734
Services, etc.	..	34,126	37,785	42,515	50,786	63,635	71,170	90,778	113,371	136,054	168,123
Gross Domestic Saving	13,424	15,502	16,781	17,881	21,756	28,006	27,941	45,007	55,843	66,664	79,430
Gross National Saving	..	16,129	17,466	18,582	22,393	28,282	27,909	44,927	56,349	67,583	81,453
					(Billions of 1987 Italian Lire)						
Gross National Product	563,661	593,055	602,259	618,128	661,700	695,040	675,074	719,552	745,273	773,460	822,097
GDP at Market Prices	560,347	590,105	599,277	615,319	659,647	695,455	677,015	721,555	745,910	773,372	819,674
Resource Balance	-6,783	-15,157	-11,801	-13,359	-19,363	-15,166	1,214	-2,319	6,989	12,596	9,736
Exports of Goods & NFServices	73,324	77,697	83,261	90,988	94,717	101,379	103,030	113,823	125,080	136,366	147,971
Imports of Goods & NFServices	80,107	92,855	95,062	104,347	114,080	116,545	101,816	116,142	118,090	123,770	138,235
Domestic Absorption	567,131	605,262	611,078	628,677	679,009	710,621	675,800	723,874	738,921	760,776	809,938
Private Consumption, etc.	316,468	336,691	345,667	356,343	381,189	397,537	402,002	421,960	440,908	456,552	488,296
General Gov't Consumption	96,373	99,544	105,275	110,593	113,424	116,312	119,176	121,937	125,292	129,695	133,586
Gross Domestic Investment	154,290	169,028	160,136	161,742	184,396	196,773	154,622	179,976	172,721	174,528	188,056
Fixed Investment	163,908	168,887	163,443	165,589	180,079	183,756	170,284	170,365	173,505	174,599	184,568
GDP at factor cost	513,365	539,677	550,687	571,380	613,905	649,590	644,206	680,910	701,548	731,025	780,274
Agriculture	..	33,807	33,805	30,939	32,871	33,257	34,714	33,392	33,117	33,782	35,806
Industry	..	209,893	210,035	217,779	237,686	254,044	236,414	255,828	265,143	273,433	292,819
Manufacturing	..	115,643	117,226	123,642	139,059	148,591	140,152	160,824	166,572	174,426	191,856
Services, etc.	..	341,890	352,140	364,607	385,769	404,685	403,280	430,454	446,188	465,112	489,454
Memo Items:											
Capacity to Import	81,436	88,389	93,609	101,616	95,644	91,643	96,276	104,484	115,663	127,414	134,682
Terms of Trade Adjustment	8,112	10,692	10,348	10,628	927	-9,736	-6,754	-9,339	-9,416	-8,952	-13,289
Gross Domestic Income	568,459	600,797	609,625	625,946	660,574	685,719	670,261	712,216	736,494	764,420	806,386
Gross National Income	571,773	603,747	612,608	628,756	662,628	685,305	668,320	710,213	735,856	764,508	808,808
DOMESTIC PRICES/DEFLATORS					*(Index 1987 = 100)*						
Overall (GDP)	10.6	11.4	12.2	13.0	14.7	17.6	20.5	24.2	28.7	32.8	37.8
Domestic Absorption	10.5	11.2	12.0	12.7	14.7	18.1	20.7	24.7	29.1	33.1	38.4
Agriculture	..	15.5	16.0	17.8	22.0	25.2	28.8	34.9	42.0	48.3	53.8
Industry	..	13.2	14.2	14.6	16.3	19.7	24.3	28.3	32.9	37.0	41.7
Manufacturing	..	15.7	16.7	17.0	18.7	23.5	27.4	32.0	37.1	40.9	45.7
Consumer Price Index	12.4	13.0	13.6	14.4	16.0	19.0	22.3	26.0	30.4	34.1	39.1
MANUFACTURING ACTIVITY											
Employment (1987=100)	111.5	114.5	121.3	121.0	124.5	125.0	124.7	122.6	120.8	117.8	117.8
Real Earnings per Empl. (1987=100)	55.8	63.9	68.5	69.8	75.0	78.0	80.2	84.2	89.6	92.3	94.9
Real Output per Empl. (1987=100)	..	39.1	38.6	41.7	50.4	57.9	52.4	60.9	62.3	64.9	73.2
Earnings as % of Value Added	39.1	41.4	43.6	42.7	39.1	36.9	39.7	36.9	39.4	39.7	37.9
MONETARY HOLDINGS					*(Billions of current Italian Lire)*						
Money Supply, Broadly Defined	49,817	56,679	66,630	79,313	95,562	110,273	135,769	163,683	199,846	246,066	298,115
Money	22,477	29,885	35,567	42,229	52,460	57,194	64,011	76,311	92,702	116,763	145,069
Currency Outside Banks	8,256	8,502	9,567	11,789	13,557	14,981	13,215	14,255	16,105	19,044	21,665
Demand Deposits	14,221	21,383	26,000	30,440	38,903	42,213	50,796	62,056	76,597	97,719	123,404
Quasi-Money	27,340	26,794	31,063	37,084	43,102	53,079	71,758	87,372	107,144	129,303	153,046
					(Billions of current Italian Lire)						
GOVERNMENT DEFICIT (-) OR SURPLUS	..	..	..	..	-8,421	-12,086	-21,492	-19,805	-24,349	-21,151	-27,452
Current Revenue	..	..	..	..	24,431	31,594	36,722	48,554	61,380	76,365	94,591
Current Expenditure	..	..	..	..	26,129	32,728	41,838	52,372	63,195	80,829	103,944
Current Budget Balance	..	..	..	..	-1,698	-1,134	-5,116	-3,818	-1,815	-4,464	-9,353
Capital Receipts	..	..	..	..	8	2	1	12	16	7	8
Capital Payments	..	..	..	..	6,731	10,954	16,377	15,999	22,550	16,694	18,107

1980	1981	1982	1983	1984	1985	1986	1987	1988	1989 estimate	NOTES	ITALY
7,480	8,030	7,920	7,550	7,610	7,720	8,570	10,410	13,350	15,150	..	CURRENT GNP PER CAPITA (US $)
56,434	56,508	56,640	56,836	57,005	57,141	57,246	57,345	57,441	57,537	..	POPULATION (thousands)

(Billions of current Italian Lire) — USE AND ORIGIN OF RESOURCES

1980	1981	1982	1983	1984	1985	1986	1987	1988	1989 estimate	NOTES	ITALY
388,521	461,828	541,547	629,122	722,415	807,254	889,348	972,836	1,075,550	1,179,990	..	Gross National Product (GNP)
790	-2,186	-3,652	-4,196	-4,736	-5,378	-6,907	-6,722	-7,345	-8,004	..	Net Factor Income from Abroad
387,731	464,014	545,199	633,318	727,151	812,632	896,255	979,558	1,082,900	1,187,990	..	GDP at Market Prices
-16,281	-15,470	-14,298	-6,081	-13,069	-15,364	3,525	-3,113	-5,936	-7,772	..	Resource Balance
77,332	99,905	114,259	126,787	150,622	168,981	167,166	175,932	193,687	227,659	..	Exports of Goods & NFServices
93,613	115,376	128,557	132,869	163,691	184,344	163,641	179,045	199,622	235,431	..	Imports of Goods & NFServices
404,013	479,485	559,497	639,399	740,220	827,995	892,730	982,671	1,088,830	1,195,760	..	Domestic Absorption
235,623	282,448	334,211	386,202	441,859	497,276	549,481	602,435	662,265	728,322	..	Private Consumption, etc.
58,028	75,306	88,798	105,142	119,994	135,486	147,682	167,877	188,270	203,838	..	General Gov't Consumption
110,361	121,731	136,488	148,054	178,367	195,233	195,567	212,358	238,297	263,604	..	Gross Domestic Investment
94,063	109,677	120,827	136,562	158,823	175,313	186,806	207,705	234,606	262,155	..	Fixed Investment
22,454	24,999	29,751	39,925	45,089	49,833	54,050	67,177	82,264	94,633	..	Indirect Taxes, net
365,277	439,015	515,448	593,393	682,062	762,799	842,205	912,381	1,000,630	1,093,360	..	GDP at factor cost
22,309	24,811	27,948	33,298	33,912	36,621	38,688	40,254	39,807	..	B	Agriculture
151,345	174,652	200,955	226,231	255,910	281,457	306,795	331,222	364,486		B	Industry
107,827	123,874	141,041	155,921	176,555	195,732	210,834	227,359	251,095	..	B	Manufacturing
214,077	264,551	316,296	373,789	437,330	494,554	550,772	608,082	678,604	..	B	Services, etc.
94,080	106,260	122,190	141,973	165,298	179,869	199,092	209,246	232,362	255,832	..	Gross Domestic Saving
96,043	105,712	120,523	139,912	163,116	177,022	194,370	204,181	226,902	..	..	Gross National Saving

(Billions of 1987 Italian Lire)

1980	1981	1982	1983	1984	1985	1986	1987	1988	1989 estimate	NOTES	ITALY
856,315	858,769	859,838	869,538	897,123	921,213	943,712	972,836	1,013,930	1,046,300	..	Gross National Product
854,404	862,594	865,406	875,144	902,809	927,147	950,971	979,558	1,020,870	1,053,160	..	GDP at Market Prices
-7,125	8,378	7,792	13,674	9,295	8,590	7,702	-3,113	-7,013	-6,711	..	Resource Balance
135,119	145,370	143,769	147,245	157,936	164,102	170,381	175,932	184,308	202,943	..	Exports of Goods & NFServices
142,244	136,992	135,977	133,571	148,641	155,512	162,679	179,045	191,320	209,655	..	Imports of Goods & NFServices
861,529	854,216	857,614	861,470	893,514	918,557	943,269	982,670	1,027,880	1,059,870	..	Domestic Absorption
513,425	523,965	530,310	534,844	545,134	561,830	582,437	602,435	626,488	648,427	..	Private Consumption, etc.
136,408	140,038	144,077	148,248	151,979	157,306	161,864	167,877	172,567	173,478	..	General Gov't Consumption
211,696	190,213	183,227	178,378	196,400	199,422	198,968	212,358	228,829	237,967	..	Gross Domestic Investment
200,636	194,304	184,221	182,510	190,641	193,352	196,381	207,705	221,717	233,088	..	Fixed Investment
806,536	818,535	820,297	821,801	848,672	872,162	894,163	912,381	943,089	968,829	..	GDP at factor cost
37,142	37,355	36,371	39,403	37,971	38,139	38,904	40,254	38,998	..	..	Agriculture
308,474	304,084	299,921	299,003	306,813	313,149	320,130	331,222	348,909	..	..	Industry
202,100	198,595	197,134	198,709	207,605	213,789	218,682	227,359	240,944	..	..	Manufacturing
506,679	520,270	529,523	536,737	558,025	575,859	591,937	608,082	632,964	..	..	Services, etc.

Memo Items:

1980	1981	1982	1983	1984	1985	1986	1987	1988	1989 estimate	NOTES	ITALY
117,505	118,623	120,854	127,458	136,774	142,551	166,183	175,932	185,632	202,734	..	Capacity to Import
-17,614	-26,747	-22,915	-19,787	-21,162	-21,551	-4,198	0	1,324	-210	..	Terms of Trade Adjustment
836,790	835,847	842,491	855,357	881,647	905,597	946,773	979,558	1,022,190	1,052,950	..	Gross Domestic Income
838,701	832,022	836,923	849,750	875,960	899,663	939,514	972,836	1,015,250	1,046,090	..	Gross National Income

(Index 1987 = 100) — DOMESTIC PRICES/DEFLATORS

1980	1981	1982	1983	1984	1985	1986	1987	1988	1989 estimate	NOTES	ITALY
45.4	53.8	63.0	72.4	80.5	87.6	94.2	100.0	106.1	112.8	..	Overall (GDP)
46.9	56.1	65.2	74.2	82.8	90.1	94.6	100.0	105.9	112.8	..	Domestic Absorption
60.1	66.4	76.8	84.5	89.3	96.0	99.4	100.0	102.1	..	..	Agriculture
49.1	57.4	67.0	75.7	83.4	89.9	95.8	100.0	104.5	..	..	Industry
53.4	62.4	71.5	78.5	85.0	91.6	96.4	100.0	104.2	..	..	Manufacturing
47.3	55.8	65.0	74.6	82.6	90.2	95.5	100.0	105.0	111.6	..	Consumer Price Index

MANUFACTURING ACTIVITY

1980	1981	1982	1983	1984	1985	1986	1987	1988	1989 estimate	NOTES	ITALY
116.0	111.0	104.5	107.7	107.9	100.1	98.9	100.0	99.8	..	..	Employment (1987 = 100)
95.7	97.9	96.8	94.2	100.4	98.0	97.1	100.0	105.6	..	..	Real Earnings per Empl. (1987 = 100)
77.5	80.0	81.5	85.4	93.7	99.0	97.6	100.0	107.3	..	..	Real Output per Empl/ (1987 = 100)
37.5	37.7	38.4	45.2	45.7	42.4	41.6	40.7	40.9	..	..	Earnings as % of Value Added

(Billions of current Italian Lire) — MONETARY HOLDINGS

1980	1981	1982	1983	1984	1985	1986	1987	1988	1989 estimate	NOTES	ITALY
336,599	372,080	444,509	498,237	563,250	629,382	695,766	762,306	846,730	952,463	D	Money Supply, Broadly Defined
164,615	181,044	212,029	239,210	269,575	297,951	331,039	357,151	386,038	432,769	..	Money
25,357	29,712	33,263	37,338	41,202	45,009	48,203	52,646	56,980	67,473	..	Currency Outside Banks
139,258	151,332	178,766	201,872	228,373	252,942	282,836	304,505	329,058	365,296	..	Demand Deposits
171,984	191,036	232,480	259,027	293,675	331,431	364,727	405,155	460,692	519,694	..	Quasi-Money

(Billions of current Italian Lire)

1980	1981	1982	1983	1984	1985	1986	1987	1988	1989 estimate	NOTES	ITALY
-41,480	-52,017	-54,081	-71,513	-95,325	-108,216	-128,056	-146,631	-115,338	..	F	GOVERNMENT DEFICIT (-) OR SURPLUS
123,676	145,292	186,105	230,751	253,130	278,495	334,360	361,513	400,103	..	..	Current Revenue
145,723	..	..	..	..	..	392,322	437,537	456,089	..	..	Current Expenditure
-22,047	..	..	..	..	..	-57,962	-76,024	-55,986	..	..	Current Budget Balance
8	..	..	..	..	..	41	147	1,416	..	..	Capital Receipts
19,441	..	..	..	..	..	70,135	70,754	60,768	..	..	Capital Payments

ITALY	1969	1970	1971	1972	1973	1974	1975	1976	1977	1978	1979
FOREIGN TRADE (CUSTOMS BASIS)					*(Billions of current US dollars)*						
Value of Exports, fob	11.73	13.21	15.11	18.55	22.22	30.25	34.83	36.97	45.06	56.05	72.24
Nonfuel Primary Products	1.42	1.56	1.77	2.18	2.52	3.32	3.79	3.78	4.90	5.26	7.36
Fuels	0.60	0.67	0.82	0.82	1.26	2.36	2.03	2.10	2.53	3.29	4.75
Manufactures	9.71	10.98	12.52	15.55	18.44	24.57	29.01	31.08	37.63	47.49	60.13
Value of Imports, cif	12.45	14.94	15.97	19.28	27.79	40.68	37.93	42.79	46.68	55.11	76.16
Nonfuel Primary Products	5.22	5.93	6.13	7.56	11.16	13.82	12.52	13.81	14.86	17.32	23.48
Fuels	1.82	2.09	2.69	2.90	3.92	10.83	10.26	11.05	12.00	13.35	18.35
Manufactures	5.41	6.91	7.15	8.82	12.71	16.03	15.15	17.93	19.82	24.45	34.33
					(Index 1987 = 100)						
Terms of Trade	126.3	130.2	127.8	122.2	108.9	86.2	96.1	86.5	89.9	90.5	88.4
Export Prices, fob	26.4	28.2	29.9	33.1	39.4	48.9	55.3	52.1	58.6	64.9	78.3
Import Prices, cif	20.9	21.7	23.4	27.1	36.2	56.7	57.5	60.3	65.2	71.6	88.6
BALANCE OF PAYMENTS					*(Billions of current US dollars)*						
Exports of Goods & Services	..	18.88	21.38	25.99	31.23	40.87	45.52	47.64	58.43	73.02	95.13
Merchandise, fob	..	13.12	14.97	18.44	22.07	30.02	34.51	36.84	44.80	55.50	71.39
Nonfactor Services	..	4.13	4.58	5.37	6.34	7.16	8.26	8.43	10.75	13.43	17.51
Factor Services	..	1.63	1.83	2.18	2.82	3.69	2.75	2.37	2.88	4.09	6.24
Imports of Goods & Services	..	18.28	20.05	24.42	33.98	48.87	46.34	50.79	56.17	66.39	90.11
Merchandise, fob	..	13.50	14.85	18.39	26.03	38.53	35.66	41.08	44.93	52.59	72.38
Nonfactor Services	..	3.44	3.66	4.14	5.30	6.25	6.99	6.57	7.85	9.54	12.30
Factor Services	..	1.35	1.53	1.89	2.65	4.10	3.69	3.14	3.40	4.27	5.44
Long-Term Interest	..	..	..	..	..	..	..	..	..	..	..
Private Current Transfers, net	..	0.51	0.56	0.63	0.63	0.57	0.59	0.52	0.83	1.11	1.42
Workers' Remittances	..	0.45	0.52	0.58	0.62	0.54	0.52	0.46	0.71	0.93	1.15
Curr. A/C Bal before Off. Transf.	..	1.10	1.90	2.20	-2.12	-7.43	-0.23	-2.62	3.09	7.73	6.44
Net Official Transfers	..	-0.30	-0.29	-0.15	-0.34	-0.57	-0.29	-0.22	-0.60	-1.48	-0.93
Curr. A/C Bal after Off. Transf.	..	0.80	1.60	2.06	-2.46	-8.00	-0.52	-2.84	2.49	6.25	5.50
Long-Term Capital, net	..	0.38	-0.08	-1.10	3.11	1.70	-0.36	-0.39	0.29	1.04	-0.40
Direct Investment	..	0.50	0.12	0.41	0.37	0.40	0.29	-0.06	0.58	0.35	-0.18
Long-Term Loans	..	..	..	..	..	..	..	..	..	..	..
Disbursements	..	..	..	..	..	..	..	..	..	..	..
Repayments	..	..	..	..	..	..	..	..	..	..	..
Other Long-Term Capital	..	-0.12	-0.20	-1.51	2.74	1.31	-0.66	-0.32	-0.30	0.69	-0.22
Other Capital, net	..	-0.79	-0.04	-1.81	-0.80	5.14	-2.43	5.11	3.07	-3.53	-2.23
Change in Reserves	..	-0.39	-1.48	0.85	0.15	1.16	3.32	-1.88	-5.85	-3.76	-2.87
Memo Item:					*(Italian Lire per US dollar)*						
Conversion Factor (Annual Avg)	625.000	625.000	619.900	583.200	583.000	650.300	652.800	832.300	882.400	848.700	830.900
				(Millions US dollars), outstanding at end of year							
EXTERNAL DEBT (Total)	..	..	..	..	..	..	..	..	..	..	..
Long-Term Debt (by debtor)	..	..	..	..	..	..	..	..	..	..	..
Central Bank, incl. IMF credit	..	..	..	..	..	..	..	..	..	..	..
Central Government	..	..	..	..	..	..	..	..	..	..	..
Rest of General Government	..	..	..	..	..	..	..	..	..	..	..
Non-financial Public Enterprises	..	..	..	..	..	..	..	..	..	..	..
Priv. Sector, incl non-guaranteed	..	..	..	..	..	..	..	..	..	..	..
Short-Term Debt	..	..	..	..	..	..	..	..	..	..	..
Memo Items:					*(Millions of US dollars)*						
Int'l Reserves Excluding Gold	2,089	2,465	3,689	2,954	2,953	3,406	1,306	3,223	8,104	11,109	18,197
Gold Holdings (at market price)	2,973	3,082	3,595	5,346	9,259	15,383	11,568	11,114	13,676	18,786	34,157
SOCIAL INDICATORS											
Total Fertility Rate	2.5	2.4	2.4	2.4	2.3	2.3	2.2	2.1	2.0	1.9	1.8
Infant Mortality Rate	30.8	29.6	28.5	27.0	26.2	22.9	21.1	19.5	18.1	17.1	15.7
Life Expectancy at Birth	71.4	71.7	71.9	72.1	72.3	72.4	72.6	72.7	73.6	74.0	74.3
Urban Population, % of total	63.8	64.3	64.6	64.8	65.1	65.3	65.6	65.8	66.0	66.1	66.3
Food Prod. per capita (1987=100)	87.7	87.7	88.3	81.3	87.4	89.9	91.7	87.6	90.4	90.0	93.8
Labor Force, Agriculture (%)	20.0	18.8	18.1	17.4	16.7	16.1	15.4	14.7	14.0	13.4	12.7
Labor Force, Female (%)	28.4	28.7	29.0	29.2	29.5	29.8	30.1	30.4	30.7	30.9	31.2
Primary Schl. Enroll. Ratio	..	110.0	..	..	..	..	106.0	105.0	103.0	102.0	102.0
Primary Schl. Enroll. Ratio, Female	..	109.0	..	..	..	..	106.0	104.0	103.0	102.0	102.0
Secondary Schl. Enroll. Ratio	..	61.0	..	..	..	..	70.0	72.0	73.0	73.0	73.0

1980	1981	1982	1983	1984	1985	1986	1987	1988	1989 estimate	NOTES	ITALY
				(Billions of current US dollars)							**FOREIGN TRADE (CUSTOMS BASIS)**
77.64	75.25	73.44	72.67	73.36	78.94	97.81	116.58	128.53	..	..	Value of Exports, fob
7.45	7.75	7.13	6.78	7.07	7.96	9.36	10.45	11.95	..	..	Nonfuel Primary Products
4.40	4.72	4.99	3.89	3.32	3.69	2.73	2.84	2.10	..	..	Fuels
65.80	62.77	61.31	62.00	62.96	67.29	85.72	103.29	114.48	..	..	Manufactures
98.12	89.00	83.83	78.32	81.97	88.59	99.77	122.21	135.51	..	..	Value of Imports, cif
26.00	20.66	20.54	19.64	20.72	22.69	25.73	30.70	34.50	..	..	Nonfuel Primary Products
27.34	30.74	27.15	24.54	23.18	23.72	17.34	16.66	11.69	..	..	Fuels
44.78	37.59	36.14	34.14	38.08	42.18	56.71	74.85	89.32	..	..	Manufactures
				(Index 1987 = 100)							
86.0	70.5	79.5	78.4	79.4	81.8	96.7	100.0	97.5	..	..	Terms of Trade
89.0	73.8	77.9	74.0	71.7	71.6	86.7	100.0	105.2	..	..	Export Prices, fob
103.5	104.7	97.9	94.5	90.3	87.5	89.7	100.0	107.9	..	..	Import Prices, cif
				(Billions of current US dollars)							**BALANCE OF PAYMENTS**
105.26	101.53	98.91	97.08	99.55	103.36	128.91	155.46	170.56	..	..	Exports of Goods & Services
77.02	76.18	72.87	72.09	73.84	76.07	96.72	115.87	128.05	..	..	Merchandise, fob
19.92	16.74	17.41	17.97	18.13	19.30	23.14	28.96	30.57	..	..	Nonfactor Services
8.32	8.61	8.62	7.01	7.58	7.98	9.05	10.64	11.94	..	..	Factor Services
116.69	112.14	106.41	97.18	103.67	107.92	124.36	156.08	174.77	..	..	Imports of Goods & Services
93.96	88.32	81.78	74.60	79.65	82.16	92.19	115.94	128.82	..	..	Merchandise, fob
15.17	13.16	13.05	12.51	13.28	14.53	17.70	23.53	27.03	..	..	Nonfactor Services
7.56	10.67	11.58	10.07	10.73	11.24	14.47	16.62	18.92	..	..	Factor Services
..	..	..	..	..	..	..	..	..	..	..	Long-Term Interest
1.37	1.44	1.47	1.41	1.45	1.33	1.47	1.28	1.45	..	..	Private Current Transfers, net
1.24	1.16	1.19	1.14	1.11	1.08	1.21	1.21	1.23	..	..	Workers' Remittances
-10.05	-9.17	-6.04	1.30	-2.67	-3.24	6.01	0.66	-2.76	-7.09	..	Curr. A/C Bal before Off. Transf.
0.10	-0.53	-0.35	0.08	0.17	-0.30	-3.10	-2.32	-2.69	-3.54	..	Net Official Transfers
-9.96	-9.70	-6.39	1.38	-2.50	-3.54	2.91	-1.66	-5.45	-10.63	..	Curr. A/C Bal after Off. Transf.
3.28	8.32	4.91	0.69	0.58	2.11	-2.92	3.38	7.68	10.57	..	Long-Term Capital, net
-0.16	-0.25	-0.38	-0.95	-0.69	-0.87	-2.85	1.75	1.27	..	..	Direct Investment
..	..	..	..	..	..	..	..	..	..	..	Long-Term Loans
..	..	..	..	..	..	..	..	..	..	..	Disbursements
..	..	..	..	..	..	..	..	..	..	..	Repayments
3.44	8.57	5.30	1.63	1.26	2.98	-0.07	1.63	6.41	10.57	..	Other Long-Term Capital
7.61	0.64	-3.09	3.75	4.57	-6.01	2.45	3.72	5.24	10.54	..	Other Capital, net
-0.93	0.74	4.56	-5.81	-2.64	7.44	-2.44	-5.43	-7.47	-10.47	..	Change in Reserves
				(Italian Lire per US dollar)							Memo Item:
856.400	1,136.800	1,352.500	1,518.900	1,757.000	1,909.400	1,490.800	1,296.100	1,301.600	1,372.100	..	Conversion Factor (Annual Avg)
				(Millions US dollars), outstanding at end of year							
..	..	..	..	..	..	..	..	..	..	..	**EXTERNAL DEBT (Total)**
..	..	..	..	..	..	..	..	..	..	..	Long-Term Debt (by debtor)
..	..	..	..	..	..	..	..	..	..	..	Central Bank, incl. IMF credit
..	..	..	..	..	..	..	..	..	..	..	Central Government
..	..	..	..	..	..	..	..	..	..	..	Rest of General Government
..	..	..	..	..	..	..	..	..	..	..	Non-financial Public Enterprises
..	..	..	..	..	..	..	..	..	..	..	Priv. Sector, incl non-guaranteed
..	..	..	..	..	..	..	..	..	..	..	Short-Term Debt
				(Millions of US dollars)							Memo Items:
23,126	20,134	14,091	20,105	20,795	15,595	19,987	30,214	34,715	46,720	..	Int'l Reserves Excluding Gold
39,302	26,501	30,462	25,435	20,555	21,801	26,062	32,275	27,352	26,735	..	Gold Holdings (at market price)
											SOCIAL INDICATORS
1.7	1.6	1.6	1.5	1.5	1.4	1.4	1.3	1.3	1.3	..	Total Fertility Rate
14.6	14.1	13.0	12.3	11.4	10.5	9.8	9.6	9.5	9.1	..	Infant Mortality Rate
74.7	75.1	75.5	75.7	76.0	76.3	76.6	76.8	77.0	77.2	..	Life Expectancy at Birth
66.5	66.7	66.9	67.0	67.2	67.4	67.6	67.9	68.1	68.4	..	Urban Population, % of total
99.7	98.9	96.3	104.5	96.0	97.2	97.3	100.0	96.8	97.0	..	Food Prod. per capita (1987=100)
12.0	..	..	..	..	..	..	..	..	..	..	Labor Force, Agriculture (%)
31.5	31.5	31.6	31.6	31.7	31.7	31.8	31.8	31.9	31.9	..	Labor Force, Female (%)
100.0	..	100.0	99.0	97.0	96.0	95.0	95.0	..	..	..	Primary Schl. Enroll. Ratio
100.0	..	100.0	99.0	97.0							Primary Schl. Enroll. Ratio, Female
72.0	..	73.0	73.0	72.0	73.0	74.0	75.0	..	..	..	Secondary Schl. Enroll. Ratio

JAMAICA	1969	1970	1971	1972	1973	1974	1975	1976	1977	1978	1979
CURRENT GNP PER CAPITA (US $)	640	720	770	910	960	1,090	1,260	1,330	1,440	1,420	1,290
POPULATION (thousands)	1,845	1,869	1,896	1,925	1,956	1,986	2,013	2,038	2,060	2,081	2,104
USE AND ORIGIN OF RESOURCES					*(Millions of current Jamaica Dollars)*						
Gross National Product (GNP)	941	1,120	1,208	1,414	1,692	2,211	2,620	2,627	2,856	3,586	4,018
Net Factor Income from Abroad	-51	-51	-74	-25	-27	52	20	-69	-98	-152	-259
GDP at Market Prices	993	1,171	1,282	1,439	1,720	2,159	2,600	2,696	2,954	3,737	4,277
Resource Balance	-67	-49	-91	-119	-165	-221	-269	-239	-44	50	-68
Exports of Goods & NFServices	365	389	434	472	543	770	917	783	928	1,575	2,065
Imports of Goods & NFServices	431	438	525	591	707	991	1,186	1,022	972	1,525	2,133
Domestic Absorption	1,059	1,220	1,374	1,558	1,885	2,380	2,869	2,935	2,998	3,687	4,344
Private Consumption, etc.	608	713	803	968	1,063	1,469	1,722	1,882	2,024	2,375	2,697
General Gov't Consumption	103	137	159	197	280	386	477	562	612	750	825
Gross Domestic Investment	349	369	412	393	542	525	670	491	361	562	823
Fixed Investment	315	367	356	367	448	478	610	451	349	499	748
Indirect Taxes, net	87	98	114	125	146	180	239	237	216	272	358
GDP at factor cost	905	1,073	1,169	1,314	1,574	1,980	2,362	2,460	2,739	3,465	3,919
Agriculture	77	78	102	107	120	154	191	214	249	297	308
Industry	419	499	511	533	633	820	956	992	1,092	1,485	1,722
Manufacturing	160	184	207	242	287	387	444	491	545	638	699
Services, etc.	497	593	670	799	968	1,185	1,453	1,490	1,613	1,956	2,246
Gross Domestic Saving	283	320	320	274	377	304	401	253	318	612	755
Gross National Saving	..	292	268	276	381	387	441	185	234	482	620
					(Millions of 1987 Jamaica Dollars)						
Gross National Product	13,836.5	15,567.9	15,809.7	17,991.1	18,124.9	18,208.1	17,796.4	15,984.9	15,404.6	15,346.4	14,765.8
GDP at Market Prices	14,532.9	16,261.3	16,760.8	18,280.8	18,351.6	17,752.0	17,617.4	16,379.1	15,927.4	15,995.7	15,670.1
Resource Balance	-419.5	-216.0	-405.8	-430.3	-639.7	-864.5	-1,990.6	-1,428.1	-656.2	-146.6	384.3
Exports of Goods & NFServices	5,896.4	6,009.2	6,568.2	6,810.3	6,729.6	6,685.3	5,947.6	5,154.4	5,231.6	5,499.8	5,611.7
Imports of Goods & NFServices	6,315.9	6,225.2	6,974.0	7,240.6	7,369.3	7,549.8	7,938.3	6,582.5	5,887.8	5,646.4	5,227.4
Domestic Absorption	14,952.4	16,477.3	17,166.6	18,711.1	18,991.3	18,616.5	19,608.0	17,807.2	16,583.6	16,142.3	15,285.8
Private Consumption, etc.	6,351.9	7,431.2	8,072.3	10,359.0	7,879.0	9,719.3	9,945.6	10,096.5	10,713.2	9,781.5	9,081.0
General Gov't Consumption	1,030.0	1,376.7	1,397.6	1,570.7	1,988.2	2,069.1	2,102.3	2,390.6	2,414.7	2,508.5	2,486.6
Gross Domestic Investment	7,570.5	7,669.3	7,696.6	6,781.4	9,124.2	6,828.2	7,560.1	5,320.0	3,455.7	3,852.2	3,718.3
Fixed Investment	7,070.5	7,830.6	6,933.1	6,481.1	7,631.9	6,377.1	7,073.2	5,051.5	3,441.9	3,499.2	3,445.9
GDP at factor cost	13,284.3	14,940.1	15,312.2	16,726.2	16,829.4	16,317.6	16,038.1	14,966.7	14,782.2	14,848.4	14,372.0
Agriculture	823.4	861.9	976.6	994.1	855.5	896.8	912.0	918.4	945.2	1,036.0	928.8
Industry	7,401.6	8,478.2	8,712.8	9,224.0	9,186.4	9,072.4	8,708.4	7,700.3	7,237.8	7,153.7	6,923.6
Manufacturing	3,522.0	3,742.2	3,829.2	4,277.1	4,304.0	4,159.0	4,253.5	4,066.6	3,764.8	3,588.6	3,404.9
Services, etc.	6,569.2	7,274.4	7,418.9	8,371.7	8,614.5	8,083.9	8,245.5	7,911.4	7,838.4	7,856.8	7,881.4
Memo Items:											
Capacity to Import	5,342.3	5,528.8	5,761.2	5,779.0	5,652.5	5,867.2	6,137.2	5,045.9	5,624.3	5,831.5	5,061.7
Terms of Trade Adjustment	-554.1	-480.4	-807.0	-1,031.3	-1,077.1	-818.1	189.6	-108.5	392.6	331.7	-550.0
Gross Domestic Income	13,978.8	15,780.8	15,953.8	17,249.5	17,274.5	16,934.0	17,807.0	16,270.6	16,320.0	16,327.4	15,120.1
Gross National Income	13,282.4	15,087.5	15,002.8	16,959.8	17,047.8	17,390.0	17,986.0	15,876.4	15,797.3	15,678.0	14,215.8
DOMESTIC PRICES/DEFLATORS					*(Index 1987 = 100)*						
Overall (GDP)	6.8	7.2	7.7	7.9	9.4	12.2	14.8	16.5	18.5	23.4	27.3
Domestic Absorption	7.1	7.4	8.0	8.3	9.9	12.8	14.6	16.5	18.1	22.8	28.4
Agriculture	9.3	9.0	10.4	10.7	14.0	17.2	21.0	23.3	26.3	28.7	33.2
Industry	5.7	5.9	5.9	5.8	6.9	9.0	11.0	12.9	15.1	20.8	24.9
Manufacturing	4.5	4.9	5.4	5.7	6.7	9.3	10.4	12.1	14.5	17.8	20.5
Consumer Price Index	6.2	7.2	7.5	8.0	9.4	11.9	14.0	15.4	17.1	23.0	29.7
MANUFACTURING ACTIVITY											
Employment (1987=100)	..	..	..	..	..	..	..	..	..	..	..
Real Earnings per Empl. (1987=100)	..	..	..	..	..	..	..	..	..	..	..
Real Output per Empl. (1987=100)	..	..	..	..	..	..	..	..	..	..	..
Earnings as % of Value Added	44.2	42.6	41.5	44.2	46.5	42.5	46.3	47.7	45.9	46.3	45.9
MONETARY HOLDINGS					*(Millions of current Jamaica Dollars)*						
Money Supply, Broadly Defined	342	393	492	581	667	868	962	1,030	1,145	1,353	1,538
Money	111	127	160	173	218	258	322	339	474	570	629
Currency Outside Banks	37	46	58	72	82	102	127	138	182	173	220
Demand Deposits	74	80	102	101	136	156	195	200	292	397	410
Quasi-Money	231	266	332	408	448	609	640	691	671	783	909
					(Millions of current Jamaica Dollars)						
GOVERNMENT DEFICIT (-) OR SURPLUS	..	..	..	..	..	..	-253.0	-394.9	-496.5	-514.1	-542.6
Current Revenue	..	..	..	..	..	..	681.9	709.9	734.1	1,129.7	1,148.5
Current Expenditure	..	..	..	..	..	..	585.1	740.2	814.2	..	..
Current Budget Balance	..	..	..	..	..	..	96.8	-30.3	-80.1	..	..
Capital Receipts	..	..	..	..	..	..	0.1	..	..	..	1.4
Capital Payments	..	..	..	..	..	..	349.9	364.6	416.4	..	..

1980	1981	1982	1983	1984	1985	1986	1987	1988	1989 estimate	NOTES	JAMAICA
1,160	1,240	1,310	1,360	1,150	910	870	960	1,080	1,260	A	CURRENT GNP PER CAPITA (US $)
2,133	2,166	2,203	2,242	2,279	2,311	2,338	2,361	2,379	2,396	..	POPULATION (thousands)
				(Millions of current Jamaica Dollars)							USE AND ORIGIN OF RESOURCES
4,432	4,999	5,578	6,745	8,453	9,685	11,758	13,869	15,331	18,562	..	Gross National Product (GNP)
-318	-293	-289	-248	-902	-1,466	-1,552	-1,848	-2,314	-2,801	..	Net Factor Income from Abroad
4,750	5,292	5,867	6,993	9,355	11,151	13,310	15,717	17,645	21,363	..	GDP at Market Prices
-99	-547	-679	-844	-624	-1,148	293	45	-1,488	-2,400	..	Resource Balance
2,426	2,510	2,240	2,621	4,956	6,521	7,294	8,618	8,609	9,454	..	Exports of Goods & NFServices
2,525	3,058	2,919	3,465	5,580	7,669	7,001	8,574	10,097	11,854	..	Imports of Goods & NFServices
4,849	5,839	6,546	7,837	9,979	12,299	13,017	15,673	19,133	..	..	Domestic Absorption
3,136	3,667	4,034	4,874	6,275	7,761	8,504	9,820	11,622	..	..	Private Consumption, etc.
966	1,095	1,288	1,406	1,550	1,752	2,045	2,295	2,732	..	..	General Gov't Consumption
748	1,077	1,224	1,557	2,155	2,786	2,468	3,558	4,779	..	..	Gross Domestic Investment
690	954	1,168	1,436	1,981	2,494	2,335	3,422	..	..	..	Fixed Investment
387	517	643	592	934	1,470	1,940	2,467	..	..	..	Indirect Taxes, net
4,363	4,774	5,225	6,401	8,421	9,681	11,370	13,251	..	..	B	GDP at factor cost
392	398	396	451	544	672	820	957	988	..	..	Agriculture
1,804	1,866	1,977	2,449	3,525	4,106	5,350	6,422	7,412	..	..	Industry
771	865	1,054	1,399	1,732	2,237	3,028	3,506	3,742	..	..	Manufacturing
2,554	3,028	3,494	4,093	5,286	6,373	7,140	8,338	9,244	..	..	Services, etc.
648	530	545	713	1,530	1,638	2,761	3,603	3,291	..	..	Gross Domestic Saving
476	457	496	647	945	1,023	1,820	2,398	3,368	..	..	Gross National Saving
				(Millions of 1987 Jamaica Dollars)							
13,743.7	14,318.1	14,499.5	15,058.9	13,932.5	12,762.6	13,149.9	13,869.1	13,678.8	14,270.4	..	Gross National Product
14,696.9	15,065.9	15,181.3	15,544.8	15,324.7	14,559.4	14,899.7	15,717.4	15,837.8	16,315.1	..	GDP at Market Prices
324.5	223.3	-330.6	-184.1	-255.5	-516.4	210.8	44.6	-1,342.7	-1,400.2	..	Resource Balance
5,527.6	5,746.3	5,035.5	5,510.2	6,483.1	7,207.8	7,692.1	8,618.1	8,789.9	9,597.4	..	Exports of Goods & NFServices
5,203.1	5,523.0	5,366.1	5,694.3	6,738.6	7,724.2	7,481.2	8,573.5	10,132.7	10,997.6	..	Imports of Goods & NFServices
14,372.4	14,842.6	15,511.9	15,729.0	15,580.2	15,075.8	14,688.9	15,672.8	17,180.5	17,715.3	..	Domestic Absorption
8,831.8	8,283.0	9,082.7	9,182.0	9,626.3	9,187.6	9,499.7	9,819.7	..	..	..	Private Consumption, etc.
2,434.6	2,487.6	2,526.2	2,501.0	2,334.4	2,270.0	2,256.1	2,294.7	..	..	..	General Gov't Consumption
3,106.0	4,071.9	3,902.9	4,045.9	3,619.5	3,618.2	2,933.0	3,558.4	3,893.8	3,191.5	..	Gross Domestic Investment
3,003.2	3,656.6	3,759.3	3,704.6	3,235.2	3,071.2	2,757.8	3,421.9	..	..	..	Fixed Investment
13,507.2	13,598.5	13,517.2	14,231.7	13,788.9	12,626.5	12,722.1	13,250.9	..	..	B	GDP at factor cost
889.2	909.0	837.4	898.0	988.2	953.3	933.5	956.8	914.9	928.6	..	Agriculture
6,265.2	6,337.1	6,209.8	6,392.4	6,161.2	5,750.6	6,008.5	6,422.3	6,498.6	6,832.7	..	Industry
3,021.5	3,052.6	3,275.0	3,338.3	3,198.7	3,214.8	3,331.9	3,505.9	3,474.8	3,613.7	..	Manufacturing
7,562.9	7,828.8	8,141.2	8,254.4	8,175.3	7,855.4	7,957.7	8,338.3	8,424.2	8,553.9	..	Services, etc.
											Memo Items:
4,998.8	4,534.4	4,117.8	4,307.5	5,984.9	6,568.2	7,794.0	8,618.1	8,639.4	8,770.8	..	Capacity to Import
-528.7	-1,211.9	-917.7	-1,202.7	-498.2	-639.6	101.9	0.0	-150.5	-826.6	..	Terms of Trade Adjustment
14,168.2	13,854.0	14,263.6	14,342.1	14,826.5	13,919.8	15,001.6	15,717.4	15,687.2	15,488.5	..	Gross Domestic Income
13,215.0	13,106.3	13,581.9	13,856.1	13,434.3	12,123.0	13,251.9	13,869.1	13,528.2	13,443.9	..	Gross National Income
				(Index 1987 = 100)							DOMESTIC PRICES/DEFLATORS
32.3	35.1	38.6	45.0	61.0	76.6	89.3	100.0	111.4	130.9	..	Overall (GDP)
33.7	39.3	42.2	49.8	64.1	81.6	88.6	100.0	111.4	..	..	Domestic Absorption
44.1	43.7	47.3	50.2	55.1	70.4	87.9	100.0	108.0	..	..	Agriculture
28.8	29.4	31.8	38.3	57.2	71.4	89.0	100.0	114.1	..	..	Industry
25.5	28.3	32.2	41.9	54.1	69.6	90.9	100.0	107.7	..	..	Manufacturing
37.8	42.7	45.4	50.7	64.8	81.5	93.8	100.0	108.3	123.8	..	Consumer Price Index
											MANUFACTURING ACTIVITY
..	..	..	..	..	..	..	..	..	..	..	Employment (1987=100)
..	..	..	..	..	..	..	..	..	..	..	Real Earnings per Empl. (1987=100)
..	..	..	..	..	..	..	..	..	..	..	Real Output per Empl. (1987=100)
46.6	..	..	..	..	..	..	..	..	..	..	Earnings as % of Value Added
				(Millions of current Jamaica Dollars)							MONETARY HOLDINGS
1,842	2,358	3,015	3,897	4,692	6,009	7,623	8,930	12,097	13,247	D	Money Supply, Broadly Defined
717	775	876	1,066	1,319	1,520	2,140	2,252	3,445	3,153	..	Money
260	282	316	375	436	540	729	844	1,288	1,378	..	Currency Outside Banks
457	492	560	691	882	980	1,410	1,407	2,157	1,775	..	Demand Deposits
1,126	1,584	2,139	2,831	3,373	4,489	5,483	6,679	8,653	10,094	..	Quasi-Money
				(Millions of current Jamaica Dollars)							
-739.3	-720.6	-893.3	-1,389.9	-177.2	..	..	..	..	..	C	GOVERNMENT DEFICIT (-) OR SURPLUS
1,381.9	1,671.7	1,719.4	1,840.8	3,231.5	..	..	..	..	..	..	Current Revenue
..	..	..	2,476.9	2,699.4	..	..	..	..	..	..	Current Expenditure
..	..	..	-636.1	532.1	..	..	..	..	..	..	Current Budget Balance
..	..	..	..	10.0	..	..	..	..	..	..	Capital Receipts
..	..	..	753.8	719.3	..	..	..	..	..	..	Capital Payments

JAMAICA	1969	1970	1971	1972	1973	1974	1975	1976	1977	1978	1979
FOREIGN TRADE (CUSTOMS BASIS)					*(Millions of current US dollars)*						
Value of Exports, fob	247.3	334.9	330.2	366.1	390.2	730.9	783.9	632.6	778.0	746.9	817.3
Nonfuel Primary Products	218.8	171.3	170.2	180.9	184.7	293.2	340.8	257.5	323.1	286.7	354.8
Fuels	7.1	8.7	9.2	10.4	9.4	10.9	12.1	17.6	17.7	18.8	33.9
Manufactures	21.4	155.0	150.8	174.7	196.1	426.8	431.1	357.5	437.2	441.4	428.5
Value of Imports, cif	436.0	525.4	550.5	620.2	664.4	935.5	1,122.5	911.2	858.8	879.9	991.5
Nonfuel Primary Products	90.2	107.9	115.6	155.6	180.9	262.8	271.4	250.5	219.3	240.6	208.7
Fuels	30.8	34.0	53.2	56.1	72.5	195.5	215.3	207.3	249.6	212.5	317.4
Manufactures	314.9	383.5	381.7	408.6	410.9	477.3	635.8	453.4	389.9	426.8	465.4
					(Index 1987 = 100)						
Terms of Trade	142.8	130.0	126.3	120.6	119.9	116.0	115.9	111.2	113.9	105.1	101.2
Export Prices, fob	34.7	33.5	33.6	36.2	44.8	68.0	69.1	69.0	76.8	78.4	91.1
Import Prices, cif	24.3	25.8	26.6	30.0	37.4	58.6	59.6	62.1	67.5	74.6	90.0
BALANCE OF PAYMENTS					*(Millions of current US dollars)*						
Exports of Goods & Services	..	537.2	558.6	630.0	649.1	1,056.2	1,122.1	942.9	1,007.0	1,169.8	1,220.9
Merchandise, fob	..	341.4	343.6	376.7	392.1	752.3	808.6	656.4	737.8	831.1	818.2
Nonfactor Services	..	157.9	174.9	206.3	199.3	238.0	242.1	222.2	211.8	281.9	346.9
Factor Services	..	37.9	40.0	47.0	57.7	65.9	71.4	64.3	57.4	56.8	55.8
Imports of Goods & Services	..	712.6	752.3	855.5	924.1	1,172.9	1,432.6	1,251.4	1,069.2	1,245.6	1,439.9
Merchandise, fob	..	449.0	475.5	528.6	570.4	811.4	969.6	791.6	666.7	750.1	882.5
Nonfactor Services	..	141.0	147.7	171.8	184.2	246.5	315.3	311.9	224.3	282.2	315.0
Factor Services	..	122.6	129.1	155.1	169.5	115.0	147.6	147.9	178.2	213.3	242.4
Long-Term Interest	..	63.5	61.4	63.1	80.9	101.7	109.9	96.1	98.8	98.4	104.4
Private Current Transfers, net	..	26.9	27.0	35.5	34.7	33.9	22.7	2.0	15.1	15.2	70.0
Workers' Remittances	..	28.8	35.9	52.1	50.8	48.8	47.4	47.5	41.0	26.5	48.7
Curr. A/C Bal before Off. Transf.	..	-148.5	-166.8	-190.0	-240.3	-82.9	-287.8	-306.5	-47.1	-60.6	-149.0
Net Official Transfers	..	-4.4	-5.4	-6.7	-7.3	-9.0	5.0	3.9	5.0	10.6	10.1
Curr. A/C Bal after Off. Transf.	..	-152.9	-172.2	-196.7	-247.6	-91.9	-282.8	-302.6	-42.1	-50.0	-138.9
Long-Term Capital, net	..	160.7	186.8	124.8	202.0	225.6	227.8	94.2	51.5	-95.5	-25.3
Direct Investment	..	161.4	174.4	97.2	71.5	23.3	-1.8	-0.6	-9.7	-26.6	-26.4
Long-Term Loans	..	9.7	26.2	34.6	149.5	229.2	193.2	-218.0	79.6	-313.0	74.0
Disbursements	..	179.9	200.3	216.2	334.5	426.8	401.7	345.6	260.7	263.4	235.8
Repayments	..	170.2	174.1	181.6	185.0	197.6	208.5	563.6	181.1	576.4	161.8
Other Long-Term Capital	..	-10.4	-13.8	-7.0	-19.1	-26.9	36.5	312.8	-18.4	244.1	-72.9
Other Capital, net	..	7.0	17.4	46.5	-3.4	-71.0	-19.6	2.1	-43.5	89.0	5.0
Change in Reserves	..	-14.9	-31.9	25.4	49.1	-62.8	74.5	206.3	34.1	56.5	159.2
Memo Item:					*(Jamaica Dollars per US dollar)*						
Conversion Factor (Annual Avg)	0.830	0.830	0.820	0.800	0.910	0.910	0.910	0.910	0.910	1.450	1.760
					(Millions of US dollars), outstanding at end of year						
EXTERNAL DEBT (Total)	..	982.0	1,013.0	1,041.1	1,205.6	1,434.6	1,614.1	1,449.5	1,678.5	1,423.4	1,707.0
Long-Term Debt (by debtor)	..	982.0	1,013.0	1,041.1	1,205.6	1,434.6	1,614.1	1,449.5	1,575.5	1,343.4	1,601.0
Central Bank, incl. IMF credit	..	0.0	0.0	0.3	17.6	54.8	60.2	166.0	185.8	257.6	424.2
Central Government	..	124.4	136.9	150.1	195.8	283.7	373.0	505.4	557.7	697.8	827.6
Rest of General Government	..	..	..	..	..	..	..	..	..	..	..
Non-financial Public Enterprises	..	30.5	42.0	55.5	105.5	137.0	196.2	242.7	239.8	212.7	200.0
Priv. Sector, incl non-guaranteed	..	827.1	834.1	835.2	886.7	959.1	984.7	535.4	592.2	175.3	149.2
Short-Term Debt	..	0.0	0.0	0.0	0.0	0.0	0.0	0.0	103.0	80.0	106.0
Memo Items:					*(Millions of US dollars)*						
Int'l Reserves Excluding Gold	117.94	139.19	179.05	159.69	127.45	190.39	125.58	32.39	47.78	58.82	63.81
Gold Holdings (at market price)	..	..	..	..	..	..	..	..	1.86	..	5.79
SOCIAL INDICATORS											
Total Fertility Rate	5.5	5.3	5.2	5.0	4.8	4.6	4.4	4.2	4.0	3.9	3.8
Infant Mortality Rate	41.4	39.6	37.8	36.0	33.8	31.6	29.4	27.2	25.0	22.8	20.6
Life Expectancy at Birth	67.2	67.7	68.2	68.6	68.9	69.2	69.5	69.8	70.1	70.3	70.6
Urban Population, % of total	40.7	41.5	42.0	42.5	43.1	43.6	44.1	44.6	45.2	45.7	46.3
Food Prod. per capita (1987=100)	92.3	95.7	103.4	102.8	96.1	96.9	93.2	95.0	97.8	110.4	102.8
Labor Force, Agriculture (%)	34.0	33.2	33.0	32.7	32.5	32.3	32.1	31.9	31.8	31.6	31.4
Labor Force, Female (%)	42.2	42.5	43.0	43.4	43.8	44.2	44.6	44.9	45.2	45.5	45.8
Primary Schl. Enroll. Ratio	..	119.0	..	..	..	..	97.0	97.0	98.0	99.0	99.0
Primary Schl. Enroll. Ratio, Female	..	119.0	..	..	..	..	98.0	97.0	98.0	100.0	100.0
Secondary Schl. Enroll. Ratio	..	46.0	..	..	..	..	58.0	58.0	58.0	60.0	60.0

1980	1981	1982	1983	1984	1985	1986	1987	1988	1989 estimate	NOTES	JAMAICA
											FOREIGN TRADE (CUSTOMS BASIS)
964.6	985.3	739.2	713.0	714.0	549.0	596.0	649.0	755.0	..	..	Value of Exports, fob
333.9	304.2	269.1	230.7	213.1	180.6	192.7	210.7	297.0	..	..	Nonfuel Primary Products
19.2	27.8	26.5	23.3	21.9	16.4	9.3	13.4	13.0	..	..	Fuels
611.5	653.4	443.6	459.0	479.0	352.0	394.0	425.0	445.0	..	..	Manufactures
1,177.7	1,487.0	1,373.3	1,531.0	1,129.9	1,123.7	964.0	1,207.2	1,449.0	..	..	Value of Imports, cif
270.1	328.1	313.9	347.7	260.1	245.8	207.5	237.9	268.0	..	..	Nonfuel Primary Products
445.5	494.4	398.8	470.9	316.0	305.6	137.3	202.8	166.0	..	..	Fuels
462.1	664.5	660.6	712.4	553.8	572.3	619.2	766.5	1,015.0	..	..	Manufactures

(Index 1987 = 100)

1980	1981	1982	1983	1984	1985	1986	1987	1988	1989	NOTES	JAMAICA
86.5	86.4	91.1	88.3	88.9	91.1	106.4	100.0	102.6	..	..	Terms of Trade
99.0	97.3	94.5	90.3	87.6	87.5	96.7	100.0	108.5	..	..	Export Prices, fob
114.4	112.7	103.8	102.3	98.5	96.1	90.9	100.0	105.7	..	..	Import Prices, cif

(Millions of current US dollars)

1980	1981	1982	1983	1984	1985	1986	1987	1988	1989	NOTES	JAMAICA
											BALANCE OF PAYMENTS
1,421.6	1,499.8	1,371.1	1,332.2	1,335.2	1,266.2	1,411.0	1,633.4	1,731.2	2,225.7	f	Exports of Goods & Services
962.7	974.0	767.4	685.7	702.3	568.6	589.5	708.4	833.5	1,017.0	..	Merchandise, fob
396.1	426.3	477.3	534.0	561.7	603.4	734.6	812.3	769.3	1,084.7	..	Nonfactor Services
62.8	99.5	126.4	112.5	71.2	94.2	86.9	112.7	128.4	124.0	..	Factor Services
1,678.3	1,960.9	1,924.8	1,788.8	1,787.9	1,789.0	1,597.5	1,941.1	2,159.8	2,735.6	f	Imports of Goods & Services
1,038.2	1,296.7	1,208.9	1,124.2	1,037.0	1,004.2	837.4	1,065.1	1,228.5	1,568.9	..	Merchandise, fob
347.7	385.1	394.4	369.4	379.7	372.6	366.1	406.9	480.9	650.2	..	Nonfactor Services
292.4	279.1	321.5	295.2	371.2	412.2	394.0	469.1	450.4	516.5	..	Factor Services
121.2	109.8	140.3	156.4	191.0	212.4	217.7	217.0	216.2	214.0	..	Long-Term Interest
81.7	123.3	134.5	94.7	80.4	153.2	111.6	117.2	435.6	141.1	..	Private Current Transfers, net
50.6	62.7	74.5	41.6	26.1	92.3	54.0	58.8	72.7	72.7	..	Workers' Remittances
-175.0	-337.8	-419.2	-361.9	-372.3	-369.6	-74.9	-190.5	7.0	-368.8	..	Curr. A/C Bal before Off. Transf.
9.0	1.0	15.8	6.8	40.2	68.0	36.5	54.4	70.0	155.4	..	Net Official Transfers
-166.0	-336.8	-403.4	-355.1	-332.1	-301.6	-38.4	-136.1	77.0	-213.4	..	Curr. A/C Bal after Off. Transf.
231.0	116.8	349.1	137.5	390.0	131.8	-182.9	255.6	12.4	239.4	f	Long-Term Capital, net
27.7	-11.5	-15.8	-18.7	12.2	-9.0	-4.6	53.4	-12.0	28.1	..	Direct Investment
248.9	292.5	442.1	287.0	277.1	219.3	-3.6	99.3	-4.7	133.6	..	Long-Term Loans
350.5	464.7	557.0	409.6	367.7	418.8	224.1	292.1	203.6	301.1	..	Disbursements
101.6	172.2	114.9	122.6	90.6	199.5	227.7	192.8	208.3	167.5	..	Repayments
-45.6	-164.2	-77.2	-130.8	100.7	-78.5	-174.7	102.9	29.1	77.7	..	Other Long-Term Capital
-2.4	-46.2	4.1	109.1	-37.7	209.8	336.4	45.4	40.2	-101.2	f	Other Capital, net
-62.6	266.2	50.3	108.4	-20.1	-40.1	-115.1	-164.9	-129.5	75.2	..	Change in Reserves

(Jamaica Dollars per US dollar)

1980	1981	1982	1983	1984	1985	1986	1987	1988	1989	NOTES	JAMAICA
											Memo Item:
1.780	1.930	1.990	2.150	3.940	5.560	5.480	5.490	5.490	5.740	..	Conversion Factor (Annual Avg)

(Millions of US dollars), outstanding at end of year

1980	1981	1982	1983	1984	1985	1986	1987	1988	1989	NOTES	JAMAICA
1,903.4	2,299.2	2,842.3	3,313.6	3,470.6	3,879.3	4,024.8	4,537.0	4,305.0	4,322.0	..	**EXTERNAL DEBT (Total)**
1,805.4	2,207.2	2,744.3	3,063.6	3,220.1	3,695.5	3,847.4	4,305.4	4,037.7	4,018.9	..	Long-Term Debt (by debtor)
477.5	816.9	1,022.5	1,170.4	1,173.0	1,255.9	1,199.3	1,097.2	855.6	760.8	..	Central Bank, incl. IMF credit
971.7	1,118.1	1,429.9	1,582.5	1,763.6	2,121.6	2,316.3	2,819.5	2,824.8	2,910.7	..	Central Government
..	..	..	..	..	..	..	..	..	..	..	Rest of General Government
192.9	166.0	150.9	152.3	155.5	186.4	186.6	225.1	215.2	227.5	..	Non-financial Public Enterprises
163.3	106.2	141.0	158.5	128.0	131.6	145.2	163.6	142.1	119.9	..	Priv. Sector, incl non-guaranteed
98.0	92.0	98.0	250.0	250.5	183.8	177.4	231.6	267.3	303.1	..	Short-Term Debt

(Millions of US dollars)

1980	1981	1982	1983	1984	1985	1986	1987	1988	1989	NOTES	JAMAICA
											Memo Items:
105.00	85.17	108.97	63.20	96.93	161.30	98.42	174.30	147.20	107.50	..	Int'l Reserves Excluding Gold
..	..	..	..	..	..	..	..	..	..	..	Gold Holdings (at market price)
											SOCIAL INDICATORS
3.7	3.6	3.6	3.4	3.2	3.0	2.8	2.6	2.6	2.5	..	Total Fertility Rate
18.4	16.2	14.0	13.4	12.8	12.2	11.6	11.0	10.7	10.4	..	Infant Mortality Rate
70.8	71.1	71.3	71.6	71.8	72.1	72.3	72.5	72.7	72.9	..	Life Expectancy at Birth
46.8	47.3	47.8	48.4	48.9	49.4	50.0	50.6	51.1	51.7	..	Urban Population, % of total
95.3	91.3	88.0	94.3	103.6	99.7	100.1	100.0	87.5	78.0	..	Food Prod. per capita (1987=100)
31.3	..	..	..	..	..	..	..	..	..	..	Labor Force, Agriculture (%)
46.0	46.0	45.9	45.9	45.8	45.8	45.8	45.8	45.8	45.8	..	Labor Force, Female (%)
101.0	104.0	106.0	106.0	..	..	105.0	..	..	..	..	Primary Schl. Enroll. Ratio
101.0	..	108.0	107.0	..	..	106.0	..	..	..	..	Primary Schl. Enroll. Ratio, Female
59.0	60.0	60.0	59.0	..	..	65.0	..	..	..	..	Secondary Schl. Enroll. Ratio

JAPAN	1969	1970	1971	1972	1973	1974	1975	1976	1977	1978	1979
CURRENT GNP PER CAPITA (US $)	1,690	1,950	2,140	2,540	3,240	3,820	4,490	4,970	5,690	7,020	8,620
POPULATION (millions)	103	104	106	107	108	110	112	113	114	115	116

USE AND ORIGIN OF RESOURCES					*(Billions of current Japanese Yen)*						
Gross National Product (GNP)	62,066	73,188	80,592	92,401	112,520	133,997	148,170	166,417	185,530	204,475	221,825
Net Factor Income from Abroad	-163	-157	-109	7	21	-247	-157	-156	-92	70	278
GDP at Market Prices	62,229	73,345	80,701	92,394	112,499	134,244	148,327	166,573	185,622	204,405	221,547
Resource Balance	835	796	2,084	2,150	47	-1,258	-112	1,162	2,931	3,629	-1,740
Exports of Goods & NFServices	6,822	8,277	9,889	10,385	12,141	19,439	20,251	23,838	25,554	24,116	27,897
Imports of Goods & NFServices	5,988	7,482	7,805	8,235	12,094	20,697	20,363	22,676	22,624	20,487	29,637
Domestic Absorption	61,231	72,393	78,617	90,244	112,452	135,502	148,439	165,410	182,691	200,776	223,287
Private Consumption, etc.	33,328	38,367	43,273	49,918	60,339	73,197	84,999	95,959	107,213	117,748	129,834
General Gov't Consumption	5,640	6,470	7,258	8,090	9,447	11,807	14,030	16,042	17,950	19,725	21,340
Gross Domestic Investment	22,263	27,555	28,085	32,236	42,666	50,498	49,411	53,410	57,528	63,303	72,113
Fixed Investment	19,532	24,170	26,440	30,694	39,026	43,506	46,830	51,656	56,890	64,129	70,541
Indirect Taxes, net	3,596	4,397	4,808	5,425	6,710	7,131	7,529	8,689	10,421	11,199	13,258
GDP at factor cost	58,633	68,948	75,893	86,969	105,789	127,113	140,798	157,884	175,201	193,206	208,289
Agriculture	4,452	4,488	4,274	5,050	6,675	7,506	8,141	8,870	9,402	9,441	9,623
Industry	28,243	34,230	37,282	42,134	52,186	59,956	62,901	70,747	76,862	85,200	92,071
Manufacturing	21,975	26,402	28,430	31,918	39,569	45,137	44,801	51,101	55,412	60,545	64,815
Services, etc.	29,533	34,627	39,145	45,209	53,638	66,782	77,285	86,956	99,358	109,764	119,853
Gross Domestic Saving	23,261	28,508	30,169	34,386	42,713	49,239	49,298	54,573	60,459	66,932	70,373
Gross National Saving	..	28,340	30,046	34,353	42,708	48,964	49,112	54,375	60,351	66,947	70,601

					(Billions of 1987 Japanese Yen)						
Gross National Product	151,567	167,987	175,548	190,607	206,212	203,286	208,724	218,735	230,406	242,368	255,179
GDP at Market Prices	151,964	168,348	175,787	190,594	206,174	203,686	208,960	218,954	230,531	242,286	254,855
Resource Balance	-2,448	-3,413	-2,405	-3,209	-6,332	-4,246	-1,938	-233	1,325	48	-1,592
Exports of Goods & NFServices	9,452	11,143	12,966	13,682	14,653	18,049	18,174	20,927	23,166	23,001	24,437
Imports of Goods & NFServices	11,901	14,556	15,371	16,891	20,985	22,295	20,112	21,160	21,841	22,954	26,029
Domestic Absorption	154,413	171,761	178,192	193,803	212,506	207,932	210,899	219,187	229,206	242,238	256,447
Private Consumption, etc.	91,199	97,910	103,582	112,825	122,161	121,874	128,041	133,050	139,276	146,298	154,396
General Gov't Consumption	15,777	16,899	17,781	18,773	19,795	20,405	21,777	22,797	23,795	25,045	26,138
Gross Domestic Investment	47,437	56,951	56,829	62,205	70,550	65,653	61,080	63,340	66,135	70,895	75,913
Fixed Investment	49,867	58,279	60,812	66,931	75,349	68,042	67,533	69,281	72,005	78,232	82,244
GDP at factor cost	142,732	157,709	164,683	178,704	193,162	192,497	198,128	207,314	217,330	228,622	239,361
Agriculture	10,490	9,308	8,775	9,948	10,587	10,358	10,316	9,834	9,630	9,585	9,723
Industry	54,543	61,986	65,895	71,504	79,122	77,151	76,052	80,996	84,077	90,236	95,216
Manufacturing	32,452	36,595	38,623	42,300	48,093	47,997	45,070	49,600	52,311	55,835	59,591
Services, etc.	87,591	97,748	101,529	109,398	115,814	115,754	122,829	128,277	137,348	142,735	150,202
Memo Items:											
Capacity to Import	13,560	16,103	19,475	21,301	21,067	20,940	20,002	22,245	24,670	27,020	24,501
Terms of Trade Adjustment	4,107	4,961	6,510	7,618	6,413	2,890	1,828	1,318	1,505	4,018	64
Gross Domestic Income	156,072	173,309	182,297	198,212	212,588	206,576	210,788	220,272	232,036	246,304	254,919
Gross National Income	155,675	172,947	182,057	198,225	212,625	206,176	210,552	220,053	231,911	246,386	255,244

DOMESTIC PRICES/DEFLATORS					*(Index 1987 = 100)*						
Overall (GDP)	40.9	43.6	45.9	48.5	54.6	65.9	71.0	76.1	80.5	84.4	86.9
Domestic Absorption	39.7	42.1	44.1	46.6	52.9	65.2	70.4	75.5	79.7	82.9	87.1
Agriculture	42.4	48.2	48.7	50.8	63.0	72.5	78.9	90.2	97.6	98.5	99.0
Industry	51.8	55.2	56.6	58.9	66.0	77.7	82.7	87.3	91.4	94.4	96.7
Manufacturing	67.7	72.1	73.6	75.5	82.3	94.0	99.4	103.0	105.9	108.4	108.8
Consumer Price Index	34.1	36.7	39.0	40.9	45.7	56.3	62.9	68.8	74.4	77.6	80.4

MANUFACTURING ACTIVITY											
Employment (1987=100)	100.7	103.3	102.0	104.0	105.8	101.5	99.9	99.0	96.3	96.2	96.1
Real Earnings per Empl. (1987=100)	58.3	63.0	68.3	73.2	79.8	83.7	83.0	83.8	85.3	87.0	89.4
Real Output per Empl. (1987=100)	33.6	36.7	38.1	40.3	47.1	54.3	51.0	56.7	61.0	62.2	70.2
Earnings as % of Value Added	31.9	31.8	34.2	34.8	33.4	35.2	40.4	38.6	38.7	37.8	35.6

MONETARY HOLDINGS					*(Billions of current Japanese Yen)*						
Money Supply, Broadly Defined	64,068	74,890	92,738	115,669	138,980	158,623	185,068	213,447	241,885	275,360	306,284
Money	18,282	21,360	27,693	34,526	40,311	44,951	49,949	56,179	60,786	68,929	71,020
Currency Outside Banks	4,319	5,098	5,958	7,706	9,113	10,731	11,579	12,858	14,122	16,259	17,052
Demand Deposits	13,963	16,262	21,735	26,820	31,198	34,220	38,370	43,321	46,664	52,670	53,968
Quasi-Money	45,786	53,530	65,045	81,143	98,669	113,672	135,119	157,268	181,099	206,431	235,264

GOVERNMENT DEFICIT (-) OR SURPLUS					*(Billions of current Japanese Yen)*						
	..	-79	-393	-1,740	-382	-3,357	-7,666	-9,417	-11,916	-15,236	-16,318
Current Revenue	..	7,963	8,741	10,409	14,204	15,993	14,690	16,635	18,560	20,719	24,219
Current Expenditure	..	6,343	6,861	8,696	11,075	14,958	17,375	20,539	23,630	27,768	31,657
Current Budget Balance	..	1,620	1,880	1,713	3,129	1,035	-2,685	-3,904	-5,070	-7,049	-7,438
Capital Receipts	..	227	276	100	102	24	11	20	33	21	51
Capital Payments	..	1,926	2,549	3,553	3,613	4,416	4,992	5,533	6,879	8,208	8,931

1980	1981	1982	1983	1984	1985	1986	1987	1988	1989 estimate	NOTES	JAPAN
9,870	10,390	10,280	10,320	10,560	11,240	12,840	15,800	20,960	23,810	..	**CURRENT GNP PER CAPITA (US $)**
117	118	118	119	120	121	121	122	123	123	..	**POPULATION (millions)**
				(Billions of current Japanese Yen)							**USE AND ORIGIN OF RESOURCES**
240,098	256,817	269,697	280,568	298,453	317,440	331,254	345,292	366,608	391,342	..	Gross National Product (GNP)
-78	-546	69	311	505	1,137	1,229	2,054	2,302	2,453	..	Net Factor Income from Abroad
240,176	257,363	269,628	280,257	297,948	316,303	330,025	343,238	364,306	388,889	..	GDP at Market Prices
-2,211	1,508	2,137	5,345	8,661	11,943	14,540	13,065	10,701	7,789	..	Resource Balance
35,724	41,824	44,490	43,486	49,996	52,090	43,441	43,804	47,578	55,759	..	Exports of Goods & NFServices
37,935	40,316	42,353	38,142	41,335	40,147	28,901	30,739	36,876	47,969	..	Imports of Goods & NFServices
242,387	255,855	267,491	274,912	289,287	304,360	315,485	330,173	353,605	381,100	..	Domestic Absorption
141,277	149,796	159,448	167,447	175,504	183,544	190,252	197,530	207,055	218,730	..	Private Consumption, etc.
23,494	25,704	26,881	28,189	29,581	30,739	32,841	32,582	33,259	34,506	..	General Gov't Consumption
77,616	80,355	81,161	79,276	84,201	90,077	92,392	100,061	113,291	127,864	..	Gross Domestic Investment
75,876	80,768	82,996	83,726	88,992	95,561	100,779	110,788	124,914	140,796	..	Fixed Investment
14,095	15,710	16,505	16,663	19,136	21,250	21,562	25,012	27,602	30,974	..	Indirect Taxes, net
226,081	241,653	253,123	263,594	278,812	295,053	308,463	318,226	336,704	357,915	..	GDP at factor cost
8,847	8,957	9,064	9,264	9,626	9,798	9,547	9,304	9,306	..	B	Agriculture
100,680	107,307	111,214	113,610	122,148	129,250	134,022	139,550	150,154	..	B	Industry
70,232	74,540	78,191	81,416	88,845	94,160	96,380	99,541	106,366	..	B	Manufacturing
130,649	141,099	149,350	157,383	166,174	177,255	186,456	194,384	204,846	..	B	Services, etc.
75,405	81,863	83,299	84,621	92,862	102,020	106,932	113,126	123,992	135,653	..	Gross Domestic Saving
75,273	81,271	83,345	84,889	93,336	103,090	108,062	115,037	126,151	..	..	Gross National Saving
				(Billions of 1987 Japanese Yen)							
266,094	275,868	284,374	293,589	307,811	322,736	331,111	345,292	364,408	382,314	..	Gross National Product
266,186	276,460	284,307	293,271	307,302	321,606	329,886	343,238	362,093	379,893	..	GDP at Market Prices
4,330	7,559	8,318	11,083	14,615	17,007	13,899	13,065	10,059	9,639	..	Resource Balance
28,758	33,236	34,437	35,867	42,143	44,515	42,183	43,804	47,342	54,014	..	Exports of Goods & NFServices
24,427	25,677	26,120	24,784	27,528	27,507	28,285	30,739	37,283	44,375	..	Imports of Goods & NFServices
261,856	268,901	275,989	282,188	292,687	304,599	315,987	330,173	352,033	370,254	..	Domestic Absorption
159,700	163,269	169,335	175,754	180,587	186,249	191,169	197,530	204,815	210,055	..	Private Consumption, etc.
26,877	28,166	28,713	29,559	30,378	30,902	32,813	32,582	33,288	33,942	..	General Gov't Consumption
75,278	77,467	77,941	76,874	81,722	87,449	92,006	100,061	113,929	126,257	..	Gross Domestic Investment
82,328	84,934	85,631	85,484	89,589	94,711	100,297	110,788	125,566	139,490	..	Fixed Investment
250,886	259,910	267,255	276,253	288,032	300,499	308,388	318,226	334,334	..	..	GDP at factor cost
9,062	8,786	9,234	9,344	9,540	9,484	9,149	9,304	9,212	..	..	Agriculture
100,679	104,432	108,439	112,799	122,085	129,220	130,898	139,550	151,125	..	..	Industry
64,936	67,880	71,798	77,549	86,514	92,567	93,016	99,541	107,473	..	..	Manufacturing
156,686	163,624	166,786	171,127	175,677	182,903	189,839	194,384	201,755	..	..	Services, etc.
											Memo Items:
23,004	26,638	27,438	28,257	33,296	35,690	42,514	43,804	48,102	51,581	..	Capacity to Import
-5,754	-6,598	-7,000	-7,610	-8,847	-8,824	330	0	760	-2,433	..	Terms of Trade Adjustment
260,432	269,862	277,307	285,661	298,455	312,782	330,216	343,238	362,852	377,459	..	Gross Domestic Income
260,340	269,269	277,374	285,979	298,964	313,912	331,442	345,292	365,168	379,881	..	Gross National Income
				(Index 1987 = 100)							**DOMESTIC PRICES/DEFLATORS**
90.2	93.1	94.8	95.6	97.0	98.4	100.0	100.0	100.6	102.4	..	Overall (GDP)
92.6	95.1	96.9	97.4	98.8	99.9	99.8	100.0	100.4	102.9	..	Domestic Absorption
97.6	101.9	98.2	99.1	100.9	103.3	104.3	100.0	101.0	..	..	Agriculture
100.0	102.8	102.6	100.7	100.1	100.0	102.4	100.0	99.4	..	..	Industry
108.2	109.8	108.9	105.0	102.7	101.7	103.6	100.0	99.0	..	..	Manufacturing
86.7	91.0	93.5	95.2	97.4	99.4	100.0	100.0	100.7	103.0	..	Consumer Price Index
											MANUFACTURING ACTIVITY
97.0	97.9	97.2	98.6	99.7	100.6	101.3	100.0	101.5	101.7	..	Employment (1987=100)
88.3	89.6	91.6	92.6	94.0	96.7	98.5	100.0	102.9	..	..	Real Earnings per Empl. (1987=100)
82.1	83.1	86.2	89.9	98.2	102.8	95.6	100.0	108.4	..	..	Real Output per Empl. (1987=100)
34.8	36.2	36.2	36.4	35.1	35.2	36.7	35.4	33.9	..	..	Earnings as % of Value Added
				(Billions of current Japanese Yen)							**MONETARY HOLDINGS**
337,202	376,528	410,689	442,707	476,216	517,999	566,186	618,383	674,813	..	D	Money Supply, Broadly Defined
69,572	76,510	80,900	80,802	86,375	88,980	98,214	102,973	111,844	114,474	..	Money
17,475	18,584	19,776	20,575	22,114	23,407	26,198	28,583	31,521	36,681	..	Currency Outside Banks
52,097	57,926	61,124	60,227	64,261	65,573	72,016	74,390	80,323	77,793	..	Demand Deposits
267,630	300,018	329,789	361,905	389,841	429,019	467,972	515,410	562,969	..	..	Quasi-Money
				(Billions of current Japanese Yen)							**GOVERNMENT DEFICIT (-) OR SURPLUS**
-16,872	-16,826	-17,583	-18,843	-17,290	-15,661	-15,928	-12,155	-9,492	..	..	
28,043	31,607	32,973	33,829	36,751	40,143	41,656	47,122	51,892	..	..	Current Revenue
35,591	38,938	41,253	43,550	45,095	47,374	48,838	49,790	52,473	..	..	Current Expenditure
-7,548	-7,331	-8,280	-9,721	-8,344	-7,231	-7,182	-2,668	-581	..	..	Current Budget Balance
62	34	65	86	84	158	136	178	154	..	..	Capital Receipts
9,386	9,529	9,368	9,208	9,030	8,588	8,882	9,665	9,065	..	..	Capital Payments

JAPAN	1969	1970	1971	1972	1973	1974	1975	1976	1977	1978	1979
FOREIGN TRADE (CUSTOMS BASIS)					*(Billions of current US dollars)*						
Value of Exports, fob	15.99	19.32	24.02	28.59	36.93	55.54	55.75	67.20	80.47	97.50	102.96
Nonfuel Primary Products	1.05	1.25	1.34	1.43	1.87	3.18	2.17	2.49	2.80	3.29	3.64
Fuels	0.05	0.05	0.06	0.07	0.09	0.25	0.22	0.12	0.16	0.26	0.36
Manufactures	14.89	18.02	22.61	27.08	34.97	52.11	53.36	64.60	77.51	93.95	98.96
Value of Imports, cif	15.02	18.88	19.71	23.47	38.31	62.09	57.86	64.50	70.56	78.73	110.11
Nonfuel Primary Products	8.46	10.20	10.03	11.72	19.92	24.51	21.75	24.04	26.17	29.14	40.03
Fuels	3.04	3.91	4.75	5.72	8.34	24.92	25.65	28.29	31.15	31.34	45.29
Manufactures	3.52	4.78	4.93	6.04	10.05	12.67	10.46	12.18	13.24	18.26	24.80
					(Index 1987 = 100)						
Terms of Trade	141.4	147.7	139.6	141.5	118.9	83.0	82.5	76.6	77.9	89.8	73.8
Export Prices, fob	28.6	30.3	31.3	34.9	42.9	55.1	53.4	53.0	57.7	69.9	75.7
Import Prices, cif	20.2	20.5	22.4	24.6	36.0	66.4	64.8	69.2	74.1	77.8	102.6
BALANCE OF PAYMENTS					*(Billions of current US dollars)*						
Exports of Goods & Services	..	22.95	28.40	34.28	44.72	66.47	68.23	80.49	94.76	114.30	126.26
Merchandise, fob	..	18.96	23.55	28.00	36.21	54.40	54.65	65.93	79.16	95.32	101.12
Nonfactor Services	..	3.23	3.81	4.60	5.80	8.41	9.83	10.93	11.58	13.29	15.69
Factor Services	..	0.76	1.03	1.67	2.72	3.67	3.76	3.62	4.02	5.69	9.45
Imports of Goods & Services	..	20.75	22.33	27.18	44.55	70.89	68.55	76.43	83.46	97.08	133.88
Merchandise, fob	..	15.00	15.79	19.07	32.56	53.05	49.71	56.13	62.00	71.02	99.38
Nonfactor Services	..	4.44	5.05	6.32	9.15	13.11	14.26	15.85	16.71	20.35	26.08
Factor Services	..	1.31	1.49	1.79	2.83	4.74	4.57	4.45	4.75	5.71	8.42
Long-Term Interest	..	..	..	..	..	..	..	..	..	..	..
Private Current Transfers, net	..	-0.03	-0.04	-0.13	-0.10	-0.10	-0.10	-0.14	-0.06	-0.26	-0.23
Workers' Remittances	..	..	..	..	..	..	..	..	..	..	..
Curr. A/C Bal before Off. Transf.	..	2.17	6.03	6.97	0.08	-4.52	-0.41	3.92	11.24	16.96	-7.85
Net Official Transfers	..	-0.18	-0.22	-0.33	-0.20	-0.20	-0.27	-0.22	-0.33	-0.42	-0.89
Curr. A/C Bal after Off. Transf.	..	1.99	5.80	6.64	-0.13	-4.72	-0.68	3.71	10.91	16.54	-8.74
Long-Term Capital, net	..	-1.46	-0.96	-3.06	-8.36	-3.59	-0.44	-1.44	-6.30	-12.39	-12.62
Direct Investment	..	-0.26	-0.15	-0.56	-1.93	-1.67	-1.53	-1.87	-1.63	-2.36	-2.66
Long-Term Loans	..	..	..	..	..	..	..	..	..	..	..
Disbursements	..	..	..	..	..	..	..	..	..	..	..
Repayments	..	..	..	..	..	..	..	..	..	..	..
Other Long-Term Capital	..	-1.20	-0.81	-2.50	-6.43	-1.92	1.09	0.43	-4.67	-10.03	-9.96
Other Capital, net	..	0.53	5.42	-0.73	2.14	9.55	0.53	1.53	1.87	5.81	8.22
Change in Reserves	..	-1.06	-10.26	-2.85	6.35	-1.25	0.59	-3.80	-6.48	-9.96	13.14
Memo Item:					*(Japanese Yen per US dollar)*						
Conversion Factor (Annual Avg)	360.000	360.000	349.330	303.170	271.700	299.080	296.800	296.550	268.510	210.440	219.140
				(Millions US dollars), outstanding at end of year							
EXTERNAL DEBT (Total)	..	..	..	..	..	..	..	..	..	..	..
Long-Term Debt (by debtor)	..	..	..	..	..	..	..	..	..	..	..
Central Bank, incl. IMF credit	..	..	..	..	..	..	..	..	..	..	..
Central Government	..	..	..	..	..	..	..	..	..	..	..
Rest of General Government	..	..	..	..	..	..	..	..	..	..	..
Non-financial Public Enterprises	..	..	..	..	..	..	..	..	..	..	..
Priv. Sector, incl non-guaranteed	..	..	..	..	..	..	..	..	..	..	..
Short-Term Debt	..	..	..	..	..	..	..	..	..	..	..
Memo Items:					*(Millions of US dollars)*						
Int'l Reserves Excluding Gold	3,241	4,308	14,622	17,564	11,355	12,614	11,950	15,746	22,341	32,407	19,521
Gold Holdings (at market price)	416	569	847	1,369	2,369	3,937	2,961	2,845	3,567	5,418	12,405
SOCIAL INDICATORS											
Total Fertility Rate	2.1	2.1	2.2	2.1	2.1	2.1	1.9	1.9	1.8	1.8	1.8
Infant Mortality Rate	14.2	13.1	12.4	11.7	11.3	10.7	10.0	9.3	8.9	8.3	7.8
Life Expectancy at Birth	71.8	71.9	72.8	73.1	73.4	73.7	74.3	74.7	75.1	75.6	75.8
Urban Population, % of total	70.4	71.2	72.1	73.0	73.9	74.8	75.7	75.8	75.9	76.0	76.1
Food Prod. per capita (1987=100)	136.8	125.6	107.9	114.4	112.4	114.7	120.8	107.6	116.2	111.3	108.1
Labor Force, Agriculture (%)	20.9	19.6	18.8	17.9	17.0	16.2	15.4	14.5	13.7	12.8	12.0
Labor Force, Female (%)	39.0	39.0	38.9	38.7	38.6	38.4	38.3	38.2	38.1	37.9	37.8
Primary Schl. Enroll. Ratio	..	99.0	..	..	..	..	99.0	99.0	99.0	99.0	101.0
Primary Schl. Enroll. Ratio, Female	..	99.0	..	..	..	..	99.0	99.0	99.0	100.0	101.0
Secondary Schl. Enroll. Ratio	..	86.0	..	..	..	..	91.0	92.0	93.0	93.0	92.0

JAPAN

1980	1981	1982	1983	1984	1985	1986	1987	1988	1989 estimate	NOTES	JAPAN
				(Billions of current US dollars)							**FOREIGN TRADE (CUSTOMS BASIS)**
129.54	151.91	138.58	146.80	170.04	175.86	209.08	229.05	264.77	..	..	Value of Exports, fob
5.01	4.72	3.96	4.32	4.38	4.17	4.60	4.94	5.78	..	..	Nonfuel Primary Products
0.50	0.55	0.41	0.43	0.50	0.54	0.59	0.78	0.64	..	..	Fuels
124.03	146.64	134.21	142.05	165.15	171.14	203.90	223.34	258.35	..	..	Manufactures
139.89	140.83	130.32	125.02	134.26	127.51	119.42	146.05	183.25	..	..	Value of Imports, cif
42.90	40.13	37.36	37.23	40.25	37.63	40.38	50.07	66.41	..	..	Nonfuel Primary Products
69.99	72.56	65.62	58.92	60.34	55.79	36.90	39.14	38.37	..	..	Fuels
27.00	28.14	27.34	28.86	33.67	34.09	42.14	56.84	78.47	..	..	Manufactures
				(Index 1987 = 100)							
59.9	62.8	63.2	65.1	67.2	69.4	96.0	100.0	102.3	..	..	Terms of Trade
80.8	85.0	79.1	77.6	77.5	75.7	91.2	100.0	110.6	..	..	Export Prices, fob
134.9	135.3	125.2	119.2	115.3	109.2	95.0	100.0	108.2	..	..	Import Prices, cif
				(Billions of current US dollars)							**BALANCE OF PAYMENTS**
158.23	189.30	178.75	183.06	210.44	219.53	259.29	304.28	371.55	..	..	Exports of Goods & Services
126.74	149.52	137.66	145.47	168.29	174.02	205.59	224.62	259.77	269.65	..	Merchandise, fob
19.89	23.35	22.00	21.24	22.48	22.47	23.54	28.85	35.03	..	..	Nonfactor Services
11.60	16.43	19.09	16.35	19.67	23.04	30.16	50.81	76.75	..	..	Factor Services
167.45	182.91	170.52	160.71	173.93	168.71	171.40	213.58	287.82	..	..	Imports of Goods & Services
124.61	129.56	119.58	114.01	124.03	118.03	112.77	128.20	164.77	192.54	..	Merchandise, fob
31.03	34.88	32.26	31.88	32.80	32.74	35.45	48.42	63.53	..	..	Nonfactor Services
11.81	18.47	18.68	14.82	17.10	17.94	23.18	36.96	59.52	..	..	Factor Services
..	..	..	..	..	..	..	..	..	..	..	Long-Term Interest
-0.24	-0.21	-0.09	-0.18	-0.13	-0.28	-0.59	-0.99	-1.12	..	..	Private Current Transfers, net
..	..	..	..	..	..	..	..	..	..	..	Workers' Remittances
-9.46	6.18	8.14	22.17	36.38	50.54	87.30	89.71	82.61	60.28	..	Curr. A/C Bal before Off. Transf.
-1.29	-1.41	-1.29	-1.37	-1.38	-1.37	-1.47	-2.69	-3.00	-3.29	..	Net Official Transfers
-10.75	4.77	6.85	20.80	35.00	49.17	85.83	87.02	79.61	56.99	..	Curr. A/C Bal after Off. Transf.
2.39	-6.45	-16.25	-18.73	-50.01	-63.26	-132.08	-133.98	-117.09	-32.62	..	Long-Term Capital, net
-2.11	-4.71	-4.10	-3.20	-5.97	-5.81	-14.25	-18.35	-34.73	..	..	Direct Investment
..	..	..	..	..	..	..	..	..	..	..	Long-Term Loans
..	..	..	..	..	..	..	..	..	..	..	Disbursements
..	..	..	..	..	..	..	..	..	..	..	Repayments
4.50	-1.74	-12.15	-15.53	-44.04	-57.45	-117.83	-115.63	-82.36	-32.62	..	Other Long-Term Capital
13.39	5.32	4.70	-0.52	17.13	13.51	61.09	84.90	54.00	-37.12	..	Other Capital, net
-5.03	-3.64	4.70	-1.55	-2.12	0.58	-14.84	-37.94	-16.52	12.75	..	Change in Reserves
				(Japanese Yen per US dollar)							**Memo Item:**
226.740	220.540	249.050	237.520	237.520	238.540	168.520	144.640	128.150	137.960	..	Conversion Factor (Annual Avg)
			(Millions US dollars), outstanding at end of year								**EXTERNAL DEBT (Total)**
..	..	..	..	..	..	..	..	..	..	..	Long-Term Debt (by debtor)
..	..	..	..	..	..	..	..	..	..	..	Central Bank, incl. IMF credit
..	..	..	..	..	..	..	..	..	..	..	Central Government
..	..	..	..	..	..	..	..	..	..	..	Rest of General Government
..	..	..	..	..	..	..	..	..	..	..	Non-financial Public Enterprises
..	..	..	..	..	..	..	..	..	..	..	Priv. Sector, incl non-guaranteed
..	..	..	..	..	..	..	..	..	..	..	Short-Term Debt
				(Millions of US dollars)							**Memo Items:**
24,637	28,208	23,334	24,602	26,429	26,719	42,257	80,973	96,728	83,957	..	Int'l Reserves Excluding Gold
14,282	9,631	11,070	9,243	7,469	7,923	9,471	11,729	9,940	9,715	..	Gold Holdings (at market price)
											SOCIAL INDICATORS
1.8	1.8	1.8	1.8	1.7	1.7	1.7	1.7	1.7	1.7	..	Total Fertility Rate
7.5	7.1	6.6	6.2	6.0	5.5	5.5	5.0	4.9	4.8	..	Infant Mortality Rate
76.0	76.4	76.9	76.9	76.9	77.3	77.7	78.2	78.4	78.5	..	Life Expectancy at Birth
76.2	76.3	76.4	76.5	76.6	76.7	76.8	76.8	76.9	76.9	..	Urban Population, % of total
96.2	97.5	98.4	97.0	105.5	105.9	104.9	100.0	95.2	96.3	..	Food Prod. per capita (1987=100)
11.2	..	..	..	..	..	..	..	..	..	..	Labor Force, Agriculture (%)
37.7	37.8	37.8	37.8	37.8	37.8	37.8	37.8	37.9	37.9	..	Labor Force, Female (%)
101.0	..	101.0	101.0	101.0	102.0	102.0	102.0	..	..	..	Primary Schl. Enroll. Ratio
101.0	100.0	101.0	101.0	101.0	102.0	102.0	102.0	..	..	..	Primary Schl. Enroll. Ratio, Female
93.0	..	95.0	94.0	94.0	96.0	95.0	96.0	..	..	..	Secondary Schl. Enroll. Ratio

JORDAN	1969	1970	1971	1972	1973	1974	1975	1976	1977	1978	1979
CURRENT GNP PER CAPITA (US $)	..	..	..	..	..	..	..	..	..	..	..
POPULATION (thousands)	2,241	2,299	2,353	2,400	2,445	2,493	2,550	2,611	2,674	2,744	2,825

USE AND ORIGIN OF RESOURCES *(Millions of current Jordan Dinars)*

	1969	1970	1971	1972	1973	1974	1975	1976	1977	1978	1979
Gross National Product (GNP)	..	..	..	..	..	..	..	..	..	..	..
Net Factor Income from Abroad	..	..	..	..	..	..	..	..	..	..	..
GDP at Market Prices	..	..	..	..	..	..	..	..	..	..	..
Resource Balance	..	..	..	..	..	..	..	..	..	..	..
Exports of Goods & NFServices	..	..	..	..	..	..	..	..	..	..	..
Imports of Goods & NFServices	..	..	..	..	..	..	..	..	..	..	..
Domestic Absorption	..	..	..	..	..	..	..	..	..	..	..
Private Consumption, etc.	..	..	..	..	..	..	..	..	..	..	..
General Gov't Consumption	..	..	..	..	..	..	..	..	..	..	..
Gross Domestic Investment	..	..	..	..	..	..	..	..	..	..	..
Fixed Investment	..	..	..	..	..	..	..	..	..	..	..
Indirect Taxes, net	..	..	..	..	..	..	..	..	..	..	..
GDP at factor cost	..	..	..	..	..	..	..	..	..	..	..
Agriculture	..	..	..	..	..	..	..	..	..	..	..
Industry	..	..	..	..	..	..	..	..	..	..	..
Manufacturing	..	..	..	..	..	..	..	..	..	..	..
Services, etc.	..	..	..	..	..	..	..	..	..	..	..
Gross Domestic Saving	..	..	..	..	..	..	..	..	..	..	..
Gross National Saving	..	..	..	..	..	..	..	..	..	..	..

(Millions of 1987 Jordan Dinars)

	1969	1970	1971	1972	1973	1974	1975	1976	1977	1978	1979
Gross National Product	..	..	..	..	..	..	..	..	..	..	..
GDP at Market Prices	..	..	..	..	..	..	..	..	..	..	..
Resource Balance	..	..	..	..	..	..	..	..	..	..	..
Exports of Goods & NFServices	..	..	..	..	..	..	..	..	..	..	..
Imports of Goods & NFServices	..	..	..	..	..	..	..	..	..	..	..
Domestic Absorption	..	..	..	..	..	..	..	..	..	..	..
Private Consumption, etc.	..	..	..	..	..	..	..	..	..	..	..
General Gov't Consumption	..	..	..	..	..	..	..	..	..	..	..
Gross Domestic Investment	..	..	..	..	..	..	..	..	..	..	..
Fixed Investment	..	..	..	..	..	..	..	..	..	..	..
GDP at factor cost	..	..	..	..	..	..	..	..	..	..	..
Agriculture	..	..	..	..	..	..	..	..	..	..	..
Industry	..	..	..	..	..	..	..	..	..	..	..
Manufacturing	..	..	..	..	..	..	..	..	..	..	..
Services, etc.	..	..	..	..	..	..	..	..	..	..	..
Memo Items:											
Capacity to Import	..	..	..	..	..	..	..	..	..	..	..
Terms of Trade Adjustment	..	..	..	..	..	..	..	..	..	..	..
Gross Domestic Income	..	..	..	..	..	..	..	..	..	..	..
Gross National Income	..	..	..	..	..	..	..	..	..	..	..

DOMESTIC PRICES/DEFLATORS *(Index 1987 = 100)*

	1969	1970	1971	1972	1973	1974	1975	1976	1977	1978	1979
Overall (GDP)	..	..	..	..	..	..	..	..	..	..	..
Domestic Absorption	..	..	..	..	..	..	..	..	..	..	..
Agriculture	..	..	..	..	..	..	..	..	..	..	..
Industry	..	..	..	..	..	..	..	..	..	..	..
Manufacturing	..	..	..	..	..	..	..	..	..	..	..
Consumer Price Index	25.0	26.5	27.8	29.9	33.3	39.7	44.5	49.6	56.8	60.7	69.4

MANUFACTURING ACTIVITY

	1969	1970	1971	1972	1973	1974	1975	1976	1977	1978	1979
Employment (1987=100)	37.3	..	25.7	..	..	35.0	43.0	43.7	47.7	55.0	48.7
Real Earnings per Empl. (1987=100)	64.1	..	72.8	..	..	68.1	61.6	63.0	62.7	77.1	97.7
Real Output per Empl. (1987=100)	..	..	..	..	..	..	..	..	..	..	..
Earnings as % of Value Added	28.1	37.2	36.9	..	..	23.5	25.7	25.6	27.1	32.8	29.5

MONETARY HOLDINGS *(Millions of current Jordan Dinars)*

	1969	1970	1971	1972	1973	1974	1975	1976	1977	1978	1979
Money Supply, Broadly Defined	118.8	129.3	135.1	146.6	176.4	219.8	288.4	387.5	473.9	607.6	767.2
Money	96.2	105.5	108.0	115.0	139.2	172.0	224.7	276.7	329.0	370.5	465.6
Currency Outside Banks	71.3	82.4	83.0	81.5	97.5	115.5	139.0	161.5	188.2	219.5	275.4
Demand Deposits	24.9	23.0	25.0	33.6	41.8	56.5	85.7	115.2	140.8	151.1	190.2
Quasi-Money	22.6	23.8	27.1	31.6	37.2	47.8	63.8	110.8	144.9	237.1	301.6

GOVERNMENT DEFICIT (-) OR SURPLUS *(Millions of current Jordan Dinars)*

	1969	1970	1971	1972	1973	1974	1975	1976	1977	1978	1979
	..	..	..	..	..	-19.37	-21.76	-40.64	-92.59	-160.35	-74.85
Current Revenue	..	..	..	..	..	125.59	179.35	169.57	259.41	230.82	386.40
Current Expenditure	..	..	..	..	..	101.58	121.89	182.96	190.90	203.58	309.75
Current Budget Balance	..	..	..	..	..	24.01	57.46	-13.39	68.51	27.24	76.65
Capital Receipts	..	..	..	..	..	0.05	0.04	0.02	0.02	0.06	0.13
Capital Payments	..	..	..	..	..	43.43	79.26	27.27	161.12	187.65	151.63

1980	1981	1982	1983	1984	1985	1986	1987	1988	1989	NOTES	JORDAN
									estimate		
..	..	..	..	..	1,880	1,940	2,040	2,000	1,730	..	**CURRENT GNP PER CAPITA** (US $)
2,923	3,025	3,137	3,256	3,380	3,506	3,635	3,767	3,903	4,041	f	**POPULATION** (thousands)
			(Millions of current Jordan Dinars)								**USE AND ORIGIN OF RESOURCES**
..	..	..	1,777.3	1,832.3	1,875.3	2,007.3	2,038.5	2,111.5	2,335.4	..	Gross National Product (GNP)
..	..	..	49.2	13.6	-4.7	-17.3	-50.0	-87.3	-190.1	..	Net Factor Income from Abroad
..	..	..	1,728.1	1,818.7	1,880.0	2,024.6	2,088.5	2,198.8	2,525.5	..	GDP at Market Prices
..	..	..	-783.8	-738.0	-690.8	-533.5	-498.3	-495.2	-503.2	..	Resource Balance
..	..	..	637.2	743.2	778.1	630.3	753.5	903.2	1,340.9	..	Exports of Goods & NFServices
..	..	..	1,421.0	1,481.2	1,468.9	1,163.8	1,251.8	1,398.4	1,844.1	..	Imports of Goods & NFServices
..	..	..	2,511.9	2,556.7	2,570.8	2,558.1	2,586.8	2,694.0	3,028.7	..	Domestic Absorption
..	..	..	1,448.7	1,472.5	1,560.9	1,558.0	1,547.0	1,693.0	1,962.6	..	Private Consumption, etc.
..	..	..	461.3	522.8	515.2	546.5	566.3	586.0	601.2	..	General Gov't Consumption
..	..	..	601.9	561.4	494.7	453.6	473.5	415.0	464.9	..	Gross Domestic Investment
..	..	..	548.5	530.4	455.6	423.8	411.8	415.0	464.9	..	Fixed Investment
..	..	..	222.6	213.9	233.7	338.3	327.2	323.2	294.2	..	Indirect Taxes, net
..	..	..	1,505.5	1,604.8	1,646.3	1,686.3	1,761.3	1,875.6	2,231.3	..	GDP at factor cost
..	..	..	97.2	79.6	87.4	100.1	125.0	124.0	137.6	..	Agriculture
..	..	..	448.3	504.1	440.1	418.7	435.0	489.5	650.0	..	Industry
..	..	..	197.6	233.7	192.9	180.0	199.6	231.4	296.1	..	Manufacturing
..	..	..	960.0	1,021.1	1,118.8	1,167.5	1,201.3	1,262.1	1,443.7	..	Services, etc.
..	..	..	-181.9	-176.6	-196.1	-79.9	-24.8	-80.2	-38.3	..	Gross Domestic Saving
..	..	..	171.2	195.9	104.4	216.3	152.3	106.0	65.4	..	Gross National Saving
			(Millions of 1987 Jordan Dinars)								
..	..	..	1,811.3	1,814.1	1,824.8	1,984.6	2,038.5	1,989.6	1,833.6	..	Gross National Product
..	..	..	1,764.9	1,801.7	1,829.1	2,002.2	2,088.5	2,073.6	1,988.5	H	GDP at Market Prices
..	..	..	-582.9	-512.3	-489.8	-596.7	-498.3	-509.3	-460.6	..	Resource Balance
..	..	..	605.3	667.6	695.5	605.7	753.5	808.9	904.6	..	Exports of Goods & NFServices
..	..	..	1,188.2	1,179.9	1,185.3	1,202.4	1,251.8	1,318.2	1,365.2	..	Imports of Goods & NFServices
..	..	..	2,359.9	2,337.7	2,334.1	2,599.4	2,586.8	2,598.0	2,481.4	..	Domestic Absorption
..	..	..	1,325.8	1,292.4	1,390.1	1,596.3	1,547.0	1,637.6	1,575.6	..	Private Consumption, etc.
..	..	..	502.0	569.0	527.0	532.4	566.3	585.9	583.0	..	General Gov't Consumption
..	..	..	532.2	476.4	417.0	470.6	473.5	374.5	322.9	..	Gross Domestic Investment
..	..	..	474.2	439.1	374.9	434.4	411.8	365.6	315.2	..	Fixed Investment
..	..	..	1,537.2	1,589.0	1,601.5	1,667.3	1,761.3	1,769.1	1,756.9	H	GDP at factor cost
..	..	..	103.4	82.0	93.9	97.0	125.0	141.9	128.0	..	Agriculture
..	..	..	417.7	455.1	403.2	432.2	435.0	435.2	448.1	..	Industry
..	..	..	200.7	223.9	200.1	191.9	199.6	212.6	221.9	..	Manufacturing
..	..	..	1,016.1	1,051.9	1,104.5	1,138.1	1,201.3	1,192.0	1,180.8	..	Services, etc.
											Memo Items:
..	..	..	532.8	592.0	627.9	651.2	753.5	851.4	992.7	..	Capacity to Import
..	..	..	-72.5	-75.6	-67.6	45.5	0.0	42.5	88.1	..	Terms of Trade Adjustment
..	..	..	1,692.4	1,726.1	1,761.5	2,047.7	2,088.5	2,116.1	2,076.6	..	Gross Domestic Income
..	..	..	1,738.8	1,738.6	1,757.2	2,030.1	2,038.5	2,032.1	1,921.7	..	Gross National Income
			(Index 1987 = 100)								**DOMESTIC PRICES/DEFLATORS**
..	..	..	97.9	100.9	102.8	101.1	100.0	106.0	127.0	..	Overall (GDP)
..	..	..	106.4	109.4	110.1	98.4	100.0	103.7	122.1	..	Domestic Absorption
..	..	..	94.0	97.0	93.1	103.2	100.0	87.4	107.5	..	Agriculture
..	..	..	107.3	110.8	109.1	96.9	100.0	112.5	145.1	..	Industry
..	..	..	98.4	104.4	96.4	93.8	100.0	108.9	133.4	..	Manufacturing
77.1	83.0	89.2	93.7	97.3	100.2	100.2	100.0	106.6	134.0	..	Consumer Price Index
											MANUFACTURING ACTIVITY
55.8	63.8	65.9	71.6	86.6	94.7	96.5	100.0	..	..	..	Employment (1987=100)
100.8	108.7	113.2	111.8	103.2	100.4	99.5	100.0	..	..	..	Real Earnings per Empl. (1987=100)
..	..	..	146.8	169.9	161.1	88.4	100.0	..	..	..	Real Output per Empl. (1987=100)
26.9	27.4	28.6	29.5	29.5	31.2	28.4	25.3		..	..	Earnings as % of Value Added
			(Millions of current Jordan Dinars)								**MONETARY HOLDINGS**
980.3	1,183.6	1,406.9	1,617.9	1,762.2	1,879.1	2,078.7	2,404.2	2,778.0	3,237.6	..	Money Supply, Broadly Defined
580.7	701.7	787.5	869.4	878.4	848.2	897.1	979.8	1,166.8	1,302.3	..	Money
351.6	412.3	470.0	516.0	530.5	531.8	583.9	655.8	811.2	871.1	..	Currency Outside Banks
229.1	289.3	317.5	353.4	347.9	316.4	313.2	324.0	355.6	431.2	..	Demand Deposits
399.5	482.0	619.4	748.5	883.8	1,030.9	1,181.7	1,424.4	1,611.2	1,935.4	..	Quasi-Money
			(Millions of current Jordan Dinars)								**GOVERNMENT DEFICIT (-) OR SURPLUS**
-109.90	-115.91	-128.22	-108.48	-139.70	-153.08	-130.00	-247.84	-208.32	..	..	Current Revenue
414.56	498.60	542.92	573.82	498.36	599.18	612.90	589.48	629.85	..	..	Current Revenue
305.40	356.14	451.13	458.34	474.30	523.43	556.10	561.23	614.79	..	..	Current Expenditure
109.16	142.46	91.79	115.48	24.06	75.75	56.80	28.25	15.06	..	..	Current Budget Balance
2.79	0.37	0.64	..	0.34	0.74	1.40	0.51	0.28	..	..	Capital Receipts
221.85	258.74	220.65	223.96	164.10	229.57	188.20	276.60	223.66	..	..	Capital Payments

JORDAN	1969	1970	1971	1972	1973	1974	1975	1976	1977	1978	1979
FOREIGN TRADE (CUSTOMS BASIS)					*(Millions of current US dollars)*						
Value of Exports, fob	33.3	34.1	32.0	47.6	57.5	154.7	153.2	209.1	249.3	296.7	402.3
Nonfuel Primary Products	28.8	22.7	19.9	27.1	33.1	100.3	104.1	134.6	147.4	162.2	244.6
Fuels	0.0	0.0	0.1	0.0	0.5	0.4	0.9	2.7	0.5	0.3	0.4
Manufactures	4.5	11.3	12.1	20.6	23.9	54.0	48.2	71.8	101.4	134.2	157.3
Value of Imports, cif	190.0	184.5	214.6	266.9	327.9	486.6	730.8	1,022.1	1,381.1	1,498.8	1,948.6
Nonfuel Primary Products	63.2	64.7	70.4	92.6	112.6	156.2	183.2	297.2	292.8	369.9	459.6
Fuels	10.7	10.5	13.7	12.8	12.6	16.2	77.8	111.9	130.9	153.0	246.7
Manufactures	116.1	109.3	130.5	161.6	202.6	314.2	469.9	613.0	957.4	975.9	1,242.3
					(Index 1987 = 100)						
Terms of Trade	138.7	132.1	122.1	111.3	108.3	144.2	151.2	122.0	117.6	108.4	111.6
Export Prices, fob	36.4	36.5	35.9	37.6	46.4	80.5	88.1	72.7	72.9	77.0	93.8
Import Prices, cif	26.3	27.6	29.4	33.8	42.9	55.8	58.3	59.6	62.0	71.0	84.0
BALANCE OF PAYMENTS					*(Millions of current US dollars)*						
Exports of Goods & Services	..	123.5	113.1	124.9	189.0	279.7	414.6	590.4	815.3	973.0	1,279.5
Merchandise, fob	..	34.1	32.0	47.6	73.7	154.3	152.9	206.9	261.5	297.6	402.7
Nonfactor Services	..	55.0	51.2	65.0	96.2	98.1	226.4	344.3	462.1	568.6	728.0
Factor Services	..	34.4	30.0	12.3	19.2	27.3	35.3	39.2	91.7	106.8	148.8
Imports of Goods & Services	..	253.9	275.2	330.1	417.9	609.1	951.2	1,309.4	1,797.3	2,071.8	2,874.2
Merchandise, fob	..	163.8	190.4	236.6	291.9	430.3	648.2	907.9	1,443.0	1,502.2	1,959.0
Nonfactor Services	..	88.3	82.1	90.7	122.0	172.3	293.3	387.4	287.5	480.6	786.4
Factor Services	..	1.8	2.7	2.8	4.0	6.5	9.7	14.2	66.8	89.0	128.8
Long-Term Interest	..	1.8	2.8	2.9	3.1	3.9	7.0	9.4	17.8	31.5	53.1
Private Current Transfers, net	..	0.0	0.0	27.2	55.4	82.0	172.0	401.8	971.8	818.2	528.6
Workers' Remittances	..	..	..	20.7	44.7	74.8	166.7	410.9	443.7	469.6	540.6
Curr. A/C Bal before Off. Transf.	..	-130.4	-162.1	-178.1	-173.5	-247.4	-364.6	-317.2	-10.2	-280.6	-1,066.1
Net Official Transfers	..	110.8	100.3	184.5	186.0	250.9	409.3	353.3	0.0	350.8	1,067.9
Curr. A/C Bal after Off. Transf.	..	-19.6	-61.8	6.4	12.5	3.4	44.7	36.1	-10.2	70.2	1.8
Long-Term Capital, net	..	3.2	21.5	17.1	19.2	32.9	137.6	-44.9	162.9	-59.6	183.7
Direct Investment	..	..	..	-1.1	-3.3	3.4	19.4	-10.2	15.0	50.0	15.7
Long-Term Loans	..	11.7	23.2	28.0	30.1	51.8	90.1	91.6	227.4	246.6	262.6
Disbursements	..	14.5	28.1	35.0	38.6	62.4	104.4	111.1	264.8	294.0	336.6
Repayments	..	2.8	4.9	7.0	8.5	10.6	14.3	19.5	37.4	47.4	74.0
Other Long-Term Capital	..	-8.5	-1.7	-9.8	-7.6	-22.3	28.1	-126.2	-79.5	-356.2	-94.6
Other Capital, net	..	10.7	1.2	-4.8	7.8	-10.4	-9.4	36.1	53.5	110.4	26.7
Change in Reserves	..	5.7	39.2	-18.7	-39.4	-26.0	-172.9	-27.4	-206.2	-121.0	-212.2
Memo Item:					*(Jordan Dinars per US dollar)*						
Conversion Factor (Annual Avg)	0.360	0.360	0.360	0.360	0.330	0.320	0.320	0.330	0.330	0.310	0.300
				(Millions of US dollars), outstanding at end of year							
EXTERNAL DEBT (Total)	..	119.5	153.8	178.7	214.1	272.4	346.1	436.5	798.3	1,167.5	1,522.6
Long-Term Debt (by debtor)	..	119.5	153.8	178.7	214.1	272.4	346.1	436.5	686.3	962.5	1,238.6
Central Bank, incl. IMF credit	..	0.0	4.9	4.9	1.9	0.0	0.0	0.0	0.0	0.0	0.0
Central Government	..	110.2	123.5	148.4	186.0	223.3	277.1	357.7	495.9	704.3	903.6
Rest of General Government	..	3.0	3.0	3.1	3.3	3.3	3.0	7.3	8.8	13.0	15.3
Non-financial Public Enterprises	..	5.0	21.2	21.2	21.4	43.8	61.1	61.8	167.9	227.0	299.2
Priv. Sector, incl non-guaranteed	..	1.3	1.2	1.1	1.5	2.0	4.9	9.7	13.7	18.2	20.5
Short-Term Debt	..	0.0	0.0	0.0	0.0	0.0	0.0	0.0	112.0	205.0	284.0
Memo Items:					*(Millions of US dollars)*						
Int'l Reserves Excluding Gold	232.9	227.8	222.9	241.0	270.7	312.8	458.9	471.5	643.2	885.6	1,166.1
Gold Holdings (at market price)	29.8	29.8	34.8	51.7	89.5	148.6	111.8	107.4	133.0	183.3	417.8
SOCIAL INDICATORS											
Total Fertility Rate	7.9	7.9	7.8	7.8	7.7	7.6	7.5	7.5	7.4	7.3	7.2
Infant Mortality Rate	94.0	90.0	86.0	82.0	78.6	75.2	71.8	68.4	65.0	62.8	60.6
Life Expectancy at Birth	53.6	54.6	55.6	56.6	57.5	58.4	59.3	60.2	61.2	61.7	62.2
Urban Population, % of total	49.7	50.5	51.5	52.5	53.4	54.4	55.4	56.3	57.3	58.2	59.2
Food Prod. per capita (1987=100)	118.6	83.0	103.9	115.2	74.6	107.7	70.7	75.5	75.8	90.9	64.9
Labor Force, Agriculture (%)	29.4	27.8	25.9	24.1	22.4	20.7	19.0	17.2	15.5	13.7	12.0
Labor Force, Female (%)	6.3	6.4	6.6	6.7	6.9	7.0	7.1	7.3	7.5	7.6	7.8
Primary Schl. Enroll. Ratio	..	..	..	..	..	..	..	..	..	98.0	102.0
Primary Schl. Enroll. Ratio, Female	..	..	..	..	..	..	..	..	..	97.0	99.0
Secondary Schl. Enroll. Ratio	..	..	..	..	..	..	..	..	..	67.0	74.0

1980	1981	1982	1983	1984	1985	1986	1987	1988	1989 estimate	NOTES	JORDAN
											FOREIGN TRADE (CUSTOMS BASIS)
				(Millions of current US dollars)							
561.4	731.8	738.9	579.0	751.9	788.6	714.0	929.6	1,019.0	..	..	Value of Exports, fob
358.9	407.2	371.8	301.2	358.5	357.2	415.0	437.2	543.9	..	..	Nonfuel Primary Products
1.7	0.3	0.2	0.4	0.3	0.3	1.0	0.1	1.1	..	..	Fuels
200.8	324.3	366.9	277.5	393.1	431.1	298.0	492.3	474.0	..	..	Manufactures
2,394.4	3,146.3	3,217.5	3,016.3	2,784.1	2,732.9	2,413.0	2,710.0	2,732.0	..	..	Value of Imports, cif
503.1	612.6	666.3	641.9	648.4	602.0	621.0	642.4	639.2	..	..	Nonfuel Primary Products
408.5	546.8	682.0	584.2	576.1	543.4	346.0	464.8	424.8	..	..	Fuels
1,482.8	1,986.8	1,869.1	1,790.2	1,559.6	1,587.5	1,446.0	1,602.8	1,668.0	..	..	Manufactures
				(Index 1987 = 100)							
108.2	101.3	95.6	95.9	97.2	94.3	108.6	100.0	106.9	..	..	Terms of Trade
105.3	98.6	92.0	89.4	89.7	85.3	98.7	100.0	111.2	..	..	Export Prices, fob
97.3	97.3	96.2	93.2	92.3	90.5	90.9	100.0	104.0	..	..	Import Prices, cif
				(Millions of current US dollars)							**BALANCE OF PAYMENTS**
1,781.5	2,214.6	2,208.9	2,042.4	2,164.6	2,181.7	2,022.5	2,376.4	2,562.3	2,454.0	f	Exports of Goods & Services
575.1	735.0	750.8	580.2	756.8	789.7	731.8	932.0	1,016.0	1,110.0	..	Merchandise, fob
997.4	1,172.8	1,142.5	1,175.2	1,180.6	1,186.7	1,069.8	1,292.2	1,415.0	1,241.0	..	Nonfactor Services
209.0	306.8	315.6	287.0	227.2	205.3	220.9	152.2	131.3	103.0	..	Factor Services
3,323.0	4,351.6	4,423.5	4,066.3	4,048.2	3,948.4	3,596.8	3,995.4	4,130.1	3,669.3	f	Imports of Goods & Services
2,397.6	3,169.7	3,239.0	3,035.9	2,783.7	2,724.2	2,423.4	2,694.1	2,716.0	2,399.0	..	Merchandise, fob
828.4	1,049.3	1,051.7	879.0	1,072.7	1,006.9	903.1	1,001.6	1,048.0	834.0	..	Nonfactor Services
97.0	132.6	132.8	151.4	191.8	217.3	270.3	299.7	366.1	436.3	..	Factor Services
79.0	94.3	101.0	139.1	143.4	205.9	238.6	281.5	303.1	253.7	..	Long-Term Interest
605.1	837.4	846.4	836.9	933.5	773.4	895.8	671.1	730.6	511.4	..	Private Current Transfers, net
714.6	929.4	975.5	999.0	1,113.0	921.1	1,066.4	844.2	804.6	561.1	..	Workers' Remittances
-936.4	-1,299.6	-1,368.2	-1,187.0	-950.1	-993.3	-678.5	-947.9	-837.2	-703.9	..	Curr. A/C Bal before Off. Transf.
1,311.0	1,258.2	1,032.4	797.7	681.4	739.0	633.0	599.0	550.0	622.0	..	Net Official Transfers
374.6	-41.4	-335.8	-389.3	-268.7	-254.3	-45.5	-348.9	-287.2	-81.9	..	Curr. A/C Bal after Off. Transf.
103.7	135.0	352.8	426.2	167.6	338.9	147.9	217.9	64.1	-166.0	f	Long-Term Capital, net
27.4	67.7	90.6	24.3	75.2	14.1	22.6	32.7	0.1	..	..	Direct Investment
266.0	329.6	413.4	568.0	291.2	396.8	620.9	450.2	292.3	829.9	..	Long-Term Loans
369.3	513.3	545.0	744.9	525.7	688.4	977.5	910.3	859.8	1,030.0	..	Disbursements
103.3	183.7	131.6	176.9	234.5	291.6	356.6	460.1	567.5	200.1	..	Repayments
-189.7	-262.3	-151.2	-166.1	-198.8	-72.0	-495.6	-265.0	-228.3	-995.9	..	Other Long-Term Capital
-121.5	-47.1	-194.2	101.7	-79.2	67.4	31.6	78.0	-264.9	490.9	f	Other Capital, net
-356.8	-46.5	177.2	-138.6	180.3	-152.0	-134.0	53.0	488.0	-243.0	..	Change in Reserves
				(Jordan Dinars per US dollar)							**Memo Item:**
0.300	0.330	0.350	0.360	0.380	0.390	0.350	0.340	0.370	0.570	..	Conversion Factor (Annual Avg)
				(Millions of US dollars), outstanding at end of year							**EXTERNAL DEBT (Total)**
1,976.8	2,291.2	2,746.6	3,207.1	3,508.3	4,153.4	5,025.8	6,373.3	6,564.1	7,418.2	..	
1,491.1	1,762.5	2,137.9	2,634.8	2,831.6	3,460.6	4,260.8	5,050.6	5,389.9	6,499.9	..	Long-Term Debt (by debtor)
0.0	0.0	0.0	0.0	0.0	63.0	71.5	181.7	166.5	271.4	..	Central Bank, incl. IMF credit
1,021.0	1,015.0	1,172.8	1,686.4	1,804.5	2,284.2	2,914.8	3,387.2	3,735.9	4,641.9	..	Central Government
14.5	15.1	28.8	28.3	25.7	24.1	21.9	21.0	19.1	16.8	..	Rest of General Government
430.0	705.8	906.3	891.7	976.4	1,060.1	1,220.5	1,423.1	1,435.2	1,517.2	..	Non-financial Public Enterprises
25.6	26.6	30.0	28.4	25.0	29.2	32.1	37.6	33.2	52.6	..	Priv. Sector, incl non-guaranteed
485.7	528.7	608.7	572.3	676.7	692.8	765.0	1,322.7	1,174.2	918.3	..	Short-Term Debt
				(Millions of US dollars)							**Memo Items:**
1,142.8	1,086.7	884.1	824.2	515.0	422.8	437.1	424.7	109.6	470.7	..	Int'l Reserves Excluding Gold
601.9	424.1	493.5	415.8	326.8	347.0	415.9	485.1	304.8	300.0	..	Gold Holdings (at market price)
											SOCIAL INDICATORS
7.2	7.1	7.0	6.9	6.8	6.7	6.6	6.5	6.4	6.3	..	Total Fertility Rate
58.4	56.2	54.0	52.0	50.0	48.0	46.0	44.0	42.6	41.2	..	Infant Mortality Rate
62.7	63.2	63.7	64.1	64.6	65.0	65.5	66.0	66.3	66.6	..	Life Expectancy at Birth
60.1	61.0	61.8	62.7	63.5	64.4	65.1	65.9	66.6	67.4	..	Urban Population, % of total
95.7	86.7	83.7	97.5	89.5	103.0	89.8	100.0	102.2	86.5	..	Food Prod. per capita (1987=100)
10.2	..	..	..	..	..	..	..	..	..	..	Labor Force, Agriculture (%)
7.9	8.2	8.5	8.7	8.9	9.1	9.4	9.6	9.9	10.1	..	Labor Force, Female (%)
104.0	..	100.0	99.0	..	..	..	..	..	..	..	Primary Schl. Enroll. Ratio
102.0	100.0	98.0	99.0	..	..	..	..	..	..	..	Primary Schl. Enroll. Ratio, Female
76.0	..	78.0	79.0	..	..	..	..	..	..	..	Secondary Schl. Enroll. Ratio

KENYA	1969	1970	1971	1972	1973	1974	1975	1976	1977	1978	1979
CURRENT GNP PER CAPITA (US $)	130	130	160	180	180	210	230	240	270	310	370
POPULATION (thousands)	11,114	11,498	11,899	12,322	12,770	13,242	13,741	14,267	14,821	15,402	16,006

USE AND ORIGIN OF RESOURCES *(Billions of current Kenya Shillings)*

	1969	1970	1971	1972	1973	1974	1975	1976	1977	1978	1979
Gross National Product (GNP)	10.05	11.03	12.32	14.62	16.69	20.37	23.01	27.71	35.62	39.17	44.93
Net Factor Income from Abroad	-0.37	-0.42	-0.38	-0.43	-0.88	-0.85	-0.93	-1.36	-1.57	-1.82	-1.68
GDP at Market Prices	10.42	11.45	12.70	15.05	17.57	21.21	23.93	29.07	37.20	40.99	46.60
Resource Balance	0.15	-0.10	-0.83	-0.32	-0.22	-1.53	-1.12	0.20	1.25	-4.00	-2.73
Exports of Goods & NFServices	3.08	3.42	3.64	4.00	4.81	7.14	7.14	9.43	13.00	11.86	12.00
Imports of Goods & NFServices	2.93	3.51	4.47	4.32	5.04	8.68	8.26	9.23	11.75	15.86	14.73
Domestic Absorption	10.27	11.55	13.53	15.37	17.79	22.75	25.06	28.87	35.95	44.99	49.33
Private Consumption, etc.	6.54	6.89	8.21	9.36	10.37	13.67	16.33	17.91	20.75	24.79	30.00
General Gov't Consumption	1.71	1.86	2.28	2.65	2.89	3.61	4.39	5.08	6.40	8.00	8.95
Gross Domestic Investment	2.02	2.79	3.04	3.36	4.53	5.46	4.34	5.88	8.80	12.20	10.39
Fixed Investment	1.87	2.25	2.88	3.28	3.59	4.06	4.84	5.81	7.80	10.28	10.87
Indirect Taxes, net	0.89	1.07	1.30	1.28	1.78	2.44	2.79	3.51	4.38	5.39	5.94
GDP at factor cost	9.53	10.38	11.40	13.78	15.79	18.78	21.14	25.56	32.81	35.60	40.66
Agriculture	3.22	3.46	3.58	4.85	5.60	6.64	7.22	9.69	13.77	13.14	14.07
Industry	1.88	2.06	2.32	2.81	3.28	3.89	4.28	4.76	5.90	7.15	8.07
Manufacturing	1.14	1.24	1.43	1.56	1.89	2.39	2.54	2.88	3.60	4.39	5.00
Services, etc.	4.43	4.86	5.50	6.12	6.92	8.25	9.64	11.12	13.15	15.31	18.52
Gross Domestic Saving	2.17	2.70	2.21	3.04	4.31	3.93	3.22	6.09	10.05	8.20	7.66
Gross National Saving	..	2.20	1.73	2.59	3.37	2.99	2.20	4.56	8.51	6.51	6.06

(Millions of 1987 Kenya Shillings)

	1969	1970	1971	1972	1973	1974	1975	1976	1977	1978	1979
Gross National Product	46,484	44,260	54,411	64,576	66,916	70,221	71,456	72,267	79,137	84,476	91,876
GDP at Market Prices	48,599	46,326	56,727	67,096	71,006	73,587	74,562	76,188	83,329	89,000	95,677
Resource Balance	-11,417	-16,636	-21,882	-17,162	-14,806	-18,802	-11,194	-9,865	-15,258	-25,569	-17,211
Exports of Goods & NFServices	21,350	21,968	22,973	20,513	22,287	25,665	22,683	23,114	23,759	24,158	23,053
Imports of Goods & NFServices	32,767	38,603	44,855	37,675	37,093	44,467	33,878	32,980	39,017	49,727	40,263
Domestic Absorption	60,015	62,961	78,609	84,258	85,813	92,389	85,756	86,053	98,587	114,569	112,888
Private Consumption, etc.	30,461	25,665	39,387	46,272	42,098	49,177	49,887	46,636	49,142	55,086	61,219
General Gov't Consumption	9,948	10,289	11,834	12,834	13,297	14,431	16,155	17,350	19,469	22,355	23,634
Gross Domestic Investment	19,607	27,008	27,388	25,152	30,418	28,781	19,714	22,067	29,975	37,128	28,035
Fixed Investment	..	..	..	..	..	..	..	..	..	..	28,626
GDP at factor cost	43,282	40,965	49,817	58,534	61,216	61,883	64,407	65,951	71,752	76,175	81,489
Agriculture	18,098	16,673	19,362	21,573	22,161	21,620	23,211	23,654	26,018	27,001	27,732
Industry	6,424	6,060	7,653	11,216	12,100	12,196	12,253	12,206	13,775	15,231	15,769
Manufacturing	3,344	3,199	4,142	5,503	6,263	6,591	6,631	6,559	7,601	8,552	9,190
Services, etc.	19,884	19,220	23,741	25,875	26,892	28,006	28,915	30,089	31,917	33,850	37,929
Memo Items:											
Capacity to Import	34,447	37,548	36,506	34,869	35,444	36,615	29,276	33,702	43,173	37,192	32,802
Terms of Trade Adjustment	13,097	15,581	13,533	14,356	13,156	10,950	6,593	10,587	19,414	13,034	9,749
Gross Domestic Income	61,695	61,906	70,260	81,452	84,163	84,537	81,154	86,775	102,743	102,034	105,427
Gross National Income	59,581	59,840	67,944	78,932	80,073	81,171	78,049	82,854	98,551	97,510	101,625

DOMESTIC PRICES/DEFLATORS *(Index 1987 = 100)*

	1969	1970	1971	1972	1973	1974	1975	1976	1977	1978	1979
Overall (GDP)	21.4	24.7	22.4	22.4	24.7	28.8	32.1	38.2	44.6	46.1	48.7
Domestic Absorption	17.1	18.3	17.2	18.2	20.7	24.6	29.2	33.5	36.5	39.3	43.7
Agriculture	17.8	20.7	18.5	22.5	25.3	30.7	31.1	41.0	52.9	48.7	50.7
Industry	29.3	34.0	30.4	25.1	27.1	31.9	34.9	39.0	42.8	46.9	51.2
Manufacturing	34.0	38.9	34.6	28.3	30.2	36.2	38.3	44.0	47.3	51.3	54.4
Consumer Price Index	15.5	15.8	16.4	17.3	19.0	22.3	26.6	29.6	34.0	39.8	43.0

MANUFACTURING ACTIVITY

	1969	1970	1971	1972	1973	1974	1975	1976	1977	1978	1979
Employment (1987=100)	31.6	37.0	40.8	50.5	56.0	61.7	59.7	64.4	71.7	77.1	82.0
Real Earnings per Empl. (1987=100)	138.6	131.1	123.7	145.8	137.0	137.2	125.2	125.3	112.0	102.6	102.1
Real Output per Empl. (1987=100)	25.3	22.7	27.0	40.1	41.8	46.2	53.1	58.6	68.5	60.0	56.5
Earnings as % of Value Added	51.6	50.2	47.5	48.0	44.4	43.6	44.0	39.4	36.2	38.9	41.6

MONETARY HOLDINGS *(Millions of current Kenya Shillings)*

	1969	1970	1971	1972	1973	1974	1975	1976	1977	1978	1979
Money Supply, Broadly Defined	3,140	4,005	4,307	4,908	6,120	6,731	8,051	9,820	14,355	16,571	19,253
Money	1,801	2,226	2,371	2,804	3,449	3,755	4,143	5,120	7,333	7,879	9,178
Currency Outside Banks	570	697	740	894	982	1,086	1,235	1,625	2,182	2,305	2,673
Demand Deposits	1,231	1,529	1,631	1,909	2,467	2,670	2,908	3,495	5,151	5,573	6,504
Quasi-Money	1,339	1,779	1,936	2,104	2,671	2,975	3,909	4,700	7,022	8,693	10,075

GOVERNMENT DEFICIT (-) OR SURPLUS *(Millions of current Kenya Shillings)*

	1969	1970	1971	1972	1973	1974	1975	1976	1977	1978	1979
GOVERNMENT DEFICIT (-) OR SURPLUS	..	..	..	-566	-902	-587	-1,151	-1,709	-1,327	-1,627	-3,015
Current Revenue	..	..	..	2,712	2,827	3,696	4,522	5,325	6,381	9,364	10,100
Current Expenditure	..	..	..	2,352	2,618	3,080	4,006	4,848	5,531	7,643	9,400
Current Budget Balance	..	..	..	360	209	616	516	477	850	1,721	700
Capital Receipts	..	..	..	..	1	..	..	..	2	1	2
Capital Payments	..	..	..	926	1,112	1,203	1,667	2,186	2,179	3,349	3,717

1980	1981	1982	1983	1984	1985	1986	1987	1988	1989 estimate	NOTES	KENYA
420	430	400	350	330	310	330	340	370	370	..	CURRENT GNP PER CAPITA (US $)
16,632	17,280	17,951	18,643	19,358	20,096	20,856	21,640	22,446	23,277	..	POPULATION (thousands)
				(Billions of current Kenya Shillings)							USE AND ORIGIN OF RESOURCES
52.23	60.07	67.52	77.11	86.25	97.08	113.29	125.50	142.99	163.16	..	Gross National Product (GNP)
-1.68	-1.94	-2.79	-2.54	-3.00	-3.66	-4.19	-4.97	-6.41	-7.26	..	Net Factor Income from Abroad
53.91	62.02	70.31	79.66	89.25	100.75	117.48	130.47	149.40	170.42	f	GDP at Market Prices
-5.99	-5.04	-2.64	-0.36	-1.23	-1.07	0.21	-6.69	-7.79	-9.89	..	Resource Balance
15.07	15.94	17.55	19.93	23.41	25.50	30.33	27.99	33.30	39.95	..	Exports of Goods & NFServices
21.05	20.97	20.19	20.28	24.64	26.57	30.13	34.68	41.09	49.85	..	Imports of Goods & NFServices
59.90	67.05	72.94	80.02	90.48	101.82	117.28	137.16	157.19	180.31	..	Domestic Absorption
33.47	38.36	44.64	48.77	56.45	58.49	70.19	81.02	93.58	104.14	..	Private Consumption, etc.
10.68	11.53	12.95	14.66	15.51	17.60	21.52	24.29	25.75	32.72	..	General Gov't Consumption
15.75	17.16	15.35	16.59	18.51	25.73	25.57	31.85	37.86	43.45	..	Gross Domestic Investment
12.42	14.49	13.36	14.35	16.14	17.61	23.06	25.73	30.44	34.24	..	Fixed Investment
7.94	8.83	9.32	10.19	11.79	12.37	15.18	18.22	21.58	23.81	..	Indirect Taxes, net
45.97	53.19	60.99	69.47	77.46	88.37	102.30	112.25	127.82	146.61	f	GDP at factor cost
14.98	17.29	20.35	23.77	26.27	28.73	33.80	35.64	40.78	45.43	..	Agriculture
9.58	10.78	12.16	13.46	14.66	16.88	19.01	20.89	24.67	29.25	..	Industry
5.90	6.56	7.45	8.16	9.22	10.37	12.17	13.05	15.06	17.11	..	Manufacturing
21.40	25.12	28.48	32.24	36.53	42.76	49.49	55.72	62.38	71.94	..	Services, etc.
9.77	12.13	12.72	16.23	17.28	24.65	25.77	25.16	30.07	33.56	..	Gross Domestic Saving
8.29	11.08	10.84	14.53	15.15	22.33	22.53	21.38	25.24	28.39	..	Gross National Saving
				(Millions of 1987 Kenya Shillings)							
97,402	101,518	102,650	104,975	106,445	110,857	118,716	125,496	132,281	138,461	..	Gross National Product
100,808	104,909	106,855	108,421	110,250	115,014	123,211	130,468	138,279	144,585	f	GDP at Market Prices
-19,980	-11,682	-5,302	-455	-4,525	-926	-2,870	-6,690	-8,544	-7,521	..	Resource Balance
24,305	23,287	24,028	23,479	23,685	25,275	27,744	27,992	29,269	32,225	..	Exports of Goods & NFServices
44,284	34,968	29,329	23,934	28,210	26,201	30,614	34,682	37,813	39,746	..	Imports of Goods & NFServices
120,788	116,591	112,157	108,877	114,775	115,940	126,081	137,158	146,822	152,106	..	Domestic Absorption
58,894	57,175	61,542	61,248	66,258	61,519	74,805	81,016	85,437	86,981	..	Private Consumption, etc.
24,171	22,867	22,526	23,283	23,045	22,345	23,981	24,290	26,564	28,025	..	General Gov't Consumption
37,723	36,548	28,089	24,345	25,471	32,076	27,294	31,852	34,821	37,101	..	Gross Domestic Investment
29,345	30,818	24,289	20,937	21,576	21,707	24,285	25,734	27,964	28,400	..	Fixed Investment
84,745	89,801	93,355	95,661	96,444	101,374	107,048	112,250	118,061	123,900	f	GDP at factor cost
28,030	29,691	31,878	32,470	31,342	32,598	34,203	35,638	37,311	38,793	..	Agriculture
16,610	17,275	17,567	17,650	18,026	19,083	19,843	20,892	22,013	23,281	..	Industry
9,671	10,018	10,244	10,706	11,165	11,669	12,346	13,050	13,834	14,651	..	Manufacturing
40,028	42,780	43,883	45,541	47,076	49,692	53,002	55,720	58,737	61,825	..	Services, etc.
											Memo Items:
31,689	26,572	25,500	23,511	26,802	25,144	30,824	27,992	30,645	31,857	..	Capacity to Import
7,385	3,285	1,472	33	3,116	-131	3,079	0	1,376	-367	..	Terms of Trade Adjustment
108,193	108,195	108,327	108,454	113,367	114,883	126,290	130,468	139,655	144,217	..	Gross Domestic Income
104,786	104,803	104,122	105,007	109,561	110,726	121,795	125,496	133,657	138,094	..	Gross National Income
				(Index 1987 = 100)							DOMESTIC PRICES/DEFLATORS
53.5	59.1	65.8	73.5	81.0	87.6	95.4	100.0	108.0	117.9	..	Overall (GDP)
49.6	57.5	65.0	73.5	78.8	87.8	93.0	100.0	107.1	118.5	..	Domestic Absorption
53.5	58.2	63.8	73.2	83.8	88.1	98.8	100.0	109.3	117.1	..	Agriculture
57.7	62.4	69.2	76.2	81.3	88.4	95.8	100.0	112.1	125.6	..	Industry
61.0	65.5	72.7	76.3	82.6	88.9	98.5	100.0	108.9	116.8	..	Manufacturing
48.9	54.7	65.9	73.4	80.9	91.5	95.1	100.0	108.3	118.9	..	Consumer Price Index
											MANUFACTURING ACTIVITY
82.4	88.2	86.8	87.9	90.1	93.7	97.1	100.0	102.4	..	G	Employment (1987=100)
97.7	103.2	99.8	97.2	97.7	91.3	94.8	100.0	103.3	..	G	Real Earnings per Empl. (1987=100)
53.7	58.5	69.4	71.2	78.2	83.6	88.4	100.0	97.5	..	G	Real Output per Empl. (1987=100)
43.0	44.5	43.4	44.4	44.7	43.5	43.8	44.1	43.8	..	..	Earnings as % of Value Added
				(Millions of current Kenya Shillings)							MONETARY HOLDINGS
20,430	23,708	27,585	30,256	35,862	39,488	49,979	55,653	60,064	68,794	D	Money Supply, Broadly Defined
8,434	9,409	10,635	11,473	13,095	12,923	17,522	18,916	19,160	21,647	..	Money
3,032	3,569	3,724	4,083	4,370	5,038	6,371	7,688	8,536	9,655	..	Currency Outside Banks
5,402	5,840	6,911	7,390	8,725	7,885	11,151	11,229	10,624	11,992	..	Demand Deposits
11,997	14,299	16,950	18,783	22,767	26,565	32,457	36,736	40,904	47,147	..	Quasi-Money
				(Millions of current Kenya Shillings)							GOVERNMENT DEFICIT (-) OR SURPLUS
-2,409	-4,002	-5,463	-3,838	-4,281	-6,245	-5,144	-8,329	-6,272	..	C	GOVERNMENT DEFICIT (-) OR SURPLUS
12,206	13,959	15,270	16,620	18,230	20,347	24,129	29,121	34,129	..	..	Current Revenue
10,455	12,851	16,400	17,002	19,339	21,782	25,093	30,004	34,187	..	..	Current Expenditure
1,751	1,108	-1,130	-382	-1,109	-1,435	-964	-883	-58	..	..	Current Budget Balance
2	15	11	2	1	1	2	6	11	..	..	Capital Receipts
4,162	5,125	4,344	3,458	3,173	4,811	4,182	7,452	6,225	..	..	Capital Payments

KENYA	1969	1970	1971	1972	1973	1974	1975	1976	1977	1978	1979
FOREIGN TRADE (CUSTOMS BASIS)					*(Millions of current US dollars)*						
Value of Exports, fob	272.0	305.0	314.0	372.0	516.0	661.0	647.0	824.0	1,195.0	1,023.0	1,107.0
Nonfuel Primary Products	216.6	230.4	228.7	284.1	402.7	460.1	427.4	483.8	842.6	682.6	709.6
Fuels	31.9	37.6	42.0	43.6	50.7	116.4	132.8	171.0	204.5	185.4	223.1
Manufactures	23.5	37.0	43.3	44.2	62.6	84.4	86.9	169.2	147.9	155.0	174.2
Value of Imports, cif	360.0	442.0	560.0	554.0	655.0	1,026.0	987.0	923.0	1,285.6	1,705.9	1,655.5
Nonfuel Primary Products	31.4	43.1	68.0	72.1	89.3	109.4	87.3	106.3	130.4	172.1	154.2
Fuels	40.1	45.3	51.0	63.8	72.7	236.6	278.2	237.5	286.1	307.5	395.8
Manufactures	288.4	353.5	441.0	418.0	493.0	680.0	621.5	579.2	869.1	1,226.3	1,105.5
					(Index 1987 = 100)						
Terms of Trade	111.9	108.5	99.7	115.1	126.6	130.6	112.6	139.6	174.6	138.6	136.5
Export Prices, fob	23.9	24.7	26.2	31.9	44.0	68.8	63.4	81.1	109.3	96.3	113.5
Import Prices, cif	21.4	22.8	26.3	27.7	34.8	52.7	56.2	58.1	62.6	69.5	83.2
BALANCE OF PAYMENTS					*(Millions of current US dollars)*						
Exports of Goods & Services	..	505.5	529.0	580.7	706.0	971.4	1,011.1	1,142.9	1,593.9	1,543.6	1,629.4
Merchandise, fob	..	285.5	293.7	337.4	469.9	581.0	633.2	745.9	1,130.9	956.0	1,031.4
Nonfactor Services	..	172.8	200.8	207.2	209.2	352.0	321.5	361.7	422.2	540.3	537.5
Factor Services	..	47.2	34.5	36.2	26.8	38.4	56.4	35.4	40.8	47.4	60.5
Imports of Goods & Services	..	580.1	699.0	686.9	861.9	1,310.6	1,280.0	1,281.7	1,632.8	2,295.1	2,219.0
Merchandise, fob	..	371.8	478.6	454.3	544.8	897.9	846.9	809.7	1,112.8	1,631.8	1,594.2
Nonfactor Services	..	138.2	161.3	162.4	188.2	273.4	283.8	294.6	320.9	428.4	376.6
Factor Services	..	70.1	59.1	70.2	128.9	139.4	149.3	177.4	199.1	234.9	248.3
Long-Term Interest	..	17.4	17.7	19.7	29.3	41.0	46.5	50.3	63.0	89.2	121.4
Private Current Transfers, net	..	-11.2	-12.9	-1.4	-8.7	-13.7	-12.5	-19.6	3.4	16.3	10.7
Workers' Remittances	..	..	..	..	..	..	..	..	..	..	..
Curr. A/C Bal before Off. Transf.	..	-85.8	-182.9	-107.6	-164.6	-353.0	-281.3	-158.4	-35.5	-735.2	-579.0
Net Official Transfers	..	36.8	71.2	39.5	38.6	45.1	62.9	34.1	63.1	74.7	80.6
Curr. A/C Bal after Off. Transf.	..	-49.0	-111.7	-68.1	-126.0	-307.9	-218.4	-124.2	27.5	-660.5	-498.4
Long-Term Capital, net	..	50.1	36.8	71.9	129.7	184.6	156.3	222.1	189.5	416.5	488.3
Direct Investment	..	13.8	12.4	..	..	..	15.8	42.1	53.9	32.1	78.1
Long-Term Loans	..	47.0	28.8	87.2	185.7	223.8	113.8	211.8	158.3	481.8	407.0
Disbursements	..	75.8	63.5	114.8	221.3	281.1	204.5	319.0	382.6	617.2	565.9
Repayments	..	28.8	34.7	27.6	35.6	57.3	90.7	107.2	224.3	135.4	158.9
Other Long-Term Capital	..	-10.7	-4.4	-15.3	-56.0	-39.2	26.7	-31.8	-22.7	-97.4	3.2
Other Capital, net	..	44.3	4.4	20.0	18.0	35.2	24.4	-12.2	59.7	44.0	200.7
Change in Reserves	..	-45.4	70.5	-23.8	-21.7	88.1	37.7	-85.7	-276.7	200.1	-190.6
Memo Item:					*(Kenya Shillings per US dollar)*						
Conversion Factor (Annual Avg)	7.140	7.140	7.140	7.140	7.000	7.140	7.340	8.370	8.280	7.730	7.480
EXTERNAL DEBT (Total)					*(Millions of US dollars), outstanding at end of year*						
	..	406.1	420.8	492.6	723.3	999.8	1,108.4	1,304.2	1,746.4	2,323.0	2,887.4
Long-Term Debt (by debtor)	..	406.1	420.8	492.6	723.3	999.8	1,108.4	1,304.2	1,443.4	1,920.0	2,458.4
Central Bank, incl. IMF credit	..	0.0	0.0	0.0	0.0	40.4	84.0	108.3	78.2	115.0	219.1
Central Government	..	283.7	293.1	330.3	381.8	439.7	476.2	528.9	709.6	806.8	1,192.0
Rest of General Government	..	2.6	3.7	4.4	4.3	4.3	4.1	4.0	3.8	3.7	3.6
Non-financial Public Enterprises	..	31.5	41.6	50.2	119.1	129.6	122.5	198.1	320.5	489.6	524.5
Priv. Sector, incl non-guaranteed	..	88.3	82.4	107.7	218.1	385.8	421.6	464.9	331.3	504.9	519.2
Short-Term Debt	..	0.0	0.0	0.0	0.0	0.0	0.0	0.0	303.0	403.0	429.0
Memo Items:					*(Millions of US dollars)*						
Int'l Reserves Excluding Gold	169.66	219.83	170.95	201.99	233.04	193.28	173.40	275.52	522.39	352.58	627.71
Gold Holdings (at market price)	..	..	..	..	0.00	0.01	0.00	0.00	3.39	16.25	40.83
SOCIAL INDICATORS											
Total Fertility Rate	8.0	8.0	8.0	8.0	8.0	8.0	8.1	8.1	8.1	8.1	8.0
Infant Mortality Rate	104.0	102.0	100.0	98.0	96.0	94.0	92.0	90.0	88.0	86.4	84.8
Life Expectancy at Birth	49.5	50.0	50.5	51.0	51.5	52.0	52.5	53.0	53.5	53.9	54.4
Urban Population, % of total	10.0	10.3	10.8	11.3	11.9	12.4	12.9	13.5	14.2	14.8	15.5
Food Prod. per capita (1987=100)	126.3	124.2	121.1	122.1	121.9	117.0	119.0	118.5	120.4	114.4	109.4
Labor Force, Agriculture (%)	85.0	84.8	84.4	84.0	83.6	83.2	82.9	82.5	82.1	81.7	81.3
Labor Force, Female (%)	42.4	42.4	42.3	42.3	42.2	42.2	42.1	42.1	42.0	42.0	41.9
Primary Schl. Enroll. Ratio	..	58.0	..	..	..	..	95.0	97.0	95.0	91.0	108.0
Primary Schl. Enroll. Ratio, Female	..	48.0	..	..	..	..	87.0	90.0	88.0	85.0	101.0
Secondary Schl. Enroll. Ratio	..	9.0	..	..	..	..	13.0	15.0	17.0	18.0	18.0

1980	1981	1982	1983	1984	1985	1986	1987	1988	1989 estimate	NOTES	KENYA
											FOREIGN TRADE (CUSTOMS BASIS)
				(Millions of current US dollars)							
1,389.0	1,183.0	1,045.0	979.0	1,083.0	987.6	1,216.8	960.6	1,071.0	1,114.9	f	Value of Exports, fob
734.1	654.7	587.7	645.0	766.7	708.3	931.1	621.4	715.1	..	..	Nonfuel Primary Products
444.6	374.8	263.3	206.0	198.5	155.9	134.8	174.8	173.3	..	..	Fuels
210.4	153.5	194.0	128.0	117.8	123.4	150.9	164.4	182.6	199.8	..	Manufactures
2,589.9	2,081.3	1,603.0	1,390.0	1,529.4	1,455.1	1,649.1	1,755.0	1,975.0	1,944.9	f	Value of Imports, cif
265.3	184.2	167.2	186.6	228.6	193.3	210.2	154.1	312.1	..	..	Nonfuel Primary Products
877.1	776.8	595.3	523.9	488.5	461.4	300.0	357.5	442.8	..	..	Fuels
1,447.6	1,120.4	840.6	679.5	812.3	800.4	1,138.8	1,243.4	1,220.1	..	..	Manufactures
				(Index 1987 = 100)							
124.2	113.3	107.1	109.1	124.6	111.9	134.3	100.0	104.0	..	f	Terms of Trade
129.3	123.0	112.2	113.0	124.6	108.6	119.7	100.0	105.5	..	f	Export Prices, fob
104.1	108.6	104.8	103.6	100.0	97.0	89.1	100.0	101.4	..	f	Import Prices, cif
											BALANCE OF PAYMENTS
				(Millions of current US dollars)							
2,061.3	1,798.6	1,630.0	1,524.8	1,663.1	1,606.6	1,902.3	1,738.6	1,879.8	1,934.6	f	Exports of Goods & Services
1,261.4	1,081.3	935.5	926.0	1,034.5	943.2	1,170.2	908.7	1,017.5	926.1	..	Merchandise, fob
745.9	680.3	672.6	569.6	589.6	625.2	695.1	784.3	854.2	984.6	..	Nonfactor Services
53.9	37.0	21.9	28.7	39.0	38.2	36.9	45.6	8.1	23.9	..	Factor Services
3,094.7	2,575.1	2,067.5	1,752.6	1,966.0	1,911.1	2,147.6	2,447.2	2,680.0	2,904.6	f	Imports of Goods & Services
2,344.8	1,834.0	1,467.7	1,197.9	1,348.2	1,269.8	1,454.6	1,622.6	1,802.2	1,963.4	..	Merchandise, fob
501.6	503.0	398.4	341.5	377.0	359.5	415.2	502.9	530.0	598.9	..	Nonfactor Services
248.2	238.1	201.4	213.2	240.8	281.8	277.8	321.7	347.8	342.3	..	Factor Services
174.5	172.1	185.9	167.2	166.9	178.4	199.7	226.6	207.7	190.7	..	Long-Term Interest
27.2	98.6	83.3	63.4	60.1	81.5	58.2	72.0	89.0	101.5	..	Private Current Transfers, net
0.0	0.0	0.0	0.0	0.0	0.0	0.0	0.0	0.0	..	..	Workers' Remittances
-1,006.2	-677.9	-354.2	-164.4	-242.8	-223.0	-187.1	-636.6	-711.2	-868.4	..	Curr. A/C Bal before Off. Transf.
120.2	119.5	52.1	119.4	119.5	112.7	150.5	142.6	257.1	281.1	..	Net Official Transfers
-886.0	-558.4	-302.1	-44.9	-123.4	-110.3	-36.6	-494.0	-454.2	-587.4	..	Curr. A/C Bal after Off. Transf.
532.2	302.4	51.8	109.5	126.6	-45.0	109.0	259.0	314.0	609.8	f	Long-Term Capital, net
77.9	8.3	3.4	9.2	3.9	12.7	27.8	40.7	-19.4	68.8	..	Direct Investment
405.0	218.6	240.3	235.7	225.0	86.5	305.3	219.6	228.7	250.1	..	Long-Term Loans
615.9	468.2	502.5	503.5	536.7	428.1	645.2	530.8	526.8	490.7	..	Disbursements
210.9	249.6	262.2	267.8	311.7	341.6	339.9	311.2	298.1	240.6	..	Repayments
49.3	75.5	-191.9	-135.4	-102.3	-144.2	-224.1	-1.3	104.7	290.9	..	Other Long-Term Capital
152.3	66.9	92.7	34.7	56.4	99.4	56.3	199.1	86.6	141.6	f	Other Capital, net
201.5	189.1	157.6	-99.4	-59.7	56.0	-128.8	35.9	53.6	-164.1	..	Change in Reserves
											Memo Item:
				(Kenya Shillings per US dollar)							
7.420	9.050	10.920	13.310	14.410	16.430	16.230	16.450	17.750	20.570	..	Conversion Factor (Annual Avg)
				(Millions of US dollars), outstanding at end of year							
											EXTERNAL DEBT (Total)
3,530.1	3,405.1	3,540.1	3,787.4	3,689.0	4,308.5	4,833.9	5,787.0	5,730.6	5,689.8	..	Long-Term Debt (by debtor)
2,888.7	2,935.2	3,202.0	3,381.3	3,315.6	3,833.5	4,456.1	5,178.7	5,166.7	5,048.8	..	Central Bank, incl. IMF credit
288.2	297.1	439.8	511.9	464.3	572.7	515.7	467.1	515.1	468.1	..	Central Bank, incl. IMF credit
1,517.0	1,655.1	1,787.7	1,823.4	2,017.8	2,264.1	2,821.9	3,402.7	3,289.1	3,248.0	..	Central Government
3.4	3.2	3.0	2.8	2.6	2.4	2.2	2.0	1.9	1.7	..	Rest of General Government
557.4	541.5	527.6	498.8	368.1	449.2	625.2	776.3	700.9	670.5	..	Non-financial Public Enterprises
522.7	438.3	443.9	544.4	462.8	545.1	491.1	530.6	659.7	660.5	..	Priv. Sector, incl non-guaranteed
641.4	469.9	338.1	406.1	373.4	475.0	377.8	608.3	563.9	641.0	..	Short-Term Debt
				(Millions of US dollars)							
											Memo Items:
491.70	231.13	211.67	376.00	389.80	390.65	413.32	255.80	263.74	284.65	..	Int'l Reserves Excluding Gold
47.01	31.70	36.44	30.42	24.59	26.08	31.17	38.61	32.72	31.98	..	Gold Holdings (at market price)
											SOCIAL INDICATORS
8.0	8.0	7.9	7.7	7.6	7.4	7.2	7.0	6.9	6.8	..	Total Fertility Rate
83.2	81.6	80.0	78.4	76.8	75.2	73.6	72.0	70.4	68.7	..	Infant Mortality Rate
54.9	55.4	55.9	56.4	56.9	57.4	57.9	58.5	58.7	59.0	..	Life Expectancy at Birth
16.1	16.8	17.5	18.3	19.0	19.7	20.7	21.7	22.3	23.0	..	Urban Population, % of total
100.6	95.2	106.4	105.7	84.6	99.2	107.7	100.0	104.0	104.4	..	Food Prod. per capita (1987=100)
81.0	..	..	..	..	..	..	..	..	..	..	Labor Force, Agriculture (%)
41.9	41.6	41.4	41.3	41.1	40.9	40.7	40.5	40.3	40.1	..	Labor Force, Female (%)
115.0	..	107.0	105.0	107.0	98.0	97.0	96.0	..	..	..	Primary Schl. Enroll. Ratio
110.0	..	102.0	101.0	104.0	96.0	94.0	93.0	..	..	..	Primary Schl. Enroll. Ratio, Female
20.0	..	18.0	20.0	21.0	21.0	21.0	23.0	..	..	..	Secondary Schl. Enroll. Ratio

KOREA, REPUBLIC OF	1969	1970	1971	1972	1973	1974	1975	1976	1977	1978	1979
CURRENT GNP PER CAPITA (US $)	230	270	310	330	390	480	580	750	910	1,190	1,520
POPULATION (thousands)	31,249	31,923	32,596	33,266	33,935	34,606	35,281	35,849	36,412	36,969	37,534

USE AND ORIGIN OF RESOURCES *(Billions of current Korean Won)*

	1969	1970	1971	1972	1973	1974	1975	1976	1977	1978	1979
Gross National Product (GNP)	2,155	2,777	3,407	4,177	5,356	7,564	10,065	13,818	17,729	23,937	30,741
Net Factor Income from Abroad	25	17	-3	-16	-41	-67	-159	-177	-257	-306	-483
GDP at Market Prices	2,130	2,760	3,410	4,194	5,397	7,631	10,224	13,996	17,985	24,243	31,224
Resource Balance	-254	-269	-354	-194	-155	-833	-873	-176	37	-726	-2,265
Exports of Goods & NFServices	288	389	524	836	1,602	2,140	2,855	4,446	5,848	7,336	8,563
Imports of Goods & NFServices	542	658	878	1,031	1,757	2,973	3,728	4,621	5,811	8,062	10,829
Domestic Absorption	2,384	3,028	3,763	4,388	5,552	8,464	11,097	14,171	17,948	24,969	33,489
Private Consumption, etc.	1,542	2,082	2,573	3,092	3,779	5,321	7,208	9,105	11,125	14,844	19,356
General Gov't Consumption	221	263	334	425	452	734	1,121	1,521	1,919	2,501	3,059
Gross Domestic Investment	621	683	857	871	1,321	2,408	2,767	3,545	4,904	7,624	11,074
Fixed Investment	556	687	765	853	1,243	1,940	2,550	3,365	4,840	7,488	10,191
Indirect Taxes, net	202	255	302	332	409	605	986	1,433	1,867	2,620	3,469
GDP at factor cost	1,929	2,505	3,108	3,862	4,988	7,026	9,238	12,563	16,118	21,622	27,755
Agriculture	595	718	906	1,096	1,322	1,857	2,504	3,244	3,958	4,890	5,878
Industry	616	805	974	1,228	1,728	2,485	3,431	4,856	6,470	9,297	12,502
Manufacturing	433	584	725	939	1,356	1,984	2,676	3,869	4,943	6,788	8,949
Services, etc.	920	1,237	1,530	1,870	2,346	3,289	4,289	5,896	7,557	10,056	12,845
Gross Domestic Saving	367	414	503	677	1,166	1,575	1,894	3,370	4,941	6,897	8,809
Gross National Saving	..	461	537	708	1,186	1,571	1,811	3,286	4,767	6,802	8,519

(Billions of 1987 Korean Won)

	1969	1970	1971	1972	1973	1974	1975	1976	1977	1978	1979
Gross National Product	23,291	25,280	27,678	29,238	33,612	36,552	39,057	44,421	49,194	54,641	58,493
GDP at Market Prices	23,077	25,131	27,645	29,258	33,714	36,707	39,519	44,851	49,788	55,232	59,344
Resource Balance	-2,284	-2,192	-2,594	-1,419	-1,058	-2,545	-1,384	-236	54	-2,107	-4,467
Exports of Goods & NFServices	2,388	2,855	3,458	4,703	7,196	7,140	8,499	12,023	14,818	16,677	16,488
Imports of Goods & NFServices	4,672	5,048	6,052	6,122	8,254	9,686	9,883	12,259	14,764	18,784	20,955
Domestic Absorption	25,361	27,323	30,239	30,677	34,772	39,253	40,903	45,088	49,733	57,338	63,812
Private Consumption, etc.	15,798	17,626	19,727	20,319	22,866	24,311	25,666	28,225	29,581	32,292	35,884
General Gov't Consumption	3,613	3,852	4,205	4,448	4,420	5,130	5,718	5,928	6,362	7,148	7,177
Gross Domestic Investment	5,950	5,845	6,307	5,910	7,486	9,811	9,518	10,935	13,790	17,898	20,751
Fixed Investment	5,144	5,194	5,345	5,388	6,684	7,663	8,243	9,832	12,597	16,765	18,203
GDP at factor cost	14,609	22,778	25,167	26,919	31,147	33,788	35,704	40,264	44,629	49,275	52,769
Agriculture	7,885	7,775	8,037	8,200	8,783	9,407	9,800	10,795	11,114	10,014	10,751
Industry	5,061	5,823	6,499	7,079	8,893	10,165	11,387	13,674	15,994	19,460	21,079
Manufacturing	2,839	3,404	4,035	4,582	5,906	6,857	7,680	9,554	11,015	13,364	14,772
Services, etc.	11,131	12,442	14,036	14,860	16,718	17,762	18,921	20,885	23,116	26,042	27,776

Memo Items:

	1969	1970	1971	1972	1973	1974	1975	1976	1977	1978	1979
Capacity to Import	2,481	2,986	3,614	4,967	7,525	6,973	7,569	11,793	14,859	17,091	16,572
Terms of Trade Adjustment	93	131	156	265	329	-167	-930	-230	40	414	84
Gross Domestic Income	23,170	25,261	27,801	29,523	34,043	36,540	38,589	44,622	49,828	55,646	59,428
Gross National Income	23,384	25,410	27,834	29,503	33,941	36,385	38,127	44,192	49,234	55,055	58,577

DOMESTIC PRICES/DEFLATORS *(Index 1987 = 100)*

	1969	1970	1971	1972	1973	1974	1975	1976	1977	1978	1979
Overall (GDP)	9.2	11.0	12.3	14.3	16.0	20.8	25.9	31.2	36.1	43.9	52.6
Domestic Absorption	9.4	11.1	12.4	14.3	16.0	21.6	27.1	31.4	36.1	43.5	52.5
Agriculture	7.5	9.2	11.3	13.4	15.1	19.7	25.5	30.0	35.6	48.8	54.7
Industry	12.2	13.8	15.0	17.3	19.4	24.5	30.1	35.5	40.5	47.8	59.3
Manufacturing	15.3	17.2	18.0	20.5	23.0	28.9	34.8	40.5	44.9	50.8	60.6
Consumer Price Index	12.8	14.9	16.9	18.8	19.4	24.2	30.3	34.9	38.4	44.0	52.0

MANUFACTURING ACTIVITY

	1969	1970	1971	1972	1973	1974	1975	1976	1977	1978	1979
Employment (1987=100)	26.8	28.0	27.6	32.1	38.2	43.2	47.3	57.3	64.1	70.5	70.7
Real Earnings per Empl. (1987=100)	28.1	30.1	31.5	31.9	38.2	39.7	41.6	46.1	54.1	65.4	72.5
Real Output per Empl. (1987=100)	22.4	24.3	29.6	29.9	37.0	40.7	43.3	44.2	47.1	51.9	54.7
Earnings as % of Value Added	24.9	25.0	23.3	23.5	22.5	23.2	23.6	24.8	26.1	27.1	31.2

MONETARY HOLDINGS *(Billions of current Korean Won)*

	1969	1970	1971	1972	1973	1974	1975	1976	1977	1978	1979
Money Supply, Broadly Defined	782	990	1,224	1,632	2,191	2,682	3,379	4,511	6,256	8,374	10,484
Money	252	308	358	519	730	946	1,182	1,544	2,173	2,714	3,275
Currency Outside Banks	111	134	162	218	311	411	507	677	953	1,364	1,604
Demand Deposits	141	174	196	302	419	535	675	867	1,219	1,349	1,671
Quasi-Money	530	683	866	1,112	1,461	1,737	2,197	2,967	4,083	5,660	7,209

GOVERNMENT DEFICIT (-) OR SURPLUS *(Billions of current Korean Won)*

	1969	1970	1971	1972	1973	1974	1975	1976	1977	1978	1979
	..	..	-10	-161	-27	-165	-201	-192	-316	-300	-545
Current Revenue	..	440	530	577	675	1,026	1,552	2,314	2,938	4,084	5,376
Current Expenditure	..	..	413	537	574	895	1,258	1,790	2,362	3,196	4,205
Current Budget Balance	..	..	117	40	101	131	294	524	576	888	1,171
Capital Receipts	..	9	8	8	20	13	13	14	20	24	70
Capital Payments	..	..	135	209	148	309	508	730	912	1,212	1,786

1980	1981	1982	1983	1984	1985	1986	1987	1988	1989 estimate	NOTES	KOREA, REPUBLIC OF
1,620	1,830	1,930	2,110	2,240	2,320	2,570	2,950	3,600	4,400	..	**CURRENT GNP PER CAPITA (US $)**
38,124	38,723	39,326	39,910	40,406	40,806	41,184	41,575	41,975	42,380	..	**POPULATION (thousands)**
				(Billions of current Korean Won)							**USE AND ORIGIN OF RESOURCES**
36,750	45,528	52,182	61,722	70,084	78,088	90,544	105,630	123,579	141,066	..	Gross National Product (GNP)
-1,291	-1,954	-2,261	-2,111	-2,560	-2,758	-2,827	-2,404	-1,730	-1,201	..	Net Factor Income from Abroad
38,041	47,482	54,443	63,833	72,644	80,847	93,371	108,034	125,309	142,267	f	GDP at Market Prices
-2,831	-2,378	-1,404	-300	87	1,018	5,669	8,695	10,681	3,923	..	Resource Balance
12,944	17,341	18,769	22,748	26,126	27,937	36,034	45,051	51,095	48,714	..	Exports of Goods & NFServices
15,774	19,719	20,174	23,049	26,039	26,919	30,365	36,356	40,414	44,791	..	Imports of Goods & NFServices
40,872	49,860	55,847	64,133	72,557	79,829	87,702	99,339	114,628	138,343	..	Domestic Absorption
24,414	30,352	34,029	38,920	43,629	48,020	51,443	57,044	64,499	74,630	..	Private Consumption, etc.
4,387	5,515	6,255	6,852	7,263	8,136	9,401	10,708	12,763	14,593	..	General Gov't Consumption
12,071	13,994	15,563	18,361	21,666	23,673	26,858	31,586	37,366	49,121	..	Gross Domestic Investment
12,226	13,275	15,446	18,669	20,998	22,837	25,764	30,738	36,087	44,778	..	Fixed Investment
4,539	5,658	6,619	8,179	8,752	9,407	10,872	12,548	14,582	16,353	..	Indirect Taxes, net
33,503	41,824	47,824	55,653	63,892	71,439	82,499	95,486	110,727	125,914	B f	GDP at factor cost
5,677	7,431	7,989	8,678	9,392	10,352	10,729	11,353	13,577	14,546	..	Agriculture
15,728	19,305	21,964	26,542	30,847	33,839	40,019	46,963	54,209	62,611	..	Industry
11,298	14,199	15,908	19,106	22,375	24,530	29,566	34,783	39,655	44,460	..	Manufacturing
16,636	20,746	24,490	28,612	32,405	36,656	42,623	49,717	57,523	65,110	..	Services, etc.
9,241	11,615	14,159	18,061	21,753	24,691	32,527	40,281	48,047	53,044	..	Gross Domestic Saving
8,192	9,949	12,225	16,389	19,609	22,415	30,606	38,864	47,344	51,978	..	Gross National Saving
				(Billions of 1987 Korean Won)							
55,499	58,845	63,098	71,269	77,748	83,152	93,822	105,630	118,522	126,966	..	Gross National Product
57,393	61,337	65,853	73,790	80,603	86,177	96,777	108,034	120,197	127,946	f	GDP at Market Prices
-1,669	-84	221	1,826	2,112	3,531	6,605	8,695	10,153	952	..	Resource Balance
18,165	20,912	21,848	26,049	28,119	29,373	37,049	45,051	50,952	48,661	..	Exports of Goods & NFServices
19,835	20,996	21,627	24,223	26,006	25,842	30,445	36,356	40,800	47,709	..	Imports of Goods & NFServices
59,062	61,420	65,632	71,964	78,490	82,647	90,173	99,339	110,044	126,994	..	Domestic Absorption
34,964	36,574	39,404	43,011	46,345	49,112	52,708	57,044	62,386	68,840	..	Private Consumption, etc.
7,640	8,076	8,155	8,434	8,559	9,041	10,016	10,708	11,977	12,629	..	General Gov't Consumption
16,458	16,770	18,073	20,518	23,586	24,494	27,448	31,586	35,681	45,524	..	Gross Domestic Investment
16,299	15,633	17,252	20,320	22,542	23,602	26,175	30,738	34,353	40,597	..	Fixed Investment
50,546	54,040	57,864	64,378	70,920	76,178	85,528	95,486	106,207	113,601	B f	GDP at factor cost
8,609	9,838	10,570	11,388	11,218	11,639	12,176	11,353	12,371	12,172	..	Agriculture
20,913	22,324	24,149	28,242	32,468	34,716	40,316	46,963	52,465	55,919	..	Industry
14,608	16,052	17,127	19,764	23,191	24,840	29,401	34,783	39,322	41,034	..	Manufacturing
28,188	29,446	31,375	34,160	36,916	39,822	44,285	49,717	55,361	59,855	..	Services, etc.
											Memo Items:
16,276	18,463	20,121	23,908	26,093	26,819	36,128	45,051	51,582	51,889	..	Capacity to Import
-1,890	-2,449	-1,727	-2,141	-2,026	-2,554	-921	0	630	3,227	..	Terms of Trade Adjustment
55,503	58,888	64,127	71,649	78,577	83,624	95,856	108,034	120,827	131,173	..	Gross Domestic Income
53,609	56,397	61,371	69,128	75,722	80,598	92,901	105,630	119,153	130,194	..	Gross National Income
				(Index 1987 = 100)							**DOMESTIC PRICES/DEFLATORS**
66.3	77.4	82.7	86.5	90.1	93.8	96.5	100.0	104.3	111.2	..	Overall (GDP)
69.2	81.2	85.1	89.1	92.4	96.6	97.3	100.0	104.2	108.9	..	Domestic Absorption
65.9	75.5	75.6	76.2	83.7	88.9	88.1	100.0	109.7	119.5	..	Agriculture
75.2	86.5	91.0	94.0	95.0	97.5	99.3	100.0	103.3	112.0	..	Industry
77.3	88.5	92.9	96.7	96.5	98.8	100.6	100.0	100.8	108.4	..	Manufacturing
67.0	81.3	87.1	90.1	92.2	94.4	97.0	100.0	107.1	113.3	..	Consumer Price Index
											MANUFACTURING ACTIVITY
68.3	68.1	69.9	73.8	78.0	81.2	91.2	100.0	104.7	104.6	G	Employment (1987=100)
69.3	68.1	71.3	75.5	82.4	86.3	88.8	100.0	106.1	107.2	G	Real Earnings per Empl. (1987=100)
60.3	68.0	69.9	74.5	83.1	84.4	88.0	100.0	115.0	116.7	G	Real Output per Empl. (1987=100)
29.3	26.8	27.5	26.3	26.3	27.1	26.2	27.0	26.5	26.0	..	Earnings as % of Value Added
				(Billions of current Korean Won)							**MONETARY HOLDINGS**
13,622	17,153	21,680	24,972	27,320	32,640	38,892	49,202	62,634	80,616	D	Money Supply, Broadly Defined
3,807	3,982	5,799	6,783	6,821	7,558	8,809	10,107	12,152	14,328	..	Money
1,856	2,025	2,574	2,874	3,109	3,286	3,679	4,443	5,133	6,140	..	Currency Outside Banks
1,951	1,957	3,226	3,909	3,711	4,272	5,130	5,665	7,018	8,188	..	Demand Deposits
9,816	13,170	15,881	18,189	20,499	25,083	30,083	39,095	50,482	66,288	..	Quasi-Money
				(Billions of current Korean Won)							**GOVERNMENT DEFICIT (-) OR SURPLUS**
-849	-1,585	-1,656	-663	-841	-943	-86	478	2,009	..	..	Current Revenue
6,738	8,534	9,875	11,418	12,511	13,738	15,721	18,510	22,558	..	..	Current Expenditure
5,641	6,931	8,297	9,145	10,213	11,523	12,829	14,325	16,746	..	..	Current Budget Balance
1,097	1,603	1,578	2,273	2,298	2,215	2,892	4,185	5,812	..	..	Capital Receipts
96	71	108	120	93	185	119	148	332	..	..	Capital Payments
2,042	3,259	3,342	3,056	3,232	3,343	3,097	3,855	4,135			

KOREA, REPUBLIC OF	1969	1970	1971	1972	1973	1974	1975	1976	1977	1978	1979
FOREIGN TRADE (CUSTOMS BASIS)					*(Millions of current US dollars)*						
Value of Exports, fob	623	835	1,068	1,624	3,225	4,460	5,081	7,715	10,016	12,695	15,052
Nonfuel Primary Products	143	186	183	246	473	559	830	801	1,391	1,435	1,624
Fuels	5	9	11	18	35	108	104	145	117	41	29
Manufactures	475	641	873	1,360	2,717	3,794	4,147	6,770	8,509	11,219	13,398
Value of Imports, cif	1,823	1,983	2,394	2,522	4,240	6,844	7,271	8,764	10,803	14,966	20,296
Nonfuel Primary Products	667	761	907	860	1,569	2,243	2,199	2,394	2,960	3,748	5,292
Fuels	111	136	189	219	312	1,054	1,387	1,747	2,179	2,453	3,785
Manufactures	1,045	1,086	1,298	1,443	2,358	3,547	3,685	4,623	5,664	8,765	11,219
					(Index 1987 = 100)						
Terms of Trade	138.1	149.8	145.1	136.9	125.6	110.7	109.7	120.0	113.1	113.8	110.3
Export Prices, fob	35.4	39.1	40.5	41.1	50.7	62.6	64.1	71.3	72.3	79.6	94.5
Import Prices, cif	25.7	26.1	27.9	30.0	40.3	56.6	58.4	59.4	63.9	69.9	85.6
BALANCE OF PAYMENTS					*(Millions of current US dollars)*						
Exports of Goods & Services	..	1,379	1,617	2,226	4,135	5,353	5,882	9,457	13,073	17,161	19,530
Merchandise, fob	..	882	1,133	1,676	3,284	4,516	5,003	7,814	10,046	12,711	14,705
Nonfactor Services	..	426	429	507	782	723	796	1,525	2,784	4,056	4,390
Factor Services	..	71	54	43	70	115	84	118	243	394	435
Imports of Goods & Services	..	2,180	2,633	2,764	4,631	7,600	7,996	10,113	13,284	18,717	24,120
Merchandise, fob	..	1,804	2,177	2,251	3,849	6,454	6,674	8,404	10,523	14,491	19,100
Nonfactor Services	..	300	336	354	568	818	869	1,190	2,022	3,193	3,502
Factor Services	..	76	119	159	214	329	452	519	739	1,033	1,518
Long-Term Interest	..	76	101	160	254	240	331	424	517	793	1,123
Private Current Transfers, net	..	95	105	119	155	154	158	193	170	434	399
Workers' Remittances	..	..	..	..	..	..	..	..	..	..	..
Curr. A/C Bal before Off. Transf.	..	-706	-911	-418	-342	-2,094	-1,956	-463	-41	-1,122	-4,191
Net Official Transfers	..	83	63	50	36	67	67	153	53	37	40
Curr. A/C Bal after Off. Transf.	..	-623	-848	-368	-306	-2,026	-1,889	-310	12	-1,085	-4,151
Long-Term Capital, net	..	558	641	501	524	891	1,350	1,332	1,400	2,111	3,071
Direct Investment	..	66	39	63	93	105	53	75	73	61	16
Long-Term Loans	..	271	536	622	662	1,019	1,351	1,361	1,604	2,425	3,404
Disbursements	..	476	774	906	1,090	1,398	1,769	1,935	2,416	3,687	5,128
Repayments	..	205	239	284	428	379	418	575	812	1,262	1,724
Other Long-Term Capital	..	221	67	-184	-230	-233	-54	-104	-277	-375	-349
Other Capital, net	..	113	167	9	132	964	904	291	-42	-295	1,954
Change in Reserves	..	-48	40	-141	-350	171	-365	-1,313	-1,370	-731	-874
Memo Item:					*(Korean Won per US dollar)*						
Conversion Factor (Annual Avg)	288.230	310.570	348.200	392.900	398.320	400.430	484.000	484.000	484.000	484.000	484.000
					(Millions of US dollars), outstanding at end of year						
EXTERNAL DEBT (Total)	..	1,991	2,570	3,203	3,924	5,091	6,489	7,983	14,343	17,301	22,886
Long-Term Debt (by debtor)	..	1,991	2,570	3,203	3,924	5,091	6,489	7,983	9,886	12,776	15,721
Central Bank, incl. IMF credit	..	117	222	230	218	484	817	936	999	949	1,287
Central Government	..	183	393	635	846	944	1,040	1,428	1,792	2,158	2,327
Rest of General Government	..	21	21	25	25	26	32	46	53	60	63
Non-financial Public Enterprises	..	443	516	664	837	987	1,081	1,270	1,589	2,148	2,698
Priv. Sector, incl non-guaranteed	..	1,227	1,419	1,650	1,998	2,650	3,519	4,303	5,453	7,461	9,346
Short-Term Debt	..	0	0	0	0	0	0	0	4,457	4,525	7,165
Memo Items:					*(Millions of US dollars)*						
Int'l Reserves Excluding Gold	550	606	434	523	885	277	781	1,970	2,967	2,764	2,959
Gold Holdings (at market price)	3	4	4	7	12	21	16	15	24	62	151
SOCIAL INDICATORS											
Total Fertility Rate	4.4	4.3	4.2	4.1	3.8	3.6	3.3	3.1	2.8	2.7	2.6
Infant Mortality Rate	53.0	51.0	49.0	47.0	44.6	42.2	39.8	37.4	35.0	34.0	33.0
Life Expectancy at Birth	59.2	59.9	60.7	61.4	62.3	63.1	63.9	64.7	65.5	66.0	66.4
Urban Population, % of total	39.0	40.7	42.2	43.6	45.1	46.5	48.0	49.8	51.6	53.3	55.1
Food Prod. per capita (1987=100)	99.3	94.1	93.4	91.8	92.6	97.0	106.2	114.7	120.2	125.8	124.6
Labor Force, Agriculture (%)	50.2	49.1	47.7	46.4	45.1	43.9	42.8	41.4	40.1	38.8	37.6
Labor Force, Female (%)	31.6	32.1	32.4	32.6	32.9	33.1	33.3	33.5	33.6	33.8	34.0
Primary Schl. Enroll. Ratio	..	103.0	..	..	..	..	107.0	108.0	107.0	109.0	109.0
Primary Schl. Enroll. Ratio, Female	..	103.0	..	..	..	..	107.0	109.0	107.0	109.0	109.0
Secondary Schl. Enroll. Ratio	..	42.0	..	..	..	..	56.0	61.0	64.0	68.0	75.0

1980	1981	1982	1983	1984	1985	1986	1987	1988	1989 estimate	NOTES	KOREA, REPUBLIC OF
				(Millions of current US dollars)							**FOREIGN TRADE (CUSTOMS BASIS)**
17,483	21,250	21,850	24,437	29,248	30,283	34,702	47,172	60,697	61,000	..	Value of Exports, fob
1,715	1,832	1,610	1,661	1,737	1,685	2,153	2,870	3,615	..	..	Nonfuel Primary Products
46	181	285	536	805	929	618	723	584	..	..	Fuels
15,722	19,237	19,955	22,240	26,707	27,669	31,931	43,579	56,498	56,100	..	Manufactures
22,228	26,028	24,236	26,174	30,609	31,119	31,518	40,925	51,811	58,000	..	Value of Imports, cif
5,978	6,965	5,440	5,820	6,319	5,910	6,586	8,743	11,964	..	..	Nonfuel Primary Products
6,648	7,775	7,593	6,958	7,274	7,333	5,024	5,993	5,987	..	..	Fuels
9,601	11,288	11,204	13,396	17,015	17,876	19,908	26,189	33,860	..	..	Manufactures
				(Index 1987 = 100)							
92.1	93.6	96.3	99.2	104.5	104.7	105.8	100.0	102.1	..	..	Terms of Trade
99.7	101.7	97.7	95.3	96.5	94.0	92.5	100.0	113.6	..	..	Export Prices, fob
108.3	108.7	101.4	96.1	92.3	89.7	87.5	100.0	111.3	..	..	Import Prices, cif
				(Millions of current US dollars)							**BALANCE OF PAYMENTS**
22,577	27,269	28,356	30,383	33,652	33,106	41,965	56,255	70,900	74,051	..	Exports of Goods & Services
17,214	20,671	20,879	23,204	26,335	26,442	33,913	46,244	59,648	61,408	..	Merchandise, fob
4,707	5,756	6,673	6,470	6,452	5,593	6,866	8,797	9,664	10,326	..	Nonfactor Services
656	842	804	709	865	1,071	1,186	1,214	1,588	2,317	..	Factor Services
28,347	32,416	31,505	32,581	35,565	34,571	38,387	47,619	58,187	69,243	..	Imports of Goods & Services
21,598	24,299	23,473	24,967	27,371	26,461	29,707	38,585	48,203	56,811	..	Merchandise, fob
4,057	4,419	4,152	4,151	4,192	4,094	4,598	5,397	6,829	9,354	..	Nonfactor Services
2,692	3,698	3,880	3,463	4,002	4,016	4,082	3,637	3,155	3,078	..	Factor Services
1,636	2,031	2,439	2,280	2,510	2,778	2,863	2,407	2,052	1,942	..	Long-Term Interest
399	422	447	566	516	555	1,028	1,199	1,404	200	..	Private Current Transfers, net
..	..	..	..	..	..	..	..	..	..	..	Workers' Remittances
-5,371	-4,725	-2,702	-1,632	-1,397	-910	4,606	9,835	14,117	5,008	..	Curr. A/C Bal before Off. Transf.
50	79	52	26	25	23	11	19	44	48	..	Net Official Transfers
-5,321	-4,646	-2,650	-1,606	-1,372	-887	4,617	9,854	14,161	5,056	..	Curr. A/C Bal after Off. Transf.
1,987	3,533	1,797	1,783	2,652	2,229	-2,571	-8,562	-3,407	-2,779	..	Long-Term Capital, net
-7	60	-76	-57	73	200	325	418	720	453	..	Direct Investment
2,426	3,821	2,423	3,397	3,476	2,649	-1,500	-9,365	-3,095	-1,707	..	Long-Term Loans
3,980	5,837	4,564	6,061	6,326	7,101	5,596	4,461	3,905	3,898	..	Disbursements
1,554	2,015	2,141	2,665	2,850	4,452	7,096	13,826	7,000	5,605	..	Repayments
-432	-348	-550	-1,557	-897	-620	-1,396	385	-1,032	-1,525	..	Other Long-Term Capital
3,645	784	858	-413	-720	-1,150	-1,969	812	-1,438	843	..	Other Capital, net
-311	329	-5	236	-560	-192	-77	-2,104	-9,316	-3,120	..	Change in Reserves
				(Korean Won per US dollar)							**Memo Item:**
607.430	681.030	731.080	775.750	805.980	870.020	881.450	822.570	731.470	671.460	..	Conversion Factor (Annual Avg)
			(Millions of US dollars), outstanding at end of year								
29,480	32,989	37,329	40,419	42,099	47,133	46,724	39,808	35,694	33,111	..	**EXTERNAL DEBT (Total)**
18,919	22,763	24,903	28,304	30,674	36,401	37,468	30,517	25,914	23,311	..	Long-Term Debt (by debtor)
1,974	3,260	3,883	4,303	5,653	7,140	6,924	3,821	2,576	1,457	..	Central Bank, incl. IMF credit
2,800	3,479	4,117	4,756	4,861	5,665	6,512	7,494	6,673	6,213	..	Central Government
73	119	133	367	601	840	907	915	854	757	..	Rest of General Government
3,581	4,115	4,692	5,194	5,660	6,382	6,690	5,595	4,849	4,161	..	Non-financial Public Enterprises
10,491	11,790	12,078	13,685	13,900	16,375	16,436	12,692	10,962	10,724	..	Priv. Sector, incl non-guaranteed
10,561	10,226	12,427	12,115	11,425	10,732	9,256	9,291	9,780	9,800	..	Short-Term Debt
				(Millions of US dollars)							**Memo Items:**
2,925	2,682	2,807	2,347	2,754	2,869	3,320	3,584	12,347	15,214	..	Int'l Reserves Excluding Gold
176	120	139	116	95	102	124	155	131	128	..	Gold Holdings (at market price)
											SOCIAL INDICATORS
2.6	2.5	2.4	2.3	2.2	2.0	1.9	1.8	1.8	1.8	..	Total Fertility Rate
32.0	31.0	30.0	29.0	28.0	27.0	26.0	25.0	24.3	23.5	..	Infant Mortality Rate
66.8	67.3	67.7	68.0	68.3	68.7	69.0	69.3	69.5	69.8	..	Life Expectancy at Birth
56.9	58.6	60.3	61.9	63.6	65.3	66.6	68.0	69.3	70.7	..	Urban Population, % of total
96.7	107.1	109.0	106.9	112.4	112.5	110.5	100.0	105.9	108.4	..	Food Prod. per capita (1987=100)
36.4	..	..	..	..	..	..	..	..	..	..	Labor Force, Agriculture (%)
34.1	34.1	34.1	34.0	34.0	34.0	34.0	33.9	33.9	33.9	..	Labor Force, Female (%)
110.0	..	..	103.0	99.0	96.0	98.0	101.0	104.0	..	..	Primary Schl. Enroll. Ratio
111.0	105.0	109.0	104.0	99.0	97.0	99.0	101.0	104.0	..	..	Primary Schl. Enroll. Ratio, Female
76.0	..	..	87.0	91.0	89.0	89.0	88.0	89.0	..	..	Secondary Schl. Enroll. Ratio

KUWAIT	1969	1970	1971	1972	1973	1974	1975	1976	1977	1978	1979
CURRENT GNP PER CAPITA (US $)	3,560	3,350	3,570	3,670	4,250	6,030	9,070	14,530	14,020	15,290	18,440
POPULATION (thousands)	690	744	796	845	894	947	1,007	1,073	1,144	1,218	1,296
USE AND ORIGIN OF RESOURCES					*(Millions of current Kuwaiti Dinars)*						
Gross National Product (GNP)	840.0	851.3	1,115.8	1,102.4	1,262.1	3,532.0	3,711.0	4,280.7	4,557.6	4,981.3	7,712.9
Net Factor Income from Abroad	-149.0	-175.0	-266.0	-361.6	-342.0	-281.0	224.0	441.0	506.0	717.0	873.0
GDP at Market Prices	989.0	1,026.3	1,381.8	1,464.0	1,604.1	3,813.0	3,487.0	3,839.7	4,051.6	4,264.3	6,839.9
Resource Balance	342.0	366.4	658.9	701.8	798.3	2,711.7	1,899.0	1,742.4	1,158.0	1,308.0	3,362.0
Exports of Goods & NFServices	628.0	613.9	916.8	1,004.3	1,153.9	3,239.5	2,806.0	2,992.4	2,918.0	3,008.0	5,333.0
Imports of Goods & NFServices	286.0	247.5	257.9	302.5	355.6	527.8	907.0	1,250.0	1,760.0	1,700.0	1,971.0
Domestic Absorption	647.0	659.9	722.9	762.2	805.8	1,101.3	1,588.0	2,097.3	2,893.6	2,956.3	3,477.8
Private Consumption, etc.	306.0	396.2	420.0	427.4	438.6	563.8	758.8	1,029.8	1,362.7	1,477.5	1,780.3
General Gov't Consumption	152.0	139.3	173.3	198.6	214.6	279.1	385.5	432.3	586.3	615.9	763.8
Gross Domestic Investment	189.0	124.4	129.6	136.2	152.6	258.4	443.7	635.2	944.6	862.9	933.7
Fixed Investment	170.0	126.5	126.6	127.3	145.8	221.7	417.6	563.1	815.2	793.9	789.6
Indirect Taxes, net	..	..	..	..	..	..	..	..	..	..	..
GDP at factor cost	..	..	..	..	..	..	..	..	..	..	..
Agriculture	5.0	2.9	3.2	3.8	4.7	5.9	8.8	10.3	7.7	10.0	11.8
Industry	636.0	689.7	995.3	1,018.3	1,118.7	3,254.1	2,727.8	2,876.5	2,882.3	2,984.3	5,201.1
Manufacturing	36.0	42.8	54.2	66.4	80.2	171.2	197.5	234.2	241.3	282.6	566.7
Services, etc.	348.0	333.7	383.3	441.9	480.7	553.0	750.4	952.9	1,161.6	1,270.0	1,627.0
Gross Domestic Saving	531.0	490.8	788.5	838.0	950.9	2,970.1	2,342.7	2,377.6	2,102.6	2,170.9	4,295.8
Gross National Saving	..	253.3	429.9	384.3	388.5	2,327.1	2,486.7	2,726.6	2,502.6	2,768.9	5,021.8
					(Millions of 1987 Kuwaiti Dinars)						
Gross National Product	6,046.8	6,093.3	6,409.8	6,364.6	6,527.5	6,879.4	7,189.9	8,188.0	8,209.5	9,159.3	10,107.0
GDP at Market Prices	7,826.7	8,075.7	8,720.6	9,239.1	9,018.4	8,127.7	7,422.1	8,074.4	8,019.9	8,622.0	9,854.6
Resource Balance	5,284.6	5,683.2	6,051.3	6,407.0	5,904.2	5,051.3	4,363.6	4,587.5	3,163.0	3,575.8	4,546.3
Exports of Goods & NFServices	5,638.2	5,999.2	6,362.8	6,762.8	6,311.6	5,558.7	5,137.9	5,592.4	5,233.5	5,613.7	6,770.0
Imports of Goods & NFServices	353.6	316.0	311.5	355.7	407.4	507.4	774.3	1,004.9	2,070.5	2,037.9	2,223.8
Domestic Absorption	..	1,894.5	1,964.3	2,025.1	2,004.9	2,352.3	3,099.3	3,797.0	4,879.5	4,718.3	5,010.7
Private Consumption, etc.	..	1,053.0	1,049.0	1,031.1	968.6	1,099.9	1,462.9	1,775.2	2,170.6	2,198.2	2,471.6
General Gov't Consumption	..	478.0	553.1	622.4	666.0	744.9	844.8	930.7	1,123.6	1,164.1	1,201.4
Gross Domestic Investment	440.5	363.5	362.1	371.6	370.3	507.6	791.6	1,091.1	1,585.3	1,356.0	1,337.7
Fixed Investment	..	..	..	..	..	..	..	..	..	..	..
GDP at factor cost	..	..	..	..	..	..	..	..	..	..	..
Agriculture	..	7.1	7.2	6.3	6.8	7.0	8.4	9.2	10.4	12.4	11.4
Industry	..	5,646.7	6,071.9	6,295.8	5,921.4	5,246.0	4,614.7	4,947.5	4,765.8	5,161.5	6,005.3
Manufacturing	..	..	..	..	..	..	..	..	532.6	610.8	607.0
Services, etc.	..	1,089.5	1,187.2	1,314.4	1,371.4	1,425.0	1,667.5	1,966.9	2,263.4	2,351.5	2,469.8
Memo Items:											
Capacity to Import	776.4	783.7	1,107.4	1,181.1	1,322.0	3,114.0	2,395.6	2,405.7	3,432.7	3,605.9	6,016.9
Terms of Trade Adjustment	-4,861.8	-5,215.4	-5,255.4	-5,581.7	-4,989.6	-2,444.7	-2,742.3	-3,186.7	-1,800.8	-2,007.8	-753.1
Gross Domestic Income	2,964.8	2,860.3	3,465.2	3,657.4	4,028.9	5,683.0	4,679.7	4,887.6	6,219.1	6,614.2	9,101.5
Gross National Income	1,184.9	877.9	1,154.4	782.9	1,537.9	4,434.7	4,447.6	5,001.2	6,408.8	7,151.6	9,353.9
DOMESTIC PRICES/DEFLATORS					*(Index 1987 = 100)*						
Overall (GDP)	12.6	12.7	15.8	15.8	17.8	46.9	47.0	47.6	50.5	49.5	69.4
Domestic Absorption	..	34.8	36.8	37.6	40.2	46.8	51.2	55.2	59.3	62.7	69.4
Agriculture	..	41.1	44.2	60.6	69.6	84.9	104.5	111.9	74.2	80.4	103.9
Industry	..	12.2	16.4	16.2	18.9	62.0	59.1	58.1	60.5	57.8	86.6
Manufacturing	..	..	..	..	..	..	..	..	45.3	46.3	93.4
Consumer Price Index	..	..	..	41.5	44.9	50.7	55.0	57.8	63.6	69.1	74.0
MANUFACTURING ACTIVITY											
Employment (1987=100)	..	..	..	..	..	..	..	..	..	..	..
Real Earnings per Empl. (1987=100)	..	..	..	..	..	..	..	..	..	..	..
Real Output per Empl. (1987=100)	..	..	..	..	..	..	..	..	..	..	..
Earnings as % of Value Added	17.5	12.2	14.5	26.3	27.5	18.1	24.8	19.6	24.6	24.7	19.5
MONETARY HOLDINGS					*(Millions of current Kuwaiti Dinars)*						
Money Supply, Broadly Defined	379.1	362.1	418.8	493.6	536.3	684.6	891.1	1,220.1	1,568.7	1,950.4	2,262.7
Money	107.6	95.2	107.7	142.0	172.4	195.6	290.3	393.7	490.7	636.4	669.4
Currency Outside Banks	44.3	44.8	50.4	57.1	71.1	81.7	101.7	129.1	150.9	177.0	215.9
Demand Deposits	63.3	50.4	57.3	84.9	101.3	113.9	188.6	264.6	339.8	459.4	453.5
Quasi-Money	271.5	266.9	311.1	351.6	363.9	489.0	600.8	826.4	1,078.0	1,314.0	1,593.3
GOVERNMENT DEFICIT (-) OR SURPLUS					*(Millions of current Kuwaiti Dinars)*						
	..	..	..	192.0	162.0	1,588.0	..	..	1,514.0	1,134.0	1,753.0
Current Revenue	..	..	..	608.0	694.0	2,724.0	..	..	2,989.0	3,045.0	3,643.0
Current Expenditure	..	..	..	303.0	368.0	737.0	..	..	989.0	1,045.0	1,117.0
Current Budget Balance	..	..	..	305.0	326.0	1,987.0	..	..	2,000.0	2,000.0	2,526.0
Capital Receipts	..	..	..	1.0	2.0	5.0	..	..	7.0	5.0	4.0
Capital Payments	..	..	..	114.0	166.0	404.0	..	..	493.0	871.0	777.0

1980	1981	1982	1983	1984	1985	1986	1987	1988	1989 estimate	NOTES	KUWAIT
17,790	20,150	18,980	18,540	17,500	15,010	15,710	14,680	14,630	16,380	..	**CURRENT GNP PER CAPITA (US $)**
1,375	1,451	1,524	1,593	1,655	1,712	1,791	1,873	1,958	2,020	..	**POPULATION (thousands)**
											USE AND ORIGIN OF RESOURCES
			(Millions of current Kuwaiti Dinars)								
9,051.2	9,122.8	7,921.3	7,585.2	7,850.8	7,305.3	7,178.0	7,658.5	7,564.0	9,365.5	..	Gross National Product (GNP)
1,310.1	2,137.0	1,709.0	1,451.0	1,470.0	1,387.0	2,180.0	1,504.0	1,978.0	2,449.1	..	Net Factor Income from Abroad
7,741.1	6,985.8	6,212.3	6,134.2	6,380.8	5,918.3	4,998.0	6,154.5	5,586.0	6,916.4	..	GDP at Market Prices
3,410.0	2,167.0	133.0	533.0	825.0	534.0	-249.0	961.5	267.0	840.4	..	Resource Balance
6,065.0	4,855.0	3,386.0	3,596.0	3,862.0	3,463.0	2,403.0	3,275.5	2,746.9	3,887.4	..	Exports of Goods & NFServices
2,655.0	2,688.0	3,253.0	3,063.0	3,037.0	2,929.0	2,652.0	2,314.0	2,479.9	3,047.0	..	Imports of Goods & NFServices
4,331.0	4,818.9	6,079.3	5,601.2	5,555.8	5,384.2	5,247.0	5,193.0	5,319.0	6,076.0	..	Domestic Absorption
2,388.5	2,663.9	3,317.0	2,795.7	2,878.7	2,668.4	2,677.0	2,813.0	3,008.0	3,206.0	..	Private Consumption, etc.
864.9	993.2	1,197.2	1,298.7	1,356.6	1,457.2	1,451.0	1,369.0	1,351.0	1,578.0	..	General Gov't Consumption
1,077.6	1,161.8	1,565.1	1,506.8	1,320.5	1,258.6	1,119.0	1,011.0	960.0	1,292.0	..	Gross Domestic Investment
972.6	1,072.8	1,436.0	1,525.1	1,306.3	1,295.5	1,096.0	..	..	..	..	Fixed Investment
..	..	..	..	..	..	..	..	..	..	..	Indirect Taxes, net
..	..	..	..	..	..	..	..	..	..	B	GDP at factor cost
14.0	24.0	28.5	28.4	34.9	39.3	51.5	56.7	63.8	70.0	..	Agriculture
5,794.6	4,798.7	3,335.6	3,688.4	3,975.5	3,559.4	2,554.4	2,841.3	2,646.0	3,842.6	..	Industry
427.3	415.1	307.9	374.9	300.3	377.2	555.5	586.6	583.0	597.0	..	Manufacturing
1,932.5	2,163.1	2,848.2	2,417.4	2,370.4	2,319.6	2,392.1	3,256.5	2,876.2	3,003.8	..	Services, etc.
4,487.7	3,328.7	1,698.1	2,039.8	2,145.5	1,792.7	870.0	1,972.5	1,227.0	2,132.4	..	Gross Domestic Saving
5,610.8	5,273.7	3,155.1	3,238.8	3,330.5	2,865.7	2,735.0	3,169.5	2,876.0	4,203.5	..	Gross National Saving
			(Millions of 1987 Kuwaiti Dinars)								
8,174.8	7,290.4	6,213.5	6,636.3	6,914.5	6,509.6	7,700.3	7,658.5	8,309.8	9,333.1	..	Gross National Product
7,670.1	6,098.1	5,327.8	5,858.2	6,122.3	5,758.1	6,148.0	6,154.5	6,698.6	7,400.4	H	GDP at Market Prices
1,825.8	784.1	-429.3	-37.5	183.2	-5.2	1,042.5	961.5	1,275.8	1,837.4	..	Resource Balance
4,678.9	3,444.0	2,450.5	2,902.1	3,188.5	2,906.3	3,263.9	3,275.5	3,588.2	4,505.7	..	Exports of Goods & NFServices
2,853.0	2,660.0	2,879.7	2,939.6	3,005.3	2,911.5	2,221.4	2,314.0	2,312.4	2,668.4	..	Imports of Goods & NFServices
5,779.9	5,906.4	6,996.2	6,294.9	6,223.1	5,937.4	4,851.0	5,193.0	4,473.7	3,551.8	..	Domestic Absorption
3,100.6	3,224.9	3,722.0	2,997.5	3,049.4	2,787.6	2,213.6	2,813.0	2,252.5	934.8	..	Private Consumption, etc.
1,279.1	1,269.3	1,447.7	1,518.3	1,565.3	1,616.6	1,520.6	1,369.0	1,281.8	1,416.3	..	General Gov't Consumption
1,400.2	1,412.2	1,826.5	1,779.1	1,608.5	1,533.2	1,116.7	1,011.0	939.4	1,200.7	..	Gross Domestic Investment
..	..	..	..	..	..	..	..	..	..	..	Fixed Investment
..	..	..	..	..	..	..	..	..	..	B H	GDP at factor cost
12.8	20.9	23.5	27.1	34.2	39.7	53.3	56.7	60.6	63.8	..	Agriculture
4,188.6	2,957.9	2,280.0	2,819.7	3,027.5	2,751.1	3,227.5	2,841.3	2,888.9	4,390.8	..	Industry
598.2	581.5	631.6	627.1	611.7	640.6	647.5	586.6	589.0	590.7	..	Manufacturing
2,936.2	3,099.1	3,338.4	3,011.4	3,060.6	2,967.4	2,867.2	3,256.5	3,749.1	2,945.8	..	Services, etc.
											Memo Items:
6,517.3	4,804.3	2,997.5	3,451.1	3,821.7	3,442.3	2,012.8	3,275.5	2,561.4	3,404.3	..	Capacity to Import
1,838.5	1,360.3	547.0	549.1	633.2	536.0	-1,251.0	0.0	-1,026.9	-1,101.4	..	Terms of Trade Adjustment
9,508.6	7,458.4	5,874.8	6,407.3	6,755.5	6,294.1	4,896.9	6,154.5	5,671.7	6,299.0	..	Gross Domestic Income
10,013.2	8,650.7	6,760.5	7,185.4	7,547.7	7,045.6	6,449.2	7,658.5	7,283.0	8,231.7	..	Gross National Income
											DOMESTIC PRICES/DEFLATORS
			(Index 1987 = 100)								
100.9	114.6	116.6	104.7	104.2	102.8	81.3	100.0	83.4	93.5	..	Overall (GDP)
74.9	81.6	86.9	89.0	89.3	90.7	108.2	100.0	118.9	171.1	..	Domestic Absorption
109.1	115.1	121.3	104.7	102.1	99.1	96.7	100.0	105.3	109.8	..	Agriculture
138.3	162.2	146.3	130.8	131.3	129.4	79.1	100.0	91.6	87.5	..	Industry
71.4	71.4	48.7	59.8	49.1	58.9	85.8	100.0	99.0	101.1	..	Manufacturing
79.1	84.9	91.5	95.8	97.0	98.4	99.3	100.0	101.5	104.9	..	Consumer Price Index
											MANUFACTURING ACTIVITY
..	..	..	..	..	..	..	..	..	..	G J	Employment (1987=100)
..	..	..	..	..	..	..	..	..	..	G J	Real Earnings per Empl. (1987=100)
..	..	..	..	..	..	..	..	..	..	G J	Real Output per Empl. (1987=100)
22.2	27.5	41.7	37.6	51.1	43.0	28.4	..	..	..	J	Earnings as % of Value Added
											MONETARY HOLDINGS
			(Millions of current Kuwaiti Dinars)								
2,857.6	3,866.0	4,182.7	4,367.8	4,475.8	4,435.3	4,546.9	4,762.1	5,067.5	5,276.8	..	Money Supply, Broadly Defined
720.8	1,290.2	1,247.6	1,179.6	968.1	943.9	979.3	1,035.7	958.0	938.8	..	Money
251.3	284.7	342.7	340.6	325.1	327.9	337.1	338.3	342.5	334.1	..	Currency Outside Banks
469.5	1,005.5	904.9	839.0	643.0	616.0	642.2	697.4	615.5	604.7	..	Demand Deposits
2,136.8	2,575.8	2,935.1	3,188.2	3,507.7	3,491.4	3,567.6	3,726.4	4,109.5	4,338.0	..	Quasi-Money
			(Millions of current Kuwaiti Dinars)								
4,545.0	3,025.0	566.0	492.0	780.0	501.0	1,690.0	..	..	..	C	**GOVERNMENT DEFICIT (-) OR SURPLUS**
6,916.0	6,338.0	4,272.0	4,145.0	4,358.0	3,794.0	4,744.0	..	..	..		Current Revenue
1,460.0	1,696.0	1,915.0	2,161.0	2,042.0	2,158.0	2,009.0	1,906.0	2,018.0	..		Current Expenditure
5,456.0	4,642.0	2,357.0	1,984.0	2,316.0	1,636.0	2,735.0	..	..	..		Current Budget Balance
7.0	13.0	8.0	10.0	9.0	12.0	7.0	..	19.0	..		Capital Receipts
918.0	1,630.0	1,799.0	1,502.0	1,545.0	1,147.0	1,052.0	..	..	..		Capital Payments

KUWAIT	1969	1970	1971	1972	1973	1974	1975	1976	1977	1978	1979
FOREIGN TRADE (CUSTOMS BASIS)					*(Millions of current US dollars)*						
Value of Exports, fob	1,372.0	1,901.4	2,572.7	3,056.4	3,784.7	10,954.1	9,186.0	9,838.2	9,753.9	10,427.5	18,404.0
Nonfuel Primary Products	20.5	22.6	23.2	28.4	45.5	48.1	46.4	71.2	76.4	84.1	134.3
Fuels	1,285.5	1,787.4	2,433.4	2,859.7	3,495.1	10,361.5	8,407.5	8,831.4	8,618.4	9,233.6	16,517.0
Manufactures	66.0	91.5	116.1	168.3	244.1	544.6	732.1	935.6	1,059.1	1,109.7	1,752.9
Value of Imports, cif	646.8	625.1	650.5	797.0	1,042.2	1,553.5	2,388.2	3,329.5	4,845.0	4,598.0	5,203.8
Nonfuel Primary Products	124.3	135.8	148.8	178.5	229.4	314.1	443.2	539.7	680.4	778.8	947.9
Fuels	6.0	4.4	6.0	7.9	9.7	18.7	14.1	24.9	34.6	27.2	36.1
Manufactures	516.6	484.9	495.7	610.6	803.2	1,220.7	1,930.9	2,764.9	4,130.0	3,792.0	4,219.9
					(Index 1987 = 100)						
Terms of Trade	28.0	26.1	32.2	33.1	39.1	126.2	115.2	124.2	124.2	107.2	129.3
Export Prices, fob	7.8	7.8	10.1	11.3	15.9	62.8	62.0	66.9	72.5	72.6	101.0
Import Prices, cif	27.8	29.8	31.4	34.2	40.7	49.7	53.9	53.8	58.3	67.7	78.1
BALANCE OF PAYMENTS					*(Millions of current US dollars)*						
Exports of Goods & Services	..	1,809	2,668	3,153	4,660	12,212	10,289	11,864	12,151	13,837	22,872
Merchandise, fob	..	1,693	2,272	2,558	3,826	10,959	8,485	9,621	9,562	10,234	18,114
Nonfactor Services	..	26	275	185	275	486	521	612	625	702	1,183
Factor Services	..	90	121	410	559	767	1,283	1,631	1,965	2,901	3,575
Imports of Goods & Services	..	781	841	1,509	2,038	2,514	3,289	4,398	6,341	6,475	7,552
Merchandise, fob	..	625	652	797	1,052	1,552	2,400	3,300	4,735	4,326	4,870
Nonfactor Services	..	69	73	317	477	621	759	975	1,406	1,854	2,265
Factor Services	..	87	116	395	509	341	131	123	199	295	416
Long-Term Interest	..	..	..	..	..	..	..	..	..	..	..
Private Current Transfers, net	..	-175	-260	-280	-743	-1,235	-276	-315	-370	-433	-532
Workers' Remittances	..	..	..	..	..	..	..	..	..	..	..
Curr. A/C Bal before Off. Transf.	..	853	1,567	1,364	1,879	8,463	6,723	7,152	5,440	6,930	14,788
Net Official Transfers	..	0	0	0	0	0	-793	-222	-879	-800	-756
Curr. A/C Bal after Off. Transf.	..	853	1,567	1,364	1,879	8,463	5,930	6,929	4,561	6,130	14,032
Long-Term Capital, net	..	-40	-90	27	24	126	-1,083	-913	-614	-505	-868
Direct Investment	..	..	-8	-40	-54	-484	-93	-109	-52	-95	-188
Long-Term Loans	..	..	..	..	..	..	..	..	..	..	..
Disbursements	..	..	..	..	..	..	..	..	..	..	..
Repayments	..	..	..	..	..	..	..	..	..	..	..
Other Long-Term Capital	..	-40	-82	67	78	610	-990	-804	-562	-411	-680
Other Capital, net	..	-792	-1,402	-1,316	-1,794	-7,728	-4,533	-5,769	-3,004	-6,067	-12,798
Change in Reserves	..	-21	-75	-75	-109	-861	-315	-247	-943	443	-366
Memo Item:					*(Kuwaiti Dinars per US dollar)*						
Conversion Factor (Annual Avg)	0.360	0.360	0.360	0.330	0.300	0.290	0.290	0.290	0.290	0.280	0.280
					(Millions of US dollars), outstanding at end of year						
EXTERNAL DEBT (Total)	..	..	..	..	..	..	..	..	..	..	..
Long-Term Debt (by debtor)	..	..	..	..	..	..	..	..	..	..	..
Central Bank, incl. IMF credit	..	..	..	..	..	..	..	..	..	..	..
Central Government	..	..	..	..	..	..	..	..	..	..	..
Rest of General Government	..	..	..	..	..	..	..	..	..	..	..
Non-financial Public Enterprises	..	..	..	..	..	..	..	..	..	..	..
Priv. Sector, incl non-guaranteed	..	..	..	..	..	..	..	..	..	..	..
Short-Term Debt	..	..	..	..	..	..	..	..	..	..	..
Memo Items:					*(Millions of US dollars)*						
Int'l Reserves Excluding Gold	95.9	117.1	193.7	269.0	380.8	1,249.2	1,491.5	1,701.8	2,883.1	2,500.4	2,870.1
Gold Holdings (at market price)	86.7	92.0	108.2	161.0	319.5	653.5	559.3	751.6	414.2	570.7	1,300.0
SOCIAL INDICATORS											
Total Fertility Rate	7.2	7.1	7.0	6.9	6.7	6.5	6.3	6.1	5.9	5.7	5.5
Infant Mortality Rate	46.6	42.4	38.2	34.0	31.8	29.6	27.4	25.2	23.0	23.3	23.6
Life Expectancy at Birth	65.5	66.1	66.7	67.3	67.7	68.2	68.6	69.1	69.5	70.0	70.4
Urban Population, % of total	77.8	77.8	79.0	80.2	81.4	82.6	83.8	85.1	86.4	87.6	88.9
Food Prod. per capita (1987=100)	..	..	..	..	..	..	..	..	..	..	..
Labor Force, Agriculture (%)	1.7	1.8	1.8	1.8	1.8	1.8	1.8	1.8	1.8	1.9	1.9
Labor Force, Female (%)	7.6	8.1	9.1	10.0	10.8	11.5	12.2	12.4	12.6	12.8	12.9
Primary Schl. Enroll. Ratio	..	89.0	..	..	..	..	92.0	97.0	100.0	98.0	98.0
Primary Schl. Enroll. Ratio, Female	..	76.0	..	..	..	..	85.0	92.0	94.0	93.0	95.0
Secondary Schl. Enroll. Ratio	..	63.0	..	..	..	..	66.0	74.0	74.0	73.0	74.0

KUWAIT

1980	1981	1982	1983	1984	1985	1986	1987	1988	1989 estimate	NOTES	KUWAIT
				(Millions of current US dollars)							**FOREIGN TRADE (CUSTOMS BASIS)**
19,663.0	16,044.0	10,864.0	11,504.0	11,623.0	10,487.0	7,383.0	8,466.0	7,661.0	..	..	Value of Exports, fob
153.6	219.8	196.8	117.9	148.0	121.0	151.6	177.1	237.0	..	..	Nonfuel Primary Products
17,385.0	13,371.0	8,219.0	9,947.0	10,395.0	9,475.0	6,382.0	7,261.7	6,750.0	..	f	Fuels
2,124.6	2,453.4	2,448.3	1,439.0	1,080.0	891.0	849.0	1,027.2	674.0	..	..	Manufactures
6,530.0	6,978.0	8,282.0	7,373.0	6,896.0	5,934.0	5,759.0	5,198.0	6,144.0	..	..	Value of Imports, cif
1,129.0	1,162.1	1,403.1	1,238.2	1,041.0	715.0	1,017.0	980.0	671.0	..	..	Nonfuel Primary Products
49.9	39.7	51.4	45.7	39.0	33.0	29.0	24.0	53.0	..	..	Fuels
5,375.3	5,767.3	6,828.9	6,036.3	5,816.0	5,186.0	4,713.0	4,194.0	5,420.0	..	..	Manufactures
				(Index 1987 = 100)							
174.6	180.0	158.5	161.0	174.2	174.5	86.2	100.0	77.2	..	..	Terms of Trade
148.3	152.5	130.8	131.4	137.5	137.0	79.0	100.0	84.0	..	..	Export Prices, fob
85.0	84.7	82.5	81.6	78.9	78.5	91.7	100.0	108.8	..	..	Import Prices, cif
				(Millions of current US dollars)							**BALANCE OF PAYMENTS**
27,344	25,819	18,450	18,029	18,847	16,791	16,380	15,119	16,493	21,550	..	Exports of Goods & Services
20,633	16,023	10,819	11,473	12,156	10,374	7,216	8,221	7,709	11,383	..	Merchandise, fob
1,225	1,392	941	868	888	1,137	1,053	1,030	1,158	1,328	..	Nonfactor Services
5,487	8,404	6,690	5,688	5,803	5,280	8,111	5,867	7,626	8,840	..	Factor Services
10,463	10,381	12,056	11,191	11,096	10,404	9,735	9,488	10,755	10,729	..	Imports of Goods & Services
6,756	6,736	7,811	6,889	6,553	5,662	5,272	4,945	6,064	5,746	..	Merchandise, fob
3,067	2,906	3,491	3,620	3,705	4,076	3,861	4,073	4,204	4,228	..	Nonfactor Services
640	739	754	683	838	665	602	470	487	756	..	Factor Services
..	..	..	..	..	..	..	..	..	..	..	Long-Term Interest
-692	-689	-875	-865	-963	-1,044	-1,084	-1,102	-1,179	-1,287	..	Private Current Transfers, net
..	..	..	..	..	..	..	..	..	..	..	Workers' Remittances
16,190	14,750	5,519	5,973	6,789	5,343	5,561	4,529	4,559	9,534	..	Curr. A/C Bal before Off. Transf.
-888	-972	-646	-686	-416	-529	-182	-158	-140	-211	..	Net Official Transfers
15,302	13,778	4,873	5,287	6,374	4,815	5,379	4,371	4,419	9,323	..	Curr. A/C Bal after Off. Transf.
-37	83	-243	-902	-1,074	-712	-1,975	-240	-620	-943	..	Long-Term Capital, net
-407	-151	-108	-240	-95	-70	-248	-115	-255	-507	..	Direct Investment
..	..	..	..	..	..	..	..	..	..	..	Long-Term Loans
..	..	..	..	..	..	..	..	..	..	..	Disbursements
..	..	..	..	..	..	..	..	..	..	..	Repayments
370	233	-136	-662	-980	-642	-1,728	-126	-366	-436	..	Other Long-Term Capital
-14,219	-13,574	-2,652	-5,372	-5,331	-3,558	-3,487	-5,977	-5,795	-7,126	..	Other Capital, net
-1,045	-286	-1,978	988	32	-545	83	1,847	1,996	-1,255	..	Change in Reserves
				(Kuwaiti Dinars per US dollar)							**Memo Item:**
0.270	0.280	0.290	0.290	0.300	0.300	0.290	0.280	0.280	0.290	..	Conversion Factor (Annual Avg)
			(Millions of US dollars), outstanding at end of year								**EXTERNAL DEBT (Total)**
..	..	..	..	..	..	..	..	..	..	..	Long-Term Debt (by debtor)
..	..	..	..	..	..	..	..	..	..	..	Central Bank, incl. IMF credit
..	..	..	..	..	..	..	..	..	..	..	Central Government
..	..	..	..	..	..	..	..	..	..	..	Rest of General Government
..	..	..	..	..	..	..	..	..	..	..	Non-financial Public Enterprises
..	..	..	..	..	..	..	..	..	..	..	Priv. Sector, incl non-guaranteed
..	..	..	..	..	..	..	..	..	..	..	Short-Term Debt
				(Millions of US dollars)							**Memo Items:**
3,928.5	4,067.5	5,913.2	5,192.1	4,590.2	5,470.7	5,501.1	4,141.6	1,923.5	3,101.9	..	Int'l Reserves Excluding Gold
1,496.7	1,009.3	1,160.1	968.6	782.8	830.3	992.5	1,229.1	1,041.6	1,018.1	..	Gold Holdings (at market price)
											SOCIAL INDICATORS
5.3	5.1	4.9	4.7	4.5	4.3	4.1	3.9	3.7	3.6	..	Total Fertility Rate
23.8	24.1	22.8	20.9	19.0	18.4	17.2	16.0	15.4	14.8	..	Infant Mortality Rate
70.8	71.2	71.6	71.9	72.3	72.6	72.9	73.2	73.5	73.7	..	Life Expectancy at Birth
90.2	90.9	91.6	92.3	93.0	93.7	94.1	94.5	94.8	95.2	..	Urban Population, % of total
..	..	..	..	..	..	..	..	..	..	f	Food Prod. per capita (1987=100)
1.9	..	..	..	..	..	..	..	..	..	..	Labor Force, Agriculture (%)
13.0	13.1	13.2	13.3	13.4	13.4	13.7	14.0	14.2	14.4	..	Labor Force, Female (%)
102.0	..	103.0	104.0	99.0	96.0	94.0	94.0	..	..	..	Primary Schl. Enroll. Ratio
100.0	100.0	101.0	102.0	97.0	94.0	92.0	92.0	..	..	..	Primary Schl. Enroll. Ratio, Female
80.0	..	82.0	82.0	86.0	86.0	83.0	82.0	..	..	..	Secondary Schl. Enroll. Ratio

LESOTHO	1969	1970	1971	1972	1973	1974	1975	1976	1977	1978	1979
CURRENT GNP PER CAPITA (US $)	80	100	110	110	150	200	230	250	290	330	360
POPULATION (thousands)	1,042	1,064	1,087	1,112	1,137	1,165	1,193	1,223	1,254	1,287	1,320

USE AND ORIGIN OF RESOURCES

(Millions of current Lesotho Maloti)

	1969	1970	1971	1972	1973	1974	1975	1976	1977	1978	1979
Gross National Product (GNP)	61.6	74.8	76.3	95.8	132.4	158.1	199.7	247.7	308.0	385.1	422.5
Net Factor Income from Abroad	11.9	22.3	25.8	31.5	44.6	60.1	89.1	119.3	139.9	153.3	178.2
GDP at Market Prices	49.7	52.5	50.5	64.3	87.8	98.0	110.6	128.4	168.1	231.8	244.3
Resource Balance	-17.9	-22.9	-29.5	-41.9	-56.6	-82.0	-98.6	-153.4	-167.3	-169.9	-246.4
Exports of Goods & NFServices	6.4	5.7	6.8	10.1	12.8	14.1	14.6	21.3	18.0	36.4	50.0
Imports of Goods & NFServices	24.3	28.6	36.3	52.0	69.4	96.1	113.2	174.7	185.3	206.3	296.4
Domestic Absorption	67.6	75.4	80.0	106.2	144.4	180.0	209.2	281.8	335.4	401.7	490.7
Private Consumption, etc.	56.0	63.2	63.7	85.6	116.0	146.9	167.2	210.5	264.2	300.7	353.7
General Gov't Consumption	6.1	6.2	8.3	10.8	12.1	15.8	21.3	24.9	29.2	40.9	52.4
Gross Domestic Investment	5.5	6.0	8.0	9.8	16.3	17.3	20.7	46.4	42.0	60.1	84.6
Fixed Investment	4.9	5.1	7.1	8.6	10.7	14.5	20.7	45.5	40.3	51.0	73.7
Indirect Taxes, net	3.7	4.7	4.4	5.2	10.9	14.0	13.2	14.3	23.6	46.3	28.8
GDP at factor cost	46.0	47.8	46.1	59.1	76.9	84.0	97.4	114.1	144.5	185.5	215.5
Agriculture	15.6	16.7	12.0	21.0	32.7	31.7	31.7	31.0	49.6	55.2	65.7
Industry	4.7	4.4	4.9	6.0	8.3	11.3	12.9	21.7	22.4	43.5	54.0
Manufacturing	1.8	2.1	2.4	2.8	3.9	4.8	5.6	6.2	7.2	10.1	11.9
Services, etc.	25.7	26.7	29.2	32.1	35.9	41.0	52.8	61.4	72.5	86.8	95.8
Gross Domestic Saving	-12.4	-16.9	-21.5	-32.1	-40.3	-64.7	-77.9	-107.0	-125.3	-109.8	-161.8
Gross National Saving	..	26.8	26.5	27.8	50.8	52.5	12.2	13.5	15.9	44.9	18.0

(Millions of 1987 Lesotho Maloti)

	1969	1970	1971	1972	1973	1974	1975	1976	1977	1978	1979
Gross National Product	364.02	426.32	471.12	506.39	655.20	754.61	808.49	914.17	1,060.49	1,152.23	1,168.19
GDP at Market Prices	262.79	268.51	285.01	312.27	405.68	450.23	389.39	432.41	526.72	623.19	641.23
Resource Balance	-148.81	-173.75	-214.97	-291.09	-342.27	-403.88	-593.49	-713.71	-737.70	-723.83	-774.19
Exports of Goods & NFServices	41.87	44.28	53.49	62.92	65.11	63.57	48.01	65.11	46.47	98.43	136.57
Imports of Goods & NFServices	190.68	218.04	268.45	354.01	407.38	467.45	641.50	778.81	784.18	822.26	910.76
Domestic Absorption	411.60	442.26	499.98	603.36	747.95	854.11	982.88	1,146.12	1,264.42	1,347.03	1,415.42
Private Consumption, etc.	341.89	371.35	409.11	494.92	604.08	708.09	790.00	892.63	918.57	1,011.97	1,027.92
General Gov't Consumption	25.10	24.56	32.27	40.52	44.47	51.28	67.24	66.34	69.21	90.19	96.28
Gross Domestic Investment	44.60	46.35	58.59	67.92	99.40	94.74	125.64	187.15	276.64	244.87	291.22
Fixed Investment	..	..	..	..	..	..	..	..	..	..	..
GDP at factor cost	228.95	229.82	247.81	271.51	338.93	372.96	326.47	364.46	433.11	499.40	518.39
Agriculture	..	170.56	175.66	139.95	163.46	200.28	152.15	143.94	180.76	201.16	208.26
Industry	..	18.06	12.57	26.06	38.87	46.87	43.90	60.81	97.40	113.40	134.43
Manufacturing	..	6.29	3.82	12.36	18.65	19.10	17.75	20.67	19.55	20.00	27.19
Services, etc.	..	84.40	98.88	115.13	142.32	137.20	136.32	163.68	167.39	197.94	193.00

Memo Items:	1969	1970	1971	1972	1973	1974	1975	1976	1977	1978	1979
Capacity to Import	50.22	43.45	50.29	68.76	75.14	68.59	82.74	94.96	76.17	145.08	153.64
Terms of Trade Adjustment	8.35	-0.83	-3.20	5.84	10.03	5.01	34.73	29.85	29.70	46.65	17.06
Gross Domestic Income	271.14	267.68	281.81	318.12	415.71	455.24	424.12	462.26	556.42	669.85	658.29
Gross National Income	372.37	425.50	467.92	512.24	665.23	759.62	843.22	944.02	1,090.19	1,198.88	1,185.25

DOMESTIC PRICES/DEFLATORS

(Index 1987 = 100)

	1969	1970	1971	1972	1973	1974	1975	1976	1977	1978	1979
Overall (GDP)	18.9	19.6	17.7	20.6	21.6	21.8	28.4	29.7	31.9	37.2	38.1
Domestic Absorption	16.4	17.0	16.0	17.6	19.3	21.1	21.3	24.6	26.5	29.8	34.7
Agriculture	..	9.8	6.8	15.0	20.0	15.8	20.8	21.5	27.4	27.4	31.5
Industry	..	24.4	39.0	23.0	21.4	24.1	29.4	35.7	23.0	38.4	40.2
Manufacturing	..	33.4	62.8	22.7	20.9	25.1	31.5	30.0	36.8	50.5	43.8
Consumer Price Index	..	..	..	..	16.0	18.2	20.7	23.1	27.0	30.3	35.2

MANUFACTURING ACTIVITY

	1969	1970	1971	1972	1973	1974	1975	1976	1977	1978	1979
Employment (1987=100)	..	..	..	..	..	..	..	..	..	..	..
Real Earnings per Empl. (1987=100)	..	..	..	..	..	..	..	..	..	..	..
Real Output per Empl. (1987=100)	..	..	..	..	..	..	..	..	..	..	..
Earnings as % of Value Added	..	..	..	..	..	..	..	..	..	..	..

MONETARY HOLDINGS

(Millions of current Lesotho Maloti)

	1969	1970	1971	1972	1973	1974	1975	1976	1977	1978	1979
Money Supply, Broadly Defined	..	..	..	..	..	..	..	..	..	..	..
Money	..	..	..	..	..	..	..	..	..	..	..
Currency Outside Banks	..	..	..	..	..	..	..	..	..	..	..
Demand Deposits	..	..	..	..	..	..	..	..	..	..	..
Quasi-Money	..	..	..	..	..	..	..	..	..	..	..

(Millions of current Lesotho Maloti)

	1969	1970	1971	1972	1973	1974	1975	1976	1977	1978	1979
GOVERNMENT DEFICIT (-) OR SURPLUS	..	..	..	..	4.70	8.72	-8.70	-12.85	-2.99	..	..
Current Revenue	..	..	14.88	14.94	23.91	32.04	32.40	40.28	70.08	..	..
Current Expenditure	..	..	..	..	15.67	16.87	26.76	31.87	43.09	..	..
Current Budget Balance	..	..	..	..	8.24	15.18	5.64	8.41	26.99	..	..
Capital Receipts	..	..	0.01	0.02	0.00	0.00	0.02	0.10	0.06	..	..
Capital Payments	..	..	..	..	3.55	6.46	14.35	21.36	30.04	..	..

1980	1981	1982	1983	1984	1985	1986	1987	1988	1989 estimate	NOTES	LESOTHO
410	480	550	510	480	390	340	340	410	470	..	**CURRENT GNP PER CAPITA (US $)**
1,355	1,391	1,427	1,465	1,505	1,545	1,587	1,630	1,676	1,722	..	**POPULATION (thousands)**
				(Millions of current Lesotho Maloti)							**USE AND ORIGIN OF RESOURCES**
491.3	583.2	744.6	814.6	941.6	1,059.0	1,202.8	1,341.2	1,672.5	2,175.6	C	Gross National Product (GNP)
205.0	254.8	372.9	423.1	487.2	514.3	583.3	615.4	702.5	983.5	..	Net Factor Income from Abroad
286.3	328.4	371.7	391.5	454.4	544.7	619.5	725.8	970.0	1,192.1	C f	GDP at Market Prices
-292.2	-365.1	-458.0	-518.8	-616.3	-699.5	-750.1	-876.6	-1,000.0	-1,447.0	..	Resource Balance
58.0	58.2	55.4	50.8	60.5	70.2	80.2	123.2	185.9	179.4	..	Exports of Goods & NFServices
350.2	423.3	513.4	569.6	676.8	769.7	830.3	999.8	1,185.9	1,626.4	..	Imports of Goods & NFServices
578.5	693.5	829.7	910.3	1,070.7	1,244.2	1,369.6	1,602.4	1,970.0	2,639.1	..	Domestic Absorption
354.6	442.8	526.4	655.0	747.3	791.2	878.2	1,051.9	1,241.9	1,619.5	..	Private Consumption, etc.
102.5	109.8	118.6	123.9	134.5	180.6	210.2	224.3	279.7	227.0	..	General Gov't Consumption
121.4	140.9	184.7	131.4	188.9	272.4	281.2	326.2	448.4	792.6	..	Gross Domestic Investment
115.6	133.2	186.8	130.8	184.5	273.3	276.2	327.0	446.4	790.0	..	Fixed Investment
39.1	45.8	64.3	82.6	89.1	93.9	127.0	148.2	187.0	..	..	Indirect Taxes, net
247.2	282.6	307.4	308.9	365.3	450.8	492.5	577.6	783.0	..	C f	GDP at factor cost
58.3	76.6	66.9	73.6	87.6	95.3	93.1	114.0	187.7	..	..	Agriculture
71.5	73.6	98.4	75.3	96.4	133.2	139.8	174.9	233.3	..	..	Industry
16.1	20.0	26.9	32.7	42.7	49.6	63.7	82.7	111.8	..	..	Manufacturing
117.4	132.4	142.1	160.0	181.3	222.3	259.6	288.7	362.0	..	..	Services, etc.
-170.8	-224.2	-273.3	-387.4	-427.4	-427.1	-468.9	-550.4	-551.6	-654.4	..	Gross Domestic Saving
35.8	32.4	102.5	38.6	64.7	91.2	119.1	65.6	157.5	337.8	..	Gross National Saving
				(Millions of 1987 Lesotho Maloti)							
1,141.08	1,197.39	1,371.84	1,343.21	1,400.74	1,353.19	1,330.27	1,341.20	1,431.49	1,516.58	C	Gross National Product
622.11	628.84	651.88	614.94	661.62	682.57	676.39	725.80	815.05	848.51	C f	GDP at Market Prices
-812.04	-898.70	-954.24	-962.42	-983.35	-955.44	-856.04	-876.60	-914.83	-948.05	..	Resource Balance
127.15	108.07	109.39	77.60	84.84	85.93	91.19	123.20	153.89	149.51	..	Exports of Goods & NFServices
939.19	1,006.77	1,063.63	1,040.03	1,068.19	1,041.37	947.24	999.80	1,068.72	1,097.55	..	Imports of Goods & NFServices
1,434.15	1,527.54	1,606.12	1,577.36	1,644.97	1,638.01	1,532.44	1,602.40	1,729.88	1,796.56	..	Domestic Absorption
896.48	985.23	1,002.90	1,138.25	1,144.30	1,046.78	991.91	1,051.90	1,099.47	950.52	..	Private Consumption, etc.
183.78	185.21	193.64	192.21	198.66	206.73	221.61	224.30	228.42	126.71	..	General Gov't Consumption
353.89	357.10	409.57	246.91	302.00	384.50	318.91	326.20	401.99	719.33	..	Gross Domestic Investment
338.11	340.75	414.16	246.57	296.00	387.25	312.67	327.00	401.00	719.52	..	Fixed Investment
489.11	489.11	504.54	490.49	506.33	529.41	537.06	577.60	653.73	680.51	C f	GDP at factor cost
129.30	137.51	110.01	147.49	118.44	113.33	108.23	114.00	144.16	116.88	..	Agriculture
163.47	140.61	183.36	99.68	137.86	163.93	154.78	174.90	204.62	248.98	..	Industry
36.18	37.53	46.74	44.50	61.13	63.60	72.81	82.70	98.21	106.07	..	Manufacturing
207.30	218.42	221.07	243.32	250.03	252.15	274.04	288.70	304.94	314.66	..	Services, etc.
											Memo Items:
155.55	138.42	114.77	92.76	95.49	94.98	91.49	123.20	167.53	121.07	..	Capacity to Import
28.40	30.35	5.38	15.15	10.65	9.04	0.30	0.00	13.64	-28.44	..	Terms of Trade Adjustment
650.51	659.19	657.26	630.09	672.27	691.62	676.70	725.80	828.69	820.07	..	Gross Domestic Income
1,169.49	1,227.74	1,377.22	1,358.37	1,411.39	1,362.24	1,330.57	1,341.20	1,445.13	1,488.14	..	Gross National Income
				(Index 1987 = 100)							**DOMESTIC PRICES/DEFLATORS**
46.0	52.2	57.0	63.7	68.7	79.8	91.6	100.0	119.0	140.5	..	Overall (GDP)
40.3	45.4	51.7	57.7	65.1	76.0	89.4	100.0	113.9	146.9	..	Domestic Absorption
45.1	55.7	60.8	49.9	74.0	84.1	86.0	100.0	130.2	..	..	Agriculture
43.7	52.3	53.7	75.5	69.9	81.3	90.3	100.0	114.0	..	..	Industry
44.5	53.3	57.5	73.5	69.9	78.0	87.5	100.0	113.8	..	..	Manufacturing
40.7	45.8	51.3	60.3	66.9	75.8	89.5	100.0	111.5	127.9	..	Consumer Price Index
											MANUFACTURING ACTIVITY
..	..	..	..	..	..	..	..	..	..	..	Employment (1987 = 100)
..	..	..	..	..	..	..	..	..	..	..	Real Earnings per Empl. (1987 = 100)
..	..	..	..	..	..	..	..	..	..	..	Real Output per Empl. (1987 = 100)
26.2	29.7	33.9	26.7	24.0	27.7	..	..	..	..	..	Earnings as % of Value Added
				(Millions of current Lesotho Maloti)							**MONETARY HOLDINGS**
116.64	144.20	185.41	217.03	250.32	310.72	352.11	387.08	490.00	555.82	..	Money Supply, Broadly Defined
48.47	58.62	77.17	84.67	103.28	133.14	154.64	156.81	219.88	245.18	..	Money
6.92	10.62	17.77	23.14	23.67	25.23	32.55	33.19	41.87	53.36	..	Currency Outside Banks
41.55	48.00	59.40	61.52	79.60	107.91	122.09	123.62	178.01	191.82	..	Demand Deposits
68.17	85.58	108.24	132.36	147.04	177.58	197.47	230.26	270.12	310.63	..	Quasi-Money
				(Millions of current Lesotho Maloti)							
..	..	..	..	..	..	..	..	..	..	C	**GOVERNMENT DEFICIT (-) OR SURPLUS**
..	..	..	..	239.45	..	287.20	..	..	..	..	Current Revenue
..	..	122.69	142.28	167.52	211.62	257.21	..	..	..	..	Current Expenditure
..	..	..	..	71.92	..	29.99	..	..	..	..	Current Budget Balance
..	..	8.29	1.13	0.03	0.04	0.14	..	..	..	..	Capital Receipts
..	..	..	..	..	..	..	..	..	..	..	Capital Payments
1980	1981	1982	1983	1984	1985	1986	1987	1988	1989		

LESOTHO	1969	1970	1971	1972	1973	1974	1975	1976	1977	1978	1979
FOREIGN TRADE (CUSTOMS BASIS)					*(Millions of current US dollars)*						
Value of Exports, fob	7.00	6.00	4.00	8.00	13.00	14.00	13.00	17.00	14.00	32.00	45.00
Nonfuel Primary Products	6.19	5.60	3.64	6.72	10.64	11.75	10.32	13.50	11.10	24.10	34.50
Fuels	0.00	0.00	0.00	0.00	0.00	0.00	0.00	0.00	0.00	0.00	0.00
Manufactures	0.81	0.40	0.36	1.28	2.36	2.25	2.68	3.50	2.90	7.90	10.50
Value of Imports, cif	34.00	32.00	39.00	56.00	87.00	120.00	160.00	207.00	229.00	273.00	373.00
Nonfuel Primary Products	10.19	10.74	10.80	15.50	24.09	33.22	44.30	57.38	63.42	75.60	111.80
Fuels	1.99	2.06	2.40	3.45	5.36	7.39	9.90	12.72	14.08	16.80	23.00
Manufactures	21.82	19.20	25.80	37.05	57.55	79.39	105.80	136.90	151.50	180.60	238.20
					(Index 1987 = 100)						
Terms of Trade	165.4	151.0	132.9	127.5	144.9	127.6	114.2	112.4	104.8	104.9	108.4
Export Prices, fob	42.2	39.7	37.8	41.5	58.8	69.1	65.4	67.6	68.7	77.1	94.2
Import Prices, cif	25.5	26.3	28.5	32.5	40.6	54.1	57.3	60.1	65.6	73.5	86.9
BALANCE OF PAYMENTS					*(Millions of current US dollars)*						
Exports of Goods & Services	..	11.00	16.00	18.00	19.00	26.00	152.53	172.62	199.99	233.34	277.43
Merchandise, fob	..	6.00	4.00	8.00	12.00	14.00	13.52	17.94	15.18	33.01	39.07
Nonfactor Services	..	2.00	5.00	5.00	6.00	6.00	12.03	11.96	14.14	16.79	18.65
Factor Services	..	3.00	7.00	5.00	1.00	6.00	126.98	142.72	170.66	183.54	219.71
Imports of Goods & Services	..	42.00	52.00	68.00	102.00	143.00	174.98	214.48	240.70	278.76	358.07
Merchandise, fob	..	31.00	37.00	53.00	83.00	113.00	151.45	189.41	210.80	243.11	316.74
Nonfactor Services	..	10.00	14.00	14.00	17.00	27.00	19.07	20.93	24.84	29.90	35.27
Factor Services	..	1.00	1.00	1.00	2.00	3.00	4.46	4.14	5.06	5.75	6.06
Long-Term Interest	..	0.20	0.10	0.20	0.20	0.20	0.20	0.20	0.20	0.40	0.60
Private Current Transfers, net	..	30.00	31.00	37.00	67.00	84.00	1.35	1.38	1.50	1.61	1.90
Workers' Remittances	..	29.00	30.00	36.00	66.00	85.00	..	..	..	..	..
Curr. A/C Bal before Off. Transf.	..	-1.00	-5.00	-13.00	-16.00	-33.00	-21.10	-40.48	-39.22	-43.82	-78.74
Net Official Transfers	..	19.00	21.00	20.00	30.00	32.00	20.01	6.32	30.02	52.33	78.74
Curr. A/C Bal after Off. Transf.	..	18.00	16.00	7.00	14.00	-1.00	-1.08	-34.16	-9.20	8.51	0.00
Long-Term Capital, net	..	0.00	0.00	0.00	0.00	2.00	3.92	2.07	9.43	8.63	22.39
Direct Investment	..	..	..	..	..	..	..	..	..	..	..
Long-Term Loans	..	0.10	0.40	0.40	-0.20	1.90	4.40	2.20	7.20	6.20	17.10
Disbursements	..	0.40	0.50	0.50	0.00	2.00	4.50	2.50	7.40	6.90	18.90
Repayments	..	0.30	0.10	0.10	0.20	0.10	0.10	0.30	0.20	0.70	1.80
Other Long-Term Capital	..	-0.10	-0.40	-0.40	0.20	0.10	-0.48	-0.13	2.23	2.42	5.29
Other Capital, net	..	-18.58	-16.00	-7.01	-14.00	-0.86	-2.14	32.04	-0.29	-17.32	-23.28
Change in Reserves	..	0.58	0.00	0.01	0.00	-0.14	-0.70	0.05	0.06	0.19	0.90
Memo Item:					*(Lesotho Maloti per US dollar)*						
Conversion Factor (Annual Avg)	0.710	0.710	0.720	0.770	0.690	0.680	0.740	0.870	0.870	0.870	0.840
				(Millions of US dollars), outstanding at end of year							
EXTERNAL DEBT (Total)	..	8.10	8.60	9.50	8.20	10.20	14.10	16.10	24.00	33.20	52.00
Long-Term Debt (by debtor)	..	8.10	8.60	9.50	8.20	10.20	14.10	16.10	24.00	30.20	52.00
Central Bank, incl. IMF credit	..	0.00	0.00	0.00	0.00	0.00	0.00	0.00	0.60	0.40	4.70
Central Government	..	7.90	8.40	8.90	7.60	9.60	13.60	15.70	23.00	28.30	44.50
Rest of General Government	..	..	..	..	..	..	..	..	..	..	..
Non-financial Public Enterprises	..	0.20	0.20	0.60	0.60	0.60	0.50	0.40	0.40	0.30	0.30
Priv. Sector, incl non-guaranteed	..	0.00	0.00	0.00	0.00	0.00	0.00	0.00	0.00	1.20	2.50
Short-Term Debt	..	0.00	0.00	0.00	0.00	0.00	0.00	0.00	0.00	3.00	0.00
Memo Items:					*(Thousands of US dollars)*						
Int'l Reserves Excluding Gold	..	..	..	..	..	..	..	..	..	..	..
Gold Holdings (at market price)	..	..	..	..	..	..	..	..	..	..	..
SOCIAL INDICATORS											
Total Fertility Rate	5.8	5.8	5.8	5.8	5.8	5.8	5.8	5.8	5.8	5.8	5.8
Infant Mortality Rate	136.0	134.0	132.0	130.0	128.6	127.2	125.8	124.4	123.0	120.6	118.2
Life Expectancy at Birth	48.9	49.0	49.1	49.2	49.6	50.0	50.4	50.8	51.2	51.5	51.9
Urban Population, % of total	8.1	8.6	9.0	9.5	9.9	10.4	10.8	11.4	11.9	12.5	13.0
Food Prod. per capita (1987=100)	152.4	145.6	160.0	128.4	136.7	178.5	132.0	125.2	154.1	160.4	136.2
Labor Force, Agriculture (%)	90.2	89.9	89.5	89.1	88.7	88.4	88.0	87.6	87.2	86.9	86.5
Labor Force, Female (%)	47.8	47.9	47.7	47.5	47.3	47.1	46.9	46.6	46.4	46.2	46.0
Primary Schl. Enroll. Ratio	..	87.0	..	..	..	..	105.0	105.0	105.0	103.0	104.0
Primary Schl. Enroll. Ratio, Female	..	101.0	..	..	..	..	123.0	125.0	125.0	124.0	123.0
Secondary Schl. Enroll. Ratio	..	7.0	..	..	..	..	13.0	14.0	14.0	14.0	17.0

1980	1981	1982	1983	1984	1985	1986	1987	1988	1989 estimate	NOTES	LESOTHO
				(Millions of current US dollars)							**FOREIGN TRADE (CUSTOMS BASIS)**
58.00	51.00	35.00	35.00	28.00	22.40	25.40	46.50	54.00	..	f	Value of Exports, fob
43.80	38.70	25.90	26.38	20.83	17.27	16.54	30.57	37.64	..	..	Nonfuel Primary Products
0.00	0.00	0.00	0.00	0.00	0.00	0.00	0.00	0.00	..	..	Fuels
14.20	12.30	9.10	8.62	7.17	5.13	8.86	15.93	16.36	..	..	Manufactures
490.00	564.00	514.00	561.00	504.00	364.00	415.00	523.00	591.00	..	f	Value of Imports, cif
152.80	177.38	133.80	228.09	211.96	133.29	152.00	192.00	212.00	..	..	Nonfuel Primary Products
30.20	34.72	31.60	34.54	24.95	21.86	25.00	32.00	31.00	..	..	Fuels
307.00	351.90	348.60	298.37	267.09	208.84	238.00	299.00	348.00	..	..	Manufactures
				(Index 1987 = 100)							
104.3	103.3	102.0	97.6	85.8	92.7	100.6	100.0	100.3	..	..	Terms of Trade
99.6	97.3	90.3	90.4	80.5	82.1	95.2	100.0	108.1	..	..	Export Prices, fob
95.5	94.2	88.6	92.6	93.8	88.5	94.7	100.0	107.8	..	..	Import Prices, cif
				(Millions of current US dollars)							**BALANCE OF PAYMENTS**
363.49	381.41	424.97	454.04	396.18	282.77	314.24	438.81	456.15	498.00	..	Exports of Goods & Services
58.16	45.24	37.35	31.09	28.33	22.43	25.39	46.53	66.03	68.54	..	Merchandise, fob
32.23	34.30	26.22	27.93	24.35	18.34	20.22	27.50	10.23	10.17	..	Nonfactor Services
273.10	301.87	361.40	395.02	343.49	242.01	268.64	364.78	379.89	419.29	..	Factor Services
482.39	512.92	508.73	545.21	489.39	348.07	398.06	490.95	606.70	675.17	..	Imports of Goods & Services
424.48	448.65	446.94	482.54	433.23	303.55	341.55	415.26	521.76	559.52	..	Merchandise, fob
50.33	55.15	46.68	50.22	45.10	35.53	46.20	60.69	70.79	72.22	..	Nonfactor Services
7.58	9.12	15.11	12.45	11.07	9.00	10.30	15.01	14.16	43.42	..	Factor Services
1.40	1.50	4.80	6.10	3.60	4.20	4.40	5.70	7.10	7.30	..	Long-Term Interest
2.05	2.05	2.66	2.60	3.31	1.82	2.05	0.31	2.90	3.33	..	Private Current Transfers, net
..	..	..	..	..	..	0.00	..	..	..	..	Workers' Remittances
-116.84	-129.45	-81.10	-88.56	-89.90	-63.48	-81.76	-51.83	-147.66	-173.84	..	Curr. A/C Bal before Off. Transf.
105.67	80.57	42.62	78.11	91.42	76.57	64.47	76.22	94.65	136.62	..	Net Official Transfers
-11.17	-48.89	-38.48	-10.46	1.52	13.09	-17.29	24.39	-53.01	-37.22	..	Curr. A/C Bal after Off. Transf.
33.86	47.27	49.82	33.56	-0.04	29.38	17.45	39.15	40.45	39.15	..	Long-Term Capital, net
4.49	4.79	3.04	4.80	2.31	4.78	2.06	5.67	12.77	12.81	..	Direct Investment
9.80	17.90	42.40	19.20	11.10	29.30	14.80	40.10	37.50	38.30	..	Long-Term Loans
13.20	20.80	46.90	34.00	28.10	42.90	23.60	48.20	53.00	52.30	..	Disbursements
3.40	2.90	4.50	14.80	17.00	13.60	8.80	8.10	15.50	14.00	..	Repayments
19.56	24.58	4.38	9.56	-13.45	-4.71	0.58	-6.62	-9.82	-11.96	..	Other Long-Term Capital
20.42	2.21	-3.29	2.88	6.67	-37.70	11.36	-63.84	3.27	-18.98	..	Other Capital, net
-43.10	-0.59	-8.05	-25.98	-8.14	-4.77	-11.51	0.30	9.29	17.05	..	Change in Reserves
				(Lesotho Maloti per US dollar)							Memo Item:
0.780	0.880	1.090	1.110	1.480	2.230	2.280	2.040	2.270	2.620	..	Conversion Factor (Annual Avg)
				(Millions of US dollars), outstanding at end of year							
70.70	83.10	120.50	135.20	136.10	173.00	194.20	255.90	285.20	323.80	..	**EXTERNAL DEBT (Total)**
62.70	77.10	117.50	131.20	132.10	169.00	190.20	251.90	279.20	321.80	..	Long-Term Debt (by debtor)
6.20	5.70	5.40	5.00	4.20	3.90	3.10	2.20	7.20	12.10	..	Central Bank, incl. IMF credit
54.10	69.50	110.50	124.70	125.70	156.80	178.50	239.10	262.90	297.00	..	Central Government
..	..	..	..	..	..	..	..	..	..	..	Rest of General Government
0.40	0.30	0.20	0.30	1.30	7.20	7.50	9.20	7.80	11.60	..	Non-financial Public Enterprises
2.00	1.60	1.40	1.20	0.90	1.10	1.10	1.40	1.30	1.10	..	Priv. Sector, incl non-guaranteed
8.00	6.00	3.00	4.00	4.00	4.00	4.00	4.00	6.00	2.00	..	Short-Term Debt
				(Thousands of US dollars)							Memo Items:
50,268	43,396	47,535	66,677	48,576	43,520	60,260	67,531	56,281	48,998	..	Int'l Reserves Excluding Gold
..	..	..	..	..	..	..	..	..	..	..	Gold Holdings (at market price)
											SOCIAL INDICATORS
5.8	5.8	5.8	5.8	5.8	5.8	5.8	5.8	5.7	5.6	..	Total Fertility Rate
115.8	113.4	111.0	108.8	106.6	104.4	102.2	100.0	98.2	96.4	..	Infant Mortality Rate
52.2	52.6	53.0	53.5	54.0	54.5	55.0	55.6	55.9	56.2	..	Life Expectancy at Birth
13.6	14.2	14.8	15.5	16.1	16.7	17.6	18.5	19.1	19.7	..	Urban Population, % of total
125.1	123.5	106.5	104.6	104.8	111.0	100.0	100.0	116.1	92.2	..	Food Prod. per capita (1987=100)
86.2	..	..	..	..	..	..	..	..	..	..	Labor Force, Agriculture (%)
45.7	45.5	45.3	45.0	44.8	44.6	44.3	44.1	43.8	43.6	..	Labor Force, Female (%)
103.0	..	110.0	111.0	111.0	113.0	..	..	..	..	..	Primary Schl. Enroll. Ratio
120.0	..	125.0	125.0	123.0	125.0	..	..	..	..	..	Primary Schl. Enroll. Ratio, Female
17.0	..	19.0	21.0	22.0	..	..	..	..	..	..	Secondary Schl. Enroll. Ratio

LIBERIA	1969	1970	1971	1972	1973	1974	1975	1976	1977	1978	1979
CURRENT GNP PER CAPITA (US $)	290	300	310	320	320	370	410	460	500	530	580
POPULATION (thousands)	1,354	1,394	1,435	1,477	1,521	1,567	1,614	1,663	1,714	1,767	1,822
USE AND ORIGIN OF RESOURCES					*(Millions of current Liberian Dollars)*						
Gross National Product (GNP)	381.4	402.3	424.4	461.9	487.9	613.5	721.0	757.2	866.2	932.9	1,053.9
Net Factor Income from Abroad	-5.5	-6.1	-5.5	-4.6	-4.7	-4.3	-4.9	-4.6	-6.7	-10.8	-13.7
GDP at Market Prices	386.9	408.4	429.9	466.5	492.6	617.8	725.9	761.8	872.9	943.7	1,067.6
Resource Balance	130.3	81.1	77.5	90.6	89.0	75.1	31.8	20.9	-62.9	-48.6	-33.8
Exports of Goods & NFServices	273.9	240.1	251.8	274.8	329.9	407.2	403.7	467.1	459.0	500.0	553.6
Imports of Goods & NFServices	143.6	159.0	174.3	184.2	240.9	332.1	371.9	446.2	521.9	548.6	587.4
Domestic Absorption	256.6	327.3	352.4	375.9	403.6	542.7	694.1	740.9	935.8	992.3	1,101.4
Private Consumption, etc.	148.0	191.6	212.9	221.8	276.0	356.4	373.9	411.8	529.8	572.8	623.3
General Gov't Consumption	45.3	45.1	53.1	55.4	56.0	64.5	73.2	89.3	120.0	139.0	156.6
Gross Domestic Investment	63.3	90.6	86.4	98.7	71.6	121.8	247.0	239.8	286.0	280.5	321.5
Fixed Investment	..	..	..	..	..	..	..	..	..	..	..
Indirect Taxes, net	27.4	30.0	29.9	35.4	39.4	47.5	49.5	63.0	84.7	103.7	114.2
GDP at factor cost	359.5	378.4	400.0	431.1	453.2	570.3	676.4	698.8	788.2	840.0	953.4
Agriculture	88.5	91.2	97.7	97.1	135.6	184.1	179.9	208.4	251.2	288.3	326.8
Industry	145.1	157.2	162.1	184.8	173.5	222.2	305.4	276.1	257.4	247.2	286.0
Manufacturing	13.0	15.2	17.1	18.0	22.6	34.6	36.3	45.2	50.2	53.7	82.0
Services, etc.	125.9	130.0	140.2	149.2	144.1	164.0	191.1	214.3	279.6	304.5	340.6
Gross Domestic Saving	193.6	171.7	163.9	189.3	160.6	196.9	278.8	260.7	223.1	231.9	287.7
Gross National Saving	..	152.3	145.3	171.9	138.6	173.2	252.2	233.7	190.9	191.2	242.0
					(Millions of 1980 Liberian Dollars)						
Gross National Product	839.6	898.7	946.2	987.9	963.0	1,008.9	985.8	1,044.5	1,070.1	1,120.9	1,154.5
GDP at Market Prices	857.4	913.4	960.2	998.8	972.9	1,016.3	993.4	1,051.7	1,079.0	1,134.1	1,169.8
Resource Balance	27.6	135.8	79.5	130.8	141.2	117.2	-67.6	-133.4	-191.4	-115.2	-68.8
Exports of Goods & NFServices	595.6	675.6	651.8	711.4	746.3	720.7	548.0	592.3	528.3	618.9	610.9
Imports of Goods & NFServices	568.0	539.8	572.3	580.5	605.1	603.5	615.6	725.6	719.7	734.2	679.7
Domestic Absorption	829.8	777.6	880.7	868.0	831.7	899.1	1,061.0	1,185.0	1,270.4	1,249.3	1,238.6
Private Consumption, etc.	544.4	409.1	518.5	379.0	561.2	579.6	585.3	695.4	779.7	772.0	718.9
General Gov't Consumption	128.6	150.4	158.4	159.3	133.1	144.1	145.6	154.6	171.0	179.0	191.0
Gross Domestic Investment	156.8	218.1	203.7	329.6	137.5	175.4	330.1	335.0	319.7	298.3	328.7
Fixed Investment	..	..	..	..	..	..	..	..	..	..	..
GDP at factor cost	787.2	842.2	883.6	912.8	887.3	931.8	914.0	961.2	971.4	1,003.9	1,041.7
Agriculture	213.0	234.6	245.4	251.4	276.3	292.4	296.7	323.5	331.8	344.4	353.7
Industry	256.3	275.6	284.8	299.3	300.2	320.8	281.1	283.5	264.2	270.4	282.0
Manufacturing	39.4	46.5	50.6	53.9	61.9	77.0	68.4	82.9	86.5	90.9	97.7
Services, etc.	317.9	332.0	353.4	362.0	310.8	318.6	336.3	354.2	375.3	389.2	406.1
Memo Items:											
Capacity to Import	1,083.5	815.1	826.8	866.0	828.7	740.0	668.3	759.6	633.0	669.1	640.6
Terms of Trade Adjustment	487.8	139.5	175.0	154.7	82.4	19.3	120.3	167.4	104.7	50.2	29.7
Gross Domestic Income	1,345.2	1,052.9	1,135.1	1,153.5	1,055.3	1,035.6	1,113.7	1,219.0	1,183.6	1,184.3	1,199.5
Gross National Income	1,327.4	1,038.2	1,121.1	1,142.6	1,045.4	1,028.2	1,106.1	1,211.9	1,174.7	1,171.1	1,184.2
DOMESTIC PRICES/DEFLATORS					*(Index 1980 = 100)*						
Overall (GDP)	45.1	44.7	44.8	46.7	50.6	60.8	73.1	72.4	80.9	83.2	91.3
Domestic Absorption	30.9	42.1	40.0	43.3	48.5	60.4	65.4	62.5	73.7	79.4	88.9
Agriculture	41.5	38.9	39.8	38.6	49.1	63.0	60.6	64.4	75.7	83.7	92.4
Industry	56.6	57.0	56.9	61.7	57.8	69.3	108.7	97.4	97.4	91.4	101.4
Manufacturing	33.0	32.7	33.8	33.4	36.5	44.9	53.1	54.5	58.1	59.1	83.9
Consumer Price Index	29.8	30.3	30.0	31.2	37.3	44.4	50.6	53.5	56.8	60.9	68.0
MANUFACTURING ACTIVITY											
Employment (1987=100)	..	..	..	..	..	..	..	..	..	..	..
Real Earnings per Empl. (1987=100)	..	..	..	..	..	..	..	..	..	..	..
Real Output per Empl. (1987=100)	..	..	..	..	..	..	..	..	..	..	..
Earnings as % of Value Added	..	..	..	..	..	..	..	..	..	..	..
MONETARY HOLDINGS					*(Millions of current Liberian Dollars)*						
Money Supply, Broadly Defined	..	..	..	..	..	75.03	73.92	108.88	122.27	150.97	154.73
Money	..	..	..	..	..	..	..	..	..	..	..
Currency Outside Banks	..	..	..	..	..	8.48	7.97	8.36	9.24	10.19	11.00
Demand Deposits	..	..	..	..	..	..	..	..	..	..	..
Quasi-Money	..	..	..	..	..	..	..	..	..	..	..
GOVERNMENT DEFICIT (-) OR SURPLUS					*(Millions of current Liberian Dollars)*						
	..	..	..	..	..	6.80	3.40	-16.00	-24.20	-56.20	-141.20
Current Revenue	..	..	..	..	..	116.70	129.20	163.70	181.10	197.50	224.10
Current Expenditure	..	..	..	..	..	84.60	88.90	111.60	119.30	126.50	152.90
Current Budget Balance	..	..	..	..	..	32.10	40.30	52.10	61.80	71.00	71.20
Capital Receipts	..	..	..	..	..	0.20	3.10	0.20	0.30	0.20	0.20
Capital Payments	..	..	..	..	..	25.50	40.00	68.30	86.30	127.40	212.60

1980	1981	1982	1983	1984	1985	1986	1987	1988	1989 estimate	NOTES	LIBERIA
580	590	550	500	470	470	450	450	..	..	..	**CURRENT GNP PER CAPITA (US $)**
1,879	1,938	2,000	2,064	2,130	2,199	2,268	2,337	2,406	2,475	..	**POPULATION (thousands)**
				(Millions of current Liberian Dollars)							**USE AND ORIGIN OF RESOURCES**
1,092.9	1,073.9	1,049.7	969.5	977.4	1,031.0	1,012.0	1,062.6	..	..	..	Gross National Product (GNP)
-23.9	-21.1	-72.3	-97.5	-116.6	-64.0	-73.0	-76.7	..	..	..	Net Factor Income from Abroad
1,116.8	1,095.0	1,122.0	1,067.0	1,094.0	1,095.0	1,085.0	1,139.3	..	..	..	GDP at Market Prices
-0.5	27.1	-20.0	-19.0	45.0	62.0	95.0	..	..	..	..	Resource Balance
613.5	588.0	539.0	487.0	471.0	467.0	464.0	..	..	..	..	Exports of Goods & NFServices
614.0	560.9	559.0	506.0	426.0	405.0	369.0	..	..	..	..	Imports of Goods & NFServices
1,117.3	1,067.9	1,142.0	1,086.0	1,049.0	1,033.0	990.0	..	..	..	..	Domestic Absorption
630.2	677.9	739.0	756.0	750.0	708.0	700.0	..	..	..	..	Private Consumption, etc.
182.0	211.0	243.0	204.0	187.0	230.0	185.0	..	..	..	..	General Gov't Consumption
305.1	179.0	160.0	126.0	112.0	95.0	105.0	..	..	..	..	Gross Domestic Investment
..	169.0	130.0	126.0	117.0	97.0	95.0	..	..	..	..	Fixed Investment
115.8	103.6	110.2	102.7	100.3	98.0	100.0	..	..	..	..	Indirect Taxes, net
1,001.0	991.4	1,011.8	964.3	993.7	997.0	985.0	..	..	..	..	GDP at factor cost
359.2	312.9	326.2	326.4	352.3	364.2	368.0	..	..	..	f	Agriculture
281.6	327.2	319.5	293.0	282.8	276.4	273.7	..	..	..	f	Industry
77.0	56.5	53.6	49.6	51.2	49.0	46.9	..	..	..	f	Manufacturing
360.2	351.3	366.1	344.9	358.6	356.4	343.3	..	..	..	f	Services, etc.
304.6	206.1	140.0	107.0	157.0	157.0	200.0	..	..	..	..	Gross Domestic Saving
251.7	155.0	22.7	-29.5	-3.2	65.0	101.6	..	..	..	..	Gross National Saving
				(Millions of 1980 Liberian Dollars)							
1,092.9	1,082.5	1,016.8	969.5	935.1	979.4	953.6	944.1	..	..	..	Gross National Product
1,116.8	1,103.1	1,081.3	1,064.3	1,047.2	1,040.4	1,023.0	1,012.8	..	..	..	GDP at Market Prices
-0.5	69.7	68.4	12.6	38.3	57.3	93.5	..	..	..	..	Resource Balance
613.5	612.5	579.6	507.4	511.8	504.5	501.7	..	..	..	..	Exports of Goods & NFServices
614.0	542.8	511.2	494.8	473.5	447.2	408.1	..	..	..	..	Imports of Goods & NFServices
1,117.3	1,033.4	1,013.0	1,051.7	1,008.9	983.1	929.5	..	..	..	..	Domestic Absorption
630.2	571.5	552.1	660.9	670.5	611.7	605.8	..	..	..	..	Private Consumption, etc.
182.0	276.6	303.1	262.6	229.7	279.9	223.5	..	..	..	..	General Gov't Consumption
305.1	185.3	157.7	128.3	108.7	91.5	100.2	..	..	..	..	Gross Domestic Investment
..	..	..	..	..	..	..	..	..	..	..	Fixed Investment
1,001.0	986.5	963.2	950.8	941.4	937.9	919.3	..	..	..	..	GDP at factor cost
359.2	345.1	342.6	353.7	364.5	373.3	374.3	..	..	..	f	Agriculture
281.6	252.4	234.7	222.1	204.7	198.2	194.6	..	..	..	f	Industry
77.0	73.5	66.3	63.4	62.5	59.2	56.3	..	..	..	f	Manufacturing
360.2	388.9	385.9	375.1	372.3	366.5	350.4	..	..	..	f	Services, etc.
											Memo Items:
613.5	569.0	492.9	476.2	523.5	515.7	513.2	..	..	..	..	Capacity to Import
0.0	-43.5	-86.7	-31.1	11.7	11.1	11.5	..	..	..	..	Terms of Trade Adjustment
1,116.8	1,059.6	994.7	1,033.2	1,059.0	1,051.6	1,034.6	..	..	..	..	Gross Domestic Income
1,092.9	1,039.0	930.1	938.3	946.8	990.5	965.2	..	..	..	..	Gross National Income
				(Index 1980 = 100)							**DOMESTIC PRICES/DEFLATORS**
100.0	99.3	103.8	100.3	104.5	105.2	106.1	112.5	..	..	..	Overall (GDP)
100.0	103.3	112.7	103.3	104.0	105.1	106.5	..	..	..	..	Domestic Absorption
100.0	90.7	95.2	92.3	96.7	97.6	98.3	..	..	..	..	Agriculture
100.0	129.6	136.1	132.0	138.2	139.5	140.6	..	..	..	..	Industry
100.0	76.9	80.8	78.3	81.9	82.7	83.3	..	..	..	..	Manufacturing
78.0	83.9	88.9	91.4	92.5	91.6	95.2	100.0	109.6	..	f	Consumer Price Index
											MANUFACTURING ACTIVITY
..	..	..	..	..	..	..	..	..	..	G	Employment (1987=100)
..	..	..	..	..	..	..	..	..	..	G	Real Earnings per Empl. (1987=100)
..	..	..	..	..	..	..	..	..	..	..	Real Output per Empl. (1987=100)
..	..	..	..	..	..	..	..	..	..	..	Earnings as % of Value Added
				(Millions of current Liberian Dollars)							**MONETARY HOLDINGS**
114.54	100.94	126.69	142.12	144.39	170.75	202.15	233.54	256.54	302.83	..	Money Supply, Broadly Defined
..	..	..	..	..	..	..	..	..	..	..	Money
11.35	11.59	15.74	19.83	28.60	46.17	66.06	..	..	..	..	Currency Outside Banks
..	..	..	..	..	..	..	..	..	..	..	Demand Deposits
..	..	..	..	..	..	..	..	..	..	..	Quasi-Money
				(Millions of current Liberian Dollars)							
-88.30	-110.30	-116.60	-102.90	-61.00	..	..	..	..	..	C	**GOVERNMENT DEFICIT (-) OR SURPLUS**
225.10	242.40	278.20	257.20	259.50	228.80	..	..	..	..	..	Current Revenue
179.70	211.80	295.40	268.70	244.70	..	205.30	..	231.60	..	..	Current Expenditure
45.40	30.60	-17.20	-11.50	14.80	..	..	..	..	..	..	Current Budget Balance
0.20	0.10	0.10	5.50	0.20	0.50	0.30	0.20	0.10	..	..	Capital Receipts
133.90	141.00	99.50	96.90	76.00	..	91.30	..	..	..	..	Capital Payments

LIBERIA	1969	1970	1971	1972	1973	1974	1975	1976	1977	1978	1979
FOREIGN TRADE (CUSTOMS BASIS)					*(Millions of current US dollars)*						
Value of Exports, fob	195.30	217.19	222.37	244.01	323.79	399.76	393.94	463.03	454.42	496.31	547.15
Nonfuel Primary Products	190.11	207.03	216.01	236.85	317.25	393.37	386.31	450.71	439.67	476.85	522.27
Fuels	0.02	0.01	0.00	0.11	0.03	0.22	0.17	0.52	0.02	0.06	0.02
Manufactures	5.17	10.15	6.36	7.05	6.51	6.17	7.46	11.80	14.73	19.40	24.86
Value of Imports, cif	114.10	149.67	162.24	178.56	193.46	288.42	331.21	399.22	463.47	480.95	506.45
Nonfuel Primary Products	18.89	27.38	31.64	32.55	37.53	48.46	50.46	57.25	77.17	87.45	100.49
Fuels	4.65	9.53	11.84	12.03	14.72	56.41	48.34	59.51	68.85	84.54	103.17
Manufactures	90.56	112.76	118.76	133.98	141.21	183.55	232.41	282.46	317.45	308.96	302.79
					(Index 1987 = 100)						
Terms of Trade	180.9	199.4	171.5	155.2	178.8	137.1	142.0	147.9	141.4	117.2	122.7
Export Prices, fob	46.9	51.1	47.5	47.5	67.4	74.9	80.5	84.0	88.7	84.1	104.9
Import Prices, cif	25.9	25.6	27.7	30.6	37.7	54.7	56.7	56.8	62.8	71.8	85.5
BALANCE OF PAYMENTS					*(Millions of current US dollars)*						
Exports of Goods & Services	..	..	..	..	..	..	..	..	..	..	..
Merchandise, fob	..	213.70	223.90	243.60	324.00	400.30	394.40	457.00	447.40	486.40	536.60
Nonfactor Services	..	3.20	4.10	3.70	5.90	6.90	9.30	10.00	11.60	13.60	17.00
Factor Services	..	..	..	..	..	..	..	..	..	..	..
Imports of Goods & Services	..	230.70	235.20	252.40	323.40	440.40	336.10	412.10	480.90	506.90	540.10
Merchandise, fob	..	149.70	162.40	174.70	193.50	289.40	290.40	358.60	417.30	430.60	457.50
Nonfactor Services	..	74.90	67.30	73.10	125.20	146.70	40.80	48.90	56.90	65.50	68.90
Factor Services	..	6.10	5.50	4.60	4.70	4.30	4.90	4.60	6.70	10.80	13.70
Long-Term Interest	..	6.00	5.90	4.90	5.30	5.00	5.10	5.90	7.20	12.90	22.80
Private Current Transfers, net	..	-13.30	-13.10	-12.80	-17.30	-19.40	-21.70	-22.40	-25.50	-29.90	-32.00
Workers' Remittances	..	..	..	..	..	..	..	..	..	..	..
Curr. A/C Bal before Off. Transf.	..	-27.10	-20.30	-17.90	-10.80	-52.60	45.90	32.50	-47.40	-36.80	-18.50
Net Official Transfers	..	10.80	13.30	9.30	19.60	22.20	27.80	32.30	28.80	29.60	34.70
Curr. A/C Bal after Off. Transf.	..	-16.30	-7.00	-8.60	8.80	-30.40	73.70	64.80	-18.60	-7.20	16.20
Long-Term Capital, net	..	35.50	30.00	29.20	57.20	50.10	88.40	69.60	83.80	53.50	102.90
Direct Investment	..	28.10	20.70	18.70	49.00	45.00	80.80	39.10	44.70	..	..
Long-Term Loans	..	-4.00	1.50	-1.40	-3.80	0.40	8.10	27.80	50.70	68.10	117.10
Disbursements	..	7.40	12.30	10.50	8.10	14.90	35.40	43.30	69.70	81.40	169.00
Repayments	..	11.40	10.80	11.90	11.90	14.50	27.30	15.50	19.00	13.30	51.90
Other Long-Term Capital	..	11.40	7.80	11.90	12.00	4.70	-0.50	2.70	-11.60	-14.60	-14.20
Other Capital, net	..	-18.27	-24.21	-20.29	-64.46	-18.10	-161.56	-131.10	-59.22	-58.19	-157.84
Change in Reserves	..	-0.93	1.21	-0.31	-1.54	-1.60	-0.54	-3.30	-5.98	11.89	38.74
Memo Item:					*(Liberian Dollars per US dollar)*						
Conversion Factor (Annual Avg)	1.000	1.000	1.000	1.000	1.000	1.000	1.000	1.000	1.000	1.000	1.000
				(Millions of US dollars), outstanding at end of year							
EXTERNAL DEBT (Total)	..	162.3	162.1	159.4	159.1	162.1	178.6	208.5	292.0	443.0	594.8
Long-Term Debt (by debtor)	..	162.3	162.0	159.3	159.0	161.9	178.6	208.4	266.9	353.7	519.5
Central Bank, incl. IMF credit	..	6.4	2.7	1.0	1.2	2.3	4.9	6.2	11.2	30.1	84.6
Central Government	..	142.3	142.1	137.1	129.6	129.3	142.2	168.3	206.5	264.7	358.6
Rest of General Government	..	..	..	..	..	..	..	..	..	..	..
Non-financial Public Enterprises	..	13.6	17.2	21.2	28.2	30.3	31.5	33.9	43.7	53.4	72.2
Priv. Sector, incl non-guaranteed	..	0.0	0.0	0.0	0.0	0.0	0.0	0.0	5.5	5.5	4.1
Short-Term Debt	..	0.0	0.1	0.1	0.1	0.2	0.0	0.1	25.1	89.3	75.3
Memo Items:					*(Thousands of US dollars)*						
Int'l Reserves Excluding Gold	..	..	..	..	..	18,719	19,189	17,170	27,345	18,021	54,979
Gold Holdings (at market price)	..	..	..	..	..	..	..	..	..	..	..
SOCIAL INDICATORS											
Total Fertility Rate	6.4	6.5	6.5	6.5	6.5	6.5	6.5	6.5	6.5	6.5	6.5
Infant Mortality Rate	169.0	167.0	165.0	163.0	161.0	159.0	157.0	155.0	153.0	151.4	149.8
Life Expectancy at Birth	43.6	43.9	44.2	44.5	44.8	45.1	45.4	45.7	46.0	46.3	46.6
Urban Population, % of total	25.2	26.0	26.9	27.8	28.6	29.5	30.4	31.3	32.2	33.1	34.0
Food Prod. per capita (1987=100)	96.0	99.7	102.2	101.9	101.5	107.0	103.7	105.0	107.0	105.3	103.5
Labor Force, Agriculture (%)	77.7	77.5	77.2	76.8	76.5	76.2	75.9	75.5	75.2	74.8	74.5
Labor Force, Female (%)	32.0	32.0	32.0	32.0	32.0	32.0	32.0	32.0	31.9	31.9	31.9
Primary Schl. Enroll. Ratio	..	56.0	..	..	..	..	62.0	..	..	60.0	71.0
Primary Schl. Enroll. Ratio, Female	..	36.0	..	..	..	..	45.0	..	..	46.0	54.0
Secondary Schl. Enroll. Ratio	..	10.0	..	..	..	..	17.0	..	..	19.0	23.0

1980	1981	1982	1983	1984	1985	1986	1987	1988	1989 estimate	NOTES	LIBERIA
				(Millions of current US dollars)							**FOREIGN TRADE (CUSTOMS BASIS)**
596.98	529.20	477.40	438.00	452.10	435.60	404.40	382.20	392.00	..	..	Value of Exports, fob
569.75	510.32	459.50	416.26	432.96	415.95	398.48	376.94	386.73	..	..	Nonfuel Primary Products
6.95	0.35	1.30	1.40	0.00	0.00	0.00	0.00	0.00	..	..	Fuels
20.28	18.53	16.60	20.34	19.13	19.65	5.92	5.26	5.27	..	..	Manufactures
534.09	477.43	422.00	412.00	368.70	284.40	234.80	208.03	216.39	..	..	Value of Imports, cif
109.25	114.24	96.32	93.99	95.06	62.71	55.21	44.50	47.26	..	..	Nonfuel Primary Products
152.10	129.26	112.61	110.98	73.76	74.57	40.13	44.19	46.67	..	..	Fuels
272.74	233.94	213.07	207.03	199.88	147.12	139.46	119.34	122.46	..	..	Manufactures
				(Index 1987 = 100)							
112.9	96.2	105.0	103.2	106.4	99.8	103.1	100.0	104.8	..	..	Terms of Trade
119.7	105.4	106.5	101.5	98.5	93.2	93.0	100.0	107.0	..	..	Export Prices, fob
106.0	109.6	101.5	98.3	92.6	93.4	90.1	100.0	102.0	..	..	Import Prices, cif
				(Millions of current US dollars)							**BALANCE OF PAYMENTS**
..	..	511.90	461.10	486.20	468.70	466.90	432.60		..	..	Exports of Goods & Services
600.40	529.20	477.40	420.80	446.70	430.40	407.90	374.90	..	..	..	Merchandise, fob
13.10	11.50	32.70	38.50	36.90	34.60	56.90	52.50	..	..	..	Nonfactor Services
..	..	1.80	1.80	2.60	3.70	2.10	5.20	..	..	..	Factor Services
574.69	503.71	556.30	638.86	547.33	475.45	522.60	574.20	..	..	..	Imports of Goods & Services
478.00	423.90	390.20	374.80	325.40	263.80	258.80	311.70	..	..	..	Merchandise, fob
72.70	58.70	92.00	108.70	92.50	80.20	80.50	74.20	..	..	..	Nonfactor Services
23.99	21.11	74.10	155.36	129.43	131.45	183.30	188.30	..	..	..	Factor Services
22.80	17.50	13.50	10.20	10.60	10.10	14.30	6.00	7.30	0.70	..	Long-Term Interest
-29.00	-30.00	-45.00	-39.00	-43.60	-28.00	-25.40	-21.40	..	..	..	Private Current Transfers, net
..	..	..	..	..	..	..	0.00	..	..	..	Workers' Remittances
9.81	6.99	-89.40	-216.76	-104.73	-34.75	-81.10	-163.00	..	..	..	Curr. A/C Bal before Off. Transf.
36.20	68.45	92.85	114.15	103.87	91.64	96.40	45.40	..	..	..	Net Official Transfers
46.01	75.44	3.45	-102.60	-0.86	56.89	15.30	-117.60	..	..	..	Curr. A/C Bal after Off. Transf.
70.50	43.90	177.90	73.13	71.84	-115.31	-218.66	-188.91	..	..	..	Long-Term Capital, net
..	..	34.80	49.10	36.20	-16.20	-16.50	38.50	..	..	..	Direct Investment
60.30	73.80	45.70	68.40	91.40	55.10	29.90	27.10	5.90	0.10	..	Long-Term Loans
75.50	81.80	65.20	77.70	100.10	63.40	43.60	31.90	15.10	1.20	..	Disbursements
15.20	8.00	19.50	9.30	8.70	8.30	13.70	4.80	9.20	1.10	..	Repayments
10.20	-29.90	97.40	-44.37	-55.76	-154.21	-232.06	-254.51	..	..	..	Other Long-Term Capital
-157.16	-173.61	-249.74	-7.34	-104.44	63.42	200.76	306.02	..	..	..	Other Capital, net
40.65	54.28	68.38	36.81	33.47	-5.00	2.60	0.49	-1.30	-10.21	..	Change in Reserves
				(Liberian Dollars per US dollar)							**Memo Item:**
1.000	1.000	1.000	1.000	1.000	1.000	1.000	1.000	1.000	..	..	Conversion Factor (Annual Avg)
			(Millions of US dollars), outstanding at end of year								
686.2	814.1	902.7	1,005.4	1,075.6	1,247.2	1,439.1	1,685.2	1,707.1	1,760.9	..	**EXTERNAL DEBT (Total)**
605.1	733.4	823.8	948.5	1,006.4	1,142.1	1,272.0	1,444.5	1,410.3	1,389.8	..	Long-Term Debt (by debtor)
106.6	152.1	211.9	249.6	247.7	271.9	301.2	348.8	329.4	319.2	..	Central Bank, incl. IMF credit
423.0	511.3	536.1	610.0	669.8	766.4	850.4	954.4	937.5	931.6	..	Central Government
..	..	..	..	..	..	..	..	..	..	..	Rest of General Government
74.1	70.0	75.8	88.9	88.9	103.8	120.4	141.3	143.4	139.0	..	Non-financial Public Enterprises
1.4	0.0	0.0	0.0	0.0	0.0	0.0	0.0	0.0	..	..	Priv. Sector, incl non-guaranteed
81.1	80.7	78.9	56.9	69.2	105.1	167.1	240.7	296.8	371.1	..	Short-Term Debt
				(Thousands of US dollars)							**Memo Items:**
5,450	8,339	6,471	20,400	3,479	1,522	2,664	513	420	7,869	..	Int'l Reserves Excluding Gold
..	..	..	..	..	..	..	..	..	..	..	Gold Holdings (at market price)
											SOCIAL INDICATORS
6.6	6.6	6.6	6.6	6.6	6.5	6.5	6.5	6.4	6.3	..	Total Fertility Rate
148.2	146.6	145.0	142.4	139.8	137.2	134.6	132.0	129.7	127.4	..	Infant Mortality Rate
46.9	47.2	47.5	47.9	48.3	48.7	49.1	49.5	49.9	50.3	..	Life Expectancy at Birth
34.9	35.8	36.7	37.7	38.6	39.5	40.7	41.8	42.5	43.3	..	Urban Population, % of total
100.7	104.6	104.2	104.0	103.1	101.5	99.6	100.0	98.9	94.4	..	Food Prod. per capita (1987=100)
74.2	..	..	..	..	..	..	..	..	..	..	Labor Force, Agriculture (%)
31.9	31.7	31.6	31.4	31.3	31.1	30.9	30.7	30.6	30.4	..	Labor Force, Female (%)
49.0	..	47.0	..	40.0	..	35.0	..	..	..	..	Primary Schl. Enroll. Ratio
34.0	..	..	..	28.0	..	..	..	..	..	..	Primary Schl. Enroll. Ratio, Female
23.0	..	..	..	18.0	..	..	..	..	..	..	Secondary Schl. Enroll. Ratio

LIBYA	1969	1970	1971	1972	1973	1974	1975	1976	1977	1978	1979
CURRENT GNP PER CAPITA (US $)	1,810	1,870	1,840	1,980	2,450	3,210	4,640	6,920	6,790	7,000	8,490
POPULATION (thousands)	1,906	1,986	2,069	2,155	2,247	2,344	2,446	2,554	2,666	2,785	2,910
USE AND ORIGIN OF RESOURCES	*(Millions of current Libyan Dinars)*										
Gross National Product (GNP)	1,195.2	1,259.6	1,469.2	1,762.4	2,152.5	3,910.3	3,781.5	4,899.8	5,403.1	5,375.9	7,594.7
Net Factor Income from Abroad	-162.8	-166.8	-157.6	-36.1	-93.7	27.1	1.5	-7.2	-359.9	-312.1	-251.7
GDP at Market Prices	1,358.0	1,426.4	1,626.8	1,798.5	2,246.2	3,883.2	3,780.0	4,907.0	5,763.0	5,688.0	7,846.4
Resource Balance	369.0	467.0	539.1	445.4	413.8	1,062.0	387.5	1,210.0	1,482.0	779.0	1,979.0
Exports of Goods & NFServices	788.0	870.0	975.1	997.8	1,240.3	2,489.9	2,053.2	2,881.4	3,431.0	2,978.0	4,801.0
Imports of Goods & NFServices	419.0	403.0	436.0	552.4	826.5	1,427.9	1,665.7	1,671.4	1,949.0	2,199.0	2,822.0
Domestic Absorption	989.0	959.4	1,087.7	1,353.1	1,832.4	2,821.2	3,392.5	3,697.0	4,281.0	4,909.0	5,867.4
Private Consumption, etc.	382.6	463.9	468.6	543.4	702.8	927.0	1,193.5	1,336.6	1,483.0	1,665.0	1,973.4
General Gov't Consumption	256.8	259.9	318.4	359.1	465.4	864.8	1,044.3	1,184.6	1,400.0	1,692.0	1,929.0
Gross Domestic Investment	349.6	235.6	300.7	450.6	664.2	1,029.4	1,154.7	1,175.8	1,398.0	1,552.0	1,965.0
Fixed Investment	342.0	232.0	288.0	437.0	636.0	971.0	1,055.0	1,226.0	1,368.0	1,532.0	1,855.0
Indirect Taxes, net	51.4	42.0	40.3	45.5	63.9	91.2	105.7	138.9	150.0	192.0	243.4
GDP at factor cost	1,306.6	1,384.4	1,586.5	1,753.0	2,182.3	3,792.0	3,674.3	4,768.1	5,613.0	5,496.0	7,603.0
Agriculture	37.4	33.1	33.0	43.6	60.0	64.7	82.9	99.7	90.0	122.0	140.4
Industry	886.4	950.3	1,078.9	1,154.2	1,459.6	2,850.8	2,499.6	3,402.3	4,058.0	3,705.0	5,539.3
Manufacturing	26.7	29.1	32.7	46.0	62.8	71.5	86.2	114.8	125.0	149.0	185.8
Services, etc.	382.8	401.0	474.6	555.2	662.7	876.5	1,091.8	1,266.1	1,465.0	1,669.0	1,923.3
Gross Domestic Saving	718.6	702.6	839.8	896.0	1,078.0	2,091.4	1,542.2	2,385.8	2,880.0	2,331.0	3,944.0
Gross National Saving	..	485.8	620.4	759.2	902.4	2,014.9	1,466.8	2,302.4	2,266.0	1,731.2	3,438.0
	(Millions of 1980 Libyan Dinars)										
Gross National Product	7,227.2	7,598.3	7,310.8	7,051.8	6,972.1	6,270.7	6,694.8	8,222.0	8,369.5	8,726.1	10,124.8
GDP at Market Prices	8,211.9	8,604.2	8,094.9	7,196.1	7,275.7	6,227.3	6,692.2	8,234.1	8,927.0	9,232.7	10,460.4
Resource Balance	10,331.3	11,061.3	8,761.8	6,955.4	6,696.6	2,770.8	2,918.1	4,612.9	4,821.9	4,264.4	4,621.8
Exports of Goods & NFServices	11,217.4	11,873.9	9,602.9	7,946.1	8,041.2	5,108.4	5,293.8	6,909.9	7,392.0	7,028.5	7,624.0
Imports of Goods & NFServices	886.1	812.5	841.0	990.7	1,344.6	2,337.6	2,375.7	2,296.9	2,570.1	2,764.0	3,002.2
Domestic Absorption	1,935.4	1,647.5	2,007.1	2,312.2	2,621.7	4,246.3	4,504.6	4,747.5	5,300.8	5,848.9	6,433.1
Private Consumption, etc.	297.0	303.2	555.0	613.2	775.3	1,164.1	1,330.1	1,456.8	1,529.5	1,872.3	2,076.1
General Gov't Consumption	497.9	508.3	604.7	642.7	804.6	1,620.7	1,554.3	1,741.1	2,031.3	2,135.8	2,211.7
Gross Domestic Investment	1,140.6	836.0	847.4	1,056.4	1,041.8	1,461.5	1,620.2	1,549.6	1,740.0	1,840.9	2,145.4
Fixed Investment	..	..	..	..	..	..	..	..	..	..	..
GDP at factor cost	8,382.8	8,787.6	8,281.7	7,351.1	7,411.7	6,282.3	6,744.1	8,270.7	9,014.1	9,249.0	10,194.3
Agriculture	66.3	49.9	58.7	78.4	90.2	92.6	110.5	126.2	106.6	136.0	150.6
Industry	10,604.3	11,137.0	10,124.1	8,534.7	8,307.7	6,350.0	6,463.3	8,198.3	8,835.4	8,765.6	9,453.4
Manufacturing	55.2	58.2	64.1	70.4	93.3	85.4	110.2	141.4	154.7	182.8	226.3
Services, etc.	386.3	411.1	512.7	598.9	702.7	832.6	1,013.0	1,151.2	1,311.9	1,435.3	1,656.2
Memo Items:											
Capacity to Import	1,666.5	1,754.1	1,881.0	1,789.4	2,017.9	4,076.2	2,928.3	3,959.8	4,524.3	3,743.2	5,107.6
Terms of Trade Adjustment	-9,550.9	-10,120.0	-7,721.9	-6,156.6	-6,023.3	-1,032.2	-2,365.4	-2,950.1	-2,867.7	-3,285.3	-2,516.5
Gross Domestic Income	-1,339.0	-1,515.5	373.0	1,039.4	1,252.4	5,195.1	4,326.8	5,284.0	6,059.3	5,947.5	7,943.9
Gross National Income	-2,323.7	-2,521.5	-411.1	895.1	948.7	5,238.4	4,329.4	5,272.0	5,501.8	5,440.8	7,608.4
DOMESTIC PRICES/DEFLATORS	*(Index 1980 = 100)*										
Overall (GDP)	16.5	16.6	20.1	25.0	30.9	62.4	56.5	59.6	64.6	61.6	75.0
Domestic Absorption	51.1	58.2	54.2	58.5	69.9	66.4	75.3	77.9	80.8	83.9	91.2
Agriculture	56.5	66.4	56.3	55.6	66.5	69.8	75.0	79.0	84.4	89.7	93.2
Industry	8.4	8.5	10.7	13.5	17.6	44.9	38.7	41.5	45.9	42.3	58.6
Manufacturing	48.3	50.0	51.1	65.3	67.3	83.7	78.2	81.2	80.8	81.5	82.1
Consumer Price Index	..	..	..	..	..	..	..	..	..	..	..
MANUFACTURING ACTIVITY											
Employment (1987=100)	..	..	..	..	..	..	..	..	..	..	..
Real Earnings per Empl. (1987=100)	..	..	..	..	..	..	..	..	..	..	..
Real Output per Empl. (1987=100)	..	..	..	..	..	..	..	..	..	..	..
Earnings as % of Value Added	35.5	37.1	33.9	37.3	36.9	31.1	32.6	30.6	35.3	35.7	47.4
MONETARY HOLDINGS	*(Millions of current Libyan Dinars)*										
Money Supply, Broadly Defined	255.5	320.8	462.9	588.6	810.9	1,334.3	1,360.5	1,694.9	2,128.1	2,373.7	3,199.8
Money	201.9	241.1	364.5	413.0	514.0	753.8	867.6	1,139.4	1,443.8	1,687.8	2,247.3
Currency Outside Banks	102.4	112.3	120.7	147.4	202.6	262.2	346.0	436.0	585.0	868.5	1,053.7
Demand Deposits	99.5	128.8	243.8	265.6	311.4	491.6	521.6	703.4	858.8	819.3	1,193.6
Quasi-Money	53.6	79.7	98.4	175.7	296.8	580.5	492.9	555.6	684.3	685.9	952.5
GOVERNMENT DEFICIT (-) OR SURPLUS	*(Millions of current Libyan Dinars)*										
Current Revenue	..	..	..	..	..	..	..	..	..	..	..
Current Expenditure	..	..	..	..	..	..	..	..	..	..	..
Current Budget Balance	..	..	..	..	..	..	..	..	..	..	..
Capital Receipts	..	..	..	..	..	..	..	..	..	..	..
Capital Payments	..	..	..	..	..	..	..	..	..	..	..

1980	1981	1982	1983	1984	1985	1986	1987	1988	1989 estimate	NOTES	LIBYA
9,740	9,280	9,260	8,590	7,230	6,560	5,500	5,340	5,410	..	..	**CURRENT GNP PER CAPITA (US $)**
3,043	3,182	3,327	3,476	3,630	3,786	3,942	4,095	4,245	4,395	..	**POPULATION (thousands)**
				(Millions of current Libyan Dinars)							**USE AND ORIGIN OF RESOURCES**
10,503.9	9,379.0	8,524.1	8,307.2	7,356.3	7,016.5	6,286.4	6,443.0	6,819.0		..	Gross National Product (GNP)
-19.3	32.5	-150.7	-223.8	-159.3	..	..	..		..	..	Net Factor Income from Abroad
10,523.2	9,346.5	8,674.8	8,531.0	7,920.7	7,203.0	6,473.0	7,086.0		..	..	GDP at Market Prices
3,658.0	1,468.0	1,596.0	1,092.0	..	..	..	..	..	..	..	Resource Balance
6,964.0	4,995.0	4,573.0	3,979.0	..	..	..	..	..	..	..	Exports of Goods & NFServices
3,306.0	3,527.0	2,977.0	2,887.0	..	..	..	..	..	..	..	Imports of Goods & NFServices
6,865.2	7,878.5	7,078.8	7,439.0	..	..	..	..	..	..	..	Domestic Absorption
2,242.2	2,478.5	1,655.8	2,172.0	..	..	..	..	..	..	..	Private Consumption, etc.
2,298.0	2,539.0	3,005.0	3,113.0	..	..	..	..	..	..	..	General Gov't Consumption
2,325.0	2,861.0	2,418.0	2,154.0	2,163.0	..	..	..	..	..	..	Gross Domestic Investment
2,230.0	2,811.0	2,362.0	2,093.0	..	..	..	..	..	..	..	Fixed Investment
297.9	385.9	315.6	390.5	395.0	..	..	..	..	..	..	Indirect Taxes, net
10,225.3	8,960.6	8,359.2	8,140.5	7,525.7	..	..	..	..	..	..	GDP at factor cost
164.9	202.3	220.3	273.8	270.4	..	..	..	..	..	..	Agriculture
7,808.1	6,156.8	5,490.0	5,092.1	4,310.5	..	..	..	..	..	..	Industry
202.0	229.1	273.5	294.2	359.9	..	..	..	..	..	..	Manufacturing
2,252.3	2,601.5	2,648.9	2,774.6	2,944.8	..	..	..	..	..	..	Services, etc.
5,983.0	4,329.0	4,014.0	3,246.0	..	..	..	..	..	..	..	Gross Domestic Saving
5,641.4	3,896.6	3,390.6	2,416.9	..	..	..	..	..	..	..	Gross National Saving
				(Millions of 1980 Libyan Dinars)							
10,503.9	8,574.5	8,119.1	7,957.5	7,235.4	6,986.6	6,359.7	6,159.3	6,187.6		..	Gross National Product
10,523.2	8,544.8	8,262.7	8,171.9	7,869.5	7,173.6	6,549.5	6,339.9	6,384.1		..	H	GDP at Market Prices
3,658.0	1,099.8	1,183.7	1,567.4	..	..	..	..	..	..	..	Resource Balance
6,964.0	4,491.4	4,426.9	4,426.9	..	..	..	..	..	..	..	Exports of Goods & NFServices
3,306.0	3,391.6	3,243.2	2,859.6	..	..	..	..	..	..	..	Imports of Goods & NFServices
6,865.2	6,619.4	6,242.6	5,681.8	..	..	..	..	..	..	..	Domestic Absorption
2,242.2	2,182.9	2,308.8	2,201.1	..	..	..	..	..	..	..	Private Consumption, etc.
2,298.0	2,128.3	2,269.7	2,100.1	..	..	..	..	..	..	..	General Gov't Consumption
2,325.0	2,308.2	1,664.1	1,380.7	1,382.1	..	..	..	..	..	..	Gross Domestic Investment
..	..	..	..	..	..	..	..	..	..	..	Fixed Investment
10,225.3	8,307.2	8,036.7	7,944.3	7,651.0	..	..	..	..	..	H	GDP at factor cost
164.9	186.0	190.1	222.4	214.1	..	..	..	..	..	..	Agriculture
7,808.1	6,051.6	5,764.1	5,496.5	5,160.6	..	..	..	..	..	..	Industry
202.0	216.1	248.5	262.7	315.7	..	..	..	..	..	..	Manufacturing
2,252.3	1,898.3	1,861.9	1,888.8	1,866.8	..	..	..	..	..	..	Services, etc.
											Memo Items:
6,964.0	4,803.2	4,982.0	3,941.2	..	..	..	..	..	..	..	Capacity to Import
0.0	311.8	555.0	-485.7	..	..	..	..	..	..	..	Terms of Trade Adjustment
10,523.2	8,856.6	8,817.8	7,686.2	..	..	..	..	..	..	..	Gross Domestic Income
10,503.9	8,886.3	8,674.2	7,471.8	..	..	..	..	..	..	..	Gross National Income
				(Index 1980 = 100)							**DOMESTIC PRICES/DEFLATORS**
100.0	109.4	105.0	104.4	100.7	100.4	98.8	111.8	..	..	..	Overall (GDP)
100.0	119.0	113.4	130.9	..	..	..	..	..	..	..	Domestic Absorption
100.0	108.8	115.9	123.1	126.3	..	..	..	..	..	..	Agriculture
100.0	101.7	95.2	92.6	83.5	..	..	..	..	..	..	Industry
100.0	106.0	110.0	112.0	114.0	..	..	..	..	..	..	Manufacturing
..	..	..	..	..	..	..	..	..	..	..	Consumer Price Index
											MANUFACTURING ACTIVITY
..	..	..	..	..	..	..	..	..	..	J	Employment (1987=100)
..	..	..	..	..	..	..	..	..	..	J	Real Earnings per Empl. (1987=100)
..	..	..	..	..	..	..	..	..	..	J	Real Output per Empl. (1987=100)
40.9	..	..	..	..	..	..	..	..	..	J	Earnings as % of Value Added
				(Millions of current Libyan Dinars)							**MONETARY HOLDINGS**
4,104.5	4,646.8	4,305.4	4,126.8	4,175.3	5,053.6	4,811.4	5,073.1	4,754.5	5,156.5	..	Money Supply, Broadly Defined
2,898.9	3,512.2	3,232.3	2,884.5	2,711.3	3,492.2	3,041.4	3,438.6	3,011.6	3,521.4	..	Money
685.7	791.1	889.9	838.2	767.5	985.0	1,023.7	1,068.2	899.6	1,131.6	..	Currency Outside Banks
2,213.2	2,721.0	2,342.4	2,046.2	1,943.8	2,507.2	2,017.7	2,370.4	2,112.0	2,389.8	..	Demand Deposits
1,205.7	1,134.7	1,073.1	1,242.3	1,464.0	1,561.4	1,770.0	1,634.5	1,742.9	1,635.0	..	Quasi-Money
				(Millions of current Libyan Dinars)							**GOVERNMENT DEFICIT (-) OR SURPLUS**
..	..	..	..	..	..	..	..	..	..	..	Current Revenue
..	..	..	..	..	..	..	..	..	..	..	Current Expenditure
..	..	..	..	..	..	..	..	..	..	..	Current Budget Balance
..	..	..	..	..	..	..	..	..	..	..	Capital Receipts
..	..	..	..	..	..	..	..	..	..	..	Capital Payments

LIBYA	1969	1970	1971	1972	1973	1974	1975	1976	1977	1978	1979
FOREIGN TRADE (CUSTOMS BASIS)					*(Millions of current US dollars)*						
Value of Exports, fob	2,167	2,366	2,695	2,943	3,995	8,268	6,840	9,562	11,423	9,907	16,085
Nonfuel Primary Products	3	2	2	7	9	3	1	0	1	0	0
Fuels	2,161	2,355	2,686	2,931	3,984	8,262	6,834	9,554	- 11,411	9,867	16,007
Manufactures	3	8	7	5	2	3	6	7	12	40	78
Value of Imports, cif	676	674	930	1,291	2,011	3,746	4,424	4,277	5,458	6,386	9,606
Nonfuel Primary Products	112	139	178	209	413	610	723	556	824	881	1,127
Fuels	21	18	23	23	36	45	69	86	21	36	39
Manufactures	543	517	729	1,059	1,562	3,091	3,632	3,635	4,613	5,469	8,440
					(Index 1987 = 100)						
Terms of Trade	..	..	..	..	..	..	..	..	..	..	..
Export Prices, fob	..	..	..	..	..	..	..	..	..	..	..
Import Prices, cif	26.3	28.6	30.4	33.2	40.5	49.2	53.7	53.8	58.4	67.3	76.7
BALANCE OF PAYMENTS					*(Millions of current US dollars)*						
Exports of Goods & Services	..	2,536	2,886	2,695	3,743	8,237	6,793	9,096	10,786	10,370	16,547
Merchandise, fob	..	2,397	2,714	2,470	3,528	7,803	6,418	8,748	10,406	9,900	15,981
Nonfactor Services	..	42	42	97	101	143	160	167	136	153	143
Factor Services	..	97	129	128	114	291	215	181	244	317	424
Imports of Goods & Services	..	1,638	1,838	2,049	3,249	5,118	5,977	5,851	7,690	8,582	11,874
Merchandise, fob	..	674	930	1,291	2,011	3,746	4,424	4,277	4,929	5,764	8,647
Nonfactor Services	..	400	337	520	811	1,173	1,343	1,368	1,301	1,448	1,953
Factor Services	..	564	572	238	427	200	210	206	1,459	1,370	1,273
Long-Term Interest	..	..	..	..	..	..	..	..	..	..	..
Private Current Transfers, net	..	-140	-174	-306	-273	-350	-260	-257	-858	-972	-859
Workers' Remittances	..										
Curr. A/C Bal before Off. Transf.	..	758	874	340	222	2,768	556	2,988	2,238	816	3,814
Net Official Transfers	..	-113	-90	-102	-156	-69	-164	-144	-79	-78	-43
Curr. A/C Bal after Off. Transf.	..	645	783	238	66	2,700	392	2,844	2,159	738	3,771
Long-Term Capital, net	..	139	130	-43	-510	-422	-1,524	-1,508	-1,066	-1,068	-930
Direct Investment	..	139	140	-4	-148	-241	-616	-521	-512	-720	-609
Long-Term Loans	..	..	..	..	..	..	..	..	..	..	..
Disbursements	..	..	..	..	..	..	..	..	..	..	..
Repayments	..	..	..	..	..	..	..	..	..	..	..
Other Long-Term Capital	..	0	-10	-39	-362	-182	-908	-987	-554	-348	-321
Other Capital, net	..	-87	-40	239	-537	48	-765	-178	581	-189	-621
Change in Reserves	..	-697	-874	-434	982	-2,325	1,897	-1,157	-1,674	519	-2,220
Memo Item:					*(Libyan Dinars per US dollar)*						
Conversion Factor (Annual Avg)	0.360	0.360	0.360	0.330	0.300	0.300	0.300	0.300	0.300	0.300	0.300
EXTERNAL DEBT (Total)				*(Millions of US dollars), outstanding at end of year*							
Long-Term Debt (by debtor)	..	..	..	..	..	..	..	..	..	..	..
Central Bank, incl. IMF credit	..	..	..	..	..	..	..	..	..	..	..
Central Government	..	..	..	..	..	..	..	..	..	..	..
Rest of General Government	..	..	..	..	..	..	..	..	..	..	..
Non-financial Public Enterprises	..	..	..	..	..	..	..	..	..	..	..
Priv. Sector, incl non-guaranteed	..	..	..	..	..	..	..	..	..	..	..
Short-Term Debt	..	..	..	..	..	..	..	..	..	..	..
Memo Items:					*(Millions of US dollars)*						
Int'l Reserves Excluding Gold	832.3	1,504.8	2,572.8	2,832.2	2,023.8	3,511.1	2,095.0	3,106.4	4,786.4	4,104.8	6,344.4
Gold Holdings (at market price)	85.8	91.1	106.3	158.2	273.6	454.6	341.9	328.5	403.8	553.3	1,261.6
SOCIAL INDICATORS											
Total Fertility Rate	7.5	7.5	7.6	7.6	7.5	7.5	7.5	7.4	7.4	7.3	7.3
Infant Mortality Rate	124.8	122.2	119.6	117.0	115.0	113.0	111.0	109.0	107.0	105.0	103.0
Life Expectancy at Birth	51.4	51.9	52.4	52.9	53.5	54.1	54.6	55.2	55.8	56.3	56.8
Urban Population, % of total	33.9	35.8	38.0	40.2	42.4	44.6	46.8	48.8	50.7	52.7	54.6
Food Prod. per capita (1987=100)	81.9	72.1	54.9	87.4	85.5	90.7	99.1	104.4	73.2	63.4	88.3
Labor Force, Agriculture (%)	31.0	28.9	27.6	26.5	25.4	24.4	23.5	22.2	21.1	20.0	19.1
Labor Force, Female (%)	6.3	6.4	6.4	6.5	6.6	6.6	6.7	6.8	6.9	7.1	7.2
Primary Schl. Enroll. Ratio	..	..	..	..	..	..	..	..	..	..	..
Primary Schl. Enroll. Ratio, Female	..	..	..	..	..	..	..	..	..	..	..
Secondary Schl. Enroll. Ratio	..	..	..	..	..	..	..	..	..	..	..

FOREIGN TRADE (CUSTOMS BASIS)

(Millions of current US dollars)

1980	1981	1982	1983	1984	1985	1986	1987	1988	1989 est.	NOTES	LIBYA
21,919	15,566	13,952	10,957	11,136	10,840	5,814	5,648	5,640	..	..	Value of Exports, fob
3	13	9	4	7	6	2	..	..	..	..	Nonfuel Primary Products
21,837	15,436	13,739	10,750	10,948	10,648	5,682	..	..	..	..	Fuels
79	117	204	203	181	186	130	..	..	..	..	Manufactures
11,520	16,181	12,195	9,976	9,404	6,339	4,926	5,984	6,386	..	..	Value of Imports, cif
1,630	1,875	1,890	1,689	1,588	1,061	829	1,009	..	..	..	Nonfuel Primary Products
49	93	83	73	70	47	37	44	..	..	..	Fuels
9,841	14,213	10,222	8,214	7,746	5,231	4,060	4,931	..	..	..	Manufactures

(Index 1987 = 100)

1980	1981	1982	1983	1984	1985	1986	1987	1988	1989 est.	NOTES	LIBYA
..	..	..	..	..	..	..	..	..	..	..	Terms of Trade
..	..	..	..	..	..	..	..	..	..	..	Export Prices, fob
84.8	83.9	82.9	81.7	79.8	79.9	91.9	100.0	..	..	..	Import Prices, cif

BALANCE OF PAYMENTS

(Millions of current US dollars)

1980	1981	1982	1983	1984	1985	1986	1987	1988	1989 est.	NOTES	LIBYA
23,366	16,521	14,732	13,185	11,748	10,879	6,443	6,673	6,533	..	..	Exports of Goods & Services
21,919	14,731	13,701	12,348	11,028	10,353	5,814	5,828	5,644	..	..	Merchandise, fob
164	163	163	161	170	63	82	114	128	..	..	Nonfactor Services
1,282	1,627	868	676	550	463	547	731	761	..	..	Factor Services
14,018	18,838	14,617	12,726	11,884	8,068	6,072	7,191	7,824	..	..	Imports of Goods & Services
10,368	14,563	10,976	8,978	8,464	5,754	4,434	5,391	5,753	..	..	Merchandise, fob
2,303	2,757	2,265	2,315	2,202	1,775	1,047	1,437	1,634	..	..	Nonfactor Services
1,347	1,517	1,376	1,433	1,218	540	591	364	437	..	..	Factor Services
..	..	..	..	..	..	..	..	..	..	..	Long-Term Interest
-1,089	-1,570	-1,597	-2,045	-1,240	-859	-490	-470	-496	..	..	Private Current Transfers, net
..	..	..	..	..	..	..	..	..	..	..	Workers' Remittances
8,259	-3,888	-1,482	-1,586	-1,376	1,952	-119	-989	-1,786	..	..	Curr. A/C Bal before Off. Transf.
-46	-76	-78	-58	-81	-45	-36	-56	-37	..	..	Net Official Transfers
8,214	-3,964	-1,560	-1,643	-1,456	1,906	-156	-1,045	-1,823	..	..	Curr. A/C Bal after Off. Transf.
-1,372	-1,705	-1,026	-557	-214	-19	-251	-2,953	-430	..	..	Long-Term Capital, net
-1,136	-769	-411	-327	-17	119	-177	-213	42	..	..	Direct Investment
..	..	..	..	..	..	..	..	..	..	..	Long-Term Loans
..	..	..	..	..	..	..	..	..	..	..	Disbursements
..	..	..	..	..	..	..	..	..	..	..	Repayments
-236	-935	-615	-231	-197	-138	-74	-2,740	-472	..	..	Other Long-Term Capital
-435	1,532	585	423	-51	475	618	2,998	863	..	..	Other Capital, net
-6,407	4,136	2,001	1,778	1,721	-2,362	-212	1,000	1,390	-25	..	Change in Reserves

Memo Item:

(Libyan Dinars per US dollar)

1980	1981	1982	1983	1984	1985	1986	1987	1988	1989 est.	NOTES	LIBYA
0.300	0.300	0.300	0.300	0.300	0.300	0.310	0.270	0.290	..	..	Conversion Factor (Annual Avg)

(Millions of US dollars), outstanding at end of year

1980	1981	1982	1983	1984	1985	1986	1987	1988	1989 est.	NOTES	LIBYA
..	..	..	..	..	..	..	..	..	..	..	**EXTERNAL DEBT (Total)**
..	..	..	..	..	..	..	..	..	..	..	Long-Term Debt (by debtor)
..	..	..	..	..	..	..	..	..	..	..	Central Bank, incl. IMF credit
..	..	..	..	..	..	..	..	..	..	..	Central Government
..	..	..	..	..	..	..	..	..	..	..	Rest of General Government
..	..	..	..	..	..	..	..	..	..	..	Non-financial Public Enterprises
..	..	..	..	..	..	..	..	..	..	..	Priv. Sector, incl non-guaranteed
..	..	..	..	..	..	..	..	..	..	..	Short-Term Debt

Memo Items:

(Millions of US dollars)

1980	1981	1982	1983	1984	1985	1986	1987	1988	1989 est.	NOTES	LIBYA
13,090.5	9,002.9	7,059.5	5,218.7	3,634.2	5,903.9	5,953.2	5,838.0	4,321.6	4,332.7	..	Int'l Reserves Excluding Gold
1,814.3	1,422.4	1,635.0	1,365.2	1,124.7	1,177.2	1,407.2	1,742.8	1,476.9	1,443.6	..	Gold Holdings (at market price)

SOCIAL INDICATORS

1980	1981	1982	1983	1984	1985	1986	1987	1988	1989 est.	NOTES	LIBYA
7.3	7.2	7.2	7.1	7.1	7.0	6.9	6.9	6.8	6.7	..	Total Fertility Rate
101.0	99.0	97.0	94.0	91.0	88.0	85.0	82.0	79.8	77.5	..	Infant Mortality Rate
57.3	57.8	58.3	58.8	59.3	59.8	60.3	60.8	61.2	61.7	..	Life Expectancy at Birth
56.6	58.2	59.8	61.3	62.9	64.5	65.6	66.8	67.9	69.1	..	Urban Population, % of total
92.9	91.0	102.1	97.6	92.0	107.1	91.4	100.0	97.7	100.1	..	Food Prod. per capita (1987=100)
18.2	..	..	..	..	..	..	..	..	..	..	Labor Force, Agriculture (%)
7.3	7.5	7.6	7.8	8.0	8.1	8.3	8.5	8.7	8.9	..	Labor Force, Female (%)
..	..	..	..	..	..	..	..	..	..	..	Primary Schl. Enroll. Ratio
..	..	..	..	..	..	..	..	..	..	..	Primary Schl. Enroll. Ratio, Female
..	..	..	..	..	..	..	..	..	..	..	Secondary Schl. Enroll. Ratio

LUXEMBOURG	1969	1970	1971	1972	1973	1974	1975	1976	1977	1978	1979
CURRENT GNP PER CAPITA (US $)	..	..	..	..	..	..	..	..	..	10,760	12,710
POPULATION (thousands)	339	340	345	348	353	357	361	362	362	362	364

USE AND ORIGIN OF RESOURCES *(Billions of current Luxembourg Francs)*

	1969	1970	1971	1972	1973	1974	1975	1976	1977	1978	1979
Gross National Product (GNP)	..	..	..	..	..	..	..	116.47	122.00	133.49	145.32
Net Factor Income from Abroad	0.40	1.92	2.21	3.42	3.48	5.68	11.87	16.67	19.45	21.30	23.19
GDP at Market Prices	..	..	..	..	..	..	..	99.80	102.56	112.20	122.14
Resource Balance	..	..	..	..	..	..	..	5.47	3.80	0.98	4.55
Exports of Goods & NFServices	..	..	..	..	..	..	..	87.97	89.07	93.94	111.00
Imports of Goods & NFServices	..	..	..	..	..	..	..	82.50	85.27	92.96	106.45
Domestic Absorption	..	..	..	..	..	..	..	94.33	98.76	111.21	117.58
Private Consumption, etc.	..	..	..	..	..	..	..	56.82	61.42	66.76	73.34
General Gov't Consumption	..	..	..	..	..	..	..	15.05	16.32	17.54	18.99
Gross Domestic Investment	..	..	..	..	..	..	..	22.46	21.02	26.91	25.25
Fixed Investment	..	..	..	..	..	..	..	23.43	24.66	26.31	28.92
Indirect Taxes, net	3.76	4.72	5.36	6.45	7.68	8.27	8.90	9.44	9.59	11.26	11.57
GDP at factor cost	..	..	..	..	..	..	..	90.37	92.97	100.94	110.56
Agriculture	..	..	..	..	..	..	..	2.81	3.05	3.48	3.62
Industry	..	..	..	..	..	..	..	42.34	40.61	44.81	48.77
Manufacturing	..	..	..	..	..	..	..	31.56	29.52	33.53	36.85
Services, etc.	..	..	..	..	..	..	..	54.65	58.89	63.91	69.75
Gross Domestic Saving	..	..	..	..	..	..	..	27.93	24.82	27.90	29.81
Gross National Saving	..	..	..	..	..	..	..	..	..	..	..

(Billions of 1987 Luxembourg Francs)

	1969	1970	1971	1972	1973	1974	1975	1976	1977	1978	1979
Gross National Product	..	..	..	..	..	..	..	203.70	209.58	218.01	223.34
GDP at Market Prices	..	..	..	..	..	..	..	170.58	173.26	180.32	184.55
Resource Balance	..	..	..	..	..	..	..	-5.52	-1.89	-6.04	-2.47
Exports of Goods & NFServices	..	..	..	..	..	..	..	136.49	142.26	146.74	160.57
Imports of Goods & NFServices	..	..	..	..	..	..	..	142.01	144.14	152.78	163.04
Domestic Absorption	..	..	..	..	..	..	..	176.11	175.15	186.36	187.02
Private Consumption, etc.	..	..	..	..	..	..	..	105.52	108.82	111.48	116.19
General Gov't Consumption	..	..	..	..	..	..	..	28.31	29.14	29.66	30.32
Gross Domestic Investment	..	..	..	..	..	..	..	42.27	37.19	45.22	40.50
Fixed Investment	..	..	..	..	..	..	..	44.06	44.03	44.49	46.17
GDP at factor cost	..	..	..	..	..	..	..	152.62	155.90	161.10	165.80
Agriculture	..	..	..	..	..	..	..	4.48	4.99	5.36	5.27
Industry	..	..	..	..	..	..	..	63.04	63.00	65.14	67.05
Manufacturing	..	..	..	..	..	..	..	44.85	45.08	46.95	48.76
Services, etc.	..	..	..	..	..	..	..	102.47	104.77	109.35	111.70
Memo Items:											
Capacity to Import	..	..	..	..	..	..	..	151.43	150.57	154.40	170.01
Terms of Trade Adjustment	..	..	..	..	..	..	..	14.95	8.31	7.66	9.44
Gross Domestic Income	..	..	..	..	..	..	..	185.53	181.57	187.98	193.99
Gross National Income	..	..	..	..	..	..	..	218.64	217.89	225.67	232.78

DOMESTIC PRICES/DEFLATORS *(Index 1987 = 100)*

	1969	1970	1971	1972	1973	1974	1975	1976	1977	1978	1979
Overall (GDP)	..	..	..	..	..	..	..	58.5	59.2	62.2	66.2
Domestic Absorption	..	..	..	..	..	..	..	53.6	56.4	59.7	62.9
Agriculture	..	..	..	..	..	..	..	62.9	61.2	64.9	68.6
Industry	..	..	..	..	..	..	..	67.2	64.5	68.8	72.7
Manufacturing	..	..	..	..	..	..	..	70.4	65.5	71.4	75.6
Consumer Price Index	35.5	37.2	38.9	40.9	43.5	47.6	52.7	57.8	61.7	63.6	66.5

MANUFACTURING ACTIVITY

	1969	1970	1971	1972	1973	1974	1975	1976	1977	1978	1979
Employment (1987=100)	114.7	117.2	120.6	123.1	127.7	132.5	129.9	126.7	123.5	116.3	113.4
Real Earnings per Empl. (1987=100)	64.5	73.3	75.1	76.9	79.4	89.4	90.1	87.9	89.5	93.3	94.8
Real Output per Empl. (1987=100)	..	..	..	..	..	..	..	57.1	59.1	62.5	71.2
Earnings as % of Value Added	46.4	42.9	55.2	56.8	48.5	46.2	63.6	66.3	76.9	67.4	62.7

MONETARY HOLDINGS *(Millions of current Luxembourg Francs)*

	1969	1970	1971	1972	1973	1974	1975	1976	1977	1978	1979
Money Supply, Broadly Defined	..	..	..	..	..	..	..	..	..	..	..
Money	..	..	..	..	..	..	..	..	..	..	..
Currency Outside Banks	..	..	..	..	..	..	..	..	..	..	..
Demand Deposits	..	..	..	..	..	..	..	..	..	..	..
Quasi-Money	..	..	..	..	..	..	..	..	..	..	..

(Millions of current Luxembourg Francs)

	1969	1970	1971	1972	1973	1974	1975	1976	1977	1978	1979
GOVERNMENT DEFICIT (-) OR SURPLUS	..	1,024	1,129	969	2,125	4,067	1,008	314	706	3,801	-294
Current Revenue	..	17,557	19,841	22,617	27,509	34,341	38,557	44,757	50,523	56,137	58,143
Current Expenditure	..	14,296	16,083	18,313	21,187	25,321	32,323	38,013	42,887	45,439	50,397
Current Budget Balance	..	3,261	3,758	4,304	6,322	9,020	6,234	6,744	7,636	10,698	7,746
Capital Receipts	..	12	3	5	5	16	6	29	9	12	107
Capital Payments	..	2,249	2,632	3,340	4,202	4,969	5,232	6,459	6,939	6,909	8,147

1980	1981	1982	1983	1984	1985	1986	1987	1988	1989 estimate	NOTES	LUXEMBOURG
14,980	15,600	15,820	14,700	14,090	14,000	15,120	17,620	22,290	24,860	..	**CURRENT GNP PER CAPITA (US $)**
365	366	366	366	366	367	370	372	375	379	..	**POPULATION (thousands)**
			(Billions of current Luxembourg Francs)								**USE AND ORIGIN OF RESOURCES**
161.57	179.02	219.82	247.65	270.96	289.21	299.32	304.53	326.90	349.88	..	Gross National Product (GNP)
28.64	37.33	61.05	72.99	77.31	83.96	81.41	78.33	85.64	91.65	..	Net Factor Income from Abroad
132.93	141.69	158.77	174.65	193.65	205.24	217.91	226.20	241.26	258.23	..	GDP at Market Prices
-1.84	-4.76	-3.42	-0.66	2.44	9.65	9.68	-0.92	3.23	1.30	..	Resource Balance
117.27	122.57	140.96	157.16	195.46	222.57	224.94	224.34	248.38	280.66	..	Exports of Goods & NFServices
119.11	127.33	144.38	157.83	193.02	212.91	215.25	225.26	245.15	279.36	..	Imports of Goods & NFServices
134.77	146.45	162.19	175.32	191.21	195.59	208.23	227.13	238.03	256.93	..	Domestic Absorption
80.99	88.92	97.84	106.90	115.38	120.51	125.88	135.94	141.26	152.20	..	Private Consumption, etc.
21.06	23.09	25.68	28.50	31.08	32.31	34.02	36.19	38.09	40.72	..	General Gov't Consumption
32.72	34.44	38.67	39.92	44.75	42.77	48.32	55.00	58.68	64.01	..	Gross Domestic Investment
35.05	35.10	38.29	36.88	39.58	37.88	49.73	54.89	57.84	62.08	..	Fixed Investment
14.03	13.86	16.53	20.46	23.62	25.89	27.98	28.71	32.58	..	..	Indirect Taxes, net
118.90	127.83	142.24	154.19	170.02	179.36	189.93	197.50	208.68	..	..	GDP at factor cost
3.45	3.89	5.41	4.94	5.17	5.56	5.56	5.49	5.62	..	B	Agriculture
51.44	53.64	61.18	65.07	73.00	77.78	78.86	76.62	84.95	..	B	Industry
37.82	39.35	46.77	49.83	57.40	61.64	61.37	57.44	63.37	..	B	Manufacturing
78.03	84.17	92.18	104.64	115.47	121.91	133.49	144.10	150.70	..	B	Services, etc.
30.88	29.68	35.24	39.26	47.19	52.43	58.01	54.08	61.91	65.31	..	Gross Domestic Saving
..	..	..	..	..	..	..	..	..	..	..	Gross National Saving
			(Billions of 1987 Luxembourg Francs)								
230.14	237.46	263.80	276.64	287.88	299.17	304.24	304.53	319.52	335.58	..	Gross National Product
186.10	185.08	187.17	192.76	204.54	210.43	219.82	226.20	235.61	243.90	..	GDP at Market Prices
-11.74	-13.36	-13.31	-6.97	-0.93	3.56	3.64	-0.92	2.07	2.02	..	Resource Balance
157.27	150.35	150.10	158.20	186.92	204.76	213.34	224.34	244.39	261.34	..	Exports of Goods & NFServices
169.01	163.71	163.41	165.17	187.85	201.20	209.70	225.26	242.33	259.33	..	Imports of Goods & NFServices
197.84	198.44	200.48	199.74	205.47	206.87	216.19	227.13	233.54	241.89	..	Domestic Absorption
118.15	119.70	120.13	121.29	123.74	127.62	130.82	135.94	138.69	143.65	..	Private Consumption, etc.
31.26	31.70	32.17	32.78	33.49	34.15	35.26	36.19	37.31	38.26	..	General Gov't Consumption
48.43	47.04	48.19	45.67	48.24	45.11	50.11	55.00	57.53	59.97	..	Gross Domestic Investment
52.04	48.18	47.95	42.42	42.65	40.04	51.53	54.89	56.66	58.33	..	Fixed Investment
165.17	165.83	166.35	169.24	179.08	183.07	190.81	197.50	203.68	..	..	GDP at factor cost
4.92	5.10	5.81	5.13	5.57	5.59	5.51	5.49	5.20	..	..	Agriculture
67.20	64.10	63.81	65.25	70.57	73.38	75.75	76.62	83.18	..	..	Industry
48.25	45.39	46.20	47.80	53.28	56.23	57.59	57.44	62.25	..	..	Manufacturing
113.51	115.71	117.48	122.38	128.40	131.47	138.56	144.10	147.23	..	..	Services, etc.
											Memo Items:
166.39	157.58	159.53	164.47	190.22	210.33	219.14	224.34	245.52	260.53	..	Capacity to Import
9.12	7.24	9.43	6.28	3.30	5.56	5.80	0.00	1.13	-0.81	..	Terms of Trade Adjustment
195.23	192.31	196.60	199.04	207.84	216.00	225.62	226.20	236.73	243.09	..	Gross Domestic Income
239.27	244.70	273.23	282.92	291.18	304.73	310.04	304.53	320.65	334.77	..	Gross National Income
			(Index 1987 = 100)								**DOMESTIC PRICES/DEFLATORS**
71.4	76.6	84.8	90.6	94.7	97.5	99.1	100.0	102.4	105.9	..	Overall (GDP)
68.1	73.8	80.9	87.8	93.1	94.5	96.3	100.0	101.9	106.2	..	Domestic Absorption
70.2	76.2	93.1	96.3	92.8	99.5	100.8	100.0	108.0	..	..	Agriculture
76.6	83.7	95.9	99.7	103.4	106.0	104.1	100.0	102.1	..	..	Industry
78.4	86.7	101.2	104.2	107.7	109.6	106.6	100.0	101.8	..	..	Manufacturing
70.7	76.4	83.6	90.8	95.9	99.8	100.1	100.0	101.5	104.9	..	Consumer Price Index
											MANUFACTURING ACTIVITY
110.2	109.0	107.4	103.1	101.8	101.4	103.1	100.0	96.8	96.6	..	Employment (1987=100)
96.5	93.9	92.7	88.7	91.2	93.8	98.5	100.0	103.4	..	..	Real Earnings per Empl. (1987=100)
73.3	68.9	71.0	77.8	92.4	99.2	100.5	100.0	113.5	..	..	Real Output per Empl. (1987=100)
65.0	65.6	57.0	52.1	49.4	50.6	49.9	58.1	53.3	..	..	Earnings as % of Value Added
			(Millions of current Luxembourg Francs)								**MONETARY HOLDINGS**
..	..	..	..	..	..	..	..	..	..	..	Money Supply, Broadly Defined
..	..	..	..	..	..	..	..	..	..	..	Money
..	..	..	..	..	..	..	..	..	..	..	Currency Outside Banks
..	..	..	..	..	..	..	..	..	..	..	Demand Deposits
..	..	..	..	..	..	..	..	..	..	..	Quasi-Money
			(Millions of current Luxembourg Francs)								**GOVERNMENT DEFICIT (-) OR SURPLUS**
1,673	-3,016	1,152	-3,560	10,253	21,431	16,336	8,081	7,610	..	..	Current Revenue
66,339	72,133	79,548	90,293	96,889	105,115	109,808	113,965	120,912	..	..	Current Expenditure
56,580	62,783	71,537	76,746	80,805	84,645	91,748	96,587	103,432	..	..	Current Budget Balance
9,759	9,350	8,011	13,547	16,084	20,470	18,060	17,378	17,480	..	..	Capital Receipts
13	98	51	96	171	65	225	210	204	..	..	Capital Payments
8,571	10,005	10,491	16,423	11,413	11,657	9,733	10,976	12,722	..	..	

LUXEMBOURG	1969	1970	1971	1972	1973	1974	1975	1976	1977	1978	1979
FOREIGN TRADE (CUSTOMS BASIS)					*(Millions of current US dollars)*						
Value of Exports, fob	..	..	..	..	..	..	..	..	..	..	..
Nonfuel Primary Products	..	..	..	..	..	..	..	..	..	..	..
Fuels	..	..	..	..	..	..	..	..	..	..	..
Manufactures	..	..	..	..	..	..	..	..	..	..	..
Value of Imports, cif	..	..	..	..	..	..	..	..	..	..	..
Nonfuel Primary Products	..	..	..	..	..	..	..	..	..	..	..
Fuels	..	..	..	..	..	..	..	..	..	..	..
Manufactures	..	..	..	..	..	..	..	..	..	..	..
					(Index 1987 = 100)						
Terms of Trade	..	..	..	..	..	..	..	..	..	..	..
Export Prices, fob	..	..	..	..	..	..	..	..	..	..	..
Import Prices, cif	..	..	..	..	..	..	..	..	..	..	..
BALANCE OF PAYMENTS					*(Millions of current US dollars)*						
Exports of Goods & Services	..	..	..	..	..	..	..	..	..	..	..
Merchandise, fob	..	..	..	..	..	..	..	..	..	..	..
Nonfactor Services	..	..	..	..	..	..	..	..	..	..	..
Factor Services	..	..	..	..	..	..	..	..	..	..	..
Imports of Goods & Services	..	..	..	..	..	..	..	..	..	..	..
Merchandise, fob	..	..	..	..	..	..	..	..	..	..	..
Nonfactor Services	..	..	..	..	..	..	..	..	..	..	..
Factor Services	..	..	..	..	..	..	..	..	..	..	..
Long-Term Interest	..	..	..	..	..	..	..	..	..	..	..
Private Current Transfers, net	..	..	..	..	..	..	..	..	..	..	..
Workers' Remittances	..	..	..	..	..	..	..	..	..	..	..
Curr. A/C Bal before Off. Transf.	..	..	..	..	..	..	..	..	..	..	..
Net Official Transfers	..	..	..	..	..	..	..	..	..	..	..
Curr. A/C Bal after Off. Transf.	..	..	..	..	..	..	..	..	..	..	..
Long-Term Capital, net	..	..	..	..	..	..	..	..	..	..	..
Direct Investment	..	..	..	..	..	..	..	..	..	..	..
Long-Term Loans	..	..	..	..	..	..	..	..	..	..	..
Disbursements	..	..	..	..	..	..	..	..	..	..	..
Repayments	..	..	..	..	..	..	..	..	..	..	..
Other Long-Term Capital	..	..	..	..	..	..	..	..	..	..	..
Other Capital, net	..	..	..	..	..	..	..	..	..	..	..
Change in Reserves	..	..	..	..	..	..	..	..	..	..	..
Memo Item:					*(Luxembourg Francs per US dollar)*						
Conversion Factor (Annual Avg)	50.000	50.000	48.870	44.010	38.980	38.950	36.780	38.610	35.840	31.490	29.320
EXTERNAL DEBT (Total)				*(Millions of US dollars), outstanding at end of year*							
Long-Term Debt (by debtor)	..	..	..	..	..	..	..	..	..	..	..
Central Bank, incl. IMF credit	..	..	..	..	..	..	..	..	..	..	..
Central Government	..	..	..	..	..	..	..	..	..	..	..
Rest of General Government	..	..	..	..	..	..	..	..	..	..	..
Non-financial Public Enterprises	..	..	..	..	..	..	..	..	..	..	..
Priv. Sector, incl non-guaranteed	..	..	..	..	..	..	..	..	..	..	..
Short-Term Debt	..	..	..	..	..	..	..	..	..	..	..
Memo Items:					*(Millions of US dollars)*						
Int'l Reserves Excluding Gold	..	..	..	..	..	..	..	..	..	..	..
Gold Holdings (at market price)	15.48	16.43	19.30	28.70	49.65	82.49	62.03	59.60	74.37	102.86	233.03
SOCIAL INDICATORS											
Total Fertility Rate	2.0	2.0	1.9	1.7	1.5	1.6	1.5	1.5	1.4	1.5	1.5
Infant Mortality Rate	17.5	24.9	22.5	14.0	15.3	13.5	14.8	17.9	10.6	10.6	13.0
Life Expectancy at Birth	70.2	70.3	70.5	70.6	70.9	71.1	71.4	71.6	71.9	72.1	72.4
Urban Population, % of total	66.8	67.8	69.0	70.2	71.3	72.5	73.7	74.6	75.6	76.5	77.5
Food Prod. per capita (1987=100)	..	..	..	..	..	..	..	..	..	..	..
Labor Force, Agriculture (%)	8.7	7.9	7.6	7.4	7.1	6.9	6.6	6.4	6.1	5.9	5.6
Labor Force, Female (%)	26.9	26.9	27.3	27.8	28.3	28.7	29.1	29.8	30.5	31.1	31.8
Primary Schl. Enroll. Ratio	..	112.0	..	..	..	..	..	98.0	98.0	98.0	94.0
Primary Schl. Enroll. Ratio, Female	..	112.0	..	..	..	..	..	..	..	..	..
Secondary Schl. Enroll. Ratio	..	48.0	..	..	..	..	59.0	62.0	64.0	65.0	66.0

1980	1981	1982	1983	1984	1985	1986	1987	1988	1989	NOTES	LUXEMBOURG
				(Millions of current US dollars)							**FOREIGN TRADE (CUSTOMS BASIS)**
..	..	..	..	..	..	..	..	..	..	f	Value of Exports, fob
..	..	..	..	..	..	..	..	..	..		Nonfuel Primary Products
..	..	..	..	..	..	..	..	..	..		Fuels
..	..	..	..	..	..	..	..	..	..		Manufactures
..	..	..	..	..	..	..	..	..	..	f	Value of Imports, cif
..	..	..	..	..	..	..	..	..	..		Nonfuel Primary Products
..	..	..	..	..	..	..	..	..	..		Fuels
..	..	..	..	..	..	..	..	..	..		Manufactures
				(Index 1987 = 100)							
..	..	..	..	..	..	..	..	..	..	f	Terms of Trade
..	..	..	..	..	..	..	..	..	..	f	Export Prices, fob
..	..	..	..	..	..	..	..	..	..	f	Import Prices, cif
				(Millions of current US dollars)							**BALANCE OF PAYMENTS**
..	..	..	..	..	..	..	..	..	..	f	Exports of Goods & Services
..	..	..	..	..	..	..	..	..	..		Merchandise, fob
..	..	..	..	..	..	..	..	..	..		Nonfactor Services
..	..	..	..	..	..	..	..	..	..		Factor Services
..	..	..	..	..	..	..	..	..	..	f	Imports of Goods & Services
..	..	..	..	..	..	..	..	..	..		Merchandise, fob
..	..	..	..	..	..	..	..	..	..		Nonfactor Services
..	..	..	..	..	..	..	..	..	..		Factor Services
..	..	..	..	..	..	..	..	..	..		Long-Term Interest
..	..	..	..	..	..	..	..	..	..	f	Private Current Transfers, net
..	..	..	..	..	..	..	..	..	..		Workers' Remittances
..	..	..	..	..	..	..	..	..	..		Curr. A/C Bal before Off. Transf.
..	..	..	..	..	..	..	..	..	..		Net Official Transfers
..	..	..	..	..	..	..	..	..	..		Curr. A/C Bal after Off. Transf.
..	..	..	..	..	..	..	..	..	..	f	Long-Term Capital, net
..	..	..	..	..	..	..	..	..	..		Direct Investment
..	..	..	..	..	..	..	..	..	..		Long-Term Loans
..	..	..	..	..	..	..	..	..	..		Disbursements
..	..	..	..	..	..	..	..	..	..		Repayments
..	..	..	..	..	..	..	..	..	..		Other Long-Term Capital
..	..	..	..	..	..	..	..	..	..		Other Capital, net
..	..	..	..	..	..	..	..	..	..		Change in Reserves
				(Luxembourg Francs per US dollar)							**Memo Item:**
29.240	37.130	45.690	51.130	57.780	59.380	44.670	37.330	36.770	39.400	..	Conversion Factor (Annual Avg)
				(Millions of US dollars), outstanding at end of year							**EXTERNAL DEBT (Total)**
..	..	..	..	..	..	..	..	..	..	..	Long-Term Debt (by debtor)
..	..	..	..	..	..	..	..	..	..		Central Bank, incl. IMF credit
..	..	..	..	..	..	..	..	..	..		Central Government
..	..	..	..	..	..	..	..	..	..		Rest of General Government
..	..	..	..	..	..	..	..	..	..		Non-financial Public Enterprises
..	..	..	..	..	..	..	..	..	..		Priv. Sector, incl non-guaranteed
..	..	..	..	..	..	..	..	..	..		Short-Term Debt
				(Millions of US dollars)							**Memo Items:**
..	..	..	..	..	..	..	..	..	..	..	Int'l Reserves Excluding Gold
268.30	180.91	207.95	173.63	132.29	140.31	167.68	207.65	175.98	172.01	..	Gold Holdings (at market price)
											SOCIAL INDICATORS
1.5	1.6	1.5	1.4	1.4	1.4	1.4	1.4	1.6	1.6	..	Total Fertility Rate
11.5	13.8	12.1	11.2	11.7	9.0	7.9	9.4	8.7	8.7	..	Infant Mortality Rate
72.7	73.0	73.3	73.5	73.7	73.9	74.2	74.4	74.5	74.7	..	Life Expectancy at Birth
78.4	79.1	79.8	80.4	81.1	81.8	82.3	82.8	83.3	83.8	..	Urban Population, % of total
..	..	..	..	..	..	..	..	..	..	..	Food Prod. per capita (1987=100)
5.4	..	..	..	..	..	..	..	..	..	..	Labor Force, Agriculture (%)
32.4	32.4	32.3	32.3	32.3	32.2	32.2	32.1	32.0	31.9	..	Labor Force, Female (%)
..	..	..	..	..	..	..	..	..	..	..	Primary Schl. Enroll. Ratio
..	..	..	..	..	..	..	..	..	..	..	Primary Schl. Enroll. Ratio, Female
71.0	..	..	74.0	74.0	75.0	76.0	..	..	..	..	Secondary Schl. Enroll. Ratio

MADAGASCAR	1969	1970	1971	1972	1973	1974	1975	1976	1977	1978	1979
CURRENT GNP PER CAPITA (US $)	170	170	170	180	190	230	280	280	300	310	370
POPULATION (thousands)	6,600	6,752	6,905	7,065	7,235	7,414	7,604	7,806	8,021	8,246	8,478

USE AND ORIGIN OF RESOURCES *(Billions of current Malagasy Francs)*

	1969	1970	1971	1972	1973	1974	1975	1976	1977	1978	1979
Gross National Product (GNP)	268.0	298.5	321.6	330.0	361.9	456.4	483.4	515.8	572.1	600.4	734.2
Net Factor Income from Abroad	-6.3	-10.3	-10.8	-8.1	-6.5	-5.1	-5.9	-5.5	-7.4	-2.0	-2.6
GDP at Market Prices	274.3	308.8	332.4	338.1	368.4	461.5	489.3	521.3	579.5	602.4	736.8
Resource Balance	-13.7	-7.5	-21.9	-13.7	-17.1	-21.6	-24.6	-12.3	-20.9	-41.6	-116.5
Exports of Goods & NFServices	49.7	59.2	48.0	48.2	52.5	71.7	77.6	79.1	95.3	103.3	107.4
Imports of Goods & NFServices	63.4	66.6	69.9	62.0	69.6	93.3	102.2	91.4	116.2	144.9	223.9
Domestic Absorption	288.1	316.3	354.3	351.8	385.5	483.1	513.9	533.6	600.4	644.0	853.3
Private Consumption, etc.	216.1	245.2	267.8	275.8	306.9	391.5	421.1	432.8	489.7	514.7	644.3
General Gov't Consumption	42.4	40.5	49.2	46.2	45.1	51.7	53.0	58.5	63.9	71.6	90.4
Gross Domestic Investment	29.6	30.6	37.3	29.8	33.5	40.0	39.8	42.4	46.8	57.8	118.6
Fixed Investment	..	28.1	32.6	27.9	31.0	33.2	37.6	40.6	46.8	55.6	112.6
Indirect Taxes, net	28.9	32.5	38.2	36.6	39.9	50.0	53.0	56.9	61.7	70.1	83.9
GDP at factor cost	245.4	276.3	294.2	301.5	328.5	411.5	436.3	464.4	517.8	532.3	652.9
Agriculture	58.7	67.5	71.5	75.4	88.0	140.8	148.5	154.7	169.8	171.6	194.3
Industry	37.4	45.0	48.5	51.2	58.9	65.3	69.1	74.6	88.0	91.7	112.1
Manufacturing	..	..	..	..	..	..	..	..	..	..	..
Services, etc.	149.3	163.7	174.2	174.9	181.6	205.4	218.6	235.1	260.0	269.1	346.4
Gross Domestic Saving	15.9	23.1	15.4	16.1	16.5	18.4	15.2	30.1	25.9	16.1	2.1
Gross National Saving	..	5.9	-2.1	0.3	4.9	11.1	4.0	20.4	14.0	10.7	-4.1

(Billions of 1987 Malagasy Francs)

	1969	1970	1971	1972	1973	1974	1975	1976	1977	1978	1979
Gross National Product	2,459.20	2,557.10	2,679.70	2,661.90	2,598.50	2,671.80	2,703.10	2,623.90	2,679.70	2,636.10	2,896.20
GDP at Market Prices	2,516.50	2,649.20	2,772.50	2,729.70	2,648.00	2,701.20	2,735.10	2,650.80	2,713.40	2,642.80	2,904.00
Resource Balance	-519.70	-512.80	-638.90	-498.20	-495.80	-356.60	-324.80	-208.90	-247.00	-293.20	-567.00
Exports of Goods & NFServices	634.00	596.20	477.60	471.30	492.30	521.60	613.00	470.20	495.40	547.90	594.10
Imports of Goods & NFServices	1,153.60	1,109.00	1,116.40	969.40	988.00	878.30	937.80	679.20	742.40	841.00	1,161.10
Domestic Absorption	3,036.10	3,162.10	3,411.40	3,227.90	3,143.80	3,057.80	3,060.00	2,859.70	2,960.50	2,935.90	3,471.00
Private Consumption, etc.	2,504.10	2,655.60	2,814.60	2,736.80	2,655.80	2,558.50	2,570.30	2,411.20	2,526.40	2,489.30	2,815.50
General Gov't Consumption	184.20	186.70	219.50	200.00	184.60	176.90	180.60	189.50	190.70	201.60	230.40
Gross Domestic Investment	347.80	319.80	377.40	291.10	303.40	322.30	309.10	259.00	243.40	245.00	425.10
Fixed Investment	..	..	..	..	..	..	..	..	..	..	..
GDP at factor cost	2,216.80	2,334.00	2,418.40	2,398.10	2,325.10	2,371.70	2,401.50	2,325.30	2,387.40	2,299.60	2,534.10
Agriculture	..	679.10	665.60	679.40	686.80	749.50	745.80	681.30	703.40	657.30	704.30
Industry	..	406.80	371.00	374.80	367.20	391.50	391.50	355.70	366.40	381.60	430.40
Manufacturing	..	..	..	..	..	..	..	..	..	..	..
Services, etc.	..	1,256.60	1,374.00	1,341.80	1,276.30	1,230.70	1,265.70	1,294.20	1,323.30	1,267.80	1,409.10

Memo Items:

	1969	1970	1971	1972	1973	1974	1975	1976	1977	1978	1979
Capacity to Import	904.00	984.40	767.00	754.60	745.70	674.80	712.00	587.70	609.00	599.60	556.90
Terms of Trade Adjustment	270.00	388.20	289.40	283.30	253.40	153.20	99.00	117.40	113.60	51.70	-37.10
Gross Domestic Income	2,786.40	3,037.40	3,062.00	3,013.10	2,901.40	2,854.30	2,834.10	2,768.20	2,827.00	2,694.50	2,866.80
Gross National Income	2,729.20	2,945.30	2,969.10	2,945.20	2,851.90	2,825.00	2,802.10	2,741.30	2,793.30	2,687.80	2,859.10

DOMESTIC PRICES/DEFLATORS *(Index 1987 = 100)*

	1969	1970	1971	1972	1973	1974	1975	1976	1977	1978	1979
Overall (GDP)	10.9	11.7	12.0	12.4	13.9	17.1	17.9	19.7	21.4	22.8	25.4
Domestic Absorption	9.5	10.0	10.4	10.9	12.3	15.8	16.8	18.7	20.3	21.9	24.6
Agriculture	..	9.9	10.7	11.1	12.8	18.8	19.9	22.7	24.1	26.1	27.6
Industry	..	11.1	13.1	13.7	16.1	16.7	17.7	21.0	24.0	24.0	26.1
Manufacturing	..	..	..	..	..	..	..	..	..	..	..
Consumer Price Index	12.2	12.6	13.2	14.0	14.8	18.1	19.6	20.6	21.2	22.6	25.8

MANUFACTURING ACTIVITY

	1969	1970	1971	1972	1973	1974	1975	1976	1977	1978	1979
Employment (1987=100)	..	..	..	..	..	..	..	..	..	..	..
Real Earnings per Empl. (1987=100)	..	..	..	..	..	..	..	..	..	..	..
Real Output per Empl. (1987=100)	..	..	..	..	..	..	..	..	..	..	..
Earnings as % of Value Added	37.3	35.6	38.5	42.1	41.9	42.5	40.7	40.3	37.5	38.5	36.7

MONETARY HOLDINGS *(Billions of current Malagasy Francs)*

	1969	1970	1971	1972	1973	1974	1975	1976	1977	1978	1979
Money Supply, Broadly Defined	49.5	57.1	60.6	67.5	70.2	85.1	86.7	100.2	122.4	144.8	169.0
Money	41.5	46.2	47.0	53.3	57.3	67.9	69.4	79.7	100.0	112.8	124.3
Currency Outside Banks	19.0	22.5	22.3	25.4	27.0	31.9	34.0	35.5	42.1	48.2	53.6
Demand Deposits	22.6	23.7	24.7	28.0	30.3	36.1	35.4	44.2	57.9	64.7	70.7
Quasi-Money	8.0	10.9	13.7	14.2	12.9	17.1	17.3	20.5	22.4	32.0	44.8

(Millions of current Malagasy Francs)

	1969	1970	1971	1972	1973	1974	1975	1976	1977	1978	1979
GOVERNMENT DEFICIT (-) OR SURPLUS	..	..	..	-6,729	-7,309	-9,035	..	..	..	..	..	..
Current Revenue	..	..	..	49,837	54,234	58,246	..	..	..	129,940	168,361
Current Expenditure	..	..	..	41,432	46,951	..	..	..	..	..	..
Current Budget Balance	..	..	..	8,405	7,283	..	..	..	..	..	..
Capital Receipts	..	..	..	..	..	..	..	..	..	..	..
Capital Payments	..	..	..	15,134	14,592	..	..	..	..	..	..

1980	1981	1982	1983	1984	1985	1986	1987	1988	1989 estimate	NOTES	MADAGASCAR
430	410	400	380	340	310	290	270	250	230	..	**CURRENT GNP PER CAPITA (US $)**
8,714	8,955	9,202	9,456	9,716	9,985	10,265	10,556	10,859	11,174	..	**POPULATION (thousands)**
				(Billions of current Malagasy Francs)							**USE AND ORIGIN OF RESOURCES**
844.3	951.9	1,198.6	1,463.1	1,611.0	1,831.3	2,124.2	2,583.2	3,285.3	3,752.6	..	Gross National Product (GNP)
-9.7	-24.9	-34.6	-48.4	-84.0	-85.4	-104.8	-186.4	-234.1	-317.7	..	Net Factor Income from Abroad
854.0	976.8	1,233.2	1,511.5	1,695.0	1,916.7	2,228.9	2,769.6	3,519.4	4,070.3	..	GDP at Market Prices
-140.0	-110.5	-116.4	-105.3	-83.2	-156.1	-102.9	-128.4	-229.7	-211.2	..	Resource Balance
113.9	112.4	138.4	159.8	223.1	220.5	263.4	453.0	559.8	705.6	..	Exports of Goods & NFServices
254.0	222.9	254.9	265.0	306.3	376.6	366.2	581.4	789.5	916.8	..	Imports of Goods & NFServices
994.0	1,087.3	1,349.6	1,616.8	1,778.2	2,072.9	2,331.8	2,898.0	3,749.1	4,281.5	..	Domestic Absorption
762.8	861.9	1,113.8	1,345.3	1,469.7	1,726.2	1,937.7	2,370.2	3,012.6	3,417.5	..	Private Consumption, etc.
103.4	113.3	131.2	145.1	162.4	184.8	195.0	250.5	279.6	327.8	..	General Gov't Consumption
127.8	112.1	104.6	126.4	146.1	161.8	199.2	277.2	457.0	536.3	..	Gross Domestic Investment
123.0	117.9	97.6	..	..	..	..	..	..	..	..	Fixed Investment
95.9	109.7	138.5	169.8	190.4	206.7	220.7	349.5	389.0	409.9	..	Indirect Taxes, net
758.1	867.1	1,094.7	1,341.7	1,504.6	1,710.0	2,008.2	2,420.1	3,130.4	3,660.4	B	GDP at factor cost
227.8	286.8	374.7	480.1	531.0	586.2	685.9	810.1	1,031.3	1,149.4	..	Agriculture
121.7	122.7	146.8	181.1	192.3	215.2	264.2	348.1	445.6	528.5	..	Industry
..	..	..	..	175.1	193.0	231.6	310.9	386.5	462.7	..	Manufacturing
408.6	457.6	573.2	680.5	781.4	908.6	1,058.1	1,261.8	1,653.5	1,982.5	..	Services, etc.
-12.2	1.6	-11.8	21.2	62.9	5.7	96.3	148.8	227.3	325.1	..	Gross Domestic Saving
-26.3	-27.5	-52.3	-31.0	-21.5	-63.7	5.4	-0.9	46.3	82.8	..	Gross National Saving
				(Billions of 1987 Malagasy Francs)							
2,895.80	2,575.20	2,518.10	2,529.50	2,526.00	2,565.90	2,604.60	2,583.20	2,685.20	2,788.20	..	Gross National Product
2,926.50	2,639.80	2,589.60	2,612.80	2,657.10	2,688.90	2,738.60	2,769.60	2,875.60	3,017.00	..	GDP at Market Prices
-565.30	-316.60	-318.30	-261.60	-201.80	-301.00	-283.10	-128.40	-145.70	-59.20	..	Resource Balance
584.60	431.40	399.90	350.60	369.50	357.20	350.60	453.00	430.60	533.10	..	Exports of Goods & NFServices
1,149.90	748.00	718.20	612.20	571.20	658.30	633.60	581.40	576.30	592.20	..	Imports of Goods & NFServices
3,491.80	2,956.40	2,907.90	2,874.40	2,858.90	2,989.90	3,021.70	2,898.00	3,021.30	3,076.10	..	Domestic Absorption
2,846.00	2,433.50	2,443.30	2,411.40	2,395.30	2,512.20	2,535.40	2,370.20	2,469.60	2,484.50	..	Private Consumption, etc.
241.30	240.90	233.60	234.40	223.50	235.30	233.80	250.50	240.00	259.60	..	General Gov't Consumption
404.50	282.00	231.00	228.60	240.10	242.40	252.40	277.20	311.80	332.00	..	Gross Domestic Investment
..	..	..	..	..	..	..	..	..	..	..	Fixed Investment
2,558.10	2,307.20	2,263.10	2,283.30	2,322.00	2,349.70	2,393.10	2,420.10	2,512.90	2,636.30	B	GDP at factor cost
721.80	689.60	717.20	735.70	758.70	768.00	792.00	810.10	829.70	875.20	..	Agriculture
419.00	324.50	278.00	281.80	316.50	319.00	331.90	348.10	352.60	357.80	..	Industry
..	..	..	..	285.40	283.90	290.90	310.90	310.80	314.40	..	Manufacturing
1,426.30	1,298.00	1,269.00	1,265.80	1,246.70	1,262.70	1,269.20	1,261.80	1,330.50	1,403.30	..	Services, etc.
											Memo Items:
515.90	377.20	390.10	369.10	416.10	385.40	455.60	453.00	408.60	455.80	..	Capacity to Import
-68.70	-54.20	-9.80	18.50	46.60	28.10	105.00	0.00	-22.00	-77.30	..	Terms of Trade Adjustment
2,857.80	2,585.60	2,579.80	2,631.30	2,703.70	2,717.00	2,843.70	2,769.60	2,853.70	2,939.70	..	Gross Domestic Income
2,827.10	2,521.00	2,508.30	2,548.00	2,572.60	2,594.10	2,709.60	2,583.20	2,663.20	2,710.90	..	Gross National Income
				(Index 1987 = 100)							**DOMESTIC PRICES/DEFLATORS**
29.2	37.0	47.6	57.9	63.8	71.3	81.4	100.0	122.4	134.9	..	Overall (GDP)
28.5	36.8	46.4	56.2	62.2	69.3	77.2	100.0	124.1	139.2	..	Domestic Absorption
31.6	41.6	52.2	65.3	70.0	76.3	86.6	100.0	124.3	131.3	..	Agriculture
29.1	37.8	52.8	64.3	60.7	67.5	79.6	100.0	126.4	147.7	..	Industry
..	..	..	..	61.4	68.0	79.6	100.0	124.4	147.2	..	Manufacturing
30.5	39.8	52.4	62.5	68.7	76.0	87.0	100.0	126.8	138.3	..	Consumer Price Index
											MANUFACTURING ACTIVITY
..	..	..	..	..	..	..	..	..	..	J	Employment (1987=100)
..	..	..	..	..	..	..	..	..	..	J	Real Earnings per Empl. (1987=100)
..	..	..	..	..	..	..	..	..	..	J	Real Output per Empl. (1987=100)
38.2	49.1	48.2	40.2	35.5	40.0	..	..	..	..	J	Earnings as % of Value Added
				(Billions of current Malagasy Francs)							**MONETARY HOLDINGS**
212.2	267.0	299.8	293.2	363.3	419.3	511.0	625.4	760.2	984.8	D	Money Supply, Broadly Defined
151.3	193.8	208.0	192.7	239.9	238.6	289.6	371.8	455.0	598.4	..	Money
70.2	83.1	90.4	75.8	89.9	96.2	113.2	140.3	171.2	216.6	..	Currency Outside Banks
81.1	110.7	117.6	116.8	150.0	142.4	176.3	231.5	283.8	381.7	..	Demand Deposits
60.9	73.1	91.8	100.6	123.4	180.7	221.4	253.6	305.2	386.4	..	Quasi-Money
				(Millions of current Malagasy Francs)							**GOVERNMENT DEFICIT (-) OR SURPLUS**
..	..	..	..	..	..	..	..	..	..	..	
133,025	142,722	145,898	..	..	..	..	..	..	..	..	Current Revenue
..	..	..	..	..	..	..	..	..	..	..	Current Expenditure
..	..	..	..	..	..	..	..	..	..	..	Current Budget Balance
..	..	..	..	..	..	..	..	..	..	..	Capital Receipts
..	..	..	..	..	..	..	..	..	..	..	Capital Payments

MADAGASCAR	1969	1970	1971	1972	1973	1974	1975	1976	1977	1978	1979
FOREIGN TRADE (CUSTOMS BASIS)					*(Millions of current US dollars)*						
Value of Exports, fob	112.95	144.84	146.82	163.81	202.70	244.18	301.42	282.55	347.28	399.32	407.48
Nonfuel Primary Products	98.44	128.70	128.72	148.35	174.94	198.07	263.20	236.98	310.34	362.69	358.34
Fuels	4.04	5.60	5.29	6.54	10.33	23.55	25.89	23.46	13.22	9.62	19.13
Manufactures	10.47	10.54	12.81	8.92	17.43	22.56	12.33	22.11	23.72	27.01	30.01
Value of Imports, cif	182.78	170.40	213.21	202.24	202.93	281.03	366.93	289.93	352.96	460.09	698.44
Nonfuel Primary Products	29.00	25.67	37.28	34.12	43.85	69.88	63.54	48.61	61.26	90.30	130.72
Fuels	12.05	12.56	13.99	17.41	19.40	50.73	73.82	57.67	53.50	63.91	112.09
Manufactures	141.73	132.17	161.94	150.71	139.68	160.42	229.57	183.65	238.20	305.88	455.63
					(Index 1987 = 100)						
Terms of Trade	125.4	138.6	124.1	130.3	133.4	108.1	101.7	141.9	176.4	135.5	132.6
Export Prices, fob	30.5	34.4	34.7	38.3	50.0	63.8	59.5	83.7	112.3	98.4	112.5
Import Prices, cif	24.3	24.8	28.0	29.4	37.5	59.0	58.4	59.0	63.7	72.6	84.9
BALANCE OF PAYMENTS					*(Millions of current US dollars)*						
Exports of Goods & Services	..	196.00	205.61	228.00	243.19	287.66	386.96	333.59	387.54	444.40	490.08
Merchandise, fob	..	145.00	147.44	166.11	200.28	240.17	319.53	289.02	350.66	405.00	413.78
Nonfactor Services	..	49.00	55.16	57.54	36.96	40.17	62.01	40.93	34.76	34.88	73.90
Factor Services	..	2.00	3.01	4.34	5.96	7.31	5.41	3.64	2.12	4.52	2.40
Imports of Goods & Services	..	213.00	260.77	248.63	287.30	370.87	502.16	413.94	455.92	584.87	958.58
Merchandise, fob	..	142.00	177.53	168.29	177.63	238.34	331.81	261.77	311.75	404.24	662.42
Nonfactor Services	..	64.00	71.21	71.66	95.37	107.39	148.06	131.66	135.38	167.65	265.09
Factor Services	..	7.00	12.04	8.69	14.31	25.13	22.30	20.51	8.79	12.98	31.07
Long-Term Interest	..	2.00	2.40	2.20	3.40	3.50	4.10	4.60	5.40	7.60	16.30
Private Current Transfers, net	..	-25.00	-24.07	-30.40	-22.65	-8.85	-24.50	-17.79	-18.60	-15.11	-16.97
Workers' Remittances	..	..	..	..	..	..	..	..	0.33	0.35	..
Curr. A/C Bal before Off. Transf.	..	-42.00	-79.24	-51.03	-66.76	-92.06	-139.70	-98.14	-86.98	-155.59	-485.47
Net Official Transfers	..	52.00	52.15	85.77	56.03	52.43	84.08	70.01	70.99	75.69	58.81
Curr. A/C Bal after Off. Transf.	..	10.00	-27.08	34.74	-10.73	-39.63	-55.62	-28.12	-16.00	-79.90	-426.66
Long-Term Capital, net	..	15.00	7.02	-8.69	27.42	24.30	30.66	17.07	22.67	16.71	225.51
Direct Investment	..	10.00	-2.01	11.94	10.73	13.71	4.57	1.38	-2.77	-3.68	-6.58
Long-Term Loans	..	5.20	8.50	10.70	20.80	15.40	31.70	17.80	36.60	43.00	314.00
Disbursements	..	10.50	14.30	16.20	30.00	22.20	39.40	25.90	45.00	54.00	330.90
Repayments	..	5.30	5.80	5.50	9.20	6.80	7.70	8.10	8.40	11.00	16.90
Other Long-Term Capital	..	-0.20	0.53	-31.33	-4.11	-4.81	-5.62	-2.11	-11.16	-22.61	-81.91
Other Capital, net	..	-10.25	20.06	-23.89	-5.96	-21.54	1.86	21.29	-14.56	65.73	70.40
Change in Reserves	..	-14.75	0.00	-2.17	-10.73	36.87	23.11	-10.25	7.88	-2.53	130.75
Memo Item:					*(Malagasy Francs per US dollar)*						
Conversion Factor (Annual Avg)	259.700	277.700	277.100	252.200	222.700	240.500	214.300	239.000	245.700	225.600	212.700
					(Millions of US dollars), outstanding at end of year						
EXTERNAL DEBT (Total)	..	89	103	90	118	143	184	200	291	361	788
Long-Term Debt (by debtor)	..	89	103	90	118	143	184	200	245	316	625
Central Bank, incl. IMF credit	..	0	1	1	1	5	18	18	20	33	28
Central Government	..	59	70	51	73	91	122	141	166	196	396
Rest of General Government	..	3	2	2	1	1	1	0	0	0	0
Non-financial Public Enterprises	..	17	19	25	31	35	35	33	50	78	185
Priv. Sector, incl non-guaranteed	..	10	11	12	13	11	10	8	9	9	16
Short-Term Debt	..	0	0	0	0	0	0	0	46	45	163
Memo Items:					*(Millions of US dollars)*						
Int'l Reserves Excluding Gold	19.4	37.1	46.4	52.2	67.9	49.4	35.6	42.2	68.9	59.2	5.0
Gold Holdings (at market price)	..	..	..	..	..	..	..	..	..	..	..
SOCIAL INDICATORS											
Total Fertility Rate	6.6	6.6	6.6	6.6	6.5	6.5	6.4	6.5	6.6	6.6	6.5
Infant Mortality Rate	185.8	181.2	176.6	172.0	167.6	163.2	158.8	154.4	150.0	146.0	142.0
Life Expectancy at Birth	44.9	45.4	45.9	46.5	47.1	47.7	48.3	48.9	49.5	49.6	49.7
Urban Population, % of total	13.7	14.1	14.5	15.0	15.4	15.9	16.3	16.8	17.3	17.9	18.4
Food Prod. per capita (1987=100)	118.6	119.2	117.4	116.3	114.0	124.8	119.6	119.0	110.9	106.8	103.9
Labor Force, Agriculture (%)	84.0	83.7	83.4	83.1	82.8	82.6	82.3	82.0	81.7	81.4	81.1
Labor Force, Female (%)	41.6	41.6	41.6	41.5	41.5	41.5	41.5	41.4	41.4	41.4	41.3
Primary Schl. Enroll. Ratio	..	90.0	..	..	..	..	95.0	..	..	100.0	..
Primary Schl. Enroll. Ratio, Female	..	82.0	..	..	..	..	88.0	..	..	..	..
Secondary Schl. Enroll. Ratio	..	12.0	..	..	..	..	12.0	..	..	..	..

1980	1981	1982	1983	1984	1985	1986	1987	1988	1989 estimate	NOTES	MADAGASCAR
				(Millions of current US dollars)							**FOREIGN TRADE (CUSTOMS BASIS)**
402.16	324.35	329.50	310.00	340.00	287.00	320.00	310.00	282.00	..	..	Value of Exports, fob
354.74	274.23	280.10	266.00	300.00	246.00	285.00	259.00	217.99	..	..	Nonfuel Primary Products
23.05	25.50	25.40	21.00	8.00	11.00	7.00	17.00	20.01	..	..	Fuels
24.37	24.62	24.00	23.00	32.00	30.00	28.00	34.00	44.00	..	..	Manufactures
676.47	473.03	438.95	411.00	412.00	465.00	374.00	386.00	386.00	..	..	Value of Imports, cif
83.79	82.78	83.95	95.00	63.59	71.00	66.91	42.15	32.12	..	..	Nonfuel Primary Products
98.98	50.56	106.35	79.00	114.41	92.00	83.10	123.41	126.88	..	..	Fuels
493.70	339.69	248.65	237.00	234.00	302.00	224.00	220.44	227.00	..	..	Manufactures
				(Index 1987 = 100)							
120.2	104.4	100.5	102.6	104.5	114.1	133.2	100.0	116.1	..	..	Terms of Trade
111.7	98.5	100.1	98.2	100.8	103.3	118.6	100.0	112.6	..	..	Export Prices, fob
93.0	94.3	99.6	95.7	96.4	90.5	89.0	100.0	97.0	..	..	Import Prices, cif
				(Millions of current US dollars)							**BALANCE OF PAYMENTS**
518.37	397.45	382.06	358.02	395.48	354.26	403.36	431.76	416.20	459.24	..	Exports of Goods & Services
436.44	331.91	327.22	309.93	337.14	291.28	322.99	326.50	284.50	313.37	..	Merchandise, fob
79.47	61.53	49.32	45.21	53.31	58.60	75.08	95.95	118.40	127.54	..	Nonfactor Services
2.46	4.01	5.52	2.88	5.03	4.38	5.29	9.31	13.30	18.33	..	Factor Services
1,121.41	827.18	752.39	671.51	666.47	636.17	696.67	725.67	761.34	789.24	..	Imports of Goods & Services
764.44	510.80	451.54	378.26	360.12	335.76	331.08	315.25	318.64	314.13	..	Merchandise, fob
310.63	224.05	200.07	172.24	155.30	167.21	205.21	226.29	249.97	257.48	..	Nonfactor Services
46.34	92.34	100.79	121.01	151.06	133.21	160.38	184.14	192.72	217.63	..	Factor Services
26.70	32.20	44.60	27.70	31.80	52.40	59.30	101.20	75.90	112.80	..	Long-Term Interest
-20.45	-15.57	-17.01	-8.87	-0.71	24.15	20.54	34.25	37.76	47.04	..	Private Current Transfers, net
0.38	0.22	0.11	0.12	5.64	4.57	4.23	3.36	3.23	3.33	..	Workers' Remittances
-623.49	-445.30	-387.34	-322.36	-271.70	-257.76	-272.77	-259.67	-307.38	-282.97	..	Curr. A/C Bal before Off. Transf.
66.78	82.25	87.89	75.27	78.30	74.10	131.63	119.87	158.05	155.20	..	Net Official Transfers
-556.71	-363.05	-299.45	-247.09	-193.40	-183.66	-141.13	-139.79	-149.33	-127.76	..	Curr. A/C Bal after Off. Transf.
374.86	280.28	121.32	179.36	188.47	150.37	223.50	240.25	394.30	218.91	..	Long-Term Capital, net
..	..	..	..	..	..	..	..	..	6.41	..	Direct Investment
344.60	251.00	212.90	187.50	102.40	124.70	152.40	245.70	157.20	101.10	..	Long-Term Loans
375.40	284.60	245.00	206.40	112.70	170.40	197.10	291.00	226.10	160.30	..	Disbursements
30.80	33.60	32.10	18.90	10.30	45.70	44.70	45.30	68.90	59.20	..	Repayments
30.26	29.28	-91.58	-8.14	86.07	25.67	71.10	-5.45	237.10	111.40	..	Other Long-Term Capital
325.15	51.66	132.71	47.09	27.76	9.40	-26.98	-58.42	-174.16	-54.31	..	Other Capital, net
-143.30	31.11	45.42	20.64	-22.82	23.89	-55.38	-42.03	-70.81	-36.84	..	Change in Reserves
				(Malagasy Francs per US dollar)							**Memo Item:**
211.300	271.700	349.700	430.500	576.600	662.500	676.300	1,069.200	1,407.100	1,603.400	..	Conversion Factor (Annual Avg)
				(Millions of US dollars), outstanding at end of year							
1,257	1,612	1,920	2,102	2,160	2,460	3,009	3,728	3,638	3,607	..	**EXTERNAL DEBT (Total)**
1,013	1,522	1,818	1,920	2,010	2,345	2,854	3,546	3,480	3,510	..	Long-Term Debt (by debtor)
91	259	343	293	618	801	1,019	1,373	1,239	1,178	..	Central Bank, incl. IMF credit
594	774	894	1,013	964	1,056	1,257	1,543	1,631	1,773	..	Central Government
0	0	0	0	0	0	0	0	0	0	..	Rest of General Government
309	366	480	521	397	447	522	555	545	481	..	Non-financial Public Enterprises
18	123	102	93	32	41	55	74	65	78	..	Priv. Sector, incl non-guaranteed
244	90	101	182	150	115	156	182	158	97	..	Short-Term Debt
				(Millions of US dollars)							**Memo Items:**
9.1	26.5	20.0	29.2	58.9	48.4	114.5	185.2	223.7	245.3	..	Int'l Reserves Excluding Gold
..	..	..	..	..	..	..	..	..	..	..	Gold Holdings (at market price)
											SOCIAL INDICATORS
6.5	6.4	6.4	6.3	6.3	6.2	6.2	6.1	6.0	5.9	..	Total Fertility Rate
109.0	134.0	130.0	126.0	126.0	124.0	122.0	120.0	118.8	117.6	..	Infant Mortality Rate
49.7	49.8	49.9	50.1	50.3	50.3	50.3	50.3	50.5	50.7	..	Life Expectancy at Birth
18.9	19.5	20.1	20.6	21.2	21.8	22.6	23.4	23.9	24.5	..	Urban Population, % of total
108.0	105.8	103.5	105.7	103.9	102.4	102.4	100.0	97.7	97.8	..	Food Prod. per capita (1987=100)
80.9	..	..	..	..	..	..	..	..	..	..	Labor Force, Agriculture (%)
41.3	41.1	40.9	40.7	40.5	40.4	40.1	39.9	39.7	39.5	..	Labor Force, Female (%)
143.0	..	136.0	128.0	118.0	..	..	..	103.0	..	..	Primary Schl. Enroll. Ratio
139.0	..	127.0	122.0	114.0	..	..	91.0	92.0	..	..	Primary Schl. Enroll. Ratio, Female
..	..	..	37.0	34.0	..	..	21.0	20.0	..	..	Secondary Schl. Enroll. Ratio

MALAWI	1969	1970	1971	1972	1973	1974	1975	1976	1977	1978	1979
CURRENT GNP PER CAPITA (US $)	60	60	80	80	90	110	120	120	130	160	170
POPULATION (thousands)	4,395	4,518	4,653	4,794	4,940	5,090	5,244	5,402	5,563	5,729	5,904
USE AND ORIGIN OF RESOURCES					*(Millions of current Malawi Kwacha)*						
Gross National Product (GNP)	215.7	236.1	300.3	321.8	364.8	473.9	537.7	594.0	705.0	796.7	830.0
Net Factor Income from Abroad	-5.8	-6.0	-3.3	-3.7	0.8	12.4	8.0	-18.0	-23.0	-4.0	-35.0
GDP at Market Prices	221.5	242.1	303.6	325.5	364.0	461.5	529.7	612.0	728.0	800.7	865.0
Resource Balance	-35.7	-36.1	-36.5	-47.7	-36.2	-50.5	-88.8	-51.6	-33.7	-143.5	-152.0
Exports of Goods & NFServices	52.0	58.7	71.2	75.8	100.6	129.3	154.3	186.3	218.4	185.7	201.0
Imports of Goods & NFServices	87.7	94.8	107.7	123.5	136.8	179.8	243.1	237.9	252.1	329.2	353.0
Domestic Absorption	257.2	278.2	340.1	373.2	400.2	512.0	618.5	663.6	761.7	944.2	1,017.0
Private Consumption, etc.	179.9	176.3	236.9	248.6	270.0	320.2	365.2	416.6	483.4	502.2	592.0
General Gov't Consumption	36.6	39.6	45.0	45.2	48.7	65.7	74.7	86.3	98.6	134.2	164.0
Gross Domestic Investment	40.7	62.3	58.2	79.4	81.5	126.1	178.6	160.7	179.7	307.8	261.0
Fixed Investment	..	..	..	..	74.3	87.3	131.8	135.3	161.6	247.1	231.9
Indirect Taxes, net	12.8	16.5	21.4	22.2	23.2	28.2	35.0	33.7	44.1	58.2	77.7
GDP at factor cost	208.7	225.6	282.2	303.3	340.8	433.3	494.7	578.3	683.9	742.5	787.3
Agriculture	92.4	99.2	125.1	138.4	141.7	178.4	184.2	226.7	285.8	294.9	311.9
Industry	34.8	39.4	44.6	52.9	57.3	73.9	100.6	107.1	127.6	143.5	148.1
Manufacturing	..	..	..	..	..	..	64.9	68.8	80.3	84.8	90.8
Services, etc.	81.5	87.0	112.5	112.0	141.8	181.0	209.9	244.5	270.5	304.1	327.3
Gross Domestic Saving	5.0	26.2	21.7	31.7	45.3	75.6	89.8	109.1	146.0	164.3	109.0
Gross National Saving	..	18.4	18.7	28.4	47.8	89.3	100.0	91.6	122.5	166.7	79.8
					(Millions of 1987 Malawi Kwacha)						
Gross National Product	1,273.4	1,278.5	1,509.6	1,600.6	1,660.6	1,825.9	1,914.4	1,912.6	2,004.1	2,268.3	2,292.7
GDP at Market Prices	1,323.7	1,329.1	1,547.1	1,640.7	1,680.2	1,799.7	1,910.8	2,002.3	2,103.3	2,312.8	2,418.7
Resource Balance	-571.6	-654.1	-669.6	-714.6	-611.3	-597.6	-710.6	-499.8	-509.4	-824.9	-554.7
Exports of Goods & NFServices	347.6	345.1	378.5	421.1	481.2	470.5	478.6	517.0	459.9	434.4	481.9
Imports of Goods & NFServices	919.2	999.2	1,048.1	1,135.7	1,092.5	1,068.0	1,189.3	1,016.8	969.3	1,259.3	1,036.7
Domestic Absorption	1,895.3	1,983.2	2,216.7	2,355.3	2,291.5	2,397.3	2,621.5	2,502.0	2,612.7	3,137.6	2,973.4
Private Consumption, etc.	1,286.4	1,147.3	1,460.6	1,437.5	1,454.5	1,435.6	1,524.7	1,579.8	1,685.0	1,639.4	1,742.4
General Gov't Consumption	183.9	182.7	192.4	191.4	188.7	215.4	226.3	237.7	239.4	325.1	365.8
Gross Domestic Investment	425.0	653.3	563.7	726.4	648.3	746.3	870.5	684.5	688.3	1,173.1	865.2
Fixed Investment	..	..	..	..	..	..	660.2	616.2	648.2	988.3	792.2
GDP at factor cost	1,227.6	1,218.7	1,415.5	1,504.0	1,547.7	1,662.8	1,754.8	1,864.0	1,944.9	2,106.6	2,176.7
Agriculture	535.6	528.6	617.6	676.9	634.4	647.4	653.4	730.8	812.8	836.7	862.5
Industry	221.6	230.4	242.3	284.8	281.4	303.3	356.6	344.7	364.3	407.7	411.1
Manufacturing	..	..	..	..	..	..	229.8	221.3	229.8	241.2	252.5
Services, etc.	470.4	460.8	554.4	543.6	631.9	712.2	744.8	788.5	767.8	862.2	903.1
Memo Items:											
Capacity to Import	545.0	618.7	692.9	697.1	803.4	768.1	754.9	796.2	839.8	710.4	590.3
Terms of Trade Adjustment	197.4	273.6	314.4	276.0	322.2	297.6	276.2	279.2	379.8	275.9	108.4
Gross Domestic Income	1,521.1	1,602.7	1,861.5	1,916.7	2,002.4	2,097.3	2,187.1	2,281.5	2,483.2	2,588.7	2,527.0
Gross National Income	1,470.8	1,552.1	1,824.0	1,876.6	1,982.8	2,123.5	2,190.6	2,191.8	2,383.9	2,544.3	2,401.0
DOMESTIC PRICES/DEFLATORS					*(Index 1987 = 100)*						
Overall (GDP)	16.7	18.2	19.6	19.8	21.7	25.6	27.7	30.6	34.6	34.6	35.8
Domestic Absorption	13.6	14.0	15.3	15.8	17.5	21.4	23.6	26.5	29.2	30.1	34.2
Agriculture	17.3	18.8	20.3	20.4	22.3	27.6	28.2	31.0	35.2	35.2	36.2
Industry	15.7	17.1	18.4	18.6	20.4	24.4	28.2	31.1	35.0	35.2	36.0
Manufacturing	..	..	..	..	..	..	28.2	31.1	34.9	35.2	36.0
Consumer Price Index	..	..	..	..	..	..	..	..	..	..	..
MANUFACTURING ACTIVITY											
Employment (1987=100)	..	..	..	..	..	..	..	..	..	..	..
Real Earnings per Empl. (1987=100)	..	..	..	..	..	..	..	..	..	..	..
Real Output per Empl. (1987=100)	..	..	..	..	..	..	..	..	..	..	..
Earnings as % of Value Added	37.0	36.5	35.0	37.1	41.0	40.4	40.0	..	..	..	43.3
MONETARY HOLDINGS					*(Millions of current Malawi Kwacha)*						
Money Supply, Broadly Defined	48.6	56.0	66.9	74.3	98.8	133.4	139.1	137.4	178.2	190.2	192.9
Money	28.5	32.7	38.8	40.6	55.1	73.4	73.6	72.8	100.1	93.8	90.6
Currency Outside Banks	12.5	13.3	14.8	17.3	21.3	28.3	27.8	23.1	24.6	29.8	32.3
Demand Deposits	15.9	19.4	24.0	23.3	33.8	45.1	45.8	49.7	75.5	64.0	58.3
Quasi-Money	20.1	23.3	28.1	33.7	43.7	60.0	65.5	64.6	78.2	96.4	102.4
					(Millions of current Malawi Kwacha)						
GOVERNMENT DEFICIT (-) OR SURPLUS	..	..	-24.9	-20.0	-20.6	-29.5	-48.6	-37.6	-45.2	-74.3	-75.5
Current Revenue	..	..	51.0	55.0	62.2	72.7	93.4	97.4	125.3	169.0	211.2
Current Expenditure	..	..	52.0	56.8	57.9	67.4	79.0	84.5	97.7	139.1	148.9
Current Budget Balance	..	..	-1.1	-1.8	4.3	5.2	14.4	12.9	27.6	29.9	62.3
Capital Receipts	..	..	0.2	0.3	0.3	0.3	0.3	0.3	0.3	0.3	0.4
Capital Payments	..	..	24.1	18.5	25.2	35.0	63.2	50.8	73.1	104.6	138.2

1980	1981	1982	1983	1984	1985	1986	1987	1988	1989 estimate	NOTES	MALAWI
180	180	190	180	180	170	160	150	160	180	..	CURRENT GNP PER CAPITA (US $)
6,091	6,289	6,498	6,718	6,948	7,188	7,437	7,695	7,960	8,230	..	POPULATION (thousands)
				(Millions of current Malawi Kwacha)							USE AND ORIGIN OF RESOURCES
924.0	1,034.0	1,172.0	1,362.0	1,629.0	1,854.0	2,084.7	2,605.8	3,414.4	4,208.6	..	Gross National Product (GNP)
-81.0	-74.0	-74.0	-75.0	-78.0	-90.9	-112.9	-125.7	-137.9	-155.4	..	Net Factor Income from Abroad
1,005.0	1,108.0	1,246.0	1,437.0	1,707.0	1,944.9	2,197.6	2,731.5	3,552.3	4,364.0	..	GDP at Market Prices
-140.0	-65.0	-79.0	-109.0	33.0	-111.0	-47.1	-59.8	-325.9	-639.5	..	Resource Balance
250.0	284.0	280.0	298.0	484.0	470.5	504.7	665.1	824.3	817.1	..	Exports of Goods & NFServices
390.0	349.0	359.0	407.0	451.0	581.5	551.8	724.9	1,150.2	1,456.6	..	Imports of Goods & NFServices
1,145.0	1,173.0	1,325.0	1,546.0	1,674.0	2,055.8	2,244.8	2,791.3	3,878.2	5,003.5	..	Domestic Absorption
702.0	780.0	840.0	982.0	1,186.0	1,350.2	1,541.6	1,901.5	2,671.8	3,541.2	..	Private Consumption, etc.
194.0	198.0	218.0	236.0	268.0	344.0	433.8	487.7	565.9	647.4	..	General Gov't Consumption
249.0	195.0	267.0	328.0	220.0	361.6	269.4	402.1	640.5	814.9	..	Gross Domestic Investment
223.1	167.8	181.7	197.3	222.7	259.5	264.0	352.9	524.0	674.4	..	Fixed Investment
103.5	107.8	116.1	139.6	178.1	216.0	216.4	268.3	349.4	468.4	..	Indirect Taxes, net
901.5	1,000.2	1,129.9	1,297.4	1,528.9	1,728.9	1,981.2	2,463.2	3,202.9	3,895.6	..	GDP at factor cost
335.3	360.3	420.8	487.7	581.8	632.9	721.8	886.6	1,138.2	1,373.1	..	Agriculture
172.8	196.4	215.9	247.3	277.9	323.4	360.1	445.1	601.4	757.5	..	Industry
104.8	127.1	139.0	165.2	191.2	213.3	247.1	303.9	395.0	496.8	..	Manufacturing
393.4	443.5	493.2	562.4	669.2	772.6	899.3	1,131.5	1,463.3	1,765.0	..	Services, etc.
109.0	130.0	188.0	219.0	253.0	250.7	222.2	342.3	314.6	175.4	..	Gross Domestic Saving
38.8	66.7	126.5	153.7	191.3	178.9	133.7	247.1	215.3	271.4	..	Gross National Saving
				(Millions of 1987 Malawi Kwacha)							
2,203.3	2,111.4	2,182.4	2,281.1	2,436.9	2,550.9	2,555.7	2,605.8	2,700.8	2,858.9	..	Gross National Product
2,430.5	2,302.0	2,359.3	2,446.8	2,585.1	2,701.4	2,688.2	2,731.5	2,810.5	2,962.5	..	GDP at Market Prices
-540.3	-390.6	-402.3	-401.6	-182.0	-330.6	-92.4	-59.8	-197.6	-353.3	..	Resource Balance
641.0	526.4	472.6	488.9	650.4	683.1	657.4	665.1	678.4	650.1	..	Exports of Goods & NFServices
1,181.3	916.9	874.9	890.5	832.4	1,013.7	749.8	724.9	876.0	1,003.4	..	Imports of Goods & NFServices
2,970.7	2,692.5	2,761.6	2,848.4	2,767.1	3,032.0	2,780.6	2,791.3	3,008.1	3,315.7	..	Domestic Absorption
1,843.3	1,800.7	1,736.7	1,757.3	1,957.1	1,981.6	1,972.5	1,901.5	2,024.4	2,283.3	..	Private Consumption, etc.
380.4	365.8	373.1	370.7	402.2	448.2	491.8	487.7	473.4	488.9	..	General Gov't Consumption
747.0	526.0	651.7	720.3	407.8	602.2	316.3	402.1	510.3	543.5	..	Gross Domestic Investment
696.2	472.1	460.1	448.1	434.1	432.1	324.1	352.9	405.3	435.7	..	Fixed Investment
2,168.4	2,054.9	2,113.9	2,188.3	2,285.6	2,387.2	2,413.3	2,463.2	2,544.3	2,653.9	..	GDP at factor cost
806.3	740.2	787.6	822.5	870.1	873.8	879.2	886.6	904.2	935.4	..	Agriculture
415.6	403.4	404.0	417.0	415.6	446.5	438.6	445.1	477.7	516.0	..	Industry
252.0	261.1	260.2	278.6	285.7	294.5	301.1	303.9	313.8	338.5	..	Manufacturing
946.5	911.3	922.4	948.8	999.9	1,066.8	1,095.5	1,131.5	1,162.4	1,202.4	..	Services, etc.
											Memo Items:
757.2	746.2	682.3	652.0	893.3	820.2	685.8	665.1	627.8	562.9	..	Capacity to Import
116.2	219.8	209.8	163.1	242.9	137.1	28.4	0.0	-50.6	-87.3	..	Terms of Trade Adjustment
2,546.7	2,521.8	2,569.1	2,609.9	2,828.0	2,838.5	2,716.6	2,731.5	2,759.9	2,875.2	..	Gross Domestic Income
2,319.6	2,331.2	2,392.2	2,444.2	2,679.9	2,688.0	2,584.1	2,605.8	2,650.2	2,771.6	..	Gross National Income
				(Index 1987 = 100)							DOMESTIC PRICES/DEFLATORS
41.4	48.1	52.8	58.7	66.0	72.0	81.7	100.0	126.4	147.3	..	Overall (GDP)
38.5	43.6	48.0	54.3	60.5	67.8	80.7	100.0	128.9	150.9	..	Domestic Absorption
41.6	48.7	53.4	59.3	66.9	72.4	82.1	100.0	125.9	146.8	..	Agriculture
41.6	48.7	53.4	59.3	66.9	72.4	82.1	100.0	125.9	146.8	..	Industry
41.6	48.7	53.4	59.3	66.9	72.4	82.1	100.0	125.9	146.8	..	Manufacturing
37.9	42.4	46.5	52.8	63.4	70.1	79.9	100.0	133.9	150.6	..	Consumer Price Index
											MANUFACTURING ACTIVITY
..	..	..	..	..	..	..	..	..	..	G	Employment (1987=100)
..	..	..	..	..	..	..	..	..	..	G	Real Earnings per Empl. (1987=100)
..	..	..	..	..	..	..	..	..	..	G	Real Output per Empl. (1987=100)
33.1	34.0	41.7	35.8	25.9	35.4	..	..	..	..	..	Earnings as % of Value Added
				(Millions of current Malawi Kwacha)							MONETARY HOLDINGS
219.0	273.2	317.5	348.0	453.6	407.7	580.7	781.6	..	..	D	Money Supply, Broadly Defined
97.2	114.8	130.8	127.8	154.3	166.9	220.8	298.0	435.9	427.0	..	Money
35.3	39.4	49.5	50.0	56.9	66.0	79.3	107.6	134.6	156.6	..	Currency Outside Banks
61.9	75.4	81.3	77.7	97.4	100.9	141.5	190.4	301.3	270.4	..	Demand Deposits
121.8	158.5	186.6	220.3	299.4	240.8	359.9	483.6	..	..	..	Quasi-Money
				(Millions of current Malawi Kwacha)							GOVERNMENT DEFICIT (-) OR SURPLUS
-160.3	-137.7	-95.0	-101.8	-88.3	-162.6	-217.7	-226.1	-204.7	..	C	GOVERNMENT DEFICIT (-) OR SURPLUS
235.5	257.2	271.6	310.7	380.4	460.9	530.9	626.5	804.7	..	..	Current Revenue
180.9	263.9	256.2	293.4	320.2	422.5	534.9	667.0	745.2	..	..	Current Expenditure
54.6	-6.7	15.4	17.3	60.1	38.4	-4.1	-40.6	59.5	..	..	Current Budget Balance
0.6	0.4	0.1	0.2	0.4	0.4	0.5	..	0.5	..	..	Capital Receipts
215.5	131.4	110.6	119.3	148.9	201.4	214.2	185.5	264.7	..	..	Capital Payments

MALAWI	1969	1970	1971	1972	1973	1974	1975	1976	1977	1978	1979
FOREIGN TRADE (CUSTOMS BASIS)					*(Millions of current US dollars)*						
Value of Exports, fob	52.75	59.15	72.08	80.56	99.29	120.73	139.13	165.55	200.04	185.27	222.80
Nonfuel Primary Products	47.41	50.83	64.96	72.28	89.66	107.96	121.75	153.81	185.51	171.11	208.09
Fuels	1.58	1.57	1.54	2.19	2.21	0.97	0.12	0.10	0.11	0.11	0.16
Manufactures	3.76	6.75	5.58	6.09	7.42	11.80	17.26	11.64	14.42	14.05	14.55
Value of Imports, cif	73.69	85.62	109.03	129.96	142.16	187.64	250.49	205.60	232.38	338.23	397.59
Nonfuel Primary Products	11.05	17.38	15.93	18.59	24.41	28.42	29.58	26.09	24.42	23.46	33.58
Fuels	4.29	4.71	10.15	11.58	12.71	19.54	24.91	27.78	30.21	40.28	57.96
Manufactures	58.35	63.53	82.95	99.79	105.04	139.68	196.00	151.73	177.75	274.49	306.05
					(Index 1987 = 100)						
Terms of Trade	173.6	169.4	182.8	174.3	169.2	174.2	163.2	153.2	168.1	145.2	146.9
Export Prices, fob	42.1	44.3	47.8	50.2	60.6	89.0	89.3	86.0	101.8	97.5	116.4
Import Prices, cif	24.2	26.2	26.1	28.8	35.8	51.1	54.7	56.2	60.5	67.2	79.2
BALANCE OF PAYMENTS					*(Millions of current US dollars)*						
Exports of Goods & Services	..	82.30	100.80	111.83	145.68	185.09	212.60	196.15	..	211.20	258.55
Merchandise, fob	..	58.90	71.71	78.61	97.87	119.30	138.66	165.33	199.79	184.53	222.43
Nonfactor Services	..	11.50	13.94	15.96	22.29	28.26	35.33	23.44	13.40	25.60	34.77
Factor Services	..	11.90	15.14	17.26	25.51	37.52	38.61	7.39	..	1.07	1.35
Imports of Goods & Services	..	126.20	142.02	169.59	184.90	228.86	301.59	266.00	..	432.71	577.93
Merchandise, fob	..	82.80	93.08	111.50	123.39	166.09	224.98	182.65	182.96	263.94	317.55
Nonfactor Services	..	31.00	36.51	42.56	45.42	46.30	59.25	66.15	117.51	119.35	133.19
Factor Services	..	12.40	12.44	15.53	16.09	16.48	17.36	17.20	..	49.42	127.19
Long-Term Interest	..	3.50	3.80	4.10	6.00	7.70	8.50	8.80	7.20	16,60	24.20
Private Current Transfers, net	..	-2.10	0.40	0.54	2.03	1.56	2.55	0.58	-0.55	7.59	7.10
Workers' Remittances	..	..	..	..	..	..	..	..	..	..	..
Curr. A/C Bal before Off. Transf.	..	-46.00	-40.82	-57.22	-37.19	-42.21	-86.45	-69.27	-87.83	-213.93	-312.29
Net Official Transfers	..	11.20	7.72	8.14	9.42	6.49	6.80	26.55	26.03	38.87	46.64
Curr. A/C Bal after Off. Transf.	..	-34.80	-33.10	-49.07	-27.78	-35.72	-79.65	-42.72	-61.80	-175.05	-265.65
Long-Term Capital, net	..	35.50	32.10	38.11	48.52	69.51	57.19	46.76	57.70	96.12	98.79
Direct Investment	..	8.60	9.63	10.10	7.75	22.73	8.62	9.70	5.54	9.13	-1.22
Long-Term Loans	..	36.70	24.80	30.30	27.80	25.40	52.00	48.80	83.40	109.90	97.30
Disbursements	..	39.60	28.40	34.70	32.70	32.10	60.60	57.80	97.90	129.80	117.00
Repayments	..	2.90	3.60	4.40	4.90	6.70	8.60	9.00	14.50	19.90	19.70
Other Long-Term Capital	..	-9.80	-2.33	-2.29	12.97	21.38	-3.43	-11.74	-31.24	-22.91	2.71
Other Capital, net	..	5.60	-0.40	13.48	13.20	-19.25	4.06	-40.07	55.53	71.97	89.62
Change in Reserves	..	-6.30	1.40	-2.52	-33.94	-14.54	18.40	36.03	-51.43	6.96	77.23
Memo Item:					*(Malawi Kwacha per US dollar)*						
Conversion Factor (Annual Avg)	0.830	0.830	0.830	0.800	0.820	0.840	0.860	0.910	0.900	0.840	0.820
				(Millions of US dollars), outstanding at end of year							
EXTERNAL DEBT (Total)	..	122.5	140.7	164.5	201.8	229.7	259.9	299.0	449.0	586.1	660.6
Long-Term Debt (by debtor)	..	122.5	140.7	164.5	201.8	229.7	259.9	299.0	380.0	511.1	545.6
Central Bank, incl. IMF credit	..	0.0	0.0	0.0	0.0	0.0	14.2	37.0	47.7	55.7	83.9
Central Government	..	107.4	124.9	144.7	176.0	197.4	216.1	233.8	266.2	347.2	325.1
Rest of General Government	..	..	..	..	..	..	..	..	..	..	..
Non-financial Public Enterprises	..	15.1	15.8	19.8	25.8	30.8	28.2	25.4	44.8	67.3	91.9
Priv. Sector, incl non-guaranteed	..	0.0	0.0	0.0	0.0	1.5	1.4	2.8	21.3	40.9	44.7
Short-Term Debt	..	0.0	0.0	0.0	0.0	0.0	0.0	0.0	69.0	75.0	115.0
Memo Items:					*(Millions of US dollars)*						
Int'l Reserves Excluding Gold	21.0	29.2	31.9	36.2	66.6	81.8	61.5	26.2	87.5	74.8	69.5
Gold Holdings (at market price)	..	..	..	..	..	..	..	..	1.1	2.2	6.6
SOCIAL INDICATORS											
Total Fertility Rate	7.8	7.8	7.8	7.8	7.7	7.7	7.7	7.6	7.6	7.6	7.6
Infant Mortality Rate	194.6	193.4	192.2	191.0	188.2	185.4	182.6	179.8	177.0	174.2	171.4
Life Expectancy at Birth	40.1	40.4	40.7	41.0	41.4	41.8	42.2	42.6	43.0	43.4	43.8
Urban Population, % of total	5.8	6.0	6.3	6.7	7.0	7.4	7.7	8.1	8.5	8.9	9.3
Food Prod. per capita (1987=100)	120.1	106.6	130.2	129.9	132.6	127.6	120.3	125.2	130.2	128.2	122.9
Labor Force, Agriculture (%)	90.8	90.5	89.8	89.0	88.3	87.6	87.0	86.2	85.4	84.7	84.0
Labor Force, Female (%)	45.3	45.3	45.2	45.0	44.9	44.8	44.7	44.5	44.3	44.2	44.0
Primary Schl. Enroll. Ratio	..	..	..	..	..	..	..	56.0	55.0	55.0	59.0
Primary Schl. Enroll. Ratio, Female	..	..	..	..	..	..	..	44.0	44.0	45.0	48.0
Secondary Schl. Enroll. Ratio	..	..	..	..	..	..	..	4.0	4.0	4.0	4.0

1980	1981	1982	1983	1984	1985	1986	1987	1988	1989 estimate	NOTES	MALAWI
											FOREIGN TRADE (CUSTOMS BASIS)
				(Millions of current US dollars)							
285.15	273.85	246.00	244.00	314.40	250.10	242.70	277.00	292.00	..	..	Value of Exports, fob
253.29	242.50	219.17	229.80	294.30	232.10	203.74	234.98	242.00	..	..	Nonfuel Primary Products
0.56	0.12	0.19	0.20	0.10	0.00	0.00	0.00	0.00	..	..	Fuels
31.30	31.23	26.64	14.00	20.00	18.00	38.96	42.02	50.00	..	..	Manufactures
440.23	350.12	311.00	311.00	269.90	286.70	260.40	295.00	402.00	..	..	Value of Imports, cif
43.69	46.05	37.45	34.00	30.77	30.79	24.21	25.08	33.00	..	..	Nonfuel Primary Products
67.47	59.29	50.93	56.00	45.13	38.91	18.45	24.92	25.00	..	..	Fuels
329.07	244.78	222.63	221.00	194.00	217.00	217.74	245.00	344.00	..	..	Manufactures
				(Index 1987 = 100)							
151.3	135.7	127.5	132.7	134.9	114.7	110.8	100.0	106.4	..	..	Terms of Trade
137.9	128.7	116.8	119.2	117.8	98.2	100.8	100.0	113.1	..	..	Export Prices, fob
91.1	94.9	91.6	89.8	87.3	85.6	91.0	100.0	106.3	..	..	Import Prices, cif
				(Millions of current US dollars)							**BALANCE OF PAYMENTS**
314.74	317.55	274.28	283.29	349.80	283.17	276.18	322.22	334.75	339.00	..	Exports of Goods & Services
280.75	272.53	239.70	246.18	311.81	245.48	248.41	278.48	296.96	301.20	..	Merchandise, fob
31.77	43.67	33.06	36.01	35.38	32.98	24.45	40.48	28.19	26.90	..	Nonfactor Services
2.22	1.34	1.52	1.11	2.62	4.71	3.33	3.26	9.60	10.90	..	Factor Services
637.86	522.51	440.17	459.75	434.63	443.49	408.42	421.37	483.35	603.00	..	Imports of Goods & Services
307.97	244.28	214.02	216.21	162.02	176.66	154.11	177.61	253.04	249.20	..	Merchandise, fob
178.55	146.77	133.21	141.90	156.29	147.93	139.44	150.95	184.87	286.50	..	Nonfactor Services
151.34	131.46	92.94	101.64	116.32	118.90	114.88	92.81	45.45	67.30	..	Factor Services
34.50	49.30	33.00	30.30	30.10	30.00	36.10	28.50	28.60	28.80	..	Long-Term Interest
13.30	11.95	11.84	8.26	11.53	11.11	13.11	13.81	15.07	91.10	..	Private Current Transfers, net
..	..	..	..	..	..	..	..	..	..	..	Workers' Remittances
-309.82	-193.01	-154.05	-168.20	-73.30	-149.21	-119.12	-85.34	-133.53	-172.90	..	Curr. A/C Bal before Off. Transf.
50.19	47.44	37.33	30.48	25.26	25.20	29.70	30.26	80.52	55.00	..	Net Official Transfers
-259.63	-145.57	-116.72	-137.73	-48.04	-124.01	-89.42	-55.08	-53.01	-117.90	..	Curr. A/C Bal after Off. Transf.
180.89	51.27	9.38	96.19	73.23	5.76	37.61	92.54	171.94	104.50	..	Long-Term Capital, net
9.48	1.12	..	2.55	..	0.52	..	0.09	..	..	..	Direct Investment
120.20	83.70	42.80	41.00	73.20	22.20	80.20	73.00	77.90	87.30	..	Long-Term Loans
153.40	122.90	73.30	64.60	111.40	68.90	146.00	110.10	112.20	115.50	..	Disbursements
33.20	39.20	30.50	23.60	38.20	46.70	65.80	37.10	34.30	28.20	..	Repayments
51.21	-33.55	-33.42	52.64	0.03	-16.96	-42.59	19.45	94.04	17.20	..	Other Long-Term Capital
62.01	69.03	89.13	3.17	1.46	97.62	51.10	27.02	-7.44	-33.80	..	Other Capital, net
16.72	25.27	18.21	38.37	-26.64	20.63	0.70	-64.48	-111.49	47.20	..	Change in Reserves
				(Malawi Kwacha per US dollar)							**Memo Item:**
0.810	0.900	1.060	1.170	1.410	1.720	1.860	2.210	2.560	2.760	..	Conversion Factor (Annual Avg)
			(Millions of US dollars), outstanding at end of year								
820.8	812.4	856.8	885.3	876.1	1,018.2	1,161.3	1,373.1	1,344.7	1,394.3	..	**EXTERNAL DEBT (Total)**
704.7	762.4	771.0	812.3	834.1	937.6	1,081.2	1,278.0	1,294.6	1,346.4	..	Long-Term Debt (by debtor)
105.7	135.1	124.6	128.4	129.0	145.5	133.3	116.9	105.7	100.5	..	Central Bank, incl. IMF credit
414.1	456.8	496.5	567.9	627.3	723.5	884.8	1,089.9	1,125.4	1,176.0	..	Central Government
..	..	..	..	..	..	..	..	..	..	..	Rest of General Government
131.5	125.4	113.1	88.7	59.1	53.8	49.2	58.5	52.4	59.6	..	Non-financial Public Enterprises
53.4	45.1	36.8	27.3	18.7	14.8	13.9	12.7	11.1	10.3	..	Priv. Sector, incl non-guaranteed
116.1	50.0	85.8	73.0	42.0	80.6	80.1	95.1	50.1	47.9	..	Short-Term Debt
				(Millions of US dollars)							**Memo Items:**
68.4	49.1	22.7	15.4	56.6	45.0	24.6	51.8	145.6	100.3	..	Int'l Reserves Excluding Gold
7.6	5.1	5.9	4.9	4.0	4.2	5.0	6.2	5.3	5.2	..	Gold Holdings (at market price)
											SOCIAL INDICATORS
7.6	7.6	7.6	7.6	7.6	7.6	7.6	7.6	7.6	7.6	..	Total Fertility Rate
168.6	165.8	163.0	160.4	157.8	155.2	152.6	150.0	148.8	147.7	..	Infant Mortality Rate
44.2	44.6	45.0	45.4	45.8	46.2	46.6	47.0	47.2	47.4	..	Life Expectancy at Birth
9.7	10.2	10.6	11.1	11.5	12.0	12.6	13.1	13.7	14.2	..	Urban Population, % of total
119.0	121.1	121.3	113.0	111.7	107.9	105.1	100.0	103.8	103.8	..	Food Prod. per capita (1987=100)
83.3	..	..	..	..	..	..	..	..	..	..	Labor Force, Agriculture (%)
43.9	43.6	43.3	43.1	42.9	42.6	42.3	42.0	41.7	41.5	..	Labor Force, Female (%)
60.0	65.0	62.0	60.0	60.0	62.0	65.0	66.0	..	..	..	Primary Schl. Enroll. Ratio
48.0	..	52.0	50.0	51.0	53.0	57.0	59.0	..	..	..	Primary Schl. Enroll. Ratio, Female
3.0	4.0	4.0	4.0	4.0	4.0	4.0	4.0	..	..	..	Secondary Schl. Enroll. Ratio

MALAYSIA	1969	1970	1971	1972	1973	1974	1975	1976	1977	1978	1979
CURRENT GNP PER CAPITA (US $)	380	390	410	450	550	700	820	920	1,010	1,150	1,400
POPULATION (thousands)	10,580	10,853	11,128	11,408	11,690	11,974	12,258	12,545	12,837	13,135	13,444

USE AND ORIGIN OF RESOURCES				*(Millions of current Malaysian Ringgit)*							
Gross National Product (GNP)	11,919	12,517	13,186	14,495	18,916	22,892	22,625	28,261	32,529	36,186	44,354
Net Factor Income from Abroad	-258	-339	-345	-358	-640	-984	-700	-1,074	-1,249	-1,700	-2,070
GDP at Market Prices	12,177	12,856	13,531	14,853	19,556	23,876	23,325	29,335	33,778	37,886	46,424
Resource Balance	1,149	539	197	-180	1,071	78	123	2,964	2,461	2,108	4,120
Exports of Goods & NFServices	5,303	5,404	5,250	5,129	7,779	11,060	10,187	14,576	16,240	18,585	26,004
Imports of Goods & NFServices	4,154	4,865	5,053	5,309	6,708	10,982	10,064	11,612	13,779	16,477	21,884
Domestic Absorption	11,028	12,317	13,334	15,033	18,485	23,798	23,202	26,371	31,317	35,778	42,304
Private Consumption, etc.	7,162	7,417	8,016	8,696	10,401	12,746	13,172	14,919	16,941	19,584	22,406
General Gov't Consumption	1,762	2,018	2,284	2,882	3,088	3,701	4,130	4,527	5,671	6,090	6,475
Gross Domestic Investment	2,104	2,882	3,034	3,455	4,996	7,351	5,900	6,925	8,705	10,104	13,423
Fixed Investment	1,890	2,430	2,989	3,553	4,669	6,416	6,199	6,868	8,261	9,381	12,250
Indirect Taxes, net	1,258	1,257	1,867	2,115	2,851	3,730	3,343	4,390	5,447	6,099	7,670
GDP at factor cost	10,919	11,599	11,664	12,738	16,705	20,146	19,982	24,945	28,331	31,787	38,754
Agriculture	3,537	3,667	3,504	3,824	5,155	7,061	6,527	7,857	8,682	9,513	10,988
Industry	2,965	3,246	3,571	4,077	5,296	7,418	7,303	9,477	11,236	13,203	16,736
Manufacturing	1,383	1,531	1,720	1,962	2,941	4,024	3,931	5,203	6,212	7,189	8,992
Services, etc.	5,675	5,943	6,456	6,952	9,105	9,397	9,495	12,001	13,860	15,170	18,700
Gross Domestic Saving	3,253	3,421	3,231	3,275	6,067	7,429	6,023	9,889	11,166	12,212	17,543
Gross National Saving	..	2,883	2,696	2,743	5,241	6,320	5,208	8,694	9,804	10,355	15,394

				(Millions of 1980 Malaysian Ringgit)							
Gross National Product	22,907	24,152	25,631	28,130	31,067	33,417	34,183	37,897	40,770	43,232	47,231
GDP at Market Prices	23,574	24,985	26,458	28,935	32,313	34,967	35,250	39,382	42,447	45,320	49,613
Resource Balance	4,321	3,387	3,639	4,270	4,611	2,734	5,062	7,022	5,516	4,988	5,385
Exports of Goods & NFServices	13,771	14,453	14,678	14,975	17,100	19,824	19,230	22,491	23,427	25,205	29,733
Imports of Goods & NFServices	9,450	11,066	11,039	10,705	12,489	17,089	14,168	15,470	17,911	20,217	24,348
Domestic Absorption	19,258	21,598	22,819	24,665	27,702	32,233	30,188	32,360	36,931	40,332	44,227
Private Consumption, etc.	12,111	12,549	13,420	14,177	15,327	16,645	16,545	17,306	19,256	21,370	23,537
General Gov't Consumption	2,983	3,377	3,660	4,278	4,474	5,141	5,490	5,956	6,542	6,924	7,043
Gross Domestic Investment	4,157	5,672	5,739	6,209	7,901	10,447	8,154	9,099	11,133	12,038	13,647
Fixed Investment	3,742	4,794	5,696	6,539	7,618	9,283	8,593	9,023	10,340	11,176	13,308
GDP at factor cost	22,148	23,623	23,971	26,074	29,017	31,030	31,737	35,209	37,473	38,414	41,633
Agriculture	..	7,381	7,488	8,059	9,008	9,630	9,338	10,481	10,729	10,905	11,532
Industry	..	8,669	9,549	10,345	11,410	11,939	11,979	14,095	15,191	16,707	18,899
Manufacturing	..	3,659	4,119	4,538	5,560	6,137	6,318	7,487	8,280	9,048	10,073
Services, etc.	..	8,934	9,421	10,531	11,895	13,398	13,933	14,806	16,528	17,708	19,182

Memo Items:											
Capacity to Import	12,064	12,292	11,470	10,342	14,483	17,211	14,341	19,418	21,111	22,803	28,932
Terms of Trade Adjustment	-1,707	-2,161	-3,209	-4,633	-2,617	-2,613	-4,889	-3,073	-2,317	-2,402	-801
Gross Domestic Income	21,865	22,824	23,249	24,302	29,696	32,354	30,362	36,309	40,131	42,918	48,811
Gross National Income	21,199	21,991	22,423	23,497	28,451	30,804	29,295	34,825	38,453	40,831	46,429

DOMESTIC PRICES/DEFLATORS				*(Index 1980 = 100)*							
Overall (GDP)	51.7	51.5	51.1	51.3	60.5	68.3	66.2	74.5	79.6	83.6	93.6
Domestic Absorption	57.3	57.0	58.4	60.9	66.7	73.8	76.9	81.5	84.8	88.7	95.7
Agriculture	..	49.7	46.8	47.5	57.2	73.3	69.9	75.0	80.9	87.2	95.3
Industry	..	37.4	37.4	39.4	46.4	62.1	61.0	67.2	74.0	79.0	88.6
Manufacturing	..	41.8	41.8	43.2	52.9	65.6	62.2	69.5	75.0	79.5	89.3
Consumer Price Index	43.4	44.2	44.9	46.4	51.3	60.2	62.9	64.5	67.6	70.9	73.5

MANUFACTURING ACTIVITY											
Employment (1987=100)	29.7	33.2	36.6	42.8	56.2	57.1	59.6	67.3	70.8	78.2	86.7
Real Earnings per Empl. (1987=100)	64.5	64.2	64.1	61.5	56.3	58.7	60.1	64.2	67.9	67.8	73.1
Real Output per Empl. (1987=100)	..	..	..	..	..	..	..	..	..	..	..
Earnings as % of Value Added	27.8	28.5	30.3	29.3	25.9	26.9	27.4	27.9	27.1	26.2	25.6

MONETARY HOLDINGS				*(Billions of current Malaysian Ringgit)*							
Money Supply, Broadly Defined	4.18	4.65	5.26	6.56	8.61	13.03	15.20	19.22	22.20	26.56	33.07
Money	1.91	2.07	2.17	2.72	3.74	4.06	4.35	5.26	6.13	7.24	8.49
Currency Outside Banks	0.93	1.00	1.06	1.27	1.72	2.03	2.24	2.63	3.11	3.58	4.09
Demand Deposits	0.98	1.07	1.11	1.45	2.02	2.03	2.11	2.63	3.02	3.66	4.39
Quasi-Money	2.27	2.58	3.09	3.85	4.87	8.97	10.85	13.97	16.08	19.31	24.59

GOVERNMENT DEFICIT (-) OR SURPLUS				*(Millions of current Malaysian Ringgit)*							
	..	..	..	-1,359	-1,094	-1,257	-1,827	-1,976	-2,407	-2,356	-1,401
Current Revenue	..	..	..	2,950	3,378	4,748	5,076	6,125	7,766	8,797	10,436
Current Expenditure	..	..	..	3,234	3,399	4,446	4,944	5,984	7,252	7,610	8,332
Current Budget Balance	..	..	..	-284	-21	302	132	141	514	1,187	2,104
Capital Receipts	..	..	..	..	..	11	13	13	28	11	30
Capital Payments	..	..	..	1,075	1,073	1,570	2,037	2,218	3,094	3,384	3,288

1980	1981	1982	1983	1984	1985	1986	1987	1988	1989 estimate	NOTES	MALAYSIA
1,690	1,880	1,900	1,900	2,040	1,970	1,850	1,830	1,930	2,160	..	**CURRENT GNP PER CAPITA (US $)**
13,764	14,130	14,510	14,887	15,272	15,682	16,109	16,528	16,921	17,340	..	**POPULATION (thousands)**

(Millions of current Malaysian Ringgit) — **USE AND ORIGIN OF RESOURCES**

1980	1981	1982	1983	1984	1985	1986	1987	1988	1989	NOTES	
51,390	55,602	59,690	65,530	74,182	72,039	66,953	74,729	85,796	97,447	..	Gross National Product (GNP)
-1,918	-2,011	-2,889	-4,411	-5,368	-5,508	-4,776	-4,982	-5,065	-4,089	..	Net Factor Income from Abroad
53,308	57,613	62,579	69,941	79,550	77,547	71,729	79,711	90,861	101,536	..	GDP at Market Prices
1,334	-3,563	-5,454	-3,998	1,518	3,976	4,364	11,092	9,424	4,351	..	Resource Balance
30,676	30,154	31,846	35,795	43,171	42,537	40,305	50,838	61,259	74,973	..	Exports of Goods & NFServices
29,342	33,717	37,300	39,793	41,653	38,561	35,941	39,746	51,835	70,622	..	Imports of Goods & NFServices
51,974	61,176	68,033	73,939	78,032	73,571	67,365	68,619	81,437	97,185	..	Domestic Absorption
26,946	30,594	33,226	36,458	39,594	40,360	36,574	37,764	44,856	52,930	..	Private Consumption, etc.
8,811	10,425	11,469	11,015	11,741	11,844	12,127	12,239	12,997	14,180	..	General Gov't Consumption
16,217	20,157	23,338	26,466	26,697	21,367	18,664	18,616	23,584	30,075	..	Gross Domestic Investment
16,597	20,759	22,745	25,213	25,391	23,124	18,865	18,280	21,922	30,248	..	Fixed Investment
9,139	8,834	8,759	10,310	..	..	..	..	..	..	..	Indirect Taxes, net
44,169	48,779	53,820	59,631	..	..	..	..	..	..	B	GDP at factor cost
11,680	11,962	12,807	13,555	..	..	..	..	..	..	..	Agriculture
20,164	21,409	21,851	24,835	..	..	..	..	..	..	..	Industry
11,002	11,542	11,419	12,935	..	..	..	..	..	..	..	Manufacturing
21,464	24,242	27,921	31,551	..	..	..	..	..	..	..	Services, etc.
17,551	16,594	17,884	22,468	28,215	25,343	23,028	29,708	33,008	34,426	..	Gross Domestic Saving
15,539	14,457	14,871	17,976	22,700	19,722	18,203	24,900	28,120	30,268	..	Gross National Saving

(Millions of 1980 Malaysian Ringgit)

1980	1981	1982	1983	1984	1985	1986	1987	1988	1989	NOTES	
51,390	55,208	57,732	60,011	64,090	63,290	65,018	68,559	75,150	83,332	..	Gross National Product
53,308	56,960	60,355	64,215	69,282	68,514	69,429	73,135	79,677	86,757	..	GDP at Market Prices
1,334	-561	-1,575	-594	2,120	6,337	13,819	17,701	15,288	12,477	..	Resource Balance
30,676	30,421	33,669	37,823	43,036	43,229	48,324	55,276	61,893	73,139	..	Exports of Goods & NFServices
29,342	30,982	35,244	38,417	40,916	36,892	34,505	37,575	46,606	60,662	..	Imports of Goods & NFServices
51,974	57,521	61,929	64,809	67,161	62,177	55,610	55,433	64,390	74,280	..	Domestic Absorption
26,946	28,530	29,333	30,056	31,684	31,663	27,561	27,506	32,232	36,748	..	Private Consumption, etc.
8,811	9,987	10,860	11,357	10,801	10,706	10,842	11,001	11,538	12,415	..	General Gov't Consumption
16,217	19,005	21,737	23,396	24,677	19,808	17,208	16,927	20,619	25,117	..	Gross Domestic Investment
16,597	19,598	21,167	22,866	23,543	21,311	17,395	16,624	19,162	25,271	..	Fixed Investment
44,169	48,190	51,583	53,780	57,612	57,193	60,122	63,783	69,154	75,643	B	GDP at factor cost
11,680	12,247	13,040	12,956	13,324	13,657	14,202	15,259	15,966	16,892	..	Agriculture
20,164	20,879	22,276	24,594	27,411	26,490	27,745	29,562	33,284	36,949	..	Industry
11,002	11,522	12,167	13,125	14,739	14,175	15,242	17,285	20,326	22,765	..	Manufacturing
21,464	23,834	25,039	26,665	28,547	28,367	27,483	28,314	30,428	32,915	..	Services, etc.

Memo Items:

1980	1981	1982	1983	1984	1985	1986	1987	1988	1989	NOTES	
30,676	27,708	30,090	34,557	42,407	40,695	38,695	48,061	55,079	64,399	..	Capacity to Import
0	-2,713	-3,579	-3,266	-629	-2,534	-9,630	-7,215	-6,814	-8,740	..	Terms of Trade Adjustment
53,308	54,247	56,776	60,949	68,653	65,981	59,800	65,919	72,863	78,017	..	Gross Domestic Income
51,390	52,495	54,153	56,745	63,461	60,756	55,388	61,344	68,336	74,593	..	Gross National Income

(Index 1980 = 100) — **DOMESTIC PRICES/DEFLATORS**

1980	1981	1982	1983	1984	1985	1986	1987	1988	1989	NOTES	
100.0	101.1	103.7	108.9	114.8	113.2	103.3	109.0	114.0	117.0	..	Overall (GDP)
100.0	106.4	109.9	114.1	116.2	118.3	121.1	123.8	126.5	130.8	..	Domestic Absorption
100.0	97.7	98.2	104.6	..	..	..	..	..	..	..	Agriculture
100.0	102.5	98.1	101.0	..	..	..	..	..	..	..	Industry
100.0	100.2	93.8	98.6	..	..	..	..	..	..	..	Manufacturing
78.4	86.0	91.0	94.4	98.1	98.4	99.1	100.0	102.0	104.8	f	Consumer Price Index

MANUFACTURING ACTIVITY

1980	1981	1982	1983	1984	1985	1986	1987	1988	1989	NOTES	
96.9	108.4	100.1	95.1	96.3	91.9	92.4	100.0	111.4	..	..	Employment (1987 = 100)
76.7	78.3	85.3	91.4	96.0	103.5	102.4	100.0	107.2	..	..	Real Earnings per Empl. (1987 = 100)
..	..	..	..	..	..	..	..	..	..	..	Real Output per Empl. (1987 = 100)
28.0	30.7	32.1	30.0	28.5	29.9	29.9	29.1	29.6	..	..	Earnings as % of Value Added

(Billions of current Malaysian Ringgit) — **MONETARY HOLDINGS**

1980	1981	1982	1983	1984	1985	1986	1987	1988	1989	NOTES	
41.30	49.36	60.90	66.64	77.07	85.03	96.34	99.21	108.89	..	D	Money Supply, Broadly Defined
9.76	11.01	12.48	13.43	13.36	14.13	14.52	16.37	18.73	21.98	..	Money
4.76	5.10	5.73	6.03	5.97	6.77	7.15	7.97	9.03	9.90	..	Currency Outside Banks
5.00	5.91	6.75	7.41	7.38	7.36	7.38	8.41	9.70	12.07	..	Demand Deposits
31.54	38.34	48.43	53.21	63.71	70.89	81.82	82.84	90.16	..	..	Quasi-Money

(Millions of current Malaysian Ringgit)

1980	1981	1982	1983	1984	1985	1986	1987	1988	1989	NOTES	
-3,185	-8,572	-10,100	-6,786	-5,158	-1,951	-6,561	-5,224	-1,145	..	..	**GOVERNMENT DEFICIT (-) OR SURPLUS**
14,016	15,781	16,595	18,542	20,532	23,352	21,497	20,271	23,297	..	..	Current Revenue
10,217	13,686	15,932	16,140	17,525	20,336	21,412	20,722	21,787	..	..	Current Expenditure
3,799	2,095	663	2,402	3,007	3,016	85	-451	1,510	..	..	Current Budget Balance
37	61	33	39	38	105	77	34	53	..	..	Capital Receipts
7,021	10,728	10,796	9,227	8,203	5,072	6,723	4,807	2,708	..	..	Capital Payments

MALAYSIA	1969	1970	1971	1972	1973	1974	1975	1976	1977	1978	1979
FOREIGN TRADE (CUSTOMS BASIS)					*(Millions of current US dollars)*						
Value of Exports, fob	1,650	1,687	1,639	1,722	3,040	4,234	3,847	5,295	6,079	7,387	11,075
Nonfuel Primary Products	1,426	1,438	1,326	1,412	2,511	3,301	2,739	3,706	4,275	4,939	7,088
Fuels	115	124	169	118	164	359	419	765	868	1,037	2,020
Manufactures	108	125	143	191	364	574	689	824	937	1,410	1,966
Value of Imports, cif	1,162	1,390	1,485	1,674	2,517	4,297	3,851	4,177	5,004	6,364	8,708
Nonfuel Primary Products	379	410	396	469	700	1,051	982	969	1,178	1,471	1,773
Fuels	157	168	194	136	167	436	463	564	638	683	1,050
Manufactures	625	812	895	1,069	1,650	2,810	2,406	2,644	3,188	4,210	5,885
					(Index 1987 = 100)						
Terms of Trade	131.8	121.7	105.9	97.8	122.4	126.4	99.8	111.5	120.2	122.6	137.8
Export Prices, fob	28.6	27.9	26.7	29.9	48.3	69.1	58.5	65.6	76.9	87.4	114.2
Import Prices, cif	21.7	22.9	25.2	30.6	39.4	54.7	58.6	58.9	63.9	71.3	82.8
BALANCE OF PAYMENTS					*(Millions of current US dollars)*						
Exports of Goods & Services	..	1,830	1,793	1,876	3,270	4,733	4,392	5,866	6,841	8,386	12,418
Merchandise, fob	..	1,640	1,600	1,680	2,972	4,164	3,784	5,245	6,035	7,311	10,994
Nonfactor Services	..	113	106	123	193	408	452	446	549	697	870
Factor Services	..	77	87	74	105	162	156	175	257	378	555
Imports of Goods & Services	..	1,763	1,857	2,068	3,103	5,233	4,855	5,246	6,373	8,233	11,482
Merchandise, fob	..	1,291	1,375	1,550	2,320	3,939	3,527	3,780	4,516	5,718	7,838
Nonfactor Services	..	279	276	309	409	718	872	864	1,086	1,402	2,162
Factor Services	..	193	206	208	374	576	456	602	771	1,114	1,482
Long-Term Interest	..	25	27	37	54	71	85	156	179	190	344
Private Current Transfers, net	..	-65	-62	-62	-76	-52	-48	-48	-46	-68	-36
Workers' Remittances	..	..	..	..	..	..	..	..	..	..	..
Curr. Λ/C Bal before Off. Transf.	..	2	-125	-254	91	-552	-511	572	422	85	901
Net Official Transfers	..	6	17	7	14	9	15	8	14	23	28
Curr. A/C Bal after Off. Transf.	..	8	-108	-248	105	-543	-496	580	436	108	929
Long-Term Capital, net	..	96	219	296	218	668	724	568	652	690	925
Direct Investment	..	94	100	114	172	571	350	381	406	500	573
Long-Term Loans	..	1	159	221	58	221	756	428	476	402	781
Disbursements	..	58	194	269	146	334	893	676	927	1,266	1,256
Repayments	..	57	35	48	89	113	137	248	451	864	475
Other Long-Term Capital	..	1	-41	-39	-11	-123	-383	-241	-230	-212	-429
Other Capital, net	..	-90	-47	-22	-99	73	-162	-350	-780	-518	-1,053
Change in Reserves	..	-14	-64	-27	-224	-198	-65	-798	-308	-279	-802
Memo Item:					*(Malaysian Ringgit per US dollar)*						
Conversion Factor (Annual Avg)	3.060	3.060	3.050	2.820	2.440	2.410	2.400	2.540	2.460	2.320	2.190
				(Millions of US dollars), outstanding at end of year							
EXTERNAL DEBT (Total)	..	440	614	823	893	1,119	1,843	2,376	3,425	4,167	4,956
Long-Term Debt (by debtor)	..	440	614	823	893	1,119	1,843	2,376	2,830	3,356	4,082
Central Bank, incl. IMF credit	..	0	0	0	0	0	0	108	0	0	0
Central Government	..	265	379	483	519	577	967	1,118	1,489	1,874	1,964
Rest of General Government	..	11	12	9	7	16	18	18	15	20	28
Non-financial Public Enterprises	..	115	144	202	203	277	355	468	500	646	1,090
Priv. Sector, incl non-guaranteed	..	50	80	130	164	249	504	664	825	816	1,000
Short-Term Debt	..	..	..	..	..	..	..	..	595	811	874
Memo Items:					*(Millions of US dollars)*						
Int'l Reserves Excluding Gold	556.6	616.3	754.7	907.1	1,275.2	1,547.1	1,456.1	2,404.1	2,783.8	3,243.3	3,914.9
Gold Holdings (at market price)	63.4	51.2	72.4	107.7	186.3	309.6	232.8	223.7	287.0	427.1	1,090.6
SOCIAL INDICATORS											
Total Fertility Rate	5.6	5.5	5.3	5.1	5.0	4.8	4.6	4.4	4.2	4.1	4.1
Infant Mortality Rate	46.8	45.2	43.6	42.0	40.4	38.8	37.2	35.6	34.0	32.8	31.6
Life Expectancy at Birth	60.8	61.6	62.3	63.0	63.5	63.9	64.4	64.8	65.3	65.8	66.3
Urban Population, % of total	26.8	27.0	27.7	28.4	29.1	29.8	30.5	31.2	32.0	32.7	33.5
Food Prod. per capita (1987=100)	46.8	49.2	53.8	56.2	57.9	62.0	66.3	68.1	68.0	65.9	71.9
Labor Force, Agriculture (%)	54.6	53.8	52.4	51.1	49.9	48.8	47.7	46.3	45.0	43.8	42.6
Labor Force, Female (%)	30.9	31.2	31.7	32.0	32.4	32.7	33.0	33.4	33.7	34.0	34.3
Primary Schl. Enroll. Ratio	..	87.0	..	..	..	..	91.0	..	91.0	92.0	92.0
Primary Schl. Enroll. Ratio, Female	..	84.0	..	..	..	..	89.0	..	89.0	91.0	90.0
Secondary Schl. Enroll. Ratio	..	34.0	..	..	..	..	42.0	47.0	48.0	49.0	51.0

1980	1981	1982	1983	1984	1985	1986	1987	1988	1989 estimate	NOTES	MALAYSIA
					(Millions of current US dollars)						**FOREIGN TRADE (CUSTOMS BASIS)**
12,939	11,734	12,027	14,100	16,484	15,632	13,830	17,911	21,110	21,548	..	Value of Exports, fob
7,277	6,251	5,798	6,534	7,146	6,432	5,518	7,273	8,344	..	..	Nonfuel Primary Products
3,199	3,124	3,448	4,048	4,933	4,930	3,160	3,572	3,233	..	..	Fuels
2,464	2,359	2,781	3,518	4,404	4,271	5,152	7,066	9,533	8,793	..	Manufactures
11,602	13,052	14,042	14,669	14,849	12,746	11,447	12,506	16,551	17,128	..	Value of Imports, cif
2,055	2,367	2,328	2,383	2,364	1,997	1,774	2,054	3,226	..	..	Nonfuel Primary Products
1,758	2,243	2,123	2,023	1,511	1,515	885	900	978	..	..	Fuels
7,789	8,441	9,591	10,263	10,974	9,234	8,788	9,552	12,347		..	Manufactures
					(Index 1987 = 100)						
141.3	123.8	116.7	122.4	132.0	120.7	93.2	100.0	99.2	..	..	Terms of Trade
134.5	120.3	107.0	108.7	111.8	102.7	84.7	100.0	108.2	..	..	Export Prices, fob
95.2	97.1	91.7	88.8	84.7	85.1	90.9	100.0	109.0	..	..	Import Prices, cif
					(Millions of current US dollars)						**BALANCE OF PAYMENTS**
14,836	13,879	14,299	16,218	19,067	17,776	16,185	20,980	24,441	28,816	f	Exports of Goods & Services
12,868	11,675	11,966	13,683	16,407	15,133	13,547	17,754	20,852	24,831	..	Merchandise, fob
1,229	1,412	1,683	1,972	2,046	2,052	2,090	2,392	2,495	2,862	..	Nonfactor Services
739	792	650	562	614	591	548	834	1,094	1,123	..	Factor Services
15,100	16,331	17,867	19,705	20,700	18,383	16,344	18,485	22,715	29,030	f	Imports of Goods & Services
10,462	11,780	12,719	13,251	13,426	11,556	10,302	11,915	15,293	21,051	..	Merchandise, fob
3,026	2,920	3,351	4,079	4,418	4,048	3,714	3,770	4,462	5,076	..	Nonfactor Services
1,612	1,630	1,797	2,375	2,856	2,779	2,329	2,801	2,960	2,903	..	Factor Services
338	515	724	945	1,320	1,479	1,402	1,474	1,487	1,221	..	Long-Term Interest
-43	-55	-53	-35	-63	-46	-19	69	68	-25	..	Private Current Transfers, net
..	..	..	..	..	..	..	..	..	..	..	Workers' Remittances
-307	-2,507	-3,622	-3,523	-1,696	-653	-179	2,563	1,793	-239	..	Curr. A/C Bal before Off. Transf.
23	21	21	26	24	40	56	69	81	94	..	Net Official Transfers
-285	-2,486	-3,601	-3,497	-1,671	-613	-122	2,633	1,875	-145	..	Curr. A/C Bal after Off. Transf.
1,021	2,574	3,605	3,966	3,143	1,582	1,120	-530	-1,275	686	f	Long-Term Capital, net
934	1,265	1,397	1,261	797	695	489	423	649	1,846	..	Direct Investment
1,111	2,332	3,916	3,161	2,366	163	527	-612	-1,827	-682	..	Long-Term Loans
1,456	2,766	4,510	3,890	3,497	3,831	2,359	2,000	1,958	2,131	..	Disbursements
345	434	594	730	1,131	3,668	1,832	2,612	3,786	2,813	..	Repayments
-1,025	-1,023	-1,708	-455	-20	725	103	-341	-97	-478	..	Other Long-Term Capital
-268	-540	-267	-485	-986	182	458	-983	-1,029	690	f	Other Capital, net
-468	452	262	15	-486	-1,151	-1,455	-1,119	430	-1,230	..	Change in Reserves
					(Malaysian Ringgit per US dollar)						**Memo Item:**
2.180	2.300	2.340	2.320	2.340	2.480	2.580	2.520	2.620	2.710	..	Conversion Factor (Annual Avg)
					(Millions of US dollars), outstanding at end of year						
6,611	9,225	13,397	17,965	18,801	20,387	21,888	22,758	20,400	18,576	..	**EXTERNAL DEBT (Total)**
5,256	7,601	11,674	14,938	16,270	17,702	19,475	20,732	18,300	15,837	..	Long-Term Debt (by debtor)
0	221	274	330	258	118	0	0	3	35	..	Central Bank, incl. IMF credit
2,740	4,120	6,260	8,375	9,448	10,353	11,907	13,074	11,396	10,750	..	Central Government
40	49	58	59	45	50	57	65	55	48	..	Rest of General Government
1,226	1,573	1,883	3,441	3,392	3,721	4,020	3,870	3,641	2,801	..	Non-financial Public Enterprises
1,250	1,639	3,200	2,733	3,128	3,460	3,492	3,723	3,205	2,204	..	Priv. Sector, incl non-guaranteed
1,355	1,624	1,723	3,027	2,531	2,685	2,413	2,026	2,100	2,738	..	Short-Term Debt
					(Millions of US dollars)						**Memo Items:**
4,387.4	4,098.0	3,767.8	3,783.7	3,723.3	4,911.8	6,027.4	7,435.3	6,526.5	7,783.0	..	Int'l Reserves Excluding Gold
1,367.6	926.2	1,064.6	888.9	718.3	765.2	914.7	1,137.6	964.1	950.4	..	Gold Holdings (at market price)
											SOCIAL INDICATORS
4.0	4.0	3.9	3.9	3.9	3.8	3.8	3.8	3.7	3.7	..	Total Fertility Rate
30.4	29.2	28.0	27.2	26.4	25.6	24.8	24.0	23.3	22.6	..	Infant Mortality Rate
66.9	67.4	68.0	68.3	68.6	68.9	69.2	69.5	69.7	69.9	..	Life Expectancy at Birth
34.2	35.0	35.8	36.6	37.4	38.2	39.0	39.8	40.7	41.5	..	Urban Population, % of total
76.3	77.8	83.2	76.5	88.4	98.1	98.8	100.0	105.6	115.1	..	Food Prod. per capita (1987=100)
41.6	..	..	..	..	..	..	..	..	..	..	Labor Force, Agriculture (%)
34.6	34.7	34.8	34.8	34.9	34.9	34.9	35.0	35.0	35.0	..	Labor Force, Female (%)
93.0	..	94.0	96.0	98.0	100.0	101.0	102.0	..	..	..	Primary Schl. Enroll. Ratio
92.0	..	93.0	95.0	97.0	100.0	..	102.0	..	..	..	Primary Schl. Enroll. Ratio, Female
48.0	..	49.0	51.0	53.0	53.0	54.0	59.0	..	..	..	Secondary Schl. Enroll. Ratio

MALI	1969	1970	1971	1972	1973	1974	1975	1976	1977	1978	1979
CURRENT GNP PER CAPITA (US $)	60	70	70	80	80	90	120	140	170	170	210
POPULATION (thousands)	5,224	5,335	5,443	5,553	5,666	5,783	5,905	6,032	6,165	6,304	6,446

USE AND ORIGIN OF RESOURCES *(Billions of current CFA Francs)*

	1969	1970	1971	1972	1973	1974	1975	1976	1977	1978	1979
Gross National Product (GNP)	82.74	92.39	102.34	115.57	118.10	121.31	165.81	210.07	243.47	262.73	317.59
Net Factor Income from Abroad	-0.60	-1.40	-0.30	-0.10	-0.40	-1.00	-2.10	-1.60	0.20	2.50	-2.50
GDP at Market Prices	83.34	93.79	102.64	115.67	118.50	122.31	167.91	211.67	243.27	260.23	320.09
Resource Balance	-6.87	-5.62	-7.43	-11.72	-15.86	-36.53	-34.98	-22.49	-17.59	-50.39	-59.04
Exports of Goods & NFServices	9.90	12.45	14.61	12.25	12.84	16.47	17.15	24.70	32.94	31.96	40.29
Imports of Goods & NFServices	16.77	18.07	22.04	23.97	28.70	53.00	52.14	47.19	50.52	82.35	99.33
Domestic Absorption	90.21	99.41	110.07	127.39	134.36	158.84	202.90	234.17	260.86	310.62	379.14
Private Consumption, etc.	66.18	74.96	82.31	92.97	103.19	126.97	158.07	187.68	198.24	240.06	294.82
General Gov't Consumption	8.72	9.27	10.36	13.47	9.97	14.33	17.21	16.51	22.43	26.71	31.82
Gross Domestic Investment	15.32	15.19	17.41	20.95	21.21	17.54	27.62	29.98	40.19	43.85	52.49
Fixed Investment	12.62	13.09	15.31	19.05	19.81	15.64	24.02	27.58	37.19	39.85	48.49
Indirect Taxes, net	5.70	6.90	7.90	5.20	5.90	6.00	6.50	10.10	11.50	13.60	16.90
GDP at factor cost	77.64	86.89	94.74	110.47	112.60	116.31	161.41	201.57	231.77	246.63	303.19
Agriculture	50.17	57.51	62.11	68.43	64.84	59.72	102.38	123.71	142.32	143.85	186.68
Industry	8.88	10.17	11.83	13.87	14.71	16.07	18.04	22.06	25.44	27.07	29.97
Manufacturing	5.35	6.85	7.22	9.47	9.57	10.03	11.44	12.10	13.41	13.32	13.79
Services, etc.	24.30	26.11	28.70	33.37	38.94	46.51	47.49	65.90	75.51	89.31	103.44
Gross Domestic Saving	8.44	9.56	9.98	9.23	5.35	-18.99	-7.36	7.49	22.60	-6.54	-6.55
Gross National Saving	..	8.25	11.12	10.66	6.35	-19.00	-6.90	8.31	27.79	3.26	-1.70

(Billions of 1987 CFA Francs)

	1969	1970	1971	1972	1973	1974	1975	1976	1977	1978	1979
Gross National Product	271.98	286.55	300.06	316.26	307.71	298.95	338.89	386.85	416.65	409.02	445.78
GDP at Market Prices	274.11	291.02	301.03	316.66	308.81	301.35	343.20	389.92	416.36	405.16	449.39
Resource Balance	-40.34	-28.22	-22.21	-35.50	-36.39	-61.05	-55.21	-38.55	-24.51	-67.91	-69.89
Exports of Goods & NFServices	34.25	33.94	46.16	41.51	37.85	41.51	42.17	48.81	60.43	57.78	64.09
Imports of Goods & NFServices	74.59	62.16	68.37	77.00	74.24	102.56	97.38	87.36	84.95	125.69	133.98
Domestic Absorption	314.45	319.24	323.24	352.16	345.20	362.40	398.40	428.47	440.87	473.07	519.28
Private Consumption, etc.	214.73	224.25	221.58	252.74	249.36	279.99	301.98	338.93	328.02	358.24	395.55
General Gov't Consumption	38.72	41.43	45.63	42.67	41.93	40.20	40.38	34.92	44.05	47.80	51.37
Gross Domestic Investment	61.00	53.56	56.04	56.75	53.91	42.21	56.04	54.62	68.81	67.03	72.35
Fixed Investment	..	..	..	..	..	..	..	..	..	..	..
GDP at factor cost	..	..	..	..	..	..	..	..	..	..	..
Agriculture	178.62	192.59	197.08	200.08	178.12	166.65	207.56	237.50	256.46	237.00	274.92
Industry	33.52	36.84	28.95	32.88	33.58	33.58	36.59	38.67	43.30	42.61	35.89
Manufacturing	..	..	..	..	..	..	..	..	..	..	..
Services, etc.	67.64	68.59	79.26	87.29	97.36	101.11	99.61	114.92	117.55	126.18	141.46
Memo Items:											
Capacity to Import	44.03	42.82	45.31	39.36	33.21	31.87	32.04	45.73	55.37	48.78	54.34
Terms of Trade Adjustment	9.78	8.88	-0.84	-2.15	-4.64	-9.64	-10.13	-3.09	-5.06	-9.00	-9.75
Gross Domestic Income	283.89	299.91	300.18	314.51	304.17	291.71	333.06	386.83	411.30	396.16	439.64
Gross National Income	281.75	295.44	299.21	314.11	303.07	289.31	328.76	383.76	411.59	400.02	436.04

DOMESTIC PRICES/DEFLATORS *(Index 1987 = 100)*

	1969	1970	1971	1972	1973	1974	1975	1976	1977	1978	1979
Overall (GDP)	30.4	32.2	34.1	36.5	38.4	40.6	48.9	54.3	58.4	64.2	71.2
Domestic Absorption	28.7	31.1	34.1	36.2	38.9	43.8	50.9	54.7	59.2	65.7	73.0
Agriculture	28.1	29.9	31.5	34.2	36.4	35.8	49.3	52.1	55.5	60.7	67.9
Industry	26.5	27.6	40.9	42.2	43.8	47.9	49.3	57.0	58.8	63.5	83.5
Manufacturing	..	..	..	..	..	..	..	..	..	..	..
Consumer Price Index	..	..	..	..	..	..	..	..	..	..	..

MANUFACTURING ACTIVITY

	1969	1970	1971	1972	1973	1974	1975	1976	1977	1978	1979
Employment (1987=100)	..	..	..	..	..	..	..	..	..	..	..
Real Earnings per Empl. (1987=100)	..	..	..	..	..	..	..	..	..	..	..
Real Output per Empl. (1987=100)	..	..	..	..	..	..	..	..	..	..	..
Earnings as % of Value Added	38.9	45.6	47.8	46.1	49.0	44.2	31.9	30.8	26.1	29.5	29.8

MONETARY HOLDINGS *(Billions of current CFA Francs)*

	1969	1970	1971	1972	1973	1974	1975	1976	1977	1978	1979
Money Supply, Broadly Defined	12.20	13.64	14.68	16.41	17.85	27.13	32.53	36.25	41.82	51.49	60.11
Money	11.06	12.95	13.97	15.62	17.54	27.00	31.95	35.62	40.66	48.48	56.77
Currency Outside Banks	7.47	8.89	9.69	10.52	11.13	15.07	18.70	22.49	27.40	30.70	38.16
Demand Deposits	3.59	4.06	4.29	5.10	6.41	11.93	13.26	13.13	13.26	17.79	18.61
Quasi-Money	1.14	0.70	0.71	0.79	0.31	0.14	0.57	0.63	1.17	3.00	3.34

(Millions of current CFA Francs)

	1969	1970	1971	1972	1973	1974	1975	1976	1977	1978	1979
GOVERNMENT DEFICIT (-) OR SURPLUS	..	..	..	..	..	..	..	..	200	-4,000	-9,100
Current Revenue	..	..	..	..	..	..	24,200	27,100	34,700	35,200	36,000
Current Expenditure	..	..	..	..	..	..	..	25,200	29,200	33,100	39,600
Current Budget Balance	..	..	..	..	..	..	..	1,900	5,500	2,100	-3,600
Capital Receipts	..	..	..	..	..	..	..	..	..	..	..
Capital Payments	..	..	..	..	..	..	..	1,900	5,300	6,100	5,500

1980	1981	1982	1983	1984	1985	1986	1987	1988	1989 estimate	NOTES	MALI
240	240	220	170	160	150	180	200	240	270	..	CURRENT GNP PER CAPITA (US $)
6,590	6,738	6,891	7,049	7,215	7,389	7,574	7,771	7,983	8,212	..	POPULATION (thousands)
				(Billions of current CFA Francs)							USE AND ORIGIN OF RESOURCES
340.59	361.90	395.70	401.20	455.00	467.00	520.00	562.32	604.00	653.80	..	Gross National Product (GNP)
-3.60	-8.90	-7.90	-10.10	-8.50	-8.40	-8.60	-8.38	-8.20	-9.10	..	Net Factor Income from Abroad
344.19	370.80	403.60	411.30	463.50	475.40	528.60	570.70	612.20	662.90	..	GDP at Market Prices
-64.82	-65.90	-69.10	-79.80	-86.40	-160.60	-127.60	-96.00	-108.50	-100.90	..	Resource Balance
55.58	54.50	61.80	78.60	101.70	98.90	89.00	96.20	93.60	107.40	..	Exports of Goods & NFServices
120.40	120.40	130.90	158.40	188.10	259.50	216.60	192.20	202.10	208.30	..	Imports of Goods & NFServices
409.01	436.70	472.70	491.10	549.90	636.00	656.20	666.70	720.70	763.80	..	Domestic Absorption
314.80	335.30	362.10	386.30	429.30	486.90	477.10	472.30	504.10	520.70	..	Private Consumption, etc.
35.82	36.60	39.60	44.90	50.10	56.20	58.10	62.80	65.10	66.80	..	General Gov't Consumption
58.39	64.80	71.00	59.90	70.50	92.90	121.00	131.60	151.50	176.30	..	Gross Domestic Investment
58.39	64.80	71.40	75.00	84.60	104.40	121.50	120.60	123.80	136.60	..	Fixed Investment
14.50	18.40	16.30	17.50	20.00	20.80	23.30	29.40	26.90	30.30	..	Indirect Taxes, net
329.69	352.40	387.30	393.80	443.50	454.60	505.30	541.30	585.30	632.60	B	GDP at factor cost
200.84	207.00	232.03	219.90	233.42	225.10	273.50	277.00	296.30	334.30	..	Agriculture
32.14	38.27	39.00	45.50	59.90	70.50	67.70	67.60	73.70	78.10	..	Industry
14.82	17.91	19.12	21.96	33.94	40.30	34.70	36.00	40.20	42.30	..	Manufacturing
111.20	125.53	132.57	145.90	170.18	179.80	187.40	226.10	242.20	250.50	..	Services, etc.
-6.44	-1.10	1.90	-19.90	-15.90	-67.70	-6.60	35.60	43.00	75.40	..	Gross Domestic Saving
-1.49	-1.20	2.20	-21.10	-15.30	-55.10	0.90	38.22	48.80	77.80	..	Gross National Saving
				(Billions of 1987 CFA Francs)							
438.97	453.01	485.50	461.24	470.43	468.97	553.53	562.32	576.38	629.03	..	Gross National Product
443.67	464.17	495.15	472.94	479.24	477.39	562.72	570.70	584.60	638.31	..	GDP at Market Prices
-66.74	-65.96	-63.09	-72.23	-82.77	-138.60	-103.25	-96.00	-102.48	-90.12	..	Resource Balance
80.36	76.13	76.51	84.67	89.64	92.73	97.51	96.20	98.54	108.86	..	Exports of Goods & NFServices
147.10	142.10	139.60	156.90	172.41	231.34	200.76	192.20	201.03	198.98	..	Imports of Goods & NFServices
510.42	530.13	558.24	545.17	562.01	615.99	665.96	666.70	687.08	728.42	..	Domestic Absorption
387.77	405.15	428.30	426.82	431.86	465.89	481.49	472.30	476.84	504.16	..	Private Consumption, etc.
53.13	48.83	50.54	56.78	61.89	63.82	63.37	62.80	62.57	63.59	..	General Gov't Consumption
69.52	76.16	79.41	61.57	68.26	86.28	121.11	131.60	147.67	160.67	..	Gross Domestic Investment
..	..	..	..	..	..	..	..	..	..	..	Fixed Investment
..	..	..	453.54	458.74	456.59	539.52	541.30	557.70	608.71	B	GDP at factor cost
265.94	261.45	281.74	246.75	226.93	213.46	281.84	277.00	279.66	322.61	..	Agriculture
35.66	45.89	48.19	51.14	60.98	64.84	71.28	67.60	71.09	74.87	..	Industry
..	..	..	26.74	34.71	34.54	38.14	36.00	35.06	36.86	..	Manufacturing
144.78	157.89	166.53	175.06	191.33	199.08	209.60	226.10	233.85	240.83	..	Services, etc.
											Memo Items:
67.90	64.32	65.91	77.85	93.22	88.17	82.49	96.20	93.10	102.59	..	Capacity to Import
-12.45	-11.81	-10.60	-6.81	3.58	-4.56	-15.02	0.00	-5.44	-6.27	..	Terms of Trade Adjustment
431.22	452.36	484.55	466.13	482.82	472.82	547.70	570.70	579.16	632.04	..	Gross Domestic Income
426.51	441.20	474.90	454.43	474.01	464.40	538.51	562.32	570.94	622.76	..	Gross National Income
				(Index 1987 = 100)							DOMESTIC PRICES/DEFLATORS
77.6	79.9	81.5	87.0	96.7	99.6	93.9	100.0	104.7	103.9	..	Overall (GDP)
80.1	82.4	84.7	90.1	97.8	103.2	98.5	100.0	104.9	104.9	..	Domestic Absorption
75.5	79.2	82.4	89.1	102.9	105.5	97.0	100.0	106.0	103.6	..	Agriculture
90.1	83.4	80.9	89.0	98.2	108.7	95.0	100.0	103.7	104.3	..	Industry
..	..	..	82.1	97.8	116.7	91.0	100.0	114.7	114.8	..	Manufacturing
..	..	..	..	..	..	..	..	..	..	..	Consumer Price Index
											MANUFACTURING ACTIVITY
..	..	..	..	..	..	..	..	..	..	..	Employment (1987=100)
..	..	..	..	..	..	..	..	..	..	..	Real Earnings per Empl. (1987=100)
..	..	..	..	..	..	..	..	..	..	..	Real Output per Empl. (1987=100)
27.6	29.5	..	..	..	..	..	..	..	..	..	Earnings as % of Value Added
				(Billions of current CFA Francs)							MONETARY HOLDINGS
62.80	64.69	72.29	87.27	117.39	127.58	135.31	129.92	140.47	141.99	..	Money Supply, Broadly Defined
59.52	60.24	68.32	81.24	107.09	113.77	117.51	109.30	114.44	110.43	..	Money
40.60	40.90	45.00	50.15	50.48	59.76	66.92	60.77	62.19	54.77	..	Currency Outside Banks
18.92	19.34	23.32	31.09	56.61	54.01	50.58	48.53	52.24	55.66	..	Demand Deposits
3.28	4.45	3.98	6.02	10.30	13.81	17.80	20.62	26.03	31.56	..	Quasi-Money
				(Millions of current CFA Francs)							
-16,000	-14,700	-31,600	-34,500	-35,000	-46,500	-43,200	-30,900	-27,600	..	F	GOVERNMENT DEFICIT (-) OR SURPLUS
61,400	72,000	83,200	95,100	107,900	119,300	116,700	127,200	149,800	..	..	Current Revenue
42,300	46,000	49,700	52,800	59,300	75,900	79,400	78,900	76,200	..	..	Current Expenditure
19,100	26,000	33,500	42,300	48,600	43,400	37,300	48,300	73,600	..	..	Current Budget Balance
..	..	..	..	..	..	..	..	..	..	..	Capital Receipts
35,100	40,700	65,100	76,800	83,600	89,900	80,500	79,200	101,200	..	..	Capital Payments

MALI	1969	1970	1971	1972	1973	1974	1975	1976	1977	1978	1979
FOREIGN TRADE (CUSTOMS BASIS)					*(Millions of current US dollars)*						
Value of Exports, fob	17.31	35.46	36.01	36.72	58.00	64.15	36.54	84.54	124.58	112.00	148.00
Nonfuel Primary Products	16.76	31.72	32.57	33.19	51.94	56.91	32.25	83.28	123.06	108.16	114.49
Fuels	0.18	0.03	0.05	0.05	0.07	0.08	0.02	0.08	0.18	0.38	0.40
Manufactures	0.37	3.71	3.39	3.48	5.99	7.16	4.27	1.18	1.34	3.46	33.11
Value of Imports, cif	38.91	44.80	59.27	73.71	126.29	179.43	190.07	150.19	158.73	285.70	360.60
Nonfuel Primary Products	8.57	15.48	21.16	19.91	65.01	104.10	57.91	32.03	23.63	71.01	61.20
Fuels	3.44	4.01	5.65	7.89	10.94	15.75	20.03	21.49	28.41	53.30	59.27
Manufactures	26.90	25.31	32.46	45.91	50.34	59.58	112.13	96.67	106.69	161.40	240.14
					(Index 1987 = 100)						
Terms of Trade	208.4	192.2	186.6	181.9	185.4	120.7	125.7	169.7	155.2	144.0	124.7
Export Prices, fob	48.8	48.9	52.5	53.7	81.6	89.8	77.4	99.4	98.0	104.9	103.0
Import Prices, cif	23.4	25.4	28.1	29.5	44.0	74.4	61.6	58.6	63.1	72.8	82.6
BALANCE OF PAYMENTS					*(Millions of current US dollars)*						
Exports of Goods & Services	..	..	..	..	..	..	..	..	..	..	..
Merchandise, fob	..	32.80	39.52	45.06	58.53	64.10	71.86	94.37	124.59	94.17	145.73
Nonfactor Services	..	17.20	16.05	22.80	18.84	17.56	22.89	17.85	23.89	37.23	45.60
Factor Services	..	..	..	..	..	..	..	..	..	..	..
Imports of Goods & Services	..	72.00	88.76	112.15	166.42	227.78	260.34	206.57	226.35	363.39	445.89
Merchandise, fob	..	37.50	49.15	63.41	106.34	129.16	136.20	111.28	111.12	199.42	270.31
Nonfactor Services	..	29.20	33.90	43.43	51.62	90.20	102.47	78.74	95.45	150.67	163.83
Factor Services	..	5.30	5.72	5.32	8.46	8.42	21.67	16.55	19.78	13.29	11.75
Long-Term Interest	..	0.40	0.50	0.50	0.60	0.80	0.80	0.80	2.30	2.90	3.00
Private Current Transfers, net	..	0.30	5.22	6.08	6.32	4.09	11.95	10.15	20.31	32.35	34.55
Workers' Remittances		5.70	6.72	8.14	9.89	14.19	23.31	17.74	26.50	44.32	54.06
Curr. A/C Bal before Off. Transf.	..	-21.70	-27.98	-38.22	-82.73	-142.03	-153.65	-84.20	-57.55	-199.64	-220.01
Net Official Transfers		19.80	18.96	26.93	54.36	105.95	97.08	41.98	62.95	100.82	106.71
Curr. A/C Bal after Off. Transf.	..	-1.90	-9.03	-11.29	-28.37	-36.08	-56.58	-42.23	5.39	-98.82	-113.29
Long-Term Capital, net	..	3.40	3.11	19.76	9.66	12.51	17.45	25.54	36.67	41.83	81.84
Direct Investment	..	..	-0.60	3.37	0.60	..	2.01	-5.04	-4.97	-9.75	-3.06
Long-Term Loans	..	22.60	5.70	17.50	14.00	28.50	28.40	29.80	54.10	49.50	64.80
Disbursements	..	22.90	6.10	17.90	18.40	30.30	30.80	33.00	58.80	53.60	69.80
Repayments	..	0.30	0.40	0.40	4.40	1.80	2.40	3.20	4.70	4.10	5.00
Other Long-Term Capital	..	-19.20	-1.99	-1.11	-4.94	-15.99	-12.96	0.79	-12.46	2.08	20.10
Other Capital, net	..	-2.96	5.48	-7.37	20.25	27.34	31.13	18.88	-40.71	52.82	37.54
Change in Reserves	..	1.46	0.44	-1.10	-1.53	-3.77	7.99	-2.20	-1.36	4.17	-6.09
Memo Item:					*(CFA Francs per US dollar)*						
Conversion Factor (Annual Avg)	259.710	277.710	277.030	252.210	222.700	240.500	214.320	238.980	245.670	225.660	212.720
				(Millions of US dollars), outstanding at end of year							
EXTERNAL DEBT (Total)	..	247.3	270.9	268.4	301.0	349.0	356.0	373.8	472.1	568.4	572.1
Long-Term Debt (by debtor)	..	246.1	268.9	265.9	299.0	348.4	355.3	372.3	451.7	549.6	547.3
Central Bank, incl. IMF credit	..	8.6	8.3	9.0	8.8	12.7	12.4	14.8	13.6	25.0	29.1
Central Government	..	232.6	255.5	248.6	276.6	316.1	321.9	331.4	401.7	480.2	494.0
Rest of General Government	..	1.2	1.3	0.1	0.1	0.1	0.0	0.0	0.0	0.0	0.0
Non-financial Public Enterprises	..	3.7	3.8	8.2	13.5	15.3	16.4	21.0	30.2	37.1	20.7
Priv. Sector, incl non-guaranteed	..	0.0	0.0	0.0	0.0	4.2	4.6	5.1	6.2	7.3	3.5
Short-Term Debt	..	1.2	2.0	2.5	2.0	0.6	0.7	1.5	20.4	18.8	24.8
Memo Items:					*(Thousands of US dollars)*						
Int'l Reserves Excluding Gold	1,100.0	900.0	2,068.0	3,749.0	4,226.0	6,110.0	4,196.0	6,895.0	5,380.0	8,161.0	5,986.0
Gold Holdings (at market price)	..	..	..	..	..	..	..	..	1,569.0	3,214.0	9,639.0
SOCIAL INDICATORS											
Total Fertility Rate	6.5	6.5	6.5	6.5	6.5	6.5	6.5	6.5	6.5	6.5	6.6
Infant Mortality Rate	204.8	204.2	203.6	203.0	200.6	198.2	195.8	193.4	191.0	188.6	186.2
Life Expectancy at Birth	40.0	40.4	40.8	41.3	41.7	42.2	42.6	43.1	43.5	43.8	44.1
Urban Population, % of total	14.0	14.3	14.7	15.1	15.4	15.8	16.2	16.4	16.6	16.9	17.1
Food Prod. per capita (1987=100)	112.1	110.2	106.9	91.8	82.3	92.0	100.4	101.4	100.5	105.7	106.2
Labor Force, Agriculture (%)	89.4	89.2	88.8	88.4	88.0	87.7	87.3	86.9	86.6	86.2	85.8
Labor Force, Female (%)	17.3	17.3	17.3	17.4	17.4	17.4	17.5	17.5	17.4	17.4	17.4
Primary Schl. Enroll. Ratio	..	22.0	..	..	..	..	24.0	26.0	27.0	27.0	27.0
Primary Schl. Enroll. Ratio, Female	..	15.0	..	..	..	..	17.0	19.0	19.0	20.0	..
Secondary Schl. Enroll. Ratio	..	5.0	..	..	..	..	7.0	8.0	9.0	9.0	..

1980	1981	1982	1983	1984	1985	1986	1987	1988	1989 estimate	NOTES	MALI
				(Millions of current US dollars)							**FOREIGN TRADE (CUSTOMS BASIS)**
205.00	154.00	146.00	167.00	192.00	180.50	191.70	216.49	252.00	..	f	Value of Exports, fob
170.68	128.44	120.85	138.52	158.46	142.11	134.24	154.39	177.34	..	..	Nonfuel Primary Products
0.57	0.44	0.41	0.47	0.57	0.60	0.49	0.62	0.59	..	..	Fuels
33.75	25.12	24.74	28.01	32.97	37.79	56.97	61.49	74.07	..	..	Manufactures
438.60	364.60	332.00	353.00	368.00	432.00	438.00	447.08	479.00	..	f	Value of Imports, cif
80.44	68.23	61.33	65.33	70.97	69.67	62.19	59.19	69.18	..	..	Nonfuel Primary Products
74.67	62.24	56.43	60.06	64.84	72.26	51.57	69.46	77.87	..	..	Fuels
283.49	234.13	214.25	227.61	232.18	290.07	324.23	318.43	331.95	..	..	Manufactures
				(Index 1987 = 100)							
124.4	116.9	104.2	116.4	115.3	101.1	89.1	100.0	97.1	..	..	Terms of Trade
120.3	114.7	98.1	107.2	106.3	89.1	81.1	100.0	99.9	..	..	Export Prices, fob
96.7	98.1	94.2	92.1	92.2	88.1	91.0	100.0	102.9	..	..	Import Prices, cif
				(Millions of current US dollars)							**BALANCE OF PAYMENTS**
..	..	..	..	..	234.70	276.92	342.72	339.44	356.42	..	Exports of Goods & Services
204.94	154.20	145.77	166.77	192.01	176.07	205.60	255.88	251.47	274.29	..	Merchandise, fob
57.74	46.19	44.43	41.99	40.74	57.29	68.15	82.52	83.60	78.05	..	Nonfactor Services
..	..	..	..	..	1.34	3.18	4.33	4.36	4.08	..	Factor Services
537.04	470.51	419.50	435.31	458.17	610.74	682.03	690.46	732.56	709.39	..	Imports of Goods & Services
308.36	269.02	232.65	240.90	257.76	328.45	347.09	335.40	359.11	345.45	..	Merchandise, fob
211.81	168.92	162.66	166.90	172.72	262.70	306.64	323.09	338.23	327.58	..	Nonfactor Services
16.88	32.58	24.20	27.50	27.69	19.59	28.30	31.97	35.23	36.36	..	Factor Services
3.30	3.40	5.60	6.60	8.30	12.50	12.60	13.50	15.40	13.70	..	Long-Term Interest
40.47	32.38	24.95	23.36	20.83	46.74	46.49	36.60	47.00	36.05	..	Private Current Transfers, net
59.40	47.66	39.41	36.48	32.50	67.00	68.44	88.18	96.02	84.95	..	Workers' Remittances
-233.89	-237.74	-204.35	-203.19	-204.60	-329.30	-358.61	-311.14	-346.13	-316.92	..	Curr. A/C Bal before Off. Transf.
109.57	97.71	89.16	100.51	90.15	196.99	185.67	215.62	255.84	236.36	..	Net Official Transfers
-124.32	-140.04	-115.19	-102.69	-114.45	-132.31	-172.94	-95.52	-90.29	-80.56	..	Curr. A/C Bal after Off. Transf.
110.61	95.61	75.32	86.13	97.35	115.66	141.38	104.15	211.15	215.36	..	Long-Term Capital, net
2.37	3.68	1.52	3.15	4.12	2.89	-8.37	-5.99	-1.34	-2.82	..	Direct Investment
89.00	106.30	114.30	147.20	105.10	84.70	161.10	118.40	108.20	161.40	..	Long-Term Loans
95.10	112.40	120.20	154.50	114.90	106.40	178.70	136.60	138.50	183.20	..	Disbursements
6.10	6.10	5.90	7.30	9.80	21.70	17.60	18.20	30.30	21.80	..	Repayments
19.25	-14.37	-40.50	-64.22	-11.87	28.06	-11.35	-8.26	104.29	56.78	..	Other Long-Term Capital
5.75	37.64	13.94	4.07	17.39	-0.19	34.18	10.23	-64.93	-59.03	..	Other Capital, net
7.95	6.79	25.93	12.49	-0.28	16.84	-2.61	-18.86	-55.93	-75.76	..	Change in Reserves
				(CFA Francs per US dollar)							**Memo Item:**
211.280	271.730	328.610	381.060	436.960	449.260	346.300	300.540	297.850	319.010	..	Conversion Factor (Annual Avg)
			(Millions of US dollars), outstanding at end of year								
732.7	835.2	879.7	992.4	1,243.9	1,468.3	1,756.1	2,067.2	2,038.7	2,156.9	..	**EXTERNAL DEBT (Total)**
708.6	762.6	861.0	971.0	1,174.5	1,399.3	1,677.3	1,991.1	1,984.4	2,110.5	..	Long-Term Debt (by debtor)
38.7	32.8	57.9	68.4	82.6	98.0	98.8	85.2	73.8	55.1	..	Central Bank, incl. IMF credit
635.1	698.5	772.6	872.8	1,063.3	1,267.9	1,537.5	1,862.3	1,877.2	2,018.7	..	Central Government
0.7	2.2	1.9	1.5	1.3	1.7	1.7	1.7	0.0	..	..	Rest of General Government
31.2	25.2	23.5	23.8	20.4	22.5	24.0	21.2	11.1	12.2	..	Non-financial Public Enterprises
2.9	3.9	5.1	4.5	6.9	9.2	15.3	20.7	22.3	24.5	..	Priv. Sector, incl non-guaranteed
24.1	72.6	18.7	21.4	69.4	69.0	78.8	76.1	54.3	46.4	..	Short-Term Debt
				(Thousands of US dollars)							**Memo Items:**
14,536.0	17,386.0	16,727.0	16,234.0	26,641.0	22,517.0	23,311.0	15,849.0	35,973.0	115,820.0	..	Int'l Reserves Excluding Gold
11,098.0	7,483.0	8,602.0	7,182.0	5,804.0	6,156.0	7,359.0	9,114.0	7,723.0	7,549.0	..	Gold Holdings (at market price)
											SOCIAL INDICATORS
6.6	6.7	6.7	6.8	6.8	6.9	6.9	7.0	7.0	7.0	..	Total Fertility Rate
183.8	181.4	179.0	177.0	175.0	173.0	171.0	169.0	168.0	167.0	..	Infant Mortality Rate
44.4	44.7	45.0	45.4	45.9	46.3	46.8	47.2	47.4	47.6	..	Life Expectancy at Birth
17.3	17.4	17.6	17.7	17.9	18.0	18.3	18.6	18.8	19.0	..	Urban Population, % of total
104.9	115.6	119.5	114.2	102.5	104.5	109.1	100.0	108.2	108.2	..	Food Prod. per capita (1987=100)
85.5	..	..	..	..	..	..	..	..	..	..	Labor Force, Agriculture (%)
17.4	17.3	17.2	17.0	16.9	16.8	16.7	16.5	16.4	16.3	..	Labor Force, Female (%)
27.0	24.0	24.0	23.0	24.0	23.0	23.0	23.0	..	..	..	Primary Schl. Enroll. Ratio
19.0	18.0	17.0	17.0	18.0	17.0	17.0	17.0	..	..	..	Primary Schl. Enroll. Ratio, Female
9.0	8.0	7.0	7.0	7.0	7.0	6.0	6.0	..	..	..	Secondary Schl. Enroll. Ratio

MALTA	1969	1970	1971	1972	1973	1974	1975	1976	1977	1978	1979
CURRENT GNP PER CAPITA (US $)	670	760	820	900	1,030	1,220	1,540	1,700	1,860	2,090	2,500
POPULATION (thousands)	325	326	324	322	322	324	328	334	343	353	360
USE AND ORIGIN OF RESOURCES					*(Millions of current Maltese Liri)*						
Gross National Product (GNP)	88.50	102.10	105.30	110.50	123.30	144.10	184.10	221.80	258.90	294.60	338.70
Net Factor Income from Abroad	6.50	7.30	7.50	8.30	7.50	12.50	18.30	18.10	19.10	16.90	12.90
GDP at Market Prices	82.00	94.80	97.80	102.20	115.80	131.60	165.80	203.70	239.80	277.70	325.80
Resource Balance	-22.40	-28.40	-25.20	-23.50	-22.70	-38.00	-22.40	-23.90	-34.60	-19.90	-16.90
Exports of Goods & NFServices	46.60	47.10	50.00	53.50	75.30	110.40	137.30	172.70	207.40	229.60	290.80
Imports of Goods & NFServices	69.00	75.50	75.20	77.00	98.00	148.40	159.70	196.60	242.00	249.50	307.70
Domestic Absorption	104.40	123.20	123.00	125.70	138.50	169.60	188.20	227.60	274.40	297.60	342.70
Private Consumption, etc.	63.90	73.80	75.10	80.40	90.10	107.00	118.70	135.70	172.40	186.40	206.00
General Gov't Consumption	13.70	18.40	19.50	19.80	22.80	26.90	30.50	35.90	39.70	46.10	53.70
Gross Domestic Investment	26.80	31.00	28.40	25.50	25.60	35.70	39.00	56.00	62.30	65.10	83.00
Fixed Investment	25.50	27.80	25.50	22.50	22.30	31.20	37.50	54.10	60.00	60.30	78.20
Indirect Taxes, net	11.20	12.60	12.60	12.60	14.90	13.00	12.90	14.30	19.90	26.40	32.10
GDP at factor cost	70.80	82.20	85.20	89.60	100.90	118.60	152.90	189.40	219.90	251.30	293.70
Agriculture	5.20	5.80	6.10	6.70	7.30	8.30	9.20	11.40	12.90	11.40	11.50
Industry	23.90	28.40	26.60	30.30	34.80	44.40	61.80	78.50	91.40	106.40	125.20
Manufacturing	15.90	17.90	17.20	22.00	26.70	33.70	46.70	61.50	72.60	84.40	100.00
Services, etc.	41.70	48.00	52.50	52.60	58.80	65.90	81.90	99.50	115.60	133.50	157.00
Gross Domestic Saving	4.40	2.60	3.20	2.00	2.90	-2.30	16.60	32.10	27.70	45.20	66.10
Gross National Saving	..	18.90	19.00	16.80	17.80	18.00	44.10	63.20	63.20	73.20	91.50
					(Millions of 1987 Maltese Liri)						
Gross National Product	165.88	187.57	193.31	203.88	220.86	247.05	299.46	343.37	381.98	418.89	456.79
GDP at Market Prices	153.31	172.66	176.92	187.21	205.48	225.89	270.08	316.03	354.54	394.11	435.46
Resource Balance	-147.87	-155.51	-139.31	-123.04	-97.76	-99.63	-65.41	-66.34	-70.27	-40.77	-21.38
Exports of Goods & NFServices	127.97	127.08	133.29	129.30	167.00	195.39	234.20	271.91	310.94	325.58	380.36
Imports of Goods & NFServices	275.84	282.60	272.60	252.34	264.77	295.02	299.62	338.25	381.21	366.35	401.74
Domestic Absorption	301.19	328.17	316.22	310.24	303.25	325.52	335.49	382.38	424.81	434.88	456.84
Private Consumption, etc.	182.69	198.59	196.94	198.00	198.38	211.90	215.27	236.95	272.14	272.99	278.49
General Gov't Consumption	32.29	42.41	42.41	42.80	43.56	44.90	51.01	59.23	59.99	66.10	72.98
Gross Domestic Investment	86.21	87.16	76.87	69.44	61.30	68.73	69.20	86.21	92.67	95.78	105.36
Fixed Investment	89.52	81.32	71.24	62.81	52.26	56.71	64.21	79.91	85.30	82.49	91.87
GDP at factor cost	..	..	..	..	..	..	..	..	..	..	..
Agriculture	..	..	..	..	..	..	..	..	..	..	..
Industry	..	..	..	..	..	..	..	..	..	..	..
Manufacturing	..	..	..	..	..	..	..	..	..	..	..
Services, etc.	..	..	..	..	..	..	..	..	..	..	..
Memo Items:											
Capacity to Import	186.29	176.30	181.25	175.33	203.44	219.48	257.59	297.13	326.70	337.13	379.68
Terms of Trade Adjustment	58.32	49.21	47.96	46.02	36.43	24.09	23.39	25.22	15.76	11.55	-0.69
Gross Domestic Income	211.64	221.87	224.87	233.23	241.92	249.98	293.46	341.26	370.30	405.66	434.77
Gross National Income	224.21	236.78	241.27	249.90	257.29	271.14	322.85	368.59	397.74	430.44	456.10
DOMESTIC PRICES/DEFLATORS					*(Index 1987 = 100)*						
Overall (GDP)	53.5	54.9	55.3	54.6	56.4	58.3	61.4	64.5	67.6	70.5	74.8
Domestic Absorption	34.7	37.5	38.9	40.5	45.7	52.1	56.1	59.5	64.6	68.4	75.0
Agriculture	..	..	..	..	..	..	..	..	..	..	..
Industry	..	..	..	..	..	..	..	..	..	..	..
Manufacturing	..	..	..	..	..	..	..	..	..	..	..
Consumer Price Index	42.4	44.0	45.0	46.5	50.1	53.7	58.5	58.8	64.7	67.7	72.6
MANUFACTURING ACTIVITY											
Employment (1987=100)	63.2	65.0	69.5	74.9	81.8	82.2	81.6	88.8	96.9	102.7	107.6
Real Earnings per Empl. (1987=100)	33.8	38.5	42.0	43.7	44.3	49.2	61.9	69.6	70.1	80.8	84.4
Real Output per Empl. (1987=100)	..	..	..	..	..	..	..	..	..	..	..
Earnings as % of Value Added	42.1	47.3	50.7	50.6	48.0	49.6	49.8	44.7	44.4	50.3	49.0
MONETARY HOLDINGS					*(Millions of current Maltese Liri)*						
Money Supply, Broadly Defined	123.9	136.3	157.9	174.8	186.6	205.2	246.8	305.4	336.0	381.9	429.7
Money	56.6	57.7	67.9	80.1	87.2	99.0	123.8	148.3	165.6	194.6	231.6
Currency Outside Banks	40.3	45.9	55.7	62.3	72.7	79.6	98.9	119.6	137.8	155.0	176.3
Demand Deposits	16.3	11.8	12.2	17.8	14.5	19.5	24.9	28.7	27.8	39.6	55.4
Quasi-Money	67.3	78.6	90.0	94.7	99.5	106.2	123.1	157.1	170.3	187.3	198.1
					(Millions of current Maltese Liri)						
GOVERNMENT DEFICIT (-) OR SURPLUS	..	..	..	-4.8	3.1	4.8	-6.2	4.5	3.5	11.8	..
Current Revenue	..	..	..	40.8	57.6	69.4	91.3	102.5	104.9	125.5	..
Current Expenditure	..	..	..	37.9	40.9	56.4	63.9	70.6	81.5	87.6	..
Current Budget Balance	..	..	..	2.9	16.7	13.1	27.4	32.0	23.4	37.9	..
Capital Receipts	..	..	..	0.1	0.0	4.8	0.9	2.6	0.7	0.1	..
Capital Payments	..	..	..	7.7	13.6	13.1	34.5	30.0	20.6	26.2	..

1980	1981	1982	1983	1984	1985	1986	1987	1988	1989 estimate	NOTES	MALTA
3,150	3,590	3,790	3,510	3,440	3,390	3,580	4,170	5,180	5,820	..	CURRENT GNP PER CAPITA (US $)
364	364	362	357	351	344	345	346	348	351	..	POPULATION (thousands)
				(Millions of current Maltese Liri)							USE AND ORIGIN OF RESOURCES
422.50	477.70	513.80	495.70	506.50	514.80	539.90	579.80	634.80	690.50	..	Gross National Product (GNP)
30.50	41.20	52.00	38.10	45.40	38.80	28.00	30.60	28.30	30.00	..	Net Factor Income from Abroad
392.00	436.50	461.80	457.60	461.10	476.00	511.90	549.20	606.50	660.50	..	GDP at Market Prices
-21.40	-36.50	-74.80	-68.50	-70.00	-75.30	-56.00	-58.40	-74.10	-88.50	..	Resource Balance
356.60	355.90	319.80	307.60	323.50	345.20	365.70	422.50	466.80	522.00	..	Exports of Goods & NFServices
378.00	392.40	394.60	376.10	393.50	420.50	421.70	480.90	540.90	610.50	..	Imports of Goods & NFServices
413.40	473.00	536.60	526.10	531.10	551.30	567.90	607.60	680.60	749.00	..	Domestic Absorption
253.50	279.40	305.80	306.70	317.50	333.20	347.90	358.30	400.80	437.60	..	Private Consumption, etc.
63.40	75.40	85.20	82.30	80.30	84.30	89.50	98.20	105.20	119.20	..	General Gov't Consumption
96.50	118.20	145.60	137.10	133.30	133.80	130.50	151.10	174.60	192.20	..	Gross Domestic Investment
87.10	105.60	120.10	131.60	126.50	125.90	122.30	153.50	166.40	186.90	..	Fixed Investment
43.40	46.00	44.10	40.50	39.70	45.40	50.10	53.70	63.80	79.60	..	Indirect Taxes, net
348.60	390.50	417.70	417.10	421.40	430.60	461.80	495.50	542.70	580.90	..	GDP at factor cost
13.30	15.00	16.80	18.70	19.30	19.40	20.40	21.40	21.10	22.20	..	Agriculture
146.70	162.10	170.40	164.60	169.40	170.00	188.30	200.00	219.90	..	..	Industry
115.40	121.40	125.00	120.00	124.70	126.90	134.70	136.40	146.60	157.90	..	Manufacturing
188.60	213.40	230.50	233.80	232.70	241.20	253.10	274.10	301.70	..	..	Services, etc.
75.10	81.70	70.80	68.60	63.30	58.50	74.50	92.70	100.50	103.70	..	Gross Domestic Saving
117.10	135.50	138.10	120.90	123.10	114.20	121.40	145.10	161.10	170.40	..	Gross National Saving
				(Millions of 1987 Maltese Liri)							
503.78	525.38	542.94	528.45	539.00	545.84	557.07	579.80	625.18	656.44	I	Gross National Product
466.15	481.59	492.59	489.58	494.19	506.97	527.20	549.20	596.76	626.57	I	GDP at Market Prices
-23.19	-37.18	-81.20	-57.74	-59.73	-71.32	-51.40	-58.40	-90.78	-102.41	..	Resource Balance
425.83	377.26	325.14	319.15	332.01	356.63	376.81	422.50	443.35	474.40	..	Exports of Goods & NFServices
449.02	414.44	406.33	376.88	391.74	427.95	428.22	480.90	534.12	576.81	..	Imports of Goods & NFServices
489.35	518.78	573.79	547.31	553.92	578.28	578.60	607.60	687.53	728.98	..	Domestic Absorption
297.93	297.87	300.94	303.19	319.09	341.74	349.01	358.30	397.35	423.50	..	Private Consumption, etc.
74.32	79.86	84.64	83.68	81.58	86.16	89.98	98.20	104.12	114.63	..	General Gov't Consumption
117.10	141.04	188.22	160.44	153.26	150.38	139.61	151.10	186.06	190.85	..	Gross Domestic Investment
92.57	108.50	124.44	144.13	134.05	128.66	117.41	153.50	162.87	175.06	..	Fixed Investment
..	..	..	..	..	..	..	..	..	..	..	GDP at factor cost
..	..	..	..	..	..	..	..	..	..	..	Agriculture
..	..	..	..	..	..	..	..	..	..	..	Industry
..	..	..	..	..	..	..	..	..	..	..	Manufacturing
..	..	..	..	..	..	..	..	..	..	..	Services, etc.
											Memo Items:
423.60	375.89	329.31	308.24	322.06	351.31	371.35	422.50	460.95	493.19	..	Capacity to Import
-2.23	-1.37	4.17	-10.91	-9.96	-5.32	-5.46	0.00	17.60	18.80	..	Terms of Trade Adjustment
463.93	480.23	496.77	478.67	484.24	501.65	521.74	549.20	614.36	645.36	..	Gross Domestic Income
501.55	524.02	547.11	517.54	529.04	540.52	551.61	579.80	642.78	675.23	..	Gross National Income
				(Index 1987 = 100)							DOMESTIC PRICES/DEFLATORS
84.1	90.6	93.7	93.5	93.3	93.9	97.1	100.0	101.6	105.4	..	Overall (GDP)
84.5	91.2	93.5	96.1	95.9	95.3	98.2	100.0	99.0	102.7	..	Domestic Absorption
..	..	..	..	..	..	..	..	..	..	..	Agriculture
..	..	..	..	..	..	..	..	..	..	..	Industry
..	..	..	..	..	..	..	..	..	..	..	Manufacturing
84.0	93.7	99.1	98.3	97.8	97.6	99.6	100.0	100.9	101.8	..	Consumer Price Index
											MANUFACTURING ACTIVITY
104.5	101.1	90.9	86.6	90.1	92.6	95.7	100.0	..	..	..	Employment (1987=100)
89.6	91.4	101.2	102.5	102.3	103.0	101.3	100.0	..	..	..	Real Earnings per Empl. (1987=100)
..	..	..	..	..	..	..	..	..	..	..	Real Output per Empl. (1987=100)
50.4	53.7	54.0	52.7	51.0	50.0	49.4	49.0	..	..	..	Earnings as % of Value Added
				(Millions of current Maltese Liri)							MONETARY HOLDINGS
463.9	513.8	544.9	587.5	629.5	662.5	700.9	770.6	837.8	924.1	..	Money Supply, Broadly Defined
258.8	293.7	306.3	324.6	325.9	321.2	323.3	354.6	364.0	368.6	..	Money
206.1	239.2	259.7	279.6	283.7	273.3	273.8	300.2	314.3	319.4	..	Currency Outside Banks
52.7	54.6	46.5	45.0	42.2	47.9	49.5	54.4	49.6	49.2	..	Demand Deposits
205.1	220.0	238.7	262.9	303.6	341.3	377.6	416.0	473.8	555.5	..	Quasi-Money
				(Millions of current Maltese Liri)							
4.3	5.6	-7.6	7.3	2.1	-19.2	-19.5	-36.7	-0.2	..	F	GOVERNMENT DEFICIT (-) OR SURPLUS
142.2	179.1	192.5	197.5	193.7	197.0	189.8	188.7	234.0	..	..	Current Revenue
106.6	134.7	153.0	149.3	151.0	152.4	158.6	170.5	184.8	..	..	Current Expenditure
35.7	44.4	39.5	48.1	42.7	44.5	31.2	18.3	49.3	..	..	Current Budget Balance
1.1	4.0	0.9	2.2	0.1	0.1	0.1	0.1	0.1	..	..	Capital Receipts
32.5	42.9	48.0	43.0	40.7	63.9	50.8	55.1	49.5	..	..	Capital Payments

MALTA	1969	1970	1971	1972	1973	1974	1975	1976	1977	1978	1979
FOREIGN TRADE (CUSTOMS BASIS)					*(Millions of current US dollars)*						
Value of Exports, fob	38.3	38.6	45.2	67.2	98.1	134.0	166.7	228.4	288.6	341.9	424.4
Nonfuel Primary Products	11.2	8.1	7.3	7.5	14.1	15.5	18.0	23.2	33.1	31.2	38.2
Fuels	3.4	3.7	3.1	2.9	3.7	14.7	19.0	16.3	16.5	13.1	17.5
Manufactures	23.7	26.8	34.7	56.8	80.3	103.7	129.7	188.9	239.0	297.6	368.7
Value of Imports, cif	147.2	160.5	156.1	174.3	239.5	357.3	374.9	420.9	512.7	569.1	753.3
Nonfuel Primary Products	48.4	48.6	52.3	55.6	81.0	109.9	111.5	114.1	132.9	146.1	181.4
Fuels	7.1	7.8	9.6	13.0	14.4	40.4	35.6	37.0	41.4	41.8	49.9
Manufactures	91.7	104.1	94.3	105.6	144.1	207.0	227.7	269.7	338.3	381.2	522.0
					(Index 1987 = 100)						
Terms of Trade	96.0	97.3	101.2	106.6	109.3	115.3	109.8	109.5	108.4	102.4	105.6
Export Prices, fob	25.9	27.3	30.5	34.0	44.9	64.2	64.0	64.5	69.2	73.5	87.9
Import Prices, cif	27.0	28.0	30.1	31.9	41.1	55.7	58.3	58.9	63.8	71.7	83.2
BALANCE OF PAYMENTS					*(Millions of current US dollars)*						
Exports of Goods & Services	..	138.9	162.1	204.2	282.5	369.9	451.9	495.1	586.1	705.3	909.1
Merchandise, fob	..	34.0	47.0	74.4	109.3	154.9	179.8	237.6	300.7	346.4	442.4
Nonfactor Services	..	79.0	86.5	97.5	138.3	167.1	208.4	195.9	215.2	280.0	364.6
Factor Services	..	25.9	28.6	32.2	35.0	48.0	63.7	61.6	70.1	78.9	102.1
Imports of Goods & Services	..	189.8	194.3	211.2	277.9	401.8	427.0	478.4	591.3	679.1	919.7
Merchandise, fob	..	143.9	142.4	155.9	212.9	313.6	332.4	376.6	456.8	507.3	674.3
Nonfactor Services	..	37.5	41.9	44.6	51.5	72.9	79.5	85.4	113.4	138.0	181.9
Factor Services	..	8.4	10.1	10.7	13.6	15.3	15.1	16.5	21.1	33.7	63.6
Long-Term Interest	..	1.7	2.3	0.4	0.5	1.3	1.3	1.0	1.0	0.9	1.8
Private Current Transfers, net	..	21.6	20.4	17.0	20.1	20.2	23.9	30.6	38.8	28.8	34.9
Workers' Remittances	..	16.8	13.5	15.2	11.9	10.6	13.5	21.6	24.6	16.3	18.1
Curr. A/C Bal before Off. Transf.	..	-29.3	-11.8	10.0	24.7	-11.7	48.9	47.3	33.6	55.0	24.3
Net Official Transfers	..	23.7	17.7	15.2	11.9	24.4	17.2	15.3	12.8	24.7	28.5
Curr. A/C Bal after Off. Transf.	..	-5.6	5.9	25.2	36.6	12.7	66.0	62.6	46.4	79.7	52.7
Long-Term Capital, net	..	2.1	-49.8	-7.1	-40.9	21.5	31.4	43.3	1.9	0.5	-0.6
Direct Investment	..	11.6	11.6	4.5	5.2	10.6	15.9	14.1	18.5	21.5	16.2
Long-Term Loans	..	-0.7	-8.0	3.9	1.8	3.7	6.9	17.1	1.5	15.7	7.3
Disbursements	..	0.0	7.1	4.7	2.6	5.0	8.3	18.1	2.6	17.1	9.1
Repayments	..	0.7	15.1	0.8	0.8	1.3	1.4	1.0	1.1	1.4	1.8
Other Long-Term Capital	..	-8.8	-53.3	-15.4	-47.9	7.2	8.7	12.1	-18.1	-36.7	-24.0
Other Capital, net	..	20.0	61.1	54.0	43.7	7.8	15.3	-11.6	11.8	45.0	3.2
Change in Reserves	..	-16.5	-17.2	-72.1	-39.3	-42.0	-112.8	-94.2	-60.1	-125.2	-55.4
Memo Item:					*(Maltese Liri per US dollar)*						
Conversion Factor (Annual Avg)	0.420	0.420	0.410	0.380	0.370	0.390	0.380	0.430	0.420	0.390	0.360
					(Millions of US dollars), outstanding at end of year						
EXTERNAL DEBT (Total)	..	24.90	18.10	21.00	22.40	25.80	30.40	44.90	70.90	89.30	115.40
Long-Term Debt (by debtor)	..	24.90	18.10	21.00	22.40	25.80	30.40	44.90	49.90	70.30	82.40
Central Bank, incl. IMF credit	..	..	..	..	..	..	..	..	..	..	..
Central Government	..	24.90	18.10	21.00	22.40	25.80	30.40	44.90	49.90	70.30	82.40
Rest of General Government	..	..	..	..	..	..	..	..	..	..	..
Non-financial Public Enterprises	..	..	..	..	..	..	..	..	..	..	..
Priv. Sector, incl non-guaranteed	..	..	..	..	..	..	..	..	..	..	..
Short-Term Debt	..	..	..	..	..	..	..	..	21.00	19.00	33.00
Memo Items:					*(Millions of US dollars)*						
Int'l Reserves Excluding Gold	127.0	148.2	184.7	261.7	310.4	386.7	485.8	607.8	719.6	925.1	1,012.7
Gold Holdings (at market price)	12.3	10.4	15.4	22.9	39.6	65.8	49.5	47.6	59.4	81.4	187.4
SOCIAL INDICATORS											
Total Fertility Rate	2.0	2.0	2.1	2.0	1.6	1.6	2.3	2.2	2.2	2.1	2.1
Infant Mortality Rate	24.3	27.9	23.9	16.7	23.1	19.9	17.5	15.0	13.5	14.4	15.7
Life Expectancy at Birth	69.9	70.1	70.4	70.6	70.6	70.6	70.6	70.6	70.6	70.8	71.0
Urban Population, % of total	76.8	77.5	78.1	78.8	79.4	80.1	80.7	81.2	81.7	82.1	82.6
Food Prod. per capita (1987=100)	80.3	83.9	80.7	90.4	89.0	83.2	78.6	90.4	99.4	109.4	87.0
Labor Force, Agriculture (%)	7.2	6.9	6.7	6.5	6.4	6.2	6.0	5.9	5.7	5.5	5.4
Labor Force, Female (%)	21.2	21.3	21.3	21.4	21.4	21.5	21.5	21.6	21.6	21.6	21.7
Primary Schl. Enroll. Ratio	..	106.0	..	..	..	..	94.0	108.0	110.0	111.0	110.0
Primary Schl. Enroll. Ratio, Female	..	106.0	..	..	..	..	92.0	110.0	109.0	111.0	109.0
Secondary Schl. Enroll. Ratio	..	50.0	..	..	..	..	75.0	72.0	71.0	70.0	74.0

1980	1981	1982	1983	1984	1985	1986	1987	1988	1989 estimate	NOTES	MALTA
				(Millions of current US dollars)							**FOREIGN TRADE (CUSTOMS BASIS)**
482.9	447.6	410.8	362.7	394.5	399.5	497.0	605.0	711.0	..	..	Value of Exports, fob
32.0	30.1	25.2	25.3	26.7	23.9	30.6	44.8	35.1	..	..	Nonfuel Primary Products
23.9	26.0	23.4	15.8	14.1	12.3	10.8	13.0	12.2	..	..	Fuels
427.0	391.4	362.1	321.6	353.7	363.3	455.7	547.2	663.7	..	..	Manufactures
938.0	855.0	789.0	733.0	717.0	759.0	879.7	1,139.0	1,343.0	..	..	Value of Imports, cif
224.3	189.5	173.4	153.9	145.4	145.1	156.9	210.6	280.2	..	..	Nonfuel Primary Products
96.5	115.0	115.3	89.2	92.6	95.0	53.4	72.7	82.9	..	..	Fuels
617.2	550.4	500.2	489.9	479.0	518.9	669.5	855.7	979.9	..	..	Manufactures
				(Index 1987 = 100)							
104.2	93.1	106.2	91.1	89.5	88.9	99.8	100.0	100.4	..	..	Terms of Trade
98.3	88.8	98.5	81.3	78.6	77.2	91.5	100.0	107.8	..	..	Export Prices, fob
94.4	95.3	92.7	89.2	87.8	86.8	91.7	100.0	107.3	..	..	Import Prices, cif
				(Millions of current US dollars)							**BALANCE OF PAYMENTS**
1,171.9	1,073.4	925.4	821.6	815.6	835.8	1,039.5	1,329.1	1,544.2	1,689.3	..	Exports of Goods & Services
509.8	470.1	421.0	388.5	410.8	421.6	521.6	631.3	758.3	866.3	..	Merchandise, fob
508.9	441.7	330.5	300.2	266.1	287.5	371.3	558.3	629.0	631.3	..	Nonfactor Services
153.1	161.6	174.0	133.0	138.6	126.6	146.6	139.5	156.9	191.7	..	Factor Services
1,185.2	1,072.7	983.9	889.6	868.9	913.3	1,111.0	1,409.3	1,682.3	1,790.0	..	Imports of Goods & Services
884.7	778.1	709.2	659.5	639.2	672.1	786.5	1,024.6	1,216.5	1,327.7	..	Merchandise, fob
240.3	240.8	243.6	204.9	208.4	217.0	278.6	357.2	410.1	416.9	..	Nonfactor Services
60.2	53.8	31.1	25.2	21.3	24.3	45.8	27.5	55.6	45.3	..	Factor Services
1.3	1.1	0.9	1.1	1.3	1.5	2.1	2.2	2.0	2.0	..	Long-Term Interest
33.3	32.6	37.1	32.8	31.2	36.0	48.1	63.1	97.6	105.3	..	Private Current Transfers, net
22.3	19.4	16.3	17.6	13.9	10.7	10.4	16.5	26.9	40.5	..	Workers' Remittances
20.0	33.4	-21.4	-35.1	-22.1	-41.6	-23.4	-17.1	-40.5	4.6	..	Curr. A/C Bal before Off. Transf.
24.6	57.7	37.6	33.5	33.4	18.8	23.2	23.4	68.6	49.1	..	Net Official Transfers
44.6	91.0	16.3	-1.6	11.3	-22.8	-0.3	6.4	28.1	53.7	..	Curr. A/C Bal after Off. Transf.
23.7	18.4	7.8	3.2	31.0	-14.9	-46.8	-18.5	-75.9	4.3	..	Long-Term Capital, net
26.6	39.0	20.9	24.5	26.2	19.0	21.9	19.4	40.8	..	..	Direct Investment
4.9	8.8	2.5	23.5	5.0	0.6	-8.8	-8.1	-7.3	-4.3	..	Long-Term Loans
6.7	11.4	4.8	32.1	12.2	7.7	3.0	0.3	0.0	3.0	..	Disbursements
1.8	2.6	2.3	8.6	7.2	7.1	11.8	8.4	7.3	7.3	..	Repayments
-7.8	-29.5	-15.6	-44.8	-0.2	-34.5	-59.9	-29.8	-109.4	..	..	Other Long-Term Capital
-16.9	38.5	28.1	102.6	-10.4	-29.4	42.5	7.6	82.6	-56.5	..	Other Capital, net
-51.4	-147.8	-52.1	-104.2	-31.9	67.1	4.6	4.5	-34.8	7.1	..	Change in Reserves
				(Maltese Liri per US dollar)							**Memo Item:**
0.350	0.390	0.410	0.430	0.460	0.470	0.390	0.350	0.330	0.350	..	Conversion Factor (Annual Avg)
				(Millions of US dollars), outstanding at end of year							
108.20	110.00	122.60	135.80	175.80	185.40	222.20	277.80	369.90	304.10	..	**EXTERNAL DEBT** (Total)
86.20	82.00	76.60	93.80	90.80	99.40	95.20	95.50	84.90	80.10	..	Long-Term Debt (by debtor)
..	..	..	..	..	..	..	..	..	..	..	Central Bank, incl. IMF credit
86.20	82.00	76.60	93.80	90.80	99.40	95.20	95.50	84.90	80.10	..	Central Government
..	..	..	..	..	..	..	..	..	..	..	Rest of General Government
..	..	..	..	..	..	..	..	..	..	..	Non-financial Public Enterprises
..	..	..	..	..	..	..	..	..	..	..	Priv. Sector, incl non-guaranteed
22.00	28.00	46.00	42.00	85.00	86.00	127.00	182.30	285.00	224.00	..	Short-Term Debt
				(Millions of US dollars)							**Memo Items:**
990.1	1,073.8	1,083.6	1,112.3	990.2	986.9	1,145.4	1,414.6	1,364.7	1,355.2	..	Int'l Reserves Excluding Gold
255.8	181.3	211.1	180.1	143.7	152.4	182.2	225.6	191.2	90.6	..	Gold Holdings (at market price)
											SOCIAL INDICATORS
2.0	2.0	2.0	2.0	2.0	2.0	2.0	2.0	2.0	2.0	..	Total Fertility Rate
15.2	13.1	13.9	14.1	11.6	13.6	11.8	10.0	9.7	9.4	..	Infant Mortality Rate
71.3	71.5	71.7	71.9	72.1	72.3	72.5	72.8	72.9	73.1	..	Life Expectancy at Birth
83.1	83.5	84.0	84.4	84.9	85.3	85.6	85.9	86.3	86.6	..	Urban Population, % of total
96.0	89.6	102.9	103.6	98.2	106.4	108.8	100.0	91.9	93.7	..	Food Prod. per capita (1987=100)
5.2	..	..	..	..	..	..	..	..	..	..	Labor Force, Agriculture (%)
21.7	21.8	22.0	22.1	22.2	22.3	22.5	22.7	22.8	23.0	..	Labor Force, Female (%)
103.0	..	..	..	105.0	107.0	107.0	107.0	..	..	..	Primary Schl. Enroll. Ratio
104.0	..	..	..	102.0	104.0	104.0	105.0	..	..	..	Primary Schl. Enroll. Ratio, Female
67.0	..	74.0	76.0	80.0	78.0	77.0	77.0	..	..	..	Secondary Schl. Enroll. Ratio

MAURITANIA	1969	1970	1971	1972	1973	1974	1975	1976	1977	1978	1979
CURRENT GNP PER CAPITA (US $)	160	180	170	180	200	260	300	340	360	360	400
POPULATION (thousands)	1,194	1,221	1,249	1,278	1,308	1,339	1,371	1,404	1,439	1,475	1,512
USE AND ORIGIN OF RESOURCES					*(Millions of current Mauritanian Ouguiyas)*						
Gross National Product (GNP)	9,428	10,878	11,513	12,646	13,913	17,903	19,419	22,089	22,890	23,332	27,464
Net Factor Income from Abroad	-942	-750	-1,071	-736	-964	-900	-1,095	-1,521	-1,756	-1,800	-2,094
GDP at Market Prices	10,370	11,628	12,585	13,382	14,877	18,803	20,514	23,610	24,646	25,132	29,558
Resource Balance	791	892	950	-379	170	-1,941	-4,395	-9,308	-9,942	-7,795	-7,727
Exports of Goods & NFServices	4,028	4,746	5,062	8,365	7,064	9,207	7,995	9,083	8,191	8,502	9,945
Imports of Goods & NFServices	3,237	3,854	4,112	8,744	6,894	11,148	12,390	18,391	18,133	16,297	17,672
Domestic Absorption	9,579	10,736	11,635	13,761	14,707	20,744	24,909	32,918	34,588	32,927	37,285
Private Consumption, etc.	5,708	6,537	6,929	7,114	10,638	14,457	13,807	15,403	16,088	16,413	20,954
General Gov't Consumption	1,544	1,640	1,832	2,581	2,785	3,264	4,033	7,512	8,870	8,731	8,793
Gross Domestic Investment	2,327	2,559	2,873	4,065	1,284	3,023	7,069	10,003	9,630	7,783	7,538
Fixed Investment	..	..	..	..	2,415	2,050	4,141	9,319	8,499	6,673	7,375
Indirect Taxes, net	1,268	700	752	953	1,400	2,317	2,041	2,461	2,217	1,915	2,100
GDP at factor cost	9,102	10,928	11,833	12,429	13,477	16,486	18,473	21,149	22,429	23,217	27,458
Agriculture	2,532	3,199	3,317	3,463	5,201	5,872	5,467	6,023	6,556	7,158	7,811
Industry	3,777	4,204	4,674	4,420	4,068	5,488	6,296	7,163	6,687	6,082	7,916
Manufacturing	552	539	579	630	..	..	..	..	..	..	..
Services, etc.	2,794	3,524	3,842	4,546	4,208	5,126	6,710	7,963	9,186	9,977	11,731
Gross Domestic Saving	3,119	3,451	3,823	3,686	1,454	1,082	2,674	695	-312	-12	-189
Gross National Saving	..	2,373	2,480	2,753	-142	-396	599	-2,105	-3,114	-2,769	-3,756
					(Millions of 1987 Mauritanian Ouguiyas)						
Gross National Product	46,291	52,408	51,793	54,316	50,340	56,326	52,162	55,324	54,433	54,493	57,250
GDP at Market Prices	49,585	54,646	55,175	55,893	52,415	57,800	54,093	58,416	57,649	57,397	60,044
Resource Balance	5,263	5,063	5,126	4,935	4,037	-4,653	-13,414	-27,528	-22,708	-13,288	-8,778
Exports of Goods & NFServices	15,889	16,591	16,852	27,870	20,134	22,046	16,094	17,529	16,620	17,960	20,447
Imports of Goods & NFServices	10,626	11,527	11,726	22,935	16,097	26,699	29,508	45,057	39,327	31,248	29,225
Domestic Absorption	44,321	49,583	50,049	50,957	48,378	62,453	67,507	85,943	80,357	70,685	68,822
Private Consumption, etc.	35,756	38,587	38,655	37,467	35,102	39,459	36,799	41,667	38,356	36,311	38,025
General Gov't Consumption	5,430	7,392	7,556	8,058	9,268	10,255	11,593	19,899	20,311	19,337	17,999
Gross Domestic Investment	3,136	3,604	3,839	5,432	4,008	12,739	19,115	24,377	21,689	15,037	12,798
Fixed Investment	..	..	..	..	8,136	9,511	10,429	22,605	19,032	12,598	12,465
GDP at factor cost	43,979	49,478	50,012	50,108	46,490	49,820	48,004	51,758	51,749	52,369	54,380
Agriculture	19,735	18,966	16,486	23,355	19,071	19,007	15,998	16,417	17,368	16,883	17,191
Industry	9,129	10,006	10,592	9,551	9,251	10,673	9,642	10,776	9,600	10,011	11,076
Manufacturing	..	..	..	..	..	..	..	..	..	..	..
Services, etc.	13,770	19,041	20,608	16,826	17,094	18,543	21,136	23,014	23,899	24,404	24,619
Memo Items:											
Capacity to Import	13,223	14,195	14,434	21,941	16,494	22,051	19,041	22,253	17,765	16,302	16,447
Terms of Trade Adjustment	-2,666	-2,396	-2,417	-5,929	-3,640	5	2,947	4,724	1,145	-1,658	-4,000
Gross Domestic Income	46,919	52,250	52,758	49,964	48,775	57,804	57,040	63,139	58,794	55,739	56,044
Gross National Income	43,625	50,012	49,375	48,388	46,700	56,331	55,109	60,047	55,578	52,835	53,250
DOMESTIC PRICES/DEFLATORS					*(Index 1987 = 100)*						
Overall (GDP)	20.9	21.3	22.8	23.9	28.4	32.5	37.9	40.4	42.8	43.8	49.2
Domestic Absorption	21.6	21.7	23.2	27.0	30.4	33.2	36.9	38.3	43.0	46.6	54.2
Agriculture	12.8	16.9	20.1	14.8	27.3	30.9	34.2	36.7	37.7	42.4	45.4
Industry	41.4	42.0	44.1	46.3	44.0	51.4	65.3	66.5	69.7	60.8	71.5
Manufacturing	..	..	..	..	..	..	..	..	..	..	..
Consumer Price Index	..	..	..	..	..	..	..	..	..	..	..
MANUFACTURING ACTIVITY											
Employment (1987=100)	..	..	..	..	..	..	..	..	..	..	..
Real Earnings per Empl. (1987=100)	..	..	..	..	..	..	..	..	..	..	..
Real Output per Empl. (1987=100)	..	..	..	..	..	..	..	..	..	..	..
Earnings as % of Value Added	..	..	..	..	..	..	..	..	..	..	..
MONETARY HOLDINGS					*(Millions of current Mauritanian Ouguiyas)*						
Money Supply, Broadly Defined	947	1,252	1,257	1,588	2,024	3,145	3,979	4,813	5,058	5,160	6,293
Money	822	1,110	1,132	1,428	1,493	2,451	2,926	3,683	4,095	4,134	5,081
Currency Outside Banks	358	445	461	618	629	954	1,214	1,464	1,529	1,728	2,311
Demand Deposits	464	665	671	810	864	1,497	1,712	2,219	2,566	2,406	2,770
Quasi-Money	124	143	125	160	531	694	1,052	1,131	964	1,025	1,212
					(Millions of current Mauritanian Ouguiyas)						
GOVERNMENT DEFICIT (-) OR SURPLUS	..	..	..	..	..	..	-532	-2,321	-1,685	-871	-1,464
Current Revenue	..	..	..	..	..	..	7,639	12,059	9,078	8,908	8,984
Current Expenditure	..	..	..	..	..	..	..	..	..	8,648	8,479
Current Budget Balance	..	..	..	..	..	..	..	..	..	260	505
Capital Receipts	..	..	..	..	..	..	3	1	327	862	679
Capital Payments	..	..	..	..	..	..	..	..	..	1,993	2,648

1980	1981	1982	1983	1984	1985	1986	1987	1988	1989 estimate	NOTES	MAURITANIA
440	480	450	460	410	400	420	410	460	490	..	**CURRENT GNP PER CAPITA (US $)**
1,551	1,591	1,633	1,676	1,721	1,766	1,812	1,859	1,906	1,954	..	**POPULATION (thousands)**
			(Millions of current Mauritanian Ouguiyas)								**USE AND ORIGIN OF RESOURCES**
30,841	34,897	36,333	40,904	43,611	51,293	57,976	61,169	68,065	78,316	..	Gross National Product (GNP)
-1,714	-1,228	-2,505	-2,308	-2,770	-3,805	-4,723	-8,002	-5,411	-5,184	..	Net Factor Income from Abroad
32,555	36,125	38,838	43,212	46,381	55,098	62,699	69,171	73,476	83,500	..	GDP at Market Prices
-9,546	-10,568	-17,121	-12,934	-12,485	-8,553	-4,727	-4,671	-8,509	-5,621	..	Resource Balance
12,154	16,506	15,776	20,038	21,437	31,527	34,782	34,689	36,906	41,466	..	Exports of Goods & NFServices
21,700	27,074	32,897	32,972	33,922	40,080	39,509	39,360	45,415	47,087	..	Imports of Goods & NFServices
42,101	46,693	55,959	56,146	58,866	63,651	67,426	73,842	81,985	89,121	..	Domestic Absorption
22,073	23,742	30,705	40,481	39,279	42,102	44,492	50,558	58,717	65,880	f	Private Consumption, etc.
8,242	7,828	6,960	7,970	7,965	8,172	8,537	9,137	10,297	10,990	..	General Gov't Consumption
11,786	15,123	18,294	7,695	11,622	13,377	14,397	14,147	12,971	12,251	..	Gross Domestic Investment
10,187	13,507	15,774	13,540	11,022	13,540	13,576	13,975	11,977	11,270	..	Fixed Investment
1,996	2,875	3,637	4,643	4,897	6,522	6,814	7,250	7,565	8,014	..	Indirect Taxes, net
30,559	33,250	35,201	38,569	41,484	48,576	55,885	61,921	65,911	75,486	..	GDP at factor cost
9,285	10,601	11,657	13,035	11,854	13,994	18,865	22,924	24,970	28,134	f	Agriculture
7,941	8,712	8,228	8,188	10,553	13,126	13,539	13,347	14,273	18,300	f	Industry
..	..	..	..	..	..	..	..	..	..	f	Manufacturing
13,333	13,937	15,316	17,346	19,077	21,456	23,481	25,650	26,668	29,052	..	Services, etc.
2,240	4,555	1,173	-5,239	-863	4,824	9,670	9,476	4,462	6,630	..	Gross Domestic Saving
-762	2,458	-2,777	-9,026	-4,936	-588	3,237	-48	-2,610	-938	..	Gross National Saving
			(Millions of 1987 Mauritanian Ouguiyas)								
60,888	64,370	60,887	64,665	59,715	61,081	64,295	61,169	63,850	66,856	..	Gross National Product
62,441	64,817	63,487	66,590	61,763	63,523	67,100	69,171	71,738	74,161	..	GDP at Market Prices
-8,055	-10,037	-19,196	-10,790	-10,500	-7,851	-5,304	-4,671	-5,717	-5,831	..	Resource Balance
21,542	26,513	24,327	31,562	29,488	32,535	34,205	34,689	34,549	35,896	..	Exports of Goods & NFServices
29,597	36,550	43,523	42,352	39,988	40,386	39,509	39,360	40,265	41,727	..	Imports of Goods & NFServices
70,496	74,854	82,683	77,380	72,263	71,374	72,404	73,842	77,455	79,992	..	Domestic Absorption
39,434	41,971	45,546	57,692	50,038	48,357	49,262	50,558	54,959	59,574	f	Private Consumption, etc.
13,256	10,903	9,403	8,788	6,998	7,191	7,695	9,137	9,157	8,309	..	General Gov't Consumption
17,805	21,980	27,734	10,900	15,227	15,826	15,447	14,147	13,340	12,110	..	Gross Domestic Investment
14,849	19,317	23,913	19,179	14,440	16,014	14,566	13,975	12,339	11,189	..	Fixed Investment
57,356	58,588	56,487	59,495	55,136	56,685	60,137	61,921	63,248	65,892	..	GDP at factor cost
19,171	20,881	21,229	24,428	19,923	20,413	22,285	22,924	22,727	23,122	f	Agriculture
10,355	10,350	9,930	9,356	12,501	13,016	13,479	13,347	13,940	15,582	f	Industry
..	..	..	..	..	..	..	..	..	..	f	Manufacturing
27,008	26,668	24,711	25,711	22,712	23,256	24,374	25,650	26,581	27,188	..	Services, etc.
											Memo Items:
16,577	22,283	20,872	25,738	25,270	31,768	34,782	34,689	32,721	36,746	..	Capacity to Import
-4,965	-4,230	-3,455	-5,823	-4,217	-767	577	0	-1,827	850	..	Terms of Trade Adjustment
57,476	60,587	60,032	60,767	57,545	62,756	67,677	69,171	69,911	75,011	..	Gross Domestic Income
55,923	60,140	57,432	58,842	55,497	60,314	64,872	61,169	62,023	67,706	..	Gross National Income
			(Index 1987 = 100)								**DOMESTIC PRICES/DEFLATORS**
52.1	55.7	61.2	64.9	75.1	86.7	93.4	100.0	102.4	112.6	..	Overall (GDP)
59.7	62.4	67.7	72.6	81.5	89.2	93.1	100.0	105.8	111.4	..	Domestic Absorption
48.4	50.8	54.9	53.4	59.5	68.6	84.7	100.0	109.9	121.7	..	Agriculture
76.7	84.2	82.9	87.5	84.4	100.8	100.4	100.0	102.4	117.4	..	Industry
..	..	..	..	..	..	..	..	..	..	..	Manufacturing
..	..	..	..	..	..	92.5	100.0	101.3	114.4	..	Consumer Price Index
											MANUFACTURING ACTIVITY
..	..	..	..	..	..	..	..	..	..	..	Employment (1987=100)
..	..	..	..	..	..	..	..	..	..	..	Real Earnings per Empl. (1987=100)
..	..	..	..	..	..	..	..	..	..	..	Real Output per Empl. (1987=100)
..	..	..	..	..	..	..	..	..	..	..	Earnings as % of Value Added
			(Millions of current Mauritanian Ouguiyas)								**MONETARY HOLDINGS**
7,080	9,429	9,572	10,085	11,322	13,848	14,864	17,642	18,003	18,624	..	Money Supply, Broadly Defined
5,677	7,653	7,135	8,090	9,641	12,173	11,392	13,397	14,032	15,062	..	Money
2,376	2,678	2,950	3,024	3,658	4,700	4,418	5,648	5,845	6,040	..	Currency Outside Banks
3,301	4,975	4,185	5,065	5,983	7,473	6,975	7,749	8,187	9,022	..	Demand Deposits
1,403	1,777	2,437	1,995	1,682	1,674	3,471	4,244	3,971	3,562	..	Quasi-Money
			(Millions of current Mauritanian Ouguiyas)								
..	..	..	..	-4,378	-9,341	431	-1,266	-2,863	..	F	**GOVERNMENT DEFICIT (-) OR SURPLUS**
..	..	..	..	16,566	18,781	19,679	21,864	22,555	..	..	Current Revenue
..	..	..	..	10,463	11,641	12,770	13,454	14,223	..	..	Current Expenditure
..	..	..	..	6,103	7,140	6,909	8,410	8,332	..	..	Current Budget Balance
..	..	..	..	..	..	..	..	..	..	..	Capital Receipts
..	..	..	..	10,481	16,481	6,478	9,676	11,195	..	..	Capital Payments

MAURITANIA	1969	1970	1971	1972	1973	1974	1975	1976	1977	1978	1979
FOREIGN TRADE (CUSTOMS BASIS)					*(Millions of current US dollars)*						
Value of Exports, fob	77.80	88.85	93.90	119.21	155.32	181.49	174.31	177.98	156.99	123.00	147.00
Nonfuel Primary Products	74.33	88.03	86.30	112.99	126.22	177.98	171.15	171.70	152.24	119.30	142.51
Fuels	0.00	0.07	0.00	0.00	8.28	1.73	1.23	2.16	1.71	1.32	1.60
Manufactures	3.47	0.75	7.60	6.22	20.82	1.78	1.93	4.12	3.04	2.38	2.89
Value of Imports, cif	70.90	72.00	72.00	85.19	135.00	188.00	235.00	304.00	334.00	302.00	323.00
Nonfuel Primary Products	14.10	18.00	19.80	20.17	40.42	52.46	76.14	95.03	104.04	94.54	101.00
Fuels	3.90	5.50	4.70	5.24	6.65	22.62	18.90	25.94	29.35	26.15	28.01
Manufactures	52.90	48.50	47.50	59.78	87.92	112.92	139.95	183.03	200.61	181.32	193.99
					(Index 1987 = 100)						
Terms of Trade	195.5	249.1	193.5	166.6	142.2	148.6	154.7	153.4	144.3	117.0	118.9
Export Prices, fob	48.6	62.8	56.0	53.3	58.7	86.2	97.7	95.3	96.4	87.8	104.5
Import Prices, cif	24.8	25.2	28.9	32.0	41.3	58.0	63.1	62.1	66.8	75.0	87.9
BALANCE OF PAYMENTS					*(Millions of current US dollars)*						
Exports of Goods & Services	..	104.80	113.60	129.30	141.98	210.22	190.33	205.68	183.03	155.60	203.98
Merchandise, fob	..	97.20	102.80	117.30	131.37	187.01	167.32	181.87	157.22	118.58	147.17
Nonfactor Services	..	5.70	9.20	10.50	9.66	16.60	18.05	19.46	21.54	33.88	45.45
Factor Services	..	1.90	1.60	1.50	0.95	6.61	4.96	4.35	4.28	3.14	11.35
Imports of Goods & Services	..	112.30	119.70	148.40	158.55	219.60	312.73	415.84	410.40	372.58	411.94
Merchandise, fob	..	72.00	91.60	115.60	119.69	166.57	208.50	272.02	295.52	267.10	286.02
Nonfactor Services	..	27.10	12.70	14.80	27.90	41.01	69.18	80.89	67.19	75.26	83.17
Factor Services	..	13.20	15.40	18.00	10.97	12.03	35.05	62.92	47.69	30.22	42.75
Long-Term Interest	..	0.40	0.80	1.80	2.00	4.30	5.40	7.80	8.90	9.60	15.40
Private Current Transfers, net	..	-5.90	-4.90	-3.90	-14.19	-12.75	-22.74	-28.41	-22.95	-20.73	-32.10
Workers' Remittances	..	0.70	0.80	0.60	0.60	4.33	0.44	0.42	0.31	0.56	2.35
Curr. A/C Bal before Off. Transf.	..	-13.40	-11.00	-23.00	-30.76	-22.13	-145.14	-238.57	-250.31	-237.70	-240.06
Net Official Transfers	..	8.50	9.80	13.10	45.06	69.39	81.94	152.63	128.08	159.49	143.12
Curr. A/C Bal after Off. Transf.	..	-4.90	-1.20	-9.90	14.31	47.26	-63.20	-85.94	-122.23	-78.21	-96.94
Long-Term Capital, net	..	14.70	14.80	9.00	-0.24	26.70	10.07	90.00	55.26	89.12	111.78
Direct Investment	..	0.80	7.50	9.80	9.78	1.92	-122.70	1.55	4.12	2.86	63.23
Long-Term Loans	..	1.30	10.60	-3.50	44.00	48.00	21.70	114.80	53.70	107.20	36.10
Disbursements	..	4.50	13.60	5.60	54.90	57.90	55.90	184.50	85.80	123.80	86.70
Repayments	..	3.20	3.00	9.10	10.90	9.90	34.20	69.70	32.10	16.60	50.60
Other Long-Term Capital	..	12.60	-3.30	2.70	-54.01	-23.23	111.07	-26.35	-2.57	-20.94	12.45
Other Capital, net	..	-11.57	-10.98	5.31	-7.45	-30.99	-2.06	8.57	16.51	4.86	13.74
Change in Reserves	..	1.77	-2.62	-4.41	-6.62	-42.97	55.19	-12.62	50.46	-15.76	-28.59
Memo Item:					*(Mauritanian Ouguiyas per US dollar)*						
Conversion Factor (Annual Avg)	51.940	55.540	55.430	50.440	44.540	45.330	43.100	45.020	45.590	46.160	45.890
				(Millions of US dollars), outstanding at end of year							
EXTERNAL DEBT (Total)	..	27.3	39.8	56.7	105.7	168.4	188.9	407.5	523.0	683.1	717.8
Long-Term Debt (by debtor)	..	27.3	39.8	56.7	105.7	168.4	188.7	407.3	481.5	629.6	666.5
Central Bank, incl. IMF credit	..	0.4	0.4	0.4	24.5	36.9	35.6	49.2	67.7	121.2	119.3
Central Government	..	19.7	27.6	30.3	38.5	75.0	100.5	308.0	351.3	438.5	477.8
Rest of General Government	..	0.0	0.0	0.0	0.0	0.0	0.0	0.0	0.0	0.0	0.0
Non-financial Public Enterprises	..	7.2	11.8	26.0	42.7	56.5	52.6	50.1	62.5	69.9	69.4
Priv. Sector, incl non-guaranteed	..	0.0	0.0	0.0	0.0	0.0	0.0	0.0	0.0	0.0	0.0
Short-Term Debt	..	0.0	0.0	0.0	0.0	0.0	0.2	0.2	41.5	53.5	51.3
Memo Items:					*(Thousands of US dollars)*						
Int'l Reserves Excluding Gold	3,570.0	3,200.0	7,505.0	13,459.0	42,243.0	103,812.0	47,725.0	81,983.0	50,017.0	79,499.0	113,673.0
Gold Holdings (at market price)	..	..	..	..	..	..	..	..	924.0	1,898.0	4,301.0
SOCIAL INDICATORS											
Total Fertility Rate	6.5	6.5	6.5	6.5	6.5	6.5	6.5	6.5	6.5	6.5	6.5
Infant Mortality Rate	168.2	165.8	163.4	161.0	158.6	156.2	153.8	151.4	149.0	146.6	144.2
Life Expectancy at Birth	38.7	39.1	39.5	40.0	40.4	40.8	41.2	41.6	42.0	42.4	42.8
Urban Population, % of total	13.1	13.9	15.0	16.2	17.3	18.5	19.6	21.1	22.5	24.0	25.4
Food Prod. per capita (1987=100)	139.1	139.5	131.6	124.4	103.2	94.8	99.2	107.2	111.6	114.0	114.7
Labor Force, Agriculture (%)	85.5	84.8	83.1	81.6	80.0	78.5	77.1	75.5	73.8	72.3	70.8
Labor Force, Female (%)	21.6	21.5	21.4	21.2	21.1	20.9	20.8	20.6	20.5	20.3	20.2
Primary Schl. Enroll. Ratio	..	14.0	..	..	..	..	19.0	23.0	26.0	32.0	32.0
Primary Schl. Enroll. Ratio, Female	..	8.0	..	..	..	..	13.0	15.0	17.0	..	24.0
Secondary Schl. Enroll. Ratio	..	2.0	..	..	..	..	4.0	4.0	6.0	9.0	9.0

1980	1981	1982	1983	1984	1985	1986	1987	1988	1989 estimate	NOTES	MAURITANIA
											FOREIGN TRADE (CUSTOMS BASIS)
				(Millions of current US dollars)							
196.00	270.00	240.00	315.00	294.00	374.30	349.00	428.00	455.00	..	..	Value of Exports, fob
190.09	246.00	235.35	305.70	285.00	363.30	339.18	416.00	442.45	..	..	Nonfuel Primary Products
2.11	17.00	0.10	3.32	3.00	3.00	0.82	2.00	2.04	..	..	Fuels
3.80	7.00	4.55	5.98	6.00	8.00	9.00	10.00	10.51	..	..	Manufactures
363.00	436.00	482.00	427.00	341.00	358.00	429.90	474.30	519.00	..	..	Value of Imports, cif
113.49	136.31	150.73	139.96	83.04	85.02	144.11	100.01	117.04	..	..	Nonfuel Primary Products
31.51	37.83	41.82	54.04	47.96	42.98	43.79	33.99	25.96	..	..	Fuels
218.00	261.87	289.44	233.00	210.00	230.00	242.00	340.30	376.00	..	..	Manufactures
				(Index 1987 = 100)							
112.2	112.9	111.9	102.9	112.6	116.4	107.5	100.0	108.0	..	..	Terms of Trade
115.8	113.3	105.4	97.4	101.1	103.2	102.6	100.0	117.5	..	..	Export Prices, fob
103.2	100.4	94.1	94.6	89.7	88.6	95.4	100.0	108.8	..	..	Import Prices, cif
				(Millions of current US dollars)							**BALANCE OF PAYMENTS**
269.76	338.95	305.78	354.74	330.28	402.57	444.80	439.44	476.99	505.60	f	Exports of Goods & Services
196.30	269.92	240.03	315.37	293.79	371.53	418.76	402.41	437.61	449.00	..	Merchandise, fob
56.48	48.91	47.25	30.25	28.02	27.09	23.73	34.54	35.25	51.50	..	Nonfactor Services
16.99	20.13	18.51	9.12	8.46	3.96	2.31	2.49	4.13	5.10	..	Factor Services
492.88	585.02	648.22	626.82	527.46	631.77	730.93	665.45	655.57	635.20	f	Imports of Goods & Services
321.27	386.22	426.57	378.24	302.12	333.90	401.20	359.18	348.85	355.00	..	Merchandise, fob
127.76	128.13	157.55	177.17	177.78	201.78	211.15	214.53	217.05	212.00	..	Nonfactor Services
43.84	70.67	64.11	71.41	47.57	96.09	118.59	91.73	89.67	68.20	..	Factor Services
12.80	18.20	22.50	22.70	23.40	27.20	31.60	29.80	32.60	24.50	..	Long-Term Interest
-28.05	-17.99	-27.91	-26.98	-20.42	-20.85	-22.99	-20.60	-22.07	-28.70	..	Private Current Transfers, net
5.58	3.71	2.32	1.22	0.96	0.79	1.86	6.70	9.30	3.50	..	Workers' Remittances
-251.16	-264.06	-370.36	-299.06	-217.61	-250.05	-309.12	-246.61	-200.65	-158.30	..	Curr. A/C Bal before Off. Transf.
117.91	116.93	93.79	86.04	106.91	134.01	114.86	99.39	104.77	269.70	..	Net Official Transfers
-133.25	-147.13	-276.57	-213.02	-110.69	-116.03	-194.27	-147.22	-95.88	111.40	..	Curr. A/C Bal after Off. Transf.
128.17	128.87	166.66	166.53	82.68	98.03	171.79	98.74	76.87	180.70	f	Long-Term Capital, net
27.09	12.44	14.97	1.37	8.53	6.98	3.13	1.43	0.98	3.30	..	Direct Investment
112.40	124.30	195.40	164.30	96.60	56.20	158.70	98.60	50.80	41.20	..	Long-Term Loans
129.50	160.00	211.20	178.50	115.00	104.60	202.00	162.20	128.80	95.80	..	Disbursements
17.10	35.70	15.80	14.20	18.40	48.40	43.30	63.60	78.00	54.60	..	Repayments
-11.32	-7.87	-43.71	0.87	-22.45	34.86	9.96	-1.29	25.08	136.20	..	Other Long-Term Capital
-32.89	13.30	61.53	14.79	-1.02	-7.07	11.35	42.64	1.64	-271.50	f	Other Capital, net
37.96	4.96	48.37	31.69	29.04	25.07	11.13	5.84	17.37	-20.60	..	Change in Reserves
				(Mauritanian Ouguiyas per US dollar)							Memo Item:
45.910	48.300	51.770	54.810	63.800	77.080	74.380	73.880	75.260	83.050	..	Conversion Factor (Annual Avg)
				(Millions of US dollars), outstanding at end of year							
844.5	973.1	1,151.3	1,296.5	1,338.4	1,502.4	1,772.7	2,044.0	2,072.2	2,010.1	..	**EXTERNAL DEBT (Total)**
779.5	874.8	1,058.3	1,189.1	1,211.3	1,394.7	1,655.9	1,924.4	1,890.3	1,845.5	..	Long-Term Debt (by debtor)
131.6	143.1	166.8	173.7	165.0	178.8	194.3	244.0	203.8	189.6	..	Central Bank, incl. IMF credit
582.3	634.4	711.1	762.6	787.7	902.8	1,094.1	1,275.0	1,320.5	1,343.6	..	Central Government
0.0	0.0	1.9	1.2	0.7	0.6	0.4	0.1	0.0	..	..	Rest of General Government
65.6	97.3	178.5	251.2	255.4	309.3	364.1	403.0	364.0	311.9	..	Non-financial Public Enterprises
0.0	0.0	0.0	0.4	2.5	3.2	3.0	2.3	2.0	0.4	..	Priv. Sector, incl non-guaranteed
65.0	98.3	93.0	107.4	127.1	107.7	116.8	119.6	181.9	164.6	..	Short-Term Debt
				(Thousands of US dollars)							Memo Items:
139,900.0	161,804.0	139,111.0	105,933.0	77,529.0	59,217.0	48,219.0	71,808.0	55,567.0	82,418.0	..	Int'l Reserves Excluding Gold
6,543.0	4,412.0	5,072.0	4,235.0	3,515.0	3,630.0	4,495.0	5,567.0	4,718.0	4,612.0	..	Gold Holdings (at market price)
											SOCIAL INDICATORS
6.5	6.5	6.5	6.5	6.5	6.5	6.5	6.5	6.5	6.5	..	Total Fertility Rate
141.8	139.4	137.0	135.0	133.0	131.0	129.0	127.0	125.3	123.6	..	Infant Mortality Rate
43.2	43.6	44.0	44.4	44.8	45.2	45.6	46.0	46.2	46.4	..	Life Expectancy at Birth
26.9	28.4	30.0	31.5	33.1	34.6	36.5	38.4	39.6	40.9	..	Urban Population, % of total
113.7	113.0	106.9	99.3	99.3	99.9	100.9	100.0	101.3	99.2	..	Food Prod. per capita (1987 = 100)
69.3	..	..	..	..	..	..	..	..	..	..	Labor Force, Agriculture (%)
20.0	20.3	20.5	20.7	20.9	21.1	21.3	21.6	21.8	22.0	..	Labor Force, Female (%)
37.0	..	37.0	40.0	46.0	49.0	51.0	52.0	..	..	..	Primary Schl. Enroll. Ratio
26.0	..	29.0	32.0	37.0	39.0	39.0	42.0	..	..	..	Primary Schl. Enroll. Ratio, Female
11.0	..	12.0	13.0	15.0	15.0	16.0	16.0	..	..	..	Secondary Schl. Enroll. Ratio

MAURITIUS	1969	1970	1971	1972	1973	1974	1975	1976	1977	1978	1979
CURRENT GNP PER CAPITA (US $)	280	280	300	340	430	590	710	860	930	1,020	1,200
POPULATION (thousands)	816	829	840	850	860	870	883	898	914	931	948
USE AND ORIGIN OF RESOURCES					*(Millions of current Mauritian Rupees)*						
Gross National Product (GNP)	1,216	1,236	1,368	1,681	2,187	3,780	4,021	4,657	5,440	6,258	7,596
Net Factor Income from Abroad	1	7	7	2	16	10	17	-47	-2	0	-44
GDP at Market Prices	1,215	1,229	1,361	1,679	2,171	3,770	4,004	4,704	5,442	6,258	7,640
Resource Balance	26	16	-60	37	-46	222	42	-324	-579	-772	-898
Exports of Goods & NFServices	475	531	523	759	991	2,124	2,269	2,388	2,656	2,705	3,260
Imports of Goods & NFServices	449	515	583	722	1,037	1,902	2,227	2,712	3,235	3,477	4,158
Domestic Absorption	1,188	1,213	1,421	1,642	2,217	3,548	3,962	5,028	6,021	7,030	8,538
Private Consumption, etc.	864	925	1,042	1,166	1,441	2,238	2,466	2,956	3,658	4,249	5,144
General Gov't Consumption	156	166	182	219	235	360	443	575	733	858	1,009
Gross Domestic Investment	169	122	197	257	541	950	1,053	1,497	1,630	1,923	2,385
Fixed Investment	144	145	184	229	480	750	1,138	1,287	1,510	1,770	1,965
Indirect Taxes, net	222	208	224	247	325	479	546	539	666	764	1,100
GDP at factor cost	993	1,020	1,137	1,431	1,846	3,291	3,458	4,165	4,776	5,494	6,540
Agriculture	167	165	195	263	368	985	770	938	939	977	1,224
Industry	217	223	262	346	436	712	855	1,041	1,213	1,436	1,697
Manufacturing	142	146	168	233	277	505	564	631	699	801	972
Services, etc.	609	632	680	823	1,043	1,594	1,833	2,186	2,624	3,081	3,619
Gross Domestic Saving	195	138	137	294	495	1,172	1,095	1,173	1,051	1,151	1,487
Gross National Saving	..	153	153	316	537	1,212	1,149	1,153	1,076	1,183	1,475
					(Millions of 1987 Mauritian Rupees)						
Gross National Product	9,237	9,246	9,591	10,314	11,754	12,742	12,824	14,166	15,434	16,315	17,126
GDP at Market Prices	9,204	9,167	9,513	10,271	11,633	12,658	12,712	14,276	15,387	16,259	17,169
Resource Balance	1,880	1,511	789	1,196	1,423	-893	-2,466	-1,735	-1,607	-1,774	-1,502
Exports of Goods & NFServices	6,224	6,536	5,935	7,264	8,111	6,980	5,678	7,290	8,270	8,243	8,514
Imports of Goods & NFServices	4,343	5,026	5,146	6,067	6,688	7,872	8,144	9,025	9,877	10,016	10,016
Domestic Absorption	7,323	7,656	8,724	9,074	10,210	13,550	15,179	16,010	16,994	18,033	18,671
Private Consumption, etc.	4,897	5,616	6,067	6,037	6,093	8,636	10,024	10,413	11,330	11,955	12,443
General Gov't Consumption	942	1,028	1,121	1,282	1,214	1,437	1,543	2,109	2,216	2,329	2,300
Gross Domestic Investment	1,485	1,012	1,536	1,755	2,903	3,477	3,612	3,488	3,448	3,749	3,928
Fixed Investment	..	..	..	..	..	..	..	4,066	4,328	4,647	4,353
GDP at factor cost	7,613	7,678	8,010	8,811	9,979	11,108	11,043	12,695	13,571	14,110	14,623
Agriculture	..	2,809	3,024	3,404	3,556	3,506	2,468	2,731	2,731	2,734	2,845
Industry	..	1,621	1,714	1,918	2,241	2,807	2,800	3,410	3,731	3,985	4,022
Manufacturing	..	1,276	1,319	1,485	1,634	2,071	1,905	2,087	2,203	2,371	2,494
Services, etc.	..	3,517	3,621	3,934	4,499	5,103	5,890	6,691	7,231	7,511	7,869
Memo Items:											
Capacity to Import	4,595	5,182	4,616	6,378	6,391	8,791	8,297	7,947	8,109	7,792	7,853
Terms of Trade Adjustment	-1,629	-1,354	-1,319	-886	-1,720	1,812	2,620	656	-161	-450	-661
Gross Domestic Income	7,575	7,812	8,194	9,385	9,914	14,469	15,332	14,932	15,226	15,809	16,508
Gross National Income	7,609	7,892	8,272	9,429	10,035	14,553	15,444	14,822	15,273	15,865	16,465
DOMESTIC PRICES/DEFLATORS					*(Index 1987 = 100)*						
Overall (GDP)	13.2	13.4	14.3	16.3	18.7	29.8	31.5	33.0	35.4	38.5	44.5
Domestic Absorption	16.2	15.8	16.3	18.1	21.7	26.2	26.1	31.4	35.4	39.0	45.7
Agriculture	..	5.9	6.5	7.7	10.3	28.1	31.2	34.3	34.4	35.7	43.0
Industry	..	13.7	15.3	18.0	19.4	25.4	30.5	30.5	32.5	36.0	42.2
Manufacturing	..	11.4	12.7	15.7	17.0	24.4	29.6	30.2	31.7	33.8	39.0
Consumer Price Index	16.2	16.4	16.5	17.3	19.7	25.4	29.2	32.9	36.0	39.0	44.7
MANUFACTURING ACTIVITY											
Employment (1987=100)	12.5	12.8	14.5	16.4	20.6	25.7	28.1	35.4	39.0	37.8	39.2
Real Earnings per Empl. (1987=100)	111.4	108.3	109.2	115.4	103.8	97.4	113.4	124.9	128.1	137.4	131.8
Real Output per Empl. (1987=100)	..	200.8	190.4	175.0	259.4	225.8	166.7	144.7	143.9	157.3	167.0
Earnings as % of Value Added	32.7	34.3	33.9	32.6	26.3	26.2	34.3	44.7	54.7	53.9	50.5
MONETARY HOLDINGS					*(Millions of current Mauritian Rupees)*						
Money Supply, Broadly Defined	432	489	566	713	921	1,634	2,009	2,163	2,445	2,968	3,218
Money	218	230	262	376	467	784	993	1,099	1,219	1,449	1,426
Currency Outside Banks	97	105	126	156	201	314	438	588	694	824	725
Demand Deposits	120	125	135	220	266	469	555	511	526	625	701
Quasi-Money	214	259	304	336	455	851	1,015	1,064	1,226	1,519	1,792
					(Millions of current Mauritian Rupees)						
GOVERNMENT DEFICIT (-) OR SURPLUS	..	..	..	..	-27	-202	-186	-209	-457	-727	-882
Current Revenue	..	..	..	..	355	460	722	1,058	1,173	1,234	1,418
Current Expenditure	..	..	..	..	286	496	669	912	1,176	1,404	1,758
Current Budget Balance	..	..	..	..	69	-36	53	147	-3	-170	-340
Capital Receipts	..	..	..	..	1	0	1	7	..	..	..
Capital Payments	..	..	..	..	97	166	240	363	454	558	542

1980	1981	1982	1983	1984	1985	1986	1987	1988	1989 estimate	NOTES	MAURITIUS
1,180	1,260	1,210	1,120	1,080	1,100	1,230	1,470	1,730	1,990	..	**CURRENT GNP PER CAPITA (US $)**
966	982	995	1,006	1,014	1,020	1,030	1,040	1,051	1,062	..	**POPULATION (thousands)**
				(Millions of current Mauritian Rupees)							**USE AND ORIGIN OF RESOURCES**
8,634	9,949	11,227	12,278	13,734	15,918	18,971	22,452	25,675	30,937	..	Gross National Product (GNP)
-63	-260	-498	-485	-626	-700	-729	-1,124	-2,128	-709	..	Net Factor Income from Abroad
8,697	10,209	11,725	12,763	14,360	16,618	19,700	23,576	27,803	31,646	..	GDP at Market Prices
-892	-1,068	-330	-46	-481	-315	1,312	498	-1,423	-2,474	..	Resource Balance
4,450	4,566	5,529	5,953	6,989	8,895	11,919	15,639	18,565	21,347	..	Exports of Goods & NFServices
5,342	5,634	5,859	5,999	7,470	9,210	10,607	15,141	19,988	23,821	..	Imports of Goods & NFServices
9,589	11,277	12,055	12,809	14,841	16,933	18,388	23,078	29,226	34,120	..	Domestic Absorption
6,562	7,277	8,301	8,874	9,841	11,118	12,000	14,395	17,215	20,925	..	Private Consumption, etc.
1,224	1,422	1,624	1,706	1,835	1,915	2,068	2,722	3,509	3,930	..	General Gov't Consumption
1,803	2,578	2,130	2,229	3,165	3,900	4,320	5,961	8,502	9,265	..	Gross Domestic Investment
2,028	2,240	2,100	2,300	2,595	3,100	3,890	5,090	7,990	8,565	..	Fixed Investment
1,308	1,444	1,705	2,150	2,310	2,738	3,250	3,881	4,622	5,076	..	Indirect Taxes, net
7,389	8,765	10,020	10,613	12,050	13,880	16,450	19,695	23,181	26,570	..	GDP at factor cost
914	1,257	1,530	1,465	1,736	2,123	2,510	2,884	3,067	3,386	..	Agriculture
1,912	2,169	2,462	2,596	3,188	4,056	5,194	6,401	7,541	8,379	..	Industry
1,127	1,377	1,560	1,678	2,183	2,864	3,830	4,841	5,627	6,052	..	Manufacturing
4,563	5,339	6,028	6,552	7,126	7,701	8,746	10,410	12,573	14,805	..	Services, etc.
911	1,510	1,800	2,183	2,684	3,585	5,632	6,459	7,079	6,791	..	Gross Domestic Saving
923	1,354	1,459	1,888	2,324	3,222	5,306	5,857	5,912	7,123	..	Gross National Saving
				(Millions of 1987 Mauritian Rupees)							
15,332	15,873	16,534	16,595	17,329	18,677	20,576	22,452	23,224	25,434	..	Gross National Product
15,391	16,215	17,151	17,198	18,011	19,337	21,333	23,576	25,116	25,986	..	GDP at Market Prices
-437	-101	1,696	1,561	1,261	1,823	2,345	498	-623	-298	..	Resource Balance
8,658	8,029	8,954	9,037	9,409	10,533	13,373	15,639	17,531	18,110	..	Exports of Goods & NFServices
9,095	8,130	7,258	7,476	8,148	8,710	11,028	15,141	18,154	18,408	..	Imports of Goods & NFServices
15,828	16,316	15,455	15,638	16,750	17,514	18,988	23,078	25,739	26,284	..	Domestic Absorption
11,235	11,205	10,781	10,940	11,501	12,080	12,559	14,395	15,576	16,465	..	Private Consumption, etc.
2,315	2,322	2,351	2,411	2,500	2,500	2,541	2,722	2,863	2,964	..	General Gov't Consumption
2,279	2,789	2,323	2,287	2,748	2,934	3,888	5,961	7,300	6,855	..	Gross Domestic Investment
3,538	3,285	2,824	2,914	3,093	3,402	4,081	5,090	7,175	6,670	..	Fixed Investment
13,114	13,965	14,813	14,857	15,567	16,703	18,253	19,695	20,857	21,581	..	GDP at factor cost
1,872	2,283	2,734	2,378	2,396	2,666	2,952	2,884	2,732	2,498	..	Agriculture
3,636	3,768	3,932	3,943	4,309	4,900	5,716	6,401	7,005	7,379	..	Industry
2,318	2,520	2,702	2,730	3,062	3,530	4,243	4,841	5,225	5,366	..	Manufacturing
7,583	7,931	8,216	8,536	8,862	9,137	9,585	10,410	11,119	11,704	..	Services, etc.
											Memo Items:
7,576	6,588	6,849	7,418	7,624	8,412	12,393	15,639	16,862	16,496	..	Capacity to Import
-1,082	-1,440	-2,105	-1,618	-1,785	-2,121	-981	0	-669	-1,614	..	Terms of Trade Adjustment
14,310	14,775	15,046	15,580	16,225	17,216	20,352	23,576	24,447	24,372	..	Gross Domestic Income
14,251	14,433	14,429	14,977	15,544	16,555	19,595	22,452	22,555	23,820	..	Gross National Income
				(Index 1987 = 100)							**DOMESTIC PRICES/DEFLATORS**
56.5	63.0	68.4	74.2	79.7	85.9	92.3	100.0	110.7	121.8	..	Overall (GDP)
60.6	69.1	78.0	81.9	88.6	96.7	96.8	100.0	113.5	129.8	..	Domestic Absorption
48.8	55.1	56.0	61.6	72.4	79.6	85.0	100.0	112.3	135.5	..	Agriculture
52.6	57.6	62.6	65.8	74.0	82.8	90.9	100.0	107.6	113.5	..	Industry
48.6	54.6	57.7	61.5	71.3	81.1	90.3	100.0	107.7	112.8	..	Manufacturing
63.4	72.6	80.9	85.4	91.7	97.9	99.5	100.0	109.2	123.0	..	Consumer Price Index
											MANUFACTURING ACTIVITY
40.1	40.6	41.8	43.6	51.6	69.7	86.5	100.0	105.5	..	G J	Employment (1987=100)
108.0	106.9	102.1	103.1	101.3	90.4	92.5	100.0	105.5	..	G J	Real Earnings per Empl. (1987=100)
144.8	157.4	163.9	156.6	139.5	115.5	104.3	100.0	98.4	..	G J	Real Output per Empl. (1987=100)
52.3	48.9	47.8	49.9	47.6	46.0	43.8	43.2	44.4	..	J	Earnings as % of Value Added
				(Millions of current Mauritian Rupees)							**MONETARY HOLDINGS**
3,939	4,093	5,048	5,556	6,342	8,315	10,705	13,851	17,797	20,542	D	Money Supply, Broadly Defined
1,720	1,533	1,741	1,804	2,050	2,039	2,432	3,304	3,820	4,511	..	Money
735	791	875	922	958	1,096	1,305	1,663	2,009	2,404	..	Currency Outside Banks
985	742	866	881	1,092	943	1,127	1,640	1,812	2,107	..	Demand Deposits
2,218	2,560	3,307	3,752	4,292	6,277	8,273	10,547	13,977	16,031	..	Quasi-Money
				(Millions of current Mauritian Rupees)							
-897	-1,293	-1,388	-978	-649	-580	-347	54	87	..	C	**GOVERNMENT DEFICIT (-) OR SURPLUS**
1,813	2,073	2,289	2,985	3,295	3,758	4,361	5,390	6,681	..	..	Current Revenue
1,972	2,471	2,892	3,208	3,360	3,626	3,843	4,147	5,257	..	..	Current Expenditure
-159	-398	-604	-223	-65	132	518	1,244	1,424	..	..	Current Budget Balance
..	..	..	..	..	..	..	..	..	..	..	Capital Receipts
737	895	785	755	583	712	864	1,190	1,337	..	..	Capital Payments

MAURITIUS	1969	1970	1971	1972	1973	1974	1975	1976	1977	1978	1979
FOREIGN TRADE (CUSTOMS BASIS)					*(Millions of current US dollars)*						
Value of Exports, fob	57.9	69.0	64.9	107.0	137.8	312.6	298.0	265.0	309.8	325.8	376.0
Nonfuel Primary Products	56.8	67.0	62.0	102.2	125.9	285.1	261.4	212.5	237.4	238.6	271.2
Fuels	0.0	0.0	0.0	0.0	0.0	0.0	0.0	0.0	0.0	0.0	0.0
Manufactures	1.1	2.0	2.9	4.8	11.8	27.4	36.5	52.5	72.4	87.1	104.7
Value of Imports, cif	75.2	75.6	83.1	119.8	169.6	308.5	330.7	357.5	444.9	498.4	566.0
Nonfuel Primary Products	28.2	29.3	30.8	39.0	49.7	111.0	97.4	97.3	121.9	150.8	174.4
Fuels	5.5	5.4	5.3	9.6	11.8	28.4	32.4	31.3	41.7	45.7	65.9
Manufactures	41.5	40.9	46.9	71.3	108.1	169.1	200.9	229.0	281.3	301.8	325.7
					(Index 1987 = 100)						
Terms of Trade	69.4	81.9	68.9	90.4	84.2	127.3	156.4	116.3	116.6	98.8	93.4
Export Prices, fob	17.9	22.0	20.4	28.4	33.8	76.4	94.0	68.4	74.3	72.5	80.4
Import Prices, cif	25.7	26.8	29.7	31.4	40.2	60.0	60.1	58.7	63.7	73.5	86.1
BALANCE OF PAYMENTS					*(Millions of current US dollars)*						
Exports of Goods & Services	..	98.2	96.9	144.7	186.2	376.4	379.3	340.1	405.7	445.4	515.4
Merchandise, fob	..	69.8	65.5	108.0	138.8	315.2	303.4	264.3	308.0	321.6	381.9
Nonfactor Services	..	25.3	28.0	33.7	42.4	56.6	65.8	61.0	92.7	118.2	129.7
Factor Services	..	3.1	3.4	3.0	5.0	4.6	10.1	14.8	5.0	5.6	3.8
Imports of Goods & Services	..	94.3	106.8	138.0	193.0	336.6	373.2	405.9	496.4	576.3	675.9
Merchandise, fob	..	64.8	74.2	98.5	143.4	267.6	278.8	307.6	368.0	418.9	482.8
Nonfactor Services	..	27.3	30.0	36.4	46.4	65.5	86.9	89.7	120.7	143.8	172.6
Factor Services	..	2.2	2.6	3.1	3.2	3.5	7.5	8.7	7.7	13.6	20.4
Long-Term Interest	..	1.7	1.5	1.4	1.2	1.6	1.6	2.5	3.4	9.0	14.9
Private Current Transfers, net	..	1.4	1.7	3.8	4.8	5.3	6.1	4.0	4.1	5.2	5.0
Workers' Remittances	..	..	..	..	..	..	..	..	..	..	..
Curr. A/C Bal before Off. Transf.	..	5.3	-8.2	10.5	-2.0	45.1	12.1	-38.6	-86.7	-125.6	-155.5
Net Official Transfers	..	2.5	2.8	5.0	2.4	9.3	5.6	2.2	8.4	8.6	7.2
Curr. A/C Bal after Off. Transf.	..	7.8	-5.4	15.5	0.4	54.4	17.7	-36.4	-78.3	-117.0	-148.3
Long-Term Capital, net	..	1.8	0.3	1.6	0.6	5.7	6.6	8.5	13.6	65.5	77.3
Direct Investment	..	1.6	1.2	-1.2	-3.2	0.6	2.2	2.7	1.5	4.3	-0.7
Long-Term Loans	..	0.8	0.1	1.1	7.3	5.8	8.5	7.2	19.5	67.2	74.6
Disbursements	..	2.2	2.8	3.1	8.8	7.8	17.1	12.9	27.7	75.1	86.1
Repayments	..	1.4	2.7	2.0	1.5	2.0	8.6	5.7	8.2	7.9	11.5
Other Long-Term Capital	..	-0.6	-1.0	1.7	-3.5	-0.7	-4.1	-1.4	-7.4	-6.0	3.4
Other Capital, net	..	3.9	3.0	4.2	-4.2	3.5	27.7	-47.9	27.0	30.4	23.9
Change in Reserves	..	-13.5	2.1	-21.4	3.2	-63.5	-52.0	75.8	37.7	21.0	47.1
Memo Item:					*(Mauritian Rupees per US dollar)*						
Conversion Factor (Annual Avg)	5.560	5.560	5.480	5.340	5.440	5.700	6.030	6.680	6.610	6.160	6.310
EXTERNAL DEBT (Total)					*(Millions of US dollars), outstanding at end of year*						
	..	31.7	33.3	35.9	42.3	47.9	52.2	64.9	142.4	251.0	373.2
Long-Term Debt (by debtor)	..	31.7	33.3	35.9	42.3	47.9	52.2	64.9	101.4	190.0	306.2
Central Bank, incl. IMF credit	..	0.0	0.0	0.0	0.0	0.0	0.0	0.0	13.4	26.4	63.8
Central Government	..	30.6	32.1	31.5	33.0	38.8	39.8	40.4	55.4	120.0	188.8
Rest of General Government	..	..	..	..	..	..	..	..	..	..	..
Non-financial Public Enterprises	..	1.1	1.2	1.3	1.7	2.2	1.8	3.4	5.5	10.1	10.3
Priv. Sector, incl non-guaranteed	..	0.0	0.0	3.1	7.6	6.9	10.6	21.1	27.1	33.5	43.3
Short-Term Debt	..	0.0	0.0	0.0	0.0	0.0	0.0	0.0	41.0	61.0	67.0
Memo Items:					*(Millions of US dollars)*						
Int'l Reserves Excluding Gold	33.1	46.2	51.7	70.1	66.8	131.1	166.0	89.5	66.3	45.8	29.2
Gold Holdings (at market price)	..	..	..	..	..	..	..	..	1.6	7.4	19.3
SOCIAL INDICATORS											
Total Fertility Rate	3.9	3.6	3.4	3.3	3.2	3.2	3.1	3.1	3.1	2.9	2.8
Infant Mortality Rate	62.2	59.8	57.4	55.0	51.6	48.2	44.8	41.4	38.0	36.0	34.0
Life Expectancy at Birth	62.1	62.4	62.7	62.9	63.3	63.7	64.1	64.5	64.9	65.1	65.2
Urban Population, % of total	41.0	42.0	42.3	42.6	43.0	43.3	43.6	43.5	43.3	43.2	43.0
Food Prod. per capita (1987=100)	109.4	95.5	98.7	111.8	110.9	109.4	84.0	113.9	105.8	106.5	106.1
Labor Force, Agriculture (%)	34.5	34.0	33.4	32.8	32.2	31.6	31.0	30.3	29.6	29.0	28.5
Labor Force, Female (%)	20.0	20.0	20.4	20.7	21.1	21.4	21.8	22.0	22.3	22.5	22.7
Primary Schl. Enroll. Ratio	..	94.0	..	..	..	..	107.0	..	109.0	109.0	103.0
Primary Schl. Enroll. Ratio, Female	..	93.0	..	..	..	..	106.0	..	107.0	107.0	102.0
Secondary Schl. Enroll. Ratio	..	30.0	..	..	..	..	39.0	43.0	46.0	48.0	50.0

1980	1981	1982	1983	1984	1985	1986	1987	1988	1989 estimate	NOTES	MAURITIUS
											FOREIGN TRADE (CUSTOMS BASIS)
				(Millions of current US dollars)							
430.6	324.0	367.0	368.0	372.3	434.5	676.0	918.0	1,131.0	..	..	Value of Exports, fob
305.9	202.5	248.5	252.1	235.9	244.7	346.0	432.0	439.0	..	..	Nonfuel Primary Products
0.0	0.0	0.0	0.0	0.0	0.0	0.0	0.0	0.0	..	..	Fuels
124.7	121.5	118.5	115.9	136.4	189.8	330.0	486.0	692.0	..	..	Manufactures
619.3	554.0	464.0	440.0	471.0	528.5	675.6	1,010.0	1,112.0	..	..	Value of Imports, cif
194.2	181.0	149.5	141.8	135.0	146.5	173.4	222.1	233.3	..	..	Nonfuel Primary Products
87.5	100.0	77.2	73.3	73.8	77.5	42.3	75.9	105.4	..	..	Fuels
337.7	273.0	237.3	224.9	262.3	304.5	460.0	712.0	773.3	..	..	Manufactures
				(Index 1987 = 100)							
90.9	81.0	80.0	80.5	79.1	81.4	95.2	100.0	103.6	..	..	Terms of Trade
90.3	84.6	78.1	76.4	71.9	72.5	87.3	100.0	109.6	..	..	Export Prices, fob
99.3	104.5	97.6	94.9	90.8	89.1	91.6	100.0	105.8	..	..	Import Prices, cif
				(Millions of current US dollars)							**BALANCE OF PAYMENTS**
578.6	508.6	510.7	508.5	506.7	580.8	892.7	1,223.8	1,402.2	1,454.8	..	Exports of Goods & Services
433.7	327.1	366.1	368.5	374.1	433.0	675.2	891.4	997.9	989.8	..	Merchandise, fob
139.9	174.2	140.7	137.5	129.7	145.9	211.8	318.4	377.7	414.1	..	Nonfactor Services
5.1	7.3	4.0	2.5	2.9	1.9	5.7	14.0	26.6	51.0	..	Factor Services
718.1	681.3	587.4	556.7	590.2	645.4	847.7	1,226.6	1,558.6	1,602.6	..	Imports of Goods & Services
515.9	478.2	396.7	385.9	415.5	458.8	617.1	907.6	1,165.7	1,170.4	..	Merchandise, fob
174.0	150.3	141.0	126.9	126.6	139.4	170.9	263.6	322.3	361.6	..	Nonfactor Services
28.2	52.8	49.7	43.9	48.0	47.3	59.7	55.4	70.6	70.7	..	Factor Services
22.6	35.4	34.8	28.5	27.1	28.1	29.8	33.4	42.0	41.9	..	Long-Term Interest
9.8	11.6	14.4	16.2	19.3	21.8	29.9	40.6	71.5	68.2	..	Private Current Transfers, net
..	..	..	..	..	..	0.0	..	0.0	..	..	Workers' Remittances
-129.7	-161.1	-62.2	-32.1	-64.1	-42.8	74.9	37.8	-84.9	-79.6	..	Curr. A/C Bal before Off. Transf.
11.1	5.1	19.6	8.9	8.9	14.2	19.7	25.4	21.5	8.5	..	Net Official Transfers
-118.7	-156.0	-42.6	-23.1	-55.2	-28.6	94.6	63.2	-63.4	-71.1	..	Curr. A/C Bal after Off. Transf.
67.6	55.9	49.3	-17.4	45.8	25.5	27.8	81.3	148.6	103.3	..	Long-Term Capital, net
1.2	0.7	1.8	1.6	4.9	8.0	7.4	17.1	23.6	25.6	..	Direct Investment
78.5	51.3	46.0	-22.3	43.3	17.5	8.5	74.4	122.3	47.2	..	Long-Term Loans
97.0	73.1	79.1	38.4	95.3	60.1	47.0	123.1	226.2	99.4	..	Disbursements
18.5	21.8	33.1	60.7	52.0	42.6	38.5	48.7	103.9	52.2	..	Repayments
-12.1	3.9	1.6	3.3	-2.4	0.0	11.9	-10.2	2.7	30.5	..	Other Long-Term Capital
69.3	-16.4	-26.7	10.1	28.2	19.7	-1.4	72.2	98.4	112.8	..	Other Capital, net
-18.3	116.5	19.9	30.5	-18.8	-16.6	-121.0	-216.7	-183.6	-145.1	..	Change in Reserves
				(Mauritian Rupees per US dollar)							Memo Item:
7.680	8.940	10.870	11.710	13.800	15.440	13.470	12.880	13.440	15.250	..	Conversion Factor (Annual Avg)
				(Millions of US dollars), outstanding at end of year							
466.5	546.4	585.4	568.3	549.8	628.6	668.1	810.6	857.2	831.9	..	**EXTERNAL DEBT (Total)**
419.3	507.4	553.4	519.3	510.8	577.6	630.1	777.5	808.9	799.8	..	Long-Term Debt (by debtor)
101.8	159.3	175.8	180.9	161.0	164.9	161.6	151.7	103.0	62.5	..	Central Bank, incl. IMF credit
255.3	286.1	319.4	283.4	299.9	347.6	385.7	478.0	446.1	433.0	..	Central Government
..	..	..	..	..	..	..	..	..	..	..	Rest of General Government
17.0	16.7	16.6	18.9	17.9	22.2	25.1	56.4	152.9	162.6	..	Non-financial Public Enterprises
45.2	45.3	41.6	36.1	32.0	42.9	57.7	91.4	106.9	141.7	..	Priv. Sector, incl non-guaranteed
47.2	39.0	32.0	49.0	39.0	51.0	38.0	33.1	48.3	32.1	..	Short-Term Debt
				(Millions of US dollars)							Memo Items:
90.7	35.1	38.0	17.9	23.6	29.9	136.0	343.5	442.0	517.8	..	Int'l Reserves Excluding Gold
22.2	15.0	17.2	14.3	11.6	12.3	14.7	18.2	21.2	24.6	..	Gold Holdings (at market price)
											SOCIAL INDICATORS
2.7	2.5	2.4	2.3	2.2	2.2	2.1	2.0	2.0	1.9	..	Total Fertility Rate
32.0	30.0	28.0	27.0	26.0	25.0	26.3	23.7	22.4	21.7	..	Infant Mortality Rate
65.4	65.5	65.7	65.7	66.1	66.3	66.5	68.0	66.8	67.0	..	Life Expectancy at Birth
42.9	42.8	42.6	42.5	42.3	42.2	42.3	42.3	42.3	42.3	..	Urban Population, % of total
80.7	91.6	108.4	90.6	87.8	94.8	100.1	100.0	90.4	87.3	..	Food Prod. per capita (1987=100)
27.9	..	..	..	..	..	..	..	..	..	..	Labor Force, Agriculture (%)
22.9	23.3	23.7	24.1	24.4	24.8	25.1	25.5	25.9	26.2	..	Labor Force, Female (%)
108.0	..	114.0	112.0	105.0	105.0	107.0	106.0	..	..	..	Primary Schl. Enroll. Ratio
108.0	114.0	114.0	112.0	106.0	106.0	107.0	107.0	..	..	..	Primary Schl. Enroll. Ratio, Female
48.0	..	49.0	51.0	51.0	51.0	50.0	51.0	..	..	..	Secondary Schl. Enroll. Ratio

MEXICO	1969	1970	1971	1972	1973	1974	1975	1976	1977	1978	1979
CURRENT GNP PER CAPITA (US $)	620	820	800	820	940	1,120	1,360	1,500	1,490	1,580	1,820
POPULATION (thousands)	51,048	52,770	54,596	56,439	58,283	60,113	61,918	63,689	65,416	67,105	68,769

USE AND ORIGIN OF RESOURCES *(Billions of current Mexican Pesos)*

	1969	1970	1971	1972	1973	1974	1975	1976	1977	1978	1979
Gross National Product (GNP)	390	461	508	586	715	930	1,137	1,410	1,899	2,402	3,142
Net Factor Income from Abroad	-12	-18	-21	-24	-31	-37	-42	-60	-73	-90	-113
GDP at Market Prices	403	479	529	610	746	966	1,179	1,471	1,972	2,491	3,255
Resource Balance	-7	-12	-10	-10	-14	-28	-39	-32	-20	-41	-78
Exports of Goods & NFServices	31	31	33	41	52	67	68	104	170	218	306
Imports of Goods & NFServices	38	43	43	50	66	96	106	136	190	259	383
Domestic Absorption	410	491	538	620	760	994	1,218	1,503	1,991	2,532	3,333
Private Consumption, etc.	302	358	402	456	549	704	845	1,048	1,372	1,728	2,205
General Gov't Consumption	28	31	36	47	61	80	110	146	193	247	324
Gross Domestic Investment	80	102	100	116	149	210	263	308	426	557	803
Fixed Investment	78	95	94	115	143	192	252	309	389	528	770
Indirect Taxes, net	19	23	26	30	38	45	67	78	114	147	220
GDP at factor cost	384	456	503	580	708	922	1,112	1,393	1,857	2,344	3,036
Agriculture	45	56	61	64	83	107	127	151	201	247	290
Industry	119	141	153	178	216	289	352	438	605	763	1,017
Manufacturing	85	106	119	135	165	217	258	317	443	553	717
Services, etc.	239	282	314	368	447	570	700	882	1,166	1,481	1,948
Gross Domestic Saving	73	90	91	106	135	182	224	276	407	516	726
Gross National Saving	..	72	70	82	105	147	183	217	336	428	616

(Billions of 1987 Mexican Pesos)

	1969	1970	1971	1972	1973	1974	1975	1976	1977	1978	1979
Gross National Product	66,271.0	94,131.3	97,956.6	105,997.0	114,577.0	121,302.0	128,055.0	132,944.0	137,772.0	149,105.0	162,129.0
GDP at Market Prices	88,416.0	94,891.7	98,829.8	107,212.0	116,038.0	123,062.0	130,081.0	135,584.0	139,977.0	151,490.0	165,508.0
Resource Balance	-3,313.3	-5,344.8	-4,283.0	-4,102.7	-5,136.1	-8,822.7	-10,092.0	-8,314.1	-3,983.5	-6,504.3	-11,631.0
Exports of Goods & NFServices	10,163.7	9,572.5	9,949.5	11,584.2	13,168.8	13,194.4	12,019.4	14,016.3	16,070.7	17,932.3	20,109.1
Imports of Goods & NFServices	13,477.0	14,917.3	14,232.5	15,686.9	18,304.9	22,017.0	22,111.6	22,330.4	20,054.2	24,436.6	31,739.8
Domestic Absorption	91,729.3	100,237.0	103,113.0	111,315.0	121,174.0	131,884.0	140,173.0	143,898.0	143,961.0	157,995.0	177,138.0
Private Consumption, etc.	64,970.0	68,426.2	71,967.8	76,710.3	81,666.8	86,373.1	91,609.6	95,619.8	95,916.7	104,418.0	115,017.0
General Gov't Consumption	5,313.5	5,698.8	6,304.7	7,150.1	7,868.0	8,365.3	9,547.4	10,154.7	10,039.8	11,037.3	12,095.2
Gross Domestic Investment	21,445.9	26,111.5	24,840.4	27,454.3	31,638.9	37,145.9	39,016.5	38,123.1	38,004.4	42,539.5	50,026.2
Fixed Investment	19,667.7	22,858.3	22,466.9	25,216.2	28,934.4	31,220.7	34,113.5	34,266.5	31,966.0	36,816.3	44,271.1
GDP at factor cost	..	..	..	..	..	..	..	..	..	..	154,304.0
Agriculture	10,144.8	10,645.2	11,255.1	11,333.5	11,793.9	12,093.4	12,337.2	12,461.9	13,398.6	14,200.6	13,904.1
Industry	30,119.0	32,983.8	33,595.4	36,965.1	41,046.0	43,982.4	46,300.8	48,728.0	49,809.8	55,087.2	61,380.8
Manufacturing	22,496.9	24,445.3	25,389.0	27,875.9	30,800.0	32,754.6	34,403.1	36,136.4	37,419.1	41,085.6	45,453.4
Services, etc.	48,104.7	51,346.7	53,906.6	58,909.2	63,401.5	67,254.1	71,654.4	74,670.6	77,003.6	82,656.6	90,815.4

Memo Items:

	1969	1970	1971	1972	1973	1974	1975	1976	1977	1978	1979
Capacity to Import	10,970.2	10,628.4	11,066.5	12,706.2	14,436.0	15,538.2	14,061.5	17,048.7	17,963.7	20,566.5	25,309.8
Terms of Trade Adjustment	806.4	1,055.9	1,117.0	1,122.0	1,267.2	2,343.9	2,042.1	3,032.4	1,892.9	2,634.2	5,200.7
Gross Domestic Income	89,222.4	95,947.7	99,946.8	108,334.0	117,305.0	125,406.0	132,123.0	138,616.0	141,870.0	154,125.0	170,709.0
Gross National Income	67,077.5	95,187.3	99,073.6	107,119.0	115,844.0	123,646.0	130,098.0	135,977.0	139,665.0	151,739.0	167,330.0

DOMESTIC PRICES/DEFLATORS *(Index 1987 = 100)*

	1969	1970	1971	1972	1973	1974	1975	1976	1977	1978	1979
Overall (GDP)	0.5	0.5	0.5	0.6	0.6	0.8	0.9	1.1	1.4	1.6	2.0
Domestic Absorption	0.4	0.5	0.5	0.6	0.6	0.8	0.9	1.0	1.4	1.6	1.9
Agriculture	0.4	0.5	0.5	0.6	0.7	0.9	1.0	1.2	1.5	1.7	2.1
Industry	0.4	0.4	0.5	0.5	0.5	0.7	0.8	0.9	1.2	1.4	1.7
Manufacturing	0.4	0.4	0.5	0.5	0.5	0.7	0.7	0.9	1.2	1.3	1.6
Consumer Price Index	0.4	0.5	0.5	0.5	0.6	0.7	0.8	1.0	1.2	1.4	1.7

MANUFACTURING ACTIVITY

	1969	1970	1971	1972	1973	1974	1975	1976	1977	1978	1979
Employment (1987=100)	..	77.5	79.6	82.2	86.5	89.7	89.9	91.9	92.1	95.8	102.9
Real Earnings per Empl. (1987=100)	..	130.9	132.4	134.5	136.6	135.5	139.0	148.5	150.4	146.5	145.0
Real Output per Empl. (1987=100)	..	72.5	71.7	75.5	80.1	84.8	87.8	89.2	89.4	93.9	96.0
Earnings as % of Value Added	..	44.0	42.7	41.4	40.6	39.2	39.1	40.1	37.6	35.8	34.7

MONETARY HOLDINGS *(Billions of current Mexican Pesos)*

	1969	1970	1971	1972	1973	1974	1975	1976	1977	1978	1979
Money Supply, Broadly Defined	115	135	150	168	209	245	296	530	566	759	1,029
Money	49	54	58	68	84	101	122	158	208	270	361
Currency Outside Banks	19	20	22	27	34	43	53	80	89	115	150
Demand Deposits	30	34	36	41	49	58	70	78	119	155	211
Quasi-Money	67	81	92	100	126	144	173	372	358	489	668

GOVERNMENT DEFICIT (-) OR SURPLUS *(Billions of current Mexican Pesos)*

	1969	1970	1971	1972	1973	1974	1975	1976	1977	1978	1979
GOVERNMENT DEFICIT (-) OR SURPLUS	..	..	..	-17	-28	-34	-54	-64	-61	-63	-102
Current Revenue	..	..	..	58	70	96	134	169	241	323	439
Current Expenditure	..	..	..	48	64	93	124	158	222	276	350
Current Budget Balance	..	..	..	10	6	3	10	11	19	47	89
Capital Receipts	..	..	..	..	..	..	..	..	..	..	..
Capital Payments	..	..	..	27	33	37	64	75	81	110	191

1980	1981	1982	1983	1984	1985	1986	1987	1988	1989 estimate	NOTES	MEXICO
2,320	3,000	2,820	2,290	2,130	2,180	1,890	1,770	1,750	1,990	..	**CURRENT GNP PER CAPITA (US $)**
70,416	72,047	73,666	75,279	76,896	78,524	80,199	81,909	83,656	85,440	..	**POPULATION (thousands)**
				(Billions of current Mexican Pesos)							**USE AND ORIGIN OF RESOURCES**
4,341	5,905	9,240	16,824	27,853	45,079	74,735	183,283	375,762	459,534	..	Gross National Product (GNP)
-129	-223	-558	-1,055	-1,618	-2,313	-4,396	-10,179	-20,120	-34,520	..	Net Factor Income from Abroad
4,470	6,128	9,798	17,879	29,472	47,392	79,131	193,462	395,882	494,054	..	GDP at Market Prices
-101	-155	491	1,713	2,307	2,408	3,630	13,420	9,015	4,657	..	Resource Balance
479	638	1,502	3,397	5,122	7,305	13,655	37,814	65,654	81,005	..	Exports of Goods & NFServices
580	793	1,011	1,684	2,815	4,897	10,025	24,394	56,639	76,348	..	Imports of Goods & NFServices
4,572	6,283	9,306	16,166	27,164	44,984	75,501	180,042	386,867	489,397	..	Domestic Absorption
2,909	3,945	6,036	10,882	18,590	30,235	53,804	126,334	272,264	349,244	..	Private Consumption, etc.
449	660	1,026	1,574	2,722	4,374	7,208	16,505	32,961	54,460	..	General Gov't Consumption
1,214	1,678	2,244	3,710	5,853	10,375	14,489	37,203	81,642	85,693	..	Gross Domestic Investment
1,107	1,617	2,249	3,137	5,287	9,076	15,415	35,630	75,057	85,589	..	Fixed Investment
371	497	974	1,383	2,435	4,627	6,319	18,713	35,724	46,441	..	Indirect Taxes, net
4,099	5,631	8,824	16,496	27,037	42,765	72,812	174,749	360,158	447,613	B	GDP at factor cost
368	503	720	1,392	2,533	4,307	7,466	16,676	33,943	44,426	..	Agriculture
1,464	1,956	3,057	6,016	9,860	15,805	26,833	69,239	139,593	157,126	..	Industry
989	1,326	2,033	3,772	6,618	11,069	19,557	50,092	106,682	121,495	f	Manufacturing
2,638	3,668	6,021	10,471	17,078	27,280	44,831	107,547	222,346	292,502	..	Services, etc.
1,112	1,523	2,736	5,423	8,160	12,783	18,119	50,623	90,657	90,350	..	Gross Domestic Saving
989	1,306	2,191	4,399	6,596	10,554	13,934	40,973	71,439	57,100	..	Gross National Saving
				(Billions of 1987 Mexican Pesos)							
173,541.0	187,272.0	182,108.0	172,970.0	180,485.0	187,694.0	178,257.0	183,283.0	187,618.0	193,573.0	..	Gross National Product
179,364.0	195,098.0	193,874.0	185,738.0	192,569.0	197,860.0	190,169.0	193,462.0	195,978.0	202,002.0	..	GDP at Market Prices
-20,522.0	-25,464.0	-1,624.2	12,658.2	10,926.9	6,752.5	11,096.6	13,420.0	5,207.6	-633.6	..	Resource Balance
21,337.3	23,807.7	28,998.2	32,931.2	34,808.5	33,261.1	34,335.8	37,814.0	38,839.6	39,999.0	..	Exports of Goods & NFServices
41,859.5	49,271.5	30,622.4	20,273.0	23,881.6	26,508.6	23,239.3	24,394.0	33,632.0	40,632.6	..	Imports of Goods & NFServices
199,886.0	220,562.0	195,498.0	173,080.0	181,642.0	191,108.0	179,073.0	180,042.0	190,771.0	202,635.0	..	Domestic Absorption
125,604.0	135,921.0	127,556.0	119,051.0	124,251.0	129,315.0	126,616.0	126,334.0	131,994.0	142,489.0	..	Private Consumption, etc.
13,248.3	14,609.4	14,907.6	15,312.1	16,321.9	16,475.5	16,711.7	16,505.0	16,445.9	16,357.4	..	General Gov't Consumption
61,033.1	70,032.1	53,034.4	38,716.3	41,069.1	45,317.3	35,745.0	37,203.0	42,331.0	43,788.9	..	Gross Domestic Investment
50,884.2	59,141.0	49,210.8	35,299.0	37,560.9	40,512.4	35,731.1	35,630.0	37,790.8	39,997.5	..	Fixed Investment
164,459.0	179,251.0	174,582.0	171,351.0	176,647.0	178,557.0	174,976.0	174,749.0	178,290.0	183,039.0	B	GDP at factor cost
14,889.8	15,800.5	15,489.5	15,802.3	16,227.7	16,728.6	16,498.0	16,676.0	16,413.0	15,640.3	..	Agriculture
67,197.6	73,226.8	71,715.4	65,300.2	68,381.3	71,687.8	67,440.0	69,239.0	70,075.6	74,407.5	..	Industry
48,722.3	51,863.7	50,442.3	46,487.9	48,818.7	51,786.9	48,840.6	50,092.0	51,175.9	55,156.9	f	Manufacturing
98,032.6	106,887.0	107,263.0	104,635.0	107,960.0	109,444.0	106,231.0	107,547.0	109,490.0	111,954.0	..	Services, etc.
											Memo Items:
34,534.1	39,642.3	45,510.9	40,890.2	43,452.2	39,543.7	31,654.1	37,814.0	38,985.0	43,111.1	..	Capacity to Import
13,196.8	15,834.6	16,512.8	7,959.0	8,643.7	6,282.5	-2,681.8	0.0	145.4	3,112.1	..	Terms of Trade Adjustment
192,560.0	210,933.0	210,387.0	193,697.0	201,213.0	204,143.0	187,488.0	193,462.0	196,124.0	205,114.0	..	Gross Domestic Income
186,738.0	203,107.0	198,620.0	180,929.0	189,129.0	193,976.0	175,575.0	183,283.0	187,763.0	196,685.0	..	Gross National Income
				(Index 1987 = 100)							**DOMESTIC PRICES/DEFLATORS**
2.5	3.1	5.1	9.6	15.3	24.0	41.6	100.0	202.0	244.6	..	Overall (GDP)
2.3	2.8	4.8	9.3	15.0	23.5	42.2	100.0	202.8	241.5	..	Domestic Absorption
2.5	3.2	4.6	8.8	15.6	25.7	45.3	100.0	206.8	284.0	..	Agriculture
2.2	2.7	4.3	9.2	14.4	22.0	39.8	100.0	199.2	211.2	..	Industry
2.0	2.6	4.0	8.1	13.6	21.4	40.0	100.0	208.5	220.3	..	Manufacturing
2.2	2.8	4.4	8.9	14.7	23.2	43.1	100.0	214.2	257.0	..	Consumer Price Index
											MANUFACTURING ACTIVITY
108.6	114.2	111.6	101.1	99.2	104.1	98.4	100.0	101.6	..	J	Employment (1987=100)
141.6	145.9	142.4	105.5	102.8	104.7	98.5	100.0	101.5	..	J	Real Earnings per Empl. (1987=100)
94.0	93.5	91.4	96.8	104.6	108.0	105.4	100.0	104.1	..	J	Real Output per Empl. (1987=100)
32.9	34.2	34.0	23.8	21.1	20.9	20.0	19.8	19.8	..	J	Earnings as % of Value Added
				(Billions of current Mexican Pesos)							**MONETARY HOLDINGS**
1,426	2,141	3,330	5,443	9,186	13,255	23,612	58,555	52,702	98,379	D	Money Supply, Broadly Defined
477	635	1,031	1,447	2,315	3,462	5,790	12,627	21,191	28,742	..	Money
195	283	505	681	1,122	1,738	3,067	7,339	13,201	18,065	..	Currency Outside Banks
282	352	526	766	1,193	1,724	2,723	5,288	7,990	10,677	..	Demand Deposits
949	1,506	2,299	3,996	6,871	9,793	17,822	45,928	31,511	69,637	..	Quasi-Money
				(Billions of current Mexican Pesos)							**GOVERNMENT DEFICIT (-) OR SURPLUS**
-134	-392	-1,454	-1,362	-2,095	-3,979	-10,407	-26,224	-40,343	..	..	Current Revenue
675	895	1,520	3,222	4,772	7,820	12,642	33,682	67,465	..	..	Current Revenue
507	843	2,191	3,660	5,451	9,669	19,670	52,636	97,031	..	..	Current Expenditure
168	52	-671	-438	-679	-1,849	-7,028	-18,954	-29,566	..	..	Current Budget Balance
..	..	..	..		1		1	1	11	..	Capital Receipts
302	444	783	924	1,417	2,130	3,380	7,271	10,788	..	..	Capital Payments

MEXICO	1969	1970	1971	1972	1973	1974	1975	1976	1977	1978	1979
FOREIGN TRADE (CUSTOMS BASIS)					*(Millions of current US dollars)*						
Value of Exports, fob	1,254	1,205	1,320	1,845	2,632	2,957	2,993	3,468	4,284	6,301	8,817
Nonfuel Primary Products	892	775	785	1,174	1,503	1,713	1,599	1,902	2,089	2,793	3,063
Fuels	40	38	31	22	25	124	463	554	1,014	1,804	3,859
Manufactures	321	392	504	649	1,103	1,120	931	1,012	1,182	1,704	1,894
Value of Imports, cif	2,078	2,461	2,407	2,935	4,146	6,057	6,572	6,033	5,589	8,053	12,587
Nonfuel Primary Products	259	397	339	421	793	1,529	1,347	887	1,142	1,548	2,204
Fuels	75	78	104	143	293	426	361	343	166	263	313
Manufactures	1,744	1,986	1,964	2,371	3,060	4,102	4,864	4,802	4,281	6,242	10,069
					(Index 1987 = 100)						
Terms of Trade	126.3	128.8	129.6	129.7	136.8	121.7	117.8	135.3	131.4	115.2	130.3
Export Prices, fob	30.7	33.8	35.4	38.7	49.6	63.5	63.9	71.9	77.6	76.9	99.3
Import Prices, cif	24.3	26.2	27.3	29.9	36.2	52.2	54.3	53.2	59.0	66.8	76.2
BALANCE OF PAYMENTS					*(Millions of current US dollars)*						
Exports of Goods & Services	..	2,935	3,171	3,816	4,840	6,368	6,358	7,203	8,211	11,425	16,003
Merchandise, fob	..	1,348	1,409	1,717	2,141	2,999	3,007	3,475	4,604	6,246	9,301
Nonfactor Services	..	1,397	1,586	1,892	2,463	3,057	3,059	3,364	3,189	4,497	5,830
Factor Services	..	190	177	207	236	311	292	363	419	682	872
Imports of Goods & Services	..	4,058	4,064	4,797	6,329	9,365	10,541	10,767	10,235	14,788	21,687
Merchandise, fob	..	2,236	2,158	2,610	3,656	5,791	6,278	5,771	5,625	7,992	12,131
Nonfactor Services	..	1,181	1,238	1,406	1,580	1,817	2,188	2,518	2,040	3,344	4,573
Factor Services	..	641	668	781	1,093	1,757	2,075	2,479	2,570	3,452	4,983
Long-Term Interest	..	283	312	353	516	813	1,104	1,360	1,588	2,258	3,357
Private Current Transfers, net	..	25	26	25	41	57	59	73	88	104	131
Workers' Remittances	..	..	..	..	..	..	..	..	..	..	..
Curr. A/C Bal before Off. Transf.	..	-1,098	-867	-955	-1,448	-2,940	-4,124	-3,492	-1,936	-3,259	-5,553
Net Official Transfers	..	30	31	39	33	65	81	83	82	88	94
Curr. A/C Bal after Off. Transf.	..	-1,068	-835	-916	-1,415	-2,876	-4,042	-3,409	-1,854	-3,171	-5,459
Long-Term Capital, net	..	626	746	827	1,819	3,046	4,656	4,994	4,611	5,118	5,144
Direct Investment	..	323	307	301	457	678	609	628	556	824	1,332
Long-Term Loans	..	358	453	602	1,819	2,669	3,746	4,504	4,709	4,537	4,081
Disbursements	..	1,375	1,502	1,780	3,173	3,979	5,255	6,489	7,819	9,442	12,140
Repayments	..	1,017	1,049	1,178	1,354	1,310	1,509	1,985	3,110	4,905	8,059
Other Long-Term Capital	..	-55	-14	-76	-456	-301	302	-138	-654	-243	-269
Other Capital, net	..	471	219	267	-247	-97	-410	-2,445	-2,135	-1,561	630
Change in Reserves	..	-29	-130	-178	-157	-74	-204	860	-622	-386	-315
Memo Item:					*(Mexican Pesos per US dollar)*						
Conversion Factor (Annual Avg)	12.500	12.500	12.500	12.500	12.500	12.500	12.500	15.400	22.600	22.800	22.800
				(Billions of US dollars), outstanding at end of year							
EXTERNAL DEBT (Total)	..	5.97	6.42	7.03	9.00	11.95	15.61	20.52	31.19	35.71	42.77
Long-Term Debt (by debtor)	..	5.97	6.42	7.03	9.00	11.95	15.61	20.52	25.74	30.77	34.75
Central Bank, incl. IMF credit	..	1.15	1.42	1.74	2.48	3.17	4.91	7.05	8.86	9.83	10.73
Central Government	..	0.35	0.32	0.36	0.45	0.93	1.37	2.58	3.96	4.69	4.31
Rest of General Government	..	0.00	0.00	0.00	0.00	0.00	0.00	0.00	0.00	0.00	0.00
Non-financial Public Enterprises	..	1.65	1.71	1.76	2.36	3.68	4.53	5.76	7.34	9.77	11.98
Priv. Sector, incl non-guaranteed	..	2.81	2.97	3.17	3.71	4.17	4.79	5.13	5.57	6.47	7.73
Short-Term Debt	..	0.00	0.00	0.00	0.00	0.00	0.00	0.00	5.45	4.95	8.02
Memo Items:					*(Millions of US dollars)*						
Int'l Reserves Excluding Gold	493	568	752	976	1,160	1,238	1,384	1,188	1,649	1,842	2,072
Gold Holdings (at market price)	170	188	229	321	520	683	513	216	289	428	1,016
SOCIAL INDICATORS											
Total Fertility Rate	6.6	6.5	6.4	6.4	6.1	5.8	5.5	5.2	4.9	4.8	4.6
Infant Mortality Rate	75.0	73.0	71.0	69.0	67.2	65.4	63.6	61.8	60.0	58.6	57.2
Life Expectancy at Birth	61.2	61.7	62.2	62.6	63.2	63.7	64.3	64.8	65.4	65.8	66.2
Urban Population, % of total	58.2	59.0	59.8	60.5	61.3	62.0	62.8	63.5	64.2	65.0	65.7
Food Prod. per capita (1987=100)	90.4	90.9	91.9	94.7	94.0	92.4	95.0	94.1	100.0	106.5	99.9
Labor Force, Agriculture (%)	45.1	44.1	43.2	42.4	41.6	40.9	40.3	39.4	38.6	37.9	37.2
Labor Force, Female (%)	17.5	17.8	18.9	20.0	20.9	21.8	22.6	23.6	24.6	25.4	26.2
Primary Schl. Enroll. Ratio	..	104.0	..	..	..	..	109.0	..	113.0	118.0	120.0
Primary Schl. Enroll. Ratio, Female	..	101.0	..	..	..	..	106.0	..	110.0	117.0	119.0
Secondary Schl. Enroll. Ratio	..	22.0	..	..	..	..	34.0	37.0	39.0	42.0	44.0

1980	1981	1982	1983	1984	1985	1986	1987	1988	1989 estimate	NOTES	MEXICO
				(Millions of current US dollars)							**FOREIGN TRADE (CUSTOMS BASIS)**
15,308	20,041	21,230	22,312	24,196	22,108	16,237	20,887	20,761	22,266	f	Value of Exports, fob
2,767	3,575	2,516	3,163	3,544	2,828	3,068	3,026	2,814	..	..	Nonfuel Primary Products
10,306	13,802	16,910	15,862	16,403	14,640	6,043	8,087	6,370	..	..	Fuels
2,234	2,664	1,804	3,287	4,249	4,640	7,126	9,774	11,577	11,592	..	Manufactures
19,517	24,161	15,041	8,023	11,788	13,994	12,032	12,731	19,592	17,098	f	Value of Imports, cif
3,490	4,079	2,128	1,732	2,803	2,893	2,286	2,441	4,878	..	..	Nonfuel Primary Products
318	486	310	161	397	611	124	119	173	..	..	Fuels
15,709	19,596	12,603	6,130	8,588	10,489	9,622	10,170	14,541	13,283	..	Manufactures
				(Index 1987 = 100)							
162.7	173.2	185.4	156.9	152.4	148.2	95.2	100.0	87.4	..	..	Terms of Trade
137.3	145.0	149.0	128.6	124.5	118.7	84.3	100.0	96.8	..	..	Export Prices, fob
84.4	83.7	80.4	82.0	81.7	80.1	88.6	100.0	110.7	..	..	Import Prices, cif
				(Millions of current US dollars)							**BALANCE OF PAYMENTS**
21,994	27,637	27,520	28,578	32,378	29,544	23,684	29,899	32,007	35,900	..	Exports of Goods & Services
15,511	20,102	21,230	22,312	24,196	21,663	16,031	20,655	20,566	22,765	..	Merchandise, fob
5,241	5,893	4,760	4,817	5,847	5,748	5,842	6,955	8,489	10,141	..	Nonfactor Services
1,242	1,642	1,530	1,449	2,335	2,133	1,811	2,289	2,952	2,994	..	Factor Services
33,028	44,001	34,130	23,477	28,594	29,414	25,821	26,579	35,017	42,019	..	Imports of Goods & Services
18,896	23,948	14,435	8,550	11,255	13,212	11,432	12,222	18,898	23,410	..	Merchandise, fob
6,221	8,129	5,711	4,213	4,940	5,170	4,875	5,009	6,049	7,604	..	Nonfactor Services
7,911	11,924	13,984	10,714	12,399	11,032	9,514	9,348	10,070	11,005	..	Factor Services
4,580	6,117	7,769	8,140	10,250	9,382	7,675	7,691	7,541	7,897	..	Long-Term Interest
245	246	232	255	325	327	345	384	397	516	..	Private Current Transfers, net
139	128	98	111	177	173	180	207	209	321	..	Workers' Remittances
-10,789	-16,118	-6,378	5,356	4,109	457	-1,792	3,704	-2,613	-5,603	..	Curr. A/C Bal before Off. Transf.
39	57	71	47	85	673	119	264	170	156	..	Net Official Transfers
-10,750	-16,061	-6,307	5,403	4,194	1,130	-1,673	3,968	-2,443	-5,447	..	Curr. A/C Bal after Off. Transf.
10,530	18,610	14,645	7,299	2,453	-410	433	4,044	-677	1,030	..	Long-Term Capital, net
2,156	2,835	1,655	461	390	491	1,523	3,246	2,594	2,241	..	Direct Investment
6,821	12,499	7,969	2,359	1,625	-25	538	3,781	-1,498	-274	..	Long-Term Loans
11,581	17,003	12,500	7,187	7,281	5,048	4,960	7,174	4,697	3,966	..	Disbursements
4,760	4,504	4,531	4,828	5,656	5,072	4,422	3,394	6,195	4,240	..	Repayments
1,553	3,276	5,021	4,479	438	-876	-1,628	-2,982	-1,773	-937	..	Other Long-Term Capital
1,038	-1,274	-13,127	-9,452	-4,497	-3,451	1,152	-2,442	-3,518	4,597	..	Other Capital, net
-818	-1,275	4,789	-3,250	-2,150	2,731	88	-5,570	6,638	-180	..	Change in Reserves
				(Mexican Pesos per US dollar)							**Memo Item:**
23.000	24.500	56.400	120.100	167.800	256.900	611.800	1,378.200	2,273.100	2,461.300	..	Conversion Factor (Annual Avg)
			(Billions of US dollars), outstanding at end of year								
57.38	78.22	86.02	92.96	94.82	96.87	100.87	109.45	100.75	95.64	..	**EXTERNAL DEBT (Total)**
41.21	53.23	59.87	82.83	88.38	91.42	94.97	103.65	91.30	85.35	..	Long-Term Debt (by debtor)
11.58	15.31	18.55	15.06	16.32	11.85	15.60	18.91	18.60	19.13	..	Central Bank, incl. IMF credit
4.92	5.57	8.88	32.39	37.38	53.31	53.54	59.66	57.41	53.51	..	Central Government
0.00	0.00	0.00	0.05	0.09	0.01	0.01	0.01	0.00	0.00	..	Rest of General Government
15.15	19.87	22.09	18.84	16.71	9.45	9.70	9.91	9.02	8.49	..	Non-financial Public Enterprises
9.57	12.49	10.35	16.49	17.88	16.79	16.13	15.16	6.25	4.21	..	Priv. Sector, incl non-guaranteed
16.16	24.98	26.15	10.14	6.44	5.45	5.90	5.80	9.46	10.30	..	Short-Term Debt
				(Millions of US dollars)							**Memo Items:**
2,960	4,074	834	3,913	7,272	4,906	5,670	12,464	5,279	6,329	..	Int'l Reserves Excluding Gold
1,215	897	944	881	747	773	1,004	1,228	1,048	411	..	Gold Holdings (at market price)
											SOCIAL INDICATORS
4.5	4.3	4.2	4.1	4.0	3.8	3.7	3.6	3.5	3.4	..	Total Fertility Rate
55.8	54.4	53.0	51.8	50.6	49.4	48.2	47.0	45.9	44.8	..	Infant Mortality Rate
66.6	67.0	67.4	67.7	68.0	68.3	68.6	68.9	69.1	69.4	..	Life Expectancy at Birth
66.4	67.0	67.7	68.3	69.0	69.6	70.2	70.8	71.4	72.0	..	Urban Population, % of total
104.1	108.1	101.4	105.6	103.9	105.6	102.5	100.0	100.9	104.4	..	Food Prod. per capita (1987=100)
36.5	..	..	..	..	..	..	..	..	..	..	Labor Force, Agriculture (%)
27.0	27.0	27.0	27.0	27.0	27.0	27.1	27.1	27.1	27.1	..	Labor Force, Female (%)
115.0	..	119.0	119.0	118.0	119.0	119.0	118.0	..	..	..	Primary Schl. Enroll. Ratio
115.0	118.0	117.0	117.0	116.0	117.0	118.0	116.0	..	..	..	Primary Schl. Enroll. Ratio, Female
46.0	..	53.0	55.0	53.0	53.0	53.0	53.0	..	..	..	Secondary Schl. Enroll. Ratio

MOROCCO	1969	1970	1971	1972	1973	1974	1975	1976	1977	1978	1979
CURRENT GNP PER CAPITA (US $)	250	260	280	300	340	410	500	560	600	650	770
POPULATION (thousands)	14,908	15,310	15,712	16,113	16,511	16,908	17,305	17,702	18,098	18,502	18,927
USE AND ORIGIN OF RESOURCES					*(Billions of current Moroccan Dirhams)*						
Gross National Product (GNP)	18.26	19.79	21.74	23.05	25.31	33.33	36.04	40.45	48.90	53.85	60.34
Net Factor Income from Abroad	-0.22	-0.23	-0.26	-0.29	-0.32	-0.27	-0.36	-0.56	-0.87	-1.30	-1.71
GDP at Market Prices	18.48	20.02	22.00	23.35	25.64	33.60	36.39	41.01	49.76	55.15	62.04
Resource Balance	-0.21	-0.79	-0.61	-0.15	-0.32	-0.21	-3.96	-7.97	-10.16	-7.55	-7.97
Exports of Goods & NFServices	3.38	3.53	3.73	4.34	5.34	9.24	8.18	7.59	8.41	9.03	10.55
Imports of Goods & NFServices	3.59	4.32	4.34	4.49	5.67	9.45	12.14	15.56	18.57	16.58	18.53
Domestic Absorption	18.69	20.81	22.61	23.50	25.96	33.81	40.35	48.98	59.93	62.71	70.02
Private Consumption, etc.	13.86	14.70	15.95	17.04	18.65	22.85	25.27	28.24	32.65	37.21	41.59
General Gov't Consumption	2.21	2.41	2.71	2.89	2.99	4.04	5.92	9.21	10.25	11.47	13.23
Gross Domestic Investment	2.62	3.70	3.95	3.57	4.32	6.92	9.17	11.53	17.03	14.03	15.20
Fixed Investment	2.43	2.99	3.27	3.18	3.47	4.93	9.04	12.18	15.90	13.73	14.88
Indirect Taxes, net	..	..	..	..	..	..	..	..	..	..	..
GDP at factor cost	..	..	..	..	..	..	..	..	..	..	..
Agriculture	3.57	3.99	4.81	4.96	5.34	6.87	6.30	7.86	8.15	10.43	11.12
Industry	5.11	5.40	6.00	6.43	7.17	11.74	12.64	13.34	16.20	17.29	20.27
Manufacturing	3.08	3.24	3.58	3.92	4.45	5.25	6.03	6.76	8.24	9.37	10.44
Services, etc.	9.80	10.63	11.19	11.95	13.13	14.99	17.45	19.82	25.41	27.43	30.66
Gross Domestic Saving	2.41	2.91	3.34	3.42	4.00	6.71	5.21	3.56	6.87	6.47	7.22
Gross National Saving	..	2.87	3.45	3.61	4.54	7.75	6.80	5.21	8.46	8.09	8.99
					(Millions of 1987 Moroccan Dirhams)						
Gross National Product	70,044	73,512	77,616	79,415	82,156	86,975	92,618	102,445	107,052	109,459	113,979
GDP at Market Prices	70,829	74,298	78,484	80,362	83,132	87,614	93,484	103,768	108,854	112,023	117,149
Resource Balance	-6	-1,785	-1,312	1,700	874	-1,105	-13,031	-18,789	-21,810	-14,559	-15,747
Exports of Goods & NFServices	18,038	18,503	18,433	21,834	25,053	24,226	20,022	21,421	23,400	24,802	24,923
Imports of Goods & NFServices	18,044	20,287	19,746	20,134	24,179	25,332	33,053	40,210	45,210	39,361	40,670
Domestic Absorption	70,835	76,082	79,796	78,662	82,258	88,719	106,516	122,557	130,664	126,582	132,896
Private Consumption, etc.	53,052	55,483	57,294	59,087	62,073	65,059	69,433	76,057	78,928	82,915	87,460
General Gov't Consumption	5,898	6,409	6,788	6,828	6,962	7,827	10,865	15,716	16,173	17,306	18,721
Gross Domestic Investment	11,884	14,190	15,714	12,747	13,224	15,833	26,218	30,784	35,563	26,360	26,715
Fixed Investment	12,434	14,396	15,805	14,012	13,551	16,558	29,115	34,504	39,325	28,961	29,361
GDP at factor cost	..	..	..	..	..	..	..	..	..	..	..
Agriculture	16,580	17,271	18,998	18,575	16,844	17,197	16,106	18,571	16,283	19,207	18,877
Industry	23,878	24,636	26,543	28,203	29,909	31,886	35,233	38,510	41,577	41,184	44,358
Manufacturing	..	..	..	..	..	..	..	..	..	..	..
Services, etc.	30,389	32,236	33,178	33,907	36,250	38,472	42,358	46,808	51,445	51,756	54,277
Memo Items:											
Capacity to Import	16,982	16,578	16,971	19,452	22,792	24,766	22,278	19,613	20,466	21,430	23,167
Terms of Trade Adjustment	-1,055	-1,924	-1,463	-2,382	-2,261	540	2,257	-1,808	-2,933	-3,372	-1,756
Gross Domestic Income	69,773	72,373	77,021	77,980	80,872	88,154	95,741	101,959	105,920	108,650	115,393
Gross National Income	68,989	71,587	76,153	77,033	79,896	87,515	94,875	100,637	104,119	106,087	112,223
DOMESTIC PRICES/DEFLATORS					*(Index 1987 = 100)*						
Overall (GDP)	26.1	26.9	28.0	29.0	30.8	38.4	38.9	39.5	45.7	49.2	53.0
Domestic Absorption	26.4	27.4	28.3	29.9	31.6	38.1	37.9	40.0	45.9	49.5	52.7
Agriculture	21.5	23.1	25.3	26.7	31.7	40.0	39.1	42.3	50.1	54.3	58.9
Industry	21.4	21.9	22.6	22.8	24.0	36.8	35.9	34.6	39.0	42.0	45.7
Manufacturing	..	..	..	..	..	..	..	..	..	..	..
Consumer Price Index	24.4	24.7	25.7	26.7	27.8	32.7	35.2	38.2	43.0	47.2	51.2
MANUFACTURING ACTIVITY											
Employment (1987=100)	40.9	..	..	..	..	..	..	53.5	57.5	54.1	59.3
Real Earnings per Empl. (1987=100)	112.6	..	..	..	..	..	..	119.5	123.1	129.0	128.0
Real Output per Empl. (1987=100)	104.6	..	..	..	..	..	..	111.6	108.3	116.1	118.0
Earnings as % of Value Added	45.7	..	..	..	..	..	..	44.0	55.1	54.1	54.5
MONETARY HOLDINGS					*(Millions of current Moroccan Dirhams)*						
Money Supply, Broadly Defined	5,946	6,510	7,347	8,677	9,998	12,875	15,421	18,153	21,732	25,670	29,677
Money	5,058	5,514	6,193	7,336	8,572	10,869	12,837	15,102	18,002	20,785	23,352
Currency Outside Banks	2,121	2,261	2,461	2,944	3,411	4,063	4,650	5,732	6,650	7,676	9,020
Demand Deposits	2,937	3,254	3,732	4,392	5,161	6,806	8,187	9,370	11,352	13,109	14,332
Quasi-Money	887	995	1,154	1,341	1,426	2,006	2,584	3,051	3,730	4,885	6,325
GOVERNMENT DEFICIT (-) OR SURPLUS					*(Millions of current Moroccan Dirhams)*						
	..	-619	-658	-897	-526	-1,348	-3,341	-7,217	-7,647	-5,773	-6,039
Current Revenue	..	3,857	3,884	4,330	5,151	8,449	9,441	9,424	12,219	13,183	15,562
Current Expenditure	..	3,326	3,472	4,035	4,373	7,582	8,025	8,782	10,080	11,403	13,383
Current Budget Balance	..	531	412	295	778	867	1,416	642	2,139	1,780	2,179
Capital Receipts	..	5	6	5	13	19	88	177	114	163	241
Capital Payments	..	1,155	1,076	1,197	1,317	2,234	4,845	8,036	9,900	7,716	8,459

1980	1981	1982	1983	1984	1985	1986	1987	1988	1989 estimate	NOTES	MOROCCO
930	870	860	730	660	610	650	680	830	880	..	**CURRENT GNP PER CAPITA (US $)**
19,382	19,865	20,375	20,912	21,475	22,061	22,706	23,376	23,960	24,567	..	**POPULATION (thousands)**
				(Billions of current Moroccan Dirhams)							**USE AND ORIGIN OF RESOURCES**
71.74	75.28	88.90	94.66	107.17	121.75	148.33	151.80	171.63	179.83	..	Gross National Product (GNP)
-2.35	-3.75	-3.99	-4.49	-5.18	-7.75	-6.40	-6.55	-8.86	-10.18	..	Net Factor Income from Abroad
74.09	79.03	92.90	99.14	112.35	129.51	154.73	158.36	180.48	190.01	..	GDP at Market Prices
-7.77	-11.53	-13.43	-8.74	-11.91	-11.64	-9.80	-6.92	-0.83	-10.60	..	Resource Balance
12.88	15.94	17.88	21.29	26.77	32.05	32.92	35.40	44.94	42.77	..	Exports of Goods & NFServices
20.66	27.47	31.31	30.03	38.68	43.68	42.72	42.32	45.77	53.37	..	Imports of Goods & NFServices
81.86	90.56	106.33	107.88	124.26	141.14	164.52	165.28	181.31	200.61	..	Domestic Absorption
50.34	54.84	63.11	67.47	78.37	85.50	105.60	107.82	114.71	124.19	..	Private Consumption, etc.
13.59	15.08	17.00	16.63	17.48	20.52	23.75	24.71	28.05	30.64	..	General Gov't Consumption
17.93	20.64	26.22	23.79	28.41	35.12	35.17	32.75	38.55	45.79	..	Gross Domestic Investment
16.48	20.51	25.38	24.23	25.95	29.93	32.99	31.63	37.24	43.71	..	Fixed Investment
..	..	..	..	..	..	..	..	..	..	..	Indirect Taxes, net
..	..	..	..	..	..	..	..	..	..	B	GDP at factor cost
13.65	10.21	14.22	15.03	16.85	21.50	29.53	23.99	30.94	31.23	..	Agriculture
22.92	26.92	29.63	32.95	37.38	43.24	49.94	51.51	60.59	64.01	..	Industry
12.47	14.30	16.09	18.22	20.74	24.03	26.59	28.59	31.97	34.58	..	Manufacturing
37.51	41.90	49.04	51.16	58.11	64.77	75.26	82.85	88.95	94.77	..	Services, etc.
10.16	9.12	12.79	15.04	16.50	23.49	25.38	25.82	37.72	35.19	..	Gross Domestic Saving
11.76	10.47	13.85	16.87	18.78	25.45	31.67	32.47	39.56	36.51	..	Gross National Saving
				(Millions of 1987 Moroccan Dirhams)							
123,867	118,658	130,707	129,631	135,050	141,449	155,192	151,805	165,567	166,858	..	Gross National Product
127,810	124,277	136,232	135,472	141,171	149,943	161,765	158,355	174,276	176,338	..	GDP at Market Prices
-11,653	-12,317	-12,228	-5,555	-6,247	-4,949	-7,064	-6,923	-3,092	-10,381	..	Resource Balance
25,820	25,878	27,136	29,346	30,171	31,451	32,143	35,395	41,964	36,058	..	Exports of Goods & NFServices
37,473	38,195	39,364	34,900	36,418	36,400	39,208	42,318	45,056	46,440	..	Imports of Goods & NFServices
139,463	136,594	148,460	141,026	147,418	154,892	168,830	165,278	177,368	186,719	..	Domestic Absorption
93,476	89,843	95,662	94,860	98,673	99,521	105,170	107,820	113,785	117,425	..	Private Consumption, etc.
18,030	18,711	20,170	19,094	19,690	22,716	26,106	24,712	24,477	26,805	..	General Gov't Consumption
27,956	28,040	32,629	27,072	29,054	32,655	37,554	32,746	39,106	42,489	..	Gross Domestic Investment
28,973	31,450	35,767	31,045	30,505	32,576	33,926	31,632	34,985	38,387	..	Fixed Investment
..	..	..	..	..	..	..	..	..	..	B	GDP at factor cost
21,523	15,364	20,737	18,587	19,273	22,829	31,214	23,992	31,326	30,733	..	Agriculture
43,794	44,925	46,193	46,815	47,463	50,204	50,677	51,511	56,036	55,434	..	Industry
22,033	22,363	23,543	24,534	25,591	27,402	27,731	28,587	30,588	30,603	..	Manufacturing
62,235	64,337	69,079	70,070	74,435	76,910	79,874	82,853	86,914	90,171	..	Services, etc.
											Memo Items:
23,370	22,168	22,481	24,741	25,202	26,703	30,216	35,395	44,237	37,213	..	Capacity to Import
-2,449	-3,710	-4,654	-4,604	-4,969	-4,748	-1,928	0	2,273	1,154	..	Terms of Trade Adjustment
125,361	120,567	131,577	130,868	136,202	145,196	159,838	158,355	176,548	177,492	..	Gross Domestic Income
121,417	114,948	126,053	125,027	130,081	136,701	153,264	151,805	167,840	168,013	..	Gross National Income
				(Index 1987 = 100)							**DOMESTIC PRICES/DEFLATORS**
58.0	63.6	68.2	73.2	79.6	86.4	95.6	100.0	103.6	107.8	..	Overall (GDP)
58.7	66.3	71.6	76.5	84.3	91.1	97.4	100.0	102.2	107.4	..	Domestic Absorption
63.4	66.4	68.6	80.9	87.4	94.2	94.6	100.0	98.8	101.6	..	Agriculture
52.3	59.9	64.1	70.4	78.8	86.1	98.5	100.0	108.1	115.5	..	Industry
56.6	63.9	68.3	74.3	81.0	87.7	95.9	100.0	104.5	113.0	..	Manufacturing
56.0	63.0	69.6	73.9	83.1	89.6	97.4	100.0	102.4	105.6	..	Consumer Price Index
											MANUFACTURING ACTIVITY
65.0	66.5	68.0	69.6	81.9	86.1	97.3	100.0	114.0	..	..	Employment (1987=100)
125.9	120.6	117.5	119.3	103.3	109.3	96.1	100.0	..	..	..	Real Earnings per Empl. (1987=100)
105.4	107.6	116.2	113.2	96.6	111.0	100.3	100.0	..	..	..	Real Output per Empl. (1987=100)
55.0	54.3	..	..	..	..	..	..	..	..	..	Earnings as % of Value Added
				(Millions of current Moroccan Dirhams)							**MONETARY HOLDINGS**
33,208	38,486	43,364	51,267	56,778	66,754	77,445	84,839	97,549	..	D	Money Supply, Broadly Defined
25,312	29,016	30,064	34,197	36,779	42,820	50,029	54,489	62,032	68,395	..	Money
9,807	11,133	12,022	13,636	14,770	16,192	18,694	20,003	21,914	24,814	..	Currency Outside Banks
15,505	17,883	18,042	20,561	22,009	26,628	31,335	34,486	40,118	43,581	..	Demand Deposits
7,896	9,470	13,300	17,071	19,999	23,934	27,416	30,350	35,517	..	..	Quasi-Money
				(Millions of current Moroccan Dirhams)							**GOVERNMENT DEFICIT (-) OR SURPLUS**
-7,184	-10,557	-10,630	-7,680	-6,762	-9,424	-11,872	-7,025	..	..	..	
17,235	20,066	24,080	24,220	26,383	29,896	32,757	36,870	..	..	..	Current Revenue
16,877	20,755	22,902	24,171	26,156	31,748	34,162	34,573	..	..	..	Current Expenditure
358	-689	1,178	49	227	-1,852	-1,405	2,297	..	..	..	Current Budget Balance
267	352	308	296	301	317	127	219	..	..	..	Capital Receipts
7,809	10,220	12,116	8,025	7,290	7,889	10,594	9,541	..	..	..	Capital Payments

MOROCCO	1969	1970	1971	1972	1973	1974	1975	1976	1977	1978	1979
FOREIGN TRADE (CUSTOMS BASIS)					*(Millions of current US dollars)*						
Value of Exports, fob	485.1	487.9	499.1	633.6	876.6	1,706.4	1,543.0	1,262.1	1,299.9	1,511.3	1,958.6
Nonfuel Primary Products	437.3	438.7	423.6	541.7	741.7	1,501.5	1,336.1	1,041.8	1,007.1	1,145.1	1,427.3
Fuels	1.6	1.9	1.8	1.3	4.7	11.9	14.2	17.7	20.3	21.2	70.9
Manufactures	46.2	47.3	73.7	90.5	130.2	193.0	192.8	202.6	272.4	345.0	460.5
Value of Imports, cif	560.3	684.3	697.0	764.4	1,098.2	1,900.8	2,547.3	2,592.9	3,168.5	2,950.3	3,673.5
Nonfuel Primary Products	166.0	211.1	241.3	248.4	416.0	711.1	914.9	710.5	778.7	811.6	1,027.1
Fuels	32.6	37.4	46.6	54.7	71.2	258.7	276.4	295.2	370.2	428.2	704.1
Manufactures	361.7	435.8	409.2	461.3	611.0	931.0	1,356.0	1,587.2	2,019.5	1,710.6	1,942.3
					(Index 1987 = 100)						
Terms of Trade	143.7	136.0	129.6	127.6	115.8	151.1	162.4	129.1	126.2	118.5	116.5
Export Prices, fob	37.0	37.3	38.4	40.7	49.4	94.5	104.8	78.3	81.4	87.0	103.7
Import Prices, cif	25.8	27.4	29.6	31.9	42.7	62.5	64.5	60.6	64.6	73.4	89.0
BALANCE OF PAYMENTS					*(Millions of current US dollars)*						
Exports of Goods & Services	..	705.0	745.2	945.7	1,301.8	2,131.1	2,026.1	1,720.2	1,870.9	2,164.4	2,711.3
Merchandise, fob	..	487.0	499.5	641.7	913.2	1,704.1	1,529.4	1,247.0	1,283.5	1,488.2	1,936.6
Nonfactor Services	..	203.0	231.7	291.0	374.3	399.3	467.8	448.9	555.4	649.5	734.9
Factor Services	..	15.0	14.0	13.0	14.3	27.7	28.9	24.2	32.0	26.6	39.8
Imports of Goods & Services	..	902.0	913.7	1,035.8	1,449.6	2,234.5	3,070.1	3,622.5	4,286.4	4,261.5	5,166.4
Merchandise, fob	..	624.0	636.9	709.0	1,037.1	1,692.1	2,265.5	2,307.6	2,821.0	2,628.7	3,245.3
Nonfactor Services	..	218.0	211.6	249.7	319.5	453.4	687.6	1,163.5	1,241.4	1,293.0	1,443.6
Factor Services	..	60.0	65.2	77.1	93.0	89.0	117.0	151.4	224.1	339.8	477.5
Long-Term Interest	..	25.0	29.5	35.5	43.7	46.0	56.8	77.2	170.8	293.3	448.6
Private Current Transfers, net	..	36.0	74.2	107.5	211.0	299.5	481.9	499.2	545.6	702.0	891.2
Workers' Remittances	..	63.0	95.3	140.1	250.3	359.6	533.0	547.1	588.9	762.2	947.9
Curr. A/C Bal before Off. Transf.	..	-161.0	-94.3	17.4	63.2	196.0	-562.1	-1,403.2	-1,869.9	-1,395.1	-1,563.9
Net Official Transfers	..	37.0	35.1	30.4	33.4	30.1	33.8	6.1	14.9	57.6	43.3
Curr. A/C Bal after Off. Transf.	..	-124.0	-59.2	47.8	96.6	226.1	-528.3	-1,397.1	-1,855.1	-1,337.5	-1,520.6
Long-Term Capital, net	..	114.0	109.3	44.5	1.2	40.9	708.9	2,347.9	2,997.7	2,288.8	1,378.8
Direct Investment	..	20.0	23.1	13.0	-1.2	-20.4	-0.2	38.0	57.1	47.5	38.5
Long-Term Loans	..	135.6	124.0	58.0	29.0	161.9	514.6	661.0	1,824.6	994.6	991.5
Disbursements	..	175.3	185.6	131.6	122.2	265.0	620.3	775.6	1,969.6	1,325.9	1,435.9
Repayments	..	39.7	61.6	73.6	93.2	103.1	105.7	114.6	145.0	331.3	444.4
Other Long-Term Capital	..	-41.6	-37.7	-26.5	-26.6	-100.6	194.5	1,648.9	1,116.1	1,246.7	348.8
Other Capital, net	..	26.1	-10.5	-36.5	-95.8	-144.8	-209.0	-968.5	-1,144.4	-979.9	67.8
Change in Reserves	..	-16.1	-39.7	-55.8	-1.9	-122.2	28.4	17.6	1.7	28.6	74.0
Memo Item:					*(Moroccan Dirhams per US dollar)*						
Conversion Factor (Annual Avg)	5.060	5.060	5.050	4.600	4.110	4.370	4.050	4.420	4.500	4.170	3.900
				(Millions of US dollars), outstanding at end of year							
EXTERNAL DEBT (Total)	..	754	888	944	1,040	1,246	1,727	2,470	4,955	6,247	8,495
Long-Term Debt (by debtor)	..	754	888	944	1,040	1,246	1,727	2,470	4,389	5,698	7,760
Central Bank, incl. IMF credit	..	55	32	44	48	60	103	291	523	690	684
Central Government	..	506	626	689	742	807	1,094	1,495	2,435	3,083	4,625
Rest of General Government	..	4	4	4	4	3	3	2	1	1	0
Non-financial Public Enterprises	..	153	185	156	180	296	422	537	1,139	1,599	2,047
Priv. Sector, incl non-guaranteed	..	36	43	52	66	80	106	144	292	325	404
Short-Term Debt	..	..	..	..	..	..	..	..	565	549	735
Memo Items:					*(Millions of US dollars)*						
Int'l Reserves Excluding Gold	93.0	119.3	150.7	213.7	240.6	391.0	352.4	467.1	505.3	618.4	557.0
Gold Holdings (at market price)	21.1	22.4	26.2	38.9	67.4	113.4	85.3	81.9	104.3	153.7	360.5
SOCIAL INDICATORS											
Total Fertility Rate	7.0	7.0	6.9	6.9	6.7	6.5	6.3	6.1	5.9	5.8	5.7
Infant Mortality Rate	131.6	128.4	125.2	122.0	119.6	117.2	114.8	112.4	110.0	106.4	102.8
Life Expectancy at Birth	51.4	51.9	52.4	52.9	53.5	54.1	54.6	55.2	55.8	56.3	56.8
Urban Population, % of total	34.1	34.6	35.2	35.9	36.5	37.2	37.8	38.5	39.2	39.9	40.6
Food Prod. per capita (1987=100)	103.6	107.0	115.6	112.5	96.2	109.2	91.1	103.9	85.9	104.1	102.0
Labor Force, Agriculture (%)	58.3	57.6	56.3	55.0	53.8	52.6	51.5	50.1	48.9	47.7	46.6
Labor Force, Female (%)	13.5	13.9	14.5	15.0	15.6	16.0	16.5	16.9	17.3	17.7	18.0
Primary Schl. Enroll. Ratio	..	52.0	..	..	..	..	62.0	66.0	69.0	72.0	75.0
Primary Schl. Enroll. Ratio, Female	..	36.0	..	..	..	..	45.0	48.0	51.0	54.0	56.0
Secondary Schl. Enroll. Ratio	..	13.0	..	..	..	..	16.0	17.0	19.0	20.0	22.0

1980	1981	1982	1983	1984	1985	1986	1987	1988	1989 estimate	NOTES	MOROCCO
											FOREIGN TRADE (CUSTOMS BASIS)
(Millions of current US dollars)											
2,403.4	2,320.3	2,058.6	2,062.0	2,171.9	2,165.1	2,427.5	2,807.0	3,625.0	3,335.6	..	Value of Exports, fob
1,721.5	1,560.7	1,264.3	1,181.8	1,200.7	1,204.8	1,308.7	1,362.0	1,742.0	..	..	Nonfuel Primary Products
116.5	105.0	87.6	81.8	85.9	84.2	61.9	77.0	75.0	..	..	Fuels
565.5	654.6	706.7	798.4	885.3	876.1	1,056.9	1,368.0	1,808.0	1,814.7	..	Manufactures
4,182.4	4,352.6	4,315.3	3,596.6	3,906.7	3,849.6	3,790.2	4,229.0	4,773.0	..	..	Value of Imports, cif
1,248.7	1,411.0	1,127.1	1,023.5	1,219.3	1,153.4	1,131.2	1,185.0	1,357.0	..	..	Nonfuel Primary Products
986.9	1,187.8	1,173.2	988.3	1,021.2	1,075.9	595.2	740.0	629.0	..	..	Fuels
1,946.8	1,753.8	2,015.0	1,584.8	1,666.2	1,620.3	2,063.8	2,304.0	2,787.0	..	..	Manufactures
(Index 1987 = 100)											
108.8	98.2	95.9	89.2	91.0	88.8	102.9	100.0	103.9	..	..	Terms of Trade
117.9	110.6	98.1	90.5	91.8	87.6	92.9	100.0	111.3	..	..	Export Prices, fob
108.3	112.6	102.3	101.4	100.8	98.6	90.3	100.0	107.1	..	..	Import Prices, cif
											BALANCE OF PAYMENTS
(Millions of current US dollars)											
3,270.4	3,083.7	2,944.4	2,931.0	3,016.0	3,160.2	3,575.9	4,192.7	5,405.8	5,012.5	..	Exports of Goods & Services
2,414.5	2,282.9	2,042.8	2,058.0	2,161.2	2,145.0	2,410.5	2,781.4	3,607.8	3,312.5	..	Merchandise, fob
817.0	762.3	875.6	860.6	837.2	993.0	1,148.2	1,392.7	1,778.5	1,659.1	..	Nonfactor Services
38.9	38.5	25.9	12.4	17.6	22.3	17.2	18.7	19.5	40.9	..	Factor Services
5,807.1	6,014.0	5,824.3	4,808.7	4,943.1	5,125.1	5,340.6	5,787.6	6,545.0	7,422.5	..	Imports of Goods & Services
3,770.0	3,839.7	3,815.2	3,300.6	3,568.9	3,513.1	3,477.0	3,850.1	4,359.8	4,991.4	..	Merchandise, fob
1,400.5	1,410.6	1,320.1	865.0	769.2	819.3	1,143.9	1,135.3	1,086.3	1,190.3	..	Nonfactor Services
636.6	763.7	689.0	643.1	605.0	792.7	719.8	802.2	1,098.9	1,240.8	..	Factor Services
618.7	671.1	614.1	561.4	530.0	491.1	623.2	620.0	810.2	1,065.8	..	Long-Term Interest
1,004.2	987.6	839.8	887.9	847.2	965.4	1,393.8	1,579.3	1,303.2	1,355.5	..	Private Current Transfers, net
1,053.7	1,013.5	849.2	916.1	871.8	967.2	1,398.3	1,587.2	1,303.4	1,336.5	..	Workers' Remittances
-1,532.5	-1,942.7	-2,040.2	-989.8	-1,080.0	-999.6	-370.9	-15.6	164.0	-1,054.5	..	Curr. A/C Bal before Off. Transf.
113.7	103.6	164.8	100.7	93.5	110.8	160.3	191.2	303.2	264.8	..	Net Official Transfers
-1,418.9	-1,839.1	-1,875.4	-889.1	-986.5	-888.8	-210.6	175.6	467.2	-789.7	..	Curr. A/C Bal after Off. Transf.
1,359.5	1,291.5	1,298.7	765.5	831.1	621.3	416.7	427.6	493.8	599.9	..	Long-Term Capital, net
89.4	58.6	79.5	46.1	47.0	20.0	0.5	59.6	84.5	167.1	..	Direct Investment
1,167.0	1,216.6	1,420.7	404.0	977.9	695.3	669.0	629.1	529.3	443.8	..	Long-Term Loans
1,757.0	1,862.9	2,244.6	1,123.0	1,222.2	1,209.1	1,353.9	1,260.6	1,046.2	1,060.6	..	Disbursements
590.0	646.3	823.9	719.0	244.3	513.8	684.9	631.5	516.9	616.8	..	Repayments
103.1	16.3	-201.5	315.4	-193.8	-94.0	-252.8	-261.1	-120.0	-11.0	..	Other Long-Term Capital
-189.2	131.7	159.2	-105.1	53.5	180.0	112.1	-258.7	-726.5	185.4	..	Other Capital, net
248.5	415.9	417.5	228.7	101.9	87.5	-318.2	-344.5	-234.5	4.4	..	Change in Reserves
											Memo Item:
(Moroccan Dirhams per US dollar)											
3.940	5.170	6.020	7.110	8.810	10.060	9.100	8.360	8.210	8.490	..	Conversion Factor (Annual Avg)
(Millions of US dollars), outstanding at end of year											
9,678	10,632	12,401	13,187	14,027	16,409	17,926	20,504	20,334	20,851	..	**EXTERNAL DEBT (Total)**
8,903	9,846	11,370	12,056	12,895	15,222	16,966	19,551	20,025	20,557	..	Long-Term Debt (by debtor)
835	923	1,278	1,284	1,282	1,509	1,380	1,417	1,219	1,084	..	Central Bank, incl. IMF credit
5,382	6,299	7,101	7,854	8,975	10,644	12,367	14,780	15,987	16,798	..	Central Government
0	0	0	0	0	1	0	0	0	..	..	Rest of General Government
2,201	2,008	2,212	2,156	1,984	2,239	2,221	2,137	1,685	1,576	..	Non-financial Public Enterprises
484	615	779	763	654	829	997	1,216	1,133	1,099	..	Priv. Sector, incl non-guaranteed
775	786	1,031	1,131	1,132	1,187	960	953	309	294	..	Short-Term Debt
(Millions of US dollars)											Memo Items:
398.6	229.7	217.6	106.7	48.7	115.1	211.4	411.1	547.5	488.5	..	Int'l Reserves Excluding Gold
415.0	279.8	321.7	268.6	217.0	230.2	275.2	340.8	288.8	282.3	..	Gold Holdings (at market price)
											SOCIAL INDICATORS
5.6	5.5	5.4	5.3	5.2	5.1	5.0	4.8	4.7	4.7	..	Total Fertility Rate
99.2	95.6	92.0	88.2	84.4	80.6	76.8	73.0	73.0	69.8	..	Infant Mortality Rate
57.3	57.8	58.3	58.8	59.3	59.8	60.3	60.8	61.0	61.3	..	Life Expectancy at Birth
41.3	42.0	42.7	43.4	44.1	44.8	45.5	46.3	47.0	47.8	..	Urban Population, % of total
103.6	83.8	105.5	95.4	95.8	106.1	126.3	100.0	125.9	120.9	..	Food Prod. per capita (1987=100)
45.6	..	..	..	..	..	..	..	..	..	..	Labor Force, Agriculture (%)
18.4	18.7	18.9	19.2	19.5	19.7	19.9	20.1	20.3	20.5	..	Labor Force, Female (%)
78.0	83.0	85.0	86.0	79.0	78.0	74.0	71.0	..	..	..	Primary Schl. Enroll. Ratio
59.0	63.0	66.0	66.0	61.0	60.0	58.0	57.0	..	..	..	Primary Schl. Enroll. Ratio, Female
25.0	26.0	28.0	29.0	33.0	34.0	36.0	27.0	..	..	..	Secondary Schl. Enroll. Ratio

MOZAMBIQUE	1969	1970	1971	1972	1973	1974	1975	1976	1977	1978	1979
CURRENT GNP PER CAPITA (US $)	..	..	..	..		..		..	..	..	..
POPULATION (thousands)	9,176	9,390	9,611	9,843	10,086	10,340	10,606	10,884	11,176	11,478	11,788
USE AND ORIGIN OF RESOURCES					*(Billions of current Mozambique Meticais)*						
Gross National Product (GNP)	..	..	..	..	..	..	..	..	..	..	..
Net Factor Income from Abroad	..	..	..	..	..	..	..	..	..	..	..
GDP at Market Prices	..	..	..	..	..	..	..	..	..	..	..
Resource Balance	..	..	..	..	..	..	..	..	..	..	..
Exports of Goods & NFServices	..	..	..	..	..	..	..	..	..	..	..
Imports of Goods & NFServices	..	..	..	..	..	..	..	..	..	..	..
Domestic Absorption	..	..	..	..	..	..	..	..	..	..	..
Private Consumption, etc.	..	..	..	..	..	..	..	..	..	..	..
General Gov't Consumption	..	..	..	..	..	..	..	..	..	..	..
Gross Domestic Investment	..	..	..	..	..	..	..	..	..	..	..
Fixed Investment	..	..	..	..	..	..	..	..	..	..	..
Indirect Taxes, net	..	..	..	..	..	..	..	..	..	..	..
GDP at factor cost	..	..	..	..	..	..	..	..	..	..	..
Agriculture	..	..	..	..	..	..	..	..	..	..	..
Industry	..	..	..	..	..	..	..	..	..	..	..
Manufacturing	..	..	..	..	..	..	..	..	..	..	..
Services, etc.	..	..	..	..	..	..	..	..	..	..	..
Gross Domestic Saving	..	..	..	..	..	..	..	..	..	..	..
Gross National Saving	..	..	..	..	..	..	..	..	..	..	..
Gross National Product					*(Millions of 1987 Mozambique Meticais)*						
	..	..	..	..	..	..	..	..	..	..	..
GDP at Market Prices	..	..	..	..	..	..	..	..	..	..	..
Resource Balance	..	..	..	..	..	..	..	..	..	..	..
Exports of Goods & NFServices	..	..	..	..	..	..	..	..	..	..	..
Imports of Goods & NFServices	..	..	..	..	..	..	..	..	..	..	..
Domestic Absorption	..	..	..	..	..	..	..	..	..	..	..
Private Consumption, etc.	..	..	..	..	..	..	..	..	..	..	..
General Gov't Consumption	..	..	..	..	..	..	..	..	..	..	..
Gross Domestic Investment	..	..	..	..	..	..	..	..	..	..	..
Fixed Investment	..	..	..	..	..	..	..	..	..	..	..
GDP at factor cost	..	..	..	..	..	..	..	..	..	..	..
Agriculture	..	..	..	..	..	..	..	..	..	..	..
Industry	..	..	..	..	..	..	..	..	..	..	..
Manufacturing	..	..	..	..	..	..	..	..	..	..	..
Services, etc.	..	..	..	..	..	..	..	..	..	..	..
Memo Items:											
Capacity to Import	..	..	..	..	..	..	..	..	..	..	..
Terms of Trade Adjustment	..	..	..	..	..	..	..	..	..	..	..
Gross Domestic Income	..	..	..	..	..	..	..	..	..	..	..
Gross National Income	..	..	..	..	..	..	..	..	..	..	..
DOMESTIC PRICES/DEFLATORS					*(Index 1987 = 100)*						
Overall (GDP)	..	..	..	..	..	..	..	..	..	..	..
Domestic Absorption	..	..	..	..	..	..	..	..	..	..	..
Agriculture	..	..	..	..	..	..	..	..	..	..	..
Industry	..	..	..	..	..	..	..	..	..	..	..
Manufacturing	..	..	..	..	..	..	..	..	..	..	..
Consumer Price Index	..	..	..	..	..	..	..	..	..	..	..
MANUFACTURING ACTIVITY											
Employment (1987=100)	66.2	76.6	78.7	85.0	89.1	..	..	..	..	..	..
Real Earnings per Empl. (1987=100)	..	..	..	..	..	..	..	..	..	..	..
Real Output per Empl. (1987=100)	..	..	..	..	..	..	..	..	..	..	..
Earnings as % of Value Added	30.4	28.8	40.9	41.2	41.4	..	..	..	..	..	..
MONETARY HOLDINGS					*(Millions of current Mozambique Meticais)*						
Money Supply, Broadly Defined	..	..	..	..	..	..	..	..	..	..	..
Money	..	..	..	..	..	..	..	..	..	..	..
Currency Outside Banks	..	..	..	..	..	..	..	..	..	..	..
Demand Deposits	..	..	..	..	..	..	..	..	..	..	..
Quasi-Money	..	..	..	..	..	..	..	..	..	..	..
GOVERNMENT DEFICIT (-) OR SURPLUS	..	..	..	..	*(Millions of current Mozambique Meticais)*			..	..	..	..
Current Revenue	..	..	..	..	..	..	..	..	..	..	..
Current Expenditure	..	..	..	..	..	..	..	..	..	..	..
Current Budget Balance	..	..	..	..	..	..	..	..	..	..	..
Capital Receipts	..	..	..	..	..	..	..	..	..	..	..
Capital Payments	..	..	..	..	..	..	..	..	..	..	..

1980	1981	1982	1983	1984	1985	1986	1987	1988	1989 estimate	NOTES	MOZAMBIQUE
..	..	190	160	180	180	220	150	100	80	..	**CURRENT GNP PER CAPITA (US $)**
12,103	12,425	12,753	13,090	13,435	13,791	14,160	14,544	14,943	15,357	..	**POPULATION (thousands)**
			(Billions of current Mozambique Meticais)								**USE AND ORIGIN OF RESOURCES**
77.18	79.19	89.24	87.06	104.58	141.45	160.09	367.80	530.47	826.78	..	Gross National Product (GNP)
-1.02	-1.51	-3.46	-4.34	-3.12	-5.15	-6.81	-60.30	-129.43	-128.12	..	Net Factor Income from Abroad
78.20	80.70	92.70	91.40	107.70	146.60	166.90	428.10	659.90	954.90	..	GDP at Market Prices
-14.41	-16.39	-20.95	-18.97	-18.11	-14.62	-18.08	-149.95	-327.70	-504.30	..	Resource Balance
12.92	13.96	12.70	8.93	6.65	6.17	5.92	50.45	99.40	149.60	..	Exports of Goods & NFServices
27.33	30.35	33.65	27.90	24.76	20.79	24.00	200.40	427.10	653.90	..	Imports of Goods & NFServices
92.61	97.09	113.65	110.37	125.81	161.22	184.98	578.05	987.60	1,459.20	..	Domestic Absorption
59.60	59.99	73.85	75.17	86.38	118.22	126.38	385.65	627.50	902.60	..	Private Consumption, etc.
18.24	20.70	21.90	26.10	28.00	32.90	42.40	90.60	145.90	238.00	..	General Gov't Consumption
14.77	16.40	17.90	9.10	11.43	10.10	16.20	101.80	214.20	318.60	..	Gross Domestic Investment
14.77	16.40	17.90	9.10	114.30	10.10	16.20	101.80	214.20	318.60	..	Fixed Investment
9.81	9.93	11.00	11.70	11.80	9.00	11.20	43.00	80.70	138.40	..	Indirect Taxes, net
68.39	70.77	81.70	79.70	95.90	137.60	155.70	385.10	579.20	816.50	..	GDP at factor cost
36.80	37.50	45.40	42.90	55.10	87.60	98.90	247.60	377.70	524.40	..	Agriculture
18.67	19.20	20.70	21.10	21.50	28.50	34.80	82.40	124.30	179.20	..	Industry
..	..	..	..	..	..	..	..	..	..	..	Manufacturing
12.92	14.07	15.60	15.70	19.30	21.50	22.00	55.10	77.20	112.90	..	Services, etc.
0.36	0.01	-3.05	-9.87	-6.68	-4.52	-1.88	-48.15	-113.50	-185.70	..	Gross Domestic Saving
-1.48	-2.54	-7.40	-15.01	-10.89	-10.75	-9.62	-108.45	-202.00	-250.51	..	Gross National Saving
			(Millions of 1987 Mozambique Meticais)								
497,350	496,989	470,569	405,560	420,199	383,325	386,679	367,800	371,950	410,284	..	Gross National Product
505,067	507,656	490,231	427,621	434,217	399,549	407,041	428,100	452,042	466,255	..	GDP at Market Prices
-92,150	-109,980	-126,831	-121,631	-123,760	-102,198	-148,021	-149,950	-160,066	-172,614	..	Resource Balance
127,807	113,760	122,663	77,159	48,472	47,498	43,526	50,450	52,656	57,661	..	Exports of Goods & NFServices
219,957	223,740	249,494	198,790	172,231	149,696	191,547	200,400	212,722	230,275	..	Imports of Goods & NFServices
597,217	617,636	617,062	549,252	557,977	501,747	555,063	578,050	612,108	638,868	..	Domestic Absorption
356,374	358,646	380,383	365,032	371,914	352,310	362,408	385,650	389,375	396,249	..	Private Consumption, etc.
121,511	134,567	117,913	125,241	116,581	91,266	104,590	90,600	99,926	116,581	..	General Gov't Consumption
119,332	124,422	118,767	58,979	69,483	58,171	88,065	101,800	122,806	126,038	..	Gross Domestic Investment
118,393	123,443	117,831	58,515	68,935	57,713	87,372	101,800	121,839	125,046	..	Fixed Investment
454,030	456,032	440,095	384,291	390,371	359,422	366,198	385,100	406,695	419,458	..	GDP at factor cost
252,401	252,401	252,401	211,935	231,139	233,197	234,568	247,600	265,433	270,234	..	Agriculture
127,345	128,026	114,406	103,511	89,210	74,909	81,719	82,400	86,486	91,253	..	Industry
..	..	..	..	..	..	..	..	..	..	..	Manufacturing
75,318	76,495	74,141	68,846	70,023	51,317	49,910	55,100	54,776	57,972	..	Services, etc.
											Memo Items:
103,983	102,913	94,163	63,627	46,258	44,426	47,248	50,450	49,507	52,683	..	Capacity to Import
-23,824	-10,847	-28,500	-13,532	-2,214	-3,072	3,723	0	-3,149	-4,979	..	Terms of Trade Adjustment
481,243	496,809	461,731	414,089	432,003	396,477	410,764	428,100	448,893	461,276	..	Gross Domestic Income
473,526	486,142	442,069	392,029	417,985	380,253	390,402	367,800	368,801	405,305	..	Gross National Income
			(Index 1987 = 100)								**DOMESTIC PRICES/DEFLATORS**
15.5	15.9	18.9	21.4	24.8	36.7	41.0	100.0	146.0	204.8	..	Overall (GDP)
15.5	15.7	18.4	20.1	22.5	32.1	33.3	100.0	161.3	228.4	..	Domestic Absorption
14.6	14.9	18.0	20.2	23.8	37.6	42.2	100.0	142.3	194.1	..	Agriculture
14.7	15.0	18.1	20.4	24.1	38.0	42.6	100.0	143.7	196.4	..	Industry
..	..	..	..	..	..	..	..	..	..	..	Manufacturing
..	..	..	..	..	..	..	..	..	..	..	Consumer Price Index
											MANUFACTURING ACTIVITY
..	..	..	..	..	..	56.0	100.0	104.2	..	..	Employment (1987 = 100)
..	..	..	..	..	..	..	..	..	..	..	Real Earnings per Empl. (1987 = 100)
..	..	..	..	..	..	134.0	100.0	..	..	..	Real Output per Empl. (1987 = 100)
..	..	..	..	..	..	..	..	..	..	..	Earnings as % of Value Added
			(Millions of current Mozambique Meticais)								**MONETARY HOLDINGS**
..	..	..	..	..	..	..	..	..	..	..	Money Supply, Broadly Defined
..	..	..	..	..	..	..	..	..	..	..	Money
..	..	..	..	..	..	..	..	..	..	..	Currency Outside Banks
..	..	..	..	..	..	..	..	..	..	..	Demand Deposits
..	..	..	..	..	..	..	..	..	..	..	Quasi-Money
			(Millions of current Mozambique Meticais)								**GOVERNMENT DEFICIT (-) OR SURPLUS**
..	..	..	..	..	..	..	..	..	..	..	Current Revenue
..	..	..	..	..	..	..	..	..	..	..	Current Expenditure
..	..	..	..	..	..	..	..	..	..	..	Current Budget Balance
..	..	..	..	..	..	..	..	..	..	..	Capital Receipts
..	..	..	..	..	..	..	..	..	..	..	Capital Payments

MOZAMBIQUE	1969	1970	1971	1972	1973	1974	1975	1976	1977	1978	1979
FOREIGN TRADE (CUSTOMS BASIS)					*(Millions of current US dollars)*						
Value of Exports, fob	142	157	160	175	227	296	202	150	149	163	254
Nonfuel Primary Products	..	..	..	..	..	..	..	..	..	..	..
Fuels	..	..	..	..	..	..	..	..	..	..	..
Manufactures	..	..	..	..	..	..	..	..	..	..	..
Value of Imports, cif	260	323	335	327	465	464	417	300	328	521	571
Nonfuel Primary Products	..	..	..	..	..	..	..	..	..	..	..
Fuels	..	..	..	..	..	..	..	..	..	..	..
Manufactures	..	..	..	..	..	..	..	..	..	..	..
					(Index 1987 = 100)						
Terms of Trade	..	..	..	..	..	..	..	..	..	..	..
Export Prices, fob	..	..	..	..	..	..	..	..	..	..	..
Import Prices, cif	..	..	..	..	..	..	..	..	..	..	..
BALANCE OF PAYMENTS					*(Millions of current US dollars)*						
Exports of Goods & Services	..	..	..	..	..	..	..	..	..	..	..
Merchandise, fob	..	..	..	..	..	..	..	..	..	..	..
Nonfactor Services	..	..	..	..	..	..	..	..	..	..	..
Factor Services	..	..	..	..	..	..	..	..	..	..	..
Imports of Goods & Services	..	..	..	..	..	..	..	..	..	..	..
Merchandise, fob	..	..	..	..	..	..	..	..	..	..	..
Nonfactor Services	..	..	..	..	..	..	..	..	..	..	..
Factor Services	..	..	..	..	..	..	..	..	..	..	..
Long-Term Interest	..	..	..	..	..	..	..	..	..	..	..
Private Current Transfers, net	..	..	..	..	..	..	..	..	..	..	..
Workers' Remittances	..	..	..	..	..	..	..	..	..	..	..
Curr. A/C Bal before Off. Transf.	..	..	..	..	..	..	..	..	..	..	..
Net Official Transfers	..	..	..	..	..	..	..	..	..	..	..
Curr. A/C Bal after Off. Transf.	..	..	..	..	..	..	..	..	..	..	..
Long-Term Capital, net	..	..	..	..	..	..	..	..	..	..	..
Direct Investment	..	..	..	..	..	..	..	..	..	..	..
Long-Term Loans	..	..	..	..	..	..	..	..	..	..	..
Disbursements	..	..	..	..	..	..	..	..	..	..	..
Repayments	..	..	..	..	..	..	..	..	..	..	..
Other Long-Term Capital	..	..	..	..	..	..	..	..	..	..	..
Other Capital, net	..	..	..	..	..	..	..	..	..	..	..
Change in Reserves	..	..	..	..	..	..	..	..	..	..	..
Memo Item:					*(Mozambique Meticais per US dollar)*						
Conversion Factor (Annual Avg)	28.750	28.750	28.320	27.010	24.670	25.410	25.550	30.220	32.930	33.000	32.560
				(Millions of US dollars), outstanding at end of year							
EXTERNAL DEBT (Total)	..	..	..	..	..	..	..	..	..	..	..
Long-Term Debt (by debtor)	..	..	..	..	..	..	..	..	..	..	..
Central Bank, incl. IMF credit	..	..	..	..	..	..	..	..	..	..	..
Central Government	..	..	..	..	..	..	..	..	..	..	..
Rest of General Government	..	..	..	..	..	..	..	..	..	..	..
Non-financial Public Enterprises	..	..	..	..	..	..	..	..	..	..	..
Priv. Sector, incl non-guaranteed	..	..	..	..	..	..	..	..	..	..	..
Short-Term Debt	..	..	..	..	..	..	..	..	..	..	..
Memo Items:					*(Millions of US dollars)*						
Int'l Reserves Excluding Gold	..	..	..	..	..	..	..	..	..	..	..
Gold Holdings (at market price)	..	..	..	..	..	..	..	..	..	..	..
SOCIAL INDICATORS											
Total Fertility Rate	6.7	6.6	6.6	6.6	6.6	6.6	6.5	6.5	6.5	6.5	6.4
Infant Mortality Rate	171.5	169.8	168.0	166.7	165.3	164.0	162.7	161.3	160.0	158.6	157.2
Life Expectancy at Birth	39.9	40.5	41.1	41.5	41.9	42.3	42.7	43.1	43.5	43.9	44.3
Urban Population, % of total	5.5	5.7	6.3	6.9	7.4	8.0	8.6	9.5	10.4	11.3	12.2
Food Prod. per capita (1987=100)	149.8	149.2	149.7	150.6	153.0	147.9	131.5	130.4	126.5	121.7	120.2
Labor Force, Agriculture (%)	86.6	86.4	86.2	86.0	85.8	85.6	85.5	85.2	85.0	84.8	84.6
Labor Force, Female (%)	50.2	50.2	50.1	50.1	50.1	50.1	50.0	50.0	49.9	49.9	49.9
Primary Schl. Enroll. Ratio	..	47.0	..	..	..	..	..	87.0	100.0	102.0	104.0
Primary Schl. Enroll. Ratio, Female	..	..	..	..	..	..	..	70.0	82.0	84.0	87.0
Secondary Schl. Enroll. Ratio	..	5.0	..	..	..	..	..	3.0	4.0	5.0	6.0

1980	1981	1982	1983	1984	1985	1986	1987	1988	1989 estimate	NOTES	MOZAMBIQUE
				(Millions of current US dollars)							**FOREIGN TRADE (CUSTOMS BASIS)**
281	281	229	132	96	77	79	97	105	..	..	Value of Exports, fob
191	201	149	96	78	70	71	86	94	..	..	Nonfuel Primary Products
67	62	42	22	6	4	4	3	3	..	..	Fuels
22	18	38	14	13	3	4	8	8	..	..	Manufactures
800	801	836	636	540	424	543	625	706	..	..	Value of Imports, cif
212	237	195	209	194	183	213	222	209	..	..	Nonfuel Primary Products
220	172	221	106	109	75	54	72	46	..	..	Fuels
368	392	420	321	237	166	276	331	451	..	..	Manufactures
				(Index 1987 = 100)							
..	..	..	..	..	..	..	..	..	..	..	Terms of Trade
..	..	..	..	..	..	..	..	..	..	..	Export Prices, fob
..	..	..	..	..	..	..	..	..	..	..	Import Prices, cif
				(Millions of current US dollars)							**BALANCE OF PAYMENTS**
452	459	401	297	214	184	192	234	260	272	f	Exports of Goods & Services
281	281	229	132	96	77	79	97	104	105	..	Merchandise, fob
118	114	108	91	61	66	63	79	85	95	..	Nonfactor Services
53	65	64	75	57	41	50	58	72	71	..	Factor Services
850	894	953	782	664	599	747	927	995	1,149	f	Imports of Goods & Services
720	721	752	573	486	381	488	592	694	761	..	Merchandise, fob
124	138	140	121	98	100	104	107	114	115	..	Nonfactor Services
6	36	60	88	81	117	155	228	187	274	..	Factor Services
0	0	0	0	0	20	31	15	24	34	..	Long-Term Interest
-25	-29	-24	-20	-26	-25	-23	0	78	85	..	Private Current Transfers, net
..	..	..	..	..	..	..	..	..	..	..	Workers' Remittances
-423	-465	-576	-505	-476	-440	-578	-693	-657	-793	..	Curr. A/C Bal before Off. Transf.
56	57	79	90	168	139	219	304	377	388	..	Net Official Transfers
-367	-407	-497	-415	-308	-301	-359	-389	-280	-405	..	Curr. A/C Bal after Off. Transf.
364	409	395	43	140	143	-52	-83	-131	-72	f	Long-Term Capital, net
0	0	0	0	0	0	0	0	0	..	..	Direct Investment
0	0	0	82	1,145	364	410	343	143	174	..	Long-Term Loans
0	0	0	82	1,145	395	477	359	157	191	..	Disbursements
0	0	0	0	0	31	67	16	14	17	..	Repayments
364	409	395	-39	-1,005	-221	-461	-426	-273	-246	..	Other Long-Term Capital
-30	-69	-39	357	191	137	434	456	385	461	f	Other Capital, net
32	67	141	15	-23	21	-24	16	25	16	..	Change in Reserves
				(Mozambique Meticais per US dollar)							**Memo Item:**
32.400	35.350	37.700	40.180	42.440	43.180	40.430	290.730	524.650	744.920	..	Conversion Factor (Annual Avg)
				(Millions of US dollars), outstanding at end of year							
..	..	..	82	1,365	2,863	3,525	4,261	4,418	4,737	..	**EXTERNAL DEBT (Total)**
..	..	..	82	1,285	2,706	3,232	3,928	4,019	4,186	..	Long-Term Debt (by debtor)
..	..	..	0	0	19	18	59	71	82	..	Central Bank, incl. IMF credit
..	..	..	82	1,271	2,177	2,526	3,193	3,323	3,409	..	Central Government
..	..	..	..	..	..	..	..	..	..	..	Rest of General Government
..	..	..	..	14	349	481	449	386	449	..	Non-financial Public Enterprises
..	..	..	..	0	161	207	228	239	245	..	Priv. Sector, incl non-guaranteed
..	..	..	..	80	157	293	332	400	551	..	Short-Term Debt
				(Millions of US dollars)							**Memo Items:**
..	..	..	..	..	..	..	..	..	..	..	Int'l Reserves Excluding Gold
..	..	..	..	..	..	..	..	..	..	..	Gold Holdings (at market price)
											SOCIAL INDICATORS
6.4	6.3	6.3	6.3	6.3	6.3	6.3	6.3	6.3	6.4	..	Total Fertility Rate
155.8	154.4	153.0	150.6	148.2	145.8	143.4	141.0	139.3	137.5	..	Infant Mortality Rate
44.7	45.0	45.4	45.9	46.5	47.0	47.4	47.8	48.2	48.6	..	Life Expectancy at Birth
13.1	14.4	15.6	16.9	18.1	19.4	21.3	23.1	24.3	25.6	..	Urban Population, % of total
119.9	118.2	114.8	107.0	104.5	103.9	103.7	100.0	100.2	98.5	..	Food Prod. per capita (1987=100)
84.5	..	..	..	..	..	..	..	..	..	..	Labor Force, Agriculture (%)
49.8	49.6	49.3	49.1	48.9	48.7	48.4	48.1	47.9	47.7	..	Labor Force, Female (%)
75.0	94.0	92.0	84.0	..	86.0	80.0	68.0	..	..	..	Primary Schl. Enroll. Ratio
84.0	..	79.0	72.0	..	75.0	74.0	59.0	..	..	..	Primary Schl. Enroll. Ratio, Female
5.0	5.0	5.0	6.0	..	7.0	8.8	5.0			..	Secondary Schl. Enroll. Ratio

NEPAL	1969	1970	1971	1972	1973	1974	1975	1976	1977	1978	1979
CURRENT GNP PER CAPITA (US $)	80	80	80	80	80	100	110	120	120	120	130
POPULATION (thousands)	11,115	11,350	11,608	11,890	12,195	12,513	12,841	13,177	13,526	13,888	14,260
USE AND ORIGIN OF RESOURCES					*(Millions of current Nepalese Rupees)*						
Gross National Product (GNP)	7,985	8,768	8,938	10,369	9,969	12,808	16,838	17,671	17,599	20,023	22,605
Net Factor Income from Abroad	0	0	0	0	0	0	267	277	319	291	390
GDP at Market Prices	7,985	8,768	8,938	10,369	9,969	12,808	16,571	17,394	17,280	19,732	22,215
Resource Balance	-256	-298	-333	-234	-375	-653	-740	-592	-437	-967	-929
Exports of Goods & NFServices	560	430	483	587	659	698	1,475	1,874	2,037	2,086	2,618
Imports of Goods & NFServices	816	728	816	821	1,034	1,351	2,215	2,466	2,474	3,053	3,547
Domestic Absorption	8,241	9,066	9,271	10,603	10,344	13,461	17,311	17,986	17,717	20,699	23,144
Private Consumption, etc.	7,854	8,543	8,578	9,843	9,429	12,339	13,652	14,060	13,688	15,621	17,741
General Gov't Consumption	..	..	..	..	..	..	1,257	1,294	1,260	1,471	1,889
Gross Domestic Investment	387	523	693	760	915	1,122	2,402	2,632	2,769	3,607	3,514
Fixed Investment	..	..	..	..	..	..	2,223	2,443	2,581	3,294	3,263
Indirect Taxes, net	161	55	163	239	204	383	635	805	1,025	1,306	1,436
GDP at factor cost	7,824	8,713	8,775	10,130	9,765	12,425	15,936	16,589	16,255	18,426	20,779
Agriculture	5,304	5,863	5,974	7,035	6,513	8,763	11,435	11,495	10,389	11,616	13,365
Industry	827	1,005	817	943	956	1,115	1,303	1,469	1,821	2,199	2,489
Manufacturing	307	323	336	409	399	526	664	690	736	794	848
Services, etc.	1,693	1,845	1,984	2,152	2,296	2,547	3,198	3,625	4,045	4,611	4,925
Gross Domestic Saving	131	225	360	526	540	469	1,662	2,040	2,332	2,640	2,585
Gross National Saving	..	225	360	526	540	469	2,109	2,558	2,862	3,131	3,265
					(Millions of 1975 Nepalese Rupees)						
Gross National Product	14,768	15,148	14,967	15,434	15,360	16,333	16,838	17,576	18,151	18,881	19,382
GDP at Market Prices	14,768	15,148	14,967	15,434	15,360	16,333	16,571	17,300	17,822	18,607	19,048
Resource Balance	..	..	..	..	..	..	..	..	..	..	..
Exports of Goods & NFServices	..	..	..	..	..	..	..	..	..	..	..
Imports of Goods & NFServices	..	..	..	..	..	..	..	..	..	..	..
Domestic Absorption	..	..	..	..	..	..	..	..	..	..	..
Private Consumption, etc.	..	..	..	..	..	..	..	..	..	..	..
General Gov't Consumption	..	..	..	..	..	..	..	..	..	..	..
Gross Domestic Investment	..	..	..	..	..	..	..	..	..	..	..
Fixed Investment	..	..	..	..	..	..	..	..	..	..	..
GDP at factor cost	14,470	15,053	14,694	15,078	15,046	15,845	15,936	16,500	16,765	17,375	17,816
Agriculture	10,231	10,585	10,660	10,738	10,647	11,246	11,435	11,498	11,017	11,013	11,346
Industry	..	..	..	..	..	..	..	..	..	..	..
Manufacturing	..	..	..	..	..	..	..	..	..	..	..
Services, etc.	..	..	..	..	..	..	..	..	..	..	..
Memo Items:											
Capacity to Import	..	..	..	..	..	..	1,474	1,527	1,397	1,407	1,457
Terms of Trade Adjustment	..	..	..	..	..	..	0	-327	-368	-260	-390
Gross Domestic Income	..	..	..	..	..	..	16,571	16,973	17,454	18,347	18,658
Gross National Income	..	..	..	..	..	..	16,838	17,249	17,783	18,621	18,992
DOMESTIC PRICES/DEFLATORS					*(Index 1975 = 100)*						
Overall (GDP)	54.1	57.9	59.7	67.2	64.9	78.4	100.0	100.5	97.0	106.0	116.6
Domestic Absorption	..	..	..	..	..	..	..	..	..	..	..
Agriculture	51.8	55.4	56.0	65.5	61.2	77.9	100.0	100.0	94.3	105.5	117.8
Industry	..	..	..	..	..	..	..	..	..	..	..
Manufacturing	..	..	..	..	..	..	..	..	..	..	..
Consumer Price Index	20.5	23.6	23.2	25.1	28.0	33.5	36.1	34.9	38.4	41.2	42.7
MANUFACTURING ACTIVITY											
Employment (1987=100)	..	..	..	..	..	..	..	..	31.3	..	..
Real Earnings per Empl. (1987=100)	..	..	..	..	..	..	..	..	93.9	..	..
Real Output per Empl. (1987=100)	..	..	..	..	..	..	..	..	..	..	..
Earnings as % of Value Added	..	..	..	..	..	..	..	..	24.8	..	..
MONETARY HOLDINGS					*(Millions of current Nepalese Rupees)*						
Money Supply, Broadly Defined	922	931	1,108	1,293	1,663	1,948	2,180	2,811	3,401	4,070	4,712
Money	739	699	784	842	1,090	1,290	1,333	1,636	1,932	2,200	2,534
Currency Outside Banks	487	525	549	596	747	882	882	996	1,212	1,379	1,627
Demand Deposits	252	174	235	245	343	408	451	640	720	821	907
Quasi-Money	183	232	324	451	573	658	847	1,175	1,468	1,870	2,178
					(Millions of current Nepalese Rupees)						
GOVERNMENT DEFICIT (-) OR SURPLUS	..	..	..	-126	-223	-248	-236	-422	-576	-582	-588
Current Revenue	..	..	..	783	783	975	1,277	1,447	1,683	1,989	2,323
Current Expenditure	..	..	..	..	..	..	..	..	..	..	..
Current Budget Balance	..	..	..	..	..	..	..	..	..	..	..
Capital Receipts	..	..	..	..	..	..	..	..	..	..	..
Capital Payments	..	..	..	..	..	..	..	..	..	..	..

1980	1981	1982	1983	1984	1985	1986	1987	1988	1989 estimate	NOTES	NEPAL
140	160	160	160	170	170	160	160	180	180	..	**CURRENT GNP PER CAPITA (US $)**
14,640	15,023	15,423	15,833	16,255	16,682	17,098	17,529	17,976	18,431	..	**POPULATION (thousands)**
				(Millions of current Nepalese Rupees)							**USE AND ORIGIN OF RESOURCES**
23,845	27,894	31,603	34,458	40,015	45,078	51,137	60,766	71,088	79,128	C	Gross National Product (GNP)
494	587	615	697	625	661	709	1,169	1,575	1,714	..	Net Factor Income from Abroad
23,351	27,307	30,988	33,761	39,390	44,417	50,428	59,597	69,513	77,414	C f	GDP at Market Prices
-1,679	-1,834	-2,236	-3,741	-3,465	-3,945	-4,712	-5,585	-6,717	-9,478	..	Resource Balance
2,695	3,523	3,592	3,455	4,196	5,372	6,506	7,563	8,747	9,878	..	Exports of Goods & NFServices
4,374	5,357	5,828	7,196	7,661	9,317	11,218	13,148	15,464	19,356	..	Imports of Goods & NFServices
25,030	29,141	33,224	37,502	42,855	48,362	55,140	65,182	76,230	86,892	..	Domestic Absorption
19,195	22,411	25,272	27,458	31,860	33,807	39,408	45,724	54,897	63,192	..	Private Consumption, etc.
1,565	1,922	2,638	3,416	3,644	4,371	5,133	6,570	7,087	8,628	..	General Gov't Consumption
4,270	4,808	5,314	6,628	7,351	10,184	10,599	12,888	14,246	15,072	..	Gross Domestic Investment
3,681	4,299	5,465	6,576	6,907	9,386	9,431	11,815	12,423	12,049	..	Fixed Investment
1,465	1,841	1,951	2,117	2,386	2,861	3,364	3,888	5,182	6,166	..	Indirect Taxes, net
21,886	25,466	29,037	31,644	37,004	41,556	47,064	55,709	64,331	71,248	C f	GDP at factor cost
13,520	15,510	17,715	19,082	22,570	23,927	26,555	30,276	35,708	41,343	..	Agriculture
2,608	3,148	3,733	4,049	4,661	5,917	7,073	9,143	10,256	9,912	..	Industry
936	1,049	1,243	1,460	1,816	1,998	2,622	3,559	3,646	3,909	..	Manufacturing
5,758	6,808	7,589	8,513	9,773	11,712	13,436	16,290	18,367	19,993	..	Services, etc.
2,591	2,974	3,078	2,887	3,886	6,239	5,887	7,303	7,529	5,594	..	Gross Domestic Saving
3,429	4,041	4,155	4,125	5,130	7,571	7,360	9,672	10,685	8,760	..	Gross National Saving
				(Millions of 1975 Nepalese Rupees)							
19,000	20,592	21,335	20,717	22,615	23,978	24,994	25,808	28,412	28,879	C	Gross National Product
18,606	20,158	20,920	20,297	22,262	23,630	24,645	25,617	27,624	28,263	C f	GDP at Market Prices
..	..	..	..	..	..	..	..	..	..	..	Resource Balance
..	..	..	..	..	..	..	..	..	..	..	Exports of Goods & NFServices
..	..	..	..	..	..	..	..	..	..	..	Imports of Goods & NFServices
..	..	..	..	..	..	..	..	..	..	..	Domestic Absorption
..	..	..	..	..	..	..	..	..	..	..	Private Consumption, etc.
..	..	..	..	..	..	..	..	..	..	..	General Gov't Consumption
..	..	..	..	..	..	..	..	..	..	..	Gross Domestic Investment
..	..	..	..	..	..	..	..	..	..	..	Fixed Investment
17,439	18,799	19,603	19,024	20,914	22,104	23,003	24,064	25,569	26,012	C f	GDP at factor cost
10,803	11,936	12,483	12,348	13,547	13,849	14,559	14,556	15,889	16,882	..	Agriculture
..	..	..	..	..	..	..	..	..	..	..	Industry
..	..	..	..	..	..	..	..	..	..	..	Manufacturing
..	..	..	..	..	..	..	..	..	..	..	Services, etc.
											Memo Items:
1,132	1,447	1,405	1,364	1,513	..	..	..	..	..	..	Capacity to Import
-662	-1,036	-1,180	-921	-789	..	..	..	..	..	..	Terms of Trade Adjustment
17,944	19,122	19,740	19,376	21,473	..	..	..	..	..	..	Gross Domestic Income
18,338	19,556	20,155	19,796	21,826	..	..	..	..	..	..	Gross National Income
				(Index 1975 = 100)							**DOMESTIC PRICES/DEFLATORS**
125.5	135.5	148.1	166.3	176.9	188.0	204.6	232.6	251.6	273.9	..	Overall (GDP)
..	..	..	..	..	..	..	..	..	..	..	Domestic Absorption
125.2	129.9	141.9	154.5	166.6	172.8	182.4	208.0	224.7	244.9	..	Agriculture
..	..	..	..	..	..	..	..	..	..	..	Industry
..	..	..	..	..	..	..	..	..	..	..	Manufacturing
48.9	54.4	60.8	68.3	70.2	75.9	90.3	100.0	109.0	118.6	f	Consumer Price Index
											MANUFACTURING ACTIVITY
..	..	52.4	..	..	..	97.7	100.0	..	..	..	Employment (1987=100)
..	..	..	..	..	..	95.3	100.0	..	..	..	Real Earnings per Empl. (1987=100)
..	..	..	..	..	..	..	..	..	..	..	Real Output per Empl. (1987=100)
..	..	..	..	..	..	22.1	25.0	..	..	..	Earnings as % of Value Added
				(Millions of current Nepalese Rupees)							**MONETARY HOLDINGS**
5,526	6,580	7,987	9,594	10,841	13,014	15,543	19,024	23,219	28,540	D	Money Supply, Broadly Defined
2,864	3,205	3,705	4,366	4,942	5,616	6,951	8,682	9,826	11,720	..	Money
1,814	2,147	2,408	2,783	3,302	3,797	4,787	5,826	6,671	7,905	..	Currency Outside Banks
1,050	1,058	1,297	1,583	1,641	1,819	2,164	2,855	3,155	3,815	..	Demand Deposits
2,661	3,375	4,283	5,228	5,899	7,398	8,592	10,343	13,393	16,820	..	Quasi-Money
				(Millions of current Nepalese Rupees)							
-705	-728	-1,591	-2,954	-2,985	-3,380	-3,637	-3,902	-4,280	..	C F	**GOVERNMENT DEFICIT (-) OR SURPLUS**
2,620	3,233	3,626	3,867	4,186	4,759	5,656	7,046	9,202	..	..	Current Revenue
..	..	..	..	..	..	3,232	3,732	4,216	..	..	Current Expenditure
..	..	..	..	..	..	2,424	3,314	4,986	..	..	Current Budget Balance
..	..	..	..	..	14	25	19	14	..	..	Capital Receipts
..	..	..	..	..	..	6,085	7,236	9,280	..	..	Capital Payments

NEPAL	1969	1970	1971	1972	1973	1974	1975	1976	1977	1978	1979
FOREIGN TRADE (CUSTOMS BASIS)					*(Millions of current US dollars)*						
Value of Exports, fob	53.00	48.00	48.00	58.00	63.00	66.00	100.00	98.00	81.00	91.00	108.00
Nonfuel Primary Products	41.80	41.00	42.40	49.70	53.90	46.50	90.00	85.60	67.33	76.28	84.26
Fuels	0.00	0.00	0.00	0.00	0.00	0.00	0.00	0.10	0.02	0.00	0.00
Manufactures	11.20	7.00	5.60	8.30	9.10	19.50	10.00	12.30	13.65	14.72	23.74
Value of Imports, cif	74.00	85.40	69.70	87.70	95.70	110.00	171.00	214.00	244.00	339.00	379.00
Nonfuel Primary Products	28.80	29.30	22.90	26.70	25.60	27.25	55.00	76.56	75.92	85.65	72.58
Fuels	3.00	6.50	6.50	9.40	11.20	23.15	38.60	55.04	62.32	88.47	125.72
Manufactures	42.20	49.60	40.30	51.60	58.90	59.60	77.40	82.40	105.77	164.87	180.70
					(Index 1987 = 100)						
Terms of Trade	127.7	139.7	144.2	161.5	160.1	124.4	120.0	110.3	106.7	114.7	112.3
Export Prices, fob	37.8	37.9	41.3	48.1	60.0	73.8	74.4	71.8	74.0	85.3	102.0
Import Prices, cif	29.6	27.2	28.6	29.8	37.5	59.3	62.0	65.1	69.3	74.4	90.8
BALANCE OF PAYMENTS					*(Millions of current US dollars)*						
Exports of Goods & Services	..	71.00	81.00	97.00	106.00	114.00	149.10	170.17	162.33	177.20	223.50
Merchandise, fob	..	42.00	48.00	58.00	63.00	66.00	83.80	102.10	81.18	86.40	101.30
Nonfactor Services	..	25.00	29.00	35.00	38.00	40.00	55.10	61.35	72.22	82.70	111.80
Factor Services	..	4.00	4.00	4.00	5.00	8.00	10.20	6.72	8.93	8.10	10.40
Imports of Goods & Services	..	96.10	109.10	109.10	132.20	171.30	209.90	198.52	212.58	248.80	302.70
Merchandise, fob	..	75.00	85.00	85.00	103.00	134.00	171.00	154.11	165.70	194.50	236.30
Nonfactor Services	..	21.00	24.00	24.00	29.00	37.00	38.40	42.80	46.03	53.20	64.30
Factor Services	..	0.10	0.10	0.10	0.20	0.30	0.50	1.62	0.85	1.10	2.10
Long-Term Interest	..	0.10	0.10	0.10	0.20	0.30	0.40	0.60	0.80	1.10	1.50
Private Current Transfers, net	..	0.00	0.00	0.00	0.00	0.00	16.40	19.26	16.85	16.50	24.20
Workers' Remittances	..	..	..	..	..	..	..	0.00	0.00	0.00	0.00
Curr. A/C Bal before Off. Transf.	..	-25.10	-28.10	-12.10	-26.20	-57.30	-44.40	-9.09	-33.41	-55.10	-55.00
Net Official Transfers	..	24.00	27.00	24.00	17.00	32.00	33.00	27.62	31.83	31.10	48.20
Curr. A/C Bal after Off. Transf.	..	-1.10	-1.10	11.90	-9.20	-25.30	-11.40	18.54	-1.58	-24.00	-6.80
Long-Term Capital, net	..	-2.00	5.00	4.00	8.00	8.00	8.40	7.14	26.79	20.40	26.80
Direct Investment	..	..	..	..	..	..	..	0.00	0.00	0.00	0.00
Long-Term Loans	..	-1.60	5.20	3.70	7.80	7.10	8.00	10.80	26.80	31.50	31.10
Disbursements	..	0.60	5.30	3.90	8.10	7.60	9.20	11.90	28.80	33.10	32.90
Repayments	..	2.20	0.10	0.20	0.30	0.50	1.20	1.10	2.00	1.60	1.80
Other Long-Term Capital	..	-0.40	-0.20	0.30	0.20	0.90	0.40	-3.66	-0.01	-11.10	-4.30
Other Capital, net	..	16.26	2.10	-14.91	9.31	19.34	-18.00	2.91	-5.63	-2.50	-42.30
Change in Reserves	..	-13.16	-6.00	-0.99	-8.11	-2.04	21.00	-28.59	-19.58	6.10	22.30
Memo Item:					*(Nepalese Rupees per US dollar)*						
Conversion Factor (Annual Avg)	10.130	10.130	10.130	10.130	10.280	10.560	10.560	11.970	12.500	12.360	12.000
					(Millions of US dollars), outstanding at end of year						
EXTERNAL DEBT (Total)	..	2.8	8.3	11.6	19.5	27.1	33.7	49.5	100.5	115.3	146.3
Long-Term Debt (by debtor)	..	2.8	8.3	11.6	19.5	27.1	33.7	49.5	77.5	99.3	134.3
Central Bank, incl. IMF credit	..	0.0	0.0	0.0	0.0	0.0	0.0	5.2	7.3	19.9	24.4
Central Government	..	1.1	6.3	9.6	15.7	22.3	27.6	37.4	63.5	74.3	105.1
Rest of General Government	..	..	..	..	..	..	..	..	..	..	..
Non-financial Public Enterprises	..	0.9	0.9	0.8	0.8	0.8	0.7	0.6	0.0	0.0	0.0
Priv. Sector, incl non-guaranteed	..	0.8	1.1	1.2	3.0	4.0	5.4	6.3	6.7	5.1	4.8
Short-Term Debt	..	0.0	0.0	0.0	0.0	0.0	0.0	0.0	23.0	16.0	12.0
Memo Items:					*(Millions of US dollars)*						
Int'l Reserves Excluding Gold	75.5	88.7	96.1	98.4	117.5	121.3	95.7	127.5	139.5	127.4	165.7
Gold Holdings (at market price)	8.2	5.5	6.2	8.8	14.6	24.3	18.3	17.5	21.9	24.8	41.3
SOCIAL INDICATORS											
Total Fertility Rate	6.3	6.4	6.5	6.5	6.5	6.5	6.5	6.5	6.5	6.5	6.4
Infant Mortality Rate	159.6	157.4	155.2	153.0	151.8	150.6	149.4	148.2	147.0	145.4	143.8
Life Expectancy at Birth	41.9	42.4	42.8	43.3	43.8	44.3	44.8	45.3	45.8	46.3	46.8
Urban Population, % of total	3.8	3.9	4.1	4.3	4.4	4.6	4.8	5.1	5.3	5.6	5.8
Food Prod. per capita (1987=100)	109.1	110.6	106.7	102.6	109.5	109.0	108.7	105.8	99.2	100.0	92.2
Labor Force, Agriculture (%)	93.7	93.6	93.6	93.5	93.4	93.4	93.3	93.2	93.2	93.1	93.0
Labor Force, Female (%)	35.1	35.1	35.0	35.0	35.0	34.9	34.9	34.9	34.9	34.9	34.9
Primary Schl. Enroll. Ratio	..	26.0	..	..	..	..	51.0	59.0	69.0	77.0	88.0
Primary Schl. Enroll. Ratio, Female	..	8.0	..	..	..	..	16.0	24.0	32.0	38.0	49.0
Secondary Schl. Enroll. Ratio	..	10.0	..	..	..	..	13.0	12.0	14.0	16.0	19.0

1980	1981	1982	1983	1984	1985	1986	1987	1988	1989 estimate	NOTES	NEPAL
											FOREIGN TRADE (CUSTOMS BASIS)
					(Millions of current US dollars)						
109.30	134.00	115.00	94.00	128.20	159.70	141.80	150.80	193.00	..	C f	Value of Exports, fob
76.00	100.25	92.15	53.39	51.35	57.86	43.71	38.91	58.00	..	..	Nonfuel Primary Products
0.00	0.00	0.10	4.86	7.30	7.98	2.60	3.15	6.00	..	..	Fuels
33.30	33.75	22.75	35.75	69.56	93.86	95.48	108.74	129.00	..	..	Manufactures
342.00	369.00	395.00	446.60	416.00	453.10	459.30	569.23	688.00	..	C f	Value of Imports, cif
56.98	62.78	67.78	84.59	71.56	60.69	53.48	75.07	85.98	..	..	Nonfuel Primary Products
152.64	161.01	169.01	49.12	52.78	54.22	36.08	46.71	56.02	..	..	Fuels
132.39	145.21	158.22	312.89	291.65	338.19	369.75	447.44	546.00	..	..	Manufactures
					(Index 1987 = 100)						
80.4	82.0	87.2	97.5	99.7	104.8	106.8	100.0	101.7	..	..	Terms of Trade
93.7	95.8	94.9	87.7	88.9	89.1	94.9	100.0	108.3	..	..	Export Prices, fob
116.5	116.8	108.7	90.0	89.1	85.1	88.9	100.0	106.5	..	..	Import Prices, cif
					(Millions of current US dollars)						**BALANCE OF PAYMENTS**
239.40	306.90	292.60	264.10	280.50	306.80	335.20	355.50	405.40	411.30	C f	Exports of Goods & Services
96.10	134.40	116.00	81.90	111.90	154.20	158.00	142.80	188.50	170.30	..	Merchandise, fob
127.40	159.20	161.50	167.30	162.50	147.40	174.00	208.00	208.00	221.40	..	Nonfactor Services
15.90	13.30	15.10	14.90	6.10	5.20	3.20	4.70	8.90	19.60	..	Factor Services
367.90	449.70	471.20	542.10	526.10	527.60	575.40	621.60	705.10	773.00	C f	Imports of Goods & Services
283.30	352.60	381.40	455.00	428.00	414.90	454.90	494.00	560.40	621.60	..	Merchandise, fob
81.30	93.80	87.10	85.40	95.10	107.50	117.20	122.00	139.40	145.70	..	Nonfactor Services
3.30	3.30	2.70	1.70	3.00	5.20	3.30	5.60	5.30	5.70	..	Factor Services
1.90	2.40	3.10	4.20	5.30	7.60	11.40	13.90	18.60	24.60	..	Long-Term Interest
28.70	38.90	34.90	37.20	37.60	36.80	36.00	55.00	67.90	53.40	..	Private Current Transfers, net
0.00	0.00	0.00	0.00	0.00	0.00	0.00	0.00	0.00	..	..	Workers' Remittances
-99.80	-103.90	-143.70	-240.80	-208.00	-184.00	-204.20	-211.10	-231.80	-308.30	..	Curr. A/C Bal before Off. Transf.
70.30	79.30	94.70	99.90	98.10	79.90	77.50	68.40	65.00	53.90	..	Net Official Transfers
-29.50	-24.60	-49.00	-140.90	-109.90	-104.10	-126.70	-142.70	-166.80	-254.40	..	Curr. A/C Bal after Off. Transf.
34.30	50.90	59.90	59.10	79.30	73.00	96.30	108.60	157.90	237.10	C f	Long-Term Capital, net
0.00	0.00	0.00	0.00	0.00	0.00	0.00	0.00	0.00	..	..	Direct Investment
48.10	64.30	66.40	68.10	88.00	96.20	128.00	169.80	188.00	212.70	..	Long-Term Loans
50.20	66.50	69.00	71.90	92.10	102.10	142.30	185.60	205.80	241.40	..	Disbursements
2.10	2.20	2.60	3.80	4.10	5.90	14.30	15.80	17.80	28.70	..	Repayments
-13.80	-13.40	-6.50	-9.00	-8.70	-23.20	-31.70	-61.20	-30.10	24.40	..	Other Long-Term Capital
-0.20	-39.30	42.10	37.60	-7.80	-16.70	54.20	49.00	118.10	0.20	C f	Other Capital, net
-4.60	13.00	-53.00	44.20	38.40	47.80	-23.80	-14.90	-109.20	17.10	..	Change in Reserves
											Memo Item:
					(Nepalese Rupees per US dollar)						
12.000	12.000	12.940	13.800	15.260	17.780	19.800	21.600	22.050	25.320	..	Conversion Factor (Annual Avg)
				(Millions of US dollars), outstanding at end of year							
204.5	278.5	352.9	452.2	470.0	589.6	740.6	980.3	1,162.9	1,352.7	..	**EXTERNAL DEBT** (Total)
197.5	256.5	313.9	372.2	446.0	566.6	720.1	961.6	1,139.9	1,335.2	..	Long-Term Debt (by debtor)
41.6	37.8	30.5	23.4	15.5	21.8	23.5	43.0	52.7	52.4	..	Central Bank, incl. IMF credit
151.2	214.2	278.6	341.9	412.7	521.4	659.5	840.7	961.7	1,164.7	..	Central Government
..	..	..	..	..	..	..	..	..	..	..	Rest of General Government
0.0	0.0	0.5	2.8	13.9	19.6	26.5	67.3	114.9	108.0	..	Non-financial Public Enterprises
4.7	4.5	4.3	4.1	3.9	3.8	10.6	10.6	10.6	10.1	..	Priv. Sector, incl non-guaranteed
7.0	22.0	39.0	80.0	24.0	23.0	20.5	18.7	23.0	17.5	..	Short-Term Debt
					(Millions of US dollars)						**Memo Items:**
177.8	174.0	221.7	170.9	124.6	68.6	101.3	125.1	241.1	229.4	..	Int'l Reserves Excluding Gold
98.9	64.5	48.0	62.9	56.4	48.1	52.5	67.7	66.3	57.0	..	Gold Holdings (at market price)
											SOCIAL INDICATORS
6.4	6.3	6.3	6.2	6.1	6.0	5.9	5.9	5.8	5.7	..	Total Fertility Rate
142.2	140.6	139.0	136.8	134.6	132.4	130.2	128.0	126.3	124.6	..	Infant Mortality Rate
47.3	47.8	48.3	48.8	49.3	49.9	50.4	50.9	51.2	51.5	..	Life Expectancy at Birth
6.1	6.4	6.7	7.1	7.4	7.7	8.1	8.5	8.8	9.2	..	Urban Population, % of total
97.5	98.5	90.4	102.7	100.5	100.0	92.5	100.0	107.8	101.8	..	Food Prod. per capita (1987=100)
93.0	..	..	..	..	..	..	..	..	..	..	Labor Force, Agriculture (%)
34.9	34.8	34.7	34.6	34.4	34.3	34.2	34.0	33.8	33.7	..	Labor Force, Female (%)
..	..	71.0	77.0	81.0	82.0	..	..	..	..	..	Primary Schl. Enroll. Ratio
..	..	41.0	45.0	49.0	..	..	..	..	..	..	Primary Schl. Enroll. Ratio, Female
22.0	..	21.0	23.0	25.0	26.0	..	..	..	..	..	Secondary Schl. Enroll. Ratio

NETHERLANDS, THE	1969	1970	1971	1972	1973	1974	1975	1976	1977	1978	1979
CURRENT GNP PER CAPITA (US $)	2,320	2,500	2,830	3,210	4,020	5,210	6,060	6,850	7,670	8,780	10,410
POPULATION (thousands)	12,878	13,039	13,195	13,329	13,439	13,545	13,666	13,774	13,856	13,942	14,038

USE AND ORIGIN OF RESOURCES

(Billions of current Netherlands Guilders)

	1969	1970	1971	1972	1973	1974	1975	1976	1977	1978	1979
Gross National Product (GNP)	108.78	120.25	136.61	155.03	177.35	201.45	219.94	252.04	275.39	296.33	315.19
Net Factor Income from Abroad	0.79	0.56	0.39	0.70	1.30	1.67	-0.02	0.12	0.49	-0.68	-0.73
GDP at Market Prices	107.99	119.69	136.22	154.33	176.05	199.78	219.96	251.92	274.90	297.01	315.92
Resource Balance	-0.27	-2.08	-0.31	4.28	5.74	5.38	7.32	8.63	3.40	0.03	-1.73
Exports of Goods & NFServices	45.86	54.06	61.92	69.40	83.44	107.75	109.68	128.54	130.78	133.33	154.90
Imports of Goods & NFServices	46.13	56.14	62.23	65.12	77.70	102.37	102.37	119.91	127.38	133.29	156.63
Domestic Absorption	108.27	121.76	136.53	150.05	170.31	194.40	212.65	243.30	271.50	296.98	317.65
Private Consumption, etc.	63.14	69.58	77.59	87.37	99.69	113.37	128.88	148.01	164.31	179.22	192.29
General Gov't Consumption	20.23	22.55	25.11	27.86	30.26	33.86	38.79	43.47	47.85	52.61	57.17
Gross Domestic Investment	24.89	29.63	33.83	34.83	40.36	47.16	44.97	51.81	59.34	65.14	68.20
Fixed Investment	28.38	31.52	36.00	38.21	42.85	45.94	48.43	51.31	60.07	64.74	66.92
Indirect Taxes, net	0.00	11.55	13.79	15.77	17.02	17.96	20.21	22.77	26.73	29.30	29.80
GDP at factor cost	107.99	108.13	122.43	138.56	159.03	181.82	199.75	229.15	248.17	267.71	286.12
Agriculture	6.63	6.61	6.98	8.02	9.10	8.29	9.75	11.29	11.41	11.77	11.33
Industry	41.23	44.65	50.43	56.96	64.37	73.09	76.96	87.97	92.61	97.71	102.76
Manufacturing	29.09	30.93	34.25	38.48	43.63	49.99	48.24	54.37	55.05	57.95	60.08
Services, etc.	60.14	68.42	78.81	89.36	102.59	118.39	133.25	152.67	170.88	187.53	201.83
Gross Domestic Saving	24.62	27.55	33.52	39.11	46.10	52.54	52.29	60.44	62.74	65.18	66.47
Gross National Saving	..	27.87	33.65	39.45	46.88	53.53	51.55	59.68	62.30	63.37	64.55

(Billions of 1987 Netherlands Guilders)

	1969	1970	1971	1972	1973	1974	1975	1976	1977	1978	1979
Gross National Product	283.53	290.14	305.16	311.44	328.56	353.57	348.63	366.31	376.17	383.77	391.68
GDP at Market Prices	281.39	288.66	304.16	309.87	325.98	350.60	348.67	366.14	375.50	384.68	392.60
Resource Balance	-6.30	-15.89	-11.03	-9.70	-7.34	7.01	7.93	7.94	1.23	-3.31	-2.09
Exports of Goods & NFServices	96.42	107.16	118.99	132.09	147.12	151.03	146.39	160.67	157.78	163.01	175.11
Imports of Goods & NFServices	102.72	123.05	130.02	141.79	154.46	144.02	138.46	152.73	156.56	166.32	177.20
Domestic Absorption	287.69	304.56	315.20	319.57	333.32	343.59	340.74	358.20	374.27	387.99	394.69
Private Consumption, etc.	161.54	170.78	177.44	183.70	193.04	203.04	208.98	220.50	229.58	238.44	245.28
General Gov't Consumption	46.72	50.55	52.03	53.10	52.89	53.99	55.94	58.08	59.95	62.34	64.15
Gross Domestic Investment	79.43	83.23	85.72	82.77	87.39	86.56	75.82	79.62	84.74	87.21	85.26
Fixed Investment	76.09	79.92	83.99	82.25	84.48	81.25	77.56	75.45	83.00	85.03	83.58
GDP at factor cost	279.76	259.29	271.98	276.00	292.36	318.86	316.31	332.63	338.52	346.17	355.37
Agriculture	8.49	8.66	9.07	9.14	10.02	11.02	10.86	10.96	11.42	12.27	12.74
Industry	96.83	101.05	107.76	112.21	119.49	126.41	122.31	127.80	128.14	128.16	128.86
Manufacturing	..	..	..	..	..	..	..	..	..	..	..
Services, etc.	177.02	179.70	187.97	188.86	196.20	212.91	215.34	227.26	235.87	244.23	251.01

Memo Items:

	1969	1970	1971	1972	1973	1974	1975	1976	1977	1978	1979
Capacity to Import	102.12	118.49	129.38	151.11	165.87	151.59	148.36	163.71	160.73	166.36	175.25
Terms of Trade Adjustment	5.70	11.34	10.39	19.01	18.75	0.56	1.97	3.04	2.95	3.35	0.13
Gross Domestic Income	287.09	300.00	314.55	328.88	344.73	351.16	350.64	369.18	378.44	388.03	392.73
Gross National Income	289.22	301.48	315.55	330.45	347.31	354.13	350.60	369.36	379.12	387.12	391.81

DOMESTIC PRICES/DEFLATORS

(Index 1987 = 100)

	1969	1970	1971	1972	1973	1974	1975	1976	1977	1978	1979
Overall (GDP)	38.4	41.5	44.8	49.8	54.0	57.0	63.1	68.8	73.2	77.2	80.5
Domestic Absorption	37.6	40.0	43.3	47.0	51.1	56.6	62.4	67.9	72.5	76.5	80.5
Agriculture	78.1	76.4	76.9	87.7	90.8	75.2	89.8	103.0	99.9	96.0	88.9
Industry	42.6	44.2	46.8	50.8	53.9	57.8	62.9	68.8	72.3	76.2	79.7
Manufacturing	..	..	..	..	..	..	..	..	..	..	..
Consumer Price Index	39.0	40.4	43.5	46.8	50.6	55.5	61.1	66.7	71.0	73.9	77.0

MANUFACTURING ACTIVITY

	1969	1970	1971	1972	1973	1974	1975	1976	1977	1978	1979
Employment (1987=100)	132.0	132.0	129.9	125.9	123.8	122.9	118.6	113.6	114.2	111.3	110.3
Real Earnings per Empl. (1987=100)	68.7	75.4	78.8	82.0	87.1	91.1	92.7	95.0	92.6	95.8	97.5
Real Output per Empl. (1987=100)	56.6	61.7	64.6	65.3	72.9	85.6	80.3	87.6	83.4	82.6	89.5
Earnings as % of Value Added	50.3	52.2	52.8	51.6	51.2	50.7	57.1	53.5	55.7	56.8	57.7

MONETARY HOLDINGS

(Billions of current Netherlands Guilders)

	1969	1970	1971	1972	1973	1974	1975	1976	1977	1978	1979
Money Supply, Broadly Defined	63.20	70.57	80.12	109.68	124.88	141.20	159.51	183.33	207.80	233.78	258.59
Money	23.23	25.95	29.85	35.12	35.14	39.43	47.20	51.05	57.77	60.19	61.87
Currency Outside Banks	9.43	9.95	10.49	11.41	11.92	12.85	14.49	15.89	17.41	18.71	19.98
Demand Deposits	13.79	16.00	19.36	23.71	23.22	26.58	32.70	35.16	40.35	41.47	41.90
Quasi-Money	39.98	44.61	50.27	74.56	89.74	101.77	112.31	132.29	150.03	173.59	196.72

GOVERNMENT DEFICIT (-) OR SURPLUS

(Billions of current Netherlands Guilders)

	1969	1970	1971	1972	1973	1974	1975	1976	1977	1978	1979
GOVERNMENT DEFICIT (-) OR SURPLUS	..	..	..	..	-0.04	-0.04	-6.35	-6.12	-8.37	-9.20	-14.53
Current Revenue	..	..	..	..	77.22	89.71	103.72	119.49	133.01	143.71	154.63
Current Expenditure	..	..	..	..	66.75	80.26	97.30	112.61	125.91	139.89	152.45
Current Budget Balance	..	..	..	..	10.47	9.45	6.42	6.88	7.10	3.82	2.18
Capital Receipts	..	..	..	..	0.05	0.21	0.21	0.23	0.22	0.15	0.13
Capital Payments	..	..	..	..	10.56	9.74	12.39	12.40	12.43	12.58	15.16

1980	1981	1982	1983	1984	1985	1986	1987	1988	1989 estimate	NOTES	NETHERLANDS, THE
12,020	11,810	10,930	10,070	9,670	9,340	10,040	11,740	14,510	16,010	..	**CURRENT GNP PER CAPITA (US $)**
14,150	14,247	14,313	14,367	14,424	14,492	14,572	14,665	14,758	14,828	..	**POPULATION (thousands)**
			(Billions of current Netherlands Guilders)								**USE AND ORIGIN OF RESOURCES**
336.16	351.92	368.52	381.62	399.76	418.84	427.63	430.50	449.26	471.81	..	Gross National Product (GNP)
-0.62	-0.96	-0.38	0.56	-0.50	0.68	-0.98	-0.72	-1.95	-2.30	..	Net Factor Income from Abroad
336.78	352.88	368.90	381.06	400.26	418.16	428.62	431.22	451.21	474.11	..	GDP at Market Prices
-1.74	12.26	15.78	14.59	20.97	19.88	19.48	13.11	18.08	19.78	..	Resource Balance
176.89	204.49	212.61	219.76	248.62	265.46	232.59	226.40	245.92	275.50	..	Exports of Goods & NFServices
178.63	192.23	196.84	205.17	227.65	245.58	213.11	213.28	227.84	255.71	..	Imports of Goods & NFServices
338.52	340.63	353.13	366.47	379.29	398.28	409.14	418.11	433.12	454.32	..	Domestic Absorption
205.68	213.28	221.95	229.86	236.78	247.86	256.09	263.19	268.28	280.57	..	Private Consumption, etc.
60.26	62.75	65.12	66.58	66.39	67.66	68.55	70.45	70.93	71.60	..	General Gov't Consumption
72.57	64.60	66.06	70.02	76.11	82.76	84.49	84.46	93.91	102.15	..	Gross Domestic Investment
70.84	66.83	67.21	70.26	75.41	81.85	88.16	88.71	98.54	104.40	..	Fixed Investment
32.02	32.90	32.70	33.92	35.38	37.19	39.80	40.55	41.82	44.19	..	Indirect Taxes, net
304.76	319.98	336.20	347.14	364.88	380.97	388.81	390.67	409.39	429.92	..	GDP at factor cost
11.68	14.56	15.93	16.13	17.26	17.14	18.45	17.43	18.17	..	B	Agriculture
110.46	116.02	121.26	124.63	133.39	140.41	137.85	130.30	138.47	..	B	Industry
60.37	59.79	64.68	67.47	72.57	75.23	83.21	83.00	89.78	..	B	Manufacturing
214.64	222.31	231.71	240.30	249.61	260.61	272.31	283.49	294.56	..	B	Services, etc.
70.83	76.86	81.84	84.62	97.08	102.64	103.97	97.58	111.99	121.93	..	Gross Domestic Saving
68.59	74.10	79.57	83.56	95.08	101.81	101.14	94.74	108.29	117.95	..	Gross National Saving
			(Billions of 1987 Netherlands Guilders)								
396.38	393.16	388.08	394.26	404.76	415.80	425.41	430.50	441.98	460.69	..	Gross National Product
397.11	394.24	388.49	393.68	405.26	415.12	426.39	431.22	443.91	462.91	..	GDP at Market Prices
2.36	15.28	13.40	13.14	18.00	16.39	16.42	13.11	15.68	18.92	..	Resource Balance
177.78	180.43	180.32	186.38	200.05	210.57	217.65	226.40	244.22	258.76	..	Exports of Goods & NFServices
175.41	165.15	166.92	173.24	182.05	194.17	201.23	213.28	228.54	239.84	..	Imports of Goods & NFServices
394.75	378.96	375.09	380.54	387.26	398.73	409.97	418.11	428.22	443.99	..	Domestic Absorption
245.96	242.30	239.08	240.85	243.36	248.59	256.22	263.19	266.57	275.87	..	Private Consumption, etc.
64.56	65.86	66.26	67.00	66.59	67.47	69.08	70.45	70.46	70.71	..	General Gov't Consumption
84.23	70.79	69.75	72.68	77.31	82.67	84.67	84.46	91.20	97.41	..	Gross Domestic Investment
82.82	74.12	71.23	72.81	76.72	81.78	88.16	88.71	97.45	101.96	..	Fixed Investment
359.65	357.75	353.84	358.52	369.26	377.97	386.57	390.67	402.56	419.76	..	GDP at factor cost
13.13	14.93	16.03	16.54	17.53	17.01	18.70	17.43	18.68	..	..	Agriculture
128.33	124.23	118.10	120.79	124.92	128.71	130.53	130.30	138.73	..	..	Industry
..	..	..	..	..	..	..	..	..	..	..	Manufacturing
255.70	255.09	254.40	256.35	262.81	269.40	277.15	283.49	286.50	..	..	Services, etc.
											Memo Items:
173.71	175.68	180.30	185.56	198.81	209.89	219.62	226.40	246.67	258.40	..	Capacity to Import
-4.07	-4.75	-0.02	-0.82	-1.24	-0.68	1.97	0.00	2.45	-0.37	..	Terms of Trade Adjustment
393.04	389.49	388.47	392.86	404.03	414.45	428.36	431.22	446.36	462.54	..	Gross Domestic Income
392.31	388.41	388.06	393.44	403.52	415.13	427.38	430.50	444.44	460.32	..	Gross National Income
			(Index 1987 = 100)								**DOMESTIC PRICES/DEFLATORS**
84.8	89.5	95.0	96.8	98.8	100.7	100.5	100.0	101.6	102.4	..	Overall (GDP)
85.8	89.9	94.1	96.3	97.9	99.9	99.8	100.0	101.1	102.3	..	Domestic Absorption
88.9	97.5	99.4	97.5	98.4	100.7	98.7	100.0	97.3	..	..	Agriculture
86.1	93.4	102.7	103.2	106.8	109.1	105.6	100.0	99.8	..	..	Industry
..	..	..	..	..	..	..	..	..	..	..	Manufacturing
82.0	87.6	92.7	95.3	98.4	100.6	100.7	100.0	100.7	101.8	..	Consumer Price Index
											MANUFACTURING ACTIVITY
109.0	105.4	100.9	96.4	95.3	97.2	99.2	100.0	100.5	..	..	Employment (1987=100)
96.5	95.2	96.5	97.2	95.4	96.1	96.2	100.0	..	..	..	Real Earnings per Empl. (1987=100)
91.0	92.4	90.3	97.5	106.0	104.3	97.3	100.0	..	..	..	Real Output per Empl. (1987=100)
57.9	58.8	56.8	54.0	50.1	50.3	46.2	47.0	..	..	..	Earnings as % of Value Added
			(Billions of current Netherlands Guilders)								**MONETARY HOLDINGS**
273.69	293.69	312.03	327.30	346.85	366.60	386.50	..	..	..	D	Money Supply, Broadly Defined
65.58	64.03	72.30	79.66	85.00	90.77	97.21	103.71	111.31	119.02	..	Money
22.00	22.34	23.39	26.35	27.80	28.60	29.77	32.85	34.61	36.00	..	Currency Outside Banks
43.59	41.70	48.91	53.31	57.20	62.17	67.44	70.86	76.70	83.02	..	Demand Deposits
208.11	229.66	239.73	247.64	261.85	275.83	289.29	..	..	..	..	Quasi-Money
			(Billions of current Netherlands Guilders)								
-15.56	-22.97	-28.05	-29.55	-29.92	-23.37	-8.21	-13.77	-19.25	..	..	**GOVERNMENT DEFICIT (-) OR SURPLUS**
169.42	179.55	189.95	201.07	206.97	217.79	223.94	225.56	230.56	..	..	Current Revenue
164.76	178.65	195.95	206.46	212.41	216.60	222.39	225.23	228.38	..	..	Current Expenditure
4.66	0.90	-6.00	-5.39	-5.44	1.19	1.55	0.33	2.18	..	..	Current Budget Balance
0.17	0.19	0.19	0.09	0.18	0.26	0.36	0.29	0.24	..	..	Capital Receipts
19.93	23.23	22.58	22.17	24.13	21.18	9.48	16.08	21.31	..	..	Capital Payments

NETHERLANDS, THE	1969	1970	1971	1972	1973	1974	1975	1976	1977	1978	1979
FOREIGN TRADE (CUSTOMS BASIS)					*(Millions of current US dollars)*						
Value of Exports, fob	9,965	11,766	13,934	17,351	24,012	32,734	34,957	40,147	43,605	50,149	63,667
Nonfuel Primary Products	3,310	3,842	4,221	5,234	7,385	9,084	10,145	11,298	12,550	14,693	17,852
Fuels	827	1,256	1,737	2,077	3,127	5,234	5,960	7,112	7,932	8,023	11,966
Manufactures	5,829	6,668	7,975	10,040	13,501	18,416	18,852	21,737	23,123	27,434	33,849
Value of Imports, cif	10,994	13,393	14,901	17,226	23,753	32,508	34,394	39,452	45,500	53,041	67,281
Nonfuel Primary Products	2,961	3,354	3,484	4,114	6,036	7,825	8,031	9,141	10,679	11,942	14,649
Fuels	1,072	1,458	1,937	2,267	3,151	5,890	6,145	7,682	8,380	8,253	13,358
Manufactures	6,960	8,581	9,481	10,845	14,566	18,792	20,219	22,630	26,440	32,846	39,274
					(Index 1987 = 100)						
Terms of Trade	122.4	121.3	117.4	124.1	140.3	115.0	112.5	110.1	107.8	114.4	120.4
Export Prices, fob	27.3	27.3	28.4	33.0	47.8	59.9	62.0	62.5	66.9	78.1	98.9
Import Prices, cif	22.3	22.5	24.1	26.6	34.0	52.1	55.1	56.7	62.1	68.3	82.1
BALANCE OF PAYMENTS					*(Billions of current US dollars)*						
Exports of Goods & Services	..	15.15	17.73	21.62	30.62	43.06	45.26	50.56	55.66	64.02	83.63
Merchandise, fob	..	10.88	12.54	15.58	21.95	30.51	32.02	36.36	39.91	45.47	58.61
Nonfactor Services	..	2.96	3.65	4.36	6.07	7.94	9.17	9.63	10.65	12.69	14.41
Factor Services	..	1.31	1.54	1.69	2.61	4.61	4.07	4.58	5.10	5.86	10.61
Imports of Goods & Services	..	15.70	17.90	20.30	28.14	39.71	42.23	46.71	53.75	64.21	82.62
Merchandise, fob	..	11.78	13.16	15.14	20.95	29.92	31.12	35.01	40.15	46.96	60.04
Nonfactor Services	..	2.76	3.32	3.69	5.05	6.55	7.27	7.96	9.27	11.48	14.07
Factor Services	..	1.16	1.42	1.47	2.14	3.24	3.83	3.74	4.32	5.77	8.52
Long-Term Interest	..	..	..	..	..	..	..	..	..	..	..
Private Current Transfers, net	..	-0.07	-0.07	-0.11	-0.19	-0.25	-0.29	-0.33	-0.38	-0.52	-0.59
Workers' Remittances	..	..	..	..	..	..	..	..	..	..	..
Curr. A/C Bal before Off. Transf.	..	-0.62	-0.24	1.21	2.29	3.10	2.75	3.52	1.54	-0.71	0.42
Net Official Transfers		0.03	0.01	-0.02	0.13	-0.06	-0.37	-0.07	-0.31	-0.50	-0.20
Curr. A/C Bal after Off. Transf.	..	-0.59	-0.23	1.18	2.42	3.04	2.37	3.45	1.23	-1.21	0.21
Long-Term Capital, net	..	0.57	0.51	-0.94	-1.82	-2.15	-1.81	-4.09	-1.87	-2.65	-5.03
Direct Investment	..	-0.01	0.09	-0.13	-0.06	-1.58	-1.05	-1.49	-2.39	-2.33	-4.44
Long-Term Loans	..	..	..	..	..	..	..	..	..	..	..
Disbursements	..	..	..	..	..	..	..	..	..	..	..
Repayments	..	..	..	..	..	..	..	..	..	..	..
Other Long-Term Capital	..	0.59	0.42	-0.81	-1.76	-0.57	-0.77	-2.61	0.51	-0.33	-0.59
Other Capital, net	..	0.63	-0.12	0.62	0.36	0.09	-0.24	0.97	0.94	2.94	4.22
Change in Reserves	..	-0.62	-0.16	-0.87	-0.96	-0.98	-0.32	-0.33	-0.30	0.92	0.59
Memo Item:					*(Netherlands Guilders per US dollar)*						
Conversion Factor (Annual Avg)	3.620	3.620	3.500	3.210	2.800	2.690	2.530	2.640	2.550	2.160	2.010
					(Millions US dollars), outstanding at end of year						
EXTERNAL DEBT (Total)	..	..	..	..	..	..	..	..	..	..	..
Long-Term Debt (by debtor)	..	..	..	..	..	..	..	..	..	..	..
Central Bank, incl. IMF credit	..	..	..	..	..	..	..	..	..	..	..
Central Government	..	..	..	..	..	..	..	..	..	..	..
Rest of General Government	..	..	..	..	..	..	..	..	..	..	..
Non-financial Public Enterprises	..	..	..	..	..	..	..	..	..	..	..
Priv. Sector, incl non-guaranteed	..	..	..	..	..	..	..	..	..	..	..
Short-Term Debt	..	..	..	..	..	..	..	..	..	..	..
Memo Items:					*(Millions of US dollars)*						
Int'l Reserves Excluding Gold	809	1,454	1,724	2,726	4,253	4,630	4,884	5,178	5,742	5,088	7,591
Gold Holdings (at market price)	1,731	1,908	2,379	3,516	6,098	10,132	7,620	7,321	9,011	12,380	22,514
SOCIAL INDICATORS											
Total Fertility Rate	2.7	2.6	2.4	2.2	1.9	1.8	1.7	1.6	1.6	1.6	1.6
Infant Mortality Rate	13.2	12.7	12.1	11.7	11.5	11.3	10.6	10.7	9.5	9.6	8.7
Life Expectancy at Birth	73.6	73.5	73.8	74.0	74.1	74.3	74.4	74.8	75.3	75.4	75.6
Urban Population, % of total	86.0	86.1	86.6	87.0	87.5	87.9	88.4	88.4	88.4	88.4	88.4
Food Prod. per capita (1987=100)	70.3	76.6	77.0	72.6	76.4	82.2	83.8	80.6	81.5	85.7	87.1
Labor Force, Agriculture (%)	7.2	6.8	6.7	6.5	6.4	6.3	6.2	6.0	5.9	5.8	5.6
Labor Force, Female (%)	26.1	26.4	26.9	27.3	27.7	28.2	28.6	29.1	29.6	30.1	30.6
Primary Schl. Enroll. Ratio	..	102.0	..	..	..	..	98.0	100.0	100.0	101.0	101.0
Primary Schl. Enroll. Ratio, Female	..	102.0	..	..	..	..	99.0	100.0	101.0	102.0	102.0
Secondary Schl. Enroll. Ratio	..	75.0	..	..	..	..	88.0	91.0	92.0	92.0	93.0

1980	1981	1982	1983	1984	1985	1986	1987	1988	1989 estimate	NOTES	NETHERLANDS, THE
				(Millions of current US dollars)							**FOREIGN TRADE (CUSTOMS BASIS)**
73,871	68,758	66,404	65,676	65,874	68,282	80,555	92,882	103,206	..	..	Value of Exports, fob
19,930	18,789	18,001	17,819	17,720	17,638	22,145	26,560	29,333	..	..	Nonfuel Primary Products
16,114	16,231	15,669	15,212	14,878	15,495	12,214	10,089	8,690	..	..	Fuels
37,827	33,738	32,734	32,645	33,275	35,149	46,197	56,232	65,183	..	..	Manufactures
76,889	66,109	62,583	61,585	62,136	65,212	75,580	91,316	99,743	..	..	Value of Imports, cif
16,602	14,092	13,381	13,163	13,271	13,341	15,440	18,460	21,355	..	..	Nonfuel Primary Products
18,252	17,258	15,986	15,129	14,470	14,181	8,738	9,936	9,055	..	..	Fuels
42,036	34,759	33,216	33,294	34,395	37,690	51,402	62,921	69,333	..	..	Manufactures
				(Index 1987 = 100)							
111.4	102.8	107.3	102.5	101.4	103.0	103.4	100.0	100.5	..	..	Terms of Trade
107.5	98.4	96.9	89.5	85.5	83.7	91.1	100.0	104.5	..	..	Export Prices, fob
96.5	95.7	90.2	87.4	84.4	81.3	88.1	100.0	103.9	..	..	Import Prices, cif
				(Billions of current US dollars)							**BALANCE OF PAYMENTS**
97.74	92.15	88.94	84.87	86.59	87.01	103.50	124.19	136.83	146.04	..	Exports of Goods & Services
67.48	63.18	60.61	59.31	60.11	62.55	73.72	86.95	98.41	101.83	..	Merchandise, fob
17.08	15.91	15.62	14.03	14.38	14.80	17.13	20.80	22.24	23.75	..	Nonfactor Services
13.18	13.06	12.71	11.53	12.11	9.66	12.64	16.44	16.19	20.46	..	Factor Services
97.56	86.95	83.00	78.92	79.03	82.00	98.14	118.24	129.69	137.14	..	Imports of Goods & Services
68.89	59.29	55.95	55.05	54.45	57.08	66.55	81.81	89.92	93.84	..	Merchandise, fob
16.94	14.91	14.62	13.39	13.71	14.38	17.87	20.64	22.36	22.90	..	Nonfactor Services
11.73	12.75	12.43	10.48	10.87	10.53	13.72	15.79	17.41	20.39	..	Factor Services
..	..	..	..	..	..	..	..	..	..	..	Long-Term Interest
-0.81	-0.72	-0.71	-0.57	-0.47	-0.45	-0.75	-1.04	-0.89	-0.80	..	Private Current Transfers, net
..	..	..	..	..	..	..	..	..	..	..	Workers' Remittances
-0.63	4.48	5.24	5.39	7.10	4.56	4.61	4.91	6.25	8.10	..	Curr. A/C Bal before Off. Transf.
-0.40	-0.79	-0.75	-0.42	-0.53	-0.53	-0.99	-1.23	-0.78	-1.14	..	Net Official Transfers
-1.04	3.70	4.49	4.97	6.57	4.03	3.62	3.68	5.47	6.96	..	Curr. A/C Bal after Off. Transf.
-2.25	-3.05	-4.04	-3.40	-5.95	-2.60	-6.61	-2.55	2.65	7.52	..	Long-Term Capital, net
-3.73	-2.98	-2.22	-2.38	-3.38	-1.79	-0.31	-5.63	0.30	-3.82	..	Direct Investment
..	..	..	..	..	..	..	..	..	..	..	Long-Term Loans
..	..	..	..	..	..	..	..	..	..	..	Disbursements
..	..	..	..	..	..	..	..	..	..	..	Repayments
1.48	-0.07	-1.82	-1.03	-2.57	-0.81	-6.29	3.08	2.36	11.33	..	Other Long-Term Capital
4.47	-1.47	1.34	-1.79	-0.58	-0.68	2.60	1.74	-6.50	-14.03	..	Other Capital, net
-1.18	0.83	-1.78	0.23	-0.04	-0.75	0.39	-2.86	-1.63	-0.45	..	Change in Reserves
				(Netherlands Guilders per US dollar)							Memo Item:
1.990	2.500	2.670	2.850	3.210	3.320	2.450	2.030	1.980	2.120	..	Conversion Factor (Annual Avg)
				(Millions US dollars), outstanding at end of year							**EXTERNAL DEBT (Total)**
..	..	..	..	..	..	..	..	..	..	..	Long-Term Debt (by debtor)
..	..	..	..	..	..	..	..	..	..	..	Central Bank, incl. IMF credit
..	..	..	..	..	..	..	..	..	..	..	Central Government
..	..	..	..	..	..	..	..	..	..	..	Rest of General Government
..	..	..	..	..	..	..	..	..	..	..	Non-financial Public Enterprises
..	..	..	..	..	..	..	..	..	..	..	Priv. Sector, incl non-guaranteed
..	..	..	..	..	..	..	..	..	..	..	Short-Term Debt
				(Millions of US dollars)							Memo Items:
11,645	9,339	10,133	10,171	9,237	10,782	11,191	16,003	16,075	16,509	..	Int'l Reserves Excluding Gold
25,904	17,467	20,077	16,764	13,547	14,369	17,177	21,272	18,027	17,621	..	Gold Holdings (at market price)
											SOCIAL INDICATORS
1.6	1.6	1.5	1.5	1.5	1.5	1.6	1.6	1.6	1.6	..	Total Fertility Rate
8.6	8.3	8.3	8.4	8.3	8.0	7.7	7.6	7.5	7.3	..	Infant Mortality Rate
75.7	75.9	76.1	76.2	76.3	76.5	76.6	76.8	76.9	77.1	..	Life Expectancy at Birth
88.4	88.4	88.4	88.4	88.4	88.4	88.4	88.4	88.5	88.5	..	Urban Population, % of total
87.0	96.4	97.3	95.0	97.1	95.2	104.2	100.0	96.5	99.9	..	Food Prod. per capita (1987=100)
5.5	..	..	..	..	..	..	..	..	..	..	Labor Force, Agriculture (%)
31.0	31.0	31.0	31.0	31.0	31.0	31.0	31.0	30.9	30.9	..	Labor Force, Female (%)
100.0	99.0	97.0	95.0	95.0	114.0	115.0	..	..	..	..	Primary Schl. Enroll. Ratio
101.0	100.0	98.0	96.0	96.0	115.0	116.0	..	..	..	..	Primary Schl. Enroll. Ratio, Female
92.0	94.0	97.0	101.0	102.0	104.0	104.0	..	..	..	..	Secondary Schl. Enroll. Ratio

NEW ZEALAND	1969	1970	1971	1972	1973	1974	1975	1976	1977	1978	1979
CURRENT GNP PER CAPITA (US $)	2,070	2,150	2,410	2,710	3,520	4,360	4,360	4,280	4,300	4,600	5,580
POPULATION (thousands)	2,804	2,820	2,854	2,902	2,956	3,024	3,087	3,111	3,120	3,121	3,109
USE AND ORIGIN OF RESOURCES					*(Millions of current New Zealand Dollars)*						
Gross National Product (GNP)	4,883	5,515	6,460	7,177	8,736	9,711	10,280	12,538	14,543	15,519	18,475
Net Factor Income from Abroad	-41	-41	-46	-54	-37	-82	-165	-265	-336	-409	-460
GDP at Market Prices	4,924	5,556	6,506	7,231	8,773	9,793	10,445	12,803	14,879	15,928	18,935
Resource Balance	67	-76	6	61	226	-970	-868	-445	-399	18	-156
Exports of Goods & NFServices	1,176	1,308	1,496	1,690	2,280	2,227	2,382	3,536	4,081	4,421	5,642
Imports of Goods & NFServices	1,109	1,384	1,490	1,629	2,053	3,197	3,251	3,981	4,480	4,403	5,798
Domestic Absorption	4,857	5,632	6,500	7,170	8,547	10,763	11,313	13,248	15,278	15,910	19,091
Private Consumption, etc.	3,276	3,655	4,076	4,603	5,257	6,123	6,769	7,936	8,964	10,014	11,597
General Gov't Consumption	728	781	906	1,021	1,129	1,303	1,568	1,861	2,227	2,622	3,041
Gross Domestic Investment	853	1,197	1,518	1,546	2,161	3,337	2,976	3,451	4,087	3,274	4,453
Fixed Investment	1,096	1,342	1,601	1,938	2,331	2,796	3,078	3,498	3,661	3,824	4,099
Indirect Taxes, net	0	0	0	0	0	0	0	..	..	..	..
GDP at factor cost	4,924	5,556	6,506	7,231	8,773	9,793	10,445	..	..	..	..
Agriculture	..	..	777	1,004	1,099	858	1,101	1,467	1,496	1,518	2,304
Industry	..	..	2,142	2,323	2,736	3,340	3,514	4,328	4,750	5,016	5,980
Manufacturing	..	..	1,540	1,648	1,920	2,365	2,459	3,081	3,281	3,563	4,272
Services, etc.	..	..	3,586	3,905	4,938	5,594	5,830	7,008	8,633	9,394	10,651
Gross Domestic Saving	920	1,120	1,524	1,607	2,387	2,366	2,108	3,006	3,688	3,292	4,296
Gross National Saving	..	1,075	1,492	1,598	2,406	2,319	1,993	2,775	3,400	2,909	3,906
					(Millions of 1980 New Zealand Dollars)						
Gross National Product	17,985	18,552	19,217	19,440	21,395	23,084	22,203	22,820	22,352	20,933	21,173
GDP at Market Prices	18,140	18,693	19,358	19,597	21,496	23,290	22,554	23,296	22,869	21,491	21,720
Resource Balance	-329	-687	-553	-1,163	-1,815	-3,554	-1,456	-536	-647	-255	-928
Exports of Goods & NFServices	4,372	4,820	5,057	4,799	5,238	5,116	5,310	6,095	6,142	6,183	6,574
Imports of Goods & NFServices	4,702	5,507	5,610	5,963	7,054	8,670	6,766	6,632	6,789	6,437	7,502
Domestic Absorption	18,469	19,380	19,911	20,760	23,311	26,844	24,010	23,832	23,516	21,746	22,648
Private Consumption, etc.	11,406	12,044	12,037	12,632	13,711	14,690	14,385	14,198	13,722	13,711	13,771
General Gov't Consumption	2,519	2,568	2,668	2,798	2,945	3,146	3,325	3,348	3,428	3,583	3,614
Gross Domestic Investment	4,544	4,769	5,206	5,331	6,656	9,008	6,299	6,286	6,366	4,452	5,263
Fixed Investment	4,161	4,615	4,907	5,618	6,380	7,015	6,545	6,292	5,635	5,225	4,871
GDP at factor cost	..	..	..	..	..	..	..	..	..	..	..
Agriculture	..	..	..	..	..	..	..	..	2,059	1,874	2,156
Industry	..	..	..	..	..	..	..	..	7,127	6,710	6,921
Manufacturing	..	..	..	..	..	..	..	..	4,892	4,673	4,966
Services, etc.	..	..	..	..	..	..	..	..	13,683	12,907	12,643
Memo Items:											
Capacity to Import	4,985	5,203	5,632	6,187	7,831	6,039	4,958	5,890	6,184	6,464	7,300
Terms of Trade Adjustment	613	383	574	1,387	2,593	923	-351	-205	43	281	726
Gross Domestic Income	18,753	19,076	19,933	20,984	24,089	24,212	22,202	23,091	22,912	21,773	22,446
Gross National Income	18,598	18,935	19,792	20,828	23,988	24,007	21,852	22,615	22,395	21,214	21,900
DOMESTIC PRICES/DEFLATORS					*(Index 1980 = 100)*						
Overall (GDP)	27.1	29.7	33.6	36.9	40.8	42.0	46.3	55.0	65.1	74.1	87.2
Domestic Absorption	26.3	29.1	32.6	34.5	36.7	40.1	47.1	55.6	65.0	73.2	84.3
Agriculture	..	..	..	..	..	..	..	..	72.6	81.0	106.9
Industry	..	..	..	..	..	..	..	..	66.6	74.8	86.4
Manufacturing	..	..	..	..	..	..	..	..	67.1	76.3	86.0
Consumer Price Index	12.5	13.3	14.7	15.8	17.0	18.9	21.7	25.4	29.0	32.5	37.0
MANUFACTURING ACTIVITY											
Employment (1987=100)	85.4	89.3	90.5	91.8	95.6	101.0	103.6	106.4	109.3	112.3	111.0
Real Earnings per Empl. (1987=100)	..	..	..	..	..	..	..	..	..	..	..
Real Output per Empl. (1987=100)	..	..	..	..	..	..	..	..	..	..	..
Earnings as % of Value Added	58.9	61.8	63.2	61.6	63.4	65.1	66.5	62.7	66.6	65.8	65.4
MONETARY HOLDINGS					*(Millions of current New Zealand Dollars)*						
Money Supply, Broadly Defined	2,819	3,066	3,351	4,060	5,011	5,236	5,833	6,793	7,807	9,506	11,108
Money	801	861	949	1,219	1,545	1,601	1,749	1,910	1,946	2,378	2,458
Currency Outside Banks	168	195	212	242	290	336	352	418	460	536	590
Demand Deposits	633	665	737	978	1,255	1,265	1,397	1,491	1,486	1,842	1,868
Quasi-Money	2,018	2,206	2,402	2,841	3,466	3,635	4,083	4,883	5,862	7,127	8,649
GOVERNMENT DEFICIT (-) OR SURPLUS					*(Millions of current New Zealand Dollars)*						
	..	-108	-93	-298	-225	-416	-1,194	-614	-789	-1,502	-1,127
Current Revenue	..	1,614	1,901	2,141	2,626	3,121	3,496	4,277	5,150	5,648	6,823
Current Expenditure	..	1,380	1,610	1,978	2,326	2,712	3,474	3,870	4,777	5,914	6,858
Current Budget Balance	..	234	291	163	300	409	22	407	373	-266	-35
Capital Receipts	..	6	7	5	6	3	7	6	3	3	4
Capital Payments	..	348	391	466	531	828	1,223	1,027	1,165	1,239	1,096

1980	1981	1982	1983	1984	1985	1986	1987	1988	1989 estimate	NOTES	NEW ZEALAND
6,520	7,230	7,320	6,970	6,530	6,600	6,700	7,990	10,190	11,800	..	**CURRENT GNP PER CAPITA (US $)**
3,113	3,145	3,183	3,227	3,260	3,290	3,305	3,336	3,292	3,343	..	**POPULATION (thousands)**
				(Millions of current New Zealand Dollars)							**USE AND ORIGIN OF RESOURCES**
21,480	25,947	29,694	31,674	35,147	41,929	48,020	55,179	61,267	65,360	C f	Gross National Product (GNP)
-511	-615	-859	-1,275	-1,914	-2,689	-2,215	-2,751	-2,730	-2,911	..	Net Factor Income from Abroad
21,991	26,562	30,553	32,949	37,061	44,618	50,235	57,930	63,997	68,270	..	GDP at Market Prices
-434	-593	-1,434	-206	-1,686	-484	-500	-302	1,638	-138	..	Resource Balance
6,775	8,002	8,785	10,299	12,296	14,628	14,651	15,875	17,337	19,041	..	Exports of Goods & NFServices
7,209	8,595	10,219	10,505	13,982	15,113	15,150	16,177	15,699	19,179	..	Imports of Goods & NFServices
22,425	27,155	31,987	33,155	38,747	45,102	50,734	58,232	62,359	68,408	..	Domestic Absorption
13,725	16,031	18,353	19,637	22,199	25,829	30,064	34,550	37,239	39,986	..	Private Consumption, etc.
3,598	4,284	4,722	5,252	5,806	6,674	7,822	8,617	8,966	9,274	..	General Gov't Consumption
5,102	6,840	8,912	8,267	10,742	12,599	12,849	15,065	16,153	19,148	..	Gross Domestic Investment
4,915	6,498	8,472	8,947	10,482	12,270	13,487	15,362	16,557	18,429	..	Fixed Investment
..	..	..	..	..	..	..	..	..	..	..	Indirect Taxes, net
..	..	..	..	..	..	..	..	..	..	..	GDP at factor cost
2,412	2,548	2,516	2,846	3,543	4,021	4,080	4,873	..	..	B	Agriculture
6,804	8,648	10,007	10,518	12,091	14,176	15,176	16,223	..	..	B	Industry
4,870	6,239	7,110	7,526	8,729	9,904	10,691	11,367	..	..	B	Manufacturing
12,775	15,367	18,029	19,586	21,427	26,421	30,979	36,834	..	..	B	Services, etc.
4,667	6,247	7,477	8,061	9,056	12,115	12,349	14,763	17,791	19,010	..	Gross Domestic Saving
4,267	5,708	6,831	7,035	7,489	9,717	10,497	12,385	15,504	16,597	..	Gross National Saving
				(Millions of 1980 New Zealand Dollars)							
21,480	22,185	22,481	22,594	23,359	24,699	24,330	24,216	24,749	24,988	C f	Gross National Product
21,991	22,711	23,134	23,503	24,626	26,259	25,450	25,472	25,910	26,101	..	GDP at Market Prices
-434	-537	-1,143	-151	-1,000	49	-217	-1,067	-606	-1,835	..	Resource Balance
6,775	7,005	6,903	7,455	7,913	8,649	8,591	8,831	9,144	9,299	..	Exports of Goods & NFServices
7,209	7,542	8,047	7,606	8,914	8,600	8,808	9,898	9,750	11,134	..	Imports of Goods & NFServices
22,425	23,249	24,277	23,653	25,626	26,210	25,668	26,539	26,517	27,936	..	Domestic Absorption
13,725	13,947	13,971	13,982	14,714	14,696	15,159	15,302	15,586	15,765	..	Private Consumption, etc.
3,598	3,671	3,590	3,744	3,845	3,875	3,956	3,936	3,817	3,802	..	General Gov't Consumption
5,102	5,631	6,716	5,927	7,067	7,639	6,553	7,301	7,114	8,369	..	Gross Domestic Investment
4,915	5,567	6,441	6,379	6,942	7,123	6,821	7,017	7,048	7,555	..	Fixed Investment
..	..	..	..	..	..	..	..	..	..	..	GDP at factor cost
2,412	2,402	2,535	2,396	2,376	2,983	2,885	..	..	..	..	Agriculture
6,804	7,342	7,578	7,760	8,407	8,779	8,513	..	..	..	..	Industry
4,870	5,291	5,395	5,484	6,019	6,040	5,870	..	..	..	..	Manufacturing
12,775	12,967	13,020	13,347	13,844	14,497	14,053	..	..	..	..	Services, etc.
											Memo Items:
6,775	7,022	6,917	7,457	7,839	8,324	8,518	9,713	10,767	11,054	..	Capacity to Import
0	17	14	2	-75	-325	-73	882	1,624	1,755	..	Terms of Trade Adjustment
21,991	22,728	23,148	23,504	24,551	25,934	25,377	26,354	27,534	27,856	..	Gross Domestic Income
21,480	22,202	22,495	22,595	23,284	24,374	24,257	25,098	26,373	26,743	..	Gross National Income
				(Index 1980 = 100)							**DOMESTIC PRICES/DEFLATORS**
100.0	117.0	132.1	140.2	150.5	169.9	197.4	227.4	247.0	261.6	..	Overall (GDP)
100.0	116.8	131.8	140.2	151.2	172.1	197.7	219.4	235.2	244.9	..	Domestic Absorption
100.0	106.1	99.3	118.8	149.1	134.8	141.4	..	..	..	..	Agriculture
100.0	117.8	132.0	135.5	143.8	161.5	178.3	..	..	..	..	Industry
100.0	117.9	131.8	137.3	145.0	164.0	182.1	..	..	..	..	Manufacturing
43.3	49.9	58.0	62.3	66.1	76.3	86.4	100.0	106.4	112.5	..	Consumer Price Index
											MANUFACTURING ACTIVITY
109.8	108.7	110.2	111.6	111.6	111.7	107.4	100.0	90.1	81.2	G	Employment (1987=100)
..	..	..	..	..	..	..	..	..	..	G	Real Earnings per Empl. (1987=100)
..	..	..	..	..	..	..	..	..	..	G	Real Output per Empl. (1987=100)
66.1	64.5	65.5	62.1	56.4	59.1	57.5	..	..	..	..	Earnings as % of Value Added
				(Millions of current New Zealand Dollars)							**MONETARY HOLDINGS**
12,400	14,456	16,254	18,147	21,478	26,601	31,019	..	..	..	..	Money Supply, Broadly Defined
2,535	2,926	3,030	3,426	3,761	4,104	4,668	6,667	..	..	..	Money
577	683	714	739	867	940	1,006	1,059	1,205	1,323	..	Currency Outside Banks
1,958	2,243	2,316	2,687	2,894	3,164	3,661	5,608	..	..	..	Demand Deposits
9,865	11,530	13,224	14,721	17,717	22,497	26,351	..	..	..	..	Quasi-Money
				(Millions of current New Zealand Dollars)							**GOVERNMENT DEFICIT (-) OR SURPLUS**
-1,541	-2,111	-2,389	-3,209	-3,234	-2,082	-1,990	642	1,354	..	C	
7,871	9,747	11,204	11,711	13,686	16,891	20,682	26,582	26,983	..	..	Current Revenue
8,246	10,432	12,171	13,313	15,239	17,195	21,443	26,505	27,170	..	..	Current Expenditure
-375	-685	-967	-1,602	-1,553	-304	-761	77	-187	..	..	Current Budget Balance
6	6	3	13	19	42	161	86	177	..	..	Capital Receipts
1,172	1,432	1,425	1,620	1,700	1,820	1,390	-479	-1,364	..	..	Capital Payments

NEW ZEALAND	1969	1970	1971	1972	1973	1974	1975	1976	1977	1978	1979
FOREIGN TRADE (CUSTOMS BASIS)					*(Millions of current US dollars)*						
Value of Exports, fob	1,182.0	1,226.9	1,361.6	1,831.0	2,607.9	2,437.3	2,170.7	2,820.0	3,203.9	3,985.6	4,668.7
Nonfuel Primary Products	1,072.7	1,066.8	1,184.6	1,586.4	2,304.7	2,075.8	1,773.2	2,230.4	2,531.1	3,074.0	3,624.5
Fuels	7.2	9.1	13.6	18.2	16.5	23.6	37.0	50.8	53.9	61.8	96.3
Manufactures	102.1	151.0	163.5	226.4	286.7	337.9	360.6	538.8	618.9	849.8	947.9
Value of Imports, cif	1,002.5	1,237.6	1,370.8	1,524.3	2,186.4	3,665.7	3,182.7	3,295.1	3,280.2	3,660.0	4,561.7
Nonfuel Primary Products	170.6	210.3	206.1	219.4	331.6	505.3	427.9	414.2	426.0	497.6	561.3
Fuels	81.3	83.2	101.9	112.7	157.4	429.6	455.2	481.7	503.0	513.7	727.0
Manufactures	750.6	944.1	1,062.7	1,192.2	1,697.4	2,730.8	2,299.6	2,399.2	2,351.2	2,648.8	3,273.3
					(Index 1987 = 100)						
Terms of Trade	128.5	120.6	119.1	138.1	149.5	96.8	85.5	92.9	88.1	94.4	100.1
Export Prices, fob	32.5	33.1	35.2	44.8	60.6	57.1	54.0	59.4	61.8	73.7	92.5
Import Prices, cif	25.3	27.4	29.6	32.5	40.6	59.0	63.2	63.9	70.1	78.1	92.4
BALANCE OF PAYMENTS					*(Millions of current US dollars)*						
Exports of Goods & Services	..	1,471	1,782	2,358	3,124	3,051	3,282	3,810	4,132	4,988	6,156
Merchandise, fob	..	1,235	1,479	1,955	2,511	2,277	2,449	3,009	3,225	4,020	4,988
Nonfactor Services	..	188	251	327	491	653	729	698	787	852	1,036
Factor Services	..	48	52	75	122	122	105	103	119	116	132
Imports of Goods & Services	..	1,688	1,810	2,230	3,293	4,894	4,504	4,614	4,814	5,457	7,024
Merchandise, fob	..	1,167	1,213	1,457	2,148	3,595	3,095	3,129	3,116	3,418	4,698
Nonfactor Services	..	389	460	549	837	1,060	1,008	962	1,144	1,339	1,677
Factor Services	..	132	137	225	307	239	401	523	554	701	649
Long-Term Interest	..	..	..	..	..	..	..	..	..	..	..
Private Current Transfers, net	..	-5	16	54	76	49	60	34	47	27	72
Workers' Remittances	..	40	56	66	79	85	95	91	112	122	159
Curr. A/C Bal before Off. Transf.	..	-222	-12	182	-92	-1,793	-1,162	-770	-636	-442	-796
Net Official Transfers	..	-10	-8	-18	-29	-49	-58	-48	-53	-47	-47
Curr. A/C Bal after Off. Transf.	..	-232	-20	164	-121	-1,842	-1,220	-818	-689	-488	-843
Long-Term Capital, net	..	220	202	158	204	1,135	1,054	627	701	577	757
Direct Investment	..	137	98	123	189	231	117	242	122	218	276
Long-Term Loans	..	..	..	..	..	..	..	..	..	..	..
Disbursements	..	..	..	..	..	..	..	..	..	..	..
Repayments	..	..	..	..	..	..	..	..	..	..	..
Other Long-Term Capital	..	83	103	35	15	904	937	385	578	359	481
Other Capital, net	..	30	7	167	-53	214	12	5	192	-289	42
Change in Reserves	..	-18	-189	-488	-30	493	154	186	-203	201	44
Memo Item:					*(New Zealand Dollars per US dollar)*						
Conversion Factor (Annual Avg)	0.890	0.890	0.870	0.820	0.720	0.730	0.890	1.030	1.010	0.960	1.000
					(Millions US dollars), outstanding at end of year						
EXTERNAL DEBT (Total)	..	..	..	..	..	..	..	..	..	..	..
Long-Term Debt (by debtor)	..	..	..	..	..	..	..	..	..	..	..
Central Bank, incl. IMF credit	..	..	..	..	..	..	..	..	..	..	..
Central Government	..	..	..	..	..	..	..	..	..	..	..
Rest of General Government	..	..	..	..	..	..	..	..	..	..	..
Non-financial Public Enterprises	..	..	..	..	..	..	..	..	..	..	..
Priv. Sector, incl non-guaranteed	..	..	..	..	..	..	..	..	..	..	..
Short-Term Debt	..	..	..	..	..	..	..	..	..	..	..
Memo Items:					*(Millions of US dollars)*						
Int'l Reserves Excluding Gold	209.0	256.9	492.0	832.2	1,045.1	638.6	426.9	490.8	442.5	451.0	450.7
Gold Holdings (at market price)	0.8	0.8	1.0	1.5	2.5	4.2	3.2	3.0	7.3	14.8	23.2
SOCIAL INDICATORS											
Total Fertility Rate	3.3	3.2	3.2	2.9	2.7	2.6	2.3	2.3	2.2	2.1	2.2
Infant Mortality Rate	16.9	16.7	16.5	15.6	16.2	15.5	15.9	14.0	14.2	13.7	12.4
Life Expectancy at Birth	71.4	71.5	71.6	71.7	71.8	72.0	72.1	72.3	72.4	72.7	72.9
Urban Population, % of total	80.7	81.1	81.4	81.8	82.1	82.5	82.8	82.9	83.0	83.1	83.2
Food Prod. per capita (1987=100)	91.3	88.1	88.2	90.9	90.6	81.7	87.6	98.2	93.1	93.0	91.6
Labor Force, Agriculture (%)	0.0	0.0	0.0	0.0	0.0	0.0	0.0	0.0	0.0	0.0	0.0
Labor Force, Female (%)	..	..	..	..	..	..	..	..	..	..	..
Primary Schl. Enroll. Ratio	..	110.0	..	..	..	..	106.0	108.0	108.0	108.0	107.0
Primary Schl. Enroll. Ratio, Female	..	109.0	..	..	..	..	106.0	107.0	108.0	108.0	106.0
Secondary Schl. Enroll. Ratio	..	77.0	..	..	..	..	81.0	82.0	81.0	80.0	81.0

1980	1981	1982	1983	1984	1985	1986	1987	1988	1989 estimate	NOTES	NEW ZEALAND
				(Millions of current US dollars)							**FOREIGN TRADE (CUSTOMS BASIS)**
5,453.7	5,567.2	5,479.3	5,269.9	5,508.1	5,731.1	5,937.0	7,179.4	8,785.0	..	..	Value of Exports, fob
4,151.5	4,176.1	4,142.4	4,102.7	4,006.4	4,148.0	4,293.8	5,335.6	6,478.0	..	..	Nonfuel Primary Products
128.2	155.7	14.6	14.3	22.5	95.3	48.3	64.4	119.0	..	..	Fuels
1,174.0	1,235.4	1,322.3	1,152.9	1,479.2	1,487.8	1,594.9	1,779.4	2,188.0	..	..	Manufactures
5,514.7	5,731.5	5,900.5	5,326.9	6,180.5	5,981.7	6,131.4	7,254.5	7,304.0	..	..	Value of Imports, cif
644.4	620.1	697.9	604.8	699.7	654.1	612.3	762.1	888.9	..	..	Nonfuel Primary Products
1,238.6	1,112.9	978.6	964.4	829.7	759.8	530.0	484.0	398.1	..	..	Fuels
3,631.7	3,998.5	4,224.0	3,757.7	4,651.1	4,567.8	4,989.1	6,008.4	6,017.0	..	..	Manufactures
				(Index 1987 = 100)							
86.9	86.4	86.3	87.8	87.0	86.0	86.9	100.0	103.5	..	..	Terms of Trade
95.7	91.2	85.4	84.5	80.2	77.9	81.7	100.0	114.0	..	..	Export Prices, fob
110.1	105.6	98.9	96.2	92.2	90.5	94.0	100.0	110.1	..	..	Import Prices, cif
				(Millions of current US dollars)							**BALANCE OF PAYMENTS**
6,503	7,068	6,788	6,918	7,116	7,360	7,990	10,265	12,121	12,259	..	Exports of Goods & Services
5,394	5,603	5,304	5,282	5,434	5,595	5,836	7,245	8,785	8,821	..	Merchandise, fob
950	1,249	1,262	1,395	1,469	1,493	1,775	2,236	2,567	2,547	..	Nonfactor Services
159	216	223	241	213	272	379	783	769	890	..	Factor Services
7,487	8,207	8,499	7,966	9,132	9,226	9,918	12,080	12,970	14,555	..	Imports of Goods & Services
5,091	5,346	5,524	4,937	5,846	5,654	5,741	6,719	6,716	7,985	..	Merchandise, fob
1,700	2,001	2,014	1,907	1,951	1,969	2,335	2,856	3,541	3,678	..	Nonfactor Services
697	860	960	1,122	1,335	1,603	1,842	2,504	2,714	2,892	..	Factor Services
..	..	..	..	..	..	..	..	..	..	..	Long-Term Interest
108	66	160	166	197	144	190	220	290	297	..	Private Current Transfers, net
201	197	215	230	291	322	353	430	501	514	..	Workers' Remittances
-876	-1,073	-1,551	-881	-1,819	-1,722	-1,738	-1,595	-559	-1,999	..	Curr. A/C Bal before Off. Transf.
-50	-43	-61	-86	-73	-60	-39	-40	-43	-40	..	Net Official Transfers
-926	-1,116	-1,612	-968	-1,893	-1,783	-1,777	-1,635	-603	-2,039	..	Curr. A/C Bal after Off. Transf.
685	1,863	2,226	821	1,495	398	2,509	-1,226	-810	-343	..	Long-Term Capital, net
71	171	-79	46	227	193	116	-203	-277	-233	..	Direct Investment
..	..	..	..	..	..	..	..	..	..	..	Long-Term Loans
..	..	..	..	..	..	..	..	..	..	..	Disbursements
..	..	..	..	..	..	..	..	..	..	..	Repayments
614	1,692	2,305	775	1,267	206	2,393	-1,023	-533	-110	..	Other Long-Term Capital
169	-304	-577	359	1,912	1,810	1,230	569	1,473	2,748	..	Other Capital, net
72	-444	-37	-212	-1,514	-425	-1,963	2,292	-60	-365	..	Change in Reserves
				(New Zealand Dollars per US dollar)							**Memo Item:**
1.040	1.200	1.370	1.520	1.930	1.960	1.890	1.620	1.550	1.670	..	Conversion Factor (Annual Avg)
				(Millions US dollars), outstanding at end of year							
..	..	..	..	..	..	..	..	..	..	..	**EXTERNAL DEBT (Total)**
..	..	..	..	..	..	..	..	..	..	..	Long-Term Debt (by debtor)
..	..	..	..	..	..	..	..	..	..	..	Central Bank, incl. IMF credit
..	..	..	..	..	..	..	..	..	..	..	Central Government
..	..	..	..	..	..	..	..	..	..	..	Rest of General Government
..	..	..	..	..	..	..	..	..	..	..	Non-financial Public Enterprises
..	..	..	..	..	..	..	..	..	..	..	Priv. Sector, incl non-guaranteed
..	..	..	..	..	..	..	..	..	..	..	Short-Term Debt
				(Millions of US dollars)							**Memo Items:**
352.1	673.9	635.9	777.6	1,786.7	1,595.7	3,771.2	3,259.6	2,836.0	3,026.8	..	Int'l Reserves Excluding Gold
13.2	8.9	10.2	8.5	6.9	7.3	8.7	10.8	9.2	0.6	..	Gold Holdings (at market price)
											SOCIAL INDICATORS
2.1	2.0	1.9	1.9	1.9	1.9	1.9	1.9	1.9	1.9	..	Total Fertility Rate
12.8	11.6	11.8	12.5	11.7	10.8	11.2	11.0	10.8	10.6	..	Infant Mortality Rate
73.2	73.5	73.7	73.9	74.1	74.4	74.6	74.8	75.0	75.1	..	Life Expectancy at Birth
83.3	83.4	83.5	83.5	83.6	83.7	83.8	83.9	84.0	84.1	..	Urban Population, % of total
93.0	96.3	97.1	98.0	96.0	104.1	99.5	100.0	104.0	96.2	..	Food Prod. per capita (1987=100)
0.0	..	..	..	..	..	..	..	..	..	..	Labor Force, Agriculture (%)
..	..	..	..	..	..	..	..	..	..	..	Labor Force, Female (%)
111.0	..	107.0	106.0	107.0	107.0	106.0	107.0	..	..	..	Primary Schl. Enroll. Ratio
111.0	..	106.0	105.0	106.0	106.0	106.0	106.0	..	..	..	Primary Schl. Enroll. Ratio, Female
83.0	..	82.0	85.0	86.0	85.0	85.0	85.0	..	..	..	Secondary Schl. Enroll. Ratio

NICARAGUA	1969	1970	1971	1972	1973	1974	1975	1976	1977	1978	1979
CURRENT GNP PER CAPITA (US $)	370	380	390	390	430	560	630	700	780	740	560
POPULATION (thousands)	1,988	2,053	2,124	2,195	2,266	2,337	2,408	2,478	2,546	2,615	2,689

USE AND ORIGIN OF RESOURCES — *(Millions of current Nicaraguan New Cordobas)*

	1969	1970	1971	1972	1973	1974	1975	1976	1977	1978	1979
Gross National Product (GNP)	5.1	5.3	5.6	5.8	7.2	10.2	10.5	12.1	14.2	13.6	13.8
Net Factor Income from Abroad	-0.2	-0.2	-0.2	-0.2	-0.3	-0.5	-0.4	-0.5	-0.5	-0.7	-0.7
GDP at Market Prices	5.2	5.5	5.8	6.1	7.6	10.6	11.0	12.6	14.7	14.3	14.5
Resource Balance	-0.1	-0.1	-0.1	0.3	-0.7	-1.4	-1.0	0.1	-0.8	0.5	2.0
Exports of Goods & NFServices	1.3	1.5	1.5	2.2	2.2	3.1	3.1	4.3	5.0	5.2	6.1
Imports of Goods & NFServices	1.5	1.6	1.7	1.8	2.9	4.5	4.1	4.1	5.9	4.7	4.1
Domestic Absorption	5.4	5.6	5.9	5.7	8.3	12.1	11.9	12.4	15.6	13.8	12.5
Private Consumption, etc.	3.9	4.1	4.3	4.3	5.9	7.9	8.6	8.9	10.2	10.1	10.7
General Gov't Consumption	0.5	0.5	0.6	0.6	0.6	0.8	1.0	1.2	1.4	1.8	2.6
Gross Domestic Investment	1.0	1.0	1.0	0.8	1.8	3.4	2.3	2.4	3.9	1.9	-0.8
Fixed Investment	0.9	0.9	0.9	0.9	1.5	2.5	2.5	2.6	3.6	2.1	1.0
Indirect Taxes, net	0.4	0.4	0.5	0.5	0.8	1.1	1.0	1.2	1.5	1.3	1.3
GDP at factor cost	4.8	5.1	5.3	5.5	6.8	9.6	9.9	11.4	13.3	12.9	13.2
Agriculture	1.3	1.4	1.4	1.5	1.9	2.9	2.5	2.9	3.6	3.7	4.1
Industry	1.3	1.4	1.5	1.7	2.0	2.9	3.3	3.7	4.2	4.2	4.2
Manufacturing	1.0	1.1	1.2	1.3	1.6	2.2	2.5	2.7	3.1	3.3	3.6
Services, etc.	2.7	2.7	2.8	2.9	3.7	4.8	5.2	6.0	7.0	6.4	6.3
Gross Domestic Saving	0.9	0.9	0.9	1.1	1.1	1.9	1.3	2.5	3.1	2.4	1.2
Gross National Saving	..	0.7	0.7	0.9	0.9	1.5	1.0	2.0	2.6	1.7	0.5

(Millions of 1987 Nicaraguan New Cordobas)

	1969	1970	1971	1972	1973	1974	1975	1976	1977	1978	1979
Gross National Product	2,531.350	2,532.100	2,608.290	2,648.610	2,769.620	3,221.320	3,272.540	3,411.640	3,701.740	3,360.310	2,425.150
GDP at Market Prices	2,619.710	2,614.780	2,700.900	2,755.690	2,935.650	3,352.360	3,347.150	3,508.500	3,817.570	3,517.010	2,585.800
Resource Balance	197.914	188.964	207.508	338.466	220.324	157.505	319.968	339.831	197.647	371.855	542.494
Exports of Goods & NFServices	591.656	447.609	464.306	608.822	602.378	611.849	656.962	683.228	663.992	723.849	828.428
Imports of Goods & NFServices	393.742	258.645	256.799	270.357	382.053	454.345	336.994	343.398	466.345	351.995	285.934
Domestic Absorption	2,421.790	2,425.810	2,493.390	2,417.220	2,715.330	3,194.850	3,027.180	3,168.670	3,619.920	3,145.150	2,043.300
Private Consumption, etc.	1,965.960	1,985.690	2,039.510	2,056.750	2,139.640	2,424.600	2,482.230	2,595.900	2,783.730	2,624.230	1,883.750
General Gov't Consumption	140.391	127.932	131.363	144.454	134.162	149.239	177.317	196.458	212.257	256.677	274.914
Gross Domestic Investment	315.447	312.195	322.516	216.015	441.530	621.010	367.637	376.314	623.933	264.242	-115.360
Fixed Investment	285.214	262.908	271.566	250.363	333.406	417.420	393.214	411.766	546.223	302.751	106.188
GDP at factor cost	..	2,416.220	2,479.040	2,526.340	2,653.850	3,031.370	3,044.170	3,197.480	3,446.360	3,201.780	2,354.820
Agriculture	747.415	822.783	854.272	854.102	931.035	1,025.500	1,043.540	1,061.920	1,121.330	1,199.110	1,014.780
Industry	469.374	538.234	556.531	587.601	613.779	725.465	719.487	756.897	861.609	765.049	505.625
Manufacturing	339.783	379.538	397.556	415.935	436.578	493.436	505.025	525.849	579.267	579.629	421.005
Services, etc.	1,395.800	1,249.240	1,286.270	1,302.230	1,385.420	1,575.400	1,564.670	1,661.210	1,778.130	1,549.770	1,118.690
Memo Items:											
Capacity to Import	360.186	236.806	236.734	321.825	285.154	310.008	255.797	355.820	399.906	387.600	427.185
Terms of Trade Adjustment	-231.470	-210.803	-227.572	-286.997	-317.224	-301.841	-401.164	-327.408	-264.086	-336.250	-401.243
Gross Domestic Income	2,388.240	2,403.980	2,473.330	2,468.690	2,618.430	3,050.510	2,945.990	3,181.100	3,553.480	3,180.760	2,184.550
Gross National Income	2,299.880	2,321.290	2,380.720	2,361.610	2,452.400	2,919.480	2,871.380	3,084.230	3,437.650	3,024.060	2,023.910

DOMESTIC PRICES/DEFLATORS — *(Index 1987 = 100)*

	1969	1970	1971	1972	1973	1974	1975	1976	1977	1978	1979
Overall (GDP)	0.20	0.20	0.20	0.20	0.30	0.30	0.30	0.40	0.40	0.40	0.60
Domestic Absorption	0.20	0.20	0.20	0.20	0.30	0.40	0.40	0.40	0.40	0.40	0.60
Agriculture	0.20	0.20	0.20	0.20	0.20	0.30	0.20	0.30	0.30	0.30	0.40
Industry	0.30	0.30	0.30	0.30	0.30	0.40	0.50	0.50	0.50	0.50	0.80
Manufacturing	0.30	0.30	0.30	0.30	0.40	0.40	0.50	0.50	0.50	0.60	0.80
Consumer Price Index	..	..	..	0.04	0.05	0.06	0.06	0.06	0.07	0.07	0.11

MANUFACTURING ACTIVITY

	1969	1970	1971	1972	1973	1974	1975	1976	1977	1978	1979
Employment (1987=100)	..	..	..	..	..	..	..	..	..	..	..
Real Earnings per Empl. (1987=100)	..	..	..	..	..	..	..	..	..	..	..
Real Output per Empl. (1987=100)	..	..	..	..	..	..	..	..	..	..	..
Earnings as % of Value Added	16.8	15.7	15.3	18.4	15.8	15.7	15.5	16.2	16.7	15.9	21.8

MONETARY HOLDINGS — *(Thousands of current Nicaraguan New Cordobas)*

	1969	1970	1971	1972	1973	1974	1975	1976	1977	1978	1979
Money Supply, Broadly Defined	721	829	949	1,226	1,734	2,016	2,030	2,699	2,855	2,652	3,427
Money	513	578	619	749	1,146	1,313	1,256	1,616	1,699	1,579	2,654
Currency Outside Banks	219	251	252	329	411	452	445	636	692	883	1,572
Demand Deposits	295	327	367	420	735	862	811	980	1,007	697	1,083
Quasi-Money	208	251	330	477	588	703	774	1,084	1,156	1,073	773

(Millions of current Nicaraguan New Cordobas)

	1969	1970	1971	1972	1973	1974	1975	1976	1977	1978	1979
GOVERNMENT DEFICIT (-) OR SURPLUS	..	-0.05	-0.14	-0.23	-0.13	-0.62	-0.62	-0.49	-0.99	-0.84	-0.94
Current Revenue	..	0.65	0.72	0.74	1.04	1.46	1.48	1.72	2.05	1.88	2.14
Current Expenditure	..	0.54	0.57	0.62	0.67	1.09	1.24	1.36	1.77	2.22	2.80
Current Budget Balance	..	0.11	0.15	0.13	0.37	0.37	0.24	0.37	0.28	-0.35	-0.66
Capital Receipts	..	0.02	0.02	0.01	0.02	0.02	0.05	0.04	0.01	0.02	..
Capital Payments	..	0.18	0.30	0.38	0.52	1.01	0.91	0.90	1.29	0.51	0.28

1980	1981	1982	1983	1984	1985	1986	1987	1988	1989 estimate	NOTES	NICARAGUA
650	760	800	810	790	760	760	800	..	..	A	**CURRENT GNP PER CAPITA (US $)**
2,771	2,859	2,954	3,055	3,161	3,272	3,387	3,504	3,623	3,740	..	**POPULATION (thousands)**
(Millions of current Nicaraguan New Cordobas)											**USE AND ORIGIN OF RESOURCES**
19.4	23.1	26.6	31.1	41.0	104.5	393.2	2,503.7	274,948.0	15,418,100.0	..	Gross National Product (GNP)
-1.3	-1.4	-1.8	-1.8	-4.0	-11.0	-42.6	-192.1	-45,210.0	-3,229,600.0	..	Net Factor Income from Abroad
20.8	24.5	28.3	32.9	45.0	115.4	435.7	2,695.8	320,158.0	18,647,700.0	..	GDP at Market Prices
-4.0	-4.8	-2.9	-3.5	-5.9	-8.1	-35.1	-53.6	-146,152.0	-6,458,200.0	..	Resource Balance
5.0	5.5	4.5	6.4	7.4	17.0	55.7	317.3	31,869.6	2,595,610.0	..	Exports of Goods & NFServices
9.0	10.2	7.4	9.9	13.3	25.2	90.8	371.0	178,022.0	9,053,820.0	..	Imports of Goods & NFServices
24.8	29.2	31.2	36.4	50.9	123.6	470.8	2,749.5	466,310.0	25,105,900.0	..	Domestic Absorption
17.2	18.1	19.2	18.7	25.0	55.6	243.2	1,400.7	253,535.0	14,837,800.0	..	Private Consumption, etc.
4.1	5.4	6.6	10.4	15.9	41.2	154.0	922.9	107,959.0	4,785,810.0	..	General Gov't Consumption
3.5	5.8	5.3	7.4	10.0	26.7	73.6	425.9	104,816.0	5,482,270.0	..	Gross Domestic Investment
3.0	5.2	4.7	6.4	8.7	23.9	60.3	355.4	95,217.6	4,618,800.0	..	Fixed Investment
1.4	3.4	4.5	6.6	10.6	24.5	89.3	504.4	59,813.5	3,483,940.0	..	Indirect Taxes, net
19.4	21.1	23.9	26.3	34.4	90.9	346.4	2,191.4	260,345.0	15,163,800.0	B	GDP at factor cost
4.8	5.0	6.1	7.6	11.2	27.3	90.6	778.4	88,852.9	5,523,480.0	..	Agriculture
6.5	8.1	9.1	10.1	14.3	40.4	146.2	623.2	70,217.0	3,798,090.0	..	Industry
5.3	6.5	7.4	8.0	11.4	31.9	120.7	505.0	54,498.0	2,863,610.0	..	Manufacturing
9.4	11.5	13.2	15.2	19.5	47.7	199.0	1,294.3	161,088.0	9,326,140.0	..	Services, etc.
-0.5	1.0	2.5	3.9	4.2	18.6	38.5	372.3	-41,336.0	-975,940.0	..	Gross Domestic Saving
-1.8	-0.2	0.8	2.1	0.2	8.1	-4.1	180.1	-86,546.0	-4,205,500.0	..	Gross National Saving
(Millions of 1987 Nicaraguan New Cordobas)											
2,548.140	2,713.690	2,679.240	2,818.980	2,673.320	2,524.140	2,469.260	2,503.710	2,144.610	2,026.220	..	Gross National Product
2,705.030	2,850.120	2,826.850	2,957.250	2,895.580	2,772.450	2,716.370	2,695.850	2,445.130	2,384.190	..	GDP at Market Prices
-27.144	68.904	158.071	134.067	24.664	-29.334	-37.893	-53.639	-74.569	77.136	..	Resource Balance
492.067	565.262	519.769	556.552	440.705	389.119	320.523	317.320	275.244	373.779	..	Exports of Goods & NFServices
519.211	496.358	361.699	422.486	416.041	418.453	358.416	370.959	349.814	296.643	..	Imports of Goods & NFServices
2,732.180	2,781.210	2,668.780	2,823.190	2,870.920	2,801.780	2,754.270	2,749.490	2,519.700	2,307.060	..	Domestic Absorption
2,042.980	1,873.580	1,775.840	1,713.100	1,640.490	1,518.690	1,442.770	1,400.710	1,169.800	1,240.880	..	Private Consumption, etc.
370.444	420.208	491.243	673.318	789.820	845.110	878.921	922.872	922.673	675.323	..	General Gov't Consumption
318.753	487.418	401.697	436.771	440.607	437.977	432.573	425.909	427.235	390.855	..	Gross Domestic Investment
267.855	428.816	346.303	362.559	370.510	374.662	351.869	355.403	348.954	281.637	..	Fixed Investment
2,538.040	2,467.100	2,391.230	2,375.140	2,219.810	2,180.060	2,158.840	2,191.450	1,995.800	1,947.850	B	GDP at factor cost
821.592	899.717	925.248	978.523	926.269	881.845	804.401	778.359	696.659	715.552	..	Agriculture
591.949	609.069	590.680	624.829	630.717	612.329	633.887	623.199	465.225	449.174	..	Industry
482.752	497.329	497.601	525.668	527.750	502.943	513.264	505.025	359.620	334.450	..	Manufacturing
1,266.120	1,328.840	1,311.950	1,353.900	1,338.590	1,278.270	1,278.080	1,294.290	1,283.250	1,219.470	..	Services, etc.
											Memo Items:
290.733	265.478	221.808	273.285	232.270	283.106	219.823	317.320	62.624	85.043	..	Capacity to Import
-201.335	-299.784	-297.961	-283.267	-208.435	-106.013	-100.700	0.000	-212.621	-288.735	..	Terms of Trade Adjustment
2,503.700	2,550.330	2,528.890	2,673.990	2,687.140	2,666.430	2,615.670	2,695.850	2,232.510	2,095.460	..	Gross Domestic Income
2,346.810	2,413.910	2,381.280	2,535.720	2,464.880	2,418.120	2,368.560	2,503.710	1,931.990	1,737.480	..	Gross National Income
(Index 1987 = 100)											**DOMESTIC PRICES/DEFLATORS**
0.80	0.90	1.00	1.10	1.60	4.20	16.00	100.00	13,093.70	782,139.00	..	Overall (GDP)
0.90	1.10	1.20	1.30	1.80	4.40	17.10	100.00	18,506.50	1,088,220.00	..	Domestic Absorption
0.60	0.60	0.70	0.80	1.20	3.10	11.30	100.00	12,754.10	771,918.00	..	Agriculture
1.10	1.30	1.50	1.60	2.30	6.60	23.10	100.00	15,093.10	845,572.00	..	Industry
1.10	1.30	1.50	1.50	2.20	6.30	23.50	100.00	15,154.30	856,214.00	..	Manufacturing
0.14	0.18	0.22	0.29	0.40	1.26	9.88	100.00	10,305.03	..	..	Consumer Price Index
											MANUFACTURING ACTIVITY
..	..	..	..	..	..	..	..	..	..	J	Employment (1987=100)
..	..	..	..	..	..	..	..	..	..	J	Real Earnings per Empl. (1987=100)
..	..	..	..	..	..	..	..	..	..	J	Real Output per Empl. (1987=100)
29.1	30.6	22.9	18.8	19.7	16.5	..	..	..	..	J	Earnings as % of Value Added
(Thousands of current Nicaraguan New Cordobas)											**MONETARY HOLDINGS**
5,747	7,927	9,895	15,190	25,900	63,600			..	..	..	Money Supply, Broadly Defined
4,102	5,206	6,546	10,937	20,844	54,775	192,925	1,421,850	..	..	..	Money
1,964	2,376	3,086	5,426	11,338	28,560	99,100	730,275	..	..	..	Currency Outside Banks
2,139	2,831	3,460	5,511	9,506	26,215	93,825	691,575	..	..	..	Demand Deposits
1,644	2,720	3,349	4,253	5,056	8,825	..	..	..	..	..	Quasi-Money
(Millions of current Nicaraguan New Cordobas)											
-1.42	-2.63	-5.74	-10.30	-10.61	-25.32	-64.18	..	..	..	..	**GOVERNMENT DEFICIT (-) OR SURPLUS**
4.97	6.93	8.16	11.89	18.08	43.22	163.09	..	..	..	..	Current Revenue
5.15	7.55	10.83	13.93	21.56	60.79	209.45	..	..	..	..	Current Expenditure
-0.18	-0.62	-2.67	-2.04	-3.48	-17.57	-46.36	..	..	..	..	Current Budget Balance
0.00	0.09	0.09	0.08	0.08	0.21	0.77	..	..	..	..	Capital Receipts
1.24	2.09	3.16	8.34	7.21	7.96	18.59	..	..	..	..	Capital Payments

NICARAGUA	1969	1970	1971	1972	1973	1974	1975	1976	1977	1978	1979
FOREIGN TRADE (CUSTOMS BASIS)					*(Millions of current US dollars)*						
Value of Exports, fob	154.64	174.79	183.40	246.27	274.65	376.99	371.47	538.54	632.99	646.00	633.22
Nonfuel Primary Products	135.84	146.44	154.99	210.33	229.63	304.88	306.85	449.41	526.65	535.90	555.96
Fuels	0.03	0.23	0.39	1.79	1.37	1.59	1.38	2.12	1.20	1.10	5.36
Manufactures	18.77	28.12	28.02	34.15	43.65	70.52	63.24	87.01	105.14	109.00	71.90
Value of Imports, cif	175.59	197.86	209.59	217.95	326.36	559.01	516.86	532.14	761.93	779.96	414.94
Nonfuel Primary Products	20.84	25.05	26.16	29.65	47.44	58.08	52.34	57.75	72.75	93.72	64.28
Fuels	10.47	12.06	15.66	15.95	23.67	60.56	73.83	69.37	105.07	118.43	88.34
Manufactures	144.28	160.75	167.77	172.35	255.25	440.37	390.69	405.02	584.11	567.81	262.32
					(Index 1987 = 100)						
Terms of Trade	155.8	165.4	155.9	154.3	175.7	148.6	121.4	162.4	171.0	140.8	136.8
Export Prices, fob	37.4	41.5	41.7	45.6	64.5	74.6	66.5	90.3	103.4	97.1	114.9
Import Prices, cif	24.0	25.1	26.7	29.6	36.7	50.2	54.8	55.6	60.5	68.9	84.0
BALANCE OF PAYMENTS					*(Millions of current US dollars)*						
Exports of Goods & Services	..	217.8	224.4	290.8	322.6	447.6	457.9	629.7	732.9	731.9	683.2
Merchandise, fob	..	178.6	187.3	249.4	278.4	381.0	374.9	541.8	636.2	646.0	615.9
Nonfactor Services	..	34.5	32.8	36.5	37.4	55.7	71.8	73.8	83.1	74.2	56.3
Factor Services	..	4.7	4.3	4.9	6.8	10.9	11.2	14.1	13.6	11.7	11.0
Imports of Goods & Services	..	263.4	273.9	297.2	446.0	720.4	659.5	678.3	926.0	773.9	594.6
Merchandise, fob	..	178.6	190.2	205.5	327.5	541.8	482.1	485.0	704.2	553.3	388.9
Nonfactor Services	..	49.9	47.6	50.2	62.9	104.9	106.4	107.4	137.1	112.0	121.8
Factor Services	..	34.9	36.1	41.5	55.6	73.7	71.0	85.9	84.7	108.6	83.9
Long-Term Interest	..	6.8	8.0	10.8	18.1	29.2	35.5	40.8	51.5	50.5	36.9
Private Current Transfers, net	..	2.5	2.6	2.6	27.5	3.4	4.1	1.0	0.7	0.1	1.4
Workers' Remittances	..	..	..	..	..	..	..	..	..	..	..
Curr. A/C Bal before Off. Transf.	..	-43.1	-46.9	17.3	-95.8	-269.4	-197.5	-47.6	-192.4	-34.3	90.0
Net Official Transfers	..	3.6	2.4	4.5	29.9	12.1	12.5	8.3	10.5	9.4	90.2
Curr. A/C Bal after Off. Transf.	..	-39.5	-44.5	21.7	-65.9	-257.2	-185.0	-39.3	-181.9	-24.9	180.2
Long-Term Capital, net	..	45.9	51.4	50.5	112.1	173.5	178.2	36.5	211.0	135.0	122.5
Direct Investment	..	15.0	13.3	10.0	13.2	13.8	10.9	12.9	10.0	7.0	2.8
Long-Term Loans	..	27.5	32.5	46.2	98.0	127.6	141.0	57.3	193.0	87.4	96.7
Disbursements	..	43.7	55.3	66.3	147.9	147.4	160.2	91.4	239.7	134.6	112.2
Repayments	..	16.2	22.8	20.1	49.9	19.8	19.2	34.1	46.7	47.2	15.5
Other Long-Term Capital	..	3.4	5.5	-5.7	0.8	32.1	26.3	-33.8	8.0	40.6	23.0
Other Capital, net	..	2.3	-1.4	-48.8	19.0	49.6	48.7	-1.2	-25.8	-183.6	-305.4
Change in Reserves	..	-8.7	-5.4	-23.4	-65.2	34.1	-41.9	4.0	-3.3	73.5	2.7
Memo Item:					*(Nicaraguan New Cordobas per US dollar)*						
Conversion Factor (Annual Avg)	0.010	0.010	0.010	0.010	0.010	0.010	0.010	0.010	0.010	0.010	0.010
					(Millions of US dollars), outstanding at end of year						
EXTERNAL DEBT (Total)	..	154.9	190.8	234.4	339.0	465.4	610.9	661.8	1,274.0	1,429.3	1,487.2
Long-Term Debt (by debtor)	..	154.9	190.8	234.4	339.0	465.4	610.9	661.8	847.0	944.3	1,142.2
Central Bank, incl. IMF credit	..	59.3	70.1	69.6	103.5	110.1	162.2	172.1	205.6	229.2	332.3
Central Government	..	36.6	45.1	76.1	133.7	193.9	270.2	279.2	381.4	418.9	503.2
Rest of General Government	..	2.4	1.8	1.3	0.9	0.7	0.6	0.2	0.2	0.2	0.2
Non-financial Public Enterprises	..	40.6	51.3	58.5	69.9	94.3	107.4	136.0	170.1	193.4	203.5
Priv. Sector, incl non-guaranteed	..	16.0	22.5	28.9	31.0	66.4	70.5	74.3	89.7	102.6	103.0
Short-Term Debt	..	0.0	0.0	0.0	0.0	0.0	0.0	0.0	427.0	485.0	345.0
Memo Items:					*(Millions of US dollars)*						
Int'l Reserves Excluding Gold	43.7	48.6	58.1	80.1	116.3	104.5	121.6	146.1	148.3	50.8	146.6
Gold Holdings (at market price)	0.5	0.6	0.8	0.6	1.7	3.5	2.5	2.3	4.3	6.1	9.2
SOCIAL INDICATORS											
Total Fertility Rate	6.9	6.9	6.8	6.7	6.6	6.6	6.5	6.4	6.3	6.2	6.2
Infant Mortality Rate	109.0	106.0	103.0	100.0	98.6	97.2	95.8	94.4	93.0	89.6	86.2
Life Expectancy at Birth	52.9	53.5	54.1	54.7	55.0	55.3	55.7	56.0	56.3	57.0	57.7
Urban Population, % of total	46.1	47.0	47.7	48.3	49.0	49.6	50.3	50.9	51.5	52.2	52.8
Food Prod. per capita (1987=100)	157.8	164.0	161.2	154.7	147.4	150.2	162.8	165.5	166.0	176.6	182.5
Labor Force, Agriculture (%)	52.5	51.5	51.0	50.5	50.0	49.5	49.1	48.5	48.0	47.5	47.0
Labor Force, Female (%)	19.6	19.8	20.0	20.1	20.3	20.4	20.6	20.8	21.0	21.2	21.4
Primary Schl. Enroll. Ratio	..	80.0	..	..	..	..	82.0	88.0	87.0	84.0	90.0
Primary Schl. Enroll. Ratio, Female	..	81.0	..	..	..	..	85.0	90.0	89.0	88.0	93.0
Secondary Schl. Enroll. Ratio	..	18.0	..	..	..	..	24.0	28.0	30.0	28.0	30.0

	1980	1981	1982	1983	1984	1985	1986	1987	1988	1989 estimate	NOTES
FOREIGN TRADE (CUSTOMS BASIS) *(Millions of current US dollars)*											
Value of Exports, fob	413.84	475.91	390.72	434.70	386.70	301.50	247.17	299.90	236.00	..	..
Nonfuel Primary Products	346.49	419.41	355.46	392.29	339.98	261.75	219.51	265.85	212.14	..	..
Fuels	10.28	9.28	4.95	6.27	7.48	6.11	3.12	3.85	2.75	..	..
Manufactures	57.07	47.22	30.31	36.14	39.24	33.64	24.53	30.20	21.11	..	..
Value of Imports, cif	881.88	994.22	774.88	799.00	848.40	964.30	856.80	922.60	892.00	..	..
Nonfuel Primary Products	148.88	184.60	103.07	117.55	141.56	155.74	135.63	152.58	248.81	..	..
Fuels	175.84	199.13	179.57	177.55	163.46	162.02	70.86	98.23	98.67	..	..
Manufactures	557.16	610.49	492.24	503.90	543.38	646.54	650.31	671.79	544.51	..	..
(Index 1987 = 100)											
Terms of Trade	128.6	111.2	112.5	117.7	118.7	111.5	121.9	100.0	102.2	..	..
Export Prices, fob	124.6	110.2	107.4	109.4	106.9	98.3	111.0	100.0	108.7	..	..
Import Prices, cif	96.9	99.1	95.4	92.9	90.1	88.1	91.1	100.0	106.4	..	..
BALANCE OF PAYMENTS *(Millions of current US dollars)*											
Exports of Goods & Services	514.0	581.6	455.5	504.5	465.4	345.9	288.0	326.0	317.1	347.8	f
Merchandise, fob	450.4	508.2	406.0	451.9	412.4	305.1	257.8	295.1	236.0	290.0	..
Nonfactor Services	44.4	45.1	40.8	46.1	48.4	39.3	29.5	29.5	79.2	50.5	..
Factor Services	19.2	28.3	8.7	6.5	4.6	1.5	0.7	1.4	2.1	6.8	..
Imports of Goods & Services	1,049.3	1,243.5	1,020.9	1,091.2	1,152.3	1,198.5	1,090.8	1,140.2	1,095.0	964.0	f
Merchandise, fob	802.9	922.4	723.5	742.3	735.3	794.1	677.4	734.4	718.0	633.0	..
Nonfactor Services	102.7	109.0	102.5	127.6	149.0	129.6	159.1	160.5	138.0	118.0	..
Factor Services	143.7	212.1	194.9	221.3	268.0	274.8	254.3	245.3	239.0	213.0	..
Long-Term Interest	37.8	90.6	109.1	37.4	34.3	28.0	21.2	11.4	17.4	9.5	..
Private Current Transfers, net	1.6	13.2	8.0	3.6	2.0	13.8	0.0	0.0	0.0	..	..
Workers' Remittances	..	..	..	..	..	..	..	..	..	..	..
Curr. A/C Bal before Off. Transf.	-533.7	-648.7	-557.4	-583.1	-684.9	-838.8	-802.8	-814.2	-778.0	-617.0	..
Net Official Transfers	122.3	57.1	43.5	75.7	87.8	113.1	115.1	135.4	189.0	169.0	..
Curr. A/C Bal after Off. Transf.	-411.4	-591.6	-513.9	-507.4	-597.1	-725.7	-687.7	-678.8	-589.0	-448.0	..
Long-Term Capital, net	558.0	675.7	473.2	873.3	617.8	783.2	387.2	80.4	2.4	-100.0	f
Direct Investment	..	..	..	7.7	..	..	..	..	..	..	..
Long-Term Loans	221.6	294.8	240.4	271.9	348.9	582.2	592.3	474.0	429.0	264.4	..
Disbursements	266.0	364.9	294.2	316.9	378.5	600.9	603.4	495.8	433.4	282.3	..
Repayments	44.4	70.1	53.8	45.0	29.6	18.7	11.1	21.8	4.4	17.9	..
Other Long-Term Capital	336.4	380.9	232.8	593.7	268.9	201.0	-205.1	-393.6	-426.6	-364.4	..
Other Capital, net	-348.1	-117.2	0.0	-223.0	285.3	-48.6	155.8	618.3	660.5	479.3	f
Change in Reserves	201.5	33.1	40.6	-142.9	-306.0	-8.9	144.7	-19.9	-73.9	68.7	..
Memo Item: *(Nicaraguan New Cordobas per US dollar)*											
Conversion Factor (Annual Avg)	0.010	0.010	0.010	0.010	0.020	0.040	0.160	0.790	..	..	..
EXTERNAL DEBT (Total) *(Millions of US dollars), outstanding at end of year*	2,170.8	2,572.2	3,330.5	4,174.3	5,105.7	5,690.7	6,181.5	7,321.8	8,052.4	9,205.5	..
Long-Term Debt (by debtor)	1,710.8	2,101.2	2,506.8	3,396.8	4,097.1	4,483.9	5,204.6	6,180.6	6,744.0	7,546.5	..
Central Bank, incl. IMF credit	304.0	448.3	547.2	1,258.8	1,555.3	1,638.6	1,658.6	1,730.5	1,765.8	1,767.2	..
Central Government	1,186.8	1,421.1	1,726.5	1,879.7	2,295.3	2,583.4	3,361.8	4,236.9	4,780.4	5,581.8	..
Rest of General Government	0.1	0.1	0.1	0.1	0.1	0.1	0.0	0.0	0.0	..	..
Non-financial Public Enterprises	177.0	189.6	191.2	213.8	197.8	213.0	164.3	193.3	179.2	179.0	..
Priv. Sector, incl non-guaranteed	42.9	42.1	41.8	44.4	48.6	48.8	19.9	19.9	18.6	18.5	..
Short-Term Debt	460.0	471.0	823.7	777.5	1,008.6	1,206.8	976.9	1,141.2	1,308.4	1,659.0	..
Memo Items: *(Millions of US dollars)*											
Int'l Reserves Excluding Gold	64.5	111.4	171.2	174.7	..	..	..	..	..	..	..
Gold Holdings (at market price)	10.6	7.2	8.2	45.8	..	..	..	..	..	..	..
SOCIAL INDICATORS											
Total Fertility Rate	6.1	6.0	5.9	5.9	5.8	5.7	5.6	5.5	5.4	5.3	..
Infant Mortality Rate	82.8	79.4	76.0	73.2	70.4	67.6	64.8	62.0	60.1	58.2	..
Life Expectancy at Birth	58.4	59.1	59.8	60.5	61.2	61.9	62.6	63.3	63.7	64.1	..
Urban Population, % of total	53.4	54.0	54.7	55.3	56.0	56.6	57.2	57.9	58.5	59.2	..
Food Prod. per capita (1987=100)	121.7	119.3	121.3	115.5	107.9	108.7	103.1	100.0	85.6	82.6	..
Labor Force, Agriculture (%)	46.6	..	..	..	..	..	..	..	..	..	..
Labor Force, Female (%)	21.6	22.0	22.4	22.8	23.1	23.4	23.8	24.2	24.6	24.9	..
Primary Schl. Enroll. Ratio	99.0	..	100.0	103.0	99.0	101.0	98.0	99.0	..	..	..
Primary Schl. Enroll. Ratio, Female	102.0	..	103.0	106.0	102.0	107.0	103.0	104.0	..	..	..
Secondary Schl. Enroll. Ratio	43.0	..	39.0	44.0	43.0	39.0	42.0	43.0	..	..	..

NIGER	1969	1970	1971	1972	1973	1974	1975	1976	1977	1978	1979
CURRENT GNP PER CAPITA (US $)	160	160	170	160	160	200	230	230	250	300	360
POPULATION (thousands)	4,058	4,146	4,238	4,340	4,451	4,572	4,704	4,845	4,996	5,159	5,331

USE AND ORIGIN OF RESOURCES *(Billions of current CFA Francs)*

	1969	1970	1971	1972	1973	1974	1975	1976	1977	1978	1979
Gross National Product (GNP)	160.60	177.14	188.28	184.20	206.74	240.60	214.55	247.87	310.09	389.29	431.99
Net Factor Income from Abroad	-2.10	-2.50	-2.70	-3.00	-4.20	-6.40	-10.20	-6.50	-7.20	-11.10	-16.70
GDP at Market Prices	162.70	179.64	190.98	187.20	210.94	247.00	224.75	254.37	317.29	400.40	448.69
Resource Balance	-11.58	-13.16	-6.17	-11.76	-17.34	-41.25	-26.40	-30.71	-30.74	-21.21	-37.38
Exports of Goods & NFServices	15.22	19.35	23.62	26.61	32.73	30.31	43.26	56.63	62.32	90.21	128.06
Imports of Goods & NFServices	26.80	32.52	29.79	38.37	50.07	71.56	69.66	87.34	93.06	111.43	165.44
Domestic Absorption	174.28	192.80	197.15	198.96	228.28	288.25	251.15	285.08	348.02	421.61	486.06
Private Consumption, etc.	149.94	159.52	166.56	160.81	178.58	230.89	194.68	215.92	240.18	283.08	318.95
General Gov't Consumption	14.21	15.59	15.74	17.42	18.19	20.17	24.30	33.01	45.39	46.46	51.20
Gross Domestic Investment	10.12	17.69	14.86	20.72	31.51	37.19	32.17	36.14	62.45	92.07	115.91
Fixed Investment	..	..	..	..	..	..	..	..	..	..	..
Indirect Taxes, net	5.50	5.50	6.00	6.50	6.90	9.10	9.60	11.90	19.00	23.90	26.00
GDP at factor cost	157.20	174.14	184.98	180.70	204.04	237.90	215.15	242.47	298.29	376.50	422.69
Agriculture	108.07	116.54	125.02	116.93	127.14	157.57	113.07	119.62	164.31	210.93	218.44
Industry	8.53	12.47	14.13	15.17	19.78	19.11	24.75	32.76	44.38	59.89	84.09
Manufacturing	4.77	8.34	9.17	9.85	13.34	12.12	12.50	14.85	16.29	18.49	19.00
Services, etc.	46.10	50.63	51.84	55.11	64.02	70.32	86.92	101.98	108.59	129.58	146.16
Gross Domestic Saving	-1.45	4.53	8.68	8.96	14.17	-4.07	5.77	5.43	31.71	70.85	78.53
Gross National Saving	..	0.97	4.37	3.74	6.41	-14.47	-8.50	-5.81	19.06	51.72	51.24

(Billions of 1987 CFA Francs)

	1969	1970	1971	1972	1973	1974	1975	1976	1977	1978	1979
Gross National Product	583.55	600.98	634.96	600.93	496.53	536.32	512.08	525.82	568.16	641.17	679.22
GDP at Market Prices	594.56	612.75	647.58	614.09	509.48	554.15	538.65	542.30	584.38	663.15	710.50
Resource Balance	6.45	20.91	44.93	29.25	31.72	-65.59	47.95	47.00	39.61	75.91	0.81
Exports of Goods & NFServices	120.93	126.36	136.44	144.96	165.89	89.92	175.97	192.25	178.30	237.99	182.17
Imports of Goods & NFServices	114.48	105.45	91.50	115.71	134.18	155.51	128.02	145.26	138.69	162.08	181.36
Domestic Absorption	589.14	599.28	608.26	600.00	516.98	616.06	535.45	549.49	585.57	647.80	738.63
Private Consumption, etc.	492.34	470.08	498.10	470.29	356.95	456.41	388.25	394.35	410.80	452.90	522.13
General Gov't Consumption	53.98	57.95	55.96	56.46	52.99	56.95	62.90	68.84	77.76	72.80	71.32
Gross Domestic Investment	42.82	71.25	54.19	73.26	107.04	102.69	84.30	86.30	97.01	122.10	145.18
Fixed Investment	..	..	..	..	..	..	..	..	..	..	..
GDP at factor cost	574.52	594.04	627.29	592.85	492.95	533.94	515.44	516.59	549.24	623.58	669.61
Agriculture	270.46	286.16	300.96	272.26	183.00	222.02	178.07	162.37	187.48	213.05	200.49
Industry	71.19	59.90	70.70	71.19	82.98	72.18	84.94	97.22	107.53	128.64	174.79
Manufacturing	..	..	..	..	..	..	..	..	..	..	..
Services, etc.	192.85	197.89	205.45	212.38	224.99	219.31	274.78	297.46	289.90	319.52	352.92

Memo Items:											
Capacity to Import	65.03	62.76	72.54	80.25	87.71	65.86	79.50	94.18	92.88	131.22	140.39
Terms of Trade Adjustment	-55.90	-63.60	-63.90	-64.71	-78.19	-24.06	-96.47	-98.07	-85.41	-106.77	-41.78
Gross Domestic Income	538.66	549.15	583.68	549.38	431.29	530.09	442.18	444.23	498.97	556.38	668.72
Gross National Income	527.65	537.38	571.06	536.21	418.34	512.26	415.61	427.74	482.75	534.40	637.43

DOMESTIC PRICES/DEFLATORS *(Index 1987 = 100)*

	1969	1970	1971	1972	1973	1974	1975	1976	1977	1978	1979
Overall (GDP)	27.4	29.3	29.5	30.5	41.4	44.6	41.7	46.9	54.3	60.4	63.2
Domestic Absorption	29.6	32.2	32.4	33.2	44.2	46.8	46.9	51.9	59.4	65.1	65.8
Agriculture	40.0	40.7	41.5	42.9	69.5	71.0	63.5	73.7	87.6	99.0	109.0
Industry	12.0	20.8	20.0	21.3	23.8	26.5	29.1	33.7	41.3	46.6	48.1
Manufacturing	..	..	..	..	..	..	..	..	..	..	..
Consumer Price Index	26.7	27.0	28.1	30.8	34.5	35.6	38.9	48.0	59.2	65.2	69.9

MANUFACTURING ACTIVITY

	1969	1970	1971	1972	1973	1974	1975	1976	1977	1978	1979
Employment (1987=100)	..	..	..	..	..	..	..	..	50.0	58.0	63.4
Real Earnings per Empl. (1987=100)	..	..	..	..	..	..	..	..	116.9	130.4	142.5
Real Output per Empl. (1987=100)	..	..	..	..	..	..	..	..	29.7	33.5	38.0
Earnings as % of Value Added	..	..	..	..	..	..	..	..	..	43.1	41.2

MONETARY HOLDINGS *(Billions of current CFA Francs)*

	1969	1970	1971	1972	1973	1974	1975	1976	1977	1978	1979
Money Supply, Broadly Defined	9.21	9.60	12.13	12.90	15.50	20.32	22.31	29.24	37.64	54.20	64.51
Money	8.54	8.83	10.57	11.38	13.62	17.64	20.13	24.78	32.33	46.39	57.27
Currency Outside Banks	4.78	4.87	5.96	6.18	6.66	9.39	9.43	13.41	14.85	19.74	27.28
Demand Deposits	3.76	3.96	4.61	5.20	6.96	8.25	10.70	11.36	17.49	26.66	29.99
Quasi-Money	0.67	0.77	1.56	1.52	1.88	2.68	2.17	4.46	5.30	7.81	7.24

(Millions of current CFA Francs)

	1969	1970	1971	1972	1973	1974	1975	1976	1977	1978	1979
GOVERNMENT DEFICIT (-) OR SURPLUS	..	..	..	..	..	..	..	-5,468	-5,261	-12,622	-12,105
Current Revenue	..	..	..	..	..	..	..	30,485	37,644	50,382	62,553
Current Expenditure	..	..	..	..	..	..	..	24,820	27,113	34,937	39,163
Current Budget Balance	..	..	..	..	..	..	..	5,665	10,531	15,445	23,390
Capital Receipts	..	..	..	..	..	..	..	4	11	7	6
Capital Payments	..	..	..	..	..	..	..	11,137	15,803	28,074	35,501

1980	1981	1982	1983	1984	1985	1986	1987	1988	1989 estimate	NOTES	NIGER
440	440	380	310	240	230	240	250	300	290	..	**CURRENT GNP PER CAPITA (US $)**
5,515	5,709	5,914	6,130	6,356	6,593	6,813	7,033	7,256	7,479	..	**POPULATION (thousands)**
				(Billions of current CFA Francs)							**USE AND ORIGIN OF RESOURCES**
528.00	582.10	618.50	649.20	621.10	629.40	622.60	626.50	672.90	633.80	..	Gross National Product (GNP)
-8.20	-7.80	-26.90	-28.10	-17.20	-17.70	-20.80	-23.40	-21.30	-18.00	..	Net Factor Income from Abroad
536.20	589.90	645.40	677.30	638.30	647.10	643.40	649.90	694.20	651.80	..	GDP at Market Prices
-75.50	-68.40	-67.20	-36.00	-30.30	-67.10	-28.90	-30.60	-29.50	-41.10	..	Resource Balance
130.80	146.70	136.60	152.50	132.10	112.60	126.60	120.80	127.20	113.00	..	Exports of Goods & NFServices
206.30	215.10	203.80	188.50	162.40	179.70	155.50	151.40	156.70	154.10	..	Imports of Goods & NFServices
611.70	658.30	712.60	713.30	668.60	714.20	672.30	680.50	723.70	692.90	..	Domestic Absorption
360.00	474.10	519.80	549.50	583.10	561.70	533.20	544.30	575.30	552.00	..	Private Consumption, etc.
55.20	64.50	75.20	77.20	65.20	70.10	74.00	76.10	72.20	78.90	..	General Gov't Consumption
196.50	119.70	117.60	86.60	20.30	82.40	65.10	60.10	76.20	62.00	..	Gross Domestic Investment
152.00	137.60	87.10	99.00	62.90	64.10	63.10	63.10	67.00	66.00	..	Fixed Investment
27.00	27.80	31.30	25.80	26.20	25.60	24.70	21.00	19.10	19.90	..	Indirect Taxes, net
509.20	562.10	614.10	651.50	612.10	621.50	618.70	628.90	675.10	631.90	B	GDP at factor cost
228.20	269.30	293.70	311.10	228.30	237.80	237.90	219.10	270.70	237.20	..	Agriculture
121.60	113.00	114.40	114.50	137.90	135.50	141.80	157.20	102.30	82.40	..	Industry
19.80	23.20	25.60	20.50	44.80	46.20	49.30	56.70	49.60	39.50	..	Manufacturing
186.40	207.60	237.30	251.70	272.10	273.80	263.70	273.60	321.20	332.20	..	Services, etc.
121.00	51.30	50.40	50.60	-10.00	15.30	36.20	29.50	46.70	20.90	..	Gross Domestic Saving
100.82	29.39	6.05	3.73	-46.13	-28.78	0.40	-8.90	15.00	-9.90	..	Gross National Saving
				(Billions of 1987 CFA Francs)							
729.73	739.66	709.09	695.71	585.37	602.90	641.55	626.50	657.09	636.72	..	Gross National Product
744.89	753.74	744.53	731.04	607.18	625.92	666.15	649.90	682.36	658.14	H	GDP at Market Prices
0.95	-7.85	-55.37	-38.53	-23.24	-61.55	-29.66	-30.60	-13.37	-0.42	..	Resource Balance
193.80	189.93	146.81	155.91	141.26	127.13	121.28	120.80	124.76	123.83	..	Exports of Goods & NFServices
192.85	197.78	202.18	194.45	164.50	188.68	150.95	151.40	138.13	124.26	..	Imports of Goods & NFServices
770.98	786.23	804.93	776.01	633.38	706.87	707.72	680.50	697.42	661.01	..	Domestic Absorption
576.64	583.75	621.17	594.08	554.64	555.21	586.86	544.30	543.96	516.37	..	Private Consumption, etc.
64.88	68.35	70.30	74.98	71.34	70.27	67.53	76.10	77.11	81.01	..	General Gov't Consumption
129.46	134.14	113.46	106.94	7.39	81.39	53.33	60.10	76.36	63.64	..	Gross Domestic Investment
..	..	..	..	..	..	..	..	..	..	..	Fixed Investment
707.64	718.51	708.57	703.53	582.31	600.63	639.92	628.90	..	..	B H	GDP at factor cost
210.81	209.01	203.70	226.88	204.18	234.40	252.69	219.10	..	..	..	Agriculture
181.67	189.52	182.65	163.15	153.10	149.12	150.61	157.20	..	..	..	Industry
..	..	..	..	..	..	..	..	..	..	..	Manufacturing
370.79	376.87	384.28	341.01	249.90	242.40	262.85	273.60	..	..	..	Services, etc.
											Memo Items:
122.27	134.89	135.52	157.31	133.81	118.23	122.89	120.80	112.13	91.12	..	Capacity to Import
-71.53	-55.04	-11.30	1.40	-7.45	-8.90	1.61	0.00	-12.63	-32.72	..	Terms of Trade Adjustment
673.36	698.70	733.23	732.44	599.73	617.02	667.76	649.90	669.73	625.43	..	Gross Domestic Income
658.21	684.63	697.79	697.11	577.92	594.00	643.16	626.50	644.46	604.00	..	Gross National Income
				(Index 1987 = 100)							**DOMESTIC PRICES/DEFLATORS**
72.0	78.3	86.7	92.6	105.1	103.4	96.6	100.0	101.7	99.0	..	Overall (GDP)
79.3	83.7	88.5	91.9	105.6	101.0	95.0	100.0	103.8	104.8	..	Domestic Absorption
108.2	128.8	144.2	137.1	111.8	101.4	94.1	100.0	..	..	..	Agriculture
66.9	59.6	62.6	70.2	90.1	90.9	94.1	100.0	..	..	..	Industry
..	..	..	..	..	..	..	..	..	..	..	Manufacturing
77.1	94.8	105.8	103.2	111.8	110.7	107.2	100.0	98.6	95.8	..	Consumer Price Index
											MANUFACTURING ACTIVITY
65.2	..	81.7	118.0	100.6	94.8	94.8	100.0	..	..	G	Employment (1987=100)
148.1	..	98.6	89.4	85.3	91.2	90.0	100.0	..	..	G	Real Earnings per Empl. (1987=100)
28.4	..	29.5	91.3	89.9	93.2	94.0	100.0	..	..	G	Real Output per Empl. (1987=100)
43.8	..	40.5	9.5	8.1	7.8	7.0	6.7	6.3	..	..	Earnings as % of Value Added
				(Billions of current CFA Francs)							**MONETARY HOLDINGS**
77.93	94.07	82.98	82.69	101.02	108.13	121.05	114.44	..	139.46	..	Money Supply, Broadly Defined
64.59	74.75	70.93	66.55	78.41	80.62	82.99	73.15	..	88.20	..	Money
31.05	34.84	35.27	31.53	30.71	33.37	40.46	35.59	..	41.81	..	Currency Outside Banks
33.54	39.91	35.66	35.01	47.69	47.25	42.54	37.55	..	46.39	..	Demand Deposits
13.34	19.32	12.05	16.14	22.62	27.51	38.06	41.30	..	51.26	..	Quasi-Money
				(Millions of current CFA Francs)							
-25,241	..	..	..	..	..	..	..	..	..	C	**GOVERNMENT DEFICIT (-) OR SURPLUS**
77,430	..	..	..	..	..	..	..	..	..	..	Current Revenue
50,581	..	..	..	..	..	..	..	..	..	..	Current Expenditure
26,849	..	..	..	..	..	..	..	..	..	..	Current Budget Balance
6	..	..	..	..	..	..	..	..	..	..	Capital Receipts
52,096	..	..	..	..	..	..	..	..	..	..	Capital Payments

NIGER	1969	1970	1971	1972	1973	1974	1975	1976	1977	1978	1979
FOREIGN TRADE (CUSTOMS BASIS)					*(Millions of current US dollars)*						
Value of Exports, fob	24.21	31.62	38.37	54.32	62.78	52.57	91.23	133.87	160.11	282.86	448.03
Nonfuel Primary Products	22.73	30.40	36.74	50.38	57.77	46.23	83.23	130.49	155.57	277.15	442.61
Fuels	0.05	0.04	0.01	0.01	0.01	0.01	0.02	0.07	0.08	0.10	0.09
Manufactures	1.43	1.18	1.62	3.93	5.00	6.33	7.98	3.31	4.46	5.61	5.33
Value of Imports, cif	48.70	58.37	52.99	65.70	86.77	96.36	98.94	127.09	196.28	305.92	461.71
Nonfuel Primary Products	8.25	10.72	8.31	12.99	19.95	26.03	28.03	15.69	32.35	61.81	83.91
Fuels	2.07	2.32	4.48	5.82	8.25	13.08	12.43	14.70	14.39	43.40	79.18
Manufactures	38.38	45.33	40.20	46.89	58.57	57.25	58.48	96.70	149.54	200.71	298.62
					(Index 1987 = 100)						
Terms of Trade	176.2	180.7	174.4	177.0	160.3	140.6	148.1	170.8	163.4	162.3	151.4
Export Prices, fob	45.6	49.6	46.9	52.5	59.6	80.6	90.0	95.6	100.4	115.9	124.4
Import Prices, cif	25.9	27.4	26.9	29.6	37.2	57.4	60.8	56.0	61.5	71.4	82.1
BALANCE OF PAYMENTS					*(Millions of current US dollars)*						
Exports of Goods & Services	..	60.20	73.52	91.31	126.84	107.57	172.13	203.07	231.65	328.45	533.06
Merchandise, fob	..	46.70	58.37	71.01	99.54	81.52	138.52	171.64	196.64	287.65	484.95
Nonfactor Services	..	12.30	13.44	18.46	23.25	17.86	23.90	23.37	26.03	31.52	35.69
Factor Services	..	1.20	1.71	1.85	4.05	8.20	9.71	8.06	8.98	9.28	12.43
Imports of Goods & Services	..	88.80	85.96	115.52	170.59	236.24	254.11	313.89	380.13	613.07	839.16
Merchandise, fob	..	55.10	53.06	67.86	112.06	144.90	147.96	198.39	241.35	410.62	527.04
Nonfactor Services	..	31.00	29.89	44.73	54.84	77.06	87.01	103.66	129.29	163.35	242.35
Factor Services	..	2.70	3.01	2.93	3.70	14.29	19.14	11.85	9.49	39.10	69.77
Long-Term Interest	..	0.80	0.60	0.70	0.70	0.60	2.30	2.40	3.10	24.70	42.00
Private Current Transfers, net	..	-3.80	-5.82	-8.79	-15.97	-16.64	-18.99	-19.83	-22.18	-35.59	-49.82
Workers' Remittances	..	..	0.60	1.85	1.79	2.07	3.00	3.36	3.26	4.66	4.59
Curr. A/C Bal before Off. Transf.	..	-32.40	-13.64	-33.01	-59.73	-122.84	-70.69	-130.65	-170.31	-320.21	-278.77
Net Official Transfers	..	32.30	30.09	45.06	84.28	95.04	82.74	110.68	74.68	119.25	141.20
Curr. A/C Bal after Off. Transf.	..	-0.10	16.45	12.05	24.56	-27.80	12.05	-19.97	-95.63	-200.96	-137.57
Long-Term Capital, net	..	20.80	7.12	6.90	10.13	16.47	36.29	52.22	90.35	156.61	189.33
Direct Investment	..	0.40	-5.72	0.76	0.83	6.60	16.38	8.35	9.19	35.90	36.08
Long-Term Loans	..	10.80	8.00	11.20	10.50	24.70	23.20	20.30	22.90	126.70	191.50
Disbursements	..	12.40	9.60	12.90	12.40	27.20	29.00	27.00	29.00	146.00	224.20
Repayments	..	1.60	1.60	1.70	1.90	2.50	5.80	6.70	6.10	19.30	32.70
Other Long-Term Capital	..	9.60	4.84	-5.06	-1.20	-14.82	-3.29	23.57	58.26	-5.99	-38.25
Other Capital, net	..	-10.41	-12.73	-12.66	-29.70	4.94	-42.63	5.52	18.67	58.16	-55.29
Change in Reserves	..	-10.29	-10.84	-6.30	-4.99	6.39	-5.72	-37.77	-13.39	-13.81	3.52
Memo Item:					*(CFA Francs per US dollar)*						
Conversion Factor (Annual Avg)	259.710	277.710	277.130	252.210	222.700	240.500	214.320	238.980	245.670	225.640	212.720
				(Millions of US dollars), outstanding at end of year							
EXTERNAL DEBT (Total)	..	31.7	41.5	54.0	64.2	91.7	111.2	129.9	170.3	606.2	628.5
Long-Term Debt (by debtor)	..	31.7	41.5	54.0	64.2	91.7	111.2	129.9	118.3	356.2	522.5
Central Bank, incl. IMF credit	..	0.0	0.0	0.0	0.0	0.0	0.0	0.0	0.0	7.0	7.1
Central Government	..	17.5	25.9	37.8	45.7	61.0	79.7	103.0	90.6	144.9	173.7
Rest of General Government	..	0.1	0.1	0.1	0.1	0.0	0.0	0.0	0.0	0.0	0.0
Non-financial Public Enterprises	..	1.7	1.7	2.4	3.2	2.8	2.9	3.5	6.4	23.4	56.1
Priv. Sector, incl non-guaranteed	..	12.4	13.8	13.7	15.2	27.9	28.6	23.4	21.3	180.9	285.6
Short-Term Debt	..	0.0	0.0	0.0	0.0	0.0	0.0	0.0	52.0	250.0	106.0
Memo Items:					*(Millions of US dollars)*						
Int'l Reserves Excluding Gold	6.7	18.7	33.6	41.4	50.8	45.5	50.3	82.5	101.1	128.4	131.7
Gold Holdings (at market price)	..	..	..	..	..	..	..	..	0.9	1.9	5.7
SOCIAL INDICATORS											
Total Fertility Rate	6.8	6.9	6.9	6.9	6.9	7.0	7.0	7.1	7.1	7.1	7.1
Infant Mortality Rate	172.0	170.0	168.0	166.0	164.2	162.4	160.6	158.8	157.0	154.8	152.6
Life Expectancy at Birth	38.1	38.4	38.7	39.0	39.3	39.6	39.9	40.2	40.5	40.9	41.3
Urban Population, % of total	8.2	8.5	8.9	9.3	9.8	10.2	10.6	11.1	11.6	12.2	12.7
Food Prod. per capita (1987=100)	142.0	124.4	125.5	118.1	82.1	99.5	92.3	113.8	125.9	129.8	131.9
Labor Force, Agriculture (%)	94.4	94.3	93.9	93.6	93.3	93.0	92.7	92.3	92.0	91.7	91.4
Labor Force, Female (%)	49.0	49.0	48.9	48.8	48.7	48.6	48.6	48.4	48.3	48.2	48.1
Primary Schl. Enroll. Ratio	..	14.0	..	..	..	..	20.0	21.0	22.0	23.0	..
Primary Schl. Enroll. Ratio, Female	..	10.0	..	..	..	..	14.0	15.0	16.0	17.0	..
Secondary Schl. Enroll. Ratio	..	1.0	..	..	..	..	2.0	3.0	3.0	4.0	..

1980	1981	1982	1983	1984	1985	1986	1987	1988	1989 estimate	NOTES	NIGER
				(Millions of current US dollars)							**FOREIGN TRADE (CUSTOMS BASIS)**
579.69	454.81	380.00	335.00	303.40	251.40	330.00	361.40	256.00	..	f	Value of Exports, fob
560.81	440.84	369.70	325.30	283.70	240.50	320.90	353.40	243.95	..	..	Nonfuel Primary Products
6.47	3.91	2.90	2.80	18.00	9.00	2.20	2.30	2.97	..	..	Fuels
12.41	10.06	7.40	6.90	1.70	1.90	6.90	5.70	9.08	..	..	Manufactures
607.69	604.00	573.00	367.00	341.00	354.00	379.00	417.00	490.00	..	f	Value of Imports, cif
108.44	139.01	108.23	87.96	71.21	77.11	135.10	149.00	149.33	..	..	Nonfuel Primary Products
158.27	75.99	76.77	64.04	49.79	50.89	20.90	31.00	37.26	..	..	Fuels
340.97	389.00	388.00	215.00	220.00	226.00	223.00	237.00	303.41	..	..	Manufactures
				(Index 1987 = 100)							
119.4	126.5	131.1	127.9	137.1	137.3	118.5	100.0	95.5	..	..	Terms of Trade
122.4	123.5	120.3	120.5	122.7	121.1	110.5	100.0	103.8	..	..	Export Prices, fob
102.5	97.6	91.8	94.2	89.5	88.2	93.3	100.0	108.7	..	..	Import Prices, cif
				(Millions of current US dollars)							**BALANCE OF PAYMENTS**
643.66	542.67	440.73	387.50	348.09	316.39	..	495.78	419.01	368.64	f	Exports of Goods & Services
576.09	484.63	381.33	335.23	303.27	259.43	331.50	411.93	368.98	310.96	..	Merchandise, fob
40.56	39.84	41.80	40.33	31.36	38.56	..	75.86	48.35	50.78	..	Nonfactor Services
27.01	18.20	17.60	11.94	13.46	18.40	..	7.99	1.68	6.90	..	Factor Services
1,016.28	873.50	817.59	537.98	461.99	533.76	411.49	654.83	578.15	571.15	f	Imports of Goods & Services
677.38	591.79	515.33	331.58	269.92	345.64	309.76	409.60	392.48	368.64	..	Merchandise, fob
278.96	194.12	212.95	153.74	124.20	127.46	84.20	152.73	112.47	139.18	..	Nonfactor Services
59.94	87.59	89.31	52.67	67.87	60.66	17.53	92.50	73.19	63.32	..	Factor Services
64.90	66.30	71.60	51.70	37.60	41.40	48.00	71.00	74.20	35.20	..	Long-Term Interest
-56.68	-51.92	-53.11	-49.25	-43.32	-58.72	-43.31	-49.91	-34.92	-40.12	f	Private Current Transfers, net
5.88	4.58	3.35	2.98	4.48	2.10	..	..	10.07	10.03	..	Workers' Remittances
-429.30	-342.08	-382.79	-197.66	-144.57	-276.09	-123.30	-208.96	-194.06	-242.63	..	Curr. A/C Bal before Off. Transf.
153.61	160.58	149.98	135.83	145.77	212.11	148.42	142.08	153.77	131.97	..	Net Official Transfers
-275.69	-181.50	-232.81	-61.83	1.20	-63.98	25.12	-66.88	-40.29	-110.66	..	Curr. A/C Bal after Off. Transf.
223.85	224.35	37.38	45.55	32.04	49.02	78.83	102.48	95.69	95.92	..	Long-Term Capital, net
43.94	-6.71	24.93	0.21	-1.05	-9.57	..	..	..	17.70	..	Direct Investment
223.10	323.00	21.20	77.50	42.60	53.10	112.80	144.50	121.00	112.20	..	Long-Term Loans
280.60	406.70	178.90	160.10	90.30	106.90	176.90	201.50	177.30	167.40	..	Disbursements
57.50	83.70	157.70	82.60	47.70	53.80	64.10	57.00	56.30	55.20	..	Repayments
-43.19	-91.94	-8.76	-32.16	-9.50	5.49	-33.97	-42.02	-25.31	-33.98	..	Other Long-Term Capital
57.69	-40.08	132.13	13.34	-1.98	17.98	-97.46	-21.46	-16.48	6.17	..	Other Capital, net
-5.85	-2.77	63.31	2.94	-31.26	-3.02	-6.49	-14.14	-38.91	8.56	f	Change in Reserves
				(CFA Francs per US dollar)							**Memo Item:**
211.300	271.730	328.620	381.070	436.960	449.260	346.300	300.540	297.850	319.010	..	Conversion Factor (Annual Avg)
				(Millions of US dollars), outstanding at end of year							
862.8	1,021.9	957.5	949.7	955.9	1,208.2	1,448.3	1,697.3	1,741.7	1,577.9	..	**EXTERNAL DEBT (Total)**
703.5	908.1	833.9	883.5	893.1	1,109.3	1,325.5	1,620.8	1,636.6	1,470.3	..	Long-Term Debt (by debtor)
16.1	14.8	14.0	45.6	56.8	78.3	106.1	122.5	94.6	84.6	..	Central Bank, incl. IMF credit
236.0	361.6	405.2	472.3	519.5	667.2	837.4	1,085.4	1,175.3	1,042.3	..	Central Government
0.0	0.0	0.0	0.0	0.0	0.0	0.0	0.0	0.0	..	..	Rest of General Government
106.2	171.8	124.8	111.6	95.7	97.4	94.4	97.3	71.2	46.8	..	Non-financial Public Enterprises
345.2	359.9	289.9	254.0	221.1	266.4	287.6	315.6	295.5	296.6	..	Priv. Sector, incl non-guaranteed
159.3	113.8	123.6	66.2	62.8	98.9	122.8	76.5	105.1	107.6	..	Short-Term Debt
				(Millions of US dollars)							**Memo Items:**
125.9	105.3	29.6	53.2	88.7	136.4	189.2	248.5	232.1	212.3	..	Int'l Reserves Excluding Gold
6.5	4.4	5.1	4.2	3.4	3.6	4.3	5.4	4.6	4.5	..	Gold Holdings (at market price)
											SOCIAL INDICATORS
7.1	7.1	7.1	7.1	7.1	7.1	7.1	7.1	7.1	7.1	..	Total Fertility Rate
150.4	148.2	146.0	143.8	141.6	139.4	137.2	135.0	132.9	130.9	..	Infant Mortality Rate
41.7	42.1	42.5	42.9	43.3	43.7	44.1	44.5	44.8	45.1	..	Life Expectancy at Birth
13.2	13.8	14.4	15.0	15.6	16.2	17.1	17.9	18.4	19.0	..	Urban Population, % of total
133.4	127.6	125.1	120.6	94.4	114.9	115.9	100.0	128.0	109.8	..	Food Prod. per capita (1987=100)
91.1	..	..	..	..	..	..	..	..	..	..	Labor Force, Agriculture (%)
48.0	47.9	47.8	47.6	47.5	47.4	47.2	47.1	47.0	46.8	..	Labor Force, Female (%)
27.0	..	..	27.0	26.0	28.0	29.0	..	..	..	..	Primary Schl. Enroll. Ratio
19.0	..	..	19.0	19.0	20.0	20.0	..	..	..	..	Primary Schl. Enroll. Ratio, Female
5.0	..	..	6.0	..	6.0	..	..	..	..	..	Secondary Schl. Enroll. Ratio

NIGERIA	1969	1970	1971	1972	1973	1974	1975	1976	1977	1978	1979
CURRENT GNP PER CAPITA (US $)	110	150	190	230	270	360	440	600	700	720	870
POPULATION (thousands)	64,568	66,182	67,892	69,619	71,361	73,116	74,884	76,715	78,613	80,580	82,619

USE AND ORIGIN OF RESOURCES *(Billions of current Nigerian Naira)*

	1969	1970	1971	1972	1973	1974	1975	1976	1977	1978	1979
Gross National Product (GNP)	4.98	9.41	10.59	11.24	12.61	21.03	24.81	31.02	36.30	39.07	46.61
Net Factor Income from Abroad	-0.15	-0.33	-0.75	-0.85	-0.87	-0.68	-0.53	-0.66	-0.87	-0.84	-1.03
GDP at Market Prices	5.13	9.74	11.34	12.09	13.48	21.71	25.34	31.67	37.16	39.90	47.63
Resource Balance	-0.03	-0.02	0.05	0.26	0.64	3.44	0.24	-0.05	-0.27	-1.45	2.45
Exports of Goods & NFServices	0.68	0.94	1.41	1.52	2.44	6.18	5.27	6.52	8.43	7.11	10.61
Imports of Goods & NFServices	0.70	0.96	1.36	1.25	1.81	2.74	5.03	6.57	8.70	8.56	8.16
Domestic Absorption	5.16	9.76	11.29	11.83	12.84	18.27	25.10	31.72	37.43	41.35	45.18
Private Consumption, etc.	4.19	7.93	8.79	8.77	9.25	13.79	17.35	20.56	23.69	26.67	30.72
General Gov't Consumption	0.42	0.57	0.66	0.84	0.98	1.31	2.24	2.58	3.83	4.79	4.88
Gross Domestic Investment	0.55	1.26	1.85	2.22	2.62	3.17	5.51	8.58	9.92	9.89	9.58
Fixed Investment	..	..	..	..	2.51	2.96	5.02	8.11	9.42	9.39	9.08
Indirect Taxes, net	0.43	0.68	0.32	0.31	0.30	0.31	0.36	0.48	0.52	0.69	0.76
GDP at factor cost	4.70	9.06	11.02	11.78	13.18	21.40	24.98	31.20	36.64	39.21	46.88
Agriculture	2.26	3.63	4.27	4.36	4.46	6.52	7.61	8.70	10.38	11.44	12.82
Industry	0.78	1.32	2.02	2.47	3.47	7.87	7.45	10.50	12.02	13.64	18.45
Manufacturing	0.35	0.39	0.43	0.53	0.62	0.82	1.45	1.81	1.93	2.94	4.72
Services, etc.	1.66	4.11	4.73	4.95	5.25	7.02	9.92	12.00	14.25	14.13	15.61
Gross Domestic Saving	0.52	1.24	1.90	2.48	3.25	6.60	5.75	8.53	9.65	8.44	12.03
Gross National Saving	..	0.92	1.13	1.60	2.35	5.87	5.15	7.77	8.67	7.44	10.80

(Millions of 1987 Nigerian Naira)

	1969	1970	1971	1972	1973	1974	1975	1976	1977	1978	1979
Gross National Product	55,466	66,086	71,140	71,756	77,761	88,406	86,387	94,644	100,257	94,913	101,835
GDP at Market Prices	59,320	71,083	79,336	80,372	86,533	96,369	93,189	102,071	108,273	102,362	109,707
Resource Balance	18,586	22,208	19,224	26,557	28,043	22,409	-5,547	-12,417	-20,472	-38,892	16,842
Exports of Goods & NFServices	34,562	43,171	46,950	51,359	58,404	60,203	51,737	51,620	76,660	61,589	91,839
Imports of Goods & NFServices	15,977	20,962	27,726	24,802	30,361	37,795	57,284	64,036	97,132	100,480	74,997
Domestic Absorption	40,734	48,875	60,112	53,815	58,491	73,960	98,736	114,488	128,745	141,253	92,865
Private Consumption, etc.	28,221	30,016	36,340	28,918	28,624	43,318	54,157	58,023	62,793	87,127	47,866
General Gov't Consumption	5,156	5,011	5,663	5,974	7,306	7,499	9,787	9,898	13,868	15,833	13,115
Gross Domestic Investment	7,357	13,848	18,110	18,924	22,561	23,144	34,792	46,567	52,084	38,294	31,884
Fixed Investment	..	..	..	..	22,466	22,969	34,432	46,287	51,802	38,033	31,644
GDP at factor cost	55,865	68,908	76,305	77,871	84,808	95,236	92,073	100,759	106,978	100,796	108,218
Agriculture	25,517	29,988	31,550	29,254	31,863	35,166	31,514	31,020	33,138	30,274	29,357
Industry	16,478	25,445	33,809	40,337	39,847	46,706	40,327	49,818	52,299	50,363	59,884
Manufacturing	1,616	2,067	2,003	2,481	2,762	2,671	3,300	4,071	4,326	4,920	7,230
Services, etc.	10,932	13,209	14,333	14,800	16,798	18,176	21,928	23,119	24,744	23,337	23,895

Memo Items:

	1969	1970	1971	1972	1973	1974	1975	1976	1977	1978	1979
Capacity to Import	15,374	20,487	28,731	30,060	41,041	85,136	59,976	63,561	94,108	83,458	97,528
Terms of Trade Adjustment	-19,188	-22,684	-18,219	-21,299	-17,363	24,933	8,240	11,941	17,448	21,869	5,690
Gross Domestic Income	40,131	48,399	61,117	59,073	69,171	121,302	101,429	114,013	125,721	124,231	115,397
Gross National Income	36,278	43,402	52,921	50,457	60,399	113,339	94,627	106,585	117,705	116,782	107,524

DOMESTIC PRICES/DEFLATORS *(Index 1987 = 100)*

	1969	1970	1971	1972	1973	1974	1975	1976	1977	1978	1979
Overall (GDP)	8.7	13.7	14.3	15.0	15.6	22.5	27.2	31.0	34.3	39.0	43.4
Domestic Absorption	12.7	20.0	18.8	22.0	22.0	24.7	25.4	27.7	29.1	29.3	48.7
Agriculture	8.9	12.1	13.5	14.9	14.0	18.5	24.1	28.0	31.3	37.8	43.7
Industry	4.7	5.2	6.0	6.1	8.7	16.8	18.5	21.1	23.0	27.1	30.8
Manufacturing	21.6	18.8	21.6	21.5	22.3	30.7	43.9	44.5	44.5	59.8	65.4
Consumer Price Index	7.9	9.0	10.5	10.8	11.4	12.9	17.2	21.4	24.4	29.7	33.2

MANUFACTURING ACTIVITY

	1969	1970	1971	1972	1973	1974	1975	1976	1977	1978	1979
Employment (1987=100)	..	..	..	..	..	..	..	..	..	..	..
Real Earnings per Empl. (1987=100)	..	..	..	..	..	..	..	..	..	..	..
Real Output per Empl. (1987=100)	..	..	..	..	..	..	..	..	..	..	..
Earnings as % of Value Added	18.1	17.6	20.1	21.6	21.8	20.7	21.8	24.5	23.6	22.3	..

MONETARY HOLDINGS *(Millions of current Nigerian Naira)*

	1969	1970	1971	1972	1973	1974	1975	1976	1977	1978	1979
Money Supply, Broadly Defined	663	979	1,042	1,204	1,508	2,730	4,178	5,843	7,813	7,521	9,849
Money	447	643	670	747	926	1,757	2,605	3,864	5,558	5,101	6,147
Currency Outside Banks	253	342	355	385	436	570	1,031	1,351	1,941	2,157	2,351
Demand Deposits	195	300	316	362	490	1,187	1,575	2,513	3,617	2,943	3,796
Quasi-Money	215	337	372	457	582	973	1,572	1,979	2,255	2,420	3,702

GOVERNMENT DEFICIT (-) OR SURPLUS *(Millions of current Nigerian Naira)*

	1969	1970	1971	1972	1973	1974	1975	1976	1977	1978	1979
GOVERNMENT DEFICIT (-) OR SURPLUS	..	..	..	-83	189	1,248	-1,436	-1,870	-2,134	-639	..
Current Revenue	..	..	..	1,054	1,830	4,308	4,740	5,449	6,659	5,933	..
Current Expenditure	..	..	..	716	885	..	2,660	2,646	4,063	2,452	..
Current Budget Balance	..	..	..	338	945	..	2,081	2,803	2,596	3,481	..
Capital Receipts	..	..	..	..	..	..	..	..	..	..	..
Capital Payments	..	..	..	420	756	..	3,517	4,673	4,731	4,120	..

1980	1981	1982	1983	1984	1985	1986	1987	1988	1989 estimate	NOTES	NIGERIA
1,030	1,090	1,110	980	900	930	710	370	280	250	..	CURRENT GNP PER CAPITA (US $)
84,732	87,352	90,214	93,261	96,432	99,669	103,011	106,497	110,068	113,665	..	POPULATION (thousands)
				(Billions of current Nigerian Naira)							USE AND ORIGIN OF RESOURCES
54.43	57.42	61.77	64.09	70.21	78.80	80.09	92.66	126.37	202.64	C	Gross National Product (GNP)
-2.06	-1.40	-0.95	-0.94	-1.10	-1.84	-1.69	-5.57	-8.56	-15.31	..	Net Factor Income from Abroad
56.49	58.82	62.72	65.03	71.31	80.65	81.78	98.23	134.93	217.95	C	GDP at Market Prices
5.11	-2.04	-3.83	-2.24	1.20	2.64	-1.89	5.36	3.30	18.40	..	Resource Balance
14.76	11.36	8.53	7.77	9.42	11.64	9.49	31.96	34.72	74.84	..	Exports of Goods & NFServices
9.65	13.40	12.36	10.00	8.21	8.99	11.38	26.60	31.42	56.44	..	Imports of Goods & NFServices
51.38	60.87	66.55	67.26	70.10	78.00	83.67	92.87	131.63	199.55	..	Domestic Absorption
34.76	42.55	49.75	51.37	56.41	63.77	66.10	68.61	99.84	152.93	f	Private Consumption, etc.
5.05	5.71	7.16	8.48	9.39	8.16	9.64	13.03	15.17	19.35	..	General Gov't Consumption
11.57	12.60	9.64	7.42	4.30	6.07	7.92	11.24	16.62	27.27	f	Gross Domestic Investment
10.98	12.39	9.46	7.28	4.22	5.43	7.79	12.36	15.87	26.15	..	Fixed Investment
1.73	2.22	2.24	1.74	1.36	1.87	2.04	1.83	3.26	4.96	..	Indirect Taxes, net
54.76	56.60	60.48	63.29	69.95	78.78	79.74	96.40	131.67	212.99	C	GDP at factor cost
14.32	14.45	17.01	20.07	25.00	27.62	28.96	28.55	45.51	65.36	..	Agriculture
22.91	22.03	22.18	19.10	19.45	23.30	21.04	42.23	48.30	93.90	..	Industry
5.04	6.11	7.45	6.32	6.66	9.36	10.14	8.43	13.56	18.73	..	Manufacturing
17.54	20.12	21.30	24.13	25.50	27.85	29.73	25.63	37.86	53.74	..	Services, etc.
16.68	10.56	5.81	5.18	5.50	8.72	6.04	16.60	19.92	45.67	..	Gross Domestic Saving
14.39	8.89	4.60	3.97	4.17	6.65	4.15	10.95	11.21	30.23	..	Gross National Saving
				(Millions of 1987 Nigerian Naira)							
102,967	99,128	99,528	93,351	85,234	90,133	97,347	92,661	95,900	101,124	C	Gross National Product
113,464	106,958	106,746	100,129	92,850	100,946	102,958	98,233	102,955	108,956	C	GDP at Market Prices
-8,271	-72,044	-63,256	-44,041	-24,664	-16,019	-1,904	5,359	9,448	12,190	..	Resource Balance
83,151	37,055	29,730	27,883	32,217	36,689	35,875	31,955	35,358	41,064	..	Exports of Goods & NFServices
91,422	109,099	92,986	71,925	56,881	52,708	37,779	26,596	25,911	28,874	..	Imports of Goods & NFServices
121,735	179,001	170,002	144,171	117,514	116,965	104,862	92,874	93,507	96,766	..	Domestic Absorption
74,273	125,589	125,367	107,231	93,928	92,221	79,353	68,605	69,965	73,394	f	Private Consumption, etc.
10,795	13,666	15,098	14,508	11,509	9,472	10,628	13,032	10,995	9,672	..	General Gov't Consumption
36,667	39,747	29,537	22,431	12,078	15,271	14,881	11,237	12,547	13,700	f	Gross Domestic Investment
36,443	39,089	29,002	22,018	11,875	13,649	14,633	12,361	11,985	13,137	..	Fixed Investment
110,250	103,116	103,116	97,610	91,189	98,750	100,512	96,404	100,593	106,476	C	GDP at factor cost
30,807	25,735	26,525	26,547	24,780	28,318	30,932	28,550	30,120	31,325	..	Agriculture
58,575	52,638	51,509	43,883	41,135	45,099	43,853	42,225	45,418	49,397	..	Industry
7,642	8,799	9,744	7,403	6,598	8,449	8,020	8,428	8,976	8,976	..	Manufacturing
25,108	26,734	26,840	27,180	25,274	25,333	25,728	25,629	25,055	25,754	..	Services, etc.
											Memo Items:
139,900	92,474	64,183	55,854	65,216	68,214	31,508	31,955	28,630	38,289	..	Capacity to Import
56,749	55,418	34,452	27,971	32,999	31,525	-4,367	0	-6,728	-2,775	..	Terms of Trade Adjustment
170,213	162,376	141,199	128,100	125,850	132,471	98,591	98,233	96,227	106,180	..	Gross Domestic Income
159,716	154,546	133,980	121,322	118,233	121,657	92,980	92,661	89,171	98,349	..	Gross National Income
				(Index 1987 = 100)							DOMESTIC PRICES/DEFLATORS
49.8	55.0	58.8	64.9	76.8	79.9	79.4	100.0	131.1	200.0	..	Overall (GDP)
42.2	34.0	39.1	46.7	59.7	66.7	79.8	100.0	140.8	206.2	..	Domestic Absorption
46.5	56.1	64.1	75.6	100.9	97.5	93.6	100.0	151.1	208.6	..	Agriculture
39.1	41.9	43.1	43.5	47.3	51.7	48.0	100.0	106.4	190.1	..	Industry
65.9	69.4	76.5	85.4	100.9	110.8	126.4	100.0	151.1	208.6	..	Manufacturing
36.5	44.1	47.5	58.5	81.6	86.1	90.7	100.0	138.3	194.8	..	Consumer Price Index
											MANUFACTURING ACTIVITY
..	..	..	..	..	..	..	..	..	..	..	Employment (1987 = 100)
..	..	..	..	..	..	..	..	..	..	..	Real Earnings per Empl. (1987 = 100)
..	..	..	..	..	..	..	..	..	..	..	Real Output per Empl. (1987 = 100)
21.9	30.1	27.7	20.5	25.2	..	..	..	..	..	..	Earnings as % of Value Added
				(Millions of current Nigerian Naira)							MONETARY HOLDINGS
14,390	15,239	16,694	19,034	21,243	23,153	23,605	28,895	38,406	42,519	..	Money Supply, Broadly Defined
9,227	9,745	10,049	11,283	12,204	13,227	12,663	14,906	21,446	25,813	..	Money
3,186	3,862	4,223	4,843	4,884	4,910	5,178	6,299	9,414	11,669	..	Currency Outside Banks
6,041	5,883	5,826	6,440	7,321	8,318	7,485	8,608	12,033	14,144	..	Demand Deposits
5,163	5,494	6,645	7,752	9,039	9,926	10,942	13,989	16,960	16,707	..	Quasi-Money
				(Millions of current Nigerian Naira)							
..	..	..	..	-2,900	-1,999	-2,773	-9,702	..	..	C	GOVERNMENT DEFICIT (-) OR SURPLUS
..	..	..	..	7,344	9,000	12,549	17,375	..	..	..	Current Revenue
..	..	..	..	6,418	5,797	8,720	17,172	..	..	..	Current Expenditure
..	..	..	..	926	3,203	3,829	203	..	..	..	Current Budget Balance
..	..	..	..	..	..	..	..	..	..	..	Capital Receipts
..	..	..	..	3,826	5,203	6,602	9,905	..	..	..	Capital Payments

NIGERIA	1969	1970	1971	1972	1973	1974	1975	1976	1977	1978	1979
FOREIGN TRADE (CUSTOMS BASIS)					*(Millions of current US dollars)*						
Value of Exports, fob	905.0	1,227.9	1,793.2	2,161.1	3,448.0	9,195.0	7,992.0	10,568.7	11,848.4	10,560.0	17,712.6
Nonfuel Primary Products	482.3	496.4	433.9	339.8	505.8	606.7	496.3	541.2	749.6	822.2	925.1
Fuels	386.6	714.0	1,335.4	1,793.6	2,889.9	8,547.4	7,452.0	9,959.3	11,019.0	9,575.9	16,650.0
Manufactures	36.1	17.5	23.9	27.7	52.3	40.9	43.7	68.1	79.7	161.9	137.4
Value of Imports, cif	696.3	1,059.0	1,510.5	1,504.9	1,861.7	2,780.6	6,041.2	8,194.6	11,020.2	12,762.8	10,274.3
Nonfuel Primary Products	84.1	118.5	172.9	195.1	255.1	389.7	747.6	1,021.8	1,625.0	2,079.7	2,038.8
Fuels	43.8	33.6	12.6	14.9	20.6	88.8	162.8	279.3	199.4	246.3	235.4
Manufactures	568.4	906.9	1,325.0	1,294.9	1,585.9	2,302.1	5,130.9	6,893.6	9,195.8	10,436.8	8,000.1
					(Index 1987 = 100)						
Terms of Trade	62.8	44.2	41.3	39.3	47.0	138.0	122.1	132.0	134.7	119.1	145.3
Export Prices, fob	14.9	11.8	12.5	13.1	18.6	69.1	66.2	72.0	80.4	81.6	114.6
Import Prices, cif	23.7	26.8	30.3	33.3	39.7	50.1	54.2	54.6	59.7	68.6	78.9
BALANCE OF PAYMENTS					*(Millions of current US dollars)*						
Exports of Goods & Services	..	1,341.0	2,010.0	2,315.8	3,763.6	10,048.1	9,130.4	10,924.1	13,278.9	11,581.0	18,108.5
Merchandise, fob	..	1,248.0	1,888.6	2,184.5	3,607.4	9,698.1	8,329.1	10,121.7	12,365.9	10,414.4	16,811.5
Nonfactor Services	..	83.0	108.3	117.3	131.1	194.8	299.9	359.1	562.7	876.3	1,027.5
Factor Services	..	10.0	13.0	14.1	25.0	155.1	501.4	443.3	350.3	290.3	269.5
Imports of Goods & Services	..	1,772.0	2,418.2	2,636.1	3,718.3	5,052.3	8,961.6	11,124.9	14,107.6	15,067.8	16,050.8
Merchandise, fob	..	939.0	1,393.1	1,365.8	1,714.3	2,479.8	5,484.3	7,477.8	9,670.1	11,583.0	11,887.3
Nonfactor Services	..	369.0	454.4	575.4	1,020.5	1,852.1	2,695.4	2,915.2	3,552.0	2,964.9	3,441.4
Factor Services	..	464.0	570.7	694.9	983.5	720.4	781.9	732.0	885.5	519.9	722.1
Long-Term Interest	..	27.8	30.1	31.5	38.2	41.7	45.4	44.3	52.1	66.2	257.6
Private Current Transfers, net	..	19.0	-25.1	-46.7	-54.8	-91.4	-111.7	-161.6	-178.5	-251.0	-350.2
Workers' Remittances	..	..	..	..	..	..	..	..	20.2	3.1	8.1
Curr. A/C Bal before Off. Transf.	..	-412.0	-433.3	-367.0	-9.5	4,904.4	57.1	-362.5	-1,007.1	-3,737.8	1,707.5
Net Official Transfers	..	44.0	27.1	25.0	1.2	-7.2	-14.6	5.8	-4.7	-18.9	-39.0
Curr. A/C Bal after Off. Transf.	..	-368.0	-406.2	-342.0	-8.3	4,897.1	42.5	-356.7	-1,011.8	-3,756.7	1,668.5
Long-Term Capital, net	..	205.0	309.9	367.0	306.4	169.6	208.8	-27.7	419.9	1,605.4	1,234.8
Direct Investment	..	205.0	285.8	305.1	373.1	257.4	417.7	339.4	439.2	211.7	304.7
Long-Term Loans	..	13.3	63.2	86.9	-99.0	-41.1	-91.3	-229.8	55.2	1,626.6	1,306.9
Disbursements	..	81.1	127.6	150.7	91.5	109.2	133.1	126.2	141.3	1,709.3	1,442.0
Repayments	..	67.8	64.4	63.8	190.5	150.3	224.4	356.0	86.1	82.7	135.1
Other Long-Term Capital	..	-13.3	-39.1	-25.0	32.2	-46.7	-117.5	-137.3	-74.5	-232.9	-376.9
Other Capital, net	..	236.0	256.8	-87.4	-96.2	-168.8	-42.1	4.6	-231.2	43.0	301.0
Change in Reserves	..	-73.0	-160.5	62.4	-201.9	-4,898.0	-209.2	379.8	823.0	2,108.4	-3,204.3
Memo Item:					*(Nigerian Naira per US dollar)*						
Conversion Factor (Annual Avg)	0.710	0.710	0.710	0.660	0.660	0.630	0.620	0.630	0.640	0.640	0.600
					(Millions of US dollars), outstanding at end of year						
EXTERNAL DEBT (Total)	..	567	651	732	1,205	1,274	1,143	906	3,146	5,091	6,259
Long-Term Debt (by debtor)	..	567	651	732	1,205	1,274	1,143	906	985	2,645	3,976
Central Bank, incl. IMF credit	..	0	0	0	0	0	0	0	0	0	0
Central Government	..	189	278	372	841	897	772	510	548	2,009	2,927
Rest of General Government	..	12	9	6	4	4	2	2	2	2	2
Non-financial Public Enterprises	..	246	247	253	252	257	262	280	299	294	334
Priv. Sector, incl non-guaranteed	..	120	117	101	108	116	108	115	137	340	713
Short-Term Debt	..	..	..	..	..	..	..	..	2,161	2,446	2,283
Memo Items:					*(Millions of US dollars)*						
Int'l Reserves Excluding Gold	112.4	202.2	408.3	355.5	558.8	5,602.5	5,585.6	5,179.8	4,232.2	1,886.7	5,547.9
Gold Holdings (at market price)	20.1	21.3	23.7	35.2	64.1	106.5	80.1	76.9	103.8	142.2	351.7
SOCIAL INDICATORS											
Total Fertility Rate	6.9	6.9	6.9	6.9	6.9	6.9	6.9	6.9	6.9	6.9	6.9
Infant Mortality Rate	162.4	157.6	152.8	148.0	143.2	138.4	133.6	128.8	124.0	122.0	120.0
Life Expectancy at Birth	43.3	43.7	44.1	44.5	44.9	45.3	45.7	46.1	46.5	46.9	47.3
Urban Population, % of total	19.4	20.0	20.7	21.4	22.0	22.7	23.4	24.1	24.9	25.6	26.4
Food Prod. per capita (1987=100)	133.4	130.7	124.7	112.7	116.1	123.7	112.7	108.4	105.6	101.2	102.4
Labor Force, Agriculture (%)	71.2	71.0	70.6	70.3	70.1	69.8	69.6	69.2	68.9	68.7	68.4
Labor Force, Female (%)	37.2	37.1	37.1	37.1	37.0	37.0	36.9	36.9	36.8	36.8	36.7
Primary Schl. Enroll. Ratio	..	37.0	..	..	..	..	51.0	71.0	82.0	92.0	98.0
Primary Schl. Enroll. Ratio, Female	..	27.0	..	..	..	..	..	..	70.0	..	..
Secondary Schl. Enroll. Ratio	..	4.0	..	..	..	..	8.0	9.0	11.0	12.0	16.0

1980	1981	1982	1983	1984	1985	1986	1987	1988	1989 estimate	NOTES	NIGERIA
											FOREIGN TRADE (CUSTOMS BASIS)
				(Millions of current US dollars)							
25,968.0	17,846.0	12,154.0	10,370.0	11,891.0	12,566.0	6,769.0	7,365.0	7,006.0	7,707.0	f	Value of Exports, fob
941.8	995.7	523.2	652.6	601.9	277.2	299.1	543.4	678.1	..	..	Nonfuel Primary Products
24,896.2	16,758.2	11,489.1	9,579.2	11,214.4	12,202.8	6,370.9	6,701.2	6,173.4	..	..	Fuels
130.0	92.1	141.7	138.2	74.6	86.0	99.0	120.4	154.5	..	..	Manufactures
16,642.0	20,877.0	16,060.0	12,254.2	9,364.0	8,890.0	7,465.6	7,816.0	7,435.0	6,862.3	f	Value of Imports, cif
3,243.4	3,873.3	846.5	2,293.6	1,736.4	1,284.5	934.0	2,363.0	1,796.6	..	..	Nonfuel Primary Products
357.4	453.6	408.7	267.0	236.9	401.8	146.4	189.6	168.6	..	..	Fuels
13,041.2	16,550.1	14,804.8	9,693.6	7,390.7	7,203.7	6,385.2	5,263.4	5,469.8	..	..	Manufactures
				(Index 1987 = 100)							
205.8	222.8	215.7	196.1	200.7	183.9	91.6	100.0	76.7	..	..	Terms of Trade
181.9	196.8	177.9	163.4	163.3	149.7	83.9	100.0	84.8	..	..	Export Prices, fob
88.4	88.3	82.5	83.3	81.4	81.4	91.6	100.0	110.5	..	..	Import Prices, cif
				(Millions of current US dollars)							**BALANCE OF PAYMENTS**
27,748.9	19,736.2	12,896.7	10,854.6	12,350.0	13,510.3	6,313.1	7,815.0	7,301.4	8,416.6	f	Exports of Goods & Services
25,928.8	18,115.0	12,162.8	10,343.8	11,859.4	13,114.7	6,014.9	7,544.6	6,897.2	8,135.4	..	Merchandise, fob
1,128.1	901.2	498.9	397.2	425.5	315.6	229.9	224.9	363.7	192.0	..	Nonfactor Services
692.0	719.9	234.9	113.7	65.2	80.0	68.3	45.5	40.6	89.2	..	Factor Services
22,043.9	25,341.6	19,752.8	14,814.1	11,908.8	10,689.1	5,833.9	7,859.4	7,483.4	8,651.5	f	Imports of Goods & Services
14,752.8	18,946.2	14,893.9	11,432.8	8,867.1	7,498.9	3,701.5	4,096.9	4,271.1	5,291.0	..	Merchandise, fob
5,238.0	4,935.1	3,418.0	2,378.4	1,790.6	1,641.5	1,194.8	870.5	839.6	888.9	..	Nonfactor Services
2,053.1	1,460.3	1,441.0	1,002.9	1,251.1	1,548.7	937.6	2,891.9	2,372.7	2,471.6	..	Factor Services
531.2	669.3	873.0	997.7	1,248.8	1,298.5	514.8	553.3	1,435.4	1,279.8	..	Long-Term Interest
-410.0	-441.6	-388.3	-374.4	-300.3	-253.7	-107.8	-19.4	-32.9	-18.6	..	Private Current Transfers, net
12.9	13.6	12.0	8.4	6.6	9.9	4.5	2.7	2.5	10.2	..	Workers' Remittances
5,295.0	-6,047.1	-7,244.5	-4,333.8	140.9	2,567.5	371.4	-63.7	-214.9	-253.5	..	Curr. A/C Bal before Off. Transf.
-168.2	-116.7	-40.9	-20.1	-26.4	-1.5	-5.3	-5.1	21.0	110.8	..	Net Official Transfers
5,126.8	-6,163.8	-7,285.4	-4,353.8	114.5	2,566.0	366.1	-68.8	-193.9	-142.8	..	Curr. A/C Bal after Off. Transf.
-81.8	1,335.2	1,522.5	1,828.3	-46.5	-508.0	-961.6	-1,788.3	-2,425.8	1,854.3	f	Long-Term Capital, net
-739.7	546.5	432.5	344.5	199.8	478.3	166.8	602.7	376.9	2,081.9	..	Direct Investment
1,509.9	2,506.0	2,882.7	1,818.5	-201.5	-1,108.5	102.0	913.7	379.8	1,040.1	..	Long-Term Loans
1,752.5	3,140.5	3,723.7	2,980.8	2,023.4	1,659.0	1,346.7	1,358.4	1,023.9	1,524.9	..	Disbursements
242.6	634.5	841.0	1,162.3	2,224.9	2,767.5	1,244.7	444.7	644.1	484.8	..	Repayments
-852.0	-1,717.2	-1,792.8	-334.7	-44.8	122.2	-1,230.4	-3,304.7	-3,182.5	-1,267.7	..	Other Long-Term Capital
-672.3	162.3	3,652.7	2,084.4	414.7	-1,569.4	117.5	3,666.6	2,182.9	-526.9	f	Other Capital, net
-4,372.7	4,666.3	2,110.2	441.1	-482.8	-488.6	477.9	-1,809.4	436.8	-1,184.7	..	Change in Reserves
				(Nigerian Naira per US dollar)							**Memo Item:**
0.550	0.620	0.670	0.720	0.770	0.890	1.750	4.020	4.540	7.360	..	Conversion Factor (Annual Avg)
				(Millions of US dollars), outstanding at end of year							
8,934	12,136	12,954	18,539	18,537	19,551	24,043	31,193	31,956	32,876	..	**EXTERNAL DEBT (Total)**
5,381	7,709	10,419	13,481	12,793	14,556	20,324	29,532	30,250	32,118	..	Long-Term Debt (by debtor)
0	0	38	2,383	1,963	905	259	259	0	..	..	Central Bank, incl. IMF credit
3,621	5,036	6,747	6,546	5,771	8,124	15,089	24,668	25,675	29,139	..	Central Government
188	581	1,492	2,187	2,639	2,914	3,038	2,775	2,852	1,431	..	Rest of General Government
455	709	779	1,013	970	1,116	1,204	1,098	1,027	985	..	Non-financial Public Enterprises
1,117	1,383	1,362	1,351	1,449	1,497	735	732	696	563	..	Priv. Sector, incl non-guaranteed
3,553	4,427	2,535	5,059	5,744	4,995	3,719	1,661	1,707	759	..	Short-Term Debt
				(Millions of US dollars)							**Memo Items:**
10,234.8	3,895.4	1,612.5	989.9	1,462.3	1,667.2	1,081.4	1,165.3	651.2	1,765.6	..	Int'l Reserves Excluding Gold
405.0	273.1	313.9	262.1	211.8	224.7	268.6	332.6	281.8	275.5	..	Gold Holdings (at market price)
											SOCIAL INDICATORS
6.9	6.9	6.9	6.9	6.8	6.8	6.7	6.7	6.6	6.5	..	Total Fertility Rate
118.0	116.0	114.0	112.2	110.4	108.6	106.8	105.0	103.1	101.2	..	Infant Mortality Rate
47.7	48.1	48.5	48.9	49.3	49.7	50.1	50.5	50.8	51.1	..	Life Expectancy at Birth
27.1	27.9	28.7	29.4	30.2	31.0	32.1	33.1	33.8	34.5	..	Urban Population, % of total
105.4	104.3	106.8	99.5	99.8	108.3	111.9	100.0	99.5	98.6	..	Food Prod. per capita (1987=100)
68.1	..	..	..	..	..	..	..	..	..	..	Labor Force, Agriculture (%)
36.7	36.5	36.3	36.1	35.9	35.7	35.5	35.3	35.1	34.9	..	Labor Force, Female (%)
97.0	91.0	92.1	92.1	88.0	77.7	75.1	..	..	..	..	Primary Schl. Enroll. Ratio
84.0	84.0	84.0	81.0	..	..	..	102.0	..	..	..	Primary Schl. Enroll. Ratio, Female
19.0	22.0	28.0	29.0	..	..	..	57.0	..	..	..	Secondary Schl. Enroll. Ratio

NORWAY	1969	1970	1971	1972	1973	1974	1975	1976	1977	1978	1979
CURRENT GNP PER CAPITA (US $)	2,530	2,750	3,090	3,560	4,240	5,290	6,610	7,650	8,550	9,510	10,990
POPULATION (thousands)	3,851	3,877	3,903	3,933	3,961	3,985	4,007	4,026	4,043	4,059	4,073

USE AND ORIGIN OF RESOURCES

(Billions of current Norwegian Kroner)

	1969	1970	1971	1972	1973	1974	1975	1976	1977	1978	1979
Gross National Product (GNP)	68.85	79.26	88.36	97.37	110.67	127.88	146.79	167.66	186.77	205.84	229.20
Net Factor Income from Abroad	-0.57	-0.62	-0.75	-1.03	-1.19	-1.85	-1.92	-3.05	-4.73	-7.18	-9.33
GDP at Market Prices	69.42	79.88	89.11	98.40	111.85	129.73	148.70	170.71	191.50	213.02	238.52
Resource Balance	1.56	-1.04	-2.88	0.68	-0.63	-3.71	-9.95	-16.30	-20.49	-1.88	6.21
Exports of Goods & NFServices	29.40	33.39	35.83	40.01	48.68	60.05	62.19	70.11	76.18	87.25	105.34
Imports of Goods & NFServices	27.84	34.43	38.71	39.34	49.31	63.76	72.13	86.42	96.67	89.14	99.13
Domestic Absorption	67.86	80.91	91.98	97.73	112.49	133.44	158.65	187.01	211.99	214.91	232.31
Private Consumption, etc.	39.25	43.03	47.87	52.49	58.37	66.29	77.53	89.44	104.07	110.74	120.15
General Gov't Consumption	11.34	13.24	14.93	16.64	18.94	21.51	25.52	34.09	38.63	43.54	46.58
Gross Domestic Investment	17.27	24.65	29.18	28.60	35.18	45.64	55.60	63.49	69.29	60.62	65.57
Fixed Investment	16.45	20.95	26.52	27.24	33.44	38.92	48.99	59.16	67.17	64.12	63.36
Indirect Taxes, net	7.62	10.45	11.88	12.96	14.35	15.23	17.20	19.39	22.22	21.50	24.36
GDP at factor cost	61.80	69.43	77.22	85.45	97.50	114.50	131.50	151.32	169.29	191.52	214.16
Agriculture	3.96	4.46	5.02	4.93	5.52	6.46	7.12	8.32	9.47	9.81	10.13
Industry	23.64	25.61	28.13	31.50	35.44	42.72	51.39	57.77	62.73	73.04	88.29
Manufacturing	15.08	17.26	18.81	21.12	24.05	28.38	32.27	34.41	35.96	37.52	43.79
Services, etc.	41.82	49.81	55.96	61.98	70.90	80.55	90.20	104.62	119.31	130.17	140.10
Gross Domestic Saving	18.83	23.61	26.30	29.27	34.55	41.93	45.65	47.19	48.81	58.74	71.79
Gross National Saving	..	23.22	25.85	28.50	33.54	40.20	43.80	44.15	43.98	51.39	62.19

(Billions of 1987 Norwegian Kroner)

	1969	1970	1971	1972	1973	1974	1975	1976	1977	1978	1979
Gross National Product	271.72	276.99	289.49	303.87	316.22	331.44	345.81	367.68	378.42	392.30	409.66
GDP at Market Prices	274.97	280.24	293.07	308.21	320.82	337.48	351.55	375.49	388.94	406.59	427.19
Resource Balance	-18.12	-32.59	-39.39	-25.37	-35.36	-41.52	-48.75	-55.97	-57.65	-20.61	-15.73
Exports of Goods & NFServices	89.07	89.16	90.17	102.88	111.40	112.16	115.63	128.64	133.32	144.50	148.23
Imports of Goods & NFServices	107.19	121.75	129.56	128.25	146.76	153.68	164.37	184.62	190.96	165.10	163.95
Domestic Absorption	293.09	312.83	332.46	333.58	356.18	379.00	400.30	431.47	446.58	427.20	442.92
Private Consumption, etc.	166.48	163.54	169.12	179.11	184.66	189.05	197.67	211.13	226.33	229.00	235.53
General Gov't Consumption	50.44	53.60	56.83	59.41	62.65	65.17	69.35	74.47	78.14	82.32	85.24
Gross Domestic Investment	76.17	95.69	106.50	95.06	108.86	124.78	133.27	145.87	142.11	115.88	122.15
Fixed Investment	71.79	82.47	97.93	93.92	106.73	112.17	125.54	138.25	143.29	127.22	120.90
GDP at factor cost	241.55	239.76	249.90	264.24	275.60	293.71	307.33	329.87	341.32	362.98	379.92
Agriculture	15.54	13.70	14.45	14.54	14.34	15.74	15.19	15.68	15.80	15.27	15.73
Industry	74.49	74.04	77.37	83.01	86.89	91.75	100.46	108.83	110.03	126.30	136.61
Manufacturing	64.43	66.67	69.04	72.35	76.46	80.29	78.53	78.71	77.07	75.18	77.59
Services, etc.	189.65	198.64	207.68	216.99	226.23	236.71	241.40	256.43	269.80	268.25	276.91

Memo Items:

	1969	1970	1971	1972	1973	1974	1975	1976	1977	1978	1979
Capacity to Import	113.20	118.08	119.93	130.45	144.88	144.74	141.71	149.79	150.49	161.61	174.23
Terms of Trade Adjustment	24.13	28.93	29.76	27.58	33.48	32.58	26.08	21.14	17.18	17.12	26.00
Gross Domestic Income	299.10	309.17	322.83	335.78	354.30	370.06	377.63	396.63	406.11	423.71	453.19
Gross National Income	295.85	305.91	319.24	331.45	349.70	364.02	371.90	388.83	395.59	409.42	435.66

DOMESTIC PRICES/DEFLATORS

(Index 1987 = 100)

	1969	1970	1971	1972	1973	1974	1975	1976	1977	1978	1979
Overall (GDP)	25.2	28.5	30.4	31.9	34.9	38.4	42.3	45.5	49.2	52.4	55.8
Domestic Absorption	23.2	25.9	27.7	29.3	31.6	35.2	39.6	43.3	47.5	50.3	52.4
Agriculture	25.5	32.5	34.7	33.9	38.5	41.1	46.8	53.1	59.9	64.2	64.4
Industry	31.7	34.6	36.4	37.9	40.8	46.6	51.1	53.1	57.0	57.8	64.6
Manufacturing	23.4	25.9	27.2	29.2	31.5	35.3	41.1	43.7	46.7	49.9	56.4
Consumer Price Index	22.5	24.9	26.4	28.4	30.5	33.3	37.2	40.6	44.3	47.9	50.2

MANUFACTURING ACTIVITY

	1969	1970	1971	1972	1973	1974	1975	1976	1977	1978	1979
Employment (1987=100)	108.9	112.1	113.3	113.6	113.6	116.5	115.9	115.8	116.4	114.7	113.3
Real Earnings per Empl. (1987=100)	74.0	73.5	76.9	77.9	80.1	84.0	89.9	93.1	93.8	93.6	92.6
Real Output per Empl. (1987=100)	63.9	63.7	65.3	64.9	69.4	76.6	75.3	77.7	79.7	76.5	78.8
Earnings as % of Value Added	47.2	50.4	52.2	57.2	55.6	54.0	57.7	60.7	63.0	63.8	59.8

MONETARY HOLDINGS

(Billions of current Norwegian Kroner)

	1969	1970	1971	1972	1973	1974	1975	1976	1977	1978	1979
Money Supply, Broadly Defined	40.59	46.70	52.93	59.57	67.61	75.09	86.59	95.66	112.16	126.01	142.83
Money	15.27	17.20	19.21	22.39	25.81	28.87	33.65	32.42	37.00	40.19	43.25
Currency Outside Banks	6.52	7.28	7.99	8.75	9.44	10.77	12.39	14.26	16.08	17.06	17.73
Demand Deposits	8.75	9.92	11.22	13.64	16.37	18.10	21.26	18.16	20.92	23.13	25.52
Quasi-Money	25.32	29.50	33.72	37.18	41.80	46.22	52.94	63.24	75.16	85.83	99.58

GOVERNMENT DEFICIT (-) OR SURPLUS

(Billions of current Norwegian Kroner)

	1969	1970	1971	1972	1973	1974	1975	1976	1977	1978	1979
GOVERNMENT DEFICIT (-) OR SURPLUS	..	..	..	-1.44	-1.03	-1.76	-4.72	-10.01	-13.13	-14.47	-14.99
Current Revenue	..	..	..	37.32	42.91	49.02	55.73	66.12	73.86	82.69	92.88
Current Expenditure	..	..	..	32.40	36.66	42.51	49.84	61.28	70.19	81.36	90.22
Current Budget Balance	..	..	..	4.93	6.24	6.51	5.90	4.84	3.66	1.33	2.67
Capital Receipts	..	..	..	0.00	0.00	0.00	0.00	..	..	..	..
Capital Payments	..	..	..	6.37	7.27	8.27	10.61	14.85	16.80	15.80	17.66

1980	1981	1982	1983	1984	1985	1986	1987	1988	1989 estimate	NOTES	NORWAY
12,880	14,130	14,390	14,160	14,170	14,470	15,420	17,350	19,550	21,850	..	**CURRENT GNP PER CAPITA (US $)**
4,091	4,100	4,115	4,133	4,140	4,153	4,169	4,187	4,196	4,215	..	POPULATION (thousands)
											USE AND ORIGIN OF RESOURCES
				(Billions of current Norwegian Kroner)							
275.55	317.05	349.55	389.21	439.27	490.67	504.51	554.01	571.81	611.15	..	Gross National Product (GNP)
-9.52	-10.58	-12.70	-13.00	-13.14	-9.51	-9.09	-9.55	-13.55	-14.50	..	Net Factor Income from Abroad
285.07	327.62	362.25	402.21	452.41	500.17	513.60	563.55	585.36	625.65	..	GDP at Market Prices
17.43	25.80	20.50	31.77	41.23	41.50	-18.20	-11.23	-3.16	24.42	..	Resource Balance
134.80	156.18	164.96	183.78	214.08	236.07	194.91	200.23	212.70	258.73	..	Exports of Goods & NFServices
117.37	130.38	144.46	152.01	172.85	194.58	213.11	211.47	215.87	234.31	..	Imports of Goods & NFServices
267.63	301.83	341.75	370.44	411.19	458.67	531.80	574.79	588.52	601.23	..	Domestic Absorption
135.44	155.10	175.20	192.93	210.82	245.41	278.84	297.24	307.70	314.80	..	Private Consumption, etc.
53.48	62.62	70.41	78.21	84.10	92.80	102.09	116.67	123.18	131.20	..	General Gov't Consumption
78.72	84.11	96.14	99.30	116.27	120.46	150.87	160.88	157.65	155.24	..	Gross Domestic Investment
68.52	90.36	89.33	101.20	117.57	107.75	143.31	157.03	170.89	170.85	..	Fixed Investment
29.06	33.90	38.09	45.29	52.49	65.06	71.51	76.79	74.27	71.13	..	Indirect Taxes, net
256.00	293.72	324.17	356.92	399.92	435.12	442.09	486.77	511.09	554.52	..	GDP at factor cost
10.97	12.96	13.44	13.14	15.04	15.15	16.02	17.76	17.68	..	B	Agriculture
112.91	129.57	142.58	163.12	190.18	206.47	178.27	196.78	198.82	..	B	Industry
45.64	48.57	51.38	56.73	64.51	70.12	75.63	84.90	89.38	..	B	Manufacturing
161.19	185.10	206.23	225.96	247.19	278.55	319.31	349.01	368.86	..	B	Services, etc.
96.15	109.91	116.64	131.07	157.49	161.96	132.67	149.65	154.48	179.65	..	Gross Domestic Saving
86.37	99.16	103.56	117.67	144.06	151.88	122.54	138.79	139.84	163.92	..	Gross National Saving
				(Billions of 1987 Norwegian Kroner)							
428.67	432.66	432.97	454.47	480.32	513.72	538.01	554.01	553.04	578.85	..	Gross National Product
445.16	449.06	450.56	471.44	496.73	524.84	547.93	563.55	565.84	594.10	..	GDP at Market Prices
-17.96	-18.39	-24.90	-13.27	-16.65	-15.92	-33.48	-11.23	6.27	35.63	..	Resource Balance
151.33	153.41	153.19	164.79	178.33	190.55	193.51	200.23	212.45	243.25	..	Exports of Goods & NFServices
169.29	171.81	178.09	178.06	194.98	206.47	226.99	211.47	206.18	207.62	..	Imports of Goods & NFServices
463.12	467.46	475.46	484.71	513.38	540.77	581.41	574.79	559.57	558.47	..	Domestic Absorption
239.43	242.51	245.84	252.66	258.70	288.05	301.19	297.24	293.01	298.74	..	Private Consumption, etc.
89.87	95.39	99.12	103.73	106.27	109.73	112.18	116.67	117.25	120.18	..	General Gov't Consumption
133.82	129.56	130.50	128.33	148.42	142.98	168.04	160.88	149.31	139.55	..	Gross Domestic Investment
119.09	140.43	124.98	132.25	146.72	126.26	156.48	157.03	161.70	154.74	..	Fixed Investment
394.06	396.00	396.96	412.32	431.19	448.70	469.84	486.77	495.66	528.64	..	GDP at factor cost
16.04	17.49	18.20	18.02	19.53	17.77	16.72	17.76	17.80	..	..	Agriculture
146.39	144.52	145.03	156.78	170.52	175.74	180.89	196.78	206.66	..	..	Industry
76.74	76.00	75.49	74.93	79.23	82.14	82.10	84.90	83.01	..	..	Manufacturing
283.50	288.70	288.84	296.65	306.68	331.33	350.33	349.01	341.38	..	..	Services, etc.
											Memo Items:
194.44	205.80	203.36	215.27	241.48	250.51	207.61	200.23	203.16	229.26	..	Capacity to Import
43.11	52.39	50.17	50.48	63.15	59.96	14.09	0.00	-9.29	-13.99	..	Terms of Trade Adjustment
488.27	501.45	500.73	521.93	559.89	584.80	562.03	563.55	556.55	580.10	..	Gross Domestic Income
471.78	485.05	483.14	504.95	543.48	573.68	552.10	554.01	543.75	564.86	..	Gross National Income
				(Index 1987 = 100)							**DOMESTIC PRICES/DEFLATORS**
64.0	73.0	80.4	85.3	91.1	95.3	93.7	100.0	103.4	105.3	..	Overall (GDP)
57.8	64.6	71.9	76.4	80.1	84.8	91.5	100.0	105.2	107.7	..	Domestic Absorption
68.4	74.1	73.8	72.9	77.0	85.3	95.8	100.0	99.3	..	..	Agriculture
77.1	89.7	98.3	104.0	111.5	117.5	98.6	100.0	96.2	..	..	Industry
59.5	63.9	68.1	75.7	81.4	85.4	92.1	100.0	107.7	..	..	Manufacturing
55.7	63.3	70.5	76.4	81.2	85.8	92.0	100.0	106.7	111.6	..	Consumer Price Index
											MANUFACTURING ACTIVITY
112.7	110.8	107.6	100.0	98.8	99.4	100.3	100.0	93.5	92.4	..	Employment (1987=100)
91.7	89.8	87.8	88.9	92.7	96.2	98.3	100.0	100.8	..	..	Real Earnings per Empl. (1987=100)
85.7	90.0	90.6	91.3	96.7	103.9	100.0	100.0	105.3	..	..	Real Output per Empl. (1987=100)
60.3	62.1	62.3	58.9	56.4	58.1	59.9	59.1	56.1	..	..	Earnings as % of Value Added
				(Billions of current Norwegian Kroner)							**MONETARY HOLDINGS**
158.52	179.99	200.29	222.58	268.10	305.65	312.94	359.74	377.40	409.00	..	Money Supply, Broadly Defined
45.56	52.38	58.81	65.92	82.00	98.65	101.76	152.63	187.11	313.45	..	Money
18.82	20.16	20.93	21.75	22.78	25.05	26.58	28.16	28.52	29.20	..	Currency Outside Banks
26.74	32.22	37.88	44.17	59.22	73.60	75.18	124.48	158.58	284.25	..	Demand Deposits
112.96	127.61	141.48	156.67	186.10	207.00	211.18	207.11	190.30	95.54	..	Quasi-Money
				(Billions of current Norwegian Kroner)							**GOVERNMENT DEFICIT (-) OR SURPLUS**
-5.40	6.82	3.89	9.44	8.96	18.28	17.32	0.32	0.07	..	..	Current Revenue
117.80	141.24	154.68	177.41	194.94	224.09	245.53	256.42	270.98	..	..	Current Revenue
104.40	119.72	135.15	150.00	163.32	178.85	199.83	223.22	243.14	..	..	Current Expenditure
13.40	21.52	19.53	27.40	31.61	45.24	45.70	33.19	27.83	..	..	Current Budget Balance
0.05	0.04	0.10	0.15	0.25	0.39	0.38	0.81	1.51	..	..	Capital Receipts
18.85	14.74	15.74	18.11	22.90	27.36	28.76	33.68	29.27	..	..	Capital Payments

NORWAY	1969	1970	1971	1972	1973	1974	1975	1976	1977	1978	1979
FOREIGN TRADE (CUSTOMS BASIS)					*(Millions of current US dollars)*						
Value of Exports, fob	2,203	2,457	2,563	3,279	4,680	6,274	7,207	7,917	8,716	10,027	13,466
Nonfuel Primary Products	941	1,041	1,061	1,230	1,709	2,061	1,827	2,231	2,424	2,623	3,175
Fuels	37	54	58	105	139	401	936	1,501	1,638	2,058	4,863
Manufactures	1,225	1,361	1,444	1,944	2,831	3,812	4,444	4,185	4,654	5,346	5,428
Value of Imports, cif	2,943	3,702	4,083	4,369	6,219	8,414	9,705	11,105	12,870	11,435	13,732
Nonfuel Primary Products	613	791	780	827	1,109	1,550	1,528	1,583	1,647	1,667	2,094
Fuels	217	285	308	326	479	1,034	955	1,241	1,424	1,353	2,071
Manufactures	2,113	2,627	2,996	3,216	4,631	5,830	7,222	8,281	9,800	8,416	9,568
					(Index 1987 = 100)						
Terms of Trade	119.2	123.3	114.2	108.8	114.7	107.3	110.6	110.4	110.3	103.6	108.2
Export Prices, fob	29.1	31.2	31.9	33.4	43.2	57.9	63.3	64.7	70.5	74.5	92.7
Import Prices, cif	24.4	25.3	27.9	30.7	37.6	54.0	57.3	58.6	63.9	72.0	85.6
BALANCE OF PAYMENTS					*(Millions of current US dollars)*						
Exports of Goods & Services	..	4,790	5,204	6,177	8,563	11,157	12,125	13,113	14,564	17,022	21,397
Merchandise, fob	..	2,480	2,587	3,307	4,729	6,329	7,270	8,047	9,152	11,033	13,747
Nonfactor Services	..	2,166	2,481	2,742	3,631	4,505	4,511	4,744	5,061	5,521	6,992
Factor Services	..	144	136	127	203	322	343	323	351	468	659
Imports of Goods & Services	..	5,021	5,729	6,216	8,879	12,174	14,444	16,661	19,305	18,757	22,005
Merchandise, fob	..	3,633	4,046	4,322	6,262	8,666	10,141	11,608	13,205	11,545	13,601
Nonfactor Services	..	1,138	1,364	1,508	2,032	2,540	3,592	4,172	4,860	5,372	5,900
Factor Services	..	250	319	385	586	968	710	882	1,240	1,840	2,504
Long-Term Interest	..	..	..	..	..	..	..	..	..	..	..
Private Current Transfers, net	..	31	41	39	31	20	12	1	-18	-31	-53
Workers' Remittances	..	..	..	..	..	..	..	4	6	6	
Curr. A/C Bal before Off. Transf.	..	-200	-484	0	-285	-997	-2,307	-3,547	-4,759	-1,766	-660
Net Official Transfers	..	-42	-41	-59	-79	-121	-171	-199	-275	-337	-384
Curr. A/C Bal after Off. Transf.	..	-242	-525	-59	-364	-1,118	-2,478	-3,746	-5,034	-2,103	-1,044
Long-Term Capital, net	..	138	354	286	850	990	2,577	2,495	4,185	3,187	2,269
Direct Investment	..	32	62	121	159	198	48	179	643	424	358
Long-Term Loans	..	..	..	..	..	..	..	..	..	..	..
Disbursements	..	..	..	..	..	..	..	..	..	..	..
Repayments	..	..	..	..	..	..	..	..	..	..	..
Other Long-Term Capital	..	106	292	165	691	792	2,529	2,316	3,542	2,763	1,912
Other Capital, net	..	175	475	-88	-242	448	242	1,223	727	-447	60
Change in Reserves	..	-71	-304	-139	-244	-321	-340	28	121	-637	-1,285
Memo Item:											
Conversion Factor (Annual Avg)	7.140	7.140	7.040	6.590	5.770	5.540	5.230	5.460	5.320	5.240	5.060
					(Norwegian Kroner per US dollar)						
EXTERNAL DEBT (Total)	..	..	..	..	*(Millions US dollars), outstanding at end of year*						
					..	..	..	..	..	..	..
Long-Term Debt (by debtor)	..	..	..	..	..	..	..	..	..	..	..
Central Bank, incl. IMF credit	..	..	..	..	..	..	..	..	..	..	..
Central Government	..	..	..	..	..	..	..	..	..	..	..
Rest of General Government	..	..	..	..	..	..	..	..	..	..	..
Non-financial Public Enterprises	..	..	..	..	..	..	..	..	..	..	..
Priv. Sector, incl non-guaranteed	..	..	..	..	..	..	..	..	..	..	..
Short-Term Debt	..	..	..	..	..	..	..	..	..	..	..
Memo Items:					*(Millions of US dollars)*						
Int'l Reserves Excluding Gold	685	788	1,118	1,288	1,533	1,887	2,196	2,189	2,196	2,861	4,215
Gold Holdings (at market price)	25	25	41	63	110	183	137	132	178	256	606
SOCIAL INDICATORS											
Total Fertility Rate	2.7	2.5	2.5	2.4	2.2	2.1	2.0	1.9	1.8	1.8	1.8
Infant Mortality Rate	13.8	12.7	12.8	11.8	11.9	10.4	11.0	10.4	9.1	8.6	8.7
Life Expectancy at Birth	74.1	74.2	74.3	74.4	74.6	74.8	75.0	75.1	75.3	75.5	75.6
Urban Population, % of total	61.3	64.8	65.5	66.2	66.8	67.5	68.2	68.7	69.1	69.6	70.0
Food Prod. per capita (1987=100)	81.1	80.1	81.7	80.9	80.6	91.4	83.6	82.2	89.0	94.2	91.0
Labor Force, Agriculture (%)	12.5	11.8	11.4	11.0	10.7	10.3	10.0	9.6	9.3	9.0	8.6
Labor Force, Female (%)	28.7	29.3	30.5	31.7	32.9	33.9	35.0	36.1	37.1	38.2	39.1
Primary Schl. Enroll. Ratio	..	89.0	..	..	..	..	101.0	101.0	100.0	100.0	100.0
Primary Schl. Enroll. Ratio, Female	..	94.0	..	..	..	..	101.0	101.0	100.0	100.0	100.0
Secondary Schl. Enroll. Ratio	..	83.0	..	..	..	..	88.0	89.0	90.0	92.0	94.0

	1980	1981	1982	1983	1984	1985	1986	1987	1988	1989 estimate	NOTES	NORWAY
					(Millions of current US dollars)							**FOREIGN TRADE (CUSTOMS BASIS)**
Value of Exports, fob	18,481	17,968	17,583	17,972	18,914	18,662	18,230	21,449	22,503	..	..	Value of Exports, fob
Nonfuel Primary Products	3,615	3,401	2,877	3,180	3,364	3,032	3,591	4,588	5,730	..	..	Nonfuel Primary Products
Fuels	8,935	9,034	9,135	9,481	10,322	10,012	7,814	8,690	8,218	..	..	Fuels
Manufactures	5,931	5,533	5,571	5,311	5,228	5,618	6,825	8,171	8,555	..	..	Manufactures
Value of Imports, cif	16,952	15,638	15,471	13,494	13,885	14,519	20,298	22,578	23,212	..	..	Value of Imports, cif
Nonfuel Primary Products	2,610	2,255	1,930	1,769	1,918	1,886	2,472	2,721	3,242	..	..	Nonfuel Primary Products
Fuels	2,957	2,253	2,030	1,402	1,421	1,265	1,192	1,193	842	..	..	Fuels
Manufactures	11,384	11,130	11,511	10,323	10,546	11,368	16,634	18,664	19,128	..	..	Manufactures
					(Index 1987 = 100)							
Terms of Trade	126.2	132.3	131.6	128.7	132.0	128.9	103.8	100.0	92.5	..	..	Terms of Trade
Export Prices, fob	125.4	124.3	116.2	109.1	109.1	104.3	95.8	100.0	101.3	..	..	Export Prices, fob
Import Prices, cif	99.4	94.0	88.3	84.8	82.7	80.9	92.3	100.0	109.5	..	..	Import Prices, cif
					(Millions of current US dollars)							**BALANCE OF PAYMENTS**
Exports of Goods & Services	28,252	28,690	27,220	26,542	27,828	29,615	29,008	32,776	36,102	41,395	..	Exports of Goods & Services
Merchandise, fob	18,649	18,494	17,664	18,055	19,115	20,059	18,143	21,191	23,024	27,162	..	Merchandise, fob
Nonfactor Services	8,525	8,676	7,898	7,061	7,068	7,428	8,100	8,478	9,732	10,718	..	Nonfactor Services
Factor Services	1,078	1,520	1,658	1,425	1,645	2,128	2,766	3,107	3,346	3,515	..	Factor Services
Imports of Goods & Services	26,658	26,028	25,997	23,977	24,403	25,998	32,749	35,899	38,838	40,210	..	Imports of Goods & Services
Merchandise, fob	16,753	15,459	15,278	13,704	13,957	15,331	20,258	21,951	23,169	23,393	..	Merchandise, fob
Nonfactor Services	6,901	7,190	7,056	7,060	7,174	7,438	8,497	9,428	10,232	10,723	..	Nonfactor Services
Factor Services	3,004	3,379	3,663	3,213	3,272	3,229	3,994	4,520	5,437	6,094	..	Factor Services
Long-Term Interest	..	..	..	..	..	..	..	..	..	..	..	Long-Term Interest
Private Current Transfers, net	-55	-29	-57	-54	-36	-66	-140	-194	-167	-178	..	Private Current Transfers, net
Workers' Remittances	13	9	11	9	10	11	11	12	9	17	..	Workers' Remittances
Curr. A/C Bal before Off. Transf.	1,539	2,633	1,166	2,510	3,389	3,551	-3,880	-3,316	-2,903	1,007	..	Curr. A/C Bal before Off. Transf.
Net Official Transfers	-441	-456	-504	-524	-469	-499	-665	-788	-812	-781	..	Net Official Transfers
Curr. A/C Bal after Off. Transf.	1,098	2,177	662	1,986	2,919	3,052	-4,545	-4,105	-3,715	226	..	Curr. A/C Bal after Off. Transf.
Long-Term Capital, net	-927	-900	292	-1,582	-600	-1,367	2,809	-13	5,028	2,874	..	Long-Term Capital, net
Direct Investment	-193	499	136	-27	-781	-1,731	-582	-687	-249	-4	..	Direct Investment
Long-Term Loans	..	..	..	..	..	..	..	..	..	..	..	Long-Term Loans
Disbursements	..	..	..	..	..	..	..	..	..	..	..	Disbursements
Repayments	..	..	..	..	..	..	..	..	..	..	..	Repayments
Other Long-Term Capital	-734	-1,399	155	-1,555	181	363	3,391	674	5,278	2,878	..	Other Long-Term Capital
Other Capital, net	1,711	-846	-246	-502	748	1,768	-1,474	3,898	-1,452	-2,135	..	Other Capital, net
Change in Reserves	-1,882	-431	-708	98	-3,068	-3,452	3,211	220	138	-965	..	Change in Reserves
					(Norwegian Kroner per US dollar)							**Memo Item:**
Conversion Factor (Annual Avg)	4.940	5.740	6.450	7.300	8.160	8.600	7.390	6.740	6.520	6.900	..	Conversion Factor (Annual Avg)
					(Millions US dollars), outstanding at end of year							**EXTERNAL DEBT (Total)**
Long-Term Debt (by debtor)	..	..	..	..	..	..	..	..	..	..	..	Long-Term Debt (by debtor)
Central Bank, incl. IMF credit	..	..	..	..	..	..	..	..	..	..	..	Central Bank, incl. IMF credit
Central Government	..	..	..	..	..	..	..	..	..	..	..	Central Government
Rest of General Government	..	..	..	..	..	..	..	..	..	..	..	Rest of General Government
Non-financial Public Enterprises	..	..	..	..	..	..	..	..	..	..	..	Non-financial Public Enterprises
Priv. Sector, incl non-guaranteed	..	..	..	..	..	..	..	..	..	..	..	Priv. Sector, incl non-guaranteed
Short-Term Debt	..	..	..	..	..	..	..	..	..	..	..	Short-Term Debt
					(Millions of US dollars)							**Memo Items:**
Int'l Reserves Excluding Gold	6,048	6,253	6,874	6,629	9,365	13,917	12,525	14,277	13,268	13,785	..	Int'l Reserves Excluding Gold
Gold Holdings (at market price)	698	471	541	452	365	387	463	573	486	475	..	Gold Holdings (at market price)
												SOCIAL INDICATORS
Total Fertility Rate	1.7	1.7	1.7	1.7	1.7	1.7	1.7	1.8	1.8	1.8	..	Total Fertility Rate
Infant Mortality Rate	8.0	7.5	8.1	7.9	8.2	8.5	7.8	8.4	8.3	8.2	..	Infant Mortality Rate
Life Expectancy at Birth	75.7	75.9	76.0	76.2	76.3	76.5	76.6	76.8	76.9	77.1	..	Life Expectancy at Birth
Urban Population, % of total	70.5	71.0	71.4	71.9	72.3	72.8	73.1	73.4	73.8	74.1	..	Urban Population, % of total
Food Prod. per capita (1987=100)	94.3	96.7	101.2	95.9	102.9	99.2	92.1	100.0	102.3	104.2	..	Food Prod. per capita (1987=100)
Labor Force, Agriculture (%)	8.3	..	..	..	..	..	..	..	..	..	..	Labor Force, Agriculture (%)
Labor Force, Female (%)	40.1	40.2	40.3	40.3	40.4	40.5	40.6	40.8	40.9	41.0	..	Labor Force, Female (%)
Primary Schl. Enroll. Ratio	100.0	..	98.0	98.0	95.0	94.0	95.0				..	Primary Schl. Enroll. Ratio
Primary Schl. Enroll. Ratio, Female	100.0	100.0	99.0	98.0	94.0	94.0	95.0				..	Primary Schl. Enroll. Ratio, Female
Secondary Schl. Enroll. Ratio	94.0	..	97.0	96.0	97.0	97.0	95.0				..	Secondary Schl. Enroll. Ratio

OMAN	1969	1970	1971	1972	1973	1974	1975	1976	1977	1978	1979
CURRENT GNP PER CAPITA (US $)	310	360	370	400	390	560	1,280	2,840	2,860	2,790	3,080
POPULATION (thousands)	623	640	658	680	705	733	766	803	844	889	936

USE AND ORIGIN OF RESOURCES — *(Millions of current Omani Rials)*

	1969	1970	1971	1972	1973	1974	1975	1976	1977	1978	1979
Gross National Product (GNP)	76.7	88.6	105.1	111.8	106.7	416.5	589.3	736.4	816.6	835.9	1,152.2
Net Factor Income from Abroad	-23.3	-18.2	-20.0	-29.0	-62.7	-152.0	-134.9	-147.9	-130.2	-111.0	-137.3
GDP at Market Prices	100.0	106.8	125.1	140.8	169.4	568.5	724.2	884.3	946.8	946.9	1,289.5
Resource Balance	62.7	57.7	42.1	22.0	21.4	147.6	122.1	144.7	135.0	90.8	262.4
Exports of Goods & NFServices	74.6	78.7	82.3	83.6	114.9	419.1	489.2	551.2	552.0	552.0	787.4
Imports of Goods & NFServices	11.9	21.0	40.2	61.6	93.5	271.5	367.1	406.5	417.0	461.2	525.0
Domestic Absorption	37.3	49.1	83.0	118.8	148.0	420.9	602.1	739.6	811.8	855.7	1,027.1
Private Consumption, etc.	22.9	20.7	21.4	35.1	40.6	49.6	115.1	181.6	253.4	309.9	337.0
General Gov't Consumption	5.1	13.7	26.0	41.7	63.0	197.2	229.0	240.9	268.5	272.3	354.7
Gross Domestic Investment	9.3	14.7	35.6	42.0	44.4	174.1	258.0	317.1	289.9	273.5	335.4
Fixed Investment	9.3	14.7	35.6	42.0	44.4	174.1	258.0	321.2	310.8	281.0	318.0
Indirect Taxes, net	1.2	1.1	1.1	1.6	1.7	2.3	0.5	4.5	4.6	4.6	8.1
GDP at factor cost	98.8	105.7	124.0	139.2	167.7	566.2	723.7	879.8	942.2	942.3	1,281.4
Agriculture	16.1	16.6	16.8	17.0	16.7	18.4	20.2	18.3	24.1	30.7	40.3
Industry	77.2	82.5	94.8	100.0	120.0	469.1	561.5	616.7	626.7	584.8	828.1
Manufacturing	0.1	0.2	0.2	0.3	0.6	2.0	2.1	4.3	6.7	8.5	9.6
Services, etc.	6.7	7.7	13.5	23.8	32.7	81.0	142.5	249.3	296.0	331.4	421.1
Gross Domestic Saving	72.0	72.4	77.7	64.0	65.8	321.7	380.1	461.8	424.9	364.7	597.8
Gross National Saving	..	..	..	..	..	131.4	173.3	238.0	218.1	180.4	374.6

(Millions of 1980 Omani Rials)

	1969	1970	1971	1972	1973	1974	1975	1976	1977	1978	1979
Gross National Product	938.7	1,157.7	1,182.3	1,219.4	1,059.1	1,040.4	1,496.2	1,847.1	1,930.6	1,903.1	1,918.4
GDP at Market Prices	1,118.3	1,273.7	1,285.1	1,411.4	1,210.3	1,349.4	1,679.1	2,024.0	2,044.4	1,969.7	1,991.0
Resource Balance	..	..	..	..	..	..	..	..	..	687.7	675.6
Exports of Goods & NFServices	..	..	..	..	..	..	..	..	..	1,319.7	1,291.7
Imports of Goods & NFServices	..	..	..	..	..	..	..	..	..	632.0	616.2
Domestic Absorption	..	..	..	..	..	..	..	..	..	1,282.1	1,315.4
Private Consumption, etc.	..	..	..	..	..	..	..	..	..	..	..
General Gov't Consumption	..	..	..	..	..	..	..	..	..	..	..
Gross Domestic Investment	..	..	..	..	..	..	..	..	..	370.5	442.4
Fixed Investment	..	..	..	..	..	..	..	..	..	..	..
GDP at factor cost	..	..	..	..	..	..	..	..	..	..	..
Agriculture	..	..	..	..	..	..	..	..	..	33.0	43.6
Industry	..	..	..	..	..	..	..	..	..	1,498.0	1,436.2
Manufacturing	..	..	..	..	..	..	..	..	..	9.1	11.3
Services, etc.	..	..	..	..	..	..	..	..	..	438.8	511.2

Memo Items:

	1969	1970	1971	1972	1973	1974	1975	1976	1977	1978	1979
Capacity to Import	..	..	..	..	..	..	..	..	..	756.5	924.1
Terms of Trade Adjustment	..	..	..	..	..	..	..	..	..	-563.2	-367.6
Gross Domestic Income	..	..	..	..	..	..	..	..	..	1,406.5	1,623.4
Gross National Income	..	..	..	..	..	..	..	..	..	1,339.9	1,550.8

DOMESTIC PRICES/DEFLATORS — *(Index 1980 = 100)*

	1969	1970	1971	1972	1973	1974	1975	1976	1977	1978	1979
Overall (GDP)	8.9	8.4	9.7	10.0	14.0	42.1	43.1	43.7	46.3	48.1	64.8
Domestic Absorption	..	..	..	..	..	..	..	..	..	66.7	78.1
Agriculture	..	..	..	..	..	..	..	..	..	93.2	92.5
Industry	..	..	..	..	..	..	..	..	..	39.0	57.7
Manufacturing	..	..	..	..	..	..	..	..	..	93.3	85.3
Consumer Price Index	..	..	..	..	..	..	..	..	..	..	..

MANUFACTURING ACTIVITY

	1969	1970	1971	1972	1973	1974	1975	1976	1977	1978	1979
Employment (1987=100)	..	..	..	..	..	..	..	..	..	..	..
Real Earnings per Empl. (1987=100)	..	..	..	..	..	..	..	..	..	..	..
Real Output per Empl. (1987=100)	..	..	..	..	..	..	..	..	..	..	..
Earnings as % of Value Added	..	..	..	..	..	..	..	..	..	61.4	..

MONETARY HOLDINGS — *(Millions of current Omani Rials)*

	1969	1970	1971	1972	1973	1974	1975	1976	1977	1978	1979
Money Supply, Broadly Defined	..	..	..	44.76	46.61	85.24	117.98	164.59	206.56	230.61	246.22
Money	..	..	..	18.96	24.95	48.41	71.64	102.12	111.22	114.32	123.14
Currency Outside Banks	..	..	..	12.29	15.17	28.88	38.53	47.76	55.07	64.38	74.28
Demand Deposits	..	..	..	6.66	9.78	19.52	33.11	54.36	56.16	49.94	48.86
Quasi-Money	..	..	..	25.80	21.66	36.83	46.34	62.48	95.33	116.30	123.08

GOVERNMENT DEFICIT (-) OR SURPLUS — *(Millions of current Omani Rials)*

	1969	1970	1971	1972	1973	1974	1975	1976	1977	1978	1979
GOVERNMENT DEFICIT (-) OR SURPLUS	..	..	..	-17.1	-23.5	-56.4	-37.7	-84.7	58.1	-75.3	85.0
Current Revenue	..	..	..	53.0	68.5	311.5	429.5	473.5	575.0	446.3	650.7
Current Expenditure	..	..	..	..	62.2	186.5	309.9	369.9	367.7	410.8	420.5
Current Budget Balance	..	..	..	..	6.3	125.0	119.6	103.6	207.3	35.5	230.2
Capital Receipts	..	..	..	..	..	..	0.8	1.8	1.1	1.3	1.8
Capital Payments	..	..	..	..	29.8	181.4	158.1	190.1	150.3	112.1	147.0

1980	1981	1982	1983	1984	1985	1986	1987	1988	1989 estimate	NOTES	OMAN
3,660	5,830	7,110	7,220	7,280	7,550	6,660	5,810	4,980	5,220	..	CURRENT GNP PER CAPITA (US $)
984	1,033	1,083	1,135	1,187	1,242	1,299	1,359	1,421	1,486	..	POPULATION (thousands)
				(Millions of current Omani Rials)							USE AND ORIGIN OF RESOURCES
1,843.6	2,269.4	2,382.7	2,429.9	2,696.7	3,056.9	2,459.7	2,804.5	2,760.0	2,935.6	..	Gross National Product (GNP)
-222.6	-237.5	-226.7	-310.0	-350.2	-399.0	-338.0	-328.1	-201.3	..	..	Net Factor Income from Abroad
2,066.2	2,506.9	2,609.4	2,739.9	3,046.9	3,455.9	2,797.7	3,132.6	2,961.3	..	..	GDP at Market Prices
516.6	666.9	401.7	427.0	387.0	437.0	-396.0	..	..	..	..	Resource Balance
1,294.6	1,621.9	1,527.7	1,470.0	1,532.0	1,722.0	1,060.2	..	..	..	..	Exports of Goods & NFServices
778.0	955.0	1,126.0	1,043.0	1,145.0	1,285.0	1,456.2	..	..	..	..	Imports of Goods & NFServices
1,549.6	1,840.0	2,207.7	2,312.9	2,659.7	3,018.9	3,193.7	2,407.6	2,626.4	..	..	Domestic Absorption
572.3	647.7	832.5	859.5	938.5	1,171.7	1,441.9	929.6	1,179.7	..	..	Private Consumption, etc.
516.7	616.7	681.2	727.8	808.0	894.1	853.4	913.7	956.0	..	..	General Gov't Consumption
460.6	575.6	694.0	725.6	913.2	953.1	898.4	564.3	490.6	..	..	Gross Domestic Investment
464.3	569.9	709.2	..	..	..	..	..	..	..	..	Fixed Investment
12.0	..	..	..	..	..	..	..	..	..	..	Indirect Taxes, net
2,054.2	..	..	..	..	..	..	..	..	..	B	GDP at factor cost
52.6	62.1	66.1	80.5	89.0	95.8	89.3	70.6	77.8	..	..	Agriculture
1,433.1	1,683.1	1,651.7	1,663.1	1,800.5	2,049.0	1,206.5	2,465.8	2,361.1	..	..	Industry
13.4	24.0	35.9	67.1	92.3	115.9	178.3	111.5	122.7	..	..	Manufacturing
580.5	761.7	891.6	996.3	1,157.4	1,311.1	1,501.9	596.2	522.4	..	..	Services, etc.
977.2	1,242.5	1,095.7	1,152.6	1,300.4	1,390.1	502.4	1,289.3	825.5	..	..	Gross Domestic Saving
629.6	846.0	677.0	602.6	667.2	678.1	-158.6	699.2	..	..	..	Gross National Saving
				(Millions of 1980 Omani Rials)							
1,843.6	2,299.1	2,552.1	3,002.8	3,480.1	4,007.2	4,283.0	4,362.6	4,249.9	4,395.7	..	Gross National Product
2,066.2	2,412.2	2,668.2	3,151.4	3,658.4	4,208.6	4,426.5	4,509.3	..	..	..	GDP at Market Prices
516.6	508.9	341.7	523.3	489.0	678.6	947.4	1,612.1	..	..	..	Resource Balance
1,294.6	1,452.9	1,504.3	1,606.1	1,701.7	1,972.6	2,180.6	2,445.8	..	..	..	Exports of Goods & NFServices
778.0	944.0	1,162.5	1,082.8	1,212.7	1,294.0	1,233.3	833.6	..	..	..	Imports of Goods & NFServices
1,549.6	1,903.2	2,326.4	2,628.1	3,169.4	3,529.9	3,479.1	2,897.2	..	..	..	Domestic Absorption
..	..	..	..	..	..	..	..	..	..	..	Private Consumption, etc.
..	..	..	..	..	..	..	..	..	..	..	General Gov't Consumption
460.6	577.2	781.4	852.4	1,283.3	1,378.1	1,056.9	541.6	..	..	..	Gross Domestic Investment
..	..	..	..	..	..	..	..	..	..	..	Fixed Investment
..	..	..	..	..	..	..	..	..	..	..	GDP at factor cost
52.6	53.4	58.1	68.9	75.6	89.2	79.1	66.9	75.6	..	..	Agriculture
1,433.1	1,660.5	1,805.2	2,185.2	2,506.7	2,938.0	3,258.0	3,287.2	..	..	..	Industry
13.4	22.1	33.4	51.2	72.4	89.4	81.8	90.4	93.5	..	..	Manufacturing
580.5	698.3	804.9	897.3	1,076.1	1,181.4	1,089.4	1,155.2	..	..	..	Services, etc.
											Memo Items:
1,294.6	1,603.2	1,577.3	1,526.1	1,622.6	1,734.0	897.9	..	..	..	..	Capacity to Import
0.0	150.3	73.0	-80.0	-79.2	-238.6	-1,282.7	..	..	..	..	Terms of Trade Adjustment
2,066.2	2,562.4	2,741.2	3,071.4	3,579.3	3,970.0	3,143.7	..	..	..	..	Gross Domestic Income
1,843.6	2,449.4	2,625.1	2,922.7	3,401.0	3,768.6	3,000.3	..	..	..	..	Gross National Income
				(Index 1980 = 100)							DOMESTIC PRICES/DEFLATORS
100.0	103.9	97.8	86.9	83.3	82.1	63.2	69.5	..	..	..	Overall (GDP)
100.0	96.7	94.9	88.0	83.9	85.5	91.8	83.1	..	..	..	Domestic Absorption
100.0	116.4	113.8	116.8	117.8	107.4	112.9	105.6	102.9	..	..	Agriculture
100.0	101.4	91.5	76.1	71.8	69.7	37.0	75.0	..	..	..	Industry
100.0	108.7	107.3	130.9	127.6	129.6	218.0	123.4	131.2	..	..	Manufacturing
..	..	..	..	..	..	..	..	..	..	f	Consumer Price Index
											MANUFACTURING ACTIVITY
..	..	..	..	..	..	..	..	..	..	..	Employment (1987=100)
..	..	..	..	..	..	..	..	..	..	..	Real Earnings per Empl. (1987=100)
..	..	..	..	..	..	..	..	..	..	..	Real Output per Empl. (1987=100)
..	..	..	..	..	..	..	..	..	..	..	Earnings as % of Value Added
				(Millions of current Omani Rials)							MONETARY HOLDINGS
325.01	450.69	570.87	704.55	774.00	936.96	873.44	919.49	974.10	1,065.78	..	Money Supply, Broadly Defined
154.73	212.65	248.79	299.07	283.92	328.60	312.82	335.19	315.29	345.44	..	Money
94.80	116.17	129.81	140.40	149.96	178.52	168.83	180.36	176.27	183.57	..	Currency Outside Banks
59.93	96.48	118.98	158.68	133.96	150.08	143.99	154.83	139.02	161.86	..	Demand Deposits
170.28	238.04	322.08	405.48	490.08	608.36	560.62	584.30	658.81	720.34	..	Quasi-Money
				(Millions of current Omani Rials)							GOVERNMENT DEFICIT (-) OR SURPLUS
9.1	48.5	-222.8	-242.3	-346.8	-364.2	-700.2	-146.2	-346.7	..	..	Current Revenue
825.2	1,123.4	999.0	1,122.2	1,212.1	1,393.2	888.2	1,197.8	1,022.2	..	..	Current Revenue
626.3	787.0	891.2	1,017.4	1,127.1	1,293.4	1,218.1	1,091.8	1,149.3	..	..	Current Expenditure
198.9	336.4	107.8	104.8	85.0	99.8	-329.9	106.0	-127.1	..	..	Current Budget Balance
3.9	2.5	2.2	2.2	2.3	4.4	6.8	1.6	3.5	..	..	Capital Receipts
193.7	290.4	332.8	349.3	434.1	468.4	377.1	253.8	223.1	..	..	Capital Payments

OMAN	1969	1970	1971	1972	1973	1974	1975	1976	1977	1978	1979
FOREIGN TRADE (CUSTOMS BASIS)					*(Millions of current US dollars)*						
Value of Exports, fob	194.4	206.0	221.1	242.0	344.0	1,211.0	1,436.0	1,566.0	1,573.0	1,598.0	2,280.0
Nonfuel Primary Products	1.6	1.0	1.0	1.0	2.0	1.0	3.0	0.0	0.0	9.2	44.0
Fuels	192.7	205.0	220.0	241.0	342.0	1,210.0	1,433.0	1,562.0	1,568.6	1,503.0	2,159.0
Manufactures	0.1	0.0	0.0	0.0	0.0	0.0	0.0	4.0	4.3	85.8	76.0
Value of Imports, cif	13.4	18.0	33.0	49.0	117.0	393.0	671.0	667.0	875.0	947.0	1,246.0
Nonfuel Primary Products	2.5	0.0	13.0	17.0	32.0	59.0	106.0	111.0	153.0	181.0	235.0
Fuels	0.5	1.0	2.0	2.0	5.0	15.0	31.0	48.0	62.0	80.0	84.0
Manufactures	10.4	17.0	17.0	29.0	79.0	318.0	533.0	508.0	659.0	686.0	928.0
					(Index 1987 = 100)						
Terms of Trade	..	..	..	..	..	..	..	..	..	..	..
Export Prices, fob	..	..	..	..	..	..	..	..	..	..	..
Import Prices, cif	..	..	..	..	..	..	..	..	..	..	..
BALANCE OF PAYMENTS					*(Millions of current US dollars)*						
Exports of Goods & Services	..	..	..	..	..	1,231.3	1,432.8	1,601.3	1,619.6	1,610.6	2,287.2
Merchandise, fob	..	..	..	..	..	1,212.2	1,416.3	1,595.8	1,619.6	1,598.1	2,279.7
Nonfactor Services	..	..	..	..	..	0.0	0.0	0.0	0.0	7.8	7.5
Factor Services	..	..	..	..	..	19.1	16.5	5.5	0.0	4.6	0.0
Imports of Goods & Services	..	..	..	..	..	965.3	1,374.6	1,397.2	1,389.4	1,468.2	1,669.1
Merchandise, fob	..	..	..	..	..	551.5	907.9	1,000.0	1,044.0	1,157.2	1,285.2
Nonfactor Services	..	..	..	..	..	103.6	154.9	176.9	185.9	193.1	234.8
Factor Services	..	..	..	..	..	310.1	311.8	220.3	159.5	117.8	149.1
Long-Term Interest	..	0.0	0.0	0.0	0.0	3.6	6.5	10.1	25.1	20.2	23.3
Private Current Transfers, net	..	..	..	..	..	-110.9	-208.2	-219.7	-221.8	-212.2	-248.7
Workers' Remittances	..	..	..	..	..	0.0	0.0	0.0	0.0	29.0	32.7
Curr. A/C Bal before Off. Transf.	..	..	..	..	..	155.2	-150.0	-15.6	8.4	-69.8	369.4
Net Official Transfers	..	..	..	..	..	24.0	207.3	52.1	268.4	20.3	179.2
Curr. A/C Bal after Off. Transf.	..	..	..	..	..	179.2	57.3	36.5	276.8	-49.5	548.6
Long-Term Capital, net	..	..	..	..	..	16.5	245.2	246.4	132.6	136.4	-25.2
Direct Investment	..	..	..	..	..	-61.1	106.3	81.4	48.1	86.3	117.5
Long-Term Loans	..	0.0	0.0	0.0	43.5	124.1	121.1	76.0	99.3	-55.0	47.7
Disbursements	..	0.0	0.0	0.0	43.5	130.0	142.2	105.9	161.2	65.5	216.2
Repayments	..	0.0	0.0	0.0	0.0	5.9	21.1	29.9	61.9	120.5	168.5
Other Long-Term Capital	..	..	..	..	..	-46.5	17.9	89.0	-14.8	105.1	-190.4
Other Capital, net	..	..	..	..	..	-145.2	-237.0	-226.3	-337.2	-135.4	-368.0
Change in Reserves	..	..	-14.1	-14.1	-5.1	-50.5	-65.5	-56.6	-72.2	48.5	-155.4
Memo Item:					*(Omani Rials per US dollar)*						
Conversion Factor (Annual Avg)	0.420	0.420	0.420	0.380	0.350	0.350	0.350	0.350	0.350	0.350	0.350
EXTERNAL DEBT (Total)				*(Millions of US dollars), outstanding at end of year*							
	..	..	..	..	41.7	175.7	287.4	349.2	654.3	631.4	660.1
Long-Term Debt (by debtor)	..	..	..	..	41.7	175.7	287.4	349.2	473.3	449.4	514.1
Central Bank, incl. IMF credit	..	..	..	..	..	..	..	..	..	..	..
Central Government	..	..	..	..	41.7	175.7	287.4	349.2	473.3	449.4	514.1
Rest of General Government	..	..	..	..	..	..	..	..	..	..	..
Non-financial Public Enterprises	..	..	..	..	0.0	0.0	0.0	0.0	0.0	0.0	0.0
Priv. Sector, incl non-guaranteed	..	..	..	..	..	..	..	..	..	..	..
Short-Term Debt	..	..	..	..	..	..	..	..	181.0	182.0	146.0
Memo Items:					*(Millions of US dollars)*						
Int'l Reserves Excluding Gold	..	10.3	24.4	36.4	47.1	92.9	161.3	219.6	289.6	254.1	415.6
Gold Holdings (at market price)	..	2.4	0.6	0.9	1.6	5.6	4.2	6.2	16.7	41.9	95.8
SOCIAL INDICATORS											
Total Fertility Rate	7.2	7.2	7.2	7.2	7.2	7.2	7.2	7.2	7.2	7.2	7.2
Infant Mortality Rate	166.0	159.0	152.0	145.0	137.0	129.0	121.0	113.0	105.0	96.0	87.0
Life Expectancy at Birth	46.6	47.4	48.2	49.0	49.8	50.6	51.4	52.2	53.0	54.2	55.4
Urban Population, % of total	4.9	5.1	5.3	5.5	5.7	5.9	6.1	6.3	6.6	6.8	7.1
Food Prod. per capita (1987=100)	..	..	..	..	..	..	..	..			
Labor Force, Agriculture (%)	57.7	56.7	55.9	55.2	54.5	53.8	53.1	52.3	51.5	50.9	50.3
Labor Force, Female (%)	6.1	6.2	6.4	6.6	6.8	6.9	7.1	7.1	7.2	7.2	7.2
Primary Schl. Enroll. Ratio	..	3.0	..	..	..	..	44.0	49.0	53.0	57.0	..
Primary Schl. Enroll. Ratio, Female	..	1.0	..	..	..	..	24.0	28.0	33.0	37.0	..
Secondary Schl. Enroll. Ratio	..	..	..	..	..	..	1.0	2.0	5.0	8.0	..

1980	1981	1982	1983	1984	1985	1986	1987	1988	1989 estimate	NOTES	OMAN
				(Millions of current US dollars)							**FOREIGN TRADE (CUSTOMS BASIS)**
3,748.0	4,696.0	4,423.0	4,256.0	4,421.0	4,971.0	2,888.0	3,805.0	3,123.0	..	..	Value of Exports, fob
32.0	47.0	36.0	41.0	51.0	62.0	60.0	..	..	..	..	Nonfuel Primary Products
3,604.0	4,420.0	4,084.0	3,914.0	4,074.0	4,647.0	2,627.0	3,464.0	2,844.0	..	f	Fuels
112.0	229.0	303.0	301.0	296.0	262.0	201.0	264.0	217.0	..	..	Manufactures
1,732.0	2,171.0	2,683.0	2,492.0	2,640.0	3,028.0	2,402.0	1,822.0	2,202.0	..	..	Value of Imports, cif
295.0	346.0	383.0	410.0	438.0	455.0	427.0	..	..	..	..	Nonfuel Primary Products
187.0	299.4	279.0	41.0	41.0	53.0	67.0	51.0	61.0	..	..	Fuels
1,250.0	1,642.9	2,021.0	2,042.0	2,161.0	2,520.0	1,908.0	1,447.0	1,749.0	..	..	Manufactures
				(Index 1987 = 100)							
..	..	..	..	..	..	..	..	..	..	..	Terms of Trade
..	..	..	..	..	..	..	..	..	..	..	Export Prices, fob
..	..	..	..	..	..	..	..	..	..	..	Import Prices, cif
				(Millions of current US dollars)							**BALANCE OF PAYMENTS**
3,852.3	4,881.0	4,753.0	4,577.3	4,780.0	5,347.5	3,471.4	4,338.1	..	..	..	Exports of Goods & Services
3,748.1	4,695.7	4,423.0	4,255.9	4,421.0	4,971.1	2,861.4	3,804.9	..	..	..	Merchandise, fob
8.7	8.7	11.6	14.5	14.5	14.5	13.1	13.0	..	..	..	Nonfactor Services
95.5	176.6	318.5	306.9	344.5	361.9	596.9	520.2	..	..	..	Factor Services
2,650.0	3,331.8	3,754.8	3,538.5	3,872.1	4,350.1	3,642.6	2,813.0	..	..	..	Imports of Goods & Services
1,780.0	2,296.2	2,582.5	2,360.5	2,639.6	3,027.8	2,309.0	1,768.5	..	..	..	Merchandise, fob
517.7	620.4	700.9	687.9	672.6	689.6	688.5	501.9	..	..	..	Nonfactor Services
352.3	415.2	471.3	490.2	559.9	632.6	645.1	542.5	..	..	..	Factor Services
43.9	34.8	33.5	52.5	85.4	113.6	168.3	175.8	183.2	225.6	..	Long-Term Interest
-361.9	-460.3	-555.9	-694.8	-819.3	-906.2	-845.6	-681.4	..	..	..	Private Current Transfers, net
34.7	40.5	43.4	43.4	43.4	43.4	39.3	39.0	..	..	..	Workers' Remittances
840.5	1,088.9	442.4	343.9	88.6	91.2	-1,016.8	843.7	..	..	..	Curr. A/C Bal before Off. Transf.
101.9	144.8	43.4	147.7	211.4	173.7	0.0	7.8	..	..	..	Net Official Transfers
942.4	1,233.6	485.8	491.6	299.9	264.9	-1,016.8	851.5	..	..	..	Curr. A/C Bal after Off. Transf.
39.4	192.5	251.6	523.7	575.3	306.3	687.2	-102.0	..	..	..	Long-Term Capital, net
98.4	62.5	182.1	154.6	158.1	161.3	140.3	33.0	..	..	..	Direct Investment
-81.4	118.6	203.0	427.9	254.2	520.7	539.6	-102.8	66.3	183.5	..	Long-Term Loans
97.7	199.0	287.0	510.9	383.0	667.7	764.8	334.2	414.3	558.5	..	Disbursements
179.1	80.4	84.0	83.0	128.8	147.0	225.2	437.0	348.0	375.0	..	Repayments
22.3	11.4	-133.5	-58.8	163.0	-375.6	7.3	-32.2	..	..	..	Other Long-Term Capital
-185.7	-178.8	7.1	-663.9	-556.6	-449.5	-292.5	-641.5	..	..	..	Other Capital, net
-796.1	-1,247.4	-744.5	-351.4	-318.6	-121.7	622.1	-108.0	345.1	-301.2	..	Change in Reserves
				(Omani Rials per US dollar)							**Memo Item:**
0.350	0.350	0.350	0.350	0.350	0.350	0.380	0.380	0.380	0.380	..	Conversion Factor (Annual Avg)
				(Millions of US dollars), outstanding at end of year							
598.6	754.2	957.9	1,488.8	1,632.8	2,330.0	2,959.0	2,847.7	2,938.1	3,064.1	..	**EXTERNAL DEBT (Total)**
435.6	537.2	723.9	1,131.8	1,339.8	1,908.0	2,463.0	2,442.7	2,486.3	2,626.1	..	Long-Term Debt (by debtor)
..	..	..	..	..	..	..	..	..	..	..	Central Bank, incl. IMF credit
435.6	537.2	723.8	1,128.3	1,320.4	1,887.2	2,438.2	2,405.2	2,456.3	2,601.7	..	Central Government
..	..	..	..	..	..	..	..	..	..	..	Rest of General Government
0.0	0.0	0.1	3.5	19.4	20.8	24.8	37.5	30.0	24.4	..	Non-financial Public Enterprises
..	..	..	..	..	..	..	..	..	..	..	Priv. Sector, incl non-guaranteed
163.0	217.0	234.0	357.0	293.0	422.0	496.0	405.0	451.8	438.0	..	Short-Term Debt
				(Millions of US dollars)							**Memo Items:**
581.4	744.3	872.4	762.6	900.2	1,090.2	967.9	1,402.2	1,054.2	1,354.3	..	Int'l Reserves Excluding Gold
123.1	108.8	127.3	109.9	89.0	94.4	112.9	139.8	118.5	115.8	..	Gold Holdings (at market price)
											SOCIAL INDICATORS
7.2	7.2	7.2	7.2	7.2	7.2	7.2	7.2	7.1	7.0	..	Total Fertility Rate
78.0	69.0	60.0	56.0	52.0	48.0	44.0	40.0	38.1	36.3	..	Infant Mortality Rate
56.6	57.8	59.0	60.0	61.0	62.0	63.0	64.0	64.4	64.9	..	Life Expectancy at Birth
7.3	7.6	7.9	8.2	8.5	8.8	9.2	9.5	9.9	10.2	..	Urban Population, % of total
..	..	..	..	..	..	..	..	..	..	..	Food Prod. per capita (1987=100)
49.8	..	..	..	..	..	..	..	..	..	..	Labor Force, Agriculture (%)
7.2	7.3	7.4	7.4	7.5	7.5	7.8	7.9	8.1	8.3	..	Labor Force, Female (%)
60.0	..	69.0	75.0	83.0	89.0	94.0	97.0	..	..	..	Primary Schl. Enroll. Ratio
42.0	..	53.0	62.0	72.0	80.0	86.0	92.0	..	..	..	Primary Schl. Enroll. Ratio, Female
14.0	..	22.0	25.0	29.0	33.0	35.0	38.0	..	..	..	Secondary Schl. Enroll. Ratio

PAKISTAN	1969	1970	1971	1972	1973	1974	1975	1976	1977	1978	1979
CURRENT GNP PER CAPITA (US $)	150	170	170	160	130	130	130	170	190	220	240
POPULATION (thousands)	58,811	60,607	62,514	64,545	66,669	68,842	71,033	73,255	75,515	77,817	80,169

USE AND ORIGIN OF RESOURCES *(Billions of current Pakistan Rupees)*

	1969	1970	1971	1972	1973	1974	1975	1976	1977	1978	1979
Gross National Product (GNP)	40.93	47.75	50.40	54.16	65.99	86.12	111.32	130.63	148.08	174.62	192.81
Net Factor Income from Abroad	-0.18	0.00	-0.08	0.10	-0.88	-0.73	-0.94	-1.42	-1.67	-1.80	-2.29
GDP at Market Prices	41.11	47.75	50.49	54.06	66.87	86.85	112.27	132.05	149.75	176.42	195.11
Resource Balance	-1.11	-3.26	-3.51	-2.66	-1.89	-6.05	-12.71	-12.38	-14.58	-16.33	-23.54
Exports of Goods & NFServices	3.44	3.71	4.00	4.00	8.93	11.91	12.21	14.17	13.90	16.31	20.86
Imports of Goods & NFServices	4.56	6.97	7.51	6.67	10.83	17.96	24.91	26.54	28.48	32.64	44.40
Domestic Absorption	42.22	51.01	53.99	56.72	68.76	92.90	124.97	144.43	164.33	192.74	218.65
Private Consumption, etc.	32.06	38.62	40.83	42.58	52.39	72.75	94.80	107.32	118.76	142.12	163.54
General Gov't Consumption	4.10	4.85	5.27	6.48	7.72	8.54	11.95	14.34	16.71	19.12	20.24
Gross Domestic Investment	6.07	7.54	7.89	7.66	8.65	11.61	18.22	22.77	28.86	31.50	34.88
Fixed Investment	5.67	6.83	7.04	6.81	7.65	10.61	16.22	22.77	27.86	30.51	33.13
Indirect Taxes, net	3.56	4.40	4.79	4.89	6.08	6.41	7.63	10.63	13.77	16.49	17.07
GDP at factor cost	37.55	43.34	45.70	49.17	60.79	80.44	104.64	121.42	135.98	159.93	178.04
Agriculture	14.04	15.96	16.24	17.93	21.91	28.08	33.53	38.34	43.97	50.57	54.15
Industry	8.21	9.67	10.57	10.63	13.33	17.64	24.53	29.47	31.10	36.46	42.01
Manufacturing	6.01	6.96	7.57	7.77	9.69	12.75	17.48	20.05	20.39	24.02	27.48
Services, etc.	15.30	17.71	18.89	20.61	25.55	34.71	46.58	53.61	60.92	72.90	81.88
Gross Domestic Saving	4.95	4.28	4.39	5.00	6.76	5.57	5.51	10.39	14.27	15.18	11.33
Gross National Saving	..	4.67	4.61	6.22	7.32	6.32	6.83	12.46	18.45	25.52	23.85

(Billions of 1987 Pakistan Rupees)

	1969	1970	1971	1972	1973	1974	1975	1976	1977	1978	1979
Gross National Product	207.95	232.53	233.28	235.90	248.86	258.67	269.48	283.00	294.11	318.15	329.33
GDP at Market Prices	209.13	232.76	233.91	235.72	252.51	261.15	271.93	286.27	297.63	321.66	333.48
Resource Balance	-42.52	-72.38	-61.42	-36.85	-27.89	-42.14	-35.01	-35.45	-48.18	-49.92	-70.00
Exports of Goods & NFServices	29.39	34.05	34.35	28.45	30.08	24.88	27.76	31.69	26.12	29.45	33.37
Imports of Goods & NFServices	71.91	106.43	95.77	65.30	57.97	67.03	62.76	67.13	74.29	79.37	103.37
Domestic Absorption	251.65	305.14	295.32	272.57	280.40	303.29	306.94	321.72	345.81	371.57	403.48
Private Consumption, etc.	188.50	231.19	220.64	196.10	200.36	230.37	225.72	237.03	253.94	274.89	303.91
General Gov't Consumption	21.50	24.87	25.53	29.98	31.87	27.08	30.15	32.67	33.61	36.15	36.04
Gross Domestic Investment	41.66	49.08	49.16	46.49	48.17	45.84	51.07	52.02	58.27	60.53	63.53
Fixed Investment	40.29	45.79	45.26	42.73	44.38	43.27	46.24	53.55	57.36	59.85	61.36
GDP at factor cost	189.30	208.96	209.60	211.92	226.97	241.17	252.85	261.43	272.11	293.18	309.60
Agriculture	70.36	77.08	74.71	77.30	78.59	81.88	80.14	83.73	85.84	88.27	91.00
Industry	38.44	43.81	45.26	43.08	47.98	52.40	53.58	56.20	60.14	65.84	70.89
Manufacturing	26.95	30.16	30.93	29.83	33.02	35.48	35.68	36.24	39.00	43.10	46.67
Services, etc.	80.26	87.69	89.19	91.30	100.09	106.51	119.09	121.35	125.90	138.91	147.53

Memo Items:

	1969	1970	1971	1972	1973	1974	1975	1976	1977	1978	1979
Capacity to Import	54.33	56.64	51.03	39.19	47.84	44.45	30.75	35.83	36.26	39.67	48.56
Terms of Trade Adjustment	24.93	22.59	16.69	10.75	17.76	19.57	2.99	4.14	10.14	10.22	15.19
Gross Domestic Income	234.06	255.36	250.59	246.47	270.27	280.71	274.93	290.42	307.77	331.88	348.67
Gross National Income	232.89	255.13	249.96	246.65	266.62	278.23	272.48	287.15	304.25	328.37	344.52

DOMESTIC PRICES/DEFLATORS *(Index 1987 = 100)*

	1969	1970	1971	1972	1973	1974	1975	1976	1977	1978	1979
Overall (GDP)	19.7	20.5	21.6	22.9	26.5	33.3	41.3	46.1	50.3	54.8	58.5
Domestic Absorption	16.8	16.7	18.3	20.8	24.5	30.6	40.7	44.9	47.5	51.9	54.2
Agriculture	20.0	20.7	21.7	23.2	27.9	34.3	41.8	45.8	51.2	57.3	59.5
Industry	21.4	22.1	23.4	24.7	27.8	33.7	45.8	52.4	51.7	55.4	59.3
Manufacturing	22.3	23.1	24.5	26.1	29.4	35.9	49.0	55.3	52.3	55.7	58.9
Consumer Price Index	19.7	20.7	21.7	22.8	28.1	35.6	43.1	46.1	50.8	53.9	58.4

MANUFACTURING ACTIVITY

	1969	1970	1971	1972	1973	1974	1975	1976	1977	1978	1979
Employment (1987=100)	..	..	..	..	..	..	..	..	..	..	..
Real Earnings per Empl. (1987=100)	..	..	..	..	..	..	..	..	..	..	..
Real Output per Empl. (1987=100)	..	..	..	..	..	..	..	..	..	..	..
Earnings as % of Value Added	21.1	20.8	21.6	22.0	23.0	24.2	25.5	26.9	23.4	22.7	23.4

MONETARY HOLDINGS *(Billions of current Pakistan Rupees)*

	1969	1970	1971	1972	1973	1974	1975	1976	1977	1978	1979
Money Supply, Broadly Defined	18.58	20.75	23.61	27.73	31.56	31.18	37.80	49.97	58.94	70.63	84.12
Money	12.62	14.02	16.49	19.94	22.19	22.52	25.62	34.04	39.97	47.19	56.83
Currency Outside Banks	7.10	8.06	8.16	9.35	10.99	11.43	11.88	13.85	17.35	21.04	26.45
Demand Deposits	5.52	5.95	8.33	10.59	11.20	11.09	13.74	20.19	22.62	26.15	30.38
Quasi-Money	5.96	6.74	7.12	7.80	9.37	8.67	12.18	15.92	18.97	23.44	27.29

GOVERNMENT DEFICIT (-) OR SURPLUS *(Billions of current Pakistan Rupees)*

	1969	1970	1971	1972	1973	1974	1975	1976	1977	1978	1979
	..	..	..	..	-4.55	-5.15	-11.47	-12.24	-12.58	-13.25	-18.00
Current Revenue	..	..	..	..	8.74	12.36	14.64	18.79	21.53	26.25	30.35
Current Expenditure	..	..	..	..	8.71	12.33	15.89	17.63	19.31	23.89	29.86
Current Budget Balance	..	..	..	..	0.04	0.03	-1.25	1.15	2.22	2.37	0.49
Capital Receipts	..	..	..	..	..	..	..	..	..	..	..
Capital Payments	..	..	..	..	4.59	5.18	10.21	13.39	14.80	15.61	18.48

1980	1981	1982	1983	1984	1985	1986	1987	1988	1989 estimate	NOTES	PAKISTAN
290	330	360	350	350	340	340	330	350	360	..	**CURRENT GNP PER CAPITA (US $)**
82,581	85,068	87,648	90,343	93,177	96,180	99,399	102,738	106,261	109,950	..	**POPULATION (thousands)**
											USE AND ORIGIN OF RESOURCES
				(Billions of current Pakistan Rupees)							
231.75	275.61	320.77	359.04	413.84	464.48	504.20	560.55	660.82	756.06	C	Gross National Product (GNP)
-2.78	-2.58	-3.38	-5.34	-5.97	-7.67	-10.33	-11.93	-14.57	-16.96	..	Net Factor Income from Abroad
234.53	278.20	324.16	364.39	419.80	472.16	514.53	572.48	675.39	773.01	C	GDP at Market Prices
-27.26	-26.42	-35.47	-37.62	-44.39	-56.84	-40.21	-30.22	-37.60	-48.46	..	Resource Balance
29.26	35.71	33.03	44.39	47.83	49.89	63.27	79.06	93.60	107.55	..	Exports of Goods & NFServices
56.52	62.13	68.50	82.02	92.22	106.73	103.47	109.27	131.20	156.00	..	Imports of Goods & NFServices
261.79	304.62	359.63	402.01	464.19	529.00	554.74	602.70	712.98	821.47	..	Domestic Absorption
194.91	224.14	263.66	291.94	336.75	385.35	392.53	415.67	486.56	556.25	..	Private Consumption, etc.
23.54	28.28	33.52	41.61	50.74	57.13	65.66	77.48	104.75	129.20	..	General Gov't Consumption
43.34	52.21	62.45	68.46	76.70	86.52	96.55	109.54	121.67	136.02	..	Gross Domestic Investment
41.34	47.71	54.59	61.76	69.21	77.92	87.55	100.04	111.27	123.62	..	Fixed Investment
23.93	30.40	32.00	36.00	45.50	47.10	48.20	57.00	74.40	86.61	..	Indirect Taxes, net
210.60	247.80	292.16	328.39	374.30	425.06	466.33	515.48	601.00	686.41	C	GDP at factor cost
62.16	76.40	92.22	99.38	104.55	121.29	128.80	135.31	156.37	185.50	..	Agriculture
52.49	56.01	65.02	72.49	84.98	95.52	108.85	123.83	146.53	165.09	..	Industry
33.55	37.45	44.20	50.20	60.40	67.60	75.88	85.85	100.92	113.49	..	Manufacturing
95.95	115.38	134.92	156.51	184.77	208.25	228.68	256.34	298.10	335.82	..	Services, etc.
16.08	25.78	26.98	30.84	32.31	29.68	56.34	79.32	84.07	87.56	..	Gross Domestic Saving
32.06	45.40	52.22	65.93	69.14	64.82	93.02	111.92	110.22	113.86	..	Gross National Saving
				(Billions of 1987 Pakistan Rupees)							
363.50	393.60	418.80	445.35	468.34	501.72	527.65	560.55	604.49	634.44	C	Gross National Product
368.20	397.42	423.29	451.88	475.07	509.97	538.37	572.48	617.74	648.42	C	GDP at Market Prices
-67.63	-37.90	-40.32	-38.83	-47.67	-56.85	-36.76	-30.22	-30.14	-29.33	..	Resource Balance
39.88	47.15	44.33	55.22	53.18	52.99	70.38	79.06	75.42	84.54	..	Exports of Goods & NFServices
107.51	85.05	84.65	94.05	100.85	109.84	107.14	109.27	105.55	113.87	..	Imports of Goods & NFServices
435.83	435.32	463.61	490.71	522.74	566.82	575.13	602.70	647.87	677.76	..	Domestic Absorption
329.01	322.11	336.70	350.85	372.50	403.59	401.07	415.67	457.54	470.66	..	Private Consumption, etc.
38.14	40.45	43.98	51.92	58.25	62.19	68.42	77.48	80.86	97.36	..	General Gov't Consumption
68.67	72.76	82.92	87.94	91.98	101.04	105.64	109.54	109.47	109.74	..	Gross Domestic Investment
66.46	66.29	72.73	79.90	83.98	91.56	96.29	100.04	100.01	99.48	..	Fixed Investment
332.43	353.64	380.49	406.21	422.63	458.28	490.70	515.48	550.25	576.75	C	GDP at factor cost
97.01	107.15	112.22	117.16	111.51	123.70	131.04	135.31	139.00	148.86	..	Agriculture
78.68	78.59	87.03	91.33	97.77	105.43	113.97	123.83	135.99	142.31	..	Industry
51.58	52.29	59.48	63.66	68.68	74.24	79.84	85.85	94.42	98.16	..	Manufacturing
156.34	167.75	181.00	197.73	213.35	229.14	245.68	256.34	275.26	285.58	..	Services, etc.
											Memo Items:
55.65	48.88	40.82	50.91	52.31	51.34	65.51	79.06	75.31	78.50	..	Capacity to Import
15.77	1.73	-3.51	-4.32	-0.87	-1.65	-4.87	0.00	-0.11	-6.04	..	Terms of Trade Adjustment
383.97	399.15	419.78	447.57	474.20	508.32	533.50	572.48	617.62	642.39	..	Gross Domestic Income
379.27	395.32	415.29	441.03	467.47	500.07	522.78	560.55	604.38	628.40	..	Gross National Income
				(Index 1987 = 100)							**DOMESTIC PRICES/DEFLATORS**
63.7	70.0	76.6	80.6	88.4	92.6	95.6	100.0	109.3	119.2	..	Overall (GDP)
60.1	70.0	77.6	81.9	88.8	93.3	96.5	100.0	110.1	121.2	..	Domestic Absorption
64.1	71.3	82.2	84.8	93.8	98.1	98.3	100.0	112.5	124.6	..	Agriculture
66.7	71.3	74.7	79.4	86.9	90.6	95.5	100.0	107.7	116.0	..	Industry
65.0	71.6	74.3	78.9	87.9	91.1	95.0	100.0	106.9	115.6	..	Manufacturing
65.4	73.1	77.4	82.4	87.4	92.3	95.5	100.0	108.8	117.4	..	Consumer Price Index
											MANUFACTURING ACTIVITY
..	..	..	..	..	..	..	..	..	..	..	Employment (1987=100)
..	..	..	..	..	..	..	..	..	..	..	Real Earnings per Empl. (1987=100)
..	..	..	..	..	..	..	..	..	..	..	Real Output per Empl. (1987=100)
20.9	19.6	19.5	21.2	20.3	19.2	19.0	..	..	..	..	Earnings as % of Value Added
				(Billions of current Pakistan Rupees)							**MONETARY HOLDINGS**
97.32	108.54	132.23	159.88	167.31	191.99	222.84	259.40	279.38	300.05	..	Money Supply, Broadly Defined
66.67	72.29	87.34	100.57	105.78	123.06	145.25	173.02	189.83	217.03	..	Money
32.48	34.49	41.15	46.42	52.00	58.68	71.58	81.77	92.17	105.22	..	Currency Outside Banks
34.19	37.80	46.19	54.14	53.78	64.38	73.67	91.25	97.67	111.80	..	Demand Deposits
30.65	36.25	44.89	59.32	61.53	68.92	77.59	86.38	89.54	83.03	..	Quasi-Money
				(Billions of current Pakistan Rupees)							**GOVERNMENT DEFICIT (-) OR SURPLUS**
-13.34	-16.14	-15.35	-24.78	-25.93	-33.78	-46.92	-48.78	-46.11	..	C E	
39.93	47.96	52.93	59.94	73.00	79.07	94.23	102.33	121.17	..	..	Current Revenue
33.93	45.44	45.97	59.25	72.47	82.51	105.72	..	..	..	..	Current Expenditure
6.00	2.52	6.96	0.68	0.53	-3.44	-11.49	..	..	..	..	Current Budget Balance
..	..	..	..	..	..	..	..	..	..	..	Capital Receipts
19.35	18.66	22.31	25.47	26.46	30.34	35.43	..	..	..	..	Capital Payments

PAKISTAN	1969	1970	1971	1972	1973	1974	1975	1976	1977	1978	1979
FOREIGN TRADE (CUSTOMS BASIS)					*(Millions of current US dollars)*						
Value of Exports, fob	681.5	723.3	666.0	698.1	947.1	1,102.4	1,048.8	1,166.8	1,174.4	1,475.1	2,056.0
Nonfuel Primary Products	289.8	289.0	288.0	294.8	341.7	485.8	453.1	461.1	422.4	567.3	758.2
Fuels	8.7	8.8	7.7	11.0	7.2	25.0	11.1	24.2	49.4	45.4	138.0
Manufactures	383.0	425.4	370.4	392.3	598.2	591.6	584.6	681.5	702.5	862.4	1,159.8
Value of Imports, cif	1,010.7	1,170.9	925.9	681.9	965.9	1,729.4	2,153.1	2,182.9	2,454.6	3,160.5	4,061.3
Nonfuel Primary Products	138.5	321.1	233.2	254.2	332.8	535.7	647.8	589.3	603.0	840.6	1,056.3
Fuels	63.4	76.0	80.3	53.1	78.2	238.8	385.5	396.9	387.6	597.3	681.9
Manufactures	808.8	773.8	612.4	374.5	554.9	955.0	1,119.7	1,196.6	1,464.1	1,722.6	2,323.1
					(Index 1987 = 100)						
Terms of Trade	135.2	119.8	123.8	120.4	163.4	138.5	104.3	111.5	124.4	119.1	120.0
Export Prices, fob	32.7	32.3	34.7	39.4	66.6	82.7	65.6	68.9	82.9	89.5	106.0
Import Prices, cif	24.2	27.0	28.1	32.7	40.8	59.7	62.9	61.8	66.6	75.2	88.3
BALANCE OF PAYMENTS					*(Millions of current US dollars)*						
Exports of Goods & Services	..	805.0	770.3	742.9	922.5	1,236.3	1,267.6	1,460.2	1,437.2	1,681.0	2,153.7
Merchandise, fob	..	672.0	661.0	626.8	768.5	1,018.0	978.8	1,161.2	1,131.7	1,282.4	1,644.2
Nonfactor Services	..	107.0	96.3	106.4	136.6	182.2	252.0	268.9	272.7	364.3	463.1
Factor Services	..	26.0	13.0	9.8	17.4	36.2	36.8	30.0	32.8	34.2	46.3
Imports of Goods & Services	..	1,591.0	1,432.3	1,157.4	1,191.5	1,932.6	2,671.3	2,758.4	3,089.9	3,507.6	4,763.8
Merchandise, fob	..	1,210.0	1,081.2	859.9	890.5	1,488.6	2,110.5	2,138.6	2,417.7	2,751.3	3,815.9
Nonfactor Services	..	261.0	274.8	197.6	200.3	334.2	428.8	445.6	459.4	541.7	669.1
Factor Services	..	120.0	76.2	99.9	100.6	109.8	132.1	174.2	212.8	214.6	278.8
Long-Term Interest	..	77.5	59.3	75.6	86.4	84.4	102.3	130.5	143.5	183.4	214.4
Private Current Transfers, net	..	81.0	65.2	129.2	144.7	149.6	228.9	352.1	590.3	1,225.8	1,496.2
Workers' Remittances	..	86.0	70.2	130.3	145.8	150.8	220.1	327.7	576.9	1,155.6	1,397.6
Curr. A/C Bal before Off. Transf.	..	-705.0	-596.8	-285.2	-124.3	-546.7	-1,174.8	-946.1	-1,062.4	-600.8	-1,113.9
Net Official Transfers	..	38.0	114.3	44.5	41.9	54.3	105.8	120.4	148.9	111.8	293.5
Curr. A/C Bal after Off. Transf.	..	-667.0	-482.4	-240.7	-82.4	-492.4	-1,069.0	-825.7	-913.5	-489.0	-820.4
Long-Term Capital, net	..	429.0	398.2	200.9	240.5	331.7	790.3	808.8	619.4	648.7	367.8
Direct Investment	..	23.0	1.0	17.4	6.3	1.2	11.2	21.7	3.5	33.7	33.5
Long-Term Loans	..	376.9	546.8	188.5	241.2	710.3	711.5	747.2	573.6	476.6	583.6
Disbursements	..	491.9	639.4	294.9	350.5	829.6	866.8	906.8	769.7	693.5	891.3
Repayments	..	115.0	92.6	106.4	109.3	119.3	155.3	159.6	196.1	216.9	307.7
Other Long-Term Capital	..	29.1	-149.6	-5.0	-7.0	-379.8	67.6	39.9	42.3	138.4	-249.3
Other Capital, net	..	120.7	32.9	28.8	-11.5	66.6	154.7	26.7	63.4	125.5	122.5
Change in Reserves	..	117.3	51.4	11.1	-146.6	94.1	124.0	-9.8	230.7	-285.2	330.1
Memo Item:					*(Pakistan Rupees per US dollar)*						
Conversion Factor (Annual Avg)	4.760	4.760	4.760	5.810	10.570	9.900	9.900	9.900	9.900	9.900	9.900
EXTERNAL DEBT (Total)				*(Millions of US dollars), outstanding at end of year*							
	..	3,114	3,660	3,928	4,407	4,946	5,553	6,571	7,581	8,344	8,933
Long-Term Debt (by debtor)	..	3,114	3,660	3,928	4,407	4,946	5,553	6,571	7,401	8,134	8,492
Central Bank, incl. IMF credit	..	45	46	120	157	292	438	553	606	642	573
Central Government	..	2,679	3,117	3,352	3,858	4,270	4,749	5,695	6,396	7,078	7,404
Rest of General Government	..	0	0	0	0	1	9	12	23	33	27
Non-financial Public Enterprises	..	241	312	276	237	234	221	203	274	264	337
Priv. Sector, incl non-guaranteed	..	149	184	179	155	149	136	109	102	118	150
Short-Term Debt	..	..	..	..	..	..	..	..	180	210	441
Memo Items:					*(Millions of US dollars)*						
Int'l Reserves Excluding Gold	278.0	136.2	129.4	220.7	412.0	392.3	340.3	466.2	448.9	407.7	213.0
Gold Holdings (at market price)	54.9	58.3	69.1	103.1	178.3	296.2	222.7	218.0	266.8	388.3	931.0
SOCIAL INDICATORS											
Total Fertility Rate	7.0	7.0	7.0	7.0	7.0	7.0	7.0	7.0	7.0	7.0	7.0
Infant Mortality Rate	143.0	142.0	141.0	140.0	138.0	136.0	134.0	132.0	130.0	128.0	126.0
Life Expectancy at Birth	47.7	48.1	48.6	49.0	49.4	49.8	50.2	50.6	51.0	51.4	51.7
Urban Population, % of total	24.6	24.9	25.2	25.5	25.8	26.1	26.4	26.7	27.1	27.4	27.8
Food Prod. per capita (1987=100)	91.0	91.9	89.7	90.0	91.5	92.3	92.6	94.4	95.9	95.6	98.0
Labor Force, Agriculture (%)	59.0	58.9	58.4	58.0	57.6	57.2	56.8	56.3	55.8	55.4	55.0
Labor Force, Female (%)	9.0	9.1	9.3	9.4	9.5	9.7	9.8	9.9	10.1	10.2	10.3
Primary Schl. Enroll. Ratio	..	40.0	..	..	..	..	46.0	51.0	50.0	54.0	42.0
Primary Schl. Enroll. Ratio, Female	..	22.0	..	..	..	..	28.0	30.0	29.0	30.0	..
Secondary Schl. Enroll. Ratio	..	13.0	..	..	..	..	15.0	16.0	..	15.0	14.0

1980	1981	1982	1983	1984	1985	1986	1987	1988	1989 estimate	NOTES	PAKISTAN
											FOREIGN TRADE (CUSTOMS BASIS)
				(Millions of current US dollars)							
2,618.4	2,779.3	2,376.5	3,074.8	2,592.0	2,738.7	3,384.0	4,178.0	4,522.0	5,321.0	..	Value of Exports, fob
1,148.7	1,120.6	819.5	1,053.5	774.4	969.0	1,074.9	1,120.0	1,371.0	..	..	Nonfuel Primary Products
184.4	179.4	139.8	57.0	25.3	38.6	23.8	28.0	32.0	..	..	Fuels
1,285.3	1,479.3	1,417.2	1,964.3	1,792.3	1,731.1	2,285.3	3,030.0	3,119.0	3,717.0	..	Manufactures
5,350.5	5,412.7	5,232.8	5,341.0	5,873.1	5,890.4	5,376.8	5,827.0	6,590.0	6,515.0	f	Value of Imports, cif
1,020.0	1,205.3	1,051.5	1,094.0	1,471.8	1,463.4	1,324.2	1,295.0	1,817.9	..	..	Nonfuel Primary Products
1,442.1	1,506.2	1,616.8	1,514.1	1,454.6	1,433.2	764.9	1,026.0	1,233.1	..	..	Fuels
2,888.4	2,701.2	2,564.5	2,733.0	2,946.7	2,993.8	3,287.7	3,506.0	3,539.0	..	..	Manufactures
				(Index 1987 = 100)							
113.3	108.3	101.3	104.1	98.6	95.4	99.9	100.0	102.1	..	..	Terms of Trade
117.2	115.2	104.5	103.5	99.1	92.9	90.3	100.0	105.3	..	..	Export Prices, fob
103.5	106.3	103.2	99.5	100.5	97.4	90.4	100.0	103.2	..	..	Import Prices, cif
				(Millions of current US dollars)							**BALANCE OF PAYMENTS**
3,010.5	3,556.7	3,185.4	3,540.4	3,644.7	3,401.8	3,907.3	4,505.7	5,347.2	5,733.3	C f	Exports of Goods & Services
2,340.8	2,811.5	2,319.7	2,635.6	2,668.8	2,460.5	2,944.6	3,491.8	4,373.6	4,645.1	..	Merchandise, fob
617.4	649.7	735.7	784.1	779.8	786.0	850.9	921.8	868.0	949.3	..	Nonfactor Services
52.3	95.5	130.0	120.7	196.1	155.3	111.8	92.1	105.6	138.9	..	Factor Services
6,042.3	6,823.0	7,137.1	7,134.4	7,687.2	7,774.6	7,982.7	7,792.7	9,294.5	9,781.8	C f	Imports of Goods & Services
4,856.6	5,563.5	5,775.0	5,619.8	5,993.8	6,016.4	6,002.2	5,797.6	6,936.3	7,225.5	..	Merchandise, fob
852.6	903.1	911.3	973.0	1,054.6	1,096.8	1,228.1	1,207.9	1,422.6	1,532.5	..	Nonfactor Services
333.1	356.4	450.8	541.6	638.8	661.4	752.4	787.2	935.6	1,023.8	..	Factor Services
248.5	199.9	253.1	315.7	315.5	310.3	353.5	394.7	437.0	455.6	..	Long-Term Interest
1,894.9	2,241.9	2,415.7	3,082.8	3,046.6	2,687.8	2,824.4	2,559.5	2,261.9	2,105.6	..	Private Current Transfers, net
1,747.6	2,097.4	2,226.6	2,888.1	2,738.4	2,456.3	2,597.0	2,280.3	2,017.7	1,901.7	..	Workers' Remittances
-1,136.9	-1,024.4	-1,536.0	-511.2	-995.9	-1,685.0	-1,251.0	-727.5	-1,685.4	-1,942.9	..	Curr. A/C Bal before Off. Transf.
268.4	275.0	419.3	333.3	307.0	402.6	477.5	393.9	521.3	592.0	..	Net Official Transfers
-868.5	-749.4	-1,116.7	-177.9	-688.9	-1,282.4	-773.5	-333.6	-1,164.1	-1,350.9	..	Curr. A/C Bal after Off. Transf.
823.3	504.0	520.3	639.6	434.6	459.6	768.7	439.0	788.7	1,528.4	C f	Long-Term Capital, net
68.1	71.5	122.1	26.1	43.3	77.6	150.1	108.1	144.5	170.4	..	Direct Investment
707.6	410.2	1,068.9	235.7	591.4	278.9	506.5	533.1	805.6	1,018.6	..	Long-Term Loans
1,060.9	768.8	1,402.6	1,024.5	1,198.8	1,013.2	1,200.9	1,292.4	1,651.8	1,830.3	..	Disbursements
353.3	358.6	333.7	788.8	607.4	734.3	694.4	759.3	846.2	811.7	..	Repayments
47.6	22.3	-670.7	377.8	-200.1	103.1	112.1	-202.2	-161.4	339.4	..	Other Long-Term Capital
54.6	262.9	64.5	241.8	192.5	-224.8	432.9	187.5	285.2	-257.5	C f	Other Capital, net
-9.4	-17.5	531.9	-703.5	61.8	1,047.6	-428.1	-292.9	90.2	80.0	..	Change in Reserves
											Memo Item:
				(Pakistan Rupees per US dollar)							
9.900	9.900	10.550	12.700	13.480	15.160	16.130	17.160	17.550	19.160	..	Conversion Factor (Annual Avg)
			(Millions of US dollars), outstanding at end of year								
9,941	10,534	11,637	11,930	12,125	13,362	14,904	16,708	16,996	18,509	..	**EXTERNAL DEBT (Total)**
9,204	9,631	10,917	11,133	11,193	12,052	13,041	14,428	14,567	15,739	..	Long-Term Debt (by debtor)
675	1,024	1,419	1,613	1,440	1,455	1,254	996	634	1,012	..	Central Bank, incl. IMF credit
7,742	7,835	8,709	8,655	8,839	9,510	10,725	12,386	12,895	13,631	..	Central Government
25	25	20	16	11	7	5	3	2	2	..	Rest of General Government
585	539	522	543	597	680	609	562	538	610	..	Non-financial Public Enterprises
178	207	247	306	306	399	449	482	498	484	..	Priv. Sector, incl non-guaranteed
737	903	720	797	932	1,310	1,863	2,280	2,429	2,770	..	Short-Term Debt
				(Millions of US dollars)							**Memo Items:**
495.8	721.5	968.5	1,972.5	1,035.5	807.5	709.1	501.9	394.6	520.5	..	Int'l Reserves Excluding Gold
1,072.0	733.8	844.3	710.3	575.0	622.0	755.8	939.0	798.1	781.7	..	Gold Holdings (at market price)
											SOCIAL INDICATORS
7.0	7.0	7.0	6.9	6.9	6.8	6.8	6.7	6.6	6.5	..	Total Fertility Rate
124.0	122.0	120.0	117.8	115.6	113.4	111.2	109.0	107.3	105.5	..	Infant Mortality Rate
52.1	52.4	52.8	53.2	53.6	54.0	54.4	54.8	55.1	55.3	..	Life Expectancy at Birth
28.1	28.4	28.8	29.1	29.5	29.8	30.2	30.7	31.1	31.6	..	Urban Population, % of total
98.3	101.5	101.3	100.8	99.2	99.2	102.8	100.0	101.9	104.6	..	Food Prod. per capita (1987=100)
54.6	..	..	..	..	..	..	..	..	..	..	Labor Force, Agriculture (%)
10.4	10.7	10.9	11.1	11.3	11.4	11.7	11.9	12.1	12.3	..	Labor Force, Female (%)
39.0	..	42.0	45.0	49.8	51.6	52.5	52.1	..	..	..	Primary Schl. Enroll. Ratio
27.0	..	28.0	30.0	34.0	36.0	36.0	35.0	..	..	..	Primary Schl. Enroll. Ratio, Female
14.0	..	15.0	16.0	17.0	16.0	18.0	19.0	..	..	..	Secondary Schl. Enroll. Ratio

PANAMA	1969	1970	1971	1972	1973	1974	1975	1976	1977	1978	1979
CURRENT GNP PER CAPITA (US $)	640	680	740	770	840	920	1,030	1,080	1,120	1,290	1,420
POPULATION (thousands)	1,488	1,531	1,574	1,618	1,662	1,705	1,748	1,790	1,832	1,873	1,915

USE AND ORIGIN OF RESOURCES					*(Millions of current Panamanian Balboas)*						
Gross National Product (GNP)	920.1	994.8	1,120.6	1,231.2	1,404.3	1,599.1	1,820.0	1,902.7	2,008.8	2,403.7	2,721.6
Net Factor Income from Abroad	-25.3	-26.4	-31.3	-33.7	-42.3	-55.0	-20.8	-53.6	-61.0	-48.8	-78.6
GDP at Market Prices	945.4	1,021.2	1,151.9	1,264.9	1,446.6	1,654.1	1,840.8	1,956.3	2,069.8	2,452.5	2,800.2
Resource Balance	-10.4	-34.2	-43.4	-62.4	-56.8	-155.3	-134.0	-137.4	-75.8	-113.8	-246.5
Exports of Goods & NFServices	362.9	388.2	426.4	460.7	528.1	761.8	865.4	837.8	921.1	986.4	1,124.8
Imports of Goods & NFServices	373.3	422.4	469.8	523.1	584.9	917.1	999.4	975.2	996.9	1,100.2	1,371.3
Domestic Absorption	955.8	1,055.4	1,195.3	1,327.3	1,503.4	1,809.4	1,974.8	2,093.7	2,145.6	2,566.3	3,046.7
Private Consumption, etc.	614.9	618.8	665.2	698.3	767.6	954.0	1,054.1	1,088.8	1,242.6	1,431.7	1,693.8
General Gov't Consumption	118.2	152.3	180.2	226.5	250.1	299.3	353.3	386.1	412.1	482.9	567.2
Gross Domestic Investment	222.7	284.3	349.9	402.5	485.7	556.1	567.4	618.8	490.9	651.7	785.7
Fixed Investment	200.7	261.9	306.3	372.2	434.8	465.0	535.5	608.6	445.9	606.3	661.2
Indirect Taxes, net	71.4	78.8	90.6	103.1	115.4	136.9	139.6	146.0	181.9	216.0	251.7
GDP at factor cost	874.0	942.4	1,061.3	1,161.8	1,331.2	1,517.2	1,701.2	1,810.3	1,887.9	2,236.5	2,548.5
Agriculture	149.2	149.1	164.2	170.9	184.9	184.5	205.6	231.1	263.5	288.5	304.2
Industry	187.7	219.2	247.5	259.8	318.3	364.0	432.1	431.3	424.1	511.9	587.1
Manufacturing	114.8	127.3	135.9	141.0	161.0	202.0	236.0	217.3	234.0	252.6	293.3
Services, etc.	608.5	652.9	740.2	834.2	943.4	1,105.6	1,203.1	1,293.9	1,382.2	1,652.1	1,908.9
Gross Domestic Saving	212.3	250.1	306.5	340.1	428.9	400.8	433.4	481.4	415.1	537.9	539.2
Gross National Saving	..	212.8	263.0	292.6	363.9	320.2	387.0	400.1	324.2	455.6	421.3

					(Millions of 1987 Panamanian Balboas)						
Gross National Product	2,308.2	2,477.5	2,715.8	2,845.1	2,997.8	3,074.5	3,178.6	3,190.8	3,222.8	3,567.6	3,714.4
GDP at Market Prices	2,378.1	2,543.5	2,788.1	2,915.9	3,072.3	3,152.0	3,204.4	3,255.8	3,291.1	3,613.9	3,781.2
Resource Balance	-225.9	-286.2	-369.1	-446.7	-389.6	-482.2	-397.2	-349.2	-196.0	-310.1	-364.7
Exports of Goods & NFServices	784.9	822.9	857.9	868.7	909.8	973.4	989.9	965.1	1,067.7	1,142.1	1,126.9
Imports of Goods & NFServices	1,010.9	1,109.1	1,226.9	1,315.4	1,299.4	1,455.6	1,387.1	1,314.4	1,263.7	1,452.2	1,491.6
Domestic Absorption	2,604.0	2,829.7	3,157.2	3,362.6	3,461.9	3,634.2	3,601.6	3,605.1	3,487.0	3,924.0	4,145.9
Private Consumption, etc.	1,585.2	1,633.8	1,731.6	1,719.3	1,767.5	1,974.5	1,910.5	1,902.8	2,051.6	2,287.0	2,420.1
General Gov't Consumption	397.2	463.2	526.5	614.1	625.9	645.4	712.6	733.0	761.6	795.3	818.4
Gross Domestic Investment	621.6	732.7	899.1	1,029.3	1,068.4	1,014.3	978.5	969.2	673.9	841.7	907.4
Fixed Investment	557.1	673.6	774.2	959.6	961.4	860.4	928.5	947.0	629.1	779.8	771.4
GDP at factor cost	..	..	..	..	..	..	..	..	..	..	..
Agriculture	354.6	352.0	379.4	366.9	370.9	349.2	374.5	394.5	414.4	446.5	427.3
Industry	518.5	565.4	635.6	660.1	734.4	712.4	734.4	761.2	702.6	790.1	849.2
Manufacturing	276.4	294.9	313.7	328.0	348.7	353.3	340.6	349.1	353.3	358.9	398.5
Services, etc.	1,509.4	1,632.7	1,781.3	1,899.0	1,979.8	2,099.6	2,106.6	2,112.9	2,184.4	2,389.2	2,516.0
Memo Items:											
Capacity to Import	982.7	1,019.3	1,113.6	1,158.5	1,173.2	1,209.1	1,201.1	1,129.2	1,167.6	1,302.0	1,223.5
Terms of Trade Adjustment	197.7	196.4	255.7	289.8	263.4	235.7	211.2	164.1	99.9	159.9	96.6
Gross Domestic Income	2,575.9	2,739.9	3,043.8	3,205.7	3,335.7	3,387.7	3,415.6	3,419.9	3,390.9	3,773.8	3,877.8
Gross National Income	2,505.9	2,673.9	2,971.6	3,134.9	3,261.2	3,310.2	3,389.8	3,354.8	3,322.7	3,727.5	3,811.0

DOMESTIC PRICES/DEFLATORS					*(Index 1987 = 100)*						
Overall (GDP)	39.8	40.1	41.3	43.4	47.1	52.5	57.4	60.1	62.9	67.9	74.1
Domestic Absorption	36.7	37.3	37.9	39.5	43.4	49.8	54.8	58.1	61.5	65.4	73.5
Agriculture	42.1	42.4	43.3	46.6	49.8	52.8	54.9	58.6	63.6	64.6	71.2
Industry	36.2	38.8	38.9	39.4	43.3	51.1	58.8	56.7	60.4	64.8	69.1
Manufacturing	41.5	43.2	43.3	43.0	46.2	57.2	69.3	62.2	66.2	70.4	73.6
Consumer Price Index	41.7	43.0	43.8	46.2	49.3	57.3	60.7	63.1	66.0	68.8	74.3

MANUFACTURING ACTIVITY											
Employment (1987=100)	51.8	57.5	66.4	68.2	72.1	70.6	70.1	69.3	70.9	74.0	78.0
Real Earnings per Empl. (1987=100)	86.7	86.9	85.1	86.2	86.1	84.0	85.8	87.5	94.7	92.0	90.8
Real Output per Empl. (1987=100)	75.4	74.6	79.6	86.2	90.5	110.9	103.9	114.2	110.3	100.0	116.1
Earnings as % of Value Added	36.0	32.0	32.8	32.8	31.3	29.1	28.1	29.5	32.9	32.8	30.6

MONETARY HOLDINGS					*(Millions of current Panamanian Balboas)*						
Money Supply, Broadly Defined	..	..	..	..	..	..	634.6	682.4	793.7	946.8	1,166.3
Money	84.8	100.5	105.4	153.6	161.1	196.3	173.1	190.0	213.2	246.0	301.3
Currency Outside Banks	..	..	..	..	..	..	..	..	..	..	..
Demand Deposits	..	..	..	..	..	..	..	..	..	..	..
Quasi-Money	..	..	..	..	..	..	461.5	492.4	580.5	700.8	865.0

GOVERNMENT DEFICIT (-) OR SURPLUS					*(Millions of current Panamanian Balboas)*						
	..	..	..	..	-91.0	-119.4	-149.5	-202.7	-119.0	-159.6	-371.8
Current Revenue	..	..	..	..	306.1	391.5	451.7	440.2	546.4	597.6	696.6
Current Expenditure	..	..	..	..	304.1	382.3	431.2	479.4	532.8	614.8	795.9
Current Budget Balance	..	..	..	..	2.0	9.2	20.5	-39.2	13.6	-17.2	-99.3
Capital Receipts	..	..	..	..	..	..	..	..	..	..	..
Capital Payments	..	..	..	..	93.0	128.6	170.0	163.5	132.6	142.4	272.5

| | 1969 | 1970 | 1971 | 1972 | 1973 | 1974 | 1975 | 1976 | 1977 | 1978 | 1979 |

1980	1981	1982	1983	1984	1985	1986	1987	1988	1989 estimate	NOTES	PANAMA
1,630	1,820	1,950	1,950	1,980	2,060	2,170	2,210	1,810	1,760	..	CURRENT GNP PER CAPITA (US $)
1,956	2,000	2,044	2,089	2,134	2,180	2,227	2,274	2,322	2,370	..	POPULATION (thousands)
				(Millions of current Panamanian Balboas)							USE AND ORIGIN OF RESOURCES
3,223.6	3,559.2	3,874.1	3,989.4	4,239.7	4,498.5	4,787.5	4,940.4	4,118.7	4,071.3	..	Gross National Product (GNP)
-335.2	-318.8	-404.8	-384.3	-325.8	-402.6	-357.6	-369.3	-432.7	-477.5	..	Net Factor Income from Abroad
3,558.8	3,878.0	4,278.9	4,373.7	4,565.5	4,901.1	5,145.1	5,309.7	4,551.4	4,548.8	..	GDP at Market Prices
-118.1	-167.7	-179.8	18.1	-74.8	24.3	187.2	99.5	542.6	395.4	..	Resource Balance
1,567.1	1,690.5	1,689.6	1,709.5	1,622.1	1,735.2	1,786.5	1,736.3	1,625.4	1,554.8	..	Exports of Goods & NFServices
1,685.2	1,858.2	1,869.4	1,691.4	1,696.9	1,710.9	1,599.3	1,636.8	1,082.8	1,159.4	..	Imports of Goods & NFServices
3,676.9	4,045.4	4,458.7	4,355.6	4,640.3	4,876.6	4,957.9	5,210.2	4,008.8	4,153.4	..	Domestic Absorption
2,009.5	2,065.4	2,311.5	2,480.0	2,878.0	3,080.0	2,970.9	3,055.3	2,683.5	3,047.6	..	Private Consumption, etc.
680.5	812.8	962.6	941.5	1,001.3	1,043.6	1,127.8	1,226.9	1,011.6	987.1	..	General Gov't Consumption
986.9	1,167.2	1,184.6	934.1	761.0	753.0	859.2	928.0	313.7	118.7	..	Gross Domestic Investment
866.4	1,079.6	1,185.4	917.8	779.9	773.1	896.7	937.0	407.7	329.7	..	Fixed Investment
268.2	281.6	307.9	331.4	353.7	384.7	427.6	444.6	318.8	340.6	..	Indirect Taxes, net
3,290.6	3,596.4	3,971.0	4,042.3	4,211.8	4,516.4	4,717.5	4,865.1	4,232.6	4,208.2	B	GDP at factor cost
320.4	359.3	371.2	408.4	415.9	450.6	478.6	505.5	478.7	493.0	..	Agriculture
735.0	821.9	934.3	833.9	836.9	867.6	915.4	936.6	676.4	661.6	f	Industry
356.0	375.6	394.0	401.0	411.0	420.0	421.8	440.4	328.7	352.4	..	Manufacturing
2,503.4	2,696.8	2,973.4	3,131.4	3,312.7	3,582.9	3,751.1	3,867.6	3,396.3	3,394.2	..	Services, etc.
868.8	999.8	1,004.8	952.2	686.2	777.5	1,046.4	1,027.5	856.3	514.1	..	Gross Domestic Saving
481.4	633.4	544.6	508.2	328.4	342.9	661.9	608.7	396.7	1.5	..	Gross National Saving
				(Millions of 1987 Panamanian Balboas)							
3,952.9	4,171.5	4,344.7	4,393.6	4,452.1	4,608.2	4,830.7	4,940.4	4,050.9	3,970.5	..	Gross National Product
4,364.0	4,545.3	4,798.6	4,816.6	4,794.3	5,020.6	5,191.5	5,309.7	4,477.2	4,437.2	..	GDP at Market Prices
-132.0	-178.3	-60.5	90.7	-139.9	-52.0	57.6	99.5	608.6	401.6	..	Resource Balance
1,620.6	1,570.1	1,687.1	1,682.9	1,575.6	1,689.0	1,769.8	1,736.3	1,686.9	1,626.7	..	Exports of Goods & NFServices
1,752.6	1,748.4	1,747.6	1,592.2	1,715.6	1,741.0	1,712.2	1,636.8	1,078.3	1,225.1	..	Imports of Goods & NFServices
4,496.0	4,723.6	4,859.1	4,725.9	4,934.2	5,072.6	5,133.8	5,210.2	3,868.6	4,035.6	..	Domestic Absorption
2,569.1	2,510.8	2,610.8	2,801.7	3,093.0	3,161.3	3,059.0	3,055.3	2,534.4	2,933.7	..	Private Consumption, etc.
866.2	1,018.6	1,099.2	1,045.6	1,059.6	1,076.7	1,168.2	1,226.9	996.7	963.2	..	General Gov't Consumption
1,060.7	1,194.2	1,149.1	878.5	781.6	834.7	906.6	928.0	337.6	138.6	..	Gross Domestic Investment
939.6	1,096.0	1,145.3	856.5	797.9	852.4	934.9	937.0	426.2	363.4	..	Fixed Investment
4,364.0	4,545.3	4,798.6	4,816.6	4,794.3	5,020.6	5,170.0	4,865.1	4,163.1	4,104.3	B	GDP at factor cost
410.1	444.1	437.3	451.0	458.5	481.4	470.8	505.5	480.0	495.1	f	Agriculture
936.3	940.0	1,026.4	906.4	852.5	873.9	912.1	936.6	673.8	661.4	f	Industry
421.9	408.0	416.8	409.4	407.3	415.4	424.6	440.4	340.8	359.5	..	Manufacturing
3,023.6	3,166.7	3,340.7	3,459.2	3,483.2	3,665.3	3,808.6	3,867.6	3,323.4	3,280.7	f	Services, etc.
											Memo Items:
1,629.8	1,590.6	1,579.5	1,609.2	1,639.9	1,765.8	1,912.6	1,736.3	1,618.7	1,642.9	..	Capacity to Import
9.2	20.5	-107.6	-73.7	64.3	76.7	142.8	0.0	-68.2	16.2	..	Terms of Trade Adjustment
4,373.2	4,565.8	4,691.0	4,742.9	4,858.6	5,097.4	5,334.2	5,309.7	4,409.0	4,453.4	..	Gross Domestic Income
3,962.1	4,192.0	4,237.1	4,319.9	4,516.5	4,684.9	4,973.5	4,940.4	3,982.7	3,986.7	..	Gross National Income
				(Index 1987 = 100)							DOMESTIC PRICES/DEFLATORS
81.5	85.3	89.2	90.8	95.2	97.6	99.1	100.0	101.7	102.5	..	Overall (GDP)
81.8	85.6	91.8	92.2	94.0	96.1	96.6	100.0	103.6	102.9	..	Domestic Absorption
78.1	80.9	84.9	90.6	90.7	93.6	101.7	100.0	99.7	99.6	..	Agriculture
78.5	87.4	91.0	92.0	98.2	99.3	100.4	100.0	100.4	100.0	..	Industry
84.4	92.1	94.5	98.0	100.9	101.1	99.3	100.0	96.5	98.0	..	Manufacturing
84.5	90.7	94.6	96.5	98.1	99.1	99.0	100.0	100.3	100.2	..	Consumer Price Index
											MANUFACTURING ACTIVITY
82.2	89.2	93.8	93.3	95.2	94.2	95.2	100.0	..	..	..	Employment (1987=100)
79.3	86.1	89.8	95.5	99.5	98.8	98.4	100.0	..	..	..	Real Earnings per Empl. (1987=100)
110.9	108.1	104.1	103.7	100.3	96.8	93.4	100.0	..	..	..	Real Output per Empl. (1987=100)
25.1	28.8	34.8	33.2	33.7	34.3	34.3	34.9	..	..	..	Earnings as % of Value Added
				(Millions of current Panamanian Balboas)							MONETARY HOLDINGS
1,458.3	1,723.8	1,949.1	1,970.8	2,108.9	2,194.9	..	..	..	..	D	Money Supply, Broadly Defined
335.3	359.7	379.3	372.6	381.0	409.5	449.5	442.1	303.8	306.9	..	Money
..	..	..	..	..	..	..	..	..	..	..	Currency Outside Banks
..	..	..	..	..	..	..	..	..	..	..	Demand Deposits
1,123.0	1,364.1	1,569.8	1,598.2	1,727.9	1,785.4	..	..	..	..	..	Quasi-Money
				(Millions of current Panamanian Balboas)							
-197.6	-334.6	-482.6	-272.5	-340.0	-155.0	-220.7	-227.9	-238.0	..	..	GOVERNMENT DEFICIT (-) OR SURPLUS
966.1	1,029.8	1,203.8	1,324.3	1,369.0	1,472.5	1,595.4	1,605.6	1,146.2	..	..	Current Revenue
952.3	1,069.9	1,401.1	1,341.7	1,457.5	1,466.4	1,619.9	1,705.4	1,279.8	..	..	Current Expenditure
13.8	-40.1	-197.3	-17.4	-88.5	6.1	-24.5	-99.8	-133.6	..	..	Current Budget Balance
..	..	..	..	5.1	5.0	2.1	..	..	..	..	Capital Receipts
211.4	294.5	285.3	255.1	256.6	166.1	198.3	128.1	104.4	..	..	Capital Payments

PANAMA	1969	1970	1971	1972	1973	1974	1975	1976	1977	1978	1979
FOREIGN TRADE (CUSTOMS BASIS)					*(Millions of current US dollars)*						
Value of Exports, fob	108.8	109.5	116.5	122.6	137.8	210.5	286.4	236.7	249.5	244.3	291.6
Nonfuel Primary Products	82.3	84.1	88.5	97.7	107.1	110.8	144.7	148.6	158.3	163.0	188.8
Fuels	24.1	21.5	25.2	21.6	24.4	86.3	128.3	66.3	68.3	60.1	72.4
Manufactures	2.5	3.9	2.8	3.3	6.3	13.4	13.5	21.8	22.9	21.1	30.4
Value of Imports, cif	293.6	357.0	395.8	440.5	502.2	822.4	892.1	848.3	858.9	942.4	1,183.8
Nonfuel Primary Products	32.9	41.7	54.9	53.0	64.8	95.9	86.5	87.9	95.0	100.7	134.5
Fuels	64.8	66.4	70.9	73.3	102.0	293.4	360.5	282.1	283.4	230.1	337.6
Manufactures	196.0	249.0	270.0	314.1	335.4	433.2	445.1	478.4	480.5	611.5	711.7
					(Index 1987 = 100)						
Terms of Trade	113.0	111.2	103.3	116.4	125.0	129.9	119.8	127.4	124.5	115.2	119.3
Export Prices, fob	19.7	21.3	23.3	29.3	38.2	70.6	68.8	74.2	79.6	80.0	101.0
Import Prices, cif	17.5	19.2	22.6	25.2	30.5	54.3	57.4	58.2	63.9	69.5	84.6
BALANCE OF PAYMENTS					*(Millions of current US dollars)*						
Exports of Goods & Services	..	394.5	446.4	495.5	603.9	1,059.8	1,222.6	1,230.7	1,388.1	1,743.6	2,590.0
Merchandise, fob	..	130.3	137.8	146.1	161.9	250.9	330.9	269.0	288.5	304.4	356.0
Nonfactor Services	..	250.3	278.9	303.8	351.6	493.9	512.4	544.9	608.3	633.6	782.0
Factor Services	..	13.9	29.7	45.6	90.5	315.0	379.4	416.8	491.3	805.6	1,450.0
Imports of Goods & Services	..	462.7	524.2	598.7	710.9	1,301.0	1,391.8	1,403.0	1,541.1	1,949.2	2,910.0
Merchandise, fob	..	331.0	363.9	408.7	458.1	760.7	823.1	783.3	790.4	862.1	1,090.0
Nonfactor Services	..	88.9	100.8	109.9	121.4	150.2	164.4	165.6	200.9	233.1	280.0
Factor Services	..	42.8	59.5	80.1	131.4	390.1	404.3	454.1	549.8	854.0	1,540.0
Long-Term Interest	..	6.9	12.3	17.3	23.6	44.1	41.2	55.9	73.2	122.0	197.8
Private Current Transfers, net	..	-10.9	-12.2	-13.8	-22.7	-25.6	-25.6	-27.7	-29.9	-33.5	-39.3
Workers' Remittances	..	..	..	..	..	..	..	..	..	..	..
Curr. A/C Bal before Off. Transf.	..	-79.1	-90.0	-116.9	-129.6	-246.4	-189.4	-200.0	-182.9	-239.1	-362.6
Net Official Transfers	..	14.9	16.5	18.5	18.5	22.0	20.8	23.8	27.5	31.4	51.6
Curr. A/C Bal after Off. Transf.	..	-64.2	-73.4	-98.5	-111.1	-224.4	-168.6	-176.2	-155.4	-207.7	-311.0
Long-Term Capital, net	..	119.8	86.2	128.1	147.7	113.4	184.4	722.0	-113.0	451.4	314.0
Direct Investment	..	33.4	21.8	13.4	35.6	34.5	7.6	-10.6	10.9	-2.5	49.8
Long-Term Loans	..	43.8	50.8	100.8	99.9	103.5	213.7	322.0	239.4	549.5	219.3
Disbursements	..	67.4	78.9	135.5	163.3	194.9	244.9	366.7	327.6	992.4	409.4
Repayments	..	23.6	28.1	34.7	63.4	91.4	31.2	44.7	88.2	442.9	190.1
Other Long-Term Capital	..	42.6	13.6	14.0	12.2	-24.6	-36.9	410.7	-363.3	-95.6	44.9
Other Capital, net	..	-56.3	-14.0	-11.3	-39.5	99.1	-38.2	-528.8	261.1	-157.5	-30.1
Change in Reserves	..	0.6	1.3	-18.3	2.9	11.9	22.4	-17.0	7.3	-86.2	27.1
Memo Item:					*(Panamanian Balboas per US dollar)*						
Conversion Factor (Annual Avg)	1.000	1.000	1.000	1.000	1.000	1.000	1.000	1.000	1.000	1.000	1.000
				(Millions of US dollars), outstanding at end of year							
EXTERNAL DEBT (Total)	..	193.9	244.7	345.4	457.4	573.9	791.2	1,142.5	1,684.4	2,312.7	2,604.3
Long-Term Debt (by debtor)	..	193.9	244.7	345.4	457.4	573.9	791.2	1,142.5	1,384.4	1,927.7	2,113.3
Central Bank, incl. IMF credit	..	6.3	12.4	18.3	17.1	26.6	63.9	134.2	173.0	175.9	161.9
Central Government	..	145.4	178.6	220.8	305.3	369.4	452.6	573.2	677.9	1,154.7	1,464.6
Rest of General Government	..	0.0	0.5	11.7	12.5	11.3	9.4	7.6	5.7	2.6	3.1
Non-financial Public Enterprises	..	42.2	53.2	94.6	122.5	166.6	265.3	427.5	522.2	589.0	469.2
Priv. Sector, incl non-guaranteed	..	0.0	0.0	0.0	0.0	0.0	0.0	0.0	5.6	5.5	14.5
Short-Term Debt	..	0.0	0.0	0.0	0.0	0.0	0.0	0.0	300.0	385.0	491.0
Memo Items:					*(Thousands of US dollars)*						
Int'l Reserves Excluding Gold	14,100	15,750	21,022	43,128	41,715	39,316	34,445	78,942	70,866	150,418	118,718
Gold Holdings (at market price)	..	..	..	..	..	..	..	..	..	..	..
SOCIAL INDICATORS											
Total Fertility Rate	5.3	5.2	5.1	4.9	4.8	4.6	4.4	4.2	4.1	3.9	3.8
Infant Mortality Rate	48.4	46.6	44.8	43.0	40.8	38.6	36.4	34.2	32.0	30.8	29.6
Life Expectancy at Birth	65.1	65.5	65.9	66.4	66.9	67.5	68.1	68.6	69.2	69.6	69.9
Urban Population, % of total	47.0	47.6	47.9	48.2	48.5	48.8	49.1	49.4	49.7	49.9	50.2
Food Prod. per capita (1987=100)	104.5	91.2	97.1	93.1	95.3	96.5	98.3	94.9	100.2	101.1	100.0
Labor Force, Agriculture (%)	42.4	41.6	40.5	39.5	38.5	37.5	36.6	35.5	34.5	33.5	32.6
Labor Force, Female (%)	24.9	25.3	25.4	25.5	25.6	25.7	25.8	25.9	25.9	26.0	26.1
Primary Schl. Enroll. Ratio	..	99.0	..	..	..	..	114.0	121.0	120.0	118.0	116.0
Primary Schl. Enroll. Ratio, Female	..	97.0	..	..	..	..	111.0	120.0	118.0	116.0	113.0
Secondary Schl. Enroll. Ratio	..	38.0	..	..	..	..	55.0	60.0	63.0	66.0	66.0

1980	1981	1982	1983	1984	1985	1986	1987	1988	1989 estimate	NOTES	PANAMA
											FOREIGN TRADE (CUSTOMS BASIS)
				(Millions of current US dollars)							
353.4	319.4	310.2	302.6	307.0	335.3	341.0	350.0	280.0	..	..	Value of Exports, fob
240.0	229.6	201.2	236.8	217.6	240.7	255.0	256.0	187.0	..	..	Nonfuel Primary Products
81.8	58.4	70.3	36.5	54.9	55.7	40.0	45.0	35.0	..	..	Fuels
31.5	31.4	38.7	29.3	34.5	38.9	46.0	49.0	58.0	..	..	Manufactures
1,447.4	1,561.9	1,567.8	1,411.4	1,411.8	1,383.3	1,229.2	1,306.0	751.0	..	..	Value of Imports, cif
166.1	162.9	164.2	167.1	165.6	185.6	124.7	25.3	80.1	..	..	Nonfuel Primary Products
441.7	439.0	417.5	392.3	367.2	293.0	127.1	117.7	160.9	..	..	Fuels
839.6	960.0	986.1	852.0	879.0	904.7	977.5	1,163.0	510.0	..	..	Manufactures
				(Index 1987 = 100)							
126.3	116.0	117.1	118.6	111.5	108.9	109.8	100.0	112.4	..	..	Terms of Trade
127.9	117.0	113.0	112.7	102.9	97.7	99.4	100.0	113.5	..	..	Export Prices, fob
101.3	100.9	96.5	95.0	92.3	89.8	90.5	100.0	100.9	..	..	Import Prices, cif
				(Millions of current US dollars)							**BALANCE OF PAYMENTS**
4,230.0	5,100.0	5,440.0	4,520.0	4,170.0	3,960.0	3,640.0	3,230.0	2,298.0	2,246.0	f	Exports of Goods & Services
526.0	496.0	489.0	426.0	432.0	417.0	414.0	443.0	364.0	366.0	..	Merchandise, fob
1,120.0	1,240.0	1,280.0	1,350.0	1,310.0	1,530.0	1,480.0	1,430.0	1,360.0	1,300.0	..	Nonfactor Services
2,590.0	3,370.0	3,670.0	2,750.0	2,420.0	2,010.0	1,740.0	1,350.0	578.0	586.0	..	Factor Services
4,570.0	5,490.0	5,890.0	4,780.0	4,420.0	4,180.0	3,700.0	3,310.0	2,094.0	2,280.0	f	Imports of Goods & Services
1,340.0	1,470.0	1,500.0	1,350.0	1,340.0	1,330.0	1,180.0	1,240.0	794.0	969.0	..	Merchandise, fob
356.0	385.0	375.0	344.0	363.0	476.0	442.0	395.0	315.0	285.0	..	Nonfactor Services
2,870.0	3,640.0	4,020.0	3,080.0	2,720.0	2,380.0	2,080.0	1,670.0	984.0	1,030.0	..	Factor Services
251.8	280.9	337.6	291.6	304.3	303.0	321.8	225.1	12.6	0.7	..	Long-Term Interest
-52.2	-47.6	-55.4	-59.7	-32.0	-32.0	-26.9	-49.5	-26.9	-35.1	..	Private Current Transfers, net
..	..	..	..	..	..	..	..	..	..		Workers' Remittances
-388.7	-438.7	-507.0	-307.0	-280.0	-260.0	-81.8	-130.4	180.0	-69.3	..	Curr. A/C Bal before Off. Transf.
66.7	78.7	101.0	104.0	144.0	140.0	122.0	114.0	112.0	108.0	..	Net Official Transfers
-322.0	-360.0	-406.0	-203.0	-136.0	-120.0	40.2	-16.4	292.0	38.7	..	Curr. A/C Bal after Off. Transf.
85.0	280.0	613.0	117.0	65.0	-224.0	-361.0	-412.0	-633.0	-508.0	f	Long-Term Capital, net
-46.6	171.0	0.8	54.9	6.5	57.3	-61.0	50.9	-35.6	11.9	..	Direct Investment
189.3	165.4	493.1	230.6	163.9	59.9	62.9	-17.3	46.3	-1.0	..	Long-Term Loans
403.9	378.7	774.0	419.2	396.6	167.2	212.6	139.3	61.4	0.6	..	Disbursements
214.6	213.3	280.9	188.6	232.7	107.3	149.7	156.6	15.1	1.6	..	Repayments
-57.7	-56.4	119.1	-168.5	-105.4	-341.2	-362.9	-445.6	-643.7	-518.9	..	Other Long-Term Capital
248.3	6.7	-222.5	75.0	-12.6	226.0	380.4	390.8	335.7	520.0	f	Other Capital, net
-11.3	73.3	15.5	11.0	83.6	118.0	-59.6	37.6	5.3	-50.7	..	Change in Reserves
				(Panamanian Balboas per US dollar)							Memo Item:
1.000	1.000	1.000	1.000	1.000	1.000	1.000	1.000	1.000	1.000	..	Conversion Factor (Annual Avg)
				(Millions of US dollars), outstanding at end of year							
2,974.0	3,366.1	3,923.2	4,388.8	4,369.0	4,759.3	4,932.5	5,301.8	5,683.1	5,800.1	..	**EXTERNAL DEBT (Total)**
2,294.0	2,523.1	3,001.2	3,338.1	3,456.3	3,635.3	3,922.5	4,046.1	4,000.9	3,894.5	..	Long-Term Debt (by debtor)
159.7	273.0	342.1	493.5	534.5	588.2	605.1	609.7	584.9	539.2	..	Central Bank, incl. IMF credit
1,679.2	1,779.8	2,082.6	2,197.8	2,255.4	2,329.5	2,541.4	2,574.6	2,556.2	2,519.6	..	Central Government
12.0	24.8	36.5	48.4	51.6	48.2	59.9	73.9	72.7	65.2	..	Rest of General Government
422.6	427.6	517.0	566.9	582.2	640.4	689.2	757.4	758.1	742.1	..	Non-financial Public Enterprises
20.5	17.9	23.0	31.5	32.6	29.0	26.9	30.5	29.0	28.4	..	Priv. Sector, incl non-guaranteed
680.0	843.0	922.0	1,050.7	912.7	1,124.0	1,010.0	1,255.7	1,682.2	1,905.6	..	Short-Term Debt
				(Thousands of US dollars)							Memo Items:
117,383	119,947	100,970	206,696	215,639	97,962	170,174	77,814	72,214	119,413	..	Int'l Reserves Excluding Gold
..	..	..	..	..	..	..	..	..	..	..	Gold Holdings (at market price)
											SOCIAL INDICATORS
3.7	3.6	3.5	3.4	3.3	3.3	3.2	3.1	3.1	3.0	..	Total Fertility Rate
28.4	27.2	26.0	25.4	24.8	24.2	23.6	23.0	22.4	21.8	..	Infant Mortality Rate
70.3	70.6	71.0	71.2	71.4	71.6	71.9	72.1	72.2	72.4	..	Life Expectancy at Birth
50.5	50.9	51.3	51.6	52.0	52.4	52.9	53.4	53.8	54.3	..	Urban Population, % of total
97.6	101.7	97.5	99.6	97.2	99.0	97.7	100.0	87.5	87.6	..	Food Prod. per capita (1987=100)
31.7	..	..	..	..	..	..	..	..	..	..	Labor Force, Agriculture (%)
26.1	26.3	26.4	26.5	26.6	26.7	26.8	26.9	27.0	27.1	..	Labor Force, Female (%)
106.0	..	104.0	104.0	105.0	105.0	106.0	..	..	..	..	Primary Schl. Enroll. Ratio
104.0	..	102.0	101.0	102.0	102.0	104.0	..	..	..	..	Primary Schl. Enroll. Ratio, Female
61.0	..	59.0	59.0	59.0	59.0	59.0	..	..	..	..	Secondary Schl. Enroll. Ratio

PAPUA NEW GUINEA	1969	1970	1971	1972	1973	1974	1975	1976	1977	1978	1979
CURRENT GNP PER CAPITA (US $)	230	260	280	300	370	450	530	520	540	650	710
POPULATION (thousands)	2,364	2,422	2,481	2,541	2,602	2,665	2,729	2,794	2,861	2,929	2,999

USE AND ORIGIN OF RESOURCES

(Millions of current Papua New Guinea Kina)

	1969	1970	1971	1972	1973	1974	1975	1976	1977	1978	1979
Gross National Product (GNP)	485.9	558.8	602.6	680.8	856.9	947.2	981.0	1,158.2	1,271.8	1,361.5	1,594.6
Net Factor Income from Abroad	-6.3	-17.6	-31.0	-36.3	-57.8	-75.1	-55.3	-40.4	-26.7	-19.4	-38.0
GDP at Market Prices	492.2	576.4	633.6	717.1	914.7	1,022.3	1,036.3	1,198.6	1,298.5	1,380.9	1,632.6
Resource Balance	-132.8	-204.4	-233.6	-122.2	92.0	72.0	-64.1	11.9	-16.8	-48.1	-1.8
Exports of Goods & NFServices	93.1	106.5	135.4	223.8	410.5	479.3	414.3	500.7	584.0	579.1	742.5
Imports of Goods & NFServices	225.9	310.9	369.0	346.0	318.5	407.3	478.4	488.8	600.8	627.2	744.3
Domestic Absorption	625.0	780.8	867.2	839.3	822.7	950.3	1,100.4	1,186.7	1,315.3	1,429.0	1,634.4
Private Consumption, etc.	324.8	367.6	401.2	422.1	432.0	473.1	545.0	600.5	697.1	763.3	879.7
General Gov't Consumption	157.2	173.4	195.1	217.6	249.1	299.1	347.7	362.7	337.7	353.3	371.4
Gross Domestic Investment	143.0	239.8	270.9	199.6	141.6	178.1	207.7	223.5	280.5	312.4	383.3
Fixed Investment	136.9	229.3	258.9	185.8	130.2	158.5	175.0	200.6	239.3	268.5	326.2
Indirect Taxes, net	21.8	28.5	33.4	35.5	39.3	48.0	57.0	67.6	83.2	82.9	95.3
GDP at factor cost	470.4	547.9	600.2	681.6	875.4	974.3	979.3	1,131.0	1,215.3	1,298.0	1,537.3
Agriculture	205.8	214.3	218.5	232.2	258.0	286.2	307.8	380.0	428.3	497.5	552.8
Industry	90.9	127.4	155.0	202.7	330.3	356.4	295.2	301.0	338.7	351.0	474.8
Manufacturing	..	31.5	36.7	40.7	51.8	68.8	83.9	101.0	99.9	134.0	152.2
Services, etc.	195.5	234.7	260.1	282.2	326.4	379.7	433.3	517.6	531.5	532.4	605.0
Gross Domestic Saving	10.2	35.4	37.3	77.4	233.6	250.1	143.6	235.4	263.7	264.3	381.5
Gross National Saving	..	26.7	8.9	45.3	172.3	165.9	83.0	148.6	192.3	182.5	275.5

(Millions of 1987 Papua New Guinea Kina)

	1969	1970	1971	1972	1973	1974	1975	1976	1977	1978	1979
Gross National Product	1,708.1	1,856.1	1,934.3	2,038.4	2,122.6	2,154.9	2,206.1	2,171.5	2,222.9	2,432.9	2,448.4
GDP at Market Prices	1,737.2	1,925.7	2,047.1	2,162.5	2,303.7	2,363.7	2,342.9	2,263.5	2,282.6	2,477.6	2,523.1
Resource Balance	-708.1	-986.9	-1,015.8	-619.9	-220.7	-239.5	-295.2	-296.6	-390.6	-338.3	-436.0
Exports of Goods & NFServices	257.5	290.4	364.9	564.2	788.8	896.4	865.0	789.6	821.0	898.6	896.1
Imports of Goods & NFServices	965.6	1,277.3	1,380.7	1,184.1	1,009.6	1,135.9	1,160.2	1,086.1	1,211.7	1,236.9	1,332.1
Domestic Absorption	2,445.3	2,912.7	3,062.9	2,782.4	2,524.4	2,603.2	2,638.1	2,560.1	2,673.3	2,815.9	2,959.0
Private Consumption, etc.	972.1	1,008.2	1,053.1	1,155.9	1,225.8	1,261.6	1,287.4	1,323.4	1,443.8	1,559.7	1,565.1
General Gov't Consumption	760.2	761.9	780.5	792.7	770.7	784.0	798.4	737.6	691.2	703.0	715.6
Gross Domestic Investment	713.0	1,142.5	1,229.3	833.9	528.0	557.6	552.3	499.0	538.3	553.1	678.3
Fixed Investment	660.1	1,057.7	1,134.0	763.4	487.7	501.8	468.5	426.2	455.5	495.7	572.7
GDP at factor cost	..	..	..	..	2,267.0	2,316.4	2,276.6	2,196.1	2,196.7	2,394.7	2,442.7
Agriculture	535.6	554.7	569.6	588.4	599.1	627.2	652.3	662.7	667.5	693.9	707.0
Industry	..	..	..	..	..	..	..	..	..	..	..
Manufacturing	..	..	..	..	..	..	..	..	..	..	..
Services, etc.	..	..	..	..	..	..	..	..	..	..	..

Memo Items:

	1969	1970	1971	1972	1973	1974	1975	1976	1977	1978	1979
Capacity to Import	397.9	437.6	506.6	765.9	1,301.2	1,336.7	1,004.7	1,112.6	1,177.8	1,142.0	1,328.9
Terms of Trade Adjustment	140.5	147.2	141.7	201.7	512.3	440.3	139.7	323.0	356.8	243.4	432.7
Gross Domestic Income	1,877.7	2,072.9	2,188.8	2,364.2	2,816.0	2,804.0	2,482.6	2,586.5	2,639.4	2,721.0	2,955.8
Gross National Income	1,848.6	2,003.3	2,076.1	2,240.1	2,635.0	2,595.2	2,345.8	2,494.5	2,579.7	2,676.3	2,881.2

DOMESTIC PRICES/DEFLATORS

(Index 1987 = 100)

	1969	1970	1971	1972	1973	1974	1975	1976	1977	1978	1979
Overall (GDP)	28.3	29.9	31.0	33.2	39.7	43.2	44.2	53.0	56.9	55.7	64.7
Domestic Absorption	25.6	26.8	28.3	30.2	32.6	36.5	41.7	46.4	49.2	50.7	55.2
Agriculture	38.4	38.6	38.4	39.5	43.1	45.6	47.2	57.3	64.2	71.7	78.2
Industry	..	..	..	..	..	..	..	..	..	..	..
Manufacturing	..	..	..	..	..	..	..	..	..	..	..
Consumer Price Index	..	..	30.3	32.2	34.9	42.9	47.4	51.1	53.4	56.5	59.7

MANUFACTURING ACTIVITY

	1969	1970	1971	1972	1973	1974	1975	1976	1977	1978	1979
Employment (1987=100)	..	..	..	..	..	..	..	..	..	..	..
Real Earnings per Empl. (1987=100)	..	..	..	..	..	..	..	..	..	..	..
Real Output per Empl. (1987=100)	..	..	..	..	..	..	..	..	..	..	..
Earnings as % of Value Added	40.0	40.1	39.0	40.3	39.7	39.1	41.7	40.7	36.0	32.5	37.2

MONETARY HOLDINGS

(Millions of current Papua New Guinea Kina)

	1969	1970	1971	1972	1973	1974	1975	1976	1977	1978	1979
Money Supply, Broadly Defined	..	..	..	..	195.64	320.04	245.46	277.82	428.46	449.03	571.71
Money	..	..	..	..	99.40	140.43	150.80	135.02	169.38	178.99	195.41
Currency Outside Banks	..	..	..	..	57.37	76.61	85.21	47.51	56.66	61.55	67.89
Demand Deposits	..	..	..	..	42.03	63.82	65.59	87.50	112.72	117.44	127.52
Quasi-Money	..	..	..	..	96.24	179.61	94.66	142.80	259.08	270.04	376.30

(Millions of current Papua New Guinea Kina)

GOVERNMENT DEFICIT (-) OR SURPLUS	1969	1970	1971	1972	1973	1974	1975	1976	1977	1978	1979
GOVERNMENT DEFICIT (-) OR SURPLUS	..	..	..	..	..	..	-56.96	-26.80	-19.36	-21.48	-62.80
Current Revenue	..	..	..	..	..	..	330.04	353.48	388.98	431.35	458.79
Current Expenditure	..	..	..	..	..	..	251.67	315.42	353.03	386.69	450.26
Current Budget Balance	..	..	..	..	..	..	78.37	38.06	35.95	44.66	8.53
Capital Receipts	..	..	..	..	..	..	0.22	0.11	0.04	0.02	0.03
Capital Payments	..	..	..	..	..	..	135.55	64.97	55.35	66.16	71.36

1980	1981	1982	1983	1984	1985	1986	1987	1988	1989	NOTES	PAPUA NEW GUINEA
									estimate		
760	820	780	760	750	740	740	760	850	890	..	CURRENT GNP PER CAPITA (US $)
3,070	3,143	3,219	3,297	3,377	3,460	3,546	3,633	3,722	3,812	..	POPULATION (thousands)

(Millions of current Papua New Guinea Kina) — **USE AND ORIGIN OF RESOURCES**

1980	1981	1982	1983	1984	1985	1986	1987	1988	1989	NOTES	
1,649.4	1,622.5	1,661.1	2,023.2	2,220.9	2,335.4	2,482.9	2,700.6	3,018.8	2,898.4	..	Gross National Product (GNP)
-58.7	-58.7	-88.0	-119.4	-72.5	-88.5	-72.1	-130.5	-122.1	-115.0	..	Net Factor Income from Abroad
1,708.1	1,681.2	1,749.1	2,142.6	2,293.4	2,423.9	2,555.0	2,831.1	3,140.9	3,013.4	f	GDP at Market Prices
-173.2	-344.7	-413.9	-369.7	-314.3	-250.3	-200.0	-185.7	-274.9	-368.5	..	Resource Balance
737.6	642.9	644.3	775.5	904.7	1,020.9	1,121.0	1,232.1	1,371.1	1,238.0	..	Exports of Goods & NFServices
910.8	987.6	1,058.2	1,145.2	1,219.0	1,271.2	1,321.0	1,417.8	1,646.0	1,606.5	..	Imports of Goods & NFServices
1,881.4	2,025.9	2,163.1	2,512.2	2,607.8	2,674.4	2,755.0	3,016.6	3,415.8	3,381.8	..	Domestic Absorption
1,039.5	1,113.4	1,132.5	1,382.4	1,455.5	1,624.5	1,656.2	1,791.7	1,890.4	1,929.0	..	Private Consumption, etc.
411.2	454.4	468.1	499.1	533.3	569.2	591.1	639.6	662.9	744.9	..	General Gov't Consumption
430.7	458.1	562.5	630.7	619.0	480.7	507.7	585.3	862.5	707.9	..	Gross Domestic Investment
394.2	450.7	576.7	636.9	547.5	446.9	539.2	551.2	737.0	791.0	..	Fixed Investment
110.0	114.6	134.4	151.9	179.2	189.7	212.0	240.7	254.2	314.0	..	Indirect Taxes, net
1,598.1	1,566.6	1,614.7	1,990.7	2,114.2	2,234.2	2,343.0	2,590.4	2,886.7	2,699.4	B f	GDP at factor cost
565.7	561.4	567.2	700.1	857.1	818.5	828.0	852.4	924.5	856.0	..	Agriculture
458.5	390.7	406.4	597.5	540.4	635.9	729.8	904.3	1,083.1	899.9	..	Industry
162.3	166.6	164.6	217.3	252.0	264.6	256.3	268.9	294.3	336.9	..	Manufacturing
683.9	729.1	775.5	845.0	895.9	969.5	997.2	1,074.4	1,133.3	1,257.5	..	Services, etc.
257.4	113.4	148.5	261.1	304.6	230.2	307.7	399.8	587.6	339.5	..	Gross Domestic Saving
127.8	-30.2	-30.1	60.3	146.7	52.9	159.2	174.4	357.5	112.7	..	Gross National Saving

(Millions of 1987 Papua New Guinea Kina)

1980	1981	1982	1983	1984	1985	1986	1987	1988	1989	NOTES	
2,365.3	2,376.9	2,353.6	2,407.5	2,455.5	2,550.6	2,660.6	2,700.6	2,801.3	2,761.7	..	Gross National Product
2,465.0	2,469.2	2,477.3	2,552.1	2,538.4	2,647.8	2,736.5	2,831.1	2,917.0	2,865.3	f	GDP at Market Prices
-565.9	-520.0	-518.1	-492.7	-437.1	-289.3	-166.5	-185.7	-325.1	-175.1	..	Resource Balance
893.2	941.5	926.1	942.3	971.9	1,091.0	1,198.1	1,232.1	1,218.7	1,213.1	..	Exports of Goods & NFServices
1,459.1	1,461.4	1,444.2	1,435.0	1,409.0	1,380.3	1,364.5	1,417.8	1,543.9	1,388.2	..	Imports of Goods & NFServices
3,030.9	2,989.1	2,995.3	3,044.8	2,975.5	2,937.1	2,902.9	3,016.8	3,242.1	3,040.4	..	Domestic Absorption
1,632.1	1,646.6	1,609.6	1,636.9	1,630.0	1,781.1	1,734.0	1,791.9	1,792.1	1,763.7	..	Private Consumption, etc.
691.6	664.9	618.3	606.3	611.8	628.5	620.6	639.6	628.7	666.3	..	General Gov't Consumption
707.2	677.7	767.4	801.6	733.6	527.5	548.3	585.3	821.3	610.3	..	Gross Domestic Investment
646.0	662.1	780.9	803.9	648.3	493.1	563.6	551.2	691.4	699.9	..	Fixed Investment
2,302.8	2,300.4	2,291.7	2,368.0	2,333.5	2,439.5	2,513.3	2,590.4	2,676.0	2,582.2	B f	GDP at factor cost
740.5	799.0	787.9	795.5	819.1	795.2	808.4	852.4	883.6	898.5	..	Agriculture
784.0	694.9	700.4	765.6	718.7	819.1	915.4	904.3	959.5	853.7	f	Industry
260.7	265.4	248.0	259.0	281.1	288.9	265.0	268.9	281.3	314.0	..	Manufacturing
950.6	964.9	980.0	991.0	1,000.5	1,033.5	1,012.6	1,074.4	1,073.8	1,113.1	f	Services, etc.

Memo Items:

1980	1981	1982	1983	1984	1985	1986	1987	1988	1989	NOTES	
1,181.7	951.3	879.3	971.7	1,045.7	1,108.5	1,158.0	1,232.1	1,286.0	1,069.8	..	Capacity to Import
288.5	9.9	-46.8	29.4	73.8	17.5	-40.1	0.0	67.3	-143.3	..	Terms of Trade Adjustment
2,753.4	2,479.1	2,430.5	2,581.6	2,612.2	2,665.3	2,696.3	2,831.1	2,984.3	2,722.0	..	Gross Domestic Income
2,653.8	2,386.7	2,306.8	2,436.9	2,529.3	2,568.1	2,620.5	2,700.6	2,868.6	2,618.4	..	Gross National Income

(Index 1987 = 100) — **DOMESTIC PRICES/DEFLATORS**

1980	1981	1982	1983	1984	1985	1986	1987	1988	1989	NOTES	
69.3	68.1	70.6	84.0	90.3	91.5	93.4	100.0	107.7	105.2	..	Overall (GDP)
62.1	67.8	72.2	82.5	87.6	91.1	94.9	100.0	105.4	111.2	..	Domestic Absorption
76.4	70.3	72.0	88.0	104.6	102.9	102.4	100.0	104.6	95.3	..	Agriculture
58.5	56.2	58.0	78.0	75.2	77.6	79.7	100.0	112.9	105.4	..	Industry
62.3	62.8	66.4	83.9	89.7	91.6	96.7	100.0	104.6	107.3	..	Manufacturing
66.9	72.3	76.3	82.4	88.5	91.8	96.8	100.0	105.4	110.2	..	Consumer Price Index

MANUFACTURING ACTIVITY

1980	1981	1982	1983	1984	1985	1986	1987	1988	1989	NOTES	
..	..	..	..	..	..	..	..	..	..	J	Employment (1987=100)
..	..	..	..	..	..	..	..	..	..	J	Real Earnings per Empl. (1987=100)
..	..	..	..	..	..	..	..	..	..	J	Real Output per Empl. (1987=100)
37.4	33.4	37.4	37.2	33.6	35.0	..	..	..	..	J	Earnings as % of Value Added

(Millions of current Papua New Guinea Kina) — **MONETARY HOLDINGS**

1980	1981	1982	1983	1984	1985	1986	1987	1988	1989	NOTES	
553.15	554.74	567.85	650.04	748.02	820.12	928.96	943.29	984.85	1,037.50	..	Money Supply, Broadly Defined
201.56	194.36	188.64	205.97	248.99	244.15	256.68	281.33	322.17	344.50	..	Money
70.49	73.39	72.41	79.95	88.90	94.26	95.74	106.35	115.20	122.03	..	Currency Outside Banks
131.06	120.98	116.23	126.02	160.09	149.90	160.94	174.98	206.97	222.48	..	Demand Deposits
351.59	360.37	379.22	444.08	499.03	575.97	672.28	661.96	662.68	693.00	..	Quasi-Money

(Millions of current Papua New Guinea Kina)

1980	1981	1982	1983	1984	1985	1986	1987	1988	1989	NOTES	
-33.02	-107.72	-97.18	-94.57	-21.13	-56.15	-76.85	-52.01	-28.18	..	F	GOVERNMENT DEFICIT (-) OR SURPLUS
566.81	555.86	555.65	616.91	723.60	703.77	751.56	810.71	888.98	..	..	Current Revenue
498.23	570.14	572.49	610.20	649.17	696.34	720.80	763.02	808.09	..	..	Current Expenditure
68.58	-14.28	-16.84	6.71	74.43	7.43	30.76	47.69	80.89	..	..	Current Budget Balance
0.13	0.32	0.84	0.27	4.73	0.79	1.21	1.29	1.27	..	..	Capital Receipts
101.73	93.76	81.18	101.55	100.29	64.37	108.82	100.99	110.34	..	..	Capital Payments

PAPUA NEW GUINEA	1969	1970	1971	1972	1973	1974	1975	1976	1977	1978	1979
FOREIGN TRADE (CUSTOMS BASIS)					*(Millions of current US dollars)*						
Value of Exports, fob	71.9	79.1	113.4	148.5	294.2	710.3	579.5	455.7	613.2	756.0	877.3
Nonfuel Primary Products	68.0	75.3	81.3	104.7	252.1	656.7	540.9	409.6	596.4	736.7	857.3
Fuels	0.2	0.0	0.0	0.0	0.0	0.1	0.1	0.1	0.0	0.1	0.1
Manufactures	3.7	3.8	32.1	43.8	42.1	53.5	38.5	46.0	16.9	19.2	19.9
Value of Imports, cif	220.1	300.3	355.9	336.4	355.9	502.7	555.7	502.3	642.1	770.3	902.7
Nonfuel Primary Products	54.7	61.0	69.8	70.4	84.6	134.8	123.8	117.2	139.8	180.2	211.3
Fuels	11.4	12.6	15.0	18.8	20.8	61.6	66.8	77.1	132.4	108.5	128.7
Manufactures	154.0	226.7	271.1	247.3	250.5	306.3	365.1	308.0	370.0	481.6	562.7
					(Index 1987 = 100)						
Terms of Trade	154.0	152.6	121.3	122.7	164.5	145.7	134.4	150.5	176.7	148.7	146.6
Export Prices, fob	40.1	41.7	35.8	38.9	64.8	82.2	77.5	88.5	114.3	107.9	124.7
Import Prices, cif	26.0	27.4	29.5	31.7	39.4	56.4	57.6	58.8	64.7	72.6	85.1
BALANCE OF PAYMENTS					*(Millions of current US dollars)*						
Exports of Goods & Services	..	123.0	159.0	305.0	613.0	718.0	560.0	639.8	751.7	788.2	1,100.4
Merchandise, fob	..	104.0	121.0	222.0	514.0	654.0	456.0	551.1	683.3	714.3	1,009.1
Nonfactor Services	..	15.0	33.0	75.0	81.0	42.0	87.0	68.9	38.0	35.7	41.8
Factor Services	..	4.0	5.0	8.0	18.0	22.0	17.0	19.8	30.3	38.3	49.4
Imports of Goods & Services	..	372.0	459.0	464.0	577.0	706.0	691.0	685.0	824.9	1,008.9	1,179.3
Merchandise, fob	..	300.0	356.0	299.0	290.0	428.0	504.0	434.2	559.9	688.4	783.3
Nonfactor Services	..	48.0	63.0	114.0	163.0	159.0	122.0	175.4	183.5	217.0	237.8
Factor Services	..	24.0	40.0	51.0	124.0	119.0	65.0	75.4	81.5	103.5	158.1
Long-Term Interest	..	9.7	17.5	25.8	32.8	35.0	32.0	32.1	33.5	35.9	37.2
Private Current Transfers, net	..	10.0	3.0	5.0	-5.0	-13.0	-7.0	-58.5	-56.4	-88.1	-95.6
Workers' Remittances	..	..	..	..	..	..	..	..	..	..	..
Curr. A/C Bal before Off. Transf.	..	-239.0	-297.0	-154.0	31.0	-1.0	-138.0	-103.7	-129.6	-308.8	-174.5
Net Official Transfers	..	150.0	175.0	160.0	184.0	222.0	116.0	144.7	228.5	254.2	252.0
Curr. A/C Bal after Off. Transf.	..	-89.0	-122.0	6.0	215.0	221.0	-22.0	41.0	98.8	-54.6	77.5
Long-Term Capital, net	..	98.0	217.0	132.0	56.0	58.0	97.0	32.7	65.1	-42.6	44.5
Direct Investment	..	..	..	19.0	89.0	52.0	34.0	18.9	18.0	34.0	41.0
Long-Term Loans	..	133.6	194.1	80.2	10.1	-8.6	9.6	-0.6	38.3	-62.8	16.6
Disbursements	..	154.0	237.3	159.8	101.5	73.3	79.2	66.9	108.3	20.3	66.9
Repayments	..	20.4	43.2	79.6	91.4	81.9	69.6	67.5	70.0	83.1	50.3
Other Long-Term Capital	..	-35.6	22.9	32.8	-43.1	14.6	53.4	14.3	8.8	-13.8	-13.1
Other Capital, net	..	65.0	-23.0	-141.4	-185.8	-179.5	-93.0	-30.9	-25.9	103.6	-9.8
Change in Reserves	..	-74.0	-72.0	3.4	-85.2	-99.5	18.0	-42.8	-138.0	-6.5	-112.2
Memo Item:					*(Papua New Guinea Kina per US dollar)*						
Conversion Factor (Annual Avg)	0.890	0.890	0.880	0.840	0.700	0.690	0.760	0.790	0.790	0.710	0.710
					(Millions of US dollars), outstanding at end of year						
EXTERNAL DEBT (Total)	..	208.7	407.2	495.0	525.5	505.3	506.1	520.8	675.8	583.2	608.7
Long-Term Debt (by debtor)	..	208.7	407.2	495.0	525.5	505.3	506.1	520.8	576.8	530.2	580.7
Central Bank, incl. IMF credit	..	0.0	0.0	0.0	0.0	0.0	0.0	28.8	30.0	30.0	23.9
Central Government	..	36.1	89.4	130.4	218.3	243.1	273.4	280.6	328.6	351.2	375.8
Rest of General Government	..	..	..	..	..	..	..	..	..	..	..
Non-financial Public Enterprises	..	0.0	0.0	0.0	0.0	0.0	0.0	0.0	0.0	0.0	0.0
Priv. Sector, incl non-guaranteed	..	172.6	317.8	364.6	307.2	262.2	232.7	211.4	218.2	149.0	181.0
Short-Term Debt	..	..	..	..	..	..	..	..	99.0	53.0	28.0
Memo Items:					*(Millions of US dollars)*						
Int'l Reserves Excluding Gold	..	..	..	..	31.26	32.45	179.67	257.20	426.63	404.72	503.55
Gold Holdings (at market price)	..	..	..	..	..	..	..	..	4.73	10.03	27.25
SOCIAL INDICATORS											
Total Fertility Rate	6.2	6.1	6.1	6.1	6.0	6.0	6.0	5.9	5.9	5.8	5.8
Infant Mortality Rate	120.0	115.0	110.0	105.0	101.0	97.0	93.0	89.0	85.0	82.8	80.6
Life Expectancy at Birth	46.2	46.7	47.2	47.7	48.1	48.5	48.9	49.3	49.7	50.2	50.6
Urban Population, % of total	8.9	9.8	10.2	10.6	11.1	11.5	11.9	12.1	12.3	12.6	12.8
Food Prod. per capita (1987=100)	104.4	103.9	104.7	105.4	103.3	106.2	107.4	106.0	104.1	103.7	101.5
Labor Force, Agriculture (%)	12.1	11.9	11.8	11.7	11.6	11.6	11.5	11.5	11.4	11.4	11.3
Labor Force, Female (%)	29.0	29.4	29.9	30.3	30.8	31.2	31.6	32.1	32.5	33.0	33.5
Primary Schl. Enroll. Ratio	..	52.0	..	..	..	..	56.0	..	57.0	58.0	60.0
Primary Schl. Enroll. Ratio, Female	..	39.0	..	..	..	..	43.0	..	45.0	47.0	50.0
Secondary Schl. Enroll. Ratio	..	8.0	..	..	..	..	12.0	12.0	11.0	11.0	11.0

1980	1981	1982	1983	1984	1985	1986	1987	1988	1989 estimate	NOTES	PAPUA NEW GUINEA
				(Millions of current US dollars)							**FOREIGN TRADE (CUSTOMS BASIS)**
1,033.0	863.6	791.1	820.0	892.0	911.9	1,033.2	1,172.2	1,448.0	..	..	Value of Exports, fob
972.9	782.9	718.7	747.3	817.4	856.3	971.7	1,104.5	1,374.0	..	..	Nonfuel Primary Products
0.1	0.1	0.5	0.5	0.6	0.6	0.5	0.8	1.0	..	..	Fuels
59.9	80.6	71.9	72.2	74.0	55.0	61.0	66.9	73.0	..	..	Manufactures
1,176.1	1,261.2	1,169.7	1,120.0	1,109.7	1,008.0	1,130.0	1,222.0	1,380.0	..	f	Value of Imports, cif
253.9	250.5	233.2	224.5	224.8	193.2	238.7	261.2	351.0	..	..	Nonfuel Primary Products
222.4	293.0	248.9	242.0	213.0	180.0	98.0	120.9	134.0	..	..	Fuels
699.8	717.7	687.7	653.5	671.9	634.8	793.3	840.0	895.0	..	f	Manufactures
				(Index 1987 = 100)							
121.9	102.4	107.6	111.2	121.8	112.7	108.9	100.0	101.1	..	..	Terms of Trade
121.8	105.5	104.0	104.4	109.8	99.7	99.1	100.0	107.3	..	..	Export Prices, fob
100.0	103.1	96.6	93.8	90.1	88.5	91.0	100.0	106.1	..	..	Import Prices, cif
				(Millions of current US dollars)							**BALANCE OF PAYMENTS**
1,087.9	971.8	925.3	953.4	1,029.0	1,041.0	1,194.6	1,399.1	1,716.2	1,499.4	..	Exports of Goods & Services
984.8	839.7	770.2	819.5	914.0	921.4	1,030.6	1,243.9	1,475.3	1,299.5	..	Merchandise, fob
43.3	84.7	95.4	75.7	64.4	64.0	72.5	97.3	122.3	112.9	..	Nonfactor Services
59.8	47.4	59.6	58.3	50.6	55.5	91.5	57.9	118.6	87.0	..	Factor Services
1,561.1	1,647.6	1,546.3	1,488.4	1,518.0	1,325.1	1,434.0	1,713.5	2,024.0	2,031.2	..	Imports of Goods & Services
1,020.5	1,096.4	1,017.6	974.8	962.8	874.8	928.8	1,129.6	1,262.7	1,340.2	..	Merchandise, fob
301.6	342.1	347.8	333.4	356.1	288.5	302.7	377.6	435.1	405.9	..	Nonfactor Services
239.0	209.2	180.9	180.3	199.2	161.8	202.5	206.3	326.2	285.1	..	Factor Services
51.7	71.1	102.0	117.2	146.6	131.6	131.4	151.7	162.3	160.4	..	Long-Term Interest
-105.7	-126.1	-122.6	-97.4	-95.0	-88.8	-78.7	-104.5	-124.6	-130.2	..	Private Current Transfers, net
..	..	..	..	..	..	..	..	..	46.1	..	Workers' Remittances
-578.8	-801.9	-743.6	-632.4	-584.0	-372.9	-318.1	-418.9	-432.4	-662.1	..	Curr. A/C Bal before Off. Transf.
266.6	280.5	260.7	256.7	261.9	218.4	212.7	204.3	217.7	217.3	..	Net Official Transfers
-312.2	-521.5	-482.9	-375.6	-322.2	-154.5	-105.4	-214.6	-214.7	-444.8	..	Curr. A/C Bal after Off. Transf.
100.4	392.2	481.4	345.6	238.8	120.7	126.4	123.3	117.8	69.8	..	Long-Term Capital, net
59.8	85.6	84.1	137.7	113.4	82.4	82.1	70.9	118.8	185.8	..	Direct Investment
63.8	337.4	448.7	376.9	159.0	229.3	269.6	112.3	112.0	223.0	..	Long-Term Loans
135.4	418.9	564.2	532.4	378.0	419.9	438.5	302.5	399.8	577.4	..	Disbursements
71.6	81.5	115.5	155.5	219.0	190.6	168.9	190.2	287.8	354.4	..	Repayments
-23.2	-30.8	-51.4	-169.1	-33.6	-191.0	-225.3	-60.0	-113.1	-339.0	..	Other Long-Term Capital
142.9	78.3	-34.4	127.2	130.4	30.9	-22.2	88.4	17.4	313.0	..	Other Capital, net
68.9	51.0	35.9	-97.2	-47.1	3.0	1.2	3.0	79.6	62.0	..	Change in Reserves
				(Papua New Guinea Kina per US dollar)							Memo Item:
0.670	0.670	0.740	0.830	0.890	1.000	0.970	0.910	0.870	0.860	..	Conversion Factor (Annual Avg)
				(Millions of US dollars), outstanding at end of year							
719.0	1,184.5	1,627.6	1,868.0	2,029.6	2,113.1	1,984.8	2,291.9	2,294.2	2,496.0	..	**EXTERNAL DEBT (Total)**
655.0	1,022.5	1,445.6	1,801.0	1,884.6	1,967.1	1,922.8	2,186.9	2,159.3	2,331.3	..	Long-Term Debt (by debtor)
30.9	75.1	71.2	67.6	33.9	28.9	15.1	12.0	6.1	3.0	..	Central Bank, incl. IMF credit
459.9	563.1	652.6	837.4	880.9	971.8	1,102.8	1,298.6	1,137.3	1,095.7	..	Central Government
..	..	..	..	..	..	..	..	..	..	..	Rest of General Government
0.0	19.1	38.4	47.6	57.8	68.8	106.0	118.8	134.8	253.7	..	Non-financial Public Enterprises
164.2	365.2	683.4	848.4	912.0	897.6	698.9	757.5	881.1	978.9	..	Priv. Sector, incl non-guaranteed
64.0	162.0	182.0	67.0	145.0	146.0	62.0	105.0	134.9	164.7	..	Short-Term Debt
				(Millions of US dollars)							Memo Items:
423.43	396.17	452.88	440.07	435.23	442.57	425.46	436.83	393.49	384.38	..	Int'l Reserves Excluding Gold
34.33	24.72	28.50	23.90	19.37	20.57	24.61	30.50	25.84	25.26	..	Gold Holdings (at market price)
											SOCIAL INDICATORS
5.7	5.6	5.6	5.5	5.4	5.4	5.3	5.3	5.2	5.1	..	Total Fertility Rate
78.4	76.2	74.0	71.8	69.6	67.4	65.2	63.0	61.4	59.9	..	Infant Mortality Rate
51.1	51.5	51.9	52.3	52.8	53.2	53.6	54.0	54.2	54.4	..	Life Expectancy at Birth
13.0	13.3	13.5	13.8	14.0	14.3	14.6	14.9	15.2	15.5	..	Urban Population, % of total
104.6	103.8	107.4	104.8	107.5	105.7	102.7	100.0	100.2	99.2	..	Food Prod. per capita (1987=100)
11.2	..	..	..	..	..	..	..	..	..	..	Labor Force, Agriculture (%)
33.9	34.0	34.2	34.3	34.4	34.5	34.6	34.7	34.7	34.8	..	Labor Force, Female (%)
59.0	..	60.0	..	..	..	..	70.0	..	..	..	Primary Schl. Enroll. Ratio
51.0	..	53.0	..	..	..	..	64.0	..	..	..	Primary Schl. Enroll. Ratio, Female
12.0	..	11.0	..	..	..	..	12.0	..	..	..	Secondary Schl. Enroll. Ratio

PARAGUAY	1969	1970	1971	1972	1973	1974	1975	1976	1977	1978	1979
CURRENT GNP PER CAPITA (US $)	240	260	270	300	350	440	550	620	720	830	1,030
POPULATION (thousands)	2,290	2,351	2,409	2,470	2,536	2,606	2,682	2,764	2,853	2,947	3,046
USE AND ORIGIN OF RESOURCES	*(Billions of current Paraguayan Guaranies)*										
Gross National Product (GNP)	68.5	73.7	82.5	94.9	123.3	166.0	188.9	212.1	261.5	319.4	428.3
Net Factor Income from Abroad	-1.5	-1.2	-1.3	-2.0	-2.1	-2.0	-1.5	-2.0	-2.1	-3.2	-2.2
GDP at Market Prices	70.1	74.9	83.7	96.9	125.4	168.0	190.4	214.1	263.6	322.5	430.5
Resource Balance	-3.2	-0.9	-2.2	-0.1	0.9	-3.8	-10.4	-7.2	-7.9	-11.9	-23.7
Exports of Goods & NFServices	9.5	11.2	11.2	13.3	18.8	26.1	25.2	31.4	51.3	59.4	69.1
Imports of Goods & NFServices	12.8	12.1	13.3	13.4	17.9	29.9	35.6	38.6	59.2	71.3	92.8
Domestic Absorption	73.3	75.8	85.9	97.0	124.6	171.8	200.8	221.3	271.5	334.5	454.2
Private Consumption, etc.	55.8	58.0	66.6	74.6	92.5	127.3	143.0	155.2	190.1	225.2	306.5
General Gov't Consumption	6.3	6.7	7.1	7.8	8.2	9.2	12.0	13.4	16.4	21.5	24.7
Gross Domestic Investment	11.2	11.0	12.2	14.6	23.9	35.3	45.9	52.7	65.1	87.7	123.0
Fixed Investment	10.8	10.9	11.8	13.3	20.4	30.9	39.5	48.7	62.9	81.3	116.1
Indirect Taxes, net	5.3	5.5	5.9	6.0	6.4	6.8	7.9	8.9	10.3	16.3	27.6
GDP at factor cost	64.8	69.4	77.9	90.9	119.0	161.2	182.6	205.1	253.3	306.2	402.9
Agriculture	22.8	24.0	27.8	33.4	47.3	59.3	70.3	74.0	89.9	103.4	135.2
Industry	14.0	15.5	17.4	19.8	25.6	38.1	40.0	47.5	60.8	76.7	102.1
Manufacturing	11.4	12.5	13.7	15.7	20.0	30.3	29.8	34.2	45.0	54.4	69.6
Services, etc.	33.3	35.4	38.5	43.7	52.6	70.7	80.1	92.6	112.9	142.4	193.2
Gross Domestic Saving	8.0	10.1	10.0	14.5	24.7	31.5	35.5	45.5	57.2	75.8	99.3
Gross National Saving	..	9.2	9.3	12.9	22.9	29.7	34.1	43.6	55.2	72.7	97.5
	(Billions of 1987 Paraguayan Guaranies)										
Gross National Product	884.68	932.63	984.76	1,042.56	1,120.45	1,220.20	1,304.61	1,390.41	1,576.37	1,720.79	1,925.19
GDP at Market Prices	905.00	948.82	1,000.39	1,064.87	1,141.23	1,236.42	1,316.04	1,405.41	1,555.17	1,725.44	1,916.50
Resource Balance	-7.12	24.27	0.48	19.10	-9.63	-36.25	-7.44	-67.82	-130.05	-130.28	76.31
Exports of Goods & NFServices	163.33	186.28	180.99	200.80	199.52	226.65	224.95	209.87	261.67	314.17	559.93
Imports of Goods & NFServices	170.44	162.01	180.51	181.69	209.15	262.90	232.39	277.69	391.72	444.44	483.62
Domestic Absorption	912.12	924.55	999.91	1,045.76	1,150.86	1,272.67	1,323.48	1,473.23	1,685.22	1,855.71	1,840.19
Private Consumption, etc.	704.38	712.63	773.10	798.48	845.61	946.42	964.38	1,046.27	1,204.03	1,251.31	1,163.15
General Gov't Consumption	71.58	76.99	77.29	77.37	70.13	63.61	77.33	82.74	94.71	110.39	102.85
Gross Domestic Investment	136.16	134.93	149.52	169.92	235.12	262.64	281.77	344.23	386.49	494.01	574.19
Fixed Investment	..	..	..	..	218.21	245.22	253.26	320.92	381.44	463.52	554.11
GDP at factor cost	837.27	879.74	930.50	999.19	1,083.58	1,186.62	1,262.11	1,347.15	1,494.44	1,638.44	1,793.74
Agriculture	299.44	317.99	322.41	334.88	356.23	391.05	423.00	438.61	467.63	491.18	523.75
Industry	182.63	198.21	213.53	228.61	251.38	271.36	278.20	303.05	361.26	418.05	480.76
Manufacturing	156.87	168.73	178.24	190.67	206.65	221.95	217.85	229.91	269.80	301.21	331.04
Services, etc.	418.26	428.44	459.18	495.13	527.04	566.12	605.39	655.64	720.04	813.46	912.25
Memo Items:											
Capacity to Import	127.15	149.91	151.44	180.74	219.31	229.34	164.43	225.68	339.58	370.20	360.27
Terms of Trade Adjustment	-36.18	-36.37	-29.55	-20.05	19.80	2.70	-60.51	15.81	77.91	56.03	-199.66
Gross Domestic Income	868.82	912.45	970.84	1,044.82	1,161.02	1,239.12	1,255.53	1,421.22	1,633.08	1,781.47	1,716.85
Gross National Income	848.50	896.26	955.21	1,022.51	1,140.25	1,222.90	1,244.09	1,406.22	1,654.27	1,776.82	1,725.54
DOMESTIC PRICES/DEFLATORS	*(Index 1987 = 100)*										
Overall (GDP)	7.7	7.9	8.4	9.1	11.0	13.6	14.5	15.2	17.0	18.7	22.5
Domestic Absorption	8.0	8.2	8.6	9.3	10.8	13.5	15.2	15.0	16.1	18.0	24.7
Agriculture	7.6	7.6	8.6	10.0	13.3	15.2	16.6	16.9	19.2	21.1	25.8
Industry	7.7	7.8	8.1	8.6	10.2	14.0	14.4	15.7	16.8	18.3	21.2
Manufacturing	7.3	7.4	7.7	8.2	9.7	13.7	13.7	14.9	16.7	18.1	21.0
Consumer Price Index	8.8	8.7	9.2	10.0	11.3	14.1	15.1	15.8	17.3	19.1	24.5
MANUFACTURING ACTIVITY											
Employment (1987=100)	..	..	..	..	..	..	..	..	..	..	..
Real Earnings per Empl. (1987=100)	..	..	..	..	..	..	..	..	..	..	..
Real Output per Empl. (1987=100)	..	..	..	..	..	..	..	..	..	..	..
Earnings as % of Value Added	..	..	..	..	..	..	..	..	..	..	..
MONETARY HOLDINGS	*(Billions of current Paraguayan Guaranies)*										
Money Supply, Broadly Defined	11.86	13.51	15.24	18.84	24.30	29.38	37.09	45.75	60.15	78.49	97.49
Money	6.56	7.31	7.85	9.42	12.49	15.12	17.83	21.59	28.57	39.81	49.54
Currency Outside Banks	3.45	4.02	4.41	5.14	6.49	7.55	8.90	10.29	13.34	18.69	24.31
Demand Deposits	3.10	3.29	3.44	4.28	6.00	7.57	8.93	11.30	15.23	21.12	25.22
Quasi-Money	5.30	6.20	7.39	9.42	11.81	14.26	19.26	24.16	31.58	38.68	47.95
GOVERNMENT DEFICIT (-) OR SURPLUS	*(Billions of current Paraguayan Guaranies)*										
	..	..	..	-1.61	-0.04	1.74	-0.56	-2.22	1.63	3.06	4.34
Current Revenue	..	..	..	10.94	13.41	18.40	21.16	23.89	31.33	40.81	51.15
Current Expenditure	..	..	..	10.25	11.29	13.82	17.09	18.79	21.79	26.36	32.41
Current Budget Balance	..	..	..	0.69	2.12	4.58	4.08	5.10	9.54	14.46	18.73
Capital Receipts	..	..	..	0.10	0.08	0.04	0.03	0.03	0.04	0.04	0.09
Capital Payments	..	..	..	2.40	2.24	2.88	4.67	7.35	7.96	11.44	14.49

1980	1981	1982	1983	1984	1985	1986	1987	1988	1989 estimate	NOTES	PARAGUAY
1,340	1,680	1,740	1,640	1,490	1,170	950	890	970	1,030	A	CURRENT GNP PER CAPITA (US $)
3,147	3,251	3,358	3,468	3,579	3,693	3,808	3,925	4,042	4,161	..	POPULATION (thousands)
			(Billions of current Paraguayan Guaranies)								USE AND ORIGIN OF RESOURCES
582.2	737.2	762.0	835.8	1,086.9	1,347.7	1,757.8	2,384.9	3,204.1	4,565.9	..	Gross National Product (GNP)
5.3	8.8	8.3	5.0	-2.4	-46.2	-76.0	-109.2	-115.1	-54.5	..	Net Factor Income from Abroad
576.9	728.4	753.7	830.8	1,089.3	1,393.9	1,833.8	2,494.1	3,319.2	4,620.4	..	GDP at Market Prices
-77.3	-84.8	-73.3	-28.1	-69.0	-123.2	-177.8	-253.5	-57.2	-294.1	..	Resource Balance
88.3	83.9	91.1	116.1	189.3	292.0	441.0	554.6	877.1	1,566.7	..	Exports of Goods & NFServices
165.6	168.7	164.4	144.2	258.4	415.2	618.8	808.1	934.2	1,860.8	..	Imports of Goods & NFServices
654.2	813.2	827.1	858.9	1,158.4	1,517.1	2,011.6	2,747.6	3,376.4	4,914.5	..	Domestic Absorption
458.3	560.3	585.9	625.6	843.6	1,120.4	1,430.9	1,959.0	2,382.6	3,664.2	..	Private Consumption, etc.
34.7	48.6	52.3	58.0	69.3	90.2	121.8	162.8	185.0	280.0	..	General Gov't Consumption
161.2	204.3	188.9	175.2	245.5	306.5	458.9	625.8	808.8	970.3	..	Gross Domestic Investment
152.7	194.2	176.9	164.5	231.2	288.0	431.8	591.4	768.2	..	..	Fixed Investment
34.5	41.9	48.2	45.1	50.7	66.2	89.5	121.7	158.9		..	Indirect Taxes, net
542.4	686.5	705.5	785.7	1,038.6	1,327.7	1,744.3	2,372.4	3,160.3	..	B	GDP at factor cost
165.1	196.8	190.6	211.6	307.1	403.3	498.9	681.9	983.3	1,362.8	..	Agriculture
158.3	203.2	208.4	226.1	288.2	357.4	481.5	641.5	735.1	1,035.0	..	Industry
92.3	118.5	121.0	134.3	172.0	226.1	296.0	404.1	556.0	788.5	..	Manufacturing
253.5	328.5	354.6	393.1	494.0	633.2	853.4	1,170.6	1,600.8	2,222.6	..	Services, etc.
83.9	119.5	115.6	147.2	176.4	183.3	281.1	372.3	751.6	676.2	..	Gross Domestic Saving
89.2	128.6	124.0	152.3	174.5	139.4	208.9	277.9	655.9	637.5	..	Gross National Saving
			(Billions of 1987 Paraguayan Guaranies)								
2,211.76	2,411.52	2,372.13	2,203.79	2,262.41	2,334.23	2,299.00	2,384.90	2,555.11	2,793.48	..	Gross National Product
2,193.93	2,383.00	2,348.35	2,231.08	2,301.00	2,392.38	2,389.59	2,494.10	2,655.32	2,816.20	..	GDP at Market Prices
-369.91	-354.50	-275.48	-109.45	-168.52	-166.54	-188.34	-253.52	-97.79	-103.88	..	Resource Balance
336.73	345.38	384.22	343.06	410.92	401.30	607.98	554.60	712.42	802.59	..	Exports of Goods & NFServices
706.64	699.87	659.70	452.51	579.44	567.84	796.32	808.12	810.21	906.47	..	Imports of Goods & NFServices
2,563.84	2,737.50	2,623.83	2,340.53	2,469.51	2,558.92	2,577.93	2,747.62	2,753.11	2,920.08	..	Domestic Absorption
1,752.94	1,785.94	1,806.75	1,641.35	1,770.62	1,848.36	1,843.32	1,959.00	1,923.73	2,120.61	..	Private Consumption, etc.
117.41	140.25	143.38	147.90	139.22	144.83	147.99	162.80	179.09	211.77	..	General Gov't Consumption
693.49	811.30	673.70	551.28	559.67	565.73	586.63	625.82	650.28	587.70	..	Gross Domestic Investment
674.84	796.31	649.76	533.35	537.97	539.81	556.56	591.42	613.31	..	..	Fixed Investment
2,062.21	2,245.64	2,198.01	2,109.94	2,193.93	2,278.78	2,272.97	2,372.40	2,528.33	..	B	GDP at factor cost
568.30	625.46	627.99	612.66	648.89	678.71	637.29	681.93	764.22	843.60	..	Agriculture
628.35	672.65	642.19	597.87	618.21	619.40	630.99	641.53	658.68	614.01	..	Industry
375.06	391.22	376.75	360.85	377.09	395.94	390.39	404.05	427.62	454.72	..	Manufacturing
1,002.51	1,089.33	1,080.73	1,020.55	1,033.89	1,094.27	1,121.32	1,170.63	1,232.42	1,358.59	..	Services, etc.
											Memo Items:
376.90	348.03	365.37	364.47	424.59	399.38	567.55	554.60	760.63	763.20	..	Capacity to Import
40.17	2.66	-18.85	21.40	13.67	-1.92	-40.43	0.00	48.21	-39.39	..	Terms of Trade Adjustment
2,234.10	2,385.66	2,329.50	2,252.48	2,314.66	2,390.46	2,349.16	2,494.10	2,703.53	2,776.81	..	Gross Domestic Income
2,251.93	2,414.18	2,353.28	2,225.19	2,276.08	2,332.31	2,258.56	2,384.90	2,603.32	2,754.09	..	Gross National Income
			(Index 1987 = 100)								DOMESTIC PRICES/DEFLATORS
26.3	30.6	32.1	37.2	47.3	58.3	76.7	100.0	125.0	164.1	..	Overall (GDP)
25.5	29.7	31.5	36.7	46.9	59.3	78.0	100.0	122.6	168.3	..	Domestic Absorption
29.1	31.5	30.4	34.5	47.3	59.4	78.3	100.0	128.7	161.5	..	Agriculture
25.2	30.2	32.5	37.8	46.6	57.7	76.3	100.0	111.6	168.6	..	Industry
24.6	30.3	32.1	37.2	45.6	57.1	75.8	100.0	130.0	173.4	..	Manufacturing
30.0	34.2	36.5	41.4	49.8	62.3	82.1	100.0	122.8	155.0	..	Consumer Price Index
											MANUFACTURING ACTIVITY
..	..	..	..	..	..	..	..	..	..	..	Employment (1987=100)
..	..	..	..	..	..	..	..	..	..	..	Real Earnings per Empl. (1987=100)
..	..	..	..	..	..	..	..	..	..	..	Real Output per Empl. (1987=100)
..	..	..	..	..	..	..	..	..	..	..	Earnings as % of Value Added
			(Billions of current Paraguayan Guaranies)								MONETARY HOLDINGS
131.26	156.79	165.69	193.42	225.94	272.94	347.65	469.34	563.22	..	..	Money Supply, Broadly Defined
62.36	62.43	60.20	75.59	97.81	125.20	158.67	243.67	328.49	..	..	Money
31.18	31.15	33.17	38.47	48.60	62.61	84.47	119.56	149.09	..	..	Currency Outside Banks
31.19	31.28	27.03	37.12	49.21	62.59	74.20	124.10	179.39	..	..	Demand Deposits
68.89	94.35	105.49	117.84	128.13	147.73	188.98	225.67	234.74	..	..	Quasi-Money
			(Billions of current Paraguayan Guaranies)								
1.81	-10.59	2.98	-7.73	-18.44	-6.91	0.52	-0.96	25.20	..	..	GOVERNMENT DEFICIT (-) OR SURPLUS
62.14	72.73	85.82	83.44	102.42	135.41	177.54	253.03	322.40	..	..	Current Revenue
43.13	57.39	72.36	72.89	90.12	106.20	133.79	179.43	218.73	..	..	Current Expenditure
19.01	15.35	13.45	10.55	12.30	29.21	43.75	73.60	103.67	..	..	Current Budget Balance
0.05	0.11	0.09	0.59	0.09	0.10	1.22	0.26	0.18	..	..	Capital Receipts
17.25	26.04	10.56	18.87	30.83	26.58	19.72	53.03	78.66	..	..	Capital Payments

PARAGUAY	1969	1970	1971	1972	1973	1974	1975	1976	1977	1978	1979
FOREIGN TRADE (CUSTOMS BASIS)					*(Millions of current US dollars)*						
Value of Exports, fob	55.2	65.3	66.5	85.6	128.0	173.2	188.0	202.0	327.0	356.0	384.5
Nonfuel Primary Products	50.3	58.1	59.3	76.3	115.0	154.8	168.6	176.8	295.1	319.7	348.0
Fuels	0.1	0.0	0.0	0.0	0.5	1.0	1.2	1.3	1.3	2.0	2.0
Manufactures	4.8	7.2	7.2	9.3	12.5	17.3	18.2	23.9	30.6	34.3	34.5
Value of Imports, cif	95.0	91.0	98.0	93.0	149.0	229.0	262.0	289.0	435.0	521.0	687.0
Nonfuel Primary Products	35.3	28.8	29.4	26.6	41.8	54.5	70.9	85.7	141.7	156.3	192.8
Fuels	10.7	13.4	13.4	13.0	15.4	63.4	57.3	74.6	88.8	122.6	173.9
Manufactures	49.0	48.9	55.2	53.3	91.8	111.1	133.8	128.7	204.5	242.1	320.3
					(Index 1987 = 100)						
Terms of Trade	168.2	202.9	190.0	194.0	251.3	168.3	139.0	139.4	137.1	128.5	127.0
Export Prices, fob	39.9	45.5	49.0	53.7	91.9	95.6	83.4	88.0	97.7	97.7	115.0
Import Prices, cif	23.7	22.4	25.8	27.7	36.5	56.8	60.0	63.1	71.3	76.0	90.6
BALANCE OF PAYMENTS					*(Millions of current US dollars)*						
Exports of Goods & Services	..	89.7	90.1	106.4	151.0	212.7	233.8	257.8	419.6	489.1	593.7
Merchandise, fob	..	65.3	66.5	85.6	128.0	173.2	188.0	202.1	327.1	356.1	384.5
Nonfactor Services	..	24.0	22.6	19.9	21.5	34.0	34.1	39.9	62.9	78.2	129.1
Factor Services	..	0.4	1.0	1.0	1.5	5.5	11.7	15.8	29.6	54.8	80.1
Imports of Goods & Services	..	111.3	120.2	118.2	172.7	269.3	320.0	330.5	479.5	607.8	807.0
Merchandise, fob	..	76.6	82.9	78.7	127.3	198.3	227.3	236.4	360.1	432.0	577.1
Nonfactor Services	..	21.8	23.5	26.5	31.8	45.3	55.1	57.8	72.1	95.6	154.2
Factor Services	..	12.9	13.7	13.0	13.6	25.6	37.6	36.3	47.3	80.2	75.7
Long-Term Interest	..	3.5	4.6	5.7	5.8	6.7	8.5	9.6	12.9	17.9	29.9
Private Current Transfers, net	..	2.3	4.4	2.6	2.3	1.8	1.0	0.9	0.7	0.6	3.1
Workers' Remittances	..	..	..	..	..	..	0.5	0.3	0.4	0.4	1.4
Curr. A/C Bal before Off. Transf.	..	-19.3	-25.7	-9.2	-19.4	-54.7	-85.2	-71.8	-59.2	-118.1	-210.2
Net Official Transfers	..	2.9	3.2	3.9	3.5	2.0	13.0	3.3	0.5	5.2	4.3
Curr. A/C Bal after Off. Transf.	..	-16.4	-22.5	-5.3	-16.0	-52.7	-72.2	-68.5	-58.7	-112.9	-205.9
Long-Term Capital, net	..	18.8	24.6	20.4	29.6	52.9	85.9	117.3	85.2	166.4	135.5
Direct Investment	..	3.8	7.1	2.9	9.2	20.7	24.4	-3.0	21.7	19.6	50.2
Long-Term Loans	..	7.3	9.4	6.7	9.0	31.0	43.3	54.4	112.6	125.7	132.5
Disbursements	..	14.4	17.8	16.3	19.9	47.0	65.0	76.2	142.6	158.0	186.5
Repayments	..	7.1	8.4	9.6	10.9	16.0	21.7	21.8	30.0	32.3	54.0
Other Long-Term Capital	..	7.7	8.1	10.8	11.4	1.2	18.2	65.9	-49.1	21.1	-47.2
Other Capital, net	..	3.2	-1.4	-7.8	7.4	30.0	15.9	-8.1	83.1	123.4	230.1
Change in Reserves	..	-5.6	-0.7	-7.3	-21.0	-30.3	-29.6	-40.7	-109.6	-176.9	-159.7
Memo Item:					*(Paraguayan Guaranies per US dollar)*						
Conversion Factor (Annual Avg)	126.000	126.000	126.000	126.000	126.000	126.000	126.000	126.000	126.000	126.000	126.000
					(Millions of US dollars), outstanding at end of year						
EXTERNAL DEBT (Total)	..	112.4	123.5	137.0	150.9	187.6	228.2	281.8	452.4	615.1	806.8
Long-Term Debt (by debtor)	..	112.4	123.5	137.0	150.9	187.6	228.2	281.8	398.4	531.1	661.8
Central Bank, incl. IMF credit	..	16.3	18.7	27.6	26.9	31.5	36.4	39.7	43.1	48.3	50.5
Central Government	..	57.9	64.8	69.0	74.2	77.7	96.5	127.7	151.2	191.3	267.4
Rest of General Government	..	0.4	0.2	0.0	0.2	0.5	1.0	2.0	2.9	2.9	2.9
Non-financial Public Enterprises	..	35.5	38.0	39.0	44.2	50.7	52.0	62.7	133.7	198.0	201.0
Priv. Sector, incl non-guaranteed	..	2.3	1.8	1.4	5.4	27.2	42.3	49.7	67.5	90.6	140.0
Short-Term Debt	..	..	..	..	..	..	..	..	54.0	84.0	145.0
Memo Items:					*(Millions of US dollars)*						
Int'l Reserves Excluding Gold	10.3	17.5	21.0	31.4	57.0	87.1	115.0	157.5	267.8	448.7	609.1
Gold Holdings (at market price)	0.1	0.1	0.1	0.2	0.3	0.4	0.3	0.3	1.0	2.4	18.0
SOCIAL INDICATORS											
Total Fertility Rate	6.1	6.0	5.8	5.7	5.5	5.4	5.3	5.2	5.1	5.0	5.0
Infant Mortality Rate	61.4	58.6	55.8	53.0	52.2	51.4	50.6	49.8	49.0	48.2	47.4
Life Expectancy at Birth	65.2	65.3	65.5	65.6	65.7	65.8	65.8	65.9	66.0	66.1	66.2
Urban Population, % of total	36.9	37.1	37.5	37.9	38.2	38.6	39.0	39.5	40.1	40.6	41.2
Food Prod. per capita (1987=100)	82.9	87.4	87.4	85.4	85.1	87.8	83.4	86.3	91.1	88.8	93.7
Labor Force, Agriculture (%)	53.0	52.6	52.1	51.7	51.3	50.9	50.6	50.1	49.7	49.3	48.9
Labor Force, Female (%)	21.2	21.3	21.2	21.2	21.1	21.1	21.0	21.0	20.9	20.9	20.8
Primary Schl. Enroll. Ratio	..	109.0	..	..	..	..	102.0	103.0	102.0	102.0	102.0
Primary Schl. Enroll. Ratio, Female	..	103.0	..	..	..	..	97.0	99.0	98.0	98.0	98.0
Secondary Schl. Enroll. Ratio	..	17.0	..	..	..	..	20.0	23.0	23.0	24.0	26.0

1980	1981	1982	1983	1984	1985	1986	1987	1988	1989 estimate	NOTES	PARAGUAY
				(Millions of current US dollars)							**FOREIGN TRADE (CUSTOMS BASIS)**
400.3	398.5	396.2	326.0	361.3	324.4	573.4	951.6	1,097.0	..	..	Value of Exports, fob
358.4	359.2	354.6	296.9	329.3	287.4	508.1	829.9	964.0	..	..	Nonfuel Primary Products
0.1	0.7	0.6	0.1	1.0	0.0	0.0	6.5	4.0	..	..	Fuels
41.8	38.6	41.0	29.0	31.0	37.0	65.3	115.2	129.0	..	..	Manufactures
803.0	915.0	822.0	629.0	741.0	530.0	830.0	1,180.0	1,271.0	..	..	Value of Imports, cif
278.2	358.6	245.1	149.7	212.8	106.9	179.0	255.8	282.9	..	..	Nonfuel Primary Products
226.1	248.1	223.1	171.3	176.8	176.9	73.8	85.7	232.3	..	..	Fuels
298.7	308.4	353.8	308.0	351.4	246.2	577.2	838.5	755.7	..	..	Manufactures
				(Index 1987 = 100)							
107.0	100.0	99.3	113.5	109.9	91.9	95.2	100.0	115.3	..	..	Terms of Trade
118.8	113.7	104.0	114.9	113.0	91.9	88.4	100.0	117.7	..	..	Export Prices, fob
111.1	113.7	104.7	101.2	102.8	100.0	92.8	100.0	102.1	..	..	Import Prices, cif
				(Millions of current US dollars)							**BALANCE OF PAYMENTS**
781.2	772.2	792.4	632.6	742.2	728.3	840.4	853.8	1,182.9	1,360.0	..	Exports of Goods & Services
582.9	561.0	492.0	506.1	544.6	466.0	575.0	595.0	826.0	1,018.8	..	Merchandise, fob
118.1	104.9	177.5	63.3	126.9	183.5	204.9	230.4	286.2	284.0	..	Nonfactor Services
80.2	106.3	122.9	63.2	70.7	78.8	60.5	28.4	70.7	57.2	..	Factor Services
1,398.8	1,429.1	1,300.1	787.4	1,008.0	957.2	1,306.3	1,394.5	1,594.2	1,461.1	..	Imports of Goods & Services
1,054.3	1,070.0	847.9	544.2	705.1	659.0	879.0	933.0	1,040.0	874.3	..	Merchandise, fob
260.0	268.9	360.9	169.0	211.3	206.6	260.0	303.3	417.0	445.6	..	Nonfactor Services
84.5	90.2	91.3	74.2	91.6	91.6	167.3	158.2	137.2	141.2	..	Factor Services
44.5	36.3	45.2	47.2	59.8	79.0	90.3	93.7	113.0	64.8	..	Long-Term Interest
-0.3	2.5	1.5	1.4	2.5	7.5	11.1	27.0	35.3	15.0	..	Private Current Transfers, net
2.0	1.7	0.8	0.2	0.4	0.1	..	..	..	..	..	Workers' Remittances
-617.9	-654.4	-506.2	-153.4	-263.3	-221.4	-454.8	-513.7	-376.0	-86.1	..	Curr. A/C Bal before Off. Transf.
4.8	3.3	3.5	4.7	6.8	0.0	0.0	0.0	0.0	..	..	Net Official Transfers
-613.1	-651.1	-502.7	-148.7	-256.5	-221.4	-454.8	-513.7	-376.0	-86.1	..	Curr. A/C Bal after Off. Transf.
560.4	602.5	623.2	551.9	395.9	163.1	100.6	12.4	-103.4	-79.0	..	Long-Term Capital, net
29.8	26.2	33.7	5.5	0.5	8.3	31.0	8.5	6.2	21.0	..	Direct Investment
126.8	107.9	243.7	228.8	163.7	164.9	112.3	95.4	-39.7	125.0	..	Long-Term Loans
205.9	201.3	304.4	282.4	239.6	243.3	244.2	226.2	141.8	202.2	..	Disbursements
79.1	93.4	60.7	53.6	75.9	78.4	131.9	130.8	181.5	77.2	..	Repayments
403.8	468.4	345.8	317.6	231.7	-10.1	-42.7	-91.5	-69.9	-225.0	..	Other Long-Term Capital
203.6	80.6	-250.7	-436.8	-235.7	-46.3	180.6	429.8	290.4	217.0	..	Other Capital, net
-150.9	-32.0	130.2	33.6	96.3	104.6	173.6	71.5	189.0	-51.9	..	Change in Reserves
				(Paraguayan Guaranies per US dollar)							Memo Item:
126.000	126.000	136.000	146.000	243.700	440.700	517.400	668.000	840.000	1,120.000	..	Conversion Factor (Annual Avg)
				(Millions of US dollars), outstanding at end of year							
954.3	1,148.2	1,295.8	1,413.7	1,469.7	1,816.0	2,086.1	2,521.2	2,497.0	2,489.6	..	**EXTERNAL DEBT (Total)**
780.3	840.2	1,069.8	1,272.7	1,357.8	1,637.8	1,912.0	2,253.4	2,124.3	2,124.7	..	Long-Term Debt (by debtor)
50.5	52.1	56.4	54.7	46.0	46.2	43.8	54.0	49.8	45.0	..	Central Bank, incl. IMF credit
346.4	377.1	471.8	525.9	609.8	861.6	1,062.0	1,410.2	1,321.2	1,387.9	..	Central Government
3.2	2.2	2.2	3.2	3.5	3.8	4.1	6.5	5.8	4.1	..	Rest of General Government
228.2	275.2	407.6	495.7	520.1	554.2	647.7	754.3	719.1	660.4	..	Non-financial Public Enterprises
152.0	133.6	131.8	193.2	178.4	172.0	154.4	28.4	28.4	27.3	..	Priv. Sector, incl non-guaranteed
174.0	308.0	226.0	141.0	111.9	178.2	174.1	267.8	372.7	364.9	..	Short-Term Debt
				(Millions of US dollars)							Memo Items:
761.9	805.7	739.0	680.2	666.3	533.6	446.7	497.0	323.7	432.6	..	Int'l Reserves Excluding Gold
20.9	14.1	16.2	13.5	10.9	11.6	13.8	17.1	14.3	14.0	..	Gold Holdings (at market price)
											SOCIAL INDICATORS
4.9	4.9	4.8	4.8	4.7	4.7	4.6	4.6	4.5	4.5	..	Total Fertility Rate
46.6	45.8	45.0	44.4	43.8	43.2	42.6	42.0	41.4	40.9	..	Infant Mortality Rate
66.3	66.4	66.4	66.5	66.6	66.7	66.8	66.9	67.0	67.1	..	Life Expectancy at Birth
41.7	42.2	42.8	43.3	43.9	44.4	45.0	45.6	46.3	46.9	..	Urban Population, % of total
92.6	95.2	94.7	95.1	99.0	103.8	91.1	100.0	111.1	112.5	..	Food Prod. per capita (1987=100)
48.6	..	..	..	..	..	..	..	..	..	..	Labor Force, Agriculture (%)
20.8	20.8	20.8	20.8	20.8	20.8	20.8	20.8	20.7	20.7	..	Labor Force, Female (%)
104.0	..	103.0	103.0	103.0	103.0	102.0	..	..	..	..	Primary Schl. Enroll. Ratio
101.0	..	99.0	100.0	100.0	100.0	99.0	..	..	..	..	Primary Schl. Enroll. Ratio, Female
26.0	..	30.0	30.0	31.0	30.0	30.0	..	..	..	..	Secondary Schl. Enroll. Ratio

PERU	1969	1970	1971	1972	1973	1974	1975	1976	1977	1978	1979
CURRENT GNP PER CAPITA (US $)	490	520	580	620	700	850	1,000	1,040	970	840	850
POPULATION (thousands)	12,828	13,193	13,568	13,952	14,347	14,750	15,161	15,580	16,008	16,440	16,870
USE AND ORIGIN OF RESOURCES					*(Billions of current Peruvian Intis)*						
Gross National Product (GNP)	2.35E-1	2.75E-1	3.09E-1	3.42E-1	4.08E-1	5.16E-1	6.57E-1	8.55E-1	1.10E+0	1.80E+0	3.30E+0
Net Factor Income from Abroad	-6.97E-3	-4.51E-3	-3.75E-3	-4.17E-3	-6.27E-3	-6.23E-3	-8.69E-3	-2.01E-2	-1.07E-1	-8.77E-2	-2.11E-1
GDP at Market Prices	2.42E-1	2.80E-1	3.12E-1	3.46E-1	4.14E-1	5.22E-1	6.65E-1	8.76E-1	1.20E+0	1.90E+0	3.50E+0
Resource Balance	1.67E-3	5.26E-3	-2.98E-3	-2.27E-3	-8.59E-3	-3.89E-2	-7.38E-2	-7.16E-2	-8.14E-2	1.28E-2	3.02E-1
Exports of Goods & NFServices	4.34E-2	5.01E-2	4.44E-2	4.89E-2	5.67E-2	7.57E-2	7.22E-2	1.06E-1	1.90E-1	3.94E-1	9.68E-1
Imports of Goods & NFServices	4.18E-2	4.48E-2	4.74E-2	5.12E-2	6.53E-2	1.15E-1	1.46E-1	1.77E-1	2.71E-1	3.81E-1	6.66E-1
Domestic Absorption	2.41E-1	2.75E-1	3.15E-1	3.48E-1	4.23E-1	5.61E-1	7.39E-1	9.47E-1	1.30E+0	1.90E+0	3.20E+0
Private Consumption, etc.	1.57E-1	1.97E-1	2.21E-1	2.50E-1	2.85E-1	3.66E-1	4.93E-1	6.48E-1	8.77E-1	1.30E+0	2.10E+0
General Gov't Consumption	2.33E-2	3.42E-2	3.88E-2	4.55E-2	5.35E-2	6.00E-2	8.22E-2	1.07E-1	1.68E-1	2.12E-1	3.01E-1
Gross Domestic Investment	6.08E-2	4.34E-2	5.59E-2	5.27E-2	8.42E-2	1.35E-1	1.64E-1	1.92E-1	2.29E-1	3.68E-1	7.57E-1
Fixed Investment	4.74E-2	4.13E-2	4.83E-2	5.36E-2	8.22E-2	1.21E-1	1.47E-1	1.81E-1	2.47E-1	3.77E-1	7.24E-1
Indirect Taxes, net	2.13E-2	2.26E-2	2.47E-2	2.79E-2	3.04E-2	2.98E-2	4.57E-2	5.46E-2	-9.94E-1	1.65E-1	4.90E-1
GDP at factor cost	2.21E-1	2.57E-1	2.88E-1	3.18E-1	3.84E-1	4.92E-1	6.20E-1	8.21E-1	2.20E+0	1.70E+0	3.00E+0
Agriculture	4.36E-2	5.23E-2	5.56E-2	5.81E-2	6.83E-2	8.31E-2	1.09E-1	1.34E-1	1.87E-1	2.49E-1	4.08E-1
Industry	7.70E-2	8.84E-2	9.92E-2	1.11E-1	1.39E-1	1.81E-1	2.11E-1	2.99E-1	4.13E-1	7.28E-1	1.50E+0
Manufacturing	4.33E-2	5.54E-2	6.44E-2	7.03E-2	8.55E-2	1.13E-1	1.33E-1	1.90E-1	2.49E-1	4.33E-1	8.20E-1
Services, etc.	1.22E-1	1.39E-1	1.58E-1	1.77E-1	2.07E-1	2.58E-1	3.45E-1	4.42E-1	5.93E-1	9.24E-1	1.60E+0
Gross Domestic Saving	6.25E-2	4.87E-2	5.29E-2	5.04E-2	7.56E-2	9.61E-2	9.03E-2	1.20E-1	1.48E-1	3.81E-1	1.10E+0
Gross National Saving	..	4.52E-2	4.94E-2	4.65E-2	6.95E-2	9.07E-2	8.23E-2	1.01E-1	4.05E-2	2.94E-1	8.47E-1
					(Billions of 1987 Peruvian Intis)						
Gross National Product	405.0	434.0	454.0	466.0	489.0	536.0	554.0	559.0	558.0	549.0	572.0
GDP at Market Prices	419.0	442.0	460.0	473.0	497.0	543.0	562.0	573.0	575.0	577.0	610.0
Resource Balance	-23.4	-11.6	-16.4	-11.0	-31.3	-50.3	-47.1	-32.1	-25.2	4.4	6.5
Exports of Goods & NFServices	56.8	57.9	56.2	61.5	50.1	52.7	53.9	55.7	63.0	71.1	86.1
Imports of Goods & NFServices	80.1	69.5	72.7	72.5	81.4	103.0	101.0	87.9	88.2	66.7	79.5
Domestic Absorption	442.0	453.0	477.0	484.0	528.0	594.0	609.0	605.0	600.0	572.0	603.0
Private Consumption, etc.	275.0	324.0	331.0	345.0	342.0	357.0	373.0	387.0	392.0	382.0	400.0
General Gov't Consumption	42.8	51.7	55.3	58.9	62.5	66.2	73.6	77.1	88.2	77.0	69.7
Gross Domestic Investment	124.0	77.5	90.2	79.5	124.0	171.0	162.0	141.0	120.0	113.0	133.0
Fixed Investment	97.9	83.8	94.6	98.2	134.0	170.0	176.0	152.0	139.0	127.0	139.0
GDP at factor cost	..	404.0	421.0	433.0	432.0	489.0	529.0	542.0	565.0	515.0	515.0
Agriculture	56.6	62.4	61.2	57.5	57.0	59.8	59.5	60.8	60.4	60.1	62.7
Industry	136.0	148.0	153.0	159.0	170.0	186.0	188.0	195.0	197.0	203.0	220.0
Manufacturing	98.0	106.0	113.0	115.0	122.0	133.0	137.0	142.0	139.0	134.0	139.0
Services, etc.	221.0	225.0	241.0	252.0	268.0	295.0	315.0	317.0	316.0	310.0	323.0
Memo Items:											
Capacity to Import	83.3	77.7	68.1	69.2	70.7	68.4	49.7	52.3	61.7	68.9	116.0
Terms of Trade Adjustment	26.6	19.8	11.9	7.8	20.6	15.7	-4.2	-3.4	-1.3	-2.2	29.5
Gross Domestic Income	445.0	461.0	472.0	480.0	518.0	559.0	558.0	570.0	574.0	574.0	639.0
Gross National Income	432.0	454.0	466.0	474.0	509.0	552.0	550.0	555.0	556.0	547.0	601.0
DOMESTIC PRICES/DEFLATORS					*(Index 1987 = 100)*						
Overall (GDP)	5.79E-2	6.34E-2	6.78E-2	7.33E-2	8.33E-2	9.61E-2	1.18E-1	1.53E-1	2.07E-1	3.30E-1	5.72E-1
Domestic Absorption	5.44E-2	6.06E-2	6.61E-2	7.21E-2	8.00E-2	9.44E-2	1.21E-1	1.57E-1	2.12E-1	3.30E-1	5.29E-1
Agriculture	7.70E-2	8.38E-2	9.08E-2	1.01E-1	1.20E-1	1.39E-1	1.83E-1	2.21E-1	3.09E-1	4.15E-1	6.50E-1
Industry	5.67E-2	5.99E-2	6.49E-2	6.97E-2	8.17E-2	9.72E-2	1.12E-1	1.54E-1	2.10E-1	3.58E-1	6.80E-1
Manufacturing	4.41E-2	5.20E-2	5.72E-2	6.12E-2	6.99E-2	8.52E-2	9.74E-2	1.34E-1	1.78E-1	3.24E-1	5.89E-1
Consumer Price Index	6.11E-2	6.41E-2	6.85E-2	7.34E-2	8.04E-2	9.40E-2	1.16E-1	1.55E-1	2.14E-1	3.38E-1	5.63E-1
MANUFACTURING ACTIVITY											
Employment (1987=100)	61.6	64.4	51.2	69.4	69.8	..	..	..	..	..	87.2
Real Earnings per Empl. (1987=100)	102.9	..	..	126.4	124.8	..	..	..	..	..	101.2
Real Output per Empl. (1987=100)	102.3	117.1	149.1	118.9	126.1	..	..	..	..	..	121.8
Earnings as % of Value Added	22.6	..	..	20.5	18.4	..	..	..	..	..	14.8
MONETARY HOLDINGS					*(Millions of current Peruvian Intis)*						
Money Supply, Broadly Defined	42	57	62	77	95	127	147	182	225	362	695
Money	28	43	47	60	76	106	123	155	185	270	461
Currency Outside Banks	12	16	19	22	27	34	43	50	61	91	162
Demand Deposits	16	27	28	38	49	72	81	106	124	179	299
Quasi-Money	15	14	16	17	19	21	23	27	40	92	235
					(Millions of current Peruvian Intis)						
GOVERNMENT DEFICIT (-) OR SURPLUS	..	-1	-6	-3	-12	-10	-18	-32	-34	-85	-19
Current Revenue	..	39	39	52	52	67	89	114	163	263	551
Current Expenditure	..	36	35	40	50	57	81	111	146	291	442
Current Budget Balance	..	3	4	12	2	10	8	3	17	-28	109
Capital Receipts	..	..	..	..	..	..	..	..	..	..	..
Capital Payments	..	4	9	15	14	20	26	35	51	57	128

1980	1981	1982	1983	1984	1985	1986	1987	1988	1989 estimate	NOTES	PERU
990	1,240	1,380	1,150	1,120	980	1,080	1,170	1,040	1,010	..	**CURRENT GNP PER CAPITA (US $)**
17,295	17,716	18,134	18,550	18,965	19,383	19,806	20,237	20,681	21,142	..	**POPULATION (thousands)**
				(Billions of current Peruvian Intis)							**USE AND ORIGIN OF RESOURCES**
5.70	10.20	17.30	31.00	69.00	184.00	357.00	707.30	4,459.80	109,000.00	..	Gross National Product (GNP)
-0.28	-0.42	-0.64	-1.40	-3.40	-13.90	-17.00	-32.10	-350.50	-6,308.70	..	Net Factor Income from Abroad
6.00	10.70	17.90	32.40	72.40	197.90	374.00	739.40	4,810.20	115,000.00	..	GDP at Market Prices
0.00	-0.64	-1.00	-0.34	2.70	9.30	-8.10	-20.70	-94.10	2,766.80	..	Resource Balance
1.30	1.70	2.80	5.90	13.50	39.60	45.40	68.50	583.20	15,248.80	..	Exports of Goods & NFServices
1.30	2.40	3.80	6.20	10.80	30.30	53.50	89.20	677.30	12,481.90	..	Imports of Goods & NFServices
6.00	11.30	18.90	32.80	69.70	188.60	382.10	760.10	4,904.30	112,000.00	..	Domestic Absorption
3.70	6.70	11.10	21.10	45.50	123.40	255.00	497.60	3,188.10	78,073.50	..	Private Consumption, etc.
0.67	1.20	2.30	4.10	8.10	22.50	43.30	93.90	481.90	11,366.90	..	General Gov't Consumption
1.60	3.30	5.60	7.60	16.10	42.70	83.80	168.70	1,234.30	22,938.80	..	Gross Domestic Investment
1.40	2.80	4.90	7.40	16.30	42.30	83.40	157.30	1,179.60	22,284.50	..	Fixed Investment
0.97	0.66	1.90	2.40	5.40	19.80	30.50	50.10	249.50	4,728.00	..	Indirect Taxes, net
5.00	10.00	16.00	30.00	67.00	178.10	343.50	689.40	4,560.70	110,000.00	B	GDP at factor cost
0.61	1.10	1.70	3.40	8.00	18.60	41.90	76.10	398.60	8,763.10	..	Agriculture
2.50	4.10	6.90	12.00	27.70	84.00	134.50	253.30	2,036.30	35,117.30	f	Industry
1.20	2.00	3.30	5.90	14.40	48.10	90.70	172.80	1,538.80	24,075.20	..	Manufacturing
2.90	5.50	9.30	17.00	36.70	95.30	197.60	410.10	2,375.30	71,265.50	f	Services, etc.
1.60	2.70	4.60	7.30	18.80	52.00	75.70	148.00	1,140.20	25,705.60	..	Gross Domestic Saving
1.40	2.30	3.90	5.80	15.40	38.10	58.60	115.80	789.70	19,396.90	..	Gross National Saving
				(Billions of 1987 Peruvian Intis)							
607.0	639.0	641.0	552.0	575.0	581.0	651.0	707.0	631.0	571.0	..	Gross National Product
637.0	666.0	667.0	583.0	610.0	624.0	681.0	739.0	680.0	603.0	..	GDP at Market Prices
-25.8	-44.1	-42.5	-14.2	8.1	17.7	-3.8	-20.7	-12.0	13.7	..	Resource Balance
78.2	75.9	80.5	72.2	78.8	82.3	73.9	68.5	64.4	76.7	..	Exports of Goods & NFServices
104.0	120.0	123.0	86.4	70.7	64.5	77.7	89.2	76.5	63.0	..	Imports of Goods & NFServices
663.0	710.0	709.0	598.0	602.0	606.0	685.0	760.0	692.0	589.0	..	Domestic Absorption
396.0	408.0	412.0	387.0	408.0	421.0	465.0	498.0	460.0	410.0	..	Private Consumption, etc.
85.3	83.9	95.1	86.8	82.8	85.7	88.6	93.9	83.0	65.1	..	General Gov't Consumption
181.0	218.0	202.0	124.0	112.0	99.2	132.0	169.0	150.0	114.0	..	Gross Domestic Investment
170.0	197.0	193.0	135.0	126.0	112.0	133.0	157.0	140.0	111.0	..	Fixed Investment
559.0	593.0	593.0	529.0	551.0	550.0	621.0	689.0	646.0	571.0	B f	GDP at factor cost
58.7	64.0	65.9	58.8	65.8	68.2	72.4	76.1	82.2	79.7	..	Agriculture
232.0	234.0	235.0	197.0	206.0	211.0	232.0	253.0	225.0	196.0	..	Industry
147.0	148.0	147.0	120.0	127.0	132.0	153.0	173.0	155.0	127.0	..	Manufacturing
343.0	365.0	364.0	328.0	338.0	344.0	377.0	410.0	373.0	327.0	..	Services, etc.
											Memo Items:
104.0	87.6	89.9	81.6	88.3	84.4	65.9	68.5	65.8	77.0	..	Capacity to Import
25.6	11.8	9.4	9.4	9.5	2.1	-8.0	0.0	1.4	0.3	..	Terms of Trade Adjustment
663.0	678.0	677.0	593.0	620.0	626.0	673.0	739.0	682.0	603.0	..	Gross Domestic Income
632.0	651.0	650.0	561.0	585.0	583.0	644.0	707.0	632.0	572.0	..	Gross National Income
				(Index 1987 = 100)							**DOMESTIC PRICES/DEFLATORS**
9.37E-1	1.60E+0	2.70E+0	5.60E+0	11.9	31.7	54.9	100.0	707.1	19,093.8	..	Overall (GDP)
9.00E-1	1.60E+0	2.70E+0	5.50E+0	11.6	31.1	55.8	100.0	708.4	19,067.8	..	Domestic Absorption
1.00E+0	1.70E+0	2.60E+0	5.80E+0	12.1	27.3	57.9	100.0	485.1	10,989.7	..	Agriculture
1.10E+0	1.70E+0	2.90E+0	6.10E+0	13.4	39.8	57.8	100.0	904.2	17,873.1	..	Industry
8.19E-1	1.30E+0	2.20E+0	5.00E+0	11.4	36.3	59.2	100.0	993.5	18,918.7	..	Manufacturing
8.97E-1	1.57E+0	2.59E+0	5.46E+0	11.5	30.2	53.8	100.0	767.0	26,835.3	..	Consumer Price Index
											MANUFACTURING ACTIVITY
90.0	78.8	92.4	87.0	85.8	86.8	91.9	100.0	..	..	G	Employment (1987=100)
105.6	115.4	108.7	87.9	84.0	78.9	91.2	100.0	..	..	G	Real Earnings per Empl. (1987=100)
142.4	129.1	107.4	97.4	100.5	93.5	90.1	100.0	..	..	G	Real Output per Empl. (1987=100)
15.5	21.1	21.6	18.9	16.6	12.6	18.2	18.2	..	..	..	Earnings as % of Value Added
				(Millions of current Peruvian Intis)							**MONETARY HOLDINGS**
1,276	2,152	3,700	7,525	17,098	43,864	67,541	139,000	1,010,000	20,300,000	..	Money Supply, Broadly Defined
730	1,075	1,509	2,965	6,059	23,098	43,424	96,390	593,000	10,400,000	..	Money
273	437	621	1,116	2,502	8,145	16,435	41,945	261,000	5,370,000	..	Currency Outside Banks
456	638	888	1,849	3,557	14,954	26,989	54,445	331,000	5,030,000	..	Demand Deposits
546	1,077	2,191	4,560	11,038	20,765	24,117	43,091	413,000	9,880,000	..	Quasi-Money
				(Millions of current Peruvian Intis)							**GOVERNMENT DEFICIT (-) OR SURPLUS**
-142	-420	-557	-2,343	-3,020	-4,072	-13,392	-42,000	-123,000	..	..	Current Revenue
1,019	1,523	2,485	3,738	9,554	27,963	45,191	66,000	403,000	..	..	Current Revenue
898	1,504	2,456	5,065	10,306	27,255	47,755	92,000	458,000	..	..	Current Expenditure
121	19	29	-1,327	-752	708	-2,564	-26,000	-55,000	..	..	Current Budget Balance
..	..	9	3	92	272	140	..	..	..	..	Capital Receipts
263	439	595	1,019	2,360	5,052	10,968	17,000	68,000	..	..	Capital Payments

PERU	1969	1970	1971	1972	1973	1974	1975	1976	1977	1978	1979

FOREIGN TRADE (CUSTOMS BASIS)

(Millions of current US dollars)

Value of Exports, fob	865.5	1,044.4	892.9	944.4	1,049.5	1,517.4	1,290.9	1,359.5	1,725.6	1,940.7	3,490.9
Nonfuel Primary Products	846.6	1,021.0	875.3	919.9	1,006.4	1,446.0	1,210.4	1,245.4	1,553.8	1,567.6	2,342.3
Fuels	6.2	7.5	5.6	8.0	12.9	18.2	43.6	53.3	53.4	177.7	651.8
Manufactures	12.7	15.9	12.0	16.5	30.3	53.2	36.9	60.8	118.3	195.5	496.8
Value of Imports, cif	600.0	621.7	749.6	796.3	1,024.2	1,595.3	2,379.6	1,798.0	1,598.3	1,601.0	1,951.0
Nonfuel Primary Products	158.5	158.0	177.7	187.3	187.1	311.0	474.0	307.1	294.5	297.7	374.5
Fuels	21.0	14.3	30.3	49.1	61.7	204.7	288.1	299.4	319.3	77.3	47.2
Manufactures	420.5	449.5	541.6	559.9	775.4	1,079.6	1,617.5	1,191.5	984.6	1,226.0	1,529.3

(Index 1987 = 100)

Terms of Trade	177.2	175.0	155.7	167.1	226.0	188.8	125.0	150.0	146.1	127.8	142.3
Export Prices, fob	48.3	51.1	46.1	52.4	86.3	102.0	72.2	87.5	93.4	89.9	114.7
Import Prices, cif	27.3	29.2	29.6	31.4	38.2	54.0	57.8	58.3	63.9	70.3	80.6

BALANCE OF PAYMENTS

(Millions of current US dollars)

Exports of Goods & Services	..	1,239	1,086	1,166	1,369	1,880	1,723	1,755	2,144	2,416	4,143
Merchandise, fob	..	1,034	890	945	1,112	1,506	1,291	1,360	1,726	1,941	3,491
Nonfactor Services	..	190	178	209	231	336	398	385	406	459	594
Factor Services	..	15	19	13	25	39	34	10	13	16	58
Imports of Goods & Services	..	1,119	1,159	1,237	1,673	2,653	3,313	3,007	3,123	2,664	3,536
Merchandise, fob	..	699	730	812	1,097	1,909	2,389	2,099	2,164	1,601	1,951
Nonfactor Services	..	272	285	291	387	534	648	526	523	470	560
Factor Services	..	148	144	134	188	211	276	381	436	594	1,025
Long-Term Interest	..	162	163	163	229	266	324	336	411	475	576
Private Current Transfers, net	..	26	4	7	4	22	17	4	3	3	0
Workers' Remittances	..	..	..	..	..	..	..	..	..	..	..
Curr. A/C Bal before Off. Transf.	..	146	-69	-64	-300	-752	-1,574	-1,249	-976	-245	607
Net Official Transfers	..	56	35	33	38	27	33	55	54	53	122
Curr. A/C Bal after Off. Transf.	..	202	-34	-32	-262	-725	-1,541	-1,193	-922	-192	729
Long-Term Capital, net	..	-17	9	106	408	720	1,293	807	955	264	541
Direct Investment	..	-70	-58	24	70	58	316	170	54	25	71
Long-Term Loans	..	54	71	96	350	1,119	1,233	1,015	603	186	444
Disbursements	..	387	424	466	888	1,669	1,754	1,538	1,318	900	1,172
Repayments	..	333	354	370	538	549	521	523	715	713	729
Other Long-Term Capital	..	-1	-3	-13	-13	-457	-256	-378	297	52	26
Other Capital, net	..	61	-26	-79	-59	410	-270	-4	14	-56	-122
Change in Reserves	..	-246	51	4	-87	-405	517	390	-46	-16	-1,148

Memo Item:

(Peruvian Intis per US dollar)

Conversion Factor (Annual Avg)	0.0387	0.0387	0.0387	0.0387	0.0387	0.0387	0.0405	0.0564	0.0838	0.1560	0.2250

EXTERNAL DEBT (Total)

(Millions of US dollars), outstanding at end of year

EXTERNAL DEBT (Total)	..	2,665	2,745	2,874	3,229	4,349	5,077	6,287	9,171	9,717	9,269
Long-Term Debt (by debtor)	..	2,665	2,745	2,874	3,229	4,349	5,077	6,287	7,071	7,619	7,695
Central Bank, incl. IMF credit	..	38	34	63	238	709	836	1,282	1,563	1,766	1,997
Central Government	..	476	478	584	685	720	1,132	1,318	1,913	2,330	2,741
Rest of General Government	..	18	15	11	7	4	1	1	1	1	0
Non-financial Public Enterprises	..	317	364	418	518	780	1,044	1,241	1,450	1,568	1,684
Priv. Sector, incl non-guaranteed	..	1,817	1,854	1,798	1,780	2,136	2,063	2,444	2,143	1,954	1,273
Short-Term Debt	..	0	0	0	0	0	0	0	2,100	2,098	1,574

Memo Items:

(Millions of US dollars)

Int'l Reserves Excluding Gold	142.2	296.3	380.9	442.5	526.1	925.2	425.5	289.4	356.8	389.7	1,520.7
Gold Holdings (at market price)	25.0	42.4	49.4	70.7	112.6	187.1	140.7	135.2	165.4	226.9	592.9

SOCIAL INDICATORS

Total Fertility Rate	6.2	6.0	5.9	5.7	5.6	5.4	5.3	5.1	5.0	4.9	4.8
Infant Mortality Rate	119.6	116.4	113.2	110.0	109.0	108.0	107.0	106.0	105.0	103.8	102.6
Life Expectancy at Birth	53.1	53.9	54.7	55.6	55.8	56.1	56.4	56.7	57.0	57.3	57.6
Urban Population, % of total	56.3	57.4	58.2	59.0	59.8	60.6	61.4	62.0	62.6	63.3	63.9
Food Prod. per capita (1987=100)	127.7	134.9	133.3	126.0	123.5	123.9	118.1	116.1	113.5	108.0	105.5
Labor Force, Agriculture (%)	47.6	47.1	46.3	45.5	44.8	44.1	43.5	42.7	42.0	41.3	40.6
Labor Force, Female (%)	20.3	20.3	20.7	21.2	21.6	21.9	22.3	22.7	23.1	23.5	23.9
Primary Schl. Enroll. Ratio	..	107.0	..	..	..	..	113.0	112.0	112.0	113.0	112.0
Primary Schl. Enroll. Ratio, Female	..	99.0	..	..	..	..	..	107.0	108.0	109.0	108.0
Secondary Schl. Enroll. Ratio	..	31.0	..	..	..	..	46.0	47.0	50.0	55.0	56.0

1980	1981	1982	1983	1984	1985	1986	1987	1988	1989 estimate	NOTES	PERU
											FOREIGN TRADE (CUSTOMS BASIS)
3,898.3	3,249.0	3,293.3	3,015.2	3,147.0	2,966.0	2,530.6	2,661.0	2,695.0	..	f	Value of Exports, fob
2,455.4	1,986.7	2,083.8	1,979.7	1,854.6	1,688.5	1,670.6	1,852.0	1,919.0	..	..	Nonfuel Primary Products
776.8	690.8	718.9	544.2	650.3	641.7	287.0	338.0	206.0	..	..	Fuels
666.1	571.4	490.6	491.3	642.1	635.8	573.0	471.0	570.0	..	..	Manufactures
3,062.0	3,803.0	3,721.0	2,722.0	2,212.0	2,023.3	2,908.8	3,562.0	3,080.0	..	..	Value of Imports, cif
675.3	795.7	604.6	575.7	424.2	367.0	453.1	654.0	706.0	..	..	Nonfuel Primary Products
63.0	40.8	49.1	78.9	43.6	36.0	20.4	29.0	31.0	..	..	Fuels
2,323.7	2,966.4	3,067.3	2,067.4	1,744.2	1,620.3	2,435.3	2,879.0	2,343.0	..	..	Manufactures
				(Index 1987 = 100)							
141.2	129.7	119.7	115.7	117.0	112.3	93.8	100.0	107.0	..	..	Terms of Trade
127.6	116.2	101.8	99.3	97.0	92.7	87.0	100.0	118.9	..	..	Export Prices, fob
90.3	89.6	85.0	85.8	82.9	82.5	92.8	100.0	111.1	..	..	Import Prices, cif
				(Millions of current US dollars)							**BALANCE OF PAYMENTS**
4,832	4,223	4,186	3,842	3,974	3,925	3,460	3,659	3,734	4,599	..	Exports of Goods & Services
3,916	3,249	3,293	3,015	3,147	2,978	2,531	2,661	2,691	3,542	..	Merchandise, fob
715	770	784	711	670	814	836	931	1,000	979	..	Nonfactor Services
202	204	109	116	157	133	93	67	43	78	..	Factor Services
5,080	6,112	5,962	4,933	4,353	3,923	4,687	5,320	4,987	4,246	..	Imports of Goods & Services
3,090	3,802	3,721	2,722	2,140	1,806	2,596	3,182	2,790	2,140	..	Merchandise, fob
880	1,087	1,098	965	891	984	1,179	1,353	1,371	1,365	..	Nonfactor Services
1,111	1,223	1,143	1,246	1,322	1,133	912	785	826	741	..	Factor Services
670	670	696	539	539	457	271	160	62	96	..	Long-Term Interest
0	0	0	0	0	0	0	0	0	..	..	Private Current Transfers, net
..	..	..	..	..	..	..	..	..	..	..	Workers' Remittances
-248	-1,889	-1,776	-1,091	-379	3	-1,227	-1,661	-1,253	353	..	Curr. A/C Bal before Off. Transf.
147	161	167	219	158	134	150	180	157	155	..	Net Official Transfers
-101	-1,728	-1,609	-872	-221	137	-1,077	-1,481	-1,096	508	..	Curr. A/C Bal after Off. Transf.
277	356	1,136	1,237	-119	-619	-1,187	-1,226	-1,271	-848	..	Long-Term Capital, net
27	125	48	38	-89	1	22	32	26	59	..	Direct Investment
365	286	1,407	1,321	1,124	197	211	449	187	425	..	Long-Term Loans
1,478	1,817	2,563	1,897	1,595	712	606	625	263	548	..	Disbursements
1,113	1,531	1,156	576	471	514	395	175	76	122	..	Repayments
-115	-55	-319	-122	-1,154	-817	-1,420	-1,707	-1,484	-1,332	..	Other Long-Term Capital
461	683	390	-399	590	669	1,968	2,039	2,377	934	..	Other Capital, net
-637	689	84	34	-250	-186	295	668	-10	-594	..	Change in Reserves
				(Peruvian Intis per US dollar)							**Memo Item:**
0.2890	0.4220	0.6980	1.6300	3.4700	11.7000	15.4600	26.9800	252.2300	4,024.5600	..	Conversion Factor (Annual Avg)
				(Millions of US dollars), outstanding at end of year							
10,038	10,319	12,305	12,061	13,099	14,279	16,154	18,645	18,998	19,876	..	**EXTERNAL DEBT (Total)**
7,954	7,840	9,281	10,526	11,349	12,383	13,399	15,010	14,730	15,017	..	Long-Term Debt (by debtor)
1,783	1,463	1,641	1,587	1,712	1,827	1,960	2,197	2,129	2,077	..	Central Bank, incl. IMF credit
3,089	3,248	4,245	5,389	6,082	6,883	7,496	8,378	8,237	8,437	..	Central Government
0	0	0	0	0	0	0	0	0	0	..	Rest of General Government
1,750	1,679	1,686	1,933	2,054	2,293	2,564	2,952	2,895	2,869	..	Non-financial Public Enterprises
1,332	1,450	1,710	1,618	1,501	1,380	1,380	1,484	1,468	1,633	..	Priv. Sector, incl non-guaranteed
2,084	2,479	3,024	1,536	1,750	1,896	2,754	3,634	4,269	4,859	..	Short-Term Debt
				(Millions of US dollars)							**Memo Items:**
1,979.9	1,199.5	1,349.7	1,365.7	1,630.5	1,842.0	1,407.2	645.8	511.0	808.4	..	Int'l Reserves Excluding Gold
824.1	555.7	638.8	533.3	431.0	639.0	835.4	724.7	702.4	788.8	..	Gold Holdings (at market price)
											SOCIAL INDICATORS
4.7	4.6	4.5	4.4	4.3	4.2	4.1	4.1	4.0	3.9	..	Total Fertility Rate
101.4	100.2	99.0	96.8	94.6	92.4	90.2	88.0	86.0	84.1	..	Infant Mortality Rate
57.9	58.3	58.6	59.2	59.7	60.3	60.9	61.4	61.8	62.1	..	Life Expectancy at Birth
64.5	65.1	65.7	66.2	66.8	67.4	68.0	68.5	69.1	69.6	..	Urban Population, % of total
93.5	100.3	104.7	95.6	103.6	96.7	94.0	100.0	103.9	97.7	..	Food Prod. per capita (1987=100)
40.0	..	..	..	..	..	..	..	..	..	..	Labor Force, Agriculture (%)
24.2	24.2	24.2	24.2	24.2	24.2	24.2	24.2	24.1	24.1	..	Labor Force, Female (%)
114.0	115.0	118.0	..	..	122.0	..	..	..	..	..	Primary Schl. Enroll. Ratio
111.0	112.0	115.0	..	..	120.0	..	..	..	..	..	Primary Schl. Enroll. Ratio, Female
59.0	61.0	61.0	..	..	65.0	..	..	..	..	..	Secondary Schl. Enroll. Ratio

PHILIPPINES	1969	1970	1971	1972	1973	1974	1975	1976	1977	1978	1979
CURRENT GNP PER CAPITA (US $)	250	230	220	220	250	300	360	420	450	510	590
POPULATION (thousands)	36,424	37,540	38,650	39,745	40,839	41,954	43,103	44,281	45,486	46,718	47,974

USE AND ORIGIN OF RESOURCES				*(Billions of current Philippine Pesos)*							
Gross National Product (GNP)	35.01	41.75	49.60	55.90	72.20	99.90	114.40	134.20	153.30	177.00	218.00
Net Factor Income from Abroad	-0.28	-0.70	-0.52	-0.60	-0.10	0.40	-0.30	-1.10	-0.90	-0.70	0.50
GDP at Market Prices	35.30	42.45	50.12	56.50	72.30	99.50	114.70	135.30	154.20	177.70	217.50
Resource Balance	-1.23	-0.14	-0.39	-0.40	2.50	-3.10	-7.80	-8.60	-5.90	-8.90	-12.10
Exports of Goods & NFServices	4.58	8.09	9.26	9.90	15.90	22.30	21.30	23.20	28.90	32.40	41.50
Imports of Goods & NFServices	5.81	8.24	9.65	10.30	13.40	25.40	29.10	31.80	34.80	41.30	53.60
Domestic Absorption	36.52	42.59	50.51	56.90	69.80	102.60	122.50	143.90	160.10	186.60	229.60
Private Consumption, etc.	26.20	30.08	35.78	40.70	49.00	68.60	77.60	88.70	101.40	119.20	143.60
General Gov't Consumption	3.12	3.51	4.27	5.30	6.20	8.90	11.10	13.20	14.30	16.10	18.30
Gross Domestic Investment	7.21	8.99	10.45	10.90	14.60	25.10	33.80	42.00	44.40	51.30	67.70
Fixed Investment	5.73	6.70	8.15	9.30	11.40	18.40	27.10	33.70	36.40	42.30	56.30
Indirect Taxes, net	2.30	3.13	3.94	4.33	6.34	10.16	11.16	11.78	13.60	16.85	22.38
GDP at factor cost	33.00	39.32	46.18	52.17	65.96	89.34	103.54	123.52	140.60	160.85	195.12
Agriculture	10.09	11.78	14.78	16.10	21.20	29.60	33.20	37.60	42.00	47.40	55.50
Industry	9.89	12.58	14.76	18.00	24.00	32.90	38.10	46.00	53.10	61.30	76.90
Manufacturing	7.32	9.57	11.42	14.00	18.20	24.30	28.20	32.90	37.40	43.70	52.10
Services, etc.	15.32	18.08	20.58	22.40	27.10	37.00	43.40	51.70	59.10	69.00	85.10
Gross Domestic Saving	5.98	8.85	10.07	10.50	17.10	22.00	26.00	33.40	38.50	42.40	55.60
Gross National Saving	..	8.33	9.76	10.44	17.64	23.23	26.90	33.40	38.70	43.15	57.79

				(Billions of 1987 Philippine Pesos)							
Gross National Product	361.10	376.93	398.14	420.49	459.82	487.10	514.66	547.81	584.04	619.66	666.44
GDP at Market Prices	362.46	379.18	397.80	419.88	455.61	478.22	509.78	549.76	584.10	616.39	655.35
Resource Balance	-29.38	-17.18	-15.60	-11.49	-4.79	-27.41	-33.00	-20.43	-13.45	-23.41	-37.64
Exports of Goods & NFServices	57.46	61.49	63.27	69.62	79.47	71.03	71.73	85.09	99.16	103.38	110.41
Imports of Goods & NFServices	86.84	78.67	78.87	81.11	84.26	98.44	104.74	105.52	112.61	126.79	148.05
Domestic Absorption	391.84	396.36	413.39	431.37	460.40	505.62	542.79	570.19	597.55	639.80	692.98
Private Consumption, etc.	273.92	279.96	291.63	307.29	322.56	339.64	345.12	349.06	374.94	402.01	432.03
General Gov't Consumption	26.47	28.18	30.35	35.32	39.32	44.65	48.65	49.32	49.98	51.31	53.31
Gross Domestic Investment	91.45	88.23	91.41	88.76	98.53	121.33	149.02	171.82	172.63	186.47	207.65
Fixed Investment	73.06	64.97	71.29	76.30	77.94	93.53	123.06	141.11	144.39	155.88	174.75
GDP at factor cost	337.25	351.33	366.61	387.79	415.74	429.44	460.30	502.03	532.72	558.12	588.15
Agriculture	91.72	93.77	98.37	102.46	108.82	112.01	116.46	126.01	132.37	137.46	143.82
Industry	107.27	114.35	123.27	136.78	154.26	162.61	177.05	196.05	212.01	224.93	242.40
Manufacturing	81.56	88.49	94.39	104.78	119.75	124.99	129.48	136.97	147.45	157.93	166.16
Services, etc.	162.37	170.25	175.18	179.61	191.64	202.87	215.70	226.92	238.95	253.38	268.62

Memo Items:											
Capacity to Import	68.46	77.32	75.70	77.96	99.98	86.42	76.66	76.99	93.52	99.46	114.63
Terms of Trade Adjustment	11.00	15.83	12.42	8.34	20.51	15.39	4.93	-8.11	-5.64	-3.91	4.22
Gross Domestic Income	373.46	395.02	410.22	428.22	476.13	493.61	514.71	541.65	578.46	612.47	659.56
Gross National Income	372.10	392.76	410.57	428.83	480.33	502.50	519.59	539.70	578.40	615.75	670.66

DOMESTIC PRICES/DEFLATORS				*(Index 1987 = 100)*							
Overall (GDP)	9.7	11.2	12.6	13.5	15.9	20.8	22.5	24.6	26.4	28.8	33.2
Domestic Absorption	9.3	10.7	12.2	13.2	15.2	20.3	22.6	25.2	26.8	29.2	33.1
Agriculture	11.0	12.6	15.0	15.7	19.5	26.4	28.5	29.8	31.7	34.5	38.6
Industry	9.2	11.0	12.0	13.2	15.6	20.2	21.5	23.5	25.0	27.3	31.7
Manufacturing	9.0	10.8	12.1	13.4	15.2	19.4	21.8	24.0	25.4	27.7	31.4
Consumer Price Index	8.3	9.6	11.7	12.6	14.7	19.7	21.1	23.0	25.3	27.1	31.9

MANUFACTURING ACTIVITY											
Employment (1987=100)	57.5	58.0	60.6	62.7	77.8	76.7	75.2	104.6	119.1	130.2	138.7
Real Earnings per Empl. (1987=100)	109.6	106.6	100.8	98.6	83.7	72.5	81.7	77.8	81.6	84.0	68.8
Real Output per Empl. (1987=100)	77.7	84.6	89.1	89.5	88.4	106.7	103.6	72.2	81.2	81.0	83.6
Earnings as % of Value Added	23.6	20.6	20.8	21.0	18.6	15.3	14.8	27.6	26.4	25.1	18.5

MONETARY HOLDINGS				*(Billions of current Philippine Pesos)*							
Money Supply, Broadly Defined	..	..	..	..	..	..	..	..	..	..	..
Money	4.02	4.31	5.01	6.47	7.27	9.01	10.31	12.07	14.94	16.95	18.84
Currency Outside Banks	2.12	2.41	2.65	3.43	3.45	4.31	4.75	5.65	6.73	8.14	9.18
Demand Deposits	1.90	1.90	2.36	3.03	3.81	4.70	5.57	6.42	8.21	8.81	9.66
Quasi-Money	..	..	..	..	..	..	..	..	..	..	..

GOVERNMENT DEFICIT (-) OR SURPLUS				*(Millions of current Philippine Pesos)*							
	..	..	..	-1,101	-843	445	-1,360	-2,352	-2,807	-2,171	-349
Current Revenue	..	..	..	6,970	9,484	12,151	16,822	18,282	19,944	23,882	29,315
Current Expenditure	..	..	..	6,546	8,506	8,762	14,651	15,798	17,719	19,215	20,777
Current Budget Balance	..	..	..	424	978	3,389	2,171	2,484	2,225	4,667	8,538
Capital Receipts	..	..	..	2	15	6	16	18	15	125	4
Capital Payments	..	..	..	1,527	1,836	2,950	3,547	4,854	5,047	6,963	8,891

1980	1981	1982	1983	1984	1985	1986	1987	1988	1989 estimate	NOTES	PHILIPPINES
680	770	790	740	630	570	560	590	630	700	..	**CURRENT GNP PER CAPITA (US $)**
49,253	50,551	51,863	53,183	54,504	55,819	57,149	58,493	59,851	61,224	..	**POPULATION (thousands)**
			(Billions of current Philippine Pesos)								**USE AND ORIGIN OF RESOURCES**
264.50	303.60	335.40	378.80	527.40	597.74	614.70	703.36	822.72	961.38	..	Gross National Product (GNP)
-0.20	-1.70	-5.20	-5.30	-13.10	-14.94	-12.43	-5.01	-2.98	-2.62	..	Net Factor Income from Abroad
264.70	305.30	340.60	384.10	540.50	612.68	627.13	708.37	825.71	964.00	..	GDP at Market Prices
-15.10	-16.60	-23.10	-26.20	-0.70	18.06	38.92	6.07	4.80	-10.68	..	Resource Balance
53.60	57.80	56.20	75.30	117.70	126.57	155.10	163.47	202.94	242.58	..	Exports of Goods & NFServices
68.70	74.40	79.30	101.50	118.40	108.51	116.19	157.40	198.14	253.26	..	Imports of Goods & NFServices
279.80	321.90	363.70	410.30	541.20	594.62	588.21	702.29	820.91	974.67	..	Domestic Absorption
177.40	203.80	238.00	278.20	413.60	465.17	458.67	533.43	604.58	706.00	..	Private Consumption, etc.
21.20	24.80	29.20	29.50	35.60	44.04	48.44	58.47	73.07	89.00	..	General Gov't Consumption
81.20	93.30	96.50	102.60	92.00	85.40	81.11	110.39	143.26	179.67	..	Gross Domestic Investment
68.00	79.30	86.00	95.30	100.10	89.97	80.82	98.59	126.41	167.14	..	Fixed Investment
25.76	25.93	28.66	34.72	43.92	49.35	52.31	70.23	64.16	78.50	..	Indirect Taxes, net
238.94	279.37	311.93	349.38	496.58	563.34	574.82	638.14	761.55	885.49	B	GDP at factor cost
61.80	69.40	76.70	84.60	139.50	162.52	155.99	170.77	189.99	226.70	..	Agriculture
96.80	111.60	122.50	138.20	186.20	200.55	204.98	232.58	277.18	322.27	..	Industry
64.60	75.20	83.10	95.20	137.30	150.53	155.17	173.54	207.45	241.26	..	Manufacturing
106.10	124.30	141.40	161.30	214.80	249.61	266.16	305.01	358.54	415.03	..	Services, etc.
66.10	76.70	73.40	76.40	91.30	103.47	120.02	116.47	148.05	169.00	..	Gross Domestic Saving
68.15	77.57	70.95	73.73	80.17	91.73	112.39	119.20	155.62	176.66	..	Gross National Saving
			(Billions of 1987 Philippine Pesos)								
698.08	718.08	724.52	735.77	680.06	649.97	661.75	703.36	750.86	793.90	..	Gross National Product
690.01	716.49	737.33	745.54	697.35	665.29	674.35	708.37	753.54	796.25	I f	GDP at Market Prices
-28.30	-22.95	-29.09	-35.95	3.66	25.88	41.25	6.07	-20.63	-62.17	..	Resource Balance
124.48	125.88	124.48	135.73	146.98	136.09	165.69	163.47	189.39	205.12	..	Exports of Goods & NFServices
152.77	148.84	153.56	171.67	143.32	110.21	124.44	157.40	210.03	267.29	..	Imports of Goods & NFServices
718.31	739.44	766.42	781.49	693.70	639.41	633.11	702.29	774.17	858.43	..	Domestic Absorption
446.39	460.64	491.61	519.93	522.75	494.04	496.21	533.43	581.78	640.52	..	Private Consumption, etc.
55.31	57.31	60.64	57.98	55.31	54.79	54.56	58.47	62.70	69.03	..	General Gov't Consumption
216.60	221.49	214.16	203.57	115.63	90.58	82.33	110.39	129.68	148.88	..	Gross Domestic Investment
186.23	192.79	194.44	188.69	127.98	97.02	82.51	98.59	113.82	138.34	..	Fixed Investment
623.10	655.90	675.53	677.80	642.79	611.56	618.20	638.14	694.70	732.19	B I	GDP at factor cost
150.83	156.55	161.64	158.46	161.64	167.07	172.53	170.77	176.87	184.47	..	Agriculture
253.64	265.96	271.28	273.56	245.44	220.37	215.78	232.58	252.55	270.01	..	Industry
173.64	179.63	183.37	187.86	174.39	161.23	162.54	173.54	189.22	201.23	..	Manufacturing
284.95	293.48	303.90	313.52	290.27	277.85	286.05	305.01	324.12	341.78	..	Services, etc.
											Memo Items:
119.20	115.63	108.83	127.36	142.48	128.56	166.12	163.47	215.11	256.02	..	Capacity to Import
-5.28	-10.25	-15.65	-8.37	-4.50	-7.53	0.43	0.00	25.72	50.91	..	Terms of Trade Adjustment
684.73	706.24	721.69	737.17	692.85	657.76	674.79	708.37	779.26	847.16	..	Gross Domestic Income
692.80	707.83	708.88	727.40	675.56	642.44	662.19	703.36	776.58	844.81	..	Gross National Income
			(Index 1987 = 100)								**DOMESTIC PRICES/DEFLATORS**
38.4	42.6	46.2	51.5	77.5	92.1	93.0	100.0	109.6	121.1	..	Overall (GDP)
39.0	43.5	47.5	52.5	78.0	93.0	92.9	100.0	106.0	113.5	..	Domestic Absorption
41.0	44.3	47.4	53.4	86.3	97.3	90.4	100.0	107.4	122.9	..	Agriculture
38.1	42.0	45.2	50.5	75.9	91.0	95.0	100.0	109.8	119.4	..	Industry
37.2	41.9	45.3	50.7	78.7	93.4	95.5	100.0	109.6	119.9	..	Manufacturing
37.7	42.6	47.0	51.7	77.7	95.6	96.3	100.0	108.8	120.3	..	Consumer Price Index
											MANUFACTURING ACTIVITY
141.4	144.6	144.4	103.8	94.1	91.2	93.2	100.0	..	..	G J	Employment (1987=100)
69.0	70.9	72.6	89.0	77.2	74.9	83.0	100.0	..	..	G J	Real Earnings per Empl. (1987=100)
83.0	74.9	81.2	104.3	99.4	87.1	93.1	100.0	..	..	G J	Real Output per Empl. (1987=100)
22.0	24.7	33.1	20.9	18.1	22.3	20.5	26.2	25.1	..	J	Earnings as % of Value Added
			(Billions of current Philippine Pesos)								**MONETARY HOLDINGS**
..	..	..	..	..	..	136.50	..	192.92	..	..	Money Supply, Broadly Defined
22.54	23.52	23.52	33.55	34.44	36.76	43.17	53.80	61.20	81.28	..	Money
10.18	11.63	12.71	19.59	21.76	24.03	29.26	35.37	40.64	52.94	..	Currency Outside Banks
12.36	11.90	10.82	13.96	12.68	12.73	13.90	18.43	20.56	28.34	..	Demand Deposits
..	..	..	..	..	..	93.33	..	131.72	..	..	Quasi-Money
			(Millions of current Philippine Pesos)								**GOVERNMENT DEFICIT (-) OR SURPLUS**
-3,385	-12,154	-14,414	-7,468	-9,957	-11,158	-30,648	-16,728	-23,244	..	..	GOVERNMENT DEFICIT (-) OR SURPLUS
34,371	35,733	37,990	45,603	56,822	68,954	79,241	101,955	106,849	..	..	Current Revenue
24,156	26,201	30,777	34,533	42,967	55,288	70,726	95,538	113,633	..	..	Current Expenditure
10,215	9,532	7,213	11,070	13,855	13,666	8,515	6,417	-6,784	..	..	Current Budget Balance
2	3	3	3	4	3	4	..	..	..	..	Capital Receipts
13,602	21,689	21,630	18,541	23,816	24,827	39,167	..	..	..	..	Capital Payments

PHILIPPINES	1969	1970	1971	1972	1973	1974	1975	1976	1977	1978	1979
FOREIGN TRADE (CUSTOMS BASIS)					*(Millions of current US dollars)*						
Value of Exports, fob	823.0	1,059.7	1,116.3	1,028.8	1,797.3	2,650.7	2,218.1	2,508.4	3,079.6	3,349.1	4,601.2
Nonfuel Primary Products	744.8	962.0	1,013.1	923.4	1,492.7	2,290.2	1,786.6	1,843.1	2,282.6	2,203.4	2,967.3
Fuels	12.6	17.2	24.2	10.3	16.2	17.5	37.5	33.8	18.9	9.7	11.0
Manufactures	65.7	80.5	79.0	95.1	288.3	343.0	394.0	631.4	778.1	1,136.0	1,622.9
Value of Imports, cif	1,256.1	1,210.4	1,318.7	1,387.7	1,789.5	3,467.6	3,776.2	3,953.3	4,269.8	5,143.3	6,613.0
Nonfuel Primary Products	257.6	237.4	284.7	320.3	391.6	626.3	588.8	600.9	703.5	750.9	907.4
Fuels	128.1	144.7	172.7	177.2	231.2	696.0	800.1	927.6	1,040.1	1,088.0	1,466.5
Manufactures	870.3	828.3	861.3	890.2	1,166.7	2,145.3	2,387.3	2,424.9	2,526.2	3,304.5	4,239.0
					(Index 1987 = 100)						
Terms of Trade	177.6	189.1	168.2	160.5	186.9	198.2	141.4	135.7	128.3	117.5	122.2
Export Prices, fob	39.6	42.1	41.5	44.4	65.6	106.4	80.3	79.1	81.7	81.8	101.6
Import Prices, cif	22.3	22.3	24.7	27.7	35.1	53.7	56.8	58.3	63.7	69.7	83.2
BALANCE OF PAYMENTS					*(Millions of current US dollars)*						
Exports of Goods & Services	..	1,322	1,402	1,480	2,455	3,527	3,170	3,389	4,236	4,910	6,256
Merchandise, fob	..	1,064	1,136	1,136	1,872	2,694	2,263	2,517	3,151	3,426	4,601
Nonfactor Services	..	248	250	322	517	663	737	745	732	1,012	1,077
Factor Services	..	10	16	22	66	171	170	127	353	472	578
Imports of Goods & Services	..	1,489	1,539	1,661	2,211	4,012	4,412	4,761	5,249	6,323	8,106
Merchandise, fob	..	1,090	1,186	1,261	1,596	3,144	3,459	3,633	3,915	4,732	6,142
Nonfactor Services	..	259	236	253	435	642	657	748	840	983	1,163
Factor Services	..	140	117	148	180	226	296	380	494	608	801
Long-Term Interest	..	44	72	84	94	110	119	167	224	309	491
Private Current Transfers, net	..	29	34	80	94	123	165	148	148	197	229
Workers' Remittances	..	..	..	..	..	..	..	..	125	154	191
Curr. A/C Bal before Off. Transf.	..	-138	-102	-101	337	-362	-1,076	-1,225	-865	-1,216	-1,621
Net Official Transfers	..	90	100	107	136	154	153	120	112	122	126
Curr. A/C Bal after Off. Transf.	..	-48	-2	6	473	-208	-923	-1,105	-753	-1,094	-1,495
Long-Term Capital, net	..	130	-9	115	132	227	517	1,137	861	884	1,106
Direct Investment	..	-29	-6	-21	54	4	97	126	211	101	7
Long-Term Loans	..	157	26	196	-14	412	532	1,095	996	958	1,130
Disbursements	..	416	283	452	389	741	831	1,438	1,365	1,907	2,087
Repayments	..	260	258	256	403	329	299	343	370	949	957
Other Long-Term Capital	..	2	-29	-61	93	-189	-112	-83	-346	-175	-31
Other Capital, net	..	-7	110	60	106	557	395	-87	-135	1,077	766
Change in Reserves	..	-75	-99	-181	-712	-577	11	54	27	-867	-377
Memo Item:					*(Philippine Pesos per US dollar)*						
Conversion Factor (Annual Avg)	3.900	5.900	6.430	6.670	6.760	6.790	7.250	7.440	7.400	7.370	7.380
				(Millions of US dollars), outstanding at end of year							
EXTERNAL DEBT (Total)	..	1,613	1,777	1,962	2,028	2,428	3,064	4,437	8,184	10,781	13,289
Long-Term Debt (by debtor)	..	1,613	1,777	1,962	2,028	2,428	3,064	4,437	5,716	6,918	7,974
Central Bank, incl. IMF credit	..	378	405	533	512	646	821	1,109	1,458	1,963	2,448
Central Government	..	153	201	222	222	258	377	449	725	1,125	1,264
Rest of General Government	..	1	1	0	0	0	0	0	0	0	0
Non-financial Public Enterprises	..	162	192	224	254	311	454	1,066	1,368	1,739	2,191
Priv. Sector, incl non-guaranteed	..	919	980	983	1,041	1,213	1,411	1,812	2,165	2,091	2,071
Short-Term Debt	..	..	..	..	..	..	..	..	2,468	3,863	5,315
Memo Items:					*(Millions of US dollars)*						
Int'l Reserves Excluding Gold	76.0	195.0	309.0	479.8	992.8	1,458.9	1,314.5	1,596.8	1,479.4	1,763.0	2,249.7
Gold Holdings (at market price)	45.3	59.8	83.5	120.5	118.6	196.9	148.1	142.3	174.2	341.9	871.4
SOCIAL INDICATORS											
Total Fertility Rate	6.5	6.4	6.3	6.1	5.9	5.7	5.5	5.2	5.0	4.9	4.9
Infant Mortality Rate	67.6	66.4	65.2	64.0	62.0	60.0	58.0	56.0	54.0	53.4	52.8
Life Expectancy at Birth	56.8	57.2	57.5	57.9	58.3	58.7	59.1	59.5	59.9	60.2	60.6
Urban Population, % of total	32.7	33.0	33.5	34.0	34.6	35.1	35.6	36.0	36.3	36.7	37.0
Food Prod. per capita (1987=100)	96.8	94.6	95.5	91.6	101.6	105.8	106.7	111.7	112.0	115.0	115.5
Labor Force, Agriculture (%)	55.3	54.8	54.4	54.1	53.8	53.6	53.3	53.0	52.7	52.3	52.0
Labor Force, Female (%)	33.3	33.2	33.2	33.1	33.0	32.9	32.8	32.9	32.9	32.9	32.9
Primary Schl. Enroll. Ratio	..	108.0	..	..	..	..	107.0	103.0	108.0	110.0	107.0
Primary Schl. Enroll. Ratio, Female	..	..	..	..	..	..	..	..	..	..	..
Secondary Schl. Enroll. Ratio	..	46.0	..	..	..	..	54.0	60.0	61.0	63.0	64.0

1980	1981	1982	1983	1984	1985	1986	1987	1988	1989 estimate	NOTES	PHILIPPINES
											FOREIGN TRADE (CUSTOMS BASIS)
				(Millions of current US dollars)							
5,787.8	5,722.1	5,020.6	5,000.6	5,391.0	4,629.0	4,841.8	5,649.0	7,074.0	7,272.6	..	Value of Exports, fob
3,596.6	3,119.5	2,512.4	2,356.5	2,329.9	1,950.6	1,972.3	2,082.9	2,530.0	..	..	Nonfuel Primary Products
50.0	42.2	16.3	110.5	82.4	34.5	61.5	80.0	144.0	..	..	Fuels
2,141.2	2,560.4	2,491.9	2,533.6	2,978.7	2,643.9	2,808.0	3,486.1	4,400.0	4,843.4	..	Manufactures
8,294.6	8,477.7	8,262.3	7,977.4	6,424.3	5,444.6	5,392.5	7,144.0	8,729.0	9,304.5	..	Value of Imports, cif
1,077.0	1,027.4	1,171.3	1,012.7	771.1	792.1	865.1	1,092.8	1,492.4	..	..	Nonfuel Primary Products
2,354.8	2,553.7	2,187.9	2,193.7	1,696.3	1,507.9	918.5	1,184.9	1,152.6	..	..	Fuels
4,862.8	4,896.6	4,903.1	4,771.0	3,956.9	3,144.6	3,608.9	4,866.3	6,084.0	6,493.7	..	Manufactures
				(Index 1987 = 100)							
110.2	97.7	92.8	98.3	103.7	94.1	99.1	100.0	110.2	..	..	Terms of Trade
110.7	101.3	91.2	93.8	95.6	87.6	88.7	100.0	114.7	..	..	Export Prices, fob
100.5	103.7	98.3	95.4	92.2	93.1	89.4	100.0	104.0	..	..	Import Prices, cif
				(Millions of current US dollars)							**BALANCE OF PAYMENTS**
7,998	8,583	8,004	8,132	8,017	7,917	8,633	9,174	10,666	12,407	f	Exports of Goods & Services
5,788	5,722	5,021	5,005	5,391	4,629	4,842	5,720	7,074	7,821	f	Merchandise, fob
1,448	1,791	1,804	1,808	1,642	2,235	2,860	2,345	2,413	3,225	..	Nonfactor Services
762	1,070	1,179	1,319	984	1,053	931	1,109	1,179	1,361	..	Factor Services
10,348	11,151	11,690	11,375	9,697	8,331	8,120	10,191	11,831	14,702	f	Imports of Goods & Services
7,727	7,946	7,667	7,487	6,070	5,111	5,044	6,737	8,159	10,419	f	Merchandise, fob
1,420	1,608	1,800	1,710	1,168	850	824	1,124	1,281	1,527	..	Nonfactor Services
1,201	1,597	2,223	2,178	2,459	2,370	2,252	2,330	2,391	2,756	..	Factor Services
574	823	923	940	928	938	1,141	1,401	1,591	1,697	..	Long-Term Interest
299	325	322	237	118	172	235	376	500	473	..	Private Current Transfers, net
205	254	239	180	59	111	163	211	388	360	..	Workers' Remittances
-2,051	-2,243	-3,364	-3,006	-1,562	-242	748	-641	-665	-1,822	..	Curr. A/C Bal before Off. Transf.
148	182	164	235	268	207	206	197	275	357	..	Net Official Transfers
-1,903	-2,061	-3,200	-2,771	-1,294	-35	954	-444	-390	-1,465	..	Curr. A/C Bal after Off. Transf.
877	1,503	1,566	1,464	308	3,094	1,249	457	459	1,003	f	Long-Term Capital, net
-106	172	16	105	9	12	127	307	936	482	..	Direct Investment
1,317	1,505	1,577	1,756	1,008	1,039	422	-77	95	718	..	Long-Term Loans
1,853	2,225	2,544	2,580	1,530	1,665	1,539	1,333	1,375	1,703	..	Disbursements
536	721	968	824	523	626	1,117	1,410	1,281	985	..	Repayments
-334	-174	-27	-396	-709	2,043	700	227	-571	-197	..	Other Long-Term Capital
1,982	226	916	-739	1,170	-3,207	-1,104	-348	557	742	f	Other Capital, net
-956	332	718	2,046	-184	148	-1,099	335	-626	-280	..	Change in Reserves
				(Philippine Pesos per US dollar)							Memo Item:
7.510	7.900	8.540	11.110	16.700	18.610	20.390	20.570	21.100	21.740	..	Conversion Factor (Annual Avg)
				(Millions of US dollars), outstanding at end of year							
17,431	20,900	24,538	24,363	24,375	26,819	28,372	30,038	29,161	28,902	..	**EXTERNAL DEBT (Total)**
9,875	11,379	13,073	14,755	14,918	17,662	22,993	26,240	25,301	24,951	..	Long-Term Debt (by debtor)
3,076	3,439	4,082	4,490	4,392	5,276	8,901	9,855	9,029	8,776	..	Central Bank, incl. IMF credit
1,737	2,325	2,736	3,539	3,827	5,383	6,721	9,291	9,958	10,709	..	Central Government
1	2	2	2	2	1	1	1	1	0	..	Rest of General Government
2,608	2,853	3,022	3,596	3,985	4,401	5,013	5,219	4,918	4,302	..	Non-financial Public Enterprises
2,454	2,761	3,230	3,127	2,713	2,601	2,358	1,874	1,396	1,163	..	Priv. Sector, incl non-guaranteed
7,556	9,521	11,465	9,608	9,456	9,157	5,379	3,798	3,860	3,951	..	Short-Term Debt
				(Millions of US dollars)							Memo Items:
2,846.1	2,065.9	887.8	746.9	602.1	614.9	1,728.2	968.3	1,003.4	1,417.0	..	Int'l Reserves Excluding Gold
1,131.8	659.5	852.6	110.3	242.3	483.3	883.0	1,343.9	1,165.5	981.2	..	Gold Holdings (at market price)
											SOCIAL INDICATORS
4.8	4.8	4.7	4.5	4.4	4.2	4.1	3.9	3.8	3.7	..	Total Fertility Rate
52.2	51.6	51.0	49.8	48.6	47.4	46.2	45.0	43.8	42.7	..	Infant Mortality Rate
61.0	61.4	61.8	62.1	62.4	62.8	63.1	63.4	63.7	63.9	..	Life Expectancy at Birth
37.4	37.8	38.3	38.7	39.2	39.6	40.2	40.7	41.3	41.8	..	Urban Population, % of total
118.1	118.9	114.3	110.9	104.9	103.0	102.7	100.0	99.9	102.9	..	Food Prod. per capita (1987=100)
51.8	..	..	..	..	..	..	..	..	..	..	Labor Force, Agriculture (%)
32.9	32.7	32.6	32.4	32.3	32.1	31.9	31.7	31.6	31.4	..	Labor Force, Female (%)
113.0	..	109.0	109.0	107.0	106.0	106.0	..	106.0	..	..	Primary Schl. Enroll. Ratio
113.0	113.0	110.0	109.0	108.0	107.0	106.0	..	107.0	..	..	Primary Schl. Enroll. Ratio, Female
65.0	..	66.0	67.0	68.0	65.0	68.0	..	66.0	..	..	Secondary Schl. Enroll. Ratio

POLAND	1969	1970	1971	1972	1973	1974	1975	1976	1977	1978	1979
CURRENT GNP PER CAPITA (US $)	..	..	..	..	..	..	..	..	..	..	..
POPULATION (thousands)	32,555	32,526	32,805	33,068	33,363	33,691	34,022	34,362	34,698	35,010	35,225

USE AND ORIGIN OF RESOURCES *(Billions of current Polish Zlotys)*

	1969	1970	1971	1972	1973	1974	1975	1976	1977	1978	1979
Gross National Product (GNP)	..	..	..	..	..	..	..	..	..	..	..
Net Factor Income from Abroad	..	..	..	..	..	..	..	..	..	..	..
GDP at Market Prices	..	..	..	..	..	..	..	..	..	..	..
Resource Balance	..	..	..	..	..	..	..	..	..	..	..
Exports of Goods & NFServices	..	..	..	..	..	..	..	..	..	..	..
Imports of Goods & NFServices	..	..	..	..	..	..	..	..	..	..	..
Domestic Absorption	..	..	..	..	..	..	..	..	..	..	..
Private Consumption, etc.	..	..	..	..	..	..	..	..	..	..	..
General Gov't Consumption	..	..	..	..	..	..	..	..	..	..	..
Gross Domestic Investment	..	..	..	..	..	..	..	..	..	..	..
Fixed Investment	..	..	..	..	..	..	..	..	..	..	..
Indirect Taxes, net	..	..	..	..	..	..	..	..	..	..	..
GDP at factor cost	..	..	..	..	..	..	..	..	..	..	..
Agriculture	..	..	..	..	..	..	..	..	..	..	..
Industry	..	..	..	..	..	..	..	..	..	..	..
Manufacturing	..	..	..	..	..	..	..	..	..	..	..
Services, etc.	..	..	..	..	..	..	..	..	..	..	..
Gross Domestic Saving	..	..	..	..	..	..	..	..	..	..	..
Gross National Saving	..	..	..	..	..	..	..	..	..	..	..

(Billions of 1987 Polish Zlotys)

	1969	1970	1971	1972	1973	1974	1975	1976	1977	1978	1979
Gross National Product	..	..	..	..	..	..	..	..	..	..	..
GDP at Market Prices	..	..	..	..	..	..	..	..	..	..	..
Resource Balance	..	..	..	..	..	..	..	..	..	..	..
Exports of Goods & NFServices	..	..	..	..	..	..	..	..	..	..	..
Imports of Goods & NFServices	..	..	..	..	..	..	..	..	..	..	..
Domestic Absorption	..	..	..	..	..	..	..	..	..	..	..
Private Consumption, etc.	..	..	..	..	..	..	..	..	..	..	..
General Gov't Consumption	..	..	..	..	..	..	..	..	..	..	..
Gross Domestic Investment	..	..	..	..	..	..	..	..	..	..	..
Fixed Investment	..	..	..	..	..	..	..	..	..	..	..
GDP at factor cost	..	..	..	..	..	..	..	..	..	..	..
Agriculture	..	..	..	..	..	..	..	..	..	..	..
Industry	..	..	..	..	..	..	..	..	..	..	..
Manufacturing	..	..	..	..	..	..	..	..	..	..	..
Services, etc.	..	..	..	..	..	..	..	..	..	..	..
Memo Items: .											
Capacity to Import	..	..	..	..	..	..	..	..	..	..	..
Terms of Trade Adjustment	..	..	..	..	..	..	..	..	..	..	..
Gross Domestic Income	..	..	..	..	..	..	..	..	..	..	..
Gross National Income	..	..	..	..	..	..	..	..	..	..	..

DOMESTIC PRICES/DEFLATORS *(Index 1987 = 100)*

	1969	1970	1971	1972	1973	1974	1975	1976	1977	1978	1979
Overall (GDP)	..	..	..	..	..	..	..	..	..	..	..
Domestic Absorption	..	..	..	..	..	..	..	..	..	..	..
Agriculture	..	..	..	..	..	..	..	..	..	..	..
Industry	..	..	..	..	..	..	..	..	..	..	..
Manufacturing	..	..	..	..	..	..	..	..	..	..	..
Consumer Price Index	..	11.0	11.1	11.1	11.4	12.2	12.4	13.0	13.6	14.7	15.8

MANUFACTURING ACTIVITY

	1969	1970	1971	1972	1973	1974	1975	1976	1977	1978	1979
Employment (1987=100)	96.3	98.1	101.6	105.9	109.4	112.4	114.6	115.2	116.5	116.0	114.9
Real Earnings per Empl. (1987=100)	..	69.0	71.9	75.5	80.6	85.3	100.3	106.1	108.8	106.3	107.9
Real Output per Empl. (1987=100)	..	..	..	..	..	..	..	..	..	..	..
Earnings as % of Value Added	..	24.1	25.1	25.2	24.7	23.3	24.1	25.7	25.0	24.0	25.2

MONETARY HOLDINGS *(Billions of current Polish Zlotys)*

	1969	1970	1971	1972	1973	1974	1975	1976	1977	1978	1979
Money Supply, Broadly Defined	..	..	..	..	..	..	..	..	..	..	1,386
Money	..	..	..	..	..	..	..	..	..	..	825
Currency Outside Banks	..	..	..	..	..	..	..	..	..	..	235
Demand Deposits	..	..	..	..	..	..	..	..	..	..	591
Quasi-Money	..	..	..	..	..	..	..	..	..	..	561

GOVERNMENT DEFICIT (-) OR SURPLUS *(Billions of current Polish Zlotys)*

	1969	1970	1971	1972	1973	1974	1975	1976	1977	1978	1979
Current Revenue	..	..	..	..	..	..	..	..	..	..	..
Current Expenditure	..	..	..	..	..	..	..	..	..	..	..
Current Budget Balance	..	..	..	..	..	..	..	..	..	..	..
Capital Receipts	..	..	..	..	..	..	..	..	..	..	..
Capital Payments	..	..	..	..	..	..	..	..	..	..	..

1980	1981	1982	1983	1984	1985	1986	1987	1988	1989 estimate	NOTES	POLAND
..	..	1,540	1,800	2,060	2,080	2,030	1,850	1,850	1,780	..	**CURRENT GNP PER CAPITA (US $)**
35,578	35,902	36,227	36,571	36,914	37,203	37,456	37,664	37,862	38,061	..	**POPULATION (thousands)**
				(Billions of current Polish Zlotys)							**USE AND ORIGIN OF RESOURCES**
2,407	2,588	5,287	6,668	8,277	10,069	12,484	16,167	28,357	94,066	..	Gross National Product (GNP)
-104	-165	-260	-256	-299	-376	-469	-773	-1,272	-4,220	..	Net Factor Income from Abroad
2,511	2,753	5,546	6,924	8,576	10,445	12,953	16,940	29,629	98,286	..	GDP at Market Prices
-74	-58	116	122	169	148	183	407	811	98	..	Resource Balance
707	638	1,078	1,192	1,516	1,901	2,357	3,625	6,744	18,085	..	Exports of Goods & NFServices
780	697	962	1,070	1,346	1,753	2,174	3,218	5,934	17,986	..	Imports of Goods & NFServices
2,585	2,811	5,430	6,802	8,407	10,297	12,770	16,533	28,818	98,188	..	Domestic Absorption
1,692	2,042	3,425	4,458	5,348	6,423	7,852	10,133	16,732	..	..	Private Consumption, etc.
231	260	455	610	801	986	1,178	1,516	2,428	..	..	General Gov't Consumption
662	508	1,551	1,734	2,257	2,888	3,740	4,884	9,657	32,336	..	Gross Domestic Investment
621	514	1,117	1,395	1,781	2,211	2,836	3,821	6,663	..	..	Fixed Investment
..	..	..	..	..	..	..	..	..	..	..	Indirect Taxes, net
..	..	..	..	..	..	..	..	..	..	..	GDP at factor cost
..	..	..	..	..	..	..	..	..	..	..	Agriculture
..	..	..	..	..	..	..	..	..	..	..	Industry
..	..	..	..	..	..	..	..	..	..	..	Manufacturing
..	..	..	..	..	..	..	..	..	..	..	Services, etc.
588	450	1,667	1,856	2,426	3,036	3,923	5,290	10,468	32,435	..	Gross Domestic Saving
510	332	1,477	1,665	2,210	2,802	3,647	4,930	9,924	29,864	..	Gross National Saving
				(Billions of 1987 Polish Zlotys)							
15,195.7	13,415.9	12,962.4	13,819.5	14,632.6	15,367.1	16,013.2	16,167.2	16,877.3	16,962.2	..	Gross National Product
15,856.1	14,274.4	13,594.7	14,350.1	15,160.6	15,941.3	16,614.3	16,939.9	17,634.5	17,722.3	..	GDP at Market Prices
-274.8	-173.9	348.7	459.1	574.6	393.8	376.4	407.1	458.3	562.2	..	Resource Balance
3,114.4	2,546.6	2,704.6	2,952.6	3,303.1	3,313.3	3,452.8	3,625.2	3,966.1	4,077.0	..	Exports of Goods & NFServices
3,389.2	2,720.6	2,356.0	2,493.6	2,728.5	2,919.6	3,076.4	3,218.1	3,507.7	3,514.8	..	Imports of Goods & NFServices
16,130.9	14,448.3	13,246.0	13,891.0	14,586.0	15,547.5	16,237.9	16,532.8	17,176.1	17,160.2	..	Domestic Absorption
9,478.5	9,045.0	7,955.1	8,343.3	8,670.2	9,378.3	9,857.7	10,132.9	10,356.1	10,321.6	..	Private Consumption, etc.
1,304.7	1,245.4	1,275.6	1,315.2	1,414.4	1,500.3	1,501.0	1,516.4	1,518.7	1,362.3	..	General Gov't Consumption
5,347.6	4,157.9	4,015.3	4,232.5	4,501.4	4,668.9	4,879.1	4,883.5	5,301.3	5,476.2	..	Gross Domestic Investment
4,002.8	3,239.7	2,796.9	3,042.5	3,341.4	3,512.7	3,671.1	3,821.0	4,054.0	..	..	Fixed Investment
..	..	..	..	..	..	..	..	..	..	..	GDP at factor cost
..	..	..	..	..	..	..	..	..	..	..	Agriculture
..	..	..	..	..	..	..	..	..	..	..	Industry
..	..	..	..	..	..	..	..	..	..	..	Manufacturing
..	..	..	..	..	..	..	..	..	..	..	Services, etc.
											Memo Items:
3,069.9	2,493.6	2,640.1	2,778.3	3,071.6	3,165.9	3,335.7	3,625.2	3,987.0	3,534.0	..	Capacity to Import
-44.4	-53.0	-64.5	-174.3	-231.5	-147.4	-117.1	0.0	21.0	-543.0	..	Terms of Trade Adjustment
15,811.6	14,221.4	13,530.1	14,175.7	14,929.1	15,793.9	16,497.2	16,939.9	17,655.4	17,179.4	..	Gross Domestic Income
15,151.3	13,362.9	12,897.9	13,645.2	14,401.0	15,219.7	15,896.1	16,167.2	16,898.3	16,419.2	..	Gross National Income
				(Index 1987 = 100)							**DOMESTIC PRICES/DEFLATORS**
15.8	19.3	40.8	48.3	56.6	65.5	78.0	100.0	168.0	554.6	..	Overall (GDP)
16.0	19.5	41.0	49.0	57.6	66.2	78.6	100.0	167.8	572.2	..	Domestic Absorption
..	..	..	..	..	..	..	..	..	..	..	Agriculture
..	..	..	..	..	..	..	..	..	..	..	Industry
..	..	..	..	..	..	..	..	..	..	..	Manufacturing
17.3	20.9	42.0	51.3	59.0	67.9	79.9	100.0	160.2	562.5	..	Consumer Price Index
											MANUFACTURING ACTIVITY
117.0	116.1	108.4	106.9	105.9	101.4	101.2	100.0	98.1	..	G	Employment (1987=100)
112.8	117.0	87.8	93.7	96.5	100.1	102.6	100.0	116.3	..	G	Real Earnings per Empl. (1987=100)
..	..	..	..	..	..	..	..	..	..	G	Real Output per Empl. (1987=100)
28.0	39.1	23.5	24.9	24.2	23.8	23.4	21.5	22.6	..	..	Earnings as % of Value Added
				(Billions of current Polish Zlotys)							**MONETARY HOLDINGS**
1,546	1,907	2,643	3,039	3,576	4,366	5,532	7,416	12,110	70,459	..	Money Supply, Broadly Defined
910	1,105	1,573	1,747	2,001	2,449	2,998	3,786	5,748	19,055	..	Money
293	402	605	718	824	1,014	1,166	1,312	2,523	9,880	..	Currency Outside Banks
618	703	968	1,029	1,177	1,435	1,832	2,474	3,225	9,175	..	Demand Deposits
636	802	1,070	1,292	1,575	1,917	2,534	3,631	6,361	51,404	..	Quasi-Money
				(Billions of current Polish Zlotys)							**GOVERNMENT DEFICIT (-) OR SURPLUS**
..	..	..	..	-39.9	-180.4	-41.3	-241.6	-673.0	..	..	
..	..	..	..	3,750.8	4,538.0	5,417.5	6,598.9	11,013.0	..	..	Current Revenue
..	..	..	..	3,573.0	4,391.3	5,009.5	6,214.7	10,771.5	..	..	Current Expenditure
..	..	..	..	177.8	146.7	408.0	384.2	241.5	..	..	Current Budget Balance
..	..	..	..	..	0.1	..	0.5	0.3	..	..	Capital Receipts
..	..	..	..	217.7	327.2	449.3	626.3	914.8	..	..	Capital Payments

POLAND	1969	1970	1971	1972	1973	1974	1975	1976	1977	1978	1979
FOREIGN TRADE (CUSTOMS BASIS)					*(Millions of current US dollars)*						
Value of Exports, fob	3,320	3,548	3,872	4,927	6,432	8,321	10,289	11,024	12,273	14,114	16,249
Nonfuel Primary Products	..	..	..	..	..	..	..	..	..	..	..
Fuels	..	..	..	..	..	..	..	..	..	..	..
Manufactures	..	..	..	..	..	..	..	..	..	..	..
Value of Imports, cif	2,856	3,210	3,593	4,745	6,953	9,327	11,155	12,898	13,420	14,744	16,142
Nonfuel Primary Products	..	..	..	..	..	..	..	..	..	..	..
Fuels	..	..	..	..	..	..	..	..	..	..	..
Manufactures	..	..	..	..	..	..	..	..	..	..	..
					(Index 1987 = 100)						
Terms of Trade	..	..	..	..	..	..	..	..	..	..	..
Export Prices, fob	..	..	..	..	..	..	..	..	..	..	..
Import Prices, cif	..	..	..	..	..	..	..	..	..	..	..
BALANCE OF PAYMENTS					*(Millions of current US dollars)*						
Exports of Goods & Services	..	..	..	..	..	..	..	10,723	11,927	13,593	15,221
Merchandise, fob	..	..	..	..	..	..	..	9,506	10,506	11,967	13,276
Nonfactor Services	..	..	..	..	..	..	..	1,180	1,385	1,586	1,874
Factor Services	..	..	..	..	..	..	..	37	36	40	71
Imports of Goods & Services	..	..	..	..	..	..	..	14,095	14,957	17,024	19,261
Merchandise, fob	..	..	..	..	..	..	..	12,263	12,724	14,259	15,660
Nonfactor Services	..	..	..	..	..	..	..	1,144	1,309	1,521	1,863
Factor Services	..	..	..	..	..	..	..	688	924	1,244	1,738
Long-Term Interest	..	0	0	1	2	16	53	91	151	183	237
Private Current Transfers, net	..	..	..	..	..	..	..	399	463	673	672
Workers' Remittances	..	..	..	..	..	..	..	..	..	..	..
Curr. A/C Bal before Off. Transf.	..	..	..	..	..	..	..	-2,973	-2,567	-2,758	-3,368
Net Official Transfers	..	..	..	..	..	..	..	180	175	213	3
Curr. A/C Bal after Off. Transf.	..	..	..	..	..	..	..	-2,793	-2,392	-2,545	-3,365
Long-Term Capital, net	..	..	..	..	..	..	..	2,785	2,619	2,195	3,621
Direct Investment	..	..	..	..	..	..	..	-6	-12	9	17
Long-Term Loans	..	24	17	36	133	166	322	857	227	675	991
Disbursements	..	30	24	43	171	235	460	1,072	506	1,015	1,515
Repayments	..	6	6	7	38	69	138	215	279	339	524
Other Long-Term Capital	..	..	..	..	..	..	..	1,934	2,404	1,511	2,613
Other Capital, net	..	..	..	..	..	..	..	193	-598	479	19
Change in Reserves	..	..	..	..	..	..	..	-185	371	-129	-275
Memo Item:					*(Polish Zlotys per US dollar)*						
Conversion Factor (Annual Avg)	..	..	..	..	..	..	..	..	..	..	..
				(Millions of US dollars), outstanding at end of year							
EXTERNAL DEBT (Total)	..	24	41	77	207	401	698	1,487	1,839	2,770	3,872
Long-Term Debt (by debtor)	..	24	41	77	207	401	698	1,487	1,839	2,770	3,872
Central Bank, incl. IMF credit	..	0	0	18	137	338	641	1,436	1,628	2,282	3,142
Central Government	..	24	41	59	69	63	57	51	211	459	577
Rest of General Government	..	..	..	..	..	..	..	..	..	..	..
Non-financial Public Enterprises	..	0	0	0	0	0	0	0	0	29	153
Priv. Sector, incl non-guaranteed	..	..	..	..	..	..	..	..	..	..	..
Short-Term Debt	..	0	0	0	0	0	0	0	0	0	0
Memo Items:					*(Millions of US dollars)*						
Int'l Reserves Excluding Gold	..	..	..	..	..	..	..	..	..	..	565.1
Gold Holdings (at market price)	..	..	..	..	..	..	..	..	..	..	657.9
SOCIAL INDICATORS											
Total Fertility Rate	2.2	2.2	2.3	2.2	2.3	2.3	2.3	2.3	2.3	2.2	2.2
Infant Mortality Rate	34.3	33.2	29.5	28.4	25.8	23.5	24.8	23.7	24.6	22.4	21.0
Life Expectancy at Birth	70.1	70.3	70.4	70.5	70.6	70.6	70.7	70.8	70.9	70.9	70.9
Urban Population, % of total	51.8	52.3	52.9	53.5	54.0	54.6	55.2	55.8	56.4	57.0	57.6
Food Prod. per capita (1987=100)	88.2	93.7	90.5	95.3	100.6	100.9	101.5	102.9	96.2	103.7	104.4
Labor Force, Agriculture (%)	39.8	38.9	37.8	36.8	35.7	34.7	33.7	32.7	31.6	30.6	29.5
Labor Force, Female (%)	45.2	45.4	45.3	45.3	45.3	45.3	45.3	45.3	45.3	45.3	45.3
Primary Schl. Enroll. Ratio	..	101.0	..	..	..	..	100.0	100.0	100.0	100.0	99.0
Primary Schl. Enroll. Ratio, Female	..	99.0	..	..	..	..	99.0	99.0	99.0	..	..
Secondary Schl. Enroll. Ratio	..	62.0	..	..	69.0	..	73.0	..	74.0	75.0	76.0

1980	1981	1982	1983	1984	1985	1986	1987	1988	1989 estimate	NOTES	POLAND
				(Millions of current US dollars)							**FOREIGN TRADE (CUSTOMS BASIS)**
13,870	10,656	11,214	11,572	11,647	11,489	12,074	12,204	13,959	..	..	Value of Exports, fob
2,479	1,575	1,793	2,025	2,125	..	..	2,563	..	..	..	Nonfuel Primary Products
2,067	1,035	1,735	2,075	2,127	1,801	1,594	1,374	..	..	..	Fuels
9,324	8,046	7,686	7,472	7,395	7,403	8,188	8,229	..	..	..	Manufactures
16,915	12,795	10,244	10,590	10,547	10,836	11,208	10,844	12,064	..	..	Value of Imports, cif
4,465	3,572	2,828	2,252	2,401	..	..	2,314	..	..	..	Nonfuel Primary Products
3,252	2,564	2,247	2,759	2,442	2,405	2,319	1,872	..	..	..	Fuels
9,198	6,659	5,169	5,579	5,704	6,152	6,727	6,647	..	..	..	Manufactures
				(Index 1987 = 100)							
..	..	..	..	..	..	..	..	..	..	..	Terms of Trade
..	..	..	..	..	..	..	..	..	..	..	Export Prices, fob
..	..	..	..	..	..	..	..	..	..	..	Import Prices, cif
				(Millions of current US dollars)							**BALANCE OF PAYMENTS**
16,200	12,626	13,482	13,789	13,866	13,222	14,129	14,459	16,589	16,480	..	Exports of Goods & Services
14,043	10,542	11,547	11,615	11,654	10,945	11,926	12,026	13,846	12,869	..	Merchandise, fob
2,018	1,913	1,842	1,990	2,017	2,104	2,015	2,216	2,472	3,201	..	Nonfactor Services
139	171	93	184	195	173	188	217	271	410	..	Factor Services
20,338	17,845	16,254	16,073	15,681	15,174	16,332	16,396	18,387	19,498	..	Imports of Goods & Services
15,819	12,723	11,631	11,312	10,995	10,598	11,459	11,236	12,757	12,822	..	Merchandise, fob
2,023	1,727	1,467	1,783	1,853	1,846	2,012	2,028	2,404	3,053	..	Nonfactor Services
2,496	3,395	3,156	2,978	2,833	2,730	2,861	3,132	3,226	3,623	..	Factor Services
704	389	423	588	912	1,477	999	971	828	767	..	Long-Term Interest
593	909	831	703	732	970	1,097	1,558	1,691	1,146	..	Private Current Transfers, net
0	0	0	0	0	0	0	0	..	..	..	Workers' Remittances
-3,545	-4,310	-1,941	-1,581	-1,083	-982	-1,106	-379	-107	-1,872	..	Curr. A/C Bal before Off. Transf.
128	324	0	0	0	0	0	0	..	887	..	Net Official Transfers
-3,417	-3,986	-1,941	-1,581	-1,083	-982	-1,106	-379	-107	-985	..	Curr. A/C Bal after Off. Transf.
2,640	988	-1,147	-2,730	-300	11,188	-1,550	4,353	747	-1,796	..	Long-Term Capital, net
-11	15	10	15	16	14	-6	4	-7	-7	..	Direct Investment
3,005	2,370	1,256	435	246	500	667	-478	-255	-402	..	Long-Term Loans
5,058	3,116	1,428	701	385	955	1,385	505	578	273	..	Disbursements
2,053	746	172	266	139	455	718	983	833	674	..	Repayments
-354	-1,397	-2,413	-3,180	-562	10,674	-2,211	4,827	1,009	-1,387	..	Other Long-Term Capital
140	3,033	3,458	4,429	1,724	-10,442	2,483	-3,177	-79	3,040	..	Other Capital, net
637	-35	-370	-118	-341	236	173	-797	-561	-259	..	Change in Reserves
				(Polish Zlotys per US dollar)							**Memo Item:**
44.280	51.250	84.820	91.550	113.240	147.140	175.290	265.080	430.500	1,439.180	..	Conversion Factor (Annual Avg)
				(Millions of US dollars), outstanding at end of year							
8,894	13,065	18,767	20,177	21,161	33,336	36,670	42,620	42,146	43,324	..	**EXTERNAL DEBT (Total)**
6,594	10,465	15,367	15,977	16,361	29,763	31,932	36,055	33,670	34,747	..	Long-Term Debt (by debtor)
4,840	6,296	6,364	6,017	5,578	5,674	5,559	5,857	5,442	4,352	..	Central Bank, incl. IMF credit
800	3,033	7,928	8,951	9,863	19,887	24,691	27,717	25,802	27,992	..	Central Government
..	..	..	..	..	..	..	..	..	..	..	Rest of General Government
954	1,136	1,075	1,009	920	4,202	1,683	2,482	2,427	2,404	..	Non-financial Public Enterprises
..	..	..	..	..	..	..	..	..	..	..	Priv. Sector, incl non-guaranteed
2,300	2,600	3,400	4,200	4,800	3,573	4,738	6,565	8,476	8,577	..	Short-Term Debt
				(Millions of US dollars)							**Memo Items:**
127.6	277.8	646.8	765.2	1,106.0	870.4	697.8	1,494.7	2,055.3	2,314.3	..	Int'l Reserves Excluding Gold
446.8	186.8	215.2	180.1	145.5	154.3	184.5	228.5	193.6	189.3	..	Gold Holdings (at market price)
											SOCIAL INDICATORS
2.3	2.3	2.3	2.3	2.3	2.3	2.2	2.2	2.2	2.2	..	Total Fertility Rate
21.2	20.6	20.2	19.2	19.2	18.4	17.5	17.5	16.2	16.2	..	Infant Mortality Rate
70.9	70.9	70.9	71.0	71.1	71.2	71.3	71.4	71.6	71.7	..	Life Expectancy at Birth
58.2	58.6	59.0	59.3	59.7	60.1	60.5	60.9	61.2	61.6	..	Urban Population, % of total
91.5	90.5	93.0	96.2	98.4	99.9	106.2	100.0	102.0	101.5	..	Food Prod. per capita (1987=100)
28.5	..	..	..	..	..	..	..	..	..	..	Labor Force, Agriculture (%)
45.3	45.3	45.4	45.4	45.4	45.4	45.5	45.5	45.5	45.6	..	Labor Force, Female (%)
100.0	..	100.0	101.0	101.0	101.0	101.0	101.0	..	..	..	Primary Schl. Enroll. Ratio
99.0	99.0	99.0	100.0	100.0	100.0	101.0	101.0	..	..	..	Primary Schl. Enroll. Ratio, Female
77.0	..	75.0	75.0	78.0	78.0	79.0	80.0	..	..	..	Secondary Schl. Enroll. Ratio

PORTUGAL	1969	1970	1971	1972	1973	1974	1975	1976	1977	1978	1979
CURRENT GNP PER CAPITA (US $)	610	700	820	940	1,200	1,420	1,540	1,700	1,830	1,890	2,090
POPULATION (thousands)	9,097	9,044	8,644	8,631	8,633	8,754	9,093	9,355	9,455	9,558	9,661

USE AND ORIGIN OF RESOURCES *(Billions of current Portuguese Escudos)*

	1969	1970	1971	1972	1973	1974	1975	1976	1977	1978	1979
Gross National Product (GNP)	160.9	178.8	199.6	232.5	284.6	343.1	376.8	464.3	617.9	771.6	971.8
Net Factor Income from Abroad	1.1	1.0	0.5	0.7	2.4	3.8	-0.4	-4.6	-7.9	-15.7	-21.5
GDP at Market Prices	159.8	177.8	199.1	231.8	282.2	339.3	377.2	468.9	625.8	787.3	993.3
Resource Balance	-6.6	-11.6	-14.0	-10.9	-19.8	-51.9	-46.7	-62.9	-94.1	-97.7	-107.6
Exports of Goods & NFServices	39.1	43.4	49.9	63.1	75.4	91.2	76.9	81.7	115.3	158.4	268.7
Imports of Goods & NFServices	45.7	55.0	63.9	74.0	95.2	143.1	123.6	144.6	209.4	256.1	376.3
Domestic Absorption	166.4	189.4	213.1	242.7	302.0	391.2	423.9	531.8	719.9	885.0	1,100.9
Private Consumption, etc.	108.2	118.3	133.9	144.8	182.1	246.5	275.8	345.8	450.4	535.3	670.3
General Gov't Consumption	20.7	24.6	26.9	31.0	36.1	47.9	56.5	64.4	87.8	109.7	137.6
Gross Domestic Investment	37.5	46.5	52.3	66.9	83.8	96.8	91.6	121.6	181.7	240.0	293.0
Fixed Investment	36.1	41.3	49.2	62.8	75.6	88.2	97.8	117.5	167.9	222.3	270.6
Indirect Taxes, net	..	..	..	..	..	..	..	..	..	..	..
GDP at factor cost	..	..	..	..	..	..	..	..	..	..	..
Agriculture	..	..	..	..	..	..	..	..	74.6	94.0	115.0
Industry	..	..	..	..	..	..	..	..	226.3	291.5	376.3
Manufacturing	..	..	..	..	..	..	..	..	..	..	..
Services, etc.	..	..	..	..	..	..	..	..	324.9	401.8	502.0
Gross Domestic Saving	30.9	34.9	38.3	56.0	64.0	44.9	44.9	58.7	87.6	142.3	185.4
Gross National Saving	..	49.9	57.1	80.5	93.3	76.9	71.8	83.3	123.1	198.4	284.8

(Billions of 1980 Portuguese Escudos)

	1969	1970	1971	1972	1973	1974	1975	1976	1977	1978	1979
Gross National Product	712.0	776.1	824.8	891.4	996.7	1,010.7	955.2	1,012.1	1,065.7	1,093.2	1,153.7
GDP at Market Prices	707.5	772.0	823.3	889.2	988.8	1,000.2	956.7	1,022.6	1,079.9	1,116.3	1,180.3
Resource Balance	-98.0	-105.4	-132.7	-130.1	-174.8	-254.0	-161.9	-175.9	-220.8	-199.1	-177.9
Exports of Goods & NFServices	259.6	255.5	280.6	332.9	346.7	292.4	246.7	246.7	237.2	254.3	323.6
Imports of Goods & NFServices	357.6	360.9	413.4	463.0	521.4	546.3	408.6	422.6	458.0	453.4	501.5
Domestic Absorption	805.3	877.3	955.9	1,019.2	1,163.5	1,254.3	1,118.5	1,198.4	1,300.7	1,315.4	1,358.2
Private Consumption, etc.	510.7	528.5	593.6	610.0	699.8	801.5	751.8	794.9	823.4	809.7	812.5
General Gov't Consumption	75.4	80.8	85.9	93.5	100.7	118.1	125.9	134.8	150.6	157.1	167.2
Gross Domestic Investment	219.2	267.9	276.4	315.6	362.9	334.6	241.0	268.8	326.7	348.7	378.5
Fixed Investment	222.0	247.6	271.7	308.5	337.9	314.3	278.9	281.1	314.9	337.0	333.6
GDP at factor cost	..	..	..	..	..	..	..	..	..	..	..
Agriculture	..	..	..	..	..	..	..	..	98.2	104.1	125.6
Industry	..	..	..	..	..	..	..	..	411.8	440.1	462.3
Manufacturing	..	..	..	..	..	..	..	..	..	..	..
Services, etc.	..	..	..	..	..	..	..	..	569.8	572.1	592.5

Memo Items:

	1969	1970	1971	1972	1973	1974	1975	1976	1977	1978	1979
Capacity to Import	306.0	284.8	322.8	394.8	413.0	348.2	254.2	238.7	252.2	280.4	358.1
Terms of Trade Adjustment	46.3	29.2	42.2	61.9	66.3	55.8	7.5	-7.9	15.0	26.1	34.5
Gross Domestic Income	753.9	801.3	865.6	951.3	1,055.3	1,056.2	964.2	1,014.6	1,094.9	1,142.5	1,214.8
Gross National Income	758.4	805.5	867.1	953.5	1,063.2	1,066.7	962.7	1,004.1	1,080.7	1,119.3	1,188.2

DOMESTIC PRICES/DEFLATORS *(Index 1980 = 100)*

	1969	1970	1971	1972	1973	1974	1975	1976	1977	1978	1979
Overall (GDP)	22.6	23.0	24.2	26.1	28.5	33.9	39.4	45.9	57.9	70.5	84.2
Domestic Absorption	20.7	21.6	22.3	23.8	26.0	31.2	37.9	44.4	55.3	67.3	81.1
Agriculture	..	..	..	..	..	..	..	..	76.0	90.3	91.6
Industry	..	..	..	..	..	..	..	..	54.9	66.2	81.4
Manufacturing	..	..	..	..	..	..	..	..	..	..	..
Consumer Price Index	5.2	5.5	5.9	6.4	7.0	9.0	10.9	12.8	16.3	20.0	24.8

MANUFACTURING ACTIVITY

	1969	1970	1971	1972	1973	1974	1975	1976	1977	1978	1979
Employment (1987=100)	71.1	71.3	77.2	88.0	94.3	95.4	97.2	100.0	101.6	104.1	107.8
Real Earnings per Empl. (1987=100)	69.3	76.7	81.4	86.9	90.5	104.3	114.8	114.5	105.6	98.3	94.0
Real Output per Empl. (1987=100)	..	..	..	..	..	..	..	..	..	..	..
Earnings as % of Value Added	32.4	33.9	39.2	41.3	40.9	46.6	61.0	60.6	53.0	49.8	46.1

MONETARY HOLDINGS *(Billions of current Portuguese Escudos)*

	1969	1970	1971	1972	1973	1974	1975	1976	1977	1978	1979
Money Supply, Broadly Defined	144.9	166.5	189.0	234.8	301.3	342.3	385.5	470.7	578.6	738.2	1,012.5
Money	93.9	100.4	104.9	122.3	165.6	182.5	227.3	256.2	286.0	326.5	414.8
Currency Outside Banks	26.7	29.7	31.9	36.1	38.3	69.7	109.8	109.2	113.3	121.4	142.1
Demand Deposits	67.2	70.7	73.0	86.2	127.3	112.8	117.4	147.0	172.7	205.1	272.6
Quasi-Money	51.0	66.1	84.1	112.5	135.7	159.8	158.2	214.5	292.6	411.7	597.8

GOVERNMENT DEFICIT (-) OR SURPLUS *(Billions of current Portuguese Escudos)*

	1969	1970	1971	1972	1973	1974	1975	1976	1977	1978	1979
GOVERNMENT DEFICIT (-) OR SURPLUS	..	..	..	..	..	..	-31.70	-54.20	-40.90	-92.80	-100.50
Current Revenue	..	..	..	..	..	..	95.70	127.40	178.20	217.30	272.30
Current Expenditure	..	..	..	..	..	..	108.20	147.50	..	239.80	300.80
Current Budget Balance	..	..	..	..	..	..	-12.50	-20.10	..	-22.50	-28.50
Capital Receipts	..	..	..	..	..	..	0.40	..	..	0.70	0.80
Capital Payments	..	..	..	..	..	..	19.60	34.00	..	71.00	72.80

1980	1981	1982	1983	1984	1985	1986	1987	1988	1989 estimate	NOTES	PORTUGAL
2,380	2,500	2,500	2,250	1,990	1,970	2,270	2,830	3,650	4,250	..	**CURRENT GNP PER CAPITA (US $)**
9,766	9,855	9,930	10,009	10,089	10,157	10,208	10,250	10,291	10,333	..	**POPULATION (thousands)**
											USE AND ORIGIN OF RESOURCES
			(Billions of current Portuguese Escudos)								
1,203.2	1,413.0	1,757.8	2,170.0	2,631.4	3,344.5	4,267.4	5,038.2	5,909.1	6,951.1	..	Gross National Product (GNP)
-31.8	-59.3	-98.8	-118.9	-174.1	-191.8	-151.4	-131.7	-120.1	-115.2	..	Net Factor Income from Abroad
1,235.0	1,472.7	1,856.9	2,289.0	2,805.5	3,536.3	4,418.8	5,169.9	6,029.2	7,066.3	..	GDP at Market Prices
-186.0	-297.3	-374.0	-282.0	-228.5	-123.3	-111.7	-337.6	-575.0	-686.5	..	Resource Balance
355.1	403.0	488.7	733.0	1,020.1	1,316.2	1,457.9	1,777.0	2,077.8	2,543.4	..	Exports of Goods & NFServices
541.1	700.3	862.7	1,015.0	1,248.6	1,439.5	1,569.6	2,114.6	2,652.8	3,229.9	..	Imports of Goods & NFServices
1,421.0	1,770.0	2,230.9	2,571.0	3,034.1	3,659.6	4,530.5	5,507.5	6,604.1	7,752.8	..	Domestic Absorption
823.1	1,020.3	1,277.5	1,570.0	1,979.1	2,388.6	2,900.8	3,388.4	4,010.4	4,681.4	..	Private Consumption, etc.
177.3	218.7	266.6	334.0	405.5	501.9	598.6	688.8	799.5	921.2	..	General Gov't Consumption
420.6	531.0	686.8	667.0	649.5	769.1	1,031.1	1,430.3	1,794.2	2,150.2	..	Gross Domestic Investment
364.2	463.0	587.5	678.0	669.9	766.7	986.4	1,307.3	1,680.4	2,025.5	..	Fixed Investment
..	..	..	..	..	..	..	..	..	..		Indirect Taxes, net
..	..	..	..	..	..	..	..	..	..	B	GDP at factor cost
126.0	123.6	159.8	200.0	265.0	331.0	371.0	448.0		..	..	Agriculture
484.1	579.6	734.6	902.0	1,117.0	1,375.0	1,669.0	1,919.0	..	..	..	Industry
..	..	..	..	..	..	..	..	..	..	..	Manufacturing
624.9	769.5	962.5	1,187.0	1,423.5	1,830.3	2,378.8	2,802.9	..	..	..	Services, etc.
234.6	233.7	312.8	385.0	420.9	645.8	919.4	1,092.7	1,219.3	1,463.7	..	Gross Domestic Saving
352.9	352.5	425.7	502.1	560.2	814.9	1,159.6	1,439.0	1,616.1	1,907.9	..	Gross National Saving
			(Billions of 1980 Portuguese Escudos)								
1,203.2	1,198.5	1,219.6	1,219.4	1,186.4	1,233.7	1,310.5	1,378.7	1,448.5	1,525.9	..	Gross National Product
1,235.0	1,247.2	1,286.1	1,284.3	1,262.0	1,303.4	1,359.4	1,417.9	1,481.7	1,555.2	..	GDP at Market Prices
-186.0	-216.8	-226.4	-114.1	-39.0	-5.5	-64.8	-171.9	-264.5	-307.1	..	Resource Balance
355.1	344.4	365.2	426.1	486.6	540.7	576.9	638.0	681.4	727.9	..	Exports of Goods & NFServices
541.1	561.2	591.6	540.2	525.6	546.1	641.7	809.9	945.9	1,035.0	..	Imports of Goods & NFServices
1,421.0	1,464.0	1,512.6	1,398.4	1,301.0	1,308.9	1,424.4	1,590.5	1,747.2	1,863.6	..	Domestic Absorption
823.1	850.0	867.9	845.1	808.7	811.9	880.9	1,042.7	1,189.6	1,268.7	..	Private Consumption, etc.
177.3	182.1	187.2	192.2	197.2	200.1	203.7	208.3	218.5	223.8	..	General Gov't Consumption
420.6	431.9	457.5	361.1	295.1	296.9	339.9	339.9	339.9	371.9	..	Gross Domestic Investment
364.2	382.8	393.8	364.4	298.7	289.7	317.3	379.5	438.8	480.1	..	Fixed Investment
..	..	..	..	..	..	..	..	..	..	B	GDP at factor cost
126.0	109.4	115.7	109.9	113.0	117.2	..	..	..	..	..	Agriculture
484.1	493.6	508.7	511.0	498.7	515.0	..	..	..	..	..	Industry
..	..	..	..	..	..	..	..	..	..	..	Manufacturing
624.9	644.2	661.7	663.3	650.3	671.2	..	..	..	..	..	Services, etc.
											Memo Items:
355.1	323.0	335.1	390.1	429.4	499.4	596.0	680.6	740.9	815.0	..	Capacity to Import
0.0	-21.4	-30.0	-35.9	-57.2	-41.3	19.2	42.6	59.5	87.2	..	Terms of Trade Adjustment
1,235.0	1,225.7	1,256.1	1,248.3	1,204.8	1,262.1	1,378.8	1,460.9	1,541.6	1,643.0	..	Gross Domestic Income
1,203.2	1,177.0	1,189.6	1,183.5	1,129.2	1,192.4	1,329.9	1,421.6	1,508.4	1,613.5	..	Gross National Income
			(Index 1980 = 100)								**DOMESTIC PRICES/DEFLATORS**
100.0	118.1	144.4	178.2	222.3	271.3	325.1	364.6	406.9	454.4	..	Overall (GDP)
100.0	120.9	147.5	183.8	233.2	279.6	318.1	346.3	378.0	416.0	..	Domestic Absorption
100.0	113.0	138.1	181.9	234.6	282.5	..	..	..	..	..	Agriculture
100.0	117.4	144.4	176.5	224.0	267.0	..	..	..	..	..	Industry
..	..	..	..	..	..	..	..	..	..	..	Manufacturing
28.9	34.7	42.5	53.2	68.6	81.9	91.4	100.0	109.6	123.4	f	Consumer Price Index
											MANUFACTURING ACTIVITY
109.5	110.1	108.5	107.0	103.1	100.2	100.2	100.0	99.6	..	..	Employment (1987=100)
100.3	101.0	99.0	94.1	87.1	89.3	94.8	100.0	107.1	..	..	Real Earnings per Empl. (1987=100)
..	..	..	..	..	..	..	..	..	..	..	Real Output per Empl. (1987=100)
43.2	45.1	46.9	43.5	38.4	39.1	38.7	36.0	36.7	..	..	Earnings as % of Value Added
			(Billions of current Portuguese Escudos)								**MONETARY HOLDINGS**
1,365.4	1,755.3	2,218.1	2,661.6	3,400.6	4,226.6	4,992.1	5,553.6	6,302.0	..	..	Money Supply, Broadly Defined
506.0	550.5	638.6	687.3	799.4	1,017.6	1,413.4	1,581.8	1,791.1	..	..	Money
165.2	188.4	219.5	240.0	267.3	319.0	399.3	457.7	509.7	..	..	Currency Outside Banks
340.8	362.1	419.2	447.3	532.1	698.6	1,014.1	1,124.1	1,281.5	..	..	Demand Deposits
859.4	1,204.9	1,579.5	1,974.3	2,601.2	3,209.0	3,578.8	3,971.8	4,510.9	..	..	Quasi-Money
			(Billions of current Portuguese Escudos)								**GOVERNMENT DEFICIT (-) OR SURPLUS**
-121.50	-179.60	-195.00	-219.70	-272.40	-522.00	-543.20	-559.20	-478.70	..	..	Current Revenue
379.10	480.90	602.30	806.40	954.80	1,177.70	1,609.60	1,773.90	2,173.80	..	..	Current Revenue
412.40	550.50	665.70	826.00	1,027.20	1,457.40	1,836.50	1,967.50	2,258.10	..	..	Current Expenditure
-33.30	-69.60	-63.40	-19.60	-72.40	-279.70	-226.90	-193.60	-84.30	..	..	Current Budget Balance
1.00	1.50	2.40	5.30	0.50	9.70	0.90	3.00	6.20	..	..	Capital Receipts
89.20	111.50	134.00	205.40	200.50	252.00	317.20	368.60	400.60	..	..	Capital Payments

PORTUGAL	1969	1970	1971	1972	1973	1974	1975	1976	1977	1978	1979
FOREIGN TRADE (CUSTOMS BASIS)					*(Millions of current US dollars)*						
Value of Exports, fob	853	949	1,053	1,294	1,862	2,302	1,940	1,820	2,013	2,410	3,480
Nonfuel Primary Products	291	321	320	390	543	633	530	551	560	609	822
Fuels	10	22	23	22	22	65	40	39	34	44	129
Manufactures	553	606	709	882	1,297	1,604	1,370	1,231	1,420	1,757	2,529
Value of Imports, cif	1,298	1,590	1,824	2,227	3,073	4,641	3,863	4,316	4,964	5,229	6,509
Nonfuel Primary Products	382	427	496	649	934	1,434	1,263	1,352	1,544	1,430	1,845
Fuels	110	145	156	154	192	584	588	692	737	826	1,267
Manufactures	806	1,017	1,172	1,425	1,947	2,623	2,012	2,272	2,683	2,973	3,397
					(Index 1987 = 100)						
Terms of Trade	124.3	126.2	120.1	120.6	122.5	104.8	106.9	98.9	93.3	99.0	97.5
Export Prices, fob	29.9	30.8	33.2	38.2	50.1	60.9	66.0	62.5	62.9	72.8	86.9
Import Prices, cif	24.1	24.4	27.7	31.7	40.9	58.1	61.7	63.2	67.4	73.6	89.1
BALANCE OF PAYMENTS					*(Millions of current US dollars)*						
Exports of Goods & Services	..	1,349	1,817	2,268	3,091	3,657	2,998	2,628	3,472	3,944	5,333
Merchandise, fob	..	956	1,057	1,307	1,843	2,289	1,942	1,791	2,534	2,738	3,549
Nonfactor Services	..	310	691	840	1,073	1,136	941	788	868	1,117	1,648
Factor Services	..	83	69	121	175	232	115	49	70	88	136
Imports of Goods & Services	..	1,995	2,317	2,795	3,847	5,597	4,794	4,874	5,562	6,042	7,864
Merchandise, fob	..	1,448	1,695	2,041	2,753	4,284	3,544	3,960	4,528	4,783	6,183
Nonfactor Services	..	495	572	674	1,015	1,211	1,110	714	765	831	1,105
Factor Services	..	52	50	79	80	102	139	200	269	428	576
Long-Term Interest	..	34	37	34	34	34	44	52	94	184	363
Private Current Transfers, net	..	488	646	881	1,097	1,109	1,070	965	1,134	1,635	2,471
Workers' Remittances	..	523	678	908	1,140	1,144	1,103	907	1,173	1,673	2,454
Curr. A/C Bal before Off. Transf.	..	-158	146	354	341	-831	-726	-1,282	-957	-463	-60
Net Official Transfers	..	0	0	..	..	..	-29	..	..	..	6
Curr. A/C Bal after Off. Transf.	..	-158	146	354	341	-831	-755	-1,282	-957	-463	-54
Long-Term Capital, net	..	278	97	-104	-141	273	-93	60	69	696	676
Direct Investment	..	15	49	66	51	69	107	58	55	60	70
Long-Term Loans	..	-46	14	18	153	94	299	356	788	1,437	1,488
Disbursements	..	38	102	117	257	204	404	536	1,066	1,841	2,075
Repayments	..	84	88	100	104	110	106	181	279	404	587
Other Long-Term Capital	..	309	34	-188	-345	111	-499	-354	-773	-801	-883
Other Capital, net	..	-88	97	106	128	-33	-197	188	553	98	-346
Change in Reserves	..	-32	-340	-356	-328	590	1,045	1,034	334	-331	-276
Memo Item:					*(Portuguese Escudos per US dollar)*						
Conversion Factor (Annual Avg)	28.750	28.750	28.310	27.050	24.670	25.410	25.550	30.230	38.280	43.940	48.620
EXTERNAL DEBT (Total)				*(Millions of US dollars), outstanding at end of year*							
	..	753	808	848	1,061	1,210	1,477	2,022	4,327	6,242	7,875
Long-Term Debt (by debtor)	..	753	808	848	1,061	1,210	1,477	2,022	3,027	4,659	6,225
Central Bank, incl. IMF credit	..	0	0	0	0	0	0	201	347	925	980
Central Government	..	193	182	207	266	255	217	260	345	794	1,271
Rest of General Government	..	4	4	3	2	1	0	0	0	0	0
Non-financial Public Enterprises	..	69	135	170	310	472	740	1,019	1,691	2,289	3,181
Priv. Sector, incl non-guaranteed	..	486	487	468	483	482	520	543	644	650	793
Short-Term Debt	..	0	0	0	0	0	0	0	1,300	1,583	1,650
Memo Items:					*(Millions of US dollars)*						
Int'l Reserves Excluding Gold	570	602	945	1,291	1,676	1,161	398	176	366	871	931
Gold Holdings (at market price)	880	963	1,148	1,745	3,091	5,192	3,887	3,729	3,977	5,002	11,331
SOCIAL INDICATORS											
Total Fertility Rate	2.8	2.8	2.8	2.7	2.7	2.6	2.5	2.6	2.4	2.2	2.1
Infant Mortality Rate	55.8	55.5	51.9	41.4	44.8	37.9	38.9	33.4	30.3	29.1	26.0
Life Expectancy at Birth	67.0	67.4	67.7	68.0	68.3	68.6	68.9	69.1	69.4	70.2	71.0
Urban Population, % of total	25.8	26.2	26.5	26.8	27.2	27.5	27.8	28.1	28.5	28.8	29.2
Food Prod. per capita (1987=100)	113.6	126.1	112.5	111.9	120.2	123.5	115.5	105.2	89.7	89.0	109.2
Labor Force, Agriculture (%)	33.1	31.8	31.0	30.2	29.5	28.8	28.1	27.6	27.1	26.6	26.2
Labor Force, Female (%)	24.0	24.8	26.2	27.4	28.6	29.8	30.9	31.9	33.0	33.9	34.8
Primary Schl. Enroll. Ratio	..	98.0	..	..	..	..	113.0	114.0	117.0	103.0	..
Primary Schl. Enroll. Ratio, Female	..	96.0	..	..	..	..	111.0	112.0	115.0	..	..
Secondary Schl. Enroll. Ratio	..	57.0	..	..	..	..	53.0	54.0	55.0	..	48.0

1980	1981	1982	1983	1984	1985	1986	1987	1988	1989 estimate	NOTES	PORTUGAL
				(Millions of current US dollars)							**FOREIGN TRADE (CUSTOMS BASIS)**
4,629	4,180	4,171	4,601	5,208	5,685	7,160	9,167	10,556	11,027	..	Value of Exports, fob
1,052	921	870	906	1,049	1,038	1,236	1,623	1,783	..	..	Nonfuel Primary Products
255	298	163	231	186	236	217	149	275	..	..	Fuels
3,322	2,961	3,138	3,464	3,973	4,412	5,707	7,395	8,498	8,742	..	Manufactures
9,293	9,946	9,605	8,257	7,975	7,650	9,393	13,438	16,108	16,353	..	Value of Imports, cif
2,247	2,491	2,149	1,918	2,169	1,974	2,129	2,819	3,471	..	..	Nonfuel Primary Products
2,243	2,396	2,546	2,218	2,286	2,026	1,439	1,563	2,265	..	..	Fuels
4,802	5,058	4,911	4,120	3,520	3,650	5,825	9,055	10,372	10,139	..	Manufactures
				(Index 1987 = 100)							
101.3	89.9	80.7	76.0	75.1	80.6	92.0	100.0	103.1	..	..	Terms of Trade
105.8	94.9	81.1	75.9	75.8	76.8	82.2	100.0	107.9	..	..	Export Prices, fob
104.5	105.6	100.6	99.9	101.0	95.2	89.3	100.0	104.7	..	..	Import Prices, cif
				(Millions of current US dollars)							**BALANCE OF PAYMENTS**
6,846	6,377	5,894	6,940	7,137	7,966	10,029	12,810	14,751	16,007	..	Exports of Goods & Services
4,582	4,061	4,122	5,224	5,206	5,685	7,209	9,170	10,708	12,787	..	Merchandise, fob
2,088	2,109	1,614	1,543	1,732	2,000	2,516	3,235	3,561	2,699	..	Nonfactor Services
176	207	158	173	199	281	304	405	483	521	..	Factor Services
10,916	11,876	11,807	10,075	9,829	9,779	11,695	15,892	19,698	20,964	..	Imports of Goods & Services
8,611	9,121	8,984	7,624	7,233	7,142	8,844	12,545	15,845	17,931	..	Merchandise, fob
1,493	1,586	1,421	1,205	1,208	1,231	1,536	2,007	2,536	1,780	..	Nonfactor Services
812	1,170	1,402	1,246	1,388	1,407	1,316	1,340	1,317	1,253	..	Factor Services
529	870	973	905	1,091	1,152	1,218	1,261	1,168	1,056	..	Long-Term Interest
2,999	2,895	2,663	2,130	2,141	2,118	2,618	3,393	3,590	3,552	..	Private Current Transfers, net
2,928	2,838	2,602	2,118	2,152	2,091	2,544	3,245	3,371	3,379	..	Workers' Remittances
-1,072	-2,605	-3,250	-1,004	-551	304	952	310	-1,356	-1,404	..	Curr. A/C Bal before Off. Transf.
7	..	..	..	36	106	192	330	725	829	..	Net Official Transfers
-1,064	-2,605	-3,250	-1,004	-514	410	1,144	640	-632	-575	..	Curr. A/C Bal after Off. Transf.
703	1,186	2,075	1,225	1,149	949	-549	-236	684	2,554	..	Long-Term Capital, net
143	155	136	123	186	232	239	308	821	1,546	..	Direct Investment
1,434	1,684	1,624	1,698	1,087	792	-203	-1,142	-381	1,259	..	Long-Term Loans
2,098	2,576	2,588	2,869	2,711	2,702	2,417	2,533	2,939	3,515	..	Disbursements
664	892	964	1,172	1,624	1,910	2,620	3,675	3,320	2,256	..	Repayments
-875	-653	315	-595	-124	-75	-585	597	244	-251	..	Other Long-Term Capital
719	1,277	1,297	-803	-632	-451	-706	1,348	826	2,673	..	Other Capital, net
-357	142	-122	582	-3	-909	111	-1,752	-878	-4,652	..	Change in Reserves
				(Portuguese Escudos per US dollar)							**Memo Item:**
50.060	61.550	79.470	110.780	146.390	170.390	149.590	140.880	143.950	157.460	..	Conversion Factor (Annual Avg)
				(Millions of US dollars), outstanding at end of year							
9,700	11,553	13,578	14,498	14,865	16,627	16,661	18,332	17,134	18,289	..	**EXTERNAL DEBT (Total)**
7,305	8,218	9,739	11,076	11,850	14,000	15,232	16,168	14,531	15,339	..	Long-Term Debt (by debtor)
896	729	568	857	925	915	838	569	51	77	..	Central Bank, incl. IMF credit
1,686	2,191	2,849	3,506	3,901	4,676	5,241	6,007	6,205	8,460	..	Central Government
0	0	0	0	0	0	0	0	0	..	..	Rest of General Government
3,944	4,637	5,287	5,851	6,331	7,707	8,391	8,652	7,404	5,875	..	Non-financial Public Enterprises
779	660	1,036	862	692	703	761	940	871	927	..	Priv. Sector, incl non-guaranteed
2,395	3,335	3,839	3,422	3,015	2,627	1,429	2,164	2,603	2,950	..	Short-Term Debt
				(Millions of US dollars)							**Memo Items:**
795	534	447	385	516	1,395	1,456	3,327	5,127	9,953	..	Int'l Reserves Excluding Gold
13,068	8,800	10,093	7,796	6,257	6,614	7,880	9,712	6,593	6,436	..	Gold Holdings (at market price)
											SOCIAL INDICATORS
2.2	2.1	2.1	1.9	1.9	1.7	1.6	1.6	1.6	1.6	..	Total Fertility Rate
24.3	21.8	19.8	19.2	16.7	17.8	15.8	14.2	13.7	13.1	..	Infant Mortality Rate
71.4	71.8	72.3	72.7	73.0	73.4	73.8	74.2	74.4	74.7	..	Life Expectancy at Birth
29.5	29.8	30.2	30.5	30.9	31.2	31.6	32.0	32.5	32.9	..	Urban Population, % of total
91.7	81.7	96.8	85.0	92.7	96.5	94.4	100.0	78.3	104.3	..	Food Prod. per capita (1987=100)
25.8	..	..	..	..	..	..	..	..	..	..	Labor Force, Agriculture (%)
35.7	35.8	35.9	36.1	36.2	36.3	36.4	36.5	36.5	36.6	..	Labor Force, Female (%)
123.0	..	121.0	119.0	126.0	124.0	..	..	..	..	..	Primary Schl. Enroll. Ratio
123.0	..	122.0	119.0	123.0	121.0	..	..	..	..	..	Primary Schl. Enroll. Ratio, Female
37.0	..	43.0	47.0	52.0	56.0	..	..	..	..	..	Secondary Schl. Enroll. Ratio

RWANDA	1969	1970	1971	1972	1973	1974	1975	1976	1977	1978	1979
CURRENT GNP PER CAPITA (US $)	60	60	60	60	70	70	90	120	160	180	210
POPULATION (thousands)	3,582	3,695	3,817	3,944	4,077	4,215	4,358	4,506	4,658	4,815	4,976

USE AND ORIGIN OF RESOURCES

(Billions of current Rwanda Francs)

	1969	1970	1971	1972	1973	1974	1975	1976	1977	1978	1979
Gross National Product (GNP)	18.97	22.03	22.38	22.78	24.49	28.48	52.76	61.84	71.82	80.57	96.20
Net Factor Income from Abroad	0.09	0.04	0.15	0.08	0.09	-0.20	-0.01	-0.03	0.19	-0.48	0.03
GDP at Market Prices	18.87	21.99	22.23	22.70	24.40	28.68	52.77	61.87	71.63	81.05	96.17
Resource Balance	-1.26	-0.82	-1.48	-1.81	-0.45	-2.63	-4.50	-2.98	-2.43	-7.31	-1.64
Exports of Goods & NFServices	1.45	2.53	2.27	1.88	2.83	3.49	4.84	9.02	10.22	11.98	20.24
Imports of Goods & NFServices	2.71	3.35	3.75	3.69	3.28	6.12	9.34	12.00	12.65	19.29	21.88
Domestic Absorption	20.13	22.81	23.71	24.51	24.85	31.31	57.27	64.85	74.06	88.36	97.81
Private Consumption, etc.	17.23	19.35	19.48	19.92	19.77	24.86	41.24	45.97	50.86	62.10	73.62
General Gov't Consumption	1.65	1.91	2.20	2.42	2.78	3.45	8.78	10.33	12.41	12.80	12.62
Gross Domestic Investment	1.25	1.55	2.03	2.17	2.30	3.00	7.25	8.55	10.79	13.46	11.57
Fixed Investment	1.23	1.58	2.01	2.16	..	..	6.96	7.99	9.14	11.32	14.27
Indirect Taxes, net	0.76	1.52	1.29	1.39	1.62	2.24	3.25	5.61	6.44	5.95	8.24
GDP at factor cost	18.10	20.47	20.94	21.31	22.78	26.44	49.52	56.26	65.19	75.10	87.93
Agriculture	12.41	13.55	13.60	13.52	14.89	16.96	25.97	30.45	33.28	34.38	47.16
Industry	1.77	1.89	1.93	2.14	2.13	2.64	10.01	11.69	15.19	17.93	18.02
Manufacturing	0.77	0.79	0.83	0.93	1.00	1.25	6.48	7.60	10.20	12.64	12.30
Services, etc.	4.68	6.55	6.70	7.04	7.38	9.08	16.79	19.73	23.16	28.74	30.99
Gross Domestic Saving	-0.01	0.73	0.55	0.36	1.85	0.37	2.75	5.57	8.36	6.15	9.93
Gross National Saving	..	0.46	0.54	0.15	1.84	-0.27	2.47	5.35	8.30	5.78	10.51

(Billions of 1987 Rwanda Francs)

	1969	1970	1971	1972	1973	1974	1975	1976	1977	1978	1979
Gross National Product	83.44	88.17	89.66	89.64	92.70	92.47	95.65	102.28	107.74	116.55	128.98
GDP at Market Prices	83.00	87.98	89.05	89.28	92.35	93.10	95.65	102.30	107.40	117.23	128.90
Resource Balance	-4.90	-3.52	-5.46	-6.22	-2.36	-7.70	-7.15	-5.26	-8.23	-9.50	-7.28
Exports of Goods & NFServices	4.30	6.83	6.14	4.99	7.23	7.65	5.92	10.07	6.46	9.28	12.56
Imports of Goods & NFServices	9.20	10.35	11.60	11.21	9.59	15.34	13.07	15.32	14.69	18.78	19.84
Domestic Absorption	87.91	91.50	94.51	95.50	94.71	100.79	102.80	107.56	115.63	126.73	136.19
Private Consumption, etc.	77.15	79.86	80.34	80.38	78.55	83.24	78.38	81.33	87.02	99.77	113.71
General Gov't Consumption	6.57	6.91	7.97	8.61	9.52	10.13	14.40	15.45	16.21	14.85	12.64
Gross Domestic Investment	4.19	4.73	6.20	6.51	6.64	7.43	10.02	10.78	12.40	12.10	9.83
Fixed Investment	..	..	..	..	..	..	..	10.07	10.47	10.11	12.56
GDP at factor cost	..	..	..	..	86.43	86.03	89.97	93.26	97.97	108.81	118.11
Agriculture	33.95	36.97	37.96	36.00	37.72	44.49	41.93	53.96	54.37	55.86	67.89
Industry	..	..	..	..	..	..	..	22.01	24.12	25.50	25.95
Manufacturing	11.36	11.68	12.01	12.34	12.84	13.13	13.41	13.78	15.29	16.22	16.07
Services, etc.	..	..	..	..	..	..	..	26.92	29.44	36.02	35.56

Memo Items:

	1969	1970	1971	1972	1973	1974	1975	1976	1977	1978	1979
Capacity to Import	4.92	7.82	7.02	5.71	8.27	8.75	6.77	11.52	11.86	11.66	18.36
Terms of Trade Adjustment	0.62	0.99	0.89	0.72	1.04	1.10	0.85	1.45	5.41	2.38	5.80
Gross Domestic Income	83.63	88.97	89.93	90.00	93.39	94.20	96.50	103.76	112.81	119.61	134.70
Gross National Income	84.06	89.16	90.54	90.36	93.75	93.57	96.50	103.73	113.14	118.93	134.77

DOMESTIC PRICES/DEFLATORS

(Index 1987 = 100)

	1969	1970	1971	1972	1973	1974	1975	1976	1977	1978	1979
Overall (GDP)	22.7	25.0	25.0	25.4	26.4	30.8	55.2	60.5	66.7	69.1	74.6
Domestic Absorption	22.9	24.9	25.1	25.7	26.2	31.1	55.7	60.3	64.0	69.7	71.8
Agriculture	36.6	36.6	35.8	37.6	39.5	38.1	61.9	56.4	61.2	61.6	69.5
Industry	..	..	..	..	..	..	..	53.1	63.0	70.3	69.4
Manufacturing	6.7	6.8	6.9	7.5	7.8	9.5	48.3	55.1	66.7	78.0	76.5
Consumer Price Index	21.3	21.4	21.5	22.2	24.3	31.8	41.4	44.4	50.5	57.2	66.1

MANUFACTURING ACTIVITY

	1969	1970	1971	1972	1973	1974	1975	1976	1977	1978	1979
Employment (1987=100)	..	..	..	..	..	..	..	..	..	..	..
Real Earnings per Empl. (1987=100)	..	..	..	..	..	..	..	..	..	..	..
Real Output per Empl. (1987=100)	..	..	..	..	..	..	..	..	..	..	..
Earnings as % of Value Added	39.4	22.0	27.9	34.2	43.7	24.5	..	..	6.1	6.6	8.7

MONETARY HOLDINGS

(Millions of current Rwanda Francs)

	1969	1970	1971	1972	1973	1974	1975	1976	1977	1978	1979
Money Supply, Broadly Defined	2,120	2,568	2,921	2,973	4,029	5,350	5,997	8,047	10,138	11,181	14,086
Money	1,825	2,165	2,472	2,520	3,565	4,288	4,850	6,516	8,035	8,961	11,255
Currency Outside Banks	1,092	1,238	1,409	1,445	2,003	2,553	2,722	3,070	3,948	4,443	5,242
Demand Deposits	733	927	1,063	1,075	1,563	1,735	2,129	3,446	4,087	4,517	6,012
Quasi-Money	295	404	449	453	464	1,063	1,147	1,530	2,104	2,220	2,831

GOVERNMENT DEFICIT (-) OR SURPLUS

(Millions of current Rwanda Francs)

	1969	1970	1971	1972	1973	1974	1975	1976	1977	1978	1979
GOVERNMENT DEFICIT (-) OR SURPLUS	..	..	..	..	-653	-728	-727	-1,225	-1,026	-1,291	-1,618
Current Revenue	..	..	..	..	2,419	3,369	5,010	6,750	8,703	9,180	12,478
Current Expenditure	..	..	..	..	2,679	3,345	4,093	4,777	6,320	6,692	8,443
Current Budget Balance	..	..	..	..	-260	24	917	1,973	2,383	2,488	4,035
Capital Receipts	..	..	..	..	..	..	..	..	..	..	..
Capital Payments	..	..	..	..	393	752	1,644	3,198	3,409	3,779	5,653

1980	1981	1982	1983	1984	1985	1986	1987	1988	1989 estimate	NOTES	RWANDA
240	260	260	270	260	270	300	310	330	320	..	**CURRENT GNP PER CAPITA (US $)**
5,139	5,306	5,477	5,653	5,836	6,026	6,225	6,434	6,656	6,893	..	**POPULATION (thousands)**
			(Billions of current Rwanda Francs)								**USE AND ORIGIN OF RESOURCES**
108.11	123.41	130.94	141.60	158.62	173.13	169.60	171.13	176.85	172.72	..	Gross National Product (GNP)
0.12	0.77	-0.02	-0.59	-0.49	-0.56	-0.74	-0.78	-1.08	-0.79	..	Net Factor Income from Abroad
107.99	122.64	130.96	142.19	159.11	173.70	170.34	171.91	177.93	173.51	..	GDP at Market Prices
-12.90	-14.63	-16.50	-13.05	-11.19	-15.82	-12.89	-15.99	-16.43	-15.62	..	Resource Balance
15.59	12.05	15.13	16.47	20.10	18.73	21.44	16.94	16.09	15.38	..	Exports of Goods & NFServices
28.49	26.68	31.63	29.52	31.29	34.54	34.33	32.94	32.53	31.00	..	Imports of Goods & NFServices
120.89	137.27	147.46	155.24	170.30	189.51	183.23	187.91	194.36	189.13	..	Domestic Absorption
89.97	96.40	107.27	119.29	128.91	139.87	135.84	138.72	143.58	138.97	..	Private Consumption, etc.
13.49	24.56	16.90	16.71	16.24	19.58	20.35	22.33	22.88	23.94	..	General Gov't Consumption
17.43	16.31	23.28	19.24	25.15	30.07	27.04	26.85	27.90	26.22	..	Gross Domestic Investment
13.19	15.98	18.78	20.74	24.66	27.05	26.80	26.92	26.97	26.84	..	Fixed Investment
8.26	7.81	9.24	9.46	11.70	13.03	14.74	16.61	15.20	15.66	..	Indirect Taxes, net
99.73	114.83	121.72	132.73	147.41	160.67	155.60	155.30	162.73	157.85	B	GDP at factor cost
49.51	49.96	52.10	54.32	64.98	72.67	63.92	65.35	67.43	63.88	..	Agriculture
23.27	25.58	28.91	35.02	37.89	40.31	40.42	37.90	38.74	39.21	f	Industry
16.48	19.30	17.66	21.83	22.20	23.83	27.13	24.68	25.11	25.58	..	Manufacturing
35.21	47.10	49.95	52.85	56.25	60.72	65.99	68.66	71.76	70.43	f	Services, etc.
4.53	1.68	6.78	6.19	1.96	14.25	14.15	10.86	11.47	10.60	..	Gross Domestic Saving
4.36	2.17	7.20	6.12	13.55	14.12	14.02	10.67	11.19	10.47	..	Gross National Saving
			(Billions of 1987 Rwanda Francs)								
142.30	155.63	157.21	166.37	158.77	163.44	171.75	171.13	170.96	159.47	..	Gross National Product
142.11	154.62	157.19	167.04	159.28	163.99	172.53	171.91	172.03	160.22	I f	GDP at Market Prices
-11.78	-11.28	-16.11	-13.71	-17.24	-19.65	-19.45	-16.00	-18.35	-16.69	..	Resource Balance
11.69	11.84	12.05	12.84	12.73	13.18	15.11	16.94	13.40	12.49	..	Exports of Goods & NFServices
23.47	23.11	28.17	26.55	29.97	32.82	34.56	32.94	31.75	29.18	..	Imports of Goods & NFServices
153.89	165.90	173.31	180.75	176.52	183.64	191.98	187.91	190.38	176.91	..	Domestic Absorption
126.80	130.43	133.95	145.95	137.38	135.29	144.40	138.72	137.78	126.32	..	Private Consumption, etc.
12.62	21.54	19.30	17.92	16.51	19.56	20.34	22.33	22.89	23.95	..	General Gov't Consumption
14.47	13.93	20.05	16.89	22.63	28.79	27.24	26.85	29.70	26.64	..	Gross Domestic Investment
10.52	13.63	18.55	21.19	25.93	25.89	26.98	26.92	28.38	27.30	..	Fixed Investment
131.47	144.90	146.29	156.16	147.77	151.74	159.20	155.30	157.30	145.68	B I f	GDP at factor cost
66.82	62.66	71.62	75.07	68.36	64.60	66.48	65.35	63.84	56.31	..	Agriculture
32.57	33.42	32.66	38.18	37.03	35.98	37.60	37.90	37.98	36.61	f	Industry
20.92	22.14	21.26	24.23	20.60	20.49	24.41	24.68	23.96	23.07	..	Manufacturing
43.01	57.65	52.59	53.80	53.88	63.41	68.45	68.66	70.20	67.30	f	Services, etc.
											Memo Items:
12.84	10.44	13.47	14.81	19.25	17.79	21.58	16.94	15.71	14.48	..	Capacity to Import
1.15	-1.40	1.42	1.97	6.52	4.62	6.47	0.00	2.31	1.99	..	Terms of Trade Adjustment
143.26	153.22	158.61	169.01	165.80	168.61	179.00	171.91	174.34	162.21	..	Gross Domestic Income
143.45	154.23	158.63	168.34	165.29	168.06	178.21	171.13	173.27	161.46	..	Gross National Income
			(Index 1987 = 100)								**DOMESTIC PRICES/DEFLATORS**
76.0	79.3	83.3	85.1	99.9	105.9	98.7	100.0	103.4	108.3	..	Overall (GDP)
78.6	82.7	85.1	85.9	96.5	103.2	95.4	100.0	102.1	106.9	..	Domestic Absorption
74.1	79.7	72.7	72.4	95.0	112.5	96.2	100.0	105.6	113.4	..	Agriculture
71.4	76.5	88.5	91.7	102.3	112.0	107.5	100.0	102.0	107.1	..	Industry
78.8	87.2	83.1	90.1	107.8	116.3	111.2	100.0	104.8	110.9	..	Manufacturing
70.9	75.5	85.0	90.6	95.5	97.1	96.1	100.0	103.0	104.0	..	Consumer Price Index
											MANUFACTURING ACTIVITY
..	..	..	..	..	..	..	..	..	..	J	Employment (1987=100)
..	..	..	..	..	..	..	..	..	..	J	Real Earnings per Empl. (1987=100)
..	..	..	..	..	..	..	..	..	..	J	Real Output per Empl. (1987=100)
..	..	..	..	19.0	10.3	9.6	..	..	..	J	Earnings as % of Value Added
			(Millions of current Rwanda Francs)								**MONETARY HOLDINGS**
15,226	15,983	16,172	18,077	19,892	23,430	26,608	29,339	31,491	30,184	..	Money Supply, Broadly Defined
12,026	11,774	11,460	12,317	13,343	14,699	17,334	17,791	18,332	16,052	..	Money
5,689	6,086	6,260	6,662	7,030	7,161	7,686	8,202	8,439	7,744	..	Currency Outside Banks
6,337	5,688	5,200	5,655	6,314	7,537	9,648	9,588	9,894	8,308	..	Demand Deposits
3,200	4,209	4,712	5,759	6,549	8,731	9,274	11,548	13,159	14,132	..	Quasi-Money
			(Millions of current Rwanda Francs)								
-1,875	..	..	..	..	..	..	..	..	..	..	**GOVERNMENT DEFICIT (-) OR SURPLUS**
13,805	..	..	..	..	..	..	..	..	..		Current Revenue
10,059	..	..	..	..	..	..	..	..	..		Current Expenditure
3,746	..	..	..	..	..	..	..	..	..		Current Budget Balance
	..	..	..	..	..	..	..	..	..		Capital Receipts
5,621	..	..	..	..	..	..	..	..	..		Capital Payments

RWANDA	1969	1970	1971	1972	1973	1974	1975	1976	1977	1978	1979
FOREIGN TRADE (CUSTOMS BASIS)					*(Millions of current US dollars)*						
Value of Exports, fob	14.10	24.54	22.33	20.20	51.30	53.60	57.60	114.20	126.50	111.70	203.00
Nonfuel Primary Products	14.05	24.27	21.65	19.12	50.66	51.07	56.42	112.45	124.79	110.27	201.74
Fuels	0.00	0.00	0.00	0.00	0.00	0.00	0.00	0.00	0.00	0.00	0.00
Manufactures	0.05	0.27	0.68	1.08	0.64	2.53	1.18	1.75	1.71	1.43	1.26
Value of Imports, cif	23.62	29.10	33.05	34.56	41.00	72.00	102.00	128.00	125.00	202.00	224.00
Nonfuel Primary Products	6.21	8.21	6.50	9.19	8.76	19.77	26.23	25.31	23.10	32.30	37.29
Fuels	1.49	1.61	1.97	2.72	3.69	11.40	13.85	14.50	11.70	15.23	18.57
Manufactures	15.92	19.28	24.57	22.65	28.55	40.84	61.92	88.19	90.20	154.47	168.14
					(Index 1987 = 100)						
Terms of Trade	143.7	157.3	137.0	141.2	152.4	109.9	105.5	171.0	205.2	149.5	161.7
Export Prices, fob	36.7	43.1	39.0	43.3	55.8	62.8	62.4	98.7	128.4	104.3	131.7
Import Prices, cif	25.5	27.4	28.5	30.7	36.6	57.1	59.2	57.8	62.6	69.8	81.5
BALANCE OF PAYMENTS					*(Millions of current US dollars)*						
Exports of Goods & Services	..	25.90	22.57	22.26	55.79	..	..	123.34	140.89	130.28	235.10
Merchandise, fob	..	24.20	20.86	20.19	51.26	53.64	57.55	114.19	126.47	111.67	202.98
Nonfactor Services	..	1.50	1.50	1.95	4.29	4.81	6.48	7.99	11.01	14.15	23.70
Factor Services	..	0.20	0.20	0.11	0.24	..	..	1.16	3.41	4.46	8.42
Imports of Goods & Services	..	35.20	41.12	47.12	62.11	90.16	127.87	159.07	184.87	270.92	319.03
Merchandise, fob	..	21.10	23.37	26.06	33.02	56.52	80.13	104.46	102.29	144.94	159.49
Nonfactor Services	..	13.90	17.45	20.95	26.23	30.79	44.35	49.41	74.68	116.36	147.60
Factor Services	..	0.20	0.30	0.11	2.86	2.85	3.38	5.20	7.90	9.62	11.95
Long-Term Interest	..	0.10	0.10	0.10	0.00	0.00	0.10	0.30	0.60	0.70	1.00
Private Current Transfers, net	..	-3.10	-1.60	-3.15	-1.19	-4.69	-2.91	-2.02	-2.69	1.17	5.90
Workers' Remittances	..	0.50	0.90	0.87	0.72	0.12	0.49	0.26	1.22	2.09	2.74
Curr. A/C Bal before Off. Transf.	..	-12.40	-20.16	-28.01	-7.51	-36.41	-66.75	-37.75	-46.67	-139.47	-78.03
Net Official Transfers	..	18.90	19.76	23.45	29.92	37.61	58.03	55.83	67.51	92.96	124.91
Curr. A/C Bal after Off. Transf.	..	6.50	-0.40	-4.56	22.41	1.20	-8.72	18.07	20.84	-46.51	46.89
Long-Term Capital, net	..	-0.40	2.11	1.09	3.34	9.26	16.66	23.23	31.24	25.52	22.69
Direct Investment	..	-0.20	1.71	0.54	2.03	2.16	3.01	5.86	4.95	4.69	12.57
Long-Term Loans	..	-0.10	-0.10	1.40	4.40	4.10	11.70	22.80	27.60	24.70	31.90
Disbursements	..	0.20	0.20	1.80	4.50	4.50	12.00	23.50	28.30	25.70	32.90
Repayments	..	0.30	0.30	0.40	0.10	0.40	0.30	0.70	0.70	1.00	1.00
Other Long-Term Capital	..	-0.10	0.50	-0.86	-3.09	3.00	1.95	-5.43	-1.32	-3.87	-21.78
Other Capital, net	..	-1.71	-2.01	0.08	-17.45	-11.12	4.83	-8.71	-17.61	21.70	0.39
Change in Reserves	..	-4.39	0.31	3.40	-8.30	0.66	-12.76	-32.60	-34.47	-0.70	-69.97
Memo Item:					*(Rwanda Francs per US dollar)*						
Conversion Factor (Annual Avg)	100.000	100.000	99.740	92.110	84.050	92.840	92.840	92.840	92.840	92.840	92.840
				(Millions of US dollars), outstanding at end of year							
EXTERNAL DEBT (Total)	..	4.80	2.00	3.40	7.90	12.30	24.10	47.70	87.50	126.80	156.10
Long-Term Debt (by debtor)	..	4.80	2.00	3.40	7.90	12.30	24.10	47.70	78.50	109.80	135.10
Central Bank, incl. IMF credit	..	2.90	0.00	0.00	0.00	0.00	0.00	0.00	0.50	0.80	8.50
Central Government	..	1.80	1.90	3.40	7.90	12.30	24.10	47.70	78.00	109.00	126.60
Rest of General Government	..	..	..	..	..	..	..	..	..	..	..
Non-financial Public Enterprises	..	0.10	0.10	0.00	0.00	0.00	0.00	0.00	0.00	0.00	0.00
Priv. Sector, incl non-guaranteed	..	..	..	..	..	..	..	..	..	..	..
Short-Term Debt	..	..	..	..	..	..	..	..	9.00	17.00	21.00
Memo Items:					*(Millions of US dollars)*						
Int'l Reserves Excluding Gold	3.0	7.7	5.8	6.4	15.2	13.0	25.6	64.3	82.9	87.6	152.3
Gold Holdings (at market price)	..	..	..	..	..	..	..	..	0.7	0.9	..
SOCIAL INDICATORS											
Total Fertility Rate	7.8	7.8	7.9	7.9	7.9	7.9	8.0	8.0	8.0	8.0	8.0
Infant Mortality Rate	140.0	140.0	140.0	140.0	140.0	140.0	140.0	140.0	140.0	138.4	136.8
Life Expectancy at Birth	48.3	47.7	47.0	46.4	45.9	45.5	45.0	44.6	44.2	44.6	45.0
Urban Population, % of total	3.1	3.2	3.4	3.5	3.7	3.8	4.0	4.2	4.4	4.6	4.8
Food Prod. per capita (1987=100)	113.1	118.6	116.2	110.8	111.8	106.5	115.5	118.5	120.1	118.5	124.8
Labor Force, Agriculture (%)	93.8	93.7	93.6	93.5	93.4	93.3	93.2	93.1	93.0	93.0	92.9
Labor Force, Female (%)	50.1	50.0	49.9	49.9	49.8	49.8	49.7	49.7	49.6	49.6	49.5
Primary Schl. Enroll. Ratio	..	68.0	..	..	..	..	56.0	64.0	66.0	71.0	70.0
Primary Schl. Enroll. Ratio, Female	..	60.0	..	..	..	..	51.0	59.0	62.0	67.0	67.0
Secondary Schl. Enroll. Ratio	..	2.0	..	..	..	..	2.0	2.0	2.0	2.0	2.0

1980	1981	1982	1983	1984	1985	1986	1987	1988	1989 estimate	NOTES	RWANDA
				(Millions of current US dollars)							**FOREIGN TRADE (CUSTOMS BASIS)**
133.60	113.30	108.50	124.10	142.60	126.10	184.00	121.40	125.00	..	..	Value of Exports, fob
132.56	112.18	107.34	122.64	141.32	125.00	182.47	120.00	123.85	..	..	Nonfuel Primary Products
0.00	0.00	0.00	0.00	0.00	0.00	0.00	0.00	0.00	..	..	Fuels
1.04	1.12	1.16	1.46	1.28	1.10	1.53	1.40	1.15	..	..	Manufactures
277.00	279.00	297.00	277.00	282.00	313.00	348.00	352.00	372.00	..	f	Value of Imports, cif
46.45	47.43	50.86	47.54	51.13	54.10	66.97	65.63	67.32	..	..	Nonfuel Primary Products
22.82	22.73	24.23	29.80	34.00	39.50	41.00	70.28	78.47	..	f	Fuels
207.73	208.84	221.91	199.66	196.87	219.40	240.03	216.09	226.22	..	..	Manufactures
				(Index 1987 = 100)							
130.9	115.8	123.9	122.2	135.0	134.5	166.5	100.0	116.7	..	..	Terms of Trade
119.4	106.2	110.5	108.0	118.0	117.7	152.7	100.0	118.8	..	..	Export Prices, fob
91.2	91.7	89.2	88.4	87.4	87.6	91.7	100.0	101.8	..	..	Import Prices, cif
				(Millions of current US dollars)							**BALANCE OF PAYMENTS**
182.43	175.87	157.83	160.62	182.72	170.15	236.80	177.85	174.73	156.90	f	Exports of Goods & Services
133.59	113.31	108.46	124.08	142.61	126.10	184.14	121.44	117.88	104.80	..	Merchandise, fob
31.79	37.33	33.25	27.89	31.93	34.89	43.30	46.15	48.18	43.20	..	Nonfactor Services
17.06	25.23	16.12	8.65	8.19	9.16	9.36	10.27	8.67	8.90	..	Factor Services
334.62	345.51	354.34	327.09	325.39	350.61	430.04	438.24	443.60	397.80	f	Imports of Goods & Services
195.79	207.13	214.66	197.64	197.52	219.33	259.21	266.98	278.58	254.20	..	Merchandise, fob
123.44	121.67	120.83	112.99	113.22	114.23	148.40	146.96	134.28	124.80	..	Nonfactor Services
15.39	16.71	18.85	16.45	14.65	17.04	22.43	24.30	30.74	18.80	..	Factor Services
1.70	2.00	2.10	2.40	3.40	4.20	5.40	7.30	8.40	7.60	..	Long-Term Interest
-3.18	-2.99	4.64	5.50	1.89	4.32	7.01	7.48	10.54	8.20	..	Private Current Transfers, net
1.09	1.66	1.49	1.60	1.19	1.33	1.72	1.90	1.12	..	..	Workers' Remittances
-155.36	-172.63	-191.87	-160.97	-140.79	-176.14	-186.24	-252.91	-258.33	-232.70	..	Curr. A/C Bal before Off. Transf.
107.46	105.68	105.25	112.31	99.21	112.09	117.00	118.56	139.30	127.60	..	Net Official Transfers
-47.90	-66.95	-86.62	-48.65	-41.58	-64.05	-69.24	-134.35	-119.03	-105.10	..	Curr. A/C Bal after Off. Transf.
44.03	45.48	41.58	36.54	51.05	74.12	85.76	110.88	87.64	60.50	f	Long-Term Capital, net
16.42	18.03	20.70	11.12	15.07	14.62	17.58	17.55	21.05	15.60	..	Direct Investment
24.60	24.20	28.60	35.80	44.20	70.90	66.20	92.30	75.90	53.70	..	Long-Term Loans
27.20	26.60	31.10	40.80	50.60	80.20	76.30	103.80	84.60	67.60	..	Disbursements
2.60	2.40	2.50	5.00	6.40	9.30	10.10	11.50	8.70	13.90	..	Repayments
3.02	3.25	-7.73	-10.38	-8.22	-11.39	1.98	1.03	-9.30	-8.80	..	Other Long-Term Capital
33.14	21.40	8.48	-6.30	-1.67	-9.97	11.21	10.15	3.62	7.10	f	Other Capital, net
-29.28	0.08	36.56	18.41	-7.80	-0.10	-27.74	13.32	27.77	37.50	..	Change in Reserves
				(Rwanda Francs per US dollar)							**Memo Item:**
92.840	92.840	92.840	94.340	100.170	101.260	87.640	79.670	76.440	79.980	..	Conversion Factor (Annual Avg)
				(Millions of US dollars), outstanding at end of year							
189.80	196.50	218.30	242.30	291.40	369.40	455.60	610.00	658.20	651.50	..	**EXTERNAL DEBT** (Total)
163.80	176.50	197.30	226.30	254.40	342.40	428.60	571.00	616.70	607.00	..	Long-Term Debt (by debtor)
14.40	12.40	11.80	11.20	10.50	10.00	8.60	6.90	3.70	0.90	..	Central Bank, incl. IMF credit
149.40	164.10	185.50	215.10	243.90	332.40	420.00	564.10	613.00	606.10	..	Central Government
..	..	..	..	..	..	..	..	..	..	..	Rest of General Government
0.00	0.00	0.00	0.00	0.00	0.00	0.00	0.00	0.00	..	..	Non-financial Public Enterprises
..	..	..	..	..	..	..	..	..	..	..	Priv. Sector, incl non-guaranteed
26.00	20.00	21.00	16.00	37.00	27.00	27.00	39.00	41.50	44.50	..	Short-Term Debt
				(Millions of US dollars)							**Memo Items:**
186.6	173.1	128.4	110.9	106.9	113.3	162.3	164.2	118.3	70.4	..	Int'l Reserves Excluding Gold
..	..	..	..	..	..	..	..	..	..	..	Gold Holdings (at market price)
											SOCIAL INDICATORS
8.0	8.0	8.0	8.0	8.0	8.0	8.0	8.0	8.0	8.0	..	Total Fertility Rate
135.2	133.6	132.0	130.0	128.0	126.0	124.0	122.0	120.4	118.8	..	Infant Mortality Rate
45.4	45.8	46.3	46.7	47.2	47.6	48.1	48.5	48.7	49.0	..	Life Expectancy at Birth
5.0	5.2	5.5	5.7	6.0	6.2	6.6	7.0	7.2	7.5	..	Urban Population, % of total
122.1	127.3	130.1	122.1	109.7	119.4	104.6	100.0	98.8	89.6	..	Food Prod. per capita (1987=100)
92.8	..	..	..	..	..	..	..	..	..	..	Labor Force, Agriculture (%)
49.5	49.3	49.1	48.9	48.8	48.6	48.4	48.2	48.0	47.9	..	Labor Force, Female (%)
63.0	..	63.0	62.0	61.0	63.0	65.0	67.0	64.0	..	..	Primary Schl. Enroll. Ratio
60.0	..	60.0	60.0	59.0	61.0	64.0	66.0	..	..	..	Primary Schl. Enroll. Ratio, Female
3.0	..	2.0	2.0	7.0	6.0	6.0	6.0	..	..	..	Secondary Schl. Enroll. Ratio

SAO TOME AND PRINCIPE	1969	1970	1971	1972	1973	1974	1975	1976	1977	1978	1979
CURRENT GNP PER CAPITA (US $)	..	..	..	270	290	350	410	380	360	360	400
POPULATION (thousands)	72	74	76	79	82	84	87	88	90	91	92

USE AND ORIGIN OF RESOURCES

(Millions of current Sao Tome & Principe Dobras)

	1969	1970	1971	1972	1973	1974	1975	1976	1977	1978	1979
Gross National Product (GNP)	..	565.30	558.70	592.00	725.20	776.00	812.30	809.30	966.80	1,096.70	1,294.30
Net Factor Income from Abroad	..	0.90	0.80	0.70	0.80	1.00	2.40	-20.60	-8.20	46.80	79.30
GDP at Market Prices	..	564.40	557.90	591.30	724.40	775.00	809.90	829.90	975.00	1,049.90	1,215.00
Resource Balance	..	-1.60	-29.10	-8.20	61.80	114.60	-92.00	-185.00	-230.00	-281.90	-463.80
Exports of Goods & NFServices	..	213.00	169.40	181.20	297.60	405.70	212.90	235.00	420.00	550.00	720.00
Imports of Goods & NFServices	..	214.60	198.50	189.40	235.80	291.10	304.90	420.00	650.00	831.90	1,183.80
Domestic Absorption	..	566.00	587.00	599.50	662.60	660.40	901.90	1,014.90	1,205.00	1,331.80	1,678.80
Private Consumption, etc.	..	394.10	411.20	426.00	493.70	480.60	684.30	769.00	759.70	1,040.00	1,278.70
General Gov't Consumption	..	70.30	70.30	70.30	70.30	70.30	70.30	70.30	70.30	70.30	70.30
Gross Domestic Investment	..	101.60	105.50	103.20	98.60	109.50	147.30	175.60	375.00	221.50	329.80
Fixed Investment	..	..	..	..	..	..	..	..	..	..	..
Indirect Taxes, net	..	65.10	58.90	67.20	77.90	82.30	88.20	125.90	188.30	298.50	229.50
GDP at factor cost	..	499.30	499.00	524.10	646.50	692.70	721.70	704.00	786.70	751.40	985.50
Agriculture	..	182.80	172.10	191.10	269.60	342.00	272.50	284.60	357.00	425.00	450.00
Industry	..	106.80	113.90	130.60	154.30	174.70	167.20	174.40	220.90	243.80	296.00
Manufacturing	..	29.20	33.70	40.40	54.00	64.40	59.60	66.00	72.10	79.40	111.20
Services, etc.	..	209.70	213.00	202.40	222.60	176.00	282.00	245.00	208.80	82.60	239.50
Gross Domestic Saving	..	100.00	76.40	95.00	160.40	224.10	55.30	-9.40	145.00	-60.40	-134.00
Gross National Saving	..	..	..	..	..	216.50	51.20	-33.20	132.90	-10.90	-44.40

(Millions of 1987 Sao Tome & Principe Dobras)

	1969	1970	1971	1972	1973	1974	1975	1976	1977	1978	1979
Gross National Product	..	2,109.50	2,196.10	2,164.40	2,114.60	2,155.50	2,315.30	2,426.00	2,754.60	3,083.50	3,439.30
GDP at Market Prices	..	2,056.20	2,135.20	2,107.80	2,056.30	2,094.00	2,242.00	2,431.80	2,704.10	2,873.10	3,202.40
Resource Balance	..	..	..	..	..	..	-755.30	-765.70	-1,067.80	-1,389.90	-1,826.30
Exports of Goods & NFServices	..	..	..	..	..	..	554.70	513.40	572.40	637.60	649.20
Imports of Goods & NFServices	..	..	..	..	..	..	1,309.90	1,279.10	1,640.20	2,027.50	2,475.50
Domestic Absorption	..	..	..	..	..	..	2,997.30	3,197.50	3,771.90	4,263.00	5,028.80
Private Consumption, etc.	..	..	..	..	..	..	1,987.10	2,134.60	2,234.60	2,881.50	3,339.20
General Gov't Consumption	..	..	..	..	..	..	863.50	890.10	1,315.80	1,131.10	1,340.50
Gross Domestic Investment	..	..	..	..	..	..	146.70	172.80	221.40	250.40	349.10
Fixed Investment	..	..	..	..	..	..	..	..	..	..	..
GDP at factor cost	..	..	..	..	..	..	..	..	..	..	..
Agriculture	..	..	..	..	..	..	..	..	..	..	2,515.00
Industry	..	..	..	..	..	..	..	..	..	..	769.80
Manufacturing	..	..	..	..	..	..	..	..	..	..	309.40
Services, etc.	..	..	..	..	..	..	..	..	..	..	1,436.30

Memo Items:

	1969	1970	1971	1972	1973	1974	1975	1976	1977	1978	1979
Capacity to Import	..	..	..	..	..	..	914.70	715.70	1,059.80	1,340.50	1,505.60
Terms of Trade Adjustment	..	..	..	..	..	..	360.00	202.30	487.40	702.80	856.50
Gross Domestic Income	..	..	..	..	..	..	2,602.00	2,634.10	3,191.50	3,576.00	4,058.90
Gross National Income	..	..	..	..	..	..	2,675.30	2,628.30	3,242.00	3,786.30	4,295.70

DOMESTIC PRICES/DEFLATORS

(Index 1987 = 100)

	1969	1970	1971	1972	1973	1974	1975	1976	1977	1978	1979
Overall (GDP)	..	27.4	26.1	28.1	35.2	37.0	36.1	34.1	36.1	36.5	37.9
Domestic Absorption	..	..	..	..	..	..	30.1	31.7	31.9	31.2	33.4
Agriculture	..	..	..	..	..	..	..	..	..	..	58.5
Industry	..	..	..	..	..	..	..	..	..	..	95.7
Manufacturing	..	..	..	..	..	..	..	..	..	..	..
Consumer Price Index	..	..	..	..	..	..	..	..	..	..	..

MANUFACTURING ACTIVITY

	1969	1970	1971	1972	1973	1974	1975	1976	1977	1978	1979
Employment (1987=100)		..	..	..		..	..	..	..	..	..
Real Earnings per Empl. (1987=100)	..	..	..	..	..	..	..	..	..	..	..
Real Output per Empl. (1987=100)	..	..	..	..	..	..	..	..	..	..	..
Earnings as % of Value Added	..	..	..	..	..	..	..	..	..	..	..

MONETARY HOLDINGS

(Millions of current Sao Tome & PrincipeDobras)

	1969	1970	1971	1972	1973	1974	1975	1976	1977	1978	1979
Money Supply, Broadly Defined	..	..	..	..	..	..	..	..	..	..	..
Money	..	..	..	..	..	..	..	..	..	..	..
Currency Outside Banks	..	..	..	..	..	..	..	..	..	..	..
Demand Deposits	..	..	..	..	..	..	..	..	..	..	..
Quasi-Money	..	..	..	..	..	..	..	..	..	..	..

GOVERNMENT DEFICIT (-) OR SURPLUS

(Millions of current Sao Tome & PrincipeDobras)

	1969	1970	1971	1972	1973	1974	1975	1976	1977	1978	1979
Current Revenue	..	..	..	..	..	..	..	..	..	..	..
Current Expenditure	..	..	..	..	..	..	..	..	..	..	..
Current Budget Balance	..	..	..	..	..	..	..	..	..	..	..
Capital Receipts	..	..	..	..	..	..	..	..	..	..	..
Capital Payments	..	..	..	..	..	..	..	..	..	..	..

1980	1981	1982	1983	1984	1985	1986	1987	1988	1989 estimate	NOTES	SAO TOME AND PRINCIPE
480	350	400	350	340	320	370	370	400	340	..	**CURRENT GNP PER CAPITA (US $)**
94	96	99	101	105	108	112	115	119	122	..	**POPULATION (thousands)**
					(Millions of current Sao Tome & Principe Dobras)						**USE AND ORIGIN OF RESOURCES**
1,590.90	1,139.20	1,435.80	1,506.40	1,549.10	1,487.00	2,353.30	2,848.90	3,990.40	5,241.30	..	Gross National Product (GNP)
92.90	68.80	-14.70	16.00	110.30	-76.00	-124.40	-155.10	-230.60	-498.70	..	Net Factor Income from Abroad
1,498.00	1,070.40	1,450.50	1,490.40	1,438.80	1,563.00	2,477.70	3,004.00	4,221.00	5,740.00	..	GDP at Market Prices
-735.00	-822.00	-1,071.00	-630.00	-861.00	-861.00	-571.40	-951.70	-1,284.80	-3,925.40	..	Resource Balance
682.40	335.70	444.00	434.00	627.00	412.00	483.60	534.20	1,252.80	1,307.50	..	Exports of Goods & NFServices
1,417.40	1,157.70	1,515.00	1,064.00	1,488.00	1,273.00	1,055.00	1,485.90	2,537.60	5,232.90	..	Imports of Goods & NFServices
2,233.00	1,892.40	2,521.50	2,120.40	2,299.80	2,424.00	3,048.70	3,955.20	5,505.90	9,664.90	..	Domestic Absorption
1,367.10	974.80	1,307.00	1,153.70	1,069.30	1,261.50	1,961.10	2,466.20	3,162.00	4,432.00	..	Private Consumption, etc.
353.80	415.00	491.40	527.70	543.40	584.00	729.40	972.50	1,155.90	1,355.90	..	General Gov't Consumption
512.10	502.60	723.10	439.00	687.10	578.50	358.20	516.50	1,188.00	3,877.00	..	Gross Domestic Investment
550.00	360.00	785.00	357.10	842.80	502.00	..	..	..	..	..	Fixed Investment
200.00	-70.60	170.50	91.30	44.60	63.10	52.00	121.90	210.00	313.20	..	Indirect Taxes, net
1,298.00	1,141.00	1,280.00	1,399.10	1,394.20	1,499.90	2,425.70	2,882.10	4,011.00	5,426.80	..	GDP at factor cost
580.00	420.00	379.00	454.00	415.10	414.50	659.00	882.00	1,220.00	1,660.00	..	Agriculture
258.00	249.00	309.00	288.00	255.50	325.20	289.00	355.00	452.00	615.00	..	Industry
118.00	95.00	112.00	130.00	93.80	140.40	..	..	..	..	..	Manufacturing
460.00	472.00	592.00	657.10	723.60	760.20	1,477.70	1,645.10	2,339.00	3,151.80	..	Services, etc.
-222.90	-319.40	-347.90	-191.00	-173.90	-282.50	-212.80	-434.70	-96.90	-47.90	..	Gross Domestic Saving
-112.60	-225.90	-343.40	-123.90	78.60	-368.30	-367.70	-606.60	-327.10	-584.00	..	Gross National Saving
					(Millions of 1987 Sao Tome & Principe Dobras)						
3,862.00	2,773.10	3,300.30	3,070.10	3,015.10	2,902.20	2,904.20	2,848.90	2,884.60	2,870.80	..	Gross National Product
3,638.30	2,626.20	3,331.70	3,038.70	2,808.40	3,042.60	3,072.50	3,004.00	3,058.20	3,108.10	..	GDP at Market Prices
-1,683.30	-1,380.80	-1,717.40	-1,179.80	-1,767.20	-1,603.90	-1,140.70	-951.70	-1,125.40	-1,622.50	..	Resource Balance
756.70	464.70	736.20	591.20	754.30	526.70	697.60	534.20	591.80	499.00	..	Exports of Goods & NFServices
2,439.90	1,845.50	2,453.50	1,771.00	2,521.50	2,130.60	1,838.30	1,485.90	1,717.10	2,121.50	..	Imports of Goods & NFServices
5,321.60	4,007.00	5,049.10	4,218.50	4,575.60	4,646.50	4,213.20	3,955.70	4,183.60	4,730.60	..	Domestic Absorption
3,723.30	2,369.80	3,062.30	2,434.20	2,593.80	2,730.70	2,524.50	2,466.70	2,367.20	1,642.70	..	Private Consumption, etc.
1,132.90	1,203.00	1,393.50	1,398.10	1,364.30	1,410.50	1,115.50	972.50	967.80	958.10	..	General Gov't Consumption
465.30	434.30	593.30	386.30	617.50	505.30	573.10	516.50	848.70	2,129.80	..	Gross Domestic Investment
..	..	..	..	..	..	..	..	..	..	..	Fixed Investment
3,194.30	2,861.70	3,018.40	2,926.90	2,773.70	2,995.80	3,023.60	2,882.10	2,919.20	2,976.70	..	GDP at factor cost
977.60	875.80	923.70	895.80	848.90	916.80	925.40	882.00	893.40	911.10	..	Agriculture
393.40	352.40	371.80	360.40	341.60	368.90	372.40	355.00	359.50	366.60	..	Industry
..	..	..	..	..	..	..	..	..	..	..	Manufacturing
1,823.20	1,633.40	1,722.90	1,670.70	1,583.20	1,710.00	1,725.80	1,645.10	1,666.40	1,699.10	..	Services, etc.
											Memo Items:
1,174.70	535.10	719.10	722.40	1,062.50	689.60	842.70	534.20	847.70	530.10	..	Capacity to Import
418.00	70.50	-17.10	131.20	308.20	162.90	145.00	0.00	256.00	31.10	..	Terms of Trade Adjustment
4,056.30	2,696.70	3,314.60	3,169.90	3,116.50	3,205.50	3,217.50	3,004.00	3,314.20	3,139.20	..	Gross Domestic Income
4,280.00	2,843.60	3,283.20	3,201.30	3,323.30	3,065.00	3,049.20	2,848.90	3,140.60	2,901.90	..	Gross National Income
					(Index 1987 = 100)						**DOMESTIC PRICES/DEFLATORS**
41.2	40.8	43.5	49.0	51.2	51.4	80.6	100.0	138.0	184.7	..	Overall (GDP)
42.0	47.2	49.9	50.3	50.3	52.2	72.4	100.0	131.6	204.3	..	Domestic Absorption
59.3	48.0	41.0	50.7	48.9	45.2	71.2	100.0	136.6	182.2	..	Agriculture
65.6	70.7	83.1	79.9	74.8	88.2	77.6	100.0	125.7	167.8	..	Industry
..	..	..	..	..	..	..	..	..	..	..	Manufacturing
..	..	..	..	..	..	..	..	..	..	..	Consumer Price Index
											MANUFACTURING ACTIVITY
..	..	..	..	..	..	..	..	..	..	..	Employment (1987=100)
..	..	..	..	..	..	..	..	..	..	..	Real Earnings per Empl. (1987=100)
..	..	..	..	..	..	..	..	..	..	..	Real Output per Empl. (1987=100)
..	..	..	..	..	..	..	..	..	..	..	Earnings as % of Value Added
					(Millions of current Sao Tome & Principe Dobras)						**MONETARY HOLDINGS**
..	..	1,094	1,454	1,641	1,717	1,845	1,945	..	..	..	Money Supply, Broadly Defined
..	..	..	..	1,326	1,408	1,569	1,712	1,610	..	..	Money
..	..	..	..	484	390	409	514	465	..	..	Currency Outside Banks
..	..	..	..	843	1,018	1,161	1,198	1,145	..	..	Demand Deposits
..	..	..	..	314	309	276	233	..	..	..	Quasi-Money
					(Millions of current Sao Tome & Principe Dobras)						
..	..	..	..	..	..	..	..	..	..	..	**GOVERNMENT DEFICIT (-) OR SURPLUS**
..	..	..	..	..	..	..	..	..	..	..	Current Revenue
..	..	..	..	..	..	..	..	..	..	..	Current Expenditure
..	..	..	..	..	..	..	..	..	..	..	Current Budget Balance
..	..	..	..	..	..	..	..	..	..	..	Capital Receipts
..	..	..	..	..	..	..	..	..	..	..	Capital Payments

SAO TOME AND PRINCIPE	1969	1970	1971	1972	1973	1974	1975	1976	1977	1978	1979
FOREIGN TRADE (CUSTOMS BASIS)					*(Thousands of current US dollars)*						
Value of Exports, fob	..	8,000	7,000	7,000	13,000	17,000	7,000	8,000	23,000	21,000	27,000
Nonfuel Primary Products	..	..	..	..	..	..	..	..	..	..	..
Fuels	..	..	..	..	..	..	..	..	..	..	..
Manufactures	..	..	..	..	..	..	..	..	..	..	..
Value of Imports, cif	8,000	9,000	8,000	8,000	10,000	10,000	11,000	9,000	14,000	18,000	20,000
Nonfuel Primary Products	..	..	..	..	..	..	..	..	..	..	..
Fuels	..	..	..	..	..	..	..	..	..	..	..
Manufactures	..	..	..	..	..	..	..	..	..	..	..
					(Index 1987 = 100)						
Terms of Trade	..	..	..	..	..	..	..	..	..	..	..
Export Prices, fob	..	..	..	..	..	..	..	..	..	..	..
Import Prices, cif	..	..	..	..	..	..	..	..	..	..	..
BALANCE OF PAYMENTS					*(Thousands of current US dollars)*						
Exports of Goods & Services	..	..	..	..	..	18	8	..	24	26	31
Merchandise, fob	..	..	..	..	..	17	7	8	23	23	27
Nonfactor Services	..	..	..	..	..	1	1	1	0	1	3
Factor Services	..	..	..	..	..	0	0	..	1	1	2
Imports of Goods & Services	..	..	..	..	..	12	12	10	16	23	23
Merchandise, fob	..	..	..	..	..	8	9	8	12	17	15
Nonfactor Services	..	..	..	..	..	3	3	2	5	6	8
Factor Services	..	..	..	..	..	0	0	0	0	0	0
Long-Term Interest	..	0	0	0	0	0	0	0	0	0	0
Private Current Transfers, net	..	..	..	..	..	0	0	0	0	0	0
Workers' Remittances	..	..	..	..	..	..	..	..	..	0	1
Curr. A/C Bal before Off. Transf.	..	..	..	..	..	6	-5	-2	8	3	8
Net Official Transfers	..	..	..	..	..	..	5	1	0	3	0
Curr. A/C Bal after Off. Transf.	..	..	..	..	..	6	0	-1	8	6	9
Long-Term Capital, net	..	..	..	..	..	-1	-1	17	4	2	2
Direct Investment	..	..	..	..	..	..	..	..	..	..	..
Long-Term Loans	..	0	0	0	0	0	0	0	2	8	4
Disbursements	..	0	0	0	0	0	0	0	2	8	4
Repayments	..	0	0	0	0	0	0	0	0	0	0
Other Long-Term Capital	..	..	..	..	..	-1	-1	16	2	-6	-2
Other Capital, net	..	..	..	..	..	-2	0	-4	-5	0	-9
Change in Reserves	..	..	..	..	..	-3	1	-12	-7	-8	-2
Memo Item:					*(Sao Tome & Principe Dobras per US dollar)*						
Conversion Factor (Annual Avg)	28.750	28.750	28.350	27.170	24.670	25.410	25.550	30.230	37.560	36.150	35.020
				(Thousands of US dollars), outstanding at end of year							
EXTERNAL DEBT (Total)	..	0.00	0.00	0.00	0.00	0.00	0.00	100.00	2,200.00	10,300.00	16,700.00
Long-Term Debt (by debtor)	..	0.00	0.00	0.00	0.00	0.00	0.00	100.00	2,200.00	10,300.00	14,700.00
Central Bank, incl. IMF credit	..	0.00	0.00	0.00	0.00	0.00	0.00	0.00	0.00	0.00	0.00
Central Government	..	0.00	0.00	0.00	0.00	0.00	0.00	100.00	2,200.00	10,300.00	14,700.00
Rest of General Government	..	..	..	..	..	..	..	..	..	..	..
Non-financial Public Enterprises	..	..	..	..	..	..	..	..	..	..	..
Priv. Sector, incl non-guaranteed	..	..	..	..	..	..	..	..	..	..	..
Short-Term Debt	..	0.00	0.00	0.00	0.00	0.00	0.00	0.00	0.00	0.00	2,000.00
Memo Items:					*(Millions of US dollars)*						
Int'l Reserves Excluding Gold	..	..	..	..	..	..	..	..	..	..	..
Gold Holdings (at market price)	..	..	..	..	..	..	..	..	..	..	..
SOCIAL INDICATORS											
Total Fertility Rate	..	..	..	..	..	..	..	..	..	..	..
Infant Mortality Rate	..	..	..	..	..	66.0	59.9	53.2	57.1	49.7	71.4
Life Expectancy at Birth	..	..	..	..	..	..	..	..	..	..	..
Urban Population, % of total	22.6	23.4	24.3	25.2	26.1	27.0	27.9	28.9	29.8	30.8	31.7
Food Prod. per capita (1987=100)	206.3	207.1	222.3	209.7	219.2	204.8	164.2	158.4	142.3	153.0	163.2
Labor Force, Agriculture (%)	..	..	..	..	..	..	..	..	..	..	..
Labor Force, Female (%)	..	..	..	..	..	..	..	..	..	..	..
Primary Schl. Enroll. Ratio	..	..	..	..	..	..	..	..	..	..	..
Primary Schl. Enroll. Ratio, Female	..	..	..	..	..	..	..	..	..	..	..
Secondary Schl. Enroll. Ratio	..	..	..	..	..	..	..	..	..	..	..

1980	1981	1982	1983	1984	1985	1986	1987	1988	1989 estimate	NOTES	SAO TOME AND PRINCIPE
				(Thousands of current US dollars)							**FOREIGN TRADE (CUSTOMS BASIS)**
17,500	7,190	9,050	8,670	12,180	7,400	9,000	7,000	..	..	..	Value of Exports, fob
..	..	..	..	..	..	..	..	..	..	..	Nonfuel Primary Products
..	..	..	..	..	..	..	..	..	..	..	Fuels
..	..	..	..	..	..	..	..	..	..	..	Manufactures
19,000	17,000	15,000	10,000	12,000	13,000	15,000	18,000	..	..	..	Value of Imports, cif
..	..	..	..	..	..	..	..	..	..	..	Nonfuel Primary Products
..	..	..	..	..	..	..	..	..	..	..	Fuels
..	..	..	..	..	..	..	..	..	..	..	Manufactures
				(Index 1987 = 100)							
..	..	..	..	..	..	..	..	..	..	..	Terms of Trade
..	..	..	..	..	..	..	..	..	..	..	Export Prices, fob
..	..	..	..	..	..	..	..	..	..	..	Import Prices, cif
				(Thousands of current US dollars)							**BALANCE OF PAYMENTS**
23	11	12	11	14	9	14	8	11	11	..	Exports of Goods & Services
17	7	9	9	12	7	10	7	10	6	..	Merchandise, fob
3	2	2	2	2	2	4	2	2	5	..	Nonfactor Services
3	2	1	1	0	0	0	0	0	0	..	Factor Services
22	30	38	26	35	30	37	23	23	46	..	Imports of Goods & Services
15	22	27	18	24	20	23	14	14	27	..	Merchandise, fob
6	8	10	7	10	9	11	9	8	15	..	Nonfactor Services
0	0	1	1	1	2	3	1	1	4	..	Factor Services
0	0	0	1	1	1	1	1	1	3	..	Long-Term Interest
1	1	0	1	3	0	-1	0	0	0	..	Private Current Transfers, net
1	1	1	1	3	0	0	0	0	..	..	Workers' Remittances
1	-18	-26	-14	-17	-21	-25	-15	-12	-35	..	Curr. A/C Bal before Off. Transf.
0	0	1	6	6	5	6	2	1	13	..	Net Official Transfers
1	-18	-25	-9	-11	-16	-19	-13	-11	-22	..	Curr. A/C Bal after Off. Transf.
0	3	15	3	14	8	5	3	2	21	..	Long-Term Capital, net
..	..	..	..	..	..	..	..	0	0	..	Direct Investment
9	7	8	7	14	7	10	8	11	16	..	Long-Term Loans
10	8	10	9	16	8	10	10	12	17	..	Disbursements
1	1	2	2	2	2	1	2	1	2	..	Repayments
-9	-4	6	-4	0	1	-4	-4	-9	5	..	Other Long-Term Capital
-13	8	8	4	-8	9	12	6	5	0	..	Other Capital, net
12	7	2	2	5	-1	1	4	4	1	..	Change in Reserves
											Memo Item:
				(Sao Tome & Principe Dobras per US dollar)							
34.770	38.400	41.000	42.330	44.160	44.600	38.590	70.500	98.200	140.400	..	Conversion Factor (Annual Avg)
				(Thousands of US dollars), outstanding at end of year							
23,500.00	34,400.00	37,800.00	43,800.00	53,900.00	62,300.00	77,000.00	92,700.00	104,100.00	130,600.00	..	**EXTERNAL DEBT (Total)**
23,500.00	29,400.00	36,800.00	42,800.00	53,900.00	61,500.00	74,800.00	86,200.00	95,900.00	110,700.00	..	Long-Term Debt (by debtor)
0.00	0.00	0.00	0.00	0.00	0.00	0.00	0.00	0.00	1,100.00	..	Central Bank, incl. IMF credit
23,500.00	29,400.00	36,800.00	42,800.00	53,900.00	61,500.00	74,800.00	86,200.00	95,900.00	109,600.00	..	Central Government
..	..	..	..	..	..	..	..	..	..	..	Rest of General Government
..	..	..	..	..	..	..	..	..	..	..	Non-financial Public Enterprises
..	..	..	..	..	..	..	..	..	..	..	Priv. Sector, incl non-guaranteed
0.00	5,000.00	1,000.00	1,000.00	0.00	800.00	2,200.00	6,500.00	8,200.00	19,900.00	..	Short-Term Debt
				(Millions of US dollars)							**Memo Items:**
..	..	..	..	..	..	..	..	..	..	..	Int'l Reserves Excluding Gold
..	..	..	..	..	..	..	..	..	..	..	Gold Holdings (at market price)
											SOCIAL INDICATORS
..	..	5.3	5.3	5.3	5.3	5.3	5.3	5.2	5.1	..	Total Fertility Rate
70.8	70.1	69.5	65.3	61.1	56.9	52.7	48.5	46.7	44.9	..	Infant Mortality Rate
..	..	63.4	63.7	64.0	64.4	64.7	65.1	65.4	65.8	..	Life Expectancy at Birth
32.7	32.4	32.0	33.9	35.7	37.6	38.8	40.0	40.8	41.5	..	Urban Population, % of total
136.7	144.5	130.9	126.9	107.6	110.4	106.7	100.0	110.3	98.7	..	Food Prod. per capita (1987=100)
..	..	..	..	..	..	..	..	..	..	..	Labor Force, Agriculture (%)
..	..	..	..	..	..	..	..	..	..	..	Labor Force, Female (%)
..	..	..	..	..	..	..	138.0	..	..	..	Primary Schl. Enroll. Ratio
..	..	..	..	..	..	..	..	..	..	..	Primary Schl. Enroll. Ratio, Female
..	..	..	..	..	..	..	..	..	..	..	Secondary Schl. Enroll. Ratio

SAUDI ARABIA	1969	1970	1971	1972	1973	1974	1975	1976	1977	1978	1979
CURRENT GNP PER CAPITA (US $)	530	560	760	980	1,140	2,070	3,290	5,410	7,120	7,720	8,790
POPULATION (thousands)	5,517	5,745	5,997	6,276	6,579	6,905	7,251	7,617	7,999	8,409	8,863
USE AND ORIGIN OF RESOURCES	*(Billions of current Saudi Arabian Riyals)*										
Gross National Product (GNP)	12.77	13.65	21.33	28.03	33.72	94.96	138.60	163.13	204.74	224.68	259.12
Net Factor Income from Abroad	-3.20	-3.75	-1.59	-0.23	-6.83	-4.35	-1.00	-1.40	-0.32	-0.72	9.58
GDP at Market Prices	15.98	17.40	22.92	28.26	40.55	99.31	139.60	164.53	205.06	225.40	249.54
Resource Balance	4.24	5.31	9.98	13.56	21.74	70.39	87.20	77.42	77.62	49.26	39.76
Exports of Goods & NFServices	9.09	10.30	15.19	19.86	30.01	85.68	114.46	120.28	140.32	140.76	147.24
Imports of Goods & NFServices	4.85	4.99	5.20	6.30	8.27	15.29	27.26	42.86	62.70	91.50	107.48
Domestic Absorption	11.74	12.09	12.94	14.70	18.81	28.93	52.40	87.11	127.43	176.14	209.78
Private Consumption, etc.	5.36	5.86	6.41	6.91	7.89	9.83	18.04	23.90	34.37	54.61	68.61
General Gov't Consumption	3.03	3.42	3.80	4.28	5.33	9.86	15.91	28.88	41.03	47.03	71.90
Gross Domestic Investment	3.35	2.81	2.73	3.50	5.58	9.23	18.45	34.32	52.03	74.50	69.27
Fixed Investment	2.63	2.60	2.93	3.40	5.69	8.40	17.70	33.54	51.19	66.89	76.65
Indirect Taxes, net	0.18	0.16	0.35	0.36	0.53	0.51	-0.52	-0.90	-0.67	-0.90	-0.93
GDP at factor cost	15.80	17.24	22.57	27.90	40.02	98.81	140.12	165.43	205.73	226.30	250.47
Agriculture	0.96	0.98	1.02	1.06	1.14	1.24	1.39	1.59	1.87	3.91	4.20
Industry	9.91	11.03	15.89	20.45	30.93	86.62	120.24	134.27	164.26	169.32	179.85
Manufacturing	1.37	1.67	1.96	1.98	2.43	5.08	7.37	8.17	9.28	9.97	12.62
Services, etc.	5.10	5.38	6.01	6.75	8.48	11.46	17.97	28.67	38.93	52.17	65.50
Gross Domestic Saving	7.59	8.12	12.71	17.06	27.32	79.62	105.65	111.74	129.65	123.76	109.03
Gross National Saving	..	3.54	10.19	15.72	19.04	73.43	102.70	106.85	124.02	113.37	105.96
	(Billions of 1980 Saudi Arabian Riyals)										
Gross National Product	97.64	106.37	146.88	183.81	188.82	249.24	257.27	275.86	320.03	333.28	366.04
GDP at Market Prices	122.58	135.70	157.66	185.27	225.01	260.07	259.05	278.15	320.51	334.33	352.59
Resource Balance	94.80	111.39	133.71	163.15	198.52	214.49	189.67	161.23	157.39	134.42	131.48
Exports of Goods & NFServices	104.77	121.05	143.24	174.43	212.56	238.34	227.49	222.64	242.86	246.60	249.03
Imports of Goods & NFServices	9.96	9.67	9.53	11.27	14.04	23.85	37.82	61.41	85.47	112.18	117.55
Domestic Absorption	27.78	24.32	23.95	22.12	26.49	45.58	69.39	116.92	163.12	199.91	221.11
Private Consumption, etc.	..	..	..	..	..	..	..	..	..	..	..
General Gov't Consumption	..	..	..	..	..	..	..	..	..	..	..
Gross Domestic Investment	6.95	5.55	5.06	6.19	9.52	14.59	29.58	51.30	71.26	91.35	75.78
Fixed Investment	..	..	..	..	..	..	..	..	..	..	..
GDP at factor cost	121.21	134.43	155.29	183.01	222.22	258.81	259.98	279.63	321.53	335.65	353.89
Agriculture	2.71	2.79	2.88	2.98	3.09	3.20	3.33	3.46	3.63	4.20	4.39
Industry	95.33	107.20	126.95	152.67	188.39	218.55	215.96	227.98	262.60	268.38	278.15
Manufacturing	8.38	10.00	11.00	11.05	11.83	12.45	12.09	13.08	14.82	16.12	17.72
Services, etc.	24.54	25.71	27.82	29.63	33.53	38.33	39.76	46.71	54.27	61.75	70.05
Memo Items:											
Capacity to Import	18.66	19.96	27.81	35.52	50.95	133.63	158.82	172.33	191.28	172.57	161.03
Terms of Trade Adjustment	-86.10	-101.10	-115.43	-138.90	-161.61	-104.71	-68.67	-50.31	-51.58	-74.03	-88.00
Gross Domestic Income	36.48	34.61	42.23	46.37	63.40	155.36	190.39	227.84	268.93	260.30	264.59
Gross National Income	11.54	5.27	31.45	44.91	27.21	144.53	188.61	225.55	268.44	259.25	278.05
DOMESTIC PRICES/DEFLATORS	*(Index 1980 = 100)*										
Overall (GDP)	13.0	12.8	14.5	15.3	18.0	38.2	53.9	59.1	64.0	67.4	70.8
Domestic Absorption	42.3	49.7	54.0	66.5	71.0	63.5	75.5	74.5	78.1	88.1	94.9
Agriculture	35.3	35.3	35.2	35.6	36.9	38.8	41.8	45.8	51.3	93.0	95.5
Industry	10.4	10.3	12.5	13.4	16.4	39.6	55.7	58.9	62.6	63.1	64.7
Manufacturing	16.4	16.7	17.8	18.0	20.5	40.8	60.9	62.5	62.6	61.9	71.2
Consumer Price Index	33.8	33.9	35.4	36.9	43.0	52.3	70.4	92.6	103.1	101.5	103.4
MANUFACTURING ACTIVITY											
Employment (1987=100)	..	..	..	..	..	..	..	..	..	..	..
Real Earnings per Empl. (1987=100)	..	..	..	..	..	..	..	..	..	..	..
Real Output per Empl. (1987=100)	..	..	..	..	..	..	..	..	..	..	..
Earnings as % of Value Added	..	..	..	..	..	..	..	..	..	..	..
MONETARY HOLDINGS	*(Billions of current Saudi Arabian Riyals)*										
Money Supply, Broadly Defined	2.97	3.14	3.59	5.04	6.81	9.78	17.78	29.61	45.56	58.03	65.98
Money	2.32	2.40	2.65	3.78	5.29	7.33	14.18	24.27	38.41	49.21	54.70
Currency Outside Banks	1.56	1.63	1.67	2.42	3.05	4.14	6.68	10.59	16.25	19.18	23.71
Demand Deposits	0.77	0.77	0.98	1.36	2.23	3.19	7.50	13.68	22.16	30.03	31.00
Quasi-Money	0.64	0.74	0.94	1.26	1.52	2.44	3.60	5.34	7.14	8.82	11.28
GOVERNMENT DEFICIT (-) OR SURPLUS	*(Millions of current Saudi Arabian Riyals)*										
Current Revenue	..	..	..	..	..	..	..	..	..	..	..
Current Expenditure	..	..	..	..	..	..	..	..	..	..	..
Current Budget Balance	..	..	..	..	..	..	..	..	..	..	..
Capital Receipts	..	..	..	..	..	..	..	..	..	..	..
Capital Payments	..	..	..	..	..	..	..	..	..	..	..

1980	1981	1982	1983	1984	1985	1986	1987	1988	1989 estimate	NOTES	SAUDI ARABIA
10,400	13,010	14,310	12,820	10,140	8,630	7,830	6,650	6,060	6,020	..	CURRENT GNP PER CAPITA (US $)
9,372	9,925	10,514	11,130	11,762	12,395	12,991	13,612	14,016	14,435	..	POPULATION (thousands)
				(Billions of current Saudi Arabian Riyals)							USE AND ORIGIN OF RESOURCES
387.56	525.18	485.00	422.08	387.80	352.56	310.42	312.42	301.48	321.48	C	Gross National Product (GNP)
1.75	4.59	26.91	44.38	36.40	38.62	39.33	36.93	19.51	18.53	..	Net Factor Income from Abroad
385.81	520.59	458.10	377.70	351.40	313.94	271.09	275.49	281.97	302.95	C	GDP at Market Prices
126.14	210.97	70.50	-7.22	-45.11	-24.73	-29.25	-20.12	-11.86	-2.28	..	Resource Balance
258.49	368.43	269.03	187.35	145.53	113.16	85.99	99.05	103.08	113.44	..	Exports of Goods & NFServices
132.35	157.46	198.53	194.57	190.64	137.89	115.24	119.17	114.94	115.72	..	Imports of Goods & NFServices
259.67	309.62	387.60	384.92	396.50	338.67	300.34	295.62	293.83	305.23	..	Domestic Absorption
102.45	114.90	147.78	160.33	159.35	158.59	140.15	135.58	138.43	143.20	..	Private Consumption, etc.
77.50	81.91	131.07	126.57	121.06	114.39	106.37	107.71	92.25	97.35	..	General Gov't Consumption
79.72	112.80	108.75	98.02	116.10	65.69	53.83	52.33	63.15	64.68	..	Gross Domestic Investment
97.07	106.38	120.99	109.87	96.49	76.31	66.14	65.20	56.99	70.94	..	Fixed Investment
..	..	..	..	..	..	..	..	..	..	..	Indirect Taxes, net
..	..	..	..	..	..	..	..	..	..	B C	GDP at factor cost
4.65	5.57	8.35	9.64	11.62	13.79	15.86	18.31	20.69	23.03	..	Agriculture
301.25	419.19	318.83	225.19	193.97	153.64	117.25	122.90	120.52	135.21	..	Industry
19.29	25.75	24.16	26.89	27.42	24.50	19.72	23.85	24.74	27.31	..	Manufacturing
79.91	95.83	130.92	142.86	145.81	146.51	137.98	134.29	140.75	144.71	..	Services, etc.
205.86	323.77	179.25	90.80	70.99	40.96	24.58	32.21	51.28	62.40	..	Gross Domestic Saving
193.99	310.27	187.83	117.09	88.77	60.75	46.11	50.66	47.73	..	..	Gross National Saving
				(Billions of 1980 Saudi Arabian Riyals)							
387.56	417.16	417.96	410.57	360.26	344.07	382.08	368.37	373.37	373.50	C	Gross National Product
385.81	413.48	393.40	363.46	322.03	300.51	327.86	318.95	346.06	345.54	C	GDP at Market Prices
126.14	113.18	..	..	..	..	..	..	..	..	..	Resource Balance
258.49	273.62	..	..	..	..	..	..	..	..	..	Exports of Goods & NFServices
132.35	160.44	..	..	..	..	..	..	..	..	..	Imports of Goods & NFServices
259.67	300.30	..	..	..	..	..	..	..	..	..	Domestic Absorption
..	..	..	..	..	..	..	..	..	..	..	Private Consumption, etc.
..	..	..	..	..	..	..	..	..	..	..	General Gov't Consumption
79.72	114.95	..	..	..	..	..	..	..	..	..	Gross Domestic Investment
..	..	..	..	..	..	..	..	..	..	..	Fixed Investment
..	..	..	..	..	..	..	..	..	..	B C	GDP at factor cost
4.65	4.92	5.72	6.45	7.67	9.05	10.41	12.12	13.42	14.36	..	Agriculture
301.25	319.30	278.87	241.71	200.12	177.59	209.58	200.52	223.95	221.94	..	Industry
19.29	20.67	24.56	27.64	29.09	32.62	32.69	36.88	40.03	40.39	..	Manufacturing
79.91	89.27	108.80	115.30	114.24	113.87	107.87	106.31	108.69	109.24	..	Services, etc.
											Memo Items:
258.49	375.40	..	..	..	..	..	..	..	..	..	Capacity to Import
0.00	101.78	..	..	..	..	..	..	..	..	..	Terms of Trade Adjustment
385.81	515.27	..	..	..	..	..	..	..	..	..	Gross Domestic Income
387.56	518.94	..	..	..	..	..	..	..	..	..	Gross National Income
				(Index 1980 = 100)							DOMESTIC PRICES/DEFLATORS
100.0	125.9	116.4	103.9	109.1	104.5	82.7	86.4	81.5	87.7	..	Overall (GDP)
100.0	103.1	..	..	..	..	..	..	..	..	..	Domestic Absorption
100.0	113.3	145.8	149.4	151.5	152.4	152.4	151.1	154.2	160.3	..	Agriculture
100.0	131.3	114.3	93.2	96.9	86.5	55.9	61.3	53.8	60.9	..	Industry
100.0	124.6	98.4	97.3	94.3	75.1	60.3	64.7	61.8	67.6	..	Manufacturing
107.3	110.1	109.5	108.9	107.6	104.1	101.0	100.0	101.1	102.2	..	Consumer Price Index
											MANUFACTURING ACTIVITY
..	..	..	..	..	..	..	..	..	..	..	Employment (1987 = 100)
..	..	..	..	..	..	..	..	..	..	..	Real Earnings per Empl. (1987 = 100)
..	..	..	..	..	..	..	..	..	..	..	Real Output per Empl. (1987 = 100)
..	..	..	..	..	..	..	..	..	..	..	Earnings as % of Value Added
				(Billions of current Saudi Arabian Riyals)							MONETARY HOLDINGS
77.44	102.99	123.79	137.09	145.35	147.01	160.56	168.40	177.89	..	..	Money Supply, Broadly Defined
58.96	72.98	83.78	84.93	82.98	81.83	86.28	91.78	93.43	..	..	Money
25.68	29.49	34.44	35.42	35.11	35.77	38.81	40.07	35.95	..	..	Currency Outside Banks
33.28	43.49	49.34	49.51	47.86	46.06	47.47	51.70	57.48	..	..	Demand Deposits
18.48	30.01	40.01	52.16	62.37	65.18	74.28	76.62	84.46	..	..	Quasi-Money
				(Millions of current Saudi Arabian Riyals)							
..	..	..	..	..	..	..	..	..	..	..	GOVERNMENT DEFICIT (-) OR SURPLUS
..	..	..	..	..	..	..	..	..	..	..	Current Revenue
..	..	..	..	..	..	..	..	..	..	..	Current Expenditure
..	..	..	..	..	..	..	..	..	..	..	Current Budget Balance
..	..	..	..	..	..	..	..	..	..	..	Capital Receipts
..	..	..	..	..	..	..	..	..	..	..	Capital Payments

SAUDI ARABIA	1969	1970	1971	1972	1973	1974	1975	1976	1977	1978	1979
FOREIGN TRADE (CUSTOMS BASIS)					*(Millions of current US dollars)*						
Value of Exports, fob	1,992	2,424	3,845	5,491	9,089	35,562	29,669	38,282	43,458	40,715	63,419
Nonfuel Primary Products	4	4	4	9	14	49	31	30	27	95	107
Fuels	1,987	2,417	3,792	5,391	8,993	35,482	29,466	38,164	43,311	40,383	62,847
Manufactures	2	2	49	91	82	31	172	89	120	237	465
Value of Imports, cif	734	692	806	1,125	1,977	2,848	4,141	8,409	14,289	20,177	24,384
Nonfuel Primary Products	224	241	256	308	480	639	743	1,233	1,830	2,639	3,583
Fuels	10	8	10	11	13	29	28	62	81	136	156
Manufactures	500	443	539	806	1,484	2,180	3,370	7,113	12,378	17,403	20,646
					(Index 1987 = 100)						
Terms of Trade	25.7	23.8	30.3	31.6	37.3	126.1	115.3	124.7	126.1	110.6	137.9
Export Prices, fob	7.5	7.5	9.9	11.1	15.7	64.5	62.7	67.4	73.7	74.4	106.8
Import Prices, cif	29.2	31.5	32.7	35.1	41.9	51.2	54.4	54.0	58.5	67.3	77.4
BALANCE OF PAYMENTS					*(Millions of current US dollars)*						
Exports of Goods & Services	..	2,372	2,926	4,381	8,264	32,735	30,569	40,272	46,447	43,461	67,766
Merchandise, fob	..	2,089	2,581	3,911	7,489	30,132	27,294	35,632	40,351	36,993	58,009
Nonfactor Services	..	222	279	364	569	1,383	1,436	1,756	2,108	2,168	4,841
Factor Services	..	61	67	106	205	1,220	1,839	2,884	3,989	4,301	4,915
Imports of Goods & Services	..	2,037	1,600	1,867	4,856	8,177	12,503	21,601	29,049	38,929	49,363
Merchandise, fob	..	829	805	1,197	1,853	3,569	6,004	10,385	14,698	20,020	20,912
Nonfactor Services	..	313	374	509	955	2,163	4,375	7,935	10,272	14,396	26,386
Factor Services	..	895	421	162	2,048	2,445	2,124	3,280	4,079	4,512	2,065
Long-Term Interest	..	..	..	..	..	..	..	..	..	..	..
Private Current Transfers, net	..	-183	-207	-268	-391	-518	-554	-989	-1,506	-2,844	-3,764
Workers' Remittances	..	..	..	..	..	..	..	..	..	..	..
Curr. A/C Bal before Off. Transf.	..	152	1,119	2,246	3,016	24,039	17,512	17,683	15,892	1,688	14,639
Net Official Transfers	..	-81	-147	-157	-496	-1,014	-3,127	-3,323	-3,901	-3,900	-3,502
Curr. A/C Bal after Off. Transf.	..	71	972	2,089	2,520	23,025	14,385	14,360	11,991	-2,212	11,137
Long-Term Capital, net	..	93	-127	27	-912	-8,873	-9,137	-11,156	-7,503	-2,733	-3,755
Direct Investment	..	20	-111	34	-626	-3,732	1,865	-397	783	556	-1,351
Long-Term Loans	..	..	..	..	..	..	..	..	..	..	..
Disbursements	..	..	..	..	..	..	..	..	..	..	..
Repayments	..	..	..	..	..	..	..	..	..	..	..
Other Long-Term Capital	..	73	-16	-7	-286	-5,141	-11,002	-10,759	-8,286	-3,289	-2,404
Other Capital, net	..	-77	-172	-1,059	-691	-3,764	3,811	523	-1,791	-1,755	-7,148
Change in Reserves	..	-87	-673	-1,057	-917	-10,388	-9,059	-3,727	-2,697	6,700	-234
Memo Item:					*(Saudi Arabian Riyals per US dollar)*						
Conversion Factor (Annual Avg)	4.500	4.500	4.490	4.150	3.710	3.550	3.520	3.530	3.520	3.400	3.360
				(Millions of US dollars), outstanding at end of year							
EXTERNAL DEBT (Total)	..	..	..	..	..	..	..	..	..	..	..
Long-Term Debt (by debtor)	..	..	..	..	..	..	..	..	..	..	..
Central Bank, incl. IMF credit	..	..	..	..	..	..	..	..	..	..	..
Central Government	..	..	..	..	..	..	..	..	..	..	..
Rest of General Government	..	..	..	..	..	..	..	..	..	..	..
Non-financial Public Enterprises	..	..	..	..	..	..	..	..	..	..	..
Priv. Sector, incl non-guaranteed	..	..	..	..	..	..	..	..	..	..	..
Short-Term Debt	..	..	..	..	..	..	..	..	..	..	..
Memo Items:					*(Millions of US dollars)*						
Int'l Reserves Excluding Gold	488	543	1,327	2,383	3,747	14,153	23,193	26,900	29,903	19,200	19,273
Gold Holdings (at market price)	120	127	135	200	346	575	432	415	508	1,026	2,338
SOCIAL INDICATORS											
Total Fertility Rate	7.3	7.3	7.3	7.3	7.3	7.3	7.3	7.3	7.3	7.3	7.3
Infant Mortality Rate	132.0	128.0	124.0	120.0	116.0	112.0	108.0	104.0	100.0	97.0	94.0
Life Expectancy at Birth	51.5	52.3	53.1	53.9	54.7	55.5	56.3	57.1	57.9	58.5	59.1
Urban Population, % of total	46.7	48.7	50.7	52.7	54.7	56.7	58.7	60.3	61.9	63.6	65.2
Food Prod. per capita (1987=100)	55.6	58.2	75.4	45.4	48.5	67.1	66.9	59.3	62.2	56.2	52.7
Labor Force, Agriculture (%)	64.8	64.2	62.3	60.5	59.0	57.6	56.3	54.3	52.6	51.0	49.7
Labor Force, Female (%)	4.9	5.0	5.2	5.4	5.6	5.7	5.9	6.0	6.1	6.1	6.2
Primary Schl. Enroll. Ratio	..	45.0	..	..	..	..	58.0	59.0	58.0	60.0	62.0
Primary Schl. Enroll. Ratio, Female	..	29.0	..	..	..	..	43.0	45.0	44.0	46.0	48.0
Secondary Schl. Enroll. Ratio	..	12.0	..	..	..	..	22.0	24.0	26.0	28.0	30.0

1980	1981	1982	1983	1984	1985	1986	1987	1988	1989 estimate	NOTES	SAUDI ARABIA
				(Millions of current US dollars)							**FOREIGN TRADE (CUSTOMS BASIS)**
109,113	119,913	79,125	45,861	37,530	27,481	20,085	23,138	24,300	..	..	Value of Exports, fob
181	153	136	153	126	90	226	260	462	..	..	Nonfuel Primary Products
108,226	119,039	78,165	44,928	36,657	26,676	18,041	20,783	20,100	..	..	Fuels
705	721	824	780	747	715	1,818	2,096	3,738	..	..	Manufactures
29,957	35,042	40,473	39,206	33,696	23,697	19,112	20,465	22,100	..	..	Value of Imports, cif
4,965	5,770	5,967	5,732	5,955	3,949	3,651	3,969	4,288	..	..	Nonfuel Primary Products
191	254	192	247	237	157	150	160	172	..	..	Fuels
24,801	29,018	34,314	33,227	27,504	19,592	15,311	16,336	17,640	..	..	Manufactures
				(Index 1987 = 100)							
203.1	228.7	213.1	195.8	193.8	187.9	87.6	100.0	80.9	..	..	Terms of Trade
174.1	195.8	176.5	159.4	156.0	150.5	80.8	100.0	88.9	..	..	Export Prices, fob
85.7	85.6	82.8	81.4	80.5	80.1	92.3	100.0	110.0	..	..	Import Prices, cif
				(Millions of current US dollars)							**BALANCE OF PAYMENTS**
114,208	130,400	92,828	65,883	55,023	43,458	34,069	36,251	37,060	..	..	Exports of Goods & Services
100,717	111,831	73,876	45,662	37,423	27,393	20,125	23,138	24,315	..	..	Merchandise, fob
6,048	7,613	4,892	4,353	4,234	3,647	2,665	2,577	2,385	..	..	Nonfactor Services
7,443	10,956	14,060	15,868	13,366	12,418	11,279	10,537	10,361	..	..	Factor Services
62,710	79,725	75,507	73,499	64,541	47,941	38,060	37,789	35,239	..	..	Imports of Goods & Services
25,563	29,889	34,444	33,218	28,557	20,364	17,066	18,283	19,805	..	..	Merchandise, fob
30,231	40,236	34,852	37,259	32,856	25,822	20,336	18,830	15,103	..	..	Nonfactor Services
6,917	9,599	6,210	3,022	3,127	1,756	659	676	331	..	..	Factor Services
..	..	..	..	..	..	..	..	..	..	..	Long-Term Interest
-4,094	-5,348	-5,347	-5,236	-5,284	-5,199	-4,804	-4,935	-6,158	..	..	Private Current Transfers, net
..	..	..	..	..	..	..	..	..	..	..	Workers' Remittances
47,404	45,327	11,974	-12,852	-14,802	-9,682	-8,795	-6,473	-4,275	..	..	Curr. A/C Bal before Off. Transf.
-5,901	-5,700	-4,399	-4,000	-3,598	-3,249	-3,000	-3,300	-2,499	..	..	Net Official Transfers
41,503	39,627	7,575	-16,852	-18,401	-12,932	-11,795	-9,773	-6,774	..	..	Curr. A/C Bal after Off. Transf.
-29,732	-27,725	1,949	-2,585	-8,556	-7,921	-10,115	-9,055	-7,423	..	..	Long-Term Capital, net
-3,192	6,498	11,128	4,944	4,850	491	967	-1,175	-2,606	..	..	Direct Investment
..	..	..	..	..	..	..	..	..	..	..	Long-Term Loans
..	..	..	..	..	..	..	..	..	..	..	Disbursements
..	..	..	..	..	..	..	..	..	..	..	Repayments
-26,539	-34,223	-9,180	-7,529	-13,406	-8,412	-11,082	-7,880	-4,817	..	..	Other Long-Term Capital
-7,834	-2,334	-11,832	17,929	25,477	20,143	14,291	21,468	12,678	..	..	Other Capital, net
-3,937	-9,568	2,308	1,508	1,480	709	7,619	-2,640	1,519	3,507	..	Change in Reserves
				(Saudi Arabian Riyals per US dollar)							Memo Item:
3.330	3.380	3.430	3.450	3.520	3.620	3.700	3.740	3.740	3.740	..	Conversion Factor (Annual Avg)
				(Millions of US dollars), outstanding at end of year							
..	..	..	..	..	..	..	..	..	..	..	**EXTERNAL DEBT (Total)**
..	..	..	..	..	..	..	..	..	..	..	Long-Term Debt (by debtor)
..	..	..	..	..	..	..	..	..	..	..	Central Bank, incl. IMF credit
..	..	..	..	..	..	..	..	..	..	..	Central Government
..	..	..	..	..	..	..	..	..	..	..	Rest of General Government
..	..	..	..	..	..	..	..	..	..	..	Non-financial Public Enterprises
..	..	..	..	..	..	..	..	..	..	..	Priv. Sector, incl non-guaranteed
..	..	..	..	..	..	..	..	..	..	..	Short-Term Debt
				(Millions of US dollars)							Memo Items:
23,437	32,236	29,549	27,287	24,748	25,004	18,324	22,684	20,553	16,747	..	Int'l Reserves Excluding Gold
2,692	1,815	2,100	1,753	1,417	1,503	1,797	2,225	1,886	1,843	..	Gold Holdings (at market price)
											SOCIAL INDICATORS
7.3	7.3	7.3	7.3	7.2	7.2	7.2	7.2	7.1	7.0	..	Total Fertility Rate
91.0	88.0	85.0	82.2	79.4	76.6	73.8	71.0	69.4	67.7	..	Infant Mortality Rate
59.7	60.3	60.9	61.4	61.9	62.4	62.9	63.4	63.7	64.0	..	Life Expectancy at Birth
66.8	68.0	69.3	70.5	71.8	73.0	73.9	74.7	75.6	76.4	..	Urban Population, % of total
42.8	33.8	44.2	51.5	71.1	100.9	100.0	100.0	113.4	108.4	..	Food Prod. per capita (1987 = 100)
48.4	..	..	..	..	..	..	..	..	..	..	Labor Force, Agriculture (%)
6.3	6.4	6.4	6.5	6.6	6.7	6.8	7.0	7.1	7.2	..	Labor Force, Female (%)
63.0	..	65.0	67.0	69.0	69.0	71.0	..	..	..	..	Primary Schl. Enroll. Ratio
50.0	53.0	54.0	58.0	60.0	61.0	65.0	..	..	..	..	Primary Schl. Enroll. Ratio, Female
30.0	..	33.0	35.0	38.0	42.0	44.0	..	..	..	..	Secondary Schl. Enroll. Ratio

SENEGAL	1969	1970	1971	1972	1973	1974	1975	1976	1977	1978	1979
CURRENT GNP PER CAPITA (US $)	210	220	210	230	240	280	350	400	400	380	460
POPULATION (thousands)	4,043	4,158	4,284	4,410	4,539	4,670	4,806	4,945	5,087	5,232	5,382
USE AND ORIGIN OF RESOURCES					*(Billions of current CFA Francs)*						
Gross National Product (GNP)	211.4	234.3	242.0	267.8	271.8	327.3	394.6	453.3	469.9	477.3	565.1
Net Factor Income from Abroad	-5.2	-5.8	-5.2	-5.8	-6.5	-11.5	-11.8	-6.0	-13.7	-17.4	-16.8
GDP at Market Prices	216.6	240.1	247.2	273.6	278.3	338.8	406.4	459.3	483.6	494.7	581.9
Resource Balance	-17.7	-11.0	-18.0	-10.0	-28.1	-22.4	-21.3	-36.9	-30.0	-62.9	-59.3
Exports of Goods & NFServices	51.5	65.8	64.0	84.2	79.5	143.7	148.6	166.7	213.0	154.9	185.3
Imports of Goods & NFServices	69.2	76.8	82.0	94.2	107.6	166.1	169.9	203.6	243.0	217.8	244.6
Domestic Absorption	234.3	251.1	265.2	283.6	306.4	361.2	427.7	496.2	513.6	557.6	641.2
Private Consumption, etc.	171.6	177.7	186.4	196.3	210.0	236.1	293.6	348.8	351.1	380.3	446.6
General Gov't Consumption	33.6	35.7	38.8	40.8	43.8	50.0	61.8	71.7	77.9	91.1	111.0
Gross Domestic Investment	29.1	37.7	40.0	46.5	52.6	75.1	72.3	75.7	84.6	86.2	83.6
Fixed Investment	..	..	..	..	..	..	..	..	..	..	82.6
Indirect Taxes, net	25.5	27.3	30.3	32.0	32.8	37.4	44.8	52.9	59.0	55.8	63.7
GDP at factor cost	191.1	212.8	216.9	241.6	245.5	301.4	361.6	406.4	424.6	438.9	518.2
Agriculture	50.7	57.8	51.8	67.4	62.8	80.7	122.8	138.0	132.5	104.6	139.6
Industry	44.5	48.6	51.2	54.5	54.7	80.2	92.7	106.9	113.1	120.4	141.1
Manufacturing	36.9	39.2	41.6	44.2	44.8	66.8	74.7	85.5	75.6	76.3	89.4
Services, etc.	121.4	133.7	144.2	151.7	160.8	177.9	190.9	214.4	238.0	269.7	301.2
Gross Domestic Saving	11.4	26.7	22.0	36.5	24.5	52.7	51.0	38.8	54.6	23.3	24.3
Gross National Saving	..	16.2	11.3	25.3	13.3	35.8	37.2	36.3	44.7	7.7	3.7
					(Billions of 1987 CFA Francs)						
Gross National Product	829.09	900.44	904.82	959.93	905.95	930.81	1,006.88	1,112.66	1,064.84	995.19	1,095.51
GDP at Market Prices	846.50	919.26	920.69	977.05	924.33	959.43	1,032.74	1,123.60	1,093.92	1,029.80	1,126.10
Resource Balance	-24.34	-31.06	-43.30	-13.40	-47.66	-40.50	-21.54	-20.15	-45.21	-101.43	-71.31
Exports of Goods & NFServices	161.76	176.23	156.62	201.53	156.22	167.98	187.73	234.53	320.82	222.09	250.62
Imports of Goods & NFServices	186.11	207.30	199.93	214.93	203.87	208.48	209.27	254.68	366.03	323.51	321.94
Domestic Absorption	870.85	950.32	964.00	990.46	971.99	999.93	1,054.28	1,143.75	1,139.13	1,131.22	1,197.41
Private Consumption, etc.	634.01	684.61	692.10	703.49	682.17	687.68	756.48	821.45	793.45	779.34	854.55
General Gov't Consumption	116.56	119.71	122.17	122.17	121.29	129.53	136.36	135.14	166.69	181.58	194.55
Gross Domestic Investment	120.28	146.00	149.73	164.80	168.53	182.72	161.43	187.16	179.00	170.30	148.31
Fixed Investment	..	..	..	..	..	..	..	..	141.75	124.38	146.35
GDP at factor cost	..	..	..	..	..	..	..	..	..	..	..
Agriculture	243.67	257.94	215.34	266.46	223.65	275.40	285.63	328.65	306.07	233.87	297.34
Industry	170.51	186.40	191.98	196.73	188.67	210.56	224.59	242.55	288.17	262.16	263.40
Manufacturing	149.10	157.37	165.64	167.71	163.80	186.78	198.72	212.28	212.74	169.78	174.37
Services, etc.	433.72	475.17	505.26	512.46	505.08	478.05	524.72	558.59	509.58	529.58	567.06
Memo Items:											
Capacity to Import	138.50	177.61	156.04	192.11	150.63	180.37	183.03	208.52	320.84	230.08	243.89
Terms of Trade Adjustment	-23.26	1.37	-0.58	-9.41	-5.59	12.38	-4.70	-26.01	0.02	8.00	-6.74
Gross Domestic Income	823.24	920.63	920.11	967.64	918.74	971.81	1,028.04	1,097.59	1,093.94	1,037.79	1,119.37
Gross National Income	805.83	901.81	904.24	950.51	900.36	943.19	1,002.18	1,086.65	1,064.86	1,003.19	1,088.77
DOMESTIC PRICES/DEFLATORS					*(Index 1987 = 100)*						
Overall (GDP)	25.6	26.1	26.8	28.0	30.1	35.3	39.4	40.9	44.2	48.0	51.7
Domestic Absorption	26.9	26.4	27.5	28.6	31.5	36.1	40.6	43.4	45.1	49.3	53.5
Agriculture	20.8	22.4	24.1	25.3	28.1	29.3	43.0	42.0	43.3	44.7	46.9
Industry	26.1	26.1	26.7	27.7	29.0	38.1	41.3	44.1	39.2	45.9	53.6
Manufacturing	24.7	24.9	25.1	26.4	27.3	35.8	37.6	40.3	35.5	44.9	51.3
Consumer Price Index	20.9	21.4	22.3	23.6	26.3	30.7	40.4	40.8	45.5	47.0	51.6
MANUFACTURING ACTIVITY											
Employment (1987=100)	..	..	..	..	..	..	..	..	..	..	..
Real Earnings per Empl. (1987=100)	..	..	..	..	..	..	..	..	..	..	..
Real Output per Empl. (1987=100)	..	..	..	..	..	..	..	..	..	..	..
Earnings as % of Value Added	..	..	..	..	..	29.7	30.4	31.3	27.8	45.9	46.6
MONETARY HOLDINGS					*(Billions of current CFA Francs)*						
Money Supply, Broadly Defined	29.73	37.27	38.05	42.83	52.37	77.26	86.10	113.65	130.97	158.83	161.12
Money	27.97	34.50	35.20	39.12	44.20	67.77	75.18	94.89	109.12	126.53	121.21
Currency Outside Banks	11.58	15.24	15.94	16.49	19.45	28.96	29.46	33.74	39.47	46.22	42.94
Demand Deposits	16.39	19.26	19.26	22.63	24.75	38.81	45.72	61.15	69.65	80.30	78.28
Quasi-Money	1.76	2.77	2.84	3.72	8.17	9.49	10.92	18.76	21.85	32.31	39.91
					(Billions of current CFA Francs)						
GOVERNMENT DEFICIT (-) OR SURPLUS	..	1.24	-1.20	..	-7.51	..	-2.15	..	-15.09	1.49	-4.26
Current Revenue	..	38.99	41.41	..	46.30	..	76.97	..	86.11	98.01	107.73
Current Expenditure	..	37.00	39.51	..	45.30	..	66.38	74.60	77.85	88.50	99.50
Current Budget Balance	..	1.99	1.90	..	1.00	..	10.59	..	8.26	9.51	8.23
Capital Receipts	..	1.00	0.03	..	1.40	..	0.08	..	0.16	0.17	0.08
Capital Payments	..	1.75	3.13	..	9.91	..	12.82	16.82	23.51	8.19	12.57

1980	1981	1982	1983	1984	1985	1986	1987	1988	1989 estimate	NOTES	SENEGAL
510	490	500	440	380	380	430	520	650	650	..	**CURRENT GNP PER CAPITA (US $)**
5,538	5,699	5,864	6,034	6,211	6,395	6,589	6,789	6,996	7,211	..	**POPULATION (thousands)**
				(Billions of current CFA Francs)							**USE AND ORIGIN OF RESOURCES**
616.2	640.0	805.8	900.1	960.4	1,085.9	1,227.9	1,314.7	1,411.8	1,416.6	f	Gross National Product (GNP)
-21.1	-29.7	-38.0	-39.2	-55.3	-66.2	-66.4	-67.6	-71.4	-71.1	..	Net Factor Income from Abroad
637.3	669.7	843.8	939.3	1,015.7	1,152.1	1,294.3	1,382.3	1,483.2	1,487.7	..	GDP at Market Prices
-100.1	-141.3	-93.4	-133.5	-104.2	-138.2	-97.0	-96.4	-78.7	-69.3	..	Resource Balance
180.2	221.4	319.5	313.2	402.3	357.9	358.2	349.9	379.4	407.6	..	Exports of Goods & NFServices
280.3	362.7	412.9	446.7	506.5	496.1	455.2	446.3	458.1	476.9	..	Imports of Goods & NFServices
737.4	811.0	937.2	1,072.8	1,119.9	1,290.3	1,391.3	1,478.7	1,561.9	1,557.0	..	Domestic Absorption
499.8	550.2	635.1	734.2	752.4	919.5	982.1	1,031.5	1,104.3	1,085.7	..	Private Consumption, etc.
140.3	150.7	169.2	186.5	206.8	213.0	219.9	236.2	241.8	243.3	..	General Gov't Consumption
97.3	110.1	132.9	152.1	160.7	157.8	189.3	211.0	215.8	228.0	..	Gross Domestic Investment
100.2	102.4	124.5	148.3	151.8	161.3	188.8	207.2	211.0	228.0	..	Fixed Investment
..	..	..	..	..	..	..	..	..	..	..	Indirect Taxes, net
..	..	..	..	..	..	..	..	..	..	B f	GDP at factor cost
120.1	121.0	185.7	204.7	174.1	218.8	292.8	301.9	327.6	327.8	..	Agriculture
156.2	171.6	205.0	235.5	280.4	330.1	366.6	397.6	428.2	462.4	..	Industry
96.3	107.8	133.0	137.8	175.4	212.8	237.2	260.8	279.8	300.2	..	Manufacturing
361.0	377.1	453.1	499.1	561.2	603.2	634.9	682.8	727.4	697.5	..	Services, etc.
-2.8	-31.2	39.5	18.6	56.5	19.6	92.3	114.6	137.1	158.7	..	Gross Domestic Saving
-28.1	-63.6	0.0	-21.2	1.3	-38.9	34.9	56.0	75.2	97.2	..	Gross National Saving
				(Billions of 1987 CFA Francs)							
1,062.09	1,044.95	1,200.57	1,235.35	1,160.11	1,199.60	1,261.33	1,314.70	1,384.44	1,363.85	f	Gross National Product
1,095.76	1,090.19	1,251.74	1,283.21	1,223.13	1,269.14	1,327.65	1,382.30	1,453.37	1,431.34	..	GDP at Market Prices
-93.54	-122.79	-29.24	-46.55	-60.02	-86.55	-69.62	-96.40	-68.91	-60.28	..	Resource Balance
214.04	213.39	307.28	287.62	296.53	249.68	357.04	349.90	363.55	361.37	..	Exports of Goods & NFServices
307.58	336.18	336.52	334.16	356.55	336.23	426.66	446.30	432.45	421.65	..	Imports of Goods & NFServices
1,189.29	1,212.97	1,280.98	1,329.75	1,283.15	1,355.70	1,397.27	1,478.70	1,522.28	1,491.62	..	Domestic Absorption
841.04	857.61	906.41	940.71	895.39	975.06	993.24	1,031.50	1,083.53	1,065.28	..	Private Consumption, etc.
198.64	203.41	211.75	219.16	222.88	228.91	227.98	236.20	235.73	220.16	..	General Gov't Consumption
149.62	151.96	162.82	169.88	164.88	151.73	176.05	211.00	203.02	206.17	..	Gross Domestic Investment
154.04	140.44	151.28	164.89	154.93	155.09	175.31	207.20	198.52	205.92	..	Fixed Investment
..	..	..	..	..	..	..	..	..	..	B f	GDP at factor cost
242.92	229.33	286.20	299.94	247.44	266.99	293.96	301.90	325.14	302.71	..	Agriculture
282.54	298.64	343.12	351.03	344.71	351.61	368.82	397.60	414.69	402.24	..	Industry
188.32	219.77	233.19	228.75	233.60	235.90	246.97	260.80	268.63	268.91	..	Manufacturing
564.99	556.50	621.07	632.24	630.98	650.55	664.87	682.80	713.54	726.39	..	Services, etc.
											Memo Items:
197.74	205.21	260.40	234.30	283.20	242.56	335.74	349.90	358.16	360.38	..	Capacity to Import
-16.30	-8.18	-46.88	-53.32	-13.33	-7.11	-21.30	0.00	-5.39	-0.99	..	Terms of Trade Adjustment
1,079.45	1,082.01	1,204.86	1,229.89	1,209.80	1,262.03	1,306.35	1,382.30	1,447.98	1,430.35	..	Gross Domestic Income
1,045.79	1,036.77	1,153.68	1,182.03	1,146.78	1,192.48	1,240.03	1,314.70	1,379.05	1,362.86	..	Gross National Income
				(Index 1987 = 100)							**DOMESTIC PRICES/DEFLATORS**
58.2	61.4	67.4	73.2	83.0	90.8	97.5	100.0	102.1	103.9	..	Overall (GDP)
62.0	66.9	73.2	80.7	87.3	95.2	99.6	100.0	102.6	104.4	..	Domestic Absorption
49.4	52.8	64.9	68.2	70.4	82.0	99.6	100.0	100.8	108.3	..	Agriculture
55.3	57.5	59.7	67.1	81.3	93.9	99.4	100.0	103.3	115.0	..	Industry
51.1	49.1	57.0	60.2	75.1	90.2	96.0	100.0	104.2	111.6	..	Manufacturing
56.1	59.4	69.7	77.8	86.9	98.2	104.3	100.0	98.2	98.6	..	Consumer Price Index
											MANUFACTURING ACTIVITY
..	..	..	..	..	..	..	..	..	..	J	Employment (1987=100)
..	..	..	..	..	..	..	..	..	..	J	Real Earnings per Empl. (1987=100)
..	..	..	..	..	..	..	..	..	..	J	Real Output per Empl. (1987=100)
43.0	49.2	44.6	43.5	43.2	43.8	43.8	..	..	..	J	Earnings as % of Value Added
				(Billions of current CFA Francs)							**MONETARY HOLDINGS**
177.69	216.92	262.33	273.00	287.12	300.11	333.67	332.83	334.49	368.94	..	Money Supply, Broadly Defined
137.94	163.23	189.00	189.15	191.65	193.49	226.99	214.42	214.91	230.83	..	Money
51.36	73.61	84.49	78.28	77.32	86.22	104.30	100.70	92.78	102.68	..	Currency Outside Banks
86.58	89.62	104.51	110.87	114.32	107.26	122.69	113.72	122.13	128.15	..	Demand Deposits
39.75	53.69	73.34	83.85	95.47	106.62	106.68	118.41	119.58	138.11	..	Quasi-Money
				(Billions of current CFA Francs)							**GOVERNMENT DEFICIT (-) OR SURPLUS**
5.44	-22.63	-52.30	-55.47	-82.44	..	..	..	..	..	C F	
153.99	151.97	180.04	196.19	217.15	..	..	..	..	..	..	Current Revenue
142.25	140.93	169.09	181.12	237.69	..	..	..	..	..	..	Current Expenditure
11.74	11.04	10.95	15.07	-20.54	..	..	..	..	..	..	Current Budget Balance
0.04	0.10	0.48	0.11	0.08	..	..	..	..	..	..	Capital Receipts
6.34	33.77	63.73	70.65	61.98	..	..	..	..	..	..	Capital Payments

SENEGAL	1969	1970	1971	1972	1973	1974	1975	1976	1977	1978	1979
FOREIGN TRADE (CUSTOMS BASIS)					*(Millions of current US dollars)*						
Value of Exports, fob	123.7	160.6	124.9	215.9	194.7	390.7	462.4	485.1	622.8	420.8	533.3
Nonfuel Primary Products	99.7	125.5	89.0	169.5	140.2	315.3	360.8	383.6	499.1	299.8	426.4
Fuels	3.0	4.7	7.3	8.7	11.4	22.1	32.4	37.3	52.0	60.3	66.2
Manufactures	21.0	30.3	28.6	37.6	43.0	53.3	69.2	64.2	71.6	60.8	40.7
Value of Imports, cif	198.6	192.4	217.8	278.5	359.0	497.4	581.4	643.9	762.3	756.1	931.2
Nonfuel Primary Products	76.2	62.9	77.7	88.8	147.7	186.9	169.2	177.6	198.7	203.8	239.0
Fuels	14.8	9.6	13.6	15.8	21.9	64.7	69.2	78.6	95.3	106.2	154.3
Manufactures	107.6	119.9	126.5	173.9	189.5	245.9	343.0	387.7	468.3	446.1	537.8
					(Index 1987 = 100)						
Terms of Trade	138.2	131.3	116.2	127.5	114.6	151.9	145.4	141.3	140.8	119.3	124.7
Export Prices, fob	33.1	34.5	32.6	39.5	47.6	92.4	85.4	82.0	89.1	84.8	103.5
Import Prices, cif	23.9	26.3	28.0	31.0	41.5	60.8	58.7	58.0	63.3	71.1	83.0
BALANCE OF PAYMENTS					*(Millions of current US dollars)*						
Exports of Goods & Services	..	242.6	238.6	343.1	364.4	608.7	696.2	703.7	865.0	686.8	832.6
Merchandise, fob	..	158.7	135.5	225.3	214.2	416.9	503.1	513.8	667.2	401.7	478.5
Nonfactor Services	..	79.1	96.5	109.7	143.8	183.0	185.1	182.1	188.0	273.4	337.6
Factor Services	..	4.8	6.6	8.1	6.4	8.8	8.1	7.7	9.7	11.7	16.5
Imports of Goods & Services	..	291.7	312.4	396.9	522.8	737.7	865.7	902.8	1,039.2	1,042.6	1,196.9
Merchandise, fob	..	203.7	221.9	283.9	374.7	552.5	611.5	659.6	772.5	744.2	813.3
Nonfactor Services	..	68.3	67.6	83.0	101.5	126.5	170.2	174.5	202.6	210.6	287.7
Factor Services	..	19.7	23.0	30.0	46.6	58.7	84.0	68.7	64.1	87.8	95.9
Long-Term Interest	..	1.9	4.5	6.2	8.3	14.4	18.9	18.3	21.9	31.4	48.5
Private Current Transfers, net	..	-17.1	-19.9	-21.4	-21.2	-22.5	-9.5	14.6	15.5	8.1	-18.0
Workers' Remittances	..	2.8	2.8	3.9	5.5	7.8	25.4	45.2	42.1	53.7	54.4
Curr. A/C Bal before Off. Transf.	..	-66.2	-93.7	-75.2	-179.6	-151.5	-179.0	-184.6	-158.8	-347.7	-382.2
Net Official Transfers	..	50.1	68.2	85.9	78.2	85.9	93.4	92.1	91.8	112.4	118.5
Curr. A/C Bal after Off. Transf.	..	-16.1	-25.5	10.7	-101.4	-65.6	-85.6	-92.5	-67.0	-235.2	-263.7
Long-Term Capital, net	..	26.1	25.7	-0.7	53.8	54.0	58.2	116.7	58.5	140.5	111.5
Direct Investment	..	4.7	9.4	12.8	4.8	7.0	15.7	35.5	25.1	-5.5	5.0
Long-Term Loans	..	12.2	23.7	11.6	67.5	55.2	58.0	65.5	96.6	157.8	126.0
Disbursements	..	20.0	36.3	22.7	99.7	79.6	80.8	91.4	133.0	232.2	211.6
Repayments	..	7.8	12.6	11.1	32.2	24.4	22.8	25.9	36.4	74.4	85.6
Other Long-Term Capital	..	9.2	-7.4	-25.1	-18.5	-8.3	-15.4	15.7	-63.2	-11.8	-19.5
Other Capital, net	..	0.0	1.2	-4.6	15.9	5.8	22.9	-43.0	11.9	53.3	139.2
Change in Reserves	..	-10.0	-1.5	-5.3	31.7	5.9	4.5	18.8	-3.4	41.5	13.1
Memo Item:					*(CFA Francs per US dollar)*						
Conversion Factor (Annual Avg)	259.710	277.710	277.130	252.210	222.700	240.500	214.320	238.980	245.670	225.640	212.720
				(Millions of US dollars), outstanding at end of year							
EXTERNAL DEBT (Total)	..	132.9	152.3	161.7	195.1	260.5	344.6	405.6	623.9	889.7	1,117.2
Long-Term Debt (by debtor)	..	132.9	152.3	161.7	195.1	260.5	344.6	405.6	513.9	748.7	914.2
Central Bank, incl. IMF credit	..	0.0	0.0	0.0	0.0	0.0	29.8	29.5	30.9	74.3	92.9
Central Government	..	82.2	99.7	111.8	125.4	184.3	231.7	284.7	371.5	531.3	637.9
Rest of General Government	..	0.3	0.2	0.2	0.1	0.1	0.0	0.0	0.0	0.4	0.3
Non-financial Public Enterprises	..	10.3	15.4	18.8	45.0	51.9	57.7	63.7	78.2	111.0	122.1
Priv. Sector, incl non-guaranteed	..	40.1	37.0	30.9	24.6	24.2	25.4	27.7	33.3	31.7	61.0
Short-Term Debt	..	..	..	..	..	..	..	..	110.0	141.0	203.0
Memo Items:					*(Thousands of US dollars)*						
Int'l Reserves Excluding Gold	6,200	22,050	29,323	38,493	12,062	6,320	31,126	25,220	33,665	18,816	19,150
Gold Holdings (at market price)	..	..	..	..	..	..	..	..	2,408	4,949	14,848
SOCIAL INDICATORS											
Total Fertility Rate	6.5	6.5	6.5	6.5	6.5	6.6	6.6	6.6	6.6	6.6	6.6
Infant Mortality Rate	118.0	116.0	114.0	112.0	109.0	106.0	103.0	100.0	97.0	95.0	93.0
Life Expectancy at Birth	42.3	42.6	42.9	43.2	43.5	43.9	44.2	44.6	44.9	45.0	45.1
Urban Population, % of total	33.3	33.4	33.6	33.7	33.9	34.0	34.2	34.3	34.5	34.6	34.8
Food Prod. per capita (1987=100)	129.4	96.8	125.9	82.1	93.9	120.7	133.1	115.2	72.7	113.6	79.4
Labor Force, Agriculture (%)	82.8	82.7	82.4	82.2	82.0	81.8	81.6	81.4	81.2	81.0	80.8
Labor Force, Female (%)	41.3	41.3	41.3	41.3	41.3	41.3	41.3	41.3	41.3	41.3	41.3
Primary Schl. Enroll. Ratio	..	41.0	..	..	..	..	41.0	..	41.0	42.0	44.0
Primary Schl. Enroll. Ratio, Female	..	32.0	..	..	..	..	34.0	..	32.0	34.0	35.0
Secondary Schl. Enroll. Ratio	..	10.0	..	..	..	..	10.0	..	10.0	10.0	10.0

1980	1981	1982	1983	1984	1985	1986	1987	1988	1989 estimate	NOTES	SENEGAL
											FOREIGN TRADE (CUSTOMS BASIS)
(Millions of current US dollars)											
476.7	500.1	547.9	581.0	613.0	498.0	584.0	645.0	740.0	..	f	Value of Exports, fob
315.0	214.7	330.9	392.0	421.0	354.0	438.0	464.0	487.2	..	..	Nonfuel Primary Products
89.5	187.1	132.0	107.0	100.0	51.0	55.0	73.0	70.8	..	..	Fuels
72.1	98.3	85.0	82.0	92.0	93.0	91.0	108.0	182.0	..	..	Manufactures
1,037.9	1,075.9	991.9	1,025.0	1,035.0	898.0	1,014.0	1,174.0	1,165.0	..	f	Value of Imports, cif
268.9	307.1	290.9	310.0	323.0	317.0	402.3	473.0	495.0	..	..	Nonfuel Primary Products
263.0	327.0	239.0	234.0	270.0	185.0	139.7	170.0	134.0	..	..	Fuels
506.0	441.8	462.0	481.0	442.0	396.0	472.0	531.0	536.0	..	..	Manufactures
(Index 1987 = 100)											
116.2	110.2	109.8	112.4	114.3	106.9	96.7	100.0	100.6	..	..	Terms of Trade
118.6	120.3	107.3	105.8	107.6	96.7	93.0	100.0	103.4	..	..	Export Prices, fob
102.0	109.2	97.7	94.2	94.2	90.5	96.2	100.0	102.8	..	..	Import Prices, cif
(Millions of current US dollars)											
											BALANCE OF PAYMENTS
830.5	1,002.2	903.5	972.3	916.1	810.0	1,051.7	1,183.9	1,293.6	1,290.8	f	Exports of Goods & Services
421.7	560.6	501.9	605.8	597.8	480.8	618.5	673.1	760.8	785.6	..	Merchandise, fob
385.1	421.2	380.6	341.0	302.6	311.2	410.0	484.1	506.0	486.4	..	Nonfactor Services
23.7	20.4	21.0	25.5	15.7	18.0	23.1	26.6	26.9	18.8	..	Factor Services
1,337.0	1,630.8	1,346.7	1,416.1	1,327.3	1,280.5	1,523.5	1,683.0	1,797.9	1,717.5	f	Imports of Goods & Services
875.1	1,020.3	815.1	917.2	818.9	792.0	892.9	942.7	1,009.6	980.3	..	Merchandise, fob
339.6	494.3	414.2	374.6	369.8	327.9	421.6	494.1	528.5	496.1	..	Nonfactor Services
122.3	116.3	117.4	124.2	138.6	160.7	209.1	246.2	259.8	241.1	..	Factor Services
66.8	49.7	37.2	41.8	59.0	50.8	98.5	121.8	117.7	147.7	..	Long-Term Interest
-19.8	-10.1	-4.6	-1.6	0.3	17.1	26.0	29.9	31.9	30.0	..	Private Current Transfers, net
74.8	64.5	62.2	55.1	50.3	43.4	57.8	69.9	73.9	..	..	Workers' Remittances
-526.3	-638.8	-447.8	-445.4	-410.9	-453.4	-445.9	-469.2	-472.4	-396.7	..	Curr. A/C Bal before Off. Transf.
140.1	177.1	182.1	157.6	138.6	133.3	176.1	213.0	205.1	217.2	..	Net Official Transfers
-386.2	-461.6	-265.7	-287.8	-272.3	-320.1	-269.7	-256.2	-267.2	-179.5	..	Curr. A/C Bal after Off. Transf.
281.9	241.7	188.1	246.8	236.0	98.2	274.6	291.1	107.8	100.6	f	Long-Term Capital, net
12.9	19.6	10.1	-36.3	27.2	51.2	..	..	..	-20.1	..	Direct Investment
170.5	222.9	270.2	332.9	161.3	124.2	321.3	267.0	110.5	178.3	..	Long-Term Loans
326.8	302.0	300.7	362.4	205.8	177.0	418.7	424.7	276.8	308.8	..	Disbursements
156.3	79.1	30.5	29.5	44.5	52.8	97.4	157.7	166.3	130.5	..	Repayments
98.5	-0.8	-92.2	-49.8	47.5	-77.2	-46.7	24.1	-2.7	-57.6	..	Other Long-Term Capital
57.9	160.1	-60.5	21.2	10.1	208.0	-0.9	-52.0	192.8	-5.9	f	Other Capital, net
46.3	59.9	138.0	19.8	26.2	13.9	-4.0	17.1	-33.3	84.8	..	Change in Reserves
(CFA Francs per US dollar)											Memo Item:
211.300	271.730	328.620	381.070	436.960	449.260	346.300	300.540	297.850	319.010	..	Conversion Factor (Annual Avg)
(Millions of US dollars), outstanding at end of year											
1,468.4	1,666.8	1,858.0	2,074.2	2,200.1	2,559.2	3,221.9	4,020.2	3,879.9	4,139.3	..	**EXTERNAL DEBT (Total)**
1,249.4	1,429.8	1,656.0	1,882.1	1,928.1	2,335.1	2,948.5	3,698.9	3,599.0	3,857.7	..	Long-Term Debt (by debtor)
140.1	186.5	220.7	230.8	230.0	267.7	289.0	342.8	318.3	316.0	..	Central Bank, incl. IMF credit
868.1	1,047.8	1,241.8	1,462.1	1,518.1	1,862.3	2,349.7	2,968.4	2,944.5	3,201.8	..	Central Government
0.2	0.1	0.0	0.0	0.0	0.0	0.0	0.0	0.0	..	..	Rest of General Government
180.7	148.4	154.0	158.7	153.2	175.8	217.6	287.6	251.2	250.2	..	Non-financial Public Enterprises
60.3	47.0	39.5	30.5	26.8	29.3	92.2	100.1	85.0	89.7	..	Priv. Sector, incl non-guaranteed
219.0	237.0	202.0	192.1	272.0	224.1	273.4	321.3	280.9	281.6	..	Short-Term Debt
(Thousands of US dollars)											Memo Items:
8,069	8,664	11,422	12,207	3,688	5,051	9,379	9,202	10,463	19,011	..	Int'l Reserves Excluding Gold
17,096	11,528	13,250	11,064	8,941	9,483	11,336	14,039	11,897	11,629	..	Gold Holdings (at market price)
											SOCIAL INDICATORS
6.6	6.6	6.6	6.6	6.6	6.6	6.5	6.5	6.5	6.5	..	Total Fertility Rate
76.5	89.0	87.0	85.6	84.2	82.8	86.4	80.0	78.4	76.7	..	Infant Mortality Rate
45.2	45.2	45.3	45.8	46.2	46.7	47.1	47.6	50.0	48.1	..	Life Expectancy at Birth
34.9	35.2	35.5	35.8	36.1	36.4	36.9	37.4	37.7	38.1	..	Urban Population, % of total
71.4	106.1	95.1	67.4	78.4	92.5	93.8	100.0	83.5	88.5	..	Food Prod. per capita (1987=100)
80.6	..	..	..	..	..	..	..	..	..	..	Labor Force, Agriculture (%)
41.3	41.1	40.9	40.7	40.5	40.3	40.1	39.9	39.7	39.5	..	Labor Force, Female (%)
46.0	..	51.0	53.0	55.0	57.0	58.0	60.0	..	..	..	Primary Schl. Enroll. Ratio
36.0	38.0	41.0	43.0	44.0	46.0	47.0	49.0	..	..	..	Primary Schl. Enroll. Ratio, Female
11.0	..	12.0	12.0	13.0	14.0	14.0	15.0	..	..	..	Secondary Schl. Enroll. Ratio

SEYCHELLES	1969	1970	1971	1972	1973	1974	1975	1976	1977	1978	1979
CURRENT GNP PER CAPITA (US $)	340	350	410	470	580	700	800	870	960	1,120	1,610
POPULATION (thousands)	52	53	55	56	57	58	59	60	61	62	62
USE AND ORIGIN OF RESOURCES					*(Millions of current Seychelles Rupees)*						
Gross National Product (GNP)	91.0	102.0	120.0	163.0	200.0	245.0	287.0	349.8	463.4	556.6	749.9
Net Factor Income from Abroad	-0.4	-0.4	-0.5	-0.6	-0.8	-1.0	-1.1	-15.8	-29.6	-38.3	-56.3
GDP at Market Prices	91.4	102.4	120.5	163.6	200.8	246.0	288.1	365.6	493.0	594.9	806.2
Resource Balance	..	..	..	..	..	..	..	-58.5	-19.9	-7.4	-48.3
Exports of Goods & NFServices	..	..	..	..	..	..	..	271.9	386.3	488.4	582.5
Imports of Goods & NFServices	..	..	..	..	..	..	..	330.4	406.2	495.8	630.8
Domestic Absorption	..	..	..	..	..	..	..	424.1	512.9	602.3	854.5
Private Consumption, etc.	..	..	..	..	..	..	..	200.3	198.5	195.3	377.6
General Gov't Consumption	..	..	..	..	..	..	..	81.5	117.1	149.5	211.4
Gross Domestic Investment	..	..	..	..	..	..	..	142.3	197.3	257.5	265.5
Fixed Investment	..	..	..	..	..	..	..	134.5	190.5	253.4	256.6
Indirect Taxes, net	..	..	..	..	..	..	..	36.9	56.8	79.0	115.5
GDP at factor cost	..	..	..	..	..	..	..	328.7	436.2	515.9	690.7
Agriculture	..	..	..	..	..	..	..	35.2	45.2	50.0	58.8
Industry	..	..	..	..	..	..	..	59.3	68.2	82.1	121.7
Manufacturing	..	..	..	..	..	..	..	20.1	26.9	36.4	48.6
Services, etc.	..	..	..	..	..	..	..	271.1	379.6	462.8	625.7
Gross Domestic Saving	..	..	..	..	..	..	..	83.8	177.4	250.1	217.2
Gross National Saving	..	..	..	..	..	..	..	65.0	143.8	206.7	154.4
					(Millions of 1980 Seychelles Rupees)						
Gross National Product	421.3	458.7	531.5	565.0	616.2	624.0	643.7	688.6	729.9	778.0	899.5
GDP at Market Prices	423.3	460.9	533.9	567.6	619.0	627.0	646.7	719.7	776.4	831.4	966.9
Resource Balance	..	..	..	..	..	..	..	14.3	-6.8	-116.7	-62.4
Exports of Goods & NFServices	..	..	..	..	..	..	..	547.6	584.9	625.0	708.4
Imports of Goods & NFServices	..	..	..	..	..	..	..	533.3	591.7	741.7	770.7
Domestic Absorption	..	..	..	..	..	..	..	705.4	783.2	948.1	1,029.3
Private Consumption, etc.	..	..	..	..	..	..	..	297.1	302.8	377.1	433.6
General Gov't Consumption	..	..	..	..	..	..	..	155.0	186.1	228.9	267.5
Gross Domestic Investment	..	..	..	..	..	..	..	253.4	294.3	342.0	328.1
Fixed Investment	..	..	..	..	..	..	..	239.4	284.2	335.3	318.7
GDP at factor cost	..	..	..	..	..	..	..	647.0	687.1	721.2	828.4
Agriculture	..	..	..	..	..	..	..	64.6	59.8	55.4	64.4
Industry	..	..	..	..	..	..	..	106.7	107.4	117.8	149.5
Manufacturing	..	..	..	..	..	..	..	35.3	42.3	49.7	54.6
Services, etc.	..	..	..	..	..	..	..	548.5	609.2	658.2	753.1
Memo Items:											
Capacity to Import	..	..	..	..	..	..	..	438.9	562.7	730.6	711.7
Terms of Trade Adjustment	..	..	..	..	..	..	..	-108.8	-22.2	105.6	3.3
Gross Domestic Income	..	..	..	..	..	..	..	611.0	754.2	937.0	970.3
Gross National Income	..	..	..	..	..	..	..	579.8	707.7	883.6	902.9
DOMESTIC PRICES/DEFLATORS					*(Index 1980 = 100)*						
Overall (GDP)	21.6	22.2	22.6	28.8	32.4	39.2	44.5	50.8	63.5	71.6	83.4
Domestic Absorption	..	..	..	..	..	..	..	60.1	65.5	63.5	83.0
Agriculture	..	..	..	..	..	..	..	54.5	75.6	90.2	91.3
Industry	..	..	..	..	..	..	..	55.6	63.5	69.7	81.4
Manufacturing	..	..	..	..	..	..	..	57.0	63.6	73.3	89.0
Consumer Price Index	..	17.4	20.0	24.2	28.6	35.7	42.3	48.6	55.8	62.4	70.2
MANUFACTURING ACTIVITY											
Employment (1987=100)	..	..	..	..	..	..	..	..	..	..	..
Real Earnings per Empl. (1987=100)	..	..	..	..	..	..	..	..	..	..	..
Real Output per Empl. (1987=100)	..	..	..	..	..	..	..	..	..	..	..
Earnings as % of Value Added	..	..	..	..	..	..	..	44.1	41.2	36.7	39.0
MONETARY HOLDINGS					*(Millions of current Seychelles Rupees)*						
Money Supply, Broadly Defined	..	..	45.30	64.80	72.00	74.50	96.40	138.30	162.10	186.90	233.30
Money	..	..	25.40	37.70	40.30	41.90	47.80	67.60	83.80	95.00	114.70
Currency Outside Banks	..	..	12.40	17.00	18.90	20.10	22.70	31.10	40.10	43.90	52.90
Demand Deposits	..	..	13.00	20.70	21.40	21.80	25.10	36.50	43.70	51.10	61.80
Quasi-Money	..	..	19.90	27.10	31.70	32.60	48.60	70.70	78.30	91.90	118.60
					(Millions of current Seychelles Rupees)						
GOVERNMENT DEFICIT (-) OR SURPLUS	..	..	..	..	..	..	..	..	..	..	..
Current Revenue	..	..	..	..	..	..	..	..	..	..	..
Current Expenditure	..	..	..	..	..	..	..	..	..	..	..
Current Budget Balance	..	..	..	..	..	..	..	..	..	..	..
Capital Receipts	..	..	..	..	..	..	..	..	..	..	..
Capital Payments	..	..	..	..	..	..	..	..	..	..	..

1980	1981	1982	1983	1984	1985	1986	1987	1988	1989 estimate	NOTES	SEYCHELLES
2,000	2,270	2,350	2,350	2,330	2,520	2,650	3,040	3,640	4,170	..	**CURRENT GNP PER CAPITA (US $)**
63	64	64	65	66	66	67	67	68	68	..	**POPULATION (thousands)**
				(Millions of current Seychelles Rupees)							**USE AND ORIGIN OF RESOURCES**
907.8	957.2	941.8	960.3	1,026.9	1,162.7	1,231.5	1,307.3	1,430.3	1,574.0	..	Gross National Product (GNP)
-34.1	-14.6	-26.4	-32.6	-41.2	-42.2	-79.9	-126.7	-93.6	-74.9	..	Net Factor Income from Abroad
941.9	971.8	968.2	992.9	1,068.1	1,204.9	1,311.4	1,434.0	1,523.9	1,648.9	..	GDP at Market Prices
-105.3	-151.5	-227.6	-220.3	-144.3	-186.7	-224.9	-158.6	..	..	..	Resource Balance
640.1	554.1	507.9	415.0	524.9	581.1	498.7	..	..	..	..	Exports of Goods & NFServices
745.4	705.6	735.5	635.3	669.2	767.8	723.6	..	..	..	..	Imports of Goods & NFServices
1,047.2	1,123.3	1,195.8	1,213.2	1,212.4	1,391.6	1,536.3	1,592.6	..	..	..	Domestic Absorption
416.3	497.7	544.6	676.8	653.2	700.7	740.2	779.5	..	..	..	Private Consumption, etc.
270.0	308.5	338.0	326.0	327.7	417.4	497.6	512.5	..	..	..	General Gov't Consumption
360.9	317.1	313.2	210.4	231.5	273.5	298.5	300.6	..	..	..	Gross Domestic Investment
344.2	329.6	302.9	219.9	226.9	273.5	292.7	..	..	..	..	Fixed Investment
152.9	167.5	183.1	186.4	190.6	204.6	213.2	..	..	..	..	Indirect Taxes, net
789.0	804.3	785.1	806.5	877.5	1,000.3	1,098.2	..	..	..	B	GDP at factor cost
64.4	76.5	62.0	76.9	68.9	69.3	77.3	86.0	..	..	..	Agriculture
147.3	166.7	150.2	156.7	176.5	221.2	227.1	242.5	..	..	..	Industry
69.5	83.4	82.6	95.6	100.3	116.4	116.3	123.8	..	..	..	Manufacturing
730.2	728.6	756.0	759.3	822.7	914.4	1,007.0	1,105.5	..	..	..	Services, etc.
255.6	165.6	85.6	-9.9	87.2	86.8	73.6	142.0	..	..	..	Gross Domestic Saving
212.2	134.3	38.1	-61.3	29.5	38.7	-37.6	2.4	..	..	..	Gross National Saving
				(Millions of 1980 Seychelles Rupees)							
907.8	863.1	839.5	852.4	877.0	962.9	964.4	996.1	1,032.5	1,109.7	..	Gross National Product
941.9	876.3	862.9	881.4	912.0	997.8	1,021.6	1,063.7	1,129.5	1,193.1	..	GDP at Market Prices
-105.3	-134.4	-265.3	..	..	..	..	..	..	..	..	Resource Balance
640.1	544.0	510.8	..	..	..	..	..	..	..	..	Exports of Goods & NFServices
745.4	678.4	776.1	..	..	..	..	..	..	..	..	Imports of Goods & NFServices
1,047.2	1,010.7	1,128.2	..	..	..	..	..	..	..	..	Domestic Absorption
416.3	409.3	451.3	..	..	..	..	..	..	..	..	Private Consumption, etc.
270.0	277.2	291.5	..	..	..	..	..	..	..	..	General Gov't Consumption
360.9	324.2	385.5	..	..	..	..	..	..	..	..	Gross Domestic Investment
344.2	314.8	373.4	..	..	..	..	..	..	..	..	Fixed Investment
789.0	725.0	700.2	716.3	749.7	828.8	855.9	..	..	..	B	GDP at factor cost
64.4	82.4	64.2	69.5	62.2	59.4	61.6	65.5	..	..	..	Agriculture
147.3	134.4	117.1	117.3	129.0	149.1	153.1	155.9	..	..	..	Industry
69.5	54.2	56.2	64.1	64.8	68.3	70.2	71.4	..	..	..	Manufacturing
730.2	659.6	681.6	694.6	720.9	789.3	806.9	842.3	..	..	..	Services, etc.
											Memo Items:
640.1	532.8	535.9	..	..	..	..	..	..	..	..	Capacity to Import
0.0	-11.3	25.1	..	..	..	..	..	..	..	..	Terms of Trade Adjustment
941.9	865.0	888.1	..	..	..	..	..	..	..	..	Gross Domestic Income
907.8	851.8	864.6	..	..	..	..	..	..	..	..	Gross National Income
				(Index 1980 = 100)							**DOMESTIC PRICES/DEFLATORS**
100.0	110.9	112.2	112.7	117.1	120.8	128.4	134.8	134.9	138.2	..	Overall (GDP)
100.0	111.1	106.0	..	..	..	..	..	..	..	..	Domestic Absorption
100.0	92.9	96.5	110.6	110.8	116.6	125.4	131.3	..	..	..	Agriculture
100.0	124.1	128.3	133.6	136.9	148.4	148.4	155.5	..	..	..	Industry
100.0	153.8	147.1	149.2	154.9	170.5	165.7	173.3	..	..	..	Manufacturing
79.7	88.1	87.4	92.7	96.5	97.2	97.5	100.0	101.8	103.4	f	Consumer Price Index
											MANUFACTURING ACTIVITY
..	..	..	..	..	..	..	..	..	..	..	Employment (1987=100)
..	..	..	..	..	..	..	..	..	..	..	Real Earnings per Empl. (1987=100)
..	..	..	..	..	..	..	..	..	..	..	Real Output per Empl. (1987=100)
29.0	30.2	31.5	30.3	30.3	30.7	30.7	..	..	..	..	Earnings as % of Value Added
				(Millions of current Seychelles Rupees)							**MONETARY HOLDINGS**
313.80	307.20	283.20	289.50	322.60	363.40	405.30	441.10	539.50	632.50	..	Money Supply, Broadly Defined
158.70	157.90	143.30	131.30	134.70	155.30	155.00	155.20	187.80	219.60	..	Money
61.70	65.30	62.60	64.30	69.90	75.80	78.10	82.40	95.60	99.50	..	Currency Outside Banks
97.00	92.60	80.70	67.00	64.80	79.50	76.90	72.80	92.20	120.10	..	Demand Deposits
155.10	149.30	139.90	158.20	187.90	208.10	250.30	285.90	351.70	412.90	..	Quasi-Money
				(Millions of current Seychelles Rupees)							**GOVERNMENT DEFICIT (-) OR SURPLUS**
..	..	..	..	..	-128	-193	-23	-56	..	..	Current Revenue
..	..	..	..	..	563	596	735	808	..	..	Current Expenditure
..	..	..	..	..	497	549	638	675	..	..	Current Budget Balance
..	..	..	..	..	67	47	98	134	..	..	Capital Receipts
..	..	..	..	..	0	0	1	0	..	..	Capital Payments
..	..	..	..	..	194	241	122	190	..	..	

SEYCHELLES	1969	1970	1971	1972	1973	1974	1975	1976	1977	1978	1979
FOREIGN TRADE (CUSTOMS BASIS)					*(Millions of current US dollars)*						
Value of Exports, fob	2.50	2.14	1.85	2.62	3.62	7.29	6.35	8.63	11.09	15.16	21.89
Nonfuel Primary Products	2.02	1.53	1.37	1.74	2.35	3.27	2.11	2.74	2.89	3.11	4.84
Fuels	0.41	0.55	0.42	0.83	1.24	4.00	4.22	5.01	7.38	11.35	16.09
Manufactures	0.07	0.06	0.06	0.05	0.03	0.02	0.02	0.88	0.82	0.70	0.96
Value of Imports, cif	7.20	10.07	15.18	20.95	24.84	28.11	31.82	43.48	45.76	52.68	89.52
Nonfuel Primary Products	2.51	2.95	4.60	5.37	7.36	9.69	9.66	11.11	11.66	13.37	17.87
Fuels	0.75	0.71	1.08	1.16	2.28	4.43	6.03	8.43	8.66	9.73	20.63
Manufactures	3.94	6.41	9.50	14.42	15.20	14.00	16.13	23.94	25.44	29.58	51.02
					(Index 1987 = 100)						
Terms of Trade	109.5	79.8	90.0	70.3	87.3	145.1	107.9	115.6	119.9	109.5	131.8
Export Prices, fob	26.0	20.9	25.9	22.5	33.5	86.7	66.1	69.7	79.3	80.4	114.0
Import Prices, cif	23.8	26.2	28.8	32.0	38.4	59.7	61.3	60.4	66.1	73.5	86.5
BALANCE OF PAYMENTS					*(Millions of current US dollars)*						
Exports of Goods & Services	..	12.10	14.10	17.10	21.20	29.30	33.50	37.73	54.65	72.72	94.76
Merchandise, fob	..	2.00	2.00	2.00	3.00	7.00	6.00	3.05	4.83	6.63	6.22
Nonfactor Services	..	10.00	12.00	15.00	18.00	22.00	27.00	33.89	48.24	63.80	83.62
Factor Services	..	0.10	0.10	0.10	0.20	0.30	0.50	0.80	1.58	2.29	4.91
Imports of Goods & Services	..	11.90	18.10	24.40	29.90	35.40	42.00	46.85	65.32	85.74	114.95
Merchandise, fob	..	10.00	15.00	21.00	25.00	28.00	32.00	33.19	38.63	51.82	71.58
Nonfactor Services	..	1.00	2.00	2.00	3.00	5.00	7.00	9.77	20.67	26.72	34.47
Factor Services	..	0.90	1.10	1.40	1.90	2.40	3.00	3.90	6.02	7.19	8.90
Long-Term Interest	..	0.00	0.00	0.00	0.00	0.00	0.00	0.00	0.00	0.00	0.10
Private Current Transfers, net	..	0.00	0.00	-0.10	-0.10	-0.30	-0.40	-0.40	-0.52	-0.73	-1.03
Workers' Remittances	..	..	..	..	..	..	..	..	..	..	..
Curr. A/C Bal before Off. Transf.	..	0.20	-4.00	-7.40	-8.80	-6.40	-8.90	-9.53	-11.20	-13.75	-21.23
Net Official Transfers	..	0.20	0.40	0.70	1.20	2.10	3.40	5.63	9.33	9.77	8.96
Curr. A/C Bal after Off. Transf.	..	0.40	-3.60	-6.70	-7.60	-4.30	-5.50	-3.90	-1.87	-3.98	-12.26
Long-Term Capital, net	..	..	..	..	..	5.80	6.30	6.43	5.26	7.77	12.08
Direct Investment	..	..	..	..	..	5.80	6.30	4.31	4.80	3.65	4.37
Long-Term Loans	..	0.00	0.00	0.00	0.00	0.00	0.00	0.00	0.50	2.60	8.10
Disbursements	..	0.00	0.00	0.00	0.00	0.00	0.00	0.00	0.50	2.70	8.20
Repayments	..	0.00	0.00	0.00	0.00	0.00	0.00	0.00	0.00	0.10	0.10
Other Long-Term Capital	..	..	..	..	..	0.00	0.00	2.12	-0.04	1.51	-0.39
Other Capital, net	..	0.00	0.00	0.00	0.00	-0.73	0.50	-1.85	-1.15	-4.66	3.81
Change in Reserves	..	-0.40	3.60	6.70	7.60	-0.77	-1.30	-0.69	-2.24	0.88	-3.63
Memo Item:					*(Seychelles Rupees per US dollar)*						
Conversion Factor (Annual Avg)	5.560	5.560	5.480	5.340	5.440	5.700	6.030	7.420	7.640	6.950	6.330
					(Millions of US dollars), outstanding at end of year						
EXTERNAL DEBT (Total)	..	0.00	0.00	0.00	0.00	0.00	0.00	0.60	109.20	385.00	473.90
Long-Term Debt (by debtor)	..	0.00	0.00	0.00	0.00	0.00	0.00	0.60	1.20	4.00	12.90
Central Bank, incl. IMF credit	..	0.00	0.00	0.00	0.00	0.00	0.00	0.00	0.00	0.00	0.00
Central Government	..	0.00	0.00	0.00	0.00	0.00	0.00	0.60	1.20	4.00	12.90
Rest of General Government	..	..	..	..	..	..	..	..	..	..	..
Non-financial Public Enterprises	..	0.00	0.00	0.00	0.00	0.00	0.00	0.00	0.00	0.00	0.00
Priv. Sector, incl non-guaranteed	..	0.00	0.00	0.00	0.00	0.00	0.00	0.00	0.00	0.00	0.00
Short-Term Debt	..	0.00	0.00	0.00	0.00	0.00	0.00	0.00	108.00	381.00	461.00
Memo Items:					*(Thousands of US dollars)*						
Int'l Reserves Excluding Gold	..	..	..	..	4,270	5,040	6,340	6,490	11,512	9,260	12,148
Gold Holdings (at market price)	..	..	..	..	..	..	..	..	..	..	..
SOCIAL INDICATORS											
Total Fertility Rate	..	..	..	..	..	..	..	4.5	4.3	4.2	4.0
Infant Mortality Rate	..	..	..	..	..	..	..	..	..	..	..
Life Expectancy at Birth	..	..	..	..	..	..	66.0	..	..	..	..
Urban Population, % of total	25.9	26.0	27.4	28.9	30.3	31.8	33.2	35.1	37.0	39.0	40.9
Food Prod. per capita (1987=100)	..	..	..	..	..	..	..	..	..	..	..
Labor Force, Agriculture (%)	..	..	..	..	..	..	..	..	..	..	..
Labor Force, Female (%)	..	..	..	..	..	..	..	..	..	..	..
Primary Schl. Enroll. Ratio	..	..	..	..	..	..	..	..	..	..	..
Primary Schl. Enroll. Ratio, Female	..	..	..	..	..	..	..	..	..	..	..
Secondary Schl. Enroll. Ratio	..	..	..	..	..	..	..	..	..	..	..

1980	1981	1982	1983	1984	1985	1986	1987	1988	1989 estimate	NOTES	SEYCHELLES
				(Millions of current US dollars)							**FOREIGN TRADE (CUSTOMS BASIS)**
21.15	17.16	15.18	20.30	25.70	28.00	18.40	22.20	31.00	..	..	Value of Exports, fob
5.07	3.91	3.17	3.85	8.57	3.00	2.26	3.07	7.37	..	..	Nonfuel Primary Products
15.39	12.41	10.91	14.76	16.27	23.00	13.14	17.76	19.14	..	..	Fuels
0.69	0.84	1.10	1.68	0.87	2.00	3.00	1.37	4.49	..	..	Manufactures
98.80	93.30	97.90	87.80	87.70	98.80	106.00	113.50	153.00	..	..	Value of Imports, cif
22.86	21.51	23.33	18.45	43.51	18.92	22.98	16.51	41.75	..	..	Nonfuel Primary Products
24.07	20.66	19.70	21.95	22.16	25.88	18.02	26.67	29.40	..	..	Fuels
51.87	51.13	54.87	47.40	22.03	54.00	65.00	70.33	81.85	..	..	Manufactures
				(Index 1987 = 100)							
153.8	160.2	150.2	149.5	135.2	148.2	88.3	100.0	95.8	..	..	Terms of Trade
158.8	163.7	144.5	144.0	196.1	138.5	80.1	100.0	98.5	..	..	Export Prices, fob
103.3	102.2	96.2	96.3	145.1	93.4	90.8	100.0	102.8	..	..	Import Prices, cif
				(Millions of current US dollars)							**BALANCE OF PAYMENTS**
102.77	97.62	84.39	84.16	102.14	118.79	129.74	155.64	184.77	201.68	..	Exports of Goods & Services
5.65	4.64	3.84	4.99	4.98	4.64	4.41	8.09	17.26	14.04	..	Merchandise, fob
91.22	88.64	77.03	76.63	94.83	111.81	123.27	144.85	164.42	184.13	..	Nonfactor Services
5.90	4.33	3.52	2.53	2.33	2.35	2.06	2.70	3.09	3.51	..	Factor Services
131.44	126.57	131.56	121.69	128.12	151.50	174.43	197.98	237.10	260.07	..	Imports of Goods & Services
83.66	79.19	83.00	74.50	73.94	84.14	89.34	96.25	134.96	138.93	..	Merchandise, fob
38.85	40.21	41.58	39.82	46.10	58.99	74.19	84.70	81.19	104.00	..	Nonfactor Services
8.93	7.17	6.97	7.38	8.08	8.37	10.90	17.03	20.95	17.14	..	Factor Services
0.20	0.30	0.80	1.30	1.70	2.30	3.70	5.10	7.20	6.60	..	Long-Term Interest
-1.46	-2.65	-3.22	-2.78	-2.34	-0.82	-5.07	-2.30	-4.93	-5.19	..	Private Current Transfers, net
..	..	..	..	..	..	..	..	..	..	..	Workers' Remittances
-30.13	-31.60	-50.39	-40.32	-28.33	-33.54	-49.76	-44.64	-57.26	-63.58	..	Curr. A/C Bal before Off. Transf.
14.51	12.80	9.75	14.27	15.04	14.34	16.46	23.53	28.85	31.67	..	Net Official Transfers
-15.62	-18.79	-40.64	-26.05	-13.29	-19.20	-33.29	-21.11	-28.41	-31.92	..	Curr. A/C Bal after Off. Transf.
17.54	10.64	29.29	16.26	17.80	16.42	34.18	17.75	20.85	27.15	..	Long-Term Capital, net
5.71	2.84	5.08	5.88	5.88	1.09	8.42	14.02	17.50	13.79	..	Direct Investment
11.60	7.10	14.10	10.80	10.30	14.60	26.10	11.60	5.70	0.30	..	Long-Term Loans
11.70	7.20	14.40	12.30	13.20	19.90	31.90	17.10	15.00	13.40	..	Disbursements
0.10	0.10	0.30	1.50	2.90	5.30	5.80	5.50	9.30	13.10	..	Repayments
0.24	0.69	10.11	-0.42	1.62	0.73	-0.34	-7.87	-2.35	13.06	..	Other Long-Term Capital
6.04	2.83	11.14	7.29	-6.05	2.73	-2.25	7.32	3.30	8.28	..	Other Capital, net
-7.96	5.33	0.21	2.50	1.54	0.06	1.36	-3.96	4.26	-3.51	..	Change in Reserves
				(Seychelles Rupees per US dollar)							Memo Item:
6.390	6.310	6.550	6.770	7.060	7.130	6.180	5.600	5.380	5.650	..	Conversion Factor (Annual Avg)
				(Millions of US dollars), outstanding at end of year							
84.10	36.80	50.70	54.50	70.50	98.10	147.50	175.10	170.70	168.40	..	**EXTERNAL DEBT (Total)**
25.10	27.80	38.70	46.50	51.40	74.10	108.10	138.60	134.40	132.80	..	Long-Term Debt (by debtor)
0.00	0.00	0.00	0.20	0.20	1.80	5.70	8.60	9.60	12.90	..	Central Bank, incl. IMF credit
22.20	25.50	34.50	42.60	45.90	62.40	89.70	111.60	108.10	102.50	..	Central Government
..	..	..	..	..	..	..	..	..	..	..	Rest of General Government
2.90	2.30	3.90	3.40	5.10	9.70	12.50	18.30	16.60	17.30	..	Non-financial Public Enterprises
0.00	0.00	0.30	0.30	0.20	0.20	0.20	0.10	0.10	0.10	..	Priv. Sector, incl non-guaranteed
59.00	9.00	12.00	8.00	19.10	24.00	39.40	36.50	36.30	35.60	..	Short-Term Debt
				(Thousands of US dollars)							Memo Items:
18,439	13,800	13,072	9,972	5,400	8,501	7,749	13,713	8,707	12,109	..	Int'l Reserves Excluding Gold
..	..	..	..	..	..	..	..	..	..	..	Gold Holdings (at market price)
											SOCIAL INDICATORS
3.8	3.7	3.5	3.4	3.4	3.3	3.3	3.2	3.1	3.1	..	Total Fertility Rate
..	..	15.0	15.6	16.2	16.8	17.4	18.4	18.2	18.0	..	Infant Mortality Rate
..	..	68.7	68.9	69.1	69.4	69.6	69.8	70.0	70.1	..	Life Expectancy at Birth
42.8	44.6	46.4	48.2	50.0	51.8	53.7	55.6	56.8	58.1	..	Urban Population, % of total
..	..	..	..	..	..	..	..	..	..	..	Food Prod. per capita (1987=100)
..	..	..	..	..	..	..	..	..	..	..	Labor Force, Agriculture (%)
..	..	..	..	..	..	..	..	..	..	..	Labor Force, Female (%)
..	..	..	..	..	..	..	..	..	..	..	Primary Schl. Enroll. Ratio
..	..	..	..	..	..	..	..	..	..	..	Primary Schl. Enroll. Ratio, Female
..	..	..	..	..	..	..	..	..	..	..	Secondary Schl. Enroll. Ratio

SIERRA LEONE	1969	1970	1971	1972	1973	1974	1975	1976	1977	1978	1979
CURRENT GNP PER CAPITA (US $)	150	160	160	160	170	190	210	210	220	220	270
POPULATION (thousands)	2,602	2,651	2,702	2,754	2,809	2,865	2,924	2,985	3,049	3,115	3,184

USE AND ORIGIN OF RESOURCES *(Millions of current Sierra Leonean Leones)*

	1969	1970	1971	1972	1973	1974	1975	1976	1977	1978	1979
Gross National Product (GNP)	304	348	343	349	387	471	564	603	730	821	987
Net Factor Income from Abroad	-7	-5	-6	-7	-6	-7	-8	-11	-14	-29	-43
GDP at Market Prices	311	353	348	356	393	478	573	613	744	850	1,029
Resource Balance	-6	-7	-4	1	-3	-34	-53	-52	-49	-63	-131
Exports of Goods & NFServices	97	104	106	110	125	144	148	150	178	216	249
Imports of Goods & NFServices	103	111	111	109	128	178	202	202	227	280	380
Domestic Absorption	316	360	352	356	396	512	626	665	793	913	1,160
Private Consumption, etc.	233	260	268	282	309	387	473	532	624	740	927
General Gov't Consumption	37	42	31	32	42	49	63	64	71	77	96
Gross Domestic Investment	46	59	53	42	46	76	90	69	98	96	138
Fixed Investment	..	..	47	43	44	57	76	72	81	100	128
Indirect Taxes, net	33	34	32	36	40	52	52	55	77	100	97
GDP at factor cost	278	319	316	320	353	426	521	559	667	750	932
Agriculture	90	90	95	97	108	130	186	213	264	282	327
Industry	73	97	91	89	97	119	123	114	130	142	204
Manufacturing	17	18	20	21	21	26	30	31	34	40	55
Services, etc.	115	133	131	134	149	177	212	232	274	327	402
Gross Domestic Saving	41	52	49	42	43	41	37	17	49	33	7
Gross National Saving	..	48	45	35	37	35	30	12	40	11	-30

(Millions of 1987 Sierra Leonean Leones)

	1969	1970	1971	1972	1973	1974	1975	1976	1977	1978	1979
Gross National Product	14,431.9	16,126.5	16,634.7	16,455.1	16,961.6	17,942.1	18,424.6	17,614.1	17,679.8	16,822.3	18,024.6
GDP at Market Prices	14,065.9	15,542.4	16,015.8	15,864.9	16,309.0	17,170.2	17,613.8	16,864.3	16,965.8	16,431.5	17,752.5
Resource Balance	-2,493.6	-2,511.5	-1,602.6	-879.4	-1,793.9	-2,286.5	-1,334.0	-821.0	-1,574.1	-2,966.7	-4,059.0
Exports of Goods & NFServices	5,513.3	5,416.3	5,240.0	5,181.3	4,633.8	4,389.7	4,491.2	4,062.9	3,130.7	2,456.0	2,557.2
Imports of Goods & NFServices	8,006.8	7,927.8	6,842.6	6,060.7	6,427.8	6,676.3	5,825.3	4,883.8	4,704.9	5,422.7	6,616.2
Domestic Absorption	16,559.5	18,053.9	17,618.4	16,744.4	18,102.9	19,456.7	18,947.8	17,685.2	18,540.0	19,398.2	21,811.5
Private Consumption, etc.	..	..	..	..	..	..	..	..	..	15,968.7	17,850.6
General Gov't Consumption	..	..	..	..	..	..	..	..	..	1,452.4	1,701.8
Gross Domestic Investment	2,757.2	3,504.9	2,422.5	1,781.2	1,887.0	2,593.9	2,667.2	1,870.7	1,862.6	1,977.1	2,259.2
Fixed Investment	..	..	..	..	..	..	..	..	..	1,937.8	2,060.5
GDP at factor cost	12,639.0	14,009.7	14,399.9	14,263.1	14,860.5	15,362.0	15,881.1	15,459.0	15,863.0	15,293.3	16,117.2
Agriculture	3,851.3	3,854.9	3,943.6	3,902.8	3,976.8	3,943.6	4,117.4	4,343.1	4,568.8	6,089.5	6,655.0
Industry	5,012.3	5,929.1	5,768.9	5,501.8	5,518.9	5,518.9	5,729.8	5,136.8	4,698.5	3,999.8	4,227.7
Manufacturing	1,180.1	1,211.6	1,205.4	1,281.9	1,358.3	1,460.7	1,594.5	1,658.0	1,613.6	931.7	963.1
Services, etc.	4,499.2	5,125.6	5,490.0	5,574.3	6,022.6	6,467.1	6,640.5	6,503.8	6,959.9	5,827.3	5,960.9

Memo Items:

	1969	1970	1971	1972	1973	1974	1975	1976	1977	1978	1979
Capacity to Import	7,571.1	7,429.7	6,576.5	6,088.5	6,286.6	5,388.9	4,288.0	3,618.1	3,690.5	4,197.0	4,336.4
Terms of Trade Adjustment	2,057.8	2,013.4	1,336.6	907.2	1,652.7	999.2	-203.2	-444.8	559.7	1,741.0	1,779.2
Gross Domestic Income	16,123.7	17,555.8	17,352.4	16,772.2	17,961.8	18,169.4	17,410.6	16,419.5	17,525.6	18,172.4	19,531.7
Gross National Income	16,489.8	18,139.8	17,971.3	17,362.3	18,614.3	18,941.2	18,221.4	17,169.3	18,239.5	18,563.3	19,803.8

DOMESTIC PRICES/DEFLATORS *(Index 1987 = 100)*

	1969	1970	1971	1972	1973	1974	1975	1976	1977	1978	1979
Overall (GDP)	2.2	2.3	2.2	2.2	2.4	2.8	3.3	3.6	4.4	5.2	5.8
Domestic Absorption	1.9	2.0	2.0	2.1	2.2	2.6	3.3	3.8	4.3	4.7	5.3
Agriculture	2.3	2.3	2.4	2.5	2.7	3.3	4.5	4.9	5.8	4.6	4.9
Industry	1.5	1.6	1.6	1.6	1.8	2.2	2.1	2.2	2.8	3.5	4.8
Manufacturing	1.4	1.5	1.7	1.6	1.6	1.8	1.9	1.9	2.1	4.3	5.7
Consumer Price Index	0.8	0.9	0.9	0.9	1.0	1.1	1.3	1.6	1.7	1.9	2.3

MANUFACTURING ACTIVITY

	1969	1970	1971	1972	1973	1974	1975	1976	1977	1978	1979
Employment (1987=100)	..	..	..	..	..	..	..	..	..	..	..
Real Earnings per Empl. (1987=100)	..	..	..	..	..	..	..	..	..	..	..
Real Output per Empl. (1987=100)	..	..	..	..	..	..	..	..	..	..	..
Earnings as % of Value Added	..	..	..	..	..	..	..	..	..	..	..

MONETARY HOLDINGS *(Millions of current Sierra Leonean Leones)*

	1969	1970	1971	1972	1973	1974	1975	1976	1977	1978	1979
Money Supply, Broadly Defined	45.8	43.3	48.0	56.5	71.3	84.5	91.6	111.9	136.2	179.3	214.5
Money	31.8	28.9	32.5	38.9	48.3	54.9	60.3	72.1	84.4	107.4	127.5
Currency Outside Banks	20.2	18.9	20.9	24.7	29.7	31.4	36.5	40.8	51.7	63.5	72.5
Demand Deposits	11.6	10.0	11.5	14.3	18.6	23.5	23.7	31.3	32.7	44.0	55.0
Quasi-Money	14.0	14.3	15.5	17.6	23.0	29.7	31.3	39.8	51.8	71.9	87.0

(Millions of current Sierra Leonean Leones)

	1969	1970	1971	1972	1973	1974	1975	1976	1977	1978	1979
GOVERNMENT DEFICIT (-) OR SURPLUS	..	..	..	..	..	-20.90	-60.00	-48.40	-51.00	-79.20	-119.00
Current Revenue	..	..	..	..	..	91.70	97.00	95.40	119.40	169.60	192.70
Current Expenditure	..	..	..	..	..	64.20	82.20	83.10	103.70	199.20	200.00
Current Budget Balance	..	..	..	..	..	27.50	14.80	12.30	15.70	-29.60	-7.30
Capital Receipts	..	..	..	..	..	..	..	..	..	..	..
Capital Payments	..	..	..	..	..	48.40	74.80	60.70	66.70	49.60	111.70

1980	1981	1982	1983	1984	1985	1986	1987	1988	1989 estimate	NOTES	SIERRA LEONE
320	370	380	380	360	360	390	280	250	220	..	**CURRENT GNP PER CAPITA (US $)**
3,255	3,329	3,406	3,487	3,570	3,657	3,747	3,841	3,938	4,040	..	**POPULATION (thousands)**
											USE AND ORIGIN OF RESOURCES
			(Millions of current Sierra Leonean Leones)								
1,122	1,259	1,561	1,835	2,669	4,703	7,542	21,548	27,145	40,819	C f	Gross National Product (GNP)
-34	-33	-43	-42	-60	-82	60	1,848	-2,048	-2,624	..	Net Factor Income from Abroad
1,156	1,292	1,604	1,876	2,729	4,785	7,481	19,700	29,193	43,443	C f	GDP at Market Prices
-197	-190	-185	-127	-44	-58	-123	130	1,069	-2,819	..	Resource Balance
281	275	230	249	377	441	822	2,461	6,252	5,584	..	Exports of Goods & NFServices
478	465	415	376	421	499	945	2,331	5,182	8,403	..	Imports of Goods & NFServices
1,352	1,482	1,789	2,003	2,773	4,843	7,605	19,571	28,124	46,262	..	Domestic Absorption
1,067	1,146	1,436	1,568	2,237	4,021	6,268	16,303	21,754	37,096	..	Private Consumption, etc.
97	90	138	167	189	345	498	1,210	2,988	4,275	..	General Gov't Consumption
187	247	215	268	347	477	839	2,058	3,382	4,891	..	Gross Domestic Investment
172	236	205	235	332	424	730	1,854	..	..	..	Fixed Investment
93	119	101	77	105	132	213	912	1,088	2,608	..	Indirect Taxes, net
1,063	1,174	1,504	1,799	2,625	4,653	7,269	18,789	28,105	40,835	C f	GDP at factor cost
351	379	539	686	1,053	2,070	2,888	7,698	11,190	18,890	..	Agriculture
233	231	256	266	358	596	1,757	3,570	4,748	4,680	..	Industry
59	54	100	108	135	166	256	907	1,355	910	..	Manufacturing
479	563	710	847	1,214	1,987	2,623	7,521	12,166	17,265	..	Services, etc.
-9	57	30	141	303	419	716	2,188	4,451	2,072	..	Gross Domestic Saving
-34	35	-7	106	262	348	800	4,036	2,412	..	..	Gross National Saving
			(Millions of 1987 Sierra Leonean Leones)								
18,857.4	20,622.2	20,533.9	20,013.3	20,439.1	19,643.1	22,525.4	21,548.1	21,492.3	21,774.5	C f	Gross National Product
18,310.2	19,894.9	19,893.8	19,282.1	19,724.3	19,059.0	18,690.2	19,700.5	19,700.1	19,570.1	C f	GDP at Market Prices
-4,602.5	-3,800.1	-2,993.8	-1,835.5	-908.9	-722.1	-713.9	129.9	327.9	-489.8	..	Resource Balance
2,786.8	2,497.7	2,059.9	1,851.3	1,860.9	1,249.7	943.8	2,460.8	2,560.0	2,097.9	..	Exports of Goods & NFServices
7,389.3	6,297.8	5,053.7	3,686.8	2,769.8	1,971.8	1,657.7	2,330.9	2,232.1	2,587.7	..	Imports of Goods & NFServices
22,912.7	23,695.0	22,887.6	21,117.6	20,633.2	19,781.1	19,404.1	19,570.6	19,372.2	20,059.9	..	Domestic Absorption
18,528.7	18,851.0	18,608.8	16,889.8	16,717.2	16,153.7	15,336.4	16,302.6	15,397.8	15,834.6	..	Private Consumption, etc.
1,487.8	1,334.9	1,623.6	1,695.2	1,330.2	1,343.8	1,191.7	1,210.0	1,587.4	1,867.5	..	General Gov't Consumption
2,896.1	3,509.2	2,655.2	2,532.6	2,585.8	2,283.6	2,876.0	2,058.0	2,387.0	2,357.8	..	Gross Domestic Investment
2,612.9	3,320.8	2,511.7	2,272.3	2,451.3	1,987.4	2,096.1	1,853.9	2,234.8	2,127.0	..	Fixed Investment
16,940.6	17,733.6	18,657.0	19,074.3	19,036.5	18,445.5	18,153.9	18,788.7	18,687.5	18,504.5	C f	GDP at factor cost
6,456.9	6,510.1	6,717.9	6,655.0	6,679.3	7,401.8	7,182.2	7,698.3	7,735.5	7,758.7	..	Agriculture
4,837.8	4,455.7	4,069.1	3,536.1	3,941.4	3,281.7	3,553.7	3,569.7	3,434.8	3,410.6	..	Industry
1,008.7	1,047.0	1,305.3	1,172.7	1,207.3	1,022.9	983.5	907.0	868.2	810.8	..	Manufacturing
6,403.0	7,274.3	8,145.5	8,883.2	8,415.8	7,762.0	7,418.0	7,520.7	7,517.2	7,335.2	..	Services, etc.
											Memo Items:
4,344.5	3,727.4	2,805.9	2,440.5	2,480.1	1,741.5	1,441.3	2,460.8	2,692.7	1,719.6	..	Capacity to Import
1,557.7	1,229.8	745.9	589.3	619.2	491.8	497.5	0.0	132.6	-378.3	..	Terms of Trade Adjustment
19,867.8	21,124.7	20,639.7	19,871.3	20,343.4	19,550.8	19,187.7	19,700.5	19,832.8	19,191.8	..	Gross Domestic Income
20,415.0	21,852.0	21,279.8	20,602.5	21,058.3	20,134.9	23,022.9	21,548.1	21,624.9	21,396.1	..	Gross National Income
											DOMESTIC PRICES/DEFLATORS
			(Index 1987 = 100)								
6.3	6.5	8.1	9.7	13.8	25.1	40.0	100.0	148.2	222.0	..	Overall (GDP)
5.9	6.3	7.8	9.5	13.4	24.5	39.2	100.0	145.2	230.6	..	Domestic Absorption
5.4	5.8	8.0	10.3	15.8	28.0	40.2	100.0	144.7	243.5	..	Agriculture
4.8	5.2	6.3	7.5	9.1	18.2	49.4	100.0	138.2	137.2	..	Industry
5.8	5.1	7.7	9.2	11.2	16.2	26.1	100.0	156.1	112.3	..	Manufacturing
2.6	3.2	4.0	6.7	11.2	19.8	35.9	100.0	134.3	215.9	..	Consumer Price Index
											MANUFACTURING ACTIVITY
..	..	..	..	..	..	..	..	..	..	..	Employment (1987=100)
..	..	..	..	..	..	..	..	..	..	..	Real Earnings per Empl. (1987=100)
..	..	..	..	..	..	..	..	..	..	..	Real Output per Empl. (1987=100)
..	22.3	..	..	..	..	..	..	..	..	..	Earnings as % of Value Added
											MONETARY HOLDINGS
			(Millions of current Sierra Leonean Leones)								
260.8	267.6	419.6	552.4	708.8	1,212.6	2,284.6	3,747.2	5,878.5	10,240.2	..	Money Supply, Broadly Defined
152.5	151.9	253.2	359.4	486.2	899.7	1,851.5	2,888.5	4,637.1	8,674.9	..	Money
86.1	86.2	121.1	197.3	260.1	442.1	1,005.6	1,364.0	2,254.6	4,058.0	..	Currency Outside Banks
66.5	65.7	132.1	162.0	226.1	457.6	845.9	1,524.5	2,382.4	4,616.9	..	Demand Deposits
108.3	115.8	166.4	193.0	222.6	312.9	433.1	858.7	1,241.4	1,565.3	..	Quasi-Money
			(Millions of current Sierra Leonean Leones)								
-148.20	-120.70	-167.40	-271.20	-205.60	-375.60	..	..	..	..	C	**GOVERNMENT DEFICIT (-) OR SURPLUS**
197.10	236.90	188.50	170.60	243.30	314.50	..	2,102.00	2,638.00	..	..	Current Revenue
..	284.30	270.40	253.10	339.60	409.00	..	..	..	..	..	Current Expenditure
..	-47.40	..	-81.90	-82.50	-96.30	-94.50	..	..	..	..	Current Budget Balance
..	..	3.00	..	22.60	12.30	..	..	..	..	..	Capital Receipts
..	73.30	88.50	188.70	131.90	293.40	..	..	..	..	..	Capital Payments

SIERRA LEONE	1969	1970	1971	1972	1973	1974	1975	1976	1977	1978	1979
FOREIGN TRADE (CUSTOMS BASIS)				*(Millions of current US dollars)*							
Value of Exports, fob	104.60	101.46	98.48	117.49	131.38	146.24	145.75	106.59	130.60	178.29	194.00
Nonfuel Primary Products	29.76	36.23	34.90	39.70	46.55	51.73	56.86	32.41	69.07	70.11	82.25
Fuels	0.17	2.64	2.98	3.34	2.52	2.33	9.89	5.85	6.48	8.90	9.09
Manufactures	74.67	62.59	60.60	74.45	82.31	92.18	79.00	68.33	55.05	99.28	102.66
Value of Imports, cif	111.63	116.88	113.12	120.97	157.67	222.39	159.26	166.28	181.00	278.00	316.00
Nonfuel Primary Products	23.49	30.49	27.83	28.01	46.86	60.77	35.67	39.47	43.13	65.80	74.91
Fuels	6.86	5.49	8.38	9.05	9.38	25.57	21.76	23.67	25.06	38.66	44.01
Manufactures	81.28	80.90	76.91	83.91	101.43	136.05	101.83	103.14	112.81	173.54	197.08
					(Index 1987 = 100)						
Terms of Trade	132.1	128.3	120.6	114.4	119.9	117.8	108.9	115.2	146.4	118.2	119.8
Export Prices, fob	32.1	34.4	33.4	34.9	47.9	66.6	64.0	68.0	93.3	84.1	100.9
Import Prices, cif	24.3	26.8	27.7	30.5	39.9	56.5	58.7	59.1	63.7	71.1	84.2
BALANCE OF PAYMENTS				*(Millions of current US dollars)*							
Exports of Goods & Services	..	121.60	113.64	131.48	147.94	170.29	151.54	134.34	162.84	211.64	243.15
Merchandise, fob	..	100.00	95.78	113.46	129.11	142.75	128.98	113.85	142.70	185.09	197.07
Nonfactor Services	..	18.50	16.85	17.15	18.00	23.33	18.69	18.33	18.32	26.17	45.79
Factor Services	..	3.10	1.00	0.87	0.83	4.21	3.87	2.16	1.83	0.38	0.28
Imports of Goods & Services	..	142.60	139.31	143.86	183.47	253.16	227.65	203.53	232.45	343.06	451.19
Merchandise, fob	..	105.30	102.51	107.70	141.03	199.64	167.58	149.80	165.02	253.00	336.34
Nonfactor Services	..	30.10	26.68	28.12	33.50	41.25	45.35	41.52	50.68	56.16	72.57
Factor Services	..	7.20	10.13	8.03	8.94	12.27	14.71	12.22	16.75	33.91	42.29
Long-Term Interest	..	2.50	2.30	2.60	3.70	4.00	4.40	5.20	4.80	7.80	9.60
Private Current Transfers, net	..	1.20	1.60	-0.33	0.00	0.48	1.66	4.31	4.45	6.78	5.30
Workers' Remittances	..	..	..	..	..	..	..	..	..	..	..
Curr. A/C Bal before Off. Transf.	..	-19.80	-24.07	-12.70	-35.53	-82.38	-74.45	-64.88	-65.16	-124.64	-202.75
Net Official Transfers	..	3.90	4.21	3.47	6.44	21.53	8.96	6.38	15.79	12.89	23.94
Curr. A/C Bal after Off. Transf.	..	-15.90	-19.86	-9.23	-29.09	-60.85	-65.49	-58.50	-49.37	-111.74	-178.81
Long-Term Capital, net	..	-0.80	7.12	9.23	15.97	34.16	35.71	24.45	10.64	42.12	43.62
Direct Investment	..	8.20	5.22	3.80	4.05	10.46	10.07	8.54	5.06	24.26	16.08
Long-Term Loans	..	-3.00	5.40	5.90	12.50	37.60	22.60	10.50	17.80	30.20	30.30
Disbursements	..	7.60	11.70	14.00	21.70	48.10	33.80	27.30	30.10	59.90	61.80
Repayments	..	10.60	6.30	8.10	9.20	10.50	11.20	16.80	12.30	29.70	31.50
Other Long-Term Capital	..	-6.00	-3.49	-0.47	-0.58	-13.91	3.05	5.41	-12.22	-12.34	-2.77
Other Capital, net	..	16.38	10.91	4.86	21.40	24.18	7.53	14.65	35.59	76.50	138.34
Change in Reserves	..	0.32	1.83	-4.86	-8.29	2.51	22.25	19.41	3.14	-6.87	-3.15
Memo Item:				*(Sierra Leonean Leones per US dollar)*							
Conversion Factor (Annual Avg)	0.830	0.830	0.830	0.820	0.820	0.840	0.880	1.000	1.140	1.090	1.050
				(Millions of US dollars), outstanding at end of year							
EXTERNAL DEBT (Total)	..	59.50	68.50	72.80	90.30	141.20	156.90	189.40	245.30	301.10	369.20
Long-Term Debt (by debtor)	..	59.50	68.50	72.80	90.30	141.00	155.20	185.80	224.80	277.10	325.00
Central Bank, incl. IMF credit	..	0.00	0.00	0.00	0.00	5.30	5.80	26.00	39.00	46.40	57.60
Central Government	..	52.90	60.70	60.70	77.80	117.60	133.10	136.40	158.10	196.90	229.70
Rest of General Government	..	..	..	..	..	..	..	..	..	..	..
Non-financial Public Enterprises	..	6.60	7.80	12.10	12.50	17.90	16.30	23.40	27.70	33.80	37.70
Priv. Sector, incl non-guaranteed	..	0.00	0.00	0.00	0.00	0.20	0.00	0.00	0.00	0.00	0.00
Short-Term Debt	..	0.00	0.00	0.00	0.00	0.20	1.70	3.60	20.50	24.00	44.20
Memo Items:				*(Thousands of US dollars)*							
Int'l Reserves Excluding Gold	35,400	39,360	38,407	46,452	51,775	54,624	28,412	25,204	33,401	34,787	46,700
Gold Holdings (at market price)	..	..	..	..	..	..	..	..	..	..	..
SOCIAL INDICATORS											
Total Fertility Rate	6.4	6.5	6.5	6.5	6.5	6.5	6.5	6.5	6.5	6.5	6.5
Infant Mortality Rate	199.6	197.4	195.2	193.0	190.2	187.4	184.6	181.8	179.0	176.4	173.8
Life Expectancy at Birth	34.0	34.3	34.6	34.9	35.3	35.7	36.1	36.5	36.9	37.3	37.7
Urban Population, % of total	17.6	18.1	18.7	19.3	19.9	20.5	21.1	21.2	21.3	21.3	21.4
Food Prod. per capita (1987=100)	122.8	117.3	115.4	115.5	112.3	113.5	118.5	116.7	115.4	118.1	107.1
Labor Force, Agriculture (%)	76.1	75.5	74.9	74.3	73.7	73.1	72.6	71.9	71.3	70.7	70.2
Labor Force, Female (%)	35.7	35.6	35.5	35.4	35.3	35.2	35.2	35.1	35.0	34.9	34.8
Primary Schl. Enroll. Ratio	..	34.0	..	..	..	..	39.0	37.0	37.0	38.0	39.0
Primary Schl. Enroll. Ratio, Female	..	27.0	..	..	..	..	30.0	..	30.0	..	..
Secondary Schl. Enroll. Ratio	..	8.0	..	..	..	..	11.0	12.0	12.0	12.0	12.0

1980	1981	1982	1983	1984	1985	1986	1987	1988	1989 estimate	NOTES	SIERRA LEONE
											FOREIGN TRADE (CUSTOMS BASIS)
				(Millions of current US dollars)							
207.00	136.00	111.00	120.00	133.00	130.30	142.70	129.40	110.00	..	..	Value of Exports, fob
80.54	60.49	56.03	63.06	69.29	57.32	57.06	47.52	41.10	..	..	Nonfuel Primary Products
10.29	6.15	4.47	5.74	8.95	11.24	4.80	5.62	4.97	..	..	Fuels
116.17	69.36	50.49	51.20	54.76	61.74	80.84	76.26	63.93	..	..	Manufactures
425.00	311.00	298.00	160.00	157.10	149.40	141.00	132.09	149.00	..	..	Value of Imports, cif
100.76	73.72	70.65	37.92	33.44	30.71	29.74	28.20	40.76	..	..	Nonfuel Primary Products
59.14	43.28	41.47	22.27	27.36	24.96	10.56	11.74	11.81	..	..	Fuels
265.10	194.00	185.88	99.80	96.30	93.73	100.71	92.15	96.43	..	..	Manufactures
				(Index 1987 = 100)							
107.8	104.0	106.5	109.0	113.9	107.9	105.6	100.0	98.2	..	..	Terms of Trade
104.5	100.8	99.3	98.8	101.6	95.7	97.7	100.0	105.5	..	..	Export Prices, fob
97.0	96.9	93.2	90.6	89.3	88.7	92.5	100.0	107.5	..	..	Import Prices, cif
				(Millions of current US dollars)							**BALANCE OF PAYMENTS**
276.05	203.61	147.98	142.10	173.95	160.07	152.67	183.01	156.62	..	f	Exports of Goods & Services
213.47	151.58	110.28	107.04	132.63	131.86	125.99	138.87	104.48	..	..	Merchandise, fob
62.01	51.51	37.54	34.79	41.08	27.97	26.54	43.97	51.97	..	..	Nonfactor Services
0.57	0.52	0.16	0.27	0.24	0.24	0.14	0.16	0.16	..	..	Factor Services
493.70	379.09	368.15	196.31	229.92	216.27	278.06	220.06	193.12	..	f	Imports of Goods & Services
385.88	282.03	260.28	132.97	149.72	141.22	111.42	114.83	138.21	..	..	Merchandise, fob
85.35	59.62	72.66	42.11	47.57	42.85	33.95	41.99	34.58	..	..	Nonfactor Services
22.46	37.44	35.21	21.22	32.63	32.20	132.69	63.24	20.34	..	..	Factor Services
7.50	9.90	2.90	3.90	4.90	2.50	2.10	1.20	2.90	0.60	..	Long-Term Interest
8.29	9.40	4.76	3.24	7.61	2.34	1.50	0.01	0.27	..	..	Private Current Transfers, net
..	..	0.00	0.00	0.00	..	..	..	..	..	..	Workers' Remittances
-209.36	-166.08	-215.41	-50.97	-48.37	-13.16	136.08	-37.04	-11.10	..	..	Curr. A/C Bal before Off. Transf.
44.58	34.34	45.61	33.42	25.42	16.88	4.62	6.77	8.43	..	..	Net Official Transfers
-164.78	-131.74	-169.79	-17.56	-22.95	3.72	140.71	-30.27	-2.67	..	..	Curr. A/C Bal after Off. Transf.
47.76	106.97	20.72	-51.56	-55.05	-78.41	-303.43	44.04	-59.44	..	f	Long-Term Capital, net
-18.67	7.51	4.68	1.70	5.86	-30.96	-140.31	39.41	-23.09	..	..	Direct Investment
55.10	31.80	75.70	17.50	12.60	29.70	11.00	2.40	14.70	5.40	..	Long-Term Loans
86.20	66.90	83.70	22.70	24.20	35.30	13.70	5.60	19.70	6.60	..	Disbursements
31.10	35.10	8.00	5.20	11.60	5.60	2.70	3.20	5.00	1.20	..	Repayments
11.33	67.67	-59.67	-70.75	-73.50	-77.16	-174.12	2.24	-51.05		..	Other Long-Term Capital
102.16	-21.19	140.66	62.29	56.90	78.44	177.93	-13.07	69.82	..	f	Other Capital, net
14.85	45.96	8.42	6.83	21.09	-3.75	-15.21	-0.71	-7.71	2.53	..	Change in Reserves
				(Sierra Leonean Leones per US dollar)							Memo Item:
1.050	1.090	1.200	1.260	2.510	3.140	5.220	31.850	25.520	46.170	..	Conversion Factor (Annual Avg)
				(Millions of US dollars), outstanding at end of year							
429.60	562.40	619.70	640.30	616.80	723.80	854.80	1,008.80	994.30	1,056.50	..	**EXTERNAL DEBT (Total)**
376.60	406.00	448.80	457.50	418.10	488.70	562.40	649.30	625.90	616.00	..	Long-Term Debt (by debtor)
59.30	84.00	78.10	92.90	95.50	100.80	101.30	115.70	108.70	104.50	..	Central Bank, incl. IMF credit
278.80	272.70	316.20	312.10	280.00	336.20	414.70	487.30	475.10	472.60	..	Central Government
..	..	..	..	..	..	..	..	..	..	..	Rest of General Government
38.50	49.30	54.50	52.50	42.60	51.70	46.40	46.30	42.10	39.10	..	Non-financial Public Enterprises
0.00	0.00	0.00	0.00	0.00	0.00	0.00	0.00	0.00	..	..	Priv. Sector, incl non-guaranteed
53.00	156.40	170.90	182.80	198.70	235.10	292.40	359.50	368.40	440.30	..	Short-Term Debt
				(Thousands of US dollars)							Memo Items:
30,600	15,950	8,430	16,205	7,749	10,822	13,655	6,328	7,427	3,726	..	Int'l Reserves Excluding Gold
..	..	..	..	..	..	..	..	..	..	..	Gold Holdings (at market price)
											SOCIAL INDICATORS
6.5	6.5	6.5	6.5	6.5	6.5	6.5	6.5	6.5	6.5	..	Total Fertility Rate
171.2	168.6	166.0	163.6	161.2	158.8	156.4	154.0	151.9	149.8	..	Infant Mortality Rate
38.1	38.5	38.9	39.4	39.9	40.3	40.8	41.3	41.7	42.1	..	Life Expectancy at Birth
21.5	22.0	22.6	23.1	23.7	24.2	24.9	25.7	26.2	26.7	..	Urban Population, % of total
108.6	107.8	115.1	114.9	101.5	97.8	103.8	100.0	93.4	94.1	..	Food Prod. per capita (1987=100)
69.6	..	..	..	..	..	..	..	..	..	..	Labor Force, Agriculture (%)
34.7	34.5	34.3	34.1	33.9	33.7	33.5	33.3	33.1	32.9	..	Labor Force, Female (%)
52.0	55.0	54.0	..	..	..	..	..	..	..	..	Primary Schl. Enroll. Ratio
43.0	45.0	44.0	..	..	..	..	..	..	..	..	Primary Schl. Enroll. Ratio, Female
14.0	15.0	17.0	..	..	..	..	..	..	..	..	Secondary Schl. Enroll. Ratio

SINGAPORE	1969	1970	1971	1972	1973	1974	1975	1976	1977	1978	1979
CURRENT GNP PER CAPITA (US $)	840	950	1,070	1,270	1,580	2,020	2,550	2,760	2,940	3,310	3,880
POPULATION (thousands)	2,043	2,075	2,113	2,152	2,193	2,230	2,263	2,293	2,325	2,353	2,384

USE AND ORIGIN OF RESOURCES *(Millions of current Singapore Dollars)*

	1969	1970	1971	1972	1973	1974	1975	1976	1977	1978	1979
Gross National Product (GNP)	5,105	5,861	6,831	8,174	10,033	12,260	13,567	14,570	15,852	17,787	20,444
Net Factor Income from Abroad	85	56	-10	-21	-224	-351	124	-81	-187	-43	-79
GDP at Market Prices	5,020	5,805	6,841	8,195	10,257	12,610	13,443	14,651	16,039	17,830	20,523
Resource Balance	-532	-1,179	-1,484	-1,378	-1,041	-2,044	-1,416	-1,199	-424	-898	-1,445
Exports of Goods & NFServices	5,782	5,929	6,655	8,804	12,227	19,097	18,726	22,281	26,442	30,132	38,801
Imports of Goods & NFServices	6,314	7,108	8,139	10,182	13,269	21,141	20,143	23,481	26,866	31,029	40,246
Domestic Absorption	5,552	6,984	8,325	9,573	11,298	14,654	14,859	15,850	16,463	18,728	21,968
Private Consumption, etc.	3,555	4,047	4,686	5,190	6,135	7,646	8,066	8,327	8,948	9,806	11,035
General Gov't Consumption	560	692	861	990	1,118	1,298	1,423	1,541	1,716	1,965	2,034
Gross Domestic Investment	1,437	2,244	2,778	3,393	4,045	5,710	5,370	5,982	5,799	6,957	8,900
Fixed Investment	1,326	1,888	2,507	3,093	3,606	4,813	4,833	5,288	5,458	6,365	7,520
Indirect Taxes, net	410	485	544	632	767	805	866	989	1,122	1,276	1,547
GDP at factor cost	4,609	5,320	6,297	7,563	9,490	11,805	12,577	13,662	14,917	16,555	18,976
Agriculture	129	135	159	161	214	230	254	257	283	274	295
Industry	1,373	1,726	2,142	2,756	3,399	4,258	4,585	5,119	5,518	6,083	7,403
Manufacturing	936	1,162	1,447	1,853	2,429	3,068	3,209	3,589	3,982	4,576	5,703
Services, etc.	3,518	3,944	4,540	5,278	6,644	8,122	8,603	9,275	10,238	11,473	12,825
Gross Domestic Saving	905	1,065	1,294	2,015	3,004	3,666	3,954	4,782	5,375	6,060	7,455
Gross National Saving	..	1,057	1,214	1,988	2,746	3,216	3,986	4,588	5,089	5,936	7,309

(Millions of 1987 Singapore Dollars)

	1969	1970	1971	1972	1973	1974	1975	1976	1977	1978	1979
Gross National Product	10,885	12,181	13,501	15,224	16,638	17,653	19,073	20,128	21,551	23,631	25,784
GDP at Market Prices	10,707	12,067	13,525	15,268	17,021	18,171	18,892	20,242	21,813	23,687	25,882
Resource Balance	..	..	..	..	..	..	-2,052	-1,774	-865	-1,330	-1,579
Exports of Goods & NFServices	..	..	..	..	..	..	20,900	23,305	26,585	29,717	36,305
Imports of Goods & NFServices	..	..	..	..	..	..	22,952	25,079	27,450	31,047	37,885
Domestic Absorption	..	..	..	..	..	..	20,944	22,016	22,678	25,018	27,461
Private Consumption, etc.	..	..	..	..	..	..	11,016	11,501	12,254	13,016	13,737
General Gov't Consumption	1,251	1,520	1,779	2,017	2,127	2,130	2,188	2,297	2,509	2,798	2,784
Gross Domestic Investment	3,531	5,083	5,959	6,506	6,982	8,397	7,740	8,217	7,915	9,203	10,940
Fixed Investment	3,056	4,069	5,068	5,812	6,304	7,058	6,791	7,120	7,253	8,275	9,342
GDP at factor cost	9,747	10,977	12,295	13,880	15,465	16,528	17,175	18,395	19,838	21,526	23,540
Agriculture	247	253	279	300	284	263	269	296	300	298	304
Industry	3,751	4,542	5,310	6,236	6,826	7,119	7,299	8,132	8,664	9,277	10,415
Manufacturing	2,577	3,130	3,705	4,372	5,079	5,278	5,173	5,779	6,318	7,033	8,004
Services, etc.	6,524	7,160	7,878	8,741	9,880	10,747	11,273	11,785	12,811	14,064	15,138

Memo Items:

	1969	1970	1971	1972	1973	1974	1975	1976	1977	1978	1979
Capacity to Import	..	..	..	..	..	..	21,338	23,798	27,016	30,149	36,524
Terms of Trade Adjustment	..	..	..	..	..	..	438	493	432	432	219
Gross Domestic Income	..	..	..	..	..	..	19,330	20,735	22,245	24,119	26,101
Gross National Income	..	..	..	..	..	..	19,511	20,620	21,983	24,063	26,003

DOMESTIC PRICES/DEFLATORS *(Index 1987 = 100)*

	1969	1970	1971	1972	1973	1974	1975	1976	1977	1978	1979
Overall (GDP)	46.9	48.1	50.6	53.7	60.3	69.4	71.2	72.4	73.5	75.3	79.3
Domestic Absorption	..	..	..	..	..	..	70.9	72.0	72.6	74.9	80.0
Agriculture	52.2	53.1	56.8	53.5	75.5	87.4	94.5	86.8	94.2	91.8	97.1
Industry	36.6	38.0	40.3	44.2	49.8	59.8	62.8	62.9	63.7	65.6	71.1
Manufacturing	36.3	37.1	39.1	42.4	47.8	58.1	62.0	62.1	63.0	65.1	71.2
Consumer Price Index	43.4	43.6	44.4	45.4	57.2	70.0	71.9	70.5	72.8	76.2	79.3

MANUFACTURING ACTIVITY

	1969	1970	1971	1972	1973	1974	1975	1976	1977	1978	1979
Employment (1987=100)	36.9	44.4	52.0	62.2	72.2	74.3	69.4	75.0	79.0	87.6	97.5
Real Earnings per Empl. (1987=100)	48.6	50.5	53.4	54.3	50.7	49.8	57.2	59.9	61.6	62.1	64.9
Real Output per Empl. (1987=100)	68.6	60.4	56.2	50.1	54.4	71.0	65.9	74.6	78.9	77.3	82.1
Earnings as % of Value Added	36.2	36.3	36.7	35.4	33.8	30.0	34.6	33.1	32.9	33.4	30.9

MONETARY HOLDINGS *(Millions of current Singapore Dollars)*

	1969	1970	1971	1972	1973	1974	1975	1976	1977	1978	1979
Money Supply, Broadly Defined	3,566	4,125	4,599	5,803	6,797	7,819	9,390	10,944	12,306	14,014	16,837
Money	1,417	1,631	1,760	2,385	2,632	2,858	3,472	4,000	4,412	4,926	5,706
Currency Outside Banks	617	727	806	1,005	1,114	1,306	1,638	1,947	2,243	2,583	2,941
Demand Deposits	800	904	954	1,380	1,518	1,552	1,834	2,053	2,169	2,343	2,765
Quasi-Money	2,149	2,494	2,839	3,418	4,165	4,961	5,918	6,944	7,894	9,088	11,131

GOVERNMENT DEFICIT (-) OR SURPLUS *(Millions of current Singapore Dollars)*

	1969	1970	1971	1972	1973	1974	1975	1976	1977	1978	1979
	..	..	..	108	-12	197	121	31	164	146	468
Current Revenue	..	1,274	1,445	1,777	2,128	2,587	3,146	3,342	3,893	4,195	4,887
Current Expenditure	..	..	..	1,213	1,335	1,472	2,005	2,288	2,677	2,797	3,191
Current Budget Balance	..	..	..	564	793	1,115	1,141	1,054	1,216	1,398	1,696
Capital Receipts	..	27	60	43	156	142	245	155	97	52	294
Capital Payments	..	..	..	499	961	1,060	1,265	1,178	1,149	1,304	1,522

1980	1981	1982	1983	1984	1985	1986	1987	1988	1989 estimate	NOTES	SINGAPORE
4,540	5,440	6,170	6,930	7,740	7,600	7,390	7,900	9,090	10,450	..	CURRENT GNP PER CAPITA (US $)
2,415	2,443	2,472	2,502	2,529	2,558	2,586	2,613	2,647	2,684	..	POPULATION (thousands)

(Millions of current Singapore Dollars) — **USE AND ORIGIN OF RESOURCES**

1980	1981	1982	1983	1984	1985	1986	1987	1988	1989	NOTES	SINGAPORE
24,189	28,191	31,776	36,561	40,815	40,330	39,602	43,192	50,359	56,347	..	Gross National Product (GNP)
-902	-1,148	-894	-172	767	1,407	949	582	994	1,037	..	Net Factor Income from Abroad
25,091	29,339	32,670	36,733	40,048	38,924	38,654	42,609	49,365	55,310	..	GDP at Market Prices
-2,216	-1,633	-1,441	-664	-1,113	-946	143	382	2,191	4,153	..	Resource Balance
52,000	59,735	62,369	62,819	64,513	61,420	60,001	73,313	95,064	105,892	..	Exports of Goods & NFServices
54,215	61,368	63,809	63,482	65,626	62,365	59,858	72,931	92,873	101,739	..	Imports of Goods & NFServices
27,307	30,973	34,111	37,397	41,161	39,869	38,510	42,228	47,174	51,157	..	Domestic Absorption
13,232	14,597	14,881	15,806	17,411	17,770	18,345	20,264	23,590	25,687	..	Private Consumption, etc.
2,447	2,789	3,570	3,995	4,333	5,548	5,270	5,327	5,380	5,901	..	General Gov't Consumption
11,628	13,587	15,659	17,596	19,417	16,551	14,895	16,637	18,204	19,569	..	Gross Domestic Investment
10,203	12,785	15,506	17,464	19,122	16,425	14,310	15,165	17,312	20,605	..	Fixed Investment
1,819	2,173	2,480	3,014	3,496	3,304	2,594	2,869	3,360	4,400	..	Indirect Taxes, net
23,272	27,167	30,190	33,719	36,552	35,619	36,059	39,740	46,005	50,910	B	GDP at factor cost
322	356	349	331	340	292	245	222	204	190	..	Agriculture
9,563	11,107	12,029	13,954	15,712	14,259	14,467	15,976	18,900	20,508	..	Industry
7,313	8,362	8,154	8,908	9,863	9,184	10,185	12,091	14,904	16,424	..	Manufacturing
15,206	17,876	20,292	22,448	23,996	24,372	23,942	26,412	30,262	34,612	..	Services, etc.
9,412	11,954	14,218	16,932	18,304	15,606	15,038	17,018	20,395	23,722	..	Gross Domestic Saving
8,288	10,499	12,909	16,323	18,616	16,561	15,613	17,244	20,969	24,263	..	Gross National Saving

(Millions of 1987 Singapore Dollars)

1980	1981	1982	1983	1984	1985	1986	1987	1988	1989	NOTES	SINGAPORE
27,368	29,874	32,289	35,781	39,721	39,647	39,889	43,192	48,323	52,719	..	Gross National Product
28,387	31,106	33,243	35,956	38,957	38,241	38,921	42,609	47,380	51,747	..	GDP at Market Prices
-1,820	-1,483	-2,404	-2,079	-1,900	-1,424	-278	382	2,339	3,435	..	Resource Balance
44,252	49,128	51,431	54,404	59,174	57,182	64,654	73,313	94,860	103,994	..	Exports of Goods & NFServices
46,072	50,612	53,834	56,482	61,074	58,606	64,932	72,931	92,521	100,558	..	Imports of Goods & NFServices
30,206	32,589	35,646	38,035	40,857	39,665	39,199	42,228	45,041	48,311	..	Domestic Absorption
14,416	15,734	16,341	16,606	17,566	17,767	18,630	20,264	23,009	24,676	..	Private Consumption, etc.
3,047	3,207	3,632	3,982	4,190	5,216	5,271	5,327	5,083	5,343	..	General Gov't Consumption
12,743	13,648	15,673	17,447	19,100	16,682	15,298	16,637	16,948	18,292	..	Gross Domestic Investment
11,228	12,927	15,546	17,223	18,848	16,574	14,673	15,165	16,415	19,317	..	Fixed Investment
25,906	28,474	30,314	32,700	35,427	34,998	36,290	39,740	44,156	47,631	B	GDP at factor cost
308	302	287	294	309	277	247	222	194	182	..	Agriculture
11,461	12,704	13,324	14,648	16,086	14,594	14,455	15,976	18,075	19,584	..	Industry
8,804	9,623	9,286	9,546	10,262	9,513	10,312	12,091	14,266	15,678	..	Manufacturing
16,597	18,096	19,610	21,013	22,562	23,370	24,219	26,412	29,110	31,981	..	Services, etc.
											Memo Items:
44,189	49,264	52,619	55,892	60,038	57,718	65,087	73,313	94,704	104,663	..	Capacity to Import
-63	136	1,188	1,488	864	536	433	0	-156	670	..	Terms of Trade Adjustment
28,323	31,242	34,431	37,444	39,821	38,777	39,354	42,609	47,223	52,417	..	Gross Domestic Income
27,305	30,010	33,478	37,269	40,585	40,183	40,322	43,192	48,167	53,389	..	Gross National Income

(Index 1987 = 100) — **DOMESTIC PRICES/DEFLATORS**

1980	1981	1982	1983	1984	1985	1986	1987	1988	1989	NOTES	SINGAPORE
88.4	94.3	98.3	102.2	102.8	101.8	99.3	100.0	104.2	106.9	..	Overall (GDP)
90.4	95.0	95.7	98.3	100.7	100.5	98.2	100.0	104.7	105.9	..	Domestic Absorption
104.6	117.8	121.6	112.4	109.9	105.6	99.0	100.0	104.7	104.5	..	Agriculture
83.4	87.4	90.3	95.3	97.7	97.7	100.1	100.0	104.6	104.7	..	Industry
83.1	86.9	87.8	93.3	96.1	96.5	98.8	100.0	104.5	104.8	..	Manufacturing
86.1	93.1	96.8	97.9	100.4	100.9	99.5	100.0	101.5	103.9	..	Consumer Price Index
											MANUFACTURING ACTIVITY
103.1	102.0	99.6	98.6	99.6	92.0	89.4	100.0	117.3	..	..	Employment (1987=100)
68.5	74.4	81.5	89.1	97.1	104.8	101.5	100.0	101.5	..	..	Real Earnings per Empl. (1987=100)
82.4	91.4	91.2	88.5	93.7	94.1	91.6	100.0	100.1	..	..	Real Output per Empl. (1987=100)
29.7	30.3	35.0	36.3	36.4	37.8	31.7	29.1	28.2	..	..	Earnings as % of Value Added

(Millions of current Singapore Dollars) — **MONETARY HOLDINGS**

1980	1981	1982	1983	1984	1985	1986	1987	1988	1989	NOTES	SINGAPORE
20,489	25,197	30,908	35,378	38,948	41,407	35,315	52,492	59,039	70,901	D	Money Supply, Broadly Defined
6,135	7,242	8,157	8,607	8,866	8,785	9,822	11,031	11,958	13,745	..	Money
3,137	3,382	3,996	4,335	4,619	4,739	5,034	5,440	5,997	6,610	..	Currency Outside Banks
2,998	3,860	4,161	4,272	4,247	4,046	4,788	5,591	5,961	7,135	..	Demand Deposits
14,354	17,956	22,751	26,771	30,082	32,622	25,493	41,461	47,081	57,156	..	Quasi-Money

(Millions of current Singapore Dollars)

1980	1981	1982	1983	1984	1985	1986	1987	1988	1989	NOTES	SINGAPORE
538	213	1,098	661	1,643	816	561	-1,165	3,485	..	C	GOVERNMENT DEFICIT (-) OR SURPLUS
6,365	7,797	9,054	10,935	11,451	10,768	10,411	12,947	13,856	..	..	Current Revenue
3,910	5,377	5,452	6,267	7,802	7,316	6,802	9,722	8,107	..	..	Current Expenditure
2,455	2,420	3,602	4,668	3,649	3,452	3,609	3,225	5,749	..	..	Current Budget Balance
255	899	1,032	782	246	3,996	4,560	858	603	..	..	Capital Receipts
2,172	3,106	3,536	4,789	2,252	6,632	7,608	5,248	2,867	..	..	Capital Payments

SINGAPORE	1969	1970	1971	1972	1973	1974	1975	1976	1977	1978	1979
FOREIGN TRADE (CUSTOMS BASIS)					*(Millions of current US dollars)*						
Value of Exports, fob	1,549	1,554	1,755	2,181	3,610	5,785	5,377	6,586	8,242	10,134	14,233
Nonfuel Primary Products	769	720	661	681	1,220	1,537	1,238	1,610	2,135	2,588	3,452
Fuels	378	360	451	536	716	1,857	1,809	1,955	2,481	2,867	3,410
Manufactures	402	474	642	964	1,673	2,391	2,331	3,020	3,625	4,679	7,372
Value of Imports, cif	2,040	2,461	2,827	3,383	5,070	8,344	8,135	9,070	10,472	13,049	17,638
Nonfuel Primary Products	667	696	708	790	1,272	1,593	1,436	1,809	2,194	2,469	3,258
Fuels	321	332	405	491	656	2,003	1,998	2,486	2,677	3,122	4,449
Manufactures	1,051	1,433	1,714	2,102	3,142	4,748	4,700	4,774	5,601	7,458	9,931
					(Index 1987 = 100)						
Terms of Trade	89.6	85.6	85.2	83.3	96.5	115.8	105.3	107.4	102.9	102.0	99.6
Export Prices, fob	18.8	18.9	20.7	22.0	34.0	62.6	59.2	63.7	67.0	72.9	85.9
Import Prices, cif	20.9	22.1	24.3	26.4	35.2	54.1	56.2	59.3	65.1	71.4	86.3
BALANCE OF PAYMENTS					*(Millions of current US dollars)*						
Exports of Goods & Services	..	2,003	2,267	3,243	5,143	8,062	8,276	9,387	11,231	13,778	18,649
Merchandise, fob	..	1,447	1,665	2,041	3,426	5,547	5,110	6,218	7,745	9,587	13,400
Nonfactor Services	..	489	519	1,090	1,550	2,289	2,787	2,800	3,094	3,664	4,443
Factor Services	..	67	83	113	167	225	380	370	391	528	806
Imports of Goods & Services	..	2,567	2,979	3,741	5,658	9,044	8,822	9,906	11,482	14,192	19,350
Merchandise, fob	..	2,302	2,655	3,127	4,735	7,764	7,511	8,442	9,729	12,090	16,450
Nonfactor Services	..	236	294	484	655	900	966	1,054	1,277	1,547	2,050
Factor Services	..	29	30	129	268	380	345	410	475	554	849
Long-Term Interest	..	..	..	..	..	..	..	..	..	..	..
Private Current Transfers, net	..	-21	-23	-2	-14	-41	-38	-46	-41	-36	-31
Workers' Remittances	..	..	..	..	..	..	..	..	..	..	..
Curr. A/C Bal before Off. Transf.	..	-585	-735	-500	-529	-1,023	-584	-564	-291	-449	-732
Net Official Transfers	..	13	11	5	10	2	0	-3	-4	-3	-4
Curr. A/C Bal after Off. Transf.	..	-572	-724	-495	-519	-1,021	-584	-567	-295	-453	-736
Long-Term Capital, net	..	140	158	213	433	353	273	305	405	299	817
Direct Investment	..	93	116	141	327	280	254	186	206	186	669
Long-Term Loans	..	..	..	..	..	..	..	..	..	..	..
Disbursements	..	..	..	..	..	..	..	..	..	..	..
Repayments	..	..	..	..	..	..	..	..	..	..	..
Other Long-Term Capital	..	47	42	73	107	73	19	119	199	113	149
Other Capital, net	..	616	885	617	499	963	719	561	203	818	435
Change in Reserves	..	-184	-320	-335	-413	-295	-407	-298	-313	-665	-516
Memo Item:					*(Singapore Dollars per US dollar)*						
Conversion Factor (Annual Avg)	3.060	3.060	3.050	2.810	2.460	2.440	2.370	2.470	2.440	2.270	2.170
EXTERNAL DEBT (Total)					*(Millions of US dollars), outstanding at end of year*						
Long-Term Debt (by debtor)	..	..	..	..	..	..	..	..	..	..	..
Central Bank, incl. IMF credit	..	..	..	..	..	..	..	..	..	..	..
Central Government	..	..	..	..	..	..	..	..	..	..	..
Rest of General Government	..	..	..	..	..	..	..	..	..	..	..
Non-financial Public Enterprises	..	..	..	..	..	..	..	..	..	..	..
Priv. Sector, incl non-guaranteed	..	..	..	..	..	..	..	..	..	..	..
Short-Term Debt	..	..	..	..	..	..	..	..	..	..	..
Memo Items:					*(Millions of US dollars)*						
Int'l Reserves Excluding Gold	827.0	1,012.0	1,452.0	1,748.0	2,286.0	2,812.0	3,007.0	3,364.0	3,858.0	5,303.0	5,818.0
Gold Holdings (at market price)	..	..	..	..	..	..	..	..	..	..	..
SOCIAL INDICATORS											
Total Fertility Rate	3.2	3.1	3.0	3.0	2.8	2.4	2.1	2.1	1.8	1.8	1.8
Infant Mortality Rate	20.7	19.7	19.7	19.0	20.1	16.7	13.9	11.6	12.4	12.6	13.2
Life Expectancy at Birth	67.3	67.7	68.1	68.5	68.9	69.3	69.7	70.1	70.5	70.9	71.2
Urban Population, % of total	100.0	100.0	100.0	100.0	100.0	100.0	100.0	100.0	100.0	100.0	100.0
Food Prod. per capita (1987=100)	105.5	124.8	139.5	128.9	128.4	119.1	121.1	110.1	134.9	118.4	107.6
Labor Force, Agriculture (%)	3.8	3.4	3.2	3.0	2.8	2.7	2.5	2.3	2.1	1.9	1.7
Labor Force, Female (%)	25.2	25.9	27.0	28.0	29.0	29.9	30.7	31.6	32.4	33.1	33.8
Primary Schl. Enroll. Ratio	..	105.0	..	..	..	..	110.0	111.0	110.0	108.0	106.0
Primary Schl. Enroll. Ratio, Female	..	101.0	..	..	..	..	107.0	108.0	107.0	106.0	105.0
Secondary Schl. Enroll. Ratio	..	46.0	..	..	..	..	52.0	54.0	55.0	57.0	59.0

1980	1981	1982	1983	1984	1985	1986	1987	1988	1989 estimate	NOTES	SINGAPORE
											FOREIGN TRADE (CUSTOMS BASIS)
				(Millions of current US dollars)							
19,376	20,968	20,788	21,833	24,055	22,815	22,428	28,592	39,205	..	..	Value of Exports, fob
4,041	3,530	3,229	3,330	4,102	3,343	3,169	3,592	5,193	..	..	Nonfuel Primary Products
4,882	5,726	5,724	6,115	6,162	6,156	4,587	4,523	4,889	..	..	Fuels
10,452	11,712	11,834	12,388	13,791	13,317	14,672	20,477	29,123	..	..	Manufactures
24,003	27,572	28,167	28,158	28,656	26,250	25,461	32,480	43,765	..	..	Value of Imports, cif
3,817	3,565	3,451	3,664	4,290	3,582	3,543	4,108	5,827	..	..	Nonfuel Primary Products
6,882	9,295	9,469	8,804	7,964	7,741	5,047	5,956	6,173	..	..	Fuels
13,303	14,712	15,248	15,691	16,402	14,927	16,871	22,416	31,765	..	..	Manufactures
				(Index 1987 = 100)							
99.4	101.5	99.4	100.8	101.8	99.8	100.3	100.0	99.9	..	..	Terms of Trade
101.5	107.1	100.0	97.7	95.6	93.1	88.9	100.0	107.6	..	..	Export Prices, fob
102.1	105.5	100.6	96.9	93.9	93.2	88.6	100.0	107.7	..	..	Import Prices, cif
				(Millions of current US dollars)							**BALANCE OF PAYMENTS**
25,239	29,366	30,386	31,029	31,847	29,730	29,775	38,060	51,664	59,703	..	Exports of Goods & Services
18,200	19,662	19,435	20,429	22,663	21,533	21,336	27,464	37,993	43,239	..	Merchandise, fob
6,085	8,612	9,709	9,299	7,582	6,383	6,220	7,348	9,246	11,058	..	Nonfactor Services
953	1,092	1,243	1,300	1,603	1,814	2,219	3,248	4,425	5,406	..	Factor Services
26,695	30,683	31,477	31,425	32,009	29,521	29,274	37,602	50,081	57,041	..	Imports of Goods & Services
22,400	25,785	26,196	26,252	26,734	24,362	23,402	29,910	40,338	45,713	..	Merchandise, fob
2,912	3,254	3,613	3,782	4,024	3,976	4,165	4,808	5,916	6,568	..	Nonfactor Services
1,382	1,644	1,668	1,390	1,252	1,183	1,707	2,884	3,827	4,760	..	Factor Services
..	..	..	..	..	..	..	..	..	..	..	Long-Term Interest
-104	-145	-194	-207	-214	-205	-172	-170	-209	-254	..	Private Current Transfers, net
..	..	..	..	..	:.	..	..	..	..	..	Workers' Remittances
-1,560	-1,462	-1,285	-602	-376	5	330	288	1,374	2,407	..	Curr. A/C Bal before Off. Transf.
-3	-8	-11	-8	-9	-8	-11	-64	-68	-69	..	Net Official Transfers
-1,563	-1,470	-1,296	-610	-385	-4	319	224	1,306	2,338	..	Curr. A/C Bal after Off. Transf.
1,463	1,682	1,834	784	772	1,017	1,167	2,480	2,497	3,583	..	Long-Term Capital, net
1,138	1,645	1,298	1,085	1,210	809	1,533	2,696	2,710	3,963	..	Direct Investment
..	..	..	..	..	..	..	..	..	..	..	Long-Term Loans
..	..	..	..	..	..	..	..	..	..	..	Disbursements
..	..	..	..	..	..	..	..	..	..	..	Repayments
325	36	536	-301	-437	208	-366	-217	-212	-380	..	Other Long-Term Capital
762	697	639	886	1,136	324	-948	-1,609	-2,144	-3,184	..	Other Capital, net
-663	-909	-1,177	-1,059	-1,524	-1,337	-538	-1,095	-1,659	-2,738	..	Change in Reserves
				(Singapore Dollars per US dollar)							Memo Item:
2.140	2.110	2.140	2.110	2.130	2.200	2.180	2.110	2.010	1.950	..	Conversion Factor (Annual Avg)
			(Millions of US dollars), outstanding at end of year								
..	..	..	..	..	..	..	..	..	..	..	**EXTERNAL DEBT (Total)**
..	..	..	..	..	..	..	..	..	..	..	Long-Term Debt (by debtor)
..	..	..	..	..	..	..	..	..	..	..	Central Bank, incl. IMF credit
..	..	..	..	..	..	..	..	..	..	..	Central Government
..	..	..	..	..	..	..	..	..	..	..	Rest of General Government
..	..	..	..	..	..	..	..	..	..	..	Non-financial Public Enterprises
..	..	..	..	..	..	..	..	..	..	..	Priv. Sector, incl non-guaranteed
..	..	..	..	..	..	..	..	..	..	..	Short-Term Debt
				(Millions of US dollars)							Memo Items:
6,567.0	7,549.0	8,480.0	9,264.0	10,416.0	12,847.0	12,939.0	15,227.0	17,073.0	20,345.0	..	Int'l Reserves Excluding Gold
..	..	..	..	..	..	..	..	..	..	..	Gold Holdings (at market price)
											SOCIAL INDICATORS
1.7	1.7	1.7	1.7	1.8	1.8	1.8	1.9	1.9	1.9	..	Total Fertility Rate
11.7	10.8	10.7	9.4	9.3	8.7	8.0	7.4	7.2	7.0	..	Infant Mortality Rate
71.5	71.8	72.1	72.4	72.6	72.9	73.2	73.5	73.7	74.0	..	Life Expectancy at Birth
100.0	100.0	100.0	100.0	100.0	100.0	100.0	100.0	100.0	100.0	..	Urban Population, % of total
103.7	121.7	95.3	96.8	117.0	105.0	100.5	100.0	83.7	103.1	..	Food Prod. per capita (1987=100)
1.6	..	..	..	..	..	..	..	..	..	..	Labor Force, Agriculture (%)
34.5	34.3	34.0	33.8	33.6	33.4	33.1	32.9	32.6	32.4	..	Labor Force, Female (%)
108.0	106.0	109.0	113.0	115.0	..	..	..	..	..	..	Primary Schl. Enroll. Ratio
106.0	105.0	107.0	111.0	113.0	..	..	..	..	..	..	Primary Schl. Enroll. Ratio, Female
58.0	62.0	65.0	69.0	71.0	..	..	..	..	..	..	Secondary Schl. Enroll. Ratio

SOLOMON ISLANDS	1969	1970	1971	1972	1973	1974	1975	1976	1977	1978	1979
CURRENT GNP PER CAPITA (US $)	..	..	..	..	..	..	290	270	300	320	440
POPULATION (thousands)	159	164	169	175	181	187	194	201	208	215	222

USE AND ORIGIN OF RESOURCES *(Millions of current Solomon Islands Dollars)*

	1969	1970	1971	1972	1973	1974	1975	1976	1977	1978	1979
Gross National Product (GNP)	..	..	..	23.20	26.70	39.90	37.80	43.30	54.10	59.60	84.30
Net Factor Income from Abroad	0.00	..	..	-0.20	-0.30	-0.50	-1.50	-3.20	-3.70	-7.40	-5.90
GDP at Market Prices	25.70	28.60	30.50	23.40	27.00	40.40	39.30	46.50	57.80	67.00	90.20
Resource Balance	..	..	..	..	..	..	..	..	..	..	..
Exports of Goods & NFServices	..	..	..	..	..	..	..	..	..	..	..
Imports of Goods & NFServices	..	..	..	..	..	..	..	..	..	..	..
Domestic Absorption	..	..	..	..	..	..	..	..	..	..	..
Private Consumption, etc.	..	..	..	..	..	..	..	..	..	..	..
General Gov't Consumption	..	..	..	..	..	..	..	..	..	..	..
Gross Domestic Investment	..	..	..	..	..	..	..	..	..	..	..
Fixed Investment	..	..	..	..	..	..	..	..	..	..	..
Indirect Taxes, net	..	2.20	2.30	2.10	2.40	4.10	3.40	4.00	5.40	6.20	10.50
GDP at factor cost	..	26.40	28.20	21.30	24.60	36.30	35.90	42.50	52.40	60.80	79.70
Agriculture	..	..	..	..	..	..	..	..	..	..	..
Industry	..	..	..	..	..	..	..	..	..	..	..
Manufacturing	..	..	..	..	..	..	..	..	..	..	..
Services, etc.	..	..	..	..	..	..	..	..	..	..	..
Gross Domestic Saving	..	1.20	1.90	1.60	0.40	2.10	-5.90	1.70	12.50	11.30	31.90
Gross National Saving	..	..	..	..	..	..	-6.00	-0.10	10.30	5.70	28.00

(Millions of 1987 Solomon Islands Dollars)

	1969	1970	1971	1972	1973	1974	1975	1976	1977	1978	1979
Gross National Product	..	..	..	..	108.12	136.44	135.89	129.09	148.39	153.73	201.54
GDP at Market Prices	111.63	117.36	120.13	86.13	96.11	121.43	107.01	121.80	139.35	151.74	189.44
Resource Balance	..	..	..	..	..	..	..	..	..	..	..
Exports of Goods & NFServices	..	..	..	..	..	..	..	..	..	..	..
Imports of Goods & NFServices	..	..	..	..	..	..	..	..	..	..	..
Domestic Absorption	..	..	..	..	..	..	..	..	..	..	..
Private Consumption, etc.	..	..	..	..	..	..	..	..	..	..	..
General Gov't Consumption	..	..	..	..	..	..	..	..	..	..	..
Gross Domestic Investment	..	..	..	..	..	..	..	..	..	..	..
Fixed Investment	..	..	..	..	..	..	..	..	..	..	..
GDP at factor cost	..	..	..	..	..	..	..	..	..	..	..
Agriculture	..	..	..	..	..	..	..	..	..	..	..
Industry	..	..	..	..	..	..	..	..	..	..	..
Manufacturing	..	..	..	..	..	..	..	..	..	..	..
Services, etc.	..	..	..	..	..	..	..	..	..	..	..
Memo Items:											
Capacity to Import	..	..	..	..	..	..	..	..	..	..	..
Terms of Trade Adjustment	..	..	..	..	..	..	..	..	..	..	..
Gross Domestic Income	..	..	..	..	..	..	..	..	..	..	..
Gross National Income	..	..	..	..	..	..	..	..	..	..	..

DOMESTIC PRICES/DEFLATORS *(Index 1987 = 100)*

	1969	1970	1971	1972	1973	1974	1975	1976	1977	1978	1979
Overall (GDP)	23.0	24.4	25.4	27.2	28.1	33.3	36.7	38.2	41.5	44.2	47.6
Domestic Absorption	..	..	..	..	..	..	..	..	..	..	..
Agriculture	..	..	..	..	..	..	..	..	..	..	..
Industry	..	..	..	..	..	..	..	..	..	..	..
Manufacturing	..	..	..	..	..	..	..	..	..	..	..
Consumer Price Index	..	..	22.0	23.5	24.3	28.8	31.7	33.1	35.9	38.2	41.3

MANUFACTURING ACTIVITY

	1969	1970	1971	1972	1973	1974	1975	1976	1977	1978	1979
Employment (1987=100)	..	..	..	..	..	..	..	..	..	..	..
Real Earnings per Empl. (1987=100)	..	..	..	..	..	..	..	..	..	..	..
Real Output per Empl. (1987=100)	..	..	..	..	..	..	..	..	..	..	..
Earnings as % of Value Added	..	..	..	..	..	..	..	..	..	..	..

MONETARY HOLDINGS *(Millions of current Solomon Islands Dollars)*

	1969	1970	1971	1972	1973	1974	1975	1976	1977	1978	1979
Money Supply, Broadly Defined	..	..	..	..	..	..	..	..	..	27.29	39.56
Money	..	..	..	..	..	..	..	..	..	7.82	10.99
Currency Outside Banks	..	..	..	..	..	..	..	..	..	3.85	4.84
Demand Deposits	..	..	..	..	..	..	..	..	..	3.96	6.15
Quasi-Money	..	..	..	..	..	..	..	..	..	19.48	28.57

GOVERNMENT DEFICIT (-) OR SURPLUS *(Thousands of current Solomon Islands Dollars)*

	1969	1970	1971	1972	1973	1974	1975	1976	1977	1978	1979
Current Revenue	..	..	..	..	..	..	40	30	-630	720	-2,940
Current Expenditure	..	..	..	..	..	..	13,020	16,760	19,800	28,060	31,140
Current Budget Balance	..	..	..	..	..	..	9,530	10,930	14,080	16,740	20,080
Capital Receipts	..	..	..	..	..	..	3,490	5,830	5,720	11,320	11,060
Capital Payments	..	..	..	..	..	..	30	30	150	70	1,180
	..	..	..	..	..	..	3,480	5,830	6,500	10,670	15,180

1980	1981	1982	1983	1984	1985	1986	1987	1988	1989 estimate	NOTES	SOLOMON ISLANDS
400	500	570	550	620	520	580	550	550	570	..	**CURRENT GNP PER CAPITA (US $)**
230	238	247	255	265	274	284	293	303	314	..	**POPULATION (thousands)**
											USE AND ORIGIN OF RESOURCES
			(Millions of current Solomon Islands Dollars)								
89.50	104.40	124.80	137.10	213.90	227.40	237.50	287.90	365.40	403.00	..	Gross National Product (GNP)
-6.90	-8.00	-1.30	-5.40	-7.80	-9.50	-15.00	-6.70	-1.10	-1.20	..	Net Factor Income from Abroad
96.40	112.40	126.10	142.50	221.70	236.90	252.50	294.60	366.50	404.20	..	GDP at Market Prices
-28.60	-36.20	-18.20	-30.70	-8.40	-44.40	-69.50	-95.10	-152.30	..	..	Resource Balance
67.70	65.30	72.00	86.70	133.40	124.20	146.30	174.60	227.00	..	..	Exports of Goods & NFServices
96.30	101.50	90.20	117.40	141.80	168.60	215.80	269.70	379.30	..	..	Imports of Goods & NFServices
124.90	148.60	144.30	173.10	230.10	281.30	322.00	389.70	518.80	..	..	Domestic Absorption
67.60	84.00	77.20	86.60	127.10	152.50	169.90	218.40	253.70	..	..	Private Consumption, etc.
22.20	26.50	29.30	34.10	52.10	66.60	84.10	90.80	123.80	..	..	General Gov't Consumption
35.10	38.10	37.80	52.40	50.90	62.20	68.00	80.50	141.30	..	..	Gross Domestic Investment
..	..	..	..	..	..	..	..	..	..	..	Fixed Investment
10.80	14.40	18.00	18.00	23.70	26.80	31.40	39.80	44.50	..	..	Indirect Taxes, net
85.60	98.00	108.10	124.50	198.00	210.10	221.10	254.80	322.00	..	..	GDP at factor cost
..	..	..	..	..	..	..	..	..	..	..	Agriculture
..	..	..	..	..	..	..	..	..	..	..	Industry
..	..	..	..	..	..	..	..	..	..	..	Manufacturing
..	..	..	..	..	..	..	..	..	..	..	Services, etc.
6.60	1.90	19.60	21.80	42.50	17.80	-1.50	-14.60	-11.00	..	..	Gross Domestic Saving
0.30	-11.10	12.80	12.00	31.50	4.30	-15.90	-21.60	-15.10	..	..	Gross National Saving
			(Millions of 1987 Solomon Islands Dollars)								
164.58	186.82	204.85	226.91	270.70	230.44	272.86	287.90	306.51	323.89	..	Gross National Product
178.16	202.01	207.92	236.75	239.71	241.74	289.61	294.60	307.35	324.73	..	GDP at Market Prices
-142.47	-126.85	-70.37	-77.00	-107.40	-113.92	-70.50	-95.10	-184.29	..	..	Resource Balance
132.37	150.55	156.81	186.14	198.26	185.74	233.45	174.60	211.55	..	..	Exports of Goods & NFServices
274.84	277.41	227.18	263.14	305.66	299.67	303.95	269.70	395.85	..	..	Imports of Goods & NFServices
320.63	328.86	278.29	313.75	347.11	355.66	360.11	389.70	491.64	..	..	Domestic Absorption
182.04	189.57	148.23	168.82	197.89	192.62	191.55	218.40	295.25	..	..	Private Consumption, etc.
64.82	66.57	65.11	70.95	76.49	82.33	87.00	90.80	96.35	..	..	General Gov't Consumption
73.77	72.72	64.95	73.98	72.72	80.71	81.55	80.50	100.05	..	..	Gross Domestic Investment
..	..	..	..	..	..	..	..	..	..	..	Fixed Investment
..	..	..	..	..	..	..	..	..	..	..	GDP at factor cost
..	..	..	..	..	..	..	..	..	..	..	Agriculture
..	..	..	..	..	..	..	..	..	..	..	Industry
..	..	..	..	..	..	..	..	..	..	..	Manufacturing
..	..	..	..	..	..	..	..	..	..	..	Services, etc.
											Memo Items:
193.21	178.47	181.34	194.33	287.55	220.75	206.06	174.60	236.90	..	..	Capacity to Import
60.85	27.92	24.53	8.19	89.30	35.01	-27.39	0.00	25.35	..	..	Terms of Trade Adjustment
239.01	229.92	232.45	244.94	329.00	276.75	262.22	294.60	332.70	..	..	Gross Domestic Income
225.42	214.74	229.38	235.10	359.99	265.44	245.47	287.90	331.86	..	..	Gross National Income
			(Index 1987 = 100)								**DOMESTIC PRICES/DEFLATORS**
54.1	55.6	60.6	60.2	92.5	98.0	87.2	100.0	119.2	124.5	..	Overall (GDP)
39.0	45.2	51.9	55.2	66.3	79.1	89.4	100.0	105.5	..	..	Domestic Absorption
..	..	..	..	..	..	..	..	..	..	..	Agriculture
..	..	..	..	..	..	..	..	..	..	..	Industry
..	..	..	..	..	..	..	..	..	..	..	Manufacturing
46.7	54.3	61.4	65.2	72.4	79.3	90.1	100.0	116.7	134.2	..	Consumer Price Index
											MANUFACTURING ACTIVITY
..	..	..	..	..	..	..	..	..	..	..	Employment (1987=100)
..	..	..	..	..	..	..	..	..	..	..	Real Earnings per Empl. (1987=100)
..	..	..	..	..	..	..	..	..	..	..	Real Output per Empl. (1987=100)
..	..	..	..	..	..	..	..	..	..	..	Earnings as % of Value Added
			(Millions of current Solomon Islands Dollars)								**MONETARY HOLDINGS**
39.04	32.19	39.77	47.90	64.64	66.35	72.67	97.59	128.57	128.14	..	Money Supply, Broadly Defined
15.14	14.23	15.77	18.43	28.32	28.33	30.38	37.23	49.03	50.90	..	Money
5.66	6.42	7.15	9.30	12.75	13.88	13.58	16.84	20.21	22.65	..	Currency Outside Banks
9.48	7.81	8.63	9.13	15.57	14.44	16.80	20.39	28.82	28.25	..	Demand Deposits
23.90	17.96	24.00	29.47	36.32	38.02	42.29	60.37	79.53	77.24	..	Quasi-Money
			(Thousands of current Solomon Islands Dollars)								**GOVERNMENT DEFICIT (-) OR SURPLUS**
-3,600	-9,210	-13,040	-13,380	-6,530	-19,330	-15,060	-34,050	-32,960	..	..	Government Deficit (-) or Surplus
36,280	37,060	38,570	40,290	51,950	54,500	82,490	99,640	119,700	..	..	Current Revenue
24,350	30,850	34,490	39,240	46,110	59,550	65,890	77,100	92,430	..	..	Current Expenditure
11,930	6,210	4,080	1,050	5,840	-5,050	16,600	22,540	27,270	..	..	Current Budget Balance
570	190	190	110	460	740	..	10	300	..	..	Capital Receipts
16,100	15,610	17,310	14,540	12,830	15,020	31,660	56,600	60,530	..	..	Capital Payments

SOLOMON ISLANDS	1969	1970	1971	1972	1973	1974	1975	1976	1977	1978	1979
FOREIGN TRADE (CUSTOMS BASIS)					*(Thousands of current US dollars)*						
Value of Exports, fob	..	..	..	..	..	..	..	..	..	..	..
Nonfuel Primary Products	..	..	..	..	..	..	..	..	..	..	..
Fuels	..	..	..	..	..	..	..	..	..	..	..
Manufactures	..	..	..	..	..	..	..	..	..	..	..
Value of Imports, cif	11,000	13,000	15,000	17,000	18,000	27,000	33,000	30,000	33,000	42,000	70,000
Nonfuel Primary Products	..	..	..	..	..	..	..	..	..	..	..
Fuels	..	..	..	..	..	..	..	..	..	..	..
Manufactures	..	..	..	..	..	..	..	..	..	..	..
					(Index 1987 = 100)						
Terms of Trade	..	..	..	..	..	..	..	..	..	..	..
Export Prices, fob	..	..	..	..	..	..	..	..	..	..	..
Import Prices, cif	..	..	..	..	..	..	..	..	..	..	..
BALANCE OF PAYMENTS					*(Millions of current US dollars)*						
Exports of Goods & Services	..	..	..	..	..	..	..	..	..	..	..
Merchandise, fob	..	..	..	..	..	..	15.45	24.32	32.82	35.03	68.48
Nonfactor Services	..	..	..	..	..	..	2.49	3.06	3.33	5.27	5.77
Factor Services	..	..	..	..	..	..	..	..	..	..	..
Imports of Goods & Services	..	..	..	..	..	..	40.32	38.74	43.36	56.20	83.84
Merchandise, fob	..	..	..	..	..	..	28.54	25.79	28.61	35.37	58.43
Nonfactor Services	..	..	..	..	..	..	9.82	9.04	10.65	17.40	20.79
Factor Services	..	..	..	..	..	..	1.96	3.91	4.10	3.43	4.62
Long-Term Interest	..	0.00	0.00	0.00	0.00	0.00	0.00	0.00	0.00	0.00	0.00
Private Current Transfers, net	..	..	..	..	..	..	1.83	1.71	1.66	2.06	2.31
Workers' Remittances	..	..	..	..	..	..	..	..	..	..	..
Curr. A/C Bal before Off. Transf.	..	..	..	..	..	..	-20.55	-9.65	-5.54	-13.85	-7.28
Net Official Transfers	..	..	..	..	..	..	7.99	11.37	11.31	17.17	17.55
Curr. A/C Bal after Off. Transf.	..	..	..	..	..	..	-12.57	1.71	5.77	3.32	10.28
Long-Term Capital, net	..	..	..	..	..	..	7.85	4.89	7.32	6.18	5.77
Direct Investment	..	..	..	..	..	..	7.85	4.89	4.44	4.58	3.46
Long-Term Loans	..	0.00	0.50	0.10	0.00	0.00	9.10	0.00	0.20	0.50	2.50
Disbursements	..	0.00	0.50	0.10	0.00	0.00	9.10	0.00	0.20	0.50	2.50
Repayments	..	0.00	0.00	0.00	0.00	0.00	0.00	0.00	0.00	0.00	0.00
Other Long-Term Capital	..	..	..	..	..	..	-9.10	0.00	2.68	1.10	-0.19
Other Capital, net	..	..	..	..	..	..	6.02	-4.77	-6.21	5.72	-8.48
Change in Reserves	..	..	..	..	..	..	-1.31	-1.83	-6.88	-15.22	-7.57
Memo Item:					*(Solomon Islands Dollars per US dollar)*						
Conversion Factor (Annual Avg)	0.890	0.890	0.880	0.840	0.700	0.700	0.760	0.820	0.900	0.870	0.870
EXTERNAL DEBT (Total)					*(Millions of US dollars), outstanding at end of year*						
	..	0.10	0.60	0.60	0.60	0.60	8.80	7.40	8.50	11.50	13.80
Long-Term Debt (by debtor)	..	0.10	0.60	0.60	0.60	0.60	8.80	7.40	8.50	9.50	12.80
Central Bank, incl. IMF credit	..	0.00	0.00	0.00	0.00	0.00	0.00	0.00	0.00	0.00	0.00
Central Government	..	0.10	0.60	0.60	0.60	0.60	8.80	7.40	8.50	9.50	12.80
Rest of General Government	..	..	..	..	..	..	..	..	..	..	..
Non-financial Public Enterprises	..	..	..	..	..	..	..	..	..	..	..
Priv. Sector, incl non-guaranteed	..	..	..	..	..	..	..	..	..	..	..
Short-Term Debt	..	..	..	..	..	..	..	..	0.00	2.00	1.00
Memo Items:					*(Thousands of US dollars)*						
Int'l Reserves Excluding Gold	..	..	..	..	..	..	..	..	2,871	29,186	36,957
Gold Holdings (at market price)	..	..	..	..	..	..	..	..	..	..	..
SOCIAL INDICATORS											
Total Fertility Rate	..	6.4	6.5	6.7	6.8	7.0	7.1	7.3	7.4	7.3	7.2
Infant Mortality Rate	..	..	..	..	..	..	..	..	46.0	49.6	53.2
Life Expectancy at Birth	..	40.3	41.5	42.7	43.9	45.2	46.4	47.6	48.8	50.0	51.0
Urban Population, % of total	8.9	8.9	8.9	9.0	9.0	9.1	9.1	9.1	9.1	9.2	9.2
Food Prod. per capita (1987=100)	97.2	99.8	98.3	94.5	93.7	90.9	90.7	100.0	105.6	114.0	122.8
Labor Force, Agriculture (%)	..	..	..	..	..	..	..	..	..	..	..
Labor Force, Female (%)	..	..	..	..	..	..	..	..	..	..	..
Primary Schl. Enroll. Ratio	..	..	..	..	..	..	..	..	..	..	..
Primary Schl. Enroll. Ratio, Female	..	..	..	..	..	..	..	..	..	..	..
Secondary Schl. Enroll. Ratio	..	..	..	..	..	..	..	..	..	..	..

1980	1981	1982	1983	1984	1985	1986	1987	1988	1989	NOTES	SOLOMON ISLANDS
											FOREIGN TRADE (CUSTOMS BASIS)
			(Thousands of current US dollars)								
73,000	66,190	58,280	61,990	93,100	70,100	66,000	..	..	..	..	Value of Exports, fob
..	..	..	..	..	..	..	..	..	..	..	Nonfuel Primary Products
..	..	..	..	..	..	..	..	..	..	..	Fuels
..	..	..	..	..	..	..	..	..	..	..	Manufactures
89,000	91,000	71,000	74,000	79,000	83,000	72,000	..	..	..	..	Value of Imports, cif
..	..	..	..	..	..	..	..	..	..	..	Nonfuel Primary Products
..	..	..	..	..	..	..	..	..	..	..	Fuels
..	..	..	..	..	..	..	..	..	..	..	Manufactures
				(Index 1987 = 100)							
..	..	..	..	..	..	..	..	..	..	..	Terms of Trade
..	..	..	..	..	..	..	..	..	..	..	Export Prices, fob
..	..	..	..	..	..	..	..	..	..	..	Import Prices, cif
			(Millions of current US dollars)								**BALANCE OF PAYMENTS**
..	..	77.64	81.84	108.27	87.32	84.18	89.05	111.69	108.58	..	Exports of Goods & Services
73.27	66.19	58.28	61.99	93.11	70.98	63.85	63.20	81.92	74.70	..	Merchandise, fob
11.69	12.99	14.83	16.37	10.52	12.29	17.23	22.61	26.22	30.00	..	Nonfactor Services
..	..	4.53	3.48	4.63	4.05	3.10	3.24	3.55	3.88	..	Factor Services
117.01	117.45	97.52	102.04	115.41	117.03	123.11	128.14	170.90	177.00	..	Imports of Goods & Services
74.11	75.85	59.11	61.47	67.60	71.85	67.53	69.39	101.56	94.36	..	Merchandise, fob
27.96	37.69	26.98	28.47	31.80	35.86	46.05	48.27	57.62	72.08	..	Nonfactor Services
14.94	3.91	11.43	12.10	16.02	9.32	9.53	10.48	11.72	10.55	..	Factor Services
0.00	0.10	0.10	0.10	1.10	1.70	1.70	2.10	3.50	3.60	..	Long-Term Interest
0.72	-5.75	-5.66	-3.83	-2.51	-2.70	0.34	-0.15	-1.44	1.22	..	Private Current Transfers, net
..	..	..	..	..	..	..	..	..	..	..	Workers' Remittances
-31.33	-44.01	-25.54	-24.03	-9.66	-32.42	-38.59	-39.24	-60.65	-67.20	..	Curr. A/C Bal before Off. Transf.
19.16	17.47	11.43	14.89	14.60	11.82	38.64	31.90	42.54	37.28	..	Net Official Transfers
-12.17	-26.55	-14.11	-9.14	4.95	-20.60	0.06	-7.34	-18.10	-29.91	..	Curr. A/C Bal after Off. Transf.
6.39	4.14	22.86	15.24	-1.96	14.59	2.93	18.47	23.58	20.58	..	Long-Term Capital, net
2.41	0.23	1.03	0.44	1.96	0.88	-2.01	8.79	3.36	5.67	..	Direct Investment
4.00	4.20	4.10	6.80	11.70	12.70	14.10	14.30	9.90	1.90	..	Long-Term Loans
4.00	4.20	4.10	6.90	12.40	13.80	15.40	15.70	13.00	7.60	..	Disbursements
0.00	0.00	0.00	0.10	0.70	1.10	1.30	1.40	3.10	5.70	..	Repayments
-0.02	-0.29	17.73	8.00	-15.63	1.01	-9.16	-4.62	10.32	13.01	..	Other Long-Term Capital
-3.25	15.77	5.94	3.46	-2.06	-3.32	-11.69	-5.21	-0.78	-2.07	..	Other Capital, net
9.04	6.64	-14.69	-9.56	-0.92	9.33	8.70	-5.92	-4.69	11.40	..	Change in Reserves
											Memo Item:
			(Solomon Islands Dollars per US dollar)								
0.830	0.870	0.970	1.150	1.270	1.480	1.740	2.000	2.080	2.290	..	Conversion Factor (Annual Avg)
		(Millions of US dollars), outstanding at end of year									
19.40	23.40	28.00	34.30	44.50	66.20	77.70	98.20	104.60	103.20	..	**EXTERNAL DEBT (Total)**
17.40	20.40	25.00	31.30	40.50	57.20	74.70	96.80	103.00	101.80	..	Long-Term Debt (by debtor)
0.00	0.90	2.70	3.50	3.10	3.00	3.50	2.20	1.70	1.40	..	Central Bank, incl. IMF credit
17.40	19.50	22.30	27.80	37.40	54.20	71.20	94.60	101.30	100.40	..	Central Government
..	..	..	..	..	..	..	..	..	..	..	Rest of General Government
..	..	..	..	..	..	..	..	..	..	..	Non-financial Public Enterprises
..	..	..	..	..	..	..	..	..	..	..	Priv. Sector, incl non-guaranteed
2.00	3.00	3.00	3.00	4.00	9.00	3.00	1.40	1.60	1.40	..	Short-Term Debt
											Memo Items:
				(Thousands of US dollars)							
29,605	21,589	37,230	47,330	44,704	35,606	29,572	36,749	39,620	26,162	..	Int'l Reserves Excluding Gold
..	..	..	..	..	..	..	..	..	..	..	Gold Holdings (at market price)
											SOCIAL INDICATORS
7.2	7.1	7.0	6.9	6.9	6.8	6.7	6.6	6.6	6.5	..	Total Fertility Rate
56.8	60.4	64.0	61.8	59.6	57.4	55.2	53.0	51.4	49.8	..	Infant Mortality Rate
52.0	53.0	60.6	61.2	61.7	62.3	62.8	63.3	63.7	64.0	..	Life Expectancy at Birth
9.2	9.3	9.4	9.5	9.6	9.7	9.9	10.1	10.2	10.4	..	Urban Population, % of total
116.9	129.3	125.9	123.0	125.1	122.5	106.2	100.0	102.9	101.1	..	Food Prod. per capita (1987=100)
..	..	..	..	..	..	..	..	..	..	..	Labor Force, Agriculture (%)
..	..	..	..	..	..	..	..	..	..	..	Labor Force, Female (%)
..	..	..	..	..	..	..	..	..	..	..	Primary Schl. Enroll. Ratio
..	..	..	..	..	..	..	..	..	..	..	Primary Schl. Enroll. Ratio, Female
..	..	..	..	..	..	..	..	..	..	..	Secondary Schl. Enroll. Ratio

SOMALIA	1969	1970	1971	1972	1973	1974	1975	1976	1977	1978	1979
CURRENT GNP PER CAPITA (US $)	90	90	90	100	110	110	160	180	170	150	130
POPULATION (thousands)	3,502	3,595	3,696	3,799	3,903	4,009	4,115	4,222	4,329	4,439	4,553
USE AND ORIGIN OF RESOURCES				*(Millions of current Somali Shillings)*							
Gross National Product (GNP)	2,139	2,260	2,357	2,913	3,195	2,956	4,477	5,090	6,866	8,166	9,031
Net Factor Income from Abroad	-6	2	-3	3	10	13	2	8	-14	-15	33
GDP at Market Prices	2,144	2,258	2,360	2,910	3,185	2,943	4,475	5,082	6,880	8,181	8,998
Resource Balance	-164	-118	-157	-140	-413	-663	-645	-702	-2,680	-2,476	-4,609
Exports of Goods & NFServices	343	260	313	458	443	514	558	510	1,394	2,114	2,187
Imports of Goods & NFServices	507	378	470	598	856	1,177	1,203	1,212	4,074	4,590	6,796
Domestic Absorption	2,309	2,376	2,517	3,050	3,598	3,606	5,120	5,784	9,560	10,657	13,607
Private Consumption, etc.	1,827	1,878	2,006	2,059	2,519	2,091	3,203	3,404	7,116	6,770	7,959
General Gov't Consumption	217	233	229	596	622	724	909	861	970	1,540	3,580
Gross Domestic Investment	265	265	282	395	457	791	1,008	1,519	1,474	2,347	2,068
Fixed Investment	..	205	218	325	361	690	684	818	1,119	1,844	2,183
Indirect Taxes, net	241	254	287	329	382	475	448	478	572	1,034	1,164
GDP at factor cost	1,904	2,005	2,074	2,581	2,803	2,468	4,026	4,603	6,308	7,147	7,834
Agriculture	1,153	1,190	1,191	1,589	1,716	1,126	2,181	2,592	3,848	4,498	4,595
Industry	283	319	355	378	370	504	504	640	759	566	794
Manufacturing	152	186	210	214	211	200	226	337	323	301	446
Services, etc.	468	495	527	614	717	839	1,342	1,371	1,701	2,083	2,445
Gross Domestic Saving	101	147	125	255	44	128	363	817	-1,206	-129	-2,541
Gross National Saving	..	154	137	270	71	163	377	832	-1,206	347	-2,282
				(Millions of 1987 Somali Shillings)							
Gross National Product	89,024	93,417	95,677	105,603	103,802	82,736	110,919	110,653	138,005	145,044	140,701
GDP at Market Prices	89,157	93,242	95,706	105,412	103,391	82,295	110,803	110,399	138,235	145,252	140,090
Resource Balance	-3,149	-2,098	-6,310	1,210	-5,795	-11,310	-12,339	-16,508	-60,342	-49,667	-66,814
Exports of Goods & NFServices	17,925	13,496	16,104	22,794	17,499	15,386	13,794	11,543	21,717	26,897	28,293
Imports of Goods & NFServices	21,074	15,595	22,413	21,584	23,294	26,696	26,134	28,051	82,059	76,565	95,107
Domestic Absorption	92,306	95,340	102,016	104,202	109,186	93,605	123,143	126,908	198,577	194,919	206,904
Private Consumption, etc.	73,804	76,362	83,211	67,689	73,345	57,779	84,918	87,993	146,982	126,978	122,663
General Gov't Consumption	8,059	8,605	8,494	22,820	22,364	22,012	23,146	19,108	19,614	28,098	52,363
Gross Domestic Investment	10,444	10,374	10,311	13,692	13,477	13,815	15,078	19,807	31,981	39,843	31,877
Fixed Investment	..	6,297	6,297	5,817	8,864	8,631	9,135	9,371	25,432	31,836	32,238
GDP at factor cost	81,515	84,877	85,630	93,048	90,503	68,197	97,580	97,978	124,406	122,647	119,508
Agriculture	..	46,582	45,799	48,661	46,508	30,071	52,069	53,938	72,974	75,649	71,200
Industry	..	17,411	18,045	18,277	15,150	15,442	14,894	16,635	18,117	11,256	13,615
Manufacturing	..	8,010	8,567	8,647	7,199	6,393	6,883	8,932	7,795	6,589	7,893
Services, etc.	..	25,228	26,560	31,542	34,200	29,685	35,251	31,238	35,540	35,528	36,016
Memo Items:											
Capacity to Import	14,247	10,726	14,926	16,531	12,055	11,658	12,116	11,804	28,078	35,263	30,606
Terms of Trade Adjustment	-3,677	-2,770	-1,177	-6,263	-5,444	-3,728	-1,678	261	6,361	8,366	2,313
Gross Domestic Income	85,480	90,472	94,529	99,149	97,947	78,567	109,125	110,661	144,596	153,618	142,403
Gross National Income	85,347	90,648	94,500	99,340	98,358	79,008	109,241	110,914	144,366	153,410	143,014
DOMESTIC PRICES/DEFLATORS				*(Index 1987 = 100)*							
Overall (GDP)	2.4	2.4	2.5	2.8	3.1	3.6	4.0	4.6	5.0	5.6	6.4
Domestic Absorption	2.5	2.5	2.5	2.9	3.3	3.9	4.2	4.6	4.8	5.5	6.6
Agriculture	..	2.6	2.6	3.3	3.7	3.7	4.2	4.8	5.3	5.9	6.5
Industry	..	1.8	2.0	2.1	2.4	3.3	3.4	3.8	4.2	5.0	5.8
Manufacturing	..	2.3	2.4	2.5	2.9	3.1	3.3	3.8	4.1	4.6	5.7
Consumer Price Index	2.2	2.3	2.2	2.2	2.3	2.7	3.3	3.7	4.1	4.6	5.7
MANUFACTURING ACTIVITY											
Employment (1987=100)	..	..	..	..	..	..	..	..	..	..	..
Real Earnings per Empl. (1987=100)	..	..	..	..	..	..	..	..	..	..	..
Real Output per Empl. (1987=100)	..	..	..	..	..	..	..	..	..	..	..
Earnings as % of Value Added	25.4	27.5	25.5	18.3	26.5	37.1	31.5	26.1	25.2	31.4	32.8
MONETARY HOLDINGS				*(Millions of current Somali Shillings)*							
Money Supply, Broadly Defined	327	465	391	518	608	783	1,005	1,200	1,545	2,047	2,813
Money	280	376	329	441	507	629	826	995	1,325	1,728	2,335
Currency Outside Banks	142	146	146	221	248	306	389	414	622	883	1,153
Demand Deposits	137	230	183	219	259	322	436	581	703	845	1,183
Quasi-Money	48	89	62	77	101	154	179	205	219	319	478
				(Millions of current Somali Shillings)							
GOVERNMENT DEFICIT (-) OR SURPLUS	..	..	..	18.5	-33.4	-59.6	-73.1	-120.3	-367.4	-700.1	..
Current Revenue	..	..	..	412.8	438.0	585.1	622.3	700.2	857.0	1,347.0	..
Current Expenditure	..	..	..	347.4	412.3	521.8	586.7	658.9	736.0	1,288.0	..
Current Budget Balance	..	..	..	65.4	25.7	63.3	35.6	41.3	121.0	59.0	..
Capital Receipts	..	..	..	..	..	..	4.6	3.8	7.7	5.5	..
Capital Payments	..	..	..	46.9	59.1	122.9	113.3	165.4	496.1	764.6	..

1980	1981	1982	1983	1984	1985	1986	1987	1988	1989 estimate	NOTES	SOMALIA
140	160	170	150	150	160	150	170	170	170	A	CURRENT GNP PER CAPITA (US $)
4,674	4,802	4,936	5,078	5,227	5,384	5,549	5,721	5,902	6,089	..	POPULATION (thousands)

(Millions of current Somali Shillings) — USE AND ORIGIN OF RESOURCES

1980	1981	1982	1983	1984	1985	1986	1987	1988	1989 estimate	NOTES	SOMALIA
17,347	21,908	28,646	34,766	58,845	82,476	113,153	159,026	270,302	575,543	..	Gross National Product (GNP)
-25	-142	-459	-291	-3,478	-4,876	-7,817	-8,510	-16,603	-43,079	..	Net Factor Income from Abroad
17,372	22,050	29,105	35,057	62,323	87,352	120,970	167,536	286,905	618,622	..	GDP at Market Prices
-9,608	-9,603	-12,248	-17,198	-28,974	-31,712	-48,687	-64,212	-71,709	-218,863	..	Resource Balance
5,764	5,473	7,558	8,283	9,092	14,040	15,162	17,525	22,236	51,809	f	Exports of Goods & NFServices
15,372	15,076	19,806	25,481	38,066	45,752	63,849	81,737	93,945	270,672	..	Imports of Goods & NFServices
26,980	31,653	41,353	52,255	91,297	119,064	169,657	231,748	358,614	837,485	..	Domestic Absorption
16,902	20,711	28,965	37,443	65,635	81,238	112,466	142,822	246,493	563,317	..	Private Consumption, etc.
2,713	4,864	3,866	6,952	10,580	16,128	28,503	41,222	58,452	141,686	..	General Gov't Consumption
7,365	6,078	8,522	7,860	15,082	21,698	28,688	47,704	53,669	132,482	..	Gross Domestic Investment
7,484	5,100	7,298	9,236	14,185	19,200	27,485	39,651	40,967	117,363	..	Fixed Investment
1,030	1,780	2,048	2,949	2,540	4,099	7,197	7,365	10,717	24,967	..	Indirect Taxes, net
16,342	20,270	27,057	32,108	59,783	83,253	113,773	160,171	276,188	593,655	..	GDP at factor cost
11,181	13,841	18,325	21,327	40,592	55,583	70,887	101,173	180,498	385,070	..	Agriculture
1,305	1,555	2,192	2,389	4,348	6,396	11,470	16,238	25,857	56,643	..	Industry
774	932	1,423	1,572	2,805	4,145	6,240	8,383	14,474	31,371	..	Manufacturing
3,856	4,874	6,540	8,392	14,843	21,274	31,416	42,760	69,833	151,942	..	Services, etc.
-2,243	-3,525	-3,726	-9,338	-13,892	-10,014	-19,999	-16,508	-18,040	-86,381	..	Gross Domestic Saving
-1,908	-3,330	-4,037	-9,327	-14,108	-14,122	-26,082	-20,849	-33,552	-130,883	..	Gross National Saving

(Millions of 1987 Somali Shillings)

1980	1981	1982	1983	1984	1985	1986	1987	1988	1989 estimate	NOTES	SOMALIA
134,086	143,993	147,516	135,038	132,646	143,147	147,428	159,026	155,719	157,889	..	Gross National Product
134,202	144,888	150,053	136,210	140,833	152,175	157,879	167,536	165,381	169,845	..	GDP at Market Prices
-64,919	-64,393	-76,534	-79,999	-78,158	-70,791	-70,423	-64,212	-39,443	-61,466	..	Resource Balance
42,998	31,682	30,872	31,635	24,388	26,117	18,043	17,525	12,850	14,410	f	Exports of Goods & NFServices
107,917	96,075	107,406	111,634	102,546	96,908	88,466	81,737	52,293	75,877	..	Imports of Goods & NFServices
199,121	209,281	226,587	216,210	218,992	222,966	228,303	231,748	204,824	231,312	..	Domestic Absorption
122,675	136,944	158,635	150,339	151,165	145,566	148,871	142,822	138,992	153,378	..	Private Consumption, etc.
19,673	31,003	20,538	26,692	23,709	28,547	37,120	41,222	33,346	38,415	..	General Gov't Consumption
56,774	41,333	47,413	39,179	44,119	48,853	42,312	47,704	32,486	39,520	..	Gross Domestic Investment
55,370	33,952	40,880	41,848	40,040	41,563	39,567	39,651	23,833	33,810	..	Fixed Investment
126,120	133,308	139,530	124,758	135,088	145,019	148,488	160,171	159,192	162,980	..	GDP at factor cost
74,156	84,800	87,203	76,547	86,489	94,707	93,488	101,173	104,981	106,737	..	Agriculture
14,213	11,953	13,671	11,378	11,713	11,993	15,475	16,238	14,796	15,393	..	Industry
8,611	7,176	8,938	7,241	6,719	7,208	7,992	8,383	7,964	8,202	..	Manufacturing
39,680	34,884	37,830	36,833	36,886	38,320	39,525	42,760	39,415	40,850	..	Services, etc.

Memo Items:

1980	1981	1982	1983	1984	1985	1986	1987	1988	1989 estimate	NOTES	SOMALIA
40,465	34,878	40,986	36,288	24,493	29,738	21,008	17,525	12,377	14,523	..	Capacity to Import
-2,532	3,196	10,115	4,653	105	3,622	2,965	0	-473	113	..	Terms of Trade Adjustment
131,670	148,084	160,167	140,864	140,939	155,797	160,844	167,536	164,908	169,958	..	Gross Domestic Income
131,554	147,189	157,631	139,692	132,751	146,768	150,393	159,026	155,246	158,002	..	Gross National Income

(Index 1987 = 100) — DOMESTIC PRICES/DEFLATORS

1980	1981	1982	1983	1984	1985	1986	1987	1988	1989 estimate	NOTES	SOMALIA
12.9	15.2	19.4	25.7	44.3	57.4	76.6	100.0	173.5	364.2	..	Overall (GDP)
13.5	15.1	18.3	24.2	41.7	53.4	74.3	100.0	175.1	362.1	..	Domestic Absorption
15.1	16.3	21.0	27.9	46.9	58.7	75.8	100.0	171.9	360.8	..	Agriculture
9.2	13.0	16.0	21.0	37.1	53.3	74.1	100.0	174.8	368.0	..	Industry
9.0	13.0	15.9	21.7	41.7	57.5	78.1	100.0	181.7	382.5	..	Manufacturing
9.0	13.0	16.0	21.8	41.7	57.5	78.0	100.0	181.9	..	..	Consumer Price Index

MANUFACTURING ACTIVITY

1980	1981	1982	1983	1984	1985	1986	1987	1988	1989 estimate	NOTES	SOMALIA
..	..	..	..	..	..	..	..	..	..	J	Employment (1987=100)
..	..	..	..	..	..	..	..	..	..	J	Real Earnings per Empl. (1987=100)
..	..	..	..	..	..	..	..	..	..	J	Real Output per Empl. (1987=100)
..	..	..	..	..	..	26.5	..	..	..	J	Earnings as % of Value Added

(Millions of current Somali Shillings) — MONETARY HOLDINGS

1980	1981	1982	1983	1984	1985	1986	1987	1988	1989 estimate	NOTES	SOMALIA
3,381	4,421	5,116	5,501	6,934	12,558	16,834	38,234	60,114	157,986	..	Money Supply, Broadly Defined
2,783	3,674	4,033	4,309	5,334	9,773	12,143	30,046	45,436	139,827	..	Money
1,508	1,891	1,456	1,355	1,900	3,787	5,209	12,327	21,033	70,789	..	Currency Outside Banks
1,275	1,783	2,577	2,954	3,434	5,986	6,934	17,719	24,403	69,038	..	Demand Deposits
598	747	1,083	1,192	1,600	2,785	4,691	8,188	14,678	18,159	..	Quasi-Money

(Millions of current Somali Shillings)

1980	1981	1982	1983	1984	1985	1986	1987	1988	1989 estimate	NOTES	SOMALIA
..	..	..	..	..	..	..	..	..	..	..	GOVERNMENT DEFICIT (-) OR SURPLUS
..	..	..	..	..	..	..	..	..	..	..	Current Revenue
..	..	..	..	..	..	..	..	..	..	..	Current Expenditure
..	..	..	..	..	..	..	..	..	..	..	Current Budget Balance
..	..	..	..	..	..	..	..	..	..	..	Capital Receipts
..	..	..	..	..	..	..	..	..	..	..	Capital Payments

SOMALIA	1969	1970	1971	1972	1973	1974	1975	1976	1977	1978	1979
FOREIGN TRADE (CUSTOMS BASIS)					*(Millions of current US dollars)*						
Value of Exports, fob	33.30	31.10	38.10	56.50	57.10	64.00	88.60	81.00	71.30	109.50	106.00
Nonfuel Primary Products	31.67	29.18	36.07	55.51	55.75	63.13	85.75	78.87	68.64	107.95	103.72
Fuels	0.00	0.00	0.00	0.01	0.03	0.00	0.02	0.05	0.18	0.32	1.24
Manufactures	1.63	1.92	2.03	0.98	1.32	0.87	2.83	2.08	2.48	1.23	1.04
Value of Imports, cif	55.50	45.60	55.80	72.20	112.00	153.60	162.30	175.90	205.70	275.10	394.00
Nonfuel Primary Products	18.59	18.19	25.08	21.98	30.24	39.47	49.08	54.15	55.86	68.90	103.46
Fuels	2.88	2.87	2.36	3.39	4.77	10.31	10.00	12.03	8.97	18.25	21.58
Manufactures	34.03	24.53	28.36	46.83	76.99	103.82	103.22	109.71	140.87	187.95	268.96
					(Index 1987 = 100)						
Terms of Trade	159.1	160.3	141.6	167.8	175.6	108.5	89.4	106.0	100.0	119.9	136.7
Export Prices, fob	42.9	44.9	46.3	56.1	72.2	60.4	55.2	64.6	64.4	86.6	114.1
Import Prices, cif	27.0	28.0	32.7	33.5	41.1	55.6	61.7	61.0	64.5	72.2	83.5
BALANCE OF PAYMENTS					*(Millions of current US dollars)*						
Exports of Goods & Services	..	43.30	49.25	66.77	73.08	84.55	115.22	111.76	104.05	151.83	153.25
Merchandise, fob	..	31.10	38.11	56.46	57.10	63.98	88.63	81.05	71.33	109.47	106.02
Nonfactor Services	..	11.20	10.23	9.34	13.59	17.92	23.31	27.59	29.71	36.46	37.71
Factor Services	..	1.00	0.90	0.98	2.38	2.65	3.28	3.12	3.02	5.91	9.52
Imports of Goods & Services	..	61.90	67.70	90.98	140.43	187.97	217.45	221.78	244.89	322.37	452.95
Merchandise, fob	..	40.40	49.55	62.75	97.52	133.73	141.08	153.09	179.05	239.43	342.86
Nonfactor Services	..	20.80	16.85	27.47	41.96	53.40	73.33	66.85	65.05	80.56	103.05
Factor Services	..	0.70	1.30	0.76	0.95	0.84	3.04	1.85	0.79	2.38	7.04
Long-Term Interest	..	0.40	0.60	0.80	0.90	1.10	1.30	0.80	1.20	1.30	1.00
Private Current Transfers, net	..	0.70	2.11	1.85	2.74	3.49	1.94	1.15	2.22	78.06	35.90
Workers' Remittances	..	..	..	..	..	..	..	..	..	..	36.65
Curr. A/C Bal before Off. Transf.	..	-17.90	-16.35	-22.37	-64.61	-99.94	-100.29	-108.87	-138.62	-92.47	-263.80
Net Official Transfers	..	12.20	17.15	15.20	25.87	48.23	100.29	39.72	105.85	27.80	58.08
Curr. A/C Bal after Off. Transf.	..	-5.70	0.80	-7.17	-38.74	-51.71	0.00	-69.16	-32.77	-64.67	-205.72
Long-Term Capital, net	..	11.00	4.31	17.70	26.11	60.97	52.82	69.62	64.32	79.76	86.10
Direct Investment	..	4.50	1.71	4.45	0.60	0.72	6.68	2.19	7.78	0.30	..
Long-Term Loans	..	3.70	5.40	15.40	15.50	46.90	59.00	55.50	77.70	93.10	86.90
Disbursements	..	4.20	6.00	16.60	17.30	48.90	61.20	57.20	79.90	96.20	90.10
Repayments	..	0.50	0.60	1.20	1.80	2.00	2.20	1.70	2.20	3.10	3.20
Other Long-Term Capital	..	2.80	-2.79	-2.15	10.01	13.35	-12.86	11.92	-21.16	-13.64	-0.80
Other Capital, net	..	-1.80	-2.27	5.19	3.53	9.84	-7.69	-1.04	22.62	12.43	12.35
Change in Reserves	..	-3.50	-2.85	-15.72	9.11	-19.10	-45.13	0.58	-54.16	-27.52	107.27
Memo Item:					*(Somali Shillings per US dollar)*						
Conversion Factor (Annual Avg)	7.14	7.14	7.13	6.98	6.28	6.30	6.30	6.30	6.30	6.30	6.30
Additional Conversion Factor	7.14	7.14	7.13	6.98	6.28	6.29	6.29	6.29	13.80	14.48	15.24
					(Millions of US dollars), outstanding at end of year						
EXTERNAL DEBT (Total)	..	77.1	84.4	101.1	124.2	174.7	228.7	287.0	392.0	515.3	571.3
Long-Term Debt (by debtor)	..	77.1	84.4	101.1	124.2	174.7	228.7	287.0	380.0	493.3	545.3
Central Bank, incl. IMF credit	..	2.2	1.8	1.3	0.8	0.4	0.1	0.1	0.1	0.2	0.2
Central Government	..	71.8	82.6	97.0	120.8	162.3	216.8	275.2	366.4	477.5	528.3
Rest of General Government	..	..	..	..	..	..	..	..	..	..	..
Non-financial Public Enterprises	..	3.1	0.0	2.8	2.6	12.0	11.8	11.7	13.5	14.6	15.8
Priv. Sector, incl non-guaranteed	..	0.0	0.0	0.0	0.0	0.0	0.0	0.0	0.0	1.0	1.0
Short-Term Debt	..	..	..	..	..	..	..	..	12.0	22.0	26.0
Memo Items:					*(Thousands of US dollars)*						
Int'l Reserves Excluding Gold	13,420	21,140	26,659	31,331	34,997	42,323	68,368	84,876	119,977	126,341	43,791
Gold Holdings (at market price)	810	112	131	195	337	492	370	355	1,777	3,350	7,589
SOCIAL INDICATORS											
Total Fertility Rate	6.7	6.7	6.7	6.7	6.7	6.7	6.7	6.7	6.7	6.7	6.7
Infant Mortality Rate	159.2	157.8	156.4	155.0	153.8	152.6	151.4	150.2	149.0	147.8	146.6
Life Expectancy at Birth	39.7	40.1	40.5	40.9	41.4	41.9	42.3	42.8	43.3	43.6	43.9
Urban Population, % of total	22.5	23.1	23.8	24.5	25.1	25.8	26.5	27.2	28.0	28.7	29.5
Food Prod. per capita (1987=100)	131.4	131.2	127.2	131.6	123.5	116.6	122.7	119.1	116.5	113.0	105.1
Labor Force, Agriculture (%)	79.7	79.4	78.9	78.5	78.1	77.8	77.5	77.0	76.6	76.2	75.9
Labor Force, Female (%)	41.2	41.2	41.1	41.1	41.0	41.0	40.9	40.9	40.8	40.7	40.7
Primary Schl. Enroll. Ratio	..	11.0	..	..	..	..	59.0	45.0	40.0	43.0	41.0
Primary Schl. Enroll. Ratio, Female	..	5.0	..	..	..	..	42.0	32.0	28.0	30.0	29.0
Secondary Schl. Enroll. Ratio	..	5.0	..	..	..	..	6.0	4.0	4.0	5.0	6.0

1980	1981	1982	1983	1984	1985	1986	1987	1988	1989 estimate	NOTES	SOMALIA
				(Millions of current US dollars)							**FOREIGN TRADE (CUSTOMS BASIS)**
133.30	175.40	170.80	98.40	54.80	90.60	88.50	94.00	59.00	..	..	Value of Exports, fob
125.81	174.39	167.42	96.28	53.44	89.23	87.07	92.34	56.00	..	..	Nonfuel Primary Products
6.43	0.37	2.46	1.59	1.03	1.02	0.80	1.00	0.00	..	..	Fuels
1.06	0.64	0.92	0.53	0.32	0.35	0.63	0.66	3.00	..	..	Manufactures
461.30	425.70	541.60	416.10	535.10	380.00	440.00	452.00	307.00	..	..	Value of Imports, cif
170.18	113.50	155.26	121.04	149.36	98.84	87.15	86.25	91.61	..	..	Nonfuel Primary Products
3.41	9.33	12.08	8.62	23.99	19.81	8.30	10.96	12.02	..	..	Fuels
287.71	302.87	374.27	286.43	361.75	261.34	344.56	354.80	203.36	..	..	Manufactures
				(Index 1987 = 100)							
114.4	111.5	108.9	116.2	110.2	105.9	96.5	100.0	97.6	..	..	Terms of Trade
109.9	103.2	98.1	102.6	96.1	91.4	90.1	100.0	107.5	..	..	Export Prices, fob
96.0	92.6	90.0	88.3	87.2	86.3	93.3	100.0	110.1	..	..	Import Prices, cif
				(Millions of current US dollars)							**BALANCE OF PAYMENTS**
204.50	255.44	256.14	177.20	106.74	127.60	116.46	141.99	81.09	94.82	f	Exports of Goods & Services
133.33	175.36	170.81	98.44	54.76	90.57	88.51	103.63	58.43	67.70	..	Merchandise, fob
66.20	74.25	83.39	77.03	51.00	35.93	25.43	35.82	22.66	27.12	..	Nonfactor Services
4.97	5.83	1.93	1.73	0.97	1.10	2.53	2.54	0.00	..	..	Factor Services
540.56	519.46	610.28	486.08	595.65	448.01	488.77	642.95	403.15	574.22	f	Imports of Goods & Services
401.52	370.53	471.35	362.09	465.67	330.74	383.04	485.18	211.01	338.30	..	Merchandise, fob
133.19	135.03	130.97	117.60	123.47	96.76	101.91	140.62	131.59	157.08	..	Nonfactor Services
5.85	13.90	7.95	6.39	6.52	20.51	3.82	17.15	60.55	78.84	..	Factor Services
1.90	3.40	6.50	9.50	3.00	2.80	3.70	3.80	2.80	10.30	..	Long-Term Interest
57.25	53.57	13.75	19.12	162.93	19.44	24.09	39.64	6.40	-2.90	..	Private Current Transfers, net
57.25	7.15	19.90	21.70	..	..	..	..	..	..	..	Workers' Remittances
-278.81	-210.45	-340.39	-289.77	-325.98	-300.96	-348.22	-461.32	-315.66	-482.30	..	Curr. A/C Bal before Off. Transf.
142.62	127.09	162.94	148.17	194.03	204.32	260.56	361.14	217.30	331.20	..	Net Official Transfers
-136.19	-83.37	-177.45	-141.59	-131.95	-96.65	-87.67	-100.17	-98.36	-151.10	..	Curr. A/C Bal after Off. Transf.
90.68	44.65	138.25	68.27	95.89	76.98	45.58	58.92	-22.50	13.49	f	Long-Term Capital, net
..	..	-0.76	-8.23	-14.94	-0.71	-0.12	-11.43	-0.05	..	..	Direct Investment
106.40	400.70	182.60	158.80	143.20	111.10	103.20	71.80	62.60	68.20	..	Long-Term Loans
113.50	443.90	187.60	166.40	146.90	113.40	106.40	75.60	63.70	75.20	..	Disbursements
7.10	43.20	5.00	7.60	3.70	2.30	3.20	3.80	1.10	7.00	..	Repayments
-15.72	-356.05	-43.59	-82.29	-32.37	-33.41	-57.49	-1.45	-85.05	-54.71	..	Other Long-Term Capital
22.47	18.65	75.19	-4.38	18.04	26.91	18.35	39.44	193.26	163.41	f	Other Capital, net
23.04	20.06	-36.00	77.70	18.02	-7.24	23.73	1.82	-72.40	-25.80	..	Change in Reserves
				(Somali Shillings per US dollar)							Memo Item:
6.30	6.30	10.75	15.79	20.02	39.49	72.00	105.18	170.45	490.68	..	Conversion Factor (Annual Avg)
28.78	31.54	37.58	47.77	79.06	99.50	129.59	163.72	274.21	546.39	..	Additional Conversion Factor
				(Millions of US dollars), outstanding at end of year							
659.8	1,055.9	1,221.8	1,410.1	1,497.9	1,639.3	1,799.7	2,009.3	2,070.9	2,136.8	..	**EXTERNAL DEBT (Total)**
613.1	1,021.7	1,169.3	1,340.0	1,394.7	1,566.0	1,710.0	1,918.8	1,944.7	1,963.6	..	Long-Term Debt (by debtor)
17.9	46.6	79.8	122.7	112.1	154.0	155.8	175.5	165.6	150.0	..	Central Bank, incl. IMF credit
546.5	912.7	1,030.2	1,160.8	1,226.2	1,383.3	1,522.4	1,720.6	1,756.2	1,792.2	..	Central Government
..	..	..	..	..	..	..	..	..	..	..	Rest of General Government
21.0	21.9	14.5	11.7	11.6	16.4	20.3	22.7	22.9	21.4	..	Non-financial Public Enterprises
27.7	40.5	44.8	44.8	44.8	12.3	11.5	0.0	0.0	..	..	Priv. Sector, incl non-guaranteed
46.7	34.2	52.5	70.1	103.2	73.3	89.7	90.5	126.2	173.2	..	Short-Term Debt
				(Thousands of US dollars)							Memo Items:
14,564	30,712	6,505	9,166	1,049	2,500	12,800	7,300	15,300	15,400	..	Int'l Reserves Excluding Gold
11,182	7,540	8,755	7,310	5,908	6,287	7,515	9,307	7,888	7,710	..	Gold Holdings (at market price)
											SOCIAL INDICATORS
6.8	6.8	6.8	6.8	6.8	6.8	6.8	6.8	6.8	6.8	..	Total Fertility Rate
145.4	144.2	143.0	140.8	138.6	136.4	134.2	132.0	130.2	128.5	..	Infant Mortality Rate
44.2	44.5	44.8	45.3	45.7	46.1	46.6	47.0	47.3	47.5	..	Life Expectancy at Birth
30.2	31.0	31.8	32.5	33.3	34.1	35.1	36.1	36.8	37.4	..	Urban Population, % of total
106.2	101.9	100.7	95.0	94.6	100.6	104.5	100.0	101.5	101.5	..	Food Prod. per capita (1987=100)
75.5	..	..	..	..	..	..	..	..	..	..	Labor Force, Agriculture (%)
40.6	40.4	40.2	40.0	39.8	39.7	39.5	39.2	39.0	38.8	..	Labor Force, Female (%)
27.0	29.0	25.0	19.0	17.0	15.0	..	..	..	..	..	Primary Schl. Enroll. Ratio
19.0	21.0	18.0	14.0	12.0	10.0	13.0	..	..	..	..	Primary Schl. Enroll. Ratio, Female
10.0	14.0	18.0	14.0	11.0	9.0	12.0	..	..	..	..	Secondary Schl. Enroll. Ratio

SOUTH AFRICA	1969	1970	1971	1972	1973	1974	1975	1976	1977	1978	1979
CURRENT GNP PER CAPITA (US $)	710	760	830	860	980	1,210	1,420	1,440	1,420	1,510	1,750
POPULATION (thousands)	21,915	22,458	23,030	23,595	24,158	24,726	25,301	25,881	26,464	27,053	27,653
USE AND ORIGIN OF RESOURCES				*(Billions of current South African Rand)*							
Gross National Product (GNP)	11.30	12.40	13.73	15.52	19.21	23.57	26.23	29.39	32.68	37.44	44.57
Net Factor Income from Abroad	-0.46	-0.51	-0.51	-0.58	-0.71	-0.90	-1.22	-1.41	-1.63	-1.86	-2.13
GDP at Market Prices	11.76	12.91	14.24	16.10	19.92	24.47	27.45	30.80	34.31	39.30	46.70
Resource Balance	0.12	-0.41	-0.59	0.45	0.64	-0.18	-0.73	-0.32	2.00	3.09	4.85
Exports of Goods & NFServices	2.74	2.76	3.02	3.98	5.01	6.66	7.39	8.48	10.47	12.96	16.72
Imports of Goods & NFServices	2.62	3.16	3.61	3.53	4.37	6.83	8.12	8.80	8.47	9.87	11.88
Domestic Absorption	11.64	13.32	14.83	15.66	19.27	24.65	28.19	31.12	32.31	36.20	41.85
Private Consumption, etc.	7.29	8.07	8.60	9.55	11.58	14.45	15.51	17.56	17.89	20.59	22.73
General Gov't Consumption	1.32	1.56	1.88	2.00	2.29	2.89	3.78	4.54	5.16	5.67	6.54
Gross Domestic Investment	3.03	3.68	4.35	4.11	5.40	7.31	8.89	9.02	9.26	9.94	12.57
Fixed Investment	..	3.19	3.74	4.32	5.03	6.16	8.11	9.22	9.57	10.34	12.25
Indirect Taxes, net	0.80	0.88	0.99	1.07	1.24	1.39	1.61	1.88	2.33	2.78	3.48
GDP at factor cost	10.96	12.02	13.25	15.04	18.67	23.08	25.85	28.92	31.98	36.52	43.22
Agriculture	1.01	0.97	1.17	1.32	1.53	2.21	2.13	2.28	2.53	2.72	2.88
Industry	4.43	4.82	5.09	5.95	7.80	9.74	11.14	12.52	13.69	16.42	20.70
Manufacturing	2.51	2.80	2.98	3.27	4.09	4.90	5.99	6.83	6.96	7.89	9.58
Services, etc.	5.52	6.23	7.00	7.77	9.34	11.13	12.57	14.13	15.76	17.37	19.64
Gross Domestic Saving	3.15	3.28	3.76	4.56	6.04	7.13	8.16	8.70	11.27	13.03	17.42
Gross National Saving	..	2.79	3.27	3.99	5.32	6.26	7.01	7.32	9.60	11.19	15.33
				(Millions of 1987 South African Rand)							
Gross National Product	96,426	101,139	108,332	111,417	115,054	122,011	124,139	126,510	127,254	130,876	135,293
GDP at Market Prices	100,420	105,562	112,420	115,651	119,559	127,118	130,198	132,707	133,425	137,246	141,801
Resource Balance	7,365	3,603	1,951	9,143	4,102	-4,123	-2,616	2,936	16,396	18,352	19,199
Exports of Goods & NFServices	31,659	32,007	33,120	35,944	34,220	32,622	32,894	34,748	48,209	50,395	50,806
Imports of Goods & NFServices	24,294	28,404	31,168	26,801	30,118	36,745	35,510	31,813	31,813	32,043	31,607
Domestic Absorption	93,055	101,959	110,468	106,508	115,457	131,241	132,813	129,772	117,028	118,894	122,602
Private Consumption, etc.	53,147	56,272	60,056	60,610	65,452	74,675	72,381	72,960	65,483	68,548	68,126
General Gov't Consumption	12,408	13,514	14,622	14,542	15,054	16,077	18,431	19,998	18,091	18,248	18,819
Gross Domestic Investment	27,500	32,173	35,791	31,356	34,952	40,489	42,001	36,813	33,454	32,097	35,658
Fixed Investment	..	28,094	31,233	32,940	34,182	36,344	40,059	39,236	34,816	33,834	35,105
GDP at factor cost	93,000	96,011	102,229	105,523	109,555	116,961	119,533	121,471	121,769	125,185	129,635
Agriculture	..	6,319	7,502	7,531	6,438	8,263	7,678	7,575	8,322	8,601	8,396
Industry	..	55,771	57,051	56,895	58,702	59,698	60,205	61,026	61,278	62,984	66,005
Manufacturing	..	16,591	18,136	19,289	21,317	23,441	24,570	25,161	23,608	25,323	27,414
Services, etc.	..	35,195	37,940	40,320	43,239	47,849	50,736	52,009	51,143	52,537	54,136
Memo Items:											
Capacity to Import	25,388	24,742	26,073	30,191	34,555	35,783	32,313	30,645	39,340	42,084	44,502
Terms of Trade Adjustment	-6,271	-7,265	-7,047	-5,753	335	3,161	-582	-4,103	-8,870	-8,311	-6,303
Gross Domestic Income	94,149	98,298	105,373	109,898	119,895	130,279	129,616	128,604	124,555	128,935	135,498
Gross National Income	90,155	93,875	101,285	105,664	115,389	125,172	123,557	122,407	118,384	122,564	128,990
DOMESTIC PRICES/DEFLATORS				*(Index 1987 = 100)*							
Overall (GDP)	11.7	12.2	12.7	13.9	16.7	19.3	21.1	23.2	25.7	28.6	32.9
Domestic Absorption	12.5	13.1	13.4	14.7	16.7	18.8	21.2	24.0	27.6	30.5	34.1
Agriculture	..	15.4	15.6	17.5	23.8	26.8	27.7	30.0	30.4	31.6	34.4
Industry	..	8.6	8.9	10.5	13.3	16.3	18.5	20.5	22.3	26.1	31.4
Manufacturing	..	16.9	16.4	16.9	19.2	20.9	24.4	27.2	29.5	31.1	34.9
Consumer Price Index	13.2	13.8	14.6	15.5	17.0	19.0	21.5	23.9	26.6	29.3	33.2
MANUFACTURING ACTIVITY											
Employment (1987=100)	..	75.2	..	79.2	82.0	85.5	87.7	94.8	92.8	92.7	94.8
Real Earnings per Empl. (1987=100)	..	73.8	..	79.1	83.3	86.1	88.3	92.3	92.8	94.7	96.1
Real Output per Empl. (1987=100)	..	46.5	..	54.3	61.9	66.7	67.1	63.4	62.7	67.6	70.1
Earnings as % of Value Added	..	45.6	..	46.8	49.0	51.3	54.1	48.7	47.8	48.1	50.7
MONETARY HOLDINGS				*(Billions of current South African Rand)*							
Money Supply, Broadly Defined	7.13	7.80	8.46	9.97	12.17	14.21	16.97	18.47	20.34	23.60	27.56
Money	2.22	2.26	2.45	2.81	3.38	4.01	4.29	4.44	4.65	5.13	6.20
Currency Outside Banks	0.46	0.51	0.57	0.63	0.75	0.88	1.03	1.11	1.15	1.28	1.46
Demand Deposits	1.77	1.75	1.88	2.18	2.64	3.13	3.26	3.33	3.50	3.85	4.74
Quasi-Money	4.91	5.54	6.01	7.17	8.78	10.20	12.68	14.03	15.69	18.46	21.36
				(Millions of current South African Rand)							
GOVERNMENT DEFICIT (-) OR SURPLUS	..	..	..	-652	-499	-1,155	-1,438	-2,023	-2,067	-2,095	-1,947
Current Revenue	..	..	..	3,295	4,185	5,114	5,988	6,669	7,599	8,956	10,764
Current Expenditure	..	..	..	2,841	3,406	4,419	5,346	6,380	7,075	8,019	9,707
Current Budget Balance	..	..	..	454	779	695	642	289	524	937	1,057
Capital Receipts	..	..	..	30	27	30	37	21	27	45	38
Capital Payments	..	..	..	1,136	1,305	1,880	2,117	2,333	2,618	3,077	3,042

1980	1981	1982	1983	1984	1985	1986	1987	1988	1989 estimate	NOTES	SOUTH AFRICA
2,190	2,750	2,710	2,570	2,550	2,170	1,920	1,970	2,280	2,460	..	CURRENT GNP PER CAPITA (US $)
28,270	28,900	29,540	30,195	30,870	31,569	32,321	33,129	33,996	34,925	..	POPULATION (thousands)

(Billions of current South African Rand) — **USE AND ORIGIN OF RESOURCES**

1980	1981	1982	1983	1984	1985	1986	1987	1988	1989	NOTES	
59.27	69.55	78.79	89.31	104.69	119.39	137.90	160.59	192.84	227.51	f	Gross National Product (GNP)
-2.74	-3.42	-3.70	-4.16	-4.89	-6.53	-7.82	-7.49	-7.74	-9.49	..	Net Factor Income from Abroad
62.01	72.96	82.49	93.48	109.58	125.92	145.72	168.08	200.58	237.00	f	GDP at Market Prices
5.26	-1.04	0.02	3.72	2.33	12.10	14.63	13.21	10.28	13.06	..	Resource Balance
22.22	20.58	21.83	23.16	28.26	40.40	46.50	48.03	57.03	66.43	..	Exports of Goods & NFServices
16.96	21.63	21.81	19.44	25.93	28.30	31.87	34.82	46.74	53.38	..	Imports of Goods & NFServices
56.75	74.01	82.47	89.76	107.25	113.82	131.09	154.87	190.29	223.95	..	Domestic Absorption
29.46	39.70	48.99	51.11	61.46	66.42	76.36	90.71	110.65	128.32	..	Private Consumption, etc.
8.45	10.27	12.84	14.67	18.58	22.07	26.61	31.74	36.55	46.36	..	General Gov't Consumption
18.84	24.03	20.63	23.97	27.21	25.33	28.12	32.43	43.09	49.26	..	Gross Domestic Investment
16.38	20.13	22.87	24.90	26.66	29.14	29.20	32.05	39.91	48.68	..	Fixed Investment
4.04	5.06	6.96	7.33	9.25	10.96	13.18	15.13	20.61	26.21	..	Indirect Taxes, net
57.96	67.91	75.53	86.15	100.33	114.96	132.54	152.95	179.97	210.79	f	GDP at factor cost
4.04	4.92	4.85	4.32	5.43	6.72	7.51	9.59	10.45	12.16	..	Agriculture
29.34	32.09	34.63	40.15	45.14	52.72	61.85	68.00	80.14	92.62	..	Industry
12.61	16.62	18.40	20.94	23.90	26.04	30.39	35.85	43.30	51.09	..	Manufacturing
24.59	30.90	36.05	41.68	49.76	55.52	63.18	75.35	89.37	106.02	..	Services, etc.
24.10	22.99	20.65	27.70	29.54	37.43	42.75	45.63	53.37	62.32	..	Gross Domestic Saving
21.44	19.65	17.08	23.69	24.83	31.09	35.11	38.34	45.84	53.17	..	Gross National Saving

(Millions of 1987 South African Rand)

1980	1981	1982	1983	1984	1985	1986	1987	1988	1989	NOTES	
142,244	156,586	150,047	148,298	156,366	155,343	155,859	160,595	168,652	167,867	f	Gross National Product
149,118	162,915	161,450	157,572	165,675	164,271	164,693	168,083	174,312	177,965	f	GDP at Market Prices
4,535	-3,767	3,773	8,278	5,030	15,589	15,802	13,209	8,127	12,929	..	Resource Balance
46,939	44,212	44,254	41,839	45,392	49,995	49,302	48,026	50,780	55,624	..	Exports of Goods & NFServices
42,405	47,978	40,480	33,561	40,362	34,406	33,500	34,817	42,653	42,695	..	Imports of Goods & NFServices
144,583	166,682	157,677	149,294	160,645	148,682	148,891	154,874	166,185	165,037	..	Domestic Absorption
70,981	87,532	89,967	79,712	88,005	84,074	87,080	90,710	96,266	94,885	..	Private Consumption, etc.
24,377	25,043	26,613	27,108	28,921	29,893	30,560	31,739	32,240	33,734	..	General Gov't Consumption
49,225	54,107	41,097	42,475	43,719	34,715	31,251	32,425	37,679	36,417	..	Gross Domestic Investment
42,668	46,329	45,431	43,755	43,126	40,015	32,849	32,046	34,810	36,201	..	Fixed Investment
136,049	147,885	146,450	142,873	150,104	149,549	149,973	152,952	158,608	161,999	f	GDP at factor cost
8,424	9,175	8,374	6,490	7,172	8,600	9,173	9,595	9,696	10,699	..	Agriculture
65,248	71,745	70,554	67,808	70,382	68,558	67,903	68,004	71,185	71,777	..	Industry
33,276	38,846	37,672	35,168	36,570	34,508	34,717	35,846	38,141	38,254	..	Manufacturing
61,829	66,258	67,033	68,575	72,550	72,392	72,898	75,353	77,727	79,523	..	Services, etc.

Memo Items:

1980	1981	1982	1983	1984	1985	1986	1987	1988	1989	NOTES	
55,557	45,664	40,517	39,988	43,989	49,112	48,884	48,026	52,037	53,137	..	Capacity to Import
8,618	1,453	-3,736	-1,851	-1,403	-883	-418	0	1,257	-2,487	..	Terms of Trade Adjustment
157,736	164,368	157,714	155,722	164,272	163,388	164,275	168,083	175,569	175,479	..	Gross Domestic Income
150,862	158,039	146,311	146,448	154,963	154,460	155,441	160,595	169,909	165,380	..	Gross National Income

(Index 1987 = 100) — **DOMESTIC PRICES/DEFLATORS**

1980	1981	1982	1983	1984	1985	1986	1987	1988	1989	NOTES	
41.6	44.8	51.1	59.3	66.1	76.7	88.5	100.0	115.1	133.2	..	Overall (GDP)
39.2	44.4	52.3	60.1	66.8	76.6	88.0	100.0	114.5	135.7	..	Domestic Absorption
47.9	53.7	58.0	66.5	75.7	78.2	81.9	100.0	107.8	113.6	..	Agriculture
45.0	44.7	49.1	59.2	64.1	76.9	91.1	100.0	112.6	129.0	..	Industry
37.9	42.8	48.9	59.5	65.4	75.5	87.5	100.0	113.5	133.6	..	Manufacturing
37.7	43.5	49.9	56.0	62.4	72.6	86.1	100.0	112.8	129.4	..	Consumer Price Index

MANUFACTURING ACTIVITY

1980	1981	1982	1983	1984	1985	1986	1987	1988	1989	NOTES	
97.3	101.5	101.7	102.8	103.4	99.5	99.0	100.0	101.3	..	G	Employment (1987=100)
99.6	102.8	105.7	106.7	108.1	105.3	100.7	100.0	104.0	..	G	Real Earnings per Empl. (1987=100)
..	105.1	100.2	93.5	97.3	93.0	91.7	100.0	103.9	..	..	Real Output per Empl. (1987=100)
47.7	49.1	48.5	50.6	50.4	50.5	49.4	49.1	47.9	..	..	Earnings as % of Value Added

(Billions of current South African Rand) — **MONETARY HOLDINGS**

1980	1981	1982	1983	1984	1985	1986	1987	1988	1989	NOTES	
33.84	39.66	45.01	51.22	61.34	70.29	76.47	91.38	116.03	139.97	D	Money Supply, Broadly Defined
8.40	11.27	13.12	16.59	23.41	21.33	23.21	32.03	39.93	43.34	..	Money
1.86	2.27	2.49	2.76	3.19	3.55	4.18	5.03	6.13	7.31	..	Currency Outside Banks
6.54	9.00	10.63	13.82	20.22	17.78	19.03	27.00	33.81	36.03	..	Demand Deposits
25.44	28.39	31.89	34.63	37.93	48.96	53.26	59.36	76.10	96.63	..	Quasi-Money

(Millions of current South African Rand)

1980	1981	1982	1983	1984	1985	1986	1987	1988	1989	NOTES	
-1,436	-2,810	-3,082	-4,771	-5,060	-4,975	-7,865	-12,001	..	..	C F	GOVERNMENT DEFICIT (-) OR SURPLUS
14,398	16,034	19,199	21,754	26,474	33,131	37,768	43,084	..	..		Current Revenue
11,709	14,644	18,231	21,936	27,203	33,130	41,131	48,956	..	..		Current Expenditure
2,689	1,390	968	-182	-729	1	-3,363	-5,872	..	..		Current Budget Balance
50	31	40	51	70	81	95	134	..	..		Capital Receipts
4,175	4,231	4,090	4,640	4,401	5,057	4,597	6,263	..	..		Capital Payments

SOUTH AFRICA	1969	1970	1971	1972	1973	1974	1975	1976	1977	1978	1979
FOREIGN TRADE (CUSTOMS BASIS)					*(Millions of current US dollars)*						
Value of Exports, fob	3,356	3,355	3,510	4,196	6,114	8,760	8,959	7,975	9,987	12,875	18,397
Nonfuel Primary Products	2,294	1,807	1,881	2,510	3,349	4,500	4,546	4,004	4,392	4,908	6,170
Fuels	26	173	189	159	39	81	114	210	463	638	1,098
Manufactures	1,036	1,375	1,440	1,528	2,726	4,179	4,299	3,761	5,132	7,329	11,129
Value of Imports, cif	3,189	3,843	4,364	3,948	5,163	7,856	8,293	7,285	6,270	7,615	8,989
Nonfuel Primary Products	282	457	452	421	660	1,010	890	835	817	799	1,016
Fuels	75	191	286	272	10	21	20	29	33	35	52
Manufactures	2,832	3,195	3,625	3,255	4,493	6,824	7,383	6,421	5,420	6,781	7,921
					(Index 1987 = 100)						
Terms of Trade	167.8	162.3	157.2	158.9	172.0	183.9	159.7	154.2	140.0	122.9	130.4
Export Prices, fob	43.5	41.8	42.4	46.6	68.7	89.8	84.1	83.1	83.5	82.9	100.7
Import Prices, cif	25.9	25.7	26.9	29.3	39.9	48.8	52.7	53.9	59.6	67.4	77.2
BALANCE OF PAYMENTS					*(Millions of current US dollars)*						
Exports of Goods & Services	..	4,019	4,402	5,379	7,577	10,073	10,343	10,027	12,290	15,282	20,471
Merchandise, fob	..	3,206	3,457	4,386	6,187	8,434	8,436	8,296	10,443	13,041	17,696
Nonfactor Services	..	457	527	557	718	921	1,112	966	1,121	1,328	1,610
Factor Services	..	356	418	435	672	718	795	765	726	913	1,165
Imports of Goods & Services	..	5,303	5,938	5,562	7,681	11,655	12,974	12,036	11,808	13,833	17,171
Merchandise, fob	..	3,615	4,088	3,698	5,130	8,482	9,164	8,559	7,913	9,222	11,589
Nonfactor Services	..	796	942	896	1,156	1,547	1,899	1,548	1,777	2,110	2,526
Factor Services	..	892	908	968	1,395	1,626	1,911	1,929	2,118	2,501	3,056
Long-Term Interest	..	..	..	..	..	..	..	..	..	..	..
Private Current Transfers, net	..	31	22	23	-25	38	87	34	-41	17	52
Workers' Remittances	..									..	..
Curr. A/C Bal before Off. Transf.	..	-1,253	-1,514	-161	-129	-1,543	-2,544	-1,975	440	1,466	3,352
Net Official Transfers	..	38	34	39	45	84	102	100	94	63	63
Curr. A/C Bal after Off. Transf.	..	-1,215	-1,479	-122	-83	-1,459	-2,442	-1,875	535	1,529	3,415
Long-Term Capital, net	..	694	743	713	215	1,632	2,158	981	183	-240	-1,634
Direct Investment	..	318	231	98	-23	578	63	-14	-190	-347	-498
Long-Term Loans	..	..	..	..	..	..	..	..	..	..	..
Disbursements	..	..	..	..	..	..	..	..	..	..	..
Repayments	..	..	..	..	..	..	..	..	..	..	..
Other Long-Term Capital	..	376	513	616	237	1,054	2,094	995	373	107	-1,136
Other Capital, net	..	98	351	-63	-325	-326	373	214	-1,224	-1,059	-1,468
Change in Reserves	..	423	385	-529	193	152	-89	680	507	-230	-313
Memo Item:					*(South African Rand per US dollar)*						
Conversion Factor (Annual Avg)	0.710	0.710	0.720	0.770	0.690	0.680	0.740	0.870	0.870	0.870	0.840
				(Millions of US dollars), outstanding at end of year							
EXTERNAL DEBT (Total)	..	..	..	..	..	..	..	..	..	..	..
Long-Term Debt (by debtor)	..	..	..	..	..	..	..	..	..	..	..
Central Bank, incl. IMF credit	..	..	..	..	..	..	..	..	..	..	..
Central Government	..	..	..	..	..	..	..	..	..	..	..
Rest of General Government	..	..	..	..	..	..	..	..	..	..	..
Non-financial Public Enterprises	..	..	..	..	..	..	..	..	..	..	..
Priv. Sector, incl non-guaranteed	..	..	..	..	..	..	..	..	..	..	..
Short-Term Debt	..	..	..	..	..	..	..	..	..	..	..
Memo Items:					*(Millions of US dollars)*						
Int'l Reserves Excluding Gold	283	346	266	609	449	377	489	425	416	423	434
Gold Holdings (at market price)	1,121	711	511	1,164	2,132	3,404	2,489	1,707	1,603	2,213	5,135
SOCIAL INDICATORS											
Total Fertility Rate	5.7	5.7	5.6	5.5	5.4	5.3	5.3	5.2	5.1	5.0	5.0
Infant Mortality Rate	116.0	114.0	112.0	110.0	107.0	104.0	101.0	98.0	95.0	92.6	90.2
Life Expectancy at Birth	52.7	53.1	53.5	53.9	54.3	54.7	55.1	55.5	55.9	56.3	56.7
Urban Population, % of total	47.8	47.9	48.4	48.9	49.5	50.0	50.5	51.0	51.6	52.1	52.7
Food Prod. per capita (1987=100)	102.9	99.0	113.1	118.8	95.7	117.4	108.8	105.2	110.5	113.8	108.3
Labor Force, Agriculture (%)	32.7	32.9	31.2	29.5	27.9	26.3	24.7	23.0	21.3	19.6	18.0
Labor Force, Female (%)	32.2	33.0	33.1	33.2	33.4	33.5	33.6	33.7	33.8	33.9	34.0
Primary Schl. Enroll. Ratio	..	99.0	..	105.0	..	..	..	..	..	..	..
Primary Schl. Enroll. Ratio, Female	..	99.0	..	105.0	..	..	..	..	..	..	..
Secondary Schl. Enroll. Ratio	..	18.0	..	20.0	..	..	..	..	..	..	..

1980	1981	1982	1983	1984	1985	1986	1987	1988	1989 estimate	NOTES	SOUTH AFRICA
				(Millions of current US dollars)							**FOREIGN TRADE (CUSTOMS BASIS)**
25,680	20,895	17,727	18,607	17,348	16,523	18,454	21,526	21,549	..	f	Value of Exports, fob
4,663	4,244	3,543	3,697	3,012	3,025	2,956	3,945	3,720	..	..	Nonfuel Primary Products
972	1,274	1,151	1,143	1,033	903	560	692	669	..	..	Fuels
20,045	15,377	13,033	13,767	13,302	12,595	14,937	16,889	17,160	..	..	Manufactures
19,246	22,619	18,575	15,704	16,234	11,469	12,989	15,329	18,757	..	f	Value of Imports, cif
1,444	1,670	1,337	1,141	1,260	785	813	914	1,027	..	..	Nonfuel Primary Products
76	72	83	65	68	58	33	41	46	..	..	Fuels
17,726	20,877	17,156	14,498	14,906	10,626	12,142	14,374	17,684	..	..	Manufactures
				(Index 1987 = 100)							
139.9	132.7	119.4	115.2	113.8	104.7	99.6	100.0	101.4	..	f	Terms of Trade
116.6	110.6	97.6	92.1	89.7	82.5	91.0	100.0	110.0	..	f	Export Prices, fob
83.3	83.3	81.7	79.9	78.8	78.8	91.4	100.0	108.5	..	f	Import Prices, cif
				(Millions of current US dollars)							**BALANCE OF PAYMENTS**
29,258	24,162	20,564	21,441	19,997	18,850	21,056	24,262	25,726	25,943	..	Exports of Goods & Services
25,698	20,632	17,328	18,241	16,948	16,244	18,330	21,088	22,432	22,399	..	Merchandise, fob
2,157	2,210	2,060	1,855	1,775	1,459	1,440	1,689	1,798	1,904	..	Nonfactor Services
1,403	1,320	1,176	1,345	1,274	1,146	1,286	1,484	1,497	1,640	..	Factor Services
25,989	28,992	24,000	21,627	21,684	16,301	17,991	21,472	24,630	24,565	..	Imports of Goods & Services
18,268	20,622	16,683	14,202	14,774	10,402	11,130	13,925	17,210	16,810	..	Merchandise, fob
3,587	3,969	3,480	3,186	3,031	2,358	2,760	3,177	3,306	3,498	..	Nonfactor Services
4,133	4,402	3,836	4,239	3,880	3,541	4,101	4,369	4,115	4,257	..	Factor Services
..	..	..	..	..	..	..	..	..	..	..	Long-Term Interest
94	90	117	140	125	84	76	97	90	129	..	Private Current Transfers, net
..	..	..	..	..	..	..	..	..	..	..	Workers' Remittances
3,363	-4,741	-3,319	-46	-1,562	2,633	3,141	2,887	1,186	1,507	..	Curr. A/C Bal before Off. Transf.
145	229	135	56	-25	-10	11	116	86	72	..	Net Official Transfers
3,508	-4,512	-3,184	10	-1,588	2,622	3,152	3,002	1,272	1,579	..	Curr. A/C Bal after Off. Transf.
-910	144	2,268	-392	1,722	-697	-1,303	-1,124	-537	-493	..	Long-Term Capital, net
-765	-579	295	-87	251	-497	-116	29	4	7	..	Direct Investment
..	..	..	..	..	..	..	..	..	..	..	Long-Term Loans
..	..	..	..	..	..	..	..	..	..	..	Disbursements
..	..	..	..	..	..	..	..	..	..	..	Repayments
-145	722	1,973	-305	1,471	-200	-1,187	-1,153	-541	-500	..	Other Long-Term Capital
-1,828	3,313	21	1,364	-660	-2,444	-2,025	-442	-1,508	-585	..	Other Capital, net
-771	1,055	895	-981	525	519	176	-1,436	774	-501	..	Change in Reserves
				(South African Rand per US dollar)							**Memo Item:**
0.780	0.880	1.080	1.110	1.440	2.190	2.290	2.040	2.270	2.620	..	Conversion Factor (Annual Avg)
			(Millions of US dollars), outstanding at end of year								
..	..	..	..	..	..	..	..	..	..	..	**EXTERNAL DEBT (Total)**
..	..	..	..	..	..	..	..	..	..	..	Long-Term Debt (by debtor)
..	..	..	..	..	..	..	..	..	..	..	Central Bank, incl. IMF credit
..	..	..	..	..	..	..	..	..	..	..	Central Government
..	..	..	..	..	..	..	..	..	..	..	Rest of General Government
..	..	..	..	..	..	..	..	..	..	..	Non-financial Public Enterprises
..	..	..	..	..	..	..	..	..	..	..	Priv. Sector, incl non-guaranteed
..	..	..	..	..	..	..	..	..	..	..	Short-Term Debt
				(Millions of US dollars)							**Memo Items:**
726	666	485	823	242	315	370	641	780	960	..	Int'l Reserves Excluding Gold
7,162	3,693	3,459	2,972	2,269	1,583	1,884	2,822	1,424	1,235	..	Gold Holdings (at market price)
											SOCIAL INDICATORS
4.9	4.8	4.8	4.7	4.7	4.6	4.5	4.5	4.4	4.3	..	Total Fertility Rate
87.8	85.4	83.0	80.8	78.6	76.4	74.2	72.0	70.1	68.3	..	Infant Mortality Rate
57.1	57.5	57.9	58.4	58.9	59.4	59.9	60.4	60.9	61.3	..	Life Expectancy at Birth
53.2	53.7	54.3	54.8	55.4	55.9	56.6	57.2	57.6	58.1	..	Urban Population, % of total
109.5	123.0	104.4	84.2	92.1	96.1	96.9	100.0	100.9	106.0	..	Food Prod. per capita (1987=100)
16.5	..	..	..	..	..	..	..	..	..	..	Labor Force, Agriculture (%)
34.1	34.3	34.5	34.6	34.8	34.9	35.1	35.2	35.4	35.5	..	Labor Force, Female (%)
..	..	..	..	..	..	..	..	..	..	..	Primary Schl. Enroll. Ratio
..	..	..	..	..	..	..	..	..	..	..	Primary Schl. Enroll. Ratio, Female
..	..	..	..	..	..	..	..	..	..	..	Secondary Schl. Enroll. Ratio

SPAIN	1969	1970	1971	1972	1973	1974	1975	1976	1977	1978	1979
CURRENT GNP PER CAPITA (US $)	1,060	1,100	1,210	1,430	1,790	2,280	2,750	3,060	3,340	3,660	4,380
POPULATION (thousands)	33,427	33,779	34,190	34,448	34,810	35,147	35,515	35,937	36,367	36,778	37,108

USE AND ORIGIN OF RESOURCES *(Billions of current Spanish Pesetas)*

	1969	1970	1971	1972	1973	1974	1975	1976	1977	1978	1979
Gross National Product (GNP)	2,344	2,607	2,946	3,459	4,179	5,130	6,005	7,207	9,135	11,164	13,078
Net Factor Income from Abroad	-16	-17	-16	-16	-12	-1	-19	-40	-62	-87	-78
GDP at Market Prices	2,360	2,624	2,962	3,476	4,190	5,131	6,023	7,248	9,197	11,251	13,156
Resource Balance	-50	-25	26	8	-32	-248	-230	-322	-194	90	44
Exports of Goods & NFServices	282	349	422	507	612	740	817	998	1,332	1,711	1,974
Imports of Goods & NFServices	332	373	396	499	644	987	1,047	1,321	1,526	1,621	1,930
Domestic Absorption	2,410	2,649	2,936	3,468	4,223	5,379	6,253	7,570	9,391	11,161	13,112
Private Consumption, etc.	1,534	1,708	1,925	2,250	2,708	3,345	3,927	4,837	6,074	7,288	8,595
General Gov't Consumption	246	276	310	351	417	537	651	788	1,019	1,292	1,575
Gross Domestic Investment	630	665	700	867	1,098	1,497	1,675	1,945	2,298	2,581	2,942
Fixed Investment	627	689	719	884	1,119	1,422	1,570	1,812	2,216	2,568	2,861
Indirect Taxes, net	169	185	194	233	297	310	338	388	485	473	598
GDP at factor cost	2,191	2,440	2,768	3,243	3,893	4,822	5,685	6,860	8,712	10,778	12,558
Agriculture	..	..	..	..	..	..	..	..	..	..	..
Industry	..	..	..	..	..	..	..	..	..	..	..
Manufacturing	..	..	..	..	..	..	..	..	..	..	..
Services, etc.	..	..	..	..	..	..	..	..	..	..	..
Gross Domestic Saving	580	640	727	874	1,066	1,249	1,445	1,622	2,105	2,671	2,986
Gross National Saving	..	669	765	914	1,137	1,315	1,494	1,660	2,150	2,712	3,029

(Billions of 1987 Spanish Pesetas)

	1969	1970	1971	1972	1973	1974	1975	1976	1977	1978	1979
Gross National Product	20,779	21,634	22,652	24,485	26,418	27,897	27,965	28,808	29,636	30,032	30,045
GDP at Market Prices	20,919	21,773	22,770	24,599	26,490	27,897	28,047	28,965	29,834	30,266	30,224
Resource Balance	-452	-277	33	-247	-489	-823	-803	-1,036	-377	74	-160
Exports of Goods & NFServices	1,971	2,315	2,644	2,998	3,297	3,265	3,250	3,413	3,825	4,233	4,472
Imports of Goods & NFServices	2,423	2,592	2,611	3,245	3,786	4,088	4,053	4,449	4,202	4,159	4,632
Domestic Absorption	21,371	22,050	22,737	24,846	26,978	28,721	28,850	30,000	30,211	30,192	30,384
Private Consumption, etc.	13,882	14,438	15,146	16,387	17,651	18,547	18,832	19,792	20,113	20,277	20,445
General Gov't Consumption	2,208	2,323	2,424	2,550	2,714	2,966	3,120	3,336	3,467	3,655	3,808
Gross Domestic Investment	5,281	5,288	5,167	5,910	6,613	7,207	6,898	6,872	6,630	6,260	6,131
Fixed Investment	5,523	5,686	5,518	6,300	7,120	7,564	7,223	7,165	7,097	6,904	6,601
GDP at factor cost	..	..	..	..	..	..	..	..	..	..	..
Agriculture	..	..	..	..	..	..	..	..	..	..	..
Industry	..	..	..	..	..	..	..	..	..	..	..
Manufacturing	..	..	..	..	..	..	..	..	..	..	..
Services, etc.	..	..	..	..	..	..	..	..	..	..	..
Memo Items:											
Capacity to Import	2,059	2,421	2,784	3,295	3,597	3,063	3,163	3,363	3,668	4,390	4,738
Terms of Trade Adjustment	88	106	141	297	299	-202	-87	-51	-156	157	266
Gross Domestic Income	21,007	21,879	22,911	24,896	26,789	27,695	27,960	28,914	29,678	30,423	30,490
Gross National Income	20,868	21,739	22,792	24,782	26,717	27,695	27,878	28,757	29,480	30,189	30,311

DOMESTIC PRICES/DEFLATORS *(Index 1987 = 100)*

	1969	1970	1971	1972	1973	1974	1975	1976	1977	1978	1979
Overall (GDP)	11.3	12.1	13.0	14.1	15.8	18.4	21.5	25.0	30.8	37.2	43.5
Domestic Absorption	11.3	12.0	12.9	14.0	15.7	18.7	21.7	25.2	31.1	37.0	43.2
Agriculture	..	..	..	..	..	..	..	..	..	..	..
Industry	..	..	..	..	..	..	..	..	..	..	..
Manufacturing	..	..	..	..	..	..	..	..	..	..	..
Consumer Price Index	11.5	12.1	13.1	14.2	15.8	18.3	21.4	24.6	30.6	36.7	42.4

MANUFACTURING ACTIVITY

	1969	1970	1971	1972	1973	1974	1975	1976	1977	1978	1979
Employment (1987=100)	104.5	106.0	107.8	110.9	115.4	119.6	120.6	121.6	120.5	133.6	130.6
Real Earnings per Empl. (1987=100)	60.3	64.1	66.6	72.5	77.1	83.6	90.7	99.6	105.2	91.4	92.8
Real Output per Empl. (1987=100)	..	..	..	..	..	..	..	..	..	..	..
Earnings as % of Value Added	50.1	51.7	52.2	51.3	50.9	51.9	59.6	63.3	65.8	44.1	44.6

MONETARY HOLDINGS *(Billions of current Spanish Pesetas)*

	1969	1970	1971	1972	1973	1974	1975	1976	1977	1978	1979
Money Supply, Broadly Defined	1,698	1,955	2,424	2,985	3,710	4,419	5,257	6,270	7,441	8,953	10,551
Money	701	743	920	1,142	1,410	1,654	1,963	2,392	2,836	3,325	3,610
Currency Outside Banks	243	263	294	328	387	447	524	614	777	946	1,039
Demand Deposits	459	480	626	814	1,023	1,208	1,439	1,778	2,058	2,379	2,571
Quasi-Money	997	1,211	1,505	1,843	2,300	2,764	3,294	3,877	4,605	5,628	6,942

GOVERNMENT DEFICIT (-) OR SURPLUS *(Billions of current Spanish Pesetas)*

	1969	1970	1971	1972	1973	1974	1975	1976	1977	1978	1979
	..	-16.8	-46.4	-18.7	-10.4	-59.4	-107.9	-65.4	-200.1	-264.3	-465.4
Current Revenue	..	479.0	554.9	683.6	833.6	1,014.1	1,259.4	1,497.2	2,080.4	2,658.8	3,183.8
Current Expenditure	..	406.7	483.5	569.4	708.0	875.0	1,096.6	1,317.6	1,856.9	2,557.9	3,170.3
Current Budget Balance	..	72.3	71.4	114.2	125.6	139.1	162.8	179.6	223.5	100.9	13.5
Capital Receipts	..	0.5	0.6	1.4	1.9	1.8	1.7	1.7	2.4	1.6	1.3
Capital Payments	..	89.6	118.4	134.3	137.9	200.3	272.4	246.7	426.0	366.8	480.2

1980	1981	1982	1983	1984	1985	1986	1987	1988	1989 estimate	NOTES	SPAIN
5,300	5,610	5,310	4,680	4,390	4,280	4,840	6,000	7,750	9,150	..	**CURRENT GNP PER CAPITA (US $)**
37,386	37,756	37,980	38,172	38,342	38,505	38,668	38,832	38,996	39,161	..	**POPULATION (thousands)**
			(Billions of current Spanish Pesetas)								**USE AND ORIGIN OF RESOURCES**
15,078	16,750	19,287	21,891	24,715	27,549	31,645	35,420	39,232	43,885	..	Gross National Product (GNP)
-130	-238	-285	-358	-397	-331	-298	-307	-428	-593	..	Net Factor Income from Abroad
15,208	16,988	19,572	22,249	25,112	27,879	31,943	35,728	39,660	44,478	..	GDP at Market Prices
-349	-355	-355	-139	585	599	711	41	-428	-1,343	..	Resource Balance
2,410	3,074	3,670	4,721	5,948	6,519	6,477	7,043	7,672	8,386	..	Exports of Goods & NFServices
2,759	3,429	4,025	4,859	5,363	5,920	5,767	7,002	8,100	9,729	..	Imports of Goods & NFServices
15,557	17,343	19,926	22,388	24,527	27,280	31,232	35,687	40,088	45,821	..	Domestic Absorption
10,078	11,454	13,142	14,829	16,367	18,138	20,424	22,846	25,071	28,206	..	Private Consumption, etc.
1,929	2,242	2,620	3,091	3,448	3,907	4,740	5,463	5,944	6,646	..	General Gov't Consumption
3,549	3,646	4,165	4,469	4,712	5,236	6,068	7,377	9,073	10,969	..	Gross Domestic Investment
3,368	3,718	4,248	4,657	4,838	5,446	6,461	7,779	9,324	11,215	..	Fixed Investment
694	909	1,033	1,324	1,568	1,948	2,812	3,119	3,331	3,672	..	Indirect Taxes, net
14,514	16,079	18,538	20,925	23,544	25,931	29,131	32,609	36,329	40,806	..	GDP at factor cost
1,073	1,038	1,226	1,371	1,643	1,744	1,814	1,942	2,102	..	B	Agriculture
5,877	6,517	7,418	8,378	9,305	10,295	12,547	..	..	..	B	Industry
4,284	4,762	5,327	6,153	6,904	7,629	9,300	..	..	..	B	Manufacturing
8,258	9,433	10,928	12,500	14,164	15,840	17,582	..	..	..	B	Services, etc.
3,200	3,292	3,810	4,330	5,297	5,835	6,779	7,418	8,644	9,626	..	Gross Domestic Saving
3,218	3,210	3,699	4,145	5,091	5,742	6,690	7,392	8,568	9,408	..	Gross National Saving
			(Billions of 1987 Spanish Pesetas)								
30,342	30,107	30,457	30,963	31,526	32,381	33,518	35,420	37,174	38,910	..	Gross National Product
30,598	30,522	30,894	31,452	32,017	32,758	33,832	35,728	37,584	39,429	..	GDP at Market Prices
-212	374	431	987	1,707	1,591	856	41	-545	-1,616	..	Resource Balance
4,574	4,958	5,194	5,721	6,392	6,568	6,652	7,043	7,444	7,772	..	Exports of Goods & NFServices
4,786	4,583	4,763	4,734	4,685	4,977	5,797	7,002	7,990	9,388	..	Imports of Goods & NFServices
30,810	30,148	30,463	30,464	30,311	31,167	32,976	35,687	38,129	41,044	..	Domestic Absorption
20,560	20,412	20,442	20,512	20,450	20,915	21,640	22,846	23,908	25,182	..	Private Consumption, etc.
3,967	4,042	4,238	4,404	4,531	4,741	5,012	5,463	5,682	5,994	..	General Gov't Consumption
6,284	5,695	5,783	5,548	5,330	5,511	6,324	7,377	8,539	9,868	..	Gross Domestic Investment
6,645	6,429	6,462	6,297	5,932	6,178	6,795	7,779	8,887	10,099	..	Fixed Investment
..	..	..	..	..	..	..	..	..	..	..	GDP at factor cost
1,837	1,663	1,638	1,740	1,890	1,948	1,771	1,942	2,019	..	..	Agriculture
..	..	..	..	..	..	..	..	..	..	..	Industry
..	..	..	..	..	..	..	..	..	..	..	Manufacturing
..	..	..	..	..	..	..	..	..	..	..	Services, etc.
											Memo Items:
4,181	4,109	4,343	4,599	5,196	5,480	6,511	7,043	7,567	8,092	..	Capacity to Import
-393	-848	-851	-1,123	-1,196	-1,088	-141	0	123	320	..	Terms of Trade Adjustment
30,205	29,674	30,043	30,329	30,821	31,671	33,690	35,728	37,706	39,749	..	Gross Domestic Income
29,949	29,259	29,606	29,840	30,330	31,294	33,376	35,420	37,297	39,230	..	Gross National Income
			(Index 1987 = 100)								**DOMESTIC PRICES/DEFLATORS**
49.7	55.7	63.4	70.7	78.4	85.1	94.4	100.0	105.5	112.8	..	Overall (GDP)
50.5	57.5	65.4	73.5	80.9	87.5	94.7	100.0	105.1	111.6	..	Domestic Absorption
58.4	62.4	74.9	78.8	86.9	89.5	102.4	100.0	104.1	..	..	Agriculture
..	..	..	..	..	..	..	..	..	..	..	Industry
..	..	..	..	..	..	..	..	..	..	..	Manufacturing
49.1	56.2	64.3	72.1	80.3	87.3	95.0	100.0	104.8	111.9	..	Consumer Price Index
											MANUFACTURING ACTIVITY
132.0	122.3	113.9	110.6	104.7	99.2	98.1	100.0	100.8	..	..	Employment (1987=100)
95.0	95.7	95.8	95.9	94.2	95.1	96.1	100.0	103.6	..	..	Real Earnings per Empl. (1987=100)
..	..	..	..	..	..	..	..	..	..	..	Real Output per Empl. (1987=100)
44.9	45.0	44.1	42.5	41.4	39.8	38.1	38.7	38.7	..	..	Earnings as % of Value Added
			(Billions of current Spanish Pesetas)								**MONETARY HOLDINGS**
12,319	14,269	16,259	16,082	16,883	18,867	22,027	24,050	27,689	30,432	..	Money Supply, Broadly Defined
4,098	4,630	4,850	5,277	5,746	6,589	7,580	8,899	10,573	12,177	..	Money
1,185	1,333	1,531	1,688	1,867	2,083	2,406	2,741	3,244	3,839	..	Currency Outside Banks
2,913	3,297	3,319	3,589	3,879	4,506	5,174	6,158	7,329	8,338	..	Demand Deposits
8,221	9,639	11,409	10,806	11,137	12,278	14,448	15,151	17,116	18,255	..	Quasi-Money
			(Billions of current Spanish Pesetas)								**GOVERNMENT DEFICIT (-) OR SURPLUS**
-635.1	-873.9	-1,093.3	-1,408.3	-2,113.2	-1,962.6	-1,463.4	-1,406.2	..	..	..	
3,674.1	4,134.6	4,996.7	5,867.3	6,611.4	7,743.1	9,437.3	11,006.2	..	..	..	Current Revenue
3,612.5	4,016.5	5,178.0	6,078.1	7,129.3	8,447.7	9,730.2	11,054.7	..	..	..	Current Expenditure
61.6	118.1	-181.3	-210.8	-517.9	-704.6	-292.9	-48.5	..	..	..	Current Budget Balance
1.8	1.3	10.4	15.2	118.1	11.5	3.6	22.5	..	..	..	Capital Receipts
698.5	993.3	922.4	1,212.7	1,713.4	1,269.5	1,174.1	1,380.2	..	..	..	Capital Payments

SPAIN	1969	1970	1971	1972	1973	1974	1975	1976	1977	1978	1979
FOREIGN TRADE (CUSTOMS BASIS)					*(Millions of current US dollars)*						
Value of Exports, fob	1,900	2,387	2,938	3,803	5,162	7,059	7,675	8,712	10,218	13,103	18,196
Nonfuel Primary Products	756	979	1,039	1,195	1,713	2,011	2,042	2,352	2,625	3,153	4,502
Fuels	122	131	126	138	242	478	252	325	378	330	347
Manufactures	1,021	1,277	1,773	2,471	3,206	4,570	5,381	6,035	7,214	9,620	13,347
Value of Imports, cif	4,202	4,714	4,936	6,754	9,536	15,291	16,100	17,288	17,648	18,630	25,370
Nonfuel Primary Products	1,440	1,536	1,657	2,181	3,141	4,529	4,664	4,473	5,000	5,397	6,941
Fuels	529	627	812	975	1,243	3,891	4,191	5,093	5,050	5,306	7,674
Manufactures	2,232	2,551	2,467	3,598	5,152	6,871	7,246	7,721	7,597	7,928	10,755
					(Index 1987 = 100)						
Terms of Trade	139.2	140.9	139.3	137.5	131.7	103.8	107.6	103.3	97.8	100.2	101.4
Export Prices, fob	31.2	32.1	34.0	38.2	48.6	60.2	64.8	64.3	67.3	74.9	93.3
Import Prices, cif	22.4	22.8	24.4	27.8	36.9	58.0	60.2	62.2	68.8	74.7	92.0
BALANCE OF PAYMENTS					*(Millions of current US dollars)*						
Exports of Goods & Services	..	4,900	5,950	7,663	10,463	12,862	13,853	14,545	17,202	22,445	29,990
Merchandise, fob	..	2,483	2,979	3,920	5,304	7,211	7,797	8,994	10,550	13,474	18,351
Nonfactor Services	..	2,367	2,863	3,577	4,817	4,989	5,443	5,110	6,182	8,189	10,266
Factor Services	..	50	108	165	342	663	613	441	471	782	1,373
Imports of Goods & Services	..	5,480	5,861	7,951	11,287	17,237	18,515	19,982	20,743	22,470	30,649
Merchandise, fob	..	4,357	4,578	6,236	8,807	14,258	15,207	16,299	16,736	17,555	24,041
Nonfactor Services	..	817	941	1,255	1,894	2,244	2,371	2,648	2,766	3,049	4,086
Factor Services	..	306	343	459	585	735	937	1,034	1,241	1,865	2,522
Long-Term Interest	..	..	..	..	..	..	..	..	..	..	..
Private Current Transfers, net	..	659	772	878	1,416	1,151	1,166	1,161	1,418	1,672	1,805
Workers' Remittances	..	469	550	599	902	859	975	1,000	1,091	1,270	1,427
Curr. A/C Bal before Off. Transf.	..	79	861	591	592	-3,224	-3,496	-4,275	-2,123	1,648	1,146
Net Official Transfers	..	..	-5	-10	-7	-8	-19	-16	-9	-14	-19
Curr. A/C Bal after Off. Transf.	..	79	856	581	585	-3,233	-3,515	-4,292	-2,133	1,634	1,128
Long-Term Capital, net	..	664	499	848	765	1,768	1,808	2,011	3,011	1,717	3,161
Direct Investment	..	179	177	231	337	273	513	285	492	1,076	1,264
Long-Term Loans	..	..	..	..	..	..	..	..	..	..	..
Disbursements	..	..	..	..	..	..	..	..	..	..	..
Repayments	..	..	..	..	..	..	..	..	..	..	..
Other Long-Term Capital	..	485	323	617	428	1,495	1,295	1,727	2,519	641	1,897
Other Capital, net	..	76	99	17	-13	753	878	1,190	267	408	-839
Change in Reserves	..	-819	-1,454	-1,446	-1,338	712	829	1,090	-1,146	-3,759	-3,450
Memo Item:					*(Spanish Pesetas per US dollar)*						
Conversion Factor (Annual Avg)	70.000	70.000	69.470	64.270	58.260	57.690	57.410	66.900	75.960	76.670	67.130
					(Millions US dollars), outstanding at end of year						
EXTERNAL DEBT (Total)	..	..	..	..	..	..	..	..	..	..	..
Long-Term Debt (by debtor)	..	..	..	..	..	..	..	..	..	..	..
Central Bank, incl. IMF credit	..	..	..	..	..	..	..	..	..	..	..
Central Government	..	..	..	..	..	..	..	..	..	..	..
Rest of General Government	..	..	..	..	..	..	..	..	..	..	..
Non-financial Public Enterprises	..	..	..	..	..	..	..	..	..	..	..
Priv. Sector, incl non-guaranteed	..	..	..	..	..	..	..	..	..	..	..
Short-Term Debt	..	..	..	..	..	..	..	..	..	..	..
Memo Items:					*(Millions of US dollars)*						
Int'l Reserves Excluding Gold	497	1,319	2,727	4,473	6,170	5,874	5,506	4,704	5,977	10,112	13,224
Gold Holdings (at market price)	789	532	621	924	1,601	2,661	2,001	1,922	2,381	3,282	7,478
SOCIAL INDICATORS											
Total Fertility Rate	2.9	2.8	2.9	2.8	2.8	2.9	2.8	2.8	2.6	2.5	2.3
Infant Mortality Rate	30.2	28.1	25.7	22.9	21.5	19.9	18.9	17.1	16.0	15.3	14.3
Life Expectancy at Birth	72.1	72.3	72.6	72.8	72.9	73.1	73.2	73.3	73.5	73.9	74.4
Urban Population, % of total	65.1	66.0	66.7	67.4	68.2	68.9	69.6	70.2	70.9	71.5	72.2
Food Prod. per capita (1987=100)	64.7	67.7	68.4	72.3	77.7	76.9	79.5	79.6	77.8	85.9	85.5
Labor Force, Agriculture (%)	27.6	26.0	25.1	24.2	23.3	22.4	21.5	20.6	19.7	18.8	18.0
Labor Force, Female (%)	19.3	19.4	19.9	20.3	20.8	21.3	21.7	22.1	22.5	22.9	23.2
Primary Schl. Enroll. Ratio	..	123.0	..	..	..	..	111.0	110.0	109.0	109.0	109.0
Primary Schl. Enroll. Ratio, Female	..	125.0	..	..	..	..	111.0	110.0	109.0	109.0	109.0
Secondary Schl. Enroll. Ratio	..	56.0	..	..	..	..	73.0	76.0	78.0	83.0	86.0

1980	1981	1982	1983	1984	1985	1986	1987	1988	1989 estimate	NOTES	SPAIN
				(Millions of current US dollars)							**FOREIGN TRADE (CUSTOMS BASIS)**
20,827	20,337	20,271	19,711	23,283	24,307	27,250	34,099	40,458	..	..	Value of Exports, fob
5,098	5,009	4,329	4,222	5,009	4,932	5,826	7,827	9,302	..	..	Nonfuel Primary Products
761	1,008	1,418	1,734	2,027	2,148	1,682	2,001	1,802	..	..	Fuels
14,967	14,320	14,525	13,755	16,247	17,227	19,742	24,271	29,354	..	..	Manufactures
33,901	32,081	31,282	28,926	28,607	30,066	35,406	49,009	60,434	..	..	Value of Imports, cif
7,835	6,730	6,542	6,325	6,384	6,354	7,973	9,648	12,037	..	..	Nonfuel Primary Products
13,116	13,641	12,474	11,671	10,826	10,865	6,696	7,993	6,881	..	..	Fuels
12,950	11,710	12,266	10,930	11,397	12,848	20,738	31,368	41,516	..	..	Manufactures
				(Index 1987 = 100)							
90.2	77.2	84.6	80.0	83.9	85.6	105.5	100.0	108.3	..	..	Terms of Trade
102.7	89.0	89.9	83.0	83.4	81.0	95.2	100.0	116.4	..	..	Export Prices, fob
113.8	115.3	106.2	103.8	99.4	94.7	90.3	100.0	107.5	..	..	Import Prices, cif
				(Millions of current US dollars)							**BALANCE OF PAYMENTS**
33,863	34,331	34,765	32,694	36,778	38,499	46,377	57,429	67,092	72,176	..	Exports of Goods & Services
20,544	20,974	21,288	19,858	22,714	23,665	26,754	33,561	39,652	43,301	..	Merchandise, fob
11,560	11,299	11,505	11,478	12,545	12,992	17,925	21,976	24,710	25,047	..	Nonfactor Services
1,759	2,058	1,972	1,357	1,519	1,843	1,698	1,891	2,730	3,828	..	Factor Services
41,089	41,011	40,590	36,604	35,855	36,776	43,544	60,296	75,380	87,716	..	Imports of Goods & Services
32,272	31,086	30,542	27,560	26,985	27,836	33,278	46,548	57,650	67,797	..	Merchandise, fob
5,563	5,579	5,803	5,222	4,940	5,205	6,471	8,931	11,084	12,673	..	Nonfactor Services
3,255	4,346	4,245	3,823	3,930	3,735	3,795	4,818	6,646	7,246	..	Factor Services
..	..	..	..	..	..	..	..	..	..	..	Long-Term Interest
2,059	1,698	1,577	1,211	1,191	1,395	1,492	2,277	3,018	3,163	..	Private Current Transfers, net
1,649	1,296	1,122	939	844	1,033	1,184	1,316	1,530	1,601	..	Workers' Remittances
-5,168	-4,982	-4,248	-2,699	2,114	3,119	4,325	-591	-5,269	-12,378	..	Curr. A/C Bal before Off. Transf.
-6	-7	3	-46	-96	-268	-360	358	1,485	1,444	..	Net Official Transfers
-5,173	-4,989	-4,245	-2,746	2,018	2,851	3,965	-233	-3,784	-10,934	..	Curr. A/C Bal after Off. Transf.
4,147	4,232	1,772	3,122	3,274	-1,549	-2,110	8,999	9,610	15,655	..	Long-Term Capital, net
1,182	1,436	1,272	1,379	1,523	1,718	3,073	3,825	5,786	6,955	..	Direct Investment
..	..	..	..	..	..	..	..	..	..	..	Long-Term Loans
..	..	..	..	..	..	..	..	..	..	..	Disbursements
..	..	..	..	..	..	..	..	..	..	..	Repayments
2,965	2,796	501	1,743	1,751	-3,267	-5,183	5,173	3,825	8,700	..	Other Long-Term Capital
231	30	-632	-642	-475	-3,576	489	3,939	2,590	-6	..	Other Capital, net
795	727	3,104	265	-4,817	2,275	-2,344	-12,706	-8,416	-4,716	..	Change in Reserves
				(Spanish Pesetas per US dollar)							**Memo Item:**
71.700	92.310	109.860	143.430	160.760	170.040	140.050	123.480	116.490	118.380	..	Conversion Factor (Annual Avg)
				(Millions US dollars), outstanding at end of year							
..	..	..	..	..	..	..	..	..	..	..	**EXTERNAL DEBT (Total)**
..	..	..	..	..	..	..	..	..	..	..	Long-Term Debt (by debtor)
..	..	..	..	..	..	..	..	..	..	..	Central Bank, incl. IMF credit
..	..	..	..	..	..	..	..	..	..	..	Central Government
..	..	..	..	..	..	..	..	..	..	..	Rest of General Government
..	..	..	..	..	..	..	..	..	..	..	Non-financial Public Enterprises
..	..	..	..	..	..	..	..	..	..	..	Priv. Sector, incl non-guaranteed
..	..	..	..	..	..	..	..	..	..	..	Short-Term Debt
				(Millions of US dollars)							**Memo Items:**
11,863	10,805	7,655	7,402	11,955	11,175	14,755	30,669	37,073	41,467	..	Int'l Reserves Excluding Gold
8,610	5,806	6,673	5,572	4,510	4,792	5,794	5,770	5,762	6,303	..	Gold Holdings (at market price)
											SOCIAL INDICATORS
2.2	2.0	1.9	1.8	1.7	1.6	1.5	1.6	1.6	1.6	..	Total Fertility Rate
12.3	12.5	11.3	10.9	9.9	8.5	8.8	8.8	8.6	8.3	..	Infant Mortality Rate
74.9	75.3	75.8	75.9	76.1	76.3	76.4	76.6	76.7	76.9	..	Life Expectancy at Birth
72.8	73.4	74.0	74.6	75.2	75.8	76.3	76.8	77.4	77.9	..	Urban Population, % of total
91.4	80.0	88.8	82.2	95.4	91.7	88.7	100.0	93.1	93.3	..	Food Prod. per capita (1987=100)
17.1	..	..	..	..	..	..	..	..	..	..	Labor Force, Agriculture (%)
23.6	23.7	23.8	23.9	24.0	24.1	24.2	24.2	24.3	24.4	..	Labor Force, Female (%)
109.0	..	..	112.0	113.0	113.0	113.0	..	..	..	..	Primary Schl. Enroll. Ratio
109.0	..	..	112.0	113.0	112.0	113.0	..	..	..	..	Primary Schl. Enroll. Ratio, Female
87.0	..	..	89.0	94.0	99.0	102.0	..	..	..	..	Secondary Schl. Enroll. Ratio

SRI LANKA	1969	1970	1971	1972	1973	1974	1975	1976	1977	1978	1979
CURRENT GNP PER CAPITA (US $)	170	170	170	160	170	200	220	230	220	220	230
POPULATION (thousands)	12,252	12,516	12,608	12,861	13,091	13,284	13,496	13,717	13,942	14,184	14,471

USE AND ORIGIN OF RESOURCES					(Billions of current Sri Lanka Rupees)						
Gross National Product (GNP)	12.33	13.44	13.86	15.07	18.22	23.59	26.36	29.92	36.15	42.43	52.15
Net Factor Income from Abroad	-0.18	-0.22	-0.19	-0.18	-0.18	-0.18	-0.21	-0.28	-0.25	-0.24	-0.24
GDP at Market Prices	12.51	13.66	14.05	15.25	18.40	23.77	26.58	30.20	36.41	42.67	52.39
Resource Balance	-1.13	-0.43	-0.28	-0.24	-0.22	-1.78	-1.98	-0.70	1.33	-2.04	-6.31
Exports of Goods & NFServices	3.34	3.48	3.46	3.40	4.48	6.28	7.31	8.77	12.31	14.83	17.66
Imports of Goods & NFServices	4.46	3.91	3.74	3.64	4.70	8.06	9.29	9.48	10.98	16.87	23.97
Domestic Absorption	13.64	14.09	14.33	15.49	18.63	25.55	28.56	30.91	35.07	44.70	58.70
Private Consumption, etc.	9.91	9.88	10.17	10.95	14.08	19.07	21.94	22.99	26.70	32.11	40.37
General Gov't Consumption	1.45	1.62	1.76	1.90	2.02	2.74	2.48	3.02	3.12	4.04	4.80
Gross Domestic Investment	2.28	2.59	2.40	2.64	2.53	3.74	4.14	4.90	5.26	8.55	13.53
Fixed Investment	2.28	2.36	2.14	2.21	2.49	2.97	3.70	4.59	5.03	8.52	13.25
Indirect Taxes, net	0.31	0.48	0.38	0.53	0.48	0.47	0.89	2.17	1.72	2.19	2.60
GDP at factor cost	12.21	13.19	13.67	14.72	17.92	23.30	25.69	28.03	34.68	40.48	49.78
Agriculture	3.52	3.73	3.70	3.88	4.89	7.73	7.80	8.13	10.64	12.33	13.41
Industry	2.80	3.14	3.38	3.56	4.55	5.84	6.79	7.59	9.95	11.03	14.05
Manufacturing	2.02	2.20	2.40	2.59	3.12	4.34	5.16	5.62	8.02	8.09	9.48
Services, etc.	5.88	6.32	6.59	7.28	8.48	9.73	11.10	12.30	14.09	17.12	22.32
Gross Domestic Saving	1.16	2.16	2.12	2.40	2.30	1.96	2.16	4.19	6.59	6.52	7.22
Gross National Saving	..	1.93	1.91	2.19	2.12	1.78	1.96	3.97	6.43	6.62	7.73

					(Millions of 1987 Sri Lanka Rupees)						
Gross National Product	90,259	92,858	95,270	93,182	102,273	106,444	113,404	117,143	123,408	130,254	138,822
GDP at Market Prices	91,582	94,436	96,597	94,331	103,327	107,248	114,258	118,261	124,335	130,997	139,426
Resource Balance	-9,017	-4,595	-1,506	811	2,189	-2,041	4,873	1,035	-2,102	-12,532	-16,890
Exports of Goods & NFServices	38,114	39,748	38,480	37,696	38,132	33,044	39,666	40,559	35,174	38,506	43,818
Imports of Goods & NFServices	47,130	44,343	39,986	36,885	35,943	35,085	34,793	39,524	37,276	51,038	60,708
Domestic Absorption	100,599	99,031	98,103	93,520	101,138	109,289	109,386	117,226	126,438	143,529	156,316
Private Consumption, etc.	77,496	73,810	73,151	66,695	78,526	79,476	82,924	84,326	95,346	100,514	103,782
General Gov't Consumption	10,352	10,733	11,572	12,323	11,128	11,840	10,018	11,528	10,466	12,309	11,964
Gross Domestic Investment	12,751	14,489	13,380	14,502	11,484	17,973	16,444	21,373	20,625	30,707	40,569
Fixed Investment	12,712	13,202	11,940	12,127	11,325	14,301	14,692	20,059	19,746	30,588	39,727
GDP at factor cost	84,943	88,183	88,520	91,778	95,328	98,176	100,713	103,813	108,038	117,077	124,500
Agriculture	29,989	31,140	30,389	31,332	31,082	32,893	32,100	32,492	35,871	37,815	38,567
Industry	23,561	25,690	25,769	25,481	27,014	26,037	26,507	28,559	27,459	31,542	34,751
Manufacturing	14,538	15,356	15,929	16,223	15,838	15,118	15,817	16,572	16,474	17,760	18,585
Services, etc.	32,197	32,644	33,320	35,435	37,365	39,566	42,270	42,806	45,083	47,926	51,168
Memo Items:											
Capacity to Import	35,234	39,464	36,981	34,455	34,239	27,357	27,360	36,584	41,798	44,876	44,729
Terms of Trade Adjustment	-2,880	-284	-1,499	-3,241	-3,893	-5,687	-12,306	-3,975	6,625	6,370	911
Gross Domestic Income	88,703	94,152	95,098	91,091	99,434	101,561	101,952	114,286	130,960	137,367	140,336
Gross National Income	87,380	92,574	93,770	89,942	98,381	100,757	101,098	113,168	130,032	136,624	139,733

DOMESTIC PRICES/DEFLATORS					(Index 1987 = 100)						
Overall (GDP)	13.7	14.5	14.5	16.2	17.8	22.2	23.3	25.5	29.3	32.6	37.6
Domestic Absorption	13.6	14.2	14.6	16.6	18.4	23.4	26.1	26.4	27.7	31.1	37.5
Agriculture	11.8	12.0	12.2	12.4	15.7	23.5	24.3	25.0	29.7	32.6	34.8
Industry	11.9	12.2	13.1	14.0	16.8	22.4	25.6	26.6	36.2	35.0	40.4
Manufacturing	13.9	14.3	15.1	16.0	19.7	28.7	32.6	33.9	48.7	45.6	51.0
Consumer Price Index	20.0	21.2	21.7	23.1	25.3	28.5	30.3	30.7	31.1	34.9	38.6

MANUFACTURING ACTIVITY											
Employment (1987=100)	43.5	46.4	51.5	52.7	54.4	52.9	60.1	65.4	71.9	69.7	78.9
Real Earnings per Empl. (1987=100)	..	..	..	..	..	..	..	..	..	..	..
Real Output per Empl. (1987=100)	50.6	53.7	54.8	58.7	48.8	53.7	..	..	..	..	53.4
Earnings as % of Value Added	..	..	..	..	..	..	..	..	..	..	..

MONETARY HOLDINGS					(Millions of current Sri Lanka Rupees)						
Money Supply, Broadly Defined	3,479	3,809	4,266	4,969	5,263	5,950	6,351	8,207	11,204	14,619	20,701
Money	1,868	1,949	2,128	2,461	2,755	2,923	3,064	4,133	5,332	5,895	7,643
Currency Outside Banks	1,084	935	1,115	1,202	1,437	1,539	1,610	2,080	2,792	3,016	3,774
Demand Deposits	784	1,014	1,013	1,259	1,319	1,384	1,454	2,053	2,540	2,879	3,868
Quasi-Money	1,612	1,860	2,138	2,508	2,508	3,027	3,287	4,074	5,872	8,724	13,058

GOVERNMENT DEFICIT (-) OR SURPLUS					(Millions of current Sri Lanka Rupees)						
GOVERNMENT DEFICIT (-) OR SURPLUS	..	-873	-1,023	..	-960	-767	-1,704	-2,518	-1,671	-5,290	-6,300
Current Revenue	..	2,750	2,650	..	3,717	4,608	5,070	5,693	6,754	11,902	13,543
Current Expenditure	..	2,781	2,909	..	3,593	4,227	4,851	5,639	6,366	11,930	12,276
Current Budget Balance	..	-31	-259	..	124	381	219	54	388	-28	1,267
Capital Receipts	..	2	2	..	2	5	3	28	23	4	5
Capital Payments	..	844	766	..	1,086	1,153	1,926	2,600	2,082	5,266	7,572

1980	1981	1982	1983	1984	1985	1986	1987	1988	1989 estimate	NOTES	SRI LANKA
260	290	330	340	350	390	410	410	420	430	..	**CURRENT GNP PER CAPITA (US $)**
14,738	14,988	15,189	15,417	15,599	15,837	16,117	16,361	16,587	16,779	..	**POPULATION (thousands)**
			(Billions of current Sri Lanka Rupees)								**USE AND ORIGIN OF RESOURCES**
66.10	83.14	100.26	120.98	149.36	161.69	178.72	195.88	221.44	250.13	..	Gross National Product (GNP)
-0.43	-1.87	-1.96	-3.21	-3.40	-3.40	-3.86	-4.34	-5.27	-5.91	..	Net Factor Income from Abroad
66.53	85.00	102.22	124.19	152.76	165.09	182.58	200.22	226.70	256.03	f	GDP at Market Prices
-15.02	-13.67	-18.76	-18.37	-9.13	-19.41	-20.84	-20.66	-23.83	-24.14	..	Resource Balance
21.43	25.89	27.15	32.02	44.29	42.24	42.57	49.56	57.88	68.47	..	Exports of Goods & NFServices
36.46	39.56	45.90	50.38	53.42	61.65	63.41	70.22	81.71	92.61	..	Imports of Goods & NFServices
81.55	98.67	120.97	142.56	161.89	184.50	203.42	220.88	250.53	280.18	..	Domestic Absorption
53.40	68.75	82.21	97.54	110.25	129.22	142.48	155.45	178.12	200.93	..	Private Consumption, etc.
5.68	6.31	8.24	9.89	11.93	16.60	18.48	19.54	21.85	24.53	..	General Gov't Consumption
22.46	23.61	30.53	35.13	39.71	38.68	42.46	45.90	50.56	54.72	..	Gross Domestic Investment
20.84	23.28	30.28	35.34	39.56	38.46	42.33	45.75	49.96	54.25	..	Fixed Investment
4.28	5.67	7.54	10.32	12.72	16.77	18.87	22.49	23.18	27.66	..	Indirect Taxes, net
62.25	79.34	94.68	113.88	140.04	148.32	163.71	177.73	203.52	228.37	f	GDP at factor cost
17.15	21.98	24.96	32.18	40.14	41.07	44.35	47.92	53.60	59.39	..	Agriculture
18.45	22.21	24.89	29.99	36.86	38.86	43.55	48.76	54.30	61.22	..	Industry
11.05	12.88	13.60	15.96	20.89	21.85	24.87	28.47	31.30	34.94	..	Manufacturing
26.64	35.15	44.83	51.71	63.05	68.39	75.81	81.05	95.62	107.77	..	Services, etc.
7.44	9.94	11.77	16.77	30.58	19.27	21.62	25.24	26.74	30.58	..	Gross Domestic Saving
9.26	11.98	15.30	20.01	34.21	23.09	26.00	30.11	31.63	35.49	..	Gross National Saving
			(Millions of 1987 Sri Lanka Rupees)								
146,575	152,326	164,243	169,413	169,457	186,477	194,576	195,883	200,617	204,873	..	Gross National Product
147,458	155,722	167,409	173,896	173,409	190,344	198,758	200,219	205,630	209,997	I f	GDP at Market Prices
-26,998	-17,403	-25,007	-30,583	-24,684	-21,154	-21,032	-20,664	-20,457	-14,351	..	Resource Balance
45,396	49,942	52,206	42,343	41,380	43,249	47,290	49,559	51,171	55,479	..	Exports of Goods & NFServices
72,394	67,345	77,212	72,927	66,064	64,403	68,322	70,223	71,628	69,830	..	Imports of Goods & NFServices
174,456	173,125	192,416	204,479	198,094	211,498	219,790	220,883	226,087	224,348	..	Domestic Absorption
113,190	118,635	133,227	143,591	137,694	150,705	155,015	155,445	161,211	159,632	..	Private Consumption, etc.
11,592	10,607	12,940	13,619	14,089	19,318	19,913	19,538	20,066	20,526	..	General Gov't Consumption
49,673	43,883	46,248	47,269	46,311	41,474	44,862	45,900	44,809	44,190	..	Gross Domestic Investment
46,091	43,268	45,873	47,552	46,136	41,233	44,717	45,752	44,277	43,808	..	Fixed Investment
131,604	139,092	145,946	153,030	160,359	168,573	175,695	177,731	182,529	186,374	I f	GDP at factor cost
39,768	42,530	43,648	45,830	45,657	49,596	50,890	47,923	48,928	48,372	..	Agriculture
36,464	37,360	38,348	39,020	41,770	43,240	45,872	48,763	50,812	52,551	..	Industry
18,739	19,710	20,654	20,819	23,371	24,590	26,663	28,470	29,797	31,112	..	Manufacturing
55,266	59,201	63,887	68,180	72,932	75,736	78,933	81,045	82,788	85,452	..	Services, etc.
											Memo Items:
42,563	44,080	45,663	46,343	54,770	44,126	45,868	49,559	50,742	51,624	..	Capacity to Import
-2,833	-5,862	-6,543	4,000	13,390	877	-1,422	0	-429	-3,854	..	Terms of Trade Adjustment
144,625	149,859	160,866	177,896	186,799	191,221	197,336	200,219	205,201	206,142	..	Gross Domestic Income
143,742	146,464	157,700	173,413	182,848	187,354	193,154	195,883	200,188	201,019	..	Gross National Income
			(Index 1987 = 100)								**DOMESTIC PRICES/DEFLATORS**
45.1	54.6	61.1	71.4	88.1	86.7	91.9	100.0	110.2	121.9	..	Overall (GDP)
46.7	57.0	62.9	69.7	81.7	87.2	92.6	100.0	110.8	124.9	..	Domestic Absorption
43.1	51.7	57.2	70.2	87.9	82.8	87.2	100.0	109.5	122.8	..	Agriculture
50.6	59.4	64.9	76.9	88.2	89.9	94.9	100.0	106.9	116.5	..	Industry
59.0	65.4	65.9	76.6	89.4	88.9	93.3	100.0	105.0	112.3	..	Manufacturing
48.8	57.5	63.7	72.6	84.7	86.0	92.8	100.0	114.0	127.2	..	Consumer Price Index
											MANUFACTURING ACTIVITY
76.7	75.9	165.8	112.4	99.9	99.4	102.3	100.0	..	..	..	Employment (1987=100)
95.1	90.3	76.9	77.1	79.6	96.5	96.7	100.0	..	..	..	Real Earnings per Empl. (1987=100)
76.9	85.5	74.8	93.3	84.9	104.0	101.2	100.0	..	..	..	Real Output per Empl. (1987=100)
25.7	24.2	19.4	17.8	..	..	..	16.6	..	..	..	Earnings as % of Value Added
			(Millions of current Sri Lanka Rupees)								**MONETARY HOLDINGS**
26,256	30,975	39,668	48,221	56,145	63,884	67,002	77,332	88,077	99,245	D	Money Supply, Broadly Defined
9,333	9,949	11,672	14,589	16,647	18,661	21,051	24,901	32,155	35,087	..	Money
4,181	4,823	5,988	7,200	8,561	9,815	11,570	13,495	18,484	19,644	..	Currency Outside Banks
5,152	5,127	5,684	7,388	8,086	8,846	9,481	11,406	13,671	15,443	..	Demand Deposits
16,923	21,026	27,996	33,632	39,498	45,223	45,952	52,431	55,922	64,158	..	Quasi-Money
			(Millions of current Sri Lanka Rupees)								
-12,157	-10,518	-13,927	-12,846	-10,482	-15,679	-18,202	-17,073	-28,197	..	..	**GOVERNMENT DEFICIT (-) OR SURPLUS**
16,057	17,482	19,565	26,782	37,342	39,540	40,968	46,808	48,277	..	..	Current Revenue
16,456	14,649	18,341	22,002	24,631	32,644	33,967	39,560	46,132	..	..	Current Expenditure
-399	2,833	1,224	4,780	12,711	6,896	7,001	7,248	2,145	..	..	Current Budget Balance
7	14	20	9	13	15	23	13	62	..	..	Capital Receipts
11,765	13,365	15,171	17,635	23,206	22,589	25,226	24,334	30,400	..	..	Capital Payments

SRI LANKA	1969	1970	1971	1972	1973	1974	1975	1976	1977	1978	1979
FOREIGN TRADE (CUSTOMS BASIS)					*(Millions of current US dollars)*						
Value of Exports, fob	321.9	337.7	326.6	325.8	405.4	523.4	559.2	566.8	762.9	845.9	980.5
Nonfuel Primary Products	311.3	327.0	316.0	304.9	349.4	451.8	494.2	485.9	661.8	730.3	760.8
Fuels	0.0	4.9	1.8	1.4	9.1	39.3	0.3	2.8	2.9	50.2	95.3
Manufactures	10.6	5.8	8.8	19.5	46.8	32.3	64.8	78.2	98.2	65.4	124.5
Value of Imports, cif	427.3	386.6	328.1	336.4	422.3	688.2	744.6	552.1	701.1	942.1	1,449.1
Nonfuel Primary Products	175.6	195.1	165.9	176.9	231.9	344.3	400.2	222.9	301.1	318.0	393.7
Fuels	27.2	10.3	5.1	6.4	45.4	137.3	124.3	137.4	169.1	155.8	254.3
Manufactures	224.5	181.1	157.2	153.1	145.0	206.5	220.1	191.9	231.0	468.3	801.2
					(Index 1987 = 100)						
Terms of Trade	181.4	147.3	135.5	119.4	121.8	100.2	90.2	112.4	146.1	132.9	127.7
Export Prices, fob	47.3	44.9	45.5	46.3	54.7	75.8	69.3	75.9	101.3	98.0	109.3
Import Prices, cif	26.1	30.5	33.6	38.7	44.9	75.6	76.8	67.5	69.3	73.8	85.6
BALANCE OF PAYMENTS					*(Millions of current US dollars)*						
Exports of Goods & Services	..	378.5	378.1	367.6	426.9	575.9	639.1	636.0	866.9	970.3	1,173.6
Merchandise, fob	..	338.8	325.3	316.5	366.3	509.3	558.4	559.6	761.6	845.7	981.1
Nonfactor Services	..	38.1	50.7	49.5	57.9	61.1	73.5	72.5	93.5	104.4	152.9
Factor Services	..	1.6	2.2	1.6	2.6	5.5	7.1	3.9	11.8	20.2	39.5
Imports of Goods & Services	..	449.0	428.9	412.6	465.2	753.8	829.2	707.1	796.3	1,115.4	1,592.0
Merchandise, fob	..	353.0	336.3	322.9	371.7	628.7	686.2	579.5	655.1	898.7	1,304.3
Nonfactor Services	..	70.6	70.0	68.8	73.6	102.9	117.5	103.4	113.7	181.5	232.8
Factor Services	..	25.4	22.6	20.8	19.9	22.1	25.5	24.1	27.5	35.2	54.8
Long-Term Interest	..	12.1	11.2	13.7	15.5	16.5	20.6	23.2	21.3	24.7	27.7
Private Current Transfers, net	..	-0.9	-3.4	-4.3	0.2	-0.2	2.7	6.7	10.7	21.9	48.4
Workers' Remittances	..	3.0	3.4	3.9	7.5	8.2	8.6	13.0	18.5	39.0	60.1
Curr. A/C Bal before Off. Transf.	..	-71.4	-54.2	-49.3	-38.0	-178.1	-187.4	-64.4	81.2	-123.2	-370.1
Net Official Transfers	..	12.6	17.8	16.7	12.9	42.2	77.3	58.5	61.0	57.6	143.7
Curr. A/C Bal after Off. Transf.	..	-58.8	-36.4	-32.6	-25.2	-135.9	-110.0	-5.9	142.2	-65.6	-226.3
Long-Term Capital, net	..	30.2	67.9	48.6	51.7	71.8	68.9	72.0	71.2	118.5	173.6
Direct Investment	..	-0.3	0.3	0.4	0.5	1.3	0.1	..	-1.2	1.5	46.9
Long-Term Loans	..	36.1	60.0	37.9	44.7	94.1	38.9	96.6	50.7	127.1	113.2
Disbursements	..	65.6	89.7	73.8	83.8	146.5	156.6	200.7	153.5	192.7	162.8
Repayments	..	29.5	29.7	35.9	39.1	52.4	117.7	104.1	102.8	65.6	49.6
Other Long-Term Capital	..	-5.6	7.6	10.3	6.6	-23.6	29.9	-24.6	21.7	-10.1	13.5
Other Capital, net	..	29.5	-34.8	-14.7	1.6	32.9	15.2	-29.2	-60.9	0.4	99.4
Change in Reserves	..	-0.9	3.3	-1.3	-28.2	31.2	25.9	-36.9	-152.5	-53.3	-46.7
Memo Item:					*(Sri Lanka Rupees per US dollar)*						
Conversion Factor (Annual Avg)	6.600	6.850	7.040	7.640	8.430	8.520	9.000	10.880	13.390	15.610	15.570
					(Millions of US dollars), outstanding at end of year						
EXTERNAL DEBT (Total)	..	395.2	471.8	502.9	574.1	712.3	743.4	847.6	1,132.2	1,372.8	1,553.7
Long-Term Debt (by debtor)	..	395.2	471.8	502.9	574.1	712.3	743.4	847.6	986.2	1,262.8	1,417.7
Central Bank, incl. IMF credit	..	78.5	78.3	85.9	97.1	133.1	154.3	165.2	216.2	305.7	412.5
Central Government	..	267.8	335.9	360.3	419.6	514.2	540.6	621.7	715.4	907.2	939.9
Rest of General Government	..	0.3	0.3	0.1	0.0	0.0	0.0	0.0	0.0	0.0	0.0
Non-financial Public Enterprises	..	43.3	52.2	52.6	52.6	60.5	45.1	56.8	51.2	46.2	59.9
Priv. Sector, incl non-guaranteed	..	5.3	5.1	4.0	4.8	4.5	3.4	3.9	3.4	3.7	5.4
Short-Term Debt	..	..	..	..	..	..	..	..	146.0	110.0	136.0
Memo Items:					*(Millions of US dollars)*						
Int'l Reserves Excluding Gold	40.00	42.74	50.33	59.46	86.60	77.59	57.43	92.33	292.59	397.64	516.90
Gold Holdings (at market price)	..	..	..	..	..	..	..	..	..	9.48	32.21
SOCIAL INDICATORS											
Total Fertility Rate	4.4	4.3	4.1	4.0	4.0	3.9	3.9	3.9	3.8	3.7	3.6
Infant Mortality Rate	55.8	53.2	50.6	48.0	46.6	45.2	43.8	42.4	41.0	38.8	36.6
Life Expectancy at Birth	64.5	64.7	64.8	65.0	65.3	65.7	66.0	66.4	66.7	67.2	67.6
Urban Population, % of total	21.5	21.9	21.9	21.9	22.0	22.0	22.0	21.9	21.8	21.8	21.7
Food Prod. per capita (1987=100)	97.5	104.7	99.7	99.8	92.5	99.9	99.8	99.9	97.7	104.5	113.1
Labor Force, Agriculture (%)	55.4	55.3	55.1	54.9	54.7	54.5	54.3	54.1	53.9	53.7	53.5
Labor Force, Female (%)	25.0	25.0	25.1	25.3	25.4	25.5	25.6	25.9	26.2	26.4	26.7
Primary Schl. Enroll. Ratio	..	99.0	..	..	..	..	77.0	79.0	82.0	89.0	94.0
Primary Schl. Enroll. Ratio, Female	..	94.0	..	..	..	..	74.0	75.0	79.0	86.0	91.0
Secondary Schl. Enroll. Ratio	..	47.0	..	..	..	..	48.0	48.0	42.0	52.0	49.0

1980	1981	1982	1983	1984	1985	1986	1987	1988	1989 estimate	NOTES	SRI LANKA
				(Millions of current US dollars)							**FOREIGN TRADE (CUSTOMS BASIS)**
1,048.7	1,035.5	1,013.8	1,066.2	1,453.7	1,333.3	1,215.0	1,392.8	1,476.0	..	..	Value of Exports, fob
689.8	659.9	605.7	649.7	929.1	738.1	652.1	760.4	780.0	..	..	Nonfuel Primary Products
161.3	133.9	131.1	102.1	126.4	133.6	58.2	72.6	73.0	..	..	Fuels
197.6	241.7	276.9	314.4	398.2	461.6	504.7	559.8	623.0	..	..	Manufactures
2,035.4	1,803.8	1,769.9	1,788.5	1,847.4	1,988.3	1,948.3	2,084.8	2,262.0	..	..	Value of Imports, cif
468.6	403.6	275.0	356.7	331.9	339.2	353.7	403.7	441.0	..	..	Nonfuel Primary Products
494.4	450.6	554.9	426.8	475.0	521.1	274.3	344.6	374.0	..	..	Fuels
1,072.4	949.6	939.9	1,004.9	1,040.5	1,128.1	1,320.3	1,336.5	1,447.0	..	..	Manufactures
				(Index 1987 = 100)							
..	102.0	100.2	114.4	132.8	106.3	102.3	100.0	103.2	..	..	Terms of Trade
..	108.2	101.7	108.6	122.6	98.2	92.7	100.0	107.4	..	..	Export Prices, fob
105.3	106.1	101.6	95.0	92.4	92.4	90.6	100.0	104.0	..	..	Import Prices, cif
				(Millions of current US dollars)							**BALANCE OF PAYMENTS**
1,340.0	1,374.9	1,348.2	1,403.8	1,795.9	1,644.5	1,581.8	1,791.4	1,875.4	1,949.1	..	Exports of Goods & Services
1,061.6	1,062.5	1,013.9	1,061.2	1,461.6	1,315.8	1,208.5	1,393.9	1,473.3	1,548.2	..	Merchandise, fob
231.1	279.4	290.6	297.9	276.2	245.4	305.3	328.2	333.5	343.1	..	Nonfactor Services
47.2	33.0	43.8	44.7	58.1	83.3	68.0	69.3	68.5	57.9	..	Factor Services
2,269.4	2,182.5	2,322.7	2,314.6	2,274.2	2,505.7	2,469.9	2,610.1	2,804.5	2,794.9	..	Imports of Goods & Services
1,845.1	1,694.5	1,794.3	1,725.6	1,698.7	1,838.5	1,764.3	1,866.0	2,017.5	2,021.0	..	Merchandise, fob
351.4	359.2	390.6	407.3	383.5	457.1	499.7	533.2	546.2	551.0	..	Nonfactor Services
72.8	128.8	137.8	181.8	191.9	210.1	206.0	210.8	240.8	222.9	..	Factor Services
32.9	49.5	69.0	92.2	106.3	116.3	121.2	126.7	124.6	107.8	..	Long-Term Interest
136.2	202.9	263.8	274.5	276.5	265.5	294.1	312.8	319.3	300.0	f	Private Current Transfers, net
151.7	229.6	289.3	294.5	300.9	291.7	326.0	350.1	357.0	337.8	..	Workers' Remittances
-793.3	-604.7	-710.6	-636.3	-201.8	-595.7	-594.0	-506.0	-609.8	-545.7	..	Curr. A/C Bal before Off. Transf.
138.0	160.3	162.3	170.3	202.6	177.2	176.9	179.9	206.1	174.1	f	Net Official Transfers
-655.3	-444.4	-548.3	-466.0	0.9	-418.4	-417.1	-326.1	-403.7	-371.6	..	Curr. A/C Bal after Off. Transf.
208.7	363.5	518.5	410.4	379.4	345.3	363.7	268.1	269.2	211.0	..	Long-Term Capital, net
43.0	49.3	63.6	37.8	32.6	24.8	29.2	58.2	43.5	26.9	..	Direct Investment
220.5	344.9	395.8	298.9	341.5	339.7	340.0	187.3	194.7	220.0	..	Long-Term Loans
271.8	390.5	470.9	373.0	432.8	451.1	488.2	392.2	400.4	404.2	..	Disbursements
51.3	45.6	75.1	74.1	91.3	111.4	148.2	204.9	205.7	184.2	..	Repayments
-54.8	-30.7	59.1	73.7	5.2	-19.2	-5.5	22.7	31.0	-35.9	..	Other Long-Term Capital
165.0	43.2	-17.5	49.0	-69.6	-41.6	-58.2	-19.9	10.0	156.1	..	Other Capital, net
281.6	37.8	47.3	6.6	-310.7	114.7	111.6	77.8	124.6	4.5	..	Change in Reserves
				(Sri Lanka Rupees per US dollar)							Memo Item:
16.530	19.250	20.810	23.530	25.440	27.160	28.020	29.450	31.810	36.040	..	Conversion Factor (Annual Avg)
				(Millions of US dollars), outstanding at end of year							
1,841.2	2,234.6	2,625.5	2,884.3	2,992.1	3,537.8	4,063.0	4,732.2	5,187.4	5,100.8	..	**EXTERNAL DEBT (Total)**
1,621.4	2,030.7	2,349.6	2,600.7	2,797.4	3,331.5	3,878.4	4,458.9	4,610.4	4,706.6	..	Long-Term Debt (by debtor)
400.9	523.9	494.3	456.2	415.0	407.5	358.9	289.1	369.5	399.0	..	Central Bank, incl. IMF credit
1,123.4	1,314.2	1,516.4	1,738.7	1,949.6	2,428.6	3,009.8	3,600.5	3,744.3	3,842.3	..	Central Government
0.0	0.0	0.0	0.0	0.0	0.0	0.0	0.0	0.0	..	..	Rest of General Government
83.4	180.7	331.0	361.8	383.0	378.3	358.1	350.3	283.4	268.5	..	Non-financial Public Enterprises
13.7	11.9	7.9	44.0	49.8	117.1	151.6	219.0	213.2	196.8	..	Priv. Sector, incl non-guaranteed
219.8	203.9	275.9	283.6	194.7	206.3	184.6	273.3	577.0	394.2	..	Short-Term Debt
				(Millions of US dollars)							Memo Items:
245.50	327.36	351.49	296.95	510.77	451.16	352.60	279.06	221.92	244.21	..	Int'l Reserves Excluding Gold
37.08	25.00	28.74	24.00	19.39	20.57	24.59	30.45	25.81	25.22	..	Gold Holdings (at market price)
											SOCIAL INDICATORS
3.5	3.4	3.3	3.1	3.0	2.9	2.7	2.6	2.5	2.5	..	Total Fertility Rate
34.4	32.2	30.0	28.3	26.5	24.8	23.0	22.0	21.3	20.5	..	Infant Mortality Rate
68.1	68.5	69.0	69.2	69.5	69.8	70.1	70.3	70.6	70.8	..	Life Expectancy at Birth
21.6	21.5	21.4	21.3	21.2	21.1	21.2	21.2	21.3	21.3	..	Urban Population, % of total
118.2	116.5	113.5	122.2	110.6	118.6	115.0	100.0	103.0	101.2	..	Food Prod. per capita (1987=100)
53.4	..	..	..	..	..	..	..	..	..	..	Labor Force, Agriculture (%)
26.9	26.9	26.9	26.9	26.9	26.9	26.9	26.8	26.8	26.8	..	Labor Force, Female (%)
103.0	..	105.0	103.0	103.0	103.0	104.0	..	..	..	..	Primary Schl. Enroll. Ratio
100.0	100.0	102.0	101.0	101.0	101.0	102.0	..	..	..	..	Primary Schl. Enroll. Ratio, Female
55.0	..	57.0	59.0	61.0	63.0	66.0	..	..	..	..	Secondary Schl. Enroll. Ratio

ST. KITTS AND NEVIS	1969	1970	1971	1972	1973	1974	1975	1976	1977	1978	1979
CURRENT GNP PER CAPITA (US $)	..	..	..	..	..	..	..	..	..	..	..
POPULATION (thousands)	46	45	45	44	44	44	44	43	44	44	44
USE AND ORIGIN OF RESOURCES				*(Millions of current Eastern Caribbean Dollars)*							
Gross National Product (GNP)	..	..	..	..	..	..	..	..	..	..	..
Net Factor Income from Abroad	..	..	..	..	..	..	..	..	..	..	..
GDP at Market Prices	31.70	32.60	38.70	44.10	47.40	64.70	72.40	78.70	81.70	93.40	108.70
Resource Balance	..	..	..	..	..	..	..	..	..	..	..
Exports of Goods & NFServices	..	..	..	..	..	..	..	..	..	..	..
Imports of Goods & NFServices	..	..	..	..	..	..	..	..	..	..	..
Domestic Absorption	..	..	..	..	..	..	..	..	..	..	..
Private Consumption, etc.	..	..	..	..	..	..	..	..	..	..	..
General Gov't Consumption	..	..	..	..	..	..	..	..	..	..	..
Gross Domestic Investment	..	..	..	..	..	..	..	..	..	..	..
Fixed Investment	..	..	..	..	..	..	..	..	..	..	..
Indirect Taxes, net	..	..	..	..	..	..	..	..	11.50	16.00	20.90
GDP at factor cost	..	..	..	..	..	..	..	..	70.20	77.40	87.80
Agriculture	..	..	..	..	..	..	..	..	13.10	12.20	13.60
Industry	..	..	..	..	..	..	..	..	19.90	19.60	21.90
Manufacturing	..	..	..	..	..	..	..	..	..	..	12.80
Services, etc.	..	..	..	..	..	..	..	..	37.20	45.60	52.30
Gross Domestic Saving	..	..	..	..	..	..	..	..	..	..	..
Gross National Saving	..	..	..	..	..	..	..	..	..	..	..
				(Millions of 1987 Eastern Caribbean Dollars)							
Gross National Product	..	..	..	..	..	..	..	..	..	..	..
GDP at Market Prices	..	..	..	..	..	..	..	..	..	..	..
Resource Balance	..	..	..	..	..	..	..	..	..	..	..
Exports of Goods & NFServices	..	..	..	..	..	..	..	..	..	..	..
Imports of Goods & NFServices	..	..	..	..	..	..	..	..	..	..	..
Domestic Absorption	..	..	..	..	..	..	..	..	..	..	..
Private Consumption, etc.	..	..	..	..	..	..	..	..	..	..	..
General Gov't Consumption	..	..	..	..	..	..	..	..	..	..	..
Gross Domestic Investment	..	..	..	..	..	..	..	..	..	..	..
Fixed Investment	..	..	..	..	..	..	..	..	..	..	..
GDP at factor cost	..	..	..	..	..	..	..	..	143.03	145.21	157.07
Agriculture	..	..	..	..	..	..	..	..	27.31	28.56	30.85
Industry	..	..	..	..	..	..	..	..	43.64	41.44	44.51
Manufacturing	..	..	..	..	..	..	..	..	..	..	..
Services, etc.	..	..	..	..	..	..	..	..	73.68	76.45	82.98
Memo Items:											
Capacity to Import	..	..	..	..	..	..	..	..	..	..	..
Terms of Trade Adjustment	..	..	..	..	..	..	..	..	..	..	..
Gross Domestic Income	..	..	..	..	..	..	..	..	..	..	..
Gross National Income	..	..	..	..	..	..	..	..	..	..	..
DOMESTIC PRICES/DEFLATORS				*(Index 1987 = 100)*							
Overall (GDP)	..	..	..	..	..	..	..	..	..	..	..
Domestic Absorption	..	..	..	..	..	..	..	..	..	..	..
Agriculture	..	..	..	..	..	..	..	..	48.0	42.7	44.1
Industry	..	..	..	..	..	..	..	..	45.6	47.3	49.2
Manufacturing	..	..	..	..	..	..	..	..	..	..	..
Consumer Price Index	..	..	..	..	..	..	..	..	..	..	66.8
MANUFACTURING ACTIVITY											
Employment (1987=100)	..	..	..	..	..	..	..	..	..	..	..
Real Earnings per Empl. (1987=100)	..	..	..	..	..	..	..	..	..	..	..
Real Output per Empl. (1987=100)	..	..	..	..	..	..	..	..	..	..	..
Earnings as % of Value Added	..	..	..	..	..	..	..	..	..	..	..
MONETARY HOLDINGS				*(Millions of current Eastern Caribbean Dollars)*							
Money Supply, Broadly Defined	..	..	..	..	..	..	..	..	..	..	83.98
Money	..	..	..	..	..	..	..	..	..	..	9.25
Currency Outside Banks	..	..	..	..	..	..	..	..	..	..	-1.55
Demand Deposits	..	..	..	..	..	..	..	..	..	..	10.81
Quasi-Money	..	..	..	..	..	..	..	..	..	..	74.73
GOVERNMENT DEFICIT (-) OR SURPLUS				*(Thousands of current Eastern Caribbean Dollars)*							
Current Revenue	..	..	..	..	..	..	..	..	..	..	..
Current Expenditure	..	..	..	..	..	..	..	..	..	..	..
Current Budget Balance	..	..	..	..	..	..	..	..	..	..	..
Capital Receipts	..	..	..	..	..	..	..	..	..	..	..
Capital Payments	..	..	..	..	..	..	..	..	..	..	..

1980	1981	1982	1983	1984	1985	1986	1987	1988	1989 estimate	NOTES	ST. KITTS AND NEVIS
..	..	1,310	1,380	1,620	1,750	2,030	2,430	2,860	..	..	**CURRENT GNP PER CAPITA (US $)**
44	44	45	45	44	43	42	42	42	41	..	**POPULATION (thousands)**
				(Millions of current Eastern Caribbean Dollars)							**USE AND ORIGIN OF RESOURCES**
127.40	148.20	160.90	163.70	192.00	202.90	252.30	290.70	328.40	..	..	Gross National Product (GNP)
-3.40	-2.80	1.60	3.00	3.20	0.50	1.90	3.80	6.50	..	..	Net Factor Income from Abroad
130.80	151.00	159.30	160.70	188.80	202.40	250.40	286.90	321.90	..	..	GDP at Market Prices
-38.30	-42.60	-49.70	-72.70	-41.30	-34.00	-33.80	-62.60	-87.80	..	..	Resource Balance
87.50	104.80	91.80	84.20	105.00	120.20	157.10	180.40	197.90	..	..	Exports of Goods & NFServices
125.80	147.40	141.50	156.90	146.30	154.20	190.90	243.00	285.70	..	..	Imports of Goods & NFServices
..	..	..	..	..	..	..	..	..	..	..	Domestic Absorption
..	..	..	..	..	..	..	..	..	..	..	Private Consumption, etc.
..	..	..	..	..	..	..	..	..	..	..	General Gov't Consumption
..	..	..	..	..	..	..	..	..	..	..	Gross Domestic Investment
..	..	..	..	..	..	..	..	..	..	..	Fixed Investment
27.70	30.50	20.40	22.00	29.50	30.60	37.20	49.30	58.70	..	..	Indirect Taxes, net
103.10	120.50	138.90	138.70	159.30	171.80	213.20	237.60	263.20	..	B	GDP at factor cost
16.50	13.80	20.30	16.20	19.20	16.40	21.80	24.60	25.90	..	..	Agriculture
27.50	30.20	34.10	34.40	37.20	39.30	54.40	60.30	67.50	..	..	Industry
15.70	17.90	18.70	17.60	22.60	21.90	32.80	35.40	38.90	..	..	Manufacturing
59.10	76.50	84.50	88.10	102.90	116.10	137.00	152.70	169.80	..	..	Services, etc.
..	..	..	..	..	..	..	..	..	..	..	Gross Domestic Saving
..	..	..	..	..	..	..	..	..	..	..	Gross National Saving
				(Millions of 1987 Eastern Caribbean Dollars)							
201.36	210.35	212.36	214.66	238.27	245.85	263.22	290.70	310.56	..	..	Gross National Product
207.46	215.59	210.64	210.48	233.71	245.09	260.94	286.90	304.10	..	..	GDP at Market Prices
..	..	..	..	..	..	..	..	..	..	..	Resource Balance
..	..	..	..	..	..	..	..	..	..	..	Exports of Goods & NFServices
..	..	..	..	..	..	..	..	..	..	..	Imports of Goods & NFServices
..	..	..	..	..	..	..	..	..	..	..	Domestic Absorption
..	..	..	..	..	..	..	..	..	..	..	Private Consumption, etc.
..	..	..	..	..	..	..	..	..	..	..	General Gov't Consumption
..	..	..	..	..	..	..	..	..	..	..	Gross Domestic Investment
..	..	..	..	..	..	..	..	..	..	..	Fixed Investment
163.50	172.04	183.64	181.84	197.30	208.07	222.07	237.60	248.66	..	B	GDP at factor cost
27.94	29.39	29.39	23.97	25.02	24.39	23.97	24.60	25.64	..	..	Agriculture
49.12	46.71	52.63	51.31	50.87	51.97	55.70	60.30	65.56	..	..	Industry
..	..	..	..	..	..	..	..	..	..	..	Manufacturing
87.74	96.45	102.39	106.55	121.41	131.71	142.40	152.70	157.45	..	..	Services, etc.
											Memo Items:
..	..	..	..	..	..	..	..	..	..	..	Capacity to Import
..	..	..	..	..	..	..	..	..	..	..	Terms of Trade Adjustment
..	..	..	..	..	..	..	..	..	..	..	Gross Domestic Income
..	..	..	..	..	..	..	..	..	..	..	Gross National Income
				(Index 1987 = 100)							**DOMESTIC PRICES/DEFLATORS**
63.0	70.0	75.6	76.4	80.8	82.6	96.0	100.0	105.9	..	..	Overall (GDP)
..	..	..	..	..	..	..	..	..	..	..	Domestic Absorption
59.1	46.9	69.1	67.6	76.7	67.2	90.9	100.0	101.0	..	..	Agriculture
56.0	64.7	64.8	67.0	73.1	75.6	97.7	100.0	103.0	..	..	Industry
..	..	..	..	..	..	..	..	..	..	..	Manufacturing
78.6	86.8	92.0	94.1	96.7	99.2	99.2	100.0	100.5	105.5	..	Consumer Price Index
											MANUFACTURING ACTIVITY
..	..	..	..	..	..	..	..	..	..	..	Employment (1987=100)
..	..	..	..	..	..	..	..	..	..	..	Real Earnings per Empl. (1987=100)
..	..	..	..	..	..	..	..	..	..	..	Real Output per Empl. (1987=100)
..	..	..	..	..	..	..	..	..	..	..	Earnings as % of Value Added
				(Millions of current Eastern Caribbean Dollars)							**MONETARY HOLDINGS**
95.32	116.84	130.92	150.69	170.90	204.21	232.56	212.22	266.00	333.40	..	Money Supply, Broadly Defined
8.01	26.42	25.49	27.58	29.26	32.90	49.81	55.26	73.92	100.19	..	Money
-1.32	10.33	11.10	11.59	12.61	9.39	12.22	13.00	16.08	22.65	..	Currency Outside Banks
9.34	16.09	14.39	15.98	16.64	23.51	37.59	42.25	57.84	77.54	..	Demand Deposits
87.31	90.41	105.43	123.11	141.64	171.31	182.75	156.96	192.08	233.21	..	Quasi-Money
				(Thousands of current Eastern Caribbean Dollars)							
..	..	..	..	..	-13,120	2,850	-47,460	..	..	..	**GOVERNMENT DEFICIT (-) OR SURPLUS**
..	..	..	..	..	62,990	76,500	88,390	99,140	..	..	Current Revenue
..	..	..	..	..	58,800	57,410	64,500	..	..	..	Current Expenditure
..	..	..	..	..	4,190	19,090	23,890	..	..	..	Current Budget Balance
..	..	..	..	..	1,030	660	1,860	1,980	..	..	Capital Receipts
..	..	..	..	..	18,340	16,900	73,210	..	..	..	Capital Payments

| 1980 | 1981 | 1982 | 1983 | 1984 | 1985 | 1986 | 1987 | 1988 | | | |

ST. KITTS AND NEVIS	1969	1970	1971	1972	1973	1974	1975	1976	1977	1978	1979
FOREIGN TRADE (CUSTOMS BASIS)				*(Thousands of current US dollars)*							
Value of Exports, fob	..	..	..	..	..	..	..	..	..	..	..
Nonfuel Primary Products	..	..	..	..	..	..	..	..	..	..	..
Fuels	..	..	..	..	..	..	..	..	..	..	..
Manufactures	..	..	..	..	..	..	..	..	..	..	..
Value of Imports, cif	..	..	..	..	..	..	..	..	..	..	..
Nonfuel Primary Products	..	..	..	..	..	..	..	..	..	..	..
Fuels	..	..	..	..	..	..	..	..	..	..	..
Manufactures	..	..	..	..	..	..	..	..	..	..	..
				(Index 1987 = 100)							
Terms of Trade	..	..	..	..	..	..	..	..	..	..	..
Export Prices, fob	..	..	..	..	..	..	..	..	..	..	..
Import Prices, cif	..	..	..	..	..	..	..	..	..	..	..
BALANCE OF PAYMENTS				*(Millions of current US dollars)*							
Exports of Goods & Services	..	..	..	..	..	..	..	..	..	..	..
Merchandise, fob	..	..	..	..	..	..	..	..	..	..	..
Nonfactor Services	..	..	..	..	..	..	..	..	..	..	..
Factor Services	..	..	..	..	..	..	..	..	..	..	..
Imports of Goods & Services	..	..	..	..	..	..	..	..	..	..	..
Merchandise, fob	..	..	..	..	..	..	..	..	..	..	..
Nonfactor Services	..	..	..	..	..	..	..	..	..	..	..
Factor Services	..	..	..	..	..	..	..	..	..	..	..
Long-Term Interest	..	..	..	..	..	..	..	..	..	..	..
Private Current Transfers, net	..	..	..	..	..	..	..	..	..	..	..
Workers' Remittances	..	..	..	..	..	..	..	..	..	..	..
Curr. A/C Bal before Off. Transf.	..	..	..	..	..	..	..	..	..	..	..
Net Official Transfers	..	..	..	..	..	..	..	..	..	..	..
Curr. A/C Bal after Off. Transf.	..	..	..	..	..	..	..	..	..	..	..
Long-Term Capital, net	..	..	..	..	..	..	..	..	..	..	..
Direct Investment	..	..	..	..	..	..	..	..	..	..	..
Long-Term Loans	..	..	..	..	..	..	..	..	..	..	..
Disbursements	..	..	..	..	..	..	..	..	..	..	..
Repayments	..	..	..	..	..	..	..	..	..	..	..
Other Long-Term Capital	..	..	..	..	..	..	..	..	..	..	..
Other Capital, net	..	..	..	..	..	..	..	..	..	..	..
Change in Reserves	..	..	..	..	..	..	..	..	..	..	..
Memo Item:				*(Eastern Caribbean Dollars per US dollar)*							
Conversion Factor (Annual Avg)	2.000	2.000	1.970	1.920	1.960	2.050	2.170	2.610	2.700	2.700	2.700
				(Millions of US dollars), outstanding at end of year							
EXTERNAL DEBT (Total)	..	..	..	..	..	..	..	..	..	..	..
Long-Term Debt (by debtor)	..	..	..	..	..	..	..	..	..	..	..
Central Bank, incl. IMF credit	..	..	..	..	..	..	..	..	..	..	..
Central Government	..	..	..	..	..	..	..	..	..	..	..
Rest of General Government	..	..	..	..	..	..	..	..	..	..	..
Non-financial Public Enterprises	..	..	..	..	..	..	..	..	..	..	..
Priv. Sector, incl non-guaranteed	..	..	..	..	..	..	..	..	..	..	..
Short-Term Debt	..	..	..	..	..	..	..	..	..	..	..
Memo Items:				*(Thousands of US dollars)*							
Int'l Reserves Excluding Gold	..	..	..	..	..	..	..	..	..	..	..
Gold Holdings (at market price)	..	..	..	..	..	..	..	..	..	..	..
SOCIAL INDICATORS											
Total Fertility Rate	..	..	..	3.5	3.5	3.5	3.4	3.4	3.4	3.4	3.4
Infant Mortality Rate	..	..	..	..	..	..	..	..	..	..	..
Life Expectancy at Birth	..	..	..	..	..	..	..	..	..	..	..
Urban Population, % of total	33.6	34.3	35.0	35.7	36.3	37.0	37.7	38.4	39.1	39.9	40.6
Food Prod. per capita (1987=100)	..	..	..	..	..	..	..	..	..	..	..
Labor Force, Agriculture (%)	..	..	..	..	..	..	..	..	..	..	..
Labor Force, Female (%)	..	..	..	..	..	..	..	..	..	..	..
Primary Schl. Enroll. Ratio	..	..	..	..	..	..	..	..	..	..	..
Primary Schl. Enroll. Ratio, Female	..	..	..	..	..	..	..	..	..	..	..
Secondary Schl. Enroll. Ratio	..	..	..	..	..	..	..	..	..	..	..

1980	1981	1982	1983	1984	1985	1986	1987	1988	1989 estimate	NOTES	ST. KITTS AND NEVIS
				(Thousands of current US dollars)							**FOREIGN TRADE (CUSTOMS BASIS)**
24,300	24,000	19,000	18,200	21,400	18,700	..	..	..	..	..	Value of Exports, fob
..	..	..	..	..	..	..	..	..	..	..	Nonfuel Primary Products
..	..	..	..	..	..	..	..	..	..	..	Fuels
..	..	..	..	..	..	..	..	..	..	..	Manufactures
45,000	48,000	44,000	52,000	50,000	49,000	..	..	..	..	..	Value of Imports, cif
..	..	..	..	..	..	..	..	..	..	..	Nonfuel Primary Products
..	..	..	..	..	..	..	..	..	..	..	Fuels
..	..	..	..	..	..	..	..	..	..	..	Manufactures
				(Index 1987 = 100)							
..	..	..	..	..	..	..	..	..	..	..	Terms of Trade
..	..	..	..	..	..	..	..	..	..	..	Export Prices, fob
..	..	..	..	..	..	..	..	..	..	..	Import Prices, cif
				(Millions of current US dollars)							**BALANCE OF PAYMENTS**
32.92	35.46	33.34	33.23	41.37	43.47	58.35	68.92	74.14	..	..	Exports of Goods & Services
24.12	24.26	18.84	18.43	20.15	20.37	25.15	27.99	27.44	..	..	Merchandise, fob
8.10	10.00	13.20	13.00	20.32	22.80	31.13	37.91	42.53	..	..	Nonfactor Services
0.70	1.20	1.30	1.80	0.90	0.30	2.07	3.01	4.17	..	..	Factor Services
48.59	52.86	53.16	58.27	57.20	58.62	72.97	91.58	107.09	..	..	Imports of Goods & Services
40.80	43.42	39.82	46.74	47.23	46.70	55.35	69.95	81.60	..	..	Merchandise, fob
5.84	7.19	12.64	10.82	9.17	10.32	14.70	17.80	20.53	..	..	Nonfactor Services
1.94	2.24	0.70	0.70	0.80	1.60	2.92	3.83	4.95	..	..	Factor Services
..	..	..	..	..	..	..	..	..	..	..	Long-Term Interest
8.20	11.10	9.00	8.20	9.80	7.12	8.52	9.15	9.85	..	..	Private Current Transfers, net
0.79	1.11	1.10	1.11	1.31	1.06	1.04	1.11	1.19	..	..	Workers' Remittances
-7.46	-6.30	-10.82	-16.84	-6.04	-8.03	-6.11	-13.51	-23.10	..	..	Curr. A/C Bal before Off. Transf.
4.80	1.60	2.10	2.10	1.70	1.35	2.37	3.08	3.73	..	..	Net Official Transfers
-2.66	-4.70	-8.72	-14.74	-4.34	-6.68	-3.74	-10.43	-19.37	..	..	Curr. A/C Bal after Off. Transf.
4.94	2.20	2.90	14.30	11.40	9.40	4.56	13.39	18.90	..	..	Long-Term Capital, net
1.00	0.90	2.20	13.50	6.00	8.00	5.96	8.73	8.17	..	..	Direct Investment
..	..	..	..	..	..	..	..	..	..	..	Long-Term Loans
..	..	..	..	..	..	..	..	..	..	..	Disbursements
..	..	..	..	..	..	..	..	..	..	..	Repayments
3.94	1.30	0.70	0.80	5.40	1.40	-1.40	4.66	10.73	..	..	Other Long-Term Capital
-3.88	2.60	2.02	1.64	-5.26	-0.78	2.30	-2.32	0.54	..	..	Other Capital, net
1.60	-0.10	3.80	-1.20	-1.80	-1.94	-3.12	-0.64	-0.07	-6.07	..	Change in Reserves
				(Eastern Caribbean Dollars per US dollar)							**Memo Item:**
2.700	2.700	2.700	2.700	2.700	2.700	2.700	2.700	2.700	2.700	..	Conversion Factor (Annual Avg)
				(Millions of US dollars), outstanding at end of year							**EXTERNAL DEBT (Total)**
..	..	..	..	..	..	..	..	..	..	..	Long-Term Debt (by debtor)
..	..	..	..	..	..	..	..	..	..	..	Central Bank, incl. IMF credit
..	..	..	..	..	..	..	..	..	..	..	Central Government
..	..	..	..	..	..	..	..	..	..	..	Rest of General Government
..	..	..	..	..	..	..	..	..	..	..	Non-financial Public Enterprises
..	..	..	..	..	..	..	..	..	..	..	Priv. Sector, incl non-guaranteed
..	..	..	..	..	..	..	..	..	..	..	Short-Term Debt
				(Thousands of US dollars)							**Memo Items:**
..	4,016	3,329	3,148	5,651	7,415	10,232	10,574	10,324	16,393	..	Int'l Reserves Excluding Gold
..	..	..	..	..	..	..	..	..	..	..	Gold Holdings (at market price)
											SOCIAL INDICATORS
3.3	3.3	3.3	3.2	3.1	3.0	2.9	2.8	2.7	2.7	..	Total Fertility Rate
..	..	45.0	43.7	42.4	41.0	39.7	40.0	39.0	38.0	..	Infant Mortality Rate
..	..	66.9	67.2	67.5	67.8	68.2	68.5	68.8	69.1	..	Life Expectancy at Birth
41.3	42.0	42.8	43.5	44.3	45.0	45.8	46.6	47.3	48.1	..	Urban Population, % of total
..	..	..	..	..	..	..	..	..	..	..	Food Prod. per capita (1987=100)
..	..	..	..	..	..	..	..	..	..	..	Labor Force, Agriculture (%)
..	..	..	..	..	..	..	..	..	..	..	Labor Force, Female (%)
..	..	..	..	..	..	..	..	..	..	..	Primary Schl. Enroll. Ratio
..	..	..	..	..	..	..	..	..	..	..	Primary Schl. Enroll. Ratio, Female
..	..	..	..	..	..	..	..	..	..	..	Secondary Schl. Enroll. Ratio

ST. LUCIA	1969	1970	1971	1972	1973	1974	1975	1976	1977	1978	1979
CURRENT GNP PER CAPITA (US $)	..	..	..	..	..	..	..	..	..	..	..
POPULATION (thousands)	100	101	103	105	107	110	112	114	117	119	121

USE AND ORIGIN OF RESOURCES *(Millions of current Eastern Caribbean Dollars)*

	1969	1970	1971	1972	1973	1974	1975	1976	1977	1978	1979
Gross National Product (GNP)	..	..	..	..	..	..	..	..	..	..	258.50
Net Factor Income from Abroad											-20.80
GDP at Market Prices	..	..	..	..	..	..	..	..	..	..	279.30
Resource Balance	..	..	..	..	..	..	..	..	..	..	-108.30
Exports of Goods & NFServices	..	..	..	..	..	..	..	..	..	..	176.30
Imports of Goods & NFServices	..	..	..	..	..	..	..	..	..	..	284.60
Domestic Absorption	..	..	..	..	..	..	..	..	..	..	..
Private Consumption, etc.	..	..	..	..	..	..	..	..	..	..	..
General Gov't Consumption	..	..	..	..	..	..	..	..	..	..	..
Gross Domestic Investment	..	..	..	..	..	..	..	..	..	..	..
Fixed Investment	..	..	..	..	..	..	..	..	..	..	..
Indirect Taxes, net	..	..	..	..	..	..	..	..	..	..	50.20
GDP at factor cost	..	..	..	..	..	..	..	..	..	..	229.10
Agriculture	..	..	..	..	..	..	..	..	..	..	34.80
Industry	..	..	..	..	..	..	..	..	..	..	52.20
Manufacturing	..	..	..	..	..	..	..	..	..	..	18.90
Services, etc.	..	..	..	..	..	..	..	..	..	..	142.10
Gross Domestic Saving	..	..	..	..	..	..	..	..	..	..	..
Gross National Saving	..	..	..	..	..	..	..	..	..	..	..

(Millions of 1987 Eastern Caribbean Dollars)

	1969	1970	1971	1972	1973	1974	1975	1976	1977	1978	1979
Gross National Product	..	..	..	..	..	..	..	..	..	..	327.76
GDP at Market Prices	..	..	..	..	..	..	..	..	..	..	442.91
Resource Balance	..	..	..	..	..	..	..	..	..	..	..
Exports of Goods & NFServices	..	..	..	..	..	..	..	..	..	..	..
Imports of Goods & NFServices	..	..	..	..	..	..	..	..	..	..	..
Domestic Absorption	..	..	..	..	..	..	..	..	..	..	..
Private Consumption, etc.	..	..	..	..	..	..	..	..	..	..	..
General Gov't Consumption	..	..	..	..	..	..	..	..	..	..	..
Gross Domestic Investment	..	..	..	..	..	..	..	..	..	..	..
Fixed Investment	..	..	..	..	..	..	..	..	..	..	..
GDP at factor cost	..	..	..	..	..	..	..	..	310.14	350.71	363.86
Agriculture	..	..	..	..	..	..	..	..	56.42	68.31	65.05
Industry	..	..	..	..	..	..	..	..	60.20	74.95	80.34
Manufacturing	..	..	..	..	..	..	..	..	24.39	28.28	23.69
Services, etc.	..	..	..	..	..	..	..	..	194.13	208.93	218.80

Memo Items:

	1969	1970	1971	1972	1973	1974	1975	1976	1977	1978	1979
Capacity to Import	..	..	..	..	..	..	..	..	..	..	..
Terms of Trade Adjustment	..	..	..	..	..	..	..	..	..	..	..
Gross Domestic Income	..	..	..	..	..	..	..	..	..	..	..
Gross National Income	..	..	..	..	..	..	..	..	..	..	..

DOMESTIC PRICES/DEFLATORS *(Index 1987 = 100)*

	1969	1970	1971	1972	1973	1974	1975	1976	1977	1978	1979
Overall (GDP)	..	..	..	..	..	..	..	..	..	..	63.1
Domestic Absorption	..	..	..	..	..	..	..	..	..	..	..
Agriculture	..	..	..	..	..	..	..	..	..	..	53.5
Industry	..	..	..	..	..	..	..	..	..	..	65.0
Manufacturing	..	..	..	..	..	..	..	..	..	..	79.8
Consumer Price Index	17.7	20.0	21.7	23.4	26.6	35.7	42.0	46.1	50.2	55.6	60.8

MANUFACTURING ACTIVITY

	1969	1970	1971	1972	1973	1974	1975	1976	1977	1978	1979
Employment (1987=100)	..	..	..	..	..	..	..	..	..	..	..
Real Earnings per Empl. (1987=100)	..	..	..	..	..	..	..	..	..	..	..
Real Output per Empl. (1987=100)	..	..	..	..	..	..	..	..	..	..	..
Earnings as % of Value Added	..	..	..	..	..	..	..	..	..	..	..

MONETARY HOLDINGS *(Millions of current Eastern Caribbean Dollars)*

	1969	1970	1971	1972	1973	1974	1975	1976	1977	1978	1979
Money Supply, Broadly Defined	..	..	..	..	..	..	82.09	100.50	106.48	127.37	149.63
Money	..	..	..	..	..	..	20.63	29.05	33.01	38.39	45.22
Currency Outside Banks	..	..	..	..	..	..	9.56	12.07	15.04	17.67	22.05
Demand Deposits	..	..	..	..	..	..	11.07	16.98	17.97	20.72	23.16
Quasi-Money	..	..	..	..	..	..	61.46	71.46	73.47	88.99	104.41

GOVERNMENT DEFICIT (-) OR SURPLUS *(Millions of current Eastern Caribbean Dollars)*

	1969	1970	1971	1972	1973	1974	1975	1976	1977	1978	1979
Current Revenue	..	..	..	..	..	..	..	..	..	-1.48	4.73
Current Expenditure	..	..	..	..	..	..	..	..	..	65.74	96.26
Current Budget Balance	..	..	..	..	..	..	..	..	..	50.57	73.97
Capital Receipts	..	..	..	..	..	..	..	..	..	15.17	22.29
Capital Payments	..	..	..	..	..	..	..	..	..	16.65	17.56

1980	1981	1982	1983	1984	1985	1986	1987	1988	1989 estimate	NOTES	ST. LUCIA
..	1,020	1,040	1,120	1,140	1,230	1,360	1,490	1,670	1,810	..	**CURRENT GNP PER CAPITA (US $)**
124	126	129	131	134	137	140	142	145	147	..	**POPULATION (thousands)**
			(Millions of current Eastern Caribbean Dollars)								**USE AND ORIGIN OF RESOURCES**
269.90	339.70	358.10	377.10	408.10	457.40	530.00	581.70	652.00	708.30	..	Gross National Product (GNP)
-36.40	-3.20	-3.20	-2.20	-8.60	-9.40	-10.80	-11.30	-11.60	-11.90	..	Net Factor Income from Abroad
306.30	342.90	361.30	379.30	416.70	466.80	540.80	593.00	663.60	720.20	..	GDP at Market Prices
-117.90	-152.00	-143.00	-68.60	-92.30	-43.20	-10.20	-51.30	-35.10	-133.90	..	Resource Balance
233.60	216.30	221.70	274.60	301.90	365.30	493.60	523.50	656.40	668.00	..	Exports of Goods & NFServices
351.50	368.30	364.70	343.20	394.20	408.50	503.80	574.80	691.50	801.90	..	Imports of Goods & NFServices
..	..	..	..	..	..	..	..	..	..	..	Domestic Absorption
..	..	..	..	..	..	..	..	..	..	..	Private Consumption, etc.
..	..	..	..	..	..	..	..	..	..	..	General Gov't Consumption
..	..	..	..	..	..	..	..	..	..	..	Gross Domestic Investment
..	..	..	..	..	..	..	..	..	..	..	Fixed Investment
42.10	43.50	48.80	55.90	63.70	78.00	97.50	121.50	144.50	172.00	..	Indirect Taxes, net
264.20	299.40	312.50	323.40	353.00	388.80	443.30	471.50	519.10	548.20	..	GDP at factor cost
31.00	28.90	36.10	42.30	46.20	58.30	82.30	87.20	97.50	87.20	..	Agriculture
65.60	74.60	71.70	63.20	70.20	77.30	84.90	91.30	104.80	120.10	..	Industry
24.70	25.30	26.80	30.20	31.10	33.00	34.00	35.00	36.30	38.40	..	Manufacturing
167.60	195.90	204.70	217.90	236.60	253.20	276.10	293.00	316.80	340.90	..	Services, etc.
..	..	..	..	..	..	..	..	..	..	..	Gross Domestic Saving
..	..	..	..	..	..	..	..	..	..	..	Gross National Saving
			(Millions of 1987 Eastern Caribbean Dollars)								
379.32	410.14	426.50	455.24	472.24	509.59	551.25	581.70	634.46	677.68	..	Gross National Product
422.03	419.57	435.61	458.47	484.96	522.91	564.16	593.00	646.37	725.51	..	GDP at Market Prices
..	..	..	..	..	..	..	..	..	..	..	Resource Balance
..	..	..	..	..	..	..	..	..	..	..	Exports of Goods & NFServices
..	..	..	..	..	..	..	..	..	..	..	Imports of Goods & NFServices
..	..	..	..	..	..	..	..	..	..	..	Domestic Absorption
..	..	..	..	..	..	..	..	..	..	..	Private Consumption, etc.
..	..	..	..	..	..	..	..	..	..	..	General Gov't Consumption
..	..	..	..	..	..	..	..	..	..	..	Gross Domestic Investment
..	..	..	..	..	..	..	..	..	..	..	Fixed Investment
361.69	366.27	376.70	390.88	410.83	435.50	462.68	471.50	506.43	525.71	..	GDP at factor cost
51.53	43.83	58.29	66.92	72.28	81.14	91.16	87.20	108.18	109.12	..	Agriculture
85.52	87.51	83.13	71.76	75.15	80.34	85.92	91.30	97.28	88.11	..	Industry
27.40	27.93	30.05	33.23	33.23	34.12	34.65	35.00	35.71	36.94	..	Manufacturing
222.22	230.76	233.79	252.20	263.40	274.02	285.60	293.00	300.97	328.49	..	Services, etc.
											Memo Items:
..	..	..	..	..	..	..	..	..	..	..	Capacity to Import
..	..	..	..	..	..	..	..	..	..	..	Terms of Trade Adjustment
..	..	..	..	..	..	..	..	..	..	..	Gross Domestic Income
..	..	..	..	..	..	..	..	..	..	..	Gross National Income
			(Index 1987 = 100)								**DOMESTIC PRICES/DEFLATORS**
72.6	81.7	82.9	82.7	85.9	89.3	95.9	100.0	102.7	99.3	..	Overall (GDP)
..	..	..	..	..	..	..	..	..	..	..	Domestic Absorption
60.2	65.9	61.9	63.2	63.9	71.9	90.3	100.0	90.1	79.9	..	Agriculture
76.7	85.2	86.3	88.1	93.4	96.2	98.8	100.0	107.7	136.3	..	Industry
90.1	90.6	89.2	90.9	93.6	96.7	98.1	100.0	101.7	103.9	..	Manufacturing
72.7	83.7	87.5	88.8	89.9	91.2	93.4	100.0	100.8	105.2	..	Consumer Price Index
											MANUFACTURING ACTIVITY
..	..	..	..	..	..	..	..	..	..	..	Employment (1987=100)
..	..	..	..	..	..	..	..	..	..	..	Real Earnings per Empl. (1987=100)
..	..	..	..	..	..	..	..	..	..	..	Real Output per Empl. (1987=100)
..	..	..	..	..	..	..	..	..	..	..	Earnings as % of Value Added
			(Millions of current Eastern Caribbean Dollars)								**MONETARY HOLDINGS**
167.24	196.44	214.62	245.78	274.03	328.64	412.21	482.34	580.44	667.11	..	Money Supply, Broadly Defined
52.67	53.53	57.57	58.39	63.06	71.05	97.62	125.58	141.40	158.63	..	Money
24.61	27.69	28.04	30.26	30.08	33.01	39.05	52.06	56.28	67.28	..	Currency Outside Banks
28.06	25.84	29.52	28.13	32.98	38.04	58.58	73.53	85.12	91.35	..	Demand Deposits
114.56	142.91	157.05	187.39	210.97	257.59	314.58	356.75	439.04	508.48	..	Quasi-Money
			(Millions of current Eastern Caribbean Dollars)								
-12.85	-7.84	-15.81	14.30	..	-11.10	-11.40	8.10	19.10	..	C	**GOVERNMENT DEFICIT (-) OR SURPLUS**
100.74	120.02	137.28	154.09	..	162.10	186.10	221.70	244.80	..	..	Current Revenue
81.59	92.32	117.00	114.52	122.85	145.20	154.20	160.50	163.30	..	..	Current Expenditure
19.15	27.70	20.28	39.57	..	16.90	31.90	61.20	81.50	..	..	Current Budget Balance
..	..	..	..	0.05	..	..	0.10	1.80	..	..	Capital Receipts
32.00	35.54	36.09	25.27	..	28.00	43.30	53.20	64.20	..	..	Capital Payments

ST. LUCIA	1969	1970	1971	1972	1973	1974	1975	1976	1977	1978	1979
FOREIGN TRADE (CUSTOMS BASIS)					*(Millions of current US dollars)*						
Value of Exports, fob	..	..	..	..	..	..	..	..	..	..	..
Nonfuel Primary Products	..	..	..	..	..	..	..	..	..	..	..
Fuels	..	..	..	..	..	..	..	..	..	..	..
Manufactures	..	..	..	..	..	..	..	..	..	..	..
Value of Imports, cif	..	..	..	..	..	..	..	..	..	..	..
Nonfuel Primary Products	..	..	..	..	..	..	..	..	..	..	..
Fuels	..	..	..	..	..	..	..	..	..	..	..
Manufactures	..	..	..	..	..	..	..	..	..	..	..
					(Index 1987 = 100)						
Terms of Trade	..	..	..	..	..	..	..	..	..	..	..
Export Prices, fob	..	..	..	..	..	..	..	..	..	..	..
Import Prices, cif	..	..	..	..	..	..	..	..	..	..	..
BALANCE OF PAYMENTS					*(Millions of current US dollars)*						
Exports of Goods & Services	..	..	..	..	..	..	..	32.10	41.30	55.80	66.70
Merchandise, fob	..	..	..	..	..	..	..	19.10	22.60	26.80	31.90
Nonfactor Services	..	..	..	..	..	..	..	12.50	17.80	27.70	33.80
Factor Services	..	..	..	..	..	..	..	0.50	0.90	1.30	1.00
Imports of Goods & Services	..	..	..	..	..	..	..	50.40	..	88.60	106.00
Merchandise, fob	..	..	..	..	..	..	..	43.63	53.90	75.27	91.99
Nonfactor Services	..	..	..	..	..	..	..	6.46	8.40	12.83	13.41
Factor Services	..	..	..	..	..	..	..	0.30	..	0.50	0.60
Long-Term Interest	..	..	..	..	..	..	..	..	..	..	..
Private Current Transfers, net	..	..	..	..	..	..	..	8.20	7.60	7.70	7.80
Workers' Remittances	..	..	..	..	..	..	..	..	..	..	..
Curr. A/C Bal before Off. Transf.	..	..	..	..	..	..	..	-10.10	-13.40	-25.10	-31.50
Net Official Transfers	..	..	..	..	..	..	..	4.70	2.50	2.10	3.40
Curr. A/C Bal after Off. Transf.	..	..	..	..	..	..	..	-5.40	-10.90	-23.00	-28.10
Long-Term Capital, net	..	..	..	..	..	..	..	5.50	14.90	23.30	28.97
Direct Investment	..	..	..	..	..	..	..	3.00	13.00	20.60	26.00
Long-Term Loans	..	..	..	..	..	..	..	..	..	..	..
Disbursements	..	..	..	..	..	..	..	..	..	..	..
Repayments	..	..	..	..	..	..	..	..	..	..	..
Other Long-Term Capital	..	..	..	..	..	..	..	2.50	1.90	2.70	2.97
Other Capital, net	..	..	..	..	..	..	..	2.42	-3.44	0.70	0.70
Change in Reserves	..	..	..	..	..	..	..	-2.52	-0.56	-1.00	-1.57
Memo Item:					*(Eastern Caribbean Dollars per US dollar)*						
Conversion Factor (Annual Avg)	2.000	2.000	1.970	1.920	1.960	2.050	2.170	2.610	2.700	2.700	2.700
EXTERNAL DEBT (Total)					*(Millions of US dollars), outstanding at end of year*						
EXTERNAL DEBT (Total)	..	..	..	..	..	..	..	..	..	..	..
Long-Term Debt (by debtor)	..	..	..	..	..	..	..	..	..	..	..
Central Bank, incl. IMF credit	..	..	..	..	..	..	..	..	..	..	..
Central Government	..	..	..	..	..	..	..	..	..	..	..
Rest of General Government	..	..	..	..	..	..	..	..	..	..	..
Non-financial Public Enterprises	..	..	..	..	..	..	..	..	..	..	..
Priv. Sector, incl non-guaranteed	..	..	..	..	..	..	..	..	..	..	..
Short-Term Debt	..	..	..	..	..	..	..	..	..	..	..
Memo Items:					*(Thousands of US dollars)*						
Int'l Reserves Excluding Gold	..	..	..	..	..	..	3,241	5,192	5,653	6,757	8,124
Gold Holdings (at market price)	..	..	..	..	..	..	..	..	..	..	..
SOCIAL INDICATORS											
Total Fertility Rate	5.9	5.7	5.6	5.5	5.4	5.3	5.2	5.1	5.0	4.9	4.8
Infant Mortality Rate	..	..	..	..	..	..	..	..	..	..	..
Life Expectancy at Birth	61.8	62.4	63.0	63.5	64.1	64.6	65.2	65.8	66.3	66.9	67.5
Urban Population, % of total	40.0	40.1	40.2	40.3	40.5	40.6	40.7	40.9	41.2	41.4	41.7
Food Prod. per capita (1987=100)	105.0	84.1	85.4	87.4	82.9	90.4	77.2	82.9	81.8	89.9	87.6
Labor Force, Agriculture (%)	..	..	..	..	..	..	..	..	..	..	..
Labor Force, Female (%)	..	..	..	..	..	..	..	..	..	..	..
Primary Schl. Enroll. Ratio	..	..	..	..	..	..	..	..	..	..	..
Primary Schl. Enroll. Ratio, Female	..	..	..	..	..	..	..	..	..	..	..
Secondary Schl. Enroll. Ratio	..	..	..	..	..	..	..	..	..	..	..

1980	1981	1982	1983	1984	1985	1986	1987	1988	1989 estimate	NOTES	ST. LUCIA
											FOREIGN TRADE (CUSTOMS BASIS)
				(Millions of current US dollars)							
46.10	42.10	41.90	47.90	47.90	52.00	83.00	..	..	..	..	Value of Exports, fob
..	..	..	..	..	..	..	..	..	..	..	Nonfuel Primary Products
..	..	..	..	..	..	..	..	..	..	..	Fuels
..	..	..	..	..	..	..	..	..	..	..	Manufactures
124.00	129.00	118.00	107.00	119.00	125.00	155.00	..	..	..	..	Value of Imports, cif
..	..	..	..	..	..	..	..	..	..	..	Nonfuel Primary Products
..	..	..	..	..	..	..	..	..	..	..	Fuels
..	..	..	..	..	..	..	..	..	..	..	Manufactures
				(Index 1987 = 100)							
..	..	..	..	..	..	..	..	..	..	..	Terms of Trade
..	..	..	..	..	..	..	..	..	..	..	Export Prices, fob
..	..	..	..	..	..	..	..	..	..	..	Import Prices, cif
				(Millions of current US dollars)							**BALANCE OF PAYMENTS**
87.50	81.60	..	102.39	..	..	166.20	..	243.50	247.70	..	Exports of Goods & Services
46.00	41.60	41.60	47.50	47.80	52.00	82.90	77.30	119.10	111.90	..	Merchandise, fob
40.50	38.50	44.70	54.20	64.00	69.50	83.30	94.50	124.00	135.50	..	Nonfactor Services
1.00	1.50	..	0.69	..	..	0.00	..	0.40	0.30	..	Factor Services
135.40	141.70	136.30	128.60	149.20	154.90	185.70	209.40	260.90	301.70	..	Imports of Goods & Services
112.55	117.17	107.35	97.08	107.72	113.63	140.72	161.89	200.98	235.17	..	Merchandise, fob
22.15	23.63	27.75	30.02	38.29	37.97	41.59	44.11	55.22	61.83	..	Nonfactor Services
0.70	0.90	1.20	1.50	3.20	3.30	3.40	3.40	4.70	4.70	..	Factor Services
..	..	..	..	..	..	..	..	..	..	..	Long-Term Interest
11.10	14.90	13.50	13.70	13.70	14.80	14.70	15.00	10.80	8.70	..	Private Current Transfers, net
..	..	..	..	..	..	0.00	..	..	..	..	Workers' Remittances
-36.80	-45.20	-36.50	-12.51	-23.70	-18.60	-4.80	-22.60	-6.60	-45.30	..	Curr. A/C Bal before Off. Transf.
3.50	5.40	5.70	7.60	10.30	6.10	6.50	9.70	4.00	3.70	..	Net Official Transfers
-33.30	-39.80	-30.80	-4.91	-13.40	-12.50	1.70	-12.90	-2.60	-41.60	..	Curr. A/C Bal after Off. Transf.
32.51	41.38	32.00	12.20	12.57	18.81	20.83	27.30	22.30	26.10	..	Long-Term Capital, net
30.90	38.20	26.50	10.00	12.00	17.00	18.50	22.00	16.00	18.00	..	Direct Investment
..	..	..	..	..	..	..	..	..	..	..	Long-Term Loans
..	..	..	..	..	..	..	..	..	..	..	Disbursements
..	..	..	..	..	..	..	..	..	..	..	Repayments
1.61	3.18	5.50	2.20	0.57	1.81	2.33	5.30	6.30	8.10	..	Other Long-Term Capital
-1.16	-6.35	1.16	-7.23	2.56	-1.57	-9.33	-5.31	-17.00	20.50	..	Other Capital, net
1.95	4.77	-2.36	-0.06	-1.73	-4.75	-13.20	-9.09	-2.70	-5.00	..	Change in Reserves
				(Eastern Caribbean Dollars per US dollar)							Memo Item:
2.700	2.700	2.700	2.700	2.700	2.700	2.700	2.700	2.700	2.700	..	Conversion Factor (Annual Avg)
				(Millions of US dollars), outstanding at end of year							**EXTERNAL DEBT (Total)**
..	..	..	..	..	..	..	..	..	..	..	Long-Term Debt (by debtor)
..	..	..	..	..	..	..	..	..	..	..	Central Bank, incl. IMF credit
..	..	..	..	..	..	..	..	..	..	..	Central Government
..	..	..	..	..	..	..	..	..	..	..	Rest of General Government
..	..	..	..	..	..	..	..	..	..	..	Non-financial Public Enterprises
..	..	..	..	..	..	..	..	..	..	..	Priv. Sector, incl non-guaranteed
..	..	..	..	..	..	..	..	..	..	..	Short-Term Debt
				(Thousands of US dollars)							Memo Items:
8,287	7,612	8,211	8,870	12,380	12,650	25,110	30,800	32,650	38,210	..	Int'l Reserves Excluding Gold
..	..	..	..	..	..	..	..	..	..	..	Gold Holdings (at market price)
											SOCIAL INDICATORS
4.4	4.2	4.0	3.9	3.8	3.7	3.6	3.5	3.4	3.3	..	Total Fertility Rate
..	..	25.0	24.1	23.3	22.4	21.5	21.0	20.4	19.8	..	Infant Mortality Rate
68.0	68.6	69.2	69.4	69.7	69.9	70.2	70.5	70.8	71.1	..	Life Expectancy at Birth
41.9	42.3	42.7	43.0	43.4	43.8	44.3	44.8	45.4	45.9	..	Urban Population, % of total
78.5	81.6	81.0	84.4	93.9	94.3	110.0	100.0	115.5	93.2	..	Food Prod. per capita (1987=100)
..	..	..	..	..	..	..	..	..	..	..	Labor Force, Agriculture (%)
..	..	..	..	..	..	..	..	..	..	..	Labor Force, Female (%)
..	..	..	..	..	..	..	..	..	..	..	Primary Schl. Enroll. Ratio
..	..	..	..	..	..	..	..	..	..	..	Primary Schl. Enroll. Ratio, Female
..	..	..	..	..	..	..	..	..	..	..	Secondary Schl. Enroll. Ratio

ST. VINCENT AND THE GRENADINES	1969	1970	1971	1972	1973	1974	1975	1976	1977	1978	1979
CURRENT GNP PER CAPITA (US $)	200	220	230	300	290	310	340	360	380	430	470
POPULATION (thousands)	87	88	89	91	92	94	95	97	98	100	101
USE AND ORIGIN OF RESOURCES					*(Millions of current Eastern Caribbean Dollars)*						
Gross National Product (GNP)	33.30	36.90	39.60	53.00	59.10	67.60	71.30	83.00	94.30	119.50	135.50
Net Factor Income from Abroad	0.00	0.00	0.00	0.00	0.00	0.00	0.00	0.00	0.00	0.00	-3.80
GDP at Market Prices	33.30	36.90	39.60	53.00	59.10	67.60	71.30	83.00	94.30	119.50	139.30
Resource Balance	..	..	..	..	..	..	..	..	-41.10	-25.20	-51.30
Exports of Goods & NFServices	..	..	..	..	..	..	..	..	44.80	78.80	88.80
Imports of Goods & NFServices	..	..	..	..	..	..	..	..	85.90	104.00	140.10
Domestic Absorption	..	..	..	..	..	..	..	..	135.30	144.60	190.40
Private Consumption, etc.	..	..	..	..	..	..	..	..	85.70	80.70	108.00
General Gov't Consumption	..	..	..	..	..	..	..	..	23.10	29.50	33.60
Gross Domestic Investment	..	..	..	..	..	..	..	..	26.50	34.40	48.80
Fixed Investment	..	..	..	..	..	..	..	..	23.90	32.50	44.40
Indirect Taxes, net	..	..	..	..	..	..	..	..	14.70	18.00	18.70
GDP at factor cost	..	..	..	..	..	..	..	..	79.60	101.50	120.60
Agriculture	..	..	..	..	..	..	..	..	14.70	20.70	19.70
Industry	..	..	..	..	..	..	..	..	18.80	24.00	31.20
Manufacturing	..	..	..	..	..	..	..	..	5.90	10.30	13.40
Services, etc.	..	..	..	..	..	..	..	..	46.10	56.80	69.70
Gross Domestic Saving	..	..	..	..	..	..	..	..	-14.50	9.30	-2.30
Gross National Saving	..	..	..	..	..	..	..	..	..	34.41	26.30
					(Millions of 1987 Eastern Caribbean Dollars)						
Gross National Product	195.72	216.75	223.18	280.83	249.66	227.63	210.31	221.94	233.33	258.47	260.49
GDP at Market Prices	194.73	215.66	222.06	279.42	248.40	226.49	209.26	220.83	232.15	257.17	262.34
Resource Balance	..	..	..	..	..	..	..	..	-55.76	-21.50	-39.38
Exports of Goods & NFServices	..	..	..	..	..	..	..	..	90.78	143.47	143.67
Imports of Goods & NFServices	..	..	..	..	..	..	..	..	146.54	164.97	183.05
Domestic Absorption	..	..	..	..	..	..	..	..	287.91	278.67	301.72
Private Consumption, etc.	..	..	..	..	..	..	..	..	..	..	..
General Gov't Consumption	..	..	..	..	..	..	..	..	..	..	..
Gross Domestic Investment	..	..	..	..	..	..	..	..	54.96	64.71	77.57
Fixed Investment	..	..	..	..	..	..	..	..	..	..	..
GDP at factor cost	..	..	..	..	..	..	..	..	170.50	189.11	204.79
Agriculture	..	..	..	..	..	..	..	..	34.64	40.53	34.41
Industry	..	..	..	..	..	..	..	..	39.14	43.10	51.43
Manufacturing	..	..	..	..	..	..	..	..	12.13	18.30	22.21
Services, etc.	..	..	..	..	..	..	..	..	96.64	105.23	119.07
Memo Items:											
Capacity to Import	..	..	..	..	..	..	..	..	76.43	124.99	116.02
Terms of Trade Adjustment	..	..	..	..	..	..	..	..	-14.36	-18.48	-27.65
Gross Domestic Income	..	..	..	..	..	..	..	..	217.80	238.70	234.69
Gross National Income	..	..	..	..	..	..	..	..	218.97	240.00	232.84
DOMESTIC PRICES/DEFLATORS					*(Index 1987 = 100)*						
Overall (GDP)	17.1	17.1	17.8	19.0	23.8	29.8	34.1	37.6	40.6	46.5	53.1
Domestic Absorption	..	..	..	..	..	..	..	..	47.0	51.9	63.1
Agriculture	..	..	..	..	..	..	..	..	42.4	51.1	57.3
Industry	..	..	..	..	..	..	..	..	48.0	55.7	60.7
Manufacturing	..	..	..	..	..	..	..	..	48.6	56.3	60.3
Consumer Price Index	..	..	..	..	..	37.4	39.9	44.4	48.9	53.1	61.3
MANUFACTURING ACTIVITY											
Employment (1987=100)	..	..	..	..	..	..	..	..	..	..	..
Real Earnings per Empl. (1987=100)	..	..	..	..	..	..	..	..	..	..	..
Real Output per Empl. (1987=100)	..	..	..	..	..	..	..	..	..	..	..
Earnings as % of Value Added	..	..	..	..	..	..	..	..	..	..	..
MONETARY HOLDINGS					*(Millions of current Eastern Caribbean Dollars)*						
Money Supply, Broadly Defined	..	..	..	..	..	..	47.11	55.79	61.31	78.20	96.43
Money	..	..	..	..	..	..	13.35	16.07	16.61	22.62	27.72
Currency Outside Banks	..	..	..	..	..	..	8.00	9.52	9.50	11.07	12.94
Demand Deposits	..	..	..	..	..	..	5.34	6.55	7.10	11.55	14.78
Quasi-Money	..	..	..	..	..	..	33.76	39.72	44.71	55.58	68.71
GOVERNMENT DEFICIT (-) OR SURPLUS					*(Thousands of current Eastern Caribbean Dollars)*						
Current Revenue	..	..	..	..	..	..	..	..	..	30,900	39,200
Current Expenditure	..	..	..	..	..	..	..	..	..	24,900	37,700
Current Budget Balance	..	..	..	..	..	..	..	..	..	6,000	1,500
Capital Receipts	..	..	..	..	..	..	..	..	..	..	..
Capital Payments	..	..	..	..	..	..	..	..	..	..	..

1980	1981	1982	1983	1984	1985	1986	1987	1988	1989 estimate	NOTES	ST. VINCENT AND THE GRENADINES
540	650	750	840	900	1,000	1,060	1,140	1,360	..	..	**CURRENT GNP PER CAPITA (US $)**
103	104	105	106	108	109	110	111	112	114	..	**POPULATION (thousands)**
			(Millions of current Eastern Caribbean Dollars)								**USE AND ORIGIN OF RESOURCES**
153.30	188.20	217.70	240.30	262.00	294.80	331.50	375.40	424.90	..	..	Gross National Product (GNP)
-2.40	-4.60	-7.30	-6.20	-8.10	-7.80	-9.40	-9.50	-10.00	..	..	Net Factor Income from Abroad
155.70	192.80	225.00	246.50	270.10	302.60	340.90	384.90	434.90	479.00	..	GDP at Market Prices
-66.70	-52.30	-69.40	-53.20	-36.40	-18.30	-37.80	-79.10	-80.50	..	..	Resource Balance
104.50	120.20	129.30	159.00	196.30	222.60	225.10	237.70	262.70	..	..	Exports of Goods & NFServices
171.20	172.50	198.70	212.20	232.70	240.90	262.90	316.80	343.20	..	..	Imports of Goods & NFServices
222.40	245.20	294.40	299.70	306.50	320.90	378.70	464.00	515.40	..	..	Domestic Absorption
121.90	136.10	176.90	180.00	172.00	175.60	229.30	..	..	..	..	Private Consumption, etc.
37.70	45.00	52.80	56.80	59.10	60.10	53.10	..	..	..	..	General Gov't Consumption
62.80	64.10	64.70	62.90	75.40	85.20	96.30	117.80	104.30	..	..	Gross Domestic Investment
57.30	58.30	58.50	56.20	70.60	76.10	96.30	..	..	..	..	Fixed Investment
20.20	24.90	34.40	33.80	37.50	50.30	56.30	66.90	76.40	85.20	..	Indirect Taxes, net
135.50	167.90	190.60	212.70	232.60	252.30	284.60	318.00	358.50	393.80	..	GDP at factor cost
19.80	27.50	31.90	36.60	43.20	49.50	54.80	54.20	65.10	67.90	..	Agriculture
36.70	44.60	49.10	49.50	54.20	59.20	69.70	78.70	90.10	98.40	..	Industry
14.50	18.80	21.20	21.70	29.50	29.30	29.40	32.70	38.20	36.20	..	Manufacturing
79.00	95.80	109.60	126.60	135.20	143.60	160.10	185.10	203.30	227.50	..	Services, etc.
-3.90	11.70	-4.70	9.70	39.00	66.90	58.50	38.70	23.80	..	..	Gross Domestic Saving
26.10	40.85	25.80	47.78	66.00	86.10	76.64	74.29	57.00	..	..	Gross National Saving
			(Millions of 1987 Eastern Caribbean Dollars)								
264.96	283.12	305.16	325.04	342.74	369.06	375.01	375.40	410.69	..	..	Gross National Product
267.75	289.47	316.73	334.33	355.13	380.83	386.99	384.90	419.78	530.91	..	GDP at Market Prices
-48.78	-35.28	-61.15	-45.46	-27.72	-23.47	-59.65	-79.10	..	..	..	Resource Balance
139.22	146.92	153.81	185.01	231.42	246.41	231.22	237.70	..	..	..	Exports of Goods & NFServices
188.00	182.20	214.95	230.48	259.14	269.89	290.87	316.80	..	..	..	Imports of Goods & NFServices
316.54	324.75	377.88	379.79	382.85	404.30	446.64	464.00	..	..	..	Domestic Absorption
..	..	..	..	..	..	..	..	..	..	..	Private Consumption, etc.
..	..	..	..	..	..	..	..	..	..	..	General Gov't Consumption
83.99	79.43	77.36	72.17	85.45	95.40	107.02	117.80	..	..	..	Gross Domestic Investment
..	..	..	..	..	..	..	..	..	..	..	Fixed Investment
210.76	227.71	239.49	253.25	267.41	279.81	299.71	318.00	346.24	366.54	..	GDP at factor cost
29.46	41.71	44.07	47.60	50.67	54.91	57.03	54.20	67.16	68.81	..	Agriculture
54.34	55.59	58.30	60.38	62.46	64.33	70.79	78.70	82.86	83.28	..	Industry
23.45	23.86	25.09	25.71	27.97	28.38	30.03	32.70	34.55	33.32	..	Manufacturing
127.45	130.39	137.10	145.27	154.29	160.57	171.89	185.10	196.21	214.45	..	Services, etc.
											Memo Items:
114.75	126.96	139.88	172.70	218.60	249.38	249.05	237.70	..	..	..	Capacity to Import
-24.46	-19.96	-13.93	-12.32	-12.82	2.97	17.83	0.00	..	..	..	Terms of Trade Adjustment
243.29	269.51	302.81	322.01	342.32	383.80	404.82	384.90	..	..	..	Gross Domestic Income
240.49	263.16	291.23	312.72	329.93	372.03	392.84	375.40	..	..	..	Gross National Income
			(Index 1987 = 100)								**DOMESTIC PRICES/DEFLATORS**
58.2	66.6	71.0	73.7	76.1	79.5	88.1	100.0	103.6	90.2	..	Overall (GDP)
70.3	75.5	77.9	78.9	80.1	79.4	84.8	100.0	..	..	..	Domestic Absorption
67.2	65.9	72.4	76.9	85.3	90.2	96.1	100.0	96.9	98.7	..	Agriculture
67.5	80.2	84.2	82.0	86.8	92.0	98.5	100.0	108.7	118.2	..	Industry
61.8	78.8	84.5	84.4	105.5	103.2	97.9	100.0	110.6	108.7	..	Manufacturing
71.9	81.1	86.9	91.7	94.1	96.1	97.2	100.0	..	..	..	Consumer Price Index
											MANUFACTURING ACTIVITY
..	..	..	..	..	..	..	..	..	..	..	Employment (1987 = 100)
..	..	..	..	..	..	..	..	..	..	..	Real Earnings per Empl. (1987 = 100)
..	..	..	..	..	..	..	..	..	..	..	Real Output per Empl. (1987 = 100)
..	..	..	..	..	..	..	..	..	..	..	Earnings as % of Value Added
			(Millions of current Eastern Caribbean Dollars)								**MONETARY HOLDINGS**
101.10	119.98	135.12	152.05	171.37	196.23	227.13	244.03	304.69	345.25	..	Money Supply, Broadly Defined
28.06	33.28	34.88	40.56	47.79	52.55	63.16	53.16	62.74	70.01	..	Money
12.85	15.35	17.61	20.14	22.53	32.03	41.42	23.27	25.15	32.12	..	Currency Outside Banks
15.21	17.93	17.26	20.42	25.27	20.52	21.74	29.89	37.59	37.89	..	Demand Deposits
73.03	86.70	100.24	111.49	123.58	143.68	163.97	190.87	241.95	275.24	..	Quasi-Money
			(Thousands of current Eastern Caribbean Dollars)								
-300	1,600	-7,100	-400	-8,300	6,100	4,400	5,200	-5,700	..	C	**GOVERNMENT DEFICIT (-) OR SURPLUS**
47,000	58,800	68,200	79,600	83,300	96,800	105,700	113,200	120,200	..	..	Current Revenue
45,000	51,200	69,000	73,400	84,300	84,600	90,400	94,500	108,000	..	..	Current Expenditure
2,000	7,600	-800	6,200	-1,000	12,200	15,300	18,700	12,200	..	..	Current Budget Balance
..	..	..	..	..	100	100	200	100	..	..	Capital Receipts
2,300	6,000	6,300	6,600	7,300	6,200	11,000	13,700	18,000	..	..	Capital Payments

ST. VINCENT AND THE GRENADINES	1969	1970	1971	1972	1973	1974	1975	1976	1977	1978	1979
FOREIGN TRADE (CUSTOMS BASIS)					*(Millions of current US dollars)*						
Value of Exports, fob	3.80	3.60	3.00	3.40	5.20	7.10	7.60	9.30	9.90	16.30	14.60
Nonfuel Primary Products	..	..	..	..	..	..	..	..	..	..	..
Fuels	..	..	..	..	..	..	..	..	..	..	..
Manufactures	..	..	..	..	..	..	..	..	..	..	..
Value of Imports, cif	12.20	15.30	18.20	18.30	19.40	25.50	24.60	23.70	30.30	36.20	46.30
Nonfuel Primary Products	..	..	..	..	..	..	..	..	..	14.70	18.40
Fuels	..	..	..	..	..	..	..	..	..	2.20	3.50
Manufactures	..	..	..	..	..	..	..	..	..	19.30	24.40
					(Index 1987 = 100)						
Terms of Trade	..	..	..	..	..	..	..	..	..	..	..
Export Prices, fob	..	..	..	..	..	..	..	..	..	..	..
Import Prices, cif	..	..	..	..	..	..	..	..	..	..	..
BALANCE OF PAYMENTS					*(Millions of current US dollars)*						
Exports of Goods & Services	..	..	..	..	..	..	..	..	..	29.40	33.40
Merchandise, fob	..	..	..	..	..	..	..	..	..	18.10	19.10
Nonfactor Services	..	..	..	..	..	..	..	..	..	11.10	13.70
Factor Services	..	..	..	..	..	..	..	..	..	0.20	0.60
Imports of Goods & Services	..	..	..	..	..	..	..	..	..	38.70	53.10
Merchandise, fob	..	..	..	..	..	..	..	..	..	32.91	42.09
Nonfactor Services	..	..	..	..	..	..	..	..	..	5.59	9.81
Factor Services	..	..	..	..	..	..	..	..	..	0.20	1.20
Long-Term Interest	..	0.00	0.10	0.00	0.10	0.10	0.10	0.10	0.10	0.10	0.20
Private Current Transfers, net	..	..	..	..	..	..	..	..	..	9.30	12.00
Workers' Remittances	..	..	..	..	..	..	..	..	..	..	..
Curr. A/C Bal before Off. Transf.	..	..	..	..	..	..	..	..	..	0.00	-7.70
Net Official Transfers	..	..	..	..	..	..	..	..	..	2.70	4.10
Curr. A/C Bal after Off. Transf.	..	..	..	..	..	..	..	..	..	2.70	-3.60
Long-Term Capital, net	..	..	..	..	..	..	..	..	..	0.60	2.80
Direct Investment	..	..	..	..	..	..	..	..	..	-0.50	0.60
Long-Term Loans	..	0.20	0.00	0.00	2.10	0.40	0.70	0.60	0.90	1.00	1.20
Disbursements	..	0.20	0.00	0.00	2.10	0.40	0.70	0.60	0.90	1.00	1.30
Repayments	..	0.00	0.00	0.00	0.00	0.00	0.00	0.00	0.00	0.00	0.10
Other Long-Term Capital	..	..	..	..	..	..	..	..	..	0.10	1.00
Other Capital, net	..	..	..	..	..	..	..	..	..	-3.15	4.64
Change in Reserves	..	..	..	..	..	..	..	..	-0.06	-0.15	-3.84
Memo Item:					*(Eastern Caribbean Dollars per US dollar)*						
Conversion Factor (Annual Avg)	2.000	2.000	1.970	1.920	1.960	2.050	2.170	2.610	2.700	2.700	2.700
				(Thousands of US dollars), outstanding at end of year							
EXTERNAL DEBT (Total)	..	700	700	800	2,800	3,100	3,500	3,700	4,700	5,700	7,300
Long-Term Debt (by debtor)	..	700	700	800	2,800	3,100	3,500	3,700	4,700	5,700	7,300
Central Bank, incl. IMF credit	..	0	0	0	100	200	500	800	1,300	1,800	2,300
Central Government	..	700	700	800	700	700	700	700	800	900	1,400
Rest of General Government	..	..	..	..	..	..	..	..	..	..	..
Non-financial Public Enterprises	..	0	0	0	2,000	2,200	2,300	2,200	2,600	3,000	3,600
Priv. Sector, incl non-guaranteed	..	..	..	..	..	..	..	..	..	..	..
Short-Term Debt	..	..	..	..	..	..	..	0	0	0	0
Memo Items:					*(Thousands of US dollars)*						
Int'l Reserves Excluding Gold	..	..	..	..	..	..	..	4,658	4,810	5,256	8,902
Gold Holdings (at market price)	..	..	..	..	..	..	..	..	..	..	..
SOCIAL INDICATORS											
Total Fertility Rate	5.6	5.4	5.2	5.0	4.8	4.7	4.5	4.3	4.1	4.0	3.8
Infant Mortality Rate	..	..	..	..	..	..	..	..	..	..	..
Life Expectancy at Birth	62.7	63.1	63.5	63.9	64.3	64.7	65.1	65.5	65.9	66.3	66.7
Urban Population, % of total	14.9	15.0	15.1	15.3	15.4	15.6	15.7	15.9	16.1	16.4	16.6
Food Prod. per capita (1987=100)	83.1	77.0	81.7	77.9	80.5	75.5	73.7	81.0	78.6	88.6	88.0
Labor Force, Agriculture (%)	..	..	..	..	..	..	..	..	..	..	..
Labor Force, Female (%)	..	..	..	..	..	..	..	..	..	..	..
Primary Schl. Enroll. Ratio	..	..	..	..	..	..	..	..	..	..	..
Primary Schl. Enroll. Ratio, Female	..	..	..	..	..	..	..	..	..	..	..
Secondary Schl. Enroll. Ratio	..	..	..	..	..	..	..	..	..	..	..

1980	1981	1982	1983	1984	1985	1986	1987	1988	1989 estimate	NOTES	ST. VINCENT AND THE GRENADINES
					(Millions of current US dollars)						**FOREIGN TRADE (CUSTOMS BASIS)**
15.70	24.00	32.20	41.00	53.60	63.30	68.10	52.30	68.10	..	..	Value of Exports, fob
13.30	21.40	27.50	34.00	35.22	47.07	49.17	37.66	55.53	..	..	Nonfuel Primary Products
0.20	0.00	0.00	0.00	0.00	0.00	0.00	0.00	0.00	..	..	Fuels
2.20	2.60	4.70	7.00	18.38	16.23	18.93	14.64	12.57	..	..	Manufactures
57.10	58.20	65.10	70.40	76.60	79.20	91.60	99.40	108.40	..	..	Value of Imports, cif
22.00	19.03	18.73	17.83	24.10	23.50	23.90	25.00	32.40	..	..	Nonfuel Primary Products
5.10	7.60	9.06	7.97	6.60	6.40	5.80	6.00	5.50	..	..	Fuels
30.00	31.57	37.31	44.60	45.90	49.30	61.90	68.40	70.50	..	..	Manufactures
					(Index 1987 = 100)						
..	..	..	..	..	..	..	..	..	..	..	Terms of Trade
..	..	..	..	..	..	..	..	..	..	..	Export Prices, fob
..	..	..	..	..	..	..	..	..	..	..	Import Prices, cif
					(Millions of current US dollars)						**BALANCE OF PAYMENTS**
39.60	50.10	48.09	59.10	72.70	82.60	87.70	72.80	87.40	..	..	Exports of Goods & Services
21.10	29.80	32.19	41.10	53.60	63.20	68.00	52.30	65.30	..	..	Merchandise, fob
17.70	18.90	15.70	17.80	19.10	19.20	19.50	20.30	21.90	..	..	Nonfactor Services
0.80	1.40	0.20	0.20	0.00	0.20	0.20	0.20	0.20	..	..	Factor Services
65.00	68.30	76.50	81.10	89.20	92.30	100.80	113.51	125.10	..	..	Imports of Goods & Services
51.91	52.91	58.59	63.36	68.94	71.28	78.30	89.47	99.27	..	..	Merchandise, fob
11.39	13.29	15.01	15.24	17.26	17.92	18.80	20.64	22.33	..	..	Nonfactor Services
1.70	2.10	2.90	2.50	3.00	3.10	3.70	3.40	3.50	..	..	Factor Services
0.30	0.40	0.60	0.60	1.10	1.20	1.20	1.20	1.30	1.40	..	Long-Term Interest
12.00	12.50	14.00	16.40	13.00	10.00	10.20	16.70	16.00	..	..	Private Current Transfers, net
..	..	..	..	..	..	..	..	..	..	..	Workers' Remittances
-13.40	-5.70	-14.41	-5.60	-3.50	0.30	-2.90	-24.01	-21.70	..	..	Curr. A/C Bal before Off. Transf.
4.10	4.90	3.60	3.00	2.50	3.40	6.70	5.50	4.20	..	..	Net Official Transfers
-9.30	-0.80	-10.81	-2.60	-1.00	3.70	3.80	-18.51	-17.50	..	..	Curr. A/C Bal after Off. Transf.
5.50	3.20	3.90	4.70	3.10	4.10	8.70	12.60	14.40	..	..	Long-Term Capital, net
1.10	0.50	1.50	2.10	1.40	1.80	3.00	3.60	3.60	..	..	Direct Investment
2.90	7.40	3.00	3.10	1.20	1.50	3.50	8.20	6.30	6.50	..	Long-Term Loans
3.00	7.70	3.80	3.80	1.90	2.70	4.90	9.60	8.10	8.30	..	Disbursements
0.10	0.30	0.80	0.70	0.70	1.20	1.40	1.40	1.80	1.80	..	Repayments
1.50	-4.70	-0.60	-0.50	0.50	0.80	2.20	0.80	4.50	..	..	Other Long-Term Capital
1.88	-2.26	3.21	-1.80	2.42	-1.42	-0.62	0.70	5.10	..	..	Other Capital, net
1.92	-0.14	3.70	-0.30	-4.52	-6.38	-11.88	5.21	-2.00	-0.95	..	Change in Reserves
					(Eastern Caribbean Dollars per US dollar)						Memo Item:
2.700	2.700	2.700	2.700	2.700	2.700	2.700	2.700	2.700	..	..	Conversion Factor (Annual Avg)
					(Thousands of US dollars), outstanding at end of year						
10,700	18,600	20,500	24,000	23,400	25,600	29,800	39,700	45,900	50,900	..	**EXTERNAL DEBT (Total)**
10,700	18,600	20,500	23,000	22,400	23,600	26,800	36,700	42,800	49,100	..	Long-Term Debt (by debtor)
3,000	5,100	5,200	5,100	4,600	4,300	4,200	4,400	4,100	4,100	..	Central Bank, incl. IMF credit
1,700	2,600	3,800	4,400	3,900	4,700	7,800	13,300	19,200	26,000	..	Central Government
..	..	..	..	..	..	..	..	..	..	..	Rest of General Government
6,000	10,900	11,500	13,500	13,900	14,600	14,800	19,000	19,500	19,000	..	Non-financial Public Enterprises
..	..	..	..	..	..	..	..	..	..	..	Priv. Sector, incl non-guaranteed
0	0	0	1,000	1,000	2,000	3,000	3,000	3,100	1,800	..	Short-Term Debt
					(Thousands of US dollars)						Memo Items:
7,270	9,005	4,783	5,697	12,820	13,800	25,832	20,220	21,820	22,770	..	Int'l Reserves Excluding Gold
..	..	..	..	..	..	..	..	..	..	..	Gold Holdings (at market price)
											SOCIAL INDICATORS
3.6	3.5	3.3	3.2	3.1	3.0	2.9	2.8	2.7	2.7	..	Total Fertility Rate
..	..	31.0	28.8	26.5	25.6	24.7	25.0	24.2	23.4	..	Infant Mortality Rate
67.1	67.5	67.9	68.2	68.5	68.7	69.0	69.3	69.6	69.9	..	Life Expectancy at Birth
16.8	17.1	17.4	17.8	18.1	18.4	18.8	19.3	19.7	20.2	..	Urban Population, % of total
84.0	85.0	88.0	91.3	111.9	131.8	129.5	100.0	129.9	127.8	..	Food Prod. per capita (1987=100)
..	..	..	..	..	..	..	..	..	..	..	Labor Force, Agriculture (%)
..	..	..	..	..	..	..	..	..	..	..	Labor Force, Female (%)
..	..	..	..	..	..	..	..	..	..	..	Primary Schl. Enroll. Ratio
..	..	..	..	..	..	..	..	..	..	..	Primary Schl. Enroll. Ratio, Female
..	..	..	..	..	..	..	..	..	..	..	Secondary Schl. Enroll. Ratio

SUDAN	1969	1970	1971	1972	1973	1974	1975	1976	1977	1978	1979
CURRENT GNP PER CAPITA (US $)	130	140	150	160	150	200	260	330	390	410	400
POPULATION (thousands)	13,511	13,859	14,243	14,652	15,083	15,537	16,012	16,507	17,019	17,550	18,104

USE AND ORIGIN OF RESOURCES *(Millions of current Sudanese Pounds)*

	1969	1970	1971	1972	1973	1974	1975	1976	1977	1978	1979
Gross National Product (GNP)	585	700	757	828	888	1,237	1,496	1,830	2,322	2,865	3,230
Net Factor Income from Abroad	0	-1	-4	-4	-9	-9	-15	-18	-18	-18	-24
GDP at Market Prices	585	701	761	832	897	1,246	1,511	1,848	2,340	2,883	3,254
Resource Balance	-7	11	-12	-13	2	-48	-173	-184	-148	-231	-217
Exports of Goods & NFServices	86	116	123	126	151	167	183	223	247	242	244
Imports of Goods & NFServices	93	105	135	139	149	215	356	407	395	473	460
Domestic Absorption	592	691	773	845	895	1,295	1,683	2,032	2,488	3,114	3,470
Private Consumption, etc.	384	447	523	623	624	885	1,210	1,374	1,810	2,369	2,632
General Gov't Consumption	133	148	160	146	166	181	208	230	278	331	407
Gross Domestic Investment	75	96	90	76	105	229	265	428	399	414	431
Fixed Investment	..	..	..	..	..	..	..	362	312	324	339
Indirect Taxes, net	79	87	96	110	110	131	169	226	256	305	358
GDP at factor cost	506	614	665	722	787	1,116	1,342	1,622	2,084	2,577	2,896
Agriculture	180	264	294	324	342	512	580	623	817	1,043	1,089
Industry	83	91	92	98	106	153	185	230	271	306	374
Manufacturing	43	49	51	52	55	71	96	109	132	148	202
Services, etc.	242	259	279	300	338	451	577	770	996	1,229	1,433
Gross Domestic Saving	68	106	78	63	107	181	93	244	251	183	215
Gross National Saving	..	105	73	59	99	173	78	279	293	249	294

(Millions of 1987 Sudanese Pounds)

	1969	1970	1971	1972	1973	1974	1975	1976	1977	1978	1979
Gross National Product	17,053.1	17,854.0	19,011.6	18,617.9	17,033.3	18,802.8	21,129.2	25,057.8	28,895.3	28,472.6	25,486.2
GDP at Market Prices	16,947.9	17,771.8	19,004.9	18,598.1	17,098.0	18,823.8	21,209.4	25,114.5	28,929.4	28,478.1	25,524.6
Resource Balance	328.1	527.9	319.1	368.9	561.0	227.3	-213.8	23.8	-102.4	-279.2	-243.1
Exports of Goods & NFServices	1,267.1	1,338.7	1,176.3	1,030.0	1,206.8	938.3	875.0	1,262.2	1,108.9	955.1	773.9
Imports of Goods & NFServices	939.0	810.8	857.3	661.1	645.8	711.0	1,088.8	1,238.5	1,211.3	1,234.4	1,017.0
Domestic Absorption	16,619.8	17,243.9	18,685.8	18,229.2	16,537.1	18,596.5	21,423.2	25,090.7	29,031.8	28,757.3	25,767.7
Private Consumption, etc.	10,963.5	11,315.6	12,715.1	13,428.6	11,637.6	12,727.6	15,064.9	16,706.1	21,133.8	21,789.8	19,518.2
General Gov't Consumption	3,679.9	3,733.8	3,945.6	3,255.5	3,084.1	2,733.8	2,989.8	3,125.8	3,437.4	3,269.8	3,192.8
Gross Domestic Investment	1,976.4	2,194.5	2,025.1	1,545.1	1,815.4	3,135.1	3,368.5	5,258.8	4,460.6	3,697.7	3,056.7
Fixed Investment	..	..	..	..	..	..	..	4,448.1	3,488.0	2,893.8	2,404.3
GDP at factor cost	14,653.1	15,559.4	16,611.9	16,139.5	14,994.8	16,852.3	18,840.4	22,047.0	25,768.4	25,460.7	22,718.9
Agriculture	5,222.8	6,680.8	7,351.1	7,241.6	6,524.2	7,727.9	8,143.9	8,461.3	10,100.8	10,298.3	8,546.8
Industry	2,409.6	2,314.8	2,303.9	2,188.9	2,018.0	2,314.0	2,596.1	3,119.8	3,347.2	3,020.5	2,930.4
Manufacturing	..	1,236.1	1,263.5	1,152.8	1,039.1	1,066.5	1,343.5	1,475.7	1,633.6	1,457.2	1,583.1
Services, etc.	7,020.6	6,563.8	6,957.0	6,709.0	6,452.6	6,810.5	8,100.5	10,465.8	12,320.4	12,141.9	11,241.7

Memo Items:

	1969	1970	1971	1972	1973	1974	1975	1976	1977	1978	1979
Capacity to Import	868.5	893.5	783.6	599.1	654.0	551.3	561.1	678.5	758.1	631.9	538.2
Terms of Trade Adjustment	-398.5	-445.2	-392.7	-430.8	-552.7	-387.0	-313.9	-583.8	-350.8	-323.2	-235.7
Gross Domestic Income	16,549.4	17,326.6	18,612.2	18,167.3	16,545.3	18,436.8	20,895.5	24,530.7	28,578.6	28,154.9	25,288.9
Gross National Income	16,654.6	17,408.9	18,618.9	18,187.1	16,480.5	18,415.8	20,815.3	24,474.1	28,544.6	28,149.4	25,250.6

DOMESTIC PRICES/DEFLATORS *(Index 1987 = 100)*

	1969	1970	1971	1972	1973	1974	1975	1976	1977	1978	1979
Overall (GDP)	3.5	3.9	4.0	4.5	5.2	6.6	7.1	7.4	8.1	10.1	12.7
Domestic Absorption	3.6	4.0	4.1	4.6	5.4	7.0	7.9	8.1	8.6	10.8	13.5
Agriculture	3.5	3.9	4.0	4.5	5.2	6.6	7.1	7.4	8.1	10.1	12.7
Industry	3.5	3.9	4.0	4.5	5.2	6.6	7.1	7.4	8.1	10.1	12.7
Manufacturing	..	3.9	4.0	4.5	5.2	6.6	7.1	7.4	8.1	10.1	12.7
Consumer Price Index	3.3	3.5	3.5	4.0	4.6	5.8	7.2	7.3	8.5	10.2	13.3

MANUFACTURING ACTIVITY

	1969	1970	1971	1972	1973	1974	1975	1976	1977	1978	1979
Employment (1987=100)	..	..	..	..	..	..	..	..	..	..	..
Real Earnings per Empl. (1987=100)	..	..	..	..	..	..	..	..	..	..	..
Real Output per Empl. (1987=100)	..	..	..	..	..	..	..	..	..	..	..
Earnings as % of Value Added	44.8	31.2	29.2	29.5	..	..	..	..	..	..	..

MONETARY HOLDINGS *(Millions of current Sudanese Pounds)*

	1969	1970	1971	1972	1973	1974	1975	1976	1977	1978	1979
Money Supply, Broadly Defined	115	130	140	166	205	278	330	412	589	751	977
Money	101	116	124	144	176	237	281	350	497	634	837
Currency Outside Banks	59	67	70	75	93	119	129	153	199	279	380
Demand Deposits	42	49	54	69	83	118	153	197	298	354	456
Quasi-Money	14	14	16	22	30	41	49	62	92	117	141

(Millions of current Sudanese Pounds)

	1969	1970	1971	1972	1973	1974	1975	1976	1977	1978	1979
GOVERNMENT DEFICIT (-) OR SURPLUS	..	..	..	-6.3	-16.2	-9.7	-74.8	-58.9	-168.4	-151.7	-135.9
Current Revenue	..	..	..	155.7	156.6	192.9	257.7	298.7	350.5	403.3	544.2
Current Expenditure	..	..	..	138.8	167.1	159.0	241.2	256.0	317.4	396.2	530.9
Current Budget Balance	..	..	..	16.9	-10.5	33.9	16.5	42.7	33.1	7.1	13.3
Capital Receipts	..	..	..	0.1	0.1	0.1	1.1	0.1	0.2	0.2	3.0
Capital Payments	..	..	..	23.3	5.8	43.7	92.4	101.7	201.7	159.0	152.2

1980	1981	1982	1983	1984	1985	1986	1987	1988	1989 estimate	NOTES	SUDAN
430	460	450	400	350	320	370	380	380	..	A	CURRENT GNP PER CAPITA (US $)
18,681	19,279	19,894	20,525	21,169	21,822	22,475	23,127	23,777	24,423	..	POPULATION (thousands)
			(Millions of current Sudanese Pounds)								USE AND ORIGIN OF RESOURCES
3,931	4,844	6,777	9,190	11,173	14,632	22,152	28,965	37,585	70,401	C	Gross National Product (GNP)
-41	-136	-264	-402	-633	-725	-918	-922	-2,706	-3,164	..	Net Factor Income from Abroad
3,972	4,980	7,040	9,592	11,807	15,357	23,070	29,887	40,291	73,565	C	GDP at Market Prices
-463	-662	-1,024	-1,384	-893	-1,283	-1,651	-974	-3,316	-5,097	..	Resource Balance
476	471	685	968	1,300	997	787	1,125	2,756	4,727	..	Exports of Goods & NFServices
938	1,134	1,709	2,352	2,193	2,280	2,438	2,100	6,072	9,824	..	Imports of Goods & NFServices
4,435	5,642	8,065	10,976	12,700	16,640	24,721	30,861	43,607	78,662	..	Domestic Absorption
3,200	4,134	5,699	8,566	9,925	14,473	18,649	23,935	33,965	61,268	..	Private Consumption, etc.
636	793	759	880	1,148	1,474	3,119	3,848	5,613	10,700	..	General Gov't Consumption
598	715	1,607	1,530	1,627	693	2,953	3,078	4,029	6,694	..	Gross Domestic Investment
458	507	1,275	1,594	1,839	1,769	2,693	2,455	3,626	5,958	..	Fixed Investment
342	460	527	734	874	1,019	1,282	1,131	1,826	2,700	..	Indirect Taxes, net
3,630	4,520	6,513	8,858	10,933	14,338	21,788	28,756	38,465	70,865	C	GDP at factor cost
1,232	1,446	2,567	3,106	3,569	4,202	7,747	9,987	11,826	25,537	..	Agriculture
492	659	917	1,334	1,696	2,342	3,331	4,398	6,110	10,334	..	Industry
249	359	459	637	868	1,236	1,867	2,505	3,396	5,784	..	Manufacturing
1,905	2,415	3,030	4,418	5,668	7,794	10,710	14,371	20,529	34,995	..	Services, etc.
136	52	582	146	734	-590	1,302	2,104	713	1,597	..	Gross Domestic Saving
199	87	652	284	614	-324	1,259	1,932	9	-230	..	Gross National Saving
			(Millions of 1987 Sudanese Pounds)								
25,657.9	25,718.0	28,657.6	29,101.0	27,226.4	25,740.0	28,443.8	28,964.7	27,508.9	30,230.9	C	Gross National Product
25,767.9	26,306.4	29,640.9	30,251.9	28,736.5	26,931.5	29,552.0	29,887.0	29,318.7	31,486.5	C	GDP at Market Prices
-284.6	-756.6	-1,023.5	-1,057.6	-1,103.2	-745.2	-787.6	-974.3	-641.5	-671.5	..	Resource Balance
1,302.3	1,113.3	922.1	1,096.8	1,188.0	977.3	966.8	1,125.3	983.7	981.4	..	Exports of Goods & NFServices
1,587.0	1,869.9	1,945.6	2,154.3	2,291.3	1,722.5	1,754.4	2,099.6	1,625.2	1,652.9	..	Imports of Goods & NFServices
26,052.6	27,063.0	30,664.4	31,309.4	29,839.7	27,676.7	30,339.6	30,861.3	29,960.2	32,158.0	..	Domestic Absorption
18,565.5	19,466.6	21,354.6	24,158.4	23,123.9	23,922.7	22,778.2	23,935.4	23,181.3	24,921.7	..	Private Consumption, etc.
4,126.2	4,191.1	3,194.0	2,765.4	2,836.2	2,614.7	3,995.3	3,847.5	4,084.5	4,579.7	..	General Gov't Consumption
3,360.8	3,405.4	6,115.7	4,385.6	3,879.7	1,139.3	3,566.0	3,078.4	2,694.3	2,656.6	..	Gross Domestic Investment
2,574.1	2,414.2	4,855.0	4,569.1	4,386.0	2,907.5	3,252.0	2,455.3	2,424.8	2,364.7	..	Fixed Investment
23,548.4	23,876.0	27,422.2	27,837.7	27,013.0	25,434.5	27,909.7	28,756.0	27,989.7	30,330.6	C	GDP at factor cost
7,993.1	7,637.0	10,805.6	9,847.3	9,393.5	8,245.8	9,923.5	9,986.7	8,605.7	10,929.8	..	Agriculture
3,195.2	3,481.9	3,861.3	4,357.7	4,102.1	4,131.6	4,267.6	4,398.1	4,446.1	4,422.9	..	Industry
1,618.0	1,895.0	1,932.1	2,081.5	2,080.7	2,175.0	2,391.4	2,505.1	2,471.4	2,475.6	..	Manufacturing
12,360.0	12,757.0	12,755.3	13,632.7	13,517.4	13,057.2	13,718.6	14,371.2	14,937.9	14,977.9	..	Services, etc.
											Memo Items:
804.8	777.4	779.5	886.3	1,358.3	753.5	566.2	1,125.3	737.7	795.3	..	Capacity to Import
-497.5	-335.9	-142.6	-210.5	170.3	-223.9	-400.6	0.0	-246.0	-186.1	..	Terms of Trade Adjustment
25,270.4	25,970.6	29,498.3	30,041.4	28,906.8	26,707.6	29,151.4	29,887.0	29,072.7	31,300.5	..	Gross Domestic Income
25,160.4	25,382.1	28,515.0	28,890.5	27,396.7	25,516.1	28,043.1	28,964.7	27,262.9	30,044.9	..	Gross National Income
			(Index 1987 = 100)								DOMESTIC PRICES/DEFLATORS
15.4	18.9	23.8	31.7	41.1	57.0	78.1	100.0	137.4	233.6	..	Overall (GDP)
17.0	20.8	26.3	35.1	42.6	60.1	81.5	100.0	145.5	244.6	..	Domestic Absorption
15.4	18.9	23.8	31.5	38.0	51.0	78.1	100.0	137.4	233.6	..	Agriculture
15.4	18.9	23.8	30.6	41.3	56.7	78.1	100.0	137.4	233.6	..	Industry
15.4	18.9	23.8	30.6	41.7	56.8	78.1	100.0	137.4	233.6	..	Manufacturing
16.7	20.8	26.2	34.2	45.8	66.6	82.9	100.0	164.7	..	..	Consumer Price Index
											MANUFACTURING ACTIVITY
..	..	..	..	..	..	..	..	..	..	..	Employment (1987=100)
..	..	..	..	..	..	..	..	..	..	..	Real Earnings per Empl. (1987=100)
..	..	..	..	..	..	..	..	..	..	..	Real Output per Empl. (1987=100)
..	..	..	..	..	..	..	..	..	..	..	Earnings as % of Value Added
			(Millions of current Sudanese Pounds)								MONETARY HOLDINGS
1,606	2,067	2,596	2,697	3,262	5,181	6,841	9,152	11,295	13,661	..	Money Supply, Broadly Defined
1,097	1,531	2,091	2,336	2,764	4,145	5,849	7,768	11,218	18,899	..	Money
508	630	820	1,022	1,247	1,930	2,760	3,625	5,601	9,240	..	Currency Outside Banks
589	901	1,271	1,314	1,517	2,214	3,089	4,144	5,617	9,658	..	Demand Deposits
508	536	505	361	498	1,036	993	1,383	77	-5,237	..	Quasi-Money
			(Millions of current Sudanese Pounds)								GOVERNMENT DEFICIT (-) OR SURPLUS
-129.9	..	-326.4	..	..	..	..	..	..	..	C	
656.6	..	1,032.8	..	..	..	..	..	..	..	..	Current Revenue
627.1	..	895.4	..	..	..	..	..	..	..	..	Current Expenditure
29.5	..	137.4	..	..	..	..	..	..	..	..	Current Budget Balance
9.2	..	0.7	..	..	..	..	..	..	..	..	Capital Receipts
168.6	..	464.5	..	..	..	..	..	..	..	..	Capital Payments

SUDAN	1969	1970	1971	1972	1973	1974	1975	1976	1977	1978	1979
FOREIGN TRADE (CUSTOMS BASIS)					*(Millions of current US dollars)*						
Value of Exports, fob	248.1	294.5	331.7	361.2	416.5	440.5	429.4	577.7	661.0	483.1	583.3
Nonfuel Primary Products	245.0	290.5	325.9	354.7	408.0	421.4	407.6	560.8	645.4	474.5	562.0
Fuels	1.7	2.4	3.5	3.7	6.6	17.1	15.4	10.0	10.0	6.3	16.7
Manufactures	1.4	1.5	2.4	2.9	1.9	2.0	6.4	6.9	5.6	2.4	4.6
Value of Imports, cif	265.6	311.2	355.2	353.5	479.5	655.8	957.0	951.8	982.6	878.0	915.8
Nonfuel Primary Products	43.8	75.4	86.0	90.6	128.1	173.5	192.4	140.6	141.1	183.7	184.0
Fuels	25.5	26.1	25.8	25.4	28.7	44.2	35.3	22.1	22.4	12.6	14.8
Manufactures	196.3	209.6	243.3	237.5	322.6	438.1	729.3	789.1	819.1	681.7	717.0
					(Index 1987 = 100)						
Terms of Trade	173.8	159.9	162.1	160.1	210.7	163.3	133.8	179.8	162.4	145.3	138.2
Export Prices, fob	39.0	39.6	45.5	50.6	84.4	93.5	77.9	100.4	98.3	102.0	110.8
Import Prices, cif	22.4	24.7	28.1	31.6	40.1	57.3	58.2	55.8	60.5	70.2	80.2
BALANCE OF PAYMENTS					*(Millions of current US dollars)*						
Exports of Goods & Services	..	325.1	352.9	371.1	483.5	448.3	508.1	640.0	713.4	705.0	708.2
Merchandise, fob	..	284.3	309.0	324.7	441.1	384.4	411.8	550.7	594.8	551.2	526.9
Nonfactor Services	..	37.6	43.3	45.8	41.2	59.4	88.8	89.3	114.8	144.9	172.5
Factor Services	..	3.2	0.6	0.5	1.2	4.6	7.5	0.0	3.8	8.9	8.8
Imports of Goods & Services	..	367.3	392.7	429.9	459.9	742.4	984.6	1,219.3	1,188.6	1,419.8	1,399.1
Merchandise, fob	..	268.2	293.6	316.7	334.4	541.7	743.2	1,062.1	985.8	1,187.9	1,115.8
Nonfactor Services	..	81.0	85.3	90.2	102.9	168.2	179.2	106.0	148.0	171.9	205.5
Factor Services	..	18.1	13.8	23.0	22.7	32.5	62.2	51.2	54.8	60.0	77.8
Long-Term Interest	..	12.1	12.4	12.0	14.9	20.4	32.1	31.2	39.1	47.8	40.5
Private Current Transfers, net	..	-1.2	-0.9	0.7	3.9	2.5	1.5	150.7	172.0	221.0	240.0
Workers' Remittances	..	..	..	..	..	..	6.1	150.7	172.0	221.0	240.0
Curr. A/C Bal before Off. Transf.	..	-43.4	-40.6	-55.4	29.9	-289.1	-475.0	-428.6	-303.2	-493.8	-450.9
Net Official Transfers	..	1.5	-1.4	6.3	-1.7	18.4	46.7	0.0	11.3	23.0	17.0
Curr. A/C Bal after Off. Transf.	..	-41.9	-42.0	-49.1	28.3	-270.7	-428.2	-428.6	-291.9	-470.8	-433.9
Long-Term Capital, net	..	0.5	5.5	14.7	4.9	253.6	32.8	470.9	304.6	310.1	605.4
Direct Investment	..	..	-1.1	0.3	..	..	..	0.0	0.0	0.0	0.0
Long-Term Loans	..	30.4	15.4	29.6	76.0	420.9	387.7	402.6	313.5	444.9	611.7
Disbursements	..	52.6	42.1	66.4	115.7	460.2	465.2	474.6	355.3	498.6	644.0
Repayments	..	22.2	26.7	36.8	39.7	39.3	77.5	72.0	41.8	53.7	32.3
Other Long-Term Capital	..	-29.9	-8.8	-15.3	-71.1	-167.3	-354.9	68.3	-8.9	-134.8	-6.3
Other Capital, net	..	26.0	50.4	25.4	-8.1	11.9	271.7	-137.7	-10.4	83.4	-161.6
Change in Reserves	..	15.4	-13.9	9.0	-25.1	5.2	123.8	95.4	-2.3	77.3	-9.9
Memo Item:					*(Sudanese Pounds per US dollar)*						
Conversion Factor (Annual Avg)	0.350	0.350	0.350	0.350	0.350	0.350	0.350	0.350	0.350	0.380	0.430
					(Millions of US dollars), outstanding at end of year						
EXTERNAL DEBT (Total)	..	337.4	343.0	391.0	488.4	983.5	1,383.5	1,809.2	2,624.1	3,158.4	4,067.1
Long-Term Debt (by debtor)	..	328.9	343.0	391.0	488.4	983.5	1,383.5	1,795.6	2,159.7	2,604.0	3,554.3
Central Bank, incl. IMF credit	..	30.9	16.5	30.5	35.0	87.7	132.7	138.4	120.8	196.3	293.0
Central Government	..	296.3	324.3	354.8	448.2	891.1	1,214.2	1,597.9	1,960.9	2,291.2	3,125.7
Rest of General Government	..	..	..	..	..	..	..	..	..	..	..
Non-financial Public Enterprises	..	1.7	2.2	5.7	5.2	4.7	34.1	48.2	66.7	104.1	133.7
Priv. Sector, incl non-guaranteed	..	0.0	0.0	0.0	0.0	0.0	2.5	11.1	11.3	12.4	1.9
Short-Term Debt	..	8.5	0.0	0.0	0.0	0.0	0.0	13.6	464.4	554.4	512.8
Memo Items:					*(Thousands of US dollars)*						
Int'l Reserves Excluding Gold	36,400	21,740	27,900	35,587	61,330	124,272	36,369	23,600	23,149	28,356	67,400
Gold Holdings (at market price)	..	..	..	..	..	..	..	..	..	..	..
SOCIAL INDICATORS											
Total Fertility Rate	6.7	6.7	6.7	6.7	6.7	6.7	6.7	6.7	6.7	6.7	6.6
Infant Mortality Rate	151.6	149.4	147.2	145.0	142.2	139.4	136.6	133.8	131.0	128.4	125.8
Life Expectancy at Birth	41.6	41.9	42.3	42.6	43.1	43.6	44.1	44.6	45.1	45.6	46.2
Urban Population, % of total	15.8	16.4	16.9	17.4	17.9	18.4	18.9	19.1	19.2	19.4	19.5
Food Prod. per capita (1987=100)	120.3	121.7	121.2	117.3	118.6	123.6	127.7	122.5	127.8	127.3	115.5
Labor Force, Agriculture (%)	77.8	77.0	76.3	75.7	75.2	74.6	74.1	73.4	72.8	72.2	71.7
Labor Force, Female (%)	20.4	20.3	20.2	20.2	20.1	20.0	20.0	19.9	19.8	19.8	19.7
Primary Schl. Enroll. Ratio	..	38.0	..	..	..	..	47.0	48.0	49.0	50.0	51.0
Primary Schl. Enroll. Ratio, Female	..	29.0	..	..	..	..	34.0	36.0	42.0	42.0	43.0
Secondary Schl. Enroll. Ratio	..	7.0	..	..	..	..	14.0	14.0	15.0	16.0	16.0

1980	1981	1982	1983	1984	1985	1986	1987	1988	1989 estimate	NOTES	SUDAN
				(Millions of current US dollars)							**FOREIGN TRADE (CUSTOMS BASIS)**
594.0	538.0	432.0	581.0	722.0	595.0	497.0	482.3	501.0	661.4	f	Value of Exports, fob
573.5	507.1	403.9	544.1	679.4	538.3	440.7	422.2	434.4	..	..	Nonfuel Primary Products
5.6	21.3	17.0	22.3	28.0	28.8	24.0	25.5	30.0	31.0	..	Fuels
15.0	9.6	11.1	14.6	14.6	27.9	32.3	34.6	36.6	40.0	..	Manufactures
1,499.3	1,518.7	1,754.0	1,534.0	1,370.0	1,114.0	990.0	694.0	975.0	1,401.8	f	Value of Imports, cif
412.3	336.0	460.7	326.5	250.8	229.2	184.1	52.2	90.7	..	..	Nonfuel Primary Products
189.4	289.6	339.0	332.8	351.0	285.8	245.6	158.7	184.3	244.0	..	Fuels
897.6	893.1	954.3	874.7	768.2	599.0	560.3	483.1	700.0	931.8	..	Manufactures
				(Index 1987 = 100)							
124.0	126.1	116.9	128.0	123.4	100.9	86.1	100.0	100.7	..	..	Terms of Trade
128.5	129.3	114.5	122.3	116.9	94.0	87.5	100.0	102.9	..	..	Export Prices, fob
103.6	102.5	97.9	95.5	94.7	93.2	101.6	100.0	102.2	..	..	Import Prices, cif
				(Millions of current US dollars)							**BALANCE OF PAYMENTS**
825.0	763.0	682.0	831.1	952.2	815.4	722.4	711.6	660.9	753.3	C f	Exports of Goods & Services
594.0	538.0	432.0	581.1	722.2	595.4	497.4	481.6	485.9	550.3	..	Merchandise, fob
216.0	210.0	235.0	240.0	220.0	205.0	205.0	220.0	175.0	200.0	..	Nonfactor Services
15.0	15.0	15.0	10.0	10.0	15.0	20.0	10.0	0.0	3.0	..	Factor Services
1,682.1	2,029.0	2,322.0	2,131.4	2,118.4	1,887.5	1,914.1	1,664.3	2,105.2	2,266.0	C f	Imports of Goods & Services
1,339.1	1,540.0	1,543.5	1,350.3	1,206.0	980.8	928.5	732.4	1,076.4	1,077.1	..	Merchandise, fob
258.0	259.0	470.5	454.1	434.4	413.7	409.6	399.9	379.8	482.9	..	Nonfactor Services
85.0	230.0	308.0	327.0	478.0	493.0	576.0	532.0	649.0	706.0	..	Factor Services
48.9	96.0	16.4	37.7	23.3	73.1	47.1	21.0	20.3	11.6	..	Long-Term Interest
209.0	305.0	350.0	415.0	395.0	430.0	350.0	250.0	445.0	297.0	..	Private Current Transfers, net
209.0	305.0	350.0	415.0	395.0	430.0	350.0	250.0	445.0	297.0	..	Workers' Remittances
-648.1	-961.0	-1,290.0	-885.3	-771.2	-642.1	-841.7	-702.7	-999.3	-1,215.7	..	Curr. A/C Bal before Off. Transf.
84.0	122.0	173.5	462.0	309.0	288.0	412.0	280.0	369.0	271.0	..	Net Official Transfers
-564.1	-839.0	-1,116.5	-423.3	-462.2	-354.1	-429.7	-422.7	-630.3	-944.7	..	Curr. A/C Bal after Off. Transf.
145.9	-105.0	-9.0	-327.0	-390.0	-322.0	-477.0	-232.0	-229.7	-328.3	C f	Long-Term Capital, net
0.0	0.0	0.0	0.0	0.0	0.0	0.0	0.0	0.0	0.0	..	Direct Investment
657.5	572.2	881.7	437.2	240.6	84.8	58.7	159.6	323.8	190.4	..	Long-Term Loans
710.9	623.6	980.6	477.2	281.1	100.9	209.9	201.2	381.8	236.6	..	Disbursements
53.4	51.4	98.9	40.0	40.5	16.1	151.2	41.6	58.0	46.2	..	Repayments
-511.6	-677.2	-890.7	-764.2	-630.6	-406.8	-535.7	-391.6	-553.5	-518.7	..	Other Long-Term Capital
261.4	729.9	786.8	844.3	845.2	567.1	919.7	434.7	580.0	1,096.0	C f	Other Capital, net
156.8	214.1	338.7	-94.0	7.0	109.0	-13.0	220.0	280.0	177.0	..	Change in Reserves
				(Sudanese Pounds per US dollar)							**Memo Item:**
0.500	0.560	0.950	1.300	1.300	2.300	2.500	3.000	4.500	4.500	..	Conversion Factor (Annual Avg)
				(Millions of US dollars), outstanding at end of year							**EXTERNAL DEBT (Total)**
5,163.2	6,191.9	7,216.4	7,600.4	8,612.4	9,127.2	9,869.8	11,562.7	11,961.3	12,964.6	..	
4,578.3	5,313.6	6,247.1	6,779.6	7,099.1	7,584.6	8,188.3	9,369.4	9,281.5	9,640.6	..	Long-Term Debt (by debtor)
431.1	564.3	578.7	698.0	664.1	738.9	822.8	954.3	905.2	884.0	..	Central Bank, incl. IMF credit
3,659.2	4,350.2	5,272.6	5,720.2	6,068.4	6,474.5	7,003.9	7,924.4	7,894.6	8,157.1	..	Central Government
..	..	..	..	..	..	..	..	..	..	..	Rest of General Government
161.1	153.2	149.9	117.4	122.6	127.2	117.6	118.7	107.7	103.5	..	Non-financial Public Enterprises
326.9	245.9	245.9	244.0	244.0	244.0	244.0	372.0	374.0	496.0	..	Priv. Sector, incl non-guaranteed
584.9	878.3	969.3	820.8	1,513.3	1,542.6	1,681.5	2,193.3	2,679.8	3,324.0	..	Short-Term Debt
				(Thousands of US dollars)							**Memo Items:**
48,726	16,970	20,500	16,563	17,200	12,200	58,512	11,714	12,114	15,913	..	Int'l Reserves Excluding Gold
..	..	..	..	..	..	..	..	..	..	..	Gold Holdings (at market price)
											SOCIAL INDICATORS
6.6	6.6	6.6	6.6	6.5	6.5	6.5	6.4	6.4	6.3	..	Total Fertility Rate
123.2	120.6	118.0	116.0	114.0	112.0	110.0	108.0	106.4	104.7	..	Infant Mortality Rate
46.7	47.2	47.8	48.2	48.6	49.0	49.4	49.8	50.0	50.2	..	Life Expectancy at Birth
19.7	19.9	20.1	20.2	20.4	20.6	20.9	21.2	21.4	21.7	..	Urban Population, % of total
124.9	138.8	117.9	116.5	105.0	121.9	118.3	100.0	124.9	104.5	..	Food Prod. per capita (1987=100)
71.1	..	..	..	..	..	..	..	..	..	..	Labor Force, Agriculture (%)
19.7	19.9	20.1	20.4	20.6	20.8	21.0	21.2	21.5	21.7	..	Labor Force, Female (%)
50.0	50.0	50.0	49.0	49.0	50.0	49.0	..	..	..	..	Primary Schl. Enroll. Ratio
41.0	41.0	42.0	41.0	40.0	41.0	..	..	..	..	..	Primary Schl. Enroll. Ratio, Female
16.0	17.0	18.0	19.0	19.0	20.0	20.0	..	..	..	..	Secondary Schl. Enroll. Ratio

SURINAME	1969	1970	1971	1972	1973	1974	1975	1976	1977	1978	1979
CURRENT GNP PER CAPITA (US $)	570	610	640	690	770	2,520	340	370	1,770	2,100	2,210
POPULATION (thousands)	364	372	378	382	384	381	365	354	362	367	365
USE AND ORIGIN OF RESOURCES					*(Millions of current Suriname Guilders)*						
Gross National Product (GNP)	387.5	417.2	452.2	491.3	540.5	693.3	909.0	945.0	1,221.0	1,416.0	1,492.0
Net Factor Income from Abroad	-79.4	-77.1	-89.1	-83.9	-70.1	-43.9	-21.0	-66.0	-61.0	-55.0	-74.0
GDP at Market Prices	466.9	494.3	541.3	575.2	610.6	737.2	930.0	1,011.0	1,282.0	1,471.0	1,566.0
Resource Balance	38.0	29.1	47.4	33.7	25.0	9.0	-53.0	-2.0	-88.0	-34.0	-5.0
Exports of Goods & NFServices	289.5	297.9	344.1	350.5	367.0	552.0	588.0	618.0	707.0	814.0	917.0
Imports of Goods & NFServices	251.5	268.8	296.7	316.8	342.0	543.0	641.0	620.0	795.0	848.0	922.0
Domestic Absorption	428.9	465.2	493.9	541.5	585.6	728.2	983.0	1,013.0	1,370.0	1,505.0	1,571.0
Private Consumption, etc.	..	..	..	..	..	..	423.0	243.0	609.0	693.0	870.0
General Gov't Consumption	..	..	..	..	..	..	193.0	251.0	282.0	335.0	343.0
Gross Domestic Investment	103.5	105.5	110.5	138.3	205.2	322.2	367.0	519.0	479.0	477.0	358.0
Fixed Investment	..	..	..	..	..	..	..	..	479.0	477.0	358.0
Indirect Taxes, net	6.0	8.1	8.2	9.8	0.1	14.9	195.8	158.6	180.6	235.1	226.3
GDP at factor cost	460.9	486.2	533.1	565.4	610.5	722.3	734.2	852.4	1,101.4	1,235.9	1,339.7
Agriculture	35.9	35.6	39.2	41.8	42.9	58.1	58.1	71.6	92.1	91.7	116.0
Industry	235.7	229.0	260.8	265.4	300.1	392.1	299.0	346.0	467.5	489.5	529.3
Manufacturing	..	..	..	..	..	..	152.3	181.2	202.9	225.3	239.6
Services, etc.	189.3	221.6	233.1	258.2	267.5	272.1	377.1	434.8	541.8	654.7	694.4
Gross Domestic Saving	141.5	134.6	157.9	172.0	230.2	331.2	314.0	517.0	391.0	443.0	353.0
Gross National Saving	..	56.9	69.7	86.4	158.6	284.5	282.4	451.0	333.8	395.0	291.5
					(Millions of 1987 Suriname Guilders)						
Gross National Product	1,643.7	1,714.0	1,775.6	1,823.2	1,879.0	20,826.3	2,425.6	2,368.8	2,610.5	2,845.1	2,602.9
GDP at Market Prices	..	2,099.6	2,180.9	2,200.4	2,206.9	2,307.6	2,354.5	2,404.4	2,600.3	2,803.7	2,592.1
Resource Balance	..	..	..	..	..	..	..	..	..	..	..
Exports of Goods & NFServices	..	..	..	..	..	..	..	..	..	..	..
Imports of Goods & NFServices	..	..	..	..	..	..	..	..	..	..	..
Domestic Absorption	..	..	..	..	..	..	..	..	..	..	..
Private Consumption, etc.	..	..	..	..	..	..	..	..	..	..	..
General Gov't Consumption	..	..	..	..	..	..	..	..	..	..	..
Gross Domestic Investment	..	..	..	..	..	..	..	..	..	..	..
Fixed Investment	..	..	..	..	..	..	..	..	..	..	..
GDP at factor cost	..	..	..	..	2,137.4	2,192.9	1,974.3	2,152.9	2,372.9	2,502.3	2,355.0
Agriculture	..	..	..	..	142.0	169.6	148.9	153.7	178.3	170.3	188.2
Industry	..	..	..	..	917.5	845.8	634.4	705.2	773.2	764.6	721.6
Manufacturing	..	..	..	..	..	..	328.0	352.6	347.0	369.1	348.4
Services, etc.	..	..	..	..	869.3	1,010.4	1,109.9	1,200.0	1,318.3	1,489.5	1,365.4
Memo Items:											
Capacity to Import	..	..	..	..	..	..	..	..	..	..	..
Terms of Trade Adjustment	..	..	..	..	..	..	..	..	..	..	..
Gross Domestic Income	..	..	..	..	..	..	..	..	..	..	..
Gross National Income	..	..	..	..	..	..	..	..	..	..	..
DOMESTIC PRICES/DEFLATORS					*(Index 1987 = 100)*						
Overall (GDP)	..	23.5	24.8	26.1	27.7	31.9	39.5	42.0	49.3	52.5	60.4
Domestic Absorption	..	..	..	..	..	..	..	..	..	..	..
Agriculture	..	..	..	..	30.2	34.2	39.0	46.6	51.7	53.9	61.6
Industry	..	..	..	..	32.7	46.4	47.1	49.1	60.5	64.0	73.3
Manufacturing	..	..	..	..	..	..	46.4	51.4	58.5	61.0	68.8
Consumer Price Index	15.0	15.4	15.4	15.9	18.0	21.0	22.8	25.1	27.5	29.9	34.4
MANUFACTURING ACTIVITY											
Employment (1987=100)	..	..	..	..	..	..	..	..	..	..	..
Real Earnings per Empl. (1987=100)	..	..	..	..	..	..	..	..	..	..	..
Real Output per Empl. (1987=100)	..	..	..	..	..	..	..	..	..	..	..
Earnings as % of Value Added	..	..	..	..	..	..	..	..	..	..	..
MONETARY HOLDINGS					*(Millions of current Suriname Guilders)*						
Money Supply, Broadly Defined	131.4	145.3	165.0	186.5	228.7	245.0	290.9	397.3	472.0	548.0	612.1
Money	80.4	86.1	98.2	103.3	133.0	140.0	168.7	198.2	219.6	246.0	273.4
Currency Outside Banks	45.4	48.6	53.2	58.2	73.5	78.8	88.6	109.6	125.3	145.1	156.3
Demand Deposits	35.0	37.5	45.0	45.0	59.6	61.2	80.1	88.6	94.3	101.0	117.1
Quasi-Money	51.0	59.3	66.9	83.3	95.6	105.0	122.3	199.0	252.3	301.9	338.6
GOVERNMENT DEFICIT (-) OR SURPLUS					*(Millions of current Suriname Guilders)*						
	..	..	-2.05	-1.76	-19.12	-8.80	-2.15	-21.85	..	..	..
Current Revenue	..	..	164.65	195.52	199.72	228.45	318.13	402.95	..	..	..
Current Expenditure	..	..	146.11	152.85	175.40	193.94	231.97	279.70	..	..	..
Current Budget Balance	..	..	18.54	42.67	24.32	34.51	86.16	123.25	..	..	..
Capital Receipts	..	..	0.41	0.41	0.20	..	..	0.15	..	..	..
Capital Payments	..	..	21.00	44.84	43.64	43.31	88.31	145.25	..	..	..

1980	1981	1982	1983	1984	1985	1986	1987	1988	1989 estimate	NOTES	SURINAME
2,420	2,950	2,840	2,580	2,500	2,450	2,380	2,260	2,600	3,020	..	**CURRENT GNP PER CAPITA (US $)**
356	356	366	376	387	398	409	418	427	436	..	POPULATION (thousands)
				(Millions of current Suriname Guilders)							**USE AND ORIGIN OF RESOURCES**
1,572.0	1,821.0	1,862.0	1,766.0	1,699.0	1,683.0	1,789.0	1,913.0	2,191.0	2,355.3	..	Gross National Product (GNP)
-30.0	23.0	13.0	-20.0	-4.0	-12.0	-4.0	-10.0	-14.0	-15.1	..	Net Factor Income from Abroad
1,602.0	1,798.0	1,849.0	1,786.0	1,703.0	1,695.0	1,793.0	1,923.0	2,205.0	2,370.4	..	GDP at Market Prices
-86.0	-248.0	-282.0	-281.0	-131.0	-75.0	-34.0	-28.0	51.0	..	..	Resource Balance
1,094.0	1,044.0	949.0	803.0	764.0	679.0	654.0	658.0	847.0	..	..	Exports of Goods & NFServices
1,180.0	1,292.0	1,231.0	1,084.0	895.0	754.0	688.0	686.0	796.0	..	..	Imports of Goods & NFServices
1,688.0	2,046.0	2,131.0	2,067.0	1,834.0	1,770.0	1,827.0	1,951.0	2,154.0	..	..	Domestic Absorption
929.0	1,060.0	1,104.0	1,179.0	1,072.0	1,029.0	997.0	1,077.0	1,201.0	..	..	Private Consumption, etc.
339.0	431.0	520.0	613.0	558.0	604.0	736.0	760.0	831.0	..	..	General Gov't Consumption
420.0	555.0	507.0	275.0	204.0	137.0	94.0	114.0	122.0	..	..	Gross Domestic Investment
420.0	555.0	507.0	275.0	204.0	137.0	94.0	114.0	122.0	..	..	Fixed Investment
247.6	269.6	245.1	226.4	172.3	136.7	149.0	139.2	166.0	..	..	Indirect Taxes, net
1,354.4	1,528.4	1,603.9	1,559.6	1,530.7	1,558.3	1,644.0	1,783.8	2,039.0	..	..	GDP at factor cost
122.7	140.1	144.3	126.9	134.5	142.7	164.2	206.1	224.0	..	..	Agriculture
521.6	575.0	538.5	483.6	484.6	464.8	460.9	450.7	525.2	..	..	Industry
249.1	271.2	225.8	195.3	197.4	206.6	226.6	210.6	305.4	..	..	Manufacturing
710.1	813.3	921.1	949.1	911.6	950.8	1,018.9	1,127.0	1,289.8	..	..	Services, etc.
334.0	307.0	225.0	-6.0	73.0	62.0	60.0	86.0	173.0	..	..	Gross Domestic Saving
315.7	336.6	233.3	-40.3	55.8	42.9	52.6	75.3	150.8	..	..	Gross National Saving
				(Millions of 1987 Suriname Guilders)							
2,502.9	2,758.8	2,580.6	2,315.0	2,225.8	2,206.6	2,157.6	1,913.0	1,985.2	2,106.5	..	Gross National Product
2,420.3	2,584.7	2,431.7	2,332.5	2,247.1	2,231.7	2,175.1	1,923.0	1,996.3	2,038.2	..	GDP at Market Prices
..	..	..	..	..	..	..	..	..	..	..	Resource Balance
..	..	..	..	..	..	..	..	..	..	..	Exports of Goods & NFServices
..	..	..	..	..	..	..	..	..	..	..	Imports of Goods & NFServices
..	..	..	..	..	..	..	..	..	..	..	Domestic Absorption
..	..	..	..	..	..	..	..	..	..	..	Private Consumption, etc.
..	..	..	..	..	..	..	..	..	..	..	General Gov't Consumption
..	..	..	..	..	..	..	..	..	..	..	Gross Domestic Investment
..	..	..	..	..	..	..	..	..	..	..	Fixed Investment
2,173.3	2,333.7	2,240.3	2,060.1	1,988.4	1,991.3	1,965.6	1,783.8	1,845.3	..	..	GDP at factor cost
189.6	214.6	208.1	189.9	197.1	199.9	196.8	206.1	208.6	..	..	Agriculture
623.4	649.0	552.3	492.9	510.1	517.4	545.4	450.7	472.9	..	..	Industry
311.7	320.5	267.8	242.3	234.6	249.8	258.9	210.6	245.1	..	..	Manufacturing
1,306.5	1,421.3	1,470.8	1,377.3	1,281.1	1,274.0	1,223.4	1,127.0	1,163.8	..	..	Services, etc.
											Memo Items:
..	..	..	..	..	..	..	..	..	..	..	Capacity to Import
..	..	..	..	..	..	..	..	..	..	..	Terms of Trade Adjustment
..	..	..	..	..	..	..	..	..	..	..	Gross Domestic Income
..	..	..	..	..	..	..	..	..	..	..	Gross National Income
				(Index 1987 = 100)							**DOMESTIC PRICES/DEFLATORS**
66.2	69.6	76.0	76.6	75.8	76.0	82.4	100.0	110.5	116.3	..	Overall (GDP)
..	..	..	..	..	..	..	..	..	..	..	Domestic Absorption
64.7	65.3	69.3	66.8	68.2	71.4	83.4	100.0	107.4	..	..	Agriculture
83.7	88.6	97.5	98.1	95.0	89.8	84.5	100.0	111.1	..	..	Industry
79.9	84.6	84.3	80.6	84.1	82.7	87.5	100.0	124.6	..	..	Manufacturing
39.2	42.8	45.9	47.9	49.7	55.3	65.2	100.0	..	..	..	Consumer Price Index
											MANUFACTURING ACTIVITY
..	..	..	..	..	..	..	..	..	..	G	Employment (1987 = 100)
..	..	..	..	..	..	..	..	..	..	G	Real Earnings per Empl. (1987 = 100)
..	..	..	..	..	..	..	..	..	..	G	Real Output per Empl. (1987 = 100)
..	..	..	..	..	..	..	..	..	..		Earnings as % of Value Added
				(Millions of current Suriname Guilders)							**MONETARY HOLDINGS**
659.5	788.4	875.7	971.3	1,168.5	1,543.8	1,934.3	2,475.0	3,060.5	3,617.6	..	Money Supply, Broadly Defined
294.2	358.0	421.2	455.0	577.3	880.2	1,228.8	1,561.9	1,945.4	2,164.6	..	Money
177.8	197.0	268.0	264.9	305.2	405.4	451.3	637.9	788.3	874.2	..	Currency Outside Banks
116.3	161.0	153.2	190.1	272.1	474.8	777.5	924.0	1,157.1	1,290.4	..	Demand Deposits
365.3	430.4	454.5	516.3	591.2	663.6	705.5	913.1	1,115.1	1,453.0	..	Quasi-Money
				(Millions of current Suriname Guilders)							**GOVERNMENT DEFICIT (-) OR SURPLUS**
..	..	..	..	-263.19	-349.18	-445.74	..	..	..	..	Current Revenue
..	..	..	..	518.87	491.62	497.57	..	..	..	..	Current Revenue
..	..	..	..	697.46	754.00	869.00	..	..	..	..	Current Expenditure
..	..	..	..	-178.59	-262.38	-371.43	..	..	..	..	Current Budget Balance
..	..	..	..	0.11	0.16	0.09	..	..	..	..	Capital Receipts
..	..	..	..	84.71	86.96	74.40	..	..	..	..	Capital Payments

SURINAME	1969	1970	1971	1972	1973	1974	1975	1976	1977	1978	1979
FOREIGN TRADE (CUSTOMS BASIS)					*(Millions of current US dollars)*						
Value of Exports, fob	131.00	144.00	157.00	171.00	179.00	270.00	277.00	276.00	310.00	411.00	444.00
Nonfuel Primary Products	126.77	131.36	152.58	164.07	153.00	233.33	258.85	270.24	..	..	432.54
Fuels	0.00	0.17	0.00	0.00	..	0.07	0.17	0.05	..	..	0.05
Manufactures	6.49	12.46	4.42	6.92	..	36.60	17.98	5.71	..	..	11.41
Value of Imports, cif	110.06	115.28	125.77	143.63	157.42	229.98	262.00	294.00	398.00	382.00	411.00
Nonfuel Primary Products	20.92	26.18	25.74	24.64	36.03	43.41	29.82	34.59	..	..	47.58
Fuels	11.96	14.25	16.95	17.76	10.77	45.68	94.57	89.40	80.00	88.00	109.00
Manufactures	77.18	74.85	83.07	101.22	110.62	140.89	137.61	170.09	..	..	184.28
					(Index 1987 = 100)						
Terms of Trade	..	..	..	..	..	..	..	..	..	..	..
Export Prices, fob	..	..	..	..	..	..	..	..	..	..	..
Import Prices, cif	..	..	..	..	..	..	..	..	..	..	..
BALANCE OF PAYMENTS					*(Millions of current US dollars)*						
Exports of Goods & Services	..	160.70	185.15	206.50	212.32	316.29	338.99	370.37	403.58	481.79	527.68
Merchandise, fob	..	136.60	157.97	175.78	180.01	269.63	277.19	303.75	346.16	411.15	444.09
Nonfactor Services	..	19.70	23.37	25.08	25.99	34.88	48.20	52.99	50.20	62.30	69.47
Factor Services	..	4.40	3.81	5.65	6.32	11.79	13.60	13.62	7.23	8.35	14.12
Imports of Goods & Services	..	185.60	205.51	223.87	240.69	336.86	380.76	396.35	486.67	513.67	571.71
Merchandise, fob	..	104.10	114.04	128.55	144.01	211.30	242.10	259.19	324.09	343.53	369.86
Nonfactor Services	..	36.90	41.72	47.99	54.84	92.48	112.92	88.21	115.07	124.43	142.46
Factor Services	..	44.60	49.75	47.34	41.84	33.07	25.74	48.95	47.51	45.71	59.38
Long-Term Interest	..	..	..	..	..	..	..	..	..	..	..
Private Current Transfers, net	..	-0.30	0.50	-0.98	-0.83	-1.56	-5.95	0.00	2.13	3.92	7.00
Workers' Remittances	..	..	..	..	..	..	..	..	0.06	..	0.34
Curr. A/C Bal before Off. Transf.	..	-25.20	-19.86	-18.35	-29.21	-22.13	-47.72	-25.98	-80.95	-27.96	-37.03
Net Official Transfers	..	12.70	12.84	12.81	13.59	22.85	178.84	89.24	77.54	55.46	80.73
Curr. A/C Bal after Off. Transf.	..	-12.50	-7.02	-5.54	-15.62	0.72	131.13	63.27	-3.42	27.51	43.70
Long-Term Capital, net	..	6.70	-4.41	16.07	20.62	5.29	-97.01	-54.61	-13.28	14.45	-16.36
Direct Investment	..	-5.00	-6.82	-1.85	14.19	-0.36	..	..	-12.66	-7.56	-15.35
Long-Term Loans	..	..	..	..	..	..	..	..	..	..	..
Disbursements	..	..	..	..	..	..	..	..	..	..	..
Repayments	..	..	..	..	..	..	..	..	..	..	..
Other Long-Term Capital	..	11.70	2.41	17.91	6.44	5.65	-97.01	-54.61	-0.62	22.02	-1.01
Other Capital, net	..	13.50	12.74	-1.63	12.64	-0.84	12.75	18.82	-1.12	-0.26	-0.62
Change in Reserves	..	-7.70	-1.30	-8.90	-17.64	-5.17	-46.87	-27.48	17.82	-41.70	-26.72
Memo Item:					*(Suriname Guilders per US dollar)*						
Conversion Factor (Annual Avg)	1.890	1.890	1.880	1.780	1.780	1.780	1.780	1.780	1.780	1.780	1.780
EXTERNAL DEBT (Total)					*(Millions of US dollars), outstanding at end of year*						
Long-Term Debt (by debtor)	..	..	..	..	..	..	..	..	..	..	..
Central Bank, incl. IMF credit	..	..	..	..	..	..	..	..	..	..	..
Central Government	..	..	..	..	..	..	..	..	..	..	..
Rest of General Government	..	..	..	..	..	..	..	..	..	..	..
Non-financial Public Enterprises	..	..	..	..	..	..	..	..	..	..	..
Priv. Sector, incl non-guaranteed	..	..	..	..	..	..	..	..	..	..	..
Short-Term Debt	..	..	..	..	..	..	..	..	..	..	..
Memo Items:					*(Thousands of US dollars)*						
Int'l Reserves Excluding Gold	23,761	27,828	33,094	37,591	56,436	67,547	91,406	110,218	94,025	132,423	169,526
Gold Holdings (at market price)	8,713	9,250	10,800	16,065	16,569	27,528	20,701	19,890	24,347	12,222	27,688
SOCIAL INDICATORS											
Total Fertility Rate	5.7	5.6	5.4	5.3	5.2	5.0	4.9	4.8	4.6	4.5	4.4
Infant Mortality Rate	53.8	53.2	52.6	52.0	51.4	50.8	50.2	49.6	49.0	48.2	47.4
Life Expectancy at Birth	63.7	63.8	63.9	64.0	64.1	64.2	64.3	64.4	64.5	64.6	64.7
Urban Population, % of total	46.1	45.9	45.7	45.5	45.2	45.0	44.8	44.8	44.8	44.8	44.8
Food Prod. per capita (1987=100)	113.2	107.5	95.3	99.0	93.8	93.1	95.9	91.6	79.4	82.5	106.9
Labor Force, Agriculture (%)	25.2	24.7	24.3	23.8	23.3	22.8	22.3	21.8	21.3	20.8	20.4
Labor Force, Female (%)	24.9	25.2	25.3	25.5	25.7	25.8	26.0	26.4	26.8	27.2	27.6
Primary Schl. Enroll. Ratio	..	126.0	..	..	..	..	108.0	106.0	103.0	120.0	115.0
Primary Schl. Enroll. Ratio, Female	..	122.0	..	..	..	..	105.0	102.0	100.0	115.0	..
Secondary Schl. Enroll. Ratio	..	41.0	..	..	..	..	46.0	49.0	50.0	50.0	51.0

1980	1981	1982	1983	1984	1985	1986	1987	1988	1989 estimate	NOTES	SURINAME
				(Millions of current US dollars)							**FOREIGN TRADE (CUSTOMS BASIS)**
514.00	480.00	429.00	367.00	357.00	329.00	241.00	301.00	282.00	..	..	Value of Exports, fob
500.00	463.40	410.50	350.50	..	..	..	..	..	..	..	Nonfuel Primary Products
0.00	2.90	2.60	2.90	..	..	..	..	..	..	..	Fuels
14.00	13.70	15.90	13.60	..	..	..	..	..	..	..	Manufactures
504.00	568.00	514.00	472.00	346.00	299.00	244.00	294.00	454.00	..	..	Value of Imports, cif
49.20	57.90	52.80	54.50	..	..	..	..	..	..	..	Nonfuel Primary Products
159.10	152.00	136.00	118.00	..	..	..	..	..	..	..	Fuels
295.70	358.10	325.20	299.50	..	..	..	..	..	..	..	Manufactures
				(Index 1987 = 100)							
..	..	..	..	..	..	..	..	..	..	..	Terms of Trade
..	..	..	..	..	..	..	..	..	..	..	Export Prices, fob
..	..	..	..	..	..	..	..	..	..	..	Import Prices, cif
				(Millions of current US dollars)							**BALANCE OF PAYMENTS**
638.60	601.96	545.32	450.98	434.34	383.08	364.37	420.90	382.41	573.84	f	Exports of Goods & Services
514.40	473.78	428.63	366.78	374.12	336.08	337.09	338.77	358.37	549.19	..	Merchandise, fob
98.60	91.93	80.90	67.68	55.24	44.26	25.66	80.90	22.69	23.70	..	Nonfactor Services
25.60	36.25	35.80	16.53	4.99	2.75	1.62	1.23	1.34	0.95	..	Factor Services
703.42	728.12	696.13	606.33	508.23	391.99	385.71	348.07	325.55	429.58	f	Imports of Goods & Services
454.00	506.44	460.34	401.63	391.60	309.52	304.09	274.29	239.44	331.65	..	Merchandise, fob
203.81	197.09	206.50	176.92	113.05	79.22	76.97	67.96	76.30	90.70	..	Nonfactor Services
45.60	24.59	29.30	27.79	3.59	3.25	4.65	5.83	9.80	7.23	..	Factor Services
..	..	..	..	..	..	..	..	..	..	..	Long-Term Interest
6.55	3.70	-2.63	-8.01	-7.39	-3.98	-1.90	-0.39	-4.59	-5.60	..	Private Current Transfers, net
0.78	0.22	..	..	..	..	..	..	..	..	..	Workers' Remittances
-58.26	-122.47	-153.45	-163.36	-81.29	-12.89	-23.25	72.44	52.27	138.66	..	Curr. A/C Bal before Off. Transf.
73.73	94.68	96.86	2.52	2.58	1.29	0.90	2.35	10.25	23.47	..	Net Official Transfers
15.46	-27.79	-56.58	-160.84	-78.71	-11.60	-22.35	74.79	62.52	162.13	..	Curr. A/C Bal after Off. Transf.
10.20	36.08	10.98	50.36	-10.25	13.67	-15.07	-59.22	-90.42	-150.87	f	Long-Term Capital, net
10.14	34.57	-6.22	45.66	-39.72	11.93	-33.84	-72.61	-95.80	-167.45	..	Direct Investment
..	..	..	..	..	..	..	..	..	..	..	Long-Term Loans
..	..	..	..	..	..	..	..	..	..	..	Disbursements
..	..	..	..	..	..	..	..	..	..	..	Repayments
0.06	1.51	17.20	4.71	29.47	1.74	18.77	13.39	5.38	16.58	..	Other Long-Term Capital
0.27	4.85	2.80	1.39	36.45	-10.56	-2.58	-24.95	22.75	-11.37	f	Other Capital, net
-25.93	-13.14	42.80	109.09	52.52	8.48	40.00	9.38	5.15	0.11	..	Change in Reserves
				(Suriname Guilders per US dollar)							Memo Item:
1.780	1.780	1.780	1.780	1.780	1.780	1.780	1.780	1.780	1.780	..	Conversion Factor (Annual Avg)
				(Millions of US dollars), outstanding at end of year							
..	..	..	..	..	..	..	..	..	..	..	**EXTERNAL DEBT** (Total)
..	..	..	..	..	..	..	..	..	..	..	Long-Term Debt (by debtor)
..	..	..	..	..	..	..	..	..	..	..	Central Bank, incl. IMF credit
..	..	..	..	..	..	..	..	..	..	..	Central Government
..	..	..	..	..	..	..	..	..	..	..	Rest of General Government
..	..	..	..	..	..	..	..	..	..	..	Non-financial Public Enterprises
..	..	..	..	..	..	..	..	..	..	..	Priv. Sector, incl non-guaranteed
..	..	..	..	..	..	..	..	..	..	..	Short-Term Debt
				(Thousands of US dollars)							Memo Items:
189,251	207,089	175,757	59,148	24,870	23,420	20,890	15,097	12,560	9,246	..	Int'l Reserves Excluding Gold
31,879	21,496	24,708	20,631	16,672	17,683	21,139	26,179	22,185	21,685	..	Gold Holdings (at market price)
											SOCIAL INDICATORS
4.3	4.2	4.1	4.0	3.9	3.8	3.8	3.7	3.6	3.5	..	Total Fertility Rate
46.6	45.8	45.0	44.4	43.8	43.2	42.6	42.0	41.1	40.2	..	Infant Mortality Rate
64.8	64.9	65.0	65.3	65.7	66.0	66.3	66.7	67.0	67.3	..	Life Expectancy at Birth
44.8	45.0	45.2	45.3	45.5	45.7	46.1	46.4	46.8	47.1	..	Urban Population, % of total
105.4	110.9	110.5	108.7	120.3	128.7	111.5	100.0	98.2	97.4	..	Food Prod. per capita (1987=100)
19.9	..	..	..	..	..	..	..	..	..	..	Labor Force, Agriculture (%)
28.0	28.1	28.3	28.5	28.7	28.8	29.0	29.2	29.3	29.4	..	Labor Force, Female (%)
125.0	..	..	132.0	133.0	..	125.0	..	..	..	..	Primary Schl. Enroll. Ratio
..	..	..	..	130.0	..	121.0	..	..	..	..	Primary Schl. Enroll. Ratio, Female
35.0	..	..	44.0	51.0	..	53.0	..	..	..	..	Secondary Schl. Enroll. Ratio

SWAZILAND	1969	1970	1971	1972	1973	1974	1975	1976	1977	1978	1979
CURRENT GNP PER CAPITA (US $)	270	270	320	330	370	460	590	580	590	600	720
POPULATION (thousands)	409	420	431	443	455	468	482	497	512	529	546
USE AND ORIGIN OF RESOURCES					*(Millions of current Swaziland Emalangeni)*						
Gross National Product (GNP)	74.8	79.4	100.1	108.9	127.7	162.7	211.6	232.4	260.7	280.6	353.9
Net Factor Income from Abroad	-9.7	-10.5	-9.0	-11.6	-20.9	-14.7	-1.8	-2.9	-2.8	-42.7	-18.9
GDP at Market Prices	84.5	89.9	109.1	120.5	148.6	177.4	213.4	235.3	263.5	323.3	372.8
Resource Balance	1.3	5.3	12.6	9.5	21.9	40.0	34.3	19.1	-8.6	-70.3	-123.5
Exports of Goods & NFServices	53.7	59.9	66.2	75.6	108.4	146.4	155.5	179.4	172.9	186.4	221.2
Imports of Goods & NFServices	52.4	54.6	53.6	66.1	86.5	106.4	121.2	160.3	181.5	256.7	344.7
Domestic Absorption	83.2	84.6	96.5	111.0	126.7	137.4	179.1	216.2	272.1	393.6	496.3
Private Consumption, etc.	54.3	48.7	57.0	59.9	64.4	53.5	105.5	104.6	146.8	181.5	273.3
General Gov't Consumption	14.9	18.6	17.8	24.2	27.6	36.1	35.6	42.0	54.2	70.2	74.9
Gross Domestic Investment	14.0	17.3	21.7	26.9	34.7	47.8	38.0	69.6	71.1	141.9	148.1
Fixed Investment	..	..	..	..	..	..	..	..	68.1	144.9	142.1
Indirect Taxes, net	18.0	17.3	20.9	24.6	32.0	41.0	52.2	49.0	49.3	62.4	73.5
GDP at factor cost	66.5	72.6	88.2	95.9	116.6	136.4	161.2	186.3	214.2	260.9	299.3
Agriculture	21.9	24.1	32.7	31.7	41.6	47.7	53.5	55.7	64.0	78.0	89.5
Industry	19.3	19.2	21.8	26.7	30.4	35.3	41.0	46.5	53.5	65.1	74.7
Manufacturing	..	..	..	..	..	..	..	..	..	..	..
Services, etc.	25.3	29.3	33.7	37.5	44.6	53.4	66.7	84.1	96.7	117.8	135.1
Gross Domestic Saving	15.3	22.6	34.3	36.4	56.6	87.8	72.3	88.7	62.5	71.6	24.6
Gross National Saving	..	..	..	..	..	73.4	71.1	85.9	59.7	27.3	4.3
					(Millions of 1980 Swaziland Emalangeni)						
Gross National Product	246.90	250.50	289.40	299.60	315.30	350.80	393.10	382.40	388.50	387.30	421.30
GDP at Market Prices	278.80	283.60	318.10	335.70	373.40	385.70	396.70	387.60	392.80	444.60	443.30
Resource Balance	-35.70	-22.40	10.10	-9.60	21.10	59.40	43.20	2.90	-20.70	-83.90	-133.50
Exports of Goods & NFServices	191.30	203.90	208.30	209.30	255.20	294.60	271.30	277.30	241.10	240.40	245.50
Imports of Goods & NFServices	227.00	226.30	198.20	218.90	234.10	235.20	228.10	274.40	261.80	324.30	379.00
Domestic Absorption	314.50	306.00	308.00	345.30	352.30	326.30	353.50	384.70	413.50	528.50	576.80
Private Consumption, etc.	206.80	177.90	176.50	183.30	173.20	116.90	197.10	173.50	202.10	209.20	294.30
General Gov't Consumption	50.50	60.40	53.40	69.40	71.50	80.90	68.60	70.60	82.10	95.70	93.20
Gross Domestic Investment	57.20	67.70	78.10	92.60	107.60	128.50	87.80	140.60	129.30	223.60	189.30
Fixed Investment	..	..	..	..	..	..	..	..	..	..	..
GDP at factor cost	219.50	228.80	257.10	267.10	293.00	296.50	299.60	306.90	318.70	353.50	354.20
Agriculture	51.12	56.02	70.53	66.83	73.33	72.93	70.13	68.33	74.83	86.93	83.33
Industry	79.28	75.68	79.28	88.68	94.78	96.48	92.08	93.58	97.08	116.37	114.77
Manufacturing	..	..	49.30	54.50	58.30	58.30	57.90	61.60	65.30	69.80	71.60
Services, etc.	89.10	97.10	107.29	111.59	124.89	127.09	137.39	144.99	146.79	150.19	156.09
Memo Items:											
Capacity to Import	232.63	248.27	244.79	250.36	293.37	323.62	292.65	307.10	249.40	235.49	243.21
Terms of Trade Adjustment	41.33	44.37	36.49	41.06	38.17	29.02	21.35	29.80	8.30	-4.91	-2.29
Gross Domestic Income	320.13	327.97	354.60	376.76	411.57	414.72	418.05	417.39	401.09	439.69	441.01
Gross National Income	288.23	294.87	325.90	340.66	353.47	379.82	414.45	412.19	396.79	382.39	419.01
DOMESTIC PRICES/DEFLATORS					*(Index 1980 = 100)*						
Overall (GDP)	30.3	31.7	34.3	35.9	39.8	46.0	53.8	60.7	67.1	72.7	84.1
Domestic Absorption	26.5	27.6	31.3	32.1	36.0	42.1	50.7	56.2	65.8	74.5	86.0
Agriculture	42.8	43.0	46.4	47.4	56.7	65.4	76.3	81.5	85.6	89.7	107.4
Industry	24.3	25.4	27.5	30.1	32.1	36.6	44.5	49.7	55.1	56.0	65.1
Manufacturing	..	..	..	..	..	..	..	..	..	..	..
Consumer Price Index	13.2	13.4	13.8	14.1	15.7	18.7	21.0	22.0	26.6	28.6	33.3
MANUFACTURING ACTIVITY											
Employment (1987=100)	..	..	..	..	..	..	..	..	..	..	..
Real Earnings per Empl. (1987=100)	..	..	..	..	..	..	..	..	..	..	..
Real Output per Empl. (1987=100)	..	..	..	..	..	..	..	..	..	..	..
Earnings as % of Value Added	..	42.5	50.6	38.7	34.3	..	..	18.2	34.4	42.8	36.5
MONETARY HOLDINGS					*(Millions of current Swaziland Emalangeni)*						
Money Supply, Broadly Defined	..	..	..	..	..	57.61	81.75	98.59	105.96	132.78	135.69
Money	..	..	..	..	..	16.93	23.42	28.79	34.16	37.21	40.91
Currency Outside Banks	..	..	..	..	..	3.33	5.11	6.52	7.31	8.90	9.59
Demand Deposits	..	..	..	..	..	13.60	18.31	22.27	26.84	28.32	31.32
Quasi-Money	..	..	..	..	..	40.68	58.32	69.80	71.81	95.57	94.78
					(Millions of current Swaziland Emalangeni)						
GOVERNMENT DEFICIT (-) OR SURPLUS	..	..	-2.02	-4.62	-10.77	1.66	17.39	-8.48	-8.56	-39.97	3.87
Current Revenue	..	..	17.46	21.35	28.56	46.23	69.99	54.66	81.13	105.19	133.93
Current Expenditure	..	..	16.03	17.79	22.48	25.64	29.67	40.22	48.53	55.37	60.21
Current Budget Balance	..	..	1.43	3.56	6.08	20.59	40.32	14.44	32.60	49.82	73.72
Capital Receipts	..	..	0.01	0.01	0.01	0.08	0.03	..	0.04	0.09	0.12
Capital Payments	..	..	3.46	8.19	16.86	19.01	22.96	22.92	41.20	89.88	69.97

1980	1981	1982	1983	1984	1985	1986	1987	1988	1989 estimate	NOTES	SWAZILAND
820	1,010	1,010	930	890	740	660	640	820	900	..	CURRENT GNP PER CAPITA (US $)
564	582	602	622	642	664	687	710	735	761	..	POPULATION (thousands)
				(Millions of current Swaziland Emalangeni)							USE AND ORIGIN OF RESOURCES
416.3	506.8	562.1	609.6	715.4	819.8	992.9	1,140.0	1,448.9	1,688.0	C	Gross National Product (GNP)
-5.8	5.9	15.4	30.0	53.1	76.5	36.9	7.2	64.7	..	..	Net Factor Income from Abroad
422.1	500.9	546.7	579.6	662.3	743.3	956.0	1,132.8	1,384.2	1,666.1	C	GDP at Market Prices
-140.2	-148.6	-165.5	-209.4	-240.0	-263.4	-113.9	4.5	-23.0	7.6	..	Resource Balance
325.7	388.0	416.7	400.6	432.8	474.6	710.7	890.0	1,000.8	1,427.5	..	Exports of Goods & NFServices
465.9	536.6	582.2	610.0	672.8	738.0	824.6	885.5	1,023.8	1,419.9	..	Imports of Goods & NFServices
562.3	649.5	712.2	789.0	902.3	1,006.7	1,069.9	1,128.3	1,407.2	..	..	Domestic Absorption
286.8	360.2	395.0	450.4	510.8	591.5	595.3	720.6	900.6	..	..	Private Consumption, etc.
103.9	133.8	141.0	135.8	182.1	177.6	240.7	237.1	286.9	..	..	General Gov't Consumption
171.6	155.5	176.2	202.8	209.4	237.6	233.9	170.6	219.7	..	..	Gross Domestic Investment
147.8	140.2	152.8	208.5	208.5	225.4	228.9	..	..	..	..	Fixed Investment
59.6	63.1	61.9	62.9	74.5	91.8	119.5	144.8	173.7	..	..	Indirect Taxes, net
362.5	437.8	484.8	516.7	587.8	651.5	836.5	988.0	1,210.5	..	C	GDP at factor cost
90.2	104.7	102.1	111.2	127.0	160.3	201.7	..	280.4	..	..	Agriculture
114.3	132.8	148.7	140.0	156.5	170.1	247.8	..	487.8	..	..	Industry
79.6	89.1	100.8	89.7	104.1	105.3	166.3	..	312.5	..	..	Manufacturing
158.0	200.3	234.0	265.5	304.3	321.1	387.0	..	442.3	..	..	Services, etc.
31.4	6.9	10.7	-6.6	-30.6	-25.8	120.0	175.1	196.7	..	..	Gross Domestic Saving
23.7	13.3	26.6	21.3	22.6	56.3	162.6	190.9	273.1	..	..	Gross National Saving
				(Millions of 1980 Swaziland Emalangeni)							
416.30	455.64	466.64	469.59	504.03	518.44	538.28	531.67	598.46	622.66	C	Gross National Product
422.10	450.33	455.69	451.94	469.27	480.53	522.82	529.09	577.76	604.72	C	GDP at Market Prices
-140.20	-133.63	-50.32	-12.08	-20.73	..	..	..	..	..	..	Resource Balance
325.70	360.93	389.08	461.52	392.03	..	..	..	..	..	..	Exports of Goods & NFServices
465.90	494.56	439.40	473.60	412.76	..	..	..	..	..	..	Imports of Goods & NFServices
562.30	583.96	506.01	464.02	490.00	..	..	..	..	..	..	Domestic Absorption
286.80	331.74	274.06	245.14	266.53	..	..	..	..	..	..	Private Consumption, etc.
103.90	122.64	104.37	80.55	95.94	..	..	..	..	..	..	General Gov't Consumption
171.60	129.58	127.59	138.34	127.53	..	..	..	..	..	..	Gross Domestic Investment
..	..	..	..	..	..	..	..	..	..	..	Fixed Investment
362.50	393.60	404.10	402.90	415.90	425.70	463.30	468.70	511.70	534.88	C	GDP at factor cost
90.23	101.59	96.50	95.20	100.22	108.64	120.95	118.45	124.85	129.22	..	Agriculture
114.27	126.57	128.87	125.37	124.77	122.87	140.67	148.40	170.32	179.86	..	Industry
79.60	88.40	93.00	94.00	93.50	92.30	109.10	115.10	132.10	140.03	..	Manufacturing
157.99	165.44	178.73	182.33	190.91	194.19	201.69	201.85	216.53	225.79	..	Services, etc.
											Memo Items:
325.70	357.60	314.49	311.02	265.52	..	..	..	..	..	..	Capacity to Import
0.00	-3.33	-74.59	-150.50	-126.51	..	..	..	..	..	..	Terms of Trade Adjustment
422.10	447.00	381.11	301.45	342.76	..	..	..	..	..	..	Gross Domestic Income
416.30	452.31	392.05	319.09	377.52	..	..	..	..	..	..	Gross National Income
				(Index 1980 = 100)							DOMESTIC PRICES/DEFLATORS
100.0	111.2	120.0	128.2	141.1	154.7	182.9	214.1	239.6	275.5	..	Overall (GDP)
100.0	111.2	140.7	170.0	184.1	..	..	..	..	..	..	Domestic Absorption
100.0	103.0	105.8	116.8	126.7	147.5	166.8	..	224.6	..	..	Agriculture
100.0	104.9	115.4	111.7	125.4	138.4	176.2	..	286.4	..	..	Industry
100.0	100.8	108.4	95.4	111.3	114.1	152.5	..	236.6	..	..	Manufacturing
39.5	47.4	53.0	58.8	66.4	79.6	88.9	100.0	111.7	..	f	Consumer Price Index
											MANUFACTURING ACTIVITY
..	..	..	..	..	..	..	..	..	..	G	Employment (1987=100)
..	..	..	..	..	..	..	..	..	..	G	Real Earnings per Empl. (1987=100)
..	..	..	..	..	..	..	..	..	..	G	Real Output per Empl. (1987=100)
40.6	43.6	47.0	53.8	40.4	48.1	..	..	..	..	..	Earnings as % of Value Added
				(Millions of current Swaziland Emalangeni)							MONETARY HOLDINGS
151.46	165.41	163.65	200.90	242.00	297.40	330.50	..	..	..	D	Money Supply, Broadly Defined
49.86	51.08	58.09	60.84	67.81	76.92	115.14	125.42	142.77	169.01	..	Money
11.90	14.41	15.03	15.22	16.77	17.45	25.21	27.19	32.20	37.20	..	Currency Outside Banks
37.96	36.67	43.06	45.62	51.04	59.47	89.93	98.23	110.57	131.82	..	Demand Deposits
101.60	114.32	105.56	140.06	174.19	220.48	215.36	..	..	..	..	Quasi-Money
				(Millions of current Swaziland Emalangeni)							GOVERNMENT DEFICIT (-) OR SURPLUS
27.55	-48.90	-31.85	-19.55	-3.63	-27.57	-48.85	21.58	59.20	..	C	GOVERNMENT DEFICIT (-) OR SURPLUS
156.38	136.06	183.92	185.57	221.46	242.45	255.62	337.29	428.09	..	..	Current Revenue
78.58	111.74	124.00	136.66	154.97	170.56	217.71	235.46	289.57	..	..	Current Expenditure
77.80	24.32	59.92	48.91	66.49	71.89	37.91	101.83	138.52	..	..	Current Budget Balance
0.07	0.05	0.08	..	..	0.05	0.06	0.03	0.10	..	..	Capital Receipts
50.32	73.27	76.89	68.46	70.12	99.51	86.82	80.28	79.42	..	..	Capital Payments

SWAZILAND	1969	1970	1971	1972	1973	1974	1975	1976	1977	1978	1979
FOREIGN TRADE (CUSTOMS BASIS)					*(Millions of current US dollars)*						
Value of Exports, fob	..	71.00	78.00	82.00	107.00	179.00	199.00	183.00	168.00	196.00	231.00
Nonfuel Primary Products	..	..	..	..	..	..	..	..	..	..	..
Fuels	..	..	..	..	..	..	..	..	..	..	..
Manufactures	..	..	..	..	..	..	..	..	..	..	..
Value of Imports, cif	50.00	60.00	67.00	69.00	96.00	138.00	180.00	·200.00	224.00	311.00	434.00
Nonfuel Primary Products	..	..	..	..	..	..	..	..	..	..	..
Fuels	..	..	..	..	..	..	..	..	..	..	..
Manufactures	..	..	..	..	..	..	..	..	..	..	..
					(Index 1987 = 100)						
Terms of Trade	..	..	..	..	..	..	..	..	..	..	..
Export Prices, fob	..	..	..	..	..	..	..	..	..	..	..
Import Prices, cif	..	..	..	..	..	..	..	..	..	..	..
BALANCE OF PAYMENTS					*(Millions of current US dollars)*						
Exports of Goods & Services	..	..	..	..	..	206.19	235.16	234.83	233.68	247.14	300.43
Merchandise, fob	..	..	..	..	..	178.81	197.02	193.43	183.89	198.72	241.63
Nonfactor Services	..	..	..	..	..	22.96	24.88	25.65	29.10	23.00	31.36
Factor Services	..	..	..	..	..	4.42	13.25	15.75	20.70	25.42	27.44
Imports of Goods & Services	..	..	..	..	..	179.55	202.97	213.67	235.75	341.32	466.50
Merchandise, fob	..	..	..	..	..	111.70	139.55	155.83	171.12	246.56	361.13
Nonfactor Services	..	..	..	..	..	29.58	40.30	42.67	46.81	64.63	84.70
Factor Services	..	..	..	..	..	38.26	23.12	15.18	17.83	30.13	20.67
Long-Term Interest	..	1.90	1.60	1.40	1.60	1.00	0.90	0.90	1.30	2.20	3.80
Private Current Transfers, net	..	..	..	..	..	0.44	0.81	0.12	0.00	-1.84	-1.66
Workers' Remittances	..	..	..	..	..	..	..	..	..	..	..
Curr. A/C Bal before Off. Transf.	..	..	..	..	..	27.08	33.00	21.28	-2.07	-96.03	-167.74
Net Official Transfers	..	..	..	..	..	14.86	17.71	8.51	12.88	26.68	47.04
Curr. A/C Bal after Off. Transf.	..	..	..	..	..	41.94	50.71	29.79	10.81	-69.35	-120.69
Long-Term Capital, net	..	..	..	..	..	7.36	20.01	15.29	27.95	69.00	90.05
Direct Investment	..	..	..	..	..	3.53	14.47	7.36	20.01	21.74	55.48
Long-Term Loans	..	2.00	-2.40	-1.10	3.10	-1.20	1.00	9.90	9.10	58.80	46.70
Disbursements	..	3.50	0.20	6.10	11.20	2.20	3.50	11.00	10.00	60.50	50.40
Repayments	..	1.50	2.60	7.20	8.10	3.40	2.50	1.10	0.90	1.70	3.70
Other Long-Term Capital	..	..	..	..	..	5.03	4.54	-1.96	-1.16	-11.53	-12.13
Other Capital, net	..	..	..	..	..	-39.30	-31.48	-17.38	-16.99	16.26	25.28
Change in Reserves	..	1.07	0.76	0.02	0.02	-10.00	-39.24	-27.70	-21.77	-15.91	5.37
Memo Item:					*(Swaziland Emalangeni per US dollar)*						
Conversion Factor (Annual Avg)	0.710	0.710	0.720	0.770	0.690	0.680	0.740	0.870	0.870	0.870	0.840
					(Millions of US dollars), outstanding at end of year						
EXTERNAL DEBT (Total)	..	37.00	34.70	32.60	37.00	36.20	33.70	40.80	61.30	134.00	180.70
Long-Term Debt (by debtor)	..	37.00	34.70	32.60	37.00	36.20	33.70	40.80	52.30	117.00	172.70
Central Bank, incl. IMF credit	..	0.00	0.00	0.00	0.00	0.00	0.00	0.00	0.00	0.00	3.20
Central Government	..	35.90	33.70	31.70	36.00	35.30	33.10	40.20	51.80	103.00	133.90
Rest of General Government	..	..	..	..	..	..	..	..	..	..	..
Non-financial Public Enterprises	..	1.10	1.00	0.90	1.00	0.90	0.60	0.60	0.50	14.00	35.60
Priv. Sector, incl non-guaranteed	..	..	..	..	..	..	..	..	..	..	..
Short-Term Debt	..	..	..	..	..	..	..	..	9.00	17.00	8.00
Memo Items:					*(Millions of US dollars)*						
Int'l Reserves Excluding Gold	..	..	..	..	..	13.47	45.61	73.39	94.71	113.61	113.71
Gold Holdings (at market price)	..	..	..	..	..	..	..	..	..	..	..
SOCIAL INDICATORS											
Total Fertility Rate	6.5	6.5	6.5	6.5	6.5	6.5	6.5	6.5	6.5	6.5	6.5
Infant Mortality Rate	145.8	145.2	144.6	144.0	143.2	142.4	141.6	140.8	140.0	137.8	135.6
Life Expectancy at Birth	45.6	46.1	46.7	47.3	47.8	48.3	48.9	49.4	49.9	50.5	51.1
Urban Population, % of total	9.1	9.7	10.6	11.4	12.3	13.1	14.0	15.2	16.3	17.5	18.6
Food Prod. per capita (1987=100)	85.4	95.7	94.3	99.2	91.4	96.9	95.7	96.2	88.8	99.3	93.2
Labor Force, Agriculture (%)	81.4	80.6	79.9	79.3	78.6	78.0	77.4	76.6	76.0	75.3	74.7
Labor Force, Female (%)	42.4	42.3	42.1	42.0	41.9	41.8	41.7	41.5	41.4	41.3	41.1
Primary Schl. Enroll. Ratio	..	87.0	..	..	..	..	99.0	99.0	100.0	101.0	103.0
Primary Schl. Enroll. Ratio, Female	..	83.0	..	..	..	..	97.0	97.0	99.0	101.0	103.0
Secondary Schl. Enroll. Ratio	..	18.0	..	..	..	..	32.0	..	36.0	37.0	38.0

1980	1981	1982	1983	1984	1985	1986	1987	1988	1989 estimate	NOTES	SWAZILAND
				(Millions of current US dollars)							**FOREIGN TRADE (CUSTOMS BASIS)**
368.37	388.00	325.00	304.00	237.00	176.00	267.00	311.00	..	..	..	Value of Exports, fob
..	..	..	..	..	..	..	..	..	..	..	Nonfuel Primary Products
..	..	..	..	..	..	..	..	..	..	..	Fuels
..	..	..	..	..	..	..	..	..	..	..	Manufactures
538.00	506.00	440.00	464.00	381.00	281.00	352.00	365.00	..	..	..	Value of Imports, cif
..	..	..	..	..	..	..	..	..	..	..	Nonfuel Primary Products
..	..	..	..	..	..	..	..	..	..	..	Fuels
..	..	..	..	..	..	..	..	..	..	..	Manufactures
				(Index 1987 = 100)							
..	..	..	..	..	..	..	..	..	..	..	Terms of Trade
..	..	..	..	..	..	..	..	..	..	..	Export Prices, fob
..	..	..	..	..	..	..	..	..	..	..	Import Prices, cif
				(Millions of current US dollars)							**BALANCE OF PAYMENTS**
450.70	496.67	409.65	410.56	344.34	271.13	377.06	568.26	600.76	624.78	..	Exports of Goods & Services
368.26	388.27	324.00	303.83	230.80	176.75	278.11	423.52	424.42	452.09	..	Merchandise, fob
36.08	39.82	31.04	39.85	42.64	26.95	29.63	46.46	53.13	54.03	..	Nonfactor Services
46.35	68.57	54.61	66.87	70.90	67.43	69.32	98.28	123.20	118.66	..	Factor Services
659.23	659.83	583.89	585.32	487.77	373.91	434.65	554.95	627.10	700.31	..	Imports of Goods & Services
537.11	501.91	437.83	463.60	371.18	271.66	295.93	369.44	444.04	466.05	..	Merchandise, fob
80.25	107.82	104.53	92.36	84.53	69.19	81.75	83.10	82.47	80.38	..	Nonfactor Services
41.86	50.09	41.54	29.35	32.06	33.06	56.98	102.40	100.60	153.89	..	Factor Services
9.00	9.20	9.00	7.90	9.10	8.30	11.10	14.90	13.70	11.70	..	Long-Term Interest
-2.44	0.57	0.46	-1.88	0.07	2.52	2.49	4.22	5.15	5.87	..	Private Current Transfers, net
..	..	..	..	..	..	..	..	..	..	..	Workers' Remittances
-210.97	-162.59	-173.79	-176.64	-143.36	-100.26	-55.10	17.53	-21.20	-69.66	..	Curr. A/C Bal before Off. Transf.
78.46	71.31	61.24	64.72	59.72	52.86	57.81	47.49	62.99	71.76	..	Net Official Transfers
-132.51	-91.28	-112.54	-111.93	-83.65	-47.40	2.71	65.03	41.79	2.10	..	Curr. A/C Bal after Off. Transf.
35.18	43.81	12.99	36.08	10.91	23.89	38.86	28.63	22.83	58.79	..	Long-Term Capital, net
17.46	31.72	-17.41	-5.74	2.71	13.41	25.86	37.82	37.61	26.00	..	Direct Investment
19.00	11.00	19.40	16.50	18.10	14.00	10.30	-9.30	-3.00	2.20	..	Long-Term Loans
26.50	20.90	31.30	29.40	28.20	29.70	27.80	20.40	18.00	22.30	..	Disbursements
7.50	9.90	11.90	12.90	10.10	15.70	17.50	29.70	21.00	20.10	..	Repayments
-1.28	1.09	10.99	25.33	-9.90	-3.52	2.70	0.12	-11.78	30.59	..	Other Long-Term Capital
134.10	7.16	93.39	92.63	95.56	41.82	-36.34	-72.30	-37.06	-8.86	..	Other Capital, net
-36.77	40.30	6.17	-16.79	-22.83	-18.31	-5.24	-21.37	-27.56	-52.03	..	Change in Reserves
				(Swaziland Emalangeni per US dollar)							**Memo Item:**
0.780	0.870	1.080	1.110	1.440	2.190	2.270	2.030	2.260	2.620	..	Conversion Factor (Annual Avg)
				(Millions of US dollars), outstanding at end of year							
205.80	185.10	198.80	235.00	191.70	238.20	278.40	308.60	269.90	281.20	..	**EXTERNAL DEBT (Total)**
190.80	179.10	184.80	198.00	184.70	223.20	261.30	291.50	262.00	260.10	..	Long-Term Debt (by debtor)
5.70	5.20	5.00	15.20	14.20	14.10	10.50	6.10	1.60	0.40	..	Central Bank, incl. IMF credit
137.10	133.80	132.50	133.90	132.80	168.40	202.20	233.40	219.70	226.50	..	Central Government
..	..	..	..	..	..	..	..	..	..	..	Rest of General Government
48.00	40.10	47.30	48.90	37.70	40.70	48.60	52.00	40.70	33.20	..	Non-financial Public Enterprises
..	..	..	..	..	..	..	..	..	..	..	Priv. Sector, incl non-guaranteed
15.00	6.00	14.00	37.00	7.00	15.00	17.10	17.10	7.90	21.10	..	Short-Term Debt
				(Millions of US dollars)							**Memo Items:**
158.74	96.36	76.12	92.50	80.10	83.42	96.45	127.16	140.01	180.61	..	Int'l Reserves Excluding Gold
..	..	..	..	..	..	..	..	..	..	..	Gold Holdings (at market price)
											SOCIAL INDICATORS
6.5	6.5	6.5	6.5	6.5	6.5	6.5	6.5	6.4	6.3	..	Total Fertility Rate
133.4	131.2	129.0	126.8	124.6	122.4	120.2	118.0	116.3	114.5	..	Infant Mortality Rate
51.7	52.3	53.0	53.5	54.0	54.5	55.0	55.5	55.8	56.1	..	Life Expectancy at Birth
19.8	21.1	22.4	23.7	25.0	26.3	28.0	29.7	30.8	32.0	..	Urban Population, % of total
103.7	104.9	102.0	101.6	102.9	94.8	106.9	100.0	98.4	93.1	..	Food Prod. per capita (1987=100)
74.1	..	..	..	..	..	..	..	..	..	..	Labor Force, Agriculture (%)
41.0	40.8	40.6	40.4	40.1	39.9	39.7	39.5	39.2	39.0	..	Labor Force, Female (%)
103.0	..	..	..	107.0	107.0	105.0	104.0	..	..	..	Primary Schl. Enroll. Ratio
102.0	..	..	..	106.0	105.0	104.0	103.0	..	..	..	Primary Schl. Enroll. Ratio, Female
38.0	40.0	42.0	44.0	42.0	43.0	42.0	43.0	..	..	..	Secondary Schl. Enroll. Ratio

SWEDEN	1969	1970	1971	1972	1973	1974	1975	1976	1977	1978	1979
CURRENT GNP PER CAPITA (US $)	3,810	4,140	4,360	4,840	5,820	6,890	8,140	8,860	9,740	10,890	12,660
POPULATION (thousands)	7,968	8,043	8,098	8,122	8,137	8,161	8,193	8,222	8,252	8,276	8,294
USE AND ORIGIN OF RESOURCES					*(Billions of current Swedish Kronor)*						
Gross National Product (GNP)	153.7	166.7	184.2	204.3	228.7	250.6	291.5	332.9	371.5	418.4	460.2
Net Factor Income from Abroad	-0.1	-0.1	0.2	0.4	0.8	0.7	0.8	0.5	-0.7	-1.4	-1.3
GDP at Market Prices	153.8	166.8	184.1	203.9	227.9	249.9	290.7	332.4	372.2	419.8	461.5
Resource Balance	-0.7	-1.0	2.1	3.1	6.4	-1.9	-0.7	-5.6	-6.5	4.3	-4.5
Exports of Goods & NFServices	35.0	41.4	45.3	49.3	62.2	82.6	84.6	94.0	101.3	116.4	140.4
Imports of Goods & NFServices	35.7	42.4	43.2	46.2	55.8	84.5	85.3	99.7	107.7	112.1	144.9
Domestic Absorption	154.5	167.7	182.0	200.8	221.5	251.8	291.4	338.0	378.7	415.5	466.1
Private Consumption, etc.	84.8	92.2	99.1	109.0	120.0	136.9	155.9	180.8	197.5	219.3	242.1
General Gov't Consumption	34.6	39.3	43.4	47.4	52.4	59.4	68.8	85.5	102.8	116.3	132.1
Gross Domestic Investment	35.1	36.2	39.5	44.5	49.2	55.5	66.8	71.7	78.4	79.9	91.8
Fixed Investment	32.8	34.3	37.6	42.4	46.9	49.3	56.4	65.4	73.4	76.4	84.8
Indirect Taxes, net	17.2	18.9	24.2	25.1	28.5	28.1	32.4	35.9	41.2	40.3	42.3
GDP at factor cost	136.6	147.8	159.8	178.9	199.4	221.8	258.3	296.5	331.1	379.5	419.2
Agriculture	..	..	..	..	..	..	..	..	..	..	..
Industry	..	..	..	..	..	..	..	..	..	..	..
Manufacturing	..	..	..	..	..	..	..	..	..	..	..
Services, etc.	..	..	..	..	..	..	..	..	..	..	..
Gross Domestic Saving	34.4	35.2	41.6	47.5	55.6	53.6	66.1	66.1	71.9	84.2	87.3
Gross National Saving	..	34.9	41.5	47.6	55.9	53.9	66.2	65.6	70.3	81.9	85.3
					(Billions of 1987 Swedish Kronor)						
Gross National Product	685.29	731.59	737.28	755.24	788.25	813.36	835.28	837.09	821.39	836.89	871.16
GDP at Market Prices	685.53	731.60	736.30	753.66	785.38	810.88	832.75	835.75	822.82	839.54	873.43
Resource Balance	-26.31	-31.66	-17.17	-14.56	-3.10	-13.12	-25.49	-37.17	-24.90	4.58	-7.41
Exports of Goods & NFServices	152.89	166.11	174.03	184.24	209.47	220.59	200.11	208.75	211.79	228.32	242.33
Imports of Goods & NFServices	179.20	197.77	191.21	198.80	212.57	233.71	225.60	245.93	236.69	223.73	249.74
Domestic Absorption	711.85	763.26	753.47	768.22	788.48	824.00	858.24	872.92	847.72	834.95	880.85
Private Consumption, etc.	396.59	409.53	411.02	424.86	436.00	449.41	461.91	479.15	475.53	476.02	485.22
General Gov't Consumption	162.82	176.00	180.43	185.21	190.49	195.98	204.90	212.06	218.39	225.38	236.15
Gross Domestic Investment	152.44	177.73	162.03	158.15	161.98	178.61	191.43	181.70	153.80	133.55	159.47
Fixed Investment	151.81	156.75	155.84	162.33	166.65	161.60	166.60	169.69	164.70	153.43	160.28
GDP at factor cost	605.87	645.04	635.71	657.59	683.78	718.73	736.90	742.50	730.49	759.01	793.72
Agriculture	..	..	..	..	..	..	..	..	..	..	..
Industry	..	..	..	..	..	..	..	..	..	..	..
Manufacturing	..	..	..	..	..	..	..	..	..	..	..
Services, etc.	..	..	..	..	..	..	..	..	..	..	..
Memo Items:											
Capacity to Import	175.75	193.15	200.48	212.03	237.02	228.40	223.74	232.09	222.50	232.35	241.91
Terms of Trade Adjustment	22.86	27.03	26.45	27.79	27.55	7.81	23.63	23.33	10.71	4.04	-0.42
Gross Domestic Income	708.40	758.63	762.75	781.44	812.93	818.69	856.38	859.08	833.53	843.57	873.02
Gross National Income	708.15	758.63	763.73	783.03	815.80	821.17	858.91	860.42	832.10	840.93	870.74
DOMESTIC PRICES/DEFLATORS					*(Index 1987 = 100)*						
Overall (GDP)	22.4	22.8	25.0	27.1	29.0	30.8	34.9	39.8	45.2	50.0	52.8
Domestic Absorption	21.7	22.0	24.1	26.1	28.1	30.6	34.0	38.7	44.7	49.8	52.9
Agriculture	..	..	..	..	..	..	..	..	..	..	..
Industry	..	..	..	..	..	..	..	..	..	..	..
Manufacturing	..	..	..	..	..	..	..	..	..	..	..
Consumer Price Index	23.2	24.8	26.6	28.2	30.1	33.1	36.3	40.1	44.7	49.1	52.7
MANUFACTURING ACTIVITY											
Employment (1987=100)	115.7	118.4	116.2	114.4	116.4	119.3	120.7	120.5	116.2	112.3	112.1
Real Earnings per Empl. (1987=100)	94.0	96.3	97.4	99.5	99.2	100.6	106.3	107.2	103.4	102.3	102.1
Real Output per Empl. (1987=100)	..	..	..	..	..	..	..	..	..	..	..
Earnings as % of Value Added	52.6	52.2	52.6	51.7	47.6	43.8	46.7	47.8	47.9	47.2	43.3
MONETARY HOLDINGS					*(Billions of current Swedish Kronor)*						
Money Supply, Broadly Defined	81.86	84.98	95.31	107.61	121.86	132.74	148.00	157.23	171.27	200.07	233.83
Money	10.94	11.40	12.82	14.15	15.38	17.32	20.15	22.19	24.43	27.58	30.97
Currency Outside Banks	10.94	11.40	12.81	14.14	15.38	17.32	20.13	22.16	24.41	27.57	30.94
Demand Deposits	0.00	0.00	0.00	0.01	0.00	0.00	0.02	0.03	0.02	0.02	0.03
Quasi-Money	70.91	73.58	82.49	93.46	106.48	115.41	127.94	135.04	146.84	172.48	202.87
GOVERNMENT DEFICIT (-) OR SURPLUS					*(Billions of current Swedish Kronor)*						
	..	-3.10	-2.44	-2.47	-3.21	-7.98	-7.55	-1.17	-6.06	-20.45	-33.22
Current Revenue	..	51.29	58.64	66.47	70.50	79.15	93.72	122.88	140.77	154.65	166.57
Current Expenditure	..	39.97	44.54	50.93	57.15	68.69	82.01	101.21	122.20	146.92	172.67
Current Budget Balance	..	11.32	14.10	15.54	13.35	10.46	11.71	21.67	18.57	7.73	-6.10
Capital Receipts	..	..	..	..	..	..	..	..	..	..	..
Capital Payments	..	14.42	16.54	18.01	16.56	18.44	19.26	22.84	24.63	28.18	27.12

1980	1981	1982	1983	1984	1985	1986	1987	1988	1989 estimate	NOTES	SWEDEN
14,330	14,990	14,210	12,620	12,040	11,940	13,270	15,810	19,300	21,710	..	CURRENT GNP PER CAPITA (US $)
8,310	8,320	8,325	8,331	8,337	8,350	8,370	8,399	8,436	8,485	..	POPULATION (thousands)
				(Billions of current Swedish Kronor)							USE AND ORIGIN OF RESOURCES
524.1	570.2	620.3	693.0	774.4	844.6	926.1	1,004.3	1,092.8	1,198.1	..	Gross National Product (GNP)
-4.0	-8.6	-13.3	-16.6	-19.8	-21.1	-20.0	-16.5	-21.1	-23.1	..	Net Factor Income from Abroad
528.2	578.9	633.6	709.6	794.2	865.7	946.1	1,020.8	1,113.9	1,221.2	..	GDP at Market Prices
-10.4	-1.1	-3.6	15.1	29.1	15.4	29.9	18.4	17.0	7.0	..	Resource Balance
156.3	174.1	204.6	253.1	289.8	306.6	311.0	332.1	361.9	397.5	..	Exports of Goods & NFServices
166.7	175.2	208.2	238.0	260.7	291.2	281.1	313.7	344.9	390.4	..	Imports of Goods & NFServices
538.5	580.0	637.2	694.5	765.1	850.3	916.2	1,002.3	1,096.9	1,214.1	..	Domestic Absorption
274.5	306.7	342.0	372.0	407.1	447.8	493.2	542.5	591.2	634.2	..	Private Consumption, etc.
153.8	170.2	185.7	203.5	221.1	239.2	257.8	271.2	289.1	319.9	..	General Gov't Consumption
110.3	103.1	109.5	119.0	137.0	163.3	165.2	188.6	216.6	260.0	..	Gross Domestic Investment
99.6	103.6	112.9	126.8	143.3	163.8	172.8	195.5	220.7	258.7	..	Fixed Investment
48.6	55.9	58.0	71.8	86.3	99.2	112.7	128.9	132.8	147.7	..	Indirect Taxes, net
479.5	522.9	575.6	637.9	708.0	766.5	833.4	891.9	981.2	1,073.4	..	GDP at factor cost
..	..	..	..	..	..	..	..	..	..	..	Agriculture
..	..	..	..	..	..	..	..	..	..	..	Industry
..	..	..	..	..	..	..	..	..	..	..	Manufacturing
..	..	..	..	..	..	..	..	..	..	..	Services, etc.
99.9	102.0	106.0	134.1	166.1	178.7	195.1	207.0	233.6	267.0	..	Gross Domestic Saving
94.6	92.2	90.9	115.2	143.7	154.2	171.6	188.2	209.7	239.4	..	Gross National Saving
				(Billions of 1987 Swedish Kronor)							
879.28	873.20	877.75	891.54	925.34	946.39	970.65	1,004.29	1,024.73	1,046.63	..	Gross National Product
885.89	886.18	896.02	912.25	948.58	969.65	991.69	1,020.76	1,044.63	1,066.64	..	GDP at Market Prices
-9.79	9.70	15.63	39.44	45.86	30.12	26.83	18.42	11.48	0.67	..	Resource Balance
241.03	245.92	259.92	285.64	305.25	309.66	319.54	332.12	343.22	354.95	..	Exports of Goods & NFServices
250.82	236.22	244.29	246.20	259.38	279.54	292.71	313.70	331.74	354.27	..	Imports of Goods & NFServices
895.68	876.48	880.39	872.82	902.72	939.52	964.86	1,002.34	1,033.15	1,065.96	..	Domestic Absorption
480.94	481.01	484.54	476.05	484.37	495.51	520.31	542.50	554.57	556.67	..	Private Consumption, etc.
241.55	247.09	249.62	251.55	257.34	263.53	267.61	271.22	274.07	279.27	..	General Gov't Consumption
173.18	148.38	146.24	145.21	161.00	180.49	176.94	188.61	204.52	230.02	..	Gross Domestic Investment
165.82	156.17	155.70	158.59	168.13	180.48	181.66	195.50	208.04	227.72	..	Fixed Investment
805.15	802.15	816.46	822.84	847.54	860.41	873.28	891.89	919.39	936.33	..	GDP at factor cost
..	..	..	..	..	..	..	..	..	..	..	Agriculture
..	..	..	..	..	..	..	..	..	..	..	Industry
..	..	..	..	..	..	..	..	..	..	..	Manufacturing
..	..	..	..	..	..	..	..	..	..	..	Services, etc.
											Memo Items:
235.20	234.73	240.11	261.85	288.33	294.33	323.82	332.12	348.13	360.65	..	Capacity to Import
-5.83	-11.19	-19.81	-23.80	-16.91	-15.33	4.28	0.00	4.91	5.71	..	Terms of Trade Adjustment
880.06	874.99	876.21	888.46	931.66	954.32	995.96	1,020.76	1,049.54	1,072.34	..	Gross Domestic Income
873.45	862.01	857.93	867.74	908.43	931.06	974.92	1,004.29	1,029.64	1,052.34	..	Gross National Income
				(Index 1987 = 100)							DOMESTIC PRICES/DEFLATORS
59.6	65.3	70.7	77.8	83.7	89.3	95.4	100.0	106.6	114.5	..	Overall (GDP)
60.1	66.2	72.4	79.6	84.8	90.5	95.0	100.0	106.2	113.9	..	Domestic Absorption
..	..	..	..	..	..	..	..	..	..	..	Agriculture
..	..	..	..	..	..	..	..	..	..	..	Industry
..	..	..	..	..	..	..	..	..	..	..	Manufacturing
59.9	67.1	72.9	79.4	85.7	92.1	95.9	100.0	105.8	112.6	..	Consumer Price Index
											MANUFACTURING ACTIVITY
111.2	107.7	102.9	99.4	99.9	100.3	100.1	100.0	98.9	98.9	..	Employment (1987=100)
97.7	95.0	94.5	93.7	95.2	95.3	98.0	100.0	100.8	101.4	..	Real Earnings per Empl. (1987=100)
..	..	..	..	..	..	..	..	..	..	..	Real Output per Empl. (1987=100)
43.7	43.5	40.4	36.8	36.6	36.7	36.5	35.4	34.3	34.0	..	Earnings as % of Value Added
				(Billions of current Swedish Kronor)							MONETARY HOLDINGS
257.16	293.61	315.06	385.16	425.11	439.39	504.66	529.78	574.12	636.66	..	Money Supply, Broadly Defined
33.61	36.11	38.46	86.98	96.85	100.42	110.42	113.49	114.86	129.79	..	Money
33.58	36.06	38.06	41.94	44.87	45.86	51.74	54.09	57.38	64.18	..	Currency Outside Banks
0.04	0.05	0.39	45.04	51.98	54.56	58.68	59.39	57.47	65.61	..	Demand Deposits
223.54	257.50	276.60	298.18	328.26	338.97	394.24	416.30	459.27	506.87	..	Quasi-Money
				(Billions of current Swedish Kronor)						C E	GOVERNMENT DEFICIT (-) OR SURPLUS
-43.03	-51.52	-52.59	-60.15	-47.98	-46.39	-26.22	20.71	31.51	..		GOVERNMENT DEFICIT (-) OR SURPLUS
186.75	213.68	241.36	272.19	309.71	350.36	377.51	439.07	476.00	..	..	Current Revenue
199.22	234.78	262.77	308.92	335.04	376.31	395.73	410.83	434.03	..	..	Current Expenditure
-12.47	-21.10	-21.41	-36.73	-25.33	-25.95	-18.22	28.24	41.97	..	..	Current Budget Balance
..	0.08	0.05	0.19	0.05	1.56	0.29	1.23	0.09	..	..	Capital Receipts
30.56	30.50	31.23	23.61	22.70	22.00	8.29	8.76	10.55	..	..	Capital Payments

SWEDEN	1969	1970	1971	1972	1973	1974	1975	1976	1977	1978	1979
FOREIGN TRADE (CUSTOMS BASIS)					*(Millions of current US dollars)*						
Value of Exports, fob	5,687	6,781	7,464	8,749	12,171	15,909	17,434	18,440	19,054	21,768	27,538
Nonfuel Primary Products	1,493	1,639	1,726	1,981	2,851	3,760	3,513	3,632	3,405	3,749	4,674
Fuels	57	64	69	90	109	213	272	283	350	409	826
Manufactures	4,137	5,078	5,670	6,678	9,212	11,936	13,649	14,525	15,299	17,610	22,039
Value of Imports, cif	5,898	7,004	7,082	8,062	10,625	15,820	18,067	19,164	20,140	20,547	28,579
Nonfuel Primary Products	1,220	1,459	1,323	1,432	1,876	2,474	2,738	2,889	3,019	3,197	4,080
Fuels	620	745	865	842	1,211	2,848	3,110	3,381	3,513	3,347	6,268
Manufactures	4,058	4,800	4,894	5,788	7,539	10,498	12,219	12,893	13,608	14,003	18,231
					(Index 1987 = 100)						
Terms of Trade	120.6	123.9	119.6	121.2	122.9	96.8	107.3	107.1	101.4	101.5	103.7
Export Prices, fob	26.8	28.6	29.7	34.0	42.4	49.6	58.2	60.4	62.9	70.0	86.2
Import Prices, cif	22.2	23.1	24.8	28.0	34.5	51.3	54.3	56.4	62.1	69.0	83.1
BALANCE OF PAYMENTS					*(Millions of current US dollars)*						
Exports of Goods & Services	..	8,256	9,166	10,768	14,840	19,144	21,041	22,404	23,350	27,083	35,004
Merchandise, fob	..	6,750	7,415	8,697	12,097	15,797	17,259	18,287	18,930	21,598	27,377
Nonfactor Services	..	1,338	1,603	1,896	2,445	3,009	3,390	3,565	3,834	4,584	6,528
Factor Services	..	168	149	174	298	338	392	552	586	902	1,099
Imports of Goods & Services	..	8,368	8,636	9,947	13,100	19,277	20,729	23,306	24,653	26,124	36,297
Merchandise, fob	..	6,447	6,520	7,479	10,066	15,405	16,182	18,124	18,654	19,023	28,072
Nonfactor Services	..	1,732	1,907	2,222	2,702	3,446	4,028	4,379	4,904	5,466	6,284
Factor Services	..	189	209	246	332	426	520	803	1,094	1,634	1,942
Long-Term Interest	..	..	..	..	..	..	..	..	..	..	..
Private Current Transfers, net	..	-48	-55	-69	-96	-90	-151	-203	-208	-209	-163
Workers' Remittances	..	..	..	..	..	..	..	..	..	..	..
Curr. A/C Bal before Off. Transf.	..	-160	475	752	1,644	-223	161	-1,105	-1,511	751	-1,456
Net Official Transfers	..	-104	-123	-185	-215	-329	-503	-543	-669	-1,001	-958
Curr. A/C Bal after Off. Transf.	..	-265	352	567	1,429	-552	-342	-1,648	-2,181	-251	-2,414
Long-Term Capital, net	..	139	-13	164	-248	423	1,569	376	3,074	548	1,410
Direct Investment	..	-104	-93	-197	-221	-349	-354	-591	-656	-346	-505
Long-Term Loans	..	..	..	..	..	..	..	..	..	..	..
Disbursements	..	..	..	..	..	..	..	..	..	..	..
Repayments	..	..	..	..	..	..	..	..	..	..	..
Other Long-Term Capital	..	244	80	361	-27	773	1,924	967	3,730	893	1,915
Other Capital, net	..	155	-91	-379	-310	-625	176	760	208	357	328
Change in Reserves	..	-29	-248	-351	-870	753	-1,404	513	-1,101	-654	676
Memo Item:					*(Swedish Kronor per US dollar)*						
Conversion Factor (Annual Avg)	5.170	5.170	5.120	4.760	4.370	4.440	4.150	4.360	4.480	4.520	4.290
					(Millions US dollars), outstanding at end of year						
EXTERNAL DEBT (Total)	..	..	..	..	..	..	..	..	..	..	..
Long-Term Debt (by debtor)	..	..	..	..	..	..	..	..	..	..	..
Central Bank, incl. IMF credit	..	..	..	..	..	..	..	..	..	..	..
Central Government	..	..	..	..	..	..	..	..	..	..	..
Rest of General Government	..	..	..	..	..	..	..	..	..	..	..
Non-financial Public Enterprises	..	..	..	..	..	..	..	..	..	..	..
Priv. Sector, incl non-guaranteed	..	..	..	..	..	..	..	..	..	..	..
Short-Term Debt	..	..	..	..	..	..	..	..	..	..	..
Memo Items:					*(Millions of US dollars)*						
Int'l Reserves Excluding Gold	470.0	561.2	892.6	1,357.9	2,284.2	1,487.0	2,838.6	2,255.5	3,414.8	4,123.7	3,513.9
Gold Holdings (at market price)	227.0	213.6	252.1	375.2	649.9	1,079.8	812.0	780.2	978.0	1,355.8	3,107.1
SOCIAL INDICATORS											
Total Fertility Rate	1.9	1.9	2.0	1.9	1.9	1.9	1.8	1.7	1.6	1.6	1.7
Infant Mortality Rate	11.7	11.0	11.1	10.8	9.9	9.5	8.6	8.3	8.0	7.7	7.4
Life Expectancy at Birth	74.4	74.5	74.6	74.7	74.8	74.9	75.0	75.1	75.2	75.4	75.6
Urban Population, % of total	80.3	81.1	81.4	81.7	82.1	82.4	82.7	82.8	82.9	82.9	83.0
Food Prod. per capita (1987=100)	84.3	90.3	91.8	93.4	90.0	106.7	96.8	101.5	102.7	105.5	103.6
Labor Force, Agriculture (%)	8.8	8.3	8.0	7.7	7.5	7.2	6.9	6.7	6.4	6.2	5.9
Labor Force, Female (%)	35.1	35.7	36.5	37.4	38.2	39.0	39.8	40.7	41.5	42.3	43.0
Primary Schl. Enroll. Ratio	..	94.0	..	..	..	..	101.0	100.0	99.0	98.0	98.0
Primary Schl. Enroll. Ratio, Female	..	95.0	..	..	..	..	102.0	101.0	99.0	99.0	98.0
Secondary Schl. Enroll. Ratio	..	86.0	..	..	..	..	78.0	78.0	80.0	84.0	85.0

1980	1981	1982	1983	1984	1985	1986	1987	1988	1989 estimate	NOTES	SWEDEN
				(Millions of current US dollars)							**FOREIGN TRADE (CUSTOMS BASIS)**
30,787	28,493	26,740	27,377	29,258	30,403	37,118	44,313	49,867	..	..	Value of Exports, fob
5,118	4,537	4,125	4,443	4,808	4,490	4,883	5,726	6,553	..	..	Nonfuel Primary Products
1,337	1,262	1,388	1,698	1,630	1,456	1,039	1,268	1,062	..	..	Fuels
24,332	22,693	21,227	21,236	22,821	24,457	31,196	37,320	42,252	..	..	Manufactures
33,426	28,842	27,533	26,090	26,331	28,538	32,493	40,621	45,793	..	..	Value of Imports, cif
4,616	3,904	3,558	3,440	3,652	3,703	4,443	5,109	6,145	..	..	Nonfuel Primary Products
8,073	7,160	6,735	5,982	5,124	5,394	3,496	3,627	3,141	..	..	Fuels
20,737	17,778	17,240	16,668	17,556	19,441	24,554	31,885	36,507	..	..	Manufactures
				(Index 1987 = 100)							
101.8	93.9	90.9	88.4	91.0	92.5	99.7	100.0	101.1	..	..	Terms of Trade
99.0	89.0	81.7	76.3	75.0	74.3	87.3	100.0	109.0	..	..	Export Prices, fob
97.3	94.7	89.8	86.3	82.5	80.3	87.6	100.0	107.8	..	..	Import Prices, cif
				(Millions of current US dollars)							**BALANCE OF PAYMENTS**
39,388	37,106	35,276	35,227	37,274	38,376	46,634	55,727	62,204	66,993	..	Exports of Goods & Services
30,662	28,389	26,576	27,203	29,121	30,174	36,845	44,010	49,327	51,002	..	Merchandise, fob
7,399	6,933	6,451	6,149	6,218	6,007	7,133	8,531	9,403	11,318	..	Nonfactor Services
1,328	1,784	2,249	1,876	1,935	2,195	2,656	3,187	3,474	4,674	..	Factor Services
42,495	38,879	37,688	35,324	36,104	38,905	45,231	55,578	63,142	70,201	..	Imports of Goods & Services
32,860	28,226	26,799	25,304	25,701	27,790	31,809	39,531	44,579	46,869	..	Merchandise, fob
6,814	6,663	6,686	6,025	6,109	6,394	8,059	9,967	11,639	14,228	..	Nonfactor Services
2,821	3,990	4,203	3,995	4,294	4,721	5,363	6,080	6,925	9,104	..	Factor Services
..	..	..	..	..	..	..	..	..	..	..	Long-Term Interest
-301	-228	-282	-296	-311	-397	-483	-381	-471	-714	..	Private Current Transfers, net
..	..	..	..	..	..	..	16	23	33	..	Workers' Remittances
-3,407	-2,001	-2,694	-392	859	-926	920	-231	-1,409	-3,922	..	Curr. A/C Bal before Off. Transf.
-997	-846	-746	-642	-614	-682	-858	-1,016	-1,140	-1,257	..	Net Official Transfers
-4,404	-2,847	-3,440	-1,034	246	-1,608	62	-1,247	-2,549	-5,179	..	Curr. A/C Bal after Off. Transf.
4,750	1,909	2,743	1,677	-510	1,305	-1,022	1,214	428	-6,179	..	Long-Term Capital, net
-374	-644	-778	-997	-882	-1,028	-2,249	-2,833	-4,399	-6,211	..	Direct Investment
..	..	..	..	..	..	..	..	..	..	..	Long-Term Loans
..	..	..	..	..	..	..	..	..	..	..	Disbursements
..	..	..	..	..	..	..	..	..	..	..	Repayments
5,123	2,554	3,522	2,674	372	2,333	1,227	4,047	4,827	32	..	Other Long-Term Capital
-451	1,141	654	44	222	1,853	1,100	916	2,787	12,581	..	Other Capital, net
105	-203	42	-687	42	-1,551	-141	-883	-667	-1,224	..	Change in Reserves
				(Swedish Kronor per US dollar)							Memo Item:
4.230	5.060	6.280	7.670	8.270	8.600	7.120	6.340	6.130	6.450	..	Conversion Factor (Annual Avg)
				(Millions US dollars), outstanding at end of year							
..	..	..	..	..	..	..	..	..	..	..	**EXTERNAL DEBT (Total)**
..	..	..	..	..	..	..	..	..	..	..	Long-Term Debt (by debtor)
..	..	..	..	..	..	..	..	..	..	..	Central Bank, incl. IMF credit
..	..	..	..	..	..	..	..	..	..	..	Central Government
..	..	..	..	..	..	..	..	..	..	..	Rest of General Government
..	..	..	..	..	..	..	..	..	..	..	Non-financial Public Enterprises
..	..	..	..	..	..	..	..	..	..	..	Priv. Sector, incl non-guaranteed
..	..	..	..	..	..	..	..	..	..	..	Short-Term Debt
				(Millions of US dollars)							Memo Items:
3,418.5	3,601.1	3,512.5	4,033.8	3,845.0	5,793.5	6,550.6	8,174.3	8,491.9	9,559.4	..	Int'l Reserves Excluding Gold
3,577.4	2,412.2	2,772.7	2,315.2	1,870.9	1,984.4	2,372.2	2,937.8	2,489.6	2,433.5	..	Gold Holdings (at market price)
											SOCIAL INDICATORS
1.7	1.7	1.6	1.6	1.7	1.7	1.8	1.9	2.0	2.0	..	Total Fertility Rate
6.9	6.9	6.7	7.8	6.3	6.8	5.9	5.7	5.8	5.6	..	Infant Mortality Rate
75.9	76.1	76.3	76.4	76.6	76.8	76.9	77.1	77.2	77.4	..	Life Expectancy at Birth
83.1	83.2	83.2	83.3	83.3	83.4	83.5	83.6	83.8	83.9	..	Urban Population, % of total
105.2	109.0	111.8	110.2	121.8	114.2	111.6	100.0	95.5	103.4	..	Food Prod. per capita (1987=100)
5.7	..	..	..	..	..	..	..	..	..	..	Labor Force, Agriculture (%)
43.8	43.9	43.9	44.0	44.1	44.1	44.2	44.3	44.4	44.5	..	Labor Force, Female (%)
97.0	..	98.0	98.0	98.0	98.0	98.0	100.0	..	..	..	Primary Schl. Enroll. Ratio
97.0	98.0	98.0	98.0	99.0	..	..	..	..	..	..	Primary Schl. Enroll. Ratio, Female
88.0	..	86.0	85.0	86.0	..	90.0	91.0	..	..	..	Secondary Schl. Enroll. Ratio

SWITZERLAND	1969	1970	1971	1972	1973	1974	1975	1976	1977	1978	1979
CURRENT GNP PER CAPITA (US $)	3,210	3,480	3,850	4,400	5,480	6,900	7,960	12,240	11,680	11,710	14,150
POPULATION (thousands)	6,136	6,267	6,324	6,385	6,431	6,443	6,405	6,346	6,327	6,337	6,357

USE AND ORIGIN OF RESOURCES *(Billions of current Swiss Francs)*

	1969	1970	1971	1972	1973	1974	1975	1976	1977	1978	1979
Gross National Product (GNP)	83.96	93.93	106.48	120.53	134.54	146.49	144.62	147.18	151.89	157.49	165.18
Net Factor Income from Abroad	2.56	3.27	3.49	3.83	4.48	5.40	4.47	5.22	6.11	5.82	6.64
GDP at Market Prices	81.39	90.66	102.99	116.71	130.06	141.10	140.15	141.96	145.78	151.67	158.54
Resource Balance	1.04	-1.54	-1.59	-1.04	-1.45	-2.73	4.00	4.69	3.73	3.68	-0.83
Exports of Goods & NFServices	26.64	29.71	32.07	35.78	40.23	45.90	44.02	47.72	53.45	53.21	55.99
Imports of Goods & NFServices	25.60	31.25	33.66	36.82	41.68	48.63	40.02	43.03	49.72	49.52	56.82
Domestic Absorption	80.35	92.21	104.59	117.75	131.51	143.83	136.16	137.27	142.05	147.99	159.37
Private Consumption, etc.	48.68	53.32	59.68	67.75	75.98	83.13	86.00	88.84	92.58	95.30	100.65
General Gov't Consumption	8.85	9.63	10.89	12.07	13.48	15.06	16.17	18.94	19.15	19.77	20.80
Gross Domestic Investment	22.83	29.24	34.01	37.92	42.06	45.64	34.00	29.50	30.32	32.92	37.92
Fixed Investment	21.70	24.95	29.66	33.85	37.85	39.39	35.97	29.45	30.23	32.26	35.07
Indirect Taxes, net	5.04	5.61	6.00	7.01	7.54	7.40	7.43	7.62	8.02	8.59	8.89
GDP at factor cost	76.35	85.05	96.99	109.70	122.52	133.70	132.72	134.34	137.76	143.08	149.65
Agriculture	..	..	..	..	..	..	..	..	..	..	..
Industry	..	..	..	..	..	..	..	..	..	..	..
Manufacturing	..	..	..	..	..	..	..	..	..	..	..
Services, etc.	..	..	..	..	..	..	..	..	..	..	..
Gross Domestic Saving	23.87	27.70	32.42	36.89	40.60	42.91	37.99	34.19	34.05	36.60	37.09
Gross National Saving	..	29.70	34.44	39.04	43.36	46.62	41.02	38.31	39.07	41.37	42.65

(Billions of 1980 Swiss Francs)

	1969	1970	1971	1972	1973	1974	1975	1976	1977	1978	1979
Gross National Product	87.93	93.92	97.58	100.63	103.85	105.69	97.43	160.51	165.07	165.62	170.16
GDP at Market Prices	85.22	90.66	94.35	97.37	100.34	101.80	94.39	154.70	158.35	159.29	163.17
Resource Balance	0.37	-1.54	-2.33	-2.78	-2.52	-1.78	1.64	1.80	2.16	-1.74	-4.42
Exports of Goods & NFServices	27.81	29.71	30.86	32.83	35.41	35.77	33.42	51.21	56.14	58.15	59.56
Imports of Goods & NFServices	27.44	31.25	33.19	35.61	37.92	37.55	31.79	49.41	53.98	59.88	63.99
Domestic Absorption	84.85	92.20	96.68	100.15	102.86	103.58	92.75	152.90	156.19	161.02	167.59
Private Consumption, etc.	50.60	53.32	55.86	58.90	60.53	60.24	58.47	98.95	101.92	104.11	105.28
General Gov't Consumption	9.19	9.63	10.19	10.49	10.74	10.91	10.99	20.92	21.01	21.43	21.77
Gross Domestic Investment	25.06	29.24	30.63	30.76	31.59	32.43	23.29	33.02	33.25	35.48	40.53
Fixed Investment	22.91	24.95	27.41	28.78	29.61	28.35	24.50	32.80	33.25	35.11	36.88
GDP at factor cost	79.90	85.04	88.80	91.41	94.44	96.47	89.32	146.21	149.53	149.94	153.82
Agriculture	..	..	..	..	..	..	..	..	..	..	..
Industry	..	..	..	..	..	..	..	..	..	..	..
Manufacturing	..	..	..	..	..	..	..	..	..	..	..
Services, etc.	..	..	..	..	..	..	..	..	..	..	..

Memo Items:

	1969	1970	1971	1972	1973	1974	1975	1976	1977	1978	1979
Capacity to Import	28.56	29.71	31.63	34.61	36.60	35.44	34.96	54.79	58.03	64.34	63.05
Terms of Trade Adjustment	0.75	0.00	0.76	1.78	1.19	-0.33	1.54	3.59	1.89	6.19	3.49
Gross Domestic Income	85.97	90.66	95.11	99.15	101.53	101.47	95.93	158.28	160.24	165.48	166.66
Gross National Income	88.68	93.92	98.34	102.40	105.04	105.36	98.97	164.10	166.96	171.81	173.64

DOMESTIC PRICES/DEFLATORS *(Index 1980 = 100)*

	1969	1970	1971	1972	1973	1974	1975	1976	1977	1978	1979
Overall (GDP)	95.5	100.0	109.2	119.9	129.6	138.6	148.5	91.8	92.1	95.2	97.2
Domestic Absorption	94.7	100.0	108.2	117.6	127.9	138.9	146.8	89.8	90.9	91.9	95.1
Agriculture	..	..	..	..	..	..	..	..	..	..	..
Industry	..	..	..	..	..	..	..	..	..	..	..
Manufacturing	..	..	..	..	..	..	..	..	..	..	..
Consumer Price Index	47.1	48.8	52.0	55.5	60.3	66.2	70.7	71.9	72.8	73.6	76.3

MANUFACTURING ACTIVITY

	1969	1970	1971	1972	1973	1974	1975	1976	1977	1978	1979
Employment (1987=100)	127.2	127.2	126.6	123.2	119.6	118.6	105.4	100.8	100.6	101.0	100.2
Real Earnings per Empl. (1987=100)	..	..	..	..	..	..	..	..	..	..	..
Real Output per Empl. (1987=100)	..	..	..	..	..	..	..	..	..	..	..
Earnings as % of Value Added	..	..	..	..	..	..	..	..	..	..	..

MONETARY HOLDINGS *(Billions of current Swiss Francs)*

	1969	1970	1971	1972	1973	1974	1975	1976	1977	1978	1979
Money Supply, Broadly Defined	94.67	104.43	115.59	128.11	135.11	117.64	128.72	140.52	149.80	166.99	182.55
Money	36.39	40.38	47.51	50.09	49.68	48.03	50.11	55.96	56.43	69.69	68.40
Currency Outside Banks	13.83	14.54	15.60	17.82	19.08	20.33	20.12	20.78	21.48	23.64	24.99
Demand Deposits	22.56	25.84	31.91	32.27	30.60	27.70	29.99	35.18	34.94	46.05	43.41
Quasi-Money	58.28	64.05	68.08	78.02	85.43	69.61	78.61	84.56	93.37	97.30	114.15

GOVERNMENT DEFICIT (-) OR SURPLUS *(Millions of current Swiss Francs)*

	1969	1970	1971	1972	1973	1974	1975	1976	1977	1978	1979
GOVERNMENT DEFICIT (-) OR SURPLUS	..	487	279	1,065	588	964	-647	-954	-752	-132	-1,087
Current Revenue	..	13,983	15,529	17,928	21,696	24,816	26,061	29,068	29,633	31,519	32,111
Current Expenditure	..	11,265	12,804	13,909	17,605	20,233	23,415	26,528	28,178	29,004	30,475
Current Budget Balance	..	2,718	2,725	4,019	4,091	4,583	2,646	2,540	1,455	2,515	1,636
Capital Receipts	..	18	5	8	19	8	21	13	48	7	7
Capital Payments	..	2,249	2,451	2,962	3,522	3,627	3,314	3,507	2,255	2,654	2,730

1980	1981	1982	1983	1984	1985	1986	1987	1988	1989 estimate	NOTES	SWITZERLAND
17,250	17,650	17,050	16,480	16,380	16,230	17,670	21,260	27,370	30,270	..	CURRENT GNP PER CAPITA (US $)
6,385	6,429	6,393	6,418	6,442	6,472	6,504	6,538	6,573	6,541	..	POPULATION (thousands)
				(Billions of current Swiss Francs)							USE AND ORIGIN OF RESOURCES
177.33	193.96	205.19	213.95	226.06	241.34	254.91	266.08	282.73	301.45	..	Gross National Product (GNP)
7.01	9.22	9.19	10.08	12.83	13.40	11.58	11.41	13.98	14.38	..	Net Factor Income from Abroad
170.32	184.74	196.00	203.86	213.23	227.94	243.33	254.68	268.75	287.07	..	GDP at Market Prices
-6.01	-1.82	0.87	-0.14	-0.67	0.89	2.74	2.13	0.79	-0.70	..	Resource Balance
62.58	69.07	69.58	71.74	80.46	89.00	89.11	90.53	97.57	110.47	..	Exports of Goods & NFServices
68.59	70.89	68.70	71.88	81.14	88.12	86.37	88.41	96.78	111.17	..	Imports of Goods & NFServices
176.33	186.56	195.13	204.00	213.90	227.05	240.59	252.55	267.96	287.77	..	Domestic Absorption
108.03	115.72	122.06	127.35	133.57	140.57	144.98	150.16	157.08	165.96	..	Private Consumption, etc.
21.98	23.88	25.93	27.77	28.93	30.88	32.33	33.02	35.04	36.80	..	General Gov't Consumption
46.32	46.96	47.13	48.88	51.40	55.60	63.28	69.37	75.84	85.01	..	Gross Domestic Investment
40.50	44.38	45.59	48.52	51.84	56.53	61.19	66.60	73.22	80.18	..	Fixed Investment
9.66	10.51	10.72	11.32	11.85	12.63	14.06	14.80	15.40	16.12	..	Indirect Taxes, net
160.66	174.23	185.28	192.54	201.38	215.31	229.27	239.88	253.34	270.94	..	GDP at factor cost
..	..	..	..	..	8.18	..	..	..	..	B	Agriculture
..	..	..	..	..	80.97	..	..	..	..	B	Industry
..	..	..	..	..	58.62	..	..	..	..	B	Manufacturing
..	..	..	..	..	138.79	..	..	..	..	B	Services, etc.
40.31	45.14	48.01	48.74	50.73	56.49	66.03	71.49	76.63	84.31	..	Gross Domestic Saving
46.15	52.63	55.33	56.93	61.62	67.83	75.43	80.59	88.10	..	..	Gross National Saving
				(Billions of 1980 Swiss Francs)							
177.33	181.41	179.33	181.65	186.82	193.44	197.14	200.69	208.20	213.88	..	Gross National Product
170.32	172.77	171.17	172.89	175.95	182.47	187.70	191.51	197.25	203.68	..	GDP at Market Prices
-6.01	-2.11	-2.22	-4.46	-5.28	-3.33	-8.52	-11.84	-12.61	-12.87	..	Resource Balance
62.58	65.59	63.72	64.40	68.48	74.17	74.45	75.69	79.65	84.39	..	Exports of Goods & NFServices
68.59	67.70	65.93	68.85	73.76	77.50	82.96	87.53	92.26	97.26	..	Imports of Goods & NFServices
176.33	174.88	173.39	177.34	181.23	185.80	196.22	203.35	209.86	216.55	..	Domestic Absorption
108.03	108.55	108.51	110.32	112.05	113.65	116.86	119.28	121.87	124.31	..	Private Consumption, etc.
21.98	22.54	22.78	23.67	23.96	24.73	25.65	26.11	26.96	27.70	..	General Gov't Consumption
46.32	43.79	42.09	43.36	45.23	47.42	53.72	57.96	61.03	64.53	..	Gross Domestic Investment
40.50	41.59	40.53	42.19	43.93	46.26	49.91	53.62	57.34	60.33	..	Fixed Investment
160.66	162.91	161.64	163.05	165.91	172.14	176.23	179.60	185.19	191.55	..	GDP at factor cost
..	..	..	..	..	..	..	..	..	..	..	Agriculture
..	..	..	..	..	..	..	..	..	..	..	Industry
..	..	..	..	..	..	..	..	..	..	..	Manufacturing
..	..	..	..	..	..	..	..	..	..	..	Services, etc.
											Memo Items:
62.58	65.97	66.77	68.71	73.15	78.28	85.60	89.63	93.01	96.65	..	Capacity to Import
0.00	0.38	3.06	4.32	4.67	4.11	11.16	13.94	13.36	12.26	..	Terms of Trade Adjustment
170.32	173.14	174.22	177.20	180.62	186.58	198.86	205.45	210.62	215.94	..	Gross Domestic Income
177.33	181.79	182.39	185.97	191.49	197.55	208.30	214.63	221.57	226.14	..	Gross National Income
				(Index 1980 = 100)							DOMESTIC PRICES/DEFLATORS
100.0	106.9	114.5	117.9	121.2	124.9	129.6	133.0	136.2	140.9	..	Overall (GDP)
100.0	106.7	112.5	115.0	118.0	122.2	122.6	124.2	127.7	132.9	..	Domestic Absorption
..	..	..	..	..	..	..	..	..	..	..	Agriculture
..	..	..	..	..	..	..	..	..	..	..	Industry
..	..	..	..	..	..	..	..	..	..	..	Manufacturing
79.3	84.5	89.3	91.9	94.6	97.8	98.6	100.0	101.9	105.1	f	Consumer Price Index
											MANUFACTURING ACTIVITY
102.2	102.4	104.8	100.8	96.1	97.8	99.6	100.0	99.8	99.6	G	Employment (1987=100)
..	..	..	..	..	..	..	..	..	..	G	Real Earnings per Empl. (1987=100)
..	..	..	..	..	..	..	..	..	..	G	Real Output per Empl. (1987=100)
..	..	..	..	..	..	..	..	..	..	..	Earnings as % of Value Added
				(Billions of current Swiss Francs)							MONETARY HOLDINGS
183.43	195.23	229.88	253.31	273.89	285.24	294.68	325.77	343.38	365.07	..	Money Supply, Broadly Defined
68.33	64.79	69.35	75.82	75.91	73.94	75.49	85.87	87.81	85.56	..	Money
25.44	24.74	24.19	26.31	28.04	27.42	28.57	28.90	30.53	30.90	..	Currency Outside Banks
42.89	40.05	45.16	49.51	47.86	46.52	46.91	56.97	57.27	54.66	..	Demand Deposits
115.10	130.44	160.54	177.49	197.99	211.30	219.20	239.91	255.57	279.51	..	Quasi-Money
				(Millions of current Swiss Francs)							
-344	197	-116	-771	-202	..	..	..	..	..	E	GOVERNMENT DEFICIT (-) OR SURPLUS
34,582	36,988	40,116	42,077	45,662	..	..	..	..	..	..	Current Revenue
32,206	33,229	37,043	39,144	42,182	..	..	..	..	..	..	Current Expenditure
2,376	3,759	3,073	2,933	3,480	..	..	..	..	..	..	Current Budget Balance
27	17	46	9	10	..	..	..	..	..	..	Capital Receipts
2,747	3,579	3,235	3,713	3,692	..	..	..	..	..	..	Capital Payments

SWITZERLAND	1969	1970	1971	1972	1973	1974	1975	1976	1977	1978	1979
FOREIGN TRADE (CUSTOMS BASIS)					*(Millions of current US dollars)*						
Value of Exports, fob	4,610	5,120	5,768	6,877	9,472	11,838	12,952	14,669	17,325	23,532	26,390
Nonfuel Primary Products	461	522	575	664	909	1,151	1,044	1,210	1,480	1,858	2,203
Fuels	8	9	5	7	15	26	24	19	24	21	23
Manufactures	4,141	4,590	5,188	6,207	8,549	10,661	11,884	13,440	15,821	21,653	24,163
Value of Imports, cif	5,266	6,471	7,154	8,471	11,615	14,411	13,272	14,763	17,962	23,792	29,306
Nonfuel Primary Products	1,161	1,407	1,441	1,671	2,329	2,885	2,751	2,896	3,323	3,950	4,488
Fuels	299	352	462	462	836	1,439	1,368	1,577	1,702	1,924	3,440
Manufactures	3,807	4,713	5,251	6,338	8,450	10,087	9,153	10,290	12,937	17,917	21,378
					(Index 1987 = 100)						
Terms of Trade	91.3	90.5	93.2	94.4	98.9	86.8	93.7	93.6	91.7	104.9	99.4
Export Prices, fob	21.9	22.8	24.8	28.0	35.0	42.1	49.0	50.3	53.3	68.2	76.1
Import Prices, cif	24.0	25.2	26.6	29.6	35.4	48.6	52.3	53.7	58.2	65.0	76.5
BALANCE OF PAYMENTS					*(Millions of current US dollars)*						
Exports of Goods & Services	..	9,361	10,484	12,728	17,365	21,460	23,812	26,670	30,234	41,348	37,883
Merchandise, fob	..	6,201	6,958	8,611	11,550	14,479	16,242	18,504	20,992	28,836	26,756
Nonfactor Services	..	1,455	1,747	2,098	2,729	2,965	3,487	3,807	4,289	5,436	5,990
Factor Services	..	1,705	1,779	2,020	3,085	4,016	4,083	4,359	4,953	7,075	5,137
Imports of Goods & Services	..	8,866	9,808	11,710	17,593	23,511	22,342	23,733	27,644	38,350	35,561
Merchandise, fob	..	7,141	7,952	9,597	14,428	19,796	17,947	19,248	22,710	31,014	29,209
Nonfactor Services	..	767	922	1,095	1,495	1,509	2,044	2,215	2,524	3,516	4,045
Factor Services	..	958	935	1,019	1,670	2,205	2,352	2,270	2,411	3,820	2,306
Long-Term Interest	..	..	..	..	..	..	..	..	..	..	..
Private Current Transfers, net	..	-291	-356	-437	-545	-565	-560	-440	-454	-587	-656
Workers' Remittances	..	..	..	..	..	..	..	..	..	..	..
Curr. A/C Bal before Off. Transf.	..	203	319	581	-772	-2,615	910	2,496	2,136	2,411	1,667
Net Official Transfers	..	-43	-22	-68	-125	-139	-134	-156	-212	-336	-400
Curr. A/C Bal after Off. Transf.	..	161	298	513	-897	-2,755	777	2,340	1,924	2,075	1,267
Long-Term Capital, net	..	-947	-2,192	-2,887	-2,756	-1,584	-3,709	-7,117	-5,757	-8,478	-13,586
Direct Investment	..	..	..	..	..	..	..	..	..	..	..
Long-Term Loans	..	..	..	..	..	..	..	..	..	..	..
Disbursements	..	..	..	..	..	..	..	..	..	..	..
Repayments	..	..	..	..	..	..	..	..	..	..	..
Other Long-Term Capital	..	-947	-2,192	-2,887	-2,756	-1,584	-3,709	-7,117	-5,757	-8,478	-13,586
Other Capital, net	..	1,455	3,090	2,960	4,031	4,769	4,453	7,760	4,864	13,043	8,384
Change in Reserves	..	-669	-1,196	-586	-378	-431	-1,521	-2,983	-1,031	-6,641	3,934
Memo Item:					*(Swiss Francs per US dollar)*						
Conversion Factor (Annual Avg)	4.370	4.370	4.130	3.820	3.170	2.980	2.580	2.500	2.400	1.790	1.660
					(Millions US dollars), outstanding at end of year						
EXTERNAL DEBT (Total)	..	..	..	..	..	..	..	..	..	..	..
Long-Term Debt (by debtor)	..	..	..	..	..	..	..	..	..	..	..
Central Bank, incl. IMF credit	..	..	..	..	..	..	..	..	..	..	..
Central Government	..	..	..	..	..	..	..	..	..	..	..
Rest of General Government	..	..	..	..	..	..	..	..	..	..	..
Non-financial Public Enterprises	..	..	..	..	..	..	..	..	..	..	..
Priv. Sector, incl non-guaranteed	..	..	..	..	..	..	..	..	..	..	..
Short-Term Debt	..	..	..	..	..	..	..	..	..	..	..
Memo Items:					*(Millions of US dollars)*						
Int'l Reserves Excluding Gold	1,783	2,401	3,808	4,399	5,007	5,446	7,019	9,606	10,289	17,763	16,435
Gold Holdings (at market price)	2,657	2,916	3,626	5,394	9,339	15,517	11,669	11,222	13,737	18,821	42,638
SOCIAL INDICATORS											
Total Fertility Rate	2.1	2.1	2.0	1.9	1.8	1.7	1.6	1.5	1.5	1.5	1.5
Infant Mortality Rate	15.4	15.4	14.4	13.3	13.2	12.4	10.7	10.7	8.7	8.6	8.4
Life Expectancy at Birth	72.8	73.2	73.5	73.8	74.1	74.4	74.7	74.9	75.2	75.4	75.6
Urban Population, % of total	54.2	54.5	54.7	55.0	55.2	55.5	55.7	56.0	56.2	56.5	56.7
Food Prod. per capita (1987=100)	82.1	82.7	83.3	81.8	85.2	83.7	85.8	92.9	93.1	93.1	99.2
Labor Force, Agriculture (%)	8.1	7.8	7.7	7.5	7.3	7.1	7.0	6.8	6.6	6.5	6.3
Labor Force, Female (%)	32.8	32.7	33.2	33.7	34.2	34.8	35.3	35.6	35.9	36.2	36.5
Primary Schl. Enroll. Ratio	..	..	..	..	..	..	..	..	..	..	..
Primary Schl. Enroll. Ratio, Female	..	..	..	..	..	..	..	..	..	..	..
Secondary Schl. Enroll. Ratio	..	..	..	..	..	..	..	..	..	..	..

1980	1981	1982	1983	1984	1985	1986	1987	1988	1989	NOTES	SWITZERLAND
				(Millions of current US dollars)							**FOREIGN TRADE (CUSTOMS BASIS)**
29,471	26,717	25,618	25,308	25,724	27,281	37,534	45,357	50,633	..	..	Value of Exports, fob
2,788	1,989	1,812	1,877	2,010	1,961	2,473	3,045	3,717	..	..	Nonfuel Primary Products
36	31	35	73	90	90	64	61	69	..	..	Fuels
26,647	24,697	23,770	23,358	23,623	25,230	34,997	42,250	46,847	..	..	Manufactures
36,148	30,607	28,577	28,934	29,625	30,626	41,188	50,557	56,325	..	..	Value of Imports, cif
6,409	4,541	4,144	4,260	4,260	4,307	5,516	6,586	6,802	..	..	Nonfuel Primary Products
4,055	3,742	3,331	3,267	3,040	3,044	2,404	2,245	2,077	..	..	Fuels
25,685	22,324	21,102	21,407	22,324	23,275	33,268	41,726	47,446	..	..	Manufactures
				(Index 1987 = 100)							
96.9	88.7	91.8	91.6	86.3	86.2	105.1	100.0	101.9	..	..	Terms of Trade
83.8	73.3	72.1	69.9	63.4	62.5	82.1	100.0	107.3	..	..	Export Prices, fob
86.5	82.6	78.5	76.3	73.5	72.5	78.1	100.0	105.3	..	..	Import Prices, cif
				(Millions of current US dollars)							**BALANCE OF PAYMENTS**
41,925	40,020	45,194	52,495	55,747	56,611	74,268	87,742	98,160	..	..	Exports of Goods & Services
29,265	27,097	26,196	33,905	36,657	37,057	48,453	55,259	62,836	..	..	Merchandise, fob
6,951	6,881	7,038	7,422	7,302	7,928	10,809	13,715	14,222	..	..	Nonfactor Services
5,709	6,042	11,959	11,167	11,788	11,627	15,007	18,768	21,102	..	..	Factor Services
42,340	37,561	40,246	50,372	48,760	49,766	68,524	79,957	88,138	..	..	Imports of Goods & Services
35,155	30,415	28,303	39,299	37,736	38,618	53,412	60,690	67,441	..	..	Merchandise, fob
4,657	4,452	4,511	4,710	4,697	4,977	6,539	8,146	9,146	..	..	Nonfactor Services
2,527	2,693	7,432	6,363	6,327	6,171	8,572	11,121	11,551	..	..	Factor Services
..	..	..	..	..	..	..	..	..	..	..	Long-Term Interest
-701	-881	-921	-901	-826	-841	-1,206	-1,550	-1,711	..	..	Private Current Transfers, net
..	..	84	85	69	66	93	112	114	..	..	Workers' Remittances
-1,116	1,578	4,026	1,221	6,161	6,005	4,539	6,235	8,311	8,511	..	Curr. A/C Bal before Off. Transf.
-439	-122	-99	-13	-9	35	116	45	16	-16	..	Net Official Transfers
-1,555	1,456	3,928	1,209	6,152	6,039	4,654	6,280	8,326	8,495	..	Curr. A/C Bal after Off. Transf.
-11,213	-9,622	-13,605	-3,991	-4,398	-7,036	3,365	-4,396	-17,240	..	..	Long-Term Capital, net
..	..	..	151	-362	-3,305	662	1,047	-6,913	..	..	Direct Investment
..	..	..	..	..	..	..	..	..	..	..	Long-Term Loans
..	..	..	..	..	..	..	..	..	..	..	Disbursements
..	..	..	..	..	..	..	..	..	..	..	Repayments
-11,213	-9,622	-13,605	-4,141	-4,035	-3,731	2,703	-5,443	-10,327	..	..	Other Long-Term Capital
13,104	7,646	13,176	3,166	-275	2,222	-6,926	1,322	6,488	-7,576	..	Other Capital, net
-337	520	-3,499	-384	-1,480	-1,225	-1,093	-3,205	2,426	-919	..	Change in Reserves
				(Swiss Francs per US dollar)							Memo Item:
1.670	1.960	2.030	2.100	2.350	2.460	1.800	1.490	1.460	1.640	..	Conversion Factor (Annual Avg)
			(Millions US dollars), outstanding at end of year								**EXTERNAL DEBT (Total)**
..	..	..	..	..	..	..	..	..	..	..	Long-Term Debt (by debtor)
..	..	..	..	..	..	..	..	..	..	..	Central Bank, incl. IMF credit
..	..	..	..	..	..	..	..	..	..	..	Central Government
..	..	..	..	..	..	..	..	..	..	..	Rest of General Government
..	..	..	..	..	..	..	..	..	..	..	Non-financial Public Enterprises
..	..	..	..	..	..	..	..	..	..	..	Priv. Sector, incl non-guaranteed
..	..	..	..	..	..	..	..	..	..	..	Short-Term Debt
				(Millions of US dollars)							Memo Items:
15,656	13,979	15,460	15,034	15,296	18,016	21,786	27,476	24,203	25,116	..	Int'l Reserves Excluding Gold
49,092	33,103	38,049	31,770	25,674	27,232	32,553	40,314	34,164	33,394	..	Gold Holdings (at market price)
											SOCIAL INDICATORS
1.6	1.6	1.6	1.5	1.5	1.5	1.5	1.6	1.6	1.6	..	Total Fertility Rate
9.0	7.5	7.7	7.6	7.3	6.9	6.9	6.8	6.7	6.5	..	Infant Mortality Rate
75.8	76.1	76.3	76.4	76.5	76.7	76.8	77.0	77.2	77.4	..	Life Expectancy at Birth
57.0	57.8	58.6	59.3	60.1	60.9	60.9	60.9	..	..	..	Urban Population, % of total
98.1	95.5	105.6	100.8	103.8	103.3	104.1	100.0	100.6	99.0	..	Food Prod. per capita (1987=100)
6.2	..	..	..	..	..	..	..	..	..	..	Labor Force, Agriculture (%)
36.7	36.7	36.7	36.7	36.7	36.7	36.7	36.7	36.6	36.6	..	Labor Force, Female (%)
..	..	..	..	..	..	..	..	..	..	..	Primary Schl. Enroll. Ratio
..	..	..	..	..	..	..	..	..	..	..	Primary Schl. Enroll. Ratio, Female
..	..	..	..	..	..	..	..	..	..	..	Secondary Schl. Enroll. Ratio

SYRIAN ARAB REPUBLIC	1969	1970	1971	1972	1973	1974	1975	1976	1977	1978	1979
CURRENT GNP PER CAPITA (US $)	370	350	390	460	460	650	890	1,020	1,010	1,120	1,200
POPULATION (thousands)	6,052	6,258	6,479	6,708	6,945	7,188	7,438	7,695	7,957	8,228	8,508
USE AND ORIGIN OF RESOURCES				*(Billions of current Syrian Pounds)*							
Gross National Product (GNP)	6.84	6.84	8.04	9.28	9.96	16.04	20.64	24.70	27.08	32.56	39.16
Net Factor Income from Abroad	-0.01	-0.01	-0.01	-0.01	0.01	0.09	0.04	-0.02	0.06	0.17	0.18
GDP at Market Prices	6.84	6.85	8.04	9.29	9.95	15.95	20.60	24.73	27.01	32.39	38.97
Resource Balance	-0.31	-0.24	-0.40	-0.51	-0.37	-1.53	-2.59	-3.65	-6.08	-5.31	-6.58
Exports of Goods & NFServices	1.15	1.19	1.39	1.67	2.18	3.82	4.41	4.83	4.91	4.81	7.46
Imports of Goods & NFServices	1.46	1.43	1.79	2.19	2.54	5.35	7.00	8.48	10.98	10.11	14.03
Domestic Absorption	7.15	7.09	8.44	9.80	10.31	17.48	23.18	28.38	33.09	37.70	45.55
Private Consumption, etc.	5.02	4.97	5.82	6.29	6.96	10.70	13.68	15.66	18.20	22.34	26.93
General Gov't Consumption	1.12	1.19	1.43	1.64	2.12	2.82	4.34	4.96	5.29	6.47	8.42
Gross Domestic Investment	1.02	0.94	1.19	1.87	1.23	3.96	5.16	7.76	9.60	8.89	10.19
Fixed Investment	1.02	0.90	1.15	1.60	1.77	3.07	5.16	7.76	9.60	8.89	10.19
Indirect Taxes, net	..	..	..	..	..	..	..	..	..	..	..
GDP at factor cost	..	..	..	..	..	..	..	..	..	..	..
Agriculture	1.62	1.38	1.61	2.32	1.68	3.22	3.71	4.81	5.00	6.85	6.86
Industry	1.63	1.76	2.05	2.16	2.40	4.17	4.98	6.22	6.60	8.13	10.55
Manufacturing	..	..	..	..	..	..	..	..	..	..	..
Services, etc.	3.59	3.70	4.38	4.80	5.86	8.56	11.92	13.69	15.41	17.41	21.57
Gross Domestic Saving	0.71	0.70	0.79	1.36	0.86	2.43	2.57	4.11	3.52	3.58	3.62
Gross National Saving	..	0.72	0.82	1.50	1.02	2.68	2.80	4.29	3.95	6.24	7.34
				(Millions of 1987 Syrian Pounds)							
Gross National Product	53,591	50,354	55,110	64,328	60,927	77,481	94,699	102,875	101,747	110,035	114,618
GDP at Market Prices	53,655	50,415	55,170	64,392	60,869	77,078	94,515	102,955	101,516	109,490	114,079
Resource Balance	7,399	8,587	6,556	8,787	6,666	-4,919	-7,228	-7,899	-12,637	-10,676	-15,118
Exports of Goods & NFServices	18,278	18,072	17,146	20,189	19,739	18,105	19,845	19,813	18,389	19,431	18,865
Imports of Goods & NFServices	10,880	9,485	10,590	11,402	13,072	23,023	27,073	27,712	31,026	30,107	33,983
Domestic Absorption	46,633	42,443	49,157	55,178	55,873	82,751	100,891	109,132	112,800	119,458	129,274
Private Consumption, etc.	32,627	29,789	34,131	36,412	39,662	54,727	65,809	68,468	68,001	76,444	80,627
General Gov't Consumption	5,820	6,204	7,299	8,294	9,835	12,505	18,071	18,214	18,576	20,230	25,523
Gross Domestic Investment	8,186	6,451	7,727	10,473	6,376	15,519	17,010	22,451	26,223	22,784	23,124
Fixed Investment	8,186	6,285	7,507	9,051	8,549	12,342	17,010	22,451	26,223	22,784	23,124
GDP at factor cost	..	..	..	..	..	..	..	..	..	..	..
Agriculture	19,843	15,230	16,254	24,192	14,507	24,691	24,879	29,668	25,770	31,829	27,117
Industry	9,861	10,829	13,091	14,348	14,279	17,309	22,260	24,245	22,701	23,388	23,891
Manufacturing	..	..	..	..	..	..	..	..	..	..	..
Services, etc.	25,977	24,780	26,018	28,212	30,964	36,279	46,572	49,194	51,933	54,813	61,265
Memo Items:											
Capacity to Import	8,562	7,882	8,223	8,728	11,189	16,431	17,062	15,779	13,863	14,312	18,060
Terms of Trade Adjustment	-9,716	-10,190	-8,922	-11,461	-8,549	-1,674	-2,783	-4,034	-4,525	-5,119	-804
Gross Domestic Income	43,939	40,224	46,248	52,931	52,320	75,405	91,732	98,922	96,990	104,371	113,275
Gross National Income	43,875	40,164	46,188	52,867	52,378	75,807	91,916	98,841	97,222	104,916	113,814
DOMESTIC PRICES/DEFLATORS					*(Index 1987 = 100)*						
Overall (GDP)	12.8	13.6	14.6	14.4	16.3	20.7	21.8	24.0	26.6	29.6	34.2
Domestic Absorption	15.3	16.7	17.2	17.8	18.5	21.1	23.0	26.0	29.3	31.6	35.2
Agriculture	8.2	9.1	9.9	9.6	11.6	13.1	14.9	16.2	19.4	21.5	25.3
Industry	16.6	16.3	15.7	15.1	16.8	24.1	22.3	25.7	29.1	34.8	44.2
Manufacturing	..	..	..	..	..	..	..	..	..	..	..
Consumer Price Index	8.8	9.2	9.7	9.9	11.9	13.8	15.4	17.1	19.2	20.1	21.0
MANUFACTURING ACTIVITY											
Employment (1987=100)	75.4	78.2	89.9	95.0	100.6	105.9	112.4	120.6	126.3	133.6	133.7
Real Earnings per Empl. (1987=100)	102.9	105.7	100.1	105.2	93.2	85.2	82.1	76.7	91.9	112.2	135.8
Real Output per Empl. (1987=100)	36.8	40.0	49.6	56.3	50.1	44.2	52.8	58.0	56.4	55.2	47.7
Earnings as % of Value Added	34.0	33.1	32.3	25.8	25.1	20.8	21.5	18.3	21.4	27.6	29.8
MONETARY HOLDINGS					*(Millions of current Syrian Pounds)*						
Money Supply, Broadly Defined	2,214	2,521	2,716	3,428	4,114	5,996	7,585	9,387	12,035	15,293	17,904
Money	2,088	2,341	2,502	3,151	3,797	5,540	6,966	8,561	10,924	13,866	16,119
Currency Outside Banks	1,577	1,795	1,846	2,245	2,757	3,413	3,944	5,259	6,797	8,459	9,903
Demand Deposits	511	546	656	906	1,040	2,127	3,021	3,302	4,127	5,407	6,216
Quasi-Money	126	180	213	277	317	456	619	826	1,111	1,427	1,785
					(Millions of current Syrian Pounds)						
GOVERNMENT DEFICIT (-) OR SURPLUS	..	..	..	-327	-574	-740	-992	-2,332	-2,928	-2,935	303
Current Revenue	..	..	..	2,333	2,759	4,824	8,688	9,713	10,410	10,397	15,572
Current Expenditure	..	..	..	1,735	2,240	3,203	5,160	6,046	6,634	7,333	9,210
Current Budget Balance	..	..	..	598	519	1,621	3,528	3,667	3,776	3,064	6,362
Capital Receipts	..	..	..	13	7	11	10	10	10	14	13
Capital Payments	..	..	..	938	1,100	2,372	4,530	6,009	6,714	6,013	6,072

1980	1981	1982	1983	1984	1985	1986	1987	1988	1989 estimate	NOTES	SYRIAN ARAB REPUBLIC
1,410	1,660	1,770	1,800	1,720	1,720	1,520	1,220	1,100	..	A	**CURRENT GNP PER CAPITA (US $)**
8,800	9,104	9,421	9,751	10,097	10,458	10,836	11,232	11,647	12,082	..	**POPULATION (thousands)**
				(Billions of current Syrian Pounds)							**USE AND ORIGIN OF RESOURCES**
51.31	65.70	68.10	72.69	74.88	82.74	99.63	125.05	165.61	..	..	Gross National Product (GNP)
0.04	-0.08	-0.69	-0.60	-0.46	-0.49	-0.67	-1.27	-2.18	..	..	Net Factor Income from Abroad
51.27	65.78	68.79	73.29	75.34	83.23	100.30	126.33	167.79	..	..	GDP at Market Prices
-8.82	-11.40	-7.58	-9.83	-8.72	-10.50	-10.02	-10.91	-6.80	..	..	Resource Balance
9.34	10.29	9.57	9.71	9.36	10.25	10.13	18.69	18.78	..	..	Exports of Goods & NFServices
18.17	21.69	17.15	19.55	18.08	20.74	20.16	29.60	25.58	..	..	Imports of Goods & NFServices
60.09	77.17	76.36	83.13	84.06	93.73	110.32	137.24	174.59	..	..	Domestic Absorption
34.11	48.26	44.99	49.69	49.12	54.16	65.55	90.82	120.14	..	f	Private Consumption, etc.
11.87	13.66	15.10	16.15	17.08	19.78	21.44	22.95	26.62	..	..	General Gov't Consumption
14.12	15.26	16.27	17.29	17.86	19.78	23.33	23.47	27.84	..	f	Gross Domestic Investment
14.12	15.26	16.27	17.29	17.86	19.78	23.33	23.47	27.84	..	..	Fixed Investment
..	..	..	..	..	..	..	..	..	..	..	Indirect Taxes, net
..	..	..	..	..	..	..	..	..	..	B	GDP at factor cost
10.37	12.76	13.85	15.63	14.81	17.46	23.82	34.37	64.29	..	..	Agriculture
11.95	16.79	15.94	16.47	17.04	18.21	22.61	23.87	26.90	..	..	Industry
..	..	..	..	..	..	..	..	..	..	..	Manufacturing
28.95	36.23	39.00	41.19	43.50	47.55	53.87	68.09	76.60	..	..	Services, etc.
5.29	3.86	8.69	7.45	9.14	9.28	13.31	12.56	21.03	..	..	Gross Domestic Saving
8.37	5.50	9.62	8.36	9.95	10.03	13.62	12.25	21.38	..	..	Gross National Saving
				(Millions of 1987 Syrian Pounds)							
123,746	135,220	137,924	140,704	135,261	139,699	138,584	125,051	141,696	..	..	Gross National Product
123,633	135,384	139,372	141,924	136,142	140,573	139,534	126,325	143,505	..	H	GDP at Market Prices
-18,244	-27,464	-19,627	-23,255	-22,446	-22,997	-16,533	-10,911	-5,571	..	..	Resource Balance
16,909	17,656	18,512	19,245	18,239	16,469	18,260	18,691	17,690	..	..	Exports of Goods & NFServices
35,153	45,120	38,139	42,500	40,685	39,466	34,793	29,602	23,261	..	..	Imports of Goods & NFServices
142,439	167,043	160,105	167,017	159,740	164,947	155,426	137,236	145,237	..	..	Domestic Absorption
88,897	111,654	102,242	106,527	96,133	101,749	97,081	90,818	96,656	..	f	Private Consumption, etc.
25,738	26,985	28,522	30,044	32,600	30,168	27,123	22,945	24,300	..	..	General Gov't Consumption
27,804	28,405	29,341	30,446	31,007	33,030	31,222	23,473	24,281	..	f	Gross Domestic Investment
27,804	28,405	29,341	30,446	31,007	33,030	31,222	23,473	24,281	..	..	Fixed Investment
..	..	..	..	..	..	..	..	..	..	B H	GDP at factor cost
38,054	39,507	38,582	38,380	35,096	37,320	39,496	34,369	45,019	..	..	Agriculture
23,647	23,471	24,896	26,256	24,049	26,078	29,241	23,871	26,412	..	..	Industry
..	..	..	..	..	..	..	..	..	..	..	Manufacturing
63,696	73,741	76,350	77,287	76,997	77,175	70,798	68,085	72,073	..	..	Services, etc.
											Memo Items:
18,082	21,408	21,288	21,118	21,059	19,491	17,492	18,691	17,076	..	..	Capacity to Import
1,173	3,752	2,776	1,874	2,820	3,022	-769	0	-615	..	..	Terms of Trade Adjustment
124,806	139,136	142,148	143,797	138,962	143,595	138,766	126,325	142,891	..	..	Gross Domestic Income
124,918	138,973	140,700	142,578	138,082	142,722	137,816	125,051	141,081	..	..	Gross National Income
				(Index 1987 = 100)							**DOMESTIC PRICES/DEFLATORS**
41.5	48.6	49.4	51.6	55.3	59.2	71.9	100.0	116.9	..	..	Overall (GDP)
42.2	46.2	47.7	49.8	52.6	56.8	71.0	100.0	120.2	..	..	Domestic Absorption
27.2	32.3	35.9	40.7	42.2	46.8	60.3	100.0	142.8	..	..	Agriculture
50.5	71.5	64.0	62.7	70.9	69.8	77.3	100.0	101.9	..	..	Industry
..	..	..	..	..	..	..	..	..	..	..	Manufacturing
25.1	29.7	33.9	36.0	39.3	46.1	62.7	100.0	134.6	149.9	..	Consumer Price Index
											MANUFACTURING ACTIVITY
139.7	150.5	151.7	154.4	143.7	130.6	120.2	100.0	92.3	..	G	Employment (1987 = 100)
143.4	151.9	142.1	143.2	130.0	130.3	124.2	100.0	92.1	..	G	Real Earnings per Empl. (1987 = 100)
55.7	57.1	69.2	75.1	77.3	82.8	93.3	100.0	..	..	G	Real Output per Empl. (1987 = 100)
27.7	28.4	29.7	30.9	30.8	34.7	34.9	31.7	..	..	..	Earnings as % of Value Added
				(Millions of current Syrian Pounds)							**MONETARY HOLDINGS**
24,030	27,841	33,511	42,182	52,774	63,493	71,121	79,349	..	..	..	Money Supply, Broadly Defined
21,854	24,832	29,518	36,978	45,606	54,976	61,214	67,821	..	..	..	Money
13,422	14,046	17,348	20,500	25,154	29,562	36,262	41,852	..	..	..	Currency Outside Banks
8,432	10,786	12,171	16,479	20,452	25,414	24,952	25,969	..	..	..	Demand Deposits
2,176	3,009	3,993	5,204	7,167	8,517	9,907	11,529	..	..	..	Quasi-Money
				(Millions of current Syrian Pounds)							**GOVERNMENT DEFICIT (-) OR SURPLUS**
-4,976	-4,157	..	..	..	..	-10,902	-3,355	..	..	..	Current Revenue
19,711	21,202	..	..	..	..	26,189	32,088	..	..	..	Current Revenue
15,546	17,174	..	..	..	..	26,801	23,029	..	..	..	Current Expenditure
4,165	4,028	..	..	..	..	-612	9,059	..	..	..	Current Budget Balance
15	1	..	..	..	..	..	..	..	..	..	Capital Receipts
9,156	8,186	..	..	..	..	10,290	12,414	..	..	..	Capital Payments

SYRIAN ARAB REPUBLIC	1969	1970	1971	1972	1973	1974	1975	1976	1977	1978	1979
FOREIGN TRADE (CUSTOMS BASIS)					*(Millions of current US dollars)*						
Value of Exports, fob	206.8	203.0	194.6	287.3	351.1	783.7	930.0	1,055.1	1,063.0	1,060.3	1,645.1
Nonfuel Primary Products	162.4	146.1	124.9	196.6	218.3	288.6	203.7	268.8	319.4	298.9	333.5
Fuels	21.9	34.0	46.7	52.6	76.3	432.5	653.9	682.6	644.0	665.9	1,186.6
Manufactures	22.5	22.9	23.0	38.1	56.5	62.7	72.4	103.6	99.6	95.5	125.0
Value of Imports, cif	367.9	350.0	438.3	539.4	613.2	1,229.4	1,669.1	1,959.1	2,655.9	2,443.7	3,324.0
Nonfuel Primary Products	82.4	123.5	180.8	165.2	205.7	414.0	432.8	416.7	451.3	571.5	601.8
Fuels	38.2	28.2	26.9	24.1	28.0	74.2	108.7	192.1	445.1	324.3	822.6
Manufactures	247.3	198.3	230.6	350.2	379.6	741.2	1,127.6	1,350.2	1,759.6	1,547.9	1,899.5
					(Index 1987 = 100)						
Terms of Trade	117.2	89.2	77.5	87.7	94.1	126.9	114.5	127.1	123.8	110.1	122.2
Export Prices, fob	26.1	22.6	23.2	28.7	38.6	70.0	64.3	71.5	76.5	77.9	104.2
Import Prices, cif	22.3	25.4	29.9	32.7	41.0	55.1	56.2	56.2	61.7	70.8	85.2
BALANCE OF PAYMENTS					*(Millions of current US dollars)*						
Exports of Goods & Services	..	326.0	371.1	471.2	631.8	1,142.5	1,314.9	1,379.6	1,453.1	1,371.1	2,077.5
Merchandise, fob	..	197.0	195.6	298.6	356.4	782.9	930.0	1,065.6	1,069.8	1,061.2	1,647.7
Nonfactor Services	..	128.0	174.5	171.5	265.8	304.3	335.1	295.6	329.5	259.2	376.3
Factor Services	..	1.0	1.0	1.1	9.5	55.3	49.8	18.5	53.8	50.7	53.5
Imports of Goods & Services	..	405.0	458.4	526.6	693.8	1,436.0	1,928.1	2,606.9	2,855.5	2,804.8	3,660.0
Merchandise, fob	..	332.0	381.1	445.1	568.6	1,039.1	1,425.4	2,102.4	2,402.0	2,203.5	3,055.1
Nonfactor Services	..	70.0	74.2	78.2	119.2	369.2	466.2	479.1	418.1	579.4	590.1
Factor Services	..	3.0	3.0	3.3	6.0	27.7	36.4	25.4	35.4	21.9	14.8
Long-Term Interest	..	6.2	6.8	6.7	8.5	10.9	17.3	22.5	28.3	55.5	71.6
Private Current Transfers, net	..	7.0	8.0	39.1	37.0	44.5	52.2	53.1	92.5	635.9	901.4
Workers' Remittances	..	7.0	8.0	39.1	37.0	44.5	52.2	53.1	92.5	635.9	901.4
Curr. A/C Bal before Off. Transf.	..	-72.0	-79.2	-16.3	-25.0	-248.9	-560.9	-1,174.1	-1,309.9	-797.8	-681.1
Net Official Transfers	..	3.0	21.1	44.5	363.6	416.1	654.4	401.8	1,143.2	782.4	1,626.8
Curr. A/C Bal after Off. Transf.	..	-69.0	-58.2	28.2	338.6	167.2	93.5	-772.4	-166.7	-15.4	945.7
Long-Term Capital, net	..	10.0	81.2	14.1	25.0	..	-9.7	270.2	227.8	359.2	74.9
Direct Investment	..	..	..	..	..	..	..	..	..	..	..
Long-Term Loans	..	29.4	42.9	42.3	56.6	73.6	190.1	319.4	466.8	205.5	250.3
Disbursements	..	60.0	75.7	77.6	94.8	135.1	277.2	404.1	545.8	382.6	449.1
Repayments	..	30.6	32.8	35.3	38.2	61.5	87.1	84.7	79.0	177.1	198.8
Other Long-Term Capital	..	-19.4	38.3	-28.2	-31.6	..	-199.8	-49.2	-239.0	153.7	-175.4
Other Capital, net	..	48.6	7.3	-20.2	-85.0	-64.7	159.6	93.7	130.4	-446.5	-826.0
Change in Reserves	..	10.4	-30.4	-22.1	-278.6	-102.4	-243.4	408.5	-191.5	102.7	-194.6
Memo Item:					*(Syrian Pounds per US dollar)*						
Conversion Factor (Annual Avg)	3.060	3.180	3.090	3.020	3.040	3.070	3.020	3.240	3.510	3.490	3.930
				(Millions of US dollars), outstanding at end of year							
EXTERNAL DEBT (Total)	..	242.0	298.7	361.3	440.3	518.5	685.1	1,003.5	1,820.4	2,025.0	2,335.8
Long-Term Debt (by debtor)	..	242.0	298.7	361.3	440.3	518.5	685.1	1,003.5	1,504.4	1,756.0	2,021.8
Central Bank, incl. IMF credit	..	9.5	5.2	24.6	21.6	6.6	0.0	0.0	0.0	0.0	0.0
Central Government	..	134.4	177.3	212.1	257.5	267.5	390.8	612.5	947.7	1,120.9	1,379.2
Rest of General Government	..	3.3	2.9	2.4	2.5	2.0	2.1	1.7	1.2	0.8	0.6
Non-financial Public Enterprises	..	94.8	113.3	118.3	150.2	229.8	280.3	381.4	547.9	631.4	641.8
Priv. Sector, incl non-guaranteed	..	0.0	0.0	3.9	8.5	12.6	11.9	7.9	7.6	2.9	0.2
Short-Term Debt	..	0.0	0.0	0.0	0.0	0.0	0.0	0.0	316.0	269.0	314.0
Memo Items:					*(Millions of US dollars)*						
Int'l Reserves Excluding Gold	31.00	27.00	58.00	105.30	378.67	466.10	701.90	293.39	483.74	381.80	580.83
Gold Holdings (at market price)	28.16	29.90	34.90	51.92	89.80	147.15	110.66	106.32	133.77	183.29	426.50
SOCIAL INDICATORS											
Total Fertility Rate	7.8	7.7	7.7	7.7	7.6	7.6	7.5	7.5	7.4	7.4	7.3
Infant Mortality Rate	99.4	95.6	91.8	88.0	84.4	80.8	77.2	73.6	70.0	67.8	65.6
Life Expectancy at Birth	55.2	55.8	56.4	57.0	57.6	58.2	58.8	59.4	60.1	60.6	61.1
Urban Population, % of total	42.6	43.3	43.7	44.1	44.6	45.0	45.4	45.8	46.2	46.6	47.0
Food Prod. per capita (1987=100)	86.4	63.0	66.6	96.4	54.4	93.7	92.8	105.8	94.8	108.5	100.5
Labor Force, Agriculture (%)	50.5	50.2	48.1	46.2	44.4	42.7	41.1	39.1	37.2	35.5	33.8
Labor Force, Female (%)	11.4	11.6	12.0	12.4	12.7	13.0	13.2	13.6	13.9	14.1	14.4
Primary Schl. Enroll. Ratio	..	78.0	..	..	..	..	96.0	90.0	98.0	98.0	99.0
Primary Schl. Enroll. Ratio, Female	..	59.0	..	..	..	..	78.0	75.0	81.0	83.0	86.0
Secondary Schl. Enroll. Ratio	..	38.0	..	..	..	..	43.0	..	44.0	46.0	46.0

1980	1981	1982	1983	1984	1985	1986	1987	1988	1989 estimate	NOTES	SYRIAN ARAB REPUBLIC
				(Millions of current US dollars)							**FOREIGN TRADE (CUSTOMS BASIS)**
2,108.0	2,103.0	2,026.0	1,922.8	1,853.5	1,637.0	1,037.0	1,357.0	1,345.0	..	..	Value of Exports, fob
307.2	260.6	313.6	307.8	438.9	225.0	234.0	358.0	393.5	..	..	Nonfuel Primary Products
1,662.2	1,661.7	1,513.4	1,323.8	1,168.6	1,212.0	564.0	698.0	616.8	..	..	Fuels
138.6	180.7	199.0	291.2	246.0	200.0	239.0	301.0	334.7	..	..	Manufactures
4,118.0	5,040.0	4,014.0	4,542.0	4,115.7	3,967.0	2,703.0	2,546.0	2,223.0	..	f	Value of Imports, cif
736.2	924.4	706.5	1,041.8	935.9	923.0	439.0	450.0	484.3	..	..	Nonfuel Primary Products
1,070.0	1,744.7	1,511.3	1,370.7	1,411.8	1,162.0	563.0	560.0	240.5	..	..	Fuels
2,311.8	2,370.9	1,796.2	2,129.5	1,768.0	1,882.0	1,701.0	1,536.0	1,498.2	..	..	Manufactures
				(Index 1987 = 100)							
153.4	150.5	136.6	133.0	126.0	131.4	92.4	100.0	77.7	..	..	Terms of Trade
155.2	164.0	143.8	131.3	125.9	125.2	81.8	100.0	89.8	..	..	Export Prices, fob
101.1	109.0	105.3	98.7	99.9	95.3	88.6	100.0	115.5	..	..	Import Prices, cif
				(Millions of current US dollars)							**BALANCE OF PAYMENTS**
2,567.5	2,736.5	2,510.7	2,493.1	2,376.1	2,281.2	1,611.7	1,944.6	1,917.3	..	..	Exports of Goods & Services
2,112.0	2,211.5	2,002.1	1,917.8	1,834.2	1,666.5	1,036.9	1,357.3	1,347.6	..	..	Merchandise, fob
364.8	431.3	483.0	559.5	512.0	588.7	565.2	562.7	547.3	..	..	Nonfactor Services
90.7	93.7	25.6	15.8	29.9	26.0	9.6	24.6	22.4	..	..	Factor Services
4,610.1	5,328.7	4,569.4	5,025.1	4,720.2	4,542.9	3,151.8	3,137.0	2,842.9	..	..	Imports of Goods & Services
4,009.7	4,404.0	3,635.5	4,024.0	3,687.2	3,543.1	2,363.2	2,225.8	1,986.3	..	..	Merchandise, fob
521.0	813.9	757.0	853.6	905.5	875.0	651.8	644.6	646.4	..	..	Nonfactor Services
79.4	110.8	176.9	147.5	127.5	124.8	136.8	266.6	210.2	..	..	Factor Services
77.3	55.4	73.1	72.9	76.4	75.6	82.2	101.2	108.8	112.6	..	Long-Term Interest
773.5	436.0	410.7	386.5	321.4	313.9	250.6	245.0	225.0	..	..	Private Current Transfers, net
773.5	436.0	410.7	386.5	321.4	313.9	250.6	245.0	225.0	..	..	Workers' Remittances
-1,269.1	-2,156.2	-1,648.0	-2,145.5	-2,022.7	-1,947.8	-1,289.5	-947.4	-700.6	..	..	Curr. A/C Bal before Off. Transf.
1,520.0	1,848.2	1,398.1	1,301.5	1,228.7	1,087.9	759.1	760.5	536.1	..	..	Net Official Transfers
250.9	-308.0	-249.9	-844.0	-794.0	-859.9	-530.4	-186.9	-164.5	..	..	Curr. A/C Bal after Off. Transf.
-25.0	-150.7	-179.1	189.1	289.7	-107.0	198.2	118.5	129.1	..	..	Long-Term Capital, net
..	..	..	..	..	..	..	0.0	0.0	0.0	..	Direct Investment
123.5	125.4	57.7	89.7	171.5	225.8	199.4	203.6	93.8	-22.6	..	Long-Term Loans
348.3	370.0	300.8	320.7	368.0	437.6	411.7	461.4	353.7	249.2	..	Disbursements
224.8	244.6	243.1	231.0	196.5	211.8	212.3	257.8	259.9	271.8	..	Repayments
-148.5	-276.1	-236.8	99.4	118.2	-332.8	-1.2	-85.1	35.3	..	..	Other Long-Term Capital
-479.8	407.9	336.7	509.6	720.7	781.3	393.2	147.2	116.4	..	..	Other Capital, net
253.9	50.8	92.3	145.3	-216.4	185.6	-61.0	-78.8	-81.0	0.0	..	Change in Reserves
				(Syrian Pounds per US dollar)							**Memo Item:**
3.930	4.220	4.200	4.140	4.280	4.900	7.040	10.150	16.620	..	..	Conversion Factor (Annual Avg)
				(Millions of US dollars), outstanding at end of year							
2,749.0	2,999.9	2,998.1	3,033.0	3,463.3	4,028.0	4,872.5	5,090.6	5,198.8	5,202.2	..	**EXTERNAL DEBT (Total)**
2,118.0	2,200.5	2,230.6	2,281.1	2,837.7	3,202.6	3,560.1	4,020.7	3,994.3	3,934.3	..	Long-Term Debt (by debtor)
0.0	0.0	0.0	0.0	0.0	0.0	0.0	0.0	0.0	..	..	Central Bank, incl. IMF credit
1,383.2	1,434.0	1,439.9	1,451.1	1,926.0	2,012.4	2,171.3	2,380.2	2,383.9	2,389.1	..	Central Government
1.1	1.3	1.0	0.7	6.8	18.4	24.0	28.0	26.7	24.7	..	Rest of General Government
733.6	765.1	789.7	829.3	904.9	1,171.8	1,364.8	1,612.5	1,583.7	1,520.5	..	Non-financial Public Enterprises
0.1	0.1	0.0	0.0	0.0	0.0	0.0	0.0	0.0	..	..	Priv. Sector, incl non-guaranteed
631.0	799.4	767.5	751.9	625.6	825.4	1,312.4	1,069.9	1,204.5	1,267.9	..	Short-Term Debt
				(Millions of US dollars)							**Memo Items:**
336.53	291.42	198.08	52.18	268.19	83.05	144.25	223.03	191.03	..	..	Int'l Reserves Excluding Gold
491.05	331.12	380.60	317.79	256.81	272.39	325.62	403.26	341.74	..	..	Gold Holdings (at market price)
											SOCIAL INDICATORS
7.3	7.2	7.2	7.1	7.0	6.9	6.8	6.8	6.7	6.6	..	Total Fertility Rate
63.4	61.2	59.0	56.8	54.6	52.4	50.2	48.0	46.5	45.0	..	Infant Mortality Rate
61.6	62.1	62.6	63.0	63.5	64.0	64.5	65.0	65.3	65.6	..	Life Expectancy at Birth
47.4	47.8	48.2	48.7	49.1	49.5	50.0	50.4	50.9	51.3	..	Urban Population, % of total
129.0	128.7	129.8	123.0	105.5	109.8	119.9	100.0	131.5	76.9	..	Food Prod. per capita (1987 = 100)
32.3	..	..	..	..	..	..	..	..	..	..	Labor Force, Agriculture (%)
14.6	14.9	15.2	15.5	15.7	16.0	16.3	16.5	16.8	17.0	..	Labor Force, Female (%)
102.0	..	103.0	105.0	107.0	108.0	111.0	110.0	..	..	..	Primary Schl. Enroll. Ratio
89.0	91.0	92.0	96.0	98.0	101.0	105.0	104.0	..	..	..	Primary Schl. Enroll. Ratio, Female
47.0	..	52.0	56.0	59.0	60.0	60.0	59.0	..	..	..	Secondary Schl. Enroll. Ratio

TANZANIA	1969	1970	1971	1972	1973	1974	1975	1976	1977	1978	1979
CURRENT GNP PER CAPITA (US $)	90	100	100	110	120	140	160	180	190	220	250
POPULATION (thousands)	13,088	13,513	13,968	14,440	14,927	15,427	15,942	16,470	17,011	17,568	18,149
USE AND ORIGIN OF RESOURCES				*(Billions of current Tanzania Shillings)*							
Gross National Product (GNP)	8.23	9.15	9.79	11.16	13.11	16.00	18.99	24.32	28.78	32.12	36.21
Net Factor Income from Abroad	-0.04	-0.02	-0.02	-0.01	0.01	0.00	-0.02	-0.10	-0.09	-0.04	-0.07
GDP at Market Prices	8.27	9.17	9.81	11.17	13.10	15.99	19.01	24.42	28.87	32.17	36.28
Resource Balance	0.02	-0.19	-0.46	-0.40	-0.80	-2.34	-2.36	-0.54	-0.94	-4.87	-4.63
Exports of Goods & NFServices	2.04	2.39	2.67	3.00	3.10	3.47	3.77	5.30	5.63	4.69	5.13
Imports of Goods & NFServices	2.02	2.58	3.13	3.40	3.90	5.80	6.14	5.84	6.57	9.56	9.76
Domestic Absorption	8.25	9.36	10.28	11.57	13.90	18.33	21.38	24.96	29.81	37.04	40.91
Private Consumption, etc.	5.97	6.31	6.55	7.73	9.24	12.05	14.10	15.38	17.98	23.36	25.50
General Gov't Consumption	1.00	0.98	1.14	1.40	1.91	2.76	3.28	3.99	4.31	5.58	5.96
Gross Domestic Investment	1.28	2.07	2.59	2.44	2.76	3.52	4.00	5.60	7.52	8.09	9.46
Fixed Investment	1.21	1.88	2.37	2.36	2.60	3.03	3.54	5.16	6.66	7.33	8.59
Indirect Taxes, net	0.81	0.96	0.96	1.14	1.61	1.98	2.02	2.77	3.17	3.59	3.97
GDP at factor cost	7.46	8.21	8.86	10.03	11.49	14.01	16.99	21.65	25.70	28.58	32.32
Agriculture	3.08	3.38	3.49	4.02	4.54	5.44	7.01	9.05	11.13	12.51	14.73
Industry	1.27	1.42	1.56	1.80	2.11	2.41	2.76	4.13	4.89	5.40	5.66
Manufacturing	0.74	0.83	0.85	1.14	1.26	1.48	1.77	2.81	3.29	3.86	3.87
Services, etc.	3.10	3.41	3.80	4.21	4.84	6.16	7.22	8.48	9.67	10.68	11.93
Gross Domestic Saving	1.31	1.88	2.13	2.04	1.96	1.18	1.64	5.05	6.58	3.22	4.83
Gross National Saving	..	1.93	2.14	1.93	1.87	1.10	1.70	5.05	6.65	3.35	5.00
				(Millions of 1987 Tanzania Shillings)							
Gross National Product	127,438	136,806	142,245	152,542	162,235	165,573	171,946	176,737	176,876	181,345	185,823
GDP at Market Prices	128,052	137,187	142,539	152,682	162,136	165,562	172,167	177,859	177,947	181,603	186,197
Resource Balance	-48,069	-60,047	-70,347	-66,420	-68,173	-75,299	-67,813	-54,812	-57,154	-85,858	-64,460
Exports of Goods & NFServices	25,001	28,222	30,714	34,419	29,927	22,050	25,420	26,407	25,525	27,913	28,676
Imports of Goods & NFServices	73,071	88,269	101,061	100,839	98,100	97,349	93,233	81,219	82,679	113,770	93,135
Domestic Absorption	176,121	197,234	212,886	219,102	230,308	240,861	239,980	232,671	235,101	267,461	250,657
Private Consumption, etc.	..	..	..	..	..	..	..	166,636	160,541	189,505	169,034
General Gov't Consumption	..	..	..	..	..	..	..	15,999	16,059	20,608	22,773
Gross Domestic Investment	28,813	43,143	51,529	41,409	43,331	48,829	44,868	50,036	58,501	57,348	58,850
Fixed Investment	27,008	39,097	46,763	39,823	40,718	41,999	38,667	46,198	52,010	52,700	54,822
GDP at factor cost	116,481	123,893	129,880	138,355	143,285	146,064	154,947	157,305	158,008	160,893	165,351
Agriculture	82,201	85,288	84,246	91,142	92,014	88,215	95,692	90,671	91,713	90,190	90,871
Industry	13,870	14,510	16,593	17,403	17,825	17,986	17,711	19,553	19,089	18,885	19,975
Manufacturing	8,056	8,582	9,398	10,191	10,645	10,790	10,826	12,744	11,973	12,376	12,789
Services, etc.	26,566	29,187	31,190	32,980	35,127	39,570	42,207	45,158	45,589	49,089	50,954
Memo Items:											
Capacity to Import	73,977	81,869	86,177	88,998	77,952	58,158	57,298	73,655	70,812	55,809	48,968
Terms of Trade Adjustment	48,975	53,647	55,462	54,579	48,025	36,108	31,878	47,247	45,287	27,896	20,292
Gross Domestic Income	177,027	190,834	198,001	207,261	210,161	201,670	204,045	225,106	223,234	209,499	206,490
Gross National Income	176,413	190,453	197,707	207,122	210,260	201,680	203,824	223,984	222,163	209,241	206,115
DOMESTIC PRICES/DEFLATORS				*(Index 1987 = 100)*							
Overall (GDP)	6.5	6.7	6.9	7.3	8.1	9.7	11.0	13.7	16.2	17.7	19.5
Domestic Absorption	4.7	4.7	4.8	5.3	6.0	7.6	8.9	10.7	12.7	13.8	16.3
Agriculture	3.7	4.0	4.1	4.4	4.9	6.2	7.3	10.0	12.1	13.9	16.2
Industry	9.2	9.8	9.4	10.4	11.8	13.4	15.6	21.1	25.6	28.6	28.3
Manufacturing	9.2	9.6	9.0	11.2	11.8	13.7	16.4	22.1	27.5	31.2	30.2
Consumer Price Index	4.1	4.2	4.4	4.7	5.2	6.3	7.9	8.4	9.4	10.5	11.9
MANUFACTURING ACTIVITY											
Employment (1987=100)	..	..	..	..	..	..	..	..	..	..	..
Real Earnings per Empl. (1987=100)	..	..	..	..	..	..	..	..	..	..	..
Real Output per Empl. (1987=100)	..	..	..	..	..	..	..	..	..	..	..
Earnings as % of Value Added	42.9	42.4	41.6	39.4	37.3	42.3	..	..	..	33.0	29.7
MONETARY HOLDINGS				*(Millions of current Tanzania Shillings)*							
Money Supply, Broadly Defined	1,981	2,220	2,624	3,090	3,653	4,462	5,553	6,947	8,347	9,396	13,807
Money	1,656	1,679	2,058	2,327	2,775	3,456	4,284	5,332	6,383	6,827	10,435
Currency Outside Banks	605	818	986	1,201	1,199	1,517	1,756	2,071	2,380	2,915	4,055
Demand Deposits	1,051	860	1,072	1,126	1,576	1,939	2,528	3,260	4,003	3,912	6,380
Quasi-Money	325	541	566	763	878	1,006	1,269	1,615	1,964	2,569	3,371
GOVERNMENT DEFICIT (-) OR SURPLUS				*(Millions of current Tanzania Shillings)*							
	..	..	..	-554	-745	-917	-1,891	-1,527	-1,542	-2,365	-5,376
Current Revenue	..	..	..	1,793	2,294	3,177	4,237	4,393	5,906	6,790	7,381
Current Expenditure	..	..	..	1,596	2,087	2,869	4,373	4,300	5,222	5,871	8,214
Current Budget Balance	..	..	..	197	207	308	-136	93	684	919	-833
Capital Receipts	..	..	..	..	..	..	..	..	..	..	..
Capital Payments	..	..	..	751	952	1,225	1,755	1,620	2,226	3,284	4,543

1980	1981	1982	1983	1984	1985	1986	1987	1988	1989 estimate	NOTES	TANZANIA
280	300	310	320	310	310	270	200	150	120	f	**CURRENT GNP PER CAPITA (US $)**
18,757	19,393	20,059	20,754	21,482	22,242	23,036	23,864	24,728	25,627	..	**POPULATION (thousands)**
			(Billions of current Tanzania Shillings)								**USE AND ORIGIN OF RESOURCES**
42.01	48.93	58.00	70.32	88.40	118.91	156.37	205.74	290.66	378.86	f	Gross National Product (GNP)
-0.11	-0.18	-0.23	-0.18	-0.49	-1.71	-3.28	-13.30	-20.82	-31.86	..	Net Factor Income from Abroad
42.12	49.10	58.23	70.51	88.89	120.62	159.65	219.04	311.48	410.72	f	GDP at Market Prices
-5.55	-4.17	-4.32	-3.65	-7.22	-10.03	-22.45	-50.07	-80.85	-112.14	..	Resource Balance
5.54	5.99	4.55	5.11	6.32	7.45	14.58	29.52	49.06	75.16	..	Exports of Goods & NFServices
11.09	10.16	8.86	8.76	13.54	17.48	37.03	79.59	129.91	187.30	..	Imports of Goods & NFServices
47.67	53.27	62.54	74.16	96.11	130.65	182.09	269.10	392.33	..	..	Domestic Absorption
32.49	37.03	42.26	55.13	68.65	93.13	127.31	189.80	288.52	..	..	Private Consumption, etc.
5.49	6.11	8.05	9.44	13.84	18.55	23.62	29.33	37.89	..	..	General Gov't Consumption
9.69	10.13	12.24	9.59	13.62	18.96	31.17	49.97	65.92	..	..	Gross Domestic Investment
8.63	8.63	10.82	7.75	11.97	16.87	28.68	46.29	61.80	..	..	Fixed Investment
4.66	5.20	5.68	7.90	10.75	12.54	18.85	26.07	39.76	47.25	..	Indirect Taxes, net
37.45	43.91	52.55	62.61	78.14	108.08	140.79	192.97	271.72	363.46	f	GDP at factor cost
16.64	20.34	26.45	32.74	41.29	61.23	84.15	120.94	178.25	..	..	Agriculture
6.35	6.84	6.91	6.88	8.48	10.05	13.64	16.42	20.34	..	..	Industry
4.10	4.50	4.36	4.87	5.93	6.66	8.55	9.41	11.03	..	..	Manufacturing
14.47	16.73	19.19	22.99	28.37	36.80	43.00	55.61	73.13	..	..	Services, etc.
4.14	5.96	7.92	5.94	6.40	8.94	8.72	-0.10	-14.93	-41.02	..	Gross Domestic Saving
4.21	5.97	7.92	5.96	6.86	11.30	13.63	1.39	-12.72	-46.72	..	Gross National Saving
			(Millions of 1987 Tanzania Shillings)								
190,775	188,736	188,132	187,499	195,488	196,778	206,083	205,741	215,118	221,575	f	Gross National Product
191,295	189,430	188,891	187,997	196,587	199,632	210,409	219,036	230,517	240,393	f	GDP at Market Prices
-54,622	-35,397	-33,760	-26,239	-40,465	-43,631	-55,364	-50,069	-48,854	-50,340	..	Resource Balance
35,635	46,184	34,972	32,051	27,544	35,795	25,939	29,523	29,792	32,527	..	Exports of Goods & NFServices
90,257	81,580	68,732	58,290	68,009	79,425	81,302	79,592	78,646	82,867	..	Imports of Goods & NFServices
245,917	224,826	222,652	214,236	237,053	243,262	265,772	269,105	279,371	290,733	..	Domestic Absorption
174,492	152,931	142,755	157,761	169,967	170,421	182,527	189,805	188,570	186,642	..	Private Consumption, etc.
16,545	18,606	21,967	16,765	20,680	22,448	31,878	29,327	30,618	31,690	..	General Gov't Consumption
54,881	53,290	57,929	39,710	46,406	50,393	51,368	49,973	60,182	72,400	..	Gross Domestic Investment
50,300	47,613	53,219	34,073	42,446	46,727	47,909	46,288	56,631	70,662	..	Fixed Investment
169,623	168,907	169,993	166,537	172,408	178,707	185,523	192,969	201,113	212,728	f	GDP at factor cost
94,939	95,331	96,614	99,371	103,360	109,565	115,839	120,941	126,384	133,335	..	Agriculture
19,908	18,383	18,218	15,338	16,309	15,679	15,779	16,418	17,138	18,409	..	Industry
12,163	10,799	10,445	9,534	9,788	9,407	9,026	9,407	9,915	10,559	..	Manufacturing
52,190	52,781	53,021	51,828	52,739	53,463	53,905	55,610	57,592	60,984	..	Services, etc.
											Memo Items:
45,100	48,120	35,258	34,005	31,742	33,865	32,015	29,523	29,700	33,252	..	Capacity to Import
9,465	1,936	286	1,955	4,198	-1,930	6,076	0	-92	724	..	Terms of Trade Adjustment
200,760	191,366	189,177	189,951	200,786	197,702	216,485	219,036	230,424	241,117	..	Gross Domestic Income
200,240	190,671	188,418	189,453	199,686	194,848	212,160	205,741	215,026	222,299	..	Gross National Income
			(Index 1987 = 100)								**DOMESTIC PRICES/DEFLATORS**
22.0	25.9	30.8	37.5	45.2	60.4	75.9	100.0	135.1	170.9	..	Overall (GDP)
19.4	23.7	28.1	34.6	40.5	53.7	68.5	100.0	140.4	..	..	Domestic Absorption
17.6	21.3	27.4	32.9	40.0	55.9	72.6	100.0	141.0	..	..	Agriculture
31.9	37.2	37.9	44.9	52.0	64.1	86.5	100.0	118.7	..	..	Industry
33.7	41.7	41.8	51.1	60.6	70.9	94.7	100.0	111.3	..	..	Manufacturing
15.6	19.5	25.2	32.0	43.3	58.1	77.0	100.0	131.2	..	..	Consumer Price Index
											MANUFACTURING ACTIVITY
..	..	..	..	..	..	..	..	..	..	..	Employment (1987 = 100)
..	..	..	..	..	..	..	..	..	..	..	Real Earnings per Empl. (1987 = 100)
..	..	..	..	..	..	..	..	..	..	..	Real Output per Empl. (1987 = 100)
32.8	34.1	33.1	34.5	33.7	35.1	..	..	..	..	..	Earnings as % of Value Added
			(Millions of current Tanzania Shillings)								**MONETARY HOLDINGS**
17,520	20,690	24,729	29,127	30,200	39,344	50,309	66,440	87,780	..	..	Money Supply, Broadly Defined
13,346	15,396	18,323	20,564	20,608	25,468	35,810	47,131	64,126	..	..	Money
5,246	6,611	7,989	8,194	10,473	12,673	18,310	24,551	31,227	..	..	Currency Outside Banks
8,100	8,785	10,334	12,370	10,136	12,795	17,500	22,580	32,898	..	..	Demand Deposits
4,174	5,293	6,406	8,563	9,591	13,876	14,499	19,309	23,655	..	..	Quasi-Money
			(Millions of current Tanzania Shillings)								
-3,537	-3,270	..	..	..	-5,463	..	..	..	..	C	**GOVERNMENT DEFICIT (-) OR SURPLUS**
8,539	10,311	..	..	..	20,149	..	..	..	..	..	Current Revenue
7,542	9,007	..	..	..	18,529	..	..	..	..	..	Current Expenditure
997	1,304	..	..	..	1,620	..	..	..	..	..	Current Budget Balance
..	..	..	..	..	..	..	..	..	..	..	Capital Receipts
4,534	4,574	..	..	..	7,083	..	..	..	..	..	Capital Payments

TANZANIA	1969	1970	1971	1972	1973	1974	1975	1976	1977	1978	1979
FOREIGN TRADE (CUSTOMS BASIS)					*(Millions of current US dollars)*						
Value of Exports, fob	232.7	238.3	250.9	300.1	343.5	387.8	348.6	490.4	559.0	472.3	511.4
Nonfuel Primary Products	184.6	190.3	184.4	231.7	265.6	292.4	283.1	412.0	491.3	402.9	397.5
Fuels	15.2	16.2	21.6	30.8	26.5	40.8	19.6	21.3	17.9	10.8	16.9
Manufactures	33.0	31.8	44.9	37.6	51.4	54.6	45.9	57.1	49.9	58.6	97.0
Value of Imports, cif	198.6	271.5	337.9	363.4	447.4	760.1	718.2	645.3	730.1	1,141.3	1,076.7
Nonfuel Primary Products	21.2	24.4	30.7	47.0	47.7	176.1	159.8	98.1	105.9	121.5	83.3
Fuels	20.1	23.2	30.1	34.0	48.3	140.7	77.4	120.0	96.9	126.3	149.1
Manufactures	157.4	223.9	277.0	282.4	351.3	443.3	481.0	427.2	527.3	893.5	844.3
					(Index 1987 = 100)						
Terms of Trade	128.0	126.3	119.3	116.2	142.5	125.5	110.7	144.2	166.9	138.6	137.7
Export Prices, fob	28.2	29.7	30.9	33.3	49.1	73.0	66.2	84.0	103.9	95.6	109.7
Import Prices, cif	22.0	23.5	25.9	28.6	34.5	58.2	59.8	58.3	62.3	69.0	79.7
BALANCE OF PAYMENTS					*(Millions of current US dollars)*						
Exports of Goods & Services	..	321.8	349.6	411.7	455.8	488.4	491.2	633.2	656.4	625.3	697.2
Merchandise, fob	..	245.9	262.0	316.2	363.6	399.2	372.9	490.4	538.5	476.0	545.7
Nonfactor Services	..	65.2	78.0	85.4	72.1	71.9	109.4	135.4	106.8	130.2	140.0
Factor Services	..	10.7	9.6	10.1	20.0	17.3	9.0	7.4	11.1	19.1	11.6
Imports of Goods & Services	..	370.2	455.3	473.3	568.2	822.8	823.6	722.2	842.5	1,262.6	1,218.5
Merchandise, fob	..	283.5	345.3	359.8	437.8	660.4	670.0	555.6	646.7	992.5	960.7
Nonfactor Services	..	72.5	97.1	101.6	111.6	145.3	141.4	141.0	163.9	245.3	237.6
Factor Services	..	14.2	12.8	11.8	18.8	17.2	12.1	25.7	31.8	24.8	20.2
Long-Term Interest	..	7.5	7.7	8.2	10.9	12.0	14.6	16.0	21.6	25.0	31.9
Private Current Transfers, net	..	11.1	3.5	-14.5	-14.4	-11.4	11.5	11.5	19.4	23.1	29.5
Workers' Remittances	..	..	..	..	..	..	..	..	..	..	..
Curr. A/C Bal before Off. Transf.	..	-37.3	-102.1	-76.1	-126.8	-345.9	-320.8	-77.6	-166.7	-614.2	-491.8
Net Official Transfers	..	1.7	2.3	10.4	19.3	60.6	90.8	43.9	96.5	142.2	146.6
Curr. A/C Bal after Off. Transf.	..	-35.6	-99.8	-65.7	-107.5	-285.3	-230.0	-33.7	-70.2	-472.0	-345.2
Long-Term Capital, net	..	71.6	137.7	108.4	139.5	124.7	206.4	102.4	96.6	136.0	225.4
Direct Investment	..	..	..	..	..	..	..	..	..	..	..
Long-Term Loans	..	45.3	49.0	72.1	88.1	136.9	222.3	354.4	216.0	203.4	280.8
Disbursements	..	58.1	63.4	118.8	120.4	164.4	254.3	382.8	252.6	239.7	331.5
Repayments	..	12.8	14.4	46.7	32.3	27.5	32.0	28.4	36.6	36.3	50.7
Other Long-Term Capital	..	26.3	88.7	36.3	51.4	-12.2	-15.9	-252.0	-119.4	-67.4	-55.4
Other Capital, net	..	-56.6	-51.2	7.3	0.0	23.0	8.9	-46.4	133.8	164.8	62.8
Change in Reserves	..	20.6	13.3	-50.0	-32.0	137.5	14.7	-22.3	-160.1	171.2	57.0
Memo Item:					*(Tanzania Shillings per US dollar)*						
Conversion Factor (Annual Avg)	7.140	7.140	7.140	7.140	7.020	7.140	7.370	8.380	8.290	7.710	8.220
				(Millions of US dollars), outstanding at end of year							
EXTERNAL DEBT (Total)	..	265.3	326.7	401.8	509.5	729.3	944.5	1,341.7	1,780.8	1,996.6	2,196.6
Long-Term Debt (by debtor)	..	265.3	326.7	401.8	509.5	729.3	944.5	1,341.7	1,621.8	1,743.6	1,946.6
Central Bank, incl. IMF credit	..	0.0	0.0	0.0	0.0	47.6	73.3	97.2	110.8	106.1	152.1
Central Government	..	214.1	256.2	309.5	391.5	540.4	722.1	1,075.2	1,279.7	1,343.2	1,387.6
Rest of General Government	..	..	..	..	..	..	..	..	..	..	..
Non-financial Public Enterprises	..	36.2	50.5	61.2	71.4	86.9	87.6	102.6	163.3	216.5	310.7
Priv. Sector, incl non-guaranteed	..	15.0	20.0	31.1	46.6	54.4	61.5	66.7	68.0	77.8	96.2
Short-Term Debt	..	0.0	0.0	0.0	0.0	0.0	0.0	0.0	159.0	253.0	250.0
Memo Items:					*(Thousands of US dollars)*						
Int'l Reserves Excluding Gold	80,260	64,970	60,253	119,587	144,617	50,232	65,446	112,267	281,827	99,860	68,041
Gold Holdings (at market price)	..	..	..	..	..	..	..	..	..	..	..
SOCIAL INDICATORS											
Total Fertility Rate	6.5	6.4	6.4	6.3	6.3	6.4	6.4	6.5	6.5	6.6	6.6
Infant Mortality Rate	133.0	132.0	131.0	130.0	129.0	128.0	127.0	126.0	125.0	123.0	121.0
Life Expectancy at Birth	44.7	45.1	45.6	46.0	46.5	46.9	47.4	47.8	48.3	48.8	49.2
Urban Population, % of total	6.4	6.7	7.4	8.1	8.7	9.4	10.1	11.4	12.7	13.9	15.2
Food Prod. per capita (1987=100)	103.0	105.7	100.2	97.2	100.6	98.0	105.4	109.1	110.6	110.7	114.4
Labor Force, Agriculture (%)	90.6	90.4	89.8	89.3	88.9	88.4	88.0	87.5	87.0	86.5	86.0
Labor Force, Female (%)	50.6	50.6	50.5	50.4	50.3	50.2	50.2	50.1	50.0	50.0	49.9
Primary Schl. Enroll. Ratio	..	34.0	..	..	..	..	53.0	70.0	99.0	96.0	100.0
Primary Schl. Enroll. Ratio, Female	..	27.0	..	..	..	..	44.0	..	88.0	87.0	93.0
Secondary Schl. Enroll. Ratio	..	3.0	..	..	..	..	3.0	4.0	4.0	4.0	4.0

1980	1981	1982	1983	1984	1985	1986	1987	1988	1989 estimate	NOTES	TANZANIA
											FOREIGN TRADE (CUSTOMS BASIS)
536.6	564.4	413.0	379.0	339.6	254.9	348.0	347.0	402.0	460.0	f	Value of Exports, fob
427.9	492.4	350.2	331.0	284.6	205.2	287.7	281.5	326.0	..	..	Nonfuel Primary Products
26.1	1.0	5.9	6.0	6.0	4.7	2.3	2.9	2.7	..	..	Fuels
82.6	70.9	56.9	42.0	49.0	45.0	58.0	62.6	73.3	79.2	..	Manufactures
1,226.6	1,176.3	1,134.0	795.0	847.3	1,028.0	1,047.5	1,150.0	1,237.0	1,363.9	f	Value of Imports, cif
197.1	102.4	118.3	86.1	81.7	88.3	55.8	94.5	95.2	..	..	Nonfuel Primary Products
257.2	362.2	297.3	209.7	209.9	246.4	128.5	185.5	176.7	..	..	Fuels
772.3	711.7	718.4	499.2	555.6	693.3	863.2	870.0	965.1	..	..	Manufactures
				(Index 1987 = 100)							
114.7	96.5	100.2	103.3	109.9	103.0	120.3	100.0	104.1	..	f	Terms of Trade
113.8	100.4	97.5	98.0	100.7	92.9	107.9	100.0	108.0	..	f	Export Prices, fob
99.2	104.1	97.3	94.9	91.6	90.3	89.7	100.0	103.7	..	f	Import Prices, cif
				(Millions of current US dollars)							**BALANCE OF PAYMENTS**
761.7	808.7	530.2	486.3	496.6	393.7	458.6	447.1	507.2	528.0	f	Exports of Goods & Services
582.7	613.0	412.9	378.7	389.2	285.6	348.4	346.8	386.5	415.1	..	Merchandise, fob
164.9	184.8	114.5	106.3	105.7	105.5	100.7	94.8	109.9	109.1	..	Nonfactor Services
14.0	10.9	2.8	1.3	1.6	2.5	9.5	5.5	10.8	3.8	..	Factor Services
1,249.1	1,186.9	1,030.4	785.7	853.4	1,036.5	1,103.8	1,419.4	1,515.9	1,338.6	f	Imports of Goods & Services
1,089.1	1,061.3	952.0	712.2	758.6	857.3	912.4	1,148.7	1,179.8	1,219.6	..	Merchandise, fob
132.3	93.4	50.7	55.6	61.2	78.8	82.5	58.4	109.1	86.7	..	Nonfactor Services
27.7	32.2	27.7	17.8	33.6	100.4	108.9	212.4	227.0	32.3	..	Factor Services
41.7	39.1	39.3	34.4	30.7	23.5	29.9	37.4	32.3	28.4	..	Long-Term Interest
21.8	22.6	25.4	18.8	62.1	233.3	250.6	230.0	231.9	182.4	..	Private Current Transfers, net
8.0	9.0	7.0	7.0	14.0	45.0	48.0	41.0	0.0	..	..	Workers' Remittances
-465.6	-355.6	-474.8	-280.6	-294.7	-409.5	-394.7	-742.4	-776.8	-628.3	..	Curr. A/C Bal before Off. Transf.
107.9	108.7	94.7	85.2	97.0	223.0	224.4	477.1	389.3	469.8	..	Net Official Transfers
-357.7	-247.0	-380.1	-195.4	-197.7	-186.5	-170.3	-265.3	-387.5	-158.5	..	Curr. A/C Bal after Off. Transf.
289.1	295.3	345.1	331.2	255.4	20.5	153.7	-36.5	30.7	26.2	f	Long-Term Capital, net
..	..	..	..	..	..	..	..	..	..	..	Direct Investment
346.6	293.4	339.7	390.0	190.6	131.6	162.9	71.5	148.1	120.2	..	Long-Term Loans
401.9	357.8	383.9	430.9	225.6	172.7	199.4	109.1	185.2	157.5	..	Disbursements
55.3	64.4	44.2	40.9	35.0	41.1	36.5	37.6	37.1	37.3	..	Repayments
-57.5	1.9	5.4	-58.8	64.8	-111.1	-9.2	-108.0	-117.4	-94.0	..	Other Long-Term Capital
2.4	-45.1	35.2	-91.5	-16.8	158.2	79.8	200.2	312.7	140.6	f	Other Capital, net
66.1	-3.3	-0.2	-44.3	-40.8	7.8	-63.2	101.6	44.1	-8.3	..	Change in Reserves
				(Tanzania Shillings per US dollar)							**Memo Item:**
8.200	8.280	9.280	11.140	15.290	17.470	32.700	64.260	99.290	143.380	..	Conversion Factor (Annual Avg)
			(Millions of US dollars), outstanding at end of year								
2,571.7	2,694.3	2,985.4	3,379.9	3,431.4	3,867.1	4,167.1	4,838.9	5,138.9	4,917.5	..	**EXTERNAL DEBT (Total)**
2,264.5	2,386.4	2,558.7	2,848.5	2,767.9	3,084.4	3,799.2	4,347.1	4,578.8	4,645.9	..	Long-Term Debt (by debtor)
171.3	146.4	126.1	92.2	59.0	57.8	71.2	113.5	141.4	128.5	..	Central Bank, incl. IMF credit
1,508.5	1,666.9	1,845.4	2,192.0	2,165.7	2,465.1	3,337.3	3,800.0	4,132.1	4,245.7	..	Central Government
..	..	..	..	..	..	..	..	..	..	..	Rest of General Government
449.5	434.5	434.1	420.4	408.9	469.5	320.5	358.5	248.7	220.2	..	Non-financial Public Enterprises
135.2	138.6	153.1	143.9	134.3	92.0	70.2	75.1	56.6	51.5	..	Priv. Sector, incl non-guaranteed
307.2	307.9	426.7	531.4	663.5	782.7	367.9	491.8	560.1	271.6	..	Short-Term Debt
				(Thousands of US dollars)							**Memo Items:**
20,300	18,828	4,822	19,415	26,869	16,000	61,090	31,799	77,714	54,213	..	Int'l Reserves Excluding Gold
..	..	..	..	..	..	..	..	..	..	..	Gold Holdings (at market price)
											SOCIAL INDICATORS
6.7	6.7	6.8	6.8	6.8	6.8	6.8	6.8	6.7	6.7	..	Total Fertility Rate
119.0	117.0	115.0	113.2	111.4	109.6	107.8	106.0	104.4	102.7	..	Infant Mortality Rate
49.7	50.1	50.6	51.1	51.6	52.1	52.6	53.2	53.4	53.7	..	Life Expectancy at Birth
16.5	18.1	19.7	21.2	22.8	24.4	26.5	28.6	30.0	31.4	..	Urban Population, % of total
109.0	109.1	106.4	106.4	104.2	103.9	101.1	100.0	98.0	99.7	..	Food Prod. per capita (1987=100)
85.6	..	..	..	..	..	..	..	..	..	..	Labor Force, Agriculture (%)
49.8	49.6	49.4	49.3	49.1	48.9	48.7	48.5	48.3	48.1	..	Labor Force, Female (%)
93.0	..	90.0	87.0	83.0	72.0	69.0	66.0	..	..	..	Primary Schl. Enroll. Ratio
86.0	..	85.0	85.0	81.0	71.0	69.0	66.0	..	..	..	Primary Schl. Enroll. Ratio, Female
3.0	..	3.0	3.0	3.0	3.0	3.0	4.0	..	..	..	Secondary Schl. Enroll. Ratio

THAILAND	1969	1970	1971	1972	1973	1974	1975	1976	1977	1978	1979
CURRENT GNP PER CAPITA (US $)	200	210	210	220	250	300	360	410	460	530	590
POPULATION (thousands)	34,678	35,745	36,884	38,017	39,142	40,257	41,359	42,450	43,532	44,602	45,659

USE AND ORIGIN OF RESOURCES

(Billions of current Thai Baht)

	1969	1970	1971	1972	1973	1974	1975	1976	1977	1978	1979
Gross National Product (GNP)	139.4	147.6	153.3	169.5	221.2	279.1	303.3	345.6	402.3	484.6	552.6
Net Factor Income from Abroad	0.1	0.2	-0.1	-0.6	-0.9	-0.1	0.0	-0.9	-1.2	-3.6	-6.3
GDP at Market Prices	139.3	147.4	153.4	170.1	222.1	279.2	303.3	346.5	403.5	488.2	558.9
Resource Balance	-5.4	-6.5	-4.4	-1.7	-3.2	-6.6	-14.0	-8.6	-21.9	-20.6	-37.5
Exports of Goods & NFServices	21.8	22.1	24.5	30.9	41.3	60.3	55.7	70.1	80.5	97.1	126.2
Imports of Goods & NFServices	27.2	28.6	28.9	32.6	44.5	66.9	69.7	78.7	102.4	117.7	163.7
Domestic Absorption	144.6	153.9	157.8	171.8	225.3	285.8	317.3	355.1	425.4	508.8	596.4
Private Consumption, etc.	93.7	99.5	103.0	116.3	143.7	185.3	204.9	234.0	274.0	316.7	377.5
General Gov't Consumption	15.0	16.7	17.7	18.6	21.6	26.1	31.3	38.0	42.9	54.6	66.8
Gross Domestic Investment	35.9	37.7	37.1	36.9	60.0	74.4	81.1	83.1	108.5	137.5	152.1
Fixed Investment	33.0	35.0	35.8	38.6	49.9	65.0	69.4	79.4	104.6	123.3	142.9
Indirect Taxes, net	15.7	16.1	16.5	18.4	23.3	32.9	32.6	36.3	44.8	52.9	64.5
GDP at factor cost	123.6	131.3	136.9	151.7	198.8	246.3	270.7	310.2	358.7	435.3	494.4
Agriculture	39.9	38.2	36.7	43.1	61.5	75.4	81.5	92.5	100.0	119.6	134.1
Industry	34.7	37.3	41.5	46.4	59.5	74.4	78.2	95.7	118.4	144.3	169.6
Manufacturing	21.7	23.5	26.9	31.3	42.6	53.5	56.6	68.2	81.4	97.7	117.6
Services, etc.	64.6	71.9	75.2	80.6	101.1	129.4	143.6	158.3	185.1	224.3	255.2
Gross Domestic Saving	30.6	31.2	32.7	35.2	56.8	67.8	67.1	74.5	86.6	116.9	114.6
Gross National Saving	..	31.5	32.7	35.2	58.3	72.1	68.2	74.2	85.8	113.4	108.8

(Billions of 1987 Thai Baht)

	1969	1970	1971	1972	1973	1974	1975	1976	1977	1978	1979
Gross National Product	394.5	432.7	453.1	471.3	517.8	544.2	568.8	620.0	679.1	745.3	778.3
GDP at Market Prices	394.8	432.7	454.1	473.0	519.5	542.0	567.9	621.0	681.0	752.8	790.7
Resource Balance	-71.3	-67.0	-35.3	-36.5	-73.3	-56.2	-58.1	-46.2	-65.7	-62.3	-91.2
Exports of Goods & NFServices	64.5	72.6	85.8	100.1	95.6	103.0	98.1	121.8	135.4	152.2	168.1
Imports of Goods & NFServices	135.9	139.5	121.1	136.6	168.9	159.2	156.3	168.0	201.1	214.5	259.4
Domestic Absorption	466.2	499.6	489.3	509.5	592.8	598.2	626.1	667.3	746.7	815.1	882.0
Private Consumption, etc.	303.5	324.5	316.1	343.5	379.6	391.4	408.4	438.9	470.5	492.0	556.5
General Gov't Consumption	38.7	43.1	45.1	46.6	50.1	49.9	56.9	67.9	74.9	84.7	98.0
Gross Domestic Investment	124.0	132.0	128.1	119.4	163.1	156.9	160.8	160.5	201.2	238.5	227.5
Fixed Investment	101.5	119.0	119.6	120.6	132.7	132.4	131.5	148.7	184.3	204.6	212.7
GDP at factor cost	348.9	384.0	403.7	420.3	463.3	476.3	505.0	553.9	602.9	668.6	696.5
Agriculture	104.1	108.2	112.8	110.8	121.3	124.9	130.3	138.2	141.3	159.1	156.0
Industry	108.1	118.8	129.4	140.6	155.1	161.8	169.4	196.9	227.8	253.6	269.9
Manufacturing	62.6	72.6	80.4	91.2	105.5	112.2	118.6	136.7	156.5	169.9	184.2
Services, etc.	176.0	198.4	204.8	214.9	235.7	247.9	260.7	279.4	307.9	335.4	362.6

Memo Items:											
Capacity to Import	109.1	107.8	102.7	129.5	156.7	143.5	124.9	149.7	158.1	177.0	199.9
Terms of Trade Adjustment	44.6	35.3	16.8	29.4	61.2	40.5	26.7	27.9	22.7	24.7	31.8
Gross Domestic Income	439.4	467.9	470.9	502.4	580.6	582.5	594.7	648.9	703.7	777.6	822.6
Gross National Income	439.1	468.0	469.9	500.6	579.0	584.7	595.6	647.9	701.8	770.0	810.2

DOMESTIC PRICES/DEFLATORS

(Index 1987 = 100)

	1969	1970	1971	1972	1973	1974	1975	1976	1977	1978	1979
Overall (GDP)	35.3	34.1	33.8	36.0	42.8	51.5	53.4	55.8	59.3	64.8	70.7
Domestic Absorption	31.0	30.8	32.2	33.7	38.0	47.8	50.7	53.2	57.0	62.4	67.6
Agriculture	38.4	35.3	32.5	38.9	50.7	60.4	62.6	66.9	70.8	75.2	86.0
Industry	32.1	31.4	32.1	33.0	38.4	46.0	46.2	48.6	52.0	56.9	62.8
Manufacturing	34.6	32.4	33.4	34.3	40.4	47.7	47.7	49.9	52.0	57.5	63.9
Consumer Price Index	29.8	29.7	29.9	31.3	36.2	45.0	47.4	49.4	53.1	57.3	63.0

MANUFACTURING ACTIVITY

	1969	1970	1971	1972	1973	1974	1975	1976	1977	1978	1979
Employment (1987=100)	..	..	..	..	..	..	..	..	..	..	..
Real Earnings per Empl. (1987=100)	..	..	..	..	..	..	..	..	..	..	..
Real Output per Empl. (1987=100)	..	..	..	..	..	..	..	..	..	..	..
Earnings as % of Value Added	..	24.5	24.6	24.7	24.7	24.8	24.7	24.7	24.6	24.5	23.2

MONETARY HOLDINGS

(Billions of current Thai Baht)

	1969	1970	1971	1972	1973	1974	1975	1976	1977	1978	1979
Money Supply, Broadly Defined	41.1	46.5	54.0	67.0	82.4	99.1	114.7	136.8	164.0	193.3	222.2
Money	17.9	19.4	21.3	24.8	30.0	32.7	34.7	41.4	45.4	54.5	63.5
Currency Outside Banks	11.0	11.9	13.1	15.3	18.7	20.5	22.3	25.8	28.7	33.2	40.8
Demand Deposits	6.9	7.4	8.2	9.5	11.2	12.2	12.4	15.5	16.8	21.3	22.7
Quasi-Money	23.2	27.1	32.7	42.2	52.5	66.4	80.0	95.5	118.6	138.8	158.6

GOVERNMENT DEFICIT (-) OR SURPLUS

(Billions of current Thai Baht)

	1969	1970	1971	1972	1973	1974	1975	1976	1977	1978	1979
GOVERNMENT DEFICIT (-) OR SURPLUS	..	..	..	-7.09	-7.04	2.46	-6.26	-13.87	-13.14	-17.77	-20.49
Current Revenue	..	..	..	22.10	26.40	37.76	38.84	42.37	52.09	63.20	76.68
Current Expenditure	..	..	..	20.20	25.53	27.77	34.97	40.81	47.13	59.54	74.59
Current Budget Balance	..	..	..	1.89	0.87	10.00	3.87	1.57	4.96	3.66	2.09
Capital Receipts	..	..	..	0.00	..	0.00	0.00	0.53	0.01	0.01	0.00
Capital Payments	..	..	..	8.99	7.91	7.53	10.13	15.96	18.11	21.43	22.58

1980	1981	1982	1983	1984	1985	1986	1987	1988	1989	NOTES	THAILAND
									estimate		
670	750	780	810	840	800	790	850	1,030	1,230	..	CURRENT GNP PER CAPITA (US $)
46,700	47,727	48,740	49,739	50,720	51,683	52,654	53,605	54,469	55,200	..	POPULATION (thousands)
			(Billions of current Thai Baht)								USE AND ORIGIN OF RESOURCES
653.1	748.2	807.1	903.4	962.0	996.8	1,072.2	1,211.4	1,482.2	1,767.4	..	Gross National Product (GNP)
-5.4	-12.0	-12.9	-6.7	-11.4	-17.6	-22.4	-22.6	-24.8	-23.4	..	Net Factor Income from Abroad
658.5	760.2	820.0	910.1	973.4	1,014.4	1,094.7	1,234.0	1,507.0	1,790.8	f	GDP at Market Prices
-41.5	-47.7	-14.4	-66.0	-42.2	-28.8	23.0	3.2	-23.0	-41.8	..	Resource Balance
159.7	181.3	192.9	185.2	216.4	245.3	290.2	371.5	515.0	650.0	..	Exports of Goods & NFServices
201.2	229.0	207.3	251.2	258.6	274.1	267.1	368.3	537.9	691.8	..	Imports of Goods & NFServices
700.0	807.9	834.4	976.1	1,015.6	1,043.2	1,071.7	1,230.8	1,530.0	1,832.6	..	Domestic Absorption
444.6	511.2	534.6	621.4	643.0	656.4	685.8	764.6	938.8	1,098.3	..	Private Consumption, etc.
81.4	97.0	110.2	118.6	130.1	142.9	144.6	147.7	156.7	178.0	..	General Gov't Consumption
174.0	199.7	189.6	236.1	242.5	243.9	241.3	318.5	434.5	556.4	..	Gross Domestic Investment
165.7	188.0	192.2	218.5	238.6	240.3	237.4	290.5	407.3	545.3	..	Fixed Investment
76.2	84.8	87.4	104.6	115.7	113.9	127.7	150.1	84.5	80.2	..	Indirect Taxes, net
582.3	675.4	732.6	805.5	857.7	900.5	967.0	1,083.9	1,422.5	1,710.6	B f	GDP at factor cost
152.9	163.0	156.8	185.6	175.2	169.9	180.8	198.3	250.4	271.4	..	Agriculture
203.0	240.1	258.7	285.8	325.7	345.1	374.7	428.6	540.1	677.3	..	Industry
139.9	169.5	176.4	194.3	218.1	224.5	255.0	295.5	373.3	455.2	..	Manufacturing
302.6	357.1	404.5	438.7	472.5	499.4	539.2	607.2	716.5	842.0	..	Services, etc.
132.5	152.0	175.2	170.1	200.3	215.1	264.3	321.7	411.5	514.6	..	Gross Domestic Saving
128.6	141.1	164.0	166.9	190.3	198.8	243.5	301.7	387.9	492.3	..	Gross National Saving
			(Billions of 1987 Thai Baht)								
822.0	864.7	899.3	976.5	1,040.6	1,068.5	1,113.3	1,211.4	1,395.7	1,576.2	..	Gross National Product
827.6	879.4	914.9	980.3	1,050.8	1,086.0	1,136.3	1,234.0	1,419.2	1,595.9	f	GDP at Market Prices
-77.9	-55.5	-3.5	-74.1	-42.9	-11.9	17.7	3.2	-70.1	-98.5	..	Resource Balance
181.1	196.3	219.0	206.7	243.3	268.8	308.0	371.5	444.4	531.4	..	Exports of Goods & NFServices
258.9	251.8	222.5	280.7	286.2	280.7	290.4	368.3	514.5	629.9	..	Imports of Goods & NFServices
905.4	934.9	918.4	1,054.4	1 093.7	1,097.9	1,118.6	1,230.8	1,489.3	1,694.5	..	Domestic Absorption
573.7	566.4	573.3	649.2	660.3	668.3	706.4	764.6	964.3	1,114.2	..	Private Consumption, etc.
100.7	114.3	118.3	127.3	136.3	145.9	146.1	147.7	153.9	180.3	..	General Gov't Consumption
231.0	254.3	226.8	277.9	297.0	283.8	266.1	318.5	371.2	399.9	..	Gross Domestic Investment
220.5	230.5	226.1	255.2	283.0	268.0	256.6	290.5	341.9	367.8	..	Fixed Investment
728.6	777.8	813.6	863.6	921.5	959.6	1,002.0	1,083.9	1,237.4	1,409.7	B f	GDP at factor cost
158.8	167.3	172.4	180.1	190.2	201.7	202.3	198.3	222.6	236.6	..	Agriculture
279.6	295.7	304.8	329.6	357.8	357.2	382.7	428.6	510.6	597.9	..	Industry
189.4	201.4	206.3	223.8	238.9	237.5	260.2	295.5	348.1	399.4	..	Manufacturing
387.6	415.1	436.4	470.6	502.8	527.1	551.2	607.2	686.0	761.4	..	Services, etc.
											Memo Items:
205.5	199.4	207.0	207.0	239.5	251.2	315.4	371.5	492.6	591.9	..	Capacity to Import
24.5	3.1	-11.9	0.3	-3.8	-17.6	7.3	0.0	48.2	60.5	..	Terms of Trade Adjustment
852.0	882.5	902.9	980.6	1,047.0	1,068.4	1,143.6	1,234.0	1,467.4	1,656.4	..	Gross Domestic Income
846.5	867.8	887.3	976.8	1,036.8	1,050.9	1,120.6	1,211.4	1,443.9	1,636.7	..	Gross National Income
			(Index 1987 = 100)								DOMESTIC PRICES/DEFLATORS
79.6	86.4	89.6	92.8	92.6	93.4	96.3	100.0	106.2	112.2	..	Overall (GDP)
77.3	86.4	90.9	92.6	92.9	95.0	95.8	100.0	102.7	108.2	..	Domestic Absorption
96.3	97.4	90.9	103.0	92.1	84.2	89.4	100.0	112.5	114.7	..	Agriculture
72.6	81.2	84.9	86.7	91.0	96.6	97.9	100.0	105.8	113.3	..	Industry
73.9	84.2	85.5	86.8	91.3	94.5	98.0	100.0	107.2	114.0	..	Manufacturing
75.4	84.9	89.4	92.7	93.6	95.8	97.6	100.0	103.9	109.4	..	Consumer Price Index
											MANUFACTURING ACTIVITY
..	..	..	..	..	..	..	..	..	..	..	Employment (1987=100)
..	..	..	..	..	..	..	..	..	..	..	Real Earnings per Empl. (1987=100)
..	..	..	..	..	..	..	..	..	..	..	Real Output per Empl. (1987=100)
23.2	23.4	23.5	23.6	23.6	23.6	23.4	23.6	23.6	..	..	Earnings as % of Value Added
			(Billions of current Thai Baht)								MONETARY HOLDINGS
272.9	315.5	393.1	485.0	581.0	650.3	734.3	873.1	1,033.8	..	D	Money Supply, Broadly Defined
71.4	73.3	78.3	81.8	88.8	85.8	102.4	132.4	148.5	174.7	..	Money
45.9	47.8	54.0	59.6	63.5	64.0	71.1	86.7	99.0	119.0	..	Currency Outside Banks
25.6	25.5	24.3	22.2	25.2	21.9	31.4	45.7	49.5	55.7	..	Demand Deposits
201.5	242.2	314.8	403.1	492.2	564.4	631.9	740.7	885.3	..	..	Quasi-Money
			(Billions of current Thai Baht)								GOVERNMENT DEFICIT (-) OR SURPLUS
-32.27	-25.67	-53.75	-36.63	-33.98	-55.71	-48.26	-28.29	14.91	..	C	GOVERNMENT DEFICIT (-) OR SURPLUS
96.70	117.30	120.61	145.82	157.03	166.38	177.28	203.37	256.91	..	..	Current Revenue
95.62	112.25	131.36	144.10	157.18	175.22	180.75	189.79	199.92	..	..	Current Expenditure
1.08	5.05	-10.75	1.73	-0.15	-8.84	-3.48	13.58	56.99	..	..	Current Budget Balance
0.01	0.01	0.01	0.01	0.01	0.01	0.01	0.01	0.02	..	..	Capital Receipts
33.36	30.73	43.01	38.37	33.83	46.88	44.80	41.88	42.10	..	..	Capital Payments

THAILAND	1969	1970	1971	1972	1973	1974	1975	1976	1977	1978	1979
FOREIGN TRADE (CUSTOMS BASIS)					*(Millions of current US dollars)*						
Value of Exports, fob	702	710	827	1,067	1,566	2,449	2,195	2,978	3,490	4,085	5,297
Nonfuel Primary Products	629	629	706	864	1,202	2,006	1,785	2,399	2,804	3,042	3,883
Fuels	4	5	7	13	21	21	13	7	3	5	12
Manufactures	69	76	113	190	343	422	397	572	683	1,039	1,402
Value of Imports, cif	1,286	1,293	1,287	1,484	2,073	3,156	3,279	3,572	4,613	5,314	7,132
Nonfuel Primary Products	154	162	188	223	316	421	402	484	664	684	1,011
Fuels	88	113	134	152	233	625	708	832	1,026	1,130	1,605
Manufactures	1,044	1,019	965	1,110	1,524	2,109	2,170	2,256	2,923	3,501	4,515
					(Index 1987 = 100)						
Terms of Trade	192.4	178.9	160.0	151.5	176.1	182.7	148.1	136.7	137.4	145.9	141.3
Export Prices, fob	44.9	41.9	40.6	42.5	60.7	94.4	81.7	78.5	85.8	100.6	117.6
Import Prices, cif	23.3	23.4	25.4	28.0	34.5	51.6	55.2	57.4	62.5	68.9	83.2
BALANCE OF PAYMENTS					*(Millions of current US dollars)*						
Exports of Goods & Services	..	1,171	1,278	1,589	2,133	3,173	2,971	3,621	4,178	5,133	6,663
Merchandise, fob	..	686	802	1,046	1,515	2,405	2,177	2,959	3,454	4,045	5,234
Nonfactor Services	..	406	407	485	547	624	603	508	531	819	1,034
Factor Services	..	79	68	59	70	143	191	154	194	269	394
Imports of Goods & Services	..	1,470	1,496	1,700	2,323	3,501	3,676	4,108	5,315	6,326	8,808
Merchandise, fob	..	1,148	1,152	1,325	1,835	2,793	2,850	3,152	4,238	4,904	6,785
Nonfactor Services	..	262	277	302	398	565	616	735	829	985	1,329
Factor Services	..	60	67	74	91	143	211	220	248	437	694
Long-Term Interest	..	33	40	41	55	85	104	107	125	195	321
Private Current Transfers, net	..	3	7	30	117	215	56	29	22	6	23
Workers' Remittances	..	..	..	..	..	..	18	24	44	104	187
Curr. A/C Bal before Off. Transf.	..	-296	-212	-80	-74	-113	-650	-458	-1,115	-1,187	-2,123
Net Official Transfers	..	46	37	29	27	26	24	18	18	34	37
Curr. A/C Bal after Off. Transf.	..	-250	-175	-51	-46	-87	-625	-440	-1,098	-1,153	-2,086
Long-Term Capital, net	..	110	80	156	51	388	190	297	412	636	1,476
Direct Investment	..	43	39	68	77	189	22	79	106	50	51
Long-Term Loans	..	90	45	107	-4	253	200	248	330	626	1,334
Disbursements	..	220	203	246	209	422	454	519	647	1,232	1,974
Repayments	..	131	157	139	212	169	254	271	317	606	640
Other Long-Term Capital	..	-23	-4	-19	-23	-53	-32	-30	-24	-39	91
Other Capital, net	..	58	84	91	211	183	384	224	694	543	574
Change in Reserves	..	82	10	-196	-216	-485	51	-81	-9	-27	36
Memo Item:					*(Thai Baht per US dollar)*						
Conversion Factor (Annual Avg)	20.800	20.800	20.800	20.800	20.620	20.380	20.380	20.400	20.400	20.340	20.420
					(Millions of US dollars), outstanding at end of year						
EXTERNAL DEBT (Total)	..	726	782	891	903	1,161	1,352	1,686	3,344	5,029	6,625
Long-Term Debt (by debtor)	..	726	782	891	903	1,161	1,352	1,686	2,080	2,935	4,285
Central Bank, incl. IMF credit	..	0	0	0	0	0	0	78	99	249	367
Central Government	..	173	198	212	239	245	237	350	409	735	1,144
Rest of General Government	..	4	7	5	4	2	1	0	0	0	0
Non-financial Public Enterprises	..	127	130	149	181	246	345	428	646	949	1,452
Priv. Sector, incl non-guaranteed	..	422	447	525	479	668	769	829	926	1,001	1,324
Short-Term Debt	..	..	..	..	..	..	..	..	1,264	2,094	2,340
Memo Items:					*(Millions of US dollars)*						
Int'l Reserves Excluding Gold	892.8	823.5	788.0	963.4	1,206.8	1,758.2	1,678.8	1,797.5	1,812.7	2,008.6	1,842.8
Gold Holdings (at market price)	92.2	87.5	102.1	151.9	262.7	436.4	328.2	315.3	395.4	548.3	1,257.0
SOCIAL INDICATORS											
Total Fertility Rate	5.7	5.4	5.1	4.9	4.7	4.6	4.5	4.4	4.3	4.1	4.0
Infant Mortality Rate	76.4	72.6	68.8	65.0	61.7	58.3	55.0	54.0	53.0	50.0	47.0
Life Expectancy at Birth	57.9	58.4	59.0	59.6	59.9	60.2	60.6	60.9	61.2	61.5	61.9
Urban Population, % of total	13.2	13.3	13.7	14.1	14.4	14.8	15.2	15.6	16.0	16.5	16.9
Food Prod. per capita (1987=100)	84.1	85.1	84.6	79.3	93.0	89.4	95.0	97.5	94.3	105.1	99.6
Labor Force, Agriculture (%)	80.1	79.8	78.8	77.8	76.9	76.1	75.3	74.3	73.4	72.5	71.7
Labor Force, Female (%)	47.4	47.3	47.3	47.2	47.2	47.1	47.1	47.1	47.1	47.1	47.1
Primary Schl. Enroll. Ratio	..	83.0	..	..	..	..	83.0	83.0	83.0	92.0	95.0
Primary Schl. Enroll. Ratio, Female	..	79.0	..	..	..	..	80.0	79.0	80.0	89.0	92.0
Secondary Schl. Enroll. Ratio	..	17.0	..	..	..	..	26.0	27.0	28.0	28.0	28.0

1980	1981	1982	1983	1984	1985	1986	1987	1988	1989 estimate	NOTES	THAILAND
											FOREIGN TRADE (CUSTOMS BASIS)
				(Millions of current US dollars)							
6,505	7,035	6,957	6,368	7,413	7,121	8,835	11,659	15,869	14,280	..	Value of Exports, fob
4,578	4,981	4,915	4,284	4,780	4,222	4,821	5,449	7,597	..	..	Nonfuel Primary Products
41	35	28	27	50	99	70	85	80	..	..	Fuels
1,886	2,019	2,014	2,058	2,583	2,800	3,944	6,125	8,192	5,650	..	Manufactures
9,450	10,055	8,527	10,279	10,518	9,239	9,124	12,955	20,285	16,100	..	Value of Imports, cif
1,169	1,218	1,029	1,218	1,337	1,216	1,348	1,823	3,323	..	..	Nonfuel Primary Products
2,876	2,994	2,645	2,488	2,471	2,093	1,230	1,729	2,185	..	..	Fuels
5,406	5,843	4,854	6,572	6,710	5,929	6,545	9,403	14,777	..	..	Manufactures
				(Index 1987 = 100)							
129.0	114.2	97.2	105.1	101.5	93.7	104.3	100.0	97.7	..	..	Terms of Trade
130.7	117.0	96.9	97.3	92.0	83.7	92.9	100.0	112.4	..	..	Export Prices, fob
101.3	102.4	99.7	92.6	90.6	89.3	89.1	100.0	115.1	..	..	Import Prices, cif
				(Millions of current US dollars)							**BALANCE OF PAYMENTS**
8,575	9,254	9,415	9,227	10,415	10,222	12,136	15,763	21,725	26,933	f	Exports of Goods & Services
6,449	6,902	6,835	6,308	7,338	7,059	8,803	11,595	15,781	19,824	..	Merchandise, fob
1,490	1,612	1,717	1,846	1,964	2,041	2,302	3,070	4,647	5,522	..	Nonfactor Services
636	740	864	1,073	1,113	1,122	1,031	1,098	1,297	1,588	..	Factor Services
10,861	11,993	10,602	12,378	12,699	11,925	12,114	16,353	23,616	29,631	f	Imports of Goods & Services
8,352	8,931	7,565	9,169	9,236	8,391	8,415	12,019	17,856	22,772	..	Merchandise, fob
1,615	1,782	1,621	1,865	1,860	1,769	1,804	2,342	3,481	4,360	..	Nonfactor Services
895	1,280	1,415	1,344	1,603	1,764	1,895	1,992	2,279	2,499	..	Factor Services
469	705	710	747	845	910	1,030	1,066	1,161	1,105	..	Long-Term Interest
75	50	75	153	59	47	64	100	47	46	..	Private Current Transfers, net
..	..	..	..	..	..	..	..	..	..	..	Workers' Remittances
-2,212	-2,688	-1,111	-2,998	-2,225	-1,656	86	-490	-1,844	-2,652	..	Curr. A/C Bal before Off. Transf.
142	119	108	124	115	118	161	125	189	197	..	Net Official Transfers
-2,070	-2,569	-1,003	-2,874	-2,109	-1,537	247	-365	-1,655	-2,455	..	Curr. A/C Bal after Off. Transf.
2,084	1,869	1,363	1,468	1,746	1,606	55	375	1,210	4,198	f	Long-Term Capital, net
187	288	189	348	400	162	261	182	1,082	1,650	..	Direct Investment
1,802	1,593	1,325	1,256	1,507	1,519	-131	39	103	1,520	..	Long-Term Loans
2,578	2,216	2,120	2,265	2,886	3,176	1,889	1,923	2,472	3,800	..	Disbursements
776	623	796	1,009	1,379	1,657	2,020	1,884	2,369	2,280	..	Repayments
95	-13	-150	-136	-161	-75	-75	154	25	1,028	..	Other Long-Term Capital
-175	744	-441	1,246	879	13	381	902	3,011	3,269	f	Other Capital, net
161	-43	81	161	-516	-82	-684	-912	-2,566	-5,012	..	Change in Reserves
				(Thai Baht per US dollar)							Memo Item:
20.480	21.820	23.000	23.000	23.640	27.160	26.300	25.720	25.290	25.700	..	Conversion Factor (Annual Avg)
				(Millions of US dollars), outstanding at end of year							
8,258	10,809	12,198	13,868	14,981	17,528	18,554	20,707	21,827	23,466	..	**EXTERNAL DEBT (Total)**
5,955	7,931	9,157	10,563	11,430	14,328	15,714	18,043	17,027	17,354	..	Long-Term Debt (by debtor)
348	858	846	1,040	903	1,122	1,249	1,256	957	562	..	Central Bank, incl. IMF credit
1,481	1,815	2,123	2,466	2,641	4,009	4,785	6,105	6,026	5,493	..	Central Government
0	0	0	0	0	0	0	0	0	..	..	Rest of General Government
2,287	2,994	3,703	4,210	4,305	5,573	6,282	7,234	6,712	6,352	..	Non-financial Public Enterprises
1,837	2,264	2,485	2,847	3,580	3,624	3,398	3,448	3,331	4,947	..	Priv. Sector, incl non-guaranteed
2,303	2,878	3,041	3,305	3,551	3,200	2,840	2,664	4,800	6,112	..	Short-Term Debt
				(Millions of US dollars)							Memo Items:
1,560.2	1,731.8	1,537.6	1,607.1	1,920.6	2,190.1	2,804.4	4,007.1	6,096.6	9,515.3	..	Int'l Reserves Excluding Gold
1,466.1	988.6	1,136.3	948.8	766.7	813.2	972.2	1,198.6	1,015.8	992.9	..	Gold Holdings (at market price)
											SOCIAL INDICATORS
3.8	3.7	3.5	3.3	3.1	3.0	2.8	2.6	2.5	2.5	..	Total Fertility Rate
44.0	41.0	38.0	36.6	35.1	33.7	32.2	30.8	29.8	28.8	..	Infant Mortality Rate
62.2	62.5	62.9	63.3	63.7	64.1	64.6	65.0	65.3	65.6	..	Life Expectancy at Birth
17.3	17.8	18.3	18.8	19.3	19.8	20.4	20.9	21.5	22.0	..	Urban Population, % of total
103.4	105.9	104.7	106.5	108.0	112.7	102.0	100.0	108.7	111.4	..	Food Prod. per capita (1987=100)
70.9	..	..	..	..	..	..	..	..	..	..	Labor Force, Agriculture (%)
47.1	46.8	46.6	46.3	46.1	45.9	45.6	45.4	45.1	44.8	..	Labor Force, Female (%)
99.0	..	..	97.0	97.0	96.0	96.0	95.0	..	..	..	Primary Schl. Enroll. Ratio
97.0	..	..	..	..	..	..	..	..	..	..	Primary Schl. Enroll. Ratio, Female
29.0	..	..	30.0	31.0	30.0	30.0	28.0	..	..	..	Secondary Schl. Enroll. Ratio

TOGO	1969	1970	1971	1972	1973	1974	1975	1976	1977	1978	1979
CURRENT GNP PER CAPITA (US $)	140	140	140	150	170	210	260	270	310	350	360
POPULATION (thousands)	1,934	2,020	2,070	2,121	2,173	2,227	2,282	2,328	2,381	2,440	2,506
USE AND ORIGIN OF RESOURCES					*(Billions of current CFA Francs)*						
Gross National Product (GNP)	67.50	69.10	77.80	83.00	89.00	134.50	131.70	147.40	189.70	183.80	188.50
Net Factor Income from Abroad	-2.10	-1.10	-1.10	-1.60	-1.60	-0.40	-0.60	-0.60	-1.30	-2.20	-1.20
GDP at Market Prices	69.60	70.20	78.90	84.60	90.60	134.90	132.30	148.00	191.00	186.00	189.70
Resource Balance	9.43	7.61	5.48	0.68	0.11	50.08	-13.61	1.15	-21.00	-24.00	-49.76
Exports of Goods & NFServices	31.94	34.84	36.94	33.23	30.00	89.05	57.43	70.01	79.21	119.00	94.85
Imports of Goods & NFServices	22.51	27.23	31.47	32.55	29.89	38.97	71.04	68.86	100.20	143.00	144.62
Domestic Absorption	60.17	62.59	73.42	83.92	90.49	84.82	145.91	146.85	212.00	210.00	239.46
Private Consumption, etc.	44.39	40.92	43.57	49.22	54.18	43.73	80.59	76.84	112.40	77.00	98.55
General Gov't Consumption	6.58	11.07	14.96	17.20	16.60	19.00	28.72	33.21	34.00	35.00	48.31
Gross Domestic Investment	9.20	10.60	14.90	17.50	19.70	22.10	36.60	36.80	65.60	98.00	92.60
Fixed Investment	..	..	..	..	..	..	..	..	..	..	..
Indirect Taxes, net	5.60	7.60	8.10	9.20	11.90	12.20	13.90	15.80	18.10	25.20	26.50
GDP at factor cost	64.00	62.60	70.80	75.40	78.70	122.70	118.40	132.20	172.90	160.80	163.20
Agriculture	29.90	23.70	25.00	26.00	29.00	33.20	35.20	47.80	67.70	44.80	48.10
Industry	14.80	14.80	17.80	17.20	18.30	44.70	35.10	30.30	37.20	42.40	47.90
Manufacturing	7.60	7.00	7.00	6.70	7.90	8.20	9.30	10.30	12.00	11.00	13.50
Services, etc.	24.90	31.70	36.10	41.40	43.30	57.00	62.00	69.90	86.10	98.80	93.70
Gross Domestic Saving	18.63	18.21	20.38	18.18	19.81	72.18	22.99	37.95	44.60	74.00	42.83
Gross National Saving	..	16.45	18.25	15.32	18.37	71.58	22.09	37.62	43.22	71.37	41.19
					(Billions of 1987 CFA Francs)						
Gross National Product	234.88	240.19	241.78	260.47	271.72	287.90	295.13	289.04	306.77	339.08	323.95
GDP at Market Prices	240.83	242.79	243.03	262.61	273.75	286.69	293.75	287.89	306.61	340.55	323.32
Resource Balance	-9.63	-16.77	26.91	26.92	25.85	22.84	17.21	-20.22	-68.10	-58.99	-75.31
Exports of Goods & NFServices	48.69	49.44	106.41	102.82	92.07	89.05	98.67	81.88	108.29	161.19	111.31
Imports of Goods & NFServices	58.32	66.21	79.49	75.90	66.21	66.21	81.46	102.10	176.39	220.18	186.62
Domestic Absorption	250.46	259.56	216.12	235.69	247.90	263.85	276.54	308.11	374.71	399.54	398.63
Private Consumption, etc.	175.59	175.06	119.09	127.76	139.34	151.26	118.64	162.54	155.01	150.72	153.76
General Gov't Consumption	25.30	29.30	35.95	40.75	38.09	40.48	52.20	59.13	66.32	68.52	74.57
Gross Domestic Investment	49.56	55.20	61.07	67.18	70.47	72.11	105.70	86.44	153.39	180.30	170.30
Fixed Investment	..	..	..	..	..	..	..	..	..	..	..
GDP at factor cost	..	..	..	..	..	..	..	..	..	..	..
Agriculture	77.88	72.35	71.86	75.93	78.37	79.50	81.78	77.72	73.00	85.68	81.46
Industry	45.58	42.55	43.63	50.98	56.16	60.91	62.42	67.76	77.96	78.19	77.92
Manufacturing	..	..	..	..	..	..	..	27.53	28.06	23.78	25.92
Services, etc.	115.69	129.72	129.13	136.39	138.93	146.15	149.37	142.10	156.17	177.23	164.22
Memo Items:											
Capacity to Import	82.75	84.73	93.33	77.48	66.46	151.30	65.86	103.81	139.43	183.22	122.40
Terms of Trade Adjustment	34.06	35.29	-13.08	-25.34	-25.60	62.25	-32.81	21.93	31.13	22.03	11.09
Gross Domestic Income	274.89	278.08	229.95	237.27	248.15	348.94	260.94	309.81	337.75	362.59	334.41
Gross National Income	268.94	275.48	228.70	235.13	246.12	350.16	262.32	310.97	337.91	361.12	335.04
DOMESTIC PRICES/DEFLATORS					*(Index 1987 = 100)*						
Overall (GDP)	28.9	28.9	32.5	32.2	33.1	47.1	45.0	51.4	62.3	54.6	58.7
Domestic Absorption	24.0	24.1	34.0	35.6	36.5	32.1	52.8	47.7	56.6	52.6	60.1
Agriculture	38.4	32.8	34.8	34.2	37.0	41.8	43.0	61.5	92.7	52.3	59.1
Industry	32.5	34.8	40.8	33.7	32.6	73.4	56.2	44.7	47.7	54.2	61.5
Manufacturing	..	..	..	..	..	..	..	37.4	42.8	46.2	52.1
Consumer Price Index	25.4	26.5	28.3	30.4	31.5	35.6	42.0	46.9	57.4	57.7	62.0
MANUFACTURING ACTIVITY											
Employment (1987=100)	..	..	..	..	..	..	..	..	..	..	..
Real Earnings per Empl. (1987=100)	..	..	..	..	..	..	..	..	..	..	..
Real Output per Empl. (1987=100)	..	..	..	..	..	..	..	..	..	..	..
Earnings as % of Value Added	..	..	..	..	..	45.5	33.2	31.0	40.5	36.0	28.4
MONETARY HOLDINGS					*(Billions of current CFA Francs)*						
Money Supply, Broadly Defined	11.49	12.68	14.11	13.90	15.91	30.47	28.28	41.21	48.08	64.94	66.53
Money	9.69	10.15	11.88	11.82	11.56	25.08	21.56	32.94	36.45	48.09	52.66
Currency Outside Banks	4.52	4.56	5.58	5.45	6.03	8.37	9.99	14.19	15.97	20.80	21.53
Demand Deposits	5.17	5.59	6.29	6.38	5.53	16.71	11.57	18.75	20.48	27.29	31.13
Quasi-Money	1.80	2.53	2.23	2.08	4.35	5.38	6.72	8.27	11.63	16.85	13.87
GOVERNMENT DEFICIT (-) OR SURPLUS					*(Millions of current CFA Francs)*						
	..	..	..	..	..	..	..	..	-39,222	-58,836	-17,942
Current Revenue	..	..	..	..	..	..	..	..	47,022	56,646	70,008
Current Expenditure	..	..	..	..	..	..	..	..	33,753	32,500	38,873
Current Budget Balance	..	..	..	..	..	..	..	..	13,269	24,146	31,135
Capital Receipts	..	..	..	..	..	..	..	..	..	..	..
Capital Payments	..	..	..	..	..	..	..	..	52,491	82,982	49,077

1980	1981	1982	1983	1984	1985	1986	1987	1988	1989 estimate	NOTES	TOGO
420	410	350	290	260	250	270	310	370	390	..	**CURRENT GNP PER CAPITA (US $)**
2,578	2,657	2,742	2,834	2,933	3,038	3,147	3,261	3,381	3,507		**POPULATION (thousands)**
			(Billions of current CFA Francs)								**USE AND ORIGIN OF RESOURCES**
236.50	256.40	263.30	284.50	296.60	324.10	347.40	360.80	392.10	414.50	..	Gross National Product (GNP)
-3.60	-5.10	-6.70	-7.30	-17.20	-14.00	-14.90	-14.10	-14.20	-12.20		Net Factor Income from Abroad
240.10	261.50	270.00	291.80	313.80	338.10	362.30	374.90	406.30	426.70	f	GDP at Market Prices
-12.70	-17.60	-23.00	-3.70	-6.60	-29.80	-42.50	-32.30	-38.70	-31.30		Resource Balance
122.60	120.90	135.40	132.70	160.80	165.80	161.30	159.70	177.40	193.10	..	Exports of Goods & NFServices
135.30	138.50	158.40	136.40	167.40	195.60	203.80	192.00	216.10	224.40	..	Imports of Goods & NFServices
252.80	279.10	293.00	295.50	320.40	367.90	404.80	407.20	445.00	458.00	..	Domestic Absorption
126.80	150.10	170.50	180.60	201.70	214.50	245.10	252.70	290.30	295.70	..	Private Consumption, etc.
53.70	49.90	51.60	50.30	52.30	56.10	72.60	78.70	72.80	74.60	..	General Gov't Consumption
72.30	79.10	70.90	64.60	66.40	97.30	87.10	75.80	81.90	87.70	..	Gross Domestic Investment
71.80	70.70	65.80	56.70	69.80	82.80	84.20	67.20	75.40	84.30	..	Fixed Investment
29.00	33.40	36.70	39.20	37.60	41.20	41.80	41.00	45.60	..	..	Indirect Taxes, net
211.10	228.10	233.30	252.60	276.20	296.90	320.50	333.90	360.70	385.00	B	GDP at factor cost
66.00	73.70	72.80	100.60	105.00	112.00	126.20	125.90	137.70	142.20	f	Agriculture
59.50	58.80	63.10	62.50	63.40	69.50	69.70	76.10	84.60	97.40	..	Industry
18.80	18.50	19.90	19.70	20.00	22.20	26.80	28.10	31.60	36.50	..	Manufacturing
114.60	129.00	134.10	128.70	145.40	156.60	166.40	172.90	184.00	187.10	..	Services, etc.
59.60	61.50	47.90	60.90	59.80	67.50	44.60	43.50	43.20	56.40	..	Gross Domestic Saving
56.11	56.20	40.55	52.61	41.77	56.95	33.18	30.30	31.50	47.70	..	Gross National Saving
			(Billions of 1987 CFA Francs)								
368.42	353.03	337.24	317.90	324.05	339.32	353.24	360.80	380.69	396.74	..	Gross National Product
370.83	358.15	344.88	327.09	346.27	357.26	369.49	374.90	393.72	408.38	I f	GDP at Market Prices
-4.24	-14.80	-20.67	-0.90	-13.56	-30.15	-54.79	-32.30	-43.46	-42.03	..	Resource Balance
162.82	142.09	142.23	125.97	126.24	130.44	146.29	159.70	168.10	171.21	..	Exports of Goods & NFServices
167.06	156.90	162.90	126.87	139.80	160.59	201.08	192.00	211.55	213.25	..	Imports of Goods & NFServices
375.07	372.96	365.55	327.99	359.83	387.40	424.28	407.20	437.17	450.42	..	Domestic Absorption
187.66	199.03	211.77	201.81	227.87	225.42	257.30	252.70	285.83	293.25	..	Private Consumption, etc.
75.37	65.19	63.63	54.42	58.73	59.32	78.31	78.70	72.04	74.20	..	General Gov't Consumption
112.04	108.73	90.15	71.75	73.22	102.66	88.68	75.80	79.30	82.98	..	Gross Domestic Investment
111.20	97.21	84.51	63.70	76.96	87.45	85.80	67.20	72.91	79.72	..	Fixed Investment
325.51	311.75	297.39	282.94	304.34	313.29	326.63	333.90	348.82	364.11	B I	GDP at factor cost
94.95	95.14	86.74	87.50	113.67	118.26	123.99	125.90	133.92	143.86	f	Agriculture
90.29	76.28	78.50	73.34	66.52	71.12	72.60	76.10	83.84	86.42	..	Industry
29.40	30.69	31.99	29.61	24.21	26.59	27.67	28.10	29.18	32.21	..	Manufacturing
185.65	187.08	180.26	166.26	166.08	167.87	172.90	172.90	175.95	178.11	..	Services, etc.
											Memo Items:
151.38	136.96	139.25	123.43	134.29	136.12	159.15	159.70	173.67	183.50	..	Capacity to Import
-11.44	-5.13	-2.98	-2.54	8.05	5.68	12.86	0.00	5.57	12.29	..	Terms of Trade Adjustment
359.39	353.02	341.90	324.55	354.32	362.94	382.35	374.90	399.29	420.67	..	Gross Domestic Income
356.98	347.90	334.26	315.35	332.10	345.01	366.10	360.80	386.26	409.03	..	Gross National Income
			(Index 1987 = 100)								**DOMESTIC PRICES/DEFLATORS**
64.7	73.0	78.3	89.2	90.6	94.6	98.1	100.0	103.2	104.5	..	Overall (GDP)
67.4	74.8	80.2	90.1	89.0	95.0	95.4	100.0	101.8	101.7	..	Domestic Absorption
69.5	77.5	83.9	115.0	92.4	94.7	101.8	100.0	102.8	98.8	..	Agriculture
65.9	77.1	80.4	85.2	95.3	97.7	96.0	100.0	100.9	112.7	..	Industry
64.0	60.3	62.2	66.5	82.6	83.5	96.9	100.0	108.3	113.3	..	Manufacturing
69.7	83.4	92.7	101.3	97.8	96.0	99.9	100.0	99.9	99.0	..	Consumer Price Index
											MANUFACTURING ACTIVITY
..	..	..	..	..	..	..	..	..	..	G J	Employment (1987=100)
..	..	..	..	..	..	..	..	..	..	G J	Real Earnings per Empl. (1987=100)
..	..	..	..	..	..	..	..	..	..	G J	Real Output per Empl. (1987=100)
..	..	..	..	..	..	..	..	..	..	J	Earnings as % of Value Added
			(Billions of current CFA Francs)								**MONETARY HOLDINGS**
72.57	100.57	117.17	117.76	136.08	143.20	165.49	163.82	144.31	145.92	..	Money Supply, Broadly Defined
55.34	79.97	90.07	83.07	90.69	82.74	89.67	91.04	64.38	63.15	..	Money
27.76	50.74	54.29	45.50	36.99	39.21	46.02	48.27	23.20	21.33	..	Currency Outside Banks
27.57	29.23	35.78	37.57	53.69	43.52	43.65	42.77	41.18	41.83	..	Demand Deposits
17.23	20.60	27.10	34.69	45.39	60.46	75.81	72.77	79.93	82.77	..	Quasi-Money
			(Millions of current CFA Francs)								
-4,689	-14,821	-4,794	-5,607	-7,862	-6,104	-16,644	-9,380	..	..	..	**GOVERNMENT DEFICIT (-) OR SURPLUS**
72,896	70,891	81,649	85,921	102,607	116,151	120,480	99,574	..	..	..	Current Revenue
..	61,928	61,505	67,943	85,921	89,204	86,854	80,993	..	..	..	Current Expenditure
..	8,963	20,144	17,978	16,686	26,947	33,626	18,581	..	..	..	Current Budget Balance
..	..	..	..	..	97	447	8,300	..	..	..	Capital Receipts
..	23,784	24,938	23,585	24,645	33,498	50,270	36,261	..	..	..	Capital Payments

TOGO	1969	1970	1971	1972	1973	1974	1975	1976	1977	1978	1979
FOREIGN TRADE (CUSTOMS BASIS)					*(Millions of current US dollars)*						
Value of Exports, fob	72.70	68.00	73.10	69.90	71.60	215.00	141.00	158.90	199.30	262.00	290.60
Nonfuel Primary Products	67.89	64.89	63.03	67.40	67.29	208.82	133.70	150.41	190.49	213.50	245.39
Fuels	0.04	0.02	0.02	0.02	0.01	0.01	0.03	0.03	0.04	31.20	24.76
Manufactures	4.77	3.09	10.05	2.48	4.30	6.17	7.27	8.46	8.77	17.30	20.45
Value of Imports, cif	67.90	75.80	85.30	93.50	94.50	116.30	269.00	218.20	304.50	497.20	558.10
Nonfuel Primary Products	20.72	22.74	24.49	23.94	20.76	21.22	78.00	49.42	66.57	74.02	97.07
Fuels	2.63	2.82	3.85	4.75	5.19	11.49	13.01	12.77	20.40	64.77	94.93
Manufactures	44.55	50.25	56.96	64.81	68.56	83.59	177.99	156.01	217.53	358.41	366.10
					(Index 1987 = 100)						
Terms of Trade	139.1	134.8	117.6	117.2	131.2	267.5	210.1	189.2	178.9	147.0	134.9
Export Prices, fob	38.1	38.6	35.4	37.8	50.2	139.7	124.4	109.6	115.3	103.7	113.8
Import Prices, cif	27.4	28.6	30.1	32.3	38.3	52.2	59.2	58.0	64.5	70.6	84.3
BALANCE OF PAYMENTS					*(Millions of current US dollars)*						
Exports of Goods & Services	..	77.00	83.55	81.75	..	235.90	175.36	189.09	233.92	305.22	345.98
Merchandise, fob	..	68.00	73.12	69.92	71.65	215.06	140.95	158.86	199.30	261.96	290.56
Nonfactor Services	..	7.10	6.92	8.58	11.92	14.49	27.93	23.77	27.65	36.00	45.23
Factor Services	..	1.90	3.51	3.26	..	6.35	6.48	6.46	6.96	7.26	10.19
Imports of Goods & Services	..	88.20	104.21	120.84	125.17	142.22	291.96	251.02	363.23	572.78	641.74
Merchandise, fob	..	67.00	75.22	81.32	83.69	98.04	211.51	180.63	252.74	410.89	464.32
Nonfactor Services	..	14.80	20.86	28.55	28.73	38.23	69.11	60.01	90.28	134.17	145.39
Factor Services	..	6.40	8.12	10.97	12.76	5.95	11.33	10.38	20.21	27.72	32.03
Long-Term Interest	..	0.80	0.70	1.10	1.20	2.00	4.50	3.50	9.70	11.10	9.50
Private Current Transfers, net	..	-2.40	-3.71	-4.99	0.72	-0.84	-1.39	1.13	-0.32	-1.90	-2.11
Workers' Remittances	..	..	..	..	3.46	4.12	4.77	7.09	8.03	9.33	7.96
Curr. A/C Bal before Off. Transf.	..	-13.60	-24.37	-44.08	-40.89	92.84	-117.99	-60.80	-129.64	-269.46	-297.87
Net Official Transfers	..	16.40	20.86	31.16	30.28	38.94	42.49	36.23	42.35	52.08	85.12
Curr. A/C Bal after Off. Transf.	..	2.80	-3.51	-12.92	-10.61	131.78	-75.49	-24.57	-87.29	-217.37	-212.75
Long-Term Capital, net	..	-6.10	6.02	0.76	5.48	-23.46	20.60	33.58	49.01	208.16	178.96
Direct Investment	..	0.40	3.91	0.22	1.79	-39.07	5.22	5.73	11.57	93.16	52.83
Long-Term Loans	..	2.90	3.70	3.20	5.10	24.60	38.90	61.50	123.40	266.70	192.30
Disbursements	..	4.50	5.40	7.40	10.50	31.10	51.00	81.00	170.40	303.30	211.00
Repayments	..	1.60	1.70	4.20	5.40	6.50	12.10	19.50	47.00	36.60	18.70
Other Long-Term Capital	..	-9.40	-1.59	-2.66	-1.40	-8.99	-23.52	-33.65	-85.96	-151.70	-66.17
Other Capital, net	..	10.23	-1.28	5.60	3.10	-74.01	65.75	-9.35	6.07	36.63	24.13
Change in Reserves	..	-6.93	-1.23	6.56	2.03	-34.31	-10.86	0.34	32.22	-27.42	9.66
Memo Item:					*(CFA Francs per US dollar)*						
Conversion Factor (Annual Avg)	259.710	277.710	277.130	252.210	222.700	240.500	214.320	238.980	245.670	225.640	212.720
					(Millions of US dollars), outstanding at end of year						
EXTERNAL DEBT (Total)	..	39.8	46.9	47.0	58.4	89.3	119.5	185.8	368.8	734.2	1,019.3
Long-Term Debt (by debtor)	..	39.8	46.9	47.0	58.4	89.3	119.5	185.8	329.8	644.2	921.3
Central Bank, incl. IMF credit	..	1.1	0.9	0.6	0.4	0.2	0.0	8.7	9.1	8.1	14.2
Central Government	..	30.4	37.0	35.1	40.2	70.9	106.1	164.9	302.7	607.6	829.9
Rest of General Government	..	0.3	0.2	0.2	0.1	0.1	0.0	0.0	0.0	0.0	0.0
Non-financial Public Enterprises	..	3.1	3.0	3.3	7.3	6.2	3.7	2.9	9.2	13.2	56.7
Priv. Sector, incl non-guaranteed	..	4.9	5.8	7.8	10.4	11.9	9.7	9.3	8.8	15.3	20.5
Short-Term Debt	..	..	..	..	..	..	..	..	39.0	90.0	98.0
Memo Items:					*(Millions of US dollars)*						
Int'l Reserves Excluding Gold	26.32	35.35	40.52	36.47	37.92	54.46	41.19	66.62	46.13	69.99	65.46
Gold Holdings (at market price)	..	..	..	..	..	..	..	..	1.06	2.17	6.40
SOCIAL INDICATORS											
Total Fertility Rate	6.5	6.5	6.5	6.5	6.6	6.6	6.7	6.7	6.8	6.8	6.8
Infant Mortality Rate	136.2	133.8	131.4	129.0	126.6	124.2	121.8	119.4	117.0	114.6	112.2
Life Expectancy at Birth	44.0	44.5	45.0	45.5	46.0	46.5	47.0	47.5	48.0	48.5	49.0
Urban Population, % of total	12.7	13.1	13.6	14.2	14.7	15.3	15.8	16.4	17.0	17.6	18.2
Food Prod. per capita (1987=100)	128.2	134.1	136.1	125.9	125.1	120.5	121.8	114.1	109.2	118.4	122.1
Labor Force, Agriculture (%)	77.0	76.7	76.3	75.9	75.6	75.2	74.9	74.5	74.1	73.7	73.3
Labor Force, Female (%)	39.1	39.0	39.0	38.9	38.9	38.8	38.8	38.7	38.6	38.6	38.5
Primary Schl. Enroll. Ratio	..	71.0	..	..	..	..	99.0	99.0	104.0	110.0	114.0
Primary Schl. Enroll. Ratio, Female	..	44.0	..	..	..	..	68.0	70.0	77.0	84.0	88.0
Secondary Schl. Enroll. Ratio	..	7.0	..	..	..	..	19.0	22.0	26.0	29.0	32.0

1980	1981	1982	1983	1984	1985	1986	1987	1988	1989 estimate	NOTES	TOGO
				(Millions of current US dollars)							**FOREIGN TRADE (CUSTOMS BASIS)**
475.80	377.70	344.80	273.80	239.50	242.50	275.00	297.00	337.00	..	f	Value of Exports, fob
353.55	351.12	312.01	237.30	204.50	209.50	258.00	275.00	307.03	..	..	Nonfuel Primary Products
86.86	2.73	3.40	3.40	0.00	0.00	0.00	0.00	0.00	..	..	Fuels
35.39	23.85	29.39	33.10	35.00	33.00	17.00	22.00	29.97	..	f	Manufactures
637.80	503.70	486.60	349.70	310.00	358.00	408.00	409.00	413.00	..	f	Value of Imports, cif
144.78	157.66	145.60	109.52	97.02	155.42	149.92	167.01	179.00	..	..	Nonfuel Primary Products
125.22	36.67	48.01	30.00	29.98	31.58	17.08	20.99	20.00	..	..	Fuels
367.80	309.38	293.00	210.18	183.00	171.00	241.00	221.00	214.00	..	f	Manufactures
				(Index 1987 = 100)							
142.4	147.7	134.2	124.3	128.0	112.3	108.2	100.0	100.3	..	..	Terms of Trade
144.5	141.8	124.0	112.3	114.9	101.8	103.3	100.0	108.7	..	..	Export Prices, fob
101.5	96.0	92.4	90.3	89.7	90.6	95.5	100.0	108.4	..	..	Import Prices, cif
				(Millions of current US dollars)							**BALANCE OF PAYMENTS**
570.35	490.39	449.77	360.23	384.89	392.51	486.01	436.55	485.48	481.49	f	Exports of Goods & Services
475.77	377.71	344.82	273.51	290.97	282.00	352.61	282.50	324.66	325.07	..	Merchandise, fob
73.87	97.07	88.29	70.63	76.76	86.97	105.90	131.10	137.65	134.79	..	Nonfactor Services
20.70	15.61	16.66	16.10	17.15	23.55	27.50	22.96	23.17	21.63	..	Factor Services
751.52	618.21	603.19	468.74	431.76	497.09	660.26	627.21	627.84	610.96	f	Imports of Goods & Services
524.12	413.94	408.16	291.78	263.20	303.75	413.49	362.02	352.19	345.13	..	Merchandise, fob
166.77	145.96	136.03	117.73	112.61	131.82	179.06	194.32	202.45	196.86	..	Nonfactor Services
60.63	58.31	59.01	59.24	55.95	61.51	67.72	70.87	73.19	68.96	..	Factor Services
19.30	20.00	23.40	27.10	36.80	38.70	43.10	28.90	68.60	32.50	..	Long-Term Interest
0.54	-0.74	-1.98	-2.61	-1.89	7.67	10.06	2.99	8.39	10.97	..	Private Current Transfers, net
9.93	7.86	6.11	6.08	6.61	15.41	21.42	14.31	14.77	14.11	..	Workers' Remittances
-180.64	-113.63	-155.39	-111.12	-48.77	-96.90	-164.19	-187.66	-133.96	-118.49	..	Curr. A/C Bal before Off. Transf.
85.64	69.48	68.56	67.73	74.96	69.48	91.71	70.54	71.51	72.10	..	Net Official Transfers
-95.00	-44.15	-86.84	-43.38	26.18	-27.42	-72.48	-117.12	-62.45	-46.39	..	Curr. A/C Bal after Off. Transf.
70.69	8.35	-38.07	52.51	10.26	32.75	11.91	-2.99	161.83	79.00	f	Long-Term Capital, net
42.34	10.09	16.10	1.52	-9.89	16.60	6.54	..	..	..	..	Direct Investment
81.50	17.60	34.00	50.10	14.70	1.70	4.50	18.00	88.90	41.30	..	Long-Term Loans
100.00	35.50	51.20	72.80	52.60	53.10	88.40	49.60	112.10	65.40	..	Disbursements
18.50	17.90	17.20	22.70	37.90	51.40	83.90	31.60	23.20	24.10	..	Repayments
-53.15	-19.33	-88.17	0.89	5.46	14.45	0.87	-20.99	72.93	37.70	..	Other Long-Term Capital
22.53	119.39	163.26	11.35	8.37	20.27	30.22	92.18	-182.25	9.42	..	Other Capital, net
1.78	-83.59	-38.35	-20.47	-44.81	-25.61	30.35	27.94	82.87	-42.02	f	Change in Reserves
				(CFA Francs per US dollar)							**Memo Item:**
211.300	271.730	328.620	381.070	436.960	449.260	346.300	300.540	297.850	319.010	..	Conversion Factor (Annual Avg)
			(Millions of US dollars), outstanding at end of year								
1,045.1	969.5	955.6	915.3	806.6	937.1	1,065.1	1,234.7	1,223.5	1,185.5	..	**EXTERNAL DEBT (Total)**
931.9	855.6	828.5	850.0	743.6	863.1	975.9	1,133.0	1,137.2	1,021.8	..	Long-Term Debt (by debtor)
32.5	38.2	36.2	54.4	62.2	74.2	90.3	85.3	77.9	75.4	..	Central Bank, incl. IMF credit
825.4	763.5	740.2	757.6	638.4	735.8	831.8	984.9	997.8	895.0	..	Central Government
0.0	0.0	0.0	0.0	0.0	0.0	0.0	0.0	0.0	..	..	Rest of General Government
67.0	48.9	45.8	33.5	39.4	48.8	49.1	56.9	56.3	46.8	..	Non-financial Public Enterprises
7.0	5.0	6.3	4.5	3.6	4.3	4.7	5.9	5.2	4.6	..	Priv. Sector, incl non-guaranteed
113.2	113.9	127.1	65.3	63.0	74.0	89.2	101.7	86.3	163.7	..	Short-Term Debt
				(Millions of US dollars)							**Memo Items:**
77.57	151.51	167.66	172.85	203.28	296.62	332.66	354.90	232.10	285.28	..	Int'l Reserves Excluding Gold
7.37	4.97	5.71	4.77	3.85	4.09	4.89	6.05	5.13	5.01	..	Gold Holdings (at market price)
											SOCIAL INDICATORS
6.8	6.8	6.8	6.8	6.8	6.8	6.8	6.8	6.7	6.6	..	Total Fertility Rate
109.8	130.0	105.0	102.8	100.6	98.4	96.2	98.0	88.0	90.4	..	Infant Mortality Rate
49.5	50.2	47.0	49.0	51.5	52.0	52.5	52.5	52.5	53.5	..	Life Expectancy at Birth
18.8	19.5	20.1	20.8	21.4	22.1	23.0	23.9	24.5	25.1	..	Urban Population, % of total
116.4	114.0	109.7	98.9	108.4	105.1	103.5	100.0	106.3	108.9	..	Food Prod. per capita (1987=100)
73.0	..	..	..	..	..	..	..			..	Labor Force, Agriculture (%)
38.5	38.3	38.0	37.8	37.6	37.5	37.2	37.0	36.8	36.6	..	Labor Force, Female (%)
71.0	72.1	68.4	63.1	55.5	52.6	57.9	85.7	86.1		..	Primary Schl. Enroll. Ratio
93.0	93.0	88.0	79.0	75.0	73.0	78.0	78.0			..	Primary Schl. Enroll. Ratio, Female
34.0	..	29.0	24.0	21.0	21.0	21.0	24.0			..	Secondary Schl. Enroll. Ratio

TONGA	1969	1970	1971	1972	1973	1974	1975	1976	1977	1978	1979
CURRENT GNP PER CAPITA (US $)	..	..	..	..	..	..	..	..	..	..	..
POPULATION (thousands)	84	86	87	88	89	89	90	91	92	93	93
USE AND ORIGIN OF RESOURCES						*(Millions of current Tongan Pa'anga)*					
Gross National Product (GNP)	..	..	..	..	..	..	..	..	..	..	..
Net Factor Income from Abroad	..	..	..	..	..	..	..	..	..	..	..
GDP at Market Prices	..	..	..	..	..	..	24.83	24.58	30.79	36.32	39.96
Resource Balance	..	..	..	..	..	..	-7.32	-7.30	-7.18	-14.19	-17.47
Exports of Goods & NFServices	..	..	..	..	..	..	10.26	6.62	10.43	10.46	10.42
Imports of Goods & NFServices	..	..	..	..	..	..	17.59	13.92	17.60	24.65	27.89
Domestic Absorption	..	..	..	..	..	..	32.15	31.88	37.96	50.51	57.43
Private Consumption, etc.	..	..	..	..	..	..	22.08	22.33	27.04	34.45	39.02
General Gov't Consumption	..	..	..	..	..	..	3.23	4.71	4.71	5.34	5.96
Gross Domestic Investment	..	..	..	..	..	..	6.85	4.83	6.22	10.72	12.45
Fixed Investment	..	..	..	..	..	..	5.66	4.86	5.90	8.96	11.24
Indirect Taxes, net	..	..	..	..	..	..	..	..	..	..	..
GDP at factor cost	..	..	..	..	..	..	21.01	21.46	26.68	31.03	34.71
Agriculture	..	..	..	..	..	..	10.53	9.82	11.71	12.97	14.48
Industry	..	..	..	..	..	..	2.18	2.27	3.03	4.34	5.25
Manufacturing	..	..	..	..	..	..	1.11	1.30	1.77	2.30	2.69
Services, etc.	..	..	..	..	..	..	8.31	9.37	11.94	13.72	14.98
Gross Domestic Saving	..	..	..	..	..	..	-0.47	-2.46	-0.96	-3.48	-5.02
Gross National Saving	..	..	..	..	..	..	..	..	..	..	..
						(Millions of 1980 Tongan Pa'anga)					
Gross National Product	..	..	..	..	..	..	..	..	..	..	..
GDP at Market Prices	..	..	..	..	..	..	..	..	..	..	..
Resource Balance	..	..	..	..	..	..	..	..	..	..	..
Exports of Goods & NFServices	..	..	..	..	..	..	..	..	..	..	..
Imports of Goods & NFServices	..	..	..	..	..	..	..	..	..	..	..
Domestic Absorption	..	..	..	..	..	..	..	..	..	..	..
Private Consumption, etc.	..	..	..	..	..	..	..	..	..	..	..
General Gov't Consumption	..	..	..	..	..	..	..	..	..	..	..
Gross Domestic Investment	..	..	..	..	..	..	..	..	..	..	..
Fixed Investment	..	..	..	..	..	..	..	..	..	..	..
GDP at factor cost	..	..	..	..	..	..	33.36	34.83	36.35	36.95	38.29
Agriculture	..	..	..	..	..	..	15.47	17.02	16.55	15.35	15.24
Industry	..	..	..	..	..	..	3.51	3.12	3.78	4.74	5.46
Manufacturing	..	..	..	..	..	..	2.15	2.17	2.59	2.73	2.80
Services, etc.	..	..	..	..	..	..	14.38	14.69	16.01	16.86	17.58
Memo Items:											
Capacity to Import	..	..	..	..	..	..	..	..	..	..	..
Terms of Trade Adjustment	..	..	..	..	..	..	..	..	..	..	..
Gross Domestic Income	..	..	..	..	..	..	..	..	..	..	..
Gross National Income	..	..	..	..	..	..	..	..	..	..	..
DOMESTIC PRICES/DEFLATORS						*(Index 1980 = 100)*					
Overall (GDP)	..	..	..	..	..	..	..	..	..	..	..
Domestic Absorption	..	..	..	..	..	..	..	..	..	..	..
Agriculture	..	..	..	..	..	..	68.1	57.7	70.7	84.5	95.0
Industry	..	..	..	..	..	..	62.1	72.7	80.2	91.6	96.2
Manufacturing	..	..	..	..	..	..	51.7	59.9	68.3	84.2	96.1
Consumer Price Index	..	..	..	..	..	..	27.0	28.9	34.0	37.2	39.2
MANUFACTURING ACTIVITY											
Employment (1987=100)	..	..	..	..	..	..	..	..	..	..	..
Real Earnings per Empl. (1987=100)	..	..	..	..	..	..	..	..	..	..	..
Real Output per Empl. (1987=100)	..	..	..	..	..	..	..	..	..	..	..
Earnings as % of Value Added	..	..	..	..	..	..	..	..	..	..	..
MONETARY HOLDINGS						*(Thousands of current Tongan Pa'anga)*					
Money Supply, Broadly Defined	..	..	..	..	..	..	..	..	..	..	..
Money	..	..	..	..	..	..	..	..	..	..	..
Currency Outside Banks	..	..	..	..	..	..	..	..	..	..	..
Demand Deposits	..	..	..	..	..	..	..	..	..	..	..
Quasi-Money	..	..	..	..	..	..	..	..	..	..	..
						(Millions of current Tongan Pa'anga)					
GOVERNMENT DEFICIT (-) OR SURPLUS	..	..	..	..	..	..	..	..	..	..	..
Current Revenue	..	..	..	..	..	..	..	..	..	..	..
Current Expenditure	..	..	..	..	..	..	..	..	..	..	..
Current Budget Balance	..	..	..	..	..	..	..	..	..	..	..
Capital Receipts	..	..	..	..	..	..	..	..	..	..	..
Capital Payments	..	..	..	..	..	..	..	..	..	..	..

1980	1981	1982	1983	1984	1985	1986	1987	1988	1989 estimate	NOTES	TONGA
..	..	..	..	..	750	760	760	800	910	..	**CURRENT GNP PER CAPITA (US $)**
94	94	95	95	95	95	95	96	97	98	..	**POPULATION (thousands)**
				(Millions of current Tongan Pa'anga)							**USE AND ORIGIN OF RESOURCES**
..	57.72	63.69	70.17	80.31	82.60	101.90	108.19	114.47	125.13	C f	Gross National Product (GNP)
..	3.36	3.01	3.23	5.83	2.60	3.02	3.19	3.47	3.63	..	Net Factor Income from Abroad
46.77	54.36	60.68	66.94	74.47	80.00	98.88	105.00	111.00	121.50	C f	GDP at Market Prices
-16.07	-20.69	-24.75	-27.36	-26.78	-41.60	..	..	..	..	..	Resource Balance
14.06	14.31	16.45	14.31	19.83	20.10	..	..	..	..	..	Exports of Goods & NFServices
30.13	35.00	41.20	41.66	46.61	61.70	..	..	..	..	..	Imports of Goods & NFServices
62.85	75.05	85.43	94.30	101.25	121.60	..	..	..	..	..	Domestic Absorption
42.56	53.58	59.53	63.10	64.23	78.60	..	..	..	..	..	Private Consumption, etc.
6.86	7.68	10.82	10.30	11.80	14.10	..	..	..	..	..	General Gov't Consumption
13.43	13.79	15.09	20.89	25.22	28.90	..	..	..	..	..	Gross Domestic Investment
12.19	12.56	14.21	20.23	24.67	28.40	..	..	..	..	..	Fixed Investment
..	..	8.40	9.31	10.10	10.86	..	..	..	..	..	Indirect Taxes, net
40.58	47.31	52.29	57.63	64.38	69.14	..	..	..	..	C f	GDP at factor cost
15.62	17.83	24.28	25.45	28.75	28.54	..	..	..	..	..	Agriculture
5.86	7.17	7.69	9.78	11.57	13.15	..	..	..	..	..	Industry
2.84	4.47	4.67	5.06	5.80	6.57	..	..	..	..	..	Manufacturing
19.10	22.31	20.32	22.41	24.06	27.44	..	..	..	..	..	Services, etc.
-2.64	-6.90	-9.66	-6.46	-1.56	-12.70	..	..	..	..	..	Gross Domestic Saving
..	10.47	18.68	13.75	22.17	13.10	..	..	..	..	..	Gross National Saving
				(Millions of 1980 Tongan Pa'anga)							
..	..	..	..	..	..	..	..	..	..	C f	Gross National Product
..	..	..	..	..	..	..	..	..	..	..	GDP at Market Prices
..	..	..	..	..	..	..	..	..	..	..	Resource Balance
..	..	..	..	..	..	..	..	..	..	..	Exports of Goods & NFServices
..	..	..	..	..	..	..	..	..	..	..	Imports of Goods & NFServices
..	..	..	..	..	..	..	..	..	..	..	Domestic Absorption
..	..	..	..	..	..	..	..	..	..	..	Private Consumption, etc.
..	..	..	..	..	..	..	..	..	..	..	General Gov't Consumption
..	..	..	..	..	..	..	..	..	..	..	Gross Domestic Investment
..	..	..	..	..	..	..	..	..	..	..	Fixed Investment
40.58	40.33	45.39	46.01	47.21	50.50	52.46	54.21	53.83	55.61	C f	GDP at factor cost
15.62	15.04	16.50	14.82	15.09	16.47	16.99	17.60	15.83	16.45	..	Agriculture
5.86	5.67	5.14	6.07	6.65	7.04	6.95	7.15	7.49	7.95	..	Industry
2.84	4.95	5.18	5.30	5.56	5.90	6.77	6.99	6.99	7.22	..	Manufacturing
19.10	19.62	23.75	25.12	25.46	26.99	28.52	29.46	30.51	31.21	..	Services, etc.
											Memo Items:
..	..	..	..	..	..	..	..	..	..	..	Capacity to Import
..	..	..	..	..	..	..	..	..	..	..	Terms of Trade Adjustment
..	..	..	..	..	..	..	..	..	..	..	Gross Domestic Income
..	..	..	..	..	..	..	..	..	..	..	Gross National Income
				(Index 1980 = 100)							**DOMESTIC PRICES/DEFLATORS**
..	..	..	..	..	..	..	..	..	..	..	Overall (GDP)
..	..	..	..	..	..	..	..	..	..	..	Domestic Absorption
100.0	118.5	147.1	171.8	190.5	173.3	..	..	..	..	..	Agriculture
100.0	126.4	149.6	161.1	173.9	186.7	..	..	..	..	..	Industry
100.0	90.3	90.1	95.5	104.4	111.3	..	..	..	..	..	Manufacturing
48.0	55.2	61.2	67.2	67.2	78.5	95.5	100.0	109.9	114.5	f	Consumer Price Index
											MANUFACTURING ACTIVITY
..	..	..	..	..	..	..	..	..	..	..	Employment (1987=100)
..	..	..	..	..	..	..	..	..	..	..	Real Earnings per Empl. (1987=100)
..	..	..	..	..	..	..	..	..	..	..	Real Output per Empl. (1987=100)
..	33.8	..	..	..	..	..	..	..	..	..	Earnings as % of Value Added
				(Thousands of current Tongan Pa'anga)							**MONETARY HOLDINGS**
..	..	..	..	..	..	27,000	36,100	..	..	..	Money Supply, Broadly Defined
..	..	7,417	9,619	10,054	10,929	13,291	15,198	15,685	17,171	..	Money
..	..	2,505	3,168	3,404	3,569	4,474	4,892	5,503	5,971	..	Currency Outside Banks
..	..	4,912	6,451	6,650	7,360	8,817	10,306	10,182	11,200	..	Demand Deposits
..	..	..	..	..	..	13,709	20,902	..	..	..	Quasi-Money
				(Millions of current Tongan Pa'anga)							
..	..	..	..	1.0	-3.0	-1.0	-4.0	2.0	..	..	**GOVERNMENT DEFICIT (-) OR SURPLUS**
..	..	..	..	34.0	38.0	39.0	56.0	53.0	..	..	Current Revenue
..	..	..	..	17.0	20.0	26.0	30.0	30.0	..	..	Current Expenditure
..	..	..	..	17.0	18.0	14.0	26.0	23.0	..	..	Current Budget Balance
..	..	..	..	..	..	..	..	..	..	..	Capital Receipts
..	..	..	..	16.0	21.0	14.0	30.0	21.0	..	..	Capital Payments

TONGA	1969	1970	1971	1972	1973	1974	1975	1976	1977	1978	1979
FOREIGN TRADE (CUSTOMS BASIS)					*(Thousands of current US dollars)*						
Value of Exports, fob	..	..	2,700	2,900	3,500	4,900	7,400	4,400	4,100	7,700	5,800
Nonfuel Primary Products	..	..	..	..	..	..	..	..	..	..	..
Fuels	..	..	..	..	..	..	..	..	..	..	..
Manufactures	..	..	..	..	..	..	..	..	..	..	..
Value of Imports, cif	..	..	7,000	9,000	11,000	17,000	18,300	16,000	20,000	26,000	29,000
Nonfuel Primary Products	..	..	..	..	..	..	..	..	..	..	..
Fuels	..	..	..	..	..	..	..	..	..	..	..
Manufactures	..	..	..	..	..	..	..	..	..	..	..
Terms of Trade					*(Index 1987 = 100)*						
Export Prices, fob	..	..	..	..	..	..	..	..	..	..	..
Import Prices, cif	..	..	..	..	..	..	..	..	..	..	..
BALANCE OF PAYMENTS					*(Thousands of current US dollars)*						
Exports of Goods & Services	..	..	3,999	4,765	5,779	8,656	15,391	9,698	10,166	14,400	13,900
Merchandise, fob	..	..	2,705	2,905	3,543	4,863	7,435	4,382	4,123	7,600	5,800
Nonfactor Services	..	..	1,025	1,413	1,970	3,461	7,603	4,661	5,367	5,800	6,200
Factor Services	..	..	269	447	266	332	353	655	676	1,000	1,900
Imports of Goods & Services	..	..	6,182	8,098	9,808	12,872	22,289	18,843	18,845	23,600	27,000
Merchandise, fob	..	..	5,236	6,691	8,243	10,801	18,277	15,699	14,840	18,500	22,700
Nonfactor Services	..	..	927	1,376	1,493	1,926	3,952	2,926	3,665	4,900	3,900
Factor Services	..	..	19	31	72	145	60	219	340	200	400
Long-Term Interest	..	..	..	..	..	..	..	..	..	..	..
Private Current Transfers, net	..	..	1,641	1,933	3,244	5,148	7,230	7,197	6,757	8,300	10,800
Workers' Remittances	..	..	694	479	1,420	4,311	6,546	5,240	5,407	0	0
Curr. A/C Bal before Off. Transf.	..	..	-543	-1,400	-785	931	333	-1,948	-1,922	-900	-2,300
Net Official Transfers	..	..	..	..	..	..	..	..	..	300	-100
Curr. A/C Bal after Off. Transf.	..	..	-543	-1,400	-785	931	333	-1,948	-1,922	-600	-2,400
Long-Term Capital, net	..	..	1,300	786	1,193	251	2,262	2,034	1,467	2,900	1,600
Direct Investment	..	..	..	..	..	..	..	..	..	0	0
Long-Term Loans	..	0	0	600	1,300	900	200	0	400	900	2,000
Disbursements	..	0	0	600	1,300	900	200	0	400	1,000	2,100
Repayments	..	0	0	0	0	0	0	0	0	100	100
Other Long-Term Capital	..	..	1,300	186	-107	-649	2,062	2,034	1,067	2,000	-400
Other Capital, net	..	..	-728	360	-445	550	-613	-2,409	2,798	-2,700	500
Change in Reserves	..	..	-28	254	37	-1,733	-1,982	2,323	-2,343	400	300
Memo Item:					*(Tongan Pa'anga per US dollar)*						
Conversion Factor (Annual Avg)	0.890	0.890	0.890	0.850	0.780	0.680	0.730	0.790	0.870	0.890	0.880
				(Thousands of US dollars), outstanding at end of year							
EXTERNAL DEBT (Total)	..	400	500	1,000	2,200	3,100	2,900	2,400	3,100	4,200	6,400
Long-Term Debt (by debtor)	..	400	500	1,000	2,200	3,100	2,900	2,400	3,100	4,200	6,400
Central Bank, incl. IMF credit	..	..	..	..	..	..	..	..	..	..	..
Central Government	..	400	500	1,000	2,200	3,100	2,900	2,400	3,100	4,200	6,400
Rest of General Government	..	..	..	..	..	..	..	..	..	..	..
Non-financial Public Enterprises	..	..	..	..	..	..	..	..	..	..	..
Priv. Sector, incl non-guaranteed	..	..	..	..	..	..	..	..	..	..	..
Short-Term Debt	..	..	..	..	..	..	..	..	..	..	..
Memo Items:					*(Thousands of US dollars)*						
Int'l Reserves Excluding Gold	..	..	..	..	..	..	..	..	9,001	10,116	12,560
Gold Holdings (at market price)	..	..	..	..	..	..	..	..	..	..	..
SOCIAL INDICATORS											
Total Fertility Rate	6.7	6.5	6.3	6.1	5.9	5.7	5.5	5.3	5.1	5.0	4.9
Infant Mortality Rate	56.8	57.2	57.6	58.0	58.4	58.8	59.2	59.6	60.0	56.6	53.2
Life Expectancy at Birth	..	..	..	..	..	..	..	58.0	58.8	59.6	60.4
Urban Population, % of total	21.3	21.4	21.2	21.0	20.9	20.7	20.5	20.3	20.2	20.0	19.9
Food Prod. per capita (1987=100)	120.1	112.0	113.8	120.0	116.0	119.7	125.7	126.6	121.2	113.8	113.8
Labor Force, Agriculture (%)	..	..	..	..	..	..	..	..	..	..	..
Labor Force, Female (%)	..	..	..	..	..	..	..	..	..	..	..
Primary Schl. Enroll. Ratio	..	..	..	..	..	..	..	..	..	..	..
Primary Schl. Enroll. Ratio, Female	..	..	..	..	..	..	..	..	..	..	..
Secondary Schl. Enroll. Ratio	..	..	..	..	..	..	..	..	..	..	..

1980	1981	1982	1983	1984	1985	1986	1987	1988	1989 estimate	NOTES	TONGA
											FOREIGN TRADE (CUSTOMS BASIS)
7,300	7,600	8,000	5,100	7,200	7,500	4,900	5,600	7,000	..	..	Value of Exports, fob
..	..	..	..	..	..	..	..	..	..	..	Nonfuel Primary Products
..	..	..	..	..	..	..	..	..	..	..	Fuels
..	..	..	..	..	..	..	..	..	..	..	Manufactures
..	..	..	38,000	42,000	41,000	40,000	48,000	55,000	..	..	Value of Imports, cif
..	..	..	..	..	..	..	..	..	..	..	Nonfuel Primary Products
..	..	..	..	4,700	4,100	4,600	4,700	..	..	..	Fuels
..	..	..	..	..	..	..	..	..	..	..	Manufactures

(Index 1987 = 100)

1980	1981	1982	1983	1984	1985	1986	1987	1988	1989 estimate	NOTES	TONGA
..	..	..	..	..	..	..	..	..	..	..	Terms of Trade
..	..	..	..	..	..	..	..	..	..	..	Export Prices, fob
..	..	..	..	..	..	..	..	..	..	..	Import Prices, cif

(Thousands of current US dollars)

1980	1981	1982	1983	1984	1985	1986	1987	1988	1989 estimate	NOTES	TONGA
											BALANCE OF PAYMENTS
17,400	20,400	23,000	16,700	22,400	25,900	23,700	29,000	31,100	..	C f	Exports of Goods & Services
7,300	7,600	8,000	3,500	7,200	7,900	5,900	7,000	6,400	..	..	Merchandise, fob
7,100	8,300	10,800	10,000	12,000	15,100	14,800	18,100	18,900	..	..	Nonfactor Services
3,000	4,500	4,200	3,200	3,200	2,900	3,000	3,900	5,800	..	..	Factor Services
32,500	42,900	44,900	47,100	44,500	46,500	49,000	52,100	69,400	..	C f	Imports of Goods & Services
27,100	37,100	38,600	37,500	33,400	31,800	32,300	35,100	44,100	..	..	Merchandise, fob
4,900	5,200	5,300	9,500	10,900	14,600	16,300	16,900	24,000	..	..	Nonfactor Services
500	600	1,000	100	200	100	400	100	1,300	..	..	Factor Services
..	100	100	200	200	200	200	400	400	1,200	..	Long-Term Interest
12,200	16,100	25,700	15,300	15,700	16,200	23,100	22,400	21,300	..	..	Private Current Transfers, net
0	0	0	15,500	13,900	14,900	20,800	20,300	20,300	..	..	Workers' Remittances
-2,900	-6,400	3,800	-15,100	-6,400	-4,400	-2,200	-700	-17,000	..	..	Curr. A/C Bal before Off. Transf.
-200	-1,200	-400	15,200	6,700	3,200	3,100	6,300	5,700	..	..	Net Official Transfers
-3,100	-7,600	3,400	100	300	-1,200	900	5,600	-11,300	..	..	Curr. A/C Bal after Off. Transf.
1,800	2,000	7,000	100	300	800	900	900	3,700	..	C f	Long-Term Capital, net
0	0	0	0	0	0	100	200	100	..	..	Direct Investment
13,100	3,900	2,300	600	1,400	800	5,000	5,800	2,500	100	..	Long-Term Loans
13,200	4,100	2,500	900	1,800	1,300	5,600	6,400	3,300	800	..	Disbursements
100	200	200	300	400	500	600	600	800	700	..	Repayments
-11,300	-1,900	4,700	-500	-1,100	0	-4,200	-5,100	1,100	..	..	Other Long-Term Capital
200	5,200	-11,900	-300	-6,600	-3,400	-2,300	-7,700	6,800	..	C f	Other Capital, net
1,100	400	1,500	100	6,000	3,800	500	1,200	800	5,646	..	Change in Reserves

(Tongan Pa'anga per US dollar)

1980	1981	1982	1983	1984	1985	1986	1987	1988	1989 estimate	NOTES	TONGA
											Memo Item:
0.900	0.860	0.910	1.070	1.100	1.300	1.430	1.510	1.370	1.230	..	Conversion Factor (Annual Avg)

(Thousands of US dollars), outstanding at end of year

1980	1981	1982	1983	1984	1985	1986	1987	1988	1989 estimate	NOTES	TONGA
18,900	20,400	21,400	20,000	19,100	24,200	32,800	44,900	44,500	45,200	..	**EXTERNAL DEBT (Total)**
18,900	20,400	21,400	20,000	19,100	23,500	32,300	44,400	43,900	44,100	..	Long-Term Debt (by debtor)
..	..	..	..	..	..	..	..	..	..	..	Central Bank, incl. IMF credit
18,900	20,400	21,400	20,000	19,100	23,500	32,300	43,200	41,300	41,700	..	Central Government
..	..	..	..	..	..	..	i ..	..	..	..	Rest of General Government
..	..	..	..	..	0	0	600	1,400	1,100	..	Non-financial Public Enterprises
..	..	..	..	..	0	0	600	1,200	1,300	..	Priv. Sector, incl non-guaranteed
..	..	..	..	..	700	500	500	600	1,100	..	Short-Term Debt

(Thousands of US dollars)

1980	1981	1982	1983	1984	1985	1986	1987	1988	1989 estimate	NOTES	TONGA
											Memo Items:
13,753	13,981	15,561	20,953	26,017	27,510	22,482	28,881	30,510	24,851	..	Int'l Reserves Excluding Gold
..	..	..	..	..	..	..	..	..	..	..	Gold Holdings (at market price)
											SOCIAL INDICATORS
4.8	4.8	4.7	4.6	4.5	4.4	4.3	4.2	4.2	4.1	..	Total Fertility Rate
49.8	46.4	43.0	39.6	36.2	32.8	29.4	26.0	24.7	23.4	..	Infant Mortality Rate
61.2	62.0	62.5	63.1	63.8	64.4	65.1	65.7	66.1	66.5	..	Life Expectancy at Birth
19.7	19.7	19.7	19.7	19.7	19.7	19.9	20.0	20.2	20.3	..	Urban Population, % of total
116.6	117.7	107.7	103.7	102.8	101.9	103.7	100.0	101.3	102.3	..	Food Prod. per capita (1987=100)
..	..	..	..	..	..	..	..	..	..	..	Labor Force, Agriculture (%)
..	..	..	..	..	..	..	..	..	..	..	Labor Force, Female (%)
..	..	..	..	..	..	..	..	..	..	..	Primary Schl. Enroll. Ratio
..	..	..	..	..	..	..	..	..	..	..	Primary Schl. Enroll. Ratio, Female
..	..	..	..	..	..	..	..	..	..	..	Secondary Schl. Enroll. Ratio

TRINIDAD AND TOBAGO	1969	1970	1971	1972	1973	1974	1975	1976	1977	1978	1979
CURRENT GNP PER CAPITA (US $)	790	810	840	960	1,100	1,340	1,920	2,440	2,770	3,310	3,740
POPULATION (thousands)	959	971	979	986	994	1,003	1,012	1,023	1,036	1,050	1,066
USE AND ORIGIN OF RESOURCES				*(Millions of current Trinidad & Tobago Dollars)*							
Gross National Product (GNP)	1,415	1,513	1,639	1,945	2,384	3,607	5,119	5,826	7,069	8,363	10,440
Net Factor Income from Abroad	-143	-130	-132	-136	-180	-586	-181	-265	-464	-187	-606
GDP at Market Prices	1,558	1,644	1,771	2,081	2,564	4,193	5,300	6,090	7,533	8,550	11,046
Resource Balance	66	18	-91	-139	148	1,028	943	956	953	375	634
Exports of Goods & NFServices	677	703	757	824	1,132	2,378	2,808	3,401	3,733	3,766	4,979
Imports of Goods & NFServices	611	685	848	963	984	1,350	1,865	2,445	2,779	3,391	4,345
Domestic Absorption	1,492	1,626	1,862	2,220	2,416	3,165	4,357	5,134	6,579	8,175	10,412
Private Consumption, etc.	1,038	986	980	1,234	1,385	1,774	2,256	2,896	3,605	4,443	5,663
General Gov't Consumption	187	215	280	334	366	475	652	743	967	1,148	1,536
Gross Domestic Investment	268	425	602	652	665	915	1,449	1,496	2,008	2,584	3,213
Fixed Investment	272	344	581	615	579	651	1,085	1,398	1,735	2,323	2,952
Indirect Taxes, net	83	94	107	127	133	76	90	62	112	49	-231
GDP at factor cost	1,475	1,550	1,664	1,954	2,432	4,117	5,210	6,029	7,421	8,501	11,276
Agriculture	76	80	85	107	111	135	174	238	261	302	322
Industry	670	684	740	885	1,199	2,474	3,159	3,587	4,389	4,686	6,430
Manufacturing	367	396	410	482	514	686	792	876	1,027	1,074	1,567
Services, etc.	729	786	839	962	1,122	1,508	1,877	2,204	2,771	3,513	4,524
Gross Domestic Saving	334	443	511	513	814	1,943	2,392	2,452	2,961	2,959	3,847
Gross National Saving	..	318	384	383	630	1,342	2,187	2,162	2,459	2,722	3,176
				(Millions of 1987 Trinidad & Tobago Dollars)							
Gross National Product	13,629	14,320	14,435	15,532	15,592	14,999	16,487	17,688	18,591	21,381	21,150
GDP at Market Prices	14,413	14,922	15,078	15,949	16,213	16,791	16,909	18,311	19,545	21,678	22,199
Resource Balance	1,772	1,766	1,071	1,511	1,807	1,595	886	664	481	188	-530
Exports of Goods & NFServices	2,776	2,927	2,500	2,902	3,231	3,182	2,866	3,158	2,989	3,010	3,234
Imports of Goods & NFServices	1,004	1,161	1,429	1,391	1,424	1,587	1,980	2,494	2,508	2,821	3,764
Domestic Absorption	12,641	13,157	14,007	14,438	14,407	15,195	16,023	17,647	19,064	21,490	22,729
Private Consumption, etc.	10,567	10,426	10,328	10,827	10,956	10,982	10,794	11,798	13,214	14,336	14,816
General Gov't Consumption	1,118	1,282	1,407	1,611	1,646	1,608	2,070	2,233	2,118	2,375	2,982
Gross Domestic Investment	956	1,448	2,272	2,001	1,805	2,606	3,159	3,615	3,733	4,779	4,931
Fixed Investment	..	..	..	..	..	..	..	..	..	..	..
GDP at factor cost	13,612	14,036	14,133	14,935	15,336	16,417	16,549	18,045	19,172	21,453	22,539
Agriculture	887	1,006	966	1,068	983	966	1,005	973	981	939	906
Industry	6,417	6,619	6,823	7,277	7,423	7,913	7,858	8,868	9,074	10,339	10,644
Manufacturing	2,257	2,362	2,350	2,468	2,422	2,526	2,198	2,607	2,531	2,669	2,738
Services, etc.	5,529	5,647	5,596	5,836	6,096	6,651	6,877	7,097	8,166	8,957	9,841
Memo Items:											
Capacity to Import	1,113	1,192	1,276	1,191	1,638	2,795	2,981	3,469	3,369	3,133	4,313
Terms of Trade Adjustment	-1,663	-1,735	-1,225	-1,711	-1,592	-387	114	311	379	124	1,079
Gross Domestic Income	12,750	13,187	13,853	14,238	14,621	16,404	17,024	18,622	19,924	21,802	23,278
Gross National Income	11,966	12,585	13,211	13,821	13,999	14,612	16,602	17,999	18,970	21,505	22,228
DOMESTIC PRICES/DEFLATORS					*(Index 1987 = 100)*						
Overall (GDP)	10.8	11.0	11.7	13.1	15.8	25.0	31.3	33.3	38.5	39.4	49.8
Domestic Absorption	11.8	12.4	13.3	15.4	16.8	20.8	27.2	29.1	34.5	38.0	45.8
Agriculture	8.5	8.0	8.8	10.0	11.3	14.0	17.3	24.5	26.6	32.2	35.6
Industry	10.4	10.3	10.8	12.2	16.1	31.3	40.2	40.4	48.4	45.3	60.4
Manufacturing	16.3	16.8	17.4	19.5	21.2	27.2	36.0	33.6	40.6	40.3	57.2
Consumer Price Index	13.4	13.7	14.2	15.5	17.8	21.7	25.4	28.2	31.5	34.7	39.8
MANUFACTURING ACTIVITY											
Employment (1987=100)	96.3	102.5	107.0	115.8	120.0	115.7	119.6	131.1	133.9	139.5	146.4
Real Earnings per Empl. (1987=100)	..	..	..	..	..	76.3	76.3	78.5	81.7	88.9	..
Real Output per Empl. (1987=100)	..	..	..	..	..	74.9	67.9	86.1	82.7	88.1	..
Earnings as % of Value Added	..	..	..	..	..	34.3	36.8	40.1	39.3	47.3	..
MONETARY HOLDINGS				*(Millions of current Trinidad & Tobago Dollars)*							
Money Supply, Broadly Defined	424	504	620	742	844	1,100	1,563	2,108	2,695	3,457	4,426
Money	140	151	177	211	213	270	392	572	725	936	1,147
Currency Outside Banks	51	57	68	81	80	99	138	177	231	296	412
Demand Deposits	89	95	108	130	133	171	254	395	494	641	735
Quasi-Money	284	353	443	531	631	830	1,171	1,536	1,969	2,521	3,279
				(Millions of current Trinidad & Tobago Dollars)							
GOVERNMENT DEFICIT (-) OR SURPLUS	..	..	..	..	..	..	..	499.9	799.7	301.6	-61.0
Current Revenue	..	..	..	..	..	..	..	2,340.5	3,037.9	3,153.0	4,118.7
Current Expenditure	..	..	..	..	..	..	..	948.5	1,069.0	1,461.4	2,108.8
Current Budget Balance	..	..	..	..	..	..	..	1,392.0	1,968.9	1,691.6	2,009.9
Capital Receipts	..	..	..	..	..	..	..	0.3	6.0	2.5	0.1
Capital Payments	..	..	..	..	..	..	..	892.4	1,175.2	1,392.5	2,071.0

1980	1981	1982	1983	1984	1985	1986	1987	1988	1989 estimate	NOTES	TRINIDAD AND TOBAGO
4,690	5,890	6,630	6,400	6,400	5,940	4,970	4,060	3,410	3,230	..	**CURRENT GNP PER CAPITA (US $)**
1,082	1,099	1,118	1,137	1,157	1,178	1,199	1,220	1,241	1,261	..	**POPULATION (thousands)**
			(Millions of current Trinidad & Tobago Dollars)								**USE AND ORIGIN OF RESOURCES**
14,219	15,948	19,335	18,764	18,282	16,927	16,403	16,219	15,907	15,874	..	Gross National Product (GNP)
-747	-490	160	-355	-804	-886	-784	-1,012	-1,310	-1,773	..	Net Factor Income from Abroad
14,966	16,438	19,176	19,119	19,086	17,813	17,188	17,231	17,217	17,647	..	GDP at Market Prices
1,716	1,590	-1,418	-1,918	-325	1,135	-1,457	210	850	1,222	..	Resource Balance
7,550	7,542	6,703	5,637	5,870	10,243	6,512	6,825	7,445	7,573	..	Exports of Goods & NFServices
5,834	5,952	8,121	7,555	6,195	9,108	7,969	6,614	6,595	6,351	..	Imports of Goods & NFServices
13,249	14,848	20,594	21,037	19,411	16,678	18,645	17,021	16,368	16,425	..	Domestic Absorption
6,865	8,197	12,041	12,748	11,676	9,091	10,713	9,766	9,906	9,946	..	Private Consumption, etc.
1,804	2,110	3,136	3,320	3,616	4,163	4,108	3,811	3,499	3,199	..	General Gov't Consumption
4,580	4,541	5,417	4,969	4,119	3,424	3,824	3,444	2,963	3,280	..	Gross Domestic Investment
4,204	4,342	5,189	4,770	3,954	3,424	4,058	3,326	2,963	3,280	..	Fixed Investment
-588	-537	-856	-664	-141	-17	436	934	-641	-197	..	Indirect Taxes, net
15,554	16,975	20,032	19,783	19,226	17,831	16,752	16,297	17,858	17,844	..	GDP at factor cost
337	386	432	815	867	376	510	514	497	501	..	Agriculture
9,358	9,799	9,564	8,364	8,158	7,214	6,504	6,925	6,607	7,378	..	Industry
1,338	1,118	1,349	1,448	1,433	1,325	1,391	1,389	1,372	1,485	..	Manufacturing
5,860	6,791	10,035	10,604	10,201	10,240	9,738	8,858	10,755	9,964	..	Services, etc.
6,297	6,131	3,999	3,051	3,794	4,559	2,367	3,654	3,813	4,502	..	Gross Domestic Saving
5,449	5,476	3,963	2,525	2,818	3,537	1,472	2,569	2,414	2,630	..	Gross National Saving
			(Millions of 1987 Trinidad & Tobago Dollars)								
22,780	24,207	23,924	21,659	19,839	18,053	17,638	16,219	15,248	14,718	..	Gross National Product
23,887	24,803	23,645	21,963	20,467	18,939	18,352	17,231	16,555	16,259	..	GDP at Market Prices
-544	-250	-1,681	-1,500	-441	22	412	210	550	623	..	Resource Balance
3,491	3,437	3,121	3,037	3,302	5,702	6,717	6,825	7,098	5,862	..	Exports of Goods & NFServices
4,035	3,686	4,801	4,536	3,743	5,681	6,305	6,614	6,548	5,239	..	Imports of Goods & NFServices
24,431	25,053	25,326	23,462	20,909	18,918	17,940	17,021	16,005	15,636	..	Domestic Absorption
15,228	16,389	16,595	15,743	13,225	10,113	9,815	9,766	9,622	9,340	..	Private Consumption, etc.
3,157	3,624	3,420	2,985	2,992	3,943	3,852	3,811	3,525	3,483	..	General Gov't Consumption
6,046	5,040	5,311	4,734	4,691	4,861	4,273	3,444	2,859	2,813	..	Gross Domestic Investment
..	..	..	..	..	..	..	..	..	..	..	Fixed Investment
24,703	25,493	24,634	22,659	19,945	18,956	17,847	16,297	17,029	16,540	..	GDP at factor cost
835	824	850	994	989	592	462	514	467	723	..	Agriculture
11,165	11,377	10,046	9,029	8,380	8,135	7,533	6,925	6,665	6,539	..	Industry
2,806	2,623	1,894	1,731	1,536	1,474	1,538	1,389	1,277	1,224	..	Manufacturing
11,756	12,408	13,538	12,636	10,575	10,229	9,852	8,858	9,897	9,278	..	Services, etc.
											Memo Items:
5,222	4,671	3,963	3,385	3,547	6,389	5,153	6,825	7,392	6,246	..	Capacity to Import
1,731	1,235	842	348	245	686	-1,565	0	294	385	..	Terms of Trade Adjustment
25,618	26,038	24,487	22,311	20,712	19,626	16,787	17,231	16,849	16,643	..	Gross Domestic Income
24,511	25,442	24,766	22,007	20,084	18,739	16,074	16,219	15,542	15,103	..	Gross National Income
			(Index 1987 = 100)								**DOMESTIC PRICES/DEFLATORS**
62.7	66.3	81.1	87.1	93.2	94.1	93.7	100.0	104.0	108.5	..	Overall (GDP)
54.2	59.3	81.3	89.7	92.8	88.2	103.9	100.0	102.3	105.1	..	Domestic Absorption
40.4	46.8	50.9	82.0	87.7	63.6	110.4	100.0	106.5	69.3	..	Agriculture
83.8	86.1	95.2	92.6	97.3	88.7	86.3	100.0	99.1	112.8	..	Industry
47.7	42.6	71.2	83.6	93.3	89.9	90.4	100.0	107.4	121.3	..	Manufacturing
46.8	53.5	59.7	68.7	77.9	83.8	90.3	100.0	107.8	120.1	..	Consumer Price Index
											MANUFACTURING ACTIVITY
145.1	152.6	144.8	132.4	125.8	109.8	103.0	100.0	99.3	..	..	Employment (1987=100)
..	102.6	112.7	120.4	108.3	111.4	110.7	100.0	..	..	..	Real Earnings per Empl. (1987=100)
..	129.5	89.3	87.5	92.4	100.6	98.1	100.0	..	..	..	Real Output per Empl. (1987=100)
..	73.8	78.3	72.0	69.3	82.2	72.2	69.6	..	..	..	Earnings as % of Value Added
			(Millions of current Trinidad & Tobago Dollars)								**MONETARY HOLDINGS**
5,159	6,672	9,027	9,990	10,481	10,791	10,622	..	..	..	D	Money Supply, Broadly Defined
1,337	1,855	2,547	2,435	2,294	2,260	2,073	2,170	1,892	2,144	..	Money
467	532	726	758	710	685	723	703	689	704	..	Currency Outside Banks
870	1,323	1,821	1,676	1,584	1,576	1,350	1,468	1,204	1,440	..	Demand Deposits
3,822	4,817	6,480	7,555	8,187	8,531	8,549	..	..	..	..	Quasi-Money
			(Millions of current Trinidad & Tobago Dollars)								
1,105.6	545.8	..	..	..	..	..	..	..	..	..	**GOVERNMENT DEFICIT (-) OR SURPLUS**
6,463.8	7,200.6	..	..	..	..	..	..	..	..	..	Current Revenue
2,815.3	3,123.1	..	..	..	..	..	..	..	..	..	Current Expenditure
3,648.5	4,077.5	..	..	..	..	..	..	..	..	..	Current Budget Balance
24.0	32.2	..	..	..	..	..	..	..	..	..	Capital Receipts
2,566.9	3,563.9	..	..	..	..	..	..	..	..	..	Capital Payments

TRINIDAD AND TOBAGO	1969	1970	1971	1972	1973	1974	1975	1976	1977	1978	1979
FOREIGN TRADE (CUSTOMS BASIS)					*(Millions of current US dollars)*						
Value of Exports, fob	474.6	481.5	520.5	557.6	695.7	2,037.7	1,772.7	2,219.3	2,179.8	2,042.7	2,610.4
Nonfuel Primary Products	44.0	46.4	44.4	53.1	52.2	88.4	117.1	89.0	77.6	66.1	83.3
Fuels	366.2	371.9	402.8	433.6	571.8	1,838.7	1,543.2	2,007.3	1,997.1	1,829.4	2,370.3
Manufactures	64.4	63.2	73.2	70.9	71.8	110.6	112.4	123.0	105.1	147.2	156.9
Value of Imports, cif	482.7	543.4	662.8	762.1	792.2	1,846.5	1,488.5	1,976.3	1,808.5	1,979.9	2,104.6
Nonfuel Primary Products	67.3	68.3	74.7	88.3	105.8	157.2	165.1	173.8	215.0	262.4	318.3
Fuels	253.6	287.6	330.4	364.1	402.1	1,327.8	752.6	1,131.4	861.0	798.1	601.9
Manufactures	161.8	187.5	257.7	309.6	284.3	361.5	570.8	671.0	732.5	919.4	1,184.4
					(Index 1987 = 100)						
Terms of Trade	78.2	78.4	77.9	76.4	78.2	107.8	108.9	109.9	112.0	104.6	123.1
Export Prices, fob	9.1	9.1	11.7	13.1	17.8	65.7	64.3	67.9	74.3	74.7	105.6
Import Prices, cif	11.6	11.7	15.0	17.1	22.7	61.0	59.1	61.8	66.4	71.4	85.8
BALANCE OF PAYMENTS					*(Millions of current US dollars)*						
Exports of Goods & Services	..	349.8	389.1	448.1	572.1	1,172.3	1,333.2	1,451.0	1,625.5	1,689.7	2,227.5
Merchandise, fob	..	225.3	217.2	254.5	333.3	928.1	987.4	1,054.3	1,175.2	1,221.9	1,648.8
Nonfactor Services	..	119.1	166.4	187.8	233.8	224.8	302.5	336.4	373.2	342.8	418.8
Factor Services	..	5.4	5.4	5.8	5.0	19.5	43.3	60.3	77.0	125.0	159.9
Imports of Goods & Services	..	456.7	553.9	568.7	593.7	880.8	980.2	1,165.5	1,420.2	1,609.0	2,215.8
Merchandise, fob	..	276.2	355.6	384.2	371.5	482.3	658.1	766.0	867.8	1,057.5	1,334.1
Nonfactor Services	..	108.8	129.2	108.7	131.8	169.3	195.6	233.8	285.1	351.9	469.3
Factor Services	..	71.7	69.2	75.8	90.4	229.2	126.5	165.7	267.3	199.6	412.4
Long-Term Interest	..	6.1	4.6	6.3	8.1	14.4	11.9	8.9	6.8	21.1	40.5
Private Current Transfers, net	..	2.6	3.0	2.9	-2.0	-7.3	-10.9	-10.5	-15.8	-20.8	-27.1
Workers' Remittances	..	2.7	3.2	3.3	2.6	2.5	2.6	1.6	1.4	1.4	1.4
Curr. A/C Bal before Off. Transf.	..	-104.3	-161.9	-117.7	-23.6	284.2	342.1	275.0	189.4	59.8	-15.4
Net Official Transfers	..	-4.3	-7.0	-6.2	-6.3	-10.1	-10.3	-19.5	-15.3	-17.1	-18.5
Curr. A/C Bal after Off. Transf.	..	-108.6	-168.9	-123.9	-29.9	274.1	331.8	255.4	174.1	42.7	-33.9
Long-Term Capital, net	..	80.3	98.3	103.1	58.8	69.4	43.1	14.1	230.7	262.3	432.0
Direct Investment	..	83.2	103.3	86.1	65.6	120.1	93.0	132.2	83.5	128.8	93.8
Long-Term Loans	..	-2.5	-1.2	22.2	28.9	4.5	-3.7	-50.8	151.3	112.5	156.8
Disbursements	..	7.5	19.4	27.1	37.3	44.7	11.2	17.1	157.6	121.4	165.8
Repayments	..	10.0	20.6	4.9	8.4	40.2	14.9	67.9	6.3	8.9	9.0
Other Long-Term Capital	..	-0.4	-3.8	-5.2	-35.7	-55.3	-46.1	-67.2	-4.1	21.0	181.4
Other Capital, net	..	9.3	83.1	0.4	-35.7	-55.5	83.2	-69.1	39.1	32.5	-54.2
Change in Reserves	..	19.0	-12.5	20.3	6.8	-288.0	-458.1	-200.5	-443.9	-337.5	-343.8
Memo Item:					*(Trinidad & Tobago Dollars per US dollar)*						
Conversion Factor (Annual Avg)	2.000	2.000	1.970	1.920	1.960	2.050	2.170	2.440	2.400	2.400	2.400
					(Millions of US dollars), outstanding at end of year						
EXTERNAL DEBT (Total)	..	100.7	101.5	122.1	150.8	155.4	148.8	96.0	339.3	486.6	680.7
Long-Term Debt (by debtor)	..	100.7	101.5	122.1	150.8	155.4	148.8	96.0	247.3	369.6	514.7
Central Bank, incl. IMF credit	..	0.0	0.0	0.0	0.0	0.0	0.0	0.0	0.0	0.0	0.0
Central Government	..	74.8	75.1	92.4	118.5	108.4	95.8	60.5	209.1	329.0	378.7
Rest of General Government	..	..	..	..	..	..	..	..	..	..	..
Non-financial Public Enterprises	..	25.9	26.4	29.7	31.7	44.8	49.6	31.5	33.8	34.9	125.7
Priv. Sector, incl non-guaranteed	..	0.0	0.0	0.0	0.6	2.2	3.4	4.0	4.4	5.7	10.3
Short-Term Debt	..	..	..	..	..	..	..	..	92.0	117.0	166.0
Memo Items:					*(Millions of US dollars)*						
Int'l Reserves Excluding Gold	44.7	43.0	69.4	58.3	47.0	390.3	751.0	1,013.6	1,481.7	1,804.8	2,140.0
Gold Holdings (at market price)	..	..	..	..	..	..	..	..	4.5	9.1	27.6
SOCIAL INDICATORS											
Total Fertility Rate	3.7	3.6	3.5	3.4	3.4	3.3	3.3	3.3	3.2	3.2	3.2
Infant Mortality Rate	36.6	34.4	32.2	30.0	29.2	28.4	27.6	26.8	26.0	24.4	22.8
Life Expectancy at Birth	66.0	66.2	66.3	66.5	66.7	66.9	67.1	67.3	67.5	67.9	68.3
Urban Population, % of total	37.0	38.8	40.7	42.6	44.6	46.5	48.4	50.1	51.8	53.5	55.2
Food Prod. per capita (1987=100)	259.3	294.1	271.2	289.3	247.6	240.6	237.1	243.1	226.5	201.7	163.2
Labor Force, Agriculture (%)	18.9	18.6	17.7	16.8	16.0	15.2	14.4	13.5	12.6	11.8	10.9
Labor Force, Female (%)	29.3	29.6	29.2	28.8	28.5	28.1	27.8	28.1	28.3	28.5	28.7
Primary Schl. Enroll. Ratio	..	106.0	..	..	..	..	99.0	96.0	94.0	91.0	91.0
Primary Schl. Enroll. Ratio, Female	..	107.0	..	..	..	..	100.0	97.0	95.0	92.0	92.0
Secondary Schl. Enroll. Ratio	..	42.0	..	..	..	..	48.0	56.0	58.0	61.0	..

1980	1981	1982	1983	1984	1985	1986	1987	1988	1989 estimate	NOTES	TRINIDAD AND TOBAGO
				(Millions of current US dollars)							**FOREIGN TRADE (CUSTOMS BASIS)**
4,080.0	3,760.0	3,090.0	2,352.7	2,173.4	2,160.9	1,385.7	1,462.0	1,412.0	..	..	Value of Exports, fob
86.8	77.1	70.9	58.4	57.1	53.2	65.2	77.0	93.9	..	..	Nonfuel Primary Products
3,787.3	3,368.1	2,697.0	1,963.9	1,760.6	1,710.0	980.4	1,040.1	853.1	..	..	Fuels
205.9	314.8	322.1	330.4	355.7	397.7	340.1	344.9	465.0	..	..	Manufactures
3,180.0	3,120.0	3,700.0	2,582.0	1,919.1	1,533.0	1,369.8	1,218.7	1,127.0	..	..	Value of Imports, cif
432.2	486.4	558.0	567.9	532.2	422.1	301.9	330.8	275.7	..	..	Nonfuel Primary Products
1,197.8	1,142.4	931.9	82.7	14.4	50.9	38.8	52.4	134.3	..	..	Fuels
1,550.0	1,491.1	2,210.1	1,931.4	1,372.5	1,060.0	1,029.1	835.5	717.0	..	..	Manufactures
				(Index 1987 = 100)							
155.8	161.4	162.5	166.2	161.8	155.8	89.9	100.0	82.3	..	..	Terms of Trade
167.4	177.3	157.5	140.6	134.5	129.4	82.8	100.0	88.8	..	..	Export Prices, fob
107.4	109.9	96.9	84.6	83.1	83.0	92.1	100.0	108.0	..	..	Import Prices, cif
				(Millions of current US dollars)							**BALANCE OF PAYMENTS**
3,371.2	3,488.3	3,146.2	2,575.9	2,581.3	2,594.3	1,738.6	1,634.9	1,747.0	1,880.9	..	Exports of Goods & Services
2,541.7	2,612.3	2,228.6	2,026.5	2,110.7	2,110.7	1,363.1	1,396.9	1,453.3	1,534.0	..	Merchandise, fob
597.3	531.3	560.6	319.1	329.0	287.8	278.8	221.2	273.3	325.3	..	Nonfactor Services
232.3	344.7	357.0	230.3	141.5	195.8	96.8	16.8	20.3	21.6	..	Factor Services
2,972.3	3,021.4	3,651.0	3,498.2	3,020.5	2,625.2	2,130.4	1,840.3	1,881.8	1,998.7	..	Imports of Goods & Services
1,789.1	1,763.5	2,486.7	2,233.3	1,704.9	1,354.6	1,209.4	1,057.6	1,064.2	1,175.3	..	Merchandise, fob
639.8	709.1	873.8	886.6	839.2	713.1	606.3	484.6	456.5	384.6	..	Nonfactor Services
543.4	548.8	290.5	378.3	476.5	557.6	314.7	298.0	361.1	438.8	..	Factor Services
50.4	83.2	74.8	122.4	75.2	96.0	118.1	122.3	107.3	138.2	..	Long-Term Interest
-42.3	-68.9	-81.5	-71.3	-71.5	-55.4	-30.8	-20.2	-23.0	-23.3	..	Private Current Transfers, net
1.4	1.4	1.4	1.4	0.3	0.2	0.2	0.3	1.7	..	..	Workers' Remittances
356.7	398.0	-586.4	-993.5	-510.7	-86.4	-422.6	-225.6	-157.8	-141.1	..	Curr. A/C Bal before Off. Transf.
-22.0	-23.5	-58.5	-9.3	-11.7	-4.0	-19.1	-16.6	-6.6	..	..	Net Official Transfers
334.7	374.5	-644.9	-1,002.9	-522.5	-90.3	-441.7	-242.2	-164.4	-141.1	..	Curr. A/C Bal after Off. Transf.
322.8	323.5	534.5	282.8	13.2	32.4	-74.3	-59.8	-37.9	156.5	..	Long-Term Capital, net
184.5	258.1	203.5	114.1	109.7	-7.0	-21.8	31.3	62.9	35.7	..	Direct Investment
187.0	99.4	126.4	129.2	66.0	143.6	156.4	-129.2	167.0	-9.5	..	Long-Term Loans
362.8	128.8	177.5	280.7	176.4	298.7	347.5	135.5	338.1	55.5	..	Disbursements
175.8	29.4	51.1	151.5	110.4	155.1	191.1	264.7	171.1	65.0	..	Repayments
-48.8	-33.9	204.6	39.5	-162.6	-104.3	-208.8	38.2	-267.8	130.3	..	Other Long-Term Capital
-9.2	-129.5	-96.6	-152.7	-183.6	-243.3	-205.7	46.3	59.4	13.4	..	Other Capital, net
-648.3	-568.6	206.9	872.8	692.9	301.3	721.6	255.6	142.8	-28.8	..	Change in Reserves
				(Trinidad & Tobago Dollars per US dollar)							**Memo Item:**
2.400	2.400	2.400	2.400	2.400	2.450	3.600	3.600	3.840	4.250	..	Conversion Factor (Annual Avg)
				(Millions of US dollars), outstanding at end of year							
828.5	1,049.8	1,202.8	1,438.2	1,221.9	1,448.2	1,857.7	1,805.1	2,039.8	2,012.0	..	**EXTERNAL DEBT (Total)**
712.5	794.8	906.8	1,026.2	1,062.9	1,299.2	1,584.7	1,639.0	1,877.3	1,885.0	..	Long-Term Debt (by debtor)
0.0	0.0	0.0	0.0	0.0	0.0	0.0	0.0	114.5	204.7	..	Central Bank, incl. IMF credit
468.6	465.4	555.3	674.2	707.0	890.8	947.9	1,032.9	1,212.3	1,323.4	..	Central Government
..	..	..	..	..	..	..	..	..	..	..	Rest of General Government
227.8	311.4	334.2	336.1	340.4	389.7	617.4	584.2	532.8	340.4	..	Non-financial Public Enterprises
16.1	18.0	17.3	15.9	15.5	18.7	19.4	21.9	17.7	16.5	..	Priv. Sector, incl non-guaranteed
116.0	255.0	296.0	412.0	159.0	149.0	273.0	166.1	162.5	127.0	..	Short-Term Debt
				(Millions of US dollars)							**Memo Items:**
2,780.8	3,347.5	3,080.5	2,104.5	1,356.7	1,128.5	474.1	187.8	127.1	246.5	..	Int'l Reserves Excluding Gold
31.8	21.4	24.6	20.6	16.6	17.6	21.1	26.1	22.1	21.6	..	Gold Holdings (at market price)
											SOCIAL INDICATORS
3.1	3.1	3.1	3.1	3.0	3.0	3.0	2.9	2.9	2.9	..	Total Fertility Rate
21.2	19.6	18.0	17.6	17.2	16.8	16.4	16.0	15.6	15.2	..	Infant Mortality Rate
68.8	69.2	69.6	69.9	70.2	70.4	70.7	70.9	71.1	71.3	..	Life Expectancy at Birth
56.9	58.3	59.7	61.1	62.5	63.9	64.9	66.0	67.0	68.1	..	Urban Population, % of total
141.8	134.2	112.9	137.0	88.3	124.6	109.1	100.0	137.9	141.0	..	Food Prod. per capita (1987=100)
10.2	..	..	..	..	..	..	..	..	..	..	Labor Force, Agriculture (%)
28.9	29.1	29.3	29.4	29.6	29.7	29.8	29.9	29.9	30.0	..	Labor Force, Female (%)
97.0	..	99.0	96.0	96.0	95.0	98.0	100.0	..	..	..	Primary Schl. Enroll. Ratio
101.0	..	102.0	98.0	98.0	96.0	99.0	100.0	..	..	..	Primary Schl. Enroll. Ratio, Female
68.0	..	73.0	76.0	77.0	79.0	81.0	82.0	..	..	..	Secondary Schl. Enroll. Ratio

TUNISIA	1969	1970	1971	1972	1973	1974	1975	1976	1977	1978	1979
CURRENT GNP PER CAPITA (US $)	260	280	320	400	430	560	710	800	850	930	1,080
POPULATION (thousands)	5,031	5,127	5,208	5,294	5,389	5,494	5,611	5,742	5,890	6,050	6,216
USE AND ORIGIN OF RESOURCES					*(Millions of current Tunisian Dinars)*						
Gross National Product (GNP)	673.2	736.2	866.5	1,042.5	1,110.1	1,506.3	1,694.0	1,862.0	2,114.9	2,395.9	2,816.0
Net Factor Income from Abroad	-16.8	-19.4	-14.7	-24.9	-41.2	-41.5	-47.4	-71.0	-77.0	-88.0	-106.0
GDP at Market Prices	690.0	755.6	881.2	1,067.4	1,151.3	1,547.8	1,741.4	1,933.0	2,191.9	2,483.9	2,922.0
Resource Balance	-30.4	-34.0	-17.8	-12.3	-28.5	5.4	-83.6	-153.7	-224.7	-239.4	-146.1
Exports of Goods & NFServices	149.9	166.2	212.4	270.6	300.0	547.4	540.6	562.2	648.4	769.0	1,139.0
Imports of Goods & NFServices	180.3	200.2	230.2	282.9	328.5	542.0	624.2	715.9	873.1	1,008.4	1,285.1
Domestic Absorption	720.4	789.6	899.0	1,079.7	1,179.8	1,542.4	1,825.0	2,086.7	2,416.6	2,723.3	3,068.1
Private Consumption, etc.	457.1	502.4	571.4	681.7	760.4	938.3	1,082.6	1,201.0	1,392.4	1,553.2	1,763.8
General Gov't Consumption	113.7	127.4	138.0	155.6	174.4	204.7	254.5	293.1	354.7	406.1	444.4
Gross Domestic Investment	149.6	159.8	189.6	242.4	245.0	399.4	487.9	592.6	669.5	764.0	859.9
Fixed Investment	145.6	155.0	175.2	211.0	236.0	321.0	448.0	563.0	672.0	771.0	892.0
Indirect Taxes, net	93.2	102.4	115.0	136.9	156.7	192.6	205.4	253.6	322.5	357.9	415.0
GDP at factor cost	596.8	653.2	766.2	930.5	994.6	1,355.2	1,536.0	1,679.4	1,869.4	2,126.0	2,507.0
Agriculture	108.4	128.7	170.8	229.0	227.3	289.9	321.8	343.2	346.7	374.8	395.7
Industry	147.3	155.5	180.7	214.1	245.5	419.4	451.4	486.4	564.4	655.0	844.3
Manufacturing	57.8	63.5	76.3	101.6	107.2	154.2	158.1	202.3	231.3	274.8	338.8
Services, etc.	341.1	369.0	414.7	487.4	521.8	645.9	762.8	849.8	958.3	1,096.2	1,267.0
Gross Domestic Saving	119.2	125.8	171.8	230.1	216.5	404.8	404.3	438.9	444.8	524.6	713.8
Gross National Saving	..	118.5	180.2	230.6	213.5	409.5	409.6	422.9	432.8	521.6	717.8
					(Millions of 1987 Tunisian Dinars)						
Gross National Product	2,747.7	2,927.7	3,281.3	3,870.2	3,804.7	4,145.2	4,440.3	4,752.7	4,920.7	5,234.7	5,568.2
GDP at Market Prices	2,819.4	3,010.0	3,340.9	3,966.2	3,949.5	4,269.4	4,572.6	4,933.9	5,101.7	5,430.7	5,787.1
Resource Balance	-109.3	-196.5	-56.0	-65.5	-158.6	-246.1	-394.5	-362.4	-548.5	-611.1	-584.3
Exports of Goods & NFServices	755.5	820.2	1,053.2	1,294.4	1,186.4	1,366.6	1,376.3	1,610.2	1,723.8	1,852.7	2,250.7
Imports of Goods & NFServices	864.8	1,016.7	1,109.2	1,359.9	1,345.0	1,612.7	1,770.7	1,972.5	2,272.4	2,463.8	2,835.0
Domestic Absorption	2,928.7	3,206.6	3,397.0	4,031.7	4,108.1	4,515.5	4,967.0	5,296.3	5,650.3	6,041.8	6,371.5
Private Consumption, etc.	1,369.6	1,640.0	1,797.5	2,141.1	2,285.3	2,429.8	2,695.5	2,854.3	3,112.9	3,285.9	3,487.3
General Gov't Consumption	434.5	476.2	491.0	531.7	564.1	606.5	701.1	768.5	830.4	864.1	874.1
Gross Domestic Investment	1,124.6	1,090.4	1,108.6	1,358.9	1,258.6	1,479.1	1,570.4	1,673.5	1,707.0	1,891.8	2,010.1
Fixed Investment	774.3	779.0	857.6	979.5	987.3	1,163.1	1,452.6	1,660.4	1,673.6	1,755.8	1,880.8
GDP at factor cost	2,548.8	2,722.9	3,046.1	3,528.0	3,468.7	3,728.2	4,109.3	4,271.5	4,331.4	4,621.9	4,939.6
Agriculture	493.5	527.9	643.6	797.4	716.4	820.3	858.6	918.0	826.2	875.0	833.3
Industry	863.3	926.7	981.7	1,106.3	1,117.9	1,159.4	1,328.4	1,315.1	1,412.9	1,537.2	1,703.8
Manufacturing	236.9	235.1	275.9	352.7	356.0	315.0	396.0	482.1	502.7	537.7	596.2
Services, etc.	1,213.3	1,292.9	1,433.5	1,633.8	1,646.4	1,765.1	1,936.7	2,057.5	2,104.3	2,220.7	2,408.1
Memo Items:											
Capacity to Import	719.0	844.1	1,023.4	1,300.7	1,228.3	1,628.8	1,533.6	1,549.1	1,687.6	1,878.8	2,512.7
Terms of Trade Adjustment	-36.6	23.9	-29.7	6.4	41.9	262.2	157.3	-61.1	-36.3	26.2	262.0
Gross Domestic Income	2,782.9	3,033.9	3,311.2	3,972.6	3,991.4	4,531.6	4,729.9	4,872.8	5,065.5	5,456.9	6,049.2
Gross National Income	2,711.1	2,951.6	3,251.6	3,876.6	3,846.6	4,407.4	4,597.6	4,691.6	4,884.4	5,260.9	5,830.3
DOMESTIC PRICES/DEFLATORS					*(Index 1987 = 100)*						
Overall (GDP)	24.5	25.1	26.4	26.9	29.2	36.3	38.1	39.2	43.0	45.7	50.5
Domestic Absorption	24.6	24.6	26.5	26.8	28.7	34.2	36.7	39.4	42.8	45.1	48.2
Agriculture	22.0	24.4	26.5	28.7	31.7	35.3	37.5	37.4	42.0	42.8	47.5
Industry	17.1	16.8	18.4	19.4	22.0	36.2	34.0	37.0	39.9	42.6	49.6
Manufacturing	24.4	27.0	27.7	28.8	30.1	49.0	39.9	42.0	46.0	51.1	56.8
Consumer Price Index	30.5	30.8	32.6	33.3	34.8	36.3	39.8	41.9	44.7	47.1	50.7
MANUFACTURING ACTIVITY											
Employment (1987=100)	..	..	..	..	..	..	..	..	..	..	..
Real Earnings per Empl. (1987=100)	..	..	..	..	..	..	..	..	..	..	..
Real Output per Empl. (1987=100)	..	..	..	..	..	..	..	..	..	..	..
Earnings as % of Value Added	46.8	43.7	43.5	43.4	43.8	41.7	48.3	49.9	50.0	49.7	46.5
MONETARY HOLDINGS					*(Millions of current Tunisian Dinars)*						
Money Supply, Broadly Defined	238.4	259.9	315.0	373.3	452.7	590.6	740.4	860.5	978.4	1,178.0	1,373.0
Money	181.5	192.7	241.2	278.2	323.1	404.3	475.4	513.8	575.7	688.1	785.8
Currency Outside Banks	64.5	67.3	80.4	94.2	111.5	139.6	163.0	185.0	213.6	249.7	265.1
Demand Deposits	116.9	125.3	160.8	184.0	211.6	264.7	312.4	328.7	362.1	438.4	520.6
Quasi-Money	56.9	67.3	73.8	95.1	129.5	186.3	264.9	346.7	402.7	489.9	587.2
GOVERNMENT DEFICIT (-) OR SURPLUS					*(Millions of current Tunisian Dinars)*						
	..	..	..	-9.5	-17.1	-15.4	-25.2	-62.4	-132.2	-101.2	-139.6
Current Revenue	..	..	..	262.5	293.6	404.3	504.5	533.9	630.6	786.7	949.9
Current Expenditure	..	..	..	197.2	226.3	276.8	351.4	385.4	463.4	559.9	728.2
Current Budget Balance	..	..	..	65.3	67.3	127.5	153.1	148.5	167.2	226.8	221.7
Capital Receipts	..	..	..	0.3	0.4	2.2	1.2	8.4	9.2	0.8	2.1
Capital Payments	..	..	..	75.1	84.8	145.1	179.5	219.3	308.6	328.8	363.4

1980	1981	1982	1983	1984	1985	1986	1987	1988	1989 estimate	NOTES	TUNISIA
1,280	1,380	1,310	1,240	1,210	1,170	1,110	1,180	1,230	1,260	..	**CURRENT GNP PER CAPITA (US $)**
6,384	6,555	6,729	6,905	7,082	7,261	7,441	7,622	7,804	7,988	..	**POPULATION (thousands)**
			(Millions of current Tunisian Dinars)								**USE AND ORIGIN OF RESOURCES**
3,435.5	4,017.0	4,630.4	5,315.4	6,043.0	6,609.0	6,662.2	7,556.0	8,195.3	9,106.9	..	Gross National Product (GNP)
-105.0	-145.0	-174.0	-182.0	-197.0	-301.0	-334.0	-403.0	-427.0	-454.0	..	Net Factor Income from Abroad
3,540.5	4,162.0	4,804.4	5,497.4	6,240.0	6,910.0	6,996.2	7,959.0	8,622.3	9,560.9	..	GDP at Market Prices
-189.9	-352.4	-505.7	-473.2	-728.8	-423.2	-509.8	-79.4	31.8	-396.4	..	Resource Balance
1,424.6	1,721.9	1,773.3	1,947.8	2,113.7	2,253.1	2,161.2	2,798.5	3,639.6	4,261.2	..	Exports of Goods & NFServices
1,614.5	2,074.3	2,279.0	2,421.0	2,842.5	2,676.3	2,671.0	2,877.9	3,607.8	4,657.6	..	Imports of Goods & NFServices
3,730.4	4,514.4	5,310.0	5,971.0	6,968.8	7,333.2	7,506.0	8,038.4	8,590.5	9,957.3	..	Domestic Absorption
2,178.7	2,553.2	2,992.0	3,419.0	3,943.8	4,356.2	4,665.0	5,113.0	5,538.0	6,165.0	..	Private Consumption, etc.
512.2	615.7	794.0	927.0	1,030.0	1,142.0	1,217.0	1,305.4	1,386.6	1,608.1	..	General Gov't Consumption
1,039.5	1,345.5	1,524.0	1,625.0	1,995.0	1,835.0	1,624.0	1,620.0	1,665.9	2,184.2	..	Gross Domestic Investment
1,002.0	1,290.0	1,635.0	1,750.0	1,920.0	1,850.0	1,685.0	1,620.0	1,689.0	2,000.0	..	Fixed Investment
476.4	521.3	577.7	737.4	821.0	865.8	935.0	1,012.0	1,097.8	1,092.6	..	Indirect Taxes, net
3,064.1	3,640.7	4,226.7	4,760.0	5,419.0	6,044.2	6,061.2	6,947.0	7,524.5	8,468.3	..	GDP at factor cost
500.3	568.8	632.0	673.0	863.0	1,048.0	933.0	1,226.0	1,018.0	1,172.0	..	Agriculture
1,101.5	1,332.5	1,491.8	1,676.4	1,903.5	2,058.2	2,002.6	2,224.7	2,439.1	2,776.4	..	Industry
417.3	493.9	534.1	615.6	733.4	818.0	920.2	1,049.6	1,210.5	1,387.3	..	Manufacturing
1,462.3	1,739.4	2,102.9	2,410.6	2,652.5	2,938.0	3,125.6	3,496.3	4,067.4	4,519.9	..	Services, etc.
849.6	993.1	1,018.4	1,151.4	1,266.2	1,411.8	1,114.2	1,540.6	1,697.7	1,787.8	..	Gross Domestic Saving
866.6	1,011.7	1,057.4	1,204.4	1,305.2	1,326.8	1,061.2	1,536.6	1,739.7	1,793.8	..	Gross National Saving
			(Millions of 1987 Tunisian Dinars)								
6,019.0	6,315.5	6,273.0	6,588.2	6,987.6	7,299.6	7,172.2	7,556.0	7,674.9	7,958.4	..	Gross National Product
6,215.9	6,559.1	6,527.0	6,832.5	7,229.3	7,645.7	7,533.2	7,959.0	8,064.8	8,346.9	..	GDP at Market Prices
-710.7	-1,018.2	-1,209.8	-1,114.0	-1,242.4	-712.7	-528.9	-79.4	127.1	-262.2	..	Resource Balance
2,251.8	2,329.8	2,168.6	2,188.9	2,248.0	2,322.3	2,443.6	2,798.5	3,458.4	3,573.0	..	Exports of Goods & NFServices
2,962.5	3,348.0	3,378.5	3,302.9	3,490.4	3,035.0	2,972.6	2,877.9	3,331.3	3,835.2	..	Imports of Goods & NFServices
6,926.6	7,577.3	7,736.8	7,946.5	8,471.7	8,358.5	8,062.1	8,038.4	7,937.7	8,609.0	..	Domestic Absorption
3,937.2	4,202.4	4,300.5	4,495.2	4,753.9	4,898.4	4,991.9	5,113.0	5,285.0	5,427.3	..	Private Consumption, etc.
960.9	1,040.9	1,118.2	1,183.8	1,253.2	1,305.8	1,315.9	1,305.4	1,309.0	1,356.2	..	General Gov't Consumption
2,028.4	2,334.0	2,318.2	2,267.5	2,464.5	2,154.3	1,754.3	1,620.0	1,343.7	1,825.5	..	Gross Domestic Investment
1,954.8	2,232.6	2,415.2	2,302.0	2,411.3	2,212.3	1,818.8	1,620.0	1,537.5	1,666.6	..	Fixed Investment
5,361.7	5,719.5	5,691.5	5,957.9	6,303.1	6,668.2	6,557.3	6,947.0	6,994.1	7,241.8	..	GDP at factor cost
915.5	975.3	874.7	896.6	1,011.9	1,187.6	1,043.0	1,226.0	935.1	988.1	..	Agriculture
1,857.6	1,984.7	1,987.3	2,120.5	2,201.3	2,240.0	2,222.0	2,224.7	2,275.6	2,383.7	..	Industry
687.1	772.0	793.6	859.1	916.6	962.0	1,008.6	1,049.6	1,121.9	1,188.4	..	Manufacturing
2,594.6	2,765.6	2,832.2	2,940.8	3,090.0	3,240.6	3,292.3	3,496.3	3,783.4	3,870.0	..	Services, etc.
											Memo Items:
2,614.0	2,779.2	2,628.8	2,657.3	2,595.5	2,555.1	2,405.2	2,798.5	3,360.7	3,508.8	..	Capacity to Import
362.3	449.4	460.2	468.5	347.5	232.8	-38.4	0.0	-97.7	-64.2	..	Terms of Trade Adjustment
6,578.2	7,008.5	6,987.2	7,300.9	7,576.8	7,878.5	7,494.7	7,959.0	7,967.1	8,282.6	..	Gross Domestic Income
6,381.3	6,764.9	6,733.2	7,056.7	7,335.1	7,532.4	7,133.8	7,556.0	7,577.2	7,894.2	..	Gross National Income
			(Index 1987 = 100)								**DOMESTIC PRICES/DEFLATORS**
57.0	63.5	73.6	80.5	86.3	90.4	92.9	100.0	106.9	114.5	..	Overall (GDP)
53.9	59.6	68.6	75.1	82.3	87.7	93.1	100.0	108.2	115.7	..	Domestic Absorption
54.6	58.3	72.3	75.1	85.3	88.2	89.5	100.0	108.9	118.6	..	Agriculture
59.3	67.1	75.1	79.1	86.5	91.9	90.1	100.0	107.2	116.5	..	Industry
60.7	64.0	67.3	71.7	80.0	85.0	91.2	100.0	107.9	116.7	..	Manufacturing
55.8	60.8	69.1	75.3	81.7	88.2	93.3	100.0	106.4	114.2	..	Consumer Price Index
											MANUFACTURING ACTIVITY
..	..	..	..	..	..	..	..	..	..	..	Employment (1987=100)
..	..	..	..	..	..	..	..	..	..	..	Real Earnings per Empl. (1987=100)
..	..	..	..	..	..	..	..	..	..	..	Real Output per Empl. (1987=100)
46.4	47.7	..	..	..	..	..	..	..	..	..	Earnings as % of Value Added
			(Millions of current Tunisian Dinars)								**MONETARY HOLDINGS**
1,610.4	1,979.2	2,378.8	2,786.1	3,121.7	3,541.7	3,781.3	..	..	..	D	Money Supply, Broadly Defined
950.7	1,164.6	1,455.1	1,699.2	1,814.3	2,059.1	2,111.6	2,125.7	2,494.4	2,524.1	..	Money
299.6	342.8	440.0	533.3	573.4	632.6	651.0	704.8	801.1	874.6	..	Currency Outside Banks
651.1	821.8	1,015.1	1,166.0	1,240.8	1,426.6	1,460.6	1,420.9	1,693.4	1,649.5	..	Demand Deposits
659.7	814.6	923.7	1,086.9	1,307.4	1,482.6	1,669.7	..	..	..	..	Quasi-Money
			(Millions of current Tunisian Dinars)								
-98.9	-105.5	-277.4	-458.8	-307.3	-354.2	-474.3	-364.3	-326.9	..	..	**GOVERNMENT DEFICIT (-) OR SURPLUS**
1,130.5	1,333.3	1,656.8	1,853.4	2,284.3	2,331.7	2,418.2	2,527.2	2,758.0	..	..	Current Revenue
784.1	909.9	1,273.7	1,514.0	1,735.2	1,781.5	1,965.2	2,053.3	2,273.0	..	..	Current Expenditure
346.4	423.4	383.1	339.4	549.1	550.2	453.0	473.9	485.0	..	..	Current Budget Balance
0.7	0.8	0.9	1.1	1.1	..	..	..	0.5	..	..	Capital Receipts
446.0	529.7	661.4	799.3	857.5	904.4	927.3	838.2	812.4	..	..	Capital Payments

TUNISIA	1969	1970	1971	1972	1973	1974	1975	1976	1977	1978	1979
FOREIGN TRADE (CUSTOMS BASIS)					*(Millions of current US dollars)*						
Value of Exports, fob	165.6	182.5	215.8	310.9	385.6	914.2	856.2	788.8	929.1	1,126.1	1,790.7
Nonfuel Primary Products	91.2	97.8	120.3	179.6	178.9	381.0	314.9	251.8	229.2	264.1	316.2
Fuels	43.1	49.7	60.0	84.3	122.7	328.3	373.3	334.1	389.1	433.5	870.0
Manufactures	31.4	35.0	35.5	47.0	83.9	205.0	168.0	202.9	310.8	428.5	604.6
Value of Imports, cif	255.2	304.6	341.9	458.5	605.6	1,120.1	1,417.8	1,525.8	1,820.9	2,157.7	2,842.1
Nonfuel Primary Products	86.6	111.5	108.0	128.3	170.4	344.0	346.2	315.7	370.6	410.1	589.0
Fuels	9.3	14.7	15.4	34.3	44.6	137.8	147.5	178.1	206.8	237.9	504.6
Manufactures	159.3	178.4	218.5	295.9	390.5	638.3	924.1	1,031.9	1,243.6	1,509.7	1,748.6
					(Index 1987 = 100)						
Terms of Trade	84.2	87.2	90.6	97.5	97.1	129.9	118.3	120.8	124.3	108.0	124.7
Export Prices, fob	23.5	25.0	27.8	30.6	38.5	74.9	69.5	70.2	78.1	76.1	106.6
Import Prices, cif	27.9	28.7	30.7	31.3	39.6	57.7	58.8	58.2	62.9	70.5	85.5
BALANCE OF PAYMENTS					*(Millions of current US dollars)*						
Exports of Goods & Services	..	332.0	416.2	564.6	736.7	1,256.8	1,325.9	1,329.4	1,342.8	1,672.4	2,607.9
Merchandise, fob	..	189.0	213.6	312.7	416.1	871.9	798.9	781.3	776.3	929.9	1,540.1
Nonfactor Services	..	136.0	188.6	238.9	299.2	345.2	486.9	522.4	550.2	723.3	1,016.1
Factor Services	..	7.0	14.0	13.0	21.5	39.7	40.1	25.7	16.3	19.2	51.7
Imports of Goods & Services	..	443.0	480.4	654.7	928.7	1,340.9	1,669.5	1,921.8	2,123.8	2,383.6	3,245.1
Merchandise, fob	..	294.0	334.0	452.7	622.3	971.7	1,238.4	1,425.0	1,603.9	1,775.7	2,470.1
Nonfactor Services	..	105.0	104.3	136.8	187.2	234.5	273.2	305.5	324.0	377.2	462.5
Factor Services	..	44.0	42.1	65.1	119.2	134.7	157.8	191.2	195.8	230.7	312.5
Long-Term Interest	..	18.3	20.2	23.2	27.6	30.3	34.8	37.0	63.9	108.3	174.7
Private Current Transfers, net	..	23.0	44.1	53.2	90.6	105.8	131.1	128.3	151.5	204.2	270.6
Workers' Remittances	..	29.0	44.1	61.9	98.9	117.9	144.5	142.3	167.9	221.1	282.9
Curr. A/C Bal before Off. Transf.	..	-88.0	-20.1	-36.9	-101.3	21.6	-212.5	-464.1	-629.4	-507.0	-366.6
Net Official Transfers	..	35.0	26.1	32.6	40.5	26.5	42.5	56.0	51.3	33.6	59.0
Curr. A/C Bal after Off. Transf.	..	-53.0	6.0	-4.3	-60.8	48.1	-170.0	-408.1	-578.2	-473.4	-307.5
Long-Term Capital, net	..	51.0	85.3	90.1	133.5	135.9	127.5	394.1	496.6	579.1	440.4
Direct Investment	..	16.0	23.1	31.5	57.2	25.3	44.9	109.6	93.3	88.9	49.2
Long-Term Loans	..	41.6	56.0	70.8	83.8	85.8	124.2	180.1	663.3	505.1	500.8
Disbursements	..	88.6	106.3	142.6	144.8	148.1	192.0	243.4	779.2	655.3	703.0
Repayments	..	47.0	50.3	71.8	61.0	62.3	67.8	63.3	115.9	150.2	202.2
Other Long-Term Capital	..	-6.6	6.2	-12.2	-7.5	24.8	-41.6	104.4	-260.0	-14.9	-109.6
Other Capital, net	..	22.0	-0.9	-15.9	5.1	-96.3	25.1	4.3	22.8	-23.4	-25.7
Change in Reserves	..	-20.0	-90.3	-69.8	-77.8	-87.7	17.4	9.6	58.8	-82.4	-107.2
Memo Item:					*(Tunisian Dinars per US dollar)*						
Conversion Factor (Annual Avg)	0.520	0.520	0.520	0.480	0.420	0.440	0.400	0.430	0.430	0.420	0.410
				(Millions of US dollars), outstanding at end of year							
EXTERNAL DEBT (Total)	..	554.7	623.2	695.4	811.4	927.3	1,027.7	1,185.7	2,232.8	2,941.1	3,398.7
Long-Term Debt (by debtor)	..	554.7	623.2	695.4	811.4	927.3	1,027.7	1,185.7	2,031.8	2,660.1	3,208.7
Central Bank, incl. IMF credit	..	55.7	44.9	24.5	27.4	29.9	27.7	25.9	89.3	100.4	110.7
Central Government	..	360.7	422.3	489.4	584.1	667.6	743.1	820.8	1,098.8	1,448.6	1,613.5
Rest of General Government	..	..	..	..	..	..	..	..	..	..	..
Non-financial Public Enterprises	..	112.5	130.4	157.0	176.1	199.6	226.5	273.0	533.8	668.1	974.7
Priv. Sector, incl non-guaranteed	..	25.8	25.6	24.5	23.8	30.2	30.4	66.0	309.9	443.0	509.8
Short-Term Debt	..	..	..	..	..	..	..	..	201.0	281.0	190.0
Memo Items:					*(Millions of US dollars)*						
Int'l Reserves Excluding Gold	32.60	55.20	142.87	217.84	301.77	412.82	379.88	365.84	351.19	443.00	579.27
Gold Holdings (at market price)	4.32	4.70	5.61	8.34	14.43	24.14	18.15	17.44	24.73	36.21	87.29
SOCIAL INDICATORS											
Total Fertility Rate	6.6	6.4	6.3	6.1	6.1	6.0	5.9	5.8	5.7	5.5	5.3
Infant Mortality Rate	130.8	127.2	123.6	120.0	113.6	107.2	100.8	94.4	88.0	82.8	77.6
Life Expectancy at Birth	53.5	54.2	54.9	55.6	56.5	57.4	58.3	59.2	60.1	60.7	61.3
Urban Population, % of total	42.7	43.5	44.3	45.1	46.0	46.8	47.6	48.5	49.4	50.4	51.3
Food Prod. per capita (1987=100)	67.3	71.4	86.8	87.4	91.7	92.8	102.5	96.0	90.8	88.4	81.8
Labor Force, Agriculture (%)	43.5	42.2	41.2	40.4	39.5	38.8	38.1	37.4	36.7	36.1	35.5
Labor Force, Female (%)	11.0	11.6	12.6	13.6	14.4	15.2	16.0	17.1	18.2	19.2	20.2
Primary Schl. Enroll. Ratio	..	100.0	..	..	..	..	97.0	99.0	100.0	100.0	102.0
Primary Schl. Enroll. Ratio, Female	..	79.0	..	..	..	..	78.0	80.0	82.0	83.0	85.0
Secondary Schl. Enroll. Ratio	..	23.0	..	..	..	..	21.0	22.0	23.0	24.0	25.0

1980	1981	1982	1983	1984	1985	1986	1987	1988	1989 estimate	NOTES	TUNISIA
											FOREIGN TRADE (CUSTOMS BASIS)
				(Millions of current US dollars)							
2,233.7	2,503.7	1,983.5	1,871.5	1,796.3	1,738.0	1,759.0	2,152.4	2,395.0	2,448.8	..	Value of Exports, fob
260.6	315.9	249.0	204.3	244.9	228.4	272.0	336.8	472.8	..	..	Nonfuel Primary Products
1,172.5	1,352.4	911.2	851.6	795.5	723.0	427.0	508.4	388.2	..	..	Fuels
800.7	835.4	823.4	815.6	755.9	786.6	1,060.0	1,307.2	1,534.0	1,696.8	..	Manufactures
3,508.7	3,770.9	3,395.7	3,099.5	3,114.9	2,756.5	2,890.0	3,021.7	3,640.0	3,701.6	..	Value of Imports, cif
756.7	834.0	680.9	741.2	770.1	635.1	727.2	690.0	1,177.9	..	..	Nonfuel Primary Products
727.6	773.9	439.3	366.5	347.8	324.1	197.2	326.7	251.0	..	..	Fuels
2,024.4	2,163.0	2,275.5	1,991.8	1,997.0	1,797.3	1,965.6	2,004.9	2,211.1	..	..	Manufactures
				(Index 1987 = 100)							
141.2	142.1	133.0	123.2	118.8	114.9	102.5	100.0	94.0		..	Terms of Trade
142.4	143.3	120.7	111.2	105.2	100.2	93.3	100.0	103.7	..	..	Export Prices, fob
100.8	100.9	90.8	90.3	88.5	87.2	91.1	100.0	110.4	..	..	Import Prices, cif
				(Millions of current US dollars)							**BALANCE OF PAYMENTS**
3,355.9	3,631.5	3,106.4	2,953.9	2,796.0	2,711.8	2,746.8	3,368.1	4,301.7	4,559.1	..	Exports of Goods & Services
2,158.3	2,448.3	1,977.4	1,850.4	1,776.4	1,700.4	1,763.2	2,101.0	2,399.2	2,930.5	..	Merchandise, fob
1,103.8	1,085.0	1,024.2	1,015.1	920.4	971.8	954.6	1,241.8	1,847.7	1,551.6	..	Nonfactor Services
93.8	98.1	105.0	88.4	99.1	39.5	29.0	25.3	54.8	76.9	..	Factor Services
4,119.0	4,396.8	4,178.2	3,918.9	3,912.0	3,605.8	3,764.3	3,947.3	4,751.7	5,417.6	..	Imports of Goods & Services
3,138.6	3,418.4	3,137.0	2,922.9	2,928.6	2,566.8	2,697.6	2,828.6	3,496.1	4,136.6	..	Merchandise, fob
627.2	586.9	641.6	639.4	630.8	638.7	617.1	607.0	703.0	725.8	..	Nonfactor Services
353.1	391.6	399.5	356.5	352.7	400.2	449.6	511.7	552.6	555.1	..	Factor Services
227.5	223.1	217.2	206.7	249.7	250.5	305.6	336.2	374.1	386.6	..	Long-Term Interest
301.3	331.2	360.6	346.2	303.8	258.8	353.9	481.5	546.7	484.6	..	Private Current Transfers, net
318.6	353.7	372.4	359.5	316.7	270.8	361.4	486.3	544.4	487.7	..	Workers' Remittances
-461.8	-434.1	-711.0	-618.8	-812.3	-635.1	-663.7	-97.7	96.8	-374.0	..	Curr. A/C Bal before Off. Transf.
101.2	46.9	44.0	41.3	42.5	47.9	45.3	37.4	116.6	214.9	..	Net Official Transfers
-360.5	-387.2	-667.0	-577.5	-769.8	-587.2	-618.4	-60.3	213.3	-159.1	..	Curr. A/C Bal after Off. Transf.
508.7	628.8	772.0	624.7	531.6	393.1	313.3	129.1	130.6	166.4	..	Long-Term Capital, net
234.6	290.8	338.6	182.7	112.0	101.9	61.7	90.5	58.3	73.7	..	Direct Investment
352.9	326.1	306.7	501.4	440.2	315.7	275.7	14.4	232.1	233.2	..	Long-Term Loans
611.2	687.2	637.6	913.4	880.7	791.3	826.5	744.4	882.8	940.3	..	Disbursements
258.3	361.1	330.9	412.0	440.5	475.6	550.8	730.0	650.7	707.1	..	Repayments
-78.8	11.9	126.7	-59.4	-20.5	-24.5	-24.1	24.2	-159.8	-140.5	..	Other Long-Term Capital
-71.7	-178.7	57.7	-11.9	137.9	-30.9	221.2	59.2	97.3	57.9	..	Other Capital, net
-76.5	-62.9	-162.7	-35.2	100.3	225.0	83.9	-127.9	-441.2	-65.3	..	Change in Reserves
				(Tunisian Dinars per US dollar)							Memo Item:
0.400	0.490	0.590	0.680	0.780	0.830	0.790	0.830	0.860	0.950	..	Conversion Factor (Annual Avg)
				(Millions of US dollars), outstanding at end of year							
3,526.9	3,607.7	3,771.7	4,059.1	4,095.5	4,880.3	5,898.1	6,740.7	6,675.1	6,899.2	..	**EXTERNAL DEBT (Total)**
3,390.6	3,474.2	3,635.4	3,927.7	3,926.3	4,698.4	5,671.4	6,515.0	6,401.7	6,580.3	..	Long-Term Debt (by debtor)
78.4	45.3	42.3	38.3	34.7	89.5	282.2	387.4	389.8	388.2	..	Central Bank, incl. IMF credit
1,717.9	1,793.5	1,913.0	2,098.7	2,140.5	2,611.3	3,153.0	3,659.8	3,817.1	4,156.8	..	Central Government
..	..	..	..	..	..	..	..	..	..	..	Rest of General Government
1,075.0	1,100.6	1,204.6	1,239.7	1,135.6	1,320.9	1,514.5	1,696.9	1,457.9	1,328.3	..	Non-financial Public Enterprises
519.3	534.8	475.5	551.0	615.5	676.7	721.7	770.9	736.9	707.0	..	Priv. Sector, incl non-guaranteed
136.3	133.5	136.3	131.4	169.2	181.9	226.7	225.7	273.4	318.9	..	Short-Term Debt
				(Millions of US dollars)							Memo Items:
590.13	536.11	606.45	567.29	406.31	232.72	305.28	525.49	899.30	961.89	..	Int'l Reserves Excluding Gold
110.03	74.19	85.28	71.21	57.54	61.03	72.96	90.36	76.57	74.85	..	Gold Holdings (at market price)
											SOCIAL INDICATORS
5.2	5.0	4.9	4.7	4.6	4.5	4.3	4.2	4.1	4.0	..	Total Fertility Rate
72.4	67.2	62.0	59.6	57.2	54.8	52.4	50.0	48.4	46.9	..	Infant Mortality Rate
61.9	62.5	63.1	63.6	64.1	64.6	65.1	65.6	65.9	66.2	..	Life Expectancy at Birth
52.2	52.4	52.5	52.7	52.8	53.0	53.3	53.5	53.8	54.0	..	Urban Population, % of total
91.5	85.7	75.2	85.5	82.8	102.5	85.0	100.0	71.6	76.8	..	Food Prod. per capita (1987=100)
35.0	..	..	..	..	..	..	..	..	..	..	Labor Force, Agriculture (%)
21.0	21.5	21.9	22.3	22.6	23.0	23.3	23.6	23.9	24.2	..	Labor Force, Female (%)
103.0	..	111.0	114.0	114.0	116.0	117.0	116.0	..	..	..	Primary Schl. Enroll. Ratio
88.0	..	98.0	102.0	103.0	106.0	107.0	107.0	..	..	..	Primary Schl. Enroll. Ratio, Female
27.0	..	31.0	34.0	36.0	39.0	39.0	40.0	..	..	..	Secondary Schl. Enroll. Ratio

TURKEY	1969	1970	1971	1972	1973	1974	1975	1976	1977	1978	1979
CURRENT GNP PER CAPITA (US $)	400	400	400	410	470	630	830	1,000	1,110	1,210	1,360
POPULATION (thousands)	34,438	35,321	36,229	37,165	38,119	39,075	40,025	40,970	41,906	42,847	43,815
USE AND ORIGIN OF RESOURCES	*(Billions of current Turkish Liras)*										
Gross National Product (GNP)	124	145	186	230	294	407	517	659	857	1,264	2,126
Net Factor Income from Abroad	-1	-1	-1	-2	-2	-3	-2	-5	-6	-11	-30
GDP at Market Prices	124	146	187	232	295	410	519	664	863	1,275	2,156
Resource Balance	-2	-3	-6	-7	-6	-26	-42	-46	-70	-47	-70
Exports of Goods & NFServices	6	9	13	18	26	29	29	41	41	67	91
Imports of Goods & NFServices	8	12	20	24	33	55	71	86	111	114	161
Domestic Absorption	126	149	194	239	302	436	561	710	933	1,322	2,226
Private Consumption, etc.	89	101	135	162	209	300	377	458	599	910	1,530
General Gov't Consumption	16	19	25	28	37	47	64	85	116	173	294
Gross Domestic Investment	22	29	33	48	56	89	120	167	218	239	402
Fixed Investment	22	27	32	47	59	76	108	154	211	280	449
Indirect Taxes, net	13	14	19	26	30	40	51	64	67	85	141
GDP at factor cost	112	131	168	207	266	370	468	600	796	1,190	2,015
Agriculture	34	39	50	59	73	105	136	177	220	301	466
Industry	32	36	45	53	68	95	118	146	200	337	584
Manufacturing	20	22	29	35	46	66	80	98	130	232	417
Services, etc.	46	57	73	94	124	169	214	276	376	551	966
Gross Domestic Saving	20	25	27	42	50	62	78	121	147	192	332
Gross National Saving	..	28	33	51	65	80	96	134	161	208	358
	(Billions of 1987 Turkish Liras)										
Gross National Product	22,627.0	23,738.0	25,918.0	27,595.1	28,791.0	31,273.0	34,112.3	36,991.5	38,731.7	39,967.9	39,377.2
GDP at Market Prices	22,825.7	23,919.8	26,121.4	27,837.9	29,017.0	31,500.8	34,301.2	37,305.5	39,046.9	40,345.6	39,980.1
Resource Balance	-1,678.6	-1,988.4	-2,570.3	-3,062.3	-2,708.4	-4,012.0	-4,703.6	-4,776.1	-5,559.0	-2,647.3	-2,533.2
Exports of Goods & NFServices	1,509.6	1,627.6	1,745.5	2,264.5	2,618.3	2,170.1	2,217.3	2,689.1	2,217.3	2,523.9	2,288.1
Imports of Goods & NFServices	3,188.3	3,616.0	4,315.8	5,326.7	5,326.7	6,182.1	6,920.9	7,465.2	7,776.3	5,171.2	4,821.3
Domestic Absorption	24,504.3	25,908.2	28,691.7	30,900.2	31,725.4	35,512.8	39,004.7	42,081.6	44,605.9	42,992.8	42,513.3
Private Consumption, etc.	17,321.7	17,586.9	19,853.7	21,872.2	21,751.5	23,539.1	24,735.1	27,026.3	28,209.3	29,301.7	28,736.3
General Gov't Consumption	2,351.3	2,398.4	2,868.6	2,570.8	2,680.5	2,868.6	3,213.5	3,511.3	3,668.1	4,028.6	4,091.3
Gross Domestic Investment	4,831.3	5,923.0	5,969.4	6,457.2	7,293.4	9,105.1	11,056.2	11,544.0	12,728.5	9,662.5	9,685.8
Fixed Investment	5,052.3	5,808.9	5,589.3	6,223.9	7,322.2	8,274.1	10,080.2	11,349.4	12,130.4	10,934.5	10,543.9
GDP at factor cost	20,967.3	22,088.6	24,073.1	25,518.6	26,517.8	28,843.7	31,387.7	34,186.1	35,928.2	37,502.3	37,249.5
Agriculture	5,367.0	5,485.6	6,213.6	6,112.0	5,485.6	6,061.2	6,721.5	7,229.4	7,144.8	7,331.0	7,534.2
Industry	6,831.6	7,099.5	7,456.7	7,903.2	8,751.6	9,421.4	10,247.4	11,252.0	12,256.7	13,015.8	12,569.2
Manufacturing	4,627.3	4,769.6	5,173.0	5,529.0	6,193.4	6,620.5	7,166.3	7,854.5	8,424.0	8,732.5	8,281.6
Services, etc.	8,556.3	9,290.2	10,082.1	11,241.0	12,245.3	13,307.6	14,350.5	15,644.6	16,533.1	17,189.8	17,131.8
Memo Items:											
Capacity to Import	2,488.4	2,616.4	2,891.8	3,880.0	4,264.7	3,253.7	2,824.6	3,521.2	2,869.0	3,045.4	2,731.1
Terms of Trade Adjustment	978.7	988.8	1,146.3	1,615.5	1,646.4	1,083.6	607.4	832.1	651.7	521.4	443.0
Gross Domestic Income	23,804.4	24,908.6	27,267.7	29,453.4	30,663.3	32,584.4	34,908.5	38,137.6	39,698.6	40,867.0	40,423.1
Gross National Income	23,605.7	24,726.8	27,064.3	29,210.6	30,437.4	32,356.6	34,719.7	37,823.6	39,383.3	40,489.3	39,820.2
DOMESTIC PRICES/DEFLATORS	*(Index 1987 = 100)*										
Overall (GDP)	0.5	0.6	0.7	0.8	1.0	1.3	1.5	1.8	2.2	3.2	5.4
Domestic Absorption	0.5	0.6	0.7	0.8	1.0	1.2	1.4	1.7	2.1	3.1	5.2
Agriculture	0.6	0.7	0.8	1.0	1.3	1.7	2.0	2.5	3.1	4.1	6.2
Industry	0.5	0.5	0.6	0.7	0.8	1.0	1.2	1.3	1.6	2.6	4.6
Manufacturing	0.4	0.5	0.6	0.6	0.7	1.0	1.1	1.2	1.5	2.7	5.0
Consumer Price Index	0.7	0.7	0.8	0.9	1.1	1.2	1.5	1.7	2.2	3.2	5.0
MANUFACTURING ACTIVITY											
Employment (1987=100)	43.9	54.9	58.9	62.9	69.9	72.1	76.7	79.4	81.9	87.7	86.7
Real Earnings per Empl. (1987=100)	75.7	79.5	81.9	83.6	84.7	94.0	105.3	109.8	130.5	135.6	139.6
Real Output per Empl. (1987=100)	58.1	63.7	64.6	67.9	69.0	70.9	75.6	78.3	82.7	66.4	56.7
Earnings as % of Value Added	27.0	25.9	26.8	27.4	27.1	26.3	32.0	31.6	37.7	37.7	38.3
MONETARY HOLDINGS	*(Billions of current Turkish Liras)*										
Money Supply, Broadly Defined	37	45	57	72	92	116	149	183	245	335	542
Money	30	36	44	54	71	91	119	152	210	289	456
Currency Outside Banks	9	12	14	16	21	26	33	42	63	94	144
Demand Deposits	21	24	30	38	50	65	86	109	147	195	313
Quasi-Money	6	9	13	18	21	25	30	32	35	46	85
GOVERNMENT DEFICIT (-) OR SURPLUS	*(Billions of current Turkish Liras)*										
GOVERNMENT DEFICIT (-) OR SURPLUS	..	-4	-6	-5	-5	-7	-7	-13	-53	-55	-137
Current Revenue	..	29	38	47	59	72	109	144	187	291	497
Current Expenditure	..	23	31	36	48	57	82	110	164	249	435
Current Budget Balance	..	6	7	12	11	14	27	33	23	43	62
Capital Receipts	..	0	..	0	0	0	0	..	..	..	0
Capital Payments	..	9	14	17	16	22	34	47	76	97	199

1980	1981	1982	1983	1984	1985	1986	1987	1988	1989 estimate	NOTES	TURKEY
1,390	1,440	1,290	1,180	1,100	1,080	1,110	1,220	1,280	1,370	..	**CURRENT GNP PER CAPITA (US $)**
44,823	45,865	46,938	48,040	49,166	50,310	51,466	52,623	53,772	54,899	..	**POPULATION (thousands)**
				(Billions of current Turkish Liras)							**USE AND ORIGIN OF RESOURCES**
4,243	6,255	8,378	11,201	17,684	26,870	38,172	56,763	97,929	163,969	f	Gross National Product (GNP)
-85	-159	-242	-331	-528	-682	-1,116	-1,536	-2,897	-3,800	..	Net Factor Income from Abroad
4,328	6,414	8,620	11,532	18,212	27,552	39,288	58,299	100,826	167,769	..	GDP at Market Prices
-339	-341	-283	-500	-763	-882	-1,170	-1,199	2,096	-1,700	..	Resource Balance
275	664	1,269	1,768	3,500	5,676	6,933	11,865	24,329	37,414	..	Exports of Goods & NFServices
615	1,005	1,552	2,268	4,263	6,558	8,103	13,064	22,233	39,114	..	Imports of Goods & NFServices
4,667	6,754	8,903	12,032	18,975	28,434	40,457	59,498	98,730	169,469	..	Domestic Absorption
3,175	4,645	6,189	8,597	13,773	20,277	27,362	39,365	65,868	113,767	..	Private Consumption, etc.
544	700	939	1,175	1,651	2,375	3,490	5,314	8,815	18,191	..	General Gov't Consumption
948	1,409	1,775	2,259	3,551	5,782	9,605	14,819	24,047	37,511	..	Gross Domestic Investment
864	1,241	1,647	2,130	3,288	5,562	9,089	14,083	24,166	38,202	..	Fixed Investment
230	390	540	714	863	2,026	3,660	5,374	9,085	15,864	..	Indirect Taxes, net
4,098	6,024	8,081	10,817	17,349	25,526	35,628	52,925	91,741	151,905	..	GDP at factor cost
925	1,325	1,679	2,118	3,397	4,790	6,586	9,532	16,023	25,156	..	Agriculture
1,237	1,858	2,549	3,544	5,807	9,012	12,763	18,999	33,290	53,622	..	Industry
865	1,310	1,813	2,583	4,206	6,409	8,998	13,597	23,885	38,254	..	Manufacturing
1,936	2,841	3,853	5,155	8,145	11,724	16,279	24,394	42,428	73,127	..	Services, etc.
609	1,068	1,492	1,760	2,788	4,900	8,436	13,620	26,143	35,811	..	Gross Domestic Saving
687	1,194	1,606	1,778	2,951	5,138	8,468	13,855	25,845	38,662	..	Gross National Saving
				(Billions of 1987 Turkish Liras)							
38,879.7	40,312.3	42,132.7	43,726.2	46,322.2	48,883.9	52,690.6	56,763.0	58,711.3	59,884.3	f	Gross National Product
39,687.3	41,346.6	43,352.9	45,009.1	47,684.6	50,108.2	54,244.2	58,299.0	60,468.3	61,238.7	..	GDP at Market Prices
-2,555.5	-1,265.7	75.8	-124.8	-716.1	-416.9	-1,686.0	-1,199.2	1,019.4	824.5	..	Resource Balance
2,382.4	4,411.0	6,180.1	7,029.3	8,421.0	9,458.9	9,317.4	11,864.9	14,200.1	14,860.6	..	Exports of Goods & NFServices
4,937.9	5,676.7	6,104.4	7,154.2	9,137.1	9,875.8	11,003.4	13,064.1	13,180.7	14,036.1	..	Imports of Goods & NFServices
42,242.8	42,612.2	43,277.2	45,133.9	48,400.7	50,525.2	55,930.2	59,498.2	59,448.9	60,414.2	..	Domestic Absorption
27,245.8	26,841.2	27,993.3	29,771.1	32,852.1	33,348.9	36,814.5	39,365.2	40,127.1	41,727.1	..	Private Consumption, etc.
4,451.8	4,436.2	4,483.2	4,608.6	4,608.6	4,749.7	5,063.2	5,314.0	5,455.1	5,470.8	..	General Gov't Consumption
10,545.2	11,334.9	10,800.7	10,754.2	10,940.0	12,426.6	14,052.5	14,819.0	13,866.7	13,216.3	..	Gross Domestic Investment
9,494.4	9,689.7	10,007.0	10,275.5	10,299.9	12,032.8	13,350.8	14,083.0	13,863.3	13,399.6	..	Fixed Investment
37,014.7	38,381.1	40,116.1	41,707.2	44,298.5	46,199.9	49,594.6	52,925.0	55,245.9	55,679.4	..	GDP at factor cost
7,669.6	7,669.6	8,160.6	8,143.7	8,431.5	8,634.7	9,328.8	9,532.0	10,327.7	9,176.5	..	Agriculture
12,011.1	12,680.9	13,172.0	13,998.1	15,181.3	16,029.7	17,436.2	18,999.0	19,423.2	20,003.6	..	Industry
7,759.5	8,471.4	8,946.0	9,705.4	10,702.0	11,295.2	12,386.8	13,597.0	13,763.1	14,237.7	..	Manufacturing
17,267.0	18,001.0	18,734.9	19,565.4	20,685.7	21,535.5	22,829.6	24,394.0	25,494.9	26,499.3	..	Services, etc.
											Memo Items:
2,211.9	3,750.2	4,991.4	5,577.6	7,501.7	8,547.4	9,415.1	11,864.9	14,423.3	13,426.1	..	Capacity to Import
-170.6	-660.9	-1,188.7	-1,451.7	-919.4	-911.5	97.7	0.0	223.2	-1,434.5	..	Terms of Trade Adjustment
39,516.8	40,685.7	42,164.2	43,557.3	46,765.3	49,196.7	54,342.0	58,299.0	60,691.5	59,804.1	..	Gross Domestic Income
38,709.1	39,651.4	40,944.0	42,274.4	45,402.9	47,972.4	52,788.3	56,763.0	58,934.5	58,449.7	..	Gross National Income
				(Index 1987 = 100)							**DOMESTIC PRICES/DEFLATORS**
10.9	15.5	19.9	25.6	38.2	55.0	72.4	100.0	166.7	274.0	..	Overall (GDP)
11.0	15.9	20.6	26.7	39.2	56.3	72.3	100.0	166.1	280.5	..	Domestic Absorption
12.1	17.3	20.6	26.0	40.3	55.5	70.6	100.0	155.1	274.1	..	Agriculture
10.3	14.6	19.3	25.3	38.3	56.2	73.2	100.0	171.4	268.1	..	Industry
11.1	15.5	20.3	26.6	39.3	56.7	72.6	100.0	173.5	268.7	..	Manufacturing
10.6	14.5	18.9	24.9	36.9	53.5	72.0	100.0	175.4	297.5	..	Consumer Price Index
											MANUFACTURING ACTIVITY
86.3	87.5	90.8	87.2	90.9	92.5	95.9	100.0	99.6	..	G	Employment (1987=100)
116.7	122.7	116.6	115.7	101.8	98.2	94.0	100.0	95.5	..	G	Real Earnings per Empl. (1987=100)
59.3	70.7	74.7	75.8	78.2	82.3	91.1	100.0	101.7	..	G	Real Output per Empl. (1987=100)
30.7	25.3	23.5	24.8	23.5	21.1	15.9	17.2	16.3	..	..	Earnings as % of Value Added
				(Billions of current Turkish Liras)							**MONETARY HOLDINGS**
945	1,779	2,688	3,487	5,534	8,593	12,357	17,992	27,881	47,958	..	Money Supply, Broadly Defined
758	1,024	1,413	2,090	2,487	3,468	5,432	8,960	11,956	20,302	..	Money
218	280	412	548	735	1,011	1,415	2,275	3,426	6,841	..	Currency Outside Banks
541	744	1,001	1,542	1,752	2,456	4,017	6,686	8,530	13,461	..	Demand Deposits
187	755	1,275	1,397	3,047	5,125	6,925	9,032	15,925	27,656	..	Quasi-Money
				(Billions of current Turkish Liras)							
-161	-117	..	-483	-1,816	-2,050	-1,259	-2,346	-3,859	..	F	**GOVERNMENT DEFICIT (-) OR SURPLUS**
945	1,444	..	2,304	2,712	4,820	7,016	10,387	17,494	..	..	Current Revenue
809	1,071	..	1,958	3,504	5,614	6,782	10,477	17,933	..	..	Current Expenditure
136	373	..	345	-792	-794	234	-90	-438	..	..	Current Budget Balance
11	3	..	5	9	15	36	58	93	..	..	Capital Receipts
308	492	..	834	1,033	1,271	1,529	2,314	3,513	..	..	Capital Payments

TURKEY	1969	1970	1971	1972	1973	1974	1975	1976	1977	1978	1979
FOREIGN TRADE (CUSTOMS BASIS)					*(Millions of current US dollars)*						
Value of Exports, fob	537	589	677	885	1,317	1,538	1,401	1,960	1,753	2,288	2,261
Nonfuel Primary Products	500	532	591	739	1,047	1,115	1,039	1,478	1,322	1,784	1,639
Fuels	4	4	3	22	49	86	36	16	0	4	2
Manufactures	33	53	83	124	222	337	326	466	431	501	620
Value of Imports, cif	747	886	1,088	1,508	2,049	3,720	4,640	4,993	5,694	4,479	4,946
Nonfuel Primary Products	86	139	120	144	205	676	639	427	400	262	341
Fuels	61	67	122	156	222	764	810	1,127	1,471	1,440	1,760
Manufactures	601	680	846	1,208	1,622	2,280	3,192	3,439	3,823	2,777	2,845
					(Index 1987 = 100)						
Terms of Trade	174.7	166.4	168.6	150.1	164.0	127.5	120.2	131.3	121.1	119.3	114.4
Export Prices, fob	40.1	41.3	42.0	41.6	55.9	71.0	68.6	74.6	75.1	82.6	98.0
Import Prices, cif	23.0	24.8	24.9	27.7	34.1	55.6	57.1	56.8	62.1	69.3	85.7
BALANCE OF PAYMENTS					*(Millions of current US dollars)*						
Exports of Goods & Services	..	776	896	1,266	1,859	2,082	2,018	2,541	2,293	2,821	2,969
Merchandise, fob	..	588	677	885	1,320	1,532	1,401	1,960	1,753	2,288	2,261
Nonfactor Services	..	183	210	367	526	549	616	580	534	467	674
Factor Services	..	5	9	14	13	1	1	1	6	66	34
Imports of Goods & Services	..	1,150	1,421	1,847	2,452	4,133	5,103	5,690	6,540	5,185	6,192
Merchandise, fob	..	830	1,030	1,367	1,829	3,589	4,502	4,872	5,506	4,369	4,815
Nonfactor Services	..	237	292	349	476	366	436	517	687	310	367
Factor Services	..	83	99	131	148	178	165	301	347	506	1,010
Long-Term Interest	..	44	56	66	84	102	119	169	187	209	292
Private Current Transfers, net	..	317	499	777	1,234	1,466	1,398	1,104	1,068	1,086	1,799
Workers' Remittances	..	273	471	740	1,184	1,426	1,312	982	982	983	1,694
Curr. A/C Bal before Off. Transf.	..	-57	-26	197	640	-585	-1,687	-2,045	-3,179	-1,278	-1,424
Net Official Transfers	..	13	69	15	20	24	39	16	39	13	11
Curr. A/C Bal after Off. Transf.	..	-44	43	212	660	-561	-1,648	-2,029	-3,140	-1,265	-1,413
Long-Term Capital, net	..	330	217	697	360	182	1,322	2,559	878	1,437	1,632
Direct Investment	..	58	45	43	79	64	114	10	27	34	75
Long-Term Loans	..	201	305	210	340	211	154	525	874	1,091	4,032
Disbursements	..	332	416	368	469	367	327	726	1,108	1,452	4,511
Repayments	..	131	112	158	129	156	173	202	235	361	480
Other Long-Term Capital	..	71	-133	444	-59	-93	1,054	2,024	-23	312	-2,475
Other Capital, net	..	-142	72	-220	-325	-172	-311	-758	1,896	-193	-371
Change in Reserves	..	-144	-332	-689	-696	551	637	228	366	22	152
Memo Item:					*(Turkish Liras per US dollar)*						
Conversion Factor (Annual Avg)	9.000	11.500	14.900	14.100	14.100	13.900	14.400	16.100	18.000	24.300	31.100
					(Millions of US dollars), outstanding at end of year						
EXTERNAL DEBT (Total)	..	1,963	2,348	2,540	3,003	3,310	4,769	5,442	11,452	14,855	15,900
Long-Term Debt (by debtor)	..	1,963	2,348	2,540	3,003	3,310	3,614	4,287	5,359	7,669	12,304
Central Bank, incl. IMF credit	..	81	74	7	8	8	251	408	448	689	3,449
Central Government	..	1,777	2,099	2,287	2,605	2,804	2,831	3,067	3,413	5,133	6,655
Rest of General Government	..	0	0	0	0	0	0	6	8	16	27
Non-financial Public Enterprises	..	38	85	113	178	225	229	402	691	949	1,229
Priv. Sector, incl non-guaranteed	..	67	89	132	213	273	303	404	799	883	945
Short-Term Debt	..	..	..	..	..	..	1,155	1,155	6,093	7,186	3,596
Memo Items:					*(Millions of US dollars)*						
Int'l Reserves Excluding Gold	128.0	304.1	631.4	1,262.1	1,985.9	1,561.7	943.8	990.5	638.0	801.3	658.2
Gold Holdings (at market price)	117.7	135.6	149.6	231.8	400.8	665.7	500.6	481.0	599.5	828.8	1,927.8
SOCIAL INDICATORS											
Total Fertility Rate	5.4	5.3	5.2	5.0	4.9	4.7	4.6	4.5	4.3	4.3	4.2
Infant Mortality Rate	147.0	144.0	141.0	138.0	134.4	130.8	127.2	123.6	120.0	114.4	108.8
Life Expectancy at Birth	56.1	56.7	57.3	57.9	58.4	58.8	59.3	59.7	60.2	60.5	60.8
Urban Population, % of total	37.5	38.4	39.0	39.7	40.3	41.0	41.6	42.0	42.5	42.9	43.4
Food Prod. per capita (1987=100)	93.0	95.7	96.4	94.9	87.9	94.0	100.2	102.0	101.2	102.5	102.1
Labor Force, Agriculture (%)	71.4	70.7	69.4	68.2	67.0	65.9	64.8	63.4	62.1	60.8	59.6
Labor Force, Female (%)	38.2	37.9	37.6	37.3	37.0	36.8	36.5	36.1	35.6	35.2	34.8
Primary Schl. Enroll. Ratio	..	110.0	..	..	..	..	108.0	107.0	105.0	105.0	104.0
Primary Schl. Enroll. Ratio, Female	..	94.0	..	..	..	..	..	97.0	95.0	96.0	94.0
Secondary Schl. Enroll. Ratio	..	27.0	..	..	..	..	29.0	32.0	34.0	34.0	37.0

1980	1981	1982	1983	1984	1985	1986	1987	1988	1989 estimate	NOTES	TURKEY
											FOREIGN TRADE (CUSTOMS BASIS)
				(Millions of current US dollars)							
2,910	4,702	5,890	5,905	7,389	8,255	7,583	10,190	11,695	13,190	..	Value of Exports, fob
2,086	2,847	2,928	2,795	2,878	2,715	2,924	3,203	3,949	..	..	Nonfuel Primary Products
42	107	345	233	407	373	181	233	256	..	..	Fuels
782	1,748	2,617	2,877	4,104	5,167	4,478	6,754	7,490	10,517	..	Manufactures
7,573	8,864	8,794	9,235	10,757	11,515	11,104	14,163	14,340	17,307	..	Value of Imports, cif
641	816	736	828	1,382	1,582	1,587	2,421	1,452	..	..	Nonfuel Primary Products
3,669	3,919	3,850	3,746	3,794	3,674	2,191	3,167	2,843	..	..	Fuels
3,262	4,129	4,208	4,661	5,581	6,259	7,326	8,575	10,045	13,514	..	Manufactures
				(Index 1987 = 100)							
92.2	88.7	84.9	88.5	87.7	86.4	102.3	100.0	107.1	..	..	Terms of Trade
106.6	101.8	92.4	90.5	87.2	83.0	90.6	100.0	108.6	..	..	Export Prices, fob
115.6	114.8	108.8	102.2	99.4	96.0	88.5	100.0	101.4	..	..	Import Prices, cif
				(Millions of current US dollars)							**BALANCE OF PAYMENTS**
3,672	6,019	7,928	7,946	9,755	11,417	10,921	14,517	17,955	18,854	..	Exports of Goods & Services
2,910	4,703	5,890	5,905	7,389	8,255	7,583	10,322	11,929	11,771	..	Merchandise, fob
711	1,264	1,918	1,939	2,157	2,618	2,696	3,520	5,176	5,863	..	Nonfactor Services
51	52	120	102	209	544	642	675	850	1,220	..	Factor Services
9,251	10,513	11,157	11,629	13,276	14,414	14,310	17,713	18,518	21,446	..	Imports of Goods & Services
7,513	8,567	8,518	8,895	10,331	11,230	10,664	13,551	13,706	15,972	..	Merchandise, fob
569	468	1,031	1,166	1,296	1,333	1,349	1,695	1,925	2,463	..	Nonfactor Services
1,169	1,478	1,608	1,568	1,649	1,851	2,297	2,467	2,887	3,011	..	Factor Services
507	989	1,171	1,235	1,184	1,319	1,496	1,898	2,427	2,667	..	Long-Term Interest
2,153	2,559	2,189	1,549	1,885	1,762	1,703	2,066	1,827	3,135	..	Private Current Transfers, net
2,071	2,490	2,140	1,513	1,807	1,714	1,634	2,021	1,776	3,040	..	Workers' Remittances
-3,426	-1,935	-1,040	-2,134	-1,636	-1,235	-1,686	-1,130	1,264	543	..	Curr. A/C Bal before Off. Transf.
18	-1	88	211	229	222	221	324	332	423	..	Net Official Transfers
-3,408	-1,936	-952	-1,923	-1,407	-1,013	-1,465	-806	1,596	966	..	Curr. A/C Bal after Off. Transf.
2,916	1,293	1,084	707	1,159	262	1,312	1,841	1,323	1,329	f	Long-Term Capital, net
18	95	55	46	113	99	125	106	354	663	..	Direct Investment
1,880	1,132	908	466	1,336	424	1,738	1,716	3,492	998	..	Long-Term Loans
2,475	1,937	2,101	1,632	2,517	2,788	3,734	4,758	7,343	4,708	..	Disbursements
595	805	1,193	1,165	1,181	2,364	1,996	3,042	3,851	3,710	..	Repayments
1,017	66	121	195	-290	-261	-551	19	-2,523	-332	..	Other Long-Term Capital
565	571	22	1,206	353	643	693	-455	-1,766	418	f	Other Capital, net
-72	72	-154	10	-105	108	-540	-580	-1,153	-2,713	..	Change in Reserves
				(Turkish Liras per US dollar)							Memo Item:
76.000	111.200	162.600	225.500	366.700	522.000	674.500	857.200	1,422.400	2,121.700	..	Conversion Factor (Annual Avg)
				(Millions of US dollars), outstanding at end of year							
19,119	19,227	19,708	20,317	21,601	26,010	32,842	40,799	40,864	41,594	..	**EXTERNAL DEBT (Total)**
16,629	17,033	17,944	18,036	18,421	21,251	26,493	33,176	34,447	35,617	..	Long-Term Debt (by debtor)
4,554	4,687	5,036	5,503	6,142	6,415	7,117	8,119	7,104	7,189	..	Central Bank, incl. IMF credit
9,457	9,654	9,911	9,627	9,408	10,921	13,825	17,559	19,307	20,005	..	Central Government
25	22	20	20	14	21	109	180	242	387	..	Rest of General Government
1,761	1,947	2,272	2,201	2,182	3,168	4,392	5,685	6,237	6,135	..	Non-financial Public Enterprises
832	723	706	685	675	726	1,050	1,633	1,557	1,901	..	Priv. Sector, incl non-guaranteed
2,490	2,194	1,764	2,281	3,180	4,759	6,349	7,623	6,417	5,977	..	Short-Term Debt
				(Millions of US dollars)							Memo Items:
1,077.0	928.2	1,080.1	1,288.1	1,270.7	1,055.9	1,411.6	1,775.8	2,344.5	4,780.5	..	Int'l Reserves Excluding Gold
2,221.0	1,497.8	1,722.2	1,440.3	1,171.5	1,261.6	1,500.9	1,854.8	1,567.9	1,517.7	..	Gold Holdings (at market price)
											SOCIAL INDICATORS
4.2	4.1	4.1	4.0	3.9	3.9	3.9	3.8	3.7	3.7	..	Total Fertility Rate
103.2	97.6	92.0	88.8	85.6	82.4	79.2	76.0	74.5	73.0	..	Infant Mortality Rate
61.0	61.3	61.6	62.1	62.6	63.1	63.6	64.1	64.4	64.7	..	Life Expectancy at Birth
43.8	44.2	44.6	45.1	45.5	45.9	46.5	47.1	47.6	48.0	..	Urban Population, % of total
101.7	102.7	104.1	100.0	97.9	98.5	101.3	100.0	103.5	94.0	..	Food Prod. per capita (1987=100)
58.4	..	..	..	..	..	..	..	..	..	..	Labor Force, Agriculture (%)
34.4	34.3	34.2	34.2	34.1	34.0	34.0	33.9	33.8	33.8	..	Labor Force, Female (%)
96.0	..	..	111.0	111.0	113.0	115.0	117.0	..	..	..	Primary Schl. Enroll. Ratio
90.0	..	..	107.0	107.0	110.0	111.0	113.0	..	..	..	Primary Schl. Enroll. Ratio, Female
35.0	..	36.0	38.0	40.0	42.0	44.0	46.0	..	..	..	Secondary Schl. Enroll. Ratio

UGANDA	1969	1970	1971	1972	1973	1974	1975	1976	1977	1978	1979
CURRENT GNP PER CAPITA (US $)	180	190	200	210	210	220	220	270	280	280	290
POPULATION (thousands)	9,446	9,759	10,036	10,305	10,570	10,835	11,105	11,383	11,673	11,977	12,297
USE AND ORIGIN OF RESOURCES					*(Millions of current Uganda Shillings)*						
Gross National Product (GNP)	82	94	106	112	129	159	225	264	543	590	878
Net Factor Income from Abroad	-1	-1	-2	-1	-1	-1	0	-1	-1	-2	-4
GDP at Market Prices	83	95	108	113	130	160	225	265	544	592	882
Resource Balance	1	3	-4	3	4	0	-5	4	7	-29	16
Exports of Goods & NFServices	18	21	20	21	20	22	18	28	46	76	166
Imports of Goods & NFServices	17	18	24	18	16	22	23	24	39	105	150
Domestic Absorption	82	92	112	110	125	161	230	260	537	621	866
Private Consumption, etc.	62	..	..	..	..	..	..	..	..	..	..
General Gov't Consumption	9	..	..	..	..	..	..	..	..	..	..
Gross Domestic Investment	12	13	16	12	11	17	17	15	30	46	56
Fixed Investment	10	12	15	13	10	16	15	12	..	..	..
Indirect Taxes, net	9	9	11	11	13	18	17	24	49	40	31
GDP at factor cost	75	85	97	102	117	143	208	240	495	552	851
Agriculture	38	46	55	58	71	89	150	176	366	410	558
Industry	11	12	12	11	11	16	17	18	35	28	35
Manufacturing	7	8	8	8	8	11	13	15	29	24	31
Services, etc.	26	28	30	32	34	38	41	46	94	114	258
Gross Domestic Saving	13	16	12	15	15	17	12	20	37	17	72
Gross National Saving	..	14	10	13	13	15	12	19	36	14	67
					(Millions of 1987 Uganda Shillings)						
Gross National Product	190,122.0	193,341.0	205,132.0	203,672.0	198,163.0	201,374.0	191,954.0	196,585.0	199,691.0	186,135.0	158,391.0
GDP at Market Prices	193,097.0	195,601.0	208,211.0	205,893.0	199,765.0	202,891.0	192,137.0	197,066.0	200,071.0	186,810.0	159,150.0
Resource Balance	..	..	..	..	..	..	..	..	..	..	..
Exports of Goods & NFServices	..	..	..	..	..	..	..	..	..	..	..
Imports of Goods & NFServices	..	..	..	..	..	..	..	..	..	..	..
Domestic Absorption	..	..	..	..	..	..	..	..	..	..	..
Private Consumption, etc.	..	..	..	..	..	..	..	..	..	..	..
General Gov't Consumption	..	..	..	..	..	..	..	..	..	..	..
Gross Domestic Investment	..	..	..	..	..	..	..	..	..	..	..
Fixed Investment	..	..	..	..	..	..	..	..	..	..	..
GDP at factor cost	172,991.0	176,509.0	187,377.0	186,159.0	180,187.0	180,338.0	177,276.0	178,763.0	181,776.0	174,209.0	153,585.0
Agriculture	117,659.0	119,046.0	116,271.0	120,623.0	126,709.0	125,479.0	125,070.0	125,889.0	129,201.0	128,570.0	110,279.0
Industry	23,747.3	23,377.7	23,744.1	22,575.3	20,726.7	20,989.8	18,047.6	16,973.8	16,621.9	13,800.0	10,400.2
Manufacturing	13,619.3	14,275.4	14,433.8	14,479.0	13,528.8	13,234.7	11,424.9	11,176.0	10,859.3	8,415.9	5,565.4
Services, etc.	32,808.3	34,487.0	42,119.0	40,029.1	34,673.8	35,956.4	35,615.9	37,181.7	37,040.4	32,087.3	33,103.2
Memo Items:											
Capacity to Import	..	..	..	..	..	..	..	..	..	..	..
Terms of Trade Adjustment	..	..	..	..	..	..	..	..	..	..	..
Gross Domestic Income	..	..	..	..	..	..	..	..	..	..	..
Gross National Income	..	..	..	..	..	..	..	..	..	..	..
DOMESTIC PRICES/DEFLATORS					*(Index 1987 = 100)*						
Overall (GDP)	0.00E+0	0.00E+0	1.00E-1	1.00E-1	1.00E-1	1.00E-1	1.00E-1	1.00E-1	3.00E-1	3.00E-1	6.00E-1
Domestic Absorption	..	..	..	..	..	..	..	..	..	..	..
Agriculture	0.00E+0	0.00E+0	0.00E+0	0.00E+0	1.00E-1	1.00E-1	1.00E-1	1.00E-1	3.00E-1	3.00E-1	5.00E-1
Industry	0.00E+0	1.00E-1	1.00E-1	1.00E-1	1.00E-1	1.00E-1	1.00E-1	1.00E-1	2.00E-1	2.00E-1	3.00E-1
Manufacturing	1.00E-1	1.00E-1	1.00E-1	1.00E-1	1.00E-1	1.00E-1	1.00E-1	1.00E-1	3.00E-1	3.00E-1	6.00E-1
Consumer Price Index	..	..	..	..	..	..	..	..	..	..	..
MANUFACTURING ACTIVITY											
Employment (1987=100)	..	..	..	..	..	..	..	..	..	..	..
Real Earnings per Empl. (1987=100)	..	..	..	..	..	..	..	..	..	..	..
Real Output per Empl. (1987=100)	..	..	..	..	..	..	..	..	..	..	..
Earnings as % of Value Added	41.6	..	39.4	..	..	..	..	..	..	..	..
MONETARY HOLDINGS					*(Millions of current Uganda Shillings)*						
Money Supply, Broadly Defined	14.0	16.7	16.5	21.3	28.8	38.5	46.6	61.9	73.8	92.7	137.1
Money	9.6	11.1	11.2	15.3	21.1	30.0	32.4	44.5	57.7	69.8	106.2
Currency Outside Banks	5.2	5.9	5.9	6.2	8.0	10.9	13.7	22.1	28.9	35.3	58.2
Demand Deposits	4.5	5.2	5.3	9.2	13.2	19.1	18.7	22.4	28.8	34.5	48.1
Quasi-Money	4.4	5.6	5.3	6.0	7.7	8.5	14.3	17.4	16.1	22.9	30.9
					(Millions of current Uganda Shillings)						
GOVERNMENT DEFICIT (-) OR SURPLUS	..	..	..	-9.0	-8.6	-15.3	-12.4	-13.2	-12.8	-1.6	-34.5
Current Revenue	..	..	..	15.4	12.4	11.8	20.9	24.6	34.4	57.9	26.3
Current Expenditure	..	..	..	..	..	..	26.9	31.4	39.2	45.5	48.5
Current Budget Balance	..	..	..	..	..	..	-6.1	-6.8	-4.8	12.4	-22.2
Capital Receipts	..	..	..	..	..	..	0.0	..	..	..	..
Capital Payments	..	..	..	..	..	..	6.3	6.4	7.9	14.0	12.3

1980	1981	1982	1983	1984	1985	1986	1987	1988	1989 estimate	NOTES	UGANDA
280	220	240	220	220	230	230	220	240	250	A	**CURRENT GNP PER CAPITA** (US $)
12,637	12,998	13,381	13,789	14,222	14,680	15,164	15,675	16,211	16,772	..	**POPULATION** (thousands)
				(Millions of current Uganda Shillings)							**USE AND ORIGIN OF RESOURCES**
1,262	2,126	3,106	4,953	9,262	23,195	53,801	184,352	512,629	1,035,519	..	Gross National Product (GNP)
-5	-373	-633	-943	-190	-373	-704	-2,175	-7,333	-15,847	..	Net Factor Income from Abroad
1,267	2,498	3,739	5,896	9,452	23,568	54,505	186,527	519,962	1,051,366	f	GDP at Market Prices
-82	-165	-248	-305	-248	-502	-2,230	-12,661	-48,313	-114,892	..	Resource Balance
242	428	818	1,019	1,508	3,147	6,130	13,739	37,069	62,798	..	Exports of Goods & NFServices
324	593	1,066	1,324	1,756	3,649	8,360	26,400	85,382	177,690	..	Imports of Goods & NFServices
1,349	2,663	3,987	6,201	9,700	24,070	56,735	199,188	568,275	1,166,258	..	Domestic Absorption
..	..	..	5,484	7,937	19,606	45,249	160,236	462,527	954,178	..	Private Consumption, etc.
..	..	..	183	920	2,132	4,676	14,400	38,735	75,341	..	General Gov't Consumption
77	150	294	534	843	2,332	6,810	24,552	67,013	136,739	..	Gross Domestic Investment
..	..	..	..	843	2,332	6,810	24,552	67,013	136,739	..	Fixed Investment
27	131	389	718	1,152	2,066	3,861	12,084	28,530	55,787	..	Indirect Taxes, net
1,240	2,367	3,350	5,178	8,300	21,502	50,644	174,443	491,432	995,579	f	GDP at factor cost
893	1,472	2,070	3,380	5,109	14,625	35,955	122,294	330,052	666,217	..	Agriculture
56	66	189	252	399	808	2,138	10,159	37,037	71,546	f	Industry
53	45	155	192	254	518	1,655	6,734	22,630	40,840	..	Manufacturing
291	829	1,091	1,546	2,792	6,069	12,551	41,990	124,343	257,816	f	Services, etc.
-5	-15	46	229	595	1,830	4,580	11,891	18,700	21,847	..	Gross Domestic Saving
-11	-388	-569	-613	524	1,925	5,261	14,429	23,997	30,317	..	Gross National Saving
				(Millions of 1987 Uganda Shillings)							
150,935.0	138,698.0	151,276.0	167,624.0	178,927.0	176,353.0	174,229.0	184,352.0	195,031.0	207,240.0	..	Gross National Product
151,569.0	163,001.0	182,097.0	199,538.0	182,598.0	179,189.0	176,508.0	186,527.0	197,821.0	210,412.0	f	GDP at Market Prices
..	..	..	..	..	..	..	..	..	..	..	Resource Balance
..	..	..	..	..	..	..	..	..	..	..	Exports of Goods & NFServices
..	..	..	..	..	..	..	..	..	..	..	Imports of Goods & NFServices
..	..	..	..	..	..	..	..	..	..	..	Domestic Absorption
..	..	..	..	..	..	..	..	..	..	..	Private Consumption, etc.
..	..	..	..	..	..	..	..	..	..	..	General Gov't Consumption
..	..	..	..	..	..	..	..	..	..	..	Gross Domestic Investment
..	..	..	..	..	..	..	..	..	..	..	Fixed Investment
148,348.0	154,426.0	163,150.0	175,239.0	160,343.0	163,481.0	164,005.0	174,443.0	186,967.0	199,247.0	f	GDP at factor cost
103,342.0	110,374.0	116,673.0	125,773.0	112,631.0	115,278.0	116,000.0	122,294.0	129,358.0	136,598.0	..	Agriculture
8,458.4	8,228.0	9,410.0	10,506.0	10,169.0	9,175.0	8,359.0	10,159.0	12,554.0	14,463.0	f	Industry
5,904.7	5,588.0	6,482.0	7,020.0	6,795.0	6,129.0	5,767.0	6,734.0	8,262.0	9,793.0	..	Manufacturing
36,759.5	35,691.0	37,043.0	38,960.0	37,543.0	39,028.0	39,646.0	41,990.0	45,055.0	48,186.0	f	Services, etc.
											Memo Items:
..	..	..	..	..	..	..	..	..	..	..	Capacity to Import
..	..	..	..	..	..	..	..	..	..	..	Terms of Trade Adjustment
..	..	..	..	..	..	..	..	..	..	..	Gross Domestic Income
..	..	..	..	..	..	..	..	..	..	..	Gross National Income
				(Index 1987 = 100)							**DOMESTIC PRICES/DEFLATORS**
8.00E-1	1.5	2.1	3.0	5.2	13.2	30.9	100.0	262.8	499.7	..	Overall (GDP)
..	..	..	..	..	..	..	..	..	..	..	Domestic Absorption
9.00E-1	1.3	1.8	2.7	4.5	12.7	31.0	100.0	255.1	487.7	..	Agriculture
7.00E-1	0.8	2.0	2.4	3.9	8.8	25.6	100.0	295.0	494.7	..	Industry
9.00E-1	0.8	2.4	2.7	3.7	8.5	28.7	100.0	273.9	417.0	..	Manufacturing
9.00E-1	1.8	2.7	3.3	4.7	11.0	29.6	100.0	283.6	539.6	..	Consumer Price Index
											MANUFACTURING ACTIVITY
..	..	..	..	..	..	..	..	..	..	G	Employment (1987=100)
..	..	..	..	..	..	..	..	..	..	G	Real Earnings per Empl. (1987=100)
..	..	..	..	..	..	..	..	..	..	G	Real Output per Empl. (1987=100)
..	..	..	..	..	..	..	..	..	..	..	Earnings as % of Value Added
				(Millions of current Uganda Shillings)							**MONETARY HOLDINGS**
184.5	345.6	385.1	544.2	1,162.9	2,622.1	7,118.1	..	..	..	..	Money Supply, Broadly Defined
139.6	283.1	297.8	435.4	986.6	2,256.1	6,061.8	..	..	..	..	Money
72.6	113.6	128.4	189.2	487.2	1,050.4	3,509.3	..	..	..	..	Currency Outside Banks
67.0	169.5	169.4	246.2	499.4	1,205.6	2,552.5	..	..	..	..	Demand Deposits
44.9	62.4	87.4	108.9	176.3	366.1	1,056.3	..	..	..	..	Quasi-Money
				(Millions of current Uganda Shillings)							
-39.1	-100.5	-146.0	-133.8	-221.2	-640.2	-1,344.9	..	..	..	C	**GOVERNMENT DEFICIT (-) OR SURPLUS**
40.1	30.9	276.5	536.8	937.6	1,668.9	3,228.2	..	..	..	..	Current Revenue
67.0	106.0	346.2	572.9	1,016.8	1,946.5	3,353.1	..	..	..	..	Current Expenditure
-26.9	-75.1	-69.7	-36.2	-79.2	-277.5	-125.0	..	..	..	..	Current Budget Balance
..	..	0.1	..	..	..	..	..	..	..	..	Capital Receipts
12.2	25.3	76.4	97.6	142.0	362.7	1,219.9	..	..	..	..	Capital Payments

UGANDA	1969	1970	1971	1972	1973	1974	1975	1976	1977	1978	1979
FOREIGN TRADE (CUSTOMS BASIS)					*(Millions of current US dollars)*						
Value of Exports, fob	195.66	245.48	235.25	260.54	299.90	315.82	263.58	351.70	588.33	350.00	436.00
Nonfuel Primary Products	194.36	242.94	233.16	258.40	298.55	314.79	262.91	347.32	582.72	346.70	431.74
Fuels	0.24	0.32	0.22	0.26	0.20	0.37	0.47	2.87	3.64	2.15	2.77
Manufactures	1.06	2.22	1.87	1.88	1.15	0.66	0.20	1.51	1.97	1.15	1.49
Value of Imports, cif	174.58	172.06	249.62	161.98	162.09	213.28	205.74	172.27	241.19	255.00	197.00
Nonfuel Primary Products	16.83	15.69	24.81	20.60	22.27	34.02	19.02	16.99	13.46	17.60	13.77
Fuels	2.38	2.70	1.54	1.07	0.95	1.49	3.12	51.07	53.22	56.60	45.39
Manufactures	155.37	153.67	223.27	140.31	138.87	177.77	183.60	104.21	174.51	180.80	137.84
					(Index 1987 = 100)						
Terms of Trade	141.7	161.2	138.4	138.0	152.3	128.0	113.1	206.9	284.8	193.7	176.6
Export Prices, fob	37.4	44.6	41.7	45.9	60.4	63.5	59.8	118.7	172.3	131.5	143.1
Import Prices, cif	26.4	27.7	30.2	33.3	39.6	49.6	52.9	57.4	60.5	67.9	81.0
BALANCE OF PAYMENTS					*(Millions of current US dollars)*						
Exports of Goods & Services	..	297.10	284.14	291.51	290.40	307.76	251.81	335.73	556.09	337.39	414.16
Merchandise, fob	..	261.60	243.93	263.83	275.14	294.04	237.25	323.61	547.80	322.96	397.21
Nonfactor Services	..	32.60	37.11	25.30	11.21	9.38	10.56	9.35	4.90	8.54	14.94
Factor Services	..	2.90	3.11	2.39	4.05	4.33	4.01	2.77	3.39	5.89	2.01
Imports of Goods & Services	..	271.40	365.08	269.26	246.06	330.61	320.54	294.63	485.34	471.84	387.09
Merchandise, fob	..	178.30	247.74	171.87	175.48	236.32	228.38	206.78	366.60	306.31	265.71
Nonfactor Services	..	75.10	91.77	78.17	52.22	73.96	84.26	78.16	104.49	152.52	108.37
Factor Services	..	18.00	25.58	19.22	18.36	20.32	7.89	9.70	14.24	13.02	13.00
Long-Term Interest	..	4.70	4.90	5.10	4.80	4.60	3.20	2.30	4.20	2.90	3.00
Private Current Transfers, net	..	-6.90	-7.42	-9.01	-3.93	-5.05	-3.40	-5.66	-4.67	-8.83	-16.70
Workers' Remittances	..	..	..	..	..	..	..	..	..	0.46	0.80
Curr. A/C Bal before Off. Transf.	..	18.80	-88.36	13.25	40.41	-27.90	-72.12	35.44	66.08	-143.28	10.37
Net Official Transfers	..	1.50	2.61	3.15	2.62	3.85	16.03	7.74	1.98	5.88	29.12
Curr. A/C Bal after Off. Transf.	..	20.30	-85.75	16.39	43.04	-24.05	-56.09	43.18	68.07	-137.40	39.49
Long-Term Capital, net	..	6.70	30.99	29.64	-14.78	16.24	8.01	-16.05	-11.91	15.86	92.88
Direct Investment	..	4.20	-1.20	-11.94	5.25	1.68	2.06	1.15	0.82	1.04	1.61
Long-Term Loans	..	23.30	20.00	28.20	-3.10	31.70	12.30	33.50	29.30	59.50	136.00
Disbursements	..	27.30	24.40	34.00	17.10	42.70	22.00	40.70	48.80	70.60	148.20
Repayments	..	4.00	4.40	5.80	20.20	11.00	9.70	7.20	19.50	11.10	12.20
Other Long-Term Capital	..	-20.80	12.20	13.38	-16.93	-17.15	-6.35	-50.70	-42.03	-44.68	-44.72
Other Capital, net	..	-28.60	10.36	-41.65	-36.89	-10.33	48.04	-24.67	-55.65	128.73	-165.03
Change in Reserves	..	1.60	44.40	-4.39	8.63	18.15	0.04	-2.46	-0.50	-7.19	32.65
Memo Item:					*(Uganda Shillings per US dollar)*						
Conversion Factor (Annual Avg)	0.050	0.050	0.050	0.050	0.060	0.070	0.090	0.100	0.170	0.230	0.400
				(Millions of US dollars), outstanding at end of year							
EXTERNAL DEBT (Total)	..	138.3	160.7	183.1	189.0	230.8	240.3	278.1	354.1	426.0	574.2
Long-Term Debt (by debtor)	..	138.3	160.7	183.1	189.0	230.8	240.3	278.1	320.1	405.0	544.2
Central Bank, incl. IMF credit	..	0.0	10.8	10.8	12.1	18.3	28.2	38.0	39.7	38.0	146.7
Central Government	..	133.5	144.2	166.8	171.2	206.1	205.2	231.3	268.2	337.4	366.2
Rest of General Government	..	..	..	..	..	..	..	..	..	..	..
Non-financial Public Enterprises	..	3.6	4.3	4.2	4.5	5.0	5.4	7.6	10.8	21.2	22.3
Priv. Sector, incl non-guaranteed	..	1.2	1.4	1.3	1.2	1.4	1.5	1.2	1.4	8.4	9.0
Short-Term Debt	..	0.0	0.0	0.0	0.0	0.0	0.0	0.0	34.0	21.0	30.0
Memo Items:					*(Thousands of US dollars)*						
Int'l Reserves Excluding Gold	52,270	56,650	26,923	35,952	29,113	16,759	31,023	44,534	47,206	52,700	22,839
Gold Holdings (at market price)	..	..	..	..	..	..	..	..	..	..	..
SOCIAL INDICATORS											
Total Fertility Rate	7.1	7.1	7.1	7.1	7.1	7.2	7.2	7.3	7.3	7.3	7.3
Infant Mortality Rate	117.2	116.8	116.4	116.0	115.6	115.2	114.8	114.4	114.0	113.6	113.2
Life Expectancy at Birth	46.4	46.6	46.8	47.0	46.8	46.6	46.4	46.2	46.0	46.0	46.0
Urban Population, % of total	7.7	8.0	8.1	8.1	8.2	8.2	8.3	8.4	8.5	8.5	8.6
Food Prod. per capita (1987=100)	129.4	141.6	138.5	137.9	131.0	137.3	143.1	138.9	136.0	134.8	111.3
Labor Force, Agriculture (%)	89.5	89.3	88.9	88.5	88.2	87.9	87.6	87.2	86.8	86.5	86.2
Labor Force, Female (%)	43.2	43.2	43.1	43.1	43.0	43.0	43.0	42.9	42.9	42.9	42.8
Primary Schl. Enroll. Ratio	..	38.0	..	..	..	..	44.0	47.0	50.0	51.0	50.0
Primary Schl. Enroll. Ratio, Female	..	30.0	..	..	..	..	35.0	39.0	41.0	43.0	42.0
Secondary Schl. Enroll. Ratio	..	4.0	..	..	..	..	4.0	4.0	5.0	5.0	5.0

1980	1981	1982	1983	1984	1985	1986	1987	1988	1989 estimate	NOTES	UGANDA
				(Millions of current US dollars)							**FOREIGN TRADE (CUSTOMS BASIS)**
345.00	243.00	349.00	372.00	399.00	348.00	395.00	320.00	369.00	..	f	Value of Exports, fob
342.03	240.91	345.99	368.80	396.17	345.41	393.42	318.32	367.12	..	..	Nonfuel Primary Products
1.93	1.36	1.95	2.08	1.89	1.77	0.72	0.60	0.67	..	..	Fuels
1.04	0.73	1.06	1.11	0.94	0.82	0.86	1.08	1.21	..	..	Manufactures
293.00	345.20	377.40	377.40	344.10	327.40	344.00	477.00	573.00	..	f	Value of Imports, cif
20.05	23.71	25.93	26.11	22.80	19.59	26.92	33.27	48.02	..	..	Nonfuel Primary Products
66.74	78.65	86.10	85.88	76.90	90.62	25.67	37.11	50.26	..	..	Fuels
206.21	242.84	265.37	265.41	244.40	217.19	291.41	406.62	474.72	..	..	Manufactures
				(Index 1987 = 100)							
143.0	116.7	126.5	126.9	141.8	131.1	172.0	100.0	111.7	..	f	Terms of Trade
134.8	112.0	118.2	114.8	125.0	119.4	155.9	100.0	117.6	..	f	Export Prices, fob
94.2	96.1	93.5	90.5	88.2	91.1	90.7	100.0	105.2	..	f	Import Prices, cif
				(Millions of current US dollars)							**BALANCE OF PAYMENTS**
330.70	274.40	382.10	384.40	406.00	399.00	398.00	365.00	323.00	272.00	f	Exports of Goods & Services
319.40	229.30	347.10	367.70	381.00	381.00	382.00	341.00	293.00	237.00	..	Merchandise, fob
9.90	44.30	35.00	11.50	25.00	18.00	16.00	24.00	30.00	35.00	..	Nonfactor Services
1.40	0.80	0.00	5.20	0.00	0.00	0.00	0.00	0.00	..	..	Factor Services
449.77	391.90	524.30	543.44	517.00	514.00	569.00	694.00	785.00	799.00	f	Imports of Goods & Services
317.60	278.30	337.60	342.50	386.00	392.00	447.00	530.00	597.00	633.00	..	Merchandise, fob
123.40	100.40	160.40	150.00	81.00	73.00	76.00	112.00	126.00	101.00	..	Nonfactor Services
8.77	13.20	26.30	50.94	50.00	49.00	46.00	52.00	62.00	65.00	..	Factor Services
2.40	2.60	10.20	15.90	32.80	20.80	16.20	16.50	15.40	27.50	..	Long-Term Interest
-2.20	-0.20	19.00	65.80	33.00	69.70	98.90	110.00	119.00	109.00	..	Private Current Transfers, net
..	..	..	..	..	..	..	..	..	..	..	Workers' Remittances
-121.27	-117.70	-123.20	-93.24	-78.00	-45.30	-72.10	-219.00	-343.00	-418.00	..	Curr. A/C Bal before Off. Transf.
38.10	149.60	107.30	103.50	68.00	48.00	35.00	66.00	129.00	178.00	..	Net Official Transfers
-83.17	31.90	-15.90	10.26	-10.00	2.70	-37.10	-153.00	-214.00	-240.00	..	Curr. A/C Bal after Off. Transf.
-59.30	-52.91	36.20	63.70	-4.00	110.00	152.00	197.00	199.00	204.00	f	Long-Term Capital, net
..	..	0.00	0.70	0.00	0.00	0.00	0.00	0.00	..	..	Direct Investment
85.10	43.90	157.50	35.30	26.20	125.60	87.70	231.30	180.90	50.20	..	Long-Term Loans
105.00	99.10	202.20	95.70	84.50	166.30	119.20	246.20	204.10	138.10	..	Disbursements
19.90	55.20	44.70	60.40	58.30	40.70	31.50	14.90	23.20	87.90	..	Repayments
-144.40	-96.81	-121.30	27.70	-30.20	-15.60	64.30	-34.30	18.10	153.80	..	Other Long-Term Capital
87.24	-73.68	-77.74	-146.76	60.00	-73.70	-105.90	-48.00	13.00	16.00	f	Other Capital, net
55.23	94.70	57.44	72.80	-46.00	-39.00	-9.00	4.00	2.00	20.00	..	Change in Reserves
				(Uganda Shillings per US dollar)							Memo Item:
0.730	1.570	2.140	2.690	3.600	6.720	14.000	42.840	106.140	223.090	..	Conversion Factor (Annual Avg)
				(Millions of US dollars), outstanding at end of year							
733.0	793.8	937.8	1,020.0	1,031.0	1,171.1	1,286.4	1,659.2	1,798.7	1,808.4	..	**EXTERNAL DEBT (Total)**
667.0	755.6	886.4	992.8	988.7	1,126.8	1,214.5	1,593.3	1,707.9	1,713.4	..	Long-Term Debt (by debtor)
253.1	371.4	420.1	474.0	420.9	391.6	340.3	370.7	351.9	259.6	..	Central Bank, incl. IMF credit
382.0	357.5	435.9	500.2	550.9	713.5	847.2	1,193.1	1,328.6	1,424.9	..	Central Government
..	..	..	..	..	..	..	..	..	..	..	Rest of General Government
22.2	19.0	23.1	12.9	10.9	14.8	19.0	19.9	18.3	20.7	..	Non-financial Public Enterprises
9.7	7.7	7.3	5.7	6.0	6.9	8.0	9.6	9.1	8.2	..	Priv. Sector, incl non-guaranteed
66.0	38.2	51.4	27.2	42.3	44.3	71.9	65.9	90.8	95.0	..	Short-Term Debt
				(Thousands of US dollars)							Memo Items:
3,000	30,003	78,324	106,496	67,907	27,288	29,206	54,600	49,300	14,100	..	Int'l Reserves Excluding Gold
..	..	..	..	..	..	..	..	..	..	..	Gold Holdings (at market price)
											SOCIAL INDICATORS
7.3	7.3	7.3	7.3	7.3	7.3	7.3	7.3	7.3	7.3	..	Total Fertility Rate
112.8	112.4	112.0	110.2	108.4	106.6	104.8	103.0	101.1	99.3	..	Infant Mortality Rate
46.0	46.0	46.0	46.4	46.8	47.3	47.7	48.2	48.4	48.6	..	Life Expectancy at Birth
8.7	8.8	9.0	9.1	9.3	9.4	9.6	9.9	10.1	10.2	..	Urban Population, % of total
109.9	114.4	118.9	120.5	98.5	104.9	96.3	100.0	96.7	94.9	..	Food Prod. per capita (1987=100)
85.9	..	..	..	..	..	..	..	..	..	..	Labor Force, Agriculture (%)
42.8	42.6	42.4	42.3	42.1	41.9	41.7	41.6	41.4	41.2	..	Labor Force, Female (%)
50.0	52.0	58.0	..	..	..	70.0	..	..	..	..	Primary Schl. Enroll. Ratio
43.0	44.0	49.0	..	..	..	63.0	..	50.0	..	..	Primary Schl. Enroll. Ratio, Female
5.0	5.0	8.0	..	..	..	13.0	..	8.0	..	..	Secondary Schl. Enroll. Ratio

UNITED ARAB EMIRATES	1969	1970	1971	1972	1973	1974	1975	1976	1977	1978	1979
CURRENT GNP PER CAPITA (US $)	..	..	..	..	..	..	13,280	20,370	22,960	21,070	25,680
POPULATION (thousands)	188	220	255	300	356	425	505	597	702	813	920

USE AND ORIGIN OF RESOURCES

(Millions of current U.A.E. Dirhams)

	1969	1970	1971	1972	1973	1974	1975	1976	1977	1978	1979
Gross National Product (GNP)	..	..	..	..	10,201	30,902	39,591	51,342	64,320	62,901	86,845
Net Factor Income from Abroad	..	..	..	..	-1,199	-198	277	514	1,210	2,516	7,212
GDP at Market Prices	..	..	..	..	11,400	31,100	39,314	50,828	63,110	60,385	79,633
Resource Balance	..	..	..	..	5,700	21,400	17,779	21,550	19,174	16,042	27,146
Exports of Goods & NFServices	..	..	..	..	9,400	29,400	29,183	36,106	41,265	40,121	56,871
Imports of Goods & NFServices	..	..	..	..	3,700	8,000	11,404	14,556	22,091	24,079	29,725
Domestic Absorption	..	..	..	..	5,700	9,700	21,535	29,278	43,936	44,343	52,487
Private Consumption, etc.	..	..	..	..	1,500	2,200	6,215	7,695	11,557	12,501	15,245
General Gov't Consumption	..	..	..	..	1,300	2,700	3,261	4,648	7,413	8,163	9,600
Gross Domestic Investment	..	..	..	..	2,900	4,800	12,059	16,935	24,966	23,679	27,642
Fixed Investment	..	..	..	..	..	..	12,059	16,585	22,686	25,779	28,442
Indirect Taxes, net	..	..	..	..	..	..	-321	-679	-785	-885	-1,164
GDP at factor cost	..	..	..	..	..	..	39,635	51,507	63,895	61,270	80,797
Agriculture	..	..	..	..	155	208	329	432	491	604	680
Industry	..	..	..	..	6,920	24,511	31,348	39,277	46,556	43,982	60,960
Manufacturing	..	..	..	..	225	301	369	593	1,853	2,197	2,533
Services, etc.	..	..	..	..	..	..	7,958	11,798	16,848	16,684	19,157
Gross Domestic Saving	..	..	..	..	8,600	26,200	29,838	38,485	44,140	39,721	54,788
Gross National Saving	..	..	..	..	6,802	24,696	27,302	35,085	40,549	36,546	54,788

(Millions of 1980 U.A.E. Dirhams)

	1969	1970	1971	1972	1973	1974	1975	1976	1977	1978	1979
Gross National Product	..	..	..	..	38,792	49,320	53,098	61,271	72,602	72,465	94,744
GDP at Market Prices	..	..	..	..	43,351	49,636	52,727	60,658	71,236	69,566	86,879
Resource Balance	..	..	..	..	..	..	22,687	22,061	17,957	16,432	29,116
Exports of Goods & NFServices	..	..	..	..	..	..	42,145	47,713	53,212	49,544	66,670
Imports of Goods & NFServices	..	..	..	..	..	..	19,458	25,652	35,255	33,112	37,554
Domestic Absorption	..	..	..	..	..	..	30,040	38,597	53,279	53,134	57,763
Private Consumption, etc.	..	..	..	..	..	..	9,344	12,231	15,621	16,785	17,550
General Gov't Consumption	..	..	..	..	..	..	4,667	6,490	8,280	8,570	10,204
Gross Domestic Investment	..	..	..	..	..	..	16,029	19,876	29,378	27,779	30,009
Fixed Investment	..	..	..	..	..	..	16,029	19,164	26,078	30,779	31,009
GDP at factor cost	..	..	..	..	..	..	53,054	61,437	71,956	70,506	88,059
Agriculture	..	..	..	..	..	..	367	480	563	649	732
Industry	..	..	..	..	..	..	41,467	45,451	51,713	50,639	66,141
Manufacturing	..	..	..	..	..	..	472	702	1,923	2,274	2,542
Services, etc.	..	..	..	..	..	..	11,220	15,506	19,680	19,218	21,186

Memo Items:

	1969	1970	1971	1972	1973	1974	1975	1976	1977	1978	1979
Capacity to Import	..	..	..	..	..	..	49,793	63,630	65,855	55,172	71,850
Terms of Trade Adjustment	..	..	..	..	..	..	7,648	15,916	12,643	5,628	5,180
Gross Domestic Income	..	..	..	..	..	..	60,375	76,574	83,879	75,194	92,059
Gross National Income	..	..	..	..	..	..	60,746	77,188	85,244	78,093	99,924

DOMESTIC PRICES/DEFLATORS

(Index 1980 = 100)

	1969	1970	1971	1972	1973	1974	1975	1976	1977	1978	1979
Overall (GDP)	..	..	..	..	26.3	62.7	74.6	83.8	88.6	86.8	91.7
Domestic Absorption	..	..	..	..	..	..	71.7	75.9	82.5	83.5	90.9
Agriculture	..	..	..	..	..	..	89.6	90.0	87.2	93.1	92.9
Industry	..	..	..	..	..	..	75.6	86.4	90.0	86.9	92.2
Manufacturing	..	..	..	..	..	..	78.2	84.5	96.4	96.6	99.6
Consumer Price Index	..	..	..	..	..	..	..	..	..	..	..

MANUFACTURING ACTIVITY

	1969	1970	1971	1972	1973	1974	1975	1976	1977	1978	1979
Employment (1987=100)	..	..	..	..	..	..	..	..	..	..	..
Real Earnings per Empl. (1987=100)	..	..	..	..	..	..	..	..	..	..	..
Real Output per Empl. (1987=100)	..	..	..	..	..	..	..	..	..	..	..
Earnings as % of Value Added	..	..	..	..	..	..	..	..	39.5	43.1	..

MONETARY HOLDINGS

(Millions of current U.A.E. Dirhams)

	1969	1970	1971	1972	1973	1974	1975	1976	1977	1978	1979
Money Supply, Broadly Defined	..	..	..	..	2,257	6,036	8,820	16,754	15,539	17,576	18,222
Money	..	..	..	..	970	1,536	2,603	4,725	5,215	5,776	6,269
Currency Outside Banks	..	..	..	..	265	429	628	1,077	1,392	1,704	1,965
Demand Deposits	..	..	..	..	704	1,107	1,975	3,648	3,822	4,072	4,303
Quasi-Money	..	..	..	..	1,287	4,499	6,217	12,028	10,325	11,800	11,954

GOVERNMENT DEFICIT (-) OR SURPLUS

(Millions of current U.A.E. Dirhams)

	1969	1970	1971	1972	1973	1974	1975	1976	1977	1978	1979
GOVERNMENT DEFICIT (-) OR SURPLUS	..	..	..	37	30	62	590	597	-211	-503	202
Current Revenue	..	..	..	201	420	800	1,773	3,102	5,995	6,984	8,862
Current Expenditure	..	..	..	148	331	569	886	1,456	4,364	6,269	7,498
Current Budget Balance	..	..	..	53	89	231	887	1,646	1,631	715	1,364
Capital Receipts	..	..	..	..	..	..	..	..	..	..	..
Capital Payments	..	..	..	16	59	169	297	1,049	1,842	1,218	1,162

1980	1981	1982	1983	1984	1985	1986	1987	1988	1989 estimate	NOTES	UNITED ARAB EMIRATES
30,130	31,660	28,830	25,310	24,250	22,220	16,320	16,700	16,420	18,430	..	**CURRENT GNP PER CAPITA (US $)**
1,015	1,100	1,176	1,242	1,299	1,349	1,399	1,448	1,496	1,544	..	**POPULATION (thousands)**
			(Millions of current U.A.E. Dirhams)								**USE AND ORIGIN OF RESOURCES**
115,023	127,814	120,495	107,753	106,048	104,700	83,341	90,905	90,254	101,906	..	Gross National Product (GNP)
5,190	6,975	7,342	5,506	4,405	5,506	4,405	4,405	4,772	565	..	Net Factor Income from Abroad
109,833	120,839	113,153	102,246	101,643	99,194	78,936	86,500	85,482	101,341	..	GDP at Market Prices
47,718	42,617	31,144	23,902	27,707	27,604	6,207	14,494	8,748	15,574	..	Resource Balance
85,592	83,662	71,576	60,874	60,008	58,266	37,901	48,562	46,744	55,661	..	Exports of Goods & NFServices
37,874	41,045	40,432	36,972	32,301	30,662	31,694	34,068	37,996	40,087	..	Imports of Goods & NFServices
62,115	78,222	82,009	78,344	73,936	71,590	72,729	72,006	76,734	85,767	..	Domestic Absorption
18,968	24,946	26,846	26,183	26,744	27,173	30,003	33,277	37,203	41,480	..	Private Consumption, etc.
11,992	21,475	22,000	19,958	17,696	19,484	18,897	17,762	17,653	19,242	..	General Gov't Consumption
31,155	31,801	33,163	32,203	29,496	24,933	23,829	20,967	21,878	25,045	..	Gross Domestic Investment
30,155	30,643	32,683	31,668	29,116	24,458	23,329	20,317	21,111	..	..	Fixed Investment
-1,637	-3,215	-2,501	-2,878	-2,861	-2,760	-2,532	-2,154	-2,059	-2,440	..	Indirect Taxes, net
111,470	124,054	115,654	105,124	104,504	101,954	81,468	88,654	87,541	103,781	..	GDP at factor cost
827	1,036	1,144	1,198	1,349	1,440	1,540	1,593	1,664	1,764	..	Agriculture
86,089	90,170	77,735	68,410	68,639	65,296	44,122	50,626	47,711	57,491	..	Industry
4,191	8,077	9,436	9,584	9,761	9,255	7,037	7,911	7,805	9,202	..	Manufacturing
24,554	32,848	36,775	35,516	34,516	35,218	35,806	36,435	38,166	44,526	..	Services, etc.
78,873	74,418	64,307	56,105	57,203	52,537	30,036	35,461	30,626	40,619	..	Gross Domestic Saving
75,907	72,950	63,573	55,738	56,102	52,170	29,669	35,461	30,626	..	..	Gross National Saving
			(Millions of 1980 U.A.E. Dirhams)								
115,023	119,473	110,358	103,324	107,013	101,145	102,160	102,131	106,886	119,403	..	Gross National Product
109,833	112,954	103,635	98,046	102,567	95,825	96,761	97,181	101,232	113,087	..	GDP at Market Prices
47,718	39,278	28,309	23,812	27,429	31,560	35,508	39,615	43,068	52,147	..	Resource Balance
85,592	77,835	66,714	58,377	60,189	61,044	66,019	69,894	74,713	83,264	..	Exports of Goods & NFServices
37,874	38,557	38,405	34,565	32,760	29,484	30,511	30,279	31,645	31,117	..	Imports of Goods & NFServices
62,115	73,676	75,326	74,234	75,138	64,265	61,253	57,566	58,164	60,940	..	Domestic Absorption
18,968	23,262	25,669	24,741	27,125	25,113	27,176	28,738	30,446	32,364	..	Private Consumption, etc.
11,992	20,300	20,042	18,976	18,007	17,273	14,672	12,714	11,935	12,248	..	General Gov't Consumption
31,155	30,114	29,615	30,517	30,006	21,879	19,405	16,114	15,783	16,328	..	Gross Domestic Investment
30,155	29,050	29,160	30,012	29,619	..	..	..	..	..	..	Fixed Investment
111,470	115,688	106,607	100,481	105,406	102,804	81,198	83,340	81,490	..	..	GDP at factor cost
827	1,020	1,079	1,236	1,400	1,525	1,617	1,640	1,702	..	..	Agriculture
86,089	84,618	74,140	66,470	70,657	66,296	43,651	47,579	44,434	..	..	Industry
4,191	7,990	9,251	9,116	9,655	9,443	7,280	7,434	7,352	..	..	Manufacturing
24,554	30,050	31,388	32,775	33,349	34,983	35,930	34,121	35,354	..	..	Services, etc.
											Memo Items:
85,592	78,591	67,988	56,911	60,860	56,027	36,486	43,161	38,931	43,206	..	Capacity to Import
0	756	1,274	-1,466	671	-5,017	-29,533	-26,733	-35,782	-40,058	..	Terms of Trade Adjustment
109,833	113,710	104,909	96,580	103,238	90,809	67,228	70,448	65,450	73,029	..	Gross Domestic Income
115,023	120,228	111,632	101,858	107,685	96,129	72,627	75,398	71,104	79,345	..	Gross National Income
			(Index 1980 = 100)								**DOMESTIC PRICES/DEFLATORS**
100.0	107.0	109.2	104.3	99.1	103.5	81.6	89.0	84.4	89.6	..	Overall (GDP)
100.0	106.2	108.9	105.5	98.4	111.4	118.7	125.1	131.9	140.7	..	Domestic Absorption
100.0	101.6	106.0	96.9	96.4	94.4	95.2	97.1	97.8	..	..	Agriculture
100.0	106.6	104.8	102.9	97.1	98.5	101.1	106.4	107.4	..	..	Industry
100.0	101.1	102.0	105.1	101.1	98.0	96.7	106.4	106.2	..	..	Manufacturing
..	..	..	..	..	..	..	..	..	..	f	Consumer Price Index
											MANUFACTURING ACTIVITY
..	..	..	..	..	..	..	..	..	..	G	Employment (1987 = 100)
..	..	..	..	..	..	..	..	..	..	G	Real Earnings per Empl. (1987 = 100)
..	..	..	..	..	..	..	..	..	..	G	Real Output per Empl. (1987 = 100)
..	34.3	..	..	..	61.2	..	..	..	..		Earnings as % of Value Added
			(Millions of current U.A.E. Dirhams)								**MONETARY HOLDINGS**
23,527	29,094	33,646	36,342	46,870	49,886	52,076	54,940	58,156	63,188	..	Money Supply, Broadly Defined
7,354	8,969	9,739	9,124	8,892	9,505	9,201	10,096	10,753	11,056	..	Money
2,143	2,771	2,990	2,879	2,929	3,161	3,246	3,511	3,600	3,612	..	Currency Outside Banks
5,212	6,198	6,749	6,245	5,963	6,344	5,955	6,585	7,154	7,444	..	Demand Deposits
16,172	20,124	23,907	27,217	37,978	40,381	42,875	44,844	47,403	52,132	..	Quasi-Money
			(Millions of current U.A.E. Dirhams)								
2,302	2,355	..	..	..	..	..	-624	-314	..	..	**GOVERNMENT DEFICIT (-) OR SURPLUS**
17,608	22,460	..	..	..	..	..	12,626	12,867	..	..	Current Revenue
12,311	17,418	17,648	14,737	14,827	..	..	13,031	13,038	..	..	Current Expenditure
5,297	5,042	..	..	..	..	..	-405	-171	..	..	Current Budget Balance
..	..	..	..	..	..	..	8	4	..	..	Capital Receipts
2,995	2,687	..	..	..	..	..	227	147	..	..	Capital Payments

UNITED ARAB EMIRATES	1969	1970	1971	1972	1973	1974	1975	1976	1977	1978	1979
FOREIGN TRADE (CUSTOMS BASIS)					*(Millions of current US dollars)*						
Value of Exports, fob	450	552	935	1,160	2,178	7,017	6,696	8,565	9,534	9,138	13,577
Nonfuel Primary Products	5	18	29	25	43	45	69	99	13	131	210
Fuels	432	532	902	1,114	2,116	6,932	6,544	8,262	9,091	8,678	12,862
Manufactures	14	3	5	21	18	40	83	204	431	330	505
Value of Imports, cif	307	271	312	496	842	1,781	2,754	3,443	5,179	5,389	6,966
Nonfuel Primary Products	59	50	56	76	126	290	343	465	676	717	965
Fuels	10	9	9	26	40	137	198	237	317	202	711
Manufactures	238	212	246	395	676	1,355	2,213	2,742	4,186	4,470	5,290
					(Index 1987 = 100)						
Terms of Trade	29.3	28.1	33.9	36.7	42.5	127.2	116.5	123.4	123.0	109.8	133.1
Export Prices, fob	7.7	7.7	10.1	11.3	15.9	64.6	62.9	67.3	73.2	74.4	106.0
Import Prices, cif	26.4	27.5	29.6	30.7	37.4	50.8	54.0	54.6	59.5	67.7	79.6
BALANCE OF PAYMENTS					*(Millions of current US dollars)*						
Exports of Goods & Services	..	..	..	..	2,160	7,250	7,950	9,820	11,120	11,460	17,740
Merchandise, fob	..	520	870	1,090	2,030	6,870	7,450	9,130	10,170	9,970	15,040
Nonfactor Services	..	..	..	..	50	100	150	230	230	280	340
Factor Services	..	..	..	..	80	280	350	460	720	1,210	2,360
Imports of Goods & Services	..	..	..	..	1,330	2,250	3,320	4,180	6,230	6,840	9,300
Merchandise, fob	..	270	310	480	730	1,490	2,300	2,810	4,300	4,680	4,080
Nonfactor Services	..	..	..	..	230	430	740	1,040	1,520	1,600	4,750
Factor Services	..	..	..	..	380	330	280	330	410	560	470
Long-Term Interest	..	..	..	..	..	..	..	..	..	..	..
Private Current Transfers, net	..	..	..	-50	-150	-330	-710	-990	-1,230	-1,470	-1,890
Workers' Remittances	..	..	..	..	..	..	..	..	..	..	..
Curr. A/C Bal before Off. Transf.	..	100	260	350	680	4,670	3,920	4,650	3,660	3,150	6,550
Net Official Transfers	..	-10	-50	-40	-280	-480	-560	-780	-870	-700	-1,020
Curr. A/C Bal after Off. Transf.	..	90	210	310	400	4,190	3,360	3,870	2,790	2,450	5,530
Long-Term Capital, net	..	..	10	..	60	-860	-790	-160	-50	340	-50
Direct Investment	..	..	..	..	..	..	..	..	..	..	..
Long-Term Loans	..	..	..	..	..	..	..	..	..	..	..
Disbursements	..	..	..	..	..	..	..	..	..	..	..
Repayments	..	..	..	..	..	..	..	..	..	..	..
Other Long-Term Capital	..	..	10	..	60	-860	-790	-160	-50	340	-50
Other Capital, net	..	-60	-30	-120	-280	-1,110	-1,060	-1,210	-1,610	-1,550	-3,070
Change in Reserves	..	-30	-190	-190	-180	-2,220	-1,510	-2,500	-1,130	-1,240	-2,410
Memo Item:					*(U.A.E. Dirhams per US dollar)*						
Conversion Factor (Annual Avg)	4.760	4.760	4.750	4.390	4.000	3.960	3.960	3.950	3.900	3.870	3.820
					(Millions of US dollars), outstanding at end of year						
EXTERNAL DEBT (Total)	..	..	..	..	..	..	..	..	..	..	..
Long-Term Debt (by debtor)	..	..	..	..	..	..	..	..	..	..	..
Central Bank, incl. IMF credit	..	..	..	..	..	..	..	..	..	..	..
Central Government	..	..	..	..	..	..	..	..	..	..	..
Rest of General Government	..	..	..	..	..	..	..	..	..	..	..
Non-financial Public Enterprises	..	..	..	..	..	..	..	..	..	..	..
Priv. Sector, incl non-guaranteed	..	..	..	..	..	..	..	..	..	..	..
Short-Term Debt	..	..	..	..	..	..	..	..	..	..	..
Memo Items:					*(Millions of US dollars)*						
Int'l Reserves Excluding Gold	..	..	..	..	91.7	452.9	987.9	1,906.5	800.3	811.8	1,432.3
Gold Holdings (at market price)	..	..	..	..	..	..	..	73.4	93.8	130.3	295.2
SOCIAL INDICATORS											
Total Fertility Rate	6.6	6.5	6.4	6.4	6.2	6.1	5.9	5.8	5.7	5.6	5.5
Infant Mortality Rate	73.8	68.2	62.6	57.0	53.2	49.4	45.6	41.8	38.0	36.8	35.6
Life Expectancy at Birth	60.4	61.1	61.8	62.5	63.4	64.2	65.1	65.9	66.7	67.2	67.7
Urban Population, % of total	42.1	42.3	49.8	57.3	64.8	72.3	79.8	80.1	80.4	80.6	80.9
Food Prod. per capita (1987=100)	..	..	..	..	..	..	..	..	..	..	..
Labor Force, Agriculture (%)	14.5	13.6	11.7	10.7	10.0	9.5	9.1	7.6	6.5	5.7	5.1
Labor Force, Female (%)	4.4	4.3	4.2	4.1	4.0	4.0	4.0	4.4	4.6	4.8	5.0
Primary Schl. Enroll. Ratio	..	93.0	..	..	..	..	101.0	..	108.0	108.0	113.0
Primary Schl. Enroll. Ratio, Female	..	71.0	..	..	..	..	97.0	..	107.0	108.0	112.0
Secondary Schl. Enroll. Ratio	..	22.0	..	..	..	..	33.0	..	39.0	43.0	47.0

1980	1981	1982	1983	1984	1985	1986	1987	1988	1989 estimate	NOTES	UNITED ARAB EMIRATES
											FOREIGN TRADE (CUSTOMS BASIS)
				(Millions of current US dollars)							
20,738	20,240	17,260	15,085	16,000	14,800	10,300	12,000	12,300	..	f	Value of Exports, fob
394	344	266	742	743	720	455	552	828	..	..	Nonfuel Primary Products
19,459	18,925	16,144	13,018	13,200	12,300	8,014	9,536	8,601	..	f	Fuels
885	971	850	1,324	2,057	1,780	1,831	1,912	2,871	..	..	Manufactures
8,746	9,646	9,440	8,356	7,043	5,649	6,422	7,226	8,522	..	..	Value of Imports, cif
1,227	1,291	1,183	1,213	957	36	148	389	460	..	..	Nonfuel Primary Products
999	1,262	709	586	507	238	381	205	241	..	..	Fuels
6,520	7,093	7,548	6,557	5,579	5,375	5,893	6,632	7,821	..	..	Manufactures
				(Index 1987 = 100)							
185.4	201.5	196.0	173.7	167.5	171.0	90.5	100.0	84.7	..	..	Terms of Trade
167.7	184.9	167.4	145.6	137.7	134.5	81.7	100.0	92.0	..	..	Export Prices, fob
90.5	91.8	85.4	83.8	82.2	78.7	90.3	100.0	108.6	..	..	Import Prices, cif
				(Millions of current US dollars)							**BALANCE OF PAYMENTS**
..	..	..	..	..	..	..	..	..	..	..	Exports of Goods & Services
22,000	21,800	18,200	15,400	16,000	14,800	10,300	12,300	12,300	..	..	Merchandise, fob
1,090	990	1,300	1,180	350	1,080	1,020	930	430	..	..	Nonfactor Services
..	..	..	..	..	..	..	..	..	..	..	Factor Services
..	..	..	..	..	..	..	..	..	..	..	Imports of Goods & Services
7,600	8,600	8,100	7,200	6,200	5,700	5,700	6,500	7,700	..	..	Merchandise, fob
2,890	3,490	3,500	3,580	2,150	2,980	2,720	2,730	2,230	..	..	Nonfactor Services
..	..	..	..	..	..	..	..	..	..	..	Factor Services
..	..	..	..	..	..	..	..	..	..	..	Long-Term Interest
-2,200	-2,300	-2,200	-1,600	-1,500	-1,600	-1,300	-1,200	-1,300	..	..	Private Current Transfers, net
..	..	..	..	..	..	..	..	..	..	..	Workers' Remittances
11,800	10,300	7,700	5,700	7,700	7,100	2,800	4,000	2,800	..	..	Curr. A/C Bal before Off. Transf.
-1,700	-1,100	-700	-400	-200	-200	-400	-300	-100	..	..	Net Official Transfers
10,100	9,200	7,000	5,300	7,500	6,900	2,400	3,700	2,700	..	..	Curr. A/C Bal after Off. Transf.
-3,700	-2,900	-1,700	-1,500	600	300	600	-1,000	-1,000	..	..	Long-Term Capital, net
..	..	..	..	..	..	..	..	..	..	..	Direct Investment
..	..	..	..	..	..	..	..	..	..	..	Long-Term Loans
..	..	..	..	..	..	..	..	..	..	..	Disbursements
..	..	..	..	..	..	..	..	..	..	..	Repayments
-3,700	-2,900	-1,700	-1,500	600	300	600	-1,000	-1,000	..	..	Other Long-Term Capital
-4,600	-4,000	-4,300	-4,200	-6,900	-5,900	-900	-2,000	-1,100	..	..	Other Capital, net
-1,800	-2,300	-1,000	400	-1,200	-1,300	-2,100	-700	-600	..	..	Change in Reserves
				(U.A.E. Dirhams per US dollar)							Memo Item:
3.710	3.670	3.670	3.670	3.670	3.670	3.670	3.670	3.670	3.670	..	Conversion Factor (Annual Avg)
			(Millions of US dollars), outstanding at end of year								
..	..	..	..	..	..	..	..	..	..	..	**EXTERNAL DEBT (Total)**
..	..	..	..	..	..	..	..	..	..	..	Long-Term Debt (by debtor)
..	..	..	..	..	..	..	..	..	..	..	Central Bank, incl. IMF credit
..	..	..	..	..	..	..	..	..	..	..	Central Government
..	..	..	..	..	..	..	..	..	..	..	Rest of General Government
..	..	..	..	..	..	..	..	..	..	..	Non-financial Public Enterprises
..	..	..	..	..	..	..	..	..	..	..	Priv. Sector, incl non-guaranteed
..	..	..	..	..	..	..	..	..	..	..	Short-Term Debt
				(Millions of US dollars)							Memo Items:
2,014.7	3,202.2	2,215.5	2,072.4	2,286.9	3,204.3	3,369.9	4,725.3	4,433.5	4,456.6	..	Int'l Reserves Excluding Gold
339.8	269.3	373.4	311.8	251.9	267.2	319.4	395.6	335.3	319.7	..	Gold Holdings (at market price)
											SOCIAL INDICATORS
5.4	5.3	5.2	5.1	5.1	5.0	4.9	4.8	4.7	4.7	..	Total Fertility Rate
34.4	33.2	32.0	30.8	29.6	28.4	27.2	26.0	25.2	24.3	..	Infant Mortality Rate
68.2	68.7	69.2	69.5	69.8	70.1	70.4	70.7	70.9	71.1	..	Life Expectancy at Birth
81.2	80.5	79.8	79.2	78.5	77.8	77.8	77.8	77.8	77.8	..	Urban Population, % of total
..	..	..	..	..	..	..	..	..	..	..	Food Prod. per capita (1987=100)
4.6	..	..	..	..	..	..	..	..	..	..	Labor Force, Agriculture (%)
5.1	5.3	5.4	5.5	5.6	5.7	5.9	6.0	6.2	6.3	..	Labor Force, Female (%)
88.0	..	97.0	97.0	93.0	95.0	96.0	99.0			..	Primary Schl. Enroll. Ratio
88.0	..	97.0	97.0	93.0	95.0	97.0	100.0			..	Primary Schl. Enroll. Ratio, Female
52.0	..	58.0	58.0	56.0	57.0	58.0	60.0			..	Secondary Schl. Enroll. Ratio

UNITED KINGDOM	1969	1970	1971	1972	1973	1974	1975	1976	1977	1978	1979
CURRENT GNP PER CAPITA (US $)	2,170	2,240	2,450	2,750	3,250	3,520	3,900	4,230	4,600	5,190	6,470
POPULATION (thousands)	55,461	55,632	55,928	56,097	56,223	56,236	56,226	56,216	56,190	56,178	56,242

USE AND ORIGIN OF RESOURCES

(Billions of current Pounds Sterling)

	1969	1970	1971	1972	1973	1974	1975	1976	1977	1978	1979
Gross National Product (GNP)	47.86	52.55	58.50	65.37	75.11	84.66	105.78	125.17	145.70	168.49	199.59
Net Factor Income from Abroad	0.28	0.36	0.38	0.40	0.79	0.83	0.14	0.19	0.00	0.37	1.76
GDP at Market Prices	47.59	52.19	58.12	64.97	74.32	83.84	105.64	124.98	145.70	168.12	197.83
Resource Balance	0.17	0.44	0.79	-0.11	-1.90	-4.28	-1.95	-1.74	0.71	1.92	0.47
Exports of Goods & NFServices	10.08	11.53	12.94	13.63	17.05	22.90	26.86	35.11	43.34	47.49	54.88
Imports of Goods & NFServices	9.91	11.08	12.15	13.74	18.95	27.18	28.80	36.85	42.63	45.57	54.40
Domestic Absorption	47.42	51.75	57.33	65.08	76.22	88.12	107.59	126.72	144.99	166.21	197.36
Private Consumption, etc.	30.20	32.54	36.12	41.48	46.50	52.98	64.78	74.30	86.56	99.94	119.28
General Gov't Consumption	10.65	11.44	12.82	14.20	16.06	19.10	24.94	27.04	29.47	33.40	38.88
Gross Domestic Investment	6.57	7.76	8.39	9.40	13.66	16.03	17.87	25.38	28.96	32.86	39.19
Fixed Investment	9.10	9.95	11.08	11.90	13.84	16.12	19.70	23.23	25.85	29.27	34.27
Indirect Taxes, net	6.88	7.47	7.71	8.03	8.55	8.27	10.26	12.71	16.45	18.98	25.03
GDP at factor cost	40.71	44.72	50.41	56.94	65.77	75.57	95.37	112.27	129.25	149.14	172.80
Agriculture	..	..	..	..	..	..	..	..	..	..	..
Industry	..	..	..	..	..	..	..	..	..	..	..
Manufacturing	..	..	..	..	..	..	..	..	..	..	..
Services, etc.	..	..	..	..	..	..	..	..	..	..	..
Gross Domestic Saving	6.74	8.21	9.18	9.30	11.76	11.75	15.92	23.64	29.67	34.78	39.66
Gross National Saving	..	8.55	9.56	9.64	12.45	12.46	15.93	23.81	29.62	35.02	41.22

(Billions of 1987 Pounds Sterling)

	1969	1970	1971	1972	1973	1974	1975	1976	1977	1978	1979
Gross National Product	286.78	293.46	298.49	308.31	332.24	325.49	319.86	329.40	336.37	349.36	361.58
GDP at Market Prices	285.08	291.41	296.48	306.36	328.76	322.43	319.43	328.90	336.37	348.60	358.41
Resource Balance	-2.04	-1.94	-1.15	-6.34	-7.19	-3.00	0.18	3.64	7.60	6.17	1.98
Exports of Goods & NFServices	51.66	54.38	58.16	58.79	65.79	70.62	68.62	75.03	80.19	81.69	84.76
Imports of Goods & NFServices	53.71	56.32	59.31	65.13	72.98	73.61	68.44	71.39	72.59	75.52	82.78
Domestic Absorption	287.12	293.35	297.64	312.70	335.95	325.43	319.25	325.26	328.78	342.43	356.43
Private Consumption, etc.	168.09	172.54	175.57	188.66	196.04	190.81	189.11	187.23	190.98	201.76	211.85
General Gov't Consumption	61.58	62.60	64.46	67.18	70.08	71.39	75.37	76.22	74.96	76.69	78.35
Gross Domestic Investment	57.45	58.21	57.61	56.87	69.82	63.23	54.76	61.81	62.83	63.98	66.24
Fixed Investment	55.07	56.46	57.51	57.38	61.12	59.64	58.45	59.43	58.37	60.13	61.81
GDP at factor cost	243.16	248.82	256.27	267.53	290.73	291.75	288.94	296.28	299.11	309.52	313.19
Agriculture	..	..	..	..	..	..	..	..	..	..	..
Industry	..	..	..	..	..	..	..	..	..	..	..
Manufacturing	..	..	..	..	..	..	..	..	..	..	..
Services, etc.	..	..	..	..	..	..	..	..	..	..	..
Memo Items:											
Capacity to Import	54.63	58.58	63.15	64.63	65.68	62.02	63.81	68.02	73.80	78.70	83.50
Terms of Trade Adjustment	2.96	4.20	4.99	5.84	-0.11	-8.59	-4.81	-7.01	-6.39	-3.00	-1.26
Gross Domestic Income	288.05	295.61	301.48	312.20	328.64	313.84	314.62	321.89	329.98	345.60	357.15
Gross National Income	289.74	297.66	303.49	314.15	332.13	316.89	315.05	322.39	329.98	346.37	360.32

DOMESTIC PRICES/DEFLATORS

(Index 1987 = 100)

	1969	1970	1971	1972	1973	1974	1975	1976	1977	1978	1979
Overall (GDP)	16.7	17.9	19.6	21.2	22.6	26.0	33.1	38.0	43.3	48.2	55.2
Domestic Absorption	16.5	17.6	19.3	20.8	22.7	27.1	33.7	39.0	44.1	48.5	55.4
Agriculture	..	..	..	..	..	..	..	..	..	..	..
Industry	..	..	..	..	..	..	..	..	..	..	..
Manufacturing	..	..	..	..	..	..	..	..	..	..	..
Consumer Price Index	17.1	18.2	19.9	21.3	23.3	27.0	33.5	39.1	45.3	49.0	55.6

MANUFACTURING ACTIVITY

	1969	1970	1971	1972	1973	1974	1975	1976	1977	1978	1979
Employment (1987=100)	162.8	164.7	160.6	154.3	156.3	159.3	153.2	149.7	149.2	145.6	141.9
Real Earnings per Empl. (1987=100)	66.7	69.1	70.5	73.2	75.6	77.7	78.9	78.6	75.3	79.9	82.3
Real Output per Empl. (1987=100)	..	..	..	..	..	..	..	..	..	..	..
Earnings as % of Value Added	51.6	52.2	53.1	51.3	48.4	47.2	51.3	48.3	46.7	46.2	45.7

MONETARY HOLDINGS

(Billions of current Pounds Sterling)

	1969	1970	1971	1972	1973	1974	1975	1976	1977	1978	1979
Money Supply, Broadly Defined	24.02	26.77	30.79	37.39	45.57	50.96	57.90	64.95	74.52	85.13	97.85
Money	8.81	9.64	11.09	12.66	13.30	14.74	17.48	19.47	23.52	27.36	29.86
Currency Outside Banks	3.01	3.32	3.59	4.08	4.38	5.08	5.81	6.58	7.56	8.73	9.51
Demand Deposits	5.81	6.31	7.50	8.58	8.93	9.65	11.68	12.89	15.96	18.63	20.35
Quasi-Money	15.21	17.13	19.70	24.74	32.27	36.22	40.42	45.48	51.00	57.76	67.99

(Billions of current Pounds Sterling)

	1969	1970	1971	1972	1973	1974	1975	1976	1977	1978	1979
GOVERNMENT DEFICIT (-) OR SURPLUS	..	0.92	-0.38	-1.74	-2.52	-3.83	-7.80	-7.25	-4.93	-8.81	-11.16
Current Revenue	..	19.07	20.15	21.29	23.14	29.42	37.63	44.14	50.15	55.00	64.33
Current Expenditure	..	14.74	16.53	19.16	21.67	28.27	38.60	45.72	50.58	58.36	68.51
Current Budget Balance	..	4.33	3.63	2.13	1.47	1.16	-0.97	-1.58	-0.43	-3.36	-4.19
Capital Receipts	..	0.01	0.01	0.02	0.03	0.04	0.08	0.05	0.09	0.15	0.22
Capital Payments	..	3.42	4.03	3.89	4.02	5.03	6.90	5.72	4.60	5.60	7.20

1980	1981	1982	1983	1984	1985	1986	1987	1988	1989 estimate	NOTES	UNITED KINGDOM
7,960	9,290	9,800	9,280	8,660	8,470	9,020	10,490	12,850	14,570	..	CURRENT GNP PER CAPITA (US $)
56,330	56,352	56,306	56,347	56,460	56,618	56,763	56,930	57,100	57,270	..	POPULATION (thousands)
			(Billions of current Pounds Sterling)								USE AND ORIGIN OF RESOURCES
231.48	254.87	279.13	305.24	326.06	356.59	382.64	418.95	466.83	509.97	..	Gross National Product (GNP)
0.20	0.58	0.66	1.60	1.63	1.34	1.72	0.36	0.93	1.11	..	Net Factor Income from Abroad
231.27	254.29	278.46	303.64	324.43	355.24	380.92	418.59	465.90	508.86	..	GDP at Market Prices
4.96	6.91	4.65	2.44	-0.80	3.46	-3.08	-5.28	-16.83	-19.25	..	Resource Balance
62.81	67.64	72.97	80.50	92.43	102.83	98.46	107.09	108.62	122.96	..	Exports of Goods & NFServices
57.85	60.74	68.32	78.06	93.23	99.37	101.54	112.37	125.45	142.20	..	Imports of Goods & NFServices
226.31	247.39	273.81	301.20	325.22	351.78	384.00	423.87	482.73	528.10	..	Domestic Absorption
138.18	153.44	169.64	185.38	199.30	217.11	239.46	263.83	297.62	326.73	..	Private Consumption, etc.
49.02	55.45	60.45	65.89	69.88	73.88	79.51	85.34	91.68	98.50	..	General Gov't Consumption
39.11	38.50	43.72	49.92	56.05	60.79	65.03	74.70	93.43	102.88	..	Gross Domestic Investment
38.41	38.64	43.95	48.42	55.07	60.27	64.41	73.24	87.83	97.48	..	Fixed Investment
30.76	36.10	40.67	43.25	45.07	49.44	56.67	62.82	69.71	74.68	..	Indirect Taxes, net
200.52	218.20	237.79	260.39	279.35	305.80	324.25	355.77	396.18	434.17	..	GDP at factor cost
..	..	..	..	..	..	..	..	..	..	..	Agriculture
..	..	..	..	..	..	..	..	..	..	..	Industry
..	..	..	..	..	..	..	..	..	..	..	Manufacturing
..	..	..	..	..	..	..	..	..	..	..	Services, etc.
44.07	45.40	48.37	52.37	55.25	64.25	61.95	69.42	76.60	83.63	..	Gross Domestic Saving
44.07	46.04	49.08	54.29	57.26	65.92	63.76	69.66	77.23	84.44	..	Gross National Saving
			(Billions of 1987 Pounds Sterling)								
350.85	346.83	352.84	366.29	373.96	387.27	401.60	418.95	438.43	448.66	..	Gross National Product
350.53	346.04	351.99	364.35	372.08	385.80	399.80	418.59	437.55	447.68	..	GDP at Market Prices
4.79	6.38	3.06	-0.18	-3.03	0.02	-2.52	-5.28	-18.65	-23.23	..	Resource Balance
84.78	84.16	84.91	86.78	92.43	97.90	101.88	107.09	107.82	112.24	..	Exports of Goods & NFServices
80.00	77.77	81.85	86.96	95.46	97.88	104.40	112.37	126.47	135.47	..	Imports of Goods & NFServices
345.75	339.66	348.93	364.54	375.10	385.78	402.32	423.87	456.20	470.92	..	Domestic Absorption
211.45	211.17	214.09	222.46	227.47	236.11	249.48	263.83	282.75	293.79	..	Private Consumption, etc.
79.59	79.82	80.46	82.05	82.85	82.83	84.43	85.34	85.69	86.12	..	General Gov't Consumption
54.70	48.66	54.38	60.02	64.79	66.84	68.41	74.70	87.75	91.00	..	Gross Domestic Investment
58.49	52.89	55.89	58.52	63.48	66.00	67.43	73.24	83.27	87.27	..	Fixed Investment
303.74	296.82	300.36	312.11	320.10	331.64	340.50	355.77	371.29	380.63	..	GDP at factor cost
..	..	..	..	..	..	..	..	..	..	..	Agriculture
..	..	..	..	..	..	..	..	..	..	..	Industry
..	..	..	..	..	..	..	..	..	..	..	Manufacturing
..	..	..	..	..	..	..	..	..	..	..	Services, etc.
											Memo Items:
86.86	86.62	87.42	89.69	94.64	101.29	101.23	107.09	109.50	117.14	..	Capacity to Import
2.07	2.46	2.51	2.90	2.21	3.39	-0.65	0.00	1.68	4.90	..	Terms of Trade Adjustment
352.61	348.50	354.51	367.26	374.29	389.19	399.15	418.59	439.23	452.58	..	Gross Domestic Income
352.92	349.29	355.35	369.19	376.17	390.66	400.95	418.95	440.11	453.56	..	Gross National Income
				(Index 1987 = 100)							DOMESTIC PRICES/DEFLATORS
66.0	73.5	79.1	83.3	87.2	92.1	95.3	100.0	106.5	113.7	..	Overall (GDP)
65.5	72.8	78.5	82.6	86.7	91.2	95.4	100.0	105.8	112.1	..	Domestic Absorption
..	..	..	..	..	..	..	..	..	..	..	Agriculture
..	..	..	..	..	..	..	..	..	..	..	Industry
..	..	..	..	..	..	..	..	..	..	..	Manufacturing
65.6	73.4	79.7	83.4	87.5	92.8	96.0	100.0	104.9	113.1	..	Consumer Price Index
											MANUFACTURING ACTIVITY
133.9	119.2	110.7	105.1	105.0	102.2	101.2	100.0	102.5	104.1	..	Employment (1987=100)
83.8	84.3	85.7	88.7	91.0	93.7	96.2	100.0	104.2	107.2	..	Real Earnings per Empl. (1987=100)
..	..	..	..	..	..	..	..	..	..	..	Real Output per Empl. (1987=100)
48.8	47.6	46.3	44.0	43.8	43.3	42.8	41.3	41.2	41.2	..	Earnings as % of Value Added
			(Billions of current Pounds Sterling)								MONETARY HOLDINGS
115.09	140.63	157.56	178.21	199.24	221.82	252.28	344.26	..	..	D	Money Supply, Broadly Defined
31.04	34.59	40.66	42.46	48.05	56.67	69.26	154.12	170.95	195.59	..	Money
10.24	10.77	11.22	11.01	9.16	9.83	10.42	14.18	15.34	16.13	..	Currency Outside Banks
20.81	23.83	29.44	31.46	38.89	46.84	58.85	139.94	155.61	179.46	..	Demand Deposits
84.05	106.04	116.90	135.75	151.20	165.14	183.01	190.14	..	..	..	Quasi-Money
			(Billions of current Pounds Sterling)								GOVERNMENT DEFICIT (-) OR SURPLUS
-10.73	-12.14	-9.51	-13.37	-10.28	-10.27	-9.11	-4.05	6.32	..	..	GOVERNMENT DEFICIT (-) OR SURPLUS
81.82	92.38	107.46	113.42	121.40	134.15	140.16	150.79	167.21	..	..	Current Revenue
84.22	98.49	108.51	116.46	124.99	133.85	140.25	148.91	153.82	..	..	Current Expenditure
-2.39	-6.11	-1.05	-3.04	-3.60	0.31	-0.09	1.88	13.39	..	..	Current Budget Balance
0.23	0.42	0.36	0.38	0.36	0.39	0.50	0.63	0.77	..	..	Capital Receipts
8.57	6.45	8.82	10.71	7.04	10.97	9.52	6.55	7.84	..	..	Capital Payments

UNITED KINGDOM	1969	1970	1971	1972	1973	1974	1975	1976	1977	1978	1979
FOREIGN TRADE (CUSTOMS BASIS)					*(Billions of current US dollars)*						
Value of Exports, fob	17.52	19.35	22.35	24.34	30.53	38.66	43.74	46.03	57.48	71.52	90.49
Nonfuel Primary Products	2.49	2.73	2.83	3.32	4.53	5.46	5.60	5.73	6.96	9.15	11.46
Fuels	0.42	0.50	0.57	0.60	0.91	1.80	1.80	2.25	3.63	4.50	9.15
Manufactures	14.61	16.12	18.95	20.43	25.10	31.40	36.34	38.05	46.88	57.87	69.88
Value of Imports, cif	19.96	21.72	23.94	27.86	38.84	54.15	53.19	55.95	63.62	78.35	102.41
Nonfuel Primary Products	9.11	9.66	9.52	10.32	14.02	17.26	16.31	16.60	18.55	20.29	25.54
Fuels	2.18	2.27	3.04	3.11	4.23	10.84	9.53	10.14	9.13	9.17	12.17
Manufactures	8.66	9.80	11.38	14.43	20.59	26.05	27.34	29.21	35.94	48.89	64.70
					(Index 1987 = 100)						
Terms of Trade	105.8	107.6	110.1	106.0	92.9	77.6	84.3	80.2	84.5	91.6	94.8
Export Prices, fob	24.2	25.5	27.4	30.1	34.1	43.3	48.3	47.4	54.2	65.1	80.4
Import Prices, cif	22.8	23.7	24.9	28.4	36.8	55.8	57.3	59.1	64.2	71.2	84.8
BALANCE OF PAYMENTS					*(Billions of current US dollars)*						
Exports of Goods & Services	..	31.20	35.19	42.52	53.88	68.06	74.00	78.07	91.01	112.60	154.02
Merchandise, fob	..	19.51	21.99	23.51	29.11	38.11	42.47	45.03	55.32	67.12	86.02
Nonfactor Services	..	7.77	9.10	10.08	12.21	14.86	16.36	17.26	19.56	23.13	29.76
Factor Services	..	3.93	4.10	8.93	12.56	15.10	15.17	15.78	16.14	22.36	38.24
Imports of Goods & Services	..	28.78	31.99	41.33	55.21	74.55	76.36	78.32	89.25	107.30	150.21
Merchandise, fob	..	19.51	21.46	25.36	35.36	50.34	49.75	52.10	59.32	70.18	93.11
Nonfactor Services	..	6.83	7.83	8.60	10.64	12.75	13.49	13.39	14.42	16.49	21.67
Factor Services	..	2.44	2.70	7.36	9.21	11.46	13.13	12.82	15.51	20.63	35.44
Long-Term Interest	..	..	..	..	..	..	..	..	..	..	..
Private Current Transfers, net	..	-0.03	0.00	-0.13	-0.24	-0.28	-0.31	-0.03	-0.08	-0.24	-0.41
Workers' Remittances	..	..	..	..	..	..	..	..	..	..	..
Curr. A/C Bal before Off. Transf.	..	2.39	3.20	1.06	-1.57	-6.77	-2.67	-0.28	1.68	5.06	3.39
Net Official Transfers	..	-0.41	-0.48	-0.55	-0.85	-0.71	-0.75	-1.40	-1.89	-3.20	-4.26
Curr. A/C Bal after Off. Transf.	..	1.98	2.72	0.51	-2.42	-7.48	-3.42	-1.68	-0.21	1.86	-0.87
Long-Term Capital, net	..	-1.07	-0.54	-2.27	-1.71	0.83	0.69	0.61	5.01	-5.51	-5.37
Direct Investment	..	-0.19	-0.22	-0.81	-2.26	0.00	0.32	-1.33	0.25	-3.03	-6.07
Long-Term Loans	..	..	..	..	..	..	..	..	..	..	..
Disbursements	..	..	..	..	..	..	..	..	..	..	..
Repayments	..	..	..	..	..	..	..	..	..	..	..
Other Long-Term Capital	..	-0.88	-0.32	-1.46	0.55	0.83	0.37	1.95	4.76	-2.48	0.70
Other Capital, net	..	1.72	1.86	0.23	4.48	3.79	2.60	0.14	9.33	1.49	-11.50
Change in Reserves	..	-2.63	-4.04	1.53	-0.35	2.87	0.12	0.93	-14.13	2.16	17.74
Memo Item:					*(Pounds Sterling per US dollar)*						
Conversion Factor (Annual Avg)	0.420	0.420	0.410	0.400	0.410	0.430	0.450	0.560	0.570	0.520	0.470
				(Millions US dollars), outstanding at end of year							
EXTERNAL DEBT (Total)	..	..	..	..	..	..	..	..	..	..	..
Long-Term Debt (by debtor)	..	..	..	..	..	..	..	..	..	..	..
Central Bank, incl. IMF credit	..	..	..	..	..	..	..	..	..	..	..
Central Government	..	..	..	..	..	..	..	..	..	..	..
Rest of General Government	..	..	..	..	..	..	..	..	..	..	..
Non-financial Public Enterprises	..	..	..	..	..	..	..	..	..	..	..
Priv. Sector, incl non-guaranteed	..	..	..	..	..	..	..	..	..	..	..
Short-Term Debt	..	..	..	..	..	..	..	..	..	..	..
Memo Items:					*(Millions of US dollars)*						
Int'l Reserves Excluding Gold	1,055	1,479	7,989	4,846	5,589	6,038	4,598	3,375	20,112	16,026	19,744
Gold Holdings (at market price)	1,480	1,440	968	1,368	2,358	3,921	2,949	2,833	3,666	5,159	9,343
SOCIAL INDICATORS											
Total Fertility Rate	2.5	2.4	2.4	2.2	2.0	1.9	1.8	1.7	1.7	1.8	1.9
Infant Mortality Rate	18.6	18.5	17.9	17.5	17.2	16.8	16.0	14.5	14.1	13.3	12.9
Life Expectancy at Birth	71.6	71.7	71.8	72.0	72.1	72.3	72.4	72.6	72.8	73.0	73.4
Urban Population, % of total	88.2	88.5	88.8	89.0	89.3	89.5	89.8	90.0	90.2	90.4	90.6
Food Prod. per capita (1987=100)	71.6	76.8	77.1	78.4	80.0	85.6	81.2	76.6	86.0	87.5	90.1
Labor Force, Agriculture (%)	2.9	2.8	2.8	2.8	2.8	2.7	2.7	2.7	2.7	2.6	2.6
Labor Force, Female (%)	35.2	35.6	35.9	36.2	36.5	36.8	37.1	37.5	37.8	38.2	38.5
Primary Schl. Enroll. Ratio	..	104.0	..	..	..	..	105.0	106.0	105.0	105.0	104.0
Primary Schl. Enroll. Ratio, Female	..	104.0	..	..	..	..	106.0	106.0	106.0	106.0	105.0
Secondary Schl. Enroll. Ratio	..	73.0	..	..	..	..	83.0	83.0	83.0	83.0	82.0

1980	1981	1982	1983	1984	1985	1986	1987	1988	1989 estimate	NOTES	UNITED KINGDOM
				(Billions of current US dollars)							**FOREIGN TRADE (CUSTOMS BASIS)**
114.38	102.14	96.58	91.77	94.31	101.17	106.63	131.13	145.08	..	..	Value of Exports, fob
15.21	12.66	11.54	11.60	11.29	11.10	13.44	15.40	16.34	..	..	Nonfuel Primary Products
14.88	19.36	19.59	19.81	20.48	21.69	12.66	14.37	10.30	..	..	Fuels
84.29	70.11	65.45	60.35	62.54	68.39	80.53	101.37	118.43	..	..	Manufactures
117.90	101.15	99.10	99.44	105.69	109.41	125.61	154.41	189.47	..	..	Value of Imports, cif
28.99	23.98	22.17	22.18	21.92	21.41	24.76	29.07	33.94	..	..	Nonfuel Primary Products
15.91	14.28	12.88	10.68	13.80	13.68	9.34	9.98	8.95	..	..	Fuels
73.00	62.90	64.04	66.59	69.97	74.32	91.50	115.35	146.58	..	..	Manufactures
				(Index 1987 = 100)							
103.7	105.0	104.6	103.4	100.3	103.2	98.8	100.0	99.6	..	..	Terms of Trade
100.2	97.4	91.0	86.7	82.6	83.1	86.2	100.0	108.4	..	..	Export Prices, fob
96.6	92.8	87.0	83.9	82.3	80.5	87.2	100.0	108.8	..	..	Import Prices, cif
				(Billions of current US dollars)							**BALANCE OF PAYMENTS**
201.46	211.21	205.14	186.43	191.49	200.31	214.43	254.53	294.37	323.31	..	Exports of Goods & Services
109.61	102.16	96.66	91.96	93.48	100.86	106.47	130.32	143.84	151.30	..	Merchandise, fob
35.63	33.00	29.90	29.01	28.34	31.10	36.65	43.46	47.26	47.60	..	Nonfactor Services
56.22	76.04	78.57	65.46	69.67	68.36	71.31	80.75	103.27	124.41	..	Factor Services
189.35	193.63	194.08	178.16	186.52	191.72	211.13	256.36	314.60	347.05	..	Imports of Goods & Services
106.27	95.00	92.95	93.64	99.59	103.51	119.27	148.25	180.81	189.26	..	Merchandise, fob
26.62	25.30	25.23	23.61	23.24	23.68	28.63	34.26	40.27	41.17	..	Nonfactor Services
56.46	73.33	75.90	60.91	63.68	64.53	63.23	73.85	93.52	116.62	..	Factor Services
..	..	..	..	..	..	..	..	..	..	..	Long-Term Interest
-0.47	0.12	0.08	0.50	0.51	0.41	0.14	-0.21	-0.53	-0.49	..	Private Current Transfers, net
..	..	..	..	..	..	..	..	..	..	..	Workers' Remittances
11.64	17.69	11.14	8.77	5.48	9.01	3.45	-2.03	-20.76	-24.23	..	Curr. A/C Bal before Off. Transf.
-4.12	-3.19	-3.10	-2.94	-2.88	-4.24	-3.29	-5.34	-5.85	-6.93	..	Net Official Transfers
7.52	14.50	8.04	5.83	2.61	4.77	0.16	-7.37	-26.61	-31.16	..	Curr. A/C Bal after Off. Transf.
-11.24	-19.61	-15.74	-15.78	-22.02	-23.20	-30.85	-4.25	-15.96	-38.71	..	Long-Term Capital, net
-1.10	-6.27	-1.75	-3.01	-8.28	-6.47	-9.39	-16.98	-20.62	0.23	..	Direct Investment
..	..	..	..	..	..	..	..	..	..	..	Long-Term Loans
..	..	..	..	..	..	..	..	..	..	..	Disbursements
..	..	..	..	..	..	..	..	..	..	..	Repayments
-10.13	-13.33	-13.99	-12.78	-13.75	-16.73	-21.46	12.74	4.65	-38.94	..	Other Long-Term Capital
2.28	4.38	13.37	8.74	8.68	15.31	36.81	6.30	40.70	53.88	..	Other Capital, net
1.44	0.73	-5.67	1.21	10.73	3.13	-6.12	5.32	1.87	15.99	..	Change in Reserves
				(Pounds Sterling per US dollar)							Memo Item:
0.430	0.500	0.570	0.660	0.750	0.780	0.680	0.610	0.560	0.610	..	Conversion Factor (Annual Avg)
				(Millions US dollars), outstanding at end of year							
..	..	..	..	..	..	..	..	..	..	..	**EXTERNAL DEBT (Total)**
..	..	..	..	..	..	..	..	..	..	..	Long-Term Debt (by debtor)
..	..	..	..	..	..	..	..	..	..	..	Central Bank, incl. IMF credit
..	..	..	..	..	..	..	..	..	..	..	Central Government
..	..	..	..	..	..	..	..	..	..	..	Rest of General Government
..	..	..	..	..	..	..	..	..	..	..	Non-financial Public Enterprises
..	..	..	..	..	..	..	..	..	..	..	Priv. Sector, incl non-guaranteed
..	..	..	..	..	..	..	..	..	..	..	Short-Term Debt
				(Millions of US dollars)							Memo Items:
20,651	15,238	12,397	11,339	9,440	12,859	18,422	41,715	44,103	34,768	..	Int'l Reserves Excluding Gold
11,104	7,565	8,686	7,253	5,867	6,223	7,431	9,203	7,796	7,613	..	Gold Holdings (at market price)
											SOCIAL INDICATORS
1.9	1.8	1.8	1.8	1.8	1.8	1.8	1.8	1.8	1.8	..	Total Fertility Rate
12.1	11.2	11.0	10.2	9.6	9.4	9.5	9.1	9.0	8.7	..	Infant Mortality Rate
73.8	73.9	74.0	74.3	74.5	74.7	75.0	75.2	75.4	75.6	..	Life Expectancy at Birth
90.8	91.0	91.2	91.3	91.5	91.7	91.9	92.0	92.2	92.3	..	Urban Population, % of total
95.5	93.9	96.4	97.7	106.4	101.8	101.5	100.0	97.5	96.8	..	Food Prod. per capita (1987=100)
2.6	..	..	..	..	..	..	..	..	..	..	Labor Force, Agriculture (%)
38.9	38.8	38.8	38.8	38.7	38.7	38.7	38.7	38.7	38.6	..	Labor Force, Female (%)
103.0	..	101.0	101.0	102.0	104.0	106.0	..	..	..	..	Primary Schl. Enroll. Ratio
103.0	..	101.0	101.0	102.0	105.0	106.0	..	..	..	..	Primary Schl. Enroll. Ratio, Female
83.0	..	86.0	84.0	84.0	84.0	83.0	..	..	..	..	Secondary Schl. Enroll. Ratio

UNITED STATES	1969	1970	1971	1972	1973	1974	1975	1976	1977	1978	1979
CURRENT GNP PER CAPITA (US $)	4,760	4,950	5,320	5,780	6,410	6,890	7,400	8,180	9,040	10,100	11,150
POPULATION (millions)	203	205	208	210	212	214	216	218	220	223	225

USE AND ORIGIN OF RESOURCES *(Billions of current US Dollars)*

	1969	1970	1971	1972	1973	1974	1975	1976	1977	1978	1979
Gross National Product (GNP)	963.9	1,015.5	1,102.7	1,212.8	1,359.3	1,472.8	1,598.4	1,782.8	1,990.5	2,249.7	2,508.2
Net Factor Income from Abroad	6.8	7.3	9.3	11.2	16.2	19.5	17.5	21.1	25.4	30.5	43.8
GDP at Market Prices	957.1	1,008.2	1,093.4	1,201.6	1,343.1	1,453.3	1,580.9	1,761.7	1,965.1	2,219.1	2,464.4
Resource Balance	5.6	8.4	6.3	3.1	16.6	16.3	31.0	18.8	1.9	4.2	18.7
Exports of Goods & NFServices	60.4	68.8	72.4	81.4	114.1	151.6	161.3	177.8	191.5	227.5	291.3
Imports of Goods & NFServices	54.8	60.4	66.1	78.3	97.5	135.3	130.3	159.0	189.6	223.3	272.6
Domestic Absorption	958.3	1,007.1	1,087.1	1,198.5	1,326.5	1,437.0	1,549.9	1,742.8	1,963.2	2,214.9	2,445.6
Private Consumption, etc.	596.7	640.8	681.0	746.0	822.9	895.2	996.2	1,107.2	1,230.4	1,374.1	1,522.7
General Gov't Consumption	242.4	245.7	254.3	266.5	280.4	313.5	343.9	363.3	392.9	432.5	476.4
Gross Domestic Investment	119.2	120.6	151.7	185.9	223.3	228.3	209.8	272.3	340.0	408.3	446.6
Fixed Investment	150.2	153.8	173.5	201.9	232.7	239.2	232.1	268.3	326.8	386.2	437.5
Indirect Taxes, net	84.4	91.1	100.8	107.4	117.3	127.7	137.7	150.7	162.6	174.2	185.9
GDP at factor cost	872.7	917.1	992.6	1,094.2	1,225.8	1,325.6	1,443.2	1,611.0	1,802.5	2,044.9	2,278.5
Agriculture	26.7	27.8	30.0	35.0	53.8	52.1	52.9	51.7	54.2	65.1	77.2
Industry	347.3	348.5	369.8	407.5	454.9	486.9	520.8	592.2	670.3	754.4	831.0
Manufacturing	258.4	253.9	267.0	293.9	328.2	340.5	359.5	411.6	468.0	522.8	566.5
Services, etc.	583.1	631.9	693.6	759.1	834.4	914.3	1,007.2	1,117.8	1,240.6	1,399.6	1,556.2
Gross Domestic Saving	118.0	121.8	158.0	189.1	239.9	244.6	240.8	291.2	341.8	412.6	465.3
Gross National Saving	..	127.9	166.2	199.1	254.8	263.1	257.4	311.4	366.4	442.2	508.2

(Billions of 1987 US Dollars)

	1969	1970	1971	1972	1973	1974	1975	1976	1977	1978	1979
Gross National Product	2,846.2	2,840.8	2,923.8	3,068.8	3,225.7	3,208.4	3,168.1	3,322.9	3,478.0	3,661.9	3,752.6
GDP at Market Prices	2,825.6	2,820.1	2,898.6	3,040.1	3,186.7	3,165.9	3,133.3	3,283.2	3,433.4	3,612.0	3,686.9
Resource Balance	-33.9	-29.0	-38.7	-48.2	-30.3	1.9	19.7	-9.8	-34.0	-25.3	4.9
Exports of Goods & NFServices	164.1	177.4	178.3	194.2	241.0	267.9	258.4	273.0	280.2	310.9	354.8
Imports of Goods & NFServices	198.0	206.4	217.0	242.4	271.3	266.0	238.7	282.8	314.2	336.3	349.9
Domestic Absorption	2,859.5	2,849.2	2,937.3	3,088.3	3,217.0	3,164.0	3,113.6	3,293.0	3,467.4	3,637.4	3,682.1
Private Consumption, etc.	1,731.6	1,773.0	1,829.8	1,928.7	2,007.3	1,985.1	2,025.7	2,134.0	2,228.6	2,323.8	2,364.1
General Gov't Consumption	708.3	686.0	678.6	683.7	677.2	686.7	695.9	695.2	705.7	723.7	729.8
Gross Domestic Investment	419.5	390.1	428.8	475.9	532.5	492.2	391.9	463.8	533.1	589.9	588.2
Fixed Investment	489.8	474.8	456.3	506.5	514.6	488.0	519.3	490.4	551.4	595.3	665.5
GDP at factor cost	2,572.3	2,561.7	2,626.6	2,763.8	2,903.0	2,885.9	2,859.1	2,999.0	3,147.2	3,327.4	3,409.1
Agriculture	62.0	65.0	66.3	66.9	67.9	66.8	69.4	66.8	66.4	67.2	71.4
Industry	965.4	921.9	921.5	978.7	1,057.6	1,018.1	953.5	1,017.1	1,075.5	1,135.5	1,152.6
Manufacturing	557.4	525.7	530.9	578.1	641.9	612.5	565.0	619.1	665.3	706.3	722.7
Services, etc.	1,770.3	1,808.0	1,887.2	1,969.4	2,032.7	2,058.7	2,096.3	2,184.0	2,275.1	2,392.5	2,445.6

Memo Items:

	1969	1970	1971	1972	1973	1974	1975	1976	1977	1978	1979
Capacity to Import	218.4	235.2	237.6	252.1	317.6	298.0	295.4	316.3	317.4	342.6	374.0
Terms of Trade Adjustment	54.2	57.8	59.3	57.9	76.6	30.2	37.0	43.3	37.1	31.7	19.2
Gross Domestic Income	2,879.8	2,877.9	2,957.9	3,098.0	3,263.3	3,196.0	3,170.3	3,326.5	3,470.5	3,643.7	3,706.1
Gross National Income	2,900.4	2,898.6	2,983.0	3,126.7	3,302.3	3,238.6	3,205.1	3,366.2	3,515.2	3,693.6	3,771.8

DOMESTIC PRICES/DEFLATORS *(Index 1987 = 100)*

	1969	1970	1971	1972	1973	1974	1975	1976	1977	1978	1979
Overall (GDP)	33.9	35.8	37.7	39.5	42.1	45.9	50.5	53.7	57.2	61.4	66.8
Domestic Absorption	33.5	35.3	37.0	38.8	41.2	45.4	49.8	52.9	56.6	60.9	66.4
Agriculture	43.1	42.8	45.2	52.4	79.2	78.1	76.3	77.4	81.7	96.9	108.1
Industry	36.0	37.8	40.1	41.6	43.0	47.8	54.6	58.2	62.3	66.4	72.1
Manufacturing	46.4	48.3	50.3	50.8	51.1	55.6	63.6	66.5	70.3	74.0	78.4
Consumer Price Index	32.2	34.2	35.6	36.8	39.1	43.4	47.3	50.1	53.3	57.4	63.8

MANUFACTURING ACTIVITY

	1969	1970	1971	1972	1973	1974	1975	1976	1977	1978	1979
Employment (1987=100)	111.0	106.0	101.0	104.4	109.3	108.4	99.5	102.5	107.2	111.5	114.4
Real Earnings per Empl. (1987=100)	92.1	90.6	92.5	96.5	96.5	93.5	93.4	95.9	97.7	98.0	94.4
Real Output per Empl. (1987=100)	51.7	51.4	54.4	59.0	65.1	70.6	67.6	72.0	74.5	76.5	80.1
Earnings as % of Value Added	46.9	47.3	45.8	45.3	44.0	42.1	43.1	41.7	41.4	41.3	39.9

MONETARY HOLDINGS *(Billions of current US Dollars)*

	1969	1970	1971	1972	1973	1974	1975	1976	1977	1978	1979
Money Supply, Broadly Defined	592.2	630.6	714.2	806.5	859.3	907.5	1,023.6	1,162.8	1,285.8	1,390.9	1,509.9
Money	211.0	222.3	236.9	258.9	272.4	284.2	298.1	318.1	343.7	372.2	397.0
Currency Outside Banks	46.6	50.0	53.4	57.8	61.8	68.1	74.3	81.6	89.9	99.1	107.0
Demand Deposits	164.4	172.3	183.4	201.0	210.6	216.1	223.8	236.5	253.8	273.1	290.0
Quasi-Money	381.2	408.3	477.3	547.6	587.0	623.3	725.4	844.7	942.1	1,018.7	1,112.9

(Billions of current US Dollars)

	1969	1970	1971	1972	1973	1974	1975	1976	1977	1978	1979
GOVERNMENT DEFICIT (-) OR SURPLUS	..	..	..	-18.70	-16.20	-4.50	-53.90	-74.90	-52.20	-58.90	-35.90
Current Revenue	..	..	..	213.90	243.90	277.60	291.60	311.10	371.30	416.60	488.60
Current Expenditure	..	..	..	221.10	246.50	268.00	317.00	352.10	389.00	425.90	473.20
Current Budget Balance	..	..	..	-7.20	-2.50	9.60	-25.40	-41.10	-17.70	-9.40	15.40
Capital Receipts	..	..	..	0.20	0.40	1.30	1.10	0.30	0.20	0.20	0.10
Capital Payments	..	..	..	11.70	14.20	15.40	29.60	34.10	34.80	49.70	51.50

1980	1981	1982	1983	1984	1985	1986	1987	1988	1989 estimate	NOTES	UNITED STATES
12,000	13,270	13,610	14,510	15,890	16,760	17,530	18,570	19,820	21,000	..	**CURRENT GNP PER CAPITA (US $)**
228	230	233	235	237	239	242	244	246	248	..	**POPULATION (millions)**
											USE AND ORIGIN OF RESOURCES
			(Billions of current US Dollars)								
2,732.0	3,052.7	3,165.9	3,405.7	3,772.2	4,014.9	4,231.7	4,524.2	4,880.6	5,176.4	..	Gross National Product (GNP)
47.6	52.1	51.2	49.9	47.4	40.7	34.4	30.5	33.3	44.4	..	Net Factor Income from Abroad
2,684.4	3,000.6	3,114.7	3,355.9	3,724.8	3,974.2	4,197.3	4,493.7	4,847.3	5,132.0	..	GDP at Market Prices
31.9	34.0	26.4	-5.8	-58.9	-77.9	-97.3	-112.9	-73.7	-51.8	..	Resource Balance
350.9	382.9	362.0	352.7	383.7	370.9	396.4	448.6	547.6	626.5	..	Exports of Goods & NFServices
319.0	348.8	335.7	358.5	442.6	448.8	493.7	561.5	621.3	678.3	..	Imports of Goods & NFServices
2,652.5	2,966.5	3,088.4	3,361.7	3,783.7	4,052.1	4,294.6	4,606.6	4,921.1	5,183.8	..	Domestic Absorption
1,685.3	1,861.6	1,999.4	2,182.9	2,385.4	2,588.9	2,764.9	2,980.8	3,200.7	3,360.9	..	Private Consumption, etc.
537.3	595.7	641.7	675.6	732.6	816.0	871.3	936.5	977.4	1,047.1	..	General Gov't Consumption
429.9	509.2	447.3	503.2	665.7	647.2	658.4	689.2	742.9	775.8	..	Gross Domestic Investment
445.5	492.5	471.8	527.8	637.2	690.1	713.4	759.5	831.7	887.0	..	Fixed Investment
207.6	244.7	250.1	268.5	304.0	326.4	336.1	350.2	375.0	407.8	..	Indirect Taxes, net
2,476.8	2,755.8	2,864.6	3,087.4	3,420.7	3,647.7	3,861.2	4,143.5	4,472.3	4,724.2	..	GDP at factor cost
70.2	83.5	81.2	66.4	85.4	85.4	86.8	89.8	..	..	B	Agriculture
901.0	1,012.2	1,007.2	1,064.6	1,192.6	1,231.0	1,256.4	1,315.7	..	..	B	Industry
585.5	647.7	639.7	690.0	778.9	798.7	831.5	868.2	..	..	B	Manufacturing
1,713.2	1,904.9	2,026.3	2,224.8	2,446.8	2,657.8	2,854.0	3,088.2	..	..	B	Services, etc.
461.8	543.3	473.7	497.4	606.8	569.3	561.1	576.3	669.1	724.0	..	Gross Domestic Saving
508.4	594.2	523.4	546.0	652.5	607.9	593.6	605.0	700.7	767.1	..	Gross National Saving
			(Billions of 1987 US Dollars)								
3,746.7	3,819.1	3,721.8	3,854.7	4,107.1	4,242.4	4,363.1	4,524.2	4,724.5	4,865.0	..	Gross National Product
3,682.0	3,754.4	3,661.9	3,798.3	4,055.2	4,199.1	4,327.3	4,493.7	4,692.3	4,823.0	..	GDP at Market Prices
58.1	50.5	27.6	-18.3	-81.8	-101.8	-126.9	-112.9	-72.1	-54.8	..	Resource Balance
387.1	390.7	360.2	346.4	369.9	365.4	395.2	448.6	527.4	584.2	..	Exports of Goods & NFServices
329.0	340.3	332.6	364.7	451.7	467.2	522.1	561.5	599.6	639.0	..	Imports of Goods & NFServices
3,623.9	3,704.0	3,634.3	3,816.6	4,137.0	4,300.9	4,454.3	4,606.6	4,764.4	4,877.7	..	Domestic Absorption
2,359.8	2,391.7	2,408.1	2,523.8	2,651.9	2,773.6	2,887.8	2,980.8	3,091.9	3,168.3	..	Private Consumption, etc.
743.3	754.4	768.8	777.5	811.9	875.9	912.4	936.5	940.5	964.2	..	General Gov't Consumption
520.8	557.9	457.4	515.4	673.2	651.4	654.1	689.2	731.9	745.3	..	Gross Domestic Investment
656.5	599.3	638.1	648.3	611.6	762.1	777.2	759.5	797.6	823.8	..	Fixed Investment
3,401.0	3,451.3	3,369.4	3,494.9	3,722.9	3,852.2	3,978.3	4,143.5	4,329.9	..	..	GDP at factor cost
69.8	80.5	81.8	66.4	75.6	86.7	90.2	89.8	..	..		Agriculture
1,114.0	1,120.1	1,061.2	1,104.4	1,221.2	1,257.5	1,267.6	1,315.7	..	..		Industry
690.8	702.1	659.3	698.2	782.3	812.6	829.8	868.2	..	..		Manufacturing
2,488.0	2,541.9	2,511.3	2,627.6	2,758.5	2,854.9	2,969.5	3,088.2	..	..		Services, etc.
											Memo Items:
361.9	373.4	358.8	358.8	391.6	386.1	419.2	448.6	528.4	590.2	..	Capacity to Import
-25.2	-17.3	-1.4	12.4	21.7	20.7	24.0	0.0	0.9	5.9	..	Terms of Trade Adjustment
3,656.8	3,737.2	3,660.4	3,810.7	4,076.9	4,219.8	4,351.4	4,493.7	4,693.3	4,828.9	..	Gross Domestic Income
3,721.4	3,801.8	3,720.3	3,867.1	4,128.7	4,263.1	4,387.1	4,524.2	4,725.5	4,870.9	..	Gross National Income
			(Index 1987 = 100)								**DOMESTIC PRICES/DEFLATORS**
72.9	79.9	85.1	88.4	91.9	94.6	97.0	100.0	103.3	106.4	..	Overall (GDP)
73.2	80.1	85.0	88.1	91.5	94.2	96.4	100.0	103.3	106.3	..	Domestic Absorption
100.5	103.7	99.2	100.1	113.0	98.5	96.3	100.0	..	..	..	Agriculture
80.9	90.4	94.9	96.4	97.7	97.9	99.1	100.0	..	..	..	Industry
84.8	92.3	97.0	98.8	99.6	98.3	100.2	100.0	..	..	..	Manufacturing
72.5	79.9	84.9	87.6	91.4	94.6	96.4	100.0	104.0	109.0	..	Consumer Price Index
											MANUFACTURING ACTIVITY
111.8	109.6	103.2	101.2	103.5	101.4	99.0	100.0	101.4	..	..	Employment (1987=100)
90.2	90.0	90.0	92.3	94.1	95.5	97.5	100.0	103.7	..	..	Real Earnings per Empl. (1987=100)
81.0	82.6	80.3	84.4	90.7	94.0	93.5	100.0	..	..	..	Real Output per Empl. (1987=100)
40.9	40.8	41.4	40.1	39.1	39.7	38.8	38.7	38.5	..	..	Earnings as % of Value Added
			(Billions of current US Dollars)								**MONETARY HOLDINGS**
1,647.3	1,832.3	2,023.4	2,259.7	2,496.9	2,724.9	2,998.4	3,122.9	3,313.2	3,514.4	D	Money Supply, Broadly Defined
424.1	451.4	490.9	538.3	570.3	641.0	746.5	767.2	812.3	824.1	..	Money
118.8	126.2	136.5	150.6	160.8	173.1	186.2	200.5	214.8	225.4	..	Currency Outside Banks
305.3	325.2	354.4	387.7	409.4	467.9	560.4	566.7	597.5	598.7	..	Demand Deposits
1,223.2	1,381.0	1,532.6	1,721.4	1,926.6	2,084.0	2,251.9	2,355.7	2,500.8	2,690.3	..	Quasi-Money
			(Billions of current US Dollars)								**GOVERNMENT DEFICIT (-) OR SURPLUS**
-76.20	-78.70	-125.70	-202.50	-178.30	-212.10	-212.60	-147.50	-155.50	..	E	
545.90	639.80	659.60	653.30	718.30	791.40	823.10	909.80	962.60	..	..	Current Revenue
558.10	647.20	722.10	805.70	843.80	931.50	985.30	1,010.90	1,065.50	..	..	Current Expenditure
-12.20	-7.40	-62.40	-152.40	-125.40	-140.00	-162.20	-101.10	-102.90	..	..	Current Budget Balance
0.20	0.10	0.30	0.10	0.20	0.20	0.10	0.10	0.10	..	..	Capital Receipts
64.10	71.40	63.60	50.30	53.00	72.30	50.50	46.60	52.80	..	..	Capital Payments

UNITED STATES	1969	1970	1971	1972	1973	1974	1975	1976	1977	1978	1979
FOREIGN TRADE (CUSTOMS BASIS)					*(Billions of current US dollars)*						
Value of Exports, fob	38.01	43.22	44.13	49.78	71.34	98.51	107.59	114.99	120.13	142.54	176.79
Nonfuel Primary Products	9.33	11.29	10.81	12.95	23.36	29.50	29.23	30.74	32.03	39.50	49.98
Fuels	1.20	1.70	1.59	1.67	1.67	3.45	4.48	4.23	4.20	3.95	5.69
Manufactures	27.47	30.24	31.72	35.16	46.31	65.56	73.88	80.02	83.91	99.08	121.12
Value of Imports, cif	36.04	39.95	45.56	55.56	69.48	101.00	96.90	121.79	147.86	182.20	217.39
Nonfuel Primary Products	10.44	11.35	11.51	13.35	16.97	21.09	18.47	22.67	26.30	32.16	37.15
Fuels	2.79	3.07	3.71	4.80	8.17	25.38	26.40	33.93	44.20	44.69	63.67
Manufactures	22.81	25.53	30.34	37.41	44.33	54.53	52.03	65.20	77.36	105.35	116.56
					(Index 1987 = 100)						
Terms of Trade	125.4	127.9	121.1	117.2	121.3	93.9	99.3	99.6	93.5	92.8	88.3
Export Prices, fob	31.9	34.0	34.6	36.4	44.8	53.6	58.9	61.9	64.0	69.1	81.0
Import Prices, cif	25.5	26.6	28.6	31.1	37.0	57.0	59.3	62.2	68.5	74.5	91.7
BALANCE OF PAYMENTS					*(Billions of current US dollars)*						
Exports of Goods & Services	..	65.65	68.81	77.50	110.19	146.71	155.73	171.63	184.29	220.01	286.79
Merchandise, fob	..	42.45	43.31	49.38	71.41	98.32	107.08	114.75	120.80	142.06	184.47
Nonfactor Services	..	9.12	10.24	10.57	13.77	16.96	18.98	23.21	26.18	29.59	31.76
Factor Services	..	14.08	15.26	17.55	25.01	31.43	29.67	33.67	37.31	48.36	70.56
Imports of Goods & Services	..	59.87	66.42	79.22	99.00	137.33	132.79	162.13	193.79	229.84	281.65
Merchandise, fob	..	39.86	45.58	55.80	70.50	103.83	98.18	124.22	151.91	176.00	212.01
Nonfactor Services	..	14.28	15.17	16.55	18.45	21.03	21.55	24.11	26.70	31.01	35.36
Factor Services	..	5.73	5.67	6.87	10.05	12.47	13.06	13.80	15.18	22.83	34.28
Long-Term Interest	..	..	..	..	..	..	..	..	..	..	..
Private Current Transfers, net	..	-1.10	-1.11	-1.11	-1.25	-1.02	-0.91	-0.91	-0.82	-0.86	-0.91
Workers' Remittances	..	..	..	..	..	..	..	..	..	..	..
Curr. A/C Bal before Off. Transf.	..	4.68	1.28	-2.83	9.94	8.36	22.03	8.59	-10.32	-10.69	4.23
Net Official Transfers	..	-2.35	-2.73	-2.95	-2.87	-6.42	-3.97	-4.41	-4.17	-4.71	-5.20
Curr. A/C Bal after Off. Transf.	..	2.33	-1.45	-5.78	7.07	1.94	18.06	4.18	-14.49	-15.40	-0.97
Long-Term Capital, net	..	-6.69	-9.09	-5.84	-6.95	-7.52	-19.70	-15.13	-12.34	-10.13	-19.93
Direct Investment	..	-6.13	-7.26	-6.80	-8.53	-4.28	-11.65	-7.60	-8.16	-8.16	-13.35
Long-Term Loans	..	..	..	..	..	..	..	..	..	..	..
Disbursements	..	..	..	..	..	..	..	..	..	..	..
Repayments	..	..	..	..	..	..	..	..	..	..	..
Other Long-Term Capital	..	-0.56	-1.83	0.96	1.58	-3.24	-8.05	-7.53	-4.18	-1.97	-6.58
Other Capital, net	..	-6.33	-19.93	0.57	-5.36	-3.23	-3.01	0.45	-8.21	-6.35	34.53
Change in Reserves	..	10.69	30.47	11.05	5.23	8.81	4.65	10.50	35.04	31.88	-13.63
Memo Item:					*(US Dollars per US dollar)*						
Conversion Factor (Annual Avg)	1.000	1.000	1.000	1.000	1.000	1.000	1.000	1.000	1.000	1.000	1.000
					(Millions US dollars), outstanding at end of year						
EXTERNAL DEBT (Total)	..	..	..	..	..	..	..	..	..	..	..
Long-Term Debt (by debtor)	..	..	..	..	..	..	..	..	..	..	..
Central Bank, incl. IMF credit	..	..	..	..	..	..	..	..	..	..	..
Central Government	..	..	..	..	..	..	..	..	..	..	..
Rest of General Government	..	..	..	..	..	..	..	..	..	..	..
Non-financial Public Enterprises	..	..	..	..	..	..	..	..	..	..	..
Priv. Sector, incl non-guaranteed	..	..	..	..	..	..	..	..	..	..	..
Short-Term Debt	..	..	..	..	..	..	..	..	..	..	..
Memo Items:					*(Millions of US dollars)*						
Int'l Reserves Excluding Gold	5,105	3,415	2,109	2,663	2,726	4,232	4,627	7,149	7,592	6,979	7,784
Gold Holdings (at market price)	11,927	11,822	12,723	17,910	30,978	51,468	38,528	37,013	45,782	62,469	135,475
SOCIAL INDICATORS											
Total Fertility Rate	2.5	2.5	2.3	2.0	1.9	1.8	1.8	1.7	1.8	1.8	1.8
Infant Mortality Rate	20.9	20.0	19.1	18.5	17.7	16.7	16.1	15.2	14.1	13.8	13.1
Life Expectancy at Birth	70.5	70.8	71.2	71.5	71.9	72.2	72.6	72.9	73.3	73.4	73.8
Urban Population, % of total	73.3	73.6	73.6	73.6	73.6	73.6	73.6	73.6	73.6	73.7	73.7
Food Prod. per capita (1987=100)	91.5	88.9	95.2	93.1	94.3	94.9	101.4	103.0	105.9	103.5	107.2
Labor Force, Agriculture (%)	4.5	4.3	4.2	4.1	4.0	3.9	3.9	3.8	3.7	3.6	3.5
Labor Force, Female (%)	36.1	36.5	37.1	37.6	38.2	38.7	39.1	39.7	40.2	40.7	41.2
Primary Schl. Enroll. Ratio	..	..	..	..	..	..	99.0	..	..	..	..
Primary Schl. Enroll. Ratio, Female	..	..	..	..	..	..	..	..	..	..	..
Secondary Schl. Enroll. Ratio	..	..	..	..	..	..	..	..	..	..	..

1980	1981	1982	1983	1984	1985	1986	1987	1988	1989 estimate	NOTES	UNITED STATES
											FOREIGN TRADE (CUSTOMS BASIS)
				(Billions of current US dollars)							
216.92	230.51	210.93	199.14	216.01	211.42	211.90	252.57	315.31	..	..	Value of Exports, fob
61.45	59.11	50.32	49.41	51.96	42.80	40.85	47.17	62.06	..	..	Nonfuel Primary Products
8.13	10.29	12.78	9.70	9.47	10.10	8.20	7.80	8.24	..	..	Fuels
147.34	161.11	147.83	140.04	154.58	158.52	162.84	197.60	245.01	..	..	Manufactures
250.28	271.21	253.03	267.97	338.19	358.70	381.36	422.41	458.68	..	..	Value of Imports, cif
38.76	38.90	33.88	38.09	43.70	42.91	45.89	47.39	51.26	..	..	Nonfuel Primary Products
82.20	84.26	67.42	60.00	63.07	55.68	39.77	46.74	44.11	..	..	Fuels
129.31	148.06	151.73	169.88	231.42	260.11	295.71	328.27	363.31	..	..	Manufactures
				(Index 1987 = 100)							
79.7	84.8	88.1	95.0	98.2	101.4	107.8	100.0	100.9	..	..	Terms of Trade
88.5	95.2	96.1	98.6	98.6	96.6	98.4	100.0	108.7	..	..	Export Prices, fob
110.9	112.3	109.1	103.8	100.4	95.3	91.3	100.0	107.8	..	..	Import Prices, cif
				(Billions of current US dollars)							**BALANCE OF PAYMENTS**
342.13	375.55	354.50	343.28	377.62	364.54	384.18	431.84	533.11	603.17	..	Exports of Goods & Services
224.27	237.09	211.20	201.81	219.90	215.93	223.36	250.28	320.34	360.46	..	Merchandise, fob
39.14	46.10	52.69	54.14	59.06	60.26	72.48	81.85	91.75	103.18	..	Nonfactor Services
78.72	92.36	90.61	87.33	98.66	88.35	88.34	99.71	121.02	139.53	..	Factor Services
333.84	365.97	354.50	376.66	469.03	477.05	520.24	583.88	647.35	698.47	..	Imports of Goods & Services
249.77	265.08	247.64	268.89	332.41	338.09	368.41	409.77	447.31	475.33	..	Merchandise, fob
40.25	46.08	48.53	51.87	65.41	71.20	79.95	86.62	88.51	91.45	..	Nonfactor Services
43.82	54.81	58.33	55.90	71.21	67.76	71.88	87.49	111.53	131.69	..	Factor Services
..	..	..	..	..	..	..	..	..	..	..	Long-Term Interest
-1.03	-1.13	-1.43	-1.28	-1.77	-2.06	-1.86	-1.84	-1.77	-1.33	..	Private Current Transfers, net
..	..	..	..	..	..	..	..	..	..	..	Workers' Remittances
7.26	8.45	-1.43	-34.66	-93.18	-114.57	-137.92	-153.88	-116.01	-96.63	..	Curr. A/C Bal before Off. Transf.
-6.55	-6.52	-7.75	-8.49	-10.70	-13.36	-13.93	-12.34	-13.29	-13.43	..	Net Official Transfers
0.71	1.93	-9.18	-43.15	-103.88	-127.93	-151.85	-166.22	-129.30	-110.06	..	Curr. A/C Bal after Off. Transf.
-7.31	-0.72	-10.73	-7.98	29.77	60.33	85.69	40.77	69.61	83.31	..	Long-Term Capital, net
-2.30	15.57	12.83	5.26	13.80	5.87	19.22	15.85	42.24	40.50	..	Direct Investment
..	..	..	..	..	..	..	..	..	..	..	Long-Term Loans
..	..	..	..	..	..	..	..	..	..	..	Disbursements
..	..	..	..	..	..	..	..	..	..	..	Repayments
-5.01	-16.29	-23.56	-13.24	15.97	54.46	66.47	24.92	27.37	42.81	..	Other Long-Term Capital
-1.29	-2.45	21.94	47.08	74.83	73.40	32.38	69.09	23.42	43.54	..	Other Capital, net
7.89	1.24	-2.03	4.05	-0.72	-5.80	33.78	56.36	36.27	-16.79	..	Change in Reserves
				(US Dollars per US dollar)							**Memo Item:**
1.000	1.000	1.000	1.000	1.000	1.000	1.000	1.000	1.000	1.000	..	Conversion Factor (Annual Avg)
				(Millions US dollars), outstanding at end of year							
..	..	..	..	..	..	..	..	..	..	..	**EXTERNAL DEBT (Total)**
..	..	..	..	..	..	..	..	..	..	..	Long-Term Debt (by debtor)
..	..	..	..	..	..	..	..	..	..	..	Central Bank, incl. IMF credit
..	..	..	..	..	..	..	..	..	..	..	Central Government
..	..	..	..	..	..	..	..	..	..	..	Rest of General Government
..	..	..	..	..	..	..	..	..	..	..	Non-financial Public Enterprises
..	..	..	..	..	..	..	..	..	..	..	Priv. Sector, incl non-guaranteed
..	..	..	..	..	..	..	..	..	..	..	Short-Term Debt
				(Millions of US dollars)							**Memo Items:**
15,596	18,924	22,809	22,627	23,838	32,095	37,452	34,720	36,745	63,550	..	Int'l Reserves Excluding Gold
155,817	104,984	120,635	100,483	81,018	85,887	102,431	127,018	107,432	105,034	..	Gold Holdings (at market price)
											SOCIAL INDICATORS
1.8	1.8	1.8	1.8	1.8	1.8	1.9	1.9	1.9	1.9	..	Total Fertility Rate
12.6	11.7	11.2	10.9	10.5	10.5	10.4	10.0	9.9	9.6	..	Infant Mortality Rate
73.7	74.0	74.4	74.5	74.6	74.9	75.1	75.4	75.6	75.8	..	Life Expectancy at Birth
73.7	73.7	73.8	73.8	73.9	73.9	73.9	73.9	74.0	74.0	..	Urban Population, % of total
102.4	111.3	109.6	92.7	104.9	109.3	102.9	100.0	92.9	101.6	..	Food Prod. per capita (1987=100)
3.5	..	..	..	..	..	..	..	..	..	..	Labor Force, Agriculture (%)
41.6	41.6	41.6	41.6	41.5	41.5	41.5	41.5	41.5	41.4	..	Labor Force, Female (%)
99.0	..	101.0	101.0	99.0	99.0	100.0	..	..	..	..	Primary Schl. Enroll. Ratio
99.0	..	100.0	100.0	99.0	100.0	100.0	..	..	..	..	Primary Schl. Enroll. Ratio, Female
89.0	..	94.0	94.0	94.0	97.0	98.0	..	..	..	..	Secondary Schl. Enroll. Ratio

URUGUAY	1969	1970	1971	1972	1973	1974	1975	1976	1977	1978	1979
CURRENT GNP PER CAPITA (US $)	650	780	910	910	990	1,140	1,370	1,440	1,450	1,650	2,110
POPULATION (thousands)	2,792	2,808	2,818	2,820	2,821	2,822	2,829	2,845	2,862	2,879	2,896
USE AND ORIGIN OF RESOURCES	*(Billions of current Uruguayan New Pesos)*										
Gross National Product (GNP)	0.500	0.595	0.717	1.200	2.500	4.500	8.00	12.40	19.60	30.50	57.20
Net Factor Income from Abroad	-0.006	-0.006	-0.005	-0.020	-0.023	-0.070	-0.19	-0.24	-0.32	-0.47	-0.45
GDP at Market Prices	0.506	0.601	0.722	1.200	2.600	4.500	8.20	12.60	19.90	30.90	57.60
Resource Balance	0.006	-0.008	-0.009	0.004	0.031	-0.122	-0.30	-0.10	-0.58	-0.76	-2.60
Exports of Goods & NFServices	0.066	0.073	0.071	0.178	0.354	0.641	1.30	2.40	3.80	5.50	9.40
Imports of Goods & NFServices	0.061	0.081	0.080	0.174	0.323	0.763	1.60	2.40	4.40	6.30	12.00
Domestic Absorption	0.501	0.609	0.731	1.200	2.500	4.700	8.50	12.70	20.50	31.70	60.20
Private Consumption, etc.	0.370	0.448	0.522	0.938	1.800	3.500	6.20	9.10	15.00	22.90	43.40
General Gov't Consumption	0.075	0.092	0.118	0.153	0.364	0.680	1.10	1.80	2.50	3.80	6.80
Gross Domestic Investment	0.055	0.069	0.091	0.147	0.322	0.525	1.10	1.90	3.00	5.00	10.00
Fixed Investment	0.056	0.069	0.083	0.121	0.229	0.465	1.10	2.00	3.00	4.90	9.30
Indirect Taxes, net	0.058	0.081	0.093	0.213	0.344	0.510	1.10	1.80	2.80	4.60	7.90
GDP at factor cost	0.448	0.520	0.629	1.000	2.200	4.000	7.10	10.90	17.10	26.30	49.80
Agriculture	0.056	0.067	0.083	0.185	0.429	0.661	0.85	1.20	2.20	2.90	6.00
Industry	0.136	0.148	0.174	0.273	0.610	1.200	2.20	3.40	5.10	8.10	16.70
Manufacturing	..	..	..	..	..	..	..	..	..	6.40	13.60
Services, etc.	0.256	0.305	0.372	0.571	1.200	2.200	4.00	6.30	9.80	15.30	27.00
Gross Domestic Saving	0.061	0.061	0.082	0.151	0.353	0.403	0.81	1.80	2.40	4.20	7.40
Gross National Saving	..	0.055	0.077	0.131	0.330	0.332	0.61	1.50	2.10	3.70	7.00
	(Billions of 1987 Uruguayan New Pesos)										
Gross National Product	1,227.9	1,303.0	1,306.6	1,286.6	1,293.2	1,336.5	1,409.5	1,465.5	1,487.7	1,566.6	1,673.5
GDP at Market Prices	1,253.0	1,328.8	1,331.9	1,313.2	1,317.5	1,358.6	1,439.7	1,497.0	1,516.2	1,597.8	1,697.1
Resource Balance	-39.7	-87.2	-101.3	-85.3	-106.2	-65.2	-55.1	-20.5	-24.7	-33.3	-79.5
Exports of Goods & NFServices	139.0	142.8	135.9	133.4	133.0	160.5	191.2	231.4	248.0	258.7	275.7
Imports of Goods & NFServices	178.7	230.0	237.2	218.8	239.2	225.7	246.3	251.9	272.7	292.1	355.2
Domestic Absorption	1,292.7	1,416.0	1,433.2	1,398.5	1,423.7	1,423.7	1,494.8	1,517.5	1,541.0	1,631.1	1,776.7
Private Consumption, etc.	1,028.4	1,130.4	1,137.9	1,148.3	1,153.5	1,138.1	1,179.2	1,156.7	1,152.5	1,193.8	1,255.2
General Gov't Consumption	137.4	142.4	143.3	122.7	149.0	159.7	155.8	167.5	161.9	178.5	201.0
Gross Domestic Investment	126.9	143.2	152.0	127.5	121.2	125.9	159.8	193.3	226.6	258.7	320.5
Fixed Investment	129.5	146.5	144.7	122.7	103.8	115.0	161.4	207.1	222.0	254.0	302.2
GDP at factor cost	1,098.1	1,122.6	1,126.0	1,110.9	1,114.3	1,148.1	1,217.6	1,266.5	1,282.2	1,351.5	1,435.7
Agriculture	146.1	161.7	151.5	135.6	139.2	143.7	151.8	154.6	159.6	149.0	148.3
Industry	356.0	360.3	358.2	363.9	355.3	364.0	398.4	414.3	435.0	475.3	512.5
Manufacturing	..	..	..	..	..	..	..	..	..	371.6	398.0
Services, etc.	600.4	606.7	619.9	614.4	621.7	642.1	670.3	700.3	692.0	732.4	780.6
Memo Items:											
Capacity to Import	195.0	207.3	210.5	223.8	262.2	189.6	201.1	242.1	236.3	256.7	278.7
Terms of Trade Adjustment	56.0	64.5	74.6	90.4	129.2	29.1	9.9	10.7	-11.7	-2.0	3.0
Gross Domestic Income	1,309.0	1,393.3	1,406.5	1,403.5	1,446.7	1,387.7	1,449.6	1,507.7	1,504.5	1,595.8	1,700.2
Gross National Income	1,283.8	1,367.5	1,381.2	1,376.9	1,422.4	1,365.6	1,419.4	1,476.2	1,476.0	1,564.6	1,676.5
DOMESTIC PRICES/DEFLATORS	*(Index 1987 = 100)*										
Overall (GDP)	0.0404	0.0452	0.0542	0.0946	0.1940	0.3350	0.5670	0.8440	1.3000	1.9000	3.4000
Domestic Absorption	0.0387	0.0430	0.0510	0.0885	0.1780	0.3280	0.5660	0.8390	1.3000	1.9000	3.4000
Agriculture	0.0380	0.0414	0.0548	0.1360	0.3080	0.4600	0.5610	0.7800	1.4000	2.0000	4.1000
Industry	0.0383	0.0411	0.0486	0.0750	0.1720	0.3260	0.5620	0.8150	1.2000	1.7000	3.3000
Manufacturing	..	..	..	..	..	..	..	..	..	1.7000	3.4000
Consumer Price Index	0.0360	0.0420	0.0520	0.0920	0.1800	0.3200	0.5800	0.8730	1.3810	1.9970	3.3310
MANUFACTURING ACTIVITY											
Employment (1987=100)	..	123.8	..	138.2	146.2	149.4	154.7	163.1	170.3	186.9	197.6
Real Earnings per Empl. (1987=100)	..	..	..	..	..	..	..	82.7	76.2	80.3	80.1
Real Output per Empl. (1987=100)	..	..	..	76.9	66.9	67.7	70.4	74.3	80.2	75.2	68.4
Earnings as % of Value Added	..	..	..	..	..	..	..	35.3	31.6	37.3	33.8
MONETARY HOLDINGS	*(Billions of current Uruguayan New Pesos)*										
Money Supply, Broadly Defined	0.100	0.100	0.200	0.300	0.500	0.900	1.600	3.300	5.900	11.300	21.000
Money	0.100	0.100	0.100	0.200	0.400	0.600	0.800	1.400	1.900	3.600	6.200
Currency Outside Banks	0.100	0.100	0.100	0.100	0.200	0.300	0.500	0.800	1.100	1.800	3.200
Demand Deposits	0.000	0.000	0.100	0.100	0.200	0.300	0.400	0.600	0.800	1.800	3.000
Quasi-Money	0.000	0.000	0.100	0.100	0.200	0.300	0.800	1.900	4.000	7.800	14.900
	(Billions of current Uruguayan New Pesos)										
GOVERNMENT DEFICIT (-) OR SURPLUS	..	..	..	-0.030	-0.030	-0.170	-0.360	-0.260	-0.260	-0.280	0.000
Current Revenue	..	..	..	0.280	0.550	0.910	1.510	2.790	4.510	6.900	12.100
Current Expenditure	..	..	..	0.280	0.530	1.060	1.810	3.100	3.920	6.310	10.180
Current Budget Balance	..	..	..	0.000	0.020	-0.150	-0.300	-0.310	0.590	0.600	1.920
Capital Receipts	..	..	..	0.000	0.000	0.000	0.010	0.010	0.030	0.020	0.090
Capital Payments	..	..	..	0.030	0.060	0.030	0.070	-0.040	0.880	0.900	2.010

1980	1981	1982	1983	1984	1985	1986	1987	1988	1989 estimate	NOTES	URUGUAY
2,800	3,590	3,410	2,450	1,940	1,680	1,910	2,210	2,440	2,620	..	**CURRENT GNP PER CAPITA (US $)**
2,914	2,932	2,951	2,970	2,989	3,008	3,025	3,042	3,060	3,077	..	**POPULATION (thousands)**
				(Billions of current Uruguayan New Pesos)							**USE AND ORIGIN OF RESOURCES**
91.30	121.70	126.10	175.10	274.10	492.60	938.80	1,690.10	2,745.40	4,884.20	..	Gross National Product (GNP)
-0.91	-0.80	-2.60	-9.90	-20.20	-35.60	-42.30	-63.70	-109.90	-213.20	..	Net Factor Income from Abroad
92.20	122.50	128.70	185.00	294.40	528.20	981.10	1,753.90	2,855.30	5,097.40	f	GDP at Market Prices
-5.20	-4.80	-4.00	3.10	12.10	21.10	47.40	30.40	112.60	297.40	..	Resource Balance
13.90	18.00	18.10	44.70	72.10	126.70	227.10	348.90	631.80	1,205.90	..	Exports of Goods & NFServices
19.00	22.80	22.10	41.60	59.90	105.70	179.70	318.50	519.20	908.60	..	Imports of Goods & NFServices
97.40	127.30	132.70	181.90	282.20	507.10	933.70	1,723.50	2,742.70	4,800.00	..	Domestic Absorption
69.90	91.10	94.10	137.80	216.30	394.80	725.70	1,333.60	2,091.90	3,664.90	..	Private Consumption, etc.
11.50	17.30	20.10	25.70	36.90	69.20	127.60	219.60	370.10	664.40	..	General Gov't Consumption
16.00	18.80	18.60	18.40	29.10	43.10	80.40	170.30	280.70	470.70	..	Gross Domestic Investment
15.40	19.20	19.40	20.30	27.30	39.20	77.90	159.90	272.60	478.30	..	Fixed Investment
12.70	16.50	16.70	22.90	38.20	70.50	147.90	270.00	452.70	754.40	..	Indirect Taxes, net
79.50	105.90	112.00	162.10	256.10	457.70	833.20	1,483.90	2,402.60	4,343.00	f	GDP at factor cost
8.90	10.00	9.90	16.70	30.40	55.70	101.80	179.50	267.50	468.10	..	Agriculture
26.00	31.90	30.80	48.20	80.90	140.80	247.00	463.40	703.80	1,224.00	..	Industry
20.60	24.20	21.70	38.30	67.30	118.10	206.30	383.20	566.70	966.10	..	Manufacturing
44.70	64.00	71.20	97.30	144.90	261.10	484.40	841.00	1,431.40	2,650.90	..	Services, etc.
10.80	14.00	14.50	21.50	41.20	64.20	127.80	200.70	393.30	768.00	..	Gross Domestic Saving
9.90	13.20	11.90	11.60	21.00	28.60	85.50	136.90	283.40	554.90	..	Gross National Saving
				(Billions of 1987 Uruguayan New Pesos)							
1,768.3	1,804.3	1,609.3	1,471.9	1,428.0	1,430.6	1,580.2	1,690.1	1,692.4	1,709.1	..	Gross National Product
1,797.4	1,829.0	1,655.0	1,555.3	1,533.6	1,534.4	1,651.5	1,753.9	1,760.2	1,783.9	f	GDP at Market Prices
-96.6	-82.9	-62.3	46.8	88.8	101.6	88.1	30.4	50.6	57.5	..	Resource Balance
285.7	303.3	271.4	313.3	315.5	332.3	381.1	348.9	361.7	382.8	..	Exports of Goods & NFServices
382.3	386.2	333.7	266.5	226.7	230.7	292.9	318.5	311.1	325.3	..	Imports of Goods & NFServices
1,894.0	1,911.8	1,717.2	1,508.5	1,444.7	1,432.8	1,563.4	1,723.5	1,709.6	1,726.4	..	Domestic Absorption
1,358.0	1,390.9	1,257.6	1,147.0	1,079.0	1,091.4	1,207.4	1,333.6	1,314.6	1,345.5	..	Private Consumption, etc.
198.3	213.2	208.0	202.0	203.1	209.5	218.5	219.6	220.6	224.6	..	General Gov't Consumption
337.7	307.7	251.6	159.5	162.6	131.9	137.4	170.3	174.5	156.4	..	Gross Domestic Investment
321.4	311.7	265.4	178.3	154.6	118.7	133.7	159.9	166.4	164.1	..	Fixed Investment
1,520.8	1,547.7	1,399.2	1,314.6	1,296.3	1,296.9	1,396.6	1,483.9	1,488.9	1,509.5	f	GDP at factor cost
172.3	181.9	168.5	172.0	160.4	167.6	174.9	179.5	180.4	183.0	..	Agriculture
527.2	512.5	443.5	390.5	392.2	371.8	412.1	463.4	453.2	446.2	..	Industry
407.6	389.1	323.3	300.6	309.0	304.1	340.9	383.2	369.0	361.1	..	Manufacturing
826.6	857.0	789.0	752.0	743.8	757.4	809.5	841.0	855.2	880.2	..	Services, etc.
											Memo Items:
278.6	304.4	272.8	286.3	272.5	276.7	370.2	348.9	378.6	431.8	..	Capacity to Import
-7.1	1.1	1.4	-27.0	-43.0	-55.5	-10.9	0.0	16.9	49.0	..	Terms of Trade Adjustment
1,790.3	1,830.0	1,656.3	1,528.4	1,490.5	1,478.9	1,640.6	1,753.9	1,777.1	1,832.9	..	Gross Domestic Income
1,761.3	1,805.4	1,610.7	1,445.0	1,385.0	1,375.1	1,569.3	1,690.1	1,709.3	1,758.1	..	Gross National Income
				(Index 1987 = 100)							**DOMESTIC PRICES/DEFLATORS**
5.10	6.70	7.80	11.90	19.20	34.40	59.40	100.00	162.20	285.70	..	Overall (GDP)
5.10	6.70	7.70	12.10	19.50	35.40	59.70	100.00	160.40	278.00	..	Domestic Absorption
5.10	5.50	5.90	9.70	19.00	33.20	58.20	100.00	148.20	255.80	..	Agriculture
4.90	6.20	6.90	12.30	20.60	37.90	59.90	100.00	155.30	274.30	..	Industry
5.10	6.20	6.70	12.80	21.80	38.80	60.50	100.00	153.60	267.60	..	Manufacturing
5.45	7.30	8.69	12.96	20.13	34.66	61.14	100.00	162.19	292.67	..	Consumer Price Index
											MANUFACTURING ACTIVITY
122.9	117.6	95.7	90.1	92.3	93.7	96.9	100.0	95.2	..	G J	Employment (1987 = 100)
86.2	93.3	102.9	87.4	72.5	82.9	93.3	100.0	101.7	..	G J	Real Earnings per Empl. (1987 = 100)
83.2	90.9	104.0	94.0	93.0	90.0	94.2	100.0	108.3	..	G J	Real Output per Empl. (1987 = 100)
32.8	32.0	32.5	28.6	21.0	22.3	24.9	25.7	25.7	..	J	Earnings as % of Value Added
				(Billions of current Uruguayan New Pesos)							**MONETARY HOLDINGS**
36.400	54.2	72.5	81.9	132.9	259.8	478.1	702.4	1,369.8	2,782.3	..	Money Supply, Broadly Defined
9.100	9.8	13.7	14.9	22.2	46.0	84.1	134.9	221.6	382.9	..	Money
5.100	6.1	7.9	8.4	12.1	23.3	43.1	76.3	125.5	219.3	..	Currency Outside Banks
4.000	3.7	5.8	6.5	10.0	22.7	41.0	58.5	96.1	163.6	..	Demand Deposits
27.400	44.4	58.8	66.9	110.7	213.8	394.0	567.5	1,148.2	2,399.4	..	Quasi-Money
				(Billions of current Uruguayan New Pesos)							
0.030	-1.8	-11.7	-7.3	-15.3	-11.7	-6.2	-14.1	-45.6	..	..	**GOVERNMENT DEFICIT (-) OR SURPLUS**
20.520	29.1	27.4	40.1	55.4	109.0	219.6	394.3	667.0	..	..	Current Revenue
18.540	28.2	35.3	43.0	63.5	111.0	212.4	379.4	650.7	..	..	Current Expenditure
1.980	0.9	-8.0	-3.0	-8.1	-2.0	7.3	15.0	16.3	..	..	Current Budget Balance
0.000	0.0	0.1	0.1	0.1	0.3	0.7	0.9	0.6	..	..	Capital Receipts
1.950	2.7	3.8	4.4	7.3	10.0	14.2	30.0	62.5	..	..	Capital Payments

URUGUAY	1969	1970	1971	1972	1973	1974	1975	1976	1977	1978	1979
FOREIGN TRADE (CUSTOMS BASIS)					*(Millions of current US dollars)*						
Value of Exports, fob	200.3	232.5	205.5	214.1	321.5	381.0	381.2	536.0	598.5	681.9	787.2
Nonfuel Primary Products	163.2	185.1	164.2	174.4	267.3	293.5	265.2	354.6	364.6	391.9	411.9
Fuels	0.2	0.1	0.0	0.1	0.9	2.2	1.9	0.1	0.0	0.0	0.0
Manufactures	37.0	47.4	41.2	39.6	53.3	85.2	114.2	181.3	234.0	289.9	375.3
Value of Imports, cif	196.9	232.9	222.1	186.8	284.8	461.1	516.5	599.0	668.8	715.7	1,173.2
Nonfuel Primary Products	52.2	57.1	51.2	48.5	84.6	104.1	98.2	87.4	114.3	113.6	226.6
Fuels	24.1	34.1	32.0	31.6	33.5	149.6	161.2	207.9	171.1	231.2	282.3
Manufactures	120.6	141.7	138.9	106.7	166.7	207.4	257.1	303.7	383.4	370.9	664.3
					(Index 1987 = 100)						
Terms of Trade	161.9	173.1	155.1	189.6	203.3	126.2	107.8	112.2	105.5	105.4	104.5
Export Prices, fob	35.4	36.9	37.5	49.1	74.0	71.3	62.0	66.9	67.8	75.3	90.6
Import Prices, cif	21.8	21.3	24.2	25.9	36.4	56.5	57.6	59.6	64.2	71.4	86.7
BALANCE OF PAYMENTS					*(Millions of current US dollars)*						
Exports of Goods & Services	..	291.5	253.5	352.0	415.5	504.5	554.7	703.0	820.1	931.3	1,244.2
Merchandise, fob	..	224.1	196.8	281.6	327.6	381.4	384.9	565.0	611.5	686.1	788.0
Nonfactor Services	..	65.9	55.9	68.9	82.1	118.5	166.1	131.2	197.0	226.8	406.0
Factor Services	..	1.5	0.8	1.4	5.7	4.7	3.8	6.8	11.6	18.4	54.2
Imports of Goods & Services	..	345.9	325.3	304.5	397.2	639.6	751.1	784.4	993.8	1,065.4	1,609.0
Merchandise, fob	..	203.1	203.0	178.7	248.6	433.6	494.0	536.6	686.7	709.8	1,170.0
Nonfactor Services	..	116.5	99.9	100.9	117.9	158.7	182.1	168.6	227.5	260.4	337.0
Factor Services	..	26.3	22.4	25.0	30.8	47.3	74.9	79.2	79.5	95.2	109.0
Long-Term Interest	..	17.4	17.6	21.0	23.9	36.1	51.6	60.6	63.0	67.0	80.9
Private Current Transfers, net	..	-0.9	-0.6	-0.2	-0.1	-1.2	-1.5	-1.0	2.1	1.4	1.5
Workers' Remittances	..	..	..	..	..	..	..	..	..	..	..
Curr. A/C Bal before Off. Transf.	..	-55.3	-72.4	47.2	18.1	-136.3	-197.8	-82.4	-171.6	-132.7	-362.6
Net Official Transfers	..	10.2	8.9	11.5	19.1	18.6	8.3	8.7	4.6	5.7	5.6
Curr. A/C Bal after Off. Transf.	..	-45.1	-63.5	58.7	37.2	-117.6	-189.5	-73.8	-167.1	-127.0	-357.0
Long-Term Capital, net	..	-4.5	52.8	18.6	-32.9	63.0	150.7	79.1	101.2	152.2	359.0
Direct Investment	..	..	..	..	..	..	..	..	66.0	128.8	216.0
Long-Term Loans	..	-1.1	31.9	28.7	6.4	251.9	36.0	81.4	66.1	34.6	253.2
Disbursements	..	50.3	79.3	125.5	86.1	383.5	284.6	240.4	264.8	417.2	321.5
Repayments	..	51.4	47.4	96.8	79.7	131.6	248.6	159.0	198.7	382.6	68.3
Other Long-Term Capital	..	-3.4	20.9	-10.1	-39.3	-188.9	114.7	-2.3	-30.8	-11.2	-110.2
Other Capital, net	..	21.1	-1.1	-51.0	22.7	26.4	-52.1	88.9	233.0	113.1	60.5
Change in Reserves	..	28.5	11.8	-26.4	-27.0	28.2	90.9	-94.2	-167.2	-138.3	-62.5
Memo Item:					*(Uruguayan New Pesos per US dollar)*						
Conversion Factor (Annual Avg)	0.250	0.250	0.250	0.540	0.870	1.200	2.250	3.340	4.680	6.060	7.860
					(Millions of US dollars), outstanding at end of year						
EXTERNAL DEBT (Total)	..	316	352	402	416	715	787	896	1,105	998	1,323
Long-Term Debt (by debtor)	..	316	352	402	416	715	787	896	939	861	1,117
Central Bank, incl. IMF credit	..	155	166	204	220	339	495	559	511	231	308
Central Government	..	79	97	119	123	134	136	152	182	394	430
Rest of General Government	..	1	0	0	0	0	0	0	0	0	0
Non-financial Public Enterprises	..	53	48	43	42	105	87	115	153	163	190
Priv. Sector, incl non-guaranteed	..	29	40	35	31	136	69	70	93	74	189
Short-Term Debt	..	0	0	0	0	0	0	0	166	137	206
Memo Items:					*(Millions of US dollars)*						
Int'l Reserves Excluding Gold	19.21	13.80	20.10	69.03	100.58	80.55	58.52	176.21	322.38	352.41	323.13
Gold Holdings (at market price)	165.83	172.43	184.51	229.49	396.92	659.46	496.34	477.55	589.86	822.64	1,694.72
SOCIAL INDICATORS											
Total Fertility Rate	2.9	2.9	3.0	3.0	3.0	3.0	2.9	2.9	2.9	2.8	2.8
Infant Mortality Rate	46.6	46.4	46.2	46.0	45.2	44.4	43.6	42.8	42.0	40.2	38.4
Life Expectancy at Birth	68.7	68.8	68.8	68.8	69.0	69.2	69.4	69.5	69.7	69.9	70.2
Urban Population, % of total	81.9	82.1	82.3	82.5	82.6	82.8	83.0	83.2	83.3	83.5	83.6
Food Prod. per capita (1987=100)	98.5	105.8	92.0	87.1	92.2	102.3	101.2	112.9	94.8	92.5	91.9
Labor Force, Agriculture (%)	18.8	18.6	18.3	18.0	17.7	17.4	17.1	16.9	16.6	16.3	16.0
Labor Force, Female (%)	26.1	26.3	26.6	27.0	27.3	27.6	27.9	28.3	28.6	29.0	29.3
Primary Schl. Enroll. Ratio	..	112.0	..	..	..	..	107.0	105.0	105.0	105.0	105.0
Primary Schl. Enroll. Ratio, Female	..	109.0	..	..	..	..	106.0	..	104.0	108.0	103.0
Secondary Schl. Enroll. Ratio	..	59.0	..	..	..	..	60.0	63.0	62.0	58.0	58.0

1980	1981	1982	1983	1984	1985	1986	1987	1988	1989 estimate	NOTES	URUGUAY

				(Millions of current US dollars)							**FOREIGN TRADE (CUSTOMS BASIS)**
1,060.0	1,220.0	1,020.0	1,050.0	925.0	855.0	1,090.0	1,190.0	1,405.0	1,488.0	..	Value of Exports, fob
655.4	844.6	684.7	747.7	575.7	550.3	700.0	662.9	740.0	..	..	Nonfuel Primary Products
0.0	12.3	2.8	0.8	3.0	1.9	5.0	2.1	4.0	..	..	Fuels
404.5	363.1	332.4	301.5	346.3	302.8	385.0	525.0	661.0	529.0	..	Manufactures
1,650.0	1,630.0	1,110.0	788.0	776.0	708.0	870.0	1,140.0	1,157.0	1,348.0	..	Value of Imports, cif
246.2	188.9	112.2	100.1	118.6	99.9	140.0	171.0	201.0	..	..	Nonfuel Primary Products
472.6	515.6	434.6	284.1	281.4	239.6	169.0	179.0	145.0	..	..	Fuels
931.2	925.5	563.2	403.8	376.0	368.5	561.0	790.0	811.0		..	Manufactures

				(Index 1987 = 100)							
100.5	101.0	89.1	91.8	88.0	87.8	99.7	100.0	99.8	..	..	Terms of Trade
102.6	105.2	93.8	92.4	88.3	84.9	89.6	100.0	104.3	..	..	Export Prices, fob
102.1	104.2	105.2	100.7	100.3	96.8	89.8	100.0	104.5	..	..	Import Prices, cif

				(Millions of current US dollars)							**BALANCE OF PAYMENTS**
1,597.7	1,846.0	1,687.0	1,472.5	1,377.2	1,327.4	1,592.7	1,653.0	1,875.0	2,193.0	..	Exports of Goods & Services
1,060.0	1,230.0	1,260.0	1,160.0	925.0	854.0	1,090.0	1,180.0	1,400.0	1,600.0	..	Merchandise, fob
468.0	471.0	281.0	255.0	365.0	399.0	412.0	365.0	358.0	396.0	..	Nonfactor Services
67.7	146.0	147.0	62.5	87.2	77.4	92.7	103.0	115.0	203.0	..	Factor Services
2,308.0	2,320.0	1,934.0	1,540.0	1,519.0	1,458.0	1,551.0	1,794.0	1,860.0	2,052.0	..	Imports of Goods & Services
1,670.0	1,590.0	1,040.0	740.0	732.0	675.0	815.0	1,080.0	1,110.0	1,140.0	..	Merchandise, fob
476.0	506.0	547.0	455.0	335.0	357.0	365.0	325.0	332.0	364.0	..	Nonfactor Services
168.0	220.0	344.0	350.0	449.0	428.0	371.0	384.0	420.0	552.0	..	Factor Services
121.3	148.0	179.2	225.6	295.3	292.1	254.6	272.8	267.3	274.1	..	Long-Term Interest
2.0	2.9	0.0	0.0	0.0	0.0	0.0	0.0	0.0	..	..	Private Current Transfers, net
..	..	..	..	..	..	..	..	..	..	..	Workers' Remittances
-715.7	-467.8	-245.4	-70.8	-139.0	-130.8	41.9	-139.0	12.5	145.0	..	Curr. A/C Bal before Off. Transf.
6.7	6.8	10.4	11.0	10.0	10.8	25.3	8.0	21.3	8.0	..	Net Official Transfers
-709.0	-461.0	-235.0	-59.8	-129.0	-120.0	67.2	-131.0	33.8	153.0	..	Curr. A/C Bal after Off. Transf.
404.0	346.0	515.0	626.0	35.1	59.5	174.0	120.0	22.1	17.5	..	Long-Term Capital, net
290.0	48.6	-13.7	-5.6	-3.4	-7.9	-5.0	5.0	-2.3	1.0	..	Direct Investment
226.3	353.3	241.7	381.3	39.5	27.0	102.3	237.5	-29.6	83.3	..	Long-Term Loans
356.2	456.0	533.2	502.0	189.4	220.0	207.9	390.6	282.9	295.3	..	Disbursements
129.9	102.7	291.5	120.7	149.9	193.0	105.6	153.1	312.5	212.0	..	Repayments
-112.3	-55.9	287.0	250.3	-1.0	40.4	76.7	-122.5	54.0	-66.8	..	Other Long-Term Capital
445.8	157.3	-694.9	-632.3	10.7	-4.0	15.0	51.4	2.3	-71.3	..	Other Capital, net
-140.8	-42.3	414.9	66.1	83.2	64.5	-256.2	-40.4	-58.2	-99.2	..	Change in Reserves

				(Uruguayan New Pesos per US dollar)							Memo Item:
9.100	10.820	13.910	34.540	56.120	101.430	151.990	226.670	359.440	605.510	..	Conversion Factor (Annual Avg)

				(Millions of US dollars), outstanding at end of year							
1,660	2,174	2,647	3,292	3,271	3,920	3,906	4,271	3,825	3,750	..	**EXTERNAL DEBT** (Total)
1,338	1,674	2,002	2,906	2,879	3,106	3,333	3,635	3,348	3,273	..	Long-Term Debt (by debtor)
367	441	826	1,855	1,858	2,007	2,213	2,304	2,304	2,067	..	Central Bank, incl. IMF credit
490	558	569	521	492	622	720	855	765	963	..	Central Government
0	0	4	4	4	51	50	50	49	39	0	..	Rest of General Government
266	341	389	359	343	360	303	276	149	135	..	Non-financial Public Enterprises
215	335	214	167	135	66	47	151	91	109	..	Priv. Sector, incl non-guaranteed
322	500	645	386	392	814	573	636	477	477	..	Short-Term Debt

				(Millions of US dollars)							Memo Items:
383.79	429.99	116.29	206.92	134.42	174.23	481.55	530.00	531.98	501.35	..	Int'l Reserves Excluding Gold
2,017.27	1,348.32	1,305.82	992.66	807.13	856.41	1,018.29	1,263.02	1,070.34	1,046.21	..	Gold Holdings (at market price)

											SOCIAL INDICATORS
2.7	2.6	2.6	2.5	2.5	2.5	2.5	2.4	2.4	2.3	..	Total Fertility Rate
36.6	34.8	33.0	31.2	29.4	27.6	25.8	24.0	23.1	22.1	..	Infant Mortality Rate
70.4	70.7	70.9	71.2	71.4	71.6	71.8	72.0	72.3	72.5	..	Life Expectancy at Birth
83.8	84.0	84.1	84.3	84.4	84.6	84.8	85.0	85.1	85.3	..	Urban Population, % of total
97.2	113.2	113.2	115.8	101.8	103.3	102.0	100.0	106.9	113.6	..	Food Prod. per capita (1987=100)
15.7	..	..	..	..	..	..	..	..	..	..	Labor Force, Agriculture (%)
29.6	29.8	29.9	30.1	30.3	30.4	30.6	30.7	30.9	31.0	..	Labor Force, Female (%)
106.0	..	..	109.0	108.0	110.0	110.0	..	..	..	..	Primary Schl. Enroll. Ratio
106.0	..	..	107.0	107.0	109.0	109.0	..	..	..	..	Primary Schl. Enroll. Ratio, Female
60.0	..	..	67.0	70.0	71.0	73.0	..	..	..	..	Secondary Schl. Enroll. Ratio

VANUATU	1969	1970	1971	1972	1973	1974	1975	1976	1977	1978	1979
CURRENT GNP PER CAPITA (US $)	..	..	..	..	..	..	..	..	..	..	..
POPULATION (thousands)	81	83	85	87	90	93	96	100	104	108	113
USE AND ORIGIN OF RESOURCES					*(Millions of current Vanuatu Vatu)*						
Gross National Product (GNP)	..	..	..	..	..	..	..	..	..	..	6,880
Net Factor Income from Abroad	..	..	..	..	..	..	..	..	..	..	-1,320
GDP at Market Prices	..	..	..	..	..	..	..	..	..	..	8,200
Resource Balance	..	..	..	..	..	..	..	..	..	..	..
Exports of Goods & NFServices	..	..	..	..	..	..	..	..	..	..	..
Imports of Goods & NFServices	..	..	..	..	..	..	..	..	..	..	..
Domestic Absorption	..	..	..	..	..	..	..	..	..	..	..
Private Consumption, etc.	..	..	..	..	..	..	..	..	..	..	..
General Gov't Consumption	..	..	..	..	..	..	..	..	..	..	..
Gross Domestic Investment	..	..	..	..	..	..	..	..	..	..	..
Fixed Investment	..	..	..	..	..	..	..	..	..	..	..
Indirect Taxes, net	..	..	..	..	..	..	..	..	..	..	..
GDP at factor cost	..	..	..	..	..	..	..	..	..	..	..
Agriculture	..	..	..	..	..	..	..	..	..	..	1,800
Industry	..	..	..	..	..	..	..	..	..	..	..
Manufacturing	..	..	..	..	..	..	..	..	..	..	320
Services, etc.	..	..	..	..	..	..	..	..	..	..	..
Gross Domestic Saving	..	..	..	..	..	..	..	..	..	..	..
Gross National Saving	..	..	..	..	..	..	..	..	..	..	..
					(Millions of 1987 Vanuatu Vatu)						
Gross National Product	..	..	..	..	..	..	..	..	..	..	..
GDP at Market Prices	..	..	..	..	..	..	..	..	..	..	11,438
Resource Balance	..	..	..	..	..	..	..	..	..	..	..
Exports of Goods & NFServices	..	..	..	..	..	..	..	..	..	..	..
Imports of Goods & NFServices	..	..	..	..	..	..	..	..	..	..	..
Domestic Absorption	..	..	..	..	..	..	..	..	..	..	..
Private Consumption, etc.	..	..	..	..	..	..	..	..	..	..	..
General Gov't Consumption	..	..	..	..	..	..	..	..	..	..	..
Gross Domestic Investment	..	..	..	..	..	..	..	..	..	..	..
Fixed Investment	..	..	..	..	..	..	..	..	..	..	..
GDP at factor cost	..	..	..	..	..	..	..	..	..	..	..
Agriculture	..	..	..	..	..	..	..	..	..	..	2,529
Industry	..	..	..	..	..	..	..	..	..	..	..
Manufacturing	..	..	..	..	..	..	..	..	..	..	..
Services, etc.	..	..	..	..	..	..	..	..	..	..	..
Memo Items:											
Capacity to Import	..	..	..	..	..	..	..	..	..	..	..
Terms of Trade Adjustment	..	..	..	..	..	..	..	..	..	..	..
Gross Domestic Income	..	..	..	..	..	..	..	..	..	..	..
Gross National Income	..	..	..	..	..	..	..	..	..	..	..
DOMESTIC PRICES/DEFLATORS					*(Index 1987 = 100)*						
Overall (GDP)	..	..	..	..	..	..	..	..	..	..	71.7
Domestic Absorption	..	..	..	..	..	..	..	..	..	..	..
Agriculture	..	..	..	..	..	..	..	..	..	..	71.2
Industry	..	..	..	..	..	..	..	..	..	..	..
Manufacturing	..	..	..	..	..	..	..	..	..	..	..
Consumer Price Index	..	..	..	..	..	..	..	43.5	45.9	48.9	50.9
MANUFACTURING ACTIVITY											
Employment (1987=100)	..	..	..	..	..	..	..	..	..	..	..
Real Earnings per Empl. (1987=100)	..	..	..	..	..	..	..	..	..	..	..
Real Output per Empl. (1987=100)	..	..	..	..	..	..	..	..	..	..	..
Earnings as % of Value Added	..	..	..	..	..	..	..	..	..	..	..
MONETARY HOLDINGS					*(Millions of current Vanuatu Vatu)*						
Money Supply, Broadly Defined	..	..	..	..	..	..	..	5,392	5,816	5,869	6,043
Money	..	..	..	..	..	..	..	1,629	1,770	1,888	2,094
Currency Outside Banks	..	..	..	..	..	..	..	494	564	699	846
Demand Deposits	..	..	..	..	..	..	..	1,135	1,206	1,189	1,248
Quasi-Money	..	..	..	..	..	..	..	3,763	4,046	3,981	3,949
GOVERNMENT DEFICIT (-) OR SURPLUS					*(Millions of current Vanuatu Vatu)*						
Current Revenue	..	..	..	..	..	..	..	..	..	..	..
Current Expenditure	..	..	..	..	..	..	..	..	..	..	..
Current Budget Balance	..	..	..	..	..	..	..	..	..	..	..
Capital Receipts	..	..	..	..	..	..	..	..	..	..	..
Capital Payments	..	..	..	..	..	..	..	..	..	..	..

1980	1981	1982	1983	1984	1985	1986	1987	1988	1989 estimate	NOTES	VANUATU
..	..	..	..	..	930	900	780	830	860	..	**CURRENT GNP PER CAPITA (US $)**
117	121	125	129	132	136	139	143	147	152	..	POPULATION (thousands)
				(Millions of current Vanuatu Vatu)							**USE AND ORIGIN OF RESOURCES**
6,546	7,218	7,942	9,653	11,940	12,936	12,661	12,278	13,714	14,789	..	Gross National Product (GNP)
-1,200	-1,454	-1,501	-497	-399	402	511	-865	-906	-943	..	Net Factor Income from Abroad
7,746	8,673	9,442	10,150	12,339	12,534	12,150	13,143	14,620	15,732	..	GDP at Market Prices
-668	-205	-239	-1,354	-667	-2,683	-3,878	-3,872	-3,202	..	..	Resource Balance
2,568	3,328	4,038	5,934	7,757	6,391	4,417	5,142	6,769	..	..	Exports of Goods & NFServices
3,236	3,533	4,277	7,288	8,424	9,074	8,295	9,014	9,971	..	..	Imports of Goods & NFServices
..	..	..	11,504	13,006	15,217	16,028	17,015	17,822	..	..	Domestic Absorption
..	..	..	5,240	5,990	7,172	7,901	7,948	7,515	..	..	Private Consumption, etc.
2,092	2,043	2,327	3,659	4,067	4,501	4,604	4,546	5,673	..	..	General Gov't Consumption
..	..	..	2,605	2,949	3,544	3,523	4,521	4,635	..	..	Gross Domestic Investment
..	..	..	2,142	2,491	2,849	2,903	4,201		..	..	Fixed Investment
..	..	..	1,551	2,156	2,419	2,360				..	Indirect Taxes, net
..	..	..	8,599	10,183	10,115	9,790	..	..	..	B	GDP at factor cost
1,464	1,852	1,886	2,649	3,543	3,693	2,983	3,020	..	..	..	Agriculture
..	..	..	771	951	1,018	1,118	1,498		..	..	Industry
327	367	425	312	431	481	471	612	..	..	..	Manufacturing
..	..	..	6,730	7,845	7,823	8,049	8,625	..	..	..	Services, etc.
..	..	..	1,251	2,282	861	-355	649	1,433	..	..	Gross Domestic Saving
..	..	..	1,351	2,570	1,979	922	426	1,548	..	..	Gross National Saving
				(Millions of 1987 Vanuatu Vatu)							
..	..	..	11,720	12,700	13,802	13,650	12,278	12,699	13,016	..	Gross National Product
10,134	10,560	11,690	12,343	13,183	13,334	13,074	13,143	13,538	13,876	..	GDP at Market Prices
..	..	..	-2,821	-3,577	-4,758	-4,317	-3,872	..	..	..	Resource Balance
..	..	..	5,730	6,096	5,499	4,769	5,142	..	..	..	Exports of Goods & NFServices
..	..	..	8,551	9,673	10,258	9,087	9,014	..	..	..	Imports of Goods & NFServices
..	..	..	15,163	16,761	18,093	17,391	17,015	..	..	..	Domestic Absorption
..	..	..	7,067	8,058	8,398	8,038	7,948	..	..	..	Private Consumption, etc.
..	..	..	4,579	4,915	5,302	5,159	4,546	..	..	..	General Gov't Consumption
..	..	..	3,518	3,788	4,393	4,194	4,521	..	..	..	Gross Domestic Investment
..	..	..	2,921	3,232	3,571	3,473	4,201	..	..	..	Fixed Investment
..	..	..	..	..	..	..	..	..	..	B	GDP at factor cost
2,071	2,531	2,235	3,088	3,300	3,230	3,037	3,020	..	..	..	Agriculture
..	..	..	903	1,055	1,098	1,197	1,498	..	..	..	Industry
..	..	..	325	436	485	485	612	..	..	..	Manufacturing
..	..	..	8,352	8,829	9,006	8,840	8,625	..	..	..	Services, etc.
											Memo Items:
..	..	..	6,962	8,907	7,225	4,839	5,142	..	..	..	Capacity to Import
..	..	..	1,232	2,811	1,725	69	0	..	..	..	Terms of Trade Adjustment
..	..	..	13,575	15,995	15,060	13,143	13,143	..	..	..	Gross Domestic Income
..	..	..	12,952	15,511	15,527	13,720	12,278	..	..	..	Gross National Income
				(Index 1987 = 100)							**DOMESTIC PRICES/DEFLATORS**
76.4	82.1	80.8	82.2	93.6	94.0	92.9	100.0	108.0	113.4	..	Overall (GDP)
..	..	..	75.9	77.6	84.1	92.2	100.0	..	..	..	Domestic Absorption
70.7	73.2	84.4	85.8	107.4	114.3	98.2	100.0	..	..	..	Agriculture
..	..	..	85.4	90.1	92.7	93.4	100.0	..	..	..	Industry
..	..	..	96.1	98.8	99.2	97.1	100.0	..	..	..	Manufacturing
56.7	72.2	76.7	77.9	82.2	83.1	87.1	100.0	..	..	..	Consumer Price Index
											MANUFACTURING ACTIVITY
..	..	..	..	..	..	..	..	..	..	..	Employment (1987=100)
..	..	..	..	..	..	..	..	..	..	..	Real Earnings per Empl. (1987=100)
..	..	..	..	..	..	..	..	..	..	..	Real Output per Empl. (1987=100)
..	..	..	..	..	..	..	..	..	..	..	Earnings as % of Value Added
				(Millions of current Vanuatu Vatu)							**MONETARY HOLDINGS**
5,261	5,322	7,935	8,626	10,952	12,391	15,638	14,605	15,348	22,767	..	Money Supply, Broadly Defined
1,882	1,448	1,743	2,273	3,026	2,642	2,810	4,219	3,395	4,307	..	Money
720	597	634	748	922	963	906	1,000	954	1,037	..	Currency Outside Banks
1,162	851	1,109	1,525	2,104	1,679	1,904	3,218	2,441	3,270	..	Demand Deposits
3,379	3,874	6,192	6,353	7,926	9,749	12,828	10,386	11,953	18,460	..	Quasi-Money
				(Millions of current Vanuatu Vatu)							
..	650.7	-338.3	-57.2	432.5	-62.3	-855.2	511.6	-418.2	..	..	**GOVERNMENT DEFICIT (-) OR SURPLUS**
..	3,122.5	2,812.1	2,904.7	3,879.9	3,694.6	3,321.6	5,750.7	5,763.3	..	..	Current Revenue
..	2,073.2	2,313.8	2,408.7	2,575.3	2,848.2	3,208.3	3,299.7	3,865.0	..	..	Current Expenditure
..	1,049.3	498.3	496.0	1,304.6	846.4	113.3	2,451.0	1,898.3	..	..	Current Budget Balance
..	..	..	..	..	..	..	1.6	103.9	..	..	Capital Receipts
..	398.6	836.6	553.2	872.1	908.7	968.5	1,941.0	2,420.4	..	..	Capital Payments

VANUATU	1969	1970	1971	1972	1973	1974	1975	1976	1977	1978	1979
FOREIGN TRADE (CUSTOMS BASIS)					*(Thousands of current US dollars)*						
Value of Exports, fob	11,000	12,000	13,000	15,000	21,000	30,000	11,000	17,000	37,000	42,000	47,000
Nonfuel Primary Products	..	..	..	..	..	..	..	..	..	..	..
Fuels	..	..	..	..	..	..	..	..	..	..	..
Manufactures	..	..	..	..	..	..	..	..	..	..	..
Value of Imports, cif	11,000	13,000	18,000	29,000	35,000	50,000	40,000	39,000	52,000	63,000	73,000
Nonfuel Primary Products	..	..	..	..	..	..	..	..	..	..	..
Fuels	..	..	..	..	..	..	..	..	..	..	..
Manufactures	..	..	..	..	..	..	..	..	..	..	..
					(Index 1987 = 100)						
Terms of Trade	..	..	..	..	..	..	..	..	..	..	..
Export Prices, fob	..	..	..	..	..	..	..	..	..	..	..
Import Prices, cif	..	..	..	..	..	..	..	..	..	..	..
BALANCE OF PAYMENTS					*(Millions of current US dollars)*						
Exports of Goods & Services	..	..	..	..	..	..	..	..	..	..	..
Merchandise, fob	..	..	..	..	..	..	..	..	..	..	..
Nonfactor Services	..	..	..	..	..	..	..	..	..	..	..
Factor Services	..	..	..	..	..	..	..	..	..	..	..
Imports of Goods & Services	..	..	..	..	..	..	..	..	..	..	..
Merchandise, fob	..	..	..	..	..	..	..	..	..	..	..
Nonfactor Services	..	..	..	..	..	..	..	..	..	..	..
Factor Services	..	..	..	..	..	..	..	..	..	..	..
Long-Term Interest	..	0.00	0.00	0.00	0.10	0.20	0.20	0.20	0.20	0.20	0.30
Private Current Transfers, net	..	..	..	..	..	..	..	..	..	..	..
Workers' Remittances	..	..	..	..	..	..	..	..	..	..	..
Curr. A/C Bal before Off. Transf.	..	..	..	..	..	..	..	..	..	..	..
Net Official Transfers	..	..	..	..	..	..	..	..	..	..	..
Curr. A/C Bal after Off. Transf.	..	..	..	..	..	..	..	..	..	..	..
Long-Term Capital, net	..	..	..	..	..	..	..	..	..	..	..
Direct Investment	..	..	..	..	..	..	..	..	..	..	..
Long-Term Loans	..	0.00	0.00	1.60	0.60	0.00	0.80	1.00	0.40	-0.30	-0.40
Disbursements	..	0.00	0.00	1.60	0.60	0.00	0.90	1.10	0.50	0.00	0.00
Repayments	..	0.00	0.00	0.00	0.00	0.00	0.10	0.10	0.10	0.30	0.40
Other Long-Term Capital	..	..	..	..	..	..	..	..	..	..	..
Other Capital, net	..	..	..	..	..	..	..	..	..	..	..
Change in Reserves	..	..	..	..	..	..	..	..	..	..	..
Memo Item:					*(Vanuatu Vatu per US dollar)*						
Conversion Factor (Annual Avg)	94.440	100.990	99.860	81.610	72.040	77.800	69.270	77.240	79.410	72.940	68.760
					(Thousands of US dollars), outstanding at end of year						
EXTERNAL DEBT (Total)	..	1,100	1,100	2,700	3,600	3,700	3,500	4,200	4,900	5,100	4,900
Long-Term Debt (by debtor)	..	1,100	1,100	2,700	3,600	3,700	3,500	4,200	4,900	5,100	4,900
Central Bank, incl. IMF credit	..	..	..	..	..	..	..	..	..	..	..
Central Government	..	1,100	1,100	2,700	3,600	3,700	3,500	4,200	4,900	5,100	4,900
Rest of General Government	..	..	..	..	..	..	..	..	..	..	..
Non-financial Public Enterprises	..	..	..	..	..	..	..	..	..	..	..
Priv. Sector, incl non-guaranteed	..	..	..	..	..	..	..	..	..	..	..
Short-Term Debt	..	..	..	..	..	..	..	..	..	..	..
Memo Items:					*(Thousands of US dollars)*						
Int'l Reserves Excluding Gold	..	..	..	..	..	..	..	..	..	..	..
Gold Holdings (at market price)	..	..	..	..	..	..	..	..	..	..	..
SOCIAL INDICATORS											
Total Fertility Rate	6.5	6.5	6.4	6.4	6.3	6.3	6.3	6.2	6.2	6.2	6.1
Infant Mortality Rate	..	..	..	..	..	..	..	..	..	..	..
Life Expectancy at Birth	..	..	..	..	..	..	..	..	..	..	..
Urban Population, % of total	12.9	13.5	14.2	14.9	15.5	16.2	16.9	17.1	17.3	17.4	17.6
Food Prod. per capita (1987=100)	137.5	127.0	130.6	98.1	106.9	130.3	112.9	126.8	135.5	137.0	130.4
Labor Force, Agriculture (%)	..	..	..	..	..	..	..	..	..	..	..
Labor Force, Female (%)	..	..	..	..	..	..	..	..	..	..	..
Primary Schl. Enroll. Ratio	..	..	..	..	..	..	..	..	..	..	..
Primary Schl. Enroll. Ratio, Female	..	..	..	..	..	..	..	..	..	..	..
Secondary Schl. Enroll. Ratio	..	..	..	..	..	..	..	..	..	..	..

1980	1981	1982	1983	1984	1985	1986	1987	1988	1989 est.	NOTES	VANUATU
				(Thousands of current US dollars)							**FOREIGN TRADE (CUSTOMS BASIS)**
36,000	32,000	23,000	30,000	44,000	30,000	14,000	17,000	19,000	..	..	Value of Exports, fob
..	..	..	..	..	..	..	..	..	..	..	Nonfuel Primary Products
..	..	..	..	..	..	..	..	..	..	..	Fuels
..	..	..	..	..	..	..	..	..	..	..	Manufactures
73,000	58,000	52,000	63,000	67,000	70,000	58,000	68,000	69,000	..	..	Value of Imports, cif
..	..	..	..	..	..	..	..	..	..	..	Nonfuel Primary Products
..	..	..	..	..	..	..	..	..	..	..	Fuels
..	..	..	..	..	..	..	..	..	..	..	Manufactures
				(Index 1987 = 100)							
..	..	..	..	..	..	..	..	..	..	..	Terms of Trade
..	..	..	..	..	..	..	..	..	..	..	Export Prices, fob
..	..	..	..	..	..	..	..	..	..	..	Import Prices, cif
				(Millions of current US dollars)							**BALANCE OF PAYMENTS**
..	..	53.26	62.54	83.75	83.56	80.22	81.02	78.73	..	..	Exports of Goods & Services
..	..	10.67	17.92	32.54	18.67	8.81	13.73	15.39	..	..	Merchandise, fob
..	..	36.99	38.11	42.43	38.16	30.58	36.15	39.97	..	..	Nonfactor Services
..	..	5.59	6.50	8.78	26.73	40.82	31.14	23.38	..	..	Factor Services
..	..	84.33	86.35	99.45	112.88	111.57	124.54	116.66	..	..	Imports of Goods & Services
..	..	43.27	45.82	51.48	52.29	46.81	57.09	57.89	..	..	Merchandise, fob
..	..	29.95	27.38	32.87	33.22	28.64	28.13	30.91	..	..	Nonfactor Services
..	..	11.11	13.14	15.10	27.36	36.13	39.31	27.87	..	..	Factor Services
0.20	0.20	0.20	0.20	0.20	0.20	0.40	0.50	0.60	0.80	..	Long-Term Interest
..	..	8.19	6.01	6.93	6.75	7.22	5.84	9.78	..	..	Private Current Transfers, net
..	..	8.32	5.64	6.86	6.89	6.88	6.71	7.02	..	..	Workers' Remittances
..	..	-22.88	-17.80	-8.78	-22.56	-24.13	-37.67	-28.16	..	..	Curr. A/C Bal before Off. Transf.
..	..	35.05	26.17	31.68	23.85	21.33	46.38	36.19	..	..	Net Official Transfers
..	..	12.17	8.36	22.91	1.29	-2.80	8.71	8.03	..	..	Curr. A/C Bal after Off. Transf.
..	..	-37.65	-1.16	59.43	-42.61	13.87	-0.97	-208.53	..	..	Long-Term Capital, net
..	..	6.93	5.87	7.44	4.63	2.02	12.89	10.81	..	..	Direct Investment
-0.40	-0.30	1.60	0.30	2.10	0.70	0.50	3.90	3.00	6.60	..	Long-Term Loans
0.00	0.00	1.90	0.60	2.50	1.10	1.10	4.90	3.90	7.50	..	Disbursements
0.40	0.30	0.30	0.30	0.40	0.40	0.60	1.00	0.90	0.90	..	Repayments
..	..	-46.18	-7.32	49.90	-47.93	11.35	-17.77	-222.34	..	..	Other Long-Term Capital
..	..	28.72	-6.23	-84.89	41.06	-6.28	5.20	201.18	..	..	Other Capital, net
..	..	-3.25	-0.98	2.55	0.26	-4.78	-12.93	-0.68	5.53	..	Change in Reserves
				(Vanuatu Vatu per US dollar)							**Memo Item:**
68.290	87.830	96.210	99.370	99.230	106.030	107.080	109.850	104.430	116.040	..	Conversion Factor (Annual Avg)
				(Thousands of US dollars), outstanding at end of year							
4,100	3,000	4,000	10,600	13,200	15,900	18,200	23,800	27,200	31,800	..	**EXTERNAL DEBT (Total)**
4,100	3,000	4,000	3,600	5,200	6,900	8,200	13,800	15,700	22,300	..	Long-Term Debt (by debtor)
..	..	..	..	..	..	..	..	..	..	..	Central Bank, incl. IMF credit
4,100	3,000	2,300	2,300	3,500	4,700	5,600	10,000	11,600	17,900	..	Central Government
..	..	..	..	..	..	..	..	..	..	..	Rest of General Government
..	..	..	..	..	..	..	..	..	..	..	Non-financial Public Enterprises
..	..	1,700	1,300	1,700	2,200	2,600	3,800	4,100	4,400	..	Priv. Sector, incl non-guaranteed
..	..	0	7,000	8,000	9,000	10,000	10,000	11,500	9,500	..	Short-Term Debt
				(Thousands of US dollars)							**Memo Items:**
..	8,463	5,669	6,595	8,087	10,610	21,420	40,174	40,670	35,082	..	Int'l Reserves Excluding Gold
..	..	..	..	..	..	..	..	..	..	..	Gold Holdings (at market price)
											SOCIAL INDICATORS
6.1	6.1	6.0	6.0	5.9	5.9	5.9	5.8	5.7	5.7	..	Total Fertility Rate
..	..	94.0	90.2	86.4	82.6	78.8	75.0	73.0	71.0	..	Infant Mortality Rate
..	..	61.1	61.6	62.0	62.5	63.0	63.4	63.8	64.2	..	Life Expectancy at Birth
17.8	18.1	18.3	18.6	18.8	19.1	19.3	19.6	19.8	20.1	..	Urban Population, % of total
107.8	126.0	106.2	111.5	118.4	105.1	108.2	100.0	96.6	93.1	..	Food Prod. per capita (1987=100)
..	..	..	..	..	..	..	..	..	..	..	Labor Force, Agriculture (%)
..	..	..	..	..	..	..	..	..	..	..	Labor Force, Female (%)
..	..	..	..	..	..	..	..	..	..	..	Primary Schl. Enroll. Ratio
..	..	..	..	..	..	..	..	..	..	..	Primary Schl. Enroll. Ratio, Female
..	..	..	..	..	..	..	..	..	..	..	Secondary Schl. Enroll. Ratio

VENEZUELA	1969	1970	1971	1972	1973	1974	1975	1976	1977	1978	1979
CURRENT GNP PER CAPITA (US $)	1,160	1,240	1,260	1,340	1,540	1,920	2,380	2,890	3,160	3,390	3,730
POPULATION (thousands)	10,246	10,604	10,981	11,377	11,791	12,221	12,665	13,121	13,588	14,063	14,542
USE AND ORIGIN OF RESOURCES					*(Billions of current Venezuelan Bolivares)*						
Gross National Product (GNP)	52.08	57.28	63.03	70.24	83.56	125.96	139.54	161.65	188.20	206.36	247.39
Net Factor Income from Abroad	-2.77	-2.49	-3.32	-2.11	-2.96	-2.73	0.43	0.89	0.38	0.16	-0.01
GDP at Market Prices	54.85	59.77	66.35	72.35	86.52	128.69	139.11	160.75	187.82	206.20	247.40
Resource Balance	2.21	2.43	3.65	2.09	7.22	28.26	9.62	1.19	-12.81	-23.04	3.26
Exports of Goods & NFServices	11.70	12.50	14.85	14.79	21.74	49.77	40.07	41.54	43.64	42.08	64.22
Imports of Goods & NFServices	9.48	10.07	11.21	12.70	14.53	21.51	30.46	40.35	56.45	65.12	60.96
Domestic Absorption	52.63	57.34	62.70	70.27	79.31	100.42	129.50	159.56	200.63	229.24	244.14
Private Consumption, etc.	30.28	31.02	33.56	37.76	42.89	54.01	67.98	81.63	96.81	114.64	134.29
General Gov't Consumption	6.14	6.63	7.76	8.50	9.59	12.77	15.94	19.78	22.96	24.06	27.76
Gross Domestic Investment	16.21	19.68	21.38	24.01	26.83	33.64	45.57	58.15	80.86	90.55	82.09
Fixed Investment	13.25	13.35	15.41	18.34	21.55	24.29	35.41	49.50	70.00	83.14	75.87
Indirect Taxes, net	2.48	2.84	2.73	2.65	2.72	3.32	4.57	4.70	5.21	4.54	6.65
GDP at factor cost	52.37	56.93	63.62	69.71	83.81	125.36	134.54	156.06	182.61	201.66	240.75
Agriculture	3.52	3.71	3.84	3.90	4.58	5.65	6.97	7.45	9.27	10.14	11.94
Industry	21.10	23.50	26.55	28.52	37.28	69.28	64.73	73.69	83.74	88.63	114.37
Manufacturing	8.41	9.63	10.88	11.57	13.91	23.35	21.81	26.32	28.69	30.71	40.20
Services, etc.	30.23	32.56	35.96	39.93	44.66	53.75	67.41	79.62	94.81	107.43	121.09
Gross Domestic Saving	18.43	22.12	25.03	26.10	34.04	61.91	55.18	59.34	68.05	67.51	85.35
Gross National Saving	..	19.25	21.36	23.59	30.63	58.60	55.00	59.51	67.44	66.08	83.67
					(Billions of 1987 Venezuelan Bolivares)						
Gross National Product	446.92	485.90	488.71	505.82	538.95	560.29	587.62	634.33	672.08	687.28	692.22
GDP at Market Prices	470.67	507.01	514.46	521.03	558.05	569.85	586.15	631.41	670.93	686.83	692.25
Resource Balance	..	..	..	..	..	132.73	56.90	11.62	-49.38	-49.68	11.60
Exports of Goods & NFServices	..	..	..	..	..	230.86	184.38	182.82	171.26	162.81	175.99
Imports of Goods & NFServices	..	..	..	..	..	98.13	127.48	171.20	220.64	212.49	164.39
Domestic Absorption	..	..	..	..	..	457.40	532.38	612.55	710.23	741.89	701.28
Private Consumption, etc.	..	..	..	..	..	251.75	287.82	321.00	352.92	390.51	406.84
General Gov't Consumption	..	..	..	..	..	49.41	50.91	58.66	62.04	59.88	62.79
Gross Domestic Investment	..	..	..	..	..	156.23	193.65	232.89	295.26	291.49	231.65
Fixed Investment	91.13	89.66	100.59	115.72	126.50	123.38	155.01	199.15	256.82	267.04	213.52
GDP at factor cost	449.38	482.95	493.31	501.97	540.54	555.13	566.89	612.96	652.31	671.70	673.65
Agriculture	24.09	25.34	25.68	25.33	26.66	28.29	30.28	29.19	31.48	32.49	33.43
Industry	231.13	261.75	258.02	252.17	270.57	259.21	240.92	254.10	264.12	273.29	280.46
Manufacturing	55.62	62.80	64.98	67.89	72.88	77.35	80.81	90.55	93.71	98.03	101.26
Services, etc.	207.19	208.44	220.63	235.14	251.73	276.54	314.21	348.41	376.84	382.01	378.29
Memo Items:											
Capacity to Import	..	..	..	..	..	227.10	167.73	176.26	170.57	137.32	173.19
Terms of Trade Adjustment	..	..	..	..	..	-3.76	-16.65	-6.55	-0.69	-25.48	-2.80
Gross Domestic Income	..	..	..	..	..	566.09	569.50	624.86	670.24	661.35	689.45
Gross National Income	..	..	..	..	..	556.53	570.97	627.77	671.38	661.80	689.42
DOMESTIC PRICES/DEFLATORS					*(Index 1987 = 100)*						
Overall (GDP)	11.7	11.8	12.9	13.9	15.5	22.6	23.7	25.5	28.0	30.0	35.7
Domestic Absorption	..	..	..	..	..	22.0	24.3	26.0	28.2	30.9	34.8
Agriculture	14.6	14.7	15.0	15.4	17.2	20.0	23.0	25.5	29.5	31.2	35.7
Industry	9.1	9.0	10.3	11.3	13.8	26.7	26.9	29.0	31.7	32.4	40.8
Manufacturing	15.1	15.3	16.7	17.0	19.1	30.2	27.0	29.1	30.6	31.3	39.7
Consumer Price Index	18.0	18.5	19.1	19.6	20.4	22.1	24.4	26.2	28.3	30.3	34.1
MANUFACTURING ACTIVITY											
Employment (1987=100)	47.0	48.8	50.7	54.1	58.0	66.4	73.3	87.4	93.3	96.4	104.9
Real Earnings per Empl. (1987=100)	74.0	74.0	73.8	74.3	83.7	89.8	93.9	93.8	97.4	104.8	107.2
Real Output per Empl. (1987=100)	88.3	85.7	83.1	78.3	74.3	68.7	76.2	77.0	77.1	80.0	74.0
Earnings as % of Value Added	28.7	30.6	30.0	31.7	35.0	28.7	27.3	25.3	27.1	30.5	28.5
MONETARY HOLDINGS					*(Billions of current Venezuelan Bolivares)*						
Money Supply, Broadly Defined	13.62	15.14	18.68	23.09	29.56	39.32	57.14	71.33	90.28	105.16	116.99
Money	6.64	7.07	8.19	9.65	11.48	16.94	25.60	29.00	37.41	44.05	46.55
Currency Outside Banks	2.03	2.16	2.34	2.58	2.87	3.81	4.72	5.82	7.38	9.01	10.01
Demand Deposits	4.61	4.91	5.85	7.07	8.62	13.13	20.88	23.18	30.03	35.04	36.53
Quasi-Money	6.98	8.07	10.49	13.43	18.07	22.38	31.53	42.32	52.87	61.11	70.44
GOVERNMENT DEFICIT (-) OR SURPLUS					*(Millions of current Venezuelan Bolivares)*						
	..	-697	233	-165	1,159	4,981	1,916	-3,987	-6,742	-6,892	3,967
Current Revenue	..	10,360	12,487	13,238	17,007	45,071	42,463	39,985	42,963	42,905	51,113
Current Expenditure	..	7,660	8,649	9,634	10,493	15,631	19,705	20,394	24,781	27,998	33,582
Current Budget Balance	..	2,700	3,838	3,604	6,514	29,440	22,758	19,591	18,182	14,907	17,531
Capital Receipts	..	1	2	290	65	2	18	..	30	..	..
Capital Payments	..	3,398	3,607	4,059	5,420	24,461	20,860	23,578	24,954	21,799	13,564

1980	1981	1982	1983	1984	1985	1986	1987	1988	1989 estimate	NOTES	VENEZUELA
4,070	4,730	4,920	4,790	4,250	3,830	3,570	3,180	3,130	2,450	..	**CURRENT GNP PER CAPITA** (US $)
15,024	15,485	15,940	16,394	16,851	17,317	17,791	18,272	18,751	19,244	..	**POPULATION** (thousands)
			(Billions of current Venezuelan Bolivares)								**USE AND ORIGIN OF RESOURCES**
299.21	337.40	333.68	340.00	405.88	448.71	477.29	676.50	850.50	1,437.89	..	Gross National Product (GNP)
1.41	2.46	-6.57	-9.08	-14.19	-16.03	-11.88	-19.92	-22.78	-82.34	..	Net Factor Income from Abroad
297.80	334.93	340.24	349.08	420.07	464.74	489.17	696.42	873.28	1,520.23	..	GDP at Market Prices
20.77	16.46	-8.92	29.02	46.91	42.89	-5.06	3.84	-60.54	209.76	..	Resource Balance
85.72	89.89	75.37	68.08	115.95	116.15	96.05	154.15	178.97	518.12	..	Exports of Goods & NFServices
64.95	73.42	84.29	39.07	69.03	73.26	101.11	150.31	239.51	308.36	..	Imports of Goods & NFServices
277.03	318.47	349.16	320.06	373.16	421.85	494.23	692.58	933.82	1,310.47	..	Domestic Absorption
163.40	194.04	212.37	236.03	256.33	287.32	337.11	450.35	597.74	974.48	..	Private Consumption, etc.
35.12	42.64	42.59	41.34	43.31	48.55	54.71	71.12	91.94	141.27	..	General Gov't Consumption
78.51	81.79	94.19	42.70	73.52	85.98	102.42	171.12	244.14	194.72	..	Gross Domestic Investment
74.24	80.77	81.21	64.06	67.29	80.55	99.82	147.91	199.33	257.19	..	Fixed Investment
8.00	8.42	9.78	20.39	24.92	30.35	17.78	41.63	26.12	48.57	..	Indirect Taxes, net
289.80	326.52	330.47	328.69	395.15	434.39	471.39	654.79	847.16	1,471.66	B	GDP at factor cost
14.44	16.41	17.68	19.54	21.50	26.93	32.45	42.57	57.88	92.04	..	Agriculture
138.12	148.69	141.35	134.96	189.21	199.63	198.26	282.05	350.32	696.38	..	Industry
47.66	49.85	54.13	57.03	89.93	101.80	113.81	143.31	179.41	317.39	..	Manufacturing
145.24	169.83	181.22	194.58	209.36	238.18	258.46	371.80	465.08	731.81	..	Services, etc.
99.28	98.25	85.28	71.72	120.43	128.87	97.35	174.96	183.60	404.48	..	Gross Domestic Saving
98.90	99.07	76.07	61.83	105.23	111.74	84.65	153.98	159.04	316.21	..	Gross National Saving
			(Billions of 1987 Venezuelan Bolivares)								
664.27	663.85	633.52	605.93	608.74	609.47	656.01	676.50	717.74	638.96	..	Gross National Product
661.26	659.12	645.42	621.20	630.03	631.24	672.34	696.42	736.96	675.55	..	GDP at Market Prices
-15.78	-42.65	-85.72	22.28	-12.79	-6.29	9.69	3.84	-12.46	59.45	..	Resource Balance
146.83	138.62	125.91	122.11	141.41	139.63	156.83	154.15	166.39	176.46	..	Exports of Goods & NFServices
162.61	181.27	211.62	99.83	154.20	145.92	147.14	150.31	178.85	117.00	..	Imports of Goods & NFServices
666.88	679.89	691.03	603.20	624.93	630.45	652.34	692.58	748.92	612.51	..	Domestic Absorption
407.41	417.08	416.00	434.99	421.06	421.81	433.57	450.35	472.81	442.28	..	Private Consumption, etc.
65.03	68.61	67.95	66.09	66.27	65.28	68.79	71.12	78.91	77.62	..	General Gov't Consumption
194.45	194.20	207.08	102.13	137.61	143.36	149.97	171.12	197.20	92.61	..	Gross Domestic Investment
182.53	188.01	180.99	133.32	126.87	135.17	147.14	147.91	161.03	118.81	..	Fixed Investment
643.51	642.56	626.87	584.92	592.65	590.02	647.90	654.79	714.92	653.97	B	GDP at factor cost
34.06	33.43	34.62	34.76	35.04	37.89	40.95	42.57	44.55	42.27	..	Agriculture
265.86	260.50	250.44	237.17	255.19	252.57	271.68	282.05	300.14	273.63	..	Industry
103.81	101.24	105.35	103.55	124.35	130.54	139.86	143.31	153.15	135.96	..	Manufacturing
361.71	366.48	362.57	352.18	339.78	341.41	359.84	371.80	391.93	359.65	..	Services, etc.
											Memo Items:
214.60	221.91	189.24	173.97	258.98	231.35	139.77	154.15	133.64	196.60	..	Capacity to Import
67.78	83.30	63.33	51.86	117.57	91.72	-17.06	0.00	-32.75	20.14	..	Terms of Trade Adjustment
729.04	742.42	708.75	673.06	747.60	722.96	655.28	696.42	704.22	695.69	..	Gross Domestic Income
732.05	747.14	696.84	657.79	726.32	701.19	638.95	676.50	684.99	659.10	..	Gross National Income
			(Index 1987 = 100)								**DOMESTIC PRICES/DEFLATORS**
45.0	50.8	52.7	56.2	66.7	73.6	72.8	100.0	118.5	225.0	..	Overall (GDP)
41.5	46.8	50.5	53.1	59.7	66.9	75.8	100.0	124.7	213.9	..	Domestic Absorption
42.4	49.1	51.1	56.2	61.4	71.1	79.3	100.0	129.9	217.8	..	Agriculture
52.0	57.1	56.4	56.9	74.1	79.0	73.0	100.0	116.7	254.5	..	Industry
45.9	49.2	51.4	55.1	72.3	78.0	81.4	100.0	117.2	233.4	..	Manufacturing
41.4	48.1	52.7	56.0	62.8	70.0	78.1	100.0	129.5	238.5	..	Consumer Price Index
											MANUFACTURING ACTIVITY
106.2	95.4	96.8	95.2	93.8	94.8	97.4	100.0	104.5	..	G	Employment (1987=100)
93.8	113.7	111.4	111.8	102.6	103.1	99.5	100.0	113.5	..	G	Real Earnings per Empl. (1987=100)
72.4	82.5	84.5	83.7	80.1	86.0	87.9	100.0	131.6	..	G	Real Output per Empl. (1987=100)
26.7	31.8	32.2	31.6	25.8	25.5	26.8	25.9	24.2	..	..	Earnings as % of Value Added
			(Billions of current Venezuelan Bolivares)								**MONETARY HOLDINGS**
139.33	163.05	181.07	220.18	254.52	275.98	296.72	346.84	388.46	585.83	D	Money Supply, Broadly Defined
54.54	58.30	60.81	76.25	96.68	105.22	109.85	122.56	145.45	169.95	..	Money
12.34	13.52	13.09	14.73	15.13	16.16	18.70	24.83	31.20	40.29	..	Currency Outside Banks
42.20	44.78	47.71	61.52	81.54	89.07	91.15	97.73	114.25	129.66	..	Demand Deposits
84.79	104.74	120.27	143.93	157.85	170.75	186.87	224.28	243.01	415.87	..	Quasi-Money
			(Millions of current Venezuelan Bolivares)								
113	-3,898	-12,670	-4,382	13,546	23,608	-9,965	..	..	..	F	**GOVERNMENT DEFICIT (-) OR SURPLUS**
66,805	97,738	84,019	77,394	104,582	126,561	108,646	..	..	..	..	Current Revenue
44,453	60,246	59,011	60,428	73,633	78,942	79,535	..	..	..	..	Current Expenditure
22,352	37,492	25,008	16,966	30,949	47,619	29,111	..	..	..	..	Current Budget Balance
1	89	1	88	42	23	14	..	..	..	..	Capital Receipts
22,240	41,479	37,679	21,436	17,445	24,034	39,090	..	..	..	..	Capital Payments

VENEZUELA	1969	1970	1971	1972	1973	1974	1975	1976	1977	1978	1979
FOREIGN TRADE (CUSTOMS BASIS)					*(Millions of current US dollars)*						
Value of Exports, fob	3,113	3,197	3,110	3,126	4,773	11,258	9,010	9,466	9,627	9,270	14,318
Nonfuel Primary Products	193	239	218	218	263	415	389	441	352	369	447
Fuels	2,875	2,909	2,846	2,848	4,433	10,701	8,509	8,860	9,132	8,757	13,633
Manufactures	45	48	46	61	77	143	112	165	142	144	238
Value of Imports, cif	1,719	1,869	2,079	2,430	2,806	4,186	6,004	7,663	10,938	11,766	10,670
Nonfuel Primary Products	276	296	297	340	515	771	981	1,221	1,791	1,829	1,822
Fuels	13	27	19	19	22	22	42	39	73	69	122
Manufactures	1,430	1,547	1,763	2,071	2,270	3,393	4,981	6,403	9,073	9,868	8,726
					(Index 1987 = 100)						
Terms of Trade	29.2	28.6	34.7	35.5	40.4	129.4	117.2	124.6	125.1	110.7	137.1
Export Prices, fob	8.1	8.2	10.6	11.9	16.6	65.8	64.1	68.7	75.2	75.7	108.4
Import Prices, cif	27.8	28.8	30.7	33.5	41.2	50.8	54.7	55.1	60.1	68.4	79.0
BALANCE OF PAYMENTS					*(Millions of current US dollars)*						
Exports of Goods & Services	..	2,833	3,339	3,418	5,279	11,971	10,092	10,376	10,947	10,855	16,305
Merchandise, fob	..	2,602	3,103	3,152	4,721	11,085	8,853	9,253	9,556	9,084	14,159
Nonfactor Services	..	177	197	209	329	530	499	430	609	719	800
Factor Services	..	54	39	57	229	356	740	693	782	1,052	1,346
Imports of Goods & Services	..	2,845	3,267	3,424	4,291	6,012	7,748	9,890	13,843	16,183	15,548
Merchandise, fob	..	1,713	1,896	2,222	2,626	3,876	5,462	7,337	10,194	11,234	10,004
Nonfactor Services	..	525	594	665	748	1,143	1,646	2,068	2,955	3,935	4,195
Factor Services	..	607	777	537	917	993	640	485	694	1,014	1,349
Long-Term Interest	..	53	61	81	124	142	119	139	266	498	824
Private Current Transfers, net	..	-86	-79	-89	-105	-135	-143	-169	-231	-371	-388
Workers' Remittances	..	..	..	..	..	..	..	..	..	..	..
Curr. A/C Bal before Off. Transf.	..	-98	-7	-95	883	5,824	2,201	317	-3,127	-5,699	369
Net Official Transfers	..	-6	-4	-6	-6	-64	-30	-63	-52	-36	-19
Curr. A/C Bal after Off. Transf.	..	-104	-11	-101	877	5,760	2,171	254	-3,179	-5,735	350
Long-Term Capital, net	..	91	374	-263	-53	-810	396	1,466	2,109	3,716	1,431
Direct Investment	..	-23	211	-376	-84	-430	418	-889	-3	67	88
Long-Term Loans	..	215	322	406	23	-260	-242	888	1,953	2,176	3,751
Disbursements	..	282	432	591	285	180	230	1,201	2,602	2,655	6,038
Repayments	..	67	110	184	263	440	472	313	649	479	2,287
Other Long-Term Capital	..	-101	-159	-293	9	-120	220	1,467	159	1,473	-2,408
Other Capital, net	..	59	55	534	-213	-482	148	623	1,869	954	2,317
Change in Reserves	..	-46	-418	-170	-611	-4,468	-2,715	-2,343	-799	1,065	-4,098
Memo Item:					*(Venezuelan Bolivares per US dollar)*						
Conversion Factor (Annual Avg)	4.500	4.500	4.500	4.400	4.300	4.280	4.280	4.290	4.290	4.290	4.290
					(Millions of US dollars), outstanding at end of year						
EXTERNAL DEBT (Total)	..	954	1,294	1,703	1,884	1,779	1,492	3,310	10,731	16,576	24,050
Long-Term Debt (by debtor)	..	954	1,294	1,703	1,884	1,779	1,492	3,310	5,305	8,576	12,282
Central Bank, incl. IMF credit	..	26	109	92	84	38	35	32	26	51	631
Central Government	..	271	238	239	207	138	138	2,063	3,685	5,803	5,618
Rest of General Government	..	0	0	0	2	2	2	2	1	1	21
Non-financial Public Enterprises	..	384	605	869	954	1,008	850	704	607	718	3,233
Priv. Sector, incl non-guaranteed	..	272	342	504	637	594	467	510	984	2,002	2,778
Short-Term Debt	..	..	..	..	..	..	..	..	5,426	8,000	11,768
Memo Items:					*(Millions of US dollars)*						
Int'l Reserves Excluding Gold	529.9	636.6	1,096.8	1,306.8	1,940.0	6,034.2	8,402.6	8,123.8	7,735.2	6,034.6	7,320.3
Gold Holdings (at market price)	405.2	409.9	487.3	724.9	1,253.8	2,085.1	1,568.0	1,506.5	1,867.2	2,574.1	5,867.5
SOCIAL INDICATORS											
Total Fertility Rate	5.5	5.3	5.2	5.0	4.9	4.8	4.7	4.6	4.4	4.4	4.3
Infant Mortality Rate	55.6	53.4	51.2	49.0	47.8	46.6	45.4	44.2	43.0	42.2	41.4
Life Expectancy at Birth	64.7	65.2	65.7	66.2	66.5	66.8	67.1	67.4	67.7	68.0	68.2
Urban Population, % of total	71.9	72.4	73.5	74.6	75.6	76.7	77.8	78.9	80.0	81.1	82.2
Food Prod. per capita (1987=100)	121.8	120.9	117.3	112.7	112.3	108.7	118.1	107.1	106.4	110.8	111.5
Labor Force, Agriculture (%)	26.6	26.0	24.7	23.6	22.6	21.7	20.9	19.7	18.7	17.7	16.8
Labor Force, Female (%)	20.5	20.7	21.4	21.9	22.4	22.9	23.3	23.9	24.4	24.9	25.4
Primary Schl. Enroll. Ratio	..	94.0	..	..	..	..	97.0	103.0	102.0	103.0	104.0
Primary Schl. Enroll. Ratio, Female	..	94.0	..	..	..	..	97.0	102.0	101.0	103.0	104.0
Secondary Schl. Enroll. Ratio	..	33.0	..	..	..	..	43.0	38.0	38.0	38.0	39.0

1980	1981	1982	1983	1984	1985	1986	1987	1988	1989 estimate	NOTES	VENEZUELA
				(Millions of current US dollars)							**FOREIGN TRADE (CUSTOMS BASIS)**
19,293	20,125	16,499	14,571	15,841	14,660	9,122	10,567	10,112	..	f	Value of Exports, fob
715	815	590	770	736	971	1,043	986	1,348	..	..	Nonfuel Primary Products
18,248	18,916	15,659	13,439	14,502	13,076	7,304	8,708	7,846	..	..	Fuels
330	394	250	361	603	613	775	873	918	..	..	Manufactures
11,827	13,106	12,944	8,710	7,594	8,234	9,565	10,567	12,662	..	f	Value of Imports, cif
2,280	2,769	2,635	1,777	1,456	1,322	1,753	1,678	1,787	..	..	Nonfuel Primary Products
193	104	129	89	79	69	35	40	31	..	..	Fuels
9,354	10,233	10,181	6,844	6,059	6,843	7,778	8,849	10,844	..	..	Manufactures
				(Index 1987 = 100)							
196.1	214.8	202.6	184.8	183.0	176.2	88.9	100.0	79.3	..	..	Terms of Trade
172.8	189.1	172.6	156.0	151.4	142.3	82.1	100.0	86.8	..	..	Export Prices, fob
88.1	88.0	85.2	84.4	82.7	80.8	92.3	100.0	109.5	..	..	Import Prices, cif
				(Millions of current US dollars)							**BALANCE OF PAYMENTS**
22,232	24,519	20,122	17,341	18,860	17,189	11,253	12,883	12,705	15,672	f	Exports of Goods & Services
19,051	19,963	16,332	14,571	15,878	14,283	8,535	10,437	10,082	12,992	..	Merchandise, fob
917	975	1,225	1,270	885	992	957	991	970	1,113	..	Nonfactor Services
2,264	3,581	2,565	1,500	2,097	1,914	1,761	1,455	1,653	1,567	..	Factor Services
17,065	20,110	23,729	12,703	14,037	13,691	13,377	14,182	18,367	12,989	f	Imports of Goods & Services
10,877	12,123	13,584	6,409	7,246	7,501	7,866	8,870	12,080	7,134	..	Merchandise, fob
4,253	4,980	6,050	2,681	2,632	2,043	2,148	2,238	2,863	1,982	..	Nonfactor Services
1,935	3,007	4,095	3,613	4,159	4,147	3,363	3,074	3,424	3,873	..	Factor Services
1,475	1,554	2,026	2,184	1,960	1,781	2,227	2,473	2,670	2,551	..	Long-Term Interest
-418	-383	-615	-187	-144	-147	-102	-73	-123	-171	..	Private Current Transfers, net
..	..	..	..	..	..	..	..	..	..	..	Workers' Remittances
4,749	4,026	-4,222	4,451	4,679	3,351	-2,226	-1,372	-5,785	2,512	..	Curr. A/C Bal before Off. Transf.
-21	-26	-24	-24	-28	-24	-19	-18	-24	-16	..	Net Official Transfers
4,728	4,000	-4,246	4,427	4,651	3,327	-2,245	-1,390	-5,809	2,496	..	Curr. A/C Bal after Off. Transf.
2,060	810	3,051	284	-686	-745	-2,043	-1,732	-565	288	f	Long-Term Capital, net
55	184	253	86	-3	57	-444	-16	21	77	..	Direct Investment
1,789	1,466	695	1,362	-455	-669	-1,537	-1,603	-668	501	..	Long-Term Loans
4,761	3,990	3,109	3,002	1,423	328	481	522	1,762	1,239	..	Disbursements
2,972	2,524	2,415	1,640	1,878	997	2,018	2,125	2,430	738	..	Repayments
216	-840	2,103	-1,164	-228	-133	-62	-113	82	-290	..	Other Long-Term Capital
-3,025	-4,831	-6,965	-4,379	-2,323	-1,289	-36	1,494	1,728	-2,665	f	Other Capital, net
-3,763	21	8,160	-332	-1,642	-1,293	4,324	1,628	4,646	-119	..	Change in Reserves
				(Venezuelan Bolivares per US dollar)							Memo Item:
4.290	4.290	4.290	4.300	7.020	7.500	8.080	14.500	14.500	34.680	..	Conversion Factor (Annual Avg)
				(Millions of US dollars), outstanding at end of year							
29,330	32,116	32,153	38,297	36,881	35,332	34,638	35,275	35,473	33,144	..	**EXTERNAL DEBT (Total)**
13,795	15,141	17,450	23,787	27,481	26,382	33,063	31,194	30,202	30,860	..	Long-Term Debt (by debtor)
330	78	33	30	24	20	18	14	9	1,003	..	Central Bank, incl. IMF credit
6,640	8,142	9,089	11,512	15,760	15,116	23,000	22,388	22,429	22,042	..	Central Government
18	11	4	1	1	1	0	0	0	..	..	Rest of General Government
3,408	3,051	3,184	3,164	2,897	2,527	2,309	2,715	2,877	3,289	..	Non-financial Public Enterprises
3,398	3,859	5,141	9,080	8,798	8,719	7,736	6,077	4,886	4,527	..	Priv. Sector, incl non-guaranteed
15,535	16,975	14,703	14,510	9,400	8,950	1,575	4,081	5,271	2,284	..	Short-Term Debt
				(Millions of US dollars)							Memo Items:
6,603.9	8,164.4	6,578.5	7,642.8	8,901.1	10,250.8	6,437.4	5,962.7	3,091.5	4,106.4	..	Int'l Reserves Excluding Gold
6,755.7	4,555.4	5,236.1	4,372.0	3,533.1	3,747.4	4,479.7	5,547.8	4,701.5	4,595.5	..	Gold Holdings (at market price)
											SOCIAL INDICATORS
4.2	4.2	4.1	4.0	4.0	3.9	3.8	3.8	3.7	3.6	..	Total Fertility Rate
40.6	39.8	39.0	38.4	37.8	37.2	36.6	36.0	35.4	34.8	..	Infant Mortality Rate
68.5	68.7	69.0	69.1	69.3	69.4	69.5	69.7	69.8	69.9	..	Life Expectancy at Birth
83.3	84.1	83.5	83.0	82.4	81.8	82.3	82.8	83.2	83.7	..	Urban Population, % of total
107.6	104.5	102.4	107.0	100.2	98.9	108.7	100.0	100.8	83.6	..	Food Prod. per capita (1987=100)
16.0	..	..	..	..	..	..	..	..	..	..	Labor Force, Agriculture (%)
25.8	26.0	26.2	26.4	26.5	26.7	26.9	27.1	27.3	27.5	..	Labor Force, Female (%)
109.0	..	111.0	108.0	109.0	108.0	107.0	..	..	..	..	Primary Schl. Enroll. Ratio
..	..	111.0	108.0	108.0	108.0	107.0	..	..	..	..	Primary Schl. Enroll. Ratio, Female
41.0	..	43.0	43.0	45.0	45.0	54.0	..	..	..	..	Secondary Schl. Enroll. Ratio

WESTERN SAMOA	1969	1970	1971	1972	1973	1974	1975	1976	1977	1978	1979
CURRENT GNP PER CAPITA (US $)	..	..	..	..	..	..	..	..	..	..	..
POPULATION (thousands)	141	143	145	147	148	149	150	151	152	153	154

USE AND ORIGIN OF RESOURCES *(Millions of current Western Samoa Tala)*

	1969	1970	1971	1972	1973	1974	1975	1976	1977	1978	1979
Gross National Product (GNP)	..	..	..	..	..	..	..	..	..	..	..
Net Factor Income from Abroad	..	..	..	..	..	..	..	..	..	..	..
GDP at Market Prices	..	..	..	..	..	..	..	..	..	71.00	90.00
Resource Balance	..	..	..	..	..	..	..	..	..	..	-57.40
Exports of Goods & NFServices	..	..	..	..	..	..	..	..	..	..	22.10
Imports of Goods & NFServices	..	..	..	..	..	..	..	..	..	..	79.50
Domestic Absorption	..	..	..	..	..	..	..	..	..	..	147.40
Private Consumption, etc.	..	..	..	..	..	..	..	..	..	..	88.70
General Gov't Consumption	..	..	..	..	..	..	..	..	..	..	16.90
Gross Domestic Investment	..	..	..	..	..	..	..	..	..	..	41.80
Fixed Investment	..	..	..	..	..	..	..	..	..	..	..
Indirect Taxes, net	..	..	..	..	..	..	..	..	..	..	12.00
GDP at factor cost	..	..	..	..	..	..	..	..	..	..	78.00
Agriculture	..	..	..	..	..	..	..	..	..	..	38.00
Industry	..	..	..	..	..	..	..	..	..	..	7.30
Manufacturing	..	..	..	..	..	..	..	..	..	..	3.40
Services, etc.	..	..	..	..	..	..	..	..	..	..	32.70
Gross Domestic Saving	..	..	..	..	..	..	..	..	..	..	-15.60
Gross National Saving	..	..	..	..	..	..	..	..	..	..	..

(Millions of 1987 Western Samoa Tala)

	1969	1970	1971	1972	1973	1974	1975	1976	1977	1978	1979
Gross National Product	..	..	..	..	..	..	..	..	..	..	..
GDP at Market Prices	..	..	..	..	..	..	..	..	..	208.16	230.86
Resource Balance	..	..	..	..	..	..	..	..	..	..	-141.54
Exports of Goods & NFServices	..	..	..	..	..	..	..	..	..	..	48.37
Imports of Goods & NFServices	..	..	..	..	..	..	..	..	..	..	189.91
Domestic Absorption	..	..	..	..	..	..	..	..	..	..	372.41
Private Consumption, etc.	..	..	..	..	..	..	..	..	..	..	167.29
General Gov't Consumption	..	..	..	..	..	..	..	..	..	..	62.31
Gross Domestic Investment	..	..	..	..	..	..	..	..	..	..	142.81
Fixed Investment	..	..	..	..	..	..	..	..	..	..	..
GDP at factor cost	..	..	..	..	..	..	..	..	..	..	..
Agriculture	..	..	..	..	..	..	..	..	..	..	..
Industry	..	..	..	..	..	..	..	..	..	..	..
Manufacturing	..	..	..	..	..	..	..	..	..	..	..
Services, etc.	..	..	..	..	..	..	..	..	..	..	..
Memo Items:											
Capacity to Import	..	..	..	..	..	..	..	..	..	..	52.79
Terms of Trade Adjustment	..	..	..	..	..	..	..	..	..	..	4.42
Gross Domestic Income	..	..	..	..	..	..	..	..	..	..	235.29
Gross National Income	..	..	..	..	..	..	..	..	..	..	..

DOMESTIC PRICES/DEFLATORS *(Index 1987 = 100)*

	1969	1970	1971	1972	1973	1974	1975	1976	1977	1978	1979
Overall (GDP)	..	..	..	..	..	..	..	..	..	34.1	39.0
Domestic Absorption	..	..	..	..	..	..	..	..	..	..	39.6
Agriculture	..	..	..	..	..	..	..	..	..	..	..
Industry	..	..	..	..	..	..	..	..	..	..	..
Manufacturing	..	..	..	..	..	..	..	..	..	..	..
Consumer Price Index	14.0	14.4	15.1	16.2	18.1	22.6	24.6	25.8	29.6	30.2	33.6

MANUFACTURING ACTIVITY

	1969	1970	1971	1972	1973	1974	1975	1976	1977	1978	1979
Employment (1987=100)	..	..	..	..	..	..	..	..	..	..	..
Real Earnings per Empl. (1987=100)	..	..	..	..	..	..	..	..	..	..	..
Real Output per Empl. (1987=100)	..	..	..	..	..	..	..	..	..	..	..
Earnings as % of Value Added	..	..	..	..	..	..	..	..	..	..	..

MONETARY HOLDINGS *(Thousands of current Western Samoa Tala)*

	1969	1970	1971	1972	1973	1974	1975	1976	1977	1978	1979
Money Supply, Broadly Defined	2,948	3,236	4,045	4,535	5,578	6,636	7,113	8,519	10,131	11,143	15,632
Money	902	1,278	1,937	2,312	2,763	3,206	3,478	4,044	4,755	5,225	5,770
Currency Outside Banks	73	87	104	119	144	169	185	218	232	251	174
Demand Deposits	829	1,191	1,833	2,193	2,619	3,037	3,293	3,826	4,523	4,974	5,596
Quasi-Money	2,046	1,958	2,108	2,223	2,815	3,430	3,635	4,475	5,376	5,918	9,862

GOVERNMENT DEFICIT (-) OR SURPLUS *(Thousands of current Western Samoa Tala)*

	1969	1970	1971	1972	1973	1974	1975	1976	1977	1978	1979
Current Revenue	..	..	..	..	..	..	..	..	..	..	..
Current Expenditure	..	..	..	..	..	..	..	..	..	..	..
Current Budget Balance	..	..	..	..	..	..	..	..	..	..	..
Capital Receipts	..	..	..	..	..	..	..	..	..	..	..
Capital Payments	..	..	..	..	..	..	..	..	..	..	..

1980	1981	1982	1983	1984	1985	1986	1987	1988	1989 estimate	NOTES	WESTERN SAMOA
..	..	..	..	..	640	630	620	670	720	..	**CURRENT GNP PER CAPITA (US $)**
155	156	156	157	157	157	157	158	159	159	..	**POPULATION (thousands)**

(Millions of current Western Samoa Tala)

1980	1981	1982	1983	1984	1985	1986	1987	1988	1989	NOTES	
											USE AND ORIGIN OF RESOURCES
..	..	135.50	161.30	177.20	192.40	206.00	220.40	241.90	250.00	..	Gross National Product (GNP)
..	..	5.10	6.90	-4.00	-4.30	-2.40	1.10	1.60	1.60	..	Net Factor Income from Abroad
103.00	108.90	130.40	154.40	181.20	196.70	208.40	219.30	240.30	248.40	f	GDP at Market Prices
-38.70	-59.90	-44.90	-46.00	-57.50	-70.10	-73.30	-91.60	-90.90	-92.60	..	Resource Balance
25.80	17.80	21.90	41.60	50.00	55.60	52.20	58.00	82.90	86.30	..	Exports of Goods & NFServices
64.50	77.70	66.80	87.60	107.50	125.70	125.50	149.60	173.80	178.90	..	Imports of Goods & NFServices
141.70	168.80	175.30	200.40	238.70	266.80	281.70	310.90	331.20	..	..	Domestic Absorption
89.40	105.90	118.10	136.20	155.10	171.70	184.50	196.90	218.50	..	..	Private Consumption, etc.
18.20	20.60	24.30	21.90	30.10	35.00	37.50	39.90	43.10	..	..	General Gov't Consumption
34.10	42.30	32.90	42.30	53.50	60.10	59.70	74.10	69.60	..	..	Gross Domestic Investment
..	..	..	..	..	..	..	..	..	..	..	Fixed Investment
13.70	13.00	14.00	14.00	..	..	..	..	..	..	..	Indirect Taxes, net
89.30	95.90	116.40	140.40	..	..	..	..	..	..	f	GDP at factor cost
41.10	44.90	59.50	..	..	..	..	..	..	..	..	Agriculture
10.90	11.40	14.30	..	..	..	..	..	..	..	..	Industry
4.90	5.20	6.90	..	..	..	..	..	..	..	..	Manufacturing
37.30	39.60	42.60	..	..	..	..	..	..	..	..	Services, etc.
-4.60	-17.60	-12.00	-3.70	-4.00	-10.00	-13.60	-17.50	-21.30	..	..	Gross Domestic Saving
..	..	15.59	34.70	29.75	38.76	47.50	60.80	54.10	..	..	Gross National Saving

(Millions of 1987 Western Samoa Tala)

1980	1981	1982	1983	1984	1985	1986	1987	1988	1989	NOTES	
..	..	..	194.71	197.24	207.25	219.22	220.40	218.82	218.67	..	Gross National Product
216.57	197.01	195.12	195.96	198.48	206.47	217.62	219.30	218.46	218.88	f	GDP at Market Prices
-93.83	-114.51	-76.03	-74.71	-88.23	-83.10	-75.29	-91.60	-89.86	-78.83	..	Resource Balance
56.47	41.15	40.71	45.52	38.30	49.03	58.00	58.00	67.19	69.60	..	Exports of Goods & NFServices
150.30	155.66	116.74	120.24	126.53	132.12	133.29	149.60	157.06	148.43	..	Imports of Goods & NFServices
310.40	311.52	271.15	270.68	286.71	289.57	292.91	310.90	308.32	297.71	..	Domestic Absorption
163.85	162.87	158.22	168.00	167.64	186.63	194.61	196.90	206.76	..	..	Private Consumption, etc.
49.74	46.73	45.37	39.08	48.10	39.63	34.98	39.90	38.53	..	..	General Gov't Consumption
96.81	101.92	67.57	63.60	70.98	63.31	63.31	74.10	63.03	..	..	Gross Domestic Investment
..	..	..	..	..	..	..	..	..	..	..	Fixed Investment
..	..	..	..	..	..	..	..	..	..	f	GDP at factor cost
..	..	..	..	..	..	..	..	..	..	..	Agriculture
..	..	..	..	..	..	..	..	..	..	..	Industry
..	..	..	..	..	..	..	..	..	..	..	Manufacturing
..	..	..	..	..	..	..	..	..	..	..	Services, etc.
											Memo Items:
60.12	35.66	38.27	57.10	58.85	58.44	55.44	58.00	74.91	71.60	..	Capacity to Import
3.65	-5.49	-2.44	11.58	20.55	9.41	-2.56	0.00	7.72	2.00	..	Terms of Trade Adjustment
220.22	191.52	192.68	207.54	219.03	215.89	215.06	219.30	226.18	220.88	..	Gross Domestic Income
..	..	..	206.29	217.79	216.66	216.66	220.40	226.54	220.68	..	Gross National Income

(Index 1987 = 100)

1980	1981	1982	1983	1984	1985	1986	1987	1988	1989	NOTES	
											DOMESTIC PRICES/DEFLATORS
47.6	55.3	66.8	78.8	91.3	95.3	95.8	100.0	110.0	113.5	..	Overall (GDP)
45.7	54.2	64.6	74.0	83.3	92.1	96.2	100.0	107.4	..	..	Domestic Absorption
..	..	..	..	..	..	..	..	..	..	..	Agriculture
..	..	..	..	..	..	..	..	..	..	..	Industry
..	..	..	..	..	..	..	..	..	..	..	Manufacturing
44.6	53.8	63.6	74.1	82.9	90.4	95.6	100.0	108.5	115.5	..	Consumer Price Index
											MANUFACTURING ACTIVITY
..	..	..	..	..	..	..	..	..	..	G	Employment (1987=100)
..	..	..	..	..	..	..	..	..	..	G	Real Earnings per Empl. (1987=100)
..	..	..	..	..	..	..	..	..	..	G	Real Output per Empl. (1987=100)
..	..	..	..	..	..	..	..	..	..	..	Earnings as % of Value Added

(Thousands of current Western Samoa Tala)

1980	1981	1982	1983	1984	1985	1986	1987	1988	1989	NOTES	
											MONETARY HOLDINGS
20,477	33,583	45,319	40,033	44,779	53,940	64,740	82,370	88,850	103,240	..	Money Supply, Broadly Defined
9,138	14,106	17,423	16,929	19,362	19,960	21,630	28,690	30,190	33,160	..	Money
3,555	5,280	6,053	6,019	7,079	8,440	9,180	10,530	10,720	12,480	..	Currency Outside Banks
5,583	8,826	11,370	10,910	12,283	11,520	12,450	18,160	19,470	20,680	..	Demand Deposits
11,339	19,477	27,896	23,104	25,417	33,980	43,110	53,680	58,660	70,080	..	Quasi-Money

(Thousands of current Western Samoa Tala)

1980	1981	1982	1983	1984	1985	1986	1987	1988	1989	NOTES	
											GOVERNMENT DEFICIT (-) OR SURPLUS
..	..	..	..	..	..	..	..	..	..	..	Current Revenue
..	..	..	..	36,781	..	..	..	..	..	..	Current Expenditure
..	..	..	..	..	..	..	..	..	..	..	Current Budget Balance
..	..	..	..	..	..	..	..	..	..	..	Capital Receipts
..	..	..	..	..	..	..	..	..	..	..	Capital Payments

WESTERN SAMOA	1969	1970	1971	1972	1973	1974	1975	1976	1977	1978	1979
FOREIGN TRADE (CUSTOMS BASIS)					*(Thousands of current US dollars)*						
Value of Exports, fob	6,700	5,000	6,600	5,200	7,000	13,000	7,500	7,000	14,700	9,740	18,100
Nonfuel Primary Products	..	..	..	..	..	..	..	..	..	..	..
Fuels	..	..	..	..	..	..	..	..	..	..	..
Manufactures	..	..	..	..	..	..	..	..	..	..	..
Value of Imports, cif	10,000	14,000	13,000	19,000	24,000	26,000	37,000	30,000	41,000	52,000	73,000
Nonfuel Primary Products	..	..	..	..	..	..	..	..	..	..	..
Fuels	..	..	..	..	..	..	..	..	..	..	..
Manufactures	..	..	..	..	..	..	..	..	..	..	..
					(Index 1987 = 100)						
Terms of Trade	..	..	..	..	..	..	..	..	..	..	..
Export Prices, fob	..	..	..	..	..	..	..	..	..	..	..
Import Prices, cif	..	..	..	..	..	..	..	..	..	..	..
BALANCE OF PAYMENTS					*(Thousands of current US dollars)*						
Exports of Goods & Services	..	7,218	9,435	10,610	11,953	20,056	15,222	12,143	..	..	..
Merchandise, fob	..	4,808	6,557	5,168	6,744	12,901	7,476	6,998	14,731	9,737	18,132
Nonfactor Services	..	2,343	2,780	5,127	5,130	7,055	7,693	5,033	2,417	3,911	3,631
Factor Services	..	67	97	315	80	101	53	113	..	..	..
Imports of Goods & Services	..	14,862	15,209	26,255	27,626	31,233	39,829	29,347	42,540	55,912	78,665
Merchandise, fob	..	12,179	12,101	20,979	21,353	23,654	33,212	26,809	37,337	47,655	67,154
Nonfactor Services	..	2,541	2,980	5,089	5,942	7,109	6,219	2,177	5,089	6,763	9,889
Factor Services	..	142	128	187	331	470	398	360	114	1,494	1,622
Long-Term Interest	..	0	0	0	200	600	500	500	1,000	1,200	1,600
Private Current Transfers, net	..	2,175	2,341	2,956	4,125	7,081	5,876	3,080	5,852	12,141	13,460
Workers' Remittances	..	2,580	2,909	4,180	6,449	9,272	8,256	5,149	5,852	12,141	13,460
Curr. A/C Bal before Off. Transf.	..	-5,469	-3,433	-12,689	-11,548	-4,095	-18,731	-14,123	-19,540	-30,122	-43,442
Net Official Transfers	..	397	700	1,219	3,928	2,702	6,345	3,891	9,808	12,019	21,400
Curr. A/C Bal after Off. Transf.	..	-5,072	-2,733	-11,469	-7,620	-1,393	-12,386	-10,233	-9,732	-18,103	-22,042
Long-Term Capital, net	..	2,427	2,513	6,925	5,958	5,892	12,308	9,616	10,304	11,381	8,269
Direct Investment	..	..	..	..	..	..	..	..	..	..	..
Long-Term Loans	..	2,300	-100	1,900	5,100	2,600	4,000	5,700	7,400	8,100	9,900
Disbursements	..	2,400	0	2,100	5,600	3,200	4,600	8,500	8,500	9,700	12,000
Repayments	..	100	100	200	500	600	600	2,800	1,100	1,600	2,100
Other Long-Term Capital	..	127	2,613	5,025	858	3,292	8,308	3,916	2,904	3,281	-1,631
Other Capital, net	..	3,252	967	1,802	172	-3,591	-483	-1,213	3,120	734	13,709
Change in Reserves	..	-607	-747	2,742	1,490	-908	561	1,829	-3,692	5,988	64
Memo Item:					*(Western Samoa Tala per US dollar)*						
Conversion Factor (Annual Avg)	0.720	0.720	0.720	0.680	0.610	0.610	0.630	0.800	0.790	0.740	0.820
				(Thousands of US dollars), outstanding at end of year							
EXTERNAL DEBT (Total)	..	2,700	2,600	4,400	9,500	13,600	17,400	22,600	31,300	41,300	52,500
Long-Term Debt (by debtor)	..	2,700	2,600	4,400	9,500	13,600	17,400	22,600	31,300	41,300	52,500
Central Bank, incl. IMF credit	..	0	0	0	0	0	1,500	2,200	2,300	4,600	6,300
Central Government	..	2,700	2,600	2,600	4,500	8,400	11,500	14,500	19,300	27,700	36,000
Rest of General Government	..	..	..	..	..	..	..	..	..	..	..
Non-financial Public Enterprises	..	0	0	1,800	5,000	5,200	4,400	5,900	9,700	9,000	10,200
Priv. Sector, incl non-guaranteed	..	0	0	0	0	0	0	0	0	0	0
Short-Term Debt	..	..	..	..	..	..	..	0	0	0	0
Memo Items:					*(Thousands of US dollars)*						
Int'l Reserves Excluding Gold	5,150	5,220	6,411	4,529	5,078	5,958	6,387	5,240	9,126	4,782	4,820
Gold Holdings (at market price)	..	..	..	..	..	..	..	..	..	..	..
SOCIAL INDICATORS											
Total Fertility Rate	6.9	6.7	6.3	5.9	5.9	5.8	5.8	5.7	5.7	5.7	5.6
Infant Mortality Rate	..	..	..	..	..	..	..	..	..	..	..
Life Expectancy at Birth	..	..	..	..	..	..	..	62.6	62.6	62.9	63.2
Urban Population, % of total	20.1	20.3	20.4	20.6	20.7	20.9	21.0	21.1	21.2	21.2	21.3
Food Prod. per capita (1987=100)	108.4	104.2	108.4	100.9	101.0	102.3	104.9	106.6	110.2	104.1	110.6
Labor Force, Agriculture (%)	..	..	..	..	..	..	..	..	..	..	..
Labor Force, Female (%)	..	..	..	..	..	..	..	..	..	..	..
Primary Schl. Enroll. Ratio	..	..	..	..	..	..	..	..	..	..	..
Primary Schl. Enroll. Ratio, Female	..	..	..	..	..	..	..	..	..	..	..
Secondary Schl. Enroll. Ratio	..	..	..	..	..	..	..	..	..	..	..

1980	1981	1982	1983	1984	1985	1986	1987	1988	1989 estimate	NOTES	WESTERN SAMOA
				(Thousands of current US dollars)							**FOREIGN TRADE (CUSTOMS BASIS)**
17,200	10,800	13,500	17,700	18,340	16,100	10,500	11,800	15,000	..	..	Value of Exports, fob
..	..	..	..	..	..	..	..	..	..	..	Nonfuel Primary Products
..	..	..	..	..	..	..	..	..	..	..	Fuels
..	..	..	..	..	..	..	..	..	..	..	Manufactures
63,000	57,000	50,000	52,000	50,000	51,000	47,000	62,000	76,000	..	..	Value of Imports, cif
..	..	..	..	..	..	..	..	..	..	..	Nonfuel Primary Products
..	..	..	..	..	..	..	..	..	..	..	Fuels
..	..	..	..	..	..	..	..	..	..	..	Manufactures
				(Index 1987 = 100)							
..	..	..	..	..	..	..	..	..	..	..	Terms of Trade
..	..	..	..	..	..	..	..	..	..	..	Export Prices, fob
..	..	..	..	..	..	..	..	..	..	..	Import Prices, cif
				(Thousands of current US dollars)							**BALANCE OF PAYMENTS**
25,672	18,383	21,784	26,964	27,214	27,137	25,101	30,951	43,529	45,203	..	Exports of Goods & Services
17,220	10,783	13,459	17,694	18,343	16,123	10,507	11,769	15,093	12,867	..	Merchandise, fob
8,430	7,475	8,241	9,134	8,532	10,333	13,338	16,430	25,548	27,861	..	Nonfactor Services
22	126	83	136	338	681	1,257	2,752	2,889	4,475	..	Factor Services
74,273	65,749	60,157	59,395	60,060	60,264	58,987	73,468	88,270	88,089	..	Imports of Goods & Services
56,858	51,379	45,315	44,115	45,551	46,600	42,844	55,789	68,490	68,496	..	Merchandise, fob
14,859	11,585	12,606	12,446	12,184	11,086	13,807	15,454	17,655	17,201	..	Nonfactor Services
2,556	2,785	2,236	2,834	2,325	2,579	2,335	2,225	2,125	2,392	..	Factor Services
2,300	1,700	1,100	1,100	1,400	1,700	1,400	1,300	1,300	1,100	..	Long-Term Interest
18,742	18,558	18,628	20,334	20,271	23,632	28,402	36,385	35,473	38,151	..	Private Current Transfers, net
18,742	18,558	18,628	20,334	20,271	23,828	28,621	36,635	37,708	40,873	..	Workers' Remittances
-29,859	-28,808	-19,746	-12,097	-12,576	-9,496	-5,484	-6,132	-9,267	-4,735	..	Curr. A/C Bal before Off. Transf.
16,948	15,714	13,708	16,900	13,231	11,424	17,001	17,377	15,429	15,232	..	Net Official Transfers
-12,912	-13,094	-6,038	4,803	655	1,929	11,517	11,245	6,162	10,497	..	Curr. A/C Bal after Off. Transf.
5,732	4,535	-522	3,208	4,451	-147	-1,315	3,389	1,043	1,277	..	Long-Term Capital, net
..	..	..	..	..	..	..	..	..	..	..	Direct Investment
8,200	3,700	5,300	2,000	7,300	-1,100	-1,200	3,300	1,300	1,700	..	Long-Term Loans
10,500	5,400	7,000	4,700	10,200	2,500	2,800	6,000	4,200	5,000	..	Disbursements
2,300	1,700	1,700	2,700	2,900	3,600	4,000	2,700	2,900	3,300	..	Repayments
-2,468	835	-5,822	1,208	-2,849	953	-115	89	-257	-423	..	Other Long-Term Capital
5,869	6,888	7,984	-5,258	-1,882	2,046	667	-2,618	4,734	715	..	Other Capital, net
1,311	1,671	-1,424	-2,753	-3,225	-3,828	-10,870	-12,016	-11,940	-12,490	..	Change in Reserves
				(Western Samoa Tala per US dollar)							**Memo Item:**
0.920	1.040	1.210	1.540	1.840	2.240	2.230	2.120	2.080	2.270	..	Conversion Factor (Annual Avg)
				(Thousands of US dollars), outstanding at end of year							
60,200	63,300	68,800	73,600	74,800	75,700	75,800	80,600	75,800	74,800	...	**EXTERNAL DEBT (Total)**
59,200	62,300	64,800	66,600	72,800	74,700	74,800	79,600	74,800	73,800	..	Long-Term Debt (by debtor)
5,800	7,500	6,300	7,900	9,800	10,900	10,100	8,200	3,800	1,600	..	Central Bank, incl. IMF credit
41,400	44,400	49,300	51,000	57,200	58,600	59,800	66,000	66,400	67,800	..	Central Government
..	..	..	..	..	..	..	..	..	..	..	Rest of General Government
11,900	9,800	8,300	7,000	5,200	4,400	3,900	4,200	3,600	3,400	..	Non-financial Public Enterprises
100	600	900	700	600	800	1,000	1,200	1,000	1,000	..	Priv. Sector, incl non-guaranteed
1,000	1,000	4,000	7,000	2,000	1,000	1,000	1,000	1,000	1,000	..	Short-Term Debt
				(Thousands of US dollars)							**Memo Items:**
2,770	3,282	3,481	7,229	10,557	14,021	23,746	37,198	49,197	55,066	..	Int'l Reserves Excluding Gold
..	..	..	..	..	..	..	..	..	..	..	Gold Holdings (at market price)
											SOCIAL INDICATORS
5.6	5.5	5.5	5.4	5.2	5.1	5.0	4.8	4.7	4.6	..	Total Fertility Rate
..	..	..	..	..	..	..	50.0	48.7	47.4	..	Infant Mortality Rate
63.5	63.7	64.0	64.3	64.6	64.9	65.2	65.4	65.7	65.9	..	Life Expectancy at Birth
21.4	21.5	21.6	21.6	21.7	21.8	22.0	22.2	22.5	22.7	..	Urban Population, % of total
98.9	95.7	102.9	94.3	91.6	98.2	102.6	100.0	97.1	101.2	..	Food Prod. per capita (1987 = 100)
..	..	..	..	..	..	..	..	..	..	..	Labor Force, Agriculture (%)
..	..	..	..	..	..	..	..	..	..	..	Labor Force, Female (%)
..	..	..	..	..	..	..	..	..	..	..	Primary Schl. Enroll. Ratio
..	..	..	..	..	..	..	..	..	..	..	Primary Schl. Enroll. Ratio, Female
..	..	..	..	..	..	..	..	..	..	..	Secondary Schl. Enroll. Ratio

YUGOSLAVIA	1969	1970	1971	1972	1973	1974	1975	1976	1977	1978	1979
CURRENT GNP PER CAPITA (US $)	600	660	740	780	870	1,150	1,380	1,620	1,970	2,400	2,880
POPULATION (thousands)	20,209	20,371	20,572	20,772	20,956	21,164	21,365	21,573	21,775	21,968	22,166
USE AND ORIGIN OF RESOURCES					*(Billions of current Yugoslav Dinars)*						
Gross National Product (GNP)	149	171	220	268	330	426	537	677	835	1,020	1,295
Net Factor Income from Abroad	1	-1	0	0	0	1	0	-1	0	-1	-7
GDP at Market Prices	148	172	220	268	329	425	537	679	836	1,021	1,302
Resource Balance	-3	-9	-14	-7	-12	-42	-42	-18	-52	-49	-90
Exports of Goods & NFServices	27	32	43	58	72	91	109	130	145	167	203
Imports of Goods & NFServices	30	41	56	65	84	133	151	148	198	216	293
Domestic Absorption	150	181	234	275	341	467	579	696	888	1,070	1,392
Private Consumption, etc.	81	95	125	154	195	264	301	361	442	542	670
General Gov't Consumption	26	30	37	45	53	74	98	119	147	178	223
Gross Domestic Investment	43	56	72	75	93	129	180	217	299	351	499
Fixed Investment	41	52	65	75	86	117	163	207	268	357	448
Indirect Taxes, net	12	15	19	20	21	46	47	61	79	97	129
GDP at factor cost	136	157	201	248	308	380	490	618	756	925	1,173
Agriculture	26	28	34	44	55	61	77	93	106	105	140
Industry	53	64	81	116	125	159	220	259	317	389	505
Manufacturing	..	..	..	..	..	..	..	..	..	..	..
Services, etc.	56	65	86	88	129	159	193	265	334	431	529
Gross Domestic Saving	41	46	58	69	82	87	138	199	247	302	409
Gross National Saving	..	46	58	68	82	88	137	198	247	300	402
					(Billions of 1987 Yugoslav Dinars)						
Gross National Product	25,667.8	26,548.0	28,921.1	29,969.9	30,841.3	35,421.6	35,555.4	37,414.2	40,600.9	44,277.9	46,421.7
GDP at Market Prices	25,242.5	26,444.5	28,781.8	29,801.3	30,579.4	35,105.0	35,336.1	37,218.3	40,322.5	44,026.9	46,351.7
Resource Balance	-808.3	-2,637.6	-3,327.3	-1,549.5	-2,206.3	-4,271.2	-3,958.3	-1,587.0	-3,971.5	-3,801.1	-5,395.7
Exports of Goods & NFServices	8,047.0	8,470.7	9,170.7	10,338.8	11,201.3	10,588.9	10,704.1	11,815.1	11,584.4	12,138.2	12,458.2
Imports of Goods & NFServices	8,855.3	11,108.3	12,498.0	11,888.4	13,407.6	14,860.1	14,662.3	13,402.1	15,555.9	15,939.2	17,853.9
Domestic Absorption	26,050.7	29,082.1	32,109.1	31,350.8	32,785.7	39,376.2	39,294.4	38,805.3	44,294.0	47,828.0	51,747.4
Private Consumption, etc.	11,032.8	13,035.6	15,315.7	14,354.0	14,898.9	20,129.0	18,971.8	17,487.9	20,920.5	24,133.6	25,370.7
General Gov't Consumption	10,241.3	10,521.7	10,748.2	11,411.4	11,667.4	12,497.1	12,889.6	13,613.8	14,330.1	14,936.8	15,628.0
Gross Domestic Investment	4,776.6	5,524.8	6,045.1	5,585.4	6,219.5	6,750.1	7,432.9	7,703.6	9,043.4	8,757.6	10,748.8
Fixed Investment	..	..	..	..	..	..	..	..	..	..	..
GDP at factor cost	21,911.9	22,802.7	24,759.5	25,953.1	26,968.2	29,510.1	30,370.3	31,895.3	34,375.7	37,558.5	39,350.3
Agriculture	4,286.1	4,039.7	4,299.2	4,471.8	4,864.1	5,130.6	4,998.9	5,319.0	5,622.2	5,320.7	5,519.4
Industry	8,717.7	9,359.1	10,033.3	12,132.6	12,571.4	13,814.4	14,819.6	15,405.6	16,867.1	18,419.6	19,671.1
Manufacturing	..	..	..	..	..	..	..	..	..	..	..
Services, etc.	8,969.9	9,466.5	10,494.6	9,419.3	9,606.9	10,611.7	10,683.3	11,285.7	12,050.1	13,782.3	14,204.6
Memo Items:											
Capacity to Import	8,111.5	8,622.1	9,409.2	10,680.8	11,509.3	10,211.3	10,577.7	11,803.2	11,448.3	12,321.0	12,372.7
Terms of Trade Adjustment	64.4	151.3	238.5	342.0	308.0	-377.5	-126.3	-11.9	-136.1	182.8	-85.5
Gross Domestic Income	25,306.9	26,595.9	29,020.3	30,143.3	30,887.4	34,727.5	35,209.8	37,206.3	40,186.4	44,209.7	46,266.2
Gross National Income	25,732.2	26,699.3	29,159.6	30,311.9	31,149.3	35,044.0	35,429.1	37,402.2	40,464.8	44,460.7	46,336.2
DOMESTIC PRICES/DEFLATORS					*(Index 1987 = 100)*						
Overall (GDP)	0.6	0.7	0.8	0.9	1.1	1.2	1.5	1.8	2.1	2.3	2.8
Domestic Absorption	0.6	0.6	0.7	0.9	1.0	1.2	1.5	1.8	2.0	2.2	2.7
Agriculture	0.6	0.7	0.8	1.0	1.1	1.2	1.5	1.7	1.9	2.0	2.5
Industry	0.6	0.7	0.8	1.0	1.0	1.2	1.5	1.7	1.9	2.1	2.6
Manufacturing	..	..	..	..	..	..	..	..	..	..	..
Consumer Price Index	0.6	0.6	0.7	0.8	1.0	1.2	1.5	1.7	1.9	2.2	2.7
MANUFACTURING ACTIVITY											
Employment (1987=100)	47.1	49.4	52.8	55.8	58.6	60.3	62.7	69.2	72.1	74.9	78.5
Real Earnings per Empl. (1987=100)	90.7	97.6	102.4	102.0	99.0	102.6	100.1	107.5	113.2	111.8	111.9
Real Output per Empl. (1987=100)	..	65.6	70.1	71.0	85.8	112.5	108.7	102.4	110.1	112.2	114.8
Earnings as % of Value Added	38.6	38.8	37.8	38.3	36.8	34.7	35.6	38.9	38.9	37.1	36.8
MONETARY HOLDINGS					*(Billions of current Yugoslav Dinars)*						
Money Supply, Broadly Defined	84	104	127	156	207	255	338	467	571	732	895
Money	30	36	42	59	81	102	135	217	247	291	341
Currency Outside Banks	12	15	18	24	29	35	42	49	58	75	91
Demand Deposits	18	21	23	35	52	67	93	168	189	216	250
Quasi-Money	54	68	85	97	125	153	203	251	324	442	554
GOVERNMENT DEFICIT (-) OR SURPLUS					*(Billions of current Yugoslav Dinars)*	-10.0	-10.0	-20.0	-10.0	-10.0	..
Current Revenue	..	30.0	40.0	60.0	70.0	90.0	120.0	140.0	80.0	90.0	120.0
Current Expenditure	..	..	..	..	..	..	..	..	80.0	90.0	120.0
Current Budget Balance	..	..	..	..	..	..	..	..	0.0	0.0	0.0
Capital Receipts	..	..	..	..	..	..	..	..	..	..	..
Capital Payments	..	..	..	..	..	..	..	..	10.0	10.0	0.0

1980	1981	1982	1983	1984	1985	1986	1987	1988	1989 estimate	NOTES	YUGOSLAVIA
3,250	3,450	3,230	2,640	2,270	2,040	2,290	2,510	2,720	2,920	..	**CURRENT GNP PER CAPITA (US $)**
22,304	22,471	22,646	22,800	22,963	23,123	23,271	23,411	23,559	23,707	..	**POPULATION (thousands)**
				(Billions of current Yugoslav Dinars)							**USE AND ORIGIN OF RESOURCES**
1,781	2,464	3,173	4,343	6,766	12,480	24,522	47,907	151,275	2,160,450	..	Gross National Product (GNP)
-20	-44	-78	-118	-208	-383	-561	-1,238	-4,533	-42,248	..	Net Factor Income from Abroad
1,801	2,507	3,251	4,460	6,974	12,863	25,083	49,145	155,808	2,202,700	..	GDP at Market Prices
-76	-62	-2	10	56	229	438	1,423	9,545	120,049	..	Resource Balance
336	497	710	1,216	2,073	3,837	5,982	12,068	56,161	758,521	..	Exports of Goods & NFServices
413	559	712	1,206	2,018	3,609	5,544	10,645	46,615	638,472	..	Imports of Goods & NFServices
1,877	2,569	3,253	4,450	6,918	12,635	24,645	47,722	146,263	2,082,650	..	Domestic Absorption
878	1,219	1,607	2,221	3,371	5,932	11,615	21,122	74,563	887,750	..	Private Consumption, etc.
281	375	489	639	952	1,713	3,399	16,300	12,970	138,711	..	General Gov't Consumption
718	975	1,157	1,591	2,595	4,990	9,630	10,300	58,730	1,056,190	..	Gross Domestic Investment
546	685	855	1,029	1,458	2,567	7,701	..	..	..	..	Fixed Investment
152	218	261	399	599	876	1,709	3,664	10,399	138,711	..	Indirect Taxes, net
1,648	2,289	2,991	4,061	6,375	11,987	23,374	45,481	145,409	2,063,980	..	GDP at factor cost
197	302	414	598	866	1,385	2,728	6,278	15,563	207,938	..	Agriculture
723	1,037	1,297	1,734	2,790	5,531	9,837	22,488	64,645	863,741	..	Industry
..	..	..	..	..	..	..	..	..	..	..	Manufacturing
728	950	1,280	1,729	2,718	5,070	10,809	16,715	65,202	992,306	..	Services, etc.
642	914	1,155	1,601	2,651	5,218	10,069	11,723	68,275	1,176,230	..	Gross Domestic Saving
622	870	1,076	1,483	2,443	4,836	9,508	10,485	63,743	1,134,000	..	Gross National Saving
				(Billions of 1987 Yugoslav Dinars)							
47,360.7	47,623.1	47,595.0	46,939.9	47,635.1	47,320.7	49,273.4	47,907.0	47,250.1	47,991.9	..	Gross National Product
47,547.8	48,128.1	48,432.6	47,880.2	48,707.7	48,396.8	50,128.8	49,145.0	48,366.2	48,734.9	..	GDP at Market Prices
-2,925.2	-1,389.2	-175.5	95.8	1,016.0	1,681.2	629.6	1,423.0	2,294.8	1,580.4	..	Resource Balance
13,359.3	12,732.7	12,001.9	11,264.9	12,076.7	12,682.2	12,301.7	12,068.0	11,979.0	12,546.1	..	Exports of Goods & NFServices
16,284.5	14,121.9	12,177.4	11,169.1	11,060.7	11,001.0	11,672.2	10,645.0	9,684.2	10,965.7	..	Imports of Goods & NFServices
50,473.0	49,517.3	48,608.1	47,784.4	47,691.8	46,715.7	49,499.3	47,722.0	46,071.4	47,154.5	..	Domestic Absorption
24,360.1	24,012.2	23,388.4	22,962.6	22,462.6	21,426.7	23,718.3	21,122.0	20,164.6	21,025.3	..	Private Consumption, etc.
15,816.7	15,082.7	15,117.2	14,783.1	14,923.0	15,161.1	15,825.3	16,300.0	16,050.0	16,176.0	..	General Gov't Consumption
10,296.3	10,422.4	10,102.4	10,038.7	10,306.2	10,127.9	9,955.7	10,300.0	9,856.8	9,953.2	..	Gross Domestic Investment
..	..	..	..	..	..	..	..	..	..	..	Fixed Investment
41,018.1	41,400.8	41,985.7	41,077.6	42,048.5	43,092.9	44,633.9	45,481.0	44,755.3	45,106.3	..	GDP at factor cost
5,519.2	5,672.4	6,092.8	6,045.0	6,179.0	5,763.5	6,167.0	6,278.0	6,054.5	6,238.3	..	Agriculture
20,297.3	20,744.9	20,386.0	20,071.9	20,751.5	21,157.6	22,003.9	22,488.0	22,332.4	22,531.6	..	Industry
..	..	..	..	..	..	..	..	..	..	..	Manufacturing
15,134.0	15,008.4	15,451.1	14,960.7	15,118.0	16,171.8	16,463.0	16,715.0	16,368.4	16,336.4	..	Services, etc.
											Memo Items:
13,268.0	12,563.5	12,141.3	11,262.0	11,366.5	11,697.8	12,595.1	12,068.0	11,667.3	13,027.5	..	Capacity to Import
-91.3	-169.2	139.4	-2.9	-710.2	-984.4	293.4	0.0	-311.7	481.4	..	Terms of Trade Adjustment
47,456.5	47,958.9	48,572.0	47,877.3	47,997.6	47,412.4	50,422.2	49,145.0	48,054.5	49,216.3	..	Gross Domestic Income
47,269.4	47,453.9	47,734.4	46,936.9	46,924.9	46,336.3	49,566.8	47,907.0	46,938.3	48,473.4	..	Gross National Income
				(Index 1987 = 100)							**DOMESTIC PRICES/DEFLATORS**
3.8	5.2	6.7	9.3	14.3	26.6	50.0	100.0	322.1	4519.8	..	Overall (GDP)
3.7	5.2	6.7	9.3	14.5	27.1	49.8	100.0	317.5	4416.6	..	Domestic Absorption
3.6	5.3	6.8	9.9	14.0	24.0	44.2	100.0	257.0	3333.3	..	Agriculture
3.6	5.0	6.4	8.6	13.5	26.1	44.7	100.0	289.5	3833.5	..	Industry
..	..	..	..	..	..	..	..	..	..	..	Manufacturing
3.5	4.9	6.4	9.0	13.9	23.9	45.3	100.0	294.1	3940.5	..	Consumer Price Index
											MANUFACTURING ACTIVITY
80.5	83.7	86.5	88.7	91.2	94.3	98.4	100.0	100.5	..	G	Employment (1987=100)
107.1	113.2	106.5	98.0	92.9	97.5	103.9	100.0	94.7	..	G	Real Earnings per Empl. (1987=100)
112.2	112.6	111.1	117.4	122.7	112.4	109.7	100.0	108.8	..	G	Real Output per Empl. (1987=100)
34.3	36.3	35.2	32.5	29.6	29.1	32.8	29.9	25.6	..	..	Earnings as % of Value Added
				(Billions of current Yugoslav Dinars)							**MONETARY HOLDINGS**
1,232	1,620	2,151	2,988	4,360	7,019	12,787	29,600	101,220	2,476,830	..	Money Supply, Broadly Defined
452	568	727	874	1,252	1,820	3,830	7,644	24,069	510,302	..	Money
116	149	196	249	327	551	1,161	2,153	5,852	123,752	..	Currency Outside Banks
336	420	531	625	925	1,269	2,669	5,490	18,218	386,550	..	Demand Deposits
781	1,052	1,424	2,114	3,108	5,199	8,957	21,956	77,151	1,966,530	..	Quasi-Money
				(Billions of current Yugoslav Dinars)							**GOVERNMENT DEFICIT (-) OR SURPLUS**
-20.0	..	..	..	..	..	-10.0	10.0	20.0	100.0	E F	
140.0	200.0	240.0	330.0	490.0	830.0	1,620.0	3,590.0	11,770.0	..	..	Current Revenue
160.0	200.0	240.0	330.0	490.0	840.0	1,600.0	3,560.0	11,650.0	..	..	Current Expenditure
-20.0	0.0	0.0	0.0	0.0	-10.0	20.0	30.0	120.0	..	..	Current Budget Balance
..	..	..	..	..	..	..	..	..	..	..	Capital Receipts
0.0	0.0	0.0	0.0	0.0	0.0	10.0	10.0	20.0	..	..	Capital Payments

625

YUGOSLAVIA	1969	1970	1971	1972	1973	1974	1975	1976	1977	1978	1979
FOREIGN TRADE (CUSTOMS BASIS)					*(Millions of current US dollars)*						
Value of Exports, fob	1,474	1,679	1,836	2,237	3,020	3,805	4,072	4,896	4,896	5,546	6,799
Nonfuel Primary Products	589	656	665	801	1,062	1,226	1,131	1,452	1,337	1,433	1,754
Fuels	14	20	20	18	23	41	30	48	144	146	204
Manufactures	871	1,003	1,151	1,419	1,935	2,538	2,911	3,395	3,415	3,967	4,841
Value of Imports, cif	2,134	2,874	3,297	3,233	4,783	7,520	7,699	7,367	8,973	9,769	14,037
Nonfuel Primary Products	522	731	856	866	1,292	2,035	1,452	1,554	1,831	1,788	2,476
Fuels	103	138	195	176	380	951	945	1,081	1,207	1,401	2,251
Manufactures	1,508	2,005	2,246	2,190	3,111	4,534	5,302	4,732	5,935	6,580	9,310
					(Index 1987 = 100)						
Terms of Trade	116.5	120.0	113.0	107.9	111.1	99.4	100.9	97.1	92.6	93.4	93.6
Export Prices, fob	29.8	32.2	32.2	34.2	42.7	54.0	55.7	56.7	58.7	65.5	77.9
Import Prices, cif	25.6	26.9	28.5	31.7	38.4	54.3	55.2	58.4	63.4	70.1	83.3
BALANCE OF PAYMENTS					*(Millions of current US dollars)*						
Exports of Goods & Services	..	2,425	2,689	3,343	4,342	5,690	6,170	6,927	7,546	8,581	10,226
Merchandise, fob	..	1,679	1,821	2,238	2,853	3,805	4,073	4,890	5,191	5,823	6,795
Nonfactor Services	..	728	851	1,088	1,440	1,785	2,034	1,949	2,218	2,586	3,242
Factor Services	..	18	17	17	49	100	63	88	137	172	189
Imports of Goods & Services	..	3,345	3,875	3,961	5,365	8,406	8,611	8,929	11,683	13,117	17,596
Merchandise, fob	..	2,637	2,993	2,965	4,137	6,922	7,058	6,753	8,973	9,591	12,853
Nonfactor Services	..	566	722	820	994	1,185	1,209	1,808	2,300	3,031	3,922
Factor Services	..	142	159	176	234	299	344	368	410	495	821
Long-Term Interest	..	104	110	138	209	246	289	301	367	578	817
Private Current Transfers, net	..	542	780	1,039	1,510	1,755	1,804	2,189	2,809	3,268	3,716
Workers' Remittances	..	441	654	889	1,310	1,500	1,575	1,885	2,508	2,957	3,395
Curr. A/C Bal before Off. Transf.	..	-378	-405	421	488	-962	-636	187	-1,328	-1,268	-3,654
Net Official Transfers	..	6	10	10	14	11	11	-1	-1	-5	-5
Curr. A/C Bal after Off. Transf.	..	-372	-395	431	502	-951	-625	186	-1,329	-1,273	-3,659
Long-Term Capital, net	..	196	539	489	607	497	951	1,099	1,404	1,609	1,299
Direct Investment	..	..	..	..	..	..	..	..	..	..	..
Long-Term Loans	..	270	484	765	831	586	949	1,311	1,696	1,753	1,656
Disbursements	..	645	1,019	1,509	1,676	1,557	2,102	2,450	2,923	3,059	3,892
Repayments	..	375	536	744	845	971	1,153	1,139	1,227	1,306	2,236
Other Long-Term Capital	..	-74	55	-277	-225	-89	1	-212	-292	-144	-357
Other Capital, net	..	93	-164	-444	-434	122	-617	-264	216	204	1,064
Change in Reserves	..	83	21	-476	-674	333	292	-1,021	-291	-540	1,296
Memo Item:					*(Yugoslav Dinars per US dollar)*						
Conversion Factor (Annual Avg)	12.500	12.500	14.900	17.000	16.200	15.900	17.300	18.200	18.300	18.600	19.000
				(Millions of US dollars), outstanding at end of year							
EXTERNAL DEBT (Total)	..	2,053	2,777	3,529	4,308	5,094	5,999	7,542	10,119	12,528	15,970
Long-Term Debt (by debtor)	..	2,053	2,777	3,529	4,308	5,094	5,999	7,542	9,216	11,357	14,181
Central Bank, incl. IMF credit	..	134	255	438	636	956	907	1,307	1,275	1,359	1,471
Central Government	..	583	683	767	682	634	652	675	712	768	838
Rest of General Government	..	0	0	0	0	0	0	1	1	1	5
Non-financial Public Enterprises	..	..	..	..	..	..	..	..	..	..	..
Priv. Sector, incl non-guaranteed	..	1,335	1,840	2,324	2,990	3,504	4,440	5,559	7,228	9,229	11,868
Short-Term Debt	..	0	0	0	0	0	0	0	903	1,171	1,789
Memo Items:					*(Millions of US dollars)*						
Int'l Reserves Excluding Gold	202.1	88.6	157.2	675.2	1,275.8	1,084.8	811.5	1,989.9	2,044.4	2,388.2	1,256.6
Gold Holdings (at market price)	51.3	54.4	63.6	96.4	163.5	274.1	205.5	197.5	249.2	368.8	881.4
SOCIAL INDICATORS											
Total Fertility Rate	2.5	2.3	2.4	2.4	2.3	2.3	2.3	2.2	2.2	2.2	2.2
Infant Mortality Rate	57.3	55.5	49.5	44.4	40.0	40.9	39.7	36.7	35.5	33.8	32.7
Life Expectancy at Birth	67.3	67.7	68.0	68.4	68.5	68.5	68.6	68.7	68.7	68.8	68.8
Urban Population, % of total	34.1	34.8	35.5	36.3	37.0	37.8	38.5	39.3	40.0	40.8	41.5
Food Prod. per capita (1987=100)	94.2	81.2	88.6	84.0	89.4	96.8	95.2	99.0	101.7	94.7	99.7
Labor Force, Agriculture (%)	51.2	49.8	48.0	46.2	44.5	42.7	41.0	39.2	37.5	35.7	34.0
Labor Force, Female (%)	36.3	36.5	36.6	36.7	36.9	37.0	37.1	37.3	37.5	37.6	37.8
Primary Schl. Enroll. Ratio	..	106.0	..	..	..	..	103.0	101.0	99.0	99.0	99.0
Primary Schl. Enroll. Ratio, Female	..	103.0	..	..	..	..	101.0	99.0	98.0	98.0	98.0
Secondary Schl. Enroll. Ratio	..	63.0	..	..	..	..	76.0	78.0	79.0	82.0	82.0

1980	1981	1982	1983	1984	1985	1986	1987	1988	1989 estimate	NOTES	YUGOSLAVIA
				(Millions of current US dollars)							**FOREIGN TRADE (CUSTOMS BASIS)**
8,977	10,929	10,752	9,913	10,254	10,641	10,297	11,397	12,580	14,461	..	Value of Exports, fob
2,176	2,136	2,161	2,128	2,023	1,923	1,774	2,235	2,534	..	..	Nonfuel Primary Products
231	219	199	245	357	297	203	220	184	..	..	Fuels
6,570	8,574	8,392	7,541	7,874	8,421	8,320	8,942	9,862	11,973	..	Manufactures
15,064	15,757	14,100	12,154	11,996	12,163	11,749	12,549	13,152	..	..	Value of Imports, cif
2,973	2,902	2,545	2,238	2,210	2,241	2,264	2,107	2,514	..	..	Nonfuel Primary Products
3,549	3,786	3,630	3,304	3,515	3,307	2,605	2,186	2,326	..	..	Fuels
8,542	9,069	7,925	6,612	6,271	6,615	6,879	8,256	8,312	..	..	Manufactures
				(Index 1987 = 100)							
88.3	90.2	97.2	98.3	95.5	94.8	100.7	100.0	107.1		..	Terms of Trade
88.5	90.3	94.2	94.4	91.4	87.8	90.6	100.0	110.0	..	..	Export Prices, fob
100.2	100.0	96.9	96.0	95.7	92.6	90.0	100.0	102.7	..	..	Import Prices, cif
				(Millions of current US dollars)							**BALANCE OF PAYMENTS**
13,833	15,737	15,358	13,224	13,447	14,080	15,385	15,890	17,681	19,404	f	Exports of Goods & Services
9,093	10,354	10,455	9,917	10,136	10,622	11,084	11,425	12,779	13,560	..	Merchandise, fob
4,541	5,012	4,621	3,128	3,098	3,236	4,116	4,312	4,712	5,441	..	Nonfactor Services
199	371	282	179	213	222	185	153	190	403	..	Factor Services
20,500	20,916	20,242	16,600	16,310	16,526	18,216	18,921	20,063	23,619	f	Imports of Goods & Services
13,992	13,517	12,477	11,148	10,925	11,210	11,786	11,343	12,000	13,502	..	Merchandise, fob
5,211	5,382	5,674	3,742	3,550	3,430	4,496	5,715	6,076	8,245	..	Nonfactor Services
1,297	2,017	2,091	1,710	1,835	1,886	1,934	1,863	1,987	1,872	..	Factor Services
1,077	1,463	1,606	1,514	2,339	1,534	1,778	1,725	1,609	1,374	..	Long-Term Interest
4,354	4,220	4,411	3,653	3,343	3,281	3,933	4,281	4,871	6,645	..	Private Current Transfers, net
4,102	3,960	4,185	3,429	3,168	3,106	3,731	4,051	4,593	6,290	..	Workers' Remittances
-2,313	-959	-473	277	480	835	1,102	1,250	2,489	2,430	..	Curr. A/C Bal before Off. Transf.
-4	..	..	-2	-2	-2	-2	-2	-2	-3	..	Net Official Transfers
-2,317	-959	-473	275	478	833	1,100	1,248	2,487	2,427	..	Curr. A/C Bal after Off. Transf.
1,954	578	-93	941	-265	78	-1,406	-892	-932	-314	f	Long-Term Capital, net
..	..	..	..	0	0	..	0	0	..	..	Direct Investment
2,209	1,227	92	861	-122	-79	-886	-841	-200	-647	..	Long-Term Loans
4,589	3,087	2,188	2,517	1,447	1,090	654	548	1,042	1,008	..	Disbursements
2,380	1,859	2,096	1,655	1,569	1,169	1,540	1,389	1,241	1,655	..	Repayments
-255	-649	-185	80	-143	157	-520	-51	-732	333	..	Other Long-Term Capital
51	-588	-865	-1,493	-110	-752	1,142	-118	398	301	f	Other Capital, net
312	969	1,431	277	-103	-159	-836	-238	-1,953	-2,414	..	Change in Reserves
				(Yugoslav Dinars per US dollar)							**Memo Item:**
24.600	35.000	50.300	92.800	152.800	270.200	379.200	737.000	2,522.600	28,764.000	..	Conversion Factor (Annual Avg)
				(Millions of US dollars), outstanding at end of year							
18,486	20,645	19,900	20,477	19,644	22,278	21,510	22,479	21,002	19,651	..	**EXTERNAL DEBT (Total)**
16,346	18,154	18,090	19,335	18,618	21,288	20,145	21,179	19,969	18,470	..	Long-Term Debt (by debtor)
2,451	3,525	4,237	6,345	7,361	9,456	9,630	10,703	10,415	10,233	..	Central Bank, incl. IMF credit
851	862	800	727	629	686	711	787	719	685	..	Central Government
25	26	30	38	39	51	56	66	68	64	..	Rest of General Government
..	..	..	..	..	..	..	..	..	..	..	Non-financial Public Enterprises
13,019	13,740	13,023	12,225	10,589	11,095	9,748	9,623	8,767	7,488	..	Priv. Sector, incl non-guaranteed
2,140	2,492	1,810	1,142	1,026	990	1,365	1,300	1,033	1,181	..	Short-Term Debt
				(Millions of US dollars)							**Memo Items:**
1,384.1	1,597.1	775.3	976.4	1,158.1	1,094.7	1,459.6	697.7	2,297.9	4,135.7	..	Int'l Reserves Excluding Gold
1,093.7	737.8	849.2	710.1	573.9	609.6	729.3	903.8	776.5	763.3	..	Gold Holdings (at market price)
											SOCIAL INDICATORS
2.1	2.1	2.1	2.1	2.1	2.1	2.0	2.0	2.0	2.0	..	Total Fertility Rate
31.4	30.6	29.9	31.7	28.9	28.8	27.3	25.4	24.8	24.0	..	Infant Mortality Rate
68.9	68.9	69.0	69.4	69.9	70.4	70.9	71.3	71.6	71.9	..	Life Expectancy at Birth
42.3	43.1	43.9	44.7	45.5	46.3	47.1	47.9	48.6	49.4	..	Urban Population, % of total
98.9	99.2	107.4	101.5	104.7	95.7	106.3	100.0	95.7	96.7	..	Food Prod. per capita (1987=100)
32.3	..	..	..	..	..	..	..	..	..	..	Labor Force, Agriculture (%)
37.9	38.0	38.1	38.2	38.3	38.4	38.5	38.6	38.7	38.8	..	Labor Force, Female (%)
100.0	..	101.0	100.0	98.0	97.0	96.0	95.0	..	..	..	Primary Schl. Enroll. Ratio
99.0	100.0	101.0	100.0	98.0	97.0	95.0	94.0	..	..	..	Primary Schl. Enroll. Ratio, Female
83.0	..	83.0	82.0	81.0	80.0	80.0	80.0	..	..	..	Secondary Schl. Enroll. Ratio

ZAIRE	1969	1970	1971	1972	1973	1974	1975	1976	1977	1978	1979
CURRENT GNP PER CAPITA (US $)	240	260	270	280	340	390	430	430	470	510	600
POPULATION (thousands)	19,243	19,769	20,320	20,891	21,482	22,093	22,726	23,392	24,068	24,760	25,476

USE AND ORIGIN OF RESOURCES
(Billions of current Zaires)

	1969	1970	1971	1972	1973	1974	1975	1976	1977	1978	1979
Gross National Product (GNP)	2.5	2.4	2.8	3.1	4.0	4.8	5.0	7.6	10.7	13.0	26.3
Net Factor Income from Abroad	0.0	-0.1	-0.1	-0.1	-0.1	-0.2	-0.2	-0.2	-0.2	-0.2	-0.4
GDP at Market Prices	2.6	2.5	2.9	3.2	4.0	4.9	5.3	7.8	10.8	13.2	26.7
Resource Balance	0.2	0.2	0.1	0.1	0.2	0.3	0.0	0.1	-0.3	0.3	0.7
Exports of Goods & NFServices	0.4	0.5	0.4	0.4	0.6	0.9	0.6	1.0	1.2	1.9	4.5
Imports of Goods & NFServices	0.2	0.3	0.3	0.3	0.4	0.6	0.6	1.0	1.5	1.6	3.7
Domestic Absorption	2.4	2.3	2.8	3.1	3.8	4.6	5.3	7.8	11.1	12.9	26.0
Private Consumption, etc.	1.9	1.7	2.0	2.3	3.0	3.5	4.0	6.2	8.5	10.6	21.1
General Gov't Consumption	0.3	0.4	0.4	0.4	0.5	0.6	0.7	0.8	1.1	1.3	2.7
Gross Domestic Investment	0.2	0.2	0.3	0.4	0.4	0.5	0.6	0.7	1.5	1.0	2.2
Fixed Investment	0.2	0.2	0.3	0.4	0.4	0.6	0.5	0.7	1.4	1.0	1.5
Indirect Taxes, net	..	0.1	0.1	0.1	0.1	0.2	0.2	0.2	0.2	0.2	0.4
GDP at factor cost	..	2.4	2.8	3.0	3.9	4.8	5.1	7.7	10.7	13.0	26.3
Agriculture	0.5	0.4	0.4	0.5	0.6	0.8	0.9	1.9	2.7	3.8	7.9
Industry	1.0	1.0	1.1	1.1	1.6	2.0	1.8	2.3	2.7	3.2	7.0
Manufacturing	..	..	..	..	..	..	..	..	..	..	..
Services, etc.	1.1	1.1	1.3	1.6	1.8	2.2	2.5	3.7	5.4	6.1	11.8
Gross Domestic Saving	0.4	0.4	0.4	0.5	0.6	0.8	0.6	0.8	1.2	1.3	2.9
Gross National Saving	..	0.3	0.3	0.3	0.5	0.6	0.3	0.6	1.0	1.1	2.5

(Millions of 1987 Zaires)

	1969	1970	1971	1972	1973	1974	1975	1976	1977	1978	1979
Gross National Product	749,773	766,148	757,742	766,143	825,705	842,836	798,483	766,447	776,790	735,567	732,952
GDP at Market Prices	708,493	731,655	778,652	779,062	846,180	875,494	832,880	787,031	790,099	746,755	745,135
Resource Balance	16,273	12,902	5,039	-3,976	-16,897	-11,803	-8,069	9,562	-44,436	34,296	4,021
Exports of Goods & NFServices	116,765	132,289	147,432	157,313	172,167	158,842	148,928	139,588	139,175	174,088	145,818
Imports of Goods & NFServices	100,491	119,387	142,393	161,289	189,064	170,646	156,997	130,026	183,610	139,792	141,797
Domestic Absorption	716,785	718,361	770,136	780,322	856,416	877,605	830,740	769,433	829,356	708,670	742,140
Private Consumption, etc.	586,991	569,824	614,001	646,565	702,858	707,096	677,672	641,326	650,137	594,197	599,448
General Gov't Consumption	86,698	104,077	97,380	75,577	90,325	102,243	90,285	79,204	85,422	70,412	68,220
Gross Domestic Investment	43,096	44,460	58,755	58,179	63,232	68,266	62,783	48,902	93,797	44,061	74,472
Fixed Investment	43,096	44,460	48,157	56,344	50,567	70,233	54,524	41,876	85,544	40,859	56,224
GDP at factor cost	..	796,366	744,623	741,512	815,160	847,187	808,215	771,204	777,943	736,337	733,023
Agriculture	215,227	186,257	191,300	194,232	201,623	205,609	202,560	213,352	206,315	206,666	213,000
Industry	182,617	217,002	232,508	232,995	254,321	271,245	259,174	235,866	230,788	212,657	197,914
Manufacturing	..	..	..	..	90,670	98,146	89,410	82,319	80,576	70,377	66,303
Services, etc.	335,214	328,004	351,367	349,118	383,575	388,948	360,936	329,777	347,818	323,642	335,246

Memo Items:

	1969	1970	1971	1972	1973	1974	1975	1976	1977	1978	1979
Capacity to Import	190,613	207,365	190,922	195,740	275,834	249,443	154,469	139,095	149,635	164,932	170,191
Terms of Trade Adjustment	73,848	75,077	43,491	38,427	103,666	90,601	5,541	-493	10,460	-9,155	24,373
Gross Domestic Income	782,340	806,732	822,142	817,489	949,846	966,095	838,422	786,537	800,560	737,600	769,508
Gross National Income	823,620	841,225	801,233	804,570	929,372	933,437	804,024	765,954	787,251	726,411	757,325

DOMESTIC PRICES/DEFLATORS
(Index 1987 = 100)

	1969	1970	1971	1972	1973	1974	1975	1976	1977	1978	1979
Overall (GDP)	0.4	0.3	0.4	0.4	0.5	0.6	0.6	1.0	1.4	1.8	3.6
Domestic Absorption	0.3	0.3	0.4	0.4	0.4	0.5	0.6	1.0	1.3	1.8	3.5
Agriculture	0.2	0.2	0.2	0.2	0.3	0.4	0.5	0.9	1.3	1.8	3.7
Industry	0.6	0.5	0.5	0.5	0.6	0.7	0.7	1.0	1.2	1.5	3.5
Manufacturing	..	..	..	..	..	..	..	..	..	..	..
Consumer Price Index	0.2	0.2	0.2	0.2	0.3	0.3	0.4	0.8	1.3	2.0	4.0

MANUFACTURING ACTIVITY

	1969	1970	1971	1972	1973	1974	1975	1976	1977	1978	1979
Employment (1987=100)	..	..	..	..	..	..	..	..	..	..	..
Real Earnings per Empl. (1987=100)	..	..	..	..	..	..	..	..	..	..	..
Real Output per Empl. (1987=100)	..	..	..	..	..	..	..	..	..	..	..
Earnings as % of Value Added	40.0	..	..	35.9	..	..	..	..	..	..	..

MONETARY HOLDINGS
(Billions of current Zaires)

	1969	1970	1971	1972	1973	1974	1975	1976	1977	1978	1979
Money Supply, Broadly Defined	0.17	0.21	0.22	0.27	0.38	0.50	0.55	0.76	1.21	1.86	1.96
Money	0.15	0.19	0.19	0.23	0.29	0.39	0.46	0.66	1.03	1.61	1.57
Currency Outside Banks	0.06	0.07	0.08	0.10	0.12	0.16	0.21	0.29	0.47	0.80	0.41
Demand Deposits	0.09	0.11	0.10	0.14	0.17	0.23	0.25	0.37	0.56	0.81	1.16
Quasi-Money	0.02	0.02	0.04	0.04	0.09	0.11	0.09	0.10	0.18	0.25	0.39

(Millions of current Zaires)

	1969	1970	1971	1972	1973	1974	1975	1976	1977	1978	1979
GOVERNMENT DEFICIT (-) OR SURPLUS	..	..	-77	-82	-141	-324	-216	-627	-450	-595	-549
Current Revenue	..	..	329	344	440	588	491	573	830	910	2,456
Current Expenditure	..	..	312	320	387	519	552	954	1,003	1,238	2,517
Current Budget Balance	..	..	17	24	53	69	-61	-381	-173	-328	-61
Capital Receipts	..	..	..	..	..	..	..	..	..	..	..
Capital Payments	..	..	94	107	193	393	155	246	276	267	488

1980	1981	1982	1983	1984	1985	1986	1987	1988	1989 estimate	NOTES	ZAIRE
630	590	540	460	340	270	240	240	260	260	..	**CURRENT GNP PER CAPITA (US $)**
26,225	27,001	27,798	28,625	29,489	30,398	31,346	32,334	33,366	34,442	..	**POPULATION (thousands)**
			(Billions of current Zaires)								**USE AND ORIGIN OF RESOURCES**
40.6	58.9	80.3	141.1	245.3	338.4	469.9	826.3	1,722.9	3,491.1	f	Gross National Product (GNP)
-0.7	-0.9	-2.1	-4.0	-14.5	-18.2	-25.3	-51.0	-92.7	-173.3	..	Net Factor Income from Abroad
41.3	59.8	82.4	145.2	259.8	356.6	495.1	877.4	1,815.6	3,664.4	..	GDP at Market Prices
4.0	5.2	4.4	7.6	28.3	27.0	19.5	-26.3	-53.4	104.5	..	Resource Balance
7.8	10.2	12.2	24.2	75.6	101.7	126.0	212.4	436.8	995.3	..	Exports of Goods & NFServices
3.8	5.1	7.8	16.6	47.3	74.7	106.6	238.7	490.3	890.8	..	Imports of Goods & NFServices
37.3	54.6	78.0	137.5	231.5	329.6	475.7	903.6	1,869.1	3,559.9	..	Domestic Absorption
31.0	44.4	64.8	114.7	188.3	271.2	376.8	688.1	1,390.3	2,742.2	..	Private Consumption, etc.
3.7	6.0	8.4	11.4	22.6	25.1	37.1	101.2	248.1	348.2	..	General Gov't Consumption
2.6	4.3	4.9	11.5	20.6	33.3	61.8	114.4	230.7	469.5	..	Gross Domestic Investment
2.6	4.3	4.9	11.5	20.6	33.3	61.8	114.4	230.7	469.5	..	Fixed Investment
1.0	1.5	1.4	1.9	2.0	7.4	16.1	22.2	39.5	91.3	..	Indirect Taxes, net
40.3	58.3	81.0	143.3	257.8	349.2	479.1	855.2	1,776.1	3,573.1	Bf	GDP at factor cost
11.4	15.1	25.1	47.2	77.4	107.9	165.3	262.2	516.0	1,085.6	..	Agriculture
13.7	21.2	24.8	43.2	81.7	113.0	135.6	236.8	511.6	1,176.7	f	Industry
7.1	12.2	16.2	25.5	31.2	40.9	50.9	82.5	183.8	379.0	..	Manufacturing
16.2	23.5	32.6	54.7	100.7	135.7	194.3	378.4	788.1	1,402.1	..	Services, etc.
6.7	9.4	9.3	19.1	48.9	60.3	81.3	88.1	177.2	574.0	..	Gross Domestic Saving
5.7	8.5	7.2	15.1	31.2	39.4	52.3	29.3	71.9	376.2	..	Gross National Saving
			(Millions of 1987 Zaires)								
747,296	775,719	764,425	774,296	767,162	789,761	826,416	826,339	857,168	842,614	f	Gross National Product
763,342	790,337	786,930	798,724	818,153	836,337	872,327	877,357	905,595	887,567	H	GDP at Market Prices
-1,851	-3,164	-46,000	-32,900	3,089	-8,675	7,459	-26,280	-70,463	-35,693	..	Resource Balance
177,246	169,572	174,605	192,803	225,538	211,368	242,227	212,448	206,160	199,498	..	Exports of Goods & NFServices
179,097	172,736	220,605	225,703	222,449	220,043	234,768	238,728	276,623	235,191	..	Imports of Goods & NFServices
764,390	790,543	832,042	831,624	815,064	845,012	864,868	903,637	976,058	923,260	..	Domestic Absorption
592,060	615,159	633,884	646,362	624,994	660,347	660,095	688,056	722,573	694,311	..	Private Consumption, etc.
74,266	81,894	84,998	84,259	88,335	78,514	83,642	101,171	122,048	102,196	..	General Gov't Consumption
98,064	93,490	113,160	101,003	101,735	106,151	121,131	114,410	131,437	126,753	..	Gross Domestic Investment
96,959	83,673	97,311	95,826	96,074	107,488	120,021	114,410	128,026	124,580	..	Fixed Investment
744,685	770,145	773,692	788,370	811,855	819,040	844,044	855,166	885,887	865,458	B H f	GDP at factor cost
218,981	223,430	230,901	235,680	241,853	248,585	254,379	262,185	267,315	274,749	..	Agriculture
207,521	221,244	212,980	213,485	225,275	222,294	238,265	236,798	241,026	227,338	f	Industry
68,634	75,131	75,282	75,525	77,082	75,520	80,246	82,550	90,124	79,926	..	Manufacturing
336,037	342,705	342,161	349,559	351,025	365,458	379,683	378,374	397,254	385,480	..	Services, etc.
											Memo Items:
371,817	347,884	346,114	329,112	355,732	299,494	277,618	212,448	246,475	262,787	..	Capacity to Import
194,571	178,312	171,509	136,309	130,194	88,126	35,390	0	40,315	63,289	..	Terms of Trade Adjustment
957,913	968,649	958,439	935,033	948,347	924,463	907,718	877,357	945,910	950,856	..	Gross Domestic Income
941,866	954,031	935,934	910,605	897,356	877,887	861,806	826,339	897,484	905,902	..	Gross National Income
			(Index 1987 = 100)								**DOMESTIC PRICES/DEFLATORS**
5.4	7.6	10.5	18.2	31.8	42.6	56.8	100.0	200.5	412.9	..	Overall (GDP)
4.9	6.9	9.4	16.5	28.4	39.0	55.0	100.0	191.5	385.6	..	Domestic Absorption
5.2	6.8	10.9	20.0	32.0	43.4	65.0	100.0	193.0	395.1	..	Agriculture
6.6	9.6	11.6	20.2	36.3	50.8	56.9	100.0	212.2	517.6	..	Industry
10.4	16.2	21.6	33.7	40.5	54.1	63.4	100.0	203.9	474.2	..	Manufacturing
5.8	7.9	10.8	19.0	28.9	35.8	52.5	100.0	182.7	372.9	..	Consumer Price Index
											MANUFACTURING ACTIVITY
..	..	..	..	..	..	..	..	..	..	..	Employment (1987=100)
..	..	..	..	..	..	..	..	..	..	..	Real Earnings per Empl. (1987=100)
..	..	..	..	..	..	..	..	..	..	..	Real Output per Empl. (1987=100)
..	..	..	..	..	..	..	..	..	..	..	Earnings as % of Value Added
			(Billions of current Zaires)								**MONETARY HOLDINGS**
3.18	4.84	8.22	13.55	18.78	24.34	38.67	75.74	175.09	293.11	..	Money Supply, Broadly Defined
2.71	4.20	7.42	12.61	17.43	22.49	35.90	68.49	150.11	263.26	..	Money
1.25	2.09	3.28	6.14	8.80	12.29	18.99	36.25	82.80	153.06	..	Currency Outside Banks
1.46	2.11	4.14	6.47	8.63	10.19	16.91	32.23	67.31	110.20	..	Demand Deposits
0.47	0.64	0.80	0.94	1.35	1.85	2.77	7.25	24.98	29.85	..	Quasi-Money
			(Millions of current Zaires)								**GOVERNMENT DEFICIT (-) OR SURPLUS**
-332	-2,158	-3,484	..	..	..	..	..	-116,759	..	..	Current Revenue
4,650	5,905	7,183	..	..	..	..	..	200,619	..	..	Current Revenue
4,005	5,783	8,243	..	..	..	..	..	254,053	..	..	Current Expenditure
645	122	-1,060	..	..	..	..	..	-53,434	..	..	Current Budget Balance
..	..	..	..	..	..	..	..	..	..	f	Capital Receipts
977	2,280	2,424	..	..	..	..	..	63,325	..	..	Capital Payments

ZAIRE	1969	1970	1971	1972	1973	1974	1975	1976	1977	1978	1979
FOREIGN TRADE (CUSTOMS BASIS)					*(Millions of current US dollars)*						
Value of Exports, fob	679.1	735.4	687.0	737.7	1,001.3	1,381.5	864.8	809.3	1,109.9	899.4	2,004.1
Nonfuel Primary Products	617.7	684.0	626.9	660.2	927.6	1,310.5	793.5	704.1	1,013.7	824.3	1,826.2
Fuels	3.2	1.3	10.9	22.0	1.8	2.2	5.8	72.3	40.5	12.6	52.2
Manufactures	58.2	50.0	49.2	55.5	72.0	68.8	65.6	32.9	55.8	62.5	125.8
Value of Imports, cif	451.8	533.0	619.0	766.4	781.9	940.0	932.8	840.3	852.3	796.7	826.4
Nonfuel Primary Products	70.8	95.2	109.8	135.0	160.3	220.9	176.0	198.5	181.3	195.1	196.4
Fuels	58.8	37.8	40.9	47.1	44.6	78.9	91.2	104.6	77.2	60.2	68.9
Manufactures	322.2	400.0	468.3	584.4	577.0	640.2	665.6	537.2	593.8	541.4	561.1
					(Index 1987 = 100)						
Terms of Trade	274.7	239.0	168.8	150.4	213.0	192.4	123.3	142.3	140.9	125.5	140.8
Export Prices, fob	57.4	59.8	47.1	46.4	81.9	102.8	69.4	83.4	87.2	88.6	115.7
Import Prices, cif	20.9	25.0	27.9	30.8	38.5	53.5	56.3	58.6	61.9	70.6	82.1
BALANCE OF PAYMENTS					*(Millions of current US dollars)*						
Exports of Goods & Services	..	812.0	708.9	699.1	1,065.9	1,570.9	1,024.9	1,177.5	1,282.9	1,923.8	1,915.3
Merchandise, fob	..	799.5	696.9	690.3	1,038.4	1,520.7	863.4	1,024.2	1,056.4	1,834.2	1,834.6
Nonfactor Services	..	1.2	4.5	5.0	21.3	35.7	157.7	149.4	218.0	64.7	70.5
Factor Services	..	11.3	7.5	3.8	6.2	14.4	3.8	3.9	8.5	24.9	10.1
Imports of Goods & Services	..	719.2	901.7	1,009.7	1,300.0	1,910.3	1,669.2	2,095.3	2,799.0	1,613.2	1,757.0
Merchandise, fob	..	583.4	684.2	752.1	977.3	1,439.3	993.5	1,293.5	1,602.4	1,024.5	1,106.9
Nonfactor Services	..	106.2	185.8	223.8	274.0	390.6	555.1	602.9	824.9	389.2	405.4
Factor Services	..	29.6	31.7	33.9	48.8	80.3	120.6	198.9	371.7	199.4	244.7
Long-Term Interest	..	8.8	7.8	17.0	33.8	60.6	62.7	51.0	71.4	92.2	96.3
Private Current Transfers, net	..	-174.9	-99.7	-95.8	-115.2	-126.8	-70.1	-14.3	-88.3	0.0	0.0
Workers' Remittances	..	2.1	8.2	8.7	9.7	10.5	26.6	15.5	30.2	..	..
Curr. A/C Bal before Off. Transf.	..	-140.9	-300.0	-410.2	-355.5	-480.6	-714.4	-932.2	-1,604.4	310.6	158.3
Net Official Transfers	..	77.2	198.0	81.2	110.6	108.2	121.7	99.4	153.2	-16.3	-11.9
Curr. A/C Bal after Off. Transf.	..	-63.7	-102.0	-329.0	-244.9	-372.3	-592.7	-832.8	-1,451.2	294.3	146.4
Long-Term Capital, net	..	-42.9	-17.9	212.5	180.0	133.1	80.0	279.6	276.9	114.9	58.8
Direct Investment	..	42.2	52.6	104.4	75.8	125.8	15.9	79.8	59.2	114.9	60.1
Long-Term Loans	..	3.2	171.1	208.8	320.7	406.9	424.2	547.0	501.4	397.6	69.3
Disbursements	..	31.6	200.8	252.7	384.2	533.3	513.0	584.6	546.8	447.9	151.6
Repayments	..	28.4	29.7	43.9	63.5	126.4	88.8	37.6	45.4	50.3	82.3
Other Long-Term Capital	..	-88.3	-241.6	-100.7	-216.5	-399.6	-360.1	-347.2	-283.7	-397.6	-70.6
Other Capital, net	..	77.9	61.2	106.1	109.3	187.0	384.9	391.1	1,217.0	-415.8	-135.4
Change in Reserves	..	28.6	58.7	10.4	-44.4	52.2	127.9	162.0	-42.7	6.5	-69.7
Memo Item:					*(Zaires per US dollar)*						
Conversion Factor (Annual Avg)	0.500	0.500	0.500	0.500	0.500	0.500	0.500	0.790	0.860	0.840	1.730
				(Millions of US dollars), outstanding at end of year							
EXTERNAL DEBT (Total)	..	311.2	363.7	603.7	937.7	1,377.3	1,804.2	2,574.4	3,519.8	4,309.8	4,837.7
Long-Term Debt (by debtor)	..	311.2	363.7	603.7	937.7	1,377.3	1,804.2	2,574.4	3,242.8	3,973.8	4,493.7
Central Bank, incl. IMF credit	..	0.0	1.5	34.5	41.8	45.1	101.2	230.5	297.8	358.8	400.5
Central Government	..	263.8	222.7	297.3	535.2	727.2	913.5	1,328.1	1,544.6	1,995.9	2,453.0
Rest of General Government	..	..	..	..	..	..	..	..	..	..	..
Non-financial Public Enterprises	..	47.4	139.0	271.5	360.4	604.8	789.4	1,015.8	1,400.4	1,619.1	1,640.2
Priv. Sector, incl non-guaranteed	..	0.0	0.5	0.4	0.3	0.2	0.1	0.0	0.0	0.0	0.0
Short-Term Debt	..	..	..	..	..	..	..	..	277.0	336.0	344.0
Memo Items:					*(Millions of US dollars)*						
Int'l Reserves Excluding Gold	144.21	136.00	90.87	123.18	172.79	118.80	47.91	50.28	133.87	125.75	206.69
Gold Holdings (at market price)	55.23	53.25	62.78	94.36	164.33	93.25	36.47	35.04	42.89	69.61	129.02
SOCIAL INDICATORS											
Total Fertility Rate	6.0	6.0	6.1	6.1	6.1	6.1	6.1	6.1	6.1	6.1	6.1
Infant Mortality Rate	133.0	131.0	129.0	127.0	125.0	123.0	121.0	119.0	117.0	115.0	113.0
Life Expectancy at Birth	44.8	45.2	45.6	46.0	46.4	46.8	47.2	47.6	48.0	48.4	48.8
Urban Population, % of total	29.5	30.3	30.7	31.1	31.4	31.8	32.2	32.6	33.0	33.4	33.8
Food Prod. per capita (1987=100)	116.8	118.4	115.7	115.0	115.5	115.6	115.1	112.7	110.4	103.7	105.0
Labor Force, Agriculture (%)	79.6	79.1	78.3	77.5	76.8	76.1	75.4	74.5	73.7	73.0	72.2
Labor Force, Female (%)	42.5	42.2	41.7	41.2	40.8	40.4	40.0	39.5	39.0	38.5	38.1
Primary Schl. Enroll. Ratio	..	88.0	..	..	..	..	88.0	89.0	89.0	89.0	..
Primary Schl. Enroll. Ratio, Female	..	65.0	..	..	..	..	72.0	74.0	74.0	74.0	..
Secondary Schl. Enroll. Ratio	..	9.0	..	..	..	..	16.0	17.0	20.0	23.0	..

1980	1981	1982	1983	1984	1985	1986	1987	1988	1989 estimate	NOTES	ZAIRE
				(Millions of current US dollars)							**FOREIGN TRADE (CUSTOMS BASIS)**
2,506.9	2,029.9	1,530.2	1,387.9	1,558.3	1,526.2	1,521.0	1,593.5	2,032.0	..	f	Value of Exports, fob
2,287.5	1,852.5	1,396.2	1,266.5	1,426.4	1,392.6	1,416.5	1,479.4	1,858.6	..	..	Nonfuel Primary Products
61.8	48.5	37.1	33.6	47.2	45.2	16.3	20.0	29.4	..	..	Fuels
157.6	128.9	96.9	87.8	84.7	88.4	88.2	94.1	144.0	..	..	Manufactures
1,117.1	1,019.1	912.5	841.7	877.4	918.6	1,008.0	1,149.1	1,190.0	..	f	Value of Imports, cif
264.3	242.2	216.6	199.8	197.0	196.1	205.0	209.6	351.7	..	..	Nonfuel Primary Products
92.2	83.6	75.1	69.2	79.5	80.0	29.0	36.7	41.0	..	..	Fuels
760.6	693.4	620.8	572.7	600.9	642.4	774.1	902.8	797.3	..	..	Manufactures
				(Index 1987 = 100)							
131.8	110.9	104.0	109.9	111.5	108.4	107.9	100.0	120.9	..	..	Terms of Trade
121.4	103.0	93.4	96.9	96.0	92.4	99.2	100.0	131.6	..	..	Export Prices, fob
92.2	92.9	89.8	88.2	86.1	85.2	91.9	100.0	108.9	..	..	Import Prices, cif
				(Millions of current US dollars)							**BALANCE OF PAYMENTS**
2,403.8	1,828.9	1,684.7	1,801.9	2,070.3	2,015.4	2,027.6	1,988.0	2,365.0	2,383.3	..	Exports of Goods & Services
2,268.6	1,677.9	1,600.8	1,685.8	1,928.2	1,861.5	1,839.2	1,727.3	2,178.6	2,190.1	..	Merchandise, fob
102.8	94.3	57.4	101.1	115.4	126.5	155.6	215.4	150.1	154.8	..	Nonfactor Services
32.4	56.6	26.5	15.0	26.7	27.4	32.8	45.3	36.3	38.4	..	Factor Services
2,883.3	2,676.7	2,426.6	2,327.2	2,479.3	2,451.0	2,548.3	2,791.5	3,283.4	3,219.2	..	Imports of Goods & Services
1,518.9	1,420.9	1,297.2	1,213.3	1,175.7	1,187.1	1,280.0	1,395.2	1,643.6	1,895.0	..	Merchandise, fob
834.3	727.5	607.2	689.5	876.1	872.2	812.0	897.1	1,107.6	831.4	..	Nonfactor Services
530.1	528.3	522.2	424.4	427.5	391.7	456.3	499.2	532.2	492.8	..	Factor Services
204.4	125.0	68.9	94.1	199.8	216.6	117.5	116.2	98.1	26.5	..	Long-Term Interest
-79.4	-3.5	-8.8	3.2	-91.2	-54.8	-62.0	-69.8	-67.2	-64.0	..	Private Current Transfers, net
..	..	..	..	..	..	0.0	..	..	..	..	Workers' Remittances
-558.9	-851.4	-750.7	-522.1	-500.2	-490.4	-582.7	-873.3	-985.6	-899.9	..	Curr. A/C Bal before Off. Transf.
266.8	247.6	160.1	173.2	174.3	199.0	183.7	210.8	194.9	257.0	..	Net Official Transfers
-292.1	-603.7	-590.6	-348.9	-325.9	-291.4	-399.0	-662.5	-790.7	-642.9	..	Curr. A/C Bal after Off. Transf.
1,567.4	198.0	-33.6	771.2	-296.6	-296.8	-210.6	-64.5	8.1	-64.1	..	Long-Term Capital, net
6.0	6.0	6.0	5.0	6.0	6.0	5.0	10.0	11.0	12.1	..	Direct Investment
264.8	270.5	143.3	111.1	49.7	48.0	147.6	310.6	268.3	214.1	..	Long-Term Loans
456.4	354.1	203.2	194.4	151.3	148.3	252.6	373.0	328.4	282.9	..	Disbursements
191.6	83.6	59.9	83.3	101.6	100.3	105.0	62.4	60.1	68.8	..	Repayments
1,296.6	-78.5	-182.9	655.1	-352.3	-350.8	-363.2	-385.1	-271.2	-290.3	..	Other Long-Term Capital
-1,240.7	170.1	465.2	-500.2	488.6	552.5	588.6	812.6	927.7	768.4	..	Other Capital, net
-34.6	235.6	159.1	77.9	133.9	35.7	21.0	-85.6	-145.1	-61.4	..	Change in Reserves
				(Zaires per US dollar)							Memo Item:
2.800	4.380	5.750	12.890	36.130	49.870	59.630	112.400	187.070	381.450	..	Conversion Factor (Annual Avg)
			(Millions of US dollars), outstanding at end of year								
4,860.4	4,976.4	4,990.0	5,146.3	5,149.7	6,026.6	7,059.9	8,744.2	8,741.8	8,842.6	..	**EXTERNAL DEBT (Total)**
4,534.6	4,587.1	4,525.7	4,881.3	4,835.1	5,622.4	6,641.9	8,063.9	7,912.9	8,199.2	..	Long-Term Debt (by debtor)
428.3	531.1	607.5	681.8	737.8	889.1	977.8	1,113.4	942.7	792.6	..	Central Bank, incl. IMF credit
2,854.8	2,850.9	2,763.2	3,247.7	3,211.5	3,786.8	4,644.9	5,815.4	5,884.7	6,299.3	..	Central Government
..	..	..	..	..	..	..	..	..	..	..	Rest of General Government
1,251.5	1,205.1	1,155.0	951.8	885.8	946.5	1,019.2	1,135.1	1,085.5	1,107.3	..	Non-financial Public Enterprises
0.0	0.0	0.0	0.0	0.0	0.0	0.0	0.0	0.0	..	..	Priv. Sector, incl non-guaranteed
325.8	389.3	464.3	265.0	314.6	404.2	418.0	680.3	828.9	643.4	..	Short-Term Debt
				(Millions of US dollars)							Memo Items:
204.11	151.55	38.87	101.57	137.37	189.71	268.62	180.77	186.94	195.09	..	Int'l Reserves Excluding Gold
175.67	142.31	187.33	167.86	143.67	145.52	182.55	236.24	184.61	86.62	..	Gold Holdings (at market price)
											SOCIAL INDICATORS
6.1	6.1	6.1	6.1	6.1	6.1	6.1	6.1	6.0	6.0	..	Total Fertility Rate
120.0	118.0	115.0	114.0	113.0	112.0	111.0	110.0	110.0	94.4	..	Infant Mortality Rate
49.2	49.6	50.0	50.4	50.8	51.2	51.6	52.0	52.2	52.5	..	Life Expectancy at Birth
34.2	34.7	35.2	35.6	36.1	36.6	37.4	38.1	38.6	39.0	..	Urban Population, % of total
104.3	102.6	103.7	102.9	102.4	102.3	102.6	100.0	97.9	95.4	..	Food Prod. per capita (1987=100)
71.5	..	..	..	..	..	..	..	..	..	..	Labor Force, Agriculture (%)
37.6	37.4	37.2	37.0	36.8	36.6	36.3	36.1	35.9	35.7	..	Labor Force, Female (%)
94.0	..	..	94.0	89.0	88.0	76.0	76.0	75.0	..	..	Primary Schl. Enroll. Ratio
79.0	..	..	82.0	71.0	70.0	70.0	64.0	..	..	..	Primary Schl. Enroll. Ratio, Female
34.0	..	49.0	47.0	..	..	50.0	21.5	..	..	..	Secondary Schl. Enroll. Ratio

ZAMBIA	1969	1970	1971	1972	1973	1974	1975	1976	1977	1978	1979
CURRENT GNP PER CAPITA (US $)	400	440	430	430	430	530	550	540	500	500	510
POPULATION (thousands)	4,039	4,159	4,289	4,423	4,561	4,702	4,846	4,993	5,143	5,299	5,466

USE AND ORIGIN OF RESOURCES *(Millions of current Zambian Kwacha)*

	1969	1970	1971	1972	1973	1974	1975	1976	1977	1978	1979
Gross National Product (GNP)	1,328	1,244	1,145	1,274	1,465	1,752	1,461	1,748	1,898	2,109	2,432
Net Factor Income from Abroad	-48	-33	-44	-74	-126	-136	-122	-154	-88	-141	-229
GDP at Market Prices	1,376	1,278	1,189	1,348	1,591	1,888	1,583	1,902	1,986	2,251	2,660
Resource Balance	437	215	-25	21	251	178	-309	96	-51	-76	239
Exports of Goods & NFServices	863	685	501	586	780	944	575	832	781	755	1,208
Imports of Goods & NFServices	426	471	526	565	529	765	884	736	833	831	969
Domestic Absorption	939	1,063	1,214	1,327	1,340	1,709	1,892	1,805	2,038	2,326	2,422
Private Consumption, etc.	500	504	493	536	530	660	814	853	1,023	1,252	1,413
General Gov't Consumption	176	199	280	315	345	358	436	501	525	538	633
Gross Domestic Investment	264	361	441	476	465	692	642	452	490	537	376
Fixed Investment	..	372	393	445	413	502	602	445	483	437	450
Indirect Taxes, net	132	122	114	129	152	180	151	182	190	246	237
GDP at factor cost	1,244	1,156	1,075	1,219	1,439	1,708	1,432	1,720	1,797	2,004	2,423
Agriculture	133	136	154	172	180	199	207	276	326	363	397
Industry	859	699	545	636	845	1,026	670	823	748	886	1,117
Manufacturing	112	129	150	181	195	240	266	319	353	430	487
Services, etc.	384	442	489	540	566	662	706	803	913	1,002	1,146
Gross Domestic Saving	701	576	416	498	716	870	333	548	439	461	615
Gross National Saving	..	437	263	326	497	648	126	308	274	252	277

(Millions of 1987 Zambian Kwacha)

	1969	1970	1971	1972	1973	1974	1975	1976	1977	1978	1979
Gross National Product	14,371.1	14,974.5	14,973.1	16,271.2	15,757.6	17,050.9	17,038.2	17,918.3	17,874.4	17,728.7	16,550.9
GDP at Market Prices	15,711.5	16,133.4	16,215.4	17,890.0	17,812.8	18,984.5	18,543.5	19,661.5	18,738.4	18,882.7	18,288.0
Resource Balance	-7,782.6	-8,756.8	-10,375.0	-9,545.5	-7,065.0	-9,149.5	-8,201.2	-1,971.1	-2,115.3	-626.5	-768.1
Exports of Goods & NFServices	9,633.1	8,868.5	8,303.1	9,432.6	8,623.9	9,143.9	8,840.4	10,743.8	10,445.7	9,773.4	8,725.5
Imports of Goods & NFServices	17,415.6	17,625.3	18,677.9	18,978.1	15,688.9	18,293.4	17,041.6	12,714.9	12,561.0	10,399.9	9,493.5
Domestic Absorption	20,904.6	24,341.7	25,958.6	26,859.7	25,488.2	29,791.0	29,203.4	22,174.5	20,287.9	19,783.5	17,922.5
Private Consumption, etc.	10,434.9	9,569.4	9,002.6	9,285.6	8,576.4	9,701.7	10,942.6	10,369.3	9,457.6	9,565.8	10,574.6
General Gov't Consumption	2,429.2	2,913.2	3,742.6	3,942.4	4,003.6	3,801.5	4,215.0	4,283.9	4,065.5	3,662.8	3,665.9
Gross Domestic Investment	8,040.4	11,859.1	13,213.4	13,631.7	12,908.3	16,287.9	14,045.9	7,521.3	6,764.8	6,554.9	3,682.0
Fixed Investment	..	13,112.6	12,507.3	13,718.0	12,750.6	12,627.4	13,859.2	8,347.7	7,255.6	5,775.9	4,682.3
GDP at factor cost	..	..	..	..	..	..	..	..	..	..	..
Agriculture	1,488.6	1,551.8	1,589.4	1,660.3	1,640.7	1,715.8	1,795.7	1,921.6	1,941.8	1,953.2	1,847.0
Industry	7,426.9	7,265.4	7,408.6	8,374.3	8,441.9	9,211.7	8,941.4	9,188.8	8,569.1	8,940.2	8,482.0
Manufacturing	3,193.1	3,449.6	3,852.7	4,344.6	4,416.1	4,805.7	4,528.3	4,784.8	4,352.0	4,567.8	4,843.9
Services, etc.	6,857.6	7,603.8	7,421.9	7,997.0	7,809.8	8,179.7	7,863.5	8,572.9	8,176.1	7,971.0	7,944.2

Memo Items:

	1969	1970	1971	1972	1973	1974	1975	1976	1977	1978	1979
Capacity to Import	35,277.0	25,675.6	17,786.1	19,697.3	23,144.8	22,556.6	11,087.3	14,378.5	11,785.9	9,453.7	11,831.9
Terms of Trade Adjustment	25,644.0	16,807.1	9,483.0	10,264.7	14,520.9	13,412.8	2,246.8	3,634.7	1,340.1	-319.7	3,106.4
Gross Domestic Income	41,355.4	32,940.4	25,698.4	28,154.7	32,333.7	32,397.3	20,790.4	23,296.3	20,078.6	18,562.9	21,394.4
Gross National Income	40,015.1	31,781.6	24,456.1	26,535.9	30,278.5	30,463.7	19,285.0	21,553.0	19,214.5	17,409.0	19,657.4

DOMESTIC PRICES/DEFLATORS *(Index 1987 = 100)*

	1969	1970	1971	1972	1973	1974	1975	1976	1977	1978	1979
Overall (GDP)	8.8	7.9	7.3	7.5	8.9	9.9	8.5	9.7	10.6	11.9	14.5
Domestic Absorption	4.5	4.4	4.7	4.9	5.3	5.7	6.5	8.1	10.0	11.8	13.5
Agriculture	8.9	8.8	9.7	10.4	10.9	11.6	11.5	14.4	16.8	18.6	21.5
Industry	11.6	9.6	7.4	7.6	10.0	11.1	7.5	9.0	8.7	9.9	13.2
Manufacturing	3.5	3.7	3.9	4.2	4.4	5.0	5.9	6.7	8.1	9.4	10.0
Consumer Price Index	6.2	6.4	6.7	7.1	7.5	8.2	9.0	10.7	12.8	14.9	16.3

MANUFACTURING ACTIVITY

	1969	1970	1971	1972	1973	1974	1975	1976	1977	1978	1979
Employment (1987=100)	..	..	..	..	..	..	..	..	..	..	..
Real Earnings per Empl. (1987=100)	..	..	..	..	..	..	..	..	..	..	..
Real Output per Empl. (1987=100)	..	..	..	..	..	..	..	..	..	..	..
Earnings as % of Value Added	34.4	33.5	33.9	27.8	30.1	29.2	30.1	28.9	27.7	26.6	25.6

MONETARY HOLDINGS *(Millions of current Zambian Kwacha)*

	1969	1970	1971	1972	1973	1974	1975	1976	1977	1978	1979
Money Supply, Broadly Defined	342.5	422.8	388.8	413.5	492.1	526.9	588.8	724.1	804.6	750.6	949.8
Money	181.3	185.9	198.6	201.3	258.9	265.7	330.6	400.4	392.8	396.8	516.6
Currency Outside Banks	40.5	42.8	58.3	61.3	69.4	79.6	102.4	121.1	118.4	130.9	126.2
Demand Deposits	140.8	143.1	140.3	140.0	189.5	186.0	228.2	279.3	274.4	266.0	390.5
Quasi-Money	161.1	236.9	190.2	212.2	233.2	261.2	258.2	323.6	411.8	353.7	433.2

GOVERNMENT DEFICIT (-) OR SURPLUS *(Millions of current Zambian Kwacha)*

	1969	1970	1971	1972	1973	1974	1975	1976	1977	1978	1979
	..	..	..	-175.6	-266.4	64.4	-340.8	-269.9	-261.4	-324.5	-241.1
Current Revenue	..	..	..	297.0	384.5	648.9	462.3	461.9	532.1	569.1	620.0
Current Expenditure	..	..	..	329.5	371.5	418.5	547.0	562.3	586.4	576.3	720.2
Current Budget Balance	..	..	..	-32.5	13.0	230.4	-84.7	-100.4	-54.3	-7.2	-100.2
Capital Receipts	..	..	..	1.1	86.3	1.1	..	..	..	6.1	..
Capital Payments	..	..	..	144.2	365.7	167.1	256.1	169.5	207.1	323.4	140.9

1980	1981	1982	1983	1984	1985	1986	1987	1988	1989 estimate	NOTES	ZAMBIA
600	720	660	560	460	370	260	240	290	390	..	**CURRENT GNP PER CAPITA (US $)**
5,647	5,842	6,050	6,271	6,506	6,753	7,011	7,280	7,555	7,837	..	**POPULATION (thousands)**
(Millions of current Zambian Kwacha)											**USE AND ORIGIN OF RESOURCES**
2,835	3,388	3,376	3,866	4,448	6,349	10,722	16,719	27,434	59,788	..	Gross National Product (GNP)
-229	-98	-219	-316	-483	-723	-2,241	-3,059	-2,472	-5,177	..	Net Factor Income from Abroad
3,064	3,485	3,595	4,181	4,931	7,072	12,963	19,778	29,907	64,965	f	GDP at Market Prices
-123	-436	-316	60	91	-1	-2	-5	-622	-2,659	..	Resource Balance
1,268	998	995	1,376	1,729	2,577	5,464	8,160	9,246	18,008	..	Exports of Goods & NFServices
1,391	1,434	1,312	1,317	1,639	2,578	5,467	8,165	9,868	20,667	..	Imports of Goods & NFServices
3,187	3,921	3,912	4,122	4,840	7,073	12,965	19,783	30,529	67,624	..	Domestic Absorption
1,692	2,262	2,313	2,538	2,876	4,782	8,006	13,760	22,926	55,070	..	Private Consumption, etc.
782	986	996	1,009	1,240	1,293	2,094	3,047	3,819	6,656	..	General Gov't Consumption
713	673	603	575	724	999	2,865	2,976	3,784	5,898	..	Gross Domestic Investment
558	610	618	615	623	671	1,164	2,397	3,679	5,632	..	Fixed Investment
221	357	344	632	667	970	2,044	2,338	3,033	2,703	..	Indirect Taxes, net
2,843	3,128	3,251	3,549	4,264	6,102	10,919	17,441	26,873	62,262	B f	GDP at factor cost
435	554	492	594	717	925	1,578	2,180	5,605	8,520	..	Agriculture
1,265	1,351	1,336	1,675	1,935	2,973	5,750	8,869	13,819	30,654	f	Industry
566	684	740	830	1,011	1,616	2,936	5,548	9,496	21,457	..	Manufacturing
1,363	1,581	1,767	1,913	2,279	3,174	5,636	8,729	10,482	25,791	f	Services, etc.
590	237	286	635	815	998	2,863	2,972	3,162	3,239	..	Gross Domestic Saving
217	3	15	258	249	171	292	-274	482	-2,321	..	Gross National Saving
(Millions of 1987 Zambian Kwacha)											
17,402.3	19,443.0	18,421.4	17,679.6	17,049.4	17,204.1	15,786.4	16,719.0	19,067.2	19,230.0	..	Gross National Product
18,838.3	19,987.4	19,452.8	19,037.0	18,836.8	19,164.7	19,210.7	19,778.4	20,870.4	20,898.3	H	GDP at Market Prices
-2,256.8	-1,616.2	1,517.0	1,782.0	1,400.3	39.0	-757.9	-4.8	-1,736.7	-1,158.6	..	Resource Balance
8,456.8	7,378.2	8,535.7	7,704.3	7,176.3	7,054.7	7,188.4	8,160.1	7,106.8	9,630.4	..	Exports of Goods & NFServices
10,713.6	8,994.4	7,018.7	5,922.3	5,776.1	7,015.7	7,946.2	8,164.9	8,843.6	10,789.0	..	Imports of Goods & NFServices
20,384.8	21,002.8	18,389.5	16,857.6	17,381.2	18,601.8	19,971.3	19,783.2	20,969.1	..	..	Domestic Absorption
10,208.4	10,877.9	10,069.7	10,210.2	10,293.7	11,432.8	11,055.8	13,759.5	14,228.5	..	..	Private Consumption, etc.
4,114.3	4,733.8	4,193.3	3,520.3	3,746.5	3,562.9	3,596.2	3,047.2	2,688.7	..	..	General Gov't Consumption
6,062.1	5,391.1	4,126.5	3,127.0	3,341.0	3,606.0	5,319.3	2,976.5	4,052.0	..	..	Gross Domestic Investment
5,184.1	5,293.7	4,649.3	3,719.4	3,183.1	2,986.4	2,532.7	2,397.5	3,576.7	..	..	Fixed Investment
..	..	..	..	..	..	..	..	..	..	B H	GDP at factor cost
1,812.4	1,960.3	1,731.3	1,876.2	1,981.2	2,050.4	2,229.3	2,180.4	2,627.1	..	..	Agriculture
8,675.6	9,106.3	9,051.3	8,766.1	8,520.9	8,622.9	8,637.8	8,869.2	9,450.0	..	f	Industry
4,728.0	5,303.8	5,117.6	4,718.2	4,737.9	5,142.3	5,243.4	5,547.9	6,381.3	..	..	Manufacturing
8,371.4	8,915.1	8,768.2	8,394.7	8,334.7	8,491.4	8,343.6	8,728.8	8,793.3	..	f	Services, etc.
											Memo Items:
9,764.9	6,259.2	5,325.5	6,189.9	6,095.8	7,011.9	7,943.0	8,160.1	8,285.9	9,400.8	..	Capacity to Import
1,308.0	-1,118.9	-3,210.2	-1,514.4	-1,080.6	-42.8	754.7	0.0	1,179.0	-229.6	..	Terms of Trade Adjustment
20,146.3	18,868.5	16,242.6	17,522.7	17,756.3	19,121.9	19,965.4	19,778.4	22,049.4	20,668.6	..	Gross Domestic Income
18,710.3	18,324.1	15,211.2	16,165.2	15,968.8	17,161.3	16,541.1	16,719.0	20,246.3	19,000.4	..	Gross National Income
(Index 1987 = 100)											**DOMESTIC PRICES/DEFLATORS**
16.3	17.4	18.5	22.0	26.2	36.9	67.5	100.0	143.3	310.9	..	Overall (GDP)
15.6	18.7	21.3	24.5	27.8	38.0	64.9	100.0	145.6	..	..	Domestic Absorption
24.0	28.3	28.4	31.6	36.2	45.1	70.8	100.0	213.4	..	..	Agriculture
14.6	14.8	14.8	19.1	22.7	34.5	66.6	100.0	146.2	..	..	Industry
12.0	12.9	14.5	17.6	21.3	31.4	56.0	100.0	148.8	..	..	Manufacturing
18.2	20.6	23.4	28.0	33.6	46.1	69.9	100.0	155.6	..	..	Consumer Price Index
											MANUFACTURING ACTIVITY
..	..	..	..	..	..	..	..	..	..	..	Employment (1987=100)
..	..	..	..	..	..	..	..	..	..	..	Real Earnings per Empl. (1987=100)
..	..	..	..	..	..	..	..	..	..	..	Real Output per Empl. (1987=100)
24.6	32.3	34.4	..	..	..	..	..	..	..	..	Earnings as % of Value Added
(Millions of current Zambian Kwacha)											**MONETARY HOLDINGS**
1,049.1	1,123.4	1,457.9	1,618.0	1,893.3	2,336.1	4,514.6	6,546.7	..	..	..	Money Supply, Broadly Defined
519.0	563.7	689.5	795.3	869.9	1,231.5	2,303.7	3,225.1	5,280.9	..	..	Money
151.1	190.1	209.5	238.8	285.6	342.5	593.4	974.2	1,759.5	..	..	Currency Outside Banks
367.9	373.6	479.9	556.5	584.3	889.0	1,710.3	2,250.9	3,521.4	..	..	Demand Deposits
530.1	559.8	768.5	822.7	1,023.4	1,104.6	2,210.9	3,321.6	..	..	..	Quasi-Money
(Millions of current Zambian Kwacha)											
-567.5	-449.6	-668.2	-327.3	-413.7	-1,072.6	-2,804.3	-2,548.8	-3,466.3	..	..	**GOVERNMENT DEFICIT (-) OR SURPLUS**
790.7	831.1	869.0	1,066.6	1,112.4	1,560.5	3,195.2	4,355.3	5,635.6	..	..	Current Revenue
1,012.1	1,142.1	1,221.5	1,176.6	1,258.2	1,845.8	4,140.6	4,739.5	6,693.1	..	..	Current Expenditure
-221.4	-311.0	-352.5	-110.0	-145.8	-285.3	-945.4	-384.2	-1,057.5	..	..	Current Budget Balance
..	..	..	0.6	1.1	14.6	0.8	3.0	1.1	..	..	Capital Receipts
346.1	138.6	315.7	217.9	269.0	801.9	1,859.7	2,167.6	2,409.9	..	..	Capital Payments

ZAMBIA	1969	1970	1971	1972	1973	1974	1975	1976	1977	1978	1979
FOREIGN TRADE (CUSTOMS BASIS)					*(Millions of current US dollars)*						
Value of Exports, fob	1,056.2	1,001.0	679.3	758.2	1,141.8	1,406.6	811.5	1,040.5	897.4	869.2	1,375.5
Nonfuel Primary Products	1,055.1	992.7	669.1	747.1	1,131.9	1,389.2	797.4	1,028.9	885.0	846.4	1,345.4
Fuels	0.0	0.2	0.3	0.5	0.6	4.0	2.6	3.4	2.7	14.3	16.7
Manufactures	1.1	8.1	9.9	10.6	9.3	13.4	11.6	8.1	9.8	8.5	13.4
Value of Imports, cif	435.6	477.0	558.9	563.4	532.0	787.3	928.7	655.1	671.2	628.3	750.2
Nonfuel Primary Products	56.3	61.5	90.3	73.1	57.1	100.3	91.9	65.6	63.9	65.8	83.1
Fuels	50.0	49.3	45.1	37.1	51.1	95.0	126.1	101.4	102.6	110.9	134.1
Manufactures	329.3	366.2	423.5	453.2	423.9	592.1	710.7	488.1	504.7	451.6	533.1
					(Index 1987 = 100)						
Terms of Trade	372.3	333.9	217.6	195.9	281.9	224.5	128.4	140.5	120.7	111.2	135.2
Export Prices, fob	79.9	76.4	58.7	58.7	98.5	115.4	70.3	78.8	73.8	77.0	110.7
Import Prices, cif	21.5	22.9	27.0	30.0	34.9	51.4	54.7	56.1	61.1	69.3	81.9
BALANCE OF PAYMENTS					*(Millions of current US dollars)*						
Exports of Goods & Services	..	999.0	727.2	829.5	1,202.9	1,479.2	880.3	1,122.2	973.7	951.6	1,534.5
Merchandise, fob	..	942.0	671.0	760.0	1,130.1	1,396.3	802.6	1,028.7	896.7	830.6	1,407.8
Nonfactor Services	..	17.0	25.1	49.9	57.2	52.9	65.6	83.1	73.6	112.6	115.6
Factor Services	..	40.0	31.1	19.5	15.5	30.1	12.1	10.4	3.5	8.4	11.1
Imports of Goods & Services	..	745.0	823.4	903.3	946.6	1,336.1	1,474.0	1,136.0	1,109.1	1,187.5	1,392.6
Merchandise, fob	..	487.0	561.7	565.7	538.8	791.3	947.0	668.5	683.0	617.9	756.0
Nonfactor Services	..	171.0	169.5	215.0	261.1	380.0	398.2	310.6	288.4	407.5	456.0
Factor Services	..	87.0	92.3	122.7	146.6	164.8	128.7	157.0	137.8	162.1	180.5
Long-Term Interest	..	30.7	38.0	40.3	93.9	51.6	53.0	68.7	75.8	88.4	93.0
Private Current Transfers, net	..	-147.0	-152.5	-136.8	-143.1	-134.7	-132.3	-118.9	-96.9	-85.2	-137.3
Workers' Remittances	..	..	..	..	..	..	..	..	..	..	..
Curr. A/C Bal before Off. Transf.	..	107.0	-248.7	-210.6	113.3	8.4	-726.1	-132.8	-232.3	-321.1	4.7
Net Official Transfers	..	1.0	1.0	2.2	16.7	7.2	4.9	8.1	15.2	23.4	32.1
Curr. A/C Bal after Off. Transf.	..	108.0	-247.7	-208.5	129.9	15.6	-721.2	-124.7	-217.2	-297.7	36.8
Long-Term Capital, net	..	-139.0	-327.0	102.1	-29.8	52.9	370.3	102.8	19.8	14.9	202.5
Direct Investment	..	-297.0	..	29.3	32.2	38.5	37.6	31.2	17.5	38.6	35.2
Long-Term Loans	..	321.4	2.8	59.4	29.7	122.5	418.6	164.1	112.1	-36.9	305.9
Disbursements	..	362.7	54.4	145.6	319.7	205.8	488.8	253.9	272.9	172.4	518.6
Repayments	..	41.3	51.6	86.2	290.0	83.3	70.2	89.8	160.8	209.3	212.7
Other Long-Term Capital	..	-163.4	-329.8	13.3	-91.7	-108.1	-85.9	-92.5	-109.8	13.2	-138.6
Other Capital, net	..	167.6	311.2	-40.0	-113.7	-42.5	280.4	-30.9	159.0	93.9	-347.2
Change in Reserves	..	-136.6	263.5	146.4	13.6	-26.0	70.5	52.8	38.3	189.0	107.9
Memo Item:					*(Zambian Kwacha per US dollar)*						
Conversion Factor (Annual Avg)	0.710	0.710	0.710	0.710	0.650	0.640	0.640	0.720	0.790	0.800	0.790
					(Millions of US dollars), outstanding at end of year						
EXTERNAL DEBT (Total)	..	653.5	689.2	758.4	823.2	956.7	1,352.5	1,525.4	2,340.8	2,585.1	3,046.6
Long-Term Debt (by debtor)	..	653.5	689.2	758.4	823.2	956.7	1,352.2	1,525.1	1,694.1	1,935.3	2,395.0
Central Bank, incl. IMF credit	..	0.0	20.6	41.2	68.7	69.8	88.9	110.7	115.9	322.3	513.4
Central Government	..	208.3	232.9	234.9	445.0	513.9	615.4	667.9	715.3	799.5	1,138.2
Rest of General Government	..	..	..	..	..	..	..	..	..	..	..
Non-financial Public Enterprises	..	415.2	400.7	442.3	250.3	285.8	525.4	629.4	683.5	658.8	608.2
Priv. Sector, incl non-guaranteed	..	30.0	35.0	40.0	59.2	87.2	122.5	117.1	179.4	154.7	135.2
Short-Term Debt	..	..	..	..	..	..	..	..	646.7	649.8	651.6
Memo Items:					*(Millions of US dollars)*						
Int'l Reserves Excluding Gold	362.94	508.00	277.09	158.40	185.52	164.36	142.00	92.66	66.31	51.09	79.96
Gold Holdings (at market price)	6.44	6.84	8.73	12.98	22.45	31.33	23.56	22.64	27.71	45.43	111.10
SOCIAL INDICATORS											
Total Fertility Rate	6.7	6.7	6.7	6.7	6.7	6.7	6.7	6.7	6.8	6.8	6.8
Infant Mortality Rate	109.0	106.0	103.0	100.0	98.8	97.6	96.4	95.2	94.0	92.8	91.6
Life Expectancy at Birth	46.1	46.5	46.9	47.3	47.7	48.1	48.5	48.9	49.3	49.6	49.8
Urban Population, % of total	29.0	30.4	31.6	32.8	33.9	35.1	36.3	37.6	38.9	40.2	41.5
Food Prod. per capita (1987=100)	113.1	108.0	116.6	129.7	116.4	123.8	142.3	155.4	143.5	130.1	111.6
Labor Force, Agriculture (%)	77.0	76.6	76.2	75.9	75.5	75.2	74.9	74.5	74.1	73.7	73.4
Labor Force, Female (%)	27.8	27.8	27.7	27.7	27.6	27.6	27.5	27.5	27.4	27.4	27.3
Primary Schl. Enroll. Ratio	..	90.0	..	..	..	..	97.0	..	95.0	95.0	95.0
Primary Schl. Enroll. Ratio, Female	..	80.0	..	..	..	..	88.0	..	88.0	88.0	89.0
Secondary Schl. Enroll. Ratio	..	13.0	..	..	..	..	15.0	16.0	16.0	16.0	16.0

1980	1981	1982	1983	1984	1985	1986	1987	1988	1989 estimate	NOTES	ZAMBIA
				(Millions of current US dollars)							**FOREIGN TRADE (CUSTOMS BASIS)**
1,359.5	998.0	932.0	997.0	884.0	815.0	689.2	869.0	1,179.0	1,048.0	..	Value of Exports, fob
1,331.0	975.7	911.1	976.5	862.9	785.6	666.3	842.1	1,150.0	..	..	Nonfuel Primary Products
15.7	12.5	11.6	11.8	10.6	9.4	3.9	3.9	4.0	..	..	Fuels
12.8	9.8	9.4	8.7	10.5	20.0	19.0	23.0	25.0	26.0	..	Manufactures
1,111.0	1,062.0	831.0	690.0	729.6	653.6	662.7	745.4	848.0	808.0	..	Value of Imports, cif
120.0	114.9	90.1	74.8	86.9	32.0	51.7	54.4	68.0	..	..	Nonfuel Primary Products
195.2	187.3	146.6	121.7	169.7	146.7	91.0	92.0	74.0	..	..	Fuels
795.9	759.8	594.3	493.6	473.0	475.0	520.0	599.0	706.0	651.0	..	Manufactures
				(Index 1987 = 100)							
129.9	104.3	91.7	100.5	86.9	90.9	87.2	100.0	135.8	..	..	Terms of Trade
121.7	98.9	84.2	90.1	79.4	80.6	78.5	100.0	143.3	..	..	Export Prices, fob
93.7	94.8	91.9	89.6	91.4	88.7	90.0	100.0	105.6	..	..	Import Prices, cif
				(Millions of current US dollars)							**BALANCE OF PAYMENTS**
1,624.6	1,169.4	1,078.7	1,024.6	972.7	867.7	740.8	895.3	1,243.5	1,515.2	..	Exports of Goods & Services
1,456.9	996.2	942.0	923.0	892.6	797.1	692.5	846.5	1,183.9	1,407.2	..	Merchandise, fob
151.5	152.8	121.6	98.7	75.4	68.2	47.0	47.7	58.1	83.1	..	Nonfactor Services
16.2	20.4	15.1	2.9	4.7	2.5	1.3	1.1	1.5	24.9	..	Factor Services
1,986.2	1,826.3	1,615.5	1,285.7	1,090.0	1,238.8	1,019.6	1,045.5	1,473.3	1,554.8	..	Imports of Goods & Services
1,114.0	1,065.3	1,003.5	711.0	612.1	571.3	517.8	585.3	686.6	868.0	..	Merchandise, fob
651.0	584.3	408.5	333.8	290.5	254.5	198.8	223.0	289.2	260.7	..	Nonfactor Services
221.2	176.6	203.4	241.0	187.3	412.9	303.0	237.2	497.5	426.1	..	Factor Services
116.0	98.9	86.9	74.6	57.4	43.2	64.8	62.8	66.8	62.7	..	Long-Term Interest
-183.1	-156.4	-55.8	-48.8	-45.4	-33.1	-42.5	-19.5	-25.1	-27.7	..	Private Current Transfers, net
..	..	..	..	..	..	0.0	1.0	..	..	..	Workers' Remittances
-544.6	-766.6	-592.6	-310.0	-162.7	-404.1	-321.3	-169.8	-255.0	-67.3	..	Curr. A/C Bal before Off. Transf.
7.2	33.0	27.6	39.1	10.1	5.6	21.8	29.1	59.3	71.8	..	Net Official Transfers
-537.4	-733.6	-565.0	-270.9	-152.6	-398.5	-299.5	-140.6	-195.7	4.5	..	Curr. A/C Bal after Off. Transf.
162.8	556.0	197.9	125.7	112.4	372.6	-178.1	-227.8	-218.4	-71.1	..	Long-Term Capital, net
61.7	-38.4	39.0	25.7	17.2	51.5	0.0	0.0	0.0	..	..	Direct Investment
395.9	171.0	252.0	133.0	205.4	272.9	235.4	74.7	121.3	47.7	..	Long-Term Loans
607.9	406.6	353.2	186.5	263.7	318.8	309.1	153.3	215.1	138.2	..	Disbursements
212.0	235.6	101.2	53.5	58.3	45.9	73.7	78.6	93.8	90.5	..	Repayments
-294.9	423.4	-93.0	-33.0	-110.2	48.2	-413.5	-302.5	-339.7	-118.8	..	Other Long-Term Capital
371.1	-231.4	429.6	76.6	-95.0	171.3	376.4	295.9	439.1	85.3	..	Other Capital, net
3.6	409.0	-62.6	68.6	135.2	-145.4	101.1	72.5	-25.1	-18.7	..	Change in Reserves
				(Zambian Kwacha per US dollar)							**Memo Item:**
0.790	0.870	0.930	1.260	1.810	3.140	7.790	9.520	8.270	13.810	..	Conversion Factor (Annual Avg)
				(Millions of US dollars), outstanding at end of year							
3,266.0	3,632.6	3,708.5	3,805.3	3,826.1	4,638.7	5,700.0	6,508.1	6,709.0	6,873.4	..	**EXTERNAL DEBT (Total)**
2,679.8	3,021.8	3,060.9	3,291.5	3,390.5	3,961.4	4,668.3	5,430.8	5,341.6	4,994.7	..	Long-Term Debt (by debtor)
496.5	805.4	715.1	747.1	774.4	856.4	934.3	1,080.5	1,026.9	985.7	..	Central Bank, incl. IMF credit
1,524.7	1,504.2	1,564.0	1,797.6	1,892.1	2,257.7	2,846.0	3,367.4	3,418.0	3,157.0	..	Central Government
..	..	..	..	..	..	..	..	..	..	..	Rest of General Government
559.0	650.7	727.4	713.9	693.8	840.6	888.0	982.9	896.7	852.0	..	Non-financial Public Enterprises
99.6	61.5	54.4	32.9	30.2	6.7	0.0	0.0	0.0	..	..	Priv. Sector, incl non-guaranteed
586.2	610.8	647.6	513.8	435.6	677.3	1,031.7	1,077.3	1,367.4	1,878.7	..	Short-Term Debt
				(Millions of US dollars)							**Memo Items:**
78.20	56.17	58.20	54.52	54.21	200.11	70.32	108.83	134.03	..	..	Int'l Reserves Excluding Gold
127.92	86.26	99.15	82.79	0.62	0.98	1.17	1.94	5.33	..	..	Gold Holdings (at market price)
											SOCIAL INDICATORS
6.8	6.8	6.8	6.8	6.8	6.8	6.8	6.8	6.7	6.7	..	Total Fertility Rate
90.4	89.2	88.0	86.4	84.8	83.2	81.6	80.0	78.3	76.6	..	Infant Mortality Rate
50.1	50.3	50.6	51.1	51.6	52.1	52.6	53.1	53.4	53.7	..	Life Expectancy at Birth
42.8	44.1	45.5	46.8	48.2	49.5	51.1	52.6	53.6	54.6	..	Urban Population, % of total
113.4	106.9	100.7	98.3	98.9	103.4	104.1	100.0	116.2	106.2	..	Food Prod. per capita (1987=100)
73.1	..	..	..	..	..	..	..	..	..	..	Labor Force, Agriculture (%)
27.3	27.5	27.7	27.8	28.0	28.2	28.4	28.5	28.7	28.9	..	Labor Force, Female (%)
90.0	..	..	93.0	96.0	99.0	97.0	..	..	..	..	Primary Schl. Enroll. Ratio
82.0	..	..	87.0	89.0	93.0	92.0	..	..	..	..	Primary Schl. Enroll. Ratio, Female
16.0	..	17.0	17.0	17.0	17.0	..	..	..	..	..	Secondary Schl. Enroll. Ratio

ZIMBABWE	1969	1970	1971	1972	1973	1974	1975	1976	1977	1978	1979
CURRENT GNP PER CAPITA (US $)	270	310	330	360	400	530	570	560	540	530	590
POPULATION (thousands)	5,081	5,249	5,414	5,574	5,732	5,895	6,065	6,241	6,418	6,602	6,798
USE AND ORIGIN OF RESOURCES					*(Millions of current Zimbabwe Dollars)*						
Gross National Product (GNP)	984.0	1,058.0	1,214.0	1,384.0	1,514.0	1,821.0	1,952.0	2,107.0	2,150.0	2,317.0	2,769.0
Net Factor Income from Abroad	-17.0	-21.0	-30.0	-35.0	-39.0	-40.0	-46.0	-59.0	-48.0	-46.0	-53.0
GDP at Market Prices	1,001.0	1,079.0	1,244.0	1,419.0	1,553.0	1,861.0	1,998.0	2,166.0	2,198.0	2,363.0	2,822.0
Resource Balance	27.0	11.0	-22.0	40.0	31.0	-10.0	-23.0	84.0	52.0	82.0	-5.0
Exports of Goods & NFServices	..	..	..	..	..	..	590.0	617.0	610.0	675.0	798.0
Imports of Goods & NFServices	..	..	..	..	..	..	613.0	533.0	558.0	593.0	803.0
Domestic Absorption	974.0	1,068.0	1,266.0	1,379.0	1,522.0	1,871.0	2,021.0	2,082.0	2,146.0	2,281.0	2,827.0
Private Consumption, etc.	667.0	722.0	844.0	848.0	947.0	1,138.0	1,240.0	1,375.0	1,344.0	1,549.0	1,932.0
General Gov't Consumption	119.0	126.0	143.0	157.0	180.0	221.0	256.0	319.0	382.0	451.0	537.0
Gross Domestic Investment	188.0	220.0	279.0	374.0	395.0	512.0	525.0	388.0	420.0	281.0	358.0
Fixed Investment	142.0	175.0	221.0	256.0	330.0	421.0	468.0	427.0	379.0	341.0	395.0
Indirect Taxes, net	68.0	68.0	76.0	83.0	103.0	70.0	96.0	102.0	129.0	104.0	172.0
GDP at factor cost	933.0	1,011.0	1,168.0	1,336.0	1,450.0	1,791.0	1,902.0	2,064.0	2,069.0	2,259.0	2,650.0
Agriculture	170.0	153.0	200.0	234.0	215.0	315.0	323.0	350.0	334.0	289.0	321.0
Industry	322.0	367.0	415.0	485.0	569.0	681.0	722.0	777.0	749.0	801.0	1,014.0
Manufacturing	175.0	209.0	251.0	297.0	343.0	421.0	447.0	480.0	460.0	515.0	625.0
Services, etc.	441.0	491.0	553.0	617.0	666.0	795.0	857.0	937.0	986.0	1,169.0	1,315.0
Gross Domestic Saving	215.0	231.0	257.0	414.0	426.0	502.0	502.0	472.0	472.0	363.0	353.0
Gross National Saving	..	199.5	214.8	366.8	373.4	443.1	407.9	363.6	414.4	305.2	262.0
					(Millions of 1987 Zimbabwe Dollars)						
Gross National Product	3,933.2	4,742.1	5,162.9	5,625.2	5,772.4	6,878.1	6,727.9	6,721.6	6,310.1	6,145.7	6,370.2
GDP at Market Prices	4,502.5	5,518.5	6,010.6	6,511.2	6,680.8	7,111.0	6,964.1	6,985.1	6,487.8	6,303.1	6,529.8
Resource Balance	..	..	..	..	..	..	..	-563.0	-667.5	-595.0	-784.0
Exports of Goods & NFServices	..	..	..	..	..	..	..	1,794.4	1,703.0	1,770.3	1,473.8
Imports of Goods & NFServices	..	..	..	..	..	..	..	2,357.4	2,370.6	2,365.3	2,257.8
Domestic Absorption	..	..	..	..	..	..	..	7,548.1	7,155.3	6,898.2	7,313.8
Private Consumption, etc.	..	..	..	..	..	..	..	5,446.9	5,263.1	5,145.7	5,459.9
General Gov't Consumption	327.4	390.7	428.7	458.1	501.4	563.6	601.6	679.4	734.7	1,035.6	1,063.2
Gross Domestic Investment	943.2	1,137.4	1,341.7	1,467.8	1,604.0	2,196.7	1,974.4	1,421.8	1,157.4	716.9	790.7
Fixed Investment	984.8	1,214.3	1,429.4	1,563.2	1,905.1	2,242.1	2,148.9	1,740.1	1,336.2	1,056.5	1,041.4
GDP at factor cost	4,115.0	5,044.7	5,513.6	5,977.8	6,098.6	6,467.5	6,459.3	6,409.8	5,948.1	5,902.8	6,003.8
Agriculture	777.7	719.3	912.7	1,031.6	834.1	985.3	926.8	1,031.6	812.0	894.6	894.6
Industry	1,891.4	2,105.4	2,232.9	2,466.3	2,721.4	2,784.1	2,762.5	2,639.3	2,440.4	2,338.8	2,468.5
Manufacturing	1,014.7	1,134.1	1,187.2	1,408.2	1,518.8	1,627.1	1,611.6	1,518.8	1,443.6	1,390.6	1,540.9
Services, etc.	1,484.5	2,211.7	2,349.6	2,471.4	2,569.3	2,719.2	2,789.1	2,751.1	2,705.2	2,673.2	2,651.2
Memo Items:											
Capacity to Import	..	..	..	..	..	..	..	2,729.0	2,591.5	2,692.4	2,243.7
Terms of Trade Adjustment	..	..	..	..	..	..	..	934.6	888.4	922.1	769.9
Gross Domestic Income	..	..	..	..	..	..	..	7,919.6	7,376.2	7,225.3	7,299.7
Gross National Income	..	..	..	..	..	..	..	7,656.2	7,198.5	7,067.8	7,140.1
DOMESTIC PRICES/DEFLATORS					*(Index 1987 = 100)*						
Overall (GDP)	22.2	19.6	20.7	21.8	23.2	26.2	28.7	31.0	33.9	37.5	43.2
Domestic Absorption	..	..	..	..	..	..	..	27.6	30.0	33.1	38.7
Agriculture	21.9	21.3	21.9	22.7	25.8	32.0	34.9	33.9	41.1	32.3	35.9
Industry	17.0	17.4	18.6	19.7	20.9	24.5	26.1	29.4	30.7	34.2	41.1
Manufacturing	17.2	18.4	21.1	21.1	22.6	25.9	27.7	31.6	31.9	37.0	40.6
Consumer Price Index	18.4	18.8	19.3	19.9	20.5	21.9	24.0	26.7	29.4	31.1	36.7
MANUFACTURING ACTIVITY											
Employment (1987=100)	59.1	63.9	71.6	77.7	81.4	87.4	89.8	86.6	83.4	81.4	87.1
Real Earnings per Empl. (1987=100)	80.8	83.6	84.7	86.7	91.9	95.2	97.5	97.0	95.1	97.8	91.3
Real Output per Empl. (1987=100)	83.5	84.9	77.6	82.3	85.5	86.1	86.0	80.2	83.7	79.2	81.5
Earnings as % of Value Added	45.4	42.9	42.3	42.6	42.0	40.5	42.3	43.9	46.5	43.6	42.8
MONETARY HOLDINGS					*(Millions of current Zimbabwe Dollars)*						
Money Supply, Broadly Defined	..	..	..	..	..	..	..	..	..	..	1,636.5
Money	..	..	..	..	..	..	324.1	351.9	374.5	415.0	463.2
Currency Outside Banks	..	..	..	..	..	..	66.9	79.1	83.9	95.2	107.6
Demand Deposits	..	..	..	..	..	..	257.2	272.8	290.6	319.8	355.6
Quasi-Money	..	..	..	..	..	..	..	..	..	..	1,173.3
					(Millions of current Zimbabwe Dollars)						
GOVERNMENT DEFICIT (-) OR SURPLUS	..	..	..	..	..	..	..	-118.3	-95.4	-253.5	-293.4
Current Revenue	..	..	..	..	..	..	..	491.7	575.1	572.7	610.8
Current Expenditure	..	..	..	..	..	..	..	479.6	621.5	751.4	835.1
Current Budget Balance	..	..	..	..	..	..	..	12.1	-46.4	-178.7	-224.3
Capital Receipts	..	..	..	..	..	..	..	0.5	0.6	0.3	0.6
Capital Payments	..	..	..	..	..	..	..	130.9	49.6	75.1	69.7

1980	1981	1982	1983	1984	1985	1986	1987	1988	1989 estimate	NOTES	ZIMBABWE
710	860	900	850	730	620	560	540	570	650	..	**CURRENT GNP PER CAPITA (US $)**
7,009	7,255	7,521	7,804	8,101	8,406	8,714	9,017	9,303	9,567	..	**POPULATION (thousands)**
				(Millions of current Zimbabwe Dollars)							**USE AND ORIGIN OF RESOURCES**
3,394.0	4,318.0	5,003.0	6,058.0	6,210.0	6,735.0	7,911.0	8,573.0	10,348.0	12,145.0	..	Gross National Product (GNP)
-47.0	-115.0	-194.0	-248.0	-195.0	-284.0	-384.0	-355.0	-292.0	-311.0	..	Net Factor Income from Abroad
3,441.0	4,433.0	5,197.0	6,306.0	6,405.0	7,019.0	8,295.0	8,928.0	10,640.0	12,456.0	..	GDP at Market Prices
-103.0	-325.0	-309.0	-197.0	35.0	86.0	357.0	366.0	521.6	85.0	..	Resource Balance
1,043.0	1,117.0	1,141.0	1,345.0	1,708.0	2,101.0	2,559.0	2,789.0	3,292.9	3,714.0	..	Exports of Goods & NFServices
1,146.0	1,442.0	1,450.0	1,542.0	1,673.0	2,015.0	2,202.0	2,423.0	2,771.3	3,629.0	..	Imports of Goods & NFServices
3,544.0	4,758.0	5,506.0	6,503.0	6,370.0	6,933.0	7,938.0	8,562.0	10,118.4	12,371.0	..	Domestic Absorption
2,219.0	2,969.0	3,377.0	4,342.0	3,792.0	3,894.0	4,521.0	4,386.0	5,533.4	6,793.0	..	Private Consumption, etc.
677.0	763.0	1,027.0	1,159.0	1,364.0	1,560.0	1,804.0	2,467.0	2,493.0	2,996.0	..	General Gov't Consumption
648.0	1,026.0	1,102.0	1,002.0	1,214.0	1,479.0	1,613.0	1,709.0	2,092.0	2,582.0	..	Gross Domestic Investment
528.0	830.0	1,039.0	1,238.0	1,186.0	1,133.0	1,312.0	1,386.0	1,435.0	1,797.0	..	Fixed Investment
217.0	384.0	540.0	874.0	756.0	792.0	945.0	1,017.0	1,207.0	1,328.0	..	Indirect Taxes, net
3,224.0	4,049.0	4,657.0	5,432.0	5,649.0	6,227.0	7,350.0	7,911.0	9,433.0	11,128.0	..	GDP at factor cost
451.0	640.0	669.0	544.0	748.0	1,038.0	1,121.0	951.0	1,309.0	1,408.0	..	Agriculture
1,248.0	1,484.0	1,601.0	2,287.0	2,142.0	2,121.0	2,675.0	3,104.0	3,540.0	4,320.0	..	Industry
802.0	1,016.0	1,121.0	1,441.0	1,475.0	1,488.0	1,832.0	2,098.0	2,397.0	2,946.0	..	Manufacturing
1,525.0	1,925.0	2,387.0	2,601.0	2,759.0	3,068.0	3,554.0	3,856.0	4,584.0	5,400.0	..	Services, etc.
545.0	701.0	793.0	805.0	1,249.0	1,565.0	1,970.0	2,075.0	2,613.6	2,667.0	..	Gross Domestic Saving
420.5	500.1	501.7	441.1	1,005.6	1,208.1	1,541.7	1,666.7	2,309.6	2,313.9	..	Gross National Saving
				(Millions of 1987 Zimbabwe Dollars)							
7,080.4	7,865.9	7,975.4	8,087.1	7,973.7	8,414.4	8,621.5	8,573.0	8,511.6	9,686.3	..	Gross National Product
7,220.1	8,124.4	8,338.4	8,470.6	8,261.8	8,817.4	9,056.4	8,928.0	8,796.4	9,975.9	..	GDP at Market Prices
-1,207.3	-1,866.6	-1,850.7	-1,483.6	-909.2	-835.0	88.7	366.0	-959.0	-1,335.9	..	Resource Balance
1,797.9	1,935.8	1,985.7	1,990.9	1,859.9	2,170.2	2,742.5	2,789.0	2,454.1	2,359.7	..	Exports of Goods & NFServices
3,005.1	3,802.3	3,836.4	3,474.5	2,769.1	3,005.1	2,653.8	2,423.0	3,413.0	3,695.7	..	Imports of Goods & NFServices
8,427.4	9,991.0	10,189.1	9,954.3	9,171.0	9,652.3	8,967.7	8,562.0	9,755.3	11,311.8	..	Domestic Absorption
5,957.6	6,906.2	7,349.0	6,823.2	5,649.3	6,292.9	5,556.5	4,386.0	5,175.6	7,000.3	..	Private Consumption, etc.
1,170.4	1,367.5	1,542.1	1,628.5	1,763.4	1,829.1	1,979.5	2,467.0	2,565.5	2,667.5	..	General Gov't Consumption
1,299.4	1,717.4	1,298.1	1,502.5	1,758.3	1,530.4	1,431.7	1,709.0	2,014.2	1,644.0	..	Gross Domestic Investment
1,262.1	1,750.9	1,932.8	1,914.4	1,752.1	1,607.8	1,485.9	1,386.0	1,399.3	1,673.3	..	Fixed Investment
6,644.7	7,289.9	7,397.0	7,133.2	7,286.6	7,816.6	7,993.0	7,911.0	8,422.5	8,840.5	..	GDP at factor cost
908.7	1,037.6	963.1	812.0	999.4	1,237.1	1,160.5	951.0	1,192.8	1,212.9	..	Agriculture
2,697.6	2,883.5	2,864.1	2,794.9	2,714.9	2,881.4	3,002.4	3,104.0	3,209.9	3,423.9	..	Industry
1,773.0	1,947.7	1,938.8	1,883.6	1,788.5	1,994.1	2,062.6	2,098.0	2,201.9	2,374.3	..	Manufacturing
3,046.8	3,372.5	3,568.3	3,526.3	3,572.3	3,698.2	3,830.0	3,856.0	4,019.8	4,203.6	..	Services, etc.
											Memo Items:
2,735.1	2,945.4	3,018.9	3,030.6	2,827.1	3,133.4	3,084.0	2,789.0	4,055.4	3,782.2	..	Capacity to Import
937.2	1,009.6	1,033.1	1,039.7	967.2	963.2	341.5	0.0	1,601.4	1,422.5	..	Terms of Trade Adjustment
8,157.3	9,134.0	9,371.6	9,510.4	9,228.9	9,780.6	9,398.0	8,928.0	10,397.7	11,398.4	..	Gross Domestic Income
8,017.6	8,875.5	9,008.6	9,126.9	8,940.9	9,377.6	8,963.1	8,573.0	10,113.0	11,108.8	..	Gross National Income
				(Index 1987 = 100)							**DOMESTIC PRICES/DEFLATORS**
47.7	54.6	62.3	74.4	77.5	79.6	91.6	100.0	121.0	124.9	..	Overall (GDP)
42.1	47.6	54.0	65.3	69.5	71.8	88.5	100.0	103.7	109.4	..	Domestic Absorption
49.6	61.7	69.5	67.0	74.8	83.9	96.6	100.0	109.7	116.1	..	Agriculture
46.3	51.5	55.9	81.8	78.9	73.6	89.1	100.0	110.3	126.2	..	Industry
45.2	52.2	57.8	76.5	82.5	74.6	88.8	100.0	108.9	124.1	..	Manufacturing
38.7	43.8	48.5	59.7	71.7	77.8	88.9	100.0	107.4	121.3	..	Consumer Price Index
											MANUFACTURING ACTIVITY
95.0	102.2	104.0	99.6	96.6	96.6	98.6	100.0	102.7	..	..	Employment (1987=100)
102.0	110.7	116.0	108.0	101.1	107.2	102.0	100.0	101.9	..	..	Real Earnings per Empl. (1987=100)
87.1	88.1	87.5	80.7	85.6	109.6	100.9	100.0	101.1	..	..	Real Output per Empl. (1987=100)
41.8	43.9	48.1	39.9	39.0	41.5	35.8	34.9	34.3	..	..	Earnings as % of Value Added
				(Millions of current Zimbabwe Dollars)							**MONETARY HOLDINGS**
..	..	..	..	2,995.3	3,607.7	3,917.2	4,843.5	5,165.1	7,455.4	D	Money Supply, Broadly Defined
632.8	678.8	826.9	751.4	865.8	1,005.2	1,102.8	1,224.6	1,602.7	1,905.1	..	Money
157.2	198.6	237.5	227.4	258.8	321.1	379.7	389.3	503.3	617.9	..	Currency Outside Banks
475.6	480.2	589.4	524.0	607.0	684.1	723.1	835.3	1,099.4	1,287.2	..	Demand Deposits
..	..	..	..	2,129.5	2,602.5	2,814.4	3,618.9	3,562.4	5,550.3	..	Quasi-Money
				(Millions of current Zimbabwe Dollars)							**GOVERNMENT DEFICIT (-) OR SURPLUS**
-376.0	-261.6	-545.3	-393.7	-647.4	-512.5	-638.1	-977.4	-1,004.9	..	..	Current Revenue
828.7	1,130.0	1,531.2	1,888.9	2,109.5	2,288.0	2,590.8	3,018.8	3,637.1	..	..	Current Revenue
1,136.9	1,233.7	1,715.6	1,905.8	2,364.8	2,412.6	2,856.7	3,492.9	3,855.9	..	..	Current Expenditure
-308.2	-103.7	-184.4	-16.9	-255.3	-124.6	-265.9	-474.1	-218.8	..	..	Current Budget Balance
0.9	1.1	0.4	0.6	0.8	17.0	17.1	15.0	6.9	..	..	Capital Receipts
68.7	159.0	361.3	377.4	392.9	404.9	389.3	518.3	793.0	..	..	Capital Payments

ZIMBABWE	1969	1970	1971	1972	1973	1974	1975	1976	1977	1978	1979
FOREIGN TRADE (CUSTOMS BASIS)					*(Millions of current US dollars)*						
Value of Exports, fob	325.0	370.0	404.0	515.0	693.0	864.0	936.0	974.0	877.0	891.0	1,217.0
Nonfuel Primary Products	273.2	310.6	331.2	411.1	562.4	684.3	711.0	723.0	659.0	660.0	853.0
Fuels	1.0	0.4	0.4	2.0	2.8	6.0	13.0	10.0	12.0	12.0	17.0
Manufactures	50.8	59.0	72.4	101.9	127.8	173.7	212.0	241.0	206.0	219.0	347.0
Value of Imports, cif	279.3	329.0	396.7	415.6	549.0	753.0	813.5	611.7	617.8	592.0	937.0
Nonfuel Primary Products	40.5	50.4	68.1	66.9	96.0	124.5	112.1	85.5	89.4	85.4	149.4
Fuels	24.5	25.8	26.6	27.0	37.1	99.8	111.9	84.0	77.1	66.9	121.4
Manufactures	214.3	252.8	301.9	321.7	415.9	528.6	589.6	442.3	451.2	439.6	666.2
					(Index 1987 = 100)						
Terms of Trade	183.2	187.8	165.5	157.1	169.1	143.4	131.1	144.3	139.1	125.3	121.8
Export Prices, fob	41.9	45.7	45.5	47.6	63.6	75.9	73.0	81.4	85.9	87.2	99.2
Import Prices, cif	22.9	24.3	27.5	30.3	37.6	52.9	55.7	56.4	61.7	69.6	81.5
BALANCE OF PAYMENTS					*(Millions of current US dollars)*						
Exports of Goods & Services	..	417.0	453.7	575.3	763.3	960.2	1,042.0	1,017.0	1,005.3	1,028.9	1,230.5
Merchandise, fob	..	370.0	404.0	516.0	687.0	867.0	922.0	900.0	901.0	923.2	1,079.6
Nonfactor Services	..	32.0	35.0	45.0	60.0	75.0	80.0	78.0	64.5	67.8	87.2
Factor Services	..	15.0	14.7	14.3	16.3	18.2	40.0	39.0	39.8	37.9	63.7
Imports of Goods & Services	..	428.4	507.8	571.8	773.8	1,037.0	1,190.8	962.1	1,004.0	974.3	1,283.4
Merchandise, fob	..	346.9	405.6	457.8	604.0	816.2	844.0	652.0	671.3	654.2	875.0
Nonfactor Services	..	45.5	57.1	64.6	115.0	149.9	243.8	198.1	217.9	222.8	266.1
Factor Services	..	36.0	45.1	49.4	54.8	70.9	103.0	112.0	114.8	97.3	142.2
Long-Term Interest	..	4.6	5.7	5.8	5.6	5.0	2.2	2.1	1.7	4.3	7.3
Private Current Transfers, net	..	-14.7	-17.2	-18.5	-23.2	-32.5	-84.4	-78.9	-15.3	-17.4	-55.9
Workers' Remittances	..	..	..	..	..	..	13.0	13.0	11.5	5.3	10.6
Curr. A/C Bal before Off. Transf.	..	-26.1	-71.3	-15.0	-33.7	-109.3	-233.2	-24.0	-14.0	37.2	-108.7
Net Official Transfers	..	12.2	12.3	12.0	12.1	11.9	13.1	13.1	..	..	..
Curr. A/C Bal after Off. Transf.	..	-13.9	-59.0	-3.0	-21.6	-97.4	-220.1	-10.9	-14.0	37.2	-108.7
Long-Term Capital, net	..	26.3	30.5	-2.4	51.6	62.6	147.0	24.0	-30.1	151.8	146.5
Direct Investment	..	..	..	..	..	..	..	..	-3.8	2.5	0.1
Long-Term Loans	..	-4.8	-4.8	-5.6	-10.6	-9.5	-5.7	-5.3	-4.2	270.3	92.4
Disbursements	..	0.0	0.0	0.0	0.0	0.0	0.0	0.0	0.0	274.4	99.7
Repayments	..	4.8	4.8	5.6	10.6	9.5	5.7	5.3	4.2	4.1	7.3
Other Long-Term Capital	..	31.1	35.3	3.2	62.2	72.1	152.7	29.3	-22.1	-121.0	54.0
Other Capital, net	..	-20.0	14.3	60.6	33.4	-19.1	82.3	-16.4	36.0	-114.0	82.1
Change in Reserves	..	7.6	14.2	-55.2	-63.4	53.9	-9.2	3.3	8.1	-75.0	-119.9
Memo Item:											
Conversion Factor (Annual Avg)	0.710	0.710	0.710	0.660	*(Zimbabwe Dollars per US dollar)* 0.590	0.580	0.570	0.630	0.630	0.680	0.680
EXTERNAL DEBT (Total)					*(Millions of US dollars), outstanding at end of year*						
EXTERNAL DEBT (Total)	..	229.1	233.7	213.7	217.5	217.5	186.9	143.9	199.5	446.1	559.2
Long-Term Debt (by debtor)	..	229.1	233.7	213.7	217.5	217.5	186.9	143.9	153.5	418.1	524.2
Central Bank, incl. IMF credit	..	0.0	0.0	0.0	0.0	0.0	0.0	0.0	0.0	0.0	0.0
Central Government	..	175.7	181.7	167.3	173.4	179.3	154.0	117.0	128.2	395.3	503.7
Rest of General Government	..	..	..	..	..	..	..	..	..	..	..
Non-financial Public Enterprises	..	53.4	52.0	46.4	44.1	38.2	32.9	26.9	25.3	22.8	20.5
Priv. Sector, incl non-guaranteed	..	0.0	0.0	0.0	0.0	0.0	0.0	0.0	0.0	0.0	0.0
Short-Term Debt	..	..	..	..	..	..	..	..	46.0	28.0	35.0
Memo Items:					*(Millions of US dollars)*						
Int'l Reserves Excluding Gold	27.89	20.27	6.05	61.27	124.72	70.79	79.95	76.64	72.56	148.02	298.90
Gold Holdings (at market price)	28.23	39.16	35.65	35.82	84.19	93.62	49.23	35.71	25.07	36.39	133.12
SOCIAL INDICATORS											
Total Fertility Rate	7.8	7.7	7.6	7.5	7.4	7.3	7.2	7.1	7.0	7.0	6.9
Infant Mortality Rate	97.8	96.2	94.6	93.0	91.6	90.2	88.8	87.4	86.0	84.8	83.6
Life Expectancy at Birth	50.0	50.5	51.0	51.5	52.0	52.4	52.9	53.3	53.8	54.2	54.6
Urban Population, % of total	16.4	16.9	17.4	17.9	18.4	18.9	19.4	19.9	20.4	20.9	21.4
Food Prod. per capita (1987=100)	153.6	133.1	172.4	194.0	132.9	174.3	154.7	166.7	160.4	156.6	122.6
Labor Force, Agriculture (%)	77.6	77.3	76.8	76.3	75.9	75.5	75.1	74.6	74.1	73.6	73.2
Labor Force, Female (%)	37.7	37.6	37.5	37.4	37.3	37.2	37.2	37.0	36.9	36.9	36.8
Primary Schl. Enroll. Ratio	..	74.0	..	..	..	..	73.0	72.0	70.0	63.0	61.0
Primary Schl. Enroll. Ratio, Female	..	66.0	..	..	..	..	67.0	66.0	65.0	59.0	57.0
Secondary Schl. Enroll. Ratio	..	7.0	..	..	..	..	9.0	9.0	9.0	9.0	8.0

1980	1981	1982	1983	1984	1985	1986	1987	1988	1989 estimate	NOTES	ZIMBABWE
				(Millions of current US dollars)							**FOREIGN TRADE (CUSTOMS BASIS)**
1,423.0	1,406.0	1,273.0	1,128.0	1,154.3	1,112.7	1,254.0	1,358.0	1,592.0	..	..	Value of Exports, fob
1,002.0	1,060.0	944.0	774.0	778.9	713.3	789.7	802.3	948.0	..	..	Nonfuel Primary Products
17.0	15.0	16.0	17.0	16.6	15.4	5.2	5.7	6.0	..	..	Fuels
404.0	331.0	313.0	337.0	358.8	384.0	459.1	550.0	638.0	..	..	Manufactures
1,448.4	1,695.7	1,638.9	1,205.1	955.0	1,030.9	1,099.0	1,054.9	1,189.0	..	f	Value of Imports, cif
255.1	324.0	304.0	235.1	152.2	149.8	155.2	137.4	131.0	..	..	Nonfuel Primary Products
245.6	350.8	334.7	220.5	176.7	186.2	71.0	87.0	75.0	..	..	Fuels
947.7	1,020.9	1,000.2	749.6	626.1	694.8	872.8	830.5	983.0	..	..	Manufactures
				(Index 1987 = 100)							
118.2	107.9	101.3	106.6	108.6	100.1	94.6	100.0	100.8	..	..	Terms of Trade
113.0	108.6	96.8	98.5	96.8	87.7	85.8	100.0	107.6	..	..	Export Prices, fob
95.6	100.6	95.6	92.3	89.2	87.6	90.7	100.0	106.8	..	..	Import Prices, cif
				(Millions of current US dollars)							**BALANCE OF PAYMENTS**
1,719.3	1,679.6	1,574.0	1,368.3	1,368.1	1,452.9	1,528.1	1,649.6	1,889.5	1,819.3	f	Exports of Goods & Services
1,445.5	1,451.4	1,312.1	1,153.7	1,173.6	1,119.6	1,322.7	1,452.0	1,668.7	1,589.7	..	Merchandise, fob
166.8	132.1	180.1	144.1	138.8	295.1	168.4	164.1	204.1	204.5	..	Nonfactor Services
107.1	96.0	81.8	70.6	55.8	38.2	36.9	33.5	16.6	25.1	..	Factor Services
1,900.3	2,281.8	2,200.4	1,755.3	1,517.8	1,548.1	1,553.1	1,649.2	1,836.0	1,984.6	..	Imports of Goods & Services
1,339.0	1,534.0	1,472.0	1,069.6	989.3	918.9	1,011.6	1,071.0	1,185.3	1,319.4	f	Merchandise, fob
382.0	522.1	420.3	417.0	350.1	457.5	310.0	343.6	410.7	449.1	..	Nonfactor Services
179.3	225.7	308.0	268.8	178.4	171.7	231.5	234.6	240.0	216.0	..	Factor Services
10.2	30.7	91.9	106.9	121.1	122.4	128.1	129.3	144.0	142.7	..	Long-Term Interest
-120.6	-124.5	-128.2	-114.4	-38.5	-45.2	-26.6	-32.1	-6.7	-19.9	..	Private Current Transfers, net
9.3	0.7	2.3	..	..	..	..	..	..	..	..	Workers' Remittances
-301.6	-726.7	-754.5	-501.3	-188.1	-140.4	-51.5	-31.7	46.8	-185.1	..	Curr. A/C Bal before Off. Transf.
57.7	90.8	45.4	41.1	88.2	64.8	58.3	79.7	66.0	78.6	..	Net Official Transfers
-243.8	-635.9	-709.2	-460.2	-100.0	-75.7	6.8	48.0	112.8	-106.6	..	Curr. A/C Bal after Off. Transf.
-53.7	80.3	369.3	160.8	90.0	16.4	8.5	-43.7	211.0	187.0	f	Long-Term Capital, net
1.6	3.6	-0.8	-2.1	-2.5	2.9	7.5	-30.5	3.9	-8.5	..	Direct Investment
92.6	295.4	470.5	442.0	61.7	29.9	52.4	3.5	-65.1	395.5	..	Long-Term Loans
132.3	329.9	517.9	775.2	212.0	221.5	273.3	292.3	263.6	649.1	..	Disbursements
39.7	34.5	47.4	333.2	150.3	191.6	220.9	288.8	328.7	253.6	..	Repayments
-147.8	-218.7	-100.3	-279.1	30.8	-16.3	-51.3	-16.7	272.2	-200.0	..	Other Long-Term Capital
211.0	547.5	317.4	125.4	-36.4	141.5	40.2	120.2	-58.4	-166.7	f	Other Capital, net
86.5	8.1	22.4	174.0	46.3	-82.2	-55.5	-124.5	-265.4	86.3	..	Change in Reserves
				(Zimbabwe Dollars per US dollar)							Memo Item:
0.640	0.690	0.760	1.010	1.260	1.610	1.670	1.660	1.810	2.120	..	Conversion Factor (Annual Avg)
				(Millions of US dollars), outstanding at end of year							
785.6	1,249.8	1,845.1	2,304.1	2,252.5	2,464.7	2,708.0	2,913.8	2,670.6	3,087.6	..	**EXTERNAL DEBT (Total)**
695.6	851.8	1,263.1	1,823.1	1,908.5	2,156.7	2,417.9	2,647.4	2,363.1	2,664.7	..	Long-Term Debt (by debtor)
0.0	43.6	41.4	200.1	256.1	264.1	233.7	156.5	70.2	29.2	..	Central Bank, incl. IMF credit
675.3	641.9	760.1	889.2	1,042.5	1,269.6	1,558.7	1,897.2	1,844.5	2,050.0	..	Central Government
..	..	..	..	..	..	..	..	..	..	..	Rest of General Government
20.3	153.1	423.6	647.4	532.3	558.0	569.9	534.5	398.0	515.8	..	Non-financial Public Enterprises
0.0	13.2	38.0	86.4	77.6	65.0	55.6	59.2	50.4	69.7	..	Priv. Sector, incl non-guaranteed
90.0	398.0	582.0	481.0	344.0	308.0	290.1	266.4	307.5	422.9	..	Short-Term Debt
				(Millions of US dollars)							Memo Items:
213.50	169.48	140.45	75.36	45.38	93.35	106.40	166.15	178.63	94.56	..	Int'l Reserves Excluding Gold
205.74	185.24	180.02	225.09	214.58	252.12	209.91	204.29	162.05	179.65	..	Gold Holdings (at market price)
											SOCIAL INDICATORS
6.8	6.7	6.6	6.4	6.1	5.9	5.6	5.4	5.3	5.1	..	Total Fertility Rate
82.4	81.2	80.0	74.3	68.6	63.0	57.3	51.6	49.1	46.5	..	Infant Mortality Rate
55.0	55.4	55.8	57.1	58.4	59.8	61.1	62.4	62.9	63.4	..	Life Expectancy at Birth
21.9	22.4	23.0	23.5	24.1	24.6	25.4	26.1	26.6	27.1	..	Urban Population, % of total
124.7	163.4	135.2	99.3	106.1	153.9	146.9	100.0	140.2	129.1	..	Food Prod. per capita (1987=100)
72.8	..	..	..	..	..	..	..	..	..	..	Labor Force, Agriculture (%)
36.7	36.5	36.2	36.0	35.8	35.7	35.4	35.2	35.0	34.8	..	Labor Force, Female (%)
85.0	..	..	130.0	132.0	135.0	136.0	..	128.0	..	..	Primary Schl. Enroll. Ratio
..	..	..	126.0	127.0	131.0	132.0	..	126.0	..	..	Primary Schl. Enroll. Ratio, Female
8.0	..	..	30.0	37.0	41.0	45.0	..	46.0	..	..	Secondary Schl. Enroll. Ratio

Codes for General and Country Notes

GENERAL

Code letters in the *Notes* column of the country pages refer to the following general footnotes:

A   GNP per capita in US$ is calculated using an alternative conversion factor.

B   GDP by industrial origin data for at least some years are in purchaser values and not at factor cost.

C   Data are for fiscal years; see Country Notes.

D   Money supply reflects total liquid liabilities.

E   State and local government accounts are thought to contribute at least 20 percent of central government tax revenue.

F   Break in comparability of data, see the IMF's Government Financial Statistics Yearbook.

G   Data are for *persons engaged*, not *employees*.

H   Partial rebasing into 1987 prices would yield a large rescaling deviation; therefore GDP has been rescaled directly from the original base year to 1987 prices.

I   Partial rebasing into 1987 prices has resulted in a rescaling deviation of more than 5 percent of private consumption.

J   Break in comparability of data; see UN *Yearbook of Industrial Statistics*.

COUNTRY

f   Indicates country-specific notes. These are listed in the pages following, under main topic headings, and in alphabetical order, by country.

Country Notes

National Accounts

ANTIGUA AND BARBUDA
BREAKS IN COMPARABILITY:
1977-84 Other services includes imputed bank service charges

BAHAMAS, THE
MISCELLANEOUS:
1984-87 Other services include tourism

BAHRAIN
SOURCES:
All Indicators
1980-88 Ministry of Finance and National Economy of Bahrain

BANGLADESH
BREAKS IN COMPARABILITY:
1960-72 Manufacturing includes mining and quarrying

BARBADOS
SOURCES:
All components in GDP by expenditure categories
1975 *Barbados Economic Report 1980*, Ministry of Finance and Planning (current prices)
1976-85 Barbados Statistical Service; Central Bank
All components in GDP by industrial origin
1975 *Barbados Economic Report 1980*, Ministry of Finance and Planning (current prices)

BENIN
SOURCES:
All Indicators
1960-67 UN Economic Commission for Africa (UNECA), 12/80

BHUTAN
SOURCES:
All Indicators
1980-88 *National Accounts Statistics 1980-88*, Central Statistical Office, March, 1990

BOLIVIA
BREAKS IN COMPARABILITY:
1970-84 Other services includes banking, insurance and real estate

BOTSWANA
SOURCES:
All Indicators
1960-63 UNECA (current prices)
1974-79 *Botswana Statistical Abstract*
1980-87 Bank of Botswana Annual Report, 1987
All components in GDP by expenditure categories
1970-71 UN, Economic Commission for Africa (UNECA) (current prices)
GDP at mp deflator
1965-72 GDP deflator from Statistical Abstracts for 1965, 1966, 1968, 1969, and 1972 (constant prices)
Net factor income from abroad
1974 Bank of Botswana annual report 1985 (current prices)
MISCELLANEOUS:
1968-89 From 1968 data are in new UNSNA concept and are in fiscal year ending June 30
1972-89 Data break in the series in 1972 and 1974
1965-89 Exports exclude non-factor services

1965-89 Imports include goods and net nonfactor services

BRAZIL
SOURCES:
All components in GDP by expenditure categories
All components in GDP by industrial origin
GNP at market prices
1969-89 IBGE, Departamento do Contas Nacionais

BURKINA FASO
SOURCES:
All Indicators
1950-69 UNECA
1970-89 Institut National de la Statistique and WB estimates
BREAKS IN COMPARABILITY:
1960-88 Net factor income from abroad includes workers' remittances

BURUNDI
BREAKS IN COMPARABILITY:
1965-66 Agriculture includes Construction (constant prices)

CAMEROON
SOURCES:
All Indicators
1960-89 Direction de la Statistique and WB estimates
BREAKS IN COMPARABILITY:
1977-89 Banking, insurance and real estate includes ownership of dwellings
MISCELLANEOUS:
1950-89 Fiscal year data refer to years ending June 30

CAPE VERDE
MISCELLANEOUS:
1970-89 Data for GDP by industrial origin are at market prices

CENTRAL AFRICAN REPUBLIC
SOURCES:
All Indicators
1960-69 UNECA
BREAKS IN COMPARABILITY:
1960-76 Private consumption includes change in stocks

CHAD
SOURCES:
All Indicators
1976 UNECA
All components in GDP by expenditure categories
1977-85 UNECA
BREAKS IN COMPARABILITY:
1982-85 Net factor income from abroad includes private transfers (current prices)
1960-85 Agriculture excludes forestry and fishing

CHILE
SOURCES:
All Indicators
1960-69 Central Bank of Chile
Consumer price index
1960-89 Base year is 1987

CHINA
SOURCES:
All Indicators
1960-77 Estimated based on *China Statistical Yearbook*

CONGO, PEOPLE'S REP
SOURCES:
All indicators
1960-66 UNECA
MISCELLANEOUS:
1973-88 Manufacturing includes other mining (except petroleum.)

COSTA RICA
BREAKS IN COMPARABILITY:
1960-89 Manufacturing includes mining and quarrying

COTE D'IVOIRE
BREAKS IN COMPARABILITY:
1960-73 Exports of goods and nonfactor services excludes nonfactor services
1960-71 Imports of goods and nonfactor services excludes nonfactor services
1960-80 Net factor income from abroad includes workers' remittances

CYPRUS
SOURCES:
All components in GDP by expenditure categories
All components in GDP by industrial origin
1976-89 Dept. of Statistics and Research, Ministry of Finance
MISCELLANEOUS:
1975-89 Data (except population and GNP per capita) relate to South Cyprus

DOMINICA
SOURCES:
All components in GDP by industrial origin
1977-89 Dominica Statistics Department, February 1989

ECUADOR
SOURCES:
All Indicators
1965-69 Central Bank of Ecuador

EGYPT, ARAB REPUBLIC OF
MISCELLANEOUS:
1960-80 Data are for calendar year
1981-88 Fiscal year ending June 30

ETHIOPIA
Consumer price index
1960-89 Base year is 1987
BREAKS IN COMPARABILITY:
1970-89 Private consumption includes change in stocks
1970-89 Gross domestic investment excludes change in stocks
MISCELLANEOUS:
1965-89 Fiscal year ending July 7

FIJI
SOURCES:
All components in GDP by expenditure categories
1975-76 Bureau of Statistics, Fiji
MISCELLANEOUS:
1960-76 Break in series from 1976-77

GABON
SOURCES:
All indicators
1950-66 UNECA
BREAKS IN COMPARABILITY:
1971-89 Other services includes gas, electricity and water (current prices)
MISCELLANEOUS:
1971-89 Mining includes oil research activities

GAMBIA, THE
MISCELLANEOUS:
1950-87 Fiscal year ending July 30

GERMANY, FEDERAL REPUBLIC OF
MISCELLANEOUS:
1969-89 Excludes the former German Democratic Republic

GREECE
SOURCES:
All Indicators
1964-79 OECD
1980-88 Ministry of National Economy and OECD publications
MISCELLANEOUS:
1950-88 Data for imports of goods and nonfactor services exclude ships operating overseas
1950-88 Data for fixed investment exclude ships operating overseas

GUATEMALA
Consumer price index
1960-89 Base year is 1987

GUINEA-BISSAU
SOURCES:
All Indicators
1970-74 UNECA
1980-81 Ministry of Planning and WB estimates
BREAKS IN COMPARABILITY:
1970-83 Private consumption includes change in stocks and discrepancy in GDP expenditure estimate

HAITI
Consumer price index
1960-89 Base year is 1987
MISCELLANEOUS:
1966-89 Fiscal year ending September 30
1970-75 Exports and imports exclude external transactions related to assembly industry
1970-75 Gross domestic fixed investment excludes imports related to assembly industry

HONG KONG
SOURCES:
All Indicators
1960-89 Estimates of GDP 1966-1989, Census and Statistics Department, (various issues)

INDIA
MISCELLANEOUS:
1950-89 Fiscal year ending March 31

ISRAEL
SOURCES:
All components in GDP by expenditure categories
1960-89 Central Bureau of Statistics
All components in GDP by industrial origin
1972-86 UN, *Monthly Bulletin of Statistics*, various issues (current prices)
Consumer price index
1960-89 Base year is 1987
MISCELLANEOUS:
1980-89 Data relate to new SNA, therefore not comparable to earlier years

JAMAICA
SOURCES:
All Indicators
1960-89 Statistical Institute, *National Income and Product Accounts*

JORDAN
MISCELLANEOUS:
1983-90 Data (except population) relate to East Bank only

KENYA
SOURCES:
All Indicators
1972-89 *Kenya Economic Survey*, various issues and WB estimates
All components in GDP by industrial origin
1979-89 *Kenya Economic Survey*, various issues and WB estimates
MISCELLANEOUS:
1950-88 Data series not strictly comparable - breaks in 1964, and 1972

KOREA, REPUBLIC OF
SOURCES:
All Indicators
1955, 1960-69: National Income Account 1984, Bank of Korea
1970-88 National Accounts, Bank of Korea
1989 Monthly Statistical Bulletin, April 90, The Bank of Korea
MISCELLANEOUS:
1955-89 Break in series from 1969-70
1989 Monthly Statistical Bulletin, April 90, The Bank of Korea

LESOTHO
SOURCES:
All Indicators
1966-79 UN *National Accounts Yearbook* 1976 and Lesotho National Accounts 1973/74, 1975/84 and 1976/86, and WB estimates (current prices)
MISCELLANEOUS:
1960-75 Fiscal year ending on March 31

LIBERIA
Consumer price index
1960-89 Base year is 1987
BREAKS IN COMPARABILITY:
1981-86 Other services includes ownership of dwellings and gas, electricity, and water
MISCELLANEOUS:
1960-86 Agriculture includes informal construction and informal manufacturing

MADAGASCAR
SOURCES:
All components by GDP by expenditure categories
1960-65 UN (UNECA)

MALAWI
BREAKS IN COMPARABILITY:
1955-63 Public administration and defense includes other services (current prices)
1955-63 Agriculture includes informal agriculture (current prices)

MALAYSIA
Consumer price index
1960-89 Base year is 1987

MALTA
SOURCES:
All Indicators
1955-72 UN, *Yearbook of National Accounts Statistics*, various issues
1973-86 *National Accounts of Maltese Islands*, various issues
1987-88 Dept. of Economic Planning, Economic Survey 1989

MAURITANIA
SOURCES:
All Indicators
1960-72 UN, Office for Development Research and Policy Analysis
BREAKS IN COMPARABILITY:
1960-89 Private consumption includes public enterprises
1960-87 Agriculture includes informal manufacturing

MEXICO
BREAKS IN COMPARABILITY:
1960-79 Manufacturing includes oil refinery

MAURITIUS
BREAKS IN COMPARABILITY:
1950-63 Private consumption includes Changes in stocks

MOROCCO
SOURCES:
All components in GDP by expenditure categories
1960-69 UN, *Yearbook of National Accounts Statistics*, various editions. (current prices)
All components in GDP by industrial origin
1960-69 UN, *Yearbook of National Accounts Statistics*, various issues. (current prices)

NEPAL
Consumer price index
1960-89 Base year is 1987
MISCELLANEOUS:
1960-89 Break in series in 1974 and 1975
1960-89 Fiscal year ending July 15

NIGER
SOURCES:
All Indicators
1960-66 UNECA
1976-77 UNECA

NIGERIA
SOURCES:
All Indicators
1950-69 Federal Office of Statistics
1973-80 Federal Office of Statistics, various issues and WB estimates
Imports of goods and nonfactor services
Exports of goods and nonfactor services
1950-80 Central Bank of Nigeria, various issues (current prices)
BREAKS IN COMPARABILITY:
1950-80 Private consumption includes change in stocks
MISCELLANEOUS:
1950-79 Fiscal year ending March 31
1967-69 Data exclude the three eastern states
1980-89 Data are for calendar year

OMAN
Consumer price index
1960-89 Base year is 1987

PAKISTAN
SOURCES:
All Indicators
1977-89 Federal Bureau of Statistics
MISCELLANEOUS:
1960-89 Fiscal year ending June 30
1981-89 Data based on new methodology adopted in 1988-89

PANAMA
SOURCES:
All Indicators
1980-89 Directorate of Statistics and Census
MISCELLANEOUS:
1980-84 Data on transport value added includes Panama Canal Commission

PAPUA NEW GUINEA
SOURCES:
All Indicators
1961-76 *Statistical Bulletin* (various issues) and *Compendium of Statistics*, PNG
1961-76 Fiscal year data adjusted to calendar year

PERU
SOURCES:
All Indicators
1979-89 National Institute of Statistics and WB estimates
BREAKS IN COMPARABILITY:
1969-78 Other services includes wholesale and retail trade

PORTUGAL
SOURCES:
All components in GDP by expenditure categories
1960-76 OECD, *National Accounts of OECD Countries*, various editions (current prices)
Consumer price index
1960-89 Base year is 1987

RWANDA
SOURCES:
All Indicators
1970-81 UN, *Yearbook of National Accounts*, and *Monthly Bulletin of Statistics* (current prices)
GDP at market prices
All components in GDP by industrial origin
1976-79 UN, *Yearbook of National Accounts* (constant prices)
Net factor income from abroad
1982-85 UN, *Yearbook of National Accounts* (current prices)
Net indirect taxes
1970-74 UNECA (current prices)
BREAKS IN COMPARABILITY:
1969-75 Services includes construction
1969-75 Services includes mining and quarrying and gas, electricity, and water (constant prices)

SAUDI ARABIA
MISCELLANEOUS:
1963-89 Fiscal years are based on the Islamic (Hijri) year
1984-89 Data not comparable, break in series 1984-89

SENEGAL
SOURCES:
All Indicators
1975 Ministere du Plan et de la Cooperation
1977-80 Direction de la provision, Ministry of Economy and Finance, 04/86

SEYCHELLES
SOURCES:
All Indicators
1976-82 UN, *Yearbook of National Accounts*
Consumer price index
1960-89 Base year is 1987

SIERRA LEONE
MISCELLANEOUS:
1960-89 Fiscal year ending June 30

SINGAPORE
SOURCES:
All Indicators
1960-89 Department of Statistics, Singapore
MISCELLANEOUS:
1969-89 Exports GNFS are BOP data (current prices)
1969-89 Imports GNFS are residual item (current prices)

SOMALIA
SOURCES:
All Indicators
1970-76 Official data and WB estimates (current prices)

SOUTH AFRICA
SOURCES:
All Indicators
1965-76 UN, *Yearbook of National Accounts*
1977-89 *South African Quarterly Bulletin*, various issues
MISCELLANEOUS:
1960-89 Data includes Namibia except GNP per capita

SRI LANKA
SOURCES:
All Indicators
1960-89 Central Bank of Ceylon, *Annual Report* and WB estimates (current prices)

MISCELLANEOUS:
1970-89 Break in series 1981-82

ST. VINCENT AND THE GRENADINES
SOURCES:
All components in GDP by expenditure categories
1977-86 Ministry of Finance, Statistical Unit; OECS Secretariat
All components in GDP by industrial origin
1977-88 Ministry of Finance, Ministry of Planning and Development, OECS Secretariat.

SUDAN
SOURCES:
All components in GDP by industrial origin
1965-69 Sudan National Accounts, various issues (current prices)
MISCELLANEOUS:
1960-89 Fiscal year ending June 30

SURINAME
BREAKS IN COMPARABILITY:
1977-88 Gross domestic fixed investment includes change in stocks (current prices)

SWAZILAND
Consumer price index
1960-89 Base year is 1987
MISCELLANEOUS:
1960-79 Fiscal year ending March 31 through 1976, June 30 from 1976 to 1979

SWITZERLAND
Consumer price index
1960-89 Base year is 1987

SYRIAN ARAB REPUBLIC
BREAKS IN COMPARABILITY:
1963-69, 1975-88 Private consumption includes change in stocks
1963-69, 1975-88 Gross domestic investment excludes change in stocks

TANZANIA
SOURCES:
All Indicators
1964-75 *National Accounts of Tanzania* and *Economic Survey* (various issues) (current prices)
1976-78 Bureau of statistics: *National Accounts of Tanzania*
MISCELLANEOUS:
1950-89 Data are for mainland Tanzania only
BREAKS IN COMPARABILITY:
1960-63 Banking, insurance and real estate includes wholesale, retail and ownership of dwellings (current prices)

TOGO
SOURCES:
All indicators
1960-65 UNECA, 12/78
1980-89 Ministry of Planning 11/90
MISCELLANEOUS:
1960-79 Data for agriculture represent food crops only

TONGA
Consumer price index
1960-89 Base year is 1987
MISCELLANEOUS:
1975-89 Break in series from 1981-82

TRINIDAD AND TOBAGO
SOURCES:
All components in GDP by industrial origin
1980-84 Central Statistical Office
BREAKS IN COMPARABILITY:
1970-89 Banking, insurance and real estate includes ownership of dwellings

TURKEY

SOURCES:

All Indicators

1950-69 Turkish State Institute of Statistics

All components in GDP by expenditure categories

1970-71 *OECD Economic Surveys*, Nov. 1978 (Except exports and imports of goods and nonfactor services)

UGANDA

SOURCES:

All components in GDP by expenditure categories

1950-62 UN

All components in GDP by industrial origin

1962-89 Central Statistical Office

Net factor income from abroad

1960-62 Background to Budget

Net Indirect

1960-62 Background to Budget and National Accounts of Uganda (current prices)

BREAKS IN COMPARABILITY:

1963-89 Services includes water

UNITED ARAB EMIRATES

Consumer price index

1960-89 Base year is 1987

URUGUAY

SOURCES:

All Indicators

1966-69 Central Bank of Uruguay, *Indicators of Economic and Financial Activity*

VANUATU

SOURCES:

All components in GDP by expenditure categories

1983-87 UN and UNDP estimates

WESTERN SAMOA

MISCELLANEOUS:

1979-85 Break in series in 1983 and 1984

ZAIRE

SOURCES:

All Indicators

1980-89 WB consultants for Bureau of Statistics & Bank of Zaire 5/90

BREAKS IN COMPARABILITY:

1960-67 Constructrion excludes informal construction

MISCELLANEOUS:

1960-79 Data not comparable due to breaks in series in 1960, 1967, 1970, and 1977

ZAMBIA

SOURCES:

All Indicators

1977-89 CSO's data from Monthly Digest of Statistics

BREAKS IN COMPARABILITY:

1955-63 Mining and quarrying includes manufacturing (current prices)

1955-64 Banking, insurance and real estate excludes real estate (current prices)

1964 Other services includes hotels and restaurants (current prices)

1965-85 Public administration and defense includes water

MISCELLANEOUS:

1950-77 Data series has breaks in 1964, 1970 and 1977 and not strictly comparable

ZIMBABWE

SOURCES:

General government consumption

Resource balance

1960-69 *Monthly Digest of Statistics*, Zwe. Nat. Act and BOP 1974,1978 (current prices)

GDP at market prices

Gross domestic investment

1960-69 *Zimbabwe National Income and Expenditure Report 1985* (current prices)

Balance of Payments

ARGENTINA
SOURCES:
All indicators
1989 WB

BAHAMAS
SOURCES:
All indicators
1989 WB

BANGLADESH
SOURCES:
All indicators
1973-1989 WB
MISCELLANEOUS:
1973-89 Fiscal year ending June 30

BARBADOS
SOURCES:
All indicators
1989 WB

BELGIUM
MISCELLANEOUS:
Includes Luxembourg

BENIN
SOURCES:
All indicators
1980-89 WB
BREAKS IN COMPARABILITY:
1974-79 Errors and omissions includes smuggling

BHUTAN
All indicators
SOURCES
1981-89 WB

BOLIVIA
SOURCES:
All indicators
1980-88 WB
MISCELLANEOUS:
1981-87 Large unrecorded transactions not included

BOTSWANA
SOURCES:
All indicators
1989 WB

BRAZIL
SOURCES:
All indicators
1988-89 WB

BURKINA FASO
SOURCES:
All indicators
1987-89 WB

BURUNDI
SOURCES:
All indicators
1970-1989 WB

CAMEROON
SOURCES:
All indicators
1980-89 WB
MISCELLANEOUS:
1980-89 Fiscal year ending June 30

CAPE VERDE
SOURCES:
All indicators
1978-89 WB

CENTRAL AFRICAN REPUBLIC
SOURCES:
All indicators
1988-89 WB

CHAD
SOURCES:
All indicators
1988-89 WB

CHILE
SOURCES:
All indicators
1989 WB

CHINA
SOURCES:
All indicators
1981-89 WB

COLOMBIA
SOURCES:
All indicators
1989 WB
1987-88 WB

CONGO, PEOPLES REPUBLIC OF THE
SOURCES:
All indicators
1987-89 WB

COSTA RICA
SOURCES:
All indicators
1988-89 WB

COTE D'IVOIRE
SOURCES:
All indicators
1989 WB

DOMINICAN REPUBLIC
SOURCES:
All indicators
1987-89 WB

ECUADOR
SOURCES:
All indicators
1980-1989 WB

EGYPT, ARAB REPUBLIC OF
SOURCES:
All indicators
1974-88 WB
MISCELLANEOUS:
1981-88 Fiscal year ending June 30

EL SALVADOR
SOURCES:
All indicators
1986-89 WB

ETHIOPIA
SOURCES:
All indicators
1975-89 WB
MISCELLANEOUS:
1975-89 Fiscal year ending July 7

GABON
SOURCES:
All indicators
1989 WB

GAMBIA
SOURCES
All indicators
1989 WB

GHANA
SOURCES:
All indicators
1988 WB

GUINEA-BISSAU
SOURCES:
All indicators
1978-89 WB

GUATEMALA
SOURCES:
All indicators
1988-89 WB

GUINEA-BISSAU
SOURCES:
All indicators
1989 WB

GUYANA
SOURCES:
All indicators
1986-89 WB

HAITI
MISCELLANEOUS:
1965-88 Fiscal year ending September 30

HONDURAS
SOURCES:
All indicators
1989 WB

HUNGARY
SOURCES:
All indicators
1982-1989 WB

INDIA
SOURCES:
All indicators
1970-89 WB
MISCELLANEOUS:
1970-89 Fiscal year ending March 31

INDONESIA
SOURCES:
All indicators
1989 WB

JAMAICA
SOURCES:
All indicators
1980-87 WB

JORDAN
SOURCES:
All indicators
1977-89 WB

LESOTHO
SOURCES:
All Indicators
1988-89 WB

LUXEMBOURG
MISCELLANEOUS:
See Belgium country page.

MALAWI
SOURCES:
All indicators
1989 WB

MALAYSIA
SOURCES:
All indicators
1989 WB

MAURITANIA
SOURCES:
All indicators
1989 WB

MEXICO
SOURCES:
All indicators
1988-89 WB

MOROCCO
SOURCES:
All indicators
1989 WB

MOZAMBIQUE
SOURCES:
All indicators
1986-89 WB

NEPAL
MISCELLANEOUS:
1973-88 Fiscal year ending July 15

NICARAGUA
SOURCES:
All indicators
1981-87 WB

NIGER
SOURCES:
All indicators
1989 WB

NIGERIA
SOURCES:
All indicators
1989 WB

PAKISTAN
MISCELLANEOUS:
1967-89 Imports includes some services

PANAMA
SOURCES:
All indicators
1978-89 WB
MISCELLANEOUS:
1980-87 Exports and imports by enterprises in the Colon Free Zone
  are not included

PAPUA NEW GUINEA
SOURCES:
All indicators
1989 WB

PARAGUAY
SOURCES:
All indicators
1980-88 WB

PERU
SOURCES:
All indicators
1989 WB

PHILIPPINES
SOURCES:
All indicators
1989 WB

RWANDA
SOURCES:
All indicators
1989 WB
BREAKS IN COMPARABILITY:
1987 Official transfer includes official transfers deemed capital
  grants (credit)

SAO TOME & PRINCIPE
SOURCES:
All indicators
1985-89 WB

SENEGAL
SOURCES:
All indicators
1989 WB

SIERRA LEONE
SOURCES:
All indicators
1989 WB

SOMALIA
SOURCES:
All indicators
1989 WB

SRI LANKA
SOURCES:
All indicators
1989 WB

SUDAN
SOURCES:
All indicators
1979-89 WB
MISCELLANEOUS:
1979-89 Fiscal year ending March 31

SYRIAN ARAB REPUBLIC
SOURCES:
All indicators
1987-89 WB

TANZANIA
SOURCES:
All indicators
1988-89 WB

THAILAND
SOURCES:
All indicators
1989 WB

TOGO
SOURCES:
All indicators
1989 WB

TONGA
MISCELLANEOUS:
Fiscal year ending June 30

TRINIDAD & TOBAGO
SOURCES:
All indicators
1989 WB

TUNISIA
SOURCES:
All indicators
1989 WB

TURKEY
SOURCES:
All indicator
1989 WB

UGANDA
SOURCES:
All indicators
1980-89 WB

URUGUAY
SOURCES:
All indicators
1979-89 WB

VENEZUELA
SOURCES:
All indicators
1989 WB

WESTERN SAMOA
SOURCES:
All indicators
1989 WB

YUGOSLAVIA
SOURCES:
All indicators
1987-89 WB

ZAMBIA
SOURCES:
All indicators
1989 WB

ZIMBABWE
SOURCES:
All indicators
1988-89 WB

Trade

ALGERIA
SOURCES:
Exports of all commodities
1965-88 IMF
MISCELLANEOUS:
1965-88 IMF BOP data.

BANGLADESH
SOURCES:
Imports of fuels
1965-88 IMF
Imports of manufactures
1965-88 IMF

BARBADOS
SOURCES:
All indicators
1987-88 WB
Exports of all commodities
1983-88 IMF
Imports of all commodities
1980-88 IMF
MISCELLANEOUS:
1965-82 Data include export of value added from improvement   and
    repair trade and exclude military goods

BELGIUM
MISCELLANEOUS:
Includes Luxembourg

BENIN
SOURCES:
All indicators
1984-88 WB

BOLIVIA
SOURCES:
Exports of all commodities
1965-88 IMF

BOTSWANA
SOURCES:
All indicators
1965-88 IMF

BURKINA FASO
SOURCES:
All indicators
1984-88 WB
Exports of food
Exports of other agricultural products
Imports of manufactures
1965-83 IMF

CAMEROON
SOURCES:
Exports of fuel
1965-89 WB

CENTRAL AFRICAN REPUBLIC
SOURCES:
Exports of all commodities
Imports of all commodities
1965-67 WB
1968-88 IMF

EGYPT, ARAB REPUBLIC OF
SOURCES:
All indicators
1965-88 WB
1980-88 WB Fiscal year ending June 30
MISCELLANEOUS
1965-88 Fiscal year ending June 30

EL SALVADOR
SOURCES:
Exports of beverages
1965-88 IMF

GABON
SOURCES:
Exports of all commodities
1971-88 IMF
Imports of all commodities
1973-88 IMF

GHANA
SOURCES:
Exports of all commodities
Imports of all commodities
1965-88 WB
MISCELLANEOUS:
1965-88 BOP data plus aluminum trade estimated from
    from partners' data

HAITI
SOURCES:
All indicators
1984-88 WB
Exports of manufactures
Imports of manufactures
1965-88 WB
MISCELLANEOUS:
1965-88 Fiscal year ending September 30

INDIA
SOURCES:
Exports of fuel
1965-88 WB
Exports of manufactures
1976-88 WB
Imports of fats and oils
1979-81 WB
Imports of manufactures
1975-88 WB
Imports of metals and minerals
1975-88 WB

KENYA
SOURCES:
All indicators
1965-76 IMF

KUWAIT
SOURCES:
Exports of fuel
1965-69 IMF

LESOTHO
SOURCES:
All indicators
1965-88 IMF

LUXEMBOURG:
MISCELLANEOUS:
See Belgium country page

MALI
SOURCES:
Exports of all commodities
1986-88 WB
Imports of all commodities
1985-88 WB
MISCELLANEOUS:
1985-88 Extrapolated via BOP data trend

MEXICO
SOURCES:
All indicators
1980-88 IMF
MISCELLANEOUS:
1980-88 Trade of in-bond industries excluded

NEPAL
SOURCES:
All export indicators
All import indicators
1965-88 WB Estimates based on trading partners' data

NIGER
SOURCES:
Exports of food
Exports of metals and minerals
Imports of manufactures
1965-88 IMF

NIGERIA
SOURCES:
Imports of all commodities
1980-85 IMF
1986-88 WB

OMAN
SOURCES:
Exports of fuel
1965-88 IMF

PAPUA NEW GUINEA
SOURCES:
Imports of manufactures
1965-88 IMF

PERU
SOURCES:
All export indicators
1975-88 IMF

RWANDA
SOURCES:
Imports of food
Imports of fuels
1973-88 IMF

SENEGAL
SOURCES:
Exports of all commodities
1981-88 IMF
Imports of all commodities
1981-82 IMF
1983-88 WB

SEYCHELLES
SOURCES:
All export indicators
1965-88 WB

SOMALIA
SOURCES:
Exports of all commodities
1965-86 IMF
Imports of all commodities
1965-88 IMF

SOUTH AFRICA
SOURCES:
All indicators
1965-88 IMF
Exports of metals and minerals
1973-88 IMF
Imports of all commodities
1965-79 IMF
MISCELLANEOUS:
1965-88 Include trades of Namibia, Lesotho, Botswana, and Swaziland with other countries

SUDAN
SOURCES:
All export indicators
Imports of all commodities
1965-88 WB

SYRIAN ARAB REPUBLIC
SOURCES:
Imports of all commodities
1985-88 WB

TANZANIA
SOURCES:
All indicators
1965-76 IMF
Imports of all commodities
1984-85 WB

TOGO
SOURCES:
Exports of manufactures
Exports of metals and minerals
Imports of food
Imports of manufactures
1965-88 WB

UGANDA
SOURCES:
All indicators
1965-76 IMF
Exports of all commodities
1965-88 IMF
All import indicators
1977-88 IMF

UNITED ARAB EMIRATES
SOURCES:
Exports of fuel
1980-82 IMF

VENEZUELA
SOURCES:
Exports of all commodities
1983-88 IMF
All import indicators
1965-88 IMF
Imports of all commodities
1985-88 WB

ZAIRE
SOURCES:
Imports of all commodities
1984-85 WB

ZIMBABWE
SOURCES:
Imports of all commodities
1980-88 IMF

Country List and Base Years for National Accounts

Algeria	1980	Greece	1970	Paraguay	1982
Antigua and Barbuda	1977	Grenada	1984	Peru	1979
Argentina	1970	Guatemala	1958	Philippines	1972
Australia	1980	Guinea-Bissau	1979	Poland	1984
Austria	1980	Guyana	1977	Portugal	1977
Bahamas, The	1977	Haiti	1976	Rwanda	1976
Bahrain	1985	Honduras	1978	São Tomé and Principe	1985
Bangladesh	1973	Hong Kong	1980	Saudi Arabia	1970
Barbados	1974	Hungary	1981	Senegal	1979
Belgium	1980	Iceland	1980	Seychelles	1976
Belize	1984	India	1980	Sierra Leone	1985
Benin	1978	Indonesia	1983	Singapore	1985
Bhutan	1980	Iran, Islamic Rep. of.	1974	Solomon Islands	1980
Bolivia	1980	Ireland	1980	Somalia	1985
Botswana	1980	Israel	1986	South Africa	1985
Brazil	1980	Italy	1980	Spain	1980
Bulgaria	1982	Jamaica	1974	Sri Lanka	1982
Burkina Faso	1979	Japan	1980	St. Kitts and Nevis	1977
Burundi	1980	Jordan	1985	St. Lucia	1977
Cameroon	1980	Kenya	1982	St. Vincent and	
Canada	1980	Korea, Rep.	1985	the Grenadines	1977
Cape Verde	1980	Kuwait	1984	Sudan	1982
Central African Rep.	1977	Lesotho	1980	Suriname	1980
Chad	1977	Liberia	1971	Swaziland	1980
Chile	1977	Libya	1975	Sweden	1980
China	1980	Luxembourg	1980	Switzerland	1980
Colombia	1975	Madagascar	1984	Syrian Arab Rep.	1980
Comoros	1985	Malawi	1978	Tanzania	1976
Congo, People's Rep.	1978	Malaysia	1978	Thailand	1972
Costa Rica	1966	Mali	1985	Togo	1978
Côte d'Ivoire	1984	Malta	1973	Tonga	1982
Cyprus	1985	Mauritania	1982	Trinidad and Tobago	1970
Denmark	1980	Mauritius	1982	Tunisia	1980
Dominica	1977	Mexico	1980	Turkey	1968
Dominican Rep.	1970	Morocco	1980	Uganda	1966
Ecuador	1975	Mozambique	1980	United Arab Emirates	1980
Egypt, Arab Rep.	1982	Nepal	1975	United Kingdom	1980
El Salvador	1962	Netherlands	1980	United States	1980
Equatorial Guinea	1986	New Zealand	1980	Uruguay	1978
Ethiopia	1981	Nicaragua	1980	Vanuatu	1983
Fiji	1977	Niger	1972	Venezuela	1984
Finland	1980	Nigeria	1984	Western Samoa	1980
France	1980	Norway	1980	Yugoslavia	1972
Gabon	1979	Oman	1978	Zaire	1987
Gambia, The	1977	Pakistan	1981	Zambia	1977
Germany, Fed. Rep.	1980	Panama	1970	Zimbabwe	1980
Ghana	1975	Papua New Guinea	1983		

Country Conversion Factors

where differences from the IMF's International Financial Statistics *annual exchange rates occur*

I. Fiscal Year Conversion Factors

Australia	1969-89	Nepal	1969-89
Bangladesh	1969-89	Nigeria	1969-79
Botswana	1969-89	New Zealand	1969-89
Cameroon	1969-89	Pakistan	1969-89
Gambia, The	1969-89	Sierra Leone	1969-89
Haiti	1969-89	Sudan	1976-89
India	1969-89	Tonga	1969-89

II. Trade-Weighted Conversion Factors

Dominican Republic	1982-84	Jamaica	1981-83
Ecuador	1982-85	Nicaragua	1982-87
Egypt, Arab Republic	1974-89	Paraguay	1982-86
El Salvador	1982-86	Syria	1983-89
Guatemala	1985-86	Peru	1986-89

III. Conversion Factors Estimated by World Bank staff

Argentina	1969-81	Guinea-Bissau	1970-86
Bolivia	1974-85	Somalia	1977-89
Ghana	1973-87	Uganda	1969-83